*Neu*

*Preiswert*

*Zuverlässig*

Dieses neue Taschenbuch ist ein ganz außergewöhnliches Wörterbuch. Sein Inhalt basiert auf den zweisprachigen Wörterbüchern des Verlages Langenscheidt — des bedeutendsten Verlages auf diesem Gebiet. Es enthält über 40 000 Stichwörter, gibt die Aussprache in beiden Teilen in Internationaler Lautschrift und besitzt besondere Anhänge für Eigennamen, Abkürzungen und Maße und Gewichte.

Neu und einzigartig ist die Fülle der grammatischen Informationen: Mehr als 15 000 deutsche Substantive und Verben haben Angaben zur Deklination und Konjugation. Über die unregelmäßigen Verben in beiden Sprachen gibt der Hauptteil und der Anhang zuverlässig Auskunft.

Dieses Wörterbuch ist somit ein modernes und handliches Nachschlagewerk für jeden, der in seinem Beruf, beim Lernen oder Lehren mit der englischen und deutschen Sprache zu tun hat.

# LANGENSCHEIDTS

# DEUTSCH-ENGLISCHES
# ENGLISCH-DEUTSCHES
## WÖRTERBUCH

Beide Teile in einem Band

Bearbeitet und herausgegeben

von der

LANGENSCHEIDT-REDAKTION

PUBLISHED BY POCKET BOOKS NEW YORK

# LANGENSCHEIDT'S

# GERMAN-ENGLISH
# ENGLISH-GERMAN
## DICTIONARY

Two Volumes in One

Edited by
## THE LANGENSCHEIDT
## EDITORIAL STAFF

PUBLISHED BY POCKET BOOKS NEW YORK

LANGENSCHEIDT'S GERMAN-ENGLISH
ENGLISH-GERMAN DICTIONARY

POCKET BOOK edition published March, 1953

New Revised and Enlarged Edition published March, 1970

5th printing........February, 1973

*Langenscheidt's German-English English-German Dictionary*
was formerly published under the imprint of Washington Square Press,
a division of Simon & Schuster, Inc.

This POCKET BOOK edition may not be sold in Germany,
Switzerland, and Austria.

This POCKET BOOK edition is printed from brand-new
plates made from completely reset, clear, easy-to-read type.
POCKET BOOK editions are published by POCKET BOOKS, a division of
Simon & Schuster, Inc., 630 Fifth Avenue, New York, N.Y. 10020.
Trademarks registered in the United States and other countries.

L

Standard Book Number: 671-77412-3.
This POCKET BOOK edition is published by arrangement with
Langenscheidt KG, Publishers, Berlin and Munich, Germany.
A hard-bound edition of this work is available in the United States from
Optimum Book Marketing Co., 171 Madison Avenue,
New York, New York, 10017.

Printed in the U.S.A.

# Preface

For over 100 years Langenscheidt's bilingual dictionaries have been an essential tool of the language student. For several decades Langenscheidt's German-English dictionaries have been used in all walks of life as well as in schools.

However, languages are in a constant process of change. To bring you abreast of these changes Langenscheidt has compiled this entirely new dictionary. Many new words which have entered the German and English languages in the last few years have been included in the vocabulary: e.g., Mondfähre, Mehrwertsteuer, Einwegflasche, Antirakete; lunar probe, heart transplant, non-violence.

Langenscheidt's German-English Dictionary contains another new and long desired feature for the English-speaking user: it provides clear answers to questions of declension and conjugation in over 15,000 German noun and verb entries (see pp. 7 to 8).

The phonetic transcription of the German and English headwords follows the principles laid down by the International Phonetic Association (IPA).

In addition to the vocabulary this Dictionary contains special quick-reference sections of proper names — up-to-date with names like Wankel, Mössbauer, Henze —, abbreviations and weights and measures.

Designed for the widest possible variety of uses, this Dictionary, with its more than 40,000 entries in all, will be of great value to students, teachers, and tourists as well as in home and office libraries.

# Contents

# Arrangement of the Dictionary and Guide for the User

**1. Arrangement.** Strict alphabetical order has been maintained throughout this Dictionary. The irregular plural forms of English nouns as well as the principal parts (infinitive, preterite, and past participle) of the irregular English and German verbs have also been given in their proper alphabetical order; e.g. *man - men; bite - bit - bitten; beißen - biß - gebissen.*

**2. Pronunciation.** Pronunciation is given in square brackets by means of the symbols of the International Phonetic Association. No transcription of compounds is given if the parts appear as separate headwords. The German suffixes as given on page 12 are not transcribed unless they are parts of catchwords.

**3. Explanatory additions** have been printed in italics; e.g. *abstract Inhalt* kurz zs.-fassen; *Abbau* pulling down (*of structure*); *abbauen* pull down (*structure*); *durchsichtig glass, etc.*: transparent.

**4. Subject Labels.** The field of knowledge from which a headword or some of its meanings are taken is, where possible, indicated by figurative or abbreviated labels or by other labels written out in full. A figurative or abbreviated label placed immediately after a headword applies to all translations. Any label preceding an individual translation refers to this only. In Part I, any abbreviated label with a colon applies to all following translations. An F placed before a German illustrative phrase or its English equivalent indicates that the phrase in question is colloquial usage. An F: placed before a German phrase applies to that phrase and its translation(s). Figurative labels have always, other labels sometimes, been placed between illustrative phrases and their translations.

**5.** Translations of similar meanings have been subdivided by **commas,** the various senses by **semicolons.**

**6. American spelling** has been given in the following ways: theat|re, *Am.* -er, defen|ce, *Am.* -se; council(l)or, hono(u)r, judg(e)ment; plough, *Am.* plow.

**7. Grammatical References in Part I.** Parts of speech (adjective, verb, etc.) have been indicated throughout. Entries have been subdivided by Arabic numerals to distinguish the various parts of speech.

**I. Nouns.** The inflectional forms (*genitive singular / nominative plural*) follow immediately after the indication of gender. No forms are given for compounds if the parts appear as separate headwords.

The horizontal stroke replaces that part of the word which remains unchanged in the inflexion: *Affe m* (-n/-n); *Affäre f* (-/-n).

The sign " indicates that an Umlaut appears in the inflected form in question: *Blatt n* (-[e]s/=er).

**II. Verbs.** Verbs have been treated in the following ways:

a) *bändigen v/t.* (ge-, h): The past participle of this verb is formed by means of the prefix ge- and the auxiliary verb *haben: er hat gebändigt.*

b) *abfassen v/t.* (sep., -ge-, h): In conjugation the prefix *ab* must be separated from the primary verb *fassen: er faßt ab; er hat abgefaßt.*

c) *verderben v/i.* (irr., no -ge-, sein): *irr.* following the verb refers the reader to the list of irregular German verbs in the appendix (p. 573) for the principal parts of this particular verb: *es verdarb; es ist verdorben.*

d) *abfallen v/i.* (irr. fallen, sep., -ge-, sein): A reference such as *irr. fallen* indicates that the compound verb *abfallen* is conjugated exactly like the primary verb *fallen* as given in the list of irregular verbs: *er fiel ab; er ist abgefallen.*

e) *sieden v/t. and v/i.* ([irr.,] ge-, h): The square brackets indicate that *sieden* can be treated as a regular or irregular verb: *er siedete or er sott; er hat gesiedet or er hat gesotten.*

**III. Prepositions.** Prepositions governing a headword are given in both languages. The grammatical construction following a German preposition is indicated only if the preposition governs two different cases. If a German preposition applies to all translations it is given only with the first whereas its English equivalents are given after each translation: *schützen* ... protect (*gegen*, *vor dat.* against, from), defend (against, from), guard (against, from); shelter (from).

**IV. Subdivision.** Entries have been subdivided by Arabic numerals

a) to distinguish the various parts of speech: *laut 1. adj.* ...; *2. adv.* ...; *3. prp.* ...; *4.* ♀ *m* ...;

b) to distinguish between the transitive and intransitive meanings of a verb if these differ in their translations;

c) to show that in case of change of meaning a noun or verb may be differently inflected or conjugated: *Bau m 1. (-[e]s/no pl.)* ...; *2. (-[e]s/-ten)* ...; *3. (-[e]s/-e)* ...; *schwimmen v/i. (irr., ge-) 1. (sein)* ...; *2. (h)* ...

If grammatical indications come

before the subdivision they refer to all translations following: *Alte (-n/-n) 1. m* ...; *2. f* ...; *humpeln v/i. (ge-) 1. (sein)* ...; *2. (h)* ...

**8. Grammatical References in Part II.** Parts of speech (adjective, verb, etc.) have been indicated only in cases of doubt. Entries have been subdivided by Arabic numerals to distinguish the various parts of speech.

a) (*~ally*) after an English adjective means that the adverb is formed by affixing ...ally: *automatic (~ally)* = *automatically*.

b) *irr.* following a verb refers the reader to the list of irregular English verbs in the appendix (p. 575) for the principal parts of this particular verb. A reference such as *irr. fall* indicates that the compound verb, e.g. *befall*, is conjugated exactly like the primary verb *fall*.

# Symbols and Abbreviations Used in This Dictionary

## 1. Symbols

The swung dash or tilde (~ ♀, ~ ♀) serves as a mark of repetition within an entry. The tilde in bold type (~) represents either the complete word at the beginning of the entry or the unchanged part of that word which is followed by a vertical line (|). The simple tilde (~) represents: a) the headword immediately preceding, which itself may contain a tilde in bold type; b) in phonetic transcrip-

tion, any part of the preceding transcription that remains unchanged.

When the initial letter changes from small to capital or vice versa, the usual tilde is replaced by ♀ or ♀.

Examples: *abandon* [ə'bændən], *~ment* [*~*nmənt = ə'bændənmənt]; *certi|ficate*, *~fication*, *~fy*, *~tude*. *Drama*, *~tiker*, *♀tisch*; *Haus|flur*, *~frau*; *fassen: sich kurz ~*.

☐ after an English adjective means that an adverb may be formed regularly from it by adding ...ly, or by changing ...le into ...ly, or ...y into ...ily; e.g.: *rich* ☐ = *richly*; *acceptable* ☐ = *acceptably*; *happy* ☐ = *happily*.

F *familiar,* familiär; *colloquial usage,* Umgangssprache.

P *low colloquialism,* populär, Sprache des Volkes.

V *vulgar,* vulgär.

† *archaic,* veraltet.

⚒ *rare, little used,* selten.

Ⓤ *scientific term,* wissenschaftlich.

♣ *botany,* Botanik.

⊕ *engineering,* Technik; *handicraft,* Handwerk.

⚒ *mining,* Bergbau.

⚔ *military term,* militärisch.

⚓ *nautical term,* Schiffahrt.

† *commercial term,* Handelswesen.

🚂 *railway, railroad,* Eisenbahn.

✈ *aviation,* Flugwesen.

✉ *postal affairs,* Postwesen.

♪ *musical term*, Musik.
△ *architecture*, Architektur.
ϟ *electrical engineering*, Elektrotechnik.
⚖ *legal term*, Rechtswissenschaft.

⚕ *mathematics*, Mathematik.
⚘ *farming*, Landwirtschaft.
🜍 *chemistry*, Chemie.
⚕ *medicine*, Medizin.

## 2. Abbreviations

*a.* *also*, auch.
*abbr.* *abbreviation*, Abkürzung.
*acc.* *accusative (case)*, Akkusativ.
*adj.* *adjective*, Adjektiv.
*adv.* *adverb*, Adverb.
*allg.* *commonly*, allgemein.
*Am.* *American English*, amerikanisches Englisch.
*anat.* *anatomy*, Anatomie.
*appr.* *approximately*, etwa.
*art.* *article*, Artikel.
*ast.* *astronomy*, Astronomie.
*attr.* *attributively*, attributiv.

*biol.* *biology*, Biologie.
*Brt.* *British English*, britisches Englisch.
*b.s.* *bad sense*, in schlechtem Sinne.
*bsd.* *especially*, besonders.

*cj.* *conjunction*, Konjunktion.
*co.* *comic(al)*, scherzhaft.
*coll.* *collectively*, als Sammelwort.
*comp.* *comparative*, Komparativ.
*contp.* *contemptuously*, verächtlich.

*dat.* *dative (case)*, Dativ.
*dem.* *demonstrative*, Demonstrativ...

*ea.* *one another, each other*, einander.
*eccl.* *ecclesiastical*, kirchlich.
*e-e, e-e, e-e a(n)*, eine.
*e-m, e-m, e-m to a(n)*, einem.
*e-n, e-n, e-n a(n)*, einen.
*engS.* *more strictly taken*, in engerem Sinne.
*e-r, e-r, e-r of a(n), to a(n)*, einer.
*e-s, e-s, e-s of a(n)*, eines.
*esp.* *especially*, besonders.
*et., et., et. something*, etwas.
*etc.* *et cetera, and so on*, und so weiter.

*f* *feminine*, weiblich.
*fig.* *figuratively*, bildlich.
*frz.* *French*, französisch.

*gen.* *genitive (case)*, Genitiv.
*geogr.* *geography*, Geographie.
*geol.* *geology*, Geologie.
*geom.* *geometry*, Geometrie.
*ger.* *gerund*, Gerundium.
*Ggs.* *antonym*, Gegensatz.
*gr.* *grammar*, Grammatik.

*h* *have*, haben.
*hist.* *history*, Geschichte.
*hunt.* *hunting*, Jagdwesen.

*ichth.* *ichthyology*, Ichthyologie.
*impers.* *impersonal*, unpersönlich.
*indef.* *indefinite*, Indefinit...
*inf.* *infinitive (mood)*, Infinitiv.
*int.* *interjection*, Interjektion.
*interr.* *interrogative*, Interrogativ...
*iro.* *ironically*, ironisch.
*irr.* *irregular*, unregelmäßig.

*j., j., j. someone*, jemand.
*j-m, j-m, j-m to s.o.* jemandem.
*j-n, j-n, j-n someone*, jemanden.
*j-s, j-s, j-s someone's*, jemandes.

*konkr.* *concretely*, konkret.

*ling.* *linguistics*, Linguistik.
*lit.* *literary*, nur in der Schriftsprache vorkommend.

*m* *masculine*, männlich.
*m-e, m-e, m-e my*, meine.
*m-r* *of my, to my*, meiner.
*metall.* *metallurgy*, Metallurgie.
*meteor.* *meteorology*, Meteorologie.
*min.* *mineralogy*, Mineralogie.
*mot.* *motoring*, Kraftfahrwesen.
*mount.* *mountaineering*, Bergsteigerei.
*mst* *mostly, usually*, meistens.
*myth.* *mythology*, Mythologie.

*n* *neuter*, sächlich.
*nom.* *nominative (case)*, Nominativ.
*npr.* *proper name*, Eigenname.

*od.* *or*, oder.
*opt.* *optics*, Optik.

| | |
|---|---|
| orn. | ornithology, Ornithologie. |
| o.s. | oneself, sich. |
| P., | person, Person. |
| p. | person, Person. |
| paint. | painting, Malerei. |
| parl. | parliamentary term, parlamentarischer Ausdruck. |
| pass. | passive voice, Passiv. |
| pers. | personal, Personal... |
| pharm. | pharmacy, Pharmazie. |
| phls. | philosophy, Philosophie. |
| phot. | photography, Photographie. |
| phys. | physics, Physik. |
| physiol. | physiology, Physiologie. |
| pl. | plural, Plural. |
| poet. | poetry, Dichtung. |
| pol. | politics, Politik. |
| poss. | possessive, Possessiv... |
| p.p. | past participle, Partizip Perfekt. |
| p.pr. | present participle, Partizip Präsens. |
| pred. | predicative, prädikativ. |
| pres. | present, Präsens. |
| pret. | preterit(e), Präteritum. |
| pron. | pronoun, Pronomen. |
| prov. | provincialism, Provinzialismus. |
| prp. | preposition, Präposition. |
| psych. | psychology, Psychologie. |
| refl. | reflexive, reflexiv. |
| rel. | relative, Relativ... |
| rhet. | rhetoric, Rhetorik. |
| S., S. | thing, Sache. |
| s. | see, refer to, siehe. |
| schott. | Scotch, schottisch. |
| s-e, s-e, s-e | his, one's, seine. |
| sep. | separable, abtrennbar. |
| sg. | singular, Singular. |

| | |
|---|---|
| sl. | slang, Slang. |
| s-m, s-m, s-m | to his, to one's, seinem. |
| s-n, s-n, s-n | his, one's, seinen. |
| s.o., s.o., s.o. | someone, jemand(en). |
| s-r, s-r, s-r | of his, of one's, to his, to one's, seiner. |
| s-s, s-s, s-s | of his, of one's, seines. |
| s.th., s.th., s.th. | something, etwas. |
| subj. | subjunctive (mood), Konjunktiv. |
| sup. | superlative, Superlativ. |
| surv. | surveying, Landvermessung. |
| tel. | telegraphy, Telegraphie. |
| teleph. | telephony, Fernsprechwesen. |
| thea. | theat\|re, Am. -er, Theater. |
| typ. | typography, Typographie. |
| u., u. | and, und. |
| univ. | university, Hochschulwesen, Studentensprache. |
| v/aux. | auxiliary verb, Hilfsverb. |
| vb. | verb, Verb. |
| vet. | veterinary medicine, Veterinärmedizin. |
| vgl. | confer, vergleiche. |
| v/i. | verb intransitive, intransitives Verb. |
| v/refl. | verb reflexive, reflexives Verb. |
| v/t. | verb transitive, transitives Verb. |
| weitS. | more widely taken, in weiterem Sinne. |
| z.B. | for example, zum Beispiel. |
| zo. | zoology, Zoologie. |
| zs. | together, zusammen. |
| Zssg(n). | compound word(s), Zusammensetzung(en). |

# Guide to Pronunciation
# for the German-English Part

The length of vowels is indicated by [:] following the vowel symbol, the stress by ['] preceding the stressed syllable. The glottal stop [ˀ] is the forced stop between one word or syllable and a following one beginning with a vowel, as in *unentbehrlich* [unˀɛntˈbeːrliç].

## A. Vowels

[a] as in French *carte*: Mann [man].

[ɑ:] as in *father*: Wagen [ˈvɑːgən].

[e] as in *bed*: Edikt [eˈdikt].

[e:] resembles the sound in *day*: Weg [veːk].

[ə] unstressed e as in *ago*: Bitte [ˈbitə].

[ɛ] as in *fair*: männlich [ˈmɛnliç], Geld [gɛlt].

[ɛ:] same sound but long: zählen [ˈtsɛːlən].

[i] as in *it*: Wind [vint].

[i:] as in *meet*: hier [hiːr].

[ɔ] as in *long*: Ort [ɔrt].

[ɔ:] same sound but long as in *draw*: Komfort [kɔmˈfɔːr].

[o] as in *molest*: Moral [moˈrɑːl].

[ʊ] resembles the English sound in *go* [gou] but without the [u]: Boot [boːt].

[ø:] as in French *feu*. The sound may be acquired by saying [e] through closely rounded lips: schön [ʃøːn].

[ø] same sound but short: Ökonomie [økonoˈmiː].

[œ] as in French *neuf*. The sound resembles the English vowel in *her*. Lips, however, must be well rounded as for [ɔ]: öffnen [ˈœfnən].

[u] as in *book*: Mutter [ˈmutər].

[u:] as in *boot*: Uhr [uːr].

[y] almost like the French u as in *sur*. It may be acquired by saying [i] through fairly closely rounded lips: Glück [glyk].

[y:] same sound but long: führen [ˈfyːrən].

## B. Diphthongs

[aɪ] as in *like*: Mai [maɪ].

[aʊ] as in *mouse*: Maus [maʊs].

[ɔʏ] as in *boy*: Beute [ˈbɔʏtə], Läufer [ˈlɔʏfər].

## C. Consonants

[b] as in *better*: besser [ˈbɛsər].

[d] as in *dance*: du [duː].

[f] as in *find*: finden [ˈfindən], Vater [ˈfɑːtər], Philosoph [filoˈzoːf].

[g] as in *gold*: Gold [gɔlt], Geld [gɛlt].

[ʒ] as in *measure*: Genie [ʒeˈniː], Journalist [ʒurnaˈlist].

[h] as in *house* but not aspirated: Haus [haʊs].

[ç] an approximation to this sound may be acquired by assuming the mouth-configuration for [i] and emitting a strong current of breath: Licht [liçt], Mönch [mœnç], lustig [ˈlustiç].

[x] as in Scotch *loch*. Whereas [ç] is pronounced at the front of the mouth, [x] is pronounced in the throat: Loch [lɔx].

[j] as in *year*: ja [jɑː].

[k] as in *kick*: keck [kɛk], Tag [tɑːk], Chronist [kroˈnist], Café [kaˈfeː].

[l] as in *lump*. Pronounced like English initial "clear l": lassen [ˈlasən].

[m] as in *mouse*: Maus [maʊs].

[n] as in *not*: nein [naɪn].

[ŋ] as in *sing, drink*: singen [ˈziŋən], trinken [ˈtriŋkən].

[p] as in *pass*: Paß [pas], Weib [vaɪp], obgleich [ɔpˈglaɪç].

[r] as in *rot*. There are two pronunciations: the frontal or lingual r and the uvular r (the latter unknown in England): *rot* [roːt].

[s] as in *miss*. Unvoiced when final, doubled, or next a voiceless consonant: *Glas* [glaːs], *Masse* ['masə], *Mast* [mast], *naß* [nas].

[z] as in *zero*. S voiced when initial in a word or syllable: *Sohn* [zoːn], *Rose* ['roːzə].

[ʃ] as in *ship*: *Schiff* [ʃif], *Charme* [ʃarm], *Spiel* [ʃpiːl], *Stein* [ʃtaɪn].

[t] as in *tea*: *Tee* [teː], *Thron* [troːn], *Stadt* [ʃtat], *Bad* [baːt], *Findling* ['fintliŋ], *Wind* [vint].

[v] as in *vast*: *Vase* ['vaːzə], *Winter* ['vintər].

[ă, ĕ, ŏ] are nasalized vowels. Examples: *Ensemble* [ă'săːbəl], *Terrain* [tɛ'rɛ̃ː], *Bonbon* [bŏ'bŏ̃ː].

# List of Suffixes

often given without phonetic transcription

| | | | | |
|---|---|---|---|---|
| -bar | [-baːr] | | -ist | [-ist] |
| -chen | [-çən] | | -keit | [-kaɪt] |
| -d | [-t] | | -lich | [-liç] |
| -de | [-də] | | -ling | [-liŋ] |
| -ei | [-aɪ] | | -losigkeit | [-loːziçkaɪt] |
| -en | [-ən] | | -nis | [-nis] |
| -end | [-ənt] | | -sal | [-zaːl] |
| -er | [-ər] | | -sam | [-zaːm] |
| -haft | [-haft] | | -schaft | [-ʃaft] |
| -heit | [-haɪt] | | -sieren | [-ziːrən] |
| -ie | [-iː] | | -ste | [-stə] |
| -ieren | [-iːrən] | | -tät | [-tɛːt] |
| -ig | [-iç] | | -tum | [-tuːm] |
| -ik | [-ik] | | -ung | [-uŋ] |
| -in | [-in] | | -ungs- | [-uŋs-] |
| -isch | [-iʃ] | | | |

# Erläuterung der phonetischen Umschrift im englisch-deutschen Teil

## A. Vokale und Diphthonge

[ɑ:] reines langes a, wie in Vater, kam, Schwan: *far* [fɑ:], *father* ['fɑ:ðə].

[ʌ] kommt im Deutschen nicht vor. Kurzes dunkles a, bei dem die Lippen nicht gerundet sind. Vorn und offen gebildet: *butter* ['bʌtə], *come* [kʌm], *colour* ['kʌlə], *blood* [blʌd], *flourish* ['flʌriʃ], *twopence* ['tʌpəns].

[æ] heller, ziemlich offener, nicht zu kurzer Laut. Raum zwischen Zunge und Gaumen noch größer als bei ä in Ähre: *fat* [fæt], *man* [mæn].

[ɛə] nicht zu offenes halblanges ä; im Englischen nur vor r, das als ein dem ä nachhallendes ə erscheint: *bare* [bɛə], *pair* [pɛə], *there* [ðɛə].

[ai] Bestandteile: helles, zwischen ɑ: und æ liegendes a und schwächeres offenes i. Die Zunge hebt sich halbwegs zur i-Stellung: *I* [ai], *lie* [lai], *dry* [drai].

[au] Bestandteile: helles, zwischen ɑ: und æ liegendes a und schwächeres offenes u: *house* [haus], *now* [nau].

[ei] halboffenes e, nach i auslautend, indem die Zunge sich halbwegs zur i-Stellung hebt: *date* [deit], *play* [plei], *obey* [ə'bei].

[e] halboffenes kurzes e, etwas geschlossener als das e in Bett: *bed* [bed], *less* [les].

[ə] flüchtiger Gleitlaut, ähnlich dem deutschen flüchtig gesprochenen e in Gelage: *about* [ə'baut], *butter* ['bʌtə], *nation* ['neiʃən], *connect* [kə'nekt].

[i:] langes i wie in lieb, Bibel, aber etwas offener einsetzend als im Deutschen; wird in Südengland doppellautig gesprochen, indem sich die Zunge allmählich zur i-Stellung hebt: *scene* [si:n], *sea* [si:], *feet* [fi:t], *ceiling* ['si:liŋ].

[i] kurzes offenes i wie in bin, mit: *big* [big], *city* ['siti].

[iə] halboffenes halblanges i mit nachhallendem ə: *here* [hiə], *hear* [hiə], *inferior* [in'fiəriə].

[ou] halboffenes langes o, in schwaches u auslautend; keine Rundung der Lippen, kein Heben der Zunge: *note* [nout], *boat* [bout], *below* [bi'lou].

[ɔ:] offener langer, zwischen a und o schwebender Laut: *fall* [fɔ:l], *nought* [nɔ:t], *or* [ɔ:], *before* [bi'fɔ:].

[ɔ] offener kurzer, zwischen a und o schwebender Laut, offener als das o in Motto: *god* [gɔd], *not* [nɔt], *wash* [wɔʃ], *hobby* ['hɔbi].

[ə:] im Deutschen fehlender Laut; offenes langes ö, etwa wie gedehnt gesprochenes ö in öffnen, Mörder; kein Heben der Zunge: *word* [wə:d], *girl* [gə:l], *learn* [lə:n], *murmur* ['mə:mə].

[ɔi] Bestandteile: offenes o und schwächeres offenes i. Die Zunge hebt sich halbwegs zur i-Stellung: *voice* [vɔis], *boy* [bɔi], *annoy* [ə'nɔi].

[u:] langes u wie in Buch, doch ohne Lippenrundung; vielfach diphthongisch als halboffenes langes u mit nachhallendem geschlossenen u: *fool* [fu:l], *shoe* [ʃu:], *you* [ju:], *rule* [ru:l], *canoe* [kə'nu:].

[uə] halboffenes halblanges u mit nachhallendem ə: *poor* [puə], *sure* [ʃuə], *allure* [ə'ljuə].

[u] flüchtiges u: *put* [put], *look* [luk], *full* [ful].

Die **Länge eines Vokals** wird durch [:] bezeichnet, z.B. *ask* [ɑ:sk], *astir* [ə'stə:].

Vereinzelt werden auch die folgenden französischen Nasallaute gebraucht: [ɑ̃] wie in frz. *blanc*, [ɔ̃] wie in frz. *bonbon* und [ɛ̃] wie in frz. *vin*.

## B. Konsonanten

[r] nur vor Vokalen gesprochen. Völlig verschieden vom deutschen Zungenspitzen- oder Zäpfchen-r. Die Zungenspitze bildet mit der oberen Zahnwulst eine Enge, durch die der Ausatmungsstrom mit Stimmton hindurchgetrieben wird, ohne den Laut zu rollen. Am Ende eines Wortes wird r nur bei Bindung mit dem Anlautvokal des folgenden Wortes gesprochen: *rose* [rouz], *pride* [praid], *there is* [ðɛərˈiz].

[ʒ] stimmhaftes sch, wie g in Genie, j in Journal: *azure* [ˈæʒə], *jazz* [dʒæz], *jeep* [dʒiːp], *large* [laːdʒ].

[ʃ] stimmloses sch, wie im Deutschen Schnee, rasch: *shake* [ʃeik], *washing* [ˈwɔʃiŋ], *lash* [læʃ].

[θ] im Deutschen nicht vorhandener stimmloser Lispellaut; durch Anlegen der Zunge an die oberen Schneidezähne hervorgebracht: *thin* [θin], *path* [paːθ], *method* [ˈmeθəd].

[ð] derselbe Laut wie θ, nur stimmhaft, d.h. mit Stimmton: *there* [ðɛə], *breathe* [briːð], *father* [ˈfaːðə].

[s] stimmloser Zischlaut, entsprechend dem deutschen ß in Spaß, reißen: *see* [siː], *hats* [hæts], *decide* [diˈsaid].

[z] stimmhafter Zischlaut wie im Deutschen sausen: *zeal* [ziːl], *rise* [raiz], *horizon* [həˈraizn].

[ŋ] wird wie der deutsche Nasenlaut in fangen, singen gebildet: *ring* [riŋ], *singer* [ˈsiŋə].

[ŋk] derselbe Laut mit nachfolgendem k wie im Deutschen senken, Wink: *ink* [iŋk], *tinker* [ˈtiŋkə].

[w] flüchtiges, mit Lippe an Lippe gesprochenes w, aus der Mundstellung für u: gebildet: *will* [wil], *swear* [swɛə], *queen* [kwiːn].

[f] stimmloser Lippenlaut wie im Deutschen flott, Pfeife: *fat* [fæt], *tough* [tʌf], *effort* [ˈefət].

[v] stimmhafter Lippenlaut wie im Deutschen Vase, Ventil: *vein* [vein], *velvet* [ˈvelvit].

[j] flüchtiger zwischen j und i schwebender Laut: *onion* [ˈʌnjən], *yes* [jes], *filial* [ˈfiljəl].

**Die Betonung der englischen Wörter** wird durch das Zeichen [ˈ] vor der zu betonenden Silbe angegeben, z.B. *onion* [ˈʌnjən]. Sind zwei Silben eines Wortes mit Tonzeichen versehen, so sind beide gleichmäßig zu betonen, z.B. *unsound* [ˈʌnˈsaund].

Um Raum zu sparen, werden die Endung -ed* und das Plural-s** der englischen Stichwörter hier im Vorwort einmal mit Lautschrift gegeben, erscheinen dann aber im Wörterverzeichnis ohne Lautschrift, sofern keine Ausnahmen vorliegen.

* [-d] nach Vokalen und stimmhaften Konsonanten; [-t] nach stimmlosen Konsonanten; [-id] nach auslautendem d und t.

** [-z] nach Vokalen und stimmhaften Konsonanten; [-s] nach stimmlosen Konsonanten.

# Numerals

## Cardinal Numbers

| | | | |
|---|---|---|---|
| 0 | null *nought, zero, cipher* | 51 | einundfünfzig *fifty-one* |
| 1 | eins *one* | 60 | sechzig *sixty* |
| 2 | zwei *two* | 61 | einundsechzig *sixty-one* |
| 3 | drei *three* | 70 | siebzig *seventy* |
| 4 | vier *four* | 71 | einundsiebzig *seventy-one* |
| 5 | fünf *five* | 80 | achtzig *eighty* |
| 6 | sechs *six* | 81 | einundachtzig *eighty-one* |
| 7 | sieben *seven* | 90 | neunzig *ninety* |
| 8 | acht *eight* | 91 | einundneunzig *ninety-one* |
| 9 | neun *nine* | 100 | hundert *a or one hundred* |
| 10 | zehn *ten* | 101 | hundert(und)eins *a hundred and one* |
| 11 | elf *eleven* | | |
| 12 | zwölf *twelve* | 200 | zweihundert *two hundred* |
| 13 | dreizehn *thirteen* | 300 | dreihundert *three hundred* |
| 14 | vierzehn *fourteen* | 572 | fünfhundert(und)zweiundsiebzig *five hundred and seventy-two* |
| 15 | fünfzehn *fifteen* | | |
| 16 | sechzehn *sixteen* | | |
| 17 | siebzehn *seventeen* | 1000 | tausend *a or one thousand* |
| 18 | achtzehn *eighteen* | 1972 | neunzehnhundertzweiundsiebzig *nineteen hundred and seventy-two* |
| 19 | neunzehn *nineteen* | | |
| 20 | zwanzig *twenty* | | |
| 21 | einundzwanzig *twenty-one* | 500 000 | fünfhunderttausend *five hundred thousand* |
| 22 | zweiundzwanzig *twenty-two* | | |
| 23 | dreiundzwanzig *twenty-three* | 1 000 000 | eine Million *a or one million* |
| 30 | dreißig *thirty* | | |
| 31 | einunddreißig *thirty-one* | 2 000 000 | zwei Millionen *two million* |
| 40 | vierzig *forty* | | |
| 41 | einundvierzig *forty-one* | 1 000 000 000 | eine Milliarde *a or one milliard (Am. billion)* |
| 50 | fünfzig *fifty* | | |

## Ordinal Numbers

| | | | |
|---|---|---|---|
| 1. | erste *first (1st)* | 16. | sechzehnte *sixteenth* |
| 2. | zweite *second (2nd)* | 17. | siebzehnte *seventeenth* |
| 3. | dritte *third (3rd)* | 18. | achtzehnte *eighteenth* |
| 4. | vierte *fourth (4th)* | 19. | neunzehnte *nineteenth* |
| 5. | fünfte *fifth (5th), etc.* | 20. | zwanzigste *twentieth* |
| 6. | sechste *sixth* | 21. | einundzwanzigste *twenty-first* |
| 7. | siebente *seventh* | 22. | zweiundzwanzigste *twenty-second* |
| 8. | achte *eighth* | | |
| 9. | neunte *ninth* | 23. | dreiundzwanzigste *twenty-third* |
| 10. | zehnte *tenth* | | |
| 11. | elfte *eleventh* | 30. | dreißigste *thirtieth* |
| 12. | zwölfte *twelfth* | 31. | einunddreißigste *thirty-first* |
| 13. | dreizehnte *thirteenth* | 40. | vierzigste *fortieth* |
| 14. | vierzehnte *fourteenth* | 41. | einundvierzigste *forty-first* |
| 15. | fünfzehnte *fifteenth* | 50. | fünfzigste *fiftieth* |

| 51. einundfünfzigste *fifty-first* | 300. dreihundertste *three hundredth* |
|---|---|
| 60. sechzigste *sixtieth* | 572. fünfhundert(und)zweiund- |
| 61. einundsechzigste *sixty-first* | siebzigste *five hundred and* |
| 70. siebzigste *seventieth* | *seventy-second* |
| 71. einundsiebzigste *seventy-first* | 1000. tausendste *(one) thousandth* |
| 80. achtzigste *eightieth* | 1970. neunzehnhundert(und)sieb- |
| 81. einundachtzigste *eighty-first* | zigste *nineteen hundred and* |
| 90. neunzigste *ninetieth* | *seventieth* |
| 100. hundertste *(one) hundredth* | 500000. fünfhunderttausendste *five* |
| 101. hundert(und)erste *(one) hundred* | *hundred thousandth* |
| *and first* | 1000000. millionste *(one) millionth* |
| 200. zweihundertste *two hundredth* | 2000000. zweimillionste *two millionth* |

# Fractional Numbers and other Numerical Values

$1/2$ halb *one* or *a half*

$1/2$ eine halbe Meile *half a mile*

$1^1/2$ anderthalb *or* eineinhalb *one and a half*

$2^1/2$ zweieinhalb *two and a half*

$1/3$ ein Drittel *one* or *a third*

$2/3$ zwei Drittel *two thirds*

$1/4$ ein Viertel *one fourth, one* or *a quarter*

$3/4$ drei Viertel *three fourths, three quarters*

$1^1/4$ ein und eine viertel Stunde *one hour and a quarter*

$1/5$ ein Fünftel *one* or *a fifth*

$3^4/5$ drei vier Fünftel *three and four fifths*

0,4 null Komma vier *point four (.4)*

2,5 zwei Komma fünf *two point five (2.5)*

einfach *single*

zweifach *double, twofold*

dreifach *threefold, treble, triple*

vierfach *fourfold, quadruple*

fünffach *fivefold, quintuple*

einmal *once*

zweimal *twice*

drei-, vier-, fünfmal *three* or *four* or *five times*

zweimal soviel(e) *twice as much* or *many*

erstens, zweitens, drittens *first(ly), secondly, thirdly; in the first* or *second* or *third place*

$2 \times 3 = 6$ zwei mal drei ist sechs, zwei multipliziert mit drei ist sechs *twice three are* or *make six, two multiplied by three are* or *make six*

$7 + 8 = 15$ sieben plus acht ist fünfzehn *seven plus eight are fifteen*

$10 - 3 = 7$ zehn minus drei ist sieben *ten minus three are seven*

$20 : 5 = 4$ zwanzig (dividiert) durch fünf ist vier *twenty divided by five make four*

# PART I

# GERMAN-ENGLISH
# DICTIONARY

# A

**Aal** *ichth.* [ɑ:l] *m* (-[e]s/-e) eel; '2-
'**glatt** *adj.* (as) slippery as an eel.
**Aas** [ɑ:s] *n* 1. (-es/⚔-e) carrion,
carcass; 2. *fig.* (-es/Äser) beast;
'**~geier** *orn.* *m* vulture.
**ab** [ap] 1. *prp.* (*dat.*): ~ Brüssel from
Brussels onwards; ~ Fabrik, Lager
*etc.* ✝ ex works, warehouse, *etc.*;
2. *prp.* (*dat.*, F *acc.*): ~ erstem or
ersten März from March 1st, on
and after March 1st; 3. ✝ *prp.* (*gen.*)
less; ~ Unkosten less charges; 4. *adv.
time:* von jetzt ~ from now on, in
future; ~ und zu from time to time,
now and then; von da ~ from that
time forward; *space: thea.* exit, *pl.*
exeunt; von da ~ from there
(on).
**abä  r|n** ['ap^?-] *v/t.* (*sep.*, -ge-, h)
al er, modify; *parl.* amend; '2**ung**
*f* alteration, modification; *parl.*
amendment (*to bill, etc.*); '2**ungs-
antrag** *parl.* *m* amendment.
**abarbeiten** ['ap^?-] *v/t.* (*sep.*, -ge-, h)
work off (*debt*); sich ~ drudge, toil.
**Abart** ['ap^?-] *f* variety.
'**Abbau** *m* 1. (-[e]s/*no pl.*) pulling
down, demolition (*of structure*);
dismantling (*of machine, etc.*); dismissal, discharge (*of personnel*);
reduction (*of staff, prices, etc.*);
cut (*of prices, etc.*); 2. ⚒ (-[e]s/-e)
working, exploitation; '2**en** *v/t.*
(*sep.*, -ge-, h) pull or take down,
demolish (*structure*); dismantle
(*machine, etc.*); dismiss, discharge
(*personnel*); reduce (*staff, prices,
etc.*); cut (*prices, etc.*); ⚒ work,
exploit.
'**ab|beißen** *v/t.* (*irr.* beißen, *sep.*,
-ge-, h) bite off; '**~bekommen** *v/t.*
(*irr.* kommen, *sep.*, no -ge-, h) get
off; s-n Teil or et. ~ get one's share;
et. ~ be hurt, get hurt.
**abberuf|en** *v/t.* (*irr.* rufen, *sep.*, no
-ge-, h) recall; '2**ung** *f* recall.
'**ab|bestellen** *v/t.* (*sep.*, no -ge-, h)
countermand, cancel one's order
for (*goods, etc.*); cancel one's subscription to, discontinue (*news-
paper, etc.*); '**~biegen** *v/i.* (*irr.* biegen, *sep.*, -ge-, sein) *p.* turn off;
*road:* turn off, bend; nach rechts
(*links*) ~ turn right (left); von e-r
Straße ~ turn off a road.
'**Abbild** *n* likeness; image; 2**en**
['~dən] *v/t.* (*sep.*, -ge-, h) figure,
repr sent; sie ist auf der ersten
Seite abgebildet her picture is on
the front page; **~ung** ['~duŋ] *f*
picture, illustration.
'**abbinden** *v/t.* (*irr.* binden, *sep.*,

-ge-, h) untie, unbind, remove; ⚕
ligate, tie up.
'**Abbitte** *f* apology; ~ leisten or tun
make one's apology (*bei j-m wegen
et.* to s.o. for s.th.); '2**n** *v/t.* (*irr.*
bitten, *sep.*, -ge-, h): j-m et. ~
apologize to s.o. for s.th.
'**ab|blasen** *v/t.* (*irr.* blasen, *sep.*,
-ge-, h) blow off (*dust, etc.*); call
off (*strike, etc.*), cancel; ⚔ break
off (*attack*); '**~blättern** *v/i.* (*sep.*,
-ge-, sein) paint, *etc.*: scale, peel
(off); ⚕ *skin:* desquamate; ♃ shed
the leaves; '**~blenden** (*sep.*, -ge-, h)
1. *v/t.* screen (*light*) *mot.* dim, dip
(*headlights*); 2. *v/i. mot.* dim or dip
the headlights; *phot.* stop down;
'**~blitzen** F *v/i.* (*sep.*, -ge-, sein)
meet with a rebuff; ~ lassen snub;
'**~brausen** (*sep.*, -ge-) 1. *v/refl.* (h)
have a shower(-bath), douche; 2. F
*v/i.* (sein) rush off; '**~brechen** (*irr.*
brechen, *sep.*, -ge-) 1. *v/t.* (h) break
off (*a. fig.*); pull down, demolish
(*building, etc.*); strike (*tent*); *fig.*
stop; das Lager ~ break up camp,
strike tents; 2. *v/i.* (sein) break off;
3. *fig. v/i.* (h) stop; '**~bremsen** *v/t.*
and *v/i.* (*sep.*, -ge-, h) slow down;
brake; '**~brennen** (*irr.* brennen,
*sep.*, -ge-) 1. *v/t.* (h) burn down
(*building, etc.*); let or set off (*firework*); 2. *v/i.* (sein) burn away or
down; *s.* abgebrannt; '**~bringen**
*v/t.* (*irr.* bringen, *sep.*, -ge-, h) get
off; j-n ~ von argue s.o. out of;
dissuade s.o. from; '**~bröckeln** *v/i.*
(*sep.*, -ge-, sein) crumble (*a.* ✝).
'**Abbruch** *m* pulling down, demolition (*of building, etc.*); rupture (*of
relations*); breaking off (*of negotia-
tions, etc.*); *fig.* damage, injury; j-m
~ tun damage s.o.
'**ab|brühen** *v/t.* (*sep.*, -ge-, h)
scald; *s.* abgebrüht; '**~bürsten** *v/t.*
(*sep.*, -ge-, h) brush off (*dirt, etc.*);
brush (*coat, etc.*); '**~büßen** *v/t.*
(*sep.*, -ge-, h) expiate, atone for
(*sin, etc.*); serve (*sentence*).    [bet.]
**Abc** [ɑ:be'tse:] *n* (-/-) ABC, alpha-}
'**abdank|en** *v/i.* (*sep.*, -ge-, h) re-
sign; *ruler:* abdicate; '2**ung** *f* (-/-en)
resignation; abdication.
'**ab|decken** *v/t.* (*sep.*, -ge-, h) un-
cover; untile (*roof*); unroof (*building*); clear (*table*); cover; '**~dichten**
*v/t.* (*sep.*, -ge-, h) make tight; seal
up (*window, etc.*); ⊕ pack (*gland,
etc.*); '**~dienen** *v/t.* (*sep.*, -ge-, h):
s-e Zeit ~ ⚔ serve one's time; '**~
drängen** *v/t.* (*sep.*, -ge-, h) push
aside; '**~drehen** (*sep.*, -ge-, h)

2*

1. *v/t.* twist off (*wire*); turn off (*water, gas, etc.*); ⚡ switch off (*light*); 2. ⚓, ✈ *v/i.* change one's course; '~drosseln *mot. v/t.* (*sep., -ge-, h*) throttle.

'**Abdruck** *m* (-[e]s/=e) impression, print, mark; cast; '**~en** *v/t.* (*sep., -ge-, h*) print; publish (*article*).

'**abdrücken** (*sep., -ge-, h*) 1. *v/t.* fire (*gun, etc.*); F hug *or* squeeze affectionately; *sich* ~ leave an impression *or* a mark; 2. *v/i.* pull the trigger.

**Abend** ['a:bənt] *m* (-s/-e) evening; *am* ~ in the evening, at night; *heute abend* tonight; *morgen* (*gestern*) *abend* tomorrow (last) night; *s. essen;* '~anzug *m* evening dress; '~blatt *n* evening paper; '~brot *n* supper, dinner; '~dämmerung *f* (evening) twilight, dusk; '~essen *n s.* Abendbrot; '~gesellschaft *f* evening party; '~kasse *f* thea. *f* box-office; '~kleid *n* evening dress *or* gown; '~land *n* (-[e]s/no *pl.*) the Occident; 2**ländisch** *adj.* ['~lɛndiʃ] western, occidental; '~mahl *eccl. n* (-[e]s/-e) the (Holy) Communion, the Lord's Supper; '~rot *n* evening *or* sunset glow.     [evening.)

**abends** *adv.* ['a:bənts] in the)
'**Abend|schule** *f* evening school, night-school; '~sonne *f* setting sun; '~toilette *f* evening dress; '~wind *m* evening breeze; '~zeitung *f* evening paper.

**Abenteu|er** ['a:bəntɔʏər] *n* (-s/-) adventure; 2**erlich** *adj.* adventurous; *fig.*: strange; wild, fantastic; **~rer** ['~ɔʏrər] *m* (-s/-) adventurer.

**aber** ['a:bər] 1. *adv.* again; *Tausende und* ~ *Tausende* thousands upon thousands; 2. *cj.* but; *oder* ~ otherwise, (or) else; 3. *int.:* ~! now then!; ~, ~! come, come!; ~ *nein!* no!, on the contrary!; 4. 2 *n* (-s/-) but.

'**Aber|glaube** *m* superstition; 2**gläubisch** *adj.* ['~glɔʏbiʃ] superstitious.

**aberkennen** ['ap⁹-] *v/t.* (*irr. kennen, sep., no -ge-, h*): *j-m et.* ~ deprive s.o. of s.th. (*a.* ⚖); dispossess s.o. of s.th.; '2ung *f* (-/-en) deprivation (*a.* ⚖); dispossession.

**aber|malig** *adj.* ['a:bərma:liç] repeated; **~mals** *adv.* ['~s] again, once more.

**ab|ernten** ['ap⁹-] *v/t.* (*sep., -ge-, h*) reap, harvest; **~essen** ['ap⁹-] (*irr. essen, sep., -ge-, h*) 1. *v/t.* clear (*plate*); 2. *v/i.* finish eating; '~fahren (*irr. fahren, sep., -ge-*) 1. *v/i.* (*sein*) leave (*nach for*), depart (for), start (for); set out *or* off (for); 2. *v/t.* (*h*) carry *or* cart away (*load*).

'**Abfahrt** *f* departure (*nach for*); start (for); setting out *or* off (for); *skiing:* downhill run; '~sbahnsteig

*m* departure platform; '~slauf *m skiing:* downhill race; '~ssignal *n* starting-signal; '~szeit *f* time of departure; ⚓ *a.* time of sailing.

'**Abfall** *m* defection (*von from*), falling away (from); *esp. pol.* secession (from); *eccl.* apostasy (from); *often* Abfälle *pl.* waste, refuse, rubbish, *Am. a.* garbage; ⊕ clippings *pl.*, shavings *pl.;* at butcher's: offal; '~eimer *m* dust-bin, *Am.* ash can; '2en *v/i.* (*irr. fallen, sep., -ge-, sein*) leaves, *etc.:* fall (off); ground, *etc.:* slope (down); *fig.* fall away (*von from*); *esp. pol.* secede (from); *eccl.* apostatize (from); ~ *gegen* come off badly by comparison with, be inferior to; '~erzeugnis *n* waste product; by-product.

'**abfällig** *adj.* judgement, *etc.:* adverse, unfavo(u)rable; *remark:* disparaging, depreciatory.

'**Abfallprodukt** *n* by-product; waste product.

'**ab|fangen** *v/t.* (*irr. fangen, sep., -ge-, h*) catch; snatch (*ball, etc.*); intercept (*letter, etc.*); ⚓, ✗ prop; ✗ check (*attack*); ✗ flatten out; *mot.*, ✗ right; '~färben *v/i.* (*sep., -ge-, h*): *der Pullover färbt ab* the colo(u)r of the pull-over runs (*auf acc.* on); ~ *auf* (*acc.*) influence, affect.

'**abfass|en** *v/t.* (*sep., -ge-, h*) compose, write, pen; catch (*thief, etc.*); '2ung *f* composition; wording.

'**ab|faulen** *v/i.* (*sep., -ge-, sein*) rot off; '~fegen *v/t.* (*sep., -ge-, h*) sweep off; '~feilen *v/t.* (*sep., -ge-, h*) file off.

**abfertig|en** ['apfertigən] *v/t.* (*sep., -ge-, h*) dispatch (*a.* ✉); *customs:* clear; serve, attend to (*customer*); *j-n kurz* ~ snub s.o.; '2ung *f* (-/-en) dispatch; *customs:* clearance; *schroffe* ~ snub.     [(off), discharge.)

'**abfeuern** *v/t.* (*sep., -ge-, h*) fire)
'**abfinden** *v/t.* (*irr. finden, sep., -ge-, h*) satisfy, pay off (*creditor*); compensate; *sich mit et.* ~ resign o.s. to s.th.; put up with s.th.; '2ung *f* (-/-en) settlement; satisfaction; compensation; '2ung(ssumme) *f* indemnity; compensation.

'**ab|flachen** *v/t. and v/refl.* (*sep., -ge-, h*) flatten; '~flauen *v/i.* (*sep., -ge-, sein*) wind, *etc.:* abate; *interest, etc.:* flag; ⛵ *business:* slacken; '~fliegen *v/i.* (*irr. fliegen, sep., -ge-, sein*) leave by plane; ✗ take off, start; '~fließen *v/i.* (*irr. fließen, sep., -ge-, sein*) drain *or* flow off *or* away.     [parture.)

'**Abflug** ✗ *m* take-off, start, de-)
'**Abfluß** *m* flowing *or* draining off *or* away; discharge (*a.* ✗); drain (*a. fig.*); sink; outlet (*of lake, etc.*).

'**abfordern** *v/t.* (*sep., -ge-, h*): *j-m et.* ~ demand s.th. of *or* from s.o.

**Abfuhr** ['apfuːr] *f* (-/-en) removal; *fig.* rebuff.

**'abführ|en** (*sep.*, *-ge-*, *h*) **1.** *v/t.* lead off *or* away; march (*prisoner*) off; pay over (*money*) (*an acc.* to); **2.** *↯ v/i.* purge (the bowels), loosen the bowels; '**~end** *↯ adj.* purgative, aperient, laxative; '**2mittel** *↯ n* purgative, aperient, laxative.

**'abfüllen** *v/t.* (*sep.*, *-ge-*, *h*) decant; *in Flaschen* **~** bottle; *Bier in Fässer* **~** rack casks with beer.

**'Abgabe** *f sports*: pass; casting (*of one's vote*); sale (*of shares*, *etc.*); *mst* **~***n pl.* taxes *pl.*, rates *pl.*, *Am.* local taxes *pl.*; duties *pl.*; '**2frei** *adj.* tax-free; duty-free; '**2npflichtig** *adj.* taxable; dutiable; liable to tax *or* duty.

**'Abgang** *m* departure; start; *thea.* exit (*a. fig.*); retirement (*from a job*); loss, wastage; deficiency (*in weight, etc.*); *↯* discharge; *↯* miscarriage; *nach* **~** *von der Schule* after leaving school.

**'abgängig** *adj.* missing.

**'Abgangszeugnis** *n* (school-)leaving certificate, *Am. a.* diploma.

**'Abgas** *n* waste gas; *esp. mot.* exhaust gas. [toil-worn, worn-out.)

**abgearbeitet** *adj.* ['apgə'?arbaItət])

**'abgeben** *v/t.* (*irr.* geben, *sep.*, *-ge-*, *h*) leave (*bei*, *an dat.* at); hand in (*paper, etc.*); deposit, leave (*luggage*); cast (*one's vote*); *sports*: pass (*ball, etc.*); sell, dispose of (*goods*); give off (*heat, etc.*); *e-e Erklärung* **~** make a statement; *s-e Meinung* **~** express one's opinion (*über acc.* on); *j-m et.* **~** von et. give s.o. some of s.th.; *e-n guten Gelehrten* **~** make a good scholar; *sich* **~** mit occupy o.s. with *s.th.*; *sie gibt sich gern mit Kindern ab* she loves to be among children.

**'abge|brannt** *adj.* burnt down; ⊦ *fig.* hard up, *sl.* broke; **~brüht** *fig. adj.* ['~bryːt] hardened, callous; '**~droschen** *adj.* trite, hackneyed; **~feimt** *adj.* ['~faImt] cunning, crafty; '**~griffen** *adj.* worn; *book*: well-thumbed; **~härtet** *adj.* ['~hɛrtət] hardened (*gegen* to), inured (*to*); **~härmt** *adj.* ['~hɛrmt] care-worn.

**'abgehen** (*irr.* gehen, *sep.*, *-ge-*) **1.** *v/i.* (sein) go off *or* away; leave, start, depart; *letter, etc.*: be dispatched; *post*: go; *thea.* make one's exit; *side-road*: branch off; *goods*: sell; *button, etc.*: come off; *stain, etc.*: come out; *↯* be discharged; (*von e-m Amt*) **~** give up a post; retire; *von der Schule* **~** leave school; **~** *von* digress from (*main subject*); deviate from (*rule*); alter, change (*one's opinion*); relinquish (*plan, etc.*); *diese Eigenschaft geht ihm ab* he lacks this quality; *gut* **~** end well, pass off well; *hiervon geht or gehen*

... *ab* ⊤ less, minus; **2.** *v/t.* (*h*) measure by steps; patrol.

**abge|hetzt** *adj.* ['apgəhɛtst] harassed; exhausted; run down; breathless; **~kartet** ⊦ *adj.* ['~kartət]: **~e** *Sache* prearranged affair, put-up job; '**~legen** *adj.* remote, distant; secluded; out-of-the-way; **~macht** *adj.* ['~maxt]: **~!** it's a bargain *or* deal!; **~magert** *adj.* ['~maɡərt] emaciated; **~neigt** *adj.* ['~naIkt] disinclined (*dat.* for *s.th.*; *zu tun* to do), averse (*to*; *from* doing), unwilling (*zu tun* to do); **~nutzt** *adj.* ['~nutst] worn-out.

**Abgeordnete** ['apgə'?ɔrdnətə] *m*, *f* (*-n/-n*) deputy, delegate; *in Germany*: member of the Bundestag *or* Landtag; *Brt.* Member of Parliament, *Am.* Representative.

**'abgerissen** *fig. adj.* ragged; shabby; *style, speech*: abrupt, broken.

**'Abgesandte** *m*, *f* (*-n/-n*) envoy; emissary; ambassador.

**'abgeschieden** *fig. adj.* isolated; secluded, retired; '**2heit** *f* (-/-en) seclusion; retirement.

**'abgeschlossen** *adj.* flat: self-contained; *training, etc.*: complete.

**abgeschmackt** *adj.* ['apgəʃmakt] tasteless; tactless; '**2heit** *f* (-/-en) tastelessness; tactlessness.

**'abgesehen** *adj.*: **~** *von* apart from, *Am. a.* aside from.

**abge|spannt** *fig. adj.* ['apgəʃpant] exhausted, tired, run down; '**~standen** *adj.* stale, flat; '**~storben** *adj.* numb; dead; **~stumpft** *adj.* ['~ʃtumpft] blunt(ed); *fig.* indifferent (*gegen* to); '**~tragen** *adj.* worn-out; threadbare, shabby.

**'abgewöhnen** *v/t.* (*sep.*, *-ge-*, *h*): *j-m et.* **~** break *or* cure s.o. of s.th.; *sich das Rauchen* **~** give up smoking.

**abgezehrt** *adj.* ['apgətseːrt] emaciated, wasted.

**'abgießen** *v/t.* (*irr.* gießen, *sep.*, *-ge-*, *h*) pour off; ⚗ decant; ⊕ cast.

**'Abglanz** *m* reflection (*a. fig.*).

**'abgleiten** *v/i.* (*irr.* gleiten, *sep.*, *-ge-*, sein) slip off; slide off; glide.

**'Abgott** *m* idol. [off.)

**abgöttisch** *adv.* ['apgœtɪʃ]: *j-n* **~** *lieben* idolize *or* worship s.o.; dote (*up*)on s.o.

**'ab|grasen** *v/t.* (*sep.*, *-ge-*, *h*) graze; *fig.* scour; '**~grenzen** *v/t.* (*sep.*, *-ge-*, *h*) mark off, delimit; demarcate (*a. fig.*); *fig.* define.

**'Abgrund** *m* abyss; precipice; chasm, gulf; *am Rande des* **~s** on the brink of disaster.

**'Abguß** *m* cast.

**'ab|hacken** *v/t.* (*sep.*, *-ge-*, *h*) chop *or* cut off; '**~haken** *fig. v/t.* (*sep.*, *-ge-*, *h*) tick *or* check off; '**~halten** *v/t.* (*irr.* halten, *sep.*, *-ge-*, *h*) hold (*meeting, examination, etc.*); keep out (*rain*); *j-n von der Arbeit* **~** keep s.o. from his work; *j-n davon* ~ *et. zu tun* keep *or* restrain s.o. from doing s.th.; *et. von j-m* ~ keep s.th. away from s.o.; '~**handeln** *v/t.* (*sep.*, *-ge-*, *h*) discuss, treat; *j-m et.* ~ bargain s.th. out of s.o.

**abhanden** *adv.* [ap'handən]: ~ *kommen* get lost.

'**Abhandlung** *f* treatise (*über acc.* [up]on), dissertation ([up]on, concerning); essay.

'**Abhang** *m* slope, incline; declivity.

'**abhängen** 1. *v/t.* (*sep.*, *-ge-*, *h*) take down (*picture, etc.*); 🎣 uncouple; 2. *v/i.* (*irr. hängen, sep.*, *-ge-*, *h*): ~ *von* depend (up)on.

**abhängig** *adj.* ['ap'hɛnjç]: ~ *von* dependent (up)on; '**2keit** *f* (*-/no pl.*) dependence (*von* [up]on).

**ab|härmen** ['aphɛrmən] *v/refl.* (*sep.*, *-ge-*, *h*) pine away (*über acc.* at); '~**härten** *v/t.* (*sep.*, *-ge-*, *h*) harden (*gegen* to), inure (to); *sich* ~ *harden* o.s. (*gegen* to), inure o.s. (to); '~**hauen** (*irr. hauen, sep.*, *-ge-*) 1. *v/t.* (*h*) cut *or* chop off; 2. F *v/i.* (*sein*) be off; *hau ab! sl.* beat it!, scram!; '~**häuten** *v/t.* (*sep.*, *-ge-*, *h*) skin, flay; '~**heben** (*irr. heben, sep.*, *-ge-*, *h*) 1. *v/t.* lift *or* take off; *teleph.* lift (*receiver*); (with)draw (*money*); *sich* ~ *von* stand out against; *fig. a.* contrast with; 2. *v/i.* cut (the cards); *teleph.* lift the receiver; '~**heilen** *v/i.* (*sep.*, *-ge-*, *sein*) heal (up); '~**helfen** *v/i.* (*irr. helfen, sep.*, *-ge-*, *h*): *e-m Übel* ~ cure *or* redress an evil; *dem ist nicht abzuhelfen* there is nothing to be done about it; '~**hetzen** *v/refl.* (*sep.*, *-ge-*, *h*) tire o.s. out; rush, hurry.

'**Abhilfe** *f* remedy, redress, relief; ~ *schaffen* take remedial measures.

'**abhobeln** *v/t.* (*sep.*, *-ge-*, *h*) plane (away, down).

**abhold** *adj.* ['apholt] averse (*dat.* to *s.th.*); ill-disposed (*towards s.o.*).

'**ab|holen** *v/t.* (*sep.*, *-ge-*, *h*) fetch; call for, come for; *j-n von der Bahn* ~ go to meet s.o. at the station; '~**holzen** *v/t.* (*sep.*, *-ge-*, *h*) fell, cut down (*trees*); deforest; '~**horchen** 🩺 *v/t.* (*sep.*, *-ge-*, *h*) auscultate, sound; '~**hören** *v/t.* (*sep.*, *-ge-*, *h*) listen in to, intercept (*telephone conversation*); *e-n Schüler* ~ hear a pupil's lesson.

**Abitur** [abi'tu:r] *n* (*-s/*⊶*-e*) school-leaving examination (*qualifying for university entrance*).

'**ab|jagen** *v/t.* (*sep.*, *-ge-*, *h*): *j-m et.* ~ recover s.th. from s.o.; '~**kanzeln** F *v/t.* (*sep.*, *-ge-*, *h*) reprimand, F tell *s.o.* off; '~**kaufen** *v/t.* (*sep.*, *-ge-*, *h*): *j-m et.* ~ buy *or* purchase s.th. from s.o.

**Abkehr** *fig.* ['apke:r] *f* (*-/no pl.*) estrangement (*von* from); withdrawal (from); '**2en** *v/t.* (*sep.*, *-ge-*, *h*) sweep off; *sich* ~ *von* turn away from; *fig.*: take no further interest in; become estranged from; withdraw from.

'**ab|klingen** *v/i.* (*irr. klingen, sep.*, *-ge-*, *sein*) fade away; *pain, etc.*: die down; *pain, illness*: ease off; '~**klopfen** (*sep.*, *-ge-*, *h*) 1. *v/t.* knock (*dust, etc.*) off; dust (*coat, etc.*); 🩺 sound, percuss; 2. *v/i. conductor*: stop the orchestra; '~**knicken** *v/t.* (*sep.*, *-ge-*, *h*) snap *or* break off; bend off; '~**knöpfen** *v/t.* (*sep.*, *-ge-*, *h*) unbutton; F *j-m Geld* ~ get money out of s.o.; '~**kochen** (*sep.*, *-ge-*, *h*) 1. *v/t.* boil; scald (*milk*); 2. *v/i.* cook in the open air (*a.* 🟩); '~**kommandieren** ✗ *v/t.* (*sep.*, *no -ge-*, *h*) detach, detail; second (*officer*).

**Abkomme** ['apkɔmə] *m* (*-n/-n*) descendant.

'**abkommen** 1. *v/i.* (*irr. kommen, sep.*, *-ge-*, *sein*) come away, get away *or* off; *von e-r Ansicht* ~ change one's opinion; *von e-m Thema* ~ digress from a topic; *vom Wege* ~ lose one's way; 2. 2 *n* (*-s/-*) agreement.

**abkömm|lich** *adj.* ['apkœmlíç] dispensable; available; *er ist nicht* ~ he cannot be spared; **2ling** ['~lɪŋ] *m* (*-s/-e*) descendant.

'**ab|koppeln** *v/t.* (*sep.*, *-ge-*, *h*) uncouple; '~**kratzen** (*sep.*, *-ge-*) 1. *v/t.* (*h*) scrape off; 2. *sl. v/i.* (*sein*) kick the bucket; '~**kühlen** *v/t.* (*sep.*, *-ge-*, *h*) cool; refrigerate; *sich* ~ cool down (*a. fig.*).

**Abkunft** ['apkunft] *f* (*-/*⊶*-e*) descent; origin, extraction; birth.

'**abkürz|en** *v/t.* (*sep.*, *-ge-*, *h*) shorten; abbreviate (*word, story, etc.*); *den Weg* ~ take a short cut; '**2ung** *f* (*-/-en*) abridgement; abbreviation; short cut.

'**abladen** *v/t.* (*irr. laden, sep.*, *-ge-*, *h*) unload; dump (*rubbish, etc.*).

'**Ablage** *f* place of deposit; filing tray; files *pl.*; cloak-room.

'**ab|lagern** (*sep.*, *-ge-*) 1. *v/t.* (*h*) season (*wood, wine*); age (*wine*); *sich* ~ settle; be deposited; 2. *v/i.* (*sein*) *wood, wine*: season; *wine*: age; '~**lassen** (*irr. lassen, sep.*, *-ge-*, *h*) 1. *v/t.* let (*liquid*) run off; let off (*steam*); drain (*pond, etc.*); 2. *v/i.* leave off (*von et.* [doing] s.th.).

'**Ablauf** *m* running off; outlet, drain; *sports*: start; *fig.* expiration, end; *nach* ~ *von* at the end of; '**2en** (*irr. laufen, sep.*, *-ge-*) 1. *v/i.* (*sein*) run off; drain off; *period of time*: expire; 🕈 *bill of exchange*: fall due; *clock, etc.*: run down; *thread, film*: unwind; *spool*: run out; *gut* ~ *end* well; 2. v/t. (h) wear out (shoes); scour (region, etc.); sich die Beine ~ run one's legs off; s. Rang.

'**Ableben** n (-s/ no pl.) death, decease (esp. ⚰), ⚰ demise.

'**ab|lecken** v/t. (sep., -ge-, h) lick (off); '**~legen** (sep., -ge-, h) 1. v/t. take off (garments); leave off (garments); give up, break o.s. of (habit); file (documents, letters, etc.); make (confession, vow); take (oath, examination); Zeugnis ~ bear witness (für to; von of); s. Rechenschaft; 2. v/i. take off one's (hat and) coat.

'**Ableger** ♣ m (-s/-) layer, shoot.

'**ablehn|en** (sep., -ge-, h) 1. v/t. decline, refuse; reject (doctrine, candidate, etc.); turn down (proposal, etc.); 2. v/i. decline; dankend ~ decline with thanks; '**~end** adj. negative; '**Qung** f (-/-en) refusal; rejection.

**ableit|en** v/t. (sep., -ge-, h) divert (river, etc.); drain off or away (water, etc.); gr., ♣, fig. derive (aus, von from); fig. infer (from); '**Qung** f diversion; drainage; gr., ♣ derivation (a. fig.).

'**ab|lenken** v/t. (sep., -ge-, h) turn aside; divert (suspicion, etc.) (von from); phys., etc.: deflect (rays, etc.); j-n von der Arbeit ~ distract s.o. from his work; '**~lesen** v/t. (irr. lesen, sep., -ge-, h) read (speech, etc.); read (off) (values from instruments); '**~leugnen** v/t. (sep., -ge-, h) deny, disavow, disown.

'**abliefer|n** v/t. (sep., -ge-, h) deliver; hand over; surrender; '**Qung** f delivery.

'**ablöschen** v/t. (sep., -ge-, h) blot (up) (ink); ⊕ temper (steel).

'**ablös|en** v/t. (sep., -ge-, h) detach; take off; ✂, etc.: relieve; supersede (predecessor in office); discharge (debt); redeem (obligation); sich ~ come off; fig. alternate, take turns; '**Qung** f detachment; ✂, etc.: relief; fig. supersession; discharge; redemption.

'**abmach|en** v/t. (sep., -ge-, h) remove, detach; fig. settle, arrange (business, etc.); agree (up)on (price, etc.); '**Qung** f (-/-en) arrangement, settlement; agreement.

'**abmager|n** v/i. (sep., -ge-, sein) lose flesh; grow lean or thin; '**Qung** f (-/-en) emaciation.

'**ab|mähen** v/t. (sep., -ge-, h) mow (off); '**~malen** v/t. (sep., -ge-, h) copy.

'**Abmarsch** m start; ✕ marching off; '**Qieren** v/i. (sep., no -ge-, sein) start; ✕ march off.

'**abmeld|en** v/t. (sep., -ge-, h): j-n von der Schule ~ give notice of the withdrawal of a pupil (from school); sich polizeilich ~ give notice to the police of one's departure (from

town, etc.); '**Qung** f notice of withdrawal; notice of departure.

'**abmess|en** v/t. (irr. messen, sep., -ge-, h) measure; '**Qung** f (-/-en) measurement.

'**ab|montieren** v/t. (sep., no -ge-, h) disassemble; dismantle, strip (machinery); remove (tyre, etc.); '**~mühen** v/refl. (sep., -ge-, h) drudge, toil; '**~nagen** v/t. (sep., -ge-, h) gnaw off; pick (bone).

**Abnahme** ['apnɑ:mə] f (-/⚙-n) taking off; removal; ⚙ amputation; ✝ taking delivery; ✝ purchase; ✝ sale; ⊕ acceptance (of machine, etc.); administering (of oath); decrease, diminution; loss (of weight).

'**abnehm|en** (irr. nehmen, sep., -ge-, h) 1. v/t. take off; remove; teleph. lift (receiver); ⚙ amputate; gather (fruit); ⊕ accept (machine, etc.); j-m et. ~ take s.th. from s.o.; ✝ a. buy or purchase s.th. from s.o.; j-m zuviel ~ overcharge s.o.; 2. v/i. decrease, diminish; decline; lose weight; moon: wane; storm: abate; days: grow shorter; '**Qer** ✝ m (-s/-) buyer; customer; consumer.

'**Abneigung** f aversion (gegen to); disinclination (to); dislike (to, of, for); antipathy (against, to).

**abnorm** adj. [ap'nɔrm] abnormal; anomalous; exceptional; **Qi'tät** f (-/-en) abnormality; anomaly.

'**abnötigen** v/t. (sep., -ge-, h): j-m et. ~ extort s.th. from s.o.

'**ab|nutzen** v/t. and v/refl. (sep., -ge-, h), '**~nützen** v/t. and v/refl. (sep., -ge-, h) wear out; '**Qnutzung** f, '**Qnützung** f (-/-en) wear (and tear).

**Abonn|ement** [abɔn(ə)'mã:] n (-s/ -s) subscription (auf acc. to); '**~ent** [~'nɛnt] m (-en/-en) subscriber; **Qieren** [~'ni:rən] v/t. (no -ge-, h) subscribe to (newspaper); '**Qiert** adj. [~'ni:rt]: ~ sein auf (acc.) take in (newspaper, etc.).

**abordn|en** ['ap⁹-] v/t. (sep., -ge-, h) depute, delegate, Am. a. deputize; '**Qung** f delegation, deputation.

**Abort** [a'bɔrt] m (-[e]s/-e) lavatory, toilet.

'**ab|passen** v/t. (sep., -ge-, h) fit, adjust; watch for, wait for (s.o., opportunity); waylay s.o.; '**~pflücken** v/t. (sep., -ge-, h) pick, pluck (off), gather; '**~plagen** v/refl. (sep., -ge-, h) toil; '**~platzen** v/i. (sep., -ge-, sein) burst off; fly off; '**~prallen** v/i. (sep., -ge-, sein) rebound, bounce (off); ricochet; '**~putzen** v/t. (sep., -ge-, h) clean (off, up); wipe off; polish; '**~raten** v/t. (irr. raten, sep., -ge-, h): j-m ~ von dissuade s.o. from, advise s.o. against; '**~räumen** v/t. (sep., -ge-, h) clear (away); '**~reagieren** v/t. (sep., no -ge-, h) work off (one's anger, etc.); sich ~ F a. let off steam.

'**abrechn|en** (*sep.*, -ge-, h) **1.** *v/t.*
deduct; settle (*account*); **2.** *v/i.*: mit
*j-m* ~ settle with s.o.; *fig.* settle (ac-
counts) with s.o., F get even with
s.o.; '**2ung** *f* settlement (of ac-
counts); deduction, discount.
'**Abrede** *f*: in ~ *stellen* deny or question *s.th.*
'**abreib|en** *v/t.* (*irr. reiben, sep.*,
-ge-, h) rub off; rub down (*body*);
polish; '**2ung** *f* rub-down; F *fig.*
beating.
'**Abreise** *f* departure (*nach* for); '**2n**
*v/i.* (*sep.*, -ge-, *sein*) depart (*nach*
for), leave (for), start (for), set out
(for).
'**abreiß|en** (*irr. reißen, sep.*, -ge-)
**1.** *v/t.* (h) tear or pull off; pull down
(*building*); *s. abgerissen*; **2.** *v/i.*
(*sein*) break off; *button, etc.*: come
off; '**2kalender** *m* tear-off calendar.
'**ab|richten** *v/t.* (*sep.*, -ge-, h) train
(*animal*), break (*horse*) (in); '**~rie-
geln** *v/t.* (*sep.*, -ge-, h) bolt, bar
(*door*); block (*road*).
'**Abriß** *m* draft; summary, abstract;
(brief) outlines *pl.*; brief survey.
'**ab|rollen** (*sep.*, -ge-) *v/t.* (h) *and*
*v/i.* (*sein*) unroll; uncoil; unwind,
unreel; roll off; '**~rücken** (*sep.*,
-ge-) **1.** *v/t.* (h) move off or away
(*von* from), remove; **2.** ✕ *v/i.* (*sein*)
march off, withdraw.
'**Abruf** *m* call; recall; *auf* ~ ✝ on
call; '**2en** *v/t.* (*irr. rufen, sep.*, -ge-,
h) call off (a. ✝), call away; recall;
🖩 call out.
'**ab|runden** *v/t.* (*sep.*, -ge-, h) round
(off); '**~rupfen** *v/t.* (*sep.*, -ge-, h)
pluck off.
**abrupt** *adj.* [ap'rupt] abrupt.
'**abrüst|en** ✕ *v/i.* (*sep.*, -ge-, h)
disarm; '**2ung** ✕ *f* disarmament.
'**abrutschen** *v/i.* (*sep.*, -ge-, *sein*)
slip off, glide down; ✈ skid.
'**Absage** *f* cancellation; refusal; '**2n**
(*sep.*, -ge-, h) **1.** *v/t.* cancel, call off;
refuse; recall (*invitation*); **2.** *v/i.*
guest: decline; *j-m* ~ cancel one's
appointment with s.o.
'**absägen** *v/t.* (*sep.*, -ge-, h) saw off;
F *fig.* sack *s.o.*
'**Absatz** *m* stop, pause; *typ.* paragraph; ✝ sale; heel (*of shoe*); landing (*of stairs*); '**2fähig** ✝ *adj.* sale-
able, marketable; '**~markt** ✝ *m*
market, outlet; '**~möglichkeit** ✝ *f*
opening, outlet.
'**abschaben** *v/t.* (*sep.*, -ge-, h)
scrape off.
'**abschaff|en** *v/t.* (*sep.*, -ge-, h)
abolish; abrogate (*law*); dismiss
(*servants*); '**2ung** *f* (-/-en) abolition;
abrogation; dismissal.
'**ab|schälen** *v/t.* (*sep.*, -ge-, h) peel
(off), pare; bark (*tree*); '**~schalten**
*v/t.* (*sep.*, -ge-, h) switch off, turn
off or out; ≠ disconnect.
'**abschätz|en** *v/t.* (*sep.*, -ge-, h) esti-

mate; value; assess; '**2ung** *f* valuation; estimate; assessment.
'**Abschaum** *m* (-[e]s/no *pl.*) scum;
*fig. a.* dregs *pl.*
'**Abscheu** *m* (-[e]s/no *pl.*) horror
(*vor dat.* of), abhorrence (of); loathing (of); disgust (for).
'**abscheuern** *v/t.* (*sep.*, -ge-, h)
scour (off); wear out; chafe, abrade.
**abscheulich** *adj.* [ap'ɔʏlɪç] abominable, detestable, horrid; **2keit** *f*
(-/-en) detestableness; atrocity.
'**ab|schicken** *v/t.* (*sep.*,-ge-, h) send
off, dispatch; ✝ post, *esp. Am.*
mail; '**~schieben** *v/t.* (*irr. schieben,
sep.*,-ge-, h) push or shove off.
**Abschied** ['apʃiːt] *m* (-[e]s/ ~-e)
departure; parting, leave-taking,
farewell; dismissal, ✕ discharge;
~ *nehmen* take leave (*von* of), bid
farewell (to); *j-m den* ~ *geben*
dismiss s.o., ✕ discharge s.o.;
*s-n* ~ *nehmen* resign, retire; '**~s-
feier** *f* farewell party; '**~sgesuch** *n*
resignation.
'**ab|schießen** *v/t.* (*irr. schießen,
sep.*, -ge-, h) shoot off; shoot, discharge, fire (off) (*fire-arm*); launch
(*rocket*); kill; shoot; (shoot or bring)
down (*aircraft*); *s. Vogel*; '**~schin-
den** *v/refl.* (*irr. schinden, sep.*, -ge-,
h) toil and moil, slave, drudge; '**~
schirmen** *v/t.* (*sep.*, -ge-, h) shield
(*gegen* from); screen (*from*), screen
off (*from*); '**~schlachten** *v/t.* (*sep.*,
-ge-, h) slaughter, butcher.
'**Abschlag** ✝ *m* reduction (*in price*);
*auf* ~ on account; **2en** ['~ɡən] *v/t.*
(*irr. schlagen, sep.*, -ge-, h) knock
off, beat off, strike off; cut off
(*head*); refuse (*request*); repel (*attack*).
**abschlägig** *adj.* ['apʃleːɡɪç] negative; ~e Antwort refusal, denial.
'**Abschlagszahlung** *f* payment on
account; instal(l)ment.
'**abschleifen** *v/t.* (*irr. schleifen, sep.*,
-ge-, h) grind off; *fig.* refine, polish.
'**Abschlepp|dienst** *mot. m* towing
service, *Am. a.* wrecking service;
'**2en** *v/t.* (*sep.*, -ge-, h) drag off;
*mot.* tow off.
'**abschließen** (*irr. schließen, sep.*,
-ge-, h) **1.** *v/t.* lock (up); ⊕ seal
(up); conclude (*letter, etc.*); settle
(*account*); balance (*the books*); effect
(*insurance*); contract (*loan*); *fig.* seclude, isolate; e-n *Handel* ~ strike
a bargain; *sich* ~ seclude o.s.; **2.** *v/i.*
conclude; '**~d 1.** *adj.* concluding;
final; **2.** *adv.* in conclusion.
'**Abschluß** *m* settlement; conclusion; ⊕ seal; '**~prüfung** *f* final
examination, finals *pl.*, *Am. a.* graduation; '**~zeugnis** *n* leaving certificate; diploma.
'**ab|schmeicheln** *v/t.* (*sep.*, -ge-, h):
*j-m et.* ~ coax s.th. out of s.o.; '**~
schmelzen** (*irr. schmelzen, sep.*,

-ge-) v/t. (h) and v/i. (sein) melt (off); ⊕ fuse; '~schmieren ⊕ v/t. (sep., -ge-, h) lubricate, grease; '~schnallen v/t. (sep., -ge-, h) unbuckle; take off (ski, etc.); '~schneiden (irr. schneiden, sep., -ge-, h) 1. v/t. cut (off); slice off; den Weg ~ take a short cut; j-m das Wort ~ cut s.o. short; 2. v/i.: gut ~ come out or off well.

'Abschnitt m ⚹ segment; ✝ coupon; typ. section, paragraph; counterfoil, Am. a. stub (of cheque, etc.); stage (of journey); phase (of development); period (of time).

'ab|schöpfen v/t. (sep., -ge-, h) skim (off); '~schrauben v/t. (sep., -ge-, h) unscrew, screw off.

'abschrecken v/t. (sep., -ge-, h) deter (von from); scare away; '~d adj. deterrent; repulsive, forbidding.

'abschreib|en (irr. schreiben, sep., -ge-, h) 1. v/t. copy; write off (debt, etc.); plagiarize; in school: crib; 2. v/i. send a refusal; '2er m copyist; plagiarist; '2ung ✝ f (-/-en) depreciation.

'abschreiten v/t. (irr. schreiten, sep., -ge-, h) pace (off); e-e Ehrenwache ~ inspect a guard of hono(u)r.

'Abschrift f copy, duplicate.

'abschürf|en v/t. (sep., -ge-, h) graze, abrade (skin); '2ung f (-/-en) abrasion.

'Abschuß m discharge (of fire-arm); launching (of rocket); hunt. shooting; shooting down, downing (of aircraft); '~rampe f launching platform.

abschüssig adj. ['apʃysiç] sloping; steep.

'ab|schütteln v/t. (sep., -ge-, h) shake off (a. fig.); fig. get rid of; '~schwächen v/t. (sep., -ge-, h) weaken, lessen, diminish; '~schweifen v/i. (sep., -ge-, sein) deviate; fig. digress; '~schwenken v/i. (sep., -ge-, sein) swerve; ⚔ wheel; '~schwören v/i. (irr. schwören, sep., -ge-, h) abjure; forswear; '~segeln v/i. (sep., -ge-, sein) set sail, sail away.

abseh|bar adj. ['apze:baːr]: in ~er Zeit in the not-too-distant future; '~en (irr. sehen, sep., -ge-, h) 1. v/t. (fore)see; j-m et. ~ learn s.th. by observing s.o.; es abgesehen haben auf (acc.) have an eye on, be aiming at; 2. v/i.: ~ von refrain from; disregard.

abseits ['apzaits] 1. adv. aside, apart; football, etc.: off side; 2. prp. (gen.) aside from; off (the road).

'absend|en v/t. (irr. senden, sep., -ge-, h) send off, dispatch; ⍟ post, esp. Am. mail; '2er ⍟ m sender.

'absengen v/t. (sep., -ge-, h) singe off.

'Absenker ⚘ m (-s/-) layer, shoot.

'absetz|en (sep., -ge-, h) 1. v/t. set or put down, deposit; deduct (sum); take off (hat); remove, dismiss (official); depose, dethrone (king); drop, put down (passenger); ✝ sell (goods); typ. set up (in type); thea.: ein Stück ~ take off a play; 2. v/i. break off, stop, pause; '2ung f (-/-en) deposition; removal, dismissal.

'Absicht f (-/-en) intention, purpose, design; '2lich 1. adj. intentional; 2. adv. on purpose.

'absitzen (irr. sitzen, sep., -ge-) 1. v/i. (sein) rider: dismount; 2. v/t. (h) serve (sentence), F do (time).

absolut adj. [apzo'luːt] absolute.

absolvieren [apzɔl'viːrən] v/t. (no -ge-, h) absolve; complete (studies); get through, graduate from (school).

'absonder|n (sep., -ge-, h) separate; ⚕ secrete; sich ~ withdraw; '2ung f (-/-en) separation; ⚕ secretion.

ab|sorbieren [apzɔr'biːrən] v/t. (no -ge-, h) absorb; '~speisen fig. v/t. (sep., -ge-, h) put s.o. off.

abspenstig adj. ['apʃpenstiç]: ~ machen entice away (von from).

'absperr|en v/t. (sep., -ge-, h) lock; shut off; bar (way); block (road); turn off (gas, etc.); '2hahn m stopcock.

'ab|spielen v/t. (sep., -ge-, h) play (record, etc.); play back (tape recording); sich ~ happen, take place; '~sprechen (irr. sprechen, sep., -ge-, h) deny; arrange, agree; '~springen (irr. springen, sep., -ge-, sein) jump down or off; ⚔ jump, bale out, (Am. only) bail out; rebound.

'Absprung m jump; sports: take-off.

'abspülen v/t. (sep., -ge-, h) wash up; rinse.

'abstamm|en v/i. (sep., -ge-, sein) be descended (von from); gr. be derived (both: von from); '2ung f (-/-en) descent; gr. derivation.

'Abstand m distance; interval; ✝ compensation, indemnification; ~ nehmen von desist from.

ab|statten ['apʃtatən] v/t. (sep., -ge-, h): e-n Besuch ~ pay a visit; Dank ~ return or render thanks; '~stauben v/t. (sep., -ge-, h) dust.

'abstech|en (irr. stechen, sep., -ge-, h) 1. v/t. cut (sods); stick (pig, sheep, etc.); stab (animal); 2. v/i. contrast (von with); '2er m (-s/-) excursion, trip; detour.

'ab|stecken v/t. (sep., -ge-, h) unpin, undo; fit, pin (dress); surv. mark out; '~stehen v/i. (irr. stehen, sep., -ge-, h) stand off; stick out, protrude; s. abgestanden; '~steigen v/i. (irr. steigen, sep., -ge-, sein) descend; alight (*von* from) (*carriage*); get off, dismount (from) (*horse*); put up (*in dat.* at) (*hotel*); '**stellen** *v/t.* (*sep.*, *-ge-*, h) put down; stop, turn off (*gas, etc.*); park (*car*); *fig.* put an end to *s.th.*; '**stempeln** *v/t.* (*sep.*, *-ge-*, h) stamp; '**sterben** *v/i.* (*irr.* sterben, *sep.*, *-ge-*, sein) die off; *limb:* mortify.

**Abstieg** ['apʃti:k] *m* (-[e]s/-e) descent; *fig.* decline.

'**abstimm|en** (*sep.*, *-ge-*, h) 1. *v/i.* vote; 2. *v/t.* tune in (*radio*) (*auf*: harmonize; time; ✝ balance (*books*); '**Qung** *f* voting; vote; tuning.

**Abstinenzler** [apsti'nɛntslər] *m* (-s/-) teetotal(l)er.

'**abstoppen** (*sep.*, *-ge-*, h) 1. *v/t.* stop; slow down; *sports:* clock, time; 2. *v/i.* stop.

'**abstoßen** *v/t.* (*irr.* stoßen, *sep.*, *-ge-*, h) knock off; push off; clear off (*goods*); *fig.* repel; *sich die Hörner* ~ sow one's wild oats; '**d** *fig. adj.* repulsive.

**abstrakt** *adj.* [ap'strakt] abstract.

'**ab|streichen** *v/t.* (*irr.* streichen, *sep.*, *-ge-*, h) take *or* wipe off; '**streifen** *v/t.* (*sep.*, *-ge-*, h) strip off; take *or* pull off (*glove, etc.*); slip off (*dress*); wipe (*shoes*); '**streiten** *v/t.* (*irr.* streiten, *sep.*, *-ge-*, h) contest, dispute; deny.

'**Abstrich** *m* deduction, cut; ⚕ swab.

'**ab|stufen** *v/t.* (*sep.*, *-ge-*, h) graduate; gradate; '**stumpfen** (*sep.*, *-ge-*) 1. *v/t.* (h) blunt; *fig.* dull (*mind*); 2. *fig. v/i.* (sein) become dull.

'**Absturz** *m* fall; ✈ crash.

'**ab|stürzen** *v/i.* (*sep.*, *-ge-*, sein) fall down; ✈ crash; '**suchen** *v/t.* (*sep.*, *-ge-*, h) search (*nach* for); scour *or* comb (*area*) (for).

**absurd** *adj.* [ap'zurt] absurd, preposterous.

**Abszeß** ⚕ [aps'tsɛs] *m* (Abszesses/ Abszesse) abscess.

**Abt** [apt] *m* (-[e]s/=e) abbot.

'**abtakeln** ⚓ *v/t.* (*sep.*, *-ge-*, h) unrig, dismantle, strip.

**Abtei** [ap'taɪ] *f* (-/-en) abbey.

**Ab|'teil** 🚃 *n* compartment; '**Qteilen** *v/t.* (*sep.*, *-ge-*, h) divide; ⚗ partition off; '**teilung** *f* division; '**teilung** *f* department; ward (*of hospital*); compartment; ✗ detachment; '**teilungsleiter** *m* head of a department.

'**abtelegraphieren** *v/i.* (*sep.*, *no -ge-*, h) cancel a visit, *etc.* by telegram.

**Äbtissin** [ɛp'tisin] *f* (-/-nen) abbess.

'**ab|töten** *v/t.* (*sep.*, *-ge-*, h) destroy, kill (*bacteria, etc.*); '**tragen** *v/t.* (*irr.* tragen, *sep.*, *-ge-*, h) carry off; pull down (*building*); wear out (*garment*) (pay (*debt*).

**abträglich** *adj.* ['aptrɛːkliç] injurious, detrimental.

'**abtreib|en** (*irr.* treiben, *sep.*, *-ge-*) 1. *v/t.* (h) drive away *or* off; *ein Kind* ~ procure abortion; 2. ⚓, ✗ *v/i.* (sein) drift off; '**Qung** *f* (-/-en) abortion.

'**abtrennen** *v/t.* (*sep.*, *-ge-*, h) detach; separate; sever (*limbs, etc.*); take (*trimmings*) off (*dress*).

'**abtret|en** (*irr.* treten, *sep.*, *-ge-*) 1. *v/t.* (h) wear down (*heels*); wear out (*steps, etc.*); *fig.* cede, transfer; 2. *v/i.* (sein) retire, withdraw; resign; *thea.* make one's exit; '**Qer** *m* (-s/-) doormat; '**Qung** *f* (-/-en) cession, transfer.

'**ab|trocknen** (*sep.*, *-ge-*) 1. *v/t.* (h) dry (up); wipe (dry); *sich* ~ dry oneself, rub oneself down; 2. *v/i.* (sein) dry up, become dry; '**tropfen** *v/i.* (*sep.*, *-ge-*, sein) *liquid:* drip; *dishes, vegetables:* drain.

**abtrünnig** *adj.* ['aptrynıç] unfaithful, disloyal; *eccl.* apostate; '**Qe** ['**gə**] *m* (-n/-n) deserter; *eccl.* apostate.

'**ab|tun** *v/t.* (*irr.* tun, *sep.*, *-ge-*, h) take off; settle (*matter*); *fig.*: dispose of; dismiss; '**urteilen** ['ap'-] *v/i.* (*sep.*, *-ge-*, h) pass sentence on *s.o.*; '**wägen** *v/t.* (*irr.* wägen,] *sep.*, *-ge-*, h) weigh (out); *fig.* consider carefully; '**wälzen** *v/t.* (*sep.*, *-ge-*, h) roll away; *fig.* shift; '**wandeln** *v/t.* (*sep.*, *-ge-*, h) vary, modify; '**wandern** *v/i.* (*sep.*, *-ge-*, sein) wander away; migrate (*von* from).

'**Abwandlung** *f* modification, variation.

'**abwarten** (*sep.*, *-ge-*, h) 1. *v/t.* wait for, await; *s-e Zeit* ~ bide one's time; 2. *v/i.* wait.

**abwärts** *adv.* ['apvɛrts] down, downward(s).

'**abwaschen** *v/t.* (*irr.* waschen, *sep.*, *-ge-*, h) wash (off, away); bathe; sponge off; wash up (*dishes, etc.*).

'**abwechseln** (*sep.*, *-ge-*, h) 1. *v/t.* vary; alternate; 2. *v/i.* vary; alternate; *mit j-m* ~ take turns; '**d** *adj.* alternate.

'**Abwechs(e)lung** *f* (-/-en) change; alternation; variation; diversion; *zur* ~ for a change.

'**Abweg** *m*: *auf* ~*e geraten* go astray; '**Qig** *adj.* ['**gıç**] erroneous, wrong.

'**Abwehr** *f* defen|ce, *Am.* -se; warding off (*of thrust, etc.*); '**dienst** ✗ *m* counter-espionage service; '**Qen** *v/t.* (*sep.*, *-ge-*, h) ward off; avert; repulse, repel, ward off (*attack, enemy*).

'**abweich|en** *v/i.* (*irr.* weichen, *sep.*, *-ge-*, sein) deviate (*von* from), swerve (from); differ (from); *compass-needle:* deviate; '**Qung** *f* (-/-en) deviation; difference; deflexion, (*Am. only*) deflection.

'**abweiden** *v/t.* (*sep.*, *-ge-*, h) graze.

'**abweis|en** *v/t.* (*irr.* weisen, *sep.*, *-ge-*, h) refuse, reject; repel (*a.* ✗);

rebuff; '～end *adj.* unfriendly, cool; '2ung *f* refusal, rejection; repulse (*a.* ✗); rebuff.

'ab|wenden *v/t.* ([*irr.* wenden,] *sep.*, -ge-, *h*) turn away; avert (*disaster, etc.*); parry (*thrust*); sich ～ turn away (von from); '～werfen *v/t.* (*irr.* werfen, *sep.*, -ge-, *h*) throw off; ✗ drop (*bombs*); shed, cast (*skin, etc.*); shed (*leaves*); yield (*profit*).

'abwert|en *v/t.* (*sep.*, -ge-, *h*) devaluate; '2ung *f* devaluation.

abwesen|d *adj.* ['apvɛːzənt] absent; '2heit *f* (-/✗ -en) absence.

'ab|wickeln *v/t.* (*sep.*, -ge-, *h*) unwind, unreel, wind off; transact (*business*); '～wiegen *v/t.* (*irr.* wiegen, *sep.*, -ge-, *h*) weigh (out) (*goods*); '～wischen *v/t.* (*sep.*, -ge-, *h*) wipe (off); '～würgen *v/t.* (*sep.*, -ge-, *h*) strangle, throttle, choke; *mot.* stall; '～zahlen *v/t.* (*sep.*, -ge-, *h*) pay off; pay by instal(l)ments; '～zählen *v/t.* (*sep.*, -ge-, *h*) count (out, over).

'Abzahlung *f* instal(l)ment, payment on account; '～sgeschäft *n* hire-purchase.

'abzapfen *v/t.* (*sep.*, -ge-, *h*) tap, draw off.

'Abzehrung *f* (-/-en) wasting away, emaciation; 🕮 consumption.

'Abzeichen *n* badge; ✗ marking.

'ab|zeichnen *v/t.* (*sep.*, -ge-, *h*) copy, draw; mark off; initial; tick off; sich ～ gegen stand out against; '～ziehen (*irr.* ziehen, *sep.*, -ge-) 1. *v/t.* (*h*) take off, remove; & subtract; strip (*bed*); bottle (*wine*); *phot.* print (*film*); *typ.* pull (*proof*); take out (*key*); das Fell ～ skin (*animal*); 2. *v/i.* (*sein*) go away; ✗ march off; *smoke:* escape; *thunderstorm, clouds:* move on.

'Abzug *m* departure; ✗ withdrawal, retreat; ⊕ drain; outlet; deduction (*of sum*); *phot.* print; *typ.* proof (-sheet).

abzüglich *prp.* (*gen.*) ['aptsyːkliç] less, minus, deducting.

'Abzugsrohr *n* waste-pipe.

abzweig|en ['aptsvaɪɡən] (*sep.*, -ge-) 1. *v/t.* (*h*) branch; divert (*money*); sich ～ branch off; 2. *v/i.* (*sein*) branch off; '2ung *f* (-/-en) branch; road-junction.

ach *int.* [ax] oh!, ah!, alas!; ～ so! oh, I see!

Achse ['aksə] *f* (-/-n) axis; ⊕: axle; shaft; axle(-tree) (*of carriage*); auf der ～ on the move.

Achsel ['aksəl] *f* (-/-n) shoulder; die ～n zucken shrug one's shoulders; '～höhle *f* armpit.

acht[1] [axt] 1. *adj.* eight; in ～ Tagen today week, this day week; vor ～ Tagen a week ago; 2. 2 *f* (-/-en) (figure) eight.

Acht[2] [～] *f* (-/*no pl.*) ban, outlawry; attention; außer acht lassen dis-

regard; sich in acht nehmen be careful; be on one's guard (vor j-m or et. against s.o. or s.th.); look out (for s.o. or s.th.).

'achtbar *adj.* respectable.

'achte *adj.* eighth; 2l ['～əl] *n* (-s/-) eighth (part).

'achten (ge-, *h*) 1. *v/t.* respect, esteem; regard; 2. *v/i.*: ～ auf (*acc.*) pay attention to; achte auf meine Worte mark or mind my words; darauf ～ daß see to it that, take care that.

ächten ['ɛçtən] *v/t.* (ge-, *h*) outlaw, proscribe; ban.

'Achter *m* (-s/-) *rowing:* eight.

achtfach *adj.* ['axtfax] eightfold.

'achtgeben *v/i.* (*irr.* geben, *sep.*, -ge-, *h*) be careful; pay attention (auf *acc.* to); take care (of); gib acht! look or watch out!, be careful!

'achtlos *adj.* inattentive, careless, heedless.

Acht'stundentag *m* eight-hour day.

'Achtung *f* (-/*no pl.*) attention; respect, esteem, regard; ～! look out!, ✗ attention!; ～ Stufe! mind the step!; 2svoll *adj.* respectful.

'achtzehn *adj.* eighteen; ～te *adj.* ['～tə] eighteenth.

achtzig *adj.* ['axtsiç] eighty; '～ste *adj.* eightieth.

ächzen ['ɛçtsən] *v/i.* (ge-, *h*) groan, moan.

Acker ['akər] *m* (-s/-) field; '～bau *m* agriculture; farming; '2bautreibend *adj.* agricultural, farming; '～geräte *n/pl.* farm implements *pl.*; '～land *n* arable land; '2n *v/t.* and *v/i.* (ge-, *h*) plough, till, *Am.* plow.

add|ieren [a'diːrən] *v/t.* (*no* -ge-, *h*) add (up); 2tion [adi'tsjoːn] *f* (-/-en) addition, adding up.

Adel ['aːdəl] *m* (-s/*no pl.*) nobility, aristocracy; '2ig *adj.* noble; '2n *v/t.* (ge-, *h*) ennoble (*a. fig.*); *Brt.* knight, raise to the peerage; '～stand *m* nobility; aristocracy; *Brt.* peerage.

Ader ['aːdər] *f* (-/-n) ✗, *wood, etc.*: vein; *anat.*: vein; artery; zur ～ lassen bleed.

adieu *int.* [a'djøː] good-bye, farewell, adieu, F cheerio.

Adjektiv *gr.* ['atjɛktiːf] *n* (-s/-ə) adjective.

Adler *orn.* ['aːdlər] *m* (-s/-) eagle; '～nase *f* aquiline nose.

adlig *adj.* ['aːdliç] noble; 2e ['～ɡə] *m* (-n/-n) nobleman, peer.

Admiral ⚓ [atmi'raːl] *m* (-s/-e, ～e) admiral.

adopt|ieren [adɔp'tiːrən] *v/t.* (*no* -ge-, *h*) adopt; 2ivkind [～'tiːf-] *n* adopted child.

Adressat [adrɛ'saːt] *m* (-en/-en) addressee; consignee (*of goods*).

Adreßbuch [a'drɛs-] *n* directory.

**Adress|e** [a'drɛsə] f (-/-n) address; direction; per ~ care of (abbr. c/o); **2ieren** [~si:rən] v/t. (no -ge-, h) address, direct; ✝ consign; falsch ~ misdirect.

**adrett** adj. [a'drɛt] smart, neat.

**Adverb** gr. [at'vɛrp] n (-s/-ien) adverb.

**Affäre** [a'fɛ:rə] f (-/-n) (love) affair; matter, business, incident.

**Affe** zo. ['afə] m (-n/-n) ape; monkey.

**Affekt** [a'fɛkt] m (-[e]s/-e) emotion; passion; **2iert** adj. [~'ti:rt] affected. **'affig** F adj. foppish; affected; silly.

**Afrikan|er** [afri'ka:nər] m (-s/-) African; **2isch** adj. African.

**After** anat. ['aftər] m (-s/-) anus.

**Agent** [a'gɛnt] m (-en/-en) agent; broker; pol. (secret) agent; **~ur** [~'tu:r] f (-/-en) agency.

**aggressiv** adj. [agrɛ'si:f] aggressive.

**Agio** ✝ ['a:ʒio] n (-s/no pl.) agio, premium.

**Agitator** [agi'ta:tɔr] m (-s/-en) agitator. [brooch.\]

**Agraffe** [a'grafə] f (-/-n) clasp;\]

**agrarisch** adj. [a'gra:riʃ] agrarian.

**Ägypt|er** [ɛ:'gyptər] m (-s/-) Egyptian; **2isch** adj. Egyptian.

**ah** int. [a:] ah!

**aha** int. ['a:ha] aha!, I see!

**Ahle** ['a:lə] f (-/-n) awl, pricker; punch.

**Ahn** [a:n] m (-[e]s/-s, -en/-en) ancestor; **~en** pl. a. forefathers pl.

**ähneln** ['ɛ:nəln] v/i. (ge-, h) be like, resemble.

**ahnen** ['a:nən] v/t. (ge-, h) have a presentiment of or that; suspect; divine.

**ähnlich** adj. ['ɛ:nliç] like, resembling; similar (dat. to); iro.: das sieht ihm ~ that's just like him; **'2keit** f (-/-en) likeness, resemblance; similarity.

**Ahnung** ['a:nuŋ] f (-/-en) presentiment; foreboding; notion, idea; **'2slos** adj. unsuspecting; **'2svoll** adj. full of misgivings.

**Ahorn** ♀ ['a:hɔrn] m (-s/-e) maple (-tree).

**Ähre** ♀ ['ɛ:rə] f (-/-n) ear, head; spike; **~n lesen** glean.

**Akademi|e** [akadə'mi:] f (-/-n) academy, society; **~ker** [~'de:mikər] m (-s/-) university man, esp. Am. university graduate; **2sch** adj. [~'de:miʃ] academic.

**Akazie** ♀ [a'ka:tsjə] f (-/-n) acacia.

**akklimatisieren** [aklimati'zi:rən] v/t. and v/refl. (no -ge-, h) acclimatize, Am. acclimate.

**Akkord** [a'kɔrt] m (-[e]s/-e) ♪ chord; ✝: contract; agreement; composition; im ~ ✝ by the piece or job; **~arbeit** f piece-work; **~arbeiter** m piece-worker; **~lohn** m piece-wages pl.

**akkredit|ieren** [akredi'ti:rən] v/t. (no -ge-, h) accredit (bei to); **2iv** [~'ti:f] n (-s/-e) credentials pl.; ✝ letter of credit.

**Akku** F ⊕ ['aku] m (-s/-s), **~mulator** ⊕ [~mu'la:tɔr] m (-s/-en) accumulator, (storage-)battery.

**Akkusativ** gr. ['akuzati:f] m (-s/-e) accusative (case). [acrobat.\]

**Akrobat** [akro'ba:t] m (-en/-en)\]

**Akt** [akt] m (-[e]s/-e) act(ion), deed; thea. act; paint. nude.

**Akte** ['aktə] f (-/-n) document, deed; file; **~n** pl. records pl., papers pl.; deeds pl., documents pl.; files pl.; zu den ~n to be filed; zu den ~n legen file; **'~ndeckel** m folder; **'~nmappe** f, **'~ntasche** f portfolio; briefcase; **'~nzeichen** n reference or file number.

**Aktie** ✝ ['aktsjə] f (-/-n) share, Am. stock; **~n besitzen** hold shares, Am. hold stock; **'~nbesitz** m shareholdings pl., Am. stockholdings pl.; **'~ngesellschaft** f appr. joint-stock company, Am. (stock) corporation; **'~nkapital** n share-capital, Am. capital stock.

**Aktion** [ak'tsjo:n] f (-/-en) action; activity; pol., etc.: campaign, drive; ✕ operation; **~är** [~'nɛ:r] m (-s/-e) shareholder, Am. stockholder.

**aktiv** adj. [ak'ti:f] active.

**Aktiva** ✝ [ak'ti:va] n/pl. assets pl.; **~posten** [~'ti:f-] m asset (a. fig.).

**aktuell** adj. [aktu'ɛl] current, present-day, up-to-date, topical.

**Akust|ik** [a'kustik] f (-/no pl.) acoustics sg., pl.; **2isch** adj. acoustic.

**akut** adj. [a'ku:t] acute.

**Akzent** [ak'tsɛnt] m (-[e]s/-e) accent; stress; **2uieren** [~u'i:rən] v/t. (no -ge-, h) accent(uate); stress.

**Akzept** ✝ [ak'tsɛpt] n (-[e]s/-e) acceptance; **~ant** [~'tant] m (-en/-en) acceptor; **2ieren** [~'ti:rən] v/t. (no -ge-, h) accept.

**Alarm** [a'larm] m (-[e]s/-e) alarm; ~ blasen or schlagen ✕ sound or give the alarm; **~bereitschaft** f: in ~ sein stand by; **2ieren** [~'mi:rən] v/t. (no -ge-, h) alarm.

**Alaun** 🜍 [a'laun] m (-[e]s/-e) alum.

**albern** adj. ['albərn] silly, foolish.

**Album** ['album] n (-s/Alben) album.

**Alge** ♀ ['algə] f (-/-n) alga, seaweed.

**Algebra** ⩜ ['algebra] f (-/no pl.) algebra.

**Alibi** 🕮 ['a:libi] n (-s/-s) alibi.

**Alimente** 🕮 [ali'mɛntə] pl. alimony.

**Alkohol** ['alkohol] m (-s/-e) alcohol; **'2frei** adj. non-alcoholic, esp. Am. soft; **~es Restaurant** temperance restaurant; **~iker** [~'ho:likər] m (-s/-) alcoholic; **2isch** adj. [~'ho:liʃ] alcoholic; **'~schmuggler** m liquor-smuggler, Am. bootlegger; **'~verbot** n prohibition; **'~vergiftung** f alcoholic poisoning.

**all¹** [al] **1.** *pron.* all; ~e everybody; ~es in ~em on the whole; vor ~em first of all; **2.** *adj.* all; every, each; any; ~e beide both of them; auf ~e Fälle in any case, at all events; ~e Tage every day; ~e zwei Minuten every two minutes.

**All²** [~] *n* (-s/no *pl.*) the universe.

**'alle** F *adj.* all gone; ~ werden come to an end; *supplies, etc.*: run out.

**Allee** [a'le:] *f* (-/-n) avenue; (tree-lined) walk.

**allein** [a'laɪn] **1.** *adj.* alone; single; unassisted; **2.** *adv.* alone; only; **3.** *cj.* yet, only, but, however; **2be-rechtigung** *f* exclusive right; **2be-sitz** *m* exclusive possession; **2herr-scher** *m* absolute monarch, auto-crat; dictator; ~ig *adj.* only, ex-clusive, sole; **2sein** *n* loneliness, solitariness, solitude; ~stehend *adj. p.:* alone in the world; single; *building, etc.:* isolated, detached; **2verkauf** *m* exclusive sale; monop-oly; **2vertreter** *m* sole represent-ative *or* agent; **2vertrieb** *m* sole distributors *pl.*

**allemal** *adv.* ['alə'ma:l] always; ein für ~ once (and) for all.

**'allen|falls** *adv.* if need be; pos-sibly, perhaps; at best.

**allenthalben** † *adv.* ['alənt'halbən] everywhere.

**'aller|'best** *adj.* best ... of all, very best; ~dings *adv.* ['~'dɪŋs] indeed; to be sure; ~! certainly!, *Am.* F sure!; '~'erst **1.** *adj.* first ... of all, very first; foremost; **2.** *adv.:* zu ~ first of all.

**Allergie** ⚕ [alɛr'gi:] *f* (-/-n) allergy.

**'aller|'hand** *adj.* of all kinds *or* sorts; F das ist ja ~! F I say!; *sl.* that's the limit!; '2'heiligen *n* (-/no *pl.*) All Saints' Day; ~lei *adj.* ['~'laɪ] of all kinds *or* sorts; '2'lei *n* (-s/-s) medley; '~'letzt **1.** *adj.* last of all, very last; latest (*news, fashion, etc.*); **2.** *adv.:* zu ~ last of all; '~'liebst **1.** *adj.* dearest of all; (most) lovely; **2.** *adv.:* am ~en best of all; '~'meist **1.** *adj.* most; **2.** *adv.:* am ~en mostly; chiefly; '~'nächst *adj.* very next; '~'neu(e)st *adj.* the very latest; '2'seelen *n* (-/no *pl.*) All Souls' Day; '~'seits *adv.* on all sides; universally; '~'wenigst *adv.:* am ~en least of all.

**'alle|'samt** *adv.* one and all, all together; '~'zeit *adv.* always, at all times, for ever.

**'all|'gegenwärtig** *adj.* omnipresent, ubiquitous; '~'ge'mein **1.** *adj.* general; common; universal; **2.** *adv.:* im ~en in general, generally; '2ge-'meinheit *f* (-/no *pl.*) generality; universality; general public; 2'heil-mittel *n* panacea, cure-all (*both a. fig.*).

**Allianz** [ali'ants] *f* (-/-en) alliance.

**alli'ier|en** *v/refl.* (*no -ge-, h*) ally o.s. (*mit* to, with); 2te *m* (-n/-n) ally.

**'all|'jährlich 1.** *adj.* annual; **2.** *adv.* annually, every year; '2macht *f* (-/no *pl.*) omnipotence; ~'mächtig *adj.* omnipotent, almighty; ~'mäh-lich [~'mɛ:liç] **1.** *adj.* gradual; **2.** *adv.* gradually, by degrees.

**Allopathie** ⚕ [alopa'ti:] allopathy.

**all|'seitig** *adj.* ['al'zaɪtiç] universal; all-round; '2strom ⚡ *m* (-[e]s/no *pl.*) alternating current/direct cur-rent (*abbr.* A.C./D.C.); '2tag *m* workday; week-day; *fig.* everyday life, daily routine; ~'täglich *adj.* daily; *fig.* common, trivial; '2tags-leben *n* (-s/no *pl.*) everyday life; '~'wissend *adj.* omniscient; '2'wis-senheit *f* (-/no *pl.*) omniscience; '~'wöchentlich *adj.* weekly; '~zu *adv.* (much) too; '~zu'viel *adv.* too much.

**Alm** [alm] *f* (-/-en) Alpine pasture, alp.

**Almosen** ['almo:zən] *n* (-s/-) alms; ~ *pl.* alms *pl.*, charity.

**Alp|druck** ['alp-] *m* (-[e]s/~e), '~drücken *n* (-s/no *pl.*) night-mare.

**Alpen** ['alpən] *pl.* Alps *pl.*

**Alphabet** [alfa'be:t] *n* (-[e]s/-e) alphabet; 2isch *adj.* alphabetic(al).

**'Alptraum** *m* nightmare.

**als** *cj.* [als] than; as, like; (in one's capacity) as; but, except; *temporal:* after, when; as; ~ ob as if, as though; so viel ~ as much as; er ist zu dumm, ~ daß er es verstehen könnte he is too stupid to under-stand it; ~'bald *adv.* immediately; ~'dann *adv.* then.

**also** ['alzo:] **1.** *adv.* thus, so; **2.** *cj.* therefore, so, consequently; na ~! there you are!

**alt¹** *adj.* [alt] old; aged; ancient, antique; stale; second-hand.

**Alt²** ♪ [~] *m* (-s/-e) alto, contralto.

**Altar** [al'ta:r] *m* (-[e]s/~e) altar.

**Alteisen** ['alt?-] *n* scrap-iron.

**'Alte** (-n/-n) **1.** *m* old man; F: der ~ the governor; *hist.:* die ~n *pl.* the ancients *pl.*; **2.** *f* old woman.

**Alter** *n* (-s/-) age; old age; seniority; er ist in meinem ~ he is my age; von mittlerem ~ middle-aged.

**älter** *adj.* ['ɛltər] older; senior; der ~e Bruder the elder brother.

**altern** ['altərn] *v/i.* (ge-, *h*, sein) grow old, age.

**Alternative** [altɛrna'ti:və] *f* (-/-n) alternative; keine ~ haben have no choice.

**'Alters|grenze** *f* age-limit; retire-ment age; '~heim *n* old people's home; '~rente *f* old-age pension; '2schwach *adj.* decrepit; senile; '~schwäche *f* decrepitude; '~ver-sorgung *f* old-age pension.

**Altertum** ['altərtu:m] *n* 1. (-s/no *pl.*) antiquity; 2. (-s/=er) *mst Altertümer pl.* antiquities *pl.*

**altertümlich** *adj.* ['altərty:mliç] ancient, antique, archaic.

**'Altertums|forscher** *m* arch(a)eologist; **'~kunde** *f* arch(a)eology.

**ältest** *adj.* ['ɛltəst] oldest; eldest (*sister, etc.*); earliest (*recollections*); **ℒe** *m* (-n/-n) elder; senior; *mein ~r* my eldest (son).

**Altistin** *♪* [al'tistin] *f* (-/-nen) altosinger, contralto-singer.

**'altklug** *adj.* precocious, forward.

**ältlich** *adj.* ['ɛltliç] elderly, oldish.

**'Alt|material** *n* junk, scrap; salvage; **'~meister** *m* doyen, dean, F Grand Old Man (*a. sports*); *sports*: ex-champion; **'ℒmodisch** *adj.* old-fashioned; **'~papier** *n* waste paper; **'~philologe** *m* classical philologist *or* scholar; **'~stadt** *f* old town *or* city; **'~warenhändler** *m* second-hand dealer; **~'weibersommer** *m* Indian summer; gossamer.

**Aluminium** ⚗ [alu'mi:njum] *n* (-s/no *pl.*) aluminium, *Am.* aluminum.

**am** *prp.* [am] = *an dem*.

**Amateur** [ama'tø:r] *m* (-s/-e) amateur.

**Amboß** ['ambɔs] *m* (*Ambosses/Ambosse*) anvil.

**ambulan|t** ♂ *adj.* [ambu'lant]: ~ Behandelter out-patient; **ℒz** [~ts] *f* (-/-en) ambulance.

**Ameise** *zo.* [a'maizə] *f* (-/-n) ant; **'~haufen** *m* ant-hill.

**Amerikan|er** [ameri'ka:nər] *m* (-s/-), **~erin** *f* (-/-nen) American; **ℒisch** *adj.* American.

**Amme** ['amə] *f* (-/-n) (wet-)nurse.

**Amnestie** [amnɛs'ti:] *f* (-/-n) amnesty, general pardon.

**Amor** ['a:mɔr] *m* (-s/no *pl.*) Cupid.

**Amortis|ation** [amɔrtiza'tsjo:n] *f* (-/-en) amortization, redemption; **ℒieren** [~'zi:rən] *v/t.* (*no -ge-, h*) amortize, redeem; pay off.

**Ampel** ['ampəl] *f* (-/-n) hanging lamp; traffic light.

**Amphibie** *zo.* [am'fi:bjə] *f* (-/-n) amphibian.

**Ampulle** [am'pulə] *f* (-/-n) ampoule.

**Amput|ation** [amputa'tsjo:n] *f* (-/-en) amputation; **ℒieren** ♂ [~'ti:rən] *v/t.* (*no -ge-, h*) amputate; **~ierte** *m* (-n/-n) amputee.

**Amsel** *orn.* ['amzəl] *f* (-/-n) blackbird.

**Amt** [amt] *n* (-[e]s/=er) office; post; charge; office, board; official duty, function; (telephone) exchange; **ℒieren** [~'ti:rən] *v/i.* (*no -ge-, h*) hold office; officiate; **ℒlich** *adj.* official; **'~mann** *m* district administrator; *hist.* bailiff.

**'Amts|arzt** *m* medical officer of health; **'~befugnis** *f* competence, authority; **'~bereich** *m*, **'~bezirk** *m* jurisdiction; **'~blatt** *n* gazette; **'~eid** *m* oath of office; **'~einführung** *f* inauguration; **'~führung** *f* administration; **'~geheimnis** *n* official secret; **'~gericht** *n appr.* district court; **'~geschäfte** *n/pl.* official duties *pl.*; **'~gewalt** *f* (official) authority; **'~handlung** *f* official act; **'~niederlegung** *f* (-/~-en) resignation; **'~richter** *m appr.* district court judge; **'~siegel** *n* official seal; **'~vorsteher** *m* head official.

**Amulett** [amu'lɛt] *n* (-[e]s/-e) amulet, charm.

**amüs|ant** *adj.* [amy'zant] amusing, entertaining; **~ieren** [~'zi:rən] *v/t.* (*no -ge-, h*) amuse, entertain; *sich ~* amuse *or* enjoy o.s., have a good time.

**an** [an] 1. *prp.* (*dat.*) at; on, upon; in; against; to; by, near, close to; ~ *der Themse* on the Thames; ~ *der Wand* on *or* against the wall; *es ist ~ dir zu inf.* it is up to you to *inf.*; *am Leben* alive; *am 1. März* on March 1st; *am Morgen* in the morning; 2. *prp.* (*acc.*) to; on; on to; at; against; about; *bis ~* as far as, up to; 3. *adv.* on; *von heute ~* from this day forth, from today; *von nun or jetzt ~* from now on.

**analog** *adj.* [ana'lo:k] analogous (*dat. or zu* to, with).

**Analphabet** [an(⁹)alfa'be:t] *m* (-en/-en) illiterate (person).

**Analys|e** [ana'ly:zə] *f* (-/-n) analysis; **ℒieren** [~'zi:rən] *v/t.* (*no -ge-, h*) analy|se, *Am.* -ze.

**Anämie** [anɛ'mi:] *f* (-/-n) an(a)emia.

**Ananas** ['ananas] *f* (-/-, -se) pineapple.

**Anarchie** [anar'çi:] *f* (-/-n) anarchy.

**Anatom|ie** [anato'mi:] *f* (-/no *pl.*) anatomy; **ℒisch** *adj.* [~'to:miʃ] anatomical.

**'anbahnen** *v/t.* (*sep., -ge-, h*) pave the way for, initiate; open up; *sich ~* be opening up.

**'Anbau** *m* 1. ✗ (-[e]s/no *pl.*) cultivation; 2. △ (-[e]s/-ten) outbuilding, annex, extension, addition; **'ℒen** *v/t.* (*sep., -ge-, h*) ✗ cultivate, grow; △ add (*an acc.* to); **'~fläche** ✗ *f* arable land.

**'anbehalten** *v/t.* (*irr. halten, sep., no -ge-, h*) keep (*garment, etc.*) on.

**an'bei** ✝ *adv.* enclosed.

**'an|beißen** (*irr. beißen, sep., -ge-, h*) 1. *v/t.* bite into; 2. *v/i. fish:* bite; **'~bellen** *v/t.* (*sep., -ge-, h*) bark at; **~berau men** ['~bəraumən] *v/t.* (*sep., no -ge-, h*) appoint, fix; **'~beten** *v/t.* (*sep., -ge-, h*) adore, worship.

**'Anbetracht** *m: in ~* considering, in consideration of.

'anbetteln v/t. (sep., -ge-, h) beg from, solicit alms of.

'Anbetung f (-/%-en) worship, adoration; ~swürdig adj. adorable.

'an|bieten v/t. (irr. bieten, sep., -ge-, h) offer; '~binden v/t. (irr. binden, sep., -ge-, h) bind, tie (up); ~ an (dat., acc.) tie to; s. angebunden; '~blasen v/t. (irr. blasen, sep., -ge-, h) blow at or (up)on.

'Anblick m look; view; sight, aspect; '2en v/t. (sep., -ge-, h) look at; glance at; view; eye.

'an|blinzeln v/t. (sep., -ge-, h) wink at; '~brechen (irr. brechen, sep., -ge-) 1. v/t. (h) break into (provisions, etc.); open (bottle, etc.); 2. v/i. (sein) begin; day: break, dawn; '~brennen (irr. brennen, sep., -ge-) 1. v/t. (h) set on fire; light (cigar, etc.); 2. v/i. (sein) catch fire; burn; '~bringen v/t. (irr. bringen, sep., -ge-, h) bring; fix (an dat. to), attach (to); place; ✝ dispose of (goods); lodge (complaint); s. angebracht.

'Anbruch m (-[e]s/no pl.) beginning; break (of day).

'anbrüllen v/t. (sep., -ge-, h) roar at.

Andacht f ['andaxt] f (-/-en) devotion(s pl.); prayers pl.

andächtig adj. ['andɛçtiç] devout.

'andauern v/i. (sep., -ge-, h) last, continue, go on.

'Andenken n (-s/-) memory, remembrance; keepsake, souvenir; zum ~ an (acc.) in memory of.

ander adj. ['andər] other; different; next; opposite; am ~en Tag (on) the next day; e-n Tag um den ~en every other day; ein ~er Freund another friend; nichts ~es nothing else.

andererseits adv. ['andərərʦaɪts] on the other hand.

ändern ['ɛndərn] v/t. (ge-, h) alter; change; ich kann es nicht ~ I can't help it; sich ~ alter; change.

'andern'falls adv. otherwise, else.

anders adv. ['andərs] otherwise; differently (als from); else; j. ~ somebody else; ich kann nicht ~, ich muß weinen I cannot help crying; ~ werden change.

'ander'seits adv. s. andererseits.

'anders'wo adv. elsewhere.

anderthalb adj. ['andərt'halp] one and a half.

'Änderung f (-/-en) change, alteration.

ander|wärts adv. ['andər'vɛrts] elsewhere; '~weitig 1. adj. other; 2. adv. otherwise.

'andeut|en v/t. (sep., -ge-, h) indicate; hint; intimate; imply; suggest; '2ung f intimation; hint; suggestion.

'Andrang m rush; ✳ congestion.

andre adj. ['andrə] s. andere.

'andrehen v/t. (sep., -ge-, h) turn on (gas, etc.); ✦ switch on (light).

'androh|en v/t. (sep., -ge-, h) j-m et. ~ threaten s.o. with s.th.; '2ung f threat.

aneignen ['an?-] v/refl. (sep., -ge-, h) appropriate; acquire; adopt; seize; usurp.

aneinander adv. [an?aɪ'nandər] together; ~geraten v/i. (irr. raten, sep., no -ge-, sein) clash (mit with).

anekeln ['an?-] v/t. (sep., -ge-, h) disgust, sicken.

Anerbieten ['an?-] n (-s/-) offer.

anerkannt adj. ['an?-] acknowledged, recognized.

anerkenn|en ['an?-] v/t. (irr. kennen, sep., no -ge-, h) acknowledge (als as), recognize; appreciate; own (child); hono(u)r (bill); '2ung f (-/-en) acknowledgement; recognition; appreciation.

'anfahr|en (irr. fahren, sep., -ge-) 1. v/i. (sein) start; ✗ descend; angefahren kommen drive up; 2. v/t. (h) run into; carry, convey; j-n ~ let fly at s.o.; '2t f approach; drive.

'Anfall m fit, attack; '2en (irr. fallen, sep., -ge-) 1. v/t. (h) attack; assail; 2. v/i. (sein) accumulate; money: accrue.

anfällig adj. ['anfeliç] susceptible (für to); prone to (diseases, etc.).

'Anfang m beginning, start, commencement; ~ Mai at the beginning of May, early in May; '2en v/t. and v/i. (irr. fangen, sep., -ge-, h) begin, start, commence.

Anfäng|er ['anfɛŋər] m (-s/-) beginner; '2lich 1. adj. initial; 2. adv. in the beginning.

anfangs adv. ['anfaŋs] in the beginning; '2buchstabe m initial (letter); großer ~ capital letter; 2gründe ['~gryndə] m/pl. elements pl.

'anfassen (sep., -ge-, h) 1. v/t. seize; touch; handle; 2. v/i. lend a hand.

anfecht|bar adj. ['anfɛçtbaːr] contestable; '~en v/t. (irr. fechten, sep., -ge-, h) contest, dispute; ✞ avoid (contract); '2ung f (-/-en) contestation; ✞ avoidance; fig. temptation.

an|fertigen ['anfɛrtigən] v/t. (sep., -ge-, h) make, manufacture; '~feuchten v/t. (sep., -ge-, h) moisten, wet, damp; '~feuern v/t. (sep., -ge-, h) fire, heat; sports: cheer; fig. encourage; '~flehen v/t. (sep., -ge-, h) implore; '~fliegen ✈ v/t. (irr. fliegen, sep., -ge-, h) approach, head for (airport, etc.); '2flug m ✈ approach (flight); fig. touch, tinge.

'anforder|n v/t. (sep., -ge-, h) demand; request; claim; '2ung f demand; request; claim.

'Anfrage f inquiry; '2n v/i. (sep., -ge-, h) ask (bei j-m s.o.); inquire (bei j-m nach et. of s.o. about s.th.).

**an|freunden** ['anfrɔyndən] *v/refl.* (*sep.*, -ge-, *h*): sich ~ *mit* make friends with; **'~frieren** *v/i.* (*irr.* frieren, *sep.*, -ge-, *sein*) freeze on (*an dat. or acc.* to); **'~fügen** *v/t.* (*sep.*, -ge-, *h*) join, attach (*an acc.* to); **'~fühlen** *v/t.* (*sep.*, -ge-, *h*) feel, touch; sich ~ feel.

**Anfuhr** ['anfu:r] *f* (-/-en) conveyance, carriage.

**'anführ|en** *v/t.* (*sep.*, -ge-, *h*) lead; allege; ✕ command; quote, cite (*authority, passage, etc.*); dupe, fool, trick; **'2er** *m* (ring)leader; **'2ungszeichen** *n/pl.* quotation marks *pl.*, inverted commas *pl.*

**'Angabe** *f* declaration; statement; instruction; F *fig.* bragging, showing off.

**'angeb|en** (*irr.* geben, *sep.*, -ge-, *h*) **1.** *v/t.* declare; state; specify; allege; give (*name, reason*); † quote (*prices*); denounce, inform against; **2.** *v/i.* cards: deal first; F *fig.* brag, show off, *Am.* blow; **'2er** *m* (-s/-) informer; F braggart, *Am.* blowhard; **~lich** *adj.* ['~pliç] supposed; pretended, alleged.

**'angeboren** *adj.* innate, inborn; ✺ congenital.

**'Angebot** *n* offer (*a.* †); *at auction sale*: bid; † supply.

**'ange|bracht** *adj.* appropriate, suitable; well-timed; **'~bunden** *adj.*: kurz ~ *sein* be short (*gegen* with).

**'angehen** (*irr.* gehen, *sep.*, -ge-) **1.** *v/i.* (sein) begin; *meat, etc.*: go bad, go off; *es geht an* it will do; **2.** *v/t.* (*h*): *j-n* ~ concern s.o.; *das geht dich nichts an* that is no business of yours.

**'angehör|en** *v/i.* (*sep.*, no -ge-, *h*) belong to; **2ige** ['~igə] *m, f* (-n/-n): *seine* ~*n pl.* his relations *pl.*; *die nächsten* ~*n pl.* the next of kin.

**Angeklagte** ⚖ ['angəkla:ktə] *m, f* (-n/-n) *the* accused; prisoner (at the bar); defendant.

**Angel** ['aŋəl] *f* (-/-n) hinge; fishing-tackle, fishing-rod.

**'angelegen** *adj.*: sich et. ~ sein lassen make s.th. one's business; **'2-heit** *f* business, concern, affair, matter.

**'Angel|gerät** *n* fishing-tackle; **'2n** (ge-, *h*) **1.** *v/i.* fish (*nach* for), angle (for) (*both a. fig.*); ~ *in* fish (*river, etc.*); **2.** *v/t.* fish (*trout*); **'~punkt** *fig. m* pivot.

**'Angel|sachse** *m* Anglo-Saxon; **'2-sächsisch** *adj.* Anglo-Saxon.

**'Angelschnur** *f* fishing-line.

**'ange|messen** *adj.* suitable, appropriate; reasonable; adequate; **'~nehm** *adj.* pleasant, agreeable, pleasing; *sehr* ~! glad *or* pleased to meet you; **~regt** *adj.* ['~re:kt] stimulated; *discussion*: animated, lively; **'~sehen** *adj.* respected, esteemed.

**'Angesicht** *n* (-[e]s/-er, -e) face, countenance; *von* ~ *zu* ~ face to face; **'2s** *prp.* (*gen.*) in view of.

**angestammt** *adj.* ['angəʃtamt] hereditary, innate.

**Angestellte** ['angəʃtɛltə] *m, f* (-n/-n) employee; *die* ~*n pl.* the staff.

**'ange|trunken** *adj.* tipsy; **'~wandt** *adj.* ['~vant] applied; **'~wiesen** *adj.*: ~ *sein auf* (*acc.*) be dependent *or* thrown (up)on.

**'angewöhnen** *v/t.* (*sep.*, -ge-, *h*): *j-m et.* ~ accustom s.o. to s.th.; sich et. ~ get into the habit of s.th.; take to (*smoking*).

**'Angewohnheit** *f* custom, habit.

**Angina** ✱ [aŋ'gi:na] *f* (-/Anginen) angina; tonsillitis.

**'angleichen** *v/t.* (*irr.* gleichen, *sep.*, -ge-, *h*) assimilate (*an acc.* to, with), adjust (to); sich ~ *an* (*acc.*) assimilate to *or* with, adjust *or* adapt o.s. to.

**Angler** ['aŋlər] *m* (-s/-) angler.

**'angliedern** *v/t.* (*sep.*, -ge-, *h*) join; annex; affiliate.

**Anglist** [aŋ'glist] *m* (-en/-en) professor *or* student of English, Angli(ci)st.

**'angreif|en** *v/t.* (*irr.* greifen, *sep.*, -ge-, *h*) touch; draw upon (*capital, provisions*); attack; affect (*health, material*); ⚗ corrode; exhaust; **'2er** *m* (-s/-) aggressor, assailant.

**'angrenzend** *adj.* adjacent; adjoining.

**'Angriff** *m* attack, assault; *in* ~ *nehmen* set about; **'~skrieg** *m* offensive war; **'2slustig** *adj.* aggressive.

**Angst** [aŋst] *f* (-/⁀e) fear; anxiety; anguish; *ich habe* ~ I am afraid (*vor dat.* of); **'~hase** *m* coward.

**ängstigen** ['ɛŋstigən] *v/t.* (ge-, *h*) frighten, alarm; sich ~ be afraid (*vor dat.* of); be alarmed (*um* about).

**ängstlich** *adj.* ['ɛŋstliç] uneasy, nervous, anxious; afraid; scrupulous; timid; **'2keit** *f* (-/no *pl.*) anxiety; scrupulousness; timidity.

**'an|haben** *v/t.* (*irr.* haben, *sep.*, -ge-, *h*) have (*garment*) on; *das kann mir nichts* ~ that can't do me any harm; **'~haften** *v/i.* (*sep.*, -ge-, *h*) stick, adhere (*dat.* to); **'~haken** *v/t.* (*sep.*, -ge-, *h*) hook on; tick (off), *Am.* check (off) (*name, item*).

**'anhalten** (*irr.* halten, *sep.*, -ge-, *h*) **1.** *v/t.* stop; *j-n* ~ *zu* et. keep s.o. to s.th.; *den Atem* ~ hold one's breath; **2.** *v/i.* continue, last; stop; *um ein Mädchen* ~ propose to a girl; **'~d** *adj.* continuous; persevering.

**'Anhaltspunkt** *m* clue.

**'Anhang** *m* appendix, supplement (*to book, etc.*); followers *pl.*, adherents *pl.*

**'anhäng|en** (*sep.*, -ge-, *h*) **1.** *v/t.* hang on; affix, attach, join; add; couple (on) (*coach, vehicle*); **2.** *v/i.*

(*irr.* hängen) adhere to; '2er *m* (-s/-) adherent, follower; pendant (*of necklace, etc.*); label, tag; trailer (*behind car, etc.*).

**anhänglich** *adj.* ['anhɛŋliç] devoted, attached; '2keit *f* (-/*no pl.*) devotion, attachment.

**Anhängsel** ['anhɛŋzəl] *n* (-s/-) appendage.

'**anhauchen** *v/t.* (*sep.,* -ge-, h) breathe on; blow (*fingers*).

'**anhäuf|en** *v/t.* and *v/refl.* (*sep.,* -ge-, h) pile up, accumulate; '2ung *f* accumulation.

'**an|heben** *v/t.* (*irr.* heben, *sep.,* -ge-, h) lift, raise; '..heften *v/t.* (*sep.,* -ge-, h) fasten (an *acc.* to); stitch (to).

**an'heim|fallen** *v/i.* (*irr.* fallen, *sep.,* -ge-, sein): j-m ~ fall to s.o.; ..stellen *v/t.* (*sep.,* -ge-, h): j-m et. ~ leave s.th. to s.o.

'**Anhieb** *m:* auf ~ at the first go.

'**Anhöhe** *f* rise, elevation, hill.

'**anhören** *v/t.* (*sep.,* -ge-, h) listen to; sich ~ sound.

**Anilin** [ani'li:n] *n* (-s/*no pl.*) anilin(e).

'**ankämpfen** *v/i.* (*sep.,* -ge-, h): ~ gegen struggle against.

'**Ankauf** *m* purchase.

**Anker** ['aŋkər] *m* (-s/-) anchor; vor ~ gehen cast anchor; '..kette *f* cable; '2n *v/t.* and *v/i.* (ge-, h) anchor; '..uhr *f* lever watch.

'**anketten** *v/t.* (*sep.,* -ge-, h) chain (an *dat. or acc.* to).

'**Anklage** *f* accusation, charge; a. indictment; '2n *v/t.* (*sep.,* -ge-, h) accuse (*gen. or wegen of*), charge (with); a. indict (for).

'**Ankläger** *m* accuser; öffentlicher ~ public prosecutor, *Am.* district attorney.

'**anklammern** *v/t.* (*sep.,* -ge-, h) clip *s.th.* on; sich ~ cling (an *dat. or acc.* to).

'**Anklang** *m:* ~ an (*acc.*) suggestion of; ~ finden meet with approval.

'**an|kleben** *v/t.* (*sep.,* -ge-, h) stick on (an *dat. or acc.* to); glue on (to); paste on (to); gum on (to); '..kleiden *v/t.* (*sep.,* -ge-, h) dress; sich ~ dress (o.s.); '..klopfen *v/i.* (*sep.,* -ge-, h) knock (an *acc.* at); '..knipsen *v/t.* (*sep.,* -ge-, h) turn or switch on; '..knüpfen (*sep.,* -ge-, h) 1. *v/t.* tie (an *dat. or acc.* to); *fig.* begin; Verbindungen ~ form connexions or (*Am. only*) connections; 2. *v/i.* refer (an *acc.* to); '..kommen *v/i.* (*irr.* kommen, *sep.,* -ge-, sein) arrive; ~ auf (*acc.*) depend (up)on; es darauf ~ lassen run the risk, risk it; darauf kommt es an that is the point; es kommt nicht darauf an it does not matter.

**Ankömmling** ['aŋkœmliŋ] *m* (-s/-e) new-comer, new arrival.

'**ankündig|en** *v/t.* (*sep.,* -ge-, h) announce; advertise; '2ung *f* announcement; advertisement.

**Ankunft** ['ankunft] *f* (-/*no pl.*) arrival.

'**an|kurbeln** *v/t.* (*sep.,* -ge-, h) *mot.* crank up; die Wirtschaft ~ F boost the economy; '..lächeln *v/t.* (*sep.,* -ge-, h), '..lachen *v/t.* (*sep.,* -ge-, h) smile at.

'**Anlage** *f* construction; installation; ⊕ plant; grounds *pl.*, park; plan, arrangement, layout; enclosure (*to letter*); † investment; talent; predisposition, tendency; öffentliche ~n *pl.* public gardens *pl.*; '..kapital † *n* invested capital.

'**anlangen** (*sep.,* -ge-) 1. *v/i.* arrive at; 2. *v/t.* F touch; concern; was mich anlangt as far as I am concerned, (speaking) for myself.

**Anlaß** ['anlas] *m* (Anlasses/Anlässe) occasion; ohne allen ~ without any reason.

'**anlass|en** *v/t.* (*irr.* lassen, *sep.,* -ge-, h) F leave or keep (garment, etc.) on; leave (*light, etc.*) on; ⊕ start, set going; sich gut ~ promise well; '2er *mot. m* (-s/-) starter.

**anläßlich** *prp.* (*gen.*) ['anlɛsliç] on the occasion of.

'**Anlauf** *m* start, run; '2en (*irr.* laufen, *sep.,* -ge-) 1. *v/i.* (sein) run up; start; tarnish, (grow) dim; ~ gegen run against; 2. ⊕ *v/t.* (h) call or touch at (*port*).

'**an|legen** (*sep.,* -ge-, h) 1. *v/t.* put (an *acc.* to, against); lay out (*garden*); invest (*money*); level (*gun*); put on (*garment*); found (*town*); apply (*dressing*); lay in (*provisions*); Feuer ~ an (*acc.*) set fire to; 2. *v/i.* ⊕: land; moor; ~ auf (*acc.*) aim at; '..lehnen *v/t.* (*sep.,* -ge-, h) lean (an *acc.* against); leave or set (*door*) ajar; sich ~ an (*acc.*) lean against or on.

**Anleihe** ['anlaɪə] *f* (-/-n) loan.

'**anleit|en** *v/t.* (*sep.,* -ge-, h) guide (zu to); instruct (in *dat.* in); '2ung *f* guidance, instruction; guide.

'**Anliegen** *n* (-s/-) desire, request.

'**an|locken** *v/t.* (*sep.,* -ge-, h) allure, entice; decoy; '..machen *v/t.* (*sep.,* -ge-, h) fasten (an *acc.* to), fix (to); make, light (*fire*); switch on (*light*); dress (*salad*); '..malen *v/t.* (*sep.,* -ge-, h) paint.

'**Anmarsch** *m* approach.

**anmaß|en** ['anma:sən] *v/refl.* (*sep.,* -ge-, h) arrogate *s.th.* to o.s.; assume (*right*); presume; '..end *adj.* arrogant; '2ung *f* (-/-en) arrogance, presumption.

'**anmeld|en** *v/t.* (*sep.,* -ge-, h) announce, notify; sich ~ bei make an appointment with; '2ung *f* announcement, notification.

**'anmerk|en** v/t. (sep., -ge-, h) mark; note down; j-m et. ~ observe or perceive s.th. in s.o.; '2ung f (-/-en) remark; note; annotation; comment.

**'anmessen** v/t. (irr. messen, sep., -ge-, h): j-m e-n Anzug ~ measure s.o. for a suit; s. angemessen.

**'Anmut** f (-/no pl.) grace, charm, loveliness; '2ig adj. charming, graceful, lovely.

**'an|nageln** v/t. (sep., -ge-, h) nail on (an acc. to); **'~nähen** v/t. (sep., -ge-, h) sew on (an acc. to).

**annäher|nd** adj. ['annɛːərnt] approximate; '2ung f (-/-en) approach.

**Annahme** ['annɑːmə] f (-/-n) acceptance; receiving-office; fig. assumption, supposition.

**'annehm|bar** adj. acceptable; price: reasonable; **'~en** (irr. nehmen, sep., -ge-, h) 1. v/t. accept; take; fig.: suppose, take it, Am. guess; assume; contract (habit); adopt (child); parl. pass (bill); sich (gen.) ~ attend to s.th.; befriend s.o.; 2. v/i. accept; '2lichkeit f (-/-en) amenity, agreeableness.

**Annexion** [anɛk'sjoːn] f (-/-en) annexation.

**Annonce** [a'nõːsə] f (-/-n) advertisement.                                    [mous.)

**anonym** adj. [ano'nyːm] anony-)

**anordn|en** ['an⁹-] v/t. (sep., -ge-, h) order; arrange; direct; '2ung f arrangement; direction; order.

**'anpacken** v/t. (sep., -ge-, h) seize, grasp; fig. tackle.

**'anpass|en** v/t. (sep., -ge-, h) fit, adapt, suit; adjust; try or fit (garment) on; sich ~ adapt o.s. (dat. to); '2ung f (-/-en) adaptation; '~ungsfähig adj. adaptable.

**'anpflanz|en** v/t. (sep., -ge-, h) cultivate, plant; '2ung f cultivation; plantation.

**Anprall** ['anpral] m (-[e]s/⁹-e) impact; '2en v/i. (sep., -ge-, sein) strike (an acc. against).

**'anpreisen** v/t. (irr. preisen, sep., -ge-, h) commend, praise; boost, push.

**'Anprobe** f try-on, fitting.

**'an|probieren** v/t. (sep., no -ge-, h) try or fit on; **'~raten** v/t. (irr. raten, sep., -ge-, h) advise; **'~rechnen** v/t. (sep., -ge-, h) charge; hoch ~ value highly.

**'Anrecht** n right, title, claim (auf acc. to).

**'Anrede** f address; '2n v/t. (sep., -ge-, h) address, speak to.

**'anreg|en** v/t. (sep., -ge-, h) stimulate; suggest; **'~end** adj. stimulative, stimulating; suggestive; '2ung f stimulation; suggestion.

**'Anreiz** m incentive; '2en v/t. (sep., -ge-, h) stimulate; incite.

**'an|rennen** v/i. (irr. rennen, sep., -ge-, sein): ~ gegen run against; angerannt kommen come running; **'~richten** v/t. (sep., -ge-, h) prepare, dress (food, salad); cause, do (damage).

**anrüchig** adj. ['anryçiç] disreputable.

**'anrücken** v/i. (sep., -ge-, sein) approach.

**'Anruf** m call (a. teleph.); '2en v/t. (irr. rufen, sep., -ge-, h) call (zum Zeugen to witness); teleph. ring up, F phone, Am. call up; hail (ship); invoke (God, etc.); appeal to (s.o.'s help).

**'anrühren** v/t. (sep., -ge-, h) touch; mix.

**'Ansage** f announcement; '2n v/t. (sep., -ge-, h) announce; **'~r** m (-s/-) announcer; compère, Am. master of ceremonies.

**'ansammeln** v/t. (sep., -ge-, h) collect, gather; accumulate, amass; sich ~ collect, gather; accumulate.

**ansässig** adj. ['anzɛsiç] resident.

**'Ansatz** m start.

**'an|schaffen** v/t. (sep., -ge-, h) procure, provide; purchase; sich et. ~ provide or supply o.s. with s.th.; **'~schalten** ⚡ v/t. (sep., -ge-, h) connect; switch on (light).

**'anschau|en** v/t. (sep., -ge-, h) look at, view; **'~lich** adj. clear, vivid; graphic.

**'Anschauung** f (-/-en) view; perception; conception; intuition; contemplation; **'~smaterial** n illustrative material; **'~sunterricht** ['anʃauʊŋs⁹-] m visual instruction, object-lessons pl.; **'~svermögen** n intuitive faculty.

**'Anschein** m (-[e]s/no pl.) appearance; '2end adj. apparent, seeming.

**'an|schicken** v/refl. (sep., -ge-, h): sich ~, et. zu tun get ready for s.th.; prepare for s.th.; set about doing s.th.; **~schirren** ['~ʃirən] v/t. (sep., -ge-, h) harness.

**'Anschlag** m ⊕ stop, catch; ♪ touch; notice; placard, poster, bill; estimate; calculation; plot; e-n ~ auf j-n verüben make an attempt on s.o.'s life; **~brett** ['~k-] n notice-board, Am. bulletin board; 2en ['~gən] (irr. schlagen, sep., -ge-, h) 1. v/t. strike (an dat. or acc. against); knock (against); post up (bill); ♪ touch; level (gun); estimate, rate; 2. v/i. strike (an acc. against), knock (against); dog: bark; ♟ take (effect); food: agree (bei with); **~säule** ['~k-] f advertising pillar; **~zettel** ['~k-] m notice; placard, poster, bill.

**'anschließen** v/t. (irr. schließen, sep., -ge-, h) fix with a lock; join, attach, annex; ⊕, ⚡ connect; sich j-m ~ join s.o.; sich e-r Meinung ~

follow an opinion; '~d adj. adjacent (an acc. to); subsequent (to).

'Anschluß m joining; 🖼, ⚡, teleph., gas, etc.: connexion, (Am. only) connection; ~ haben an (acc.) 🖼, boat: connect with; 🚂 run in connexion with; ~ finden make friends (an acc. with), F pal up (with); teleph.: ~ bekommen get through; '~dose ⚡ f (wall) socket; '~zug 🚂 m connecting train, connexion.

'an|schmiegen v/refl. (sep., -ge-, h): sich ~ an (acc.) nestle to; '~schmieren v/t. (sep., -ge-, h) (be)smear, grease; F fig. cheat; '~schnallen v/t. (sep., -ge-, h) buckle on; bitte ~l 🚗 fasten seat-belts, please!; '~schnauzen F v/t. (sep., -ge-, h) snap at, blow s.o. up, Am. a. bawl s.o. out; '~schneiden v/t. (irr. schneiden, sep., -ge-, h) cut; broach (subject).

'Anschnitt m first cut or slice.

'an|schrauben v/t. (sep., -ge-, h) screw on (an dat. or acc. to); '~schreiben v/t. (irr. schreiben, sep., -ge-, h) write down; sports, games: score; et. ~ lassen have s.th. charged to one's account; buy s.th. on credit; '~schreien v/t. (irr. schreien, sep., -ge-, h) shout at.

'Anschrift f address.

an|schuldigen ['anʃuldigən] v/t. (sep., -ge-, h) accuse, incriminate; '~schwärzen v/t. (sep., -ge-, h) blacken; fig. a. defame.

'anschwell|en (irr. schwellen, sep., -ge-) 1. v/i. (sein) swell; increase, rise; 2. v/t. (h) swell; '2ung f swelling.

anschwemm|en ['anʃvɛmən] v/t. (sep., -ge-, h) wash ashore; geol. deposit (alluvium); '2ung f (-/-en) wash; geol. alluvial deposits pl., alluvium.

'ansehen 1. v/t. (irr. sehen, sep., -ge-, h) (take a) look at; view; regard, consider (als as); et. mit ~ witness s.th.; ~ für take for; man sieht ihm sein Alter nicht an he does not look his age; 2. 2 n (-s/no pl.) authority, prestige; respect; F appearance, aspect.

ansehnlich adj. ['anze:nliç] considerable; good-looking.

'an|seilen mount. v/t. and v/refl. (sep., -ge-, h) rope; '~sengen v/t. (sep., -ge-, h) singe; '~setzen (sep., -ge-, h) 1. v/t. put (an acc. to); add (to); fix, appoint (date); rate; fix, quote (prices); charge; put forth (leaves, etc.); put on (flesh); put (food) on (to boil); Rost ~ rust; 2. v/i. try; start; get ready.

'Ansicht f (-/-en) sight, view; fig. view, opinion; meiner ~ nach in my opinion; zur ~ ✝ on approval; '~s-(post)karte f picture postcard; '~ssache f matter of opinion.

'ansied|eln v/t. and v/refl. (sep., -ge-, h) settle; '2ler m settler; '2lung f settlement.

'Ansinnen n (-s/-) request, demand.

'anspann|en v/t. (sep., -ge-, h) stretch; put or harness (horses, etc.) to the carriage, etc.; fig. strain, exert; '2ung fig. f strain, exertion.

'anspeien v/t. (irr. speien, sep., -ge-, h) spit (up)on or at.

'anspiel|en v/i. (sep., -ge-, h) cards: lead; sports: lead off; football: kick off; ~ auf (acc.) allude to, hint at; '2ung f (-/-en) allusion, hint.

anspitzen v/t. (sep., -ge-, h) point, sharpen.

'Ansporn m (-[e]s/🔔 -e) spur; '2en v/t. (sep., -ge-, h) spur s.o. on.

'Ansprache f address, speech; e-e ~ halten deliver an address.

'ansprechen v/t. (irr. sprechen, sep., -ge-, h) speak to, address; appeal to; '~d adj. appealing.

'an|springen (irr. springen, sep., -ge-) 1. v/i. (sein) engine: start; 2. v/t. (h) jump (up)on, leap at; '~spritzen v/t. (sep., -ge-, h) splash (j-n mit et. s.th. on s.o.); (be-) sprinkle.

'Anspruch m claim (a. ⚖) (auf acc. to), pretension (to); ⚖ title (to); ~ haben auf (acc.) be entitled to; in ~ nehmen claim s.th.; Zeit in ~ nehmen take up time; '2slos adj. unpretentious; unassuming; '2svoll adj. pretentious.

'an|spülen v/t. (sep., -ge-, h) s. anschwemmen; '~stacheln v/t. (sep., -ge-, h) goad (on).

Anstalt ['anʃtalt] f (-/-en) establishment, institution; ~en treffen zu make arrangements for.

'Anstand m 1. (-[e]s/⚔e) hunt. stand; objection; 2. (-[e]s/🔔-e) good manners pl.; decency, propriety.

anständig adj. ['anʃtɛndiç] decent; respectable; price: fair, handsome; '2keit f (-/🔔-en) decency.

'Anstands|gefühl n sense of propriety; tact; '2los adv. unhesitatingly.

'anstarren v/t. (sep., -ge-, h) stare or gaze at.

anstatt prp. (gen.) and cj. [an'ʃtat] instead of.

'anstaunen v/t. (sep., -ge-, h) gaze at s.o. or s.th. in wonder.

'ansteck|en v/t. (sep., -ge-, h) pin on; put on (ring); 🔥 infect; set on fire; kindle (fire); light (candle, etc.); '~end adj. infectious; contagious; fig. a. catching; '2ung 🔥 f (-/-en) infection; contagion.

'an|stehen v/i. (irr. stehen, sep., -ge-, h) queue up (nach for), Am. stand in line (for); '~steigen v/i. (irr. steigen, sep., -ge-, sein) ground: rise, ascend; fig. increase.

'anstell|en v/t. (sep., -ge-, h) engage, employ, hire; make (ex-

*periments*); draw (*comparison*); turn on (*light, etc.*); manage; *sich* ~ queue up (*nach* for), *Am.* line up (for); *sich dumm* ~ set about *s.th.* stupidly; '~**ig** *adj.* handy, skil(l)ful; '**⏀ung** *f* place, position, job; employment.

**Anstieg** ['anʃtiːk] *m* (-[e]s/-e) ascent.

'**anstift|en** *v/t.* (*sep., -ge-, h*) instigate; '**⏀er** *m* instigator; '**⏀ung** *f* instigation.

'**anstimmen** *v/t.* (*sep., -ge-, h*) strike up (*tune*).

'**Anstoß** *m football*: kick-off; *fig.* impulse; offen|ce, *Am.* -se; ~ erregen give offence (*bei* to); ~ nehmen *an* (*dat.*) take offence at; ~ geben zu et. start s.th., initiate s.th.; '**⏀en** (*irr. stoßen, sep., -ge-*) 1. *v/t.* (h) push, knock (*acc. or an* against); nudge; 2. *v/i.* (*sein*) knock (*an acc.* against); border (on, upon); adjoin; 3. *v/i.* (h): *mit der Zunge* ~ lisp; *auf j-s Gesundheit* ~ drink (to) s.o.'s health; '**⏀end** *adj.* adjoining.

**anstößig** *adj.* ['anʃtøːsiç] shocking.

'**an|strahlen** *v/t.* (*sep., -ge-, h*) illuminate; floodlight (*building, etc.*); *fig.* beam at *s.o.*; '~**streben** *v/t.* (*sep., -ge-, h*) aim at, aspire to, strive for.

'**anstreich|en** *v/t.* (*irr. streichen, sep., -ge-, h*) paint; whitewash; mark; underline (*mistake*); '**⏀er** *m* (-s/-) house-painter; decorator.

**anstreng|en** ['anʃtrɛŋən] *v/t.* (*sep., -ge-, h*) exert; try (*eyes*); fatigue; *Prozeß* ~ bring an action (*gegen j-n* against s.o.); *sich* ~ exert o.s.; '~**end** *adj.* strenuous; trying (*für* to); '**⏀ung** *f* (-/-en) exertion, strain, effort.

'**Anstrich** *m* paint, colo(u)r; coat (-ing); *fig.*: tinge; air.

'**Ansturm** *m* assault; onset; ~ *auf* (*acc.*) rush for; ✝ run on (*bank*).

'**anstürmen** *v/i.* (*sep., -ge-, sein*) storm, rush.

'**Anteil** *m* share, portion; ~ *nehmen an* (*dat.*) take an interest in; sympathize with; ~**nahme** ['~naːmə] *f* (-/*no pl.*) sympathy; interest; '~**schein** ✝ *m* share-certificate.

**Antenne** [an'tɛnə] *f* (-/-n) aerial.

**Antialkoholiker** [anti⁹alko'hoːlikər, '~] *m* (-s/-) teetotaller.

**antik** *adj.* [an'tiːk] antique.

**Antilope** *zo.* [anti'loːpə] *f* (-/-n) antelope.

**Antipathie** [antipa'tiː] *f* (-/-n) antipathy.

'**antippen** F *v/t.* (*sep., -ge-, h*) tap.

**Antiquar** [anti'kvaːr] *m* (-s/-e) second-hand bookseller; ~**iat** [~ar-'jaːt] *n* (-[e]s/-e) second-hand bookshop; '**⏀isch** *adj. and adv.* [~'kvaːriʃ] second-hand.

**Antiquitäten** [antikvi'tɛːtən] *f/pl.* antiques *pl.*

'**Anti-Rakete** *f* anti-ballistic missile.

**antiseptisch** ✷ *adj.* [anti'zɛptiʃ] antiseptic.

**Antlitz** ['antlits] *n* (-es/✸ -e) face, countenance.

**Antrag** ['antraːk] *m* (-[e]s/⁼e) offer, proposal; application, request; *parl.* motion; ~ *stellen auf* (*acc.*) make an application for; *parl.* put a motion for; '~**steller** *m* (-s/-) applicant; *parl.* mover; ⟂ petitioner.

'**an|treffen** *v/t.* (*irr. treffen, sep., -ge-, h*) meet with. find; '~**treiben** (*irr. treiben, sep., -ge-*) 1. *v/i.* (*sein*) drift ashore; 2. *v/t.* (h) drive (on); *fig.* impel; '~**treten** (*irr. treten, sep., -ge-*) 1. *v/t.* (h) enter upon (*office*); take up (*position*); set out on (*journey*); enter upon take possession of (*inheritance*); 2. *v/i.* (*sein*) take one's place; ✖ fall in.

'**Antrieb** *m* motive, impulse; ⊕ drive, propulsion.

'**Antritt** *m* (-[e]s/✸ -e) entrance (*into office*); taking up (*of position*); setting out (*on journey*); entering into possession (*of inheritance*).

'**antun** *v/t.* (*irr. tun, sep., -ge-, h*): *j-m et.* ~ do s.th. to s.o.; *sich et.* ~ lay hands on o.s.

'**Antwort** *f* (-/-en) answer, reply (*auf acc.* to); '**⏀en** (*ge-, h*) 1. *v/i.* answer (*j-m* s.o.), reply (*j-m* to s.o.; *both*: *auf acc.* to); 2. *v/t.* answer (*auf acc.* to), reply (to); '~**schein** *m* (international) reply coupon.

'**an|vertrauen** *v/t.* (*sep., no -ge-, h*): *j-m et.* ~ (en)trust s.o. with s.th., entrust s.th. to s.o.; confide s.th. to s.o.; '~**wachsen** *v/i.* (*irr. wachsen, sep., -ge-, sein*) take root; *fig.* increase; ~ *an* (*acc.*) grow on to.

**Anwalt** ['anvalt] *m* (-[e]s/⁼e) lawyer; solicitor, *Am.* attorney; counsel; barrister, *Am.* counsel(l)or; *fig.* advocate.

'**Anwandlung** *f* fit; impulse.

'**Anwärter** *m* candidate, aspirant; expectant.

**Anwartschaft** ['anvartʃaft] *f* (-/-en) expectancy; candidacy; prospect (*auf acc.* of).

'**anweis|en** *v/t.* (*irr. weisen, sep., -ge-, h*) assign; instruct; direct; *s. angewiesen*; '**⏀ung** *f* assignment; instruction; direction; ✝: cheque, *Am.* check; draft; *s. Postanweisung.*

'**anwend|en** *v/t.* ([*irr. wenden,*] *sep., -ge-, h*) employ, use; apply (*auf acc.* to); *s. angewandt*; '**⏀ung** *f* application.

'**anwerben** *v/t.* (*irr. werben, sep., -ge-, h*) ✖ enlist, enrol(l); engage.

'**Anwesen** *n* estate; property.

'**anwesen|d** *adj.* present; '**⏀heit** *f* (-/*no pl.*) presence.

'**Anzahl** *f* (-/*no pl.*) number; quantity.

'anzahl|en v/t. (sep., -ge-, h) pay on account; pay a deposit; '⊊ung f (first) instal(l)ment; deposit.
'anzapfen v/t. (sep., -ge-, h) tap.
'Anzeichen n symptom; sign.
Anzeige ['antsaɪgə] f (-/-n) notice, announcement; ✝ advice; advertisement; ⚡ information; '⊊n v/t. (sep., -ge-, h) announce, notify; ✝ advise; advertise; indicate; ⊕ instrument: indicate, show; thermometer: read (degrees); j-n ~ denounce s.o., inform against s.o.
'anziehen (irr. ziehen, sep., -ge-, h) 1. v/t. draw, pull; draw (rein); tighten (screw); put on (garment); dress; fig. attract; 2. v/i. draw; prices: rise; '~d adj. attractive, interesting.
'Anziehung f attraction; '~skraft f attractive power; attraction.
'Anzug m 1. (-[e]s/-e) dress; suit; 2. (-[e]s/no pl.): im ~ sein storm: be gathering; danger: be impending.
anzüglich adj. ['antsy:kliç] personal; '⊊keit f (-/-en) personality.
'anzünden v/t. (sep., -ge-, h) light, kindle; strike (match); set (building) on fire.
apathisch adj. [a'pɑːtiʃ] apathetic.
Apfel ['apfəl] m (-s/-) apple; '~mus n apple-sauce; ~sine [~'ziːnə] f (-/-n) orange; '~wein m cider.
Apostel [a'pɔstəl] m (-s/-) apostle.
Apostroph [apɔ'stroːf] m (-s/-e) apostrophe.
Apotheke [apo'teːkə] f (-/-n) chemist's shop, pharmacy, Am. drugstore; ~r m (-s/-) chemist, Am. druggist, pharmacist.
Apparat [apa'rɑːt] m (-[e]s/-e) apparatus; device; teleph.: am ~l speaking!; teleph.: am ~ bleiben hold the line.
Appell [a'pɛl] m (-s/-e) ✕: roll-call; inspection; parade; fig. appeal (an acc. to); ⊊ieren [~'liːrən] v/i. (no -ge-, h) appeal (an acc. to).
Appetit [ape'tiːt] m (-[e]s/-e) appetite; ⊊lich adj. appetizing, savo(u)ry, dainty.
Applaus [a'plaus] m (-es/✕ -e) applause.
Aprikose [apri'koːzə] f (-/-n) apricot.
April [a'pril] m (-[s]/-e) April.
Aquarell [akva'rɛl] n (-s/-e) watercolo(u)r (painting), aquarelle.
Aquarium [a'kvɑːrium] n (-s/Aquarien) aquarium
Äquator [ɛ'kvɑːtɔr] m (-s/✕ -en) equator.
Ära ['ɛːra] f (-/✕ Ären) era.
Arab|er ['arabər] m (-s/-) Arab; ⊊isch adj. [a'rɑːbiʃ] Arabian, Arab(ic).
Arbeit ['arbaɪt] f (-/-en) work; labo(u)r, toil; employment; job;

task; paper; workmanship; bei der ~ at work; sich an die ~ machen, an die ~ gehen set to work; (keine) ~ haben be in (out of) work; die ~ niederlegen stop work, down tools; '⊊en (ge-, h) 1. v/i. work; labo(u)r, toil; 2. v/t. work; make.
'Arbeiter m (-s/-) worker; workman, labo(u)rer, hand; '~in f (-/-nen) female worker; working woman, workwoman; '~klasse f working class(es pl.); '~partei f Labo(u)r Party; '~schaft f (-/-en), '~stand m working class(es pl.), labo(u)r.
'Arbeit|geber m (-s/-), '~geberin f (-/-nen) employer; '~nehmer m (-s/-), '~nehmerin f (-/-nen) employee.
'arbeitsam adj. industrious.
'Arbeits|amt n labo(u)r exchange; '~anzug m overall; '~beschaffung f (-/-en) provision of work; '~bescheinigung f certificate of employment; '~einkommen n earned income; '⊊fähig adj. able to work; '~gericht n labo(u)r or industrial court; '~kleidung f working clothes pl.; '~kraft f working power; worker, hand; Arbeitskräfte pl. a. labo(u)r; '~leistung f efficiency; power (of engine); output (of factory); '~lohn m wages pl., pay; '⊊los adj. out of work, unemployed; '~lose m (-n/-n): die ~n pl. the unemployed pl.; '~losenunterstützung f unemployment benefit; ~ beziehen F be on the dole; '~losigkeit f (-/no pl.) unemployment; '~markt m labo(u)r market; '~minister m Minister of Labour, Am. Secretary of Labour; '~nachweis(stelle f) m employment registry office, Am. labor registry office; '~niederlegung f (-/-en) strike, Am. F a. walkout; '~pause f break, intermission; '~platz m place of work; job; '~raum m workroom; '⊊scheu adj. work-shy; '~scheu f aversion to work; '~schutzgesetz n protective labo(u)r law; '~tag m working day, workday; '⊊unfähig adj. incapable of working; disabled; '~weise f practice, method of working; '~willige m (-n/-n) non-striker; '~zeit f working time; working hours pl.; '~zeug n tools pl.; '~zimmer n workroom; study.
Archäo|loge [arçeo'loːgə] m (-n/-n) arch(a)eologist; ~logie [~o'giː] f (-/no pl.) arch(a)eology.
Arche ['arçə] f (-/-n) ark.
Architekt [arçi'tɛkt] m (-en/-en) architect; ~ur [~'tuːr] f (-/-en) architecture.
Archiv [ar'çiːf] n (-s/-e) archives pl.; record office.
Areal [are'ɑːl] n (-s/-e) area.

**Arena** [a'reːna] f (-/Arenen) arena; bullring; (circus-)ring.

**arg** adj. [ark] bad; wicked; gross.

**Ärger** ['ɛrgər] m (-s/no pl.) vexation, annoyance; anger; **'⁀lich** adj. vexed, F mad, angry (auf, über acc. at s.th., with s.o.); annoying, vexatious; **'⁀n** v/t. (ge-, h) annoy, vex, irritate, fret; bother; sich ~ feel angry or vexed (über acc. at, about s.th.; with s.o.); **'⁀nis** n (-ses/-se) scandal, offen|ce, Am. -se.

**'Arg|list** f (-/no pl.) cunning, craft (-iness); **'⁀listig** adj. crafty, cunning; **'⁀los** adj. guileless; artless, unsuspecting; **⁀wohn** ['⁀voːn] m (-[e]s/no pl.) suspicion; **⁀wöhnen** ['⁀vøːnən] v/t. (ge-, h) suspect; **'⁀wöhnisch** adj. suspicious.

**Arie** ♪ ['aːrjə] f (-/-n) aria.

**Aristokrat** [aristo'kraːt] m (-en/-en), **⁀in** f (-/-nen) aristocrat; **⁀ie** [⁀kra'tiː] f (-/-n) aristocracy.

**Arkade** [ar'kaːdə] f (-/-n) arcade.

**arm¹** adj. [arm] poor.

**Arm²** [⁀] m (-[e]s/-e) arm; branch (of river, etc.); F: j-n auf den ~ nehmen pull s.o.'s leg.

**Armaturenbrett** [arma'tuːrənbret] n instrument board, dash-board.

**'Arm|band** ♭ bracelet; **⁀banduhr** ['armbantʔ-] f wrist watch; **'⁀bruch** m fracture of the arm.

**Armee** [ar'meː] f (-/-n) army.

**Ärmel** ['ɛrməl] m (-s/-) sleeve; **'⁀kanal m the** (English) Channel.

**'Armen|haus** n alms-house, Brt. a. workhouse; **'⁀pflege** f poor relief; **'⁀pfleger** m guardian of the poor; welfare officer; **'⁀unterstützung** f poor relief.

**ärmlich** adj. ['ɛrmliç] s. armselig.

**'armselig** adj. poor; wretched; miserable; shabby; paltry.

**Armut** ['armuːt] f (-/no pl.) poverty.

**Aroma** [a'roːma] n (-s/Aromen, Aromata, -s) aroma, flavo(u)r; fragrance.

**Arrest** [a'rest] m (-es/-e) arrest; confinement; seizure (of goods); detention (of pupil, etc.); ~ bekommen be kept in.

**Art** [aːrt] f (-/-en) kind, sort; ♀, zo. species; manner, way; nature; manners pl.; breed, race (of animals); auf die(se) ~ in this way; **'⁀en** v/i. (ge-, sein): ~ nach take after. [artery.]

**Arterie** anat. [ar'teːrjə] f (-/-n)⌐

**artig** adj. ['aːrtiç] good, well-behaved; civil, polite; **'2keit** f (-/-en) good behavio(u)r; politeness; civility, a. civilities pl.

**Artikel** [ar'tiːkəl] m (-s/-) article; commodity.

**Artillerie** [artilə'riː] f (-/-n) artillery.

**Artist** [ar'tist] m (-en/-en), **⁀in** f (-/-nen) circus performer.

**Arznei** [arts'naɪ] f (-/-en) medicine, F physic; **⁀kunde** f (-/no pl.) pharmaceutics; **⁀mittel** n medicine, drug.

**Arzt** [aːrtst] m (-es/⁀e) doctor, medical man; physician.

**Ärztin** ['ɛːrtstin] f (-/-nen) woman or lady doctor.

**ärztlich** adj. ['ɛːrtstliç] medical.

**As** [as] n (-ses/-se) ace.

**Asche** ['aʃə] f (-/-n) ash(es pl.); **'⁀nbahn** f sports: cinder-track, mot. dirt-track; **'⁀nbecher** m ash-tray; **⁀nbrödel** ['⁀nbrøːdəl] n (-s/no pl.), **⁀nputtel** ['⁀nputəl] n 1. (-s/no pl.) Cinderella; 2. (-s/-) drudge.

**Aschermittwoch** m Ash Wednesday.

**'asch'grau** adj. ash-grey, ashy, Am. ash-gray.

**äsen** hunt. ['ɛːzən] v/i. (ge-, h) graze, browse.

**Asiat** [az'jaːt] m (-en/-en), **⁀in** f (-/-nen) Asiatic, Asian; **2isch** adj. Asiatic, Asian.

**Asket** [as'keːt] m (-en/-en) ascetic.

**Asphalt** [as'falt] m (-[e]s/-e) asphalt; **2ieren** [⁀'tiːrən] v/t. (no -ge-, h) asphalt.

**aß** [aːs] pret. of essen.

**Assistent** [asis'tent] m (-en/-en), **⁀in** f (-/-nen) assistant.

**Ast** [ast] m (-es/⁀e) branch, bough; knot (in timber); **'⁀loch** n knot-hole.

**Astro|naut** [astro'naut] m (-en/-en) astronaut; **⁀nom** [⁀'noːm] m (-en/-en) astronomer.

**Asyl** [a'zyːl] n (-s/-e) asylum; fig. sanctuary.

**Atelier** [atə'ljeː] n (-s/-s) studio.

**Atem** ['aːtəm] m (-s/no pl.) breath; außer ~ out of breath; **'2los** adj. breathless; **'⁀not** ♭ f difficulty in breathing; **'⁀pause** f breathing-space; **'⁀zug** m breath, respiration.

**Äther** ['ɛːtər] m 1. (-s/no pl.) the ether; 2. ♣ (-s/-) ether; **2isch** adj. [ɛ'teːriʃ] ethereal, etheric.

**Athlet** [at'leːt] m (-en/-en), **⁀in** f (-/-nen) athlete; **⁀ik** f (-/no pl.) athletics mst sg.; **2isch** adj. athletic.

**atlantisch** adj. [at'lantiʃ] Atlantic.

**Atlas** ['atlas] m 1. geogr. (-/no pl.) Atlas; 2. (-, -ses/-se, Atlanten) maps: atlas; 3. (-, -ses/-se) textiles: satin.

**atmen** ['aːtmən] v/i. and v/t. (ge-, h) breathe.

**Atmosphär|e** [atmo'sfɛːrə] f (-/-n) atmosphere; **2isch** adj. atmospheric.

**'Atmung** f (-/-en) breathing, respiration.

**Atom** [a'toːm] n (-s/-e) atom; **2ar** adj. [ato'maːr] atomic; **⁀bombe** f atomic bomb, atom-bomb, A-bomb; **⁀energie** f atomic or nuclear energy; **⁀forschung** f atomic or nuclear research; **⁀kern** m atomic nucleus; **⁀kraftwerk** n nuclear power station; **~meiler** *m* atomic pile, nuclear reactor; **~phy-siker** *m* atomic physicist; **~reaktor** *m* nuclear reactor, atomic pile; **~versuch** *m* atomic test; **~waffe** *f* atomic *or* nuclear weapon; **~wissenschaftler** *m* atomic scientist; **~zeitalter** *n* atomic age.

**Attentlat** [atɛn'taːt] *n* (-[e]s/-e) (attempted) assassination; *fig.* outrage; **~äter** [~ɛːtər] *m* (-s/-) assailant, assassin.

**Attest** [a'tɛst] *n* (-es/-e) certificate; **Sieren** [~'tiːrən] *v/t.* (*no* -ge-, h) attest, certify.

**Attraktion** [atrak'tsjoːn] *f* (-/-en) attraction.

**Attrappe** [a'trapə] *f* (-/-n) dummy.

**Attribut** [atri'buːt] *n* (-[e]s/-e) attribute; *gr.* attributive.

**ätzlen** ['ɛtsən] *v/t.* (ge-, h) corrode; ⚒ cauterize; etch (*metal plate*); **~end** *adj.* corrosive; caustic (*a. fig.*); **Sung** *f* (-/-en) corrosion; ⚒ cauterization; etching.

**au** *int.* [aʊ] oh!; ouch!

**auch** *cj.* [aʊx] also, too, likewise; even; ~ *nicht* neither, nor; *wo* ~ (*immer*) wher(eso)ever; *ist es* ~ *wahr?* is it really true?

**Audienz** [aʊdi'ɛnts] *f* (-/-en) audience, hearing.

**auf** [aʊf] 1. *prp.* (*dat.*) (up)on; in; at; of; by; ~ *dem Tisch* (up)on the table; ~ *dem Markt* in the market; ~ *der Universität* at the university; ~ *e-m Ball* at a ball; 2. *prp.* (*acc.*) on; in; at; to; towards (*a.* ~ *zu*); up; ~ *deutsch* in German; ~ *e-e Entfernung von* at a range of; ~ *die Post etc. gehen* go to the post-office; ~ *ein Pfund gehen 20 Schilling* 20 shillings go to a pound; *es geht* ~ *neun* it is getting on to nine; ~ ... *hin* on the strength of; 3. *adv.* up(wards); ~ *und ab gehen* walk up and down *or* to and fro; 4. *cj.:* ~ *daß* (in order) that; ~ *daß nicht* that not, lest; 5. *int.:* ~! up!

**auflarbeiten** ['aʊf⁹-] *v/t.* (*sep.*, -ge-, h) work off (*arrears of work*); furbish up; F do up (*garments*); **~atmen** *fig.* ['aʊf⁹-] *v/i.* (*sep.*, -ge-, h) breathe again.

**'Aufbau** *m* (-[e]s/*no pl.*) building up; construction (*of play, novel*); F *esp. Am.* setup (*of organization*); *mot.* body (*of car, etc.*); **Sen** *v/t.* (*sep.*, -ge-, h) erect, build up; construct.

**'auflbauschen** *v/t.* (*sep.*, -ge-, h) puff out; *fig.* exaggerate; **~beißen** *v/t.* (*irr.* beißen, *sep.*, -ge-, h) crack; **~bekommen** *v/t.* (*irr.* kommen, *sep.*, *no* -ge-, h) get open (*door*); be given (*a task*); **~bessern** *v/t.* (*sep.*, -ge-, h) raise (*salary*); **~bewahren** *v/t.* (*sep.*, *no* -ge-, h) keep; preserve;

**~bieten** *v/t.* (*irr.* bieten, *sep.*, -ge-, h) summon; exert; ✗ raise; **~binden** *v/t.* (*irr.* binden, *sep.*, -ge-, h) untie; **~bleiben** *v/i.* (*irr.* bleiben, *sep.*, -ge-, sein) sit up; door, *etc.*: remain open; **~blenden** (*sep.*, -ge-, h) 1. *mot.* *v/i.* turn up the headlights; 2. *v/t.* fade in (*scene*)**;** **~blicken** *v/i.* (*sep.*, -ge-, h) look up; raise one's eyes; **~blitzen** *v/i.* (*sep.*, -ge-, h, sein) flash (up); **~blühen** *v/i.* (*sep.*, -ge-, sein) bloom; flourish.

**'auflbrausen** *fig.* *v/i.* (*sep.*, -ge-, sein) fly into a passion; **~d** *adj.* hottempered.

**'auflbrechen** (*irr.* brechen, *sep.*, -ge-) 1. *v/t.* (h) break open; force open; 2. *v/i.* (sein) burst open; set out (*nach for*); **~bringen** *v/t.* (*irr.* bringen, *sep.*, -ge-, h) raise (*money, troops*); capture (*ship*); rouse *or* irritate *s.o.*

**'Aufbruch** *m* departure, start.

**'auflbügeln** *v/t.* (*sep.*, -ge-, h) iron; **~bürden** *v/t.* (*sep.*, -ge-, h): *j-m et.* ~ impose s.th. on *s.o.*; **~decken** *v/t.* (*sep.*, -ge-, h) uncover; spread (*cloth*), *fig.* disclose; **~drängen** *v/t.* (*sep.*, -ge-, h) force, obtrude (*j-m* [up]on *s.o.*); **~drehen** *v/t.* (*sep.*, -ge-, h) turn on (*gas, etc.*).

**'aufdringlich** *adj.* obtrusive.

**'Aufdruck** *m* (-[e]s/-e) imprint; surcharge.

**'aufdrücken** *v/t.* (*sep.*, -ge-, h) impress.

**aufeinander** *adv.* [aʊf⁹aɪ'nandər] one after *or* upon another; **Sfolge** *f* succession; **~folgend** *adj.* successive.

**Aufenthalt** ['aʊfɛnthalt] *m* (-[e]s/-e) stay; residence; delay; ⚌ stop; **~s-genehmigung** *f* residence permit.

**auferlegen** ['aʊf⁹ɛrleːgən] *v/t.* (*sep.*, *no* -ge-, h) impose (*j-m* on *s.o.*).

**auferstehlen** ['aʊf⁹ɛrʃteːən] *v/i.* (*irr.* stehen, *sep.*, *no* -ge-, sein) rise (from the dead); **Sung** *f* (-/-en) resurrection.

**auflessen** ['aʊf⁹-] *v/t.* (*irr.* essen, *sep.*, -ge-, h) eat up; **~fahren** *v/i.* (*irr.* fahren, *sep.*, -ge-, sein) ascend; start up; *fig.* fly out; ⚓ run aground; *mot.* drive *or* run (*auf acc.* against, into).

**'Auffahrt** *f* ascent; driving up; approach; drive, *Am.* driveway; **~srampe** *f* ramp.

**'auflfallen** *v/i.* (*irr.* fallen, *sep.*, -ge-, sein) be conspicuous; *j-m* ~ strike *s.o.*; **~fallend** *adj.*, **~fällig** *adj.* striking; conspicuous; flashy.

**'auffangen** *v/t.* (*irr.* fangen, *sep.*, -ge-, h) catch (up); parry (*thrust*).

**'auffasslen** *v/t.* (*sep.*, -ge-, h) conceive; comprehend; interpret; **Sung** *f* conception; interpretation; grasp.

**'auffinden** *v/t.* (*irr.* finden, sep., -ge-, h) find, trace, discover, locate.

**'aufforder|n** *v/t.* (sep., -ge-, h) ask, invite; call (up)on; *esp. ₃₁₂* summon; **'2ung** *f* invitation; *esp. ₃₁₂* summons.

**'auffrischen** (sep., -ge-) **1.** *v/t.* (h) freshen up, touch up; brush up (*knowledge*); revive; **2.** *v/i.* (sein) *wind*: freshen.

**'aufführ|en** *v/t.* (sep., -ge-, h) *thea.* represent, perform, act; enumerate; enter (*in list*); einzeln ~ specify, *Am.* itemize; sich ~ behave; **'2ung** *f thea.* performance; enumeration; entry; specification; conduct.

**'Aufgabe** *f* task; problem; *school:* homework; posting, *Am.* mailing (*of letter*); booking (*of luggage*), *Am.* checking (*of baggage*); resignation (*from office*); abandonment; giving up (*business*); es sich zur ~ machen make it one's business.

**'Aufgang** *m* ascent; *ast.* rising; staircase.

**'aufgeben** (*irr.* geben, sep., -ge-, h) **1.** *v/t.* give up, abandon; resign from (*office*); insert (*advertisement*); post, *Am.* mail (*letter*); book (*luggage*), *Am.* check (*baggage*); hand in, send (*telegram*); † give (*order*); set, *Am.* assign (*homework*); set (*riddle*); **2.** *v/i.* give up or in.

**'Aufgebot** *n* public notice; ✕ levy; *fig.* array; banns *pl.* (*of marriage*).

**'aufgehen** *v/i.* (*irr.* gehen, sep., -ge-, sein) open; ♫ leave no remainder; *sewing:* come apart; *paste, star, curtain:* rise; *seed:* come up; ~ in (*dat.*) be merged in; *fig.* be devoted to (*work*); in Flammen ~ go up in flames.

**aufgeklärt** *adj.* ['aufgəklɛːrt] enlightened; **'2heit** *f* (*-/no pl.*) enlightenment.

**'Aufgeld** † *n* agio, premium.

**aufge|legt** *adj.* ['aufgəleːkt] disposed (*zu for*); in the mood (*zu inf.* for *ger.*; *zu inf.*); gut (*schlecht*) ~ in a good (bad) humo(u)r; **'~schlossen** *fig. adj.* open-minded; **~weckt** *fig. adj.* ['~vɛkt] bright.

**'auf|gießen** *v/t.* (*irr.* gießen, sep., -ge-, h) pour (on); make (*tea*); **'~greifen** *v/t.* (*irr.* greifen, sep., -ge-, h) snatch up, *fig.* take up;

**'Aufguß** *m* infusion. [seize.]

**'auf|haben** (*irr.* haben, sep., -ge-, h) **1.** *v/t.* have on (*hat*); have open (*door*); have to do (*task*); **2.** F *v/i.: das Geschäft hat auf* the shop is open; **'~haken** *v/t.* (sep., -ge-, h) unhook; **'~halten** *v/t.* (*irr.* halten, sep., -ge-, h) keep open; stop, detain, delay; hold up (*traffic*); sich ~ stay; sich ~ bei dwell on; sich ~ mit spend one's time on; **'~hängen** *v/t.* (*irr.* hängen, sep., -ge-, h) hang (up); ⊕ suspend.

**'aufheb|en** *v/t.* (*irr.* heben, sep., -ge-, h) lift (up), raise; pick up; raise (*siege*); keep, preserve; cancel, annul, abolish; break off (*engagement*); break up (*meeting*); sich ~ neutralize; *die Tafel* ~ rise from the table; *gut aufgehoben sein* be well looked after; *viel Aufhebens machen* make a fuss (*von* about); **'2ung** *f* (*-/-en*) raising; abolition; annulment; breaking up.

**'auf|heitern** *v/t.* (sep., -ge-, h) cheer up; sich ~ *weather:* clear up; *face:* brighten; **'~hellen** *v/t. and v/refl.* (sep., -ge-, h) brighten.

**'aufhetz|en** *v/t.* (sep., -ge-, h) incite, instigate *s.o.*; **'2ung** *f* (*-/-en*) instigation, incitement.

**'auf|holen** (sep., -ge-, h) **1.** *v/t.* make up (for); ♪ haul up; **2.** *v/i.* gain (*gegen* on); pull up (to); **'~hören** *v/i.* (sep., -ge-, h) cease, stop; *Am.* quit (*all: zu tun doing*); F: *da hört (sich) doch alles auf!* that's the limit!, *Am.* that beats everything!; **'~kaufen** *v/t.* (sep., -ge-, h) buy up.

**'aufklär|en** *v/t.* (sep., -ge-, h) clear up; enlighten (*über acc.* on); ✕ reconnoit|re, *Am.* -er; sich ~ clear up; **'2ung** *f* enlightenment; ✕ reconnaissance.

**'auf|kleben** *v/t.* (sep., -ge-, h) paste on, stick on, affix on; **'~klinken** *v/t.* (sep., -ge-, h) unlatch; **'~knöpfen** *v/t.* (sep., -ge-, h) unbutton.

**'aufkommen 1.** *v/i.* (*irr.* kommen, sep., -ge-, sein) rise; recover (*from illness*); come up; come into fashion or use; *thought:* arise; ~ für et. answer for s.th.; ~ gegen prevail against *s.o.*; **2.** 2 *n* (*-s/no pl.*) rise; recovery.

**auf|krempeln** ['aufkrɛmpəln] *v/t.* (sep., -ge-, h) turn up, roll up; tuck up; **'~lachen** *v/i.* (sep., -ge-, h) burst out laughing; **'~laden** *v/t.* (*irr.* laden, sep., -ge-, h) load; ⨍ charge.

**'Auflage** *f* edition (*of book*); circulation (*of newspaper*); ⊕ support.

**'auf|lassen** *v/t.* (*irr.* lassen, sep., -ge-, h) F leave open (*door, etc.*); F keep on (*hat*); ₃₁₂ cede; **'~lauern** *v/i.* (sep., -ge-, h): j-m ~ lie in wait for s.o.

**'Auflauf** *m* concourse; riot; *dish:* soufflé; **'2en** *v/i.* (*irr.* laufen, sep., -ge-, sein) *interest:* accrue; ♪ run aground.

**'auflegen** (sep., -ge-, h) **1.** *v/t.* put on, lay on; apply (*auf acc.* to); print, publish (*book*); *teleph.* hang up; **2.** *teleph. v/i.* ring off.

**'auflehn|en** *v/t.* (sep., -ge-, h) lean (on); sich ~ lean (on); *fig.* rebel, revolt (*gegen* against); **'2ung** *f* (*-/-en*) rebellion.

**'auf|lesen** v/t. (irr. lesen, sep., -ge-, h) gather, pick up; **'~leuchten** v/i. (sep., -ge-, h) flash (up); **'~liegen** v/i. (irr. liegen, sep., -ge-, h) lie (auf dat. on).

**'auflös|bar** adj. (dis)soluble; **'~en** v/t. (sep., -ge-, h) undo (knot); break up (meeting); dissolve (salt, etc.; marriage, business, Parliament, etc.); solve (&, riddle); disintegrate; fig. aufgelöst upset; **'2ung** f (dis-)solution; disintegration.

**'aufmach|en** v/t. (sep., -ge-, h) open; undo (dress, parcel); put up (umbrella); make up, get up; sich ~ wind: rise; set out (nach acc. for); make for; die Tür ~ answer the door; **'2ung** f (-/-en) make-up, get-up.

**'aufmarschieren** v/i. (sep., no -ge-, sein) form into line; ~ lassen ✗ deploy.

**'aufmerksam** adj. attentive (gegen to); j-n ~ machen auf (acc.) call s.o.'s attention to; **'2keit** f (-/-en) attention; token.

**'aufmuntern** v/t. (sep., -ge-, h) rouse; encourage; cheer up.

**Aufnahme** ['aufnaːmə] f (-/-n) taking up (of work); reception; admission; phot.: taking; photograph, shot; shooting (of a film); **'2fähig** adj. capable of absorbing; mind: receptive (für of); **'~gebühr** f admission fee; **'~gerät** n phot. camera; recorder; **'~prüfung** f entrance examination.

**'aufnehmen** v/t. (irr. nehmen, sep., -ge-, h) take up; pick up; take s.o. in; take down (dictation, etc.); take s.th. in (mentally); receive (guests); admit; raise, borrow (money); draw up, record, shoot (film); phot. take (picture); gut (übel) ~ take well (ill); es ~ mit be a match for.

**aufopfer|n** ['aufʔ-] v/t. (sep., -ge-, h) sacrifice; **'2ung** f sacrifice.

**'auf|passen** v/i. (sep., -ge-, h) attend (auf acc. to); watch; at school: be attentive; look out; ~ auf (acc.) take care of; **'~platzen** v/i. (sep., -ge-, sein) burst (open); **'~polieren** v/t. (sep., no -ge-, h) polish up; **'~prallen** v/i. (sep., -ge-, sein): auf den Boden ~ strike the ground; **'~pumpen** v/t. (sep., -ge-, h) blow up (tyre, etc.); **'~raffen** v/t. (sep., -ge-, h) snatch up; sich ~ rouse o.s. (zu for); muster up one's energy; **'~räumen** (sep., -ge-, h) 1. v/t. put in order; tidy (up), Am. straighten up; clear away; 2. v/i. tidy up; ~ mit do away with.

**'aufrecht** adj. and adv. upright (a. fig.), erect; **'~erhalten** v/t. (irr. halten, sep., no -ge-, h) maintain, uphold; **'2erhaltung** f (-/no pl.) maintenance.

**'aufreg|en** v/t. (sep., -ge-, h) stir up, excite; sich ~ get excited or upset (über acc. about); aufgeregt excited; upset; **'2ung** f excitement, agitation.

**'auf|reiben** v/t. (irr. reiben, sep., -ge-, h) chafe (skin, etc.); fig.: destroy; exhaust, wear s.o. out; **'~reißen** (irr. reißen, sep., -ge-) 1. v/t. (h) rip or tear up or open; fling open (door); open (eyes) wide; 2. v/i. (sein) split open, burst.

**'aufreiz|en** v/t. (sep., -ge-, h) incite, stir up; **'~end** adj. provocative; **'2ung** f instigation.

**'aufrichten** v/t. (sep., -ge-, h) set up, erect; sich ~ stand up; straighten; sit up (in bed).

**'aufrichtig** adj. sincere, candid; **'2keit** f sincerity, cando(u)r.

**'aufriegeln** v/t. (sep., -ge-, h) unbolt.

**'Aufriß** △ m elevation.

**'aufrollen** v/t. and v/refl. (sep., -ge-, h) roll up; unroll.

**'Aufruf** m call, summons; **'2en** v/t. (irr. rufen, sep., -ge-, h) call up; call on s.o.

**Aufruhr** ['aufruːr] m (-[e]s/-e) uproar, tumult; riot, rebellion.

**'aufrühr|en** v/t. (sep., -ge-, h) stir up; revive; fig. rake up; **'2er** m (-s/-) rebel; **'~erisch** adj. rebellious.

**'Aufrüstung** ✗ f (re)armament.

**'auf|rütteln** v/t. (sep., -ge-, h) shake up; rouse; **'~sagen** v/t. (sep., -ge-, h) say, repeat; recite.

**aufsässig** adj. ['aufzɛsiç] rebellious.

**'Aufsatz** m essay; composition; ⊕ top.

**'auf|saugen** v/t. (sep., -ge-, h) suck up; ✍ absorb; **'~scheuchen** v/t. (sep., -ge-, h) scare (away); disturb; rouse; **'~scheuern** v/t. (sep., -ge-, h) scour; ⚙ chafe; **'~schichten** v/t. (sep., -ge-, h) pile up; **'~schieben** v/t. (irr. schieben, sep., -ge-, h) slide open; fig.: put off; defer, postpone; adjourn.

**'Aufschlag** m striking; impact; additional or extra charge; facing (on coat), lapel (of coat); cuff (on sleeve); turn-up (on trousers); tennis: service; **'2en** ['~ɡən] (irr. schlagen, sep., -ge-) 1. v/t. (h) open; turn up (sleeve, etc.); take up (abode); pitch (tent); raise (prices); cut (one's knee) open; 2. v/i. (sein) strike, hit; ✝ rise, go up (in price); tennis: serve.

**'auf|schließen** v/t. (irr. schließen, sep., -ge-, h) unlock, open; **'~schlitzen** v/t. (sep., -ge-, h) slit or rip open.

**'Aufschluß** fig. m information.

**'auf|schnallen** v/t. (sep., -ge-, h) unbuckle; **'~schnappen** (sep., -ge-) 1. v/t. (h) snatch; fig. pick up; 2. v/i. (sein) snap open; **'~schnei-**

**den** (*irr. schneiden, sep., -ge-, h*)
1. *v/t.* cut open; cut up (*meat*);
2. *fig. v/i.* brag, boast.
**'Aufschnitt** *m* (slices *pl.* of) cold
meat, *Am.* cold cuts *pl.*
**'auf|schnüren** *v/t.* (*sep., -ge-, h*)
untie; unlace; **'~schrauben** *v/t.*
(*sep., -ge-, h*) screw (*auf acc.* on);
unscrew; **'~schrecken** (*sep., -ge-*)
1. *v/t.* (*h*) startle; 2. *v/i.* (*irr.
schrecken, sein*) start (up).
**'Aufschrei** *m* shriek, scream; *fig.*
outcry.
**'auf|schreiben** *v/t.* (*irr. schreiben,
sep., -ge-, h*) write down; **'~
schreien** *v/i.* (*irr. schreien, sep.,
-ge-, h*) cry out, scream.
**'Aufschrift** *f* inscription; address,
direction (*on letter*); label.
**'Aufschub** *m* deferment; delay;
adjournment; respite.
**'auf|schürfen** *v/t.* (*sep., -ge-, h*)
graze (*skin*); **'~schwingen** *v/refl.*
(*irr. schwingen, sep., -ge-, h*) soar,
rise; *sich zu et. ~* bring o.s. to do
s.th.
**'Aufschwung** *m fig.* rise, *Am.* up-
swing; ✝ boom.
**'aufsehen** 1. *v/i.* (*irr. sehen, sep.,
-ge-, h*) look up; 2. ⚘ *n* (*-s/no pl.*)
sensation; *~ erregen* cause a sensation; **'~erregend** *adj.* sensational.
**'Aufseher** *m* overseer; inspector.
**'aufsetzen** (*sep., -ge-, h*) 1. *v/t.* set
up; put on (*hat, countenance*); draw
up (*document*); *sich ~* sit up; 2. ✈
*v/i.* touch down.
**'Aufsicht** *f* (*-/-en*) inspection, supervision; *store*: shopwalker, *Am.* floor-
walker; **'~behörde** *f* board of control; **'~srat** *m* board of directors.
**'auf|sitzen** *v/i.* (*irr. sitzen, sep.,
-ge-, h*) *rider*: mount; **'~spannen**
*v/t.* (*sep., -ge-, h*) stretch; put up
(*umbrella*); spread (*sails*); **'~sparen**
*v/t.* (*sep., -ge-, h*) save; *fig.* reserve;
**'~speichern** *v/t.* (*sep., -ge-, h*)
store up; **'~sperren** *v/t.* (*sep., -ge-,
h*) open wide; **'~spielen** (*sep., -ge-,
h*) 1. *v/t. and v/i.* strike up; 2. *v/refl.*
show off; *sich ~ als* set up for; **'~
spießen** *v/t.* (*sep., -ge-, h*) pierce;
*with horns*: gore; run through,
spear; **'~springen** *v/i.* (*irr. springen, sep., -ge-, sein*) jump up; *door*:
fly open; crack; *skin*: chap; **'~spü-
ren** *v/t.* (*sep., -ge-, h*) hunt up;
track down; **'~stacheln** *fig. v/t.*
(*sep., -ge-, h*) goad; incite, instigate;
**'~stampfen** *v/i.* (*sep., -ge-, h*)
stamp (one's foot).
**'Aufstand** *m* insurrection; rebellion;
uprising, revolt.
**aufständisch** *adj.* ['aufʃtendiʃ] rebellious; **'2e** *m* (*-n/-n*) insurgent,
rebel.
**'auf|stapeln** *v/t.* (*sep., -ge-, h*) pile
up; ✝ store (up); **'~stechen** *v/t.*
(*irr. stechen, sep., -ge-, h*) puncture,

prick open; ⚔ lance; **'~stecken** *v/t.*
(*sep., -ge-, h*) pin up; put up (*hair*);
**'~stehen** *v/i.* (*irr. stehen, sep., -ge-*)
1. (*sein*) stand up; rise, get up; revolt; 2. F (*h*) stand open; **'~steigen**
*v/i.* (*irr. steigen, sep., -ge-, sein*) rise,
ascend; ✈ take off; *rider*: mount.
**'aufstell|en** *v/t.* (*sep., -ge-, h*) set
up, put up; ✗ draw up; post (*sen-
tries*); make (*assertion*); set (*example*); erect (*column*); set (*trap*);
nominate (*candidate*); draw up
(*bill*); lay down (*rule*); make out
(*list*); set up, establish (*record*);
**'2ung** *f* putting up; drawing up;
erection; nomination; ✝ statement;
list.

**Aufstieg** ['aufʃti:k] *m* (*-[e]s/-e*)
ascent, *Am. a.* ascension; *fig.* rise.
**'auf|stöbern** *fig. v/t.* (*sep., -ge-, h*)
hunt up; **'~stoßen** (*irr. stoßen, sep.,
-ge-*) 1. *v/t.* (*h*) push open; *~ auf*
(*acc.*) knock against; 2. *v/i.* (*h, sein*)
*of food*: rise, repeat; belch; **'~strei-
chen** *v/t.* (*irr. streichen, sep., -ge-,
h*) spread (*butter*).
**'Aufstrich** *m* spread (*for bread*).
**'auf|stützen** *v/t.* (*sep., -ge-, h*) prop
up, support *s.th.*; *sich ~ auf* (*acc.*)
lean on; **'~suchen** *v/t.* (*sep., -ge-, h*)
visit (*places*); go to see *s.o.*, look
*s.o.* up.
**'Auftakt** *m* ♪ upbeat; *fig.* prelude,
preliminaries *pl.*
**'auf|tauchen** *v/i.* (*sep., -ge-, sein*)
emerge, appear, turn up; **'~tauen**
(*sep., -ge-*) 1. *v/t.* (*h*) thaw; 2. *v/i.*
(*sein*) thaw (*a. fig.*); **'~teilen** *v/t.*
(*sep., -ge-, h*) divide (up), share.

**Auftrag** ['auftra:k] *m* (*-[e]s/=e*)
commission; instruction; mission;
⚖ mandate; ✝ order; **2en** ['~gən]
*v/t.* (*irr. tragen, sep., -ge-, h*) serve
(up) (*meal*); lay on (*paint*); wear
out (*dress*); *j-m et. ~* charge *s.o.*
with *s.th.*; **'~geber** ['-k-] *m* (*-s/-*)
employer; customer; principal; **'~
erteilung** ['-ks'ertailuŋ] *f* (*-/-en*)
placing of an order.
**'auf|treffen** *v/i.* (*irr. treffen, sep.,
-ge-, sein*) strike, hit; **'~treiben** *v/t.*
(*irr. treiben, sep., -ge-, h*) hunt up;
raise (*money*); **'~trennen** *v/t.* (*sep.,
-ge-, h*) rip; unstitch (*seam*).
**'auftreten** 1. *v/i.* (*irr. treten, sep.,
-ge-, sein*) tread; *thea., witness, etc.*:
appear (*als* as); behave, act; *difficulties*: arise; 2. ⚘ *n* (*-s/no pl.*) appearance; occurrence (*of events*);
behavio(u)r.
**'Auftrieb** *m phys. and fig.* buoyancy; ✈ lift; *fig.* impetus.
**'Auftritt** *m thea.* scene (*a. fig.*);
appearance (*of actor*).
**'auf|trumpfen** *fig. v/i.* (*sep., -ge-, h*)
put one's foot down; **'~tun** *v/t.* (*irr.
tun, sep., -ge-, h*) open; *sich ~ open;
chasm*: yawn; *society*: form; **'~tür-
men** *v/t.* (*sep., -ge-, h*) pile *or* heap

up; *sich* ~ tower up; pile up; *difficulties*: accumulate; '~**wachen** *v/i.* (*sep.*, -ge-, *sein*) awake, wake up; '~**wachsen** *v/i.* (*irr.* wachsen, *sep.*, -ge-, *sein*) grow up.

'**Aufwallung** *f* ebullition, surge.

**Aufwand** ['aufvant] *m* (-[e]s/*no pl.*) expense, expenditure (*an dat.* of); pomp; splendid *or* great display (*of words*, *etc.*).

'**aufwärmen** *v/t.* (*sep.*, -ge-, *h*) warm up.

'**Aufwarte|frau** *f* charwoman, *Am. a.* cleaning woman; '**2n** *v/i.* (*sep.*, -ge-, *h*) wait (up)on *s.o.*, attend on *s.o.*; wait (at table).

**aufwärts** *adv.* ['aufverts] upward(s).

'**Aufwartung** *f* attendance; visit; *j-m* ~ *e machen* pay one's respects to s.o., call on s.o.

'**aufwasch|en** *v/t.* (*irr.* waschen, *sep.*, -ge-, *h*) wash up; '**2wasser** *n* dish-water.

'**auf|wecken** *v/t.* (*sep.*, -ge-, *h*) awake(n), wake (up); '~**weichen** (*sep.*, -ge-) 1. *v/t.* (*h*) soften; soak; 2. *v/i.* (*sein*) soften, become soft; '~**weisen** *v/t.* (*irr.* weisen, *sep.*, -ge-, *h*) show, exhibit; produce; '~**wenden** *v/t.* [*irr.* wenden,] *sep.*, -ge-, *h*) spend; *Mühe* ~ take pains; '~**werfen** *v/t.* (*irr.* werfen, *sep.*, -ge-, *h*) raise (*a.* question).

'**aufwert|en** *v/t.* (*sep.*, -ge-, *h*) revalorize; revalue; '**2ung** *f* revalorization; revaluation.

'**aufwickeln** *v/t. and v/refl.* (*sep.*, -ge-, *h*) wind up, roll up.

**aufwiegel|n** ['aufvi:gəln] *v/t.* (*sep.*, -ge-, *h*) stir up, incite, instigate; '**2ung** *f* (-/-*en*) instigation.

'**aufwiegen** *fig.* *v/t.* (*irr.* wiegen, *sep.*, -ge-, *h*) make up for.

**Aufwiegler** ['aufvi:glər] *m* (-s/-) agitator; instigator.

'**aufwirbeln** (*sep.*, -ge-) 1. *v/t.* (*h*) whirl up; raise (*dust*); *fig.* viel Staub ~ create a sensation; 2. *v/i.* (*sein*) whirl up.

'**aufwisch|en** *v/t.* (*sep.*, -ge-, *h*) wipe up; '**2lappen** *m* floor-cloth.

'**aufwühlen** *v/t.* (*sep.*, -ge-, *h*) turn up; *fig.* stir.

'**aufzähl|en** *v/t.* (*sep.*, -ge-, *h*) count up; *fig.* enumerate, *Am. a.* call off; specify, *Am.* itemize; '**2ung** *f* (-/-*en*) enumeration; specification.

'**auf|zäumen** *v/t.* (*sep.*, -ge-, *h*) bridle; '~**zehren** *v/t.* (*sep.*, -ge-, *h*) consume.

'**aufzeichn|en** *v/t.* (*sep.*, -ge-, *h*) draw; note down; record; '**2ung** *f* note; record.

'**auf|zeigen** *v/t.* (*sep.*, -ge-, *h*) show; demonstrate; point out (*mistakes*, *etc.*); disclose; '~**ziehen** (*irr.* ziehen, *sep.*, -ge-) 1. *v/t.* (*h*) draw *or* pull up; (pull) open; hoist (*flag*); bring up (*child*); mount (*picture*);

wind (up) (*clock*, *etc.*); *j-n* ~ tease s.o., pull s.o.'s leg; *Saiten auf e-e Violine* ~ string a violin; 2. *v/i.* (*sein*) ✕ draw up; *storm*: approach.

'**Aufzucht** *f* rearing, breeding.

'**Aufzug** *m* ⊕ hoist; lift, *Am.* elevator; *thea.* act; attire; show.

'**aufzwingen** *v/t.* (*irr.* zwingen, *sep.*, -ge-, *h*): *j-m et.* ~ force s.th. upon s.o.

**Augapfel** ['auk*ʔ*-] *m* eyeball.

**Auge** ['augə] *n* (-*s*/-*n*) eye; sight; ⚘ bud; *in meinen* ~*n* in my view; *im* ~ *behalten* keep an eye on; keep in mind; *aus den* ~*n verlieren* lose sight of; *ein* ~ *zudrücken* turn a blind eye (*bei* to); *ins* ~ *fallen* strike the eye; *große* ~*n machen* open one's eyes wide; *unter vier* ~*n* face to face, privately; *kein* ~ *zutun* not to get a wink of sleep.

'**Augen|arzt** *m* oculist, eye-doctor; '~**blick** *m* moment, instant; '**2-blicklich** 1. *adj.* instantaneous; momentary; present; 2. *adv.* instant(aneous)ly; at present; '~**braue** *f* eyebrow; '~**entzündung** ♂ *f* inflammation of the eye; '~**heilkunde** *f* ophthalmology; '~**klinik** *f* ophthalmic hospital; '~**leiden** ♂ *n* eye-complaint; '~**licht** *n* eyesight; '~**lid** *n* eyelid; '~**maß** *n*: *ein gutes* ~ *a sure eye*; *nach dem* ~ by eye; '~**merk** ['~merk] *n* (-[e]s/*no pl.*): *sein* ~ *richten auf* (*acc.*) turn one's attention to; have *s.th.* in view; '~**schein** *m* appearance; *in* ~ *nehmen* examine, view, inspect; '**2-scheinlich** *adj.* evident; '~**wasser** *n* eyewash, eye-lotion; '~**wimper** *f* eyelash; '~**zeuge** *m* eyewitness.

**August** [au'gust] *m* (-[e]s, - /-*e*) August.

**Auktion** [auk'tsjo:n] *f* (-/-*en*) auction; ~**ator** [*-*o'na:tər] *m* (-s/-*en*) auctioneer.

**Aula** ['aula] *f* (-/*Aulen*, -*s*) (assembly) hall, *Am.* auditorium.

**aus** [aus] 1. *prp.* (*dat.*) out of; from; of; by; for; in; ~ *Achtung* out of respect; ~ *London* kommen come from London; ~ *diesem Grunde* for this reason; ~ *Ihrem Brief ersehe ich* I see from your letter; 2. *adv.* out; over; *die Schule ist* ~ school is over; F: *von mir* ~ for all I care; *auf et.* ~ *sein* be keen on s.th.; *es ist* ~ *mit ihm* it is all over with him; *das Spiel ist* ~*!* the game is up!; *er weiß weder ein noch* ~ he is at his wit's end; *on instruments*, *etc.*: *an* — ~ on — off.

**ausarbeit|en** ['aus*ʔ*-] *v/t.* (*sep.*, -ge-, *h*) work out; elaborate; '**2ung** *f* (-/-*en*) working-out; elaboration; composition.

**aus|arten** ['aus*ʔ*-] *v/i.* (*sep.*, -ge-, *sein*) degenerate; get out of hand; ~**atmen** ['aus*ʔ*-] (*sep.*, -ge-, *h*)

**1.** v/i. breathe out; **2.** v/t. breathe out; exhale (*vapour, etc.*); '~**baggern** v/t. (*sep., -ge-, h*) dredge (*river, etc.*); excavate (*ground*).

'**Ausbau** m (*-[e]s/-ten*) extension; completion; development; '**2en** v/t. (*sep., -ge-, h*) develop; extend; finish, complete; ⊕ dismantle (*engine*).

'**ausbedingen** v/t. (*irr. bedingen, sep., no -ge-, h*) stipulate.

'**ausbesser|n** v/t. (*sep., -ge-, h*) mend, repair, *Am.* F *a.* fix; '**2ung** f repair, mending.

'**Ausbeut|e** f (*-/~-n*) gain, profit; yield; ⚒ output; '**2en** v/t. (*sep., -ge-, h*) exploit; sweat (*workers*); '~**ung** f (*-/-en*) exploitation.

'**ausbild|en** v/t. (*sep., -ge-, h*) form, develop; train; instruct, educate; ✗ drill; '**2ung** f development; training; instruction; education; ✗ drill.

'**ausbitten** v/t. (*irr. bitten, sep., -ge-, h*): sich et. ~ request s.th.; insist on s.th.

'**ausbleiben 1.** v/i. (*irr. bleiben, sep., -ge-, sein*) stay away, fail to appear; **2.** 2 n (*-s/no pl.*) non-arrival, non-appearance; absence.

'**Ausblick** m outlook (*auf acc.* over, on), view (of), prospect (of); *fig.* outlook (on).

'**aus|bohren** v/t. (*sep., -ge-, h*) bore, drill; '~**brechen** (*irr. brechen, sep., -ge-*) **1.** v/t. (h) break out; vomit; **2.** v/i. (sein) break out; *fig.* burst out (*laughing, etc.*).

'**ausbreit|en** v/t. (*sep., -ge-, h*) spread (out); stretch (out) (*arms, wings*); display; sich ~ spread; '**2ung** f (*-/~-en*) spreading.

'**ausbrennen** v. brennen, sep., -ge-) **1.** v/t. (h) burn out; ✄ cauterize; **2.** v/i. (sein) burn out.

'**Ausbruch** m outbreak; eruption (*of volcano*); escape (*from prison*); outburst (*of emotion*).

'**aus|brüten** v/t. (*sep., -ge-, h*) hatch (*a. fig.*); '~**bürgern** v/t. (*sep., -ge-, h*) denationalize, expatriate.

'**Ausdauer** f perseverance; '**2nd** adj. persevering; ♧ perennial.

'**ausdehn|en** v/t. and v/refl. (*sep., -ge-, h*) extend (*auf acc.* to); expand; stretch; '**2ung** f expansion; extension; extent.

'**aus|denken** v/t. (*irr. denken, sep., -ge-, h*) think s.th. out, *Am. a.* think s.th. up, contrive, devise, invent; imagine; '~**dörren** v/t. (*sep., -ge-, h*) dry up; parch; '~**drehen** v/t. (*sep., -ge-, h*) turn off (*radio, gas*); ✄ turn out, switch off (*light*).

'**Ausdruck** m **1.** (*-[e]s/no pl.*) expression; **2.** (*-[e]s/~e*) expression; term.

'**ausdrück|en** v/t. (*sep., -ge-, h*) press, squeeze (out); stub out (*cig-*

*arette*); *fig.* express; '~**lich** adj. express, explicit.

'**ausdrucks|los** adj. inexpressive, expressionless; blank; '~**voll** adj. expressive; '**2weise** f mode of expression; style.

'**Ausdünstung** f (*-/-en*) exhalation; perspiration; odo(u)r, smell.

**auseinander** adv. [aus?ar'nandər] asunder, apart; separate(d); ~**bringen** v/t. (*irr. bringen, sep., -ge-, h*) separate, sever; ~**gehen** v/i. (*irr. gehen, sep., -ge-, sein*) meeting, *crowd:* break up; *opinions:* differ; *friends:* part; *crowd:* disperse; *roads:* diverge; ~**nehmen** v/t. (*irr. nehmen, sep., -ge-, h*) take apart or to pieces; ⊕ disassemble, dismantle; ~**setzen** *fig.* v/t. (*sep., -ge-, h*) explain; sich mit j-m ~ ✝ compound with s.o.; argue with s.o.; have it out with s.o.; sich mit e-m Problem ~ get down to a problem; come to grips with a problem; '**2setzung** f (*-/-en*) explanation; discussion; settlement (*with creditors, etc.*); kriegerische ~ armed conflict.

**auserlesen** adj. ['aus?-] exquisite, choice; select(ed).

**auserwählen** ['aus?-] v/t. (*sep., no -ge-, h*) select, choose.

'**ausfahr|en** (*irr. fahren, sep., -ge-*) **1.** v/i. (sein) drive out, go for a drive; ♒ leave (*port*); **2.** v/t. (h) take (*baby*) out (*in pram*); take *s.o.* for a drive; rut (*road*); ✈ lower (*undercarriage*); '**2t** f drive; excursion; way out, exit (*of garage, etc.*); gateway; departure.

'**Ausfall** m falling out; ✝: loss; deficit; '**2en** v/i. (*irr. fallen, sep., -ge-, sein*) fall out; not to take place; turn out, prove; ~ **lassen** drop; cancel; die Schule fällt aus there is no school; '**2end** adj. offensive, insulting.

'**aus|fasern** v/i. (*sep., -ge-, sein*) ravel out, fray; '~**fegen** v/t. (*sep., -ge-, h*) sweep (out).

**ausfertig|en** ['ausfertigən] v/t. (*sep., -ge-, h*) draw up (*document*); make out (*bill, etc.*); issue (*passport*); '**2ung** f (*-/-en*) drawing up; issue; draft; copy; in doppelter ~ in duplicate. [*chen* find out; discover.]

**ausfindig** adj. ['ausfindiç]: ~ **ma-**]

'**Ausflucht** f (*-/~e*) excuse, evasion, shift, subterfuge.

'**Ausflug** m trip, excursion, outing.

**Ausflügler** ['ausfly:klər] m (*-s/-*) excursionist, tripper, tourist.

'**Ausfluß** m flowing out; discharge (*a.* ✄); outlet, outfall.

'**aus|fragen** v/t. (*sep., -ge-, h*) interrogate, *Am. a.* quiz; sound; '~**fransen** v/i. (*sep., -ge-, sein*) fray.

**Ausfuhr** ✝ ['ausfu:r] f (*-/-en*) export(ation); '~**artikel** ✝ m export (article).

'**ausführ|bar** adj. practicable; ✝ exportable; '**~en** v/t. (sep., -ge-, h) execute, carry out, perform, Am. a. fill; ✝ export; explain; j-n ~ take s.o. out.

'**Ausfuhr|genehmigung** f export permit; '**~handel** m export trade.

'**ausführlich 1.** adj. detailed; comprehensive; circumstantial; **2.** adv. in detail, at (some) length; '**♀keit** f (-/no pl.) minuteness of detail; particularity; comprehensiveness; copiousness.

'**Ausführung** f execution, performance; workmanship; type, make; explanation; '**~sbestimmungen** ✝ f/pl. export regulations pl.

'**Ausfuhr|verbot** n embargo on exports; '**~waren** f/pl. exports pl.; '**~zoll** m export duty.

'**ausfüllen** v/t. (sep., -ge-, h) fill out or up; fill in, complete (form); Am. fill out (blank).

'**Ausgabe** f distribution; edition (of book); expense, expenditure; issue (of shares, etc.); issuing office.

'**Ausgang** m going out; exit; way out; outlet; end; result; '**~skapital** ✝ n original capital; '**~spunkt** m starting-point; '**~sstellung** f starting-position.

'**ausgeben** v/t. (irr. geben, sep., -ge-, h) give out; spend (money); issue (shares, etc.); sich ~ für pass o.s. off for, pretend to be.

**ausge|beult** adj. ['**ausgəbɔylt**] baggy; '**~bombt** adj. ['**~bɔmpt**] bombed out; **~dehnt** adj. ['**~de:nt**] expansive, vast, extensive; **~dient** adj. ['**~di:nt**] worn out; superannuated; retired, pensioned off; **~er** Soldat ex-serviceman, veteran; '**~fallen** fig. adj. odd, queer, unusual.

'**ausgehen** v/i. (irr. gehen, sep., -ge-, sein) go out; take a walk; end; colour: fade; hair: fall out; money, provisions: run out; uns gehen die Vorräte aus we run out of provisions; darauf ~ aim at; gut etc. ~ turn out well, etc.; leer ~ come away empty-handed; von et. ~ start from s.th.

'**ausge|lassen** fig. adj. frolicsome, boisterous; '**~nommen** prp. **1.** (acc.) except (for); **2.** (nom.): Anwesende ~ present company excepted; **~prägt** adj. ['**~prɛ:kt**] marked, pronounced; **~rechnet** fig. adv. ['**~rɛçnət**] just; ~ er he of all people; ~ heute today of all days; '**~schlossen** fig. adj. impossible.

'**ausgestalten** v/t. (sep., no -ge-, h) arrange (celebration); et. zu et. ~ develop or turn s.th. into s.th.

**ausge|sucht** fig. adj. ['**ausgəzu:xt**] exquisite, choice; '**~wachsen** adj. full-grown; '**~zeichnet** fig. adj. ['**~tsaiçnət**] excellent.

**ausgiebig** adj. ['**ausgi:biç**] abundant, plentiful; meal: substantial.

'**ausgießen** v/t. (irr. gießen, sep., -ge-, h) pour out.

**Ausgleich** ['**ausglaiç**] m (-[e]s/-e) compromise; compensation; ✝ settlement; sports: equalization (of score); tennis: deuce (score of 40 all); '**♀en** v/t. (irr. gleichen, sep., -ge-, h) equalize; compensate (loss); ✝ balance.

'**aus|gleiten** v/i. (irr. gleiten, sep., -ge-, sein) slip, slide; '**~graben** v/t. (irr. graben, sep., -ge-, h) dig out or up (a. fig.); excavate; exhume (body).

**Ausguck** ⚓ ['**ausguk**] m (-[e]s/-e) look-out.

'**Ausguß** m sink; '**~eimer** m slop-pail.

'**aus|haken** v/t. (sep., -ge-, h) unhook; '**~halten** (irr. halten, sep., -ge-, h) **1.** v/t. endure, bear, stand; ♪ sustain (note); **2.** v/i. hold out; last; **~händigen** ['**~hɛndigən**] v/t. (sep., -ge-, h) deliver up, hand over, surrender.

'**Aushang** m notice, placard, poster.

'**aushänge|n 1.** v/t. (sep., -ge-, h) hang or put out; unhinge (door); **2.** v/i. (irr. hängen, sep., -ge-, h) have been hung or put out; '**♀schild** n signboard.

**aus|harren** ['**ausharən**] v/i. (sep., -ge-, h) persevere; hold out; '**~hauchen** v/t. (sep., -ge-, h) breathe out, exhale; '**~heben** v/t. (irr. heben, sep., -ge-, h) dig (trench); unhinge (door); recruit, levy (soldiers); excavate (earth); rob (nest); clean out, raid (nest of criminals); '**~helfen** v/i. (irr. helfen, sep., -ge-, h) help out.

'**Aushilf|e** f (temporary) help or assistance; sie hat e-e ~ she has s.o. to help out; '**♀sweise** adv. as a makeshift; temporarily.

'**aushöhl|en** v/t. (sep., -ge-, h) hollow out; '**♀ung** f hollow.

'**aus|holen** (sep., -ge-, h) **1.** v/i. raise one's hand (as if to strike); weit ~ go far back (in narrating s.th.); **2.** v/t. sound, pump s.o.; '**~horchen** v/t. (sep., -ge-, h) sound, pump s.o.; '**~hungern** v/t. (sep., -ge-, h) starve (out); '**~husten** v/t. (sep., -ge-, h) cough up; '**~kennen** v/refl. (irr. kennen, sep., -ge-, h) know one's way (about place); be well versed, be at home (in subject); er kennt sich aus he knows what's what; '**~kleiden** v/t. (sep., -ge-, h) undress; ⊕ line, coat; sich ~ undress; '**~klopfen** v/t. (sep., -ge-, h) beat (out); dust (garment); knock out (pipe); '**~klügeln** ['**~kly:gəln**] v/t. (sep., -ge-, h) work s.th. out; contrive; puzzle s.th. out.

'**auskommen 1.** v/i. (irr. kommen, sep., -ge-, sein) get out; escape; ~

*mit* manage with *s.th.*; get on with *s.o.*; ~ *ohne* do without; *mit dem Geld* ~ make both ends meet; **2.** 2 *n* (-s/*no pl.*) competence, competency.

'**auskundschaften** *v/t.* (*sep.*, -ge-, *h*) explore; ✕ reconnoit|re, *Am.* -er, scout.

**Auskunft** ['auskunft] *f* (-/-e) information; inquiry office, inquiries *pl.*, *Am.* information desk; '~sstelle *f* inquiry office, inquiries *pl.*, *Am.* information bureau.

'**aus|lachen** *v/t.* (*sep.*, -ge-, *h*) laugh at, deride; '~laden *v/t.* (*irr.* laden, *sep.*, -ge-, *h*) unload; discharge (*cargo from ship*); cancel *s.o.'s* invitation, put off (*guest*).

'**Auslage** *f* display, show (*of goods*); *in der* ~ in the (shop) window; ~n *pl.* expenses *pl.*

'**Ausland** *n* (-[e]s/*no pl.*): *das* ~ foreign countries *pl.*; *ins* ~, *im* ~ abroad.

**Ausländ|er** ['auslɛndər] *m* (-s/-), '~erin *f* (-/-nen) foreigner; alien; 2isch *adj.* foreign; 2, *zo.* exotic.

'**Auslandskorrespondent** *m* foreign correspondent.

'**auslass|en** *v/t.* (*irr.* lassen, *sep.*, -ge-, *h*) let out (*water*); melt (down) (*butter*); render down (*fat*); let out (*garment*); let down (*hem*); leave out, omit (*word*); cut *s.th.* out; miss *or* cut out (*meal*); miss (*dance*); s-n *Zorn an j-m* ~ vent one's anger on *s.o.*; *sich* ~ *über* (*acc.*) say *s.th.* about; express one's opinion about; '2ung *f* (-/-en) omission; remark, utterance; '2ungszeichen *gr. n* apostrophe.

'**aus|laufen** *v/i.* (*irr.* laufen, *sep.*, -ge-, *sein*) run *or* leak out (*aus et.* of *s.th.*); leak; end (*in s.th.*); *machine:* run down; ⏚ (set) sail; '~leeren *v/t.* (*sep.*, -ge-, *h*) empty; 🗲 evacuate (*bowels*).

'**ausleg|en** *v/t.* (*sep.*, -ge-, *h*) lay out; display (*goods*); explain, interpret; advance (*money*); '2ung *f* (-/-en) explanation, interpretation.

'**aus|leihen** *v/t.* (*irr.* leihen, *sep.*, -ge-, *h*) lend (out), *esp. Am.* loan; '~lernen *v/i.* (*sep.*, -ge-, *h*) finish one's apprenticeship; *man lernt nie aus* we live and learn.

'**Auslese** *f* choice, selection; *fig.* pick; '2n *v/t.* (*irr.* lesen, *sep.*, -ge-, *h*) pick out, select; finish reading (*book*).

'**ausliefer|n** *v/t.* (*sep.*, -ge-, *h*) hand *or* turn over, deliver (up); extradite (*criminal*); *ausgeliefert sein* (*dat.*) be at the mercy of; '2ung *f* delivery; extradition.

'**aus|liegen** *v/i.* (*irr.* liegen, *sep.*, -ge-, *h*) be displayed, be on show; '~löschen *v/t.* (*sep.*, -ge-, *h*) put out, switch off (*light*); extinguish (*fire*) (*a. fig.*); efface (*word*); wipe

out, erase; '~losen *v/t.* (*sep.*, -ge-, *h*) draw (lots) for.

'**auslös|en** *v/t.* (*sep.*, -ge-, *h*) ⊕ release; redeem, ransom (*prisoner*); redeem (*from pawn*); *fig.* cause, start; arouse (*applause*); '2er *m* (-s/-) ⊕ release, *esp. phot.* trigger.

'**aus|lüften** *v/t.* (*sep.*, -ge-, *h*) air, ventilate; '~machen *v/t.* (*sep.*, -ge-, *h*) make out, sight, spot; *sum:* amount to; constitute, make up; put out (*fire*); 🗲 turn out, switch off (*light*); agree on, arrange; settle; *es macht nichts aus* it does not matter; *würde es Ihnen et.* ~, *wenn ...?* would you mind (*ger.*) ...?; '~malen *v/t.* (*sep.*, -ge-, *h*) paint; *sich et.* ~ picture *s.th.* to o.s., imagine *s.th.*

'**Ausmaß** *n* dimension(s *pl.*), measurement(s *pl.*); *fig.* extent.

**aus|mergeln** ['ausmɛrgəln] *v/t.* (*sep.*, -ge-, *h*) emaciate; exhaust; ~merzen ['~mɛrtsən] *v/t.* (*sep.*, -ge-, *h*) eliminate; eradicate; '~messen *v/t.* (*irr.* messen, *sep.*, -ge-, *h*) measure.

**Ausnahm|e** ['ausna:mə] *f* (-/-n) exception; '2sweise *adv.* by way of exception; exceptionally.

'**ausnehmen** *v/t.* (*irr.* nehmen, *sep.*, -ge-, *h*) take out; draw (*fowl*); F fleece *s.o.*; *fig.* except, exempt; '~d **1.** *adj.* exceptional; **2.** *adv.* exceedingly.

'**aus|nutzen** *v/t.* (*sep.*, -ge-, *h*) utilize; take advantage of; *esp.* 🜨, ✕ exploit; '~packen (*sep.*, -ge-, *h*) **1.** *v/t.* unpack; **2.** F *fig. v/i.* speak one's mind; '~pfeifen *thea. v/t.* (*irr.* pfeifen, *sep.*, -ge-, *h*) hiss; '~plaudern *v/t.* (*sep.*, -ge-, *h*) blab *or* let out; '~polstern *v/t.* (*sep.*, -ge-, *h*) stuff, pad; wad; '~probieren *v/t.* (*sep.*, -ge-, *h*) try, test.

**Auspuff** *mot.* ['auspuf] *m* (-[e]s/-e) exhaust; '~gas *mot. n* exhaust gas; '~rohr *mot. n* exhaust-pipe; '~topf *mot. m* silencer, *Am.* muffler.

'**aus|putzen** *v/t.* (*sep.*, -ge-, *h*) clean; '~quartieren *v/t.* (*sep.*, *no* -ge-, *h*) dislodge; ✕ billet out; '~radieren *v/t.* (*sep.*, *no* -ge-, *h*) erase; '~rangieren *v/t.* (*sep.*, *no* -ge-, *h*) discard; '~rauben *v/t.* (*sep.*, -ge-, *h*) rob; ransack; '~räumen *v/t.* (*sep.*, -ge-, *h*) empty, clear (out); remove (*furniture*); '~rechnen *v/t.* (*sep.*, -ge-, *h*) calculate, compute; reckon (out), *Am.* figure out *or* up (*all a. fig.*).

'**Ausrede** *f* excuse, evasion, subterfuge; '2n (*sep.*, -ge-, *h*) **1.** *v/i.* finish speaking; ~ *lassen* hear *s.o.* out; **2.** *v/t.*: j-m *et.* ~ dissuade *s.o.* from *s.th.*

'**ausreichen** *v/i.* (*sep.*, -ge-, *h*) suffice; '~d *adj.* sufficient.

'**Ausreise** *f* departure; ⏚ voyage out.

'ausreiß|en (irr. reißen, sep., -ge-) 1 .v/t. (h) pull or tear out; 2. v/i. (sein) run away; '2er m runaway.

aus|renken ['ausrɛŋkən] v/t. (sep., -ge-, h) dislocate; '⌐richten v/t. (sep., -ge-, h) straighten; ✗ dress; adjust; deliver (message); do, effect; accomplish; obtain; arrange (feast); richte ihr e-n Gruß von mir aus! remember me to her!; ⌐rotten ['⌐rɔtən] v/t. (sep., -ge-, h) root up; fig. extirpate, exterminate.

'Ausruf m cry; exclamation; '2en (irr. rufen, sep., -ge-,h) 1. v/i. cry out, exclaim; 2. v/t. proclaim; '⌐zeichen n exclamation mark, Am. a. exclamation point; '⌐ung f (-/-en) proclamation; '⌐ungszeichen n s. Ausrufezeichen. [-ge-, h) rest.\
'ausruhen v/i.,v/t. and v/refl. (sep.,)
'ausrüst|en v/t. (sep., -ge-, h) fit out; equip; '2ung f outfit, equipment, fittings pl. [disseminate.\
'aussäen v/t. (sep., -ge-, h) sow; fig.)
'Aussage f statement; declaration; ᵗᵗ evidence; gr. predicate; '2n (sep., -ge-, h) 1. v/t. state, declare; ᵗᵗ depose; 2. ᵗᵗ v/i. give evidence.

'Aussatz ᵗ m (-es/no pl.) leprosy.

'aus|saugen v/t. (sep., -ge-, h) suck (out); fig. exhaust (land); '⌐schalten v/t. (sep., -ge-, h) eliminate; ∉ cut out, switch off, turn off or out (light).

Ausschank ['ausʃaŋk] m (-[e]s/⌐e) retail (of alcoholic drinks); public house, F pub.

'Ausschau f (-/no pl.): ⌐ halten nach be on the look-out for, watch for.

'ausscheid|en (irr. scheiden, sep., -ge-) 1. v/t. (h) separate; ?⌐, ?⌐, physiol. eliminate; ℰ secrete; 2. v/i. (sein) retire; withdraw; sports: drop out; '2ung f separation; elimination (a. sports); ℰ secretion.

'aus|schiffen v/t. and v/refl. (sep., -ge-, h) disembark; '⌐schimpfen v/t. (sep., -ge-, h) scold, tell s.o. off, berate; '⌐schirren v/t. (sep., -ge-, h) unharness; '⌐schlachten v/t. (sep., -ge-, h) cut up; cannibalize (car, etc.); fig. exploit, make the most of; '⌐schlafen (irr. schlafen, sep., -ge-, h) 1. v/i. sleep one's fill; 2. v/t. sleep off (effects of drink, etc.).

'Ausschlag m ℰ eruption, rash; deflexion (of pointer); den ⌐ geben settle it; '2en ['⌐gən] (irr. schlagen, sep., -ge-) 1. v/t. (h) knock or beat out; line; refuse, decline; 2. v/i. (h) horse: kick; pointer: deflect; 3. v/i. (h, sein) bud; '2gebend adj. ['⌐k-] decisive.

'ausschließ|en v/t. (irr. schließen, sep., -ge-, h) shut or lock out; fig.: exclude; expel; sports: disqualify; '⌐lich adj. exclusive.

'Ausschluß m exclusion; expulsion; sports: disqualification.

'ausschmücken v/t. (sep., -ge-, h) adorn, decorate; fig. embellish.

'Ausschnitt m cut; décolleté, (low) neck (of dress); cutting, Am. clipping (from newspaper); fig. part, section.

'ausschreib|en v/t. (irr. schreiben, sep., -ge-, h) write out; copy; write out (word) in full; make out (invoice); announce; advertise; '2ung f (-/-en) announcement; advertisement.

'ausschreit|en (irr. schreiten, sep., -ge-) 1. v/i. (sein) step out, take long strides; 2. v/t. (h) pace (room), measure by steps; '2ung f (-/-en) excess; ⌐en pl. riots pl.

'Ausschuß m refuse, waste, rubbish; committee, board.

'aus|schütteln v/t. (sep., -ge-, h) shake out; '⌐schütten v/t. (sep., -ge-, h) pour out; spill; † distribute (dividend); j-m sein Herz ⌐ pour out one's heart to s.o.; '⌐schwärmen v/i. (sep., -ge-, sein) swarm out; ⌐ (lassen) ✗ extend, deploy.

'ausschweif|end adj. dissolute; '2ung f (-/-en) debauchery, excess.

'ausschwitzen v/t. (sep., -ge-, h) exude.

'aussehen 1. v/i. (irr. sehen, sep., -ge-, h) look; wie sieht er aus? what does he look like?; es sieht nach Regen aus it looks like rain; 2. 2 n (-s/ no pl.) look(s pl.), appearance.

außen adv. ['ausən] (on the) outside; von ⌐ her from (the) outside; nach ⌐ (hin) outward(s); '2aufnahme f film: outdoor shot; '2bordmotor m outboard motor.

'aussenden v/t. ([irr. senden,] sep., -ge-, h) send out.

'Außen|hafen m outport; '⌐handel m foreign trade; '⌐minister m foreign minister; Foreign Secretary, Am. Secretary of State; '⌐ministerium n foreign ministry; Foreign Office, Am. State Department; '⌐politik f foreign policy; '2politisch adj. of or referring to foreign affairs; '⌐seite f outside, surface; '⌐seiter m (-s/-) outsider; '⌐stände † ['⌐ʃtɛndə] pl. outstanding debts pl., Am. accounts pl. receivable; '⌐welt f outer or outside world.

außer ['ausər] 1. prp. (dat.) out of; beside(s), Am. aside from; except; ⌐ sich sein be beside o.s. (vor Freude with joy); 2. cj.: ⌐ daß except that; ⌐ wenn unless; '⌐dem cj. besides, moreover.

äußere ['ɔysərə] 1. adj. exterior, outer, external, outward; 2. 2 n (Äußer[e]n/no pl.) exterior, outside, outward appearance.

'außer|gewöhnlich adj. extraordinary; exceptional; **'~halb 1.** *prp.* (*gen.*) outside, out of; beyond; **2.** *adv.* on the outside.

**äußerlich** *adj.* ['ɔysərliç] external, outward; **'2keit** *f* (*-/-en*) superficiality; formality.

**äußern** ['ɔysərn] *v/t.* (*ge-, h*) utter, express; advance; *sich ~ matter*: manifest itself; *p.* express o.s.

**'außer'ordentlich** *adj.* extraordinary.

**äußerst** ['ɔysərst] **1.** *adj.* outermost; *fig.* utmost, extreme; **2.** *adv.* extremely, highly.

**außerstande** *adj.* [ausər'ʃtandə] unable, not in a position.

**'Äußerung** *f* (*-/-en*) utterance, remark.

**'aussetz|en** (*sep., -ge-, h*) **1.** *v/t.* set or put out; lower (*boat*); promise (*reward*); settle (*pension*); bequeath; expose (*child*); expose (*dat.* to); et. ~ *an* (*dat.*) find fault with; **2.** *v/i.* intermit; fail; *activity*: stop; suspend; *mot.* misfire; **'2ung** *f* (*-/-en*) exposure (*of child, to weather, etc.*) (*a.* ⚰).

**'Aussicht** *f* (*-/-en*) view (*auf acc.* of); *fig.* prospect (of), chance (of); *in ~ haben* have in prospect; **'2slos** *adj.* hopeless, desperate; **'2sreich** *adj.* promising, full of promise.

**aussöhn|en** ['ausˌzø:nən] *v/t.* (*sep., -ge-, h*) reconcile *s.o.* (*mit* to *s.th.*, with *s.o.*); *sich ~* reconcile o.s. (to *s.th.*, with *s.o.*); **'2ung** *f* (*-/-en*) reconciliation.

**'aussondern** *v/t.* (*sep., -ge-, h*) single out; separate.

**'aus|spannen** (*sep., -ge-, h*) **1.** *v/t.* stretch, extend; F *fig.* steal (*s.o.'s girl friend*); unharness (*draught animal*); **2.** *fig.* *v/i.* (take a) rest, relax; **'~speien** *v/t. and v/i.* (*irr. speien, sep., -ge-, h*) spit out.

**'aussperr|en** *v/t.* (*sep., -ge-, h*) shut out; lock out (*workmen*); **'2ung** *f* (*-/-en*) lock-out.

**'aus|spielen** (*sep., -ge-, h*) **1.** *v/t.* play (*card*); **2.** *v/i.* *at cards*: lead; *er hat ausgespielt* he is done for; **'~spionieren** *v/t.* (*sep., no -ge-, h*) spy out.　　　　[cent; discussion.]

**'Aussprache** *f* pronunciation, ac-|

**'aussprechen** (*irr. sprechen, sep., -ge-, h*) **1.** *v/t.* pronounce, express; *sich ~ für* (*gegen*) declare o.s. for (against); **2.** *v/i.* finish speaking.

**'Ausspruch** *m* utterance; saying; remark.

**'aus|spucken** *v/i. and v/t.* (*sep., -ge-, h*) spit out; **'~spülen** *v/t.* (*sep., -ge-, h*) rinse.

**'Ausstand** *m* strike, *Am.* F *a.* walkout; *in den ~ treten* go on strike, *Am.* F *a.* walk out.

**ausstatt|en** ['ausˌʃtatən] *v/t.* (*sep., -ge-, h*) fit out, equip; furnish; supply (*mit* with); give a dowry to

(*daughter*); get up (*book*); **'2ung** *f* (*-/-en*) outfit, equipment; furniture; supply; dowry; get-up (*of book*).

**'aus|stechen** *v/t.* (*irr. stechen, sep., -ge-, h*) cut out (*a. fig.*); put out (*eye*); **'~stehen** (*irr. stehen, sep., -ge-, h*) **1.** *v/i.* *payments*: be outstanding; **2.** *v/t.* endure, bear; **'~steigen** *v/i.* (*irr. steigen, sep., -ge-, sein*) get out *or* off, alight.

**'ausstell|en** *v/t.* (*sep., -ge-, h*) exhibit; make out (*invoice*); issue (*document*); draw (*bill*); **'2er** *m* (*-s/-*) exhibitor; drawer; **'2ung** *f* exhibition, show; **'2ungsraum** *m* show-room.

**'aussterben** *v/i.* (*irr. sterben, sep., -ge-, sein*) die out; become extinct.

**'Aussteuer** *f* trousseau, dowry.

**'ausstopfen** *v/t.* (*sep., -ge-, h*) stuff; wad, pad.

**'ausstoß|en** *v/t.* (*irr. stoßen, sep., -ge-, h*) thrust out, eject; expel; utter (*cry*); heave (*sigh*); ✕ cashier; **'2ung** *f* (*-/-en*) expulsion.

**'aus|strahlen** *v/t. and v/i.* (*sep., -ge-, h*) radiate; **'~strecken** *v/t.* (*sep., -ge-, h*) stretch (out); **'~streichen** *v/t.* (*irr. streichen, sep., -ge-, h*) strike out; smooth (down); **'~streuen** *v/t.* (*sep., -ge-, h*) scatter; spread (*rumours*); **'~strömen** (*sep., -ge-*) **1.** *v/i.* (*sein*) stream out; *gas, light*: emanate; *gas, steam*: escape; **2.** *v/t.* (*h*) pour (out); **'~suchen** *v/t.* (*sep., -ge-, h*) choose, select.

**'Austausch** *m* exchange; **'2bar** *adj.* exchangeable; **'2en** *v/t.* (*sep., -ge-, h*) exchange.

**'austeil|en** *v/t.* (*sep., -ge-, h*) distribute; deal out (*blows*); **'2ung** *f* distribution.

**Auster** *zo.* ['austər] *f* (*-/-n*) oyster.

**'austragen** *v/t.* (*irr. tragen, sep., -ge-, h*) deliver (*letters, etc.*); hold (*contest*).

**Austral|ier** [au'strɑ:liər] *m* (*-s/-*) Australian; **2isch** *adj.* Australian.

**'austreib|en** *v/t.* (*irr. treiben, sep., -ge-, h*) drive out; expel; **'2ung** *f* (*-/-en*) expulsion.

**'aus|treten** (*irr. treten, sep., -ge-*) **1.** *v/t.* (*h*) tread *or* stamp out; wear out (*shoes*); wear down (*steps*); **2.** *v/i.* (*sein*) emerge, come out; *river*: overflow its banks; retire (*aus* from); F ease o.s.; ~ *aus* leave (*society, etc.*); **'~trinken** *v/t. and v/i.* (*irr. trinken, sep., -ge-, h*) **1.** *v/t.* drink up; empty; drain; **2.** *v/i.* finish drinking; **'2tritt** *m* leaving; retirement; **'~trocknen** (*sep., -ge-*) **1.** *v/t.* (*h*) dry up; drain (*land*); parch (*throat, earth*); **2.** *v/i.* (*sein*) dry up.

**ausüb|en** ['ausˌʔy:-] *v/t.* (*sep., -ge-, h*) exercise; practi|se, *Am.* -ce (*profession*); exert (*influence*); **'2ung** *f* practice; exercise.

'Ausverkauf ✝ m selling off or out (of stock); sale; 'Qt ✝, thea. adj. sold out; theatre notice: 'full house'.
'Auswahl f choice; selection; ✝ assortment. [choose, select.]
'auswählen v/t. (sep., -ge-, h))
'Auswander|er m emigrant; 'Qn v/i. (sep.,-ge-, sein) emigrate; '~ung f emigration.
auswärt|ig adj. ['ausvertiç] out-of-town; non-resident; foreign; das Auswärtige Amt s. Außenministerium; ~s adv. ['~s] outward(s); out of doors; out of town; abroad; ~ essen dine out.
'auswechseln 1. v/t. (sep., -ge-, h) exchange; change; replace; 2. Q n (-s/no pl.) exchange; replacement.
'Ausweg m way out (a. fig.); outlet; fig. expedient.
'ausweichen v/i. (irr. weichen, sep., -ge-, sein) make way (for); fig. evade, avoid; '~d adj. evasive.
Ausweis ['ausvais] m (-es/-e) (bank) return; identity card, Am. identification (card); Qen ['~zən] v/t. (irr. weisen, sep., -ge-, h) turn out, expel; evict; deport; show, prove; sich ~ prove one's identity; '~papiere n/pl. identity papers pl.; '~ung ['~zuŋ] f expulsion; '~ungsbefehl m expulsion order.
'ausweiten v/t. and v/refl. (sep., -ge-, h) widen, stretch, expand.
'auswendig 1. adj. outward, outside; 2. adv. outwardly, outside; fig. by heart.
'aus|werfen v/t. (irr. werfen, sep., -ge-, h) throw out, cast; eject; ⚕ expectorate; allow (sum of money); '~werten v/t. (sep., -ge-, h) evaluate; analyze, interpret; utilize, exploit; '~wickeln v/t. (sep., -ge-, h) unwrap; '~wiegen v/t. (irr. wiegen, sep., -ge-, h) weigh out; '~wirken v/refl. (sep., -ge-, h) take effect, operate; sich ~ auf (acc.) affect; 'Qwirkung f effect; '~wischen v/t. (sep., -ge-, h) wipe out, efface; '~wringen v/t. (irr. wringen, sep., -ge-, h) wring out.
'Auswuchs m excrescence, outgrowth (a. fig.), protuberance.
'Auswurf m ⚕ expectoration; fig. refuse, dregs pl.
'aus|zahlen v/t. (sep., -ge-, h) pay out; pay s.o. off; '~zählen v/t. (sep., -ge-, h) count out.

'Auszahlung f payment.
'Auszehrung f (-/-en) consumption.
'auszeichn|en v/t. (sep., -ge-, h) mark (out); fig. distinguish (sich o.s.); 'Qung f marking; distinction; hono(u)r; decoration.
'auszieh|en (irr. ziehen, sep., -ge-) 1. v/t. (h) draw out, extract; take off (garment); sich ~ undress; 2. v/i. (sein) set out; move (out), remove, move house; 'Qplatte f leaf (of table).
'Auszug m departure; ✗ marching out; removal; extract, excerpt (from book); summary; ✝ statement (of account). [tic, genuine.]
authentisch adj. [au'tɛntiʃ] authen-)
Auto ['auto] n (-s/-s) (motor-)car, Am. a. automobile; ~ fahren drive, motor; '~bahn f motorway, autobahn; ~biogra'phie f autobiography; ~bus ['~bus] m (-ses/-se) (motor-)bus; (motor) coach; '~bushaltestelle f bus stop; '~didakt [~di'dakt] m (-en/-en) autodidact, self-taught person; '~droschke f taxi(-cab), Am. cab; '~fahrer m motorist; ~'gramm n autograph; ~'grammjäger m autograph hunter; '~händler m car dealer; '~kino n drive-in cinema; ~krat ['krat] m (-en/-en) autocrat; ~kratie [~a-'ti:] f (-/-n) autocracy; ~mat [~'ma:t] m (-en/-en) automaton; slot-machine, vending machine; ~'matenrestaurant n self-service restaurant, Am. automat; ~'mation ⊕ [~ma'tsjo:n] f (-/no pl.) automation; Q'matisch adj. automatic; '~mechaniker m car mechanic; ~mobil ['~mo'bi:l] n (-s/-e) s. Auto; Qnom adj. ['~'no:m] autonomous; ~nomie [~o'mi:] f (-/-n) autonomy.
Autor ['auto:r] m (-s/-en) author.
'Autoreparaturwerkstatt f car repair shop, garage. [thor(ess).]
Autorin [au'to:rin] f (-/-nen) au-)
autori|sieren [autori'zrən] v/t. (no -ge-, h) authorize; ~tär adj. [~'tɛ:r] authoritarian; Q'tät f (-/-en) authority.
'Auto|straße f motor-road; '~vermietung f (-/-en) car hire service.
avisieren ✝ [avi'zi:rən] v/t. (no -ge-, h) advise.
Axt [akst] f (-/-e) ax(e).
Azetylen ⚗ [atsety'le:n] n (-s/no pl.) acetylene. [Qn adj. azure.]
Azur [a'tsu:r] m (-s/no pl.) azure;)

# B

Bach [bax] m (-[e]s/-e) brook, Am. a. run. [port.]
Backbord ⚓ ['bak-] n (-[e]s/-e))
Backe ['bakə] f (-/-n) cheek.
backen ['bakən] (irr., ge-, h) 1.

v/t. bake; fry; dry (fruit); 2. v/i. bake; fry.
'Backen|bart m (side-)whiskers pl., Am. a. sideburns pl.; '~zahn m molar (tooth), grinder.

**Bäcker** ['bɛkər] *m* (-s/-) baker; **.ei** [.'raɪ] *f* (-/-en) baker's (shop), bakery.

'**Back|fisch** *m* fried fish; *fig.* girl in her teens, teenager, *Am. a.* bobby soxer; '**.obst** *n* dried fruit; '**.ofen** *m* oven; '**.pflaume** *f* prune; '**.pulver** *n* baking-powder; '**.stein** *m* brick; '**.ware** *f* baker's ware.

**Bad** [baːt] *n* (-[e]s/*≈*er) bath; *in river, etc.*: *a.* bathe; *s. Badeort; ein* **.** *nehmen* take *or* have a bath.

**Bade|anstalt** ['baːdəʔ-] *f* (public swimming) baths *pl.*; '**.anzug** *m* bathing-costume, bathing-suit; '**.hose** *f* bathing-drawers *pl.*, (bathing) trunks *pl.*; '**.kappe** *f* bathing-cap; '**.kur** *f* spa treatment; '**.mantel** *m* bathing-gown, *Am.* bathrobe; '**.meister** *m* bath attendant; swimming-instructor; '**2n** (*ge-, h*) 1. *v/t.* bath (*baby, etc.*); bathe (*eyes, etc.*); 2. *v/i.* bath, tub; have *or* take a bath; *in river, etc.*: bathe; **.** *gehen* go swimming; '**.ofen** *m* geyser, boiler, *Am. a.* water heater; '**.ort** *m* watering-place; spa; seaside resort; '**.salz** *n* bath-salt; '**.strand** *m* bathing-beach; '**.tuch** *n* bathtowel; '**.wanne** *f* bath-tub; '**.zimmer** *n* bathroom.

**Bagatell|e** [baga'tɛlə] *f* (-/-n) trifle, trifling matter, bagatelle; **2i'sieren** *v/t.* (*no -ge-, h*) minimize (the importance of), *Am. a.* play down.

**Bagger** ['bagər] *m* (-s/-) excavator; dredge(r); '**2n** *v/i. and v/t.* (*ge-, h*) excavate; dredge.

**Bahn** [baːn] *f* (-/-en) course; path; ██ railway, *Am.* railroad; *mot.* lane; trajectory (*of bullet, etc.*); *ast.* orbit; *sports*: track, course, lane; *skating*: rink; *bowling*: alley; '**2brechend** *adj.* pioneer(ing), epoch-making; *art*: avant-gardist; '**.damm** *m* railway embankment, *Am.* railroad embankment; '**2en** *v/t.* (*ge-, h*) clear, open (up) (*way*); *den Weg* **.** *prepare or pave the way* (*dat.* for); *sich e-n Weg* **.** *force or work or elbow one's way;* '**.hof** *m* (railway-) station, *Am.* (railroad-)station; '**.linie** *f* railway-line, *Am.* railroad line; '**.steig** *m* platform; '**.steigkarte** *f* platform ticket; '**.übergang** *m* level crossing, *Am.* grade crossing.

**Bahre** ['baːrə] *f* (-/-n) stretcher, litter; bier.

**Bai** [baɪ] *f* (-/-en) bay; creek.

**Baisse** ✝ ['bɛːs(ə)] *f* (-/-n) depression (on the market); fall (in prices); *auf* **.** *spekulieren* ✝ bear, speculate for a fall, *Am.* sell short; '**.spekulant** *m* bear.

**Bajonett** ✗ [bajo'nɛt] *n* (-[e]s/-e) bayonet; *das* **.** *aufpflanzen* fix the bayonet.

**Bake** ['baːkə] *f* (-/-n) ⚓ beacon; ▒ warning-sign.

**Bakterie** [bak'teːrjə] *f* (-/-n) bacterium, microbe, germ.

**bald** *adv.* [balt] soon; shortly; before long; F almost, nearly; early; *so* **.** *als möglich* as soon as possible; **.** *hier,* **.** *dort* now here, now there; **.ig** *adj.* ['.dɪç] speedy; **.e** Antwort ✝ early reply.

**Baldrian** ['baldriaːn] *m* (-s/-e) valerian.

**Balg** [balk] 1. *m* (-[e]s/*≈*e) skin; body (*of doll*); bellows *pl.*; 2. F *m, n* (-[e]s/*≈*er) brat, urchin; **2en** ['balgən] *v/refl.* (*ge-, h*) scuffle (*um* for), wrestle (for).

**Balken** ['balkən] *m* (-s/-) beam; rafter.

**Balkon** [bal'kõː; .'koːn] *m* (-s/-s; -s/-e) balcony; *thea.* dress circle, *Am.* balcony; **.tür** *f* French window.

**Ball** [bal] *m* (-[e]s/*≈*e) ball; *geogr., ast. a.* globe; ball, dance; *auf dem* **.** at the ball.

**Ballade** [ba'laːdə] *f* (-/-n) ballad.

**Ballast** ['balast] *m* (-es/*≈*-e) ballast; *fig.* burden, impediment; dead weight.

'**ballen**[1] *v/t.* (*ge-, h*) (form into a) ball; clench (*fist*); *sich* **.** (form into a) ball; cluster.

'**Ballen**[2] *m* (-s/-) bale; *anat.* ball; **.** *Papier* ten reams *pl.*

**Ballett** [ba'lɛt] *n* (-[e]s/-e) ballet; **.änzer** [ba'lɛttɛntsər] *m* (-s/-) ballet-dancer.

**ball|förmig** *adj.* ['balfœrmiç] ball-shaped, globular; '**2kleid** *n* ball-dress.

**Ballon** [ba'lõː; .'oːn] *m* (-s/-s; -s/-s, -e) balloon.

'**Ball|saal** *m* ball-room; '**.spiel** *n* ball-game, game of ball.

**Balsam** ['balzaːm] *m* (-s/-e) balsam, balm (*a. fig.*); **2ieren** [.a'miːrən] *v/t.* (*no -ge-, h*) embalm.

**Balz** [balts] *f* (-/-en) mating season; display (*by cock-bird*).

**Bambus** ['bambus] *m* (-ses/-se) bamboo; '**.rohr** *n* bamboo, cane.

**banal** *adj.* [ba'naːl] commonplace, banal, trite; trivial; **3.** *ität* [.ali'tɛːt] *f* (-/-en) banality; commonplace; triviality.

**Banane** [ba'naːnə] *f* (-/-n) banana; **.nstecker** ⚡ *m* banana plug.

**Band** [bant] 1. *m* (-[e]s/*≈*e) volume; 2. *n* (-[e]s/*≈*er) band; ribbon; tape; *anat.* ligament; 3. *fig. n* (-[e]s/-e) bond, tie; 4. 2 *pret.* of binden.

**Bandag|e** [ban'daːʒə] *f* (-/-n) bandage; **2ieren** [.a'ʒiːrən] *v/t.* (*no -ge-, h*) (apply a) bandage.

**Bande** ['bandə] *f* (-/-n) *billiards*: cushion; *fig.* gang, band.

**bändigen** ['bɛndigən] *v/t.* (*ge-, h*)

tame; break in (*horse*); subdue (*a. fig.*); *fig.* restrain, master.

**Bandit** [ban'di:t] *m* (-*en*/-*en*) bandit.

**'Band|maß** *n* tape measure; '~**säge** *f* band-saw; '~**scheibe** *anat. f* intervertebral disc; '~**wurm** *zo. m* tapeworm.

**bang** *adj.* [baŋ], ~**e** *adj.* ['~ə] anxious (*um* about), uneasy (about), concerned (for); *mir ist* ~ I am afraid (*vor dat.* of); *j-m bange machen* frighten *or* scare s.o.; '~**en** *v/i.* (*ge-*, *h*) be anxious *or* worried (*um* about).

**Bank** [baŋk] *f* 1. (-/~e) bench; *school*: desk; F *durch die* ~ without exception, all through; *auf die lange* ~ *schieben* put off, postpone; shelve; 2. ✝ (-/-*en*) bank; *Geld auf der* ~ money in the bank; '~**anweisung** *f* cheque, *Am.* check; '~**ausweis** *m* bank return *or* statement; '~**beamte** *m* bank clerk *or* official; '~**einlage** *f* deposit.

**Bankett** [baŋ'kɛt] *n* (-[*e*]*s*/-*e*) banquet.

**'Bank|geheimnis** *n* banker's duty of secrecy; '~**geschäft** ✝ *n* bank(-ing) transaction, banking operation; '~**haus** *n* bank(ing-house).

**Bankier** [baŋk'je:] *m* (-*s*/-*s*) banker.

**'Bank|konto** *n* bank(ing) account; '~**note** *f* (bank) note, *Am.* (bank) bill.

**bankrott** [baŋ'krɔt] 1. *adj.* bankrupt; 2. ♀ *m* (-[*e*]*s*/-*e*) bankruptcy, insolvency, failure; ~ *machen* fail, go *or* become bankrupt.

**'Bankwesen** *n* banking.

**Bann** [ban] *m* (-[*e*]*s*/-*e*) ban; *fig.* spell; *eccl.* excommunication; '2**en** *v/t.* (*ge-*, *h*) banish (*a. fig.*); exorcize (*devil*); avert (*danger*); *eccl.* excommunicate; spellbind.

**Banner** ['banər] *n* (-*s*/-) banner (*a. fig.*); standard; '~**träger** *m* standard-bearer.

**'Bann|fluch** *m* anathema; '~**meile** *f* precincts *pl.*; ⟨t⟩ area around government buildings within which processions and meetings are prohibited.

**bar**[1] [ba:r] 1. *adj.*: *e-r Sache* ~ destitute *or* devoid of s.th.; ~*es Geld* ready money, cash; ~*er Unsinn* sheer nonsense; 2. *adv.*: ~ *bezahlen* pay in cash, pay money down.

**Bar**[2] [ˌ] *f* (-/-*s*) bar; night-club.

**Bär** [bɛ:r] *m* (-*en*/-*en*) bear; *j-m e-n* ~*en aufbinden* hoax s.o.

**Baracke** [ba'rakə] *f* (-/-*n*) barrack; ~*nlager n* hutment.

**Barbar** [bar'ba:r] *m* (-*en*/-*en*) barbarian; ~*ei* [~a'raɪ] *f* (-/-*en*) barbarism; barbarity; 2*isch* [~'ba:rɪʃ] *adj.* barbarian; barbarous; *art*, *taste*: barbaric.

**'Bar|bestand** *m* cash in hand; '~**betrag** *m* amount in cash.

**'Bärenzwinger** *m* bear-pit.

**barfuß** *adj. and adv.* ['ba:r-], ~**füßig** *adj. and adv.* ['~fy:sɪç] barefoot.

**barg** [bark] *pret. of bergen.*

**'Bar|geld** *n* cash, ready money; '2**geldlos** *adj.* cashless; ~*er Zahlungsverkehr* cashless money transfers *pl.*; 2**häuptig** *adj. and adv.* ['~hɔyptɪç] bare-headed, uncovered.

**Bariton** ♪ ['ba:ritɔn] *m* (-*s*/-*e*) baritone.
[launch.]

**Barkasse** ⚓ [bar'kasə] *f* (-/-*n*)

**barmherzig** *adj.* [barm'hɛrtsɪç] merciful, charitable; *der* ~*e Samariter* the good Samaritan; 2*e Schwester* Sister of Mercy *or* Charity; 2*keit* *f* (-/-*en*) mercy, charity.

**Barometer** [baro'-] *n* barometer.

**Baron** [ba'ro:n] *m* (-*s*/-*e*) baron; ~*in* *f* (-/-*nen*) baroness.

**Barre** ['barə] *f* (-/-*n*) bar.

**Barren** ['barən] *m* (-*s*/-) *metall.* bar, ingot, bullion; *gymnastics*: parallel bars *pl.*

**Barriere** [bar'jɛ:rə] *f* (-/-*n*) barrier.

**Barrikade** [bari'ka:də] *f* (-/-*n*) barricade; ~*n errichten* raise barricades.

**barsch** *adj.* [barʃ] rude, gruff, rough.

**'Bar|schaft** *f* (-/-*en*) ready money, cash; '~**scheck** ✝ *m* open cheque, *Am.* open check.

**barst** [barst] *pret. of bersten.*

**Bart** [ba:rt] *m* (-[*e*]*s*/~*e*) beard; bit (*of key*); *sich e-n* ~ *wachsen lassen* grow a beard.

**bärtig** *adj.* ['bɛ:rtɪç] bearded.

**'bartlos** *adj.* beardless.

**'Barzahlung** *f* cash payment; *nur gegen* ~ ✝ terms strictly cash.

**Basis** ['ba:zɪs] *f* (-/*Basen*) base; *fig.* basis.

**Baß** ♪ [bas] *m* (*Basses/Bässe*) bass; '~**geige** *f* bass-viol.

**Bassist** [ba'sɪst] *m* (-*en*/-*en*) bass (singer).

**Bast** [bast] *m* (-*es*/-*e*) bast; velvet (*on antlers*).

**Bastard** ['bastart] *m* (-[*e*]*s*/-*e*) bastard; half-breed; *zo.*, ♀ hybrid.

**bast|eln** ['bastəln] (*ge-*, *h*) 1. *v/t.* build, F rig up; 2. *v/i.* build; '2**ler** *m* (-*s*/-) amateur craftsman, do-it-yourself man.

**bat** [ba:t] *pret. of bitten.*

**Bataillon** [batal'jo:n] *n* (-*s*/-*e*) battalion.

**Batist** [ba'tɪst] *m* (-[*e*]*s*/-*e*) cambric.

**Batterie** ⚔, ⚡ [batə'ri:] *f* (-/-*n*) battery.

**Bau** [bau] *m* 1. (-[*e*]*s*/*no pl.*) building, construction; build, frame; 2. (-[*e*]*s*/-*ten*) building, edifice; 3. (-[*e*]*s*/-*e*) burrow, den (*a. fig.*), earth.

**'Bau|arbeiter** *m* workman in the building trade; '~**art** *f* architecture, style; method of construction; *mot.* type, model.

**Bauch** [baux] *m* (-[e]s/*̈e) *anat.*
abdomen, belly; paunch; *ship:*
bottom; '2ig *adj.* big-bellied, bulgy;
'~landung *f* belly landing; '~red-
ner *m* ventriloquist; '~schmerzen
*m/pl.*, '~weh *n* (-s/*no pl.*) belly-ache,
stomach-ache.

**bauen** ['bauən] (*ge-, h*) **1.** *v/t.* build,
construct; erect, raise; build, make
(*nest*); make (*violin, etc.*); **2.** *v/i.*
build; ~ *auf* (*acc.*) trust (in); rely
*or* count *or* depend on.

**Bauer** ['bauər] **1.** *m* (-n, -s/-n)
farmer; peasant, countryman; *chess:*
pawn; **2.** *n, m* (-s/-) (bird-)cage.

**Bäuerin** ['bɔyərin] *f* (-/-nen) farmer's wife; peasant woman.

**Bauerlaubnis** ['bauʔ-] *f* building
permit.

**bäuerlich** *adj.* ['bɔyərliç] rural,
rustic.

**Bauern|fänger** *contp.* ['bauərn-
fɛŋər] *m* (-s/-) trickster, confidence
man; '~haus *n* farm-house; '~hof
*m* farm.

'**bau|fällig** *adj.* out of repair,
dilapidated; '2gerüst *n* scaffold
(-ing); '2handwerker *m* craftsman
in the building trade; '2herr *m*
owner; '2holz *n* timber, *Am.* lumber; '2jahr *n* year of construction;
~ 1969 1969 model *or* make; '2ka-
sten *m* box of bricks; '2kunst *f*
architecture.

'**baulich** *adj.* architectural, struc-
tural; *in gutem ~en Zustand* in good
repair.

**Baum** [baum] *m* (-[e]s/*̈e) tree.

'**Baumeister** *m* architect.

**baumeln** ['bauməln] *v/i.* (*ge-, h*)
dangle, swing; *mit den Beinen* ~
dangle *or* swing one's legs.

'**Baum|schere** *f* (*eine a pair of*)
pruning-shears *pl.*; '~schule *f*
nursery (*of young trees*); '~stamm
*m* trunk; '~wolle *f* cotton; '2wol-
len *adj.* (made of) cotton.

'**Bau|plan** *m* architect's *or* building
plan; '~platz *m* building plot *or* site,
*Am.* location; '~polizei *f* Board of
Surveyors.

**Bausch** [bauʃ] *m* (-es/-e, *̈e) pad;
bolster; wad; *in ~ und Bogen* altogether, wholesale, in the lump;
'2en *v/t.* (*ge-, h*) swell; *sich ~* bulge,
swell out, billow (out).

'**Bau|stein** *m* brick, building stone;
building block; *fig.* element; '~
stelle *f* building site; '~stil *m* (architectural) style; '~stoff *m* building material; '~unternehmer *m*
building contractor; '~zaun *m*
hoarding.

**Bay|er** ['baɪər] *m* (-n/-n) Bavarian;
'2(e)risch *adj.* Bavarian.

**Bazill|enträger** ⚕ [ba'tsilən-] *m*
(germ-)carrier; ~us [~us] *m* (-/Ba-
zillen) bacillus, germ.

**beabsichtigen** [bə'apziçtigən] *v/t.*

(*no -ge-, h*) intend, mean, propose
(*zu tun* to do, doing).

**be'acht|en** *v/t.* (*no -ge-, h*) pay at-
tention to; notice; observe; ~ens-
wert *adj.* noteworthy, remarkable;
~lich *adj.* remarkable; considerable; 2ung *f* attention, consideration; notice; observance.

**Beamte** [bə'amtə] *m* (-n/-n) official,
officer, *Am. a.* officeholder; functionary; Civil Servant.

**be'ängstigend** *adj.* alarming, dis-
quieting.

**beanspruch|en** [bə'anʃpruxən] *v/t.*
(*no -ge-, h*) claim, demand; require
(*efforts, time, space, etc.*); ⊕ stress;
2ung *f* (-/-en) claim; demand (*gen.*
on); ⊕ stress, strain.

**beanstand|en** [bə'anʃtandən] *v/t.*
(*no -ge-, h*) object to; 2ung *f* (-/-en)
objection (*gen.* to).

**beantragen** [bə'antra:gən] *v/t.* (*no
-ge-, h*) apply for; ⚖, *parl.* move,
make a motion; propose.

**be'antwort|en** *v/t.* (*no -ge-, h*) an-
swer (*a. fig.*), reply to; 2ung *f*
(-/-en) answer, reply; *in ~* (*gen.*) in
answer *or* reply to.

**be'arbeit|en** *v/t.* (*no -ge-, h*) work;
⚒ till; dress (*leather*); hew (*stone*);
process; ⚒ treat; ⚖ be in charge
of (*case*); edit, revise (*book*); adapt
(*nach* from); *esp.* ♪ arrange; *j-n ~*
work on s.o.; batter s.o.; 2ung *f*
(-/-en) working; revision (*of book*);
*thea.* adaptation; *esp.* ♪ arrangement; processing; ⚒ treatment.

**be'argwöhnen** *v/t.* (*no -ge-, h*) suspect, be suspicious of.

**beaufsichtig|en** [bə'aufziçtigən]
*v/t.* (*no -ge-, h*) inspect, superin-
tend, supervise, control; look after
(*child*); 2ung *f* (-/-en) inspection,
supervision, control.

**be'auftrag|en** *v/t.* (*no -ge-, h*) com-
mission (*zu inf.* to inf.), charge (*mit*
with); 2te [~ktə] *m* (-n/-n) commissioner; representative; deputy;
proxy.

**be'bauen** *v/t.* (*no -ge-, h*) ⚠ build
on; ⚒ cultivate.

**beben** ['be:bən] *v/i.* (*ge-, h*) shake
(*vor dat.* with), tremble (with);
shiver (with); *earth:* quake.

**Becher** ['bɛçər] *m* (-s/-) cup (*a.
fig.*).

**Becken** ['bɛkən] *n* (-s/-) basin, *Am.
a.* bowl; ♪ cymbal(s *pl.*); *anat.*
pelvis.

**bedacht** *adj.* [bə'daxt]: ~ *sein auf*
(*acc.*) look after, be concerned
about, be careful *or* mindful of;
*darauf ~ sein zu inf.* be anxious
to *inf.*

**bedächtig** *adj.* [bə'dɛçtiç] deliberate.

**bedang** [bə'daŋ] *pret. of* **bedingen.**

**be'danken** *v/refl.* (*no -ge-, h*): *sich
bei j-m für et.* ~ thank s.o. for s.th.

**Bedarf** [bə'darf] *m* (-[e]s/*no pl.*) need (*an dat.* of), want (of); † demand (for); **~sartikel** [bə'darfs⁹-] *m/pl.* necessaries *pl.*, requisites *pl.*

**bedauerlich** *adj.* [bə'dauərliç] regrettable, deplorable.

**be'dauern 1.** *v/t.* (*no* -ge-, *h*) feel *or* be sorry for *s.o.*; pity *s.o.*; regret, deplore *s.th.*; **2.** Ձ *n* (-s/*no pl.*) regret; pity; **~swert** *adj.* pitiable, deplorable.

**be'deck|en** *v/t.* (*no* -ge-, *h*) cover; ⚔ escort; ⚓ convoy; **~t** *adj. sky*: overcast; Ձung *f* cover(ing); ⚔ escort; ⚓ convoy.

**be'denken 1.** *v/t.* (*irr.* denken, *no* -ge-, *h*) consider; think *s.th.* over; *j-n in s-m Testament* ~ remember s.o. in one's will; **2.** Ձ *n* (-s/-) consideration; objection; hesitation; scruple; **~los** *adj.* unscrupulous.

**be'denklich** *adj.* doubtful; *character*: a. dubious; *situation, etc.*: dangerous, critical; delicate; risky.

**Be'denkzeit** *f* time for reflection; *ich gebe dir e-e Stunde* ~ I give you one hour to think it over.

**be'deut|en** *v/t.* (*no* -ge-, *h*) mean, signify; stand for; **~end** *adj.* important, prominent; *sum, etc.* considerable; **~sam** *adj.* significant.

**Be'deutung** *f* meaning, significance; importance; Ձslos *adj.* insignificant; meaningless; Ձsvoll *adj.* significant; **~swandel** *ling. m* semantic change.

**be'dien|en** (*no* -ge-, *h*) **1.** *v/t.* serve; wait on; ⊕ operate, work (*machine*); ⚔ serve (*gun*); answer (*telephone*); *sich* ~ *at table*: help o.s.; **2.** *v/i.* serve; wait (at table); *cards*: follow suit; Ձung *f* (-/-en) service, *esp.* † attendance; *in restaurant, etc.*: service; waiter, waitress; shop assistant(s *pl.*).

**beding|en** [bə'diŋən] *v/t.* ([*irr.*,] *no* -ge-, *h*) condition; stipulate; require; cause; imply; **~t** *adj.* conditional (*durch* on); restricted; ~ *sein durch* be conditioned by; Ձung *f* (-/-en) condition; stipulation; **~en** *pl.* † terms *pl.*; **~ungslos** *adj.* unconditional.

**be'dräng|en** *v/t.* (*no* -ge-, *h*) press hard, beset; Ձnis *f* (-/-se) distress.

**be'droh|en** *v/t.* (*no* -ge-, *h*) threaten; menace; **~lich** *adj.* threatening; Ձung *f* threat, menace (*gen.* to).

**be'drück|en** *v/t.* (*no* -ge-, *h*) oppress; depress; deject; Ձung *f* (-/-en) oppression; depression; dejection.

**bedungen** [bə'duŋən] *p.p.* of bedingen.

**be'dürf|en** *v/i.* (*irr.* dürfen, *no* -ge-, *h*): *e-r Sache* ~ need *or* want *or* require *s.th.*; Ձnis *n* (-ses/-se) need, want, requirement; *sein* ~ *verrichten* relieve o.s. *or* nature; Ձnisan-

**stalt** [bə'dyrfnis⁹-] *f* public convenience, *Am.* comfort station; **~tig** *adj.* needy, poor, indigent.

**be'ehren** *v/t.* (*no* -ge-, *h*) hono(u)r, favo(u)r; *ich beehre mich zu inf.* I have the hono(u)r to *inf.*

**be'eilen** *v/refl.* (*no* -ge-, *h*) hasten, hurry, make haste, *Am.* F *a.* hustle.

**beeindrucken** [bə'aindrukən] *v/t.* (*no* -ge-, *h*) impress, make an impression on.

**beeinfluss|en** [bə'ainflussən] *v/t.* (*no* -ge-, *h*) influence; affect; *parl.* lobby; Ձung *f* (-/-en) influence; *parl.* lobbying.

**beeinträchtig|en** [bə'aintreçtigən] *v/t.* (*no* -ge-, *h*) impair, injure, affect (adversely); Ձung *f* (-/-en) impairment (*gen.* of); injury (to).

**be'end|en** *v/t.* (*no* -ge-, *h*), **~igen** [~igən] *v/t.* (*no* -ge-, *h*) (bring to an) end, finish, terminate; Ձigung [~iguŋ] *f* (-/-en) ending, termination.

**beengt** *adj.* [bə'ɛŋkt] *space*: narrow, confined, cramped; *sich* ~ *fühlen* feel cramped (for room); feel oppressed *or* uneasy.

**be'erben** *v/t.* (*no* -ge-, *h*): *j-n* ~ be s.o.'s heir.

**beerdig|en** [bə'e:rdigən] *v/t.* (*no* -ge-, *h*) bury; Ձung *f* (-/-en) burial, funeral.

**Beere** ['be:rə] *f* (-/-n) berry.

**Beet** ✗ [be:t] *n* (-[e]s/-e) bed.

**befähig|en** [bə'fɛ:igən] *v/t.* (*no* -ge-, *h*) enable (*zu inf.* to *inf.*); qualify (*für, zu* for); **~t** *adj.* [~çt] (cap)able; Ձung *f* (-/-en) qualification; capacity.

**befahl** [bə'fɑ:l] *pret.* of befehlen.

**befahr|bar** *adj.* [bə'faːrbaːr] passable, practicable, trafficable; ⚓ navigable; *~en v/t.* (*irr.* fahren, *no* -ge-, *h*) drive *or* travel on; ⚓ navigate (*river*).

**be'fallen** *v/t.* (*irr.* fallen, *no* -ge-, *h*) attack; befall; *disease*: a. strike; *fear*: seize.

**be'fangen** *adj.* embarrassed; self-conscious; prejudiced (*a.* ✗); ✗ bias(s)ed; Ձheit *f* (-/-en) embarrassment; self-consciousness; ✗ bias, prejudice.

**be'fassen** *v/refl.* (*no* -ge-, *h*): *sich* ~ *mit* occupy o.s. with; engage in; attend to; deal with.

**Befehl** [bə'fe:l] *m* (-[e]s/-e) command (*über acc.* of); order; Ձen (*irr.*, *no* -ge-, *h*) **1.** *v/t.* command; order; **2.** *v/i.* command; Ձigen [~igən] *v/t.* (*no* -ge-, *h*) command. **Be'fehlshaber** *m* (-s/-) commander(-in-chief); Ձisch *adj.* imperious.

**be'festig|en** *v/t.* (*no* -ge-, *h*) fasten (*an dat.* to), fix (to), attach (to); ✗ fortify; *fig.* strengthen; Ձung *f* (-/-en) fixing, fastening; ✗ fortification; *fig.* strengthening.

**be'feuchten** v/t. (no -ge-, h) moisten, damp; wet.

**be'finden 1.** v/refl. (irr. finden, no -ge-, h) be; **2.** 2 n (-s/no pl.) (state of) health.

**be'flaggen** v/t. (no -ge-, h) flag.

**be'flecken** v/t. (no -ge-, h) spot, stain (a. fig.); fig. sully.

**beflissen** adj. [bə'flisən] studious; **2heit** f (-/no pl.) studiousness, assiduity.

**befohlen** [bə'fo:lən] p.p. of befehlen.

**be'folg|en** v/t. (no -ge-, h) follow, take (advice); obey (rule); adhere to (principle); **2ung** f (-/⸚-en) observance (of); adherence (to).

**be'förder|n** v/t. (no -ge-, h) convey, carry; haul (goods), transport; forward; ✝ ship (a. ⚓); promote (to be) (a. ✕); **2ung** f conveyance, transport(ation), forwarding; promotion; **2ungsmittel** n (means of) transport, Am. (means of) transportation.

**be'fragen** v/t. (no -ge-, h) question, interview; interrogate.

**be'frei|en** v/t. (no -ge-, h) (set) free (von from); liberate (nation, mind, etc.) (from); rescue (captive) (from); exempt s.o. (from); deliver s.o. (aus, von from); **2er** m liberator; **2ung** f (-/-en) liberation, deliverance; exemption.

**Befremden** [bə'frɛmdən] n (-s/ no pl.) surprise.

**befreund|en** [bə'frɔyndən] v/refl. (no -ge-, h): sich mit j-m ⁓ make friends with s.o.; sich mit et. ⁓ get used to s.th., reconcile o.s. to s.th.; **⁓et** adj. friendly; on friendly terms; **⁓ sein** be friends.

**befriedig|en** [bə'fri:digən] v/t. (no -ge-, h) satisfy; appease (hunger); meet (expectations, demand); pay off (creditor); **⁓end** adj. satisfactory; **2ung** f (-/-en) satisfaction.

**be'fristen** v/t. (no -ge-, h) set a time-limit.

**be'frucht|en** v/t. (no -ge-, h) fertilize; fructify; fecundate; impregnate; **2ung** f (-/-en) fertilization; fructification; fecundation; impregnation.

**Befug|nis** [bə'fu:knis] f (-/-se) authority, warrant; esp. ⚖ competence; **2t** adj. authorized; competent.

**be'fühlen** v/t. (no -ge-, h) feel; touch, handle, finger.

**Be'fund** m (-[e]s/-e) result; finding(s pl.); ⚕ diagnosis.

**be'fürcht|en** v/t. (no -ge-, h) fear, apprehend; suspect; **2ung** f (-/-en) fear, apprehension, suspicion.

**befürworten** [bə'fy:rvɔrtən] v/t. (no -ge-, h) plead for, advocate.

**begab|t** adj. [bə'ga:pt] gifted, talented; **2ung** f (-/-en) gift, talent(s pl.).

**begann** [bə'gan] pret. of beginnen.

**be'geben** v/t. (irr. geben, no -ge-, h) ✝ negotiate (bill of exchange); sich ⁓ happen; sich ⁓ nach go to, make for; sich in Gefahr ⁓ expose o.s. to danger.

**begegn|en** [bə'ge:gnən] v/i. (no -ge-, sein) meet s.o. or s.th., meet with; incident: happen to; anticipate, prevent; **2ung** f (-/-en) meeting.

**be'gehen** v/t. (irr. gehen, no -ge-, h) walk (on); inspect; celebrate (birthday, etc.); commit (crime); make (mistake); ein Unrecht ⁓ do wrong.

**begehr|en** [bə'ge:rən] v/t. (no -ge-, h) demand, require; desire, crave (for); long for; **⁓lich** adj. desirous, covetous.

**begeister|n** [bə'gaistərn] v/t. (no -ge-, h) inspire, fill with enthusiasm; sich ⁓ für feel enthusiastic about; **2ung** f (-/no pl.) enthusiasm, inspiration.

**Be'gier** f, **⁓de** [⁓də] f (-/-n) desire (nach for), appetite (for); concupiscence; **2ig** adj. eager (nach for, auf acc. for; zu inf. to inf.), desirous (nach of; zu inf. to inf.), anxious (zu inf. to inf.).

**be'gießen** v/t. (irr. gießen, no -ge-, h) water; baste (roasting meat); F wet (bargain).

**Beginn** [bə'gin] m (-[e]s/no pl.) beginning, start, commencement; origin; **2en** v/t. and v/i. (irr. no -ge-, h) begin, start, commence.

**beglaubig|en** [bə'glaubigən] v/t. (no -ge-, h) attest, certify; legalize, authenticate; **2ung** f (-/-en) attestation, certification; legalization; **2ungsschreiben** n credentials pl.

**be'gleichen** ✝ v/t. (irr. gleichen, no -ge-, h) pay, settle (bill, debt).

**be'gleit|en** v/t. (no -ge-, h) accompany (a. ♪ auf dat. on), escort; attend (a. fig.); see (s.o. home, etc.); **2er** m (-s/-) companion, attendant; escort; ♪ accompanist; **2erscheinung** f attendant symptom; **2schreiben** n covering letter; **2ung** f (-/-en) company; attendants pl., retinue (of sovereign, etc.); esp. ✕ escort; ⚓, ✕ convoy; ♪ accompaniment.

**be'glückwünschen** v/t. (no -ge-, h) congratulate (zu on).

**begnadig|en** [bə'gna:digən] v/t. (no -ge-, h) pardon; pol. amnesty; **2ung** f (-/-en) pardon; pol. amnesty.

**begnügen** [bə'gny:gən] v/refl. (no -ge-, h): sich ⁓ mit content o.s. with, be satisfied with.

**begonnen** [bə'gɔnən] p.p. of beginnen.

**be'graben** v/t. (irr. graben, no -ge-, h) bury (a. fig.); inter.

**Begräbnis** [bə'grɛ:pnis] n (-ses/-se) burial; funeral, obsequies pl.

**begradigen** [bə'grɑːdigən] v/t. (no -ge-, h) straighten (road, frontier, etc.).

**be'greif|en** v/t. (irr. greifen, no -ge-, h) comprehend, understand; **~lich** adj. comprehensible.

**be'grenz|en** v/t. (no -ge-, h) bound, border; fig. limit; **2theit** f (-/-en) limitation (of knowledge); narrowness (of mind); **2ung** f (-/-en) boundary; bound, limit, limitation.

**Be'griff** m idea, notion, conception; comprehension; im ~ sein zu inf. be about or going to inf.

**be'gründ|en** v/t. (no -ge-, h) establish, found; give reasons for, substantiate (claim, charge); **2ung** f establishment, foundation; fig. substantiation (of claim or charge); reason.

**be'grüß|en** v/t. (no -ge-, h) greet, welcome; salute; **2ung** f (-/-en) greeting, welcome; salutation.

**begünstig|en** [bə'gynstigən] v/t. (no -ge-, h) favo(u)r; encourage; patronize; **2ung** (-/-en) f favo(u)r; encouragement; patronage.

**begutachten** [bə'guːtʔ-] v/t. (no -ge-, h) give an opinion on; examine; ~ lassen obtain expert opinion on, submit s.th. to an expert.

**begütert** adj. [bə'gyːtərt] wealthy, well-to-do.

**be'haart** adj. hairy.

**behäbig** adj. [bə'hɛːbiç] phlegmatic, comfort-loving; figure: portly.

**be'haftet** adj. afflicted (with disease, etc.).

**behag|en** [bə'hɑːgən] **1.** v/i. (no -ge-, h) please or suit s.o.; **2.** 2 n (-s/no pl.) comfort, ease; **~lich** adj. [-k-] comfortable; cosy, snug.

**be'halten** v/t. (irr. halten, no -ge-, h) re'tain; keep (für sich to o.s.); remember.

**Behälter** [bə'hɛltər] m (-s/-) container, receptacle; box; for liquid: reservoir; for oil, etc.: tank.

**be'hand|eln** v/t. (no -ge-, h) treat; deal with (a. subject); ⊕ process; 𝔰 treat; dress (wound); **2lung** f treatment; handling; ⊕ processing.

**be'hängen** v/t. (no -ge-, h) hang, drape (mit with); sich ~ mit cover or load o.s. with (jewellery).

**beharr|en** [bə'harən] v/i. (no -ge-, h) persist (auf dat. in); **~lich** adj. persistent; **2lichkeit** f (-/no pl.) persistence.

**be'hauen** v/t. (no -ge-, h) hew; trim (wood).

**behaupt|en** [bə'hauptən] v/t. (no -ge-, h) assert; maintain; **2ung** f (-/-en) assertion; statement.

**Behausung** [bə'hauzuŋ] f (-/-en) habitation; lodging.

**Be'helf** m (-[e]s/-e) expedient, (make)shift; s. Notbehelf; **2en** v/refl. (irr. helfen, no -ge-, h): sich ~ mit make shift with; sich ~ ohne do without; **~sheim** n temporary home.

**behend** adj. [bə'hɛnt], **~e** adj. [~də] nimble, agile; smart; **2igkeit** [~d-] f (-/no pl.) nimbleness, agility; smartness. [lodge, shelter.)

**be'herbergen** v/t. (no -ge-, h))

**be'herrsch|en** v/t. (no -ge-, h) rule (over), govern; command (situation, etc.); have command of (language); sich ~ control o.s.; **2er** m ruler (gen. over, of); **2ung** f (-/-en) command, control.

**beherzigen** [bə'hɛrtsigən] v/t. (no -ge-, h) take to heart, (bear in) mind.

**be'hexen** v/t. (no -ge-, h) bewitch.

**be'hilflich** adj.: j-m ~ sein help s.o. (bei in).

**be'hindern** v/t. (no -ge-, h) hinder, hamper, impede; handicap; obstruct (a. traffic, etc.).

**Behörde** [bə'høːrdə] f (-/-n) authority, mst authorities pl.; board; council.

**be'hüten** v/t. (no -ge-, h) guard, preserve (vor dat. from).

**behutsam** adj. [bə'huːtzɑːm] cautious, careful; **2keit** f (-/no pl.) caution.

**bei** prp. (dat.) address: ~ Schmidt care of (abbr. c/o) Schmidt; **~m** Buchhändler at the bookseller's; ~ uns with us; ~ der Hand nehmen take by the hand; ich habe kein Geld ~ mir I have no money about or on me; ~ der Kirche near the church; ~ guter Gesundheit in good health; wie es ~ Schiller heißt as Schiller says; die Schlacht ~ Waterloo the Battle of Waterloo; **e-m** Glase Wein over a glass of wine; ~ alledem for all that; Stunden nehmen ~ take lessons from or with; ~ günstigem Wetter weather permitting.

**'beibehalten** v/t. (irr. halten, sep., no -ge-, h) keep up, retain.

**'Beiblatt** n supplement (zu to).

**'beibringen** v/t. (irr. bringen, sep., -ge-, h) bring forward; produce (witness, etc.); j-m et. ~ impart (news, etc.) to s.o.; teach s.o. s.th.; inflict (defeat, wound, etc.) on s.o.

**Beichte** ['baiçtə] f (-/-n) confession; **2n** v/t. and v/i. (ge-, h) confess.

**beide** adj. ['baidə] both; nur wir ~ just the two of us; in ~n Fällen in either case.

**beider|lei** adj. ['baidərlai] of both kinds; ~ Geschlechts of either sex; **'~seitig 1.** adj. on both sides; mutual; **2.** adv. mutually; **'~seits 1.** prp. on both sides (gen. of); **2.** adv. mutually.

**'Beifahrer** m (-s/-) (front-seat) passenger; assistant driver; motor racing: co-driver.

'**Beifall** m (-[e]s/no pl.) approbation; applause; cheers pl.
'**beifällig** adj. approving; favo(u)rable.
'**Beifallsruf** m acclaim; ~e pl. cheers pl.
'**beifügen** v/t. (sep., -ge-, h) add; enclose.
'**Beigeschmack** m (-[e]s/no pl.) slight flavo(u)r; smack (of) (a. fig.).
'**Beihilfe** f aid; allowance; for study: grant; for project: subsidy; ₫₫ aiding and abetting; j-m ~ leisten ₫₫ aid and abet s.o.
'**beikommen** v/i. (irr. kommen, sep., -ge-, sein) get at.
**Beil** [bail] n (-[e]s/-e) hatchet; chopper; cleaver; ax(e).
'**Beilage** f supplement (to newspaper); F trimming. pl. (of meal); vegetables pl.
**beiläufig** adj. ['bailɔyfiç] casual; incidental.
'**beileg|en** v/t. (sep., -ge-, h) add (dat. to); enclose; settle (dispute); '♀ung f (-/-en) settlement.
**Beileid** ['bailait] n condolence; j-m sein ~ bezeigen condole with s.o. (zu on, upon).
'**beiliegen** v/i. (irr. liegen, sep., -ge-, h) be enclosed (dat. with).
'**beimessen** v/t. (irr. messen, sep., -ge-, h) attribute (dat. to), ascribe (to); attach (importance) (to).
'**beimisch|en** v/t. (sep., -ge-, h): e-r Sache et. ~ mix s.th. with s.th.; '♀ung f admixture.
**Bein** [bain] n (-[e]s/-e) leg; bone.
'**beinah(e)** adv. almost, nearly.
'**Beiname** m appellation; nickname.
'**Beinbruch** m fracture of the leg.
**beiordnen** ['bai?-] v/t. (sep., -ge-, h) adjoin; co-ordinate (a. gr.).
'**beipflichten** v/i. (sep., -ge-, h) agree with s.o.; assent to s.th.
'**Beirat** m (-[e]s/ːe) adviser, counsel(l)or; advisory board.
**be'irren** v/t. (no -ge-, h) confuse.
**beisammen** adv. [bai'zamən] together.
'**Beisein** n presence; im ~ (gen.) or von in the presence of s.o., in s.o.'s presence.
**bei'seite** adv. aside ‚apart; Spaß ~! joking apart!
'**beisetz|en** v/t. (sep., -ge-, h) bury, inter; '♀ung f (-/-en) burial, funeral.
'**Beisitzer** ₫₫ m (-s/-) assessor; associate judge; member (of committee).
'**Beispiel** n example, instance; zum ~ for example or instance; '♀haft adj. exemplary; '♀los adj. unprecedented, unparalleled; unheard of.
**beißen** ['baisən] (irr., ge-, h) 1. v/t. bite; fleas, etc.: bite, sting; 2. v/i. bite (auf acc. on; in acc. into); fleas, etc.: bite, sting; smoke: bite, burn (in dat. in); pepper, etc.: bite,

burn (auf dat. on); '~d adj. biting, pungent (both a. fig.); pepper, etc.: hot.
'**Beistand** m assistance.
'**beistehen** v/i. (irr. stehen, sep., -ge-, h): j-m ~ stand by or assist or help s.o.
'**beisteuern** v/t. and v/i. (sep., -ge-, h) contribute (zu to).
**Beitrag** ['baitraːk] m (-[e]s/ːe) contribution; share; subscription, Am. dues pl.; article (in newspaper, etc.).
'**bei|treten** v/i. (irr. treten, sep., -ge-, sein) join (political party, etc.); '♀tritt m joining.
'**Beiwagen** m side-car (of motorcycle); trailer (of tram).
'**Beiwerk** n accessories pl.
'**beiwohnen** v/i. (sep., -ge-, h) assist or be present at, attend.
**bei'zeiten** adv. early; in good time.
**beizen** ['baitsən] v/t. (ge-, h) corrode; metall. pickle; bate (hides); stain (wood); ❀ cauterize; hunt. hawk.
**bejahen** [bəˈjaːən] v/t. (no -ge-, h) answer in the affirmative, affirm; ~d adj. affirmative.
**be'jahrt** adj. aged.
**Bejahung** f (-/-en) affirmation, affirmative answer; fig. acceptance.
**be'jammern** s. beklagen.
**be'kämpfen** v/t. (no -ge-, h) fight (against), combat; fig. oppose.
**bekannt** adj. [bəˈkant] known (dat. to); j-n mit j-m ~ machen introduce s.o. to s.o.; ♀e m, f (-n/-n) acquaintance, mst friend; ~lich adv. as you know; ~machen v/t. (sep., -ge-, h) make known; ♀machung f (-/-en) publication; public notice; ♀schaft f (-/-en) acquaintance.
**be'kehr|en** v/t. (no -ge-, h) convert; ♀te m, f (-n/-n) convert; ♀ung f (-/-en) conversion (zu to).
**be'kenn|en** v/t. (irr. kennen, no -ge-, h) admit; confess; sich schuldig ~ ₫₫ plead guilty; sich ~ zu declare o.s. for; profess s.th.; ♀tnis n (-ses/-se) confession; creed.
**be'klagen** v/t. (no -ge-, h) lament, deplore; sich ~ complain (über acc. of, about); ~swert adj. deplorable, pitiable.
**Beklagte** [bəˈklaːktə] m, f (-n/-n) civil case: defendant, the accused.
**be'klatschen** v/t. (no -ge-, h) applaud, clap.
**be'kleben** v/t. (no -ge-, h) glue or stick s.th. on s.th.; mit Etiketten ~ label s.th.; mit Papier ~ paste s.th. up with paper; e-e Mauer mit Plakaten ~ paste (up) posters on a wall.
**bekleckern** F [bəˈklɛkərn] v/t. (no -ge-, h) stain (garment); sich ~ soil one's clothes.
**be'klecksen** v/t. (no -ge- h) stain, daub; blot.

be'kleid|en v/t. (no -ge-, h) clothe, dress; hold, fill (office, etc.); ~ mit invest with; 2ung f clothing, clothes pl.

be'klemm|en v/t. (no -ge-, h) oppress; 2ung f (-/-en) oppression; anguish, anxiety.

be'kommen (irr. kommen, no -ge-) 1. v/t. (h) get, receive; obtain; get, catch (illness); have (baby); catch (train, etc.); Zähne ~ teethe, cut one's teeth; 2. v/i. (sein): j-m (gut) ~ agree with s.o.; j-m nicht or schlecht ~ disagree with s.o.

bekömmlich adj. [bə'kœmliç] wholesome (dat. to).

beköstig|en [bə'kœstigən] v/t. (no -ge-, h) board, feed; 2ung f (-/-en) board(ing).

be'kräftig|en v/t. (no -ge-, h) confirm; 2ung f (-/-en) confirmation.

be'kränzen v/t. (no-ge-, h) wreathe, festoon.

be'krittel|n v/t. (no -ge-, h) carp at, criticize.

be'kümmern v/t. (no -ge-, h) afflict, grieve; trouble; s. kümmern.

be'laden v/t. (irr. laden, no -ge-, h) load; fig. burden.

Belag [bə'la:k] m (-[e]s/~e) covering; ⊕ coat(ing); surface (of road); foil (of mirror); ⚓ fur (on tongue); (slices of) ham, etc. (on bread); filling (of roll).

Belager|er [bə'la:gərər] m (-s/-) besieger; 2n v/t. (no -ge-, h) besiege, beleaguer; ~ung f siege.

Belang [bə'laŋ] m (-[e]s/-e) importance; ~e pl. interests pl.; 2en v/t. (no -ge-, h) concern; ⚖ sue; 2los adj. unimportant; ~losigkeit f (-/-en) insignificance.

be'lasten v/t. (no -ge-, h) load; fig. burden; ⚖ incriminate; mortgage (estate, etc.); j-s Konto (mit e-r Summe) ~ ✝ charge or debit s.o.'s account (with a sum).

belästig|en [bə'lɛstigən] v/t. (no -ge-, h) molest; trouble, bother; 2ung f molestation; trouble.

Be'lastung f (-/-en) load (a. ⚡, ⊕); fig. burden; ✝ debit; encumbrance; ⚖ incrimination; erbliche ~ hereditary taint; ~szeuge ⚖ m witness for the prosecution.

be'laufen v/refl. (irr. laufen, no -ge-, h): sich ~ auf (acc.) amount to.

be'lauschen v/t. (no -ge-, h) overhear, eavesdrop on s.o.

be'leb|en fig. v/t. (no -ge-, h) enliven, animate; stimulate; ~t adj. street: busy, crowded; stock exchange: brisk; conversation: lively, animated.

Beleg [bə'le:k] m (-[e]s/-e) proof; ⚖ (supporting) evidence; document; voucher; 2en [~gən] v/t. (no -ge-, h) cover; reserve (seat, etc.); prove, verify; univ. enrol(l) or register for,

Am. a. sign up for (course of lectures, term); ein Brötchen mit et. ~ put s.th. on a roll, fill a roll with s.th.; ~schaft f (-/-en) personnel, staff; labo(u)r force; ~stelle f reference; 2t adj. engaged, occupied; hotel, etc.: full; voice: thick, husky; tongue: coated, furred; ~es Brot (open) sandwich.

be'lehr|en v/t. (no -ge-, h) instruct, inform; sich ~ lassen take advice; ~end adj. instructive; 2ung f (-/-en) instruction; information; advice.

beleibt adj. [bə'laɪpt] corpulent, stout, bulky, portly.

beleidig|en [bə'laɪdigən] v/t. (no -ge-, h) offend (s.o.; ear, eye, etc.); insult; ~end adj. offensive; insulting; 2ung f (-/-en) offen|ce, Am. -se; insult.

be'lesen adj. well-read.

be'leucht|en v/t. (no -ge-, h) light (up), illuminate (a. fig.); fig. shed or throw light on; 2ung f (-/-en) light(ing); illumination; 2ungskörper m lighting appliance.

be'licht|en phot. v/t. (no -ge-, h) expose; 2ung phot. f exposure.

Be'lieb|en n (-s/no pl.) will, choice; nach ~ at will; es steht in Ihrem ~ I leave it you to; 2ig 1. adj. any; jeder ~e anyone; 2. adv. at pleasure; ~ viele as many as you like; 2t adj. [~pt] popular (bei with); ~theit f (-/no pl.) popularity.

be'liefer|n v/t. (no -ge-, h) supply, furnish (mit with); 2ung f (-/no pl.) supply.

bellen ['bɛlən] v/i. (ge-, h) bark.

belobigen [bə'lo:bigən] v/t. (no -ge-, h) commend, praise.

be'lohn|en v/t. (no -ge-, h) reward; recompense; 2ung f (-/-en) reward; recompense.

be'lügen v/t. (irr. lügen, no -ge-, h): j-n ~ lie to s.o.

belustig|en [bə'lustigən] v/t. (no -ge-, h) amuse, entertain; sich ~ amuse o.s.; 2ung f (-/-en) amusement, entertainment.

bemächtigen [bə'mɛçtigən] v/refl. (no -ge-, h): sich e-r Sache ~ take hold of s.th., seize s.th.; sich e-r Person ~ lay hands on s.o., seize s.o.

be'malen v/t. (no -ge-, h) cover with paint; paint; daub.

bemängeln [bə'mɛŋəln] v/t. (no -ge-, h) find fault with, cavil at.

be'mannen v/t. (no -ge-, h) man.

be'merk|bar adj. perceptible; ~en v/t. (no -ge-, h) notice, perceive; remark, mention; ~enswert adj. remarkable (wegen for); 2ung f (-/-en) remark.

bemitleiden [bə'mitlaɪdən] v/t. (no -ge-, h) pity, commiserate (with); ~swert adj. pitiable.

be'müh|en v/t. (no -ge-, h) trouble (j-n in or wegen et. s.o. about s.th.);

sich ~ trouble o.s.; endeavo(u)r; sich um e-e Stelle ~ apply for a position; 2ung f (-/-en) trouble; endeavo(u)r, effort.

be'nachbart adj. neighbo(u)ring; adjoining, adjacent (to).

benachrichtig|en [bəˈnɑːxriçtigən] v/t. (no -ge-, h) inform, notify; ✝ advise; 2ung f (-/-en) information; notification; ✝ advice.

benachteilig|en [bəˈnɑːxtailigən] v/t. (no -ge-, h) place s.o. at a disadvantage, discriminate against s.o.; handicap; sich benachteiligt fühlen feel handicapped or at a disadvantage; 2ung f (-/-en) disadvantage; discrimination; handicap.

be'nehmen 1. v/refl. (irr. nehmen, no -ge-, h) behave (o.s.); 2. 2 n (-s/no pl.) behavio(u)r, conduct.

be'neiden v/t. (no -ge-, h) envy (j-n um et. s.o. s.th.); ~swert adj. enviable.

be'nennen v/t. (irr. nennen, no -ge-, h) name. [rascal; urchin.)

Bengel ['bɛŋəl] m (-s/-) (little))

benommen adj. [bəˈnɔmən] bemused, dazed, stunned; ~ sein be in a daze.

be'nötigen v/t. (no -ge-, h) need, require, want.

be'nutz|en v/t. (no -ge-, h) use (a. patent, etc.); make use of; avail o.s. of (opportunity); take (tram, etc.); 2ung f use.

Benzin [bɛnˈtsiːn] n (-s/-e) 🜛 benzine; mot. petrol, F juice, Am. gasoline, F gas; ~motor m petrol engine, Am. gasoline engine; s. Tank.

beobacht|en [bəˈʔoːbaxtən] v/t. (no -ge-, h) observe; watch; police: shadow; 2er m (-s/-) observer; 2ung f (-/-en) observation.

beordern [bəˈʔɔrdərn] v/t. (no -ge-, h) order, command.

be'packen v/t. (no -ge-, h) load (mit with). [(mit with).)

be'pflanzen v/t. (no -ge-, h) plant)

bequem adj. [bəˈkveːm] convenient; comfortable; p.: easy-going; lazy; ~en v/refl. (no -ge-, h): sich ~ zu condescend to; consent to; 2lichkeit f (-/-en) convenience; comfort, ease; indolence.

be'rat|en (irr. raten, no -ge-, h) 1. v/t. advise s.o.; consider, debate, discuss s.th.; sich ~ confer (mit j-m with s.o.; über et. on or about s.th.); 2. v/i. confer; über et. ~ consider, debate, discuss s.th., confer on or about s.th.; 2er m (-s/-) adviser, counsel(l)or; consultant; ~schlagen (no -ge-, h) 1. v/i. s. beraten 2; 2. v/refl. confer (mit j-m with s.o.; über et. on or about s.th.); 2ung f (-/-en) advice; debate; consultation; conference; 2ungsstelle f advisory bureau.

be'raub|en v/t. (no -ge-, h) rob, deprive (gen. of); 2ung f (-/-en) robbery, deprivation.

be'rauschen v/t. (no -ge-, h) intoxicate (a. fig.).

be'rechn|en v/t. (no -ge-, h) calculate; ✝ charge (zu at); ~end adj. calculating, selfish; 2ung f calculation.

berechtig|en [bəˈrɛçtigən] v/t. (no -ge-, h) j-n ~ zu entitle s.o. to; authorize s.o. to; ~t adj. [~çt] entitled (zu to); qualified (to); claim: legitimate; 2ung f (-/-en) title (zu to); authorization.

be'red|en v/t. (no -ge-, h) talk s.th. over; persuade s.o.; gossip about s.o.; 2samkeit [~tza:mkait] f (-/no pl.) eloquence; ~t adj. [~t] eloquent (a. fig.).

Be'reich m, n (-[e]s/-e) area; reach; fig. scope, sphere; science, etc.: field, province; 2ern v/t. (no -ge-, h) enrich; sich ~ enrich o.s.; ~erung f (-/-en) enrichment.

be'reif|en v/t. (no -ge-, h) hoop (barrel); tyre, (Am. only) tire (wheel); 2ung f (-/-en) (set of) tyres pl., (Am. only) (set of) tires pl.

be'reisen v/t. (no -ge-, h) tour (in), travel (over); commercial traveller: cover (district).

bereit adj. [bəˈrait] ready, prepared; ~en v/t. (no -ge-, h) prepare; give (joy, trouble, etc.); ~s adv. already; 2schaft f (-/-en) readiness; police: squad; ~stellen v/t. (sep., -ge-, h) place s.th. ready; provide; 2ung f (-/-en) preparation; ~willig adj. ready, willing; 2willigkeit f (-/no pl.) readiness, willingness.

be'reuen v/t. (no -ge-, h) repent (of); regret, rue.

Berg m [bɛrk] m (-[e]s/-e) mountain; hill; ~e pl. von F heaps pl. of, piles pl. of; über den ~ sein be out of the wood, Am. be out of the woods; über alle ~e off and away; die Haare standen ihm zu ~e his hair stood on end; 2'ab adv. downhill (a. fig.); 2'an adv. s. bergauf; '~arbeiter m miner; 2'auf adv. uphill (a. fig.); '~bahn 🚞 f mountain railway; '~bau m (-[e]s/pl.) mining.

bergen ['bɛrgən] v/t. (irr., ge-, h) save; rescue s.o.; ⚓ salvage, salve.

bergig adj. ['bɛrgiç] mountainous, hilly.

'Berg|kette f mountain chain or range; '~mann ⚒ m (-[e]s/Bergleute) miner; '~predigt f (-/no pl.) the Sermon on the Mount; '~recht n mining laws pl.; '~rennen mot. n mountain race; '~rücken m ridge; '~rutsch m landslide, landslip; '~spitze f mountain peak; '~steiger m (-s/-) mountaineer; '~sturz m s. Bergrutsch.

**'Bergung** f (-/-en) ⚓ salvage; rescue; **~sarbeiten** ['bɛrguŋsʔ-] f/pl. salvage operations pl.; rescue work.

**'Bergwerk** n mine; **~saktien** ['berkverksʔ-] f/pl. mining shares pl.

**Bericht** [bə'riçt] m (-[e]s/-e) report (über acc. on); account (of); 2en (no -ge-, h) 1. v/t. report; j-m et. ~ inform s.o. of s.th.; tell s.o. about s.th.; 2. v/i. report (über acc. on); **journalist**: a. cover (über et. s.th.); **~erstatter** m (-s/-) reporter; correspondent; **~erstattung** f reporting; report(s pl.).

**berichtig|en** [bə'riçtigən] v/t. (no -ge-, h) correct (s.o.; error, mistake, etc.); put right (mistake); emend (corrupt text); † settle (claim, debt, etc.); 2ung f (-/-en) correction; emendation; settlement.

**be'riechen** v/t. (irr. riechen, no -ge-, h) smell or sniff at.

**Berliner** [ber'li:nər] 1. m (-s/-) Berliner; 2. adj. (of) Berlin.

**Bernstein** ['bɛrnʃtain] m amber; **schwarzer ~** jet.

**bersten** ['bɛrstən] v/i. (irr., ge-, sein) burst (fig. vor dat. with).

**berüchtigt** adj. [bə'ryçtiçt] notorious (wegen for), ill-famed.

**berücksichtig|en** [bə'rykziçtigən] v/t. (no -ge-, h) take s.th. into consideration, pay regard to s.th.; consider s.o.; 2ung f (-/-en) consideration; regard.

**Beruf** [bə'ru:f] m (-[e]s/-e) calling; profession; vocation; trade; occupation; 2en 1. v/t. (irr. rufen, no -ge-, h): j-n zu e-m Amt ~ appoint s.o. to an office; sich auf j-n ~ refer to s.o.; 2. adj. competent; qualified; 2lich adj. professional; vocational.

**Be'rufs|ausbildung** f vocational or professional training; **~beratung** f vocational guidance; **~kleidung** f work clothes pl.; **~krankheit** f occupational disease; **~schule** f vocational school; **~spieler** m sports: professional (player); 2tätig adj. working; **~tätige** [~gə] pl. working people pl.

**Be'rufung** f (-/-en) appointment (zu to); ⚖ appeal (bei dat. to); reference (auf acc. to); **~sgericht** n court of appeal.

**be'ruhen** v/i. (no -ge-, h): ~ auf (dat.) rest or be based on; et. auf sich ~ lassen let a matter rest.

**beruhig|en** [bə'ru:igən] v/t. (no -ge- h) quiet, calm; soothe; sich ~ calm down; 2ung f (-/-en) calming (down); soothing; comfort; 2ungsmittel ⚕ n sedative.

**berühmt** adj. [bə'ry:mt] famous (wegen for); celebrated; 2heit f (-/-en) fame, renown; famous or celebrated person, celebrity; person of note.

**be'rühr|en** v/t. (no -ge-, h) touch (a. fig.); touch (up)on (subject); 2ung f (-/-en) contact; touch; in ~ kommen mit come into contact with.

**be'sag|en** v/t. (no -ge-, h) say; mean, signify; **~t** adj. [~kt] (afore-) said; above(-mentioned).

**besänftigen** [bə'zɛnftigən] v/t. (no -ge-, h) appease, calm, soothe.

**Be'satz** m (-es/⁀e) trimming; braid.

**Be'satzung** f ✕ occupation troops pl.; ✕ garrison; ⚓, ✈ crew; **~s-macht** ✕ f occupying power.

**be'schädig|en** v/t. (no -ge-, h) damage, injure; 2ung f damage, injury (gen. to).

**be'schaffen** 1. v/t. (no -ge-, h) procure; provide; raise (money); 2. adj.: gut (schlecht) ~ sein be in good (bad) condition or state; 2heit f (-/-en) state, condition; properties pl.

**beschäftig|en** [bə'ʃɛftigən] v/t. (no -ge-, h) employ, occupy; keep busy; sich ~ occupy or busy o.s.; 2ung f (-/-en) employment; occupation.

**be'schäm|en** v/t. (no -ge-, h) (put to) shame, make s.o. feel ashamed; **~end** adj. shameful; humiliating; **~t** adj. ashamed (über acc. of); 2ung f (-/-en) shame; humiliation.

**beschatten** [bə'ʃatən] v/t. (no -ge-, h) shade; fig. shadow s.o., Am. sl. tail s.o.

**be'schau|en** v/t. (no -ge-, h) look at, view; examine, inspect (goods, etc.); **~lich** adj. contemplative, meditative.

**Bescheid** [bə'ʃait] m (-[e]s/-e) answer; ⚖ decision; information (über acc. on, about); ~ geben let s.o. know; ~ bekommen be informed or notified; ~ hinterlassen leave word (bei with, at); ~ wissen be informed, know, F be in the know.

**bescheiden** adj. [bə'ʃaidən] modest, unassuming; 2heit f (-/no pl.) modesty.

**bescheinig|en** [bə'ʃainigən] v/i. (no -ge-, h) certify, attest; den Empfang ~ acknowledge receipt; es wird hiermit bescheinigt, daß this is to certify that; 2ung f (-/-en) certification, attestation; certificate; receipt; acknowledgement.

**be'schenken** v/t. (no -ge-, h): j-n ~ make s.o. a present; j-n mit et. ~ present s.o. with s.th.; j-n reichlich ~ shower s.o. with gifts.

**be'scher|en** v/t. (no -ge-, h): j-n ~ give s.o. presents (esp. for Christmas); 2ung f (-/-en) presentation of gifts; F fig. mess.

**be'schieß|en** v/t. (irr. schießen, no -ge-, h) fire or shoot at or on; bombard (a. phys.), shell; 2ung f (-/-en) bombardment.

**be'schimpf|en** v/t. (no -ge-, h) abuse, insult; call s.o. names; 2ung f (-/-en) abuse; insult, affront.

**be'schirmen** v/t. (no -ge-, h) shelter, shield, guard, protect (vor dat. from); defend (against).

**be'schlafen** v/t. (irr. schlafen, no -ge-, h): et. ~ sleep on a matter, take counsel of one's pillow.

**Be'schlag** m ⊕ metal fitting(s pl.); furnishing(s pl.) (of door, etc.); shoe (of wheel, etc.); (horse)shoe; seizure, confiscation; in ~ nehmen, mit ~ belegen seize; ⚖ seize, attach (real estate, salary, etc.); confiscate (goods, etc.); monopolize s.o.'s attention.

**be'schlagen 1.** v/t. (irr. schlagen, no -ge-, h) cover (mit with); ⊕ fit, mount (horse); hobnail (shoe); 2. v/i. (irr. schlagen, no -ge-, h) window, wall, etc.: steam up; mirror, etc.: cloud or film over; 3. adj. windows, etc.: steamed-up; fig. well versed (auf, in dat. in).

**Beschlagnahme** [bə'ʃlaːknaːmə] f (-/-n) seizure; confiscation (of contraband goods, etc.); ⚖ sequestration, distraint (of property); ✗ requisition (of houses, etc.); embargo, detention (of ship); **2n** v/t. (no -ge-, h) seize; attach (real estate); confiscate; ⚖ sequestrate, distrain upon (property); ✗ requisition; ⚓ embargo.

**beschleunig|en** [bə'ʃlɔynigən] v/t. (no -ge-, h) mot. accelerate; hasten, speed up; s-e Schritte ~ quicken one's steps; **2ung** f (-/-en) acceleration.

**be'schließen** v/t. (irr. schließen, no -ge-, h) end, close, wind up; resolve, decide.

**Be'schluß** m decision, resolution, Am. a. resolve; ⚖ **2fähig** adj.: ~ sein form or have a quorum; **~fassung** f (passing of a) resolution.

**be'schmieren** v/t. (no -ge-, h) (be)smear (with grease, etc.).

**be'schmutzen** v/t. (no -ge-, h) soil (a. fig.), dirty; bespatter.

**be'schneiden** v/t. (irr. schneiden, no -ge-, h) clip, cut; lop (tree); trim, clip (hair, hedge, etc.); dress (vinestock, etc.); fig. cut down, curtail, F slash.

**beschönig|en** [bə'ʃøːnigən] v/t. (no -ge-, h) gloss over, palliate; **2ung** f (-/-en) gloss, palliation.

**beschränk|en** [bə'ʃrɛŋkən] v/t. (no -ge-, h) confine, limit, restrict, Am. a. curb; sich ~ auf (acc.) confine o.s. to; **~t** fig. adj. of limited intelligence; **2ung** f (-/-en) limitation, restriction.

**be'schreib|en** v/t. (irr. schreiben, no -ge-, h) write on (piece of paper, etc.), cover with writing; describe; give a description of; **2ung** f (-/-en) description; account.

**be'schrift|en** v/t. (no -ge-, h) in-scribe; letter; **2ung** f (-/-en) inscription; lettering.

**beschuldig|en** [bə'ʃuldigən] v/t. (no -ge-, h) accuse (gen. of [doing] s.th.), esp. ⚖ charge (with); **2te** [~ktə] m, f (-n/-n) the accused; **2ung** f (-/-en) accusation, charge.

**Be'schuß** m (Beschusses/no pl.) bombardment.

**be'schütz|en** v/t. (no -ge-, h) protect, shelter, guard (vor dat. from); **2er** m (-s/-) protector; **2ung** f (-/-en) protection.

**be'schwatzen** v/t. (no -ge-, h) talk s.o. into (doing) s.th., coax s.o. into (doing s.th.).

**Beschwerde** [bə'ʃveːrdə] f (-/-n) trouble; ⚕ complaint; complaint (über acc. about); ⚖ objection (gegen to); **~buch** n complaints book.

**beschwer|en** [bə'ʃveːrən] v/t. (no -ge-, h) burden (a. fig.); weight (loose sheets, etc.); lie heavy on (stomach); weigh on (mind, etc.); sich ~ complain (über acc. about, of; bei to); **~lich** adj. troublesome.

**beschwichtigen** [bə'ʃviçtigən] v/t. (no -ge-, h) appease, calm (down), soothe.

**be'schwindeln** v/t. (no -ge-, h) tell a fib or lie; cheat, F diddle (um out of).

**be'schwipst** F adj. tipsy.

**be'schwör|en** v/t. (irr. schwören, no -ge-, h) take an oath on s.th.; implore or entreat s.o.; conjure (up), invoke (spirit); **2ung** f (-/-en) conjuration.

**be'seelen** v/t. (no -ge-, h) animate, inspire.

**be'sehen** v/t. (irr. sehen, no -ge-, h) look at; inspect; sich et. ~ look at s.th.; inspect s.th.

**beseitig|en** [bə'zaɪtigən] v/t. (no -ge-, h) remove, do away with; **2ung** f (-/-en) removal.

**Besen** ['beːzən] m (-s/-) broom; **~stiel** m broomstick.

**besessen** adj. [bə'zesən] obsessed, possessed (von by, with); wie ~ like mad; **2e** m, f (-n/-n) demoniac.

**be'setz|en** v/t. (no -ge-, h) occupy (seat, table, etc.); fill (post, etc.); man (orchestra); thea. cast (play); ✗ occupy; trim (dress, etc.); set (crown with jewels, etc.); **~t** adj. engaged, occupied; seat: taken; F bus, etc.: full up; hotel: full; teleph. engaged, Am. busy; **2ung** f (-/-en) thea. cast; ✗ occupation.

**besichtig|en** [bə'ziçtigən] v/t. (no -ge-, h) view, look over; inspect (a. ✗); visit; **2ung** f (-/-en) sightseeing; visit (gen. to); inspection (a. ✗).

**be'sied|eln** v/t. (no -ge-, h) colonize, settle; populate; **2lung** f (-/-en) colonization, settlement.

be'siegeln v/t. (no -ge-, h) seal (a. fig.).

be'siegen v/t. (no -ge-, h) conquer; defeat, beat (a. sports).

be'sinn|en v/refl. (irr. sinnen, no -ge-, h) reflect, consider; sich ~ auf (acc.) remember, think of; ~lich adj. reflective, contemplative.

Be'sinnung f (-/no pl.) reflection; consideration; consciousness; (wieder) zur ~ kommen recover consciousness; fig. come to one's senses; 2slos adj. unconscious.

Be'sitz m possession; in ~ nehmen, ~ ergreifen von take possession of; 2anzeigend gr. adj. possessive; 2en v/t. (irr. sitzen, no -ge-, h) possess; ~er m (-s/-) possessor, owner, proprietor; den ~ wechseln change hands; ~ergreifung f taking possession (von of), occupation; ~tum n (-s/=er), ~ung f (-/-en) possession; property; estate.

be'sohlen v/t. (no -ge-, h) sole.

besold|en [bə'zɔldən] v/t. (no -ge-, h) pay a salary to (civil servant, etc.); pay (soldier); 2ung f (-/-en) pay; salary.

besonder adj. [bə'zɔndər] particular, special; peculiar; separate; 2heit f (-/-en) particularity; peculiarity; ~s adv. especially, particularly; chiefly, mainly; separately.

besonnen adj. [bə'zɔnən] sensible, considerate, level-headed; prudent; discreet; 2heit f (-/no pl.) considerateness; prudence; discretion; presence of mind.

be'sorg|en v/t. (no -ge-, h) get (j-m et. s.o. s.th.), procure (s.th. for s.o.); do, manage; 2nis [~knis] f (-/-se) apprehension, fear, anxiety, concern (über acc. about, at); ~niserregend adj. alarming; ~t adj. [~kt] uneasy (um about); worried (about), concerned (about); anxious (um for, about); 2ung f (-/-en) procurement; management; errand; ~en machen go shopping.

be'sprech|en v/t. (irr. sprechen, no -ge-, h) discuss, talk s.th. over; arrange; review (book, etc.); sich ~ mit confer with (über acc. about); 2ung f (-/-en) discussion; review; conference.

be'spritzen v/t. (no -ge-, h) splash, (be)spatter.

besser ['besər] 1. adj. better; superior; 2. adv. better; '~n v/t. (no -ge-, h) (make) better, improve; reform; sich ~ get or become better, improve, change for the better; mend one's ways; '2ung f (-/-en) improvement; change for the better; reform (of character); ﾟ improvement, recovery; gute ~! I wish you a speedy recovery!

best [best] 1. adj. best; der erste ~e (just) anybody; ~en Dank thank you very much; sich von s-r ~en Seite zeigen be on one's best behavio(u)r; 2. adv. best; am ~en best; aufs ~e, ~ens in the best way possible; zum ~en geben recite (poem), tell (story), oblige with (song); j-n zum ~en haben or halten make fun of s.o., F pull s.o.'s leg; ich danke ~ens! thank you very much!

Be'stand m (continued) existence; continuance; stock; † stock-in-trade; † cash in hand; ~ haben be lasting, last.

be'ständig adj. constant, steady; lasting; continual; weather: settled; 2keit f (-/-en) constancy, steadiness; continuance.

Bestand|saufnahme † [bə-'ʃtants?-] f stock-taking, Am. inventory; ~teil m component, constituent; elemen., ingredient; part.

be'stärken v/t. (no -ge-, h) confirm, strengthen, encourage (in dat. in).

be'stätig|en [bə'ʃtɛːtigən] v/t. confirm (a. ﾟﾟ verdict, † order); attest; verify (statement, etc.); ratify (law, treaty); † acknowledge (receipt); 2ung f (-/-en) confirmation; attestation; verification; ratification; acknowledgement.

bestatt|en [bə'ʃtatən] v/t. (no -ge-, h) bury, inter; 2ung f (-/-en) burial, interment; funeral; 2ungsinstitut [bə'ʃtatuŋs?-] n undertakers pl.

'Beste 1. n (-n/no pl.) the best (thing); zu deinem ~n in your interest; zum ~n der Armen for the benefit of the poor; das ~ daraus machen make the best of it; 2. m, f (-n/-n): er ist der ~ in s-r Klasse he is the best in his class.

Besteck [bə'ʃtɛk] n (-[e]s/-e) ﾟ (case or set of) surgical instruments pl.; (single set of) knife, fork and spoon; (complete set of) cutlery, Am. a. flatware.

be'stehen 1. v/t. (irr. stehen, no -ge-, h) come off victorious in (combat, etc.); have (adventure); stand, undergo (well) (test, trial); pass (test, examination); 2. v/i. (irr. stehen, no -ge-, h) be, exist; continue, last; ~ auf (dat.) insist (up)on; ~ aus consist of; 3. 2 n (-s/no pl.) existence; continuance; passing.

be'stehlen v/t. (irr. stehlen, no -ge-, h) steal from, rob.

be'steig|en v/t. (irr. steigen, no -ge-, h) climb (up) (mountain, tree, etc.); mount (horse, bicycle, etc.); ascend (throne); get into or on, board (bus, train, plane); 2ung f ascent; accession (to throne).

be'stell|en v/t. (no -ge-, h) order; † a. place an order for; subscribe to (newspaper, etc.); book, reserve (room, seat, etc.); make an appointment with s.o.; send for (taxi, etc.); cultivate, till (soil, etc.); give (mes-

*sage, greetings*); *j-n zu sich* ~ send for s.o.; ℒung *f* order; subscription (to); booking, *esp. Am.* reservation; ✗ cultivation; message.

**'besten'falls** *adv.* at (the) best.

**be'steuer|n** *v/t.* (*no -ge-, h*) tax; ℒung *f* taxation.

**besti|alisch** *adj.* [best'ja:liʃ] bestial; brutal; inhuman; *weather, etc.*: F beastly; ℒe ['~jə] *f* (*-/-n*) beast; *fig.* brute, beast, inhuman person.

**be'stimmen** (*no -ge-, h*) **1.** *v/t.* determine, decide; fix (*date, place, price, etc.*); appoint (*date, time, place, etc.*); prescribe; define (*species, word, etc.*); *j-n für or zu et.* ~ designate *or* intend s.o. for s.th.; **2.** *v/i.:* ~ *über* (*acc.*) dispose of.

**be'stimmt 1.** *adj. voice, manner, etc.:* decided, determined, firm; *time, etc.:* appointed, fixed; *point, number. etc.:* certain; *answer, etc.:* positive; *tone, answer, intention, idea:* definite (*a. gr.*); ~ *nach* ⚓ ✈ bound for; **2.** *adv.* certainly, surely; ℒheit *f* (*-/-en*) determination, firmness; certainty.

**Be'stimmung** *f* determination; destination (*of s.o. for the church, etc.*); designation, appointment (*of s.o. as successor, etc.*); definition; ⚖ provision (*in document*) (*amtliche*) ~en *pl.* (official) regulations *pl.*; ~sort [bə'ʃtimuŋs⁹-] *m* destination.

**be'straf|en** *v/t.* (*no -ge-, h*) punish (*wegen, für for; mit with*); ℒung *f* (*-/-en*) punishment.

**be'strahl|en** *v/t.* (*no -ge-, h*) irradiate (*a. ✗*); ℒung *f* irradiation; ✗ ray treatment, radiotherapy.

**Be'streb|en** *n* (*-s/no pl.*), ~ung *f* (*-/-en*) effort, endeavo(u)r.

**be'streichen** *v/t.* (*irr. streichen, no -ge-, h*) coat, cover; spread; *mit Butter* ~ butter.

**be'streiten** *v/t.* (*irr. streiten, no -ge-, h*) contest, dispute, challenge (*point, right, etc.*); deny (*facts, guilt, etc.*); defray (*expenses, etc.*); fill (*programme*).

**be'streuen** *v/t.* (*no -ge-, h*) strew, sprinkle (*mit with*); *mit Mehl* ~ flour; *mit Zucker* ~ sugar.

**be'stürmen** *v/t.* (*no -ge-, h*) storm, assail (*a. fig.*); pester, plague (*s.o. with questions, etc.*).

**be'stürz|t** *adj.* dismayed, struck with consternation (*über acc.* at); ℒung *f* (*-/-en*) consternation, dismay.

**Besuch** [bə'zu:x] *m* (*-[e]s/-e*) visit (*gen., bei, in dat.* to); call (*bei on; in dat.* at); attendance (*gen.* at) (*lecture, church, etc.*); visitor(s *pl.*), company; ℒen *v/t.* (*no -ge-, h*) visit; call on, go to see; attend (*school, etc.*); frequent; ~er *m* visitor, caller; ~szeit *f* visiting hours *pl.*

**be'tasten** *v/t.* (*no -ge-, h*) touch, feel, finger; ✗ palpate.

**betätigen** [bə'tɛ:tigən] *v/t.* (*no -ge-, h*) ⊕ operate (*machine, etc.*); put on, apply (*brake*); *sich* ~ *als* act *or* work as; *sich poli⁺isch* ~ dabble in politics.

**betäub|en** [bə'tɔybən] *v/t.* (*no -ge-, h*) stun (*a. fig.*), daze (*by blow, noise, etc.*); deafen (*by noise, etc.*); slaughtering: stun (*animal*); ✗ an(a)esthetize; ℒung *f* (*-/-en*) ✗ an(a)esthetization; ✗ an(a)esthesia; *fig.* stupefaction; ℒungsmittel ✗ *n* narcotic, an(a)esthetic.

**beteilig|en** [bə'tailigən] *v/t.* (*no -ge-, h*): *j-n* ~ give s.o. a share (*an dat.* in); *sich* ~ take part (*an dat., bei* in), participate (*a. ⚖*) (in); ℒte [~çtə] *m, f* (*-n/-n*) person *or* party concerned; ℒung *f* (*-/-en*) participation (*a. ⚖, ✝*), partnership; share, interest (*a. ✝*).

**beten** ['be:tən] *v/i.* (*ge-, h*) pray (*um* for), say one's prayers; *at table:* say grace

**be'teuer|n** *v/t.* (*no -ge- h*) protest (*one's innocence*); swear (*to s.th.;* that); ℒung *f* protestation; solemn declaration.

**be'titeln** *v/t.* (*no -ge-, h*) entitle (*book, etc.*); style (*s.o. 'baron', etc.*).

**Beton** ⊕ [be'tõ:; be'tɔ:n] *m* (*-s/-s; -s/-e*) concrete.

**be'tonen** *v/t.* (*no -ge-, h*) stress; *fig. a.* emphasize.

**betonieren** [beto'ni:rən] *v/t.* (*no -ge-, h*) concrete.

**Be'tonung** *f* (*-/-en*) stress; emphasis.

**betör|en** [bə'tø:rən] *v/t.* (*no -ge-, h*) dazzle; infatuate, bewitch; ℒung *f* (*-/-en*) infatuation.

**Betracht** [bə'traxt] *m* (*-[e]s/no pl.*): *in* ~ *ziehen* take into consideration; (*nicht*) *in* ~ *kommen* (not to) come into question; ℒen *v/t.* (*no -ge-, h*) view; contemplate; *fig. a.* consider.

**beträchtlich** *adj.* [bə'trɛçtliç] considerable.

**Be'trachtung** *f* (*-/-en*) view; contemplation; consideration.

**Betrag** [bə'tra:k] *m* (*-[e]s/=e*) amount, sum; ℒen [~gən] **1.** *v/t.* (*irr. tragen, no -ge-, h*) amount to; **2.** *v/refl.* (*irr. tragen, no -ge-, h*) behave (*o.s.*); **3.** ℒ *n* (*-s/no pl.*) behavio(u)r, conduct.

**be'trauen** *v/t.* (*no -ge-, h*): *j-n mit et.* ~ entrust *or* charge s.o. with s.th.

**be'trauern** *v/t.* (*no -ge-, h*) mourn (for, over).

**Betreff** [bə'trɛf] *m* (*-[e]s/-e*) *at head of letter:* reference; ℒen *v/t.* (*irr. treffen, no -ge-, h*) befall; refer to; concern; *was ... betrifft* as for, as to; ℒend *adj.* concerning; *das* ~e *Geschäft* the business referred to or in question; ℒs *prp.* (*gen.*) concerning; as to.

**be'treiben 1.** *v/t.* (*irr. treiben, no -ge-, h*) carry on (*business, etc.*); pursue (*one's studies*); operate (*railway line, etc.*); **2.** 2 *n* (*-s/no pl.*): auf ~ von at or by *s.o.'s* instigation.

**be'treten 1.** *v/t.* (*irr. treten, no -ge-, h*) step on; enter (*room, etc.*); **2.** *adj.* embarrassed, abashed.

**betreu|en** [bə'trɔyən] *v/t.* (*no -ge-, h*) look after; attend to; care for; 2ung *f* (*-/no pl.*) care (*gen.* of, for).

**Betrieb** [bə'tri:p] *m* (*-[e]s/-e*) working, running, *esp. Am.* operation; business, firm, enterprise; plant, works *sg.*; workshop, *Am. a.* shop; *fig.* bustle; in ~ working; 2sam *adj.* active; industrious.

**Be'triebs|anleitung** *f* operating instructions *pl.*; ~ausflug *m* firm's outing; ~ferien *pl.* (firm's, works) holiday; ~führer *m s. Betriebsleiter*; ~kapital *n* working capital; ~kosten *pl.* working expenses *pl.*, *Am.* operating costs *pl.* ~leiter *m* (works) manager, superintendent; ~leitung *f* management; ~material *n* working materials *pl.*; 錢 rolling stock; ~rat *m* works council; 2sicher *adj.* safe to operate; foolproof; ~störung *f* breakdown; ~unfall *m* industrial accident, accident while at work.

**be'trinken** *v/refl.* (*irr. trinken, no -ge-, h*) get drunk.

**betroffen** *adj.* [bə'trɔfən] afflicted (*von* by), stricken (with); *fig.* disconcerted.

**be'trüben** *v/t.* (*no -ge-, h*) grieve, afflict.

**Be'trug** *m* cheat(ing); fraud (*a.* 錢); deceit.

**be'trüg|en** *v/t.* (*irr. trügen, no -ge-, h*) deceive; cheat (*a. at games*); defraud; F skin; 2er *m* (*-s/-*) cheat, deceiver, impostor, confidence man, swindler, trickster; ~erisch *adj.* deceitful, fraudulent.

**be'trunken** *adj.* drunken; *pred.* drunk; 2e *m* (*-n/-n*) drunk(en man).

**Bett** [bɛt] *n* (*-[e]s/-en*) bed; ~bezug *m* plumeau case; ~decke *f* blanket; bedspread, coverlet.

**Bettel|brief** ['bɛtəl-] *m* begging letter; ~ei [~'laɪ] *f* (*-/-en*) begging, mendicancy; 2n *v/i.* (*ge-, h*) beg (*um* for); ~ gehen go begging; ~stab *m*: an den ~ bringen reduce to beggary.

**'Bett|gestell** *n* bedstead; 2lägerig *adj.* ['~lɛ:gəriç] bedridden, confined to bed, *Am. a.* bedfast; '~laken *n* sheet.

**Bettler** ['bɛtlər] *m* (*-s/-*) beggar, *Am. sl.* panhandler.

**'Bett|überzug** *m* plumeau case; ~uch ['bɛttu:x] *n* sheet; '~vorleger *m* bedside rug; '~wäsche *f* bedlinen; '~zeug *n* bedding.

**be'tupfen** *v/t.* (*no -ge-, h*) dab.

**beug|en** ['bɔygən] *v/t.* (*ge-, h*) bend, bow; *fig.* humble, break (*pride*); *gr.* inflect (*word*), decline (*noun, adjective*); sich ~ bend (*vor dat.* to), bow (to); '2ung *f* (*-/-en*) bending; *gr.* inflection, declension.

**Beule** ['bɔylə] *f* (*-/-n*) bump, swelling; boil; *on metal, etc.*: dent.

**beunruhig|en** [bə'unru:igən] *v/t.* (*no -ge-, h*) disturb, trouble, disquiet, alarm; sich ~ über (*acc.*) be uneasy about, worry about; 2ung *f* (*-/no pl.*) disturbance; alarm; uneasiness.

**beurkund|en** [bə'u:rkundən] *v/t.* (*no -ge-, h*) attest, certify, authenticate; 2ung *f* (*-/-en*) attestation, certification, authentication.

**beurlaub|en** [bə'u:rlaubən] *v/t.* (*no -ge-, h*) give *or* grant *s.o.* leave (of absence); give *s.o.* time off; suspend (*civil servant, etc.*); 2ung *f* (*-/-en*) leave (of absence); suspension.

**beurteil|en** [bə'urtaɪlən] *v/t.* (*no -ge-, h*) judge (*nach* by); 2ung *f* (*-/-en*) judg(e)ment.

**Beute** ['bɔytə] *f* (*-/no pl.*) booty, spoil(s *pl.*); loot; prey; *hunt.* bag; *fig.* prey, victim (*gen.* to).

**Beutel** ['bɔytəl] *m* (*-s/-*) bag; purse; pouch.

**'Beutezug** *m* plundering expedition.

**bevölker|n** [bə'fœlkərn] *v/t.* (*no -ge-, h*) people, populate; 2ung *f* (*-/-en*) population.

**bevollmächtig|en** [bə'fɔlmɛçtigən] *v/t.* (*no -ge-, h*) authorize, empower; 2te [~çtə] *m, f* (*-n/-n*) authorized person *or* agent, deputy; *pol.* plenipotentiary; 2ung *f* (*-/-en*) authorization.

**be'vor** *cj.* before.

**bevormund|en** *fig.* [bə'fo:rmundən] *v/t.* (*no -ge-, h*) patronize, keep in tutelage; 2ung *fig. f* (*-/-en*) patronizing, tutelage.

**be'vorstehen** *v/i.* (*irr. stehen, sep., -ge-, h*) be approaching, be near; *crisis, etc.*: be imminent; *j-m* ~ be in store for *s.o.*, await *s.o.*; ~d *adj.* approaching; imminent.

**bevorzug|en** [bə'fo:rtsu:gən] *v/t.* (*no -ge-, h*) prefer; favo(u)r; 錢 privilege; 2ung *f* (*-/-en*) preference.

**be'wach|en** *v/t.* (*no -ge-, h*) guard, watch; 2ung *f* (*-/-en*) guard; escort.

**bewaffn|en** [bə'vafnən] *v/t.* (*no -ge-, h*) arm; 2ung *f* (*-/-en*) armament; arms *pl.*

**be'wahren** *v/t.* (*no -ge-, h*) keep, preserve (*mst fig.*: secret, silence, etc.).

**be'währen** *v/refl.* (*no -ge-, h*) stand the test, prove a success; sich ~ als prove o.s. (as) (*a good teacher, etc.*); sich ~ in prove o.s. efficient in (*one's profession, etc.*); sich nicht ~ prove a failure.

be'wahrheiten v/refl. (no -ge-, h) prove (to be) true; prophecy, etc.: come true.

be'währt adj. friend, etc.: tried; solicitor, etc.: experienced; friendship, etc.: long-standing; remedy, etc.: proved, proven.

Be'währung f 🕇🕇 probation; in Zeiten der ~ in times of trial; s. bewähren; ~sfrist 🕇🕇 f probation.

bewaldet adj. [bə'valdət] wooded, woody, Am. a. timbered.

bewältigen [bə'vɛltigən] v/t. (no -ge-, h) overcome (obstacle); master (difficulty); accomplish (task).

be'wandert adj. (well) versed (in dat. in), proficient (in); in e-m Fach gut ~ sein have a thorough knowledge of a subject.

be'wässer|n v/t. (no -ge-, h) water (garden, lawn, etc.); irrigate (land, etc.); 2ung f (-/-en) watering; irrigation.

bewegen¹ [bə've:gən] v/t. (irr., no -ge-, h): j-n ~ zu induce or get s.o. to.

beweg|en² [~] v/t. and v/refl. (no -ge-, h) move, stir; 2grund [~k-] m motive (gen., für for); ~lich adj. [~k-] movable; p., mind, etc.: agile, versatile; active; 2lichkeit [~k-] f (-/no pl.) mobility; agility, versatility; ~t adj. [~kt] sea: rough, heavy; fig. moved, touched; voice: choked, trembling; life: eventful; times, etc.: stirring, stormy; 2ung f (-/-en) movement; motion (a. phys.); fig. emotion; in ~ setzen set going or in motion; ~ungslos adj. motionless, immobile.

be'weinen v/t. (no -ge-, h) weep or cry over; lament (for, over).

Beweis [bə'vais] m (-es/-e) proof (für of); ~(e pl.) evidence (esp. 🕇🕇); 2en [~zən] v/t. (irr. weisen, no -ge-, h) prove; show (interest, etc.); ~führung f argumentation; ~grund m argument; ~material n evidence; ~stück n (piece of) evidence; 🕇🕇 exhibit.                     [leave it at that.]

be'wenden vb.: es dabei ~ lassen|

be'werb|en v/refl. (irr. werben, no -ge-, h): sich ~ um apply for, Am. run for; stand for; compete for (prize); court (woman); 2er m (-s/-) applicant (um for); candidate; competitor; suitor; 2ung f application; candidature; competition; courtship; 2ungsschreiben n (letter of) application.

bewerkstelligen [bə'vɛrkʃtɛligən] v/t. (no -ge-, h) manage, effect, bring about.

be'wert|en v/t. (no -ge-, h) value (auf acc. at; nach by); 2ung f valuation.

bewillig|en [bə'viligən] v/t. (no -ge-, h) grant, allow; 2ung f (-/-en) grant, allowance.

be'wirken v/t. (no -ge-, h) cause; bring about, effect.

be'wirt|en v/t. (no -ge-, h) entertain; ~schaften v/t. (no -ge-, h) farm (land); ~' cultivate (field); manage (farm, etc.); ration (food, etc.); control (foreign exchange, etc.); 2ung f (-/-en) entertainment; hospitality.

bewog [bə'vo:k] pret. of bewegen¹; ~en [bə'vo:gən] p.p. of bewegen¹.

be'wohn|en v/t. (no -ge-, h) inhabit, live in; occupy; 2er m (-s/-) inhabitant; occupant.

bewölk|en v/refl. (no -ge-, h) sky: cloud up or over; brow: cloud over, darken; ~t adj. sky: clouded, cloudy, overcast; brow: clouded, darkened; 2ung f (-/no pl.) clouds pl.

be'wunder|n v/t. (no -ge-, h) admire (wegen for); ~nswert adj. admirable; 2ung f (-/-en) admiration.

bewußt adj. [bə'vust] deliberate, intentional; sich e-r Sache ~ sein be conscious or aware of s.th.; die ~e Sache the matter in question; ~los adj. unconscious; 2sein n (-s/no pl.) consciousness.

be'zahl|en v/t. (no -ge-, h) 1. v/t. pay; pay for (s.th. purchased); pay off, settle (debt); 2. v/i. pay (für for); 2ung f payment; settlement.

be'zähmen v/t. (no -ge-, h) tame (animal); restrain (one's anger, etc.); sich ~ control or restrain o.s.

be'zauber|n v/t. (no -ge-, h) bewitch, enchant (a. fig.); fig. charm, fascinate; 2ung f (-/-en) enchantment, spell; fascination.

be'zeichn|en v/t. (no -ge-, h) mark; describe (als as), call; ~end adj. characteristic, typical (für of); 2ung f indication (of direction, etc.); mark, sign, symbol; name, designation, denomination.

be'zeugen v/t. (no -ge-, h) 🕇🕇 testify to, bear witness to (both a. fig.); attest.

be'zieh|en v/t. (irr. ziehen, no -ge-, h) cover (upholstered furniture, etc.); put cover on (cushion, etc.); move into (flat, etc.); enter (university); draw (salary, pension, etc.); get, be supplied with (goods); take in (newspaper, etc.); sich ~ sky: cloud over; sich ~ auf (acc.) refer to; 2er m (-s/-) subscriber (gen. to).

Be'ziehung f relation (zu et. to s.th.; zu j-m with s.o.); connexion, (Am. only) connection (zu with); in dieser ~ in this respect; 2sweise adv. respectively; or rather.

Bezirk [bə'tsirk] m (-[e]s/-e) district, Am. a. precinct; s. Wahlbezirk.

Bezogene 🕇 [bə'tso:gənə] m (-n/-n) drawee.

Bezug [bə'tsu:k] m cover(ing), case; purchase (of goods); subscription (*to newspaper*); in ~ auf (*acc.*) with regard or reference to, as to; ~ *nehmen auf* (*acc.*) refer to, make reference to.

**bezüglich** [bə'tsy:kliç] **1.** *adj.* relative, relating (*both: auf acc.* to); **2.** *prp.* (*gen.*) regarding, concerning.

**Be'zugsbedingungen** † *f/pl.* terms *pl.* of delivery.

**be'zwecken** *v/t.* (*no -ge-, h*) aim at; ~ *mit* intend by.

**be'zweifeln** *v/t.* (*no -ge-, h*) doubt, question.

**be'zwing|en** *v/t.* (*irr. zwingen, no -ge-, h*) conquer (*fortress, mountain, etc.*); overcome, master (*feeling, difficulty, etc.*); sich ~ keep o.s. under control, restrain o.s.; **2ung** *f* (*-/-en*) conquest; mastering.

**Bibel** ['bi:bəl] *f* (*-/-n*) Bible.

**Biber** *zo.* ['bi:bər] *m* (*-s/-*) beaver.

**Bibliothek** [biblio'te:k] *f* (*-/-en*) library; **~ar** [~e'ka:r] *m* (*-s/-e*) librarian.

**biblisch** *adj.* ['bi:bliʃ] biblical, scriptural; **~e** *Geschichte* Scripture.

**bieder** *adj.* ['bi:dər] honest, upright, worthy (*a. iro.*); simple-minded; **2keit** *f* (*-/no pl.*) honesty, uprightness; simple-mindedness.

**bieg|en** ['bi:gən] (*irr., ge-*) **1.** *v/t.* (*h*) bend; **2.** *v/refl.* (*h*) bend; *sich vor Lachen ~* double up with laughter; **3.** *v/i.* (*sein*): *um e-e Ecke ~* turn (round) a corner; **~sam** *adj.* ['bi:kza:m] *wire, etc.*: flexible; *body*: lithe, supple; pliant (*a. fig.*); **2samkeit** *f* (*-/no pl.*) flexibility; suppleness; pliability; **2ung** *f* (*-/-en*) bend, wind (*of road, river*); curve (*of road, arch*).

**Biene** *zo.* ['bi:nə] *f* (*-/-n*) bee; **~n-königin** *f* queen bee; **~nkorb** *m* (bee)hive; **~nschwarm** *m* swarm of bees; **~nstock** *m* (bee)hive; **~n-zucht** *f* bee-keeping; **~nzüchter** *m* bee-keeper.

**Bier** [bi:r] *n* (*-[e]s/-e*) beer; *helles ~* pale beer, ale; *dunkles ~* dark beer; stout, porter; ~ *vom Faß* beer on draught; **~brauer** *m* brewer; **~brauerei** *f* brewery; **~garten** *m* beer-garden; **~krug** *m* beer-mug, *Am.* stein.

**Biest** [bi:st] *n* (*-es/-er*) beast, brute.

**bieten** ['bi:tən] (*irr., ge-, h*) **1.** *v/t.* offer; † *at auction sale:* bid; *sich ~ opportunity, etc.*: offer itself, arise, occur; **2.** *v/i. at auction sale:* bid.

**Bigamie** [biga'mi:] *f* (*-/-n*) bigamy.

**Bilanz** [bi'lants] *f* (*-/-en*) balance; balance-sheet, *Am. a.* statement; *fig.* result, outcome; *die ~ ziehen* strike a balance; *fig.* take stock (*of one's life, etc.*).

**Bild** [bilt] *n* (*-[e]s/-er*) picture; image; illustration; portrait; *fig.* idea, notion; **~bericht** *m* *press:* picture story.

**bilden** ['bildən] *v/t.* (*ge-, h*) form; shape; *fig.:* educate, train (*s.o., mind, etc.*); develop (*mind, etc.*); form, be, constitute (*obstacle, etc.*); *sich ~* form; *fig.* educate o.s., improve one's mind; *sich e-e Meinung ~* form an opinion.

**Bilder|buch** ['bildər-] *n* picture-book; **~galerie** *f* picture-gallery; **~rätsel** *n* rebus.

**'Bild|fläche** *f:* F *auf der ~ erscheinen* appear on the scene; F *von der ~ verschwinden* disappear (from the scene); **~funk** *m* radio picture transmission; television; **~hauer** *m* (*-s/-*) sculptor; **~hauerei** [~'rai] *f* (*-/-en*) sculpture; **~lich** *adj.* pictorial; *word, etc.:* figurative; **~nis** *n* (*-ses/-se*) portrait; **~röhre** *f* picture *or* television tube; **~säule** *f* statue; **~schirm** *m* (television) screen; **~schön** *adj.* most beautiful; **~seite** *f* face, head (*of coin*); **~streifen** *m* picture *or* film strip; **~telegraphie** *f* (*-/no pl.*) phototelegraphy.

**'Bildung** *f* (*-/-en*) forming, formation (*both a. gr.: of plural, etc.*); constitution (*of committee, etc.*); education; culture; (good) breeding. [*sg.;* billiard-table.]

**Billard** ['biljart] *n* (*-s/-e*) billiards)

**billig** *adj.* ['biliç] just, equitable; fair; *price:* reasonable, moderate; *goods:* cheap, inexpensive; *recht und ~* right and proper; **~en** ['~gən] *v/t.* (*ge-, h*) approve of, *Am. a.* approbate; **2keit** *f* (*-/no pl.*) justness, equity; fairness; reasonableness, moderateness; **2ung** ['~guŋ] *f* (*-/~-en*) approval, sanction.

**Binde** ['bində] *f* (*-/-n*) band; tie; 🦺 bandage; (arm-)sling; *s. Damenbinde;* **~gewebe** *anat. n* connective tissue; **~glied** *n* connecting link; **~haut** *anat. f* conjunctiva; **~hautentzündung** 🦺 *f* conjunctivitis; **2n** (*irr., ge-, h*) **1.** *v/t.* bind, tie (*an acc.* to); hind (*book, etc.*); make (*broom, wreath, etc.*); knot (*tie*); *sich ~* bind *or* commit *or* engage o.s.; **2.** *v/i.* bind; unite; ⊕ *cement, etc.:* set, harden; **~strich** *m* hyphen; **~wort** *gr. n* (*-[e]s/~er*) conjunction.

**Bindfaden** ['bint-] *m* string; pack-thread.

**'Bindung** *f* (*-/-en*) binding (*a. of ski*); ♪ slur, tie, ligature; *fig.* commitment (*a. pol.*); engagement; **~en** *pl.* bonds *pl.*, ties *pl.*

**binnen** *prp.* (*dat., a. gen.*) ['binən] within; ~ *kurzem* before long.

**'Binnen|gewässer** *n* inland water; **~hafen** *m* close port; **~handel** *m* domestic *or* home trade, *Am.* domestic commerce; **~land** *n* inland, interior; **~verkehr** *m* inland traffic *or* transport.

**Binse** ♣ ['binzə] f (-/-n) rush; F: *in die ~n gehen* go to pot; '~**nwahrheit** f, '~**nweisheit** f truism.

**Biochemie** [bioçe'mi:] f (-/*no pl.*) biochemistry.

**Biograph|ie** [biogra'fi:] f (-/-n) biography; **2isch** *adj.* [~'gra:fiʃ] biographic(al).

**Biolog|ie** [biolo'gi:] f (-/*no pl.*) biology; **2isch** *adj.* [~'lo:giʃ] biological.

**Birke** ♣ ['birkə] f (-/-n) birch(-tree).

**Birne** ['birnə] f (-/-n) ♣ pear; ⚡ (electric) bulb; *fig. sl.* nob, *Am.* bean.

**bis** [bis] **1.** *prp.* (*acc.*) *space:* to, as far as; *time:* till, until, by; *zwei ~ drei* two or three, two to three; *~ auf weiteres* until further orders, for the meantime; *~ vier zählen* count up to four; *alle ~ auf drei* all but *or* except three; **2.** *cj.* till, until.

**Bisamratte** *zo.* ['bi:zam-] f muskrat.

**Bischof** ['biʃɔf] m (-s/⁼e) bishop.

**bischöflich** *adj.* ['biʃøfliç] episcopal.

**bisher** *adv.* [bis'he:r] hitherto, up to now, so far; ~**ig** *adj.* until now; hitherto existing; former.

**Biß** [bis] **1.** m (*Bisses/Bisse*) bite; **2.** 2 *pret.* of *beißen.*

**bißchen** ['bisçən] **1.** *adj.*: *ein ~* a little, a (little) bit of; **2.** *adv.*: *ein ~* a little (bit).

**Bissen** ['bisən] m (-s/-) mouthful; morsel; bite.

**bissig** *adj.* biting (*a. fig.*); *remark:* cutting; *Achtung, ~er Hund!* beware of the dog!

**Bistum** ['bistu:m] n (-s/⁼er) bishopric, diocese.

**bisweilen** *adv.* [bis'vailən] sometimes, at times, now and then.

**Bitte** ['bitə] f (-/-n) request (*um* for); entreaty; *auf j-s ~* (hin) at s.o.'s request.

**'bitten** (*irr.*, ge-, h) **1.** *v/t.*: *j-n um et. ~* ask *or* beg s.o. for s.th.; *j-n um Entschuldigung ~* beg s.o.'s pardon; *dürfte ich Sie um Feuer ~?* may I trouble you for a light?; *bitte* please; (wie) *bitte?* (I beg your) pardon?; *bitte! offering s.th.:* (please,) help yourself, (please,) do take some *or* one; *danke (schön)* — *bitte (sehr)!* thank you — not at all, you're welcome, don't mention it, F that's all right; **2.** *v/i.*: *um et. ~* ask *or* beg for s.th.

**bitter** *adj.* ['bitər] bitter (*a. fig.*); *frost:* sharp; '2**keit** f (-/-en) bitterness; *fig. a.* acrimony; '~**lich** *adv.* bitterly.

**'Bitt|gang** *eccl.* m procession; '~**schrift** f petition; '~**steller** m (-s/-) petitioner.

**bläh|en** ['blɛ:ən] (ge-, h) **1.** *v/t.* inflate, distend, swell out; belly (out),

swell out (*sails*); *sich ~ sails:* belly (out), swell out; *skirt:* balloon out; **2.** ⚕ *v/i.* cause flatulence; '~**end** ⚕ *adj.* flatulent; '2**ung** ⚕ f (-/-en) flatulence, F wind.

**Blam|age** [bla'ma:ʒə] f (-/-n) disgrace, shame; **2ieren** [~'mi:rən] *v/t.* (*no* -ge-, h) make a fool of s.o., disgrace; *sich ~* make a fool of o.s.

**blank** *adj.* [blaŋk] shining, shiny, bright; polished; F *fig.* broke.

**blanko** ⸸ ['blaŋko] **1.** *adj.* form, *etc.*: blank, not filled in; in blank; **2.** *adv.*: ~ *verkaufen stock exchange:* sell short; '2**scheck** m blank cheque, *Am.* blank check; '2**unterschrift** f blank signature; '2**vollmacht** f full power of attorney, carte blanche.

**Bläschen** ⚕ ['blɛ:sçən] n (-s/-) vesicle, small blister.

**Blase** ['bla:zə] f (-/-n) bubble; blister (*a.* ⚕); *anat.* bladder; bleb (*in glass*); ⊕ flaw; '~**balg** m (*ein a pair of*) bellows *pl.*; '2**n** (*irr.*, ge-, h) **1.** *v/t.* blow; blow, sound; play (*wind-instrument*); **2.** *v/i.* blow.

**Blas|instrument** ♪ ['bla:s-] n wind-instrument; '~**kapelle** f brass band.

**blaß** *adj.* [blas] pale (*vor dat.* with); ~ *werden* turn pale; *keine blasse Ahnung* not the faintest idea.

**Blässe** ['blɛsə] f (-/*no pl.*) paleness.

**Blatt** [blat] n (-[e]s/⁼er) leaf (*of book,* ♣); petal (*of flower*); leaf, sheet (*of paper*); ♪ sheet; blade (*of oar, saw, airscrew, etc.*); sheet (*of metal*); *cards:* hand; (news)paper.

**Blattern** ⚕ ['blatərn] *pl.* smallpox.

**blättern** ['blɛtərn] *v/i.* (ge-, h): *in e-m Buch ~* leaf through a book, thumb a book.

**'Blatternarb|e** f pock-mark; '2**ig** *adj.* pock-marked.

**'Blätterteig** m puff paste.

**'Blatt|gold** n gold-leaf, gold-foil; '~**laus** *zo.* f plant-louse; '~**pflanze** f foliage plant.

**blau** [blau] **1.** *adj.* blue; F *fig.* drunk, tight, boozy; ~**er Fleck** bruise; ~**es Auge** black eye; *mit e-m ~en Auge davonkommen* get off cheaply; **2.** 2 n (-s/*no pl.*) blue (colo[u]r); *Fahrt ins ~e* mystery tour. [blue.]

**bläuen** ['blɔyən] *v/t.* (ge-, h) (dye)

**'blau|grau** *adj.* bluish grey; '2**jacke** ♣ f bluejacket, sailor.

**'bläulich** *adj.* bluish.

**'Blausäure** ⚗ f (-/*no pl.*) hydrocyanic *or* prussic acid.

**Blech** [blɛç] n (-[e]s/-e) sheet metal; metal sheet, plate; F *fig.* balderdash, rubbish, *Am. sl. a.* baloney; '~**büchse** f tin, *Am.* can; '2**ern** *adj.* (of) tin; *sound:* brassy; *voice:* tinny; '~**musik** f brass-band music; '~**waren** f/pl. tinware.

**Blei** [blai] n (-[e]s/-e) **1.** n lead; **2.** F n, m (lead) pencil.

**bleiben** ['blaɪbən] v/i. (irr., ge-, sein) remain, stay; be left; ruhig ~ keep calm; ~ bei keep to s.th., stick to s.th.; bitte bleiben Sie am Apparat teleph. hold the line, please; '~d adj. lasting, permanent; '~lassen v/t. (irr. lassen, sep., no -ge-, h) leave s.th. alone; laß das bleiben! don't do it!; leave it alone!; stop that (noise, etc.)!

**bleich** adj. [blaɪç] pale (vor dat. with); '~en (ge-) 1. v/t. (h) make pale; bleach; blanch; 2. v/i. (irr., sein) bleach; lose colo(u)r, fade; '~süchtig ⚕ adj. chlorotic, greensick.

**'bleiern** adj. (of) lead, leaden (a. fig.).

**'Blei|rohr** n lead pipe; '~soldat m tin soldier; '~stift m (lcad) pencil; '~stifthülse f pencil cap; '~stiftspitzer m (-s/-) pencil-sharpener; '~vergiftung ⚕ f lead-poisoning.

**Blend|e** ['blɛndə] f (-/-n) phot. diaphragm, stop; ⚔ blind or sham window; '2en (ge-, h) 1. v/t. blind; dazzle (both a. fig.); 2. v/i. light: dazzle the eyes; ~laterne ['blɛnt-] f dark lantern.

**blich** [blɪç] pret. of bleichen 2.

**Blick** [blɪk] m (-[e]s/-e) glance, look; view (auf acc. of); auf den ersten ~ at first sight; ein böser ~ an evil or angry look; '2en v/i. (ge-, h) look, glance (auf acc., nach at); '~fang m eye-catcher.

**blieb** [bli:p] pret. of bleiben.

**blies** [bli:s] pret. of blasen.

**blind** adj. [blɪnt] blind (a. fig.: gegen, für to; vor dat. with); metal: dull, tarnished; window: opaque (with age, dirt); mirror: clouded, dull; cartridge: blank; ~er Alarm false alarm; ~er Passagier stowaway; auf e-m Auge ~ blind in one eye.

**'Blinddarm** anat. m blind gut; appendix; '~entzündung ⚕ f appendicitis.

**Blinde** ['blɪndə] (-n/-n) 1. m blind man; 2. f blind woman; ~nanstalt ['blɪndən?-] f institute for the blind; '~nheim n home for the blind; '~nhund m guide dog, Am. a. seeing-eye dog; '~nschrift f braille.

**'blind|fliegen** ✈ (irr. fliegen, sep., -ge-) v/t. (h) and v/i. (sein) fly blind or on instruments; '2flug ✈ m blind flying or flight; '2gänger m ✕ blind shell, dud; F fig. washout; '2heit f (-/no pl.) blindness; '~lings adv. ['~lɪŋs] blindly; at random; '2schleiche zo. f (-/-n) slow-worm, blind-worm; '~schreiben v/t. and v/i. (irr. schreiben, sep., -ge-, h) touch-type.

**blink|en** ['blɪŋkən] v/i. (ge-, h) star, light: twinkle; metal, leather, glass, etc.: shine; signal (with lamps),

flash; '2er mot. m (-s/-) flashing indicator; '2feuer n flashing light.

**blinzeln** ['blɪntsəln] v/i. (ge-, h) blink (at light, etc.); wink.

**Blitz** [blɪts] m (-es/-e) lightning; '~ableiter m (-s/-) lightning-conductor; '2en v/i. (ge-, h) flash; es blitzt it is lightening; '~gespräch teleph. n special priority call; '~licht phot. n flash-light; '2schnell adv. with lightning speed; '~strahl m flash of lightning.

**Block** [blɔk] m 1. (-[e]s/≈e) block; slab (of cooking chocolate); block, log (of wood); ingot (of metal); parl., pol., ♱ bloc; 2. (-[e]s/≈e, -s) block (of houses); pad, block (of paper); ~ade ✕, ♱ ['~'ka:də] f (-/-n) blockade; ~adebrecher m (-s/-) blockade-runner; '~haus n log cabin; 2ieren ['~ki:rən] (no -ge-, h) 1. v/t. block (up); lock (wheel); 2. v/i. brakes, etc.: jam.

**blöd** adj. [blø:t], ~e adj. ['~də] imbecile; stupid, dull; silly; '2heit f (-/-en) imbecility; stupidity, dullness; silliness; '2sinn m imbecility; rubbish, nonsense; '~sinnig adj. imbecile; idiotic, stupid, foolish.

**blöken** ['blø:kən] v/i. (ge-, h) sheep, calf: bleat.

**blond** adj. [blɔnt] blond, fair (-haired).

**bloß** [blo:s] 1. adj. bare, naked; mere; ~e Worte mere words; mit dem ~en Auge wahrnehmbar visible to the naked eye; 2. adv. only, merely, simply, just.

**Blöße** ['blø:sə] f (-/-n) bareness, nakedness; fig. weak point or spot; sich e-e ~ geben give o.s. away; lay o.s. open to attack; keine ~ bieten be invulnerable.

**'bloß|legen** v/t. (sep., -ge-, h) lay bare, expose; '~stellen v/t. (sep., -ge-, h) expose, compromise, unmask; sich ~ compromise o.s.

**blühen** ['bly:ən] v/i. (ge-, h) blossom, flower, bloom; fig. flourish, thrive, prosper; ♱ boom.

**Blume** ['blu:mə] f (-/-n) flower; wine: bouquet; beer: froth.

**'Blumen|beet** n flower-bed; '~blatt n petal; '~händler m florist; '~strauß m bouquet or bunch of flowers; '~topf m flowerpot; '~zucht f floriculture.

**Bluse** ['blu:zə] f (-/-n) blouse.

**Blut** [blu:t] n (-[e]s/no pl.) blood; ~ vergießen shed blood; böses ~ machen breed bad blood; '~andrang ⚕ m congestion; '2arm adj. bloodless; ⚕ an(a)emic; '~armut ⚕ f an(a)emic; '~bad n carnage, massacre; '~bank f blood bank; '~blase f blood blister; '~druck m blood pressure; '2dürstig adj. ['~dyrstiç] bloodthirsty.

**Blüte** ['bly:tə] f (-/-n) blossom,

5*

bloom, flower; *esp. fig.* flower; prime, heyday (*of life*).

**Blutegel** ['blu:t⁹e:gəl] *m* (-s/-) leech.

**'bluten** *v/i.* (ge-, *h*) bleed (*aus from*); *aus der Nase* ~ bleed at the nose.

**Bluterguß** ⚕ ['blu:t⁹-] *m* effusion of blood.

**'Blütezeit** *f* flowering period *or* time; *fig. a.* prime, heyday.

**'Blut|gefäß** *anat. n* blood-vessel; **~gerinnsel** ⚕ ['~gərinzəl] *n* (-s/-) clot of blood; **'~gruppe** *f* blood group; **'~hund** *zo. m* bloodhound.

**'blutig** *adj.* bloody, blood-stained; *es ist mein ~er Ernst* I am dead serious; *~er Anfänger* mere beginner, F greenhorn.

**Blut|körperchen** ['blu:tkœrpərçən] *n* (-s/-) blood corpuscle; **'~kreislauf** *m* (blood) circulation; **'~lache** *f* pool of blood; **'₂leer** *adj.*, **'₂los** *adj.* bloodless; **'~probe** *f* blood test; **'~rache** *f* blood feud *or* revenge *or* vengeance, vendetta; **'₂-'rot** *adj.* blood-red; crimson; **₂rünstig** *adj.* ['~rynstiç] bloodthirsty; bloody; **'~schande** *f* incest; **~spender** *m* blood-donor; **'₂stillend** *adj.* blood-sta(u)nching; **'~sturz** ⚕ *m* h(a)emorrhage; **'₂sverwandt** *adj.* related by blood (*mit* to); **'~sverwandtschaft** *f* blood-relationship, consanguinity; **'~übertragung** *f* blood-transfusion; **'~ung** *f* (-/-en) bleeding, h(a)emorrhage; **'₂unterlaufen** *adj.* eye: blood-shot; **'~vergießen** *n* bloodshed; **'~vergiftung** *f* blood-poisoning.

**Bö** [bø] *f* (-/-en) gust, squall.

**Bock** [bɔk] *m* (-[e]s/⁹e) *deer, hare, rabbit:* buck; he-goat, F billy-goat; *sheep:* ram; *gymnastics:* buck; *e-n* ~ *schießen* commit a blunder, *sl.* commit a bloomer; *den* ~ *zum Gärtner machen* set the fox to keep the geese; **'₂en** *v/i.* (ge-, *h*) *horse:* buck; *child:* sulk; *p.* be obstinate *or* refractory; *mot.* move jerkily, *Am.* F *a.* buck; **'₂ig** *adj.* stubborn, obstinate, pigheaded; **'~sprung** *m* leap-frog; *gymnastics:* vault over the buck; *Bocksprünge machen* caper, cut capers.

**Boden** ['bo:dən] *m* (-s/⁹) ground; ✿ soil; bottom; floor; loft; **'~kammer** *f* garret, attic; **'₂los** *adj.* bottomless; *fig.* enormous; unheard-of; **'~personal** ✈ *n* ground personnel *or* staff, *Am.* ground crew; **'~reform** *f* land reform; **'~satz** *m* grounds *pl.*, sediment; **~schätze** ['~ʃɛtsə] *m/pl.* mineral resources *pl.*; **'₂ständig** *adj.* native, indigenous.

**bog** [bo:k] *pret. of* biegen.

**Bogen** ['bo:gən] *m* (-s/-, ⁹) bow, bend, curve; Å arc; ⚒ arch; *skiing:* turn; *skating:* curve; sheet (*of*

---

*paper*); **'₂förmig** *adj.* arched; **'~gang** ⚒ *m* arcade; **'~lampe** ⚡ *f* arc-lamp; **'~schütze** *m* archer, bowman.

**Bohle** ['bo:lə] *f* (-/-n) thick plank, board.

**Bohne** ['bo:nə] *f* (-/-n) bean; *grüne* ~*n pl.* French beans *pl.*, *Am.* string beans *pl.*; *weiße* ~*n pl.* haricot beans *pl.*; F *blaue* ~*n pl.* bullets *pl.*; **'~nstange** *f* beanpole (*a.* F *fig.*).

**bohnern** ['bo:nərn] *v/t.* (ge-, *h*) polish (*floor, etc.*), (bees)wax (*floor*).

**bohr|en** ['bo:rən] (ge-, *h*) **1.** *v/t.* bore, drill (*hole*); sink, bore (*well, shaft*); bore, cut, drive (*tunnel, etc.*); **2.** *v/i.* drill (*a. dentistry*); bore; **'₂er** ⊕ *m* (-s/-) borer, drill.

**'böig** *adj.* squally, gusty; 🛩 bumpy.

**Boje** ['bo:jə] *f* (-/-n) buoy.

**Bollwerk** 🛡 ['bɔlvɛrk] *n* bastion, bulwark (*a. fig.*).

**Bolzen** ⊕ ['bɔltsən] *m* (-s/-) bolt.

**Bombard|ement** [bɔmbardə'mã:] *n* (-s/-s) bombardment; bombing; shelling; **₂ieren** ['di:rən] *v/t.* (no -ge-, *h*) bomb; shell; bombard (*a. fig.*).

**Bombe** ['bɔmbə] *f* (-/-n) bomb; *fig.* bomb-shell; **'₂nsicher** *adj.* bomb-proof; F *fig.* dead sure; **'~nschaden** *m* bomb damage; **'~r** 🛩 ➟ *m* (-s/-) bomber.

**Bon** ✝ [bõ:] *m* (-s/-s) coupon; voucher; credit note.

**Bonbon** [bõ'bõ:] *m*, *n* (-s/-s) sweet (-meat), bon-bon, F goody, *Am.* candy.

**Bonze** F ['bɔntsə] *m* (-n/-n) bigwig, *Am. a.* big shot.

**Boot** [bo:t] *n* (-[e]s/-e) boat; **'~shaus** *n* boat-house; **'~smann** *m* (-[e]s/ *Bootsleute*) boatswain.

**Bord** [bɔrt] (-[e]s/-e) **1.** *n* shelf; **2.** ⚓, ➟ *m:* *an* ~ on board, aboard (*ship, aircraft, etc.*); *über* ~ overboard; *von* ~ *gehen* go ashore; **'~funker** ⚓, ➟ *m* wireless *or* radio operator; **'~stein** *m* kerb, *Am.* curb.

**borgen** ['bɔrgən] *v/t.* (ge-, *h*) borrow (*von, bei from, of*); lend, *Am. a.* loan (*j-m et. s.th. to s.o.*).

**Borke** ['bɔrkə] *f* (-/-n) bark (*of tree*).

**borniert** *adj.* narrow-minded, of restricted intelligence.

**Borsalbe** ['bo:r-] *f* boracic ointment.

**Börse** ['bœrzə] *f* (-/-n) purse; ✝ stock exchange; stock-market; money-market; **'~nbericht** *m* market report; **'₂nfähig** *adj.* stock: negotiable on the stock exchange; **'~nkurs** *m* quotation; **'~nmakler** *m* stock-broker; **'~nnotierung** *f* (official, stock exchange) quotation; **'~npapiere** *n/pl.* listed securities *pl.*; **'~nspekulant** *m* stock-jobber; **'~nzeitung** *f* financial newspaper.

**Borst|e** ['bɔrstə] f (-/-n) bristle (*of hog or brush, etc.*); '**2ig** *adj.* bristly.

**Borte** ['bɔrtə] f (-/-n) border (*of carpet, etc.*); braid, lace.

'**bösartig** *adj.* malicious, vicious; ♂ malignant; '**2keit** f (-/-en) viciousness; ♂ malignity.

**Böschung** ['bœʃuŋ] f (-/-en) slope; embankment (*of railway*); bank (*of river*).

**böse** ['bøːzə] **1.** *adj.* bad, evil, wicked; malevolent, spiteful; angry (*über acc.* at, about; *auf j-n* with s.o.); *er meint es nicht* ~ he means no harm; **2.** ~ n (-n/no pl.) evil; **2wicht** ['~viçt] m (-[e]s/-er, -e) villain, rascal.

**bos|haft** *adj.* ['boːshaft] wicked; spiteful; malicious; '**2heit** f (-/-en) wickedness; malice; spite.

'**böswillig** *adj.* malevolent; ~e *Absicht* ⚖ malice prepense; ~es *Verlassen* ⚖ wilful desertion; '**2keit** f (-/-en) malevolence.

**bot** [boːt] *pret. of* bieten.

**Botan|ik** [boˈtɑːnik] f (-/no pl.) botany; **~iker** m (-s/-) botanist; **2isch** *adj.* botanical.

**Bote** ['boːtə] m (-n/-n) messenger; '**~ngang** m errand; *Botengänge machen* run errands.

'**Botschaft** f (-/-en) message; *pol.* embassy; '**~er** m (-s/-) ambassador; *in British Commonwealth countries:* High Commissioner.

**Bottich** ['bɔtiç] m (-[e]s/-e) tub; wash-tub; *brewing:* tun. vat.

**Bouillon** [buˈljõː] f (-/-s) beef tea.

**Bowle** ['boːlə] f (-/-n) vessel: bowl; *cold drink consisting of fruit, hock and champagne or soda-water: appr.* punch.

**box|en** ['bɔksən] **1.** *v/i.* (ge-, h) box; **2.** *v/t.* (ge-, h) punch *s.o.*; **2.** ~ n (-s/no pl.) boxing; pugilism; '**2er** m (-s/-) boxer; pugilist; '**2handschuh** m boxing-glove; '**2kampf** m boxing-match, bout, fight; '**2sport** m boxing.

**Boykott** [bɔyˈkɔt] (-[e]s/-e) boycott; **2ieren** [~ˈtiːrən] *v/t.* (no -ge-, h) boycott.

**brach** [brɑːx] **1.** *pret. of* brechen; **2.** ~ *adv.* fallow; uncultivated (*both a. fig.*).

**brachte** ['braxtə] *pret. of* bringen.

**Branche** ✝ ['brɑ̃ːʃə] f (-/-n) line (of business), trade; branch.

**Brand** [brant] m (-[e]s/=e) burning; fire, blaze; ♂ gangrene; ♫, ♪ blight, smut, mildew; ♪ blase f blister; '**~bombe** f incendiary bomb; **2en** ['~dən] *v/i.* (ge-, h) surge (*a. fig.*), break (*an acc.*, gegen against); '**~fleck** m burn; **2ig** *adj.* ['~diç] ♪, ♪ blighted, smutted; ♂ gangrenous; '**~mal** n brand; *fig.* stigma, blemish; '**2marken** *v/t.* (ge-, h) brand (*animal*); *fig.* brand

*or* stigmatize *s.o.*; '**~mauer** f fire(-proof) wall; '**~schaden** m damage caused by *or* loss suffered by fire; '**2schatzen** *v/t.* (ge-, h) lay (*town*) under contribution; sack, pillage; '**~stätte** f, '**~stelle** f scene of fire; '**~stifter** m incendiary, *Am.* F a. firebug; '**~stiftung** f arson; **~ung** ['~duŋ] f (-/-en) surf, surge, breakers *pl.*; '**~wache** f fire-watch; '**~wunde** f burn; scald; '**~zeichen** n brand.

**brannte** ['brantə] *pret. of* brennen.

**Branntwein** ['brantvaɪn] m brandy, spirits *pl.*; whisk(e)y; gin; '**~brennerei** f distillery.

**braten** ['brɑːtən] **1.** *v/t.* (*irr.*, ge-, h) *in oven:* roast; grill; *in frying-pan:* fry; bake (*apple*); *am Spieß* ~ roast on a spit, barbecue; **2.** *v/i.* (*irr.*, ge-, h) roast; grill; fry; *in der Sonne* ~ *p.* roast *or* grill in the sun; **3.** **2** m (-s/-) roast (meat); joint; '**2fett** n dripping; '**2soße** f gravy.

'**Brat|fisch** m fried fish; '**~hering** m grilled herring; '**~huhn** n roast chicken; '**~kartoffeln** *pl.* fried potatoes *pl.*; '**~ofen** m (kitchen) oven; '**~pfanne** f frying-pan; *Am. a.* skillet; '**~röhre** f *s.* Bratofen.

**Brauch** [braux] m (-[e]s/=e) custom, usage; use, habit; practice; '**2bar** *adj. p.*, *thing:* useful; *p.* capable, able; *thing:* serviceable; '**2en** (h) **1.** *v/t.* (ge-) need, want; require; take (*time*); use; **2.** *v/aux.* (no -ge-): *du brauchst es nur zu sagen* you only have to say so; *er hätte nicht zu kommen* ~ he need not have come; '**~tum** n (-[e]s/=er) custom; tradition; folklore.

**Braue** ['brauə] f (-/-n) eyebrow.

**brau|en** ['brauən] *v/t.* (ge-, h) brew; '**2er** m (-s/-) brewer; **2erei** [~ˈraɪ] f (-/-en) brewery; '**2haus** n brewery.

**braun** *adj.* [braun] brown; *horse:* bay; ~ *werden* get a tan (*on one's skin*).

**Bräune** ['brɔynə] f (-/no pl.) brown colo(u)r; (sun) tan; **2n** (ge-, h) **1.** *v/t.* make *or* dye brown; *sun:* tan; **2.** *v/i.* tan.

'**Braunkohle** f brown coal, lignite.

'**bräunlich** *adj.* brownish.

**Brause** ['brauzə] f (-/-n) rose, sprinkling-nozzle (*of watering can*); *s.* Brausebad; *s.* Brauselimonade; '**~bad** n shower(-bath); '**~limonade** f fizzy lemonade; '**2n** *v/i.* (ge-, h) *wind, water, etc.:* roar; rush; have a shower(-bath); '**~pulver** n effervescent powder.

**Braut** [braut] f (-/=e) fiancée; *on wedding-day:* bride; '**~führer** m best man.

**Bräutigam** ['brɔytigam] m (-s/-e) fiancé; *on wedding-day:* bridegroom, *Am. a.* groom.

'**Braut|jungfer** f bridesmaid; '**~**

**kleid** n wedding-dress; '**~kranz** m bridal wreath; '**~leute** pl., '**~paar** n engaged couple; on wedding-day: bride and bridegroom; '**~schleier** m bridal veil.

**brav** adj. [brɑːf] honest, upright; good, well-behaved; brave.

**bravo** int. ['brɑːvo] bravo!, well done!

**Bravour** [bra'vuːr] f (-/no pl.) bravery, courage; brilliance.

**Brecheisen** ['brɛç?-] n crowbar; (burglar's) jemmy, Am. a. jimmy. '**brechen** (irr., ge-) 1. v/t. (h) break; pluck (flower); refract (ray, etc.); fold (sheet of paper); quarry (stone); vomit; die Ehe ~ commit adultery; sich ~ break (one's leg, etc.); opt. be refracted; 2. v/i. (h) break; vomit; mit j-m ~ break with s.o.; 3. v/i. (sein) break, get broken; bones: break, fracture.

'**Brech|mittel** ⚕ n emetic; F fig. sickener; '**~reiz** m nausea; '**~stange** f crowbar, Am. a. pry; '**~ung** opt. f (-/-en) refraction.

**Brei** [braɪ] m (-[e]s/-e) paste; pulp; mash; pap (for babies); made of oatmeal: porridge; (rice, etc.) pudding; '**2ig** adj. pasty; pulpy; pappy.

**breit** adj. [braɪt] broad, wide; zehn Meter ~ ten metres wide; ~e Schichten der Bevölkerung large sections of or the bulk of the population; '**~beinig** 1. adj. with legs wide apart; 2. adv.: ~ gehen straddle. **Breite** ['braɪtə] f (-/-n) breadth, width; ast., geogr. latitude; '2n v/t. (ge-, h) spread; '**~ngrad** m degree of latitude; '**~nkreis** m parallel (of latitude).

'**breit|machen** v/refl. (sep., -ge-, h) spread o.s.; take up room; '**~schlagen** v/t. (irr. schlagen, sep., -ge-, h): F j-n ~ persuade s.o.; F j-n zu et. ~ talk s.o. into (doing) s.th.; '2seite ⚓ f broadside.

**briet** [briːt] pret. of braten.

**Bremse** ['brɛmzə] f (-/-n) zo. gad-fly; horse-fly; ⊕ brake; '2n (ge-, h) v/i. brake, put on the brakes; slow down; 2. v/t. brake, put on the brakes to; slow down; fig. curb.

'**Brems|klotz** m brake-block; ⚒ wheel chock; '**~pedal** n brake pedal; '**~vorrichtung** f brake-mechanism; '**~weg** m braking distance.

**brenn|bar** adj. ['brɛnbaːr] combustible, burnable; '2**dauer** f burning time; '**~en** (irr., ge-, h) 1. v/t. burn; distil(l) (brandy); roast (coffee); bake (brick, etc.); 2. v/i. burn; be ablaze, be on fire; wound, eye: smart, burn; nettle: sting; vor Ungeduld ~ burn with impatience; F darauf ~ zu inf. be burning to inf.; es brennt! fire!

'**Brenn|er** m (-s/-) p. distiller; fixture: burner; **~essel** ['brɛnnɛsəl] f

stinging nettle; '**~glas** n burning glass; '**~holz** n firewood; '**~material** n fuel; '**~öl** n lamp-oil; fuel-oil; '**~punkt** m focus, focal point; in den ~ rücken bring into focus (a. fig.); im ~ des Interesses stehen be the focus of interest; '**~schere** f curling-tongs pl.; '**~spiritus** m methylated spirit; '**~stoff** m combustible; mot. fuel.

**brenzlig** ['brɛntslɪç] 1. adj. burnt; matter: dangerous; situation: precarious; ~er Geruch burnt smell, smell of burning; 2. adv.: es riecht ~ it smells of burning.

**Bresche** ['brɛʃə] f (-/-n) breach (a. fig.), gap; in die ~ springen help s.o. out of a dilemma.

**Brett** [brɛt] n (-[e]s/-er) board; plank; shelf; spring-board; '**~spiel** n game played on a board.

**Brezel** ['breːtsəl] f (-/-n) pretzel.

**Brief** [briːf] m (-[e]s/-e) letter; '**~aufschrift** f address (on a letter); '**~beschwerer** m (-s/-) paperweight; '**~bogen** m sheet of notepaper; '**~geheimnis** n secrecy of correspondence; '**~karte** f correspondence card (with envelope); '**~kasten** m letter-box; pillar-box; Am. mailbox; '2lich adj. and adv. by letter, in writing; '**~marke** f (postage) stamp; '**~markensammlung** f stamp-collection; '**~öffner** m letter-opener; '**~ordner** m letter-file; '**~papier** n notepaper; '**~porto** n postage; '**~post** f mail, post; '**~tasche** f wallet, Am. a. billfold; '**~taube** f carrier pigeon, homing pigeon, homer; '**~träger** m postman, Am. mailman; '**~umschlag** m envelope; '**~waage** f letter-balance; '**~wechsel** m correspondence; '**~zensur** f postal censorship.

**Brikett** [bri'kɛt] n (-[e]s/-s) briquet (-te).

**Brillant** [bril'jant] 1. m (-en/-en) brilliant, cut diamond; 2. ♀ adj. brilliant; **~ring** m diamond ring.

**Brille** ['brilə] f (-/-n) (eine a pair of) glasses pl. or spectacles pl.; goggles pl.; lavatory seat; '**~nfutteral** n spectacle-case; '**~nträger** m person who wears glasses.

**bringen** ['brɪŋən] v/t. (irr., ge-, h) bring; take; see (s.o. home, etc.); put (in order); make (sacrifice); yield (interest); an den Mann ~ dispose of, get rid of; j-n dazu ~, et. zu tun make or get s.o. to do s.th.; et. mit sich ~ involve s.th., j-n um et. ~ deprive s.o. of s.th.; j-n zum Lachen ~ make s.o. laugh.

**Brise** ['briːzə] f (-/-n) breeze.

**Brit|e** ['briːtə] m (-n/-n) Briton, Am. a. Britisher; die **~n** pl. the British pl.; '2**isch** adj. British.

**bröckeln** ['brœkəln] v/i. (ge-, h) crumble; become brittle.

**Brocken** ['brɔkən] 1. m (-s/-) piece; lump (of earth or stone, etc.); morsel (of food); F ein harter ~ a hard nut; 2. ♀ v/t. (ge-, h): Brot in die Suppe ~ break bread into soup.

**brodeln** ['bro:dəln] v/i. (ge-, h) bubble, simmer.

**Brombeer|e** ['brɔm-] f blackberry; **~strauch** m blackberry bush.

**Bronch|ialkatarrh** ♂ [brɔnçi'a:l-katar] m bronchial catarrh; **~ien** anat. f/pl. bronchi(a) pl.; **~itis** ♂ [~çi:tis] f (-/Bronchitiden) bronchitis.

**Bronze** ['brõ:sə] f (-/-n) bronze; **~medaille** f bronze medal.

**Brosche** ['brɔʃə] f (-/-n) brooch.

**broschier|en** [brɔ'ʃi:rən] v/t. (no -ge-, h) sew, stitch (book); **~t** adj. book: paper-backed, paper-bound; fabric: figured.

**Broschüre** [brɔ'ʃy:rə] f (-/-n) booklet; brochure; pamphlet.

**Brot** [bro:t] n (-[e]s/-e) bread; loaf; sein ~ verdienen earn one's living; **~aufstrich** m spread.

**Brötchen** ['brø:tçən] n (-s/-) roll.

**'Brot|korb** m: j-m den ~ höher hängen put s.o. on short allowance; **'2los** fig. adj. unemployed; unprofitable; **~rinde** f crust; **~schneidemaschine** f bread-cutter; **~schnitte** f slice of bread; **~studium** n utilitarian study; **~teig** m bread dough.

**Bruch** [brux] (-[e]s/⸚e) break(ing); breach; ♂ fracture (of bones); ♂ hernia; crack; fold (in paper); crease (in cloth); split (in silk); Ⱥ fraction; breach (of promise); violation (of oath, etc.); violation, infringement (of law, etc.); **~band** n truss.

**brüchig** adj. ['bryçiç] fragile; brittle, voice: cracked.

**'Bruch|landung** ⚡ f crash-landing; **~rechnung** f fractional arithmetic, F fractions pl.; **~strich** Ⱥ m fraction bar; **~stück** n fragment (a. fig.); **~teil** m fraction; im ~ e-r Sekunde in a split second; **~zahl** f fraction(al) number.

**Brücke** ['brykə] f (-/-n) bridge; carpet: rug; sports: bridge; e-e ~ schlagen über (acc.) build or throw a bridge across, bridge (river); **~n-kopf** ✕ m bridge-head; **~npfeiler** m pier (of bridge).

**Bruder** ['bru:dər] m (-s/⸚) brother; eccl. (lay) brother, friar; **~krieg** m fratricidal or civil war; **~kuß** m fraternal kiss.

**brüderlich** ['bry:dərliç] 1. adj. brotherly, fraternal; 2. adv.: ~ teilen share and share alike; **2keit** f (-/no pl.) brotherliness, fraternity.

**Brühe** ['bry:ə] f (-/-n) broth; stock;

beef tea; F dirty water; drink: F dishwater; **'2heiß** adj. scalding hot; **~würfel** m beef cube.

**brüllen** ['brylən] v/i. (ge-, h) roar; bellow; cattle: low; bull: bellow; vor Lachen ~ roar with laughter; ~des Gelächter roar of laughter.

**brumm|en** ['brumən] v/i. (ge-, h) p. speak in a deep voice, mumble; growl (a. fig.); insect: buzz; engine: buzz, boom; fig. grumble, Am. F grouch; mir brummt der Schädel my head is buzzing; **'2bär** fig. m grumbler, growler, Am. F grouch; **2er** m (-s/-) bluebottle; dung-beetle; **~ig** adj. grumbling. Am. F grouchy.

**brünett** adj. [bry'nɛt] woman: brunette.

**Brunft** hunt. [brunft] f (-/⸚e) rut; **~zeit** f rutting season.

**Brunnen** ['brunən] m (-s/-) well; spring; fountain (a. fig.); e-n ~ graben sink a well; **~wasser** n pump-water, well-water.

**Brunst** [brunst] f (-/⸚e) rut (of male animal), heat (of female animal); lust, sexual desire.

**brünstig** adj. ['brynstiç] zo. rutting, in heat; lustful.

**Brust** [brust] f (-/⸚e) chest, anat. thorax; breast; (woman's) breast(s pl.), bosom; aus voller ~ at the top of one's voice, lustily; **~bild** n half-length portrait.

**brüsten** ['brystən] v/refl. (ge-, h) boast, brag.

**'Brust|fell** anat. n pleura; **~fell-entzündung** ♂ f pleurisy; **~ka-sten** m, **~korb** m chest, anat. thorax; **~schwimmen** n (-s/no pl.) breast-stroke.

**Brüstung** ['brystuŋ] f (-/-en) balustrade, parapet.

**'Brustwarze** anat. f nipple.

**Brut** [bru:t] f (-/-en) brooding, sitting; brood; hatch; fry, spawn (of fish); fig. F brood, (bad) lot.

**brutal** adj. [bru'ta:l] brutal; **2ität** [~ali'tɛ:t] f (-/-en) brutality.

**Brutapparat** zo. f ['bru:t?-] m incubator.

**brüten** ['bry:tən] v/i. (ge-, h) brood, sit (on egg); incubate; ~ über (dat.) brood over.

**'Brutkasten** ♂ m incubator.

**brutto** ✝ adv. ['bruto] gross; **'2ge-wicht** n gross weight; **'2register-tonne** f gross register ton; **'2ver-dienst** m gross earnings pl.

**Bube** ['bu:bə] m (-n/-n) boy, lad; knave, rogue; cards: knave, jack; **~nstreich** m, **~nstück** n boyish prank; knavish trick.

**Buch** [bu:x] n (-[e]s/⸚er) book; volume; **~binder** m (book-)binder; **~drucker** m printer; **~druckerei** [~'raɪ] f printing; printing-office, Am. print shop.

**Buche** ♀ ['buːxə] *f* (-/-n) beech.
**buchen** ['buːxən] *v/t.* (ge-, h) book, reserve (*passage, flight, etc.*); *bookkeeping*: book (*item, sum*), enter (*transaction*) in the books; et. als Erfolg ~ count s.th. as a success.
**Bücher|abschluß** ✝ ['byːçər-] *m* closing of *or* balancing of books; '~brett *n* bookshelf; ~ei [~'raɪ] *f* (-/-en) library; '~freund *m* booklover, bibliophil(e); '~revisor ✝ *m* (-s/-en) auditor; accountant; '~schrank *m* bookcase; '~wurm *m* bookworm.
'**Buch|fink** *orn. m* chaffinch; '~halter *m* (-s/-) book-keeper; '~haltung *f* book-keeping; '~handel *m* book-trade; '~händler *m* bookseller; '~handlung *f* bookshop, *Am.* bookstore.
**Büchse** ['byksə] *f* (-/-n) box, case; tin, *Am.* can; rifle; '~nfleisch *n* tinned meat, *Am.* canned meat; '~nöffner ['byksən?-] *m* tin-opener, *Am.* can opener.
**Buchstab|e** ['buːxʃtaːbə] *m* (-n/-n) letter, character; *typ.* type; 2ieren [~ə'biːrən] *v/t.* (no -ge-, h) spell.
**buchstäblich** ['buːxʃtɛːpliç] 1. *adj.* literal; 2. *adv.* literally; word for word.
**Bucht** [buxt] *f* (-/-en) bay; bight; creek, inlet.
'**Buchung** *f* (-/-en) booking, reservation; *book-keeping*: entry.
**Buckel** ['bukəl] 1. *m* (-s/-) hump, hunch; humpback, hunchback; boss, stud, knob; 2. *f* (-/-n) boss, stud, knob.
'**buckelig** *adj. s.* bucklig.
**bücken** ['bykən] *v/refl.* (ge-, h) bend (down), stoop.
**bucklig** *adj.* ['bukliç] humpbacked, hunchbacked.
**Bückling** ['byklɪŋ] *m* (-s/-e) bloater, red herring; *fig.* bow.
**Bude** ['buːdə] *f* (-/-n) stall, booth; hut, cabin, *Am.* shack; F: place; den; (*student's, etc.*) digs *pl.*
**Budget** [by'dʒeː] *n* (-s/-s) budget.
**Büfett** [by'feː; by'fɛt] *n* (-[e]s/-s; -[e]s/-e) sideboard, buffet; buffet, bar, *Am. a.* counter; kaltes ~ buffet supper *or* lunch.
**Büffel** ['byfəl] *m* (-s/-) *zo.* buffalo; F *fig.* lout, blockhead.
**Bug** [buːk] *m* (-[e]s/-e) ✈ bow; 🔫 nose; fold; (sharp) crease.
**Bügel** ['byːɡəl] *m* (-s/-) bow (*of spectacles, etc.*); handle (*of handbag, etc.*); coat-hanger; stirrup; '~brett *n* ironing-board; '~eisen *n* (flat-) iron; '~falte *f* crease; 2n *v/t.* (ge-, h) iron (*shirt, etc.*), press (*suit, skirt, etc.*).
**Bühne** ['byːnə] *f* (-/-n) platform (*a.* ⊕); scaffold; *thea.* stage; *fig.*: die ~ the stage; die politische ~ the political scene; ~nanweisungen ['byː-

nən?-] *f/pl.* stage directions *pl.*; '~nbild *n* scene(ry); décor; stage design; '~ndichter *m* playwright, dramatist; '~nlaufbahn *f* stage career; '~nstück *n* stage play.
**buk** [buːk] *pret. of* backen.
**Bull|auge** ⚓ ['bul-] *n* porthole, bull's eye; '~dogge *zo. f* bulldog.
**Bulle** ['bulə] 1. *zo. m* (-n/-n) bull; 2. *eccl. f* (-/-n) bull.
**Bummel** F ['buməl] *m* (-s/-) stroll; spree, pub-crawl, *sl.* binge; ~ei [~'laɪ] *f* (-/-en) dawdling; negligence; 2n *v/i.* (ge-) 1. (sein) stroll, saunter; pub-crawl; 2. (h) dawdle (*on way, at work*), waste time; '~streik *m* go-slow (strike), *Am.* slowdown; '~zug *m* slow train, *Am.* way train.
**Bummler** ['bumlər] *m* (-s/-) saunterer, stroller; loafer, *Am.* F *a.* bum; dawdler.
**Bund** [bunt] 1. *m* (-[e]s/-e) *pol.* union, federation, confederacy; (waist-, neck-, wrist)band; 2. *n* (-[e]s/-e) bundle (*of faggots*); bundle, truss (*of hay or straw*); bunch (*of radishes, etc.*).
**Bündel** ['byndəl] *n* (-s/-) bundle, bunch; 2n *v/t.* (ge-, h) make into a bundle, bundle up.
**Bundes|bahn** ['bundəs-] *f* Federal Railway(s *pl.*); '~bank *f* Federal Bank; '~genosse *m* ally; '~gerichtshof *m* Federal Supreme Court; '~kanzler *m* Federal Chancellor; '~ministerium *n* Federal Ministry; '~post *f* Federal Postal Administration; '~präsident *m* President of the Federal Republic; '~rat *m* Bundesrat, Upper House of German Parliament; '~republik *f* Federal Republic; '~staat *m* federal state; confederation; '~tag *m* Bundestag, Lower House of German Parliament.
**bündig** *adj.* ['byndiç] *style, speech*: concise, to the point, terse.
**Bündnis** ['byntnis] *n* (-ses/-se) alliance; agreement.
**Bunker** ['bunkər] *m* (-s/-) ⚒, coal, fuel, etc.: bunker; bin; air-raid shelter; ⚒ bunker, pill-box; ⚓ (submarine) pen.
**bunt** *adj.* [bunt] (multi-)colo(u)red, colo(u)rful; motley; *bird, flower, etc.*: variegated; bright, gay; *fig.* mixed, motley; full of variety; '2druck *m* colo(u)r-print(ing); '2stift *m* colo(u)red pencil, crayon.
**Bürde** ['byrdə] *f* (-/-n) burden (*a. fig.*: für j-n to s.o.), load.
**Burg** [burk] *f* (-/-en) castle; fortress; citadel (*a. fig.*).
**Bürge** ⚖ ['byrɡə] *m* (-n/-n) guarantor, security, surety, bailsman; sponsor; '2n *v/i.* (ge-, h): für j-n ~ stand guarantee *or* surety *or* security for s.o., *Am. a.* bond s.o.; stand

bail for s.o.; vouch or answer for s.o.; sponsor s.o.; für et. ~ stand security for s.th. guarantee s.th.; vouch or answer for s.th.

**Bürger** ['byrgər] m (-s/-) citizen; townsman; '~krieg m civil war.

**'bürgerlich** adj. civic, civil; ~e Küche plain cooking; Verlust der ~en Ehrenrechte loss of civil rights; Bürgerliches Gesetzbuch German Civil Code; '2e m (-n/-n) commoner.

**'Bürger|meister** m mayor; in Germany: a. burgomaster; in Scotland: provost; '~recht n civic rights pl.; citizenship; '~schaft f (-/-en) citizens pl.; '~steig m pavement, Am. sidewalk; '~wehr f militia.

**Bürgschaft** ['byrkʃaft] f (-/-en) security; bail; guarantee.

**Büro** [by'ro:] n (-s/-s) office; ~angestellte m, f (-n/-n) clerk; ~arbeit f office-work; ~klammer f paper-clip; ~krat [~o'kra:t] m (-en/-en) bureaucrat; ~kratie [~okra'ti:] f (-/-n) bureaucracy; red tape; 2kratisch adj. [~o'kra:tiʃ] bureaucratic; ~stunden f/pl. office hours pl.; ~vorsteher m head or senior clerk.

**Bursch** [burʃ] m (-en/-en), ~e ['~ə] m (-n/-en) boy, lad, youth; F chap, Am. a. guy; ein übler ~ a bad lot, F a bad egg.

**burschikos** adj. [burʃi'ko:s] free and easy; esp. girl: boyish, unaffected, hearty.

**Bürste** ['byrstə] f (-/-n) brush; '2n v/t. (ge-, h) brush.

**Busch** [buʃ] m (-es/=e) bush, shrub.

**Büschel** ['byʃəl] n (-s/-) bunch,

tuft, handful (of hair); wisp (of straw or hair).

**'Busch|holz** n brushwood, underwood; '2ig adj. hair, eyebrows, etc.: bushy, shaggy; covered with bushes or scrub, bushy; '~messer n bushknife; machete; '~neger m maroon; '~werk n bushes pl., shrubbery, Am. a. brush.

**Busen** ['bu:zən] m (-s/-) bosom, breast (esp. of woman); fig. bosom, heart; geog. bay, gulf; '~freund m bosom friend.

**Bussard** orn. ['busart] m (-[e]s/-e) buzzard.

**Buße** ['bu:sə] f (-/-n) atonement (for sins), penance; repentance; satisfaction; fine; ~ tun do penance.

**büßen** ['by:sən] (ge-, h) 1. v/t. expiate, atone for (sin, crime); er mußte es mit s-m Leben ~ he paid for it with his life; das sollst du mir ~! you'll pay for that!; 2. v/i. atone, pay (für for).

**'Büßer** m (-s/-) penitent.

**'buß|fertig** adj. penitent, repentant, contrite; '2fertigkeit f (-/no pl.) repentance, contrition; '2tag m day of repentance; Buß- und Bettag day of prayer and repentance.

**Büste** ['bystə] f (-/-n) bust; '~nhalter m (-s/-) brassière, F bra.

**Büttenpapier** ['bytən-] n handmade paper.

**Butter** ['butər] f (-/no pl.) butter; '~blume ♀ f buttercup; '~brot n (slice or piece of) bread and butter; F: für ein ~ for a song; '~brotpapier n greaseproof paper; '~dose f butter-dish; '~faß n butter-churn; '~milch f buttermilk; '2n v/i. (ge-, h) churn.

# C

**Café** [ka'fe:] n (-s/-s) café, coffeehouse.

**Cape** [ke:p] n (-s/-s) cape.

**Cell|ist** ♪ [tʃe'list] m (-en/-en) violoncellist, (')cellist; ~o ♪ ['~o] n (-s/-s, Celli) violoncello, (')cello.

**Celsius** ['tselzius]: 5 Grad ~ (abbr. 5° C) five degrees centigrade.

**Chaiselongue** [ʃɛz(ə)'lõ:] f (-/-n, -s) chaise longue, lounge, couch.

**Champagner** [ʃam'panjər] m (-s/-) champagne.

**Champignon** ♀ ['ʃampinjõ] m (-s/-s) champignon, (common) mushroom.

**Chance** ['ʃã:s(ə)] f (-/-n) chance; keine ~ haben not to stand a chance; sich eine ~ entgehen lassen miss a chance or an opportunity; die ~n sind gleich the chances or odds are even.

**Chaos** ['ka:os] n (-/no pl.) chaos.

**Charakter** [ka'raktər] m (-s/-e) character; nature; ~bild n character (sketch); ~darsteller thea. m character actor; ~fehler m fault in s.o.'s character; 2fest adj. of firm or strong character; 2i'sieren v/t. (no -ge-, h) characterize, describe (als acc. as); ~i'sierung f (-/-en), ~istik [~'ristik] f (-/-en) characterization; 2istisch adj. [~'ristiʃ] characteristic or typical (für of); 2lich adj. of or concerning (the) character; 2los adj. characterless, without (strength of) character, spineless; ~rolle thea. f character role; ~zug m characteristic, feature, trait.

**charm|ant** adj. [ʃar'mant] charming, winning; 2e [ʃarm] m (-s/no pl.) charm, grace.

**Chassis** [ʃaˈsiː] *n* (-/-) *mot.*, *radio*: frame, chassis.

**Chauffeur** [ʃɔˈføːr] *m* (-s/-e) chauffeur, driver.

**Chaussee** [ʃoˈseː] *f* (-/-n) highway, (high) road.

**Chauvinismus** [ʃoviˈnismus] *m* (-/ no pl.) jingoism; chauvinism.

**Chef** [ʃɛf] *m* (-s/-s) head, chief; ✝ principal, F boss; senior partner.

**Chem|ie** [çeˈmiː] *f* (-/no pl.) chemistry; **~iefaser** *f* chemical fib|re, *Am.* -er; **~ikalien** [~iˈkaːljən] *f/pl.* chemicals *pl.*; **~iker** [ˈçeːmikər] *m* (-s/-) (analytical) chemist; **2isch** *adj.* [ˈçeːmiʃ] chemical.

**Chiffr|e** [ˈʃifər] *f* (-/-n) number; cipher; *in advertisement*: box number; **2ieren** [ʃiˈfriːrən] *v/t.* (no -ge-, h) cipher, code (*message, etc.*); write in code *or* cipher.

**Chines|e** [çiˈneːzə] *m* (-n/-n) Chinese, *contp.* Chinaman; **2isch** *adj.* Chinese.

**Chinin** ⚗ [çiˈniːn] *n* (-s/no pl.) quinine.

**Chirurg** [çiˈrurk] *m* (-en/-en) surgeon; **~ie** [~ˈgiː] *f* (-/-n) surgery; **2isch** *adj.* [~ˈgiʃ] surgical.

**Chlor** ⚗ [kloːr] *n* (-s/no pl.) chlorine; **2en** *v/t.* (ge-, h) chlorinate (*water*); **~kalk** ⚗ *m* chloride of lime.

**Chloroform** ⚗ [kloroˈfɔrm] *n* (-/no pl.) chloroform; **2ieren** 🗲 [~ˈmiː-rən] *v/t.* (no -ge-, h) chloroform.

**Cholera** ⚕ [ˈkoːlərə] *f* (-/no pl.) cholera.

**cholerisch** *adj.* [koˈleːriʃ] choleric, irascible.

**Chor** [koːr] *m* **1.** ⚖ *a. n* (-[e]s/-e, ¨e) chancel, choir; (organ-)loft; **2.** (-[e]s/¨e) *in drama*: chorus; singers: choir, chorus; *piece of music*: chorus; **~al** [koˈraːl] *m* (-s/¨e) cho-

ral(e); hymn; **~gesang** *m* choral singing, chorus; **~sänger** *m* member of a choir; chorister.

**Christ** [krist] *m* (-en/-en) Christian; **~baum** *m* Christmas-tree; **~enheit** *f* (-/no pl.): die ~ Christendom; **~entum** *n* (-s/no pl.) Christianity; **~kind** *n* (-[e]s/no pl.) Christ-child, Infant Jesus; **2lich** *adj.* Christian.

**Chrom** [kroːm] *n* (-s/no pl.) *metal*: chromium; *pigment*: chrome.

**chromatisch** 🎵, *opt. adj.* [kroˈmaː-tiʃ] chromatic.

**Chronik** [ˈkroːnik] *f* (-/-en) chronicle.

**chronisch** *adj.* [ˈkroːniʃ] *disease*: chronic (*a. fig.*).

**Chronist** [kroˈnist] *m* (-en/-en) chronicler.

**chronologisch** *adj.* [kronoˈloːgiʃ] chronological.

**circa** *adv.* [ˈtsirka] about, approximately.

**Clique** [ˈkliːkə] *f* (-/-n) clique, set, group, coterie; **~nwirtschaft** *f* (-/no pl.) cliquism.

**Conférencier** [kõferãˈsjeː] *m* (-s/-s) compère, *Am.* master of ceremonies.

**Couch** [kautʃ] *f* (-/-es) couch.

**Coupé** [kuˈpeː] *n* (-s/-s) *mot.* coupé; 🔧 🚃 compartment.

**Couplet** [kuˈpleː] *n* (-s/-s) comic *or* music-hall song.

**Coupon** [kuˈpõː] *m* (-s/-s) coupon; dividend-warrant; counterfoil.

**Courtage** ✝ [kurˈtaːʒə] *f* (-/-n) brokerage.

**Cousin** [kuˈzɛ̃] *m* (-s/-s), **~e** [~iˈnə] *f* (-/-n) cousin.

**Creme** [krɛːm, kreːm] *f* (-/-s) cream (*a. fig.*: only sg.).

**Cut** [kœt, kat] *m* (-s/-s), **~away** [ˈkœtəveː, ˈkatəveː] *m* (-s/-s) cutaway (coat), morning coat.


# D

**da** [daː] **1.** *adv. space*: there; ~ wo where; hier und ~ here and there; ~ bin ich here I am; ~ haben wir's! there we are!; von ~ an from there; *time*: ~ erst only then, not till then; von ~ an from that time (on), since then; hier und ~ now and then *or* again; **2.** *cj. time*: as, when, while; nun, ~ du es einmal gesagt hast now (that) you have mentioned it; *causal*: as, since, because; ~ ich krank war, konnte ich nicht kommen as *or* since I was ill I couldn't come.

**dabei** *adv.* [daˈbaɪ, *when emphatic*: ˈdaːbaɪ] near (at hand), by; about, going (zu *inf.* to *inf.*), on the point

(of *ger.*); besides; nevertheless, yet, for all that; was ist schon ~? what does it matter?; lassen wir es ~ let's leave it at that; ~ bleiben stick to one's point, persist in it.

**da'bei|bleiben** *v/i.* (*irr. bleiben, sep.*, -ge-, sein) stay with it *or* them; **~sein** *v/i.* (*irr. sein, sep.*, -ge-, sein) be present *or* there; **~stehen** *v/i.* (*irr. stehen, sep.*, -ge-, h) stand by *or* near.

**'dableiben** *v/i.* (*irr. bleiben, sep.*, -ge-, sein) stay, remain.

**da capo** *adv.* [daˈkaːpo] at opera, *etc.*: encore.

**Dach** [dax] *n* (-[e]s/¨er) roof; *fig.* shelter; **~antenne** *f* roof aerial;

'**⁓decker** m (-s/-) roofer; tiler; slater; '**⁓fenster** n skylight; dormer window; '**⁓garten** m roof-garden; '**⁓gesellschaft † ƒ** holding company; '**⁓kammer** ƒ attic, garret; '**⁓pappe** ƒ roofing felt; '**⁓rinne** ƒ gutter, eaves pl.

**dachte** ['daxtə] pret. of denken.

**Dachs** zo. [daks] m (-es/-e) badger; '**⁓bau** m (-[e]s/-e) badger's earth.

'**Dach|sparren** m rafter; '**⁓stube** ƒ attic, garret; '**⁓stuhl** m roof frame-work; '**⁓ziegel** m (roofing) tile.

**dadurch** [da'durç, when emphatic: 'da:durç] 1. adv. for this reason, in this manner or way, thus; by it or that; 2. cj.: ⁓, daß owing to (the fact that), because; by ger.

**dafür** adv. [da'fy:r, when emphatic: 'da:fy:r] for it or that; instead (of it); in return (for it), in exchange; ⁓ sein to be in favo(u)r of it; ⁓ sein zu inf. be for ger., to be in favo(u)r of ger.; er kann nichts ⁓ it is not his fault; ⁓ sorgen, daß see to it that.

**Da'fürhalten** n (-s/no pl.): nach meinem ⁓ in my opinion.

**dagegen** [da'ge:gən, when emphatic: 'da:ge:gən] 1. adv. against it or that; in comparison with it, compared to it; ⁓ sein be against it, be opposed to it; ich habe nichts ⁓ I have no objection (to it); 2. cj. on the other hand, however.

**daheim** adv. [da'haɪm] at home.

**daher** [da'he:r, when emphatic: 'da:he:r] 1. adv. from there; prefixed to verbs of motion: along; fig. from this, hence; ⁓ kam es, daß thus it happened that; 2. cj. therefore; that is (the reason) why.

**dahin** adv. [da'hin, when emphatic: 'da:hin] there, to that place; gone, past; prefixed to verbs of motion: along; j-n ⁓ bringen, daß induce s.o. to inf.; m-e Meinung geht ⁓, daß my opinion is that.

**da'hingestellt** adj.: es ⁓ sein lassen (,ob) leave it undecided (whether).

**dahinter** adv. [da'hintər, when emphatic: 'da:hintər] behind it or that, at the back of it; es steckt nichts ⁓ there is nothing in it.

**da'hinterkommen** v/i. (irr kommen, sep., -ge-, sein) find out about it.

**damal|ig** adj. ['da:ma:liç] then, of that time; der ⁓e Besitzer the then owner; '**⁓s** adv. then, at that time.

**Damast** [da'mast] m (-es/-e) damask.

**Dame** ['da:mə] ƒ (-/-n) lady; dancing, etc.: partner; cards, chess: queen; s. Damespiel; '**⁓brett** n draught-board, Am. checkerboard.

'**Damen|binde** ƒ (woman's) sanitary towel, Am. sanitary napkin; '**⁓doppel** n tennis: women's doubles pl.; '**⁓einzel** n tennis: women's

singles pl.; '**⁓haft** adj. ladylike; '**⁓konfektion** ƒ ladies' ready-made clothes pl.; '**⁓mannschaft** ƒ sports: women's team; '**⁓schneider** m ladies' tailor, dressmaker.

'**Damespiel** n (game of) draughts pl., Am. (game of) checkers pl.

**damit** 1. adv. [da'mit, when emphatic: 'da:mit] with it or that, therewith, herewith; by it or that; was will er ⁓ sagen? what does he mean by it?; wie steht es ⁓? how about it?; ⁓ einverstanden sein agree to it; 2. cj. (in order) that, in order to inf.; so (that); ⁓ nicht lest, (so as) to avoid that; for fear that (all with subjunctive).

**dämlich** F adj. ['dɛ:mliç] silly, asinine.

**Damm** [dam] m (-[e]s/⁓e) dam; dike, dyke; ⚕ embankment; embankment, Am. levee (of river); roadway; fig. barrier; '**⁓bruch** m bursting of a dam or dike.

**dämmer|ig** adj. ['dɛməriç] dusky; '**⁓licht** n twilight; '**⁓n** v/i. (ge-, h) dawn (a. fig.: F j-m on s.o.); grow dark or dusky; '**⁓ung** ƒ (-/-en) twilight, dusk; in the morning: dawn.

**Dämon** ['dɛ:mɔn] m (-s/-en) demon; **⁓isch** adj. [dɛ'mo:nɪʃ] demoniac(al).

**Dampf** [dampf] m (-[e]s/⁓e) steam; vapo(u)r; '**⁓bad** n vapo(u)r-bath; '**⁓boot** n steamboat; '**⁓en** v/i. (ge-, h) steam.

**dämpfen** ['dɛmpfən] v/t. (ge-, h) deaden (pain, noise, force of blow); muffle (bell, drum, oar); damp (sound, oscillation, fig. enthusiasm); ƒ mute (stringed instrument); soften (colour, light); attenuate (wave); steam (cloth, food); stew (meat, fruit); fig. suppress, curb (emotion).

'**Dampfer** m (-s/-) steamer, steam-ship.

'**Dämpfer** m (-s/-) damper (a. ƒ of piano); ƒ mute (for violin, etc.).

'**Dampf|heizung** ƒ steam-heating; '**⁓kessel** m (steam-)boiler; '**⁓maschine** ƒ steam-engine; '**⁓schiff** n steamer, steamship; '**⁓walze** ƒ steam-roller.

**danach** adv. [da'na:x, when emphatic: 'da:na:x] after it or that; afterwards; subsequently; accordingly; ich fragte ihn ⁓ I asked him about it; iro. er sieht ganz ⁓ aus he looks very much like it.

**Däne** ['dɛ:nə] m (-n/-n) Dane.

**daneben** adv. [da'ne:bən, when emphatic: 'da:ne:bən] next to it or that, beside it or that; besides, moreover; beside the mark.

**da'nebengehen** F v/i. (irr. gehen, sep., -ge-n, sein) bullet, etc.: miss the target or mark; remark, etc.: miss one's effect, F misfire.

**daniederliegen** [da'ni:dər-] v/i.

*(irr. liegen, sep., -ge-* h) be laid up *(an dat.* with); *trade:* be depressed.

**dänisch** *adj.* ['dɛːniʃ] Danish.

**Dank** [daŋk] **1.** *m* (-[e]s/*no pl.*) thanks *pl.*, gratitude; reward; *j-m* ~ *sagen* thank s.o.; *Gott sei* ~*!* thank God!; **2.** ⌀ *prp.* (*dat.*) owing *or* thanks to; **'⌀bar** *adj.* thankful, grateful (*j-m* to s.o.; *für* for); profitable; **'~barkeit** *f* (-/*no pl.*) gratitude; **'⌀en** *v/i.* (ge-, h) thank (*j-m für* e. s.o. for s.th.); *danke (schön)!* thank you (very much)!; *danke* thank you; *nein, danke* no, thank you; *nichts zu* ~ don't mention it; **'⌀enswert** *adj. thing:* one can be grateful for; *efforts, etc.:* kind; *task, etc.:* rewarding, worth-while; '~gebet *n* thanksgiving (prayer); '~schreiben *n* letter of thanks.

**dann** *adv.* [dan] then; ~ *und wann* (every) now and then.

**daran** *adv.* [da'ran, *when emphatic:* 'daːran] at (*or* by, in, on, to) it *or* that; *sich* ~ *festhalten* hold on tight to it; ~ *festhalten* stick to it; *nahe* ~ *sein zu inf.* be on the point *or* verge of *ger.*

**da'rangehen** *v/i.* (*irr. gehen, sep., -ge-,* sein) set to work; set about *ger.*

**darauf** *adv.* [da'rauf, *when emphatic:* 'daːrauf] *space:* on (top of) it *or* that; *time:* thereupon; after it *or* that; *am Tage* ~ the day after, the next *or* following day; *zwei Jahre* ~ two years later; ~ *kommt es an* that's what matters; ~**hin** *adv.* [darauf'hin, *when emphatic:* 'daːraufhin] thereupon.

**daraus** *adv.* [da'raus, *when emphatic:* 'daːraus] out of it *or* that, from it *or* that; ~ *folgt* hence it follows; *was ist* ~ *geworden?* what has become of it?; *ich mache mir nichts* ~ I don't care *or* mind (about it).

**darben** ['darbən] *v/i.* (ge-, h) suffer want; starve.

**darbiet|en** ['daːr-] *v/t.* (*irr. bieten, sep., -ge-,* h) offer, present; perform; **'⌀ung** *f* (-/-en) *thea., etc.:* performance.

**'darbringen** *v/t.* (*irr. bringen, sep., -ge-,* h) offer; make (*sacrifice*).

**darein** *adv.* [da'rain, *when emphatic:* 'daːrain] into it *or* that, therein.

**da'rein|finden** *v/refl.* (*irr. finden, sep., -ge-,* h) put up with it; ~**mischen** *v/refl.* (*sep., -ge-,* h) interfere (with it); ~**reden** *v/i.* (*sep., -ge-,* h) interrupt; *fig.* interfere.

**darin** *adv.* [da'rin, *when emphatic:* 'daːrin] in it *or* that; therein; *es war nichts* ~ there was nothing in it *or* them.

**darleg|en** ['daːr-] *v/t.* (*sep., -ge-,* h)

lay open, expose, disclose; show; explain; demonstrate; point out; **'⌀ung** *f* (-/-en) exposition; explanation; statement.

**Darlehen** ['daːrleːən] *n* (-s/-) loan.

**Darm** [darm] *m* (-[e]s/~e) gut, *anat.* intestine; (sausage-)skin; *Därme pl.* intestines *pl.*, bowels *pl.*

**'darstell|en** *v/t.* (*sep., -ge-,* h) represent; show, depict; delineate; describe; *actor:* interpret (*character, part*), represent (*character*); *graphic arts:* graph, plot (*curve, etc.*); **'⌀er** *thea. m* (-s/-) interpreter (*of a part*); actor; **'⌀ung** *f* representation; *thea.* performance.

**'dartun** *v/t.* (*irr. tun, sep., -ge-,* h) prove; demonstrate; set forth.

**darüber** *adv.* [da'ryːbər, *when emphatic:* 'daːryːbər] over it *or* that; across it; in the meantime; ~ *werden Jahre vergehen* it will take years; *wir sind* ~ *hinweg* we got over it; *ein Buch* ~ *schreiben* write a book about it.

**darum** *adv.* [da'rum, *when emphatic:* 'daːrum] **1.** *adv.* around it *or* that; *er kümmert sich nicht* ~ he does not care; *es handelt sich* ~ *zu inf.* the point is to *inf.*; **2.** *cj.* therefore, for that reason; ~ *ist er nicht gekommen* that's (the reason) why he hasn't come.

**darunter** *adv.* [da'runtər, *when emphatic:* 'daːruntər] under it *or* that; beneath it; among them; less; *zwei Jahre und* ~ two years and under; *was verstehst du* ~? what do you understand by it?

**das** [das] *s. der.*

**dasein** ['daː-] **1.** *v/i.* (*irr. sein, sep., -ge-,* sein) be there *or* present; exist; **2.** ⌀ *n* (-s/*no pl.*) existence; life; being.

**daß** *cj.* [das] that; ~ *nicht* less; *es sei denn,* ~ unless; *ohne* ~ without *ger.*; *nicht* ~ *ich wüßte* not that I know of.

**'dastehen** *v/i.* (*irr. stehen, sep., -ge-,* h) stand (there).

**Daten** ['daːtən] *pl.* data *pl.* (*a.* ⊕), facts *pl.*; particulars *pl.*; **'~verarbeitung** *f* (-/-en) data processing.

**datieren** [da'tiːrən] *v/t. and v/i.* (*no -ge-,* h) date.  [(case).\

**Dativ** *gr.* ['daːtiːf] *m* (-s/-e) dative]

**Dattel** ['datəl] *f* (-/-n) date.

**Datum** ['daːtum] *n* (-s/*Daten*) date.

**Dauer** ['dauər] *f* (-/*no pl.*) length, duration; continuance; *auf die* ~ in the long run; *für die* ~ *von* for a period *or* term of; *von* ~ *sein* last well; **'⌀haft** *adj.* peace, *etc.*: lasting; *material, etc.*: durable; *colour, dye:* fast; **'~karte** *f* season ticket, *Am.* commutation ticket; **'~lauf** *m* jog-trot; endurance-run; **'⌀n** *v/i.* (ge-, h) continue, last; take (*time*); **'~welle** *f* permanent wave, F perm.

**Daumen** ['daumən] m (-s/-) thumb; j-m den ~ halten keep one's fingers crossed (for s.o.); '~abdruck m (-[e]s/~e) thumb-print.

**Daune** ['daunə] f (-/-n): ~(n pl.) down; '~ndecke f eiderdown (quilt).

**davon** adv. [da'fɔn, when emphatic: 'da:fɔn] of it or that; thereof; from it or that; off, away; was habe ich ~? what do I get from it?; das kommt ~! it serves you right!

**da'von|kommen** v/i. (irr. kommen, sep., -ge-, sein) escape, get off; ~laufen v/i. (irr. laufen, sep., -ge-, sein) run away.

**davor** adv. [da'fo:r, when emphatic: 'da:fo:r] space: before it or that, in front of it or that; er fürchtet sich ~ he is afraid of it.

**dazu** adv. [da'tsu:, when emphatic: 'da:tsu:] to it or that; for it or that; for that purpose; in addition to that; noch ~ at that; ~ gehört Zeit it requires time.

**da'zu|gehörig** adj. belonging to it; ~kommen v/i. (irr. kommen, sep., -ge-, sein) appear (on the scene); find time.

**dazwischen** adv. [da'tsviʃən] between (them), in between; ~kommen v/i. (irr. kommen, sep., -ge-, sein) thing: intervene, happen.

**Debatt|e** [de'batə] f (-/-n) debate; **2ieren** [~'ti:rən] (no -ge-, h) 1. v/t. discuss; debate; 2. v/i. debate (über acc. on).

**Debüt** [de'by:] n (-s/-s) first appearance, début.

**dechiffrieren** [deʃi'fri:rən] v/t. (no -ge-, h) decipher, decode.

**Deck** ⚓ [dɛk] n (-[e]s/-s, ~-e) deck; '~adresse f cover (address); '~bett n feather bed.

**Decke** ['dɛkə] f (-/-n) cover(ing); blanket; (travel[l]ing) rug; ceiling; '~l m (-s/-) lid, cover (of box or pot, etc.); lid (of piano); (book-)cover; '2n (ge-, h) 1. v/t. cover; den Tisch ~ lay the table; 2. v/i. paint: cover.

**'Deck|mantel** m cloak, mask, disguise; '~name m assumed name, pseudonym; '~ung f (-/-en) cover; security.

**defekt** [de'fɛkt] 1. adj. defective, faulty; 2. 2 m (-[e]s/-e) defect, fault.

**defin|ieren** [defi'ni:rən] v/t. (no -ge-, h) define; **2ition** [~i'tsjo:n] f (-/-en) definition; ~itiv adj. [~i'ti:f] definite; definitive.

**Defizit** † ['de:fitsit] n (-s/-e) deficit, deficiency.

**Degen** ['de:gən] m (-s/-) sword; fencing: épée.

**degradieren** [degra'di:rən] v/t. (no -ge-, h) degrade, Am. a. demote.

**dehn|bar** adj. ['de:nba:r] extensible; elastic; metal: ductile; notion, etc.: vague; '~en v/t. (ge-, h) extend; stretch; '2ung f (-/-en) extension; stretch(ing).

**Deich** [daiç] m (-[e]s/-e) dike, dyke.

**Deichsel** ['daiksəl] f (-/-n) pole, shaft.

**dein** poss. pron. [dain] your; der (die, das) ~e yours; ich bin ~ I am yours; die Deinen pl. your family; ~erseits adv. ['~ər'zaits] for or on your part; '~esgleichen pron. your like, your (own) kind, F the like(s) of you.

**Dekan** eccl. and univ. [de'ka:n] m (-s/-e) dean.

**Deklam|ation** [deklama'tsjo:n] f (-/-en) declamation; reciting; **2ieren** [~'mi:rən] v/t. and v/i. (no -ge-, h) recite; declaim.

**Deklin|ation** gr. [deklina'tsjo:n] f (-/-en) declension; **2ieren** gr. [~'ni:rən] v/t. (no -ge-, h) decline.

**Dekor|ateur** [dekora'tø:r] m (-s/-e) decorator; window-dresser; thea. scene-painter; ~ation [~'tsjo:n] f (-/-en) decoration; (window-)dressing; thea. scenery; **2ieren** [~'ri:rən] v/t. (no -ge-, h) decorate; dress (window).

**Dekret** [de'kre:t] n (-[e]s/-e) decree.

**delikat** adj. [deli'ka:t] delicate (a. fig.); delicious; fig. ticklish; **2esse** [~a'tɛsə] f (-/-n) delicacy; dainty.

**Delphin** zo. [dɛl'fi:n] m (-s/-e) dolphin.

**Dement|i** [de'mɛnti] n (-s/-s) (formal) denial; **2ieren** [~'ti:rən] v/t. (no -ge-, h) deny, give a (formal) denial of.

**'dem|entsprechend** adv., '~gemäß adv. correspondingly, accordingly; '~nach adv. therefore, hence; accordingly; '~nächst adv. soon, shortly, before long.

**demobili'sier|en** (no -ge-, h) 1. v/t. demobilize; disarm; 2. v/i. disarm; **2ung** f (-/-en) demobilization.

**Demokrat** [demo'kra:t] m (-en/-en) democrat; ~ie [~a'ti:] f (-/-n) democracy; **2isch** adj. [~'kra:tiʃ] democratic.

**demolieren** [demo'li:rən] v/t. (no -ge-, h) demolish.

**Demonstr|ation** [demɔnstra'tsjo:n] f (-/-en) demonstration; **2ieren** [~'stri:rən] v/t. and v/i. (no -ge-, h) demonstrate.

**Demont|age** [demɔn'ta:ʒə] f (-/-n) disassembly; dismantling; **2ieren** [~'ti:rən] v/t. (no -ge-, h) disassemble; dismantle.

**Demut** ['de:mu:t] f (-/no pl.) humility, humbleness.

**demütig** adj. ['de:my:tiç] humble; ~en ['~gən] v/t. (ge-, h) humble, humiliate.

**denk|bar** ['dɛŋkba:r] 1. adj. conceivable; thinkable, imaginable; 2. adv.: ~ einfach most simple;

'~en (*irr.*, ge-, h) **1.** *v/i.* think; ~ *an* (*acc.*) think of; remember; ~ *über* (*acc.*) think about; j-m zu ~ geben set s.o. thinking; **2.** *v/t.* think; sich et. ~ imagine *or* fancy s.th.; das habe ich mir gedacht I thought as much; '2mal *n* monument; memorial; '2schrift *f* memorandum; memoir; '2stein *m* memorial stone; '~würdig *adj.* memorable; 2zettel *fig. m* lesson.

**denn** [dɛn] **1.** *cj.* for; mehr ~ je more than ever; **2.** *adv.* then; es sei ~, daß unless, except; wieso ~? how so.

**dennoch** *cj.* ['dɛnɔx] yet, still, nevertheless; though.

**Denunz|iant** [denun'tsjant] *m* (-en/-en) informer; ~iation [~'tsjoːn] *f* (-/-en) denunciation; 2ieren [~'tsiːrən] *v/t.* (*no* -ge-, h) inform against, denounce.

**Depesche** [de'pɛʃə] *f* (-/-n) dispatch; telegram, F wire; wireless.

**deponieren** [depo'niːrən] *v/t.* (*no* -ge-, h) deposit.

**Deposit|en** † [depo'ziːtən] *pl.* deposits *pl.*; ~bank *f* deposit bank.

**der** [deːr], **die** [diː], **das** [das] **1.** *art.* the; **2.** *dem. pron.* that, this; he, she, it; die *pl.* these, those, they, them; **3.** *rel. pron.* who, which, that.

'**der'artig** *adj.* such, of such a kind of this *or* that kind.

**derb** *adj.* [dɛrp] *cloth*: coarse, rough; *shoes, etc.*: stout, strong; *ore, etc.*: massive; *p.*: sturdy; rough; *food*: coarse; *p., manners*: rough, coarse; *way of speaking*: blunt, unrefined; *joke*: crude; *humour*: broad.

**der'gleichen** *adj.* such, of that kind; *used as a noun*: the like, such a thing; und ~ and the like; nichts ~ nothing of the kind.

**der-** ['deːrjeːnigə], '**die-**, '**dasjenige** *dem. pron.* he *who*, she *who*, that *which*; diejenigen *pl.* those *who*, those *which*.

**der-** [deːr'zɛlbə], **die-**, **das'selbe** *dem. pron.* the same; he, she, it.

**Desert|eur** [dezɛr'tøːr] *m* (-s/-e) deserter; 2ieren [~'tiːrən] *v/i.* (*no* -ge-, sein) desert.

**desgleichen** [dɛs'glaɪçən] **1.** *dem. pron.* such a thing; **2.** *cj.* likewise.

**deshalb** ['dɛshalp] **1.** *cj.* for this *or* that reason; therefore; **2.** *adv.*: ich tat es nur ~, weil I did it only because.

**desinfizieren** [dɛsʔinfi'tsiːrən] *v/t.* (*no* -ge-, h) disinfect.

**Despot** [dɛs'poːt] *m* (-en/-en) despot; 2isch *adj.* despotic.

**destillieren** [dɛsti'liːrən] *v/t.* (*no* -ge-, h) distil.

**desto** *adv.* ['dɛsto] (all, so much) the; ~ besser all the better; ~ erstaunter (all) the more astonished.

**deswegen** *cj. and adv.* ['dɛs'veːgən] *s.* deshalb.

**Detail** [de'taɪ] *n* (-s/-s) detail.

**Detektiv** [detɛk'tiːf] *m* (-s/-e) detective.

**deuten** ['dɔʏtən] (ge-, h) **1.** *v/t.* interpret; read (*stars, dream, etc.*); **2.** *v/i.*: ~ *auf* (*acc.*) point at.

'**deutlich** *adj.* clear, distinct, plain.

**deutsch** *adj.* [dɔʏtʃ] German; '2e *m*, *f* (-n/-n) German.

'**Deutung** *f* (-/-en) interpretation, explanation.

**Devise** [de'viːzə] *f* (-/-n) motto; ~n *pl.* † foreign exchange *or* currency.

**Dezember** [de'tsɛmbər] *m* (-[s]/-) December.

**dezent** *adj.* [de'tsɛnt] attire, etc.: decent, modest; *literature, etc.*: decent; *behaviour*: decent, proper; *music, colour*: soft, restrained; *lighting, etc.*: subdued.

**Dezernat** [detsɛr'naːt] *n* (-[e]s/-e) (administrative) department.

**dezimal** *adj.* [detsi'maːl] decimal; 2bruch *m* decimal fraction; 2stelle *f* decimal place.

**dezi'mieren** *v/t.* (*no* -ge-, h) decimate; *fig. a.* reduce (drastically).

**Diadem** [dia'deːm] *n* (-s/-e) diadem.

**Diagnose** [dia'gnoːzə] *f* (-/-n) diagnosis.

**diagonal** *adj.* [diago'naːl] diagonal; 2e *f* (-/-n) diagonal.

**Dialekt** [dia'lɛkt] *m* (-[e]s/-e) dialect; 2isch *adj.* dialectical.

**Dialog** [dia'loːk] *m* (-[e]s/-e) dialogue, Am. *a.* dialog.

**Diamant** [dia'mant] *m* (-en/-en) diamond.

**Diät** [di'ɛːt] *f* (-/*no pl.*) diet; diät leben live on a diet. [yourself.]

**dich** *pers. pron.* [diç] you; ~ (*selbst*)

**dicht** [diçt] **1.** *adj.* fog, rain, etc.: dense; *fog, forest, hair*: thick; *eyebrows*: bushy, thick; *crowd*: dense; *shoe, etc.*: (water)tight; **2.** *adv.*: ~ *an* (*dat.*) *or* bei close to.

'**dichten**[1] *v/t.* (ge-, h) make tight.

'**dicht|en**[2] (ge-, h) **1.** *v/t.* compose, write; **2.** *v/i.* compose *or* write poetry; '2er *m* (-s/-) poet; author; '~erisch *adj.* poetic(al); '2kunst *f* poetry.

'**Dichtung**[1] ⊕ *f* (-/-en) seal(ing).

'**Dichtung**[2] *f* (-/-en) poetry; fiction; poem, poetic work.

**dick** *adj.* [dik] wall, material, etc.: thick; *book*: thick, bulky; *p.* fat, stout; '2e *f* (-/-n) thickness; bulkiness; *p.* fatness, stoutness; '~fellig *adj. p.* thick-skinned; '~flüssig *adj.* thick; viscid, viscous, syrupy; 2icht ['~içt] *n* (-[e]s/-e) thicket; '2kopf *m* stubborn person, F pig-headed person; ~leibig *adj.* ['~laɪbiç] corpulent; *fig.* bulky.

**die** [diː] *s. der.*

**Dieb** [diːp] *m* (-[e]s/-e) thief, *Am.* F *a.* crook; ~erei [diːbə'raɪ] *f* (-/-en) thieving, thievery.

**Diebes|bande** ['di:bəs-] f band of thieves; '~gut n stolen goods pl.

**dieb|isch** adj. ['di:biʃ] thievish; fig. malicious; **2stahl** ['di:p-] m (-[e]s/ ~e) theft, ſ̷t̷ mst larceny.

**Diele** ['di:lə] f (-/-n) board, plank; hall, Am. a. hallway.

**dienen** ['di:nən] v/i. (ge-, h) serve (j-m s.o.; als as; zu for; dazu, zu inf. to inf.); womit kann ich ~? what can I do for you?

**'Diener** m (-s/-) (man-, domestic) servant; fig. bow (vor dat. to); '~in f (-/-nen) (woman-)servant, maid; '~schaft f (-/-en) servants pl.

**'dienlich** adj. useful, convenient; expedient, suitable.

**Dienst** [di:nst] m (-es/-e) service; duty; employment; ~ haben be on duty; im (außer) ~ on (off) duty.

**Dienstag** ['di:nsta:k] m (-[e]s/-e) Tuesday.

**'Dienst|alter** n seniority, length of service; **2bar** adj. subject (j-m to s.o.); subservient (to); '~bote m domestic (servant), Am. help; '2eifrig adj. (over-)eager (in one's duty); **2frei** adj. off duty; ~er Tag day off; '~herr m master; employer; '~leistung f service; **2lich** adj. official; '~mädchen n maid, Am. help; '~mann m (street-)porter; '~stunden f/pl. office hours pl.; '2tauglich adj. fit for service or duty; **2tuend** adj. ['~tu:ənt] on duty; '2untauglich adj. unfit for service or duty; '~weg m official channels pl.; '~wohnung f official residence.

**dies** [di:s], ~er ['di:zər], ~e ['di:zə], ~es ['di:zəs] adj. and dem. pron. this; diese pl. these; dieser Tage one of these days; used as a noun: this one; he, she, it; diese pl. they.

**Dieselmotor** ['di:zəl-] m Diesel engine.

**dies|jährig** adj. ['di:sje:riç] of this year, this year's; '~mal adv. this time; for (this) once; ~seits ['~zaits] 1. adv. on this side; 2. prp. (gen.) on this side of.

**Dietrich** ['di:triç] m (-s/-e) skeleton key; picklock.

**Differenz** [difə'rɛnts] f (-/-en) difference; disagreement.

**Diktat** [dik'ta:t] n (-[e]s/-e) dictation; nach ~ at or from dictation; ~or [~ɔr] m (-s/-en) dictator; **2orisch** adj. [~a'to:riʃ] dictatorial; ~ur [~a'tu:r] f (-/-en) dictatorship.

**dik'tieren** v/t. and v/i. (no -ge-, h) dictate.

**Dilettant** [dile'tant] m (-en/-en) dilettante, dabbler; amateur.

**Ding** [diŋ] n (-[e]s/-e) thing; guter ~e in good spirits; vor allen ~en first of all, above all.

**Diphtherie** ♃ [difte'ri:] f (-/-n) diphtheria.

**Diplom** [di'plo:m] n (-[e]s/-e) diploma, certificate.

**Diplomat** [diplo'ma:t] m (-en/-en) diplomat; diplomatist; ~ie [~a'ti:] f (-/no pl.) diplomacy; **2isch** adj. [~'ma:tiʃ] diplomatic (a. fig.).

**dir** pers. pron. [di:r] (to) you.

**direkt** [di'rɛkt] 1. adj. direct; ~er Wagen 🚂 through carriage, Am. through car; 2. adv. direct(ly); **2ion** [~'tsjo:n] f (-/-en) direction; management; board of directors; **2or** [di'rɛktɔr] m (-s/-en) director; manager; headmaster, Am. principal; **2orin** [~'to:rin] f (-/-nen) headmistress, Am. principal; **2rice** [~'tri:s(ə)] f (-/-n) directress; manageress.

**Dirigent** ♪ [diri'gɛnt] m (-en/-en) conductor; **2ieren** ♪ [~'gi:rən] v/t. and v/i. (no -ge-, h) conduct.

**Dirne** ['dirnə] f (-/-n) prostitute.

**Disharmon|ie** ♪ [disharmo'ni:] f (-/-n) disharmony, dissonance (both a. fig.); **2isch** adj. [~'mo:niʃ] discordant, dissonant.

**Diskont** 🕀 [dis'kɔnt] m (-s/-e) discount; **2ieren** [~'ti:rən] v/t. (no -ge-, h) discount.

**diskret** adj. [dis'kre:t] discreet; **2ion** [~e'tsjo:n] f (-/no pl.) discretion.

**Disku|ssion** [disku'sjo:n] f (-/-en) discussion, debate; **2'tieren** (no -ge-, h) 1. v/t. discuss, debate; 2. v/i.: ~ über (acc.) have a discussion about, debate (up)on.

**dispo|nieren** [dispo'ni:rən] v/i. (no -ge-, h) make arrangements; plan ahead; dispose (über acc. of); **2si-tion** [~zi'tsjo:n] f (-/-en) disposition; arrangement; disposal.

**Distanz** [di'stants] f (-/-en) distance (a. fig.); **2ieren** [~'tsi:rən] v/refl. (no -ge-, h): sich ~ von dis(as)so-ciate o.s. from.

**Distel** ♣ ['distəl] f (-/-n) thistle.

**Distrikt** [di'strikt] m (-[e]s/-e) district; region; area.

**Disziplin** [distsi'pli:n] f (-/-en) discipline.

**Divid|ende** 🕀 [divi'dɛndə] f (-/-n) dividend; **2ieren** [~'di:rən] v/t. (no -ge-, h) divide (durch by).

**Diwan** ['di:va:n] m (-s/-e) divan.

**doch** [dɔx] 1. cj. but, though; however, yet; 2. adv. in answer to negative question: yes; bist du noch nicht fertig? — ~! aren't you ready yet? — yes, I am; also ~! I knew it!, I was right after all!; komm ~ herein! do come in!; nicht ~! I don't!

**Docht** [dɔxt] m (-[e]s/-e) wick.

**Dock** ⚓ [dɔk] n (-[e]s/-e) dock.

**Dogge** zo. ['dɔgə] f (-/-n) Great Dane.

**Dohle** orn. ['do:lə] f (-/-n) (jack)daw.

**Doktor** ['dɔktɔr] m (-s/-en) doctor.

**Dokument** [doku'mɛnt] ● (-[e]s/-e)

document; Ⴒ instrument; **~arfilm** [~'ta:r-] *m* documentary (film).

**Dolch** [dɔlç] *m* (-[e]s/-e) dagger; poniard; **~stoß** *m* dagger-thrust.

**Dollar** ['dɔlar] *m* (-s/-s) dollar.

**dolmetsch|en** ['dɔlmɛtʃən] *v/i.* and *v/t.* (ge-, h) interpret; '**2er** *m* (-s/-) interpreter.

**Dom** [do:m] *m* (-[e]s/-e) cathedral.

**Domäne** [do'mɛ:nə] *f* (-/-n) domain (*a. fig.*); province.

**Domino** ['do:mino] (-s/-s) **1.** *m* domino; **2.** *n* (game of) dominoes *pl.*

**Donner** ['dɔnər] *m* (-s/-) thunder; '**2n** *v/i.* (ge-, h) thunder (*a. fig.*); '**~schlag** *m* thunderclap (*a. fig.*); '**~stag** *m* Thursday; '**~wetter** *n* thunderstorm; F *fig.* telling off; F *~l* my word!, by Jove!; F *zum ~l* F confound it!, *sl.* damn it.

**Doppel** ['dɔpəl] *n* (-s/-) duplicate; *tennis, etc.*: double, *Am.* doubles *pl.*; '**~bett** *n* double bed; '**~decker** *m* (-s/-) 🪶 biplane; double-decker (bus); '**~ehe** *f* bigamy; **~gänger** ['~gɛŋər] *m* (-s/-) double; '**~punkt** *m* colon; '**~sinn** *m* double meaning, ambiguity; '**2sinnig** *adj.* ambiguous, equivocal; '**~stecker** ∮ *m* two-way adapter; '**2t 1.** *adj.* double; **2.** *adv.* doubly; twice; '**~zentner** *m* quintal; **2züngig** *adj.* ['~tsyŋiç] two-faced.

**Dorf** [dɔrf] *n* (-[e]s/=er) village; '**~bewohner** *m* villager.

**Dorn** [dɔrn] *m* **1.** (-[e]s/-en) thorn (*a. fig.*), prickle, spine; *j-m ein ~ im Auge sein* be a thorn in s.o.'s flesh or side; **2.** (-[e]s/-e) tongue (*of buckle*); spike (*of running-shoe, etc.*); ⊕ punch; '**2ig** *adj.* thorny (*a. fig.*).

**dörr|en** ['dœrən] *v/t.* (ge-, h) dry; '**2fleisch** *n* dried meat; '**2gemüse** *n* dried vegetables *pl.*; '**2obst** *n* dried fruit.

**Dorsch** *ichth.* [dɔrʃ] *m* (-es/-e) cod(fish).

**dort** *adv.* [dɔrt] there; over there; '**~her** *adv.* from there; '**~hin** *adv.* there, to that place; '**~ig** *adj.* there, in or of that place.

**Dose** ['do:zə] *f* (-/-n) box; tin, *Am.* can; **~nöffner** ['do:zən?-] *m* (-s/-) tin-opener, *Am.* can opener.

**Dosis** ['do:zis] *f* (-/Dosen) dose (*a. fig.*).

**dotieren** [do'ti:rən] *v/t.* (*no* -ge-, h) endow.

**Dotter** ['dɔtər] *m*, *n* (-s/-) yolk.

**Dozent** [do'tsɛnt] *m* (-en/-en) (university) lecturer, *Am.* assistant professor.

**Drache** ['draxə] *m* (-n/-n) dragon; '**~n** *m* (-s/-) kite; *fig.* termagant, shrew, battle-axe.

**Dragoner** [dra'go:nər] *m* (-s/-) 🪶 dragoon (*a. fig.*).

**Draht** [dra:t] *m* (-[e]s/=e) wire; '**2en** *v/t.* (ge-, h) telegraph, wire; '**~geflecht** *n* (-[e]s/-e) wire netting; '**~hindernis** 🪶 *n* wire entanglement; '**2ig** *adj.* *p.* wiry; '**2los** *adj.* wireless; '**~seilbahn** *f* funicular (railway); '**~stift** *m* wire tack; '**~zieher** F *fig. m* (-s/-) wire-puller.

**drall** *adj.* [dral] *girl, legs, etc.*: plump; *woman*: buxom.

**Drama** ['dra:ma] *n* (-s/Dramen) drama; **~tiker** [dra'ma:tikər] *m* (-s/-) dramatist; **2tisch** *adj.* [dra'ma:tiʃ] dramatic.

**dran** F *adv.* [dran] *s. daran*; *er ist gut (übel) ~* he's well (badly) off; *ich bin ~* it's my turn.

**Drang** [draŋ] **1.** *m* (-[e]s/⁖=e) pressure, rush; *fig.* urge; **2.** 2 *pret. of dringen*.

**drängen** ['drɛŋən] (ge-, h) **1.** *v/t.* press (*a. fig.*), push; *fig.* urge; *creditor:* dun; *sich ~* crowd, throng; **2.** *v/i.* press, be pressing or urgent.

**drangsalieren** [draŋza'li:rən] *v/t.* (*no* -ge-, h) harass, vex, plague.

**drastisch** *adj.* ['drastiʃ] drastic.

**drauf** F *adv.* [drauf] *s. darauf*; *~ und dran sein zu inf.* be on the point of *ger.*; **2gänger** ['~gɛŋər] *m* (-s/-) dare-devil, *Am. sl. a.* go-getter.

**draus** F *adv.* [draus] *s. daraus*.

**draußen** *adv.* ['drausən] outside; out of doors; abroad; out at sea.

**drechs|eln** ['drɛksəln] *v/t.* (ge-, h) turn (*wood, etc.*); **2ler** ['~slər] *m* (-s/-) turner.

**Dreck** F [drɛk] *m* (-[e]s/*no pl.*) dirt; mud; filth (*a. fig.*); *fig.* trash; F *~ am Stecken haben* not to have a clean slate; F *das geht dich einen ~ an* that's none of your business; '**2ig** *adj.* dirty; filthy.

**Dreh|bank** ['dre:-] *f* (-/=e) (turning-) lathe; '**2bar** *adj.* revolving, rotating; '**~bleistift** *m* propelling pencil; '**~buch** *n* scenario; script; '**~bühne** *thea. f* revolving stage; '**2en** *v/t.* (ge-, h) turn; shoot (*film*); roll (*cigarette*); *es dreht sich darum zu inf.* it is a matter of *ger.*; *sich ~* turn; '**~kreuz** *n* turnstile; '**~orgel** *f* barrel-organ; '**~punkt** *m* ⊕ centre of rotation, *Am.* center of rotation, pivot (*a. fig.*); '**~strom** ∮ *m* three-phase current; '**~stuhl** *m* swivel-chair; '**~tür** *f* revolving door; '**~ung** *f* (-/-en) turn; rotation.

**drei** *adj.* [drai] three; '**~beinig** *adj.* three-legged; '**2eck** *n* triangle; '**~eckig** *adj.* triangular; **~erlei** *adj.* ['~ər'lai] of three kinds or sorts; **~fach** *adj.* ['~fax] threefold, treble; triple; '**~farbig** *adj.* three-col(u)r(ed); '**2fuß** *m* tripod; '**~jährig** *adj.* ['~jɛ:riç] three-year-old; triennial; '**~mal** *adv.* three times; '**~malig** *adj.* done or repeated three times; three; **2'meilenzone** ⚓, Ⴒ *f* three-mile limit; '**2rad** *n* tricycle;

'**~seitig** adj. three-sided; trilateral;
'**~silbig** adj. trisyllabic.
**dreißig** adj. ['draɪsɪç] thirty; '**~ste**
adj. thirtieth.
**dreist** adj. [draɪst] bold, audacious;
cheeky, saucy; '**2igkeit** f (-/-en)
boldness, audacity; cheek, sauciness.
'**drei|stimmig** ♪ adj. for or in three
voices; **~tägig** adj. ['~tɛ:gɪç] three-
day; '**~teilig** adj. in three parts,
tripartite; '**~zehn(te)** adj. thir-
teen(th).
**dresch|en** ['drɛʃən] v/t. and v/i.
(irr., ge-, h) thresh; thrash; '**2flegel**
m flail; '**2maschine** f threshing-
machine.
**dressieren** [drɛ'si:rən] v/t. (no -ge-,
h) train; break in (horse).
**drillen** ✕, ✍ ['drɪlən] v/t. (ge-, h)
drill.
**Drillinge** ['drɪlɪŋə] m/pl. triplets pl.
**drin** F adv. [drɪn] s. darin.
**dringen** ['drɪŋən] v/i. (irr., ge-)
1. (sein): ~ durch force one's way
through s.th., penetrate or pierce
s.th.; ~ aus break forth from s.th.;
noise: come from; ~ in (acc.) penetrate into; in j-n ~ urge or press s.o.;
an die Öffentlichkeit ~ get abroad;
2. (h): ~ auf (acc.) insist on, press
for; '**~d** adj. urgent, pressing;
suspicion: strong.
'**dringlich** adj. urgent, pressing;
'**2keit** f (-/no pl.) urgency.
**drinnen** adv. ['drɪnən] inside; indoors.
**dritt|e** adj. ['drɪtə] third; '**2el** n
(-s/-) third; '**~ens** adv. thirdly;
'**~letzt** adj. last but two.
**Drog|e** F ['dro:gə] f (-/-n) drug;
**~erie** [drogə'ri:] f (-/-n) chemist's
(shop), Am. drugstore; '**~ist** [dro-
'gɪst] m (-en/-en) (retail pharma-
ceutical) chemist.
**drohen** ['dro:ən] v/i. (ge-, h) threat-
en, menace.
**Drohne** ['dro:nə] f (-/-n) zo. drone
(a. fig.).
**dröhnen** ['drø:nən] v/i. (ge-, h)
voice, etc.: resound; cannon, drum,
etc.: roar; voice, cannon: boom.
**Drohung** ['dro:uŋ] f (-/-en) threat,
menace.
**drollig** adj. ['drɔlɪç] amusing, quaint,
comical.
**Dromedar** zo. [drome'da:r] n (-s/-e)
dromedary.
**drosch** [drɔʃ] pret. of dreschen.
**Droschke** ['drɔʃkə] f (-/-n) taxi
(-cab), Am. a. cab, hack; '**~kut-
scher** m cabman, driver, Am. a.
hackman.
**Drossel** orn. ['drɔsəl] f (-/-n) thrush;
'**2n** ⊕ v/t. (ge-, h) throttle.
**drüben** adv. ['dry:bən] over there,
yonder.
**drüber** F adv. ['dry:bər] s. darüber.
**Druck** [druk] m 1. (-[e]s/ⁿe) pres-

sure; squeeze (of hand, etc.); 2. typ.
(-[e]s/-e) print(ing); '**~bogen** m
printed sheet; '**~buchstabe** m
block letter.
**drucken** ['drukən] v/t. (ge-, h) print;
~ lassen have s.th. printed, publish.
**drücken** ['drykən] (ge-, h) 1. v/t.
press; squeeze (hand, etc.); force
down (prices, wages, etc.); lower
(record); press, push (button, etc.).
F sich ~ vor (dat.) or von shirk
(work, etc.); 2. v/i. shoe: pinch.
'**Drucker** m (-s/-) printer.
'**Drücker** m (-s/-) door-handle;
trigger.
**Drucker|ei** [drukə'raɪ] f (-/-en)
printing office, Am. printery, print
shop; '**~schwärze** f printer's or
printing-ink.
'**Druck|fehler** m misprint; '**~fch-
lerverzeichnis** n errata pl.; '**2fer-
tig** adj. ready for press; '**~kammer**
f pressurized cabin; '**~knopf** m
patent fastener, snap-fastener; ⚡
push-button; '**~luft** f compressed
air; '**~pumpe** f pressure pump;
'**~sache(n** pl.) ✆ f printed matter,
Am. a. second-class or third-class
matter; '**~schrift** f block letters;
publication; '**~taste** f press key.
**drum** F adv., cj. [drum] s. darum.
**drunter** F adv. ['druntər] s. darunter.
**Drüse** anat. ['dry:zə] f (-/-n) gland.
**du** pers. pron. [du:] you.
**Dublette** [du'blɛtə] f (-/-n) duplicate.
**ducken** ['dukən] v/refl. (ge-, h)
duck, crouch; fig. cringe (vor dat.
to, before).
**Dudelsack** ♪ ['du:dəl-] m bagpipes
pl.
**Duell** [du'ɛl] n (-s/-e) duel; **2ieren**
[due'li:rən] v/refl. (no -ge-, h)
(fight a) duel (mit with).
**Duett** ♪ [du'ɛt] n (-[e]s/-e) duet.
**Duft** [duft] m (-[e]s/ⁿe) scent, fragrance, perfume; '**2en** v/i. (ge-, h)
smell, have a scent, be fragrant;
'**2end** adj. fragrant; '**2ig** adj. dainty,
fragrant.
**duld|en** ['duldən] (ge-, h) 1. v/t.
bear, stand, endure, suffer (pain,
grief, etc.); tolerate, put up with;
2. v/i. suffer; **~sam** adj. ['~t-] tol-
erant; '**2samkeit** f (-/no pl.) tol-
erance; **2ung** ['~duŋ] f (-/✍-en)
toleration; sufferance.
**dumm** adj. [dum] stupid, dull, Am.
F dumb; '**2heit** f (-/-en) stupidity,
dullness; stupid or foolish action;
'**2kopf** m fool, blockhead, Am. sl. a.
dumbbell.
**dumpf** adj. [dumpf] smell, air, etc.:
musty, fusty; atmosphere: stuffy,
heavy; sound, sensation, etc.: dull;
'**~ig** adj. cellar, etc.: damp, musty.
**Düne** ['dy:nə] f (-/-n) dune, sand-
hill.

**Dung** [duŋ] m (-[e]s/no pl.) dung, manure.

**dünge|n** ['dyŋən] v/t. (ge-, h) dung, manure; fertilize; **'2r** m (-s/-) s. Dung; fertilizer.

**dunkel** ['duŋkəl] **1.** adj. dark; dim; fig. obscure; idea, etc.: dim, faint, vague; **2.** 2 n (-s/no pl.) s. Dunkelheit.

**Dünkel** ['dyŋkəl] m (-s/no pl.) conceit, arrogance; **'2haft** adj. conceited, arrogant.

**'Dunkel|heit** f (-/no pl.) darkness (a. fig.); fig. obscurity; **'~kammer** phot. f dark-room; **'2n** v/i. (ge-, h) grow dark, darken.

**dünn** adj. [dyn] paper, material, voice, etc.: thin; hair, population, etc.: thin, sparse; liquid: thin, watery; air: rare(fied).

**Dunst** [dunst] m (-es/⸗e) vapo(u)r; haze, mist; fume.

**dünsten** ['dynstən] (ge-, h) **1.** v/t. steam (fish, etc.); stew (fruit, etc.); **2.** v/i. steam.

**'dunstig** adj. vaporous; hazy.

**Duplikat** [dupli'ka:t] n (-[e]s/-e) duplicate.

**Dur** ♩ [du:r] n (-/-) major.

**durch** [durç] **1.** prp. (acc.) through; **2.** adv.: die ganze Nacht ~ all night long; ~ und ~ through and through; thoroughly.

**durcharbeiten** ['durç⸗] (sep., -ge-, h) **1.** v/t. study thoroughly; sich ~ durch work through (book, etc.); **2.** v/i. work without a break.

**durch'aus** adv. through and through; thoroughly; by all means; absolutely, quite; ~ nicht not at all, by no means.

**'durch|biegen** v/t. (irr. biegen, sep., -ge-, h) bend; deflect (beam, etc.); sich ~ beam, etc.: deflect, sag; **'~blättern** v/t. (sep., -ge-, h) glance or skim through (book, etc.), Am. thumb through, skim; **'2blick** m: ~ auf (acc.) view through to, vista over, view of; **'~blicken** v/i. (sep., -ge-, h) look through; ~ lassen, daß give to understand that.

**durch|'bluten** v/t. (no -ge-, h) supply with blood; **~'bohren** v/t. (no -ge-, h) pierce, perforate; mit Blicken ~ look daggers at s.o.

**'durch|braten** v/t. (irr. braten, sep., -ge-, h) roast thoroughly; **~brechen** (irr. brechen) **1.** ['~breçən] v/i. (sep., -ge-, sein) break through or apart; **2.** ['~] v/t. (sep., -ge-, h) break apart or in two; **3.** [~'breçən] v/t. (no -ge-, h) break through, breach; run (blockade); crash (sound barrier); **'~brennen** v/i. (irr. brennen, sep., -ge-, sein) ⚡ fuse: blow; F fig. run away; woman: elope; **'~bringen** v/t. (irr. bringen, sep., -ge-, h) bring or get through; dissipate, squander (money); **'2bruch** m ⚡ break,

through; rupture; breach; fig. ultimate success.

**durch'denken** v/t. (irr. denken, no -ge-, h) think s.th. over thoroughly.

**'durch|drängen** v/refl. (sep., -ge-,h) force or push one's way through; **~dringen** (irr. dringen) **1.** ['~driŋən] v/i. (sep., -ge-, sein) penetrate (through); win acceptance (mit for) (proposal); **2.** [~'driŋən] v/t. (no -ge-, h) penetrate, pierce; water, smell, etc.: permeate.

**durcheinander** [durç⸗ai'nandər] **1.** adv. in confusion or disorder; pell-mell; **2.** 2 n (-s/-) muddle, mess, confusion; **~bringen** v/t. (irr. bringen, sep., -ge-, h) confuse s.o.; fig. mix (things) up; **~werfen** v/t. (irr. werfen, sep., -ge-, h) throw into disorder; fig. mix up.

**durchfahr|en** (irr. fahren) **1.** ['~fa:rən] v/i. (sep., -ge-, sein) go or pass or drive through; **2.** [~'fa:rən] v/t. (no -ge-, h) go or pass or travel or drive through; traverse (tract of country, etc.); **'2t** f passage (through); gate(way); ~ verboten! no thoroughfare!

**'Durchfall** m ⚕ diarrh(o)ea; F fig. failure, Am. a. flunk; **2en** (irr. fallen) **1.** ['~falən] v/i. (sep., -ge-, sein) fall through; fail, F get ploughed (in examination); thea. be a failure, sl. be a flop; ~ lassen reject, F plough; **2.** [~'falən] v/t. (no -ge-, h) fall or drop through (space).

**'durch|fechten** v/t. (irr. fechten, sep., -ge-, h) fight or see s.th. through; **'~finden** v/refl. (irr. finden, sep., -ge-, h) find one's way (through).

**durch|'flechten** v/t. (irr. flechten, no -ge-, h) interweave, intertwine; **~'forschen** v/t. (no -ge-, h) search through, investigate; explore (region, etc.).

**'Durchfuhr** † f (-/-en) transit.

**durchführ|bar** adj. ['durçfy:rba:r] practicable, feasible, workable; **'~en** v/t. (sep., -ge-, h) lead or take through or across; fig. carry out or through; realize; **'2ungsbestimmung** f (implementing) regulation.

**'Durchgang** m passage; † transit; sports: run; **'~sverkehr** m through traffic; † transit traffic; **'~szoll** m transit duty.

**'durchgebraten** adj. well done.

**'durchgehen** (irr. gehen, sep., -ge-) **1.** v/i. (sein) go or walk through; bill: pass, be carried; run away or off; abscond; woman: elope; horse: bolt; **2.** v/t. (sein) go through (street, etc.); **3.** v/t. (h, sein) go or look or read through (work, book, etc.); **'~d 1.** adj. continuous; ~er Zug through train; **2.** adv. generally; throughout.

**durch'geistigt** adj. spiritual.

**'durch|greifen** v/i. (irr. greifen,

sep., -ge-, h) put one's hand through; fig. take drastic measures or steps; '∼greifend adj. drastic; radical, sweeping; '∼halten (irr. halten, sep., -ge-, h) 1. v/t. keep up (pace, etc.); 2. v/i. hold out; '∼hauen v/t. (irr. hauen, sep., -ge-, h) cut or chop through; fig. give s.o. a good hiding; '∼helfen v/i. (irr. helfen, sep., -ge-, h) help through (a. fig.); '∼kämpfen v/t. (sep., -ge-, h) fight out; sich ∼ fight one's way through; '∼kneten v/t. (sep., -ge-, h) knead or work thoroughly; '∼kommen v/i. (irr. kommen, sep., -ge-, sein) come or get or pass through; sick person: pull through; in examination: pass.

durch'kreuzen v/t. (no -ge-, h) cross, foil, thwart (plan, etc.).

Durch|laß ['durçlas] m (Durchlasses/Durchlässe) passage; '∼lassen v/t. (irr. lassen, sep., -ge-, h) let pass, allow to pass, let through; Wasser ∼ leak; '∼lässig adj. pervious (to), permeable (to); leaky.

durchlaufen (irr. laufen) 1. ['∼laufən] v/i. (sep., -ge-, sein) run or pass through; 2. ['∼] v/t. (sep., -ge-, h) wear out (shoes, etc.); 3. [∼'laufən] v/t. (no -ge-, h) pass through (stages, departments, etc.); sports: cover (distance).

durch'leben v/t. (no -ge-, h) go or live through.

'durchlesen v/t. (irr. lesen, sep., -ge-, h) read through.

durchleuchten (h) 1. ['∼lɔʏçtən] v/i. (sep., -ge-) shine through; 2. [∼'lɔʏçtən] v/t. (no -ge-) ⚕ X-ray; fig. investigate.

durchlöchern [durç'lœçərn] v/t. (no -ge-, h) perforate, make holes into s.th.

'durchmachen v/t. (sep., -ge-, h) go through (difficult times, etc.); undergo (suffering).

'Durchmarsch m march(ing) through.

'Durchmesser m (-s/-) diameter.

durch'nässen v/t. (no -ge-, h) wet through, soak, drench.

'durch|nehmen v/t. (irr. nehmen, sep., -ge-, h) go through or over (subject); '∼pausen v/t. (sep., -ge-, h) trace, calk (design, etc.).

durchqueren [durç'kveːrən] v/t. (no -ge-, h) cross, traverse.

'durch|rechnen v/t. (sep., -ge-, h) (re)calculate, check; '2reise f journey or way through; '∼reisen 1. ['∼raɪzən] v/i. (sep., -ge-, sein) travel or pass through; 2. [∼'raɪzən] v/t. (no -ge-, h) travel over or through or across; '2reisende m, f (-n/-n) person travel(l)ing through. Am. a. transient; ⛟ through passenger; '∼reißen (irr. reißen, sep., -ge-) 1. v/i. (sein) tear, break; 2. v/t. (h) tear

asunder, tear in two; ∼schauen (h) 1. ['∼ʃaʊən] v/i. and v/t. (sep., -ge-) look through; 2. fig. [∼'ʃaʊən] v/t. (no -ge-) see through.

'durchscheinen v/i. (irr. scheinen, sep., -ge-, h) shine through; '∼d adj. translucent; transparent.

'durchscheuern v/t. (sep., -ge-, h) rub through; ∼schießen (irr. schießen) 1. ['∼ʃiːsən] v/i. (sep., -ge-, h) shoot through; 2. ['∼] v/i. (sep., -ge-, sein) water: shoot or race through; 3. [∼'ʃiːsən] v/t. (no -ge-, h) shoot s.th. through; typ.: space out (lines); interleave (book).

'Durchschlag m colander, strainer; carbon copy; 2en (irr. schlagen) 1. ['∼ʃlaːgən] v/t. (sep., -ge-, h) break or pass through; strain (peas, etc.); sich ∼ get along, make one's way; 2. ['∼] v/i. (sep., -ge-, h) typ. come through; take or have effect; 3. [∼'ʃlaːgən] v/t. (no -ge-, h) pierce; bullet: penetrate; 2end adj. effective, telling; ∼papier ['∼k-] n copying paper.

durchschneiden v/t. (irr. schneiden, h) 1. ['∼ʃnaɪdən] (sep., -ge-) cut through; 2. [∼'ʃnaɪdən] (no -ge-) cut through, cut in two.

'Durchschnitt m cutting through; ⊕ section, profile; A intersection; fig. average; im ∼ on an average; '2lich 1. adj. average; normal; 2. adv. on an average; normally; '∼swert m average value.

'durch|sehen (irr. sehen, sep., -ge-, h) 1. v/i. see or look through; 2. v/t. see or look through s.th.; look s.th. over, go over s.th.; '∼seihen v/t. (sep., -ge-, h) filter, strain; ∼setzen v/t. (h) 1. ['∼zetsən] (sep., -ge-) put (plan, etc.) through; force through; seinen Kopf ∼ have one's way; sich ∼ opinion, etc.: gain acceptance; 2. [∼'zetsən] (no -ge-) intersperse.

'Durchsicht f looking through or over; examination; correction; typ. reading; '2ig adj. glass, water, etc.: transparent; fig. clear, lucid; '∼igkeit f (-/no pl.) transparency; fig. clarity, lucidity.

'durch|sickern v/i. (sep., -ge-, sein) seep or ooze through; news, etc.: leak out; ∼sieben v/t. (h) 1. ['∼ziːbən] (sep., -ge-) sieve, sift; bolt (flour); 2. [∼'ziːbən] (no -ge-) riddle (with bullets); '∼sprechen v/t. (irr. sprechen, sep., -ge-, h) discuss, talk over; ∼stechen v/t. (irr. stechen, h) 1. ['∼ʃtɛçən] (sep., -ge-) stick (needle, etc.) through s.th.; stick through s.th.; 2. [∼'ʃtɛçən] (no -ge-) pierce; cut through (dike, etc.); '∼stecken v/t. (sep., -ge-, h) pass or stick through.

'Durchstich m cut(ting).

durch'stöbern v/t. (no -ge-, h) ransack (room, pockets, etc.); rummage through (*drawers*, *papers*, etc.).

**'durchstreichen** v/t. (*irr. streichen*, *sep.*, -*ge*-. *h*) strike *or* cross out, cancel.

**durch'streifen** v/t. (*no -ge*-, *h*) roam *or* wander through *or* over *or* across.

**durch'such|en** v/t. (*no -ge*-, *h*) search (*a.* 🔫); 2**ung** *f* (-/-*en*) search.

**durchtrieben** *adj.* [durç'tri:bən] cunning, artful; 2**heit** *f* (-/*no pl.*) cunning, artfulness.

**durch'wachen** v/t. (*no -ge*-, *h*) pass (*the night*) waking.

**durch'wachsen** *adj. bacon*: streaky.

**durchwandern 1.** ['~vandərn] v/i. (*sep.*, -*ge*-, *sein*) walk *or* pass through; **2.** [~'vandərn] v/t. (*no -ge*-, *h*) walk *or* pass through (*place*, *area*, etc.).

**durch'weben** v/t. (*no -ge*-, *h*) interweave; *fig. a.* intersperse.

**durch|weichen 1.** ['~vaiçən] v/i. (*sep.*, -*ge*-, *sein*) soak; **2.** [~'vaiçən] v/t. (*no -ge*-, *h*) soak, drench; '~**winden** v/refl. (*irr. winden*, *sep.*, -*ge*-, *h*) worm *or* thread one's way through; **~wühlen** (*h*) **1.** *fig.* ['~vy:lən] v/refl. (*sep.*, -*ge*-) work one's way through; **2.** [~'vy:lən] v/t. (*no -ge*-) rummage; '~**zählen** v/t. (*sep.*, -*ge*-, *h*) count; **~ziehen** (*irr. ziehen*) **1.** ['~tsi:ən] v/i. (*sep.*, -*ge*-, *sein*) pass *or* go *or* come *or* march through; **2.** [~] v/t. (*sep.*, -*ge*-, *h*) pull (*thread*, etc.) through; **3.** [~'tsi:ən] v/t. (*no -ge*-, *h*) go *or* travel through; *scent*, etc.: fill, pervade (*room*, etc.).

**durch'zucken** v/t. (*no -ge*-, *h*) flash through.

**'Durchzug** *m* passage through; draught, *Am.* draft.

**'durchzwängen** v/refl. (*sep.*, -*ge*-, *h*) squeeze o.s. through.

**dürfen** ['dyrfən] (*irr.*, *h*) **1.** v/i. (*ge*-): *ich darf* (*nicht*) I am (not) allowed to; **2.** v/aux. (*no -ge*-): ich darf *inf.* I am permitted *or* allowed to *inf.*; I may *inf.*; du darfst nicht *inf.* you must not *inf.*; *iro.*: wenn ich bitten darf if you please.

**durfte** ['durftə] *pret. of* dürfen.

**dürftig** *adj.* ['dyrftiç] poor; scanty.

**dürr** *adj.* [dyr] *wood, leaves*, etc.: dry; *land*: barren, arid; *p.* gaunt, lean, skinny; 2**e** *f* (-/-*n*) dryness; barrenness; leanness.

**Durst** [durst] *m* (-*es*/*no pl.*) thirst (*nach* for); ~ haben be thirsty.

**dürsten** ['dyrstən] v/i. (*ge*-, *h*): ~ *nach* thirst for.

**'durstig** *adj.* thirsty (*nach* for).

**Dusche** ['duʃə] *f* (-/-*n*) shower (-*bath*); 2**n** v/refl. *and* v/i. (*ge*-, *h*) have a shower(-bath).

**Düse** ['dy:zə] *f* (-/-*n*) ⊕ nozzle; ✈ jet; **~nantrieb** ['~n?-] *m* jet propulsion; *mit* ~ jet-propelled; '~**n-flugzeug** *n* jet(-propelled) aircraft, F jet; '~**njäger** ✈ *m* jet fighter.

**düster** *adj.* ['dy:stər] dark, gloomy (*both a. fig.*); *light*: dim; *fig.*: sad; depressing; 2**heit** *f* (-/*no pl.*), 2**keit** *f* (-/*no pl.*) gloom(iness).

**Dutzend** ['dutsənt] *n* (-*s*/-*e*) dozen; *ein* ~ *Eier* a dozen eggs; ~*e von Leuten* dozens of people; 2**weise** *adv.* by the dozen, in dozens.

**Dynam|ik** [dy'na:mik] *f* (-/*no pl.*) dynamics; 2**isch** *adj.* dynamic(al).

**Dynamit** [dyna'mi:t] *n* (-*s*/*no pl.*) dynamite.

**Dynamo** [dy'na:mo] *m* (-*s*/-*s*), **~ma-schine** *f* dynamo, generator.

**D-Zug** ['de:tsu:k] *m* express train.

# E

**Ebbe** ['ɛbə] *f* (-/-*n*) ebb(-tide); low tide; 2**n** v/i. (*ge*-, *sein*) ebb.

**eben** ['e:bən] **1.** *adj.* even, plain, level; ✈ plane; *zu* ~*er Erde* on the ground floor, *Am.* on the first floor; **2.** *adv.* exactly; just; ~ *erst* just now; 2**bild** *n* image, likeness; **~bürtig** *adj.* ['~byrtiç] of equal birth; *j-m* ~ *sein* be a match for s.o., be s.o.'s equal; '~**da** *adv.*, '~**daselbst** *adv.* at the very (same) place, just there; *quoting books*: ibidem (*abbr.* ib., ibid.); ~**der**, '~**die**, '~**das** *dem. pron.* = '~**der-selbe**, '~**die'selbe**, '~**das'selbe** *dem. pron.* the very (same); '~

**des'wegen** *adv.* for that very reason.

**Ebene** ['e:bənə] *f* (-/-*n*) plain; ✈ plane; *fig.* level.

**'eben|erdig** *adj. and adv.* at street level; on the ground floor, *Am.* on the first floor; '~**falls** *adv.* likewise; 2**holz** *n* ebony; '~**maß** *n* symmetry; harmony; regularity (*of features*); '~**mäßig** *adj.* symmetrical; harmonious; regular; '~**so** *adv.* just so; just as ...; likewise; '~**sosehr** *adv.*, '~**soviel** *adv.* just as much; '~**sowenig** *adv.* just as little *or* few (*pl.*), no more.

**Eber** zo. ['e:bər] m (-s/-) boar; '~esche ♀ f mountain-ash.

**ebnen** ['e:bnən] v/t. (ge-, h) level; fig. smooth.

**Echo** ['εço] n (-s/-s) echo.

**echt** adj. [εçt] genuine; true; pure; real; colour: fast; document: authentic; '2heit f (-/no pl.) genuineness, purity; reality; fastness; authenticity.

**Eck** [εk] n (-[e]s/-e) s. Ecke; '~ball m sports: corner-kick; '~e f (-/-n) corner; edge; '2ig adj. angular; fig. awkward; '~platz m corner-seat; '~stein m corner-stone; '~zahn m canine tooth.

**edel** adj. ['e:dəl] noble; min. precious; organs of the body: vital; '~denkend adj. noble-minded; '2-mann m nobleman; '2mut m generosity; ~mütig adj. ['~my:tiç] noble-minded, generous; '2stein m precious stone; gem.

**Edikt** [e'dikt] n (-[e]s/-e) edict.

**Efeu** ♀ ['e:fɔy] m (-s/no pl.) ivy.

**Effekt** [ε'fεkt] m (-[e]s/-e) effect; ~en pl. effects pl.; ✝: securities pl.; stocks pl., ~enhandel m dealing in stocks; ~hascherei [~haʃə'raɪ] f (-/-en) claptrap; 2iv adj. [~'ti:v] effective; 2uieren [~u'i:rən] v/t. (no -ge-, h) effect; execute, Am. a. fill; 2voll adj. effective, striking.

**egal** adj. [e'gɑ:l] equal; F all the same.

**Egge** ['εgə] f (-/-n) harrow; '2n v/t. (ge-, h) harrow.

**Egois|mus** [ego'ismus] m (-/Egoismen) ego(t)ism; ~t m (-en/-en) ego-(t)ist; 2tisch adj. selfish, ego(t)istic(al).

**ehe**[1] cj. ['e:ə] before.

**Ehe**[2] [~ə] f (-/-n) marriage; matrimony; '~anbahnung f (-/-en) matrimonial agency; '~brecher m (-s/-) adulterer; '~brecherin f (-/-nen) adulteress; '2brecherisch adj. adulterous; '~bruch m adultery; '~frau f wife; '~gatte m, '~gattin f spouse; '~leute pl. married people pl.; '2lich adj. conjugal; child: legitimate; '~losigkeit f (-/no pl.) celibacy; single life.

**ehemal**|ig adj. ['e:əma:liç] former, ex-...; old; '~s adv. formerly.

**'Ehe|mann** m husband; '~paar n married couple.

**'eher** adv. sooner; rather; more likely; je ~ desto besser the sooner the better.

**'Ehering** m wedding ring.

**ehern** adj. ['e:ərn] brazen, of brass.

**'Ehe|scheidung** f divorce; '~schließung f (-/-en) (contraction of) marriage; '~stand m (-[e]s/no pl.) married state, matrimony; '~stifter m, '~stifterin f (-/-nen) matchmaker; '~vermittlung f s. Eheanbahnung; '~versprechen n promise of marriage; '~vertrag m marriage contract.

**Ehrabschneider** ['e:r⁹apʃnaɪdər] m (-s/-) slanderer.

**'ehrbar** adj. hono(u)rable, respectable; modest; '2keit f (-/no pl.) respectability; modesty.

**Ehre** ['e:rə] f (-/-n) hono(u)r; zu ~n (gen.) in hono(u)r of; '2n v/t. (ge-, h) hono(u)r; esteem.

**'ehren|amtlich** adj. honorary; '2-bürger m honorary citizen; '2doktor m honorary doctor; '2erklärung f (full) apology; '2gast m guest of hono(u)r; '2gericht n court of hono(u)r; '~haft adj. hono(u)rable; '2kodex m code of hono(u)r; 2legion ['~legio:n] f (-/no pl.) Legion of Hono(u)r; '2mann m man of hono(u)r; '2mitglied n honorary member; '2platz m place of hono(u)r; '2recht n: bürgerliche ~e pl. civil rights pl.; '2rettung f rehabilitation; '~rührig adj. defamatory; '2sache f affair of hono(u)r; point of hono(u)r; '~voll adj. hono(u)rable; '~wert adj. hono(u)rable; '2wort n (-[e]s/-e) word of hono(u)r.

**ehr|erbietig** adj. ['e:r⁹εrbi:tiç] respectful; '2erbietung f (-/-en) reverence; '2furcht f (-/♀ ~en) respect; awe; '~furchtgebietend adj. awe-inspiring, awesome; '~fürchtig adj. ['~fyrçtiç] respectful; '2gefühl n (-[e]s/no pl.) sense of hono(u)r; '2geiz m ambition; '~geizig adj. ambitious.

**'ehrlich** adj. honest; commerce, game: fair; opinion: candid; ~ währt am längsten honesty is the best policy; '2keit f (-/no pl.) honesty; fairness.

**'ehrlos** adj. dishono(u)rable, infamous; '2igkeit f (-/-en) dishonesty, infamy.

**'ehr|sam** adj. s. ehrbar; '2ung f (-/-en) hono(u)r (conferred on s.o.); '~vergessen adj. dishono(u)rable, infamous; '2verlust ₺₺ m (-es/no pl.) loss of civil rights; '~würdig adj. venerable, reverend.

**ei**[1] int. [aɪ] ah! indeed!

**Ei**[2] [~] n (-[e]s/-er) egg; physiol.ovum.

**Eibe** ♀ ['aɪbə] f (-/-n) yew(-tree).

**Eiche** ♀ ['aɪçə] f (-/-n) oak(-tree); ~l ['~l] f (-/-n) ♀ acorn; cards: club; '2häher orn. ['~hε:ər] m (-s/-) jay.

**eichen**[1] ['aɪçən] v/t. (ge-, h) ga(u)ge.

**eichen**[2] adj. [~] oaken, of oak.

**Eich|hörnchen** zo. ['aɪçhœrnçən] n (-s/-) squirrel; '~maß n standard.

**Eid** [aɪt] m (-[e]s/-e) oath; '2brüchig adj.: ~ werden break one's oath.

**Eidechse** zo.['aɪdεksə] f (-/-n) lizard.

**eidesstattlich** ₺₺ adj. ['aɪdəs-] in lieu of (an) oath; ~e Erklärung statutory declaration.

**'eidlich 1.** *adj.* sworn; **2.** *adv.* on oath.

**'Eidotter** *m, n* yolk.

**'Eier|kuchen** *m* omelet(te), pancake; **'~schale** *f* egg-shell; **'~stock** *anat. m* ovary; **'~uhr** *f* egg-timer.

**Eifer** ['aifər] *m* (-s/no pl.) zeal; eagerness; ardo(u)r; **'~er** *m* (-s/-) zealot; **'~sucht** *f* (-/no pl.) jealousy; **'2süchtig** *adj.* jealous (auf acc. of).

**eifrig** *adj.* ['aifriç] zealous, eager; ardent.

**eigen** *adj.* ['aigən] own; particular; strange, odd; *in compounds:* ...-owned; peculiar (dat. to); **'2art** *f* peculiarity; **'~artig** *adj.* peculiar; singular; **2brötler** ['~brø:tlər] *m* (-s/-) odd *or* eccentric person, crank; **'2gewicht** *n* dead weight; **~händig** *adj. and adv.* ['~hɛndiç] with one's own hands; **'2heim** *n* house of one's own; homestead; **'2heit** *f* (-/-en) peculiarity; oddity; *of language:* idiom; **'2liebe** *f* self-love; **'2lob** *n* self-praise; **'~mächtig** *adj.* arbitrary; **'2name** *m* proper name; **~nützig** *adj.* ['~nytsiç] self-interested; selfish; **'~s** *adv.* expressly, specially; on purpose.

**'Eigenschaft** *f* (-/-en) quality (of s.o.); property (of s.th.); *in* s-r **~** als in his capacity as; **'~swort** *gr. n* (-[e]s/~er) adjective.

**'Eigensinn** *m* (-[e]s/no pl.) obstinacy; **'2ig** *adj.* wil(l)ful, obstinate.

**'eigentlich 1.** *adj.* proper; actual; true, real; **2.** *adv.* properly (speaking).

**'Eigentum** *n* (-s/~er) property.

**Eigentüm|er** ['aigənty:mər] *m* (-s/-) owner, proprietor; **'2lich** *adj.* peculiar; odd; **'~lichkeit** *f* (-/-en) peculiarity.

**'Eigentums|recht** *n* ownership; copyright; **'~wohnung** *f* freehold flat.

**'eigenwillig** *adj.* self-willed; *fig.* individual.

**eign|en** ['aignən] *v/refl.* (ge-, h): sich **~** für be suited for; **'2ung** *f* (-/-en) aptitude, suitability.

**'Eil|bote** ℀ *m* express messenger; durch **~**n by special delivery; **'~brief** ℀ *m* express letter, *Am.* special delivery letter.

**Eile** ['ailə] *f* (-/no pl.) haste, speed; hurry; **'2n** *v/i.* (ge-. sein) hasten, make haste; hurry; *letter, affair:* be urgent; **2nds** *adv.* ['~ts] quickly, speedily.

**'Eil|fracht** *f,* **~gut** *n* express goods *pl., Am.* fast freight; **'2ig** *adj.* hasty, speedy; urgent; es **~** haben be in a hurry.

**Eimer** ['aimər] *m* (-s/-) bucket, pail.

**ein** [ain] **1.** *adj.* one; **2.** *indef. art.* a, an.

**einander** *adv.* [ai'nandər] one another; each other.

**ein|arbeiten** ['ain?-] *v/t.* (sep., -ge-, h): j-n **~** in (acc.) make s.o. acquainted with; **~armig** *adj.* ['ain?-] one-armed; **~äschern** ['ain?ɛʃərn] *v/t.* (sep., -ge-, h) burn to ashes; cremate (dead body); **'2äscherung** *f* (-/-en) cremation; **~atmen** ['ain?-] *v/t.* (sep., -ge-, h) breathe, inhale; **~äugig** *adj.* ['ain?ɔygiç] one-eyed.

**'Einbahnstraße** *f* one-way street.

**'einbalsamieren** *v/t.* (sep., no -ge-, h) embalm.

**'Einband** *m* (-[e]s/~e) binding; cover.

**'ein|bauen** *v/t.* (sep., -ge-, h) build in; install (engine, etc.); **'~behalten** *v/t.* (irr. halten, sep., no -ge- h) detain; **'~berufen** *v/t.* (irr. rufen, sep., no -ge-, h) convene; ℀ call up, *Am.* induct.

**'einbett|en** *v/t.* (sep., -ge-, h) embed; **'2zimmer** *n* single(-bedded) room.

**'einbild|en** *v/refl.* (sep., -ge-, h) fancy, imagine; **'2ung** *f* imagination, fancy; conceit.

**'einbinden** *v/t.* (irr. binden, sep., -ge-, h) bind (books).

**'Einblick** *m* insight (in acc. into).

**'einbrechen** (irr. brechen, sep., -ge-) **1.** *v/t.* (h) break open; **2.** *v/i.* (sein) break in; of night, etc.: set in; **~** in (acc.) break into (house).

**'Einbrecher** *m at night:* burglar; *by day:* housebreaker.

**'Einbruch** *m* ℀ invasion; house-breaking, burglary; bei **~** der Nacht at nightfall; **'~(s)diebstahl** *m* house-breaking, burglary.

**einbürger|n** ['ainbyrgərn] *v/t.* (sep., -ge-, h) naturalize; **'2ung** *f* (-/-en) naturalization.

**'Ein|buße** *f* loss; **'2büßen** *v/t.* (sep., -ge-, h) lose, forfeit.

**ein|dämmen** ['aindɛmən] *v/t.* (sep., -ge-, h) dam (up); embank (river); *fig.* check; **'~deutig** *adj.* unequivocal; clear, plain.

**'eindring|en** *v/i.* (irr. dringen, sep., -ge-, sein) enter; penetrate; intrude; **~** in (acc.) penetrate (into); force one's way into; invade (country); **'~lich** *adj.* urgent; **2ling** ['~liŋ] *m* (-s/-e) intruder; invader.

**'Eindruck** *m* (-[e]s/~e) impression.

**'ein|drücken** *v/t.* (sep., -ge-, h) press in; crush (in) (hat); break (pane); **'~drucksvoll** *adj.* impressive; **~engen** ['ain?-] *v/t.* (sep., -ge-, h) narrow; *fig.* limit.

**einer¹** ['ainər], **'~e, '~(e)s** *indef. pron.* one.

**Einer²** [~] *m* (-s/-) ℀ unit, digit; *rowing:* single sculler, skiff.

**einerlei** ['ainər'lai] **1.** *adj.* of the same kind; immaterial; es ist mir **~** it is all the same to me; **2.** **2** *n* (-s/no pl.) sameness; monotony; humdrum (of one's existence).

**einerseits** *adv.* ['aɪnər'zaɪts] on the one hand.

**einfach** *adj.* ['aɪnfax] simple; single; plain; *meal:* frugal; *ticket:* single, *Am.* one-way; '**2heit** *f* (-/no *pl.*) simplicity.

**einfädeln** ['aɪnfɛːdəln] *v/t.* (*sep.*, -ge-, *h*) thread; *fig.* start, set on foot; contrive.

'**Einfahrt** *f* entrance, entry.

'**Einfall** *m* ✕ invasion; idea, inspiration; '**2en** *v/i.* (*irr. fallen, sep.*, -ge-, *sein*) fall in, collapse; break in (*on a conversation*), interrupt, cut short; chime in; ♪ join in; invade; *j-m* ~ occur to s.o.

**Ein|falt** ['aɪnfalt] *f* (-/no *pl.*) simplicity, silliness; **2fältig** *adj.* ['~fɛltiç] simple; silly; '**~faltspinsel** *m* simpleton, *Am.* F sucker.

**ein|farbig** *adj.* one-colo(u)red, uni-colo(u)red; plain; '**~fassen** *v/t.* (*sep.*, -ge-, *h*) border; set (*precious stone*); '**2fassung** *f* border; setting; '**~fetten** *v/t.* (*sep.*, -ge-, *h*) grease; oil; '**~finden** *v/refl.* (*irr. finden, sep.*, -ge-, *h*) appear; arrive; '**~flechten** *fig. v/t.* (*irr. flechten, sep.*, -ge-, *h*) put in, insert; '**~fließen** *v/i.* (*irr. fließen, sep.*, -ge-, *sein*) flow in; ~ *in* (*acc.*) flow into; ~ *lassen* mention in passing; '**~flößen** *v/t.* (*sep.*, -ge-, *h*) infuse.

'**Einfluß** *m* influx; *fig.* influence; '**2reich** *adj.* influential.

**ein|förmig** *adj.* ['aɪnfœrmiç] uniform; monotonous; **~frieden** ['~friːdən] *v/t.* (*sep.*, -ge-, *h*) fence, enclose; '**2friedung** *f* (-/-en) enclosure; '**~frieren** (*irr. frieren, sep.*, -ge-) **1.** *v/i.* (*sein*) freeze (in); **2.** *v/t.* (*h*) freeze (*food*); '**~fügen** *v/t.* (*sep.*, -ge-, *h*) put in; *fig.* insert; *sich* ~ fit in.

**Einfuhr** † ['aɪnfuːr] *f* (-/-en) import(ation); '**~bestimmungen** *f/pl.* import regulations *pl.*

'**einführen** *v/t.* (*sep.*, -ge-, *h*) † import; introduce (*s.o., custom*); insert; initiate; install (*s.o. in an office*).

'**Einfuhrwaren** † *f/pl.* imports *pl.*

'**Eingabe** *f* petition; application.

'**Eingang** *m* entrance; entry; arrival (*of goods*); *nach* ~ on receipt; '**~buch** † *n* book of entries.

'**eingeben** *v/t.* (*irr. geben, sep.*, -ge-, *h*) give, administer (*medicine*) (*dat. to*); prompt, suggest (*to*).

'**einge|bildet** *adj.* imaginary; conceited (*auf acc. of*); '**~boren** *adj.* native; '**2borene** *m, f* (-*n*/-*n*) native.

**Eingebung** ['aɪngeːbuŋ] *f* (-/-en) suggestion; inspiration.

**einge|denk** *adj.* ['aɪngədɛŋk] mindful (*gen. of*); '**~fallen** *adj.* *eyes, cheeks:* sunken, hollow; emaciated; **~fleischt** *fig. adj.* ['~gəflaɪʃt] inveterate; confirmed; ~*er Junggeselle* confirmed bachelor.

'**eingehen** (*irr. gehen, sep.*, -ge-) **1.** *v/i.* (*sein*) mail, *goods:* come in, arrive; ♀, *animal:* die; cease (to exist); *material:* shrink; ~ *auf* (*acc.*) agree to; enter into; **2.** *v/t.* (*h, sein*) enter into (*relationship*); contract (*marriage*); *ein Risiko* ~ run a risk, *esp. Am.* take a chance; *e-n Vergleich* ~ come to terms; *Verbindlichkeiten* ~ incur liabilities; *e-e Wette* ~ make a bet; *eingegangene Gelder* *n/pl.* receipts *pl.*; '**~d** *adj.* detailed; thorough; *examination:* close.

**Eingemachte** ['aɪngəmaxtə] *n* (-*n*/ no *pl.*) preserves *pl.*; pickles *pl.*

'**eingemeinden** *v/t.* (*sep., no* -ge-, *h*) incorporate (*dat.* into).

'**einge|nommen** *adj.* partial (*für* to); prejudiced (*gegen* against); *von sich* ~ conceited; '**2sandt** ✎ *n* (-*s*/-*s*) letter to the editor; **~schnappt** F *fig. adj.* ['~ʃnapt] offended, touchy; '**~sessen** *adj.* long-established; '**2ständnis** *n* confession, avowal; '**~stehen** *v/t.* (*irr. stehen, sep., no* -ge-, *h*) confess, avow.

**Eingeweide** *anat.* ['aɪngəvaɪdə] *pl.* viscera *pl.*; intestines *pl.*; bowels *pl.*; *esp. of animals:* entrails *pl.*

'**einge|wöhnen** *v/refl.* (*sep., no* -ge-, *h*) accustom o.s. (*in acc.* to); acclimatize o.s., *Am.* acclimate o.s. (*to*); get used (to).

**eingewurzelt** *adj.* ['~gəvurtsəlt] deep-rooted, inveterate.

'**eingießen** *v/t.* (*irr. gießen, sep.*, -ge-, *h*) pour in *or* out.

**eingleisig** *adj.* ['aɪnglaɪziç] single-track.

'**ein|graben** *v/t.* (*irr. graben, sep.*, -ge-, *h*) dig in; bury; engrave; *sich* ~ ✕ dig o.s. in, entrench o.s.; *fig.* engrave itself (*on one's memory*); '**~gravieren** *v/t.* (*sep., no* -ge-, *h*) engrave.

'**eingreifen 1.** *v/i.* (*irr. greifen, sep.*, -ge-, *h*) intervene; ~ *in* (*acc.*) interfere with; encroach on (*s.o.'s rights*); *in die Debatte* ~ join in the debate; **2.** ♀ *n* (-*s*/no *pl.*) intervention.

'**Eingriff** *m* *fig.* encroachment; ✂ operation.

'**einhaken** *v/t.* (*sep.*, -ge-, *h*) fasten; *sich bei j-m* ~ take s.o.'s arm.

'**Einhalt** *m* (-[e]*s*/no *pl.*): ~ *gebieten* (*dat.*) put a stop to; '**2en** *fig.* (*irr. halten, sep.*, -ge-, *h*) **1.** *v/t.* observe, keep; **2.** *v/i.* stop, leave off (*zu tun* doing).

'**ein|hängen** [*irr. hängen,*] *v/t.* (*sep.*, -ge-, *h*) **1.** *v/t.* hang in; hang up, replace (*receiver*); *sich bei j-m* ~ take s.o.'s arm, link arms with s.o.; **2.** *teleph.* *v/i.* hang up; '**~heften** *v/t.* (*sep.*, -ge-, *h*) sew *or* stitch in.

'**einheimisch** *adj.* native (*in dat.*

to), indigenous (to) (*a.* &); ✠ endemic; *product*: home-grown; '²e *m, f* (*-n/-n*) native; resident.

**'Einheit** *f* (*-/-en*) unity; oneness; ℞, *phys.*, ⚒ unit; '²lich *adj.* uniform; '~preis ✝ *m* standard price.

**'einheizen** (*sep.*, *-ge-, h*) 1. *v/i.* make a fire; 2. *v/t.* heat (*stove*).

**einhellig** *adj.* ['aɪnhɛlɪç] unanimous.

**'einholen** (*sep.*, *-ge-, h*) 1. *v/t.* catch up with, overtake; make up for (*lost time*); make (*inquiries*); take (*order*); seek (*advice*); ask for (*permission*); buy; 2. *v/i.*: ~ gehen go shopping.

**'Einhorn** *zo. n* unicorn.

**'einhüllen** *v/t.* (*sep.*, *-ge-, h*) wrap (up *or* in), envelop.

**einig** *adj.* ['aɪnɪç] united; ~ *sein* agree; *nicht* ~ *sein* differ (*über acc.* about); ~e *indef. pron.* ['~gə] several; some; '~en ['~ɪgən] *v/t.* (*ge-, h*) unite; *sich* ~ come to terms; ~ermaßen *adv.* ['~gər'ma:sən] in some measure; somewhat; '~es *indef. pron.* ['~gəs] some(thing); '²keit *f* (*-/no pl.*) unity; concord; ²ung ['~g-] *f* (*-/-en*) union; agreement.

**ein|impfen** ['aɪn²-] *v/t.* (*sep.*, *-ge-, h*) ✠ inoculate (*a. fig.*); '~jagen *v/t.* (*sep.*, *-ge-, h*): *j-m Furcht* ~ scare s.o.

**einjährig** *adj.* ['aɪnje:rɪç] one-yearold; *esp.* ♀ annual; *animal*: yearling.

**'ein|kalkulieren** *v/t.* (*sep.*, *no -ge-, h*) take into account, allow for; '~kassieren *v/t.* (*sep.*, *no -ge-, h*) cash; collect.

**'Einkauf** *m* purchase; *Einkäufe machen s.* einkaufen 2; '²en (*sep.*, *-ge-, h*) 1. *v/t.* buy, purchase; 2. *v/i.* make purchases, go shopping.

**'Einkäufer** *m* buyer.

**'Einkaufs|netz** *n* string bag; '~preis ✝ *m* purchase price; '~tasche *f* shopping-bag.

**'ein|kehren** *v/i.* (*sep.*, *-ge-, sein*) put up *or* stay (*at an inn*); '~kerben *v/t.* (*sep.*, *-ge-, h*) notch; '~kerkern *v/t.* (*sep.*, *-ge-, h*) imprison; '~klagen *v/t.* (*sep.*, *-ge-, h*) sue for; '~klammern *v/t.* (*sep.*, *-ge-, h*) *typ.* bracket; put in brackets.

**'Einklang** *m* unison; harmony.

**'ein|kleiden** *v/t.* (*sep.*, *-ge-, h*) clothe; fit out; '~klemmen *v/t.* (*sep.*, *-ge-, h*) squeeze (in); jam; '~klinken (*sep.*, *-ge-*) 1. *v/t.* (*h*) latch; 2. *v/i.* (*sein*) latch; engage; '~knicken (*sep.*, *-ge-*) *v/t.* (*h*) *and v/i.* (*sein*) bend in, break; '~kochen (*sep.*, *ge-*) 1. *v/t.* (*h*) preserve; 2. *v/i.* (*sein*) boil down *or* away.

**'Einkommen** *n* (*-s/-*) income, revenue; '~steuer *f* income-tax.

**'einkreisen** *v/t.* (*sep.*, *-ge-, h*) encircle.

**Einkünfte** ['aɪnkynftə] *pl.* income, revenue.

**'einlad|en** *v/t.* (*irr. laden*, *sep.*, *-ge-, h*) load (in) (*goods*); *fig.* invite; '²ung *f* invitation.

**'Einlage** *f* enclosure (*in letter*); ✝ investment; deposit (*of money*); *gambling*: stake; inserted piece; ♫ arch-support; temporary filling (*of tooth*); '²rn ✝ *v/t.* (*sep.*, *-ge-, h*) store (up).

**Einlaß** ['aɪnlas] *m* (*Einlasses/Einlässe*) admission, admittance.

**'einlassen** *v/t.* (*irr. lassen*, *sep.*, *-ge-, h*) let in, admit; ~ in (*acc.*) ⊕ imbed in; *sich* ~ in *or* auf (*both acc.*) engage in, enter into.

**'ein|laufen** *v/i.* (*irr. laufen*, *sep.*, *-ge-, sein*) come in, arrive; *ship*: enter; *material*: shrink; '~leben *v/refl.* (*sep.*, *-ge-, h*) accustom o.s. (in *acc.* to).

**'einlege|n** *v/t.* (*sep.*, *-ge-, h*) lay *or* put in; insert; ⊕ inlay; deposit (*money*); pickle; preserve (*fruit*); *Berufung* ~ lodge an appeal (*bei* to); *Ehre* ~ *mit* gain hono(u)r *or* credit by; '²sohle *f* insole, sock.

**'einleit|en** *v/t.* (*sep.*, *-ge-, h*) start; introduce; '~end *adj.* introductory; '²ung *f* introduction.

**'ein|lenken** *fig. v/i.* (*sep.*, *-ge-, h*) come round; '~leuchten *v/i.* (*sep.*, *-ge-, h*) be evident *or* obvious; '~liefern *v/t.* (*sep.*, *-ge-, h*) deliver (up); *in ein Krankenhaus* ~ take to a hospital, *Am.* hospitalize; '~lösen *v/t.* (*sep.*, *-ge-, h*) ransom (*prisoner*); redeem (*pledge*); ✝ hono(u)r (*bill*); cash (*cheque*); ✝ meet (*bill*); '~machen *v/t.* (*sep.*, *-ge-, h*) preserve (*fruit*); tin, *Am.* can.

**'einmal** *adv.* once; one day; *auf* ~ all at once; *es war* ~ once (upon a time) there was; *nicht* ~ not even; '²eins *n* (*-/-*) multiplication table; '~ig *adj.* single; unique.

**'Einmarsch** *m* marching in, entry; '²ieren *v/i.* (*sep.*, *no -ge-, sein*) march in, enter.

**'ein|mengen** *v/refl.* (*sep.*, *-ge-, h*), '~mischen *v/refl.* (*sep.*, *-ge-, h*) meddle, interfere (*in acc.* with), *esp. Am. sl.* butt in.

**'Einmündung** *f* junction (*of roads*); mouth (*of river*).

**einmütig** *adj.* ['aɪnmy:tɪç] unanimous; '²keit *f* (*-/no pl.*) unanimity.

**Einnahme** ['aɪnna:mə] *f* (*-/-n*) ⚒ taking, capture; *mst* ~n *pl.* takings *pl.*, receipts *pl.*

**'einnehmen** *v/t.* (*irr. nehmen*, *sep.*, *-ge-, h*) take (*meal*, *position*, ⚒); ✝ take (*money*); ✝ earn, make (*money*); take up, occupy (*room*); *fig.* captivate; '~d *adj.* taking, engaging, captivating.

**'einnicken** *v/i.* (*sep.*, *-ge-, sein*) doze *or* drop off.

**Einöde** ['aɪnʲ-] *f* desert, solitude.
**ein|ordnen** ['aɪnʲ-] *v/t.* (*sep.*, -ge-, *h*) arrange in proper order; classify; file (*letters*, *etc.*); '**~packen** *v/t.* (*sep.*, -ge-, *h*) pack up; wrap up; '**~pferchen** *v/t.* (*sep.*, -ge-, *h*) pen in; *fig.* crowd, cram; '**~pflanzen** *v/t.* (*sep.*, -ge-, *h*) plant; *fig.* implant; '**~pökeln** *v/t.* (*sep.*, -ge-, *h*) pickle, salt; '**~prägen** *v/t.* (*sep.*, -ge-, *h*) imprint; impress; *sich* **~** imprint itself; commit *s.th.* to one's memory; '**~quartieren** *v/t.* (*sep.*, *no* -ge-, *h*) quarter, billet; '**~rahmen** *v/t.* (*sep.*, -ge-, *h*) frame; '**~räumen** *fig. v/t.* (*sep.*, -ge-, *h*) grant, concede; '**~rechnen** *v/t.* (*sep.*, -ge-, *h*) comprise, include; '**~reden** (*sep.*, -ge-, *h*) **1.** *v/t.*: *j-m* **~** persuade *or* talk *s.o.* into (*doing*) *s.th.*; **2.** *v/i.*: *auf j-n* **~** talk insistently to s.o.; '**~reichen** *v/t.* (*sep.*, -ge-, *h*) hand in, send in, present; '**~reihen** *v/t.* (*sep.*, -ge-, *h*) insert (*unter acc.* in); class (with); place (among); *sich* **~** take one's place.
**einreihig** *adj.* ['aɪnraiç] *jacket:* single-breasted.
**'Einreise** *f* entry; '**~erlaubnis** *f*, '**~genehmigung** *f* entry permit.
**'ein|reißen** (*irr.* reißen, *sep.*, -ge-) **1.** *v/t.* (*h*) tear; pull down (*building*); **2.** *v/i.* (*sein*) tear; *abuse, etc.*: spread; '**~renken** ['~rɛŋkən] *v/t.* (*sep.*, -ge-, *h*) ⚕ set; *fig.* set right.
**'einricht|en** *v/t.* (*sep.* -ge-, *h*) establish; equip; arrange; set up (*shop*); furnish (*flat*); es **~** manage; *sich* **~** establish o.s., settle down; economize; *sich* **~** *auf* (*acc.*) prepare for; '**Qung** *f* establishment; arrangement, *esp. Am.* setup; equipment; furniture; fittings *pl.* (*of shop*); institution.
**'ein|rollen** *v/t.* (*sep.*, -ge-, *h*) roll up *or* in; *sich* **~** roll up; curl up; '**~rosten** *v/i.* (*sep.*, -ge-, *sein*) rust; screw, *etc.*: rust in; '**~rücken** (*sep.*, -ge-) **1.** *v/i.* (*sein*) enter, march in; ✕ join the army; **2.** *v/t.* (*h*) insert (*advertisement in a paper*); *typ.* indent (*line*, *word*, *etc.*); '**~rühren** *v/t.* (*sep.*, -ge-, *h*) stir (in).
**eins** *adj.* [aɪns] one.
**'einsam** *adj.* lonely, solitary; **'Qkeit** *f* (-/⚬, -en) loneliness, solitude.
**'einsammeln** *v/t.* (*sep.*, -ge-, *h*) gather; collect.
**'Einsatz** *m* inset; insertion (*of piece of material*); gambling: stake, pool; ♪ striking in, entry; employment; engagement (*a.* ✕); ✕ action, operation; *unter* **~** *s-s Lebens* at the risk of one's life.
**'ein|saugen** *v/t.* (*sep.*, -ge-, *h*) suck in; *fig.* imbibe; '**~schalten** (*sep.*, -ge-, *h*) insert; ⚡ switch *or* turn on; *den ersten Gang* **~** *mot.* go into first *or* bottom gear; *sich* **~**

intervene; '**~schärfen** *v/t.* (*sep.*, -ge-, *h*) inculcate (*dat.* upon); '**~schätzen** *v/t.* (*sep.*, -ge-, *h*) assess, appraise, estimate (*auf acc.* at); value (*a. fig.*); '**~schenken** *v/t.* (*sep.*, -ge-, *h*) pour in *or* out; '**~schicken** *v/t.* (*sep.*, -ge-, *h*) send in; '**~schieben** *v/t.* (*irr.* schieben, *sep.*, -ge-, *h*) insert; '**~schiffen** *v/t.* and *v/refl.* (*sep.*, -ge-, *h*) embark; **'Qschiffung** *f* (-/-en) embarkation; '**~schlafen** *v/i.* (*irr.* schlafen, *sep.*, -ge-, *sein*) fall asleep; **~schläfern** ['~ʃlɛːfərn] *v/t.* (*sep.*, -ge-, *h*) lull to sleep; ✊ narcotize.
**'Einschlag** *m* striking (*of lightning*); impact (*of missile*); *fig.* touch; '**Qen** (*irr.* schlagen, *sep.*, -ge-, *h*) **1.** *v/t.* drive in (*nail*); break (*in*); smash (*in*); wrap up; take (*road*), tuck in (*hem, etc.*); enter upon (*career*); **2.** *v/i.* shake hands; *lightning, missile:* strike; *fig.* be a success; *nicht* **~** fail; (*wie e-e Bombe*) **~** cause a sensation; *auf j-n* **~** belabour *s.o.*
**einschlägig** *adj.* ['aɪnʃlɛːgiç] relevant, pertinent.
**'Einschlagpapier** *n* wrapping-paper.
**'ein|schleichen** *v/refl.* (*irr.* schleichen, *sep.*, -ge-, *h*) creep *or* sneak in; '**~schleppen** *v/t.* (*sep.*, -ge-, *h*) ⚓ tow in; import (*disease*); '**~schleusen** *fig. v/t.* (*sep.*, -ge-, *h*) channel *or* let in; '**~schließen** *v/t.* (*irr.* schließen, *sep.*, -ge-, *h*) lock in *or* up; enclose; ✕ surround, encircle; *fig.* include; '**~schließlich** *prp.* (*gen.*) inclusive of; including, comprising; '**~schmeicheln** *v/refl.* (*sep.*, -ge-, *h*) ingratiate o.s. (*bei with*); '**~schmeichelnd** *adj.* insinuating; '**~schmuggeln** *v/t.* (*sep.*, -ge-, *h*) smuggle in; '**~schnappen** *v/i.* (*sep.*, -ge-, *sein*) catch; *fig. s.* eingeschnappt; '**~schneidend** *fig. adj.* incisive, drastic.
**'Einschnitt** *m* cut, incision; notch.
**'ein|schnüren** *v/t.* (*sep.*, -ge-, *h*) lace (up); '**~schränken** ['~ʃrɛŋkən] *v/t.* (*sep.*, -ge-, *h*) restrict, confine; reduce (*expenses*); *sich* **~** economize; **'Qschränkung** *f* (-/-en) restriction; reduction.
**'Einschreibe|brief** *m* registered letter; **'Qn** *v/t.* (*irr.* schreiben, *sep.*, -ge-, *h*) enter; book; enrol(l); ✕ enlist, enrol(l); ✉ register; *~ lassen* have registered; *sich* **~** enter one's name.
**'einschreiten 1.** *fig. v/i.* (*irr.* schreiten, *sep.*, -ge-, *sein*) step in, interpose, intervene; take action (*gegen* against); **2.** ⚥ *n* (-s/*no pl.*) intervention.
**'ein|schrumpfen** *v/i.* (*sep.*, -ge-, *sein*) shrink; '**~schüchtern** *v/t.* (*sep.*, -ge-, *h*) intimidate; bully; **'Qschüchterung** *f* (-/-en) intim-

idation; '~schulen *v/t.* (*sep., -ge-, h*) put to school.

'**Einschuß** *m* bullet-hole; ✝ invested capital.

'**ein|segnen** *v/t.* (*sep., -ge-, h*) consecrate; confirm (*children*); '**⁀segnung** *f* consecration; confirmation.

'**einsehen 1.** *v/t.* (*irr. sehen, sep., -ge-, h*) look into; *fig.*: see, comprehend; realize; **2.** ⁀ *n* (*-s/no pl.*): *ein ~ haben* show consideration.

'**einseifen** *v/t.* (*sep., -ge-, h*) soap; lather (*beard*); F *fig.* humbug (*s.o.*).

**einseitig** *adj.* ['aɪnzaɪtɪç] one-sided; 🜊, *pol.*, 🜊 unilateral.

'**einsend|en** *v/t.* ([*irr. senden*], *sep., -ge-, h*) send in; '**⁀er** *m* (*-s/-*) sender; contributor (*to a paper*).

'**einsetz|en** (*sep., -ge-, h*) **1.** *v/t.* set *or* put in; stake (*money*); insert; institute; instal(l), appoint (*s.o.*); *fig.* use, employ; risk (*one's life*); *sich ~ für* stand up for; **2.** *v/i. fever, flood, weather*: set in; 🜊 strike in; '**⁀ung** *f* (*-/-en*) insertion; appointment, installation.

'**Einsicht** *f* (*-/-en*) inspection; *fig.* insight, understanding; judiciousness; '**⁀ig** *adj.* judicious; sensible.

'**einsickern** *v/i.* (*sep., -ge-, sein*) soak in; infiltrate.

'**Einsiedler** *m* hermit.

**einsilbig** *adj.* ['aɪnzɪlbɪç] monosyllabic; *fig.* taciturn; '**⁀keit** *f* (*-/no pl.*) taciturnity.

'**einsinken** *v/i.* (*irr. sinken, sep., -ge-, sein*) sink (in).

**Einspänn|er** *m* (*-s/-*) one-horse carriage; '**⁀ig** *adj.* one-horse.

'**ein|sparen** *v/t.* (*sep., -ge-, h*) save, economize; '**⁀sperren** *v/t.* (*sep., -ge-, h*) imprison; lock up, confine; '**⁀springen** *v/i.* (*irr. springen, sep., -ge-, sein*) ⊕ catch; *fig.* step in, help out; *für j-n ~* substitute for s.o.; '**⁀spritzen** *v/t.* (*sep., -ge-, h*) inject; '**⁀spritzung** *f* (*-/-en*) injection.

'**Einspruch** *m* objection, protest, veto; appeal; '**⁀srecht** *n* veto.

'**einspurig** *adj.* single-track.

**einst** *adv.* [aɪnst] once; one *or* some day.

'**Einstand** *m* entry; *tennis:* deuce.

'**ein|stecken** *v/t.* (*sep., -ge-, h*) put in; pocket; plug in; '**⁀steigen** *v/i.* (*irr. steigen, sep., -ge-, sein*) get in; *~!* ⊛ take your seats!, *Am.* all aboard!

'**einstell|en** *v/t.* (*sep., -ge-, h*) put in; ✕ enrol(l), enlist, *Am.* muster in; engage, employ, *Am. a.* hire; give up; stop, cease, *Am. a.* quit (*payment, etc.*); adjust (*mechanism*) (*auf acc.* to); tune in (*radio*) (to); opt., focus (on) (*a. fig.*); *die Arbeit ~* cease working; strike, *Am. a.* walk out; *sich ~* appear; *sich ~ auf* (*acc.*) be prepared for; adapt o.s. to; '**⁀ung** *f* ✕ enlistment; engagement; adjustment; focus; (*mental*) attitude, mentality.

'**einstimm|en** 🜊 *v/i.* (*sep., -ge-, h*) join in; '**⁀ig** *adj.* unanimous; '**⁀igkeit** *f* (*-/no pl.*) unanimity.

**einstöckig** *adj.* ['aɪnstœkɪç] one-storied.

'**ein|streuen** *fig. v/t.* (*sep., -ge-, h*) intersperse; '**⁀studieren** *v/t.* (*sep., no -ge-, h*) study; *thea.* rehearse; '**⁀stürmen** *v/i.* (*sep., -ge-, sein*): *auf j-n ~* rush at s.o.; '**⁀sturz** *m* falling in, collapse; '**⁀stürzen** *v/i.* (*sep., -ge-, sein*) fall in, collapse.

**einst|weilen** *adv.* ['aɪnst'vaɪlən] for the present; in the meantime; '**⁀'weilig** *adj.* temporary.

'**ein|tauschen** *v/t.* (*sep., -ge-, h*) exchange (*gegen* for); '**⁀teilen** *v/t.* (*sep., -ge-, h*) divide (*in acc.* into); classify; '**⁀teilig** *adj.* one-piece; '**⁀teilung** *f* division; classification.

**eintönig** *adj.* ['aɪntøːnɪç] monotonous; '**⁀keit** *f* (*-/🜊, -en*) monotony.

'**Eintopf(gericht** *n*) *m* hot-pot; stew.

'**Eintracht** *f* (*-/no pl.*) harmony, concord.

**einträchtig** *adj.* ['aɪntrɛçtɪç] harmonious.

'**eintragen** *v/t.* (*irr. tragen, sep., -ge-, h*) enter; register; bring in, yield (*profit*); *sich ~ in* (*acc.*) sign.

**einträglich** *adj.* ['aɪntrɛːklɪç] profitable.

'**Eintragung** *f* (*-/-en*) entry; registration.

'**ein|treffen** *v/i.* (*irr. treffen, sep., -ge-, sein*) arrive; happen; come true; '**⁀treiben** *v/t.* (*irr. treiben, sep., -ge-, h*) drive in *or* home; collect (*debts, taxes*); '**⁀treten** (*irr. treten, sep., -ge-*) **1.** *v/i.* (*sein*) enter; occur, happen, take place; *~ für* stand up for; *~ in* (*acc.*) enter into (*rights*); enter upon (*possession*); enter (*room*); join (*the army, etc.*); **2.** *v/t.* (*h*) kick in (*door*); *sich ~: ~ run s.th. into one's foot.

'**Eintritt** *m* entry, entrance; admittance; beginning, setting-in (*of winter, etc.*); *~ frei!* admission free!; *~ verboten!* no admittance!; '**⁀sgeld** *n* entrance *or* admission fee; *sports:* gate money; '**⁀skarte** *f* admission ticket.

'**ein|trocknen** *v/i.* (*sep., -ge-, sein*) dry (up); '**⁀trüben** *v/refl.* (*sep., -ge-, h*) become cloudy *or* overcast; '**⁀üben** ['aɪn⁀-] *v/t.* (*sep., -ge-, h*) practi|se, *Am. -ce s.th.*; train *s.o.*

**einver|leiben** ['aɪnfɛrlaɪbən] *v/t.* ([*sep.,*] *no -ge-, h*) incorporate (*dat.* in); annex (to); F *sich et. ~* eat *or* drink s.th.; '**⁀nehmen** *n* (*-s/no pl.*) agreement, understanding; *in gutem ~* on friendly terms; '**⁀standen**

*adj.:* ~ *sein* agree; '**ⱵStändnis** *n* agreement.

'**Einwand** *m* (-[e]s/ɛe) objection (*gegen* to).

'**Einwander|er** *m* immigrant; '**Ⱶn** *v/i.* (*sep.*, -ge-, *sein*) immigrate; '**Ⱶung** *f* immigration.

'**einwandfrei** *adj.* unobjectionable; perfect; faultless; *alibi:* sound.

**einwärts** *adv.* ['aɪnvɛrts] inward(s).

'**Einwegflasche** *f* one-way bottle, non-return bottle.

'**einweih|en** *v/t.* (*sep.*, -ge-, h) *eccl.* consecrate; inaugurate; ~ *in* (*acc.*) initiate *s.o.* into; '**Ⱶung** *f* (-/-en) consecration; inauguration; initiation.

'**einwend|en** *v/t.* ([*irr. wenden,*] *sep.*, -ge-, h) object; '**Ⱶung** *f* objection.

'**einwerfen** (*irr. werfen, sep.*, -ge-, h) **1.** *v/t.* throw in (*a. fig.*); smash, break (*window-pane*); post, *Am.* mail (*letter*); interject (*remark*); **2.** *v/i. football:* throw in.

'**einwickel|n** *v/t.* (*sep.*, -ge-, h) wrap (up), envelop; '**Ⱶpapier** *n* wrapping-paper.

**einwillig|en** ['aɪnvɪlɪgən] *v/i.* (*sep.*, -ge-, h) consent, agree (*in acc.* to); '**Ⱶung** *f* (-/-en) consent, agreement.

'**einwirk|en** *v/i.* (*sep.*, -ge-, h): ~ *auf* (*acc.*) act (up)on; influence; effect; '**Ⱶung** *f* influence; effect.

**Einwohner** ['aɪnvoːnər] *m* (-s/-), '**Ⱶin** *f* (-/-nen) inhabitant, resident.

'**Einwurf** *m* throwing in; *football:* throw-in; *fig.* objection; slit (*for letters, etc.*); slot (*for coins*).

'**Einzahl** *gr. f* (-/ꞏ-en) singular (number); '**Ⱶen** *v/t.* (*sep.*, -ge-, h) pay in; '**Ⱶung** *f* payment; deposit (*at bank*).

**einzäunen** ['aɪntsɔʏnən] *v/t.* (*sep.*, -ge-, h) fence in.

**Einzel** ['aɪntsəl] *n* (-s/-) *tennis:* single, *Am.* singles *pl.*; **Ⱶgänger** ['ꞏgɛŋər] *m* (-s/-) outsider; F lone wolf; '**Ⱶhandel** ✝ *m* retail trade; '**Ⱶhändler** ✝ *m* retailer, retail dealer; '**Ⱶheit** *f* (-/-en) detail, item; ~*en pl.* particulars *pl.*, details *pl.*; '**Ⱶn 1.** *adj.* single; particular; individual; separate; *of shoes, etc.:* odd; *im* ~*en* in detail; **2.** *adv.:* ~ *angeben* or *aufführen* specify, *esp. Am.* itemize; '**Ⱶne** *m* (-n/-n) the individual; '**Ⱶverkauf** *m* retail sale; '**Ⱶwesen** *n* individual.

'**einziehen** (*irr. ziehen, sep.*, -ge-) **1.** *v/t.* (h) draw in; *esp.* ⊕ retract; ✗ call up, *Am.* draft, induct; ⅋ seize, confiscate; make (*inquiries*) (*über acc.* on, about); **2.** *v/i.* (*sein*) enter; move in; *liquid:* soak in; ~ *in* (*acc.*) move into (*flat, etc.*).

**einzig** *adj.* ['aɪntsɪç] only; single; sole; unique; '**Ⱶartig** *adj.* unique, singular.

'**Einzug** *m* entry, entrance; moving in.

'**einzwängen** *v/t.* (*sep.*, -ge-, h) squeeze, jam.

**Eis** [aɪs] *n* (-es/no pl.) ice; ice-cream; '**Ⱶbahn** *f* skating-rink; '**Ⱶbär** *zo. m* polar bear; '**Ⱶbein** *n* pickled pork shank; '**Ⱶberg** *m* iceberg; '**Ⱶdecke** *f* sheet of ice; '**Ⱶdiele** *f* ice-cream parlo(u)r.

**Eisen** ['aɪzən] *n* (-s/-) iron.

'**Eisenbahn** *f* railway, *Am.* railroad; *mit der* ~ by rail, by train; '**Ⱶer** *m* (-s/-) railwayman; '**Ⱶfahrt** *f* railway journey; '**Ⱶknotenpunkt** *m* (railway) junction; '**Ⱶunglück** *n* railway accident; '**Ⱶwagen** *m* railway carriage, *Am.* railroad car; coach.

'**Eisen|blech** *n* sheet-iron; '**Ⱶerz** *n* iron-ore; '**Ⱶgießerei** *f* iron-foundry; '**Ⱶhaltig** *adj.* ferruginous; '**Ⱶhütte** *f* ironworks *sg., pl.*; '**Ⱶwaren** *f/pl.* ironmongery, *esp. Am.* hardware; '**Ⱶwarenhändler** *m* ironmonger, *esp. Am.* hardware dealer.

**eisern** *adj.* ['aɪzərn] iron, of iron.

'**Eis|gang** *m* breaking up of the ice; ice-drift; '**Ⱶgekühlt** *adj.* ['ꞏgəkyːlt] iced; '**Ⱶgrau** *adj.* hoary; '**Ⱶhockey** *n* ice-hockey; '**Ⱶig** *adj.* ['aɪzɪç] icy; '**Ⱶkalt** *adj.* icy (cold); '**Ⱶkunstlauf** *m* figure-skating; '**Ⱶlauf** *m,* '**Ⱶlaufen** *n* (-s/no pl.) skating; skate; '**Ⱶläufer** *m* skater; '**Ⱶmeer** *n* polar sea; '**Ⱶschnellauf** *m* speed-skating; '**Ⱶscholle** *f* ice-floe; '**Ⱶschrank** *m s.* Kühlschrank; '**Ⱶvogel** *orn. m* kingfisher; '**Ⱶzapfen** *m* icicle; '**Ⱶzeit** *geol. f* ice-age.

**eitel** *adj.* ['aɪtəl] vain (*auf acc.* of); conceited; mere; '**Ⱶkeit** *f* (-/-en) vanity.

**Eiter** ⚕ ['aɪtər] *m* (-s/no pl.) matter, pus; '**Ⱶbeule** ⚕ *f* abscess; '**Ⱶig** ⚕ *adj.* purulent; '**Ⱶn** ⚕ *v/i.* (-ge-, h) fester, suppurate; '**Ⱶung** ⚕ *f* (-/-en) suppuration.

**eitrig** ⚕ *adj.* ['aɪtrɪç] purulent.

'**Eiweiß** *n* (-es/-e) white of egg; ⚕ albumen; '**Ⱶhaltig** ⚕ *adj.* albuminous.

'**Eizelle** *f* egg-cell, ovum.

**Ekel** ['eːkəl] **1.** *m* (-s/no pl.) disgust (*vor dat.* at), loathing; aversion; ⚕ nausea; **2.** F *n* (-s/-) nasty person; '**Ⱶerregend** *adj.* nauseating, sickening; '**Ⱶhaft** *adj.*, '**Ⱶig** *adj.* revolting; *fig.* disgusting; '**Ⱶn** *v/refl.* (ge-, h): *sich* ~ be nauseated (*vor dat.* at); *fig.* be or feel disgusted (at).

**eklig** *adj.* ['eːklɪç] *s.* ekelhaft.

**elasti|sch** *adj.* [eˈlastɪʃ] elastic; **Ⱶzität** [ꞏtsiˈtɛːt] *f* (-/no pl.) elasticity.

**Elch** *zo.* [ɛlç] *m* (-[e]s/-e) elk, moose.

**Elefant** *zo.* [eleˈfant] *m* (-en/-en) elephant.

**elegan|t** *adj.* [ele'gant] elegant; smart; **2z** [ʦ] *f* (-/*no pl.*) elegance.

**elektrifizier|en** [elektrifi'tsi:rən] *v/t.* (*no -ge-, h*) electrify; **2ung** *f* (-/-en) electrification.

**Elektri|ker** [e'lɛktrikər] *m* (-s/-) electrician; **2sch** *adj.* electric(al); **2sieren** [ʌ'zi:rən] *v/t.* (*no -ge-, h*) electrify.

**Elektrizität** [elɛktritsi'tɛːt] *f* (-/*no pl.*) electricity; **ʌsgesellschaft** *f* electricity supply company; **ʌs-werk** *n* (electric) power station, power-house, *Am.* power plant.

**Elektrode** [elɛk'tro:də] *f* (-/-n) electrode.

**Elektro|gerät** [e'lɛktro-] *n* electric appliance; **ʌlyse** [ʌ'ly:zə] *f* (-/-n) electrolysis.

**Elektron** *ɛ* [e'lɛktrɔn] *n* (-s/-en) electron; **ʌengehirn** [ʌ'tro:nən-] *n* electronic brain; **ʌik** [ʌ'tro:nik] *f* (-/*no pl.*) electronics *sg.*

**Elektro'technik** *f* electrical engineering; **ʌer** *m* electrical engineer.

**Element** [ele'mɛnt] *n* (-[e]s/-e) element.

**elementar** [elemen'taːr] elementary; **2schule** elementary *or* primary school, *Am.* grade school.

**Elend** ['e:lɛnt] **1.** *n* (-[e]s/*no pl.*) misery; need, distress; **2. 2** *adj.* miserable, wretched; needy, distressed; **ʌsviertel** *n* slums *pl.*

**elf**¹ [ɛlf] **1.** *adj.* eleven; **2. 2** *f* (-/-en) eleven (*a.* sports).

**Elf**² [ʌ] *m* (-en/-en), **ʌe** ['ɛlfə] *f* (-/-n) elf, fairy.

**'Elfenbein** *n* (-[e]s/ʌ-e) ivory; **'2ern** *adj.* ivory.

**Elf'meter** *m* football: penalty kick; **ʌmarke** *f* penalty spot.

**'elfte** *adj.* eleventh.

**Elite** [e'li:tə] *f* (-/-n) élite.

**'Ellbogen** anat. *m* (-s/-) elbow.

**Elle** ['ɛlə] *f* (-/-n) yard; anat. ulna.

**Elster** orn. ['ɛlstər] *f* (-/-n) magpie.

**elter|lich** ['ɛltərlɪç] parental; **'2n** *pl.* parents *pl.*; **'ʌnlos** *adj.* parentless, orphaned; **'2nteil** *m* parent.    [(-/-n) enamel.\

**Email** [e'maːj] *n* (-s/-s), **ʌle** [ʌ] *f\*

**Emanzipation** [emantsipa'tsjo:n] *f* (-/-en) emancipation.

**Embargo** [ɛm'bargo] *n* (-s/-s) embargo.

**Embolie** *ɛ* [ɛmbo'li:] *f* (-/-n) embolism.

**Embryo** biol. ['ɛmbryo] *m* (-s/-s, -nen) embryo.

**Emigrant** [emi'grant] *m* (-en/-en) emigrant.

**empfahl** [ɛm'pfaːl] pret. of empfehlen.

**Empfang** [ɛm'pfaŋ] *m* (-[e]s/ʌe) reception *or* receipt (of s.th.); nach *or* bei ʌ on receipt; **'2en** *v/t.* (irr. fangen, no -ge-, h) receive; welcome; conceive (child).

**Empfänger** [ɛm'pfɛŋər] *m* (-s/-) receiver, recipient; payee (of money); addressee (of letter); ✝ consignee (of goods).

**em'pfänglich** *adj.* susceptible (für to); **2keit** *f* (-/*no pl.*) susceptibility.

**Em'pfangs|dame** *f* receptionist; **ʌgerät** *n* receiver, receiving set; **ʌschein** *m* receipt; **ʌzimmer** *n* reception-room.

**empfehl|en** [ɛm'pfe:lən] *v/t.* (irr., no -ge-, h) recommend; commend; ʌ Sie mich (dat.) please remember me to; **ʌenswert** *adj.* (re)commendable; **2ung** *f* (-/-en) recommendation; compliments *pl.*

**empfinden** [ɛm'pfindən] *v/t.* (irr. finden, no -ge-, h) feel; perceive.

**empfindlich** *adj.* [ɛm'pfintlɪç] sensitive (*a.* phot., ✍) (für, gegen to); pred. *a.* susceptible (gegen to); delicate; tender; *p.:* touchy, sensitive; cold: severe; pain, loss, etc.: grievous; pain: acute; **2keit** *f* (-/-en) sensitivity; sensibility; touchiness; delicacy.

**empfindsam** *adj.* [ɛm'pfintzaːm] sensitive; sentimental; **2keit** *f* (-/-en) sensitiveness; sentimentality.

**Empfindung** [ɛm'pfindʊŋ] *f* (-/-en) perception; sensation; sentiment; **2slos** *adj.* insensible; esp. fig. unfeeling; **ʌsvermögen** *n* faculty of perception.

**empfohlen** [ɛm'pfo:lən] *p.p.* of empfehlen.

**empor** *adv.* [ɛm'po:r] up, upwards.

**empören** [ɛm'pøːrən] *v/t.* (*no -ge-, h*) incense; shock; sich ʌ revolt (*a.* fig.), rebel; grow furious (über acc. at); empört indignant, shocked (both: über acc. at).

**em'por|kommen** *v/i.* (irr. kommen, sep., -ge-, sein) rise (in the world); **2kömmling** [ʌkœmlɪŋ] *m* (-s/-e) upstart; **ʌragen** *v/i.* (sep., -ge-, h) tower, rise; **ʌsteigen** *v/i.* (irr. steigen, sep., -ge-, sein) rise, ascend.

**Em'pörung** *f* (-/-en) rebellion, revolt; indignation.

**emsig** *adj.* ['ɛmzɪç] busy, industrious, diligent; **2keit** *f* (-/*no pl.*) busyness, industry, diligence.

**Ende** ['ɛndə] *n* (-s/-n) end; am ʌ at *or* in the end; after all; eventually; zu ʌ gehen end; expire; run short; **'2n** *v/i.* (ge-, h) end; cease, finish.

**end|gültig** *adj.* ['ɛntgyltɪç] final, definitive; **'ʌlich** *adv.* finally, at last; **ʌlos** *adj.* ['ʌlo:s] endless; **'2punkt** *m* final point; **'2runde** *f* sports: final; **'2station** ⛿ *f* terminus, *Am.* terminal; **'2summe** *f* (sum) total.

**Endung** ling. ['ɛndʊŋ] *f* (-/-en) ending, termination.

**Endzweck** ['ɛnt-] *m* ultimate object.

**Energie** [enɛr'giː] *f* (-/-n) energy; **2los** *adj.* lacking (in) energy.

**e'nergisch** *adj.* vigorous; energetic.

**eng** *adj.* [ɛŋ] narrow; *clothes:* tight; close; intimate; *im ~eren Sinne* strictly speaking.

**engagieren** [ãgaʒiːrən] *v/t.* (*no -ge-, h*) engage, *Am. a.* hire.

**Enge** ['ɛŋə] *f* (-/-n) narrowness; *fig.* straits *pl.*

**Engel** ['ɛŋəl] *m* (-s/-) angel.

**'engherzig** *adj.* ungenerous, petty.

**Engländer** ['ɛŋlɛndər] *m* (-s/-) Englishman; *die ~ pl.* the English *pl.*; '**~in** *f* (-/-nen) Englishwoman.

**englisch** *adj.* ['ɛŋliʃ] English; British.

**'Engpaß** *m* defile, narrow pass, *Am. a.* notch; *fig.* bottle-neck.

**en gros** † *adv.* [ã'groː] wholesale.

**En'groshandel** † *m* wholesale trade.

**'engstirnig** *adj.* narrow-minded.

**Enkel** ['ɛŋkəl] *m* (-s/-) grandchild; grandson; *~in f* (-/-nen) granddaughter.

**enorm** *adj.* [e'nɔrm] enormous; F *fig.* tremendous.

**Ensemble** *thea.,* ♪ [ã'sãːbəl] *n* (-s/-s) ensemble; company.

**entart|en** [ɛnt'aːrtən] *v/i.* (*no -ge-, sein*) degenerate; **2ung** *f* (-/-en) degeneration.

**entbehr|en** [ɛnt'beːrən] *v/t.* (*no -ge-, h*) lack; miss; want; do without; **~lich** *adj.* dispensable; superfluous; **2ung** *f* (-/-en) want, privation.

**ent'bind|en** (*irr. binden, no -ge-, h*) **1.** *v/t.* dispense, release (*von* from); deliver (*of a child*); **2.** *v/i.* be confined; **2ung** *f* dispensation, release; delivery; **2ungsheim** *n* maternity hospital.

**ent'blöß|en** *v/t.* (*no -ge-, h*) bare, strip; uncover (*head*); **~t** *adj.* bare.

**ent'deck|en** *v/t.* (*no -ge-, h*) discover; detect; disclose; **~er** *m* (-s/-) discoverer; **2ung** *f* discovery.

**Ente** ['ɛntə] *f* (-/-n) *orn.* duck; *false report:* F canard, hoax.

**ent'ehr|en** *v/t.* (*no -ge-, h*) dishono(u)r; **2ung** *f* degradation; rape.

**ent'eign|en** *v/t.* (*no -ge-, h*) expropriate; dispossess; **2ung** *f* expropriation; dispossession.

**ent'erben** *v/t.* (*no -ge-, h*) disinherit.

**entern** ['ɛntərn] *v/t.* (*ge-, h*) board, grapple (*ship*).

**ent|'fachen** *v/t.* (*no -ge-, h*) kindle; *fig. a.* rouse (*passions*); **~'fallen** *v/i.* (*irr. fallen, no -ge-, sein*): *j-m ~* escape s.o.; *fig.* slip s.o.'s memory; *auf j-n ~* fall to s.o.'s share; *s. wegfallen;* **~'falten** *v/t.* (*no -ge-, h*) unfold; *fig.:* develop; display; *sich ~* unfold; *fig.* develop (*zu* into).

**ent'fern|en** *v/t.* (*no -ge-, h*) remove; *sich ~* withdraw; **~t** *adj.* distant,

remote (*both a. fig.*); **2ung** *f* (-/-en) removal; distance; range; **2ungsmesser** *phot. m* (-s/-) range-finder.

**ent'flammen** (*no -ge-*) *v/t.* (*h*) *and v/i.* (*sein*) inflame; **~'fliehen** *v/i.* (*irr. fliehen, no -ge-, sein*) flee, escape (*aus or dat.* from); **~'fremden** *v/t.* (*no -ge-, h*) estrange, alienate (*j-m* from s.o.).

**ent'führ|en** *v/t.* (*no -ge-, h*) abduct, kidnap; run away with; **2er** *m* abductor, kidnap(p)er; **2ung** *f* abduction, kidnap(p)ing.

**ent'gegen 1.** *prp.* (*dat.*) in opposition to, contrary to; against; **2.** *adv.* towards; **~gehen** *v/i.* (*irr. gehen, sep., -ge-, sein*) go to meet; **~gesetzt** *adj.* opposite; *fig.* contrary; **~halten** *v/t.* (*irr. halten, sep., -ge-, h*) hold out; *fig.* object; **~kommen** *v/i.* (*irr. kommen, sep., -ge-, sein*) come to meet; *fig.* meet s.o.('s wishes) halfway; **2kommen** *n* (-s/no pl.) obligingness; **~kommend** *adj.* obliging; **~nehmen** *v/t.* (*irr. nehmen, sep., -ge-, h*) accept, receive; **~sehen** *v/i.* (*dat.*) (*irr. sehen, sep., -ge-, h*) await; look forward to; **~setzen** *v/t.* (*sep., -ge-, h*) oppose; **~stehen** *v/i.* (*irr. stehen, sep., -ge-, h*) be opposed (*dat.* to); **~strecken** *v/t.* (*sep., -ge-, h*) hold or stretch out (*dat.* to); **~treten** *v/i.* (*dat.*) (*irr. treten, sep., -ge-, sein*) step up to s.o.; oppose; face (*danger*).

**entgegn|en** [ɛnt'geːgnən] *v/i.* (*no -ge-, h*) reply; return; retort; **2ung** *f* (-/-en) reply; retort.

**ent'gehen** *v/i.* (*irr. gehen, no -ge-, sein*) escape.

**entgeistert** *adj.* [ɛnt'gaɪstərt] aghast, thunderstruck, flabbergasted.

**Entgelt** [ɛnt'gɛlt] *n* (-[e]s/no pl.) recompense; **2en** *v/t.* (*irr. gelten, no -ge-, h*) atone or suffer or pay for.

**entgleis|en** [ɛnt'glaɪzən] *v/i.* (*no -ge-, sein*) run off the rails, be derailed; *fig.* (make a) slip; **2ung** *f* (-/-en) derailment; *fig.* slip.

**ent'gleiten** *v/i.* (*irr. gleiten, no -ge-, sein*) slip (*dat.* from).

**ent'halt|en** *v/t.* (*irr. halten, no -ge-, h*) contain, hold; include; *sich ~* (*gen.*) abstain or refrain from; **~sam** *adj.* abstinent; **2samkeit** *f* (-/no pl.) abstinence; **2ung** *f* abstention.

**ent'haupten** *v/t.* (*no -ge-, h*) behead, decapitate.

**ent'hüll|en** *v/t.* (*no -ge-, h*) uncover; unveil; *fig.* reveal, disclose; **2ung** *f* (-/-en) uncovering; unveiling; *fig.* revelation, disclosure.

**Enthusias|mus** [ɛntuzi'asmus] *m* (-/no pl.) enthusiasm; **~t** *m* (-en/-en) enthusiast; *film, sports:* F fan; **2tisch** *adj.* enthusiastic.

**ent'kleiden** *v/t. and v/refl.* (*no -ge-, h*) undress.

**ent'kommen 1.** v/i. (irr. kommen, no -ge-, sein) escape (j-m s.o.; aus from), get away or off; **2.** ⚲ n (-s/no pl.) escape.

**entkräft|en** [ɛnt'krɛftən] v/t. (no -ge-, h) weaken, debilitate; fig. refute; **2ung** f (-/-en) weakening; debility; fig. refutation.

**ent'lad|en** v/t. (irr. laden, no -ge-, h) unload; esp. ⚡ discharge; explode; sich ~ esp. ⚡ discharge; gun: go off; anger: vent itself; **2ung** f unloading; esp. ⚡ discharge; explosion.

**ent'lang 1.** prp. (dat.; acc.) along; **2.** adv. along; er geht die Straße ~ he goes along the street.

**ent'larven** v/t. (no -ge-, h) unmask; fig. a. expose.

**ent'lass|en** v/t. (irr. lassen, no -ge-, h) dismiss, discharge; F give s.o. the sack, Am. a. fire; **2ung** f (-/-en) dismissal, discharge; **2ungsgesuch** n resignation.

**ent'lasten** v/t. (no -ge-, h) unburden; ⚖ exonerate, clear (from suspicion).

**Ent'lastung** f (-/-en) relief; discharge; exoneration; ~sstraße f by-pass (road); ~szeuge m witness for the defen[c]e, Am. -se.

**ent'|laufen** v/i. (irr. laufen, no -ge-, sein) run away (dat. from); ~ledigen [~'le:digən] v/refl. (gen.) (no -ge-, h): rid o.s. of s.th., get rid of s.th.; acquit o.s. of (duty); execute (orders); ~'leeren v/t. (no -ge-, h) empty. [of-the-way.\]

**ent'legen** adj. remote, distant, out-\
**ent'|lehnen** v/t. (no -ge-, h) borrow (dat. or aus from); ~'locken v/t. (no -ge-, h) draw, elicit (dat. from); ~'lohnen v/t. (no -ge-, h) pay (off); ~'lüften v/t. (no -ge-, h) ventilate; ~militarisieren [~militari'zi:rən] v/t. (no -ge-, h) demilitarize; ~mutigen [~'mu:tigən] v/t. (no -ge-, h) discourage; ~'nehmen v/t. (irr. nehmen, no -ge- h) take (dat. from); ~ aus (with)draw from; fig. gather or learn from; ~'rätseln v/t. (no -ge-, h) unriddle; ~'reißen v/t. (irr. reißen, no -ge-, h) snatch away (dat. from); ~'richten v/t. (no -ge-, h) pay; ~'rinnen v/i. (irr. rinnen, no -ge-, sein) escape (dat. from); ~'rollen v/t. (no -ge-, h) unroll; ~'rücken v/t. (no -ge-, h) remove (dat. from), carry off or away; ~'rückt adj. entranced; lost in thought.

**ent'rüst|en** v/t. (no -ge-, h) fill with indignation; sich ~ become angry or indignant (über acc. at s.th., with s.o.); ~et adj. indignant (über acc. at s.th., with s.o.); **2ung** f indignation.

**ent'sag|en** v/i. (no -ge-, h) renounce, resign; **2ung** f (-/-en) renunciation, resignation.

**ent'schädig|en** v/t. (no -ge-, h) indemnify, compensate; **2ung** f indemnification, indemnity; compensation.

**ent'scheid|en** (irr. scheiden, no -ge-, h) **1.** v/t. decide; sich ~ question, etc.: be decided; p.: decide (für for; gegen against; über acc. on); come to a decision; **2.** v/i. decide; ~end adj. decisive; crucial; **2ung** f decision.

**entschieden** adj. [ɛnt'ʃi:dən] decided; determined, resolute; **2heit** f (-/no pl.) determination.

**ent'schließen** v/refl. (irr. schließen, no -ge-, h) resolve, decide, determine (zu on s.th.; zu inf. to inf.), make up one's mind (zu inf. to inf.).

**ent'schlossen** adj. resolute, determined (zu to); **2heit** f (-/no pl.) resoluteness.

**ent'schlüpfen** v/i. (no -ge-, sein) escape, slip (dat. from).

**Ent'schluß** m resolution, resolve, decision, determination.

**entschuldig|en** [ɛnt'ʃuldigən] v/t. (no -ge-, h) excuse; sich ~ apologize (bei to; für for); sich ~ lassen beg to be excused; **2ung** f (-/-en) excuse; apology; ich bitte (Sie) um ~ I beg your pardon.

**ent'senden** v/t. (irr. senden, no -ge-, h) send off, dispatch; delegate, depute.

**ent'setz|en 1.** v/t. (no -ge-, h) dismiss (from a position); ✗ relieve; frighten; sich ~ be terrified or shocked (über acc. at); **2.** ⚲ n (no pl.) horror, fright; ~lich adj. horrible, dreadful, terrible, shocking.

**ent'sinnen** v/refl. (gen.) (irr. sinnen, no -ge-, h) remember or recall s.o., s.th.

**ent'spann|en** v/t. (no -ge-, h) relax; unbend; sich ~ relax; political situation: ease; **2ung** f relaxation; pol. détente.

**ent'sprech|en** v/i. (irr. sprechen, no -ge-, h) answer (description, etc.); correspond to; meet (demand); ~end adj. corresponding; appropriate; **2ung** f (-/-en) equivalent.

**ent'springen** v/i. (irr. springen, no -ge-, sein) escape (dat. from); river: rise, Am. head; s. entstehen.

**ent'stammen** v/i. (no -ge-, sein) be descended from; come from or of, originate from.

**ent'steh|en** v/i. (irr. stehen. no -ge-, sein) arise, originate (both: aus from); **2ung** f (-/-en) origin.

**ent'stell|en** v/t. (no -ge-, h) disfigure; deface, deform; distort; **2ung** f disfigurement; distortion, misrepresentation.

**ent'täusch|en** v/t. (no -ge-, h) disappoint; **2ung** f disappointment.

**ent'thronen** v/t. (no -ge-, h) dethrone.

**entvölker|n** [ɛnt'fœlkərn] v/t. (no

-ge-, h) depopulate; 2ung f (-/-en) depopulation.

ent'wachsen v/i. (irr. wachsen, no -ge-, sein) outgrow.

entwaffn|en [ɛnt'vafnən] v/t. (no -ge-, h) disarm; 2ung f (-/-en) disarmament.

ent'warnen v/i. (no -ge-, h) civil defence: sound the all-clear (signal).

ent'wässer|n v/t. (no -ge-, h) drain; 2ung f (-/-en) drainage; ~ dehydration.

ent'weder cj.: ~ ... oder either ... or.

ent|'weichen v/i. (irr. weichen, no -ge-, sein) escape (aus from); ~'weihen v/t. (no -ge-, h) desecrate, profane; ~'wenden v/t. (no -ge-, h) pilfer, purloin (j-m et. s.th. from s.o.); ~'werfen v/t. (irr. werfen, no -ge-, h) draft, draw up (document); design; sketch, trace out, outline; plan.

ent'wert|en v/t. (no -ge-, h) depreciate, devaluate; cancel (stamp); 2ung f depreciation, devaluation; cancellation.

ent'wickeln v/t. (no -ge-, h) develop (a. phot.); evolve; sich ~ develop.

Entwicklung [ɛnt'viklun] f (-/-en) development; evolution; ~shilfe f development aid.

ent|'wirren v/t. (no -ge-, h) disentangle, unravel; ~'wischen v/i. (no -ge-, sein) slip away, escape (j-m [from] s.o.; aus from), j-m give s.o. the slip; ~'wöhnen [~'vø:nən] v/t. (no -ge-, h) wean.

Ent'wurf m sketch; design; plan; draft.

ent|'wurzeln v/t. (no -ge-, h) uproot; ~'ziehen v/t. (irr. ziehen, no -ge-, h) deprive (j-m et s.o. of s.th.); withdraw (dat. from), sich ~ avoid, elude; evade (responsibility); ~'ziffern v/t. (no -ge-, h) decipher, make out; tel. decode

ent'zücken 1. v/t. (no -ge-, h) charm, delight; 2. 2 n (-s/no pl.) delight, rapture; transport(s pl.).

ent'zückend adj. delightful; charming.

Ent'zug m (-[e]s/no pl.) withdrawal; cancellation (of licence); deprivation.

entzünd|bar adj. [ɛnt'tsyntba:r] (in)flammable; ~en v/t. (no -ge-, h) inflame (a. phot.); kindle; sich ~ catch fire; ~ become inflamed; 2ung f inflammation.

ent'zwei adv. asunder, in two, to pieces; ~en v/t. (no -ge-, h) disunite, set at variance; sich ~ quarrel, fall out (both: mit with); ~gehen v/i. (irr. gehen, sep., -ge-, sein) break, go to pieces; 2ung f (-/-en) disunion.

Enzian [ˈɛntsjaːn] m (-s/-e) gen-

Enzyklopädie [ɛntsyklopeˈdiː] f (-/-n) (en)cyclop(a)edia.

Epidemie [epideˈmiː] f (-/-n) epidemic (disease).

Epilog [epiˈloːk] m (-s/-e) epilog(ue).

episch adj. [ˈeːpiʃ] epic.

Episode [epiˈzoːdə] f (-/-n) episode.

Epoche [eˈpɔxə] f (-/-n) epoch.

Epos [ˈeːpɔs] n (-/Epen) epic (poem).

er pers. pron. [eːr] he.

erachten [ɛr'-] 1.v/t. (no -ge-, h) consider, think, deem; 2. 2 n (-s/no pl.) opinion; m-s ~s in my opinion.

erbarmen [ɛr'barmən] 1. v/refl. (gen.) (no -ge-, h) pity or commiserate s.o.; 2. 2 n (-s/no pl.) pity, compassion, commiseration; mercy; ~swert adj. pitiable.

erbärmlich adj. [ɛr'bɛrmliç] pitiful, pitiable; miserable; behaviour: mean.

er'barmungslos adj. pitiless, merciless, relentless.

er'bau|en v/t. (no -ge-, h) build (up), construct, raise; fig. edify; 2er m (-s/-) builder; constructor; ~lich adj. edifying; 2ung fig. f (-/-en) edification, Am. uplift.

Erbe [ˈɛrbə] 1. m (-n/-n) heir; 2. n (-s/no pl.) inheritance, heritage.

er'beben v/i. (no -ge-, sein) tremble, shake, quake.

'erben v/t. (ge-, h) inherit.

er'beuten v/t. (no -ge-, h) capture.

er'bieten v/refl. (irr. bieten, no -ge-, h) offer, volunteer.

'Erbin f (-/-nen) heiress.

er'bitten v/t. (irr. bitten, no -ge-, h) beg or ask for, request, solicit.

er'bitter|n v/t. (no -ge-, h) embitter, exasperate; 2ung f (-/~ -en) bitterness, exasperation.

Erbkrankheit f [ˈɛrp-] f hereditary disease.

erblassen [ɛr'blasən] v/i. (no -ge-, sein) grow or turn pale, lose colo(u)r.

Erblasser [ˈɛrblasər] m (-s/-) testator; ~in f (-/-nen) testatrix.

er'bleichen v/i. (no -ge-, sein) s. erblassen.

erblich adj. [ˈɛrpliç] hereditary; 2keit physiol. f (-/no pl.) heredity.

er'blicken v/t. (no -ge-, h) perceive, see; catch sight of.

erblind|en [ɛr'blindən] v/i. (no -ge-, sein) grow blind; 2ung f (-/-en) loss of sight.

er'brechen 1. v/t. (irr. brechen, no -ge-, h) break or force open; vomit; sich ~ vomit; 2. 2 n (-s/no pl.) vomiting.

Erbschaft [ˈɛrpʃaft] f (-/-en) inheritance, heritage.

Erbse [ˈɛrpsə] f (-/-n) pea; ~nbrei m pease-pudding, Am. pea purée; ~nsuppe f pea-soup.

Erb|stück [ˈɛrp-] n heirloom; ~sünde f original sin; ~teil n (portion of an) inheritance.

**Erd|arbeiter** ['eːrt-] *m* digger, navvy; '~ball *m* globe; '~beben *n* (-*s*/-) earthquake; '~beere ♀ *f* strawberry; '~boden *m* earth; ground, soil; ~e ['eːrdə] *f* (-/~ -*n*) earth; ground; soil; world; ♀en ⚹ *v/t.* (ge-, *h*) earth, ground.

**er'denklich** *adj.* imaginable.

**Erdgeschoß** ['eːrt-] *n* ground-floor, *Am.* first floor.

**er'dicht|en** *v/t.* (*no* -ge-, *h*) invent, feign; ~et *adj.* fictitious.

**erdig** *adj.* ['eːrdiç] earthy.

**Erd|karte** ['eːrt-] *f* map of the earth; '~kreis *m* earth, world; '~kugel *f* globe; '~kunde *f* geography; '~leitung ⚡ *f* earth-connexion, earth-wire, *Am.* ground wire; '~nuß *f* peanut; '~öl *n* mineral oil, petroleum.

**er'dolchen** *v/t.* (*no* -ge-, *h*) stab (with a dagger).

**Erdreich** ['eːrt-] *n* ground, earth.

**er'dreisten** *v/refl.* (*no* -ge-, *h*) dare, presume.

**er'drosseln** *v/t.* (*no* -ge-, *h*) strangle, throttle.

**er'drücken** *v/t.* (*no* -ge-, *h*) squeeze *or* crush to death; ~d *fig. adj.* overwhelming.

**Erd|rutsch** ['eːrt-] *m* landslip; landslide (*a. pol.*); '~schicht *f* layer of earth, stratum; '~teil *m* part of the world; *geogr.* continent.

**er'dulden** *v/t.* (*no* -ge-, *h*) suffer, endure.

**er'eifern** *v/refl.* (*no* -ge-, *h*) get excited, fly into a passion.

**er'eignen** *v/refl.* (*no* -ge-, *h*) happen, come to pass, occur.

**Ereignis** [er'aiknis] *n* (-*ses*/-*se*) event, occurrence; ♀reich *adj.* eventful.

**Eremit** [ere'miːt] *m* (-*en*/-*en*) hermit, anchorite.

**ererbt** *adj.* [er'erpt] inherited.

**er'fahr|en 1.** *v/t.* (*irr.* fahren, *no* -ge-, *h*) learn; hear; experience; **2.** *adj.* experienced, expert, skil(l)ful; ♀ung *f* (-/-*en*) experience; practice; skill.

**er'fassen** *v/t.* (*no* -ge-, *h*) grasp (*a. fig.*), seize, catch; cover; register; record.

**er'find|en** *v/t.* (*irr.* finden, *no* -ge-, *h*) invent; ♀er *m* inventor; ~erisch *adj.* inventive; ♀ung *f* (-/-*en*) invention.

**Erfolg** [er'folk] *m* (-[*e*]*s*/-*e*) success; result; ♀en [-gən] *v/i.* (*no* -ge-, *sein*) ensue follow; happen; ♀los *adj.* [-k-] unsuccessful; vain; ♀reich *adj.* [-k-] successful.

**er'forder|lich** *adj.* necessary, required; ~n *v/t.* (*no* -ge-, *h*) require, demand; ♀nis *n* (-*ses*/-*se*) requirement, demand, exigence, exigency.

**er'forsch|en** *v/t.* (*no* -ge-, *h*) inquire into, investigate; explore

(*country*); ♀er *m* investigator; explorer; ♀ung *f* investigation; exploration.

**er'freu|en** *v/t.* (*no* -ge-, *h*) please; delight; gratify; rejoice; *sich* e-*r* *Sache* ~ enjoy s.th.; ~lich *adj.* delightful, pleasing, pleasant, gratifying.

**er'frier|en** *v/i.* (*irr.* frieren, *no* -ge-, *sein*) freeze to death; ♀ung *f* (-/-*en*) frost-bite.

**er'frisch|en** *v/t.* (*no* -ge-, *h*) refresh; ♀ung *f* (-/-*en*) refreshment.

**er'froren** *adj. limb:* frost-bitten.

**er'füll|en** *v/t.* (*no* -ge-, *h*) fill; *fig.* fulfil(l); perform (*mission*); comply with (*s.o.'s wishes*); meet (*requirements*); ♀ung *f* fulfil(l)ment; performance; compliance; ♀ungsort ↑, ⚹ [er'fylun̩s?-] *m* place of performance (*of contract*).

**ergänz|en** [er'gentsən] *v/t.* (*no* -ge-, *h*) complete, complement; supplement; replenish (*stores, etc.*); ~end *adj.* complementary, supplementary; ♀ung *f* (-/-*en*) completion; supplement; replenishment; *gr.* complement; ♀ungsband *m* (-[*e*]*s*/~e) supplementary volume.

**er'geb|en 1.** *v/t.* (*irr.* geben, *no* -ge-, *h*) yield, give; prove; *sich* ~ surrender; *difficulties:* arise; devote o.s. to *s.th.*; *sich* ~ *aus* result from; *sich* ~ *in* (*acc.*) resign o.s. to; **2.** *adj.* devoted (*dat.* to); ~st *adv.* respectfully; ♀heit *f* (-/*no pl.*) devotion.

**Ergeb|nis** [er'geːpnis] *n* (-*ses*/-*se*) result, outcome; *sports:* score; ~ung [-bun̩] *f* (-/-*en*) resignation; ✗ surrender.

**er'gehen** *v/i.* (*irr.* gehen, *no* -ge-, *sein*) be issued; ~ *lassen* issue, publish; *über sich* ~ *lassen* suffer, submit to; *wie ist es ihm ergangen?* how did he come off?; *sich* ~ *in* (*dat.*) indulge in.

**ergiebig** *adj.* [er'giːbiç] productive, rich.

**er'gießen** *v/refl.* (*irr.* gießen, *no* -ge-, *h*) flow (*in acc.* into; *über acc.* over).

**er'götz|en 1.** *v/t.* (*no* -ge-, *h*) delight; *sich* ~ *an* (*dat.*) delight in; **2.** ♀ *n* (-*s*/*no pl.*) delight; ~lich *adj.* delightful.

**er'greif|en** *v/t.* (*irr.* greifen, *no* -ge-, *h*) seize; grasp; take (*possession, s.o.'s part, measures, etc.*); take to (*flight*); take up (*profession, pen, arms*); *fig.* move, affect, touch; ♀ung *f* (-/~ -*en*) seizure.

**Er'griffenheit** *f* (-/*no pl.*) emotion.

**er'gründen** *v/t.* (*no* -ge-, *h*) fathom; *fig.* penetrate, get to the bottom of.

**Er'guß** *m* outpouring; effusion.

**er'haben** *adj.* elevated; *fig.* exalted, sublime; ~ *sein über* (*acc.*) be above; ♀heit *f* (-/~ -*en*) elevation; *fig.* sublimity.

er'halt|en 1. v/t. (irr. halten, no -ge-, h) get; obtain; receive; preserve, keep; support, maintain; sich ~ von subsist on; 2. adj.: gut ~ in good repair or condition; 2ung f preservation; maintenance.

erhältlich adj. [ɛr'hɛltliç] obtainable.

er|'hängen v/t. (no -ge-, h) hang; ~'härten v/t. (no -ge-, h) harden; fig. confirm; ~'haschen v/t. (no -ge-, h) snatch, catch.

er'heb|en v/t. (irr. heben, no -ge-, h) lift, raise; elevate; exalt; levy, raise, collect (taxes, etc.); Klage ~ bring an action; sich ~ rise; question, etc.: arise; ~end fig. adj. elevating; ~lich adj. [~p-] considerable; 2ung [~buŋ] f (-/-en) elevation; levy (of taxes); revolt; rising ground.

er|'heitern v/t. (no -ge-, h) cheer up, amuse; ~'hellen v/t. (no -ge-, h) light up; fig. clear up; ~'hitzen v/t. (no -ge-, h) heat; sich ~ get or grow hot; ~'hoffen v/t. (no -ge-, h) hope for.

er'höh|en v/t. (no -ge-, h) raise; increase; 2ung f (-/-en) elevation; rise (in prices, wages); advance (in prices); increase.

er'hol|en v/refl. (no -ge-, h) recover; (take a) rest, relax; 2ung f (-/-en) recovery; recreation; relaxation; 2ungsurlaub [ɛr'ho:luŋsʔ-] m holiday, Am. vacation; recreation leave; ✠ convalescent leave, sick-leave. [(request).]

er'hören v/t. (no -ge-, h) hear; grant.

erinner|n [ɛr'inərn] v/t. (no -ge-, h): j-n ~ an (acc.) remind s.o. of; sich ~ (gen.), sich ~ an (acc.) remember s.o. or s.th., recollect s.th.; 2ung f (-/-en) remembrance; recollection; reminder; ~en pl. reminiscences pl.

er'kalten v/i. (no -ge-, sein) cool down (a. fig.), get cold.

erkält|en [ɛr'kɛltən] v/refl. (no -ge-, h): sich (sehr) ~ catch (a bad) cold; 2ung f (-/-en) cold.

er'kennen v/t. (irr. kennen, no -ge-, h) recognize (an dat. by); perceive, discern; realize.

er'kenntlich adj. perceptible; sich ~ zeigen show one's appreciation; 2keit f (-/-en) gratitude; appreciation.

Er'kenntnis 1. f perception; realization; 2. ✞ n (-ses/-se) decision, sentence, finding.

Erker ['ɛrkər] m (-s/-) bay; '~fenster n bay-window.

er'klär|en v/t. (no -ge-, h) explain; account for; declare, state; sich ~ declare (für for; gegen against); ~lich adj. explainable, explicable; ~t adj. professed, declared; 2ung f explanation; declaration.

er'klingen v/i. (irr. klingen, no -ge-, sein) (re)sound, ring (out).

erkoren adj. [ɛr'ko:rən] (s)elect, chosen.

er'krank|en v/i. (no -ge-, sein) fall ill, be taken ill (an dat. of, with); become affected; 2ung f (-/-en) illness, sickness, falling ill.

er|'kühnen v/refl. (no -ge-, h) venture, presume, make bold (zu inf. to inf.); ~'kunden v/t. (no -ge-, h) explore; ✠ reconnoit|re, Am. -er.

erkundig|en [ɛr'kundigən] v/refl. (no -ge-, h) inquire (über acc. after; nach after or for s.o.; about s.th.); 2ung f (-/-en) inquiry.

er|'lahmen fig. v/i. (no -ge-, sein) grow weary, tire; slacken; interest: wane, flag; ~'langen v/t. (no -ge-, h) obtain, get.

Er|laß [ɛr'las] m (Erlasses/Erlasse) dispensation, exemption; remission (of debt, penalty, etc.); edict, decree; 2'lassen v/t. (irr. lassen, no -ge-, h) remit (debt, penalty, etc.); dispense (j-m et. s.o. from s.th.); issue (decree); enact (law).

erlauben [ɛr'laubən] v/t. (no -ge-, h) allow, permit; sich et. ~ indulge in s.th.; sich ~ zu inf. ✝ beg to inf.

Erlaubnis [ɛr'laupnis] f (-/no pl.) permission; authority; ~schein m permit.

er'läuter|n v/t. (no -ge-, h) explain, illustrate; comment (up)on; 2ung f explanation, illustration; comment.

Erle ✿ ['ɛrlə] f (-/-n) alder.

er'leb|en v/t. (no -ge-, h) (live to) see; experience; go through; 2nis [~pnis] n (-ses/-se) experience; adventure.

erledig|en [ɛr'le:digən] v/t. (no -ge-, h) dispatch; execute; settle (matter); ~t adj. [~çt] finished, settled; fig.: played out; F done for; F: du bist für mich ~ I am through with you; 2ung [~guŋ] f (-/✠ -en) dispatch; settlement.

er'leichter|n v/t. (no -ge-, h) lighten (burden); fig.: make easy, facilitate; relieve; 2ung f (-/-en) ease; relief; facilitation; ~en pl. facilities pl.

er|'leiden v/t. (irr. leiden, no -ge-, h) suffer, endure; sustain (damage, loss); ~'lernen v/t. (no -ge-, h) learn, acquire.

er'leucht|en v/t. (no -ge-, h) illuminate; fig. enlighten; 2ung f (-/-en) illumination; fig. enlightenment.

er'liegen v/i. (irr. liegen, no -ge-, sein) succumb (dat. to).

erlogen adj. [ɛr'lo:gən] false, untrue.

Erlös [ɛr'lø:s] m (-es/-e) proceeds pl.

erlosch [ɛr'lɔʃ] pret. of erlöschen; ~en 1. p.p. of erlöschen; 2. adj. extinct.

er'löschen v/i. (irr., no -ge-, sein) go out; fig. become extinct; contract: expire.

er'lös|en v/t. (no -ge-, h) redeem;

deliver; 2er *m* (-s/-) redeemer, deliverer; *eccl.* Redeemer, Saviour; 2ung *f* redemption; deliverance.

**ermächtig|en** [ɛr'mɛçtigən] *v/t.* (no -ge-, h) authorize; 2ung *f* (-/-en) authorization; authority; warrant.

**er'mahn|en** *v/t.* (no -ge-, h) admonish; 2ung *f* admonition.

**er'mangel|n** *v/i.* (no -ge-, h) be wanting (gen. in); 2ung *f* (-/no pl.): in ~ (gen.) in default of, for want of, failing.

**er'mäßig|en** *v/t.* (no -ge-, h) abate, reduce, cut (down); 2ung *f* (-/-en) abatement, reduction.

**er'matt|en** (no -ge-) 1. *v/t.* (h) fatigue, tire, exhaust; 2. *v/i.* (sein) tire, grow weary; *fig.* slacken; 2ung *f* (-/ᴚ -en) fatigue, exhaustion.

**er'messen** 1. *v/t.* (irr. messen, no -ge-, h) judge; 2. 2 *n* (-s/no pl.) judg(e)ment; discretion.

**er'mitt|eln** *v/t.* (no -ge-, h) ascertain, find out; ᵗᵗ investigate; 2(e)-lung [~(ə)luŋ] *f* (-/-en) ascertainment; inquiry; ᵗᵗ investigation.

**er'möglichen** *v/t.* (no -ge-, h) render or make possible.

**er'mord|en** *v/t.* (no -ge-, h) murder; assassinate; 2ung *f* (-/-en) murder; assassination.

**er'müd|en** (no -ge-) 1. *v/t.* (h) tire, fatigue; 2. *v/i.* (sein) tire, get tired or fatigued; 2ung *f* (-/ᴚ -en) fatigue, tiredness.

**er'munter|n** *v/t.* (no -ge-, h) rouse, encourage; animate; 2ung *f* (-/-en) encouragement, animation.

**ermutig|en** [ɛr'mu:tigən] *v/t.* (no -ge-, h) encourage; 2ung *f* (-/-en) encouragement.

**er'nähr|en** *v/t.* (no -ge-, h) nourish, feed; support; 2er *m* (-s/-) breadwinner, supporter; 2ung *f* (-/ᴚ -en) nourishment; support; *physiol.* nutrition.

**er'nenn|en** *v/t.* (irr. nennen, no -ge-, h) nominate, appoint; 2ung *f* nomination, appointment.

**er'neu|ern** *v/t.* (no -ge-, h) renew, renovate; revive; 2erung *f* renewal, renovation; revival; ~t *adv.* once more.

**erniedrig|en** [ɛr'ni:drigən] *v/t.* (no -ge-, h) degrade; humiliate, humble; 2ung *f* (-/-en) degradation; humiliation.

**Ernst** [ɛrnst] 1. *m* (-es/no pl.) seriousness; earnest(ness); gravity; im ~ in earnest; 2. 2 *adj.* = '2haft *adj.*, '2lich *adj.* serious, earnest, grave.

**Ernte** ['ɛrntə] *f* (-/-n) harvest; crop; ~'dankfest *n* harvest festival; '2n *v/t.* (ge-, h) harvest, gather (in), reap (a. fig.).

**er'nüchter|n** *v/t.* (no -ge-, h) (make) sober; *fig.* disillusion; 2ung *f* (-/-en) sobering; *fig.* disillusionment.

**Er'ober|er** *m* (-s/-) conqueror; 2n *v/t.* (no -ge-, h) conquer; ~ung *f* (-/-en) conquest.

**er'öffn|en** *v/t.* (no -ge-, h) open; inaugurate; disclose (j-m et. s.th. to s.o.); notify; 2ung *f* opening; inauguration; disclosure.

**erörter|n** [ɛr'œrtərn] *v/t.* (no -ge-, h) discuss; 2ung *f* (-/-en) discussion.

**Erpel** *orn.* ['ɛrpəl] *m* (-s/-) drake.

**erpicht** *adj.* [ɛr'piçt]: ~ auf (acc.) bent or intent or set or keen on.

**er'press|en** *v/t.* (no -ge-, h) extort (von from); blackmail; 2er *m* (-s/-), 2erin *f* (-/-nen) extort(ion)er; blackmailer; 2ung *f* (-/-en) extortion; blackmail.

**er'proben** *v/t.* (no -ge-, h) try, test.

**erquick|en** [ɛr'kvikən] *v/t.* (no -ge-, h) refresh; 2ung *f* (-/-en) refreshment.

**er|'raten** *v/t.* (irr. raten, no -ge-, h) guess, find out; ~'rechnen *v/t.* (no -ge-, h) calculate, compute, work out.

**erreg|bar** *adj.* [ɛr're:kba:r] excitable; ~en [~gən] *v/t.* (no -ge-, h) excite; cause; 2er *m* (-s/-) exciter (a. ♂); ♂ germ, virus; 2ung [~guŋ] *f* excitation; excitement.

**er'reich|bar** *adj.* attainable; within reach or call; ~en *v/t.* (no -ge-, h) reach; *fig.* achieve, attain; catch (train); come up to (certain standard).

**er'rett|en** *v/t.* (no -ge-, h) rescue; 2ung *f* rescue.

**er'richt|en** *v/t.* (no -ge-, h) set up, erect; establish; 2ung *f* erection; establishment.

**er|'ringen** *v/t.* (irr. ringen, no -ge-, h) gain, obtain; achieve (success); ~'röten *v/i.* (no -ge-, sein) blush.

**Errungenschaft** [ɛr'ruŋənʃaft] *f* (-/-en) acquisition; achievement.

**Er'satz** *m* (-es/no pl.) replacement; substitute; compensation, amends sg., damages pl.; indemnification; s. Ersatzmann, Ersatzmittel; ~ leisten make amends; ~mann *m* substitute; ~mine *f* refill (for pencil); ~mittel *n* substitute, surrogate; ~reifen *mot.* *m* spare tyre, (Am. only) spare tire; ~teil ⊕ *n, m* spare (part).

**er'schaff|en** *v/t.* (irr. schaffen, no -ge-, h) create; 2ung *f* (-/no pl.) creation.

**er'schallen** *v/i.* ([irr. schallen,] no -ge-, sein) (re)sound; ring.

**er'schein|en** 1. *v/i.* (irr. scheinen, no -ge-, sein) appear; 2. 2 *n* (-s/no pl.) appearance; 2ung *f* (-/-en) appearance; apparition; vision.

**er|'schießen** *v/t.* (irr. schießen, no -ge-, h) shoot (dead); ~'schlaffen *v/i.* (no -ge-, sein) tire; relax; *fig.* languish, slacken; ~'schlagen *v/t.* (irr. schlagen, no -ge-, h) kill, slay;

~'schließen v/t. (irr. schließen, no -ge-, h) open; open up (new market); develop (district).

er'schöpf|en v/t. (no -ge-, h) exhaust; ℒung f exhaustion.

erschrak [er'ʃraːk] pret. of erschrecken 2.

er'schrecken 1. v/t. (no -ge-, h) frighten, scare; 2. v/i. (irr., no -ge-, sein) be frightened (über acc. at); ~d adj. alarming, startling.

erschrocken [er'ʃrɔkən] 1. p.p. of erschrecken 2; 2. adj. frightened, terrified.

erschütter|n [er'ʃytərn] v/t. (no -ge-, h) shake; fig. shock, move; ℒung f (-/-en) shock; fig. emotion; ℱ concussion; ⊕ percussion.

er'schweren v/t. (no -ge-, h) make more difficult; aggravate.

er'schwing|en v/t. (irr. schwingen, no -ge-, h) afford; ~lich adj. within s.o.'s means; prices: reasonable.

er'|sehen v/t. (irr. sehen, no -ge-, h) see, learn, gather (all: aus from); ~'sehnen v/t. (no -ge-, h) long for; ~'setzen v/t. (no -ge-, h) repair; make up for, compensate (for); replace; refund.

er'sichtlich adj. evident, obvious.

er'sinnen v/t. (irr. sinnen, no -ge-, h) contrive, devise.

er'spar|en v/t. (no -ge-, h) save; j-m et. ~ spare s.o. s.th.; ℒnis f (-/-se) saving.

er'sprießlich adj. useful, beneficial.

erst [eːrst] 1. adj.: der (die, das) ~e the first; 2. adv. first; at first; only; not ... till or until.

er'starr|en v/i. (no -ge-, sein) stiffen; solidify; congeal; set; grow numb; fig. blood: run cold; ~t adj. benumbed; ℒung f (-/-en) numbness; solidification; congealment; setting.

erstatt|en [er'ʃtatən] v/t. (no -ge-, h) restore; s. ersetzen; Bericht ~ (make a) report; ℒung f (-/-en) restitution.

'Erstaufführung f thea. first night or performance, premiere; film: a. first run.

er'staun|en 1. v/i. (no -ge-, sein) be astonished (über acc. at); 2. v/t. (no -ge-, h) astonish; 3. ℒ n astonishment; in ~ setzen astonish; ~lich adj. astonishing, amazing.

er'stechen v/t. (irr. stechen, no -ge-, h) stab.

er'steig|en v/t. (irr. steigen, no -ge-, h) ascend, climb; ℒung f ascent.

erstens adv. ['eːrstəns] first, firstly.

er'stick|en (no -ge-) v/t. (h) and v/i. (sein) choke, suffocate; stifle; ℒung f (-/-en) suffocation. [rate, F A 1.}

'erstklassig adj. first-class, first-}

er'streben v/t. (no -ge-, h) strive after or for; ~swert adj. desirable.

er'strecken v/refl. (no -ge-, h) extend; sich ~ über (acc.) cover.

er'suchen 1. v/t. (no -ge-, h) request; 2. ℒ n (-s/-) request.

er|'tappen v/t. (no -ge-, h) catch, surprise; s. frisch; ~'tönen v/i. (no -ge-, sein) (re)sound.

Ertrag [er'traːk] m (-[e]s/-e) produce, yield; proceeds pl., returns pl.; ✗ output; ℒen [~gən] v/t. (irr. tragen, no -ge-, h) bear, endure; suffer; stand.

erträglich adj. [er'treːkliç] tolerable.

er|'tränken v/t. (no -ge-, h) drown; ~'trinken v/i. (irr. trinken, no -ge-, sein) be drowned, drown; ~übrigen [er'yːbrigən] v/t. (no -ge-, h) save; spare (time); sich ~ be unnecessary; ~'wachen v/i. (no -ge-, sein) awake, wake up.

er'wachsen 1. v/i. (irr. wachsen, no -ge-, sein) arise (aus from); 2. adj. grown-up, adult; ℒe m, f (-/-n) grown-up, adult.

er'wäg|en v/t. (irr. wägen, no -ge-, h) consider, think s.th. over; ℒung f (-/-en) consideration.

er'wählen v/t. (no -ge-, h) choose, elect.

er'wähn|en v/t. (no -ge-, h) mention; ℒung f (-/-en) mention.

er'wärmen v/t. (no -ge-, h) warm, heat; sich ~ warm (up).

er'wart|en v/t. (no -ge-, h) await, wait for; fig. expect; ℒung f expectation.

er|'wecken v/t. (no -ge-, h) wake, rouse; fig. awake; cause (fear); arouse (suspicion); ~'wehren v/refl. (gen.) (no -ge-, h) keep or ward off; ~'weichen v/t. (no -ge-, h) soften; fig. move; ~'weisen v/t. (irr. weisen, no -ge-, h) prove; show (respect); render (service); do, pay (honour); do (favour).

er'weiter|n v/t. and v/refl. (no -ge-, h) expand, enlarge, extend, widen; ℒung f (-/-en) expansion, enlargement, extension.

Erwerb [er'verp] m (-[e]s/-e) acquisition; living; earnings pl.; business; ℒen [~bən] v/t. (irr. werben, no -ge-, h) acquire; gain; earn.

erwerbs|los adj. [er'verpsloːs] unemployed; ~tätig adj. (gainfully) employed; ~unfähig adj. [er-'verpsʔ-] incapable of earning one's living; ℒzweig m line of business.

Erwerbung [er'verbuŋ] f acquisition.

erwider|n [er'viːdərn] v/t. (no -ge-, h) return; answer, reply; retort; ℒung f (-/-en) return; answer, reply.

er'wischen v/t. (no -ge-, h) catch, trap, get hold of.

er'wünscht adj. desired; desirable; welcome.

er'würgen v/t. (no -ge-, h) strangle, throttle.

**Erz** ⚒ [e:rts] *n* (-es/-e) ore; *poet.* brass.

**er'zähl|en** *v/t.* (*no* -ge-, *h*) tell; relate; narrate; 2er *m*, 2erin *f* (-/-nen) narrator; writer; 2ung *f* (-/-en) narration; (short) story, narrative.

**'Erz|bischof** *eccl. m* archbishop; '~bistum *eccl. n* archbishopric; '~engel *eccl. m* archangel.

**er'zeug|en** *v/t.* (*no* -ge-, *h*) beget; produce; make, manufacture; 2er *m* (-s/-) father (*of child*); ⚭ producer; 2nis *n* produce; production; ⊕ product; 2ung *f* production.

**'Erz|feind** *m* arch-enemy; '~herzog *m* archduke; '~herzogin *f* archduchess; '~herzogtum *n* archduchy.

**er'zieh|en** *v/t.* (*irr.* ziehen, *no* -ge-, *h*) bring up, rear, raise; educate; 2er *m* (-s/-) educator; teacher, tutor; 2rin *f* (-/-nen) teacher; governess; ~risch *adj.* educational, pedagogic(-al).

**Er'ziehung** *f* (-/⚭ -en) upbringing; breeding; education; ~sanstalt [er'tsi:uns�ʔ-] *f* reformatory, approved school; ~swesen *n* (-s/*no pl.*) educational matters *pl.* or system.

**er'|zielen** *v/t.* (*no* -ge-, *h*) obtain; realize (*price*); achieve (*success*); *sports:* score (*points, goal*); ~'zürnen *v/t.* (*no* -ge-, *h*) make angry, irritate, enrage; ~'zwingen *v/t.* (*irr.* zwingen, *no* -ge-, *h*) force; compel; extort (*von* from).

**es** *pers. pron.* [es] **1.** *pers.:* it, he, she; *wo ist das Buch?* — ~ *ist auf dem Tisch* where is the book? — it is on the table; *das Mädchen blieb stehen, als* ~ *seine Mutter sah* the girl stopped when she saw her mother; **2.** *impers.:* it; ~ *gibt* there is, there are; ~ *ist kalt* it is cold; ~ *klopft* there is a knock at the door.

**Esche** 🌿 ['ɛʃə] *f* (-/-n) ash(-tree).

**Esel** *zo.* ['e:zəl] *m* (-s/-) donkey; *esp. fig.* ass; ~ei [~'laɪ] *f* (-/-en) stupidity, stupid thing, folly; '~sbrücke *f at school:* crib, *Am.* pony; ~sohr ['e:zəls⁹-] *n* dog's ear (*of book*).

**Eskorte** [ɛs'kɔrtə] *f* (-/-n) ⚔ escort; ⚓ convoy.

**Espe** 🌿 ['ɛspə] *f* (-/-n) asp(en).

**'eßbar** *adj.* eatable, edible.

**Esse** ['ɛsə] *f* (-/-n) chimney.

**essen** ['ɛsən] **1.** *v/i.* (*irr.*, ge-, *h*) eat; *zu Mittag* ~ (have) lunch; dine, have dinner; *zu Abend* ~ dine, have dinner; *esp. late at night:* sup, have supper; *auswärts* ~ eat *or* dine out; **2.** *v/t.* (*irr.*, ge-, *h*) eat; *et. zu Mittag etc.* ~ have s.th. for lunch, *etc.*; **3.** 2 *n* (-s/-) eating; food; meal; dish; *midday meal:* lunch, dinner; *evening meal:* dinner; *last meal of the day:* supper; '2szeit *f* lunch-time; dinner-time; supper-time.

**Essenz** [ɛ'sɛnts] *f* (-/-en) essence.

**Essig** ['ɛsiç] *m* (-s/-e) vinegar; '~gurke *f* pickled cucumber, gherkin.

**'Eß|löffel** *m* soup-spoon; '~nische *f* dining alcove, *Am.* dinette; '~tisch *m* dining-table; '~waren *f/pl.* eatables *pl.*, victuals *pl.*, food; '~zimmer *n* dining-room.

**etablieren** [eta'bli:rən] *v/t.* (*no* -ge-, *h*) establish, set up.

**Etage** [e'ta:ʒə] *f* (-/-n) floor, stor(e)y; ~nwohnung *f* flat, *Am. a.* apartment.

**Etappe** [e'tapə] *f* (-/-n) ⚔ base; *fig.* stage, leg.

**Etat** [e'ta:] *m* (-s/-s) budget, *parl. the* Estimates *pl.*; ~sjahr *n* fiscal year. [*or sg.*]

**Ethik** ['e:tik] *f* (-/⚭ -en) ethics *pl.*]

**Etikett** [eti'kɛt] *n* (-[e]s/-e, -s) label, ticket; tag; *gummed: Am. a.* sticker; ~e *f* (-/-n) etiquette; 2ieren [~'ti:rən] *v/t.* (*no* -ge-, *h*) label.

**etliche** *indef. pron.* ['ɛtliçə] some, several.

**Etui** [e'tvi:] *n* (-s/-s) case.

**etwa** *adv.* ['ɛtva] perhaps, by chance; about, *Am. a.* around; ~ig *adj.* ['~⁹iç] possible, eventual.

**etwas** ['ɛtvas] **1.** *indef. pron.* something; anything; **2.** *adj.* some; any; **3.** *adv.* somewhat; **4.** 2 *n* (-/-): *das gewisse* ~ that certain something.

**euch** *pers. pron.* [ɔyç] you; ~ (*selbst*) yourselves.

**euer** *poss. pron.* ['ɔyər] your; *der* (*die, das*) *eu(e)re* yours.

**Eule** *orn.* ['ɔylə] *f* (-/-n) owl; ~n *nach Athen tragen* carry coals to Newcastle.

**euresgleichen** *pron.* ['ɔyrəs'glaɪçən] people like you, F the likes of you.

**Europä|er** [ɔyro'pɛ:ər] *m* (-s/-) European; 2isch *adj.* European.

**Euter** ['ɔytər] *n* (-s/-) udder.

**evakuieren** [evaku'i:rən] *v/t.* (*no* -ge-, *h*) evacuate.

**evangeli|sch** *adj.* [evan'ge:liʃ] evangelic(al); Protestant; Lutheran; 2um [~jum] *n* (-s/Evangelien) gospel.

**eventuell** [eventu'ɛl] **1.** *adj.* possible; **2.** *adv.* possibly, perhaps.

**ewig** *adj.* ['e:viç] eternal; everlasting; perpetual; *auf* ~ for ever; '2keit *f* (-/-en) eternity; F: *seit e-r* ~ for ages.

**exakt** *adj.* [ɛ'ksakt] exact; 2heit *f* (-/-en) exactitude, exactness; accuracy.

**Exam|en** [ɛ'ksa:mən] *n* (-s/-, Examina) examination, F exam; 2inieren [~ami'ni:rən] *v/t.* (*no* -ge-, *h*) examine.

**Exekutive** [ɛksəku'ti:və] *f* (-/*no pl.*) executive power.

**Exempel** [ɛ'ksɛmpəl] *n* (-s/-) example, instance.

**Exemplar** [ɛksɛm'plɑːr] *n* (-s/-e) specimen; copy (*of book*).
**exerzier|en** ✕ [ɛksɛr'tsiːrən] *v/i.* *and v/t.* (*no* -ge-, *h*) drill; **2platz** ✕ *m* drill-ground, parade-ground.
**Exil** [ɛ'ksiːl] *n* (-s/-e) exile.
**Existenz** [ɛksis'tɛnts] *f* (-/-en) existence; living, livelihood; **∼minimum** *n* subsistence minimum.
**exis'tieren** *v/i.* (*no* -ge-, *h*) exist; subsist.
**exotisch** *adj.* [ɛ'ksoːtiʃ] exotic.
**exped|ieren** [ɛkspe'diːrən] *v/t.* (*no* -ge-, *h*) dispatch; **2ition** [∼i'tsjoːn] *f* (-/-en) dispatch, forwarding; expedition; ✝ dispatch *or* forwarding office.
**Experiment** [ɛksperi'mɛnt] *n* (-[e]s/-e) experiment; **2ieren** [∼'tiːrən] *v/i.* (*no* -ge-, *h*) experiment.

**explo|dieren** [ɛksplo'diːrən] *v/i.* (*no* -ge-, *sein*) explode, burst; **2sion** [∼'zjoːn] *f* (-/-en) explosion; **∼siv** *adj.* [∼'ziːf] explosive.
**Export** [ɛks'pɔrt] *m* (-[e]s/-e) export(ation); **2ieren** [∼'tiːrən] *v/t.* (*no* -ge-, *h*) export.
**extra** *adj.* ['ɛkstra] extra; special; **2blatt** *n* extra edition (*of newspaper*), *Am.* extra.
**Extrakt** [ɛks'trakt] *m* (-[e]s/-e) extract.
**Extrem** [ɛks'treːm] **1.** *n* (-s/-e) extreme; **2.** 2 *adj.* extreme.
**Exzellenz** [ɛkstsɛ'lɛnts] *f* (-/-en) Excellency.
**exzentrisch** *adj.* [ɛks'tsɛntriʃ] eccentric.
**Exzeß** [ɛks'tsɛs] *m* (*Exzesses/Exzesse*) excess.

# F

**Fabel** ['fɑːbəl] *f* (-/-n) fable (*a. fig.*); plot (*of story, book, etc.*); **2haft** *adj.* fabulous; marvellous; **2n** *v/i.* (ge-, *h*) tell (tall) stories.
**Fabrik** [fa'briːk] *f* (-/-en) factory, works *sg.*, *pl.*, mill; **∼ant** [∼i'kant] *m* (-en/-en) factory-owner, mill-owner; manufacturer; **∼arbeit** *f* factory work; *s.* Fabrikware; **∼arbeiter** *m* factory worker *or* hand; **∼at** [∼i'kaːt] *n* (-[e]s/-e) make; product; **∼ationsfehler** [∼a'tsjoːns-] *m* flaw; **∼besitzer** *m* factory-owner; **∼marke** *f* trade mark; **∼stadt** *f* factory *or* industrial town; **∼ware** *f* manufactured article; **∼zeichen** *n s.* Fabrikmarke.
**Fach** [fax] *n* (-[e]s/∼er) section, compartment, shelf (*of bookcase, cupboard, etc.*); pigeon-hole (*in desk*); drawer; *fig.* subject; *s.* Fachgebiet; **∼arbeiter** *m* skilled worker; **∼arzt** *m* specialist (*für* in); **∼ausbildung** *f* professional training; **∼ausdruck** *m* technical term.
**fächeln** ['fɛçəln] *v/t.* (ge-, *h*) fan *s.o.*
**Fächer** ['fɛçər] *m* (-s/-) fan; **2förmig** *adj.* ['∼fœrmiç] fan-shaped.
**'Fach|gebiet** *n* branch, field, province; **∼kenntnisse** *f/pl.* specialized knowledge; **∼kreis** *m*: *in* ∼en among experts; **2kundig** *adj.* competent, expert; **∼literatur** *f* specialized literature; **∼mann** *m* expert; **2männisch** *adj.* ['∼mɛniʃ] expert; **∼schule** *f* technical school; **∼werk** △ *n* framework.
**Fackel** ['fakəl] *f* (-/-n) torch; **2n** F *v/i.* (ge-, *h*) hesitate, F shilly-shally; **∼zug** *m* torchlight procession.
**fad** *adj.* [fɑːt], **∼e** *adj.* ['fɑːdə] food:

insipid, tasteless; stale; *p.* dull, boring.
**Faden** ['fɑːdən] *m* (-s/∺) thread (*a. fig.*); *fig.*: *an e-m ∼ hängen* hang by a thread; **∼nudeln** *f/pl.* vermicelli *pl.*; **2scheinig** *adj.* ['∼ʃainiç] threadbare; *excuse, etc.*: flimsy, thin.
**fähig** *adj.* ['fɛːiç] capable (*zu inf.* of *ger.*; *gen.* of); able (*to inf.*); **2keit** *f* (-/-en) (cap)ability; talent, faculty.
**fahl** *adj.* [fɑːl] pale, pallid; *colour*: faded; *complexion*: leaden, livid.
**fahnd|en** ['fɑːndən] *v/i.* (ge-, *h*): *nach j-m ∼* search for s.o.; **2ung** *f* (-/-en) search.
**Fahne** ['fɑːnə] *f* (-/-n) flag; standard; banner; ⚓, ✕, *fig.* colo(u)rs *pl.*; *typ.* galley-proof.
**'Fahnen|eid** *m* oath of allegiance; **∼flucht** *f* desertion; **2flüchtig** *adj.*: *∼ werden* desert (the colo[u]rs); **∼stange** *f* flagstaff, *Am. a.* flagpole.
**'Fahr|bahn** *f*, **∼damm** *m* roadway.
**Fähre** ['fɛːrə] *f* (-/-n) ferry(-boat).
**fahren** ['fɑːrən] (*irr.*, ge-) **1.** *v/i.* (*sein*) driver, *vehicle*, *etc.*: drive, go, travel; *cyclist*: ride, cycle; ⚓ sail; *mot.* motor; *mit der Eisenbahn ∼* go by train *or* rail; *spazieren* ∼ go for *or* take a drive; *mit der Hand ∼ über* (*acc.*) pass one's hand over; *∼ lassen* let go *or* slip; *gut* (*schlecht*) *∼ bei* do *or* fare well (badly) at *or* with; *er ist gut dabei gefahren* he did very well out of it; **2.** *v/t.* (*h*) carry, convey; drive (*car, train, etc.*); ride (*bicycle, etc.*).
**'Fahrer** *m* (-s/-) driver; **∼flucht** *f* (-/*no pl.*) hit-and-run offence, *Am.* hit-and-run offense.

'**Fahr|gast** *m* passenger; *in taxi:*
fare; '**~geld** *n* fare; '**~gelegenheit**
*f* transport facilities *pl.*; '**~gestell** *n*
*mot.* chassis; 🜖 undercarriage,
landing gear; '**~karte** *f* ticket;
'**~kartenschalter** *m* booking-office, *Am.* ticket office; '**2lässig** *adj.*
careless, negligent; '**~lässigkeit** *f*
(-/**~**-en) carelessness, negligence;
'**~lehrer** *mot. m* driving instructor;
'**~plan** *m* timetable, *Am. a.* schedule; '**2planmäßig 1.** *adj.* regular,
*Am.* scheduled; **2.** *adv.* on time,
*Am. a.* on schedule; '**~preis** *m* fare;
'**~rad** *n* bicycle, F bike; '**~schein**
*m* ticket; '**~schule** *mot. f* driving
school, school of motoring; '**~stuhl**
*m* lift, *Am.* elevator; '**~stuhlführer**
*m* lift-boy, lift-man, *Am.* elevator
operator; '**~stunde** *mot. f* driving
lesson.

**Fahrt** [faːrt] *f* (-/-en) ride, drive,
journey; voyage, passage; trip; **~**
*ins Blaue* mystery tour; *in voller* **~**
(at) full speed.

**Fährte** ['fɛːrtə] *f* (-/-n) track (*a. fig.*);
*auf der falschen* **~** *sein* be on the
wrong track.

'**Fahr|vorschrift** *f* rule of the road;
'**~wasser** *n* 🜄 navigable water;
*fig.* track; '**~weg** *m* roadway; '**~zeug**
*n* vehicle; 🜄 vessel.

**Fakt|or** ['faktɔr] *m* (-s/-en) factor;
**~otum** [~'toːtum] *n* (-s/-s, *Faktoten*)
factotum; **~ur** [~'tuːr] *f* (-/-en),
**~ura** † [~'tuːra] *f* (-/*Fakturen*)
invoice.

**Fakultät** *univ.* [fakul'tɛːt] *f* (-/-en)
faculty.

**Falke** *orn.* ['falkə] *m* (-n/-n) hawk,
falcon.

**Fall** [fal] *m* (-[e]s/**~**e) fall (*of body,
stronghold, city, etc.*); *gr.,* 🜃🜃, ♂
case; *gesetzt den* **~** suppose; *auf
alle Fälle* at all events; *auf jeden* **~**
in any case, at any rate; *auf keinen* **~**
on no account, in no case.

**Falle** ['falə] *f* (-/-n) trap (*a. fig.*);
pitfall (*a. fig.*); *e-e* **~** *stellen* set a
trap (*j-m* for s.o.).

**fallen** ['falən] **1.** *v/i.* (*irr.,* ge-, sein)
fall, drop; 🜖 be killed in action;
*shol:* be heard; *flood water:* subside; *auf j-n* **~** *suspicion, etc.:* fall
on s.o.; **~** *lassen* drop (*plate, etc.*);
**2.** **2** *n* (-s/*no pl.*) fall(ing).

**fällen** ['fɛlən] *v/t.* (ge-, h) fell, cut
down (*tree*); 🜖 lower (*bayonet*); 🜃🜃
pass (*judgement*), give (*decision*).

'**fallenlassen** *v/t.* (*irr.* lassen, sep.,
*no* -ge-, h) drop (*plan, claim, etc.*).

**fällig** *adj.* ['fɛliç] due; payable;
'**2keit** *f* (-/**~**-en) maturity; '**2keits-
termin** *m* date of maturity.

'**Fall|obst** *n* windfall; '**~reep** 🜄
['~reːp] *n* (-[e]s/-e) gangway.

**falls** *cj.* [fals] if; in the event of *ger.*;
in case.

'**Fall|schirm** *m* parachute; '**~**-

'**~schirmspringer** *m* parachutist;
'**~strick** *m* snare; '**~tür** *f* trap door.

**falsch** [falʃ] **1.** *adj.* false; wrong;
*bank-note, etc.:* counterfeit; *money:*
base; *bill of exchange, etc.:* forged;
*p.* deceitful; **2.** *adv.:* **~** *gehen watch:*
go wrong; **~** *verbunden! teleph.*
sorry, wrong number.

**fälsch|en** ['fɛlʃən] *v/t.* (ge-, h) fal-
sify, forge, fake (*document, etc.*);
counterfeit (*bank-note, coin, etc.*);
fake (*calculations, etc.*); tamper
with (*financial account*); adulterate
(*food, wine*); '**2er** *m* (-s/-) forger,
faker; adulterator.

'**Falsch|geld** *n* counterfeit or bad or
base money; '**~heit** *f* (-/**~**-en) false-
ness, falsity, duplicity, deceitful-
ness; '**~meldung** *f* false report;
'**~münzer** *m* (-s/-) coiner; '**~mün-
zerwerkstatt** *f* coiner's den;
'**2spielen** *v/i.* (*sep.,* -ge-, h) cheat
(at cards); '**~spieler** *m* card-
sharper.

'**Fälschung** *f* (-/-en) forgery; fal-
sification; fake; adulteration.

**Falt|boot** ['falt-] *n* folding canoe,
*Am.* foldboat, faltboat; **~e** ['~ə] *f*
(-/-n) fold; pleat (*in skirt, etc.*);
crease (*in trousers*); wrinkle (*on
face*); '**2en** *v/t.* (ge-, h) fold; clasp
or join (*one's hands*); '**2ig** *adj.*
folded; pleated; wrinkled.

**Falz** [falts] *m* (-es/-e) fold; rabbet
(*for woodworking, etc.*); bookbind-
*ing:* guard; '**2en** *v/t.* (ge-, h) fold;
rabbet.

**familiär** *adj.* [famil'jɛːr] familiar;
informal.

**Familie** [fa'miːljə] *f* (-/-n) family
(*a. zo.,* ♣).

**Fa'milien|angelegenheit** *f* family
affair; **~anschluß** *m:* **~** *haben* live
as one of the family; **~nachrichten**
*f/pl. in newspaper:* birth, marriage
and death announcements *pl.*;
**~name** *m* family name, surname,
*Am. a.* last name; **~stand** *m* marital
status.

**Fanati|ker** [fa'naːtikər] *m* (-s/-)
fanatic; **2sch** *adj.* fanatic(al).

**Fanatismus** [fana'tismus] *m* (-/*no
pl.*) fanaticism.

**fand** [fant] *pret. of* finden.

**Fanfare** [fan'faːrə] *f* (-/-n) fanfare,
flourish (of trumpets).

**Fang** [faŋ] *m* (-[e]s/**~**e) capture,
catch(ing); *hunt.* bag; '**2en** *v/t.* (*irr.*
ge-, h) catch (*animal, ball, thief,
etc.*); '**~zahn** *m* fang (*of dog, wolf,
etc.*); tusk (*of boar*).

**Farb|band** ['farp-] *n* (typewriter)
ribbon; **~e** ['~bə] *f* (-/-n) colo(u)r;
paint; dye; complexion; *cards:*
suit; **2echt** *adj.* ['farpʔ-] colo(u)r-
fast.

**färben** ['fɛrbən] *v/t.* (ge-, h) col-
o(u)r (*glass, food, etc.*); dye (*material,
hair, Easter eggs, etc.*); tint (*hair,*

*paper*, *glass*); stain (*wood, fabrics, glass, etc.*); *sich ~* take on *or* assume a colo(u)r; *sich rot ~* turn *or* go red.

'**farben|blind** adj. colo(u)r-blind; '2druck m (-[e]s/-e) colo(u)r print; '~prächtig adj. splendidly colo(u)rful.

**Färber** ['fɛrbər] m (-s/-) dyer.

**Farb|fernsehen** ['farp-] n colo(u)r television; '~film m colo(u)r film; 2ig adj. ['~biç] colo(u)red; glass: tinted, stained; fig. colo(u)rful; 2los adj. ['~p-] colo(u)rless; '~photographie f colo(u)r photography; '~stift m colo(u)red pencil; '~stoff m colo(u)ring matter; '~ton m tone; shade, tint.

**Färbung** ['fɛrbuŋ] f (-/-en) colo(u)ring (a. fig.); shade (a. fig.).

**Farnkraut** ♣ ['farnkraut] n fern.

**Fasan** orn. [fa'zaːn] m (-[e]s/-e[n]) pheasant.

**Fasching** ['faʃiŋ] m (-s/-e, -s) carnival.

**Fasel|ei** [faːzə'laɪ] f (-/-en) drivelling, waffling; twaddle; '2n v/i. (ge-, h) blather; F waffle.

**Faser** ['faːzər] f (-/-n) anat., ♣, fig. fib|re, Am. -er; cotton, wool, etc.: staple; '2ig adj. fibrous; '2n v/i. (ge-, h) wool: shed fine hairs.

**Faß** [fas] n (Fasses/Fässer) cask, barrel; tub; vat; '~bier n draught beer.

**Fassade** ⚠ [fa'saːdə] f (-/-n) façade, front (a. fig.); ~nkletterer m (-s/-) cat burglar.

**fassen** ['fasən] (ge-, h) 1. v/t. seize, take hold of; catch, apprehend (criminal); hold; s. einfassen; fig. grasp, understand, believe; pluck up (courage); form (plan); make (decision); sich ~ compose o.s.; sich kurz ~ be brief; 2. v/i.: ~ nach reach for. [ceivable.\]

'**faßlich** adj. comprehensible, con-

'**Fassung** f (-/-en) setting (of jewels); ⚡ socket; fig.: composure; draft (-ing); wording, version; die ~ verlieren lose one's self-control; aus der ~ bringen disconcert; '~skraft f (powers of) comprehension, mental capacity; '~svermögen n (holding) capacity; fig. s. Fassungskraft.

**fast** adv. [fast] almost, nearly; ~ nichts next to nothing; ~ nie hardly ever.

**fasten** ['fastən] v/i. (ge-, h) fast; abstain from food and drink; '2zeit f Lent.

'**Fast|nacht** f (-/no pl.) Shrovetide; carnival; '~tag m fast-day.

**fatal** adj. [fa'taːl] situation, etc.: awkward; business, etc.: unfortunate; mistake, etc.: fatal.

**fauchen** ['fauxən] v/i. (ge-, h) cat, etc.: spit; F p. spit (with anger); locomotive, etc.: hiss.

**faul** adj. [faul] fruit, etc.: rotten, bad; fish, meat: putrid, bad; fig. lazy, indolent, idle; fishy; ~e Ausrede lame excuse; '~en v/i. (ge-, h) rot, go bad, putrefy.

**faulenze|n** ['faulɛntsən] v/i. (ge-, h) idle; laze, loaf; '2r m (-s/-) idler, sluggard, F lazy-bones.

'**Faul|heit** f (-/no pl.) idleness, laziness; '2ig adj. putrid.

**Fäulnis** ['fɔʏlnis] f (-/no pl.) rottenness; putrefaction; decay.

'**Faul|pelz** m s. Faulenzer; '~tier n zo. sloth (a. fig.).

**Faust** [faust] f (-/~e) fist; auf eigene ~ on one's own initiative; '~handschuh m mitt(en); '~schlag m blow with the fist, punch, Am. F a. slug.

**Favorit** [favo'riːt] m (-en/-en) favo(u)rite.

**Faxe** ['faksə] f (-/-n): ~n machen (play the) fool; ~n schneiden pull or make faces.

**Fazit** ['faːtsit] n (-s/-e, -s) result, upshot; total; das ~ ziehen sum or total up.

**Februar** ['feːbruaːr] m (-[s]/-e) February.

**fecht|en** ['fɛçtən] v/i. (irr., ge-, h) fight; fenc. fence; '2er m (-s/-) fencer.

**Feder** ['feːdər] f (-/-n) feather; (ornamental) plume; pen; ⊕ spring; '~bett n feather bed; '~busch m tuft of feathers; plume; '~gewicht n boxing, etc.: featherweight; '~halter m (-s/-) penholder; '~kiel m quill; '~kraft f elasticity, resilience; '~krieg m paper war; literary controversy; '2leicht adj. (as) light as a feather; '~lesen n (-s/no pl.) nicht viel ~s machen mit make short work of; '~messer n penknife; '2n v/i. (ge-, h) be elastic; '2nd adj. springy, elastic; '~strich m stroke of the pen; '~vieh n poultry; '~zeichnung f pen-and-ink drawing.

**Fee** [fe:] f (-/-n) fairy.

**Fegefeuer** ['feːgə-] n purgatory.

**fegen** ['feːgən] v/t. (ge-, h) sweep; clean.

**Fehde** ['feːdə] f (-/-n) feud; private war; in ~ liegen be at feud; F be at daggers drawn.

**Fehl** [fe:l] m: ohne ~ without fault or blemish; '~betrag m deficit, deficiency.

**fehlen** ['feːlən] v/i. (ge-, h) be absent; be missing or lacking; do wrong; es fehlt ihm an (dat.) he lacks; was fehlt Ihnen? what is the matter with you?; weit gefehlt! far off the mark!

**Fehler** ['feːlər] m (-s/-) mistake, error, F slip; fault; ⊕ defect, flaw; '2frei adj., '2los adj. faultless, perfect; ⊕ flawless; '2haft adj. faulty; defective; incorrect.

'**Fehl|geburt** f miscarriage, abortion; '⊾gehen v/i. (irr. gehen, sep., -ge-, sein) go wrong; '⊾griff fig. m mistake, blunder; '⊾schlag fig. m failure; '⊾schlagen fig. v/i. (irr. schlagen, sep., -ge-, sein) fail, miscarry; '⊾schuß m miss; '⊾treten v/i. (irr. treten, sep., -ge-, sein) make a false step; '⊾tritt m false step; slip; fig. slip, fault; '⊾urteil ⚖ n error of judg(e)ment; '⊾zündung mot. f misfire, backfire.

**Feier** ['faɪər] f (-/-n) ceremony; celebration; festival; festivity; '⊾abend m finishing or closing time; ⊾ machen finish, F knock off; '⊾lich adj. promise, oath, etc.: solemn; act: ceremonial; '⊾lichkeit f (-/-en) solemnity; ceremony; '⊾n (ge-, h) 1. v/t. hold (celebration); celebrate, observe (feast, etc.); 2. v/i. celebrate; rest (from work), make holiday; '⊾tag m holiday; festive day.

**feig** adj. [faɪk] cowardly.
**feige**[1] adj. ['faɪgə] cowardly.
**Feige**[2] [⊾] f (-/-n) fig; '⊾nbaum ♀ m fig-tree; '⊾nblatt n fig-leaf.
**Feig|heit** ['faɪkhaɪt] f (-/no pl.) cowardice, cowardliness; ⊾ling ['⊾klɪŋ] m (-s/-e) coward.
**feil** adj. [faɪl] for sale, to be sold; fig. venal; '⊾bieten v/t. (irr. bieten, sep., -ge-, h) offer for sale.
**Feile** ['faɪlə] f (-/-n) file; '⊾n (ge-, h) 1. v/t. file (a. fig.); fig. polish; 2. v/i.: ⊾ an (dat.) file (at); fig. polish (up).
**feilschen** ['faɪlʃən] v/i. (ge-, h) bargain (um for), haggle (for, about), Am. a. dicker (about).
**fein** adj. [faɪn] fine; material, etc.: high-grade; wine, etc.: choice; fabric, etc.: delicate, dainty; manners: polished; p. polite; distinction: subtle.
**Feind** [faɪnt] m (-[e]s/-e) enemy (a. ✕); '⊾lich adj. hostile, inimical; '⊾schaft f (-/-en) enmity; animosity, hostility; '⊾selig adj. hostile (gegen to); '⊾seligkeit f (-/-en) hostility; malevolence.
'**fein|fühlend** adj., '⊾fühlig adj. sensitive; '⊾gefühl n sensitiveness; delicacy; '⊾gehalt m (monetary) standard; '⊾heit f (-/-en) fineness; delicacy, daintiness; politeness; elegance; '⊾kost f high-class groceries pl., Am. delicatessen; '⊾mechanik f precision mechanics; '⊾schmecker m (-s/-) gourmet, epicure; '⊾sinnig adj. subtle.
**feist** adj. [faɪst] fat, stout.
**Feld** [felt] n (-[e]s/-er) field (a. ✕, ♞, sports); ground, soil; plain; chess: square; △, ⊕ panel, compartment; ins ⊾ ziehen take the field; '⊾arbeit f agricultural work; '⊾bett n camp-bed; '⊾blume f wild flower; '⊾dienst ✕ m field service; '⊾flasche f water-bottle;

'⊾frucht f fruit of the field; '⊾geschrei n war-cry, battle-cry; '⊾herr m general; '⊾kessel m camp-kettle; '⊾lazarett ✕ n field-hospital; '⊾lerche orn. f skylark; '⊾marschall m Field Marshal; '⊾marschmäßig ✕ adj. in full marching order; '⊾maus zo. f field-mouse; '⊾messer m (land) survey-or; '⊾post ✕ f army postal service; '⊾schlacht ✕ f battle; '⊾stecher m (-s/-) (ein a pair of) field-glasses pl.; '⊾stuhl m camp-stool; ⊾webel ['⊾ve:bəl] m (-s/-) sergeant; '⊾weg m (field) path; '⊾zeichen ✕ n standard; '⊾zug m ✕ campaign (a. fig.), (military) expedition; Am. fig. a. drive.
**Felge** ['felgə] f (-/-n) felloe (of cart-wheel); rim (of car wheel, etc.).
**Fell** [fel] n (-[e]s/-e) skin, pelt, fur (of dead animal); coat (of cat, etc.); fleece (of sheep).
**Fels** [fels] m (-en/-en), ⊾en ['⊾zən] m (-s/-) rock; ⊾block ['fels-] m rock; boulder; ⊾ig adj. ['⊾zɪç] rocky.
**Fenchel** ♀ ['fençəl] m (-s/no pl.) fennel.
**Fenster** ['fenstər] n (-s/-) window; '⊾brett n window-sill; '⊾flügel m casement (of casement window); sash (of sash window); '⊾kreuz n cross-bar(s pl.); '⊾laden m shutter; '⊾rahmen m window-frame; '⊾riegel m window-fastener; '⊾scheibe f (window-)pane; '⊾sims m, n window-sill.
**Ferien** ['fe:rjən] pl. holiday(s pl.), esp. Am. vacation; leave, Am. a. furlough; parl. recess; ⚖ vacation, recess; '⊾kolonie f children's holiday camp.
**Ferkel** ['ferkəl] n (-s/-) young pig; contp. p. pig.
**fern** [fern] 1. adj. far (off), distant; remote; 2. adv. far (away); von ⊾ from a distance.
'**Fernamt** teleph. n trunk exchange, Am. long-distance exchange.
'**fernbleiben** 1. v/i. (irr. bleiben, sep., -ge-, sein) remain or stay away (dat. from); 2. ⊾ n (-s/no pl.) absence (from school, etc.); absentee-ism (from work).
**Fern|e** ['fernə] f (-/-n) distance; remoteness; aus der ⊾ from or at a distance; '⊾er 1. adj. farther; fig.: further; future; 2. adv. further (-more), in addition, also; ⊾ liefen ... also ran ...; '⊾flug ⊾ m long-distance flight; ⊾gelenkt adj. ['⊾gə-leŋkt] missile: guided; aircraft, etc.: remote-control(l)ed; '⊾gespräch teleph. n trunk call, Am. long-distance call; '⊾gesteuert adj. s. fern-gelenkt; '⊾glas n binoculars pl.; '⊾halten v/t. and v/refl. (irr. halten, sep., -ge-, h) keep away (von from); '⊾heizung f district heating; '⊾la-

ster F *mot. m* long-distance lorry, *Am.* long haul truck; '~lenkung *f* (-/-en) remote control; '2liegen *v/i.* (irr. liegen, sep., -ge-, h): es liegt mir fern zu inf. I am far from ger.; '~rohr *n* telescope; '~schreiber *m* teleprinter, *Am.* teletypewriter; '~sehen 1. *n* (-s/no pl.) television; 2. 2 *v/i.* (irr. sehen, sep., -ge-, h) watch television; '~seher *m* television set; *p.* television viewer, televiewer; '~sehsendung *f* television broadcast, telecast; '~sicht *f* visual range.

'Fernsprech|amt *n* telephone exchange, *Am. a.* central; '~anschluß *m* telephone connection; '~er *m* telephone; '~leitung *f* telephone line; '~zelle *f* telephone box.

'fern|stehen *v/i.* (irr. stehen, sep., -ge-, h) have no real (point of) contact (dat. with); '2steuerung *f* s. Fernlenkung; '2unterricht *m* correspondence course or tuition; '2verkehr *m* long-distance traffic.

Ferse ['fɛrzə] *f* (-/-n) heel.

fertig adj. ['fɛrtiç] ready; *article*, etc.: finished; *clothing*: ready-made; mit et. ~ werden get s.th. finished; mit et. ~ sein have finished s.th.; '~bringen *v/t.* (irr. bringen, sep., -ge-, h) bring about; manage; '2keit *f* (-/-en) dexterity; skill; fluency (in the spoken language); '~machen *v/t.* (sep., -ge-, h) finish, complete; get s.th. ready; *fig.* finish, settle *s.o.'s* hash; sich ~ get ready; '2stellung *f* completion; '2waren *f/pl.* finished goods *pl.* or products *pl.*

fesch F adj. [fɛʃ] hat, dress, etc.: smart, stylish, chic; dashing.

Fessel ['fɛsəl] *f* (-/-n) chain, fetter, shackle; *vet.* fetlock; *fig.* bond, fetter, tie; '~ballon *m* captive balloon; '2n *v/t.* (ge-, h) chain, fetter, shackle; j-n ~ hold or arrest *s.o.'s* attention; fascinate *s.o.*

fest [fɛst] 1. adj. firm; solid; fixed; fast; *principle*: firm, strong; *sleep*: sound; *fabric*: close; 2. 2 *n* (-es/-e) festival, celebration; holiday, eccl. feast; '~binden *v/t.* (irr. binden, sep., -ge-, h) fasten, tie (an dat. to); '2essen *n* banquet, feast; '~fahren *v/refl.* (irr. fahren, sep., -ge-, h) get stuck; *fig.* reach a deadlock; '2halle *f* (festival) hall; '~halten (irr. halten, sep., -ge-, h) 1. *v/i.* hold fast or tight; ~ an (dat.) adhere or keep to; 2. *v/t.* hold on to; hold tight; sich ~ an (dat.) hold on to; ~igen ['~igən] *v/t.* (ge-, h) consolidate (one's position, etc.); strengthen (friendship, etc.); stabilize (currency); 2igkeit ['~ç-] *f* (-/no pl.) firmness; solidity; '2land *n* mainland, continent; '~legen *v/t.* (sep., -ge-, h) fix, set; sich auf et. ~

commit *o.s.* to s.th.; '~lich adj. meal, day, etc.: festive; *receptions* etc.: ceremonial; '2lichkeit *f* (-/-en) festivity; festive character; '~machen (sep., -ge-, h) 1. *v/t.* fix, fasten, attach (an dat. to); ⚓ moor; 2. ⚓ *v/i.* moor; put ashore; '2mahl *n* banquet, feast; 2nahme ['~na:mə] *f* (-/-n) arrest; '~nehmen *v/t.* (irr. nehmen, sep., -ge-, h) arrest, take into custody; '2rede *f* speech of the day; '~setzen *v/t.* (sep., -ge-, h) fix, set; sich ~ dust, etc.: become ingrained; *p.* settle (down); '2spiel *n* festival; '~stehen *v/i.* (irr. stehen, sep., -ge-, h) stand firm; *fact*: be certain; '~stehend adj. fixed, stationary; *fact*: established; '~stellen *v/t.* (sep., -ge-, h) establish (fact, identity, etc.); ascertain, find out (fact, *s.o.'s* whereabouts, etc.); state; see, perceive (fact, etc.); '2stellung *f* establishment; ascertainment; statement; '2tag *m* festive day; festival, holiday; eccl. feast; '2ung ⚔ *f* (-/-en) fortress; '2zug *m* festive procession.

fett [fɛt] 1. adj. fat; fleshy; *voice*: oily; *land*, etc.: rich; 2. 2 *n* (-[e]s/-e) fat; grease (a. ⊕); '2druck *typ. m* bold type; '2fleck *m* grease-spot; '~ig adj. hair, skin, etc.: greasy, oily; *fingers*, etc.: greasy; *substance*: fatty.

Fetzen ['fɛtsən] *m* (-s/-) shred; rag, *Am. a.* frazzle; scrap (of paper); in ~ in rags.

feucht adj. [fɔyçt] climate, air, etc.: damp, moist; air, zone, etc.: humid; '2igkeit *f* (-/no pl.) moisture (of substance); dampness (of place, etc.); humidity (of atmosphere, etc.).

Feuer ['fɔyər] *n* (-s/-) fire; light; *fig.* ardo(u)r; ~ fangen catch fire; *fig.* fall for (girl); '~alarm *m* fire alarm; '2beständig adj. fire-proof, fire-resistant; '2bestattung *f* cremation; '~eifer *m* ardo(u)r; '2fest adj. s. feuerbeständig; '2gefährlich adj. inflammable; '~haken *m* poker; '~löscher *m* (-s/-) fire extinguisher; '~melder *m* (-s/-) fire-alarm; '2n (ge-, h) 1. ⚔ *v/i.* shoot, fire (auf acc. at, on); 2. F *fig. v/t.* hurl; '~probe *fig. f* crucial test; '2rot adj. fiery (red), (as) red as fire; '~brunst *f* conflagration; '~schiff ⚓ *n* lightship; '~schutz *m* fire prevention; ⚔ covering fire; '~sgefahr *f* danger or risk of fire; '2speiend adj.: ~er Berg volcano; '~spritze *f* fire engine; '~stein *m* flint; '~versicherung *f* fire insurance (company); '~wache *f* fire station, *Am. a.* firehouse; '~wehr *f* fire-brigade, *Am. a.* fire department; '~wehrmann *m* fireman; '~werk *n* (display of) fireworks *pl.*; '~werkskörper *m* firework; '~

zange f (e-e a pair of) firetongs pl.; '~zeug n lighter.

feurig adj. ['fɔyriç] fiery (a. fig.); fig. ardent.

Fiasko ['fiasko] n (-s/-s) (complete) failure, fiasco; sl. flop.

Fibel ['fi:bəl] f (-/-n) spelling-book, primer.

Fichte ♀ ['fiçtə] f (-/-n) spruce; '~nnadel f pine-needle.

fidel adj. [fi'de:l] cheerful, merry, jolly, Am. F a. chipper.

Fieber ['fi:bər] n (-s/-) temperature, fever; ~ haben have or run a temperature; '~anfall m attack or bout of fever; '2haft adj. feverish (a. fig.); febrile; '2krank adj. ill with fever; '~mittel n febrifuge; '2n v/i. (ge-, h) have or run a temperature; ~ nach crave or long for; '~schauer m chill, shivers pl.; '~tabelle f temperature-chart; '~thermometer n clinical thermometer.

fiel [fi:l] pret. of fallen.

Figur [fi'gu:r] f (-/-en) figure; chess: chessman, piece.

figürlich adj. [fi'gy:rliç] meaning, etc.: figurative.

Filet [fi'le:] n (-s/-s) fillet (of beef, pork, etc.).

Filiale [fi'ja:lə] f (-/-n) branch.

Filigran(arbeit f) [fili'grɑ:n(ˀ-)] n (-s/-e) filigree.

Film [film] m (-[e]s/-e) film, thin coating (of oil, wax, etc.); phot. film; film, (moving) picture, Am. a. motion picture, F movie; e-n ~ einlegen phot. load a camera; '~atelier n film studio; '~aufnahme f filming, shooting (of a film); film (of sporting event, etc.); '2en (ge-, h) 1. v/t. film, shoot (scene, etc.); 2. v/i. film; make a film; '~gesellschaft f film company, Am. motion-picture company; '~kamera f film camera, Am. motion-picture camera; '~regisseur m film director; '~reklame f screen advertising; '~schauspieler m film or screen actor, Am. F movie actor; '~spule f (film) reel; '~streifen m film strip; '~theater n cinema, Am. motion-picture or F movie theater; '~verleih m (-[e]s/-e) film distributors pl.; '~vorführer m projectionist; '~vorstellung f cinema performance, Am. F movie performance.

Filter ['filtər] (-s/-) 1. m (coffee-, etc.) filter; 2. ⊕ n filter; '2n v/t. (ge-, h) filter (water, air, etc.); filtrate (water, impurities, etc.); strain (liquid); '~zigarette f filter-tipped cigarette.

Filz [filts] m (-es/-e) felt; fig. F skinflint; '2ig adj. felt-like; of felt; fig. F niggardly, stingy; '~laus f crab louse.

Finanz|amt [fi'nantsˀamt] n (inland) revenue office, office of the Inspector of Taxes; ~en f/pl. finances pl.; 2iell adj. [~'tsjel] financial; 2ieren [~'tsi:rən] v/t. (no -ge-, h) finance (scheme, etc.); sponsor (radio programme, etc.); '~lage f financial position; '~mann m financier; '~minister m minister of finance; Chancellor of the Exchequer, Am. Secretary of the Treasury; '~ministerium n ministry of finance; Exchequer, Am. Treasury Department; '~wesen n (-s/no pl.) finances pl.; financial matters pl.

Findelkind ['findəl-] n foundling.

finden ['findən] (irr., ge-, h) 1. v/t. find; discover, come across; find, think, consider; wie ~ Sie ...? how do you like ...?; sich ~ thing: be found; 2. v/i.: ~ zu find one's way to.

'Finder m (-s/-) finder; '~lohn m finder's reward.

'findig adj. resourceful, ingenious.

Findling ['fintliŋ] m (-s/-e) foundling; geol. erratic block, boulder.

fing [fiŋ] pret. of fangen.

Finger ['fiŋər] m (-s/-) finger; sich die ~ verbrennen burn one's fingers; er rührte keinen ~ he lifted no finger; '~abdruck m fingerprint; '~fertigkeit f manual skill; '~hut m thimble; ♀ foxglove; '2n v/i. (ge-, h): ~ nach fumble for; '~spitze f finger-tip; '~spitzengefühl fig. n sure instinct; '~übung ♪ f finger exercise; '~zeig ['~tsaık] m (-[e]s/-e) hint, F pointer.

Fink orn. [fiŋk] m (-en/-en) finch.

finster adj. ['finstər] night, etc.: dark; shadows, wood, etc.: sombre; night, room, etc.: gloomy, murky; person, nature: sullen; thought, etc.: sinister, sombre, gloomy; '2nis f (-/no pl.) darkness, gloom.

Finte ['fintə] f (-/-n) feint; fig. a. ruse, trick.

Firma ♰ ['firma] f (-/-Firmen) firm, business, company.

firmen eccl. ['firmən] v/t. (ge-, h) confirm.

'Firmen|inhaber m owner of a firm; '~wert m goodwill.

Firn [firn] m (-[e]s/-e) firn, névé.

First △ [first] m (-es/-e) ridge; '~ziegel m ridge tile.

Fisch [fiʃ] m (-es/-e) fish; '~dampfer m trawler; '2en v/t. and v/i. (ge-, h) fish; '~er m (-s/-) fisherman; '~erboot n fishing-boat; '~erdorf n fishing-village; '~erei [~'raı] f (-/-en) fishery; fishing; '~fang m fishing; '~geruch m fishy smell; '~gräte f fish-bone; '~grätenmuster n herring-bone pattern; '~händler m fishmonger, Am. fish dealer; '2ig adj. fishy; '~laich m spawn; '~leim m fish-glue; '~mehl n fish-meal; '~schuppe f scale; '~tran m train-oil; '~vergiftung

&# f fish-poisoning; '~zucht f pisci-culture, fish-hatching; '~zug m catch, haul, draught (of fish).

**fiskalisch** adj. [fis'ka:liʃ] fiscal, governmental.

**Fiskus** ['fiskus] m (-/~, -se, Fisken) Exchequer, esp. Am. Treasury; government.

**Fistel** ['fistəl] f (-/-n) fistula; '~stimme ♪ f falsetto.

**Fittich** ['fitiç] m (-[e]s/-e) poet. wing; j-n unter s-e ~e nehmen take s.o. under one's wing.

**fix** adj. [fiks] salary, price, etc.: fixed; quick, clever, smart; e-e ~e Idee an obsession; ein ~er Junge a smart fellow; ♀ierbad phot. [fi-'ksi:rba:t] n fixing bath; ~ieren [fi'ksi:rən] v/t. (no -ge-, h) fix (a. phot.); fix one's eyes (up)on, stare at s.o.; '♀stern ast. m fixed star; '♀um n (-s/Fixa) fixed or basic salary.

**flach** adj. [flax] roof, etc.: flat; ground, etc.: flat, level, even; water, plate, fig.: shallow; ♀ plane.

**Fläche** ['fleçə] f (-/-n) surface, ♀ a. plane; sheet (of water, snow, etc.); geom. area; tract, expanse (of land, etc.); ~inhalt ♀ ['fleçən?-] m (surface) area; '~nmaß n square or surface measure.

'**Flach|land** n plain, flat country; '~rennen n turf: flat race.

**Flachs** ♀ [flaks] m (-es/no pl.) flax.

**flackern** ['flakərn] v/i. (ge-, h) light, flame, eyes, etc.: flicker, wave; voice: quaver, shake.

**Flagge** ✕ ['flagə] f (-/-n) flag, colo(u)rs pl.; '♀n v/i. (ge-, h) fly or hoist a flag; signal (with flags).

**Flak** ✕ [flak] f (-/-, -s) anti-aircraft gun; anti-aircraft artillery.

**Flamme** ['flamə] f (-/-n) flame; blaze; '~nmeer n sea of flames; '~nwerfer ✕ m (-s/-) flame-thrower.

**Flanell** [fla'nɛl] m (-s/-e) flannel; ~anzug m flannel suit; ~hose f flannel trousers pl., flannels pl.

**Flank|e** ['flaŋkə] f (-/-n) flank (a. △, ⊕, ✕, mount.); side; ♀ieren [~'ki:rən] v/t. (no -ge-, h) flank.

**Flasche** ['flaʃə] f (-/-n) bottle; flask.

'**Flaschen|bier** n bottled beer; '~hals m neck of a bottle; '~öffner m (-s/-) bottle-opener; '~zug ⊕ m block and tackle.

**flatter|haft** adj. ['flatərhaft] girl, etc.: fickle, flighty; mind: fickle, volatile; '~n v/i. (ge-) 1. (h, sein) bird, butterfly, etc.: flutter (about); bird, bat, etc.: flit (about); 2. (h) hair, flag, garment, etc.: stream, fly; mot. wheel: shimmy, wobble; car steering: judder; 3. (sein): auf den Boden ~ flutter to the ground.

**flau** adj. [flau] weak, feeble, faint; sentiment, reaction, etc.: lukewarm;

drink: stale; colour: pale, dull; ✝ market, business, etc.: dull, slack; ~e Zeit slack period.

**Flaum** [flaum] m (-[e]s/no pl.) down, fluff; fuzz.

**Flau|s** [flaus] m (-es/-e), ~sch [~ʃ] m (-es/-e) tuft (of wool, etc.); napped coating.

**Flausen** F ['flauzən] f/pl. whims pl., fancies pl., (funny) ideas pl.; F fibs pl.; j-m ~ in den Kopf setzen put funny ideas into s.o.'s head; j-m ~ vormachen tell s.o. fibs.

**Flaute** ['flautə] f (-/-n) ♀ dead calm; esp. ✝ dullness, slack period.

**Flecht|e** ['flɛçtə] f (-/-n) braid, plait (of hair); ♀ lichen; ♀ herpes; '~en v/t. (irr., ge-, h) braid, plait (hair, ribbon, etc.); weave (basket, wreath, etc.); wreath (flowers); twist (rope, etc.); '~werk n wickerwork.

**Fleck** [flɛk] m (-[e]s/-e, -en) 1. mark (of dirt, grease, etc.; zo.); spot (of grease, paint, etc.); smear (of oil, blood, etc.); stain (of wine, coffee, etc.); blot (of ink); place, spot; fig. blemish, spot, stain; 2. patch (of material); bootmaking: heel-piece; '~en m (-s/-) s. Fleck 1; small (market-)town, townlet; '~enwasser n spot or stain remover; '~fieber ♀ n (epidemic) typhus; '♀ig adj. spotted; stained.

**Fledermaus** zo. ['fle:dər-] f bat.

**Flegel** ['fle:gəl] m (-s/-) flail; fig. lout, boor; ~ei [~'lai] f (-/-en) rude, ness; loutishness; '♀haft adj. rude-ill-mannered; loutish; '~jahre pl. awkward age.

**flehen** ['fle:ən] 1. v/i. (ge-, h) en-treat, implore (zu j-m s.o.; um et. s.th.); 2. ♀ n (-s/no pl.) supplication; imploration, entreaty.

**Fleisch** [flaiʃ] n (-es/no pl.) flesh; meat; ♀ pulp; '~brühe f meat-broth; beef tea; '~er m (-s/-) butcher; ~erei [~'rai] f (-/-en) butcher's (shop), Am. butcher shop; '~extrakt m meat extract; '♀fressend adj. carnivorous; '~hackmaschine f mincing machine, mincer, Am. meat grinder; '♀ig adj. fleshy; ♀ pulpy; '~konserven f/pl. tinned or potted meat, Am. canned meat; '~kost f meat (food); '♀lich adj. desires, etc.: carnal, fleshly; '♀los adj. meatless; '~pastete f meat pie, Am. a. potpie; '~speise f meat dish; '~vergiftung f meat or ptomaine poisoning; '~ware f meat (product); '~wolf m s. Fleischhackmaschine.

**Fleiß** [flais] m (-es/no pl.) diligence, industry; '♀ig adj. diligent, indus-trious, hard-working.

**fletschen** ['fletʃən] v/t. (ge-, h): die Zähne ~ animal: bare its teeth; p. bare one's teeth.

**Flicken** ['flikən] 1. m (-s/-) patch;

2. ⚲ v/t. (ge-, h) patch (dress, tyre, etc.); repair (shoe, roof, etc.); cobble (shoe).

'Flick|schneider m jobbing tailor; '~schuster m cobbler; '~werk n (-[e]s/no pl.) patchwork.

Flieder ♀ ['fli:dər] m (-s/-) lilac.

Fliege ['fli:gə] f (-/-n) zo. fly; bow-tie.

'fliegen 1. v/i. (irr., ge-, sein) fly; go by air; 2. v/t. (irr., ge-, h) fly, pilot (aircraft, etc.); convey (goods, etc.) by air; 3. ⚲ n (-s/no pl.) flying; ✈ a. aviation.

Fliegen|fänger ['fli:gənfeŋər] m (-s/-) fly-paper; '~fenster n fly-screen; '~gewicht n boxing, etc.: flyweight; '~klappe f fly-flap, Am. fly swatter; '~pilz ♀ m fly agaric.

'Flieger m (-s/-) flyer; ✈ airman, aviator; pilot; F plane, bomber; cycling: sprinter; '~abwehr ✕ f anti-aircraft defen|ce, Am. -se; '~alarm ✕ m air-raid alarm or warning; '~bombe ✕ f aircraft bomb; '~offizier ✕ m air-force officer.

flieh|en ['fli:ən] (irr., ge-) 1. v/i. (sein) flee (vor dat. from), run away; 2. v/t. (h) flee, avoid, keep away from; '2kraft phys. f centrifugal force. [(floor-)tile.)

Fliese ['fli:zə] f (-/-n) (wall-)tile.

Fließ|band ['fli:s-] n (-[e]s/~er) conveyor-belt; assembly-line; '2en v/i. (irr., ge-, sein) river, traffic, etc.: flow; tap-water, etc.: run; '2end 1. adj. water: running; traffic: moving; speech, etc.: fluent; 2. adv.: ~ lesen (sprechen) read (speak) fluently; '~papier n blotting-paper.

Flimmer ['flimər] m (-s/-) glimmer, glitter; '2n v/i. (ge-, h) glimmer, glitter; television, film: flicker; es flimmert mir vor den Augen everything is dancing in front of my eyes.

flink adj. [flink] quick, nimble, brisk.

Flinte ['flintə] f (-/-n) shotgun; die ~ ins Korn werfen throw up the sponge.

Flirt [flœrt] m (-es/-s) flirtation; '2en v/i. (ge-, h) flirt (mit with).

Flitter ['flitər] m (-s/-) tinsel (a. fig.), spangle; '~kram m cheap finery; '~wochen pl. honeymoon.

flitzen F ['flitsən] v/i. (ge-, sein) whisk, scamper; dash (off, etc.).

flocht [flɔxt] pret. of flechten.

Flock|e ['flɔkə] f (-/-n) flake (of snow, soap, etc.); flock (of wool); '2ig adj. fluffy, flaky.

flog [flo:k] pret. of fliegen.

floh[1] [flo:] pret. of fliehen.

Floh[2] zo. [~] m (-[e]s/~e) flea.

Flor [flo:r] m (-s/-e) bloom, blossom; fig. bloom, prime; gauze; crêpe, crape.

Florett fenc. [flo'ret] n (-[e]s/-e) foil.

florieren [flo'ri:rən] v/i. (no -ge-, h)

business, etc.: flourish, prosper, thrive.

Floskel ['flɔskəl] f (-/-n) flourish; empty phrase.

floß[1] [flɔs] pret. of fließen.

Floß[2] [flo:s] n (-es/~e) raft, float.

Flosse ['flɔsə] f (-/-n) fin; flipper (of penguin, etc.).

flöß|en ['flø:sən] v/t. (ge-, h) raft, float (timber, etc.); '2er m (-s/-) rafter, raftsman.

Flöte ♪ ['flø:tə] f (-/-n) flute; '2n (ge-, h) 1. v/i. (play the) flute; 2. v/t. play on the flute.

flott adj. [flɔt] ♧ floating, afloat; pace, etc.: quick, brisk; music, etc.: gay, lively; dress, etc.: smart, stylish; car, etc.: sporty, racy; dancer, etc.: excellent.

Flotte ['flɔtə] f (-/-n) ♧ fleet; ✕ navy; '~nstützpunkt ✕ m naval base.

Flotille ♧ [flɔ'tiljə] f (-/-n) flotilla.

Flöz geol., ✕ [flø:ts] n (-es/-e) seam; layer, stratum.

Fluch [flu:x] m (-[e]s/~e) curse, malediction; eccl. anathema; curse, swear-word; '2en v/i. (ge-, h) swear, curse.

Flucht [fluxt] f (-/-en) flight (vor dat. from); escape (aus dat. from); line (of windows, etc.); suite (of rooms); flight (of stairs).

flücht|en ['flyçtən] (ge-) v/i. (sein) and v/refl. (h) flee (nach, zu to); run away; escape; '~ig adj. fugitive (a. fig.); thought, etc.: fleeting; fame, etc.: transient; p. careless, superficial; ♠ volatile; 2ling ['~liŋ] m (-s/-e) fugitive; pol. refugee; '2lingslager n refugee camp.

Flug [flu:k] m (-[e]s/~e) flight; im ~(e) rapidly; quickly; '~abwehrrakete f anti-aircraft missile; '~bahn f trajectory of (rocket, etc.); ✕ flight path; '~ball m tennis, etc.: volley; '~blatt n handbill, leaflet, Am. a. flier; '~boot ✕ n flying-boat; '~dienst ✕ m air service.

Flügel ['fly:gəl] m (-s/-) wing (a. ♧, ✕, ✕); blade, vane (of propeller, etc.); s. Fensterflügel, Türflügel, Lungenflügel; sail (of windmill, etc.); ♪ grand piano; '~fenster ♠ n casement-window; '2lahm adj. brokenwinged; '~mann ✕ m marker; flank man; '~tür ♠ f folding door.

Fluggast ['flu:k-] m (air) passenger.

flügge adj. ['flygə] fledged; ~ werden fledge; fig. begin to stand on one's own feet.

'Flug|hafen m airport; '~linie f ✈ air route; airline; '~platz m airfield, aerodrome, Am. a. airdrome; airport; '~sand geol. m wind-blown sand; '~schrift f pamphlet; '~sicherung f air traffic control; '~sport m sporting aviation; '~wesen n aviation, aeronautics.

**'Flugzeug** *n* aircraft, aeroplane, F plane, *Am. a.* airplane; '**∽bau** *m* aircraft construction; '**∽führer** *m* pilot; '**∽halle** *f* hangar; '**∽rumpf** *m* fuselage, body; '**∽träger** *m* aircraft carrier, *Am. sl.* flattop; '**∽unglück** *n* air crash *or* disaster.

**Flunder** *ichth.* ['flundər] *f* (-/-n) flounder.

**Flunker|ei** F [fluŋkə'raɪ] *f* (-/-en) petty lying, F fib(bing); '**2n** *v/i.* (ge-, *h*) F fib, tell fibs.

**fluoreszieren** [fluores'tsi:rən] *v/i.* (*no* -ge-, *h*) fluoresce.

**Flur** [flu:r] 1. *f* (-/-en) field, meadow; *poet.* lea; 2. *m* (-[e]s/-e) (entrance-)hall.

**Fluß** [flus] *m* (*Flusses/Flüsse*) river, stream; flow(ing); *fig.* fluency, flux; 2'**abwärts** *adv.* downriver, downstream; 2'**aufwärts** *adv.* upriver, upstream; '**∽bett** *n* river bed.

**flüssig** *adj.* ['flysiç] fluid, liquid; *metal:* molten, melted; ✝ *money, capital, etc.*: available, in hand; *style:* fluent, flowing; '**2keit** *f* (-/-en) fluid, liquid; fluidity, liquidity; availability; fluency.

**'Fluß|lauf** *m* course of a river; '**∽mündung** *f* mouth of a river; '**∽pferd** *zo.* *n* hippopotamus; '**∽schiffahrt** *f* river navigation *or* traffic.

**flüstern** ['flystərn] *v/i. and v/t.* (ge-, *h*) whisper.

**Flut** [flu:t] *f* (-/-en) flood; high tide, (flood-)tide; *fig.* flood, torrent, deluge; '**2en** (ge-) 1. *v/i.* (sein) water, crowd, *etc.*: flood, surge (*über acc.* over); 2. *v/t.* (*h*) flood (*dock, etc.*); '**∽welle** *f* tidal wave.

**focht** [fɔxt] *pret. of* **fechten.**

**Fohlen** *zo.* ['fo:lən] 1. *n* (-s/-) foal; *male:* colt; *female:* filly; 2. 2 *v/i.* (ge-, *h*) foal.

**Folge** ['fɔlgə] *f* (-/-n) sequence, succession (*of events*); instalment, part (*of radio series, etc.*); consequence, result; series; set, suit; future; **∽n** *pl.* aftermath.

**'folgen** *v/i.* (*dat.*) (ge-, sein) follow; succeed (*j-m* s.o.; *auf acc.* to); follow, ensue (*aus* from); obey (*j-m* s.o.); **∽dermaßen** *adv.* ['∽dərmaːsən] as follows; '**∽schwer** *adj.* of grave consequence, grave.

**'folgerichtig** *adj.* logical, consistent.

**folger|n** ['fɔlgərn] *v/t.* (ge-, *h*) infer, conclude, deduce (*aus* from); '**2ung** *f* (-/-en) inference, conclusion, deduction.

**'folgewidrig** *adj.* illogical; inconsistent.

**folglich** *cj.* ['fɔlkliç] therefore, consequently.

**folgsam** *adj.* ['fɔlkzaːm] obedient; '**2keit** *f* (-/*no pl.*) obedience.

**Folie** ['fo:ljə] *f* (-/-n) foil.

**Folter** ['fɔltər] *f* (-/-n) torture; *auf die ∽ spannen* put to the rack; *fig.* F *a.* keep on tenterhooks; '**2n** *v/t.* (ge-, *h*) torture, torment; '**∽qual** *f* torture, *fig. a.* torment.

**Fonds** ✝ [fõ:] *m* (-/-) fund (*a. fig.*); funds *pl.*

**Fontäne** [fɔn'tɛːnə] *f* (-/-n) fountain.

**foppen** ['fɔpən] *v/t.* (ge-, *h*) tease, F pull s.o.'s leg; hoax, fool.

**forcieren** [fɔr'siːrən] *v/t.* (*no* -ge-, *h*) force (up).

**'Förder|band** *n* (-[e]s/∼er) conveyor-belt; '**2lich** *adj.* conducive (*dat.* to), promotive (*of*); '**∽korb** ⚒ *m* cage.

**fordern** ['fɔrdərn] *v/t.* (ge-, *h*) demand; claim (*compensation, etc.*); ask (*price, etc.*); challenge (*to duel*).

**fördern** ['fœrdərn] *v/t.* (ge-, *h*) further, advance, promote; ⚒ haul, raise (*coal, etc.*); *zutage ∽* reveal, bring to light.

**'Forderung** *f* (-/-en) demand; claim; charge; challenge.

**'Förderung** *f* (-/-en) furtherance, advancement, promotion; ⚒ haulage; output.                         [trout.]

**Forelle** *ichth.* [fo'rɛlə] *f* (-/-n)

**Form** [fɔrm] *f* (-/-en) form; figure, shape; model; ⊕ mo(u)ld; *sports:* form, condition; **2al** *adj.* [∽'maːl] formal; **∽alität** [∽ali'tɛːt] *f* (-/-en) formality; **∽at** [∽'maːt] *n* (-[e]s/-e) size; *von ∽* of distinction; **∽el** ['∽əl] *f* (-/-n) formula; **2ell** *adj.* [∽'mɛl] formal; '**2en** *v/t.* (ge-, *h*) form (*object, character, etc.*); shape, fashion (*wood, metal, etc.*); mo(u)ld (*clay, character, etc.*); '**∽enlehre** *gr.* *f* accidence; '**∽fehler** *m* informality; ⚖ flaw; **2ieren** [∽'miːrən] *v/t.* (*no* -ge-, *h*) form; draw up, line up; *sich ∽* line up.

**förmlich** *adj.* ['fœrmliç] formal; ceremonious; '**2keit** *f* (-/-en) formality; ceremoniousness.

**'formlos** *adj.* formless, shapeless; *fig.* informal.

**Formular** [fɔrmu'laːr] *n* (-s/-e) form, *Am. a.* blank.

**formu'lieren** *v/t.* (*no* -ge-, *h*) formulate (*question, etc.*); word, phrase (*question, contract, etc.*).

**forsch** *adj.* [fɔrʃ] vigorous, energetic; smart, dashing.

**forsch|en** ['fɔrʃən] *v/i.* (ge-, *h*): ∼ *nach* (*dat.*) search for *or* after; ∼ *in* (*dat.*) search (through); '**2er** *m* (-s/-) researcher, research worker.

**'Forschung** *f* (-/-en) research (work); '**∽sreise** *f* (exploring) expedition; '**∽sreisende** *m* explorer.

**Forst** [fɔrst] *m* (-es/-e[n]) forest; '**∽aufseher** *m* (forest-)keeper, gamekeeper.

**Förster** ['fœrstər] *m* (-s/-) forester; ranger.

**'Forst|haus** n forester's house; **'~revier** n forest district; **'~wesen** n, **'~wirtschaft** f forestry.

**Fort¹** ⚔ [fo:r] n (-s/-s) fort.

**fort²** adv. [fɔrt] away, gone; on; gone, lost; in e-m ~ continuously; und so ~ and so on or forth; s. a. weg.

**'fort|bestehen** v/i. (irr. stehen, sep., no -ge-, h) continue, persist; **'~bewegen** v/t. (sep., no -ge-, h) move (on, away); sich ~ move, walk; **'2dauer** f continuance; **'~dauern** v/i. (sep., -ge-, h) continue, last; **'~fahren** v/i. (irr. fahren, sep., -ge-) 1. (sein) depart, leave; drive off; 2. (h) continue, keep on (et. zu tun doing s.th.); **'~führen** v/t. (sep., -ge-, h) continue, carry on; **2gang** m departure, leaving; continuance; **'~gehen** v/i. (irr. gehen, sep., -ge-, sein) go (away), leave; **'~geschritten** adj. advanced; **'2kommen** n (-s/no pl.) progress; **'~laufend** adj. consecutive, continuous; **'~pflanzen** v/t. (sep., -ge-, h) propagate; sich ~ biol. propagate, reproduce; phys., disease, rumour: be propagated; **'2pflanzung** f propagation; reproduction; **'~reißen** v/t. (irr. reißen, sep., -ge-, h) avalanche, etc.: sweep or carry away; **'~schaffen** v/t. (sep., -ge-, h) get or take away, remove; **'~schreiten** v/i. (irr. schreiten, sep., -ge-, sein) advance, proceed, progress; **'~schreitend** adj. progressive; **'2schritt** m progress; **'~schrittlich** adj. progressive; **'~setzen** v/t. (sep., -ge-, h) continue, pursue; **'2setzung** f (-/-en) continuation, pursuit; ~ folgt to be continued; **'~während 1.** adj. continual, continuous; perpetual; **2.** adv. constantly, always.

**Forum** ['fo:rum] n (-s/Foren, Fora and -s) forum.

**Foto...** ['fo:to-] s. Photo...

**Foyer** [foa'je:] n (-s/-s) thea. foyer, Am. and parl. lobby; hotel: foyer, lounge.

**Fracht** [fraxt] f (-/-en) goods pl.; 🚃 carriage, freight; ⚓, ✈ freight (-age), cargo; **'~brief** m 🚃 consignment note, Am., ⚓ bill of lading; **'~dampfer** m cargo steamer, freighter; **'~er** m (-s/-) freighter; **'2frei** adj. carriage or freight paid; **'~führer** m carrier, Am. a. teamster; **'~geld** n carriage charges pl., ✈, ⚓, Am. freight; **'~gut** n goods pl., freight; **'~stück** n package.

**Frack** [frak] m (-[e]s/⸚e, -s) dress coat, tail-coat, F tails; **'~anzug** m dress-suit.

**Frag|e** ['fra:gə] f (-/-n) question; gr., reth. interrogation; problem, point; e-e ~ stellen ask a question; in ~ stellen question; **'~ebogen** m questionnaire; form; **'2en** (ge-, h)

1. v/t. ask; question; es fragt sich, ob it is doubtful whether; 2. v/i. ask; **'~er** m (-s/-) questioner; **'~ewort** gr. n (-[e]s/⸚er) interrogative; **'~ezeichen** n question-mark, point of interrogation, Am. mst interrogation point; **2lich** adj. ['fra:k-] doubtful, uncertain; in question; **2los** adv. ['fra:k-] undoubtedly, unquestionably.

**Fragment** [frag'mɛnt] n (-[e]s/-e) fragment.

**fragwürdig** adj. ['fra:k-] doubtful, dubious, questionable.

**Fraktion** parl. [frak'tsjo:n] f (-/-en) (parliamentary) group.

**frank|ieren** [fraŋ'ki:rən] v/t. (no -ge-, h) prepay, stamp; **~o** adv. ['~o] free; post(age) paid; parcel: carriage paid.

**Franse** ['franzə] f (-/-n) fringe.

**Franz|ose** [fran'tso:zə] m (-n/-n) Frenchman; die ~n pl. the French pl.; **~ösin** [~ø:zin] f (-/-nen) Frenchwoman; **2ösisch** adj. [~ø:zif] French.

**fräs|en** ⊕ ['frɛ:zən] v/t. (ge-, h) mill; **2maschine** ['frɛ:s-] f milling-machine.

**Fraß** [fra:s] 1. F m (-es/-e) sl. grub; 2. 2 pret. of fressen.

**Fratze** ['fratsə] f (-/-n) grimace, F face; **~n schneiden** make grimaces.

**Frau** [frau] f (-/-en) woman; lady; wife; ~ X Mrs X.

**'Frauen|arzt** m gyn(a)ecologist; **'~klinik** f hospital for women; **'~rechte** n/pl. women's rights pl.; **'~stimmrecht** pol. n women's suffrage; **'~zimmer** mst contp. n female, woman.

**Fräulein** ['frɔylaɪn] n (-s/-, F -s) young lady; teacher; shop-assistant; waitress; ~ X Miss X.

**fraulich** adj. womanly.

**frech** adj. [freç] impudent, insolent, F saucy, cheeky, Am. F a. sassy, sl. fresh; lie, etc.: brazen; thief, etc.: bold, daring; **'2heit** f (-/-en) impudence, insolence; F sauciness; cheek; boldness.

**frei** adj. [frai] free (von from, of); position: vacant; field: open; parcel: carriage-paid; journalist, etc.: freelance; liberal; candid, frank; licentious; ~ Haus ✝ franco domicile; ~er Tag day off; im Freien in the open air.

**'Frei|bad** n open-air bath; **~beuter** ['~bɔytər] m (-s/-) freebooter; **2bleibend** ✝ adj. price, etc.: subject to alteration; offer: conditional; **'~brief** m charter; fig. warrant; **'~denker** m (-s/-) freethinker.

**Freier** ['fraiər] m (-s/-) suitor.

**'Frei|exemplar** n free or presentation copy; **'~frau** f baroness; **'~gabe** f release; **'2geben** (irr. geben, sep., -ge-, h) 1. v/t. release; give *(s.o. an hour, etc.)* off; **2.** *v/i.*: j-m ~ give s.o. time off; **'2gebig** *adj.* generous, liberal; **'~gebigkeit** *f* (-/-en) generosity, liberality; **'~gepäck** *n* free luggage; **'2haben** *v/i.* *(irr. haben, sep., -ge-, h)* have a holiday; have a day off; **'~hafen** *m* free port; **'2halten** *v/t.* *(irr. halten, sep., -ge-, h)* keep free *or* clear; *in restaurant, etc.:* treat; **'~handel** *m* free trade.

**'Freiheit** *f* (-/-en) liberty; freedom; *dichterische* ~ poetic licence, *Am.* poetic license.

**'Frei|herr** *m* baron; **'~karte** *f* free *(thea. a.* complimentary) ticket; **'2lassen** *v/t.* *(irr. lassen, sep., -ge-, h)* release, set free *or* at liberty; *gegen Kaution* ~ $\frac{1}{2}$ release on bail; **'~lassung** *f* (-/-en) release; **'~lauf** *m* free-wheel.

**'freilich** *adv.* indeed, certainly, of course; admittedly.

**'Frei|lichtbühne** *f* open-air stage or theat|re, *Am.* -er; **'2machen** *v/t.* *(sep., -ge-, h)* ✆ prepay, stamp *(letter, etc.);* sich ~ undress, take one's clothes off; **'~marke** *f* stamp; **'~maurer** *m* freemason; **~maurerei** [~'raɪ] *f* (-/no pl.) freemasonry; **'~mut** *m* frankness; **2mütig** *adj.* ['~myːtɪç] frank; **'2schaffend** *adj.*: **~er** *Künstler* free-lance artist; **~schärler** ✗ ['~ʃɛːrlər] *m* (-s/-) volunteer, irregular; **'~schein** *m* licen|ce, *Am.* -se; **'2sinnig** *adj.* liberal; **'2sprechen** *v/t.* *(irr. sprechen, sep., -ge-, h)* *esp. eccl.* absolve *(von* from); $\frac{1}{2}$ acquit *(of);* release *(apprentice)* from his articles; **'~sprechung** *f* (-/-en) *esp. eccl.* absolution; release from articles; = **'~spruch** $\frac{1}{2}$ *m* acquittal; **'~staat** *pol. m* free state; **'2stehen** *v/i.* *(irr. stehen, sep., -ge-, h)* house, *etc.*: stand empty; *es steht Ihnen frei zu inf.* you are free *or* at liberty to *inf.;* **'2stellen** *v/t.* *(sep., -ge-, h):* j-n ~ exempt s.o. *(von* from) *(a.* ✗); j-m et. ~ leave s.th. open to s.o.; **'~stoß** *m* football: free kick; **'~tag** *m* Friday; **'~tod** *m* suicide; **'2tragend** △ *adj.* cantilever; **'~treppe** *f* outdoor staircase; **'2willig 1.** *adj.* voluntary; **2.** *adv. a.* of one's own free will; **'~willige** ['~vɪligə] *m* (-n/-n) volunteer; **'~zeit** *f* free *or* spare *or* leisure time; **2zügig** *adj.* ['~tsyːgɪç] free to move; **'~zügigkeit** *f* (-/no pl.) freedom of movement.

**fremd** *adj.* [fremt] strange; foreign; alien; extraneous; **'~artig** *adj.* strange; exotic.

**Fremde** ['fremdə] **1.** *f* (-/no pl.) distant *or* foreign parts; *in der* ~ far away from home, abroad; **2.** *m, f* (-n/-n) stranger; foreigner; **'~buch** *n* visitors' book; **'~nführer** *m* guide, cicerone; **~nheim** *n*

boarding house; **~nindustrie** ['fremdən⁹-] *f* tourist industry; **~nlegion** ✗ *f* Foreign Legion; **'~nverkehr** *m* tourism, tourist traffic; **'~nzimmer** *n* spare (bed-) room; *tourism:* room.

**'Fremd|herrschaft** *f* foreign rule; **'~körper** 🖋 *m* foreign body; **2ländisch** *adj.* ['~lɛndɪʃ] foreign, exotic; **'~sprache** *f* foreign language; **'2sprachig** *adj.,* **'2sprachlich** *adj.* foreign-language; **'~wort** *n* (-[e]s/╌er) foreign word.

**Frequenz** *phys.* [fre'kvɛnts] *f* (-/-en) frequency.

**fressen** ['fresən] **1.** *v/t.* *(irr., ge-, h)* eat; *beast of prey:* devour; F *p.* devour, gorge; **2.** *v/i.* *(irr., ge-, h)* eat; F *p.* gorge; **3.** ♀ *n* (-s/no pl.) feed, food.

**'Freß|gier** *f* voracity, gluttony; **'~napf** *m* feeding dish.

**Freude** ['frɔydə] *f* (-/-n) joy, gladness; delight; pleasure; ~ *haben an (dat.)* find *or* take pleasure in.

**'Freuden|botschaft** *f* glad tidings *pl.;* **'~fest** *n* happy occasion; **'~feuer** *n* bonfire; **'~geschrei** *n* shouts *pl.* of joy; **'~tag** *m* day of rejoicing, red-letter day; **'~taumel** *m* transports *pl.* of joy.

**'freud|estrahlend** *adj.* radiant with joy; **'~ig** *adj.* joyful; happy; **~es** *Ereignis* happy event; **~los** *adj.* ['frɔytloːs] joyless, cheerless.

**freuen** ['frɔyən] *v/t.* *(ge-, h):* es freut mich, daß I am glad *or* pleased (that); sich ~ *über (acc.)* be pleased about *or* with, be glad about; sich ~ *auf (acc.)* look forward to.

**Freund** [frɔynt] *m* (-es/-e) (boy-) friend; **~in** ['~dɪn] *f* (-/-nen) (girl-) friend; **2lich** *adj.* friendly, kind, nice; cheerful, bright; *climate:* mild; **'~lichkeit** *f* (-/-en) friendliness, kindness; **'~schaft** *f* (-/-en) friendship; ~ *schließen* make friends *(mit* with); **2schaftlich** *adj.* friendly.

**Frevel** ['freːfəl] *m* (-s/-) outrage *(an dat., gegen* on), crime *(against);* **2haft** *adj.* wicked, outrageous; impious; **'2n** *v/i.* *(ge-, h)* commit a crime *or* outrage *(gegen* against).

**Frevler** ['freːflər] *m* (-s/-) evil-doer, offender; blasphemer.

**Friede(n)** ['friːdə(n)] *m* (Friedens/ Frieden) peace; *im Frieden* in peacetime; *laß mich in Frieden!* leave me alone!

**'Friedens|bruch** *m* violation of (the) peace; **'~stifter** *m* peacemaker; **'~störer** *m* (-s/-) disturber of the peace; **'~verhandlungen** *f/pl.* peace negotiations *pl.;* **'~vertrag** *m* peace treaty.

**fried|fertig** *adj.* ['friːt-] peaceable, peace-loving; **'2hof** *m* cemetery, graveyard; churchyard; **'~lich** *adj.*

s. friedfertig; peaceful; '~liebend *adj.* peace-loving.

**frieren** ['fri:rən] *v/i.* (*irr.*, ge-) **1.** (sein) *liquid:* freeze, become frozen; *river, etc.:* freeze (over, up); *window-pane, etc.:* freeze over; **2.** (h) be *or* feel cold; *mich friert or ich friere an den Füßen* my feet are cold.

**Fries** ⚠ [fri:s] *m* (-es/-e) frieze.

**frisch** [friʃ] **1.** *adj.* food, flowers, *etc.:* fresh; *egg:* new-laid; *linen, etc.:* clean; *auf ~er Tat ertappen* catch red-handed; **2.** *adv.:* ~ *gestrichen!* wet paint!, *Am.* fresh paint!; 2e ['~ə] *f* (-/*no pl.*) freshness.

**Friseu|r** [fri'zø:r] *m* (-s/-e) hairdresser; (*men's*) barber; '~se [~zə] *f* (-/-n) (woman) hairdresser.

**fri'sier|en** *v/t.* (*no* -ge-, h): *j-n* ~ do *or* dress s.o.'s hair; *F: einen Wagen* ~ *mot.* tune up *or* soup up *or* hot up a car; *sich* ~ do one's hair; 2**kommode** *f* dressing-table; 2**salon** *m* hairdressing saloon; 2**tisch** *m s.* Frisierkommode.

**Frist** [frist] *f* (-/-en) (fixed *or* limited) period of time; time allowed; term; ⅛ prescribed time; ⅛, ✝ respite, grace; '2en *v/t.* (ge-, h): *sein Dasein* ~ scrape along, scrape a living.

**Frisur** [fri'zu:r] *f* (-/-en) hair-style, hair-do, coiffure.

**frivol** [fri'vo:l] frivolous, flippant; 2**ität** [~oli'tɛ:t] *f* (-/-en) frivolity, flippancy.

**froh** *adj.* [fro:] joyful, glad; cheerful; happy; gay (*a. colour*).

**fröhlich** *adj.* ['frø:lɪç] gay, merry, cheerful, happy, *Am.* F a. chipper; '2**keit** *f* (-/~, -en) gaiety, cheerfulness; merriment.

**froh|'locken** *v/i.* (*no* -ge-, h) shout for joy, be jubilant; exult (*über acc.* at, in); gloat (over); '2**sinn** *m* (-[e]s/*no pl.*) gaiety, cheerfulness.

**fromm** *adj.* [frɔm] *p.* pious, religious; *life, etc.:* godly; *prayer, etc.:* devout; *horse, etc.:* docile; ~*e Lüge* white lie; ~*er Wunsch* wishful thinking, idle wish.

**Frömmelei** [frœmə'laɪ] *f* (-/-en) affected piety, bigotry.

'**Frömmigkeit** *f* (-/-en) piety, religiousness; godliness; devoutness.

**Fron** [fro:n] *f* (-/-en), '~**arbeit** *f*, '~**dienst** *hist.* *m* forced *or* compulsory labo(u)r *or* service; *fig.* drudgery.

**frönen** ['frø:nən] *v/i.* (*dat.*) (ge-, h) indulge in; be a slave to.

**Front** [frɔnt] *f* (-/-en) ⚠ front, façade, face; ✕ front (line), line; *pol.*, ✝, *etc.:* front.

**fror** [fro:r] *pret. of* frieren.

**Frosch** *zo.* [frɔʃ] *m* (-es/-e) frog; '~**perspektive** *f* worm's-eye view.

**Frost** [frɔst] *m* (-es/-e) frost; chill; '~**beule** *f* chilblain.

**frösteln** ['frœstəln] *v/i.* (ge-, h) feel chilly, shiver (with cold).

'**frostig** *adj.* frosty (*a. fig.*); *fig.* cold, frigid, icy.

'**Frost|salbe** ⚕ *f* chilblain ointment; '~**schaden** *m* frost damage; '~**schutzmittel** *mot.* *n* anti-freezing mixture; '~**wetter** *n* frosty weather.

**frottier|en** [frɔ'ti:rən] *v/t.* (*no* -ge-, h) rub; 2(**hand**)**tuch** *n* Turkish towel.

**Frucht** [fruxt] *f* (-/-e) ⚕ fruit (*a. fig.*); corn; crop; *fig.* reward, result; '2**bar** *adj.* fruitful (*esp. fig.*); fertile (*a. biol.*); '~**barkeit** *f* (-/*no pl.*) fruitfulness; fertility; 2**bringend** *adj.* fruit-bearing; *fig.* fruitful; '2en *fig. v/i.* (ge-, h) be of use; '~**knoten** ⚕ *m* ovary; 2**los** *adj.* fruitless; *fig. a.* ineffective.

**früh** [fry:] **1.** *adj.* early; *am ~en Morgen* in the early morning; *~es Aufstehen* early rising; *~e Anzeichen* early symptoms; *~er former;* **2.** *adv.* in the morning; ~ *aufstehen* rise early; *heute* ~ this morning; *morgen* ~ tomorrow morning; *~er earlier;* formerly, in former times; *~estens* at the earliest; '2**aufsteher** *m* (-s/-) early riser, F early bird; '2e *f* (-/*no pl.*): *in aller* ~ very early in the morning; '2**geburt** *f* premature birth; premature baby *or* animal; '2**gottesdienst** *m* early service; '2**jahr** *n*, 2**ling** ['~lɪŋ] *m* (-s/-e) spring; '~**morgens** *adv.* early in the morning; '~**reif** *fig. adj.* precocious; '2**sport** *m* early morning exercises; '2**stück** *n* breakfast; '~**stücken** *v/i.* **1.** *v/i.* (have) breakfast; **2.** *v/t.* have *s.th.* for breakfast; '2**zug** 🚂 *m* early train.

**Fuchs** [fuks] *m* (-es/-e) *zo.* fox (*a. fig.*); *horse:* sorrel.

**Füchsin** *zo.* ['fyksɪn] *f* (-/-nen) she-fox, vixen.

'**Fuchs|jagd** *f* fox-hunt(ing); '~**pelz** *m* fox-fur; '2**rot** *adj.* foxy-red, sorrel; '~**schwanz** *m* foxtail; ⊕ pad-saw; ⚕ amarant(h); '2'**teufels-wild** F *adj.* mad with rage, F hopping mad.

**fuchteln** ['fuxtəln] *v/i.* (ge-, h): ~ *mit* (*dat.*) wave (*one's hands*) about.

**Fuder** ['fu:dər] *n* (-s/-) cart-load; tun (*of wine*). [🎵 fugue.]

**Fuge** ['fu:gə] *f* (-/-n) ⊕ joint; seam;

**füg|en** ['fy:gən] *v/refl.* (ge-, h) submit, give in, yield (*dat.*, *in acc.* to); comply (with); '~**sam** *adj.* ['fy:k-] (com)pliant; manageable.

**fühl|bar** *adj.* ['fy:lba:r] tangible, palpable; *fig.* sensible, noticeable; '~**en** (ge-, h) **1.** *v/t.* feel; be aware of; *sich glücklich* ~ feel happy; **2.** *v/i.:* *mit j-m* ~ feel for *or* sympathize with s.o.; '2**er** *m* (-s/-) feeler

(a. fig.); '²ung f (-/-en) touch, contact (a. ⚔); ~ haben be in touch (mit with); ~ verlieren lose touch.
fuhr [fu:r] pret. of fahren.
Fuhre ['fu:rə] f (-/-n) cart-load.
führen ['fy:rən] (ge-, h) 1. v/t. lead, guide (blind person, etc.); show (zu dat. to); wield (paint-brush, etc.); ⚔ command (regiment, etc.); have, bear (title, etc.); carry on (conversation, etc.); conduct (campaign, etc.); † run (shop, etc.); deal in (goods); lead (life); keep (diary, etc.); ⚖ try (case); wage (war) (mit, gegen against); ~ durch show round; sich ~ conduct o.s., behave (o.s.); 2. v/i. path, etc.: lead, run, go (nach, zu to); sports, etc.: (hold the) lead, be ahead; ~ zu lead to, result in; '~d adj. leading, prominent, Am. a. banner.
'Führer m (-s/-) leader (a. pol., sports); guide(-book); '~raum ⚔ m cockpit; '~schein mot. m driving licence, Am. driver's license; '~sitz m mot. driver's seat, ⚔ pilot's seat; '~stand ⛟ m (driver's) cab.
'Fuhr|geld n, '~lohn m cartage, carriage; '~mann m (-[e]s/~er, Fuhrleute) carter, carrier, wag(g)oner; driver; '~park m fleet (of lorries), Am. fleet (of trucks).
'Führung f (-/-en) leadership; conduct, management; guidance; conduct, behavio(u)r; sports, etc.: lead; '~szeugnis n certificate of good conduct.
'Fuhr|unternehmer m carrier, haulage contractor, Am. a. trucker, teamster; '~werk n (horse-drawn) vehicle; cart, wag(g)on.
Fülle ['fylə] f (-/no pl.) fullness (a. fig.); corpulence, plumpness, stoutness; fig. wealth, abundance, profusion.
füllen¹ ['fylən] v/t. (ge-, h) fill (a. tooth); stuff (cushion, poultry, etc.).
Füllen² zo. [..] n (-s/-) foal; male: colt; female: filly.
'Füll|er F m (-s/-), '~feder(halter m) f fountain-pen; '~horn n horn of plenty; '~ung f (-/-en) filling; panel (of door, etc.).
Fund [funt] m (-[e]s/-e) finding, discovery; find.
Fundament [funda'mɛnt] n (-[e]s/-e) ⚒ foundation; fig. basis.
'Fund|büro n lost-property office; '~gegenstand m object found; '~grube fig. f rich source, mine.
fünf adj. [fynf] five; '²eck n pentagon; '~fach adj. ['~fax] fivefold, quintuple; '²kampf m sports: pentathlon; ²linge ['~liŋə] m/pl. quintuplets pl.; '~te adj. fifth; '²tel n (-s/-) fifth; '~tens adv. fifthly, in the fifth place; '~zehn(te) adj. fifteen(th); ~zig adj. ['~tsiç] fifty; '~zigste adj. fiftieth.

fungieren [fuŋ'gi:rən] v/i. (no -ge-, h): ~ als officiate or act as.
Funk [funk] m (-s/no pl.) radio, wireless; '~anlage f radio or wireless installation or equipment; '~bastler m do-it-yourself radio ham; '~bild n photo-radiogram.
Funke ['funkə] m (-ns/-n) spark; fig. a. glimmer.
'funkeln v/i. (ge-, h) sparkle, glitter; star: twinkle, sparkle.
'Funken¹ esp. fig. m (-s/-) s. Funke.
'funken² v/t. (ge-, h) radio, wireless, broadcast.
'Funk|er m (-s/-) radio or wireless operator; '~gerät n radio (communication) set; '~spruch m radio or wireless message; '~station f radio or wireless station; '~stille f radio or wireless silence; '~streifenwagen m radio patrol car.
Funktion [funk'tsjo:n] f (-/-en) function; ~är [~tsjo'nɛ:r] m (-s/-e) functionary, official; ²ieren [~o'ni:rən] v/i. (no -ge-, h) function, work.
'Funk|turm m radio or wireless tower; '~verkehr m radio or wireless communication; '~wagen m radio car; '~wesen n (-s/no pl.) radio communication.
für prp. (acc.) [fy:r] for; in exchange or return for; in favo(u)r of; in s.o.'s place; Schritt ~ Schritt step by step; Tag ~ Tag day after day; ich ~ meine Person ... as for me, I ...; das Für und Wider the pros and cons pl.
'Fürbitte f intercession.
Furche ['furçə] f (-/-n) furrow (a. in face); rut; ⊕ groove; ²n v/t. (ge-, h) furrow (a. face); ⊕ groove.
Furcht [furçt] f (-/no pl.) fear, dread; aus ~ vor for fear of; '²bar adj. awful, terrible, dreadful.
fürchten ['fyrçtən] (ge-, h) 1. v/t. fear, dread; sich ~ vor (dat.) be afraid or scared of; 2. v/i.: ~ um fear for.
'fürchterlich adj. s. furchtbar.
'furcht|los adj. fearless; '²losigkeit f (-/no pl.) fearlessness; '~sam adj. timid, timorous; '²samkeit f (-/no pl.) timidity.
Furie fig. ['fu:rjə] f (-/-n) fury.
Furnier ⊕ [fur'ni:r] n (-s/-e) veneer; ²en v/t. (no -ge-, h) veneer.
'Für|sorge f care; öffentliche ~ public welfare work; '~sorgeamt n welfare department; '~sorgeerziehung f corrective training for juvenile delinquents; '~sorger m (-s/-) social or welfare worker; '²sorglich adj. considerate, thoughtful, solicitous; '~sprache f intercession (für for, bei with); '~sprecher m intercessor.
Fürst [fyrst] m (-en/-en) prince; sovereign; '~enhaus n dynasty;

'**∼enstand** m prince's rank; '**∼entum** n (-s/∼er) principality; '**²lich**
1. adj. princely (a. fig.), royal; fig. magnificent, sumptuous; 2. adv.: ∼ leben live like a lord or king; '**∼lichkeiten** f/pl. royalties pl.

**Furt** [furt] f (-/-en) ford.

**Furunkel** ♣ [fu'ruŋkəl] m (-s/-) boil, furuncle.

'**Fürwort** gr. n (-[e]s/∼er) pronoun.

**Fusel** F ['fu:zəl] m (-s/-) low-quality spirits, F rotgut.

**Fusion** ♣ [fu'zjo:n] f (-/-en) merger, amalgamation.

**Fuß** [fu:s] m (-es/∼e) foot; ∼ fassen find a foothold; fig. become established; auf gutem (schlechtem) ∼ stehen mit be on good (bad) terms with; zu ∼ on foot; zu ∼ gehen walk; gut zu ∼ sein be a good walker; '**∼abstreifer** m (-s/-) door-scraper, door-mat; '**∼angel** f mantrap; '**∼ball** m (association) football, F and Am. soccer; '**∼ballspieler** m football player, footballer; '**∼bank** f footstool; '**∼bekleidung** f footwear, footgear; '**∼boden** m floor (-ing); '**∼bodenbelag** m floor covering; '**∼bremse** mot. f foot-brake;

'**²en** v/i. (ge-, h): ∼ auf (dat.) be based or founded on; **∼gänger** ['∼gεŋər] m (-s/-) pedestrian; '**∼gelenk** anat. n ankle joint; '**∼note** f footnote; '**∼pfad** m footpath; '**∼sack** m foot-muff; '**∼sohle** anat. f sole of the foot; '**∼soldat** ⚔ m foot-soldier, infantryman; '**∼spur** f footprint; track; '**∼stapfe** ['∼ʃtapfə] f (-/-n) footprint, fig. a. footstep; '**∼steig** m footpath; '**∼tritt** m kick; '**∼wanderung** f walking tour, hike; '**∼weg** m footpath.

**Futter** ['futər] n 1. (-s/no pl.) food, sl. grub, Am. F a. chow; feed, fodder; 2. (-s/-) lining; ⚙ casing.

**Futteral** [futə'ra:l] n (-s/-e) case (for spectacles, etc.); cover (of umbrella); sheath (of knife).

'**Futtermittel** n feeding stuff.

**füttern** ['fytərn] v/t. (ge-, h) feed; line (dress, etc.); ⚙ case.

'**Futter|napf** m feeding bowl or dish; '**∼neid** fig. m (professional) jealousy; '**∼stoff** m lining (material).

'**Fütterung** f (-/-en) feeding; lining; ⚙ casing.

**Futur** gr. [fu'tu:r] n (-s/-e) future (tense).

# G

**gab** [ga:p] pret. of geben.

**Gabe** ['ga:bə] f (-/-n) gift, present; alms; donation; ⚕ dose; talent.

**Gabel** ['ga:bəl] f (-/-n) fork; '**²n** v/refl. (ge-, h) fork, bifurcate; '**∼ung** f (-/-en) bifurcation.

**gackern** ['gakərn] v/i. (ge-, h) cackle.

**gaffen** ['gafən] v/i. (ge-, h) gape; stare.

**Gage** ['ga:ʒə] f (-/-n) salary, pay.

**gähnen** ['gɛ:nən] 1. v/i. (ge-, h) yawn; 2. ² n (-s/no pl.) yawning.

**Gala** ['gala] f (-/no pl.) gala; in ∼ in full dress.

**galant** adj. [ga'lant] gallant; courteous; **²erie** [∼ə'ri:] f (-/-n) gallantry; courtesy.

**Galeere** ⚓ [ga'le:rə] f (-/-n) galley.

**Galerie** [galə'ri:] f (-/-n) gallery.

**Galgen** ['galgən] m (-s/-) gallows, gibbet; '**∼frist** f respite; '**∼gesicht** n gallows-look, hangdog look; '**∼humor** m grim humo(u)r; '**∼strick** m, '**∼vogel** m gallows-bird, hangdog.

**Galle** anat. ['galə] f (-/-n) bile (of person); gall (of animal) (a. fig.); '**∼nblase** anat. f gall-bladder; '**∼nleiden** ⚕ n bilious complaint; '**∼nstein** ⚕ m gall-stone, bile-stone.

**Gallert** ['galərt] n (-[e]s/-e), **∼e** [ga'lɛrtə] f (-/-n) gelatine, jelly.

'**gallig** fig. adj. bilious.

**Galopp** [ga'lɔp] m (-s/-s, -e) gallop; canter; **²ieren** [∼'pi:rən] v/i. (no -ge-, sein) gallop; canter.

**galt** [galt] pret. of gelten.

**galvani|sch** adj. [gal'va:niʃ] galvanic; **∼sieren** [∼ani'-] v/t. (no -ge-, h) galvanize.

**Gang¹** [gaŋ] m (-[e]s/∼e) walk; s. Gangart; fig. motion; running, working (of machine); errand; way; course (of events), of a meal, etc.); passage(-way); alley; corridor, gallery; in vehicle, between seats: gangway, esp. Am. aisle; ⛟ corridor, Am. aisle; fencing: pass; anat. duct; mot. gear; erster (zweiter, dritter, vierter) ∼ low or bottom (second, third, top) gear; in ∼ bringen or setzen set going or in motion, Am. operate; in ∼ kommen get going, get started; im ∼ sein be in motion; ⊕ be working or running; fig. be in progress; in vollem ∼ in full swing.

**gang²** adj. [∼]: ∼ und gäbe customary, traditional.

'**Gang|art** f gait, walk (of person); pace (of horse); **²bar** adj. road: practicable, passable; money: current; ♣ goods: marketable; s. gängig.

**Gängelband** ['gɛŋəl-] n leading-strings *pl.*; *am ~ führen* keep in leading-strings, lead by the nose.

**gängig** *adj.* ['gɛŋiç] *money*: current; ✝ *goods*: marketable; *~er Ausdruck* current word *or* phrase.

**Gans** *orn.* [gans] *f* (-/-e) goose.

**Gänse|blümchen** ❦ ['gɛnzəblyːmçən] *n* (-s/-) daisy; '*~braten* m roast goose; '*~feder* *f* goose-quill; *~füßchen* ['~fyːsçən] *n/pl.* quotation marks *pl.*, inverted commas *pl.*; '*~haut* *f* goose-skin; *fig. a.* gooseflesh, *Am. a.* goose pimples *pl.*; '*~klein* n (-s/*no pl.*) (goose-)giblets *pl.*; '*~marsch* m single *or* Indian file; *~rich orn.* ['~riç] *m* (-s/-e) gander; '*~schmalz* n goose-grease.

**ganz** [gants] **1.** *adj.* all; entire, whole; complete, total, full; *den ~en Tag* all day (long); **2.** *adv.* quite; entirely, *etc.* (s. 1.); very; *~ Auge (Ohr)* all eyes (ears); *~ und gar* wholly, totally; *~ und gar nicht* not at all; *im ~en* on the whole, generally; in all; ✝ *im* the lump; '2e *n* (-n/*no pl.*) whole; totality; *aufs ~ gehen* go all out, *esp. Am. sl.* go the whole hog.

**gänzlich** *adj.* ['gɛntsliç] complete, total, entire.

'**Ganztagsbeschäftigung** *f* full-time job *or* employment.

**gar** [gaːr] **1.** *adj. food*: done; **2.** *adv.* quite, very; even; *~ nicht* not at all.

**Garage** [ga'raːʒə] *f* (-/-n) garage.

**Garantie** [garan'tiː] *f* (-/-n) guarantee, warranty, ♫♫ guaranty; 2*ren v/t.* (*no -ge-*, h) guarantee, warrant.

**Garbe** ['garbə] *f* (-/-n) sheaf.

**Garde** ['gardə] *f* (-/-n) guard.

**Garderobe** [gardə'roːbə] *f* (-/-n) wardrobe; cloakroom, *Am.* check-room; *thea.* dressing-room; *~nfrau f* cloak-room attendant, *Am.* hat-check girl; *~nmarke f* check; *~n-schrank m* wardrobe; *~nständer m* coat-stand, hat-stand, hall-stand.

**Garderobiere** [gardəro'bjɛːrə] *f* (-/-n) *s. Garderobenfrau; thea.* wardrobe mistress.

**Gardine** [gar'diːnə] *f* (-/-n) curtain.

**gär|en** ['gɛːrən] *v/i.* (*irr.*, ge-, h, sein) ferment; 2*mittel n* ferment.

**Garn** [garn] *n* (-[e]s/-e) yarn; thread; cotton; net; *j-m ins ~ gehen* fall into s.o.'s snare.

**Garnele** *zo.* [gar'neːlə] *f* (-/-n) shrimp.

**garnieren** [gar'niːrən] *v/t.* (*no -ge-*, h) trim; garnish (*esp. a dish*).

**Garnison** ✕ [garni'zoːn] *f* (-/-en) garrison, post.

**Garnitur** [garni'tuːr] *f* (-/-en) trimming; ⊕ fittings *pl.*; set.

**garstig** *adj.* ['garstiç] nasty, bad; ugly.

'**Gärstoff** m ferment.

**Garten** ['gartən] *m* (-s/ä) garden; '*~anlage f* gardens *pl.*, park; '*~ar-*

---

*beit* *f* gardening; '*~bau* m horti-culture; '*~erde f* (garden-)mo(u)ld; '*~fest* n garden-party, *Am. a.* lawn party; '*~geräte n/pl.* gardening-tools *pl.*; '*~stadt f* garden city.

**Gärtner** ['gɛrtnər] *m* (-s/-) gardener; *~ei* [~'rai] *f* (-/-en) gardening, horti-culture; nursery; '*~in f* (-/-nen) gardener.

**Gärung** ['gɛːruŋ] *f* (-/-en) fermen-tation.

**Gas** [gaːs] *n* (-es/-e) gas; *~ geben mot.* open the throttle, *Am.* step on the gas; '*~anstalt f* gas-works, *Am. a.* gas plant; '*~behälter m* gasometer, *Am.* gas tank *or* con-tainer; '*~beleuchtung f* gaslight; '*~brenner m* gas-burner; 2*förmig adj.* ['~fœrmiç] gaseous; '*~hahn m* gas-tap; '*~herd m* gas-stove, *Am.* gas range; '*~leitung f* gas-mains *pl.*; '*~messer m* (-s/-) gas-meter; *~ofen m* gas-oven; '*~pedal mot. n* accelerator (pedal), *Am.* gas pedal.

**Gasse** ['gasə] *f* (-/-n) lane, by-street, alley(-way); '*~nhauer m* (-s/-) street ballad, popular song; '*~n-junge m* street arab.

**Gast** [gast] *m* (-es/ä) guest; visitor; customer (*of public house, etc.*); *thea.*: guest (artist); guest star; '*~arbeiter m* foreign worker; '*~bett n* spare bed.

**Gäste|buch** ['gɛstə-] *n* visitors' book; '*~zimmer n* guest-room; spare (bed)room; *s. Gaststube.*

'**gast|freundlich** *adj.* hospitable; '2*freundschaft f* hospitality; '2*ge-ber m* (-s/-) host; '2*geberin f* (-/-nen) hostess; '2*haus n,* '2*hof m* restaurant; inn, hotel; '2*hörer univ. m* guest student, *Am. a.* auditor.

**gastieren** *thea.* [gas'tiːrən] *v/i.* (*no -ge-*, h) appear as a guest.

'**gast|lich** *adj.* hospitable; '2*mahl n* feast, banquet; '2*recht n* right of *or* to hospitality; '2*rolle thea. f* guest part; starring part *or* role; '2*spiel thea. n* guest appearance *or* performance; starring (perform-ance); '2*stätte f* restaurant; '2*stube f* taproom; restaurant; '2*wirt m* innkeeper, landlord; '2*wirtin f* innkeeper, landlady; '2*wirtschaft f* inn, public house, restaurant; '2*zimmer n s. Gästezimmer.*

'**Gas|uhr** *f* gas-meter; '*~werk n s. Gasanstalt.*

**Gatte** ['gatə] *m* (-n/-n) husband; spouse, consort.

**Gatter** ['gatər] *n* (-s/-) lattice; rail-ing, grating.

'**Gattin** *f* (-/-nen) wife; spouse, con-sort.

**Gattung** ['gatuŋ] *f* (-/-en) kind; sort; type; species; genus.

**gaukeln** ['gaukəln] *v/i.* (ge-, h) juggle; *birds, etc.*: flutter.

**Gaul** [gaul] *m* (-[e]s/ᵘe) (old) nag.
**Gaumen** *anat.* ['gaumən] *m* (-s/-) palate.
**Gauner** ['gaunər] *m* (-s/-) scoundrel, swindler, sharper, *sl.* crook; ᴗei [ᴗ'rai] *f* (-/-en) swindling, cheating, trickery.
**Gaze** ['gɑːzə] *f* (-/-n) gauze.
**Gazelle** *zo.* [ga'tsɛlə] *f* (-/-n) gazelle.
**Geächtete** [gə'ɛçtətə] *m, f* (-n/-n) outlaw.
**Gebäck** [gə'bɛk] *n* (-[e]s/-e) baker's goods *pl.*; pastry; fancy cakes *pl.*
**ge'backen** *p.p. of* backen.
**Gebälk** [gə'bɛlk] *n* (-[e]s/no *pl.*) framework, timber-work; beams *pl.*
**gebar** [gə'baːr] *pret. of* gebären.
**Gebärde** [gə'bɛːrdə] *f* (-/-n) gesture; ᴗn *v/refl.* (no -ge-, h) conduct o.s., behave; ᴗnspiel *n* (-[e]s/no *pl.*) gesticulation; dumb show, pantomime; ᴗnsprache *f* language of gestures.
**Gebaren** [gə'bɑːrən] *n* (-s/no *pl.*) conduct, deportment, behavio(u)r.
**gebären** [gə'bɛːrən] *v/t.* (*irr.*, no -ge-, h) bear, bring forth (*a. fig.*); give birth to.
**Ge|bäude** [gə'bɔydə] *n* (-s/-) building, edifice, structure; ᴗbell [ᴗ'bɛl] *n* (-[e]s/no *pl.*) barking.
**geben** ['geːbən] *v/t.* (*irr.*, ge-, h) give (*j-m et. s.o. s.th.*); present (*s.o. with s.th.*); put; yield *s.th.*; deal (*cards*); pledge (*one's word*); *von sich* ᴗ emit; utter (*words*); bring up, vomit (*food*); *et.* (*nichts*) ᴗ *auf* (*acc.*) set (no) great store by; *sich* geschlagen ᴗ give in; *sich zufrieden* ᴗ content o.s. (*mit with*); *sich zu* erkennen ᴗ make o.s. known; *es gibt* there is, there are; *was gibt es?* what is the matter?; *thea.*: gegeben werden be on.
**Gebet** [gə'beːt] *n* (-[e]s/-e) prayer.
**ge'beten** *p.p. of* bitten.
**Gebiet** [gə'biːt] *n* (-[e]s/-e) territory; district; region; area; *fig.*: field; province; sphere.
**ge'giet|en** (*irr. bieten, no* -ge-, h) **1.** *v/t.* order, command; **2.** *v/i.* rule; 2er *m* (-s/-) master, lord, governor; 2erin *f* (-/-nen) mistress; ᴗerisch *adj.* imperious; commanding.
**Gebilde** [gə'bildə] *n* (-s/-) form, shape; structure; 2t *adj.* educated; cultured, cultivated.
**Gebirg|e** [gə'birgə] *n* (-s/-) mountains *pl.*; mountain chain *or* range; 2ig *adj.* mountainous; ᴗsbewohner *m* mountaineer; ᴗszug *m* mountain range.
**Ge'biß** *n* (Gebisses/Gebisse) (set of) teeth; (set of) artificial *or* false teeth, denture; *harness*: bit.
**ge|'bissen** *p.p. of* beißen; ᴗ'blasen *p.p. of* blasen; ᴗ'blichen *p.p. of* bleichen 2; ᴗ'blieben [ᴗ'bliːbən] *p.p. of* bleiben; ᴗblümt *adj.*

[ᴗ'blyːmt] *pattern, design:* flowered; *material:* sprigged; ᴗ'bogen **1.** *p.p. of* biegen; **2.** *adj.* bent, curved; ᴗboren [ᴗ'boːrən] **1.** *p.p. of* gebären; **2.** *adj.* born; *ein* ᴗer *Deutscher* German by birth; ᴗe *Schmidt* née Smith.
**ge'borgen 1.** *p.p. uf* bergen; **2.** *adj.* safe, sheltered; 2heit *f* (-/no *pl.*) safety, security.
**geborsten** [gə'bɔrstən] *p.p. of* bersten.
**Ge'bot** *n* (-[e]s/-e) order; command; bid(ding), offer; *eccl.*: die Zehn ᴗe *pl.* the Ten Commandments *pl.*; 2en *p.p. of* bieten.
**ge|bracht** [gə'braxt] *p.p. of* bringen; ᴗbrannt [ᴗ'brant] *p.p. of* brennen; ᴗ'braten *p.p. of* braten.
**Ge'brauch** *m* **1.** (-[e]s/no *pl.*) use; *application*; **2.** (-[e]s/ᵘe) usage, practice; custom; 2en *v/t.* (no -ge-, h) use, employ; 2t *adj.* clothes, *etc.*: second-hand.
**gebräuchlich** [gə'brɔyçliç] *adj.* in use; usual, customary.
**Ge'brauchs|anweisung** *f* directions *pl. or* instructions *pl.* for use; ᴗartikel *m* commodity, necessary, requisite; personal article; 2fertig *adj.* ready for use; *coffee, etc.*: instant; ᴗmuster † *n* sample; registered design.
**Ge'braucht|wagen** *mot. m* used car; ᴗwaren *f/pl.* second-hand articles *pl.*
**Ge'brechen** *n* (-s/-) defect, infirmity; affliction.
**ge'brechlich** *adj.* fragile; *p.*: frail, weak; infirm; 2keit *f* (-/-en) fragility; infirmity.
**gebrochen** [gə'brɔxən] *p.p. of* brechen.
**Ge|brüder** [gə'bryːdər] *pl.* brothers *pl.*; ᴗbrüll [ᴗ'bryl] *n* (-[e]s/no *pl.*) roaring; lowing (*of cattle*).
**Gebühr** [gə'byːr] *f* (-/-en) due; duty; charge; rate; fee; ᴗen *pl.* fee(s *pl.*), dues *pl.*; 2en *v/i.* (no -ge-, h) be due (*dat.* to); *sich* ᴗ be proper *or* fitting; 2end *adj.* due; becoming; proper; 2enfrei *adj.* free of charge; 2enpflichtig *adj.* liable to charges, chargeable.
**gebunden** [gə'bundən] **1.** *p.p. of* binden; **2.** *adj.* bound.
**Geburt** [gə'buːrt] *f* (-/-en) birth; ᴗenkontrolle *f*, ᴗenregelung *f* birth-control; ᴗenziffer *f* birthrate.
**gebürtig** *adj.* [gə'byrtiç]: ᴗ *aus a* native of.
**Ge'burts|anzeige** *f* announcement of birth; ᴗfehler *m* congenital defect; ᴗhelfer *m* obstetrician; ᴗhilfe *f* obstetrics, midwifery; ᴗjahr *n* year of birth; ᴗland *n* native country; ᴗort *m* birth-place; ᴗschein *m* birth certificate; ᴗtag *m*

birthday; **~urkunde** f birth certificate.

**Gebüsch** [gə'byʃ] n (-es/-e) bushes pl., undergrowth, thicket.

**gedacht** [gə'daxt] p.p. of denken.

**Gedächtnis** [gə'dɛçtnis] n (-ses/-se) memory; remembrance, recollection; im ~ behalten keep in mind; zum ~ (gen.) in memory of; **~feier** f commemoration.

**Gedanke** [gə'daŋkə] m (-ns/-n) thought; idea; in ~n (versunken or verloren) absorbed in thought; sich ~n machen über (acc.) worry about.

**Ge'danken|gang** m train of thought; **~leser** m, **~leserin** f (-/-nen) thought-reader; **2los** adj. thoughtless; **~strich** m dash; **2voll** adj. thoughtful, pensive.

**Ge|därm** [gə'dɛrm] n (-[e]s/-e) mst pl. entrails pl., bowels pl., intestines pl.; **~deck** [~'dɛk] n (-[e]s/-e) cover; menu; ein ~ auflegen lay a place.

**gedeihen** [gə'daɪən] 1. v/i. (irr., no -ge-, sein) thrive, prosper; 2. 2 n (-s/no pl.) thriving, prosperity.

**ge'denken** v/i. (gen.) (irr. denken, no -ge-, h) think of; remember, recollect; commemorate; mention; ~ zu inf. intend to inf.; 2. 2 n (-s/no pl.) memory, remembrance (an acc. of).

**Ge'denk|feier** f commemoration; **~stein** m memorial stone; **~tafel** f commemorative or memorial tablet.

**Ge'dicht** n (-[e]s/-e) poem.

**gediegen** adj. [gə'di:gən] solid; pure; **2heit** f (-/no pl.) solidity; purity.

**gedieh** [gə'di:] pret. of gedeihen; **~en** p.p. of gedeihen.

**Gedräng|e** [gə'drɛŋə] n (-s/no pl.) crowd, throng; **2t** adj. crowded, packed, crammed; style: concise.

**ge|droschen** [gə'drɔʃən] p.p. of dreschen; **~drückt** fig. adj. depressed; **~drungen** [~'druŋən] 1. p.p. of dringen; 2. adj. compact; squat, stocky, thickset.

**Geduld** [gə'dult] f (-/no pl.) patience; **2en** [~dən] v/refl. (no -ge-, h) have patience; **2ig** adj. [~diç] patient.

**ge|dunsen** adj. [gə'dunzən] bloated; **~durft** [~'durft] p.p. of dürfen 1; **~ehrt** adj. [~'e:rt] hono(u)red; correspondence: Sehr ~er Herr N.! Dear Sir, Dear Mr N.; **~eignet** adj. [~'aignət] fit (für, zu, als for s.th.); suitable (to, for); qualified (for).

**Gefahr** [gə'fɑ:r] f (-/-en) danger, peril; risk; auf eigene ~ at one's own risk; ~ laufen zu inf. run the risk of ger.

**gefährden** [gə'fɛːrdən] v/t. (no -ge-, h) endanger; risk.

**ge'fahren** p.p. of fahren.

**gefährlich** adj. [gə'fɛːrliç] dangerous.

**ge'fahrlos** adj. without risk, safe.

**Gefährt|e** [gə'fɛːrtə] m (-en/-en), **~in** f (-/-nen) companion, fellow.

**Gefälle** [gə'fɛlə] n (-s/-) fall, slope, incline, descent, gradient, esp. Am. a. grade; fall (of river, etc.).

**Ge'fallen** 1. m (-s/-) favo(u)r; 2. n (-s/no pl.) finden an (dat.) take (a) pleasure in, take a fancy to or for; 3. 2 v/i. (irr. fallen, no -ge-, h) please (j-m s.o.); er gefällt mir I like him; sich et. ~ lassen put up with s.th.; 4. 2 p.p. of fallen.

**gefällig** adj. [gə'fɛliç] pleasing, agreeable, p.: complaisant, obliging; kind; **2keit** f (-/~-en) complaisance, kindness; favo(u)r; **~st** adv. (if you) please.

**ge'fangen** 1. p.p. of fangen; 2. adj. captive, imprisoned; **2e** m (-n/-n), f (-n/-n) prisoner, captive; **2en-lager** n prison(ers') camp; **2en-nahme** f (-/no pl.) capture; seizure, arrest; **~nehmen** v/t. (irr. nehmen, sep., -ge-, h) take prisoner; fig. captivate; **2schaft** f (-/no pl.) captivity, imprisonment; **~setzen** v/t. (sep., -ge-, h) put in prison.

**Gefängnis** [gə'fɛŋnis] n (-ses/-se) prison, jail, gaol, Am. a. penitentiary; **~direktor** m governor, warden; **~strafe** f (sentence or term of) imprisonment; **~wärter** m warder, gaoler, jailer, (prison) guard.

**Gefäß** [gə'fɛːs] n (-es/-e) vessel.

**gefaßt** adj. [gə'fast] composed; ~ auf (acc.) prepared for.

**Ge|fecht** [gə'fɛçt] n (-[e]s/-e) engagement; combat, fight; action; **~fieder** [~'fi:dər] n (-s/-) plumage, feathers pl.

**ge|fleckt** adj. spotted; **~flochten** [~'flɔxtən] p.p. of flechten; **~flogen** [~'flo:gən] p.p. of fliegen; **~flohen** [~'flo:ən] p.p. of fliehen; **~flossen** [~'flɔsən] p.p. of fließen.

**Ge|'flügel** n (-s/no pl.) fowl; poultry; **~flüster** [~'flystər] n (-s/no pl.) whisper(ing).

**gefochten** [gə'fɔxtən] p.p. of fechten.

**Ge'folg|e** n (-s/no pl.) retinue, train, followers pl.; attendants pl.; **~schaft** [~kʃaft] f (-/-en) followers pl.

**gefräßig** adj. [gə'frɛːsiç] greedy, voracious; **2keit** f (-/no pl.) greediness, gluttony, voracity.

**ge'fressen** p.p. of fressen.

**ge'frier|en** v/i. (irr. frieren, no -ge-, sein) congeal, freeze; **2fleisch** n frozen meat; **2punkt** m freezing-point; **2schutz(mittel** n) m antifreeze.

**gefroren** [gə'fro:rən] p.p. of frieren; **2e** [~ə] n (-n/no pl.) ice-cream.

**Gefüge** [gə'fy:gə] n (-s/-) structure; texture.

ge'fügig *adj.* pliant; 2keit *f* (-/*no pl.*) pliancy.

Gefühl [gə'fy:l] *n* (-[e]s/-e) feeling; touch; sense (für of); sensation; 2los *adj.* unfeeling, insensible (gegen to); 2sbetont *adj.* emotional; 2voll *adj.* (full of) feeling; tender; sentimental.

ge|funden [gə'fundən] *p.p. of* finden; ~gangen [~'gaŋən] *p.p. of* gehen.

ge'geben *p.p. of* geben; ~enfalls *adv.* in that case; if necessary.

gegen *prp.* (*acc.*) ['ge:gən] *space, time*: towards; against, ⚕ versus; about, *Am.* around; by; compared with; (in exchange) for; *remedy*: for; *freundlich sein* ~ be kind to (-wards); ~ *bar* for cash.

'Gegen|angriff *m* counter-attack; '~antrag *m* counter-motion; '~antwort *f* rejoinder; '~befehl *m* counter-order; '~beschuldigung *f* countercharge; '~besuch *m* return visit; '~bewegung *f* counter-movement; '~beweis *m* counter-evidence.

Gegend ['ge:gənt] *f* (-/-en) region; area.

'Gegen|dienst *m* return service, service in return; '~druck *m* counter-pressure; *fig.* reaction; 2ei'nander *adv.* against one another *or* each other; '~erklärung *f* counterstatement; '~forderung *f* counterclaim; '~frage *f* counter-question; '~geschenk *n* return present; '~gewicht *n* counterbalance, counterpoise; '~gift ⚕ *n* antidote; '~kandidat *m* rival candidate; '~klage *f* countercharge; '~leistung *f* return (service), equivalent; ~lichtaufnahme *phot.* ['ge:gənliçt?-] *f* back-lighted shot; '~liebe *f* requited love; *keine* ~ *finden* meet with no sympathy *or* enthusiasm; '~maßnahme *f* counter-measure; '~mittel *n* remedy (gegen for), antidote (against, for); '~partei *f* opposite party; '~probe *f* checktest; '~satz *m* contrast; opposition; *im* ~ *zu* in contrast to *or* with, in opposition to; 2sätzlich *adj.* ['~zetsliç] contrary, opposite; '~seite *f* opposite side; '2seitig *adj.* mutual, reciprocal; '~seitigkeit *f* (-/*no pl.*): *auf* ~ *assurance*: mutual; *auf* ~ *beruhen* be mutual; '~spieler *m* *games, sports*: opponent; antagonist; '~spionage *f* counter-espionage; '~stand *m* object; subject, topic; '~strömung *f* counter-current; '~stück *n* counterpart; match; '~teil *n* contrary, reverse; *im* ~ *on the contrary*; '2teilig *adj.* contrary, opposite; 2'über 1. *adv.* opposite; 2. *prp.* (*dat.*) opposite (to); to (-wards); as against; face to face with; ~'über *n* (-s/-) vis-à-vis;

2'überstehen *v/i.* (*irr. stehen, sep.,* -ge-, h) (*dat.*) be faced with; face; ~'überstellung *esp.* ⚕ *f* confrontation; '~vorschlag *m* counter-proposal; ~wart ['~vart] *f* (-/*no pl.*) presence; present time; *gr.* present tense; 2wärtig ['~vertiç] 1. *adj.* present; actual; 2. *adv.* at present; '~wehr *f* defen|ce, *Am.* -se; resistance; '~wert *m* equivalent; '~wind *m* contrary wind, head wind; '~wirkung *f* counter-effect, reaction; '2zeichnen *v/t.* (*sep.*, -ge-, h) countersign; '~zug *m* counter-move (*a. fig.*); 🚂 corresponding train.

ge|gessen [gə'gesən] *p.p. of* essen; ~glichen [~'gliçən] *p.p. of* gleichen; ~'gliedert *adj.* articulate, jointed; ~glitten [~'glitən] *p.p. of* gleiten; ~glommen [~'glɔmən] *p.p. of* glimmen.

Gegner ['ge:gnər] *m* (-s/-) adversary, opponent; ~schaft *f* (-/-en) opposition.

ge|golten [gə'gɔltən] *p.p. of* gelten; ~goren [~'go:rən] *p.p. of* gären; ~gossen [~'gɔsən] *p.p. of* gießen; ~'graben *p.p. of* graben; ~griffen [~'grifən] *p.p. of* greifen; ~habt [~'ha:pt] *p.p. of* haben.

Gehalt [gə'halt] 1. *m* (-[e]s/-e) contents *pl.*; capacity; merit; 2. *n* (-[e]s/-er) salary; 2en *p.p. of* halten; 2los *adj.* [~lo:s] *adj.* empty; ~sempfänger [gə'halts?-] *m* salaried employee *or* worker; ~serhöhung [gə'halts?-] *f* rise (in salary), *Am.* raise; 2voll *adj.* rich; substantial; *wine*: racy.

gehangen [gə'haŋən] *p.p. of* hängen 1.

gehässig *adj.* [gə'hɛsiç] malicious, spiteful; 2keit *f* (-/-en) malice, spitefulness.

ge'hauen *p.p. of* hauen.

Ge|häuse [gə'hɔyzə] *n* (-s/-) case, box; cabinet; shell; core (*of apple, etc.*); ~hege [~'he:gə] *n* (-s/-) enclosure.

geheim *adj.* [gə'haim] secret; 2dienst *m* secret service.

Ge'heimnis *n* (-ses/-se) secret; mystery; ~krämer *m* mystery-monger; 2voll *adj.* mysterious.

Ge'heim|polizei *f* secret police; ~polizist *m* detective; plain-clothes man; ~schrift *f* cipher; *tel.* code.

ge'heißen *p.p. of* heißen.

gehen ['ge:ən] *v/i.* (*irr.*, ge-, sein) go; walk; leave; *machine*: go, work; *clock, watch*: go; *merchandise*: sell; *wind*: blow; *paste*: rise; *wie geht es Ihnen?* how are you (getting on)?; *das geht nicht* that won't do; *in sich* ~ repent; *wieviel Pfennige* ~ *auf e-e Mark?* how many pfennigs go to a mark?; *das Fenster geht nach Norden* the window faces *or* looks north; *es geht nichts über* (acc.) there is nothing like; *wenn es nach mir ginge* if I had my way.

**Geheul** [gə'hɔʏl] n (-[e]s/no pl.) howling.

**Ge'hilf|e** m (-n/-n), **～in** f (-/-nen) assistant; fig. helpmate.

**Ge'hirn** n (-[e]s/-e) brain(s pl.); **～erschütterung** ♀ f concussion (of the brain); **～schlag** ♀ m cerebral apoplexy.

**gehoben** [gə'ho:bən] 1. p.p. of he ben; 2. adj. speech, style: elevated; **～e** Stimmung elated mood.

**Gehöft** [gə'hø:ft] n (-[e]s/-e) farm (-stead).

**geholfen** [gə'hɔlfən] p.p. of helfen.

**Gehölz** [gə'hœlts] n (-es/-e) wood, coppice, copse.

**Gehör** [gə'hø:r] n (-[e]s/no pl.) hearing; ear; *nach dem ～* by ear; *j-m ～ schenken* lend an ear to s.o.; *sich ～ verschaffen* make o.s. heard.

**ge'horchen** v/i. (no -ge-, h) obey (j-m s.o.).

**ge'hör|en** v/i. (no -ge-, h) belong (dat. or zu to); *es gehört sich* it is proper or fit or right or suitable; *das gehört nicht hierher* that's not to the point; **～ig** 1. adj. belonging (dat. or zu to); fit, proper, right; due; F good; 2. adv. duly; F thoroughly.

**gehorsam** [gə'ho:rza:m] 1. adj. obedient; 2. ♀ m (-s/no pl.) obedience.

**'Geh|steig** m, **'～weg** m pavement, Am. sidewalk; **'～werk** ⊕ n clockwork, works pl.

**Geier** orn. ['gaɪər] m (-s/-) vulture.

**Geige** ♪ ['gaɪgə] f (-/-n) violin, F fiddle; (auf der) *～ spielen* play (on) the violin; **～nbogen** ♪ m (violin-bow; **～nkasten** ♪ m violin-case; **'～r** ♪ m (-s/-), **'～rin** ♪ f (-/-nen) violinist.

**'Geigerzähler** phys. m Geiger counter.

**geil** adj. lascivious, wanton; luxuriant.

**Geisel** ['gaɪzəl] f (-/-n) hostage.

**Geiß** zo. [gaɪs] f (-/-en) (she-, nanny-)goat; **'～blatt** ♀ n (-[e]s/no pl.) honeysuckle, woodbine; **'～bock** zo. m he-goat, billy-goat.

**Geißel** ['gaɪsəl] f (-/-n) whip, lash; fig. scourge; **'♀n** v/t. (ge-, h) whip, lash; fig. castigate.

**Geist** [gaɪst] m (-es/-er) spirit; mind, intellect; wit; ghost; sprite.

**'Geister|erscheinung** f apparition; **'♀haft** adj. ghostly.

**'geistes|abwesend** adj. absent-minded; **'♀arbeiter** m brain-worker, white-collar worker; **'♀blitz** m brain-wave, flash of genius; **'♀gabe** f talent; **'♀gegenwart** f presence of mind; **'～gegenwärtig** adj. alert; quick-witted; **'～gestört** adj. mentally disturbed; **'～krank**

adj. insane, mentally ill; **'♀krankheit** f insanity, mental illness; **'～schwach** adj. feeble-minded, imbecile; **'～verwandt** adj. congenial; **'♀wissenschaften** f/pl. *the* Arts pl., *the* Humanities pl.; **'♀zustand** m state of mind.

**'geistig** adj. intellectual, mental; spiritual; **～e** Getränke n/pl. spirits pl.

**'geistlich** adj. spiritual; clerical; sacred; **'♀e** m (-n/-n) clergyman; minister; **'♀keit** f (-/no pl.) clergy.

**'geist|los** adj. spiritless; dull; stupid; **'～reich** adj., **'～voll** adj. ingenious, spirited.

**Geiz** [gaɪts] m (-es/no pl.) avarice; **'～hals** m miser, niggard; **'♀ig** adj. avaricious, stingy, mean.

**Gejammer** [gə'jamər] n (-s/no pl.) lamentation(s pl.), wailing.

**gekannt** [gə'kant] p.p. of kennen.

**Geklapper** [gə'klapər] n (-s/no pl.) rattling.

**Geklirr** [gə'klɪr] n (-[e]s/no pl.), **～e** [~ə] n (-s/no pl.) clashing, clanking.

**ge|klungen** [~'kluŋən] p.p. of klingen; **～kniffen** [~'knɪfən] p.p. of kneifen; **～kommen** p.p. of kommen; **～konnt** [~'kɔnt] p.p. of können 1, 2.

**Ge|kreisch** [gə'kraɪʃ] n (-es/no pl.) screaming, screams pl.; shrieking; **～kritzel** [~'krɪtsəl] n (-s/no pl.) scrawl(ing), scribbling, scribble.

**ge|krochen** [gə'krɔxən] p.p. of kriechen; **～künstelt** adj. [~'kynstəlt] artificial.

**Gelächter** [gə'lɛçtər] n (-s/-) laughter.

**ge'laden** p.p. of laden.

**Ge'lage** n (-s/-) feast; drinking-bout.

**Gelände** [gə'lɛndə] n (-s/-) ground; terrain; country; area; **♀gängig** mot. adj. cross-country; **♀lauf** m sports: cross-country race or run.

**Geländer** [gə'lɛndər] n (-s/-) railing, balustrade; banisters pl.

**ge'lang** pret. of gelingen.

**ge'langen** v/i. (no -ge-, sein): *～ an* (acc.) or *in* (acc.) arrive at, get or come to; *～ zu* attain (to), gain.

**ge'lassen** 1. p.p. of lassen; 2. adj. calm, composed.

**Gelatine** [ʒela'ti:nə] f (-/no pl.) gelatin(e).

**ge'laufen** p.p. of laufen; **～läufig** adj. [~'lɔʏfɪç] current; fluent, easy; tongue: voluble; familiar; **～launt** adj. [~'lɔʏnt] in a (good, etc.) humo(u)r or Am. mood.

**Geläut** [gə'lɔʏt] n (-[e]s/-e), **～e** [~ə] n (-s/-) ringing (of bells); chimes pl. (of church bells).

**gelb** adj. [gɛlp] yellow; **'～lich** adj. yellowish; **♀sucht** ♀ f (-/no pl.) jaundice.

**Geld** [gɛlt] n (-[e]s/-er) money; *im*

~ **schwimmen** be rolling in money; **zu ~ machen** turn into cash; '**~angelegenheit** f money-matter; '**~anlage** f investment; '**~ausgabe** f expense; '**~beutel** m purse; '**~entwertung** f devaluation of the currency; '**~erwerb** m money-making; '**~geber** m (-s/-) financial backer, investor; '**~geschäfte** n/pl. money transactions pl.; '**2gierig** adj. greedy for money, avaricious; '**~mittel** n/pl. funds pl., resources pl.; '**~schein** m bank-note, Am. bill; '**~schrank** m strong-box, safe; '**~sendung** f remittance; '**~strafe** f fine; '**~stück** n coin; '**~tasche** f money-bag; notecase, Am. billfold; '**~überhang** m surplus money; '**~umlauf** m circulation of money; '**~umsatz** m turnover (of money); '**~verlegenheit** f pecuniary embarrassment; '**~wechsel** m exchange of money; '**~wert** m (-[e]s/no pl.) value of money, money value.

**Gelee** [ʒə'leː] n, m (-s/-s) jelly.

**ge'legen 1.** p.p. of liegen; **2.** adj. situated, Am. a. located; convenient, opportune; **2heit** f (-/-en) occasion; opportunity; chance; facility; **bei ~** on occasion.

**Ge'legenheits|arbeit** f casual or odd job, Am. a. chore; **~arbeiter** m casual labo(u)rer, odd-job man; **~kauf** m bargain.

**ge'legentlich 1.** adj. occasional; **2.** prp. (gen.) on the occasion of.

**ge'lehrig** adj. docile; **2igkeit** f (-/no pl.) docility; **2samkeit** f (-/no pl.) learning; **~t** adj. [⌐t] learned; **2te** [⌐ə] m (-n/-n) learned man, scholar.

**Geleise** [gə'laɪzə] n (-s/-) rut, track; ⚙ rails pl., line, esp. Am. tracks pl.

**Geleit** [gə'laɪt] n (-[e]s/-e) escort; attendance; **j-m das ~ geben** accompany s.o.; **2en** v/t. (no -ge-, h) accompany, conduct; escort; **~zug** ⚓ m convoy.

**Gelenk** anat., ⊕, ⚙ [gə'lɛŋk] n (-[e]s/-e) joint; **2ig** adj. pliable, supple.

**ge'lernt** adj. worker: skilled; trained; **~'lesen** p.p. of lesen.

**Geliebte** [gə'liːptə] (-n/-n) **1.** m lover; **2.** f mistress, sweetheart.

**geliehen** [gə'liːən] p.p. of leihen.

**ge'linde 1.** adj. soft, smooth; gentle; **2.** adv.: **gelinde gesagt** to put it mildly, to say the least.

**gelingen** [gə'lɪŋən] **1.** v/i. (irr., no -ge-, sein) succeed; **es gelingt mir zu** inf. I succeed in ger.; **2.** 2 n (-s/no pl.) success.

**ge'litten** p.p. of leiden.

**gellen** ['gɛlən] (ge- h) **1.** v/i. shrill; yell; of ears: ring, tingle; **2.** v/t. shrill; yell; '**~d** adj. shrill, piercing.

**ge'loben** v/t. (no -ge-, h) vow, promise.

**Gelöbnis** [gə'løːpnɪs] n (-ses/-se) promise, pledge; vow.

**ge'logen** p.p. of lügen.

**gelt|en** ['gɛltən] (irr., ge-, h) **1.** v/t. be worth; **2.** v/i. be of value; be valid; go; count; money: be current; maxim, etc.: hold (good or true); et. ~ **have** credit or influence; **j-m ~ concern** s.o.; ~ **für** or **als** pass for, be reputed or thought or supposed to be; ~ **für** apply to; ~ **lassen** let pass, allow; **~d machen** maintain, assert; **s-n Einfluß bei j-m ~d machen** bring one's influence to bear on s.o.; **das gilt nicht** that is not fair; that does not count; **es galt unser Leben** our life was at stake; **2ung** f (-/**~** -en) validity; value; currency; authority (of person); **zur ~ kommen** tell; take effect; show; [ise; vow.] **2ungsbedürfnis** n desire to show off.

**Gelübde** [gə'lypdə] n (-s/-) prom-]

**gelungen** [gə'lʊŋən] **1.** p.p. of gelingen; **2.** adj. successful; amusing, funny; F: **das ist ja ~!** that beats everything!

**gemächlich** adj. [gə'mɛːçlɪç] comfortable, easy; **2keit** f (-/no pl.) ease, comfort.

**Gemahl** [gə'maːl] m (-[e]s/-e) consort; husband.

**ge'mahlen** p.p. of mahlen.

**Gemälde** [gə'mɛːldə] n (-s/-) painting, picture; **~galerie** f picture-gallery.

**gemäß** prp. (dat.) [gə'mɛːs] according to; **~igt** adj. moderate; temperate (a. geogr.).

**gemein** adj. [gə'maɪn] common; general; low, vulgar, mean, coarse; **et. ~ haben mit** have s.th. in common with.

**Gemeinde** [gə'maɪndə] f (-/-n) community; parish; municipality; eccl. congregation; **~bezirk** m district; municipality; **~rat** m municipal council; **~steuer** f rate, Am. local tax; **~vorstand** m district council.

**ge'mein|gefährlich** adj. dangerous to the public; **~er Mensch** public danger, Am. public enemy; **2heit** f (-/-en) vulgarity; meanness; mean trick; **~nützig** adj. of public utility; **2platz** m commonplace; **~sam** adj. common; joint; mutual; **2schaft** f (-/-en) community; intercourse; **~schaftlich** adj. s. gemeinsam; **2schaftsarbeit** [gə'maɪnʃafts⁹-] f team-work; **2sinn** m (-[e]s/no pl.) public spirit; **~verständlich** adj. popular; **2wesen** n community; **2wohl** n public welfare.

**Ge'menge** n (-s/-) mixture.

**ge'messen 1.** p.p. of messen; **2.** adj. measured; formal; grave.

**Gemetzel** [gə'mɛtsəl] n (-s/-) slaughter, massacre.

**gemieden** [gə'mi:dən] *p.p. of mei-den.*

**Gemisch** [gə'miʃ] *n* (-es/-e) mix-ture; ∿ compound, composition.

**ge|mocht** [gə'mɔxt] *p.p. of mögen;* ∿**molken** [gə'mɔlkən] *p.p. of mel-ken.*

**Gemse** *zo.* ['gɛmzə] *f* (-/-n) chamois.

**Gemurmel** [gə'murməl] *n* (-s/no *pl.)* murmur(ing).

**Gemüse** [gə'my:zə] *n* (-s/-) vegetable(s *pl.)*; greens *pl.*; ∿**anbau** *m* vegetable gardening, *Am.* truck farming; ∿**garten** *m* kitchen garden; ∿**händler** *m* greengrocer.

**gemußt** [gə'must] *p.p. of müssen* 1.

**Gemüt** [gə'my:t] *n* (-[e]s/-er) mind; feeling; soul; heart; disposition, temper; 2**lich** *adj.* good-natured; genial; comfortable, snug, cosy, cozy; ∿**lichkeit** *f* (-/no *pl.)* snugness, cosiness; easy-going; genial temper.

**Ge'müts|art** *f* disposition, nature, temper, character; ∿**bewegung** *f* emotion; 2**krank** *adj.* emotionally disturbed; melancholic; depressed; ∿**krankheit** *f* mental disorder; melancholy; ∿**ruhe** *f* composure; ∿**verfassung** *f*, ∿**zustand** *m* state of mind, humo(u)r.

**ge'mütvoll** *adj.* emotional; full of feeling.

**genannt** [gə'nant] *p.p. of nennen.*

**genas** [gə'nɑ:s] *pret. of genesen.*

**genau** *adj.* [gə'nau] exact, accurate; precise; strict; es ∿ nehmen (mit) be particular (about); 2**eres** full particulars *pl.*; 2**igkeit** *f* (-/-en) accuracy, exactness; precision; strictness.

**genehm** *adj.* [gə'ne:m] agreeable, convenient; ∿**igen** [∿igən] *v/t.* (no -ge-, h) grant; approve (of); 2**igung** *f* (-/-en) grant; approval; licen|ce, *Am.* -se; permit; permission; consent.

**geneigt** *adj.* [gə'naikt] well disposed (*j-m* towards s.o.); inclined (zu to).

**General** ⚔ [genə'rɑ:l] *m* (-s/-e, ✻e) general; ∿**bevollmächtigte** *m* chief representative *or* agent; ∿**direktor** *m* general manager, managing director; ∿**feldmarschall** ⚔ *m* field-marshal; ∿**intendant** *thea. m* (artistic) director; ∿**konsul** *m* consul-general; ∿**konsulat** *n* consulate-general; ∿**leutnant** ⚔ *m* lieutenant-general; ∿**major** ⚔ *m* major-general; ∿**probe** *thea. f* dress rehearsal; ∿**stab** ⚔ *m* general staff; ∿**stabskarte** ⚔ *f* ordnance (survey) map, *Am.* strategic map; ∿**streik** *m* general strike; ∿**versammlung** *f* general meeting; ∿**vertreter** *m* general agent; ∿**vollmacht** *f* full power of attorney.

**Generation** [genəra'tsjo:n] *f* (-/-en) generation.

**generell** *adj.* [genə'rɛl] general.

**genes|en** [gə'ne:zən] 1. *v/i.* (*irr., no* -ge-, sein) recover (von from); 2. *p.p. of* 1; 2**ende** *m, f* (-n/-n) convalescent; 2**ung** *f* (-/✻ -en) recovery.

**genial** *adj.* [gen'jɑ:l] highly gifted, ingenious; 2**ität** [∿ali'tɛːt] *f* (-/no *pl.)* genius.

**Genick** [gə'nik] *n* (-[e]s/-e) nape (of the neck), (back of the) neck.

**Genie** [ʒe'ni:] *n* (-s/-s) genius.

**ge'nieren** *v/t.* (no -ge-, h) trouble, bother; sich ∿ feel *or* be embarrassed *or* shy; be self-conscious.

**genießen** [gə'ni:sən] *v/t. (irr., no* -ge-, h) enjoy; eat; drink; et. ∿ take some food *or* refreshments; *j-s* Vertrauen ∿ be in s.o.'s confidence.

**Genitiv** *gr.* ['ge:niti:f] *m* (-s/-e) genitive (case); possessive (case).

**ge|nommen** [gə'nɔmən] *p.p. of nehmen;* ∿**normt** *adj.* standardized; ∿**noß** [∿nɔs] *pret. of genießen.*

**Genoss|e** [gə'nɔsə] *m* (-n/-n) companion, mate; comrade (a. *pol.*); 2**en** *p.p. of genießen;* ∿**enschaft** *f* (-/-en) company, association; co(-)operative (society); ∿**in** *f* (-/-nen) (female) companion; comrade (a. *pol.*).

**genug** *adj.* [gə'nu:k] enough, sufficient.

**Genüg|e** [gə'ny:gə] *f* (-/no *pl.*): zur ∿ enough, sufficiently; 2**en** *v/i.* (no -ge-, h) be enough, suffice; das genügt that will do; *j-m* ∿ satisfy s.o.; 2**end** *adj.* sufficient; 2**sam** *adj.* [∿k-] easily satisfied; frugal; ∿**samkeit** [∿k-] *f* (-/no *pl.*) modesty; frugality.

**Genugtuung** [gə'nu:ktu:uŋ] *f* (-/-en) satisfaction.      [gender.\
**Genus** *gr.* ['ge:nus] *n* (-/Genera)\
**Genuß** [gə'nus] *m* (Genusses/Genüsse) enjoyment; pleasure; use; consumption; taking (*of food*); *fig.* treat; ∿**mittel** *n* semi-luxury; ∿**sucht** *f* (-/no *pl.*) thirst for pleasure; 2**süchtig** *adj.* pleasure-seeking.

**Geo|graph** [geo'grɑːf] *m* (-en/-en) geographer; ∿**graphie** [∿a'fi:] *f* (-/no *pl.*) geography; 2**graphisch** *adj.* [∿'grɑːfiʃ] geographic(al); ∿**loge** [∿'lo:gə] *m* (-n/-n) geologist; ∿**logie** [∿lo'gi:] *f* (-/no *pl.*) geology; 2**logisch** *adj.* [∿'lo:giʃ] geologic(al); ∿**metrie** [∿me'tri:] *f* (-/-n) geometry; 2**metrisch** *adj.* [∿'me:triʃ] geometric(al).

**Gepäck** [gə'pɛk] *n* (-[e]s/no *pl.*) luggage, ⚔ *or Am.* baggage; ∿**annahme** *f* luggage (registration) counter, *Am.* baggage (registration) counter; ∿**aufbewahrung** *f* (-/-en) left-luggage office, *Am.* checkroom; ∿**ausgabe** *f* luggage delivery office, *Am.* baggage room; ∿**netz** *n* luggage-rack, *Am.* baggage rack; ~schein *m* luggage-ticket, *Am.* baggage check; ~träger *m* porter, *Am. a.* redcap; *on bicycle:* carrier; ~wagen *m* luggage van, *Am.* baggage car.

ge|pfiffen [gə'pfifən] *p.p. of* pfeifen; ~pflegt *adj.* [~'pfle:kt] *appearance:* well-groomed; *hands, garden, etc.:* well cared-for; *garden, etc.:* well-kept.

Gepflogenheit [gə'pflo:gənhaɪt] *f* (-/-en) habit; custom; usage.

Ge|plapper [gə'plapər] *n* (-s/*no pl.*) babbling, chattering; ~plauder [~'plaudər] *n* (-s/*no pl.*) chatting, small talk; ~polter [~'pɔltər] *n* (-s/*no pl.*) rumble; ~präge [~'prɛ:gə] *n* (-s/-) impression; stamp (*a. fig.*).

ge|priesen [gə'pri:zən] *p.p. of* preisen; ~quollen [~'kvɔlən] *p.p. of* quellen.

gerade [gə'ra:də] 1. *adj.* straight (*a. fig.*); *number, etc.:* even; direct; *bearing:* upright, erect; 2. *adv.* just; *er schrieb* ~ he was (just) writing; *nun* ~ now more than ever; ~ *an dem Tage* on that very day; 3. ♀ *f* (-/-n) ♈ straight line; straight (*of race-course*); linke(rechte) ~ *boxing:* straight left (right); ~'aus *adv.* straight on *or* ahead; ~he'raus *adv.* frankly; ~nwegs *adv.* [~nve:ks] directly; ~stehen *v/i.* (*irr.* stehen, *sep.,* -ge-, *h*) stand erect; ~ *für* answer *for s.th.*; ~wegs *adv.* [~ve:ks] straight, directly; ~'zu *adv.* straight; almost; downright.

ge'rannt *p.p. of* rennen.

Gerassel [gə'rasəl] *n* (-s/*no pl.*) clanking; rattling.

Gerät [gə'rɛ:t] *n* (-[e]s/-e) tool, implement, utensil; ⊕ gear; *teleph., radio:* set; apparatus; equipment; *elektrisches* ~ electric(al) appliance.

ge'raten 1. *v/i.* (*irr.* raten, *no* -ge-, *sein*) come *or* fall *or* get (*an acc.* by, upon; *auf acc.* on, upon; *in acc.* in, into); (*gut*) ~ succeed, turn out well; *in Brand* ~ catch fire; *ins Stocken* ~ come to a standstill; *in Vergessenheit* ~ fall *or* sink into oblivion; *in Zorn* ~ fly into a passion; 2. *p.p. of* raten.

Gerate'wohl *n: aufs* ~ at random.

geräumig *adj.* [gə'rɔymiç] spacious.

Geräusch [gə'rɔyʃ] *n* (-es/-e) noise; ♀los *adj.* noiseless; ♀voll *adj.* noisy.

gerb|en ['gɛrbən] *v/t.* (ge-, *h*) tan; '♀er *m* (-s/-) tanner; ♀erei [~'raɪ] *f* (-/-en) tannery.

ge'recht *adj.* just; righteous; ~ *werden* (*dat.*) do justice to; be fair to; meet; please *s.o.*; fulfil (*requirements*); ♀igkeit *f* (-/*no pl.*) justice; righteousness; *j-m* ~ *widerfahren lassen* do *s.o.* justice.

Ge'rede *n* (-s/*no pl.*) talk; gossip; rumo(u)r.

ge'reizt *adj.* irritable, irritated; ♀heit *f* (-/*no pl.*) irritation.

ge'reuen *v/t.* (*no* -ge-, *h*): *es gereut mich* I repent (of) it, I am sorry for it.

Gericht [gə'riçt] *n* (-[e]s/-e) dish; course; *s.* Gerichtshof; *mst rhet. and fig.* tribunal; ♀lich *adj.* judicial, legal.

Ge'richts|barkeit *f* (-/-en) jurisdiction; ~bezirk *m* jurisdiction; ~diener *m* (court) usher; ~gebäude *n* court-house; ~hof *m* lawcourt, court of justice; ~kosten *pl.* (law-)costs *pl.*; ~saal *m* courtroom; ~schreiber *m* clerk (of the court); ~stand *m* (legal) domicile; venue; ~tag *m* court-day; ~verfahren *n* legal proceedings *pl.*, lawsuit; ~verhandlung *f* (court) hearing; trial; ~vollzieher *m* (-s/-) (court-)bailiff.

gerieben [gə'ri:bən] *p.p. of* reiben.

gering *adj.* [gə'riŋ] little, small; trifling, slight; mean, low; poor; inferior; ~achten *v/t.* (*sep.,* -ge-, *h*) think little of; disregard; ~er *adj.* inferior less, minor; ~fügig *adj.* insignificant, trifling, slight; ~schätzen *v/t.* (*sep.,* -ge-, *h*) *s.* geringachten; ~schätzig *adj.* disdainful, contemptuous, slighting; ♀schätzung *f* (-/*no pl.*) disdain; disregard; ~st *adj.* least; *nicht im* ~en not in the least.

ge'rinnen *v/i.* (*irr.* rinnen, *no* -ge-, *sein*) curdle (*a. fig.*); congeal; coagulate clot.

Ge'rippe *n* (-s/-) skeleton (*a. fig.*); ⊕ framework.

ge|rissen [gə'risən] 1. *p.p. of* reißen; 2. *fig. adj.* cunning, crafty, smart; ~ritten [~'ritən] *p.p. of* reiten.

germanis|ch *adj.* [gɛr'ma:niʃ] Germanic, Teutonic; ♀t [~a'nist] *m* (-en/-en) Germanist, German scholar; student of German.

gern(e) *adv.* ['gɛrn(ə)] willingly, gladly; ~ *haben or mögen* be fond of, like; *er singt* ~ he is fond of singing, he likes to sing.

ge'rochen *p.p. of* riechen.

Geröll [gə'rœl] *n* (-[e]s/-e) boulders *pl.*

geronnen [gə'rɔnən] *p.p. of* rinnen.

Gerste ♀ ['gɛrstə] *f* (-/-n) barley; ~nkorn *n* barleycorn; 🦟 sty(e).

Gerte ['gɛrtə] *f* (-/-n) switch, twig.

Geruch [gə'rux] *m* (-[e]s/⸚e) smell, odo(u)r; scent; *fig.* reputation; ♀los *adj.* odo(u)rless, scentless; ~ssinn *m* (-[e]s/ *no pl.*) sense of smell.

Gerücht [gə'ryçt] *n* (-[e]s/-e) rumo(u)r.

ge'ruchtilgend *adj.:* ~es *Mittel* deodorant.

ge'rufen *p.p. of* rufen.

ge'ruhen *v/i.* (*no* -ge-, *h*) deign, condescend, be pleased.

Gerümpel [gə'rympəl] n (-s/no pl.) lumber, junk.

Gerundium gr. [gə'rundjum] n (-s/Gerundien) gerund.

gerungen [gə'ruŋən] p.p. of ringen.

Gerüst [gə'ryst] n (-[e]s/-e) scaffold(ing); stage; trestle.

ge'salzen p.p. of salzen.

gesamt adj. [gə'zamt] whole, entire, total, all; ‿ausgabe f complete edition; ‿betrag m sum total; ‿deutsch adj. all-German.

gesandt [gə'zant] p.p. of senden; ‿e [‿ə] m (-n/-n) envoy; ‿schaft f (-/-en) legation.

Ge'sang m (-[e]s/-e) singing; song; ‿buch eccl. h-ymn-book; ‿lehrer m singing-teacher; ‿verein m choral society, Am. glee club.

Gesäß anat. [gə'zɛːs] n (-es/-e) seat, buttocks pl., posterior, F bottom, behind.

ge'schaffen p.p. of schaffen 1.

Geschäft [gə'ʃɛft] n (-[e]s/-e) business; transaction; affair; occupation; shop, Am. store; ‿ig adj. busy, active; ‿igkeit f (-/no pl.) activity; ‿lich 1. adj. business ...; commercial; 2. adv. on business.

Ge'schäfts|bericht m business report; ‿brief m business letter; ‿frau f business woman; ‿freund m business friend, correspondent; ‿führer m manager; ‿haus n business firm; office building; ‿inhaber m owner or holder of a business; shopkeeper; ‿jahr m financial or business year, Am. fiscal year; ‿lage f business situation; ‿leute pl. businessmen pl.; ‿mann m businessman; ‿mäßig adj. business-like; ‿ordnung f standing orders pl.; rules pl. (of procedure); ‿papiere n/pl. commercial papers pl.; ‿partner m (business) partner; ‿räume m/pl. business premises pl.; ‿reise f business trip; ‿reisende m commercial travel(l)er, Am. travel(l)ing salesman; ‿schluß m closing-time; nach ‿ a. after business hours; ‿stelle f office; ‿träger m pol. chargé d'affaires; † agent, representative; ‿tüchtig adj. efficient, smart; ‿unternehmen n business enterprise; ‿verbindung f business connexion or connection; ‿viertel n business cent|re, Am. -er; Am. downtown; shopping cent|re, Am. -er; ‿zeit f office hours pl., business hours pl.; ‿zimmer n office, bureau; ‿zweig m branch (of business), line (of business).

geschah [gə'ʃaː] pret. of geschehen.

geschehen [gə'ʃeːən] 1. v/i. (irr., no -ge-, sein) happen, occur, take place; be done; es geschieht ihm recht it serves him right; 2. p.p. of

1; 3. 2 n (-s/-) events pl., happenings pl.

gescheit adj. [gə'ʃaɪt] clever, intelligent, bright.

Geschenk [gə'ʃɛŋk] n (-[e]s/-e) present, gift; ‿packung f gift-box.

Geschicht|e [gə'ʃɪçtə] f 1. (-/-n) story; tale; fig. affair; 2. (-/no pl.) history; 2lich adj. historical; ‿sforscher m, ‿sschreiber m historian.

Ge'schick n 1. (-[e]s/-e) fate; destiny; 2. (-[e]s/no pl.) = ‿lichkeit f (-/-en) skill; dexterity; aptitude; 2t adj. skil(l)ful; dexterous; apt; clever.

ge|schieden [gə'ʃiːdən] p.p. of scheiden; ‿schienen [‿'ʃiːnən] p.p. of scheinen.

Geschirr [gə'ʃɪr] n (-[e]s/-e) vessel; dishes pl.; china; earthenware, crockery; service; horse: harness.

ge'schlafen p.p. of schlafen; ‿'schlagen p.p. of schlagen.

Ge'schlecht n (-[e]s/-er) sex; kind, species; race; family; generation; gr. gender; 2lich adj. sexual.

Ge'schlechts|krankheit ♂ f venereal disease; ‿reife f puberty; ‿teile anat. n/pl. genitals pl.; ‿trieb m sexual instinct or urge; ‿verkehr m (-[e]s/no pl.) sexual intercourse; ‿wort gr. n (-[e]s/‿er) article.

ge|schlichen [gə'ʃlɪçən] p.p. of schleichen; ‿schliffen [‿'ʃlɪfən] 1. p.p. of schleifen; 2. adj. jewel: cut; fig. polished; ‿schlossen [‿'ʃlɔsən] 1. p.p. of schließen; 2. adj. formation: close; collective; ‿e Gesellschaft private party; ‿schlungen [‿'ʃluŋən] p.p. of schlingen.

Geschmack [gə'ʃmak] m (-[e]s/‿e, co. ‿er) taste (a. fig.); flavo(u)r; ‿ finden an (dat.) take a fancy to; 2los adj. tasteless; pred. fig. in bad taste; ‿(s)sache f matter of taste; 2voll adj. tasteful; pred. fig. in good taste.

ge|schmeidig adj. [gə'ʃmaɪdɪç] supple, pliant; ‿schmissen [‿'ʃmɪsən] p.p. of schmeißen; ‿schmolzen [‿'ʃmɔltsən] p.p. of schmelzen.

Geschnatter [gə'ʃnatər] n (-s/no pl.) cackling (of geese); chatter(ing) (of girls, etc.).

ge|schnitten [gə'ʃnɪtən] p.p. of schneiden; ‿schoben [‿'ʃoːbən] p.p. of schieben; ‿scholten [‿'ʃɔltən] p.p. of schelten.

Geschöpf [gə'ʃœpf] n (-[e]s/-e) creature.

ge'schoren p.p. of scheren.

Geschoß [gə'ʃɔs] n (Geschosses/Geschosse) projectile; missile; stor(e)y, floor.

geschossen [gə'ʃɔsən] p.p. of schießen.

**Ge'schrei** n (-[e]s/no pl.) cries pl.; shouting; fig. noise, fuss.

**ge|schrieben** [gə'ʃriːbən] p.p. of schreiben; **~schrie(e)n** [~'ʃriː(ə)n] p.p. of schreien; **~schritten** [~'ʃritən] p.p. of schreiten; **~schunden** [~'ʃundən] p.p. of schinden.

**Geschütz** ✕ [gə'ʃyts] n (-es/-e) gun, cannon; ordnance.

**Geschwader** ✕ [gə'ʃvaːdər] n (-s/-) ⚓ squadron; ✈ wing, Am. group.

**Geschwätz** [gə'ʃvɛts] n (-es/no pl.) idle talk; gossip; **2ig** adj. talkative.

**geschweige** cj. [gə'ʃvaɪgə]: ~ (denn) not to mention; let alone, much less.

**geschwiegen** [gə'ʃviːgən] p.p. of schweigen.

**geschwind** adj. [gə'ʃvint] fast, quick, swift; **2igkeit** [~diçkaɪt] f (-/-en) quickness; speed, pace; phys. velocity; rate; mit e-r ~ von ... at the rate of ...; **2igkeitsbegrenzung** f speed limit.

**Geschwister** [gə'ʃvistər] n (-s/-): ~ pl. brother(s pl.) and sister(s pl.).

**ge|schwollen** [gə'ʃvɔlən] 1. p.p. of schwellen; 2. adj. language: bombastic, pompous; **~schwommen** [~'ʃvɔmən] p.p. of schwimmen.

**geschworen** [gə'ʃvoːrən] p.p. of schwören; **2e** [~ə] m, f (-n/-n) juror; die ~n pl. the jury; **2engericht** n jury.

**Geschwulst** ✎ [gə'ʃvulst] f (-/⸚e) swelling; tumo(u)r.

**ge|schwunden** [gə'ʃvundən] p.p. of schwinden; **~schwungen** [~'ʃvuŋən] p.p. of schwingen.

**Geschwür** ✎ [gə'ʃvyːr] n (-[e]s/-e) abscess, ulcer.

**ge'sehen** p.p. of sehen.

**Gesell** ⚒ [gə'zɛl] m (-en/-en), **~e** [~ə] m (-n/-n) companion, fellow; ⊕ journeyman; **2en** v/refl. (no -ge-, h) associate, come together; sich zu j-m ~ join s.o.; **2ig** adj. social; sociable.

**Ge'sellschaft** f (-/-en) society; company (a. ↑); party; j-m ~ leisten keep s.o. company; **~er** m (-s/-) companion; ↑ partner; **~erin** f (-/-nen) (lady) companion; ↑ partner; **2lich** adj. social.

**Ge'sellschafts|dame** f (lady) companion; **~reise** f party tour; **~spiel** n party or round game; **~tanz** m ball-room dance.

**gesessen** [gə'zɛsən] p.p. of sitzen.

**Gesetz** [gə'zɛts] n (-es/-e) law; statute; **~buch** n code; statute-book; **~entwurf** m bill; **~eskraft** f legal force; **~essammlung** f code; **2gebend** adj. legislative; **~geber** m (-s/-) legislator; **~gebung** f (-/-en) legislation; **2lich 1.** adj. lawful, legal; 2. adv.: ~ geschützt patented, registered; **2los** adj. lawless; **2mäßig** adj. legal; lawful.

**ge'setzt 1.** adj. sedate, staid; sober; mature; 2. cj.: ~ den Fall, (daß) ... suppose or supposing (that) ...

**ge'setzwidrig** adj. unlawful, illegal.

**Ge'sicht** n (-[e]s/-er) face; countenance; fig. character; zu ~ bekommen catch sight or a glimpse of; set eyes on.

**Ge'sichts|ausdruck** m (facial) expression; **~farbe** f complexion; **~kreis** m horizon; **~punkt** m point of view, viewpoint, aspect, esp. Am. angle; **~zug** m mst Gesichtszüge pl. feature(s pl.), lineament(s pl.).

**Ge'sims** n ledge.

**Gesinde** [gə'zində] n (-s/-) (domestic) servants pl.; **~l** [~l] n (-s/no pl.) rabble, mob.

**ge'sinn|t** adj. in compounds: ...-minded; wohl ~ well disposed (j-m towards s.o.); **2ung** f (-/-en) mind; conviction; sentiment(s pl.); opinions pl.

**gesinnungs|los** adj. [gə'zinuŋslɔːs] unprincipled; **~treu** adj. loyal; **2wechsel** m change of opinion; esp. pol. volte-face.

**ge|sittet** adj. [gə'zitət] civilized; well-bred, well-mannered; **~'soffen** p.p. of saufen; **~sogen** [~'zoːgən] p.p. of saugen; **~sonnen** [~'zɔnən] 1. p.p. of sinnen; 2. adj. minded, disposed; **~sotten** [~'zɔtən] p.p. of sieden; **~'spalten** p.p. of spalten.

**Ge'spann** n (-[e]s/-e) team, Am. a. span; oxen: yoke; fig. pair, couple.

**ge'spannt** adj. tense (a. fig.); rope: tight, taut; fig. attention; close; relations: strained; ~ sein auf (acc.) be anxious for; auf ~em Fuß on bad terms; **2heit** f (-/no pl.) tenseness, tension.

**Gespenst** [gə'ʃpɛnst] n (-es/-er) ghost, spect|re, Am. -er; **2isch** adj. ghostly.

**Ge'spiel|e** m (-n/-n), **~in** f (-/-nen) playmate.

**gespien** [gə'ʃpiːn] p.p. of speien.

**Gespinst** [gə'ʃpinst] n (-es/-e) web, tissue (both a. fig.); spun yarn.

**gesponnen** [gə'ʃpɔnən] p.p. of spinnen.

**Gespött** [gə'ʃpœt] n (-[e]s/no pl.) mockery, derision, ridicule; zum ~ der Leute werden become a laughing-stock.

**Gespräch** [gə'ʃprɛːç] n (-[e]s/-e) talk; conversation; teleph. call; dialogue; **2ig** adj. talkative.

**ge|sprochen** [gə'ʃprɔxən] p.p. of sprechen; **~'sprossen** p.p. of sprießen; **~sprungen** [~'ʃpruŋən] p.p. of springen.

**Gestalt** [gə'ʃtalt] f (-/-en) form, figure, shape; stature; **2en** v/t. and v/refl. (no -ge-, h) form, shape; **~ung** f (-/-en) formation; arrangement, organization.

**gestanden** [gə'ʃtandən] p.p. of stehen.

ge'ständ|ig *adj.*: ~ sein confess; 2nis [~t-] *n* (-ses/-se) confession.

Ge'stank *m* (-[e]s/no *pl.*) stench.

gestatten [gə'ʃtatən] *v/t.* (no -ge-, h) allow, permit.

Geste ['gɛstə] *f* (-/-n) gesture.

ge'stehen (*irr. stehen, no -ge-, h*) 1. *v/t.* confess, avow; 2. *v/i.* confess.

Ge|'stein *n* (-[e]s/-e) rock, stone; ~stell [~'ʃtɛl] *n* (-[e]s/-e) stand, rack, shelf; frame; trestle, horse.

gestern *adv.* ['gɛstərn] yesterday; ~ abend last night.

gestiegen [gə'ʃtiːgən] *p.p. of steigen*.

Ge'stirn *n* (-[e]s/-e) star; *astr.* constellation; 2t *adj.* starry.

ge|stoben [gə'ʃtoːbən] *p.p. of stieben*; ~stochen [~'ʃtɔxən] *p.p. of stechen*; ~stohlen [~'ʃtoːlən] *p.p. of stehlen*; ~storben [~'ʃtɔrbən] *p.p. of sterben*; ~'stoßen *p.p. of stoßen*; ~strichen [~'ʃtriçən] *p.p. of streichen*.

gestrig *adj.* ['gɛstriç] of yesterday, yesterday's ...

ge'stritten *p.p. of streiten*.

Gestrüpp [gə'ʃtryp] *n* (-[e]s/-e) brushwood; undergrowth.

gestunken [gə'ʃtuŋkən] *p.p. of stinken*.

Gestüt [gə'ʃtyːt] *n* (-[e]s/-e) stud farm; *horses kept for breeding, etc.*: stud.

Gesuch [gə'zuːx] *n* (-[e]s/-e) application, request; petition; 2t *adj.* wanted; sought-after; *politeness*: studied.

gesund *adj.* [gə'zunt] sound, health-y; salubrious; wholesome (*a. fig.*); ~er Menschenverstand common sense; ~en [~dən] *v/i.* (no -ge-, sein) recover.

Ge'sundheit *f* (-/no *pl.*) health (-iness); wholesomeness (*a. fig.*); *auf j-s ~ trinken* drink (to) s.o.'s health; 2lich *adj.* sanitary; ~ geht es ihm gut he is in good health.

Ge'sundheits|amt *n* Public Health Department; ~pflege *f* hygiene; public health service; 2schädlich *adj.* injurious to health, unhealthy, unwholesome; ~wesen *n* Public Health; ~zustand *m* state of health, physical condition.

ge|sungen [gə'zuŋən] *p.p. of singen*; ~sunken [~'zuŋkən] *p.p. of sinken*; ~tan [~'taːn] *p.p. of tun*.

Getöse [gə'tøːzə] *n* (-s/no *pl.*) din, noise.

ge'tragen 1. *p.p. of tragen*; 2. *adj.* solemn.

Getränk [gə'trɛŋk] *n* (-[e]s/-e) drink, beverage.

ge'trauen *v/refl.* (no -ge-, h) dare, venture.

Getreide [gə'traidə] *n* (-s/-) corn, *esp. Am.* grain; cereals *pl.*; ~(an)bau *m* corn-growing, *esp. Am.* grain growing; ~pflanze *f* cereal plant;

~speicher *m* granary, grain silo, *Am.* elevator.

ge'treten *p.p. of treten*.

ge'treu(lich) *adj.* faithful, loyal; true.

Getriebe [gə'triːbə] *n* (-s/-) bustle; ⊕ gear(ing); ⊕ drive.

ge|trieben [gə'triːbən] *p.p. of treiben*; ~troffen [~'trɔfən] *p.p. of treffen*; ~trogen [~'troːgən] *p.p. of trügen*.

ge'trost *adv.* confidently.

ge'trunken *p.p. of trinken*.

Ge|tue [gə'tuːə] *n* (-s/no *pl.*) fuss; ~tümmel [~'tyməl] *n* (-s/-) turmoil; ~viert *n* (-[e]s/-e) square.

Gewächs [gə'vɛks] *n* (-es/-e) growth (*a. ♣*); plant; vintage; ~haus *n* greenhouse, hothouse, conservatory.

ge|'wachsen 1. *p.p. of wachsen*; 2. *adj.*: *j-m ~ sein* be a match for s.o.; *e-r Sache ~ sein* be equal to s.th.; *sich der Lage ~ zeigen* rise to the occasion; ~wagt *adj.* [~'vaːkt] risky; bold; ~wählt *adj.* [~'vɛːlt] *style*: refined; ~'wahr *adj.*: ~ werden (*acc. or gen.*) perceive *s.th.*; become aware of *s.th.*; ~ werden, daß become aware that.

Gewähr [gə'vɛːr] *f* (-/no *pl.*) guarantee, warrant, security; 2en *v/t.* (no -ge-, h) grant, allow; give, yield, afford; *j-n ~ lassen* let s.o. have his way; leave s.o. alone; 2leisten *v/t.* (no -ge-, h) guarantee.

Ge'wahrsam *m* (-s/-e) custody, safe keeping.

Ge'währsmann *m* informant, source.

Gewalt [gə'valt] *f* (-/-en) power; authority; control; force, violence; *höhere ~* act of God; *mit ~* by force; ~herrschaft *f* despotism, tyranny; 2ig *adj.* powerful, mighty; vehement; vast; ~maßnahme *f* violent measure; 2sam 1. *adi.* violent; 2. *adv. a.* forcibly; ~ öffnen force open; open by force; ~tat *f* act of violence; 2tätig *adj.* violent.

Gewand [gə'vant] *n* (-[e]s/₌er) garment; robe; *esp. eccl.* vestment.

ge'wandt 1. *p.p. of wenden* 2; 2. *adj.* agile, nimble, dexterous, adroit; clever; 2heit *f* (-/no *pl.*) agility, nimbleness; adroitness, dexterity; cleverness.

ge'wann *pret. of gewinnen*.

Gewäsch F [gə'vɛʃ] *n* (-es/no *pl.*) twaddle, nonsense.

ge'waschen *p.p. of waschen*.

Gewässer [gə'vɛsər] *n* (-s/-) water(s *pl.*).

Gewebe [gə'veːbə] *n* (-s/-) tissue (*a. anat. and fig.*); fabric, web; texture.

Ge'wehr *n* gun; rifle; ~kolben *m* (rifle-)butt; ~lauf *m* (rifle-, gun-) barrel.

**Geweih** [gə'vaɪ] n (-[e]s/-e) horns pl., head, antlers pl.

**Gewerbe** [gə'verbə] n (-s/-) trade, business; industry; **~freiheit** f freedom of trade; **~schein** m trade licen|ce, Am. -se; **~schule** f technical school; **~steuer** f trade tax; 2treibend adj. carrying on a business, engaged in trade; **~treibende** m (-n/-n) tradesman.

**gewerb|lich** adj. [gə'verplɪç] commercial, industrial; **~smäßig** adj. professional.

**Ge'werkschaft** f (-/-en) trade(s) union, Am. labor union; **~ler** m (-s/-) trade(s)-unionist; 2lich adj. trade-union; **~sbund** m Trade Union Congress, Am. Federation of Labor.

**ge|wesen** [gə've:zən] p.p. of sein; **~wichen** [~'vɪçən] p.p. of weichen.

**Gewicht** [gə'vɪçt] n (-[e]s/-e) weight, Am. F a. heft; e-r Sache ~ beimessen attach importance to s.th.; ~ haben carry weight (bei dat. with); ~ legen auf et. lay stress on s.th.; ins ~ fallen be of great weight, count, matter; 2ig adj. weighty (a. fig.).

**ge|wiesen** [gə'vi:zən] p.p. of weisen; **~willt** adj. [~'vɪlt] willing.

**Ge|wimmel** [gə'vɪməl] n (-s/no pl.) swarm; throng; **~winde** ⊕ [~'vɪndə] n (-s/-) thread.

**Gewinn** [gə'vɪn] m (-[e]s/-e) gain; ✝ gains pl.; profit; lottery ticket: prize; game: winnings pl.; **~anteil** m dividend; **~beteiligung** f profit-sharing; 2bringend adj. profitable; 2en (irr., no ge-, h) 1. v/t. win; gain; get; 2. v/i. win; gain; fig. improve; 2end adj. manner, smile: winning, engaging; **~er** m (-s/-) winner.

**Ge'wirr** n (-[e]s/-e) tangle, entanglement; streets: maze; voices: confusion.

**gewiß** [gə'vɪs] 1. adj. certain; ein gewisser Herr N. a certain Mr. N., one Mr. N.; 2. adv.: ~! certainly!, to be sure!, Am. sure!

**Ge'wissen** n (-s/-) conscience; 2haft adj. conscientious; 2los adj. unscrupulous; **~sbisse** m/pl. remorse, pangs pl. of conscience; **~sfrage** f question of conscience.

**gewissermaßen** adv. [gəvɪsər-'ma:sən] to a certain extent.

**Ge'wißheit** f (-/-en) certainty; certitude.

**Gewitter** [gə'vɪtər] n (-s/-) (thunder)storm; 2n v/i. (no -ge-, h): es gewittert there is a thunderstorm; **~regen** m thunder-shower; **~wolke** f thundercloud.

**ge|woben** [gə'vo:bən] p.p. of weben; **~wogen** 1. p.p. of wägen and wiegen¹; 2. adj. (dat.) well or kindly disposed towards, favo(u)rably inclined towards.

**gewöhnen** [gə'vø:nən] v/t. (no -ge-, h) accustom, get used (an acc. to).

**Gewohnheit** [gə'vo:nhaɪt] f (-/-en) habit; custom; 2smäßig adj. habitual.

**ge'wöhnlich** adj. common; ordinary; usual, customary; habitual; common, vulgar.

**ge'wohnt** adj. customary, habitual; (es) ~ sein zu inf. be accustomed or used to inf.

**Gewölbe** [gə'vœlbə] n (-s/-) vault.

**ge|wonnen** [gə'vɔnən] p.p. of gewinnen; **~worben** [~'vɔrbən] p.p. of werben; **~worden** [~'vɔrdən] p.p. of werden; **~worfen** [~'vɔrfən] p.p. of werfen; **~wrungen** [~'vrʊŋən] p.p. of wringen.

**Gewühl** [gə'vy:l] n (-[e]s/no pl.) bustle; milling crowd.

**gewunden** [gə'vʊndən] 1. p.p. of winden; 2. adj. twisted; winding.

**Gewürz** [gə'vyrts] n (-es/-e) spice; condiment; **~nelke** ♀ f clove.

**ge'wußt** p.p. of wissen.

**Ge|'zeit** f: mst **~en** pl. tide(s pl.); **~'zeter** n (-s/no pl.) (shrill) clamo(u)r.

**ge|'ziert** adj. affected; **~zogen** [~'tso:gən] p.p. of ziehen.

**Gezwitscher** [gə'tsvɪtʃər] n (-s/no pl.) chirping, twitter(ing).

**gezwungen** [gə'tsvʊŋən] 1. p.p. of zwingen; 2. adj. forced, constrained.

**Gicht** ♫ [gɪçt] f (-/no pl.) gout; 2isch adj. gouty; **~knoten** ♫ m gouty knot.

**Giebel** ['gi:bəl] m (-s/-) gable(-end).

**Gier** [gi:r] f (-/no pl.) greed(iness) (nach for); 2ig adj. greedy (nach for, of).

**'Gießbach** m torrent.

**gieß|en** ['gi:sən] (irr., ge-, h) 1. v/t. pour; ⊕ cast, found; water (flowers); 2. v/i.: es gießt it is pouring (with rain); 2er m (-s/-) founder; 2erei [~'raɪ] f (-/-en) foundry; 2kanne f watering-can or -pot.

**Gift** [gɪft] n (-[e]s/-e) poison; venom (esp. of snakes) (a. fig.); malice, spite; 2ig adj. poisonous; venomous; malicious, spiteful; **~schlange** f venomous or poisonous snake; **~zahn** m poison-fang.

**Gigant** [gi'gant] m (-en/-en) giant.

**Gimpel** orn. ['gɪmpəl] m (-s/-) bullfinch.

**ging** [gɪŋ] pret. of gehen.

**Gipfel** ['gɪpfəl] m (-s/-) summit, top; peak; **~konferenz** pol. f summit meeting or conference; 2n v/i. (ge-, h) culminate.

**Gips** [gɪps] m (-es/-e) min. gypsum; ⊕ plaster (of Paris); **~abdruck** m, **~abguß** m plaster cast; 2en v/t. (ge-, h) plaster; **~verband** ♫ m plaster (of Paris) dressing.

**Giraffe** zo. [gi'rafə] f (-/-n) giraffe.

**girieren** † [ʒi'riːrən] v/t. (no -ge-, h) endorse, indorse (bill of exchange).

**Girlande** [gir'landə] f (-/-n) garland.

**Giro** † ['ʒiːro] n (-s/-s) endorsement, indorsement; '~bank f clearing-bank; '~konto n current account.

**girren** ['girən] v/i. (ge-, h) coo.

**Gischt** [giʃt] m (-es/~ -e) and f (-/~ -en) foam, froth; spray; spindrift.

**Gitarre** ♪ [gi'tarə] f (-/-n) guitar.

**Gitter** ['gitər] n (-s/-) grating; lattice; trellis; railing; '~bett n crib; '~fenster n lattice-window.

**Glacéhandschuh** [gla'seː-] m kid glove.

**Glanz** [glants] m (-es/no pl.) brightness; lust|re, Am. -er; brilliancy; splendo(u)r.

**glänzen** ['glɛntsən] v/i. (ge-, h) glitter, shine; '~d adj. bright, brilliant; fig. splendid.

**'Glanz|leistung** f brilliant achievement or performance; '~papier n glazed paper; '~punkt m highlight; '~zeit f golden age, heyday.

**Glas** [glaːs] n (-es/~er) glass; ~er ['~zər] m (-s/-) glazier.

**gläsern** adj. ['glɛːzərn] of glass; fig. glassy.

**'Glas|glocke** f (glass) shade or cover; globe; bell-glass; '~hütte f glassworks sg., pl.

**glasieren** [gla'ziːrən] v/t. (no -ge-, h) glaze; ice, frost (cake).

**glasig** adj. ['glaːziç] glassy, vitreous.

**'Glasscheibe** f pane of glass.

**Glasur** [gla'zuːr] f (-/-en) glaze, glazing; enamel; icing, frosting (on cakes).

**glatt** [glat] 1. adj. smooth (a. fig.); even; lie, etc.: flat, downright; road, etc.: slippery; 2. adv. smoothly; evenly; ~ anliegen fit closely or tightly; ~ rasiert clean-shaven; et. ~ ableugnen deny s.th. flatly.

**Glätte** ['glɛtə] f (-/-n) smoothness; road, etc.: slipperiness.

**'Glatteis** n glazed frost, icy glaze, Am. glaze; F: j-n aufs ~ führen lead s.o. up the garden path.

**glätten** v/t. (ge-, h) smooth.

**Glatze** ['glatsə] f (-/-n) bald head.

**Glaube** ['glaubə] m (-ns/~ n) faith, belief (an acc. in); '2n (ge-, h) 1. v/t. believe; think, suppose, Am. a. guess; 2. v/i. believe (j-m s.o.; an acc. in).

**'Glaubens|bekenntnis** n creed, profession or confession of faith; '~lehre f, '~satz m dogma, doctrine.

**glaubhaft** adj. ['glaup-] credible; plausible; authentic.

**gläubig** adj. ['glɔybiç] believing, faithful; 2e ['~gə] m, f (-n/-n)

believer; 2er † ['~gər] m (-s/-) creditor.

**glaubwürdig** adj. ['glaup-] credible.

**gleich** [glaiç] 1. adj. equal (an dat. in); the same; like; even, level; in ~er Weise likewise; zur ~en Zeit at the same time; es ist mir ~ it's all the same to me; das ~e the same; as much; er ist nicht (mehr) der ~e he is not the same man; 2. adv. alike, equally; immediately, presently, directly, at once; just; es ist ~ acht (Uhr) it is close on or nearly eight (o'clock); ~altrig adj. ['~altriç] (of) the same age; '~artig adj. homogeneous; similar; uniform; '~bedeutend adj. synonymous; equivalent (to); tantamount (mit to); '~berechtigt adj. having equal rights; '~bleibend adj. constant, steady; '~en v/i. (irr., ge-, h) equal; resemble.

**'gleich|falls** adv. also, likewise; ~förmig adj. ['~fœrmiç] uniform; ~gesinnt adj. like-minded; '2gewicht n balance (a. fig.); equilibrium, equipoise; pol.: ~ der Kräfte balance of power; '~gültig adj. indifferent (gegen to); es ist mir ~ I don't care; ~, was du tust no matter what you do; '2gültigkeit f indifference; '2heit f (-/-en) equality; likeness; 2klang m unison; consonance, harmony; '~kommen v/i. (irr. kommen, sep., -ge-, sein): e-r Sache ~ amount to s.th.; j-m ~ equal s.o.; '~laufend adj. parallel; '~lautend adj. consonant; identical; '~machen v/t. (sep., -ge-, h) make equal (dat. to), equalize (to or with); '2maß n regularity; evenness; fig. equilibrium; '~mäßig adj. equal; regular; constant; even; '2mut m equanimity; '~mütig adj. even-tempered; calm; '~namig adj. ['~naːmiç] of the same name; '2nis n (-ses/-se) parable; rhet. simile; '~sam adv. as it were, so to speak; '~schalten v/t. (sep., -ge-, h) ⊕ synchronize; pol. co-ordinate, unify; '~seitig adj. equilateral; '~setzen v/t. (sep., -ge-, h) equate (dat. or mit with); '~stehen v/i. (irr. stehen, sep., -ge-, h) be equal; '~stellen v/t. (sep., -ge-, h) equalize, equate (dat. with); put s.o. on an equal footing (with); '2stellung f equalization, equation; '2strom ≰ m direct current; '2ung ⅄ f (-/-en) equation; '~wertig adj. equivalent, of the same value, of equal value; '~zeitig adj. simultaneous; synchronous; contemporary.

**Gleis** [glais] n (-es/-e) s. Geleise.

**gleiten** ['glaitən] v/i. (irr., ge-, sein) glide, slide.

**'Gleit|flug** m gliding flight, glide, ✈ volplane; '~schutzreifen m non-skid tyre, (*Am. only*) non-skid tire; '~schutz(vorrichtung *f*) *m* anti-skid device.

**Gletscher** ['glɛtʃər] *m* (-s/-) glacier; '~spalte *f* crevasse.

**glich** [gliç] *pret. of* gleichen.

**Glied** [gli:t] *n* (-[e]s/-er) *anat.* limb; member (*a. anat.*); link; ✕ rank, file; ℚ**ern** ['~dərn] *v/t.* (ge-, h) joint, articulate; arrange; divide (*in acc.* into); '~**erung** *f* (-/-en) articulation; arrangement; division; formation; ~**maßen** ['~tmɑ:sən] *pl.* limbs *pl.*, extremities *pl.*

**glimmen** ['glimən] *v/i.* ([*irr.*,] ge-, h) *fire:* smo(u)lder (*a. fig.*); glimmer; glow.

**glimpflich** ['glimpfliç] **1.** *adj.* lenient, mild; **2.** *adv.:* ~ davonkommen get off lightly.

**glitschig** *adj.* ['glitʃiç] slippery.

**glitt** [glit] *pret. of* gleiten.

**glitzern** ['glitsərn] *v/i.* (ge-, h) glitter, glisten.

**Globus** ['glo:bus] *m* (-, -ses/Globen, Globusse) globe.

**Glocke** ['glɔkə] *f* (-/-n) bell; shade; (glass) cover.

'**Glocken|schlag** *m* stroke of the clock; '~spiel *n* chime(s *pl.*); '~stuhl *m* bell-cage; '~turm *m* bell tower, belfry.

**Glöckner** ['glœknər] *m* (-s/-) bell-ringer.

**glomm** [glɔm] *pret. of* glimmen.

**Glorie** ['glo:rjə] *f* (-/-n) glory; '~n~schein *m* halo, aureola.

**glorreich** *adj.* ['glo:r-] glorious.

**glotzen** F ['glɔtsən] *v/i.* (ge-, h) stare.

**Glück** [glyk] *n* (-[e]s/*no pl.*) fortune; good luck; happiness, bliss, felicity; prosperity; *auf gut* ~ on the off chance; ~ haben be lucky, succeed; *das* ~ *haben zu inf.* have the good fortune to *inf.*; *j-m* ~ *wünschen* congratulate s.o. (*zu* on); *viel* ~! good luck!; *zum* ~ fortunately; ℚ**bringend** *adj.* lucky.

**Glucke** *orn.* ['glukə] *f* (-/-n) sitting hen. [*gen.*]

'**glücken** *v/i.* (ge-, sein) s. gelin-]

**gluckern** ['glukərn] *v/i.* (ge-, h) *water, etc.:* gurgle.

'**glücklich** *adj.* fortunate; happy; lucky; '~er'weise *adv.* fortunately.

'**Glücksbringer** *m* (-s/-) mascot.

**glück'selig** *adj.* blissful, blessed, happy.

**glucksen** ['gluksən] *v/i.* (ge-, h) gurgle.

'**Glücks|fall** *m* lucky chance, stroke of (good) luck; '~göttin *f* Fortune; '~kind *n* lucky person; ~pfennig *m* lucky penny; '~pilz *m* lucky person; '~spiel *n* game of chance; *fig.* gamble; '~stern *m* lucky star; '~tag *m* happy or lucky day, red-letter day.

'**glück|strahlend** *adj.* radiant(ly happy); 'ℚwunsch *m* congratulation, good wishes *pl.*; compliments *pl.*; ~ *zum Geburtstag* many happy returns (of the day).

'**Glüh|birne** ⚡ ['gly-] *f* (electric-light) bulb; 'ℚen *v/i.* (ge-, h) glow; 'ℚend *adj.* glowing; *iron:* red-hot; *coal:* live; *fig.* ardent, fervid; 'ℚ(end)'heiß *adj.* burning hot; '~lampe *f* incandescent lamp; '~wein *m* mulled wine; ~würmchen *zo.* ['~vyrmçən] *n* (-s/-) glow-worm.

**Glut** [glu:t] *f* (-/-en) heat, glow (*a. fig.*); glowing fire, embers *pl.*; *fig.* ardo(u)r.

**Gnade** ['gnɑ:də] *f* (-/-n) grace; favo(u)r; mercy; clemency; pardon; ✕ quarter.

'**Gnaden|akt** *m* act of grace; '~brot *n* (-[e]s/*no pl.*) bread of charity; '~frist *f* reprieve; '~gesuch *n* petition for mercy.

**gnädig** *adj.* ['gnɛ:diç] gracious, merciful; *address:* ℚe Frau Madam.

**Gnom** [gno:m] *m* (-en/-en) gnome, goblin.

**Gobelin** [gobə'lɛ̃:] *m* (-s/-s) Gobelin tapestry.

**Gold** [gɔlt] *n* (-[e]s/*no pl.*) gold; '~barren *m* gold bar, gold ingot, bullion; '~borte *f* gold lace; ℚen *adj.* ['~dən] gold; *fig.* golden; '~feder *f* gold nib; '~fisch *m* goldfish; 'ℚgelb *adj.* golden-(yellow); ~gräber ['~grɛ:bər] *m* (-s/-) gold-digger; '~grube *f* gold-mine; 'ℚhaltig *adj.* gold-bearing, containing gold; ℚig *fig. adj.* ['~diç] sweet, lovely, *Am.* F *a.* cute; '~mine *f* gold-mine; '~münze *f* gold coin; '~schmied *m* goldsmith; '~schnitt *m* gilt edge; *mit* ~ gilt-edged; '~stück *n* gold coin; '~waage *f* gold-balance; '~währung *f* gold standard.

**Golf**[1] *geogr.* [gɔlf] *m* (-[e]s/-e) gulf.

**Golf**[2] [~] *n* (-s/*no pl.*) golf; '~platz *m* golf-course, (golf-)links *pl.*; '~schläger *m* golf-club; '~spiel *n* golf; '~spieler *m* golfer.

**Gondel** ['gɔndəl] *f* (-/-n) gondola; ✈ *mst* car.

**gönnen** ['gœnən] *v/t.* (ge-, h): *j-m et.* ~ allow *or* grant *or* not to grudge s.o. s.th.

'**Gönner** *m* (-s/-) patron; *Am. a.* sponsor; 'ℚhaft *adj.* patronizing.

**gor** [go:r] *pret. of* gären.

**Gorilla** *zo.* [go'rila] *m* (-s/-s) gorilla.

**goß** [gɔs] *pret. of* gießen.

**Gosse** ['gɔsə] *f* (-/-n) gutter (*a. fig.*).

**Gott** [gɔt] *m* (-es, ✕ -s/ᵘer) God; god, deity; 'ℚergeben *adj.* resigned (to the will of God).

'**Gottes|dienst** *eccl. m* (divine) service; 'ℚfürchtig *adj.* godfearing; '~haus *n* church, chapel; '~läste-

**rer** *m* (-s/-) blasphemer; '~**läste-rung** *f* blasphemy.

'**Gottheit** *f* (-/-en) deity, divinity.

**Göttin** ['gœtin] *f* (-/-nen) goddess.

**göttlich** *adj.* ['gœtliç] divine.

**gott|'lob** *int.* thank God *or* goodness!; '~**los** *adj.* godless; impious; F *fig. deed*: unholy, wicked; '**2ver-trauen** *n* trust in God.

**Götze** ['gœtsə] *m* (-n/-n) idol; '~**nbild** *n* idol; '~**ndienst** *m* idolatry.

**Gouvern|ante** [guvɛr'nantə] *f* (-/-n) governess; ~**eur** [~'nø:r] *m* (-s/-e) governor.

**Grab** [gra:p] *n* (-[e]s/~er) grave, tomb, sepulch|re, *Am.* -er.

**Graben** ['gra:bən] 1. *m* (-s/~) ditch; ⚔ trench; 2. ♀ *v/t.* (*irr.*, ge-, *h*) dig; *animal*: burrow.

**Grab|gewölbe** ['gra:p-] *n* vault, tomb; '~**mal** *n* monument; tomb, sepulch|re, *Am.* -er; '~**rede** *f* funeral sermon; funeral oration *or* address; '~**schrift** *f* epitaph; '~**stätte** *f* burial-place; grave, tomb; '~**stein** *m* tombstone; gravestone.

**Grad** [gra:t] *m* (-[e]s/-e) degree; grade, rank; 15 ~ Kälte 15 degrees below zero; '~**einteilung** *f* graduation; '~**messer** *m* (-s/-) graduated scale, graduator; *fig.* criterion; '~**netz** *n* map: grid.

**Graf** [gra:f] *m* (-en/-en) *in Britain*: earl; count.

**Gräfin** ['grɛ:fin] *f* (-/-nen) countess.

'**Grafschaft** *f* (-/-en) county.

**Gram** [gra:m] 1. *m* (-[e]s/no pl.) grief, sorrow; 2. ♀ *adj.*: *j-m ~ sein* bear s.o. ill will *or* a grudge.

**grämen** ['grɛ:mən] *v/t.* (ge-, *h*) grieve; *sich ~* grieve (*über acc.* at, for, over).

**Gramm** [gram] *n* (-s/-e) gramme, *Am.* gram.

**Grammati|k** [gra'matik] *f* (-/-en) grammar; **2sch** *adj.* grammatical.

**Granat** *min.* [gra'na:t] *m* (-[e]s/-e) garnet; ~**e** ⚔ *f* (-/-n) shell; grenade; ~**splitter** ⚔ *m* shell-splinter; ~**trichter** ⚔ *m* shell-crater; ~**wer-fer** ⚔ *m* (-s/-) mortar.

**Granit** *min.* [gra'ni:t] *m* (-s/-e) granite.

**Granne** ♀ ['granə] *f* (-/-n) awn, beard.

**Graphi|k** ['gra:fik] *f* (-/-en) graphic arts *pl.*; '**2sch** *adj.* graphic(al).

**Graphit** *min.* ['gra'fi:t] *m* (-s/-e) graphite.

**Gras** ♀ [gra:s] *n* (-es/~er) grass; **2bewachsen** *adj.* ['~bəvaksən] grass-grown, grassy; **2en** ['~zən] *v/i.* (ge-, *h*) graze; '~**halm** *m* blade of grass; '~**narbe** *f* turf, sod; '~**platz** *m* grass-plot, green.

**grassieren** [gra'si:rən] *v/i.* (*no -ge-, h*) rage, prevail.

**gräßlich** *adj.* ['grɛsliç] horrible; hideous, atrocious.

**Grassteppe** ['gra:s-] *f* prairie, savanna(h).

**Grat** [gra:t] *m* (-[e]s/-e) edge, ridge.

**Gräte** ['grɛ:tə] *f* (-/-n) (fish-)bone.

**Gratifikation** [gratifika'tsjo:n] *f* (-/-en) gratuity, bonus.

**gratis** *adv.* ['gra:tis] gratis, free of charge.

**Gratul|ant** [gratu'lant] *m* (-en/-en) congratulator; ~**ation** [~'tsjo:n] *f* (-/-en) congratulation; **2ieren** [~'li:rən] *v/i.* (*no -ge-, h*) congratulate (*j-m zu et.* s.o. on s.th.); *j-m zum Geburtstag ~* wish s.o. many happy returns (of the day).

**grau** *adj.* [grau] grey, *esp. Am.* gray.

'**grauen**[1] *v/i.* (ge-, *h*) *day*: dawn.

'**grauen**[2] 1. *v/i.* (ge-, *h*): *mir graut vor* (*dat.*) I shudder at, I dread; 2. ♀ *n* (-s/no pl.) horror (*vor dat.* of); '~**erregend** *adj.*, '~**haft** *adj.*, '~**voll** *adj.* horrible, dreadful.

**gräulich** *adj.* ['grɔyliç] greyish, *esp. Am.* grayish.

**Graupe** ['graupə] *f* (-/-n) (peeled) barley, pot-barley; '~**ln** 1. *f/pl.* sleet; 2. ♀ *v/i.* (ge-, *h*) sleet.

'**grausam** *adj.* cruel; '**2keit** *f* (-/-en) cruelty.

**grausen** ['grauzən] 1. *v/i.* (ge-, *h*) *s.* grauen[2] 1; 2. ♀ *n* (-s/no pl.) horror (*vor dat.* of).

'**grausig** *adj.* horrible. [graver.]

**Graveur** [gra'vø:r] *m* (-s/-e) en-]

**gravieren** [gra'vi:rən] *v/t.* (*no -ge-, h*) engrave; '~**d** *fig. adj.* aggravating.

**Grazie** ['gra:tsjə] *f* (-/-n) grace(ful-ness).

**graziös** *adj.* [gra'tsjø:s] graceful.

**greifen** ['graifən] (*irr.*, ge-, *h*) 1. *v/t.* seize, grasp, catch hold of; ♪ touch (*string*); 2. *v/i.*: *an den Hut ~* touch one's hat; ~ *nach* grasp *or* snatch at; *um sich ~* spread; *j-m unter die Arme ~* give s.o. a helping hand; *zu strengen Mitteln ~* resort to severe measures; *zu den Waffen ~* take up arms.

**Greis** [grais] *m* (-es/-e) old man; **2enhaft** *adj.* ['~zən-] senile (*a.* 𝔰); ~**in** ['~zin] *f* (-/-nen) old woman.

**grell** *adj.* [grɛl] *light*: glaring; *colour.* loud; *sound*: shrill.

**Grenze** ['grɛntsə] *f* (-/-n) limit; *territory*: boundary; *state*: frontier, borders *pl.*; *e-e ~ ziehen* draw the line; '**2n** *v/i.* (ge-, *h*): ~ *an* (*acc.*) border on (*a. fig.*); *fig.* verge on; '**2nlos** *adj.* boundless.

'**Grenz|fall** *m* border-line case; '~**land** *n* borderland; '~**linie** *f* boundary *or* border line; '~**schutz** *m* frontier *or* border protection; frontier *or* border guard; '~**stein** *m* boundary stone; '~**übergang** *m* frontier *or* border crossing(-point).

**Greuel** ['grɔyəl] *m* (-s/-) horror;

**abomination;** atrocity; **'~tat** f atrocity.

**Griech|e** ['gri:çə] m (-n/-n) Greek; **'2isch** adj. Greek; △, features: Grecian.

**griesgrämig** adj. ['gri:sgre:miç] morose, sullen.

**Grieß** [gri:s] m (-es/-e) gravel (a. ⚕), grit; semolina; **'~brei** m semolina pudding.

**Griff** [grif] 1. m (-[e]s/-e) grip, grasp, hold; ♪ touch; handle (of knife, etc.); hilt (of sword); 2. 2 pret. of greifen.

**Grille** ['grilə] f (-/-n) zo. cricket; fig. whim, fancy; **'2nhaft** adj. whimsical.

**Grimasse** [gri'masə] f (-/-n) grimace; **~n schneiden** pull faces.

**Grimm** [grim] m (-[e]s/no pl.) fury, rage; **'2ig** adj. furious, fierce, grim.

**Grind** [grint] m (-[e]s/-e) scab, scurf.

**grinsen** ['grinzən] 1. v/i. (ge-, h) grin (über acc. at); sneer (at); 2. 2 n (-s/no pl.) grin; sneer.

**Grippe** ⚕ ['gripə] f (-/-n) influenza, F flu(e), grippe.

**grob** adj. [grɔp] coarse; gross; rude; work, skin: rough; **'2heit** f (-/-en) coarseness; grossness; rudeness; **~en** pl. rude things pl.

**grölen** F ['grø:lən] v/t. and v/i. (ge-, h) bawl.

**Groll** [grɔl] m (-[e]s/no pl.) grudge, ill will; **'2en** v/i. (ge-, h) thunder: rumble; j-m **~** bear s.o. ill will or a grudge.

**Gros¹** ✝ [grɔs] n (-ses/-se) gross.
**Gros²** [gro:] n (-/-) main body.

**Groschen** ['grɔʃən] m (-s/-) penny.

**groß** adj. [gro:s] great; large; big; figure: tall; huge; fig. great, grand; heat: intense; cold: severe; loss: heavy; die **2en** pl. the grown-ups pl.; im **~en** wholesale, on a large scale; im **~en (und) ganzen** on the whole; **~er Buchstabe** capital (letter); das **~e Los** the first prize; ich bin kein **~er Tänzer** I am not much of a dancer; **'~artig** adj. great, grand, sublime; first-rate; **'2aufnahme** f film: close-up.

**Größe** ['grø:sə] f (-/-n) size; largeness; height, tallness; quantity (esp. Å); importance: greatness; p. celebrity; thea. star.

**'Großeltern** pl. grandparents pl.
**'großenteils** adv. to a large or great extent, largely.

**'Größenwahn** m megalomania.

**'Groß|grundbesitz** m large landed property; **'~handel** ✝ m wholesale trade; **'~handelspreis** ✝ m wholesale price; **'~händler** ✝ m wholesale dealer, wholesaler; **'~handlung** ✝ f wholesale business; **'~herzog** m grand duke; **'~industrielle** m big industrialist.

**Grossist** [grɔ'sist] m (-en/-en) s. Großhändler.

**groß|jährig** adj. ['gro:sje:riç] of age; **~ werden** come of age; **'2jährigkeit** f (-/no pl.) majority, full (legal) age; **'2kaufmann** m wholesale merchant; **'2kraftwerk** ⚡ n superpower station; **'2macht** f great power; **'2maul** n braggart; **'2mut** f (-/no pl.) generosity; **'~mütig** adj. ['~my:tiç] magnanimous, generous; **'2mutter** f grandmother; **'2neffe** m great-nephew, grandnephew; **'2nichte** f great-niece, grand-niece; **'2onkel** m great-uncle, grand-uncle; **'2schreibung** f (-/-en) use of capital letters; capitalization; **'~sprecherisch** adj. boastful; **'~spurig** adj. arrogant; **'2stadt** f large town or city; **'~städtisch** adj. of or in a large town or city; **'2tante** f great-aunt, grand-aunt.

**größtenteils** adv. ['grø:stəntaıls] mostly, chiefly, mainly.

**'groß|tun** v/i. (irr. tun, sep., -ge-, h) swagger, boast; sich mit et. **~** boast or brag of or about s.th.; **'2vater** m grandfather; **'2verdiener** m (-s/-) big earner; **'2wild** n big game; **'~ziehen** v/t. (irr. ziehen, sep., -ge-, h) bring up (child); rear, raise (child, animal); **'~zügig** adj. ['~tsy:giç] liberal; generous; broad-minded; planning: a. on a large scale.

**grotesk** adj. [gro'tesk] grotesque.
**Grotte** ['grɔtə] f (-/-n) grotto.
**grub** [gru:p] pret. of graben.
**Grübchen** ['gry:pçən] n (-s/-) dimple.

**Grube** ['gru:bə] f (-/-n) pit; ⚒ mine, pit.

**Grübel|ei** [gry:bə'laı] f (-/-en) brooding, musing, meditation; **2n** ['~ln] v/i. (ge-, h) muse, meditate, ponder (all: über acc. on, over); Am. F a. mull (over).

**'Gruben|arbeiter** ⚒ m miner; **'~gas** ⚒ n fire-damp; **'~lampe** ⚒ f miner's lamp.

**Gruft** [gruft] f (-/=e) tomb, vault.

**grün** [gry:n] 1. adj. green; **~er Hering** fresh herring; **~er Junge** greenhorn; **~ und blau schlagen** beat s.o. black and blue; vom **~en Tisch aus** armchair (strategy, etc.); 2. 2 n (-s/no pl.) green; verdure.

**Grund** [grunt] m (-[e]s/=e) ground; soil; bottom (a. fig.); land, estate; foundation; fig.: motive; reason; argument; von **~ auf** thoroughly, fundamentally; **'~ausbildung** f basic instruction; ⚔ basic (military) training; **'~bedeutung** f basic or original meaning; **'~bedingung** f basic or fundamental condition; **'~begriff** m fundamental or basic idea; **~e** pl. principles pl.; rudiments pl.; **'~besitz** m land(ed property); '~besitzer *m* landowner; '~buch *n* land register.

gründ|en ['gryndən] *v/t.* (ge-, h) establish; † promote; sich ~ auf (acc.) be based or founded on; '2er *m* (-s/-) founder; † promoter.

'grund|falsch *adj.* fundamentally wrong; '2farbe *f* ground-colo(u)r; *opt.* primary colo(u)r; '2fläche *f* base; area (of room, etc.); '2gebühr *f* basic rate or fee; flat rate; '2gedanke *m* basic or fundamental idea; '2gesetz *n* fundamental law; ⅛ *appr.* constitution; '2kapital † *n* capital (fund); '2lage *f* foundation, basis; '~legend *adj.* fundamental, basic.

gründlich *adj.* ['gryntliç] thorough; *knowledge:* profound.

'Grund|linie *f* base-line; '2los *adj.* bottomless; *fig.:* groundless; unfounded; '~mauer *f* foundation-wall. [Thursday.]

Grün'donnerstag *eccl.* *m* Maundy]

'Grund|regel *f* fundamental rule; '~riß *m* △ ground-plan; outline; compendium; '~satz *m* principle; 2sätzlich ['~zetsliç] 1. *adj.* fundamental; 2. *adv.* in principle; on principle; '~schule *f* elementary or primary school; '~stein *m* △ foundation-stone; *fig.* corner-stone; '~steuer *f* land-tax; '~stock *m* basis, foundation; '~stoff *m* element; '~strich *m* down-stroke; '~stück *n* plot (of land); ⅞ (real) estate; premises *pl.*; '~stücksmakler *m* real estate agent, *Am.* realtor; '~ton *m* ♪ keynote; ground shade.

'Gründung *f* (-/-en) foundation, establishment.

'grund|ver'schieden *adj.* entirely different; '2wasser *geol.* *n* (under-)ground water; '2zahl *gr.* *f* cardinal number; '2zug *m* main feature, characteristic.

'grünlich *adj.* greenish.

'Grün|schnabel *fig.* *m* greenhorn; whipper-snapper; '~span *m* (-[e]s/no pl.) verdigris.

grunzen ['gruntsən] *v/i.* and *v/t.* (ge-, h) grunt.

Grupp|e ['grupə] *f* (-/-n) group; ✕ section, *Am.* squad; 2ieren [~'pi:rən] *v/t.* (no -ge-, h) group, arrange in groups; sich ~ form groups.

Gruselgeschichte ['gru:zəl-] *f* tale of horror, spine-chilling story or tale, F creepy story or tale.

Gruß [gru:s] *m* (-es/~e) salutation; greeting; *esp.* ✕, ♣ salute; *mst* Grüße *pl.* regards *pl.*; respects *pl.*, compliments *pl.*

grüßen ['gry:sən] *v/t.* (ge-, h) greet, *esp.* ✕ salute; hail; ~ Sie ihn von mir remember me to him; j-n ~ lassen send one's compliments or regards to s.o.

9*

Grütze ['grytsə] *f* (-/-n) grits *pl.*, groats *pl.*

guck|en ['gukən] *v/i.* (ge-, h) look; peep, peer; '2loch *n* peep- or spyhole.

Guerilla ✕ [ge'ril(j)a] *f* (-/-s) guer(r)illa war.

gültig *adj.* ['gyltiç] valid; effective, in force; legal; *coin:* current; *ticket:* available; '2keit *f* (-/no pl.) validity; currency (of money); availability (of ticket).

Gummi ['gumi] *n*, *m* (-s/-s) gum; (india-)rubber; '~ball *m* rubber ball; '~band *n* elastic (band); rubber band; '~baum ♀ *m* gum-tree; (india-)rubber tree.

gum'mieren *v/t.* (no -ge-, h) gum.

'Gummi|handschuh *m* rubber glove; '~knüppel *m* truncheon, *Am.* club; '~schuhe *m/pl.* rubber shoes *pl.*, *Am.* rubbers *pl.*; '~sohle *f* rubber sole; '~stiefel *m* wellington (boot), *Am.* rubber boot; '~zug *m* elastic; elastic webbing.

Gunst [gunst] *f* (-/no pl.) favo(u)r, goodwill; zu ~en (gen.) in favo(u)r of.

günst|ig *adj.* ['gynstiç] favo(u)rable; *omen:* propitious; *im* ~sten Fall at best; zu ~en Bedingungen † on easy terms; 2ling ['~liŋ] *m* (-s/-e) favo(u)rite.

Gurgel ['gurgəl] *f* (-/-n): j-m an die ~ springen leap or fly at s.o.'s throat; '2n *v/i.* (ge-, h) ✗ gargle; gurgle.

Gurke ['gurkə] *f* (-/-n) cucumber; *pickled:* gherkin.

gurren ['gurən] *v/i.* (ge-, h) coo.

Gurt [gurt] *m* ( [e]s/-e) girdle; *harness:* girth; strap; belt.

Gürtel ['gyrtəl] *m* (-s/-) belt; girdle; *geogr.* zone.

Guß [gus] *m* (Gusses/Güsse) ⊕ founding, casting; *typ.* fount, *Am.* font; *rain:* downpour, shower; '~eisen *n* cast iron; '2eisern *adj.* cast-iron; '~stahl *m* cast steel.

gut¹ [gu:t] 1. *adj.* good; ~e Worte fair words; ~es Wetter fine weather; ~er Dinge or ~en Mutes sein be of good cheer; ~e Miene zum bösen Spiel machen grin and bear it; ~ sol good!, well done!; ~ werden get well, heal; *fig.* turn out well; ganz ~ not bad; schon ~! never mind!, all right!; sei so ~ und ... (will you) be so kind as to *inf.*; auf ~ deutsch in plain German; j-m ~ sein love or like s.o.; 2. *adv.* well; ein ~ gehendes Geschäft a flourishing business; du hast ~ lachen it's easy or very well for you to laugh; es ~ haben be lucky; be well off.

Gut² [~] *n* (-[e]s/~er) possession, property; (landed) estate; † goods *pl.*

'Gut|achten n (-s/-) (expert) opinion; '~achter m (-s/-) expert; consultant; '2artig adj. good-natured; ℣ benign; ~dünken ['~dynkən] n (-s/no pl.): nach ~ at discretion or pleasure.

Gute 1. n (-n/no pl.) the good; ~s tun do good; 2. m, f (-n/-n): die ~n pl. the good pl.

Güte ['gy:tə] f (-/no pl.) goodness, kindness; ♰ class, quality; in ~ amicably; F: meine ~! good gracious!; haben Sie die ~ zu inf. be so kind as to inf.

'Güter|abfertigung f dispatch of goods; = '~annahme f goods office, Am. freight office; '~bahnhof m goods station, Am. freight depot or yard; '~gemeinschaft ℔ f community of property; '~trennung ℔ f separation of property; '~verkehr m goods traffic, Am. freight traffic; '~wagen m (goods) wag(g)on, Am. freight car; offener ~ (goods) truck; geschlossener ~ (goods) van, Am. boxcar; '~zug m goods train, Am. freight train.

'gut|gelaunt adj. good-humo(u)red; '~gläubig adj. acting or done in good faith; s. leichtgläubig; '~haben v/t. (irr. haben, sep., -ge-, h) have credit for (sum of money); '2haben ♰ n credit (balance); '~heißen v/t. (irr. heißen, sep., -ge-, h)

approve (of); '~herzig adj. good-natured, kind-hearted.

'gütig adj. good, kind(ly).

'gütlich adv.: sich ~ einigen settle s.th. amicably; sich ~ tun an (dat.) regale o.s. on.

'gut|machen v/t. (sep., -ge-, h) make up for, compensate, repair; ~mütig adj. ['~my:tiç] good-natured; '2mütigkeit f (-/℔ -en) good nature.

'Gutsbesitzer m landowner; owner of an estate.

'Gut|schein m credit note, coupon; voucher; '2schreiben v/t. (irr. schreiben, sep., -ge-, h): j-m e-n Betrag ~ put a sum to s.o.'s credit; '~schrift ♰ f credit(ing).

'Guts|haus n farm-house; manor house; '~herr m lord of the manor; landowner; '~hof m farmyard; estate, farm; '~verwalter m (landlord's) manager or steward.

'gutwillig adj. willing; obliging.

Gymnasi|albildung [gymna'zja:l-] f classical education; '~ast [~ast] m (-en/-en) appr. grammar-school boy; ~um [~'na:zjum] n (-s/Gymnasien) appr. grammar-school.

Gymnasti|k [gym'nastik] f (-/no pl.) gymnastics pl.; 2sch adj. gymnastic.

Gynäkologe ℣ [gyne:ko'lo:gə] m (-n/-n) gyn(a)ecologist.

# H

Haar [ha:r] n (-[e]s/-e) hair; sich die ~e kämmen comb one's hair; sich die ~e schneiden lassen have one's hair cut; aufs ~ to a hair; um ein ~ by a hair's breadth; '~ausfall m loss of hair; '~bürste f hairbrush; '2en v/i. and v/refl. (ge-, h) lose or shed one's hairs; '~esbreite f: um ~ by a hair's breadth; '2'fein adj. (as) fine as a hair; fig. subtle; '~gefäß anat. n capillary (vessel); '2ge'nau adj. exact to a hair; '2ig adj. hairy; in compounds: ...-haired; '2'klein adv. to the last detail; '~klemme f hair grip, Am. bobby pin; '~nadel f hairpin; '~nadelkurve f hairpin bend; '~netz n hair-net; '~öl n hair-oil;'2'scharf 1. adj. very sharp; fig. very precise; 2. adv. by a hair's breadth; '~schneidemaschine f (e-e a pair of) (hair) clippers pl.; '~schneider m barber, (men's) hairdresser; '~schnitt m haircut; '~schwund m loss of hair; '~spalte'rei f (-/-en) hair-splitting; '2sträubend adj. hair-raising, horrifying; '~tracht f hair-style, coiffure; '~wäsche f hair-wash,

shampoo; '~wasser n hair-lotion; '~wuchs m growth of the hair; '~wuchsmittel n hair-restorer.

Habe ['ha:bə] f (-/no pl.) property; belongings pl.

haben ['ha:bən] 1. v/t. (irr., ge-, h) have; F fig.: sich ~ (make a) fuss; etwas (nichts) auf sich ~ be of (no) consequence; unter sich ~ be in control of, command; zu ~ ♰ goods: obtainable, to be had; da ~ wir's! there we are!; 2. ♀ ♰ n (-s/-) credit (side).

Habgier ['ha:p-] f avarice, covetousness; '2ig adj. avaricious, covetous.

habhaft adj. ['ha:phaft]: ~ werden (gen.) get hold of; catch, apprehend.

Habicht orn. ['ha:biçt] m (-[e]s/-e) (gos)hawk.

Hab|seligkeiten ['ha:p-] f/pl. property, belongings pl.; '~sucht f s. Habgier; '2süchtig adj. s. habgierig.

Hacke ['hakə] f (-/-n) ♂ hoe, mattock; (pick)axe; heel.

Hacken ['hakən] 1. m (-s/-) heel; die ~ zusammenschlagen ⚔ click one's heels; 2. ♀ v/t. (ge-, h) ♂

hack (*soil*); mince (*meat*); chop (*wood*).

'Hackfleisch *n* minced meat, *Am.* ground meat.

Häcksel ['hɛksəl] *n*, *m* (-s/*no pl.*) chaff, chopped straw.

Hader ['haːdər] *m* (-s/*no pl.*) dispute, quarrel; discord; '~n *v/i.* (ge-, h) quarrel (*mit* with).

Hafen ['haːfən] *m* (-s/*⁀*) harbo(u)r; port; '~anlagen *f/pl.* docks *pl.*; '~arbeiter *m* docker, *Am. a.* longshoreman; '~damm *m* jetty; pier; '~stadt *f* seaport.

Hafer ['haːfər] *m* (-s/-) oats *pl.*; '~brei *m* (oatmeal) porridge; '~flocken *f/pl.* porridge oats *pl.*; '~grütze *f* groats *pl.*, grits *pl.*; '~schleim *m* gruel.

Haft *r⁀z* [haft] *f* (-/*no pl.*) custody; detention, confinement; '2bar *adj.* responsible, *r⁀z* liable (für for); '~befehl *m* warrant of arrest; '2en *v/i.* (ge-, h) stick, adhere (*an dat.* to); ~ für *r⁀z* answer for, be liable for.

Häftling ['hɛftliŋ] *m* (-s/-e) prisoner.

'Haftpflicht *r⁀z* *f* liability; '2ig *adj.* liable (für for); '~versicherung *f* third-party insurance.

'Haftung *f* (-/-en) responsibility, *r⁀z* liability; *mit beschränkter* ~ limited.

Hagel ['haːgəl] *m* (-s/-) hail; *fig. a.* shower, volley; '~korn *n* hailstone; '2n *v/i.* (ge-, h) hail (*a. fig.*); '~schauer *m* shower of hail, (brief) hailstorm.

hager *adj.* ['haːgər] lean, gaunt; scraggy, lank.

Hahn [haːn] *m* 1. *orn.* (-[e]s/⁀e) cock; rooster; 2. ⊕ (-[e]s/⁀e, -en) (stop)cock, tap, *Am. a.* faucet; '~enkampf *m* cock-fight; '~enschrei *m* cock-crow.

Hai *ichth.* [haɪ] *m* (-[e]s/-e), '~fisch *m* shark.

Hain *poet.* [haɪn] *m* (-[e]s/-e) grove; wood.

häkel|n ['hɛːkəln] *v/t. and v/i.* (ge-, h) crochet; '2nadel *f* crochet needle or hook.

Haken ['haːkən] *m* 1. *m* (-s/-) hook (*a.* boxing); peg; *fig.* snag, catch; 2. ♀ *v/i.* (ge-, h) get stuck, jam.

'hakig *adj.* hooked.

halb [halp] 1. *adj.* half; *eine* ~e *Stunde* half an hour, a half-hour; *eine* ~e *Flasche Wein* a half-bottle of wine; *ein* ~es *Jahr* half a year; ~e *Note* ♪ *minim*, *Am. a.* half note; ~er *Ton* ♪ semitone, *Am. a.* half tone; 2. *adv.* half; ~ *voll* half full; ~ *soviel* half as much; *es schlug* ~ it struck the half-hour.

'halb|amtlich *adj.* semi-official; '2bruder *m* half-brother; '2dunkel *n* semi-darkness; dusk, twilight; ~er *prp.* (*gen.*) ['halbər] on account of; for the sake of; '2fabri-

kat ⊕ *n* semi-finished product; '~gar *adj.* underdone, *Am. a.* rare; '2gott *m* demigod; '2heit *f* (-/-en) half-measure.

halbieren [hal'biːrən] *v/t.* (*no* -ge-, h) halve, divide in half; *A* bisect.

'Halb|insel *f* peninsula; '~jahr *n* half-year, six months *pl.*; '2jährig *adj.* ['~jɛːriç] half-year, six months; of six months; '2jährlich 1. *adj.* half-yearly; 2. *adv. a.* twice a year; '~kreis *m* semicircle; '~kugel *f* hemisphere; '2laut *adj.* low, subdued; 2. *adv.* in an undertone; '2mast *adv.* (at) half-mast, *Am. a.* (at) half-staff; '~messer *A* *m* (-s/-) radius; '~mond *m* half-moon, crescent; '2part *adv.*: ~ *machen* go halves, F go fifty-fifty; '~schuh *m* (low) shoe; '~schwester *f* half-sister; '~tagsbeschäftigung *f* part-time job *or* employment; '2tot *adj.* half-dead; '2wegs *adv.* ['~'veːks] half-way; *fig.* to some extent, tolerably; '~welt *f* demi-monde; '2wüchsig *adj.* ['~vyːksiç] adolescent, *Am. a.* teen-age; '~zeit *f* *sports:* half(-time).

Halde ['haldə] *f* (-/-n) slope; ⚒ dump.

half [half] *pret. of helfen.*

Hälfte ['hɛlftə] *f* (-/-n) half, *r⁀z* moiety; *die* ~ *von* half of.

Halfter ['halftər] *m*, *n* (-s/-) halter.

Halle ['halə] *f* (-/-n) hall; *hotel:* lounge; *tennis:* covered court; ✈ hangar.

hallen ['halən] *v/i.* (ge-, h) (re)sound, ring, (re-)echo.

'Hallen|bad *n* indoor swimming-bath, *Am. a.* natatorium; '~sport *m* indoor sports *pl.*

hallo [ha'loː] 1. *int.* hallo!, hello!, hullo!; 2. ♀ *fig. n* (-s/-s) hullabaloo.

Halm ♀ [halm] *m* (-[e]s/-e) blade; stem, stalk; straw.

Hals [hals] *m* (-es/⁀e) neck; throat; ~ *über Kopf* head over heels; *auf dem* ~e *haben* have on one's back, be saddled with; *sich den* ~ *verrenken* crane one's neck; '~abschneider *fig. m* extortioner, F shark; '~band *n* necklace; collar (*for dog, etc.*); '~entzündung *♂ f* sore throat; '~kette *f* necklace; string; chain; '~kragen *m* collar; '~schmerzen *m/pl.*: ~ *haben* have a sore throat; '2starrig *adj.* stubborn, obstinate; '~tuch *n* neckerchief; scarf; '~weite *f* neck size.

Halt [halt] *m* (-[e]s/-e) hold; foot-hold, handhold; support (*a. fig.*); *fig.*: stability; security, mainstay.

halt 1. *int.* stop!; ✕ halt!; 2. F *adv.* just; *das ist* ~ *so* that's the way it is.

'haltbar *adj.* material, *etc.*: durable, lasting; *colour:* fast; *fig. theory, etc.*: tenable.

'halten (*irr.*, ge-, h) 1. *v/t.* hold (*fort,*

*position, water, etc.*); maintain (*position, level, etc.*); keep (*promise, order, animal, etc.*); make, deliver (*speech*); give, deliver (*lecture*); take in (*newspaper*); ~ *für* regard as, take to be; take for; es ~ *mit* side with; be fond of; *kurz.*~ keep *s.o.* short; *viel* (*wenig*) ~ *von* think highly (little) of; *sich* ~ hold out; last; *food:* keep; *sich gerade* ~ hold o.s. straight; *sich gut* ~ *in examination, etc.*: do well; *p.* be well preserved; *sich* ~ *an* (*acc.*) adhere *or* keep to; **2.** *v/i.* stop, halt; *ice:* bear; *rope, etc.*: stand the strain; ~ zu stick to *or* by; ~ *auf* (*acc.*) set store by, value; *auf sich* ~ pay attention to one's appearance; have self-respect.

**'Halte|punkt** m 🚂, *etc.*: wayside stop, halt; *shooting:* point of aim; *phys.* critical point; '**~r** m (-s/-) keeper; *a.* owner; *devices:* ... holder; '**~stelle** f stop; 🚂 station, stop; '**~signal** 🚂 n stop signal.

**halt|los** adj. ['haltlo:s] *p.* unsteady, unstable; *theory, etc.*: baseless, without foundation; '**~machen** v/i. (*sep., -ge-, h*) stop, halt; *vor nichts* ~ stick *or* stop; at nothing; '**2ung** f (-/-en) deportment, carriage; pose; *fig.* attitude (*gegenüber* towards); self-control; *stock exchange:* tone.

**hämisch** adj. ['hɛ:miʃ] spiteful, malicious.

**Hammel** ['haməl] m (-s/-, ⸗) wether; '**~fleisch** n mutton; '**~keule** f leg of mutton; '**~rippchen** n (-s/-) mutton chop.

**Hammer** ['hamər] m (-s/⸗) hammer; (*auctioneer's*) gavel; *unter den* ~ *kommen* come under the hammer.

**hämmern** ['hemərn] (*ge-, h*) **1.** v/t. hammer; **2.** v/i. hammer (*a. an dat. et door, etc.*); hammer away (*auf dat. at piano*); *heart, etc.*: throb (violently), pound.

**Hämorrhoiden** 🔬 [hɛ:mɔrɔ'i:dən] f/pl. h(a)emorrhoids pl., piles pl.

**Hampelmann** ['hampəlman] m jumping-jack; *fig.* (mere) puppet.

**Hamster** zo. ['hamstər] m (-s/-) hamster; '**2n** v/t. and v/i. (*ge-, h*) hoard.

**Hand** [hant] f (-/⸗e) hand; *j-m die* ~ *geben* shake hands with s.o.; *an* ~ (*gen.*) *or von* with the help *or* aid of; *aus erster* ~ first-hand, at first hand; *bei der* ~, *zur* ~ at hand; ~ *und Fuß haben* be sound, hold water; *seine* ~ *im Spiele haben* have a finger in the pie; '**~arbeit** f manual labo(u)r *or* work; (*handi*)craft; needlework; '**~arbeiter** m manual labo(u)rer; '**~bibliothek** f reference library; '**~breit 1.** f (-/-) hand's breadth; **2.** ⚲ adj. a hand's breadth across; '**~bremse** mot. f hand-brake; '**~buch** n manual, handbook.

**Hände|druck** ['hendə-] m (-[e]s/⸗e)

handshake; '**~klatschen** n (-s/no pl.) (hand-)clapping; applause.

**Handel** ['handəl] m **1.** (-s/no pl.) commerce; trade; business; market; traffic; transaction, deal, bargain; **2.** (-s/⸗): *Händel pl.* quarrels pl., contention; '**2n** v/i. (*ge-, h*) act, take action; **†** trade (*mit* with *s.o., in goods*), deal (*in goods*); bargain (*um for*), haggle (*over*); ~ *von* treat of, deal with; es *handelt sich um* it concerns, it is a matter of.

**'Handels|abkommen** n trade agreement; '**~bank** f commercial bank; '**2einig** adj.: ~ *werden* come to terms; '**~genossenschaft** f traders' co-operative association; '**~gericht** n commercial court; '**~gesellschaft** f (trading) company; '**~haus** n business house, firm; '**~kammer** f Chamber of Commerce; '**~marine** f mercantile marine; '**~minister** m minister of commerce; President of the Board of Trade, *Am.* Secretary of Commerce; '**~ministerium** n ministry of commerce; Board of Trade, *Am.* Department of Commerce; '**~reisende** m commercial traveller, *Am.* traveling salesman, F drummer; '**~schiff** n merchantman; '**~schiffahrt** f merchant shipping; '**~schule** f commercial school; '**~stadt** f commercial town; '**2üblich** adj. customary in trade; '**~vertrag** m commercial treaty, trade agreement.

**'handeltreibend** adj. trading.

**'Hand|feger** m (-s/-) hand-brush; '**~fertigkeit** f manual skill; '**2fest** adj. sturdy, strong; *fig.* well-founded, sound; '**~feuerwaffen** f/pl. small arms pl.; '**~fläche** f flat of the hand, palm; '**2gearbeitet** adj. hand-made; '**~geld** n earnest money; ✗ bounty; '**~gelenk** anat. n wrist; '**~gemenge** n scuffle, mêlée; '**~gepäck** n hand luggage, *Am.* hand baggage; '**~granate** ✗ f hand-grenade; '**2greiflich** adj. violent; *fig.* tangible, palpable; ~ *werden* turn violent, *Am.* a. get tough; '**~griff** m grasp; handle, grip; *fig.* manipulation; '**~habe** *fig.* f handle; '**2haben** v/t. (*ge-, h*) handle, manage; operate (*machine, etc.*); administer (*law*); '**~karren** m hand-cart; '**~koffer** m suitcase, *Am.* a. valise; '**~kuß** m kiss on the hand; '**~langer** m (-s/-) hodman, handy man; *fig.* dog's-body, henchman.

**Händler** ['hendlər] m (-s/-) dealer, trader.

**'handlich** adj. handy; manageable.

**Handlung** ['handluŋ] f (-/-en) act, action; deed; *thea.* action, plot; **†** shop, *Am.* store.

**'Handlungs|bevollmächtigte** m proxy; '**~gehilfe** m clerk; shop-

assistant, *Am.* salesclerk; '~reisen-
de *m s.* Handelsreisende; '~weise *f*
conduct; way of acting.
'Hand|rücken *m* back of the hand;
'~schelle *f* handcuff, manacle;
'~schlag *m* handshake; '~schrei-
ben *n* autograph letter; '~schrift
*f* handwriting; manuscript; '2-
schriftlich 1. *adj.* hand-written;
2. *adv.* in one's own handwriting;
'~schuh *m* glove; '~streich ⚔ *m*
surprise attack, coup de main; *im ~
nehmen* take by surprise; '~tasche
*f* handbag, *Am. a.* purse; '~tuch *n*
towel; '~voll *f* (-/-) handful; '~wa-
gen *m* hand-cart; '~werk *n*
(handi)craft, trade; '~werker *m*
(-s/-) (handi)craftsman, artisan;
workman; '~werkzeug *n* (kit of)
tools *pl.*; '~wurzel *anat. f* wrist;
'~zeichnung *f* drawing.
Hanf ♀ [hanf] *m* (-[e]s/*no pl.*) hemp.
Hang [haŋ] *m* (-[e]s/-e) slope,
incline, declivity, hillside; *fig.*
inclination, propensity (*zu* for; *zu
inf.* to *inf.*); tendency (to).
Hänge|boden ['hɛŋə-] *m* hanging-
loft; ~brücke △ *f* suspension
bridge; '~lampe *f* hanging lamp;
'~matte *f* hammock.
hängen ['hɛŋən] 1. *v/i.* (*irr.*, ge-, h)
hang, be suspended; adhere, stick,
cling (*an dat.* to); ~ *an* (*dat.*) be
attached *or* devoted to; 2. *v/t.* (ge-,
h) hang, suspend; '~bleiben *v/i.*
(*irr.* bleiben, *sep.*, -ge-, *sein*) get
caught (up) (*an dat.* on, in); *fig.*
stick (in the memory).
hänseln ['hɛnzəln] *v/t.* (ge-, h)
tease (*wegen* about), F rag.
Hansestadt ['hanzə-] *f* Hanseatic
town.
Hanswurst [hans'-] *m* (-es/-e, F ~e)
merry andrew; Punch; *fig. contp.*
clown, buffoon.
Hantel ['hantəl] *f* (-/-n) dumb-bell.
hantieren [han'ti:rən] *v/i.* (*no* -ge-,
h) be busy (*mit* with); work (*an dat.*
on).
Happen ['hapən] *m* (-s/-) morsel,
mouthful, bite; snack.
Harfe ♪ ['harfə] *f* (-/-n) harp.
Harke ♪ ['harkə] *f* (-/-n) rake; '2n
*v/t. and v/i.* (ge-, h) rake.
harmlos *adj.* ['harmlo:s] harmless,
innocuous; inoffensive.
Harmon|ie [harmo'ni:] *f* (-/-n)
harmony (*a.* ♪); 2ieren *v/i.* (*no*
-ge-, h) harmonize (*mit* with); *fig.
a.* be in tune (with); ~ika ♪ [~'mo:-
nika] *f* (-/-s, Harmoniken) accordion;
mouth-organ; 2isch *adj.* [~'mo:niʃ]
harmonious.
Harn [harn] *m* (-[e]s/-e) urine;
'~blase *anat. f* (urinary) bladder;
'2en *v/i.* (ge-, h) pass water, urinate.
Harnisch ['harniʃ] *m* (-es/-e)
armo(u)r; *in ~ geraten* be up in
arms (*über acc.* about).

'Harnröhre *anat. f* urethra.
Harpun|e [har'pu:nə] *f* (-/-n) har-
poon; 2ieren [~u'ni:rən] *v/t.* (*no
-ge-, h*) harpoon.
hart [hart] 1. *adj.* hard; *fig. a.*
harsh; heavy, severe; 2. *adv.* hard;
~ *arbeiten* work hard.
Härte ['hɛrtə] *f* (-/-n) hardness; *fig.
a.* hardship; severity; '2n (ge-, h)
1. *v/t.* harden (metal); temper (steel);
case-harden (iron, steel); 2. *v/i. and
v/refl.* harden, become *or* grow
hard; steel: temper.
'Hart|geld *n* coin(s *pl.*), specie;
'~gummi *m* hard rubber; ✝ ebon-
ite, vulcanite; '2herzig *adj.* hard-
hearted; 2köpfig *adj.* ['~kœpfiç]
stubborn, headstrong; 2näckig *adj.*
['~nɛkiç] *p.* obstinate, obdurate;
*effort:* dogged, tenacious; ✙ *ail-
ment:* refractory.
Harz [ha:rts] *n* (-es/-e) resin; ♪
rosin; *mot.* gum; '2ig *adj.* resinous.
Hasardspiel [ha'zart-] *n* game of
chance; *fig.* gamble.
haschen ['haʃən] (ge-, h) 1. *v/t.*
catch (hold of), snatch; *sich ~
children:* play tag; 2. *v/i.: ~ nach*
snatch at; *fig.* strain after (*effect*),
fish for (*compliments*).
Hase ['ha:zə] *m* (-n/-n) zo. hare; *ein
alter ~* an old hand, an old-timer.
Haselnuß ♀ ['ha:zəlnus] *f* hazel-
nut.
'Hasen|braten *m* roast hare; '~fuß
F *fig. m* coward, F funk; '~panier F
*n: das ~ ergreifen* take to one's
heels; '~scharte ✙ *f* hare-lip.
Haß [has] *m* (Hasses/*no pl.*) hatred.
'hassen *v/t.* (ge-, h) hate.
häßlich *adj.* ['hɛsliç] ugly; *fig. a.*
nasty, unpleasant.
Hast [hast] *f* (-/*no pl.*) hurry, haste;
rush; *in wilder ~* in frantic haste;
'2en *v/i.* (ge-, *sein*) hurry, hasten;
rush; '2ig *adj.* hasty, hurried.
hätscheln ['hɛːtʃəln] *v/t.* (ge-, h)
caress, fondle, pet; pamper, coddle.
hatte ['hatə] *pret.* of haben.
Haube ['haubə] *f* (-/-n) bonnet (*a.*
⊕, *mot.*); cap; *orn.* crest, tuft; *mot.
Am. a.* hood.
Haubitze ⚔ [hau'bitsə] *f* (-/-n)
howitzer.
Hauch [haux] *m* (-[e]s/✎ ~-e) breath;
*fig.:* waft, whiff (*of perfume, etc.*);
touch, tinge (*of irony, etc.*); '2en
(ge-, h) 1. *v/i.* breathe; 2. *v/t.*
breathe, whisper; *gr.* aspirate.
Haue ['hauə] *f* (-/-n) ✎ hoe, mattock; pick; F hiding, spanking; '2n
([*irr.*,] ge-, h) 1. *v/t.* hew (coal,
stone); cut up (meat); chop (wood),
cut (hole, steps, etc.); beat (child);
*sich ~* (have a) fight; 2. *v/i.: ~ nach*
cut at, strike out at.
Haufen ['haufən] *m* (-s/-) heap, pile
(*both* F *a. fig.*); *fig.* crowd.
häufen ['hɔyfən] *v/t.* (ge-, h) heap

(up), pile (up); accumulate; *sich* ~ pile up, accumulate; *fig.* become more frequent, increase.

'häufig *adj.* frequent; '2keit *f* (-/*no pl.*) frequency.

'Häufung *fig. f* (-/-en) increase, *fig.* accumulation.

Haupt [haupt] *n* (-[e]s/=er) head; *fig.* chief, head, leader; '~altar *m* high altar; '~anschluß *teleph. m* subscriber's main station; '~bahnhof ⚅ *m* main *or* central station; '~beruf *m* full-time occupation; '~buch † *n* ledger; '~darsteller *thea. m* leading actor; '~fach *univ. n* main *or* principal subject, *Am. a.* major; '~film *m* feature (film); '~geschäft *n* main transaction; main shop; '~geschäftsstelle *f* head *or* central office; '~gewinn *m* first prize; '~grund *m* main reason; '~handelsartikel † ['haupthandəls?-] *m* staple.

Häuptling ['hɔyptliŋ] *m* (-s/-e) chief(tain).

'Haupt|linie ⚅ *f* main *or* trunk line; '~mann ⚔ *m* (-[e]s/Hauptleute) captain; '~merkmal *n* characteristic feature; '~postamt *n* general post office, *Am.* main post office; '~punkt *m* main *or* cardinal point; '~quartier *n* headquarters *sg. or pl.*; '~rolle *thea. f* lead(ing part); '~sache *f* main thing *or* point; '2sächlich *adj.* main, chief, principal; '~satz *gr. m* main clause; '~stadt *f* capital; '2städtisch *adj.* metropolitan; '~straße *f* main street; major road; '~treffer *m* first prize, jackpot; '~verkehrsstraße *f* main road; arterial road; '~verkehrsstunden *f/pl.*, '~verkehrszeit *f* rush hour(s *pl.*), peak hour(s *pl.*); '~versammlung *f* general meeting; '~wort *gr. n* (-[e]s/=er) substantive, noun.

Haus [haus] *n* (-es/=er) house; building; home, family, household; dynasty; † (business) house, firm; *parl.* House; *nach* ~e home; *zu* ~e at home, F in; '~angestellte *f* (-n/-n) (house-)maid; '~apotheke *f* (household) medicine-chest; '~arbeit *f* housework; '~arrest *m* house arrest; '~arzt *m* family doctor; '~aufgaben *f/pl.* homework, F prep; '2backen *fig. adj.* homely; '~bar *f* cocktail cabinet; '~bedarf *m* household requirements *pl.*; '~besitzer *m* house-owner; '~diener *m* (man-)servant; *hotel*: porter, boots *sg.*

hausen ['hauzən] *v/i.* (ge-, h) live; play *or* work havoc (*in a place*).

'Haus|flur *m* (entrance-)hall, *esp. Am.* hallway; '~frau *f* housewife; '~halt *m* household; '2halten *v/i.* (*irr.* halten, *sep.*, -ge-, h) be economical (*mit* with), economize (on);

'~hälterin ['~heltərin] *f* (-/-nen) housekeeper; '~halt(s)plan *parl. m* budget; '~haltung *f* housekeeping; household, family; '~haltwaren *f/pl.* household articles *pl.*; '~herr *m* master of the family; landlord.

hausier|en [hau'ziːrən] *v/i.* (*no* -ge-, h) hawk, peddle (*mit et.* s.th.); ~ gehen be a hawker *or* pedlar; 2er *m* (-s/-) hawker, pedlar.

'Haus|kleid *n* house dress; '~knecht *m* boots; '~lehrer *m* private tutor.

häuslich *adj.* ['hɔyslic] domestic; domesticated; '2keit *f* (-/*no pl.*) domesticity; family life; home.

'Haus|mädchen *n* (house-)maid; '~mannskost *f* plain fare; '~meister *m* caretaker; janitor; '~mittel *n* popular medicine; '~ordnung *f* rules *pl.* of the house; '~rat *m* household effects *pl.*; '~recht *n* domestic authority; '~sammlung *f* house-to-house collection; '~schlüssel *m* latchkey; front-door key; '~schuh *m* slipper.

Hausse ['hoːsə)] *f* (-/-n) rise, boom; ~ier [hos'je:] *m* (-s/-s) speculator for a rise, bull.

'Haus|stand *m* household; *e-n* ~ gründen set up house; '~suchung ⚖ *f* house search, domiciliary visit, *Am. a.* house check; '~tier *n* domestic animal; '~tür *f* front door; '~verwalter *m* steward; '~wirt *m* landlord; '~wirtin *f* (-/-nen) landlady.

Haut [haut] *f* (-/=e) skin; hide; film; *bis auf die* ~ to the skin; *aus der* ~ *fahren* jump out of one's skin; F *e-e ehrliche* ~ an honest soul; '~abschürfung ⚕ *f* skin abrasion; '~arzt *m* dermatologist; '~ausschlag ⚕ *m* rash; '2eng *adj.* garment: skin-tight; '~farbe *f* complexion.

Hautgout [o'gu] *m* (-s/*no pl.*) high taste.

häutig *adj.* ['hɔytiç] membranous; covered with skin.

'Haut|krankheit *f* skin disease; '~pflege *f* care of the skin; '~schere *f* (*e-e* a pair of) cuticle scissors *pl.*

Havarie ⚓ [hava'ri:] *f* (-/-n) average.

H-Bombe ⚔ ['ha:-] *f* H-bomb.

he *int.* [he:] hi!, hi there!, I say!

Hebamme ['he:p?amə] *f* midwife.

Hebe|baum ['he:bə-] *m* lever (*for raising heavy objects*); '~bühne *mot. f* lifting ramp; '~eisen *n* crowbar; '~kran *m* lifting crane.

Hebel ⊕ ['he:bəl] *m* (-s/-) lever; '~arm *m* lever arm.

heben ['he:bən] *v/t.* (*irr.*, ge-, h) lift (*a. sports*), raise (*a. fig.*); heave (*heavy load*); hoist; recover (*treas-*

*ure*); raise (*sunken ship*); *fig.* promote, improve, increase; sich ~ rise, go up.

**Hecht** *ichth.* [hɛçt] *m* (-[e]s/-e) pike.

**Heck** [hɛk] *n* (-[e]s/-e, -s) ⚓ stern; *mot.* rear; ⚞ tail.

**Hecke** ['hɛkə] *f* (-/-n) ⚟ hedge; *zo.* brood, hatch; '⚟en *v/t. and v/i.* (ge-, h) breed, hatch; '~nrose ⚟ *f* dog-rose.                      [(hallo!)

**heda** *int.* ['he:dɑ:] hi (there)!,)

**Heer** [he:r] *n* (-[e]s/-e) ⚔ army; *fig. a.* host; '~dienst *m* military service; '~esmacht *f* military force(s *pl.*); '~eszug *m* military expedition; '~führer *m* general; '~lager *n* (army) camp; '~schar *f* army, host; '~straße *f* military road; highway; '~zug *m s.* Heereszug.

**Hefe** ['he:fə] *f* (-/-n) yeast; barm.

**Heft** [hɛft] *n* (-[e]s/-e) dagger, *etc.*: haft; *knife*: handle; *fig.* reins *pl.*; exercise book; *periodical, etc.*: issue, number.

**'heft|en** *v/t.* (ge-, h) fasten, fix (*an acc.* on to); affix, attach (to); pin on (to); tack, baste (*seam, etc.*); stitch, sew (*book*); '⚟faden *m* basting thread.

**'heftig** *adj. storm, anger, quarrel, etc.*: violent, fierce; *rain, etc.*: heavy; *pain, etc.*: severe; *speech, desire, etc.*: vehement, passionate; *p.* irascible; '⚟keit *f* (-/⚟-en) violence, fierceness; severity; vehemence; irascibility.

**'Heft|klammer** *f* paper-clip; '~pflaster *n* sticking plaster.

**hegen** ['he:gən] *v/t.* (ge-, h) preserve (*game*); nurse, tend (*plants*); have, entertain (*feelings*); harbo(u)r (*fears, suspicions, etc.*).

**Hehler** ⚖ ['he:lər] *m* (-s/-) receiver (of stolen goods); '~ei [~'raı] *f* (-/-en) receiving (of stolen goods).

**Heide** ['haıdə] **1.** *m* (-n/-n) heathen; **2.** *f* (-/-n) heath(-land); = '~kraut ⚟ *n* heather; '~land *n* heath(-land).

**'Heiden|geld** F *n* pots *pl.* of money; '~lärm F *m* hullabaloo; '~spaß F *m* capital fun; '~tum *n* (-s/no *pl.*) heathenism.                          [(-ish).)

**heidnisch** *adj.* ['haıdnıʃ] heathen)

**heikel** *adj.* ['haıkəl] *p.* fastidious, particular; *problem, etc.*: delicate, awkward.

**heil** [haıl] **1.** *adj. p.* safe, unhurt; whole, sound; **2.** ⚟ *n* (-[e]s/no *pl.*) welfare, benefit; *eccl.* salvation; **3.** *int.* hail!

**Heiland** *eccl.* ['haılant] *m* (-[e]s/-e) Saviour, Redeemer.

**'Heil|anstalt** *f* sanatorium, *Am. a.* sanitarium; spa; '~bad *n* medicinal bath; spa; '⚟bar *adj.* curable; '⚟en (ge-) **1.** *v/t.* (h) cure, heal; ~ *von* cure *s.o.* of; **2.** *v/i.* (sein) heal (up); '~gehilfe *m* male nurse.

**heilig** *adj.* ['haılıç] holy; sacred; solemn; ⚟er Abend Christmas Eve; ⚟e ['~gə] *m, f* (-n/-n) saint; ~en ['~gən] *v/t.* (ge-, h) sanctify (*a. fig.*), hallow; '⚟keit *f* (-/no *pl.*) holiness; sacredness, sanctity; '~sprechen *v/t.* (*irr.* sprechen, *sep., -ge-,* h) canonize; '⚟sprechung *f* (-/-en) canonization; '⚟tum *n* (-[e]s/⚟er) sanctuary; sacred relic; ⚟ung ['~gʊŋ] *f* (-/-en) sanctification (*a. fig.*), hallowing.

**'Heil|kraft** *f* healing *or* curative power; '⚟kräftig *adj.* healing, curative; '~kunde *f* medical science; '⚟los *fig. adj.* confusion: utter, great; '~mittel *n* remedy, medicament; '~praktiker *m* non-medical practitioner; '~quelle *f* medicinal spring; '⚟sam *adj.* curative; *fig.* salutary.                          [Army.)

**Heilsarmee** ['haıls⁹-] *f* Salvation)

**'Heil|ung** *f* (-/-en) cure, healing, successful treatment; '~verfahren *n* therapy.

**heim** [haım] **1.** *adv.* home; **2.** ⚟ *n* (-[e]s/-e) home; hostel; '⚟arbeit *f* homework, outwork.

**Heimat** ['haımɑ:t] *f* (-/⚟ -en) home; own country; native land; '~land *n* own country, native land; '⚟lich *adj.* native; '⚟los *adj.* homeless; '~ort *m* home town *or* village; '~vertriebene *m* expellee.

**Heimchen** *zo.* ['haımçən] *n* (-s/-) cricket.

**'heimisch** *adj. trade, industry, etc.*: home, local, domestic; ⚟, *zo., etc.*: native, indigenous; ~ *werden* settle down; become established; sich ~ *fühlen* feel at home.

**Heim|kehr** ['haımke:r] *f* (-/no *pl.*) return (home), homecoming; '⚟kehren *v/i.* (*sep., -ge-,* sein), '⚟kommen *v/i.* (*irr.* kommen, *sep., -ge-,* sein) return home.

**'heimlich** *adj. plan, feeling, etc.*: secret; *meeting, organisation, etc.*: clandestine; *glance, movement, etc.*: stealthy, furtive.

**'Heim|reise** *f* homeward journey; '⚟suchen *v/t.* (*sep., -ge-,* h) disaster, *etc.*: afflict, strike; *ghost*: haunt; *God*: visit, punish; '~tücke *f* underhand malice, treachery; '⚟tückisch *adj.* malicious, treacherous, insidious; '⚟wärts *adv.* ['~verts] homeward(s); '~weg *m* way home; '~weh *n* homesickness, nostalgia; ~ *haben* be homesick.

**Heirat** ['haırɑ:t] *f* (-/-en) marriage; '⚟en (ge-, h) **1.** *v/t.* marry; **2.** *v/i.* marry, get married.

**'Heirats|antrag** *m* offer *or* proposal of marriage; '⚟fähig *adj.* marriageable; '~kandidat *m* possible marriage partner; '~schwindler *m* marriage impostor; '~vermittler *m* matrimonial agent.

**heiser** adj. ['haɪzər] hoarse; husky; **ˈ⸰keit** f (-/no pl.) hoarseness; huskiness.

**heiß** adj. [haɪs] hot; fig. a. passionate, ardent; mir ist ~ I am or feel hot.

**heißen** ['haɪsən] (irr., ge-, h) 1. v/t.: e-n Lügner ~ call s.o. a liar; willkommen ~ welcome; 2. v/i. be called; mean; wie ~ Sie? what is your name?; was heißt das auf englisch? what's that in English?

**heiter** adj. ['haɪtər] day, weather: bright; sky: bright, clear; p., etc.: cheerful, gay; serene; **ˈ⸰keit** f (-/no pl.) brightness; cheerfulness, gaiety; serenity.

**heiz|en** ['haɪtsən] (ge-, h) 1. v/t. heat (room, etc.); light (stove); fire (boiler); 2. v/i. stove, etc.: give out heat; turn on the heating; mit Kohlen ~ burn coal; **ˈ⸰er** m (-s/-) stoker, fireman; **ˈ⸰kissen** n electric heating pad; **ˈ⸰körper** m central heating: radiator; ⚡ heating element; **ˈ⸰material** n fuel; **ˈ⸰ung** f (-/-en) heating.

**Held** [hɛlt] m (-en/-en) hero.

**ˈHelden|gedicht** n epic (poem); **ˈ⸰haft** adj. heroic, valiant; **ˈ⸰mut** m heroism, valo(u)r; **ˈ⸰mütig** adj. ['⸰my:tiç] heroic; **ˈ⸰tat** f heroic or valiant deed; **ˈ⸰tod** m hero's death; **ˈ⸰tum** n (-[e]s/no pl.) heroism.

**helfen** ['hɛlfən] v/i. (dat.) (irr., ge-, h) help, assist, aid; ~ gegen be good for; sich nicht zu ~ wissen be helpless.

**ˈHelfer** m (-s/-) helper, assistant; **ˈ⸰shelfer** m accomplice.

**hell** adj. [hɛl] sound, voice, light, etc.: clear; light, flame, etc.: bright; hair: fair; colour: light; ale: pale; **ˈ⸰blau** adj. light-blue; **ˈ⸰blond** adj. very fair; **ˈ⸰hörig** adj. p. quick of hearing; fig. perceptive; △ poorly sound-proofed; **ˈ⸰seher** m clairvoyant.

**Helm** [hɛlm] m ([-e]s/-e) ✕ helmet; △ dome, cupola; ⚓ helm; **ˈ⸰busch** m plume.

**Hemd** [hɛmt] n (-[e]s/-en) shirt; vest; **ˈ⸰bluse** f shirt-blouse; Am. shirtwaist.

**Hemisphäre** [he:mi'sfɛːrə] f (-/-n) [hemisphere.]

**hemm|en** ['hɛmən] v/t. (ge-, h) check, stop (movement, etc.); stem (stream, flow of liquid); hamper (free movement, activity); be a hindrance to; psych.: gehemmt sein be inhibited; **ˈ⸰nis** n (-ses/-se) hindrance, impediment; **ˈ⸰schuh** m slipper; fig. hindrance, F drag (für acc. on); **ˈ⸰ung** f (-/-en) stoppage, check; psych.: inhibition.

**Hengst** zo. [hɛŋst] m (-es/-e) stallion.

**Henkel** ['hɛŋkəl] m (-s/-) handle, ear.

**Henker** ['hɛŋkər] m (-s/-) hangman, executioner; F: zum ~! hang it (all)!

**Henne** zo. ['hɛnə] f (-/-n) hen.

**her** adv. [he:r] here; hither; es ist schon ein Jahr ~, daß ... or seit ... it is a year since ...; wie lange ist es ~, seit ... how long is it since ...; hinter (dat.) ~ sein be after; ~ damit! out with it!

**herab** adv. [he'rap] down, downward; **ˈ⸰lassen** v/t. (irr. lassen, sep., -ge-, h) let down, lower; fig. sich ~ condescend; **ˈ⸰lassend** adj. condescending; **ˈ⸰setzen** v/t. (sep., -ge-, h) take down; fig. belittle, disparage s.o.; ↑ reduce, lower, cut (price, etc.); **ˈ⸰setzung** fig. f (-/-en) reduction; disparagement; **ˈ⸰steigen** v/i. (irr. steigen, sep., -ge-, sein) climb down, descend; **ˈ⸰würdigen** v/t. (sep., -ge-, h) degrade, belittle, abase.

**heran** adv. [he'ran] close, near; up; nur ~! come on!; **ˈ⸰bilden** v/t. (sep., -ge-, h) train, educate (zu as s.th., to be s.th.); **ˈ⸰kommen** v/i. (irr. kommen, sep., -ge-, sein) come or draw near; approach; ~ an (acc.) come up to s.o.; measure up to; **ˈ⸰wachsen** v/i. (irr. wachsen, sep., -ge-, sein) grow (up) (zu into).

**herauf** adv. [he'rauf] up(wards), up here; upstairs; **ˈ⸰beschwören** v/t. (irr. schwören, sep., no -ge-, h) evoke, call up, conjure up (spirit, etc.); fig. a. bring about, provoke, give rise to (war, etc.); **ˈ⸰steigen** v/i. (irr. steigen, sep., -ge-, sein) climb up (here), ascend; **ˈ⸰ziehen** v/t. ziehen, sep., -ge-) 1. v/t. (h) pull or hitch up (trousers, etc.); 2. v/i. (sein) cloud, etc.: come up.

**heraus** adv. [he'raus] out, out here; zum Fenster ~ out of the window; ~ mit der Sprache! speak out!; **ˈ⸰bekommen** v/t. (irr. kommen, sep., no -ge-, h) get out; get (money) back; fig. find out; **ˈ⸰bringen** v/t. (irr. bringen, sep., -ge-, h) bring or get out; thea. stage; **ˈ⸰finden** v/t. (irr. finden, sep., -ge-, h) find out; fig. a. discover; **ˈ⸰forderer** m (-s/-) challenger; **ˈ⸰fordern** v/t. (sep., -ge-, h) challenge (to a fight); provoke; **ˈ⸰forderung** f (-/-en) challenge; provocation; **ˈ⸰geben** (irr. geben, sep., -ge-, h) 1. v/t. surrender; hand over; restore; edit (periodical, etc.); publish (book, etc.); issue (regulations, etc.); 2. v/i. give change (auf acc. for); **ˈ⸰geber** m (-s/-) editor; publisher; **ˈ⸰kommen** v/i. (irr. kommen, sep., -ge-, sein) come out; fig. a. appear, be published; **ˈ⸰nehmen** v/t. (irr. nehmen, sep., -ge-, h) take out; sich viel ~ take liberties; **ˈ⸰putzen** v/t. (sep., -ge-, h) dress up; sich ~ dress (o.s.)

up; ~reden v/refl. (sep., -ge-, h) talk one's way out; ~stellen v/t. (sep., -ge-, h) put out; fig. emphasize, set forth; sich ~ emerge, turn out; ~strecken v/t. (sep., -ge-, h) stretch out; put out; ~streichen v/t. (irr. streichen, sep., -ge-, h) cross out, delete (word, etc.); fig. extol, praise; ~winden fig. v/refl. (irr. winden, sep., -ge-, h) extricate o.s. (aus from).

herb adj. [hɛrp] fruit, flavour, etc.: tart; wine, etc.: dry; features, etc.: austere; criticism, etc.: harsh; disappointment, etc.: bitter.

herbei adv. [hɛr'baɪ] here; ~! come here!; ~eilen [hɛr'baɪ⁹-] v/i. (sep., -ge-, seln) come hurrying; ~führen fig. v/t. (sep., -ge-, h) cause, bring about, give rise to; ~schaffen v/t. (sep., -ge-, h) bring along; procure.

Herberge ['hɛrbɛrgə] f (-/-n) shelter, lodging; inn.

'Herbheit f (-/no pl.) tartness; dryness; fig.: austerity; harshness, bitterness.

Herbst [hɛrpst] m (-[e]s/-e) autumn, Am. a. fall.

Herd [he:rt] m (-[e]s/-e) hearth, fireplace; stove; fig. seat, focus.

Herde ['he:rdə] f (-/-n) herd (of cattle, pigs, etc.) (contp. a. fig.); flock (of sheep, geese, etc.).

herein adv. [he'raɪn] in (here); ~! come in!; ~brechen fig. v/i. (irr. brechen, sep., -ge-, sein) night: fall; ~ über (acc.) misfortune, etc.: befall; ~fallen fig. v/i. (irr. fallen, sep., -ge-, sein) be taken in.

'her|fallen v/i. (irr. fallen, sep., -ge-, sein): ~ über (acc.) attack (a. fig.), fall upon; F fig. pull to pieces; '2~gang m course of events, details pl.; '~geben v/t. (irr. geben, sep., -ge-, h) give up, part with, return; yield; sich ~ zu lend o.s. to; '~gebracht fig. adj. traditional; customary; '~halten (irr. halten, sep., -ge-, h) 1. v/t. hold out; 2. v/i.: ~ müssen be the one to pay or suffer (für for).

Hering ichth. ['he:rɪŋ] m (-s/-e) herring.

'her|kommen v/i. (irr. kommen, sep., -ge-, sein) come or get here; come or draw near; ~ von come from; fig. a. be due to, be caused by; ~kömmlich adj. ['-kœmlɪç] traditional; customary; 2kunft ['-kunft] f (-/no pl.) origin; birth, descent; '~leiten v/t. (sep., -ge-, h) lead here; fig. derive (von from); '2leitung fig. f derivation.

Herold ['he:rɔlt] m (-[e]s/-e) herald.

Herr [hɛr] m (-n, ~ -en/-en) lord, master; eccl. the Lord; gentleman; ~ Maier Mr Maier; mein ~ Sir; m-e ~en gentlemen; ~ der Situation master of the situation.

'Herren|bekleidung f men's cloth-

ing; '~einzel n tennis: men's singles pl.; '~haus n manor-house; 2~los adj. ['-lo:s] ownerless; '~reiter m sports: gentleman-jockey; '~schneider m men's tailor; '~zimmer n study; smoking-room.

herrichten ['he:r-] v/t. (sep., -ge-, h) arrange, prepare.

'herrisch adj. imperious, overbearing; voice, etc.: commanding, peremptory.

'herrlich adj. excellent, glorious, magnificent, splendid; '2keit f (-/-en) glory, splendo(u)r.

'Herrschaft f (-/-en) rule, dominion (über acc. of); fig. mastery; master and mistress; m-e ~en! ladies and gentlemen!; '2lich adj. belonging to a master or landlord; fig. high-class, elegant.

herrsch|en ['hɛrʃən] v/i. (ge-, h) rule (über acc. over); monarch: reign (over); govern; fig. prevail, be; '2er m (-s/-) ruler; sovereign, monarch; '2sucht f thirst for power; '~süchtig adj. thirsting for power; imperious.

'her|rühren v/i. (sep., -ge-, h): ~ von come from, originate with; '~sagen v/t. (sep., -ge-, h) recite; say (prayer); ~stammen v/i. (sep., -ge-, h): ~ von or aus be descended from; come from; be derived from; '~stellen v/t. (sep., -ge-, h) place here; ⚙ make, manufacture, produce; '2stellung f (-/-en) manufacture, production.

herüber adv. [he'ry:bər] over (here), across.

herum adv. [he'rum] (a)round; about; ~führen v/t. (sep., -ge-, h) show (a)round; ~ in (dat.) show over; ~lungern v/i. (sep., -ge-, h) loaf or loiter or hang about; ~reichen v/t. (sep., -ge-, h) pass or hand round; ~sprechen v/refl. (irr. sprechen, sep., -ge-, h) get about, spread; ~treiben v/refl. (irr. treiben, sep., -ge-, h) F gad or knock about.

herunter adv. [he'runtər] down (here); downstairs; von oben ~ down from above; ~bringen v/t. (irr. bringen, sep., -ge-, h) bring down; fig. a. lower, reduce; ~kommen v/i. (irr. kommen, sep., -ge-, sein) come down(stairs); fig.: come down in the world; deteriorate; ~machen v/t. (sep., -ge-, h) take down; turn (collar, etc.) down; fig. give s.o. a dressing-down; fig. pull to pieces; ~reißen v/t. (irr. reißen, sep., -ge-, h) pull or tear down; fig. pull to pieces; ~sein F fig. v/i. (irr. sein, sep., -ge-, sein) be low in health; ~wirtschaften v/t. (sep., -ge-, h) run down.

hervor adv. [hɛr'fo:r] forth, out; ~bringen v/t. (irr. bringen, sep.,

-ge-, *h*) bring out, produce (*a. fig.*); yield (*fruit*); *fig.* utter (*word*); ~gehen *v/i.* (*irr.* gehen, *sep.*, -ge-, *sein*) *p.* come (*aus* from); come off (*victorious*) (from); *fact, etc.*: emerge (from); be clear *or* apparent (from); ~heben *fig. v/t.* (*irr.* heben, *sep.*, -ge-, *h*) stress, emphasize; give prominence to; ~holen *v/t.* (*sep.*, -ge-, *h*) produce; ~ragen *v/i.* (*sep.*, -ge-, *h*) project (*über acc.* over); *fig.* tower (above); ~ragend *adj.* projecting, prominent; *fig.* outstanding, excellent; ~rufen *v/t.* (*irr.* rufen, *sep.*, -ge-, *h*) *thea.* call for; *fig.* arouse, evoke; ~stechend *fig. adj.* outstanding; striking; conspicuous.

**Herz** [hɛrts] *n* (-ens/-en) *anat.* heart (*a. fig.*); *cards*: hearts *pl.*; *fig.* courage, spirit; *sich ein ~ fassen* take heart; *mit ganzem ~en* whole-heartedly; *sich et. zu ~en nehmen* take s.th. to heart; *es nicht übers ~ bringen zu inf.* not to have the heart to *inf.*; ~anfall *m* heart attack.

**'Herzens|brecher** *m* (-s/-) ladykiller; **'~lust** *f*: *nach ~* to one's heart's content; **'~wunsch** *m* heart's desire.

**'herz|ergreifend** *fig. adj.* heart-moving; **2fehler** ♂ *m* cardiac defect; **2gegend** *anat. f* cardiac region; **'~haft** *adj.* hearty, good; **'~ig** *adj.* lovely, *Am. a.* cute; **2infarkt** ♂ [~ˀınfarkt] *m* (-[e]s/-e) cardiac infarction; **2klopfen** ♂ *n* (-s/*no pl.*) palpitation; **'~krank** *adj.* having heart trouble; **'~lich 1.** *adj.* heartfelt; cordial, hearty; **~es Beileid** sincere sympathy; **2.** *adv.*: *~ gern* with pleasure; **'~los** *adj.* heartless; unfeeling.

**Herzog** ['hɛrtsoːk] *m* (-[e]s/~e, -e) duke; **'~in** *f* (-/-nen) duchess; **'~tum** *n* (-[e]s/~er) dukedom; duchy.

**'Herz|schlag** *m* heartbeat; ♂ heart failure; **'~schwäche** ♂ *f* cardiac insufficiency; **'~verpflanzung** ♂ *f* heart transplant; **2zerreißend** *adj.* heart-rending.

**Hetz|e** ['hɛtsə] *f* (-/-n) hurry, rush; instigation (*gegen acc.* against); baiting (of); **2en** (ge-) **1.** *v/t.* (*h*) course (*hare*); bait (*bear, etc.*); *hound*: hunt, chase (*animal*); *fig.* hurry, rush; *sich ~* hurry, rush; *e-n Hund auf j-n ~* set a dog at s.o.; **2.** *v/i.* (*h*) *fig.*: cause discord; agitate (*gegen* against); **3.** *fig. v/i.* (*sein*) hurry, rush; **'~er** *fig. m* (-s/-) instigator; agitator; **2erisch** *adj.* virulent, inflammatory; **'~jagd** *f* hunt(ing); *fig.*: virulent campaign; rush, hurry; **'~presse** *f* yellow press.

**Heu** [hɔy] *n* (-[e]s/*no pl.*) hay; **'~boden** *m* hayloft.

**Heuchel|ei** [hɔyçə'laı] *f* (-/-en) hypocrisy; **2n** (ge-, *h*) **1.** *v/t.* sim-

ulate, feign, affect; **2.** *v/i.* feign, dissemble; play the hypocrite.

**'Heuchler** *m* (-s/-) hypocrite; **'2isch** *adj.* hypocritical.

**heuer** ['hɔyər] **1.** *adv.* this year; **2.** ♀ ♂ *f* (-/-n) pay, wages *pl.*; **'~n** *v/t.* (ge-, *h*) hire; ♂ engage, sign on (*crew*), charter (*ship*).

**heulen** ['hɔylən] *v/i.* (ge-, *h*) *wind, etc.*: howl; *storm, wind, etc.*: roar; *siren*: wail; *F p.* howl, cry.

**'Heu|schnupfen** ♂ *m* hay-fever; **~schrecke** *zo.* ['~ʃrɛkə] *f* (-/-n) grasshopper, locust.

**heut|e** ['hɔytə] today; *~ abend* this evening, tonight; *~ früh, ~ morgen* this morning; *~ in acht Tagen* today *or* this day week; *~ vor acht Tagen* a week ago today; **'~ig** *adj.* this day's, today's; present; **~zutage** *adv.* ['hɔytsuːtaːgə] nowadays, these days.

**Hexe** ['hɛksə] *f* (-/-n) witch, sorceress; *fig.*: hell-cat; hag; **2n** *v/i.* (ge-, *h*) practice witchcraft; *F fig.* work miracles; **'~nkessel** *fig. m* inferno; **'~nmeister** *m* wizard, sorcerer; **'~nschuß** ♂ *m* lumbago; **~rei** [~'raı] *f* (-/-en) witchcraft, sorcery, magic.

**Hieb** [hiːp] **1.** *m* (-[e]s/-e) blow, stroke; lash, cut (*of whip, etc.*); *a.* punch (*with fist*); *fenc.* cut; *~e pl.* hiding, thrashing; **2.** ♀ *pret.* of hauen.

**hielt** [hiːlt] *pret.* of halten.

**hier** *adv.* [hiːr] here; in this place; *~! present!*; *~ entlang!* this way!

**hier|an** *adv.* ['hiːˀran, *when emphatic* 'hiːran] at *or* by *or* in *or* on *or* to it *or* this; **~auf** *adv.* ['hiːˀrauf, *when emphatic* 'hiːrauf] on it *or* this; after this *or* that, then; **~aus** *adv.* ['hiːˀraus, *when emphatic* 'hiːraus] from *or* out of it *or* this; **~bei** *adv.* ['hiːˀbaɪ, *when emphatic* 'hiːrbaɪ] here; in this case, in connection with this; **~durch** *adv.* ['hiːr'durç, *when emphatic* 'hiːrdurç] through here; by this, hereby; **~für** *adv.* ['hiːˀfyːr, *when emphatic* 'hiːrfyːr] for it *or* this; **~her** *adv.* ['hiːr'heːr, *when emphatic* 'hiːrheːr] here, hither; *bis ~* as far as here; **~in** *adv.* ['hiːˀrin, *when emphatic* 'hiːrin] in it *or* this; in here; **~mit** *adv.* ['hiːr'mit, *when emphatic* 'hiːrmit] with it *or* this, herewith; **~nach** *adv.* ['hiːr'naːx, *when emphatic* 'hiːrnaːx] after it *or* this; according to this; **~über** *adv.* ['hiːˀryːbər, *when emphatic* 'hiːryːbər] over it *or* this; over here; on this (subject); **~unter** *adv.* ['hiːˀruntər, *when emphatic* 'hiːruntər] under it *or* this; among these; by this *or* that; **~von** *adv.* ['hiːr'fɔn, *when emphatic* 'hiːrfɔn] of *or* from it *or* this; **~zu** *adv.* ['hiːr'tsuː, *when emphatic* 'hiːrtsuː]

with it *or* this; (in addition) to this.

**hiesig** *adj.* ['hi:zɪç] of *or* in this place *or* town, local.

**hieß** [hi:s] *pret. of* heißen.

**Hilfe** ['hilfə] *f* (-/-n) help; aid, assistance; succour; relief (*für* to); **~!** help!; *mit* ~ *von* with the help *or* aid of; '**~ruf** *m* shout *or* cry for help.

**'hilf|los** *adj.* helpless; '**~reich** *adj.* helpful.

**'Hilfs|aktion** *f* relief measures *pl.*; '**~arbeiter** *m* unskilled worker *or* labo(u)rer; '**2bedürftig** *adj.* needy, indigent; '**~lehrer** *m* assistant teacher; '**~mittel** *n* aid; device; remedy; expedient; '**~motor** *m*: *Fahrrad mit* ~ motor-assisted bicycle; '**~quelle** *f* resource; '**~schule** *f* elementary school for backward children; '**~werk** *n* relief organization. [berry.]

**Himbeere** ♀ ['himbe:rə] *f* rasp-)

**Himmel** ['hɪməl] *m* (-s/-) sky, heavens *pl.*; *eccl.*, *fig.* heaven; '**~bett** *n* tester-bed; '**2blau** *adj.* sky-blue; '**~fahrt** *eccl.* *f* ascension (of Christ); Ascension-day; '**2schreiend** *adj.* crying.

**'Himmels|gegend** *f* region of the sky; cardinal point; '**~körper** *m* celestial body; '**~richtung** *f* point of the compass, cardinal point; direction; '**~strich** *m* region, climate zone.

**'himmlisch** *adj.* celestial, heavenly.

**hin** *adv.* [hɪn] there; gone, lost; ~ *und her* to and fro, *Am.* back and forth; ~ *und wieder* now and again *or* then; ~ *und zurück* there and back.

**hinab** *adv.* [hi'nap] down; **~steigen** *v/i.* (*irr.* steigen, *sep.*, -ge-, *sein*) climb down, descend.

**hinarbeiten** ['hɪnⁱ-] *v/i.* (*sep.*, -ge-, h): ~ *auf* (*acc.*) work for *or* towards.

**hinauf** *adv.* [hi'nauf] up (there); upstairs; **~gehen** *v/i.* (*irr.* gehen, *sep.*, -ge-, *sein*) go up(stairs); *prices, wages, etc.*: go up, rise; **~steigen** *v/i.* (*irr.* steigen, *sep.*, -ge-, *sein*) climb up, ascend.

**hinaus** *adv.* [hi'naus] out; ~ *mit euch!* out with you!; *auf (viele) Jahre* ~ for (many) years (to come); **~gehen** *v/i.* (*irr.* gehen, *sep.*, -ge-, *sein*) go *or* walk out; ~ *über* (*acc.*) go beyond, exceed; ~ *auf* (*acc.*) *window, etc.*: look out on, overlook; *intention, etc.*: drive *or* aim at; **~laufen** *v/i.* (*irr.* laufen, *sep.*, -ge-, *sein*) run *or* rush out; ~ *auf* (*acc.*) come *or* amount to; **~schieben** *fig.* *v/t.* (*irr.* schieben, *sep.*, -ge-, h) put off, postpone, defer; **~werfen** *v/t.* (*irr.* werfen, *sep.*, -ge-, h) throw out (*aus* of); turn *or* throw *or* F chuck *s.o.* out.

**'Hin|blick** *m*: *im* ~ *auf* (*acc.*) in view of, with regard to; '**2bringen** *v/t.* (*irr.* bringen, *sep.*, -ge-, h) take there; while away, pass (*time*).

**hinder|lich** *adj.* ['hɪndərlɪç] hindering, impeding; *j-m* ~ *sein* be in s.o.'s way; '**~n** *v/t.* (ge-, h) hinder, hamper (*bei, in* at, in); ~ *an* (*dat.*) prevent from; '**2nis** *n* (-ses/-se) hindrance; *sports*: obstacle; *turf, etc.*: fence; '**2nisrennen** *n* obstacle-race.

**hin'durch** *adv.* through; all through, throughout; across.

**hinein** *adv.* [hi'naɪn] in; ~ *mit dir!* in you go!; **~gehen** *v/i.* (*irr.* gehen, *sep.*, -ge-, *sein*) go in; ~ *in* (*acc.*) go into; *in den Topf gehen ... hinein* the pot holds *or* takes ...

**'Hin|fahrt** *f* journey *or* way there; '**2fallen** *v/i.* (*irr.* fallen, *sep.*, -ge-, *sein*) fall (down); '**2fällig** *adj.* p. frail; *regulation, etc.*: invalid; ~ *machen* invalidate, render invalid.

**hing** [hɪŋ] *pret. of* hängen 1.

**'Hin|gabe** *f* devotion (*an acc.* to); '**2geben** *v/t.* (*irr.* geben, *sep.*, -ge-, h) give up *or* away; *sich* ~ (*dat.*) give o.s. to; devote o.s. to; '**~gebung** *f* (-/-en) devotion; '**2gehen** *v/i.* (*irr.* gehen, *sep.*, -ge-, *sein*) go *or* walk there; go (*zu* to); *path, etc.*: lead there; lead (*zu* to *a place*); '**2halten** *v/t.* (*irr.* halten, *sep.*, -ge-, h) hold out (*object, etc.*); put *s.o.* off.

**hinken** ['hɪŋkən] *v/i.* (ge-) 1. (h) limp (*auf dem rechten Fuß* with one's right leg), have a limp; 2. (*sein*) limp (along).

**'hin|länglich** *adj.* sufficient, adequate; '**~legen** *v/t.* (*sep.*, -ge-, h) lay *or* put down; *sich* ~ lie down; '**~nehmen** *v/t.* (*irr.* nehmen, *sep.*, -ge-, h) accept, take; put up with; '**~raffen** *v/t.* (*sep.*, -ge-, h) *death, etc.*: snatch *s.o.* away, carry *s.o.* off; '**~reichen** (*sep.*, -ge-, h) 1. *v/t.* reach *or* stretch *or* hold out (*dat.* to); 2. *v/i.* suffice; '**~reißen** *fig.* *v/t.* (*irr.* reißen, *sep.*, -ge-, h) carry away; enrapture, ravish; '**~reißend** *adj.* ravishing, captivating; '**~richten** *v/t.* (*sep.*, -ge-, h) execute, put to death; '**2richtung** *f* execution; '**~setzen** *v/t.* (*sep.*, -ge-, h) set *or* put down; *sich* ~ sit down; '**2sicht** *f* regard, respect; *in* ~ *auf* (*acc.*) = '**~sichtlich** *prp.* (*gen.*) with regard to, as to, concerning; '**~stellen** *v/t.* (*sep.*, -ge-, h) place; put; put down; *et.* ~ *als* represent s.th. as; make s.th. appear (as).

**hintan|setzen** [hɪnt'an-] *v/t.* (*sep.*, -ge-, h) set aside; **2setzung** *f* (-/-en) setting aside; **~stellen** *v/t.* (*sep.*, -ge-, h) set aside; **2stellung** *f* (-/-en) setting aside.

**hinten** *adv.* ['hɪntən] behind, at the

back; in the background; in the rear.

**hinter** *prp.* ['hintər] **1.** (*dat.*) behind, *Am. a.* back of; ~ *sich lassen* outdistance; **2.** (*acc.*) behind; '2bein *n* hind leg; 2bliebenen *pl.* [~'bli:bə-nən] *the* bereaved *pl.*; surviving dependants *pl.*; ~'bringen *v/t.* (*irr.* bringen, *no* -ge-, *h*): *j-m et.* ~ inform s.o. of s.th. (secretly); ~ei'nander *adv.* one after the other; in succession; '2gedanke *m* ulterior motive; ~'gehen *v/t.* (*irr.* gehen, *no* -ge-, *h*) deceive, F doublecross; 2'gehung *f* (-/-en) deception; '2grund *m* background (*a. fig.*); '2halt *m* ambush; ~hältig *adj.* ['~hɛltiç] insidious; underhand; '2haus *n* back *or* rear building; ~'her *adv.* behind; afterwards; '2hof *m* backyard; '2kopf *m* back of the head; ~'lassen *v/t.* (*irr.* lassen, *no* -ge-, *h*) leave (behind); 2'lassenschaft *f* (-/-en) property (left), estate; ~'legen *v/t.* (*no* -ge-, *h*) deposit, lodge (*bei* with); 2'legung *f* (-/-en) deposit(ion); '2list *f* deceit; craftiness; insidiousness; '2listig *adj.* deceitful; crafty; insidious; '2mann *m* ✕ rear-rank man; *fig.*: † subsequent endorser; *pol.* backer; wire-puller; instigator; '2n F *m* (-s/-) backside, behind, bottom; '2rad *n* rear wheel; ~rücks *adv.* ['~ryks] from behind; *fig.* behind his, *etc.* back; '2seite *f* back; '2teil *n* back (part); rear (part); F *s.* Hintern; ~'treiben *v/t.* (*irr.* treiben, *no* -ge-, *h*) thwart, frustrate; '2treppe *f* backstairs *pl.*; '2tür *f* back door; ~'ziehen ⚖ *v/t.* (*irr.* ziehen, *no* -ge-, *h*) evade (*tax, duty, etc.*); 2'ziehung *f* evasion.

**hinüber** *adv.* [hi'ny:bər] over (there); across.

**Hin- und 'Rückfahrt** *f* journey there and back, *Am.* round trip.

**hinunter** *adv.* [hi'nuntər] down (there); downstairs; ~schlucken *v/t.* (*sep.*, -ge-, *h*) swallow (down); *fig.* swallow.

'**Hinweg**[1] *m* way there *or* out.

**hinweg**[2] *adv.* [hin'vɛk] away, off; ~gehen *v/i.* (*irr.* gehen, *sep.*, -ge-sein): ~ *über* (*acc.*) go *or* walk over *or* across; *fig.* pass over, ignore; ~kommen *v/i.* (*irr.* kommen, *sep.*, -ge-, *sein*): ~ *über* (*acc.*) get over (*a. fig.*); ~sehen *v/i.* (*irr.* sehen, *sep.*, -ge-, *h*): ~ *über* (*acc.*) see *or* look over; *fig.* overlook, shut one's eyes to; ~setzen *v/refl.* (*sep.*, -ge-, *h*): *sich* ~ *über* (*acc.*) ignore, disregard, make light of.

**Hin|weis** ['hinvaıs] *m* (-es/-e) reference (*auf acc.* to); hint (at); indication (of); 2weisen (*irr.* weisen, *sep.*, -ge-, *h*) **1.** *v/t.*: *j-n* ~ *auf* (*acc.*) draw *or* call s.o.'s attention to; **2.** *v/i.*: ~

*auf* (*acc.*) point at *or* to, indicate (*a. fig.*); *fig.*: point out; hint at; '2werfen *v/t.* (*irr.* werfen, *sep.*, -ge-, *h*) throw down; *fig.*: dash off (*sketch, etc.*); say *s.th.* casually; '2wirken *v/i.* (*sep.*, -ge-, *h*): ~ *auf* (*acc.*) work towards; use one's influence to; '2ziehen (*irr.* ziehen, *sep.*, -ge-) **1.** *fig. v/t.* (*h*) attract *or* draw there; *sich* ~ *space:* extend (*bis zu* to), stretch (to); *time:* drag on; **2.** *v/i.* (*sein*) go *or* move there; '2zielen *v/i.* (*sep.*, -ge-, *h*): ~ *auf* (*acc.*) aim *or* drive at.

**hin'zu** *adv.* there; near; in addition; ~fügen *v/t.* (*sep.*, -ge-, *h*) add (zu to) (*a. fig.*); 2fügung *f* (-/-en) addition; ~kommen *v/i.* (*irr.* kommen, *sep.*, -ge-, *sein*) come up (zu to); supervene; be added; *es kommt (noch) hinzu, daß* add to this that, (and) moreover; ~rechnen *v/t.* (*sep.*, -ge-, *h*) add (zu to), include (in, among); ~setzen *v/t.* (*sep.*, -ge-, *h*) *s. hinzufügen*; ~treten *v/i.* (*irr.* treten, *sep.*, -ge-, *sein*) *s. hinzukommen*; join; ~ziehen *v/t.* (*irr.* ziehen, *sep.*, -ge-, *h*) call in (*doctor, etc.*).

**Hirn** [hirn] *n* (-[e]s/-e) *anat.* brain; *fig.* brains *pl.*, mind; '~gespinst *n* figment of the mind, chimera; '~los *fig. adj.* brainless, senseless; '~schale *anat. f* brain-pan, cranium; '~schlag ⚕ *m* apoplexy; '2verbrannt *adj.* crazy, F crack-brained, cracky.

**Hirsch** *zo.* [hirʃ] *m* (-es/-e) *species:* deer; stag, hart; '~geweih *n* (stag's) antlers *pl.*; '~kuh *f* hind; '~leder *n* buckskin, deerskin.

**Hirse** ♣ ['hirzə] *f* (-/-n) millet.

**Hirt** [hirt] *m* (-en/-en), ~e ['~ə] *m* (-n/-n) herdsman; shepherd.

**hissen** ['hisən] *v/t.* (ge-, *h*) hoist, raise (*flag*); ⚓ *a.* trice up (*sail*).

**Histori|ker** [hi'sto:rikər] *m* (-s/-) historian; 2sch *adj.* historic(al).

**Hitz|e** ['hitsə] *f* (-/*no pl.*) heat; 2ebeständig *adj.* heat-resistant, heat-proof; '~ewelle *f* heat-wave, hot spell; '2ig *adj. p.* hot-tempered, hot-headed; *discussion:* heated; '~kopf *m* hothead; '~schlag ⚕ *m* heat-stroke.

**hob** [ho:p] *pret. of* heben.

**Hobel** ⊕ ['ho:bəl] *m* (-s/-) plane; '~bank *f* carpenter's bench; '2n *v/t.* (ge-, *h*) plane.

**hoch** [ho:x] **1.** *adj.* high; *church spire, tree, etc.:* tall; *position, etc.:* high, important; *guest, etc.:* distinguished; *punishment, etc.:* heavy, severe; *age:* great, old; *hohe See* open sea, high seas *pl.*; **2.** *adv.:* ~ *lebe ...!* long live ...! **3.** 2 *n* (-s/-s) cheer; toast; *meteorology:* high (-pressure area).

'**hoch|achten** *v/t.* (*sep.*, -ge-, *h*) esteem highly; '2achtung *f* high esteem *or* respect; '~achtungsvoll **1.** *adj.* (most) respectful; **2.** *adv.* correspondence: yours faithfully *or* sincerely, *esp. Am.* yours truly; '²adel *m* greater *or* higher nobility; '²amt *eccl. n* high mass; '²antenne *f* overhead aerial; '²bahn *f* elevated *or* overhead railway, *Am.* elevated railroad; '²betrieb *m* intense activity, rush; '²burg *fig. f* stronghold; '~deutsch *adj.* High *or* standard German; '²druck *m* high pressure (*a. fig.*); *mit* ~ *arbeiten* work at high pressure; '²ebene *f* plateau, tableland; '~fahrend *adj.* highhanded, arrogant; '~fein *adj.* superfine; '²form *f*: *in* ~ in top form; '²frequenz *≠ f* high frequency; '²gebirge *n* high mountains *pl.*; '²genuß *m* great enjoyment; '²glanz *m* high polish; '²haus *n* multi-stor(e)y building, skyscraper; '~herzig *adj.* nobleminded; generous; '²herzigkeit *f* (-/-en) noble-mindedness; generosity; '²konjunktur *† f* boom, business prosperity; '²land *n* upland(s *pl.*), highlands *pl.*; '²mut *m* arrogance, haughtiness; ~mütig *adj.* ['~my:tiç] arrogant, haughty; ~näsig F *adj.* ['~nɛ:ziç] stuck-up; '²ofen ⊕ *m* blast-furnace; '~'rot *adj.* bright red; '²saison *f* peak season, height of the season; '~schätzen *v/t.* (*sep.*, *-ge-*, *h*) esteem highly; '²schule *f* university; academy; '²seefischerei *f* deep-sea fishing; '²sommer *m* midsummer; '²spannung *≠ f* high tension *or* voltage; '²sprung *m sports*: high jump.

**höchst** [hø:çst] **1.** *adj.* highest; *fig. a.*: supreme; extreme; **2.** *adv.* highly, most, extremely.

**Hochstap|elei** [ho:xʃtɑːpəˈlaɪ] *f* (-/-en) swindling; '~ler *m* (-s/-) confidence man, swindler.

**höchstens** *adv.* ['hø:çstəns] at (the) most, at best.

'**Höchst|form** *f sports*: top form; '~geschwindigkeit *f* maximum speed; speed limit; '~leistung *f sports*: record (performance); ⊕ maximum output (*of machine, etc.*); '~lohn *m* maximum wages *pl.*; '~maß *n* maximum; '~preis *m* maximum price.

'**hoch|trabend** *fig. adj.* high-flown; pompous; '²verrat *m* high treason; '²wald *m* high forest; '²wasser *n* high tide *or* water; flood; '~wertig *adj.* high-grade, high-class; '²wild *n* big game; '²wohlgeboren *m* (-s/-) Right Hono(u)rable.

**Hochzeit** ['hɔxtsaɪt] *f* (-/-en) wedding; marriage; '²lich *adj.* bridal, nuptial; '~sgeschenk *n* wedding present; '~sreise *f* honeymoon (trip).

**Hocke** ['hɔkə] *f* (-/-n) *gymnastics*: squat-vault; *skiing*: crouch; '²n *v/i.* (ge-, h) squat, crouch; '~r *m* (-s/-) stool.

**Höcker** ['hœkər] *m* (-s/-) *surface, etc.*: bump; *camel, etc.*: hump; *p.* hump, hunch; '²ig *adj. animal*: humped; *p.* humpbacked, hunchbacked; *surface, etc.*: bumpy, rough, uneven.

**Hode** *anat.* ['ho:də] *m* (-n/-n), *f* (-/-n), '~n *anat. m* (-s/-) testicle.

**Hof** [ho:f] *m* (-[e]s/∹e) court(yard); farm; *king, etc.*: court; *ast.* halo; *j-m den* ~ *machen* court s.o.; '~dame *f* lady-in-waiting; '²fähig *adj.* presentable at court.

**Hoffart** ['hɔfart] *f* (-/*no pl.*) arrogance, haughtiness; pride.

**hoffen** ['hɔfən] (ge-, h) **1.** *v/i.* hope (*auf acc.* for); trust (in); **2.** *v/t.*: *das Beste* ~ hope for the best; '~t-lich *adv.* it is to be hoped that, I hope, let's hope.

**Hoffnung** ['hɔfnʊŋ] *f* (-/-en) hope (*auf acc.* for, of); *in der* ~ *zu inf.* in the hope of *ger.*, hoping to *inf.*; *s-e* ~ *setzen auf* (*acc.*) pin one's hopes on; '²slos *adj.* hopeless; '²svoll *adj.* hopeful; promising.

'**Hofhund** *m* watch-dog.

**höfisch** *adj.* ['hø:fiʃ] courtly.

**höflich** *adj.* ['hø:fliç] polite, civil, courteous (*gegen* to); '²keit *f* (-/-en) politeness, civility, courtesy.

'**Hofstaat** *m* royal *or* princely household; suite, retinue.

**Höhe** ['hø:ə] *f* (-/-n) height; 久, ℬ, *ast.*, *geogr.* altitude; hill; peak; amount (*of bill, etc.*); size (*of sum, fine, etc.*); level (*of price, etc.*); severity (*of punishment, etc.*); ♪ pitch; *in gleicher* ~ *mit* on a level with; *auf der* ~ *sein* be up to the mark; *in die* ~ up(wards).

**Hoheit** ['ho:haɪt] *f* (-/-en) *pol.* sovereignty; *title*: Highness; '~sgebiet *n* (sovereign) territory; '~sgewässer *n/pl.* territorial waters *pl.*; '~szeichen *n* national emblem.

'**Höhen|kurort** *m* high-altitude health resort; '~luft *f* mountain air; '~sonne *f* mountain sun; ⚡ ultra-violet lamp; '~steuer ⚡ *n* elevator; '~zug *m* mountain range.

'**Höhepunkt** *m* highest point; *ast.*, *fig.* culmination, zenith; *fig. a.*: climax; summit, peak.

**hohl** *adj.* [ho:l] hollow (*a. fig.*); *cheeks, etc.*: sunken; *hand*: cupped; *sound*: hollow, dull.

**Höhle** ['hø:lə] *f* (-/-n) cave, cavern; den, lair (*of bear, lion, etc.*) (*both a. fig.*); hole, burrow (*of fox, rabbit, etc.*); hollow, cavity.

'**Hohl|maß** *n* dry measure; '~raum *m* hollow, cavity; '~spiegel *m* concave mirror.

**Höhlung** ['høːluŋ] *f* (-/-en) excavation; hollow, cavity.

'**Hohlweg** *m* defile.

**Hohn** [hoːn] *m* (-[e]s/*no pl.*) scorn, disdain; derision.

**höhnen** ['høːnən] *v/i.* (ge-, *h*) sneer, jeer, mock, scoff (*über acc.* at).

'**Hohngelächter** *n* scornful *or* derisive laughter.

'**höhnisch** *adj.* scornful; sneering, derisive.

**Höker** ['høːkər] *m* (-s/-) hawker, huckster; '**2n** *v/i.* (ge-, *h*) huckster, hawk about.

**holen** ['hoːlən] *v/t.* (ge-, *h*) fetch; go for; *a. ~ lassen* send for; draw (*breath*); *sich e-e Krankheit ~* catch a disease; *sich bei j-m Rat ~* seek s.o.'s advice.

**Holländer** ['hɔlɛndər] *m* (-s/-) Dutchman.

**Hölle** ['hœlə] *f* (-/°-n) hell.

'**Höllen|angst** *fig. f:* e-e ~ *haben* be in a mortal fright *or* F blue funk; '**_lärm** F *fig. m* infernal noise; '**_maschine** *f* infernal machine, time bomb; '**_pein** F *fig. f* torment of hell.

'**höllisch** *adj.* hellish, infernal (*both a. fig.*).

**holper|ig** *adj.* ['hɔlpəriç] *surface, road, etc.:* bumpy, rough, uneven; *vehicle, etc.:* jolty, jerky; *verse, style, etc.:* rough, jerky; '**_n** (ge-) 1. *v/i.* (sein) *vehicle:* jolt, bump; 2. *v/i.* (*h*) *vehicle:* jolt, bump; be jolty *or* bumpy.

**Holunder** & [hɔ'lundər] *m* (-s/-) elder.

**Holz** [hɔlts] *n* (-es/°er) wood; timber, *Am.* lumber; '**_bau** ⚠ *m* wooden structure; '**_bildhauer** *m* woodcarver; '**_blasinstrument** ♪ *n* woodwind instrument; '**_boden** *m* wood(en) floor; wood-loft.

**hölzern** *adj.* ['hœltsərn] wooden; *fig. a.* clumsy, awkward.

'**Holz|fäller** *m* (-s/-) woodcutter, woodman, *Am. a.* lumberjack, logger; '**_hacker** *m* (-s/-) woodchopper, woodcutter, *Am.* lumberjack; '**_händler** *m* wood *or* timber merchant, *Am.* lumberman; '**_haus** *n* wooden house, *Am.* frame house; '**2ig** *adj.* woody; '**_kohle** *f* charcoal; '**_platz** *m* wood *or* timber vard, *Am.* lumberyard; '**_schnitt** *m* woodcut, wood-engraving; '**_schnitzer** *m* wood-carver; '**_schuh** *m* wooden shoe, clog; '**_stoß** *m* pile *or* stack of wood; stake; '**_weg** *fig. m: auf dem ~ sein* be on the wrong track; '**_wolle** *f* wood-wool; fine wood shavings *pl., Am. a.* excelsior.

**Homöopath** ♪ [homøo'paːt] *m* (-en/-en) hom(o)eopath(ist); **_ie** [__a'tiː] *f* (-/*no pl.*) hom(o)eopathy; **2isch** *adj.* [__'paːtiʃ] hom(o)eopathic.

**Honig** ['hoːniç] *m* (-s/-e) honey; '**_kuchen** *m* honey-cake; gingerbread; '**2süß** *adj.* honey-sweet, honeyed (*a. fig.*); '**_wabe** *f* honeycomb.

**Honor|ar** [hono'raːr] *n* (-s/-e) fee; royalties *pl.*; salary; **_atioren** [__a-'tsjoːrən] *pl.* notabilities *pl.*; **2ieren** [__'riːrən] *v/t.* (*no* -ge-, *h*) fee, pay a fee to; ✝ hono(u)r, meet (*bill of exchange*).

**Hopfen** ['hɔpfən] *m* (-s/-) & hop; *brewing:* hops *pl.*

**hops|a** *int.* ['hɔpsa] (wh)oops!; upsadaisy!; '**_en** F *v/i.* (ge-, sein) hop, jump.

**hörbar** *adj.* ['høːrbaːr] audible.

**horch|en** ['hɔrçən] *v/i.* (ge-, *h*) listen (*auf acc.* to); eavesdrop; '**2er** *m* (-s/-) eavesdropper.

**Horde** ['hɔrdə] *f* (-/-n) horde, gang.

**hör|en** ['høːrən] (ge-, *h*) 1. *v/t.* hear; listen (in) to (*radio*); attend (*lecture, etc.*); hear, learn; 2. *v/i.* hear (*von dat.* from); listen; ~ *auf* (*acc.*) listen to; *schwer ~* be hard of hearing; ~ *Sie mal!* look here!; I say!; '**2er** *m* (-s/-) hearer; *radio:* listener(-in); *univ.* student; *teleph.* receiver; '**2erschaft** *f* (-/-en) audience; '**2gerät** *n* hearing aid; '**2ig** *adj.: j-m ~ sein* be enslaved to s.o.; '**2igkeit** *f* (-/*no pl.*) subjection.

**Horizont** [hori'tsɔnt] *m* (-[e]s/-e) horizon; skyline; *s-n ~ erweitern* broaden one's mind; *das geht über meinen ~* that's beyond me; **2al** *adj.* [__'taːl] horizontal.

**Hormon** [hɔr'moːn] *n* (-s/-e) hormone.

**Horn** [hɔrn] *n* 1. (-[e]s/°er) horn (*of bull*); ♪, *mot., etc.:* horn; ⚔ bugle; peak; 2. (-[e]s/-e) horn, horny matter; '**_haut** *f* horny skin; *anat.* cornea (*on eye*).

**Hornisse** *zo.* [hɔr'nisə] *f* (-/-n) hornet.

**Hornist** ♪ [hɔr'nist] *m* (-en/-en) horn-player; ⚔ bugler.

**Horoskop** [horo'skoːp] *n* (-s/-e) horoscope; *j-m das ~ stellen* cast s.o.'s horoscope.

'**Hör|rohr** *n* ear-trumpet; ⚕ stethoscope; '**_saal** *m* lecture-hall; '**_spiel** *n* radio play; '**_weite** *f: in ~* within earshot.

**Hose** ['hoːzə] *f* (-/-n) (e-e a pair of) trousers *pl. or Am.* pants *pl.*; slacks *pl.*

'**Hosen|klappe** *f* flap; '**_latz** ['__lats] *m* (-es/°e) flap; fly; '**_tasche** *f* trouser-pocket; '**_träger** *m:* (*ein Paar*) ~ *pl.* (a pair of) braces *pl. or Am.* suspenders *pl.*

**Hospital** [hɔspi'taːl] *n* (-s/-e, °er) hospital.

**Hostie** *eccl.* ['hɔstjə] *f* (-/-n) host, consecrated *or* holy wafer.

**Hotel** [ho'tɛl] *n* (-s/-s) hotel; **_besitzer** *m* hotel owner *or* proprietor;

~gewerbe *n* hotel industry; ~ier [~'je:] *m* (-s/-s) hotel-keeper.

Hub ⊕ [hu:p] *m* (-[e]s/=e) *mot.* stroke (*of piston*); lift (*of valve, etc.*); '~raum *mot. m* capacity.

hübsch *adj.* [hypʃ] pretty, nice; good-looking, handsome; attractive.

'Hubschrauber ✈ *m* (-s/-) helicopter.

Huf [hu:f] *m* (-[e]s/-e) hoof; '~eisen *n* horseshoe; '~schlag *m* hoof-beat; (horse's) kick; '~schmied *m* farrier.

Hüft|e *anat.* ['hyftə] *f* (-/-n) hip; *esp. zo.* haunch; '~gelenk *n* hip-joint; '~gürtel *m* girdle; suspender belt, *Am.* garter belt.

Hügel ['hy:gəl] *m* (-s/-) hill(ock); 'Qig *adj.* hilly.

Huhn *orn.* [hu:n] *n* (-[e]s/=er) fowl, chicken; hen; *junges* ~ chicken.

Hühnchen ['hy:nçən] *n* (-s/-) chicken; *ein* ~ *zu rupfen haben* have a bone to pick (*mit* with).

Hühner|auge ✱ ['hy:nər-] *n* corn; '~ei *n* hen's egg; '~hof *m* poultry-yard, *Am.* chicken yard; '~hund *zo. m* pointer, setter; '~leiter *f* chicken-ladder.

Huld [hult] *f* (-/*no pl.*) grace, favo(u)r; Qigen ['~digən] *v/i.* (*dat.*) (ge-, *h*) pay homage to (*sovereign, lady, etc.*); indulge in (*vice, etc.*); '~igung *f* (-/-en) homage; Qreich *adj.*, 'Qvoll *adj.* gracious.

Hülle ['hylə] *f* (-/-n) cover(ing), wrapper; *letter, balloon, etc.*: envelope; *book, etc.*: jacket; *umbrella, etc.*: sheath; 'Qn *v/t.* (ge-, *h*) wrap, cover, envelope (*a. fig.*); *sich in Schwelgen* ~ wrap o.s. in silence.

Hülse ['hylzə] *f* (-/-n) legume, pod (*of leguminous plant*); husk, hull (*of rice, etc.*); skin (*of pea, etc.*); ✱ case; '~nfrucht *f* legume(n); leguminous plant; '~nfrüchte *f/pl.* pulse.

human *adj.* [hu'ma:n] humane; Qität [~ani'tɛ:t] *f* (-/*no pl.*) humanity.

Hummel *zo.* ['huməl] *f* (-/-n) bumble-bee.

Hummer *zo.* ['humər] *m* (-s/-) lobster.

Humor [hu'mo:r] *m* (-s/✱-e) humo(u)r; ~ist [~o'rist] *m* (-en/-en) humorist; Qistisch *adj.* [~o'ristiʃ] humorous.

humpeln ['humpəln] *v/i.* (ge-) 1. (*sein*) hobble (along), limp (along); 2. (*h*) (have a) limp, walk with a limp.

Hund [hunt] *m* (-[e]s/-e) *zo.* dog; ✱ tub; *ast.* dog, canis; *auf den* ~ *kommen* go to the dogs.

'Hunde|hütte *f* dog-kennel, *Am. a.* doghouse; '~kuchen *m* dog-biscuit; '~leine *f* (dog-)lead *or* leash; '~peitsche *f* dog-whip.

hundert ['hundərt] 1. *adj.* a *or* one hundred; 2. Q *n* (-s/-e) hundred; *fünf vom* ~ *five per cent; zu* ~*en by hundreds*; '~fach *adj.*, '~fältig *adj.* hundredfold; Q'jahrfeier *f* centenary, *Am. a.* centennial; '~jährig *adj.* ['~jɛ:riç] centenary, a hundred years old; '~st *adj.* hundredth.

'Hunde|sperre *f* muzzling-order; '~steuer *f* dog tax.

Hündi|n *zo.* ['hyndin] *f* (-/-nen) bitch, she-dog; 'Qsch *adj.* doggish; *fig.* servile, cringing.

'hunds|ge'mein F *adj.* dirty, mean, scurvy; '~mise'rabel F *adj.* rotten, wretched, lousy; 'Qtage *m/pl.* dogdays *pl.*

Hüne ['hy:nə] *m* (-n/-n) giant.

Hunger ['huŋər] *m* (-s/*no pl.*) hunger (*fig. nach* for); ~ *bekommen* get hungry; ~ *haben* be *or* feel hungry; '~kur *f* starvation cure; '~leider F *m* (-s/-) starveling, poor devil; '~lohn *m* starvation wages *pl.*; 'Qn *v/i.* (ge-, *h*) hunger (*fig. nach* after, for); go without food; ~ *lassen* starve *s.o.*; '~snot *f* famine; '~streik *m* hunger-strike; '~tod *m* death from starvation; '~tuch *fig. n*: *am* ~ *nagen* have nothing to bite.

'hungrig *adj.* hungry (*fig. nach* for).

Hupe *mot.* ['hu:pə] *f* (-/-n) horn, hooter; klaxon; 'Qn *v/i.* (ge-, *h*) sound one's horn, hoot.

hüpfen ['hypfən] *v/i.* (ge-, *sein*) hip, skip; gambol, frisk (about).

Hürde ['hyrdə] *f* (-/-n) hurdle; fold, pen; '~nrennen *n* hurdle-race.

Hure ['hu:rə] *f* (-/-n) whore, prostitute.

hurtig *adj.* ['hurtiç] quick, swift; agile, nimble.

Husar ✕ [hu'za:r] *m* (-en/-en) hussar.

husch *int.* [huʃ] in *or* like a flash; shoo!; '~en *v/i.* (ge-, *sein*) slip, dart; *small animal*: scurry, scamper; *bat, etc.*: flit.

hüsteln ['hy:stəln] 1. *v/i.* (ge-, *h*) cough slightly; 2. Q *n* (-s/*no pl.*) slight cough.

husten ['hu:stən] 1. *v/i.* (ge-, *h*) cough; 2. Q *m* (-s/✱-) cough.

Hut [hu:t] 1. *m* (-[e]s/=e) hat; *den* ~ *abnehmen* take off one's hat; ~ *ab vor* (*dat.*)! hats off to ...!; 2. *f* (-/*no pl.*) care, charge; guard; *auf der* ~ *sein* be on one's guard (*vor dat.* against).

hüte|n ['hy:tən] *v/t.* (ge-, *h*) guard, protect, keep watch over; keep (*secret*); tend (*sheep, etc.*); *das Bett* ~ be confined to (one's bed); *sich* ~ *vor* (*dat.*) beware of; 'Qr *m* (-s/-) keeper, guardian; herdsman.

'Hut|futter *n* hat-lining; '~krempe *f* hat-brim; '~macher *m* (-s/-) hatter; '~nadel *f* hat-pin.

Hütte ['hytə] *f* (-/-n) hut; cottage, cabin; ⊕ metallurgical plant; *mount.*

refuge; '~nwesen ⊕ *n* metallurgy, metallurgical engineering.
**Hyäne** *zo.* [hy'ɛ:nə] *f* (-/-n) hy(a)ena.
**Hyazinthe** ⚘ [hya'tsintə] *f* (-/-n) hyacinth.
**Hydrant** [hy'drant] *m* (-en/-en) hydrant.
**Hydrauli|k** *phys.* [hy'draulik] *f* (-/no pl.) hydraulics *pl.*; **2sch** *adj.* hydraulic.
**Hygien|e** [hy'gje:nə] *f* (-/no pl.) hygiene; **2isch** *adj.* hygienic(al).
**Hymne** ['hymnə] *f* (-/-n) hymn.
**Hypno|se** [hyp'no:zə] *f* (-/-n) hypnosis; **2tisieren** [~oti'zi:rən] *v/t.* and *v/i.* (no -ge-, h) hypnotize.
**Hypochond|er** [hypo'xɔndər] *m* (-s/-) hypochondriac; **2risch** *adj.* hypochondriac.
**Hypotenuse** ⩓ [hypote'nu:zə] *f* (-/-n) hypotenuse.
**Hypothek** [hypo'te:k] *f* (-/-en) mortgage; e-e ~ *aufnehmen* raise a mortgage; **2arisch** *adj.* [~e'ka:riʃ]: ~e *Belastung* mortgage.
**Hypothe|se** [hypo'te:zə] *f* (-/-n) hypothesis; **2tisch** *adj.* hypothetical.
**Hyster|ie** *psych.* [hyste'ri:] *f* (-/-n) hysteria; **2isch** *psych. adj.* [~'te:riʃ] hysterical.

# I

**ich** [iç] 1. *pers. pron.* I; 2. 2 *n* (-[s]/-[s]) self; *psych. the* ego.
**Ideal** [ide'a:l] 1. *n* (-s/-e) ideal; 2. 2 *adj.* ideal; **2isieren** [~ali'zi:rən] *v/t.* (no -ge-, h) idealize; **~ismus** [~a'lismus] *m* (-/Idealismen) idealism; **~ist** [~a'list] *m* (-en/-en) idealist.
**Idee** [i'de:] *f* (-/-n) idea, notion.
**identi|fizieren** [idɛntifi'tsi:rən] *v/t.* (no -ge-, h) identify; *sich* ~ identify o.s.; **~sch** *adj.* [i'dɛntiʃ] identical; **2tät** [~'te:t] *f* (-/no pl.) identity.
**Ideolog|ie** [ideolo'gi:] *f* (-/-n) ideology; **2isch** *adj.* [~'lo:giʃ] ideological.
**Idiot** [idi'o:t] *m* (-en/-en) idiot; **~ie** [~o'ti:] *f* (-/-n) idiocy; **2isch** *adj.* [~'o:tiʃ] idiotic.
**Idol** [i'do:l] *n* (-s/-e) idol.
**Igel** *zo.* ['i:gəl] *m* (-s/-) hedgehog.
**Ignor|ant** [igno'rant] *m* (-en/-en) ignorant person, ignoramus; **~anz** [~ts] *f* (-/no pl.) ignorance; **2ieren** *v/t.* (no -ge-, h) ignore, take no notice of.
**ihm** *pers. pron.* [i:m] *p.* (to) him; *thing*: (to) it.
**ihn** *pers. pron.* [i:n] *p.* him; *thing*: it.
'**ihnen** *pers. pron.* (to) them; *Ihnen sg. and pl.* (to) you.
**ihr** [i:r] 1. *pers. pron.*: (*2nd pl. nom.*) you; (*3rd sg. dat.*) (to) her; 2. *poss. pron.*: her; their; *Ihr sg. and pl.* your; *der (die, das)* ~e hers; theirs; *der (die, das) Ihre sg. and pl.* yours; **~erseits** ['~ər'zaits] *adv.* on her part; on their part; *Ihrerseits sg. and pl.* on your part; '**~es'gleichen** *pron.* (of) her *or* their kind, her *or* their equal; *Ihresgleichen sg.* (of) your kind, your equal; *pl.* (of) your kind, your equals; '**~et'wegen** *adv.* for her *or* their sake, on her *or* their account; *Ihretwegen sg. or pl.* for your sake, on your account; '**~etwillen** *adv.*: *um* ~ *s. ihretwegen*; **~ige** *poss. pron.* ['~igə]: *der (die, das)* ~ hers; theirs; *der (die, das) Ihrige* yours.
**illegitim** *adj.* [ilegi'ti:m] illegitimate.
**illusorisch** *adj.* [ilu'zo:riʃ] illusory, deceptive.
**illustrieren** [ilu'stri:rən] *v/t.* (no -ge-, h) illustrate.
**Iltis** *zo.* ['iltis] *m* (-ses/-se) fitchew, polecat.
**im** *prp.* [im] = *in dem.*
**imaginär** *adj.* [imagi'nɛ:r] imaginary.
'**Imbiß** *m* light meal, snack; '**~stube** *f* snack bar.
**Imker** ['imkər] *m* (-s/-) bee-master, bee-keeper.
**immatrikulieren** [imatriku'li:rən] *v/t.* (no -ge-, h) matriculate, enrol(l); *sich* ~ *lassen* matriculate, enrol(l).
**immer** *adv.* ['imər] always; ~ *mehr* more and more; ~ *wieder* again *or* time and again; *für* ~ for ever, for good; '**2grün** ⚘ *n* (-s/-e) evergreen; '**~'hin** *adv.* still, yet; '**~'zu** *adv.* always, continually.
**Immobilien** [imo'bi:ljən] *pl.* immovables *pl.*, real estate; **~händler** *m s. Grundstücksmakler.*
**immun** *adj.* [i'mu:n] immune (*gegen* against, from); **2ität** [~uni'tɛ:t] *f* (-/no pl.) immunity.
**Imperativ** *gr.* ['imperati:f] *m* (-s/-e) imperative (mood).
**Imperfekt** *gr.* ['impɛrfɛkt] *n* (-s/-e) imperfect (tense), past tense.
**Imperialis|mus** [imperia'lismus] *m* (-/no pl.) imperialism; **~t** *m* (-en/-en) imperialist; **2tisch** *adj.* imperialistic.
**impertinent** *adj.* [impɛrti'nɛnt] impertinent, insolent.
**impf|en** ⚕ ['impfən] *v/t.* (ge-, h) vaccinate; inoculate; '**2schein** *m* certificate of vaccination *or* inoculation; '**2stoff** ⚕ *m* vaccine;

serum; '**2ung** f (-/-en) vaccination; inoculation.

**imponieren** [impo'ni:rən] v/i. (no -ge-, h): j-m ~ impress s.o.

**Import** ✝ [im'pɔrt] m (-[e]s/-e) import(ation); **~eur** ✝ [~'tø:r] m (-s/-e) importer; **2ieren** [~'ti:rən] v/t. (no -ge-, h) import.

**imposant** adj. [impo'zant] imposing, impressive.

**imprägnieren** [imprɛ'gni:rən] v/t. (no -ge-, h) impregnate; (water-) proof (raincoat, etc.).

**improvisieren** [improvi'zi:rən] v/t. and v/i. (no -ge-, h) improvise.

**Im'puls** m (-es/-e) impuls; **2iv** adj. [~'zi:f] impulsive. [be able.]

**imstande** adj. [im'ʃtandə]: ~ sein

**in** prp. (dat.; acc.) [in] **1.** place: in, at; within; into, in; with names of important towns: in, **ſ** at, of; with names of villages and less important towns: at; im Hause in the house, indoors, in; im ersten Stock on the first floor; ~ der Schule (im Theater) at school (the theat[re, Am. -er); ~ die Schule (~s Theater) to school (the theat[rc, Am. -er); ~ England in England; waren Sie schon einmal in England? have you ever been to England?; **2.** time: in, at, during; within; ~ drei Tagen (with)in three days; heute ~ vierzehn Tagen today fortnight; im Jahre 1960 in 1960; im Februar in February; im Frühling in (the) spring; ~ der Nacht at night; ~ letzter Zeit lately, of late, recently; **3.** mode: ~ großer Eile in great haste; ~ Frieden leben live at peace; ~ Reichweile within reach; **4.** condition, state: im Alter von fünfzehn Jahren at (the age of) fifteen; ~ Behandlung under treatment.

**'Inbegriff** m (quint)essence; embodiment, incarnation; paragon; **2en** adj. included, inclusive (of).

**'Inbrunst** f (-/no pl.) ardo(u)r, fervo(u)r.

**'inbrünstig** adj. ardent, fervent.

**in'dem** cj. whilst, while; by (ger.); ~ er mich ansah, sagte er looking at me he said.

**Inder** ['indər] m (-s/-) Indian.

**in'des(sen) 1.** adv. meanwhile; **2.** cj. while; however.

**Indianer** [in'dja:nər] m (-s/-) (American or Red) Indian.

**Indikativ** gr. ['indikati:f] m (-s/-e) indicative (mood).

**'indirekt** adj. indirect.

**indisch** adj. ['indiʃ] Indian.

**'indiskret** adj. indiscreet; **2ion** [~e'tsjo:n] f (-/-en) indiscretion.

**indiskutabel** adj. ['indiskuta:bəl] out of the question.

**individu|ell** adj. [individu'ɛl] individual; **2um** [~'vi:duum] n (-s/ Individuen) individual.

**10***

**Indizienbeweis** ** [in'di:tsjən-] m circumstantial evidence.

**Indoss|ament** ✝ [indɔsa'mɛnt] n (-s/-e) endorsement, indorsement; **2ieren** ✝ [~'si:rən] v/t. (no -ge-, h) indorse, endorse.

**Industrialisierung** [industriali'zi:ruŋ] f (-/-en) industrialization.

**Industrie** [indus'tri:] f (-/-n) industry; **~anlage** f industrial plant; **~arbeiter** m industrial worker; **~ausstellung** f industrial exhibition; **~erzeugnis** n industrial product; **~gebiet** n industrial district or area; **2ll** adj. [~i'ɛl] industrial; **~lle** [~i'ɛlə] m (-n/-n) industrialist; **~staat** m industrial country.

**ineinander** adv. [in'ʔaɪ'nandər] into one another; **~greifen** ⊕ v/i. (irr. greifen, sep., -ge-, h) gear into one another, interlock.

**infam** adj. [in'fa:m] infamous.

**Infanter|ie** ✗ [infantə'ri:] f (-/-n) infantry; **~ist** ✗ m (-en/-en) infantryman.

**Infektion** ** [infɛk'tsjo:n] f (-/-en) infection; **~skrankheit** ** f infectious disease.

**Infinitiv** gr. ['infiniti:f] m (-s/-e) infinitive (mood).

**infizieren** [infi'tsi:rən] v/t. (no -ge-, h) infect. [flation.]

**Inflation** [infla'tsjo:n] f (-/-en) in-]

**in'folge** prp. (gen.) in consequence of, owing or due to; **~'dessen** adv. consequently.

**Inform|ation** [infɔrma'tsjo:n] f (-/-en) information; **2ieren** [~'mi:rən] v/t. (no -ge-, h) inform; falsch ~ misinform.

**Ingenieur** [inʒe'njø:r] m (-s/-e) engineer.

**Ingwer** ['inʋər] m (-s/no pl.) ginger.

**Inhaber** ['inha:bər] m (-s/-) owner, proprietor (of business or shop); occupant (of flat); keeper (of shop); holder (of office, share, etc.); bearer (of cheque, etc.).

**'Inhalt** m (-[e]s/-e) contents pl. (of bottle, book, etc.); tenor (of speech); geom. volume; capacity (of vessel). **'Inhalts|angabe** f summary; **2los** adj. empty, devoid of substance; **2reich** adj. full of meaning; life: rich, full; **'~verzeichnis** n on parcel: list of contents; in book: table of contents.

**Initiative** [initsja'ti:və] f (-/no pl.) initiative; die ~ ergreifen take the initiative.

**Inkasso** ✝ [in'kaso] n (-s/-s, Inkassi) collection.

**'inkonsequen|t** adj. inconsistent; **2z** ['~ts] f (-/-en) inconsistency.

**In'krafttreten** n (-s/no pl.) coming into force, taking effect (of new law, etc.).

**'Inland** n (-[e]s/no pl.) home (country); inland.

**inländisch** *adj.* ['inlɛndiʃ] native; inland; home; domestic; *product*: home-made.

**Inlett** ['inlɛt] *n* (-[e]s/-e) bedtick.

**in'mitten** *prp.* (*gen.*) in the midst of, amid(st).

**'inne|haben** *v/t.* (*irr. haben, sep., -ge-, h*) possess, hold (*office, record, etc.*); occupy (*flat*); **~halten** *v/i.* (*irr. halten, sep., -ge-, h*) stop, pause.

**innen** *adv.* ['inən] inside, within; indoors; *nach* ~ inwards.

**'Innen|architekt** *m* interior decorator; **~ausstattung** *f* interior decoration, fittings *pl.*, furnishing; **~minister** *m* minister of the interior; Home Secretary, *Am.* Secretary of the Interior; **~ministerium** *n* ministry of the interior; Home Office, *Am.* Department of the Interior; **~politik** *f* domestic policy; **~seite** *f* inner side, inside; **~stadt** *f* city, *Am.* downtown.

**inner** *adj.* ['inər] interior; inner; ℰ, *pol.* internal; **¹**ℒe *n* (-n/no *pl.*) interior; *Minister(ium) des Innern s. Innenminister(ium)*; ℒeien [ˌ'raɪən] *f/pl.* offal(s *pl.*); **~halb 1.** *prp.* (*gen.*) within; **2.** *adv.* within, inside; **~lich** *adv.* inwardly; *esp.* ℰ internally.

**innig** *adj.* ['iniç] intimate, close; affectionate.

**Innung** ['inuŋ] *f* (-/-en) guild, corporation.

**inoffiziell** *adj.* ['inⁱ-] unofficial.

**ins** *prp.* [ins] = *in das*.

**Insasse** ['inzasə] *m* (-n/-n) inmate; occupant, passenger (*of car*).

**'Inschrift** *f* inscription; legend (*on coin, etc.*).

**Insekt** *zo.* [in'zɛkt] *n* (-[e]s/-en) insect.

**Insel** ['inzəl] *f* (-/-n) island; **~bewohner** *m* islander.

**Inser|at** [inzə'raːt] *n* (-[e]s/-e) advertisement, F ad; ℒieren [ˌ'riːrən] *v/t. and v/i.* (*no -ge-, h*) advertise.

**insge'heim** *adv.* secretly; **~samt** *adv.* altogether.

**in'sofern** *cj.* so far; ~ *als* in so far as.

**insolvent** † *adj.* ['inzɔlvɛnt] insolvent.

**Inspekt|ion** [inspɛk'tsjoːn] *f* (-/-en) inspection; **~or** [in'spɛktɔr] *m* (-s/-en) inspector; surveyor; overseer.

**inspirieren** [inspi'riːrən] *v/t.* (*no -ge-, h*) inspire.

**inspizieren** [inspi'tsiːrən] *v/t.* (*no -ge-, h*) inspect (*troops, etc.*); examine (*goods*); survey (*buildings*).

**Install|ateur** [instala'tøːr] *m* (-s/-e) plumber; (gas- *or* electrical) fitter; ℒieren [ˌ'liːrən] *v/t.* (*no -ge-, h*) install.

**instand** *adv.* [in'ʃtant]: ~ *halten* keep in good order; keep up; ⊕

maintain; ~ *setzen* repair; ℒhaltung *f* maintenance; upkeep.

**'inständig** *adv.*: *j-n* ~ *bitten* implore *or* beseech s.o.

**Instanz** [in'stants] *f* (-/-en) authority; ℒ instance; **~enweg** ℒ *m* stages of appeal; *auf dem* ~ through the prescribed channels.

**Instinkt** [in'stiŋkt] *m* (-[e]s/-e) instinct; ℒiv *adv.* [ˌ'tiːf] instinctively.

**Institut** [insti'tuːt] *n* (-[e]s/-e) institute.

**Instrument** [instru'mɛnt] *n* (-[e]s/-e) instrument.

**inszenier|en** *esp. thea.* [instse'niːrən] *v/t.* (*no -ge-, h*) (put on the) stage; ℒung *thea.* *f* (-/-en) staging, production.

**Integr|ation** [integra'tsjoːn] *f* (-/-en) integration; ℒieren [ˌ'griːrən] *v/t.* (*no -ge-, h*) integrate.

**intellektuell** [intɛlɛktu'ɛl] intellectual, highbrow; ℒe *m* (-n/-n) intellectual, highbrow.

**intelligen|t** *adj.* [inteli'gɛnt] intelligent; ℒz [ˌts] *f* (-/-en) intelligence.

**Intendant** *thea.* [intɛn'dant] *m* (-en/-en) director.

**intensiv** *adj.* [intɛn'ziːf] intensive; intense.

**interess|ant** *adj.* [intɛrɛ'sant] interesting; ℒe [ˌ'rɛsə] *n* (-s/-n) interest (*an dat., für* in); ℒengebiet [ˌ'rɛsən-] *n* field of interest; ℒengemeinschaft [ˌ'rɛsən-] *f* community of interests; combine, pool, trust; ℒent [ˌ'sɛnt] *m* (-en/-en) interested person *or* party; † prospective buyer, *esp. Am.* prospect; ℒieren [ˌ'siːrən] *v/t.* (*no -ge-, h*) interest (*für* in); *sich* ~ *für* take an interest in.

**intern** *adj.* [in'tɛrn] internal; ℒat [ˌ'naːt] *n* (-[e]s/-e) boarding-school.

**international** *adj.* [internatsjo'naːl] international.

**inter|'nieren** *v/t.* (*no -ge-, h*) intern; ℒ'nierung *f* (-/-en) internment; ℒ'nist ℰ *m* (-en/-en) internal specialist, *Am.* internist.

**inter|pretieren** [intɛrpre'tiːrən] *v/t.* (*no -ge-, h*) interpret; ℒpunktion [ˌpuŋk'tsjoːn] *f* (-/-en) punctuation; ℒvall [ˌ'val] *n* (-s/-e) interval; **~venieren** [ˌve'niːrən] *v/i.* (*no -ge-, h*) intervene; ℒ'zonenhandel *m* interzonal trade; ℒ'zonenverkehr *m* interzonal traffic.

**intim** *adj.* [in'tiːm] intimate (*mit* with); ℒität [ˌimi'tɛːt] *f* (-/-en) intimacy.

**'intoleran|t** *adj.* intolerant; ℒz [ˌts] *f* (-/-en) intolerance.

**intransitiv** *gr. adj.* ['intranzitiːf] intransitive.

**I:.trig|e** [in'triːgə] *f* (-/-n) intrigue, scheme, plot; ℒieren [ˌi'giːrən] *v/i.* (*no -ge-, h*) intrigue, scheme, plot.

**Invalid|e** [inva'li:də] *m* (-n/-n) invalid; disabled person; **~enrente** *f* disability pension; **~ität** [~idi-'tɛ:t] *f* (-/no pl.) disablement, disability.

**Inventar** [invɛn'tɑ:r] *n* (-s/-e) inventory, stock.

**Inventur** † [invɛn'tu:r] *f* (-/-en) stock-taking; **~ machen** take stock.

**invest|ieren** † [invɛs'ti:rən] *v/t.* (no -ge-, h) invest; **2ition** † [~i'tsjo:n] *f* (-/-en) investment.

**inwie'fern** *cj.* to what extent; in what way *or* respect; **~'weit** *cj.* how far, to what extent.

**in'zwischen** *adv.* in the meantime, meanwhile.

**Ion** *phys.* [i'o:n] *n* (-s/-en) ion.

**ird|en** *adj.* ['irdən] earthen; **~isch** *adj.* earthly; worldly; mortal.

**Ire** ['i:rə] *m* (-n/-n) Irishman; *die* **~n** *pl.* the Irish *pl.*

**irgend** *adv.* ['irgənt] *in compounds:* some; any (*a. negative and in questions*); *wenn ich* **~** *kann* if I possibly can; **~'ein(e)** *indef. pron. and adj.* some(one); any(one); **~'einer** *indef. pron. s.* irgend jemand; **~'ein(e)s** *indef. pron.* some; any; **~ etwas** *indef. pron.* something; anything; **~ jemand** *indef. pron.* someone; anyone; **~'wann** *adv.* some time (or other); **~'wie** *adv.* somehow; anyhow; **~'wo** *adv.* somewhere; anywhere; **~'wo'her** *adv.* from somewhere; from anywhere; **~'wo'hin** *adv.* somewhere; anywhere.

**'irisch** *adj.* Irish.

**Iron|ie** [iro'ni:] *f* (-/-en) irony; **2isch** *adj.* [i'ro:niʃ] ironic(al).

**irre** ['irə] **1.** *adj.* confused; **2** insane; mad; **2.** **2** *f* (-/no pl.): *in die* **~** *gehen* go astray; **3.** **2** *m,* *f* (-n/-n) lunatic; mental patient; *wie ein* **~r** like a madman; **~führen** *v/t.* (*sep.,* -ge-, h) lead astray; *fig.* mislead; **~gehen** *v/i.* (*irr. gehen, sep.,* -ge-, *sein*) go astray, stray; lose one's way; **~machen** *v/t.* (*sep.,* -ge-, h) puzzle, bewilder; perplex; confuse;

**~n 1.** *v/i.* (ge-, h) err; wander; **2.** *v/refl.* (ge-, h) be mistaken (*in dat.* in *s.o.,* about *s.th.*); be wrong.

**'Irren|anstalt** **2** *f* lunatic asylum, mental home *or* hospital; **'~arzt** **2** *m* alienist, mental specialist; **'~haus** **2** *n s.* Irrenanstalt.

**'irrereden** *v/i.* (*sep.,* -ge-, h) rave.

**'Irr|fahrt** *f* wandering; Odyssey; **'~garten** *m* labyrinth, maze; **'~glaube** *m* erroneous belief; false doctrine, heterodoxy; heresy; **'2-gläubig** *adj.* heterodox; heretical; **'2ig** *adj.* erroneous, mistaken, false, wrong.

**irritieren** [iri'ti:rən] *v/t.* (no -ge-, h) irritate, annoy; confuse.

**'Irr|lehre** *f* false doctrine, heterodoxy; heresy; **'~licht** *n* will-o'-the-wisp, jack-o'-lantern; **'~sinn** *m* insanity; madness; **'2sinnig** *adj.* insane; mad; *fig.:* fantastic; terrible; **'~sinnige** *m, f* (-n/-n) *s.* irre 3; **'~tum** *m* (-s/-er) error, mistake; *im* **~** *sein* be mistaken; **2tümlich** ['~ty:mlıç] **1.** *adj.* erroneous; **2.** *adv.* = **'2tümlicherweise** *adv.* by mistake; mistakenly, erroneously; **'~wisch** *m s.* Irrlicht; *p.* flibbertigibbet.

**Ischias** **2** ['iʃias] *f,* F *a.: n, m* (-/no *pl.*) sciatica.

**Islam** ['islam, is'lɑ:m] *m* (-s/no *pl.*) Islam.

**Isländ|er** ['i:slɛndər] *m* (-s/-) Icelander; **'2isch** *adj.* Icelandic.

**Isolator** **2** [izo'lɑ:tɔr] *m* (-s/-en) insulator.

**Isolier|band** **2** [izo'li:r-] *n* insulating tape; **2en** *v/t.* (no -ge-, h) isolate; **~masse** **2** *f* insulating compound; **~schicht** **2** *f* insulating layer; **~ung** *f* (-/-en) isolation (*a. **2***); **2** quarantine; **2** insulation.

**Isotop** **2,** *phys.* [izo'to:p] *n* (-s/-e) isotope.

**Israeli** [isra'e:li] *m* (-s/-s) Israeli.

**Italien|er** [ital'je:nər] *m* (-s/-) Italian; **2isch** *adj.* Italian.

**I-Tüpfelchen** *fig.* ['i:typfəlçən] *n* (-s/-): *bis aufs* **~** to a T.

# J

**ja** [jɑ:] **1.** *adv.* yes; **⚓,** *parl.* aye, *Am. parl. a.* yea; **~** *doch,* **~** *freilich* yes, indeed; to be sure; *da ist er* **~***l* well, there he is!; *ich sagte es Ihnen* **~** I told you so; *tut es* **~** *nicht!* don't you dare do it!; *vergessen Sie es* **~** *nicht!* be sure not to forget it!; **2.** *cj.:* **~** *sogar,* **~** *selbst* nay (even); *wenn* **~** if so; *er ist* **~** *mein Freund* why, he is my friend; **3.** *int.:* **~,** *weißt du*

*denn nicht, daß* why, don't you know that.

**Jacht** **⚓** [jaxt] *f* (-/-en) yacht; **'~klub** *m* yacht-club.

**Jacke** ['jakə] *f* (-/-n) jacket.

**Jackett** [ʒa'kɛt] *n* (-s/-e, -s) jacket.

**Jagd** [jɑ:kt] *f* (-/-en) hunt(ing); *with a gun:* shoot(ing); chase; *s. Jagd-revier; auf* (dis) **~** *gehen* go hunting *or* shooting, *Am. a.* be gunning; **~** *machen auf* (*acc.*) hunt after *or* for;

'‿aufseher m gamekeeper, Am. game warden; '‿bomber ✕ m (-s/-) fighter-bomber; '‿büchse f sporting rifle; '‿flinte f sporting gun; fowling-piece; '‿flugzeug ✕ n fighter (aircraft); '‿geschwader ✕ n fighter wing, Am. fighter group; '‿gesellschaft f hunting or shooting party; '‿haus n shooting-box or -lodge, hunting-box or -lodge; '‿hund m hound; '‿hütte f shooting-box, hunting-box; '‿pächter m game-tenant; '‿rennen n steeplechase; '‿revier n hunting-ground, shoot; '‿schein m shooting licen|ce, Am. -se; '‿schloß n hunting seat; '‿tasche f game-bag.

jagen ['ja:gən] (ge-, h) 1. v/i. go hunting or shooting, hunt; shoot; rush, dash; 2. v/t. hunt; chase; aus dem Hause ‿ turn s.o. out (of doors).

Jäger ['je:gər] m (-s/-) hunter, huntsman, sportsman; ✕ rifleman; '‿latein F fig. n huntsmen's yarn, tall stories pl. [jaguar.]

Jaguar zo. ['ja:gua:r] m (-s/-e)]

jäh adj. [je:] sudden, abrupt; precipitous, steep.

Jahr [ja:r] n (-[e]s/-e) year; ein halbes ‿ half a year, six months pl.; einmal im ‿ once a year; im ‿e 1900 in 1900; mit 18 ‿en, im Alter von 18 ‿en at (the age of) eighteen; letztes ‿ last year; das ganze ‿ hindurch or über all the year round; ‿aus adv.: ‿, jahrein year in, year out; year after year; '‿buch n year-book, annual; '‿ein adv. s. jahraus.

'Jahrelang 1. adv. for years; 2. adj.: ‿e Erfahrung (many) years of experience.

jähren ['je:rən] v/refl. (ge-, h): es jährt sich heute, daß ... it is a year ago today that ..., it is a year today since ...

'Jahres|abonnement n annual subscription (to magazine, etc.); thea. yearly season ticket; '‿abschluß m annual statement of accounts; '‿anfang m beginning of the year; zum ‿ die besten Wünsche! best wishes for the New Year; '‿bericht m annual report; '‿einkommen n annual or yearly income; '‿ende n end of the year; '‿gehalt n annual salary; '‿tag m anniversary; '‿wechsel m turn of the year; '‿zahl f date, year; '‿zeit f season, time of the year.

'Jahrgang m volume, year (of periodical, etc.); p. age-group; univ., school: year, class; wine: vintage.

Jahr'hundert n (-s/-e) century; '‿feier f centenary, Am. centennial; ‿wende f turn of the century.

jährig adj. ['je:riç] one-year-old.

jährlich ['je:rliç] 1. adj. annual, yearly; 2. adv. every year; yearly, once a year.

Jahr|markt m fair; '‿tausend n (-s/-e) millennium; '‿tausend-feier f millenary; '‿zehnt n (-[e]s/-e) decade.

'Jähzorn m violent (fit of) temper; irascibility; 'ℨig adj. hot-tempered; irascible.

Jalousie [ʒalu'zi:] f (-/-n) (Venetian) blind, Am. a. window shade.

Jammer ['jamər] m (-s/no pl.) lamentation; misery; es ist ein ‿ it is a pity.

jämmerlich adj. ['jemərliç] miserable, wretched; piteous; pitiable (esp. contp.).

jammer|n ['jamərn] v/i. (ge-, h) lament (nach, um for; über acc. over); moan; wail, whine; '‿schade adj.: es ist ‿ it is a thousand pities, it is a great shame.

Januar ['janua:r] m (-[s]/-e) January.

Japan|er [ja'pɑ:nər] m (-s/-) Japanese; die ‿ pl. the Japanese pl.; ℨisch adj. Japanese.

Jargon [ʒar'gõ] m (-s/-s) jargon, cant, slang.

Jasmin ♀ [jas'mi:n] m (-s/-e) jasmin(e), jessamine.

'Jastimme parl. f aye, Am. a. yea.

jäten ['je:tən] v/t. (ge-, h) weed.

Jauche ['jauxə] f (-/-n) 🖋 liquid manure; sewage.

jauchzen ['jauxtsən] v/i. (ge-, h) exult, rejoice, cheer; vor Freude ‿ shout for joy.

jawohl adv. [ja'vo:l] yes; yes, indeed; yes, certainly; that's right; ✕, etc.: yes, Sir!

'Jawort n consent; j-m das ‿ geben accept s.o.'s proposal (of marriage).

je [je:] 1. adv. ever, at any time; always; ohne ihn ‿ gesehen zu haben without ever having seen him; seit eh und ‿ since time immemorial, always; distributive with numerals: ‿ zwei two at a time, two each, two by two, by or in twos; sie bekamen ‿ zwei Äpfel they received two apples each; für ‿ zehn Wörter for every ten words; in Schachteln mit or zu ‿ zehn Stück verpackt packed in boxes of ten; 2. cj.: ‿ nach Größe according to or depending on size; ‿ nachdem it depends; ‿ nachdem, was er für richtig hält according as he thinks fit; ‿ nachdem, wie er sich fühlt depending on how he feels; ‿ mehr, desto besser the more the better; ‿ länger, ‿ lieber the longer the better; 3. prp.: die Birnen kosten e-e Mark ‿ Pfund the pears cost one mark a pound; s. pro.

jede|(r, -s) indef. pron. ['je:də(r, -s)] every; any; of a group: each; of two persons: either; jeder, der whoever; jeden zweiten Tag every other day; '‿n'falls adv. at all events, in any case; '⹂rmann *indef. pron.* everyone, everybody; '⹂r'zeit *adv.* always, at any time; '⹂s'mal *adv.* each *or* every time; ~ wenn whenever.

**jedoch** *cj.* [je'dɔx] however, yet, nevertheless.

'**jeher** *adv.*: von or seit ~ at all times, always, from time immemorial.

**jemals** *adv.* ['je:mɑːls] ever, at any time.

**jemand** *indef. pron.* ['je:mant] someone, somebody; *with questions and negations*: anyone, anybody.

**jene|(r, -s)** *dem. pron.* ['je:nə(r, -s)] that (one); jene *pl.* those *pl.*

**jenseitig** *adj.* ['jɛnzaitiç] opposite.

'**jenseits** 1. *prp.* (*gen.*) on the other side of, beyond, across; 2. *adv.* on the other side, beyond; 3. ♀ n (-/no *pl.*) *the* other *or* next world, *the* world to come, *the* beyond.

**jetzig** *adj.* ['jɛtsiç] present, existing; *prices, etc.*: current.

**jetzt** *adv.* [jɛtst] now, at present; bis ~ until now; so far; eben ~ just now; erst ~ only now; für ~ for the present; gleich ~ at once, right away; noch ~ even now; von ~ an from now on.

**jeweil|ig** *adj.* ['je:vailiç] respective; ~s *adv.* ['⹂s] respectively, at a time; from time to time (*esp. ♔*).

**Joch** [jɔx] *n* (-[e]s/-e) yoke; *in mountains*: col, pass, saddle; ⚠ bay; '⹂bein *anat.* n cheek-bone.

**Jockei** ['dʒɔki] *m* (-s/-s) jockey.

**Jod** ♔ [jo:t] *n* (-[e]s/no *pl.*) iodine.

**jodeln** ['jo:dəln] *v/i.* (ge-, h) yodel.

**Johanni** [jo'hani] *n* (-/no *pl.*), ~s [⹂s] *n* (-/no *pl.*) Midsummer day; ~s-beere *f* currant; rote ~ red currant; ~stag *m eccl.* St John's day; Midsummer day.

**johlen** ['jo:lən] *v/i.* (ge-, h) bawl, yell, howl.

**Jolle** ⚓ ['jɔlə] *f* (-/-n) jolly-boat, yawl, dinghy.

**Jongl|eur** [ʒõ'glø:r] *m* (-s/-e) juggler; ♀ieren *v/t. and v/i.* (no -ge-, h) juggle.

**Journal** [ʒur'nɑːl] *n* (-s/-e) journal; newspaper; magazine; diary; ⚓ log-book; ~ist [⹂a'list] *m* (-en/-en) journalist, *Am. a.* newspaperman.

**Jubel** ['ju:bəl] *m* (-s/no *pl.*) jubilation, exultation, rejoicing; cheering; '♀n *v/i.* (ge-, h) jubilate; exult, rejoice (über *acc.* at).

**Jubil|ar** [jubi'lɑːr] *m* (-s/-e) person celebrating his jubilee, *etc.*; ~äum [⹂ɛ:um] *n* (-s/ *Jubiläen*) jubilee.

**Juchten** ['juxtən] *m*, *n* (-s/no *pl.*), '⹂leder *n* Russia (leather).

**jucken** ['jukən] (ge-, h) 1. *v/i.* itch; 2. *v/t.* irritate, (make) itch; F *sich* ~ scratch (o.s.).

**Jude** ['ju:də] *m* (-n/-n) Jew; '♀n-feindlich *adj.* anti-Semitic; '⹂n-

**tum** *n* (-s/no *pl.*) Judaism; '⹂nver-folgung *f* persecution of Jews, Jew-baiting; pogrom.

**Jüd|in** ['jy:din] *f* (-/-nen) Jewess; '♀isch *adj.* Jewish.

**Jugend** ['ju:gənt] *f* (-/no *pl.*) youth; '⹂amt *n* youth welfare department; '⹂buch *n* book for the young; '⹂freund *m* friend of one's youth; school-friend; '⹂fürsorge *f* youth welfare; '⹂gericht *n* juvenile court; '⹂herberge *f* youth hostel; '⹂jahre *n/pl.* early years, youth; '⹂krimi-nalität *f* juvenile delinquency; '♀-lich *adj.* youthful, juvenile, young; '⹂liche *m, f* (-n/-n) young person; juvenile; young man, youth; young girl; teen-ager; '⹂liebe *f* early *or* first love, calf-love, *Am. a.* puppy love; old sweetheart *or* flame; '⹂schriften *f/pl.* books for the young; '⹂schutz *m* protection of children and young people; '⹂streich *m* youthful prank; '⹂werk *n* early work (*of author*); ~e *pl. a.* juvenilia *pl.*; '⹂zeit *f* (time *or* days of) youth.

**Jugoslav|e** [jugo'slɑːvə] *m* (-en/-en) Jugoslav, Yugoslav; ♀isch *adj.* Jugoslav, Yugoslav.

**Juli** ['ju:li] *m* (-[s]/-s) July.

**jung** *adj.* [juŋ] young; youthful; *peas*: green; *beer, wine*: new; ~es Gemüse young *or* early vegetables *pl.*; F *fig.* young people, small fry.

'**Junge** 1. *m* (-n/-n) boy, youngster; lad; fellow, chap, *Am.* guy; *cards*: knave, jack; 2. *n* (-n/-n) young; puppy (*of dog*); kitten (*of cat*); calf (*of cow, elephant, etc.*); cub (*of beast of prey*); ~ werfen bring forth young; ein ~s a young one; '♀nhaft *adj.* boyish; '⹂nstreich *m* boyish prank *or* trick.

**jünger** ['jyŋər] 1. *adj.* younger, junior; er ist drei Jahre ~ als ich he is my junior by three years, he is three years younger than I; 2. ♀ *m* (-s/-) disciple.

**Jungfer** ['juŋfər] *f* (-/-n): alte ~ old maid *or* spinster.

'**Jungfern|fahrt** ⚓ *f* maiden voyage *or* trip; '⹂flug ✈ *m* maiden flight; '⹂rede *f* maiden speech.

'**Jung|frau** *f* maid(en), virgin; ♀-fräulich *adj.* ['⹂frɔyliç] virginal; *fig.* virgin; '⹂fräulichkeit *f* (-/no *pl.*) virginity, maidenhood; '⹂ge-selle *m* bachelor; '⹂gesellenstand *m* bachelorhood; '⹂gesellin *f* (-/-nen) bachelor girl.

**Jüngling** ['jyŋliŋ] *m* (-s/-e) youth, young man.

**jüngst** [jyŋst] 1. *adj.* youngest; *time*: (most) recent, latest; das ♀e Ge-richt, der ♀e Tag Last Judg(e)ment, Day of Judg(e)ment; 2. *adv.* recently, lately.

'**jungverheiratet** *adj.* newly married; '♀en *pl.* the newlyweds *pl.*

Juni ['juːni] m (-[s]/-s) June; '~käfer zo. m cockchafer, June-bug.

junior ['juːnjɔr] 1. adj. junior; 2. ♀ m (-s/-en) junior (a. sports).

Jura ['juːra] n/pl.: ~ studieren read or study law.

Jurist [ju'rist] m (-en/-en) lawyer; law-student; ♀isch adj. legal.

Jury [ʒy'riː] f (-/-s) jury.

justier|en ⊕ [jus'tiːrən] v/t. (no -ge-, h) adjust; ♀ung ⊕ f (-/-en) adjustment.

Justiz [ju'stiːts] f (-/no pl.) (administration of) justice; ~beamte m judicial officer; ~gebäude n courthouse; ~inspektor m judicial officer; ~irrtum m judicial error; ~minister m minister of justice; Lord Chancellor, Am. Attorney General; ~ministerium n ministry of justice; Am. Department of Justice; ~mord m judicial murder.

Juwel [ju've:l] m, n (-s/-en) jewel, gem; ~en pl. jewel(le)ry; ~ier [~e'liːr] m (-s/-e) jewel(l)er.

Jux F [juks] m (-es/-e) (practical) joke, fun, spree, lark; prank.

# K

(Compare also C and Z)

Kabel ['kaːbəl] n (-s/-) cable.

Kabeljau ichth. ['kaːbəljau] m (-s/-e, -s) cod(fish).

'kabeln v/t. and v/i. (ge-, h) cable.

Kabine [ka'biːnə] f (-/-n) cabin; at hairdresser's, etc.: cubicle; cage (of lift).

Kabinett pol. [kabi'net] n (-s/-e) cabinet, government.

Kabriolett [kabrio'let] n (-s/-e) cabriolet, convertible.

Kachel ['kaxəl] f (-/-n) (Dutch or glazed) tile; '~ofen m tiled stove.

Kadaver [ka'daːvər] m (-s/-) carcass.

Kadett [ka'det] m (-en/-en) cadet.

Käfer zo. ['kɛːfər] m (-s/-) beetle, chafer.

Kaffee ['kafe, ka'feː] m (-s/-s) coffee; (')~bohne ♀ f coffee-bean; (')~kanne f coffee-pot; (')~mühle f coffee-mill or -grinder; (')~satz m coffee-grounds pl.; (')~tasse f coffee-cup.

Käfig ['kɛːfiç] m (-s/-e) cage (a.fig.).

kahl adj. [kaːl] p. bald; tree, etc.: bare; landscape, etc.: barren, bleak; rock, etc.: naked; '♀kopf m baldhead, baldpate; '~köpfig adj. ['~kœpfiç] bald(-headed).

Kahn [kaːn] m (-[e]s/=e) boat; riverbarge; ~ fahren go boating; '~fahren v (-s/no pl.) boating.

Kai [kai] m (-s/-e, -s) quay, wharf.

Kaiser ['kaizər] m (-s/-) emperor; '~krone f imperial crown; '♀lich adj. imperial; '~reich n, '~tum n (-[e]s/=er) empire; '~würde f imperial status.

Kajüte ⊕ [ka'jyːtə] f (-/-n) cabin.

Kakao [ka'kaːo] m (-s/-s) cocoa; ♀ a. cacao.

Kakt|ee ♀ [kak'teː(ə)] f (-/-n), ~us ♀ ['~us] m (-/Kakteen, F Kaktusse) cactus.

Kalauer ['kaːlauər] m (-s/-) stale joke; pun.

Kalb [kalp] n (-[e]s/=er) calf; ♀en ['~bən] v/i. (ge-, h) calve; '~fell n calfskin; '~fleisch n veal; '~leder n calf(-leather).

'Kalbs|braten m roast veal; '~keule f leg of veal; '~leder n s. Kalbleder; '~nierenbraten m loin of veal.

Kalender [ka'lendər] m (-s/-) calendar; almanac; '~block m dateblock; ~jahr n calendar year; ~uhr f calendar watch or clock.

Kali 🜹 ['kaːli] n (-s/-s) potash.

Kaliber [ka'liːbər] n (-s/-) calib|re, Am. -er (a. fig.), bore (of firearm).

Kalk [kalk] m (-[e]s/-e) lime; geol. limestone; '~brenner m limeburner; '♀en v/t. (ge-, h) whitewash (wall, etc.); ✒ lime (field); '♀ig adj. limy; '~ofen m limekiln; '~stein m limestone; '~steinbruch m limestone quarry.

Kalorie [kalo'riː] f (-/-n) calorie.

kalt adj. [kalt] climate, meal, sweat, etc.: cold; p., manner, etc.: cold, chilly, frigid; mir ist ~ I am cold; ~e Küche cold dishes pl. or meat, etc.; j-m die ~e Schulter zeigen give s.o. the cold shoulder; ~blütig adj. ['~blyːtiç] cold-blooded (a. fig.).

Kälte ['kɛltə] f (-/no pl.) cold; chill; coldness, chilliness (both a. fig.); vor ~ zittern shiver with cold; fünf Grad ~ five degrees below zero; '~grad m degree below zero; '~welle f cold spell.

'kalt|stellen fig. v/t. (sep., -ge-, h) shelve, reduce to impotence; '♀welle f cold wave.

kam [kaːm] pret. of kommen.

Kamel zo. [ka'meːl] n (-[e]s/-e) camel; ~haar n textiles: camel hair.

Kamera phot. ['kaməra] f (-/-s) camera.

**Kamerad** [kamə'rɑːt] m (-en/-en) comrade; companion; mate, F pal, chum; ~schaft f (-/-en) comradeship, companionship; 2schaftlich adj. comradely, companionable.

**Kamille** ♧ [ka'milə] f (-/-n) camomile; ~ntee m camomile tea.

**Kamin** [ka'miːn] m (-s/-e) chimney (a. mount.); fireplace, fireside; ~sims m, n mantelpiece; ~vorleger m hearth-rug; ~vorsetzer m (-s/-) fender.

**Kamm** [kam] m (-[e]s/⁓e) comb; crest (of bird or wave); crest, ridge (of mountain).

**kämmen** ['kɛmən] v/t. (ge-, h) comb; sich (die Haare) ~ comb one's hair.

**Kammer** ['kamər] f (-/-n) (small) room; closet; pol. chamber; board; ⅔ division (of court); '~diener m valet; '~frau f lady's maid; '~gericht ⅔ n supreme court; '~herr m chamberlain; '~jäger m vermin exterminator; '~musik f chamber music; '~zofe f chambermaid.

**'Kamm|garn** n worsted (yarn); '~rad ⊕ n cogwheel.

**Kampagne** [kam'panjə] f (-/-n) campaign.

**Kampf** [kampf] m (-[e]s/⁓e) combat, fight (a. fig.); struggle (a. fig.); battle (a. fig.); fig. conflict; sports: contest, match; boxing: fight, bout; '~bahn f sports: stadium, arena; '2bereit adj. ready for battle.

**kämpfen** ['kɛmpfən] v/i. (ge-, h) fight (gegen against; mit with; um for) (a. fig.); struggle (a. fig.); fig. contend, wrestle (mit with).

**Kampfer** ['kampfər] m (-s/no pl.) camphor.

**Kämpfer** ['kɛmpfər] m (-s/-) fighter (a. fig.); ⚔ combatant, warrior.

**'Kampf|flugzeug** n tactical aircraft; '~geist m fighting spirit; '~platz m battlefield; fig., sports: arena; '~preis m sports: prize; ✝ cut-throat price; '~richter m referee, judge, umpire; '2unfähig adj. disabled.

**kampieren** [kam'piːrən] v/i. (no -ge-, h) camp.

**Kanal** [ka'nɑːl] m (-s/⁓e) canal; channel (a. ⊕, fig.); geogr. the Channel; sewer, drain; ~isation [~aliza'tsjoːn] f (-/-en) river: canalization; town, etc.: sewerage; drainage; 2isieren [~ali'ziːrən] v/t. (no -ge-, h) canalize; sewer.

**Kanarienvogel** orn. [ka'nɑːrjən-] m canary(-bird).

**Kandare** [kan'dɑːrə] f (-/-n) curb (-bit).

**Kandid|at** [kandi'dɑːt] m (-en/-en) candidate; applicant; ~atur [~a'tuːr] f (-/-en) candidature, candidacy; 2ieren [~'diːrən] v/i. (no -ge-, h) be a candidate (für for);

~ für apply for, stand for, Am. run for (office, etc.).

**Känguruh** zo. ['kɛŋguruː] n (-s/-s) kangaroo.

**Kaninchen** zo. [ka'niːnçən] n (-s/-) rabbit; ~bau m rabbit-burrow.

**Kanister** [ka'nistər] m (-s/-) can.

**Kanne** ['kanə] f (-/-n) milk, etc.: jug; coffee, tea: pot; oil, milk: can; ~gießer F fig. m political wiseacre.

**Kannibal|e** [kani'bɑːlə] m (-n/-n) cannibal; 2isch adj. cannibal.

**kannte** ['kantə] pret. of kennen.

**Kanon** ♩ ['kɑːnɔn] m (-s/-s) canon.

**Kanon|ade** ⚔ [kano'nɑːdə] f (-/-n) cannonade; ~e [~'noːnə] f (-/-n) ⚔ cannon, gun; F fig.: big shot; esp. sports: ace, crack.

**Ka'nonen|boot** ⚔ n gunboat; ~donner m boom of cannon; ~futter fig. n cannon-fodder; ~kugel f cannon-ball; ~rohr n gun barrel.

**Kanonier** ⚔ [kano'niːr] m (-s/-e) gunner.

**Kant|e** ['kantə] f (-/-n) edge; brim; '~en m (-s/-) end of loaf; '2en v/t. (ge-, h) square (stone, etc.); set on edge; tilt; edge (skis); '2ig adj. angular, edged; square(d).

**Kantine** [kan'tiːnə] f (-/-n) canteen.

**Kanu** ['kɑːnu] n (-s/-s) canoe.

**Kanüle** ⚕ [ka'nyːlə] f (-/-n) tubule, cannula.

**Kanzel** ['kantsəl] f (-/-n) eccl. pulpit; ✈ cockpit; ⚔ (gun-)turret.; '~redner m preacher.

**Kanzlei** [kants'lai] f (-/-en) office.

**'Kanzler** m (-s/-) chancellor.

**Kap** geogr. [kap] n (-s/-s) headland.

**Kapazität** [kapatsi'tɛːt] f (-/-en) capacity; fig. authority.

**Kapell|e** [ka'pɛlə] f (-/-n) eccl. chapel; ♩ band; ~meister m bandleader, conductor.

**kaper|n** ⚓ ['kɑːpərn] v/t. (ge-, h) capture, seize; '2schiff n privateer.

**kapieren** F [ka'piːrən] v/t. (no -ge-, h) grasp, get.

**Kapital** [kapi'tɑːl] 1. n (-s/-e, -ien) capital, stock, funds pl.; ~ und Zinsen principal and interest; 2. 2 adj. capital; ~anlage f investment; ~flucht f flight of capital; ~gesellschaft f joint-stock company; 2isieren [~ali'ziːrən] v/t. (no -ge-, h) capitalize; ~ismus [~a'lismus] m (-/no pl.) capitalism; ~ist [~a'list] m (-en/-en) capitalist; ~markt [~'tɑːl-] m capital market; ~verbrechen n capital crime.

**Kapitän** [kapi'tɛːn] m (-s/-e) captain; ~ zur See naval captain; ~leutnant m (senior) lieutenant.

**Kapitel** [ka'pitəl] n (-s/-) chapter (a. fig.).

**Kapitul|ation** ⚔ [kapitula'tsjoːn] f (-/-en) capitulation, surrender; 2ieren [~'liːrən] v/i. (no -ge-, h) capitulate, surrender.

**Kaplan** *eccl.* [ka'plɑːn] *m* (-s/ᵘe) chaplain.

**Kappe** ['kapə] *f* (-/-n) cap; hood (*a.* ⊕); bonnet; '2n *v/t.* (ge-, h) cut (*cable*); lop, top (*tree*).

**Kapriole** [kapri'oːlə] *f* (-/-n) equitation: capriole; *fig.*: caper; prank.

**Kapsel** ['kapsəl] *f* (-/-n) case, box; ♀, ♂, *anat.*, *etc.*: capsule.

**kaputt** *adj.* [ka'put] broken; *elevator*, *etc.*: out of order; *fruit*, *etc.*: spoilt; *p.*: ruined; tired out, F fagged out; **gehen** *v/i.* (*irr. gehen*, *sep.*, -ge-, *sein*) break, go to pieces; spoil.

**Kapuze** [ka'puːtsə] *f* (-/-n) hood; *eccl.* cowl.

**Karabiner** [kara'biːnər] *m* (-s/-) carbine.

**Karaffe** [ka'rafə] *f* (-/-n) carafe (*for wine or water*); decanter (*for liqueur*, *etc.*).

**Karambol|age** [karambo'lɑːʒə] *f* (-/-n) collision, crash; *billiards*: cannon, *Am. a.* carom; 2ieren *v/i.* (*no* -ge-, *sein*) cannon, *Am. a.* carom; F *fig.* collide.

**Karat** [ka'rɑːt] *n* (-[e]s/-e) carat.

**Karawane** [kara'vɑːnə] *f* (-/-n) caravan.

**Karbid** [kar'biːt] *n* (-[e]s/-e) carbide.

**Kardinal** *eccl.* [kardi'nɑːl] *m* (-s/ᵘe) cardinal.

**Karfreitag** *eccl.* [kɑr'-] *m* Good Friday.

**karg** *adj.* [kark] *soil*: meagre; *vegetation*: scant, sparse; *meal*: scanty, meagre, frugal; **en** ['gən] *v/i.* (ge-, h): ~ *mit* be sparing of.

**kärglich** *adj.* ['kerkliç] scanty, meagre; poor.

**kariert** *adj.* [ka'riːrt] check(ed), chequered, *Am.* checkered.

**Karik|atur** [karika'tuːr] *f* (-/-en) caricature, cartoon; 2ieren [.'kiːrən] *v/t.* (*no* -ge-, h) caricature, cartoon.

**karmesin** *adj.* [karme'ziːn] crimson.

**Karneval** ['karnəval] *m* (-s/-e, -s) Shrovetide, carnival.

**Karo** ['kɑːro] *n* (-s/-s) square, check; *cards*: diamonds *pl.*

**Karosserie** *mot.* [karɔsə'riː] *f* (-/-n) body.

**Karotte** ♀ [ka'rɔtə] *f* (-/-n) carrot.

**Karpfen** *ichth.* ['karpfən] *m* (-s/-) carp.

**Karre** ['karə] *f* (-/-n) cart; wheelbarrow.

**Karriere** [kar'jeːrə] *f* (-/-n) (successful) career.

**Karte** ['kartə] *f* (-/-n) card; postcard; map; chart; ticket; menu, bill of fare; list.

**Kartei** [kar'tai] *f* (-/-en) card-index; **karte** *f* index-card, filing-card; **schrank** *m* filing cabinet.

**Kartell** ✝ [kar'tel] *n* (-s/-e) cartel.

'**Karten|brief** *m* letter-card; '**haus** *n* ♣ chart-house; *fig.* house of cards; '**legerin** *f* (-/-nen) fortune-teller from the cards; '**spiel** *n* card-playing; card-game.

**Kartoffel** [kar'tɔfəl] *f* (-/-n) potato, F spud; **brei** *m* mashed potatoes *pl.*; **käfer** *m* Colorado *or* potato beetle, *Am. a.* potato bug; **schalen** *f/pl.* potato peelings *pl.*

**Karton** [kar'tõ, kar'toːn] *m* (-s/-s, -e) cardboard, pasteboard; cardboard box, carton. [*Kartei.*)

**Kartothek** [karto'teːk] *f* (-/-en) s.)

**Karussell** [karu'sel] *n* (-s/-s, -e) roundabout, merry-go-round, *Am. a.* car(r)ousel.

**Karwoche** *eccl.* ['kɑːr-] *f* Holy *or* Passion Week.

**Käse** ['kɛːzə] *m* (-s/-) cheese.

**Kasern|e** ⚔ [ka'zernə] *f* (-/-n) barracks *pl.*; **enhof** *m* barrack-yard *or* -square; 2ieren [.'niːrən] *v/t.* (*no* -ge-, h) quarter in barracks, barrack.

'**käsig** *adj.* cheesy; *complexion*: pale, pasty.

**Kasino** [ka'ziːno] *n* (-s/-s) casino, club(-house); (officers') mess.

**Kasperle** ['kasperlə] *n*, *m* (-s/-) Punch; **theater** *n* Punch and Judy show.

**Kasse** ['kasə] *f* (-/-n) cash-box; till (*in shop*, *etc.*); cash-desk, pay-desk (*in bank*, *etc.*); pay-office (*in firm*); *thea.*, *etc.*: box-office, booking-office; cash; *bei* ~ in cash.

'**Kassen|abschluß** ✝ *m* balancing of the cash (accounts); '**anweisung** *f* disbursement voucher; '**bestand** *m* cash in hand; '**bote** *m* bank messenger; '**buch** *n* cash book; '**erfolg** *m* *thea.*, *etc.*: box-office success; '**patient** ✝ *m* panel patient; '**schalter** *m* *bank*, *etc.*: teller's counter.

**Kasserolle** [kasə'rɔlə] *f* (-/-n) stew-pan, casserole.

**Kassette** [ka'setə] *f* (-/-n) box (*for money*, *etc.*); casket (*for jewels*, *etc.*); slip-case (*for books*); *phot.* plate-holder.

**kassiere|n** [ka'siːrən] (*no* -ge-, h) **1.** *v/i.* waiter, *etc.*: take the money (*für* for); **2.** *v/t.* take (*sum of money*); collect (*contributions*, *etc.*); annul; ⚖ quash (*verdict*); 2r *m* (-s/-) cashier; *bank*: *a.* teller; collector.

**Kastanie** ♀ [ka'stɑːnjə] *f* (-/-n) chestnut.

**Kasten** ['kastən] *m* (-s/ᵘ, ⚔ -) box; chest (*for tools*, *etc.*); case (*for violin*, *etc.*); bin (*for bread*, *etc.*).

**Kasus** *gr.* ['kɑːsus] *m* (-/-) case.

**Katalog** [kata'loːk] *m* (-[e]s/-e) catalogue, *Am. a.* catalog; 2isieren [.ogi'ziːrən] *v/t.* (*no* -ge-, h) catalogue, *Am. a.* catalog.

**Katarrh** ✤ [ka'tar] *m* (-s/-e) (common) cold, catarrh.

**katastroph|al** adj. [katastro'fɑ:l] catastrophic, disastrous; **2e** [ˌˈstro:-fə] f (-/-n) catastrophe, disaster.

**Katechismus** eccl. [kate'çismus] m (-/Katechismen) catechism.

**Katego|rie** [katego'ri:] f (-/-n) category; **2risch** adj. [ˌˈgo:riʃ] categorical.

**Kater** ['kɑːtər] m (-s/-) zo. male cat, tom-cat; fig. s. Katzenjammer.

**Katheder** [ka'te:dər] n, m (-s/-) lecturing-desk.　　　[cathedral.]

**Kathedrale** [kɑte'drɑːlə] f (-/-n)

**Katholi|k** [kato'li:k] m (-en/-en) (Roman) Catholic; **2sch** adj. [ˌˈto:liʃ] (Roman) Catholic.

**Kattun** [ka'tuːn] m (-s/-e) calico; cotton cloth or fabric; chintz.

**Katze** zo. ['katsə] f (-/-n) cat; '**ˌn-jammer** F fig. m hangover, morn-ing-after feeling.

**Kauderwelsch** ['kaudərvɛlʃ] n (-[s]/no pl.) gibberish, F double Dutch; '**2en** v/i. (ge-, h) gibber, F talk double Dutch.

**kauen** ['kauən] v/t. and v/i. (ge-, h) chew.

**kauern** ['kauərn] (ge-, h) 1. v/i. crouch; squat; 2. v/refl. crouch (down); squat (down); duck (down).

**Kauf** [kauf] m (-[e]s/ˈˌe) purchase; bargain, F good buy; acquisition; purchasing, buying; '**ˌbrief** m deed of purchase; '**2en** v/t. (ge-, h) buy, purchase; acquire (by purchase); sich et. ˌ buy o.s. s.th., buy s.th. for o.s.

**Käufer** ['kɔyfər] m (-s/-) buyer, purchaser; customer.

'**Kauf|haus** n department store; '**ˌladen** m shop, Am. a. store.

**käuflich** ['kɔyfliç] 1. adj. for sale; purchasable; fig. open to bribery, bribable; venal; 2. adv.: ˌ erwerben (acquire by) purchase; ˌ überlassen transfer by way of sale.

'**Kauf|mann** m (-[e]s/Kaufleute) businessman; merchant; trader; deal-er, shopkeeper; Am. a. storekeeper; **2männisch** adj. ['ˌmɛniʃ] com-mercial, mercantile; '**ˌvertrag** m contract of sale.

'**Kaugummi** m chewing-gum.

**kaum** adv. [kaum] hardly, scarcely, barely; ˌ glaublich hard to believe.

'**Kautabak** m chewing-tobacco.

**Kaution** [kau'tsjoːn] f (-/-en) security, surety; ᵗᵗᵗ mst bail.

**Kautschuk** ['kautʃuk] m (-s/-e) caoutchouc, pure rubber.

**Kavalier** [kava'liːr] m (-s/-e) gentle-man; beau, admirer.

**Kavallerie** ✕ [kavalə'riː] f (-/-n) cavalry, horse.

**Kaviar** ['kɑːviar] m (-s/-e) caviar(e).

**keck** adj. [kɛk] bold; impudent, saucy, cheeky; '**2heit** f (-/-en) bold-ness; impudence, sauciness, cheek-iness.

**Kegel** ['keːgəl] m (-s/-) games: skittle, pin; esp. Ⱥ, ⊕ cone; ˌ schieben s. kegeln; '**ˌbahn** f skittle-alley, Am. bowling alley; **2förmig** adj. ['ˌfœrmiç] conic(al), coniform; tapering; '**2n** v/i. (ge-, h) play (at) skittles or ninepins, Am. bowl.

**Kegler** ['keːglər] m (-s/-) skittle-player, Am. bowler.

**Kehl|e** ['keːlə] f (-/-n) throat; '**ˌkopf** anat. m larynx.

**Kehre** ['keːrə] f (-/-n) (sharp) bend, turn; '**2n** v/t. (ge-, h) sweep, brush; turn (nach oben upwards); j-m den Rücken ˌ turn one's back on s.o.

**Kehricht** ['keːriçt] m, n (-[e]s/no pl.) sweepings pl., rubbish.

'**Kehrseite** f wrong side, reverse; esp. fig. seamy side.

'**kehrtmachen** v/i. (sep., -ge-, h) turn on one's heel; ✕ turn or face about.

**keifen** ['kaifən] v/i. (ge-, h) scold, chide.

**Keil** [kail] m (-[e]s/-e) wedge; gore, gusset; '**ˌe** F f (-/no pl.) thrashing, hiding; '**ˌer** zo. m (-s/-) wild-boar; '**ˌerei** f [ˌˈrai] f (-/-en) row, scrap; **2förmig** adj. ['ˌfœrmiç] wedge-shaped, cuneiform; '**ˌkissen** n wedge-shaped bolster; '**ˌschrift** f cuneiform characters pl.

**Keim** [kaim] m (-[e]s/-e) ♀, biol. germ; ♀: seed-plant; shoot; sprout; fig. seeds pl., germ, bud; '**2en** v/i. (ge-, h) seeds, etc.: germinate; seeds, plants, potatoes, etc.: sprout; fig. b(o)urgeon; '**2frei** adj. sterilized, sterile; '**ˌträger** ꝰ m (germ-)car-rier; '**ˌzelle** f germ-cell.

**kein** indef. pron. [kain] as adj.: ˌ(e) no, not any; ˌ anderer als none other but; as noun: ˌer, ˌe, ˌ(e)s none, no one, nobody; ˌer von beiden neither (of the two); ˌer von uns none of us; '**ˌes'falls** adv., ˌes-wegs adv. ['ˌve:ks] by no means, not at all; '**ˌmal** adv. not once, not a single time.

**Keks** [ke:ks] m, n (-, -es/-, -e) bis-cuit, Am. cookie; cracker.

**Kelch** [kɛlç] m (-[e]s/-e) cup, goblet; eccl. chalice, communion-cup; ♀ calyx.

**Kelle** ['kɛlə] f (-/-n) scoop; ladle; tool: trowel.

**Keller** ['kɛlər] m (-s/-) cellar; base-ment; '**ˌei** [ˌˈrai] f (-/-en) wine-vault; '**ˌgeschoß** n basement; '**ˌmeister** m cellarman.

**Kellner** ['kɛlnər] m (-s/-) waiter; '**ˌin** f (-/-nen) waitress.

**Kelter** ['kɛltər] f (-/-n) winepress; '**2n** v/t. (ge-, h) press.

**kenn|en** ['kɛnən] v/t. (irr., ge-, h) know, be acquainted with; have knowledge of s.th.; '**ˌenlernen** v/t. (sep., -ge-, h) get or come to know;

make *s.o.*'s acquaintance, meet *s.o.*; '2er *m* (-s/-) expert; connoisseur; '.tlich *adj.* recognizable (*an dat.* by); ~ *machen* mark; label; '2tnis *f* (-/-se) knowledge; ~ *nehmen von* take not(ic)e of; '2zeichen *n* mark, sign; *mot.* registration (number), *Am.* license number; *fig.* hallmark, criterion; '.zeichnen *v/t.* (ge-, h) mark, characterize.

kentern ⚓ ['kɛntərn] *v/i.* (ge-, sein) capsize, keel over, turn turtle.

Kerbe ['kɛrbə] *f* (-/-n) notch, nick; slot; '2n *v/t.* (ge-, h) notch, nick, indent.

Kerker ['kɛrkər] *m* (-s/-) gaol, jail, prison; '.meister *m* gaoler, jailer.

Kerl F [kɛrl] *m* (-s, ⌖ -es/-e, F -s) man; fellow, F chap, bloke, *esp. Am.* guy.

Kern [kɛrn] *m* (-[e]s/-e) kernel (*of nut, etc.*); stone, *Am.* pit (*of cherry, etc.*); pip (*of orange, apple, etc.*); core (*of the earth*); *phys.* nucleus; *fig.* core, heart, crux; *Kern... s. a.* Atom...; '.energie *f* nuclear energy; '.forschung *f* nuclear research; '.gehäuse *n* core; '2ge'sund *adj.* thoroughly healthy, F as sound as a bell; '2ig *adj.* full of pips; *fig.*: pithy; solid; '.punkt *m* central *or* crucial point; '.spaltung *f* nuclear fission.

Kerze ['kɛrtsə] *f* (-/-n) candle; '.n-licht *n* candle-light; '.nstärke *f* candle-power.

keß F *adj.* [kes] pert, jaunty; smart.

Kessel ['kɛsəl] *m* (-s/-) kettle; cauldron; boiler; hollow.

Kette ['kɛtə] *f* (-/-n) chain; range (*of mountains, etc.*); necklace; '2n *v/t.* (ge-, h) chain (*an acc. to*).

'Ketten|hund *m* watch-dog; '.raucher *m* chain-smoker; '.reaktion *f* chain reaction.

Ketzer ['kɛtsər] *m* (-s/-) heretic; ~ei [.'raɪ] *f* (-/-en) heresy; '2isch *adj.* heretical.

keuch|en ['kɔʏçən] *v/i.* (ge-, h) pant, gasp; '2husten ♂ *m* (w)hooping cough.

Keule ['kɔʏlə] *f* (-/-n) club; leg (*of mutton, pork, etc.*).

keusch *adj.* [kɔʏʃ] chaste, pure; '2heit *f* (-/no *pl.*) chastity, purity.

kichern ['kiçərn] *v/i.* (ge-, h) giggle, titter.

Kiebitz ['kiːbits] *m* (-es/-e) *orn.* pe(e)wit; F *fig.* kibitzer; '2en F *fig. v/i.* (ge-, h) kibitz.

Kiefer ['kiːfər] 1. *anat. m* (-s/-) jaw(-bone); 2. ♀ *f* (-/-n) pine.

Kiel [kiːl] *m* (-[e]s/-e) ⚓ keel; quill; '.raum *m* bilge, hold; '.wasser *n* wake (*a. fig.*).

Kieme *zo.* ['kiːmə] *f* (-/-n) gill.

Kies [kiːs] *m* (-es/-e) gravel; *sl. fig.* dough; ~el ['.zəl] *m* (-s/-) pebble, flint; '.weg *m* gravel-walk.

Kilo ['kiːlo] *n* (-s/-[s]), ~gramm [kilo'gram] *n* kilogram(me); ~hertz [.'hɛrts] *n* (-/no *pl.*) kilocycle per second; ~'meter *m* kilomet|re, *Am.* -er; ~'watt *n* kilowatt.

Kimme ['kimə] *f* (-/-n) notch.

Kind [kint] *n* (-[e]s/-er) child; baby.

'Kinder|arzt *m* p(a)ediatrician; ~ei [.'raɪ] *f* (-/-en) childishness; childish trick; trifle; '.frau *f* nurse; '.fräulein *n* governess; '.funk *m* children's program(me); '.garten *m* kindergarten, nursery school; '.lähmung ♂ *f* infantile paralysis, polio(myelitis); '2leicht *adj.* very easy *or* simple, F as easy as winking *or* as ABC; '.lied *n* children's song; '2los *adj.* childless; '.mädchen *n* nurse(maid); '.spiel *n* children's game; *ein ~ s.* kinder-leicht; '.stube *f* nursery; *fig.* manners *pl.*, upbringing; '.wagen *m* perambulator, F pram, *Am.* baby carriage; '.zeit *f* childhood; '.zimmer *n* children's room.

'Kindes|alter *n* childhood, infancy; '.beine *n/pl.*: *von ~n an* from childhood, from a very early age; '.kind *n* grandchild.

'Kind|heit *f* (-/no *pl.*) childhood; 2isch *adj.* ['.dɪʃ] childish; '2lich *adj.* childlike.

Kinn *anat.* [kin] *n* (-[e]s/-e) chin; '.backe *f*, '.backen *m* (-s/-) jaw (-bone); '.haken *m boxing*: hook to the chin; uppercut; '.lade *f* jaw(-bone).

Kino ['kiːno] *n* (-s/-s) cinema, F the pictures *pl.*, *Am.* motion-picture theater, F the movies *pl.*; *ins ~ gehen* go to the cinema *or* F pictures, *Am.* F go to the movies; '.besucher *m* cinema-goer, *Am.* F moviegoer; '.vorstellung *f* cinema-show, *Am.* motion-picture show.

Kippe F ['kipə] *f* (-/-n) stub, fag-end, *Am. a.* butt; *auf der ~ stehen or sein* hang in the balance; '2n (ge-) 1. *v/i.* (sein) tip (over), topple (over), tilt (over); 2. *v/t.* (h) tilt, tip over *or* up.

Kirche ['kirçə] *f* (-/-n) church.

'Kirchen|älteste *m* (-n/-n) churchwarden, elder; '.buch *n* parochial register; '.diener *m* sacristan, sexton; '.gemeinde *f* parish; '.jahr *n* ecclesiastical year; '.lied *n* hymn; '.musik *f* sacred music; '.schiff △ *n* nave; '.steuer *f* church-rate; '.stuhl *m* pew; '.vorsteher *m* churchwarden.

'Kirch|gang *m* church-going; ~gänger [.gɛŋər] *m* (-s/-) church-goer; '.hof *m* churchyard; '2lich *adj.* ecclesiastical; '.spiel *n* parish; '.turm *m* steeple; '.weih ['.vaɪ] *f* (-/-en) parish fair.

Kirsche ['kirʃə] *f* (-/-n) cherry.

**Kissen** ['kisən] *n* (-s/-) cushion; pillow; bolster, pad.

**Kiste** ['kistə] *f* (-/-n) box, chest; crate.

**Kitsch** [kitʃ] *m* (-es/*no pl.*) trash, rubbish; '2ig *adj.* shoddy, trashy.

**Kitt** [kit] *m* (-[e]s/-e) cement; putty.

**Kittel** ['kitəl] *m* (-s/-) overall; smock, frock.

'**kitten** *v/t.* (ge-, h) cement; putt.

**kitz|eln** ['kitsəln] (ge-, h) 1. *v/t.* tickle; 2. *v/i.*: meine Nase kitzelt my nose is tickling; '~lig *adj.* ticklish (*a. fig.*).

**Kladde** ['kladə] *f* (-/-n) rough note-book, waste-book.

**klaffen** ['klafən] *v/i.* (ge-, h) gape, yawn.

**kläffen** ['klɛfən] *v/i.* (ge-, h) yap, yelp.

**klagbar** ʒ⅔ *adj.* ['kla:kba:r] *matter*, *etc.*: actionable; *debt*, *etc.*: suable.

**Klage** ['kla:gə] *f* (-/-n) complaint; lament; ʒ⅔ action, suit; '2n (ge-, h) 1. *v/i.* complain (*über acc.* of, about; *bei* to); lament; ʒ⅔ take legal action (*gegen* against); 2. *v/t.*: j-m et. ~ complain to s.o. of *or* about s.th.

**Kläger** ʒ⅔ ['klɛ:gər] *m* (-s/-) plaintiff; complainant.

**kläglich** *adj.* ['klɛ:kliç] pitiful, piteous, pitiable; *cries*, *etc.*: plaintive; *condition*: wretched, lamentable; *performance*, *result*, *etc.*: miserable, poor; *failure*, *etc.*: lamentable, miserable.

**klamm** [klam] 1. *adj.* hands, *etc.*: numb *or* stiff with cold, clammy; 2. 2 *f* (-/-en) ravine, gorge, canyon.

**Klammer** ['klamər] *f* (-/-n) ⊕ clamp, cramp; (paper-)clip; *gr.*, *typ.*, Å bracket, parenthesis; '2n (ge-, h) 1. *v/t.* clip together; ⚓ close (*wound*) with clips; *sich ~ an* (*acc.*) cling to (*a. fig.*); 2. *v/i. boxing*: clinch.

**Klang** [klaŋ] 1. *m* (-[e]s/⁓e) sound, tone (*of voice, instrument, etc.*); tone (*of radio*, *etc.*); clink (*of glasses*, *etc.*); ringing (*of bells*, *etc.*); timbre; 2. 2 *pret. of* klingen; '~fülle *f* sonority; '2los *adj.* toneless; '2voll *adj.* sonorous.

**Klappe** ['klapə] *f* (-/-n) flap, flap, drop leaf (*of table*, *etc.*); shoulder strap (*of uniform*, *etc.*); tailboard (*of lorry*, *etc.*); ⊕, ⚓, *anat.* valve; ♪ key; F *fig.*: bed; trap; '2n (ge-, h) 1. *v/t.*: nach oben ~ tip up; nach unten ~ lower, put down; 2. *v/i.* clap, flap; *fig.* come off well, work out fine, *Am. sl. a.* click.

**Klapper** ['klapər] *f* (-/-n) rattle; '2ig *adj.* vehicle, *etc.*: rattly, ramshackle; *furniture*: rickety; *person*, *horse*, *etc.*: decrepit; '~kasten F *m* wretched piano; rattletrap; '2n *v/i.* (ge-, h) clatter, rattle (*mit et. s.th.*); er klapperte vor Kälte mit den Zäh-

nen his teeth were chattering with cold; '~schlange *zo. f* rattlesnake, *Am. a.* rattler.

'**Klapp|kamera** *phot. f* folding camera; '~messer *n* clasp-knife, jack-knife; '~sitz *m* tip-up *or* flap seat; '~stuhl *m* folding chair; '~tisch *m* folding table, *Am. a.* gate-leg(ged) table; ~ult ['klappult] *n* folding desk.

**Klaps** [klaps] *m* (-es/-e) smack, slap; '2en *v/t.* (ge-, h) smack, slap.

**klar** *adj.* [kla:r] clear; bright; transparent, limpid; pure; *fig.*: clear, distinct; plain; evident, obvious; *sich ~ sein über* (*acc.*) be clear about; ~*en Kopf bewahren* keep a clear head.

**klären** ['klɛ:rən] *v/t.* (ge-, h) clarify; *fig.* clarify, clear up, elucidate.

'**klar|legen** *v/t.* (*sep.*, -ge-, h), '~stellen *v/t.* (*sep.*, -ge-, h) clear up.

'**Klärung** *f* (-/-en) clarification; *fig. a.* elucidation.

**Klasse** ['klasə] *f* (-/-n) class, category; *school*: class, form, *Am. a.* grade; (social) class.

'**Klassen|arbeit** *f* (test) paper; '2bewußt *adj.* class-conscious; '~bewußtsein *n* class-consciousness; '~buch *n* class-book; '~haß *m* class-hatred; '~kamerad *m* classmate; '~kampf *m* class-war(fare); '~zimmer *n* classroom, schoolroom.

**klassifizier|en** [klasifi'tsi:rən] *v/t.* (*no* -ge-, h) classify; 2ung *f* (-/-en) classification.

**Klass|iker** ['klasikər] *m* (-s/-) classic; '2isch *adj.* classic(al).

**klatsch** [klatʃ] 1. *int.* smack!, slap!; 2. 2 *m* (-es/-e) smack, slap; F *fig.*: gossip; scandal; 2base ['~ba:zə] *f* (-/-n) gossip; '2e *f* (-/-n) fly-flap; '~en (ge-, h) 1. *v/t.* fling, hurl; *Beifall* ~ clap, applaud (*j-m* s.o.) 2. *v/i.* splash; applaud, clap; F *fig.* gossip; '~haft *adj.* gossiping, gossipy; '2maul F *n s. Klatschbase*; '~naß *adj.* soaking wet.

**Klaue** ['klauə] *f* (-/-n) claw; paw; *fig.* clutch.

**Klause** ['klauzə] *f* (-/-n) hermitage; cell.

**Klausel** ʒ⅔ ['klauzəl] *f* (-/-n) clause; proviso; stipulation.

**Klaviatur** ♪ [klavja'tu:r] *f* (-/-en) keyboard, keys *pl.*

**Klavier** ♪ [kla'vi:r] *n* (-s/-e) piano (-forte); '~konzert *n* piano concert *or* recital; '~lehrer *m* piano teacher; '~sessel *m* music-stool; '~stimmer *m* (-s/-) piano-tuner; '~stunde *f* piano-lesson.

**kleb|en** ['kle:bən] (ge-, h) 1. *v/t.* glue, paste, stick; 2. *v/i.* stick, adhere (*an dat.* to); '~end *adj.* adhesive; '2epflaster *n* adhesive *or* sticking plaster; '~rig *adj.* adhesive, sticky; '2stoff *m* adhesive; glue.

**Klecks** [klɛks] *m* (-es/-e) blot (*of ink*); mark (*of dirt, grease, paint, etc.*); stain (*of wine, coffee, etc.*); **'2en** (ge-) 1. *v/t.* (h) make a mark *or* spot *or* stain; 2. *v/i.* (sein) ink, *etc.*: drip (down); 3. *v/t.* (h): et. auf et. ∼ splash *or* spill s.th. on s.th.

**Klee** ♧ [kle:] *m* (-s/*no pl.*) clover, trefoil.

**Kleid** [klaɪt] *n* (-[e]s/-er) garment; dress, frock; gown; ∼*er pl.* clothes *pl.*; **2en** ['dən] *v/t.* (ge-, h) dress, clothe; *sich* ∼ dress (o.s.); *j-n gut* ∼ suit *or* become s.o.

**Kleider|ablage** ['klaɪdər-] *f* cloakroom, *Am. a.* checkroom; 'bügel *m* coat-hanger; 'bürste *f* clothesbrush; 'haken *m* clothes-peg; 'schrank *m* wardrobe; 'ständer *m* hat and coat stand; 'stoff *m* dress material.

**'kleidsam** *adj.* becoming.

**Kleidung** ['klaɪdʊŋ] *f* (-/-en) clothes *pl.*, clothing; dress; 'stück *n* piece *or* article of clothing; garment.

**Kleie** ['klaɪə] *f* (-/-n) bran.

**klein** [klaɪn] 1. *adj.* little (*only attr.*), small; *fig. a.* trifling, petty; 2. *adv.*: ∼ schreiben write with a small (initial) letter; ∼ anfangen start in a small *or* modest way; 3. *noun*: von ∼ auf from an early age; '2auto *n* baby *or* small car; '2bahn *f* narrow-ga(u)ge railway; '2bildkamera *f* miniature camera; '2geld *n* (small) change; 'gläubig *adj.* of little faith; '2handel ♰ *m* retail trade; '2händler *m* retailer; '2heit *f* (-/*no pl.*) smallness, small size; '2holz *n* firewood, matchwood, kindling.

**'Kleinigkeit** *f* (-/-en) trifle, triviality; 'skrämer *m* pettifogger.

**'Klein|kind** *n* infant; '2laut *adj.* subdued; 'lich *adj.* paltry; pedantic, fussy; 'mut *m* pusillanimity; despondency; 2mütig *adj.* ['my:tiç] pusillanimous; despondent; '2schneiden *v/t.* (*irr. schneiden, sep., -ge-*, h) cut into small pieces; 'staat *m* small *or* minor state; 'stadt *f* small town; 'städter *m* small-town dweller, *Am. a.* smalltowner; '2städtisch *adj.* smalltown, provincial; 'vieh *n* small livestock.

**Kleister** ['klaɪstər] *m* (-s/-) paste; '2n *v/t.* (ge-, h) paste.

**Klemm|e** ['klɛmə] *f* (-/-n) ⊕ clamp; ⚡ terminal; F *in der* ∼ *sitzen* be in a cleft stick, F be in a jam; '2en *v/t.* (ge-, h) jam, squeeze, pinch; 'er *m* (-s/-) pince-nez; 'schraube ⊕ *f* set screw.

**Klempner** ['klɛmpnər] *m* (-s/-) tinman, tin-smith, *Am. a.* tinner; plumber.

**Klerus** ['kle:rʊs] *m* (-/*no pl.*) clergy.

**Klette** ['klɛtə] *f* (-/-n) ♧ bur(r); *fig. a.* leech.

**Kletter|er** ['klɛtərər] *m* (-s/-) climber; '2n *v/i.* (ge-, sein) climb, clamber (*auf e-n Baum* [up] a tree); 'pflanze *f* climber, creeper.

**Klient** [kli'ɛnt] *m* (-en/-en) client.

**Klima** ['kli:ma] *n* (-s/-s, -te) climate; *fig. a.* atmosphere; 'anlage *f* airconditioning plant; 2tisch *adj.* [∼'ma:tɪʃ] climatic.

**klimpern** ['klɪmpərn] *v/i.* (ge-, h) jingle, chink (*mit et. s.th.*); F strum *or* tinkle away (*auf acc.* on, at *piano, guitar*).

**Klinge** ['klɪŋə] *f* (-/-n) blade.

**Klingel** ['klɪŋəl] *f* (-/-n) bell, handbell; 'knopf *m* bell-push; '2n *v/i.* (ge-, h) ring (the bell); doorbell, *etc.*: ring; *es klingelt* the doorbell is ringing; 'zug *m* bell-pull.

**klingen** ['klɪŋən] *v/i.* (*irr.*, ge-, h) sound; bell, metal, *etc.*: ring; glasses, *etc.*: clink; *musical instrument*: speak.

**Klini|k** ['kli:nɪk] *f* (-/-en) nursing home; private hospital; clinic(al hospital); '2sch *adj.* clinical.

**Klinke** ['klɪŋkə] *f* (-/-n) latch; (door-) handle.

**Klippe** ['klɪpə] *f* (-/-n) cliff; reef; crag; rock; *fig.* rock, hurdle.

**klirren** ['klɪrən] *v/i.* (ge-, h) windowpane, chain, *etc.*: rattle; chain, swords, *etc.*: clank, jangle; keys, spurs, *etc.*: jingle; glasses, *etc.*: clink, chink; *pots, etc.*: clatter; ∼ *mit* rattle; jingle.

**Klistier** ⚕ [kli'sti:r] *n* (-s/-e) enema.

**Kloake** [klo'a:kə] *f* (-/-n) sewer, cesspool (*a. fig.*).

**Klob|en** ['klo:bən] *m* (-s/-) ⊕ pulley, block; log; '2ig *adj.* clumsy (*a. fig.*).

**klopfen** ['klɔpfən] (ge-, h) 1. *v/i.* heart, pulse: beat, throb; knock (*at door, etc.*); tap (*on shoulder*); pat (*on cheek*); *es klopft* there's a knock at the door; 2. *v/t.* knock, drive (*nail, etc.*).

**Klöppel** ['klœpəl] *m* (-s/-) clapper (*of bell*); lacemaking: bobbin; beetle; 'spitze *f* pillow-lace, bonelace.

**Klops** [klɔps] *m* (-es/-e) meat ball.

**Klosett** [klo'zɛt] *n* (-s/-e, -s) lavatory, (water-)closet, W.C., toilet; ∼*papier n* toilet-paper.

**Kloß** [klo:s] *m* (-es/⸚e) earth, clay, *etc.*: clod, lump; *cookery*: dumpling.

**Kloster** ['klo:stər] *n* (-s/⸚) cloister; monastery; convent, nunnery; 'bruder *m* friar; 'frau *f* nun; 'gelübde *n* monastic vow.

**Klotz** [klɔts] *m* (-es/⸚e) block, log (*a. fig.*).

**Klub** [klʊp] *m* (-s/-s) club; 'kamerad *m* clubmate; 'sessel *m* loungechair.

**Kluft** [klʊft] *f* 1. (-/⸚e) gap (*a. fig.*),

crack; cleft; gulf, chasm (*both a. fig.*); 2. F (-/-en) outfit, F togs *pl.*; uniform.

**klug** *adj.* [klu:k] clever; wise, intelligent, sensible; prudent; shrewd; cunning; '2heit *f* (-/no *pl.*) cleverness; intelligence; prudence; shrewdness; good sense.

**Klump|en** ['klumpən] *m* (-s/-) lump (*of earth, dough, etc.*); clod (*of earth, etc.*); nugget (*of gold, etc.*); heap; '~fuß *m* club-foot; '2ig *adj.* lumpy; cloddish.

**knabbern** ['knabərn] (ge-, h) 1. *v/t.* nibble, gnaw; 2. *v/i.* nibble, gnaw (*an dat.* at).

**Knabe** ['knɑ:bə] *m* (-n/-n) boy; lad; F *alter* ~ F old chap.

**'Knaben|alter** *n* boyhood; '~chor *m* boys' choir; '2haft *adj.* boyish.

**Knack** [knak] *m* (-[e]s/-e) crack, snap, click; '2en (ge-, h) 1. *v/i. wood:* crack; *fire:* crackle; click; 2. *v/t.* crack (*nut, etc.*); F crack open (*safe*); e-e harte Nuß zu ~ haben have a hard nut to crack; ~s [~s] *m* (-es/-e) s. Knack; F *fig.* defect; '2en *v/i.* (ge-, h) s. knacken 1.

**Knall** [knal] *m* (-[e]s/-e) crack, bang (*of shot*); bang (*of explosion*); crack (*of rifle or whip*); report (*of gun*); detonation, explosion, report; '~bonbon *m, n* cracker; '~effekt *fig. m* sensation; '2en *v/i.* (ge-, h) *rifle, whip:* crack; *fireworks, door, etc.:* bang; *gun:* fire; *cork, etc.:* pop; *explosive, etc.:* detonate.

**knapp** *adj.* [knap] *clothes:* tight, close-fitting; *rations, etc.:* scanty; scarce; *style, etc.:* concise; *lead, victory, etc.:* narrow; *majority, etc.:* bare; *mit ~er* Not entrinnen have a narrow escape; ~ werden run short; '2e ⚔ *m* (-n/-n) miner; '~halten *v/t.* (*irr.* halten, *sep.*, -ge-, h) keep *s.o.* short; '2heit *f* (-/no *pl.*) scarcity, shortage; conciseness; '~schaft ⚔ *f* (-/-en) miners' society.

**Knarre** ['knarə] *f* (-/-n) rattle; F rifle, gun; '2n *v/i.* (ge-, h) creak; *voice:* grate.

**knattern** ['knatərn] *v/i.* (ge-, h) crackle; *machine-gun, etc.:* rattle; *mot.* roar.

**Knäuel** ['knɔʏəl] *m, n* (-s/-) clew, ball; *fig.* bunch, cluster.

**Knauf** [knauf] *m* (-[e]s/ᵘe) knob, pommel (*of sword*).

**Knauser** ['knauzər] *m* (-s/-) niggard, miser, skinflint; '~ei [~'rai] *f* (-/-en) niggardliness, miserliness; '2ig *adj.* niggardly, stingy; '2n *v/i.* (ge-, h) be stingy.

**Knebel** ['kne:bəl] *m* (-s/-) gag; '2n *v/t.* (ge-, h) gag; *fig.* muzzle (*press*).

**Knecht** [knɛçt] *m* (-[e]s/-e) servant; farm-labo(u)rer, farm-hand; slave; '2en *v/t.* (ge-, h) enslave; tyrannize;

subjugate; '~schaft *f* (-/no *pl.*) servitude, slavery.

**kneif|en** ['knaifən] (*irr.*, ge-, h) 1. *v/t.* pinch, nip; 2. *v/i.* pinch; F *fig.* back out, *Am.* F *a.* crawfish; '2er *m* (-s/-) pince-nez; '2zange *f* (e-e a pair of) pincers *pl. or* nippers *pl.*

**Kneipe** ['knaipə] *f* (-/-n) public house, tavern, F pub, *Am. a.* saloon; '2n *v/i.* (ge-, h) carouse, tipple, F booze; '~rei *f* (-/-en) drinking-bout, carousal.

**kneten** ['kne:tən] *v/t.* (ge-, h) knead (*dough, etc.*); ⚕ *a.* massage (*limb, etc.*).

**Knick** [knik] *m* (-[e]s/-e) *wall, etc.:* crack; *paper, etc.:* fold, crease; *path, etc.:* bend; '2en *v/t.* (ge-, h) fold, crease; bend; break.

**Knicker** F ['knikər] *m* (-s/-) s. Knauser.

**Knicks** [kniks] *m* (-es/-e) curts(e)y; e-n ~ machen = '2en *v/i.* (ge-, h) (drop a) curts(e)y (*vor dat.* to).

**Knie** [kni:] *n* (-s/-) knee; '2fällig *adv.* on one's knees; '~kehle *anat. f* hollow of the knee; '2n *v/i.* (ge-, h) kneel, be on one's knees; '~scheibe *anat. f* knee-cap, knee-pan; '~strumpf *m* knee-length sock.

**Kniff** [knif] 1. *m* (-[e]s/-e) crease, fold; *fig.* trick, knack; 2. 2 *pret. of* kneifen; '2(e)lig *adj.* ['~(ə)liç] tricky; intricate.

**knipsen** ['knipsən] (ge-, h) 1. *v/t.* clip, punch (*ticket, etc.*); F *phot.* take a snapshot of, snap; 2. F *phot. v/i.* take snapshots.

**Knirps** [knirps] *m* (-es/-e) little man; little chap, F nipper; '2ig *adj.* very small.

**knirschen** ['knirʃən] *v/i.* (ge-, h) *gravel, snow, etc.:* crunch, grind; *teeth, etc.:* grate; *mit den Zähnen* ~ grind *or* gnash one's teeth.

**knistern** ['knistərn] *v/i.* (ge-, h) *woodfire, etc.:* crackle; *dry leaves, silk, etc.:* rustle.

**knitter|frei** *adj.* ['knitər-] crease-resistant; '2n *v/t. and v/i.* (ge-, h) crease, wrinkle.

**Knoblauch** ♣ ['kno:plaux] *m* (-[e]s/no *pl.*) garlic.

**Knöchel** *anat.* ['knœçəl] *m* (-s/-) knuckle; ankle.

**Knoch|en** *anat.* ['knɔxən] *m* (-s/-) bone; '~enbruch *m* fracture (of a bone); '2ig *adj.* bony.

**Knödel** ['knø:dəl] *m* (-s/-) dumpling.

**Knolle** ♣ ['knɔlə] *f* (-/-n) tuber; bulb.

**Knopf** [knɔpf] *m* (-[e]s/ᵘe) button.

**knöpfen** ['knœpfən] *v/t.* (ge-, h) button.

**'Knopfloch** *n* buttonhole.

**Knorpel** ['knɔrpəl] *m* (-s/-) cartilage, gristle.

**Knorr|en** ['knɔrən] *m* (-s/-) knot,

knag, gnarl; '**&ig** *adj.* gnarled, knotty.

**Knospe** ♀ ['knɔspə] *f* (-/-n) bud; '**&n** *v/i.* (ge-, h) (be in) bud.

**Knot|en** ['kno:tən] 1. *m* (-s/-) knot (*a. fig.*, ♣); 2. ♀ *v/t.* (ge-, h) knot; '**&npunkt** *m* 🚂 junction; intersection; '**&ig** *adj.* knotty.

**Knuff** F [knuf] *m* (-[e]s/-e) poke, cuff, nudge; '**&en** F *v/t.* (ge-, h) poke, cuff, nudge.

**knülle|n** ['knylən] *v/t. and v/i.* (ge-, h) crease, crumple; '**&r** F *m* (-s/-) hit.

**knüpfen** ['knypfən] *v/t.* (ge-, h) make, tie (*knot, etc.*); make (*net*); knot (*carpet, etc.*); tie (*shoe-lace, etc.*); strike up (*friendship, etc.*); attach (*condition, etc.*) (*an acc.* to).

**Knüppel** ['knypəl] *m* (-s/-) cudgel.

**knurren** ['knurən] *v/i.* (ge-, h) growl, snarl; *fig.* grumble (*über acc.* at, over about); *stomach*: rumble.

**knusp(e)rig** *adj.* ['knusp(ə)riç] crisp, crunchy.

**Knute** ['knu:tə] *f* (-/-n) knout.

**Knüttel** ['knytəl] *m* (-s/-) cudgel.

**Kobold** ['ko:bɔlt] *m* (-[e]s/-e) (hob)goblin, imp.

**Koch** [kɔx] *m* (-[e]s/=e) cook; '**&buch** *n* cookery-book, *Am.* cookbook; '**&en** (ge-, h) 1. *v/t.* boil (*water, egg, fish, etc.*); cook (*meat, vegetables, etc.*) (*by boiling*); make (*coffee, tea, etc.*); 2. *v/i. water, etc.*: boil (*a. fig.*); do the cooking; be a (*good, etc.*) cook; '**&er** *m* (-s/-) cooker.

**Köcher** ['kœçər] *m* (-s/-) quiver.

'**Koch|kiste** *f* haybox; '**&löffel** *m* wooden spoon; '**&nische** *f* kitchenette; '**&salz** *n* common salt; '**&topf** *m* pot, saucepan.

**Köder** ['ko:dər] *m* (-s/-) bait (*a. fig.*); lure (*a. fig.*); '**&n** *v/t.* (ge-, h) bait; lure; *fig. a.* decoy.

**Kodex** ['ko:dɛks] *m* (-es, -/-e, Kodizes) code.

**Koffer** ['kɔfər] *m* (-s/-) (suit)case; trunk; '**&radio** *n* portable radio (set).

**Kognak** ['kɔnjak] *m* (-s/-s, ⚗-e) French brandy, cognac.

**Kohl** ♀ [ko:l] *m* (-[e]s/-e) cabbage.

**Kohle** ['ko:lə] *f* (-/-n) coal, charcoal; ⚗ carbon; *wie auf* (*glühenden*) **&n** *sitzen* be on tenterhooks.

'**Kohlen|bergwerk** *n* coal-mine, coal-pit, colliery; '**&eimer** *m* coalscuttle; '**&händler** *m* coal-merchant; '**&kasten** *m* coal-box; '**&revier** ⚒ *n* coal-district; '**&säure** *f* carbonic acid; '**&stoff** 🧪 *m* carbon.

'**Kohle|papier** *n* carbon paper; '**&zeichnung** *f* charcoal-drawing.

'**Kohl|kopf** ♀ *m* (head of) cabbage; '**&rübe** ♀ *f* Swedish turnip.

**Koje** ⚓ ['ko:jə] *f* (-/-n) berth, bunk.

**Kokain** [koka'i:n] *n* (-s/no *pl.*) cocaine, *sl.* coke, snow.

**kokett** *adj.* [ko'kɛt] coquettish; **&erie** [~ə'ri:] *f* (-/-n) coquetry, coquettishness; **&ieren** [~'ti:rən] *v/i.* (no -ge-, h) coquet, flirt (*mit* with; *a. fig.*).

**Kokosnuß** ♀ ['ko:kɔs-] *f* coconut.

**Koks** [ko:ks] *m* (-es/-e) coke.

**Kolben** ['kɔlbən] *m* (-s/-) butt (*of rifle*); ⊕ piston; '**&stange** *f* piston-rod.

**Kolchose** [kɔl'ço:zə] *f* (-/-n) collective farm, kolkhoz.

**Kolleg** *univ.* [kɔ'le:k] *n* (-s/-s, -ien) course of lectures; **&e** [~gə] *m* (-n/-n) colleague; **&ium** [~gjum] *n* (-s/Kollegien) council, board; teaching staff.

**Kollekt|e** *eccl.* [kɔ'lɛktə] *f* (-/-n) collection; **&ion** ✝ [~'tsjo:n] *f* (-/-en) collection, range.

**Koller** ['kɔlər] *m* (-s/-) *vet.* staggers *pl.*; F *fig.* rage, tantrum; '**&n** *v/i.* 1. (h) *turkey-cock*: gobble; *pigeon*: coo; *bowels*: rumble; *vet.* have the staggers; 2. (sein) *ball, tears, etc.*: roll.

**kolli|dieren** [kɔli'di:rən] *v/i.* (no -ge-, sein) collide; *fig.* clash; **&sion** [~'zjo:n] *f* (-/-en) collision; *fig.* clash, conflict.

**Kölnischwasser** ['kœlniʃ-] *n* eau-de-Cologne.

**Kolonialwaren** [kolo'nja:l-] *f/pl.* groceries *pl.*; **&händler** *m* grocer; **&handlung** *f* grocer's (shop), *Am.* grocery.

**Kolon|ie** [kolo'ni:] *f* (-/-n) colony; **&isieren** [~izi'rən] *v/t.* (no -ge-, h) colonize.

**Kolonne** [ko'lɔnə] *f* (-/-n) column; convoy; gang (*of workers, etc.*).

**kolorieren** [kolo'ri:rən] *v/t.* (no -ge-, h) colo(u)r.

**Kolo|ß** [ko'lɔs] *m* (Kolosses/Kolosse) colossus; **&ssal** [~'sa:l] *adj.* colossal, huge (*both a. fig.*).

**Kombin|ation** [kɔmbina'tsjo:n] *f* (-/-en) combination; overall; F flying-suit; *football, etc.*: combined attack; **&ieren** [~'ni:rən] (no -ge-, h) 1. *v/t.* combine; 2. *v/i.* reason, deduce; *football, etc.*: combine, move.

**Kombüse** ⚓ [kɔm'by:zə] *f* (-/-n) galley, caboose.

**Komet** *ast.* [ko'me:t] *m* (-en/-en) comet.

**Komfort** [kɔm'fɔːr] *m* (-s/no *pl.*) comfort; **&abel** *adj.* [~ɔr'ta:bəl] comfortable.

**Komik** ['ko:mik] *f* (-/no *pl.*) humo(u)r, fun(niness); '**&er** *m* (-s/-) comic actor, comedian.

**komisch** *adj.* ['ko:miʃ] comic(al), funny; *fig.* funny, odd, queer.

**Komitee** [komi'te:] *n* (-s/-s) committee.

**Kommand|ant** ✕ [kɔman'dant] *m* (-en/-en), **~eur** ✕ [~'døːr] *m* (-s/-e) commander, commanding officer; **2ieren** [~'diːrən] (*no* -ge-, *h*) **1.** *v/i.* order, command, be in command; **2.** *v/t.* ✕ command, be in command of; order; **~itgesellschaft** † [~'diːt-] *f* limited partnership; **~o** [~'mando] *n* (-s/-s) ✕ command, order; order(s *pl.*), directive(s *pl.*); ✕ detachment; **~obrücke** ⚓ *f* navigating bridge.

**kommen** ['kɔmən] *v/i.* (*irr.*, *ge-*, *sein*) come; arrive; **~ lassen** send for *s.o.*, order *s.th.*; *et.* **~ sehen** foresee; *an die Reihe* **~** it is one's turn; **~ auf** (*acc.*) think of, hit upon; remember; *zu dem Schluß* **~**, *daß* decide that; *hinter et.* **~** find s.th. out; *um et.* **~** lose s.th.; *zu et.* **~** come by s.th.; *wieder zu sich* **~** come round *or* to; *wie* **~** *Sie dazu!* how dare you!

**Komment|ar** [kɔmɛn'taːr] *m* (-s/-e) commentary, comment; **~ator** [~tɔr] *m* (-s/-en) commentator; **2ieren** [~'tiːrən] *v/t.* (*no* -ge-, *h*) comment on.

**Kommissar** [kɔmi'saːr] *m* (-s/-e) commissioner; superintendent; *pol.* commissar.

**Kommißbrot** F [kɔ'mis-] *n* army *or* ration bread, *Am. a.* G.I. bread.

**Kommission** [kɔmi'sjoːn] *f* (-/-en) commission (*a.* †); committee; **~är** † [~o'nɛːr] *m* (-s/-e) commission agent.

**Kommode** [kɔ'moːdə] *f* (-/-n) chest of drawers, *Am.* bureau.

**Kommunis|mus** *pol.* [kɔmu'nismus] *m* (-/*no pl.*) communism; **~t** *m* (-en/-en) communist; **2tisch** *adj.* communist(ic).

**Komöd|iant** [kømø'djant] *m* (-en/-en) comedian; *fig.* play-actor; **2ie** [~'møːdjə] *f* (-/-n) comedy; **~spielen** play-act.

**Kompagnon** † [kɔmpan'jõː] *m* (-s/-s) (business-)partner, associate.

**Kompanie** ✕ [kɔmpa'niː] *f* (-/-n) company.

**Kompaß** ['kɔmpas] *m* (Kompasses/Kompasse) compass.

**kompetent** *adj.* [kɔmpe'tɛnt] competent.

**komplett** *adj.* [kɔm'plɛt] complete.

**Komplex** [kɔm'plɛks] *m* (-es/-e) complex (*a. psych.*); block (*of houses*).

**Kompliment** [kɔmpli'mɛnt] *n* (-[e]s/-e) compliment.

**Komplize** [kɔm'pliːtsə] *m* (-n/-n) accomplice.

**komplizier|en** [kɔmpli'tsiːrən] *v/t.* (*no* -ge-, *h*) complicate; **~t** *adj.* machine, *etc.*: complicated; *argument, situation, etc.*: complex; **~er Bruch** 𝓰 compound fracture.

**Komplott** [kɔm'plɔt] *n* (-[e]s/-e) plot, conspiracy.

**kompo|nieren** ♪ [kɔmpo'niːrən] *v/t. and v/i.* (*no* -ge-, *h*) compose; **2nist** *m* (-en/-en) composer; **2sition** [~zi'tsjoːn] *f* (-/-en) composition.

**Kompott** [kɔm'pɔt] *n* (-[e]s/-e) compote, stewed fruit, *Am. a.* sauce.

**komprimieren** [kɔmpri'miːrən] *v/t.* (*no* -ge-, *h*) compress.

**Kompromi|ß** [kɔmpro'mis] *m* (Kompromisses/Kompromisse) compromise; **2ßlos** *adj.* uncompromising; **2ttieren** [~'tiːrən] *v/t.* (*no* -ge-, *h*) compromise.

**Kondens|ator** [kɔndɛn'zaːtɔr] *m* (-s/-en) ⚡ capacitor, condenser (*a.* 🜁); **2ieren** [~'ziːrən] *v/t.* (*no* -ge-, *h*) condense.

**Kondens|milch** [kɔn'dɛns-] *f* evaporated milk; **~streifen** ✈ *m* condensation *or* vapo(u)r trail; **~wasser** *n* water of condensation.

**Konditor** [kɔn'diːtɔr] *m* (-s/-en) confectioner, pastry-cook; **~ei** [~ito'raɪ] *f* (-/-en) confectionery, confectioner's (shop); **~eiwaren** *f/pl.* confectionery.

**Konfekt** [kɔn'fɛkt] *n* (-[e]s/-e) sweets *pl.*, sweetmeat, *Am. a.* soft candy; chocolates *pl.*

**Konfektion** [kɔnfɛk'tsjoːn] *f* (-/-en) (manufacture of) ready-made clothing; **~sanzug** [kɔnfɛk'tsjoːns?-] *m* ready-made suit; **~sgeschäft** *n* ready-made clothes shop.

**Konfer|enz** [kɔnfe'rɛnts] *f* (-/-en) conference; **2ieren** [~'iːrən] *v/i.* (*no* -ge-, *h*) confer (*über acc.* on).

**Konfession** [kɔnfe'sjoːn] *f* (-/-en) confession, creed; denomination; **2ell** *adj.* [~o'nɛl] confessional, denominational; **~sschule** [~'sjoːns-] *f* denominational school.

**Konfirm|and** *eccl.* [kɔnfir'mant] *m* (-en/-en) candidate for confirmation, confirmee; **~ation** [~'tsjoːn] *f* (-/-en) confirmation; **2ieren** [~'miːrən] *v/t.* (*no* -ge-, *h*) confirm.

**konfiszieren** ⚖ [kɔnfis'tsiːrən] *v/t.* (*no* -ge-, *h*) confiscate, seize.

**Konfitüre** [kɔnfi'tyːrə] *f* (-/-n) preserve(s *pl.*), (whole-fruit) jam.

**Konflikt** [kɔn'flikt] *m* (-[e]s/-e) conflict.

**konform** *adv.* [kɔn'fɔrm]: **~ gehen mit** agree *or* concur with.

**konfrontieren** [kɔnfrɔn'tiːrən] *v/t.* (*no* -ge-, *h*) confront (*mit* with).

**konfus** *adj.* [kɔn'fuːs] *p., a. ideas:* muddled; *p.* muddle-headed.

**Kongreß** [kɔn'grɛs] *m* (Kongresses/Kongresse) congress; *Am. parl.* Congress; **~halle** *f* congress hall.

**König** ['køːniç] *m* (-s/-e) king; **2lich** *adj.* ['~k-] royal; regal; **~reich** ['~k-] *n* kingdom; **~swürde** ['~ks-] *f* royal dignity, kingship; **~tum** *n* (-s/~er) monarchy; kingship.

**Konjug|ation** *gr.* [kɔnjuga'tsjoːn] *f*

(-/-en); 2ieren [~'gi:rən] v/t. (no -ge-, h) conjugate.

**Konjunkt|iv** gr. ['konjuŋkti:f] m (-s/-e) subjunctive (mood); **~ur ✝** [~'tu:r] f (-/-en) trade or business cycle; economic or business situation.

**konkret** adj. [kɔn'kre:t] concrete.

**Konkurrent** [kɔnku'rɛnt] m (-en/ -en) competitor, rival.

**Konkurrenz** [kɔnku'rɛnts] f (-/-en) competition; competitors pl., rivals pl.; sports: event; 2fähig adj. able to compete; competitive; **~geschäft** n rival business or firm; **~kampf** m competition.

**konkur'rieren** v/i. (no -ge-, h) compete (mit with; um for).

**Konkurs ✝**, ⚖ [kɔn'kurs] m (-es/-e) bankruptcy, insolvency, failure; **~** anmelden file a petition in bankruptcy; in **~** gehen or geraten become insolvent, go bankrupt; **~er-klärung** ⚖ f declaration of insolvency; **~masse** ⚖ f bankrupt's estate; **~verfahren** ⚖ n bankruptcy proceedings pl.; **~verwalter** ⚖ m trustee in bankruptcy; liquidator.

**können** ['kœnən] 1. v/i. (irr., ge-, h): ich kann nicht I can't, I am not able to; 2. v/t. (irr., ge-, h) know, understand; e-e Sprache **~** know a language, have command of a language; 3. v/aux. (irr., no -ge-, h) be able to inf., be capable of ger.; be allowed or permitted to inf.; es kann sein it may be; du kannst hingehen you may go there; er kann schwimmen he can swim, he knows how to swim; 4. 2 n (-s/no pl.) ability; skill; proficiency.

**Konnossement ✝** [kɔnɔsə'mɛnt] n (-[e]s/-é) bill of lading.

**konnte** ['kɔntə] pret. of können.

**konsequen|t** adj. [kɔnze'kvɛnt] consistent; 2z [~ts] f (-/-en) consistency; consequence; die **~en** ziehen do the only thing one can.

**konservativ** adj. [kɔnzerva'ti:f] conservative.

**Konserven** [kɔn'zervən] f/pl. tinned or Am. canned foods pl.; **~büchse** f, **~dose** f tin, Am. can; **~fabrik** f tinning factory, esp. Am. cannery.

**konservieren** [kɔnzer'vi:rən] v/t. (no -ge-, h) preserve.

**Konsonant** gr. [kɔnzo'nant] m (-en/ -en) consonant.

**Konsortium ✝** [kɔn'zɔrtsjum] n (-s/Konsortien) syndicate.

**konstruieren** [kɔnstru'i:rən] v/t. (no -ge-, h) gr. construe; ⊕: construct; design.

**Konstruk|teur** ⊕ [kɔnstruk'tø:r] m (-s/-e) designer; **~tion** ⊕ [~'tsjo:n] f (-/-en) construction; **~'tionsfehler** ⊕ m constructional defect.

**Konsul** pol. ['kɔnzul] m (-s/-n) con-

sul; **~at** pol. [~'la:t] n (-[e]s/-e) consulate; 2'tieren v/t. (no -ge-, h) consult, seek s.o.'s advice.

**Konsum** [kɔn'zu:m] m 1. (-s/no pl.) consumption; 2. (-s/-s) co-operative shop, Am. co-operative store, F co-op; 3. (-s/no pl.) consumers' co-operative society, F co-op; **~ent** [~u'mɛnt] m (-en/-en) consumer; 2ieren [~u'mi:rən] v/t. (no -ge-, h) consume; **~verein** m s. Konsum 3.

**Kontakt** [kɔn'takt] m (-[e]s/-e) contact (a. ⚡); in **~** stehen mit be in contact or touch with.

**Kontinent** ['kɔntinɛnt] m (-[e]s/-e) continent.

**Kontingent** [kɔntiŋ'gɛnt] n (-[e]s/ -e) ✗ contingent, quota (a. ✝).

**Konto ✝** ['kɔnto] n (-s/Konten, Kontos, Konti) account; **'~auszug ✝** m statement of account; **~korrent-konto ✝** [~kɔ'rɛnt-] n current account.

**Kontor** [kɔn'to:r] n (-s/-e) office; **~ist** [~o'rist] m (-en/-en) clerk.

**Kontrast** [kɔn'trast] m (-es/-e) contrast.

**Kontroll|e** [kɔn'trɔlə] f (-/-n) control; supervision; check; 2ieren [~'li:rən] v/t. (no -ge-, h) control; supervise; check.

**Kontroverse** [kɔntro'verzə] f (-/-n) controversy.

**konventionell** adj. [kɔnvɛntsjo'nɛl] conventional.

**Konversation** [kɔnverza'tsjo:n] f (-/-en) conversation; **~slexikon** n encyclop(a)edia.

**Konzentr|ation** [kɔntsɛntra'tsjo:n] f (-/-en) concentration; 2ieren [~-'tri:rən] v/t. (no -ge-, h) concentrate, focus (attention, etc.) (auf acc. on); sich **~** concentrate (auf acc. on).

**Konzern ✝** [kɔn'tsern] m (-s/-e) combine, group.

**Konzert ♪** [kɔn'tsɛrt] n (-[e]s/-e) concert; recital; concerto; **~saal ♪** m concert-hall.

**Konzession** [kɔntse'sjo:n] f (-/-en) concession; licen|ce, Am. -se; 2ieren [~o'ni:rən] v/t. (no -ge-, h) license.

**Kopf** [kɔpf] m (-[e]s/⸚e) head; top; brains pl.; pipe: bowl; ein fähiger **~** a clever fellow; **~** hoch! chin up!; j-m über den **~** wachsen outgrow s.o.; fig. get beyond s.o.; **~arbeit** f brain-work; '**~bahnhof 🚂** m terminus, Am. terminal; **~bedeckung** f headgear, headwear.

**köpfen** ['kœpfən] v/t. (ge-, h) behead, decapitate; football: head (ball).

'**Kopf|ende** n head; '**~hörer** n headphone, headset; '**~kissen** n pillow; '2los adj. headless; fig. confused; '**~nicken** n (-s/no pl.) nod; '**~rechnen** n (-s/no pl.) mental arithmetic; '**~salat** m cabbage-lettuce;

'**~schmerzen** m/pl. headache; '**~sprung** m headcr; '**~tuch** n scarf; ²**über** adv. head first, headlong; '**~weh** n (-[e]s/-e) s. Kopfschmerzen; '**~zerbrechen** n (-s/no pl.): j-m ~ machen puzzle s.o.

**Kopie** [ko'pi:] f(-/-n) copy; duplicate; phot., film: print; **~rstift** m indelible pencil.

**Koppel** ['kɔpəl] **1.** f (-/-n) hounds: couple; horses: string; paddock; **2.** ✕ n (-s/-) belt; '²n v/t. (ge-, h) couple (a. ⊕, ⚡).

**Koralle** [ko'ralə] f (-/-n) coral; **~nfischer** m coral-fisher.

**Korb** [kɔrp] m (-[e]s/⸚e) basket; fig. refusal; Hahn im ~ cock of the walk; '**~möbel** n/pl. wicker furniture.

**Kordel** ['kɔrdəl] f (-/-n) string, twine; cord.

**Korinthe** [ko'rintə] f (-/-n) currant.

**Kork** [kɔrk] m (-[e]s/-e), '**~en** m (-s/-) cork; '**~(en)zieher** m (-s/-) corkscrew.

**Korn** [kɔrn] **1.** n (-[e]s/⸚er) seed; grain; n (-[e]s/-e) corn, cereals pl.; **3.** n (-[e]s/⚡-e) front sight; **4.** F m (-[e]s/-) (German) corn whisky.

**körnig** adj. ['kœrniç] granular; in compounds: ...-grained.

**Körper** ['kœrpər] m (-s/-) body (a. phys., 🜂); ⚕ solid; '**~bau** m build, physique; ²**behindert** adj. ['**~bə**hindərt] (physically) disabled, handicapped; '**~beschaffenheit** f constitution, physique; '**~fülle** f corpulence; '**~geruch** m body-odo(u)r; **~größe** f stature; '**~kraft** f physical strength; ²**lich** adj. physical; corporal; bodily; '**~pflege** f care of the body, hygiene; '**~schaft** f (-/-en) body (corporate), corporation; '**~verletzung** ⚖ f bodily harm, physical injury.

**korrekt** adj. [kɔ'rekt] correct; ²**or** [**~ɔr**] m (-s/-en) (proof-)reader; ²**ur** [**~'tu:r**] f (-/-en) correction; ²**ur**-**bogen** m proof-sheet.

**Korrespond|ent** [kɔrespɔn'dent] m (-en/-en) correspondent; **~enz** [**~ts**] f (-/-en) correspondence; ²**ieren** [**~'di:rən**] v/i. (no -ge-, h) correspond (mit with).

**korrigieren** [kɔri'gi:rən] v/t. (no -ge-, h) correct.

**Korsett** [kɔr'zet] n (-[e]s/-e, -s) corset, stays pl.

**Kosename** ['ko:zə-] m pet name.

**Kosmetik** [kɔs'me:tik] f (-/no pl.) beauty culture; **~erin** f (-/-nen) beautician, cosmetician.

**Kost** [kɔst] f (-/no pl.) food, fare; board; diet; '²**bar** adj. present, etc.: costly, expensive; health, time, etc.: valuable; mineral, etc.: precious.

'**kosten¹** v/t. (ge-, h) taste, try, sample.

'**Kosten²** **1.** pl. cost(s pl.); expense(s pl.), charges pl.; auf ~ (gen.) at the expense of; **2.** ⚡ v/t. (ge-, h) cost; take, require (time, etc.); '**~anschlag** m estimate, tender; '²**frei** **1.** adj. free; **2.** adv. free of charge; '²**los** s. kostenfrei.

**Kost|gänger** ['kɔstgeŋər] m (-s/-) boarder; '**~geld** n board-wages pl.

**köstlich** adj. ['kœstliç] delicious.

'**Kost|probe** f taste, sample (a. fig.); ²**spielig** adj. ['**~ʃpi:liç**] expensive, costly.

**Kostüm** [kɔs'ty:m] n (-s/-e) costume, dress; suit; **~fest** n fancy-dress ball.

**Kot** [ko:t] m (-[e]s/no pl.) mud, mire; excrement.

**Kotelett** [kɔt(ə)'let] n (-[e]s/-s, ✎ -e) pork, veal, lamb: cutlet; pork, veal, mutton: chop; **~en** pl. sidewhiskers pl., Am. a. sideburns pl.

'**Kot|flügel** mot. m mudguard, Am. a. fender; '²**ig** adj. muddy, miry.

**Krabbe** zo. ['krabə] f (-/-n) shrimp; crab.

**krabbeln** ['krabəln] v/i. (ge-, sein) crawl.

**Krach** [krax] m (-[e]s/-e, -s) crack, crash (a. ✝); quarrel, sl. bust-up; F row; ~ machen kick up a row; '²**en** v/i. (ge-) **1.** (h) thunder: crash; cannon: roar, thunder; **2.** (sein) crash (a. ✝), smash.

**krächzen** ['kreçtsən] v/t. and v/i. (ge-, h) croak.

**Kraft** [kraft] **1.** f (-/⸚e) strength; force (a. ✕); power (a. ⚡, ⊕); energy; vigo(u)r; efficacy; in ~ sein (setzen, treten) be in (put into, come into) operation or force; außer ~ setzen repeal, abolish (law); **2.** ⚡ prp. (gen.) by virtue of; '**~anlage** ⚡ f power plant; '**~brühe** f beef tea; '**~fahrer** m driver, motorist; '**~fahrzeug** n motor vehicle.

**kräftig** adj. ['kreftiç] strong (a. fig.), powerful; fig. nutritious, rich; **~en** ['**~gən**] (ge-, h) **1.** v/t. strengthen; **2.** v/i. give strength.

'**kraft|los** adj. powerless; feeble; weak; '²**probe** f trial of strength; '²**rad** n motor cycle; '²**stoff** mot. m fuel; '**~voll** adj. powerful (a. fig.); ²**wagen** m motor vehicle; ²**werk** ⚡ n power station.

**Kragen** ['kra:gən] m (-s/-) collar; '**~knopf** m collar-stud, Am. collar button.

**Krähe** orn. ['kre:ə] f (-/-n) crow; '²**n** v/i. (ge-, h) crow.

**Kralle** ['kralə] f (-/-n) claw (a. fig.); talon, clutch.

**Kram** [kra:m] m (-[e]s/no pl.) stuff, odds and ends pl.; fig. affairs pl., business.

**Krämer²** ['kre:mər] m (-s/-) shop-keeper.

**Krampf** ♂ [krampf] *m* (-[e]s/⸗e) cramp; spasm, convulsion; '⸗ader ♂ *f* varicose vein; '2haft *adj.* ♂ spasmodic, convulsive; *laugh*: forced.

**Kran** ⊕ [kra:n] *m* (-[e]s/⸗e, -e) crane.

**krank** *adj.* [kraŋk] sick; *organ, etc.*: diseased; ~ *sein p.* be ill, *esp. Am.* be sick; *animal*: be sick *or* ill; ~ werden *p.* fall ill *or esp. Am.* sick; *animal*: fall sick; '2e *m, f* (-n/-n) sick person, patient, invalid.

**kränkeln** ['krɛŋkəln] *v/i.* (ge-, h) be sickly, be in poor health.

**'kranken** *fig. v/i.* (ge-, h) suffer (*an dat.* from).

**kränken** ['krɛŋkən] *v/t.* (ge-, h) offend, injure; wound *or* hurt *s.o.'s* feelings; *sich* ~ feel hurt (*über acc.* at, about).

**'Kranken|bett** *n* sick-bed; '⸗geld *n* sick-benefit; '⸗haus *n* hospital; '⸗kasse *f* health insurance (fund); '⸗kost *f* invalid diet; '⸗lager *n s. Krankenbett*; '⸗pflege *f* nursing; '⸗pfleger *m* male nurse; '⸗schein *m* medical certificate; '⸗schwester *f* (sick-)nurse; '⸗versicherung *f* health *or* sickness insurance; '⸗wagen *m* ambulance; '⸗zimmer *n* sick-room.

**'krank|haft** *adj.* morbid, pathological; '2heit *f* (-/-en) illness, sickness; disease.

**'Krankheits|erreger** ♂ *m* pathogenic agent; '⸗erscheinung *f* symptom (*a. fig.*).

**'kränklich** *adj.* sickly, ailing.

**'Kränkung** *f* (-/-en) insult, offen|ce, *Am.* -se.

**Kranz** [krants] *m* (-es/⸗e) wreath; garland.

**Kränzchen** *fig.* ['krɛntsçən] *n* (-s/-) tea-party, F hen-party.

**kraß** *adj.* [kras] crass, gross.

**kratzen** ['kratsən] (ge-, h) 1. *v/i.* scratch; 2. *v/t.* scratch; *sich* ~ scratch (o.s.).

**kraulen** ['kraulən] (ge-) 1. *v/t.* (h) scratch gently; 2. *v/i.* (sein) *sports*: crawl.

**kraus** *adj.* [kraus] curly, curled; crisp; frizzy; *die Stirn* ~ *ziehen* knit one's brow; '2e *f* (-/-n) ruff(le), frill.

**kräuseln** ['krɔyzəln] *v/t.* (ge-, h) curl, crimp (*hair, etc.*); pucker (*lips*); *sich* ~ *hair*: curl; *waves, etc.*: ruffle; *smoke*: curl *or* wreath up.

**Kraut** ♀ [kraut] *n* 1. (-[e]s/⸗er) plant; herb; 2. (-[e]s/*no pl.*) tops *pl.*; cabbage; weed.

**Krawall** [kra'val] *m* (-[e]s/-e) riot; shindy, F row, *sl.* rumpus.

**Krawatte** [kra'vatə] *f* (-/-n) (neck-)tie.

**Kreatur** [krea'tu:r] *f* (-/-en) creature.

**Krebs** [kre:ps] *m* (-es/-e) *zo.* crayfish, *Am. a.* crawfish; *ast.* Cancer, Crab; ♂ cancer; ~e *pl.* ♱ returns *pl.*

**Kredit** ♱ [kre'di:t] *m* (-[e]s/-e) credit; *auf* ~ on credit; 2fähig ♱ *adj.* credit-worthy.

**Kreide** ['kraidə] *f* (-/-n) chalk; *paint.* crayon.

**Kreis** [krais] *m* (-es/-e) circle (*a. fig.*); *ast.* orbit; ♂ circuit; district, *Am.* county; *fig.*: sphere, field; range.

**kreischen** ['kraiʃən] (ge-, h) 1. *v/i.* screech, scream; squeal, shriek; *circular saw, etc.*: grate (on the ear); 2. *v/t.* shriek, screech (*insult, etc.*).

**Kreisel** ['kraizəl] *m* (-s/-) (whipping-)top; '⸗kompaß *m* gyro-compass.

**kreisen** ['kraizən] *v/i.* (ge-, h) (move in a) circle; revolve, rotate; ♍, *bird*: circle; *bird*: wheel; *blood, money*: circulate.

**kreis|förmig** *adj.* ['kraisfœrmiç] circular; '2lauf *m physiol., money, etc.*: circulation; *business, trade*: cycle; '2laufstörungen ♂ *f/pl.* circulatory trouble; '⸗rund *adj.* circular; 2säge ♂ *f* circular saw, *Am. a.* buzz saw; '2verkehr *m* roundabout (traffic).

**Krempe** ['krɛmpə] *f* (-/-n) brim (*of hat*).

**Krempel** F ['krɛmpəl] *m* (-s/*no pl.*) rubbish, stuff, lumber.

**krepieren** [kre'pi:rən] *v/i.* (*no* -ge-, sein) *shell*: burst, explode; *sl.* kick the bucket, peg *or* snuff out; *animal*: die, perish.

**Krepp** [krep] *m* (-s/-s, -e) crêpe; crape; ⸗apier ['krɛppapi:r] *n* crêpe paper; '⸗sohle *f* crêpe(-rubber) sole.

**Kreuz** [krɔyts] 1. *n* (-es/-e) cross (*a. fig.*); crucifix; *anat.* small of the back; ♂ sacral region; *cards*: club(s *pl.*); ♪ sharp; *zu* ~(e) *kriechen* eat humble pie; 2. 2 *adv.*: ~ *und quer* in all directions; criss-cross.

**'kreuzen** (ge-, h) 1. *v/t.* cross, fold (*arms, etc.*); ♀, *zo.* cross(-breed), hybridize; *sich* ~ *roads*: cross, intersect; *plans, etc.*: clash; 2. ⚓ *v/i.* cruise.

**'Kreuzer** ⚓ *m* (-s/-) cruiser.

**'Kreuz|fahrer** *hist. m* crusader; '⸗fahrt *f hist.* crusade; ⚓ cruise; '⸗feuer *n* ✕ cross-fire (*a. fig.*); 2igen ['⸗igən] *v/t.* (ge-, h) crucify; ⸗igung ['⸗iguŋ] *f* (-/-en) crucifixion; ⸗otter *zo. f* common viper; '⸗ritter *hist. m* knight of the Cross; '⸗schmerzen *m/pl.* back ache; '⸗spinne *zo. f* garden- *or* cross-spider; '⸗ung *f* (-/-en) ♞, roads, *etc.*: crossing, intersection; *roads*: crossroads; ♀, *zo.* cross-breeding, hybridization; '⸗verhör ♎ *n* cross-examination; *ins* ~ *nehmen* cross-examine; '**~weise** adv. crosswise, crossways; '**~worträtsel** n crossword (puzzle); '**~zug** hist. m crusade.

**kriech|en** ['kri:çən] v/i. (irr., ge-, sein) creep, crawl; fig. cringe (vor dat. to, before); '**~er** contp. m (-s/-) toady; **~erei** contp. [~'raɪ] f (-/-en) toadyism.

**Krieg** [kri:k] m (-[e]s/-e) war; im ~ at war; s. führen.

**kriegen** F ['kri:gən] v/t. (ge-, h) catch, seize; get.

**Krieg|er** ['kri:gər] m (-s/-) warrior; '**~erdenkmal** n war memorial; '**~erisch** adj. warlike; militant; '**~führend** adj. belligerent; '**~führung** f warfare.

'**Kriegs|beil** fig. n: das ~ begraben bury the hatchet; **~beschädigt** adj. ['~bəʃɛ:dɪçt] war-disabled; '**~beschädigte** m (-n/-n) disabled ex-serviceman; '**~dienst** ✕ m war service; '**~dienstverweigerer** ✕ m (-s/-) conscientious objector; '**~erklärung** f declaration of war; '**~flotte** f naval force; '**~gefangene** m prisoner of war; '**~gefangenschaft** ✕ f captivity; '**~gericht** ✕ n court martial; **~gewinnler** ['~gəvɪnlər] m (-s/-) war profiteer; '**~hafen** m naval port; '**~kamerad** m wartime comrade; '**~list** f stratagem; '**~macht** f military forces pl.; '**~minister** hist. m minister of war; Secretary of State for War, Am. Secretary of War; '**~ministerium** hist. n ministry of war; War Office, Am. War Department; '**~rat** m council of war; '**~schauplatz** ✕ m theatre or Am. -er of war; '**~schiff** n warship; '**~schule** f military academy; '**~teilnehmer** m combatant; ex-serviceman, Am. veteran; '**~treiber** m (-s/-) warmonger; '**~verbrecher** m war criminal; '**~zug** m (military) expedition, campaign.

**Kriminal|beamte** [krimi'na:l-] m criminal investigator, Am. plain-clothes man; **~film** m crime film; thriller; **~polizei** f criminal investigation department; **~roman** m detective or crime novel, thriller, sl. whodun(n)it.

**kriminell** adj. [krimi'nɛl] criminal; **2e** m (-n/-n) criminal.

**Krippe** ['krɪpə] f (-/-n) crib, manger; crèche.

**Krise** ['kri:zə] f (-/-n) crisis.

**Kristall** [krɪs'tal] 1. m (-s/-e) crystal; 2. n (-s/no pl.) crystal(-glass); **2isieren** [~i'zi:rən] v/i. and v/refl. (no -ge-, h) crystallize.

**Kriti|k** [kri'ti:k] f (-/-en) criticism; ♪, thea., etc.: review, criticism; F unter aller ~ beneath contempt; ~ üben an (dat.) s. kritisieren; **~ker** ['kri:tikər] m (-s/-) critic; books: re-

viewer; **2sch** adj. ['kri:tiʃ] critical (gegenüber of); **2sieren** [kriti'zi:rən] v/t. (no -ge-, h) criticize; review (book).

**kritt|eln** ['krɪtəln] v/t. (ge-, h) find fault (an dat. with), cavil (at); **2ler** ['~lər] m (-s/-) fault-finder, caviller.

**Kritzel|ei** [krɪtsə'laɪ] f (-/-en) scrawl(ing), scribble, scribbling; '**2n** v/t. and v/i. (ge-, h) scrawl, scribble.

**kroch** [krɔx] pret. of kriechen.

**Krokodil** zo. [kroko'di:l] n (-s/-e) crocodile.

**Krone** ['kro:nə] f (-/-n) crown; coronet (of duke, earl, etc.).

**krönen** ['krø:nən] v/t. (ge-, h) crown (zum König king) (a. fig.).

'**Kron|leuchter** m chandelier; lust|re, Am. -er; electrolier; '**~prinz** m crown prince; '**~prinzessin** f crown princess.

'**Krönung** f (-/-en) coronation, crowning; fig. climax, culmination.

'**Kronzeuge** ✟✟ m chief witness; King's evidence, Am. State's evidence.

**Kropf** ✞ [krɔpf] goit|re, Am. -er.

**Kröte** zo. ['krø:tə] f (-/-n) toad.

**Krücke** ['krykə] f (-/-n) crutch.

**Krug** [kru:k] m (-[e]s/=e) jug, pitcher; jar; mug; tankard.

**Krume** ['kru:mə] f (-/-n) crumb; ✗ topsoil.

**Krümel** ['kry:məl] m (-s/-) small crumb; '**2n** v/t. and v/i. (ge-, h) crumble.

**krumm** adj. [krum] p. bent, stooping; limb, nose, etc.: crooked; spine: curved; deal, business, etc.: crooked; '**~beinig** adj. bandy- or bow-legged.

**krümmen** ['krymən] v/t. (ge-, h) bend (arm, back, etc.); crook (finger, etc.); curve (metal sheet, etc.); sich ~ person, snake, etc.: writhe; worm, etc.: wriggle; sich vor Schmerzen ~ writhe with pain; sich vor Lachen ~ be convulsed with laughter.

'**Krümmung** f (-/-en) road, etc.: bend; arch, road, etc.: curve; river, path, etc.: turn, wind, meander; earth's surface, spine, etc.: curvature.

**Krüppel** ['krypəl] m (-s/-) cripple.

**Kruste** ['krustə] f (-/-n) crust.

**Kübel** ['ky:bəl] m (-s/-) tub; pail, bucket.

**Kubik|meter** [ku'bi:k-] n, m cubic met|re, Am. -er; **~wurzel** ♐ f cube root.

**Küche** ['kyçə] f (-/-n) kitchen; cuisine, cookery; s. kalt.

**Kuchen** ['ku:xən] m (-s/-) cake, flan; pastry.

'**Küchen|gerät** n, '**~geschirr** n kitchen utensils pl.; '**~herd** m (kitchen-)range; cooker, stove; '**~schrank** m kitchen cupboard or cabinet; '**~zettel** *m* bill of fare, menu.

**Kuckuck** *orn.* ['kukuk] *m* (-s/-e) cuckoo.

**Kufe** ['ku:fə] *f* (-/-n) ≋ skid; *sleigh, etc.*: runner.

**Küfer** ['ky:fər] *m* (-s/-) cooper; cellarman.

**Kugel** ['ku:gəl] *f* (-/-n) ball; ✕ bullet; Å, *geogr.* sphere; *sports*: shot, weight; **2förmig** *adj.* ['~fœrmiç] spherical, ball-shaped, globular; **~gelenk** ⊕, *anat.* *n* ball-and-socket joint; '**~lager** ⊕ *n* ball-bearing; '2n (ge-) 1. *v/i.* (*sein*) *ball, etc.*: roll; 2. *v/t.* (h) roll (*ball, etc.*); *sich ~ children, etc.*: roll about; F double up (*vor* with *laughter*); '**~schreiber** *m* ball-(point)-pen; '**~stoßen** *n* (-s/*no pl.*) *sports*: putting the shot *or* weight.

**Kuh** *zo.* [ku:] *f* (-/≈e) cow.

**kühl** *adj.* [ky:l] cool (*a. fig.*); '2**anlage** *f* cold-storage plant; '2e *f* (-/*no pl.*) cool(ness); '**~en** *v/t.* (ge-, h) cool (*wine, wound, etc.*); chill (*wine, etc.*); '2er *mot.* *m* (-s/-) radiator; '2**raum** *m* cold-storage chamber; '2**schrank** *m* refrigerator, F fridge.

**kühn** *adj.* [ky:n] bold (*a. fig.*), daring; audacious.

'**Kuhstall** *m* cow-house, byre, *Am. a.* cow barn.

**Küken** *orn.* ['ky:kən] *n* (-s/-) chick.

**kulant** ✝ *adj.* [ku'lant] firm, *etc.*: accommodating, obliging; *price, terms, etc.*: fair, easy.

**Kulisse** [ku'lisə] *f* (-/-n) *thea.* wing, side-scene; *fig.* front; *~n pl. a.* scenery; *hinter den ~n* behind the scenes.

**Kult** [kult] *m* (-[e]s/-e) cult, worship.

**kultivieren** [kulti'vi:rən] *v/t.* (*no -ge-, h*) cultivate (*a. fig.*).

**Kultur** [kul'tu:r] *f* (-/-en) ✗ cultivation; *fig.*: culture; civilization; 2ell *adj.* [~'rel] cultural; **~film** [~'tu:r-] *m* educational film; **~geschichte** *f* history of civilization; **~volk** *n* civilized people.

**Kultus** ['kultus] *m* (-/*Kulte*) *s.* Kult; '**~minister** *m* minister of education and cultural affairs; '**~ministerium** *n* ministry of education and cultural affairs.

**Kummer** ['kumər] *m* (-s/*no pl.*) grief, sorrow; trouble, worry.

**kümmer|lich** *adj.* ['kymərliç] *life, etc.*: miserable, wretched; *conditions, etc.*: pitiful, pitiable; *result, etc.*: poor; *resources*: scanty; '**~n** *v/t.* (ge-, h): es kümmert mich I bother, I worry; *sich ~ um* look after, take care of; see to; meddle with.

'**kummervoll** *adj.* sorrowful.

**Kump|an** F [kum'pa:n] *m* (-s/-e) companion; F mate, chum, *Am.* F *a.*

buddy; **~el** ['~pəl] *m* (-s/-, F -s) ✕ pitman, collier; F work-mate; F *s.* Kumpan.

**Kunde** ['kundə] 1. *m* (-n/-n) customer, client; 2. *f* (-/-n) knowledge.

**Kundgebung** ['kunt-] *f* (-/-en) manifestation; *pol.* rally.

**kündig|en** ['kyndigən] (ge-, h) 1. *v/i.*: *j-m ~* give s.o. notice; 2. *v/t.* ✝ call in (*capital*); ✝✝ cancel (*contract*); *pol.* denounce (*treaty*); '2**ung** *f* (-/-en) notice; ✝ calling in; ✝✝ cancellation; *pol.* denunciation.

'**Kundschaft** *f* (-/-en) customers *pl.*, clients *pl.*; custom, clientele; '**~er** ✕ *m* (-s/-) scout; spy.

**künftig** ['kynftiç] 1. *adj. event, years, etc.*: future; *event, programme, etc.*: coming; *life, world, etc.*: next; 2. *adv.* in future, from now on.

**Kunst** [kunst] *f* (-/≈e) art; skill; '**~akademie** *f* academy of arts; '**~ausstellung** *f* art exhibition; '**~druck** *m* art print(ing); '**~dünger** *m* artificial manure, fertilizer; '2**fertig** *adj.* skilful, skilled; '**~fertigkeit** *f* artistic skill; '**~gegenstand** *m* objet d'art; '2**gerecht** *adj.* skilful; professional, expert; '**~geschichte** *f* history of art; '**~gewerbe** *n* arts and crafts *pl.*; applied arts *pl.*; '**~glied** *n* artificial limb; '**~griff** *m* trick, dodge; artifice, knack; '**~händler** *m* art-dealer; '**~kenner** *m* connoisseur of *or* in art; '**~leder** *n* imitation *or* artificial leather.

**Künstler** ['kynstlər] *m* (-s/-) artist; ♪, *thea.* performer; '2**isch** *adj.* artistic.

**künstlich** *adj.* ['kynstliç] *eye, flower, light, etc.*: artificial; *teeth, hair, etc.*: false; *fibres, dyes, etc.*: synthetic.

'**Kunst|liebhaber** *m* art-lover; '**~maler** *m* artist, painter; '**~reiter** *m* equestrian; circus-rider; '**~schätze** ['~ʃɛtsə] *m/pl.* art treasures *pl.*; '**~seide** *f* artificial silk; rayon; '**~stück** *n* feat, trick, F stunt; '**~tischler** *m* cabinet-maker; '**~verlag** *m* art publishers *pl.*; '2**voll** *adj.* artistic, elaborate; '**~werk** *n* work of art.

**kunterbunt** F *fig. adj.* ['kuntər-] higgledy-piggledy.

**Kupfer** ['kupfər] *n* (-s/*no pl.*) copper; '**~geld** *n* copper coins *pl.*, F coppers *pl.*; '2n *adj.* (of) copper; '2**rot** *adj.* copper-colo(u)red; '**~stich** *m* copper-plate engraving.

**Kupon** [ku'põ:] *m* (-s/-s) *s.* Coupon.

**Kuppe** ['kupə] *f* (-/-n) rounded hilltop; *nail*: head.

**Kuppel** △ ['kupəl] *f* (-/-n) dome, cupola; **~ei** ✝✝ ['~'lai] *f* (-/-en) procuring; '2n (ge-, h) 1. *v/t. s.* koppeln; 2. *mot. v/i.* declutch.

**Kuppl|er** ['kuplər] *m* (-s/-) pimp, procurer; '**~ung** *f* (-/-en) ⊕ coupling (*a.* ☸); *mot.* clutch.

**Kur** [ku:r] f (-/-en) course of treatment, cure.

**Kür** [ky:r] f (-/-en) sports: s. Kürlauf; voluntary exercise.

**Kuratorium** [kura'to:rium] n (-s/ Kuratorien) board of trustees.

**Kurbel** ⊕ ['kurbəl] f (-/-n) crank, winch, handle; '~n (ge-, h) 1. v/t. shoot (film); in die Höhe ~ winch up (load, etc.); wind up (car window, etc.); 2. v/i. crank.

**Kürbis** ♦ ['kyrbis] m (-ses/-se) pumpkin.

**'Kur|gast** m visitor to or patient at a health resort or spa; '~haus n spa hotel.

**Kurier** [ku'ri:r] m (-s/-e) courier, express (messenger).

**kurieren** ♂ [ku'ri:rən] v/t. (no -ge-, h) cure.

**kurios** adj. [kur'jo:s] curious, odd, strange, queer.                [skating.]

**'Kürlauf** m sports: free (roller))

**'Kur|ort** m health resort; spa; '~pfuscher** m quack (doctor); ~pfusche'rei f (-/-en) quackery.

**Kurs** [kurs] m (-es/-e) ♦ currency; ♦ rate, price; ♦ and fig. course; course, class; '~bericht** ♦ m market-report; '~buch 🚂 n railway guide, Am. railroad guide.

**Kürschner** ['kyrʃnər] m (-s/-) furrier.

**kursieren** [kur'zi:rən] v/i. (no -ge-, h) money, etc.: circulate, be in circulation; rumour, etc.: circulate, be afloat, go about.

**Kursivschrift** typ. [kur'zi:f-] f italics pl.

**Kursus** ['kurzus] m (-/Kurse) course, class.

**'Kurs|verlust** ♦ m loss on the stock exchange; '~wert** ♦ m market value; '~zettel** ♦ m stock exchange list.

**Kurve** ['kurvə] f (-/-n) curve; road, etc.: a. bend, turn.

**kurz** [kurts] 1. adj. space: short; time, etc.: short, brief; ~ und bündig brief, concise; ~e Hose shorts pl.; mit ~en Worten with a few words; den kürzeren ziehen get the worst of it; 2. adv. in short; ~ angebunden sein be curt or sharp; ~ und gut in short, in a word; ~ vor London short of London; sich ~ fassen be brief or concise; in ~em before long, shortly; vor ~em a short time ago; zu ~ kommen come off badly, get a raw deal; um es ~ zu sagen to cut a long story short; '2arbeit ♦ f short-

time work; '2arbeiter ♦ m short-time worker; ~atmig adj. [.'~ʔa:tmiç] short-winded.

**Kürze** ['kyrtsə] f (-/no pl.) shortness; brevity; in ~ shortly, before long; '2n v/t. (ge-, h) shorten (dress, etc.) (um by); abridge, condense (book, etc.); cut, reduce (expenses, etc.).

**'kurz|er'hand** adv. without hesitation; on the spot; '2film m short (film); '2form f shortened form; '~fristig adj. short-term; ♦ bill, etc.: short-dated; '2geschichte f (short) short story; ~lebig adj. ['.~le:biç] short-lived; '2nachrichten f/pl. news summary.

**kürzlich** adv. ['kyrtsliç] lately, recently, not long ago.

**'Kurz|schluß** ♂ m short circuit, F short; '~schrift f shorthand, stenography; '2sichtig adj. shortsighted, near-sighted; 2'um adv. in short, in a word.

**'Kürzung** f (-/-en) shortening (of dress, etc.); abridg(e)ment, condensation (of book, etc.); cut, reduction (of expenses, etc.).

**'Kurz|waren** f/pl. haberdashery, Am. dry goods pl., notions pl.; '~weil f (-/no pl.) amusement, entertainment; '2weilig adj. amusing, entertaining; '~welle ♦ f short wave; radio: short-wave band.

**Kusine** [ku'zi:nə] f (-/-n) s. Cousine.

**Kuß** [kus] m (Kusses/Küsse) kiss; '2echt adj. kiss-proof.

**küssen** ['kysən] v/t. and v/i. (ge-, h) kiss.

**'kußfest** adj. s. kußecht.

**Küste** ['kystə] f (-/-n) coast; shore.

**'Küsten|bewohner** m inhabitant of a coastal region; '~fischerei f inshore fishery or fishing; '~gebiet n coastal area or region; '~schiffahrt f coastal shipping.

**Küster** eccl. ['kystər] m (-s/-) verger, sexton, sacristan.

**Kutsch|bock** ['kutʃ-] m coach-box; '~e f (-/-n) carriage, coach; '~enschlag m carriage-door, coach-door; '~er m (-s/-) coachman; 2ieren [.~'tʃi:rən] (no -ge-) 1. v/t. (h) drive s.o. in a coach; 2. v/i. (h) (drive a) coach; 3. v/i. (sein) (drive or ride in a) coach.

**Kutte** ['kutə] f (-/-n) cowl.

**Kutter** ♦ ['kutər] m (-s/-) cutter.

**Kuvert** [ku'vert; ku've:r] n (-[e]s/-e; -s/-s) envelope; at table: cover.

**Kux** ⚒ [kuks] m (-es/-e) mining share.

# L

**Lab** zo. [lɑːp] n (-[e]s/-e) rennet.
**labil** adj. [la'biːl] unstable (a. ⊕, ✗); phys., ♫ labile.
**Labor** [la'boːr] n (-s/-s, -e) s. Laboratorium; ⟋ant [labo'rant] m (-en/-en) laboratory assistant; ⟋atorium [labora'toːrjum] n (-s/ Laboratorien) laboratory; 2ieren [⟋o'riːrən] v/i. (no -ge-, h): ⟋ an (dat.) labo(u)r under, suffer from.
**Labyrinth** [laby'rint] n (-[e]s/-e) labyrinth, maze.
**Lache** ['laxə] f (-/-n) pool, puddle.
**lächeln** ['lɛçəln] 1. v/i. (ge-, h) smile (über acc. at); höhnisch ⟋ sneer (über acc. at); 2. 2 n (-s/no pl.) smile; höhnisches ⟋ sneer.
**lachen** ['laxən] 1. v/i. (ge-, h) laugh (über acc. at); 2. 2 n (-s/no pl.) laugh(ter).
**lächerlich** adj. ['lɛçərliç] ridiculous, laughable, ludicrous; absurd; derisory, scoffing; ⟋ machen ridicule; sich ⟋ machen make a fool of o.s.
**Lachs** ichth. [laks] m (-es/-e) salmon.
**Lack** [lak] m (-[e]s/-e) (gum-)lac; varnish; lacquer, enamel; 2ieren [la'kiːrən] v/t. (no -ge-, h) lacquer, varnish; enamel; ⟋leder n patent leather; ⟋schuhe m/pl. patent leather shoes pl., F patents pl.
**Lade|fähigkeit** ['laːdə-] f loading capacity; ⟋fläche f loading area; ⟋hemmung ✗ f jam, stoppage; ⟋linie ♫ f load-line.
**laden¹** ['laːdən] v/t. (irr., ge-, h) load; load (gun), charge (a. ⚡); freight, ship; ⚖ cite, summon; invite, ask (guest).
**Laden²** [⟋] m (-s/⸚) shop, Am. store; shutter; ⟋besitzer m s. Ladeninhaber; ⟋dieb m shop-lifter; ⟋diebstahl m shop-lifting; ⟋hüter m drug on the market; ⟋inhaber m shopkeeper, Am. storekeeper; ⟋kasse f till; ⟋preis m selling-price, retail price; ⟋schild n shopsign; ⟋schluß m closing time; nach ⟋ after hours; ⟋tisch m counter.
**'Lade|platz** m loading-place; ⟋rampe f loading platform or ramp; ⟋raum m loading space; ♫ hold; ⟋schein ♫ m bill of lading.
**Ladung** f (-/-en) loading; load, freight; ♫ cargo; ⚡ charge (a. of gun); ⚖ summons.
**lag** [laːk] pret. of liegen.
**Lage** ['laːgə] f (-/-n) situation, position; site, location (of building); state, condition; attitude; geol. layer, stratum; round (of beer, etc.); in der ⟋ sein zu inf. be able to inf., be in a position to inf.; versetzen

Sie sich in meine ⟋ put yourself in my place.
**Lager** ['laːgər] n (-s/-) couch, bed; den, lair (of wild animals); geol. deposit; ⊕ bearing; warehouse, storehouse, depot; store, stock (♱ pl. a. Läger); ✗, etc.: camp, encampment; auf ⟋ ♱ on hand, in stock; ⟋buch n stock-book; ⟋feuer n camp-fire; ⟋geld n storage; ⟋haus n warehouse; 2n (ge-, h) 1. v/i. lie down, rest; ✗ (en)camp; ♱ be stored; 2. v/t. lay down; ✗ (en)camp; ♱ store, warehouse; sich ⟋ lie down, rest; ⟋platz m ♱ depot; resting-place; ✗, etc.: camp-site; ⟋raum m store-room; ⟋ung f (-/-en) storage (of goods).
**Lagune** [la'guːnə] f (-/-n) lagoon.
**lahm** adj. [laːm] lame; ⟋en v/i. (ge-, h) be lame.
**lähmen** ['lɛːmən] v/t. (ge-, h) (make) lame; paraly|se, Am. -ze (a. fig.).
**'lahmlegen** v/t. (sep., -ge-, h) paraly|se, Am. -ze; obstruct.
**'Lähmung** ♫ f (-/-en) paralysis.
**Laib** [laɪp] m (-[e]s/-e) loaf.
**Laich** [laɪç] m (-[e]s/-e) spawn; 2en v/i. (ge-, h) spawn.
**Laie** ['laɪə] m (-n/-n) layman; amateur; ⟋nbühne f amateur theat|re, Am. -er.
**Lakai** [la'kaɪ] m (-en/-en) lackey (a. fig.), footman.
**Lake** ['laːkə] f (-/-n) brine, pickle.
**Laken** ['laːkən] n (-s/-) sheet.
**lallen** ['lalən] v/i. and v/t. (ge-, h) stammer; babble.
**Lamelle** [la'mɛlə] f (-/-n) lamella, lamina; ♀ gill (of mushrooms).
**lamentieren** [lamen'tiːrən] v/i. (no -ge-, h) lament (um for; über acc. over).
**Lamm** zo. [lam] n (-[e]s/⸚er) lamb; ⟋fell n lambskin; 2fromm adj. (as) gentle or (as) meek as a lamb.
**Lampe** ['lampə] f (-/-n) lamp.
**'Lampen|fieber** n stage fright; ⟋licht n lamplight; ⟋schirm m lamp-shade.
**Lampion** [lɑ̃'pjõ] m, n (-s/-s) Chinese lantern.
**Land** [lant] n (-[e]s/⸚er, poet. -e) land; country; territory; ground, soil; an ⟋ gehen go ashore; auf dem ⟋e in the country; aufs ⟋ gehen go into the country; außer ⟋es gehen go abroad; zu ⟋e by land; ⟋arbeiter m farm-hand; ⟋besitz m landed property; ⚖ real estate; ⟋besitzer m landowner, landed proprietor; ⟋bevölkerung f rural population.
**Lande|bahn** ✈ ['landə-] f runway; ⟋deck ✈ n flight-deck.

**land'einwärts** adv. upcountry, inland.

**landen** ['landən] (ge-) **1.** v/i. (sein) land; **2.** v/t. (h) ⚓ disembark (troups); ✈ land, set down (troups).

**'Landenge** f neck of land, isthmus.

**Landeplatz** ✈ ['landə-] m landing-field.

**Ländereien** [lɛndə'raiən] pl. landed property, lands pl., estates pl.

**Länderspiel** ['lɛndər-] n sports: international match.

**Landes|grenze** ['landəs-] f frontier, boundary; '~innere n interior, inland, upcountry; '~kirche f national church; Brt. Established Church; '~regierung f government; in Germany: Land government; '~sprache f native language, vernacular; '2üblich adj. customary; '~verrat m treason; '~verräter m traitor to his country; '~verteidigung f national defen|ce, Am. -se.

**'Land|flucht** f rural exodus; '~friedensbruch ⚖ m breach of the public peace; '~gericht n appr. district court; '~gewinnung f (-/-en) reclamation of land; '~gut n country-seat, estate; '~haus n country-house, cottage; '~karte f map; '~kreis m rural district; 2läufig adj. ['~bʏfiç] customary, current, common.

**ländlich** adj. ['lɛntliç] rural, rustic.

**'Land|maschinen** f/pl. agricultural or farm equipment; '~partie f picnic, outing, excursion into the country; '~plage iro. f nuisance; '~rat m (-[e]s/~e) appr. district president; '~ratte ⚓ f landlubber; '~recht n common law; '~regen m persistent rain.

**'Landschaft** f (-/-en) province, district, region; countryside, scenery; esp. paint. landscape; '2lich adj. provincial; scenic (beauty, etc.).

**'Landsmann** m (-[e]s/Landsleute) (fellow-)countryman, compatriot; was sind Sie für ein ~? what's your native country?

**'Land|straße** f highway, high road; '~streicher m (-s/-) vagabond, tramp, Am. sl. hobo; '~streitkräfte f/pl. land forces pl., the Army; ground forces pl.; '~strich m tract of land, region; '~tag m Landtag, Land parliament.

**Landung** ['landuŋ] f (-/-en) ⚓, ✈ landing; disembarkation; arrival; '~sbrücke ⚓ f floating: landing-stage; pier; '~ssteg ⚓ m gangway, gang-plank.

**'Land|vermesser** m (-s/-) surveyor; '~vermessung f land-surveying; 2wärts adv. ['~vɛrts] landward(s); '~weg m: auf dem ~e by land; '~wirt m farmer, agriculturist; '~wirtschaft f agriculture, farming; '2wirtschaftlich adj. agri-

cultural; '~e Maschinen f/pl. s. Landmaschinen; '~zunge f spit.

**lang** [laŋ] **1.** adj. long; p. tall; er machte ein ~es Gesicht his face fell; **2.** adv. long; e-e Woche ~ for a week; über kurz oder ~ sooner or later; ~(e) anhaltend continuous; ~(e) entbehrt long-missed; ~(e) ersehnt long-wished-for; das ist schon ~(e) her that was a long time ago; ~ und breit at (full or great) length; noch ~(e) nicht not for a long time yet; far from ger.; wie ~e lernen Sie schon Englisch? how long have you been learning English?; '~atmig adj. ['~a:tmiç] long-winded; '~e adv. s. lang 2.

**Länge** ['lɛŋə] f (-/-n) length; tallness; geogr., ast. longitude; der ~ nach (at) full length, lengthwise.

**langen** ['laŋən] v/i. (ge-, h) suffice, be enough; ~ nach reach for.

**'Längen|grad** m degree of longitude; '~maß n linear measure.

**'länger 1.** adj. longer; '~e Zeit (for) some time; **2.** adv. longer; ich kann es nicht ~ ertragen I cannot bear it any longer; je ~, je lieber the longer the better.

**'Langeweile** f (-, Langeweile/no pl.) boredom, tediousness, ennui.

**'lang|fristig** adj. long-term; '~jährig adj. of long standing; ~e Erfahrung (many) years of experience; '2lauf m skiing: cross-country run or race.

**'länglich** adj. longish, oblong.

**'Langmut** f (-/no pl.) patience, forbearance.

**längs** [lɛŋs] **1.** prp. (gen., dat.) along(side of); ~ der Küste fahren ⚓ (sail along the) coast; **2.** adv. lengthwise; '2achse f longitudinal axis.

**'lang|sam** adj. slow; 2schläfer ['~ʃlɛ:fər] m (-s/-) late riser, lie-abed; '2spielplatte f long-playing record.

**längst** adv. [lɛŋst] long ago or since; ich weiß es ~ I have known it for a long time; '~ens adv. at the longest; at the latest; at the most.

**'lang|stielig** adj. long-handled; ♀ long-stemmed, long-stalked; '2streckenlauf m long-distance run or race; '2weile f (-, Langeweile/no pl.) s. Langeweile; '~weilen v/t. (ge-, h) bore; sich ~ be bored; '~weilig adj. tedious, boring, dull; ~e Person bore; '2welle f ∮ long wave; radio: long wave band; ~wierig adj. ['~vi:riç] protracted, lengthy; ✗ lingering.

**Lanze** ['lantsə] f (-/-n) spear, lance.

**Lappalie** [la'pɑ:ljə] f (-/-n) trifle.

**Lapp|en** ['lapən] m (-/-) patch; rag; duster; (dish- or floor-)cloth; anat., ♀ lobe; '2ig adj. flabby.

**läppisch** adj. ['lɛpiʃ] foolish, silly.

**Lärche** ♀ ['lɛrçə] f (-/-n) larch.
**Lärm** [lɛrm] m (-[e]s/no pl.)
noise; din; ~ *schlagen* give the
alarm; '**2en** v/i. (ge-, h) make a
noise; '**2end** adj. noisy.
**Larve** ['larfə] f (-/-n) mask; face
(*often iro.*); zo. larva, grub.
**las** [lɑːs] pret. of lesen.
**lasch** F adj. [laʃ] limp, lax.
**Lasche** ['laʃə] f (-/-n) strap; tongue
(*of shoe*).
**lassen** ['lasən] (*irr.*, ge-) **1.** v/t. (ge-)
let; leave; *laß das!* don't!; *laß das
Weinen!* stop crying!; *ich kann es
nicht* ~ I cannot help (doing) it;
*sein Leben* ~ *für* sacrifice one's life
for; **2.** v/i. (ge-): *von et.* ~ desist
from s.th., renounce s.th.; do without s.th.; **3.** v/aux. (no -ge-) allow,
permit, let; make, cause; *drucken*
~ *have s. th.* printed; *gehen* ~ let s.o.
go; *ich habe ihn dieses Buch lesen* ~
I have made him read this book;
*von sich hören* ~ send word; *er läßt
sich nichts sagen* he won't take
advice; *es läßt sich nicht leugnen*
there is no denying (the fact).
**lässig** adj. ['lɛsiç] indolent, idle;
sluggish; careless.
**Last** [last] f (-/-en) load; burden;
weight; cargo, freight; *fig.* weight,
charge, trouble; *zu* ~ *en von* ✝ to
the debit of; *j-m zur* ~ *fallen* be a
burden to s.o.; *j-m et. zur* ~ *legen*
lay s.th. at s.o.'s door *or* to s.o.'s
charge; '**~auto** n s. Lastkraftwagen.
'**lasten** v/i. (ge-, h): ~ *auf* (*dat.*)
weigh *or* press (up)on; '**2aufzug** m
goods lift, *Am.* freight elevator.
**Laster** ['lastər] n (-s/-) vice.
**Lästerer** ['lɛstərər] m (-s/-) slanderer, backbiter.
'**lasterhaft** adj. vicious; corrupt.
**Läster|maul** ['lɛstər-] n s. Lästerer;
'**2n** v/i. (ge-, h) slander, calumniate,
defame; abuse; '**~ung** f (-/-en)
slander, calumny.
**lästig** adj. ['lɛstiç] troublesome;
annoying; uncomfortable, inconvenient.
'**Last|kahn** m barge, lighter; '**~
kraftwagen** m lorry, *Am.* truck;
'**~schrift** ✝ f debit; '**~tier** n pack
animal; '**~wagen** m s. Lastkraftwagen.
**Latein** [la'taɪn] n (-s/no pl.) Latin;
**2isch** adj. Latin.
**Laterne** [la'tɛrnə] f (-/-n) lantern;
street-lamp; '**~npfahl** m lamp-post.
**latschen** F ['lɑːtʃən] v/i. (ge-, sein)
shuffle (along).
**Latte** ['latə] f (-/-n) pale; lath;
*sports:* bar; '**~nkiste** f crate; '**~n-
verschlag** m latticed partition;
'**~nzaun** m paling, *Am.* picket
fence.
**Lätzchen** ['lɛtsçən] n (-s/-) bib,
feeder.

**lau** adj. [lau] tepid, lukewarm (*a.
fig.*).
**Laub** [laup] n (-[e]s/no pl.) foliage,
leaves pl.; '**~baum** m deciduous
tree.
**Laube** ['laubə] f (-/-n) arbo(u)r,
bower; '**~ngang** m arcade.
'**Laub|frosch** zo. m tree-frog;
'**~säge** f fret-saw.
**Lauch** ♀ [laux] m (-[e]s/-e) leek.
**Lauer** ['lauər] f (-/no pl.): *auf der* ~
*liegen or sein* lie in wait *or* ambush,
be on the look-out; '**2n** v/i. (ge-, h)
lurk (*auf acc.* for); ~ *auf* (*acc.*)
watch for; '**2nd** adj. louring, low-
ering.
**Lauf** [lauf] m (-[e]s/⁼e) run(ning);
*sports:* a. run, heat; race; current
(*of water*); course; barrel (*of gun*)
♪ run; *im* ~ *der Zeit* in (the) course
of time; '**~bahn** f career; '**~bursche**
m errand-boy, office-boy; '**~diszi-
plin** f sports: running event.
'**laufen** (*irr.*, ge-) **1.** v/i. (sein) run;
walk; flow; *time:* pass, go by,
elapse; leak; *die Dinge* ~ *lassen* let
things slide; *j-n* ~ *lassen* let s.o. go;
**2.** v/t. (sein, h) run; walk; '**~d** adj.
running; current; regular; *~en Monats* ✝ instant; *auf dem* ~*en sein*
be up to date, be fully informed.
**Läufer** ['lɔyfər] m (-s/-) runner (*a.
carpet*); *chess:* bishop; *football:*
half-back.
'**Lauf|masche** f ladder, *Am.* a. run;
'**~paß** F m sack, *sl.* walking papers
pl.; '**~planke** ✠ f gang-board,
gang-plank; '**~schritt** m: *im* ~ running; '**~steg** m footbridge; ✠ gangway.
**Lauge** ['laugə] f (-/-n) lye.
**Laun|e** ['launə] f (-/-n) humo(u)r;
mood; temper; caprice, fancy,
whim; *guter* ~ in (high) spirits;
'**2enhaft** adj. capricious; '**2isch**
adj. moody; wayward.
**Laus** zo. [laus] f (-/⁼e) louse; '**~bub**
['~buːp] m (-en/-en) young scamp, F
young devil, rascal.
**lausch|en** ['lauʃən] v/i. (ge-, h)
listen; eavesdrop; '**~ig** adj. snug,
cosy; peaceful.
**laut** [laut] **1.** adj. loud (*a. fig.*);
noisy; **2.** adv. aloud, loud(ly);
(*sprechen Sie*) ~*er!* speak up!, *Am.*
louder!; **3.** prp. (*gen., dat.*) according
to; ✝ as per; **4.** **2** m (-[e]s/-e) sound;
'**2e** ♪ f (-/-n) lute; '**~en** v/i. (ge-,
h) sound; *words, etc.*: run; read;
~ *auf* (*acc.*) passport, *etc.*: be issued
to.
**läuten** ['lɔytən] (ge-) **1.** v/i. ring;
toll; *es läutet* the bell is ringing;
**2.** v/t. ring; toll.
'**lauter** adj. pure; clear; genuine;
sincere; mere, nothing but, only.
**läuter|n** ['lɔytərn] v/t. (ge-, h)
purify; ⊕ cleanse; refine; '**2ung** f
(-/-en) purification; refining.

**'laut|los** adj. noiseless; mute; silent; *silence*: hushed; **'2schrift** f phonetic transcription; **'2sprecher** m loud-speaker; **'2stärke** f sound intensity; *radio*: (sound-)volume; **2stärkeregler** ['~re:glər] m (-s/-) volume control.

**'lauwarm** adj. tepid, lukewarm.

**Lava** geol. ['la:va] f (-/*Laven*) lava.

**Lavendel** ♀ [la'vendəl] m (-s/-) lavender.

**lavieren** [la'vi:rən] v/i. (*no -ge-, h, sein*) ⚓ tack (a. fig.).

**Lawine** [la'vi:nə] f (-/-n) avalanche.

**lax** adj. [laks] lax, loose; *morals*: a. easy.

**Lazarett** [latsa'rɛt] n (-[e]s/-e) (military) hospital.

**leben¹** ['le:bən] (ge-, h) **1.** v/i. live; be alive; ~ *Sie wohl!* good-bye!, farewell!; *j-n hochleben lassen* cheer s.o.; *at table*: drink s.o.'s health; *von et.* ~ live on s.th.; *hier lebt es sich gut* it is pleasant living here; **2.** v/t. live (*one's life*).

**Leben²** [~] n (-s/-) life; stir, animation, bustle; *am* ~ *bleiben* remain alive, survive; *am* ~ *erhalten* keep alive; *ein neues* ~ *beginnen* turn over a new leaf; *ins* ~ *rufen* call into being; *sein* ~ *aufs Spiel setzen* risk one's life; *sein* ~ *lang* all one's life; *ums* ~ *kommen* lose one's life; perish.

**lebendig** adj. [le'bendiç] living, *pred.*: alive; quick; lively.

**'Lebens|alter** n age; **'~anschauung** f outlook on life; **'~art** f manners pl., behavio(u)r; **'~auffassung** f philosophy of life; **'~bedingungen** f/pl. living conditions pl.; **'~beschreibung** f life, biography; **'~dauer** f span of life; ⊕ durability; **'2echt** adj. true to life; **'~erfahrung** f experience of life; **'2fähig** adj. ♀ *and fig.* viable; **'~gefahr** f danger of life; **~!** danger (of death)!; *unter* ~ at the risk of one's life; **'2gefährlich** adj. dangerous (to life), perilous; **'~gefährte** m life's companion; **'~größe** f life-size; *in* ~ at full length; **'~kraft** f vital power, vigo(u)r, vitality; **'2länglich** adj. for life, lifelong; **'~lauf** m course of life; personal record, curriculum vitae; **'2lustig** adj. gay, merry; **'~mittel** pl. food (-stuffs pl.), provisions pl., groceries pl.; **'2müde** adj. weary or tired of life; **'2notwendig** adj. vital, essential; **'~retter** m life-saver, rescuer; **'~standard** m standard of living; **'~unterhalt** m livelihood; *s-n* ~ *verdienen* earn one's living; **'~versicherung** f life-insurance; **'~wandel** m life, (moral) conduct; **'~weise** f mode of living, habits pl.; *gesunde* ~ regimen; **'~weisheit** f worldly wisdom; **'2wichtig** adj. vital, essential; *~e Organe* pl. vitals

pl.; **'~zeichen** n sign of life; **'~zeit** f lifetime; *auf* ~ for life.

**Leber** anat. ['le:bər] f (-/-n) liver; **'~fleck** m mole; **'2krank** adj., **'2leidend** adj. suffering from a liver-complaint; **'~tran** m cod-liver oil; **'~wurst** f liver-sausage, *Am.* liverwurst.

**'Lebewesen** n living being, creature.

**Lebe'wohl** n (-[e]s/-e, -s) farewell.

**leb|haft** adj. ['le:phaft] lively; vivid; spirited; *interest*: keen; *traffic*: busy; **'2kuchen** m gingerbread; **'~los** adj. lifeless; **'2zeiten** pl.: *zu s-n* ~ in his lifetime.

**lechzen** ['lɛçtsən] v/i. (ge-, h): ~ *nach* languish or yearn or pant for.

**Leck** [lɛk] **1.** n (-[e]s/-s) leak; **2.** 2 adj. leaky; ~ *werden* ⚓ spring a leak.

**lecken** ['lɛkən] (ge-, h) **1.** v/t. lick; **2.** v/i. lick; leak.

**lecker** adj. ['lɛkər] dainty; delicious; **'2bissen** m dainty, delicacy.

**Leder** ['le:dər] n (-s/-) leather; *in* ~ *gebunden* leather-bound; **'2n** adj. leathern, of leather.

**ledig** adj. ['le:diç] single, unmarried; *child*: illegitimate; **'~lich** adv. ['~k-] solely, merely.

**Lee** ⚓ [le:] f (-/*no pl.*) lee (side).

**leer** [le:r] **1.** adj. empty; vacant; void; vain; blank; **2.** adv.: ~ *laufen* ⊕ idle; **'2e** f (-/*no pl.*) emptiness, void (*a. fig.*); *phys.* vacuum; **'~en** v/t. (ge-, h) empty; clear (out); pour out; **'2gut** ♀ n empties pl.; **'2lauf** m ⊕ idling; *mot.* neutral gear; *fig.* waste of energy; **'~stehend** adj. *flat*: empty, unoccupied, vacant.

**legal** adj. [le'ga:l] legal, lawful.

**Legat** [le'ga:t] **1.** m (-en/-en) legate; **2.** ♀ n (-[e]s/-e) legacy.

**legen** ['le:gən] (ge-, h) **1.** v/t. lay; place, put; *sich* ~ *wind, etc.*: calm down, abate; cease; *Wert* ~ *auf (acc.)* attach importance to; **2.** v/i. hen: lay.

**Legende** [le'gendə] f (-/-n) legend.

**legieren** [le'gi:rən] v/t. (*no -ge-, h*) ⊕ alloy; *cookery*: thicken (*mit* with).

**Legislative** [le:gisla'ti:və] f (-/-n) legislative body or power.

**legitim** adj. [legi'ti:m] legitimate; **~ieren** [~i'mi:rən] v/t. (*no -ge-, h*) legitimate; authorize; *sich* ~ prove one's identity.

**Lehm** [le:m] m (-[e]s/-e) loam; mud; **'2ig** adj. loamy.

**Lehn|e** ['le:nə] f (-/-n) support; arm, back (*of chair*); **'2en** (ge-, h) **1.** v/i. lean (*an dat.* against); **2.** v/t. lean, rest (*an acc., gegen* against); *sich* ~ *an (acc.)* lean against; *sich* ~ *auf (acc.)* rest or support o.s. (up-)on; *sich aus dem Fenster* ~ lean out of the window; **'~sessel** m, **'~stuhl** m armchair, easy chair.

**Lehrbuch** ['le:r-] *n* textbook.
**Lehre** ['le:rǝ] *f* (-/-n) rule, precept; doctrine; system; science; theory; lesson, warning; moral (*of fable*); instruction, tuition; ⊕ ga(u)ge; ⊕ pattern; *in der ~ sein* be apprenticed (*bei* to); *in die ~ geben* apprentice, article (*both: bei, zu* to); '2n *v/t.* (*ge-. h*) teach, instruct; show.
'**Lehrer** *m* (-s/-) teacher; master, instructor; '~in *f* (-/-nen) (lady) teacher; (school)mistress; '~kollegium *n* staff (of teachers).
'**Lehr|fach** *n* subject; '~film *m* instructional film; '~gang *m* course (of instruction); '~geld *n* premium; '~herr *m* master, *sl.* boss; '~jahre *n/pl.* (years *pl.* of) apprenticeship; '~junge *m s.* Lehrling; '~körper *m* teaching staff; *univ.* professoriate, faculty; '~kraft *f* teacher; professor; '~ling *m* (-s/-e) apprentice; '~mädchen *n* girl apprentice; '~meister *m* master; '~methode *f* method of teaching; '~plan *m* curriculum, syllabus; '2reich *adj.* instructive; '~satz *m* ♉ theorem; doctrine; *eccl.* dogma; '~stoff *m* subject-matter, subject(*s pl.*); '~stuhl *m* professorship; '~vertrag *m* articles *pl.* of apprenticeship, indenture(s *pl.*); '~zeit *f* apprenticeship.
**Leib** [laɪp] *m* (-[e]s/-er) body; belly, *anat.* abdomen; womb; *bei lebendigem ~e* alive; *mit ~ und Seele* body and soul; *sich j-n vom ~e halten* keep s.o. at arm's length; '~arzt *m* physician in ordinary, personal physician; '~chen *n* (-s/-) bodice.
**Leibeigen|e** ['laɪpˀaɪgǝnǝ] *m* (-n/-n) bond(s)man, serf; '~schaft *f* (-/*no pl.*) bondage, serfdom.
**Leibes|erziehung** ['laɪbǝs-] *f* physical training; '~frucht *f* (o)etus; '~kraft *f*: *aus Leibeskräften pl.* with all one's might; '~übung *f* bodily *or* physical exercise.
'**Leib|garde** *f* body-guard; '~gericht *n* favo(u)rite dish; 2haftig *adj.* ['~haftiç]: *der ~e Teufel* the devil incarnate; '2lich *adj.* bodily, corpor(e)al; '~rente *f* life-annuity; '~schmerzen *m/pl.* stomach-ache, belly-ache, ♉ colic; '~wache *f* body-guard; '~wäsche *f* underwear.
**Leiche** ['laɪçǝ] *f* (-/-n) (dead) body, corpse.
**Leichen|beschauer** ♉ ['laɪçǝnbǝʃauǝr] *m* (-s/-) *appr.* coroner; '~bestatter *m* (-s/-) undertaker, *Am. a.* mortician; '~bittermiene F *f* woebegone look *or* countenance; '2²blaß *adj.* deadly pale; '~halle *f* mortuary; '~schau *f* *appr.* (coroner's) inquest; '~schauhaus *n* morgue; '~tuch *n* (-[e]s/-er) shroud; '~verbrennung *f* cremation; '~wagen *m* hearse.

**Leichnam** ['laɪçnaːm] *m* (-[e]s/-e) *s.* Leiche.
**leicht** [laɪçt] **1.** *adj.* light; easy; slight; *tobacco:* mild; **2.** *adv.:* *es ~ nehmen* take it easy; '2athlet *m* athlete; '2athletik *f* athletics *pl.*, *Am.* track and field events *pl.*; '~fertig *adj.* light(-minded); careless; frivolous, flippant; '2fertigkeit *f* levity; carelessness; frivolity, flippancy; '2gewicht *n* boxing: lightweight; '~gläubig *adj.* credulous; '~hin *adv.* lightly, casually; 2igkeit ['~iç-] *f* (-/-en) lightness; ease, facility; '~lebig *adj.* easy-going; '2metall *n* light metal; '2sinn *m* (-[e]s/*no pl.*) frivolity, levity; carelessness; '~sinnig *adj.* light-minded, frivolous; careless; '~verdaulich *adj.* easy to digest; '~verständlich *adj.* easy to understand.
**leid** [laɪt] **1.** *adv.:* *es tut mir ~* I am sorry (*um* for), I regret; **2.** 2 *n* (-[e]s/*no pl.*) injury, harm; wrong; grief, sorrow; '~en ['~dǝn] (*irr., ge-, h*) **1.** *v/i.* suffer (*an dat.* from); **2.** *v/t.:* (*nicht*) ~ *können* (dis)like; 2en ['~dǝn] *n* (-s/-) suffering; ♉ complaint; '~end *adj.* ['~dǝnt] ailing.
'**Leidenschaft** *f* (-/-en) passion; '2lich *adj.* passionate; ardent; vehement; '2slos *adj.* dispassionate.
'**Leidens|gefährte** *m*, '~gefährtin *f* fellow-sufferer.
**leid|er** *adv.* ['laɪdǝr] unfortunately; *int.* alas!; ~ *muß ich inf.* I'm (so) sorry to *inf.*; *ich muß ~ gehen* I am afraid I have to go; '~ig *adj.* disagreeable; '~lich *adj.* ['laɪt-] tolerable; fairly well; 2tragende ['laɪt-] *m, f* (-n/-n) mourner; *er ist der ~ dabei* he is the one who suffers for it; 2wesen ['laɪt-] *n* (-s/*no pl.*): *zu meinem ~* to my regret.
**Leier** ♪ ['laɪǝr] *f* (-/-n) lyre; '~kasten *m* barrel-organ; '~kastenmann *m* organ-grinder.
**Leih|bibliothek** (-/-n) *f*, '~bücherei *f* lending *or* circulating library, *Am. a.* rental library; '2en *v/t.* (*irr., ge-, h*) lend; borrow (*von* from); '~gebühr *f* lending fee(s *pl.*); '~haus *n* pawnshop, *Am. a.* loan office; '2weise *adv.* as a loan.
**Leim** [laɪm] *m* (-[e]s/-e) glue; F *aus dem ~ gehen* get out of joint; F: *auf den ~ gehen* fall for it, fall into the trap; '2en *v/t.* (*ge-, h*) glue; size.
**Lein** ♉ [laɪn] *m* (-[e]s/-e) flax.
**Leine** ['laɪnǝ] *f* (-/-n) line, cord; (dog-)lead, leash.
**leinen** ['laɪnǝn] **1.** *adj.* (of) linen; **2.** 2 *n* (-s/-) linen; *in ~ gebunden* cloth-bound; '2schuh *m* canvas shoe.
'**Lein|öl** *n* linseed-oil; '~samen *m* linseed; '~wand *f* (-/*no pl.*) linen (cloth); *paint.* canvas; *film:* screen.

**leise** adj. ['laɪzə] low, soft; gentle; slight, faint; ~r stellen turn down (radio).

**Leiste** ['laɪstə] f (-/-n) border, ledge; ⚕ fillet; anat. groin.

**leisten** ['laɪstən] 1. v/t. (ge-, h) do; perform; fulfil(l); take (oath); render (service); ich kann mir das ~ I can afford it; 2. ♀ ⊕ m (-s/-) last; boot-tree, Am. a. shoetree; **'2-bruch** ♉ m inguinal hernia.

**'Leistung** f (-/-en) performance; achievement; work(manship); result(s pl.); ⊕ capacity; output (of factory); benefit (of insurance company); **'2sfähig** adj. productive; efficient, ⊕ a. powerful; **'sfähig-keit** f efficiency; ⊕ productivity; ⊕ capacity, producing-power.

**Leit|artikel** ['laɪt-] m leading article, leader, editorial; **'~bild** n image; example.

**leiten** ['laɪtən] v/t. (ge-, h) lead, guide; conduct (a. phys., ♪); fig. direct, run, manage, operate; preside over (meeting); **'~d** adj. leading; phys. conductive; **~e Stellung** key position.

**'Leiter** 1. m (-s/-) leader; conductor (a. phys., ♪); guide; manager; 2. f (-/-n) ladder; **'~in** f (-/-nen) leader; conductress, guide; manageress; **'~wagen** m rack-wag(g)on.

**'Leit|faden** m manual, textbook, guide; **'~motiv** ♪ n leit-motiv; **'~spruch** m motto; **'~tier** n leader; **'~ung** f (-/-en) lead(ing), conducting, guidance; management, direction, administration, Am. a. operation; phys. conduction; ⚡ lead; circuit; tel. line; mains pl. (for gas, water, etc.); pipeline; die ~ ist besetzt teleph. the line is engaged or Am. busy.

**'Leitungs|draht** m conducting wire, conductor; **'~rohr** n conduit(-pipe); main (for gas, water, etc.); **'~wasser** n (-s/=) tap water.

**'Leitwerk** ✈ n tail unit or group, empennage.

**Lekt|ion** [lɛk'tsjoːn] f (-/-en) lesson; **~or** ['lɛktɔr] m (-s/-en) lecturer; reader; **~üre** [~'tyːrə] f 1. (-/no pl.) reading; 2. (-/-n) books pl.

**Lende** anat. ['lɛndə] f (-/-n) loin(s pl.).

**lenk|bar** adj. ['lɛŋkbaːr] guidable, manageable, tractable; docile; ⊕ steerable, dirigible; **'~en** v/t. (ge-, h) direct, guide; turn; rule; govern; drive (car); ⚓ steer; Aufmerksam-keit ~ auf (acc.) draw attention to; **'2rad** mot. n steering wheel; **'2-säule** mot. f steering column; **'2-stange** f handle-bar (of bicycle); **'2ung** mot. f (-/-en) steering-gear.

**Lenz** [lɛnts] m (-es/-e) spring.

**Leopard** zo. [leo'part] m (-en/-en) leopard.

**Lepra** ♉ ['leːpra] f (-/no pl.) leprosy.

**Lerche** orn. ['lɛrçə] f (-/-n) lark.

**lern|begierig** adj. ['lɛrn-] eager to learn, studious; **'~en** v/t. and v/i. (ge-, h) learn; study.

**Lese** ['leːzə] f (-/-n) gathering; s. Weinlese; **'~buch** n reader; **'~lam-pe** f reading-lamp.

**lesen** ['leːzən] (irr., ge-, h) 1. v/t. read; ✷ gather; Messe ~ eccl. say mass; 2. v/i. read; univ. (give a) lecture (über acc. on); **'~swert** adj. worth reading.

**'Leser** m (-s/-), **'~in** f (-/-nen) reader; ✷ gatherer; vintager; **'2lich** adj. legible; **'~zuschrift** f letter to the editor.

**'Lesezeichen** n book-mark.

**'Lesung** parl. f (-/-en) reading.

**letzt** adj. [lɛtst] last; final; ultimate; **~e Nachrichten** pl. latest news pl.; **~e Hand anlegen** put the finishing touches (an acc. to); das **~e** the last thing; der **~ere** the latter; der (die, das) Letzte the last (one); zu guter Letzt last but not least; finally; **'~ens** adv., **'~hin** adv. lately, of late; **'~lich** adv. s. letztens; finally; ultimately.]

**Leucht|e** ['lɔʏçtə] f (-/-n) (fig. shining) light, lamp (a. fig.); luminary (a. fig., esp. p.); **'2en** v/i. (ge-, h) (give) light, shine (forth); beam, gleam; **'~en** n (-s/no pl.) shining, light, luminosity; **'2end** adj. shining, bright; luminous; brilliant (a. fig.); **'~er** m (-s/-) candlestick; s. Kronleuchter; **'~feuer** n ⚓, ✈, etc.: beacon(-light), flare (light); **'~käfer** zo. m glow-worm; **'~kugel** ✖ f Very light; flare; **'~turm** m light-house; **'~ziffer** f luminous figure.

**leugnen** ['lɔʏgnən] v/t. (ge-, h) deny; disavow; contest.

**Leukämie** ♉ [lɔʏkɛ'miː] f (-/-n) leuk(a)emia.

**Leumund** ['lɔʏmʊnt] m (-[e]s/no pl.) reputation, repute; character; **'~szeugnis** ⚖ n character reference.

**Leute** ['lɔʏtə] pl. people pl.; persons pl.; ✖, pol. men pl.; workers: hands pl.; F folks pl.; domestics pl., servants pl.

**Leutnant** ✖ ['lɔʏtnant] m (-s/-s, ✖ -e) second lieutenant.

**leutselig** adj. ['lɔʏtzeːlɪç] affable.

**Lexikon** ['lɛksikɔn] n (-s/Lexika, Lexiken) dictionary; encyclop(a)e-dia.

**Libelle** zo. [li'bɛlə] f (-/-n) dragon-fly.

**liberal** adj. [libe'raːl] liberal.

**Licht** [lɪçt] 1. n (-[e]s/-er) light; brightness; lamp; candle; Pupil. eye; ~ machen ⚡ switch or turn on the light(s pl.); das ~ der Welt er-blicken see the light, be born; 2. 2 adj. light, bright; clear; **~er Augen-blick** ♉ lucid interval; **'~anlage** f lighting plant; '~bild n photo (-graph); '~bildervortrag m slide lecture; '~blick fig. m bright spot; '~bogen ⚡ m arc; '²durchlässig adj. translucent; '²echt adj. fast (to light), unfading; '²empfindlich adj. sensitive to light, phot. sensitive; ~ machen sensitize.

'lichten v/t. (ge-, h) clear (forest); den Anker ~ ⚓ weigh anchor; sich ~ hair, crowd: thin.

lichterloh adv. ['liçtər'lo:] blazing, in full blaze.

'Licht|geschwindigkeit f speed of light; '~hof m glass-roofed court; patio; halo (a. phot.); '~leitung f lighting mains pl.; '~maschine mot. f dynamo, generator; '~pause f blueprint; '~quelle f light source, source of light; '~reklame f neon sign; '~schacht m well; '~schalter m (light) switch; '~schein m gleam of light; '²scheu adj. shunning the light; '~signal n light or luminous signal; '~spieltheater n s. Filmtheater, Kino; '~strahl m ray or beam of light (a. fig.); '²undurchlässig adj. opaque.

'Lichtung f (-/-en) clearing, opening, glade.

'Lichtzelle f s. Photozelle.

Lid [li:t] n (-[e]s/-er) eyelid.

lieb adj. [li:p] dear; nice, kind; child: good; in letters: ~er Herr N. dear Mr N.; ~er Himmel! good Heavens!, dear me!; es ist mir ~ daß I am glad that; '²chen n (-s/-) sweetheart.

Liebe ['li:bə] f (-/no pl.) love (zu of, for); aus ~ for love; aus ~ zu for the love of; '²n (ge-, h) 1. v/t. love; be in love with, be fond of, like; 2. v/i. (be in) love; '~nde m, f (-n/-n): die ~n pl. the lovers pl.

'liebens|wert adj. lovable; charming; '~würdig adj. lovable, amiable; das ist sehr ~ von Ihnen that is very kind of you; '²würdigkeit f (-/-en) amiability, kindness.

'lieber 1. adj. dearer; 2. adv. rather, sooner; ~ haben prefer, like better.

'Liebes|brief m love-letter; '~dienst m favo(u)r, kindness; good turn; '~erklärung f: e-e ~ machen declare one's love; '~heirat f lovematch; '~kummer m lover's grief; '~paar n (courting) couple, lovers pl.; '~verhältnis n love-affair.

'liebevoll adj. loving, affectionate.

lieb|gewinnen ['li:p-] v/t. (irr. gewinnen, sep., no -ge-, h) get or grow fond of; '~haben v/t. (irr. haben, sep., -ge-, h) love, be fond of; '²haber m (-s/-) lover; beau; fig. amateur; '²haberei fig. [~'raɪ] f (-/-en) hobby; '²haberpreis m fancy price; '²haberwert m sentimental value; '~kosen v/t. (no -ge-, h) caress, fondle; '²kosung f (-/-en) caress;

'~lich adj. lovely, charming, delightful.

Liebling ['li:plɪŋ] m (-s/-e) darling; favo(u)rite; esp. animals: pet; esp. form of address: darling, esp. Am. honey; '~sbeschäftigung f favo(u)rite occupation, hobby.

lieb|los adj. ['li:p-] unkind; careless; '²schaft f (-/-en) (love-)affair; '²ste m, f (-n/-n) sweetheart; darling.

Lied [li:t] n (-[e]s/-er) song; tune.

liederlich adj. ['li:dərliç] slovenly, disorderly; careless; loose, dissolute.

lief [li:f] pret. of laufen.

Lieferant [li:fə'rant] m (-en/-en) supplier, purveyor; caterer.

Liefer|auto ['li:fər-] n s. Lieferwagen; '²bar adj. to be delivered; available; '~bedingungen f/pl. terms pl. of delivery; '~frist f term of delivery; '²n v/t. (ge-, h) deliver; j-m et. ~ furnish or supply s.o. with s.th.; '~schein m delivery note; '~ung f (-/-en) delivery; supply; consignment; instal(l)ment (of book); '~ungsbedingungen f/pl. s. Lieferbedingungen; '~wagen m deliveryvan, Am. delivery wagon.

Liege ['li:gə] f (-/-n) couch; bedchair.

liegen ['li:gən] v/i. (irr., ge-, h) lie; house, etc.: be (situated); room: face; an wem liegt es? whose fault is it? es liegt an or bei ihm zu inf. it is for him to inf.; es liegt daran, daß the reason for it is that; es liegt mir daran zu inf. I am anxious to inf.; es liegt mir nichts daran it does not matter or it is of no consequence to me; '~bleiben v/i. (irr. bleiben, sep., -ge-, sein) stay in bed; break down (on the road, a. mot., etc.); work, etc.: stand over; fall behind; ✝ goods: remain on hand; '~lassen v/t. (irr. lassen, sep., [-ge-,] h) leave; leave behind; leave alone; leave off (work); j-n links ~ ignore s.o., give s.o. the cold shoulder; '²schaften f/pl. real estate.

'Liege|stuhl m deck-chair; '~wagen 🚃 m couchette coach.

lieh [li:] pret. of leihen.

ließ [li:s] pret. of lassen.

Lift [lɪft] m (-[e]s/-e, -s) lift, Am. elevator.

Liga ['li:ga] f (-/Ligen) league.

Likör [li'kø:r] m (-s/-e) liqueur, cordial.

lila adj. ['li:la] lilac.

Lilie ⚘ ['li:liə] f (-/-n) lily.

Limonade [limo'nɑ:də] f (-/-n) soft drink, fruit-juice; lemonade.

Limousine mot. [limu'zi:nə] f (-/-n) limousine, saloon car, Am. sedan.

lind adj. [lɪnt] soft, gentle; mild.

Linde ⚘ ['lɪndə] f (-/-n) lime(-tree), linden(-tree).

**linder|n** ['lindərn] v/t. (ge-, h) soften; mitigate; alleviate, soothe; allay, ease (pain); '2ung f (-/⸗-en) softening; mitigation; alleviation; easing.

**Lineal** [line'a:l] n (-s/-e) ruler.

**Linie** ['li:njə] f (-/-n) line; '⸗npapier n ruled paper; '⸗nrichter m sports: linesman; '2ntreu pol. adj.: ⸗ sein follow the party line.

**lin(i)ieren** [li'ni:rən; lini'i:rən] v/t. (no -ge-, h) rule, line.

**link** adj. [liŋk] left; ⸗e Seite left (-hand) side, left; of cloth: wrong side; '2e f (-n/-n) the left (hand); pol. the Left (Wing); boxing: the left; '⸗isch adj. awkward, clumsy.

**links** adv. on or to the left; 2händer ['⸗hɛndər] m (-s/-) left-hander, Am. a. southpaw.

**Linse** ['linzə] f (-/-n) ♀ lentil; opt. lens.

**Lippe** ['lipə] f (-/-n) lip; '⸗nstift m lipstick.

**liquidieren** [likvi'di:rən] v/t. (no -ge-, h) liquidate (a. persn.); wind up (business company); charge (fee).

**lispeln** ['lispəln] v/i. and v/t. (ge-, h) lisp; whisper.

**List** [list] f (-/-en) cunning, craft; artifice, ruse, trick; stratagem.

**Liste** ['listə] f (-/-n) list, roll.

'**listig** adj. cunning, crafty, sly.

**Liter** ['li:tər] n, m (-s/-) lit|re, Am. -er.

**literarisch** adj. [lite'ra:riʃ] literary.

**Literatur** [litera'tu:r] f (-/-en) literature; ⸗beilage f literary supplement (in newspaper); ⸗geschichte f history of literature; ⸗verzeichnis n bibliography.

**litt** [lit] pret. of leiden.

**Litze** ['litsə] f (-/-n) lace, cord, braid; ∉ strand(ed wire).

**Livree** [li'vre:] f (-/-n) livery.

**Lizenz** [li'tsɛnts] f (-/-en) licen|ce, Am. -se; ⸗inhaber m licensee.

**Lob** [lo:p] n (-[e]s/no pl.) praise; commendation; 2en ['lo:bən] v/t. (ge-, h) praise; 2enswert adj. ['lo:bəns-] praise-worthy, laudable; ⸗gesang ['lo:p-] m hymn, song of praise; ⸗hudelei [lo:phu:də'lai] f (-/-en) adulation, base flattery.

**löblich** adj. ['lø:pliç] s. lobenswert.

**Lobrede** ['lo:p-] f eulogy, panegyric.

**Loch** [lɔx] n (-[e]s/⸗er) hole; '2en v/t. (ge-, h) perforate, pierce; punch (ticket, etc.); '⸗er m (-s/-) punch, perforator; '⸗karte f punch(ed) card.

**Locke** ['lɔkə] f (-/-n) curl, ringlet.

'**locken**[1] v/t. and v/refl. (ge-, h) curl.

'**locken**[2] v/t. (ge-, h) hunt.: bait; decoy (a. fig.); fig. allure, entice.

'**Locken|kopf** m curly head; ⸗wickler ['⸗viklər] m (-s/-) curler, roller.

**locker** adj. ['lɔkər] loose; slack; '⸗n

v/t. (ge-, h) loosen; slacken; relax (grip); break up (soil); sich ⸗ loosen, (be)come loose; give way; fig. relax.

'**lockig** adj. curly.

'**Lock|mittel** n s. Köder; '⸗vogel m decoy (a. fig.); Am. a. stool pigeon (a. fig.).

**lodern** ['lo:dərn] v/i. (ge-, h) flare, blaze.

**Löffel** ['lœfəl] m (-s/-) spoon; ladle; '2n v/t. (ge-, h) spoon up; ladle out; '⸗voll m (-/-) spoonful.

**log** [lo:k] pret. of lügen.

**Loge** ['lo:ʒə] f (-/-n) thea. box; freemasonry: lodge; '⸗nschließer thea. m (-s/-) box-keeper.

**logieren** [lo'ʒi:rən] v/i. (no -ge-, h) lodge, stay, Am. a. room (all: bei with; in dat. at).

**logisch** adj. ['lo:giʃ] logical; '⸗erweise adv. logically.

**Lohn** [lo:n] m (-[e]s/⸗e) wages pl., pay(ment); hire; fig. reward; '⸗büro n pay-office; '⸗empfänger m wage-earner; '2en v/t. (ge-, h) compensate, reward; sich ⸗ pay; es lohnt sich zu inf. it is worth while ger., it pays to inf.; '2end adj. paying; advantageous; fig. rewarding; '⸗erhöhung f increase in wages, rise, Am. raise; '⸗forderung f demand for higher wages; '⸗steuer f tax on wages or salary; '⸗stopp m (-s/no pl.) wage freeze; '⸗tarif m wage rate; '⸗tüte f pay envelope.

**lokal** [lo'ka:l] 1. adj. local; 2. 2 n (-[e]s/-e) locality, place; restaurant; public house, F pub, F local, Am. saloon.

**Lokomotiv|e** [lokomo'ti:və] f (-/-n) (railway) engine, locomotive; ⸗führer [⸗'ti:f-] m engine-driver, Am. engineer.

**Lorbeer** ♀ ['lɔrbeɪr] m (-s/-en) laurel, bay.

**Lore** ['lo:rə] f (-/-n) lorry, truck.

**Los**[1] [lo:s] n (-es/-e) lot; lottery ticket; fig. fate, destiny, lot; das Große ⸗ ziehen win the first prize, Am. sl. hit the jackpot; durchs ⸗ entscheiden decide by lot.

**los**[2] [lo:s] 1. pred. adj. loose; free; was ist ⸗? what is the matter?, F what's up?, Am. F what's cooking?; ⸗ sein be rid of; 2. int.: ⸗! go (on or ahead)!

**losarbeiten** ['lo:s⸗-] v/i. (sep., -ge-, h) start work(ing).

**lösbar** adj. ['lø:sba:r] soluble, ♀ a. solvable.

'**los|binden** v/t. (irr. binden, sep., -ge-, h) untie, loosen; '⸗brechen (irr. brechen, sep., -ge-) 1. v/t. (h) break off; 2. v/i. (sein) break or burst out.

**Lösch|blatt** ['lœʃ-] n blotting-paper; '2en v/t. (ge-, h) extinguish, put out (fire, light); blot out (writing);

erase (*tape recording*); cancel (*debt*); quench (*thirst*); slake (*lime*); ⚓ unload; '**~er** m (*-s/-*) blotter; '**~papier** n blotting-paper.

**lose** adj. ['loːzə] loose.

'**Lösegeld** n ransom.

**losen** ['loːzən] v/i. (ge-, h) cast or draw lots (um for).

**lösen** ['løːzən] v/t. (ge-, h) loosen, untie; buy, book (*ticket*); solve (*task, doubt, etc.*); break off (*engagement*); annul (*agreement, etc.*); 🜋 dissolve; *ein Schuß löste sich* the gun went off.

'**los|fahren** v/i. (irr. fahren, sep., -ge-, sein) depart, drive off; '**~gehen** v/i. (irr. gehen, sep., -ge-, sein) go or be off; come off, get loose; *gun*: go off; begin, start; F *auf j-n ~* fly at s.o.; '**~haken** v/t. (sep., -ge-, h) unhook; '**~kaufen** v/t. (sep., -ge-, h) ransom, redeem; '**~ketten** v/t. (sep., -ge-, h) unchain; '**~kommen** v/i. (irr. kommen, sep., -ge-, sein) get loose or free; '**~lachen** v/i. (sep., -ge-, h) laugh out; '**~lassen** v/t. (irr. lassen, sep., -ge-, h) let go; release.

**löslich** 🜋 adj. ['løːsliç] soluble.

'**los|lösen** v/t. (sep., -ge-, h) loosen, detach; sever; '**~machen** v/t. (sep., -ge-, h) unfasten, loosen; *sich ~* disengange (o.s.) (*von* from); '**~reißen** v/t. (irr. reißen, sep., -ge-, h) tear off; *sich ~* break away, esp. fig. tear o.s. away (*both: von* from); '**~sagen** v/refl. (sep., -ge-, h): *sich ~ von* renounce; '**~schlagen** (irr. schlagen, sep., -ge-, h) 1. v/t. knock off; 2. v/i. open the attack; *auf j-n ~* attack s.o.; '**~schnallen** v/t. (sep., -ge-, h) unbuckle; '**~schrauben** v/t. (sep., -ge-, h) unscrew, screw off; '**~sprechen** v/t. (irr. sprechen, sep., -ge-, h) absolve (*von* of, from); acquit (of); free (from, of); '**~stürzen** v/i. (sep., -ge-, sein): *~ auf* (*acc.*) rush at.

**Losung** ['loːzuŋ] f 1. (*-/-en*) ✗ password, watchword; fig. slogan; 2. hunt. (*-/no pl.*) droppings pl., dung.

**Lösung** ['løːzuŋ] f (*-/-en*) solution; '**~smittel** n solvent.

'**los|werden** v/t. (irr. werden, sep., -ge-, sein) get rid of, dispose of; '**~ziehen** v/i. (irr. ziehen, sep., -ge-, sein) set out, take off, march away.

**Lot** [loːt] n (*-[e]s/-e*) plumb(-line), plummet.

**löten** ['løːtən] v/t. (ge-, h) solder.

**Lotse** ⚓ ['loːtsə] m (*-n/-n*) pilot; '**2n** v/t. (ge-, h) ⚓ pilot (a. fig.).

**Lotterie** [lɔtə'riː] f (*-/-n*) lottery; **~gewinn** m prize; **~los** n lottery ticket.

**Lotto** ['lɔto] n (*-s/-s*) numbers pool, lotto.

**Löwe** zo. ['løːvə] m (*-n/-n*) lion.

'**Löwen|anteil** F m lion's share; '**~maul** ♣ n (*-[e]s/no pl.*) snapdragon; '**~zahn** ♣ m (*-[e]s/no pl.*) dandelion.

'**Löwin** zo. f (*-/-nen*) lioness.

**loyal** adj. [loa'jaːl] loyal.

**Luchs** zo. [luks] m (*-es/-e*) lynx.

**Lücke** ['lykə] f (*-/-n*) gap; blank, void (a. fig.); '**~nbüßer** m stopgap; '**2nhaft** adj. full of gaps; fig. defective, incomplete; '**2nlos** adj. without a gap; fig.: unbroken; complete; *~er Beweis* close argument.

**lud** [luːt] pret. of laden.

**Luft** [luft] f (*-/⁻e*) air; breeze; breath; *frische ~ schöpfen* take the air; *an die ~ gehen* go for an airing; *aus der ~ gegriffen* (totally) unfounded, fantastic; *es liegt et. in der ~* there is s.th. in the wind; *in die ~ fliegen* be blown up, explode; *in die ~ gehen* explode, sl. blow one's top; *in die ~ sprengen* blow up; F *j-n an die ~ setzen* turn s.o. out, Am. sl. give s.o. the air; *sich Luft machen* give vent to one's feelings.

'**Luft|alarm** m air-raid alarm; '**~angriff** m air raid; '**~aufnahme** f aerial photograph; '**~ballon** m (air-)balloon; '**~bild** n aerial photograph, airview; '**~blase** f air-bubble; '**~brücke** f air-bridge; for supplies, etc.: air-lift.

**Lüftchen** ['lyftçən] n (*-s/-*) gentle breeze.

'**luft|dicht** adj. air-tight; '**2druck** phys. m (*-[e]s/no pl.*) atmospheric or air pressure; '**2druckbremse** ⊕ f air-brake; '**~durchlässig** adj. permeable to air.

**lüften** ['lyftən] (ge-, h) 1. v/i. air; 2. v/t. air; raise (*hat*); lift (*veil*); disclose (*secret*).

'**Luft|fahrt** f aviation, aeronautics; '**~feuchtigkeit** f atmospheric humidity; '**2gekühlt** ⊕ adj. air-cooled; '**~hoheit** f air sovereignty; '**2ig** adj. airy; breezy; flimsy; '**~kissen** n air-cushion; '**~klappe** f air-valve; '**~korridor** m air corridor; '**~krankheit** f airsickness; '**~krieg** m aerial warfare; '**~kurort** m climatic health resort; '**~landetruppen** f/pl. airborne troops pl.; '**2leer** adj. void of air, evacuated; *~er Raum* vacuum; '**~linie** f air line, bee-line; '**~loch** n ✈ air-pocket; vent(-hole); '**~post** f air mail; '**~pumpe** f air-pump; '**~raum** m airspace; '**~röhre** anat. f windpipe, trachea; '**~schacht** m air-shaft; '**~schaukel** f swing-boat; '**~schiff** n airship; '**~schloß** n castle in the air or in Spain; '**~schutz** m air-raid protection; '**~schutzkeller** m air-raid shelter; '**~sprünge** ['∼ʃpryŋə] m/pl.: *~ machen* cut capers pl.; gambol; '**~stützpunkt** ✗ m air base.

**'Lüftung** f (-/-en) airing; ventilation.

**'Luft|veränderung** f change of air; **'~verkehr** m air-traffic; **'~verkehrsgesellschaft** f air transport company, airway, Am. airline; **'~verteidigung** ✖ f air defen|ce, Am. -se; **'~waffe** ✖ f air force; **'~weg** m airway; auf dem ~ by air; **'~zug** m draught, Am. draft.

**Lüge** ['ly:gə] f (-/-n) lie, falsehood; j-n ~n strafen give the lie to s.o.

**'lügen** v/i. (irr., ge-, h) (tell a) lie; **'~haft** adj. lying, mendacious; untrue, false.

**Lügner** ['ly:gnər] m (-s/-), **'~in** f (-/-nen) liar; **'2isch** adj. s. lügenhaft.

**Luke** ['lu:kə] f (-/-n) dormer- or garret-window; hatch.

**Lümmel** ['lyməl] m (-s/-) lout, boor; saucy fellow; **'2n** v/refl. (ge-, h) loll, lounge, sprawl.

**Lump** [lump] m (-en/-en) ragamuffin, beggar; cad, Am. sl. rat, heel; scoundrel.

**'Lumpen 1.** m (-s/-) rag; **2.** 2 vb.: sich nicht ~ lassen come down handsomely; **'~pack** n rabble, riffraff; **'~sammler** m rag-picker.

**'lumpig** adj. ragged; fig.: shabby, paltry; mean.

**Lunge** ['luŋə] f (-/-n) anat. lungs pl.; of animals: a. lights pl.

**'Lungen|entzündung** ✖ f pneumonia; **'~flügel** anat. m lung; **'2krank** ✖ adj. suffering from consumption, consumptive; **'~kranke** ✖ m, f consumptive (patient); **'~krankheit** ✖ f lung-disease; **'~schwindsucht** ✖ f (pulmonary) consumption.

**lungern** ['luŋərn] v/i. (ge-, h) s. herumlungern.

**Lupe** ['lu:pə] f (-/-n) magnifying-glass; unter die ~ nehmen scrutinize, take a good look at.

**Lust** [lust] f (-/̈e) pleasure, delight; desire; lust; ~ haben zu inf. have a mind to inf., feel like ger.; haben Sie ~ auszugehen? would you like to go out?

**lüstern** adj. ['lystərn] desirous (nach of), greedy (of, for); lewd, lascivious, lecherous.

**'lustig** adj. merry, gay; jolly, cheerful; amusing, funny; sich ~ machen über (acc.) make fun of; **'2keit** f (-/no pl.) gaiety, mirth; jollity, cheerfulness; fun.

**Lüstling** ['lystliŋ] m (-s/-e) voluptuary, libertine.

**'lust|los** adj. dull, spiritless; † flat; **'2mord** m rape and murder; **'2spiel** n comedy.

**lutschen** ['lutʃən] v/i. and v/t. (ge-, h) suck.

**Luv** ⏚ [lu:f] f (-/no pl.) luff, windward.

**luxuriös** adj. [luksu'rjø:s] luxurious.

**Luxus** ['luksus] m (-/no pl.) luxury (a. fig.); **'~artikel** m luxury; **'~ausgabe** f de luxe edition (of books); **'~ware** f luxury (article); fancy goods pl.

**Lymph|drüse** anat. ['lymf-] f lymphatic gland; **'~e** f (-/-n) lymph; ✖ vaccine; **'~gefäß** anat. n lymphatic vessel.

**lynchen** ['lynçən] v/t. (ge-, h) lynch.

**Lyrik** ['ly:rik] f (-/no pl.) lyric verses pl., lyrics pl.; **'~er** m (-s/-) lyric poet.

**'lyrisch** adj. lyric; lyrical (a. fig.).

# M

**Maat** ⏚ [ma:t] m (-[e]s/-e[n]) (ship's) mate.

**Mache** F ['maxə] f (-/no pl.) make-believe, window-dressing, sl. eye-wash; et. in der ~ haben have s.th. in hand.

**machen** ['maxən] (ge-, h) **1.** v/t. make; do; produce, manufacture; give (appetite, etc.); sit for, undergo (examination); come or amount to; make (happy, etc.); was macht das (aus)? what does that matter?; das macht nichts! never mind!, that's (quite) all right!; da(gegen) kann man nichts ~ that cannot be helped; ich mache mir nichts daraus I don't care about it; mach, daß du fortkommst! off with you!; j-n ~ lassen, was er will let s.o. do as he pleases; sich ~ an (acc.) go or set

about; sich et. ~ lassen have s.th. made; **2.** v/i.: na, mach schon! hurry up!; **'2schaften** f/pl. machinations pl.

**Macht** [maxt] f (-/̈e) power; might; authority; control (über acc. of); an der ~ pol. in power; **'~befugnis** f authority, power; **'~haber** pol. m (-s/-) ruler.

**mächtig** adj. ['meçtiç] powerful (a. fig.); mighty; immense, huge; ~ sein (gen.) be master of s.th.; have command of (language).

**'Macht|kampf** m struggle for power; **'2los** adj. powerless; **'~politik** f power politics sg., pl.; policy of the strong hand; **'~spruch** m authoritative decision; **'2voll** adj. powerful (a. fig.); **'~vollkommenheit** f authority; **'~wort** n (-[e]s/-e) word of command; *ein ~ sprechen* put one's foot down.

**'Machwerk** *n* concoction, F put-up job; *elendes ~* bungling work.

**Mädchen** ['mɛːtçən] *n* (-s/-) girl; maid(-servant); *~ für alles* maid of all work; *fig. a.* jack of all trades; **'2haft** *adj.* girlish; '*~name* *m* girl's name; maiden name; '*~schule* *f* girls' school.

**Made** *zo.* ['maːdə] *f* (-/-n) maggot, mite; *fruit:* worm.

**Mädel** ['mɛːdəl] *n* (-s/-, F -s) girl, lass(ie).

**madig** *adj.* ['maːdiç] maggoty, full of mites; *fruit:* wormeaten.

**Magazin** [maga'tsiːn] *n* (-s/-e) store, warehouse; ⚔, *in rifle, periodical:* magazine.

**Magd** [maːkt] *f* (-/⸚e) maid(-servant).

**Magen** ['maːgən] *m* (-s/⸚, *a.* -) stomach, F tummy; *animals:* maw; '*~beschwerden* *f/pl.* stomach *or* gastric trouble, indigestion; '*~bitter* *m* (-s/-) bitters *pl.*; '*~geschwür* ⚔ *n* gastric ulcer; '*~krampf* *m* stomach cramp; '*~krebs* ⚔ *m* stomach cancer; '*~leiden* *n* gastric complaint; '*~säure* *f* gastric acid.

**mager** *adj.* ['maːgər] meag|re, *Am.* -er (*a. fig.*); *p., animal, meat:* lean, *Am. a.* scrawny; '2milch *f* skim milk.

**Magie** [ma'giː] *f* (-/no *pl.*) magic; *~r* ['maːgjər] *m* (-s/-) magician.

**magisch** *adj.* ['maːgiʃ] magic(al).

**Magistrat** [magis'traːt] *m* (-[e]s/-e) municipal *or* town council.

**Magnet** [ma'gneːt] *m* (-[e]s, -en/ -e[n]) magnet (*a. fig.*); lodestone; **2isch** *adj.* magnetic; **2isieren** [~eti'ziːrən] *v/t.* (*no* -ge-, h) magnetize; '*~nadel* [~'gneːt-] *f* magnetic needle.

**Mahagoni** [maha'goːni] *n* (-s/no *pl.*) mahogany (wood).

**mähen** ['mɛːən] *v/t.* (ge-, h) cut, mow, reap.

**Mahl** [maːl] *n* (-[e]s/⸚er, -e) meal, repast.

**'mahlen** (*irr.*, ge-, h) 1. *v/t.* grind, mill; 2. *v/i. tyres:* spin.

**'Mahlzeit** *f* *s.* Mahl; F feed.

**Mähne** ['mɛːnə] *f* (-/-n) mane.

**mahn|en** ['maːnən] *v/t.* (ge-, h) remind, admonish (*both: an acc.* of); *j-n wegen e-r Schuld ~* press s.o. for payment, dun s.o.; '2mal *n* (-[e]s/-e) memorial; '2ung *f* (-/-en) admonition; ✝ reminder, dunning; '2zettel *m* reminder.

**Mai** [maɪ] *m* (-[e]s, -/-e) May; '*~baum* *m* maypole; '*~glöckchen* ⚘ ['~glœkçən] *n* (-s/-) lily of the valley; '*~käfer* *zo.* *m* cockchafer, may-beetle, may-bug.

**Mais** ⚘ [maɪs] *m* (-es/-e) maize, Indian corn, *Am.* corn.

**Majestät** [maje'stɛːt] *f* (-/-en) majesty; *2isch adj.* majestic; *~s-beleidigung* *f* lese-majesty.

**Major** ⚔ [ma'joːr] *m* (-s/-e) major.

**Makel** ['maːkəl] *m* (-s/-) stain, spot; *fig. a.* blemish, fault; '2los *adj.* stainless, spotless; *fig. a.* unblemished, faultless, immaculate.

**mäkeln** F ['mɛːkəln] *v/i.* (ge-, h) find fault (*an dat.* with), carp (at), F pick (at).

**Makler** ✝ ['maːklər] *m* (-s/-) broker; '*~gebühr* ✝ *f* brokerage.

**Makulatur** ⊕ [makula'tuːr] *f* (-/-en) waste paper.

**Mal¹** [maːl] *n* (-[e]s/-e, ⸚er) mark, sign; *sports:* start(ing-point), goal; spot, stain; mole.

**Mal²** [~] 1. *n* (-[e]s/-e) time; *für dieses ~* this time; *zum ersten ~e* for the first time; *mit e-m ~e* all at once, all of a sudden; 2. ⚖ *adv.* times, multiplied by; *drei ~ fünf ist fünfzehn* three times five is *or* are fifteen; F *s. einmal*.

**'malen** *v/t.* (ge-, h) paint; portray.

**'Maler** *m* (-s/-) painter; artist; *~ei* [~'raɪ] *f* (-/-en) painting; *2isch adj.* pictorial, painting; *fig.* picturesque.

**'Malkasten** *m* paint-box.

**'malnehmen** ⚖ *v/t.* (*irr. nehmen, sep.,* -ge-, h) multiply (*mit* by).

**Malz** [malts] *n* (-es/no *pl.*) malt; '*~bier* *n* malt beer.

**Mama** [ma'maː, F 'mama] *f* (-/-s) mamma, mammy, F ma, *Am.* F *a.* mummy, mom.

**man** *indef. pron.* [man] one, you, we; they, people; *~ sagte mir* I was told.

**Manager** ['mɛnidʒər] *m* (-s/-) [manager.]

**manch** [manç], '*~er, ~e, ~es adj. and indef. pron.* many a; *~e pl.* some, several; *~erlei adj.* ['~ər'laɪ] diverse, different; all sorts of, ... of several sorts; *auf ~ Art* in various ways; *used as a noun:* many *or* various things; '*~mal adv.* sometimes, at times.

**Mandant** ⚖ [man'dant] *m* (-en/-en) client.

**Mandarine** ⚘ [manda'riːnə] *f* (-/-n) tangerine.

**Mandat** [man'daːt] *n* (-[e]s/-e) authorization; ⚖ brief; *pol.* mandate; *parl.* seat.

**Mandel** ['mandəl] *f* (-/-n) ⚘ almond; *anat.* tonsil; '*~baum* ⚘ *m* almond-tree; '*~entzündung* ⚕ *f* tonsillitis.

**Manege** [ma'nɛːʒə] *f* (-/-n) (circus-) ring, manège.

**Mangel¹** ['maŋəl] *m* 1. (-s/no *pl.*) want, lack, deficiency; shortage; penury; *aus ~ an* for want of; *~ leiden an (dat.)* be in want of; 2. (-s/⸚) defect, shortcoming.

**Mangel²** [~] *f* (-/-n) mangle; calender.

'mangelhaft adj. defective; deficient; unsatisfactory; 'Ꞩigkeit f (-/no pl.) defectiveness; deficiency.

'mangeln¹ v/i. (ge-, h): es mangelt an Brot there is a lack or shortage of bread, bread is lacking or wanting; es mangelt ihm an (dat.) he is in need of or short of or wanting in, he wants or lacks.

'mangeln² v/t. (ge-, h) mangle (clothes, etc.); ⊕ calender (cloth, paper).

'mangels prp. (gen.) for lack or want of; esp. ⅔ in default of.

'Mangelware † f scarce commodity; goods pl. in short supply.

Manie [ma'ni:] f (-/-n) mania.

Manier [ma'ni:r] f (-/-en) manner; Ꞩlich adj. well-behaved; polite, mannerly. [manifesto.]

Manifest [mani'fɛst] n (-es/-e)

Mann [man] m (-[e]s/ᵘer) man; husband.

'mannbar adj. marriageable; 'Ꞩkeit f (-/no pl.) puberty, manhood.

Männchen ['mɛnçən] n (-s/-) little man; zo. male; birds: cock.

'Mannesalter n virile age, manhood; 'ꞩkraft f virility.

mannigꞩfach adj. ['maniç-], 'ꞩfaltig adj. manifold, various, diverse; 'Ꞩfaltigkeit f (-/no pl.) manifoldness, variety, diversity.

männlich adj. ['mɛnliç] male; gr. masculine; fig. manly; 'Ꞩkeit f (-/no pl.) manhood, virility.

'Mannschaft f (-/-en) (body of) men; ⚓ crew; sports: team, side; 'ꞩführer m sports: captain; 'ꞩgeist m (-es/no pl.) sports: team spirit.

Manöver [ma'nø:vər] n (-s/-) manœuvre, Am. maneuver; Ꞩrieren [ᴧ'ri:rən] v/i. (no -ge-, h) manœuvre, Am. maneuver.

Mansarde [man'zardə] f (-/-n) attic, garret; ꞩnfenster n dormer-window.

manscheꞩn F ['manʃən] (ge-, h) 1. v/t. mix, work; 2. v/i. dabble (in dat. in); Ꞩrei F f (-/-en) mixing, F mess; dabbling.

Manschette [man'ʃɛtə] f (-/-n) cuff; ꞩnknopf m cuff-link.

Mantel ['mantəl] m (-s/ᵘ) coat; overcoat, greatcoat; cloak, mantle (both a. fig.); ⊕ case, jacket; (outer) cover (of tyre).

Manuskript [manu'skript] n (-[e]s/-e) manuscript; typ. copy.

Mappe ['mapə] f (-/-n) portfolio, brief-case; folder; s. a. Schreibmappe, Schulmappe.

Märchen ['mɛːrçən] n (-s/-) fairy-tale; fig. (cock-and-bull) story, fib; 'ꞩbuch n book of fairy-tales; 'Ꞩhaft adj. fabulous (a. fig.).

Marder zo. ['mardər] m (-s/-) marten.

12*

Marine [ma'ri:nə] f (-/-n) marine; ⚔ navy, naval forces pl.; ꞩminister m minister of naval affairs; First Lord of the Admiralty, Am. Secretary of the Navy; ꞩministerium n ministry of naval affairs; the Admiralty, Am. Department of the Navy.

marinieren [mari'ni:rən] v/t. (no -ge-, h) pickle, marinade.

Marionette [mario'nɛtə] f (-/-n) puppet, marionette; ꞩntheater n puppet-show.

Mark [mark] 1. f (-/-) coin: mark; 2. n (-[e]s/no pl.) anat. marrow; ⚘ pith; fig. core.

markant adj. [mar'kant] characteristic; striking; (well-)marked.

Marke ['markə] f (-/-n) mark, sign, token; ⚘, etc.: stamp; † brand, trade-mark; coupon; ꞩnartikel † m branded or proprietary article.

mar'kierꞩen (no -ge-, h) 1. v/t. mark (a. sports); brand (cattle, goods, etc.); 2. F fig. v/i. put it on; Ꞩung f (-/-en) mark(ing).

'markig adj. marrowy; fig. pithy.

Markise [mar'ki:zə] f (-/-n) blind, (window-)awning.

'Markstein m boundary-stone, landmark (a. fig.).

Markt [markt] m (-[e]s/ᵘe) † market; s. Marktplatz; fair; auf den ꞩ bringen † put on the market; 'ꞩflecken m small market-town; 'ꞩplatz m market-place; 'ꞩschreier m (-s/-) quack; puffer.

Marmelade [marmə'la:də] f (-/-n) jam; marmalade (made of oranges).

Marmor ['marmor] m (-s/-e) marble; Ꞩieren [ᴧo'ri:rən] v/t. (no -ge-, h) marble, vein, grain; Ꞩn adj. ['ᴧorn] (of) marble. [whim, caprice.]

Marotte [ma'rɔtə] f (-/-n) fancy,

Marsch [marʃ] 1. m (-es/ᵘe) march (a. ♪); 2. f (-/-en) marsh, fen.

Marschall ['marʃal] m (-s/ᵘe) marshal.

'Marschꞩbefehl ⚔ m marching orders pl.; Ꞩieren [ᴧ'ʃi:rən] v/i. (no -ge-, sein) march; 'ꞩland n marshy land.

Marter ['martər] f (-/-n) torment, torture; Ꞩn v/t. (ge-, h) torment, torture; 'ꞩpfahl m stake.

Märtyrer ['mɛrtyrər] m (-s/-) martyr; 'ꞩtod m martyr's death; 'ꞩtum n (-s/no pl.) martyrdom.

Marxisꞩmus pol. [mar'ksismus] m (-/no pl.) Marxism; ꞩt pol. m (-en/-en) Marxian, Marxist; Ꞩtisch pol. adj. Marxian, Marxist.

März [mɛrts] m (-[e]s/-e) March.

Marzipan [martsi'pa:n] n, ⚘ m (-s/-e) marzipan, marchpane.

Masche ['maʃə] f (-/-n) mesh; knitting: stitch; F fig. trick, line; 'Ꞩnfest adj. ladder-proof, Am. run-proof.

**Maschine** [ma'ʃi:nə] f (-/-n) machine; engine.

**maschinell** adj. [maʃi'nɛl] mechanical; ~e Bearbeitung machining.

**Ma'schinen|bau** m ⊕ (-[e]s/no pl.) mechanical engineering; ~gewehr ✗ n machine-gun; 2mäßig adj. mechanical; automatic; ~pistole ✗ f sub-machine-gun; ~schaden m engine trouble; ~schlosser m (engine) fitter; ~schreiberin f (-/-nen) typist; ~schrift f typescript.

**Maschin|erie** [maʃinə'ri:] f (-/-n) machinery; ~ist [~'nist] m (-en/-en) machinist.

**Masern** ♂ ['ma:zərn] pl. measles pl.

**Mask|e** ['maskə] f (-/-n) mask (a. fig.); ~enball m fancy-dress or masked ball; ~erade [~'ra:də] f (-/-n) masquerade; 2ieren [~'ki:rən] v/t. (no -ge-, h) mask; sich ~ put on a mask; dress o.s. up (als as).

**Maß** [ma:s] 1. n (-es/-e) measure; proportion; fig. moderation; ~e pl. und Gewichte pl. weights and measures pl.; ~e pl. room, etc.: measurements pl.; 2. f (-/-[e]) appr. quart (of beer); 3. 2 pret. of messen.

**Massage** [ma'sa:ʒə] f (-/-n) massage.

**'Maßanzug** m tailor-made or bespoke suit, Am. a. custom(-made) suit.

**Masse** ['masə] f (-/-n) mass; bulk; substance; multitude; crowd; ⚖️ assets pl., estate; die breite ~ the rank and file; F e-e ~ a lot of, F lots pl. or heaps pl. of.

**'Maßeinheit** f measuring unit.

**'Massen|flucht** f stampede; '~grab n common grave; ~güter ✝ ['~gy:tər] n/pl. bulk goods pl.; '2haft adj. abundant; '~produktion ✝ f mass production; '~versammlung f mass meeting, Am. a. rally; '2~weise adv. in masses, in large numbers.

**Masseu|r** [ma'sø:r] m (-s/-e) masseur; ~se [~zə] f (-/-n) masseuse.

**'maß|gebend** adj. standard; authoritative, decisive; board: competent; circles: influential, leading; '~halten v/i. (irr. halten, sep., -ge-, h) keep within limits, be moderate.

**mas'sieren** v/t. (no -ge-, h) massage, knead.

**'massig** adj. massy, bulky; solid.

**mäßig** adj. ['mɛ:siç] moderate; food, etc.: frugal; ✝ price: moderate, reasonable; result, etc.: poor; ~en ['~gən] v/t. (ge-, h) moderate; sich ~ moderate or restrain o.s.; '2ung f (-/-en) moderation; restraint.

**massiv** [ma'si:f] 1. adj. massive, solid; 2. 2 geol. n (-s/-e) massif.

**'Maß|krug** m beer-mug, Am. a. stein; '2los adj. immoderate; boundless; exorbitant, excessive;

extravagant; ~nahme ['~na:mə] f (-/-n) measure, step, action; '2regeln v/t. (ge-, h) reprimand; inflict disciplinary punishment on; '~schneider m bespoke or Am. custom tailor; '~stab m measure, rule(r); maps, etc.: scale; fig. yardstick, standard; '2voll adj. moderate.

**Mast**[1] ⚓ [mast] m (-es/-e[n]) mast.

**Mast**[2] ✗ [~] f (-/-en) fattening; mast, food; '~darm anat. m rectum.

**mästen** ['mɛstən] v/t. (ge-, h) fatten, feed; stuff (geese, etc.).

**'Mastkorb** ⚓ m mast-head, crows-nest.

**Material** [mater'ja:l] n (-s/-ien) material; substance; stock, stores pl.; fig.: material, information; evidence; ~ismus phls. [~a'lismus] m (-/no pl.) materialism; ~ist [~a'list] m (-en/-en) materialist; 2istisch adj. [~a'listiʃ] materialistic.

**Materie** [ma'te:rjə] f (-/-n) matter (a. fig.), stuff; fig. subject; 2ll adj. [~er'jɛl] material.

**Mathemati|k** [matema'ti:k] f (-/no pl.) mathematics sg.; ~ker [~'ma:tikər] m (-s/-) mathematician; 2sch adj. [~'ma:tiʃ] mathematical.

**Matinee** thea. [mati'ne:] f (-/-n) morning performance.

**Matratze** [ma'tratsə] f (-/-n) mattress.

**Matrone** [ma'tro:nə] f (-/-n) matron; 2nhaft adj. matronly.

**Matrose** ⚓ [ma'tro:zə] m (-n/-n) sailor, seaman.

**Matsch** [matʃ] m (-es/no pl.), ~e F ['~ə] f (-/no pl.) pulp, squash; mud, slush; '2ig adj. pulpy, squashy; muddy, slushy.

**matt** adj. [mat] faint, feeble; voice, etc.: faint; eye, colour, etc.: dim; colour, light, ✝ stock exchange, style, etc.: dull; metal: tarnished; gold, etc.: dead, dull; chess: mated; ⚡ bulb: non-glare; ~ geschliffen glass: ground, frosted, matted; ~ setzen at chess: (check)mate s.o.

**Matte** ['matə] f (-/-n) mat.

**'Mattigkeit** f (-/no pl.) exhaustion, feebleness; faintness.

**'Mattscheibe** f phot. focus(s)ing screen; television: screen.

**Mauer** ['mauər] f (-/-n) wall; ~blümchen fig. ['~bly:mçən] n (-s/-) wall-flower; '2n (ge-, h) 1. v/i. make a wall, lay bricks; 2. v/t. build (in stone or brick); '~stein m brick; '~werk n masonry, brickwork.

**Maul** [maul] n (-[e]s/¨er) mouth; sl.: halt's ~! shut up!; '2en F v/i. (ge-, h) sulk, pout; '~esel zo. m mule, hinny; '~held F m braggart; '~korb m muzzle; '~schelle F f box on the ear; '~tier zo. n mule;

'**~wurf** zo. m mole; '**~wurfshügel** m molehill.

**Maurer** ['maurər] m (-s/-) bricklayer, mason; '**~meister** m master mason; '**~polier** m bricklayers' foreman.

**Maus** zo. [maus] f (-/⁓e) mouse; **~efalle** ['⁓zə-] f mousetrap; **2en** ['⁓zən] (ge-, h) 1. v/i. catch mice; 2. F v/t. pinch, pilfer, F swipe.

**Mauser** ['mauzər] f (-/no pl.) mo(u)lt(ing); in der ~ sein be mo(u)lting; '**2n** v/refl. (ge-, h) mo(u)lt.

**Maximum** ['maksimum] n (-s/Maxima) maximum.

**Mayonnaise** [majo'nɛ:zə] f (-/-n) mayonnaise.

**Mechani|k** [me'ça:nik] f 1. (-/no pl.) mechanics mst sg.; 2. ⊕ (-/-en) mechanism; **~ker** m (-s/-) mechanic; **2sch** adj. mechanical; **2sieren** [⁓ani'zi:rən] v/t. (no -ge-, h) mechanize; **~smus** ⊕ [⁓a'nismus] m (-/Mechanismen) mechanism; clock, watch, etc.: works pl.

**meckern** ['mɛkərn] v/i. (ge-, h) bleat; fig. grumble (über acc. over, at, about), carp (at); nag (at); sl. grouse, Am. sl. gripe.

**Medaill|e** [me'daljə] f (-/-n) medal; **~on** [⁓'jõ:] n (-s/-s) medallion; locket.

**Medikament** [medika'mɛnt] n (-[e]s/-e) medicament, medicine.

**Medizin** [medi'tsi:n] f 1. (-/no pl.) (science of) medicine; 2. (-/-en) medicine, F physic; **~er** m (-s/-) medical man; medical student; **2isch** adj. medical; medicinal.

**Meer** [me:r] n (-[e]s/-e) sea (a. fig.), ocean; '**~busen** m gulf, bay; '**~enge** f strait(s pl.); '**~esspiegel** m sea level; '**~rettich** ♀ m horse-radish; '**~schweinchen** zo. n guinea-pig.

**Mehl** [me:l] n (-[e]s/-e) flour; meal; '**~brei** m pap; '**2ig** adj. floury, mealy; farinaceous; '**~speise** f sweet dish, pudding; '**~suppe** f gruel.

**mehr** [me:r] 1. adj. more; er hat ~ Geld als ich he has (got) more money than I; 2. adv. more; nicht ~ no more, no longer, not any longer; ich habe nichts ~ I have nothing left; '**2arbeit** f additional work; overtime; '**2ausgaben** f/pl. additional expenditure; '**2betrag** m surplus; '**2deutig** adj. ambiguous; '**2einnahme(n** pl.) f additional receipts pl.; '**~en** v/t. (ge-, h) augment, increase; sich ~ multiply, grow; '**~ere** adj. and indef. pron. several, some; '**~fach** 1. adj. manifold, repeated; 2. adv. repeatedly, several times; '**2gebot** n higher bid; '**2heit** f (-/-en) majority, plurality; '**2kosten** pl. additional expense; '**~malig** adj. repeated, reiterated;

**~mals** adv. ['⁓ma:ls] several times, repeatedly; '**~sprachig** adj. polyglot; '**~stimmig** ♪ adj.: ~er Gesang part-song; '**2verbrauch** m excess consumption; '**2wertsteuer** ☨ f (-/no pl.) value-added tax; '**2zahl** f majority; gr. plural (form); die ~ (gen.) most of.

**meiden** ['maidən] v/t. (irr., ge-, h) avoid, shun, keep away from.

**Meile** ['mailə] f (-/-n) mile; '**~stein** m milestone.

**mein** poss. pron. [main] my; der (die, das) ~e my; die **2en** pl. my family, F my people or folks pl.; ich habe das ~e getan I have done all I can; ~e Damen und Herren! Ladies and Gentlemen!

**Meineid** ♂♀ ['main?-] m perjury; '**2ig** adj. perjured.

**meinen** ['mainən] v/t. (ge-, h) think, believe, be of (the) opinion, Am. a. reckon, guess; say; mean; wie ~ Sie das? what do you mean by that?; ~ Sie das ernst? do you (really) mean it?; es gut ~ mean well.

**meinetwegen** adv. ['mainət'-] for my sake; on my behalf; because of me, on my account; for all I care; I don't mind or care.

'**Meinung** f (-/-en) opinion (über acc., von about, of); die öffentliche ~ (the) public opinion; meiner ~ nach in my opinion, to my mind; j-m (gehörig) die ~ sagen give s.o. a piece of one's mind; '**~saustausch** ['mainuŋs?-] m exchange of views (über acc. on); '**~sverschiedenheit** f difference of opinion (über acc. on); disagreement.

**Meise** orn. ['maizə] f (-/-n) titmouse.

**Meißel** ['maisəl] m (-s/-) chisel; '**2n** v/t. and v/i. (ge-, h) chisel; carve.

**meist** [maist] 1. adj. most; die ~en Leute most people; die ~e Zeit most of one's time; 2. adv.: s. meistens; am ~en most (of all); '**2bietende** ['⁓bi:təndə] m (-n/-n) highest bidder; **~ens** adv. ['⁓əns], '**~en'teils** adv. mostly, in most cases; usually.

**Meister** ['maistər] m (-s/-) master, sl. boss; sports: champion; '**2haft** 1. adj. masterly; 2. adv. in a masterly manner or way; '**2n** v/t. (ge-, h) master; '**~schaft** f 1. (-/no pl.) mastery; 2. (-/-en) sports: championship, title; '**~stück** n, '**~werk** n masterpiece.

'**Meistgebot** n highest bid, best offer.

**Melancholi|e** [melaŋko'li:] f (-/-n) melancholy; **2sch** adj. [⁓'ko:lif] melancholy; ~ sein F have the blues.

**Melde|amt** ['mɛldə-] n registration office; '**~liste** f sports: list of entries; '**2n** v/t. (ge-, h) announce; j-m et. ~ inform s.o. of s.th.; officially: notify s.th. to s.o.; j-n ~

enter s.o.'s name (für, zu for); sich ~ report o.s. (bei to); school, etc.: put up one's hand; answer the telephone; enter (one's name) (für, zu for examination, etc.); sich ~ zu apply for; sich auf ein Inserat ~ answer an advertisement.

'Meldung f (-/-en) information, advice; announcement; report; registration; application; sports: entry.

melke|n ['mɛlkən] v/t. ([irr.,] ge-, h) milk; '2r m (-s/-) milker.

Melod|ie ♪ [melo'di:] f (-/-n) melody; tune, air; 2isch adj. [~'lo:diʃ] melodious, tuneful.

Melone [me'lo:nə] f (-/-n) ♀ melon; F bowler(-hat), Am. derby.

Membran [mɛm'braːn] f (-/-en), ~e f (-/-n) membrane; teleph. a. diaphragm.

Memme F ['mɛmə] f (-/-n) coward; poltroon.

Memoiren [memo'aːrən] pl. memoirs pl.

Menagerie [menaʒə'riː] f (-/-n) menagerie.

Menge ['mɛŋə] f (-/-n) quantity; amount; multitude; crowd; in großer ~ in abundance; persons, animals: in crowds; e-e ~ Geld plenty of money, F lots pl. of money; e-e ~ Bücher a great many books; '2n v/t. (ge-, h) mix, blend; sich ~ mix (unter acc. with), mingle (with); sich ~ in (acc.) meddle or interfere with.

Mensch [mɛnʃ] m (-en/-en) human being; man; person, individual; die ~en pl. people pl., the world, mankind; kein ~ nobody.

'Menschen|affe zo. m anthropoid ape; '~alter n generation, age; '~feind m misanthropist; '2feindlich adj. misanthropic; '~fresser m (-s/-) cannibal, man-eater; '~freund m philanthropist; '2freundlich adj. philanthropic; '2gedenken n (-s/no pl.): seit ~ from time immemorial, within the memory of man; '~geschlecht n human race, mankind; '~haß m misanthropy; '~kenner m judge of men or human nature; '~kenntnis f knowledge of human nature; '~leben n human life; '2leer adj. deserted; '~liebe f philanthropy; '~menge f crowd (of people), throng; '2möglich adj. humanly possible; '~raub m kidnap(p)ing; '~rechte n/pl. human rights pl.; '2scheu adj. unsociable, shy; '~seele f: keine ~ not a living soul; '~verstand m human understanding; gesunder ~ common sense, F horse sense; '~würde f dignity of man.

'Menschheit f (-/no pl.) human race, mankind.

'menschlich adj. human; fig. hu-

mane; '2keit f (-/no pl.) human nature; humanity, humaneness.

Mentalität [mɛntali'tɛːt] f (-/-en) mentality.

merk|bar adj. ['mɛrkbaːr] s. merklich; '2blatt n leaflet, instructional pamphlet; '2buch n notebook; '~en (ge-, h) 1. v/i.: ~ auf (acc.) pay attention to, listen to; 2. v/t. notice, perceive; find out, discover; sich et. ~ remember s.th.; bear s.th. in mind; '~lich adj. noticeable, perceptible; '2mal n (-[e]s/-e) mark, sign; characteristic, feature.

'merkwürdig adj. noteworthy, remarkable; strange, odd, curious; ~erweise adv. ['~gər'-] strange to say, strangely enough; '2keit f (-/-en) remarkableness; curiosity; peculiarity.

meßbar adj. ['mɛsbaːr] measurable.

Messe ['mɛsə] f (-/-n) ♱ fair; eccl. mass; ⚓, ♻ mess.

messen ['mɛsən] v/t. (irr., ge-, h) measure; ⚓ sound; sich mit j-m ~ compete with s.o.; sich nicht mit j-m ~ können be no match for s.o.; gemessen an (dat.) measured against, compared with.

Messer ['mɛsər] n (-s/-) knife; ⚕ scalpel; bis aufs ~ to the knife; auf des ~s Schneide on a razor-edge or razor's edge; '~griff m knife-handle; '~held m stabber; '~klinge f knife-blade; '~schmied m cutler; '~schneide f knife-edge; '~stecher m (-s/-) stabber; '~stecherei f [~ʃtɛçə'raɪ] f (-/-en) knifing, knife-battle; '~stich m stab with a knife.

Messing ['mɛsiŋ] n (-s/no pl.) brass; '~blech n sheet-brass.

'Meß|instrument n measuring instrument; '~latte f surveyor's rod; '~tisch m surveyor's or plane table.

Metall [me'tal] n (-s/-e) metal; ~arbeiter m metal worker; 2en adj. (of) metal, metallic; ~geld n coin(s pl.), specie; ~glanz m metallic lust|re, Am. -er; 2haltig adj. metalliferous; ~industrie f metallurgical industry; ~waren f/pl. hardware.

Meteor ast. [mete'oːr] m (-s/-e) meteor; ~ologe [~oro'lo:gə] m (-n/-n) meteorologist; ~ologie [~orolo'giː] f (-/no pl.) meteorology.

Meter ['me:tər] n, m (-s/-) met|re, Am. -er; '~maß n tape-measure.

Method|e [me'to:də] f (-/-n) method; ⊕ a. technique; 2isch adj. methodical.

Metropole [metro'po:lə] f (-/-n) metropolis.

Metzel|ei [mɛtsə'laɪ] f (-/-en) slaughter, massacre; '2n v/t. (ge-, h) butcher, slaughter, massacre.

Metzger ['mɛtsgər] m (-s/-) butcher; ~ei [~'raɪ] f (-/-en) butcher's (shop).

Meuchel|mord ['mɔʏçəl-] m assassination; '~mörder m assassin.

**Meute** ['mɔʏtə] f (-/-n) pack of hounds; fig. gang; ~**rei** [~'raɪ] f (-/-en) mutiny; ~**rer** m (-s/-) mutineer; **2risch** adj. mutinous; **2rn** v/i. (ge-, h) mutiny (gegen against).

**mich** pers. pron. [miç] me; ~ (selbst) myself.

**mied** [mi:t] pret. of meiden.

**Mieder** ['mi:dər] n (-s/-) bodice; corset; '~**waren** f/pl. corsetry.

**Miene** ['mi:nə] f (-/-n) countenance, air; feature; gute ~ zum bösen Spiel machen grin and bear it; ~ machen zu inf. offer or threaten to inf.

**mies** F adj. [mi:s] miserable, poor; out of sorts, seedy.

**Miet|e** ['mi:tə] f (-/-n) rent; hire; zur ~ wohnen live in lodgings, be a tenant; '2en v/t. (ge-, h) rent (land, building, etc.); hire (horse, etc.); (take on) lease (land, etc.); ⚓, ✈ charter; '~**er** m (-s/-) tenant; lodger, Am. a. roomer; ✍ lessee; '2**frei** adj. rent-free; '~**shaus** n block of flats, Am. apartment house; '~**vertrag** m tenancy agreement; lease; '~**wohnung** f lodgings pl., flat, Am. apartment.

**Migräne** 🩺 [mi'grɛ:nə] f (-/-n) migraine, megrim; sick headache.

**Mikrophon** [mikro'fo:n] n (-s/-e) microphone, F mike.

**Mikroskop** [mikro'sko:p] n (-s/-e) microscope; **2isch** adj. microscopic(al).

**Milbe** zo. ['milbə] f (-/-n) mite.

**Milch** [milç] f (-/no pl.) milk; milt, soft roe (of fish); '~**bar** f milk-bar; '~**bart** fig. m stripling; '~**brötchen** n (French) roll; '~**gesicht** n baby face; '~**glas** n frosted glass; '2**ig** adj. milky; '~**kanne** f milk-can; '~**kuh** f milk cow (a. fig.); '~**mädchen** n milkmaid, dairymaid; '~**mann** F m milkman, dairyman; '~**pulver** n milk-powder; '~**reis** m rice-milk; '~**straße** ast. f Milky Way, Galaxy; '~**wirtschaft** f dairy-farm(ing); '~**zahn** m milk-tooth.

**mild** [milt] 1. adj. weather, punishment, etc.: mild; air, weather, light, etc.: soft; wine, etc.: mellow, smooth; reprimand, etc.: gentle; 2. adv.: et. ~ beurteilen take a lenient view of s. th.

**milde** ['mildə] 1. adj. s. mild 1; 2. adv.: ~ gesagt to put it mildly; 3. 2 f (-/no pl.) mildness; softness; smoothness; gentleness.

**milder|n** ['mildərn] v/t. (ge-, h) soften, mitigate; soothe, alleviate (pain, etc.); ~**de Umstände** ✍ extenuating circumstances; '2**ung** f (-/-en) softening, mitigation; alleviation.

'**mild|herzig** adj. charitable; '2**herzigkeit** f (-/no pl.) charitableness;

'~**tätig** adj. charitable; '2**tätigkeit** f charity.

**Milieu** [mil'jø:] n (-s/-s) surroundings pl., environment; class, circles pl.; local colo(u)r.

**Militär** [mili'tɛ:r] 1. n (-s/no pl.) military, armed forces pl.; army; 2. m (-s/-s) military man, soldier; ~**attaché** [~ata∫e:] m (-s/-s) military attaché; ~**dienst** m military service; **2isch** adj. military; ~**musik** f military music; ~**regierung** f military government; ~**zeit** f (-/no pl.) term of military service.

**Miliz** ✖ [mi'li:ts] f (-/-en) militia; ~**soldat** ✖ m militiaman.

**Milliarde** [mil'jardə] f (-/-n) thousand millions, milliard, Am. billion.

**Millimeter** [mili'-] n, m millimet|re, Am. -er.

**Million** [mil'jo:n] f (-/-en) million; ~**är** [~o'nɛ:r] m (-s/-e) millionaire.

**Milz** anat. [milts] f (-/-en) spleen, milt.

**minder** ['mindər] 1. adv. less; nicht ~ no less, likewise; 2. adj. less(er); smaller; minor; inferior; '~**begabt** adj. less gifted; ~**bemittelt** adj. ['~bəmitəlt] of moderate means; **2betrag** m deficit, shortage; **2einnahme** f shortfall in receipts; **2gewicht** n short weight; '2**heit** f (-/-en) minority; '~**jährig** adj. ['~jɛ:riç] under age, minor; '2**jährigkeit** f (-/no pl.) minority; '~**n** v/t. and v/refl. (ge-, h) diminish, lessen, decrease; **2ung** f (-/-en) decrease, diminution; '~**wertig** adj. inferior, of inferior quality; '2**wertigkeit** f (-/no pl.) inferiority; † inferior quality; **2wertigkeitskomplex** m inferiority complex.

**mindest** adj. ['mindəst] least; slightest; minimum; nicht die ~e Aussicht not the slightest chance; nicht im ~en not in the least, by no means; zum ~en at least; '2**alter** n minimum age; '2**anforderungen** f/pl. minumum requirements pl.; '2**betrag** m lowest amount; '2**einkommen** n minimum income; '~**ens** adv. at least; '2**gebot** n lowest bid; '2**lohn** m minimum wage; '2**maß** n minimum; auf ein ~ herabsetzen minimize; '2**preis** m minimum price.

**Mine** ['mi:nə] f (-/-n) ✖, ✖, ⚓ mine; pencil: lead; ball-point-pen: refill.

**Mineral** [minə'ra:l] n (-s/-e, -ien) mineral; **2isch** adj. mineral; ~**ogie** [~alo'gi:] f (-/no pl.) mineralogy; ~**wasser** n (-s/⁀) mineral water.

**Miniatur** [minia'tu:r] f (-/-en) miniature; ~**gemälde** n miniature.

**Minirock** ['mini-] m miniskirt.

**Minister** [mi'nistər] m (-s/-) minister; Secretary (of State), Am. Secretary; ~ium [~'te:rjum] n (-s/Mi-nisterien) ministry; Office, Am. Department; ~präsident m prime minister, premier; in Germany, etc.: minister president; ~rat m (-[e]s/~e) cabinet council.

**minus** adv. ['mi:nus] minus, less, deducting.

**Minute** [mi'nu:tə] f (-/-n) minute; ~nzeiger m minute-hand.

**mir** pers. pron. [mi:r] (to) me.

**Misch|ehe** ['miʃ?-] f mixed mar-riage; intermarriage; '2en v/t. (ge-, h) mix, mingle; blend (coffee, to-bacco, etc.); alloy (metal); shuffle (cards); sich ~ in (acc.) interfere in; join in (conversation); sich ~ unter (acc.) mix or mingle with (the crowd); ~ling ['~liŋ] m (-s/-e) half-breed, half-caste; ♀, zo. hybrid; ~masch F ['~maʃ] m (-es/-e) hotch-potch, jumble; '~ung f (-/-en) mixture; blend; alloy.

**miß|achten** ['mis'-] v/t. (no -ge-, h) disregard, ignore, neglect; slight, despise; '2achtung f disregard, neglect; '~behagen 1. v/i. (no -ge-, h) displease; 2. ♀ n discomfort, uneasiness; '2bildung f malforma-tion, deformity; 'billigen v/t. (no -ge-, h) disapprove (of); '2billi-gung f disapproval; '2brauch m abuse; misuse; '~brauchen v/t. (no -ge-, h) abuse; misuse; ~bräuchlich adj. ['~brɔyçliç] abu-sive; improper; ~'deuten v/t. (no -ge-, h) misinterpret; '2deutung f misinterpretation.

**missen** ['misən] v/t. (ge-, h) miss; do without, dispense with.

**'Miß|erfolg** m failure; fiasco; '~ ernte f bad harvest, crop failure.

**Misse|tat** ['misə-] f misdeed; crime; '~täter m evil-doer, offender; criminal.

**miß|'fallen** v/i. (irr. fallen, no -ge-, h): j-m ~ displease s.o.; '2fallen n (-s/no pl.) displeasure, dislike; '~fällig 1. adj. displeasing; shock-ing; disparaging; 2. adv.: sich ~ äußern über (acc.) speak ill of; '2ge-burt f monster, freak (of nature), deformity; '2geschick n bad luck, misfortune, mishap; ~gestimmt fig. adj. ['~gəʃtimt] s. mißmutig; ~glücken v/i. (no -ge-, sein) fail; ~gönnen v/t. (no -ge-, h): j-m et. ~ envy or grudge s.o. s.th.; '2griff m mistake, blunder; '2gunst f envy, jealousy; '~günstig adj. envious, jealous; ~handeln v/t. (no -ge-, h) ill-treat; maul, sl. manhandle; 2'handlung f ill-treatment; maul-ing, sl. manhandling; ₮₷ assault and battery; '2heirat f misalliance; '~hellig adj. dissonant, dissentient; '2helligkeit f (-/-en) dissonance, dissension, discord.

**Mission** [mis'jo:n] f (-/-en) mission

(a. pol. and fig.); ~ar [~o'na:r] m (-s/-e) missionary.

**'Miß|klang** m dissonance, discord (both a. fig.); '~kredit fig. m (-[e]s/no pl.) discredit; in ~ bringen bring discredit upon s.o.

**miß|'lang** pret. of mißlingen; '~ lich adj. awkward; unpleasant; ~liebig adj. ['~li:biç] unpopular; ~lingen [~'liŋən] v/i. (irr., no -ge-, sein) fail; 2'lingen n (-s/no pl.) failure; '2mut m ill humo(u)r; discontent; '2mutig adj. ill-humo(u)red; discontented; ~'raten 1. v/i. (irr. raten, no -ge-, sein) fail; turn out badly; 2. adj. way-ward; ill-bred; '2stand m nuisance; grievance; '2stimmung f ill humo(u)r; '2ton m (-[e]s/-e) disso-nance, discord (both a. fig.); ~'trau-en v/i. (no -ge-, h): j-m ~ distrust or mistrust s.o.; '2trauen n (-s/no pl.) distrust, mistrust; '~trauisch adj. distrustful; suspicious; '2ver-gnügen n (-s/no pl.) displeasure; '~vergnügt adj. displeased; discon-tented; '2verhältnis n dispropor-tion; incongruity; '2verständnis n misunderstanding; dissension; '~verstehen v/t. (irr. stehen, no -ge-, h) misunderstand, mistake (intention, etc.); '2wirtschaft f mal-administration, mismanagement.

**Mist** [mist] m (-es/-e) dung, manure; dirt; F fig. trash, rubbish; '~beet n hotbed.

**Mistel** ♀ ['mistəl] f (-/-n) mistle-toe.

**'Mist|gabel** f dung-fork; '~haufen m dung-hill.

**mit** [mit] 1. prp. (dat.) with; ~ 20 Jahren at (the age of) twenty; ~ e-m Schlage at a blow; ~ Gewalt by force; ~ der Bahn by train; 2. adv. also, too; ~ dabeisein be there too, be (one) of the party.

**Mit|arbeiter** ['mit'-] m co-worker; writing, art, etc.: collaborator; colleague; newspaper, etc.: contrib-utor (an dat. to); '2benutzen v/t. (sep., no -ge-, h) use jointly or in common; '~besitzer m joint owner; '~bestimmungsrecht n right of co-determination; '~bewerber m competitor; '~bewohner m co-inhabitant, fellow-lodger; '2brin-gen v/t. (irr. bringen, sep., -ge-, h) bring along (with one); ~bringsel ['~briŋzəl] n (-s/-) little present; '~bürger m fellow-citizen; 2ein-ander adv. [mit?ai'nandər] to-gether, jointly; with each other, with one another; ~empfinden ['mit'-] n (-s/no pl.) sympathy; ~erbe ['mit'-] m co-heir; ~esser ♂ ['mit'-] m (-s/-) blackhead; '2fah-ren v/i. (irr. fahren, sep., -ge-, sein): mit j-m ~ drive or go with s.o.; j-n ~ lassen give s.o. a lift; '2fühlen v/i. (sep., -ge-, h) sympathize (mit with); '⁂geben v/t. (irr. geben, sep., -ge-, h) give along (dat. with); '⁂gefühl n sympathy; '⁂gehen v/i. (irr. gehen, sep., -ge-, sein): mit j-m ~ go with s.o.; '⁂gift f (-/-en) dowry, marriage portion.

'**Mitglied** n member; '⁂erversammlung f general meeting; '⁂erzahl f membership; '⁂sbeitrag m subscription; '⁂schaft f (-/no pl.) membership.

**mit|'hin** adv. consequently, therefore; ⁂inhaber ['mit?-] m copartner; '⁂kämpfer m fellow-combatant; '⁂kommen v/i. (irr. kommen, sep., -ge-, sein) come along (mit with); fig. be able to follow; '⁂läufer pol. m nominal member; contp. trimmer.

'**Mitleid** n (-[e]s/no pl.) compassion, pity; sympathy; aus ~ out of pity; ~ haben mit have or take pity on; '⁂enschaft f (-/no pl.): in ~ ziehen affect; implicate, involve; damage; '⁂ig adj. compassionate, pitiful; ⁂(s)los adj. ['⁂t-] pitiless, merciless; ⁂(s)voll adj. ['⁂t-] pitiful, compassionate.

'**mit|machen** (sep., -ge-, h) 1. v/i. make one of the party; 2. v/t. take part in, participate in; follow, go with (fashion); go through (hardships); '⁂mensch m fellow creature; '⁂nehmen v/t. (irr. nehmen, sep., -ge-, h) take along (with one); fig. exhaust, wear out; j-n (im Auto) ~ give s.o. a lift; ⁂nichten adv. [⁂'niçtən] by no means, not at all; '⁂rechnen v/t. (sep., -ge-, h) include (in the account); nicht ~ leave out of account; nicht mitgerechnet not counting; '⁂reden (sep., -ge-, h) 1. v/i. join in the conversation; 2. v/t.: ein Wort or Wörtchen mitzureden haben have a say (bei in); '⁂reißen v/t. (irr. reißen, sep., -ge-, h) tear or drag along; fig. sweep along.

'**Mitschuld** f complicity (an dat. in); '⁂ig adj. accessary (an dat. to crime); '⁂ige m accessary, accomplice.

'**Mitschüler** m schoolfellow.

'**mitspiel|en** (sep., -ge-, h) 1. v/i. play (bei with); sports: be on the team; thea. appear, star (in a play); join in a game; matter: be involved; j-m arg or übel ~ play s.o. a nasty trick; 2. fig. v/t. join in (game); '⁂er m partner.

'**Mittag** m midday, noon; heute ⁂ at noon today; zu ~ essen lunch, dine; '⁂essen n lunch(eon); dinner; '⁂s adv. at noon.

'**Mittags|pause** f lunch hour; '⁂ruhe f midday rest; '⁂schlaf m, '⁂schläfchen n after-dinner nap, siesta; '⁂stunde f noon; '⁂tisch fig. m lunch, dinner; '⁂zeit f noontide; lunch-time, dinner-time.

**Mitte** ['mitə] f (-/-n) middle; cent|re, Am. -er; die goldene ~ the golden or happy mean; aus unserer ~ from among us; ~ Juli in the middle of July; ~ Dreißig in the middle of one's thirties.

'**mitteil|en** v/t. (sep., -ge-, h): j-m et. ~ communicate s.th. to s.o.; impart s.th. to s.o.; inform s.o. of s.th.; make s.th. known to s.o.; '⁂sam adj. communicative; '⁂ung f (-/-en) communication; information; communiqué.

**Mittel** ['mitəl] n (-s/-) means sg., way; remedy (gegen for); average; Å mean; phys. medium; ~ pl. a. means pl., funds pl., money; ~ pl. und Wege ways and means pl.; '⁂alter n Middle Ages pl.; '⁂alterlich adj. medi(a)eval; '⁂bar adj. mediate, indirect; '⁂ding n: ein ~ zwischen ... und ... something between ... and ...; '⁂finger m middle finger; '⁂gebirge n highlands pl.; '⁂groß adj. of medium height; medium-sized; '⁂läufer m sports: centre half back, Am. center half back; '⁂los adj. without means, destitute; '⁂mäßig adj. middling; mediocre; '⁂mäßigkeit f (-/no pl.) mediocrity; '⁂punkt m cent|re, Am. -er; fig. a. focus; '⁂s prp. (gen.) by (means of), through; '⁂schule f intermediate school, Am. high school; '⁂smann m (-[e]s/=er, Mittelsleute) mediator, go-between; '⁂stand m middle classes pl.; '⁂stürmer m sports: centre forward, Am. center forward; '⁂weg fig. m middle course; '⁂wort gr. n (-[e]s/=er) participle.

**mitten** adv. ['mitən]: ~ in or an or auf or unter (acc./dat.) in the midst or middle of; ~ entzwei right in two; ~ im Winter in the depth of winter; ~ in der Nacht in the middle or dead of night; ~ ins Herz right into the heart; ~'drin F adv. right in the middle; ~'durch F adv. right through or across.

**Mitter|nacht** ['mitər-] f midnight; um ~ at midnight; ⁂nächtig adj. ['⁂nɛçtiç], ⁂nächtlich adj. midnight.

**Mittler** ['mitlər] 1. m (-s/-) mediator, intercessor; 2. ⁂ adj. middle, central; average, medium; '⁂weile adv. meanwhile, (in the) meantime.

**Mittwoch** ['mitvɔx] m (-[e]s/-e) Wednesday; '⁂s adv. on Wednesday(s), every Wednesday.

**mit|'unter** adv. now and then, sometimes; '⁂verantwortlich adj. jointly responsible; '⁂welt f (-/no pl.): die ~ our, etc. contemporaries pl.

'mitwirk|en v/i. (sep., -ge-, h) co-operate (bei in), contribute (to), take part (in); '2ende m (-n/-n) thea. performer, actor, player (a. ♪); die ~n pl. the cast; '2ung f (-/no pl.) co(-)operation, contribution.

'Mitwisser m (-s/-) confidant; ₰₤ accessary.                       [rechnen.\
'mitzählen v/t. (sep., -ge-, h) s. mit-\
Mix|becher ['miks-] m (cocktail-)shaker; '2en v/t. (ge-, h) mix; ~tur [.'tu:r] f (-/-en) mixture.

Möbel ['mø:bəl] n (-s/-) piece of furniture; ~ pl. furniture; '~händ-ler m furniture-dealer; '~spedi-teur m furniture-remover; '~stück n piece of furniture; '~tischler m cabinet-maker; '~wagen m pan-technicon, Am. furniture truck.

mobil adj. [mo'bi:l] ⚔ mobile; F active, nimble; ~ machen ⚔ mobi-lize; 2iar [.il'ja:r] n (-s/-e) furni-ture; movables pl.; ~isieren [.ili-'zi:rən] v/t. (no -ge-, h) ⚔ mobilize; ✝ realize (property, etc.); 2ma-chung ⚔ [mo'bi:lmaxuŋ] f (-/-en) mobilization.

möblieren [mø'bli:rən] v/t. (no -ge-, h) furnish; möbliertes Zimmer furnished room, F bed-sitter.

mochte ['mɔxtə] pret. of mögen.

Mode ['mo:də] f (-/-en) fashion, vogue; use, custom; die neueste ~ the latest fashion; in ~ in fashion or vogue; aus der ~ kommen grow or go out of fashion; die ~ bestimmen set the fashion; '~artikel m/pl. fancy goods pl., novelties pl.; '~far-be f fashionable colo(u)r.

Modell [mo'dɛl] n (-s/-e) ⊕, fashion, paint.: model; pattern, design; ⊕ mo(u)ld; j-m ~ stehen paint. pose for s.o.; ~eisenbahn f model rail-way; 2ieren [.'li:rən] v/t. (no -ge-, h) model, mo(u)ld, fashion.

'Moden|schau f dress parade, fashion-show; '~zeitung f fashion magazine.

Moder ['mo:dər] m (-s/no pl.) must, putrefaction; '~geruch m musty smell; '2ig adj. musty, putrid.

modern¹ ['mo:dərn] v/i. (ge-, h) putrefy, rot, decay.

modern² adj. [mo'dɛrn] modern, progressive; up-to-date; fashion-able; ~isieren [.i'zi:rən] v/t. (no -ge-, h) modernize, bring up to date.

'Mode|salon m fashion house; '~schmuck m costume jewel(le)ry; '~waren f/pl. fancy goods pl.; '~zeichner m fashion-designer.

modifizieren [modifi'tsi:rən] v/t. (no -ge-, h) modify.

modisch adj. ['mo:diʃ] fashionable, stylish.                        [liner.\
Modistin [mo'distin] f (-/-nen) mil-\
Mogel|ei [mo:gə'lai] f (-/-en) cheat; '2n F v/i. (ge-, h) cheat.

mögen ['mø:gən] (irr., h) 1. v/i. (ge-) be willing; ich mag nicht I don't like to; 2. v/t. (ge-) want, wish; like, be fond of; nicht ~ dislike; not to be keen on (food, etc.); lieber ~ like better, prefer; 3. v/aux. (no -ge-) may, might; ich möchte wissen I should like to know; ich möchte lieber gehen I would rather go; das mag (wohl) sein that's (well) pos-sible; wo er auch sein mag wherever he may be; mag er sagen, was er will let him say what he likes.

möglich ['mø:kliç] 1. adj. possible; practicable, feasible; market, crim-inal, etc.: potential; alle ~en all sorts of; alles ~e all sorts of things; sein ~stes tun do one's utmost or level best; nicht ~! you don't say (so)!; so bald etc. wie ~ = 2. adv.: ~st bald etc. as soon, etc., as possible; '~er'weise adv. possibly, if pos-sible; perhaps; '2keit f (-/-en) pos-sibility; chance; nach ~ if possible.

Mohammedan|er [mohame'da:-nər] m (-s/-) Muslim, Moslem, Mohammedan; 2isch adj. Muslim, Moslem, Mohammedan.

Mohn ♀ [mo:n] m (-[e]s/-e) poppy.

Möhre ♀ ['mø:rə] f (-/-n) carrot.

Mohrrübe ♀ ['mo:r-] f carrot.

Molch zo. [mɔlç] m (-[e]s/-e) sala-mander; newt.

Mole ⚓ ['mo:lə] f (-/-n) mole, jetty.

molk [mɔlk] pret. of melken.

Molkerei [mɔlkə'rai] f (-/-en) dairy; ~produkte n/pl. dairy products pl.

Moll ♪ [mɔl] n (-/-) minor (key).

mollig F adj. ['mɔliç] snug, cosy; plump, rounded.

Moment [mo'mɛnt] (-[e]s/-e) 1. m moment, instant; im ~ at the moment; 2. n motive; fact(or); ⊕ momentum; ⊕ impulse (a. fig.); 2an [.'ta:n] 1. adj. momentary; 2. adv. at the moment, for the time being; ~aufnahme phot. f snapshot, instantaneous photograph.

Monarch [mo'narç] m (-en/-en) monarch; ~ie [.'çi:] f (-/-n) mon-archy.

Monat ['mo:nat] m (-[e]s/-e) month; 2elang 1. adj. lasting for months; 2. adv. for months; '2lich 1. adj. monthly; 2. adv. monthly, a month.

Mönch [mœnç] m (-[e]s/-e) monk, friar.

'Mönchs|kloster n monastery; '~-kutte f (monk's) frock; '~leben n monastic life; '~orden m monastic order; '~zelle f monk's cell.

Mond [mo:nt] m (-[e]s/-e) moon; hinter dem ~ leben be behind the times; '~fähre f lunar module; '~finsternis f lunar eclipse; '2l'hell adj. moonlit; '~schein m (-[e]s/no pl.) moonlight; '~sichel f crescent; '2süchtig adj. moonstruck.

Mono|log [mono'lo:k] m (-s/-e)

monologue, *Am. a.* monolog;
soliloquy; ~'**pol** ✝ *n* (-s/-e) monop-
oly; **2polisieren** [~oli'zi:rən] *v/t.*
(*no* -ge-, *h*) monopolize; 2'**ton** *adj.*
monotonous; ~**tonie** [~to'ni:] *f*
(-/-n) monotony.

**Monstrum** ['mɔnstrum] *n* (-s/*Mon-
stren, Monstra*) monster.

**Montag** ['mo:n-] *m* Monday; '2s
*adv.* on Monday(s), every Monday.

**Montage** ⊕ [mɔn'ta:ʒə] *f* (-/-n)
mounting, fitting; setting up; as-
semblage, assembly.

**Montan|industrie** [mɔn'ta:n-] *f*
coal and steel industries *pl.*; ~**union**
*f* European Coal and Steel Community.

**Mont|eur** [mɔn'tø:r] *m* (-s/-e) ⊕
fitter, assembler; *esp. mot.*, ✈
mechanic; ~**euranzug** *m* overall;
2**ieren** [~'ti:rən] *v/t.* (*no* -ge-, *h*)
mount, fit; set up; assemble; ~**ur**
✈ [~'tu:r] *f* (-/-en) regimentals *pl.*

**Moor** [mo:r] *n* (-[e]s/-e) bog; swamp;
'~**bad** *n* mud-bath; '2**ig** *adj.* boggy,
marshy.

**Moos** ⚘ [mo:s] *n* (-es/-e) moss; '2**ig**
*adj.* mossy.

**Moped** *mot.* ['mo:pɛt] *n* (-s/-s)
moped.

**Mops** *zo.* [mɔps] *m* (-es/ṳe) pug;
'2**en** *v/t.* (ge-, *h*) F pilfer, pinch; *sl.*:
*sich* ~ be bored stiff.

**Moral** [mo'ra:l] *f* (-/⚘ -en) morality; morals *pl.*; moral; ✖, *etc.*:
morale; 2**isch** *adj.* moral; 2**isieren**
[~ali'zi:rən] *v/i.* (*no* -ge-, *h*) moral-
ize.

**Morast** [mo'rast] *m* (-es/-e, ṳe)
slough, morass; *s. Moor*; mire, mud;
2**ig** *adj.* marshy; muddy, miry.

**Mord** [mɔrt] *m* (-[e]s/-e) murder
(*an dat.* of); e-n ~ *begehen* commit
murder; '~**anschlag** *m* murderous
assault; 2**en** ['~dən] *v/i.* (ge-, *h*)
commit murder(s).

**Mörder** ['mœrdər] *m* (-s/-) mur-
derer; '2**isch** *adj.* murderous;
*climate, etc.*: deadly; ✝ *competition*:
cut-throat.

'**Mord|gier** *f* lust of murder, blood-
thirstiness; '2**gierig** *adj.* bloodthirsty; '~**kommission** *f* homicide
squad; '~**prozeß** 🕮 *m* murder trial.

'**Mords|'angst** F *f* blue funk, *sl.*
mortal fear; '~**glück** F *n* stupendous
luck; '~'**kerl** F *m* devil of a fellow;
'~**spek'takel** F *m* hullabaloo.

**Morgen** ['mɔrgən] **1.** *m* (-s/-) morning; *measure*: acre; *am* ~ *s.* morgens;
**2.** 2 *adv.* tomorrow; ~ *früh* (*abend*)
tomorrow morning (evening *or*
night); ~ *in acht Tagen* tomorrow
week; '~**ausgabe** *f* morning edition; '~**blatt** *n* morning paper;
'~**dämmerung** *f* dawn, daybreak;
'~**gebet** *n* morning prayer; '~**gym-
nastik** *f* morning exercises *pl.*;
'~**land** *n* (-[e]s/*no pl.*) Orient, East;

'~**rock** *m* peignoir, dressing-gown,
wrapper (*for woman*); '~**röte** *f*
dawn; '2s *adv.* in the morning; '~**
zeitung** *f* morning paper.

'**morgig** *adj.* of tomorrow.

**Morphium** *pharm.* ['mɔrfium] *n*
(-s/*no pl.*) morphia, morphine.

**morsch** *adj.* [mɔrʃ] rotten, decayed;
brittle.

**Mörser** ['mœrzər] *m* (-s/-) mortar
(*a.* ✖).

**Mörtel** ['mœrtəl] *m* (-s/-) mortar.

**Mosaik** [moza'i:k] *n* (-s/-en) mosaic;
~**fußboden** *m* mosaic *or* tessellated
pavement.

**Moschee** [mɔ'ʃe:] *f* (-/-n) mosque.

**Moschus** ['mɔʃus] *m* (-/*no pl.*) musk.

**Moskito** *zo.* [mɔs'ki:to] *m* (-s/-s)
mosquito; ~**netz** *n* mosquito-net.

**Moslem** ['mɔslɛm] *m* (-s/-s) Mus-
lim, Moslem.

**Most** [mɔst] *m* (-es/-e) must, grape-
juice; *of apples*: cider; *of pears*:
perry.

**Mostrich** ['mɔstriç] *m* (-[e]s/*no pl.*)
mustard.

**Motiv** [mo'ti:f] *n* (-s/-e) motive,
reason; *paint.*, ♪ motif; 2**ieren**
[~i'vi:rən] *v/t.* (*no* -ge-, *h*) motivate.

**Motor** ['mo:tɔr] *m* (-s/-en) engine,
*esp.* ⚡ motor; '~**boot** *n* motor boat;
'~**defekt** *m* engine *or* ⚡ motor
trouble; '~**haube** *f* bonnet, *Am.*
hood; 2**isieren** [motori'zi:rən] *v/t.*
(*no* -ge-, *h*) motorize; ~**isierung**
[motori'zi:ruŋ] *f* (-/*no pl.*) motor-
ization; '~**rad** *n* motor (bi)cycle;
'~**radfahrer** *m* motor cyclist; '~**roller** *m* (motor) scooter; '~**sport** *m*
motoring.

**Motte** *zo.* ['mɔtə] *f* (-/-n) moth.

'**Motten|kugel** *f* moth-ball; '2**si-
cher** *adj.* mothproof; '2**zerfressen**
*adj.* moth-eaten.

**Motto** ['mɔto] *n* (-s/-s) motto.

**Möwe** *orn.* ['mø:və] *f* (-/-n) sea-gull,
(sea-)mew.

**Mücke** *zo.* ['mykə] *f* (-/-n) midge,
gnat, mosquito; *aus e-r* ~ *e-n Elefanten machen* make a mountain
out of a molehill; '~**nstich** *m* gnat-
bite.

**Mucker** ['mukər] *m* (-s/-) bigot,
hypocrite.

**müd|e** *adj.* ['my:də] tired, weary;
*e-r Sache* ~ *sein* be weary *or* tired
of s.th.; '2**igkeit** *f* (-/*no pl.*) tired-
ness, weariness.

**Muff** [muf] *m* **1.** (-[e]s/-e) muff;
**2.** (-[e]s/*no pl.*) mo(u)ldy *or* musty
smell; '~**e** ⊕ *f* (-/-n) sleeve, socket;
'2**eln** F *v/i.* (ge-, *h*) munch; mumble; '2**ig** *adj.* smell, *etc.*: musty,
fusty; *air*: close; *fig.* sulky, sullen.

**Mühe** ['my:ə] *f* (-/-n) trouble, pains
*pl.*; (*nicht*) *der* ~ *wert* (not) worth
while; *j-m* ~ *machen* give s.o.
trouble; *sich* ~ *geben* take pains
(*mit* over, *with s.th.*); '2**los** *adj.*

effortless, easy; '2n v/refl. (ge-, h)
take pains, work hard; '2voll adj.
troublesome, hard; laborious.
Mühle ['my:lə] f (-/-n) mill.
'Müh|sal f (-/-e) toil, trouble;
hardship; '2sam, '2selig 1. adj.
toilsome, troublesome; difficult;
2. adv. laboriously; with difficulty.
Mulatte [mu'latə] m (-n/-n) mulatto.
Mulde ['muldə] f (-/-n) trough;
depression, hollow.
Mull [mul] m (-[e]s/-e) mull.
Müll [myl] m (-[e]s/no pl.) dust,
rubbish, refuse, Am. a. garbage;
'_abfuhr f removal of refuse;
'_eimer m dust-bin, Am. garbage
can.
Müller ['mylər] m (-s/-) miller.
'Müll|fahrer m dust-man, Am.
garbage collector; '_haufen m dust-
heap; '_kasten m s. Mülleimer;
'_kutscher m s. Müllfahrer; '_wa-
gen m dust-cart, Am. garbage cart.
Multipli|kation Ⱥ [multiplika-
'tsjo:n] f (-/-en) multiplication;
2zieren Ⱥ [~'tsi:rən] v/t. (no -ge-,
h) multiply (mit by).
Mumie ['mu:mjə] f (-/-n) mummy.
Mumps ⚕ [mumps] m, F f (-/no pl.)
mumps.
Mund [munt] m (-[e]s/⁓er) mouth;
den ⁓ halten hold one's tongue;
den ⁓ voll nehmen talk big; sich den ⁓
verbrennen put one's foot in it;
nicht auf den ⁓ gefallen sein have a
ready or glib tongue; j-m über den ⁓
fahren cut s.o. short; '_art f
dialect; '2artlich adj. dialectal.
Mündel ['myndəl] m, n (-s/-), girl:
a. f (-/-n) ward, pupil; 2sicher
adj.: ⁓e Papiere n/pl. ✝ gilt-edged
securities pl.
münden ['myndən] v/i. (ge-, h): ⁓ in
(acc.) river, etc.: fall or flow into;
street, etc.: run into.
'mund|faul adj. too lazy to speak;
'_gerecht adj. palatable (a. fig.);
'2harmonika ♪ f mouth-organ;
'2höhle anat. f oral cavity.
mündig ['myndiç] adj. of age;
⁓ werden come of age; '2keit f
(-/no pl.) majority.
mündlich ['myntliç] 1. adj. oral,
verbal; 2. adv. a. by word of mouth.
'Mund|pflege f oral hygiene; '_-
raub ⚖ m theft of comestibles;
'_stück n mouthpiece (of musical
instrument, etc.); tip (of cigarette);
'2tot adj.: ⁓ machen silence or gag
s.o.
'Mündung f (-/-en) mouth; a. estuary (of river); muzzle (of fire-arms).
'Mund|vorrat m provisions pl.,
victuals pl.; '_wasser n (-s/⁓) mouth-
wash, gargle; '_werk F fig. n: ein
gutes ⁓ haben have the gift of the
gab.
Munition [muni'tsjo:n] f (-/-en)
ammunition.

munkeln F ['muŋkəln] (ge-, h)
1. v/i. whisper; 2. v/t. whisper,
rumo(u)r; man munkelt there is a
rumo(u)r afloat.     [lively; merry.)
munter adj. ['muntər] awake; fig.:)
Münz|e ['myntsə] f (-/-n) coin,
(small) change; medal; mint; für
bare ⁓ nehmen take at face value;
j-m et. mit gleicher ⁓ heimzahlen
pay s.o. back in his own coin; '_ein-
heit f (monetary) unit, standard of
currency; '2en v/t. (ge-, h) coin,
mint; gemünzt sein auf (acc.) be
meant for, be aimed at; '_fern-
sprecher teleph. m coin-box telephone; '_fuß m standard (of coin-
age); '_wesen n monetary system.
mürbe adj. ['myrbə] tender; pastry,
etc.: crisp, short; meat: well-
cooked; material: brittle; F fig.
worn-out, demoralized; F j-n ⁓
machen break s.o.'s resistance; F ⁓
werden give in.
Murmel ['murməl] f (-/-n) marble;
'2n v/t. and v/i. (ge-, h) mumble,
murmur; '_tier zo. n marmot.
murren ['murən] v/i. (ge-, h)
grumble, F grouch (both: über acc.
at, over, about).
mürrisch adj. ['myriʃ] surly, sullen.
Mus [mu:s] n (-es/-e) pap; stewed
fruit.
Muschel ['muʃəl] f (-/-n) zo.: mussel; shell, conch; teleph. ear-piece.
Museum [mu'ze:um] n (-s/Museen)
museum.
Musik [mu'zi:k] f (-/no pl.) music;
_alienhandlung [~i'ka:ljən-] f
music-shop; 2alisch adj. [~'ka:-
liʃ] musical; _ant [~i'kant] m (-en/
-en) musician; _automat m juke-
box; _er ['mu:zikər] m (-s/-)
musician; bandsman; _instru-
ment n musical instrument; _leh-
rer m music-master; _stunde f
music-lesson; _truhe f radio-
gram(ophone), Am. radio-phono-
graph.
musizieren [muzi'tsi:rən] v/i. (no
-ge-, h) make or have music.
Muskat ♀ [mus'ka:t] m (-[e]s/-e)
nutmeg; _nuß ♀ f nutmeg.
Muskel ['muskəl] m (-s/-n) muscle;
'_kater F m stiffness and soreness,
Am. a. charley horse; '_kraft f
muscular strength; '_zerrung ⚕ f
pulled muscle.
Muskul|atur [muskula'tu:r] f (-/-en)
muscular system, muscles pl.; 2ös
adj. [~'lø:s] muscular, brawny.
Muß [mus] n (-/no pl.) necessity;
es ist ein ⁓ it is a must.
Muße ['mu:sə] f (-/no pl.) leisure;
spare time; mit ⁓ at one's leisure.
Musselin [musə'li:n] m (-s/-e)
muslin.
müssen ['mysən] (irr., h) 1. v/i.
(ge-): ich muß I must; 2. v/aux.
(no -ge-): ich muß I must, I have to;

I am obliged *or* compelled *or* forced to; I am bound to; *ich habe gehen ~* I had to go; *ich müßte (eigentlich) wissen* I ought to know.

**müßig** *adj.* ['myːsiç] idle; superfluous; useless; '⁀gang *m* idleness, laziness; ⁀gänger ['⁀gɛŋər] *m* (-s/-) idler, loafer; lazy-bones.

**mußte** ['mustə] *pret. of* müssen.

**Muster** ['mustər] *n* (-s/-) model; example, paragon; design, pattern; specimen; sample; '⁀betrieb *m* model factory *or* ✗ farm; '⁀gatte *m* model husband; '⁀gültig, '⁀haft **1.** *adj.* model, exemplary, perfect; **2.** *adv.: sich ~ benehmen* be on one's best behavio(u)r; '⁀kollektion ✝ *f* range of samples; '⁀n *v/t.* (ge-, h) examine; eye; ✗ inspect, review; figure, pattern (*fabric, etc.*); '⁀schutz *m* protection of patterns and designs; '⁀ung *f* (-/-en) examination; ✗ review; pattern (*of fabric, etc.*); '⁀werk *n* standard work.

**Mut** [muːt] *m* (-[e]s/*no pl.*) courage; spirit; pluck; *~ fassen* pluck up courage, summon one's courage; *den ~ sinken lassen* lose courage *or* heart; *guten ~(e)s sein* be of good cheer; '⁀ig *adj.* courageous; plucky; '⁀los *adj.* discouraged; despondent; '⁀losigkeit *f* (-/*no pl.*) discouragement; despondency; ⁀maßen ['⁀maːsən] *v/t.* (ge-, h) suppose, guess, surmise; '⁀maßlich *adj.* presumable; supposed; *heir:* presumptive; '⁀maßung *f* (-/-en) supposition, surmise; *bloße ~en pl.* guesswork.

**Mutter** ['mutər] *f* **1.** (-/⁀) mother; **2.** ⊕ (-/-n) nut; '⁀brust *f* mother's breast; '⁀leib *m* womb.

**mütterlich** *adj.* ['mytərliç] motherly; maternal; ⁀erseits *adv.* ['⁀ər-'zarts] on *or* from one's mother's side; *uncle, etc.:* maternal.

'**Mutter|liebe** *f* motherly love; '⁀los *adj.* motherless; '⁀mal *n* birth-mark; mole; '⁀milch *f* mother's milk; '⁀schaft *f* (-/*no pl.*) maternity, motherhood; '⁀seelenal'lein *adj.* all *or* utterly alone; ⁀söhnchen ['⁀zøːnçən] *n* (-s/-) milksop, *sl.* sissy; '⁀sprache *f* mother tongue; '⁀witz *m* (-es/*no pl.*) mother wit.

'**Mutwill|e** *m* wantonness; mischievousness; '⁀ig *adj.* wanton; mischievous; wilful.

**Mütze** ['mytsə] *f* (-/-n) cap.

**Myrrhe** ['myrə] *f* (-/-n) myrrh.

**Myrte** ♀ ['myrtə] *f* (-/-n) myrtle.

**mysteri|ös** *adj.* [mysterˈjøːs] mysterious; ⁀um [⁀ˈteːrjum] *n* (-s/ *Mysterien*) mystery.

**Mystifi|kation** [mystifikaˈtsjoːn] *f* (-/-en) mystification; ⁀zieren [⁀ˈtsiːrən] *v/t.* (*no* -ge-, h) mystify.

**Mysti|k** ['mystik] *f* (-/*no pl.*) mysticism; '⁀sch *adj.* mystic(al).

**Myth|e** ['myːtə] *f* (-/-n) myth; '⁀isch *adj.* mythic; *esp. fig.* mythical; ⁀ologie [mytoloˈgiː] *f* (-/-n) mythology; ⁀ologisch *adj.* [myto-'loːgiʃ] mythological; ⁀os ['⁀ɔs] *m* (-/*Mythen*), ⁀us ['⁀us] *m* (-/*Mythen*) myth.

# N

**na** *int.* [na] now!, then!, well!, *Am. a.* hey!

**Nabe** ['naːbə] *f* (-/-n) hub.

**Nabel** *anat.* ['naːbəl] *m* (-s/-) navel.

**nach** [naːx] **1.** *prp.* (*dat.*) *direction, striving:* after; to(wards), for (*a. ~ ... hin or zu*); *succession:* after; *time:* after, past; *manner, measure, example:* according to; *~ Gewicht* by weight; *~ deutschem Geld* in German money; *e-r ~ dem andern* one by one; *fünf Minuten ~ eins* five minutes past one; **2.** *adv.* after; *~ und ~* little by little, gradually; *~ wie vor* now as before, still.

**nachahm|en** ['naːx⁀aːmən] *v/t.* (*sep.*, -ge-, h) imitate, copy; counterfeit; '⁀ens'wert *adj.* worthy of imitation, exemplary; '⁀er *m* (-s/-) imitator; '⁀ung *f* (-/-en) imitation; copy; counterfeit, fake.

**Nachbar** ['naxbaːr] *m* (-n, -s/-n), '⁀in *f* (-/-nen) neighbo(u)r; '⁀schaft *f* (-/-en) neighbo(u)rhood, vicinity.

'**Nachbehandlung** ✗ *f* after-treatment.

'**nachbestell|en** *v/t.* (*sep.*, *no* -ge-, h) repeat one's order for *s.th.*; '⁀ung *f* repeat (order).

'**nachbeten** *v/t.* (*sep.*, -ge-, h) echo.

'**Nachbildung** *f* copy, imitation; replica; dummy.

'**nachblicken** *v/i.* (*sep.*, -ge-, h) look after.

**nachdem** *cj.* [naːx'deːm] after, when; *je ~* according as.

'**nachdenk|en** *v/i.* (*irr.* denken, *sep.*, -ge-, h) think (*über acc.* over, about); reflect, meditate (*über acc.* on); '⁀en *n* (-s/*no pl.*) reflection, meditation; musing; '⁀lich *adj.* meditative, reflecting; pensive.

'**Nachdichtung** *f* free version.

'**Nachdruck** *m* **1.** (-[e]s/*no pl.*) stress, emphasis; **2.** *typ.* (-[e]s/-e) reprint; *unlawfully*: piracy, pirated edition; '2en *v/t.* (*sep.*, -ge-, h) reprint; *unlawfully*: pirate.

**nachdrücklich** ['nɑːxdryklɪç] 1. *adj.* emphatic, energetic; forcible; positive; 2. *adv.*: ~ betonen emphasize.

**nacheifern** ['nɑːxˀ-] *v/i.* (*sep.*, -ge-, h) emulate *s.o.*

**nacheinander** *adv.* [nɑːxˀaɪˀnandər] one after another, successively; by *or* in turns.

**nachempfinden** ['nɑːxˀ-] *v/t.* (*irr.* empfinden, sep., no -ge-, h) s. nachfühlen.

**nacherzähl|en** ['nɑːxˀ-] *v/t.* (*sep.*, no -ge-, h) repeat; retell; *dem Englischen nacherzählt* adapted from the English; 2ung ['nɑːxˀ-] *f* repetition; story retold, reproduction.

'**Nachfolge** *f* succession; '2n *v/i.* (*sep.*, -ge-, sein) follow *s.o.*; *j-m im Amt* ~ succeed s.o. in his office; '~r *m* (-s/-) follower; successor.

'**nachforsch|en** *v/i.* (*sep.*, -ge-, h) investigate; search for; 2ung *f* investigation, inquiry, search.

'**Nachfrage** *f* inquiry; ✝ demand; '2n *v/i.* (*sep.*, -ge-, h) inquire (*nach* after).

'**nach|fühlen** *v/t.* (*sep.*, -ge-, h): es *j-m* ~ feel *or* sympathize with s.o.; '~füllen *v/t.* (*sep.*, -ge-, h) fill up, refill; '~geben *v/i.* (*irr.* geben, sep., -ge-, h) give way (*dat.* to); *fig.* give in, yield (to); 2gebühr ✆ *f* surcharge; '~gehen *v/i.* (*irr.* gehen, sep., -ge-, sein) follow (*s.o.*, *business, trade, etc.*); pursue (*pleasure*); attend to (*business*); investigate *s.th.*; *watch*: be slow; 2geschmack *m* (-[e]s/*no pl.*) after-taste.

**nachgiebig** *adj.* ['nɑːxgiːbɪç] elastic, flexible; *fig. a.* yielding, compliant; '2keit *f* (-/-en) flexibility; compliance.

'**nachgrübeln** *v/i.* (*sep.*, -ge-, h) ponder, brood (*both*: über *acc.* over), muse (on).

**nachhaltig** *adj.* ['nɑːxhaltɪç] lasting, enduring.

**nach'her** *adv.* afterwards; then; *bis* ~! see you later!, so long!

'**Nachhilfe** *f* help, assistance; '~lehrer *m* coach, private tutor; '~unterricht *m* private lesson(s *pl.*), coaching.

'**nach|holen** *v/t.* (*sep.*, -ge-, h) make up for, make good; '2hut ⚔ *f* (-/-en) rear(-guard); *die* ~ *bilden* bring up the rear (*a. fig.*); '~jagen *v/i.* (*sep.*, -ge-, sein) chase *or* pursue *s.o.*; '~klingen *v/i.* (*irr.* klingen, sep., -ge-, h) resound, echo.

'**Nachkomme** *m* (-n/-n) descendant; ~n *pl. esp.* ⚖ issue; '2n *v/i.* (*irr.* kommen, sep., -ge-, sein) follow; come later; obey (*order*); meet (*liabilities*); '~nschaft *f* (-/-en) descendants *pl.*, *esp.* ⚖ issue.

'**Nachkriegs...** post-war.

**Nachlaß** ['nɑːxlas] *m* (*Nachlasses/ Nachlasse, Nachlässe*) ✝ reduction, discount; assets *pl.*, estate, inheritance (*of deceased*).

'**nachlassen** (*irr.* lassen, sep., -ge-, h) 1. *v/t.* reduce (*price*); 2. *v/i.* deteriorate; slacken, relax; diminish; *pain, rain, etc.*: abate; *storm*: calm down; *strength*: wane; *interest*: flag.

'**nachlässig** *adj.* careless, negligent.

'**nach|laufen** *v/i.* (*irr.* laufen, sep., -ge-, sein) run (*dat.* after); '~lesen *v/t.* (*irr.* lesen, sep., -ge-, h) *in book*: look up; ↗ glean; '~liefern ✝ *v/t.* (*sep.*, -ge-, h) deliver subsequently; repeat delivery of; '~lösen *v/t.* (*sep.*, -ge-, h): *e-e Fahrkarte* ~ take a supplementary ticket; buy a ticket en route; '~machen *v/t.* (*sep.*, -ge-, h) imitate (*j-m et. s.o.* in s.th.); copy; counterfeit, forge; '~messen *v/t.* (*irr.* messen, sep., -ge-, h) measure again.

'**Nachmittag** *m* afternoon; '2s *adv.* in the afternoon; '~svorstellung *thea. f* matinée.

**Nach|nahme** ['nɑːxnɑːmə] *f* (-/-n) cash on delivery, *Am.* collect on delivery; *per* ~ *schicken* send C.O.D.; '~name *m* surname, last name; '~porto *m* ✉ surcharge.

'**nach|prüfen** *v/t.* (*sep.*, -ge-, h) verify; check; '~rechnen *v/t.* (*sep.*, -ge-, h) reckon over again; check (*bill*).

'**Nachrede** *f*: *üble* ~ ⚖ defamation (*of character*); *oral*: slander, *written*: libel; 2n *v/t.* (*sep.*, -ge-, h): *j-m Übles* ~ slander s.o.

**Nachricht** ['nɑːxrɪçt] *f* (-/-en) news; message; report; information, notice; ~ *geben s. benachrichtigen*; '~enagentur *f* news agency; '~endienst *m* news service; ⚔ intelligence service; '~ensprecher *m* newscaster; '~enwesen *n* (-s/*no pl.*) communications *pl.*

'**nachrücken** *v/i.* (*sep.*, -ge-, sein) move along.

'**Nach|ruf** *m* obituary (notice); '~ruhm *m* posthumous fame.

'**nachsagen** *v/t.* (*sep.*, -ge-, h) repeat; *man sagt ihm nach, daß he is* said to *inf.*

'**Nachsaison** *f* dead *or* off season.

'**nachschicken** *v/t.* (*sep.*, -ge-, h) s. nachsenden.

'**nachschlage|n** *v/t.* (*irr.* schlagen, sep., -ge-, h) consult (*book*); look up (*word*); 2werk *n* reference-book.

'**Nach|schlüssel** *m* skeleton key; '~schrift *f in letter*: postscript; '~schub *esp.* ⚔ *m* supplies *pl.*; '~schubweg ⚔ *m* supply line.

'**nach|sehen** (*irr.* sehen, sep., -ge-, h) 1. *v/i.* look after; ~, *ob* (go and) see whether; 2. *v/t.* look after; examine, inspect; check; overhaul (*machine*); s. *nachschlagen*; *j-m* et. ~ indulge s.o. in s.th.; '~**senden** *v/t.* ([*irr.* *senden*,] *sep.*, *-ge-*, *h*) send after; send on, forward (*letter*) (*j-m* to s.o.).

'**Nachsicht** *f* indulgence; '2**ig** *adj.*, '2**svoll** *adj.* indulgent, forbearing.

'**Nachsilbe** *gr. f* suffix.

'**nach|sinnen** *v/i.* (*irr.* *sinnen*, *sep.*, *-ge-*, *h*) muse, meditate (*über acc.* [*up*]*on*); '~**sitzen** *v/i.* (*irr.* *sitzen*, *sep.*, *-ge-*, *h*) pupil: be kept in.

'**Nach|sommer** *m* St. Martin's summer, *esp. Am.* Indian summer; '~**speise** *f* dessert; '~**spiel** *fig. n* sequel.

'**nach|spionieren** *v/i.* (*sep.*, *no -ge-*, *h*) spy (*dat.* on); '~**sprechen** (*sep.*, *-ge-*, *h*) repeat; '~**spülen** *v/t.* (*sep.*, *-ge-*, *h*) rinse; '~**spüren** *v/i.* (*sep.*, *-ge-*, *h*) (*dat.*) track, trace.

**nächst** [nɛ:çst] **1.** *adj.* succession; *time*: next; *distance*, *relation*: nearest; **2.** *prp.* (*dat.*) next to, next after; '2**beste** *m, f, n* (*-n*/*-n*): der (*die*) ~ anyone; *das* ~ anything; er fragte den ~n he asked the next person he met.

'**nachstehen** *v/i.* (*irr.* *stehen*, *sep.*, *-ge-*, *h*): *j-m* in nichts ~ be in no way inferior to s.o.

'**nachstell|en** (*sep.*, *-ge-*, *h*) **1.** *v/t.* place behind; put back (*watch*); ⊕ adjust (*screw*, etc.); **2.** *v/i.*: *j-m* ~ be after s.o.; '2**ung** *fig. f* persecution.

'**Nächstenliebe** *f* charity.

'**nächstens** *adv.* shortly, (very) soon, before long.

'**nach|streben** *v/i.* (*sep.*, *-ge-*, *h*) s. *nacheifern*; '~**suchen** *v/i.* (*sep.*, *-ge-*, *h*): ~ um apply for, seek.

**Nacht** [naxt] *f* (-/⁼e) night; *bei* ~, *des* ~s *s. nachts*; '~**arbeit** *f* nightwork; '~**asyl** *n* night-shelter; '~**ausgabe** *f* night edition (*of newspaper*); '~**dienst** *m* night-duty.

'**Nachteil** *m* disadvantage, drawback; *im* ~ *sein* be at a disadvantage; '2**ig** *adj.* disadvantageous.

'**Nacht|essen** *n* supper; '~**falter** *zo.* *m* (*-s*/-) moth; '~**gebet** *n* evening prayer; '~**geschirr** *n* chamberpot; '~**hemd** *n* night-gown, *Am. a.* night robe; *for men*: nightshirt.

**Nachtigall** *orn.* ['naxtigal] *f* (-/-en) nightingale.

'**Nachtisch** *m* (-es/*no pl.*) sweet, dessert.

'**Nachtlager** *n* (*a*) lodging for the night; bed.

**nächtlich** *adj.* ['nɛçtliç] nightly, nocturnal.

'**Nacht|lokal** *n* night-club; '~**mahl** *n* supper; '~**portier** *m* night-porter; '~**quartier** *n* night-quarters *pl.*

**Nachtrag** ['nɑːxtrɑːk] *m* (-[e]s/⁼e) supplement; '2**en** *v/t.* (*irr.* *tragen*, *sep.*, *-ge-*, *h*) carry (*j-m* et. s.th. after s.o.); add; † post up (*ledger*); *j-m* et. ~ bear s.o. a grudge; '2**end** *adj.* unforgiving, resentful.

**nachträglich** *adj.* ['nɑːxtrɛːkliç] additional; subsequent.

**nachts** *adv.* [naxts] at *or* by night.

'**Nacht|schicht** *f* night-shift; '2**schlafend** *adj.*: zu ~er Zeit in the middle of the night; '~**schwärmer** *fig. m* night-reveller; '~**tisch** *m* bedside table; '~**topf** *m* chamberpot; '~**vorstellung** *thea. f* night performance; '~**wache** *f* nightwatch; '~**wächter** *m* (night-) watchman; ~**wandler** ['~vandlər] *m* (*-s*/-) sleep-walker; '~**zeug** *n* night-things *pl.*

'**nachwachsen** *v/i.* (*irr.* *wachsen*, *sep.*, *-ge-*, *sein*) grow again.

'**Nachwahl** *parl. f* by-election.

**Nachweis** ['nɑːxvaɪs] *m* (-es/-e) proof, evidence; '2**bar** *adj.* demonstrable; traceable; '2**en** ['~zən] *v/t.* (*irr.* *weisen*, *sep.*, *-ge-*, *h*) point out, show; trace; prove; '2**lich** *adj.* s. *nachweisbar*.

'**Nach|welt** *f* posterity; '~**wirkung** *f* after-effect; consequences *pl.*; aftermath; '~**wort** *n* (-[e]s/-e) epilog(ue); '~**wuchs** *m* (-[e]s/*no pl.*) rising generation.

'**nach|zahlen** *v/t.* (*sep.*, *-ge-*, *h*) pay in addition; '~**zählen** *v/t.* (*sep.*, *-ge-*, *h*) count over (again), check; '2**zahlung** *f* additional payment.

**Nachzügler** ['nɑːxtsyːklər] *m* (*-s*/-) straggler, late-comer.

**Nacken** ['nakən] *m* (*-s*/-) nape (of the neck), neck.

**nackt** *adj.* [nakt] naked, nude; bare (*a. fig.*); *young birds*: unfledged; *truth*: plain.

**Nadel** ['nɑːdəl] *f* (-/-n) needle; pin; brooch; '~**arbeit** *f* needlework; '~**baum** ♣ *m* conifer(ous tree); '~**stich** *m* prick; stitch; *fig.* pinprick.

**Nagel** ['nɑːgəl] *m* (*-s*/⁼) *anat.*, ⊕ nail; *of wood*: peg; spike; stud; *die Arbeit brennt mir auf den Nägeln* it's a rush job; '~**haut** *f* cuticle; '~**lack** *m* nail varnish; '2**n** *v/t.* (ge-, h) nail (*an or auf acc.* to); '~**necessaire** ['~nesesɛːr] *n* (*-s*/-s) manicure-case; '2**neu** F *adj.* bran(d)-new; '~**pflege** *f* manicure.

**nage|n** ['nɑːgən] (ge-, h) **1.** *v/i.* gnaw; ~ an (*dat.*) gnaw at; pick (*bone*); **2.** *v/t.* gnaw; '2**tier** *zo. n* rodent, gnawer.

**nah** *adj.* [nɑː] near, close (*bei* to); nearby; *danger*: imminent.

**Näharbeit** ['nɛː⁹-] *f* needlework, sewing.

'**Nahaufnahme** *f film*: close-up.

**nahe** *adj.* ['nɑːə] s. *nah*.

**Nähe** ['nɛːə] f (-/no pl.) nearness, proximity; vicinity; *in der* ~ close by.

'**nahe|gehen** v/i. (*irr.* gehen, *sep.*, -ge-, sein) (*dat.*) affect, grieve; '~**kommen** v/i. (*irr.* kommen, *sep.*, -ge-, sein) (*dat.*) approach; get at (*truth*); '~**legen** v/t. (*sep.*, -ge-, h) suggest; '~**liegen** v/i. (*irr.* liegen, *sep.*, -ge-, h) suggest itself, be obvious.

**nahen** ['naːən] **1.** v/i. (ge-, sein) approach; **2.** v/refl. (ge-, h) approach (j-m s.o.).

**nähen** ['nɛːən] v/t. and v/i. (ge-, h) sew, stitch.

**näher** adj. ['nɛːər] nearer, closer; *road:* shorter; *das Nähere* (further) particulars pl. or details pl.

'**Näherin** f (-/-nen) seamstress.

'**nähern** v/t. (ge-, h) approach (*dat.* to); *sich* ~ approach (j-m s.o.).

'**nahe'zu** adv. nearly, almost.

'**Nähgarn** n (sewing-)cotton.

'**Nahkampf** ✗ m close combat.

**nahm** [naːm] *pret.* of nehmen.

'**Näh|maschine** f sewing-machine; '~**nadel** f (sewing-)needle.

**nähren** ['nɛːrən] v/t. (ge-, h) nourish (a. fig.), feed; nurse (*child*); *sich* ~ *von* live or feed on.

**nahrhaft** adj. ['naːrhaft] nutritious, nourishing.

'**Nahrung** f (-/no pl.) food, nourishment, nutriment.

'**Nahrungs|aufnahme** f intake of food; '~**mittel** n/pl. food(-stuff), victuals pl.

'**Nährwert** m nutritive value.

**Naht** [naːt] f (-/-e) seam; ✗ suture.

'**Nahverkehr** m local traffic.

'**Nähzeug** n sewing-kit.

**naiv** adj. [na'iːf] naïve, naive, simple; **2ität** [naivi'tɛːt] f (-/no pl.) naïveté, naivety, simplicity.

**Name** ['naːmə] m (-ns/-n) name; *im* ~*n* (*gen.*) on behalf of; *dem* ~*n nach* nominal(ly), in name only; *dem* ~*n nach kennen* know by name; *die Dinge beim rechten* ~*n nennen* call a spade a spade; *darf ich um Ihren* ~*n bitten?* may I ask your name?

'**namen|los** adj. nameless, anonymous; *fig.* unutterable; '~s **1.** adv. named, by the name of, called; **2.** prp. (*gen.*) in the name of.

'**Namens|tag** m name-day; '~**vetter** m namesake; '~**zug** m signature.

**namentlich** ['naːməntliç] **1.** adj. nominal; **2.** adv. by name; especially, in particular.

'**namhaft** adj. notable; considerable; ~ *machen* name.

**nämlich** ['nɛːmliç] **1.** adj. the same; **2.** adv. namely, that is (to say).

**nannte** ['nantə] *pret.* of nennen.

**Napf** [napf] m (-[e]s/-e) bowl, basin.

**Narb|e** ['narbə] f (-/-n) scar; '2**ig** adj. scarred; *leather:* grained.

**Narko|se** ✗ [nar'koːzə] f (-/-n) narcosis; **2tisieren** [~oti'ziːrən] v/t. (no -ge-, h) narcotize.

**Narr** [nar] m (-en/-en) fool; jester; *zum* ~*en halten* = '2**en** v/t. (ge-, h) make a fool of, fool.

'**Narren|haus** F n madhouse; '~**kappe** f fool's-cap; '2**sicher** adj. foolproof.

'**Narrheit** f (-/-en) folly.

**Närrin** ['nerin] f (-/-nen) fool, foolish woman.

'**närrisch** adj. foolish, silly; odd.

**Narzisse** ♀ [nar'tsisə] f (-/-n) narcissus; *gelbe* ~ daffodil.

**nasal** adj. [na'zaːl] nasal; ~*e Sprechweise* twang.

**nasch|en** ['naʃən] (ge-, h) **1.** v/i. nibble (*an dat.* at); *gern* ~ have a sweet tooth; **2.** v/t. nibble; eat *s.th.* on the sly; **2erei** [~'raɪən] f/pl. dainties pl., sweets pl.; '~**haft** adj. fond of dainties or sweets.

**Nase** ['naːzə] f (-/-n) nose; *die* ~ *rümpfen* turn up one's nose (*über acc.* at).

**näseln** ['nɛːzəln] v/i. (ge-, h) speak through the nose, nasalize; snuffle.

'**Nasen|bluten** n (-s/no pl.) nosebleeding; '~**loch** n nostril; '~**spitze** f tip of the nose.

**naseweis** adj. ['naːzəvaɪs] pert, saucy.

**nasführen** ['naːs-] v/t. (ge-, h) fool, dupe.

**Nashorn** zo. ['naːs-] n rhinoceros.

**naß** adj. [nas] wet; damp, moist.

**Nässe** ['nɛsə] f (-/no pl.) wet(ness); moisture; ♀ humidity; '2**n** (ge-, h) **1.** v/t. wet; moisten; **2.** ✗ v/i. discharge.

'**naßkalt** adj. damp and cold, raw.

**Nation** [na'tsjoːn] f (-/-en) nation.

**national** adj. [natsjo'naːl] national; **2hymne** f national anthem; **2ismus** [~a'lismus] m (-/Nationalismen) nationalism; **2ität** [~ali'tɛːt] f (-/-en) nationality; **2mannschaft** f national team.

**Natter** ['natər] f (-/-n) zo. adder, viper; *fig.* serpent.

**Natur** [na'tuːr] f **1.** (-/no pl.) nature; **2.** (-/-en) constitution; temper(ament), disposition, nature; *von* ~ by nature.

**Naturalien** [natu'raːljən] pl. natural produce sg.; *in* ~ in kind.

**naturalisieren** [naturali'ziːrən] v/t. (no -ge-, h) naturalize.

**Naturalismus** [natura'lismus] m (-/no pl.) naturalism.

**Naturanlage** [na'tuːr ?-] f (natural) disposition.

**Naturell** [natu'rel] n (-s/-e) natural disposition, nature, temper.

**Na'tur|ereignis** n, ~**erscheinung** f phenomenon; ~**forscher** m naturalist, scientist; 2gemäß *adj.* natural; ~geschichte *f* natural history; ~gesetz *n* law of nature, natural law; 2getreu *adj.* true to nature; life-like; ~kunde *f* (natural) science.

natürlich [na'ty:rliç] **1.** *adj.* natural; genuine; innate; unaffected; **2.** *adv.* naturally, of course.

Na'tur|produkte *n/pl.* natural products *pl.* or produce *sg.*; ~schutz *m* wild-life conservation; ~schutzgebiet *n*, ~schutzpark *m* national park, wild-life (p)reserve; ~trieb *m* instinct; ~wissenschaft *f* (natural) science; ~wissenschaftler *m* (natural) scientist.

Nebel ['ne:bəl] *m* (-s/-) fog; mist; haze; smoke; 2haft *fig. adj.* nebulous, hazy, dim; '~horn *n* fog-horn.

neben *prp.* (*dat.*, *acc.*) ['ne:bən] beside, by (the side of); near to; against, compared with; apart *or Am. a.* aside from, besides.

neben|'an *adv.* next door; close by; 2anschluß *teleph.* ['ne:bən?-] *m* extension (line); 2arbeit ['ne:bən?-] *f* extra work; 2ausgaben ['ne:bən?-] *f/pl.* incidental expenses *pl.*, extras *pl.*; 2ausgang ['ne:bən?-] *m* side-exit, side-door; 2bedeutung *f* secondary meaning, connotation; ~bei *adv.* by the way; besides; 2beruf *m* side-line; '~beruflich *adv.* as a side-line; in one's spare time; 2beschäftigung *f s.* Nebenberuf; 2buhler ['~bu:lər] *m* (-s/-) rival; ~ei'nander *adv.* side by side; ~ bestehen co-exist; 2eingang ['ne:bən?-] *m* side-entrance; 2einkünfte ['ne:bən?-] *pl.*, 2einnahmen ['ne:bən?-] *f/pl.* casual emoluments *pl.*, extra income; 2erscheinung ['ne:bən?-] *f* accompaniment; '2fach *n* subsidiary subject, *Am.* minor (subject); '2fluß *m* tributary (river); '2gebäude *n* annex(e); outhouse; '2geräusch *n radio:* atmospherics *pl.*, interference, jamming; 2gleis ⊞ *n* siding, side-track; 2handlung *thea. f* underplot; 2haus *n* adjoining house; ~her *adv.*, ~hin *adv.* by his *or* her side; *s. nebenbei;* 2kläger *t́ǵ m* co-plaintiff; 2kosten *pl.* extras *pl.*; 2mann *m* person next to one; 2produkt *n* by-product; 2rolle *f* minor part (*a. thea.*); 2sache *f* minor matter, side issue; '~sächlich *adj.* subordinate, incidental, unimportant; 2satz *gr. m* subordinate clause; '~stehend *adj.* in the margin; 2stelle *f* branch; agency; *teleph.* extension; '2straße *f* bystreet, by-road; '2strecke ⊞ *f* branch line; '2tisch *m* next table; '2tür *f* side-door; '2verdienst *m* incidental *or* extra earnings *pl.*; '2zimmer *n* adjoining room.

'neblig *adj.* foggy, misty, hazy.

nebst *prp.* (*dat.*) [ne:pst] together with, besides; including.

neck|en ['nekən] *v/t.* (ge-, h) tease, banter, *sl.* kid; 2erei ['~'raɪ] *f* (-/-en) teasing, banter; '~isch *adj.* playful; droll, funny.

Neffe ['nɛfə] *m* (-n/-n) nephew.

negativ [nega'ti:f] **1.** *adj.* negative; **2.** 2 *n* (-s/-e) negative.

Neger ['ne:gər] *m* (-s/-) negro; '~in *f* (-/-nen) negress.

nehmen ['ne:mən] *v/t.* (*irr.*, ge-, h) take; receive; charge (*money*); zu sich ~ take, have (*meal*); j-m et. ~ take s.th. from s.o.; *ein Ende ~* come to an end; *es sich nicht ~ lassen zu inf.* insist upon *ger.*; *streng genommen* strictly speaking.

Neid [naɪt] *m* (-[e]s/*no pl.*) envy; 2en ['naɪdən] *v/t.* (ge-, h): j-m et. ~ envy s.o. s.th.; ~er ['~dər] *m* (-s/-) envious person; ~hammel F ['naɪt-] *m* dog in the manger; 2isch *adj.* ['~dɪʃ] envious (auf *acc.* of); 2los *adj.* ['naɪt-] ungrudging.

Neige ['naɪgə] *f* (-/-n) decline; *barrel:* dregs *pl.; glass:* heeltap; *zur ~ gehen* (be on the) decline; *esp.* ⚓ run short; 2n ['ge-] **1.** *v/t.* and *v/refl.* bend, incline; **2.** *v/i.:* *er neigt zu Übertreibungen* he is given to exaggeration.

'Neigung *f* (-/-en) inclination (*a. fig.*); slope, incline.

nein *adv.* [naɪn] no.

Nektar ['nɛkta:r] *m* (-s/*no pl.*) nectar.

Nelke ♀ ['nɛlkə] *f* (-/-n) carnation, pink; *spice:* clove.

nennen ['nɛnən] *v/t.* (*irr.*, ge-, h) name; call; term; mention; nominate (*candidate*); *sports:* enter (für for); *sich ... ~ be called ...;* '~swert *adj.* worth mentioning.

'Nenn|er *ᵬ m* (-s/-) denominator; '~ung *f* (-/-en) naming; mentioning; nomination (of *candidates*); *sports:* entry; '~wert *m* nominal *or* face value; *zum ~* ⚓ at par.

Neon ♋ ['ne:ɔn] *n* (-s/*no pl.*) neon; '~röhre *f* neon tube.

Nerv [nɛrf] *m* (-s/-en) nerve; *j-m auf die ~en fallen or gehen* get on s.o.'s nerves.

'Nerven|arzt *m* neurologist; '2aufreibend *adj.* trying; '~heilanstalt *f* mental hospital; '~kitzel *m* (-s/*no pl.*) thrill, sensation; '2krank *adj.* neurotic; '2leidend *adj.* neuropathic, neurotic; '~schwäche *f* nervous debility; '2stärkend *adj.* tonic; '~system *n* nervous system; '~zusammenbruch *m* nervous breakdown.

nerv|ig *adj.* ['nɛrviç] sinewy; ~ös *adj.* ['~vø:s] nervous; 2osität [~ozi-'tɛ:t] *f* (-/*no pl.*) nervousness.

Nerz *zo.* [nɛrts] *m* (-es/-e) mink.

**Nessel** ♀ ['nɛsəl] *f* (-/-n) nettle.

**Nest** [nɛst] *n* (-es/-er) nest; F *fig.* bed; F *fig.* hick *or* one-horse town.

**nett** *adj.* [nɛt] nice; neat, pretty, *Am. a.* cute; pleasant; kind.

**netto** ✝ *adv.* ['nɛto] net, clear.

**Netz** [nɛts] *n* (-es/-e) net; *fig.* network; '⸰anschluß ∉ *m* mains connection, power supply; '⸰haut *anat. f* retina; '⸰spannung ∉ *f* mains voltage.

**neu** *adj.* [nɔʏ] new; fresh; recent; modern; ⸰ere Sprachen modern languages; ⸰este Nachrichten latest news; von ⸰em anew, afresh; ein ⸰es Leben beginnen turn over a new leaf; was gibt es Neues? what is the news?, *Am.* what is new?

**'Neu|anschaffung** *f* (-/-en) recent acquisition; '⸰artig *adj.* novel; '⸰auflage *typ. f*, '⸰ausgabe *typ. f* new edition; reprint; '⸰bau *m* (-[e]s/-ten) new building; '⸰bearbeitet *adj.* revised; '⸰e *m* (-n/-n) new man; new-comer; novice; '⸰entdeckt *adj.* recently discovered.

**neuer|dings** *adv.* ['nɔʏər'dɪŋs] of late, recently; '⸰er *m* (-s/-) innovator.

**Neuerscheinung** ['nɔʏ?-] *f* new book *or* publication.

**'Neuerung** *f* (-/-en) innovation.

**'neu|geboren** *adj.* new-born; '⸰gestalten *v/t.* (*sep.*, -ge-, *h*) reorganize; '⸰gestaltung *f* reorganization; '⸰gier *f*, ⸰gierde ['⸰də] *f* (-/*no pl.*) curiosity, inquisitiveness; '⸰gierig *adj.* curious (*auf acc.* about, of), inquisitive, *sl.* nos(e)y; ich bin ⸰, ob I wonder whether *or* if; '⸰heit *f* (-/-en) newness, freshness; novelty.

**'Neu|jahr** *n* New Year('s Day); '⸰land *n* (-[e]s/*no pl.*): ⸰ erschließen break fresh ground (*a. fig.*), '⸰lich *adv.* the other day, recently; '⸰ling *m* (-s/-e) novice; *contp* greenhorn; '⸰modisch *adj.* fashionable; '⸰mond *m* (-[e]s/*no pl.*) new moon.

**neun** *adj.* [nɔʏn] nine; '⸰te *adj.* ninth; '⸰tel *n* (-s/-) ninth part; '⸰tens *adv.* ninthly; '⸰zehn *adj.* nineteen; '⸰zehnte *adj.* nineteenth; ⸰zig *adj.* ['⸰tsɪç] ninety; '⸰zigste *adj.* ninetieth.

**'Neu|philologe** *m* student *or* teacher of modern languages; '⸰regelung *f* reorganization, rearrangement.

**neutr|al** *adj.* [nɔʏ'trɑːl] neutral; ⸰alität [⸰ali'tɛːt] *f* (-/*no pl.*) neutrality; ⸰um *gr.* ['nɔʏtrʊm] *n* (-s/Neutra, Neutren) neuter.

**'neu|vermählt** *adj.* newly married; die ⸰en *pl.* the newly-weds *pl.*; '⸰wahl *parl. f* new election; '⸰wertig *adj.* as good as new; '⸰zeit *f* (-/*no pl.*) modern times *pl.*

**nicht** *adv.* [nɪçt] not; *auch* ⸰ nor; ⸰ anziehend unattractive; ⸰ besser no better; ⸰ bevollmächtigt non-commissioned; ⸰ einlösbar ✝ inconvertible; ⸰ erscheinen fail to attend.

**'Nicht|achtung** *f* disregard; '⸰amtlich *adj.* unofficial; '⸰angriffspakt *pol. m* non-aggression pact; '⸰annahme *f* non-acceptance; '⸰befolgung *f* non-observance.

**Nichte** ['nɪçtə] *f* (-/-n) niece.

**'nichtig** *adj.* null, void; invalid; vain, futile; für ⸰ erklären declare null and void, annul; '⸰keit *f* (-/-en) 🏛 nullity; vanity, futility.

**'Nichtraucher** *m* non-smoker.

**nichts** [nɪçts] **1.** *indef. pron.* nothing, naught, not anything; **2.** ⸰ *n* (-/*no pl.*) nothing(ness); *fig.*: nonentity; void; '⸰ahnend *adj.* unsuspecting; ⸰desto'weniger *adv.* nevertheless; ⸰nutzig *adj.* ['⸰nutsɪç] good-for-nothing, worthless; '⸰sagend *adj.* insignificant; ⸰tuer ['⸰tuːər] *m* (-s/-) idler; '⸰würdig *adj.* vile, base, infamous.

**'Nicht|vorhandensein** *n* absence; lack; '⸰wissen *n* ignorance.

**nick|en** ['nɪkən] *v/i.* (*ge-*, *h*) nod; bow; '⸰erchen F *n* (-s/-): ein ⸰ machen take a nap, have one's forty winks.

**nie** *adv.* [niː] never, at no time.

**nieder** ['niːdər] **1.** *adj.* low; base, mean, vulgar; *value, rank*: inferior; **2.** *adv.* down.

**'Nieder|gang** *m* decline; '⸰gedrückt *adj.* dejected, downcast; '⸰gehen *v/i.* (*irr. gehen, sep., -ge-, sein*) go down; ✈ descend; *storm*: break; '⸰geschlagen *adj.* dejected, downcast; '⸰hauen *v/t.* (*irr. hauen, sep., -ge-, h*) cut down; '⸰kommen *v/i.* (*irr. kommen, sep., -ge-, sein*) be confined; be delivered (*mit* of); ⸰kunft ['⸰kunft] *f* (-/⸰e) confinement, delivery; '⸰lage *f* defeat; ✝ warehouse; branch; '⸰lassen *v/t.* (*irr. lassen, sep., -ge-, h*) let down; sich ⸰ settle (down); *bird*: alight; sit down; establish o.s.; settle (*in dat.* at); '⸰lassung *f* (-/-en) establishment; settlement; branch, agency; '⸰legen *v/t.* (*sep., -ge-, h*) lay *or* put down; resign (*position*); retire from (*business*); abdicate; die Arbeit ⸰ (go on) strike, down tools, *Am.* F *a.* walk out; sich ⸰ lie down, go to bed; '⸰machen *v/t.* (*sep., -ge-, h*) cut down; massacre; '⸰schlag *m* 🜄 precipitate; sediment; precipitation (*of rain, etc.*); *radio-active*: fall-out; *boxing*: knock-down, knock-out; '⸰schlagen *v/t.* (*irr. schlagen, sep., -ge-, h*) knock down; *boxing*: a. floor; cast down (*eyes*); suppress; put down, crush (*rebellion*); 🏛 quash; sich ⸰

**♏ precipitate; '♀schmettern** *fig.* *v/t.* (*sep.*, *-ge-*, *h*) crush; '♀setzen *v/t.* (*sep.*, *-ge-*, *h*) set *or* put down; *sich ~* sit down; *birds:* perch, alight; '♀strecken *v/t.* (*sep.*, *-ge-*, *h*) lay low, strike to the ground, floor; '♀trächtig *adj.* base, mean; *F* beastly; '~ung *f* (*-/-en*) lowlands *pl.*

**niedlich** *adj.* ['ni:tliç] neat, nice, pretty, *Am. a.* cute.

**Niednagel** ['ni:t-] *m* agnail, hangnail.

**niedrig** *adj.* ['ni:driç] low (*a. fig.*); moderate; *fig.* mean, base.

**niemals** *adv.* ['ni:ma:ls] never, at no time.

**niemand** *indef. pron.* ['ni:mant] nobody, no one, none; '♀sland *n* (*-[e]s/no pl.*) no man's land.

**Niere** ['ni:rə] *f* (*-/-n*) kidney; '~n-braten *m* loin of veal.

**nieseln** F ['ni:zəln] *v/i.* (*ge-*, *h*) drizzle; '♀regen F *m* drizzle.

**niesen** ['ni:zən] *v/i.* (*ge-*, *h*) sneeze.

**Niet** ⊕ [ni:t] *m* (*-[e]s/-e*) rivet; '~e *f* (*-/-n*) lottery: blank; F *fig.* washout; '♀en ⊕ *v/t.* (*ge-*, *h*) rivet.

**Nilpferd** *zo.* ['ni:l-] *n* hippopotamus.

**Nimbus** ['nimbus] *m* (*-/-se*) halo (*a. fig.*), nimbus.

**nimmer** *adv.* ['nimər] never; '~mehr *adv.* nevermore; '♀satt *m* (*-*, *-[e]s/-e*) glutton; ♀'wiedersehen F *n:* auf ~ never to meet again; *er verschwand auf ~* he left for good. [*dat.* at).\

**nippen** ['nipən] *v/i.* (*ge-*, *h*) sip (*an*)

**Nipp|es** ['nipəs] *pl.*, '~sachen *pl.* (k)nick-(k)nacks *pl.*

**nirgends** *adv.* ['nirgənts], '~(n)wo *adv.* nowhere.

**Nische** ['ni:ʃə] *f* (*-/-n*) niche, recess.

**nisten** ['nistən] *v/i.* (*ge-*, *h*) nest.

**Niveau** [ni'vo:] *n* (*-s/-s*) level; *fig. a.* standard.

**nivellieren** [nive'li:rən] *v/t.* (*no -ge-*, *h*) level, grade.

**Nixe** ['niksə] *f* (*-/-n*) water-nymph, mermaid.

**noch** [nɔx] **1.** *adv.* still; yet; ~ *ein* another, one more; ~ *einmal* once more *or* again; ~ *etwas* something more; ~ *etwas?* anything else?; ~ *heute* this very day; ~ *immer* still; ~ *nicht* not yet; ~ *nie* never before; ~ *so ever so*; ~ *im 19. Jahrhundert* as late as the 19th century; *es wird* ~ *2 Jahre dauern* it will take two more *or* another two years; **2.** *cj.*: *s. weder;* ~malig *adj.* ['~ma:liç] repeated; ~mals *adv.* ['~ma:ls] once more *or* again.

**Nomad|e** [no'ma:də] *m* (*-n/-n*) nomad; ♀isch *adj.* nomadic.

**Nominativ** *gr.* ['no:minati:f] *m* (*-s/-e*) nominative (case).

**nominieren** [nomi'ni:rən] *v/t.* (*no -ge-*, *h*) nominate.

**Nonne** ['nɔnə] *f* (*-/-n*) nun; '~n-kloster *n* nunnery, convent.

**Nord** *geogr.* [nɔrt], ~en ['~dən] *m* (*-s/no pl.*) north; ♀isch *adj.* ['~diʃ] northern.

**nördlich** *adj.* ['nœrtliç] northern, northerly.

'**Nord|licht** *n* northern lights *pl.*; ~'ost(en *m*) north-east; '~pol *m* North Pole; ♀wärts *adv.* ['~verts] northward(s), north; ~'west(en *m*) north-west.

**nörg|eln** ['nœrgəln] *v/i.* (*ge-*, *h*) nag, carp (*an dat.* at); grumble; ♀ler ['~lər] *m* (*-s/-*) faultfinder, grumbler.

**Norm** [nɔrm] *f* (*-/-en*) standard; rule; norm.

**normal** *adj.* [nɔr'ma:l] normal; regular; *measure*, *weight*, *time*: standard; ~isieren [~ali'zi:rən] *v/refl.* (*no -ge-*, *h*) return to normal.

'**norm|en** *v/t.* (*ge-*, *h*), ~ieren [~'mi:rən] *v/t.* (*no -ge-*, *h*) standardize.

**Not** [no:t] *f* (*-/-̈e*) need, want; necessity; difficulty; trouble; misery; danger, emergency, distress (*a.* ♋); ~ *leiden* suffer privations; *in* ~ *geraten* become destitute, get into trouble; *in* ~ *sein* be in trouble; *zur* ~ at a pinch; *es tut not, daß es is* necessary that.

**Notar** [no'ta:r] *m* (*-s/-e*) (public) notary.

'**Not|ausgang** *m* emergency exit; '~behelf *m* makeshift, expedient, stopgap; '~bremse *f* emergency brake; '~brücke *f* temporary bridge; '~durft ['~durft] *f* (*-/no pl.*): *s-e* ~ *verrichten* relieve o.s.; '♀dürftig *adj.* scanty, poor; temporary.

**Note** ['no:tə] *f* (*-/-n*) note (*a.* ♪); *pol.* note, memorandum; *school:* mark.

'**Noten|bank** ✝ *f* bank of issue; '~schlüssel* ♪ *m* clef; '~system* ♪ *n* staff.

'**Not|fall** *m* case of need, emergency; '♀falls *adv.* if necessary; '♀gedrungen *adv.* of necessity, needs.

**notier|en** [no'ti:rən] *v/t.* (*no -ge-*, *h*) make a note of, note (down); ✝ quote; ♀ung ✝ *f* (*-/-en*) quotation.

**nötig** *adj.* ['nø:tiç] necessary; ~ *haben* need; ~en ['~gən] *v/t.* (*ge-*, *h*) force, oblige, compel; press, urge (*guest*); '~en'falls *adv.* if necessary; '♀ung *f* (*-/-en*) compulsion; pressing; ♋ intimidation.

**Notiz** [no'ti:ts] *f* (*-/-en*) notice, note, memorandum; ~ *nehmen von* take notice of; *pay attention to*; *keine* ~ *nehmen von* ignore; *sich* ~en *machen* take notes; ~block *m* pad, *Am. a.* scratch pad; ~buch *n* notebook.

'**Not|lage** *f* distress; emergency; '♀landen ✈ *v/i.* (*-ge-*, *sein*) make

a forced or emergency landing; '~landung ✠ f forced or emergency landing; '2leidend adj. needy, destitute; distressed; '~lösung f expedient; '~lüge f white lie.
**notorisch** adj. [no'to:riʃ] notorious.
'**Not|ruf** teleph. m emergency call; '~signal n emergency or distress signal; '~sitz mot. m dick(e)y(-seat), Am. a. rumble seat; '~stand m emergency; '~standsarbeiten f/pl. relief works pl.; '~standsgebiet n distressed area; '~standsgesetze n/pl. emergency laws pl.; '~verband m first-aid dressing; '~verordnung f emergency decree; '~wehr f self-defen|ce, Am. -se; '2wendig adj. necessary; '~wendigkeit f (-/-en) necessity; '~zucht f (-/no pl.) rape.
**Novelle** [no'vɛlə] f (-/-n) short story, novella; parl. amendment.
**November** [no'vɛmbər] m (-[s]/-) November.
**Nu** [nu:] m (-/no pl.): im ~ in no time.
**Nuance** [ny'ã:sə] f (-/-n) shade.
**nüchtern** adj. ['nyçtərn] empty, fasting, sober (a. fig.); matter-of-fact; writings: jejune; prosaic; cool; plain; '2heit f (-/no pl.) sobriety; fig. soberness.
**Nudel** ['nu:dəl] f (-/-n) noodle.
**null** [nul] 1. adj. null; nil; tennis: love; ~ und nichtig null and void; 2. 2 f (-/-en) nought, cipher (a. fig.); zero; '2punkt m zero.
**numerieren** [numə'ri:rən] v/t. (no -ge-, h) number; numerierter Platz reserved seat.
**Nummer** ['numər] f (-/-n) number

(a. newspaper, thea.); size (of shoes, etc.); thea. turn; sports: event; '~nschild mot. n number-plate.
**nun** [nu:n] 1. adv. now, at present; then; ~? well?; ~ also well then; 2. int. now then!; '~'mehr adv. now.
**nur** adv. [nu:r] only; (nothing) but; merely; ~ noch only.
**Nuß** [nus] f (-/Nüsse) nut; '~kern m kernel; '~knacker m (-s/-) nutcracker; '~schale f nutshell.
**Nüstern** ['ny:stərn] f/pl. nostrils pl.
**nutz** adj. [nuts] s. nütze; '2anwendung f practical application; '~bar adj. useful; '~bringend adj. profitable.
**nütze** adj. ['nytsə] useful; zu nichts ~ sein be of no use, be good for nothing.
**Nutzen** ['nutsən] 1. m (-s/-) use; profit, gain; advantage; utility; 2. 2 v/i. and v/t. (ge-, h) s. nützen.
**nützen** ['nytsən] (ge-, h) 1. v/i.: zu et. ~ be of use or useful for s.th.; j-m ~ serve s.o.; es nützt nichts zu inf. it is no use ger.; 2. v/t. use, make use of; put to account; avail o.s. of, seize (opportunity).
'**Nutz|holz** n timber; '~leistung f capacity.
**nützlich** adj. ['nytsliç] useful, of use; advantageous.
'**nutz|los** adj. useless; 2nießer ['~ni:sər] m (-s/-) usufructuary; '2-nießung f (-/-en) usufruct.
'**Nutzung** f (-/-en) using; utilization.
**Nylon** ['naɪlɔn] n (-s/no pl.) nylon; ~strümpfe ['~ʃtrympfə] m/pl. nylons pl., nylon stockings pl.
**Nymphe** ['nymfə] f (-/-n) nymph.

# O

**o** int. [o:] oh!, ah!; ~ weh! alas!, oh dear (me)!
**Oase** [o'a:zə] f (-/-n) oasis.
**ob** cj. [ɔp] whether, if; als ~ as if, as though.
**Obacht** ['o:baxt] f (-/no pl.): ~ geben auf (acc.) pay attention to, take care of, heed.
**Obdach** ['ɔpdax] n (-[e]s/no pl.) shelter, lodging; '2los adj. unsheltered, homeless; '~lose m, f (-n/-n) homeless person; '~losenasyl n casual ward.
**Obdu|ktion** ✠ [ɔpduk'tsjo:n] f (-/-en) post-mortem (examination), autopsy; 2zieren ✠ [~'tsi:rən] v/t. (no -ge-, h) perform an autopsy on.
**oben** adv. ['o:bən] above; mountain: at the top; house: upstairs; on the surface; von ~ from above; von ~ bis unten from top to bottom;

von ~ herab behandeln treat haughtily; '~'an adv. at the top; '~'auf adv. on the top; on the surface; ~drein adv. ['~'draɪn] into the bargain, at that; ~erwähnt adj. ['o:bən'ɛrvɛ:nt], '~genannt adj. above-mentioned, aforesaid; '~'hin adv. superficially, perfunctorily.
**ober** ['o:bər] 1. adj. upper, higher; fig. a. superior; 2. 2 m (-s/-) (head) waiter; German cards: queen.
**Ober|arm** ['o:bər°-] m upper arm; ~arzt ['o:bər°-] m head physician; ~aufseher ['o:bər°-] m superintendent; ~aufsicht ['o:bər°-] f superintendence; '~befehl ✠ m supreme command; '~befehlshaber ✠ m commander-in-chief; '~bekleidung f outer garments pl., outer wear; '~bürgermeister m chief burgomaster; Lord Mayor;

'‿deck ⚓ n upper deck; '‿fläche f surface; ℒflächlich adj. ['‿flɛçliç] superficial; fig. a. shallow; 'ℒhalb prp. (gen.) above; '‿hand fig. f: die ~ gewinnen über (acc.) get the upper hand of; '‿haupt n head, chief; '‿haus Brt. parl. n House of Lords; '‿hemd n shirt; '‿herrschaft f supremacy.

'Oberin f (-/-nen) eccl. Mother Superior; at hospital: matron.

ober|irdisch adj. ['o:bər?-] overground, above ground; ≠ overhead; 'ℒkellner m head waiter; 'ℒkiefer anat. m upper jaw; 'ℒkörper m upper part of the body; 'ℒland n upland; 'ℒlauf m upper course (of river); 'ℒleder n upper; 'ℒleitung f chief management; ≠ overhead wires pl.; 'ℒleutnant ✗ m (Am. first) lieutenant; 'ℒlicht n skylight; 'ℒlippe f upper lip; 'ℒschenkel m thigh; 'ℒschule f secondary school, Am. a. high school.

'oberst 1. adj. uppermost, topmost, top; highest (a. fig.); fig. chief, principal; rank, etc.: supreme; 2. ℒ ✗ m (-en, -s/-en, -e) colonel; 'Ober|staatsanwalt ⚖ m chief public prosecutor; '‿stimme ♪ f treble, soprano.

'Oberst'leutnant ✗ m lieutenant-colonel.

'Ober|tasse f cup; '‿wasser fig. n: ~ bekommen get the upper hand.

obgleich cj. [ɔp'glaiç] (al)though.

'Obhut f (-/no pl.) care, guard; protection; custody; in (seine) ~ nehmen take care or charge of.

obig adj. ['o:biç] above(-mentioned), aforesaid.

Objekt [ɔp'jɛkt] n (-[e]s/-e) object (a. gr.); project; ✝ a. transaction.

objektiv [ɔpjɛk'ti:f] 1. adj. objective; impartial, detached; actual, practical; 2. ℒ n (-s/-e) object-glass, objective; phot. lens; ℒität [‿ivi-'tɛ:t] f (-/no pl.) objectivity; impartiality.

obligat adj. [obli'gɑ:t] obligatory; indispensable; inevitable; ℒion ✝ [‿a'tsjo:n] f (-/-en) bond, debenture; ‿orisch adj. [‿a'to:riʃ] obligatory (für on), compulsory, mandatory.

'Obmann m chairman; ⚖ foreman (of jury); umpire; ✝ shop-steward, spokesman.

Oboe ♪ [o'bo:ə] f (-/-n) oboe, hautboy.

Obrigkeit ['o:briçkait] f (-/-en) the authorities pl.; government; 'ℒlich adj. magisterial, official; '‿sstaat m authoritarian state.

ob'schon cj. (al)though.

Observatorium ast. [ɔpzɛrva'to:rjum] n (-s/Observatorien) observatory.

Obst [o:pst] n (-es/no pl.) fruit;

'‿bau m fruit-culture, fruit-growing; '‿baum m fruit-tree; '‿ernte f fruit-gathering; fruit-crop; '‿garten m orchard; '‿händler m fruiterer, Am. fruitseller; '‿züchter m fruiter, fruit-grower.

obszön adj. [ɔps'tsø:n] obscene, filthy.

ob'wohl cj. (al)though.

Ochse zo. ['ɔksə] m (-n/-n) ox; bullock; '‿nfleisch n beef.

öde ['ø:də] 1. adj. deserted, desolate; waste; fig. dull, tedious; 2. ℒ f (-/-n) desert, solitude; fig. dullness, tedium.

oder cj. ['o:dər] or.

Ofen ['o:fən] m (-s/ᵘ) stove; oven; kiln; furnace; '‿heizung f heating by stove; '‿rohr n stove-pipe.

offen adj. ['ɔfən] open (a. fig.); position: vacant; hostility: overt; fig. frank, outspoken.

'offen'bar adj. obvious, evident; apparent; 2. adv. a. it seems that; ‿en [ɔfən'-] v/t. (no -ge-, h) reveal, disclose; manifest; sich j-m ~ open one's heart to s.o.; ℒung [ɔfən'-] f (-/-en) manifestation; revelation; ℒungseid ⚖ [ɔfən'ba:runs?-] m oath of manifestation.

'Offenheit fig. f (-/no pl.) openness, frankness.

'offen|herzig adj. open-hearted, sincere; frank; '‿kundig adj. public; notorious; '‿sichtlich adj. manifest, evident, obvious.

offensiv adj. [ɔfɛn'zi:f] offensive; ℒe [‿və] f (-/-n) offensive.

'offenstehen v/i. (irr. stehen, sep., -ge-, h) stand open; ✝ bill: be outstanding; fig. be open (j-m to s.o.); es steht ihm offen zu inf. he is free or at liberty to inf.

öffentlich ['œfəntliç] 1. adj. public; ‿es Ärgernis public nuisance; ‿er Dienst Civil Service; 2. adv. publicly, in public; ~ auftreten make a public appearance; 'ℒkeit f (-/no pl.) publicity; the public; in aller ~ in public.

offerieren [ɔfə'ri:rən] v/t. (no -ge-, h) offer.

Offerte [ɔ'fɛrtə] f (-/-n) offer; tender.

offiziell adj. [ɔfi'tsjɛl] official.

Offizier ✗ [ɔfi'tsi:r] m (-s/-e) (commissioned) officer; ‿skorps ✗ [‿sko:r] n (-/-) body of officers, the officers pl.; ‿smesse f ✗ officers' mess; ⚓ a. wardroom.

offiziös adj. [ɔfi'tsjø:s] officious, semi-official.

öffn|en ['œfnən] v/t. (ge-, h) open; a. uncork (bottle); ⚕ dissect (body); sich ~ open; '‿er m (-s/-) opener; 'ℒung f (-/-en) opening, aperture; 'ℒungszeiten f/pl. hours pl. of opening, business hours pl.

oft adv. [ɔft] often, frequently.

**öfters** adv. ['œftərs] s. oft.

**'oftmal|ig** adj. frequent, repeated; **~s** adv. s. oft.

**oh** int. [o:] o(h)!

**ohne** ['o:nə] 1. prp. (acc.) without; 2. cj.: ~ daß, ~ zu inf. without ger.; **~'dies** adv. anyhow, anyway; **~'gleichen** adv. unequal(l)ed, matchless; **~'hin** adv. s. ohnedies.

**'Ohn|macht** f (-/-en) powerlessness; impotence; ⚕ faint, unconsciousness; in ~ fallen faint, swoon; **~machtsanfall** ⚕ ['o:nmaxts⁹-] m fainting fit, swoon; **'2mächtig** adj. powerless; impotent; ⚕ unconscious; ~ werden faint, swoon.

**Ohr** [o:r] n (-[e]s/-en) ear; fig. a. hearing; ein ~ haben für have an ear for; ganz ~ sein be all ears; F j-n übers ~ hauen cheat s.o., sl. do s.o. (in the eye); bis über die ~en up to the ears or eyes.

**Öhr** [ø:r] n (-[e]s/-e) eye (of needle). **'Ohren|arzt** m aurist, ear specialist; **'2betäubend** adj. deafening; **'~leiden** n ear-complaint; **'~schmalz** n ear-wax; **'~schmaus** m treat for the ears; **'~schmerzen** m/pl. earache; **'~zeuge** m ear-witness.

**'Ohr|feige** f box on the ear(s), slap in the face (a. fig.); **'2feigen** v/t. (ge-, h): j-n ~ box s.o.'s ear(s), slap s.o.'s face; **~läppchen** ['~lɛpçən] n (-s/-) lobe of ear; **'~ring** m earring.

**Ökonom|ie** [økono'mi:] f (-/-n) economy; **2isch** adj. [~'no:miʃ] economical.

**Oktav** [ɔk'ta:f] n (-s/-e) octavo; **~e** ♩ [~və] f (-/-n) octave.

**Oktober** [ɔk'to:bər] m (-[s]/-) October.

**Okul|ar** opt. [oku'la:r] n (-s/-e) eyepiece, ocular; **2ieren** ♪ v/t. (no -ge-, h) inoculate, graft.

**Öl** [ø:l] n (-[e]s/-e) oil; ~ ins Feuer gießen add fuel to the flames; ~ auf die Wogen gießen pour oil on the (troubled) waters; **'~baum** ♣ m olive-tree; **'~berg** eccl. m (-[e]s/no pl.) Mount of Olives; **'2en** v/t. (ge-, h) oil; ⊕ a. lubricate; **'~farbe** f oil-colo(u)r, oil-paint; **'~gemälde** n oil-painting; **'~heizung** f oil heating; **'2ig** adj. oily (a. fig.).

**Oliv|e** ♣ [o'li:və] f (-/-n) olive; **~enbaum** ♣ m olive-tree; **2grün** adj. olive(-green).

**Öl|male'rei** f oil-painting; **'~quelle** f oil-spring, gusher; oil-well; **'~ung** f (-/-en) oiling; ⊕ a. lubrication; Letzte ~ eccl. extreme unction.

**Olympi|ade** [olymp'ja:də] f (-/-n) Olympiad; die Olympic Games pl.; **2sch** adj. [o'lympiʃ] Olympic; Olympische Spiele pl. Olympic Games pl.

**'Ölzweig** m olive-branch.

**Omelett** [ɔm(ə)'lɛt] n (-[e]s/-e, -s), **~e** [~'lɛt] f (-/-n) omelet(te).

**Om|en** ['o:mən] n (-s/-, Omina) omen, augury; **2inös** adj. [omi'nø:s] ominous.

**Omnibus** ['ɔmnibus] m (-ses/-se) (omni)bus; (motor-)coach; **'~haltestelle** f bus-stop.

**Onkel** ['ɔŋkəl] m (-s/-, F -s) uncle.

**Oper** ['o:pər] f (-/-n) ♪ opera; operahouse.

**Operat|eur** [opəra'tø:r] m (-s/-e) operator; ⚕ surgeon; **~ion** ⚕, ✖ [~'tsjo:n] f (-/-en) operation; **~ionssaal** ⚕ m operating room, Am. surgery; **2iv** ⚕ adj. [~'ti:f] operative.

**Operette** ♪ [opə'rɛtə] f (-/-n) operetta.

**operieren** [opə'ri:rən] (no -ge-, h) 1. v/t.: j-n ~ ⚕ operate (up)on s.o. (wegen for); 2. ⚔, ✖ v/i. operate; sich ~ lassen ⚕ undergo an operation.

**'Opern|glas** n, **~gucker** F ['~gukər] m (-s/-) opera-glass(es pl.); **'~haus** n opera-house; **'~sänger** m operasinger, operatic singer; **'~text** m libretto, book (of an opera).

**Opfer** ['ɔpfər] n (-s/-) sacrifice; offering; victim (a. fig.); ein ~ bringen make a sacrifice; j-m zum ~ fallen be victimized by s.o.; **'~gabe** f offering; **'2n** (ge-, h) 1. v/t. sacrifice; immolate; sich für et. ~ sacrifice o.s. for s.th.; 2. v/i. (make a) sacrifice (dat. to); **'~stätte** f place of sacrifice; **'~tod** m sacrifice of one's life; **'~ung** f (-/-en) sacrificing, sacrifice; immolation.

**Opium** ['o:pjum] n (-s/no pl.) opium.

**opponieren** [ɔpo'ni:rən] v/i. (no -ge-, h) be opposed (gegen to), resist.

**Opposition** [ɔpozi'tsjo:n] f (-/-en) opposition (a. parl.); **~sführer** parl. m opposition leader; **~spartei** parl. f opposition party.

**Optik** ['ɔptik] f (-/~, -en) optics; phot. lens system; fig. aspect; **'~er** m (-s/-) optician.

**Optim|ismus** [ɔpti'mismus] m (-/no pl.) optimism; **~ist** m (-en/-en) optimist; **2istisch** adj. optimistic.

**'optisch** adj. optic(al); **~e** Täuschung optical illusion.

**Orakel** [o'ra:kəl] n (-s/-) oracle; **2haft** adj. oracular; **2n** v/i. (no -ge-, h) speak oracularly; **'~spruch** m oracle.

**Orange** [o'rã:ʒə] f (-/-n) orange; **2farben** adj. orange(-colo[u]red); **~nbaum** ♣ m orange-tree.

**Oratorium** ♪ [ora'to:rjum] n (-s/ Oratorien) oratorio.

**Orchester** ♪ [ɔr'kɛstər] n (-s/-) orchestra.

**Orchidee** ♣ [ɔrçi'de:ə] f (-/-n) orchid.

**Orden** ['ɔrdən] *m* (-s/-) order (*a. eccl.*); order, medal, decoration.

**'Ordens|band** *n* ribbon (of an order); **'~bruder** *eccl. m* brother, friar; **'~gelübde** *eccl. n* monastic vow; **'~schwester** *f* sister, nun; **'~verleihung** *f* conferring (of) an order.

**ordentlich** *adj.* ['ɔrdentliç] tidy; orderly; proper; regular; respectable; good, sound; **~er** *Professor univ.* professor in ordinary.

**ordinär** *adj.* [ɔrdi'nɛːr] common, vulgar, low.

**ordn|en** ['ɔrdnən] *v/t.* (ge-, h) put in order; arrange, fix (up); settle (*a. † liabilities*); **'2er** *m* (-s/-) at festival, etc.: steward; *for papers, etc.*: file.

**'Ordnung** *f* (-/-en) order; arrangement; system; rules *pl.*, regulations *pl.*; class; *in ~ bringen* put in order.

**'ordnungs|gemäß**, **'~mäßig 1.** *adj.* orderly, regular; **2.** *adv.* duly; **'2ruf** *parl. m* call to order; **'2strafe** *f* disciplinary penalty; fine; **'~widrig** *adj.* contrary to order, irregular; **'2zahl** *f* ordinal number.

**Ordonnanz** ✕ [ɔrdɔ'nants] *f* (-/-en) orderly.

**Organ** [ɔr'gaːn] *n* (-s/-e) organ.

**Organisat|ion** [ɔrganiza'tsjoːn] *f* (-/-en) organization; **~ionstalent** *n* organizing ability; **~or** [~'zaːtɔr] *m* (-s/-en) organizer; **2orisch** *adj.* [~a'toːriʃ] organizational, organizing.

**or'ganisch** *adj.* organic.

**organi'sieren** *v/t.* (no -ge-, h) organize; *sl.* scrounge; *(nicht) organisiert(er Arbeiter)* (non-)unionist.

**Organismus** [ɔrga'nismus] *m* (-/Organismen) organism; ♂ *a.* system.

**Organist** ♪ [ɔrga'nist] *m* (-en/-en) organist.

**Orgel** ♪ ['ɔrgəl] *f* (-/-n) organ, *Am. a.* pipe organ; **'~bauer** *m* organ-builder; **'~pfeife** *f* organ-pipe; **'~spieler** ♪ *m* organist.

**Orgie** ['ɔrgjə] *f* (-/-n) orgy.

**Oriental|e** [orien'taːlə] *m* (-n/-n) oriental; **2isch** *adj.* oriental.

**orientier|en** [orien'tiːrən] *v/t.* (no -ge-, h) inform, instruct; *sich ~ orient(ate) o.s.* (*a. fig.*); inform o.s. (*über acc.* of); *gut orientiert sein über* (*acc.*) be well informed about, be familiar with; **2ung** *f* (-/-en) orientation; *fig. a.* information; *die ~ verlieren* lose one's bearings.

**Origin|al** [origi'naːl] **1.** *n* (-s/-e) original; **2.** ♀ *adj.* original; **~alität** [~ali'tɛːt] *f* (-/-en) originality; **2ell** *adj.* [~'nɛl] original; *design, etc.*: ingenious.

**Orkan** [ɔr'kaːn] *m* (-[e]s/-e) hurricane; typhoon; **2artig** *adj. storm:* violent; *applause:* thunderous, frenzied.

**Ornat** [ɔr'naːt] *m* (-[e]s/-e) robe(s *pl.*), vestment.

**Ort** [ɔrt] *m* (-[e]s/-e) place; site; spot, point; locality; place, village, town; *~ der Handlung thea.* scene (of action); *an ~ und Stelle* on the spot; *höher(e)n ~(e)s* at higher quarters; **'2en** *v/t.* (ge-, h) locate.

**ortho|dox** *adj.* [ɔrto'dɔks] orthodox; **2graphie** [~gra'fiː] *f* (-/-n) orthography; **~graphisch** *adj.* [~'graːfiʃ] orthographic(al); **2päde** ♂ [~'pɛːdə] *m* (-n/-n) orthop(a)edist; **2pädie** ♂ [~pɛ'diː] *f* (-/no pl.) orthop(a)edics, orthop(a)edy; **~pädisch** *adj.* [~'pɛːdiʃ] orthop(a)edic.

**örtlich** *adj.* ['œrtliç] local; ♂ *a.* topical; **'2keit** *f* (-/-en) locality.

**'Orts|angabe** *f* statement of place; **'2ansässig** *adj.* resident, local; **~ansässige** ['~gə] *m* (-n/-n) resident; **'~beschreibung** *f* topography; **'~besichtigung** *f* local inspection.

**'Ortschaft** *f* (-/-en) place, village.

**'Orts|gespräch** *teleph. n* local call; **'~kenntnis** *f* knowledge of a place; **'2kundig** *adj.* familiar with the locality; **'~name** *m* place-name; **'~verkehr** *m* local traffic; **'~zeit** *f* local time.

**Öse** ['øːzə] *f* (-/-n) eye, loop; eyelet (*of shoe*).

**Ost** *geogr.* [ɔst] east; **'~en** *m* (-s/no pl.*) east; *the East; der Ferne* (*Nahe*) *~ the Far* (*Near*) *East.*

**ostentativ** *adj.* [ɔstenta'tiːf] ostentatious.

**Oster|ei** ['oːstar?-] *n* Easter egg; **'~fest** *n* Easter; **'~hase** *m* Easter bunny *or* rabbit; **'~lamm** *n* paschal lamb; **'~n** *n* (-/-) Easter.

**Österreich|er** ['øːstəraiçər] *m* (-s/-) Austrian; **'2isch** *adj.* Austrian.

**östlich** ['œstliç] **1.** *adj.* eastern; *wind, etc.*: easterly; **2.** *adv.*: *~ von* east of.

**ost|wärts** *adv.* ['ɔstverts] eastward(s); **'2wind** *m* east(erly) wind.

**Otter** *zo.* ['ɔtər] **1.** *m* (-s/-) otter; **2.** *f* (-/-n) adder, viper.

**Ouvertüre** ♪ [uver'tyːrə] *f* (-/-n) overture.

**oval** [o'vaːl] **1.** *adj.* oval; **2.** ♀ *n* (-s/-e) oval.

**Ovation** [ova'tsjoːn] *f* (-/-en) ovation; *j-m ~en bereiten* give s.o. ovations.

**Oxyd** ♠ [ɔ'ksyːt] *n* (-[e]s/-e) oxide; **2ieren** [~y'diːrən] (no -ge-) **1.** *v/t.* (h) oxidize; **2.** *v/i.* (sein) oxidize.

**Ozean** ['oːtseaːn] *m* (-s/-e) ocean.

# P

**Paar** [pɑːr] 1. *n* (-[e]s/-e) pair; couple; 2. ♀ *adj.*: *ein* ~ a few, some; *j-m ein* ~ *Zeilen schreiben* drop s.o. a few lines; '♀**en** *v/t.* (ge-, h) pair, couple; mate (*animals*); *sich* ~ (form a) pair; *animals*: mate; *fig.* join, unite; '~**lauf** *m sports*: pairskating; '~**läufer** *m sports*: pairskater; '♀**mal** *adv.*: *ein* ~ several *or* a few times; '~**ung** *f* (-/-en) coupling; mating, copulation; *fig.* union; '♀**weise** *adv.* in pairs *or* couples, by twos.

**Pacht** [paxt] *f* (-/-en) lease, tenure, tenancy; *money payment*: rent; '♀**en** *v/t.* (ge-, h) (take on) lease; rent.

**Pächter** ['pɛçtər] *m* (-s/-), '~**in** *f* (-/-nen) lessee, lease-holder; tenant.

'**Pacht|ertrag** *m* rental; '~**geld** *n* rent; '~**gut** *n* farm; '~**vertrag** *m* lease; '♀**weise** *adv.* on lease.

**Pack** [pak] 1. *m* (-[e]s/-e, *ⁿe*) *s.* **Packen²**; 2. *n* (-[e]s/*no pl.*) rabble.

**Päckchen** ['pɛkçən] *n* (-s/-) small parcel, *Am. a.* package; *ein* ~ *Zigaretten* a pack(et) of cigarettes.

**packen¹** ['pakən] (ge-, h) 1. *v/t.* pack (up); seize, grip, grasp, clutch; collar; *fig.* grip, thrill; *F pack dich!* F clear out!, *sl.* beat it!; 2. *v/i.* pack (up); 3. ♀ *n* (-s/*no pl.*) packing.

**Packen²** [~] *m* (-s/-) pack(et), parcel; bale.

'**Packer** *m* (-s/-) packer; ~**ei** [~'raɪ] *f* 1. (-/-en) packing-room; 2. (-/*no pl.*) packing.

'**Pack|esel** *fig. m* drudge; '~**material** *n* packing materials *pl.*; '~**papier** *n* packing-paper, brown paper; '~**pferd** *n* pack-horse; '~**ung** *f* (-/-en) pack(age), packet; ♂ pack; *e-e* ~ *Zigaretten* a pack(et) of cigarettes; '~**wagen** *m s. Gepäckwagen.*

**Pädagog|e** [pɛda'goːgə] *m* (-n/-n) pedagog(ue), education(al)ist; ~**ik** *f* (-/*no pl.*) pedagogics, pedagogy; ♀**isch** *adj.* pedagogic(al).

**Paddel** ['padəl] *n* (-s/-) paddle; '~**boot** *n* canoe; '♀**n** *v/i.* (ge-, h, *sein*) paddle, canoe.

**Page** ['pɑːʒə] *m* (-n/-n) page.

**pah** *int.* [pɑː] pah!, pooh!, pshaw!

**Paket** [pa'keːt] *n* (-[e]s/-e) parcel, packet, package; ~**annahme** ❦ *f* parcel counter; ~**karte** ❦ *f* dispatch-note; ~**post** *f* parcel post; ~**zustellung** ❦ *f* parcel delivery.

**Pakt** [pakt] *m* (-[e]s/-e) pact, agreement; treaty.

**Palast** [pa'last] *m* (-es/*ⁿe*) palace.

**Palm|e** ♀ ['palmə] *f* (-/-n) palm (-tree); '~**öl** *n* palm-oil; ~'**sonntag** *eccl. m* Palm Sunday.

**panieren** [pa'niːrən] *v/t.* (*no -ge-*, h) crumb.

**Pani|k** ['pɑːnik] *f* (-/-en) panic; stampede; '♀**sch** *adj.* panic; *von* ~*em Schrecken erfaßt* panic-stricken.

**Panne** ['panə] *f* (-/-n) breakdown, *mot. a.* engine trouble; *tyres*: puncture; *fig.* blunder.

**panschen** ['panʃən] (ge-, h) 1. *v/i.* splash (about); 2. *v/t.* adulterate (*wine, etc.*).

**Panther** *zo.* ['pantər] *m* (-s/-) panther.

**Pantine** [pan'tiːnə] *f* (-/-n) clog.

**Pantoffel** [pan'tɔfəl] *m* (-s/-n, F -) slipper; *unter dem* ~ *stehen* be henpecked; ~**held** F *m* henpecked husband.

**pantschen** ['pantʃən] *v/i. and v/t.* (ge-, h) *s.* **panschen.**

**Panzer** ['pantsər] *m* (-s/-) armo(u)r; ✕ tank; *zo.* shell; '~**abwehr** ✕ *f* anti-tank defen|ce, *Am.* -se; '~**glas** *n* bullet-proof glass; '~**hemd** *n* coat of mail; '~**kreuzer** ✕ *m* armo(u)red cruiser; '♀**n** *v/t.* (ge-, h) armo(u)r; '~**platte** *f* armo(u)r-plate; '~**schiff** ✕ *n* ironclad; '~**schrank** *m* safe; '~**ung** *f* (-/-en) armo(u)r-plating; '~**wagen** *m* armo(u)red car; ✕ tank.

**Papa** [pa'pɑː, F 'papa] *m* (-s/-s) papa, F pa, dad(dy), *Am. a.* pop.

**Papagei** *orn.* [papa'gaɪ] *m* (-[e]s, -en/-e[n]) parrot.

**Papier** [pa'piːr] *n* (-s/-e) paper; ~*e pl.* papers *pl.*, documents *pl.*; papers *pl.*, identity card; *ein Bogen* ~ a sheet of paper; ♀**en** *adj.* (of) paper; *fig.* dull; ~**fabrik** *f* paper-mill; ~**geld** *n* (-[e]s/*no pl.*) paper-money; banknotes *pl., Am.* bills *pl.*; ~**korb** *m* waste-paper-basket; ~**schnitzel** F *n or m/pl.* scraps *pl.* of paper; ~**tüte** *f* paper-bag; ~**waren** *f/pl.* stationery.

'**Papp|band** *m* (-[e]s/*ⁿe*) paperback; '~**deckel** *m* pasteboard, cardboard.

**Pappe** ['papə] *f* (-/-n) pasteboard, cardboard.

**Pappel** ♀ ['papəl] *f* (-/-n) poplar.

**päppeln** F ['pɛpəln] *v/t.* (ge-, h) feed (with pap).

**papp|en** F ['papən] (ge-, h) 1. *v/t.* paste; 2. *v/i.* stick; '♀**ig** *adj.* sticky; '♀**karton** *m*, '♀**schachtel** *f* cardboard box, carton.

**Papst** [pɑːpst] *m* (-es/*ⁿe*) pope.

**päpstlich** *adj.* ['pɛːpstliç] papal.

'**Papsttum** *n* (-s/*no pl.*) papacy.

**Parade** [pa'rɑːdə] *f* (-/-n) parade; ✕ review; *fencing*: parry.

**Paradies** [para'diːs] *n* (-es/-e) paradise; ♀**isch** *fig. adj.* [~'diːziʃ] heavenly, delightful.

**paradox** *adj.* [para'dɔks] paradoxical.

**Paragraph** [para'grɑːf] *m* (-en, -s/-en) article, section; paragraph; section-mark.

**parallel** *adj.* [para'leːl] parallel; ℒe *f* (-/-n) parallel.

**Paralys|e** ⚕ [para'lyːzə] *f* (-/-n) paralysis; ℒieren ⚕ [͜y'ziːrən] *v/t.* (*no* -ge-, *h*) paralyse.

**Parasit** [para'ziːt] *m* (-en/-en) parasite.

**Parenthese** [parɛn'teːzə] *f* (-/-n) parenthesis.

**Parforcejagd** [par'fɔrs-] *f* hunt (-ing) on horseback (with hounds), *after hares:* coursing.

**Parfüm** [par'fyːm] *n* (-s/-e, -s) perfume, scent; ͜erie [͜ymə'riː] *f* (-/-n) perfumery; ℒieren [͜y'miːrən] *v/t.* (*no* -ge-, *h*) perfume, scent.

**pari** † *adv.* ['paːri] par; *al* ͜ at par.

**parieren** [pa'riːrən] (*no* -ge-, *h*) **1.** *v/t.* fencing: parry (*a. fig.*); pull up (*horse*); **2.** *v/i.* obey (*j-m s.o.*).

**Park** [park] *m* (-s/-s, -e) park; '͜anlage *f* park; '͜aufseher *m* parkkeeper; ℒen (ge-, *h*) **1.** *v/i.* park; ͜ verboten! no parking!; **2.** *v/t.* park.

**Parkett** [par'kɛt] *n* (-[e]s/-e) parquet; *thea.* (orchestra) stalls *pl.*, *esp. Am.* orchestra *or* parquet.

**'Park|gebühr** *f* parking-fee; '͜licht *n* parking light; '͜platz *m* (car-) park, parking lot; '͜uhr *mot. f* parking meter.

**Parlament** [parla'ment] *n* (-[e]s/-e) parliament; ℒarisch *adj.* [͜'taːriʃ] parliamentary.

**Parodie** [paro'diː] *f* (-/-n) parody; ℒren *v/t.* (*no* -ge-, *h*) parody.

**Parole** [pa'roːlə] *f* (-/-n) ⚔ password, watchword; *fig.* slogan.

**Partei** [par'taɪ] *f* (-/-en) party (*a. pol.*); *j-s* ͜ ergreifen take s.o.'s part, side with s.o.; ͜apparat *pol. m* party machinery; ͜gänger [͜gɛŋər] *m* (-s/-) partisan; ℒisch *adj.*, ℒlich *adj.* partial (*für* to); prejudiced (*gegen* against); ͜los *pol. adj.* independent; ͜mitglied *pol. n* party member; ͜programm *pol. n* platform; ͜tag *pol. m* convention; ͜zugehörigkeit *pol. f* party membership.

**Parterre** [par'tɛr] *n* (-s/-s) ground floor, *Am.* first floor; *thea.:* pit, *Am.* parterre, *Am.* parquet circle.

**Partie** [par'tiː] *f* (-/-n) † parcel, lot; outing, excursion; *cards, etc.:* game; ♪ part; *marriage:* match.

**Partitur** ♪ [parti'tuːr] *f* (-/-en) score.

**Partizip** *gr.* [parti'tsiːp] *n* (-s/-ien) participle.

**Partner** ['partnər] *m* (-s/-), '͜in *f* (-/-nen) partner; *film:* a. co-star; '͜schaft *f* (-/-en) partnership.

**Parzelle** [par'tsɛlə] *f* (-/-n) plot, lot, allotment.

**Paß** [pas] *m* (Passes/Pässe) pass; passage; *football, etc.:* pass; passport.

**Passage** [pa'saːʒə] *f* (-/-n) passage; arcade.

**Passagier** [pasa'ʒiːr] *m* (-s/-e) passenger, *in taxis:* a. fare; ͜flugzeug *n* air liner.

**Passah** ['pasa] *n* (-s/*no pl.*), '͜fest *n* Passover.

**Passant** [pa'sant] *m* (-en/-en), ͜in *f* (-/-nen) passer-by.

**'Paßbild** *n* passport photo(graph).

**passen** ['pasən] (ge-, *h*) **1.** *v/i.* fit (*j-m s.o.;* auf acc. *or* für *or* zu et. s.th.); suit (*j-m s.o.*), be convenient; *cards, football:* pass; ͜ zu go with, match (with); **2.** *v/refl.* be fit *or* proper; '͜d *adj.* fit, suitable; convenient (*für* for).

**passier|bar** *adj.* [pa'siːrbaːr] passable, practicable; ͜en (*no* -ge-) **1.** *v/i.* (*sein*) happen; **2.** *v/t.* (*h*) pass (over *or* through); ℒschein *m* pass, permit.

**Passion** [pa'sjoːn] *f* (-/-en) passion; hobby; *eccl.* Passion.

**passiv** ['pasiːf] **1.** *adj.* passive; **2.** ℒ *gr. n* (-s/͜-e) passive (voice); ℒa † [pa'siːva] *f.* liabilities *pl.*

**Paste** ['pastə] *f* (-/-n) paste.

**Pastell** [pa'stɛl] *n* (-[e]s/-e) pastel.

**Pastete** [pa'steːtə] *f* (-/-n) pie; ͜bäcker *m* pastry-cook.

**Pate** ['paːtə] **1.** *m* (-n/-n) godfather; godchild; **2.** *f* (-/-n) godmother; '͜nkind *n* godchild; '͜nschaft *f* (-/-nen) sponsorship.

**Patent** [pa'tent] *n* (-[e]s/-e) patent; ⚔ commission; *ein* ͜ anmelden apply for a patent; ͜amt *n* Patent Office; ͜anwalt *m* patent agent; ℒieren [͜'tiːrən] *v/t.* (*no* -ge-, *h*) patent; et. ͜ lassen take out a patent for s.th.; ͜inhaber *m* patentee; ͜urkunde *f* letters patent.

**Patient** [pa'tsjent] *m* (-en/-en), ͜in *f* (-/-nen) patient.

**Patin** ['paːtin] *f* (-/-nen) godmother.

**Patriot** [patri'oːt] *m* (-en/-en), ͜in *f* (-/-nen) patriot.

**Patron** [pa'troːn] *m* (-s/-e) patron, protector; *contp.* fellow, bloke, customer; ͜at [͜o'naːt] *n* (-[e]s/-e) patronage; ͜e [pa'troːnə] *f* (-/-n) cartridge, *Am. a.* shell.

**Patrouill|e** ⚔ [pa'truljə] *f* (-/-n) patrol; ℒieren ⚔ [͜'jiːrən] *v/i.* (*no* -ge-, *h*) patrol.

**Patsch|e** F *fig.* ['patʃə] *f* (-/*no pl.*): *in der* ͜ *sitzen* be in a fix *or* scrape; 'ℒen F (ge-) **1.** *v/i.* (*h, sein*) splash; **2.** *v/t.* (*h*) slap; 'ℒnaß *adj.* dripping wet, drenched.

**patzig** F *adj.* ['patsiç] snappish.

**Pauke** ♪ ['paukə] *f* (-/-n) ♪ kettledrum; 'ℒn F *v/i. and v/t.* (ge-, *h*) *school:* cram.

**Pauschal|e** [pau'ʃaːlə] *f* (-/-n), ͜summe *f* lump sum.

**Pause** ['pauzə] f (-/-n) pause, stop, interval; *school:* break, *Am.* recess; *thea.* interval, *Am.* intermission; ♪ rest; *drawing:* tracing; '~n v/t. (ge-, h) trace; '~nlos *adj.* uninterrupted, incessant; '~nzeichen n *wireless:* interval signal.

**pau'sieren** v/i. (*no* -ge-, h) pause.

**Pavian** zo. ['pa:via:n] m (-s/-e) baboon.

**Pavillon** ['paviljõ] m (-s/-s) pavilion.

**Pazifist** [patsi'fist] m (-en/-en) pacif(ic)ist.

**Pech** [pɛç] n 1. (-[e]s /-e) pitch; 2. F *fig.* (-[e]s/no pl.) bad luck; '~strähne F f run of bad luck; '~vogel F m unlucky fellow.

**pedantisch** *adj.* [pe'dantiʃ] pedantic; punctilious, meticulous.

**Pegel** ['pe:gəl] m (-s/-) water-ga(u)ge.

**peilen** ['pailən] v/t. (ge-, h) sound (*depth*); take the bearings of (*coast*).

**Pein** [pain] f (-/no pl.) torment, torture, anguish; **2igen** ['~igən] v/t. (ge-, h) torment; ~iger ['~igər] m (-s/-) tormentor.

**'peinlich** *adj.* painful, embarrassing; particular, scrupulous, meticulous.

**Peitsche** ['paitʃə] f (-/-n) whip; '2n v/t. (ge-, h) whip; '~nhieb m lash.

**Pelikan** orn. ['pe:lika:n] m (-s/-e) pelican.

**Pell|e** ['pɛlə] f (-/-n) skin, peel; '2en v/t. (ge-, h) skin, peel; '~kartoffeln f/pl. potatoes pl. (boiled) in their jackets or skins.

**Pelz** [pɛlts] m (-es/-e) fur; *garment:* mst furs pl.; '2gefüttert *adj.* fur-lined; '~händler m furrier; '~handschuh m furred glove; '2ig *adj.* furry; ♪ *tongue:* furred; '~mantel m fur coat; '~stiefel m fur-lined boot; '~tiere n/pl. fur-covered animals pl.

**Pendel** ['pɛndəl] n (-s/-) pendulum; '2n v/i. (ge-, h) oscillate, swing; ♪ shuttle, *Am.* commute; '~tür f swing-door; '~verkehr ⚅ m shuttle service.

**Pension** [pã'sjõ:, pɛn'zjo:n] f (-/-en) (old-age) pension, retired pay; board; boarding-house; ~är [~o'nɛ:r] m (-s/-e) (old-age) pensioner; boarder; ~at [~o'na:t] n (-[e]s/-e) boarding-school; 2ieren [~o'ni:rən] v/t. (*no* -ge-, h) pension (off); sich ~ lassen retire; ~sgast m boarder.

**Pensum** ['pɛnzum] n (-s/Pensen, Pensa) task, lesson.

**perfekt** 1. *adj.* [pɛr'fɛkt] perfect; *agreement:* settled; 2. 2 *gr.* ['~] n (-[e]s/-e) perfect (tense).

**Pergament** [pɛrga'mɛnt] n (-[e]s/-e) parchment.

**Period|e** [per'jo:də] f (-/-n) period; ♪ periods pl.; 2isch *adj.* periodic (-al).

**Peripherie** [perife'ri:] f (-/-n)

circumference; outskirts pl. (*of town*).

**Perle** ['pɛrlə] f (-/-n) pearl; *of glass:* bead; '2n v/i. (ge-, h) sparkle; '~nkette f pearl necklace; '~nschnur f string of pearls or beads.

**'Perl|muschel** zo. f pearl-oyster; ~mutt ['~mut] n (-s/no pl.), ~'mutter f (-/no pl.) mother-of-pearl.

**Person** [pɛr'zo:n] f (-/-en) person; *thea.* character.

**Personal** [pɛrzo'na:l] n (-s/no pl.) staff, personnel; ~abteilung f personnel office; ~angaben f/pl. personal data pl.; ~ausweis m identity card; ~chef m personnel officer or manager or director; ~ien [~jən] pl. particulars pl., personal data pl.; ~pronomen gr. n personal pronoun.

**Per'sonen|verzeichnis** n list of persons; *thea.* dramatis personae pl.; ~wagen m ⚅ (passenger-)carriage or *Am.* car, coach; *mot.* (motor-)car; ~zug ⚅ m passenger train.

**personifizieren** [pɛrzonifi'tsi:rən] v/t. (*no* -ge-, h) personify.

**persönlich** *adj.* [pɛr'zø:nliç] personal; *opinion, letter:* a. private; 2keit f (-/-en) personality; personage.

**Perücke** [pe'rykə] f (-/-n) wig.

**Pest** ♪ [pɛst] f (-/no pl.) plague.

**Petersilie** ♀ [petər'zi:ljə] f (-/-n) parsley.

**Petroleum** [pe'tro:leum] n (-s/no pl.) petroleum; *for lighting, etc.:* paraffin, *esp. Am.* kerosene.

**Pfad** [pfa:t] m (-[e]s/-e) path, track; '~finder m boy scout; '~finderin f (-/-nen) girl guide, *Am.* girl scout.

**Pfahl** [pfa:l] m (-[e]s/=e) stake, pale, pile.

**Pfand** [pfant] n (-[e]s/=er) pledge; ✝ deposit, security; *real estate:* mortgage; *game:* forfeit; '~brief ✝ m debenture (bond).

**pfänden** ♪ ['pfɛndən] v/t. (ge-, h) seize s.th.; distrain upon s.o. or s.th.

**'Pfand|haus** n s. Leihhaus; '~leiher m (-s/-) pawnbroker; '~schein m pawn-ticket.

**'Pfändung** ♪ f (-/-en) seizure; distraint.

**Pfann|e** ['pfanə] f (-/-n) pan; '~kuchen m pancake.

**Pfarr|bezirk** ['pfar-] m parish; '~er m (-s/-) parson; *Church of England:* rector, vicar; *dissenters:* minister; '~gemeinde f parish; '~haus n parsonage; *Church of England:* rectory, vicarage; '~kirche f parish church; '~stelle f (church) living.

**Pfau** orn. [pfau] m (-[e]s/-en) peacock.

**Pfeffer** ['pfɛfər] m (-s/-) pepper; '~gurke f gherkin; '2ig *adj.* peppery; '~kuchen m gingerbread;

**~minze** ⚔ ['~mintsə] f (-/no pl.)
peppermint; '**~minzplätzchen** n
peppermint; '**2n** v/t. (ge-, h) pepper; '**~streuer** m (-s/-) pepperbox,
pepper-castor, pepper-caster.

**Pfeife** ['pfaɪfə] f (-/-n) whistle; ⚔
fife; pipe (of organ, etc.); (tobacco-)
pipe; '**2n** (irr., ge-, h) 1. v/i. whistle
(dat. to, for); radio: howl; pipe;
2. v/t. whistle; pipe; '**~nkopf** m
pipe-bowl.

**Pfeil** [pfaɪl] m (-[e]s/-e) arrow.

**Pfeiler** ['pfaɪlər] m (-s/-) pillar (a.
fig.); pier (of bridge, etc.).

'**pfeil**|'**schnell** adj. (as) swift as an
arrow; '**2spitze** f arrow-head.

**Pfennig** ['pfɛnɪç] m (-[e]s/-e) coin:
pfennig; fig. penny, farthing.

**Pferch** [pfɛrç] m (-[e]s/-e) fold, pen;
'**2en** v/t. (ge-, h) fold, pen; fig.
cram.

**Pferd** zo. [pfeːrt] n (-[e]s/-e) horse;
zu ~e on horseback.

**Pferde**|**geschirr** ['pfeːrdə-] n har-
ness; '**~koppel** f (-/-n) paddock,
Am. a. corral; '**~rennen** n horse-
race; '**~schwanz** m horse's tail;
hair-style: pony-tail; '**~stall** m
stable; '**~stärke** ⊕ f horsepower.

**pfiff**[1] [pfif] pret. of pfeifen.

**Pfiff**[2] m (-[e]s/-e) whistle; fig. trick;
'**2ig** adj. cunning, artful.

**Pfingst**|**en** eccl. ['pfiŋstn] n (-/-),
'**~fest** eccl. n Whitsun(tide); '**~**
**montag** eccl. m Whit Monday;
'**~rose** ⚔ f peony; '**~sonntag** eccl.
m Whit Sunday.

**Pfirsich** ['pfirzɪç] m (-[e]s/-e) peach.

**Pflanz**|**e** ['pflantsə] f (-/-n) plant;
'**2en** v/t. (ge-, h) plant, set; pot;
'**~enfaser** f vegetable fib[re], Am.
-er; '**~enfett** n vegetable fat; '**2en-**
**fressend** adj. herbivorous; '**~er** m
(-s/-) planter; '**~ung** f (-/-en) plantation.

**Pflaster** ['pflastər] n (-s/-) ⚕ plaster;
road: pavement; '**~er** m (-s/-)
paver, pavio(u)r; '**2n** v/t. (ge-, h) ⚕
plaster; pave (road); '**~stein** m
paving-stone; cobble.

**Pflaume** ['pflaumə] f (-/-n) plum;
dried: prune.

**Pflege** ['pfleːgə] f (-/-n) care; ⚕
nursing; cultivation (of art, garden,
etc.); ⊕ maintenance; in ~ geben
put out (child) to nurse; in ~ nehmen take charge of; '**2bedürftig**
adj. needing care; **~befohlene**
['~bəfoːlənə] m, f (-n/-n) charge;
'**~eltern** pl. foster-parents pl.;
'**~heim** ⚕ n nursing home; '**~kind**
n foster-child; '**2n** (ge-, h) 1. v/t.
take care of; attend (to); foster
(child); ⚕ nurse; maintain; cultivate (art, garden); 2. v/i.: ~ zu inf.
be accustomed or used or wont to
inf., be in the habit of ger.; sie
pflegte zu sagen she used to say;
'**~r** m (-s/-) fosterer; ⚕ male nurse;

trustee; ⚕ guardian, curator; '**~rin**
f (-/-nen) nurse.

**Pflicht** [pflɪçt] f (-/-en) duty (gegen
to); obligation; '**2bewußt** adj.
conscious of one's duty; '**2eifrig**
adj.zealous; '**~erfüllung** f performance of one's duty; '**~fach** n
school, univ.: compulsory subject;
'**~gefühl** n sense of duty; '**2gemäß**
adj. dutiful; '**2getreu** adj. dutiful,
loyal; '**2schuldig** adj. in duty
bound; '**2vergessen** adj. undutiful,
disloyal; '**~verteidiger** ⚕ m as-
signed counsel.

**Pflock** [pflɔk] m (-[e]s/-e) plug, peg.

**pflücken** ['pflʏkən] v/t. (ge-, h)
pick, gather, pluck.

**Pflug** [pfluːk] m (-[e]s/-e) plough,
Am. plow.

**pflügen** ['pflyːgən] v/t. and v/i.
(ge-, h) plough, Am. plow.

**Pforte** ['pfortə] f (-/-n) gate, door.

**Pförtner** ['pfœrtnər] m (-s/-) gate-
keeper, door-keeper, porter, janitor.

**Pfosten** ['pfostən] m (-s/-) post.

**Pfote** ['pfoːtə] f (-/-n) paw.

**Pfropf** [pfrɔpf] m (-[e]s/-e) s.
Pfropfen.

'**Pfropfen 1.** m (-s/-) stopper; cork;
plug; ⚕ clot (of blood); 2. ⚔ v/t.
(ge-, h) stopper; cork; fig. cram; ⚔
graft.

**Pfründe** eccl. ['pfryndə] f (-/-n)
prebend; benefice, (church) living.

**Pfuhl** [pfuːl] m (-[e]s/-e) pool,
puddle; fig. sink, slough.

**pfui** int. [pfui] fie!, for shame!

**Pfund** [pfunt] n (-[e]s/-e) pound;
⚖ F adj. '**~dɪç**] great, Am. swell;
'**2weise** adv. by the pound.

**pfusch**|**en** F ['pfuʃən] (ge-, h) 1. v/i.
bungle; 2. v/t. bungle, botch; **2erei**
F [~'raɪ] f (-/-en) bungle, botch.

**Pfütze** ['pfʏtsə] f (-/-n) puddle, pool.

**Phänomen** [fɛnoˈmeːn] n (-s/-e)
phenomenon; **2al** adj. [~ˈnɑːl]
phenomenal.

**Phantasie** [fantaˈziː] f (-/-n) imagination, fancy, vision; ♪ fantasia;
**2ren** (no -ge-, h) 1. v/i. dream;
ramble; ⚕ be delirious or raving;
♪ improvise; 2. v/t. dream; ♪ improvise.

**Phantast** [fanˈtast] m (-en/-en)
visionary, dreamer; **2isch** adj.
fantastic; F great, terrific.

**Phase** ['fɑːzə] f (-/-n) phase (a. ⚡),
stage.

**Philanthrop** [filanˈtroːp] m (-en/-en)
philanthropist.

**Philolog**|**e** [filoˈloːgə] m (-n/-n),
'**~in** f (-/-nen) philologist; '**~ie** [~o-
ˈgiː] f (-/-n) philology.

**Philosoph** [filoˈzoːf] m (-en/-en)
philosopher; '**~ie** [~oˈfiː] f (-/-n)
philosophy; **2ieren** [~oˈfiːrən] v/i.
(no -ge-, h) philosophize (über acc.
on); **2isch** adj. [~'zoːfiʃ] philosoph-
ical.

**Phlegma** ['flɛgma] n (-s/no pl.) phlegm; 2tisch adj. [,~'ma:tiʃ] phlegmatic.

**phonetisch** adj. [fo'ne:tiʃ] phonetic.

**Phosphor** ♟ ['fɔsfɔr] m (-s/no pl.) phosphorus.

**Photo** F ['fo:to] 1. n (-s/-s) photo; 2. m (-s/-s) = '~apparat m camera.

**Photograph** [foto'gra:f] m (-en/-en) photographer; ~ie [,~a'fi:] f 1. (-/-n) photograph, F: photo, picture; 2. (-/no pl.) as an art: photography; 2ieren [,~a'fi:rən] (no -ge-, h) 1. v/t. photograph; take a picture of; sich ~ lassen have one's photo(graph) taken; 2. v/i. photograph; 2isch adj. [,~'gra:fiʃ] photographic.

**Photo|kopie** f photostat; ~ko'piergerät n photostat; '~zelle f photoelectric cell.

**Phrase** ['fra:zə] f (-/-n) phrase.

**Physik** [fy'zi:k] f (-/no pl.) physics sg.; 2alisch adj. [,~i'ka:liʃ] physical; ~er ['fy:zikər] m (-s/-) physicist.

**physisch** adj. ['fy:ziʃ] physical.

**Pian|ist** [pia'nist] m (-en/-en) pianist; ~o [pi'a:no] n (-s/-s) piano.

**Picke** ⊕ ['pikə] f (-/-n) pick(axe).

**Pickel** ['pikəl] m (-s/-) ⚕ pimple; ⊕ pick(axe); ice-pick; '2ig adj. pimpled, pimply.

**picken** ['pikən] v/i. and v/t. (ge-, h) pick, peck.

**picklig** adj. ['pikliç] s. pickelig.

**Picknick** ['piknik] n (-s/-e, -s) picnic.

**piekfein** F adj. ['pi:k'-] smart, tiptop, slap-up.

**piep(s)en** ['pi:p(s)ən] v/i. (ge-, h) cheep, chirp, peep; squeak.

**Pietät** [pie'tɛ:t] f (-/no pl.) reverence; piety; 2los adj. irreverent; 2voll adj. reverent.

**Pik** [pi:k] 1. m (-s/-e, -s) peak; 2. F m (-s/-e): e-n ~ auf j-n haben bear s.o. a grudge; 3. n (-s/-s) cards: spade(s pl.).

**pikant** adj. [pi'kant] piquant, spicy (both a. fig.); das Pikante the piquancy.

**Pike** ['pi:kə] f (-/-n) pike; von der ~ auf dienen rise from the ranks.

**Pilger** ['pilgər] m (-s/-) pilgrim; '~fahrt f pilgrimage; '2n v/i. (ge-, sein) go on or make a pilgrimage; wander.

**Pille** ['pilə] f (-/-n) pill.

**Pilot** [pi'lo:t] m (-en/-en) pilot.

**Pilz** ⚕ [pilts] m (-es/-e) fungus, edible: mushroom, inedible: toadstool.

**pimp(e)lig** F adj. ['pimp(ə)liç] sickly; effeminate.

**Pinguin** orn. ['piŋgui:n] m (-s/-e) penguin.

**Pinsel** ['pinzəl] m (-s/-) brush; F fig. simpleton; '2n v/t. and v/i. (ge-, h) paint; daub; '~strich m stroke of the brush.

**Pinzette** [pin'tsetə] f (-/-n) (e-e a pair of) tweezers pl.

**Pionier** [pio'ni:r] m (-s/-e) pioneer, Am. a. trail blazer; ✂ engineer.

**Pirat** [pi'ra:t] m (-en/-en) pirate.

**Pirsch** hunt. [pirʃ] f (-/no pl.) deerstalking, Am. a. still hunt.

**Piste** ['pistə] f (-/-n) skiing, etc.: course; ✈ runway.

**Pistole** [pis'to:lə] f (-/-n) pistol, Am. F a. gun, rod; ~ntasche f holster.

**placieren** [pla'si:rən] v/t. (no -ge-, h) place; sich ~ sports: be placed (second, etc.).

**Plackerei** F [plakə'raɪ] f (-/-en) drudgery.

**plädieren** [plɛ'di:rən] v/i. (no -ge-, h) plead (für for).

**Plädoyer** ⚖ [pledoa'je:] n (-s/-s) pleading.

**Plage** ['pla:gə] f (-/-n) trouble, nuisance, F plague; torment; '2n v/t. (ge-, h) torment; trouble, bother; F plague; sich ~ toil, drudge.

**Plagiat** [plag'ja:t] n (-[e]s/-e) plagiarism; ein ~ begehen plagiarize.

**Plakat** [pla'ka:t] n (-[e]s/-e) poster, placard, bill; ~säule f advertisement pillar.

**Plakette** [pla'kɛtə] f (-/-n) plaque.

**Plan** [pla:n] m (-[e]s/ʺe) plan; design, intention; scheme.

**Plane** ['pla:nə] f (-/-n) awning, tilt.

**'planen** v/t. (ge-, h) plan; scheme.

**Planet** [pla'ne:t] m (-en/-en) planet.

**planieren** ⊕ [pla'ni:rən] v/t. (no -ge-, h) level.

**Planke** ['plaŋkə] f (-/-n) plank, board.

**plänkeln** ['plɛŋkəln] v/i. (ge-, h) skirmish (a. fig.).

**'plan|los** 1. adj. planless, aimless, desultory; 2. adv. at random; '~mäßig 1. adj. systematic, planned; 2. adv. as planned.

**planschen** ['planʃən] v/i. (ge-, h) splash, paddle.

**Plantage** [plan'ta:ʒə] f (-/-n) plantation.

**Plapper|maul** F ['plapər-] n chatterbox; '2n F v/i. (ge-, h) chatter, prattle, babble.

**plärren** F ['plɛrən] v/i. and v/t. (ge-, h) blubber; bawl.

**Plasti|k** [plastik] 1. f (-/no pl.) plastic art; 2. f (-/-en) sculpture; ✂ plastic; 3. ⊕ n (-s/-s) plastic; '2sch adj. plastic; three-dimensional.

**Platin** [pla'ti:n] n (-s/no pl.) platinum.

**plätschern** ['plɛtʃərn] v/i. (ge-, h) dabble, splash; water: ripple, murmur.

**platt** adj. [plat] flat, level, even; fig. trivial, commonplace, trite; F fig. flabbergasted.

**Plättbrett** ['plɛt-] n ironing-board.

**Platte** ['platə] *f* (-/-n) plate; dish; sheet (*of metal, etc.*); flag, slab (*of stone*); *mountain:* ledge; top (*of table*); tray, salver; disc, record; F *fig.* bald pate; *kalte* ~ cold meat.

**plätten** ['plɛtən] *v/t.* (ge-, h) iron.

**'Platten|spieler** *m* record-player; **'~teller** *m* turn-table.

**'Platt|form** *f* platform; **'~fuß** *m* ⚕ flat-foot; F *mot.* flat; **'~heit** *fig.* *f* (-/-en) triviality; commonplace, platitude, *Am. sl.* a. bromide.

**Platz** [plats] *m* (-es/⸚e) place; spot, *Am. a.* point; room, space; site; seat; square; *round:* circus; *sports:* ground; *tennis:* court; ~ *behalten* remain seated; ~ *machen* make way or room (*dat.* for); ~ *nehmen* take a seat, sit down, *Am. a.* have a seat; *ist hier noch* ~? is this seat taken or engaged or occupied?; *den dritten* ~ *belegen sports:* be placed third, come in third; **'~anweiserin** *f* (-/-nen) usherette.

**Plätzchen** ['plɛtsçən] *n* (-s/-) snug place; spot; biscuit, *Am.* cookie.

**'platzen** *v/i.* (ge-, sein) burst; explode; crack, split.

**'Platz|patrone** *f* blank cartridge; **'~regen** *m* downpour.

**Plauder|ei** [plaudə'raɪ] *f* (-/-en) chat; talk; small talk; **'2n** *v/i.* (ge-, h) (have a) chat (*mit* with), talk (to); chatter.

**plauz** *int.* [plauts] bang!

**Pleite** F ['plaɪtə] **1.** *f* (-/-n) smash; *fig.* failure; **2.** 2 F *adj.* (dead) broke, *Am. sl.* bust.

**Plissee** [pli'se:] *n* (-s/-s) pleating; **~rock** *m* pleated skirt.

**Plomb|e** ['plɔmbə] *f* (-/-n) (lead) seal; stopping, filling (*of tooth*); **2ieren** [~'bi:rən] *v/t.* (no -ge-, h) seal; stop, fill (*tooth*).

**plötzlich** *adj.* ['plœtslɪç] sudden.

**plump** *adj.* [plump] clumsy; **~s** *int.* plump, plop; **'~sen** *v/i.* (ge-, sein) plump, plop, flop.

**Plunder** F ['plundər] *m* (-s/no pl.) lumber, rubbish, junk.

**plündern** ['plyndərn] (ge-, h) **1.** *v/t.* plunder, pillage, loot, sack; **2.** *v/i.* plunder, loot.

**Plural** *gr.* ['plu:ra:l] *m* (-s/-e) plural (number).

**plus** *adv.* [plus] plus.

**Plusquamperfekt** *gr.* ['pluskvamperfɛkt] *n* (-s/-e) pluperfect (tense), past perfect.

**Pöbel** ['pø:bəl] *m* (-s/no pl.) mob, rabble; **2haft** *adj.* low, vulgar.

**pochen** ['pɔxən] *v/i.* (ge-, h) knock, rap, tap; *heart:* beat, throb, thump; *auf sein Recht* ~ stand on one's rights.

**Pocke** ⚕ ['pɔkə] *f* (-/-n) pock; **~n** ⚕ *pl.* smallpox; **2nnarbig** *adj.* pock-marked.

**Podest** [po'dɛst] *n*, *m* (-es/-e) pedestal (*a. fig.*).

**Podium** ['po:dium] *n* (-s/Podien) podium, platform, stage.

**Poesie** [poe'zi:] *f* (-/-n) poetry.

**Poet** [po'e:t] *m* (-en/-en) poet; **2isch** *adj.* poetic(al).

**Pointe** [po'ɛ̃:tə] *f* (-/-n) point.

**Pokal** [po'ka:l] *m* (-s/-e) goblet; *sports:* cup; **~endspiel** *n sports:* cup final; **~spiel** *n football:* cup-tie.

**Pökel|fleisch** ['pø:kəl-] *n* salted meat; **'2n** *v/t.* (ge-, h) pickle, salt.

**Pol** [po:l] *m* (-s/-e) pole; ⚡ *a.* terminal; **2ar** *adj.* [po'la:r] polar (*a. ⚡*).

**Pole** ['po:lə] *m* (-n/-n) Pole.

**Polemi|k** [po'le:mik] *f* (-/-en) polemic(s *pl.*); **2sch** *adj.* polemic (-al); **2sieren** [~emi'zi:rən] *v/i.* (no -ge-, h) polemize.

**Police** [po'li:s(ə)] *f* (-/-n) policy.

**Polier** ⊕ [po'li:r] *m* (-s/-e) foreman; **2en** *v/t.* (no -ge-, h) polish, burnish; furbish.

**Politi|k** [poli'ti:k] *f* (-/~-en) policy; politics *sg., pl.*; **~ker** [po'li:tikər] *m* (-s/-) politician; statesman; **2sch** *adj.* [po'li:tiʃ] political; **2sieren** [~iti'zi:rən] *v/i.* (no -ge-, h) talk politics.

**Politur** [poli'tu:r] *f* (-/-en) polish; lust|re, *Am.* -er, finish.

**Polizei** [poli'tsaɪ] *f* (-/~-en) police; **~beamte** *m* police officer; **~knüppel** *m* truncheon, *Am.* club; **~kommissar** *m* inspector; **2lich** *adj.* (of or by the) police; *Brt.* **~präsident** *m* president of police, *Am.* Chief Constable, *Am.* Chief of Police; **~präsidium** *n* police headquarters *pl.*; **~revier** *n* police-station; police precinct, *Am.* police guard; **~schutz** *m:* *unter* ~ under police guard; **~streife** *f* police patrol; police squad; **~stunde** *f* (-/no pl.) closing-time; **~verordnung** *f* police regulation(s *pl.*); **~wache** *f* police-station.

**Polizist** [poli'tsist] *m* (-en/-en) policeman, constable, *sl.* bobby, cop; **~in** *f* (-/-nen) policewoman.

**polnisch** *adj.* ['pɔlnɪʃ] Polish.

**Polster** ['pɔlstər] *n* (-s/-) pad; cushion; bolster; *s.* Polsterung; **'~möbel** *n/pl.* upholstered furniture; upholstery; **'2n** *v/t.* (ge-, h) upholster, stuff; pad, wad; **'~sessel** *m*, **'~stuhl** *m* upholstered chair; **'~ung** *f* (-/-en) padding, stuffing; upholstery.

**poltern** ['pɔltərn] *v/i.* (ge-, h) make a row; rumble; *p.* bluster.

**Polytechnikum** [poly'tɛçnikum] *n* (-s/Polytechnika, Polytechniken) polytechnic (school).

**Pommes frites** [pɔm'frit] *pl.* chips *pl.*, *Am.* French fried potatoes *pl.*

**Pomp** [pɔmp] *m* (-[e]s/no pl.) pomp, splendo(u)r; **2haft** *adj.*, **2ös** *adj.* [~'pø:s] pompous, splendid.

**Pony** ['pɔni] 1. *zo. n* (-s/-s) pony;
2. *m* (-s/-s) *hairstyle*: bang, fringe.
**popul|är** *adj.* [popu'lɛ:r] popular;
**Ωarität** [ˌari'tɛ:t] *f* (-/*no pl.*)
popularity.
**Por|e** ['po:rə] *f* (-/-n) pore; **Ωös** *adj.*
[po'rø:s] porous; permeable.
**Portemonnaie** [pɔrtmɔ'nɛ:] *n* (-s/-s)
purse.
**Portier** [pɔr'tje:] *m* (-s/-s) *s.* Pförtner.
**Portion** [pɔr'tsjo:n] *f* (-/-en) portion, share; ✗ ration; helping, serving; *zwei* ⸺*en Kaffee* coffee for two.
**Porto** ['pɔrto] *n* (-s/-s, Porti) postage; **Ωfrei** *adj.* post-free; prepaid,
*esp. Am.* postpaid; **Ωpflichtig** *adj.*
subject to postage.
**Porträt** [pɔr'trɛ:; ⸺t] *n* (-s/-s;
-[e]s/-e) portrait, likeness; **Ωieren**
[ˌɛ'ti:rən] *v/t.* (*no -ge-, h*) portray.
**Portugies|e** [pɔrtu'gi:zə] *m* (-n/-n)
Portuguese; *die* ⸺*n pl.* the Portuguese *pl.*; **Ωisch** *adj.* Portuguese.
**Porzellan** [pɔrtsɛ'la:n] *n* (-s/-e)
porcelain, china.
**Posaune** [po'zaunə] *f* (-/-n) ♩
trombone; *fig.* trumpet.
**Pose** ['po:zə] *f* (-/-n) pose, attitude;
*fig. a.* air.
**Position** [pozi'tsjo:n] *f* (-/-en)
position; social standing; ♣ station.
**positiv** *adj.* ['po:ziti:f] positive.
**Positur** [pozi'tu:r] *f* (-/-en) posture;
*sich in* ⸺ *setzen* strike an attitude.
**Posse** *thea.* ['pɔsə] *f* (-/-n) farce.
**'Possen** *m* (-s/-) trick, prank; **Ωhaft**
*adj.* farcical, comical; **'⸺reißer** *m*
(-s/-) buffoon, clown.
**possessiv** *gr. adj.* ['pɔsesi:f] possessive.
**pos'sierlich** *adj.* droll, funny.
**Post** [pɔst] *f* (-/-en) post, *Am.* mail;
mail, letters *pl.*; post office; *mit
der ersten* ⸺ by the first delivery;
**'⸺amt** *n* post office; **'⸺anschrift** *f*
mailing address; **'⸺anweisung** *f*
postal order; **'⸺beamte** *m* post-
office clerk; **'⸺bote** *m* postman,
*Am.* mailman; **'⸺dampfer** *m*
packet-boat.
**Posten** ['pɔstən] *m* (-s/-) post, place,
station; job; ✗ sentry, sentinel;
item; entry; *goods*: lot, parcel.
**'Postfach** *n* post-office box.
**pos'tieren** *v/t.* (*no -ge-, h*) post,
station, place; *sich* ⸺ station o.s.
**'Post|karte** *f* postcard, *with printed
postage stamp*: *Am. a.* postal card;
**'⸺kutsche** *f* stage-coach; **Ωlagernd**
*adj.* to be (kept until) called for,
poste restante, *Am.* (in care of)
general delivery; **'⸺leitzahl** *f* post-
code; **'⸺minister** *m* minister of
post; *Brt. a.* *Am.* Postmaster
General; **'⸺paket** *n* postal parcel;
**'⸺schalter** *m* (post-office) window;
**'⸺scheck** *m* postal cheque, *Am.*
postal check; **'⸺schließfach** *n*

post-office box; **'⸺sparbuch** *n*
post-office savings-book; **'⸺stem-
pel** *m* postmark; **Ωwendend** *adv.*
by return of post; **'⸺wertzeichen**
*n* (postage) stamp; **'⸺zug** 🚂 *m*
mail-train.
**Pracht** [praxt] *f* (-/✗ -en, ⸻e) splen-
do(u)r, magnificence; luxury.
**prächtig** *adj.* ['prɛçtiç] splendid,
magnificent; gorgeous; grand.
**'prachtvoll** *adj. s.* prächtig.
**Prädikat** [prɛdi'ka:t] *n* (-[e]s/-e) *gr.*
predicate; *school, etc.*: mark.
**prägen** ['prɛ:gən] *v/t.* (ge-, h)
stamp; coin (*word, coin*).
**prahlen** ['pra:lən] *v/i.* (ge-, h) brag,
boast (*mit of*); ⸺ *with* show off *s.th.*
**'Prahler** *m* (-s/-) boaster, braggart;
**⸺ei** [ˌ'rai] *f* (-/-en) boasting,
bragging; **Ωisch** *adj.* boastful;
ostentatious.
**Prakti|kant** [prakti'kant] *m* (-en/-en)
probationer; **'⸺ker** *m* (-s/-) practical man; expert; **⸺kum** ['⸺kum] *n*
(-s/Praktika, Praktiken) practical
course; **Ωsch** *adj.* practical; useful,
handy; **⸺er Arzt** general practitioner;
**Ωzieren** ✗, ⚕ [ˌ'tsi:rən] *v/i.* (*no
-ge-, h*) practi|se, *Am.* -ce medicine
or the law. [prelate.]
**Prälat** *eccl.* [prɛ'la:t] *m* (-en/-en)
**Praline** [pra'li:nə] *f* (-/-n): ⸺*n pl.*
chocolates *pl.*
**prall** *adj.* [pral] tight; plump; *sun*:
blazing; **'⸺en** *v/i.* (ge-, h) bounce
*or* bound (*auf acc., gegen* against).
**Prämi|e** ['prɛ:mjə] *f* (-/-n) ✦
premium; prize; bonus; **Ω(i)eren**
[prɛ'mi:rən, premi'i:rən] *v/t.* (*no
-ge-, h*) award a prize to.
**prang|en** ['praŋən] *v/i.* (ge-, h)
shine, make a show; **Ωer** *m* (-s/-)
pillory.
**Pranke** ['praŋkə] *f* (-/-n) paw.
**pränumerando** *adv.* [prɛ:numə-
'rando] beforehand, in advance.
**Präpa|rat** [prepa'ra:t] *n* (-[e]s/-e)
preparation; *microscopy*: slide;
**Ω'rieren** *v/t.* (*no -ge-, h*) prepare.
**Präposition** *gr.* [prɛpozi'tsjo:n] *f*
(-/-en) preposition.
**Prärie** [prɛ'ri:] *f* (-/-n) prairie.
**Präsens** *gr.* ['prɛ:zɛns] *n* (-/Präsen-
tia, Präsenzien) present (tense).
**Präsi|dent** [prɛzi'dɛnt] *m* (-en/-en)
president; chairman; **Ω'dieren** *v/i.*
(*no -ge-, h*) preside (*über acc.* over);
be in the chair; **⸺dium** [ˌ'zi:djum]
*n* (-s/Präsidien) presidency, chair.
**prasseln** ['prasəln] *v/i.* (ge-, h)
*fire*: crackle; *rain*: patter.
**prassen** ['prasən] *v/i.* (ge-, h) feast,
carouse.
**Präteritum** *gr.* [prɛ'te:ritum] *n*
(-s/Präterita) preterite (tense); past
tense.
**Praxis** ['praksis] *f* 1. (-/*no pl.*)
practice; 2. (-/Praxen) practice (*of
doctor or lawyer*).

**Präzedenzfall** [prɛtse'dɛnts-] *m* precedent; ꝗ *a.* case-law.

**präzis** *adj.* [prɛ'tsiːs], ~e *adj.* [~zə] precise.

**predig|en** ['preːdigən] *v/i. and v/t.* (ge-, h) preach; '2er *m* (-s/-) preacher; clergyman; 2t ['~diçt] *f* (-/-en) sermon (*a. fig.*); *fig.* lecture.

**Preis** [praɪs] *m* (-es/-e) price; cost; *competition*: prize; award; reward; praise; *um jeden* ~ at any price *or* cost; '~ausschreiben *n* (-s/-) competition.

**preisen** ['praɪzən] *v/t.* (irr., ge-, h) praise.

'**Preis|erhöhung** *f* rise *or* increase in price(s); '~gabe *f* abandonment; revelation (*of secret*); '2geben *v/t.* (*irr. geben, sep.*, -ge-, h) abandon; reveal, give away (*secret*); disclose, expose; '2gekrönt *adj.* prize-winning, prize (*novel, etc.*); '~gericht *n* jury; '~lage *f* range of prices; '~liste *f* price-list; '~nachlaß *m* price cut; discount; '~richter *m* judge, umpire; '~schießen *n* (-s/-) shooting competition; '~stopp *m* (-s/*no pl.*) price freeze; '~träger *m* prize-winner; '2wert *adj.*: ~ *sein* be a bargain.

**prell|en** ['prɛlən] *v/t.* (ge-, h) *fig.* cheat, defraud (*um of*); *sich et.* ~ ⚕ contuse *or* bruise s.th.; '2ung ⚕ *f* (-/-en) contusion.

**Premier|e** *thea.* [prəm'jɛːrə] *f* (-/-n) première, first night; ~minister [~'je:-] *m* prime minister.

**Presse** ['prɛsə] *f* 1. (-/-n) ⊕, *typ.* press; squeezer; 2. (-/*no pl.*) newspapers generally: the press; '~amt *n* public relations office; '~freiheit *f* freedom of the press; '~meldung *f* news item; '2n *v/t.* (ge-, h) press; squeeze; '~photograph *m* press-photographer; '~vertreter *m* reporter; public relations officer.

**Preßluft** ['prɛs-] *f* (-/*no pl.*) compressed air.

**Prestige** [prɛs'tiːʒə] *n* (-s/*no pl.*) prestige; ~ *verlieren a.* lose face.

**Preuß|e** ['prɔʏsə] *m* (-n/-n) Prussian; '2isch *adj.* Prussian.

**prickeln** ['prɪkəln] *v/i.* (ge-, h) prick(le), tickle; itch; *fingers*: tingle.

**Priem** [priːm] *m* (-[e]s/-e) quid.

**pries** [priːs] *pret. of* preisen.

**Priester** ['priːstər] *m* (-s/-) priest; '~in *f* (-/-nen) priestess; '2lich *adj.* priestly, sacerdotal; '~rock *m* cassock.

**prim|a** F *adj.* ['priːma] first-rate, F A 1; ✝ *a.* prime; F swell; ~är *adj.* [pri'mɛːr] primary.

**Primel** ✿ ['priːməl] *f* (-/-n) primrose.

**Prinz** [prɪnts] *m* (-en/-en) prince; ~essin [~'tsesin] *f* (-/-nen) princess; '~gemahl *m* prince consort.

**Prinzip** [prɪn'tsiːp] *n* (-s/-ien) principle; *aus* ~ on principle; *im* ~ in principle, basically.

**Priorität** [priori'tɛːt] *f* 1. (-/-en) priority; 2. (-/*no pl.*) *time*: priority.

**Prise** ['priːzə] *f* (-/-n) ⚓ prize; e-e ~ a pinch of (*salt, snuff*).

**Prisma** ['prɪsma] *n* (-s/Prismen) prism.

**Pritsche** ['prɪtʃə] *f* (-/-n) bat; plank-bed.

**privat** *adj.* [pri'vaːt] private; 2adresse *f* home address; 2mann *m* (-[e]s/Privatmänner, Privatleute) private person *or* gentleman; 2patient ⚕ *m* paying patient; 2person *f* private person; 2schule *f* private school.

**Privileg** [privi'leːk] *n* (-[e]s/-ien, -e) privilege.

**pro** *prp.* [proː] per; ~ *Jahr* per annum; ~ *Kopf* per head; ~ *Stück* a piece.

**Probe** ['proːbə] *f* (-/-n) experiment; trial, test; *metall.* assay; sample; specimen; proof; probation; check; *thea.* rehearsal; audition; *auf* ~ on probation, on trial; *auf die* ~ *stellen* (put to the) test; '~abzug *typ.*, *phot. m* proof; '~exemplar *n* specimen copy; '~fahrt *f* ⚓ trial trip; *mot.* trial run; '~flug *m* test *or* trial flight; '2n *v/t.* (ge-, h) exercise; *thea.* rehearse; '~nummer *f* specimen copy *or* number; '~seite *typ. f* specimen page; '~sendung *f* goods on approval; '2weise *adv.* on trial; *p. a.* on probation; '~zeit *f* time of probation.

**probieren** [pro'biːrən] *v/t.* (*no* -ge-, h) try, test; taste (*food.*)

**Problem** [pro'bleːm] *n* (-s/-e) problem; 2atisch *adj.* [~e'maːtiʃ] problematic(al).

**Produkt** [pro'dukt] *n* (-[e]s/-e) product (*a, Ⓐ*); ✸ produce; result; ~ion [~'tsjoːn] *f* (-/-en) production; output; 2iv *adj.* [~'tiːf] productive.

**Produz|ent** [produ'tsɛnt] *m* (-en/ -en) producer; 2ieren [~'tsiːrən] *v/t.* (*no* -ge-, h) produce; *sich* ~ perform; *contp.* show off.

**professionell** *adj.* [profesio'nɛl] professional, by trade.

**Profess|or** [pro'fɛsɔr] *m* (-s/-en) professor; ~ur [~'suːr] *f* (-/-en) professorship, chair.

**Profi** ['proːfi] *m* (-s/-s) *sports*: professional, F pro. [*on tyre*: tread.]

**Profil** [pro'fiːl] *n* (-s/-e) profile;]

**Profit** [pro'fiːt] *m* (-[e]s/-e) profit; 2ieren [~'tiːrən] *v/i.* (*no* -ge-, h) profit (*von* by).

**Prognose** [pro'gnoːzə] *f* (-/-n) ⚕ prognosis; *meteor.* forecast.

**Programm** [pro'gram] *n* (-s/-e) program(me); *politisches* ~ political program(me), *Am.* platform.

**Projektion** [projɛk'tsjoːn] *f* (-/-en) projection; ~sapparat [projɛk-'tsjoːns⁹-] *m* projector.

**proklamieren** [prokla'mi:rən] v/t. (no -ge-, h) proclaim.

**Prokur|a** ✝ [pro'ku:ra] f (-/Prokuren) procuration; **~ist** [~ku'rist] m (-en/-en) confidential clerk.

**Proletari|er** [prole'ta:rjər] m (-s/-) proletarian; **2sch** adj. proletarian.

**Prolog** [pro'lo:k] m (-[e]s/-e) prolog(ue).

**prominen|t** adj. [promi'nent] prominent; **2z** [~ts] f (-/no pl.) notables pl., celebrities pl.; high society.

**Promo|tion** univ. [promo'tsjo:n] f (-/-en) graduation; **2vieren** [~'vi:rən] v/i. (no -ge-, h) graduate (an dat. from), take one's degree.

**Pronomen** gr. [pro'no:mɛn] n (-s/-, Pronomina) pronoun.

**Propeller** [pro'pɛlər] m (-s/-) ⚓, ✈ (screw-)propeller, screw; ✈ airscrew.

**Prophe|t** [pro'fe:t] m (-en/-en) prophet; **2tisch** adj. prophetic; **2zeien** [~e'tsaiən] v/t. (no -ge-, h) prophesy; predict, foretell; **~'zeiung** f (-/-en) prophecy; prediction.

**Proportion** [propɔr'tsjo:n] f (-/-en) proportion.

**Prosa** ['pro:za] f (-/no pl.) prose.

**prosit** int. ['pro:zit] your health!, here's to you!, cheers!

**Prospekt** [pro'spɛkt] m (-[e]s/-e) prospectus; brochure, leaflet, folder.

**prost** int. [pro:st] s. prosit.

**Prostituierte** [prostitu'i:rtə] f (-n/-n) prostitute.

**Protest** [pro'tɛst] m (-es/-e) protest; **~ einlegen** or **erheben gegen** (enter a) protest against.

**Protestant** eccl. [protɛs'tant] m (-en/-en) Protestant; **2isch** adj. Protestant.

**protes'tieren** v/i. (no -ge-, h): **gegen et. ~** protest against s.th., object to s.th.

**Prothese** ⚕ [pro'te:zə] f (-/-n) pro(s)thesis; dentistry: a. denture; artificial limb.

**Protokoll** [proto'kɔl] n (-s/-e) record, minutes pl. (of meeting); diplomacy: protocol; das **~ aufnehmen** take down the minutes; das **~ führen** keep the minutes; zu **~ geben** ⚖ depose, state in evidence; zu **~ nehmen** take down, record; **2ieren** [~'li:rən] (no -ge-, h) 1. v/t. record, take down (on record); 2. v/i. keep the minutes.

**Protz** contp. [prɔts] m (-en, -es/ -e[n]) braggart, F show-off; **'2en** v/i. (ge-, h) show off (mit dat. with); **'2ig** adj. ostentatious, showy.

**Proviant** [pro'vjant] m (-s/⚓ -e) provisions pl., victuals pl.

**Provinz** [pro'vints] f (-/-en) province; fig. the provinces pl.; **2ial** adj. [~'tsja:l], **2iell** adj. [~'tsjɛl] provincial.

**Provis|ion** ✝ [provi'zjo:n] f (-/-en) commission; **2orisch** adj. [~'zo:riʃ] provisional, temporary.

**provozieren** [provo'tsi:rən] v/t. (no -ge-, h) provoke.

**Prozent** [pro'tsɛnt] n (-[e]s/-e) per cent; **~satz** m percentage; proportion; **2ual** adj. [~u'a:l] percental; **~er Anteil** percentage.

**Prozeß** [pro'tsɛs] m (Prozesses/Prozesse) process; ⚖: action, lawsuit; trial; (legal) proceedings pl.; e-n **~ gewinnen** win one's case; e-n **~ gegen j-n anstrengen** bring an action against s.o., sue s.o.; j-m den **~ machen** try s.o., put s.o. on trial; **kurzen ~ machen** mit make short work of.

**prozessieren** [protsɛ'si:rən] v/i. (no -ge-, h): mit j-m **~** go to law against s.o., have the law of s.o.

**Prozession** [protsɛ'sjo:n] f (-/-en) procession.

**prüde** adj. ['pry:də] prudish.

**prüf|en** ['pry:fən] v/t. (ge-, h) examine; try, test; quiz; check, verify; **'~end** adj. look: searching, scrutinizing; **'2er** m (-s/-) examiner; **'2ling** m (-s/-e) examinee; **'2stein** fig. m touchstone; **'2ung** f (-/-en) examination; school, etc.: a. F exam; test; quiz; verification, checking, check-up; e-e **~ machen** go in for or sit for or take an examination.

**'Prüfungs|arbeit** f, **'~aufgabe** f examination-paper; **'~ausschuß** m, **'~kommission** f board of examiners.

**Prügel** ['pry:gəl] 1. m (-s/-) cudgel, club, stick; 2. f fig. pl. beating, thrashing; **~ei** f [~'lai] f (-/-en) fight, row; **'~knabe** m scapegoat; **'2n** F v/t. (ge-, h) cudgel, flog; beat (up), thrash; sich **~** (have a) fight.

**Prunk** [pruŋk] m (-[e]s/no pl.) splendo(u)r; pomp, show; **'2en** v/i. (ge-, h) make a show (mit of), show off (mit et. s.th.); **'2voll** adj. splendid, gorgeous.

**Psalm** eccl. [psalm] m (-s/-en) psalm.

**Pseudonym** [psɔydo'ny:m] n (-s/-e) pseudonym.

**pst** int. [pst] hush!

**Psychi|ater** [psyçi'a:tər] m (-s/-) psychiatrist, alienist; **2sch** adj. ['psy:çiʃ] psychic(al).

**Psycho|analyse** [psyço°ana'ly:zə] f (-/no pl.) psychoanalysis; **~analytiker** [~tikər] m (-s/-) psychoanalist; **~loge** [~'lo:gə] m (-n/-n) psychologist; **~se** [~'ço:zə] f (-/-n) psychosis; panic.

**Pubertät** [puber'tɛ:t] f (-/no pl.) puberty.

**Publikum** ['pu:blikum] n (-s/no pl.) the public; audience; spectators pl., crowd; readers pl.

**publiz|ieren** [publi'tsi:rən] v/t. (no

-ge-, h) publish; **2ist** m (-en/-en) publicist; journalist.

**Pudding** ['pudiŋ] m (-s/-e, -s) cream.

**Pudel** zo. ['pu:dəl] m (-s/-) poodle; **'2'naß** F adj. dripping wet, drenched.

**Puder** ['pu:dər] m (-s/-) powder; **'~dose** f powder-box; compact; **'2n** v/t. (ge-, h) powder; sich ~ powder o.s. or one's face; **'~quaste** f powder-puff; **'~zucker** m powdered sugar.

**Puff** F [puf] m (-[e]s/~e, -e) poke, nudge; **'2en** (ge-, h) 1. F v/t. nudge; 2. v/i. pop; **'~er** ⚙ m (-s/-) buffer.

**Pullover** [pu'lo:vər] m (-s/-) pull-over, sweater.

**Puls** ⚙ [puls] m (-es/-e) pulse; **'~ader** anat. f artery; **2ieren** [~'zi:-rən] v/i. (no -ge-, h) pulsate, throb; **'~schlag** ⚙ m pulsation.

**Pult** [pult] n (-[e]s/-e) desk.

**Pulv|er** ['pulfər] n (-s/-) powder; gunpowder; F fig. cash, sl. brass, dough; **'2erig** adj. powdery; **2eri-sieren** [~vəri'zi:rən] v/t. (no -ge-, h) pulverize; **2rig** adj. ['~friç] powdery.

**Pump** F [pump] m (-[e]s/-e): auf ~ on tick; **'~e** f (-/-n) pump; **'2en** (ge-, h) 1. v/i. pump; 2. v/t. pump; F fig.: give s.th. on tick; borrow (et. von j-m s.th. from s.o.).

**Punkt** [puŋkt] m (-[e]s/-e) point (a. fig.); dot; typ., gr. full stop, period; spot, place; fig. item; article, clause (of agreement); der springende ~ the point; toter ~ deadlock, dead end; wunder ~ tender subject, sore point; ~ zehn Uhr on the stroke of ten, at 10 (o'clock) sharp; in vielen ~en on many points, in many respects; nach ~en siegen sports: win on points; **2ieren** [~'ti:rən] v/t. (no -ge-, h) dot, point; ⚙ puncture, tap; drawing, painting: stipple.

**pünktlich** adj. ['pyŋktliç] punctual; ~ sein be on time; **'2keit** f (-/no pl.) punctuality.

**Punsch** [punʃ] m (-es/-e) punch.

**Pupille** anat. [pu'pilə] f (-/-n) pupil.

**Puppe** ['pupə] f (-/-n) doll (a. fig.); puppet (a. fig.); tailoring: dummy; zo. chrysalis, pupa; **'~nspiel** n puppet-show; **'~nstube** f doll's room; **'~nwagen** m doll's pram, Am. doll carriage or buggy.

**pur** adj. [pu:r] pure, sheer.

**Püree** [py're:] n (-s/-s) purée, mash.

**Purpur** ['purpur] m (-s/no pl.) purple; **'2farben** adj., **'2n** adj., **'2rot** adj. purple.

**Purzel|baum** ['purtsəl-] m somersault; e-n ~ schlagen turn a somersault; **'2n** v/i. (ge-, sein) tumble.

**Puste** F ['pu:stə] f (-/no pl.) breath; ihm ging die ~ aus he got out of breath.

**Pustel** ⚙ ['pustəl] f (-/-n) pustule, pimple.

**pusten** ['pu:stən] v/i. (ge-, h) puff, pant; blow.

**Pute** orn. ['pu:tə] f (-/-n) turkey (-hen); **'~r** orn. m (-s/-) turkey (-cock); **'2r'rot** adj. (as) red as a turkey-cock.

**Putsch** [putʃ] m (-es/-e) putsch, insurrection; riot; **'2en** v/i. (ge-, h) revolt, riot.

**Putz** [puts] m (-es/-e) on garments: finery; ornaments pl.; trimming; △ roughcast, plaster; **'2en** v/t. (ge-, h) clean, cleanse; polish, wipe; adorn; snuff (candle); polish, Am. shine (shoes); sich ~ smarten or dress o.s. up; sich die Nase ~ blow or wipe one's nose; sich die Zähne ~ brush one's teeth; **'~frau** f char-woman, Am. a. scrubwoman; **'2ig** adj. droll, funny; **'~lappen** m cleaning rag; **'~zeug** n cleaning utensils pl.

**Pyjama** [pi'dʒa:ma] m (-s/-s) (ein a suit of) pyjamas pl. or Am. a. pajamas pl.

**Pyramide** [pyra'mi:də] f (-/-n) pyramid (a. Å); ✕ stack (of rifles); **2nförmig** adj. [~nfœrmiç] pyramidal.

# Q

**Quacksalber** ['kvakzalbər] m (-s/-) quack (doctor); **~ei** F [~'rai] f (-/-en) quackery; **'2n** v/i. (ge-, h) (play the) quack.

**Quadrat** [kva'dra:t] n (-[e]s/-e) square; 2 Fuß im ~ 2 feet square; ins ~ erheben square; **2isch** adj. square; Å equation: quadratic; **~meile** f square mile; **~meter** n, m square met|re, Am. -er; **~wurzel** Å f square root; **~zahl** Å f square number.

**quaken** ['kva:kən] v/i. (ge-, h) duck: quack; frog: croak.

**quäken** ['kvɛ:kən] v/i. (ge-, h) squeak.

**Quäker** ['kvɛ:kər] m (-s/-) Quaker, member of the Society of Friends.

**Qual** [kva:l] f (-/-en) pain; torment; agony.

**quälen** ['kvɛ:lən] v/t. (ge-, h) torment (a. fig.); torture; agonize; fig. bother, pester; sich ~ toil, drudge.

**Qualifikation** [kvalifika'tsjo:n] f (-/-en) qualification.

**qualifizieren** [kvalifi'tsi:rən] v/t. and v/refl. (no -ge-, h) qualify (zu for).

**Qualit|ät** [kvali'tɛ:t] f (-/-en) quality; **ℒativ** [ˌa'ti:f] 1. adj. qualitative; 2. adv. as to quality.

**Quali'täts|arbeit** f work of high quality; **̱stahl** m high-grade steel; **̱ware** f high-grade or quality goods pl.

**Qualm** [kvalm] m (-[e]s/no pl.) dense smoke; fumes pl.; vapo(u)r, steam; **ℒen** (ge-, h) 1. v/i. smoke, give out vapo(u)r or fumes; F p. smoke heavily; 2. F v/t. puff (away) at (cigar, pipe, etc.); **ℒig** adj. smoky.

**'qualvoll** adj. very painful; pain: excruciating; fig. agonizing, harrowing.

**Quantit|ät** [kvanti'tɛ:t] f (-/-en) quantity; **ℒativ** [ˌa'ti:f] 1. adj. quantitative; 2. adv. as to quantity.

**Quantum** ['kvantum] n (-s/Quanten) quantity, amount; quantum (a. phys.).

**Quarantäne** [karan'tɛ:nə] f (-/-n) quarantine; in ~ legen (put in) quarantine. [(curd(s pl.).)]

**Quark** [kvark] m (-[e]s/no pl.)]

**Quartal** [kvar'ta:l] n (-s/-e) quarter (of a year); univ. term.

**Quartett** [kvar'tɛt] n (-[e]s/-e) quartet(te); cards: four.

**Quartier** [kvar'ti:r] n (-s/-e) accommodation; ✗ quarters pl., billet.

**Quaste** ['kvastə] f (-/-n) tassel; (powder-)puff.

**Quatsch** F [kvatʃ] m (-es/no pl.) nonsense, fudge, sl. bosh, rot, Am. sl. a. baloney; **ℒen** F v/i. (ge-, h) twaddle, blether, sl. talk rot; (have a) chat; **̱kopf** F m twaddler.

**Quecksilber** ['kvɛk-] n mercury, quicksilver.

**Quelle** ['kvelə] f (-/-n) spring, source (a. fig.); oil: well; fig. fountain, origin; **ℒn** v/i. (irr., ge-, sein) gush, well; **̱nangabe** ['kvelənˀ-] f

mention of sources used; **'̱n-forschung** f original research.

**Quengel|ei** F [kvɛŋə'laɪ] f (-/-en) grumbling, whining; nagging; **'ℒn** F v/i. (ge-, h) grumble, whine; nag.

**quer** adv. [kve:r] crossways, crosswise; F fig. wrong; F ~ gehen go wrong; ~ über (acc.) across.

**'Quer|e** f (-/no pl.): der ~ nach crossways, crosswise; F j-m in die ~ kommen cross s.o.'s path; fig. thwart s.o.'s plans; **'̱frage** f cross-question; **'̱kopf** fig. m wrong-headed fellow; **'ℒschießen** F v/i. (irr. schießen, sep., -ge-, h) try to foil s.o.'s plans; **'̱schiff** ⚠ n transept; **'̱schläger** ✗ m ricochet; **'̱schnitt** m cross-section (a. fig.); **'̱straße** f cross-road; zweite ~ rechts second turning to the right; **'̱treiber** m (-s/-) schemer; **̱trei-be'rei** f (-/-en) intriguing, machination.

**Querulant** [kveru'lant] m (-en/-en) querulous person, grumbler, Am. sl. a. griper.

**quetsch|en** ['kvetʃən] v/t. (ge-, h) squeeze; ✗ bruise, contuse; sich den Finger ~ jam one's finger; **'ℒung** ✗ f (-/-en), **'ℒwunde** ✗ f bruise, contusion.

**quick** adj. [kvik] lively, brisk.

**quieken** ['kvi:kən] v/i. (ge-, h) squeak, squeal.

**quietsch|en** ['kvi:tʃən] v/i. (ge-, h) squeak, squeal; door-hinge, etc.: creak, squeak; brakes, etc.: screech; **'̱ver'gnügt** F adj. (as) jolly as a sandboy.

**Quirl** [kvirl] m (-[e]s/-e) twirling-stick; **'ℒen** v/t. (ge-, h) twirl.

**quitt** adj. [kvit]: ~ sein mit j-m be quits or even with s.o.; jetzt sind wir ~ that leaves us even; **̱ieren** [ˌ'ti:rən] v/t. (no -ge-, h) receipt (bill, etc.); quit, abandon (post, etc.); **'ℒung** f (-/-en) receipt; fig. answer; gegen ~ against receipt.

**quoll** [kvɔl] pret. of quellen.

**Quot|e** ['kvo:tə] f (-/-n) quota, share, portion; **̱ient** ⅄ [kvo'tsjɛnt] m (-en/-en) quotient.

# R

**Rabatt** ✝ [ra'bat] m (-[e]s/-e) discount, rebate.

**Rabe** orn. ['ra:bə] m (-n/-n) raven; **'ℒn'schwarz** F adj. raven, jet-black.

**rabiat** adj. [ra'bjɑ:t] rabid, violent.

**Rache** ['raxə] f (-/no pl.) revenge, vengeance; retaliation.

**Rachen** anat. ['raxən] m (-s/-) throat, pharynx; jaws pl.

**rächen** ['rɛçən] v/t. (ge-, h) avenge,

revenge; sich ~ an (dat.) revenge o.s. or be revenged on.

**'Rachen|höhle** anat. f pharynx; **'̱katarrh** ✗ m cold in the throat.

**'rach|gierig** adj., **'̱süchtig** adj. revengeful, vindictive.

**Rad** [ra:t] n (-[e]s/ˈeʳ) wheel; (bi)cycle, F bike; (ein) ~ schlagen peacock: spread its tail; sports: turn cart-wheels; unter die Räder

kommen go to the dogs; '⁓achse f
axle(-tree).

Radar ['rɑːdɑːr, raˈdɑːr] m, n (-s/-s)
radar.

Radau F [raˈdau] m (-s/no pl.) row,
racket, hubbub.

radebrechen ['rɑːdə-] v/t. (ge-, h)
speak (language) badly, murder
(language).

radeln ['rɑːdəln] v/i. (ge-, sein)
cycle, pedal, F bike.

Rädelsführer ['rɛːdəls-] m ring-
leader.

Räderwerk ⊕ ['rɛːdər-] n gearing.

'rad|fahren v/i. (irr. fahren, sep.,
-ge-, sein) cycle, (ride a) bicycle,
pedal, F bike; '⁓fahrer m cyclist,
Am. a. cycler or wheelman.

radier|en [raˈdiːrən] v/t. (no -ge-, h)
rub out, erase; art: etch; ⁓gummi
m (india-)rubber, esp. Am. eraser;
⁓messer n eraser; ⁓ung f (-/-en)
etching.

Radieschen ♀ [raˈdiːsçən] n (-s/-)
(red) radish.

radikal adj. [radiˈkɑːl] radical.

Radio ['rɑːdjo] n (-s/-s) radio, wireless; im ⁓ on the radio, on the air;
⁓aktiv phys. adj. [radjoakˈtiːf]
radio(-)active; ⁓er Niederschlag
fall-out; '⁓apparat m radio or
wireless (set).

Radium ♒ ['rɑːdjum] n (-s/no pl.)
radium.

Radius ♀ ['rɑːdjus] m (-/Radien)
radius.

'Rad|kappe f hub cap; '⁓kranz m
rim; '⁓rennbahn f cycling track;
'⁓rennen n cycle race; '⁓sport m
cycling; '⁓spur f rut, track.

raffen ['rafən] v/t. (ge-, h) snatch
up; gather (dress).

raffiniert adj. [rafiˈniːrt] refined;
fig. clever, cunning.

ragen ['rɑːgən] v/i. (ge-, h) tower,
loom.

Ragout [raˈguː] n (-s/-s) ragout,
stew, hash.

Rahe ⚓ ['rɑːə] f (-/-n) yard.

Rahm [rɑːm] m (-[e]s/no pl.) cream.

Rahmen ['rɑːmən] 1. m (-s/-) frame;
fig.: frame, background, setting;
scope; aus dem ⁓ fallen be out of
place; 2. ♀ v/t. (ge-, h) frame.

Rakete [raˈkeːtə] f (-/-n) rocket;
e-e ⁓ abfeuern or starten launch a
rocket; dreistufige ⁓ three-stage
rocket; ⁓nantrieb [raˈkeːtənᵈ-] m
rocket propulsion; mit ⁓ rocket-
propelled; ⁓nflugzeug n rocket
(-propelled) plane; ⁓ntriebwerk
n propulsion unit.

Ramm|bär ⊕ ['ram-] m, '⁓bock m,
'⁓e f (-/-n) ram(mer); '⁓en v/t.
(ge-, h) ram.

Rampe ['rampə] f (-/-n) ramp,
ascent; '⁓nlicht n footlights pl.;
fig. limelight.

Ramsch [ramʃ] m (-es/♀-e) junk,

trash; im ⁓ kaufen buy in the lump;
'⁓verkauf m jumble-sale; '⁓ware
f job lot.

Rand [rant] m (-[e]s/⁼er) edge, brink
(a. fig.); fig. verge; border; brim
(of hat, cup, etc.); rim (of plate,
etc.); margin (of book, etc.); lip (of
wound); Ränder pl. under the eyes:
rings pl., circles pl.; vor Freude
außer ⁓ und Band geraten be beside
o.s. with joy; er kommt damit nicht
zu ⁓e he can't manage it; '⁓be-
merkung f marginal note; fig.
comment.

rang[1] [raŋ] pret. of ringen.

Rang[2] [⁓] m (-[e]s/⁼e) rank, order; ✕
rank; position; thea. tier; erster ⁓
thea. dress-circle, Am. first balcony;
zweiter ⁓ thea. upper circle, Am.
second balcony; ersten ⁓es first-
class, first-rate; j-m den ⁓ ablaufen
get the start or better of s.o.

Range ['raŋə] m (-n/-n), f (-/-n)
rascal; romp.

rangieren [rɑˈʒiːrən] (no -ge-, h)
1. 🚂 v/t. shunt, Am. a. switch;
2. fig. v/i. rank.

'Rang|liste f sports, etc.: ranking
list; ✕ army-list, navy or air-force
list; '⁓ordnung f order of precedence.

Ranke ♀ ['raŋkə] f (-/-n) tendril;
runner.

Ränke ['rɛŋkə] m/pl. intrigues pl.

'ranken v/refl. (ge-, h) creep, climb.

rann [ran] pret. of rinnen.

rannte ['rantə] pret. of rennen.

Ranzen ['rantsən] m (-s/-) knapsack; satchel.

ranzig adj. ['rantsiç] rancid, rank.

Rappe zo. ['rapə] m (-n/-n) black
horse.

rar adj. [rɑːr] rare, scarce.

Rarität [rariˈtɛːt] f (-/-en) rarity;
curiosity, curio.

rasch adj. [raʃ] quick, swift, brisk;
hasty; prompt.

rascheln ['raʃəln] v/i. (ge-, h) rustle.

rasen[1] ['rɑːzən] v/i. (ge-) 1. (h)
rage, storm; rave; 2. (sein) race,
speed; '⁓d adj. raving; frenzied;
speed: tearing; pains: agonizing;
headache: splitting; j-n ⁓ machen
drive s.o. mad.

Rasen[2] [⁓] m (-s/-) grass; lawn;
turf; '⁓platz m lawn, grass-plot.

Raserei [rɑːzəˈrai] f (-/-en) rage,
fury; frenzy, madness; F mot.
scorching; j-n zur ⁓ bringen drive
s.o. mad.

Rasier|apparat [raˈziːr-] m (safety)
razor; ⁓en v/t. (no -ge-, h) shave;
sich ⁓ (lassen get a) shave; ⁓klinge
f razor-blade; ⁓messer n razor;
⁓pinsel m shaving-brush; ⁓seife f
shaving-soap; ⁓wasser n after-
shave lotion; ⁓zeug n shaving kit.

Rasse ['rasə] f (-/-n) race; zo. breed.

rasseln ['rasəln] v/i. (ge-, h) rattle.

'Rassen|frage f (-/no pl.) racial issue; '~kampf m race conflict; '~problem n racial issue; '~schranke f colo(u)r bar; '~trennung f (-/no pl.) racial segregation; '~unruhen f/pl. race riots pl.

'rasserein adj. thoroughbred, purebred.

'rassig adj. thoroughbred; fig. racy.

Rast [rast] f (-/-en) rest, repose; break, pause; '2en v/i. (ge-, h) rest, repose; '2los adj. restless; '~platz m resting-place; mot. picnic area.

Rat [ra:t] m 1. (-[e]s/no pl.) advice, counsel; suggestion; fig. way out; zu ~e ziehen consult; j-n um ~ fragen ask s.o.'s advice; 2. (-[e]s/~e) council, board; council(l)or, alderman.

Rate ['ra:tə] f (-/-n) instal(l)ment (a. ✝); auf ~n ✝ on hire-purchase.

'raten (irr., ge-, h) 1. v/i. advise, counsel (j-m zu inf. s.o. to inf.); 2. v/t. guess, divine.

'raten|weise adv. by instal(l)ments; '2zahlung ✝ f payment by instal(l)ments.

'Rat|geber m (-s/-) adviser, counsel(l)or; '~haus n town hall,` Am. a. city hall.

ratifizieren [ratifi'tsi:rən] v/t. (no -ge-, h) ratify.

Ration [ra'tsjo:n] f (-/-en) ration, allowance; 2ell adj. [~o'nel] rational; efficient; economical; 2ieren [~o'ni:rən] v/t. (no -ge-, h) ration.

'rat|los adj. puzzled, perplexed, at a loss; '~sam adj. advisable; expedient; '2schlag m (piece of) advice, counsel.

Rätsel ['rɛ:tsəl] n (-s/-) riddle, puzzle; enigma, mystery; '2haft adj. puzzling; enigmatic(al), mysterious.

Ratte zo. ['ratə] f (-/-n) rat.

rattern ['ratərn] v/i. (ge-, h, sein) rattle, clatter.

Raub [raup] m (-[e]s/no pl.) robbery; kidnap(p)ing; piracy (of intellectual property); booty, spoils pl.; '~bau m (-[e]s/no pl.): ~ treiben 🗡 exhaust the land; 🗡 rob a mine; ~ treiben mit undermine (one's health); 2en ['~bən] v/t. (ge-, h) rob, take by force, steal; kidnap; j-m et. ~ rob or deprive s.o. of s.th.

Räuber ['rɔybər] m (-s/-) robber; '~bande f gang of robbers; '2isch adj. rapacious, predatory.

'Raub|fisch ichth. m ʇish of prey; '~gier f rapacity; '2gierig adj. rapacious; '~mord m murder with robbery; '~mörder m murderer and robber; '~tier zo. n beast of prey; '~überfall m hold-up, armed robbery; '~vogel orn. m bird of prey; '~zug m ʇaid.

Rauch [raux] m (-[e]s/no pl.) smoke; fume; '2en (ge-, h) 1. v/i. smoke;

fume; p. (have a) smoke; 2. v/t. smoke (cigarette); '~er m (-s/-) smoker; s. Raucherabteil.

Räucheraal ['rɔyçər⁹-] m smoked eel.

Raucherabteil 🚃 ['rauxər⁹-] n smoking-car(riage), smoking-compartment, smoker.

'Räucher|hering m red or smoked herring, kipper; '2n (ge-, h) 1. v/t. smoke, cure (meat, fish); 2. v/i. burn incense.

'Rauch|fahne f trail of smoke; '~fang m chimney, flue; '~fleisch n smoked meat; '2ig adj. smoky; '~tabak m tobacco; '~waren f/pl. tobacco products pl.; furs pl.; '~zimmer n smoking-room.

Räud|e ['rɔydə] f (-/-n) mange, scab; '2ig adj. mangy, scabby.

Rauf|bold contp. ['raufbɔlt] m (-[e]s/-e) brawler, rowdy, Am. sl. tough; '2en (ge-, h) 1. v/t. pluck, pull; sich die Haare ~ tear one's hair; 2. v/i. fight, scuffle; ~erei [~ɔ'rai] f (-/-en) fight, scuffle.

rauh adj. [rau] rough; rugged; weather: inclement, raw; voice: hoarse; fig.: harsh; coarse, rude; F: in ~en Mengen galore; '2reif m (-[e]s/no pl.) hoar-frost, poet. rime.

Raum [raum] m (-[e]s/~e) room, space; expanse; area; room; premises pl.; '~anzug m space suit.

räumen ['rɔymən] v/t. (ge-, h) remove, clear (away); leave, give up, esp. 🗡 evacuate; vacate (flat).

'Raum|fahrt f astronautics; '~flug m space flight; '~inhalt m volume, capacity; '~kapsel f capsule.

räumlich adj. ['rɔymliç] relating to space, of space, spatial.

'Raum|meter n, m cubic met|re, Am. -er; '~schiff n space craft or ship; '~sonde f space probe; '~station f space station.

'Räumung f (-/-en) clearing, removal; esp. ✝ clearance; vacating (of flat), by force: eviction; 🗡 evacuation (of town); '~sverkauf ✝ m clearance sale.

raunen ['raunən] (ge-, h) 1. v/i. whisper, murmur; 2. v/t. whisper, murmur; man raunt rumo(u)r has it.

Raupe zo. ['raupə] f (-/-n) caterpillar; '~nschlepper ⊕ m caterpillar tractor.

raus int. [raus] get out!, sl. beat it!, scram!

Rausch [rauʃ] m (-es/~e) intoxication, drunkenness; fig. frenzy, transport(s pl.); e-n ~ haben be drunk; '2en v/i. (ge-, h) 1. (h) leaves, rain, silk: rustle; water, wind: rush; surf: roar; applause: thunder; 2. (sein) movement: sweep; '~gift n narcotic (drug), F dope.

**räuspern** ['rɔyspərn] v/refl. (ge-, h) clear one's throat.

**Razzia** ['ratsja] f (-/Razzien) raid, round-up.

**reagieren** [rea'giːrən] v/i. (no -ge-, h) react (auf acc. [up]on; to); fig. and ⊕ a. respond (to).

**Reaktion** [reak'tsjoːn] f (-/-en) reaction (a. pol.); fig. a. response (auf acc. to); **~är** [~o'nɛːr] **1.** m (-s/-e) reactionary; **2.** ♀ adj. reactionary.

**Reaktor** phys. [re'aktɔr] m (-s/-en) (nuclear) reactor, atomic pile.

**real** adj. [re'aːl] real; concrete; **~isieren** [reali'ziːrən] v/t. (no -ge-, h) realize; **♀ismus** [rea'lismus] m (-/no pl.) realism; **~istisch** adj. [rea'listiʃ] realistic; **♀ität** [reali'tɛːt] f (-/-en) reality; **♀schule** f non-classical secondary school.

**Rebe** ♀ ['reːbə] f (-/-n) vine.

**Rebell** [re'bɛl] m (-en/-en) rebel; **♀ieren** [~'liːrən] v/i. (no -ge-, h) rebel, revolt, rise; **♀isch** adj. rebellious.

**Reb|huhn** orn. ['rɛp-] n partridge; **~laus** no. ['rɛp-] f vine-fretter, phylloxera; **~stock** ♀ ['reːp-] m vine.

**Rechen** ['rɛçən] m (-s/-) rake; grid.

**Rechen|aufgabe** ['rɛçən-] f sum, (arithmetical) problem; **~fehler** m arithmetical error, miscalculation; **~maschine** f calculating-machine; **~schaft** f (-/no pl.): ~ ablegen give or render an account (über acc. of), account or answer (for); zur ~ ziehen call to account (wegen for); **~schieber** ♀ m slide-rule.

**rechne|n** ['rɛçnən] (ge-, h) **1.** v/t. reckon, calculate; estimate, value; charge; ~ zu rank with or among(st); **2.** v/i. count; ~ auf (acc.) or mit count or reckon or rely (up)on; **~risch** adj. arithmetical.

**Rechnung** f (-/-en) calculation, sum, reckoning; account, bill; invoice (of goods); in restaurant: bill, Am. check; score; auf ~ on account; ~ legen render an account (über acc. of); e-r Sache ~ tragen make allowance for s.th.; es geht auf meine ~ in restaurants: it is my treat, Am. F this is on me; **~sprüfer** m auditor.

**recht¹** [rɛçt] **1.** adj. right; real; legitimate; right, correct; zur ~en Zeit in due time, at the right moment; ein ~er Narr a regular fool; mir ist es ~ I don't mind; ~ haben be right; j-m ~ geben agree with s.o.; **2.** adv. right(ly), well; very; rather; really; correctly; ganz ~! quite (so)!; es geschieht ihm ~ it serves him right; ~ gern gladly, with pleasure; ~ gut quite good or well; ich weiß nicht ~ I wonder.

**Recht²** [~] n (-[e]s/-e) right (auf

acc. to), title (to), claim (on), interest (in); privilege; power, authority; ♀ law; justice; ~ sprechen administer justice; mit ~ justly.

**'Rechte** f (-n/-n) right hand; boxing: right; pol. the Right.

**Rechteck** ['rɛçt?-] n (-[e]s/-e) rectangle; **♀ig** adj. rectangular.

**recht|fertigen** ['rɛçtfɛrtigən] v/t. (ge-, h) justify; defend, vindicate; **♀fertigung** f (-/-en) justification; vindication, defen|ce, Am. -se; **~gläubig** adj. orthodox; **~haberisch** adj. ['~haːbəriʃ] dogmatic; **~lich** adj. legal, lawful, legitimate; honest, righteous; **~los** adj. without rights; outlawed; **♀losigkeit** f (-/no pl.) outlawry; **~mäßig** adj. legal, lawful, legitimate; **♀mäßigkeit** f (-/no pl.) legality, legitimacy.

**rechts** adv. [rɛçts] on or to the right (hand).

**'Rechts|anspruch** m legal right or claim (auf acc. on, to), title (to); **~anwalt** m lawyer, solicitor; barrister, Am. attorney (at law); **~außen** m ( / ) football: outside right; **~beistand** m legal adviser, counsel.

**'recht|schaffen 1.** adj. honest, righteous; **2.** adv. thoroughly, downright, F awfully; **♀schreibung** f (-/-en) orthography, spelling.

**'Rechts|fall** m case, cause; **~frage** f question of law; issue of law; **~gelehrte** m jurist, lawyer; **♀gültig** adj. s. rechtskräftig; **~kraft** f (-/no pl.) legal force or validity; **♀kräftig** adj. valid, legal; judgement: final; **~kurve** f right-hand bend; **~lage** f legal position or status; **~mittel** n legal remedy; **~nachfolger** m assign, assignee; **~person** f legal personality; **~pflege** f administration of justice, judicature.

**'Rechtsprechung** f (-/-en) jurisdiction.

**'Rechts|schutz** m legal protection; **~spruch** m legal decision; judg(e)-ment; sentence; verdict (of jury); **~steuerung** mot. f (-/-en) right-hand drive; **~streit** m action, lawsuit; **~verfahren** n (legal) proceedings pl.; **~verkehr** mot. m right-hand traffic; **~verletzung** f infringement; **~vertreter** m s. Rechtsbeistand; **~weg** m: den ~ beschreiten take legal action, go to law; unter Ausschluß des ~es eliminating legal proceedings; **♀widrig** adj. illegal, unlawful; **~wissenschaft** f jurisprudence.

**'recht|wink(e)lig** adj. right-angled; **~zeitig 1.** adj. punctual; opportune; **2.** adv. in (due) time, punctually, Am. on time.

**Reck** [rɛk] n (-[e]s/-e) *sports*: horizontal bar.

**recken** ['rɛkən] v/t. (ge-, h) stretch; *sich* ~ stretch o.s.

**Redakt|eur** [redak'tøːr] m (-s/-e) editor; **~ion** [~'tsjoːn] f (-/-en) editorship; editing, wording; editorial staff, editors *pl.*; editor's *or* editorial office; **2ionell** adj. [~tsjo'nɛl] editorial.

**Rede** ['reːdə] f (-/-n) speech; oration; language; talk, conversation; discourse; *direkte* ~ *gr.* direct speech; *indirekte* ~ *gr.* reported *or* indirect speech; *e-e* ~ *halten* make *or* deliver a speech; *zur* ~ *stellen* call to account (*wegen* for); *davon ist nicht die* ~ that is not the point; *davon kann keine* ~ *sein* that's out of the question; *es ist nicht der* ~ *wert* it is not worth speaking of; **2gewandt** adj. eloquent; **~kunst** f rhetoric; **2n** (ge-, h) 1. v/t. speak; talk; 2. v/i. speak (*mit* to); talk (to), chat (with); discuss (*über et.* s.th.); *sie läßt nicht mit sich* ~ she won't listen to reason.

**Redensart** ['reːdəns?-] f phrase, expression; idiom; proverb, saying.

**redigieren** [redi'giːrən] v/t. (*no* -ge-, h) edit; revise.

**redlich** ['reːtlɪç] 1. adj. honest, upright; sincere; 2. adv.: *sich* ~ *bemühen* take great pains.

**Redner** ['reːdnər] m (-s/-) speaker; orator; **~bühne** f platform; **2isch** adj. oratorical, rhetorical; **~pult** n speaker's desk.

**redselig** adj. ['reːtzeːlɪç] talkative.

**reduzieren** [redu'tsiːrən] v/t. (*no* -ge-, h) reduce (*auf acc.* to).

**Reede** ⚓ ['reːdə] f (-/-n) roads *pl.*, roadstead; **~r** m (-s/-) shipowner; **~'rei** f (-/-en) shipping company *or* firm.

**reell** [re'ɛl] 1. adj. respectable, honest; *business firm*: solid; *goods*: good; *offer*: real; 2. adv.: ~ *bedient werden* get good value for one's money.

**Refer|at** [refe'raːt] n (-[e]s/-e) report; lecture; paper; *ein* ~ *halten esp. univ.* read a paper; **~endar** [~ɛn'daːr] m (-s/-e) ⚖ junior lawyer; *at school*: junior teacher; **~ent** [~'rɛnt] m (-en/-en) reporter, speaker; **~enz** [~'rɛnts] f (-/-en) reference; **2ieren** [~'riːrən] v/i. (*no* -ge-, h) report (*über acc.* [up]on); (give a) lecture (on); *esp. univ.* read a paper (on).

**reflektieren** [reflɛk'tiːrən] (*no* -ge-, h) 1. *phys.* v/t. reflect; 2. v/i. reflect (*über acc.* [up]on); ~ *auf* (*acc.*) † think of buying; be interested in.

**Reflex** [re'flɛks] m (-es/-e) *phys.* reflection *or* reflexion; ⚡ reflex (action); **2iv** *gr.* adj. [~'ksiːf] reflexive.

**Reform** [re'fɔrm] f (-/-en) reform; **~er** m (-s/-) reformer; **2ieren** [~'miːrən] v/t. (*no* -ge-, h) reform.

**Refrain** [rə'frɛ̃ː] m (-s/-s) refrain, chorus, burden.

**Regal** [re'gaːl] n (-s/-e) shelf.

**rege** adj. ['reːgə] active, brisk, lively; busy.

**Regel** ['reːgəl] f (-/-n) rule; regulation; standard; *physiol.* menstruation, menses *pl.*; *in der* ~ *as a rule*; **2los** adj. irregular; disorderly; **2mäßig** adj. regular; **2n** v/t. (ge-, h) regulate, control; arrange, settle; put in order; **2recht** adj. regular; **~ung** f (-/-en) regulation, control; arrangement, settlement; **2widrig** adj. contrary to the rules, irregular; abnormal; *sports*: foul.

**regen**[1] ['reːgən] v/t. *and* v/refl. (ge-, h) move, stir.

**Regen**[2] [~] m (-s/-) rain; *vom* ~ *in die Traufe kommen* jump out of the frying-pan into the fire, get from bad to worse; **2arm** adj. dry; **~bogen** m rainbow; **~bogenhaut** *anat.* f iris; **2dicht** adj. rain-proof; **~guß** m downpour; **~mantel** m waterproof, raincoat, mac(k)intosh, F mac; **2reich** adj. rainy; **~schauer** m shower (of rain); **~schirm** m umbrella; **~tag** m rainy day; **~tropfen** m raindrop; **~wasser** n rain-water; **~wetter** n rainy weather; **~wolke** f rain-cloud; **~wurm** *zo.* m earthworm, *Am. a.* angleworm; **~zeit** f rainy season.

**Regie** [re'ʒiː] f (-/-n) management; *thea.*, *film*: direction; *unter der* ~ *von* directed by.

**regier|en** [re'giːrən] (*no* -ge-, h) 1. v/i. reign; 2. v/t. govern (*a. gr.*), rule; **2ung** f (-/-en) government, *Am.* administration; reign.

**Re'gierungs|antritt** m accession (to the throne); **~beamte** m government official; *Brt.* Civil Servant; **~bezirk** m administrative district; **~gebäude** n government offices *pl.*

**Regiment** [regi'mɛnt] n 1. (-[e]s/-e) government, rule; 2. ⚔ (-[e]s/-er) regiment.

**Regisseur** [reʒi'søːr] m (-s/-e) *thea.* stage manager, director; *film*: director.

**Regist|er** [re'gistər] n (-s/-) register (*a. ♪*), record; index; **~ratur** [~ra-'tuːr] f (-/-en) registry; registration.

**registrier|en** [regis'triːrən] v/t. (*no* -ge-, h) register, record; **2kasse** f cash register.

**reglos** adj. ['reːkloːs] motionless.

**regne|n** ['reːgnən] v/i. (ge-, h) rain; *es regnet in Strömen* it is pouring with rain; **~risch** adj. rainy.

**Regreß** ⚖, † [re'grɛs] m (*Regresses/Regresse*) recourse; **2flichtig** ⚖, † adj. liable to recours :.

**regulär** adj. [regu'lɛːr] regular.

**regulier|bar** adj. [regu'li:rbɑːr] adjustable, controllable; **~en** v/t. (no -ge-, h) regulate, adjust; control.

**Regung** ['reːguŋ] f (-/-en) movement, motion; emotion; impulse; **²slos** adj. motionless.

**Reh** zo. [reː] n (-[e]s/-e) deer, roe; female: doe.

**rehabilitieren** [rehabili'tiːrən] v/t. (no -ge-, h) rehabilitate.

**'Reh|bock** zo. m roebuck; **'²braun** adj., **'²farben** adj. fawn-colo(u)red; **'~geiß** zo. f doe; **'~kalb** zo. n, **'~kitz** zo. ['~kits] n (-es/-e) fawn.

**Reib|e** ['raɪbə] f (-/-n), **~eisen** ['raɪp⁹-] n grater.

**reib|en** ['raɪbən] (irr., ge-, h) **1.** v/i. rub (an dat. [up]on); **2.** v/t. rub, grate; pulverize; wund ~ chafe, gall; **²erei** F fig. ['~raɪ] f (-/-en) (constant) friction; **'²ung** f (-/-en) friction; **~ungslos** adj. frictionless; fig. smooth.

**reich¹** adj. [raɪç] rich (an dat. in); wealthy, ample, abundant, copious.

**Reich²** [~] n (-es/-e) empire; kingdom (of animals, vegetables, minerals); poet., rhet., fig. realm.

**reichen** ['raɪçən] (ge-, h) **1.** v/t. offer; serve (food); j-m et. ~ hand or pass s.th. to s.o.; sich die Hände ~ join hands; **2.** v/i. reach; extend; suffice; das reicht! that will do!

**reich|haltig** adj. ['raɪçhaltɪç] rich; abundant, copious; **'~lich 1.** adj. ample, abundant, copious, plentiful; ~ Zeit plenty of time; **2.** F adv. rather, fairly, F pretty, plenty; **'²tum** m (-s/ᵘer) riches pl.; wealth (an dat. of).

**'Reichweite** f reach; ✗ range; in ~ within reach, near at hand.

**reif¹** adj. [raɪf] ripe, mature.

**Reif²** [~] m (-[e]s/no pl.) white or hoar-frost, poet. rime.

**'Reife** f (-/no pl.) ripeness, maturity.

**'reifen¹** v/i. (ge-) **1.** (sein) ripen, mature; **2.** (h): es hat gereift there is a white or hoar-frost.

**'Reifen²** m (-s/-) hoop; ring; tyre, (Am. only) tire; as ornament: circlet; ~ wechseln mot. change tyres; **'~panne** mot. f puncture, Am. a. blowout.

**'Reife|prüfung** f s. Abitur; **'~zeugnis** n s. Abschlußzeugnis.

**'reiflich** adj. mature, careful.

**Reihe** ['raɪə] f (-/-n) row; line; rank; series; number; thea. row, tier; der ~ nach by turns; ich bin an der ~ it is my turn.

**'Reihen|folge** f succession, sequence; alphabetische ~ alphabetical order; **'~haus** n terrace-house, Am. row house; **'²weise** adv. in rows.

**Reiher** orn. ['raɪər] m (-s/-) heron.

**Reim** [raɪm] m (-[e]s/-e) rhyme; **'²en** (ge-, h) **1.** v/i. rhyme; **2.** v/t. and v/refl. rhyme (auf acc. with).

**rein** adj. [raɪn] pure; clean; clear; ~e Wahrheit plain truth; **'²ertrag** m net proceeds pl.; **'~fall** F m letdown; **'²gewicht** n net weight; **'²gewinn** m net profit; **'²heit** f (-/no pl.) purity; cleanness.

**'reinig|en** v/t. (ge-, h) clean(se); fig. purify; **'²ung** f (-/-en) clean(s)ing; fig. purification; cleaners pl.; chemische ~ dry cleaning; **'²ungsmittel** n detergent, cleanser.

**'rein|lich** adj. [~lɪç] clean; cleanly; neat, tidy; **'²machefrau** f charwoman; **'~rassig** adj. pedigree, thoroughbred, esp. Am. purebred; **'²schrift** f fair copy.

**Reis¹** ♀ [raɪs] m (-es/-e) rice.

**Reis²** [~] n (-es/-er) twig, sprig.

**Reise** ['raɪzə] f (-/-n) journey; ♇, ✈ voyage; travel; tour; trip; passage; **'~büro** n travel agency or bureau; **'~decke** f travel(l)ing-rug; **'²fertig** adj. ready to start; **'~führer** m guide(-book); **'~gepäck** n luggage, Am. baggage; **'~gesellschaft** f tourist party; **'~kosten** pl. travel(l)ing-expenses pl.; **'~leiter** m courier; **'²n** v/i. (ge-, sein) travel, journey; ~ nach go to; ins Ausland ~ go abroad; **~nde** m, f (-/-n) (✝ commercial) travel(l)er; in trains: passenger; for pleasure: tourist; **~necessaire** ['~neseseːr] n (-s/-s) dressing-case; **'~paß** m passport; **'~scheck** m traveller's cheque, Am. traveler's check; **'~schreibmaschine** f portable typewriter; **'~tasche** f travel(l)ing-bag, Am. grip(sack).

**Reisig** ['raɪzɪç] n (-s/no pl.) brushwood.

**Reißbrett** ['raɪs-] n drawing-board.

**reißen** ['raɪsən] **1.** v/t. (irr., ge-, h) tear; pull; an sich ~ seize; sich ~ scratch o.s. (an dat. with); sich ~ um scramble for; **2.** v/i. (irr., ge-, sein) break; burst; split; tear; mir riß die Geduld I lost (all) patience; **3.** ♀ F ✗ n (-s/no pl.) rheumatism; **'~d** adj. rapid; animal: rapacious; pain: acute; ~en Absatz finden sell like hot cakes.

**'Reiß|er** F m (-s/-) draw, box-office success; thriller; **'~feder** f drawing-pen; **'~leine** ✈ f rip-cord; **'~nagel** m s. Reißzwecke; **'~schiene** f (T-)square; **'~verschluß** m zipfastener, zipper, Am. a. slide fastener; **'~zeug** n drawing instruments pl.; **'~zwecke** f drawing-pin, Am. thumbtack.

**Reit|anzug** ['raɪt-] m riding-dress; **'~bahn** f riding-school, manège; riding-track; **'²en** (irr., ge-) **1.** v/i. (sein) ride, go on horseback; **2.** v/t. (h) ride; **'~er** m (-s/-) rider, horseman; ✗ police: trooper; filing: tab; **~e'rei** f (-/-en) cavalry; **~erin** f (-/-nen) horsewoman; **'~gerte** f riding-whip; '~hose f (riding-) breeches pl.; '~knecht m groom; '~kunst f horsemanship; '~lehrer m riding master; '~peitsche f riding-whip; '~pferd zo. n riding-horse, saddle-horse; '~schule f riding-school; '~stiefel m/pl. riding-boots pl.; '~weg m bridle-path.

Reiz [raɪts] m (-es/-e) irritation; charm, attraction; allurement; '2-bar adj. sensitive; irritable, excitable, Am. sore; '2en (ge-, h) 1. v/t. irritate (a. ♂); excite; provoke; nettle; stimulate, rouse; entice, (al)lure, tempt, charm, attract; 2. v/i. cards: bid; '2end adj. charming, attractive; Am. cute; lovely; '2los adj. unattractive; '~mittel n stimulus; ♂ stimulant; '~ung f (-/-en) irritation; provocation; '2-voll adj. charming, attractive.

rekeln F ['re:kəln] v/refl. (ge-, h) loll, lounge, sprawl.

Reklamation [reklama'tsjo:n] f (-/-en) claim; complaint, protest.

Reklame [re'kla:mə] f (-/-n) advertising; advertisement, F ad; publicity; ~ machen advertise; ~ machen für et. advertise s.th.

reklamieren (no -ge-, h) 1. v/t. (re)claim; 2. v/i. complain (wegen about).

Rekonvaleszen|t [rekɔnvales'tsɛnt] m (-en/-en), ~tin f (-/-nen) convalescent; ~z [~ts] f (-/no pl.) convalescence.

Rekord [re'kɔrt] m (-[e]s/-e) sports, etc.: record.

Rekrut ⚔ [re'kru:t] m (-en/-en) recruit; 2ieren ⚔ [~u'ti:rən] v/t. (no -ge-, h) recruit.

Rektor ['rɛktɔr] m (-s/-en) headmaster, rector, Am. principal; univ. chancellor, rector, Am. president.

relativ adj. [rela'ti:f] relative.

Relief [rel'jɛf] n (-s/-s, -e) relief.

Religi|on [reli'gjo:n] f (-/-en) religion; 2ös adj. [~ø:s] religious; pious, devout; ~osität [~ozi'tɛ:t] f (-/no pl.) religiousness; piety.

Reling ⚓ ['re:lɪŋ] f (-/-s, -e) rail.

Reliquie [re'li:kviə] f (-/-n) relic.

Ren zo. [ren; re:n] n (-s/-s; -s/-e) reindeer.

Renn|bahn ['ren-] f racecourse, Am. race track, horse-racing: a. the turf; mot. speedway; '~boot n racing boat, racer.

rennen ['renən] 1. v/i. (irr., ge-, sein) run; race; 2. v/t. (irr., ge-, h): j-n zu Boden ~ run s.o. down; 3. 2 n (-s/-) run(ning); race; heat.

'Renn|fahrer m mot. racing driver, racer; racing cyclist; '~läufer m ski racer; '~mannschaft f raccrew; '~pferd zo. n racehorse, racer; '~rad n racing bicycle, racer; '~sport m racing; horse-racing: a. the turf; '~stall m racing stable;

'~strecke f racecourse, Am. race track; mot. speedway; distance (to be run); '~wagen m racing car, racer.

renommiert adj. [renɔ'mi:rt] famous, noted (wegen for).

renovieren [reno'vi:rən] v/t. (no -ge-, h) renovate, repair; redecorate (interior of house).

rent|abel adj. [rɛn'ta:bəl] profitable, paying; '2e f (-/-n) income, revenue; annuity; (old-age) pension; rent; 2enempfänger ['rɛntən⁹-] m s. Rentner; rentier.

Rentier zo. ['ren-] n s. Ren.

rentieren [ren'ti:rən] v/refl. (no -ge-, h) pay.

Rentner ['rɛntnər] m (-s/-) (old-age) pensioner.

Reparatur [repara'tu:r] f (-/-en) repair; ~werkstatt f repair-shop; mot. a. garage, service station.

repa'rieren v/t. (no -ge-, h) repair, Am. F fix.

Report|age [repɔr'ta:ʒə] f (-/-n) reporting, commentary, coverage; ~er [re'pɔrtər] m (-s/-) reporter.

Repräsent|ant [reprɛzen'tant] m (-en/-en) representative; ~antenhaus Am. parl. n House of Representatives; 2ieren (no -ge-, h) 1. v/t. represent; 2. v/i. cut a fine figure.

Repressalie [reprɛ'sa:ljə] f (-/-n) reprisal.

reproduzieren [reprodu'tsi:rən] v/t. (no -ge-, h) reproduce.

Reptil zo. [rep'ti:l] n (-s/-ien, ⚹ -e) reptile.

Republik [repu'bli:k] f (-/-en) republic; ~aner pol. [~i'ka:nər] m (-s/-) republican; 2anisch adj. [~i'ka:niʃ] republican.

Reserve [re'zervə] f (-/-n) reserve; ~rad mot. n spare wheel.

reser'vier|en v/t. (no -ge-, h) reserve; ~ lassen book (seat, etc.); ~t adj. reserved (a. fig.).

Resid|enz [rezi'dɛnts] f (-/-en) residence; 2ieren v/i. (no -ge-, h) reside.

resignieren [rezi'gni:rən] v/i. (no -ge-, h) resign.

Respekt [re'spɛkt] m (-[e]s/no pl.) respect; 2ieren [~'ti:rən] v/t. (no -ge-, h) respect; 2los adj. irreverent, disrespectful; 2voll adj. respectful.

Ressort [rɛ'so:r] n (-s/-s) department; province.

Rest [rɛst] m (-es/-e, ♱ -er) rest, remainder; residue (a. ♠); esp. ♱ remnant (of cloth); leftover (of food); das gab ihm den ~ that finished him (off).

Restaurant [rɛsto'rã:] n (-s/-s) restaurant.

'Rest|bestand m remnant; '~betrag m remainder, balance; '2lich adj. remaining; '2los adv. completely; entirely; '~zahlung f payment of balance; final payment.

**Resultat** [rezul'ta:t] n (-[e]s/-e) result, outcome; *sports:* score.

**retten** ['rɛtən] v/t. (ge-, h) save; deliver, rescue.

**Rettich** ♀ ['rɛtiç] m (-s/-e) radish.

**Rettung** f (-/-en) rescue; deliverance; escape.

**'Rettungs|boot** n lifeboat; '~gürtel m lifebelt; '♀los adj. irretrievable, past help or hope, beyond recovery; '~mannschaft f rescue party; '~ring m life-buoy.

**Reu|e** ['rɔyə] f (-/no pl.) repentance (über acc. of), remorse (at); '♀en v/t.: et. reut mich I repent (of) s.th.; '♀evoll adj. repentant; ♀(müt)ig adj. ['~(my:t)iç] repentant.

**Revanche** [re'vã:ʃ(ə)] f (-/-n) revenge; ~spiel n return match.

**revan'chieren** v/refl. (no -ge-, h) take or have one's revenge (an dat. on); return (für et. s.th.).

**Revers** 1. [re'vɛ:r] n, m (-/-) lapel (of coat); 2. [re'vɛrs] m (-es/-e) declaration; ☆ bond.

**revidieren** [revi'di:rən] v/t. (no -ge-, h) revise; check; † audit.

**Revier** [re'vi:r] n (-s/-e) district, quarter; s. Jagdrevier.

**Revision** [revi'zjo:n] f (-/-en) revision (a. typ.); † audit; ☆ appeal; ~ einlegen ☆ lodge an appeal.

**Revolt|e** [re'vɔltə] f (-/-n) revolt, uprising; ♀ieren [~'ti:rən] v/i. (no -ge-, h) revolt, rise (in revolt).

**Revolution** [revolu'tsjo:n] f (-/-en) revolution; ~är [~o'nɛ:r] 1. m (-s/-e) revolutionary; 2. ♀ adj. revolutionary.

**Revolver** [re'vɔlvər] m (-s/-) revolver, Am. F a. gun.

**Revue** [rə'vy:] f (-/-n) review; thea. revue, (musical) show; ~ passieren lassen pass in review.

**Rezens|ent** [retsɛn'zɛnt] m (-en/-en) critic, reviewer; ♀ieren v/t. (no -ge-, h) review, criticize; ~ion [~'zjo:n] f (-/-en) review, critique.

**Rezept** [re'tsɛpt] n (-[e]s/-e) ♣ prescription; cooking: recipe (a. fig.).

**Rhabarber** ♀ [ra'barbər] m (-s/no pl.) rhubarb.

**rhetorisch** adj. [re'to:riʃ] rhetorical.

**rheumati|sch** ♣ adj. [rɔY'ma:tiʃ] rheumatic; ♀smus ♣ [~a'tismus] m (-/Rheumatismen) rheumatism.

**rhythm|isch** adj. ['rytmiʃ] rhythmic(al); ♀us ['~us] m (-/Rhythmen) rhythm.

**richten** ['riçtən] v/t. (ge-, h) set right, arrange, adjust; level, point (gun) (auf acc. at); direct (gegen at); ☆ judge; execute; zugrunde ~ ruin, destroy; in die Höhe ~ raise, lift up; sich ~ nach conform to, act according to; take one's bearings from;

gr. agree with; depend on; price: be determined by; ich richte mich nach Ihnen I leave it to you.

**'Richter** m (-s/-) judge; '♀lich adj. judicial; '~spruch m judg(e)ment, sentence.

**'richtig** 1. adj. right, correct, accurate; proper; true; just; ein ~er Londoner a regular cockney; 2. adv.: ~ gehen clock: go right; '♀keit f (-/no pl.) correctness; accuracy; justness; '~stellen v/t. (sep., -ge-, h) put or set right, rectify.

**'Richt|linien** f/pl. (general) directions pl., rules pl.; '~preis m standard price; '~schnur f ⊕ plumb-line; fig. rule (of conduct), guiding principle.

**'Richtung** f (-/-en) direction; course, way; fig. line; ~anzeiger mot. ['riçtuŋs?-] m (-s/-) flashing indicator, trafficator; '♀weisend adj. directive, leading, guiding.

**'Richtwaage** ⊕ f level.

**rieb** [ri:p] pret. of reiben.

**riechen** ['ri:çən] (irr., ge-, h) 1. v/i. smell (nach of; an dat. at); sniff (an dat. at); 2. v/t. smell; sniff.

**rief** [ri:f] pret. of rufen.

**riefeln** ['ri:fəln] v/t. (ge-, h) flute, groove.

**Riegel** ['ri:gəl] m (-s/-) bar, bolt; bar, cake (of soap); bar (of chocolate).

**Riemen** ['ri:mən] m (-s/-) strap, thong; belt; ♣ oar.

**Ries** [ri:s] n (-es/-e) ream.

**Riese** ['ri:zə] m (-n/-n) giant.

**rieseln** ['ri:zəln] v/i. (ge-) 1. (sein) small stream: purl, ripple, trickle; 2. (h): es rieselt it drizzles.

**ries|engroß** adj. ['ri:zən'-], '~enhaft adj., '~ig adj. gigantic, huge; '♀in f (-/-nen) giantess.

**riet** [ri:t] pret. of raten.

**Riff** [rif] n (-[e]s/-e) reef.

**Rille** ['rilə] f (-/-n) groove; ⊕ a. flute.

**Rimesse** † [ri'mɛsə] f (-/-n) remittance.

**Rind** zo. [rint] n (-[e]s/-er) ox; cow; neat; ~er pl. (horned) cattle pl.; zwanzig ~er twenty head of cattle.

**Rinde** ['rində] f (-/-n) ♀ bark; rind (of fruit, bacon, cheese); crust (of bread).

**'Rinder|braten** m roast beef; '~herde f herd of cattle; '~hirt m cowherd, Am. cowboy.

**'Rind|leder** n beef; '~(s)leder n neat's-leather, cow-hide; '~vieh n (horned) cattle pl., neat pl.

**Ring** [riŋ] m (-[e]s/-e) ring; circle; link (of chain); † ring, pool, trust, Am. F combine; '~bahn f circular railway.

**ringel|n** ['riŋəln] v/refl. (ge-, h) curl, coil; '♀natter zo. f ringsnake.

ring|en ['riŋən] (irr., ge-, h) 1. v/i. wrestle; struggle (um for); nach Atem ~ gasp (for breath); 2. v/t. wring (hands, washing); '2er m (-s/-) wrestler.

ring|förmig adj. ['riŋfœrmiç] annular, ring-like; '2kampf m sports: wrestling(-match); '2richter m boxing: referee.

rings adv. [riŋs] around; '~he'rum adv., '~um adv., '~um'her adv. round about, all (a)round.

Rinn|e ['rinə] f (-/-n) groove, channel; gutter (of roof or street); gully; '2en v/i. (irr., ge-, sein) run, flow; drip; leak; '~sal ['~za:l] n (-[e]s/-e) watercourse, streamlet; '~stein m gutter; sink (of kitchen unit).

Rippe ['ripə] f (-/-n) rib; ⚕ groin; bar (of chocolate); '2n v/t. (ge-, h) rib; '~nfell anat. n pleura; '~nfell-entzündung ✠ f pleurisy; '~n-stoß m dig in the ribs; nudge.

Risiko ['ri:ziko] n (-s/-s, Risiken) risk; ein ~ eingehen take a risk.

risk|ant adj. [ris'kant] risky, ~ieren v/t. (no -ge-, h) risk.

Riß [ris] 1. m (Risses/Risse) rent, tear; split (a. fig.); crack; in skin: chap; scratch; ⊕ draft, plan; fig. rupture; 2. 2 pret. of reißen.

rissig adj. ['risiç] full of rents; skin, etc.: chappy; '~ werden crack.

Rist [rist] m (-es/-e) instep; back of the hand; wrist.

Ritt [rit] 1. m (-[e]s/-e) ride; 2. 2 pret. of reiten.

'Ritter m (-s/-) knight; zum ~ schlagen knight; '~gut n manor; '2lich adj. knightly, chivalrous; '~lich-keit f (-/-en) gallantry, chivalry.

rittlings adv. ['ritliŋs] astride (auf e-m Pferd a horse).

Ritz [rits] m (-es/-e) crack, chink; scratch; '~e f (-/-n) crack, chink; fissure; '2en v/t. (ge-, h) scratch; cut.

Rival|e [ri'va:lə] m (-n/-n), ~in f (-/-nen) rival; 2isieren [~ali'zi:rən] v/i. (no -ge-, h) rival (mit j-m s.o.); ~ität [~ali'tɛ:t] f (-/-en) rivalry.

Rizinusöl ['ri:tsinus⁹-] n (-[e]s/no pl.) castor oil.

Robbe zo. ['rɔbə] f (-/-n) seal.

Robe ['ro:bə] f (-/-n) gown; robe.

Roboter ['rɔbɔtər] m (-s/-) robot.

robust adj. [ro'bust] robust, sturdy, vigorous.

roch [rɔx] pret. of riechen.

röcheln ['rœçəln] (ge-, h) 1. v/i. rattle; 2. v/t. gasp out (words).

Rock [rɔk] m (-[e]s/-e) skirt; coat, jacket; '~schoß m coat-tail.

Rodel|bahn ['ro:dəl-] f toboggan-run; '2n v/i. (ge-, h, sein) toboggan, Am. a. coast; '~schlitten m sled(ge), toboggan.

roden ['ro:dən] v/t. (ge-, h) clear (land); root up, stub (roots).

Rogen ichth. ['ro:gən] m (-s/-) roe, spawn.

Roggen ♃ ['rɔgən] m (-s/-) rye.

roh adj. [ro:] raw; fig.: rough, rude; cruel, brutal; oil, metal: crude; '2bau m (-[e]s/-ten) rough brick-work; '2eisen n pig-iron.

Roheit ['ro:hait] f (-/-en) rawness; roughness (a. fig.); fig.: rudeness; brutality.

'Roh|ling m (-s/-e) brute, ruffian; '~material n raw material; '~pro-dukt n raw product.

Rohr [ro:r] n (-[e]s/-e) tube, pipe; duct; ♃: reed; cane.

Röhre ['rø:rə] f (-/-n) tube, pipe; duct; radio: valve, Am. (electron) tube.

'Rohr|leger m (-s/-) pipe fitter, plumber; '~leitung f plumbing; pipeline; '~post f pneumatic dispatch or tube; '~stock m cane; '~zucker m cane-sugar.

'Rohstoff m raw material.

Rolladen ['rɔlla:dən] m (-s/=, -) rolling shutter.

'Rollbahn ✈ f taxiway, taxi-strip.

Rolle ['rɔlə] f (-/-n) roll; roller; coil (of rope, etc.); pulley; beneath furniture: cast|or, -er; mangle; thea. part, role; fig. figure; ~ Garn reel of cotton, Am. spool of thread; das spielt keine ~ that doesn't matter, it makes no difference; Geld spielt keine ~ money (is) no object; aus der ~ fallen forget o.s.

'rollen (ge-) 1. v/i. (sein) roll; ✈ taxi; 2. v/t. (h) roll; wheel; mangle (laundry).

'Rollenbesetzung thea. f cast.

'Roller m (-s/-) children's toy: scooter; mot. (motor) scooter.

'Roll|feld ✈ n man(o)euvring area, Am. maneuvering area; '~film phot. m roll film; '~kragen m turtle neck; '~schrank m roll-fronted cabinet; '~schuh m roller-skate; '~schuhbahn f roller-skating rink; '~stuhl m wheel chair; '~treppe f escalator; '~wagen m lorry, truck.

Roman [ro'ma:n] m (-s/-e) novel, (work of) fiction; novel of adventure and fig.: romance; ~ist [~a'nist] m (-en/-en) Romance scholar or student; '~schriftsteller m novel-ist.

Romanti|k [ro'mantik] f (-/no pl.) romanticism; '2sch adj. romantic.

Röm|er ['rø:mər] m (-s/-) Roman; '2isch adj. Roman.

röntgen ['rœntgən] v/t. (ge-, h) X-ray; '2aufnahme f, '2bild n X-ray; '2strahlen m/pl. X-rays pl.

rosa adj. ['ro:za] pink.

Rose ['ro:zə] f (-/-n) ♃ rose; ✠ erysipelas.

'Rosen|kohl ♃ m Brussels sprouts pl.; '~kranz eccl. m rosary; '2rot *adj.* rose-colo(u)red, rosy; '**~stock** ♀ *m* (-[e]s/~e) rose-bush.

'**rosig** *adj.* rosy (*a. fig.*), rose-colo(u)red, roseate.

**Rosine** [ro'zi:nə] *f* (-/-n) raisin.

**Roß** *zo.* [rɔs] *n* (Rosses/Rosse, F Rösser) horse, *poet.* steed; '**~haar** *n* horsehair.

**Rost** [rɔst] *m* 1. (-es/*no pl.*) rust; 2. (-es/-e) grate; gridiron; grill; '**~braten** *m* roast joint.

'**rosten** *v/i.* (ge-, h, sein) rust.

**rösten** ['rø:stən] *v/t.* (ge-, h) roast, grill; toast (*bread*); fry (*potatoes*).

'**Rost|fleck** *m* rust-stain; *in cloth:* iron-mo(u)ld; '**2frei** *adj.* rustless, rustproof; *esp. steel:* stainless; '**2ig** *adj.* rusty, corroded.

**rot** [ro:t] 1. *adj.* red; 2. ♀ *n* (-s/-, F -s) red.

**Rotationsmaschine** *typ.* [rota-'tsjo:ns-] *f* rotary printing machine.

'**rot|backig** *adj.* ruddy; '**~blond** *adj.* sandy.

**Röte** ['rø:tə] *f* (-/*no pl.*) redness, red (colo[u]r); blush; '**2n** *v/t.* (ge-, h) redden; paint *or* dye red; *sich ~* redden; flush, blush.

'**rot|gelb** *adj.* reddish yellow; '**~glühend** *adj.* red-hot; '**2haut** *f* redskin.

**rotieren** [ro'ti:rən] *v/i.* (*no* -ge-, h) rotate, revolve.

**Rot|käppchen** ['ro:tkɛpçən] *n* (-s/-) Little Red Riding Hood; '**~kehlchen** *orn. n* (-s/-) robin (redbreast).

**rötlich** *adj.* ['rø:tlíç] reddish.

'**Rot|stift** *m* red crayon *or* pencil; '**~tanne** ♀ *f* spruce (fir).

**Rotte** ['rɔtə] *f* (-/-n) band, gang.

'**Rot|wein** *m* red wine; claret; '**~wild** *zo. n* red deer.

**Rouleau** [ru'lo:] *n* (-s/-s) *s.* Rolladen; blind, *Am.* (window) shade.

**Route** ['ru:tə] *f* (-/-n) route.

**Routine** [ru'ti:nə] *f* (-/*no pl.*) routine, practice.

**Rübe** ♀ *f* ['ry:bə] *f* (-/-n) beet; *weiße ~* (Swedish) turnip, *Am. a.* rutabaga; *rote ~* red beet, beet(root); *gelbe ~* carrot.

**Rubin** [ru'bi:n] *m* (-s/-e) ruby.

**ruch|bar** *adj.* ['ru:xba:r]; *~ werden* become known, get about *or* abroad; '**~los** *adj.* wicked, profligate.

**Ruck** [ruk] *m* (-[e]s/-e) jerk, *Am.* F yank; jolt (*of vehicle*).

**Rück|antwort** ['ryk?-] *f* reply; *Postkarte mit ~* reply postcard; *mit bezahlter ~ telegram:* reply paid; '**2bezüglich** *gr. adj.* reflexive; '**~blick** *m* retrospect(ive view) (*auf acc.* at); reminiscences *pl.*

**rücken**[1] ['rykən] (ge-) 1. *v/t.* (h) move, shift; 2. *v/i.* (sein) move; *näher ~* near, approach.

**Rücken**[2] [~] *m* (-s/-) back; ridge (*of mountain*); '**~deckung** *fig. f* backing, support; '**~lehne** *f* back (*of chair, etc.*); '**~mark** *anat. n* spinal cord; '**~schmerzen** *m*/*pl.* pain in the back, back ache; '**~schwimmen** *n* (-s/*no pl.*) backstroke swimming; '**~wind** *m* following *or* tail wind; '**~wirbel** *anat. m* dorsal vertebra.

**Rück|erstattung** ['ryk?-] *f* restitution; refund (*of money*), reimbursement (*of expenses*); '**~fahrkarte** *f* return (ticket), *Am. a.* round-trip ticket; '**~fahrt** *f* return journey *or* voyage; *auf der ~* on the way back; '**~fall** *m* relapse; '**2fällig** *adj.*: *~ werden* relapse; '**~flug** *m* return flight; '**~frage** *f* further inquiry; '**~gabe** *f* return, restitution; '**~gang** *fig. m* retrogression; ♀ recession, decline; '**2gängig** *adj.* retrograde; *~ machen* cancel; '**~grat** *anat. n* (-[e]s/-e) spine, backbone (*both a. fig.*); '**~halt** *m* support; '**2haltlos** *adj.* unreserved, frank; '**~hand** *f* (-/*no pl.*) *tennis:* backhand (stroke); '**~kauf** *m* repurchase; '**~kehr** ['~ke:r] *f* (-/*no pl.*) return; '**~kopp(e)lung** ♀ *f* (-/-en) feedback; '**~lage** *f* reserve(s *pl.*); savings *pl.*; **2läufig** *fig. adj.* ['~lɔyfiç] retrograde; '**~licht** *mot. n* tail-light, tail-lamp, rear-light; '**~lings** *adv.* backwards; from behind; '**~marsch** *m* march back *or* home; retreat; '**~porto** ♀ *n* return postage; '**~reise** *f* return journey, journey back *or* home.

'**Rucksack** *m* knapsack, rucksack.

'**Rück|schlag** *m* backstroke; *fig.* setback; '**~schluß** *m* conclusion, inference; '**~schritt** *fig. m* retrogression, set-back; *pol.* reaction; '**~seite** *f* back, reverse; *a.* tail (*of coin*); '**~sendung** *f* return; '**~sicht** *f* respect, regard, consideration (*auf j-n* for s.o.); '**2sichtslos** *adj.* inconsiderate (*gegen of*), regardless (of); ruthless; reckless; *~es Fahren mot.* reckless driving; '**2sichtsvoll** *adj.* regardful (*gegen of*); considerate, thoughtful; '**~sitz** *mot. m* back-seat; '**~spiegel** *mot. m* rear-view mirror; '**~spiel** *n sports:* return match; '**~sprache** *f* consultation; *~ nehmen mit* consult (*lawyer*), consult with (*fellow workers*); *nach ~ mit* on consultation with; '**~stand** *m* arrears *pl.*; backlog; ♀ residue; *im ~ sein* mit be in arrears *or* behind with; '**2ständig** *fig. adj.* old-fashioned, backward; *~e Miete* arrears of rent; '**~stoß** *m* recoil; kick (*of gun*); '**~strahler** *m* (-s/-) rear reflector, cat's eye; '**~tritt** *m* withdrawal, retreat; resignation; '**~trittbremse** *f* back-pedal brake, *Am.* coaster brake; '**~versicherung** *f* reinsurance; 2**wärts** *adv.* ['~verts] back, backward(s); '**~wärtsgang** *mot. m* reverse (gear); '**~weg** *m* way back, return.

'**ruckweise** *adv.* by jerks.

'**rück|wirkend** *adj.* reacting; *z̄g̃,* *etc.*: retroactive, retrospective; '**~wirkung** *f* reaction; '**~zahlung** *f* repayment; '**~zug** *m* retreat.

**Rüde** ['ry:də] **1.** *zo. m* (*-n/-n*) male dog *or* fox *or* wolf; large hound; **2.** ⒉ *adj.* rude, coarse, brutal.

**Rudel** ['ru:dəl] *n* (*-s/-*) troop; pack (*of wolves*); herd (*of deer*).

**Ruder** ['ru:dər] *n* (*-s/-*) oar; rudder (*a. 🕭*); helm; '**~boot** *n* row(ing)-boat; '**~er** *m* (*-s/-*) rower, oarsman; '**~fahrt** *f* row; '**⒉n** (ge-) **1.** *v/i.* (*h, sein*) row; **2.** *v/t.* (*h*) row; **~regatta** ['~regata] *f* (*-/Ruderregatten*) boat race, regatta; '**~sport** *m* rowing.

**Ruf** [ru:f] *m* (*-[e]s/-e*) call; cry, shout; summons, *univ.* call; reputation, repute; fame; standing, credit; '**⒉en** (*irr.*, ge-) **1.** *v/i.* call; cry, shout; **2.** *v/t.* call; **~** *lassen* send for.

'**Ruf|name** *m* Christian *or* first name; '**~nummer** *f* telephone number; '**~weite** *f* (*-/no pl.*): *in ~* within call *or* earshot.

**Rüge** ['ry:gə] *f* (*-/-n*) rebuke, censure, reprimand; '**⒉n** *v/t.* (ge-, h) rebuke, censure, blame.

**Ruhe** ['ru:ə] *f* (*-/no pl.*) rest, repose; sleep; quiet, calm; tranquillity; silence; peace; composure; *sich zur ~ setzen* retire; *~!* quiet!, silence!; *immer mit der ~!* take it easy!; *lassen Sie mich in ~!* let me alone!; '**⒉bedürftig** *adj.*: *~ sein* want *or* need rest; '**~gehalt** *n* pension; '**⒉los** *adj.* restless; '**⒉n** *v/i.* (ge-, h) rest, repose; sleep; *laß die Vergangenheit ~!* let bygones be bygones!; '**~pause** *f* pause; lull; '**~platz** *m* resting-place; '**~stand** *m* (*-[e]s/no pl.*) retirement; *im ~* retired; *in den ~ treten* retire; *in den ~ versetzen* superannuate, pension off, retire; '**~stätte** *f*: *letzte ~* last resting-place; '**~störer** *m* (*-s/-*) disturber of the peace, peacebreaker; '**~störung** *f* disturbance (of the peace), disorderly behavio(u)r, riot.

'**ruhig** *adj.* quiet; *mind, water:* tranquil, calm; silent; ⊕ smooth.

**Ruhm** [ru:m] *m* (*-[e]s/no pl.*) glory; fame, renown.

**rühm|en** ['ry:mən] *v/t.* (ge-, h) praise, glorify; *sich e-r Sache ~* boast of s.th.; '**~lich** *adj.* glorious, laudable.

'**ruhm|los** *adj.* inglorious; '**~reich** *adj.* glorious.

**Ruhr** ⚡ [ru:r] *f* (*-/no pl.*) dysentery.

**Rühr|ei** ['ry:r⁹-] *n* scrambled egg; '**⒉en** (ge-, h) **1.** *v/t.* stir, move; *fig.* touch, move, affect; *sich ~* stir, move, bustle; **2.** *v/i.*: *an et. ~* touch s.th.; *wir wollen nicht daran ~* let sleeping dogs lie; '**⒉end**

*adj.* touching, moving; '**⒉ig** *adj.* active, busy; enterprising; nimble; '**⒉selig** *adj.* sentimental; '**~ung** *f* (*-/no pl.*) emotion, feeling.

**Ruin** [ru'i:n] *m* (*-s/no pl.*) ruin; decay; **~e** *f* (*-/-n*) ruin(s *pl.*); *fig.* ruin, wreck; **⒉ieren** [rui'ni:rən] *v/t.* (*no* -ge-, h) ruin; destroy, wreck; spoil; *sich ~* ruin o.s.

**rülpsen** ['rylpsən] *v/i.* (ge-, h) belch.

**Rumän|e** [ru'mɛ:nə] *m* (*-n/-n*) Ro(u)manian; **⒉isch** *adj.* Ro(u)manian.

**Rummel** 𝔽 ['ruməl] *m* (*-s/no pl.*) hurly-burly, row; bustle; revel; *in publicity:* 𝔽 ballyhoo; '**~platz** *m* fun fair, amusement park.

**rumoren** [ru'mo:rən] *v/i.* (*no* -ge-, h) make a noise *or* row; *bowels:* rumble.

**Rumpel|kammer** 𝔽 ['rumpəl-] *f* lumber-room; '**⒉n** 𝔽 *v/i.* (ge-, h, sein) rumble.

**Rumpf** [rumpf] *m* (*-[e]s/⸚e*) *anat.* trunk, body; torso (*of statue*); ⚓ hull, frame, body; 🕭 fuselage, body.

**rümpfen** ['rympfən] *v/t.* (ge-, h): *die Nase ~* turn up one's nose, sniff (*über acc. at*).

**rund** [runt] **1.** *adj.* round (*a. fig.*); circular; **2.** *adv.* about; '**⒉blick** *m* panorama, view all (a)round; **⒉e** ['rundə] *f* (*-/-n*) round; *sports:* lap; *boxing:* round; round, patrol; beat (*of policeman*); *in der or die ~* (a)round; **~en** ['~dən] *v/refl.* (ge-, h) (grow) round; '**⒉fahrt** *f* drive round (*town, etc.*); *s. Rundreise*; '**⒉flug** *m* circuit (*über of*); '**⒉frage** *f* inquiry, poll.

'**Rundfunk** *m* broadcast(ing); broadcasting service; broadcasting company; radio, wireless; *im ~* over the wireless, on the radio *or* air; '**~anstalt** *f* broadcasting company; '**~ansager** *m* (radio) announcer; '**~gerät** *n* radio *or* wireless set; '**~gesellschaft** *f* broadcasting company; '**~hörer** *m* listener(-in); ~ *pl. a.* (radio) audience; '**~programm** *n* broadcast *or* radio program(me); '**~sender** *m* broadcast transmitter; broadcasting *or* radio station; '**~sendung** *f* broadcast; '**~sprecher** *m* broadcaster, broadcast speaker, (radio) announcer; '**~station** *f* broadcasting *or* radio station; '**~übertragung** *f* radio transmission, broadcast(ing); broadcast (*of programme*).

'**Rund|gang** *m* tour, round, circuit; '**~gesang** *m* glee, catch; '**⒉he'raus** *adv.* in plain words, frankly, plainly; '**⒉he'rum** *adv.* round about, all (a)round; '**⒉lich** *adj.* round(ish); rotund, plump; '**~reise** *f* circular tour *or* trip, sight-seeing trip, *Am. a.* round trip; '**~schau** *f* panorama;

*newspaper*: review; '**~schreiben** n circular (letter); '**Ｑweg** adv. flatly, plainly.

**Runz|el** ['runtsəl] f (-/-n) wrinkle; '**Ｑelig** adj. wrinkled; '**Ｑeln** v/t. (ge-, h) wrinkle; *die Stirn* ~ knit one's brows, frown; '**Ｑlig** adj. wrinkled.

**Rüpel** ['ry:pəl] m (-s/-) boor, lout; '**Ｑhaft** adj. coarse, boorish, rude.

**rupfen** ['rupfən] v/t. (ge-, h) pull up *or* out, pick; pluck (*fowl*) (a. fig.).

**ruppig** adj. ['rupiç] ragged, shabby; fig. rude.

**Rüsche** ['ry:ʃə] f (-/-n) ruffle, frill.

**Ruß** [ru:s] m (-es/*no* pl.) soot.

**Russe** ['rusə] m (-n/-n) Russian.

**Rüssel** ['rysəl] m (-s/-) trunk (*of elefant*); snout (*of pig*).

'**ruß|en** v/i. (ge-, h) smoke; '**~ig** adj. sooty.

'**russisch** adj. Russian.

**rüsten** ['rystən] (ge-, h) **1.** v/t. *and* v/refl. prepare, get ready (*zu* for); **2.** *esp.* ⚔ v/i. arm.

**rüstig** adj. ['rystiç] vigorous, strong; '**Ｑkeit** f (-/*no* pl.) vigo(u)r.

'**Rüstung** f (-/-en) preparations pl.; ⚔ arming, armament; armo(u)r; **~sindustrie** ['rystuŋsʔ-] f armament industry.

'**Rüstzeug** n (set of) tools pl., implements pl.; fig. equipment.

**Rute** ['ru:tə] f (-/-n) rod; switch; *fox's tail*: brush.

**Rutsch** [rutʃ] m (-es/-e) (land)slide; F short trip; '**~bahn** f, '**~e** f (-/-n) slide, chute; '**Ｑen** v/i. (ge-, sein) glide, slide; slip; *vehicle*: skid; '**Ｑig** adj. slippery.

**rütteln** ['rytəln] (ge-, h) **1.** v/t. shake, jog; jolt; **2.** v/i. shake, jog; *car*: jolt; *an der Tür* ~ rattle at the door; *daran ist nicht zu* ~ that's a fact.

# S

**Saal** [za:l] m (-[e]s/*Säle*) hall.

**Saat** 🖈 [za:t] f (-/-en) sowing; standing *or* growing crops pl.; seed (a. fig.); '**~feld** 🖈 n cornfield; '**~gut** 🖈 n (-[e]s/*no* pl.) seeds pl.; '**~kartoffel** 🖈 f seed-potato.

**Sabbat** ['zabat] m (-s/-e) Sabbath.

**sabbern** F ['zabərn] v/i. (ge-, h) slaver, slobber, *Am. a.* drool; twaddle, *Am. sl. a.* drool.

**Säbel** ['zɛ:bəl] m (-s/-) sab|re, *Am.* -er; *mit dem* ~ *rasseln* pol. rattle the sabre; '**~beine** n/pl. bandy legs pl.; '**Ｑbeinig** adj. bandy-legged; '**~hieb** m sabre-cut; '**Ｑn** F fig. v/t. (ge-, h) hack.

**Sabot|age** [zabo'ta:ʒə] f (-/-n) sabotage; **~eur** [~ø:r] m (-s/-e) saboteur; **Ｑieren** v/t. (*no* -ge-, h) sabotage.

**Sach|bearbeiter** ['zax-] m (-s/-) official in charge; *social work*: case worker; '**~beschädigung** f damage to property; '**Ｑdienlich** adj. relevant, pertinent; useful, helpful.

'**Sache** f (-/-n) thing; affair, matter, concern; ⚖ case; point; issue; **~n** pl. things pl.; *beschlossene* ~ foregone conclusion; *e-e* ~ *für sich* a matter apart; (*nicht*) *zur* ~ *gehörig* (ir)relevant, *pred. a.* to (off) the point; *bei der* ~ *bleiben* stick to the point; *gemeinsame* ~ *machen mit* make common cause with.

'**sach|gemäß** adj. appropriate, proper; '**Ｑkenntnis** f expert knowledge; '**~kundig** adj. s. sachverständig; '**Ｑlage** f state of affairs, situation; '**~lich 1.** adj. relevant,

pertinent, pred. a. to the point; matter-of-fact, business-like; unbias(s)ed; objective; **2.** adv.: ~ *einwandfrei od. richtig* factually correct.

**sächlich** gr. adj. ['zɛçliç] neuter.

'**Sachlichkeit** f (-/*no* pl.) objectivity; impartiality; matter-of-factness.

'**Sach|register** n (subject) index; '**~schaden** m damage to property.

**Sachse** ['zaksə] m (-n/-n) Saxon.

**sächsisch** adj. ['zɛksiʃ] Saxon.

**sacht** adj. [zaxt] soft, gentle; slow.

**Sach|verhalt** ['zaxfɛrhalt] m (-[e]s/-e) facts pl. (of the case); '**Ｑverständig** adj. expert; '**~verständige** m (-n/-n) expert, authority; ⚖ expert witness; '**~wert** m real value.

**Sack** [zak] m (-[e]s/ːe) sack; bag; *mit* ~ *und Pack* with bag and baggage; '**~gasse** f blind alley, cul-de-sac, impasse (a. fig.), *Am. a.* dead end (a. fig.); fig. deadlock; '**~leinwand** f sackcloth.

**Sadis|mus** [za'dismus] m (-/*no* pl.) sadism; **~t** m (-en/-en) sadist; **Ｑtisch** adj. sadistic.

**säen** ['zɛ:ən] v/t. *and* v/i. (ge-, h) sow (a. fig.).

**Saffian** ['zafja:n] m (-s/*no* pl.) morocco.

**Saft** [zaft] m (-[e]s/ːe) juice (*of vegetables or fruits*); sap (*of plants*) (a. fig.); '**Ｑig** adj. fruits, *etc.*: juicy; meadow, *etc.*: lush; plants: sappy (a. fig.); joke, *etc.*: spicy, coarse; '**Ｑlos** adj. juiceless; sapless (a. fig.).

**Sage** ['za:gə] f (-/-n) legend, myth; *die* ~ *geht* the story goes.

**Säge** ['zɛːgə] f (-/-n) saw; '**~blatt** n saw-blade; '**~bock** m saw-horse, Am. a. sawbuck; '**~fisch** ichth. m sawfish; '**~mehl** n sawdust.

**sagen** ['zaːgən] (ge-, h) 1. v/t. say; j-m et. ~ tell s.o. s.th., say s.th. to s.o.; j-m ~ lassen, daß send s.o. word that; er läßt sich nichts ~ he will not listen to reason; das hat nichts zu ~ that doesn't matter; j-m gute Nacht ~ bid s.o. good night; 2. v/i. say; es ist nicht zu ~ it is incredible or fantastic; wenn ich so ~ darf if I may express myself in these terms; sage und schreibe believe it or not; no less than, as much as.

'**sägen** v/t. and v/i. (ge-, h) saw.

'**sagenhaft** adj. legendary, mythical; F fig. fabulous, incredible.

**Säge|späne** ['zɛːgəʃpɛːnə] m/pl. sawdust; '**~werk** n sawmill.

**sah** [zaː] pret. of sehen.

**Sahne** ['zaːnə] f (-/no pl.) cream.

**Saison** [zɛˈzõː] f (-/-s) season; 2**bedingt** adj. seasonal.

**Saite** ['zaɪtə] f (-/-n) string, chord (a. fig.); **~ninstrument** ['zaɪtɛnʔ-] n stringed instrument.

**Sakko** ['zako] m, n (-s/-s) lounge coat; '**~anzug** m lounge suit.

**Sakristei** [zakrisˈtaɪ] f (-/-en) sacristy, vestry.

**Salat** [zaˈlaːt] m (-[e]s/-e) salad; ♀ lettuce.

**Salb|e** ['zalbə] f (-/-n) ointment; 2**en** v/t. (ge-, h) rub with ointment; anoint; '**~ung** f (-/-en) anointing, unction (a. fig.); 2**ungsvoll** fig. adj. unctuous.

**saldieren** ✝ [zalˈdiːrən] v/t. (no -ge-, h) balance, settle.

**Saldo** ✝ ['zaldo] m (-s/Salden, Saldos, Saldi) balance; den ~ ziehen strike the balance; '**~vortrag** ✝ m balance carried down.

**Saline** [zaˈliːnə] f (-/-n) salt-pit, salt-works.

**Salmiak** ['zalˈmjak] m, n (-s/no pl.) sal-ammoniac, ammonium chloride; **~geist** m (-es/no pl.) liquid ammonia.

**Salon** [zaˈlõː] m (-s/-s) drawing-room, Am. a. parlor; ⚓ saloon; 2**fähig** adj. presentable; '**~löwe** fig. m lady's man, carpet-knight; **~wagen** 🚃 m salooncar, saloon carriage, Am. parlor car.

**Salpeter** 🜍 [zalˈpeːtər] m (-s/no pl.) saltpet|er Am. -er; nit|re, Am. -er.

**Salto** ['zalto] m (-s/-s, Salti) somersault; ~ mortale break-neck leap; e-n ~ schlagen turn a somersault.

**Salut** [zaˈluːt] m (-[e]s/-e) salute; ~ schießen fire a salute; 2**ieren** [~uˈtiːrən] v/i. (no -ge-, h) (stand at the) salute.

**Salve** ['zalvə] f (-/-n) volley; ⚓ broadside; salute.

**Salz** [zalts] n (-es/-e) salt; '**~bergwerk** n salt-mine; 2**en** v/t. ([irr.,] ge-, h) salt; '**~faß** n, **~fäßchen** ['~fɛsçən] n (-s/-) salt-cellar; '**~gurke** f pickled cucumber; 2**haltig** adj. saline, saliferous; '**~hering** m pickled herring; 2**ig** adj. salt(y); s. salzhaltig; '**~säure** 🜍 f hydrochloric or muriatic acid; '**~wasser** n (-s/⸚) salt water, brine; '**~werk** n salt-works, saltern.

**Same** ['zaːmə] m (-ns/-n), '**~n** m (-s/-) ♀ seed (a. fig.); biol. sperm, semen; '**~nkorn** ♀ n grain of seed.

**Sammel|büchse** ['zaməl-] f collecting-box; '**~lager** n collecting point; refugees, etc.: assembly camp; 2**n** (ge-, h) 1. v/t. gather; collect (stamps, etc.); sich ~ gather; fig.: concentrate; compose o.s.; 2. v/i. collect money (für for); '**~platz** m meeting-place, place of appointment; ✕, ⚓ rendezvous.

**Samml|er** ['zamlər] m (-s/-) collector; '**~ung** f 1. (-/-en) collection; 2. fig. (-/no pl.) composure; concentration.

**Samstag** ['zams-] m Saturday.

**samt**[1] [zamt] 1. adv.: ~ und sonders one and all; 2. prp. (dat.) together or along with.

**Samt**[2] [~] m (-[e]s/-e) velvet.

**sämtlich** ['zɛmtliç] 1. adj. all (together); complete; 2. adv. all (together or of them).

**Sanatorium** [zanaˈtoːrjum] n (-s/Sanatorien) sanatorium, Am. a. sanitarium.

**Sand** [zant] m (-[e]s/-e) sand; j-m ~ in die Augen streuen throw dust into s.o.'s eyes; im ~e verlaufen end in smoke, come to nothing.

**Sandale** [zanˈdaːlə] f (-/-n) sandal.

'**Sand|bahn** f sports: dirt-track; '**~bank** f sandbank; '**~boden** m sandy soil; '**~grube** f sand-pit; 2**ig** adj. ['~diç] sandy; '**~korn** n grain of sand; '**~mann** fig. m (-[e]s/no pl.) sandman, dustman; '**~papier** n sandpaper; '**~sack** m sand-bag; '**~stein** m sandstone.

**sandte** ['zantə] pret. of senden.

'**Sand|torte** f Madeira cake; '**~uhr** f sand-glass; '**~wüste** f sandy desert.

**sanft** adj. [zanft] soft; gentle, mild; smooth; slope, death, etc.: easy; **~er** Zwang non-violent coercion; mit **~er** Stimme softly, gently; '**~mütig** adj. ['~myːtiç] gentle, mild; meek.

**sang** [zaŋ] pret. of singen.

**Sänger** ['zɛŋər] m (-s/-) singer.

**Sanguini|ker** [zaŋguˈiːnikər] m (-s/-) sanguine person; 2**sch** adj. sanguine.

**sanier|en** [zaˈniːrən] v/t. (no -ge-, h) improve the sanitary conditions of; esp. ✝: reorganize; readjust; 2**ung** f (-/-en) sanitation; esp. ✝: reorganization; readjustment.

**sanitär** adj. [zani'tɛːr] sanitary.
**Sanität|er** [zani'tɛːtər] m (-s/-) ambulance man; ⚔ medical orderly.
**sank** [zaŋk] pret. of sinken.
**Sankt** [zaŋkt] Saint, St.
**sann** [zan] pret. of sinnen.
**Sard|elle** ichth. [zar'dɛlə] f (-/-n) anchovy; **~ine** ichth. [~i:nə] f (-/-n) sardine.
**Sarg** [zark] m (-[e]s/=e) coffin, Am. a. casket; **~deckel** m coffin-lid.
**Sarkas|mus** [zar'kasmus] m (-/~, Sarkasmen) sarcasm; **2tisch** adj. [~tiʃ] sarcastic.
**saß** [zaːs] pret. of sitzen.
**Satan** ['zɑːtan] m (-s/-e) Satan; fig. devil; **2isch** fig. adj. [za'tɑːniʃ] satanic.
**Satellit** ast.,pol. [zatə'liːt] m (-en/-en) satellite; **~enstaat** pol. m satellite state.
**Satin** [sa'tɛ̃ː] m (-s/-s) satin; sateen.
**Satir|e** [za'tiːrə] f (-/-n) satire; **~iker** [~ikər] m (-s/-) satirist; **2isch** adj. satiric(al).
**satt** adj. [zat] satisfied, satiated, full; colour: deep, rich; sich ~ essen eat one's fill; ich bin ~ I have had enough; F et. ~ haben be tired or sick of s.th., sl. be fed up with s.th.
**Sattel** ['zatəl] m (-s/=) saddle; **~gurt** m girth; **2n** v/t. (ge-, h) saddle.
**'Sattheit** f (-/no pl.) satiety, fullness; richness, intensity (of colours).
**sättig|en** ['zɛtigən] (ge-, h) 1. v/t. satisfy, satiate; ⚗, phys. saturate; 2. v/i. food: be substantial; **2ung** f (-/-en) satiation; ⚗, fig. saturation.
**Sattler** ['zatlər] m (-s/-) saddler; **~ei** [~'rai] f (-/-en) saddlery.
**'sattsam** adv. sufficiently.
**Satz** [zats] m (-es/=e) gr. sentence, clause; phls. maxim; ♪ proposition, theorem; ♪ movement; tennis, etc.: set; typ. setting, composition; sediment, dregs pl., grounds pl.; rate (of prices, etc.); set (of stamps, tools, etc.); leap, bound
**'Satzung** f (-/-en) statute, by-law; **2sgemäß** adj. statutory.
**'Satzzeichen** gr. n punctuation mark.
**Sau** [zau] f 1. (-/=e) zo. sow; fig. contp. filthy swine; 2. hunt. (-/-en) wild sow.
**sauber** adj. ['zaubər] clean; neat (a. fig.), tidy; attitude decent; iro. fine, nice; **2keit** f (-/no pl.) clean(li)ness; tidiness, neatness, decency (of attitude).
**säuber|n** ['zɔybərn] v/t. (ge-, h) clean(se); tidy, clean up (room, etc.); clear (von of); purge (of, from) (a. fig., pol.); **2ungsaktion** pol. f purge.
**sauer** ['zauər] 1. adj. sour (a. fig.), acid (a. ⚗); cucumber: pickled; task, etc.: hard, painful; fig. morose,

surly; 2. adv.: ~ reagieren auf et. take s.th. in bad part.
**säuer|lich** adj. ['zɔyərliç] sourish, acidulous; **~n** v/t. (ge-, h) (make) sour, acidify (a. ⚗); leaven (dough).
**'Sauer|stoff** ⚗ m (-[e]s/no pl.) oxygen; **~teig** m leaven.
**saufen** ['zaufən] v/t. and v/i. (irr., ge-, h) animals: drink; F p. sl. soak, lush.
**Säufer** F ['zɔyfər] m (-s/-) sot, sl. soak.
**saugen** ['zaugən] ([irr.,] ge-, h) 1. v/i. suck (an et. s.th.); 2. v/t. suck.
**säuge|n** ['zɔygən] v/t. (ge-, h) suckle, nurse; **2tier** n mammal.
**Säugling** ['zɔyklɪŋ] m (-s/-e) baby, suckling; **~sheim** n baby-farm, baby-nursery.
**'Saug|papier** n absorbent paper; **~pumpe** f suction-pump; **'~wirkung** f suction-effect.
**Säule** ['zɔylə] f (-/-n) 🏛, anat. column (a. of smoke, mercury, etc.); pillar, support (both a. fig.); **~ngang** m colonnade; **~nhalle** f pillared hall; portico.
**Saum** [zaum] m (-[e]s/=e) seam, hem; border, edge.
**säum|en** ['zɔymən] v/t. (ge-, h) hem; border, edge; die Straßen ~ line the streets; **~ig** adj. payer: dilatory.
**'Saum|pfad** m mule-track; **~tier** n sumpter-mule.
**Säure** ['zɔyrə] f (-/-n) sourness; acidity (a. ♨ of stomach); ⚗ acid.
**Saure'gurkenzeit** f silly or slack season.
**säuseln** ['zɔyzəln] (ge-, h) 1. v/i. leaves, wind: rustle, whisper; 2. v/i. p. say airily, purr.
**sausen** ['zauzən] v/i. (ge-) 1. (sein) ⱶ rush, dash; bullet, etc. whiz(z), whistle; 2. (h) wind: whistle, sough.
**'Saustall** m pigsty; F fig. a. horrid mess.
**Saxophon** ♪ [zakso'foːn] n (-s/-e) saxophone.
**Schab|e** ['ʃaːbə] f (-/-n) zo. cockroach; ⊕ s. Schabeisen; **~efleisch** n scraped meat; **~eisen** ⊕ n scraper, shaving-tool; **~emesser** ⊕ n scraping-knife; **2en** v/t. (ge-, h) scrape (a. ⊕); grate, rasp; scratch; **~er** ⊕ m (-s/-) scraper.
**Schabernack** ['ʃaːbərnak] m (-[e]s/-e) practical joke, hoax, prank.
**schäbig** adj. ['ʃɛːbiç] shabby (a. fig.), F seedy, Am. F a. dowdy, tacky; fig. mean.
**Schablone** [ʃa'bloːnə] f (-/-n) model, pattern; stencil; fig.: routine; cliché; **2nhaft** adj., **2nmäßig** adj. according to pattern; fig.: mechanical; attr. a. routine.
**Schach** [ʃax] n (-s/-s) chess; **~!** check!; **~ und matt!** checkmate!;

*in* or **im** ~ *halten* keep *s.o.* in check; '~**brett** *n* chessboard.

**schachern** ['ʃaxərn] *v/i.* (ge-, h) haggle (*um* about, over), chaffer (about, over), *Am. a.* dicker; ~ *mit* barter (away).

'**Schach|feld** *n* square; '~**figur** *f* chess-man, piece; *fig.* pawn; '2**matt** *adj.* (check)mated; *fig.* tired out, worn out; '~**spiel** *n* game of chess. [*a.* pit.]

**Schacht** [ʃaxt] *m* (-[e]s/=e) shaft; 父

**Schachtel** ['ʃaxtəl] *f* (-/-n) box; F *alte* ~ old frump.

'**Schachzug** *m* move (at chess); *ge-schickter* ~ clever move (*a. fig.*).

**schade** *pred. adj.* ['ʃaːdə]: *es ist* ~ it is a pity; *wie* ~! what a pity!; *zu* ~ *für* too good for.

**Schädel** ['ʃɛːdəl] *m* (-s/-) skull; cranium; '~**bruch** 父 *m* fracture of the skull.

**schaden** ['ʃaːdən] 1. *v/i.* (ge-, h) damage, injure, harm, hurt (*j-m s.o.*); be detrimental (to *s.o.*); *das schadet nichts* it does not matter, never mind; 2. ♀ *m* (-s/=) damage (*an dat.* to); injury, harm; infirmity; hurt; loss; '2**ersatz** *m* indemnification, compensation; damages *pl.*; ~ *verlangen* claim damages; ~ *leisten* pay damages; *auf* ~ (*ver*)*klagen* 父 sue for damages; '2**freude** *f* malicious enjoyment of others' misfortunes, schadenfreude; '2**froh** *adj.* rejoicing over others' misfortunes.

**schadhaft** *adj.* ['ʃaːthaft] damaged; defective, faulty; *building, etc.*: dilapidated; *pipe, etc.*: leaking; *tooth, etc.*: decayed.

**schädig|en** ['ʃɛːdigən] *v/t.* (ge-, h) damage, impair; wrong, harm; '2**ung** *f* (-/-en) damage (*gen.* to), impairment (of); prejudice (to).

**schädli|ch** *adj.* ['ʃɛːtliç] harmful, injurious; noxious; detrimental, prejudicial; 2**ng** ['~ŋ] *m* (-s/-e) *zo.* pest; ♀ destructive weed; noxious person; ~*e pl.* 父 *a.* vermin.

**schadlos** *adj.* ['ʃaːtloːs]: *sich* ~ *halten* recoup or idemnify *o.s.* (*für* for).

**Schaf** [ʃaːf] *n* (-[e]s/-e) *zo.* sheep; *fig.* simpleton; '~**bock** *zo. m* ram.

**Schäfer** ['ʃɛːfər] *m* (-s/-) shepherd; '~**hund** *m* sheep-dog; Alsatian (wolf-hound).

**Schaffell** ['ʃaːfˀ-] *n* sheepskin.

**schaffen** ['ʃafən] 1. *v/t.* (*irr.*, ge-, h) create, produce; 2. *v/t.* (ge-, h) convey, carry, move; take, bring; cope with, manage; 3. *v/i.* (ge-, h) be busy, work.

**Schaffner** ['ʃafnər] *m* (-s/-) 🚋 guard, *Am.* conductor; *tram, bus:* conductor.

'**Schafhirt** *m* shepherd.

**Schafott** [ʃaˈfɔt] *n* (-[e]s/-e) scaffold.

'**Schaf|pelz** *m* sheepskin coat; '~**stall** *m* fold.

**Schaft** [ʃaft] *m* (-[e]s/=e) shaft (*of lance, column, etc.*); stick (*of flag*); stock (*of rifle*); shank (*of tool, key, etc.*); leg (*of boot*); '~**stiefel** *m* high boot; ~ *pl. a.* Wellingtons *pl.*

'**Schaf|wolle** *f* sheep's wool; '~**zucht** *f* sheep-breeding, sheep-farming.

**schäkern** ['ʃɛːkərn] *v/i.* (ge-, h) jest, joke; flirt.

**schal**[1] *adj.* [ʃaːl] insipid; stale; *fig. a.* flat.

**Schal**[2] [~] *m* (-s/-e, -s) scarf, muffler; comforter.

**Schale** ['ʃaːlə] *f* (-/-n) bowl; ⊕ scale (*of scales*); shell (*of eggs, nuts, etc.*); peel, skin (*of fruit*); shell, crust (*of tortoise*); paring, peeling; F: *sich in* ~ *werfen* doll *o.s.* up.

**schälen** ['ʃɛːlən] *v/t.* (ge-, h) remove the peel or skin from; pare, peel (*fruit, potatoes, etc.*); *sich* ~ *skin*: peel or come off.

**Schalk** [ʃalk] *m* (-[e]s/-e, ²e) rogue, wag; '2**haft** *adj.* roguish, waggish.

**Schall** [ʃal] *m* (-[e]s/⁀-e, ²e) sound; '~**dämpfer** *m* sound absorber; *mot.* silencer, *Am.* muffler; silencer (*on fire-arms*); '2**dicht** *adj.* soundproof; '2**en** *v/i.* (*irr.*, ge-, h) sound; ring, peal; '2**end** *adj.*: ~*es Gelächter* roars *pl.* or a peal of laughter; '~**mauer** *f* sound barrier; '~**platte** *f* record, disc, disk; '~**welle** *f* sound-wave.

**schalt** [ʃalt] *pret. of* schelten.

'**Schaltbrett** ⚡ *n* switchboard.

**schalten** ['ʃaltən] (ge-, h) 1. *v/i.* ⚡ switch; *mot.* change or shift gears; direct, rule; 2. *v/t.* ⊕ actuate; operate, control.

'**Schalter** *m* (-s/-) 🚋, *theatre, etc.:* booking-office; 🏦, *bank, etc.:* counter; ⚡ switch; ⊕, *mot.* controller.

'**Schalt|hebel** *m* *mot.* gear lever; ⊕, ⚞ control lever; ⚡ switch lever; '~**jahr** *n* leap-year; '~**tafel** ⚡ *f* switchboard, control panel; '~**tag** *m* intercalary day.

**Scham** [ʃaːm] *f* (-/no *pl.*) shame; bashfulness, modesty; *anat.* privy parts *pl.*, genitals *pl.*

**schämen** ['ʃɛːmən] *v/refl.* (ge-, h) be or feel ashamed (*gen.* or *wegen* of).

'**Scham|gefühl** *n* sense of shame; '2**haft** *adj.* bashful, modest; '~**haftigkeit** *f* (-/no *pl.*) bashfulness, modesty; '2**los** *adj.* shameless; impudent; '~**losigkeit** *f* (-/-en) shamelessness; impudence; '2**rot** *adj.* blushing; ~ *werden* blush; '~**röte** *f* blush; '~**teile** *anat. m/pl.* privy parts *pl.*, genitals *pl.*

**Schande** ['ʃandə] *f* (-/⁀-n) shame, disgrace.

**schänden** ['ʃɛndən] *v/t.* (ge-, h)

dishono(u)r; disgrace; desecrate, profane; rape, violate; disfigure.

**Schandfleck** *fig.* ['ʃant-] *m* blot, stain; eyesore.

**schändlich** *adj.* ['ʃentliç] shameful, disgraceful, infamous; '**2keit** *f* (-/-en) infamy.

'**Schandtat** *f* infamous act(ion).

'**Schändung** *f* (-/-en) dishono(u)r-ing; profanation, desecration; rape, violation; disfigurement.

**Schanze** ['ʃantsə] *f* (-/-n) ✕ entrenchment; ⚓ quarter-deck; *sports:* ski-jump; '**2n** *v/i.* (ge-, h) throw up entrenchments, entrench.

**Schar** [ʃaːr] *f* (-/-en) troop, band; *geese, etc.:* flock; ⚶ ploughshare, *Am.* plowshare; '**2en** *v/t.* (ge-, h) assemble, collect; *sich ~ a.* flock (*um round*).

**scharf** [ʃarf] **1.** *adj.* sharp; *edge:* keen; *voice, sound:* piercing, shrill; *smell, taste:* pungent; *pepper, etc.:* hot; *sight, hearing, intelligence, etc.:* keen; *answer, etc.:* cutting; ✕ *ammunition:* live; *~ sein auf* (*acc.*) be very keen on; **2.** *adv.:* ~ *ansehen* look sharply at; ~ *reiten* ride hard; '**2blick** *fig. m* (-[e]s/*no pl.*) clear-sightedness.

**Schärfe** ['ʃerfə] *f* (-/-n) sharpness; keenness; pungency; '**2n** *v/t.* (ge-, h) put an edge on, sharpen; strengthen (*memory*); sharpen (*sight, hearing, etc.*).

'**Scharf|macher** *fig. m* (-s/-) fire-brand, agitator; '**~richter** *m* ex-ecutioner; '**~schütze** ✕ *m* sharp-shooter, sniper; '**2sichtig** *adj.* sharp-sighted; *fig.* clear-sighted; '**~sinn** *m* (-[e]s/*no pl.*) sagacity; acumen; '**2sinnig** *adj.* sharp-witted, shrewd; sagacious.

**Scharlach** ['ʃarlax] *m* **1.** (-s/-e) scarlet; **2.** ♏ (-s/*no pl.*) scarlet fever; '**2rot** *adj.* scarlet.

**Scharlatan** ['ʃarlatan] *m* (-s/-e) charlatan, quack (doctor); mounte-bank.

**Scharmützel** [ʃar'mytsəl] *n* (-s/-) skirmish.

**Scharnier** ⊕ [ʃar'niːr] *n* (-s/-e) hinge, joint.

**Schärpe** ['ʃerpə] *f* (-/-n) sash.

**scharren** ['ʃarən] (ge-, h) **1.** *v/i.* scrape (*mit den Füßen* one's feet); *hen, etc.:* scratch; *horse:* paw; **2.** *v/t. horse:* paw (*ground*).

**Schart|e** ['ʃartə] *f* (-/-n) notch, nick; *mountains:* gap, *Am.* notch; *e-e ~ auswetzen* repair a fault; wipe out a disgrace; '**2ig** *adj.* jagged, notchy.

**Schatten** ['ʃatən] *m* (-s/-) shadow (*a. fig.*); shade (*a. paint.*); '**~bild** *n* silhouette; '**2haft** *adj.* shadowy; '**~kabinett** *pol. n* shadow cabinet; '**~riß** *m* silhouette; '**~seite** *f* shady side; *fig.* seamy side.

**schattier|en** [ʃa'tiːrən] *v/t.* (*no -ge-, h*) shade, tint; **2ung** *f* (-/-en) shading; shade (*a. fig.*), tint.

'**schattig** *adj.* shady.

**Schatz** [ʃats] *m* (-es/ᵘe) treasure; *fig.* sweetheart, darling; '**~amt** ♏ *n* Exchequer, *Am.* Treasury (Department); '**~anweisung** *f* Treasury Bond, *Am. a.* Treasury Note.

**schätzen** ['ʃetsən] *v/t.* (ge-, h) esti-mate; value (*auf acc.* at); price (at); rate; appreciate; esteem; *sich glück-lich ~ zu inf.* be delighted to *inf.*; '**~swert** *adj.* estimable.

'**Schatz|kammer** *f* treasury; '**~meister** *m* treasurer.

'**Schätzung** *f* **1.** (-/-en) estimate, valuation; rating; **2.** (-/*no pl.*) ap-preciation, estimation; esteem.

'**Schatzwechsel** ♏ *m* Treasury Bill.

**Schau** [ʃau] *f* (-/-en) inspection; show, exhibition; *zur ~ stellen* exhibit, display.

**Schauder** ['ʃaudər] *m* (-s/-) shud-der(ing), shiver, tremor; *fig.* horror, terror; '**2haft** *adj.* horrible, dread-ful; *F fig. a.* awful; '**2n** *v/i.* (ge-, h) shudder, shiver (*both:* vor *dat.* at).

**schauen** ['ʃauən] *v/i.* (ge-, h) look (*auf acc.* at).

**Schauer** ['ʃauər] *m* (-s/-) rain, etc.: shower (*a. fig.*); shudder(ing), shiver; attack, fit; thrill; '**2lich** *adj.* dreadful, horrible; '**2n** *v/i.* (ge-, h) *s. schaudern*; '**~roman** *m* penny dreadful, thriller.

**Schaufel** ['ʃaufəl] *f* (-/-n) shovel; dust-pan; '**2n** *v/t. and v/i.* (ge-, h) shovel.

'**Schaufenster** *n* shop window, *Am. a.* show-window; '**~bummel** *m:* e-n ~ *machen* go window-shopping; '**~dekoration** *f* window-dressing; '**~einbruch** *m* smash-and-grab raid.

**Schaukel** ['ʃaukəl] *f* (-/-n) swing; '**2n** (ge-, h) **1.** *v/i.* swing; *ship, etc.:* rock; **2.** *v/t.* rock (*baby, etc.*); '**~pferd** *n* rocking-horse; '**~stuhl** *m* rocking-chair, *Am. a.* rocker.

**Schaum** [ʃaum] *m* (-[e]s/ᵘe) foam; *beer, etc.:* froth, head; *soap:* lather; '**~bad** *n* bubble bath.

**schäumen** ['ʃɔymən] *v/i.* (ge-, h) foam, froth; lather; *wine, etc.:* sparkle.

'**Schaum|gummi** *n, m* foam rub-ber; '**2ig** *adj.* foamy, frothy; '**~wein** *m* sparkling wine.

'**Schau|platz** *m* scene (of action), *theat|re, Am.* -er; '**~prozeß** ♏ *m* show trial.

**schaurig** *adj.* ['ʃauriç] horrible, horrid.

'**Schau|spiel** *n* spectacle; *thea.* play; '**~spieler** *m* actor, player; '**~spiel-haus** *n* playhouse, *theat|re, Am.* -er; '**~spielkunst** *f* (-/*no pl.*) dramatic art, *the* drama; '**.steller** *m* (-s/-) showman.

**Scheck** † [ʃɛk] *m* (-s/-s) cheque, *Am.* check; '**.buch** *n*, '**.heft** *n* cheque-book, *Am.* checkbook.

'**scheckig** *adj.* spotted; *horse:* piebald.

**scheel** [ʃeːl] **1.** *adj.* squint-eyed, cross-eyed; *fig.* jealous, envious; **2.** *adv.:* j-n ~ ansehen look askance at s.o.

**Scheffel** ['ʃɛfəl] *m* (-s/-) bushel; '**2n** *v/t.* (ge-, h) amass (*money, etc.*).

**Scheibe** ['ʃaɪbə] *f* (-/-n) disk, disc (*a. of sun, moon*); *esp. ast.* orb; slice (*of bread, etc.*); pane (*of window*); *shooting:* target; '**.nhonig** *m* honey in combs; '**.nwischer** *mot. m* (-s/-) wind-screen wiper, *Am.* windshield wiper.

**Scheide** ['ʃaɪdə] *f* (-/-n) sword, *etc.:* sheath, scabbard; border, boundary; '**.münze** *f* small coin; '**2n** (*irr.*, ge-) **1.** *v/t.* (h) separate; *ʔ* analyse; *ʒ* divorce; *sich ~ lassen von ʒ* divorce (*one's husband or wife*); **2.** *v/i.* (sein) depart; part (*von* with); *aus dem Dienst ~* retire from service; *aus dem Leben ~* depart from this life; '**.wand** *f* partition; '**.weg** *fig. m* cross-roads *sg.*

'**Scheidung** *f* (-/-en) separation; *ʒ* divorce; '**.sgrund** *ʒ* *m* ground for divorce; '**.sklage** *ʒ* *f* divorce-suit; *die ~ einreichen* file a petition for divorce.

**Schein** [ʃaɪn] *m* **1.** (-[e]s/no pl.) shine; *sun, lamp, etc.:* light; *fire:* blaze; *fig.* appearance; **2.** (-[e]s/-e) certificate; receipt; bill; (bank-)note; '**2bar** *adj.* seeming, apparent; '**2en** *v/i.* (*irr.*, ge-, h) shine; *fig.* seem, appear, look; '**.grund** *m* pretext, preten|ce, *Am.* -se; '**2heilig** *adj.* sanctimonious, hypocritical; '**.tod** *ʒ m* suspended animation; '**2tot** *adj.* in a state of suspended animation; '**.werfer** *m* (-s/-) reflector, projector; ⚓, ✈, ⚔ searchlight; *mot.* headlight; *thea.* spotlight.

**Scheit** [ʃaɪt] *n* (-[e]s/-e) log, billet.

**Scheitel** ['ʃaɪtəl] *m* (-s/-) crown *or* top of the head; *hair:* parting; summit, peak; *esp.* ⚔ vertex; '**2n** *v/t.* (ge-, h) part (*hair*).

**Scheiterhaufen** ['ʃaɪtər-] *m* (funeral) pile; stake.

'**scheitern** *v/i.* (ge-, sein) ⚓ run aground, be wrecked; *fig.* fail, miscarry. [box on the ear.]

**Schelle** ['ʃɛlə] *f* (-/-n) (little) bell;] '**Schellfisch** *ichth. m* haddock.

**Schelm** [ʃɛlm] *m* (-[e]s/-e) rogue; '**.enstreich** *m* roguish trick; '**2isch** *adj.* roguish, arch.

**Schelte** ['ʃɛltə] *f* (-/-n) scolding; '**2n** (*irr.*, ge-, h) **1.** *v/t.* scold, rebuke; **2.** *v/i.* scold.

**Schema** ['ʃeːma] *n* (-s/-s, -ta, Schemen) scheme; model, pattern; arrangement; **2tisch** *adj.* [ʃe'maːtiʃ] schematic.

**Schemel** ['ʃeːməl] *m* (-s/-) stool.

**Schemen** ['ʃeːmən] *m* (-s/-) phantom, shadow; '**2haft** *adj.* shadowy.

**Schenke** ['ʃɛŋkə] *f* (-/-n) public house, F pub; tavern, inn.

**Schenkel** ['ʃɛŋkəl] *m* (-s/-) *anat.* thigh; *anat.* shank; *triangle, etc.:* leg; ⚔ *angle:* side.

**schenken** ['ʃɛŋkən] *v/t.* (ge-, h) give; remit (*penalty, etc.*); j-m et. ~ give s.o. s.th., present s.o. with s.th., make s.o. a present of s.th.

'**Schenkung** *ʒ f* (-/-en) donation; '**.surkunde** *ʒ* ['ʃɛŋkuŋs²-] *f* deed of gift.

**Scherbe** ['ʃɛrbə] *f* (-/-n), '**.n** *m* (-s/-) (broken) piece, fragment.

**Schere** ['ʃeːrə] *f* (-/-n) (e-e a pair of) scissors *pl.*; *zo.* crab, *etc.:* claw; '**2n** *v/t.* (*irr.*, ge-, h) shear (*a. sheep*), clip; shave (*beard*); cut (*hair*); clip, prune (*hedge*); **2.** (ge-, h): *sich um et. ~* trouble about s.th.; '**.nschleifer** *m* (-s/-) knife-grinder; '**.rei** *f* (-/-en) trouble, bother.

**Scherz** [ʃɛrts] *m* (-es/-e) jest, joke; ~ *beiseite* joking apart; *im ~, zum ~* in jest *or* joke; ~ *treiben mit* make fun of; '**2en** *v/i.* (ge-, h) jest, joke; '**2haft** *adj.* joking, sportive.

**scheu** [ʃɔy] **1.** *adj.* shy, bashful, timid; *horse:* skittish; ~ *machen* frighten; **2.** *2 f* (-/no pl.) shyness, timidity; aversion (*vor dat.* to).

**scheuchen** ['ʃɔyçən] *v/t.* (ge-, h) scare, frighten (away).

'**scheuen** (ge-, h) **1.** *v/i.* shy (*vor dat.* at), take fright (at); **2.** *v/t.* shun, avoid; fear; *sich ~ vor (dat.)* shy at, be afraid of.

**Scheuer|lappen** ['ʃɔyər-] *m* scouring-cloth, floor-cloth; '**.leiste** *f* skirting-board; '**2n** (ge-, h) **1.** *v/t.* scour, scrub; chafe; **2.** *v/i.* chafe.

'**Scheuklappe** *f* blinker, *Am. a.* blinder.

**Scheune** ['ʃɔynə] *f* (-/-n) barn.

**Scheusal** ['ʃɔyzaːl] *n* (-[e]s/-e) monster.

**scheußlich** ['ʃɔyslɪç] hideous, atrocious (F *a. fig.*), abominable (F *a. fig.*); '**2keit** *f* **1.** (-/no pl.) hideousness; **2.** (-/-en) abomination; atrocity.

**Schi** [ʃiː] *m* (-s/-er) *etc. s.* Ski, *etc.*

**Schicht** [ʃɪçt] *f* (-/-en) layer; *geol.* stratum (*a. fig.*); *at work:* shift; (social) class, rank, walk of life; '**2en** *v/t.* (ge-, h) arrange *or* put in layers, pile up; classify; '**2weise** *adv.* in layers; *work:* in shifts.

**Schick** [ʃɪk] **1.** *m* (-[e]s/no pl.) chic, elegance, style; **2.** 2 *adj.* chic, stylish, fashionable.

**schicken** ['ʃɪkən] *v/t.* (ge-, h) send

(nach, zu to); remit (money); nach j-m ~ send for s.o.; sich ~ für become, suit, befit s.o.; sich ~ in put up with, resign o.s. to s.th.

'schicklich adj. becoming, proper, seemly; '²keit f (-/no pl.) propriety, seemliness.

'Schicksal n (-[e]s/-e) fate, destiny.

Schiebe|dach mot. ['ʃiːbə-] n sliding roof; '~fenster n sash-window; '²n (irr., ge-, h) 1. v/t. push, shove; shift (blame) (auf acc. on to); F fig. sell on the black market; 2. F fig. v/i. profiteer; '~r m (-s/-) bolt (of door); ⊕ slide; fig. profiteer, black marketeer, sl. spiv; '~tür f sliding door.

'Schiebung fig. f (-/-en) black marketeering, profiteering; put-up job.

schied [ʃiːt] pret. of scheiden.

Schieds|gericht ['ʃiːts-] n court of arbitration, arbitration committee; '~richter m arbitrator; tennis, etc.: umpire; football, etc.: referee; '²richterlich adj. arbitral; '~spruch m award, arbitration.

schief [ʃiːf] 1. adj. sloping, slanting; oblique; face, mouth: wry; fig. false, wrong; ~e Ebene ⚙ inclined plane; 2. adv.: j-n ~ ansehen look askance at s.o.

Schiefer ['ʃiːfər] m (-s/-) slate; splinter; '~stift m slate-pencil; '~tafel f slate.

'schiefgehen v/i. (irr. gehen, sep., -ge-, sein) go wrong or awry.

schielen ['ʃiːlən] v/i. (ge-, h) squint, be cross-eyed; ~ auf (acc.) squint at; leer at.

schien [ʃiːn] pret. of scheinen.

Schienbein ['ʃiːn-] n shin(-bone), tibia.

Schiene ['ʃiːnə] f (-/-n) 🚂, etc.: rail; ⚕ splint; '²n ⚕ v/t. (ge-, h) splint.

schießen ['ʃiːsən] (irr., ge-) 1. v/t. (h) shoot; tot ~ shoot dead; ein Tor ~ score (a goal); Salut ~ fire a salute; 2. v/i. (h): auf j-n ~ shoot or fire at; gut ~ be a good shot; 3. v/i. (sein) shoot, dart, rush.

'Schieß|pulver n gunpowder; '~scharte ⚙ f loop-hole, embrasure; '~scheibe f target; '~stand m shooting-gallery or -range.

Schiff [ʃif] n (-[e]s/-e) ⚓ ship, vessel; 🏛 church: nave.

Schiffahrt ['ʃiffaːrt] f (-/-en) navigation.

'schiff|bar adj. navigable; '²bau m shipbuilding; '²bauer m (-s/-) shipbuilder; '²bruch m shipwreck (a. fig.); ~ erleiden be shipwrecked; fig. make or suffer shipwreck; '~brüchig adj. shipwrecked; '²brücke f pontoon-bridge; '~en v/i. (ge-, sein) navigate, sail; '²er

m (-s/-) sailor; boatman; navigator; skipper.

'Schiffs|junge m cabin-boy; '~kapitän m (sea-)captain; '~ladung f shipload; cargo; '~makler m shipbroker; '~mannschaft f crew; '~raum m hold; tonnage; '~werft f shipyard, esp. ⚓ dockyard, Am. a. navy yard.

Schikan|e [ʃiˈkaːnə] f (-/-n) vexation, nasty trick; ²ieren [~ka'niːrən] v/t. (no -ge-, h) vex, ride.

Schild [ʃilt] 1. ⚔ m (-[e]s/-e) shield, buckler; 2. n (-[e]s/-er) shop, etc.: sign(board), facia; name-plate; traffic: signpost; label; cap: peak; '~drüse anat. f thyroid gland.

'Schilder|haus ⚔ n sentry-box; '~maler m sign-painter; '²n (ge-, h) describe, delineate; '~ung f (-/-en) description, delineation.

'Schild|kröte f tortoise; turtle; '~wache ⚔ f sentinel, sentry.

Schilf ⚘ [ʃilf] n (-[e]s/-e) reed; '²ig adj. reedy; '~rohr n reed.

schillern ['ʃilərn] v/i. (ge-, h) show changing colo(u)rs; be iridescent.

Schimmel ['ʃiməl] m 1. zo. (-s/-) white horse; 2. ⚘ (-s/no pl.) mo(u)ld, mildew; '²ig adj. mo(u)ldy, musty; '²n v/i. (ge-, h) become mo(u)ldy, Am. a. mo(u)ld.

Schimmer ['ʃimər] m (-s/no pl.) glimmer, gleam (a. fig.); '²n v/i. (ge-, h) glimmer, gleam.

Schimpanse zo. [ʃim'panzə] m (-n/-n) chimpanzee.

Schimpf [ʃimpf] m (-[e]s/-e) insult; disgrace; mit ~ und Schande ignominiously; '²en (ge-, h) 1. v/i. rail (über acc., auf acc. at, against); 2. v/t. scold; j-n e-n Lügner ~ call s.o. a liar; '²lich adj. disgraceful (für to), ignominious (to); '~name m abusive name; '~wort n term of abuse; ~e pl. a. invectives pl.

Schindel ['ʃindəl] f (-/-n) shingle.

schinden ['ʃindən] v/t. (irr., ge-, h) flay, skin (rabbit, etc.); sweat (worker); sich ~ drudge, slave, sweat.

'Schinder m (-s/-) knacker; fig. sweater, slave-driver; '~ei fig. [~'rai] f (-/-en) sweating, drudgery, grind.

Schinken ['ʃiŋkən] m (-s/-) ham.

Schippe ['ʃipə] f (-/-n) shovel; '²n v/t. (ge-, h) shovel.

Schirm [ʃirm] m (-[e]s/-e) umbrella, parasol, sunshade; wind, television, etc.: screen; lamp: shade; cap: peak, visor; '~futteral n umbrella-case; '~herr m protector; patron; '~herrschaft f protectorate; patronage; unter der ~ von event: under the auspices of; '~mütze f peaked cap; '~ständer m umbrella-stand.

Schlacht ⚔ [ʃlaxt] f (-/-en) battle (bei of); '~bank f shambles; '²en v/t. (ge-, h) slaughter, butcher.

**Schlächter** ['ʃlɛçtər] m (-s/-) butcher.

**'Schlacht|feld** ⚔ n battle-field; **'~haus** n, **'~hof** m slaughter-house, abattoir; **'~kreuzer** ♱ m battle-cruiser; **'~plan** ⚔ m plan of action (a. fig.); **'~schiff** ♱ n battleship; **'~vieh** n slaughter cattle.

**Schlack|e** ['ʃlakə] f (-/-n) wood, coal: cinder; metall. dross (a. fig.), slag; geol. scoria; **'2ig** adj. drossy, slaggy; F weather: slushy.

**Schlaf** [ʃlaːf] m (-[e]s/no pl.) sleep; im ~ in one's sleep; e-n leichten (festen) ~ haben be a light (sound) sleeper; in tiefem ~ liegen be fast asleep; **'~abteil** 🚃 n sleeping-compartment; **'~anzug** m (ein a pair of) pyjamas pl. or Am. pajamas pl.

**Schläfchen** ['ʃlɛːfçən] n (-s/-) doze, nap, F forty winks pl.; ein ~ machen take a nap, F have one's forty winks.

**'Schlafdecke** f blanket.

**Schläfe** ['ʃlɛːfə] f (-/-n) temple.

**'schlafen** v/i. (irr., ge-, h) sleep; ~ gehen, sich ~ legen go to bed.

**schlaff** adj. [ʃlaf] slack, loose; muscles, etc.: flabby, flaccid; plant, etc.: limp; discipline, morals, etc.: lax; **'2heit** f (-/no pl.) slackness; flabbiness; limpness; fig. laxity.

**'Schlaf|gelegenheit** f sleeping accommodation; **'~kammer** f bedroom; **'~krankheit** 🞉 f sleeping-sickness; **'~lied** n lullaby; **'2los** adj. sleepless; **'~losigkeit** f (-/no pl.) sleeplessness, 🞉 insomnia; **'~mittel** 🞉 n soporific; **'~mütze** f nightcap; fig. sleepyhead.

**schläfrig** adj. ['ʃlɛːfriç] sleepy, drowsy; **'2keit** f (-/no pl.) sleepiness, drowsiness.

**'Schlaf|rock** m dressing-gown, Am. a. robe; **'~saal** m dormitory; **'~sack** m sleeping-bag; **'~stelle** f sleeping-place; night's lodging; **'~tablette** 🞉 f sleeping-tablet; **'2trunken** adj. very drowsy; **'~wagen** 🚃 m sleeping-car(riage), Am. 🚃 a. sleeper; **~wandler** ['~vandlər] m (-s/-) sleep-walker, somnambulist; **'~zimmer** n bedroom.

**Schlag** [ʃlaːk] m (-[e]s/ᵘe) blow (a. fig.); stroke (of clock, piston) (a. tennis, etc.); slap (with palm of hand); punch (with fist); kick (of horse's hoof); 🗲 shock; beat (of heart or pulse); clap (of thunder); warbling (of bird); door (of carriage); 🞉 apoplexy; fig. race, kind, sort; breed (esp. of animals); Schläge bekommen get a beating; ~ sechs Uhr on the stroke of six; **'~ader** anat. f artery; **'~anfall** 🞉 m (stroke of) apoplexy, stroke; **'2artig 1.** adj. sudden, abrupt; **2. adv.** all of a sudden; **'~baum** m turnpike.

**schlagen** ['ʃlaːgən] (irr., ge-, h) **1.** v/t. strike, beat, hit; punch; slap;

beat, defeat; fell (trees); fight (battle); Alarm ~ sound the alarm; zu Boden ~ knock down; in den Wind ~ cast or fling to the winds; sich ~ (have a) fight; sich et. aus dem Kopf or Sinn ~ put s.th. out of one's mind, dismiss s.th. from one's mind; **2.** v/i. strike, beat; heart, pulse: beat, throb; clock: strike; bird: warble; das schlägt nicht in mein Fach that is not in my line; um sich ~ lay about one; **'~d** fig. adj. striking.

**Schlager** ['ʃlaːgər] m (-s/-) ♪ song hit; thea. hit, draw, box-office success; book: best seller.

**Schläger** ['ʃlɛːgər] m (-s/-) rowdy, hooligan; cricket, etc.: batsman; horse: kicker; cricket, etc.: bat; golf: club; tennis, etc.: racket; hockey, etc.: stick; **~ei** [~'rai] f (-/-en) tussle, fight.

**'schlag|fertig** fig. adj. quick at repartee; **~e** Antwort repartee; **'2fertigkeit** fig. f (-/no pl.) quickness at repartee; **'2instrument** ♪ n percussion instrument; **'2kraft** f (-/no pl.) striking power (a. ⚔); **'2loch** n pot-hole; **'2mann** m rowing: stroke; **'2ring** m knuckle-duster, Am. a. brass knuckles pl.; **'2sahne** f whipped cream; **'2-schatten** m cast shadow; **'2seite** f list; ~ haben ♱ list; F fig. be half-seas-over; **'2uhr** f striking clock; **'2werk** n clock: striking mechanism; **'2wort** n catchword, slogan; **'2zeile** f headline; banner headline, Am. banner; **'2zeug** ♪ n in orchestra: percussion instruments pl.; in band: drums pl., percussion; **'2zeuger** ♪ m (-s/-) in orchestra: percussionist; in band: drummer.

**schlaksig** adj. ['ʃlaːksiç] gawky.

**Schlamm** [ʃlam] m (-[e]s/ᵉ, ᵉe, ᵘe) mud, mire; **'~bad** n mud-bath; **'2ig** adj. muddy, miry.

**Schlämmkreide** ['ʃlɛm-] f (-/no pl.) whit(en)ing.

**Schlamp|e** ['ʃlampə] f (-/-n) slut, slattern; **'2ig** adj. slovenly, slipshod.

**schlang** [ʃlaŋ] pret. of schlingen.

**Schlange** ['ʃlaŋə] f (-/-n) zo. snake, rhet. serpent (a. fig.); fig.: snake in the grass; queue, Am. a. line; ~ stehen queue up (um for), Am. line up (for).

**schlängeln** ['ʃlɛŋəln] v/refl. (ge-, h): sich ~ durch person: worm one's way or o.s. through; path, river, etc.: wind (one's way) through, meander through.

**'Schlangenlinie** f serpentine line.

**schlank** adj. [ʃlaŋk] slender, slim; **'2heit** f (-/no pl.) slenderness, slimness; **'2heitskur** f: e-e ~ machen slim.

**schlapp** F adj. [ʃlap] tired, exhausted,

worn out; '2e F f (-/-n) reverse, setback; defeat; '~machen F v/i. (sep., -ge-, h) break down, faint.

**schlau** adj. [ʃlaʊ] sly, cunning; crafty, clever, F cute.

**Schlauch** [ʃlaʊx] m (-[e]s/ue) tube; hose; car, etc.: inner tube; '~boot n rubber dinghy, pneumatic boat.

**Schlaufe** ['ʃlaʊfə] f (-/-n) loop.

**schlecht** [ʃlɛçt] 1. adj. bad; wicked; poor; temper: ill; quality: inferior; ~e Laune haben be in a bad temper; ~e Aussichten poor prospects; ~e Zeiten hard times; mir ist ~ I feel sick; 2. adv. badly, ill; ~erdings adv. ['~ʔɛr'dɪŋs] absolutely, downright, utterly; ~gelaunt adj. ['~gə-laʊnt] ill-humo(u)red, in a bad temper; '~hin adv. plainly, simply; '2igkeit f (-/-en) badness; wickedness; ~en pl. base acts pl., mean tricks pl.; '~machen v/t. (sep., -ge-, h) run down, backbite; ~weg adv. ['~vɛk] plainly, simply.

**schleich|en** ['ʃlaɪçən] v/i. (irr., ge-, sein) creep (a. fig.); sneak, steal; '2er m (-s/-) creeper; fig. sneak; '2handel m illicit trade; smuggling, contraband; '2händler m smuggler, contrabandist; black marketeer; '2weg m secret path.

**Schleier** ['ʃlaɪər] m (-s/-) veil (a. fig.); mist: a. haze; den ~ nehmen take the veil; '2haft fig. adj. mysterious, inexplicable.

**Schleife** ['ʃlaɪfə] f (-/-n) loop (a. ꭓ); slip-knot; bow; wreath: streamer; loop, horse-shoe bend.

'**schleif|en** 1. v/t. (irr., ge-, h) whet (knife, etc.); cut (glass, precious stones); polish (a. fig.); 2. v/t. (ge-, h) ♪ slur; drag, trail; ꭓ raze (fortress, etc.); 3. v/i. (ge-, h) drag, trail; '2stein m grindstone, whetstone.

**Schleim** [ʃlaɪm] m (-[e]s/-e) slime; ꭓ mucus, phlegm; '~haut anat. f mucous membrane; '2ig adj. slimy (a. fig.); mucous.

**schlemm|en** ['ʃlɛmən] v/i. (ge-, h) feast, gormandize; '2er m (-s/-) glutton, gormandizer; 2erei [~'raɪ] f (-/-en) feasting; gluttony.

**schlen|dern** ['ʃlɛndərn] v/i. (ge-, sein) stroll, saunter; 2drian ['~driːan] m (-[e]s/no pl.) jogtrot; beaten track.

**schlenkern** ['ʃlɛŋkərn] (ge-, h) 1. v/t. dangle, swing; 2. v/i.: mit den Armen ~ swing one's arms.

**Schlepp|dampfer** ['ʃlɛp-] m steam tug, tug(boat); '~e f (-/-n) train (of woman's dress); '2en (ge-, h) 1. v/t. carry with difficulty, haul, Am. F a. tote; ⚓, ꭓ, mot. tow, haul; ⚓ tug; ✝ tout (customers); sich ~ drag o.s.; 2. v/i. dress: drag, trail; '2end adj. speech: drawling; gait: shuffling; style: heavy; con-

versation, etc.: tedious; '~er ⚓ m (-s/-) steam tug, tug(boat); '~tau n tow(ing)-rope; ins ~ nehmen take in or on tow (a. fig.).

**Schleuder** ['ʃlɔʏdər] f (-/-n) sling, catapult (a. ꭓ), Am. a. slingshot; spin drier; '2n (ge-, h) 1. v/t. fling, hurl (a. fig.); sling, catapult (a. ꭓ); spin-dry (washing); 2. mot. v/i. skid; '~preis ✝ m ruinous or giveaway price; zu ~en dirt-cheap.

**schleunig** adj. ['ʃlɔʏnɪç] prompt, speedy, quick.

**Schleuse** ['ʃlɔʏzə] f (-/-n) lock, sluice; '2n v/t. (ge-, h) lock (boat) (up or down); fig. manœuvre, Am. maneuver.

**schlich** [ʃlɪç] pret. of schleichen.

**schlicht** adj. [ʃlɪçt] plain, simple; modest, unpretentious; hair: smooth, sleek; '2en v/t. (ge-, h) settle, adjust; settle by arbitration; '2er fig. m (-s/-) mediator; arbitrator.

**schlief** [ʃliːf] pret. of schlafen.

**schließ|en** ['ʃliːsən] (irr., ge-, h) 1. v/t. shut, close; shut down (factory, etc.); shut up (shop); contract (marriage); conclude (treaty, speech, etc.); parl. close (debate); in die Arme ~ clasp in one's arms; in sich ~ comprise, include; Freundschaft ~ make friends (mit with); 2. v/i. shut, close; school: break up; aus et. ~ auf (acc.) infer or conclude s.th. from s.th.; '2fach n post-office box; '~lich adv. finally, eventually; at last; after all.

**Schliff** [ʃlɪf] m (-[e]s/-e) polish (a. fig.); precious stones, glass: cut; 2. pret. of schleifen 1.

**schlimm** [ʃlɪm] 1. adj. bad; evil, wicked, nasty; serious; F ꭓ bad, sore; ~er worse; am ~sten, das 2ste the worst; es wird immer ~er things are going from bad to worse; 2. adv.: ~ daran sein to be badly off; '~stenfalls adv. at (the) worst.

**Schling|e** ['ʃlɪŋə] f (-/-n) loop, sling (a. ꭓ); noose; coil (of wire or rope); hunt. snare (a. fig.); den Kopf in die ~ stecken put one's head in the noose; '~el m (-s/-) rascal, naughty boy; '2en v/t. (irr., ge-, h) wind, twist; plait; die Arme ~ um (acc.) fling one's arms round; sich um et. ~ wind round; '~pflanze ♀ f creeper, climber.

**Schlips** [ʃlɪps] m (-es/-e) (neck)tie.

**Schlitten** ['ʃlɪtən] m (-s/-) sled(ge); sleigh; sports: toboggan.

'**Schlittschuh** m skate; ~ laufen skate; '~läufer m skater.

**Schlitz** [ʃlɪts] m (-es/-e) slit, slash; slot; '2en v/t. (ge-, h) slit, slash.

**Schloß** [ʃlɔs] 1. n (Schlosses/Schlösser) lock (of door, gun, etc.); castle; palace; ins ~ fallen door: snap to;

hinter ~ und Riegel behind prison bars; 2. ♀ *pret. of* schließen.

**Schlosser** ['ʃlɔsər] *m* (-s/-) locksmith; mechanic, fitter.

**Schlot** [ʃloːt] *m* (-[e]s/-e, ⸗e) chimney; flue; ♨, 🚢 funnel; '~feger *m* (-s/-) chimney-sweep(er).

**schlotter|ig** *adj.* ['ʃlɔtəriç] shaky, tottery; loose; '~n *v/i.* (ge-, h) *garment:* hang loosely; *p.* shake, tremble (*both: vor dat.* with).

**Schlucht** [ʃluxt] *f* (-/-en) gorge, mountain cleft; ravine, *Am. a.* gulch.

**schluchzen** ['ʃluxtsən] *v/i.* (ge-, h) sob.

**Schluck** [ʃluk] *m* (-[e]s/-e, ⸗e) draught, swallow; mouthful, sip; '~auf *m* (-s/no pl.) hiccup(s *pl.*).

**'schlucken 1.** *v/t. and v/i.* (ge-, h) swallow (*a. fig.*); 2. ♀ *m* (-s/no pl.) hiccup(s *pl.*).

**schlug** [ʃluːk] *pret. of* schlagen.

**Schlummer** ['ʃlumər] *m* (-s/no pl.) slumber; '~n *v/i.* (ge-, h) slumber.

**Schlund** [ʃlunt] *m* (-[e]s/⸗e) *anat.* pharynx; *fig.* abyss, chasm, gulf.

**schlüpf|en** ['ʃlypfən] *v/i.* (ge-, sein) slip, slide; *in die Kleider* ~ slip on one's clothes; *aus den Kleidern* ~ slip out of *or* slip off one's clothes; '♀er *m* (-s/-) (*ein a pair of*) knickers *pl. or* drawers *pl. or* F panties *pl.*; briefs *pl.*

**Schlupfloch** ['ʃlupf-] *n* loop-hole.

**'schlüpfrig** *adj.* slippery; *fig.* lascivious.

**'Schlupfwinkel** *m* hiding-place.

**schlurfen** ['ʃlurfən] *v/i.* (ge-, sein) shuffle, drag one's feet.

**schlürfen** ['ʃlyrfən] *v/t. and v/i.* (ge-, h) drink *or* eat noisily; sip.

**Schluß** [ʃlus] *m* (Schlusses/Schlüsse) close, end; conclusion; *parl.* closing (*of debate*).

**Schlüssel** ['ʃlysəl] *m* (-s/-) key (*zu of*; *fig.* to); ♪ clef; *fig.*: code; quota; '~bart *m* key-bit; '~bein *n* anat. collar-bone, clavicle; '~bund *m, n* (-[e]s/-e) bunch of keys; '~industrie *fig. f* key industry; '~loch *n* keyhole; '~ring *m* key-ring.

**'Schluß|folgerung** *f* conclusion, inference; '~formel *f in letter*: complimentary close.

**schlüssig** *adj.* ['ʃlysiç] *evidence:* conclusive; *sich* ~ *werden* make up one's mind (*über acc.* about).

**'Schluß|licht** *n* 🚢, *mot., etc.*: taillight; *sports*: last runner; bottom club; '~runde *f sports*: final; '~schein ♼ *m* contract-note.

**Schmach** [ʃmaːx] *f* (-/no pl.) disgrace; insult; humiliation.

**schmachten** ['ʃmaxtən] *v/i.* (ge-, h) languish (*nach* for), pine (for).

**schmächtig** *adj.* ['ʃmɛçtiç] slender, slim; *ein* ~*er Junge* a (mere) slip of a boy.

**'schmachvoll** *adj.* disgraceful; humiliating.

**schmackhaft** *adj.* ['ʃmakhaft] palatable, savo(u)ry.

**schmäh|en** ['ʃmɛːən] *v/t.* (ge-, h) abuse, revile; decry, disparage; slander, defame; '~lich *adj.* ignominious, disgraceful; '♀schrift *f* libel, lampoon; '♀ung *f* (-/-en) abuse; slander, defamation.

**schmal** *adj.* [ʃmaːl] narrow; *figure:* slender, slim; *face:* thin; *fig.* poor, scanty.

**schmäler|n** ['ʃmɛːlərn] *v/t.* (ge-, h) curtail; impair; belittle; '♀ung *f* (-/-en) curtailment; impairment; detraction.

**'Schmal|film** *phot. m* substandard film; '~spur 🚢 *f* narrow ga(u)ge; '~spurbahn 🚢 *f* narrow-ga(u)ge railway; '♀spurig 🚢 *adj.* narrow-ga(u)ge.

**Schmalz** [ʃmalts] *n* (-es/-e) grease; lard; '♀ig *adj.* greasy; lardy; F *fig.* soppy, sentimental.

**schmarotz|en** [ʃma'rɔtsən] *v/i.* (no -ge-, h) sponge (*bei* on); ♀er *m* (-s/-) ⚘, *zo.* parasite; *fig. a.* sponge.

**Schmarre** F ['ʃmarə] *f* (-/-n) slash, cut; scar.

**Schmatz** [ʃmats] *m* (-es/-e) smack, loud kiss; '♀en *v/i.* (ge-, h) smack (*mit den Lippen* one's lips); eat noisily.

**Schmaus** [ʃmaus] *m* (-es/⸗e) feast, banquet; *fig.* treat; ♀en ['~zən] *v/i.* (ge-, h) feast, banquet.

**schmecken** ['ʃmɛkən] (ge-, h) **1.** *v/t.* taste, sample; **2.** *v/i.*: ~ *nach* taste *or* smack of (*both a. fig.*); *dieser Wein schmeckt mir* I like *or* enjoy this wine.

**Schmeichel|ei** [ʃmaiçə'lai] *f* (-/-en) flattery; cajolery; '♀haft *adj.* flattering; '♀n *v/i.* (ge-, h): *j-m* ~ flatter s.o.; cajole s.o.

**Schmeichler** ['ʃmaiçlər] *m* (-s/-) flatterer; '♀isch *adj.* flattering; cajoling.

**schmeiß|en** F ['ʃmaisən] (*irr.,* ge-, h) **1.** *v/t.* throw, fling, hurl; slam, bang (*door*); **2.** *v/i.*: *mit Geld um sich* ~ squander one's money; '♀fliege *zo. f* blowfly, bluebottle.

**Schmelz** [ʃmɛlts] *m* **1.** (-es/-e) enamel; **2.** *fig.* (-es/no pl.) bloom; ♪ sweetness, mellowness; '♀en (*irr.,* ge-) **1.** *v/i.* (sein) melt (*a. fig.*); liquefy; *fig.* waste away, dwindle; **2.** *v/t.* (h) melt; smelt, fuse (*ore, etc.*); liquefy; ~erei [~'rai] *f* (-/-en), '~hütte *f* foundry; '~ofen *m* smelting furnace; '~tiegel *m* melting-pot, crucible.

**Schmerbauch** ['ʃmeːr-] *m* paunch, pot-belly, F corporation, *Am. sl. a.* bay window.

**Schmerz** [ʃmerts] *m* (-es/-en) pain (*a. fig.*); ache; *fig.* grief, sorrow;

'²en (ge-, h) 1. v/i. pain (a. fig.), hurt; ache; 2. v/t. pain (a. fig.); hurt; fig. grieve, afflict; '²haft adj. painful; '²lich adj. painful, grievous; '²lindernd adj. soothing; '²los adj. painless.

Schmetter|ling zo. ['ʃmɛtərliŋ] m (-s/-e) butterfly; '²n (ge-, h) 1. v/t. dash (zu Boden to the ground; in Stücke to pieces); 2. v/i. crash; trumpet, etc.: bray, blare; bird: warble.

Schmied [ʃmiːt] m (-[e]s/-e) (black-) smith; ⁓e ['⁓də] f (-/-n) forge, smithy; ⁓eeisen ['⁓dəˀ-] n wrought iron; '⁓ehammer m sledge(-hammer); ²en ['⁓dən] v/t. (ge-, h) forge; make, devise, hatch (plans).

schmiegen ['ʃmiːgən] v/refl. (ge-, h) nestle (an acc. to).

schmiegsam adj. ['ʃmiːkzaːm] pliant, flexible; supple (a. fig.); '²keit f (-/no pl.) pliancy, flexibility; suppleness (a. fig.).

Schmier|e ['ʃmiːrə] f (-/-n) grease; thea. contp. troop of strolling players, sl. penny gaff; '²en v/t. (ge-, h) smear; ⊕ grease, oil, lubricate; butter (bread); spread (butter, etc.); scrawl, scribble; painter: daub; ⁓enkomödiant ['⁓kɔmødjant] m (-en/-en) strolling actor, barnstormer, sl. ham (actor); ⁓erei [⁓'raɪ] f (-/-en) scrawl; paint. daub; '²ig adj. greasy; dirty; fig.: filthy; F smarmy; '⁓mittel ⊕ n lubricant.

Schminke ['ʃmiŋkə] f (-/-n) make-up (a. thea.), paint; rouge; thea. grease-paint; '²n v/t. and v/refl. (ge-, h) paint, make up; rouge (o.s.); put on lipstick.

Schmirgel ['ʃmirgəl] m (-s/no pl.) emery; '²n v/t. (ge-, h) (rub with) emery; '⁓papier n emery-paper.

Schmiß [ʃmɪs] 1. m (Schmisses/ Schmisse) gash, cut; (duelling-) scar; 2. F m (Schmisses/no pl.) verve, go, Am. sl. a. pep; 3. ♀ pret. of schmeißen.

schmoll|en ['ʃmɔlən] v/i. (ge-, h) sulk, pout; '²winkel m sulking-corner.

schmolz [ʃmɔlts] pret. of schmelzen.

Schmor|braten ['ʃmoːr-] m stewed meat; '²en v/t. and v/i. (ge-, h) stew (a. fig.).

Schmuck [ʃmʊk] 1. m (-[e]s/⁊-e) ornament; decoration; jewel(le)ry, jewels pl.; 2. ♀ adj. neat, smart, spruce, trim.

schmücken ['ʃmʏkən] v/t. (ge-, h) adorn, trim; decorate.

'schmuck|los adj. unadorned; plain; '²sachen f/pl. jewel(le)ry, jewels pl.

Schmuggel ['ʃmʊgəl] m (-s/no pl.), ⁓ei [⁓'laɪ] f (-/-en) smuggling; '²n v/t. and v/i. (ge-, h) smuggle; '⁓ware f contraband, smuggled goods pl.

Schmuggler ['ʃmʊglər] m (-s/-) smuggler.

schmunzeln ['ʃmʊntsəln] v/i. (ge-, h) smile amusedly.

Schmutz [ʃmʊts] m (-es/no pl.) dirt; filth; fig. a. smut; '²en v/i. (ge-, h) soil, get dirty; '⁓fink fig. m mudlark; '⁓fleck m smudge, stain; fig. blemish; '²ig adj. dirty; filthy; fig. a. mean, shabby.

Schnabel ['ʃnaːbəl] m (-s/⁊-) bill, esp. bird of prey: beak.

Schnalle ['ʃnalə] f (-/-n) buckle; '²n v/t. (ge-, h) buckle; strap.

schnalzen ['ʃnaltsən] v/i. (ge-, h): mit den Fingern ⁓ snap one's fingers; mit der Zunge ⁓ click one's tongue.

schnappen ['ʃnapən] (ge-, h) 1. v/i. lid, spring, etc.: snap; lock: catch; nach et. ⁓ snap or snatch at; nach Luft ⁓ gasp for breath; 2. F v/t. catch, sl. nab (criminal).

'Schnapp|messer n flick-knife; '⁓schloß n spring-lock; '⁓schuß phot. m snapshot.

Schnaps [ʃnaps] m (-es/⁊-e) strong liquor, Am. hard liquor; brandy; ein (Glas) ⁓ a dram.

schnarch|en ['ʃnarçən] v/i. (ge-, h) snore; '²er m (-s/-) snorer.

schnarren ['ʃnarən] v/i. (ge-, h) rattle; jar.

schnattern ['ʃnatərn] v/i. (ge-, h) cackle; fig. a. chatter, gabble.

schnauben ['ʃnaʊbən] (ge-, h) 1. v/i. snort; vor Wut ⁓ foam with rage; 2. v/t.: sich die Nase ⁓ blow one's nose.

schnaufen ['ʃnaʊfən] v/i. (ge-, h) pant, puff, blow; wheeze.

Schnauz|bart ['ʃnaʊts-] m m(o)ustache; '⁓e f (-/-n) snout, muzzle; ⊕ nozzle; teapot, etc.: spout; sl. fig. potato-trap; '²en F v/i. (ge-, h) jaw.

Schnecke zo. ['ʃnɛkə] f (-/-n) snail; slug; '⁓nhaus n snail's shell; '⁓ntempo n: im ⁓ at a snail's pace.

Schnee [ʃneː] m (-s/no pl.) snow; '⁓ball m snowball; '⁓ballschlacht f pelting-match with snowballs; ²bedeckt adj. ['⁓bədɛkt] snow-covered, mountain-top: snow-capped; '²blind adj. snow-blind; '⁓blindheit f snow-blindness; '⁓brille f (-e a pair of) snow-goggles pl.; '⁓fall m snow-fall; '⁓flocke f snow-flake; '⁓gestöber n (-s/-) snow-storm; '⁓glöckchen ['⁓glœkçən] n (-s/-) snowdrop; '⁓grenze f snow-line; '⁓mann m snow man; '⁓pflug m snow-plough, Am. snowplow; '⁓schuh m snow-shoe; '⁓sturm m snow-storm, blizzard; '⁓wehe f (-/-n) snow-drift; '²weiß adj. snow-white.

Schneid F [ʃnaɪt] m (-[e]s/no pl.) pluck, dash, sl. guts pl.

Schneide ['ʃnaɪdə] f (-/-n) edge; '⁓mühle f sawmill; '²n (irr., ge-, h)

**1.** *v/t.* cut; carve (*meat*); pare, clip (*finger-nails, etc.*); **2.** *v/i.* cut.

'**Schneider** *m* (-s/-) tailor; **~ei** [~'raɪ] *f* **1.** (-/*no pl.*) tailoring; dressmaking; **2.** (-/-en) tailor's shop; dressmaker's shop; '**~in** *f* (-/-nen) dressmaker; '**~meister** *m* master tailor; '**2n** (ge-, h) **1.** *v/i.* tailor; do tailoring; do dressmaking; **2.** *v/t.* make, tailor.

'**Schneidezahn** *m* incisor.

'**schneidig** *fig. adj.* plucky; dashing, keen; smart, *Am. sl. a.* nifty.

**schneien** ['ʃnaɪən] *v/i.* (ge-, h) snow.

**schnell** [ʃnɛl] **1.** *adj.* quick, fast; rapid; swift, speedy; *reply, etc.*: prompt; sudden; **2.** *adv.*: **~** *fahren* drive fast; **~** *handeln* act promptly *or* without delay; (*mach*) **~**! be quick!, hurry up!

**Schnelläufer** ['ʃnɛlɔ ʏfər] *m* sprinter; speed skater.

'**schnell|en** (ge-) *v/t.* (h) *and v/i.* (sein) jerk; '**2feuer** ✗ *n* rapid fire; '**2hefter** *m* (-s/-) folder.

'**Schnelligkeit** *f* (-/*no pl.*) quickness, fastness; rapidity; swiftness; promptness; speed, velocity.

'**Schnell|imbiß** *m* snack (bar); '**~imbißstube** *f* snack bar; **~kraft** *f* (-/*no pl.*) elasticity; '**~verfahren** *n* ½½ summary proceeding; ⊕ highspeed process; '**~zug** 🚂 *m* fast train, express (train).

**schneuzen** ['ʃnɔ ʏtsən] *v/refl.* (ge-, h) blow one's nose.

**schniegeln** ['ʃniːgəln] *v/refl.* (ge-, h) dress *or* smarten *or* spruce (o.s.)

**Schnipp|chen** ['ʃnɪpçən] *n*: F *j-m ein ~ schlagen* outwit *or* overreach s.o.; '**2isch** *adj.* pert, snappish, *Am.* F *a.* snippy.

**Schnitt** [ʃnɪt] **1.** *m* (-[e]s/-e) cut; *dress, etc.*: cut, make, style; pattern; *book*: edge; ⅄ (inter)section; *fig.*: average; F profit; **2.** ⊊ *pret. of schneiden*; '**~blumen** *f/pl.* cut flowers *pl.*; '**~e** *f* (-/-n) slice; '**~er** *m* (-s/-) reaper, mower; '**~fläche** ⅄ *f* section(al plane); '**2ig** *adj.* streamline(d); '**~muster** *n* pattern; '**~punkt** *m* (point of) intersection; '**~wunde** *f* cut, gash.

**Schnitzel** ['ʃnɪtsəl] **1.** *n* (-s/-) schnitzel; **2.** F *n, m* (-s/-) chip; *paper*: scrap; **~** *pl.* ⊕ parings *pl.*, shavings *pl.*; *paper*: *a.* clippings *pl.*; '**2n** *v/t.* (ge-, h) chip, shred, whittle.

**schnitzen** ['ʃnɪtsən] *v/t.* (ge-, h) carve, cut (in wood).

'**Schnitzer** *m* (-s/-) carver; F *fig.* blunder, *Am. a.* boner; **~ei** [~'raɪ] *f* **1.** (-/-en) carving, carved work; **2.** (-/*no pl.*) carving.

**schnöde** *adj.* ['ʃnøːdə] contemptuous; disgraceful; base, vile; **~r** *Mammon* filthy lucre.

**Schnörkel** ['ʃnœrkəl] *m* (-s/-) flourish (*a. fig.*), scroll (*a.* △).

**schnorr|en** F ['ʃnɔrən] *v/t. and v/i.* (ge-, h) cadge; '**2er** *m* (-s/-) cadger.

**schnüff|eln** ['ʃnʏfəln] *v/i.* (ge-, h) sniff, nose (*both: an dat.* at); *fig.* nose about, *Am.* F *a.* snoop around; '**2ler** *fig. m* (-s/-) spy, *Am.* F *a.* snoop; F sleuth(-hound).

**Schnuller** ['ʃnʊlər] *m* (-s/-) dummy, comforter.

**Schnulze** F ['ʃnʊltsə] *f* (-/-n) sentimental song *or* film *or* play, F tearjerker.

**Schnupf|en** ['ʃnʊpfən] **1.** *m* (-s/-) cold, catarrh; **2.** ⊊ *v/i.* (ge-, h) take snuff; '**~er** *m* (-s/-) snuff-taker; '**~tabak** *m* snuff.

**schnuppe** F ['ʃnʊpə] *adj.*: *das ist mir* **~** I don't care (F *a damn*); '**~rn** *v/i.* (ge-, h) sniff, nose (*both: an dat.* at).

**Schnur** [ʃnuːr] *f* (-/ ⊔e, ✎ -en) cord; string, twine; line; ⚡ flex.

**Schnür|band** ['ʃnyːr-] *n* lace; **~chen** ['~çən] *n* (-s/-): *wie am* **~** like clockwork; '**2en** *v/t.* (ge-, h) lace (up); (bind with) cord, tie up.

'**schnurgerade** *adj.* dead straight.

**Schnurr|bart** ['ʃnʊr-] *m* m(o)ustache; '**2en** (ge-, h) **1.** *v/i.* wheel, *etc.*: whir(r); *cat*: purr (*a. fig.*); F *fig.* cadge; **2.** F *fig. v/t.* cadge.

**Schnür|senkel** ['ʃnyːrzɛŋkəl] *m* (-s/-) shoe-lace, shoe-string; '**~stiefel** *m* lace-boot.

**schnurstracks** *adv.* ['ʃnuːr'ʃtraks] direct, straight; on the spot; at once, *sl.* straight away.

**schob** [ʃoːp] *pret. of schieben.*

**Schober** ['ʃoːbər] *m* (-s/-) rick, stack.

**Schock** [ʃɔk] **1.** *n* (-[e]s/-e) threescore; **2.** *m* (-[e]s/-e, ✎ -e) shock; '**2ieren** [~'kiːrən] *v/t.* (*no* -ge-, h) shock, scandalize.

**Schokolade** [ʃoko'laːdə] *f* (-/-n) chocolate.

**scholl** [ʃɔl] *pret. of schallen.*

**Scholle** ['ʃɔlə] *f* (-/-n) clod (*of earth*), *poet.* glebe; floe (*of ice*); *ichth.* plaice.

**schon** *adv.* [ʃoːn] already; **~** *lange* for a long time; **~** *gut!* all right!; **~** *der Gedanke* the very idea; **~** *der Name* the bare name; *hast du* **~** *ein-mal ...?* have you ever ...?; *mußt du* **~** *gehen?* need you go yet?; **~** *um 8 Uhr* as early as 8 o'clock.

**schön** [ʃøːn] **1.** *adj.* beautiful; *man*: handsome (*a. fig.*); *weather*: fair, fine (*a. iro.*); *das* **~e** *Geschlecht* the fair sex; *die* **~en** *Künste* the fine arts; **~e** *Literatur* belles-lettres *pl.*; **2.** *adv.*: **~** *warm* nice and warm; *du hast mich* ... *erschreckt* you gave me quite a start.

**schonen** ['ʃoːnən] *v/t.* (ge-, h) spare (*j-n s.o.*; *j-s Leben s.o.*'s life); take care of; husband (*strength, etc.*); sich ~ take care of o.s., look after o.s.

'**Schönheit** f 1. (-/no pl.) beauty; of woman: a. pulchritude; 2. (-/-en) beauty; beautiful woman, belle; '~spflege f beauty treatment.

'**schöntun** v/i. (irr. tun, sep., -ge-, h) flatter (j-m s.o.); flirt (dat. with).

'**Schonung** f 1. (-/no pl.) mercy; sparing, forbearance; careful treatment; 2. (-/-en) tree-nursery; '**2slos** adj. unsparing, merciless, relentless.

**Schopf** [ʃɔpf] m (-[e]s/¨e) tuft; orn. a. crest.

**schöpfen** ['ʃœpfən] v/t. (ge-, h) scoop, ladle; draw (*water at well*); draw, take (*breath*); take (*courage*); neue Hoffnung ~ gather fresh hope; Verdacht ~ become suspicious.

'**Schöpf|er** m (-s/-) creator; '**2erisch** adj. creative; '~ung f (-/-en) creation.

**schor** [ʃoːr] pret. of scheren.

**Schorf** [ʃɔrf] m (-[e]s/-e) scurf; scab, crust; '2ig adj. scurfy; scabby.

**Schornstein** ['ʃɔrn-] m chimney; ♨, ⌀ funnel; '~feger m (-s/-) chimney-sweep(er).

**Schoß** 1. [ʃoːs] m (-es/¨e) lap; womb; coat: tail; 2. ⌀ [ʃɔs] pret. of schießen.

**Schote** ⚓ ['ʃoːtə] f (-/-n) pod, husk.

**Schott|e** ['ʃɔtə] m (-n/-n) Scot, Scotchman, Scotsman; die ~n pl. the Scotch pl.; '~er m (-s/-) gravel; (road-)metal; '2isch adj. Scotch, Scottish.

**schräg** [ʃrɛːk] 1. adj. oblique, slanting; sloping; 2. adv.: ~ gegenüber diagonally across (von from).

**schrak** [ʃraːk] pret. of schrecken 2.

**Schramme** ['ʃramə] f (-/-n) scratch; skin: a. abrasion; '2n v/t. (ge-, h) scratch; graze, abrade (skin).

**Schrank** [ʃraŋk] m (-[e]s/¨e) cupboard, esp. Am. closet; wardrobe.

'**Schranke** f (-/-n) barrier (a. fig.); ♨ a. (railway-)gate; ꭗ bar; ~n pl. fig. bounds pl., limits pl.; '2nlos fig. adj. boundless; unbridled; '~nwärter m gate-keeper.

'**Schrankkoffer** m wardrobe trunk.

**Schraube** ['ʃraubə] f (-/-n) ⊕ screw; ♨ screw(-propeller); '2n v/t. (ge-, h) screw.

'**Schrauben|dampfer** ♨ m screw (steamer); '~mutter ⊕ f nut; '~schlüssel ⊕ m spanner, wrench; '~zieher ⊕ m screwdriver.

**Schraubstock** ⊕ ['ʃraup-] m vice, Am. vise.

**Schrebergarten** ['ʃreːbər-] m allotment garden.

**Schreck** [ʃrɛk] m (-[e]s/-e) fright, terror; consternation; '~bild n bugbear; '~en m (-s/-) fright, terror; consternation; '2en (ge-) 1. v/t. (h) frighten, scare; 2. v/i. (irr., sein):

only in compounds; '~ensbotschaft f alarming or terrible news; '~ensherrschaft f reign of terror; '2haft adj. fearful, timid; '2lich adj. terrible, dreadful (both a. F fig.); '~schuß m scare shot; fig. warning shot.

**Schrei** [ʃrai] m (-[e]s/-e) cry; shout; scream.

**schreiben** ['ʃraibən] 1. v/t. and v/i. (irr., ge-, h) write (j-m to s.o.; über acc. on); mit der Maschine ~ type(write); 2. v/t. (irr., ge-, h) spell; 3. ⌀ n (-s/-) letter.

'**Schreiber** m (-s/-) writer; secretary, clerk.

**schreib|faul** adj. ['ʃraip-] lazy in writing; '2feder f pen; '2fehler m mistake in writing or spelling, slip of the pen; '2heft n exercise-book; '2mappe f writing-case; '2maschine f typewriter; (mit der) ~ schreiben type(write); '2material n writing-materials pl., stationery; '2papier n writing-paper; '2schrift typ. f script; '2tisch m (writing-)desk; 2ung f (-/-en) spelling; '2unterlage f desk pad; '2waren f/pl. writing-materials pl., stationery; '2warenhändler m stationer; '2zeug n writing-materials pl.

'**schreien** (irr., ge-, h) 1. v/t. shout; scream; 2. v/i. cry (out) (vor dat. with pain, etc.); nach for bread, etc.); shout (vor with); scream (with); '~d adj. colour: loud; injustice: flagrant.

**schreiten** ['ʃraitən] v/i. (irr., ge-, sein) step, stride (über acc. across); fig. proceed (zu to).

**schrie** [ʃriː] pret. of schreien.

**schrieb** [ʃriːp] pret. of schreiben.

**Schrift** [ʃrift] f (-/-en) (hand-) writing, hand; typ. type; character, letter; writing; publication; die Heilige ~ the (Holy) Scriptures pl.; '~art f type; '2deutsch adj. literary German; '~führer m secretary; '~leiter m editor; '2lich 1. adj. written, in writing; 2. adv. in writing; '~satz m ꭗ pleadings pl.; typ. composition, type-setting; '~setzer m compositor, type-setter; '~sprache f literary language; '~steller m (-s/-) author, writer; '~stück n piece of writing, paper, document; '~tum n (-s/no pl.) literature; '~wechsel m exchange of letters, correspondence; '~zeichen n character, letter.

**schrill** adj. [ʃril] shrill, piercing.

**Schritt** [ʃrit] m (-[e]s/-e) step (a. fig.); pace (a. fig.); ~e unternehmen take steps; 2. ⌀ pret. of schreiten; '~macher m (-s/-) sports: pace-maker; '2weise 1. adj. gradual; 2. adv. a. step by step.

**schroff** adj. [ʃrɔf] rugged, jagged;

steep, precipitous; *fig.* harsh, gruff; ~er *Widerspruch* glaring contradiction.
**schröpfen** ['ʃrœpfən] *v/t.* (ge-, h) ⚕ cup; *fig.* milk, fleece.
**Schrot** [ʃro:t] *m, n* (-[e]s/-e) crushed grain; small shot; '**~brot** *n* wholemeal bread; '**~flinte** *f* shotgun.
**Schrott** [ʃrɔt] *m* (-[e]s/-e) scrap (-iron *or* -metal).
**schrubben** ['ʃrubən] *v/t.* (ge-, h) scrub.
**Schrulle** ['ʃrulə] *f* (-/-n) whim, fad.
**schrumpf|en** ['ʃrumpfən] *v/i.* (ge-, *sein*) shrink (*a.* ⊕, ⚕, *fig.*); '**2ung** *f* (-/-en) shrinking; shrinkage.
**Schub** [ʃu:p] *m* (-[e]s/ᵘe) push, shove; *phys.*, ⊕ thrust; *bread, people, etc.*: batch; '**~fach** *n* drawer; '**~karren** *m* wheelbarrow; '**~kasten** *m* drawer; '**~kraft** *phys.*, ⊕ *f* thrust; '**~lade** *f* (-/-n) drawer.
**Schubs** F [ʃups] *m* (-es/-e) push; '**2en** F *v/t.* (ge-, h) push.
**schüchtern** *adj.* ['ʃyçtərn] shy, bashful, timid; *girl*: coy; '**2heit** *f* (-/*no pl.*) shyness, bashfulness, timidity; coyness (*of girl*).
**schuf** [ʃu:f] *pret. of schaffen* 1.
**Schuft** [ʃuft] *m* (-[e]s/-e) scoundrel, rascal; cad; '**2en** F *v/i.* (ge-, h) drudge, slave, plod; '**2ig** *adj.* scoundrelly, rascally; caddish.
**Schuh** [ʃu:] *m* (-[e]s/-e) shoe; *j-m et. in die ~e schieben* put the blame for s.th. on s.o.; *wissen, wo der ~ drückt* know where the shoe pinches; '**~anzieher** *m* (-s/-) shoehorn; '**~band** *n* shoe-lace *or* -string; '**~creme** *f* shoe-cream, shoe-polish; '**~geschäft** *n* shoe-shop; '**~löffel** *m* shoehorn; '**~macher** *m* (-s/-) shoemaker; '**~putzer** *m* (-s/-) shoeblack, *Am. a.* shoeshine; '**~sohle** *f* sole; '**~spanner** *m* (-s/-) shoetree; '**~werk** *n*, '**~zeug** F *n* foot-wear, boots and shoes *pl.*
'**Schul|amt** *n* school-board; '**~arbeit** *f* homework; '**~bank** *f* (school-) desk; '**~beispiel** *n* test-case, typical example; '**~besuch** *m* (-[e]s/*no pl.*) attendance at school; '**~bildung** *f* education; *höhere ~* secondary education; '**~buch** *n* school-book.
**Schuld** [ʃult] *f* 1. (-/*no pl.*) guilt; fault, blame; *es ist s-e ~* it is his fault, he is to blame for it; 2. (-/-en) debt; *~en machen* contract *or* incur debts; '**2bewußt** *adj.* conscious of one's guilt; **2en** ['~dən] *v/t.* (ge-, h): *j-m et. ~* owe s.o. s.th.; *j-m Dank ~* be indebted to s.o. (*für* for); **2haft** *adj.* ['~thaft] culpable.
'**Schuldiener** *m* school attendant *or* porter.
**schuldig** *adj.* ['ʃuldiç] guilty (*e-r Sache* of s.th.); *respect, etc.*: due; *j-m et. ~ sein* owe s.o. s.th.; *Dank ~ sein* be indebted *to s.o.* (*für* for); *für ~ befinden* ⚖ find guilty; **2e** ['~gə] *m, f* (-n/-n) guilty person; culprit; '**2keit** *f* (-/*no pl.*) duty, obligation.
'**Schuldirektor** *m* headmaster, *Am. a.* principal.
'**schuld|los** *adj.* guiltless, innocent; '**2losigkeit** *f* (-/*no pl.*) guiltlessness, innocence; **2ner** ['~dnər] *m* (-s/-) debtor; '**2schein** *m* evidence of debt, certificate of indebtedness, IOU (= I owe you); '**2verschreibung** *f* bond, debt certificate.
**Schule** ['ʃu:lə] *f* (-/-n) school; *höhere ~* secondary school, *Am. a.* high school; *auf or in der ~* at school; *in die ~ gehen* go to school; '**2n** *v/t.* (ge-, h) train, school; *pol.* indoctrinate.
**Schüler** ['ʃy:lər] *m* (-s/-) schoolboy, pupil; *phls., etc.*: disciple; '**~austausch** *m* exchange of pupils; '**~in** *f* (-/-nen) schoolgirl.
'**Schul|ferien** *pl.* holidays *pl.*, vacation; '**~fernsehen** *n* educational TV; '**~funk** *m* educational broadcast; '**~gebäude** *n* school(house); '**~geld** *n* school fee(s *pl.*), tuition; '**~hof** *m* playground, *Am. a.* schoolyard; '**~kamerad** *m* schoolfellow; '**~lehrer** *m* schoolmaster, teacher; '**~mappe** *f* satchel; '**2meistern** *v/t.* (ge-, h) censure pedantically; '**~ordnung** *f* school regulations *pl.*; '**2pflichtig** *adj.* schoolable; '**~rat** *m* supervisor of schools, school inspector; '**~schiff** *n* training-ship; '**~schluß** *m* end of school; end of term; '**~schwänzer** *m* (-s/-) truant; '**~stunde** *f* lesson.
**Schulter** ['ʃultər] *f* (-/-n) shoulder; '**~blatt** *anat. n* shoulder-blade; '**2n** *v/t.* (ge-, h) shoulder.
'**Schul|unterricht** *m* school, lessons *pl.*; school instruction; '**~versäumnis** *f* (-/*no pl.*) absence from school; '**~wesen** *n* educational system; '**~zeugnis** *n* report.
**schummeln** F ['ʃuməln] *v/i.* (ge-, h) cheat, *Am.* F *a.* chisel.
**Schund** [ʃunt] 1. *m* (-[e]s/*no pl.*) trash, rubbish (*both a. fig.*); 2. **2** *pret. of schinden*; '**~literatur** *f* trashy literature; '**~roman** *m* trashy novel, *Am. a.* dime novel.
**Schupp|e** ['ʃupə] *f* (-/-n) scale; *~n pl. on head*: dandruff; '**~en** 1. *m* (-s/-) shed; *mot.* garage; ✈ hangar; 2. **2** *v/t.* (ge-, h) scale (*fish*); *sich ~ skin*: scale off; '**2ig** *adj.* scaly.
**Schür|eisen** ['ʃy:rˀ-] *n* poker; '**2en** *v/t.* (ge-, h) poke; stoke; *fig.* fan, foment.
**schürfen** ['ʃyrfən] (ge-, h) 1. ⚒ *v/i.* prospect (*nach* for); 2. *v/t.* ⚒ prospect for; *sich den Arm ~* graze one's arm.
**Schurk|e** ['ʃurkə] *m* (-n/-n) scoundrel, knave; **~erei** [~'raɪ] *f* (-/-en)

rascality, knavish trick; '2isch adj.
scoundrelly, knavish.

**Schürze** ['ʃyrtsə] f (-/-n) apron;
*children*: pinafore; '2n v/t. (ge-, h)
tuck up (*skirt*); tie (*knot*); purse
(*lips*); '~njäger m skirt-chaser, *Am.
sl.* wolf.

**Schuß** [ʃus] m (Schusses/Schüsse)
shot (*a. sports*); *ammunition*: round;
*sound*: report; charge; *wine, etc.*:
dash (*a. fig.*); in ~ sein be in full
swing, be in full working order.

**Schüssel** ['ʃysəl] f (-/-n) basin (*for
water, etc.*); bowl, dish, tureen
(*for soup, vegetables, etc.*).

'**Schuß|waffe** f fire-arm; '~weite f
range; '~wunde f gunshot wound.

**Schuster** ['ʃuːstər] m (-s/-) shoemaker; '2n fig. v/i. (ge-, h) s. pfuschen.

**Schutt** [ʃut] m (-[e]s/no pl.) rubbish,
refuse; rubble, debris.

**Schüttel|frost** ['ʃytəl-] m shiver-
ing-fit; '2n v/t. (ge-, h) shake; den
Kopf ~ shake one's head; j-m die
Hand ~ shake hands with s.o.

**schütten** ['ʃytən] (ge-, h) 1. v/t.
pour; spill (*auf acc.* on); 2. v/i.:
es schüttet it is pouring with rain.

**Schutz** [ʃuts] m (-es/no pl.) protection (gegen, vor dat. against),
defen|ce, *Am.* -se (against, from);
shelter (from); safeguard; cover;
'~brille f (e-e a pair of) goggles pl.

**Schütze** ['ʃytsə] m (-n/-n) marksman,
shot; ✕ rifleman; '2n v/t. (ge-, h)
protect (gegen, vor dat. against,
from), defend (against, from),
guard (against, from); shelter
(from); safeguard (*rights, etc.*).

**Schutzengel** ['ʃuts?-] m guardian
angel.

'**Schützen|graben** ✕ m trench;
'~könig m champion shot.

'**Schutz|haft** ŧ'ŧ f protective cus-
tody; '~heilige m patron saint;
'~herr m patron, protector; '~imp-
fung ✻ f protective inoculation;
*smallpox*: vaccination.

**Schützling** ['ʃytslin] m (-s/-e) pro-
tégé, *female*: protégée.

'**schutz|los** adj. unprotected; de-
fen|celess, *Am.* -seless; '2mann m
(-[e]s/=er, Schutzleute) policeman,
(police) constable, *sl.* bobby, *sl.* cop;
'2marke f trade mark, brand; '2-
mittel n preservative; ✻ prophylactic; '2patron m patron saint;
'2umschlag m (dust-)jacket, wrapper; '~zoll m protective duty.

**Schwabe** ['ʃvaːbə] m (-n/-n) Swabian.

**schwäbisch** adj. ['ʃveːbiʃ] Swabian.

**schwach** adj. [ʃvax] resistance, team,
knees (*a. fig.*), eyes, heart, voice,
character, tea, gr. verb, ✻ demand,
etc.: weak; person, etc.: infirm;
person, recollection, etc.: feeble;
sound, light, hope, idea, etc.: faint;

consolation, attendance, etc.: poor;
light, recollection, etc.: dim; *resemblance*: remote; das ~e Geschlecht
the weaker sex; ~e Seite weak point
or side.

**Schwäche** ['ʃveçə] f (-/-n) weakness
(*a. fig.*); infirmity; fig. foible; e-e ~
haben für have a weakness for; '2n
v/t. (ge-, h) weaken (*a. fig.*); impair
(*health*).

'**Schwach|heit** f (-/-en) weakness;
fig. a. frailty; '~kopf m simpleton,
soft(y), *Am.* F a. sap(head); 2köp-
fig adj. ['~kœpfiç] weak-headed,
soft, *Am. sl. a.* sappy.

**schwäch|lich** adj. ['ʃveçliç] weakly,
feeble; delicate, frail; '2ling m
(-s/-e) weakling (*a. fig.*).

'**schwach|sinnig** adj. weak- or
feeble-minded; '2strom ✻ m
(-[e]s/no pl.) weak current.

**Schwadron** ✕ [ʃva'droːn] f (-/-en)
squadron; 2ieren [~o'niːrən] v/t.
(no -ge-, h) swagger, vapo(u)r.

**Schwager** ['ʃvaːgər] m (-s/=) broth-
er-in-law.

**Schwägerin** ['ʃveːgərin] f (-/-nen)
sister-in-law. [swallow.\

**Schwalbe** orn. ['ʃvalbə] f (-/-n)]

**Schwall** [ʃval] m (-[e]s/-e) swell,
flood; words: torrent.

**Schwamm** [ʃvam] 1. m (-[e]s/=e)
sponge; ✻ fungus; ✻ dry-rot; 2. 2
pret. of schwimmen; '2ig adj.
spongy; face, etc.: bloated.

**Schwan** orn. [ʃvaːn] m (-[e]s/=e)
swan.

**schwand** [ʃvant] pret. of schwinden.

**schwang** [ʃvaŋ] pret. of schwingen.

**schwanger** adj. ['ʃvaŋər] pregnant,
with child, in the family way.

**schwängern** ['ʃveŋərn] v/t. (ge-, h)
get with child, impregnate (*a. fig.*).

'**Schwangerschaft** f (-/-en) preg-
nancy.

**schwanken** ['ʃvaŋkən] v/i. (ge-)
1. (h) earth, etc.: shake, rock; ✻
prices: fluctuate; branches, etc.:
sway; fig. waver, oscillate, vacillate;
2. (sein) stagger, totter.

**Schwanz** [ʃvants] m (-es/=e) tail (*a.
✻, ast.*); fig. train.

**schwänz|eln** ['ʃventsəln] v/i. (ge-, h)
wag one's tail; fig. fawn (um [up]on);
'~en v/t. (ge-, h) cut (lecture, etc.);
die Schule ~ play truant, *Am. a.*
play hooky.

**Schwarm** [ʃvarm] m (-[e]s/=e) bees,
etc.: swarm; birds: a. flight, flock;
fish: school, schoal; birds, girls,
etc.: bevy; F fig. fancy, craze; p.:
idol, hero; flame.

**schwärmen** ['ʃvermən] v/i. (ge-, h)
bees, etc.: swarm; fig.: revel; rave
(von about, of), gush (over); ~ für
be wild about, adore s.o.

'**Schwärmer** m (-s/-) enthusiast;
esp. eccl. fanatic; visionary; fireworks: cracker, squib; zo. hawk-

moth; ~ei [~'rai] f (-/-en) enthusiasm (für for); idolization; ecstasy; *esp. eccl.* fanaticism; '2isch *adj.* enthusiastic; gushing, raving; adoring; *esp. eccl.* fanatic(al).

Schwarte ['ʃvartə] f (-/-n) bacon: rind; F *fig.* old book.

schwarz *adj.* [ʃvarts] black (*a. fig.*); dark; dirty; ~es Brett notice-board, *Am.* bulletin board; ~es Brot brown bread; ~er Mann bog(e)y; ~er Markt black market; ~ *auf weiß* in black and white; *auf die* ~e *Liste setzen* blacklist; '2arbeit f illicit work; '2brot *n* brown bread; '2e *m, f* (-n/-n) black.

Schwärze ['ʃvɛrtsə] f (-/no pl.) blackness (*a. fig.*); darkness; '2n *v/t.* (ge-, h) blacken.

'schwarz|fahren F *v/i.* (*irr. fahren, sep., -ge-, sein*) travel without a ticket; *mot.* drive without a licence; '2fahrer *m* fare-dodger; *mot.* person *driving* without a licence; '2fahrt f ride without a ticket; *mot.* drive without a licence; '2handel *m* illicit trade, black marketeering; '2händler *m* black marketeer; '2hörer *m* listener without a licence.

'schwärzlich *adj.* blackish.

'Schwarz|markt *m* black market; '~seher *m* pessimist; *TV*: viewer without a licence; '~sender *m* pirate broadcasting station; ~'weiß-film *m* black-and-white film.

schwatzen ['ʃvatsən] *v/i.* (ge-, h) chat; chatter, tattle.

schwätz|en ['ʃvɛtsən] *v/i.* (ge-, h) *s. schwatzen*; '2er *m* (-s/-) chatterbox; tattler, prattler; gossip.

'schwatzhaft *adj.* talkative, garrulous.

Schwebe *fig.* ['ʃveːbə] f (-/no pl.): *in der* ~ *sein* be in suspense; *law, rule, etc.*: be in abeyance; '~bahn f aerial railway *or* ropeway; '2n *v/i.* (ge-, h) be suspended; *bird:* hover (*a. fig.*); glide; *fig.* be pending (*a. ɡ̇*); *in Gefahr* ~ be in danger.

Schwede ['ʃveːdə] *m* (-n/-n) Swede; '2isch *adj.* Swedish.

Schwefel ['ʃveːfəl] *m* (-s/no pl.) sulphur, *Am. a.* sulfur; '~säure ⚗ f (-/no pl.) sulphuric acid, *Am. a.* sulfuric acid.

Schweif [ʃvaif] *m* (-[e]s/-e) tail (*a. ast.*); *fig.* train; '2en (ge-) 1. *v/i.* (sein) rove, ramble; 2. ⊕ *v/t.* (h) curve; scallop.

schweigen ['ʃvaɪɡən] 1. *v/i.* (*irr., ge-, h*) be silent; 2. 2 *n* (-s/no pl.) silence; '~d *adj.* silent.

schweigsam *adj.* ['ʃvaɪkzaːm] taciturn; '2keit f (-/no pl.) taciturnity.

Schwein [ʃvain] *n* 1. (-[e]s/-e) zo. pig, hog, swine (*all a. contp. fig.*); 2. F (-[e]s/no pl.): ~ *haben* be lucky.

'Schweine|braten *m* roast pork;

'~fleisch *n* pork; '~hund F *contp. m* swine; ~rei [~'rai] f (-/-en) mess; dirty trick; smut(ty story); '~stall *m* pigsty (*a. fig.*).

'schweinisch *fig. adj.* swinish; smutty.

'Schweinsleder *n* pigskin.

Schweiß [ʃvais] *m* (-es/-e) sweat, perspiration; '2en ⊕ *v/t.* (ge-, h) weld; '~er ⊕ *m* (-s/-) welder; '~fuß *m* perspiring foot; '2ig *adj.* sweaty, damp with sweat.

Schweizer ['ʃvaɪtsər] *m* (-s/-) Swiss; *on farm:* dairyman.

schwelen ['ʃveːlən] *v/i.* (ge-, h) smo(u)lder (*a. fig.*).

schwelg|en ['ʃvɛlɡən] *v/i.* (ge-, h) lead a luxurious life; revel; *fig.* revel (*in dat.* in); '2er *m* (-s/-) revel(l)er; epicure; 2erei [~'rai] f (-/-en) revel(ry), feasting; '~erisch *adj.* luxurious; revel(l)ing.

Schwell|e ['ʃveːlə] f(-/-n) sill, threshold (*a. fig.*); ⛴ sleeper, *Am.* tie; '2en 1. *v/i.* (*irr., ge-, sein*) swell (out); 2. *v/t.* (ge-, h) swell; '~ung f (-/-en) swelling.

Schwemme ['ʃvɛmə] f (-/-n) watering-place; horse-pond; *at tavern, etc.:* taproom; † glut (*of fruit, etc.*).

Schwengel ['ʃvɛŋəl] *m* (-s/-) clapper (*of bell*); handle (*of pump*).

schwenk|en ['ʃvɛŋkən] (ge-) 1. *v/t.* (h) swing; wave (*hat, etc.*); brandish (*stick, etc.*); rinse (*washing*); 2. *v/i.* (sein) turn, wheel; '2ung f (-/-en) turn; *fig.* change of mind.

schwer [ʃveːr] 1. *adj.* heavy; *problem, etc.:* hard, difficult; *illness, mistake, etc.:* serious; *punishment, etc.:* severe; *fault, etc.:* grave; *wine, cigar, etc.:* strong; ~e *Zeiten* hard times; 2 *Pfund* ~ *sein* weigh two pounds; 2. *adv.:* ~ *arbeiten* work hard; ~ *hören* be hard of hearing; '2e f (-/no pl.) heaviness; *phys.* gravity (*a. fig.*); severity; '2fällig *adj.* heavy, slow; clumsy; '2gewicht *n sports:* heavy-weight; *fig.* main emphasis; '2gewichtler *m* (-s/-) *sports:* heavy-weight; '~hörig *adj.* hard of hearing; '2industrie f heavy industry; '2kraft *phys.* f (-/no pl.) gravity; '~lich *adv.* hardly, scarcely; '2mut f (-/no pl.) melancholy; ~mütig *adj.* ['~my:tiç] melancholy; '2punkt *m* centre of gravity, *Am.* center of gravity; *fig.:* crucial point; emphasis.

Schwert [ʃveːrt] *n* (-[e]s/-er) sword.

'Schwer|verbrecher *m* felon; '2verdaulich *adj.* indigestible, heavy; '2verständlich *adj.* difficult *or* hard to understand; '2verwundet *adj.* seriously wounded; '2wiegend *fig. adj.* weighty, momentous.

**Schwester** ['ʃvɛstər] f (-/-n) sister; nurse.

**schwieg** [ʃviːk] pret. of schweigen.

**Schwieger|eltern** ['ʃviːgər-] pl. parents-in-law pl.; **'~mutter** f mother-in-law; **'~sohn** m son-in-law; **'~tochter** f daughter-in-law; **'~vater** m father-in-law.

**Schwiel|e** ['ʃviːlə] f (-/-n) callosity; **'2ig** adj. callous.

**schwierig** adj. ['ʃviːriç] difficult, hard; **'2keit** f (-/-en) difficulty, trouble.

**Schwimm|bad** ['ʃvim-] n swimming-bath, Am. swimming pool; **'2en** v/i. (irr., ge-) 1. (sein) swim; thing: float; ich bin über den Fluß geschwommen I swam across the river; in Geld ~ be rolling in money; 2. (h) swim; ich habe lange unter Wasser geschwommen I swam under water for a long time; **'~gürtel** m swimming-belt; lifebelt; **'~haut** f web; **'~lehrer** m swimming-instructor; **'~weste** f life-jacket.

**Schwindel** ['ʃvindəl] m (-s/no pl.) ✗ vertigo, giddiness, dizziness; F fig.: swindle, humbug, sl. eyewash; cheat, fraud; **'~anfall** ✗ m fit of dizziness; **'2erregend** adj. dizzy (a. fig.); **'~firma** ✝ f long firm, Am. wildcat firm; **'2n** v/i. (ge-, h) cheat, humbug, swindle.

**schwinden** ['ʃvindən] v/i. (irr., ge-, sein) dwindle, grow less; strength, colour, etc.: fade.

**'Schwindl|er** m (-s/-) swindler, cheat, humbug; liar; **'2ig** ✗ adj. giddy, dizzy.

**Schwind|sucht** ✗ ['ʃvint-] f (-/no pl.) consumption; **'2süchtig** ✗ adj. consumptive.

**Schwing|e** ['ʃviŋə] f (-/-n) wing, poet. pinion; swingle; **'2en** (irr., ge-, h) 1. v/t. swing; brandish (weapon); swingle (flax); 2. v/i. swing; ⊕ oscillate; sound, etc.: vibrate; **'~ung** f (-/-en) oscillation; vibration.

**Schwips** F [ʃvips] m (-es/-e): e-n ~ haben be tipsy, have had a drop too much.

**schwirren** ['ʃvirən] v/i. (ge-) 1. (sein) whir(r); arrow, etc.: whiz(z); insects: buzz; rumours, etc.: buzz, circulate; 2. (h): mir schwirrt der Kopf my head is buzzing.

**'Schwitz|bad** n sweating-bath, hot-air bath, vapo(u)r bath; **'2en** (ge-, h) 1. v/i. sweat, perspire; 2. F fig. v/t.: Blut und Wasser ~ be in great anxiety.

**schwoll** [ʃvɔl] pret. of schwellen.

**schwor** [ʃvoːr] pret. of schwören.

**schwören** ['ʃvøːrən] (irr., ge-, h) 1. v/t. swear; e-n Meineid ~ commit perjury; j-m Rache ~ vow vengeance against s.o.; 2. v/i. swear (bei by);

~ auf (acc.) have great belief in, F swear by.

**schwül** adj. [ʃvyːl] sultry, oppressively hot; **'2e** f (-/no pl.) sultriness.

**Schwulst** [ʃvulst] m (-es/ꞏe) bombast.

**schwülstig** adj. ['ʃvylstiç] bombastic, turgid.

**Schwund** [ʃvunt] m (-[e]s/no pl.) dwindling; wireless, etc.: fading; ✗ atrophy.

**Schwung** [ʃvuŋ] m (-[e]s/ꞏe) swing; fig. verve, go; flight (of imagination); buoyancy; **'2haft** ✝ adj. flourishing, brisk; **'~rad** ⊕ n fly-wheel; watch, clock: balance-wheel; **'2voll** adj. full of energy or verve; attack, translation, etc.: spirited; style, etc.: racy.

**Schwur** [ʃvuːr] m (-[e]s/ꞏe) oath; **'~gericht** ⚖ n England, Wales: appr. court of assize.

**sechs** [zɛks] 1. adj. six; 2. 2 f (-/-en) six; **'2eck** n (-[e]s/-e) hexagon; **'~eckig** adj. hexagonal; **'~fach** adj. sixfold, sextuple; **'~mal** adv. six times; **'~monatig** adj. lasting or of six months, six-months ...; **'~monatlich** 1. adj. six-monthly; 2. adv. every six months; **'~stündig** adj. ['~ʃtyndiç] lasting or of six hours, six-hour ...; 2'**tagerennen** n cycling: six-day race; **'~tägig** adj. ['~tɛːgiç] lasting or of six days.

**sechs|te** adj. ['zɛkstə] sixth; **'2tel** n (-s/-) sixth (part); **'~tens** adv. sixthly, in the sixth place.

**sech|zehn(te)** adj. ['zɛç-] sixteen(th); **~zig** adj. ['~tsiç] sixty; **'~zigste** adj. sixtieth.

**See** [zeː] 1. m (-s/-n) lake; 2. f (-/no pl.) sea; an die ~ gehen go to the seaside; in ~ gehen or stechen put to sea; auf ~ at sea; auf hoher ~ on the high seas; zur ~ gehen go to sea; 3. f (-/-n) sea, billow; **'~bad** n seaside resort; **'~fahrer** m sailor, navigator; **'~fahrt** f navigation; voyage; **'2fest** adj. seaworthy; ~ sein be a good sailor; **'~gang** m (motion of the) sea; **'~hafen** m seaport; **'~handel** ✝ m maritime trade; **'~herrschaft** f naval supremacy; **'~hund** zo. m seal; **'2krank** adj. seasick; **'~krankheit** f (-/no pl.) seasickness; **'~krieg** m naval war(fare).

**Seele** ['zeːlə] f (-/-n) soul (a. fig.); mit or von ganzer ~ with all one's heart.

**'Seelen|größe** f (-/no pl.) greatness of soul or mind; **'~heil** n salvation, spiritual welfare; **'2los** adj. soulless; **'~qual** f anguish of mind, (mental) agony; **'~ruhe** f peace of mind; coolness.

**'seelisch** adj. psychic(al), mental.

**'Seelsorge** f (-/no pl.) cure of souls;

ministerial work; '⁓r m (-s/-) pastor, minister.

'**See|macht** f naval power; '⁓**mann** m (-[e]s/Seeleute) seaman, sailor; '⁓**meile** f nautical mile; '⁓**not** f (-/no pl.) distress (at sea); '⁓**räuber** m pirate; ⁓**räuberei** [⁓'rai] f (-/-en) piracy; '⁓**recht** n maritime law; '⁓**reise** f voyage; '⁓**schiff** n seagoing ship; '⁓**schlacht** f naval battle; '⁓**schlange** f sea serpent; '⁓**sieg** m naval victory; '⁓**stadt** f seaside town; '⁓**streitkräfte** f/pl. naval forces pl.; '⁓**tüchtig** adj. seaworthy; '⁓**warte** f naval observatory; '⁓**weg** m sea-route; auf dem ⁓ by sea; '⁓**wesen** n (-s/no pl.) maritime or naval affairs pl.

**Segel** ['ze:gəl] n (-s/-) sail; unter ⁓ gehen set sail; '⁓**boot** n sailing-boat, Am. sailboat; sports: yacht; '⁓**fliegen** n (-s/no pl.) gliding, soaring; '⁓**flug** m gliding flight, glide; '⁓**flugzeug** n glider; '⁓**n** (ge-) 1. v/i. (h, sein) sail; sports: yacht; 2. v/t. (h) sail; '⁓**schiff** n sailing-ship, sailing-vessel; '⁓**sport** m yachting; '⁓**tuch** n (-[e]s/-e) sail-cloth, canvas.

**Segen** ['ze:gən] m (-s/-) blessing (a. fig.), esp. eccl. benediction; '⁓**sreich** adj. blessed.

**Segler** ['ze:glər] m (-s/-) sailing-vessel, sailing-ship; fast, good, etc. sailer; yachtsman.

**segn|en** ['ze:gnən] v/t. (ge-, h) bless; '⁓**ung** f (-/-en) s. Segen.

**sehen** ['ze:ən] (irr., ge-, h) 1. v/i. see; gut ⁓ have good eyes; ⁓ auf (acc.) look at; be particular about; ⁓ nach look for; look after; 2. v/t. see; notice; watch, observe; '⁓**swert** adj. worth seeing; '⁓**swürdigkeit** f (-/-en) object of interest, curiosity; ⁓en pl. sights pl. (of a place).

**Seher** ['ze:ər] m (-s/-) seer, prophet; '⁓**blick** m (-[e]s/no pl.) prophetic vision; '⁓**gabe** f (-/no pl.) gift of prophecy.

'**Seh|fehler** m visual defect; '⁓**kraft** f vision, eyesight.

**Sehne** ['ze:nə] f (-/-n) anat. sinew, tendon; string (of bow); Å chord.

'**sehnen** v/refl. (ge-, h) long (nach for), yearn (for, after); sich danach ⁓ zu inf. be longing to inf.

'**Sehnerv** anat. m visual or optic nerve.

'**sehnig** adj. sinewy (a. fig.), stringy.

'**sehn|lich** adj. longing; ardent; passionate; '⁓**sucht** f longing, yearning; '⁓**süchtig** adj., '⁓**suchtsvoll** adj. longing, yearning; eyes, etc.: a. wistful.

**sehr** adv. [ze:r] before adj. and adv.: very, most; with vb.: (very) much, greatly.

'**Seh|rohr** ♣ n periscope; '⁓**weite** f

range of sight, visual range; in ⁓ within eyeshot or sight.

**seicht** adj. [zaiçt] shallow; fig. a. superficial.

**Seide** ['zaidə] f (-/-n) silk.

'**seiden** adj. silk, silken (a. fig.); '⁓**flor** m silk gauze; '⁓**glanz** m silky lust|re, Am. -er; '⁓**händler** m mercer; '⁓**papier** n tissue(-paper); '⁓**raupe** zo. f silkworm; '⁓**spinnerei** f silk-spinning mill; '⁓**stoff** m silk cloth or fabric.

'**seidig** adj. silky.

**Seife** ['zaifə] f (-/-n) soap.

'**Seifen|blase** f soap-bubble; '⁓**kistenrennen** n soap-box derby; '⁓**lauge** f (soap-)suds pl.; '⁓**pulver** n soap-powder; '⁓**schale** f soapdish; '⁓**schaum** m lather.

'**seifig** adj. soapy.

**seih|en** ['zaiən] v/t. (ge-, h) strain, filter; '⁓**er** m (-s/-) strainer, colander.

**Seil** [zail] n (-[e]s/-e) rope; '⁓**bahn** f funicular or cable railway; '⁓**er** m (-s/-) rope-maker; '⁓**tänzer** m ropedancer.

**sein¹** [zain] 1. v/i. (irr., ge-, sein) be; exist; 2. ⁓ n (-s/no pl.) being; existence.

**sein²** poss. pron. [⁓] his, her, its (in accordance with gender of possessor); der (die, das) ⁓e his, hers, its; ⁓ Glück machen make one's fortune; die Seinen pl. his family or people.

'**seiner**|'**seits** adv. for his part; '⁓**zeit** adv. then, at that time; in those days.

'**seines**|'**gleichen** pron. his equal(s pl.); j-n wie ⁓ behandeln treat s.o. as one's equal; er hat nicht ⁓ he has no equal; there is no one like him.

**seit** [zait] 1. prp. (dat.): ⁓ 1945 since 1945; ⁓ drei Wochen for three weeks; 2. cj. since; es ist ein Jahr her, ⁓ ... it is a year now since ...; ⁓**dem** [⁓'de:m] 1. adv. since or from that time, ever since; 2. cj. since.

**Seite** ['zaitə] f (-/-n) side (a. fig.); flank (a. ✕, △); page (of book).

'**Seiten|ansicht** f profile, side-view; '⁓**blick** m side-glance; '⁓**flügel** △ m wing; '⁓**hieb** fig. m innuendo, sarcastic remark; '⁓**s** prp. (gen.) on the part of; by; '⁓**schiff** △ n church: aisle; '⁓**sprung** fig. m extra-marital adventure; '⁓**straße** f bystreet; '⁓**stück** fig. n counterpart (zu of); '⁓**weg** m by-way.

**seit'her** adv. since (then, that time).

'**seit|lich** adj. lateral; '⁓**wärts** adv. [⁓verts] sideways; aside.

**Sekret|är** [zekre'tε:r] m (-s/-e) secretary; bureau; '⁓**ariat** [⁓ari'a:t] n (-[e]s/-e) secretary's office; secretariat(e); ⁓**ärin** f (-/-nen) secretary.

**Sekt** [zɛkt] *m* (-[e]s/-e) champagne.

**Sekt|e** ['zɛktə] *f* (-/-n) sect; **~ierer** [~'tiːrər] *m* (-s/-) sectarian.

**Sektor** ['zɛktɔr] *m* (-s/-en) ♈, ♋, *pol.* sector; *fig.* field, branch.

**Sekunde** [ze'kundə] *f* (-/-n) second; **~ubruchteil** *m* split second; **~n-zeiger** *m* second-hand.

**selb** *adj.* [zɛlp] same; **~er** F *pron.* ['~bər] *s.* selbst 1.

**selbst** [zɛlpst] **1.** *pron.* self; personally; *ich* ~ I myself; *von* ~ *p.* of one's own accord; *thing:* by itself, automatically; **2.** *adv.* even; **3.** ♈ *n* (-/no *pl.*) (one's own) self; ego.

**selbständig** *adj.* ['zɛlpʃtɛndiç] independent; *sich* ~ *machen* set up for o.s.; **♈keit** *f* (-/no *pl.*) independence.

**'Selbst|anlasser** *mot. m* self-starter; **~anschluß** *teleph. m* automatic connection; **~bedienungsladen** *m* self-service shop; **~beherrschung** *f* self-command, self-control; **~bestimmung** *f* self-determination; **~betrug** *m* self-deception; **♈bewußt** *adj.* self-confident, self-reliant; **~bewußtsein** *n* self-confidence, self-reliance; **~binder** *m* (-s/-) tie; **~erhaltung** *f* self-preservation; **~erkenntnis** *f* self-knowledge; **~erniedrigung** *f* self-abasement; **♈gefällig** *adj.* (self-)complacent; **~gefälligkeit** *f* (-/no *pl.*) (self-)complacency; **~gefühl** *n* (-[e]s/no *pl.*) self-reliance; **♈gemacht** *adj.* ['~gəmaxt] home-made; **♈gerecht** *adj.* self-righteous; **~gespräch** *n* soliloquy, monolog(ue); **♈herrlich 1.** *adj.* high-handed, autocratic(al); **2.** *adv.* with a high hand; **~hilfe** *f* self-help; **~kostenpreis** † *m* cost price; **~laut** *gr. m* vowel; **♈los** *adj.* unselfish, disinterested; **~mord** *m* suicide; **~mörder** *m* suicide; **♈mörderisch** *adj.* suicidal; **♈sicher** *adj.* self-confident, self-assured; **~sucht** *f* (-/no *pl.*) selfishness, ego(t)ism; **♈süchtig** *adj.* selfish, ego(t)istic(al); **♈tätig** ⊕ *adj.* self-acting, automatic; **~täuschung** *f* self-deception; **~überwindung** *f* (-/no *pl.*) self-conquest; **~unterricht** *m* self-instruction; **~verleugnung** *f* self-denial; **~versorger** *m* (-s/-) self-supporter; **♈verständlich 1.** *adj.* self-evident, obvious; **2.** *adv.* of course, naturally; ~! *a.* by all means!; **~verständlichkeit** *f* **1.** (-/-en) matter of course; **2.** (-/no *pl.*) matter-of-factness; **~verteidigung** *f* self-defen|ce, *Am.* -se; **~vertrauen** *n* self-confidence, self-reliance; **~verwaltung** *f* self-government, autonomy; **♈zufrieden** *adj.* self-satisfied; **~zufriedenheit** *f* self-

satisfaction; **~zweck** *m* (-[e]s/no *pl.*) end in itself.

**selig** *adj.* ['zeːliç] *eccl.* blessed; late, deceased; *fig.* blissful, overjoyed; **♈keit** *fig. f* (-/-en) bliss, very great joy.

**Sellerie** ♧['zɛləri:] *m* (-s/-[s]), *f* (-/-) celery.

**selten** ['zɛltən] **1.** *adj.* rare; scarce; **2.** *adv.* rarely, seldom; **'♈heit** *f* (-/-en) rarity, scarcity; rarity, curio(sity); **'♈heitswert** *m* (-[e]s/no *pl.*) scarcity value.

**Selterswasser** ['zɛltərs-] *n* (-s/⁛) seltzer (water), soda-water.

**seltsam** *adj.* ['zɛltzaːm] strange, odd.

**Semester** *univ.* [ze'mɛstər] *n* (-s/-) term.

**Semikolon** *gr.* [zemi'koːlɔn] *n* (-s/-s, Semikola) semicolon.

**Seminar** [zemi'naːr] *n* (-s/-e) *univ.* seminar; seminary (*for priests*).

**Senat** [ze'naːt] *m* (-[e]s/-e) senate; *parl.* Senate.

**send|en** ['zɛndən] *v/t.* **1.** ([*irr.*,] ge-, h) send; forward; **2.** (ge-, h) transmit; broadcast; *Am. a.* radio(broadcast); telecast; **'♈er** *m* (-s/-) transmitter; broadcasting station.

**'Sende|raum** *m* (broadcasting) studio; **~zeichen** *n* interval signal.

**'Sendung** *f* (-/-en) † consignment, shipment; broadcast; telecast; *fig.* mission. [♧).\

**Senf** [zɛnf] *m* (-[e]s/-e) mustard (*a.*)

**sengen** ['zɛŋən] *v/t.* (ge-, h) singe, scorch; **~d** *adj. heat:* parching.

**senil** *adj.* [ze'niːl] senile; **♈ität** [~ili'tɛːt] *f* (-/no *pl.*) senility.

**senior** *adj.* ['zeːniɔr] senior.

**Senk|blei** ['zɛŋk-] *n* ♈ plumb, plummet; ♣ *a.* sounding-lead; **'♈e** *geogr. f* (-/-n) depression, hollow; **'♈en** *v/t.* (ge-, h) lower; sink (*a. voice*); let down; bow (*head*); cut (*prices, etc.*); *sich* ~ *land, buildings, etc.:* sink, subside; *ceiling, etc.:* sag; **'~fuß** ♨ *m* flat-foot; **'~fußeinlage** *f* arch support; **'~grube** *f* cesspool; **♈recht** *adj.* vertical, *esp.* ♈ perpendicular; **'~ung** *f* (-/-en) *geogr.* depression, hollow; lowering, reduction (*of prices*); ♨ sedimentation.

**Sensation** [zɛnza'tsjoːn] *f* (-/-en) sensation; **♈ell** *adj.* [~ɔ'nɛl] sensational; **~slust** *f* (-/no *pl.*) sensationalism; **~spresse** *f* yellow press.

**Sense** ['zɛnzə] *f* (-/-n) scythe.

**sensi|bel** *adj.* [zɛn'ziːbəl] sensitive; **♈bilität** [~ibili'tɛːt] *f* (-/no *pl.*) sensitiveness.

**sentimental** *adj.* [zɛntimɛn'taːl] sentimental; **♈ität** [~ali'tɛːt] *f* (-/no *pl.*) sentimentality.

**September** [zɛp'tɛmbər] *m* (-[s]/-) September.

**Serenade** ♪ [zere'na:də] f (-/-n) serenade.

**Serie** ['ze:rjə] f (-/-n) series; set; billiards: break; '2nmäßig 1. adj. standard; 2. adv.: ~ herstellen produce in mass; '~nproduktion f mass production.

**seriös** adj. [ze'rjø:s] serious; trustworthy, reliable.

**Serum** ['ze:rum] n (-s/Seren, Sera) serum.

**Service**[1] [zər'vi:s] n (-s/-) service, set.

**Service**[2] ['zø:rvis] m, n (-/-s) service.

**servier|en** [zər'vi:rən] v/t. (no -ge-, h) serve; '2wagen m trolley(-table).

**Serviette** [zər'vjɛtə] f (-/-n) (table-) napkin.

**Sessel** ['zesəl] m (-s/-) armchair, easy chair; '~lift m chair-lift.

**seßhaft** adj. ['zɛshaft] settled, established; resident.

**Setzei** ['zɛts?-] n fried egg.

**'setzen** (ge-) 1. v/t. (h) set, place, put; typ. compose; ♪ plant; erect, raise (monument); stake (money) (auf acc. on); sich ~ sit down, take a seat; bird: perch; foundations of house, sediment, etc.: settle; 2. v/i. (h): ~ auf (acc.) back (horse, etc.); 3. v/i. (sein): ~ über (acc.) leap (wall, etc.); clear (hurdle, etc.); take (ditch, etc.).

**'Setzer** typ. m (-s/-) compositor, type-setter; ~ei typ. [~'rai] f (-/-en) composing-room.

**Seuche** ['zɔyçə] f (-/-n) epidemic (disease).

**seufz|en** ['zɔyftsən] v/i. (ge-, h) sigh; '2er m (-s/-) sigh.

**sexuell** adj. [zɛksu'ɛl] sexual.

**sezieren** [ze'tsi:rən] v/t. (no -ge-, h) dissect (a. fig.).

**sich** refl. pron. [ziç] oneself; sg. himself, herself, itself; pl. themselves; sg. yourself, pl. yourselves; each other, one another; sie blickte ~ um she looked about her.

**Sichel** ['ziçəl] f (-/-n) sickle; s. Mondsichel.

**sicher** ['ziçər] 1. adj. secure (vor dat. from), safe (from); proof (against); hand: steady; certain, sure; positive; aus ~er Quelle from a reliable source; e-r Sache ~ sein be sure of s.th.; 2. adv. s. sicherlich; um ~ zu gehen to be on the safe side, to make sure.

**'Sicherheit** f (-/-en) security; safety; surety, certainty; positiveness; assurance (of manner); in ~ bringen place in safety; '~snadel f safety-pin; '~sschloß n safety-lock.

**'sicher|lich** adv. surely, certainly; undoubtedly; er wird ~ kommen he is sure to come; '~n v/t. (ge-, h) secure (a. ✕, ⊕); guarantee (a. ✝); protect, safeguard; sich et. ~ secure

(prize, seat, etc.); '~stellen v/t. (sep., -ge-, h) secure; '2ung f (-/-en) securing; safeguard(ing); ✝ security, guaranty; ⊕ safety device; ⚡ fuse.

**Sicht** [ziçt] f (-/no pl.) visibility; view; in ~ kommen come in(to) view or sight; auf lange ~ in the long run; auf or bei ~ ✝ at sight; '2bar adj. visible; '2en v/t. (ge-, h) ⚓ sight; fig. sift; '2lich adv. visibly; '~vermerk m visé, visa (on passport).

**sickern** ['zikərn] v/i. (ge-, sein) trickle, ooze, seep.

**sie** pers. pron. [zi:] nom.: sg. she, pl. they; acc.: sg. her, pl. them; Sie nom. and acc.: sg. and pl. you.

**Sieb** [zi:p] n (-[e]s/-e) sieve; riddle (for soil, gravel, etc.).

**sieben**[1] ['zi:bən] v/t. (ge-, h) sieve, sift; riddle.

**sieben**[2] [~] 1. adj. seven; 2. 2 f (-/-) (number) seven; böse ~ shrew, vixen; '~fach adj. sevenfold; '~mal adv. seven times; '2sachen F f/pl. belongings pl., F traps pl.; '~te adj. seventh; '2tel n (-s/-) seventh (part); '~tens adv. seventhly, in the seventh place.

**sieb|zehn(te)** adj. ['zi:p-] seventeen(th); '~zig adj. ['~tsiç] seventy; '~zigste adj. seventieth.

**siech** adj. [zi:ç] sickly; '2tum n (-s/no pl.) sickliness, lingering illness.

**Siedehitze** ['zi:də-] f boiling-heat.

**siedeln** ['zi:dəln] v/i. (ge-, h) settle; Am. a. homestead.

**siede|n** ['zi:dən] v/t. and v/i. ([irr.,] ge-, h) boil, simmer; '2punkt m boiling-point (a. fig.).

**Siedler** ['zi:dlər] m (-s/-) settler; Am. a. homesteader; '~stelle f settler's holding; Am. a. homestead.

**'Siedlung** f (-/-en) settlement; housing estate.

**Sieg** [zi:k] m (-[e]s/-e) victory (über acc. over); sports: a. win; den ~ davontragen win the day, be victorious.

**Siegel** ['zi:gəl] n (-s/-) seal (a. fig.); signet; '~lack m sealing-wax; '2n v/t. (ge-, h) seal; '~ring m signetring.

**sieg|en** ['zi:gən] v/i. (ge-, h) be victorious (über acc. over), conquer s.o.; sports: win; '2er m (-s/-) conqueror, rhet. victor; sports: winner.

**Siegeszeichen** ['zi:gəs-] n trophy.

**'siegreich** adj. victorious, triumphant.

**Signal** [zi'gna:l] n (-s/-e) signal; 2isieren [~ali'zi:rən] v/t. (no -ge-, h) signal.

**Silbe** ['zilbə] f (-/-n) syllable; '~ntrennung f syllabi(fi)cation.

**Silber** ['zilbər] n (-s/no pl.) silver; s. Tafelsilber; '2n adj. (of) silver;

'⹁zeug F *n* silver plate, *Am. a.* silverware.

**Silhouette** [zilu'ɛtə] *f* (-/-n) silhouette; skyline.

**Silvester** [zil'vɛstər] *n* (-s/-), ⹁abend *m* new-year's eve.

**simpel** ['zimpəl] **1.** *adj.* plain, simple; stupid, silly; **2.** ⚥ *m* (-s/-) simpleton.

**Sims** [zims] *m, n* (-es/-e) ledge; sill (*of window*); mantelshelf (*of fireplace*); shelf; ⚠ cornice.

**Simul|ant** [zimu'lant] *m* (-en/-en) *esp.* ✗, ⚓ malingerer; **2ieren** (*no* -ge-, *h*) **1.** *v/t.* sham, feign, simulate (*illness, etc.*); **2.** *v/i.* sham, feign; *esp.* ✗, ⚓ malinger.

**Sinfonie** ♪ [zinfo'ni:] *f* (-/-n) symphony.

**sing|en** ['ziŋən] *v/t. and v/i.* (*irr.*, *ge-*, *h*) sing; *vom Blatt* ⹁ sing at sight; *nach Noten* ⹁ sing from music; '**2sang** F *m* (-[e]s/*no pl.*) singsong; '**2spiel** *n* musical comedy; '**2stimme** ♪ *f* vocal part.

**Singular** *gr.* ['ziŋgulaːr] *m* (-s/-e) singular (number).

'**Singvogel** *m* song-bird, songster.

**sinken** ['ziŋkən] *v/i.* (*irr.*, *ge-*, *sein*) sink; *ship:* a. founder, go down; ✝ *prices:* fall, drop, go down; *den Mut* ⹁ *lassen* lose courage.

**Sinn** [zin] *m* (-[e]s/-e) sense; taste (*für for*); tendency; sense, meaning; *von* ⹁*en sein* be out of one's senses; *im* ⹁ *haben* have in mind; *in gewissem* ⹁*e* in a sense; '⹁**bild** *n* symbol, emblem; '**2bildlich** *adj.* symbolic(al), emblematic; '**2en** *v/i.* (*irr.*, *ge-*, *h*): *auf Rache* ⹁ meditate revenge.

'**Sinnen|lust** ⟨*sensuality*⟩; '⹁**mensch** *m* sensualist; '⹁**rausch** *m* intoxication of the senses.

**sinnentstellend** *adj.* ['zin⁹-] garbling, distorting. [world.]

'**Sinnenwelt** *f* (-/*no pl.*) material)

'**Sinnes|änderung** *f* change of mind; '⹁**art** *f* disposition, mentality; '⹁**organ** *n* sense-organ; '⹁**täuschung** *f* illusion, hallucination.

'**sinn|lich** *adj.* sensual; material; '**2lichkeit** *f* (-/*no pl.*) sensuality; '⹁**los** *adj.* senseless; futile, useless; '**2losigkeit** *f* (-/-en) senselessness; futility, uselessness; '⹁**reich** *adj.* ingenious; '⹁**verwandt** *adj.* synonymous.

**Sipp|e** ['zipə] *f* (-/-n) tribe; (blood-)relations *pl.*; family; '⹁**schaft** *contp.* *f* (-/-en) relations *pl.*; *fig.* clan, clique; *die ganze* ⹁ the whole lot.

**Sirene** [zi'reːnə] *f* (-/-n) siren.

**Sirup** ['ziːrup] *m* (-s/-e) syrup, *Am.* sirup; treacle, molasses *sg.*

**Sitte** ['zitə] *f* (-/-n) custom; habit; usage; ⹁*n pl.* morals *pl.*; manners *pl.*

'**Sitten|bild** *n*, '⹁**gemälde** *n* genre (-painting); *fig.* picture of manners and morals; '⹁**gesetz** *n* moral law; '⹁**lehre** *f* ethics *pl.*; '**2los** *adj.* immoral; '⹁**losigkeit** *f* (-/-en) immorality; '⹁**polizei** *f* *appr.* vice squad; '⹁**prediger** *m* moralizer; '⹁**richter** *fig.* *m* censor, moralizer; '**2streng** *adj.* puritanic(al).

'**sittlich** *adj.* moral; '**2keit** *f* (-/*no pl.*) morality; '**2keitsverbrechen** *n* sexual crime.

'**sittsam** *adj.* modest; '**2keit** *f* (-/*no pl.*) modesty.

**Situation** [zitua'tsjoːn] *f* (-/-en) situation.

**Sitz** [zits] *m* (-es/-e) seat (*a. fig.*); fit (*of dress, etc.*).

'**sitzen** *v/i.* (*irr.*, *ge-*, *h*) sit, be seated; *dress, etc.*: fit; *blow, etc.*: tell; F *fig.* do time; ⹁ *bleiben* remain seated, keep one's seat; '⹁**bleiben** *v/i.* (*irr.* bleiben, *sep.*, -ge-, *sein*) *girl at dance:* F be a wallflower; *girl:* be left on the shelf; *at school:* not to get one's remove; ⹁ *auf (dat.)* be left with (*goods*) on one's hands; '⹁**d** *adj.:* ⹁*e Tätigkeit* sedentary work; '⹁**lassen** *v/t.* (*irr.* lassen, *sep.*, [*no*] -ge-, *h*) leave *s.o.* in the lurch, let *s.o.* down; *girl:* jilt (*lover*); leave (*girl*) high and dry; *auf sich* ⹁ pocket (*insult, etc.*).

'**Sitz|gelegenheit** *f* seating accommodation, seat(s *pl.*); ⹁ *bieten für* seat; '⹁**platz** *m* seat; '⹁**streik** *m* sit-down or stay-in strike.

'**Sitzung** *f* (-/-en) sitting (*a. parl.*, *paint.*); meeting, conference; '⹁**periode** *f* session.

**Skala** ['skaːla] *f* (-/Skalen, Skalas) scale (*a. ♪*); dial (*of radio set*); *fig.* gamut; *gleitende* ⹁ sliding scale.

**Skandal** [skan'daːl] *m* (-s/-e) scandal; row, riot; **2ös** [⹁a'løːs] *adj.* [⹁a'loːs] scandalous.

**Skelett** [ske'lɛt] *n* (-[e]s/-e) skeleton.

**Skep|sis** ['skɛpsis] *f* (-/*no pl.*) scepticism, *Am. a.* skepticism; ⹁**tiker** [⹁'tikər] *m* (-s/-) sceptic, *Am. a.* skeptic; '**2tisch** *adj.* sceptical, *Am. a.* skeptical.

**Ski** [ʃiː] *m* (-s/-e, ⹁-) ski; ⹁ *laufen or fahren* ski; '⹁**fahrer** *m*, '⹁**läufer** *m* skier; '⹁**lift** *m* ski-lift; '⹁**sport** *m* (-[e]s/*no pl.*) skiing.

**Skizz|e** ['skitsə] *f* (-/-n) sketch (*a. fig.*); **2ieren** [⹁'tsiːrən] *v/t.* (*no* -ge-, *h*) sketch, outline (*both a. fig.*).

**Sklav|e** ['sklaːvə] *m* (-n/-n) slave (*a. fig.*); '⹁**enhandel** *m* slave-trade; '⹁**enhändler** *m* slave-trader; ⹁**e'rei** *f* (-/-en) slavery; '**2isch** *adj.* slavish.

**Skonto** ✝ ['skonto] *m, n* (-s/-s, ⚓ Skonti) discount.

**Skrupel** ['skruːpəl] *m* (-s/-) scruple; '**2los** *adj.* unscrupulous.

**Skulptur** [skulp'tuːr] *f* (-/-en) sculpture.

**Slalom** ['sla:lɔm] *m* (-s/-s) *skiing, etc.*: slalom.

**Slaw|e** ['sla:və] *m* (-n/-n) Slav; **ℚisch** *adj.* Slav(onic).

**Smaragd** [sma'rakt] *m* (-[e]s/-e) emerald; **ℚgrün** *adj.* emerald.

**Smoking** ['smo:kiŋ] *m* (-s/-s) dinner-jacket, *Am. a.* tuxedo, F tux.

**so** [zo:] **1.** *adv.* so, thus; like this *or* that; as; ~ *ein* such a; ~ ... *wie* as ... as; *nicht* ~ ... *wie* not so ... as; ~ *oder* ~ by hook or by crook; **2.** *cj.* so, therefore, consequently; ~ *daß* so that; **ℚbald** *cj.* [zo'-]: ~ (*als*) as soon as.

**Socke** ['zɔkə] *f* (-/-n) sock; **ℚl** *m* (-s/-) ▲ pedestal, socle; socket (*of lamp*); **ℚn** *m* (-s/-) sock; **ℚnhalter** *m/pl.* suspenders *pl.*, *Am.* garters *pl.*

**Sodawasser** ['zo:da-] *n* (-s/≈) soda(-water).

**Sodbrennen** ✿ ['zo:t-] *n* (-s/*no pl.*) heartburn.

**soeben** *adv.* [zo'-] just (now).

**Sofa** ['zo:fa] *n* (-s/-s) sofa.

**sofern** *cj.* [zo'-] if, provided that; ~ *nicht* unless.

**soff** [zɔf] *pret. of saufen.*

**sofort** *adv.* [zo'-] at once, immediately, directly, right *or* straight away; **ℚig** *adj.* immediate, prompt.

**Sog** [zo:k] **1.** *m* (-[e]s/-e) suction; ⚓ wake (*a. fig.*), undertow; **2.** ℚ *pret. of saugen.*

**so|gar** *adv.* [zo'-] even; **ℚgenannt** *adj.* ['zo:-] so-called; **ℚgleich** *adv.* [zo'-] *s.* sofort.

**Sohle** ['zo:lə] *f* (-/-n) sole; bottom (*of valley, etc.*); ⚒ floor.

**Sohn** [zo:n] *m* (-[e]s/≈e) son.

**solange** *cj.* [zo'-]: ~ (*als*) so *or* as long as. [such.)

**solch** *pron.* [zɔlç] such; *als* ~*e*(*r*) as)

**Sold** ⚔ [zɔlt] *m* (-[e]s/-e) pay.

**Soldat** [zɔl'da:t] *m* (-en/-en) soldier; *der unbekannte* ~ the Unknown Warrior *or* Soldier.

**Söldner** ['zœldnər] *m* (-s/-) mercenary.

**Sole** ['zo:lə] *f* (-/-n) brine, salt water.

**solid** *adj.* [zo'li:t] solid (*a. fig.*); *basis, etc.*: sound; ✝ firm, *etc.*: sound, solvent; *prices*: reasonable, fair; *p.* steady, staid, respectable.

**solidarisch** *adj.* [zoli'da:riʃ]: *sich* ~ *erklären mit* declare one's solidarity with.

**solide** *adj.* [zo'li:də] *s.* solid.

**Solist** [zo'list] *m* (-en/-en) soloist.

**Soll** ✝ [zɔl] *n* (-[s]/-[s]) debit; (output) target.

**'sollen** (*h*) **1.** *v/i.* (ge-): *ich sollte* (*eigentlich*) I ought to; **2.** *v/aux.* (*irr., no -ge-*): *er soll* he shall; he is to; he is said to; *ich sollte* I should; *er sollte (eigentlich) zu Hause sein* he ought to be at home; *er sollte seinen Vater niemals wiedersehen* he was never to see his father again.

**Solo** ['zo:lo] *n* (-s/-s, *Soli*) solo.

**somit** *cj.* [zo'-] thus; consequently.

**Sommer** ['zɔmər] *m* (-s/-) summer; **ℚfrische** *f* (-/-n) summer-holidays *pl.*; summer-resort; **ℚlich** *adj.* summer-like, summer(l)y; **ℚsprosse** *f* freckle; **ℚsprossig** *adj.* freckled; **ℚwohnung** *f* summer residence, *Am.* cottage, summer house; **ℚzeit** *f* **1.** (-/-en) *season*: summertime; **2.** (-/*no pl.*) summer time, *Am.* daylight-saving time.

**Sonate** ♪ [zo'na:tə] *f* (-/-n) sonata.

**Sonde** ['zɔndə] *f* (-/-n) probe.

**Sonder|angebot** ✝ ['zɔndər-] *n* special offer; **ℚausgabe** *f* special (edition); **ℚbar** *adj.* strange, odd; **ℚbeilage** *f* inset, supplement (*of newspaper*); **ℚberichterstatter** *m* special correspondent; **ℚlich 1.** *adj.* special, peculiar; **2.** *adv.*: *nicht* ~ not particularly; **ℚling** *m* (-s/-e) crank, odd person; **ℚn 1.** *cj.* but; *nicht nur,* ~ *auch* not only, but (also); **2.** *v/t.* (ge-, h): *die Spreu vom Weizen* ~ sift the chaff from the wheat; **ℚrecht** *n* privilege; **ℚzug** ☸ *m* special (train).

**sondieren** [zɔn'di:rən] (*no -ge-, h*) **1.** *v/t.* ✿ probe (*a. fig.*); **2.** *fig. v/i.* make tentative inquiries.

**Sonn|abend** ['zɔn⁹-] *m* (-s/-e) Saturday; **ℚe** *f* (-/-n) sun; **ℚen** *v/t.* (ge-, h) (expose to the) sun; *sich* ~ sun o.s. (*a. fig. in dat.* in), bask in the sun.

**'Sonnen|aufgang** *m* sunrise; **ℚbad** *n* sun-bath; **ℚbrand** *m* sunburn; **ℚbräune** *f* sunburn, tan, *Am.* (sun)tan; **ℚbrille** *f* (e-e a pair of) sunglasses *pl.*; **ℚfinsternis** *f* solar eclipse; **ℚfleck** *m* sun-spot; **ℚklar** *fig. adj.* (as) clear as daylight; **ℚlicht** *n* (-[e]s/*no pl.*) sunlight; **ℚschein** *m* (-[e]s/*no pl.*) sunshine; **ℚschirm** *m* sunshade, parasol; **ℚsegel** *n* awning; **ℚseite** *f* sunny side (*a. fig.*); **ℚstich** ✿ *m* sunstroke; **ℚstrahl** *m* sunbeam; **ℚuhr** *f* sun-dial; **ℚuntergang** *m* sunset, sundown; **ℚverbrannt** *adj.* sunburnt, tanned; **ℚwende** *f* solstice.

**'sonnig** *adj.* sunny (*a. fig.*).

**'Sonntag** *m* Sunday.

**'Sonntags|anzug** *m* Sunday suit *or* best; **ℚfahrer** *mot. contp. m* Sunday driver; **ℚkind** *n* person born on a Sunday; *fig.* person born under a lucky star; **ℚrückfahrkarte** ☸ *f* week-end ticket; **ℚruhe** *f* Sunday rest; **ℚstaat** F *co. m* (-[e]s/*no pl.*) Sunday go-to-meeting clothes *pl.*

**sonor** *adj.* [zo'no:r] sonorous.

**sonst** [zɔnst] **1.** *adv.* otherwise, *with pron.* else; usually, normally; *wer* ~? who else? *wie* ~ as usual; ~ *nichts* nothing else; **2.** *cj.* otherwise, or else; **ℚig** *adj.* other; **ℚwie** *adv.*

in some other way; **'~wo** adv. elsewhere, somewhere else.

**Sopran** ♪ [zo'prɑ:n] m (-s/-e) soprano; sopranist; **~istin** ♪ [~a'nistin] f (-/-nen) soprano, sopranist.

**Sorge** ['zɔrgə] f (-/-n) care; sorrow; uneasiness, anxiety; ~ tragen für take care of; sich ~n machen um be anxious or worried about; mach dir keine ~n don't worry.

**'sorgen** (ge-, h) 1. v/i.: ~ für care for, provide for; take care of, attend to; dafür ~, daß take care that; 2. v/refl.: sich ~ um be anxious or worried about; **'~frei** adj., **'~los** adj. carefree, free from care; **'~voll** adj. full of cares; face: worried, troubled.

**Sorg|falt** ['zɔrkfalt] f (-/no pl.) care(fulness); **2fältig** adj. ['~fɛltiç] careful; **'2lich** adj. careful, anxious; **'2los** adj. carefree; thoughtless; negligent; careless; **'2sam** adj. careful.

**Sort|e** ['zɔrtə] f (-/-n) sort, kind, species, Am. a. stripe; **2ieren** [~'ti:rən] v/t. (no -ge-, h) (as)sort; arrange; **~iment** [~i'mɛnt] n (-[e]s/-e) assortment.

**Soße** ['zo:sə] f (-/-n) sauce; gravy, **sott** [zɔt] pret. of sieden.

**Souffl|eurkasten** thea. [su'flø:r-] m prompt-box, promter's box; **~euse** thea. [~zə] f (-/-n) prompter; **2ieren** thea. (no -ge-, h) 1. v/i. prompt (j-m s.o.); 2. v/t. prompt.

**Souverän** [suvə're:n] 1. m (-s/-e) sovereign; 2. ♀ adj. sovereign; fig. superior; **~ität** [~eni'tɛ:t] f (-/no pl.) sovereignty.

**so|viel** [zo'-] 1. cj. so or as far as; ~ ich weiß so far as I know; 2. adv.: doppelt ~ twice as much; **~'weit** 1. cj. : ~ es mich betrifft in so far as it concerns me, so far as I am concerned; 2. adv.: ~ ganz gut not bad (for a start); **~'wieso** adv. [zovi'zo:] in any case, anyhow, anyway.

**Sowjet** [zɔ'vjɛt] m (-s/-s) Soviet; **2isch** adj. Soviet.

**sowohl** cj. [zo'-]: ~ ... als (auch) ... both ... and ..., ... as well as ...

**sozial** adj. [zo'tsja:l] social; **2demokrat** m social democrat; **~isieren** [~ali'zi:rən] v/t. (no -ge-, h) socialize; **2isierung** [~ali'zi:ruŋ] f (-/-en) socialization; **2ist** [~a'list] m (-en/-en) socialist; **~istisch** adj. [~a'listiʃ] socialist.

**Sozius** ['zo:tsjus] m (-/-se) ♀ partner; mot. pillion-rider; **'~sitz** mot. m pillion.

**sozusagen** adv. [zotsu'zɑ:gən] so to speak, as it were.

**Spachtel** ['ʃpaxtəl] m (-s/-), f (-/-n) spatula.

**spähe|n** ['ʃpɛ:ən] v/i. (ge-, h) look

*16\**

out (nach for); peer; **'2r** m (-s/-) look-out; ✕ scout.

**Spalier** [ʃpa'li:r] n (-s/-e) trellis, espalier; fig. lane; ~ bilden form a lane.

**Spalt** [ʃpalt] m (-[e]s/-e) crack, split, rift, crevice, fissure; **'~e** f (-/-n) s. Spalt; typ. column; **2en** v/t. ([irr.,] ge-, h) split (a. fig. hairs), cleave (block of wood, etc.); sich ~ split (up); **'~ung** f (-/-en) splitting, cleavage; fig. split; eccl. schism.

**Span** [ʃpɑ:n] m (-[e]s/⁼e) chip, shaving, splinter.

**Spange** ['ʃpaŋə] f (-/-n) clasp; buckle; clip; slide (in hair); strap (of shoes); bracelet.

**Span|ier** ['ʃpɑ:njər] m (-s/-) Spaniard; **'2isch** adj. Spanish.

**Spann** [ʃpan] 1. m (-[e]s/-e) instep; 2. ♀ pret. of spinnen; **~e** f (-/-n) span; ✕, orn. spread (of wings); ✝ margin; **2en** (ge-, h) 1. v/t. stretch (rope, muscles, etc.); cock (rifle); bend (bow, etc.); tighten (spring, etc.); vor den Wagen ~ harness to the carriage; s. gespannt; 2. v/i. be (too) tight; **2end** adj. exciting, thrilling, gripping; **'~kraft** f (-/no pl.) elasticity; fig. energy; **'~ung** f (-/-en) tension (a. fig.); ⚡ voltage; ⊕ strain, stress; ⚠ span; fig. close attention.

**Spar|büchse** ['ʃpɑ:r-] f money-box; **'2en** (ge-, h) 1. v/t. save (money, strength, etc.); put by; 2. v/i. save; economize, cut down expenses; ~ mit be chary of (praise, etc.); **'~er** m (-s/-) saver.

**Spargel** ♀ ['ʃpargəl] m (-s/-) asparagus.

**'Spar|kasse** f savings-bank; **'~konto** n savings-account.

**spärlich** adj. ['ʃpɛːrliç] crop, dress, etc.: scanty; population, etc.: sparse; hair: thin.

**Sparren** ['ʃparən] m (-s/-) rafter, spar.

**'sparsam** 1. adj. saving, economical (mit of); 2. adv.: ~ leben lead a frugal life, economize; ~ umgehen mit use sparingly, be frugal of; **'2keit** f (-/no pl. ) economy, frugality.

**Spaß** [ʃpɑ:s] m (-es/⁼e) joke, jest; fun, lark; amusement; aus or im or zum ~ in fun; ~ beiseite joking apart; er hat nur ~ gemacht he was only joking; **'2en** v/i. (ge-, h) joke, jest, make fun; damit ist nicht zu ~ that is no joking matter; **'2haft** adj., **'2ig** adj. facetious, waggish; funny; **'~macher** m (-s/-), **'~vogel** m wag, joker.

**spät** [ʃpɛ:t] 1. adj. late; advanced; zu ~ too late; am ~en Nachmittag late in the afternoon; wie ~ ist es? what time is it?; 2. adv. late; er kommt 5 Minuten zu ~ he is five minutes late (zu for); ∼ in der Nacht late at night.

**Spaten** ['ʃpɑːtən] m (-s/-) spade.

**'späte|r 1.** adj. later; **2.** adv. later on; afterward(s); früher oder ∼ sooner or later; ∼stens adv. ['∼stəns] at the latest.

**Spatz** orn. [ʃpats] m (-en, -es/-en) sparrow.

**spazieren** [ʃpa'tsiːrən] v/i. (no -ge-, sein) walk, stroll; ∼fahren (irr. fahren, sep., -ge-) **1.** v/i. (sein) go for a drive; **2.** v/t. (h) take for a drive; take (baby) out (in pram); ∼gehen v/i. (irr. gehen, sep., -ge-, sein) go for a walk.

**Spa'zier|fahrt** f drive, ride; ∼gang m walk, stroll; e-n ∼ machen go for a walk; ∼gänger [∼gɛŋər] m (-s/-) walker, stroller; ∼weg m walk.

**Speck** [ʃpɛk] m (-[e]s/-e) bacon.

**Spedi|teur** [ʃpedi'tøːr] m (-s/-e) forwarding agent; (furniture) remover; ∼tion [∼'tsjoːn] f (-/-en) forwarding agent or agency.

**Speer** [ʃpeːr] m (-[e]s/-e) spear; sports: javelin; ∼werfen n (-s/no pl.) javelin-throw(ing); ∼werfer m (-s/-) javelin-thrower.

**Speiche** ['ʃpaɪçə] f (-/-n) spoke.

**Speichel** ['ʃpaɪçəl] m (-s/no pl.) spit(tle), saliva; ∼lecker fig. m (-s/-) lickspittle, toady.

**Speicher** ['ʃpaɪçər] m (-s/-) granary; warehouse; garret, attic.

**speien** ['ʃpaɪən] (irr., ge-, h) **1.** v/t. spit out (blood, etc.); volcano, etc.: belch (fire, etc.); **2.** v/i. spit; vomit, be sick.

**Speise** ['ʃpaɪzə] f (-/-n) food, nourishment; meal; dish; ∼eis n ice-cream; ∼kammer f larder, pantry; ∼karte f bill of fare, menu; '2n (ge-, h) **1.** v/i. s. essen 1; at restaurants: take one's meals; **2.** v/t. feed; ⊕, ⚡ a. supply (mit with); ∼nfolge f menu; ∼röhre anat. f gullet, (o)esophagus; ∼saal m dining-hall; ∼schrank m (meat-)safe; ∼wagen 🚂 m dining-car, diner; ∼zimmer n dining-room.

**Spektakel** F [ʃpɛk'tɑːkəl] m (-s/-) noise, din.

**Spekul|ant** [ʃpeku'lant] m (-en/-en) speculator; ∼ation [∼a'tsjoːn] f (-/-en) speculation; ✝ a. venture; 2ieren [∼'liːrən] v/i. (no -ge-, h) speculate (auf acc. on).

**Spelunke** [ʃpe'luŋkə] f (-/-n) den; drinking-den, Am. F a. dive.

**Spende** ['ʃpɛndə] f (-/-n) gift; alms pl.; contribution; '2n v/t. (ge-, h) give; donate (money to charity, blood, etc.); eccl. administer (sacraments); bestow (praise) (dat. on); '∼r m (-s/-) giver; donor.

**spen'dieren** v/t. (no -ge-, h): j-m et. ∼ treat s.o. to s.th., stand s.o. s.th.

**Sperling** orn. ['ʃpɛrliŋ] m (-s/-e) sparrow.

**Sperr|e** ['ʃpɛrə] f (-/-n) barrier; 🚂 barrier, Am. gate; toll-bar; ⊕ lock(ing device), detent; barricade; ✝, ⚓ embargo; ⚔ blockade; sports: suspension; '2en (ge-, h) **1.** v/t. close; ✝, ⚓ embargo; cut off (gas supply, electricity, etc.); stop (cheque, etc.); sports: suspend; **2.** v/i. jam, be stuck; '∼holz n plywood; '∼konto ✝ n blocked account; '∼kreis ⚡ m wave-trap; '∼sitz thea. m stalls pl., Am. orchestra; '∼ung f (-/-en) closing; stoppage (of cheque, etc.); ✝, ⚓ embargo; ⚔ blockade; '∼zone f prohibited area.

**Spesen** ['ʃpeːzən] pl. expenses pl., charges pl.

**Spezial|ausbildung** [ʃpe'tsjaːl-] f special training; ∼fach n special(i)ty; ∼geschäft ✝ n one-line shop, Am. specialty store; 2isieren [∼ali'ziːrən] v/refl. (no -ge-, h) specialize (auf acc. in); ∼ist [∼a'list] m (-en/-en) specialist; ∼ität [∼ali-'tɛːt] f (-/-en) special(i)ty.

**speziell** adj. [ʃpe'tsjɛl] specific, special, particular.

**spezifisch** adj. [ʃpe'tsiːfiʃ]: ∼es Gewicht specific gravity.

**Sphäre** ['sfɛːrə] f (-/-n) sphere (a. fig.).

**Spick|aal** ['ʃpik-] m smoked eel; '2en (ge-, h) **1.** v/t. lard; fig. (inter)lard (mit with); F: j-n ∼ grease s.o.'s palm; **2.** F fig. v/i. crib.

**spie** [ʃpiː] pret. of speien.

**Spiegel** ['ʃpiːgəl] m (-s/-) mirror (a. fig.), looking-glass; '∼bild n reflected image; '2'blank adj. mirror-like; '∼ei [∼'ʃpiːgəlʔ-] n fried egg; '2'glatt adj. water: glassy, unrippled; road, etc.: very slippery; '2n (ge-, h) **1.** v/i. shine; **2.** v/refl. be reflected; '∼schrift f mirror-writing.

**Spieg(e)lung** ['ʃpiːg(ə)luŋ] f (-/-en) reflection, reflexion; mirage.

**Spiel** [ʃpiːl] n (-[e]s/-e) play (a. fig.); game (a. fig.); match; ♪ playing; ein ∼ Karten a pack of playing-cards, Am. a. a deck; auf dem ∼ stehen be at stake; aufs ∼ setzen jeopardize, stake; '∼art ♀, zo. f variety; '∼ball m tennis: game ball; billiards: red ball; fig. plaything, sport; '∼bank f (-/-en) gaming-house; '2en (ge-, h) **1.** v/i. play; gamble; ∼ mit play with; fig. a. toy with; **2.** v/t. play (tennis, violin, etc.); thea. act, play (part); mit j-m Schach ∼ play s.o. at chess; den Höflichen ∼ do the polite; '2end fig. adv. easily; '∼er m (-s/-) player; gambler; '∼erei f (-/-en) pastime; child's amusement; '∼ergebnis n sports: result, score; '∼feld n sports: (playing-)field; pitch; '∼film m feature film or picture; '~gefährte *m* playfellow, playmate; '~karte *f* playing-card; '~leiter *m thea.* stage manager; *cinematography:* director; *sports:* referee; '~marke *f* counter, *sl.* chip; '~plan *m thea., etc.*: program(me); repertory; '~platz *m* playground; '~raum *fig. m* play, scope; '~regel *f* rule (of the game); '~sachen *f/pl.* playthings *pl.*, toys *pl.*; '~schuld *f* gambling-debt; '~schule *f* infant-school, kindergarten; '~tisch *m* card-table; gambling-table; '~uhr *f* musical box, *Am.* music box; '~verderber *m* (-s/-) spoil-sport, killjoy, wet blanket; '~waren *f/pl.* playthings *pl.*, toys *pl.*; '~zeit *f thea.* season; *sports:* time of play; '~zeug *n* toy(s *pl.*), plaything(s *pl.*).

Spieß [ʃpiːs] *m* (-es/-e) spear, pike; spit; den ~ umdrehen turn the tables; '~bürger *m* bourgeois, Philistine, *Am. a.* Babbit; 2bürgerlich *adj.* bourgeois, Philistine; '~er *m* (-s/-) *s.* Spießbürger; '~geselle *m* accomplice; '~ruten *f/pl.*: ~ laufen run the gauntlet (*a. fig.*).

spinal *adj.* [ʃpiˈnaːl]: ~e Kinderlähmung *&* infantile paralysis, poliomyelitis, F polio.

Spinat *&* [ʃpiˈnaːt] *m* (-[e]s/-e) spinach.

Spind [ʃpint] *n, m* (-[e]s/-e) wardrobe, cupboard; *⚔, sports, etc.*: locker.

Spindel [ˈʃpindəl] *f* (-/-n) spindle; '2dürr *adj.* (as) thin as a lath.

Spinn|e *zo.* [ˈʃpinə] *f* (-/-n) spider; '2en (*irr., ge-, h*) 1. *v/t.* spin (*a. fig.*); hatch (*plot, etc.*); 2. *v/i. cat:* purr; F *fig.* be crazy, *sl.* be nuts; '~engewebe *n* cobweb; '~er *m* (-s/-) spinner; F *fig.* silly; ~e'rei *f* (-/-en) spinning; spinning-mill; '~maschine *f* spinning-machine; '~webe *f* (-/-n) cobweb.

Spion [ʃpiˈoːn] *m* (-s/-e) spy, intelligencer; *fig.* judas; '~age [~oˈnaːʒə] *f* (-/no *pl.*) espionage; 2ieren [~oˈniːrən] *v/i.* (no -ge-, h) (play the) spy.

Spiral|e [ʃpiˈraːlə] *f* (-/-n) spiral (*a. ⊕*), helix; 2förmig *adj.* [~fœrmiç] spiral, helical.

Spirituosen [ʃpirituˈoːzən] *pl.* spirits *pl.*

Spiritus [ˈʃpiːritus] *m* (-/-se) spirit, alcohol; '~kocher *m* (-s/-) spirit stove.

Spital [ʃpiˈtaːl] *n* (-s/=er) hospital; alms-house; home for the aged.

spitz [ʃpits] 1. *adj.* pointed (*a. fig.*); *&* angle: acute; *fig.* poignant; ~e Zunge sharp tongue; 2. *adv.*: ~ zulaufen taper (off); '2bube *m* thief; rogue, rascal (*both a. co.*); 2büberei [~byːbəˈraɪ] *f* (-/-en) roguery, ras-

cality (*both a. co.*); ~bübisch *adj.* ['~byːbiʃ] eyes, smile, *etc.*: roguish.

'Spitz|e *f* (-/-n) point (*of pencil, weapon, jaw, etc.*); tip (*of nose, finger, etc.*); nib (*of tool, etc.*); spire; head (*of enterprise, etc.*); lace; an der ~ liegen *sports:* be in the lead; j-m die ~ bieten make head against s.o.; auf die ~ treiben carry to an extreme; '~el *m* (-s/-) (common) informer; 2en *v/t.* (ge-, h) point, sharpen; den Mund ~ purse (up) one's lips; die Ohren ~ prick up one's ears (*a. fig.*).

'Spitzen|leistung *f* top performance; ⊕ maximum capacity; '~lohn *m* top wages *pl.*

'spitz|findig *adj.* subtle, captious; '2findigkeit *f* (-/-en) subtlety, captiousness; '2hacke *f* pickax(e), pick; '~ig *adj.* pointed; *fig. a.* poignant; '2marke *typ. f* head(ing); '2name *m* nickname.

Splitter [ˈʃplitər] *m* (-s/-) splinter, shiver; chip; '2frei *adj. glass:* shatterproof; '2ig *adj.* splintery; '2n *v/i.* (ge-, h, sein) splinter, shiver; '2'nackt F *adj.* stark naked, *Am. a.* mother-naked; '~partei *pol. f* splinter party.

spontan *adj.* [ʃpɔnˈtaːn] spontaneous.

sporadisch *adj.* [ʃpoˈraːdiʃ] sporadic.

Sporn [ʃpɔrn] *m* (-[e]s/Sporen) spur; die Sporen geben put or set spurs to (*horse*); sich die Sporen verdienen win one's spurs; '2en *v/t.* (ge-, h) spur.

Sport [ʃpɔrt] *m* (-[e]s/*⚒*-e) sport; *fig.* hobby; ~ treiben go in for sports; '~ausrüstung *f* sports equipment; '~geschäft *n* sporting-goods shop; '~kleidung *f* sport clothes *pl.*, sportswear; '~lehrer *m* games-master; '2lich *adj.* sporting, sportsmanlike; *figure:* athletic; '~nachrichten *f/pl.* sports news *sg., pl.*; '~platz *m* sports field; stadium.

Spott [ʃpɔt] *m* (-[e]s/no *pl.*) mockery; derision; scorn; (*s-n*) ~ treiben mit make sport of; '2billig F *adj.* dirt-cheap.

Spötte|lei [ʃpœtəˈlaɪ] *f* (-/-en) raillery, sneer, jeer; '2ln *v/i.* (ge-, h) sneer (*über acc.* at), jeer (at).

'spotten *v/i.* (ge-, h) mock (*über acc.* at); jeer (at); jeder Beschreibung ~ beggar description.

Spötter [ˈʃpœtər] *m* (-s/-) mocker, scoffer; ~ei [~ˈraɪ] *f* (-/-en) mockery.

'spöttisch *adj.* mocking; sneering; ironical.

'Spott|name *m* nickname; '~preis *m* ridiculous price; für e-n ~ for a mere song; '~schrift *f* lampoon, satire.

sprach [ʃpraːx] *pret. of* sprechen.

'Sprache *f* (-/-n) speech; language

(*a. fig.*); diction; *zur ~ bringen* bring up, broach; *zur ~ kommen* come up (for discussion).

'**Sprach|eigentümlichkeit** *f* idiom; '**~fehler** ⚡ *m* impediment (in one's speech); '**~führer** *m* language guide; '**~gebrauch** *m* usage; '**~gefühl** *n* (-[e]s/*no pl.*) linguistic instinct; 2**kundig** *adj.* ['~kundiç] versed in languages; '**~lehre** *f* grammar; '**~lehrer** *m* teacher of languages; '2**lich** *adj.* linguistic; grammatical; '2**los** *adj.* speechless; '**~rohr** *n* speaking-trumpet, megaphone; *fig.*: mouthpiece; organ; '**~schatz** *m* vocabulary; '**~störung** ⚡ *f* impediment (in one's speech); '**~wissenschaft** *f* philology, science of language; linguistics *pl.*; '**~wissenschaftler** *m* philologist; linguist; '2**wissenschaftlich** *adj.* philological; linguistic.

**sprang** [ʃpraŋ] *pret. of* springen.

**Sprech|chor** ['ʃpreç-] *m* speaking chorus; '2**en** (*irr.*, ge-, h) **1.** *v/t.* speak (*language, truth, etc.*); 𝔱𝔱 pronounce (*judgement*); say (*prayer*); *j-n zu ~ wünschen* wish to see s.o.; *j-n schuldig ~* 𝔱𝔱 pronounce s.o. guilty; F *Bände ~* speak volumes (*für for*); **2.** *v/i.* speak; talk (*both*: *mit* to, with; *über acc., von* of, about); *er ist nicht zu ~* you cannot see him; '**~er** *m* (-s/-) speaker; *radio*: announcer; spokesman; '**~fehler** *m* slip of the tongue; '**~stunde** *f* consulting-hours *pl.*; '**~übung** *f* exercise in speaking; '**~zimmer** *n* consulting-room, surgery.

**spreizen** ['ʃpraɪtsən] *v/t.* (ge-, h) spread (out); *a.* straddle (*legs*); *sich ~* pretend to be unwilling.

**Spreng|bombe** ✕ ['ʃprɛŋ-] *f* high-explosive bomb, demolition bomb; '**~el** *eccl. m* (-s/-) diocese, see; parish; '2**en** (ge-) **1.** *v/t.* (h) sprinkle, water (*road, lawn, etc.*); blow up, blast (*bridge, rocks, etc.*); burst open (*door, etc.*); spring (*mine, etc.*); *gambling*: break (*bank*); break up (*meeting, etc.*); **2.** *v/i.* (sein) gallop; '**~stoff** *m* explosive; '**~ung** *f* (-/-en) blowing-up, blasting; explosion; '**~wagen** *m* water(ing)-cart.

**Sprenkel** ['ʃprɛŋkəl] *m* (-s/-) speckle, spot; '2**n** *v/t.* (ge-, h) speckle, spot.

**Spreu** [ʃprɔy] *f* (-/*no pl.*) chaff; *s. sondern 2.*

**Sprich|wort** ['ʃpriç-] *n* (-[e]s/*~er) proverb, adage; '2**wörtlich** *adj.* proverbial (*a. fig.*).

**sprießen** ['ʃpriːsən] *v/i.* (*irr.*, ge-, sein) sprout; germinate.

**Spring|brunnen** ['ʃpriŋ-] *m* fountain; '2**en** *v/i.* (*irr.*, ge-, sein) jump, leap; *ball, etc.*: bounce; *swimming*: dive; burst, crack, break; *in die Augen ~* strike the eye; *~ über* (*acc.*)

jump (over), leap, clear; '**~er** *m* (-s/-) jumper; *swimming*: diver; *chess*: knight; '**~flut** *f* spring tide.

**Sprit** [ʃprit] *m* (-[e]s/-e) spirit, alcohol; F *mot.* fuel, petrol, *sl.* juice, *Am.* gasoline, F gas.

**Spritz|e** ['ʃpritsə] *f* (-/-n) syringe (*a.* ⚕), squirt; ⊕ fire-engine; *j-m e-e ~ geben* ⚕ give s.o. an injection; '2**en** (ge-) **1.** *v/t.* (h) sprinkle, water (*road, lawn, etc.*); splash (*water, etc.*) (*über acc.* on, over); **2.** *v/i.* (h) splash; *pen*: splutter; **3.** *v/i.* (sein) F *fig.* dash, flit; *~ aus blood, etc.*: spurt *or* spout from (*wound, etc.*); '**~er** *m* (-s/-) splash; '**~tour** *f* F: *e-e ~ machen* go for a spin.

**spröde** *adj.* ['ʃprøːdə] *glass, etc.*: brittle; *skin*: chapped, chappy; *esp. girl*: prudish, prim, coy.

**Sproß** [ʃprɔs] **1.** *m* (Sprosses/Sprosse) ♀ shoot, sprout, scion (*a. fig.*); *fig.* offspring; **2.** 2 *pret. of* sprießen.

**Sprosse** ['ʃprɔsə] *f* (-/-n) rung, round, step.

**Sprößling** ['ʃprœsliŋ] *m* (-s/-e) ♀ *s.* Sproß 1.; *co.* son.

**Spruch** [ʃprux] *m* (-[e]s/*~e) saying; dictum; 𝔱𝔱 sentence; 𝔱𝔱 verdict; '**~band** *n* banner; '2**reif** *adj.* ripe for decision.

**Sprudel** ['ʃpruːdəl] *m* (-s/-) mineral water; '2**n** *v/i.* (ge-) **1.** (h) bubble, effervesce; **2.** (sein): *~ aus or von* gush from.

**sprüh|en** ['ʃpryːən] (ge-) **1.** *v/t.* (h) spray, sprinkle (*liquid*); throw off (*sparks*); *Feuer ~ eyes*: flash fire; **2.** *v/i.* (h): *~ vor* sparkle with (*wit, etc.*); *es sprüht* it is drizzling; **3.** *v/i.* (sein) *sparks*: fly; '2**regen** *m* drizzle.

**Sprung** [ʃpruŋ] *m* (-[e]s/*~e) jump, leap, bound; *swimming*: dive; crack, fissure; '**~brett** *n sports*: springboard; *fig.* stepping-stone; '**~feder** *f* spiral spring.

**Spuck|e** F ['ʃpukə] *f* (-/*no pl.*) spit(tle); '2**en** (ge-, h) **1.** *v/t.* spit (out) (*blood, etc.*); **2.** *v/i.* spit; *engine*: splutter; '**~napf** *m* spittoon, *Am. a.* cuspidor.

**Spuk** [ʃpuːk] *m* (-[e]s/-e) apparition, ghost, *co.* spook; F *fig.* noise; '2**en** *v/i.* (ge-, h): *~ in* (*dat.*) haunt (*a place*); *hier spukt es* this place is haunted.

**Spule** ['ʃpuːlə] *f* (-/-n) spool, reel; bobbin; ∦ coil; '2**n** *v/t.* (ge-, h) spool, reel.

**spülen** ['ʃpyːlən] (ge-, h) **1.** *v/t.* rinse (*clothes, mouth, cup, etc.*); wash up (*dishes, etc.*); *an Land ~* wash ashore; **2.** *v/i.* flush the toilet.

**Spund** [ʃpunt] *m* (-[e]s/*~e) bung; plug; '**~loch** *n* bunghole.

**Spur** [ʃpuːr] *f* (-/-en) trace (*a. fig.*); track (*a. fig.*); print (*a. fig.*); rut (*of wheels*); *j-m auf der ~ sein* be on s.o.'s track.

**spür|en** ['ʃpy:rən] v/t. (ge-, h) feel; sense; perceive; **'⸰sinn** m (-[e]s/no pl.) scent; fig. a. flair (für for).
**Spurweite** 🚗 f ga(u)ge.
**sputen** ['ʃpu:tən] v/refl. (ge-, h) make haste, hurry up.
**Staat** [ʃta:t] m **1.** F (-[e]s/no pl.) pomp, state; finery; ∼ machen mit make a parade of; **2.** (-[e]s/-en) state; government; **'⸰enbund** m (-[e]s/⸰e) confederacy, confederation; **'⸰enlos** adj. stateless; **'⸰lich** adj. state; national; political; public.
**'Staats|angehörige** m, f (-n/-n) national, citizen, esp. Brt. subject; **'⸰angehörigkeit** f (-/no pl.) nationality, citizenship; **'⸰anwalt** ⚖ m public prosecutor, Am. prosecuting attorney; **'⸰beamte** m Civil Servant, Am. a. public servant; **'⸰begräbnis** n state or national funeral; **'⸰besuch** m official or state visit; **'⸰bürger** m citizen; **'⸰bürgerkunde** f (-/no pl.) civics sg.; **'⸰bürgerschaft** f (-/-en) citizenship; **'⸰dienst** m Civil Service; **'⸰eigen** adj. state-owned; **'⸰feind** m public enemy; **'⸰feindlich** adj. subversive; **'⸰gewalt** f (-/no pl.) supreme power; **'⸰haushalt** m budget; **'⸰hoheit** f (-/no pl.) sovereignty; **'⸰kasse** f treasury, Brt. exchequer; **'⸰klugheit** f political wisdom; **'⸰kunst** f (-/no pl.) statesmanship; **'⸰mann** m statesman; **⸰männisch** adj. ['⸰meniʃ] statesmanlike; **'⸰oberhaupt** n head of (the) state; **'⸰papiere** n/pl. Government securities pl.; **'⸰rat** m Privy Council; **'⸰recht** n public law; **'⸰schatz** m s. Staatskasse; **'⸰schulden** f/pl. national debt; **'⸰sekretär** m under-secretary of state; **'⸰streich** m coup d'état; **'⸰trauer** f national mourning; **'⸰vertrag** m treaty; **'⸰wesen** n polity; **'⸰wirtschaft** f public sector of the economy; **'⸰wissenschaft** f political science; **'⸰wohl** n public weal.
**Stab** [ʃta:p] m (-[e]s/⸰e) staff (a. fig.); bar (of metal, wood); crosier, staff (of bishop); wand (of magician); relay-race, ♪ conducting: baton; pole-vaulting: pole.
**stabil** adj. [ʃta'bi:l] stable (a. ✝); health: robust.
**stabilisier|en** [ʃtabili'zi:rən] v/t. (no -ge-, h) stabilize (a. ✝); **⸰ung** f (-/-en) stabilization (a. ✝).
**stach** [ʃtax] pret. of stechen.
**Stachel** ['ʃtaxəl] m (-s/-n) prickle (of plant, hedgehog, etc.); sting (of bee, etc.); tongue (of buckle); spike (of sports shoe); fig.: sting; goad; **'⸰beere** ♀ f gooseberry; **'⸰draht** m barbed wire; **'⸰ig** adj. prickly, thorny.
**'stachlig** adj. s. stachelig.

**Stadi|on** ['ʃta:djɔn] n (-s/Stadien) stadium; **⸰um** ['⸰um] n (-s/Stadien) stage, phase.
**Stadt** [ʃtat] f (-/⸰e) town; city.
**Städt|chen** ['ʃtɛːtçən] n (-s/-) small town; **'⸰ebau** m (-[e]s/no pl.) town-planning; **'⸰er** m (-s/-) townsman; ∼ pl. townspeople pl.
**'Stadt|gebiet** n urban area; **'⸰gespräch** n teleph. local call; fig. town talk, talk of the town; **'⸰haus** n town house.
**städtisch** adj. ['ʃtɛːtiʃ] municipal.
**'Stadt|plan** m city map; plan (of a town); **'⸰planung** f town-planning; **'⸰rand** m outskirts pl. (of a town); **'⸰rat** m (-[e]s/⸰e) town council; town council(l)or; **'⸰teil** m, **'⸰viertel** n quarter.
**Staffel** ['ʃtafəl] f (-/-n) relay; relay-race; **⸰ei** paint. [⸰'laɪ] f (-/-en) easel; **'⸰lauf** m relay-race; **'⸰n** v/t. (ge-, h) graduate (taxes, etc.); stagger (hours of work, etc.).
**Stahl¹** [ʃta:l] m (-[e]s/⸰e, -e) steel.
**stahl²** [⸰] pret. of stehlen.
**stählen** ['ʃtɛːlən] v/t. (ge-, h) ⊕ harden (a. fig.), temper.
**'Stahl|feder** f steel pen; steel spring; **'⸰kammer** f strong-room; **'⸰stich** m steel engraving.
**stak** [ʃta:k] pret. of stecken 2.
**Stall** [ʃtal] m (-[e]s/⸰e) stable (a. fig.); cow-house, cowshed; pigsty, Am. a. pigpen; shed; **'⸰knecht** m stableman; **'⸰ung** f (-/-en) stabling; ∼en pl. stables pl.
**Stamm** [ʃtam] m (-[e]s/⸰e) ♀ stem (a. gr.), trunk; fig.: race; stock; family; tribe; **'⸰aktie** ✝ f ordinary share, Am. common stock; **'⸰baum** m family or genealogical tree, pedigree (a. zo.); **'⸰buch** n album; book that contains the births, deaths, and marriages in a family; zo. studbook; **'⸰eln** (ge-, h) **1.** v/t. stammer (out); **2.** v/i. stammer; **'⸰eltern** pl. ancestors pl., first parents pl.; **'⸰en** v/i. (ge-, sein): ∼ von or aus come from (town, etc.), Am. a. hail from; date from (certain time); gr. be derived from; aus gutem Haus ∼ be of good family; **'⸰gast** m regular customer or guest, F regular.
**stämmig** adj. ['ʃtɛmiç] stocky, thickset, squat(ty).
**'Stamm|kapital** ✝ n share capital, Am. capital stock; **'⸰kneipe** F f one's favo(u)rite pub, local; **'⸰kunde** m regular customer, patron; **'⸰tisch** m table reserved for regular guests; **⸰utter** ['ʃtammʊtər] f (-/⸰) ancestress; **'⸰vater** m ancestor; **⸰verwandt** adj. cognate, kindred; pred. of the same race.
**stampfen** ['ʃtampfən] (ge-) **1.** v/t. (h) mash (potatoes, etc.); aus dem Boden ∼ conjure up; **2.** v/i. (h) stamp (one's foot); horse: paw;

**3.** v/i. (sein): ~ durch plod through; ⚓ pitch through.

**Stand** [ʃtant] **1.** m (-[e]s/=e) stand (-ing), standing or upright position; footing, foothold; s. Standplatz; stall; fig.: level; state; station, rank, status; class; profession; reading (of thermometer, etc.); ast. position; sports: score; auf den neuesten ~ bringen bring up to date; e-n schweren ~ haben have a hard time (of it); **2.** ♀ pret. of stehen.

**Standarte** [ʃtanˈdartə] f (-/-n) standard, banner.

**'Standbild** n statue.

**Ständchen** ['ʃtɛntçən] n (-s/-) serenade; j-m ein ~ bringen serenade s.o.

**Ständer** ['ʃtɛndər] m (-s/-) stand; post, pillar, standard.

**'Standes|amt** n registry (office), register office; '♀amtlich adj.: ~e Trauung civil marriage; '♀beamte m registrar; '♀dünkel m pride of place; '♀gemäß adj., '♀mäßig adj. in accordance with one's rank; '♀person f person of rank or position; '♀unterschied m social difference.

**'standhaft** adj. steadfast; firm; constant; ~ bleiben stand pat; resist temptation; '♀igkeit f (-/no pl.) steadfastness; firmness.

**'standhalten** v/i. (irr. halten, sep., -ge-, h) hold one's ground; j-m or e-r Sache ~ resist s.o. or s.th.

**ständig** adj. ['ʃtɛndiç] permanent; constant; income, etc.: fixed.

**'Stand|ort** m position (of ship, etc.); ✗ garrison, post; '♀platz m stand; '♀punkt fig. m point of view, standpoint, angle, Am. a. slant; '♀quartier ✗ n fixed quarters pl.; '♀recht ✗ n martial law; '♀uhr f grandfather's clock.

**Stange** ['ʃtaŋə] f (-/-n) pole; rod, bar (of iron, etc.); staff (of flag); Anzug or Kleid von der ~ sl. reach-me-down, Am. F hand-me-down.

**stank** [ʃtaŋk] pret. of stinken.

**Stänker|(er)** contp. ['ʃtɛŋkər(ər)] m (-s/-) mischief-maker, quarrel(l)er; '♀n F v/i. (ge-, h) make mischief.

**Stanniol** [ʃtaˈnjoːl] n (-s/-e) tin foil.

**Stanze** ['ʃtantsə] f (-/-n) stanza; ⊕ punch, stamp, die; '♀n ⊕ v/t. (ge-, h) punch, stamp.

**Stapel** ['ʃtaːpəl] m (-s/-) pile, stack; ⚓ stocks pl.; vom or von ~ lassen ⚓ launch; vom or von ~ laufen ⚓ be launched; '♀lauf ⚓ m launch; '♀n v/t. (ge-, h) pile (up), stack; '♀platz m dump; emporium.

**stapfen** ['ʃtapfən] v/i. (ge-, sein) plod (durch through).

**Star 1.** [ʃtaːr] m (-[e]s/-e) orn. starling; ✗ cataract; j-m den ~ stechen open s.o.'s eyes; **2.** [staːr] m (-s/-s) thea., etc.: star.

**starb** [ʃtarp] pret. of sterben.

**stark** [ʃtark] **1.** adj. strong (a. fig.); stout, corpulent; fig.: intense; large; ~e Erkältung bad cold; ~er Raucher heavy smoker; ~e Seite strong point, forte; **2.** adv. very much; ~ erkältet sein have a bad cold; ~ übertrieben grossly exaggerated.

**Stärke** ['ʃtɛrkə] f (-/-n) strength (a. fig.); stoutness, corpulence; fig.: intensity; largeness; strong point, forte; 🔥 starch; '♀n v/t. (ge-, h) strengthen (a. fig.); starch (linen, etc.); sich ~ take some refreshment(s).

**'Starkstrom** ⚡ m heavy current.

**'Stärkung** f (-/-en) strengthening; fig. a. refreshment; '♀smittel n restorative; ♪ a. tonic.

**starr** [ʃtar] **1.** adj. rigid (a. fig.), stiff; gaze: fixed; ~ vor (dat.) numb with (cold, etc.); transfixed with (horror, etc.); dumbfounded with (amazement, etc.); **2.** adv.: j-n ~ ansehen stare at s.o.; '♀en v/i. (ge-, h) stare (auf acc. at); vor Schmutz ~ be covered with dirt; '♀heit f (-/no pl.) rigidity (a. fig.), stiffness; '♀kopf m stubborn or obstinate fellow; '♀köpfig adj. ['♀kœpfiç] stubborn, obstinate; '♀krampf ♪ m (-[e]s/no pl.) tetanus; '♀sinn m (-[e]s/no pl.) stubbornness, obstinacy; '♀sinnig adj. stubborn, obstinate.

**Start** [ʃtart] m (-[e]s/-s, ✈ -e) start (a. fig.); ✈ take-off; '♀bahn ✈ f runway; '♀bereit adj. ready to start; ✈ ready to take off; '♀en (ge-) **1.** v/i. (sein) start; ✈ take off; **2.** v/t. (h) start; fig. a. launch; '♀er m (-s/-) sports: starter; '♀platz m starting-place.

**Station** [ʃtaˈtsjoːn] f (-/-en) station; ward (of hospital); (gegen) freie ~ board and lodging (found); ~ machen break one's journey; '♀svorsteher 🚂 m station-master, Am. a. station agent.

**Statist** [ʃtaˈtist] m (-en/-en) thea. supernumerary (actor), F super; film: extra; '♀ik f (-/-en) statistics pl., sg.; '♀iker m (-s/-) statistician; '♀isch adj. statistic(al).

**Stativ** [ʃtaˈtiːf] n (-s/-e) tripod.

**Statt** [ʃtat] **1.** f (-/no pl.): an Eides ~ in lieu of an oath; an Kindes ~ annehmen adopt; **2.** ♀ prp. (gen.) instead of; ~ zu inf. instead of ger.; ~ meiner in my place.

**Stätte** ['ʃtɛtə] f (-/-n) place, spot; scene (of events).

**'statt|finden** v/i. (irr. finden, sep., -ge-, h) take place, happen; '♀haft adj. admissible, allowable; legal.

**'Statthalter** m (-s/-) governor.

**'stattlich** adj. stately; impressive; sum of money, etc.: considerable.

**Statue** ['ʃtaːtuə] f (-/-n) statue.

**statuieren** [ʃtatuˈiːrən] v/t. (no -ge-,

*h*): *ein Exempel* ~ make an example (*an dat.* of).

**Statur** [ʃtaˈtuːr] *f* (-/-en) stature, size.

**Statut** [ʃtaˈtuːt] *n* (-[e]s/-en) statute; ~en *pl.* regulations *pl.*; ♰ articles *pl.* of association.

**Staub** [ʃtaʊp] *m* (-[e]s/⊕ -e, ⁼e) dust; powder.

**Staubecken** ['ʃtaʊ ̯-] *n* reservoir.

**stauben** ['ʃtaʊbən] *v/i.* (ge-, h) give off dust, make *or* raise a dust.

**stäuben** ['ʃtɔybən] (ge-, h) **1.** *v/t.* dust; **2.** *v/i.* spray.

'**Staub|faden** ♀ *m* filament; 2ig *adj.* ['-biç] dusty; ~**sauger** ['-p-] *m* (-s/-) vacuum cleaner; ~**tuch** ['-p-] *n* (-[e]s/⁼er) duster.

**stauchen** ⊕ ['ʃtaʊxən] *v/t.* (ge-, h) upset, jolt.

'**Staudamm** *m* dam.

**Staude** ♀ ['ʃtaʊdə] *f* (-/-n) perennial (plant); head (of lettuce).

**stau|en** ['ʃtaʊən] *v/t.* (ge-, h) dam (up) (*river, etc.*); ♻ stow; *sich* ~ *waters, etc.*: be dammed (up); *vehicles*: be jammed; '2er ♻ *m* (-s/-) stevedore.

**staunen** ['ʃtaʊnən] **1.** *v/i.* (ge-, h) be astonished (*über acc.* at); **2.** 2 *n* (-s/*no pl.*) astonishment; '~**swert** *adj.* astonishing.  [temper.\

**Staupe** *vet.* ['ʃtaʊpə] *f* (-/-n) dis-\

'**Stau|see** *m* reservoir; '~**ung** *f* (-/-en) damming (up) (*of water*); stoppage; ♨ congestion (*a. of traffic*); jam; ♻ stowage.

**stechen** ['ʃtɛçən] (*irr.*, ge-, h) **1.** *v/t.* prick; *insect, etc.*: sting; *flea, mosquito, etc.*: bite; *card*: take, trump (*other card*); ⊕ engrave (*in or auf acc.* on); cut (*lawn, etc.*); *sich in den Finger* ~ prick one's finger; **2.** *v/i.* prick; stab (*nach* at); *insect, etc.*: sting; *flea, mosquito, etc.*: bite; *sun*: burn; *j-m in die Augen* ~ strike s.o.'s eye; '~**d** *adj.* pain, look, *etc.*: piercing; *pain*: stabbing.

**Steck|brief** ♰ ['ʃtɛk-] *m* warrant of apprehension; '2**brieflich** ♰ *adv.*: *er wird* ~ *gesucht* a warrant is out against him; '~**dose** ∮ *f* (wall) socket; '2**en 1.** *v/t.* (ge-, h) put; *esp.* ⊕ insert (*in acc.* into); F stick; pin (*an acc.* to, on); ⚹ set, plant; **2.** *v/i.* ([*irr.*,] ge-, h) be; stick, be stuck; *tief in Schulden* ~ be deeply in debt; '~**en** *m* (-s/-) stick; '2**en- bleiben** *v/i.* (*irr.* bleiben, sep., -ge-, sein) get stuck; *speaker, etc.*: break down; '~**enpferd** *n* hobby-horse; *fig.* hobby; '~**er** ∮ *m* (-s/-) plug; '~**kontakt** ∮ *m* s. Steckdose; '~**na- del** *f* pin.

**Steg** [ʃteːk] *m* (-[e]s/-e) foot-bridge; ♻ landing-stage; '~**reif** *m* (-[e]s/-e): *aus dem* ~ extempore, offhand (*both a. attr.*); *aus dem* ~ *sprechen* extemporize, F ad-lib.

**stehen** ['ʃteːən] *v/i.* (*irr.*, ge-, h) stand; be; be written; *dress*: suit, become (*j-m s.o.*); ~ *vor* be faced with; *gut* ~ *mit* be on good terms with; *es kam ihm or ihn teuer zu* ~ it cost him dearly; *wie steht's mit* ...? what about ...?; *wie steht das Spiel?* what's the score?; ~ *bleiben* remain standing; '~**bleiben** *v/i.* (*irr.* bleiben, sep., -ge-, sein) stand (still), stop; leave off reading, *etc.*; '~**lassen** *v/t.* (*irr.* lassen, sep., [*no*] -ge-, h) turn one's back (up)on; leave (*meal*) untouched; leave (behind); forget; leave alone.

'**Steher** *m* (-s/-) *sports*: stayer.

'**Steh|kragen** *m* stand-up collar; '~**lampe** *f* standard lamp; '~**leiter** *f* (⊝-e a pair of) steps *pl.*, step-ladder.

**stehlen** ['ʃteːlən] (*irr.*, ge-, h) **1.** *v/t.* steal; *j-m Geld* ~ steal s.o.'s money; **2.** *v/i.* steal.

'**Stehplatz** *m* standing-room; '~**in- haber** *m* Am. F standee; *in bus, etc.*: straphanger.

**steif** *adj.* [ʃtaɪf] stiff (*a. fig.*); numb (*vor Kälte* with cold); '~**halten** *v/t.* (*irr.* halten, sep. -ge-, h): F *die Ohren* ~ keep a stiff upper lip.

**Steig** [ʃtaɪk] *m* (-[e]s/-e) steep path; '~**bügel** *m* stirrup.

**steigen** ['ʃtaɪgən] **1.** *v/i.* (*irr.*, ge-, sein) flood, barometer, spirits, prices, *etc.*: rise; *mists, etc.*: ascend; blood, tension, *etc.*: mount; prices, *etc.*: increase; *auf e-n Baum* ~ climb a tree; **2.** 2 *n* (-s/*no pl.*) rise; *fig. a.* increase.

**steigern** ['ʃtaɪgərn] *v/t.* (ge-, h) raise; increase; enhance; *gr.* compare.

'**Steigerung** *f* (-/-en) raising; increase; enhancement; *gr.* comparison; '~**sstufe** *gr. f* degree of comparison.

**Steigung** ['ʃtaɪgʊŋ] *f* (-/-en) rise, gradient, ascent, grade.

**steil** *adj.* [ʃtaɪl] steep; precipitous.

**Stein** [ʃtaɪn] *m* (-[e]s/-e) stone (*a.* ♀, 🜨), *Am.* F *a.* rock; *s. Edel*♀; '2**alt** *adj.* (as) old as the hills; '~**bruch** *m* quarry; '~**druck** *m* **1.** (-[e]s/*no pl.*) lithography; **2.** (-[e]s/-e) lithograph; '~**drucker** *m* lithographer; '2**ern** *adj.* stone-..., of stone; *fig.* stony; '~**gut** *n* (-[e]s/-e) crockery, stoneware, earthenware; '2**ig** *adj.* stony; 2**igen** ['-gən] *v/t.* (ge-, h) stone; '~**igung** *f* (-/-en) stoning; '~**kohle** *f* mineral coal; pit-coal; '~**metz** *m* (-en/-en) stonemason; '~**obst** *n* stone-fruit; '2**reich** F *adj.* immensely rich; '~**salz** *n* (-es/*no pl.*) rock-salt; '~**setzer** *m* (-s/-) pavio(u)r; '~**wurf** *m* throwing of a stone; *fig.* stone's throw; '~**zeit** *f* (-/*no pl.*) stone age.

**Steiß** [ʃtaɪs] *m* (-es/-e) buttocks *pl.*, rump; '~**bein** *anat. n* coccyx.

**Stelldichein** *co.* ['ʃtɛldiçˀaɪn] *n* (-[s]/-[s]) meeting, appointment, rendezvous, *Am.* F *a.* date.

**Stelle** ['ʃtɛlə] *f* (-/-n) place; spot; point; employment, situation, post, place, F job; agency, authority; passage (*of book, etc.*); *freie* ~ vacancy; *an deiner* ~ in your place, if I were you; *auf der* ~ on the spot; *zur* ~ *sein* be present.

**'stellen** *v/t.* (ge-, h) put, place, set, stand; regulate (*watch, etc.*); set (*watch, trap, task, etc.*); stop (*thief, etc.*); hunt down (*criminal*); furnish, supply, provide; *Bedingungen* ~ make conditions; e-e *Falle* ~ *a.* lay a snare; *sich* ~ give o.s. up (to the police); stand, place o.s. (*somewhere*); *sich krank* ~ feign *or* pretend to be ill.

**'Stellen|angebot** *n* position offered, vacancy; **'~gesuch** *n* application for a post; **'2weise** *adv.* here and there, sporadically.

**'Stellung** *f* (-/-en) position, posture; position, situation, (place of) employment; position, rank, status; arrangement (*a. gr.*); ⚔ position; ~ *nehmen* give one's opinion (*zu* on), comment (upon); **~nahme** ['~nɑːmə] *f* (-/-n) attitude (*zu* to[wards]); opinion (on); comment (on); **'2slos** *adj.* unemployed.

**'stellvertret|end** *adj.* vicarious, representative; acting, deputy; **~er** *Vorsitzender* vice-chairman, deputy chairman; **'2er** *m* representative; deputy; proxy; **'2ung** *f* representation; substitution; proxy.

**Stelz|bein** *contp.* ['ʃtɛlts-] *n* wooden leg; **'~e** *f* (-/-n) stilt; **'2en** *mst iro. v/i.* (ge-, *sein*) stalk.

**stemmen** ['ʃtɛmən] *v/t.* (ge-, *h*) lift (*weight*); *sich* ~ press (*gegen* against); *fig.* resist *or* oppose *s.th.*

**Stempel** ['ʃtɛmpəl] *m* (-s/-) stamp; ⊕ piston; ⚘ pistil; **'~geld** F *n the* dole; **'~kissen** *n* ink-pad; **'2n** (ge-, *h*) **1.** *v/t.* stamp; hallmark (*gold, silver*); **2.** *v/i.* F: ~ *gehen* be on the dole.

**Stengel** ⚘ ['ʃtɛŋəl] *m* (-s/-) stalk, stem.

**Steno** F ['ʃteno] *f* (-/*no pl.*) *s. Stenographie*; **~'gramm** *n* (-s/-e) stenograph; **~graph** [~'grɑːf] *m* (-en/-en) stenographer; **~graphie** [~a'fiː] *f* (-/-n) stenography, shorthand; **2graphieren** [~a'fiːrən] (*no* -ge-, *h*) **1.** *v/t.* take down in shorthand; **2.** *v/i.* know shorthand; **2graphisch** [~'grɑːfiʃ] **1.** *adj.* shorthand, stenographic; **2.** *adv.* in shorthand; **~typistin** [~ty'pistin] *f* (-/-nen) shorthand-typist.

**Stepp|decke** ['ʃtɛp-] *f* quilt, *Am. a.* comforter; **'2en** (ge-, *h*) **1.** *v/t.* quilt; stitch; **2.** *v/i.* tap-dance.

**Sterbe|bett** ['ʃtɛrbə-] *n* deathbed; **'~fall** *m* (case of) death; **'~kasse** *f* burial-fund.

**'sterben 1.** *v/i.* (*irr.*, ge-, *sein*) die (*a. fig.*) (*an dat.* of); *esp.* ⚖ decease; **2. 2** *n* (-s/*no pl.*): *im* ~ *liegen* be dying.

**sterblich** ['ʃtɛrpliç] **1.** *adj.* mortal; **2.** *adv.*: ~ *verliebt sein* be desperately in love (*in acc.* with); **'2keit** *f* (-/*no pl.*) mortality; **'2keitsziffer** *f* death-rate, mortality.

**stereotyp** *adj.* [stereo'tyːp] *typ.* stereotyped (*a. fig.*); **~ieren** *typ.* [~y'piːrən] *v/t.* (*no* -ge-, *h*) stereotype.

**steril** *adj.* [ʃte'riːl] sterile; **~isieren** [~ili'ziːrən] *v/t.* (*no* -ge-, *h*) sterilize.

**Stern** [ʃtɛrn] *m* (-[e]s/-e) star (*a. fig.*); **'~bild** *ast. n* constellation; **'~deuter** *m* (-s/-) astrologer; **'~deutung** *f* astrology; **'~enbanner** *n* Star-Spangled Banner, Stars and Stripes *pl.*, Old Glory; **'~fahrt** *mot. f* motor rally; **'~gucker** F *m* (-s/-) star-gazer; **'2hell** *adj.* starry, starlit; **'~himmel** *m* (-s/*no pl.*) starry sky; **'~kunde** *f* (-/*no pl.*) astronomy; **'~schnuppe** *f* (-/-n) shooting star; **'~warte** *f* observatory.

**stet** *adj.* [ʃteːt], **'~ig** *adj.* continual, constant; steady; **'2igkeit** *f* (-/*no pl.*) constancy, continuity; steadiness; **~s** *adv.* always; constantly.

**Steuer** ['ʃtɔʏər] **1.** *n* (-s/-) ⚓ helm, rudder; steering-wheel; **2.** *f* (-/-n) tax; duty; rate, local tax; **'~amt** *n s. Finanzamt*; **'~beamte** *m* revenue officer; **'~berater** *m* (-s/-) tax adviser; **'~bord** ⚓ *n* (-[e]s/-e) starboard; **'~erhebung** *f* levy of taxes; **'~erklärung** *f* tax-return; **'~ermäßigung** *f* tax allowance; **'2frei** *adj.* tax-free; *goods*: duty-free; **'~freiheit** *f* (-/*no pl.*) exemption from taxes; **'~hinterziehung** *f* tax-evasion; **'~jahr** *n* fiscal year; **'~klasse** *f* tax-bracket; **'~knüppel** ✈ *m* control lever *or* stick; **'~mann** *m* (-[e]s/⸚er, *Steuerleute*) ⚓ helmsman, steersman, *Am. a.* wheelsman; coxwain (*a. rowing*); **'2n** (ge-) **1.** *v/t.* (*h*) ⚓, ✈ steer, navigate, pilot; ⊕ control; *fig.* direct, control; **2.** *v/i.* (*h*) check *s.th.*; **3.** *v/i.* (*sein*): ~ *in* (*acc.*) ⚓ enter (*harbour, etc.*); ~ *nach* ⚓ be bound for; **'2pflichtig** *adj.* taxable; *goods*: dutiable; **'~rad** *n* steering-wheel; **'~ruder** ⚓ *n* helm, rudder; **'~satz** *m* rate of assessment; **'~ung** *f* (-/-en) ⚓, ✈ steering; ⊕, ⚡ control (*a. fig.*); ✈ controls *pl.*; **'~veranlagung** *f* tax assessment; **'~zahler** *m* (-s/-) taxpayer; ratepayer.

**Steven** ⚓ ['ʃteːvən] *m* (-s/-) stem; stern-post.

**Stich** [ʃtiç] *m* (-[e]s/-e) prick (*of needle, etc.*); sting (*of insect, etc.*);

stab (of knife, etc.); sewing: stitch; cards: trick; ⊕ engraving; ⚓ stab; ~ halten hold water; im ~ lassen abandon, desert, forsake.

**Stichel|ei** fig. [ʃtiçə'laɪ] f (-/-en) gibe, jeer; **2n** fig. v/i. (ge-, h) gibe (gegen at), jeer (at).

**'Stich|flamme** f flash; **2haltig** adj. valid, sound; ~ sein hold water; **'~probe** f random test or sample, Am. a. spot check; **'~tag** m fixed day; **'~wahl** f second ballot; **'~wort** n 1. typ. (-[e]s/~er) headword; 2. thea. (-[e]s/-e) cue; **'~wunde** f stab.

**sticken** ['ʃtɪkən] v/t. and v/i. (ge-, h) embroider.

**'Stick|garn** n embroidery floss; **'~husten** ⚕ m (w)hooping cough; **'2ig** adj. stuffy, close; **'~stoff** ⚛ m (-[e]s/no pl.) nitrogen.

**stieben** ['ʃtiːbən] v/i. ([irr.,] ge-, h, sein) sparks, etc.: fly about.

**Stief...** ['ʃtiːf-] step...

**Stiefel** ['ʃtiːfəl] m (-s/-) boot; **'~knecht** m bootjack; **'~schaft** m leg of a boot.

**'Stief|mutter** f (-/⸚) stepmother; **~mütterchen** ♣ ['~mʏtərçən] n (-s/-) pansy; **'~vater** m stepfather.

**stieg** [ʃtiːk] pret. of steigen.

**Stiel** [ʃtiːl] m (-[e]s/-e) handle; helve (of weapon, tool); haft (of axe); stick (of broom); ♣ stalk.

**Stier** [ʃtiːr] 1. zo. m (-[e]s/-e) bull; 2. 2 adj. staring; **2en** v/i. (ge-, h) stare (auf acc. at); **'~kampf** m bullfight.

**stieß** [ʃtiːs] pret. of stoßen.

**Stift** [ʃtɪft] 1. m (-[e]s/-e) pin; peg; tack; pencil, crayon; F fig.: youngster; apprentice; 2. n (-[e]s/-e, -er) charitable institution; **2en** v/t. (ge-, h) endow, give, Am. a. donate; found; fig. cause; make (mischief, peace); **'~er** m (-s/-) donor; founder; fig. author; **'~ung** f (-/-en) (charitable) endowment, donation; foundation.

**Stil** [ʃtiːl] m (-[e]s/-e) style (a. fig.); **'2gerecht** adj. stylish; **2isieren** [ʃtili'ziːrən] v/t. (no -ge-, h) stylize; **2istisch** adj. [ʃti'listiʃ] stylistic.

**still** adj. [ʃtɪl] still, quiet; silent; ♰ dull, slack; secret; ~! silence!; im ~en secretly; ~er Gesellschafter ♰ sleeping or silent partner; der 2e Ozean the Pacific (Ocean); **'2e** f (-/no pl.) stillness, quiet(ness); silence; in aller ~ quietly, silently, privately; **2eben** paint. ['ʃtile:bən] n (-s/-) still life; **2egen** ['ʃtile:gən] v/t. (sep., -ge-, h) shut down (factory, etc.); stop (traffic); **'~en** v/t. (ge-, h) soothe (pain); appease (appetite); quench (thirst); sta(u)nch (blood); nurse (baby); **'~halten** v/i. (irr. halten, sep., -ge-, h) keep still; **~iegen** ['ʃtili:gən] v/i.

(irr. liegen, sep., -ge-, h) factory, etc.: be shut down; traffic: be suspended; machines, etc.: be idle.

**stillos** adj. ['ʃtiːloːs] without style.

**'stillschweigen** 1. v/i. (irr. schweigen, sep., -ge-, h) be silent; ~ zu et. ignore s.th.; 2. 2 n (-s/no pl.) silence; secrecy; ~ bewahren observe secrecy; et. mit ~ übergehen pass s.th. over in silence; **'~d** adj. silent; agreement, etc.: tacit.

**'Still|stand** m (-[e]s/no pl.) standstill; fig.: stagnation (a. ♰); deadlock; **2stehen** v/i. (irr. stehen, sep., -ge-, h) stop; be at a standstill; stillgestanden! ⚔ attention!

**'Stil|möbel** n/pl. period furniture; **2voll** adj. stylish.

**Stimm|band** anat. ['ʃtɪm-] n (-[e]s/⸚er) vocal c(h)ord; **'2berechtigt** adj. entitled to vote; **'~e** f (-/-n) voice (a. ♪, fig.); vote; comment; ♪ part; **2en** (ge-, h) 1. v/t. tune (piano, etc.); j-n fröhlich ~ put s.o. in a merry mood; 2. v/i. be true or right; sum, etc.: be correct; ~ für vote for; **'~enmehrheit** f majority or plurality of votes; **'~enthaltung** f abstention; **'~enzählung** f counting of votes; **'~gabel** ♪ f tuning-fork; **'~recht** n right to vote; pol. franchise; **'~ung** f (-/-en) ♪ tune; fig. mood, humo(u)r; **'2ungsvoll** adj. impressive; **'~zettel** m ballot, voting-paper.

**stinken** ['ʃtɪŋkən] v/i. (irr., ge-, h) stink (nach of); F fig. be fishy.

**Stipendium** univ. [ʃti'pɛndjum] n (-s/Stipendien) scholarship; exhibition.

**stipp|en** ['ʃtɪpən] v/t. (ge-, h) dip, steep; **'2visite** f F flying visit.

**Stirn** [ʃtɪrn] f (-/-en) forehead, brow; fig. face, cheek; j-m die ~ bieten make head against s.o.; s. runzeln; **'~runzeln** n (-s/no pl.) frown(ing).

**stob** [ʃtoːp] pret. of stieben.

**stöbern** F ['ʃtøːbərn] v/i. (ge-, h) rummage (about) (in dat. in).

**stochern** ['ʃtɔxərn] v/i. (ge-, h): ~ in (dat.) poke (fire); pick (teeth).

**Stock** [ʃtɔk] m 1. (-[e]s/⸚e) stick; cane; ♪ baton; beehive; ♀ stock; 2. (-[e]s/-) stor(e)y, floor; im ersten ~ on the first floor, Am. on the second floor; **'2be'trunken** F adj. dead drunk; **'2'blind** F adj. stone-blind; **'2'dunkel** F adj. pitch-dark.

**Stöckelschuh** ['ʃtœkəl-] m high-heeled shoe.

**'stocken** v/i. (ge-, h) stop; liquid: stagnate (a. fig.); speaker: break down; voice: falter; traffic: be blocked; ihm stockte das Blut his blood curdled.

**'Stock|engländer** F m thorough or true-born Englishman; **'2'finster** F adj. pitch-dark; **'~fleck** m spot of mildew; '⚫(fleck)ig adj. foxy, mildewy; '⚫'nüchtern F adj. (as) sober as a judge; '⚫schnupfen ✠ m chronic rhinitis; '⚫'taub F adj. stone-deaf; '⚫ung f (-/-en) stop (-page); stagnation (of liquid) (a. fig.); block (of traffic); '⚫werk n stor(e)y, floor.

Stoff [ʃtɔf] m (-[e]s/-e) matter, substance; material, fabric, textile; material, stuff; fig.: subject(-matter); food; '⚫lich adj. material.

stöhnen ['ʃtøːnən] v/i. (ge-, h) groan, moan.

Stolle ['ʃtɔlə] f (-/-n) loaf-shaped Christmas cake; '⚫n m (-s/-) s. Stolle; ⚒ tunnel, gallery (a. ⚒).

stolpern ['ʃtɔlpərn] v/i. (ge-, sein) stumble (über acc. over), trip (over) (both a. fig.).

stolz [ʃtɔlts] 1. adj. proud (auf acc. of) (a. fig.); haughty; 2. ⚫ m (-es/no pl.) pride (auf acc. in); haughtiness; '⚫ieren [⚫'tsiːrən] v/i. (no -ge-, sein) strut, flaunt.

stopfen ['ʃtɔpfən] (ge-, h) 1. v/t. stuff; fill (pipe); cram (poultry, etc.); darn (sock, etc.); j-m den Mund ⚫ stop s.o.'s mouth; 2. ✠ v/i. cause constipation.

'Stopf|garn n darning-yarn; '⚫nadel f darning-needle.

Stoppel ['ʃtɔpəl] f (-/-n) stubble; '⚫bart F m stubbly beard; '⚫ig adj. stubbly.

stopp|en ['ʃtɔpən] (ge-, h) 1. v/t. stop; time, F clock; 2. v/i. stop; '⚫licht mot. n stop-light; '⚫uhr f stop-watch.

Stöpsel ['ʃtœpsəl] m (-s/-) stopper, cork; plug (a. ⚡); F fig. whippersnapper; '⚫n v/t. (ge-, h) stopper, cork; plug (up).

Storch orn. [ʃtɔrç] m (-[e]s/ᵘe) stork.

stören ['ʃtøːrən] (ge-, h) 1. v/t. disturb; trouble; radio: jam (reception); lassen Sie sich nicht ⚫! don't let me disturb you!; darf ich Sie kurz ⚫? may I trouble you for a minute?; 2. v/i. be intruding; be in the way; ⚫fried ['⚫friːt] m (-[e]s/-e) troublemaker; intruder.

störr|ig adj. ['ʃtœːrɪç], '⚫isch adj. stubborn, obstinate; a. horse: restive.

'Störung f (-/-en) disturbance; trouble (a. ⊕); breakdown; radio: jamming, interference.

Stoß [ʃtoːs] m (-es/ᵘe) push, shove; thrust (a. fencing); kick; butt; shock; knock, strike; blow; swimming, billiards: stroke; jolt (of car, etc.); pile, stock, heap; '⚫dämpfer mot. m shock-absorber; ⚫en (irr., ge-) 1. v/t. (h) push, shove; thrust (weapon, etc.); kick; butt; knock, strike; pound (pepper, etc.); sich ⚫ an (dat.) strike or knock against; fig. take offence at; 2. v/i. (h) thrust

(nach at); kick (at); butt (at); goat, etc.: butt; car: jolt; ⚫ an (acc.) adjoin, border on; 3. v/i. (sein): F ⚫ auf (acc.) come across; meet with (opposition, etc.); ⚫ gegen or an (acc.) knock or strike against.

'Stoß|seufzer m ejaculation; '⚫stange mot. f bumper; ⚫weise adv. by jerks; by fits and starts; '⚫zahn m tusk.

stottern ['ʃtɔtərn] (ge-, h) 1. v/t. stutter (out); stammer; 2. v/i. stutter; stammer; F mot. conk (out).

Straf|anstalt ['ʃtraːf⚫-] f penal institution; prison; Am. penitentiary; '⚫arbeit f imposition, F impo(t); ⚫bar adj. punishable, penal; '⚫e f (-/-n) punishment; ⚫⚫, ♱, sports, fig. penalty; fine; bei ⚫ von on or under pain of; zur ⚫ as a punishment; ⚫en v/t. (ge-, h) punish.

straff adj. [ʃtraf] tight; rope: a. taut; fig. strict, rigid.

'straf|fällig adj. liable to prosecution; ⚫gesetz n penal law; ⚫gesetzbuch n penal code.

sträf|lich adj. ['ʃtrɛːflɪç] culpable; reprehensible; inexcusable; ⚫ling ['⚫lɪŋ] m (-s/-e) convict, Am. sl. a. lag.

'straf|los adj. unpunished; ⚫losigkeit f (-/no pl.) impunity; ⚫porto n surcharge; ⚫predigt f severe lecture; j-m e-e ⚫ halten lecture s.o. severely; ⚫prozeß m criminal action; ⚫raum m football: penalty area; ⚫stoß m football: penalty kick; ⚫verfahren n criminal proceedings pl.

Strahl [ʃtraːl] m (-[e]s/-en) ray (a. fig.); beam; flash (of lightning, etc.); jet (of water, etc.); ⚫en v/i. (ge-, h) radiate; shine (vor dat. with); fig. beam (vor dat. with), shine (with); '⚫ung f (-/-en) radiation, rays pl.

Strähne ['ʃtrɛːnə] f (-/-n) lock, strand (of hair); skein, hank (of yarn); fig. stretch.

stramm adj. [ʃtram] tight; rope: a. taut; stalwart; soldier: smart.

strampeln ['ʃtrampəln] v/i. (ge-, h) kick.

Strand [ʃtrant] m (-[e]s/⚫-e, ᵘe) beach; '⚫anzug m beach-suit; ⚫en ['⚫dən] v/i. (ge-, sein) ⚓ strand, run ashore; fig. fail, founder; '⚫gut n stranded goods pl.; fig. wreckage; '⚫korb m roofed wicker chair for use on the beach; ⚫promenade ['⚫promənaːdə] f (-/-n) promenade, Am. boardwalk.

Strang [ʃtraŋ] m (-[e]s/ᵘe) cord (a. anat.); rope; halter (for hanging s.o.); trace (of harness); ⚒ track; über die Stränge schlagen kick over the traces.

Strapaz|e [ʃtra'paːtsə] f (-/-n) fatigue; toil; ⚫ieren [⚫ɑ'tsiːrən] v/t.

(no -ge-, h) fatigue, strain (a. fig.); wear out (fabric, etc.); 2ierfähig adj. [ˌaˈtsiːr-] long-lasting; 2lös adj. [ˌaˈtsjøːs] fatiguing.

Straße [ˈʃtraːsə] f (-/-n) road, highway; street (of town, etc.); strait; auf der ~ on the road; in the street.

'Straßen|anzug m lounge-suit, Am. business suit; '~bahn f tram(way), tram-line, Am. street railway, streetcar line; s. Straßenbahnwagen; '~bahnhaltestelle f tram stop, Am. streetcar stop; '~bahnwagen m tram(-car), Am. streetcar; '~beleuchtung f street lighting; '~damm m roadway; '~händler m hawker; '~junge m street arab, Am. street Arab; '~kehrer m (-s/-) scavenger, street orderly; '~kreuzung f crossing, cross roads; '~reinigung f street-cleaning, scavenging; '~rennen n road-race.

strategisch adj. [ʃtraˈteːgiʃ] strategic(al).

sträuben [ˈʃtrɔʏbən] v/t. (ge-, h) ruffle up (its feathers, etc.); sich ~ hair: stand on end; sich ~ gegen kick against or at.

Strauch [ʃtraux] m (-[e]s/=er) shrub; bush.

straucheln [ˈʃtrauxəln] v/i. (ge-, sein) stumble (über acc. over, at), trip (over) (both a. fig.).

Strauß [ʃtraus] m 1. orn. (-es/-e) ostrich; 2. (-es/=e) bunch (of flowers), bouquet; strife, combat.

Strebe [ˈʃtreːbə] f (-/-n) strut, support, brace.

'streben 1. v/i. (ge-, h): ~ nach strive for or after, aspire to or after; 2. 2 n (-s/no pl.) striving (nach for, after), aspiration (for, after); effort, endeavo(u)r.

'Streber m (-s/-) pusher, careerist; at school: sl. swot.

strebsam adj. [ˈʃtreːpzaːm] assiduous; ambitious; '2keit f (-/no pl.) assiduity; ambition.

Strecke [ˈʃtrɛkə] f (-/-n) stretch; route; tract, extent; distance (a. sports); course; 🚂, etc.: section, line; hunt. bag; zur ~ bringen hunt. bag, hunt down (a. fig.); '2n v/t. (ge-, h) stretch, extend; dilute (fluid); sich ~ stretch (o.s.); die Waffen ~ lay down one's arms; fig. a. give in.

Streich [ʃtraiç] m (-[e]s/-e) stroke; blow; fig. trick, prank; j-m e-n ~ spielen play a trick on s.o.; 2eln [ˈ~əln] v/t. (ge-, h) stroke; caress; pat; '2en (irr., ge-) 1. v/t. (h) rub; spread (butter, etc.); paint; strike out, delete, cancel (a. fig.); strike, lower (flag, sail); 2. v/i. (sein) prowl (um round); 3. v/i. (h): mit der Hand über et. ~ pass one's hand over s.th.; '~holz n match; '~instrument ♪ n stringed instrument;

'~orchester n string band; '~riemen m strop.

Streif [ʃtraif] m (-[e]s/-e) s. Streifen; '~band n (-[e]s/=er) wrapper; '~e f (-/-n) patrol; patrolman; raid.

'streifen (ge-) 1. v/t. (h) stripe, streak; graze, touch lightly in passing, brush; touch (up)on (subject); 2. v/i. (sein): ~ durch rove, wander through; 3. v/i. (h): ~ an (acc.) graze, brush; fig. border or verge on; 4. 2 m (-s/-) strip; stripe; streak.

'streif|ig adj. striped; '2licht n sidelight; '2schuß 💥 m grazing shot; '2zug m ramble; 💥 raid.

Streik [ʃtraik] m (-[e]s/-s) strike, Am. F a. walkout; in den ~ treten go on strike, Am. F a. walk out; '~brecher m (-s/-) strike-breaker, blackleg, scab; '2en v/i. (ge-, h) (be on) strike; go on strike, Am. F a. walk out; ~ende [ˈ~əndə] m, f (-n/-n) striker; '~posten m picket.

Streit [ʃtrait] m (-[e]s/-e) quarrel; dispute; conflict; ⅔ litigation; '2bar adj. pugnacious; '2en v/i. and v/refl. (irr., ge-, h) quarrel (mit with; wegen for; über acc. about); '~frage f controversy, (point of) issue; '2ig adj. debatable, controversial; j-m et. ~ machen dispute s.o.'s right to s.th.; '~igkeiten f/pl. quarrels pl.; disputes pl.; '~kräfte 💥 [ˈ~krɛftə] f/pl. (military or armed) forces pl.; '2lustig adj. pugnacious, aggressive; '2süchtig adj. quarrelsome; pugnacious.

streng [ʃtrɛŋ] 1. adj. severe; stern; strict; austere; discipline, etc.: rigorous; weather, climate: inclement; examination: stiff; 2. adv.: ~ vertraulich in strict confidence; '2e f (-/no pl.) s. streng 1: severity; sternness; strictness; austerity; rigo(u)r; inclemency; stiffness; '~genommen adv. strictly speaking; '~gläubig adj. orthodox.

Streu [ʃtrɔʏ] f (-/-en) litter; '2en v/t. (ge-, h) strew, scatter; '~zucker m castor sugar.

Strich [ʃtriç] m (-[e]s/-e) stroke; line; dash; tract (of land); j-m e-n ~ durch die Rechnung machen queer s.o.'s pitch; 2. 2 pret. of streichen; '~regen m local shower; '2weise adv. here and there.

Strick [ʃtrik] m (-[e]s/-e) cord; rope; halter; rope (for hanging s.o.); F fig. (young) rascal; '2en v/t. and v/i. (ge-, h) knit; '~garn n knitting-yarn; '~jacke f cardigan, jersey; '~leiter f rope-ladder; '~nadel f knitting-needle; '~waren f/pl. knit-wear; '~zeug n knitting(-things pl.).

Striemen [ˈʃtriːmən] m (-s/-) weal, wale.

Strippe F [ˈʃtripə] f (-/-n) band; string; shoe-lace; an der ~ hängen be on the phone.

**stritt** [ʃtrit] *pret. of* streiten; '~ig *adj.* debatable, controversial; ~er Punkt (point of) issue.

**Stroh** [ʃtro:] *n* (-[e]s/*no pl.*) straw; thatch; '~dach *n* thatch(ed roof); '~halm *m* straw; *nach e-m* ~ greifen catch at a straw; '~hut *m* straw hat; '~mann *m* man of straw; scarecrow; *fig.* dummy; '~sack *m* straw mattress; '~witwe F *f* grass widow.

**Strolch** [ʃtrɔlç] *m* (-[e]s/-e) scamp, F vagabond; '~en *v/i.* (ge-, sein): ~ durch rove.

**Strom** [ʃtro:m] *m* (-[e]s/ͤe) stream (*a. fig.*); (large) river; ⚡ current (*a. fig.*); *es regnet in Strömen* it is pouring with rain; ⚡'ab(wärts) *adv.* down-stream; ⚡'auf(wärts) *adv.* up-stream.

**strömen** ['ʃtrø:mən] *v/i.* (ge-, sein) stream; flow, run; *rain:* pour; *people:* stream, pour (*aus* out of; *in* acc. into).

'**Strom|kreis** ⚡ *m* circuit; '~linienform *f* (-/*no pl.*) streamline shape; ⚡'linienförmig *adj.* streamline(d); '~schnelle *f* (-/-n) rapid, Am. *a.* riffle; '~sperre ⚡ *f* stoppage of current.

'**Strömung** *f* (-/-en) current; *fig. a.* trend, tendency.

'**Stromzähler** ⚡ *m* electric meter.

**Strophe** ['ʃtro:fə] *f* (-/-n) stanza, verse.

**strotzen** ['ʃtrɔtsən] *v/i.* (ge-, h): ~ von abound in; teem with (*blunders*, *etc.*); burst with (*health, etc.*).

**Strudel** ['ʃtru:dəl] *m* (-s/-) eddy, whirlpool; *fig.* whirl; '~n *v/i.* (ge-, h) swirl, whirl. [ture.)

**Struktur** [ʃtruk'tu:r] *f* (-/-en) struc-)

**Strumpf** [ʃtrumpf] *m* (-[e]s/ͤe) stocking; '~band *n* (-[e]s/ͤer) garter; '~halter *m* (-s/-) suspender, Am. garter; '~waren *f/pl.* hosiery.

**struppig** *adj.* ['ʃtrupiç] *hair:* rough, shaggy; *dog, etc.:* shaggy.

**Stube** ['ʃtu:bə] *f* (-/-n) room.

'**Stuben|hocker** *fig. m* (-s/-) stay-at-home; '~mädchen *n* chambermaid; ⚡'rein *adj.* house-trained.

**Stück** [ʃtyk] *n* (-[e]s/-e) piece (*a. ♪*); fragment; head (*of cattle*); lump (*of sugar*); *thea.* play; *aus freien* ~en of one's own accord; *in* ~e gehen *or* schlagen break to pieces; '~arbeit *f* piece-work; ⚡'weise *adv.* piece by piece; (by) piecemeal; ✝ by the piece; '~werk *fig. n* patchwork.

**Student** [ʃtu'dɛnt] *m* (-en/-en), ~in *f* (-/-nen) student, undergraduate.

**Studie** ['ʃtu:djə] *f* (-/-n) study (*über* acc., *zu* of, in) (*a. art, literature*); *paint, etc.:* sketch; '~nrat *m* (-[e]s/ͤe) *appr.* secondary-school teacher; '~nreise *f* study trip.

**studier|en** [ʃtu'di:rən] (*no* -ge-, h) **1.** *v/t.* study, read (*law, etc.*); **2.** *v/i.*

study; be a student; ⚡'zimmer *n* study.

**Studium** ['ʃtu:djum] *n* (-s/Studien) study (*a. fig.*); studies *pl.*

**Stufe** ['ʃtu:fə] *f* (-/-n) step; *fig.:* degree; grade; stage.

'**Stufen|folge** *fig. f* gradation; '~leiter *f* step-ladder; *fig.* scale; ⚡'weise **1.** *adj.* gradual; **2.** *adv.* gradually, by degrees.

**Stuhl** [ʃtu:l] *m* (-[e]s/ͤe) chair, seat; *in a church:* pew; *weaving:* loom; 𝔰 *s.* Stuhlgang; '~bein *n* leg of a chair; '~gang 𝔰 *m* (-[e]s/*no pl.*) stool; motion; '~lehne *f* back of a chair.

**stülpen** ['ʃtylpən] *v/t.* (ge-, h) put (*über* acc. over); clap (*hat*) (*auf* acc. on).

**stumm** *adj.* [ʃtum] dumb, mute; *fig. a.* silent; *gr.* silent, mute.

**Stummel** ['ʃtuməl] *m* (-s/-) stump; stub.

'**Stummfilm** *m* silent film.

**Stümper** F ['ʃtympər] *m* (-s/-) bungler; ~ei F [~'rai] *f* (-/-en) bungling; bungle; ⚡'haft *adj.* bungling; ⚡n F *v/i.* (ge-, h) bungle, botch.

**stumpf** [ʃtumpf] **1.** *adj.* blunt; Ⱥ *angle:* obtuse; *senses:* dull, obtuse; apathetic; **2.** 2 *m* (-[e]s/ͤe) stump, stub; *mit* ~ *und Stiel* root and branch; ⚡'sinn *m* (-[e]s/*no pl.*) stupidity, dul(l)ness; '~sinnig *adj.* stupid, dull.

**Stunde** ['ʃtundə] *f* (-/-n) hour; lesson, Am. *a.* period; ⚡n *v/t.* (ge-, h) grant respite for.

'**Stunden|kilometer** *m* kilometre per hour, Am. kilometer per hour; ⚡'lang **1.** *adj.:* nach ~em Warten after hours of waiting; **2.** *adv.* for hours (and hours); '~lohn *m* hourly wage; '~plan *m* time-table, Am. schedule; ⚡'weise **1.** *adj.:* ~ Beschäftigung part-time employment; **2.** *adv.* by the hour; '~zeiger *m* hour-hand.

**stündlich** ['ʃtyntliç] **1.** *adj.* hourly; **2.** *adv.* hourly, every hour; at any hour.

'**Stundung** *f* (-/-en) respite.

**stur** F *adj.* [ʃtu:r] *gaze:* fixed, staring; *p.* pigheaded, mulish.

**Sturm** [ʃturm] *m* (-[e]s/ͤe) storm (*a. fig.*); ⚔ gale.

**stürm|en** ['ʃtyrmən] (ge-) **1.** *v/t.* (h) ⚔ storm (*a. fig.*); **2.** *v/i.* (h) *wind:* storm, rage; *es stürmt* it is stormy weather; **3.** *v/i.* (sein) rush; ⚡'er *m* (-s/-) football, *etc.*: forward; '~isch *adj.* stormy; *fig.:* impetuous; tumultuous.

'**Sturm|schritt** ⚔ *m* double-quick step; '~trupp ⚔ *m* storming-party; '~wind *m* storm-wind.

**Sturz** [ʃturts] *m* (-es/ͤe) fall, tumble; overthrow (*of government, etc.*);

*fig.* ruin; ✝ slump; '**~bach** *m* torrent.

**stürzen** ['ʃtyrtsən] (ge-) **1.** *v/i.* (sein) (have a) fall, tumble; *fig.* rush, plunge (*in acc.* into); **2.** *v/t.* (h) throw; overthrow (*government, etc.*); *fig.* plunge (*in acc.* into), precipitate (into); *j-n ins Unglück ~* ruin s.o.; *sich in Schulden ~* plunge into debt.

'**Sturz**|**flug** 🛪 *m* (nose)dive; '**~helm** *m* crash-helmet.

**Stute** *zo.* ['ʃtuːtə] *f* (-/-n) mare.

**Stütze** ['ʃtytsə] *f* (-/-n) support, prop, stay (*all a. fig.*).

**stutzen** ['ʃtutsən] (ge-, h) **1.** *v/t.* cut (*hedge*); crop (*ears, tail, hair*); clip (*hedge, wing*); trim (*hair, beard, hedge*); dock (*tail*); lop (*tree*); **2.** *v/i.* start (*bei* at); stop dead *or* short.

'**stützen** *v/t.* (ge-, h) support, prop, stay (*all a. fig.*); *~ auf (acc.)* base *or* found on; *sich ~ auf (acc.)* lean on; *fig.* rely (up)on; *argument, etc.:* be based on.

'**Stutz**|**er** *m* (-s/-) dandy, fop, *Am. a.* dude; **2ig** *adj.* suspicious; *~ machen* make suspicious.

'**Stütz**|**pfeiler** 🏛 *m* abutment; '**~punkt** *m phys.* fulcrum; ✕ base.

**Subjekt** [zup'jekt] *n* (-[e]s/-e) *gr.* subject; *contp.* individual; **2iv** *adj.* [.'~tiːf] subjective; **~ivität** [.~ivi'tɛːt] *f* (-/*no pl.*) subjectivity.

**Substantiv** *gr.* ['zupstanti:f] *n* (-s/-e) noun, substantive; **2isch** *gr. adj.* ['~viʃ] substantival.

**Substanz** [zup'stants] *f* (-/-en) substance (*a. fig.*).

**subtra**|**hieren** 🏛 [zuptra'hiːrən] *v/t.* (*no -ge-*, h) subtract; **2ktion** 🏛 [~k'tsjoːn] *f* (-/-en) subtraction.

**Such**|**dienst** ['zuːx-] *m* tracing service; '**~e** *f* (-/*no pl.*) search (*nach* for); *auf der ~ nach* in search of; '**2en** (ge-, h) **1.** *v/t.* seek (*advice, etc.*); search for; look for; *Sie haben hier nichts zu ~* you have no business to be here; **2.** *v/i.:* *~ nach* seek for *or* after; search for; look for; '**~er** *phot. m* (-s/-) view-finder.

**Sucht** [zuxt] *f* (-/ᵕe) mania (*nach* for), rage (for), addiction (to).

**süchtig** *adj.* ['zyçtiç] having a mania (*nach* for); *~ sein* be a drug addict; **2e** ['~gə] *m, f* (-n/-n) drug addict *or* fiend.

**Süd** *geogr.* [zyːt], **~en** ['~dən] *m* (-s/*no pl.*) south; **~früchte** ['zyːt-fryçtə] *f/pl.* fruits from the south; '**2lich 1.** *adj.* south(ern); southerly; **2.** *adv.:* *~ von* to the south of; **~'ost** *geogr.*, **~'osten** *m* (-s/*no pl.*) south-east; **2'östlich** *adj.* south-east(ern); '**~pol** *geogr. m* (-s/*no pl.*) South Pole; **2wärts** *adv.* ['~vɛrts] southward(s); **~'west** *geogr.*, **~'westen** *m* (-s/*no pl.*) south-west;

**2'westlich** *adj.* south-west(ern); '**~wind** *m* south wind.

**süffig** F *adj.* ['zyfiç] palatable, tasty.

**suggerieren** [zuge'riːrən] *v/t.* (*no -ge-*, h) suggest.

**suggestiv** *adj.* [zuges'tiːf] suggestive.

**Sühne** ['zyːnə] *f* (-/-n) expiation, atonement; '**2n** *v/t.* (ge-, h) expiate, atone for.

**Sülze** ['zyltsə] *f* (-/-n) jellied meat.

**summ**|**arisch** *adj.* [zu'maːriʃ] summary (*a.* 🏛); '**2e** *f* (-/-n) sum (*a. fig.*); (sum) total; amount.

'**summen** (ge-, h) **1.** *v/i. bees, etc.:* buzz, hum; **2.** *v/t.* hum (*song, etc.*).

**sum'mieren** *v/t.* (*no -ge-*, h) sum *or* add up; *sich ~* run up.

**Sumpf** [zumpf] *m* (-[e]s/ᵕe) swamp, bog, marsh; '**2ig** *adj.* swampy, boggy, marshy.

**Sünd**|**e** ['zyndə] *f* (-/-n) sin (*a. fig.*); '**~enbock** F *m* scapegoat; '**~er** *m* (-s/-) sinner; **2haft** ['~t-] **1.** *adj.* sinful; **2.** *adv.:* F *~ teuer* awfully expensive; **2ig** ['~diç] *adj.* sinful; **2igen** ['~digən] *v/i.* (ge-, h) (commit a) sin.

**Superlativ** ['zuːpərlatiːf] *m* (-s/-e) *gr.* superlative degree; *in ~en sprechen* speak in superlatives.

**Suppe** ['zupə] *f* (-/-n) soup; broth.

'**Suppen**|**löffel** *m* soup-spoon; '**~schöpfer** *m* soup ladle; '**~schüssel** *f* tureen; '**~teller** *m* soup-plate.

**surren** ['zurən] *v/i.* (ge-, h) whir(r); *insects:* buzz.

**Surrogat** [zuro'gaːt] *n* (-[e]s/-e) substitute.

**suspendieren** [zuspen'diːrən] *v/t.* (*no -ge-*, h) suspend.

**süß** *adj.* [zyːs] sweet (*a. fig.*); '**2e** *f* (-/*no pl.*) sweetness; '**~en** *v/t.* (ge-, h) sweeten; '**2igkeiten** *pl.* sweets *pl.*, sweetmeats *pl.*, *Am. a.* candy; '**~lich** *adj.* sweetish; mawkish (*a. fig.*); '**2stoff** *m* saccharin(e); '**2wasser** *n* (-s/-) fresh water.

**Symbol** [zym'boːl] *n* (-s/-e) symbol; **~ik** *f* (-/*no pl.*) symbolism; **2isch** *adj.* symbolic(al).

**Symmetr**|**ie** [zyme'triː] *f* (-/-n) symmetry; **2isch** *adj.* [~'meːtriʃ] symmetric(al).

**Sympath**|**ie** [zympa'tiː] *f* (-/-n) liking; **2isch** *adj.* [~'paːtiʃ] likable; *er ist mir ~* I like him; **2isieren** [~i'ziːrən] *v/i.* (*no -ge-*, h) sympathize (*mit* with).

**Symphonie** ♪ [zymfo'niː] *f* (-/-n) symphony; **~orchester** *n* symphony orchestra.

**Symptom** [zymp'toːm] *n* (-s/-e) symptom; **2atisch** *adj.* [~o'maːtiʃ] symptomatic (*für* of).

**Synagoge** [zyna'goːgə] *f* (-/-n) synagogue.

**synchronisieren** [zynkroni'ziːrən] *v/t.* (*no -ge-*, h) synchronize; dub.

**Syndik|at** [zyndi'ka:t] *n* (-[e]s/-e) syndicate; **~us** ['zyndikus] *m* (-/-se, *Syndizi*) syndic.

**Synkope** ♪ [zyn'ko:pə] *f* (-/-n) syncope.

**synonym** [zyno'ny:m] **1.** *adj.* synonymous; **2.** **2** *n* (-s/-e) synonym.

**Syntax** *gr.* ['zyntaks] *f* (-/-en) syntax.

**synthetisch** *adj.* [zyn'te:tiʃ] .synthetic.

**System** [zys'te:m] *n* (-s/-e) system; scheme; **2atisch** *adj.* [~e'ma:tiʃ] systematic(al), methodic(al).

**Szene** ['stse:nə] *f* (-/-n) scene (*a. fig.*); *in* ~ *setzen* stage; **~rie** [stsenə'ri:] *f* (-/-n) scenery.

# T

**Tabak** ['ta:bak, 'tabak, ta'bak] *m* (-s/-e) tobacco; (')**~händler** *m* tobacconist; (')**~sbeutel** *m* tobacco-pouch; (')**~sdose** *f* snuff-box; (')**~waren** *pl.* tobacco products *pl.*, F smokes *pl.*

**tabellarisch** [tabε'la:riʃ] **1.** *adj.* tabular; **2.** *adv.* in tabular form.

**Tabelle** [ta'bεlə] *f* (-/-n) table; schedule.

**Tablett** [ta'blεt] *n* (-[e]s/-e, -s) tray; *of metal*: salver; **~e** *pharm. f* (-/-n) tablet; lozenge.

**Tachometer** [taxo'-] *n, m* (-s/-) ⊕ tachometer; *mot. a.* speedometer.

**Tadel** ['ta:dəl] *m* (-s/-) blame; censure; reprimand, rebuke, reproof; reproach; *at school*: bad mark; **2los** *adj.* faultless, blameless; excellent, splendid; **2n** *v/t.* (ge-, *h*) blame (*wegen dat.*); censure; reprimand, rebuke, reprove; scold; find fault with.

**Tafel** ['ta:fəl] *f* (-/-n) table; plate (*a. book illustration*); slab; *on houses, etc.*: tablet, plaque; slate; blackboard; signboard, notice-board, *Am.* billboard; cake, bar (*of chocolate, etc.*); dinner-table; dinner; **2förmig** *adj.* ['~fœrmiç] tabular; **'~geschirr** *n* dinner-service, dinner-set; **'~land** *n* table-land, plateau; **'2n** *v/i.* (ge-, *h*) dine; feast, banquet; **'~service** *n s. Tafelgeschirr*; **'~silber** *n* silver plate, *Am.* silverware.

**Täf(e)lung** ['tε:f(ə)luŋ] *f* (-/-en) wainscot, panelling.

**Taft** [taft] *m* (-[e]s/-e) taffeta.

**Tag** [ta:k] *m* (-[e]s/-e) day; *officially*: *a.* date; *am or bei* ~e by day; *e-s* ~es one day; *den ganzen* ~ all day long; ~ *für* ~ day by day; *über* ~e ⚒ aboveground; *unter* ~e ⚒ underground; *heute vor acht* ~en a week ago; *heute in acht* (*vierzehn*) ~en today *or* this day week (fortnight), a week (fortnight) today; *denkwürdiger or freudiger* ~ red-letter day; *freier* ~ day off; *guten* ~! how do you do?; good morning!; good afternoon!; F hallo!, hullo!, *Am.* hello!; *am hellichten* ~e in broad daylight; *es wird* ~ it dawns; *an den*

~ *bringen* (*kommen*) bring (come) to light; *bis auf den heutigen* ~ to this day; **2'aus** *adv.*: ~, *tagein* day in, day out.

**Tage|blatt** ['ta:gə-] *n* daily (paper); **'~buch** *n* journal, diary.

**tagein** *adv.* [ta:k'ain] *s. tagaus.*

**tage|lang** *adv.* ['ta:gə-] day after day, for days together; **'2lohn** *m* day's *or* daily wages *pl.*; **2löhner** ['~lø:nər] *m* (-s/-) day-labo(u)rer; **'~n** *v/i.* (ge-, *h*) dawn; hold a meeting, meet, sit; ⚖ be in session; **'2reise** *f* day's journey.

**Tages|anbruch** ['ta:gəs?-] *m* daybreak, dawn; *bei* ~ at daybreak *or* dawn; **'~befehl** ⚔ *m* order of the day; **'~bericht** *m* daily report, bulletin; **'~einnahme** ✝ *f* receipts *pl. or* takings *pl.* of the day; **'~gespräch** *n* topic of the day; **'~kasse** *f thea.* box-office, booking-office; *s. Tageseinnahme*; **'~kurs** ✝ *m* current rate; *stock exchange*: quotation of the day; **'~licht** *n* daylight; **'~ordnung** *f* order of the day, agenda; *das ist an der* ~ that is the order of the day, that is quite common; **'~presse** *f* daily press; **'~zeit** *f* time of day; daytime; *zu jeder* ~ at any hour, at any time of the day; **'~zeitung** *f* daily (paper).

**tage|weise** *adv.* ['ta:gə-] by the day; **'2werk** *n* day's work; man-day.

**täglich** *adj.* ['tε:kliç] daily.

**tags** *adv.* [ta:ks]: ~ *darauf* the following day, the day after; ~ *zuvor* (on) the previous day, the day before.

**'Tagschicht** *f* day shift.

**tagsüber** *adv.* ['ta:ks?-] during the day, in the day-time.

**Tagung** ['ta:guŋ] *f* (-/-en) meeting.

**Taille** ['taljə] *f* (-/-n) waist; bodice (*of dress*).

**Takel** ⚓ ['ta:kəl] *n* (-s/-) tackle; **~age** ⚓ [takə'la:ʒə] *f* (-/-n) rigging, tackle; **'2n** ⚓ *v/t.* (ge-, *h*) rig (*ship*); **'~werk** ⚓ *n s. Takelage.*

**Takt** [takt] *m* **1.** (-[e]s/-e) ♪ time, measure; bar; *mot.* stroke; *den* ~ *halten* ♪ keep time; *den* ~ *schlagen* ♪ beat time; **2.** (-[e]s/*no pl.*) tact; **2fest** *adj.* steady in keeping time;

*fig.* firm; '⌣ik ✕ *f* (-/-en) tactics *pl.* and *sg.* (*a. fig.*); '⌣iker *m* (-s/-) tactician; '2isch *adj.* tactical; '2los *adj.* tactless; '⌣stock *m* baton; '⌣strich ♪ *m* bar; '2voll *adj.* tactful.

**Tal** [tɑ:l] *n* (-[e]s/=er) valley, *poet. a.* dale; *enges* ⌣ *glen.*

**Talar** [ta'lɑ:r] *m* (-s/-e) ꭗꞁꞁ, *eccl., univ.* gown; ꭗꞁꞁ robe.

**Talent** [ta'lɛnt] *n* (-[e]s/-e) talent, gift, aptitude, ability; 2iert *adj.* [⌣'ti:rt] talented, gifted.

'**Talfahrt** *f* downhill journey; ♨ passage downstream.

**Talg** [talk] *m* (-[e]s/-e) suet; *melted:* tallow; '⌣drüse *anat. f* sebaceous gland; 2ig *adj.* ['⌣ɡɪç] suety; tallowish, tallowy; '⌣licht *n* tallow candle.

**Talisman** ['tɑ:lɪsman] *m* (-s/-e) talisman, (good-luck) charm.

'**Talsperre** *f* barrage, dam.

**Tampon** 🗲 [tãˈpõ:, 'tampɔn] *m* (-s/-s) tampon, plug.

**Tang** ⚘ [taŋ] *m* (-[e]s/-e) seaweed.

**Tank** [taŋk] *m* (-[e]s/-s, -e) tank; '2en *v/i.* (ge-, *h*) get (some) petrol, *Am.* get (some) gasoline; '⌣er ⚓ *m* (-s/-) tanker; '⌣stelle *f* petrol station, *Am.* gas or filling station; '⌣wagen *m* mot. tank truck, *Am. a.* gasoline truck, tank trailer; 🚋 tank-car; '⌣wart ['⌣vart] *m* (-[e]s/-e) pump attendant.

**Tanne** ⚘ ['tanə] *f* (-/-n) fir(-tree).

'**Tannen|baum** *m* fir-tree; '⌣nadel *f* fir-needle; '⌣zapfen *m* fir-cone.

**Tante** ['tantə] *f* (-/-n) aunt.

**Tantieme** [tãˈtjɛ:mə] *f* (-/-n) royalty, percentage, share in profits.

**Tanz** [tants] *m* (-es/=e) dance.

**tänzeln** ['tɛntsəln] *v/i.* (ge-, *h*, *sein*) dance, trip, frisk.

'**tanzen** (ge-) *v/i.* (*h*, *sein*) and *v/t.* (*h*) dance.

**Tänzer** ['tɛntsər] *m* (-s/-), '⌣in *f* (-/-nen) dancer; *thea.* ballet-dancer; partner.

'**Tanz|lehrer** *m* dancing-master; '⌣musik *f* dance-music; '⌣saal *m* dancing-room, ball-room, dance-hall; '⌣schule *f* dancing-school; '⌣stunde *f* dancing-lesson.

**Tapete** [ta'pe:tə] *f* (-/-n) wallpaper, paper-hangings *pl.*

**tapezier|en** [tape'tsi:rən] *v/t.* (*no* -ge-, *h*) paper; 2er *m* (-s/-) paperhanger; upholsterer.

**tapfer** *adj.* ['tapfər] brave; valiant, heroic; courageous; '2keit *f* (-/*no pl.*) bravery, valo(u)r; heroism; courage.

**tappen** ['tapən] *v/i.* (ge-, *sein*) grope (about), fumble. [awkward.]

**täppisch** *adj.* ['tɛpɪʃ] clumsy,/

**tapsen** F ['tapsən] *v/i.* (ge-, *sein*) walk clumsily.

**Tara** ✝ ['tɑ:ra] *f* (-/Taren) tare.

**Tarif** [ta'ri:f] *m* (-s/-e) tariff, (table of) rates *pl.*, price-list; 2lich *adv.* according to tariff; '⌣lohn *m* standard wage(s *pl.*); '⌣vertrag *m* collective *or* wage agreement.

**tarn|en** ['tarnən] *v/t.* (ge-, *h*) camouflage; *esp. fig.* disguise; '2ung *f* (-/-en) camouflage.

**Tasche** ['taʃə] *f* (-/-n) pocket (*of garment*); (hand)bag; pouch; *s. Aktentasche, Schultasche.*

'**Taschen|buch** *n* pocket-book; '⌣dieb *m* pickpocket, *Am. sl.* dip; '⌣geld *n* pocket-money; *monthly:* allowance; '⌣lampe *f* (electric) torch, *esp. Am.* flashlight; '⌣messer *n* pocket-knife; '⌣spielerei *f* juggle(ry); '⌣tuch *n* (pocket) handkerchief; '⌣uhr *f* (pocket-)watch; '⌣wörterbuch *n* pocket dictionary.

**Tasse** ['tasə] *f* (-/-n) cup.

**Tastatur** [tasta'tu:r] *f* (-/-en) keyboard, keys *pl.*

**Tast|e** ['tastə] *f* (-/-n) key; '2en (ge-, *h*) **1.** *v/i.* touch; grope (*nach* for, after), fumble (for); **2.** *v/t.* touch, feel; *sich* ⌣ feel *or* grope one's way; '⌣sinn *m* (-[e]s/*no pl.*) sense of touch.

**Tat** [tɑ:t] **1.** *f* (-/-en) action, deed; offen|ce, *Am.* -se, crime; *in der* ⌣ indeed, in fact, as a matter of fact, really; *auf frischer* ⌣ *ertappen* catch *s.o.* red-handed; *zur* ⌣ *schreiten* proceed to action; *in die* ⌣ *umsetzen* implement, carry into effect; **2.** 2 *pret. of* tun; '⌣bestand ꭗꞁꞁ *m* facts *pl.* of the case; '2enlos *adj.* inactive, idle.

**Täter** ['tɛ:tər] *m* (-s/-) perpetrator; offender; culprit.

**tätig** *adj.* ['tɛ:tɪç] active; busy; ⌣ *sein bei* work at; be employed with; ⌣en ✝ ['⌣ɡən] *v/t.* (ge-, *h*) effect, transact; conclude; '2keit *f* (-/-en) activity; occupation, business, job; profession.

'**Tat|kraft** *f* (-/*no pl.*) energy; enterprise; '2kräftig *adj.* energetic, active.

**tätlich** *adj.* ['tɛ:tlɪç] violent; ⌣ *werden gegen* assault; '2keiten *f/pl.* (acts *pl.* of) violence; ꭗꞁꞁ assault (and battery).

**Tatort** ꭗꞁꞁ ['tɑ:tɁ-] *m* (-[e]s/-e) place *or* scene of a crime.

**tätowieren** [tɛto'vi:rən] *v/t.* (*no* -ge-, *h*) tattoo.

'**Tat|sache** *f* (matter of) fact; '⌣sachenbericht *m* factual *or* documentary report, matter-of-fact account; '2sächlich *adj.* actual, real. [pat.]

**tätscheln** ['tɛtʃəln] *v/t.* (ge-, *h*) pet,/

**Tatze** ['tatsə] *f* (-/-n) paw, claw.

**Tau**[1] [tau] *n* (-[e]s/-e) rope, cable.

**Tau**[2] [⌣] *m* (-[e]s/*no pl.*) dew.

**taub** *adj.* [taup] deaf (*fig.:* gegen to); *fingers, etc.*: benumbed, numb; *nut:*

deaf, empty; *rock*: dead; ~es Ei
addle egg; *auf e-m Ohr* ~ *sein* be
deaf of or in one ear.
**Taube** *orn.* ['tauba] *f* (-/-n) pigeon;
'~nschlag *m* pigeon-house.
'**Taub|heit** *f* (-/no *pl.*) deafness;
numbness; '2stumm *adj.* deaf and
dumb; '~stumme *m*, *f* (-/-n) deaf
mute.
**tauch|en** ['tauxən] (ge-) **1.** *v/t.*
(h) dip, plunge; **2.** *v/i.* (h, sein) dive,
plunge; dip; *submarine*: submerge;
'2er *m* (-s/-) diver; '2sieder *m* (-s/-)
immersion heater.
**tauen** ['tauən] *v/i.* (ge-) **1.** (h, sein):
*der Schnee or es taut* the snow or
it is thawing; *der Schnee ist von
den Dächern getaut* the snow has
melted off the roofs; **2.** (h): *es taut*
dew is falling.
**Taufe** ['taufə] *f* (-/-n) baptism,
christening; '2n *v/t.* (ge-, h) baptize,
christen.
**Täufling** ['tɔyfliŋ] *m* (-s/-e) child or
person to be baptized.
'**Tauf|name** *m* Christian name, *Am.
a.* given name; '~pate **1.** *m* godfather; **2.** *f* godmother; '~patin *f*
godmother; '~schein *m* certificate
of baptism.
**taug|en** ['taugən] *v/i.* (ge-, h) be
good, be fit, be of use (*all:* zu for);
(*zu*) *nichts* ~ be good for nothing,
be no good, be of no use; '2enichts
*m* (-, -es/-e) good-for-nothing, *Am.
sl.* dead beat; '~lich *adj.* ['tauk-]
good, fit, useful (*all:* für, zu for, to
*inf.*); able; ⚓, ⚒ able-bodied.
**Taumel** ['tauməl] *m* (-s/no *pl.*)
giddiness; rapture, ecstasy; '2ig
*adj.* reeling, giddy; '2n *v/i.* (ge-,
sein) reel, stagger; be giddy.
**Tausch** [tauʃ] *m* (-es/-e) exchange;
barter; '2en *v/t.* (ge-, h) exchange;
barter (gegen for).
**täuschen** ['tɔyʃən] *v/t.* (ge-, h)
deceive, delude, mislead (on purpose); cheat; *sich* ~ *deceive o.s.*; be
mistaken; *sich* ~ *lassen* let o.s. be
deceived; '~d *adj.* deceptive, delu-
sive; *resemblance*: striking.
'**Tauschhandel** *m* barter.
'**Täuschung** *f* (-/-en) deception,
delusion.
**tausend** *adj.* ['tauzənt] a thousand;
'~fach *adj.* thousandfold; '2fuß *zo.
m*, 2füß(l)er *zo.* [-'fy:s(l)ər] *m*
(-s/-) millepede, milliped(e), *Am. a.*
wireworm; '~st *adj.* thousandth;
'2stel *n* (-s/-) thousandth (part).
'**Tau|tropfen** *m* dew-drop; '~wetter
*n* thaw.
**Taxameter** [taksa'-] *m* taximeter.
**Taxe** ['taksə] *f* (-/-n) rate; fee;
estimate; *s.* Taxi.
**Taxi** ['taksi] *n* (-[s]/-[s]) taxi(-cab),
cab *Am. a.* hack.
**ta'xieren** *v/t.* (no -ge-, h) rate,
estimate; *officially:* value, appraise.

'**Taxistand** *m* cabstand.
**Technik** ['tɛçnik] *f* **1.** (-/no *pl.*)
technology; engineering; **2.** (-/-en)
skill, workmanship; technique,
practice; ♪ execution; '~er *m* (-s/-)
(technical) engineer; technician;
'~um ['~um] *n* (-s/*Technika*, *Tech-
niken*) technical school.
'**technisch** *adj.* technical; ~e *Hochschule* school of technology.
**Tee** [te:] *m* (-s/-s) tea; '~büchse *f*
tea-caddy; '~gebäck *n* scones *pl.*,
biscuits *pl.*, *Am. a.* cookies *pl.*;
'~kanne *f* teapot; '~kessel *m* tea-
kettle; '~löffel *m* tea-spoon.
**Teer** [te:r] *m* (-[e]s/-e) tar; '2en *v/t.*
(ge-, h) tar.
'**Tee|rose** ♀ *f* tea-rose; '~sieb *n*
tea-strainer; '~tasse *f* teacup;
'~wärmer *m* (-s/-) tea-cosy.
**Teich** [taiç] *m* (-[e]s/-e) pool,
pond.
**Teig** [taik] *m* (-[e]s/-e) dough, paste;
2ig *adj.* ['~giç] doughy, pasty;
'~waren *f/pl.* farinaceous food;
noodles *pl.*
**Teil** [tail] *m*, *n* (-[e]s/-e) part; portion, share; component; zⁱᵣ party;
*zum* ~ partly, in part; *ich für mein*
~ ... for my part I ...; '2bar *adj.*
divisible; '~chen *n* (-s/-) particle;
'2en *v/t.* (ge-, h) divide; *fig.* share;
'2haben *v/i.* (*irr.* haben, sep., -ge-,
h) participate, (have a) share (*both:*
an dat. in); '~haber ♈ *m* (-s/-)
partner; '~nahme ['~na:mə] *f* (-/no
*pl.*) participation (*an dat.* in); *fig.:*
interest (in); sympathy (with);
2nahmslos *adj.* ['~na:mslo:s] indifferent, unconcerned; passive;
apathetic; '~nahmslosigkeit *f*
(-/no *pl.*) indifference; passiveness,
apathy; '2nehmen *v/i.* (*irr. nehmen,
sep., -ge-, h*): ~ *an* (*dat.*) take part or
participate in; join in; be present
at, attend at; *fig.* sympathize with;
'~nehmer *m* (-s/-) participant;
member; *univ., etc.:* student; con-
testant; *sports:* competitor; *teleph.*
subscriber; 2s *adv.* [~s] partly;
'~strecke *f* section; stage, leg; ⚐
fare stage; '~ung *f* (-/-en) division;
'2weise *adv.* partly, partially, in
part; '~zahlung *f* (payment by)
instal(l)ments.
**Teint** [tɛ̃:] *m* (-s/-s) complexion.
**Tele|fon** [tele'fo:n] *n* (-s/-e) *etc. s.*
*Telephon, etc.*; ~gr f [~'gra:f] *m*
(-en/-en) *etc. s. Telegraph, etc.*;
~gramm [~'gram] *n* (-s/-e) telegram, wire; *overseas:* cable(gram).
**Telegraph** [tele'gra:f] *m* (-en/-en)
telegraph; ~enamt [~ənʔ-] *n* telegraph office; 2ieren [~a'fi:rən] *v/t.
and v/i.* (no -ge-, h) telegraph, wire;
*overseas:* cable; 2isch [~'gra:fiʃ]
**1.** *adj.* telegraphic; **2.** *adv.* by telegram, by wire; by cable; ~ist
[~a'fist] *m* (-en/-en), ~istin *f* (-/-nen)

telegraph operator, telegrapher, telegraphist.
**Teleobjektiv** *phot.* ['teːle-] *n* telephoto lens.
**Telephon** [tele'foːn] *n* (-s/-e) telephone, F phone; *am* ~ *on the* (tele)phone; *ans* ~ *gehen* answer the (tele)phone; ~ *haben* be on the (tele)phone; **~anschluß** *m* telephone connexion *or* connection; **~buch** *n* telephone directory; **~gespräch** *n* (tele)phone call; conversation *or* chat over the (tele)phone; **~hörer** *m* (telephone) receiver, handset; **2ieren** [~o'niːrən] *v/i.* (*no -ge-, h*) telephone, F phone; *mit j-m* ~ ring s.o. up, *Am.* call s.o. up; **2isch** *adv.* [~'foːniʃ] by (tele)phone, over the (tele)phone; **~ist** [~o'nist] *m* (-en/-en), **~istin** *f* (-/-nen) (telephone) operator, telephonist; **~vermittlung** *f s.* Telephonzentrale; **~zelle** *f* telephone kiosk *or* box, call-box, *Am.* telephone booth; **~zentrale** *f* (telephone) exchange.
**Teleskop** *opt.* [tele'skoːp] *n* (-s/-e) telescope.
**Teller** ['tɛlər] *m* (-s/-) plate.
**Tempel** ['tempəl] *m* (-s/-) temple.
**Temperament** [tempəra'ment] *n* (-[e]s/-e) temper(ament); *fig.* spirit(s *pl.*); **2los** *adj.* spiritless; **2voll** *adj.* (high-)spirited.
**Temperatur** [tempəra'tuːr] *f* (-/-en) temperature; *j-s* ~ *messen* take s.o.'s temperature.
**Tempo** ['tempo] *n* (-s/-s, Tempi) time; pace; speed; rate.
**Tendenz** [tɛn'dɛnts] *f* (-/-en) tendency; trend; **2iös** *adj.* [~'tsjøːs] tendentious.
**Tennis** ['tenis] *n* (-/*no pl.*) (lawn) tennis; **~ball** *m* tennis-ball; **~platz** *m* tennis-court; **~schläger** *m* (tennis-)racket; **~spieler** *m* tennis player; **~turnier** *n* tennis tournament.
**Tenor** ♪ [te'noːr] *m* (-s/-e) tenor.
**Teppich** ['tɛpiç] *m* (-s/-e) carpet; **~kehrmaschine** *f* carpet-sweeper.
**Termin** [tɛr'miːn] *m* (-s/-e) appointed time *or* day; ⚖️, ✝ date, term; *sports:* fixture; *äußerster* ~ final date, dead(-)line; **~geschäfte** ✝ *n/pl.* futures *pl.*; **~kalender** *m* appointment book *or* pad; ⚖️ causelist, *Am.* calendar; **~liste** ⚖️ *f* causelist, *Am.* calendar.
**Terpentin** [tɛrpən'tiːn] *n* (-s/-e) turpentine.
**Terrain** [tɛ'rɛ̃ː] *n* (-s/-s) ground; plot; building site.
**Terrasse** [tɛ'rasə] *f* (-/-n) terrace; **2nförmig** *adj.* [~nfœrmiç] terraced, in terraces.
**Terrine** [tɛ'riːnə] *f* (-/-n) tureen.
**Territorium** [teri'toːrjum] *n* (-s/ Territorien) territory.

**Terror** ['tɛrɔr] *m* (-s/*no pl.*) terror; **2isieren** [~ori'ziːrən] *v/t.* (*no -ge-, h*) terrorize.
**Terz** ♪ [tɛrts] *f* (-/-en) third; **~ett** ♪ [~'tsɛt] *n* (-[e]s/-e) trio.
**Testament** [tɛsta'ment] *n* (-[e]s/-e) (last) will, (*often:* last will and) testament; *eccl.* Testament; **2arisch** [~'taːriʃ] **1.** *adj.* testamentary; **2.** *adv.* by will; **~svollstrecker** *m* (-s/-) executor; *officially:* administrator.
**testen** ['tɛstən] *v/t.* (*ge-, h*) test.
**teuer** *adj.* ['tɔyər] dear (*a. fig.*), expensive; *wie* ~ *ist es?* how much is it?
**Teufel** ['tɔyfəl] *m* (-s/-) devil; *der* ~ the Devil, Satan; *zum* ~! F dickens!, hang it!; *wer zum* ~? F who the devil *or* deuce?; *der* ~ *ist los* the fat's in the fire; *scher dich zum* ~! F go to hell!, go to blazes!; **~ei** [~'lai] *f* (-/-en) devilment, mischief, devilry, *Am.* deviltry; **~skerl** F *m* devil of a fellow.
**'teuflisch** *adj.* devilish, diabolic(al).
**Text** [tɛkst] *m* (-es/-e) text; words *pl.* (*of song*); book, libretto (*of opera*); **~buch** *n* book; libretto.
**Textil|ien** [tɛks'tiːljən] *pl.*, **~waren** *pl.* textile fabrics *pi.*, textiles *pi.*
**'textlich** *adv.* concerning the text.
**Theater** [te'aːtər] *n* **1.** (-s/-) theat|re, *Am.* -er; stage; **2.** F (-s/*no pl.*) playacting; **~besucher** *m* playgoer; **~karte** *f* theatre ticket; **~kasse** *f* box-office; **~stück** *n* play; **~vorstellung** *f* theatrical performance; **~zettel** *m* playbill.
**theatralisch** *adj.* [tea'traːliʃ] theatrical, stagy.
**Theke** ['teːkə] *f* (-/-n) *at inn:* bar, *Am. a.* counter; *at shop:* counter.
**Thema** ['teːma] *n* (-s/Themen, Themata) theme, subject; topic (*of discussion*).
**Theolog|e** [teo'loːgə] *m* (-n/-n) theologian, divine; **~ie** [~o'giː] *f* (-/-n) theology.
**Theoret|iker** [teo'reːtikər] *m* (-s/-) theorist; **2isch** *adj.* theoretic(al).
**Theorie** [teo'riː] *f* (-/-n) theory.
**Therapie** 🗲 [tera'piː] *f* (-/-n) therapy. [spa.]
**Thermalbad** [tɛr'maːl-] *n* thermal]
**Thermometer** [tɛrmo'-] *n* (-s/-) thermometer; **~stand** *m* (thermometer) reading.
**Thermosflasche** ['tɛrmɔs-] *f* vacuum bottle *or* flask, thermos (flask).
**These** ['teːzə] *f* (-/-n) thesis.
**Thrombose** 🗲 [trɔm'boːzə] *f* (-/-n) thrombosis.
**Thron** [troːn] *m* (-[e]s/-e) throne; **~besteigung** *f* accession to the throne; **~erbe** *m* heir to the throne, heir apparent; **~folge** *f* succession to the throne; **~folger** *m* (-s/-) successor to the throne; **~rede** *parl.* *f* Queen's *or* King's Speech.

**Thunfisch** *ichth.* ['tu:n-] *m* tunny, tuna.

**Tick** F [tik] *m* (-[e]s/-s, -e) crotchet, fancy, kink; e-n ~ haben have a bee in one's bonnet.

**ticken** ['tikən] *v/i.* (ge-, h) tick.

**tief** [ti:f] **1.** *adj.* deep (*a. fig.*); *fig.*: profound; low; *im ~sten Winter* in the dead *or* depth of winter; **2.** *adv.*: *bis ~ in die Nacht* far into the night; *das läßt ~ blicken* that speaks volumes; *zu ~ singen* sing flat; **3.** ♀ *meteor.* n (-[e]s/-s) depression, low(-pressure area); '♀**bau** *m* civil *or* underground engineering; '♀**druckgebiet** *meteor.* n s. Tief; '♀**e** *f* (-/-n) depth (*a. fig.*); *fig.* profundity; '♀**ebene** *f* low plain, lowland; '♀**enschärfe** *phot.* *f* depth of focus; '♀**flug** *m* low-level flight; '♀**gang** ⚓ *m* draught, *Am.* draft; ~**gebeugt** *fig. adj.* ['~gəbɔʏkt] deeply afflicted, bowed down; '~**gekühlt** *adj.* deep-frozen; '~**greifend** *adj.* fundamental, radical; '♀**land** *n* lowland(s *pl.*); '~**liegend** *adj.* eyes: sunken; *fig.* deep-seated; '♀**schlag** *m boxing*: low hit; '~**schürfend** *fig. adj.* profound; thorough; '♀**see** *f* deep sea; '~**sinnig** *adj.* thoughtful, pensive; F melancholy; '♀**stand** *m* (-[e]s/*no pl.*) low level.

**Tiegel** ['ti:gəl] *m* (-s/-) saucepan, stew-pan; ⊕ crucible.

**Tier** [ti:r] *n* (-[e]s/-e) animal; beast; brute; *großes ~ fig. sl.* bigwig, big bug, *Am.* big shot; '~**arzt** *m* veterinary (surgeon), F vet, *Am. a.* veterinarian; '~**garten** *m* zoological gardens *pl.*, zoo; '~**heilkunde** *f* veterinary medicine; '♀**isch** *adj.* animal; *fig.* bestial, brutish, savage; '~**kreis** *ast. m* zodiac; '~**quälerei** [~kvɛ:lə'raɪ] *f* (-/-en) cruelty to animals; '~**reich** *n* (-[e]s/*no pl.*) animal kingdom; '~**schutzverein** *m* Society for the Prevention of Cruelty to Animals.

**Tiger** *zo.* ['ti:gər] *m* (-s/-) tiger; '~**in** *zo. f* (-/-nen) tigress.

**tilg|en** ['tilgən] *v/t.* (ge-, h) extinguish; efface; wipe *or* blot out, erase; *fig.* obliterate; annul, cancel; discharge, pay (*debt*); redeem (*mortgage*, etc.); '♀**ung** *f* (-/-en) extinction; extermination; cancel(l)ing; discharge, payment; redemption.

**Tinktur** [tiŋk'tu:r] *f* (-/-en) tincture. [*sitzen* F be in a scrape.]

**Tinte** ['tintə] *f* (-/-n) ink; *in der ~*] '**Tinten|faß** *n* ink-pot, *desk*: inkwell; '~**fisch** *ichth. m* cuttle-fish; '~**fleck** *m*, '~**klecks** *m* (ink-)blot; '~**stift** *m* indelible pencil.

**Tip** [tip] *m* (-s/-s) hint, tip; '♀**pen** (ge-, h) **1.** *v/i.* F type; *fig.* guess; *j-m auf die Schulter ~* tap s.o. on his shoulder; **2.** *v/t.* tip; foretell, predict; F type.

**Tiroler** [ti'ro:lər] **1.** *m* (-s/-) Tyrolese; **2.** *adj.* Tyrolese.

**Tisch** [tiʃ] *m* (-es/-e) table; *bei ~* at table; *den ~ decken* lay the table *or* cloth, set the table; *reinen ~ machen* make a clean sweep (*damit of it*); *zu ~ bitten* invite *or* ask to dinner *or* supper; *bitte zu ~!* dinner is ready!; '~**decke** *f* table-cloth; '♀**fertig** *adj. food*: ready-prepared; '~**gast** *m* guest; '~**gebet** *n*: *das ~ sprechen* say grace; '~**gesellschaft** *f* dinner-party; '~**gespräch** *n* table-talk; '~**lampe** *f* table-lamp; desk lamp.

**Tischler** ['tiʃlər] *m* (-s/-) joiner; carpenter; cabinet-maker; '~**ei** [~'raɪ] *f* (-/-en) joinery; joiner's workshop.

'**Tisch|platte** *f* top (of a table), table top; leaf (*of extending table*); '~**rede** *f* toast, after-dinner speech; '~**tennis** *n* table tennis, ping-pong; '~**tuch** *n* table-cloth; '~**zeit** *f* dinner-time.

**Titan** [ti'ta:n] *m* (-en/-en) Titan; ♀**isch** *adj.* titanic.

**Titel** ['ti:təl] *m* (-s/-) title; e-n ~ (*inne*)*haben sports*: hold a title; '~**bild** *n* frontispiece; cover picture (*of magazine*, etc.); '~**blatt** *n* title-page; cover (*of magazine*); '~**halter** *m* (-s/-) *sports*: title-holder; '~**kampf** *m boxing*: title fight; '~**rolle** *thea. f* title-role.

**titulieren** [titu'li:rən] *v/t.* (*no -ge-*, h) style, call, address as.

**Toast** [to:st] *m* (-es/-e, -s) toast (*a. fig.*).

**tob|en** ['to:bən] *v/i.* (ge-, h) rage, rave, storm, bluster; *children*: romp; ♀**sucht** ⚕ ['to:p-] *f* (-/*no pl.*) raving madness, frenzy; '~**süchtig** *adj.* ['to:p-] raving mad, frantic.

**Tochter** ['tɔxtər] *f* (-/⁻) daughter; '~**gesellschaft** † *f* subsidiary company.

**Tod** [to:t] *m* (-[e]s/⁻, -e) death; ⚖ decease.

**Todes|angst** ['to:dəs?-] *f* mortal agony; *fig.* mortal fear; *Todesängste ausstehen* be scared to death, be frightened out of one's wits; '~**anzeige** *f* obituary (notice); '~**fall** *m* (case of) death; *Todesfälle pl.* deaths *pl.*, ⚔ casualties *pl.*; '~**kampf** *m* death throes *pl.*, mortal agony; '~**strafe** *f* capital punishment, death penalty; *bei ~ verboten* forbidden on *or* under pain *or* penalty of death; '~**ursache** *f* cause of death; '~**urteil** *n* death *or* capital sentence, death-warrant.

'**Tod|feind** *m* deadly *or* mortal enemy; '♀**krank** *adj.* dangerously ill.

**tödlich** *adj.* ['tø:tliç] deadly; fatal; *wound*: a. mortal.

'**tod|'müde** *adj.* dead tired; '~

'schick F *adj.* dashing, gorgeous; '~'sicher F *adj.* cock-sure; '2sünde *f* deadly *or* mortal sin.

Toilette [toa'lɛtə] *f* (-/-n) dress(ing): toilet; lavatory, gentlemen's *or* ladies' room, *esp. Am.* toilet.

Toi'letten|artikel *m/pl.* toilet articles *pl., Am. a.* toiletry; ~papier *n* toilet-paper; ~tisch *m* toilet (-table), dressing-table, *Am. a.* dresser.

toleran|t *adj.* [tole'rant] tolerant (gegen of); 2z [~ts] *f* 1. (-/*no pl.*) tolerance, toleration (*esp. eccl.*); 2. ⊕ (-/-en) tolerance, allowance.

toll [tɔl] 1. *adj.* (raving) mad, frantic; mad, crazy, wild (*all a. fig.*); fantastic; *noise, etc.*: frightful, F awful; *das ist ja ~ F* that's (just) great; 2. *adv.*: es ~ treiben carry on like mad; es zu ~ treiben go too far; '~en *v/i.* (ge-, h, sein) *children*: romp; '2haus *fig. n* bedlam; '2heit *f* (-/-en) madness; mad trick; '~kühn *adj.* foolhardy, rash; '2wut *vet. f* rabies.

Tolpatsch F ['tɔlpatʃ] *m* (-es/-e) awkward *or* clumsy fellow; '2ig F *adj.* awkward, clumsy.

Tölpel F ['tœlpəl] *m* (-s/-) awkward *or* clumsy fellow; boob(y).

Tomate 🜨 [to'maːtə] *f* (-/-n) tomato.

Ton¹ [toːn] *m* (-[e]s/-e) clay.

Ton² [~] *m* (-[e]s/-e) tone (*a. of language*); ♪ single: note; accent, stress; *fig.* tone; *paint.* tone, tint, shade; guter ~ good form; den ~ angeben set the fashion; zum guten ~ gehören be the fashion; große Töne reden *or* F spucken F talk big, boast; '~abnehmer *m* pick-up; '2angebend *adj.* setting the fashion, leading; '~arm *m* pick-up arm (*of record-player*); '~art ♪ *f* key; '~band *n* recording tape; '~bandgerät *n* tape recorder.

tönen ['tøːnən] (ge-, h) 1. *v/i.* sound, ring; 2. *v/t.* tint, tone, shade.

tönern *adj.* ['tøːnɔrn] (of) clay, earthen.

'Ton|fall *m in speaking*: intonation, accent; '~film *m* sound film; '~lage *f* pitch; '~leiter ♪ *f* scale, gamut; '2los *adj.* soundless; *fig.* toneless; '~meister *m* sound engineer.

Tonne ['tɔnə] *f* (-/-n) large: tun; smaller: barrel, cask; 🜨 *measure of weight*: ton.

Tonsilbe *gr. f* accented syllable.

Tonsur [tɔn'zuːr] *f* (-/-en) tonsure.

'Tönung *paint. f* (-/-en) tint, tinge, shade.

'Tonwaren *f/pl. s.* Töpferware.

Topf [tɔpf] *m* (-[e]s/-e) pot.

Töpfer ['tœpfər] *m* (-s/-) potter; stove-fitter; ~ei [~'raɪ] *f* (-/-en) pottery; '~ware *f* pottery, earthenware, crockery.

topp¹ *int.* [tɔp] done!, agreed!

Topp² ⚓ [~] *m* (-s/-e, -s) top, masthead.

Tor¹ [toːr] *n* (-[e]s/-e) gate; gateway (*a. fig.*); *football*: goal; *skiing*: gate.

Tor² [~] *m* (-en/-en) fool.

Torf [tɔrf] *m* (-[e]s/*no pl.*) peat.

Torheit ['toːrhaɪt] *f* (-/-en) folly.

'Torhüter *m* gate-keeper; *sports*: goalkeeper.

töricht *adj.* ['tøːriçt] foolish, silly.

Törin ['tøːrin] *f* (-/-nen) fool(ish woman).

torkeln ['tɔrkəln] *v/i.* (ge-, h, sein) reel, stagger, totter.

'Tor|latte *f sports*: cross-bar; '~lauf *m skiing*: slalom; '~linie *f sports*: goal-line.

Tornister [tɔr'nistər] *m* (-s/-) knapsack; satchel.

torpedieren [tɔrpe'diːrən] *v/t.* (*no* -ge-, h) torpedo (*a. fig.*).

Torpedo [tɔr'peːdo] *m* (-s/-s) torpedo; ~boot *n* torpedo-boat.

'Tor|pfosten *m* gate-post; *sports*: goal-post; '~schuß *m* shot at the goal; '~schütze *m sports*: scorer.

Torte ['tɔrtə] *f* (-/-n) fancy cake, *Am.* layer cake; tart, *Am.* pie.

Tortur [tɔr'tuːr] *f* (-/-en) torture; *fig.* ordeal.

'Tor|wart ['toːrvart] *m* (-[e]s/-e) *sports*: goalkeeper; '~weg *m* gateway.

tosen ['toːzən] *v/i.* (ge-, h, sein) roar, rage; '~d *adj.* applause: thunderous.

tot *adj.* [toːt] dead (*a. fig.*); deceased; ~er Punkt ⊕ dead cent|re, *Am.* -er; *fig.*: deadlock; fatigue; ~es Rennen *sports*: dead heat.

total *adj.* [to'taːl] total, complete.

'tot|arbeiten *v/refl.* (sep., -ge-, h) work o.s. to death; '2e (-n/-n) 1. *m* dead man; (dead) body, corpse; die ~n *pl.* the dead *pl.*, the deceased *pl. or* departed *pl.*; ✕ casualties *pl.*; 2. *f* dead woman.

töten ['tøːtən] *v/t.* (ge-, h) kill; destroy; murder; deaden (*nerve, etc.*).

'Toten|bett *n* deathbed; '2blaß *adj.* deadly *or* deathly pale; '~blässe *f* deadly paleness *or* pallor; '2bleich *adj. s.* totenblaß; '~gräber ['~grɛːbər] *m* (-s/-) grave-digger (*a. zo.*); '~hemd *n* shroud; '~kopf *m* death's-head (*a. zo.*); *emblem of death*: *a.* skull and cross-bones; '~liste *f* death-roll (*a.* ✕), *esp.* ✕ casualty list; '~maske *f* death-mask; '~messe *eccl. f* mass for the dead, requiem; '~schädel *m* death's-head, skull; '~schein *m* death certificate; '2still *adj.* (as) still as the grave; '~stille *f* dead(ly) silence, deathly stillness.

'tot|geboren *adj.* still-born; '2geburt *f* still birth; '~lachen *v/refl.* (sep., -ge-, h) die of laughing.

**Toto** ['to:to] *m*, F *a. n* (-s/-s) football pools *pl.*

**'tot|schießen** *v/t.* (*irr. schießen, sep.,* -ge-, *h*) shoot dead, kill; **'²schlag** ɀᵗ̷ʑ *m* manslaughter, homicide; **'~schlagen** *v/t.* (*irr. schlagen, sep.,* -ge-, *h*) kill (*a. time*), slay; **'~schweigen** *v/t.* (*irr. schweigen, sep.,* -ge-, *h*) hush up; **'~stechen** *v/t.* (*irr. stechen, sep.,* -ge-, *h*) stab to death; **'~stellen** *v/refl.* (*sep.,* -ge-, *h*) feign death.

**'Tötung** *f* (-/-en) killing, slaying; ɀᵗ̷ʑ homicide; *fahrlässige* ~ ɀᵗ̷ʑ manslaughter.

**Tour** [tu:r] *f* (-/-en) tour; excursion, trip; ⊕ turn, revolution; *auf ~en kommen mot.* pick up speed; **'~enwagen** *mot. m* touring car.

**Tourist** [tu'rist] *m* (-en/-en), **~in** *f* (-/-nen) tourist.

**Tournee** [tur'ne:] *f* (-/-s, -n) tour.

**Trab** [tra:p] *m* (-[e]s/*no pl.*) trot.

**Trabant** [tra'bant] *m* (-en/-en) satellite.

**trab|en** ['tra:bən] *v/i.* (ge-, *h, sein*) trot; **²rennen** ['tra:p-] *n* trotting race.

**Tracht** [traxt] *f* (-/-en) dress, costume; uniform; fashion; load; *e-e* (*gehörige*) ~ *Prügel* a (sound) thrashing; **'²en** *v/i.* (ge-, *h*): ~ *nach et.* strive for; *j-m nach dem Leben* ~ seek s.o.'s life.

**trächtig** *adj.* ['trɛçtiç] (big) with young, pregnant. [tradition.|

**Tradition** [tradi'tsjo:n] *f* (-/-en)|

**traf** [tra:f] *pret. of* treffen.

**Trag|bahre** ['tra:k-] *f* stretcher, litter; **'²bar** *adj.* portable; *dress:* wearable; *fig.:* bearable; reasonable; **~e** ('~gə] *f*(-/-n) hand-barrow; *s. Tragbahre.*

**träge** *adj.* ['trɛ:gə] lazy, indolent; *phys.* inert (*a. fig.*).

**tragen** ['tra:gən] (*irr.,* ge-, *h*) 1. *v/t.* carry; bear (*costs, name, responsibility, etc.*); bear, endure; support; bear, yield (*fruit,* ✝ *interest, etc.*); wear (*dress, etc.*); *bei sich* ~ have about one; *sich gut* ~ *material:* wear well; *zur Schau* ~ show off; 2. *v/i. tree:* bear, yield; *gun, voice:* carry; *ice:* bear.

**Träger** ['trɛ:gər] *m* (-s/-) carrier; porter (*of luggage*); holder, bearer (*of name, licence, etc.*); wearer (*of dress*); (shoulder-)strap (*of slip, etc.*); ⊕ support; △ girder.

**Trag|fähigkeit** ['tra:k-] *f* carrying or load capacity; ⚓ tonnage; **'~fläche** ↗ *f*, **'~flügel** ↗ *m* wing, plane.

**Trägheit** ['trɛ:khait] *f* (-/*no pl.*) laziness, indolence; *phys.* inertia (*a. fig.*).

**tragisch** *adj.* ['tra:giʃ] tragic (*a. fig.*); *fig.* tragical.

**Tragödie** [tra'gø:djə] *f* (-/-n) tragedy.

**Trag|riemen** ['tra:k-] *m* (carrying) strap; sling (*of gun*); **'~tier** *n* pack animal; **'~tüte** *f* carrier-bag; **'~weite** *f* range; *fig.* import(ance), consequences *pl.*; *von großer* ~ of great moment.

**Train|er** ['trɛ:nər] *m* (-s/-) trainer; coach; **²ieren** [~'ni:rən] (*no* -ge-, *h*) 1. *v/t.* train; coach; 2. *v/i.* train; **~ing** ['~iŋ] *n* (-s/-s) training; **'~ingsanzug** *m sports:* track suit.

**traktieren** [trak'ti:rən] *v/t.* (*no* -ge-, *h*) treat (badly).

**Traktor** ⊕ ['traktɔr] *m* (-s/-en) tractor.

**trällern** ['trɛlərn] *v/t. and v/i.* (ge-, *h*) troll.

**trampel|n** ['trampəln] *v/i.* (ge-, *h*) trample, stamp; **'²pfad** *m* beaten track.

**Tran** [tra:n] *m* (-[e]s/-e) train-oil, whale-oil.

**Träne** ['trɛ:nə] *f* (-/-n) tear; *in* ~*n ausbrechen* burst into tears; **'²n** *v/i.* (ge-, *h*) water; **'~ngas** *n* tear-gas.

**Trank** [traŋk] 1. *m* (-[e]s/⁼e) drink, beverage; ✽ potion; 2. ♀ *pret. of* trinken.

**Tränke** ['trɛŋkə] *f* (-/-n) watering-place; **'²n** *v/t.* (ge-, *h*) water (*animals*); soak, impregnate (*material*).

**Trans|formator** ⚡ [transfɔr'ma:tɔr] *m* (-s/-en) transformer; **~fusion** ✽ [~u'zjo:n] *f* (-/-en) transfusion.

**Transistorradio** [tran'zistɔr-] *n* transistor radio or set.

**transitiv** *gr. adj.* ['tranziti:f] transitive.

**transparent** [transpa'rɛnt] 1. *adj.* transparent; 2. ♀ *n* (-[e]s/-e) transparency; *in political processions, etc.:* banner.

**transpirieren** [transpi'ri:rən] *v/i.* (*no* -ge-, *h*) perspire.

**Transplantation** ✽ [transplanta'tsjo:n] *f* transplant (operation).

**Transport** [trans'pɔrt] *m* (-[e]s/-e) transport(ation), conveyance, carriage; **²abel** *adj.* [~'ta:bəl] (trans-) portable; **~er** *m* (-s/-) ⚓, ✈ (troop-)transport; ✈ transport (aircraft *or* plane); **²fähig** *adj.* transportable, *sick person:* a. transferable; **²ieren** [~'ti:rən] *v/t.* (*no* -ge-, *h*) transport, convey, carry; **~unternehmen** *n* carrier.

**Trapez** [tra'pe:ts] *n* (-es/-e) ⅄ trapezium, *Am.* trapezoid; *gymnastics:* trapeze.

**trappeln** ['trapəln] *v/i.* (ge-, *sein*) *horse:* clatter; *children, etc.:* patter.

**Trass|ant** ✝ [tra'sant] *m* (-en/-en) drawer; **~at** ✝ [~'sa:t] *m* (-en/-en) drawee; **~e** ⊕ *f* (-/-n) line; **²ieren** [~'si:rən] *v/t.* (*no* -ge-, *h*) ⊕ lay *or* trace out; ~ *auf* (*acc.*) ✝ draw on.

**trat** [tra:t] *pret. of* treten.
**Tratte** ✝ ['tratə] *f* (-/-n) draft.
**Traube** ['traubə] *f* (-/-n) bunch of grapes; grape; cluster; '~nsaft *m* grape-juice; '~nzucker *m* grape-sugar, glucose.
**trauen** ['trauən] (ge-, *h*) **1.** *v/t.* marry; *sich ~ lassen* get married; **2.** *v/i.* trust (*j-m* s.o.), confide (*dat.* in); *ich traute meinen Ohren nicht* I could not believe my ears.
**Trauer** ['trauər] *f* (-/*no pl.*) sorrow, affliction; *for dead person:* mourning; '~botschaft *f* sad news; '~fall *m* death; '~feier *f* funeral ceremonies *pl.*, obsequies *pl.*; '~flor *m* mourning-crape; '~geleit *n* funeral procession; '~gottesdienst *m* funeral service; '~kleid *n* mourning (-dress); '~marsch *m* funeral march; '2n *v/i.* (ge-, *h*) mourn (*um* for); be in mourning; '~spiel *n* tragedy; '~weide ♀ *f* weeping willow; '~zug *m* funeral procession.
**Traufe** ['traufə] *f* (-/-n) eaves *pl.*; gutter; *s.* Regen².
**träufeln** ['trɔyfəln] *v/t.* (ge-, *h*) drop, drip, trickle. [cosy, snug.]
**traulich** *adj.* ['traulɪç] intimate;]
**Traum** [traum] *m* (-[e]s/ä̃e) dream (*a. fig.*); reverie; *das fällt mir nicht im ~ ein!* I would not dream of (doing) it!; '~bild *n* vision; '~deuter *m* (-s/-) dream-reader.
**träum|en** ['trɔymən] *v/i. and v/t.* (ge-, *h*) dream; '2er *m* (-s/-) dreamer (*a. fig.*); 2erei [~'raɪ] *f* (-/-en) dreaming; *fig. a.* reverie (*a. ♪*), day-dream, musing; '~erisch *adj.* dreamy; musing.
**traurig** *adj.* ['trauriç] sad (*über acc.* at), *Am.* F blue; wretched.
'**Trau|ring** *m* wedding-ring; '~schein *m* marriage certificate *or* lines *pl.*; '~ung *f* (-/-en) marriage, wedding; '~zeuge *m* witness to a marriage.
**Trecker** ⊕ ['trekər] *m* (-s/-) tractor.
**Treff** [tref] *n* (-s/-s) *cards:* club(s *pl.*).
**treffen¹** ['trefən] (*irr.*, ge-) **1.** *v/t.* (*h*) hit (*a. fig.*), strike; concern, *disadvantageously:* affect; meet; *nicht ~ miss*; *e-e Entscheidung ~* come to a decision; *Maßnahmen ~* take measures *or* steps; *Vorkehrungen ~* take precautions *or* measures; *sich ~* happen; meet; gather, assemble; *e-e* have an appointment (*mit* with), F have a date (with); *das trifft sich gut!* that's lucky!; *how fortunate!*; *sich getroffen fühlen* feel hurt; *wen trifft die Schuld?* who is to blame?; *das Los traf ihn* the lot fell on him; *du bist gut getroffen paint.*, *phot.* this is a good likeness of you; *vom Blitz getroffen* struck by lightning; **2.** *v/i.* (*h*) hit; **3.** *v/i.* (*sein*): *~ auf* (*acc.*) meet with; encounter (*a. ✗*).

**Treffen²** [~] *n* (-s/-) meeting; rally; gathering; ✗ encounter; '2d *adj.* *remark:* appropriate, to the point.
'**Treff|er** *m* (-s/-) hit (*a. fig.*); prize; '~punkt *m* meeting-place.
**Treibeis** ['traɪp?-] *n* drift-ice.
**treiben¹** ['traɪbən] (*irr.*, ge-) **1.** *v/t.* (*h*) drive; ⊕ put in motion, propel; drift (*smoke, snow*); put forth (*leaves*); force (*plants*); *fig.* impel, urge, press (*j-n zu inf.* s.o. to *inf.*); carry on (*business, trade*); *Musik (Sport) ~* go in for music (sports); *Sprachen ~* study languages; *es zu weit ~* go too far; *wenn er es weiterhin so treibt* if he carries *or* goes on like that; *was treibst du da?* what are you doing there?; **2.** *v/i.* (*sein*) drive; float, drift; **3.** *v/i.* (*h*) ♀ shoot; *dough:* ferment, work.
**Treiben²** [~] *n* (-s/*no pl.*) driving; doings *pl.*, goings-on *pl.*; *geschäftiges ~* bustle; '2d *adj.*: *~e Kraft* driving force.
**Treib|haus** ['traɪp-] *n* hothouse; '~holz *n* drift-wood; '~jagd *f* battue; '~riemen *m* driving-belt; '~stoff *m* fuel; propell|ant, -ent (*of rocket*).
**trenn|en** ['trenən] *v/t.* (ge-, *h*) separate, sever; rip (*seam*); *teleph.*, ✗ cut off, disconnect; isolate, segregate; *sich ~* separate (*von* from), part (*from or* with s.o.; *with* s.th.); '2schärfe *f* radio: selectivity; '2ung *f* (-/-en) separation; disconne|xion, -ction; segregation (*of races, etc.*); '2(ungs)wand *f* partition (wall). [(-bit).]
**Trense** ['trenzə] *f* (-/-n) snaffle]
**Treppe** ['trepə] *f* (-/-n) staircase, stairway, (e-e a flight *or* pair of) stairs *pl.*; *zwei ~n hoch* on the second floor, *Am.* on the third floor.
'**Treppen|absatz** *m* landing; '~geländer *n* banisters *pl.*; '~haus *n* staircase; '~stufe *f* stair, step.
**Tresor** [tre'zo:r] *m* (-s/-e) safe; *bank:* strong-room, vault.
**treten** ['tre:tən] (*irr.*, ge-) **1.** *v/i.* (*h*) tread, step (*j-n or j-m auf die Zehen* on s.o.'s toes); **2.** *v/i.* (*sein*) tread, step (*j-m auf die Zehen* on s.o.'s toes); walk; *ins Haus ~* enter the house; *j-m unter die Augen ~* appear before s.o., face s.o.; *j-m zu nahe ~* offend s.o.; *zu j-m ~* step *or* walk up to s.o.; *über die Ufer ~* overflow its banks; **3.** *v/t.* (*h*) tread; kick; *mit Füßen ~* trample upon.
**treu** *adj.* [trɔy] faithful, loyal; '2bruch *m* breach of faith, perfidy; '2e *f* (-/*no pl.*) fidelity, faith(fulness), loyalty; 2händer [~'hendər] *m* (-s/-) trustee; '~herzig *adj.* guileless; ingenuous, simpleminded; '~los *adj.* faithless (*gegen* to), disloyal (to); perfidious.

**Tribüne** [tri'byːnə] *f* (-/-n) platform; *sports, etc.*: (grand) stand.

**Tribut** [tri'buːt] *m* (-[e]s/-e) tribute.

**Trichter** ['triçtər] *m* (-s/-) funnel; *made by bomb, shell, etc.*: crater; horn (*of wind instruments, etc.*).

**Trick** [trik] *m* (-s/-e, -s) trick; '~film *m* animation, animated cartoon.

**Trieb** [triːp] 1. *m* (-[e]s/-e) ♀ sprout, (new) shoot; driving force; impulse; instinct; (sexual) urge; desire; 2. ♀ *pret. of* treiben; '~feder *f* main-spring; *fig.* driving force, motive; '~kraft *f* motive power; *fig.* driving force, motive; '~wagen ⛟ *m* rail-car, rail-motor; '~werk ⊕ *n* gear (drive), (driving) mechanism, transmission; engine.

**triefen** ['triːfən] *v/i.* ([*irr.*,] ge-, h) drip (*von* with); *eye:* run.

**triftig** *adj.* ['triftiç] valid.

**Trigonometrie** ⟨ [trigonome'triː] *f* (-/*no pl.*) trigonometry.

**Trikot** [tri'koː] (-s/-s) 1. *m* stockinet; 2. *n* tights *pl.*; vest; ~agen [~o'taː-ʒən] *f/pl.* hosiery.

**Triller** ♪ ['trilər] *m* (-s/-) trill, shake, quaver; '♀n *f* *v/i. and v/t.* (ge-, h) trill, shake, quaver; *bird:* a. warble.

**trink|bar** *adj.* ['triŋkbaːr] drinkable; '♀becher *m* drinking-cup; '~en (*irr.*, ge-, h) 1. *v/t.* drink; take, have (*tea, etc.*); 2. *v/i.* drink; ~ *auf* (*acc.*) drink to, toast; '♀er *m* (-s/-) drinker; drunkard; '♀gelage *n* drinking-bout; '♀geld *n* tip, gratuity; *j-m e-e Mark ~ geben* tip s.o. one mark; '♀glas *n* drinking-glass; '♀halle *f* *at spa:* pump-room; '♀kur *f: e-e ~ machen* drink the waters; '♀spruch *m* toast; '♀wasser *n* (-s/*no pl.*) drinking-water.

**Trio** ['triːo] *n* (-s/-s) trio (*a. ♪*).

**trippeln** ['tripəln] *v/i.* (ge-, sein) trip.

**Tritt** [trit] *m* (-[e]s/-e) tread, step; footprint; *noise:* footfall, (foot)step; kick; ⊕ treadle; *s. Trittbrett, Trittleiter; im (falschen) ~ in* (out of) step; ~ *halten* keep step; '~brett *n* step, footboard; *mot.* running-board; '~leiter *f* stepladder, (e-e a pair *or* set of) steps *pl.*

**Triumph** [tri'umf] *m* (-[e]s/-e) triumph; ♀al *adj.* ['~'faːl] triumphant; ~bogen *m* triumphal arch; ♀ieren [~'iːrən] *v/i.* (*no* -ge-, h) triumph (*über acc.* over).

**trocken** *adj.* ['trɔkən] dry (*a. fig.*); *soil, land:* arid; '♀dock ⛴ *n* dry dock; '♀haube *f* (hood of) hairdrier; '♀heit *f* (-/*no pl.*) dryness; drought, aridity; '~legen *v/t.* (*sep.*, -ge-, h) dry up; drain (*land*), change the napkins of, *Am.* change the diapers of (*baby*); '♀obst *n* dried fruit.

**trocknen** ['trɔknən] (ge-) 1. *v/i.* (sein) dry; 2. *v/t.* (h) dry.

**Troddel** ['trɔdəl] *f* (-/-n) tassel.

**Trödel** F ['trøːdəl] *m* (-s/*no pl.*) second-hand articles *pl.*; lumber, *Am.* junk; rubbish; '♀n F *fig. v/i.* (ge-, h) dawdle, loiter.

**Trödler** ['trøːdlər] *m* (-s/-) second-hand dealer, *Am.* junk dealer, junkman; *fig.* dawdler, loiterer.

**troff** [trɔf] *pret. of* triefen.

**Trog¹** [troːk] *m* (-[e]s/⸚e) trough.

**trog²** [~] *pret. of* trügen.

**Trommel** ['trɔməl] *f* (-/-n) drum; ⊕ *a.* cylinder, barrel; '~fell *n* drumskin; *anat.* ear-drum; '♀n *v/i. and v/t.* (ge-, h) drum.

**Trommler** ['trɔmlər] *m* (-s/-) drummer.

**Trompete** [trɔm'peːtə] *f* (-/-n) trumpet; ♀n *v/i. and v/t.* (*no* -ge-, h) trumpet; ~r *m* (-s/-) trumpeter.

**Tropen** ['troːpən] *die ~ pl.* the tropics *pl.*

**Tropf** F [trɔpf] *m* (-[e]s/⸚e) simpleton; *armer ~* poor wretch.

**tröpfeln** ['trœpfəln] (ge-) 1. *v/i.* (h) drop, drip, trickle; *tap:* a. leak; *es tröpfelt rain:* a few drops are falling; 2. *v/i.* (sein): ~ *aus or von* trickle *or* drip from; 3. *v/t.* (h) drop, drip.

**tropfen¹** ['trɔpfən] (ge-) 1. *v/i.* (h) drop, drip, trickle; *tap:* a. leak; *candle:* gutter; 2. *v/i.* (sein): ~ *aus or von* trickle *or* drip from; 3. *v/t.* (h) drop, drip.

**Tropfen²** [~] *m* (-s/-) drop; *ein ~ auf den heißen Stein* a drop in the ocean *or* bucket; ♀förmig *adj.* ['~fœrmiç] drop-shaped; ♀weise *adv.* drop by drop, by drops.

**Trophäe** [tro'fɛːə] *f* (-/-n) trophy.

**tropisch** *adj.* ['troːpiʃ] tropical.

**Trosse** ['trɔsə] *f* (-/-n) cable; ⚓ *a.* hawser.

**Trost** [troːst] *m* (-es/*no pl.*) comfort, consolation; *das ist ein schlechter ~* that is cold comfort; *du bist wohl nicht (recht) bei ~!* F you must be out of your mind!

**tröst|en** ['trøːstən] *v/t.* (ge-, h) console, comfort; *sich ~* console o.s. (*mit* with); ~ *Sie sich!* be of good comfort!, cheer up!; '~lich *adj.* comforting.

**'trost|los** *adj.* disconsolate, inconsolable; *land, etc.*: desolate; *fig.* wretched; '♀losigkeit *f* (-/*no pl.*) desolation; *fig.* wretchedness; '♀preis *m* consolation prize, booby prize; '~reich *adj.* consolatory, comforting.

**Trott** [trɔt] *m* (-[e]s/-e) trot; F *fig.* jogtrot, routine; '~el *F* *m* (-s/-) idiot, fool, ninny; '♀en *v/i.* (ge-, sein) trot.

**trotz** [trɔts] 1. *prp.* (*gen.*) in spite of, despite; ~ *alledem* for all that; 2. ♀ *m* (-es/*no pl.*) defiance; obstinacy; **~dem** cj. ['~de:m] nevertheless; (al)though; '~en v/i. (ge-, h) (dat.) defy, dare; brave (danger); be obstinate; sulk; '~ig adj. defiant; obstinate; sulky.

**trüb** adj. [try:p], **~e** adj. ['~bə] liquid: muddy, turbid, thick; mind, thinking: confused, muddy, turbid; eyes, etc.: dim, dull; weather: dull, cloudy, dreary (all a. fig.); experiences: sad.

**Trubel** ['tru:bəl] m (-s/no pl.) bustle.

**trüben** ['try:bən] v/t. (ge-, h) make thick or turbid or muddy; dim; darken; spoil (pleasures, etc.); blur (view); dull (mind); sich ~ liquid: become thick or turbid or muddy; dim, darken; relations: become strained.

**Trüb|sal** ['try:pza:l] f (-/⚥-e): ~ blasen mope, F be in the dumps, have the blues; '2selig adj. sad, gloomy, melancholy; wretched, miserable; dreary; '~sinn m (-[e]s/ no pl.) melancholy, sadness, gloom; '2sinnig adj. melancholy, gloomy, sad; ~ung ['~buŋ] f (-/-en) liquid: muddiness, turbidity (both a. fig.); dimming, darkening.

**Trüffel** ⚘ ['tryfəl] f (-/-n), F m (-s/-) truffle.

**Trug**[1] [tru:k] m (-[e]s/no pl.) deceit, fraud; delusion (of senses).

**trug**[2] [~] pret. of tragen.

'**Trugbild** n phantom; illusion.

**trüg|en** ['try:gən] (irr., ge-, h) 1. v/t. deceive; 2. v/i. be deceptive; '~erisch adj. deceptive, delusive; treacherous.

'**Trugschluß** m fallacy, false conclusion.

**Truhe** ['tru:ə] f (-/-n) chest, trunk; radio, etc.: cabinet, console.

**Trümmer** ['trymər] pl. ruins pl.; rubble, debris; ⚓, ✈ wreckage; '~haufen m heap of ruins or rubble.

**Trumpf** [trumpf] m (-[e]s/⚥e) cards: trump (card) (a. fig.); s-n ~ ausspielen play one's trump card.

**Trunk** [truŋk] m (-[e]s/⚥e) drink; draught; drinking; '2en adj. drunken; pred. drunk (a. fig. von, vor with); intoxicated; ~enbold contp. ['~bɔlt] m (-[e]s/-e) drunkard, sot; '~enheit f (-/no pl.) drunkenness, intoxication; ~ am Steuer 🚗 drunken driving, drunkenness at the wheel; '~sucht f alcoholism, dipsomania; '2süchtig adj. addicted to drink, given to drinking.

**Trupp** [trup] m (-s/-s) troop, band, gang; ⚔ detachment.

'**Truppe** f (-/-n) ⚔ troop, body; ⚔ unit; thea. company, troupe; ~n pl. ⚔ troops pl., forces pl.; die ~n pl. ⚔ the (fighting) services pl., the armed forces pl.

'**Truppen|gattung** f arm, branch, division; '~schau f military review;

'**~transporter** ⚓, ✈ m (troop-) transport; '~übungsplatz m training area.

**Truthahn** orn. ['tru:t-] m turkey (-cock).

**Tschech|e** ['tʃɛçə] m (-n/-n), '~in f (-/-nen) Czech; '2isch adj. Czech.

**Tube** ['tu:bə] f (-/-n) tube.

**tuberkul|ös** 🩺 adj. [tuberku'lø:s] tuberculous, tubercular; 2ose 🩺 [~o:zə] f (-/-n) tuberculosis.

**Tuch** [tu:x] n 1. (-[e]s/-e) cloth; fabric; 2. (-[e]s/⚥er) head covering: kerchief; shawl, scarf; round neck: neckerchief; duster; rag; '~fühlung f (-/no pl.) close touch.

**tüchtig** ['tyçtiç] 1. adj. able, fit; clever; proficient; efficient; excellent; good; thorough; 2. adv. vigorously; thoroughly; F awfully; '2keit f (-/no pl.) ability, fitness; cleverness; proficiency; efficiency; excellency.

'**Tuchwaren** f/pl. drapery, cloths pl.

**Tück|e** ['tykə] f (-/-n) malice, spite; '2isch adj. malicious, spiteful; treacherous.

**tüfteln** F ['tyftəln] v/i. (ge-, h) puzzle (an dat. over).

**Tugend** ['tu:gənt] f (-/-en) virtue; ~bold ['~bɔlt] m (-[e]s/-e) paragon of virtue; '2haft adj. virtuous.

**Tüll** [tyl] m (-s/-e) tulle.

**Tulpe** ⚘ ['tulpə] f (-/-n) tulip.

**tummel|n** ['tuməln] v/refl. (ge-, h) children: romp; hurry; bestir o.s.; '2platz m playground; fig. arena.

**Tümmler** ['tymlər] m (-s/-) orn. tumbler; zo. porpoise.

**Tumor** 🩺 ['tu:mɔr] m (-s/-en) tumo(u)r.

**Tümpel** ['tympəl] m (-s/-) pool.

**Tumult** [tu'mult] m (-[e]s/-e) tumult; riot, turmoil, uproar; row.

**tun** [tu:n] 1. (irr., ge-, h) do; make; put (to school, into the bag, etc.); dazu ~ add to it; contribute; ich kann nichts dazu ~ I cannot help it; es ist mir darum zu ~ I am anxious about (it); zu ~ haben have to do; be busy; es tut nichts it doesn't matter; 2. v/i. (irr., ge-, h) do; make; so ~ als ob make as if; pretend to inf.; das tut gut! that is a comfort!; that's good!; 3. ♀ n (-s/no pl.) doings pl.; proceedings pl.; action; ~ und Treiben ways and doings pl.

**Tünche** ['tynçə] f (-/-n) whitewash (a. fig.); '2n v/t. (ge-, h) whitewash.

**Tunichtgut** ['tu:niçtgu:t] m (-, -[e]s/-e) ne'er-do-well, good-fornothing.

**Tunke** ['tuŋkə] f (-/-n) sauce; '2n v/t. (ge-, h) dip, steep.

**tunlichst** adv. ['tu:nliçst] if possible.

**Tunnel** ['tunəl] m (-s/-, -s) tunnel; subway.

**Tüpfel** ['typfəl] *m*, *n* (*-s/-*) dot, spot; '⁓n *v/t.* (*ge-*, *h*) dot, spot.

**tupfen** ['tupfən] **1.** *v/t.* (*ge-*, *h*) dab; dot, spot; **2.** ♀ *m* (*-s/-*) dot, spot.

**Tür** [tyːr] *f* (*-/-en*) door; *mit der ⁓ ins Haus fallen* blurt (things) out; *j-n vor die ⁓ setzen* turn s.o. out; *vor der ⁓ stehen* be near *or* close at hand; *zwischen ⁓ und Angel in passing;* '⁓angel *f* (door-)hinge.

**Turbine** ⊕ [tur'biːnə] *f* (*-/-n*) turbine; ⁓**nflugzeug** *n* turbo-jet.

**Turbo-Prop-Flugzeug** ['turbo-'prɔp-] *n* turbo-prop.

**'Tür|flügel** *m* leaf (of a door); '⁓füllung *f* (door-)panel; '⁓griff *m* door-handle.

**Türk|e** ['tyrkə] *m* (*-n/-n*) Turk; '⁓in *f* (*-/-nen*) Turk(ish woman); ⁓is *min.* [⁓'kiːs] *m* (*-es/-e*) turquoise; '♀isch *adj.* Turkish.

**'Türklinke** *f* door-handle; latch.

**Turm** [turm] *m* (*-[e]s/⁼e*) tower; *a.* steeple (*of church*); *chess*: castle, rook.

**Türm|chen** ['tyrmçən] *n* (*-s/-*) turret; '♀en (*ge-*) **1.** *v/t.* (*h*) pile up; *sich ⁓* tower; **2.** F *v/i.* (*sein*) bolt, F skedaddle, *Am. sl. a.* skiddoo.

**'turm|hoch** *adv.*: *j-m ⁓ überlegen sein* stand head and shoulders above s.o.; '♀spitze *f* spire; '♀springen *n* (*-s/no pl.*) *swimming*: high diving; '♀uhr *f* tower-clock, church-clock.

**turnen** ['turnən] **1.** *v/i.* (*ge-*, *h*) do gymnastics; **2.** ♀ *n* (*-s/no pl.*) gymnastics *pl.*

**'Turn|er** *m* (*-s/-*), '⁓erin *f* (*-/-nen*) gymnast; '⁓gerät *n* gymnastic apparatus; '⁓halle *f* gym(nasium); '⁓hemd *n* (gym-)shirt; '⁓hose *f* shorts *pl.*

**Turnier** [tur'niːr] *n* (*-s/-e*) tournament.

**'Turn|lehrer** *m* gym master; '⁓lehrerin *f* gym mistress; '⁓schuh *m* gym-shoe; '⁓stunde *f* gym lesson; '⁓unterricht *m* instruction in gymnastics; '⁓verein *m* gymnastic *or* athletic club.

**'Tür|pfosten** *m* door-post; '⁓rahmen *m* door-case, door-frame; '⁓schild *n* door-plate.

**Tusche** ['tuʃə] *f* (*-/-n*) India(n) *or* Chinese ink; '♀n *v/i.* (*ge-*, *h*) whisper; '♀n *v/t.* (*ge-*, *h*) draw in India(n) ink.

**Tüte** ['tyːtə] *f* (*-/-n*) paper-bag.

**tuten** ['tuːtən] *v/i.* (*ge-*, *h*) toot(le); *mot.* honk, blow one's horn.

**Typ** [tyːp] *m* (*-s/-en*) type; ⊕ *a.* model; '⁓e *f* (*-/-n*) *typ.* type; F *fig.* (queer) character.

**Typhus** ♨ ['tyːfus] *m* (*-/no pl.*) typhoid (fever).

**'typisch** *adj.* typical (*für* of).

**Tyrann** [ty'ran] *m* (*-en/-en*) tyrant; ⁓**ei** [⁓'nai] *f* (*-/no pl.*) tyranny; ♀isch *adj.* [ty'raniʃ] tyrannical; ♀isieren [⁓i'ziːrən] *v/t.* (*no -ge-*, *h*) tyrannize (over) *s.o.*, oppress, bully.

# U

**U-Bahn** ['uː-] *f s.* Untergrundbahn.

**übel** ['yːbəl] **1.** *adj.* evil, bad; *nicht ⁓* not bad, pretty good; *mir ist ⁓* I am *or* feel sick; **2.** *adv.* ill; *⁓ gelaunt sein* be in a bad mood; *es gefällt mir nicht ⁓* I rather like it; **3.** ♀ *n* (*-s/-*) evil; *s. Übelstand; das kleinere ⁓ wählen* choose the lesser evil; '⁓gelaunt *adj.* ill-humo(u)red; '♀keit *f* (*-/-en*) sickness, nausea; '⁓nehmen *v/t.* (*irr. nehmen, sep.*, *-ge-*, *h*) take *s.th.* ill *or* amiss; '♀stand *m* grievance; '♀täter *m* evil-doer, wrongdoer.

**'übelwollen** **1.** *v/i.* (*sep.*, *-ge-*, *h*): *j-m ⁓* wish s.o. ill; be ill-disposed towards s.o.; **2.** ♀ *n* (*-s/no pl.*) ill will, malevolence; '⁓d *adj.* malevolent.

**üben** ['yːbən] (*ge-*, *h*) **1.** *v/t.* exercise; practi|se, *Am. a.* -ce; *Geduld ⁓* exercise patience; *Klavier ⁓* practise the piano; **2.** *v/i.* exercise; practi|se, *Am. a.* -ce.

**über** ['yːbər] **1.** *prp.* (*dat.*; *acc.*) over, above; across (*river, etc.*); via,

by way of (*Munich, etc.*); *sprechen ⁓* (*acc.*) talk about *or* of; *⁓ Politik sprechen* talk politics; *nachdenken ⁓* (*acc.*) think about *or* of; *ein Buch schreiben ⁓* (*acc.*) write a book on; *⁓ Nacht bleiben bei* stay overnight at; *⁓ s-e Verhältnisse leben* live beyond one's income; *⁓ kurz oder lang* sooner *or* later; **2.** *adv.*: *die ganze Zeit ⁓* all along; *j-m in et. ⁓ sein* excel s.o. in s.th.

**über'all** *adv.* everywhere, anywhere, *Am. a.* all over.

**über|'anstrengen** *v/t.* (*no -ge-*, *h*) overstrain; *sich ⁓* overstrain o.s.; ⁓**'arbeiten** *v/t.* (*no -ge-*, *h*) retouch (*painting, etc.*); revise (*book, etc.*); *sich ⁓* overwork o.s.

**überaus** *adv.* ['yːbərʔ-] exceedingly, extremely.

**'überbelichten** *phot. v/t.* (*no -ge-*, *h*) over-expose.

**über'bieten** *v/t.* (*irr. bieten*, *no -ge-*, *h*) *at auction*: outbid; *fig.*: beat; surpass.

**Überbleibsel** ['yːbərblaipsəl] *n*

(-s/-) remnant, *Am.* F *a.* holdover; ~ *pl. a.* remains *pl.*

**'Überblick** *fig. m* survey, general view (*both: über acc.* of).

**über|'blicken** *v/t.* (*no -ge-, h*) overlook; *fig.* survey, have a general view of; ~'**bringen** *v/t.* (*irr. bringen, no -ge-, h*) deliver; 2'**bringer** *m* (-s/-) bearer; ~'**brücken** *v/t.* (*no -ge-, h*) bridge; *fig.* bridge over *s.th.*; ~'**dachen** *v/t.* (*no -ge-, h*) roof over; ~'**dauern** *v/t.* (*no -ge-, h*) outlast, outlive; ~'**denken** *v/t.* (*irr. denken, no -ge-, h*) think *s.th.* over.

**über'dies** *adv.* besides, moreover.

**über'drehen** *v/t.* (*no -ge-, h*) overwind (*watch, etc.*); strip (*screw*).

**'Überdruck** *m* **1.** (-[e]s/-e) overprint; ⚙ *a.* surcharge; **2.** ⊕ (-[e]s/~e) overpressure.

**Über|druß** ['y:bərdrus] *m* (*Überdrusses/no pl.*) satiety; *bis zum ~* to satiety; 2**drüssig** *adj.* (*gen.*) ['~y-siç] disgusted with, weary *or* sick of.

**Übereif|er** ['y:bər⁹-] *m* over-zeal; 2**rig** *adj.* ['y:bər⁹-] over-zealous.

**über'eil|en** *v/t.* (*no -ge-, h*) precipitate, rush; *sich ~* hurry too much; ~*t adj.* precipitate, rash.

**übereinander** *adv.* [y:bər⁹ai'nandər] one upon the other; ~**schlagen** *v/t.* (*irr. schlagen, sep., -ge-, h*) cross (*one's legs*).

**über'ein|kommen** *v/i.* (*irr. kommen, sep., -ge-, sein*) agree; 2**kommen** *n* (-s/-), 2**kunft** [~kunft] *f* (-/~e) agreement; ~**stimmen** *v/i.* (*sep., -ge-, h*) p. agree (*mit* with); *thing:* correspond (with, to); 2**stimmung** *f* agreement; correspondence; *in ~ mit* in agreement *or* accordance with.

**über|fahren 1.** ['~faɪrən] *v/i.* (*irr. fahren, sep., -ge-, sein*) cross; **2.** [~'faːrən] *v/t.* (*irr. fahren, no -ge-, h*) run over; disregard (*traffic sign, etc.*); 2**fahrt** *f* passage; crossing.

**'Überfall** *m* ✗ surprise; ✗ invasion (*auf acc.* of); ✗ raid; hold-up; assault ([up]on).

**über'fallen** *v/t.* (*irr. fallen, no -ge-, h*) ✗ surprise; ✗ invade; ✗ raid; hold up; assault.

**'über|fällig** *adj.* overdue; '2**fallkommando** *n* flying squad, *Am.* riot squad.

**über'fliegen** *v/t.* (*irr. fliegen, no -ge-, h*) fly over *or* across; *fig.* glance over, skim (through); *den Atlantik ~* fly (across) the Atlantic.

**'überfließen** *v/i.* (*irr. fließen, sep., -ge-, sein*) overflow.

**über'flügeln** *v/t.* (*no -ge-, h*) ✗ outflank; *fig.* outstrip, surpass.

**'Über|fluß** *m* (*Überflusses/no pl.*) abundance (*an dat.* of); superfluity (*of*); ~**haben** *an* (*dat.*) abound in;

**'2flüssig** *adj.* superfluous; redundant.

**über'fluten** *v/t.* (*no -ge-, h*) overflow, flood (*a. fig.*).

**'Überfracht** *f* excess freight.

**über|führen 1.** ['~fy:rən] (*sep., -ge-, h*) convey (*dead body*); **2.** [~'fy:rən] (*no -ge-, h*) *s.* **1**; ⚖ convict (*gen.* of); 2**führung** *f* (-/-en) conveyance (*of dead body*); bridge, *Am.* overpass; ⚖ conviction (*gen.* of). [*dat.* of).\

**'Überfülle** *f* superabundance (*an*)

**über|'füllen** *v/t.* (*no -ge-, h*) overfill; cram; overcrowd; *sich den Magen ~* glut o.s.; ~'**füttern** *v/t.* (*no -ge-, h*) overfeed.

**'Übergabe** *f* delivery; handing over; surrender (*a.* ✗).

**'Übergang** *m* bridge; 🚇 crossing; *fig.* transition (*a.* ♩); *esp.* ⚖ devolution; ~**sstadium** *n* transition stage.

**über|'geben** *v/t.* (*irr. geben, no -ge-, h*) deliver up; hand over; surrender (*a.* ✗); *sich ~* vomit, be sick; ~**gehen 1.** ['~ge:ən] *v/i.* (*irr. gehen, sep., -ge-, sein*) pass over; *work, duties:* devolve (*auf acc.* [up]on); *~ in* (*acc.*) pass into; *~ zu* et. proceed to s.th.; **2.** [~'ge:ən] *v/t.* (*irr. gehen, no -ge-, h*) pass over, ignore.

**'Übergewicht** *n* (-[e]s/*no pl.*) overweight; *fig. a.* preponderance (*über acc.* over).

**über'gießen** *v/t.* (*irr. gießen, no -ge-, h*): *mit Wasser ~* pour water over *s.th.*; *mit Fett ~* baste (*roasting meat*).

**'über|greifen** *v/i.* (*irr. greifen, sep., -ge-, h*): *~ auf* (*acc.*) encroach (up-)on (*s.o.'s rights*); *fire, epidemic, etc.*: spread to; '2**griff** *m* encroachment (*auf acc.* [up]on), inroad (on); '~**haben** F *v/t.* (*irr. haben, sep., -ge-, h*) have (*coat, etc.*) on; *fig.* have enough of, *sl.* be fed up with.

**über'handnehmen** *v/i.* (*irr. nehmen, sep., -ge-, h*) be rampant, grow *or* wax rife.

**'überhängen 1.** *v/i.* (*irr. hängen, sep., -ge-, h*) overhang; **2.** *v/t.* (*sep., -ge-, h*) put (*coat, etc.*) round one's shoulders; sling (*rifle*) over one's shoulder.

**über'häufen** *v/t.* (*no -ge-, h*): *~ mit* swamp with (*letters, work, etc.*); overwhelm with (*inquiries, etc.*).

**über'haupt** *adv.*: *wer will denn ~, daß er kommt?* who wants him to come anyhow?; *wenn ~* if at all; *~ nicht* not at all; *~ kein no* ... whatever.

**überheblich** *adj.* [y:bər'he:pliç] presumptuous, arrogant; 2**keit** *f* (-/~ -en) presumption, arrogance.

**über|'hitzen** *v/t.* (*no -ge-, h*) overheat (*a.* ⚒); ⊕ superheat; ~'**holen** *v/t.* (*no -ge-, h*) overtake (*a. mot.*);

**esp. sports:** outstrip (*a. fig.*); overhaul, *esp. Am. a.* service; **~'holt** *adj.* outmoded; *pred. a.* out of date; **~'hören** *v/t.* (*no -ge-, h*) fail to hear, miss; ignore.

**'überirdisch** *adj.* supernatural; unearthly.

**'überkippen** *v/i.* (*sep., -ge-, sein*) *p.* overbalance, lose one's balance.

**über'kleben** *v/t.* (*no -ge-, h*) paste over.

**'Überkleidung** *f* outer garments *pl.*

**'überklug** *adj.* would-be wise, sapient.

**'überkochen** *v/i.* (*sep., -ge-, sein*) boil over; F *leicht ~* be very irritable.

**über'kommen** *v/t.* (*irr. kommen, no -ge-, h*): *Furcht überkam ihn* he was seized with fear; **~'laden** *v/t.* (*irr. laden, no -ge-, h*) overload; overcharge (*battery, picture, etc.*).

**'Überland|flug** *m* cross-country flight; **'~zentrale** *⚡ f* long-distance power-station.

**über'lassen** *v/t.* (*irr. lassen, no -ge-, h*): *j-m et. ~* let s.o. have s.th.; *fig.* leave s.th. to s.o.; *j-n sich selbst ~* leave s.o. to himself; *j-n s-m Schicksal ~* leave or abandon s.o. to his fate; **~'lasten** *v/t.* (*no -ge-, h*) overload; *fig.* overburden.

**über|laufen 1.** ['~laufən] *v/i.* (*irr. laufen, sep., -ge-, sein*) run over; boil over; ⚔ desert (*zu* to); **2.** [~'laufən] *v/t.* (*irr. laufen, no -ge-, h*): *es überlief mich kalt a shudder passed over me; überlaufen werden von doctor, etc.*: be besieged by (*patients, etc.*); **3.** *adj.* [~'laufən] *place, profession, etc.*: overcrowded; **'2läufer** *m* ⚔ deserter; *pol.* renegade, turncoat.

**'überlaut** *adj.* too loud.

**über'leben** (*no -ge-, h*) **1.** *v/t.* survive, outlive; **2.** *v/i.* survive; **2de** *m, f* (*-n/-n*) survivor.

**'überlebensgroß** *adj.* bigger than life-size(d).

**überlebt** *adj.* [y:bər'le:pt] outmoded, disused, out of date.

**'überlegen[1]** F *v/t.* (*sep., -ge-, h*) give (*child*) a spanking.

**über'leg|en[2] 1.** *v/t. and v/refl.* (*no -ge-, h*) consider, reflect upon, think about; *ich will es mir ~* I will think it over; *es sich anders ~* change one's mind; **2.** *v/i.* (*no -ge-, h*): *er überlegt noch* he hasn't made up his mind yet; **3.** *adj.* superior (*dat.* to; *an dat.* in); **2enheit** *f* (*-/no pl.*) superiority; preponderance; **~t** *adj.* [~kt] deliberate; prudent; **2ung** [~guŋ] *f* (*-/-en*) consideration, reflection; *nach reiflicher ~* after mature deliberation.

**über'lesen** *v/t.* (*irr. lesen, no -ge-, h*) read s.th. through quickly, run over s.th.; overlook.

**über'liefer|n** *v/t.* (*no -ge-, h*) hand down or on (*dat.* to); **2ung** *f* tradition.

**über'listen** *v/t.* (*no -ge-, h*) outwit, F outsmart.

**'Über|macht** *f* (*-/no pl.*) superiority; *esp.* ⚔ superior forces *pl.*; *in der ~ sein* be superior in numbers; **'2mächtig** *adj.* superior.

**über'malen** *v/t.* (*no -ge-, h*) paint out; **~'mannen** *v/t.* (*no -ge-, h*) overpower, overcome, overwhelm (*all. a. fig.*).

**'Über|maß** *n* (*-es/no pl.*) excess (*an dat.* of); **'2mäßig 1.** *adj.* excessive; immoderate; **2.** *adv.* excessively, *Am. a.* overly; *~ trinken* drink to excess.

**'Übermensch** *m* superman; **'2lich** *adj.* superhuman.

**über'mitt|eln** *v/t.* (*no -ge-, h*) transmit; convey; **2lung** *f* (*-/-en*) transmission; conveyance.

**'übermorgen** *adv.* the day after tomorrow.

**über'müd|et** *adj.* overtired; **2ung** *f* (*-/⚓-en*) overfatigue.

**'Über|mut** *m* wantonness; frolicsomeness; **2mütig** *adj.* ['~my:tiç] wanton; frolicsome.

**'übernächst** *adj. the* next but one; *~e Woche* the week after next.

**über'nacht|en** *v/i.* (*no -ge-, h*) stay overnight (*bei at a friend's* [*house*], *with friends*), spend the night (at, with); **2ung** *f* (*-/-en*) spending the night; *~ und Frühstück* bed and breakfast.

**Übernahme** ['y:bərna:mə] *f* (*-/-n*) field of application *s.* übernehmen 1: taking over; undertaking; assumption; adoption.

**'übernatürlich** *adj.* supernatural.

**übernehmen** *v/t.* **1.** [~'ne:mən] (*irr. nehmen, no -ge-, h*) take over (*business, etc.*); undertake (*responsibility, etc.*); take (*lead, risk, etc.*); assume (*direction of business, office, etc.*); adopt (*idea, custom, etc.*); *sich ~* overreach o.s.; **2.** ⚔ ['~ne:mən] (*irr. nehmen, sep., -ge-, h*) slope, shoulder (*arms*).

**'über|ordnen** *v/t.* (*sep., -ge-, h*): *j-n j-m ~* set s.o. over s.o.; **'~parteilich** *adj.* non-partisan; **'2produktion** *f* over-production.

**über'prüf|en** *v/t.* (*no -ge-, h*) reconsider; verify; check; review; screen *s.o.*; **2ung** *f* reconsideration; checking; review.

**über|'queren** *v/t.* (*no -ge-, h*) cross; **~'ragen** *v/t.* (*no -ge-, h*) tower above (*a. fig.*), overtop; *fig.* surpass.

**überrasch|en** [y:bər'raʃən] *v/t.* (*no -ge-, h*) surprise; catch (*bei at, in*); **2ung** *f* (*-/-en*) surprise.

**über'red|en** *v/t.* (*no -ge-, h*) persuade (*zu inf.* to *inf.*, *into ger.*);

talk (into *ger.*); ⚲ung *f* (-/⚲ -en) persuasion.

**über'reich|en** *v/t.* (*no -ge-, h*) present; ⚲ung *f* (-/⚲ -en) presentation.

**über|'reizen** *v/t.* (*no -ge-, h*) overexcite; ⚲'reizt *adj.* overstrung; ⚲'rennen *v/t.* (*irr. rennen, no -ge-, h*) overrun.

**'Überrest** *m* remainder; ⚲e *pl.* remains *pl.*; sterbliche ⚲e *pl.* mortal remains *pl.*

**über'rump|eln** *v/t.* (*no -ge-, h*) (take by) surprise; ⚲(e)lung *f* (-/⚲ -en) surprise.

**über'rund|en** *v/t.* (*no -ge-, h*) *sports:* lap; *fig.* surpass; ⚲ung *f* (-/-en) lapping.

**übersät** *adj.* [y:bər'zɛːt] studded, dotted.

**über'sättig|en** *v/t.* (*no -ge-, h*) surfeit (*a. fig.*); ⌐ supersaturate; ⚲ung *f* (-/-en) surfeit (*a. fig.*); ⌐ supersaturation.

**'Überschallgeschwindigkeit** *f* supersonic speed.

**über|'schatten** *v/t.* (*no -ge-, h*) overshadow (*a. fig.*); ⚲'schätzen *v/t.* (*no -ge-, h*) overrate, overestimate.

**'Überschlag** *m gymnastics:* somersault; ⚡ loop; ⚡ flashover; *fig.* estimate, approximate calculation; ⚲en (*irr. schlagen*) 1. ['⚲ʃlaːgən] *v/t.* (*sep., -ge-, h*) cross (*one's legs*); 2. ['⚲ʃlaːgən] *v/i.* (*sep., -ge-, sein*) *voice:* become high-pitched; 3. [⚲'ʃlaːgən] *v/t.* (*no -ge-, h*) skip (*page, etc.*); make a rough estimate of (*cost, etc.*); sich ⚲ *fall head over heels; car, etc.:* (be) turn(ed) over; ⚡ loop the loop; *voice:* become high-pitched; sich ⚲ vor (*dat.*) outdo (*one's friendliness, etc.*); 4. *adj.* [⚲'ʃlaːgən] lukewarm, tepid.

**'überschnappen** *v/i.* (*sep., -ge-, sein*) *voice:* become high-pitched; F *p.* go mad, turn crazy.

**über|'schneiden** *v/refl.* (*irr. schneiden, no -ge-, h*) overlap; intersect; ⚲'schreiben *v/t.* (*irr. schreiben, no -ge-, h*) superscribe, entitle; make s.th. over (*dat.* to); ⚲'schreiten *v/t.* (*irr. schreiten, no -ge-, h*) cross; transgress (*limit, bound*); infringe (*rule, etc.*); exceed (*speed limit, one's instructions, etc.*); sie hat das 10 bereits überschritten she is on the wrong side of 40.

**'Über|schrift** *f* heading, title; headline; ⚲'schuh *m* overshoe.

**'Über|schuß** *m* surplus, excess; profit; ⚲schüssig *adj.* ['⚲ʃysiç] surplus, excess.

**über'schütten** *v/t.* (*no -ge-, h*): ⚲ mit pour (*water, etc.*) on; *fig.:* overwhelm with (*inquiries, etc.*); shower (*gifts, etc.*) upon.

**überschwemm|en** [y:bər'ʃvɛmən]

*v/t.* (*no -ge-, h*) inundate, flood (*both a. fig.*); ⚲ung *f* (-/-en) inundation, flood(ing).

**überschwenglich** *adj.* ['y:bər-ʃvɛŋliç] effusive, gushy.

**'Übersee:** nach ⚲ gehen go overseas; '⚲dampfer ⚓ *m* transoceanic steamer; '⚲handel *m* (-s/*no pl.*) oversea(s) trade.

**über'sehen** *v/t.* (*irr. sehen, no -ge-, h*) survey; overlook (*printer's error, etc.*); *fig.* ignore, disregard.

**über'send|en** *v/t.* ([*irr. senden,*] *no -ge-, h*) send, transmit; consign; ⚲ung *f* sending, transmission; ✝ consignment.

**'übersetzen**[1] (*sep., -ge-*) 1. *v/i.* (*sein*) cross; 2. *v/t.* (*h*) ferry.

**über'setz|en**[2] *v/t.* (*no -ge-, h*) translate (*in acc.* into), render (*into*); ⊕ gear; ⚲er *m* (-s/-) translator; ⚲ung *f* (-/-en) translation (*aus* from; *in acc.* into); rendering; ⊕ gear(ing), transmission.

**'Übersicht** *f* (-/-en) survey (*über acc.* of); summary; ⚲lich *adj.* clear(ly arranged).

**über|siedeln** ['y:bərzi:dəln] *v/i.* (*sep., -ge-, sein*) and [⚲'zi:dəln] *v/i.* (*no -ge-, sein*) remove (*nach* to); ⚲siedelung [⚲'zi:dəluŋ] *f* (-/-en), ⚲siedlung ['⚲zi:dluŋ, ⚲'zi:dluŋ] *f* (-/-en) removal (*nach* to).

**'übersinnlich** *adj.* transcendental; *forces:* psychic.

**über'spann|en** *v/t.* (*no -ge-, h*) cover (*mit* with); den Bogen ⚲ go too far; ⚲t *adj.* extravagant; *p.* eccentric; *claims, etc.:* exaggerated; ⚲theit *f* (-/⚲ -en) extravagance, eccentricity.

**über'spitzt** *adj.* oversubtle; exaggerated.

**überspringen** 1. ['⚲ʃpriŋən] *v/i.* (*irr. springen, sep., -ge-, sein*) ⚡ spark: jump; *in a speech, etc.:* ⚲ von ... zu ... jump or skip from (*one subject*) to (*another*); 2. [⚲'ʃpriŋən] *v/t.* (*irr. springen, no -ge-, h*) jump, clear; skip (*page, etc.*); jump (*class*).

**überstehen** (*irr. stehen*) 1. ['⚲ʃte:ən] *v/i.* (*sep., -ge-, h*) jut (*out or forth*), project; 2. [⚲'ʃte:ən] *v/t.* (*no -ge-, h*) survive (*misfortune, etc.*); weather (*crisis*); get over (*illness*).

**über|'steigen** *v/t.* (*irr. steigen, no -ge-, h*) climb over; *fig.* exceed; ⚲'stimmen *v/t.* (*no -ge-, h*) outvote, vote down.

**'überstreifen** *v/t.* (*sep., -ge-, h*) slip s.th. over.

**überströmen** 1. ['⚲ʃtrøːmən] *v/i.* (*sep., -ge-, sein*) overflow (*vor dat.* with); 2. [⚲'ʃtrøːmən] *v/t.* (*no -ge-, h*) flood, inundate.

**'Überstunden** *f/pl.* overtime; ⚲ machen work overtime.

**über'stürz|en** *v/t.* (*no -ge-, h*) rush, hurry (*up or on*); sich ⚲ act rashly; *events*: follow in rapid succession; ~t *adj.* precipitate, rash; 2ung *f* (-/~-en) precipitancy.

**über|'teuern** *v/t.* (*no -ge-, h*) overcharge; ~'tölpeln *v/t.* (*no -ge-, h*) dupe, take in; ~'tönen *v/t.* (*no -ge-, h*) drown.

**Übertrag** † ['y:bərtraːk] *m* (-[e]s/ ~e) carrying forward; sum carried forward.

**über'trag|bar** *adj.* transferable; † negotiable; ♫ communicable; ~en [~gən] 1. *v/t.* (*irr. tragen, no -ge-, h*) † carry forward; make over (*property*) (*auf acc.* to); ♫ transfuse (*blood*); delegate (*rights, etc.*) (*dat.* to); render (*book, etc.*) (*in acc.* into); transcribe (*s.th. written in shorthand*); ♫, ⊕, *phys., radio*: transmit; *radio*: *a.* broadcast; *im Fernsehen* ~ televise; *ihm wurde eine wichtige Mission* ~ he was charged with an important mission; 2. *adj.* figurative; 2ung [~guŋ] *f* (-/-en) *field of application s.* übertragen 1: carrying forward; making over; transfusion; delegation; rendering, free translation; transcription; transmission; broadcast; ~ *im Fernsehen* telecast.

**über'treffen** *v/t.* (*irr. treffen, no -ge-, h*) excel *s.o.* (*an dat. in; in dat. in, at*); surpass (*in*), exceed (*in*).

**über'treib|en** (*irr. treiben, no -ge-, h*) 1. *v/t.* overdo; exaggerate, overstate; 2. *v/i.* exaggerate, draw the long bow; 2ung *f* (-/-en) exaggeration, overstatement.

**'übertreten**[1] *v/i.* (*irr. treten, sep., -ge-, sein*) *sports*: cross the take-off line; *fig.* go over (*zu* to); *zum Katholizismus* ~ turn Roman Catholic.

**über'tret|en**[2] *v/t.* (*irr. treten, no -ge-, h*) transgress, violate, infringe (*law, etc.*); *sich den Fuß* ~ sprain one's ankle; 2ung *f* (-/-en) transgression, violation, infringement.

**'Übertritt** *m* going over (*zu* to); *eccl.* conversion (*to*).

**übervölker|n** [y:bər'fœlkərn] *v/t.* (*no -ge-, h*) over-populate; 2ung *f* (-/~-en) over-population.

**über'vorteilen** *v/t.* (*no -ge-, h*) overreach, † do.

**über'wach|en** *v/t.* (*no -ge-, h*) supervise, superintend; control; *police*: keep under surveillance, shadow; 2ung *f* (-/~-en) supervision, superintendence; control; surveillance.

**überwältigen** [y:bər'vɛltigən] *v/t.* (*no -ge-, h*) overcome, overpower, overwhelm (*all a. fig.*); ~d *fig. adj.* overwhelming.

**über'weis|en** *v/t.* (*irr. weisen, no -ge-, h*) remit (*money*) (*dat. or an acc.* to); (*zur Entscheidung etc.*) ~ refer (to); 2ung *f* (-/-en) remittance;

reference (*an acc.* to); *parl.* devolution.

**überwerfen** (*irr. werfen*) 1. ['~verfən] *v/t.* (*sep., -ge-, h*) slip (*coat*) on; 2. [~'verfən] *v/refl.* (*no -ge-, h*) fall out (*mit with*).

**über|'wiegen** (*irr. wiegen, no -ge-, h*) 1. *v/t.* outweigh; 2. *v/i.* preponderate; predominate; ~'wiegend *adj.* preponderant; predominant; ~'winden *v/t.* (*irr. winden, no -ge-, h*) overcome (*a. fig.*), subdue; *sich* ~ *zu inf.* bring *o.s.* to *inf.*; ~'wintern *v/i.* (*no -ge-, h*) (pass the) winter.

**'Über|wurf** *m* wrap; ~'zahl *f* (-/~-en) numerical superiority; *in der* ~ superior in numbers; 2'zählig *adj.* ['~tseːliç] supernumerary; surplus.

**über'zeug|en** *v/t.* (*no -ge-, h*) convince (*von* of); satisfy (*of*); 2ung *f* (-/-en) conviction.

**überziehe|n** *v/t.* (*irr. ziehen*) 1. ['~tsiːən] (*sep., -ge-, h*) put on; 2. [~'tsiːən] (*no -ge-, h*) cover; put clean sheets on (*bed*); † overdraw (*account*); *sich* ~ *sky*: become overcast; 2r *m* (-s/-) overcoat, topcoat.

**'Überzug** *m* cover; case, tick; ⊕ coat(ing). [*ary*] normal.)

**üblich** *adj.* ['y:pliç] usual, custom-}

**U-Boot** ⚓, ✕ ['u:-] *n* submarine, *in Germany*: *a.* U-boat.

**übrig** *adj.* ['y:briç] left, remaining; *die* ~*e Welt* the rest of the world; *die* ~*en pl.* the others *pl.*, the rest; *im* ~*en* for the rest; by the way; ~ *haben* have *s.th.* left; *keine Zeit* ~ *haben* have no time to spare; *etwas* ~ *haben für* care for, have a soft spot for; *ein* ~*es tun* go out of one's way; '~*bleiben* *v/i.* (*irr. bleiben, sep., -ge-, sein*) be left; remain; *es blieb ihm nichts anderes übrig* he had no (other) alternative (*als but*); ~*ens adv.* ['~gəns] by the way; ~*lassen* ['~sə-] *v/t.* (*irr. lassen, sep., -ge-, h*) leave; *viel zu wünschen* ~ leave much to be desired.

**'Übung** *f* (-/-en) exercise; practice; drill; '~*shang* *m* *skiing*: nursery slope.

**Ufer** ['u:fər] *n* (-s/-) shore (*of sea, lake*); bank (*of river, etc.*).

**Uhr** [u:r] *f* (-/-en) clock; watch; *um vier* ~ at four o'clock; '~*armband* *n* (-[e]s/~er) watch-strap; '~*feder* *f* watch-spring; '~*macher* *m* (-s/-) watch-maker; '~*werk* *n* clockwork; watch-work; '~*zeiger* *m* hand (*of clock or watch*); '~*zeigersinn* *m* (-[e]s/*no pl.*): *im* ~ clockwise; *entgegen dem* ~ counter-clockwise.

**Uhu** *orn.* ['u:hu:] *m* (-s/-s) eagle-owl.

**Ulk** [ulk] *m* (-[e]s/-e) fun, lark; '2en *v/i.* (*ge-, h*) (sky)lark, joke; '2ig *adj.* funny.

**Ulme** ♣ ['ulmə] *f* (-/-n) elm.

**Ultimatum** [ulti'maːtum] *n* (-s/Ul-

*timaten, -s)* ultimatum; *j-m ein ~ stellen* deliver an ultimatum to s.o.

**Ultimo** † ['ultimo] *m (-s/-s)* last day of the month.

**Ultrakurzwelle** *phys.* [ultra'-] *f* ultra-short wave, very-high-frequency wave.

**um** [um] **1.** *prp. (acc.)* round, about; *~ vier Uhr* at four o'clock; *~ sein Leben laufen* run for one's life; *et. ~ einen Meter verfehlen* miss s.th. by a metre; *et. ~ zwei Mark verkaufen* sell s.th. at two marks; **2.** *prp. (gen.)*: *~ seinetwillen* for his sake; **3.** *cj.*: *~ so besser* all the better, so much the better; *~ so mehr (weniger)* all the more (less); *~ zu* (in order) to; **4.** *adv.*: *er drehte sich ~* he turned round.

**um|ändern** ['um⁹-] *v/t. (sep., -ge-, h)* change, alter; **~arbeiten** ['um⁹-] *v/t. (sep., -ge-, h)* make over *(coat, etc.)*; revise *(book, etc.)*; *~ zu* make into.

**um'arm|en** *v/t. (no -ge-, h)* hug, embrace; *sich ~* embrace; **~ung** *f (-/-en)* embrace, hug.

**'Umbau** *m (-[e]s/-e, -ten)* rebuilding; reconstruction; **~en** *v/t. (sep., -ge-, h)* rebuild; reconstruct.

**'umbiegen** *v/t. (irr. biegen, sep., -ge-, h)* bend; turn up *or* down.

**'umbild|en** *v/t. (sep., -ge-, h)* remodel, reconstruct; reorganize, reform; reshuffle *(cabinet)*; **~ung** *f (-/-en)* remodel(l)ing, reconstruction; reorganization, pol. reshuffle.

**um|binden** *v/t. (irr. binden, sep., -ge-, h)* put on *(apron, etc.)*; **~blättern** *(sep., -ge-, h)* **1.** *v/t.* turn over; **2.** *v/i.* turn over the page; **~brechen** *v/t. (irr. brechen)* **1.** ~ ['~brɛçən] *(sep., -ge-, h)* dig, break up *(ground)*; **2.** *typ.* ~ ['~brɛçən] *(no -ge-, h)* make up; **~bringen** *v/t. (irr. bringen, sep., -ge-, h)* kill; *sich ~* kill o.s.; **'2bruch** *m (-[e]s/-e, fig.:* upheaval; radical change; **~buchen** *v/t. (sep., -ge-, h)* † transfer *or* switch to another account; book for another date; **~disponieren** *v/i. (sep., no -ge-, h)* change one's plans.

**'umdreh|en** *v/t. (sep., -ge-, h)* turn; *s. Spieß*; *sich ~* turn round; **2ung** *f* [um'-] *f (-/-en)* turn; *phys.*, ⊕ rotation, revolution.

**um|fahren** *(irr. fahren)* **1.** ['~faːrən] *v/t. (sep., -ge-, h)* run down; **2.** ['~faːrən] *v/i. (sep., -ge-, sein)* go a roundabout way; **3.** [~'faːrən] *v/t. (no -ge-, h)* drive round; ⊕ sail round; ⚓ double *(cape)*; **~fallen** *v/i. (irr. fallen, sep., -ge-, sein)* fall; collapse; *tot ~* drop dead.

**'Umfang** *m (-[e]s/no pl.)* circumference, circuit; perimeter; girth *(of body, tree, etc.)*; *fig.*: extent; volume; *in großem ~* on a large

scale; **'2reich** *adj.* extensive; voluminous; spacious.

**um'fassen** *v/t. (no -ge-, h)* clasp; embrace *(a. fig.)*; ⚔ envelop; *fig.* comprise, cover, comprehend; **~d** *adj.* comprehensive, extensive; sweeping, drastic.

**'umform|en** *v/t. (sep., -ge-, h)* remodel, recast, transform *(a. ⚡)*; ⚡ convert; **'2er** ⚡ *m (-s/-)* transformer; converter.

**'Umfrage** *f* poll; *öffentliche ~* public opinion poll.

**'Umgang** *m* **1.** *(-[e]s/÷e)* ⚠ gallery, ambulatory; *eccl.* procession *(round the fields, etc.)*; **2.** *(-[e]s/no pl.)* intercourse *(with mit)*; company; *~ haben mit* associate with.

**umgänglich** *adj.* ['umgɛnliç] sociable, companionable, affable.

**'Umgangs|formen** *f/pl.* manners *pl.*; **~sprache** *f* colloquial usage; *in der deutschen ~* in colloquial German.

**um'garnen** *v/t. (no -ge-, h)* ensnare.

**um'geb|en** **1.** *v/t. (irr. geben, no -ge-, h)* surround; *mit e-r Mauer ~* wall in; **2.** *adj.* surrounded *(von* with, by) *(a. fig.)*; **2ung** *f (-/-en)* environs *pl. (of town, etc.)*; surroundings *pl.*, environment *(of place, person, etc.)*.

**umgeh|en** *(irr. gehen)* **1.** ['~geːən] *v/i. (sep., -ge-, sein)* make a detour; *rumour, etc.*: go about, be afloat; *ghost*: walk; *~ mit* use s.th.; deal with *s.o.*; keep company with; *ein Gespenst soll im Schlosse ~* the castle is said to be haunted; **2.** [~'geːən] *v/t. (no -ge-, h)* go round; ⚔ flank; bypass *(town, etc.)*; *fig.* avoid, evade; circumvent, elude *(law, etc.)*; **~end** *adj.* immediate; **2ungsstraße** [um'geːuŋs-] *f* bypass.

**umgekehrt** ['umgəkeːrt] **1.** *adj.* reverse, inverse, inverted; *in ~er Reihenfolge* in reverse order; *im ~en Verhältnis zu* in inverse proportion to; **2.** *adv.* vice versa.

**'umgraben** *v/t. (irr. graben, sep., -ge-, h)* dig (up).

**um'grenzen** *v/t. (no -ge-, h)* encircle; enclose; *fig.* circumscribe, limit.

**'umgruppier|en** *v/t. (sep., no -ge-, h)* regroup; **'2ung** *f (-/-en)* regrouping.

**'um|haben** F *v/t. (irr. haben, sep., -ge-, h)* have *(coat, etc.)* on; **'2hang** *m* wrap; cape; **~hängen** *v/t. (sep., -ge-, h)* rehang *(pictures)*; sling *(rifle)* over one's shoulder; *sich den Mantel ~* put one's coat round one's shoulders; **~hauen** *v/t. (irr. hauen, sep., -ge-, h)* fell, cut down; F: *die Nachricht hat mich umgehauen* I was bowled over by the news.

**um'her|blicken** v/i. (sep., -ge-, h) look about (one); **~streifen** v/i. (sep., -ge-, sein) rove.

**um'hinkönnen** v/i. (irr. können, sep., -ge-, h): ich kann nicht umhin, zu sagen I cannot help saying.

**um'hüll|en** v/t. (no -ge-, h) wrap up (mit in), envelop (in); **2ung** f (-/-en) wrapping, wrapper, envelopment.

**Umkehr** ['umke:r] f (-/no pl.) return; (sein, sep., -ge-) 1. v/i. (sein) return, turn back; 2. v/t. (h) turn out (one's pocket, etc.); invert (a. ♪); reverse (a. ♫, ♀); **~ung** f (-/-en) reversal; inversion.

**'umkippen** (sep., -ge-) 1. v/t. (h) upset, tilt; 2. v/i. (sein) upset, tilt (over); F faint.

**um'klammer|n** v/t. (no -ge-, h) clasp; boxing: clinch; **2ung** f (-/-en) clasp; boxing: clinch.

**'umkleid|en** v/refl. (sep., -ge-, h) change (one's clothes); **2eraum** m dressing-room.

**'umkommen** v/i. (irr. kommen, sep., -ge-, sein) be killed (bei in), die (in), perish (in); vor Langeweile ~ die of boredom.

**'Umkreis** m (-es/no pl.) ♀ circumscribed circle; im ~ von within a radius of.                 [round.)

**um'kreisen** v/t. (no -ge-, h) circle)

**'umkrempeln** v/t. (sep., -ge-, h) tuck up (shirt-sleeves, etc.); change (plan, etc.); (völlig) ~ turn s.th. inside out; **~laden** v/t. (irr. laden, sep., -ge-, h) reload; ♥, ♣ tranship.

**'Umlauf** m circulation; phys., ⊕ rotation; circular (letter); in ~ setzen or bringen circulate, put into circulation; im ~ sein circulate, be in circulation; rumours: a. be afloat; außer ~ setzen withdraw from circulation; **~bahn** f orbit; **2en** (irr. laufen) 1. ['~laufən] v/t. (sep., -ge-, h) knock over; 2. ['~laufən] v/i. (sep., -ge-, sein) circulate; make a detour; 3. [~'laufən] v/t. (no -ge-, h) run round.

**'Umlege|kragen** m turn-down collar; **2n** v/t. (sep., -ge-, h) lay down; ⊕ throw (lever); storm, etc.: beat down (wheat, etc.); re-lay (cable, etc.); put (coat, etc.) round one's shoulders; apportion (costs, etc.); fig. sl. do s.o. in.

**'umleit|en** v/t. (sep., -ge-, h) divert; **2ung** f diversion, detour.

**'umliegend** adj. surrounding; circumjacent.

**um'nacht|et** adj.: geistig ~ mentally deranged; **2ung** f (-/~-en): geistige ~ mental derangement.

**'um|packen** v/t. (sep., -ge-, h) repack; **~pflanzen** v/t. 1. ['~pflantsən] (sep., -ge-, h) transplant; 2. [~'pflantsən] (no -ge-, h): ~ mit

plant s.th. round with; **~pflügen** v/t. (sep., -ge-, h) plough, Am. plow.

**um'rahmen** v/t. (no -ge-, h) frame; musikalisch ~ put into a musical setting.

**umrand|en** [um'randən] v/t. (no -ge-, h) edge, border; **2ung** f (-/-en) edge, border.

**um'ranken** v/t. (no -ge-, h) twine (mit with).

**'umrechn|en** v/t. (sep., -ge-, h) convert (in acc. into); **'2ung** f (-/no pl.) conversion; **'2ungskurs** m rate of exchange.

**umreißen** v/t. (irr. reißen) 1. ['~raisən] (sep., -ge-, h) pull down; knock s.o. over; 2. [~'raisən] (no -ge-, h) outline.   [round (a. fig.).)

**um'ringen** v/t. (no -ge-, h) sur-)

**'Um|riß** m outline (a. fig.), contour; **'2rühren** v/t. (sep., -ge-, h) stir; **'2satteln** (sep., -ge-, h) 1. v/t. resaddle; 2. F fig. v/i. change one's studies or occupation; ~ von ... auf (acc.) change from ... to ...; **'~satz** ♥ m turnover; sales pl.; return(s pl.); stock exchange: business done.

**'umschalt|en** (sep., -ge-, h) 1. v/t. ⊕ change over; ♪ commutate; ♪, ⊕ switch; 2. ♪, ⊕ v/i. switch over; **'2er** m ⊕ change-over switch; ♪ commutator; **'2ung** f (-/-en) ⊕ change-over; ♪ commutation.

**'Umschau** f (-/no pl.): ~ halten nach look out for, be on the look-out for; **'2en** v/refl. (sep., -ge-, h) look round (nach for); look about (for) (a. fig.), look about one.

**'umschicht|en** v/t. (sep., -ge-, h) pile afresh; fig. regroup (a. ♥); **'~ig** adv. by or in turns; **2ung** fig. f (-/-en) regrouping; soziale **~en** pl. social upheavals pl.

**um'schiff|en** v/t. (no -ge-, h) circumnavigate; double (cape); **2ung** f (-/~-en) circumnavigation; doubling.

**'Umschlag** m envelope; cover, wrapper; jacket; turn-up, Am. a. cuff (of trousers); ♥ compress; ♥ poultice; trans-shipment (of goods); fig. change, turn; **'2en** (irr. schlagen, sep., -ge-, h) 1. v/t. (h) knock s.o. down; cut down, fell (tree); turn (leaf); turn up (sleeves, etc.); turn down (collar); trans-ship (goods); 2. v/i. (sein) turn over, upset; ♣ capsize, upset; wine, etc.: turn sour; fig. turn (in acc. into); **'~hafen** m port of trans-shipment.

**um|'schließen** v/t. (irr. schließen, no -ge-, h) embrace, surround (a. ♀), enclose; ♀ invest; **'schlingen** v/t. (irr. schlingen, no -ge-, h) embrace.

**'um|schmeißen** F v/t. (irr. schmeißen, sep., -ge-, h) s. umstoßen; **'~**

**schnallen** v/t. (sep., -ge-, h) buckle on.

**umschreib|en** v/t. (irr. schreiben) **1.** ['˷ʃraɪbən] (sep., -ge-, h) rewrite; transfer (property, etc.) (auf acc. to); **2.** [˷'ʃraɪbən] (no -ge-, h) ⅋ circumscribe; paraphrase; **2ung** f (-/-en) **1.** ['˷ʃraɪbʊŋ] rewriting; transfer (auf acc. to); **2.** [˷'ʃraɪbʊŋ] ⅋ circumscription; paraphrase.

**'Umschrift** f circumscription; phonetics: transcription.

**'umschütten** v/t. (sep., -ge-, h) pour into another vessel; spill.

**'Um|schweife** pl.: ˷ machen beat about the bush; ohne ˷ point-blank; **'2schwenken** fig. v/i. (sep., -ge-, sein) veer or turn round; **'˷-schwung** fig. m revolution; revulsion (of public feeling, etc.); change (in the weather, etc.); reversal (of opinion, etc.).

**um'seg|eln** v/t. (no -ge-, h) sail round; double (cape); circumnavigate (globe, world); **2(e)lung** f (-/-en) sailing round (world, etc.); doubling; circumnavigation.

**'um|sehen** v/refl. (irr. sehen, sep., -ge-, h) look round (nach for); look about (for) (a. fig.), look about one; **'˷sein** F v/i. (irr. sein, sep., -ge-, sein) time: be up; holidays, etc.: be over; **'˷setzen** v/t. (sep., -ge-, h) transpose (a. ♪); ♪ transplant; ♱ turn over; spend (money) (in acc. on books, etc.); in die Tat ˷ realize, convert into fact.

**'Umsicht** f (-/no pl.) circumspection; **'2ig** adj. circumspect.

**'umsied|eln** (sep., -ge-) **1.** v/t. (h) resettle; **2.** v/i. (sein) (re)move (nach, in acc. to); **'2lung** f (-/˷ -en) resettlement; evacuation; removal.

**um'sonst** adv. gratis, free of charge; in vain; to no purpose; nicht ˷ not without good reason.

**umspann|en** v/t. **1.** ['˷ʃpanən] (sep., -ge-, h) change (horses); ⚡ transform; **2.** [˷'ʃpanən] (no -ge-, h) span; fig. a. embrace; **'2er** ⚡ m (-s/-) transformer.

**'umspringen** v/i. (irr. springen, sep., -ge-, sein) shift, veer (round); ˷ mit treat badly, etc.

**'Umstand** m circumstance; fact, detail; unter diesen Umständen in or under the circumstances; unter keinen Umständen in or under no circumstances, on no account; unter Umständen possibly; ohne Umstände without ceremony; in anderen Umständen sein be in the family way.

**umständlich** adj. ['umʃtɛntlɪç] story, etc.: long-winded; method, etc.: roundabout; p. fussy; das ist (mir) viel zu ˷ that is far too much trouble (for me); **'2kelt** f (-/˷ -en) long-windedness; fussiness.

**'Umstands|kleid** n maternity robe; **'˷wort** gr. n (-[e]s/˷er) adverb.

**'umstehend 1.** adj.: auf der ˷en Seite overleaf; **2.** adv. overleaf; **2en** ['˷dən] pl. the bystanders pl.

**'Umsteige|karte** f transfer; **'2n** v/i. (irr. steigen, sep., -ge-, sein) change (nach for); 🚃 a. change trains (1or).

**Umsteigkarte** ['umʃtaɪk-] f s. Umsteigekarte.

**umstell|en** v/t. **1.** ['˷ʃtɛlən] (sep., -ge-, h) transpose (a. gr.); shift (furniture) about or round; convert (currency, production) (auf acc. to); sich ˷ change one's attitude; accommodate o.s. to new conditions; adapt o.s. (auf acc. to); **2.** [˷'ʃtɛlən] (no -ge-, h) surround; **2ung** ['˷ʃtɛlʊŋ] f transposition; fig.: conversion; adaptation; change.

**'um|stimmen** v/t. (sep., -ge-, h) ♪ tune to another pitch; j-n ˷ change s.o.'s mind, bring s.o. round; **'˷stoßen** v/t. (irr. stoßen, sep., -ge-, h) knock over; upset; fig. annul; ⅊ overrule, reverse; upset (plan).

**um|'stricken** fig. v/t. (no -ge-, h) ensnare; **˷stritten** adj. [˷'ʃtrɪtən] disputed, contested; controversial.

**'Um|sturz** m subversion, overturn; **'2stürzen** (sep., -ge-) **1.** v/t. (h) upset, overturn (a. fig.); fig. subvert; **2.** v/i. (sein) upset; fall down; **2stürzlerisch** adj. ['˷lərɪʃ] subversive.

**'Umtausch** m (-es/˷ -e) exchange; ♱ conversion (of currency, etc.); **'2en** v/t. (sep., -ge-, h) exchange (gegen for); ♱ convert.

**'umtun** F v/t. (irr. tun, sep., -ge-, h) put (coat, etc.) round one's shoulders; sich ˷ nach look about for.

**'umwälz|en** v/t. (sep., -ge-, h) roll round; fig. revolutionize; **'˷end** adj. revolutionary; **'2ung** fig. f (-/-en) revolution, upheaval.

**'umwand|eln** v/t. (sep., -ge-, h) transform (in acc. into); ⚡, ♱ convert (into); ⅊ commute (into); **'2lung** f transformation; ⚡, ♱ conversion; ⅊ commutation.

**'um|wechseln** v/t. (sep., -ge-, h) change; **'2weg** m roundabout way or route; detour; auf ˷en in a roundabout way; **'˷wehen** v/t. (sep., -ge-, h) blow down or over; **'2welt** f (-/˷ -en) environment; **'˷wenden 1.** v/t. (sep., -ge-, h) turn over; **2.** v/refl. ([irr. wenden,] sep., -ge-, h) look round (nach for).

**um'werben** v/t. (irr. werben, no -ge-, h) court, woo.

**umwerfen** v/t. (irr. werfen, sep., -ge-, h) upset (a. fig.), overturn; sich e-n Mantel ˷ throw a coat round one's shoulders.

**um|'wickeln** v/t. (no -ge-, h): et. mit Draht ˷ wind wire round s.th.;

**~wölken** [~'vœlkən] v/refl. (no -ge-, h) cloud over (a. fig.); **~zäunen** [~'tsɔynən] v/t. (no -ge-, h) fence (in).

**umziehen** (irr. ziehen) **1.** ['~tsi:ən] v/i. (sep., -ge-, sein) (re)move (nach to); move house; **2.** ['~tsi:ən] v/refl. (sep., -ge-, h) change (one's clothes); **3.** [~'tsi:ən] v/refl. (no -ge-, h) cloud over.

**umzingeln** [um'tsiŋəln] v/t. (no -ge-, h) surround, encircle.

'**Umzug** m procession; move (nach to), removal (to); change of residence.

**unab|änderlich** adj. [un⁹ap'ɛndərliç] unalterable; **~hängig** ['~hɛŋiç] **1.** adj. independent (von of); **2.** adv.: ~ von irrespective of; '**2hängigkeit** f (-/no pl.) independence (von of); **~kömmlich** adj. ['~kœmliç]: er ist im Moment ~ we cannot spare him at the moment, we cannot do without him at the moment; **~'lässig** adj. incessant, unremitting; **~sehbar** adj. [~'ze:ba:r] incalculable; in ~er Ferne in a distant future; **~'sichtlich** adj. unintentional; inadvertent; **~wendbar** adj. [~'vɛntba:r] inevitable, inescapable.

**unac~tsam** adj. ['un⁹-] careless, heedless; '**2keit** f (-/⸜-en) carelessness, heedlessness.

**unähnlich** adj. ['un⁹-] unlike, dissimilar (dat. to).

**unan|fechtbar** adj. [un⁹an'-] unimpeachable, unchallengeable, incontestable; **~gebracht** adj. inappropriate; pred. a. out of place; '**~gefochten 1.** adj. undisputed; unchallenged; **2.** adv. without any hindrance; '**~gemessen** adj. unsuitable; improper; inadequate; '**~genehm** adj. disagreeable, unpleasant; awkward; troublesome; **~'nehmbar** adj. unacceptable (für to); '**2nehmlichkeit** f (-/-en) unpleasantness; awkwardness; troublesomeness; **~en** pl. trouble, inconvenience; '**~sehnlich** adj. unsightly; plain; '**~ständig** adj. indecent; obscene; '**2ständigkeit** f (-/-en) indecency; obscenity; **~'tastbar** adj. unimpeachable; inviolable.

**unan~petitlich** adj. ['un⁹-] food, etc.: unappetizing; sight, etc.: distasteful, ugly.

**Unart** ['un⁹-] **1.** f bad habit; **2.** m (-[e]s/-e) naughty child; '**2ig** adj. naughty; '**~igkeit** f (-/-en) naughty behavio(u)r, naughtiness.

**unauf|dringlich** adj. ['un⁹auf-] unobtrusive; unostentatious; '**~fällig** adj. inconspicuous; unobtrusive; **~'findbar** adj. [~'fintba:r] undiscoverable, untraceable; **~gefordert** ['~gəfɔrdərt] **1.** adj. un-

asked; **2.** adv. without being asked, of one's own accord; **~'hörlich** adj. incessant, continuous, uninterrupted; '**~merksam** adj. inattentive; '**2merksamkeit** f (-/-en) inattention, inattentiveness; '**~richtig** adj. insincere; '**2richtigkeit** f (-/-en) insincerity; **~schiebbar** adj. [~'ʃi:pba:r] urgent; ~ sein brook no delay.

**unaus|bleiblich** adj. [un⁹aus'blaipliç] inevitable; das war ~ that was bound to happen; **~'führbar** adj. impracticable; **~geglichen** adj. ['~gəgliçən] unbalanced (a. ✝); **~'löschlich** adj. indelible; fig. a. inextinguishable; **~'sprechlich** adj. unutterable; unspeakable; inexpressible; **~'stehlich** adj. unbearable, insupportable.

'**unbarmherzig** adj. merciless, unmerciful; '**2keit** f (-/no pl.) mercilessness, unmercifulness.

**unbe|absichtigt** adj. ['unbə⁹apziçtiçt] unintentional, undesigned; '**~achtet** adj. unnoticed; **~anstandet** adj. ['unbə⁹-] unopposed, not objected to; '**~baut** adj. ✔ untilled; land: undeveloped; '**~dacht** adj. inconsiderate; imprudent; '**~denklich 1.** adj. unobjectionable; **2.** adv. without hesitation; '**~deutend** adj. insignificant; slight; '**~dingt 1.** adj. unconditional; obedience, etc.: implicit; **2.** adv. by all means; under any circumstances; **~'fahrbar** adj. impracticable, impassable; '**~fangen** adj. unprejudiced, unbias(s)ed; ingenuous; unembarrassed; '**~friedigend** adj. unsatisfactory; **~friedigt** adj. ['~çt] dissatisfied; disappointed; '**~fugt** adj. unauthorized; incompetent; '**2fugte** m (-n/-n) unauthorized person; ~n ist der Zutritt verboten! no trespassing!; '**~gabt** adj. untalented; **~'greiflich** adj. inconceivable, incomprehensible; '**~grenzt** adj. unlimited; boundless; '**~gründet** adj. unfounded; '**2hagen** n uneasiness; discomfort; '**~haglich** adj. uneasy; uncomfortable; **~helligt** adj. [~'hɛliçt] unmolested; '**~herrscht** adj. lacking self-control; '**2herrschtheit** f (-/no pl.) lack of self-control; '**~hindert** adj. unhindered, free; '**~holfen** adj. ['~bəhɔlfən] clumsy, awkward; '**2holfenheit** f (-/no pl.) clumsiness, awkwardness; **~'irrt** adj. unswerving; '**~kannt** adj. unknown; **~e Größe** ⅍ unknown quantity (a. fig.); **~'kümmert** adj. unconcerned (um, wegen about), careless (of, about); '**~lebt** adj. inanimate; street, etc.: unfrequented; **~'lehrbar** adj.: ~ sein take no advice; '**~liebt** adj. unpopular; sich ~ machen get o.s. disliked; '**~mannt** adj. unmanned;

'~merkt adj. unnoticed; '~mittelt adj. impecunious, without means; ~nommen adj. [~'nɔmən]: es bleibt ihm ~ zu inf. he is at liberty to inf.; '~nutzt adj. unused; '~quem adj. uncomfortable; inconvenient; '2quemlichkeit f lack of comfort; inconvenience; '~rechtigt adj. unauthorized; unjustified; ~schadet prp. (gen.) [~'ʃɑːdət] without prejudice to; ~schädigt adj. ['~çt] uninjured, undamaged; '~scheiden adj. immodest; ~scholten adj. ['~ʃɔltən] blameless, irreproachable; '~schränkt adj. unrestricted; absolute; ~schreiblich adj. [~'ʃraɪplɪç] indescribable; ~'sehen adv. unseen; without inspection; '~setzt adj. unoccupied; vacant; ~siegbar adj. [~'ziːkbaːr] invincible; '~sonnen adj. thoughtless, imprudent; rash; '2sonnenheit f (-/-en) thoughtlessness, rashness; '~ständig adj. inconstant; unsteady; weather: changeable, unsettled (a. ✝); p. erratic; '2ständigkeit f (-/no pl.) inconstancy; changeability; ~stätigt adj. ['~çt] unconfirmed; letter, etc.: unacknowledged; ~'stechlich adj. incorruptible, unbribable; 2'stechlichkeit f (-/no pl.) incorruptibility; '~stimmt adj. indeterminate (a. ♀); indefinite (a. gr.); uncertain; feeling, etc.: vague; '2~stimmtheit f (-/no pl.) indeterminateness, indetermination; indefiniteness; uncertainty; vagueness; ~'streitbar adj. incontestable; indisputable; '~st~ritten adj. uncontested, undisputed; '~teiligt adj. unconcerned (an dat. in); indifferent; ~'trächtlich adj. inconsiderable, insignificant. [flexible.]

**unbeugsam** adj. [un'bɔʏkzaːm] in-

'**unbe**|**wacht** adj. unwatched, unguarded (a. fig.); '~**waffnet** adj. unarmed; eye: naked; '~**weglich** adj. immovable; motionless; '~**wiesen** adj. unproven; '~**wohnt** adj. uninhabited; unoccupied, vacant; '~**wußt** adj. unconscious; ~'**zähmbar** adj. indomitable.

'**Un**|**bilden** pl.: ~ der Witterung inclemency of the weather; '~**bildung** f lack of education.

'**un**|**billig** adj. unfair; '~**blutig** 1. adj. bloodless; 2. adv. without bloodshed.

**unbotmäßig** adj. ['unboːt-] insubordinate; '2keit f (-/-en) insubordination.

'**un**|**brauchbar** adj. useless; '~**christlich** adj. unchristian.

**und** cj. [unt] and; F: na ~? so what?

'**Undank** m ingratitude; '2**bar** adj. ungrateful (gegen to); task, etc.: thankless; '~**barkeit** f ingratitude, ungratefulness; fig. thanklessness.

**un**|'**denkbar** adj. unthinkable; inconceivable; ~'**denklich** adj.: seit ~en Zeiten from time immemorial; '~**deutlich** adj. indistinct; speech: a. inarticulate; fig. vague, indistinct; '~**deutsch** adj. un-German; '~**dicht** adj. leaky; '2**ding** n: es wäre ein ~, zu behaupten, daß ... it would be absurd to claim that ...

'**unduldsam** adj. intolerant; '2**keit** f intolerance.

**undurch**|'**dringlich** adj. impenetrable; countenance: impassive; ~'**führbar** adj. impracticable; '~**lässig** adj. impervious, impermeable; '~**sichtig** adj. opaque; fig. mysterious.

'**uneben** adj. ['un⁹-] ground: uneven, broken; way, etc.: bumpy; '2**heit** f 1. (-/no pl.) unevenness; 2. (-/-en) bump.

**un**|'**echt** adj. ['un⁹-] jewellery, etc.: imitation; hair, teeth, etc.: false; money, jewellery, etc.: counterfeit; picture, etc.: fake; ♂ fraction: improper; '~**ehelich** adj. illegitimate.

**Unehr**|**e** ['un⁹-] f dishono(u)r; j-m ~ machen discredit s.o.; '2**ehaft** adj. dishono(u)rable; '2**lich** adj. dishonest; '~**lichkeit** f dishonesty.

'**uneigennützig** adj. ['un⁹-] disinterested, unselfish.

'**uneinig** adj. ['un⁹-]: ~ sein be at variance (mit with); disagree (über acc. on); '2**keit** f variance, disagreement.

**un**|'**ein**'**nehmbar** adj. impregnable; '~**empfänglich** adj. insusceptible (für of, to).

**unempfindlich** adj. ['un⁹-] insensitive (gegen to); '2**keit** f insensitiveness (gegen to).

**un**|'**endlich** 1. adj. endless, infinite (both a. fig.); 2. adv. infinitely (a. fig.); ~ lang endless; ~ viel no end of (money, etc.); '2**keit** f (-/no pl.) endlessness, infinitude, infinity (all a. fig.).

**unent**|**behrlich** adj. [un⁹ɛnt'beːrlɪç] indispensable; ~'**geltlich** 1. adj. gratuitous, gratis; 2. adv. gratis, free of charge; ~'**rinnbar** adj. ineluctable; '~**schieden** 1. adj. undecided; ~ enden game: end in a draw or tie; 2. ♀ n (-s/-) draw, tie; '~**schlossen** adj. irresolute; '2**schlossenheit** f irresoluteness, irresolution; ~'**schuldbar** adj. [~'ʃultbaːr] inexcusable; ~'**wegt** adv. [~'veːkt] untiringly; continuously; ~'**wirrbar** adj. inextricable.

**uner**|**bittlich** adj. [un⁹ɛr'bɪtlɪç] inexorable; fact: stubborn; '~**fahren** adj. inexperienced; ~**findlich** adj. [~'fɪntlɪç] incomprehensible; '~**forschlich** adj. inscrutable; '~**freulich** adj. unpleasant; ~'**füllbar** adj. unrealizable; ~'**giebig** adj. unproductive (an dat. of); '~**heb-**

**lich** *adj.* irrelevant (*für* to); inconsiderable; **~hört** *adj.* **1.** ['~hø:rt] unheard; **2.** [~'hø:rt] unheard-of; outrageous; **~kannt** *adj.* unrecognized; **~'klärlich** *adj.* inexplicable; **~läßlich** *adj.* [~'lesliç] indispensable (*für* to, for); **~laubt** *adj.* ['~laupt] unauthorized; illegal, illicit; **~e** *Handlung* s̷s̷ tort; **~ledigt** *adj.* ['~le:diçt] unsettled (*a.* ⌖); **~meßlich** *adj.* [~'mesliç] immeasurable, immense; **~müdlich** *adj.* [~'my:tliç] *p.* indefatigable, untiring; *efforts, etc.*: untiring, unremitting; **~quicklich** *adj.* unpleasant, unedifying; **~'reichbar** *adj.* inattainable; inaccessible; *pred. a.* above or beyond *or* out of reach; **~'reicht** *adj.* unrival(l)ed, unequal(l)ed; **~sättlich** *adj.* [~'zetliç] insatiable, insatiate; **~'schöpflich** *adj.* inexhaustible.

**unerschrocken** *adj.* ['un⁹-] intrepid, fearless; **'2heit** *f* (-/*no pl.*) intrepidity, fearlessness.

**uner|schütterlich** *adj.* [un⁹er'ʃytərliç] unshakable; **~'schwinglich** *adj.* *price*: prohibitive; *pred. a.* above or beyond *or* out of reach (*für* of); **~'setzlich** *adj.* irreplaceable; *loss, etc.*: irreparable; **~'träglich** *adj.* intolerable, unbearable; **~wartet** *adj.* unexpected; **~wünscht** *adj.* undesirable, undesired.

**'unfähig** *adj.* incapable (*zu inf.* of *ger.*); unable (to *inf.*); inefficient; **2keit** *f* incapability (*zu inf.* of *ger.*); inability (to *inf.*); inefficiency.

**'Unfall** *m* accident; *e-n* ~ *haben* meet with *or* have an accident; **'~station** *f* emergency ward; **'~versicherung** *f* accident insurance.

**un'faßlich** *adj.* incomprehensible, inconceivable; *das ist mir* ~ that is beyond me.

**un'fehlbar 1.** *adj.* infallible (*a. eccl.*); *decision, etc.*: unimpeachable; *instinct, etc.*: unfailing; **2.** *adv.* without fail; inevitably; **2keit** *f* (-/*no pl.*) infallibility.

**'un|fein** *adj.* indelicate; *pred. a.* lacking in refinement; **'~fern** *prp.* (*gen. or von*) not far from; **'~fertig** *adj.* unfinished; *fig. a.* half-baked; **~flätig** *adj.* ['~fle:tiç] dirty, filthy.

**'unfolgsam** *adj.* disobedient; **'2keit** *f* disobedience.

**un|'förmig** *adj.* ['unfœrmiç] misshapen; shapeless; **'~frankiert** *adj.* unstamped; **'~frei** *adj.* not free; ✂ unstamped; **'~freiwillig** *adj.* involuntary; *humour*: unconscious; **'~freundlich** *adj.* unfriendly (*zu* with), unkind (to); *climate, weather*: inclement; *room, day*: cheerless; **'2friede(n)** *m* discord.

**'unfruchtbar** *adj.* unfruitful; ster-

ile; **'2keit** *f* (-/*no pl.*) unfruitfulness; sterility.

**Unfug** ['unfu:k] *m* (-[e]s/*no pl.*) mischief.

**Ungar** ['uŋar] *m* (-n/-n) Hungarian; **'2isch** *adj.* Hungarian.

**'ungastlich** *adj.* inhospitable.

**unge|achtet** *prp.* (*gen.*) ['uŋə⁹axtət] regardless of; despite; **~ahnt** *adj.* ['uŋə⁹-] undreamt-of; unexpected; **~bärdig** *adj.* ['~be:rdiç] unruly; **'~beten** *adj.* uninvited, unasked; **~er** *Gast* intruder, *sl.* gatecrasher; **~bildet** *adj.* uneducated; **'~bräuchlich** *adj.* unusual; **'~braucht** *adj.* unused; **'~bührlich** *adj.* improper, undue, unseemly; **'~bunden** *adj. book*: unbound; *fig.*: free; single; **'~deckt** *adj. table*: unlaid; *sports,* ✕, ⌖: uncovered; *paper currency*: fiduciary.

**'Ungeduld** *f* impatience; **'2ig** *adj.* impatient.

**'ungeeignet** *adj.* unfit (*für* for *s.th.*, *to do s.th.*); *p. a.* unqualified; *moment*: inopportune.

**ungefähr** ['uŋəfe:r] **1.** *adj.* approximate, rough; **2.** *adv.* approximately, roughly, about, *Am.* F *a.* around; *von* ~ by chance; **'~det** *adj.* unendangered, safe; **'~lich** *adj.* harmless; *pred. a.* not dangerous.

**'unge|fällig** *adj.* disobliging; **'~halten** *adj.* displeased (*über acc.* at); **'~hemmt 1.** *adj.* unchecked; **2.** *adv.* without restraint; **'~heuchelt** *adj.* unfeigned.

**ungeheuer** ['uŋəhɔʏər] **1.** *adj.* vast, huge, enormous; **2.** ♀ *n* (-s/-) monster; **~lich** *adj.* [~'hɔʏrliç] monstrous.

**'ungehobelt** *adj.* not planed; *fig.* uncouth, rough.

**'ungehörig** *adj.* undue, improper; **'2keit** *f* (-/-en) impropriety.

**'ungehorsam 1.** *adj.* disobedient; **2.** ♀ *m* disobedience.

**'unge|künstelt** *adj.* unaffected; **'~kürzt** *adj.* unabridged.

**'ungelegen** *adj.* inconvenient, inopportune; **'2heiten** *f/pl.* inconvenience; trouble; *j-m* ~ *machen* put *s.o.* to inconvenience.

**'unge|lehrig** *adj.* indocile; **'~lenk** *adj.* awkward, clumsy; **'~lernt** *adj.* unskilled; **'~mütlich** *adj.* uncomfortable; *room*: *a.* cheerless; *p.* nasty; **'~nannt** *adj.* unnamed; *p.* anonymous.

**'ungenau** *adj.* inaccurate, inexact; **'2igkeit** *f* inaccuracy, inexactness.

**'ungeniert** *adj.* free and easy, unceremonious; undisturbed.

**'unge|nießbar** *adj.* ['uŋəni:sba:r] uneatable; undrinkable; F *p.* unbearable, *pred. a.* in a bad humo(u)r; **'~nügend** *adj.* insufficient; **~pflegt** *adj.* unkempt; **'~rade** *adj.* odd; **'~raten** *adj.* spoilt, undutiful.

**'ungerecht** adj. unjust (gegen to); **'2igkeit** f (-/-en) injustice.

**'un|gern** adv. unwillingly, grudgingly; reluctantly; **'~geschehen** adj.: ~ machen undo s.th.

**'Ungeschick** n (-[e]s/no pl.), **'~lichkeit** f awkwardness, clumsiness, maladroitness; **'2t** adj. awkward, clumsy, maladroit.

**unge|schlacht** adj. ['ungəʃlaxt] hulking; uncouth; **'~schliffen** adj. unpolished, rough (both a. fig.); **'~schminkt** adj. not made up; fig. unvarnished.

**'ungesetzlich** adj. illegal, unlawful, illicit; **2keit** f (-/-en) illegality, unlawfulness.

**'unge|sittet** adj. uncivilized; unmannerly; **'~stört** adj. undisturbed, uninterrupted; **'~straft 1.** adj. unpunished; **2.** adv. with impunity; ~ davonkommen get off or escape scot-free.

**ungestüm** ['ungəʃty:m] **1.** adj. impetuous; violent; **2.** 2 n (-[e]s/no pl.) impetuosity; violence.

**'unge|sund** adj. climate: unhealthy; appearance: a. unwholesome; food: unwholesome; **'~teilt** adj. undivided (a. fig.); **~trübt** adj. ['~try:pt] untroubled; unmixed; **2tüm** ['~ty:m] n (-[e]s/-e) monster; **~übt** adj. ['~'y:pt] untrained; inexperienced; **'~waschen** adj. unwashed.

**'ungewiß** adj. uncertain; j-n im ungewissen lassen keep s.o. in suspense; **'2heit** f (-/~-en) uncertainty; suspense.

**'unge|wöhnlich** adj. unusual, uncommon; **'~wohnt** adj. unaccustomed; unusual; **'~zählt** adj. numberless, countless; **2ziefer** ['~tsi:fər] n (-s/-) vermin; **'~ziemend** adj. improper, unseemly; **'~zogen** adj. ill-bred, rude, uncivil; child: naughty; **'~zügelt** adj. unbridled.

**'ungezwungen** adj. unaffected, easy; **'2heit** f (-/~-en) unaffectedness, ease, easiness.

**'Unglaube(n)** m unbelief, disbelief.

**'ungläubig** adj. incredulous, unbelieving (a. eccl.); infidel; **'2e** m, f unbeliever; infidel.

**unglaub|lich** adj. [un'glauplic] incredible; **'~würdig** adj. p. untrustworthy; thing: incredible; **~e Geschichte** cock-and-bull story.

**'ungleich 1.** adj. unequal, different; uneven; unlike; **2.** adv. (by) far, much; **'~artig** adj. heterogeneous; **'2heit** f difference, inequality; unevenness; unlikeness; **'~mäßig** adj. uneven; irregular.

**'Unglück** n (-[e]s/~-e) misfortune; bad or ill luck; accident; calamity, disaster; misery; **'2lich** adj. unfortunate, unlucky; unhappy; **2~licher'weise** adv. unfortunately;

unluckily; **'2selig** adj. unfortunate; disastrous.

**'Unglücks|fall** m misadventure; accident; **'~rabe** F m unlucky fellow.

**'Un|gnade** f (-/no pl.) disgrace, disfavo(u)r; in ~ fallen bei fall into disgrace with, incur s.o.'s disfavo(u)r; **'2gnädig** adj. ungracious, unkind.

**'ungültig** adj. invalid; ticket: not available; money: not current; **~** (null and) void; **'2keit** f invalidity; **~** a. voidness.

**'Un|gunst** f disfavo(u)r; inclemency (of weather); zu meinen ~en to my disadvantage; **'2günstig** adj. unfavo(u)rable; disadvantageous.

**'un|gut** adj.: ~es Gefühl misgiving; nichts für ~! no offen|ce, Am. -se!; **'~haltbar** adj. shot: unstoppable; theory, etc.: untenable; **'~handlich** adj. unwieldy, bulky.

**'Unheil** n mischief; disaster, calamity; **'2bar** adj. incurable; **'2voll** adj. sinister, ominous.

**'unheimlich 1.** adj. uncanny (a. fig.), weird; sinister; F fig. tremendous, terrific; **2.** F fig. adv.: ~ viel heaps of, an awful lot of.

**'unhöflich** adj. impolite, uncivil; **'2keit** f impoliteness, incivility.

**Unhold** ['unholt] m (-[e]s/-e) fiend.

**'un|hörbar** adj. inaudible; **'~hygienisch** adj. unsanitary, insanitary.

**Uni** ['uni] f (-/-s) F varsity.

**Uniform** [uni'fɔrm] f (-/-en) uniform.

**Unikum** ['u:nikum] n (-s/Unika, -s) unique (thing); queer fellow.

**uninteress|ant** adj. ['unʔ-] uninteresting, boring; **'~iert** adj. uninterested (an dat. in).

**Universität** [univerzi'tɛ:t] f (-/-en) university.

**Universum** [uni'verzum] n (-s/no pl.) universe.

**Unke** ['unkə] f (-/-n) zo. fire-bellied toad; F fig. croaker; **'2n** F v/i. (ge-, h) croak.

**'unkennt|lich** adj. unrecognizable; **'2lichkeit** f (-/no pl.): bis zur ~ past all recognition; **'2nis** f (-/no pl.) ignorance.

**'unklar** adj. not clear; meaning, etc.: obscure; answer, etc.: vague; im ~en sein be in the dark (über acc. about); **'2heit** f want of clearness; vagueness; obscurity.

**'unklug** adj. imprudent, unwise.

**'Unkosten** pl. cost(s pl.), expenses pl.; sich in (große) ~ stürzen go to great expense.

**'Unkraut** n weed.

**un|kündbar** adj. ['unkyntbɑːr] loan, etc.: irredeemable; employment: permanent; **~kundig** adj. ['~kundiç] ignorant (gen. of); **'~längst**

*adv.* lately, recently, the other day; '~lauter *adj. competition*: unfair; '~leidlich *adj.* intolerable, insufferable; '~leserlich *adj.* illegible; ~leugbar *adj.* ['~ɔykba:r] undeniable; '~logisch *adj.* illogical; '~lösbar *adj.* unsolvable, insoluble.

'Unlust *f* (*-/no pl.*) reluctance (*zu inf.* to *inf.*); '2ig *adj.* reluctant.

'un|manierlich *adj.* unmannerly; '~männlich *adj.* unmanly; ~maßgeblich *adj.* ['~ge:plɪç]: *nach m-r ~en Meinung* in my humble opinion; '~mäßig *adj.* immoderate; intemperate; '2menge *f* enormous *or* vast quantity *or* number.

'Unmensch *m* monster, brute; '2lich *adj.* inhuman, brutal; '~lichkeit *f* inhumanity, brutality.

'un|mißverständlich *adj.* unmistakable; '~mittelbar *adj.* immediate, direct; '~möbliert *adj.* unfurnished; '~modern *adj.* unfashionable, outmoded.

'unmöglich *adj.* impossible; '2keit *f* impossibility.

'Unmoral *f* immorality; '2isch *adj.* immoral.

'unmündig *adj.* under age.

'un|musikalisch *adj.* unmusical; '2mut *m* (*-[e]s/no pl.*) displeasure (*über acc.* at, over); '~nachahmlich *adj.* inimitable; '~nachgiebig *adj.* unyielding; '~nachsichtig *adj.* strict, severe; inexorable; ~'nahbar *adj.* inaccessible, unapproachable; '~natürlich *adj.* unnatural; affected; '~nötig *adj.* unnecessary; needless; '~nütz *adj.* useless; ~ordentlich *adj.* ['un⁹-] untidy; *room, etc.*: *a.* disorderly; 2ordnung ['un⁹-] *f* disorder, mess.

'unpartei|isch *adj.* impartial, unbias(s)ed; '2ische *m* (*-n/-n*) referee; umpire; '2lichkeit *f* impartiality.

'un|passend *adj.* unsuitable; improper; inappropriate; '~passierbar *adj.* impassable.

unpäßlich *adj.* ['unpeslɪç] indisposed, unwell; '2keit *f* (*-/-en*) indisposition.

'un|persönlich *adj.* impersonal (*a. gr.*); '~politisch *adj.* unpolitical; '~praktisch *adj.* unpractical, *Am. a.* impractical; '~rat *m* (*-[e]s/no pl.*) filth; rubbish; ~ *wittern* smell a rat.

'unrecht **1.** *adj.* wrong; ~ *haben* be wrong; *j-m* ~ *tun* wrong s.o.; **2.** 2 *n* (*-[e]s/no pl.*): *mit or zu* ~ wrongly; *ihm ist* ~ *geschehen* he has been wronged; '~mäßig *adj.* unlawful; '2mäßigkeit *f* unlawfulness.

'unreell *adj.* dishonest; unfair.

'unregelmäßig *adj.* irregular (*a. gr.*); '2keit *f* (*-/-en*) irregularity.

'unreif *adj.* unripe, immature (*both a. fig.*); '2e *f* unripeness, immaturity (*both a. fig.*).

'un|rein *adj.* impure (*a. eccl.*); unclean (*a. fig.*); '~reinlich *adj.* uncleanly; ~'rettbar *adv.*: ~ *verloren* irretrievably lost; '~richtig *adj.* incorrect, wrong.

Unruh ['unru:] *f* (*-/-en*) balance (-wheel); '~e *f* (*-/-n*) restlessness, unrest (*a. pol.*); uneasiness; disquiet(ude); flurry; alarm; ~n *pl.* disturbances *pl.*, riots *pl.*; '2ig *adj.* restless; uneasy; *sea*: rough, choppy.

'unrühmlich *adj.* inglorious.

uns *pers. pron.* [uns] us; *dat.*: *a.* to us; ~ (*selbst*) ourselves, *after prp.*: us; *ein Freund von* ~ a friend of ours.

'un|sachgemäß *adj.* inexpert; '~sachlich *adj.* not objective; personal; ~säglich *adj.* [~'ze:klɪç] unspeakable; untold; '~sanft *adj.* ungentle; '~sauber *adj.* dirty; *fig. a.* unfair (*a. sports*); '~schädlich *adj.* innocuous, harmless; '~scharf *adj.* blurred; *pred. a.* out of focus; ~'schätzbar *adj.* inestimable, invaluable; '~scheinbar *adj.* plain, *Am. a.* homely.

'unschicklich *adj.* improper, indecent; '2keit *f* (*-/-en*) impropriety, indecency.

unschlüssig *adj.* ['unʃlysɪç] irresolute; '2keit *f* (*-/no pl.*) irresoluteness, irresolution.

'un|schmackhaft *adj.* insipid; unpalatable, unsavo(u)ry; '~schön *adj.* unlovely, unsightly; *fig.* unpleasant.

'Unschuld *f* (*-/no pl.*) innocence; '2ig *adj.* innocent (*an dat.* of).

'unselbständig *adj.* dependent (on others); '2keit *f* (lack of in)dependence.

unser ['unzər] **1.** *poss. pron.* our; *der* (*die, das*) ~*e* ours; *die* ~*en pl.* our relations *pl.*; **2.** *pers. pron.* of us; *wir waren* ~ *drei* there were three of us.

'unsicher *adj.* unsteady; unsafe, insecure; uncertain; '2heit *f* unsteadiness; insecurity, unsafeness; uncertainty.

'unsichtbar *adj.* invisible.

'Unsinn *m* (*-[e]s/no pl.*) nonsense; '2ig *adj.* nonsensical.

'Unsitt|e *f* bad habit; abuse; '2lich *adj.* immoral; indecent (*a. 𝔷𝔷*); '~lichkeit *f* (*-/-en*) immorality.

'un|solid(e) *adj. p.* easy-going; *life*: dissipated; † unreliable; '~sozial *adj.* unsocial, antisocial; '~sportlich *adj.* unsportsmanlike; unfair (*gegenüber* to).

'unstatthaft *adj.* inadmissible.

'unsterblich *adj.* immortal.

'Un'sterblichkeit *f* immortality.

'un|stet *adj.* unsteady; *character, life*: unsettled; 2stimmigkeit ['~ʃtimiçkaıt] *f* (*-/-en*) discrepancy; dissension; ~'sträflich *adj.* blameless; '**.streitig** *adj.* incontestable; '**.sympathisch** *adj.* disagreeable; er ist mir ~ I don't like him; '**.tätig** *adj.* inactive; idle.

'**untauglich** *adj.* unfit (a. ⚔); unsuitable; '**2keit** *f* (-/no *pl.*) unfitness (a. ⚔).

**un'teilbar** *adj.* indivisible.

**unten** *adv.* ['untən] below; downstairs; *von oben bis* ~ from top to bottom.

**unter** ['untər] **1.** *prp.* (*dat.*; *acc.*) below, under; among; ~ *anderem* among oth·r things; ~ *zehn Mark* (for) less than ten marks; ~ *Null* below zero; ~ *aller Kritik* beneath contempt; ~ *diesem Gesichtspunkt* from this point of view; **2.** *adj.* lower; interio·; *die* ~*en Räume* the downstair(s) rooms.

**Unter|abteilung** ['untər⁹-] *f* subdivision; **.arm** ['untər⁹-] *m* forearm; '**.bau** *m* (-[e]s/-ten) △ substructure (a. 🏛), foundation.

**unter|'bieten** *v/t.* (*irr.* bieten, no -ge-, h) underbid; ✝ undercut; undersell (*competitor*); lower (*record*); '**.binden** *v/t.* (*irr.* binden, no -ge-, h) ✂ ligature; *fig.* stop; **.'bleiben** *v/t.* (*irr.* bleiben, no -ge-, sein) remain undone; not to take place.

**unter'brech|en** *v/t.* (*irr.* brechen, no -ge-, h) interrupt (a. ✂); break, *Am. a.* stop over; ✂ break (*circuit*); **2ung** *f* (-/-en) interruption; break, *Am. a.* stopover. [mit.|

**unter'breiten** *v/t.* (no -ge-, h) sub-|

'**unterbring|en** *v/t.* (*irr.* bringen, sep., -ge-, h) place (a. ✝); accommodate, lodge; **2ung** *f* ( / un) accommodation; ✝ placement.

**unterdessen** *adv.* [untər'desən] (in the) meantime, meanwhile.

**unter'drück|en** *v/t.* (no -ge-, h) oppress (*subjects*, *etc.*); repress (*revolt*, *sneeze*, *etc.*); suppress (*rising*, *truth*, *yawn*, *etc.*); put down (*rebellion*, *etc.*); **2ung** *f* (-/-en) oppression; repression; suppression; putting down.

**unterernähr|t** *adj.* ['untər⁹-] underfed, undernourished; '**2ung** *f* (-/no *pl.*) underfeeding, malnutrition.

**Unter'führung** *f* subway, *Am.* underpass.

'**Untergang** *m* (-[e]s/⚓ ~e) *ast.* setting; ⚓ sinking; *fig.* ruin.

**Unter'gebene** *m* (-n/-n) inferior, subordinate; *contp.* underling.

'**untergehen** *v/i.* (*irr.* gehen, sep., -ge-, sein) *ast.* set; ⚓ sink, founder; *fig.* be ruined.

**untergeordnet** *adj.* [untərgə⁹ordnət] subordinate; *importance*: secondary.

'**Untergewicht** *n* (-[e]s/no *pl.*) underweight.

**unter'graben** *fig. v/t.* (*irr.* graben, no -ge-, h) undermine.

'**Untergrund** *m* (-[e]s/no *pl.*) subsoil; '**.bahn** *f* underground (railway), *in London*: tube; *Am.* subway; '**.bewegung** *f* underground movement.

'**unterhalb** *prp.* (*gen.*) below, underneath.

'**Unterhalt** *m* (-[e]s/no *pl.*) support, subsistence, livelihood; maintenance.

**unter'halt|en** *v/t.* (*irr.* halten, no -ge-, h) maintain; support; entertain, amuse; *sich* ~ converse (*mit* with; *über* acc. on, about), talk (with; on, about); *sich gut* ~ enjoy o.s.; **2ung** *f* maintenance, upkeep; conversation, talk; entertainment.

'**Unterhändler** *m* negotiator; ⚔ Parlementär.

'**Unter|haus** *parl. n* (-es/no *pl.*) House of Commons; '**.hemd** *n* vest, undershirt; '**.holz** *n* (-es/no *pl.*) underwood, brushwood; '**.hose** *f* (e-e a pair of) drawers *pl.*, pants *pl.*; **2irdisch** *adj.* subterranean, underground (*both a. fig.*).

**unter'joch|en** *v/t.* (no -ge-, h) subjugate, subdue; **2ung** *f* (-/-en) subjugation.

'**Unter|kiefer** *m* lower jaw; '**.kleid** *n* slip; '**.kleidung** *f* underclothes *pl.*, underclothing, underwear.

'**unterkommen 1.** *v/i.* (*irr.* kommen, sep., -ge-, sein) find accommodation; find employment; **2.** **2** *n* (-s/⚓ ~) accommodation; employment, situation.

'**unter|kriegen** **F** *v/t.* (sep., -ge-, h) bring to heel; *sich nicht* ~ *lassen* not to knuckle down *or* under; **2kunft** ['-kunft] *f* (-/⚓ -künfte) accommodation, lodging; ⚔ quarters *pl.*; '**2lage** *f* base; pad; *fig.*: voucher; ~*n pl.* documents *pl.*; data *pl.*

**unter'lass|en** *v/t.* (*irr.* lassen, no -ge-, h) omit (zu tun doing, to do); neglect (to do, doing); fail (to do); **2ung** *f* (-/-en) omission; neglect; failure; **2ungssünde** *f* sin of omission.

'**unterlegen¹** *v/t.* (sep., -ge-, h) lay *or* put under; give (*another meaning*).

**unter'legen²** *adj.* inferior (*dat.* to); **2e** *m* (-n/-n) loser; underdog; **2heit** *f* (-/no *pl.*) inferiority.

'**Unterleib** *m* abdomen, belly.

**unter'liegen** *v/i.* (*irr.* liegen, no -ge-, sein) be overcome (*dat.* by); be defeated (by); *sports*: a. lose (to); *fig.*: be subject to; be liable to; *es unterliegt keinem Zweifel, daß* ... there is no doubt that ...

'**Unter|lippe** *f* lower lip; '**.mieter** *m* subtenant, lodger, *Am. a.* roomer.

**unter'nehmen 1.** *v/t.* (*irr.* nehmen, no -ge-, h) undertake; take (*steps*);

2. 2 *n* (-s/-) enterprise; ✝ *a.* business; ✕ operation.

**unter'nehm|end** *adj.* enterprising; **2er** ✝ *m* (-s/-) entrepreneur; contractor; employer; **2ung** *f* (-/-en) enterprise, undertaking; ✕ operation; **~ungslustig** *adj.* enterprising.

**'Unter|offizier** ✕ *m* non-commissioned officer; **2ordnen** *v/t.* (*sep.*, *-ge-*, h) subordinate (*dat.* to); **sich ~** submit (to).

**Unter'redung** *f* (-/-en) conversation, conference.

**Unterricht** ['untərriçt] *m* (-[e]s/✕ -e) instruction, lessons *pl.*

**unter'richten** *v/t.* (*no -ge-*, h): **~ in** (*dat.*) instruct in, teach (*English*, etc.); **~ von** inform *s.o.* of.

**'Unterrichts|ministerium** *n* ministry of education; **'~stunde** *f* lesson, (teaching) period; **'~wesen** *n* (-s/*no pl.*) education; teaching.

**'Unterrock** *m* slip.

**unter'sagen** *v/t.* (*no -ge-*, h) forbid (*j-m et. s.o. to do s.th.*).

**'Untersatz** *m* stand; saucer.

**unter'schätzen** *v/t.* (*no -ge-*, h) undervalue; underestimate, underrate.

**unter'scheid|en** *v/t. and v/i.* (*irr. scheiden*, *no -ge-*, h) distinguish (*zwischen* between; *von* from); **sich ~** differ (*von* from); **2ung** *f* distinction.

**'Unterschenkel** *m* shank.

**'unterschieb|en** *v/t.* (*irr. schieben*, *sep.*, *-ge-*, h) push under; *fig.*: attribute (*dat.* to); substitute (*statt* for); **2ung** *f* substitution.

**Unterschied** ['untərʃiːt] *m* (-[e]s/-e) difference; distinction; **zum ~ von** in distinction from *or* to; **2lich** *adj.* different; differential; variable, varying; **2slos** *adj.* indiscriminate; undiscriminating.

**unter'schlag|en** *v/t.* (*irr. schlagen*, *no -ge-*, h) embezzle; suppress (*truth*, etc.); **2ung** *f* (-/-en) embezzlement; suppression.

**'Unterschlupf** *m* (-[e]s/ᵘe, -e) shelter, refuge.

**unter'schreiben** *v/t. and v/i.* (*irr. schreiben*, *no -ge-*, h) sign.

**'Unterschrift** *f* signature.

**'Untersee|boot** ⚓, ✕ *n s.* U-Boot; **'~kabel** *n* submarine cable.

**unter'setzt** *adj.* thick-set, squat.

**unterst** *adj.* ['untərst] lowest, undermost.

**'Unterstand** ✕ *m* shelter, dug-out.

**unter'stehen** (*irr. stehen*, *no -ge-*, h) 1. *v/i.* (*dat.*) be subordinate to; be subject to (*law*, etc.); 2. *v/refl.* dare; *untersteh dich!* don't you dare!; **~stellen** *v/t.* 1. ['~ʃtelən] (*sep.*, *-ge-*, h) put *or* place under; garage (*car*); **sich ~** take shelter (*vor dat.* from); 2. [~'ʃtelən] (*no -ge-*, h) (pre)suppose, assume; impute (*dat.*

to); *j-m ~* ✕ put (*troops*, etc.) under *s.o.*'s command; **2'stellung** *f* (-/-en) assumption, supposition; imputation; **~streichen** *v/t.* (*irr. streichen*, *no -ge-*, h) underline, underscore (*both a. fig.*).

**unter'stütz|en** *v/t.* (*no -ge-*, h) support; back up; **2ung** *f* (-/-en) support (*a.* ✕); assistance, aid; relief.

**unter'such|en** *v/t.* (*no -ge-*, h) examine (*a.* ⚕); inquire into, investigate (*a.* ⚕); explore; ⚕ try; analy|se, *Am.* -ze (*a.* ⚗); **2ung** *f* (-/-en) examination (*a.* ⚕); inquiry (*gen.* into), investigation (*a.* ⚕); exploration; analysis (*a.* ⚗).

**Unter'suchungs|gefangene** *m* prisoner on remand; **~gefängnis** *n* remand prison; **~haft** *f* detention on remand; **~richter** *m* investigating judge.

**Untertan** ['untərtaːn] *m* (-s, -en/ -en) subject.

**untertänig** *adj.* ['untərtɛːniç] submissive.

**'Unter|tasse** *f* saucer; **2tauchen** (*sep.*, *-ge-*) 1. *v/i.* (*sein*) dive, dip; duck; *fig.* disappear; 2. *v/t.* (h) duck.

**'Unterteil** *n*, *m* lower part.

**unter'teil|en** *v/t.* (*no -ge-*, h) subdivide; **2ung** *f* subdivision.

**'Unter|titel** *m* subheading; subtitle; *a.* caption (*of film*); **'~ton** *m* undertone; **2vermieten** *v/t.* (*no -ge-*, h) sublet.

**unter'wander|n** *pol. v/t.* (*no -ge-*, h) infiltrate; **2ung** *pol. f* infiltration.

**'Unterwäsche** *f s.* Unterkleidung.

**unterwegs** *adv.* [untər've:ks] on the *or* one's way.

**unter'weis|en** *v/t.* (*irr. weisen*, *no -ge-*, h) instruct (*in dat.* in); **2ung** *f* instruction.

**'Unterwelt** *f* underworld (*a. fig.*).

**unter'werf|en** *v/t.* (*irr. werfen*, *no -ge-*, h) subdue (*dat.* to), subjugate (to); subject (to); submit (to); **sich ~** submit (to); **2ung** *f* (-/-en) subjugation, subjection; submission (*unter acc.* to).

**unterworfen** *adj.* [untər'vɔrfən] subject (*dat.* to).

**unterwürfig** *adj.* [untər'vyrfiç] submissive; subservient; **2keit** *f* (-/*no pl.*) submissiveness; subservience.

**unter'zeichn|en** *v/t.* (*no -ge-*, h) sign; **2er** *m* signer, *the* undersigned; subscriber (*gen.* to); signatory (*gen.* to *treaty*); **2erstaat** *m* signatory state; **2ete** *m*, *f* (-n/-n) *the* undersigned; **2ung** *f* signature, signing.

**unter'ziehen** *v/t.* (*irr. ziehen*) 1. ['~tsiːən] (*sep.*, *-ge-*, h) put on underneath; 2. [~'tsiːən] (*no -ge-*, h) subject (*dat.* to); *sich e-r Operation ~* undergo an operation; *sich e-r Prüfung ~* go in *or* sit for an examination; *sich der Mühe ~ zu inf.* take the trouble to *inf.*

'**Untiefe** *f* shallow, shoal.
'**Untier** *n* monster (*a. fig.*).
**un|tilgbar** *adj.* [un'tilkbɑːr] indelible; † *government annuities*: irredeemable; ~'**tragbar** *adj.* unbearable, intolerable; *costs*: prohibitive; ~'**trennbar** *adj.* inseparable.
'**untreu** *adj.* untrue (*dat.* to), disloyal (to); *husband*, *wife*: unfaithful (to); '~e *f* disloyalty; unfaithfulness, infidelity.
**un|'tröstlich** *adj.* inconsolable, disconsolate; ~**trüglich** *adj.* [~'tryːk-liç] infallible, unerring.
'**Untugend** *f* vice, bad habit.
**unüber|legt** *adj.* [ˈunˀyːbər-] inconsiderate, thoughtless; ~**sicht-lich** *adj.* badly arranged; difficult to survey; involved; *mot. corner*: blind; ~'**trefflich** *adj.* unsurpassable; ~**windlich** *adj.* [~'vintliç] invincible; *fortress*: impregnable; *obstacle*, *etc.*: insurmountable; *difficulties*, *etc.*: insuperable.
**unum|gänglich** *adj.* [unˀumˈgɛnliç] absolutely necessary; ~**schränkt** *adj.* [~'frɛŋkt] absolute; ~**stößlich** *adj.* [~'ʃtøːsliç] irrefutable; incontestable; irrevocable; ~**wunden** *adj.* [ˈ~vundən] frank, plain.
**ununterbrochen** *adj.* [ˈunˀuntər-brɔxən] uninterrupted; incessant.
**unver|'änderlich** *adj.* unchangeable; invariable; ~'**antwortlich** *adj.* irresponsible; inexcusable; ~'**besserlich** *adj.* incorrigible; '~**bindlich** *adj.* not binding *or* obligatory; *answer*, *etc.*: non-committal; ~**blümt** *adj.* [~'blyːmt] plain, blunt; ~**bürgt** *adj.* [~'byrkt] unwarranted; *news*: unconfirmed; '~**dächtig** *adj.* unsuspected; '~**daulich** *adj.* indigestible (*a. fig.*); ~**dient** *adj.* undeserved; '~**dorben** *adj.* unspoiled, unspoilt; *fig.*: uncorrupted; pure, innocent; '~**drossen** *adj.* indefatigable, unflagging; '~**dünnt** *adj.* undiluted, *Am. a.* straight; ~'**einbar** *adj.* incompatible; '~**fälscht** *adj.* unadulterated; *fig.* genuine; ~**fänglich** *adj.* [ˈ~fɛn-liç] not captious; ~**froren** *adj.* [ˈ~froːrən] unabashed, impudent; '**Qfrorenheit** *f* (-/-*en*) impudence, F check; '~**gänglich** *adj.* imperishable; '~**geßlich** *adj.* unforgettable; ~'**gleichlich** *adj.* incomparable; '~**hältnismäßig** *adj.* disproportionate; '~**heiratet** *adj.* unmarried, single; '~**hofft** *adj.* unhoped-for, unexpected; ~**hohlen** *adj.* unconcealed; '~**käuflich** *adj.* unsal(e)able; not for sale; '~**kennbar** *adj.* unmistakable; ~'**letzbar** *adj.* invulnerable; *fig. a.* inviolable; ~**meidlich** *adj.* [~'martliç] inevitable; '~**mindert** *adj.* undiminished; '~**mittelt** *adj.* abrupt.

'**Unvermögen** *n* (-*s/no pl.*) inability; impotence; '**Qd** *adj.* impecunious, without means.
'**unvermutet** *adj.* unexpected.
'**Unver|nunft** *f* unreasonableness, absurdity; '**Qnünftig** *adj.* unreasonable, absurd; '**Qrichteterdinge** *adv.* without having achieved one's object.
'**unverschämt** *adj.* impudent, impertinent; '**Qheit** *f* (-/-*en*) impudence, impertinence.
'**unver|schuldet** *adj.* not in debt; through no fault of mine, *etc.*; '~**sehens** *adv.* unawares, suddenly, all of a sudden; ~**sehrt** *adj.* [ˈ~zeːrt] uninjured; ~**söhnlich** *adj.* implacable, irreconcilable; ~**sorgt** *adj.* unprovided for; '**Qstand** *m* injudiciousness; folly, stupidity; '~**ständig** *adj.* injudicious; foolish; ~**ständlich** *adj.* unintelligible; incomprehensible; *das ist mir* ~ that is beyond me; '~**sucht** *adj.*: *nichts* ~ *lassen* leave nothing undone; '~**träglich** *adj.* unsociable; quarrelsome; '~**wandt** *adj.* steadfast; ~**wundbar** *adj.* [~'vuntbɑːr] invulnerable; ~**wüstlich** *adj.* [~'vyːstliç] indestructible; *fig.* irrepressible; ~**zagt** *adj.* [ˈ~tsɑːkt] intrepid, undaunted; ~'**zeihlich** *adj.* unpardonable; ~'**zinslich** *adj.* bearing no interest; non-interest-bearing; ~**züglich** *adj.* [~'tsyːkliç] immediate, instant.
'**unvollendet** *adj.* unfinished.
'**unvollkommen** *adj.* imperfect; '**Qheit** *f* imperfection.
'**unvollständig** *adj.* incomplete; '**Qkeit** *f* (-/*no pl.*) incompleteness.
'**unvorbereitet** *adj.* unprepared; extempore.
'**unvoreingenommen** *adj.* unbias(s)ed, unprejudiced; '**Qheit** *f* freedom from prejudice.
'**unvor|hergesehen** *adj.* unforeseen; ~**schriftsmäßig** *adj.* irregular.
'**unvorsichtig** *adj.* incautious; imprudent; '**Qkeit** *f* incautiousness; imprudence.
**unvor|'stellbar** *adj.* unimaginable; '~**teilhaft** *adj.* unprofitable; *dress*, *etc.*: unbecoming.
'**unwahr** *adj.* untrue; '**Qheit** *f* untruth.
'**unwahrscheinlich** *adj.* improbable, unlikely; '**Qkeit** *f* (-/-*en*) improbability, unlikelihood.
'**un|wegsam** *adj.* pathless, impassable; '~**weit** *prp.* (*gen. or von*) not far from; '**Qwesen** *n* (-*s/no pl.*) nuisance; *sein* ~ *treiben* be up to one's tricks; '~**wesentlich** *adj.* unessential, immaterial (*für* to); '**Q-wetter** *n* thunderstorm; '~**wichtig** *adj.* unimportant, insignificant.
**unwider|legbar** *adj.* [unviːdər'leːk-

ba:r] irrefutable; ~'ruflich *adj.* irrevocable (a. ✝).

unwider'stehlich *adj.* irresistible; ♀keit *f* (-/no *pl.*) irresistibility.

unwieder'bringlich *adj.* irretrievable.

'Unwill|e *m* (-ns/no *pl.*), '~en *m* (-s/no *pl.*) indignation (*über acc.* at), displeasure (at, over); '♀ig *adj.* indignant (*über acc.* at), displeased (at, with); unwilling; '♀kürlich *adj.* involuntary.

'unwirklich *adj.* unreal.

'unwirksam *adj.* ineffective, inefficient; *laws, rules, etc.*: inoperative; ♀ inactive; '♀keit *f* (-/no *pl.*) ineffectiveness, inefficiency; ♀ inactivity.

unwirsch *adj.* ['unvirʃ] testy.

'unwirt|lich *adj.* inhospitable, desolate; '~schaftlich *adj.* uneconomic(al).

'unwissen|d *adj.* ignorant; '♀heit *f* (-/no *pl.*) ignorance; '~tlich *adj.* unwitting, unknowing.

'unwohl *adj.* unwell, indisposed; '♀sein *n* (-s/no *pl.*) indisposition.

'unwürdig *adj.* unworthy (*gen.* of).

un|'zählig *adj.* [un'tse:liç] innumerable; '♀zart *adj.* indelicate.

Unze ['untsə] *f* (-/-n) ounce.

'Unzeit *f:* zur ~ inopportunely; '♀gemäß *adj.* old-fashioned; inopportune; '♀ig *adj.* untimely; unseasonable; *fruit*: unripe.

unzer'brechlich *adj.* unbreakable; ~'reißbar *adj.* untearable; ~'störbar *adj.* indestructible; ~'trennlich *adj.* inseparable.

'un|ziemlich *adj.* unseemly; '♀zucht *f* (-/no *pl.*) lewdness; ⚥ sexual offen|ce, *Am.* -se; '~züchtig *adj.* lewd; obscene.

'unzufrieden *adj.* discontented (*mit* with), dissatisfied (with, at); '♀heit *f* discontent, dissatisfaction.

'unzugänglich *adj.* inaccessible.

unzulänglich *adj.* ['untsulɛŋliç] insufficient; '♀keit *f* (-/-en) insufficiency; shortcoming.

'unzulässig *adj.* inadmissible; *esp.* ⚥ *influence*: undue.

'unzurechnungsfähig *adj.* irresponsible; '♀keit *f* irresponsibility.

'unzu|reichend *adj.* insufficient; '~sammenhängend *adj.* incoherent; '~träglich *adj.* unwholesome; '~treffend *adj.* incorrect; inapplicable (*auf acc.* to).

'unzuverlässig *adj.* unreliable, untrustworthy; *friend*: a. uncertain; '♀keit *f* unreliability, untrustworthiness.

'unzweckmäßig *adj.* inexpedient; '♀keit *f* inexpediency.

'un|zweideutig *adj.* unequivocal; unambiguous; '~zweifelhaft 1. *adj.* undoubted, undubitable; 2. *adv.* doubtless.

üppig *adj.* ['ypiç] ♀ luxuriant, exuberant, opulent; *food*: luxurious, opulent; *figure*: voluptuous; '♀keit *f* (-/♀ -en) luxuriance, luxuriancy, exuberance; voluptuousness.

ur|alt *adj.* ['u:r⁹alt] very old; (as) old as the hills; ♀aufführung ['u:r⁹-] *f* world première.

Uran [u'ra:n] *n* (-s/no *pl.*) uranium.

urbar *adj.* ['u:rbɑ:r] arable, cultivable; ~ machen reclaim; '♀machung *f* (-/-en) reclamation.

'Ur|bevölkerung *f* aborigines *pl.*; '~bild *n* original, prototype; '♀-eigen *adj.* one's very own; '~enkel *m* great-grandson; '~großeltern *pl.* great-grandparents *pl.*; '~großmutter *f* great-grandmother; '~großvater *m* great-grandfather.

'Urheber *m* (-s/-) author; '~recht *n* copyright (*an dat.* in); '~schaft *f* (-/no *pl.*) authorship.

Urin [u'ri:n] *m* (-s/-e) urine; ♀ieren [.i'ni:rən] *v/i.* (no -ge-, h) urinate.

'Urkund|e *f* document; deed; '~enfälschung *f* forgery of documents; ♀lich *adj.* ['.tliç] documentary.

Urlaub ['u:rlaup] *m* (-[e]s/-e) leave (of absence) (*a.* ⚥); holiday(s *pl.*), *esp. Am.* vacation; '~er ['.bər] *m* (-s/-) holiday-maker, *esp. Am.* vacationist, vacationer.

Urne ['urnə] *f* (-/-n) urn; ballotbox.

'ur|plötzlich 1. *adj.* very sudden, abrupt; 2. *adv.* all of a sudden; '♀sache *f* cause; reason; *keine ~l* don't mention it, *Am. a.* you are welcome; '~sächlich *adj.* causal; '♀schrift *f* original (text); '♀sprung *m* origin, source; ~ sprünglich *adj.* ['.ʃpryŋliç] original; '♀stoff *m* primary matter.

Urteil ['urtail] *n* (-s/-e) judg(e)-ment; ⚥ *a.* sentence; *meinem ~ nach* in my judg(e)ment; *sich ein ~ bilden* form a judg(e)ment (*über acc.* of, on); '♀en *v/i.* (ge-, h) judge (*über acc.* of; *nach* by, from); '~s-kraft *f* (-/♀ -e) discernment.

'Ur|text *m* original (text); '~wald *m* primeval or virgin forest; ♀-wüchsig *adj.* ['~vy:ksiç] original; *fig.*: natural; rough; '~zeit *f* primitive times *pl.*

Utensilien [uten'zi:ljən] *pl.* utensils *pl.*

Utop|ie [uto'pi:] *f* (-/-n) Utopia; ♀isch *adj.* [u'to:piʃ] Utopian, utopian.

# V

**Vagabund** [vaga'bunt] m (-en/-en) vagabond, vagrant, tramp, *Am.* hobo, F bum.

**Vakuum** ['va:ku⁹um] n (-s/*Vakua, Vakuen*) vacuum.

**Valuta** ✝ [va'lu:ta] f (-/*Valuten*) value; currency.

**Vanille** [va'niljə] f (-/*no pl.*) vanilla.

**variabel** adj. [vari'a:bəl] variable.

**Varia|nte** [vari'antə] f (-/-n) variant; **~tion** [~'tsjo:n] f (-/-en) variation.

**Varieté** [varie'te:] n (-s/-s), **~theater** n variety theatre, music-hall, *Am.* vaudeville theater.

**variieren** [vari'i:rən] v/i. and v/t. (*no -ge-, h*) vary.

**Vase** ['va:zə] f (-/-n) vase.

**Vater** ['fɑ:tər] m (-s/⸚) father; '**~land** n native country *or* land, mother country; '**~landsliebe** f patriotism.

**väterlich** adj. ['fɛ:tərliç] fatherly, paternal.

'**Vater|schaft** f (-/*no pl.*) paternity, fatherhood; '**~uuser** eccl. n (-s/-) Lord's Prayer.

**Vati** ['fɑ:ti] m (-s/-s) dad(dy).

**Veget|arier** [vege'tɑ:rjər] m (-s/-) vegetarian; **~arisch** adj. vegetarian; **~ation** [~a'tsjo:n] f (-/-en) vegetation; **~ieren** [~'ti:rən] v/i. (*no -ge-, h*) vegetate.

**Veilchen** ♀ ['faɪlçən] n (-s/-) violet.

**Vene** anat. ['ve:nə] f (-/-n) vein.

**Ventil** [vɛn'ti:l] n (-s/-e) valve (a. ♪); ♪ stop (*of organ*); fig. vent, outlet; **~ation** [~ila'tsjo:n] f (-/-en) ventilation; **~ator** [~i'lɑ:tər] m (-s/-en) ventilator, fan.

**verab|folgen** [fɛr'ap-] v/t. (*no -ge-, h*) deliver, ✗ administer (*medicine*); **~reden** v/t. (*no -ge-, h*) agree upon, arrange; appoint, fix (*time, place*); *sich* ~ make an appointment, *Am.* F (have a) date; ♀**redung** f (-/-en) agreement; arrangement; appointment, *Am.* F date; **~reichen** v/t. (*no -ge-, h*) s. verabfolgen; **~scheuen** v/t. (*no -ge-, h*) abhor, detest, loathe; **~schieden** [~ʃi:dən] v/t. (*no -ge-, h*) dismiss; retire (*officer*); ✗ discharge (*troops*); parl. pass (*bill*); *sich* ~ take leave (von of), say goodbye (to); ♀**schiedung** f (-/-en) dismissal; discharge; passing.

**ver|'achten** v/t. (*no -ge-, h*) despise; **~ächtlich** adj. [~'ɛçtliç] contemptuous; contemptible; ♀'**achtung** f contempt; **~allgemeinern** [~⁹algə'maɪnərn] v/t. (*no -ge-, h*) generalize; **~'altet** adj. antiquated, obsolete, out of date.

**Veranda** [ve'randa] f (-/*Veranden*) veranda(h), *Am. a.* porch.

**veränder|lich** adj. [fɛr'ɛndərliç] changeable; variable (a. ♉, gr.); **~n** v/t. and v/refl. (*no -ge-, h*) alter, change; vary; ♀**ung** f change, alteration (*in dat.* in; *an dat.* to); variation.

**verängstigt** [fɛr'ɛŋstiçt] intimidated, scared.

**ver'anlag|en** v/t. (*no -ge-, h*) of *taxation*: assess; **~t** adj. [~kt] talented; ♀**ung** f (-/-en) assessment; fig. talent(s *pl.*); 💉 predisposition.

**ver'anlass|en** v/t. (*no -ge-, h*) cause, occasion; arrange; ♀**ung** f (-/-en) occasion, cause; *auf m-e* ~ at my request *or* suggestion.

**ver|'anschaulichen** v/t. (*no -ge-, h*) illustrate; **~'anschlagen** v/t. (*no -ge-, h*) rate, value, estimate (*all: auf acc.* at).

**ver'anstalt|en** v/t. (*no -ge-, h*) arrange, organize; give (*concert, ball, etc.*); ♀**ung** f (-/-en) arrangement; event; *sports*: event, meeting, *Am.* meet.

**ver'antwort|en** v/t. (*no -ge-, h*) take the responsibility for; account for; **~lich** adj. responsible; *j-n* ~ *machen für* hold s.o. responsible for.

**Ver'antwortung** f (-/-en) responsibility; *die* ~ *tragen* be responsible; *zur* ~ *ziehen* call to account; ♀**slos** adj. irresponsible.

**ver|'arbeiten** v/t. (*no -ge-, h*) work up; ⊕ process, manufacture (*both: zu* into); digest (*food*) (a. fig.); **~'ägern** v/t. (*no -ge-, h*) vex, annoy.

**ver'arm|en** v/i. (*no -ge-, sein*) become poor; **~t** adj. impoverished.

**ver|'ausgaben** v/t. (*no -ge-, h*) spend (*money*); *sich* ~ run short of money; fig. spend o.s.; **~'äußern** v/t. (*no -ge-, h*) sell; alienate.

**Verb** gr. [vɛrp] n (-s/-en) verb.

**Ver'band** m (-[e]s/⸚e) 💉 dressing, bandage; association, union; ✗ formation, unit; **~(s)kasten** m first-aid box; **~(s)zeug** n dressing (material).

**ver'bann|en** v/t. (*no -ge-, h*) banish (a. fig.), exile; ♀**ung** f (-/-en) banishment, exile.

**ver|barrikadieren** [fɛrbarika'di:rən] v/t. (*no -ge-, h*) barricade; block (*street, etc.*); **~'bergen** v/t. (*irr.* bergen, *no -ge-, h*) conceal, hide.

**ver'besser|n** v/t. (*no -ge-, h*) improve; correct; ♀**ung** f improvement; correction.

**ver'beug|en** v/refl. (*no -ge-, h*) bow (*vor dat.* to); ♀**ung** f bow.

**ver|'biegen** v/t. (*irr.* biegen, *no*

-ge-, h) bend, twist, distort; ~
'**bieten** v/t. (irr. bieten, no -ge-, h)
forbid, prohibit; ~'**billigen** v/t.
(no -ge-, h) reduce in price,
cheapen.

ver'**bind|en** v/t. (irr. binden, no
-ge-, h) ⚕ dress; tie (together);
bind (up); link (mit to); join, unite,
combine; connect (a. teleph.);
teleph. put s.o. through (mit to);
j-m die Augen ~ blindfold s.o.; sich
~ join, unite, combine (a. 🜪); ich
bin Ihnen sehr verbunden I am
greatly obliged to you; falsch verbunden! wrong number!;
~lich adj. [~tliç] obligatory; obliging; 2lichkeit f (-/-en) obligation,
liability; obligingness, civility.

Ver'**bindung** f union; alliance;
combination; association (of ideas);
connexion, (Am. only) connection
(a. teleph., 🖂, ⚓, ⊕); relation;
communication (a. teleph.); 🜪
compound; geschäftliche ~ business relations pl.; teleph.: ~ bekommen (haben) get (be) through;
die ~ verlieren mit lose touch with;
in ~ bleiben (treten) keep (get) in
touch (mit with); sich in ~ setzen
mit communicate with, esp. Am.
contact s.o.; ~sstraße f communication road, feeder road; ~stür f
communication door.

ver|**bissen** adj. [fɛr'bisən] dogged;
crabbed; ~'**bitten** v/refl. (irr. bitten,
no -ge-, h): das verbitte ich mir!
I won't suffer or stand that!

ver'**bitter|n** v/t. (no -ge-, h) em-
bitter; 2ung f (-/~-en) bitterness
(of heart).

ver**blassen** [fɛr'blasən] v/i. (no
-ge-, sein) fade (a. fig.).

Ver**bleib** [fɛr'blaip] m (-[e]s/no pl.)
whereabouts sg., pl.; 2en [~bən] v/i.
(irr. bleiben, no -ge-, sein) be left,
remain.

ver'**blend|en** v/t. (no -ge-, h) △
face (wall, etc.); fig. blind, delude;
2ung f (-/~-en) △ facing; fig.
blindness, delusion. [faded.]

ver**blichen** adj. [fɛr'bliçən] colour:]

ver**blüff|en** [fɛr'blyfən] v/t. (no
-ge-, h) amaze; perplex; puzzle;
dumbfound; 2ung f (-/~-en)
amazement, perplexity.

ver|'**blühen** v/i. (no -ge-, sein) fade,
wither; ~'**bluten** v/i. (no -ge-, sein)
bleed to death.

ver'**borgen** adj. hidden; secret;
2heit f (-/no pl.) concealment;
secrecy.

Ver**bot** [fɛr'bo:t] n (-[e]s/-e) prohibition; 2en adj. forbidden, pro-
hibited; Rauchen ~ no smoking.

Ver'**brauch** m (-[e]s/~e) consumption (an dat. of); 2en v/t. (no
-ge-, h) consume, use up; wear out;
~er m (-s/-) consumer; 2t adj. air:
stale; p. worn out.

ver'**brechen 1.** v/t. (irr. brechen,
no -ge-, h) commit; was hat er ver-
brochen? what is his offen|ce, Am.
-se?, what has he done?; 2. 2 n
(-s/-) crime, offen|ce, Am. -se.

Ver'**brecher** m (-s/-) criminal;
2isch adj. criminal; ~tum n (-s/no
pl.) criminality.

ver'**breit|en** v/t. (no -ge-, h) spread,
diffuse; shed (light, warmth, happiness); sich ~ spread; sich ~ über
(acc.) enlarge (up)on (theme); ~ern
v/t. and v/refl. (no -ge-, h) widen,
broaden; 2ung f (-/~-en) spread
(-ing), diffusion.

ver'**brenn|en** (irr. brennen, no -ge-)
1. v/i. (sein) burn; 2. v/t. (h) burn
(up); cremate (corpse); 2ung f
(-/-en) burning, combustion;
cremation (of corpse); wound: burn.

ver'**bringen** v/t. (irr. bringen, no
-ge-, h) spend, pass.

ver**brüder|n** [fɛr'bry:dərn] v/refl.
(no -ge-, h) fraternize; 2ung f
(-/-en) fraternization.

ver|'**brühen** v/t. (no -ge-, h) scald;
sich ~ scald o.s.; ~'**buchen** v/t.
(no -ge-, h) book.

Ver**bum** gr. ['vɛrbum] n (-s/Verba)
verb.

ver**bünden** [fɛr'byndən] v/refl. (no
-ge-, h) ally o.s. (mit to, with).

Ver**bundenheit** [fɛr'bundənhaɪt] f
(-/no pl.) bonds pl., ties pl.; solidarity; affection.

Ver'**bündete** m, f (-n/-n) ally, con-
federate; die ~n pl. the allies pl.

ver|'**bürgen** v/t. (no -ge-, h) guar-
antee, warrant; sich ~ für answer
or vouch for; ~'**büßen** v/t. (no -ge-,
h): e-e Strafe ~ serve a sentence,
serve (one's) time.

Ver**dacht** [fɛr'daxt] m (-[e]s/no pl.)
suspicion; in ~ haben suspect.

ver**dächtig** adj. [fɛr'dɛçtiç] sus-
pected (gen. of); pred. suspect;
suspicious; ~en v/t. (no
-ge-, h) suspect s.o. (gen. of); cast
suspicion on; 2ung f (-/-en)
suspicion; insinuation.

ver**damm|en** [fɛr'damən] v/t. (no
-ge-, h) condemn, damn (a. eccl.);
2nis f (-/no pl.) damnation; ~t
1. adj. damned; F: ~! damn (it)!,
confound it!; 2. F adv.: ~ kalt
beastly cold; 2ung f (-/~-en) condemnation, damnation.

ver|'**dampfen** (no -ge-) v/t. (h) and
v/i. (sein) evaporate; ~'**danken** v/t.
(no -ge-, h): j-m et. ~ owe s.th. to
s.o.

ver**darb** [fɛr'darp] pret. of verderben.

ver**dau|en** [fɛr'dauən] v/t. (no -ge-,
h) digest; ~lich adj. digestible;
leicht ~ easy to digest, light; 2ung
f (-/no pl.) digestion; 2ungsstö-
rung f indigestion.

Ver'**deck** n (-[e]s/-e) ⚓ deck;

hood (of carriage, car, etc.); top (of vehicle); 2en v/t. (no -ge-, h) cover; conceal, hide.

ver'denken v/t. (irr. denken, no -ge-, h): ich kann es ihm nicht ~, daß I cannot blame him for ger.

Verderb [fer'dɛrp] m (-[e]s/no pl.) ruin; 2en [~bən] 1. v/i. (irr., no -ge-, sein) spoil (a. fig.); rot; meat, etc.: go bad; fig. perish; 2. v/t. (irr., no -ge-, h) spoil; fig. a.: corrupt; ruin; er will es mit niemandem ~ he tries to please everybody; sich den Magen ~ upset one's stomach; ~en [~bən] n (-s/no pl.) ruin; 2lich adj. [~pliç] pernicious; food: perishable; ~nis [~pnis] f (-/~-se) corruption; depravity; 2t adj. [~pt] corrupted, depraved.

ver|'deutlichen v/t. (no -ge-, h) make plain or clear; ~'dichten v/t. (no -ge-, h) condense; sich ~ condense; suspicion: grow stronger; ~'dicken v/t. and v/refl. (no -ge-, h) thicken; ~'dienen v/t. (no -ge-, h) merit, deserve; earn (money).

Ver'dienst (-es/-e) 1. m gain, profit; earnings pl.; 2. n merit; es ist sein ~, daß it is owing to him that; 2voll adj. meritorious, deserving; ~spanne † f profit margin.

ver|'dient adj. p. of merit; (well-) deserved; sich ~ gemacht haben um deserve well of; ~'dolmetschen v/t. (no -ge-, h) interpret (a. fig.); ~'doppeln v/t. and v/refl. (no -ge-, h) double.

verdorben [fer'dɔrbən] 1. p.p. of verderben; 2. adj. meat: tainted; stomach: disordered, upset; fig. corrupt, depraved.

ver|'dorren v/i. (no -ge-, sein) wither (up); ~'drängen v/t. (no -ge-, h) push away, thrust aside; fig. displace; psych. repress; ~'drehen v/t. (no -ge-, h) distort, twist (both a. fig.); roll (eyes); fig. pervert; j-m den Kopf ~ turn s.o.'s head; ~'dreht F fig. adj. crazy; ~'dreifachen v/t. and v/refl. (no -ge-, h) triple.

verdrieß|en [fer'dri:sən] v/t. (irr., no -ge-, h) vex, annoy; ~lich adj. vexed, annoyed, sulky; thing: annoying.

ver|droß [fer'drɔs] pret. of verdrießen; ~'drossen [~'drɔsən] 1. p.p. of verdrießen; 2. adj. sulky; listless.

ver'drucken typ. v/t. (no -ge-, h) misprint.

Verdruß [fer'drus] m (Verdrusses/~ Verdrusse) vexation, annoyance.

ver'dummen (no -ge-) 1. v/t. (h) make stupid; 2. v/i. (sein) become stupid.

ver'dunk|eln v/t. (no -ge-, h) darken, obscure (both a. fig.); black out (window); sich ~ darken;

2(e)lung f (-/~ -en) darkening; obscuration; black-out; ⚖ collusion.

ver|'dünnen v/t. (no -ge-, h) thin; dilute (liquid); ~'dunsten v/i. (no -ge-, sein) volatilize, evaporate; ~'dursten v/i. (no -ge-, sein) die of thirst; ~dutzt adj. [~'dutst] nonplussed.

ver'ed|eln v/t. (no -ge-, h) ennoble; refine; improve; ✿ graft; process (raw materials); 2(e)lung f (-/~ -en) refinement; improvement; processing.

ver'ehr|en v/t. (no -ge-, h) revere, venerate; worship; admire, adore; 2er m (-s/-) worship(p)er; admirer, adorer; 2ung f (-/~ -en) reverence, veneration; worship; adoration.

vereidigen [fer'aidigən] v/t. (no -ge-, h) swear (witness); at entrance into office: swear s.o. in.

Verein [fer'ain] m (-[e]s/-e) union; society, association; club.

ver'einbar adj. compatible (mit with), consistent (with); ~en v/t. (no -ge-, h) agree upon, arrange; 2ung f (-/-en) agreement, arrangement.

ver'einen v/t. (no -ge-, h) s. vereinigen.

ver'einfach|en v/t. (no -ge-, h) simplify; 2ung f (-/-en) simplification.

ver'einheitlichen v/t. (no -ge-, h) unify, standardize.

ver'einig|en v/t. (no -ge-, h) unite, join; associate; sich ~ unite, join; associate o.s.; 2ung f 1. (-/~ -en) union; 2. (-/-en) union; society, association.

ver'ein|samen v/i. (no -ge-, sein) grow lonely or solitary; ~zelt adj. isolated; sporadic.

ver|'eiteln v/t. (no -ge-, h) frustrate; ~'ekeln v/t. (no -ge-, h): er hat mir das Essen verekelt he spoilt my appetite; ~'enden v/i. (no -ge-, sein) animals: die, perish; ~enge(r)n [~'eŋə(r)n] v/t. and v/refl. (no -ge-, h) narrow.

ver'erb|en v/t. (no -ge-, h) leave, bequeath; biol. transmit; sich ~ be hereditary; sich ~ auf (acc.) descend (up)on; 2ung f (-/~ -en) biol. transmission; physiol. heredity; 2ungslehre f genetics.

verewig|en [fer'e:vigən] v/t. (no -ge-, h) perpetuate; ~t adj. [~çt] deceased, late.

ver'fahren 1. v/i. (irr. fahren, no -ge-, sein) proceed; ~ mit deal with; 2. v/t. (irr. fahren, no -ge-, h) mismanage, muddle, bungle; sich ~ miss one's way; 3. 2 n (-s/-) procedure; proceeding(s pl. ⚖); ⊕ process.

Ver'fall m (-[e]s/no pl.) decay, decline; dilapidation (of house, etc.);

**2/3** forfeiture; expiration; maturity (*of bill of exchange*); **2en 1.** *v/i.* (*irr. fallen, no -ge-, sein*) decay; *house*: dilapidate; *document, etc.*: expire; *pawn*: become forfeited; *right*: lapse; *bill of exchange*: fall due; *sick person*: waste away; ~ auf (*acc.*) hit upon (*idea, etc.*); ~ in (*acc.*) fall into; *j-m* ~ become s.o.'s slave; **2.** *adj.* ruinous; addicted (*dat.* to *drugs, etc.*); **~serscheinung** [fɛr'fals?-] *f* symptom of decline; **~tag** *m* day of payment.

ver|'fälschen *v/t.* (*no -ge-, h*) falsify; adulterate (*wine, etc.*); **~fänglich** *adj.* [~'fɛŋlɪç] *question*: captious, insidious; risky; embarrassing; **~'färben** *v/refl.* (*no -ge-, h*) change colo(u)r.

ver'fass|en *v/t.* (*no -ge-, h*) compose, write; **2er** *m* (*-s/-*) author.

Ver'fassung *f* state, condition; *pol.* constitution; disposition (*of mind*); **2smäßig** *adj.* constitutional; **2swidrig** *adj.* unconstitutional.

ver|'faulen *v/i.* (*no -ge-, sein*) rot, decay; **~'fechten** *v/t.* (*irr. fechten, no -ge-, h*) defend, advocate.

ver'fehl|en *v/t.* (*no -ge-, h*) miss; **2ung** *f* (*-/-en*) offen|ce, *Am.* -se.

ver|'feinden [fɛr'faɪndən] *v/t.* (*no -ge-, h*) make enemies of; *sich* ~ mit make an enemy of; **~feinern** [~'faɪnərn] *v/t. and v/refl.* (*no -ge-, h*) refine; **~'fertigen** [~'fɛrtɪgən] *v/t.* (*no -ge-, h*) make, manufacture; compose.

ver'film|en *v/t.* (*no -ge-, h*) film, screen; **2ung** *f* (*-/-en*) filmversion.

ver|'finstern *v/t.* (*no -ge-, h*) darken, obscure; *sich* ~ darken; **~'flachen** (*no -ge-*) *v/i.* (*sein*) *and v/refl.* (*h*) (become) shallow (*a. fig.*); **~'flechten** *v/t.* (*irr. flechten, no -ge-, h*) interlace; *fig.* involve; **~'fliegen** (*irr. fliegen, no -ge-*) **1.** *v/i.* (*sein*) evaporate; *time*: fly; *fig.* vanish; **2.** *v/refl.* (*h*) *bird*: stray; **⚡** lose one's bearings, get lost; **~'fließen** *v/i.* (*irr. fließen, no -ge-, sein*) *colours*: blend; *time*: elapse; **~flossen** *adj.* [~'flɔsən] *time*: past; **F** ein ~er Freund a late friend, an ex-friend.

ver'fluch|en *v/t.* (*no -ge-, h*) curse, *Am.* **F** cuss; **~t** *adj.* damned; **~!** damn (it)!, confound it!

ver|'flüchtigen [fɛr'flyçtɪgən] *v/t.* (*no -ge-, h*) volatilize; *sich* ~ evaporate (*a. fig.*); **F** *fig.* vanish; **~flüssigen** [~'flysɪgən] *v/t. and v/refl.* (*no -ge-, h*) liquefy.

ver'folg|en *v/t.* (*no -ge-, h*) pursue; persecute; follow (*tracks*); trace; *thoughts, dream*: haunt; *gerichtlich* ~ prosecute; **2er** *m* (*-s/-*) pursuer; persecutor; **2ung** *f* (*-/-en*) pursuit; persecution; pursuance; gericht

liche ~ prosecution; **2ungswahn** **♂** *m* persecution mania.

ver|'frachten [fɛr'fraxtən] *v/t.* (*no -ge-, h*) freight, *Am. a.* ship (*goods*); **⚓** ship; **F** *j-n* ~ in (*acc.*) bundle s.o. in(to) (*train, etc.*); **~'froren** *adj.* chilled through; **~'früht** *adj.* premature.

verfüg|bar *adj.* [fɛr'fy:kba:r] available; **~en** [~gən] (*no -ge-, h*) **1.** *v/t.* decree, order; **2.** *v/i.*: ~ über (*acc.*) have at one's disposal; dispose of; **2ung** [~guŋ] *f* (*-/-en*) decree, order; disposal; *j-m zur* ~ stehen (*stellen*) be (place) at s.o.'s disposal.

ver'führ|en *v/t.* (*no -ge-, h*) seduce; **2er** *m* (*-s/-*) seducer; **~erisch** *adj.* seductive; enticing, tempting; **2ung** *f* seduction.

vergangen *adj.* [fɛr'gaŋən] gone, past; *im* ~en *Jahr* last year; **2heit** *f* (*-/-en*) past; *gr.* past tense.

vergänglich *adj.* [fɛr'gɛŋlɪç] transient, transitory.

vergas|en [fɛr'ga:zən] *v/t.* (*no -ge-, h*) gasify; gas *s.o.*; **2er** *mot. m* (*-s/-*) carburet(t)or.

vergaß [fɛr'ga:s] *pret.* of vergessen.

ver'geb|en *v/t.* (*irr. geben, no -ge-, h*) give away (*an j-n* to s.o.); confer (on), bestow (on); place (*order*); forgive; *sich* et. ~ compromise one's dignity; **~ens** *adv.* [~s] in vain; **~lich** [~plɪç] **1.** *adj.* vain; **2.** *adv.* in vain; **2ung** [~buŋ] *f* (*-/*~*-en*) bestowal, conferment (*both*: an *acc.* on); forgiveness; pardon.

vergegenwärtigen [fɛrge:gən'vɛrtigən] *v/t.* (*no -ge-, h*) represent; *sich* et. ~ visualize s.th.

ver'gehen **1.** *v/i.* (*irr. gehen, no -ge-, sein*) pass (away); fade (away); ~ vor (*dat.*) die of; **2.** *v/refl.* (*irr. gehen, no -ge-, h*): sich an *j-m* ~ assault s.o.; violate s.o.; *sich gegen das Gesetz* ~ offend against or violate the law; **3.** **2** *n* (*-s/-*) offen|ce, *Am.* -se.

ver'gelt|en *v/t.* (*irr. gelten, no -ge-, h*) repay, requite; reward; retaliate; **2ung** *f* (*-/-en*) requital; retaliation, retribution.

vergessen [fɛr'gɛsən] **1.** *v/t.* (*irr., no -ge-, h*) forget; leave; **2.** *p.p.* of **1**; **2heit** *f* (*-/no pl.*): in ~ geraten sink or fall into oblivion.

vergeßlich *adj.* [fɛr'gɛslɪç] forgetful.

vergeud|en [fɛr'gɔydən] *v/t.* (*no -ge-, h*) dissipate, squander, waste (*time, money*); **2ung** *f* (*-/*~*-en*) waste.

vergewaltig|en [fɛrgə'valtɪgən] *v/t.* (*no -ge-, h*) violate; rape; **2ung** *f* (*-/-en*) violation; rape.

ver|gewissern [fɛrgə'wɪsərn] *v/refl.* (*no -ge-, h*) make sure (*e-r Sache* of s.th.); ~'**gießen** v/t. (irr. gießen, no -ge-, h) shed (tears, blood); spill (liquid).

ver'**gift|en** v/t. (no -ge-, h) poison (a. fig.); sich ~ take poison; 2ung f (-/-en) poisoning.

**Vergißmeinnicht** ♀ [fɛr'gɪsmannɪçt] n (-[e]s/-[e]) forget-me-not.

ver'**gittern** [fɛr'gɪtərn] v/t. (no -ge-, h) grate.

**Vergleich** [fɛr'glaɪç] m (-[e]s/-e) comparison; ♣ agreement; compromise, composition; 2bar adj. comparable (mit to); 2en v/t. (irr. gleichen, no -ge-, h) compare (mit with, to); sich ~ mit ♣ come to terms with; verglichen mit as against, compared to; 2sweise adv. comparatively.

ver'**gnügen** [fɛr'gny:gən] 1. v/t. (no -ge-, h) amuse; sich ~ enjoy o.s.; 2. 2 n (-s/-) pleasure, enjoyment; entertainment; ~ finden an (dat.) take pleasure in; viel ~! have a good time! [gay.\
ver'**gnügt** adj. [fɛr'gny:kt] merry,\
**Ver'gnügung** f (-/-en) pleasure, amusement, entertainment; ~sreise f pleasure-trip, tour; 2ssüchtig adj. pleasure-seeking.

ver'**golden** [fɛr'gɔldən] v/t. (no -ge-, h) gild; ~göttern fig. [~'gœtərn] v/t. (no -ge-, h) idolize, adore; ~graben v/t. (irr. graben, no -ge-, h) bury (a. fig.); sich ~ bury o.s.; ~greifen v/refl. (irr. greifen, no -ge-, h) sprain (one's hand, etc.); sich ~ an (dat.) lay (violent) hands on, attack, assault; embezzle (money); encroach upon (s.o.'s property); ~griffen adj. [~'grɪfən] goods: sold out; book: out of print.

ver'**größer|n** [fɛr'grø:sərn] v/t. (no -ge-, h) enlarge (a. phot.); opt. magnify; sich ~ enlarge; 2ung f 1. (-/-en) phot. enlargement; opt. magnification; 2. (-/♣-en) enlargement; increase; extension; 2ungsglas n magnifying glass.

**Vergünstigung** [fɛr'gʏnstɪgʊŋ] f (-/-en) privilege.

ver'**güt|en** [fɛr'gy:tən] v/t. (no -ge-, h) compensate (j-m et. s.o. for s.th.); reimburse (money spent); 2ung f (-/-en) compensation; reimbursement.

ver'**haft|en** v/t. (no -ge-, h) arrest; 2ung f (-/-en) arrest.

ver'**halten** 1. v/t. (irr. halten, no -ge-, h) keep back; catch or hold (one's breath); suppress, check; sich ~ thing: be; p. behave; sich ruhig ~ keep quiet; 2. 2 n (-s/no pl.) behavio(u)r, conduct.

**Verhältnis** [fɛr'hɛltnɪs] n (-ses/-se) proportion, rate; relation(s pl.) (zu with); F liaison, love-affair; F mistress; ~se pl. conditions pl., circumstances pl.; means pl.; 2mäßig

adv. in proportion; comparatively; ~wort gr. n (-[e]s/♣er) preposition.

**Ver'haltungsmaßregeln** f/pl. instructions pl.

ver'**hand|eln** (no -ge-, h) 1. v/i. negotiate, treat (über acc., wegen for); ♣ try (über et. s.th.); 2. v/t. discuss; 2lung f negotiation; discussion; ♣ trial, proceedings pl.

ver'**häng|en** v/t. (no -ge-, h) cover (over), hang; inflict (punishment) (über acc. upon); 2nis n (-ses/-se) fate; ~nisvoll adj. fatal; disastrous.

ver'**härmt** adj. [fɛr'hɛrmt] careworn; ~harren [~'harən] v/i. (no -ge-, h, sein) persist (auf dat., bei, in dat. in), stick (to); ~härten v/t. and v/refl. (no -ge-, h) harden; ~haßt adj. [~'hast] hated; hateful; odious; ~hätscheln v/t. (no -ge-, h) coddle, pamper, spoil; ~'hauen v/t. (irr. hauen, no -ge-, h) thrash.

ver'**heer|en** [fɛr'he:rən] v/t. (no -ge-, h) devastate, ravage, lay waste; ~end fig. adj. disastrous; 2ung f (-/-en) devastation.

ver'**hehlen** [fɛr'he:lən] v/t. (no -ge-, h) s. verheimlichen; ~'heilen v/i. (no -ge-, sein) heal (up).

ver'**heimlich|en** v/t. (no -ge-, h) hide, conceal; 2ung f (-/♣-en) concealment.

ver'**heirat|en** v/t. (no -ge-, h) marry (mit to); sich ~ marry; 2ung f (-/♣-en) marriage.

ver'**heiß|en** v/t. (irr. heißen, no -ge-, h) promise; 2ung f (-/-en) promise; ~ungsvoll adj. promising.

ver'**helfen** v/i. (irr. helfen, no -ge-, h): j-m zu et. ~ help s.o. to s.th.

ver'**herrlich|en** v/t. (no -ge-, h) glorify; 2ung f (-/♣-en) glorification.

ver'**hetzen** v/t. (no -ge-, h) instigate; ~'hexen v/t. (no -ge-, h) bewitch.

ver'**hinder|n** v/t. (no -ge-, h) prevent; 2ung f (-/♣-en) prevention.

ver'**höhn|en** v/t. (no -ge-, h) deride, mock (at), taunt; 2ung f (-/-en) derision, mockery.

**Verhör** ♣ [fɛr'hø:r] n (-[e]s/-e) interrogation, questioning (of prisoners, etc.); examination; 2en v/t. (no -ge-, h) examine, hear; interrogate; sich ~ hear it wrong.

ver'**hüllen** v/t. (no -ge-, h) cover, veil; ~'hungern v/i. (no -ge-, sein) starve; ~'hüten v/t. (no -ge-, h) prevent.

ver'**irr|en** v/refl. (no -ge-, h) go astray, lose one's way; ~t adj.: ~es Schaf stray sheep; 2ung fig. f (-/-en) aberration; error.

ver'**jagen** v/t. (no -ge-, h) drive away.

ver'**jähr|en** ♣ [fɛr'je:rən] v/i. (no -ge-, sein) become prescriptive;

**Θung** f (-/-en) limitation, (negative) prescription.

**verjüngen** [fɛrˈjyŋən] v/t. (no -ge-, h) make young again, rejuvenate; reduce (scale); sich ~ grow young again, rejuvenate; taper off.

**Verˈkauf** m sale; Θen v/t. (no -ge-, h) sell; zu ~ for sale; sich gut ~ sell well.

**Verˈkäufˌer** m seller; vendor; shop-assistant, salesman, Am. a. (sales-) clerk; **~erin** f (-/-nen) seller; vendor; shop-assistant, saleswoman, shop girl, Am. a. (sales)clerk; Θlich adj. sal(e)able; for sale.

**Verˈkaufsˌautomat** m slot-machine, vending machine; **~schlager** m best seller.

**Verkehr** [fɛrˈkeːr] m (-[e]s/⚥ -e) traffic; transport(ation); communication; correspondence; ⚓, ✈, ✉, etc.: service; commerce, trade; intercourse (a. sexually); aus dem ~ ziehen withdraw from service; withdraw (money) from circulation; Θen (no -ge-, h) 1. v/t. convert (in acc. into), turn (into); 2. v/i. ship, bus, etc.: run, ply (zwischen dat. between); bei j-m ~ go to or visit s.o.'s house; ~ in (dat.) frequent (public house, etc.); ~ mit associate or mix with; have (sexual) intercourse with.

**Verˈkehrsˌader** f arterial road; **~ampel** f traffic lights pl., traffic signal; **~büro** n tourist bureau; **~flugzeug** n air liner; **~insel** f refuge, island; **~minister** m minister of transport; **~mittel** n (means of) conveyance or transport, Am. transportation; **~polizist** m traffic policeman or constable, sl. traffic cop; Θreich adj. congested with traffic, busy; **~schild** n traffic sign; **~schutzmann** m s. Verkehrspolizist; **~stauung** f, **~stockung** f traffic block, traffic jam; **~störung** f interruption of traffic; ⚒, etc.: breakdown; **~straße** f thoroughfare; **~teilnehmer** m road user; **~unfall** m traffic accident; **~verein** m tourist agency; **~verhältnisse** pl. traffic conditions pl.; **~vorschrift** f traffic regulation; **~wesen** n (-s/no pl.) traffic; **~zeichen** n traffic sign.

**verˈkehrt** adj. inverted, upside down; fig. wrong; **~kennen** v/t. (irr. kennen, no -ge-, h) mistake; misunderstand, misjudge.

**Verˈkettung** f (-/-en) concatenation (a. fig.).

**verˈklagen** ⚖ v/t. (no -ge-, h) sue (auf acc., wegen for); bring an action against s.o.; **~kleben** v/t. (no -ge-, h) paste s.th. up.

**verˈkleidˌen** v/t. (no -ge-, h) disguise; ⊕: line; face; wainscot; encase; sich ~ disguise o.s.; Θung f

(-/-en) disguise; ⊕: lining; facing; panel(l)ing, wainscot(t)ing.

**verˈkleinerˌn** [fɛrˈklaɪnərn] v/t. (no -ge-, h) make smaller, reduce, diminish; fig. belittle, derogate; Θung f (-/-en) reduction, diminution; fig. derogation.

**verˈklingen** v/i. (irr. klingen, no -ge-, sein) die away; **~knöchern** [~ˈknœçərn] (no -ge-) 1. v/t. (h) ossify; 2. v/i. (sein) ossify; fig. a. fossilize; **~knoten** v/t. (no -ge-, h) knot; **~knüpfen** v/t. (no -ge-, h) knot or tie (together); fig. connect, combine; **~kohlen** (no -ge-) 1. v/t. (h) carbonize; char; F: j-n ~ pull s.o.'s leg; 2. v/i. (sein) char; **~kommen** 1. v/i. (irr. kommen, no -ge-, sein) decay; p.: go downhill or to the dogs; become demoralized; 2. adj. decayed; depraved, corrupt; **~korken** v/t. (no -ge-, h) cork (up).

**verˈkörperˌn** v/t. (no -ge-, h) personify, embody; represent; esp. thea. impersonate; Θung f (-/-en) personification, embodiment; impersonation.

**verˈkrachen** F v/refl. (no -ge-, h) fall out (mit with); **~krampft** adj. cramped; **~kriechen** v/refl. (irr. kriechen, no -ge-, h) hide; **~krümmt** adj. crooked; **~krüppelt** adj. [~ˈkrypəlt] crippled; stunted; **~krustet** adj. [~ˈkrustət] (en)crusted; caked; **~kühlen** v/refl. (no -ge-, h) catch (a) cold.

**verˈkümmerˌn** v/i. (no -ge-, sein) ⚘, ⚕ become stunted; ⚕ atrophy; fig. waste away; **~t** adj. stunted; atrophied; rudimentary (a. biol.).

**verkündˌen** [fɛrˈkyndən] v/t. (no -ge-, h), **~igen** v/t. (no -ge-, h) announce; publish, proclaim; pronounce (judgement); Θigung f, Θung f (-/-en) announcement; proclamation; pronouncement.

**verˈkuppeln** v/t. (no -ge-, h) ⊕ couple; fig. pander; **~kürzen** v/t. (no -ge-, h) shorten; abridge; beguile (time, etc.); **~lachen** v/t. (no -ge-, h) laugh at; **~laden** v/t. (irr. laden, no -ge-, h) load; ship; ⚒ entrain (esp. troops).

**Verlag** [fɛrˈlaːk] m (-[e]s/-e) publishing house, the publishers pl.; im ~ von published by.

**verˈlagern** v/t. (no -ge-, h) displace, shift; sich ~ shift.

**Verˈlagsˌbuchhändler** m publisher; **~buchhandlung** f publishing house; **~recht** n copyright.

**verˈlangen** 1. v/t. (no -ge-, h) demand; require; desire; 2. v/i. (no -ge-, h): ~ nach ask for; long for; 3. Θ n (-s/⚥ -) desire; longing (nach for); demand, request; auf ~ by request, ✝ on demand; auf ~ von at the request of, at s.o.'s request.

**verˈlängerˌn** [fɛrˈlɛŋərn] v/t. (no

-ge-, h) lengthen; prolong, extend;
**2ung** *f* (-/-en) lengthening; prolongation, extension.
**ver'langsamen** *v/t.* (no -ge-, h) slacken, slow down.
**ver'lassen** *v/t.* (irr. lassen, no -ge-, h) leave; forsake, abandon, desert; sich ~ auf (acc.) rely on; **2heit** *f* (-/no pl.) abandonment; loneliness.
**verläßlich** *adj.* [fɛr'lɛsliç] reliable.
**Ver'lauf** *m* lapse, course (of time); progress, development (of matter); course (of disease, etc.); im ~ (gen.) or von in the course of; e-n schlimmen ~ nehmen take a bad turn; **2en** (irr. laufen, no -ge-) **1.** *v/i.* (sein) time: pass, elapse; matter: take its course; turn out, develop; road, etc.: run, extend; **2.** *v/refl.* (h) lose one's way, go astray; crowd: disperse; water: subside.
**ver'lauten** *v/i.* (no -ge-, sein): ~ lassen give to understand, hint; wie verlautet as reported.
**ver'leb|en** *v/t.* (no -ge-, h) spend, pass; ~t *adj.* [~pt] worn out.
**ver'leg|en 1.** *v/t.* (no -ge-, h) mislay; transfer, shift, remove; ⊕ lay (cable, etc.); bar (road); put off, postpone; publish (book); sich ~ auf (acc.) apply o.s. to; **2.** *adj.* embarrassed; at a loss (um for answer, etc.); **2enheit** *f* (-/~-en) embarrassment; difficulty; predicament; **2er** *m* (-s/-) publisher; **2ung** *f* (-/-en) transfer, removal; ⊕ laying; time: postponement.
**ver'leiden** *v/t.* (no -ge-, h) s. verekeln.
**ver'leih|en** *v/t.* (irr. leihen, no -ge-, h) lend, Am. a. loan; hire or let out; bestow (right, etc.) (j-m on s.o.); award (prize, etc.); **2ung** *f* (-/-en) lending, loan; bestowal.
**ver'leiten** *v/t.* (no -ge-, h) mislead; induce; seduce; zu suborn; **~'lernen** *v/t.* (no -ge-, h) unlearn, forget; **~'lesen** *v/t.* (irr. lesen, no -ge-, h) read out; call (names) over; pick (vegetables, etc.); sich ~ read wrong.
**verletz|en** [fɛr'lɛtsən] *v/t.* (no -ge-, h) hurt, injure; fig. a.: offend; violate; **~end** *adj.* offensive; **2te** [~tə] *m, f* (-n/-n) injured person; die ~n *pl.* the injured *pl.*; **2ung** *f* (-/-en) hurt, injury, wound; fig. violation.
**ver'leugn|en** *v/t.* (no -ge-, h) deny; disown; renounce (belief, principle, etc.); sich ~ lassen have o.s. denied (vor j-m to s.o.); **2ung** *f* (-/-en) denial; renunciation.
**verleumd|en** [fɛr'lɔymdən] *v/t.* (no -ge-, h) slander, defame; **~erisch** *adj.* slanderous; **2ung** *f* (-/-en) slander, defamation, in writing: libel.
**ver'lieb|en** *v/refl.* (no -ge-, h): sich ~ in (acc.) fall in love with; **~t** *adj.*

[~pt] in love (in acc. with); amorous; **2theit** *f* (-/~-en) amorousness.
**verlieren** [fɛr'li:rən] (irr., no -ge-, h) **1.** *v/t.* lose; shed (leaves, etc.); sich ~ lose o.s.; disappear; **2.** *v/i.* lose.
**ver'lob|en** *v/t.* (no -ge-, h) engage (mit to); sich ~ become engaged; **2te** [~ptə] (-n/-n) **1.** *m* fiancé; die ~n *pl.* the engaged couple sg.; **2.** *f* fiancée; **2ung** [~buŋ] *f* (-/-en) engagement.
**ver'lock|en** *v/t.* (no -ge-, h) allure, entice; tempt; **~end** *adj.* tempting; **2ung** *f* (-/-en) allurement, enticement.
**verlogen** *adj.* [fɛr'lo:gən] mendacious; **2heit** *f* (-/~-en) mendacity.
**verlor** [fɛr'lo:r] pret. of verlieren; **~en 1.** p.p. of verlieren; **2.** *adj.* lost; fig. forlorn; **~e** Eier poached eggs; **~engehen** *v/i.* (irr. gehen, sep., -ge-, sein) be lost.
**ver'los|en** *v/t.* (no -ge-, h) raffle; **2ung** *f* (-/-en) lottery, raffle.
**ver'löten** *v/t.* (no -ge-, h) solder.
**Verlust** [fɛr'lust] *m* (-es/-e) loss; **~e** *pl.* ✕ casualties *pl.*
**ver'machen** *v/t.* (no -ge-, h) bequeath, leave s.th. (dat. to).
**Vermächtnis** [fɛr'mɛçtnis] *n* (-ses/-se) will; legacy, bequest.
**vermähl|en** [fɛr'mɛ:lən] *v/t.* (no -ge-, h) marry (mit to); sich ~ (mit) marry (s.o.); **2ung** *f* (-/-en) wedding, marriage.
**ver'mehr|en** *v/t.* (no -ge-, h) increase (um by), augment; multiply; add to; durch Zucht ~ propagate; breed; sich ~ increase, augment; multiply (a. biol.); propagate (itself), zo. breed; **2ung** *f* (-/~-en) increase; addition (gen. to); propagation.
**ver'meid|en** *v/t.* (irr. meiden, no -ge-, h) avoid; **2ung** *f* (-/~-en) avoidance.
**ver|meintlich** *adj.* [fɛr'maıntliç] supposed; **~'mengen** *v/t.* (no -ge-, h) mix, mingle, blend.
**Vermerk** [fɛr'mɛrk] *m* (-[e]s/-e) note, entry; **2en** *v/t.* (no -ge-, h) note down, record.
**ver'mess|en 1.** *v/t.* (irr. messen, no -ge-, h) measure; survey (land); **2.** *adj.* presumptuous; **2enheit** *f* (-/~-en) presumption; **2ung** *f* (-/-en) measurement; survey (of land).
**ver'miete|n** *v/t.* (no -ge-, h) let, esp. Am. rent; hire (out); 🏠 lease; zu ~ on or for hire; Haus zu ~ house to (be) let; **2r** *m* landlord, 🏠 lessor; letter, hirer.
**ver'mindern** *v/t.* (no -ge-, h) diminish, lessen; reduce, cut.
**ver'misch|en** *v/t.* (no -ge-, h) mix, mingle, blend; **~t** *adj.* mixed; news,

*etc.*: miscellaneous; 2ung *f* (-/﬇ -en) mixture.

**ver'mi|ssen** *v/t.* (*no* -ge-, h) miss; ﬈t *adj.* [ﬗ'mist] missing; 2﬈te *m, f* (-n/-n) missing person; *die* ﬗn *pl.* the missing *pl.*

**vermitt|eln** [fɛr'mitəln] (*no* -ge-, h) 1. *v/t.* mediate (*settlement, peace*); procure, get; give (*impression, etc.*); impart (*knowledge*) (*j-m* to *s.o.*); 2. *v/i.* mediate (*zwischen dat.* between); intercede (*bei* with, *für* for), intervene; 2ler *m* mediator; go-between; ☂ agent; 2lung *f* (-/-en) mediation; intercession, intervention; *teleph.* (telephone) exchange.

**ver'modern** *v/i.* (*no* -ge-, sein) mo(u)lder, decay, rot.

**ver'mögen** 1. *v/t.* (*irr.* mögen, *no* -ge-, h): ﬗ *zu inf.* be able to *inf.*; et. ﬗ *bei j-m* have influence with s.o.; 2. 2 *n* (-s/-) ability, power; property; fortune; means *pl.*; ﬓ assets *pl.*; ﬗd *adj.* wealthy; *pred.* well off; 2sverhältnisse *pl.* pecuniary circumstances *pl.*

**vermut|en** [fɛr'mu:tən] *v/t.* (*no* -ge-, h) suppose, presume, *Am. a.* guess; conjecture, surmise; ﬗlich 1. *adj.* presumable; 2. *adv.* presumably; I suppose; 2ung *f* (-/-en) supposition, presumption; conjecture, surmise.

**vernachlässig|en** [fɛr'na:xlɛsigən] *v/t.* (*no* -ge-, h) neglect; 2ung *f* (-/﬇ -en) neglect(ing).

**ver'narben** *v/i.* (*no* -ge-, sein) cicatrize, scar over. [with.]

**ver'narrt** *adj.*: ﬗ *in* (*acc.*) infatuated]

**ver'nehm|en** *v/t.* (*irr.* nehmen, *no* -ge-, h) hear, learn; examine, interrogate; ﬗlich *adj.* audible, distinct; 2ung ﬓ *f* (-/-en) interrogation, questioning; examination.

**ver'neig|en** *v/refl.* (*no* -ge-, h) bow (*vor dat.* to); 2ung *f* bow.

**vernein|en** [fɛr'naɪnən] (*no* -ge-, h) 1. *v/t.* answer in the negative; deny; 2. *v/i.* answer in the negative; ﬗend *adj.* negative; 2ung *f* (-/-en) negation; denial; *gr.* negative.

**vernicht|en** [fɛr'nɪçtən] *v/t.* (*no* -ge-, h) annihilate; destroy; dash (*hopes*); ﬗend *adj.* destructive (*a. fig.*); *look:* withering; *criticism:* scathing; *defeat, reply:* crushing; 2ung *f* (-/﬇ -en) annihilation; destruction.

**ver|nickeln** [fɛr'nɪkəln] *v/t.* (*no* -ge-, h) nickel(-plate); ﬗ'nieten *v/t.* (*no* -ge-, h) rivet.

**Vernunft** [fɛr'nʊnft] *f* (-/*no pl.*) reason; ﬗ annehmen listen to *or* hear reason; *j-n zur* ﬗ bringen bring s.o. to reason *or* to his senses.

**vernünftig** *adj.* [fɛr'nynftɪç] rational; reasonable; sensible.

**ver'öden** (*no* -ge-) 1. *v/t.* (h) make

---

desolate; 2. *v/i.* (sein) become desolate.

**ver'öffentlich|en** *v/t.* (*no* -ge-, h) publish; 2ung *f* (-/-en) publication.

**ver'ordn|en** *v/t.* (*no* -ge-, h) decree; order (*a.* ☂); ☂ prescribe (*j-m* to *or* for s.o.); 2ung *f* decree, order; ☂ prescription.

**ver'pachten** *v/t.* (*no* -ge-, h) rent, ﬓ lease (*building, land*).

**Ver'pächter** *m* landlord, ﬓ lessor.

**ver'pack|en** *v/t.* (*no* -ge-, h) pack (up); wrap up; 2ung *f* packing (material); wrapping.

**ver|'passen** *v/t.* (*no* -ge-, h) miss (*train, opportunity, etc.*); ﬗpatzen F [ﬗ'patsən] *v/t.* (*no* -ge-, h) *s.* verpfuschen; ﬗ'pesten *v/t.* (*no* -ge-, h) *fumes:* contaminate (*the air*); ﬗ 'pfänden *v/t.* (*no* -ge-, h) pawn, pledge (*a. fig.*); mortgage.

**ver'pflanz|en** *v/t.* (*no* -ge-, h) transplant (*a.* ☂); 2ung *f* transplantation; ☂ *a.* transplant.

**ver'pfleg|en** *v/t.* (*no* -ge-, h) board; supply with food, victual; 2ung *f* (-/﬇ -en) board; food-supply; provisions *pl.*

**ver'pflicht|en** *v/t.* (*no* -ge-, h) oblige; engage; 2ung *f* (-/-en) obligation; duty; ☂, ﬓ liability; engagement; commitment.

**ver'pfusch|en** F *v/t.* (*no* -ge-, h) bungle, botch; make a mess of; ﬗt *adj. life:* ruined, wrecked.

**ver|pönt** *adj.* [fɛr'pø:nt] taboo; ﬗ'prügeln F *v/t.* (*no* -ge-, h) thrash, flog, F wallop; ﬗ'puffen *fig. v/i.* (*no* -ge-, sein) fizzle out.

**Ver'putz** ▲ *m* (-es/﬇ -e) plaster; 2en ▲ *v/t.* (*no* -ge-, h) plaster.

**ver|quicken** [fɛr'kvɪkən] *v/t.* (*no* -ge-, h) mix up; ﬗ'quollen *adj. wood:* warped; *face:* bloated; *eyes:* swollen; ﬗrammeln [ﬗ'raməln] *v/t.* (*no* -ge-, h) bar(ricade).

**Verrat** [fɛr'ra:t] *m* (-[e]s/*no pl.*) betrayal (*an dat.* of); treachery (to); ﬓ treason (to); 2en *v/t.* (*irr.* raten, *no* -ge-, h) betray, give s.o. away; give away (*secret*); *sich* ﬗ betray o.s., give o.s. away.

**Verräter** [fɛr're:tər] *m* (-s/-) traitor (*an dat.* to); 2isch *adj.* treacherous; *fig.* telltale.

**ver'rechn|en** *v/t.* (*no* -ge-, h) reckon up; charge; settle; set off (*mit* against); account for; ﬗ *mit* offset against; *sich* ﬗ miscalculate, make a mistake (*a. fig.*); *fig.* be mistaken; *sich um s-e* Mark ﬗ be one mark out; 2ung *f* settlement; clearing; booking *or* charging (*to account*); 2ungsscheck *m* collection-only cheque *or Am.* check.

**ver'regnet** *adj.* rainy, rain-spoilt.

**ver'reis|en** *v/i.* (*no* -ge-, sein) go on a journey; ﬗt *adj.* out of town; (*geschäftlich*) ﬗ away (on business).

**verrenk|en** [fɛr'rɛŋkən] *v/t.* (*no -ge-, h*) 🟎: wrench; dislocate, luxate; *sich et.* ~ 🟎 dislocate *or* luxate s.th.; *sich den Hals* ~ crane one's neck; **2ung** 🟎 *f* (-/-en) dislocation, luxation.

**ver|'richten** *v/t.* (*no -ge-, h*) do, perform; execute; *sein Gebet* ~ say one's prayer(s); ~'**riegeln** *v/t.* (*no -ge-, h*) bolt, bar.

**verringer|n** [fɛr'riŋərn] *v/t.* (*no -ge-, h*) diminish, lessen; reduce, cut; *sich* ~ diminish, lessen; **2ung** *f* (-/-en) diminution; reduction, cut.

**ver|'rosten** *v/i.* (*no -ge-, sein*) rust; ~**rotten** [~'rɔtən] *v/i.* (*no -ge-, sein*) rot.

**ver'rück|en** *v/t.* (*no -ge-, h*) displace, (re)move, shift; ~**t** *adj.* mad, crazy (*both a. fig.: nach about*); *wie* ~ like mad; *j-n* ~ *machen* drive s.o. mad; **2te** (-*n*/-*n*) 1. *m* lunatic, madman; 2. *f* lunatic, madwoman; **2theit** *f* (-/-en) madness; foolish action; craze.

**Ver'ruf** *m* (-[e]s/*no pl.*): *in* ~ *bringen* bring discredit (up)on; *in* ~ *kommen* get into discredit; **2en** *adj.* ill-reputed, ill-famed.

**ver'rutsch|en** *v/i.* (*no -ge-, sein*) slip; ~**t** *adj.* not straight.

**Vers** [fɛrs] *m* (-es/-e) verse.

**ver'sagen** 1. *v/t.* (*no -ge-, h*) refuse, deny (*j-m et. s.o.* s.th.); *sich et.* ~ deny o.s. s.th.; 2. *v/i.* (*no -ge-, h*) fail, break down; *gun:* misfire; 3. **2** *n* (-s/*no pl.*) failure. [*ure.*\]

**Ver'sager** *m* (-s/-) misfire; *p.* fail-\]

**ver'salzen** *v/t.* ([*irr. salzen,*] *no -ge-, h*) oversalt; F *fig.* spoil.

**ver'samm|eln** *v/t.* (*no -ge-, h*) assemble; *sich* ~ assemble, meet; **2lung** *f* assembly, meeting.

**Versand** [fɛr'zant] *m* (-[e]s/*no pl.*) dispatch, Am. a. shipment; mailing; ~ *ins Ausland a.* export(ation); ~**abteilung** *f* forwarding department; ~**geschäft** *n*, ~**haus** *n* mailorder business *or* firm *or* house.

**ver'säum|en** *v/t.* (*no -ge-, h*) neglect (*one's duty, etc.*); miss (*opportunity, etc.*); lose (*time*); ~ *zu inf.* fail *or* omit to *inf.*; **2nis** *n* (-ses/-se) neglect, omission, failure.

**ver|'schachern** F *v/t.* (*no -ge-, h*) barter (away); ~'**schaffen** *v/t.* (*no -ge-, h*) procure, get; *sich* ~ obtain, get; raise (*money*); *sich Respekt* ~ make o.s. respected; ~'**schämt** *adj.* bashful; ~'**schanzen** *v/refl.* (*no -ge-, h*) entrench o.s.; *sich* ~ *hinter* (*dat.*) (take) shelter behind; ~'**schärfen** *v/t.* (*no -ge-, h*) heighten, intensify; aggravate; *sich* ~ get worse; ~'**scheiden** *v/i.* (*irr. scheiden, no -ge-, sein*) pass away; ~'**schenken** *v/t.* (*no -ge-, h*) give s.th. away; make a present of; ~'**scherzen** *v/t. and v/refl.* (*no*

~*-ge-, h*) forfeit (*von* from); ~'**scheuchen** *v/t.* (*no -ge-, h*) frighten *or* scare away; *fig.* banish; ~'**schicken** *v/t.* (*no -ge-, h*) send (away), dispatch, forward.

**ver'schieb|en** *v/t.* (*irr. schieben, no -ge-, h*) displace, shift, (re)move; 🚂 shunt; put off, postpone; F *fig.* 🟎 sell underhand; *sich* ~ shift; **2ung** *f* shift(ing); postponement.

**verschieden** *adj.* [fɛr'ʃiːdən] different (*von* from); dissimilar, unlike; *aus* ~*en Gründen* for various *or* several reasons; *Verschiedenes* various things *pl., esp.* 🟎 sundries *pl.*; ~**artig** *adj.* of a different kind, various; **2heit** *f* (-/-en) difference; diversity, variety; ~**tlich** *adv.* repeatedly; at times.

**ver'schiff|en** *v/t.* (*no -ge-, h*) ship; **2ung** *f* (-/🟎-en) shipment.

**ver|'schimmeln** *v/i.* (*no -ge-, sein*) get mo(u)ldy, Am. mo(u)ld; ~'**schlafen** 1. *v/t.* (*irr. schlafen, no -ge-, h*) miss by sleeping; sleep (*afternoon, etc.*) away; sleep off (*headache, etc.*); 2. *v/i.* (*irr. schlafen, no -ge-, h*) oversleep (o.s.); 3. *adj.* sleepy, drowsy.

**Ver'schlag** *m* shed; box; crate; **2en** [~gən] 1. *v/t.* (*irr. schlagen, no -ge-, h*) board up; nail up; *es verschlug ihm die Sprache* it dum(b)founded him; 2. *adj.* cunning; *eyes: a.* shifty; ~**enheit** *f* (-/*no pl.*) cunning.

**verschlechter|n** [fɛr'ʃlɛçtərn] *v/t.* (*no -ge-, h*) deteriorate, make worse; *sich* ~ deteriorate, get worse; **2ung** *f* (-/🟎-en) deterioration; change for the worse.

**ver'schleiern** *v/t.* (*no -ge-, h*) veil (*a. fig.*).

**Verschleiß** [fɛr'ʃlaɪs] *m* (-es/🟎-e) wear (and tear); **2en** *v/t.* ([*irr.,*] *no -ge-, h*) wear out.

**ver|'schleppen** *v/t.* (*no -ge-, h*) carry off; *pol.* displace (*person*); abduct, kidnap; delay, protract; neglect (*disease*); ~'**schleudern** *v/t.* (*no -ge-, h*) dissipate, waste; 🟎 sell at a loss, sell dirt-cheap; ~'**schließen** *v/t.* (*irr. schließen, no -ge-, h*) shut, close; lock (*door*); lock up (*house*).

**verschlimmern** [fɛr'ʃlimərn] *v/t.* (*no -ge-, h*) make worse, aggravate; *sich* ~ get worse.

**ver'schlingen** *v/t.* (*irr. schlingen, no -ge-, h*) devour; wolf (down) (*one's food*); intertwine, entwine, interlace; *sich* ~ intertwine, entwine, interlace.

**verschli|ß** [fɛr'ʃlis] *pret. of verschleißen,* ~**ssen** [~sən] *p.p. of verschleißen.*

**verschlossen** *adj.* [fɛr'ʃlɔsən] closed, shut; *fig.* reserved; **2heit** *f* (-/*no pl.*) reserve.

19*

ver'schlucken v/t. (no -ge-, h) swallow (up); sich ~ swallow the wrong way.

Ver'schluß m lock; clasp; lid; plug; stopper (of bottle); seal; fastener, fastening; phot. shutter; unter ~ under lock and key.

ver|'schmachten v/i. (no -ge-, sein) languish, pine away; vor Durst ~ die or be dying of thirst, be parched with thirst; ~'schmähen v/t. (no -ge-, h) disdain, scorn.

ver'schmelz|en (irr. schmelzen, no -ge-) v/t. (h) and v/i. (sein) melt, fuse (a. fig.); blend; fig.: amalgamate; merge (mit in, into); 2ung f (-/%-en) fusion; † merger; fig. amalgamation.

ver|'schmerzen v/t. (no -ge-, h) get over (the loss of); ~'schmieren v/t. (no -ge-, h) smear (over); blur; ~schmitzt adj. [~'∫mitst] cunning, roguish; arch; ~'schmutzen (no -ge-) 1. v/t. (h) soil, dirty; pollute (water); 2. v/i. (sein) get dirty; ~'schnaufen F v/i. and v/refl. (no -ge-, h) stop for breath; ~'schneiden v/t. (irr. schneiden, no -ge-, h) cut badly; blend (wine, etc.); geld, castrate; ~'schneit adj. covered with snow; mountains: a. snow-capped; roofs: a. snow-covered.

Ver'schnitt m (-[e]s/no pl.) blend.

ver'schnupf|en F fig. v/t. (no -ge-, h) nettle, pique; ~t adj.: ~ sein have a cold.

ver|'schnüren v/t. (no -ge-, h) tie up, cord; ~schollen adj. [~'∫ɔlən] not heard of again; missing; ⅔ presumed dead; ~'schonen v/t. (no -ge-, h) spare; j-n mit et. ~ spare s.o. s.th.

verschöne|(r)n [fɛr'∫øːnə(r)n] v/t. (no -ge-, h) embellish, beautify; 2rung f (-/-en) embellishment.

ver|schossen adj. [fɛr'∫ɔsən] colour: faded; F ~ sein in (acc.) be madly in love with; ~schränken [~'∫rɛŋkən] v/t. (no -ge-, h) cross, fold (one's arms).

ver'schreib|en v/t. (irr. schreiben, no -ge-, h) use up (in writing); 𝕤 prescribe (j-m for s.o.); ⅔ assign (j-m to s.o.); sich ~ make a slip of the pen; sich e-r Sache ~ devote o.s. to s.th.; 2ung f (-/-en) assignment; prescription.

ver|schroben adj. [fɛr'∫roːbən] eccentric, queer, odd; ~'schrotten v/t. (no -ge-, h) scrap; ~schüchtert adj. [~'∫yçtərt] intimidated.

ver'schulden 1. v/t. (no -ge-, h) be guilty of; be the cause of; 2. 2 n (-s/no pl.) fault.

ver|'schuldet adj. indebted, in debt; ~'schütten v/t. (no -ge-, h) spill (liquid); block (up) (road); bury s.o. alive; ~schwägert adj. [~'∫vɛːgərt] related by marriage;

~'schweigen v/t. (irr. schweigen, no -ge-, h) conceal (j-m et. s.th. from s.o.).

verschwend|en [fɛr'∫vɛndən] v/t. (no -ge-, h) waste, squander (an acc. on); lavish (on); 2er m (-s/-) spendthrift, prodigal; ~erisch adj. prodigal, lavish (both: mit of); wasteful; 2ung f (-/%-en) waste; extravagance.

verschwiegen adj. [fɛr'∫viːgən] discreet; place: secret, secluded; 2heit f (-/no pl.) discretion; secrecy.

ver|'schwimmen v/i. (irr. schwimmen, no -ge-, sein) become indistinct or blurred; ~'schwinden v/i. (irr. schwinden, no -ge-, sein) disappear, vanish; F verschwinde! go away!, sl. beat it!; 2'schwinden n (-s/no pl.) disappearance; ~schwommen adj. [~'∫vɔmən] vague (a. fig.); blurred; fig. woolly.

ver'schwör|en v/refl. (irr. schwören, no -ge-, h) conspire; 2er m (-s/-) conspirator; 2ung f (-/-en) conspiracy, plot.

ver'sehen 1. v/t. (irr. sehen, no -ge-, h) fill (an office); look after (house, etc.); mit et. ~ furnish or supply with; sich ~ make a mistake; ehe man sich's versieht all of a sudden; 2. 2 n (-s/-) oversight, mistake, slip; aus ~ = ~tlich adv. by mistake; inadvertently.

Versehrte [fɛr'zeːrtə] m (-n/-n) disabled person.

ver'send|en v/t. ([irr. senden,] no -ge-, h) send, dispatch, forward, Am. ship; by water: ship; ins Ausland ~ a. export; 2ung f (-/%-en) dispatch, shipment, forwarding.

ver|'sengen v/t. (no -ge-, h) singe, scorch; ~'senken v/t. (no -ge-, h) sink; sich ~ in (acc.) immerse o.s. in; ~sessen adj. [~'zɛsən]: ~ auf (acc.) bent on, mad after.

ver'setz|en v/t. (no -ge-, h) displace, remove; transfer (officer); at school: remove, move up, Am. promote; transplant (tree, etc.); pawn, pledge; F fig. stand (lover, etc.) up; ~ in (acc.) put or place into (situation, condition); j-m e-n Schlag ~ give or deal s.o. a blow; in Angst ~ frighten or terrify s.o.; in den Ruhestand ~ pension s.o. off, retire s.o.; versetzt werden be transferred; at school: go up; ~ Sie sich in m-e Lage put or place yourself in my position; Wein mit Wasser ~ mix wine with water, add water to wine; et. ~ reply s.th.; 2ung f (-/-en) removal; transfer; at school: remove, Am. promotion.

ver'seuch|en v/t. (no -ge-, h) infect; contaminate; 2ung f (-/%-en) infection; contamination.

ver'sicher|n v/t. (no -ge-, h) assure

(*a. one's life*); protest, affirm; insure (*one's property or life*); *sich* ~ insure *or* assure o.s.; *sich* ~ (, *daß*) make sure (that); 2te *m*, *f* (-n/-n) insurant, the insured *or* assured, policy-holder; 2ung *f* assurance, affirmation; insurance; (life-)assurance; insurance company.

**Ver'sicherungs|gesellschaft** *f* insurance company; ~police *f*, ~schein *m* policy of assurance, insurance policy.

**ver'|sickern** *v/i.* (*no* -ge-, *sein*) trickle away; ~'siegeln *v/t.* (*no* -ge-, *h*) seal (up); ~'siegen *v/i.* (*no* -ge-, *sein*) dry up, run dry; ~'silbern *v/t.* (*no* -ge-, *h*) silver; F *fig.* realize, convert into cash; ~'sinken *v/i.* (*irr.* sinken, *no* -ge-, *sein*) sink; *s.* versunken; *s.* ~sinnbildlichen *v/t.* (*no* -ge-, *h*) symbolize.

**Version** [ver'zjo:n] *f* (-/-en) version.

**'Versmaß** *n* met|re, *Am.* -er.

**versöhn|en** [fɛr'zøːnən] *v/t.* (*no* -ge-, *h*) reconcile (*mit* to, with); *sich* (*wieder*) ~ become reconciled; ~lich *adj.* conciliatory; 2ung *f* (-/-en) reconciliation.

**ver'sorg|en** *v/t.* (*no* -ge-, *h*) provide (*mit* with), supply (with); take care of, look after; ~t *adj.* [~kt] provided for; 2ung [~guŋ] *f* (-/-en) providing (*mit* with), supplying (with); supply, provision.

**ver'spät|en** *v/refl.* (*no* -ge-, *h*) be late; ~et *adj.* belated, late, *Am.* tardy; 2ung *f* (-/-en) lateness, *Am.* tardiness; ~ haben be late; *mit* 2 *Stunden* ~ two hours behind schedule.

**ver'sp|eisen** *v/t.* (*no* -ge-, *h*) eat (up); ~'sperren *v/t.* (*no* -ge-, *h*) lock (up); bar, block (up), obstruct (*a. view*); ~'spielen *v/t.* (*no* -ge-, *h*) at cards, *etc.*: lose (*money*); ~'spielt *adj.* playful; ~'spotten *v/t.* (*no* -ge-, *h*) scoff at, mock (at), deride, ridicule; ~'sprechen *v/t.* (*irr.* sprechen, *no* -ge-, *h*) promise; *sich* ~ make a mistake in speaking; *sich viel* ~ *von* expect much of; 2'sprechen *n* (-s/%-) promise; ~'sprühen *v/t.* (*no* -ge-, *h*) spray; ~'spüren *v/t.* (*no* -ge-, *h*) feel; perceive, be conscious of.

**ver'staatlich|en** *v/t.* (*no* -ge-, *h*) nationalize; 2ung *f* (-/%-en) nationalization.

**Verstand** [fɛr'ʃtant] *m* (-[e]s/*no pl.*) understanding; intelligence, intellect, brains *pl.*; mind, wits *pl.*; reason; (common) sense.

**Verstandes|kraft** [fɛr'ʃtandəs-] *f* intellectual power *or* faculty; 2mäßig *adj.* rational; intellectual; ~mensch *m* matter-of-fact person.

**verständ|ig** [fɛr'ʃtɛndiç] intelligent; reasonable, sensible; judi-

cious; ~igen [~gən] *v/t.* (*no* -ge-, *h*) inform (*von* of), notify (of); *sich mit j-m* ~ make o.s. understood to s.o.; come to an understanding with s.o.; 2igung [~guŋ] *f* (-/%-en) information; understanding, agreement; *teleph.* communication; ~lich *adj.* [~tliç] intelligible; understandable; *j-m et.* ~ *machen* make s.th. clear to s.o.; *sich* ~ *machen* make o.s. understood.

**Verständnis** [fɛr'ʃtɛntnis] *n* (-ses/%-se) comprehension, understanding; insight; appreciation (*für* of); ~ *haben für* appreciate; 2los *adj.* uncomprehending; *look, etc.*: blank; unappreciative; 2voll *adj.* understanding; appreciative; sympathetic; *look*: knowing.

**ver'stärk|en** *v/t.* (*no* -ge-, *h*) strengthen, reinforce (*a.* ⊕, ✗); amplify (*radio signals, etc.*); intensify; 2er *m* (-s/-) in radio, *etc.*: amplifier; 2ung *f* (-/%-en) strengthening, reinforcement (*a.* ✗); amplification; intensification.

**ver'staub|en** *v/i.* (*no* -ge-, *sein*) get dusty; ~t *adj.* [~pt] dusty.

**ver'stauch|en** ✗ *v/t.* (*no* -ge-, *h*) sprain; *sich den Fuß* ~ sprain one's foot; 2ung ✗ *f* (-/-en) sprain.

**ver'stauen** *v/t.* (*no* -ge-, *h*) stow away.

**Versteck** [fɛr'ʃtɛk] *n* (-[e]s/-e) hiding-place; *for gangsters, etc.: Am.* F *a.* hide-out; ~ *spielen* play at hide-and-seek; 2en *v/t.* (*no* -ge-, *h*) hide, conceal; *sich* ~ hide.

**ver'stehen** *v/t.* (*irr.* stehen, *no* -ge-, *h*) understand, see, F get; comprehend; realize; know (*language*); *es* ~ *zu inf.* know how to *inf.*; 2paß ~ take a joke; *zu* ~ *geben* intimate; ~ *Sie?* do you see?; *ich* ~! I see!; *verstanden?* (do you) understand?, F (do you) get me?; *falsch* ~ misunderstand; ~ *Sie mich recht!* don't misunderstand me!; *was* ~ *Sie unter* (*dat.*)? what do you mean *or* understand by ...?; *er versteht et. davon* he knows a thing or two about it; *sich* ~ understand one another; *sich* ~ *auf* (*acc.*) know well, be an expert at *or* in; *sich mit j-m gut* ~ get on well with s.o.; *es versteht sich von selbst* it goes without saying.

**ver'steifen** *v/t.* (*no* -ge-, *h*) ⊕ strut, brace; stiffen; *sich* ~ stiffen; *sich* ~ *auf* (*acc.*) make a point of, insist on.

**ver'steiger|n** *v/t.* (*no* -ge-, *h*) (sell by *or Am.* at) auction; 2ung *f* (sale by *or Am.* at) auction, auction-sale.

**ver'steinern** (*no* -ge-, *h*) *and v/i.* (*sein*) turn into stone, petrify (*both a. fig.*).

**ver'stell|bar** *adj.* adjustable; ~en *v/t.* (*no* -ge-, *h*) shift; adjust; disarrange; bar, block (up), obstruct; disguise (*voice, etc.*); *sich* ~ play or act a part; dissemble, feign; **2ung** *f* (-/~-en) disguise; dissimulation.

**ver'|steuern** *v/t.* (*no -ge-, h*) pay duty or tax on; **~stiegen** *fig. adj.* [~'ʃti:gən] eccentric.

**ver'stimm|en** *v/t.* (*no -ge-, h*) put out of tune; *fig.* put out of humo(u)r; **~t** *adj.* out of tune; *fig.* out of humo(u)r, F cross; **2ung** *f* ill humo(u)r; disagreement; ill feeling.

**ver'stockt** *adj.* stubborn, obdurate; **2heit** *f* (-/*no pl.*) obduracy.

**verstohlen** *adj.* [fer'ʃto:lən] furtive.

**ver'stopf|en** *v/t.* (*no -ge-, h*) stop (up); clog, block (up), obstruct; jam, block (*passage, street*); *§* constipate; **2ung** *§ f* (-/~-en) constipation.

**verstorben** *adj.* [fer'ʃtɔrbən] late, deceased; **2e** *m*, *f* (-*n*/-*n*) the deceased, *Am.* *§* *a.* decedent; *die ~n* *pl.* the deceased *pl.*, the departed *pl.*

**ver'stört** *adj.* scared; distracted, bewildered; **2heit** *f* (-/*no pl.*) distraction, bewilderment.

**Ver'stoß** *m* offen|ce, *Am.* -se; contravention (*gegen of law*); infringement (*on trade name, etc.*); blunder; **2en** (*irr. stoßen, no -ge-, h*) **1.** *v/t.* expel (*aus from*); repudiate, disown (*wife, child, etc.*); **2.** *v/i.*: ~ *gegen* offend against; contravene (*law*); infringe (*rule, etc.*).

**ver'|streichen** (*irr. streichen, no -ge-*) **1.** *v/i.* (*sein*) time: pass, elapse; expire; **2.** *v/t.* (*h*) spread (*butter, etc.*); **~'streuen** *v/t.* (*no -ge-, h*) scatter.

**verstümmel|n** *v/t.* [fer'ʃtyməln] (*no -ge-, h*) mutilate; garble (*text, etc.*); **2ung** *f* (-/-en) mutilation.

**ver'stummen** *v/i.* (*no -ge-, sein*) grow silent or dumb.

**Verstümmlung** *f* [fer'ʃtymluŋ] *f* (-/-en) mutilation.

**Versuch** [fer'zu:x] *m* (-[e]s/-e) attempt, trial; *phys., etc.*: experiment; *e-n ~ machen mit* give *s.o.* or *s.th.* a trial; try one's hand at *s.th.*, have a go at *s.th.*; **2en** *v/t.* (*no -ge-, h*) try, attempt; taste; *j-n ~* tempt *s.o.*; *es ~ mit* give *s.o.* or *s.th.* a trial.

**Ver'suchs|anstalt** *f* research institute; **~kaninchen** *fig. n* guinea-pig; **2weise** *adv.* by way of trial or (*an*) experiment; on trial; **~zweck** *m*: *zu ~en pl.* for experimental purposes *pl.*

**Ver'suchung** *f* (-/-en) temptation; *j-n in ~ bringen* tempt *s.o.*; *in ~ sein* be tempted.

**ver'|sündigen** *v/refl.* (*no -ge-, h*) sin (*an dat.* against); **~sunken** *fig. adj.* [~'zuŋkən]: ~ *in* (*acc.*) absorbed

or lost in; **~'süßen** *v/t.* (*no -ge-, h*) sweeten.

**ver'tag|en** *v/t.* (*no -ge-, h*) adjourn; *parl.* prorogue; *sich* ~ adjourn, *Am. a.* recess; **2ung** *f* adjournment; *parl.* prorogation.

**ver'tauschen** *v/t.* (*no -ge-, h*) exchange (*mit* for).

**verteidig|en** [fer'taidigən] *v/t.* (*no -ge-, h*) defend; *sich* ~ defend o.s.; **2er** *m* (-*s*/-) defender; *§§, fig.* advocate; *§§* counsel for the defen|ce, *Am.* -se, *Am.* attorney for the defendant or defense; *football*: fullback; **2ung** *f* (-/~-en) defen|ce, *Am.* -se.

**Ver'teidigungs|bündnis** *n* defensive alliance; **~minister** *m* minister of defence; *Brt.* Minister of Defence, *Am.* Secretary of Defense; **~ministerium** *n* ministry of defence; *Brt.* Ministry of Defence, *Am.* Department of Defense.

**ver'teil|en** *v/t.* (*no -ge-, h*) distribute; spread (*colour, etc.*); **2er** *m* (-*s*/-) distributor; **2ung** *f* (-/~-en) distribution.

**ver'teuern** *v/t.* (*no -ge-, h*) raise or increase the price of.

**ver'tief|en** *v/t.* (*no -ge-, h*) deepen (*a. fig.*); *sich* ~ deepen; *sich* ~ *in* (*acc.*) plunge in(to); become absorbed in; **2ung** *f* (-/-en) hollow, cavity; recess.

**vertikal** *adj.* [verti'ka:l] vertical.

**ver'tilg|en** *v/t.* (*no -ge-, h*) exterminate; F consume, eat (up) (*food*); **2ung** *f* (-/~-en) extermination.

**ver'tonen** *♪ v/t.* (*no -ge-, h*) set to music.

**Vertrag** [fer'tra:k] *m* (-[e]s/~e) agreement, contract; *pol.* treaty; **2en** [~gən] *v/t.* (*irr. tragen, no -ge-, h*) endure, bear, stand; *diese Speise kann ich nicht* ~ this food does not agree with me; *sich* ~ *things*: be compatible or consistent; *colours*: harmonize; *p.*: agree; get on with one another; *sich wieder* ~ be reconciled, make it up; **2lich** [~kliç] **1.** *adj.* contractual, stipulated; **2.** *adv.* as stipulated; ~ *verpflichtet sein* to be bound by contract; *sich* ~ *verpflichten* contract (*zu für s.th.*; *zu inf.* to *inf.*).

**verträglich** *adj.* [fer'tre:kliç] sociable.

**Ver'trags|bruch** *m* breach of contract; **2brüchig** *adj.*: ~ *werden* commit a breach of contract; **~entwurf** *m* draft agreement; **~partner** *m* party to a contract.

**ver'trauen** **1.** *v/i.* (*no -ge-, h*) trust (*j-m s.o.*); ~ *auf* (*acc.*) trust or confide in; **2.** **2** *n* (-*s*/*no pl.*) confidence, trust; *im* ~ confidentially, between you and me; **~erweckend** *adj.* inspiring confidence; promising.

**Ver'trauens|bruch** *m* breach or

betrayal of trust; **~frage** *parl. f*: *die ~ stellen* put the question of confidence; **~mann** *m* (-[e]s/~er, *Vertrauensleute*) spokesman; shopsteward; confidential agent; **~sache** *f*: *das ist ~* that is a matter of confidence; **~stellung** *f* position of trust; **2voll** *adj.* trustful, trusting; **~votum** *parl. n* vote of confidence; **2würdig** *adj.* trustworthy, reliable.

**ver'traulich** *adj.* confidential, in confidence; intimate, familiar; **2keit** *f* (-/-en) confidence; intimacy, familiarity.

**ver'traut** *adj.* intimate, familiar; **2e** (-n/-n) **1.** *m* confidant, intimate friend; **2.** *f* confidante, intimate friend; **2heit** *f* (-/~ -en) familiarity.

**ver'treiben** *v/t.* (*irr.* treiben, no -ge-, h) drive away; expel (*aus* from); turn out; † sell, distribute (*goods*); slide the Zeit ~ pass one's time, kill time; **2ung** *f* (-/~-en) expulsion.

**ver'tret|en** *v/t.* (*irr.* treten, no -ge-, h) represent (*s.o., firm, etc.*); substitute for *s.o.*; attend to, look after (*s.o.'s interests*); hold (*view*); *parl.* sit for (*borough*); answer for *s.th.*; *j-s Sache ~* ⚖ plead s.o.'s case *or* cause; *sich den Fuß ~* sprain one's foot; *F sich die Beine ~* stretch one's legs; **2er** *m* (-s/-) representative; † *a.* agent; proxy, agent; substitute, deputy; exponent; (sales) representative; door-to-door salesman; commercial travel(l)er, *esp. Am.* travel(l)ing salesman; **2ung** *f* (-/-en) representation (*a. pol.*); † agency; *in office*: substitution; *in ~* by proxy; *gen.*: acting for.

**Vertrieb** † [fɛr'triːp] *m* (-[e]s/-e) sale; distribution; **~ene** [~bənə] *m,f* (-n/-n) expellee.

**ver'trocknen** *v/i.* (no -ge-, sein) dry up; **~'trödeln** F *v/t.* (no -ge-, h) dawdle away, waste (*time*); **~'trösten** *v/t.* (no -ge-, h) put off; **~'tuschen** F *v/t.* (no -ge-, h) hush up; **~'übeln** *v/t.* (no -ge-, h) take *s.th.* amiss; **~'üben** *v/t.* (no -ge-, h) commit, perpetrate.

**ver'unglück|en** *v/i.* (no -ge-, sein) meet with *or* have an accident; F *fig.* fail, go wrong; *tödlich ~* be killed in an accident; **2te** *m,f* (-n/-n) casualty.

**verun|reinigen** [fɛr'unrainigən] *v/t.* (no -ge-, h) soil, dirty; defile; contaminate (*air*); pollute (*water*); **~stalten** [~ʃtaltən] *v/t.* (no -ge-, h) disfigure.

**ver'untreu|en** *v/t.* (no -ge-, h) embezzle; **2ung** *f* (-/-en) embezzlement.

**ver'ursachen** *v/t.* (no -ge-, h) cause.

**ver'urteil|en** *v/t.* (no -ge-, h) condemn (*zu* to) (*a. fig.*), sentence (to);

convict (*wegen* of); **2te** *m,f* (-n/-n) convict; **2ung** *f* (-/-en) condemnation (*a. fig.*), conviction.

**ver'vielfältigen** [fɛr'fiːlfɛltigən] *v/t.* (no -ge-, h) manifold; **~vollkommnen** [~'fɔlkɔmnən] *v/t.* (no -ge-, h) perfect; *sich ~* perfect o.s.

**vervollständig|en** [fɛr'fɔlʃtɛndigən] *v/t.* (no -ge-, h) complete; **2ung** *f* (-/~ -en) completion.

**ver|'wachsen 1.** *v/i.* (*irr.* wachsen, no -ge-, sein): *miteinander ~* grow together; **2.** *adj.* deformed; ⚕ humpbacked, hunchbacked; **~'wackeln** *phot. v/t.* (no -ge-, h) blur.

**ver'wahr|en** *v/t.* (no -ge-, h) keep; *sich ~ gegen* protest against; **~lost** *adj.* [~loːst] *child, garden, etc.*: uncared-for, neglected; degenerate; **2ung** *f* keeping; charge; custody; *fig.* protest; *j-m et. in ~ geben* give s.th. into s.o.'s charge; *in ~ nehmen* take charge of.

**verwaist** *adj.* [fɛr'vaist] orphan(ed); *fig.* deserted.

**ver'walt|en** *v/t.* (no -ge-, h) administer, manage; **2er** *m* (-s/-) administrator, manager; steward (*of estate*); **2ung** *f* (-/-en) administration; management.

**ver'wand|eln** *v/t.* (no -ge-, h) change, turn, transform; *sich ~* change (*all: in acc.* into); **2lung** *f* (-/-en) change; transformation.

**verwandt** *adj.* [fɛr'vant] related (*mit* to); *languages, tribes, etc.*: kindred; *languages, sciences*: cognate (with); *pred.* akin (to) (*a. fig.*); **2e** *m, f* (-n/-n) relative, relation; **2schaft** *f* (-/-en) relationship; relations *pl.*; *geistige ~* congeniality.

**ver'warn|en** *v/t.* (no -ge-, h) caution; **2ung** *f* caution.

**ver'wässern** *v/t.* (no -ge-, h) water (down), dilute; *fig.* water down, dilute.

**ver'wechs|eln** *v/t.* (no -ge-, h) mistake (*mit* for); confound, mix up, confuse (*all: mit* with); **2(e)lung** *f* (-/-en) mistake; confusion.

**verwegen** *adj.* [fɛr've:gən] daring, bold, audacious; **2heit** *f* (-/~-en) boldness, audacity, daring.

**ver|'wehren** *v/t.* (no -ge-, h): *j-m et. ~* (de)bar s.o. from (doing) s.th.; *den Zutritt ~* deny *or* refuse admittance (*zu* to); **~'weichlicht** *adj.* effeminate, soft.

**ver'weiger|n** *v/t.* (no -ge-, h) deny, refuse; disobey (*order*); **2ung** *f* denial, refusal.

**ver'weilen** *v/i.* (no -ge-, h) stay, linger; *bei et. ~* dwell (up)on s.th.

**Verweis** [fɛr'vais] *m* (-es/-e) reprimand; rebuke, reproof; reference (*auf acc.* to); **2en** [~zən] *v/t.* (*irr.* weisen, no -ge-, h): *j-n des Landes ~* expel s.o. from Germany, *etc.*;

*j-m et.* ~ reprimand s.o. for s.th.; *j-n* ~ *auf (acc.) or an (acc.)* refer s.o. to.

ver'welk|en *v/i. (no -ge-, sein)* fade, wither (up).

ver'wend|en *v/t. ([irr. wenden,] no -ge-, h)* employ, use; apply *(für for);* spend *(time, etc.) (auf acc. on); sich bei j-m* ~ *für* intercede with s.o. for; **2ung** *f (-/%-en)* use, employment; application; *keine* ~ *haben für* have no use for.

ver'werf|en *v/t. (irr. werfen, no -ge-, h)* reject; ➡ quash *(verdict);* **~lich** *adj.* abominable.

ver'werten *v/t. (no -ge-, h)* turn to account, utilize.

verwes|en [fɛr've:zən] *v/i. (no -ge-, sein)* rot, decay; **2ung** *f (-/%-en)* decay.

ver'wick|eln *v/t. (no -ge-, h)* entangle *(in acc. in); sich* ~ entangle o.s. (in) *(a. fig.);* **~elt** *fig. adj.* complicated; **2(e)lung** *f (-/-en)* entanglement; *fig. a.* complication.

ver'wilder|n *v/i. (no -ge-, sein)* run wild; **~t** *adj.* garden, *etc.:* uncultivated, weed-grown; *fig.* wild, unruly.

ver'winden *v/t. (irr. winden, no -ge-, h)* get over *s.th.*

ver'wirklich|en *v/t. (no -ge-, h)* realize; *sich* ~ be realized, *esp. Am.* materialize; come true; **2ung** *f (-/%-en)* realization.

ver'wirr|en *v/t. (no -ge-, h)* entangle; *j-n* ~ confuse s.o.; embarrass s.o.; **~t** *fig. adj.* confused; embarrassed; **2ung** *fig. f (-/-en)* confusion.

ver'wischen *v/t. (no -ge-, h)* wipe or blot out; efface *(a. fig.);* blur, obscure; cover up *(one's tracks).*

ver'witter|n *geol. v/i. (no -ge-, sein)* weather; **~t** *adj. geol.* weathered; weather-beaten *(a. fig.).*

ver'witwet *adj.* widowed.

verwöhn|en [fɛr'vø:nən] *v/t. (no -ge-, h)* spoil; **~t** *adj.* fastidious, particular.

verworren *adj.* [fɛr'vɔrən] ideas, *etc.:* confused; *situation, plot:* intricate.

verwund|bar *adj.* [fɛr'vuntba:r] vulnerable *(a. fig.);* **~en** [~dən] *v/t. (no -ge-, h)* wound.

ver'wunder|lich *adj.* astonishing; **2ung** *f (-/%-en)* astonishment.

Ver'wund|ete ⚔ *m (-n/-n)* wounded (soldier); casualty; **~ung** *f (-/-en)* wound, injury.

ver'wünsch|en *v/t. (no -ge-, h)* curse; **2ung** *f (-/-en)* curse.

ver'wüst|en *v/t. (no -ge-, h)* lay waste, devastate, ravage *(a. fig.);* **2ung** *f (-/-en)* devastation, ravage.

verzag|en [fɛr'tsa:gən] *v/i. (no -ge-, h)* despond *(an dat.* of); **~t** *adj.* [~kt] despondent; **2theit** [~kt-] *f (-/no pl.)* desponden|ce, -cy.

ver|'zählen *v/refl. (no -ge-, h)* miscount; **~zärteln** [~'tsɛ:rtəln] *v/t. (no -ge-, h)* coddle, pamper; **~'zaubern** *v/t. (no -ge-, h)* bewitch, enchant, charm; **~'zehren** *v/t. (no -ge-, h)* consume *(a. fig.).*

ver'zeichn|en *v/t. (no -ge-, h)* note down; record; list; *fig.* distort; ~ *können, zu* ~ *haben* score *(success, etc.);* **~et** *paint. adj.* out of drawing; **2is** *n (-ses/-se)* list, catalog(ue); register; inventory; index *(of book);* table, schedule.

verzeih|en [fɛr'tsaɪən] *(irr., no -ge-, h)* **1.** *v/t.* pardon, forgive; ~ *Sie!* I beg your pardon!; excuse me!; sorry!; **2.** *v/t.* pardon, forgive *(j-m et. s.o. s.th.);* **~lich** *adj.* pardonable; **2ung** *f (-/no pl.)* pardon; ~*!* I beg your pardon!, sorry!

ver'zerr|en *v/t. (no -ge-, h)* distort; *sich* ~ become distorted; **2ung** *f* distortion.

ver'zetteln *v/t. (no -ge-, h)* enter on cards; *sich* ~ fritter away one's energies.

Verzicht [fɛr'tsɪçt] *m (-[e]s/-e)* renunciation *(auf acc.* of); **2en** *v/i. (no -ge-, h)* renounce *(auf et. s.th.);* do without (s.th.).

verzieh [fɛr'tsi:] *pret. of* verzeihen.

ver'ziehen[1] *(irr. ziehen, no -ge-)* **1.** *v/i. (sein)* (re)move *(nach to);* **2.** *v/t. (h)* spoil *(child);* distort; *das Gesicht* ~ make a wry face, screw up one's face, grimace; *ohne e-e Miene zu* ~ without betraying the least emotion; *sich* ~ *wood:* warp; *crowd, clouds:* disperse; *storm, clouds:* blow over; F disappear.

ver'ziehen[2] *p.p. of* verzeihen.

ver'zier|en *v/t. (no -ge-, h)* adorn, decorate; **2ung** *f (-/-en)* decoration; ornament.

verzins|en [fɛr'tsɪnzən] *v/t. (no -ge-, h)* pay interest on; *sich* ~ yield interest; **2ung** *f (-/%-en)* interest.

ver'zöger|n *v/t. (no -ge-, h)* delay, retard; *sich* ~ be delayed; **2ung** *f (-/-en)* delay, retardation.

ver'zollen *v/t. (no -ge-, h)* pay duty on; *haben Sie et. zu* ~*?* have you anything to declare?

verzück|t *adj.* [fɛr'tsykt] ecstatic, enraptured; **2ung** *f (-/%-en)* ecstasy, rapture; *in* ~ *geraten* go into ecstasies *(wegen* over).

Ver'zug *m (-[e]s/no pl.)* delay; ✝ default; *in* ~ *geraten* ✝ come in default; *im* ~ *sein* (be in) default.

ver'zweif|eln *v/i. (no -ge-, h, sein)* despair *(an dat.* of); *es ist zum Verzweifeln* it is enough to drive one mad; **~elt** *adj.* hopeless; desperate; **2lung** *f (-/no pl.)* despair; *j-n zur* ~ *bringen* drive s.o. to despair.

verzweig|en [fɛr'tsvaɪgən] *v/refl. (no -ge-, h)* ramify; *trees:* branch (out); *road:* branch; *business firm, etc.*: branch out; 2ung *f* (-/-en) ramification; branching.

**verzwickt** *adj.* [fɛr'tsvikt] intricate, complicated.

**Veteran** [vete'raːn] *m* (-en/-en) ✕ veteran (*a. fig.*), ex-serviceman.

**Veterinär** [veteri'nɛːr] *m* (-s/-e) veterinary (surgeon), F vet.

**Veto** ['veːto] *n* (-s/-s) veto; *ein ~ einlegen gegen* put a veto on, veto *s.th.*

**Vetter** ['fɛtər] *m* (-s/-n) cousin; '~nwirtschaft *f* (-/no *pl.*) nepotism.

**vibrieren** [vi'briːrən] *v/i.* (*no* -ge-, h) vibrate.

**Vieh** [fiː] *n* (-[e]s/no *pl.*) livestock, cattle; animal, brute, beast; F *fig.* brute, beast; '~bestand *m* livestock; '~händler *m* cattle-dealer; '~hof *m* stockyard; '2isch *adj.* bestial, beastly, brutal; '~wagen 🚃 *m* stock-car; '~weide *f* pasture; '~zucht *f* stock-farming, cattle-breeding; '~züchter *m* stockbreeder, stock-farmer, cattle-breeder, *Am. a.* rancher.

**viel** [fiːl] **1.** *adj.* much; ~e *pl.* many; a lot (of), lots of; plenty of (*cake, money, room, time, etc.*); *das ~e Geld* all that money; *seine ~en Geschäfte pl.* his numerous affairs *pl.*; *sehr ~e pl.* a great many *pl.*; *ziemlich ~* a good deal of; *ziemlich ~e pl.* a good many *pl.*; *~ zuviel* far too much; *sehr ~* a great *or* good deal; **2.** *adv.* much; *~ besser* much *or* a good deal *or* a lot better; *et. ~ lieber tun* prefer to do *s.th.*

**viel|beschäftigt** *adj.* ['fiːlbəʃɛftiçt] very busy; '~deutig *adj.* ambiguous; ~erlei *adj.* ['~ər'laɪ] of many kinds, many kinds of; multifarious; ~fach ['~fax] **1.** *adj.* multiple; **2.** *adv.* in many cases, frequently; ~fältig *adj.* ['~fɛltiç] multiple, manifold, multifarious; ~'leicht *adv.* perhaps, maybe; ~mals *adv.* ['~maːls]: *ich danke Ihnen ~* many thanks, thank you very much; *sie läßt (dich) ~ grüßen* she sends you her kind regards; *ich bitte ~ um Entschuldigung* I am very sorry, I do beg your pardon; ~'mehr *cj.* rather; '~sagend *adj.* significant, suggestive; ~seitig *adj.* ['~zaɪtiç] many-sided, versatile; '~versprechend *adj.* (very) promising.

**vier** *adj.* [fiːr] four; *zu ~t* four of us *or* them; *auf allen ~en* on all fours; *unter ~ Augen* confidentially, privately; *um halb ~* at half past three; '~beinig *adj.* four-legged; '2eck *n* square, quadrangle; '~eckig *adj.* square, quadrangular; ~erlei *adj.* ['~ər'laɪ] of four different kinds, four kinds of; ~fach *adj.* ['~fax] fourfold; ~e *Ausfertigung* four copies; 2füßer *zo.* ['~fyːsər] *m* (-s/-) quadruped; ~füßig *adj.* ['~fyːsiç]

four-footed; *zo.* quadruped; 2füßler *zo.* ['~fyːslər] *m* (-s/-) quadruped; ~händig *f adv.* ['~hendiç]: *~ spielen* play a duet; ~jährig *adj.* ['~jɛːriç] four-year-old, of four; 2linge ['~liŋə] *m/pl.* quadruplets *pl.*, F quads *pl.*; '~mal *adv.* four times; ~schrötig *adj.* ['~ʃrøːtiç] square-built, thickset; ~seitig *adj.* ['~zaɪtiç] four-sided; ⅋ quadrilateral; '2sitzer *esp. mot. m* (-s/-) four-seater; ~stöckig *adj.* ['~ʃtœkiç] four-storeyed, four-storied; '2taktmotor *mot. m* four-stroke engine; '~te *adj.* fourth; '~teilen *v/t.* (ge-, h) quarter.

**Viertel** ['firtəl] *n* (-s/-) fourth (part); quarter; ~ *fünf*, (*ein*) ~ *nach vier* a quarter past four; *drei ~ vier* a quarter to four; '~jahr *n* three months *pl.*, quarter (of a year); '2jährlich, 2'jährlich **1.** *adj.* quarterly; **2.** *adv.* every three months, quarterly; '~note *f* crotchet, *Am. a.* quarter note; '~pfund *n*, ~'pfund *n* quarter of a pound; ~'stunde *f* quarter of an hour, *Am.* quarter hour.

**vier|tens** *adv.* ['fiːrtəns] fourthly; 2'vierteltakt *f m* common time. **vierzehn** *adj.* ['firtseːn] fourteen; ~ *Tage pl.* a fortnight, *Am.* two weeks *pl.*; '~te *adj.* fourteenth.

**vierzig** *adj.* ['firtsiç] forty; '~ste *adj.* fortieth.

**Vikar** *eccl.* [vi'kaːr] *m* (-s/-e) curate; vicar.

**Villa** ['vila] *f* (-/Villen) villa.

**violett** *adj.* [vio'lɛt] violet.

**Violine** *f* [vio'liːnə] *f* (-/-n) violin.

**Viper** *zo.* ['viːpər] *f* (-/-n) viper.

**virtuos** *adj.* [virtu'oːs] masterly; 2e [~zə] *m* (-n/-n), 2in [~zin] *f* (-/-nen) virtuoso; 2ität [~ozi'tɛːt] *f* (-/no *pl.*) virtuosity.

**Virus** 🔬 ['viːrus] *n, m* (-/Viren) virus.

**Vision** [vi'zjoːn] *f* (-/-en) vision.

**Visitation** [vizita'tsjoːn] *f* (-/-en) search; inspection.

**Visite** *f* [vi'ziːtə] *f* (-/-n) visit; ~nkarte *f* visiting-card, *Am.* calling card.

**Visum** ['viːzum] *n* (-s/Visa, Visen) visa, visé.

**Vitalität** [vitali'tɛːt] *f* (-/no *pl.*) vitality. [min.]

**Vitamin** [vita'miːn] *n* (-s/-e) vita-]

**Vize|kanzler** ['fiːtsə-] *m* vice-chancellor; '~könig *m* viceroy; '~konsul *m* vice-consul; '~präsident *m* vice-president.

**Vogel** ['foːgəl] *m* (-s/~) bird; F *e-n ~ haben* have a bee in one's bonnet, *sl.* have bats in the belfry; *den ~ abschießen* carry off the prize, *Am. sl.* take the cake; '~bauer *n, m* (-s/-) bird-cage; '~flinte *f* fowling-piece; '2frei *adj.* outlawed; '~futter *n* food for birds, bird-seed; '~kunde *f* (-/*no pl.*) ornithology; '~lieb-haber *m* bird-fancier; '~nest *n* bird's nest, bird-nest; '~perspek-tive *f* (-/*no pl.*), '~schau *f* (-/*no pl.*) bird's-eye view; '~scheuche *f* (-/-*n*) scarecrow (*a. fig.*); ~'Strauß-Politik *f* ostrich policy; ~ betreiben hide one's head in the sand (like an ostrich); '~warte *f* ornithological station; '~zug *m* passage *or* migration of birds.

**Vokab|el** [vo'ka:bəl] *f* (-/-*n*) word; ~ular [~abu'la:r] *n* (-*s*/-*e*) vocabulary.

**Vokal** *ling.* [vo'ka:l] *m* (-*s*/-*e*) vowel.

**Volk** [fɔlk] *n* 1. (-[*e*]*s*/-*er*) people; nation; swarm (*of bees*); covey (*of partridges*); 2. (-[*e*]*s*/*no pl.*) populace, *the* common people; *contp. the* common *or* vulgar herd; *der Mann aus dem* ~*e* the man in the street *or Am.* on the street.

**Völker|bund** ['fœlkər-] *m* (-[*e*]*s*/*no pl.*) League of Nations; '~kunde *f* (-/*no pl.*) ethnology; '~recht *n* (-[*e*]*s*/*no pl.*) international law, law of nations; '~wanderung *f* age of national migrations.

'**Volks|abstimmung** *pol. f* plebi-scite; '~ausgabe *f* popular edition (*of book*); '~bücherei *f* free *or* pub-lic library; '~charakter *m* national character; '~dichter *m* popular *or* national poet; '~entscheid *pol.* ['~entʃaɪt] *m* (-[*e*]*s*/-*e*) referendum; plebiscite; '~fest *n* fun fair, amuse-ment park *or* grounds *pl.*; public merry-making; national festival; '~gunst *f* popularity; '~herr-schaft *f* democracy; '~hochschule *f* adult education (*courses pl.*); '~lied *n* folk-song; '~menge *f* crowd (*of people*), multitude; '~partei *f* people's party; '~republik *f* people's republic; '~schule *f* elementary *or* primary school, *Am. a.* grade school; '~schullehrer *m* elementary *or* primary teacher, *Am.* grade teacher; '~sprache *f* vernac-ular; '~stamm *m* tribe, race; '~stück *thea. n* folk-play; '~tanz *m* folk-dance; '~tracht *f* national costume; ~tümlich *adj.* ['~ty:mliç] national; popular; '~versamm-lung *f* public meeting; '~vertreter *parl. m* deputy, representative; member of parliament; *Brt.* Mem-ber of Parliament, *Am.* Represent-ative; '~vertretung *parl. f* repre-sentation of the people; parliament; '~wirt *m* (political) economist; '~wirtschaft *f* economics, political economy; ~wirtschaftler ['~tlər] *m* (-*s*/-) *s.* Volkswirt; '~zählung *f* census.

**voll** [fɔl] 1. *adj.* full; filled; whole, complete, entire; *figure, face:* full, round; *figure:* buxom; *~er Knospen* full of buds; *aus* ~*em Halse* at the top of one's voice; *aus* ~*em Herzen* from the bottom of one's heart; *in* ~*er Blüte* in full blossom; *in* ~*er Fahrt* at full speed; *mit* ~*en Händen* lavishly, liberally; *mit* ~*em Recht* with perfect right; *um das Unglück* ~*zumachen* to make things worse; 2. *adv.* fully, in full; ~ *und ganz* fully, entirely; *j-n nicht für* ~ *an-sehen or nehmen* have a poor opinion of s.o., think little of s.o.

'**voll|auf** *adv.*, ~'auf *adv.* abundant-ly, amply, F plenty; '~automatisch *adj.* fully automatic; '2bad *n* bath; '2bart *m* beard; '2beschäftigung *f* full employment; '2besitz *m* full possession; '2blut(pferd) *zo. n* thoroughbred (horse); '~bringen *v/t.* (*irr.* bringen, *no* -ge-, *h*) ac-complish, achieve; perform; '2-dampf *m* full steam; F: *mit* ~ at *or* in full blast; ~'enden *v/t.* (*no* -ge-, *h*) finish, complete; ~'endet *adj.* perfect; ~ends *adv.* ['~ɛnts] entirely, wholly, altogether; 2'endung *f* (-/~-*en*) finishing, completion; *fig.* perfection.

**Völlerei** [fœlə'raɪ] *f* (-/~-*en*) gluttony.

**voll|'führen** *v/t.* (*no* -ge-, *h*) ex-ecute, carry out; '~füllen *v/t.* (*sep.*, -ge-, *h*) fill (up); '2gas *mot. n*: ~ geben open the throttle; *mit* ~ with the throttle full open; at full speed; ~gepfropft *adj.* ['~gəpfrɔpft] crammed, packed; '~gießen *v/t.* (*irr.* gießen, *sep.*, -ge-, *h*) fill (up); '2gummi *n*, *m* solid rubber.

**völlig** *adj.* ['fœliç] entire, complete; *silence, calm, etc.*: dead.

**voll|jährig** *adj.* ['fɔljɛ:riç]: ~ *sein* be of age; ~ *werden* come of age; '2jährigkeit *f* (-/*no pl.*) majority; '~kommen *adj.* perfect; 2'kom-menheit *f* (-/~-*en*) perfection; '2kornbrot *n* whole-meal bread; '~machen *v/t.* (*sep.*, -ge-, *h*) fill (up); F soil, dirty; *um das Unglück vollzumachen* to make things worse; '2macht *f* (-/-*en*) full power, authority; ±±± power of attorney; ~ *haben* be authorized; '2matrose ♧ *m* able-bodied seaman; '2milch *f* whole milk; '2mond *m* full moon; '~packen *v/t.* (*sep.*, -ge-, *h*) stuff, cram; '2pension *f* (-/-*en*) full board; '~schenken *v/t.* (*sep.*, -ge-, *h*) fill (up); '~schlank *adj.* stout, corpu-lent; '~ständig *adj.* complete; '~stopfen *v/t.* (*sep.*, -ge-, *h*) stuff, cram; *sich* ~ stuff o.s.; *sich die Taschen* ~ stuff one's pockets; ~'strecken *v/t.* (*no* -ge-, *h*) execute; 2'streckung *f* (-/-*en*) execution; '~tönend *adj.* sonorous, rich; '2treffer *m* direct hit; '2versamm-lung *f* plenary meeting *or* assembly; General Assembly (*of the United Nations*); '~wertig *adj.* equivalent, equal in value; full; '**‿zählig** adj. complete; **‿'ziehen** v/t. (irr. ziehen, no -ge-, h) execute; consummate (marriage); sich ‿ take place; **2'ziehung** f (-/‿‸-en), **2'zug** m (-[e]s/no pl.) execution.

**Volontär** [volɔn'tɛːr] m (-s/-e) unpaid assistant.

**Volt** ⚡ [volt] n (-, -[e]s/-) volt.

**Volumen** [vo'luːmən] n (-s/-, Volumina) volume.

**vom** prp. [fɔm] = von dem

**von** prp. (dat.) [fɔn] space, time: from; instead of gen.: of; passive: by; ‿ Hamburg from Hamburg; ‿ nun an from now on; ‿ morgen an from tomorrow (on), beginning tomorrow; ein Freund ‿ mir a friend of mine; die Einrichtung ‿ Schulen the erection of schools; ‿ dem or vom Apfel essen eat (some) of the apple; der Herzog ‿ Edinburgh the Duke of Edinburgh; ein Gedicht ‿ Schiller a poem by Schiller; ‿ selbst by itself; ‿ selbst, ‿ sich aus by oneself; ‿ drei Meter Länge three metres long; ein Betrag ‿ 300 Mark a sum of 300 marks; e-e Stadt ‿ 10 000 Einwohnern a town of 10,000 inhabitants; reden ‿ talk of or about s.th.; speak in (scientific subject); ‿ mir aus as far as I am concerned; I don't mind, for all I care; das ist nett ‿ ihm that is nice of him; ich habe ‿ ihm gehört I have heard of him; **‿statten** adv. [‿'ʃtatən]: gut ‿ gehen go well.

**vor** prp. (dat.; acc.) [foːr] space: in front of, before; time: before; ‿ langer Zeit a long time ago; ‿ einigen Tagen a few days ago; (heute) ‿ acht Tagen a week ago (today); am Tage ‿ (on) the day before, on the eve of; 5 Minuten ‿ 12 five minutes to twelve, Am. five minutes of twelve; fig. at the eleventh hour; ‿ der Tür stehen be imminent, be close at hand; ‿ e-m Hintergrund against a background; ‿ Zeugen in the presence of witnesses; ‿ allen Dingen above all; (dicht) ‿ dem Untergang stehen be on the brink or verge of ruin; ‿ Hunger sterben die of hunger; ‿ Kälte zittern tremble with cold; schützen (verstecken) ‿ protect (hide) from or against; ‿ sich gehen take place, pass off; ‿ sich hin lächeln smile to o.s.; sich fürchten ‿ be afraid of, fear.

**Vor|abend** ['foːr‸-] m eve; '**‿ahnung** f presentiment, foreboding.

**voran** adv. [fo'ran] at the head (dat. of), in front (of); before; Kopf ‿ head first; **‿gehen** v/i. (irr. gehen, sep., -ge-, sein) lead the way; precede; **‿kommen** v/i. (irr. kommen, sep., -ge-, sein) make progress; fig. get on (in life).

**Voran|schlag** ['foːr‸an-] m (rough)

estimate; '**‿zeige** f advance notice; film: trailer.

**vorarbeite|n** ['foːr‸-] v/t. and v/i. (sep., -ge-, h) work in advance; '**2r** m foreman.

**voraus** adv. [fo'raus] in front (dat. of), ahead (of); im ‿ in advance, beforehand; **‿bestellen** v/t. (sep., no -ge-, h) s. vorbestellen; **‿bezahlen** v/t. (sep., no -ge-, h) pay in advance, prepay; **‿gehen** v/i. (irr. gehen, sep., -ge-, sein) go on before; s. vorangehen; **2sage** f prediction; prophecy; forecast (of weather); **‿sagen** v/t. (sep., -ge-, h) foretell, predict; prophesy; forecast (weather, etc.); **‿schicken** v/t. (sep., -ge-, h) send on in advance; fig. mention beforehand, premise; **‿sehen** v/t. (irr. sehen, sep., -ge-, h) foresee; **‿setzen** v/t. (sep., -ge-, h) (pre)suppose, presume, assume; vorausgesetzt, daß provided that; **2setzung** f (-/-en) (pre)supposition, assumption; prerequisite; **2sicht** f foresight; aller ‿ nach in all probability; **‿sichtlich** adj. presumable, probable, likely; **2zahlung** f advance payment or instal(l)ment.

**'Vor|bedacht 1.** m (-[e]s/no pl.): mit ‿ deliberately, on purpose; **2.** 2 adj. premeditated; '**‿bedeutung** f foreboding, omen, portent; '**‿bedingung** f prerequisite.

**Vorbehalt** ['foːrbəhalt] m (-[e]s/-e) reservation, reserve; '**2en 1.** v/t. (irr. halten, sep., no -ge-, h): sich ‿ reserve (right, etc.); **2.** adj.: Änderungen ‿ subject to change (without notice); '**2los** adj. unreserved, unconditional.

**vorbei** adv. [foːr'baɪ] space: along, by, past (all: an dat. s.o., s.th.); time: over, gone; 3 Uhr ‿ past three (o'clock); **‿fahren** v/i. (irr. fahren, sep., -ge-, sein) drive past; **‿gehen** v/i. (irr. gehen, sep., -ge-, sein) pass, go by; pain: pass (off); storm: blow over; ‿ an (dat.) pass; im Vorbeigehen in passing; **‿kommen** v/i. (irr. kommen, sep., -ge-, sein) pass by; F drop in; F ‿ an (dat.) get past (obstacle, etc.); **‿lassen** v/t. (irr. lassen, sep., -ge-, h) let pass.

**'Vorbemerkung** f preliminary remark or note.

**'vorbereit|en** v/t. (sep., no -ge-, h) prepare (für, auf acc. for); '**2ung** f preparation (für, auf acc. for).

**'Vorbesprechung** f preliminary discussion or talk.

**'vor|bestellen** v/t. (sep., no -ge-, h) order in advance; book (room, etc.); '**‿bestraft** adj. previously convicted.

**'vorbeug|en** (sep., -ge-, h) **1.** v/i. prevent (e-r Sache s.th.); **2.** v/t. and v/refl. bend forward; '**‿end**

*adj.* preventive; ⚕ *a.* prophylactic; **'≈ung** *f* prevention.

**'Vorbild** *n* model; pattern; example; prototype; **'≈lich** *adj* exemplary; **≈ung** ['≈dʊŋ] *f* preparatory training.

**'vor|bringen** *v/t.* (*irr. bringen, sep.,* -ge-, *h*) bring forward, produce; advance (*opinion*); ⟵ prefer (*charge*); utter, say, state; **'≈datieren** *v/t.* (*sep., no* -ge-, *h*) post-date.

**vorder** *adj.* ['fɔrdər] front, fore.

**'Vorder|achse** *f* front axle; **'≈ansicht** *f* front view; **'≈bein** *n* foreleg; **'≈fuß** *m* forefoot; **'≈grund** *m* foreground (*a. fig.*); **'≈haus** *n* front building; **'≈mann** *m* man in front (*of s.o.*); **'≈rad** *n* front wheel; **≈radantrieb** *mot.* ['fɔrdərraːtˀ-] *m* front-wheel drive; **'≈seite** *f* front (side); obverse (*of coin*); **'≈sitz** *m* front seat; **'≈st** *adj.* foremost; **'≈teil** *n, m* front (part); **'≈tür** *f* front door; **'≈zahn** *m* front tooth; **'≈zimmer** *n* front room.

**'vordrängen** *v/refl.* (*sep.,* -ge-, *h*) press *or* push forward.

**'vordring|en** *v/i.* (*irr. dringen, sep.,* -ge-, *sein*) advance; **'≈lich** *adj.* urgent. [blank.⟩

**'Vordruck** *m* (-[e]s/-e) form, *Am. a.*⟩

**voreilig** *adj.* ['foːr'-] hasty, rash, precipitate; **≈e** *Schlüsse ziehen* jump to conclusions.

**voreingenommen** *adj.* ['foːrˀ-] prejudiced, bias(s)ed; **'≈heit** *f* (-/*no pl.*) prejudice, bias.

**vor|enthalten** ['foːrˀ-] *v/t.* (*irr. halten, sep., no* -ge-, *h*) keep back, withhold (*j-m et. s.th. from s.o.*); **≈entscheidung** ['foːrˀ-] *f* preliminary decision; **≈erst** *adv.* ['foːrˀ-] for the present, for the time being.

**Vorfahr** ['foːrfaːr] *m* (-en/-en) ancestor.

**'vorfahr|en** *v/i.* (*irr. fahren, sep.,* -ge-, *sein*) drive up; pass; *den Wagen* **≈** *lassen* order the car; **'≈t(srecht** *n*) *f* right of way, priority.

**'Vorfall** *m* incident, occurrence, event; **'≈en** *v/i.* (*irr. fallen, sep.,* -ge-, *sein*) happen, occur.

**'vorfinden** *v/t.* (*irr. finden, sep.,* -ge-, *h*) find.

**'Vorfreude** *f* anticipated joy.

**'vorführ|en** *v/t.* (*sep.,* -ge-, *h*) bring forward, produce; bring (*dat.* before); show, display, exhibit; demonstrate (*use of s.th.*); show, present (*film*); **'≈er** *m* projectionist (*in cinema theatre*); **'≈ung** *f* presentation, showing; ⊕ demonstration; ⟵ production (*of prisoner*); *thea., film:* performance.

**'Vor|gabe** *f* sports: handicap; *athletics:* stagger; *golf, etc.:* odds *pl.*; **'≈gang** *m* incident, occurrence, event; facts *pl.*; file, record(s *pl.*); *biol.,* ⊕ process; **≈gänger** ['≈gɛŋər]

*m* (-s/-), **'≈gängerin** *f* (-/-nen) predecessor; **'≈garten** *m* front garden.

**'vorgeben** *v/t.* (*irr. geben, sep.,* -ge-, *h*) *sports:* give (*j-m s.o.*); *fig.* pretend, allege.

**'Vor|gebirge** *n* promontory, cape, headland; foot-hills *pl.*; **'≈gefühl** *n* presentiment, foreboding.

**'vorgehen** **1.** *v/i.* (*irr. gehen, sep.,* -ge-, *sein*) ⚔ advance; F lead the way; go on before; *watch, clock:* be fast, gain (*fünf Minuten* five minutes); take precedence (*dat.* of, over), be more important (than); take action, act; proceed (*a. ⟵*; *gegen against*); go on, happen, take place; **2.** ≈ *n* (-s/*no pl.*) action, proceeding.

**'Vor|geschmack** *m* (-[e]s/*no pl.*) foretaste; **≈gesetzte** ['≈gəzɛtstə] *m* (-n/-n) superior; *esp. Am.* F boss; **'≈gestern** *adv.* the day before yesterday; **'≈greifen** *v/i.* (*irr. greifen, sep.,* -ge-, *h*) anticipate (*j-m or e-r Sache s.o. or s.th.*).

**'vorhaben** **1.** *v/t.* (*irr. haben, sep.,* -ge-, *h*) intend, mean; be going to do *s.th.*; *nichts* **≈** be at a loose end; *haben Sie heute abend et. vor?* have you anything on tonight?; *was hat er jetzt wieder vor?* what is he up to now?; *was hast du mit ihm vor?* what are you going to do with him?; **2.** ≈ *n* (-s/-) intention, purpose, ⟵ intent; plan; project.

**'Vorhalle** *f* vestibule, (entrance-) hall; lobby; porch.

**'vorhalt|en** (*irr. halten, sep.,* -ge-, *h*) **1.** *v/t.*: *j-m et.* **≈** hold s.th. before s.o.; *fig.* reproach s.o. with s.th.; **2.** *v/i.* last; **'≈ung** *f* remonstrance; *j-m* **≈en** *machen* remonstrate with s.o. (*wegen on*).

**vorhanden** *adj.* [for'handən] at hand, present; available (*a.* ✝); ✝ on hand, in stock; **≈** *sein* exist; **≈-sein** *n* presence, existence.

**'Vor|hang** *m* curtain; **'≈hänge-schloß** *n* padlock.

**'vorher** *adv.* before, previously; in advance, beforehand.

**vor'her|bestellen** *v/t.* (*sep., no* -ge-, *h*) *s.* vorbestellen; **≈bestimmen** *v/t.* (*sep., no* -ge-, *h*) determine beforehand, predetermine; **≈gehen** *v/i.* (*irr. gehen, sep.,* -ge-, *sein*) precede; **≈ig** *adj.* preceding, previous.

**'Vorherr|schaft** *f* predominance; **'≈schen** *v/i.* (*sep.,* -ge-, *h*) predominate, prevail; **'≈schend** *adj.* predominant, prevailing.

**Vor'her|sage** *f s.* Voraussage; **≈sa-gen** *v/t.* (*sep.,* -ge-, *h*) *s.* voraus-sagen; **≈sehen** *v/t.* (*irr. sehen, sep.,* -ge-, *h*) foresee; **≈wissen** *v/t.* (*irr. wissen, sep.,* -ge-, *h*) know beforehand, foreknow.

'vor|hin *adv.*, ~'hin *adv.* a short while ago, just now.

'Vor|hof *m* outer court, forecourt; *anat.* auricle (*of heart*); '~hut ⚔ *f* vanguard.

'vor|ig *adj.* last; ~jährig *adj.* [~je:riç] of last year, last year's.

'Vor|kämpfer *m* champion, pioneer; '~kehrung *f* (-/-en) precaution; ~en treffen take precautions; '~kenntnisse *f/pl.* preliminary *or* basic knowledge (*in dat.* of); mit guten ~n in (*dat.*) well grounded in.

'vorkommen **1.** *v/i.* (*irr.* kommen, *sep.*, -ge-, *sein*) be found; occur, happen; es kommt mir vor it seems to me; **2.** ♀ *n* (-s/-) occurrence.

'Vor|kommnis *n* (-ses/-se) occurrence; event; '~kriegszeit *f* prewar times *pl.*

'vorlad|en ɫʰʰ *v/t.* (*irr.* laden, *sep.*, -ge-, *h*) summon; '♀ung ɫʰʰ *f* summons.

'Vorlage *f* copy; pattern; *parl.* bill; presentation; production (*of document*); *football:* pass.

'vorlassen *v/t.* (*irr.* lassen, *sep.*, ~ge-, *h*) let *s.o.* pass, allow *s.o.* to pass; admit.

'Vorläuf|er *m*, '~erin *f* (-/-nen) forerunner; '♀ig **1.** *adj.* provisional, temporary; **2.** *adv.* provisionally, temporarily; for the present, for the time being.

'vorlaut *adj.* forward, pert.

'Vorleben *n* past (life), antecedents *pl.*

'vorleg|en *v/t.* (*sep.*, -ge-, *h*) put (*lock*) on; produce (*document*); submit (*plans, etc.* for discussion, *etc.*); propose (*plan, etc.*); present (*bill, etc.*); j-m et. ~ lay *or* place *or* put o.th. before *s.o.*; show *s.o.* s.th.; at table: help s.o. to s.th.; j-m e-e Frage ~ put a question to *s.o.*; sich ~ lean forward; '♀r *m* (-ɛ/-) rug.

'vorles|en *v/t.* (*irr.* lesen, *sep.*, -ge-, *h*) read aloud; j-m et. ~ read (out) s.th. to *s.o.*; '♀ung *f* lecture (*über acc.* on; vor *dat.* to); e-e ~ halten (give a) lecture.

'vorletzt *adj.* last but one; ~e Nacht the night before last.

'Vorlieb|e *f* (-/no *pl.*) predilection, preference; ♀nehmen [~'li:p~] *v/i.* (*irr.* nehmen, *sep.*, -ge-, *h*) be satisfied (*mit* with); ~ mit dem, was da ist at meals: take pot luck.

'vorliegen *v/i.* (*irr.* liegen, *sep.*, -ge-, *h*) lie before *s.o.*; be there, exist; da muß ein Irrtum ~ there must be a mistake; was liegt gegen ihn vor? what is the charge against him?; '~d *adj.* present, in question.

'vor|lügen *v/t.* (*irr.* lügen, *sep.*, -ge-, *h*): j-m et. ~ tell *s.o.* lies; '~machen *v/t.* (*sep.*, -ge-, *h*): j-m et. ~ show s.o. how to do s.th.; *fig.* impose upon *s.o.*; sich (*selbst*) et. ~ fool o.s.

'Vormacht *f* (-/~⚔e), '~stellung *f* predominance; supremacy; hegemony.

'Vormarsch ⚔ *m* advance.

'vormerken *v/t.* (*sep.*, -ge-, *h*) note down, make a note of; reserve; sich ~ lassen für put one's name down for.

'Vormittag *m* morning, forenoon; '♀s *adv.* in the morning.

'Vormund *m* (-[e]s/-e, ~er) guardian; '~schaft *f* (-/-en) guardianship.

vorn *adv.* [fɔrn] in front; nach ~ forward; von ~ from the front; ich sah sie von ~ I saw her face; von ~ anfangen begin at the beginning; noch einmal von ~ anfangen begin anew, make a new start.

'Vorname *m* Christian name, first name, *Am. a.* given name.

vornehm ['fo:rne:m] **1.** *adj.* of (superior) rank, distinguished; aristocratic; noble; fashionable; ~e Gesinnung high character; **2.** *adv.:* ~ tun give o.s. airs; '~en *v/t.* (*irr.* nehmen, *sep.*, -ge-, *h*) take s.th. in hand; deal with; make (*changes, etc.*); take up (*book*); F sich j-n ~ take s.o. to task (wegen for, about); sich ~ resolve (up)on s.th.; resolve (zu *inf.* to *inf.*), make up one's mind (to *inf.*); sich vorgenommen haben a. be determined (zu *inf.* to *inf.*); '♀heit *f* (-/no *pl.*) refinement; elegance; high-mindedness.

'vorn|herein *adv.*, ~he'rein *adv.:* von ~ from the first *or* start *or* beginning.

Vorort ['fo:rʔ~] *m* (-[e]s/-e) suburb; '~(s)verkehr *m* suburban traffic; '~(s)zug *m* local (train).

'Vor|posten *m* outpost (*a.* ⚔); '~rang *m* (-[e]s/no *pl.*) precedence (vor *dat.* of, over), priority (over); '~rat *m* store, stock (*an dat.* of); Vorräte *pl.* a. provisions *pl.*, supplies *pl.*; ♀rätig *adj.* ['~re:tiç] available; * *a.* on hand, in stock; '♀rechnen *v/t.* (*sep.*, -ge-, *h*) reckon up (j-m to *s.o.*); '~recht *n* privilege; '~rede *f* preface, introduction; '~redner *m* previous speaker; '~richtung ⊕ *f* contrivance, device; '♀rücken (*sep.*, -ge-) **1.** *v/t.* (*h*) move (*chair, etc.*) forward; **2.** *v/i.* (*sein*) advance; '~runde *f* *sports:* preliminary round; '♀sagen *v/i.* (*sep.*, -ge-, *h*): j-m ~ prompt *s.o.*; '~saison *f* off *or* dead season; '~satz *m* intention, purpose; design; ♀sätzlich *adj.* ['~zetsliç] intentional, deliberate; ~er Mord ɫʰʰ wil(l)ful murder; '~schein *m:* zum ~ bringen bring forward, produce; zum ~ kommen appear, turn up; '♀schieben *v/t.* (*irr.* schieben, *sep.*, -ge-, *h*) push s.th. forward; slip (*bolt*); s. vorschützen; '♀schießen *v/t.* (*irr. schießen, sep.,* -ge-, *h*) advance (*money*).

**'Vorschlag** *m* proposition, proposal; suggestion; offer; **Ωen** ['⁓ɡən] *v/t.* (*irr. schlagen, sep.,* -ge-, *h*) propose; suggest; offer.

**'Vor|schlußrunde** *f sports:* semifinal; **Ωschnell** *adj.* hasty, rash; **Ωschreiben** *v/t.* (*irr. schreiben, sep.,* -ge-, *h*): *j-m* et. ⁓ write s.th. out for s.o.; *fig.* prescribe.

**'Vorschrift** *f* direction, instruction; prescription (*esp.* ⚕); order (*a.* ⚔); regulation(s *pl.*); **Ωsmäßig** *adj.* according to regulations; ⁓e *Kleidung* regulation dr ss; **Ωswidrig** *adj. and adv.* contrary to regulations.

**'Vor|schub** *m:* ⁓ *leisten* (*dat.*) countenance (*fraud, etc.*); further, encourage; ⚖ aid and abet; **'⁓schule** *f* preparatory school; **'⁓schuß** *m* advance; *for barrister:* retaining fee, retainer; **Ωschützen** *v/t.* (*sep.,* -ge-, *h*) pretend, pl ad (*sickness, etc. as excuse*); **Ωschweben** *v/i.* (*sep.,* -ge-, *h*): *mir schwebt* et. *vor* I have s.th. in mind.

**'vorseh|en** *v/t.* (*irr. sehen, sep.,* -ge-, *h*) plan; design; ⚖ provide; *sich* ⁓ take care, be careful; *sich* ⁓ *vor* (*dat.*) guard against; **Ωung** *f* (-/⚖ -en) providence.

**'vorsetzen** *v/t.* (*sep.,* -ge-, *h*) put forward; place *or* put *or* set before, offer.

**'Vorsicht** *f* caution; care; ⁓*!* caution!; danger!; look out!, be careful!; ⁓, *Glas!* Glass, with care!; ⁓, *Stufe!* mind the step!; **Ωig** *adj.* cautious; careful; ⁓*!* F steady!

**'vorsichts|halber** *adv.* as a precaution; **Ωmaßnahme** *f,* **Ωmaßregel** *f* precaution(ary measure); ⁓*n treffen* take precautions.

**'Vorsilbe** *gr. f* prefix.

**'vorsingen** *v/t.* (*irr. singen, sep.,* -ge-, *h*): *j-m* et. ⁓ sing s.th. to s.o.

**'Vorsitz** *m* (-es/*no pl.*) chair, presidency; *den* ⁓ *führen or haben* be in the chair, preside (*bei* over; at); *den* ⁓ *übernehmen* take the chair; ⁓ende ['⁓ɔndə] (-n/-n) 1. *m* chairman, president; 2. *f* chairwoman.

**'Vorsorg|e** *f* (-/*no pl.*) provision; providence; precaution; ⁓ *treffen* make provision; **Ωen** *v/i.* (*sep.,* -ge-, *h*) provide; **Ωlich** ['⁓klɪç] 1. *adj.* precautionary; 2. *adv.* as a precaution.

**'Vorspeise** *f* appetizer, hors d'œuvre.

**'vorspieg|eln** *v/t.* (*sep.,* -ge-, *h*) pretend; *j-m* et. ⁓ delude s.o. (with false hopes, *etc.*); **Ω(e)lung** *f* preten|ce, *Am.* -se.

**'Vorspiel** *n* prelude; **Ωen** *v/t.* (*sep.,* -ge-, *h*): *j-m* et. ⁓ play s.th. to s.o.

**'vor|sprechen** (*irr. sprechen, sep.,* -ge-, *h*) 1. *v/t.* pronounce (*j-m* et.

s.th. to *or* for s.o.); 2. *v/i.* call (*bei* on s.o.; at *an office*); *thea.* audition; **'⁓springen** *v/i.* (*irr. springen, sep.,* -ge-, *sein*) jump forward; project; **Ωsprung** *m* △ projection; *sports:* lead; *fig.* start, advantage (*vor dat.* of); **Ωstadt** *f* suburb; '⁓städtisch *adj.* suburban; **Ωstand** *m* board of directors, managing directors *pl.*

**'vorsteh|en** *v/i.* (*irr. stehen, sep.,* -ge-, *h*) project, protrude; *fig.:* direct; manage (*both:* e-r *Sache* s.th.); **Ωer** *m* director, manager; head, chief.

**'vorstell|en** *v/t.* (*sep.,* -ge-, *h*) put forward; put (*clock*) on; introduce (*j-n* j-m s.o. to s.o.); mean, stand for; represent; *sich* ⁓ *bei* have an interview with; *sich* et. ⁓ imagine *or* fancy s.th.; **Ωung** *f* introduction, presentation; interview (*of applicant for post*); *thea.* performance; *fig.:* remonstrance; idea, conception; imagination; **Ωungsvermögen** *n* imagination.

**'Vor|stoß** ⚔ *m* thrust, advance; **'⁓strafe** *f* previous conviction; **Ωstrecken** *v/t.* (*sep.,* -ge-, *h*) thrust out, stretch forward; advance (*money*); **'⁓stufe** *f* first step *or* stage; **Ωtäuschen** *v/t.* (*sep.,* -ge-, *h*) feign, pretend.

**Vorteil** ['fɔrtaɪl] *m* advantage (*a. sports*); profit; *tennis:* (ad)vantage; **Ωhaft** *adj.* advantageous (*für* to), profitable (to).

**Vortrag** ['foːrtraːk] *m* (-[e]s/⁓e) performance; execution (*of a piece* ♪); recitation (*of poem*); ♪ recital; lecture; report; ♦ balance carried forward; e-n ⁓ *halten* (give a) lecture (*über acc.* on); **Ωen** ['⁓ɡən] *v/t.* (*irr. tragen, sep.,* -ge-, *h*) ♦ carry forward; report on; recite (*poem*); perform, *esp.* ♪ execute; lecture on; state, express (*opinion*); ⁓ende ['⁓ɡəndə] *m* (-n/-n) performer; lecturer; speaker.

**vor|trefflich** *adj.* [foːr'treflɪç] excellent; **'⁓treten** *v/i.* (*irr. treten, sep.,* -ge-, *sein*) step forward; *fig.* project, protrude, stick out; **Ωtritt** *m* (-[e]s/*no pl.*) precedence.

**vorüber** [fo'ryːbər] *space:* by, past; *time:* gone by, over; ⁓gehen *v/i.* (*irr. gehen, sep.,* -ge-, *sein*) pass, go by; ⁓gehend *adj.* passing; temporary; **Ωgehende** [⁓də] *m* (-n/-n) passer-by; ⁓ziehen *v/i.* (*irr. ziehen, sep.,* -ge-, *sein*) march past, pass by; *storm:* blow over.

**Vor|übung** ['foːr⁓-] *f* preliminary practice; ⁓untersuchung ⚖ ['foːr⁓-] *f* preliminary inquiry.

**Vorurteil** ['foːr⁓-] *n* prejudice; **Ωslos** *adj.* unprejudiced, unbias(s)ed.

**'Vor|verkauf** *thea. m* booking in advance; *im* ⁓ bookable (*bei* at);

'**Qverlegen** v/t. (sep., no -ge-, h) advance; '~wand m (-[e]s/~e) pretext, preten|ce, Am. -se.

**vorwärts** adv. ['fo:rverts] forward, onward, on; ~! go ahead!; '~kommen v/i. (irr. kommen, sep., -ge-, sein) (make) progress; fig. make one's way, get on (in life).

**vorweg** adv. [for'vek] beforehand; ~nehmen v/t. (irr. nehmen, sep., -ge-, h) anticipate.

**vor|weisen** v/t. (irr. weisen, sep., -ge-, h) produce, show; '~werfen v/t. (irr. werfen, sep., -ge-, h) throw or cast before; j-m et. ~ reproach s.o. with s.th.; '~wiegend 1. adj. predominant, preponderant; 2. adv. predominantly, chiefly, mainly, mostly; '~witzig adj. forward, pert; inquisitive.

'**Vorwort** n (-[e]s/-e) preface (by author); foreword.

'**Vorwurf** m reproach; subject (of drama, etc.); j-m e-n ~ or Vorwürfe machen reproach s.o. (wegen with); '**Qsvoll** adj. reproachful.

'**vor|zählen** v/t. (sep., -ge-, h) enu-merate, count out (both: j-m to s.o.); '**Qzeichen** n omen; '~zeichnen v/t. (sep., -ge-, h): j-m et. ~ draw or sketch s.th. for s.o.; show s.o. how to draw s.th.; fig. mark out, destine; '~zeigen v/t. (sep., -ge-, h) produce, show.

'**Vorzeit** f antiquity; in literature often: times of old, days of yore; '**Qig** adj. premature.

'**vor|ziehen** v/t. (irr. ziehen, sep., -ge-, h) draw forth; draw (curtains); fig. prefer; '**Qzimmer** n antechamber, anteroom; waiting-room; '**Q-zug** fig. m preference; advantage; merit; priority; ~**züglich** adj. [~'tsy:kliç] excellent, superior, exquisite.

'**Vorzugs|aktie** f preference share or stock, Am. preferred stock; '~preis m special price; '**Qweise** adv. preferably; chiefly.

**Votum** ['vo:tum] n (-s/Voten, Vota) vote.

**vulgär** adj. [vul'ge:r] vulgar.

**Vulkan** [vul'ka:n] m (-s/-e) volcano; **Qisch** adj. volcanic.

# W

**Waag|e** ['va:gə] f (-/-n) balance, (e-e a pair of) scales pl.; die ~ halten (dat.) counterbalance; '**Qerecht** adj., **Qrecht** adj. ['va:k-] horizontal, level; ~**schale** ['va:k-] f scale.

**Wabe** ['va:bə] f (-/-n) honeycomb.

**wach** adj. [vax] awake; hell~ wide awake; ~ werden awake, wake up; '**Qe** f (-/-n) watch; guard; guardhouse, guardroom; police-station; sentry, sentinel; ~ haben be on guard; ~ halten keep watch; '~en v/i. (ge-, h) (keep) watch (über acc. over); sit up (bei with); '**Qhund** m watch-dog.

**Wacholder** 💠 [va'xɔldər] m (-s/-) juniper.

'**wach|rufen** v/t. (irr. rufen, sep., -ge-, h) rouse, evoke; '~rütteln v/t. (sep., -ge-, h) rouse (up); fig. rouse, shake up.

**Wachs** [vaks] n (-es/-e) wax.

'**wachsam** adj. watchful, vigilant; '**Qkeit** f (-/no pl.) watchfulness, vigilance.

**wachsen**[1] ['vaksən] v/i. (irr., ge-, sein) grow; fig. increase.

**wachsen**[2] [~] v/t. (ge-, h) wax.

**wächsern** adj. ['veksərn] wax; fig. waxen, waxy.

'**Wachs|kerze** f, '~licht n wax candle; '~tuch n waxcloth, oilcloth.

**Wachstum** ['vakstu:m] n (-s/no pl.) growth; fig. increase.

**Wächte** mount. ['veçtə] f (-/-n) cornice.

**Wachtel** orn. ['vaxtəl] f (-/-n) quail.

**Wächter** ['veçtər] m (-s/-) watcher, guard(ian); watchman.

'**Wacht|meister** m sergeant; '~turm m watch-tower.

**wackel|ig** adj. ['vakəliç] shaky (a. fig.), tottery; furniture, etc.: rickety; tooth, etc.: loose; '**Qkontakt** ∮ m loose connexion or (Am. only) connection; '~n v/t. (ge-, h) shake; table, etc.: wobble; tooth, etc.: be loose; tail, etc.: wag; ~ mit wag s.th.

**wacker** adj. ['vakər] honest, upright; brave, gallant.

**wacklig** adj. ['vakliç] s. wackelig.

**Wade** ['va:də] f (-/-n) calf; '~nbein anat. n fibula.

**Waffe** ['vafə] f (-/-n) weapon (a. fig.); ~n pl. a. arms pl.

**Waffel** ['vafəl] f (-/-n) waffle; wafer.

'**Waffen|fabrik** f armaments factory, Am. a. armory; '~gattung f arm; '~gewalt f (-/no pl.): mit ~ by force of arms; '**Qlos** adj. weaponless, unarmed; '~schein m firearm certificate, Am. gun license; '~stillstand m armistice (a. fig.), truce.

**Wage|hals** ['va:gəhals] m daredevil; '**Qhalsig** adj. daring, foolhardy; attr. a. daredevil; '~mut m daring

wagen¹ ['vɑːgən] v/t. (ge-, h) venture; risk, dare; sich ~ venture (an acc. [up]on).

Wagen² [~] m (-s/-, ⸚) carriage (a. 🐎); Am. 🚗 car; 🚃 coach; wag(g)on; cart; car; lorry, truck; van.

wägen ['vɛːgən] v/t. ([irr.,] ge-, h) weigh (a. fig.).

'Wagen|heber m (-s/-) (lifting) jack; '⸚park m (-[e]s/no pl.) fleet of vehicles; '⸚schmiere f grease; '⸚spur f rut.

Waggon 🚃 [va'gõː] m (-s/-s) (railway) carriage, Am. (railroad) car.

wag|halsig adj. ['vɑːkhalsiç] s. wagehalsig; '2nis n (-ses/-se) venture, risk.

Wahl [vɑːl] f (-/-en) choice; alternative; selection; pol. election; e-e ~ treffen make a choice; s-e ~ treffen take one's choice; ich hatte keine (andere) ~ I had no choice.

wählbar adj. ['vɛːlbɑːr] eligible; '2keit f (-/no pl.) eligibility.

wahl|berechtigt adj. ['vɑːlbəreçtiçt] entitled to vote; '2beteiligung f percentage of voting, F turn-out; '2bezirk m constituency.

'wählen (ge-, h) 1. v/t. choose; pol. elect; teleph. dial; 2. v/i. choose, take one's choice; teleph. dial (the number).

'Wahlergebnis n election return.

'Wähler m (-s/-) elector, voter; '2isch adj. particular (in dat. in, about, as to); nice (about), fastidious, F choosy; '⸚schaft f (-/-en) constituency, electorate.

'Wahl|fach n optional subject, Am. a. elective; '2fähig adj. having a vote; eligible; '⸚gang m ballot; '⸚kampf m election campaign; '⸚kreis m constituency; '⸚lokal n polling station; '2los adj. indiscriminate; '⸚recht n (-[e]s/no pl.) franchise; '⸚rede f electoral speech.

'Wählscheibe teleph. f dial.

'Wahl|spruch m device, motto; '⸚stimme f vote; '⸚urne f ballot-box; '⸚versammlung f electoral rally; '⸚zelle f polling-booth; '⸚zettel m ballot, voting-paper.

Wahn [vɑːn] m (-[e]s/no pl.) delusion, illusion; mania; '⸚sinn m (-[e]s/no pl.) insanity, madness (both a. fig.); '2sinnig adj. insane, mad (vor dat. with) (both a. fig.); '⸚sinnige ['⸚gə] m (-n/-n) madman, lunatic; '⸚vorstellung f delusion, hallucination; '⸚witz m (-es/no pl.) madness, insanity; '2witzig adj. mad, insane.

wahr adj. [vɑːr] true; real; genuine; '⸚en v/t. (ge-, h) safeguard (interests, etc.); maintain (one's dignity); den Schein ~ keep up or save appearances.

währen ['vɛːrən] v/i. (ge-, h) last, continue.

'während 1. prp. (gen.) during; pending; 2. cj. while, whilst; while, whereas.

'wahrhaft adv. really, truly, indeed; '2ig [⸚'haftiç] 1. adj. truthful, veracious; 2. adv. really, truly, indeed.

'Wahrheit f (-/-en) truth; in ~ in truth; j-m die ~ sagen give s.o. a piece of one's mind; '2sgetreu adj. true, faithful; '⸚sliebe f (-/no pl.) truthfulness, veracity; '2sliebend adj. truthful, veracious.

'wahr|lich adv. truly, really; '⸚nehmbar adj. perceivable, perceptible; '⸚nehmen v/t. (irr. nehmen, sep., -ge-, h) perceive, notice, avail o.s. of (opportunity); safeguard (interests); '2nehmung f (-/-en) perception, observation; '⸚sagen v/i. (sep., -ge-, h) tell or read fortunes; sich ~ lassen have one's fortune told; '2sagerin f (-/-nen) fortune-teller; '⸚'scheinlich 1. adj. probable; likely; 2. adv.: ich werde ~ gehen I am likely to go; 2'scheinlichkeit f (-/⸚-en) probability, likelihood; aller ~ nach in all probability or likelihood.

'Wahrung f (-/no pl.) maintenance; safeguarding.

Währung ['vɛːruŋ] f (-/-en) currency; standard; '⸚sreform f currency or monetary reform.

'Wahrzeichen n landmark.

Waise ['vaɪzə] f (-/-n) orphan; '⸚haus n orphanage.

Wal zo. [vɑːl] m (-[e]s/-e) whale.

Wald [valt] m (-[e]s/⸚er) wood, forest; '⸚brand m forest fire; 2ig adj. ['⸚diç] wooded, woody; 2reich adj. ['⸚t-] rich in forests; ⸚ung ['⸚duŋ] f (-/-en) forest.

Walfänger ['vɑːlfɛŋər] m (-s/-) whaler.

walken ['valkən] v/t. (ge-, h) full (cloth); mill (cloth, leather).

Wall [val] m (-[e]s/⸚e) ⚔ rampart (a. fig.); dam; mound.

Wallach ['valax] m (-[e]s/-e) gelding.

wallen ['valən] v/i. (ge-, h, sein) hair, articles of dress, etc.: flow; simmer; boil (a. fig.).

wall|fahren ['valfɑːrən] v/i. (ge-, sein) (go on a) pilgrimage; '2fahrer m pilgrim; '2fahrt f pilgrimage; '⸚fahrten v/i. (ge-, sein) (go on a) pilgrimage.

'Wallung f (-/-en) ebullition; 🔬 congestion; (Blut) in ~ bringen make s.o.'s blood boil, enrage.

Walnuß ['val-] f walnut; '⸚baum ♣ m walnut(-tree).

Walroß zo. ['val-] n walrus.

walten ['valtən] v/i. (ge-, h): s-s Amtes ~ attend to one's duties; Gnade ~ lassen show mercy.

Walze ['valtsə] f (-/-n) roller, cylinder; ⊕ a. roll; ⊕, ♪ barrel; '2n v/t. (ge-, h) roll (a. ⊕).

**wälzen** ['vɛltsən] v/t. (ge-, h) roll; roll (*problem*) round in one's mind; shift (*blame*) (*auf acc.* [up]on); *sich* ~ roll; wallow (*in mud, etc.*); welter (*in blood, etc.*).

**Walzer** ♪ ['valtsər] m (-s/-) waltz.

**Wand** [vant] 1. f (-/ᵘe) wall; partition; 2. 2 *pret. of* winden.

**Wandel** ['vandəl] m (-s/no pl.) change; '2bar adj. changeable; variable; '~gang m, '~halle f lobby; '2n (ge-) 1. v/i. (sein) walk; 2. v/refl. (h) change.

**Wander|er** ['vandərər] m (-s/-) wanderer; hiker; '~leben n (-s/no pl.) vagrant life; '2n v/t. (ge-, sein) wander; hike; '~niere ♀ f floating kidney; '~prediger m itinerant preacher; '~preis m challenge trophy; '~schaft f (-/no pl.) wanderings pl.; *auf (der)* ~ on the tramp; '~ung f (-/-en) walking-tour; hike.

**'Wand|gemälde** n mural (painting); '~kalender m wall-calendar; '~karte f wall-map.

**Wandlung** ['vandluŋ] f (-/-en) change, transformation; eccl. transubstantiation; ⅗ redhibition.

**'Wand|schirm** m folding-screen; '~schrank m wall-cupboard; '~spiegel m wall-mirror; '~tafel f blackboard; '~teppich m tapestry; '~uhr f wall-clock.

**wandte** ['vantə] *pret. of* wenden 2.

**Wange** ['vaŋə] f (-/-n) cheek.

**Wankel|mut** ['vaŋkəlmuːt] m fickleness, inconstancy; 2mütig adj. ['~myːtiç] fickle, inconstant.

**wanken** ['vaŋkən] v/i. (ge-, h, sein) totter, stagger (a. fig.); house, etc.: rock; fig. waver.

**wann** adv. [van] when; s. dann; seit ~? how long?; since when?

**Wanne** ['vanə] f (-/-n) tub; bath (-tub), F tub; '~nbad n bath, F tub.

**Wanze** zo. ['vantsə] f (-/-n) bug, Am. a. bedbug.

**Wappen** ['vapən] n (-s/-) (coat of) arms pl.; '~kunde f (-/no pl.) heraldry; '~schild m, n escutcheon; '~tier n heraldic animal.

**wappnen** fig. ['vapnən] v/refl. (ge-, h): sich ~ gegen be prepared for; sich mit Geduld ~ have patience.

**war** [vaːr] *pret. of* sein¹.

**warb** [varp] *pret. of* werben.

**Ware** ['vaːrə] f (-/-n) commodity, article of trade; ~n pl. a. goods pl., merchandise, wares pl.

**'Waren|aufzug** m hoist; '~bestand m stock (on hand); '~haus n department store; '~lager n stock; warehouse, Am. a. stock room; '~probe f sample; '~zeichen n trade mark.

**warf** [varf] *pret. of* werfen.

**warm** adj. [varm] warm (a. fig.); meal: hot; schön ~ nice and warm.

**Wärme** ['vɛrmə] f (-/⚛-n) warmth; phys. heat; '~grad m degree of heat; '2n v/t. (ge-, h) warm; sich die Füße ~ warm one's feet.

**'Wärmflasche** f hot-water bottle.

**'warmherzig** adj. warm-hearted.

**'Warm|wasser|heizung** f hot-water heating; '~versorgung f hot-water supply.

**warn|en** ['varnən] v/t. (ge-, h) warn (vor dat. of, against), caution (against); '2signal n danger-signal (a. fig.); '2streik m token strike; '2ung f (-/-en) warning, caution; 2ungstafel ['varnuŋs-] f notice-board.

**Warte** fig. ['vartə] f (-/-n) point of view.

**warten** ['vartən] v/i. (ge-, h) wait (auf acc. for); be in store (for s.o.); j-n ~ lassen keep s.o. waiting.

**Wärter** ['vɛrtər] m (-s/-) attendant; keeper; (male) nurse.

**'Warte|saal** m, '~zimmer n waiting-room.

**Wartung** ⊕ ['vartuŋ] f (-/⚛-en) maintenance.

**warum** adv. [va'rum] why.

**Warze** ['vartsə] f (-/-n) wart; nipple.

**was** [vas] 1. interr. pron. what; ~ kostet das Buch? how much is this book?; F ~ rennst du denn so (schnell)? why are you running like this?; ~ für (ein) ...! what a(n) ...!; ~ für ein ...? what ...?; 2. rel. pron. what; ~ (auch immer), alles ~ what(so)ever; ..., ~ ihn völlig kalt ließ ... which left him quite cold; 3. F indef. pron. something; ich will dir mal ~ sagen I'll tell you what.

**wasch|bar** adj. ['vaʃbaːr] washable; '2becken n wash-basin, Am. wash-bowl.

**Wäsche** ['vɛʃə] f (-/-n) wash(ing); laundry; linen (a. fig.); underwear; in der ~ sein at the wash; sie hat heute große ~ she has a large wash today.

**waschecht** adj. ['vaʃ?-] washable; colour: a. fast; fig. dyed-in-the-wool.

**'Wäsche|klammer** f clothes-peg, clothes-pin; '~leine f clothes-line.

**'waschen** v/t. (irr., ge-, h) wash; sich ~ (lassen) a. wash; sich das Haar or den Kopf ~ wash or shampoo one's hair or head; sich gut ~ (lassen) wash well.

**Wäscher|ei** [vɛʃə'raɪ] f (-/-en) laundry; '~in f (-/-nen) washer-woman, laundress.

**'Wäscheschrank** m linen closet.

**'Wasch|frau** f s. Wäscherin; '~haus n wash house; '~kessel m copper; '~korb m clothes-basket;

'**.küche** f wash-house; '**.lappen** m face-cloth, Am. washrag, wash-cloth; '**.maschine** f washing machine, washer; '**.pulver** n washing powder; '**.raum** m lavatory, Am. a. washroom; '**.schüssel** f wash-basin; '**.tag** m wash(ing)-day; '**.ung** f (-/-en) ♣ wash; ablution; '**.weib** contp. n gossip; '**.wanne** f wash-tub.

**Wasser** ['vasər] n (-s/-, =) water; ~ lassen make water; zu ~ und zu Land(e) by sea and land; '**.ball** m 1. beach-ball; water-polo ball; 2. (-[e]s/no pl.) water-polo; '**.ball-spiel** n 1. (-[e]s/no pl.) water-polo; 2. water-polo match; '**.behälter** m reservoir, water-tank; '**.blase** ♣ f water-blister; '**.dampf** m steam; '2**dicht** adj. waterproof; water-tight; '**.eimer** m water-pail, bucket; '**.fall** m waterfall, cascade; cataract; '**.farbe** f water-colo(u)r; '**.flugzeug** n waterplane, seaplane; '**.glas** n 1. tumbler; 2. 🦀 (-es/no pl.) water-glass; '**.graben** m ditch; '**.hahn** m tap, Am. a. faucet; '**.hose** f waterspout.

**wässerig** adj. ['vesəriç] watery, washy (a. fig.); j-m den Mund ~ machen make s.o.'s mouth water.

'**Wasser|kanne** f water-jug, ewer; '**.kessel** m kettle; '**.klosett** n water-closet, W.C.; '**.kraft** f water-power; '**.kraftwerk** n hydroelectric power station or plant, water-power station; '**.krug** m water-jug, ewer; '**.kur** f water-cure, hydropathy; '**.lauf** m water-course; '**.leitung** f water-supply; '**.leitungsrohr** n water-pipe; '**.mangel** m shortage of water; '2**n** v/i. (ge-, h) alight on water; splash down. [(salted herring, etc.).]

**wässern** ['vesərn] v/t. (ge-, h) soak]

'**Wasser|pflanze** f aquatic plant; '**.rinne** f gutter; '**.rohr** n water-pipe; '**.schaden** m damage caused by water; '**.scheide** f watershed, Am. a. divide; '2**scheu** adj. afraid of water; '**.schlauch** m water-hose; '**.spiegel** m water-level; '**.sport** m aquatic sports pl.; '**.spülung** f (-/-en) flushing (system); '**.stand** m water-level; '**.standsanzeiger** ['vasərʃtants⁹-] m water-gauge; '**.stiefel** m/pl. waders pl.; '**.stoff** 🦀 m (-[e]s/no pl.) hydrogen; '**.stoff-bombe** f hydrogen bomb, H-bomb; '**.strahl** m jet of water; '**.straße** f waterway; '**.tier** n aquatic animal; '**.verdrängung** f (-/-en) displacement; '**.versorgung** f water-supply; '**.waage** f spirit-level, water-level; '**.weg** m waterway; auf dem ~ by water; '**.welle** f water-wave; '**.werk** n waterworks sg., pl.; '**.zeichen** n watermark.

---

**wäßrig** adj. ['vesriç] s. wässerig.

**waten** ['va:tən] v/i. (ge-, sein) wade.

**watscheln** ['va:tʃəln] v/i. (ge-, sein, h) waddle.

**Watt** ⚡ [vat] n (-s/-) watt.

**Watt|e** ['vatə] f (-/-n) cotton-wool; surgical cotton; wadding; '**.e-bausch** m wad; 2**ieren** [~'ti:rən] v/t. wad, pad.

**weben** ['ve:bən] v/t. and v/i. ([irr.,] ge-, h) weave.

'**Weber** m (-s/-) weaver; '**.ei** [~'raɪ] f 1. (-/no pl.) weaving; 2. (-/-en) weaving-mill.

**Webstuhl** ['ve:pʃtu:l] m loom.

**Wechsel** ['vɛksəl] m (-s/-) change; allowance; ✝ bill (of exchange); hunt. runway; eigener ~ ✝ promissory note; '**.beziehung** f correlation; '**.fälle** ['~fɛlə] pl. vicissitudes pl.; '**.fieber** ♣ n (-s/no pl.) intermittent fever; malaria; '**.frist** ✝ f usance; '**.geld** n change; '**.kurs** m rate of exchange; '**.makler** ✝ m bill-broker; '2**n** (ge-, h) 1. v/t. change; vary; exchange (words, etc.); den Besitzer ~ change hands; die Kleider ~ change (one's clothes); 2. v/i. change; vary; alternate; '**.nehmer** ✝ m (-s/-) payee; 2**seitig** adj. ['~zaitiç] mutual, reciprocal; '**.strom** ⚡ m alternating current; '**.stube** f exchange office; '2**weise** adv. alternately, by or in turns; '**.wirkung** f interaction.

**wecke|n** ['vɛkən] v/t. (ge-, h) wake (up), waken; arouse (a. fig.); '2**r** m (-s/-) alarm-clock.

**wedeln** ['ve:dəln] v/i. (ge-, h): ~ mit wag (tail).

**weder** cj. ['ve:dər]: ~ ... noch neither ... nor.

**Weg¹** [ve:k] m (-[e]s/-e) way (a. fig.); road (a. fig.); path; route; walk; auf halbem ~ half-way; am ~e by the roadside; aus dem ~e gehen steer clear of; aus dem ~e räumen remove (a. fig.); in die ~e leiten set on foot, initiate.

**weg²** adv. [vɛk] away, off; gone; geh ~! be off (with you)!; ~ mit ihm! off with him!; Hände ~! hands off!; F ich muß ~ I must be off; F ganz ~ sein be quite beside o.s.; '**.bleiben** F v/i. (irr. bleiben, sep., -ge-, sein) stay away; be omitted; '**.bringen** v/t. (irr. bringen, sep., -ge-, h) take away; a. remove (things).

**wegen** prp. (gen.) ['ve:gən] because of, on account of, owing to.

**weg|fahren** ['vɛk-] (irr. fahren, sep., -ge-) 1. v/t. (h) remove; cart away; 2. v/i. (sein) leave; '**.fallen** v/i. (irr. fallen, sep., -ge-, sein) be omitted; be abolished; '2**gang** m (-[e]s/no pl.) going away, departure; '**.gehen** v/i. (irr. gehen, sep., -ge-, sein) go away or off; merchandise:

sell; '**~haben** F *v/t.* (*irr.* haben, *sep.*, -ge-, h): e-n ~ be tight; have a screw loose; *er hat noch nicht weg, wie man es machen muß* he hasn't got the knack of it yet; '**~jagen** *v/t.* (*sep.*, -ge-, h) drive away; '**~kommen** F *v/i.* (*irr.* kommen, *sep.*, -ge-, sein) get away; be missing; *gut* (*schlecht*) ~ come off well (badly); *mach, daß du wegkommst!* be off (with you)!; '**~lassen** *v/t.* (*irr.* lassen, *sep.*, -ge-, h) let *s.o.* go; leave out, omit; '**~laufen** *v/i.* (*irr.* laufen, *sep.*, -ge-, sein) run away; '**~legen** *v/t.* (*sep.*, -ge-, h) put away; '**~machen** F *v/t.* (*sep.*, -ge-, h) remove; *a.* take out (*stains*); '**~müssen** F *v/i.* (*irr.* müssen 1, *sep.*, -ge-, h): *ich muß weg* I must be off; **2nahme** [*'~na:mə*] *f* (-/-n) taking (away); '**~nehmen** *v/t.* (*irr.* nehmen, *sep.*, -ge-, h) take up, occupy (*time, space*); *j-m et.* ~ take s.th. away from *s.o.*; '**~raffen** *fig. v/t.* (*sep.*, -ge-, h) carry off.

**Wegrand** ['ve:k-] *m* wayside.

**weg|räumen** ['vɛk-] *v/t.* (*sep.*, -ge-, h) clear away, remove; '**~schaffen** *v/t.* (*sep.*, -ge-, h) remove; '**~schikken** *v/t.* (*sep.*, -ge-, h) send away *or* off; '**~sehen** *v/i.* (*irr.* sehen, *sep.*, -ge-, h) look away; ~ *über* (*acc.*) overlook, shut one's eyes to; '**~setzen** *v/t.* (*sep.*, -ge-, h) put away; *sich* ~ *über* (*acc.*) disregard, ignore; '**~streichen** *v/t.* (*irr.* streichen, *sep.*, -ge-, h) strike off *or* out; '**~tun** *v/t.* (*irr.* tun, *sep.*, -ge-, h) put away *or* aside.

**Wegweiser** ['ve:kvaızər] *m* (-s/-) signpost, finger-post; *fig.* guide.

**weg|wenden** ['vɛk-] *v/t.* ([*irr.* wenden,] *sep.*, -ge-, h) turn away, avert (*one's eyes*); *sich* ~ turn away; '**~werfen** *v/t.* (*irr.* werfen, *sep.*, -ge-, h) throw away; '**~werfend** *adj.* disparaging; '**~wischen** *v/t.* (*sep.*, -ge-, h) wipe off; '**~ziehen** (*irr.* ziehen, *sep.*, -ge-) 1. *v/t.* (h) pull *or* draw away; 2. *v/i.* (sein) (re)move.

**weh** [ve:] 1. *adj.* sore; 2. *adv.*: ~ *tun* ache, hurt; *j-m* ~ *tun* pain *or* hurt *s.o.*; *fig. a.* grieve *s.o.*; *sich* ~ *tun* hurt *o.s.*; *mir tut der Finger* ~ my finger hurts.

**Wehen¹** [ˈveːən] *f/pl.* labo(u)r, travail.

**wehen²** [~] (ge-, h) 1. *v/t.* blow; 2. *v/i.* blow; *es weht ein starker Wind* it is blowing hard.

**weh|klagen** *v/i.* (ge-, h) lament (*um* for, over); '**~leidig** *adj.* snivel(l)ing; *voice:* plaintive; '**2mut** *f* (-/*no pl.*) wistfulness; '**~mütig** *adj.* ['~my:tiç] wistful.

**Wehr** [ve:r] 1. *f* (-/-en): *sich zur* ~ *setzen* offer resistance (*gegen* to), show fight; 2. *n* (-[e]s/-e) weir;

'**~dienst** ✗ *m* military service; '**2en** *v/refl.* (ge-, h) defend *o.s.*; offer resistance (*gegen* to); '**2fähig** ✗ *adj.* able-bodied; '**2los** *adj.* defenceless, *Am.* defenseless; '**~pflicht** ✗ *f* (-/*no pl.*) compulsory military service, conscription; '**2pflichtig** ✗ *adj.* liable to military service.

**Weib** [vaip] *n* (-[e]s/-er) woman; wife; '**~chen** *zo. n* (-s/-) female.

**Weiber|feind** ['vaibər-] *m* woman-hater; '**~held** *contp. m* ladies' man; '**~volk** F *n* (-[e]s/*no pl.*) womenfolk.

**weib|lisch** *adj.* womanish, effeminate; '**~lich** *adj.* ['~p-] female; *gr.* feminine; womanly, feminine.

**weich** *adj.* [vaiç] soft (*a. fig.*); *meat, etc.:* tender; *egg:* soft-boiled; ~ *werden* soften; *fig.* relent.

**Weiche¹** 🚆 ['vaiçə] *f* (-/-n) switch; ~ *n pl.* points *pl.*

**Weiche²** *anat.* [~] *f* (-/-n) flank, side.

**weichen¹** ['vaiçən] *v/i.* (*irr.*, ge-, sein) give way, yield (*dat.* to); *nicht von der Stelle* ~ not to budge an inch; *j-m nicht von der Seite* ~ stick to *s.o.*

**weichen²** [~] *v/i.* (ge-, h, sein) soak.

'**Weichensteller** 🚆 *m* (-s/-) pointsman, switch-man.

'**weich|herzig** *adj.* soft-hearted, tender-hearted; '**~lich** *adj.* somewhat soft; *fig.* effeminate; **2ling** ['~liŋ] *m* (-s/-e) weakling, milksop, molly(-coddle), *sl.* sissy; '**2tier** *n* mollusc.

**Weide¹** 🌳 ['vaidə] *f* (-/-n) willow.

**Weide²** 🐄 [~] *f* (-/-n) pasture; *auf der* ~ out at grass; '**~land** *n* pasture(-land); '**2n** (ge-, h) 1. *v/t.* feed, pasture, graze; *sich* ~ an (*dat.*) gloat over; feast on; 2. *v/i.* pasture, graze.

'**Weiden|korb** *m* wicker basket, osier basket; '**~rute** *f* osier switch.

**weidmännisch** *hunt. adj.* ['vait-meniʃ] sportsmanlike.

**weiger|n** ['vaigərn] *v/refl.* (ge-, h) refuse, decline; '**2ung** *f* (-/-en) refusal.

**Weihe** *eccl.* ['vaiə] *f* (-/-n) consecration; ordination; '**2n** *eccl. v/t.* (ge-, h) consecrate; *j-n zum Priester* ~ ordain *s.o.* priest.

**Weiher** ['vaiər] *m* (-s/-) pond.

'**weihevoll** *adj.* solemn.

**Weihnachten** ['vainaxtən] *n* (-s/*no pl.*) Christmas, Xmas.

'**Weihnachts|abend** *m* Christmas eve; '**~baum** *m* Christmas-tree; '**~ferien** *pl.* Christmas holidays *pl.*; '**~fest** *n* Christmas; '**~geschenk** *n* Christmas present; '**~gratifikation** *f* Christmas bonus; '**~karte** *f* Christmas card; '**~lied** *n* carol, Christmas hymn; '**~mann** *m* Father Christmas, Santa Claus; '**~markt** *m* Christmas fair; '**~zeit** *f*

(-/*no pl.*) Christmas(-tide) (*in Germany beginning on the first Advent Sunday*).

'**Weih|rauch** *eccl. m* incense; '**~wasser** *eccl. n* (-s/*no pl.*) holy water.

**weil** *cj.* [vaɪl] because, since, as.

**Weil|chen** ['vaɪlçən] *n* (-s/-): ein ~ a little while, a spell; '**~e** *f* (-/*no pl.*): e-e ~ a while.

**Wein** [vaɪn] *m* (-[e]s/-e) wine; ♣ vine; wilder ~ ♣ Virginia creeper; '**~bau** *m* (-[e]s/*no pl.*) vine-growing, viticulture; '**~beere** *f* grape; '**~berg** *m* vineyard; '**~blatt** *n* vine-leaf.

**wein|en** ['vaɪnən] *v/i.* (ge-, h) weep (um, *vor dat.* for), cry (*vor dat.* for joy, *vor etc.*, with hunger, *etc.*); '**~erlich** *adj.* tearful, lachrymose; whining.

'**Wein|ernte** *f* vintage; '**~essig** *m* vinegar; '**~faß** *n* wine-cask; '**~flasche** *f* wine-bottle; '**~geist** *m* (-[e]s/-e) spirit(s *pl.*) of wine; '**~glas** *n* wineglass; '**~handlung** *f* wine-merchant's shop; '**~karte** *f* wine-list; '**~keller** *m* wine-vault; '**~kelter** *f* winepress; '**~kenner** *m* connoisseur of *or* in wines.

'**Weinkrampf** ♣ *m* paroxysm of weeping.

'**Wein|kühler** *m* wine-cooler; '**~lese** *f* vintage; '**~presse** *f* winepress; '**~ranke** *f* vine-tendril; '**~rebe** *f* vine; '**2rot** *adj.* claret-colo(u)red; '**~stock** *m* vine; '**~traube** *f* grape, bunch of grapes.

**weise**[1] ['vaɪzə] **1.** *adj.* wise; sage; **2.** ♀ *m* (-n/-n) wise man, sage.

**Weise**[2] [~] *f* (-/-n) ♪ melody, tune; *fig.* manner, way; auf diese ~ in this way.

**weisen** ['vaɪzən] (*irr.*, ge-, h) **1.** *v/t.*: j-m die Tür ~ show s.o. the door; von der Schule ~ expel from school; von sich ~ reject (idea, *etc.*); deny (charge, *etc.*); **2.** *v/i.*: ~ auf (*acc.*) point at *or* to.

**Weis|heit** ['vaɪshaɪt] *f* (-/~-en) wisdom; am Ende s-r ~ sein be at one's wit's end; '**~heitszahn** *m* wisdom-tooth; '**2machen** *v/t.* (sep., -ge-, h): j-m et. ~ make s.o. believe s.th.

**weiß** *adj.* [vaɪs] white; '**2blech** *n* tin(-plate); '**2brot** *n* white bread; '**2e** *m* (-n/-n) white (man); '**~en** *v/t.* (ge-, h) whitewash; '**~glühend** *adj.* white-hot, incandescent; '**2kohl** *m* white cabbage; '**~lich** *adj.* whitish; '**2waren** *pl.* linen goods *pl.*; '**2wein** *m* white wine.

**Weisung** ['vaɪzʊŋ] *f* (-/-en) direction, directive.

**weit** [vaɪt] **1.** *adj.* distant (von from); world, garment: wide; area, *etc.*: vast; garment: loose; journey, way: long; conscience: elastic; **2.** *adv.*: ~ entfernt far away; ~ entfernt von a. a long distance from; *fig.* far from;

~ und breit far and wide; ~ über sechzig (Jahre alt) well over sixty; bei ~em (by) far; von ~em from a distance.

**weit|ab** *adv.* ['vaɪt-] far away (von from); '**~aus** *adv.* (by) far, much; '**2blick** *m* (-[e]s/*no pl.*) far-sightedness; '**~blickend** *adj.* far-sighted, far-seeing; '**~en** *v/t.* and *v/refl.* (ge-, h) widen.

'**weiter 1.** *adj.* particulars, *etc.*: further; charges, *etc.*: additional, extra; ~e fünf Wochen another five weeks; bis auf ~es until further notice; ohne ~es without any hesitation; off-hand; **2.** *adv.* furthermore, moreover; ~! and so on; nichts ~ nothing more; und so ~ and so on; bis hierher und nicht ~ so far and no farther; '**2e** *n* (-n/*no pl.*) the rest; further details *pl.*

'**weiter|befördern** *v/t.* (sep., no -ge-, h) forward; '**~bestehen** *v/i.* (irr. stehen, sep., no -ge-, h) continue to exist; survive; '**~bilden** *v/t.* (sep., -ge-, h) give *s.o.* further education; sich ~ improve one's knowledge; continue one's education; '**~geben** *v/t.* (irr. geben, sep., -ge-, h) pass (dat., an *acc.* to); '**~gehen** *v/i.* (irr. gehen, sep., -ge-, sein) pass *or* move on, walk along; *fig.* continue, go on; '**~hin** *adv.* in (the) future; furthermore; et. ~ tun continue doing *or* to do s.th.; '**~kommen** *v/i.* (irr. kommen, sep., -ge-, sein) get on; '**~können** *v/i.* (irr. können, sep., -ge-, h) be able to go on; '**~leben** *v/i.* (sep., -ge-, h) live on, survive (a. *fig.*); '**~machen** *v/t.* and *v/i.* (sep., -ge-, h) carry on.

'**weit|gehend** *adj.* powers: large; support: generous; '**~gereist** *adj.* travel(l)ed; '**~greifend** *adj.* far-reaching; '**~herzig** *adj.* broad-minded; '**~hin** *adv.* far off; '**~läufig** ['~lɔyfɪç] *adj.* house, *etc.*: spacious; story, *etc.*: detailed; relative: distant; **2.** *adv.*: ~ erzählen (tell in) detail; er ist ~ verwandt mit mir he is a distant relative of mine; '**~reichend** *adj.* far-reaching; '**~schweifig** *adj.* diffuse, prolix; '**~sichtig** *adj.* ♣ far-sighted; *fig.* a. far-seeing; '**2sichtigkeit** ♣ *f* (-/~-en) far-sightedness; '**2sprung** *m* (-[e]s/*no pl.*) long jump, *Am.* broad jump; '**~tragend** *adj.* ✗ long-range; *fig.* far-reaching; '**~verbreitet** *adj.* widespread.

**Weizen** ♣ ['vaɪtsən] *m* (-s/-) wheat; '**~brot** *n* wheaten bread; '**~mehl** *n* wheaten flour.

**welch** [vɛlç] **1.** *interr. pron.* what; which; ~er? which one?; ~er von beiden? which of the two?; **2.** *rel. pron.* who, that; which, that; **3.** *F indef. pron.*: es gibt ~e, die sagen, daß ... there are some who say that ...; *es sollen viele Ausländer hier sein, hast du schon ~e gesehen?* many foreigners are said to be here, have you seen any yet?

**welk** *adj.* [vɛlk] faded, withered; *skin:* flabby, flaccid; '~**en** *v/i.* (ge-, sein) fade, wither.

**Wellblech** ['vɛlbleç] *n* corrugated iron.

**Welle** ['vɛlə] *f* (-/-n) wave (*a. fig.*); ⊕ shaft.

'**wellen** *v/t. and v/refl.* (ge-, h) wave; '**2bereich** *m* wave-range; ~**förmig** *adj.* ['~fœrmɪç] undulating, undulatory; '**2länge** ⚡ *f* wavelength; '**2linie** *f* wavy line; '**2reiten** *n* (-s/no *pl.*) surf-riding.

'**wellig** *adj.* wavy.

'**Wellpappe** *f* corrugated cardboard *or* paper.

**Welt** [vɛlt] *f* (-/-en) world; *die ganze ~* the whole world, all the world; *auf der ~* in the world, *auf der ganzen ~* all over the world; *zur ~ bringen* give birth to, bring into the world.

'**Welt|all** *n* universe, cosmos; '~**anschauung** *f* Weltanschauung; '~**ausstellung** *f* world fair; '**2bekannt** *adj.* known all over the world; '**2berühmt** *adj.* worldfamous; '**2bürger** *m* cosmopolite; '**2erschütternd** *adj.* world-shaking; '**2fremd** *adj.* wordly innocent; '~**friede(n)** *m* universal peace; '~**geschichte** *f* (-/no *pl.*) universal history; '**2gewandt** *adj.* knowing the ways of the world; '~**handel** ✝ *m* (-s/no *pl.*) world trade; '~**karte** *f* map of the world; '**2klug** *adj.* wordly-wise; '~**krieg** *m* world war; *der zweite ~* World War II; '~**lage** *f* international situation; '~**lauf** *m* course of the world; '**2lich** 1. *adj.* wordly; secular, temporal; 2. *adv.*: *~ gesinnt* wordly-minded; '~**literatur** *f* world literature; '~**macht** *f* world-power; '**2männisch** *adj.* ['~menɪʃ] man-of-the-world; '~**markt** *m* (-[e]s/no *pl.*) world market; '~**meer** *n* ocean; '~**meister** *m* world champion; '~**meisterschaft** *f* world championship; '~**raum** *m* (-[e]s/no *pl.*) (outer) space; '~**reich** *n* universal empire; *das Britische ~* the British Empire; '~**reise** *f* journey round the world; '~**rekord** *m* world record; '~**ruf** *m* (-[e]s/no *pl.*) world-wide reputation; '~**schmerz** *m* Weltschmerz; '~**sprache** *f* world *or* universal language; '~**stadt** *f* metropolis; '**2weit** *adj.* world-wide; '~**wunder** *n* wonder of the world.

**Wende** ['vɛndə] *f* (-/-n) turn (*a. swimming*); *fig. a.* turning-point; '~**kreis** *m geogr.* tropic; *mot.* turning-circle.

**Wendeltreppe** ['vɛndəl-] *f* winding

staircase, (e-e a flight of) winding stairs *pl.*, spiral staircase.

'**Wende|marke** *f sports:* turningpoint; '**2n** 1. *v/t.* (ge-, h) turn (*coat, etc.*); turn (*hay*) about; 2. *v/refl.* ([*irr.,*] ge-, h): *sich ~ an* (*acc.*) turn to; address o.s. to; apply to (*wegen* for); 3. *v/i.* (ge-, h) ⚓, *mot.* turn; *bitte ~!* please turn over!; '~**punkt** *m* turning-point.

'**wend|ig** *adj.* nimble, agile (*both a. fig.*); *mot.,* ⚓ easily steerable; *mot.* flexible; '**2ung** *f* (-/-en) turn (*a. fig.*); ✂ facing; *fig.:* change; expression; idiom.

**wenig** ['ve:nɪç] 1. *adj.* little; ~*e pl.* few *pl.*; ~*er* less; ~*er pl.* fewer; *ein klein ~ Geduld* a little bit of patience; *das ~e* the little; 2. *adv.* little; ~*er* less; & *a.* minus; *am ~sten* least (of all); '**2keit** *f* (-/-en): *meine ~* my humble self; '~**stens** *adv.* ['~stəns] at least.

**wenn** *cj.* [vɛn] when; if; ~ ... *nicht* if ... not, unless; ~ *auch* (al)though, even though; ~ *auch noch so* however; *und ~ nun ...?* what if ...?; *wie wäre es, ~ wir jetzt heimgingen?* what about going home now?

**wer** [ve:r] 1. *interr. pron.* who; which; ~ *von euch?* which of you?; 2. *rel. pron.* who; ~ *auch (immer)* who(so)ever; 3. F *indef. pron.* somebody; anybody; *ist schon ~ gekommen?* has anybody come yet?

**Werbe|abteilung** ['vɛrbə-] *f* advertising *or* publicity department; '~**film** *m* advertising film.

'**werb|en** (*irr.,* ge-, h) 1. *v/t.* canvass (*votes, subscribers, etc.*); ✂ recruit, enlist; 2. *v/i.*: ~ *für* advertise, *Am. a.* advertize; make propaganda for; canvass for; '**2ung** *f* (-/-en) advertising, publicity, *Am. a.* advertizing; propaganda; canvassing; ✂ enlistment, recruiting.

**Werdegang** ['ve:rdə-] *m* career; ⊕ process of manufacture.

'**werden** 1. *v/i.* (*irr.,* ge-, sein) become, get; grow; turn (*pale, sour, etc.*); *was ist aus ihm geworden?* what has become of him?; *was will er (einmal) ~?* what is he going to be?; 2. & *n* (-s/no *pl.*): *noch im ~ sein* be in embryo.

**werfen** ['vɛrfən] (*irr.,* ge-, h) 1. *v/t.* throw (*nach at*); *zo.* throw (*young*); cast (*shadow, glance, etc.*); *Falten ~* fall in folds; set badly; 2. *v/i.* throw; *zo.* litter; ~ *mit* throw (*auf acc., nach at*).

**Werft** ⚓ [vɛrft] *f* (-/-en) shipyard, dockyard.

**Werk** [vɛrk] *n* (-[e]s/-e) work; act; ⊕ works *sg., pl.,* factory; *das ~ e-s Augenblicks* the work of a moment; *zu ~e gehen* proceed; '~**bank** ⊕ *f* work-bench; '~**meister** *m* foreman; ~**statt** ['~ʃtat] *f*

(-/~en) workshop; '~tag *m* workday; '2tätig *adj.* working; '~zeug *n* tool; implement; instrument.
**Wermut** ['ve:rmu:t] *m* (-[e]s/no *pl.*) ❦ wormwood; verm(o)uth.
**wert** [ve:rt] **1.** *adj.* worth; worthy (*gen.* of); ~, *getan zu werden* worth doing; **2.** ⚥ *m* (-[e]s/-e) value (*a.* ⚗, ⚘, *phys., fig.*); worth (*a. fig.*); *Briefmarken im ~ von 2 Schilling* 2 shillings' worth of stamps; *großen ~ legen auf* (*acc.*) set a high value (up)on.
'**Wert|brief** *m* money-letter; '2en *v/t.* (ge-, *h*) value; appraise; '~gegenstand *m* article of value; '2los *adj.* worthless, valueless; '~papiere *n/pl.* securities *pl.*; '~sachen *pl.* valuables *pl.*; '~ung *f* (-/-en) valuation; appraisal; *sports:* score; '2voll *adj.* valuable, precious.
**Wesen** ['ve:zən] *n* **1.** (-s/no *pl.*) entity, essence; nature, character; *viel ~s machen um* make a fuss of; **2.** (-s/-) being, creature; '2los *adj.* unreal; '2tlich *adj.* essential, substantial.
**weshalb** [vɛs'halp] **1.** *interr. pron.* why; **2.** *cj.* that's why.
**Wespe** *zo.* ['vɛspə] *f* (-/-n) wasp.
**West** *geogr.* [vɛst] west; '~en *m* (-s/no *pl.*) west; *the* West.
**Weste** ['vɛstə] *f* (-/-n) waistcoat, ✝ *and Am.* vest; *e-e reine ~ haben* have a clean slate.
'**west|lich** *adj.* west; westerly; western; '2wind *m* west(erly) wind.
**Wett|bewerb** ['vɛtbəvɛrp] *m* (-[e]s/-e) competition (*a.* ✝); '~büro *n* betting office; '~e *f* (-/-n) wager, bet; *e-e ~ eingehen* lay *or* make a bet; '~eifer *m* emulation, rivalry; 2eifern *v/i.* (ge-, *h*) vie (*mit* with; *in dat.* in; *um* for); '2en (ge-, *h*) **1.** *v/t.* wager, bet; **2.** *v/i.: mit j-m um et. ~* wager *or* bet s.o. s.th.; *~ auf* (*acc.*) wager *or* bet on, back.
**Wetter**[1] ['vɛtər] *n* (-s/-) weather.
**Wetter**[2] [~] *m* (-s/-) better.
'**Wetter|bericht** *m* weather-forecast; '2fest *adj.* weather-proof; '~karte *f* weather-chart; '~lage *f* weather-conditions *pl.*; '~leuchten *n* (-s/no *pl.*) sheet-lightning; '~vorhersage *f* (-/-n) weather-forecast; '~warte *f* weather-station.
'**Wett|kampf** *m* contest, competition; '~kämpfer *m* contestant; '~lauf *m* race; '~läufer *m* racer, runner; '2machen *v/t.* (*sep.*, -ge-, *h*) make up for; '~rennen *n* race; '~rüsten *n* (-s/no *pl.*) armament race; '~spiel *n* match, game; '~streit *m* contest. [sharpen.]
**wetzen** ['vɛtsən] *v/t.* (ge-, *h*) whet,]
**wich** [viç] *pret. of weichen*[1].
**Wichse** ['viksə] *f* **1.** (-/-n) blacking; polish; **2.** F *fig.* (-/no *pl.*) thrashing; '2n *v/t.* (ge-, *h*) black; polish.

**wichtig** *adj.* ['viçtiç] important; *sich ~ machen* show off; '2keit *f* (-/~-en) importance; 2tuer ['~tu:ər] *m* (-s/-) pompous fellow; '~tuerisch *adj.* pompous.
**Wickel** ['vikəl] *m* (-s/-) roll(er); ☤ compress; packing; '2n *v/t.* (ge-, *h*) wind; swaddle (*baby*); wrap.
**Widder** *zo.* ['vidər] *m* (-s/-) ram.
**wider** *prp.* (*acc.*) ['vi:dər] against, contrary to; '~borstig *adj.* crossgrained; ~fahren *v/i.* (*irr. fahren, no -ge-, sein*) happen (*dat.* to); '2haken *m* barb; 2hall ['~hal] *m* (-[e]s/-e) echo, reverberation; *fig.* response; ~hallen *v/i.* (*sep.*, -ge-, *h*) (re-)echo (*von* with), resound (with); '~legen *v/t.* (*no -ge-, h*) refute, disprove; '~lich *adj.* repugnant, repulsive; disgusting; '~natürlich *adj.* unnatural; '~rechtlich *adj.* illegal, unlawful; '2rede *f* contradiction; 2ruf *m* ⚥ revocation; retraction; ~rufen *v/t.* (*irr. rufen, no -ge-, h*) revoke; retract (*a.* ⚥); '~ruflich *adj.* revocable; 2sacher ['~zaxər] *m* (-s/-) adversary; 2schein *m* reflection; '~setzen *v/refl.* (*no -ge-, h*): *sich e-r Sache ~* oppose *or* resist s.th.; '~setzlich *adj.* refractory; insubordinate; '~sinnig *adj.* absurd; ~spenstig *adj.* ['~ʃpɛnstiç] refractory; 2spenstigkeit *f* (-/~-en) refractoriness; ~spiegeln *v/t.* (*sep.*, -ge-, *h*) reflect (*a. fig.*); *sich ~ in* (*dat.*) be reflected in; '~sprechen *v/i.* (*irr. sprechen, no -ge-, h*): *j-m ~* contradict s.o.; 2spruch *m* contradiction; opposition; *im ~ zu* in contradiction to; ~sprüchlich *adj.* ['~ʃpry:çliç] contradictory; '~spruchslos **1.** *adj.* uncontradicted; **2.** *adv.* without contradiction; 2stand *m* resistance (*a.* ⚡); opposition; *~ leisten* offer resistance (*dat.* to); *auf heftigen ~ stoßen* meet with stiff opposition; '~standsfähig *adj.* resistant (*a.* ⊕); '~stehen *v/i.* (*irr. stehen, no -ge-, h*) resist (*e-r Sache* s.th.); ~streben *v/i.* (*no -ge-, h*): *es widerstrebt mir, dies zu tun* I hate doing *or* to do that, I am reluctant to do that; ~strebend *adv.* reluctantly; '2streit *m* (-[e]s/~-e) antagonism; *fig.* conflict; ~wärtig *adj.* ['~vɛrtiç] unpleasant, disagreeable; disgusting; '2wille *m* aversion (*gegen* to, for, from); dislike (*to, of, for*); disgust (*at, for*); reluctance, unwillingness; '~willig *adj.* reluctant, unwilling.
**widm|en** ['vitmən] *v/t.* (ge-, *h*) dedicate; '2ung *f* (-/-en) dedication.
**widrig** *adj.* ['vi:driç] adverse; ~enfalls *adv.* ['~gən'-] failing which, in default of which.

**wie** [vi:] **1.** *adv.* how; ~ *alt ist er?* what is his age?; ~ *spät ist es?* what is the time?; **2.** *cj.*: *ein Mann ~ er* a man such as he, a man like him; ~ *er dies hörte* hearing this; *ich hörte, ~ er es sagte* I heard him saying so.

**wieder** *adv.* ['vi:dər] again, anew; *immer ~* again and again; 2'**aufbau** *m* (-[e]s/*no pl.*) reconstruction; rebuilding; ~'**aufbauen** *v/t.* (*sep.*, -ge-, *h*) reconstruct; ~'**aufleben** *v/i.* (*sep.*, -ge-, *sein*) revive; 2'**aufleben** *n* (-s/*no pl.*) revival; 2'**aufnahme** *f* resumption; ~'**aufnehmen** *v/t.* (*irr.* nehmen, *sep.*, -ge-, *h*) resume; '2**beginn** *m* recommencement; re-opening; ~'**bekommen** *v/t.* (*irr.* kommen, *sep.*, *no* -ge-, *h*) get back; ~'**beleben** *v/t.* (*sep.*, *no* -ge-, *h*) resurrect; 2'**belebung** *f* (-/-en) revival; *fig. a.* resurrection; 2'**belebungsversuch** *m* attempt at resuscitation; ~'**bringen** *v/t.* (*irr.* bringen, *sep.*, -ge-, *h*) bring back; restore, give back; ~'**einsetzen** *v/t.* (*sep.*, -ge-, *h*) restore; ~'**einstellen** *v/t.* (*sep.*, -ge-, *h*) re-engage; 2**er**'**greifung** *f* reseizure; ~'**erkennen** *v/t.* (*irr.* kennen, *sep.*, *no* -ge-, *h*) recognize (*an dat.* by); ~'**erstatten** *v/t.* (*sep.*, *no* -ge-, *h*) restore; reimburse, refund (*money*); ~'**geben** *v/t.* (*irr.* geben, *sep.*, -ge-, *h*) give back, return; render, reproduce; ~'**gutmachen** *v/t.* (*sep.*, -ge-, *h*) make up for; 2'**gutmachung** *f* (-/-en) reparation; ~'**herstellen** *v/t.* (*sep.*, -ge-, *h*) restore; ~**holen** *v/t.* (*h*) **1.** [~'ho:lən] (*no* -ge-) repeat; **2.** [~'ho:lən] (*sep.*, -ge-) fetch back; 2'**holung** *f* (-/-en) repetition; ~'**käuen** [~'kɔʏən] (*sep.*, -ge-, *h*) **1.** *v/i.* ruminate, chew the cud; **2.** *fig. v/t.* repeat over and over; 2**kehr** ['~ke:r] *f* (-/*no pl.*) return; recurrence; '~**kehren** *v/i.* (*sep.*, -ge-, *sein*) return; recur; '~**kommen** *v/i.* (*irr.* kommen, *sep.*, -ge-, *sein*) come back, return; '~**sehen** *v/t. and v/refl.* (*irr.* sehen, *sep.*, -ge-, *h*) see or meet again; '2**sehen** *n* (-s/*no pl.*) meeting again; *auf ~!* good-bye!; '~**tun** *v/t.* (*irr.* tun, *sep.*, -ge-, *h*) do again, repeat; '~**um** *adv.* again, anew; '~**vereinigen** *v/t.* (*sep.*, *no* -ge-, *h*) reunite; '2**vereinigung** *f* reunion; *pol.* reunification; '2**verheiratung** *f* remarriage; '2**verkäufer** *m* reseller; retailer; '2**wahl** *f* re-election; '~**wählen** *v/t.* (*sep.*, -ge-, *h*) re-elect; 2'**zulassung** *f* readmission.

**Wiege** ['vi:gə] *f* (-/-n) cradle.

**wiegen**[1] ['vi:gən] *v/t. and v/i.* (*irr.*, ge-, *h*) weigh.

**wiegen**[2] [~] *v/t.* (ge-, *h*) rock; *in Sicherheit ~* rock into security, lull *into* (a false sense of) security.

'**Wiegenlied** *n* lullaby.

**wiehern** ['vi:ərn] *v/i.* (ge-, *h*) neigh.

**Wiener** ['vi:nər] *m* (-s/-) Viennese; '2**isch** *adj.* Viennese.

**wies** [vi:s] *pret. of* weisen.

**Wiese** ['vi:zə] *f* (-/-n) meadow.

**wie**'**so** *interr. pron.* why; why so.

**wie**'**viel** *adv.* how much; ~ *pl.* how many *pl.*; ~**te** *adv.* [~tə]: *den ~ten haben wir heute?* what's the date today?

**wild** [vilt] **1.** *adj.* wild; savage; ~*es Fleisch* ⚚ proud flesh; ~*e Ehe* concubinage; ~*er Streik* ✦ wildcat strike; **2.** 2 *n* (-[e]s/*no pl.*) game. '**Wild**|**bach** *m* torrent; '~**bret** ['~brɛt] *n* (-s/*no pl.*) game; venison.

**Wilde** ['vildə] *m* (-n/-n) savage.

**Wilder**|**er** ['vildərər] *m* (-s/-) poacher; '2**n** *v/i.* (ge-, *h*) poach. '**Wild**|**fleisch** *n s.* Wildbret; '2-'**fremd** F *adj.* quite strange; '~**hüter** *m* gamekeeper; '~**leder** *n* buckskin; '2**ledern** *adj.* buckskin; doeskin; '~**nis** *f* (-/-se) wilderness, wild (*a. fig.*); '~**schwein** *n* wildboar.

**Wille** ['vilə] *m* (~ns/\~-n) will; *s-n ~n durchsetzen* have one's way; *gegen s-n ~n* against one's will; *j-m s-n ~n lassen* let s.o. have his (own) way; '2**nlos** *adj.* lacking will-power. '**Willens**|**freiheit** *f* (-/*no pl.*) freedom of (the) will; '~**kraft** *f* (-/*no pl.*) will-power; '~**schwäche** *f* (-/*no pl.*) weak will; '2**stark** *adj.* strong-willed; '~**stärke** *f* (-/*no pl.*) strong will, will-power.

'**will**|**ig** *adj.* willing, ready; '~**kommen** *adj.* welcome; 2**kür** ['~ky:r] *f* (-/*no pl.*) arbitrariness; '~**kürlich** *adj.* arbitrary.

**wimmeln** ['viməln] *v/i.* (ge-, *h*) swarm (*von* with), teem (with).

**wimmern** ['vimərn] *v/i.* (ge-, *h*) whimper, whine.

**Wimpel** ['vimpəl] *m* (-s/-) pennant, pennon, streamer.

**Wimper** ['vimpər] *f* (-/-n) eyelash. **Wind** [vint] *m* (-[e]s/-e) wind; '~**beutel** *m* cream-puff; F *fig.* windbag.

**Winde** ['vində] *f* (-/-n) windlass; reel.

**Windel** ['vindəl] *f* (-/-n) diaper, (baby's) napkin; ~*n pl. a.* swaddling-clothes *pl.*

**winden** *v/t.* (*irr.*, ge-, *h*) wind; twist, twirl; make, bind (*wreath*); *sich ~ vor* (*dat.*) writhe with.

'**Wind**|**hose** *f* whirlwind, tornado; '~**hund** *m* greyhound; 2**ig** *adj.* ['~diç] windy; F *fig. excuse:* thin, lame; '~**mühle** *f* windmill; '~**pokken** *pl.* chicken-pox; '~**richtung** *f* direction of the wind; '~**rose** ⚓ *f* compass card; '~**schutzscheibe** *f* wind-screen, *Am.* windshield; '~**stärke** *f* wind velocity; '₂still *adj.* calm; '₋stille *f* calm; '₋stoß *m* blast of wind, gust.

'Windung *f* (-/-en) winding, turn; bend (*of way, etc.*); coil (*of snake, etc.*).

Wink [viŋk] *m* (-[e]s/-e) sign; wave; wink; *fig.*: hint; tip.

Winkel ['viŋkəl] *m* (-s/-) &̸ angle; corner, nook; '₂ig *adj.* angular; *street*: crooked; '₋zug *m* subterfuge, trick, shift.

'winken *v/i.* (ge-, h) make a sign; beckon; *mit dem Taschentuch* ~ wave one's handkerchief.

winklig *adj.* ['viŋkliç] *s.* winkelig.

winseln ['vinzəln] *v/i.* (ge-, h) whimper, whine.

Winter ['vintər] *m* (-s/-) winter; *im* ~ in winter; '₂lich *adj.* wintry; '₋schlaf *m* hibernation; '₋sport *m* winter sports *pl.*

Winzer ['vintsər] *m* (-s/-) vine-dresser; vine-grower; vintager.

winzig *adj.* ['vintsiç] tiny, diminutive.

Wipfel ['vipfəl] *m* (-s/-) top.

Wippe ['vipə] *f* (-/-n) seesaw; '₂n *v/i.* (ge-, h) seesaw.

wir *pers. pron.* [vi:r] we; ~ *drei* the three of us.

Wirbel ['virbəl] *m* (-s/-) whirl, swirl; eddy; flurry (*of blows, etc.*); *anat.* vertebra; '₂ig *adj.* giddy, vertiginous; wild; '₂n *v/i.* (ge-, h) whirl; *drums*: roll; '₋säule *anat. f* spinal *or* vertebral column; '₋sturm *m* cyclone, tornado, *Am. a.* twister; '₋tier *n* vertebrate; '₋wind *m* whirlwind (*a. fig.*).

wirk|en ['virkən] (ge-, h) 1. *v/t.* knit, weave; work (*wonders*); 2. *v/i.*: ~ *als* act *or* function as; ~ *auf* (*acc.*) produce an impression on; *beruhigend* ~ have a soothing effect; '₋lich *adj.* real, actual; true, genuine; '₂lichkeit *f* (-/-en) reality; *in* ~ in reality; '₋sam *adj.* effective, efficacious; '₂samkeit *f* (-/‿-en) effectiveness, efficacy; '₂ung *f* (-/-en) effect.

'Wirkungs|kreis *m* sphere *or* field of activity; '₂los *adj.* ineffective, inefficacious; '₋losigkeit *f* (-/*no pl.*) ineffectiveness, inefficacy; '₂voll *adj. s.* wirksam.

wirr *adj.* [vir] confused; *speech*: incoherent; *hair*: dishevel(l)ed; '₂en *pl.* disorders *pl.*; troubles *pl.*; ₂warr ['₋var] *m* (-s/*no pl.*) confusion, muddle.

'Wirsingkohl ['virziŋ-] *m* (-[e]s/*no pl.*) savoy.

Wirt [virt] *m* (-[e]s/-e) host; landlord; innkeeper.

'Wirtschaft *f* (-/-en) housekeeping; economy; trade and industry; economics *pl.*; *s.* Wirtshaus; F mess; '₂en *v/i.* (ge-, h) keep house; economize; F bustle (about); '₋erin

*f* (-/-nen) housekeeper; '₂lich *adj.* economic; economical.

'Wirtschafts|geld *n* housekeeping money; '₋jahr *n* financial year; '₋krise *f* economic crisis; '₋politik *f* economic policy; '₋prüfer *m* (-s/-) chartered accountant, *Am.* certified public accountant.

'Wirtshaus *n* public house, F pub.

Wisch [viʃ] *m* (-es/-e) wisp (*of straw, etc.*); *contp.* scrap of paper; '₂en *v/t.* (ge-, h) wipe.

wispern ['vispərn] *v/t. and v/i.* (ge-, h) whisper.

Wiß|begierde ['vis-] *f* (-/*no pl.*) thirst for knowledge; '₂begierig *adj.* eager for knowledge.

wissen ['visən] 1. *v/t.* (*irr.*, ge-, h) know; *man kann nie* ~ you never know, you never can tell; 2. ⚙ *n* (-s/*no pl.*) knowledge; *meines* ~s to my knowledge, as far as I know.

'Wissenschaft *f* (-/-en) science; knowledge; '₋ler *m* (-s/-) scholar; scientist; researcher; '₂lich *adj.* scientific.

'Wissens|drang *m* (-[e]s/*no pl.*) urge *or* thirst for knowledge; '₂-wert *adj.* worth knowing.

'wissentlich *adj.* knowing, conscious.

wittern ['vitərn] *v/t.* (ge-, h) scent, smell; *fig. a.* suspect.

'Witterung *f* (-/‿-en) weather; *hunt.* scent; '₋sverhältnisse ['₋sfer-həltnisə] *pl.* meteorological conditions *pl.*   [*m* (-s/-) widower.]

Witwe ['vitvə] *f* (-/-n) widow; '₋r|

Witz [vits] *m* 1. (-es/*no pl.*) wit; 2. (-es/-e) joke; ~*e reißen* crack jokes; '₋blatt *n* comic paper; '₂ig *adj.* witty; funny.

wo [vo:] 1. *adv.* where?; 2. *cj.*: *ach* ~! nonsense!

wob [vo:p] *pret. of* weben.

wo'bei *adv.* at what?; at which; in doing so.

Woche ['vɔxə] *f* (-/-n) week; *heute in e-r* ~ today week.

'Wochen|bett *n* childbed; '₋blatt *n* weekly (paper); '₋ende *n* weekend; '₂lang 1. *adj.*: *nach* ~*em Warten* after (many) weeks of waiting; 2. *adv.* for weeks; '₋lohn *m* weekly pay *or* wages *pl.*; '₋markt *m* weekly market; '₋schau *f* news-reel; '₋tag *m* week-day.

wöchentlich ['vœçəntliç] 1. *adj.* weekly; 2. *adv.* weekly, every week; *einmal* ~ once a week.

Wöchnerin ['vœçnərin] *f* (-/-nen) woman in childbed.

wo|'durch *adv.* by what?, how?; by which, whereby; ~'für *adv.* for what?, what ... for?; (in return) for which.   [*gen*¹.]

wog [vo:k] *pret. of* wägen *and* wie-⟩

Woge ['vo:gə] *f* (-/-n) wave (*a. fig.*), billow; *die* ~*n glätten* pour oil on troubled waters; '⟨n *v/i.* (ge-, h) surge (*a. fig.*), billow; *wheat: a.* wave; heave.

**wo|'her** *adv.* from where?, where ... from?; ~ *wissen Sie das?* how do you (come to) know that?; ~'**hin** *adv.* where (... to)?

**wohl** [vo:l] **1.** *adv.* well; *sich nicht ~ fühlen* be unwell; ~ *oder übel* willy-nilly; *leben Sie ~!* farewell!; *er wird ~ reich sein* he is rich, I suppose; **2.** ⟨n *n* (-[e]s/no *pl.*): ~ *und Wehe* weal and woe; *auf Ihr ~!* your health!, here is to you!

'**Wohl|befinden** *n* well-being; good health; '⟨behagen *n* comfort, ease; '⟨behalten *adv.* safe; '⟨bekannt *adj.* well-known; '⟨ergehen *n* (-s/no *pl.*) welfare, prosperity; ⟨erzogen *adj.* ['⟨ʔɛrtso:gən] well-bred, well-behaved; '⟨fahrt *f* (-/no *pl.*) welfare; public assistance; '⟨gefallen *n* (-s/no *pl.*) pleasure; *sein ~ haben an* (*dat.*) take delight in; '⟨gemeint *adj.* well-meant, well-intentioned; ⟨gemut *adj.* ['⟨gə-mu:t] cheerful; '⟨genährt *adj.* well-fed; '⟨geruch *m* scent, perfume; '⟨gesinnt *adj.* well-disposed (*j-m towards s.o.*); '⟨habend *adj.* well-to-do; '⟨ig *adj.* comfortable; cosy, snug; '⟨klang *m* (-[e]s/no *pl.*) melodious sound, harmony; '⟨klingend *adj.* melodious, harmonious; '⟨laut *m s. Wohlklang;* '⟨leben *n* (-s/no *pl.*) luxury; '⟨riechend *adj.* fragrant; '⟨schmeckend *adj.* savo(u)ry; '⟨sein *n* well-being; good health; '⟨stand *m* (-[e]s/no *pl.*) prosperity, wealth; '⟨tat *f* kindness, charity, *fig.* comfort, treat; '⟨täter *m* benefactor; '⟨tätig *adj.* charitable, beneficent; '⟨tätigkeit *f* charity; ⟨tuend *adj.* ['⟨tu:-ənt] pleasant, comfortable; '⟨tun *v/i. irr. tun, sep., -ge-, h)* do good; '⟨verdient *adj.* well-deserved; *p.* of great merit; '⟨wollen *n* (-s/no *pl.*) goodwill; benevolence; favo(u)r; '⟨wollen *v/i.* (*sep., -ge-, h)* be well-disposed (*j-m towards s.o.*).

**wohn|en** ['vo:nən] *v/i.* (ge-, h) live (*in dat.* in, at; *bei j-m* with s.o.); reside (in, at; with); '⟨haus *n* dwelling-house; block of flats, *Am.* apartment house; '⟨haft *adj.* resident, living; '⟨lich *adj.* comfortable; cosy, snug; '⟨ort *m* dwelling-place, residence; *esp. ⁂* domicile; '⟨sitz *m* residence; *mit ~ in* resident in *or* at; *ohne festen ~* without fixed abode; '⟨ung *f* (-/-en) dwelling, habitation; flat, *Am.* apartment.

'**Wohnungs|amt** *n* housing office; '⟨not *f* housing shortage; '⟨problem *n* housing problem.

'**Wohn|wagen** *m* caravan, trailer; '⟨zimmer *n* sitting-room, *esp. Am.* living room.

**wölb|en** ['vœlbən] *v/t.* (ge-, h) vault; arch; *sich ~* arch; '⟨ung *f* (-/-en) vault, arch; curvature.

**Wolf** *zo.* [vɔlf] *m* (-[e]s/ue) wolf.

**Wolke** ['vɔlkə] *f* (-/-n) cloud.

'**Wolken|bruch** *m* cloud-burst; '⟨kratzer *m* (-s/-) skyscraper; '⟨los *adj.* cloudless.

'**wolkig** *adj.* cloudy, clouded.

**Woll|decke** ['vɔl-] *f* blanket; '⟨e *f* (-/-n) wool.

**wollen**[1] ['vɔlən] (h) **1.** *v/t.* (ge-) wish, desire; want; *lieber ~* prefer; *nicht ~* refuse; *er weiß, was er will* he knows his mind; **2.** *v/i.* (ge-): *ich will schon, aber ...* I want to, but ...; **3.** *v/aux.* (no -ge-) be willing; intend, be going to; be about to; *lieber ~* prefer; *nicht ~* refuse; *er hat nicht gehen ~* he refused to go.

**woll|en**[2] *adj.* [~] wool(l)en; '⟨ig *adj.* wool(l)y; '⟨stoff *m* wool(l)en.

**Wol|lust** ['vɔlust] *f* (-/ue) voluptuousness; ⟨lüstig *adj.* ['⟨lystiç] voluptuous.

'**Wollwaren** *f* wool(l)en goods *pl.*

**wo|'mit** *adv.* with what?, what ... with?; with which; ~'**möglich** *adv.* perhaps, maybe.

**Wonn|e** ['vɔnə] *f* (-/-n) delight, bliss; '⟨ig *adj.* delightful, blissful.

**wo|ran** *adv.* [vo:'ran]: ~ *denkst du?* what are you thinking of?; *ich weiß nicht, ~ ich mit ihm bin* I don't know what to make of him; ~ *liegt es, daß ...?* how is it that ...?; ~'**rauf** *adv.* on what?, what ... on?; whereupon, after which; ~ *wartest du?* what are you waiting for?; ~'**raus** *adv.* from what?; what ... of?; from which; ~**rin** *adv.* [~'rin] in what?; in which.

**Wort** [vɔrt] *n* **1.** (-[e]s/uer) word; *er kann seine Wörter noch nicht* he hasn't learnt his words yet; **2.** (-[e]s/-e) word; term, expression; *ums ~ bitten* ask permission to speak; *das ~ ergreifen* begin to speak; *parl.* rise to speak, address the House, *esp. Am.* take the floor; *das ~ führen* be the spokesman; ~ *halten* keep one's word; '⟨brüchig *adj.*: *er ist ~ geworden* he has broken his word.

**Wörter|buch** ['vœrtər-] *n* dictionary; '⟨verzeichnis *n* vocabulary, list of words.

'**Wort|führer** *m* spokesman; '⟨getreu *adj.* literal; '⟨karg *adj.* taciturn; '⟨klauberei** [~klaubə'raɪ] *f* (-/-en) word-splitting; '⟨laut *m* (-[e]s/no *pl.*) wording; text. [eral.⟩

**wörtlich** *adj.* ['vœrtliç] verbal, lit-⟩

'**Wort|schatz** *m* (-es/no *pl.*) vocabulary; '⟨schwall *m* (-[e]s/no *pl.*) verbiage; '⟨spiel *n* pun (*über acc., mit* [up]on), play upon words; '⟨stellung *gr. f* word order, order of words; '⟨stamm *ling. m* stem; '⟨streit *m*, '⟨wechsel *m* dispute.

**wo|rüber** adv. [vo:'ry:bər] over or upon what?, what ... over or about or on?; over or upon which, about which; **~rum** adv. [~'rum] about what?, what ... about?; about or for which; ~ handelt es sich? what is it about?; **~runter** adv. [~'run-tər] under or among what?, what ... under?; under or among which; **~'von** adv. of or from what?, what ... from or of?; about what?, what ... about?; of or from which; **~'vor** adv. of what?, what ... of?; of which; **~zu** adv. for what?, what ... for?; for which.

**Wrack** [vrak] n (-[e]s/-e, -s) ⚓ wreck (a. fig.).

**wrang** [vraŋ] pret. of wringen.

**wring|en** ['vriŋən] v/t. (irr., ge-, h) wring; **2maschine** f wringing-machine.

**Wucher** ['vu:xər] m (-s/no pl.) usury; ~ treiben practise usury; **~er** m (-s/-) usurer; **~gewinn** m excess profit; **2isch** adj. usurious; **2n** v/i. (ge-, h) grow exuberantly; **~ung** f (-/-en) ♀ exuberant growth; ♣ growth; **~zinsen** m/pl. usurious interest.

**Wuchs** [vu:ks] 1. m (-es/=e) growth; figure, shape; stature; 2. ♀ pret. of wachsen.

**Wucht** [vuxt] f (-/♣-en) weight; force; **2ig** adj. heavy.

**Wühl|arbeit** fig. ['vy:l-] f insidious agitation, subversive activity; **2en** v/i. (ge-, h) dig; pig: root; fig. agitate; ~ in (dat.) rummage (about) in; **~er** m (-s/-) agitator.

**Wulst** [vulst] m (-es/=e), f (-/=e) pad; bulge; ⚠ roll(-mo[u]lding); ⊕ bead; **2ig** adj. lips: thick.

**wund** adj. [vunt] sore; ~e Stelle sore; **~er** Punkt tender spot; **2e** ['~də] f (-/-n) wound; alte ~n wieder auf-reißen reopen old sores.

**Wunder** ['vundər] n (-s/-) miracle; fig. a. wonder, marvel; ~ wirken pills, etc.: work marvels; kein ~, wenn man bedenkt ... no wonder, considering ...; **2bar** adj. miracu-lous; fig. a. wonderful, marvel-(l)ous; **~kind** n infant prodigy; **2lich** adj. queer, odd; **2n** v/t. (ge-, h) surprise, astonish; sich ~ be sur-prised or astonished (über acc. at); **2schön** adj. very beautiful; **~tat** f wonder, miracle; **~täter** m won-der-worker; **2tätig** adj. wonder-working; **2voll** adj. wonderful; **~werk** n marvel, wonder.

**Wund|fieber** ♣ n wound-fever; **~starrkrampf** ♣ m tetanus.

**Wunsch** [vunʃ] m (-es/=e) wish, de-sire; request; auf ~ by or on re-quest; if desired; nach ~ as desired; mit den besten Wünschen zum Fest with the compliments of the season.

**Wünschelrute** ['vynʃəl-] f divin-ing-rod, dowsing-rod; **~ngänger** ['~gɛŋər] m (-s/-) diviner, dowser.

**wünschen** ['vynʃən] v/t. (ge-, h) wish, desire; wie Sie ~ as you wish; was ~ Sie? what can I do for you?; **~swert** adj. desirable.

**'wunsch|gemäß** adv. as requested or desired, according to one's wishes; **2zettel** m list of wishes.

**wurde** ['vurdə] pret. of werden.

**Würde** ['vyrdə] f (-/-n) dignity; unter seiner ~ beneath one's dig-nity; **2los** adj. undignified; **~n-träger** m dignitary; **2voll** adj. dignified; grave.

**'würdig** adj. worthy (gen. of); dig-nified; grave; **~en** ['~gən] v/t. (ge-, h) appreciate, value; mention hono(u)rably; laud, praise; j-n keines Blickes ~ ignore s.o. com-pletely; **2ung** ['~gun] f (-/-en) ap-preciation, valuation.

**Wurf** [vurf] m (-[e]s/=e) throw, cast; zo. litter.

**Würfel** ['vyrfəl] m (-s/-) die; cube (a. ♱); **~becher** m dice-box; **2n** v/i. (ge-, h) (play) dice; **~spiel** n game of dice; **~zucker** m lump sugar. [tile.\]

**'Wurfgeschoß** n missile, projec-\]

**würgen** ['vyrgən] (ge-, h) 1. v/t. choke, strangle; 2. v/i. choke; retch.

**Wurm** zo. [vurm] m (-[e]s/=er) worm; **2en** F v/t. (ge-, h) vex; rankle (j-n in s.o.'s mind); **2-stichig** adj. worm-eaten.

**Wurst** [vurst] f (-/=e) sausage; F das ist mir ganz ~ I don't care a rap.

**Würstchen** ['vyrstçən] n (-s/-) sau-sage; heißes ~ hot sausage, Am. hot dog.

**Würze** ['vyrtsə] f (-/-n) seasoning, flavo(u)r; spice, condiment; fig. salt.

**Wurzel** ['vurtsəl] f (-/-n) root (a. gr., ♱); ~ schlagen strike or take root (a. fig.); **2n** v/i. (ge-, h) (strike or take) root; ~ in (dat.) take one's root in, be rooted in.

**'würz|en** v/t. (ge-, h) spice, season, flavo(u)r; **~ig** adj. spicy, well-seasoned, aromatic.

**wusch** [vu:ʃ] pret. of waschen.

**wußte** ['vustə] pret. of wissen.

**Wust** F [vu:st] m (-es/no pl.) tangled mass; rubbish; mess.

**wüst** adj. [vy:st] desert, waste; con-fused; wild, dissolute; rude; **2e** f (-/-n) desert, waste; **2ling** ['~liŋ] m (-s/-e) debauchee, libertine, rake.

**Wut** [vu:t] f (-/no pl.) rage, fury; in ~ in a rage; **~anfall** m fit of rage.

**wüten** ['vy:tən] v/i. (ge-, h) rage (a. fig.); **~d** adj. furious, enraged (über acc. at; auf acc. with), esp. Am. F a. mad (über acc., auf acc. at).

**Wüterich** ['vy:tərɪç] m (-[e]s/-e) berserker; bloodthirsty man.

**'wutschnaubend** adj. foaming with rage.

# X, Y

**X-Beine** ['iks-] *n/pl.* knock-knees *pl.*; '**X-beinig** *adj.* knock-kneed.
**x-beliebig** *adj.* [iksbə'li:biç] any (... you please); *jede(r, -s)* ~*e* ... any ...
**x-mal** *adv.* ['iks-] many times, *sl.* umpteen times.
**X-Strahlen** ['iks-] *m/pl.* X-rays *pl.*
**x-te** *adj.* ['ikstə]: *zum* ~*n Male* for the umpteenth time.
**Xylophon** ♪ [ksylo'fo:n] *n* (-*s*/-*e*) xylophone.
**Yacht** ⚓ [jaxt] *f* (-/-*en*) yacht.

# Z

**Zacke** ['tsakə] *f* (-/-*n*) *s. Zacken.*
'**Zacken 1.** *m* (-*s*/-) (sharp) point; prong; tooth (*of comb, saw, rake*); jag (*of rock*); **2.** ♀ *v/t.* (ge-, *h*) indent, notch; jag.
'**zackig** *adj.* indented, notched; *rock*: jagged; pointed; ⚔ F *fig.* smart.
**zaghaft** *adj.* ['tsa:khaft] timid; '♀**igkeit** *f* (-/*no pl.*) timidity.
**zäh** *adj.* [tsɛ:] tough, tenacious (*both a. fig.*); *liquid*: viscid, viscous; *fig.* dogged; '~**flüssig** *adj.* viscid, viscous, sticky; '♀**igkeit** *f* (-/*no pl.*) toughness, tenacity (*both a. fig.*); viscosity; *fig.* doggedness.
**Zahl** [tsa:l] *f* (-/-*en*) number; figure, cipher; '♀**bar** *adj.* payable.
'**zählbar** *adj.* countable.
**zahlen** ['tsa:lən] (ge-, *h*) **1.** *v/i.* pay; *at restaurant*: ~ (, *bitte*)! the bill, please!, *Am.* the check, please!; **2.** *v/t.* pay.
**zählen** ['tsɛ:lən] (ge-, *h*) **1.** *v/t.* count, number; ~ *zu* count or number among; **2.** *v/i.* count; ~ *auf* (*acc.*) count (up)on, rely (up)on.
'**Zahlen|lotto** *n s. Lotto*; '♀**mäßig 1.** *adj.* numerical; **2.** *adv.*: *j-m* ~ *überlegen sein* outnumber s.o.
'**Zähler** *m* (-*s*/-) counter; ✠ numerator; *for gas, etc.*: meter.
'**Zahl|karte** *f* money-order form (*for paying direct into the postal cheque account*); '♀**los** *adj.* numberless, innumerable, countless; '~**meister** ⚔ *m* paymaster; '♀**reich 1.** *adj.* numerous; **2.** *adv.* in great number; '~**tag** *m* pay-day; '~**ung** *f* (-/-*en*) payment.
'**Zählung** *f* (-/-*en*) counting.
'**Zahlungs|anweisung** *f* order to pay; '~**aufforderung** *f* request for payment; '~**bedingungen** *f/pl.* terms *pl.* of payment; '~**befehl** *m* order to pay; '~**einstellung** *f* suspension of payment; '♀**fähig** *adj.* solvent; '~**fähigkeit** *f* solvency; '~**frist** *f* term for payment; '~**mittel** *n* currency; *gesetzliches* ~ legal tender; '~**schwierigkeiten** *f/pl.* financial or pecuniary difficulties *pl.*; '~**termin** *m* date of payment; '♀**unfähig** *adj.* insolvent; '~**unfähigkeit** *f* insolvency.
'**Zahlwort** *gr. n* (-[e]*s*/⸗*er*) numeral.
**zahm** *adj.* [tsa:m] tame (*a. fig.*), domestic(ated).
**zähm|en** ['tsɛ:mən] *v/t.* (ge-, *h*) tame (*a. fig.*), domesticate; '♀**ung** *f* (-/ ⁓ -*en*) taming (*a. fig.*), domestication.
**Zahn** [tsa:n] *m* (-[e]*s*/⸗*e*) tooth; ⊕ tooth, cog; *Zähne bekommen* cut one's teeth; '~**arzt** *m* dentist, dental surgeon; '~**bürste** *f* tooth-brush; '~**creme** *f* tooth-paste; '♀**en** *v/i.* (ge-, *h*) teethe, cut one's teeth; '~**ersatz** *m* denture; ~**fäule** ⚕ ['~fɔʏlə] *f* (-/*no pl.*) dental caries; '~**fleisch** *n* gums *pl.*; '~**füllung** *f* filling, stopping; '~**geschwür** ⚕ *n* gumboil; '~**heilkunde** *f* dentistry; '♀**los** *adj.* toothless; '~**lücke** *f* gap between the teeth; ~**pasta** ['~pasta] *f* (-/*Zahnpasten*), '~**paste** *f* tooth-paste; '~**rad** ⊕ *n* cog-wheel; '~**radbahn** *f* rack-railway; '~**schmerzen** *m/pl.* toothache; '~**stocher** *m* (-*s*/-) toothpick.
**Zange** ['tsaŋə] *f* (-/-*n*) (e-e a pair of) tongs *pl.* or pliers *pl.* or pincers *pl.*; ⚕, *zo.* forceps *sg.*, *pl.*
**Zank** [tsaŋk] *m* (-[e]*s*/*no pl.*) quarrel, F row; '~**apfel** *m* bone of contention; '♀**en** (ge-, *h*) **1.** *v/i.* scold (*mit j-m* s.o.); **2.** *v/refl.* quarrel, wrangle.
**zänkisch** *adj.* ['tsɛŋkiʃ] quarrelsome.
**Zäpfchen** ['tsɛpfçən] *n* (-*s*/-) small peg; *anat.* uvula.
**Zapfen** ['tsapfən] **1.** *m* (-*s*/-) plug; peg, pin; bung (*of barrel*); pivot; ⚘ cone; **2.** ♀ *v/t.* (ge-, *h*) tap; '~**streich** ⚔ *m* tattoo, retreat, *Am. a.* taps *pl.*
'**Zapf|hahn** *m* tap, *Am.* faucet; '~**säule** *mot. f* petrol pump.
**zappel|ig** *adj.* ['tsapəliç] fidgety; '~**n** *v/i.* (ge-, *h*) struggle; fidget.
**zart** *adj.* [tsa:rt] tender; soft; gentle; delicate; '~**fühlend** *adj.* delicate; '♀**gefühl** *n* (-[e]*s*/*no pl.*) delicacy (of feeling).

**zärtlich** *adj.* ['tsɛːrtliç] tender; fond, loving; '2keit *f* 1. (-/*no pl.*) tenderness; fondness; 2. (-/-en) caress.

**Zauber** ['tsaubər] *m* (-s/-) spell, charm, magic (*all a. fig.*); *fig.*: enchantment; glamo(u)r; ~ei [~'raɪ] *f* (-/-en) magic, sorcery; witchcraft; conjuring; '~er *m* (-s/-) sorcerer, magician; conjurer; '~flöte *f* magic flute; '~formel *f* spell; '2-haft *adj.* magic(al); *fig.* enchanting; '~in *f* (-/-nen) sorceress, witch; *fig.* enchantress; '~kraft *f* magic power; '~kunststück *n* conjuring trick; '2n (ge-, h) 1. *v/i.* practise magic or witchcraft; do conjuring tricks; 2. *v/t.* conjure; '~spruch *m* spell; '~stab *m* (magic) wand; '~wort *n* (-[e]s/-e) magic word, spell.

**zaudern** ['tsaudərn] *v/i.* (ge-, h) hesitate; linger, delay.

**Zaum** [tsaum] *m* (-[e]s/ᵘe) bridle; *im* ~ *halten* keep in check.

**zäumen** ['tsɔʏmən] *v/t.* (ge-, h) bridle.

**'Zaumzeug** *n* bridle.

**Zaun** [tsaun] *m* (-[e]s/ᵘe) fence; '~gast *m* deadhead; '~könig *orn. m* wren; '~pfahl *m* pale.

**Zebra** *zo.* ['tseːbra] *n* (-s/-s) zebra; '~streifen *m* zebra crossing.

**Zech|e** ['tsɛçə] *f* (-/-n) score, reckoning, bill; ⚒ mine; coal-pit, colliery; F *die* ~ *bezahlen* foot the bill, F stand treat; '2en *v/i.* (ge-, h) carouse, tipple; '~gelage *n* carousal, carouse; '~preller *m* (-s/-) bilk(er).

**Zeh** [tseː] *m* (-[e]s/-en), '~e *f* (-/-n) toe; '~enspitze *f* point or tip of the toe; *auf* ~ on tiptoe.

**zehn** *adj.* [tseːn] ten; '2er *m* (-s/-) ten; *coin:* F ten-pfennig piece; ~fach *adj.* ['~fax] tenfold; '~jährig *adj.* ['~jɛːrɪç] ten-year-old, of ten (years); '2kampf *m sports:* decathlon; '~mal *adv.* ten times; ~te ['~tə] 1. *adj.* tenth; 2. 2 † *m* (-n/-n) tithe; 2tel ['~təl] *n* (-s/-) tenth (part); '~tens *adv.* (-/~əns) tenthly.

**zehren** ['tseːrən] *v/i.* (ge-, h) make thin; ~ *von* live on *s.th.*; *fig.* live off (*the capital*); ~ *an* prey (up)on (*one's mind*); undermine (*one's health*).

**Zeichen** ['tsaɪçən] *n* (-s/-) sign; token; mark; indication, symptom; signal; *zum* ~ (*gen.*) in sign of, as a sign of; '~block *m* drawing-block; '~brett *n* drawing-board; '~lehrer *m* drawing-master; '~papier *n* drawing-paper; '~setzung *gr. f* (-/*no pl.*) punctuation; '~sprache *f* sign-language; '~stift *m* pencil, crayon; '~trickfilm *m* animation, animated cartoon; '~unterricht *m* drawing-lessons *pl.*

**zeichn|en** ['tsaɪçnən] (ge-, h) 1. *v/t.*

draw (*plan, etc.*); design (*pattern*); mark; sign; subscribe (*sum of money*) (*zu* to); subscribe for (*shares*); 2. *v/i.* draw; *sie zeichnet gut* she draws well; '2er *m* (-s/-) draftsman, draughtsman; designer; subscriber (*gen.* for *shares*); '2ung *f* (-/-en) drawing; design; illustration; *zo.* marking (*of skin, etc.*); subscription.

**Zeige|finger** ['tsaɪgə-] *m* forefinger, index (finger); '2n (ge-, h) 1. *v/t.* show; point out; indicate; demonstrate; *sich* ~ appear; 2. *v/i.*: ~ *auf* (*acc.*) point at; ~ *nach* point to; '~r *m* (-s/-) hand (*of clock, etc.*); pointer (*of dial, etc.*); '~stock *m* pointer.

**Zeile** ['tsaɪlə] *f* (-/-n) line; row; *j-m ein paar* ~n *schreiben* drop s.o. a line *or* a few lines.            [siskin.]

**Zeisig** *orn.* ['tsaɪzɪç] *m* (-[e]s/-e)┘

**Zeit** [tsaɪt] *f* (-/-en) time; epoch, era, age; period, space (of time); term; *freie* ~ spare time; *mit der* ~ in the course of time; *von* ~ *zu* ~ from time to time; *vor langer* ~ long ago, a long time ago; *zur* ~ (*gen.*) in the time of; *at* (the) present; *zu meiner* ~ in my time; *zu s-r* ~ in due course (of time); *das hat* ~ there is plenty of time for that; *es ist höchste* ~ it is high time; *j-m* ~ *lassen* give s.o. time; *laß dir* ~! take your time!; *sich die* ~ *vertreiben* pass the time, kill time.

**'Zeit|abschnitt** *m* epoch, period; '~alter *n* age; '~angabe *f* exact date and hour; date; '~aufnahme *phot. f* time-exposure; '~dauer *f* length of time, period (of time); '~enfolge *gr. f* sequence of tenses; '~geist *m* (-es/*no pl.*) spirit of the time(s), zeitgeist; '2gemäß *adj.* modern, up-to-date; '~genosse *m* contemporary; 2genössisch *adj.* ['~gənœsiʃ] contemporary; '~geschichte *f* contemporary history; '~gewinn *m* gain of time; '2ig 1. *adj.* early; 2. *adv.* on time; '~karte *f* season-ticket, *Am.* commutation ticket; '~lang *f*: *e-e* ~ for some time, for a while; 2'lebens *adv.* for life, all one's life; '2lich 1. *adj.* temporal; 2. *adv.* as to time; ~ *zusammenfallen* coincide; '2los *adj.* timeless; '~lupe *phot. f* slow motion; '~lupenaufnahme *phot. f* slow-motion picture; '2nah *adj.* current, up-to-date; '~ordnung *f* chronological order; '~punkt *m* moment; time; date; '~rafferaufnahme *phot. f* time-lapse photography; '2raubend *adj.* time-consuming; *pred. a.* taking up much time; '~raum *m* space (of time), period; '~rechnung *f* chronology; era; '~schrift *f* journal, periodical, magazine; review; '~tafel *f* chronological table.

**'Zeitung** f (-/-en) (news)paper, journal.
**'Zeitungs|abonnement** n subscription to a paper; **'~artikel** m newspaper article; **'~ausschnitt** m (press or newspaper) cutting, (Am. only) (newspaper) clipping; **~kiosk** ['~kiɔsk] m (-[e]s/-e) news-stand; **'~notiz** f press item; **'~papier** n newsprint; **'~verkäufer** m newsvendor; news-boy, news-man; **'~wesen** n journalism, the press.
**'Zeit|verlust** m loss of time; **'~verschwendung** f waste of time; **~vertreib** ['~fɛrtraɪp] m (-[e]s/-e) pastime; zum ~ to pass the time; **2weilig** adj. ['~vaɪlɪç] temporary; **'2weise** adv. for a time; at times, occasionally; **'~wort** gr. n (-[e]s/~er) verb; **'~zeichen** n time-signal.
**Zell|e** ['tsɛlə] f (-/-en) cell; **'~stoff** m, **~ulose** ⊕ [~u'lo:zə] f (-/-n) cellulose.
**Zelt** [tsɛlt] n (-[e]s/-e) tent; **2en** v/i. (ge-, h) camp; **'~leinwand** f canvas; **'~platz** m camping-ground.
**Zement** [tse'mɛnt] m (-[e]s/-e) cement; **2ieren** [~'ti:rən] v/t. (no -ge-, h) cement.
**Zenit** [tse'ni:t] m (-[e]s/no pl.) zenith (a. fig.).
**zens|ieren** [tsɛn'zi:rən] v/t. (no -ge-, h) censor (book, etc.); at school: mark, Am. a. grade; **2or** ['~ɔr] m (-s/-en) censor; **2ur** [~'zu:r] f 1. (-/no pl.) censorship; 2. (-/-en) at school: mark, Am. a. grade; (school) report, Am. report card.
**Zentimeter** [tsɛnti'-] n, m centimet|re, Am. -er.
**Zentner** ['tsɛntnər] m (-s/-) (Brt. appr.) hundredweight.
**zentral** adj. [tsɛn'traːl] central; **2e** f (-/-n) central office; teleph. (telephone) exchange, Am. u. central; **2heizung** f central heating.
**Zentrum** ['tsɛntrʊm] n (-s/Zentren) cent|re, Am. -er. [Am. -er.\
**Zepter** ['tsɛptər] n (-s/-) 2cept|re,\
**zer|beißen** [tsɛr'-] v/t. (irr. beißen, no -ge-, h) bite to pieces; **~'bersten** v/i. (irr. bersten, no -ge-, sein) burst asunder.
**zer'brech|en** (irr. brechen, no -ge-) 1. v/t. (h) break (to pieces); sich den Kopf ~ rack one's brains; 2. v/i. (sein) break; **~lich** adj. breakable, fragile.
**zer|'bröckeln** v/t. (h) and v/i. (sein) (no -ge-) crumble; **~'drücken** v/t. (no -ge-, h) crush; crease (dress).
**Zeremon|ie** [tseremo'ni:, ~'mo:njə] f (-/-n) ceremony; **2iell** adj. [~o'njɛl] ceremonial; **~iell** [~o'njɛl] n (-s/-e) ceremonial.
**zer'fahren** adj. road: rutted; p.: flighty, giddy; scatter-brained; absent-minded.
**Zer'fall** m (-[e]s/no pl.) ruin, decay;

disintegration; **2en** v/i. (irr. fallen, no -ge-, sein) fall to pieces, decay; disintegrate; in mehrere Teile ~ fall into several parts.
**zer|'fetzen** v/t. (no -ge-, h) tear in or to pieces; **~'fleischen** v/t. (no -ge-, h) mangle; lacerate; **~'fließen** v/i. (irr. fließen, no -ge-, sein) melt (away); ink, etc.: run; **~'fressen** v/t. (irr. fressen, no -ge-, h) eat away; **🜊** corrode; **~'gehen** v/i. (irr. gehen, no -ge-, sein) melt, dissolve; **~'gliedern** v/t. (no -ge-, h) dismember; anat. dissect; fig. analy|se, Am. -ze; **~'hacken** v/t. (no -ge-, h) cut (in)to pieces; mince; chop (up) (wood, meat); **~'kauen** v/t. (no -ge-, h) chew; **~'kleinern** v/t. (no -ge-, h) mince (meat); chop up (wood); grind.
**zer'knirsch|t** adj. contrite; **2ung** f (-/% -en) contrition.
**zer|'knittern** v/t. (no -ge-, h) (c)rumple, wrinkle, crease; **~'knüllen** v/t. (no -ge-, h) crumple up (sheet of paper); **~'kratzen** v/t. (no -ge-, h) scratch; **~'krümeln** v/t. (no -ge-, h) crumble; **~'lassen** v/t. (irr. lassen, no -ge-, h) melt; **~'legen** v/t. (no -ge-, h) take apart or to pieces; carve (joint); **🜊**, gr., fig. analy|se, Am. -ze; **~'lumpt** adj. ragged, tattered; **~'mahlen** v/t. (irr. mahlen, no -ge-, h) grind; **~malmen** [~'malmən] v/t. (no -ge-, h) crush; crunch; **~'mürben** v/t. (no -ge-, h) wear down or out; **~'platzen** v/i. (no -ge-, sein) burst; explode; **~'quetschen** v/t. (no -ge-, h) crush, squash; mash (esp. potatoes).
**Zerrbild** ['tsɛr-] n caricature.
**zer|'reiben** v/t. (irr. reiben, no -ge-, h) rub to powder, grind down, pulverize; **~'reißen** (irr. reißen, no -ge-) 1. v/t. (h) tear, rip up; in Stücke ~ tear to pieces; 2. v/i. (sein) tear; rope, string: break.
**zerren** ['tsɛrən] (ge-, h) 1. v/t. tug, pull; drag; **🜊** strain; 2. v/i.: ~ an (dat.) pull at.
**zer'rinnen** v/i. (irr. rinnen, no -ge-, sein) melt away; fig. vanish.
**'Zerrung** **🜊** f (-/-en) strain.
**zer|'rütten** [tsɛr'rytən] v/t. (no -ge-, h) derange, unsettle; disorganize; ruin, shatter (one's health or nerves); wreck (marriage); **~'sägen** v/t. (no -ge-, h) saw up; **~schellen** [~'ʃɛlən] v/i. (no -ge-, sein) be dashed or smashed; **⚓** be wrecked; **🜊** crash; **~'schlagen** 1. v/t. (irr. schlagen, no -ge-, h) break or smash (to pieces); sich ~ come to nothing; 2. adj. battered; fig. knocked up; **~'schmettern** v/t. (no -ge-, h) smash, dash, shatter; **~'schneiden** v/t. (irr. schneiden, no -ge-, h) cut in two; cut up, cut to pieces.

**zer'setz|en** v/t. and v/refl. (no -ge-, h) decompose; **Sung** f (-/ℜ-en) decomposition.

**zer|'spalten** v/t. ([irr. spalten,] no -ge-, h) cleave, split; **~'splittern** (no -ge-) **1.** v/t. (h) split (up), splinter; fritter away (one's energy, etc.); **2.** v/i. (sein) split (up), splinter; **~'sprengen** v/t. (no -ge-, h) burst (asunder); disperse (crowd); **~'springen** v/i. (irr. springen, no -ge-, sein) burst; glass: crack; mein Kopf zerspringt mir I've got a splitting headache; **~'stampfen** v/t. (no -ge-, h) crush; pound.

**zer'stäub|en** v/t. (no -ge-, h) spray; **Ser** m (-s/-) sprayer, atomizer.

**zer'stör|en** v/t. (no -ge-, h) destroy; **Ser** m (-s/-) destroyer (a. ⚓); **Sung** f destruction.

**zer'streu|en** v/t. (no -ge-, h) disperse, scatter; dissipate (doubt, etc.); fig. divert; sich ~ disperse, scatter; fig. amuse o.s.; **~t** fig. adj. absent(-minded); **Stheit** f (-/ℜ-en) absent-mindedness; **Sung** f **1.** (-/-en) dispersion; diversion, amusement; **2.** phys. (-/no pl.) dispersion (of light).

**zerstückeln** [tsɛr'ʃtykəln] v/t. (no -ge-, h) cut up, cut (in)to pieces; dismember (body, etc.).

**zer|'teilen** v/t. and v/refl. (no -ge-, h) divide (in acc. into); **~'trennen** v/t. (no -ge-, h) rip (up) (dress); **~'treten** v/t. (irr. treten, no -ge-, h) tread down; crush; tread or stamp out (fire); **~'trümmern** v/t. (no -ge-, h) smash.

**Zerwürfnis** [tsɛr'vyrfnis] n (-ses/-se) dissension, discord.

**Zettel** ['tsɛtəl] m (-s/-) slip (of paper), scrap of paper; note; ticket; label, sticker; tag; s. Anschlagzettel; s. Theaterzettel; '~kartei f, '~kasten m card index.

**Zeug** [tsɔyk] n (-[e]s/-e) stuff (a. fig. contp.), material; cloth; tools pl.; things pl.

**Zeuge** ['tsɔygə] m (-n/-n) witness; **Sn** (ge-, h) **1.** v/i. witness; ⚖ give evidence; für (gegen, von) et. ~ testify for (against, of) s.th.; ~ von be evidence of, bespeak (courage, etc.); **2.** v/t. beget.

**'Zeugen|aussage** ⚖ f testimony, evidence; '~bank f (-/⸚e) witness-box, Am. witness stand.

**Zeugin** ['tsɔygin] f (-/-nen) (female) witness.

**Zeugnis** ['tsɔyknis] n (-ses/-se) ⚖ testimony, evidence; certificate; (school) report, Am. report card.

**Zeugung** ['tsɔyguŋ] f (-/-en) procreation; '**Ssfähig** adj. capable of begetting; '~**skraft** f generative power; '**Ssunfähig** adj. ['tsɔyguns²-] impotent.

**Zick|lein** zo. ['tsiklaɪn] n (-s/-) kid;

**~zack** ['~tsak] m (-[e]s/-e) zigzag; im ~ fahren etc. zigzag.

**Ziege** zo. ['tsi:gə] f (-/-n) (she-)goat, nanny(-goat).

**Ziegel** ['tsi:gəl] m (-s/-) brick; tile (of roof); '~**dach** n tiled roof; **~ei** [~'laɪ] f (-/-en) brickworks sg., pl., brickyard; '~stein m brick.

**'Ziegen|bock** zo. m he-goat; '~**fell** n goatskin; '~**hirt** m goatherd; '~leder n kid(-leather); '~**peter** ⚕ m (-s/-) mumps.

**Ziehbrunnen** ['tsi:-] m draw-well.

**ziehen** ['tsi:ən] (irr., ge-) **1.** v/t. (h) pull, draw; draw (line, weapon, lots, conclusion, etc.); drag; ⚘ cultivate; zo. breed; take off (hat); dig (ditch); draw, extract (tooth); ⚕ extract (root of number); Blasen ~ ⚕ raise blisters; e-n Vergleich ~ draw or make a comparison; j-n ins Vertrauen ~ take s.o. into one's confidence; in Erwägung ~ take into consideration; in die Länge ~ draw out; fig. protract; Nutzen ~ aus derive profit or benefit from; an sich ~ draw to one; Aufmerksamkeit etc. auf sich ~ attract attention, etc.; et. nach sich ~ entail or involve s.th.; **2.** v/i. (h) pull (an dat. at); chimney, cigar, etc.: draw; puff (an e-r Zigarre at a cigar); tea: infuse, draw; play: draw (large audiences); F ⚘ goods: draw (customers), take; es zieht there is a draught, Am. there is a draft; **3.** v/i. (sein) move, go; march; (re)move (nach to); birds: migrate; **4.** v/refl. (h) extend, stretch, run; wood: warp; sich in die Länge ~ drag on.

**'Zieh|harmonika** ♪ f accordion; '~ung f (-/-en) drawing (of lots).

**Ziel** [tsi:l] n (-[e]s/-e) aim (a. fig.); mark; sports: winning-post, goal (a. fig.); target; ✕ objective; destination (of voyage); fig. end, purpose, target, object(ive); term; sein ~ erreichen gain one's end(s pl.); über das ~ hinausschießen overshoot the mark; zum ~e führen succeed; be successful; sich zum ~ setzen zu inf. aim at ger., Am. aim to inf.; '~**band** n sports: tape; '**Sbewußt** adj. purposeful; '**Sen** v/i. (ge-, h) (take) aim (auf acc. at); '~**fernrohr** n telescopic sight; '**Slos** adj. aimless, purposeless; '~**scheibe** f target, butt; ~ des Spottes butt or target (of derision); '**Sstrebig** adj. purposive.

**ziemlich** ['tsi:mlɪç] **1.** adj. fair, tolerable; considerable; **2.** adv. pretty, fairly, tolerably; rather; about.

**Zier** [tsi:r] f (-/no pl.), **~de** ['~də] f (-/-n) ornament; fig. a. hono(u)r (für to); '**Sen** v/t. (ge-, h) ornament, adorn; decorate; sich ~ be affected; esp. of woman: be prudish; refuse; '⌐lich adj. delicate; neat; graceful, elegant; '‿lichkeit f (-/-, -en) delicacy; neatness; gracefulness, elegance; '‿pflanze f ornamental plant.

**Ziffer** ['tsifər] f (-/-n) figure, digit; '‿blatt n dial(-plate), face.

**Zigarette** [tsiga'retə] f (-/-n) cigaret(te); ‿nautomat [‿n⁹-] m cigarette slot-machine; ‿netui [‿n⁹-] n cigarette-case; ‿nspitze f cigaretteholder; ‿nstummel m stub, Am. a. butt.

**Zigarre** [tsi'garə] f (-/-n) cigar.

**Zigeuner** [tsi'gɔʏnər] m (-s/-), ‿in f (-/-nen) gipsy, gypsy.

**Zimmer** ['tsimər] n (-s/-) room; apartment; '‿antenne f radio, etc.: indoor aerial, Am. a. indoor antenna; '‿einrichtung f furniture; '‿flucht f suite (of rooms); '‿mädchen n chamber-maid; '‿mann m (-[e]s/Zimmerleute) carpenter; 'Ǝn (ge-, h) 1. v/t. carpenter; fig. frame; 2. v/i. carpenter; '‿pflanze f indoor plant; '‿vermieterin f (-/-nen) landlady.

**zimperlich** adj. ['tsimpərliç] prim; prudish; affected.

**Zimt** [tsimt] m (-[e]s/-e) cinnamon.

**Zink** [tsiŋk] n (-[e]s/no pl.) zinc; '‿blech n sheet zinc.

**Zinke** ['tsiŋkə] f (-/-n) prong; tooth (of comb or fork); '‿n m (-s/-) s. Zinke.

**Zinn** [tsin] n (-[e]s/no pl.) tin.

**Zinne** ['tsinə] f (-/-n) ⚔ pinnacle; ✕ battlement.

**Zinnober** [tsi'no:bər] m (-s/-) cinnabar; Ǝrot adj. vermilion.

**Zins** [tsins] m (-es/-en) rent; tribute; mst ‿en pl. interest; ‿en tragen yield or bear interest; 'Ǝbringend adj. bearing interest; ‿eszins ['‿zəs-] m compound interest; 'Ǝfrei adj. rent-free; free of interest; '‿fuß m, '‿satz m rate of interest.

**Zipf|el** ['tsipfəl] m (-s/-) tip, point, end; corner (of handkerchief, etc.); lappet (of garment); 'Ǝelig adj. having points or ends; '‿elmütze f jelly-bag cap; nightcap.

**Zirkel** ['tsirkəl] m (-s/-) circle (a. fig.); ⚓ (ein a pair of) compasses pl. or dividers pl.

**zirkulieren** [tsirku'li:rən] v/i. (no -ge-, h) circulate.

**Zirkus** ['tsirkus] m (-/-se) circus.

**zirpen** ['tsirpən] v/i. (ge-, h) chirp, cheep.

**zisch|eln** ['tsiʃəln] v/t. and v/i. (ge-, h) whisper; '‿en v/i. (ge-, h) hiss; whiz(z).

**ziselieren** [tsize'li:rən] v/t. (no -ge-, h) chase.

**Zit|at** [tsi'ta:t] n (-[e]s/-e) quotation; Ǝieren [‿'ti:rən] v/t. (no -ge-, h) summon; quote.

**Zitrone** [tsi'tro:nə] f (-/-n) lemon;

‿nlimonade f lemonade; lemon squash; ‿npresse f lemon-squeezer; ‿nsaft m lemon juice.

**zittern** ['tsitərn] v/i. (ge-, h) tremble, shake (vor dat. with).

**zivil** [tsi'vi:l] 1. adj. civil; civilian; price: reasonable; 2. Ǝ n (-s/no pl.) civilians pl.; s. Zivilkleidung; Ǝbevölkerung f civilian population, civilians pl.; Ǝisation [‿iliza'tsjo:n] f (-/-, -en) civilization; ‿isieren [‿ili'zi:rən] v/t. (no -ge-, h) civilize; Ǝist [‿i'list] m (-en/-en) civilian; Ǝkleidung f civilian or plain clothes pl.

**Zofe** ['tso:fə] f (-/-n) lady's maid.

**zog** [tso:k] pret. of ziehen.

**zögern** ['tsø:gərn] 1. v/i. (ge-, h) hesitate; linger; delay; 2. Ǝ n (-s/no pl.) hesitation; delay.

**Zögling** ['tsø:kliŋ] m (-s/-e) pupil.

**Zoll** [tsɔl] m 1. (-[e]s/-) inch; 2. (-[e]s/‿e) customs pl., duty; the Customs pl.; '‿abfertigung f customs clearance; '‿amt n customhouse; '‿beamte m customs officer; '‿behörde f the Customs pl.; '‿erklärung f customs declaration; 'Ǝfrei adj. duty-free; '‿kontrolle f customs examination; 'Ǝpflichtig adj. liable to duty; '‿stock m footrule; '‿tarif m tariff.

**Zone** ['tso:nə] f (-/-n) zone.

**Zoo** [tso:] m (-[s]/-s) zoo.

**Zoolog|e** [tso⁹o'lo:gə] m (-n/-n) zoologist; ‿ie [‿o'gi:] f (-/no pl.) zoology; Ǝisch adj. [‿'lo:giʃ] zoological.

**Zopf** [tsɔpf] m (-[e]s/‿e) plait, tress; pigtail; alter ‿ antiquated ways pl. or custom.

**Zorn** [tsɔrn] m (-[e]s/no pl.) anger; Ǝig adj. angry (auf j-n with s.o.; auf et. at s.th.).

**Zote** ['tso:tə] f (-/-n) filthy or smutty joke, obscenity.

**Zott|el** ['tsɔtəl] f (-/-n) tuft (of hair); tassel; 'Ǝ(e)lig adj. shaggy.

**zu** [tsu:] 1. prp. (dat.) direction: to, towards, up to; at, in; on; in addition to, along with; purpose: for; ‿ Beginn at the beginning or outset; ‿ Weihnachten at Christmas; zum ersten Mal for the first time; ‿ e-m ... Preise at a ... price; ‿ meinem Erstaunen to my surprise; ‿ Tausenden by thousands; ‿ Wasser by water; ‿ zweien by twos; zum Beispiel for example; 2. adv. too; direction: towards, to; F closed, shut; with inf.: to; ich habe ‿ arbeiten I have to work.

**'zubauen** v/t. (sep., -ge-, h) build up or in; block.

**Zubehör** ['tsu:bəhø:r] n, m (-[e]s/-e) appurtenances pl., fittings pl., Am. F fixings pl.; esp. ⊕ accessories pl.

**'zubereit|en** v/t. (sep., no -ge-, h) prepare; 'Ǝung f preparation.

'zu|billigen *v/t.* (*sep.*, -ge-, *h*) grant; '**.binden** *v/t.* (*irr. binden*, *sep.*, -ge-, *h*) tie up; '**.blinzeln** *v/i.* (*sep.*, -ge-, *h*) wink at *s.o.*; '**.bringen** *v/t.* (*irr. bringen*, *sep.*, -ge-, *h*) pass, spend (*time*).

Zucht [tsuxt] *f* 1. (-/*no pl.*) discipline; breeding, rearing; *rearing of bees, etc.*: culture; ♣ cultivation; 2. (-/-en) breed, race; '**.bulle** *zo. m* bull (for breeding).

züch|en ['tsyçtən] *v/t.* (*ge-, h*) breed (*animals*), grow, cultivate (*plants*); '♀er *m* (-s/-) breeder (*of animals*); grower (*of plants*); '**Zucht|haus** *n* penitentiary; *punishment*: penal servitude; **.häusler** ['.hɔyslər] *m* (-s/-) convict; '**.hengst** *zo. m* stud-horse, stallion.

züchtig *adj.* ['tsyçtiç] chaste, modest; **.en** ['.gən] *v/t.* (*ge-, h*) flog. 'zucht|los *adj.* undisciplined; '**.losigkeit** *f* (-/♣ -en) want of discipline; '♀stute *zo. f* brood-mare.

zucken ['tsukən] *v/i.* (*ge-, h*) jerk; move convulsively, twitch (*all*: mit et. s.th.); *with pain*: wince; *lightning*: flash.

zücken ['tsykən] *v/t.* (*ge-, h*) draw (*sword*); ♣ pull out (*purse, pencil*).

Zucker ['tsukər] *m* (-s/*no pl.*) sugar; '**.dose** *f* sugar-basin, *Am.* sugar bowl; '**.erbse** ♣ *f* green pea; '**.guß** *m* icing, frosting; '**.hut** *m* sugarloaf; '♀ig *adj.* sugary; '♀krank *adj.* diabetic; '♀n *v/t.* (*ge-, h*) sugar; '**.rohr** ♣ *n* sugar-cane; '**.rübe** ♣ *f* sugar-beet; '♀süß *adj.* (as) sweet as sugar; '**.wasser** *n* sugared water; '**.zange** *f* (e-e a pair of) sugar-tongs *pl.*

zuckrig *adj.* ['tsukriç] sugary. 'Zuckung ♣ *f* (-/-en) convulsion. 'zudecken *v/t.* (*sep.*, -ge-, *h*) cover (up).

zudem *adv.* [tsu'de:m] besides, moreover.

'zu|drehen *v/t.* (*sep.*, -ge-, *h*) turn off (*tap*); *j-m den Rücken* ~ turn one's back on *s.o.*; '**.dringlich** *adj.* importunate, obtrusive; '**.drücken** *v/t.* (*sep.*, -ge-, *h*) close, shut; '**.erkennen** *v/t.* (*irr. kennen*, *sep.*, *no* -ge-, *h*) award (*a.* ✍); adjudge (*dat.* to) (*a.* ✍).

zuerst *adv.* [tsu'-] first (of all); at first; *er kam* ~ *an* he was the first to arrive.

'zufahr|en *v/i.* (*irr. fahren*, *sep.*, -ge-, *sein*) drive on; ~ *auf* (*acc.*) drive to (-wards); *fig.* rush at *s.o.*; '♀t *f* approach; drive, *Am.* driveway; '♀tsstraße *f* approach (road).

'Zufall *m* chance, accident; *durch* ~ by chance, by accident; '♀en *v/i.* (*irr. fallen*, *sep.*, -ge-, *sein*) *eyes*: be closing (with sleep); *door*: shut (of) itself; *j-m* ~ fall to *s.o.*('s share). 'zufällig 1. *adj.* accidental; *attr.*

chance; casual; 2. *adv.* accidentally, by chance.

'zufassen *v/i.* (*sep.*, -ge-, *h*) seize (hold of) *s.th.*; (*mit*) ~ lend *or* give a hand.

'Zuflucht *f* (-/♣ -e) refuge, shelter, resort; *s-e* ~ *nehmen zu* have recourse to *s.th.*, take refuge in *s.th.*

'Zufluß *m* afflux; influx (*a.* ♈); affluent, tributary (*of river*); ♈ supply.

'zuflüstern *v/t.* (*sep.*, -ge-, *h*): *j-m* et. ~ whisper s.th. to *s.o.*

zufolge *prp.* (*gen.*; *dat.*) [tsu'fɔlgə] according to.

zufrieden *adj.* [tsu'-] content(ed), satisfied; ♀heit *f* (-/*no pl.*) contentment, satisfaction; **.lassen** *v/t.* (*irr. lassen*, *sep.*, -ge-, *h*) let *s.o.* alone; **.stellen** *v/t.* (*sep.*, -ge-, *h*) satisfy; **.stellend** *adj.* satisfactory.

'zu|frieren *v/i.* (*irr. frieren*, *sep.*, -ge-, *sein*) freeze up *or* over; '**.fügen** *v/t.* (*sep.*, -ge-, *h*) add; do, cause; inflict (*wound*, *etc.*) (*j-m* [up]on *s.o.*); ♀fuhr ['.fu:r] *f* (-/-en) supply; supplies *pl.*; influx; '**.führen** *v/t.* (*sep.*, -ge-, *h*) carry, lead, bring; ⊕ feed; supply (*a.* ⊕).

Zug [tsu:k] *m* (-[-e]s/♣e) draw(ing), pull(ing); ⊕ traction; ✂ expedition, campaign; procession; migration (*of birds*); drift (*of clouds*); range (*of mountains*); ▓ train; feature; trait (*of character*); bent, tendency, trend; draught, *Am.* draft (*of air*); *at chess*: move; *drinking*: draught, *Am.* draft; *at cigarette, etc.*: puff.

'Zu|gabe *f* addition; extra; *thea.* encore; '**.gang** *m* entrance; access; approach; ♀gänglich *adj.* ['.gɛnliç] accessible (*für* to); '♀geben *v/t.* (*irr. geben*, *sep.*, -ge-, *h*) add; *fig.*: allow; confess; admit.

zugegen *adj.* [tsu'-] present (*bei* at.). 'zugehen *v/i.* (*irr. gehen*, *sep.*, -ge-, *sein*) *door, etc.*: close, shut; *p.* move on, walk faster; happen; *auf j-n* ~ go up to *s.o.*, move *or* walk towards *s.o.*

'Zugehörigkeit *f* (-/*no pl.*) membership (zu to) (*society, etc.*); belonging (to).

Zügel ['tsy:gəl] *m* (-s/-) rein; bridle (*a. fig.*); '♀los *adj.* unbridled; *fig.*: unrestrained; licentious; '♀n *v/t.* (*ge-, h*) rein (in); *fig.* bridle, check.

'Zuge|ständnis *n* concession; '♀stehen *v/t.* (*irr. stehen*, *sep.*, -ge-, *h*) concede.

zugetan *adj.* attached (*dat.* to).

Zugführer ▓ *m* guard, *Am.* conductor. [-ge-, *h*) add.)

zugießen *v/t.* (*irr. gießen*, *sep.*,) zug|ig *adj.* ['tsu:giç] draughty, *Am.* drafty; ♀kraft ['.k-] *f* ⊕ traction; *fig.* attraction, draw, appeal; **.kräftig** *adj.* ['.k-]: ~ *sein* be a draw.

**zugleich** adv. [tsu'-] at the same time; together.

'**Zug**|**luft** f (-/no pl.) draught, Am. draft; '**~maschine** f traction-engine, tractor; '**~pflaster** 🞐 n blister.

'**zu**|**greifen** v/i. (irr. greifen, sep., -ge-, h) grasp or grab at s.th.; at table: help o.s.; lend a hand; '**♀griff** m grip, clutch.

**zugrunde** adv. [tsu'grundə]: **~ gehen** perish; **~ richten** ruin.

'**Zugtier** n draught animal, Am. draft animal.

**zu**|**gunsten** prp. (gen.) [tsu'gunstən] in favo(u)r of; **~'gute** adv.: j-m et. **~ halten** give s.o. credit for s.th.; **~ kommen** be for the benefit (dat. of).

'**Zugvogel** m bird of passage.

'**zuhalten** v/t. (irr. halten, sep., -ge-, h) hold (door) to; sich die Ohren **~** stop one's ears. [home.]

**Zuhause** [tsu'hauzə] n (-/no pl.)]

'**zu**|**heilen** v/i. (sep., -ge-, sein) heal up, skin over; '**~hören** v/i. (sep., -ge-, h) listen (dat. to).

'**Zuhörer** m hearer, listener; **~** pl. audience; '**~schaft** f (-/🞐-en) audience.

'**zu**|**jubeln** v/i. (sep., -ge-, h) cheer; '**~kleben** v/t. (sep., -ge-, h) paste or glue up; gum (letter) down; '**~knallen** v/t. (sep., -ge-, h) bang, slam (door, etc.); '**~knöpfen** v/t. (sep., -ge-, h) button (up); '**~kommen** v/i. (irr. kommen, sep., -ge-, sein): auf j-n **~** come up to s.o.; j-m **~** be due to s.o.; j-m et. **~ lassen** let s.o. have s.th.; send s.o. s.th.; '**~korken** v/t. (sep., -ge-, h) cork (up).

**Zu**|**kunft** ['tsu:kunft] f (-/no pl.) future; gr. future (tense); '**♀künftig** 1. adj. future; **~er Vater** father-to-be; 2. adv. in future.

'**zu**|**lächeln** v/i. (sep., -ge-, h) smile at or up(on); '**♀lage** f extra pay, increase; rise, Am. raise (in salary or wages); '**~langen** v/i. (sep., -ge-, h) at table: help o.s.; '**~lassen** v/t. (irr. lassen, sep., -ge-, h) leave (door) shut; keep closed; fig.: admit s.o.; license; allow, suffer; admit of (only one interpretation, etc.); '**~lässig** adj. admissible, allowable; '**♀lassung** f (-/-en) admission; permission; licen|ce, Am. -se.

'**zulegen** v/t. (sep., -ge-, h) add; F sich et. **~** get o.s. s.th.

**zuleide** adv. [tsu'laɪdə]: j-m et. **~ tun** do s.o. harm, harm or hurt s.o.

'**zuleiten** v/t. (sep., -ge-, h) let in (water, etc.); conduct to; pass on to s.o.

**zu**|**letzt** adv. [tsu'-] finally, at last; er kam **~** an he was the last to arrive; **~'liebe** adv.: j-m **~** for s.o.'s sake.

**zum** prp. [tsum] = zu dem.

'**zumachen** v/t. (sep., -ge-, h) close, shut; button (up) (coat); fasten.

**zumal** cj. [tsu'-] especially, particularly. [up.]

'**zumauern** v/t. (sep., -ge-, h) wall]

**zumut**|**en** ['tsu:mu:tən] v/t. (sep., -ge-, h): j-m et. **~** expect s.th. of s.o.; sich zuviel **~** overtask o.s., overtax one's strength, etc.; '**♀ung** f (-/-en) exacting demand, exaction; fig. impudence.

**zunächst** [tsu'-] 1. prp. (dat.) next to; 2. adv. first of all; for the present.

'**zu**|**nageln** v/t. (sep., -ge-, h) nail up; '**~nähen** v/t. (sep., -ge-, h) sew up; '**♀nahme** ['~na:mə] f (-/-n) increase, growth; '**♀name** m surname.

**zünden** ['tsyndən] v/i. (ge-, h) kindle; esp. mot. ignite; fig. arouse enthusiasm.

**Zünd**|**holz** ['tsynt-] n match; '**~kerze** mot. f spark(ing)-plug, Am. spark plug; '**~schlüssel** mot. m ignition key; '**~schnur** f fuse; '**~stoff** fig. m fuel; **~ung** mot. ['~duŋ] f (-/-en) ignition.

'**zunehmen** v/i. (irr. nehmen, sep., -ge-, h) increase (an dat. in); grow; put on weight; moon: wax; days: grow longer.

'**zuneig**|**en** (sep., -ge-, h) 1. v/i. incline to(wards); 2. v/refl. incline to(wards); sich dem Ende **~** draw to a close; '**♀ung** f (-/🞐-en) affection.

**Zunft** [tsunft] f (-/≈e) guild, corporation.

**Zunge** ['tsuŋə] f (-/-n) tongue.

**züngeln** ['tsyŋəln] v/i. (ge-, h) play with its tongue; flame: lick.

'**zungen**|**fertig** adj. voluble; '**♀fertigkeit** f (-/no pl.) volubility; '**♀spitze** f tip of the tongue.

**zunichte** adv. [tsu'niçtə]: **~ machen** or werden bring or come to nothing.

'**zunicken** v/i. (sep., -ge-, h) nod to.

**zu**|**nutze** adv. [tsu'nutsə]: sich et. **~ machen** turn s.th. to account, utilize s.th.; **~'oberst** adv. at the top, uppermost.

**zupfen** ['tsupfən] (ge-, h) 1. v/t. pull, tug, twitch; 2. v/i. pull, tug, twitch (all: an dat. at).

**zur** prp. [tsu:r] = zu der.

'**zurechnungsfähig** adj. of sound mind; ⅛ responsible; '**♀keit** ⅛ f (-/no pl.) responsibility.

**zurecht**|**finden** [tsu'-] v/refl. (irr. finden, sep., -ge-, h) find one's way; **~kommen** v/i. (irr. kommen, sep., -ge-, sein) arrive in time; **~** (mit) get on (well) (with); manage s.th.; **~legen** v/t. (sep., -ge-, h) arrange; sich e-e Sache **~** think s.th. out; **~machen** F v/t. (sep., -ge-, h) get ready, prepare, Am. F fix; adapt (für to, for purpose); sich **~** of *woman*: make (o.s.) up; **~weisen** *v/t.* (*irr.* weisen, *sep.*, -ge-, *h*) reprimand; **2weisung** *f* reprimand.

**'zu|reden** *v/i.* (*sep.*, -ge-, *h*): *j-m* ~ try to persuade s.o.; encourage s.o.; **'~reiten** *v/t.* (*irr.* reiten, *sep.*, -ge-, *h*) break in; **'~riegeln** *v/t.* (*sep.*, -ge-, *h*) bolt (up).

**zürnen** ['tsyrnən] *v/i.* (ge-, *h*) be angry (*j-m* with s.o.).

**zurück** *adv.* [tsu'ryk] back; backward(s); behind; **~behalten** *v/t.* (*irr.* halten, *sep.*, *no* -ge-, *h*) keep back, retain; **~bekommen** *v/t.* (*irr.* kommen, *sep.*, *no* -ge-, *h*) get back; **~bleiben** *v/i.* (*irr.* bleiben, *sep.*, -ge-, *sein*) remain *or* stay behind; fall behind, lag; **~blicken** *v/i.* (*sep.*, -ge-, *h*) look back; **~bringen** *v/t.* (*irr.* bringen, *sep.*, -ge-, *h*) bring back; **~datieren** *v/t.* (*sep.*, *no* -ge-, *h*) date back, antedate; **~drängen** *v/t.* (*sep.*, -ge-, *h*) push back; *fig.* repress; **~erobern** *v/t.* (*sep.*, *no* -ge-, *h*) reconquer; **~erstatten** *v/t.* (*sep.*, *no* -ge-, *h*) restore, return; refund (*expenses*); **~fahren** (*irr.* fahren, *sep.*, -ge-) **1.** *v/i.* (*sein*) drive back; *fig.* start; **2.** *v/t.* (*h*) drive back; **~fordern** *v/t.* (*sep.*, -ge-, *h*) reclaim; **~führen** *v/t.* (*sep.*, -ge-, *h*) lead back; ~ *auf* (*acc.*) reduce to (*rule, etc.*); refer to (*cause, etc.*); **~geben** *v/t.* (*irr.* geben, *sep.*, -ge-, *h*) give back, return, restore; **~gehen** *v/i.* (*irr.* gehen, *sep.*, -ge-, *sein*) go back; return; **~gezogen** *adj.* retired; **~greifen** *fig.* *v/i.* (*irr.* greifen, *sep.*, -ge-, *h*): ~ *auf* (*acc.*) fall back (up)on; **~halten** (*irr.* halten, *sep.*, -ge-, *h*) **1.** *v/t.* hold back; **2.** *v/i.*: ~ *mit* keep back; **~haltend** *adj.* reserved; **2haltung** *f* (-/~-en) reserve; **~kehren** *v/i.* (*sep.*, -ge-, *sein*) return; **~kommen** *v/i.* (*irr.* kommen, *sep.*, -ge-, *sein*) come back; return (*fig. auf acc.* to); **~lassen** *v/t.* (*irr.* lassen, *sep.*, -ge-, *h*) leave (behind); **~legen** *v/t.* (*sep.*, -ge-, *h*) lay aside; cover (*distance, way*); **~nehmen** *v/t.* (*irr.* nehmen, *sep.*, -ge-, *h*) take back; withdraw, retract (*words, etc.*); **~prallen** *v/i.* (*sep.*, -ge-, *sein*) rebound; start; **~rufen** *v/t.* (*irr.* rufen, *sep.*, -ge-, *h*) call back; *sich ins Gedächtnis* ~ recall; **~schicken** *v/t.* (*sep.*, -ge-, *h*) send back; **~schlagen** (*irr.* schlagen, *sep.*, -ge-, *h*) **1.** *v/t.* drive (*ball*) back; repel (*enemy*); turn down (*blanket*); **2.** *v/i.* strike back; **~schrecken** *v/i.* (*sep.*, -ge-, *sein*) **1.** (*irr.* schrecken) shrink back (*vor dat.* from *spectacle, etc.*); **2.** shrink (*vor dat.* from *work, etc.*); **~setzen** *v/t.* (*sep.*, -ge-, *h*) put back; *fig.* slight, neglect; **~stellen** *v/t.* (*sep.*, -ge-, *h*) put back (*a. clock*); *fig.* defer, postpone; **~strahlen** *v/t.* (*sep.*, -ge-, *h*) reflect;

**~streifen** *v/t.* (*sep.*, -ge-, *h*) turn *or* tuck up (*sleeve*); **~treten** *v/i.* (*irr.* treten, *sep.*, -ge-, *sein*) step *or* stand back; *fig.*: recede; resign; withdraw; **~weichen** *v/i.* (*irr.* weichen, *sep.*, -ge-, *sein*) fall back; recede (*a. fig.*); **~weisen** *v/t.* (*irr.* weisen, *sep.*, -ge-, *h*) decline, reject; repel (*attack*); **~zahlen** *v/t.* (*sep.*, -ge-, *h*) pay back (*a. fig.*); **~ziehen** (*irr.* ziehen, *sep.*, -ge-) **1.** *v/t.* (*h*) draw back; *fig.* withdraw; *sich* ~ retire, withdraw; ✕ retreat; **2.** *v/i.* (*sein*) move *or* march back.

**'Zuruf** *m* call; **'2en** *v/t.* (*irr.* rufen, *sep.*, -ge-, *h*) call (out), shout (*j-m et. s.th.* to s.o.).

**'Zusage** *f* promise; assent; **'2n** (*sep.*, -ge-, *h*) **1.** *v/t.* promise; **2.** *v/i.* promise to come; *j-m* ~ *food, etc.*: agree with s.o.; accept s.o.'s invitation; suit s.o.

**zusammen** *adv.* [tsu'zamən] together; at the same time; *alles* ~ (all) in all; ~ *betragen* amount to, total (up to); **2arbeit** *f* (-/*no pl.*) co-operation; team-work; **~arbeiten** *v/i.* (*sep.*, -ge-, *h*) work together; co-operate; **~beißen** *v/t.* (*irr.* beißen, *sep.*, -ge-, *h*): *die Zähne* ~ set one's teeth; **~brechen** *v/i.* (*irr.* brechen, *sep.*, -ge-, *sein*) break down; collapse; **2bruch** *m* breakdown; collapse; **~drücken** *v/t.* (*sep.*, -ge-, *h*) compress, press together; **~fahren** *fig.* *v/i.* (*irr.* fahren, *sep.*, -ge-, *sein*) start (*bei at*; *vor dat.* with); **~fallen** *v/i.* (*irr.* fallen, *sep.*, -ge-, *sein*) fall in, collapse; coincide; **~falten** *v/t.* (*sep.*, -ge-, *h*) fold up; **~fassen** *v/t.* (*sep.*, -ge-, *h*) summarize, sum up; **2fassung** *f* (-/-en) summary; **~fügen** *v/t.* (*sep.*, -ge-, *h*) join (together); **~halten** (*irr.* halten, *sep.*, -ge-, *h*) **1.** *v/t.* hold together; **2.** *v/i.* hold together; *friends*: F stick together; **2hang** *m* coherence, coherency, connection; context; **~hängen** (*sep.*, -ge-, *h*) **1.** *v/i.* (*irr.* hängen) cohere; *fig.* be connected; **2.** *v/t.* hang together; **~klappen** *v/t.* (*sep.*, -ge-, *h*) fold up; close (*clasp-knife*); **~kommen** *v/i.* (*irr.* kommen, *sep.*, -ge-, *sein*) meet; **2kunft** [-kunft] *f* (-/-̈e) meeting; **~laufen** *v/i.* (*irr.* laufen, *sep.*, -ge-, *sein*) run *or* crowd together; ✕ converge; *milk*: curdle; **~legen** *v/t.* (*sep.*, -ge-, *h*) lay together; fold up; club (*money*) (together); **~nehmen** *fig.* *v/t.* (*irr.* nehmen, *sep.*, -ge-, *h*) collect (*one's wits*); *sich* ~ be on one's good behavio(u)r; pull o.s. together; **~packen** *v/t.* (*sep.*, -ge-, *h*) pack up; **~passen** *v/i.* (*sep.*, -ge-, *h*) match, harmonize; **~rechnen** *v/t.* (*sep.*, -ge-, *h*) add up; **~reißen** F *v/refl.* (*irr.* reißen, *sep.*, -ge-, *h*) pull o.s. together; **~rollen**

*v/t. and v/refl.* (*sep.*, -ge-, *h*) coil (up); **~rotten** *v/refl.* (*sep.*, -ge-, *h*) band together; **~rücken** (*sep.*, -ge-) 1. *v/t.* (*h*) move together; 2. *v/i.* (*sein*) close up; **~schlagen** (*irr. schlagen, sep.*, -ge-) 1. *v/t.* (*h*) clap (*hands*) (together); F smash to pieces; beat *s.o.* up; 2. *v/i.* (*sein*): **~ über** (*dat.*) close over; **~schließen** *v/refl.* (*irr. schließen, sep.*, -ge-, *h*) join; unite; **2schluß** *m* union; **~schrumpfen** *v/i.* (*sep.*, -ge-, *sein*) shrivel (up), shrink; **~setzen** *v/t.* (*sep.*, -ge-, *h*) put together; compose; compound (*a.* 🔊, *word*); ⊕ assemble; *sich* **~** aus consist of; **2set-zung** *f* (-/-en) composition; compound; ⊕ assembly; **~stellen** *v/t.* (*sep.*, -ge-, *h*) put together; compile; combine; **2stoß** *m* collision (*a. fig.*); ⚔ encounter; *fig.* clash; **~stoßen** *v/i.* (*irr. stoßen, sep.*, -ge-, *sein*) collide (*a. fig.*); adjoin; *fig.* clash; **~** mit knock (*heads, etc.*) together; **~stürzen** *v/i.* (*sep.*, -ge-, *sein*) collapse; *house, etc.*: fall in; **~tra-gen** *v/t.* (*irr. tragen, sep.*, -ge-, *h*) collect; compile (*notes*); **~treffen** *v/i.* (*irr. treffen, sep.*, -ge-, *sein*) meet; coincide; **2treffen** *n* (-s/*no pl.*) meeting; encounter (*of enemies*); coincidence; **~treten** *v/i.* (*irr. tre-ten, sep.*, -ge-, *sein*) meet; *parl. a.* convene; **~wirken** *v/i.* (*sep.*, -ge-, *h*) co-operate; **2wirken** *n* (-s/*no pl.*) co-operation; **~zählen** *v/t.* (*sep.*, -ge-, *h*) add up, count up; **~ziehen** *v/t.* (*irr. ziehen, sep.*, -ge-, *h*) draw together; contract; concentrate (*troops*); *sich* **~** contract.

'**Zusatz** *m* addition; admixture, *metall.* alloy; supplement.

**zusätzlich** *adj.* ['tsu:zɛtsliç] additional.

'**zuschau|en** *v/i.* (*sep.*, -ge-, *h*) look on (*e-r Sache at s.th.*); *j-m* **~** watch s.o. (*bei s.th. doing s.th.*); '**2er** *m* (-s/-) spectator, looker-on, onlooker; '**2erraum** *thea. m* auditorium.

'**zuschicken** *v/t.* (*sep.*, -ge-, *h*) send (*dat.* to); mail; consign (*goods*).

'**Zuschlag** *m* addition; extra charge; excess fare; 🎫 surcharge; *at auction:* knocking down; **2en** ['~gən] (*irr. schlagen, sep.*, -ge-) 1. *v/t.* (*h*) strike; 2. *v/i.* (*sein*) *door:* slam (to); 3. *v/t.* (*h*) bang, slam (*door*) (to); *at auction:* knock down (*dat.* to).

'**zu|schließen** *v/t.* (*irr. schließen, sep.*, -ge-, *h*) lock (up); '**~schnallen** *v/t.* (*sep.*, -ge-, *h*) buckle (up); '**~schnappen** (*sep.*, -ge-) 1. *v/i.* (*h*) *dog:* snap; 2. *v/i.* (*sein*) *door:* snap to; '**~schneiden** *v/t.* (*irr. schneiden, sep.*, -ge-, *h*) cut up; cut (*suit*) (to size); '**2schnitt** *m* (-[e]s/-e) cut; style; '**~schnüren** *v/t.* (*sep.*, -ge-, *h*) lace up; cord up; '**~schrauben** *v/t.*

(*sep.*, -ge-, *h*) screw up *or* tight; '**~schreiben** *v/t.* (*irr. schreiben, sep.*, -ge-, *h*): *j-m et.* **~** ascribe *or* attribute s.th. to s.o.; '**2schrift** *f* letter.

**zuschulden** *adv.* [tsu'-]: *sich et.* **~** *kommen lassen* make o.s. guilty of s.th.

'**Zu|schuß** *m* allowance; subsidy, grant (*of government*); '**2schütten** *v/t.* (*sep.*, -ge-, *h*) fill up (*ditch*); F add; '**2sehen** *v/i.* (*irr. sehen, sep.*, -ge-, *h*) s. zuschauen; **~,** *daß* see (to it) that; '**2sehends** *adv.* ['~ts] visibly; '**2senden** *v/t.* (*[irr. senden,] sep.*, -ge-, *h*) s. zuschicken; '**2setzen** (*sep.*, -ge-, *h*) 1. *v/t.* add; lose (*money*); 2. *v/i.* lose money; *j-m* **~** press s.o. hard.

'**zusicher|n** *v/t.* (*sep.*, -ge-, *h*): *j-m et.* **~** assure s.o. of s.th.; promise s.o. s.th.; '**2ung** *f* promise, assurance.

'**zu|spielen** *v/t.* (*sep.*, -ge-, *h*) *sports:* pass (*ball*) (*dat.* to) '**~spitzen** *v/t.* (*sep.*, -ge-, *h*) point; *sich* **~** taper (off); *fig.* come to a crisis; '**2spruch** *m* (-[e]s/*no pl.*) encouragement; consolation; † custom; '**2stand** *m* condition, state; *in gutem* **~** *house:* in good repair.

**zustande** *adv.* [tsu'ʃtandə]: **~** bringen bring about; **~** kommen come about; *nicht* **~** kommen not to come off.

'**zuständig** *adj.* competent; '**2keit** *f* (-/-en) competence.

**zustatten** *adv.* [tsu'ʃtatən]: *j-m* **~** kommen be useful to s.o.

'**zustehen** *v/i.* (*irr. stehen, sep.*, -ge-, *h*) be due (*dat.* to).

'**zustell|en** *v/t.* (*sep.*, -ge-, *h*) deliver (*a. ⚖*); ⚖ serve (*j-m on s.o.*); '**2ung** *f* delivery; ⚖ service.

'**zustimm|en** *v/i.* (*sep.*, -ge-, *h*) agree (*dat.* to s.th.; with s.o.); consent (*to s.th.*); '**2ung** *f* consent.

'**zustoßen** *fig. v/i.* (*irr. stoßen, sep.*, -ge-, *sein*): *j-m* **~** happen to s.o.

**zutage** *adv.* [tsu'ta:gə]: **~** treten come to light.

**Zutaten** ['tsu:ta:tən] *f/pl.* ingredients *pl.* (*of food*); trimmings *pl.* (*of dress*). [fall to s.o.'s share.)

**zuteil** *adv.* [tsu'taɪl]: *j-m* **~** werden)

'**zuteil|en** *v/t.* (*sep.*, -ge-, *h*) allot, apportion; '**2ung** *f* allotment, apportionment; ration.

'**zutragen** *v/refl.* (*irr. tragen, sep.*, -ge-, *h*) happen.

'**zutrauen** 1. *v/t.* (*sep.*, -ge-, *h*): *j-m et.* **~** credit s.o. with s.th.; *sich zu-viel* **~** overrate o.s.; 2. **2** *n* (-s/*no pl.*) confidence (*zu* in).

'**zutraulich** *adj.* confiding, trustful, trusting; *animal:* friendly, tame.

'**zutreffen** *v/i.* (*irr. treffen, sep.*, -ge-, *h*) be right, be true; **~** *auf* (*acc.*) be true of; '**~d** *adj.* right, correct; applicable.

'**zutrinken** v/i. (irr. trinken, sep., -ge-, h): j-m ~ drink to s.o.

'**Zutritt** m (-[e]s/no pl.) access; admission; ~ verboten! no admittance! [bottom.]

**zuunterst** adv. [tsu'-] right at the]

**zuverlässig** adj. ['tsu:ferlɛsiç] reliable; certain; '**2keit** f (-/no pl.) reliability; certainty.

**Zuversicht** ['tsu:ferziçt] f (-/no pl.) confidence; '**2lich** adj. confident.

**zuviel** adv. [tsu'-] too much; e-r ~ one too many.

**zuvor** adv. [tsu'-] before, previously; first; ~**kommen** v/i. (irr. kommen, sep., -ge-, sein): j-m ~ anticipate s.o.; e-r Sache ~ anticipate or prevent s.th.; ~**kommend** adj. obliging; courteous.

**Zuwachs** ['tsu:vaks] m (-es/no pl.) increase; '**2en** v/i. (irr. wachsen, sep., -ge-, sein) become overgrown; wound: close.

**zu|wege** adv. [tsu've:gə]: ~ bringen bring about; ~'**weilen** adv. sometimes.

'**zu|weisen** v/t. (irr. weisen, sep., -ge-, h) assign; '~**wenden** v/t. ([irr. wenden,] sep., -ge-, h) (dat.) turn to(wards); fig.: give; bestow on; sich ~ (dat.) turn to(wards).

**zuwenig** adv. [tsu'-] too little.

'**zuwerfen** v/t. (irr. werfen, sep., -ge-, h) fill up (pit); slam (door) (to); j-m ~ throw (ball, etc.) to s.o.; cast (look) at s.o.

**zuwider** prp. (dat.) [tsu'-] contrary to, against; repugnant, distasteful; ~**handeln** v/i. (sep., -ge-, h) (dat.) act contrary or in opposition to; esp. ₜ₅ contravene; **2handlung** ₜ₅ f contravention.

'**zu|winken** v/i. (sep., -ge-, h) (dat.) wave to; beckon to; '~**zahlen** v/t. (sep., -ge-, h) pay extra; '~**ziehen** v/t. (sep., -ge-, h) add; '~**ziehen** (irr. ziehen, sep., -ge-) **1.** v/t. (h) draw together; draw (curtains); consult (doctor, etc.); sich ~ incur (s.o.'s displeasure, etc.); ⚕ catch (disease); **2.** v/i. (sein) move in; ~**züglich** prp. (gen.) ['~tsy:k-] plus.

**Zwang** [tsvaŋ] **1.** m (-[e]s/✎, ⸚e) compulsion, coercion; constraint; ₜ₅ duress(e); force; sich ~ antun check or restrain o.s.; **2.** ⸚ pret. of zwingen.

**zwängen** ['tsvɛŋən] v/t. (ge-,h) press, force.

'**zwanglos** fig. adj. free and easy, informal; '**2igkeit** f (-/-en) ease, informality.

'**Zwangs|arbeit** f hard labo(u)r; '~**jacke** f strait waistcoat or jacket; '~**lage** f embarrassing situation; **2läufig** fig. adj. ['~lɔyf-] necessary; '~**maßnahme** f coercive measure; '~**vollstreckung** ₜ₅ f distraint, execution; '~**vorstellung** ✎ f

obsession, hallucination; '**2weise** adv. by force; '~**wirtschaft** f (-/✎ -en) controlled economy.

**zwanzig** adj. ['tsvantsiç] twenty; ~**ste** adj. ['~stə] twentieth.

**zwar** cj. [tsva:r] indeed, it is true; und ~ and that, that is.

**Zweck** [tsvɛk] m (-[e]s/-e) aim, end, object, purpose; design; keinen ~ haben be of no use; s-n ~ erfüllen answer its purpose; zu dem ~ (gen.) for the purpose of; '**2dienlich** adj. serviceable, useful, expedient.

**Zwecke** ['tsvɛkə] f (-/-n) tack; drawing-pin, Am. thumbtack.

'**zweck|los** adj. aimless, purposeless; useless; '~**mäßig** adj. expedient, suitable; '**2mäßigkeit** f (-/no pl.) expediency.

**zwei** adj. [tsvaɪ] two; '~**beinig** adj. two-legged; '**2bettzimmer** n double (bedroom); ~**deutig** adj. ['~dɔy-tiç] ambiguous; suggestive; ~**erlei** adj. ['~ər'laɪ] of two kinds, two kinds of; ~**fach** adj. ['~fax] double, twofold.

**Zweifel** ['tsvaɪfəl] m (-s/-) doubt; '**2haft** adj. doubtful, dubious; '**2los** adj. doubtless; '**2n** v/i. (ge-, h) doubt (an e-r Sache s.th.; an j-m s.o.).

**Zweig** [tsvaɪk] m (-[e]s/-e) branch (a. fig.); kleiner ~ twig; '~**geschäft** n, '~**niederlassung** f, '~**stelle** f branch.

**zwei|jährig** adj. ['tsvaɪjɛ:riç] two-year-old, of two (years); '**2kampf** m duel, single combat; '~**mal** adv. twice; '~**malig** adj. (twice) repeated; ~**motorig** adj. ['~moto:riç] two- or twin-engined; '~**reihig** adj. having two rows; suit: double-breasted; '~**schneidig** adj. double- or two-edged (both a. fig.); '~**seitig** adj. two-sided; contract, etc.: bilateral; fabric: reversible, **2sitzer** esp. mot. m (-s/-) two-seater; '~**sprachig** adj. bilingual; '~**stimmig** adj. for two voices; ~**stöckig** adj. ['~stœkiç] two-stor|eyed, -ied; '~**stufig** adj. two-stage; ~**stündig** adj. ['~ʃtyndiç] of or lasting two hours, two-hour.

**zweit** adj. [tsvaɪt] second; ein ~er another; aus ~er Hand second-hand; zu ~ by twos; wir sind zu ~ there are two of us. [engine.]

'**Zweitaktmotor** mot. m two-stroke]

'**zweit'best** adj. second-best.

'**zweiteilig** adj. garment: two-piece.

**zweitens** adv. ['tsvaɪtəns] secondly.

'**zweitklassig** adj. second-class, second-rate.

**Zwerchfell** anat. ['tsvɛrç-] n diaphragm.

**Zwerg** [tsvɛrk] m (-[e]s/-e) dwarf; **2enhaft** adj. ['~gən-] dwarfish.

**Zwetsch(g)e** ['tsvɛtʃ(g)ə] f (-/-n) plum.

**Zwick|el** ['tsvikəl] *m* (-s/-) *sewing*: gusset; '**2en** *v/t. and v/i.* (*ge-*, *h*) pinch, nip; '**₊er** *m* (-s/-) (*ein a pair of*) eye-glasses *pl.*, pince-nez; '**₊mühle** *fig. f* dilemma, quandary, fix.

**Zwieback** ['tsvi:bak] *m* (-[e]s/⁼e, -e) rusk, zwieback.

**Zwiebel** ['tsvi:bəl] *f* (-/-n) onion; bulb (*of flowers, etc.*).

**Zwie|gespräch** ['tsvi:-] *n* dialog(ue); '**₊licht** *n* (-[e]s/no pl.) twilight; '**₊spalt** *m* (-[e]s/-e, ⁼e) disunion; conflict; **2spältig** *adj.* ['₊ʃpɛltiç] disunited; *emotions*: conflicting; '**₊tracht** *f* (-/no pl.) discord.

**Zwilling|e** ['tsviliŋə] *m/pl.* twins *pl.*; '**₊sbruder** *m* twin brother; '**₊sschwester** *f* twin sister.

**Zwinge** ['tsviŋə] *f* (-/-n) ferrule (*of stick, etc.*); ⊕ clamp; '**2n** *v/t.* (*irr.*, *ge-*, *h*) compel, constrain; force; '**2nd** *adj.* forcible; *arguments*: cogent, compelling; imperative; '**₊r** *m* (-s/-) outer court; kennel(s *pl.*); bear-pit.

**zwinkern** ['tsviŋkərn] *v/i.* (*ge-*, *h*) wink, blink.

**Zwirn** [tsvirn] *m* (-[e]s/-e) thread, cotton; '**₊sfaden** *m* thread.

**zwischen** *prp.* (*dat.; acc.*) ['tsviʃən] between (*two*); among (*several*); '**2bilanz** ✝ *f* interim balance; '**2deck** ⚓ *n* steerage; **₊'durch** F *adv.* in between; for a change; '**2ergebnis** *n* provisional result; '**2fall** *m* incident; '**2händler** ✝ *m* middleman; '**2landung** ✈ *f* intermediate landing, stop, *Am. a.* stopover; (*Flug*) ohne ₊ non-stop (flight);

'**2pause** *f* interval, intermission; '**2prüfung** *f* intermediate examination; '**2raum** *m* space, interval; '**2ruf** *m* (loud) interruption; '**2spiel** *n* interlude; '**₊staatlich** *adj.* international; *Am. between States*: interstate; '**2station** *f* intermediate station; '**2stecker** ⚡ *m* adapter; '**2stück** *n* intermediate piece, connexion, (*Am. only*) connection; '**2stufe** *f* intermediate stage; '**2wand** *f* partition (wall); '**2zeit** *f* interval; *in der* ₊ in the meantime.

**Zwist** [tsvist] *m* (-es/-e), '**₊igkeit** *f* (-/-en) discord; disunion; quarrel.

**zwitschern** ['tsvitʃərn] *v/i.* (*ge-*, *h*) twitter, chirp.

**Zwitter** ['tsvitər] *m* (-s/-) hermaphrodite.

**zwölf** *adj.* [tsvœlf] twelve; *um* ₊ (*Uhr*) at twelve (o'clock); (*um*) ₊ *Uhr mittags* (at) noon; (*um*) ₊ *Uhr nachts* (at) midnight; **2'finger-darm** *anat. m* duodenum; **₊te** *adj.* ['₊tə] twelfth.

**Zyankali** [tsyan'ka:li] *n* (-s/no pl.) potassium cyanide.

**Zyklus** ['tsy:klus, 'tsyk-] *m* (-/Zyklen) cycle; course, set (*of lectures, etc.*).

**Zylind|er** [tsi'lindər, tsy'-] *m* (-s/-) ⚲, ⊕ cylinder; chimney (*of lamp*); top hat; **2risch** *adj.* [₊driʃ] cylindrical.

**Zyni|ker** ['tsy:nikər] *m* (-s/-) cynic; '**2sch** *adj.* cynical; **₊smus** [tsy-'nismus] *m* (-/Zynismen) cynicism.

**Zypresse** ♀ [tsy'prɛsə] *f* (-/-n) cypress.

**Zyste** ⚕ ['tsystə] *f* (-/-n) cyst.

# PART II

## ENGLISH-GERMAN
## DICTIONARY

# A

**a** [ei, ə] *Artikel:* ein(e); per, pro, je; *all of a size* alle gleich groß; *twice a week* zweimal wöchentlich.

**A 1** F ['ei'wʌn] Ia, prima.

**aback** [ə'bæk] rückwärts; *taken ~ fig.* überrascht, verblüfft, bestürzt.

**abandon** [ə'bændən] auf-, preisgeben; verlassen; überlassen; **~ed** verworfen; **~ment** [~nmənt] Auf-, Preisgabe *f*; Unbeherrschtheit *f*.

**abase** [ə'beis] erniedrigen, demütigen; **~ment** [~smənt] Erniedrigung *f*.

**abash** [ə'bæʃ] beschämen, verlegen machen; **~ment** [~ʃmənt] Verlegenheit *f*.

**abate** [ə'beit] *v/t.* verringern; *Mißstand* abstellen; *v/i.* abnehmen, nachlassen; **~ment** [~tmənt] Verminderung *f*; Abschaffung *f*.

**abattoir** ['æbətwɑ:] Schlachthaus *n*.

**abb|ess** ['æbis] Äbtissin *f*; **~ey** ['æbi] Abtei *f*; **~ot** ['æbət] Abt *m*.

**abbreviat|e** [ə'bri:vieit] (ab)kürzen; **~ion** [əbri:vi'eiʃən] Abkürzung *f*.

**ABC** ['eibi:'si:] Abc *n*, Alphabet *n*.

**ABC weapons** *pl.* ABC-Waffen *f/pl.*

**abdicat|e** ['æbdikeit] entsagen (*dat.*); abdanken; **~ion** [æbdi'keiʃən] Verzicht *m*; Abdankung *f*.

**abdomen** ['æbdəmen] Unterleib *m*, Bauch *m*.

**abduct** [æb'dʌkt] entführen.

**aberration** [æbə'reiʃən] Abweichung *f*; *fig.* Verirrung *f*.

**abet** [ə'bet] aufhetzen; anstiften; unterstützen; **~tor** [~tə] Anstifter *m*; (Helfers)Helfer *m*.

**abeyance** [ə'beiəns] Unentschiedenheit *f*; *in ~ 🖾* in der Schwebe.

**abhor** [əb'hɔ:] verabscheuen; **~rence** [əb'hɔrəns] Abscheu *m* (*of vor dat.*); **~rent** [~nt] zuwider (*to dat.*); abstoßend.

**abide** [ə'baid] [*irr.*] *v/i.* bleiben (*by* bei); *v/t.* erwarten; (v)ertragen.

**ability** [ə'biliti] Fähigkeit *f*.

**abject** □ ['æbdʒekt] verächtlich, gemein.

**abjure** [əb'dʒuə] abschwören; entsagen (*dat.*).

**able** □ ['eibl] fähig, geschickt; *be ~* imstande sein, können; **~-bodied** kräftig.

**abnegat|e** ['æbnigeit] ableugnen; verzichten auf (*acc.*); **~ion** [æbni'geiʃən] Ableugnung *f*; Verzicht *m*.

**abnormal** □ [æb'nɔ:məl] abnorm.

**aboard** [ə'bɔ:d] 🕂 an Bord (*gen.*); *all ~! Am.* 🚂 *etc.* einsteigen!

**abode** [ə'boud] **1.** *pret. u. p.p. von abide;* **2.** Aufenthalt *m*; Wohnung *f*.

**abolish** [ə'bɔliʃ] abschaffen, aufheben; **~tion** [æbə'liʃən] Abschaffung *f*, Aufhebung *f*; **~tionist** [~nist] Gegner *m* der Sklaverei.

**A-bomb** ['eibɔm] = *atomic bomb.*

**abomina|ble** □ [ə'bɔminəbl] abscheulich; **~te** [~neit] verabscheuen; **~tion** [əbɔmi'neiʃən] Abscheu *m*.

**aboriginal** □ [æbə'ridʒənl] einheimisch; Ur...

**abortion** 🗲 [ə'bɔ:ʃən] Fehlgeburt *f*; Abtreibung *f*.

**abortive** □ [ə'bɔ:tiv] vorzeitig; erfolglos, fehlgeschlagen; verkümmert.

**abound** [ə'baund] reichlich vorhanden sein; Überfluß haben (*in an dat.*).

**about** [ə'baut] **1.** *prp.* um (...herum); bei; im Begriff; über (*acc.*); *I had no money ~* me ich hatte kein Geld bei mir; *what are you ~?* was macht ihr da?; **2.** *adv.* herum, umher; in der Nähe; etwa; ungefähr um, gegen; *bring ~* zustande bringen.

**above** [ə'bʌv] **1.** *prp.* über; *fig.* erhaben über; **~** *all* vor allem; **~** *ground fig.* am Leben; **2.** *adv.* oben; darüber; **3.** *adj.* obig.

**abreact** [æbri'ækt] abreagieren.

**abreast** [ə'brest] nebeneinander.

**abridg|e** [ə'bridʒ] (ver)kürzen; **~(e)ment** [~dʒmənt] (Ver)Kürzung *f*; Auszug *m*.

**abroad** [ə'brɔ:d] im (ins) Ausland; überall(hin); *there is a report ~* es geht das Gerücht; *all ~* ganz im Irrtum.

**abrogate** ['æbrougeit] aufheben.

**abrupt** □ [ə'brʌpt] jäh; zs.-hanglos; schroff.

**abscess** 🗲 ['æbsis] Geschwür *n*.

**abscond** [əb'skɔnd] sich davonmachen.

**absence** ['æbsəns] Abwesenheit *f*; Mangel *m*; *~ of mind* Zerstreutheit *f*.

**absent 1.** □ ['æbsənt] abwesend; nicht vorhanden; **2.** [æb'sent]: *~ o.s.* fernbleiben; **~-minded** □ ['æbsənt'maindid] zerstreut, geistesabwesend.

**absolut|e** □ ['æbsəlu:t] absolut; umschränkt; vollkommen; unvermischt; unbedingt; **~ion** [æbsə'lu:ʃən] Lossprechung *f*.

**absolve** [əb'zɔlv] frei-, lossprechen.

**absorb** [əb'sɔ:b] aufsaugen; *fig.* ganz in Anspruch nehmen.

**absorption** [əb'sɔ:pʃən] Aufsaugung *f*; *fig.* Vertieftsein *n*.

**abstain** [əb'stein] sich enthalten.

**abstemious** □ [æb'sti:mjəs] enthaltsam; mäßig.

**abstention** [æb'stenʃən] Enthaltung f.

**abstinen|ce** ['æbstinəns] Enthaltsamkeit f; ~t □ [~nt] enthaltsam.

**abstract 1.** □ ['æbstrækt] abstrakt; **2.** [~] Auszug m; gr. Abstraktum n; **3.** [æb'strækt] abstrahieren; ablenken; entwenden; Inhalt kurz zs.-fassen; ~ed □ zerstreut; ~ion [~kʃən] Abstraktion f; (abstrakter) Begriff.

**abstruse** □ [æb'stru:s] fig. dunkel, schwer verständlich; tiefgründig.

**absurd** □ [əb'sə:d] absurd, sinnwidrig; lächerlich.

**abundan|ce** [ə'bʌndəns] Überfluß m; Fülle f; Überschwang m; ~t □ [~nt] reich(lich).

**abus|e 1.** [ə'bju:s] Mißbrauch m; Beschimpfung f; **2.** [~u:z] mißbrauchen; beschimpfen; ~ive □ [~u:siv] schimpfend; Schimpf...

**abut** [ə'bʌt] (an)grenzen (upon an).

**abyss** [ə'bis] Abgrund m.

**academic|(al** [ækə'demik(əl)] akademisch; ~ian [əkædə'miʃən] Akademiemitglied n.

**academy** [ə'kædəmi] Akademie f.

**accede** [æk'si:d]: ~ to beitreten (dat.); Amt antreten; Thron besteigen.

**accelerat|e** [æk'seləreit] beschleunigen; fig. ankurbeln; ~or [ək'seləreitə] Gaspedal n.

**accent 1.** ['æksənt] Akzent m (a. gr.); **2.** [æk'sent] v/t. akzentuieren, betonen; ~uate [~tjueit] akzentuieren, betonen.

**accept** [ək'sept] annehmen; ✝ akzeptieren; hinnehmen; ~able □ [~təbl] annehmbar; ~ance [~əns] Annahme f; ✝ Akzept n.

**access** ['ækses] Zugang m; 𝕤 Anfall m; easy of ~ zugänglich; ~ road Zufahrtsstraße f; ~ary [æk'sesəri] Mitwisser(in), Mitschuldige(r m) f; = accessory 2; ~ible [ [~səbl] zugänglich; ~ion [~eʃən] Antritt m (to gen.); Eintritt m (to in acc.); ~ to the throne Thronbesteigung f.

**accessory** [æk'sesəri] **1.** □ zusätzlich; **2.** Zubehörteil n.

**accident** ['æksidənt] Zufall m; Un(glücks)fall m; ~al □ [æksi'dentl] zufällig; nebensächlich.

**acclaim** [ə'kleim] j-m zujubeln.

**acclamation** [æklə'meiʃən] Zuruf m.

**acclimatize** [ə'klaimətaiz] akklimatisieren, eingewöhnen.

**acclivity** [ə'kliviti] Steigung f; Böschung f.

**accommodat|e** [ə'kɔmədeit] anpassen; unterbringen; Streit schlichten; versorgen; j-m aushelfen (with mit Geld); ~ion [əkɔmə'deiʃən] Anpassung f; Aushilfe f; Bequemlich-

keit f; Unterkunft f; Beilegung f; ~ seating ~ Sitzgelegenheit f; ~ train Am. Personenzug m.

**accompan|iment** [ə'kʌmpənimənt] Begleitung f; ~y [ə'kʌmpəni] begleiten; accompanied with verbunden mit.

**accomplice** [ə'kɔmplis] Komplice m.

**accomplish** [ə'kɔmpliʃ] vollenden; ausführen; ~ed vollendet, perfekt; ~ment [~ʃmənt] Vollendung f; Ausführung f; Tat f, Leistung f; Talent n.

**accord** [ə'kɔ:d] **1.** Übereinstimmung f; with one ~ einstimmig; **2.** v/i. übereinstimmen; v/t. gewähren; ~ance [~dəns] Übereinstimmung f; ~ant □ [~nt] übereinstimmend; ~ing [~diŋ]: ~ to gemäß (dat.); ~ingly [~ŋli] dementsprechend.

**accost** [ə'kɔst] j-n bsd. auf der Straße ansprechen.

**account** [ə'kaunt] **1.** Rechnung f; Berechnung f; ✝ Konto n; Rechenschaft f; Bericht m; of no ~ ohne Bedeutung; on no ~ auf keinen Fall; on ~ of wegen; take into ~, take ~ of in Betracht ziehen, berücksichtigen; turn to ~ ausnutzen; keep ~s die Bücher führen; call to ~ zur Rechenschaft ziehen; give a good ~ of o.s. sich bewähren; make ~ of Wert auf et. (acc.) legen; **2.** v/i.: ~ for Rechenschaft über et. (acc.) ablegen; (sich) erklären; be much ~ed of hoch geachtet sein; v/t. ansehen als; ~able □ [~təbl] verantwortlich; erklärlich; ~ant [~ənt] Buchhalter m; chartered ~, Am. certified public ~, vereidigter Bücherrevisor; ~ing [~tiŋ] Buchführung f.

**accredit** [ə'kredit] beglaubigen.

**accrue** [ə'kru:] erwachsen (from aus).

**accumulat|e** [ə'kju:mjulcit] (sich) (an)häufen; ansammeln; ~ion [əkju:mju'leiʃən] Anhäufung f.

**accura|cy** ['ækjurəsi] Genauigkeit f; ~te □ [~rit] genau; richtig.

**accurs|ed** [ə'kə:sid], ~t [~st] verflucht, verwünscht.

**accus|ation** [ækju:(:)'zeiʃən] Anklage f, Beschuldigung f; ~ative gr. [ə'kju:zətiv] a. ~ case Akkusativ m; ~e [ə'kju:z] anklagen, beschuldigen; ~er [~zə] Kläger(in).

**accustom** [ə'kʌstəm] gewöhnen (to an acc.); ~ed gewohnt, üblich; gewöhnt (to an acc., zu inf.).

**ace** [eis] As n (a. fig.); ~ in the hole Am. F fig. Trumpf m in Reserve; within an ~ um ein Haar.

**acerbity** [ə'sə:biti] Herbheit f.

**acet|ic** [ə'si:tik] essigsauer; ~ify [ə'setifai] säuern.

**ache** [eik] **1.** schmerzen; sich sehnen (for nach; to do zu tun); **2.** anhaltende Schmerzen m/pl.

achieve [ə'tʃiːv] ausführen; erreichen; **ment** [ˌvmənt] Ausführung *f*; Leistung *f*.

acid ['æsid] 1. sauer; 2. Säure *f*; **ity** [ə'siditi] Säure *f*.

acknowledg|e [ək'nɔlidʒ] anerkennen; zugeben; ✝ bestätigen; **(e)ment** [ˌdʒmənt] Anerkennung *f*; Bestätigung *f*; Eingeständnis *n*.

acme ['ækmi] Gipfel *m*; ✚ Krisis *f*.

acorn ♀ ['eikɔːn] Eichel *f*.

acoustics [ə'kuːstiks] *pl*. Akustik *f*.

acquaint [ə'kweint] bekannt machen; *j-m* mitteilen; be **ed with** kennen; **ance** [ˌtəns] Bekanntschaft *f*; Bekannte(r *m*) *f*.

acquiesce [ækwi'es] (*in*) hinnehmen (*acc*.); einwilligen (in *acc*.).

acquire [ə'kwaiə] erwerben; **ment** [ˌəmənt] Fertigkeit *f*.

acquisition [ækwi'ziʃən] Erwerbung *f*; Errungenschaft *f*.

acquit [ə'kwit] freisprechen; ∼ *o.s.* of *Pflicht* erfüllen; ∼ *o.s.* well s-e Sache gut machen; **tal** [ˌtl] Freisprechung *f*, Freispruch *m*; **tance** [ˌtəns] Tilgung *f*.

acre ['eikə] Morgen *m* (*4047 qm*).

acrid ['ækrid] scharf, beißend.

across [ə'krɔs] 1. *adv*. hin-, herüber; (quer) durch; drüben; überkreuz; 2. *prp*. (quer) über (*acc*.); jenseits (*gen*.), über (*dat*.); come ∼, run ∼ stoßen auf (*acc*.).

act [ækt] 1. *v/i*. handeln; sich benehmen; wirken; funktionieren; *thea*. spielen; *v/t. thea*. spielen; 2. Handlung *f*, Tat *f*; *thea*. Akt *m*; Gesetz *n*; Beschluß *m*; Urkunde *f*, Vertrag *m*; **ing** ['æktiŋ] 1. Handeln *n*; *thea*. Spiel(en) *n*; 2. tätig, amtierend.

action ['ækʃən] Handlung *f* (*a. thea*.); Tätigkeit *f*; Tat *f*; Wirkung *f*; Klage *f*, Prozeß *m*; Gang *m* (*Pferd etc*.); Gefecht *n*; Mechanismus *m*; take ∼ Schritte unternehmen.

activ|e □ ['æktiv] aktiv; tätig; rührig, wirksam; ✝ lebhaft; **ity** [æk'tiviti] Tätigkeit *f*; Betriebsamkeit *f*; *bsd*. ✝ Lebhaftigkeit *f*.

act|or ['æktə] Schauspieler *m*; **ress** ['æktris] Schauspielerin *f*.

actual □ ['æktjuəl] wirklich, tatsächlich, eigentlich.

actuate ['æktjueit] in Gang bringen.

acute □ [ə'kjuːt] spitz; scharf(sinnig); brennend (*Frage*); ♪ akut.

ad F [æd] = *advertisement*.

adamant *fig*. ['ædəmənt] unerbittlich.

adapt [ə'dæpt] anpassen (*to, for dat*.); *Text* bearbeiten (*from nach*); zurechtmachen; **ation** [ædæp'teiʃən] Anpassung *f*, Bearbeitung *f*.

add [æd] *v/t*. hinzufügen; addieren; *v/i*.: ∼ to vermehren; hinzukommen zu.

addict ['ædikt] Süchtige(r *m*) *f*; **ed** [ə'diktid] ergeben (*to dat*.); ∼ *to e-m Laster* verfallen.

addition [ə'diʃən] Hinzufügen *n*; Zusatz *m*; An-, Ausbau *m*; Addition *f*; *in* ∼ außerdem; *in* ∼ *to* außer, zu; **al** □ [ˌnl] zusätzlich.

address [ə'dres] 1. *Worte* richten (*to an acc*.); sprechen zu; 2. Adresse *f*; Ansprache *f*; Anstand *m*, Manieren *f/pl*.; pay one's **es** *to a lady* e-r Dame den Hof machen; **ee** [ædre'siː] Adressat *m*, Empfänger *m*.

adept ['ædept] 1. erfahren; geschickt; 2. Eingeweihte(r *m*) *f*; Kenner *m*.

adequa|cy ['ædikwəsi] Angemessenheit *f*; **te** □ [ˌkwit] angemessen.

adhere [əd'hiə] (*to*) haften (an *dat*.); *fig*. festhalten (an *dat*.); **nce** [ˌərəns] Anhaften *n*, Festhalten *n*; **nt** [ˌnt] Anhänger(in).

adhesion [əd'hiːʒən] = *adherence*; *fig*. Einwilligung *f*.

adhesive [əd'hiːsiv] 1. □ klebend; ∼ *plaster*, ∼ *tape* Heftpflaster *n*; 2. Klebstoff *m*.

adjacent □ [ə'dʒeisənt] (*to*) anliegend (*dat*.); anstoßend (an *acc*.); benachbart.

adjective *gr*. ['ædʒiktiv] Adjektiv *n*, Eigenschaftswort *n*.

adjoin [ə'dʒɔin] angrenzen an (*acc*.).

adjourn [ə'dʒəːn] aufschieben; (*v/i*. sich) vertagen; **ment** [ˌnmənt] Aufschub *m*; Vertagung *f*.

adjudge [ə'dʒʌdʒ] zuerkennen; verurteilen.

adjust [ə'dʒʌst] in Ordnung bringen; anpassen; *Streit* schlichten; *Mechanismus u. fig*. einstellen (*to auf acc*.); **ment** [ˌtmənt] Anordnung *f*; Einstellung *f*; Schlichtung *f*.

administ|er [əd'ministə] verwalten; spenden; ♪ verabfolgen; ∼ *justice* Recht sprechen; **ration** [ədminis'treiʃən] Verwaltung *f*; Regierung *f*; *bsd. Am*. Amtsperiode *f e-s Präsidenten*; **rative** [əd'ministrətiv] Verwaltungs...; **rator** [ˌreitə] Verwalter *m*.

admir|able □ ['ædmərəbl] bewundernswert; (vor)trefflich; **ation** [ædmə'reiʃən] Bewunderung *f*; **e** [əd'maiə] bewundern; verehren.

admiss|ible □ [əd'misəbl] zulässig; **ion** [ˌiʃən] Zulassung *f*; F Eintritt(sgeld *n*) *m*; Eingeständnis *n*.

admit [əd'mit] *v/t*. (her)einlassen (*to, into in acc*.), eintreten lassen; zulassen (*to zu*); zugeben; **tance** [ˌtəns] Einlaß *m*, Zutritt *m*.

admixture [əd'mikstʃə] Beimischung *f*, Zusatz *m*.

admon|ish [əd'mɔniʃ] ermahnen; warnen (*of, against vor dat*.); **ition** [ædmə'niʃən] Ermahnung *f*; Warnung *f*.

**ado** [ə'du:] Getue *n*; Lärm *m*; Mühe *f*.

**adolescen|ce** [ædou'lesns] Adoleszenz *f*, Reifezeit *f*; **~t** [~nt] **1.** jugendlich, heranwachsend; **2.** Jugendliche(r *m*) *f*.

**adopt** [ə'dɔpt] adoptieren; sich aneignen; **~ion** [~pʃən] Annahme *f*.

**ador|able** □ [ə'dɔ:rəbl] verehrungswürdig; **~ation** [ædɔ:'reiʃən] Anbetung *f*; **~e** [ə'dɔ:] anbeten.

**adorn** [ə'dɔ:n] schmücken, zieren; **~ment** [~nmənt] Schmuck *m*.

**adroit** □ [ə'drɔit] gewandt.

**adult** ['ædʌlt] **1.** erwachsen; **2.** Erwachsene(r *m*) *f*.

**adulter|ate** [ə'dʌltəreit] (ver)fälschen; **~er** [~rə] Ehebrecher *m*; **~ess** [~ris] Ehebrecherin *f*; **~ous** □ [~rəs] ehebrecherisch; **~y** [~ri] Ehebruch *m*.

**advance** [əd'vɑ:ns] **1.** *v/i.* vorrücken, vorgehen; steigen; Fortschritte machen; *v/t.* vorrücken; vorbringen; vorausbezahlen; vorschießen; (be)fördern; *Preis* erhöhen; beschleunigen; **2.** Vorrücken *n*; Fortschritt *m*; Angebot *n*; Vorschuß *m*; Erhöhung *f*; in **~** im voraus; **~d** vor-, fortgeschritten; **~** *in years* in vorgerücktem Alter; **~ment** [~smənt] Förderung *f*; Fortschritt *m*.

**advantage** [əd'vɑ:ntidʒ] Vorteil *m*; Überlegenheit *f*; Gewinn *m*; *take* **~** *of* ausnutzen; **~ous** □ [ædvən'teidʒəs] vorteilhaft.

**adventur|e** [əd'ventʃə] Abenteuer *n*, Wagnis *n*; Spekulation *f*; **~er** [~ərə] Abenteurer *m*; Spekulant *m*; **~ous** □ [~rəs] abenteuerlich; wagemutig.

**adverb** *gr.* ['ædvə:b] Adverb *n*, Umstandswort *n*.

**advers|ary** ['ædvəsəri] Gegner *m*, Feind *m*; **~e** □ ['ædvə:s] widrig; feindlich; ungünstig, nachteilig (*to* für); **~ity** [əd'və:siti] Unglück *n*.

**advertis|e** ['ædvətaiz] ankündigen; inserieren; Reklame machen (für); **~ement** [əd'və:tismənt] Ankündigung *f*, Inserat *n*; Reklame *f*; **~ing** ['ædvətaiziŋ] Reklame *f*, Werbung *f*; **~** *agency* Annoncenbüro *n*; **~** *designer* Reklamezeichner *m*; **~** *film* Reklamefilm *m*; **~** *screen* **~** Filmreklame *f*.

**advice** [əd'vais] Rat(schlag) *m*; (*mst pl.*) Nachricht *f*, Meldung *f*; *take medical* **~** e-n Arzt zu Rate ziehen.

**advis|able** □ [əd'vaizəbl] ratsam; **~e** [əd'vaiz] *v/t. j-n* beraten; *j-m* raten; † benachrichtigen, avisieren; *v/i.* (sich) beraten; **~er** [~zə] Ratgeber(in).

**advocate 1.** ['ædvəkit] Anwalt *m*; Fürsprecher *m*; **2.** [~keit] verteidigen, befürworten.

**aerial** ['ɛəriəl] **1.** □ luftig; Luft...;

**~** *view* Luftaufnahme *f*; **2.** *Radio*, *Fernsehen*: Antenne *f*.

**aero|...** ['ɛərou] Luft...; **~cab** *Am.* F ['ɛərəkæb] Lufttaxi *n* (*Hubschrauber als Zubringer*); **~drome** [~ədroum] Flugplatz *m*; **~naut** [~ənɔ:t] Luftschiffer *m*; **~nautics** [ɛərə'nɔ:tiks] *pl.* Luftfahrt *f*; **~plane** ['ɛərəplein] Flugzeug *n*; **~stat** ['ɛəroustæt] Luftballon *m*.

**aesthetic** [i:s'θetik] ästhetisch; **~s** *sg.* Ästhetik *f*.

**afar** [ə'fɑ:] fern, weit (weg).

**affable** □ ['æfəbl] leutselig.

**affair** [ə'fɛə] Geschäft *n*; Angelegenheit *f*, Sache *f*; F Ding *n*; Liebschaft *f*.

**affect** [ə'fekt] (ein- *od.* sich aus-) wirken auf (*acc.*); (be)rühren; *Gesundheit* angreifen; gern mögen; vortäuschen, nachahmen; **~ation** [æfek'teiʃən] Vorliebe *f*; Ziererei *f*; Verstellung *f*; **~ed** □ gerührt; befallen (*von Krankheit*); angegriffen (*Augen etc.*); geziert, affektiert; **~ion** [~kʃən] Gemütszustand *m*; (Zu)Neigung *f*; Erkrankung *f*; **~ionate** □ [~ʃnit] liebevoll.

**affidavit** [æfi'deivit] *schriftliche beeidigte Erklärung.*

**affiliate** [ə'filieit] *als Mitglied* aufnehmen; angliedern; **~d** *company* Tochtergesellschaft *f*.

**affinity** [ə'finiti] *fig.* (geistige) Verwandtschaft; ⚗ Affinität *f*.

**affirm** [ə'fə:m] bejahen; behaupten; bestätigen; **~ation** [æfə:'meiʃən] Behauptung *f*; Bestätigung *f*; **~ative** [ə'fə:mətiv] **1.** □ bejahend; **2.**: *answer in the* **~** bejahen.

**affix** [ə'fiks] (*to*) anheften (*an acc.*); befestigen (*an dat.*); *Siegel* aufdrücken (*dat.*); bei-, zufügen (*dat.*).

**afflict** [ə'flikt] betrüben; plagen; **~ion** [~kʃən] Betrübnis *f*; Leiden *n*.

**affluen|ce** ['æfluəns] Überfluß *m*; Wohlstand *m*; **~t** [~nt] **1.** □ reich (-lich); **~** *society* Wohlstandsgesellschaft *f*; **2.** Nebenfluß *m*.

**afford** [ə'fɔ:d] liefern; erschwingen; *I can* **~** *it* ich kann es mir leisten.

**affront** [ə'frʌnt] **1.** beleidigen; trotzen (*dat.*); **2.** Beleidigung *f*.

**afield** [ə'fi:ld] im Felde; (weit) weg.

**afloat** [ə'flout] ⚓ *u. fig.* flott; schwimmend; auf See; umlaufend; *set* **~** flottmachen; *fig.* in Umlauf setzen.

**afraid** [ə'freid] bange; *be* **~** *of* sich fürchten *od.* Angst haben vor (*dat.*).

**afresh** [ə'freʃ] von neuem.

**African** ['æfrikən] **1.** afrikanisch; **2.** Afrikaner(in); *Am. a.* Neger(in).

**after** ['ɑ:ftə] **1.** *adv.* hinterher; nachher; **2.** *prp.* nach; hinter (... her); **~** *all* schließlich (doch); **3.** *cj.* nachdem; **4.** *adj.* später; Nach...; **~crop** Nachernte *f*; **~glow** Abendrot *n*; **~math** [~mæθ]

Nachwirkung(en *pl.*) *f*, Folgen *f/pl.*; **~noon** [.~'nu:n] Nachmittag *m*; **~ season** Nachsaison *f*; **~taste** Nachgeschmack *m*; **~thought** nachträglicher Einfall; **~wards** [.~wədz] nachher; später.

**again** [ə'gen] wieder(um); ferner; dagegen; ~ *and* ~, *time and* ~ immer wieder; *as much* ~ noch einmal soviel.

**against** [ə'genst] gegen; *räumlich*: gegen; an, vor (*dat. od. acc.*); *fig.* in Erwartung (*gen.*), für; *as* ~ verglichen mit.

**age** [eidʒ] 1. (Lebens)Alter *n*; Zeit (-alter *n*) *f*; Menschenalter *n*; (*old*) ~ Greisenalter *n*; *of* ~ mündig; *over* ~ zu alt; *under* ~ unmündig; *wait for* ~s F e-e Ewigkeit warten; 2. alt werden *od.* machen; **~d** ['eidʒid] alt; [eidʒd]: ~ *twenty* 20 Jahre alt.

**agency** ['eidʒənsi] Tätigkeit *f*; Vermittlung *f*; Agentur *f*, Büro *n*.

**agenda** [ə'dʒendə] Tagesordnung *f*.

**agent** ['eidʒənt] Handelnde(r *m*) *f*; Agent *m*; wirkende Kraft, Agens *n*.

**age-worn** ['eidʒwɔ:n] altersschwach.

**agglomerate** [ə'glɔməreit] (sich) zs.-ballen; (sich) (an)häufen.

**agglutinate** [ə'glu:tineit] zs.-, an-, verkleben.

**aggrandize** [ə'grændaiz] vergrößern; erhöhen.

**aggravate** ['ægrəveit] erschweren; verschlimmern; F ärgern.

**aggregate 1.** ['ægrigeit] (sich) anhäufen; vereinigen (*to* mit); sich belaufen auf (*acc.*); 2. □ [.~git] gehäuft; gesamt; 3. [.~] Anhäufung *f*, Aggregat *n*.

**aggress|ion** [ə'greʃən] Angriff *m*; **~or** [.~esə] Angreifer *m*.

**aggrieve** [ə'gri:v] kränken; schädigen. [setzt.]

**aghast** [ə'gɑ:st] entgeistert, ent-]

**agil|e** □ ['ædʒail] flink, behend; **~ity** [ə'dʒiliti] Behendigkeit *f*.

**agitat|e** ['ædʒiteit] *v/t.* bewegen, schütteln; *fig.* erregen; erörtern; *v/i.* agitieren; **~ion** [ædʒi'teiʃən] Bewegung *f*, Erschütterung *f*; Aufregung *f*; Agitation *f*; **~or** ['ædʒiteitə] Agitator *m*, Aufwiegler *m*.

**ago** [ə'gou]: *a year* ~ vor e-m Jahr.

**agonize** ['ægənaiz] (sich) quälen.

**agony** ['ægəni] Qual *f*, Pein *f*; Ringen *n*; Todeskampf *m*.

**agree** [ə'gri:] *v/i.* übereinstimmen; sich vertragen; einig werden (*on, upon* über *acc.*); übereinkommen; ~ *to* zustimmen (*dat.*); einverstanden sein mit; **~able** □ [ə'griəbl] (*to*) angenehm (*für*); übereinstimmend (mit); **~ment** [ə'gri:mənt] Übereinstimmung *f*; Vereinbarung *f*, Abkommen *n*; Vertrag *m*.

**agricultur|al** [ægri'kʌltʃərəl] land-

wirtschaftlich; **~e** ['ægrikʌltʃə] Landwirtschaft *f*; **~ist** [ægri'kʌltʃərist] Landwirt *m*.

**aground** ⚓ [ə'graund] gestrandet; *run* ~ stranden, auflaufen.

**ague** ⚕ ['eigju:] Wechselfieber *n*; Schüttelfrost *m*.

**ahead** [ə'hed] vorwärts; voraus; vorn; *straight* ~ geradeaus.

**aid** [eid] 1. helfen (*dat.*; *in* bei *et.*); fördern; 2. Hilfe *f*, Unterstützung *f*.

**ail** [eil] *v/i.* kränkeln; *v/t.* schmerzen, weh(e) tun (*dat.*); *what* ~s *him?* was fehlt ihm?; **~ing** ['eiliŋ] leidend; **~ment** ['eilmənt] Leiden *n*.

**aim** [eim] 1. *v/i.* zielen (*at* auf *acc.*); ~ *at fig.* streben nach; ~ *to do bsd. Am.* beabsichtigen *od.* versuchen zu tun, tun wollen; *v/t.* ~ *at Waffe etc.* richten auf *od.* gegen (*acc.*); 2. Ziel *n*; Absicht *f*; **~less** □ ['eimlis] ziellos.

**air**[1] [ɛə] 1. Luft *f*; Luftzug *m*; *by* ~ auf dem Luftwege; *in the open* ~ im Freien; *be in the* ~ *fig.* in der Luft liegen; ungewiß sein; *on the* ~ im Rundfunk (*senden*); *be on* (*off*) *the* ~ in (außer) Betrieb sein (*Sender*); *put on the* ~ im Rundfunk senden; 2. (aus)lüften; *fig.* an die Öffentlichkeit bringen; erörtern.

**air**[2] [.~] Miene *f*; Aussehen *n*; *give o.s.* ~s vornehm tun.

**air**[3] ♩ [.~] Arie *f*, Weise *f*, Melodie *f*.

**air|-base** ✈ ['ɛəbeis] Luftstützpunkt *m*; **~bed** Luftmatratze *f*; **~borne** ✈ in der Luft (*Flugzeug*); ✕ Luftlande...; **~brake** Druckluftbremse *f*; **~conditioned** mit Klimaanlage; **~craft** Flugzeug (-e *pl.*) *n*; **~field** ✈ Flugplatz *m*; **~force** ✈ Luftwaffe *f*; **~hostess** ✈ Stewardess *f*; **~jacket** Schwimmweste *f*; **~lift** Luftbrücke *f*; **~liner** ✈ Verkehrsflugzeug *n*; **~mail** Luftpost *f*; **~man** ✈ ['ɛəmæn] Flieger *m*; **~plane** *Am.* Flugzeug *n*; **~pocket** ✈ Luftloch *n*; **~port** ✈ Flughafen *m*; **~raid** ✕ Luftangriff *m*; **~raid precautions** *pl.* Luftschutz *m*; **~raid shelter** Luftschutzraum *m*; **~route** ✈ Luftweg *m*; **~tight** luftdicht; **~case** *sl.* todsicherer Fall; **~tube** Luftschlauch *m*; **~umbrella** ✕ Luftsicherung *f*; **~way** ✈ Luftverkehrslinie *f*.

**airy** □ ['ɛəri] luftig; leicht(fertig).

**aisle** △ [ail] Seitenschiff *n*; Gang *m*.

**ajar** [ə'dʒɑ:] halb offen, angelehnt.

**akin** [ə'kin] verwandt (*to* mit).

**alacrity** [ə'lækriti] Munterkeit *f*; Bereitwilligkeit *f*, Eifer *m*.

**alarm** [ə'lɑ:m] 1. Alarm(zeichen *n*) *m*; Angst *f*; 2. alarmieren; beunruhigen; **~clock** Wecker *m*.

**albuminous** [æl'bju:minəs] eiweißartig, -haltig.

**alcohol** ['ælkəhɔl] Alkohol *m*; **~ic**

[ælkə'hɔlik] alkoholisch; **~ism** ['æl-kəhɔlizəm] Alkoholvergiftung f.

**alcove** ['ælkouv] Nische f; Laube f.

**alderman** ['ɔːldəmən] Stadtrat m.

**ale** [eil] Ale n (Art engl. Bier).

**alert** [ə'ləːt] 1. □ wachsam; munter; 2. Alarm(bereitschaft f) m; on the ~ auf der Hut; in Alarmbereitschaft.

**alibi** ['ælibai] Alibi n; Am. F Entschuldigung f; Ausrede f.

**alien** ['eiljən] 1. fremd, ausländisch; 2. Ausländer(in); **~able** [~nəbl] veräußerlich; **~ate** [~neit] veräußern; fig. entfremden (from dat.); **~ist** [~nist] Irrenarzt m, Psychiater m.

**alight** [ə'lait] 1. brennend; erhellt; 2. ab-, aussteigen; 🛬 niedergehen, landen; sich niederlassen.

**align** [ə'lain] (sich) ausrichten (with nach); surv. abstecken; ~ o.s. with sich anschließen an (acc.).

**alike** [ə'laik] 1. adj. gleich, ähnlich; 2. adv. gleich; ebenso.

**aliment** ['ælimənt] Nahrung f; **~ary** [æli'mentəri] nahrhaft; ~ canal Verdauungskanal m.

**alimony** ⚤ ['æliməni] Unterhalt m.

**alive** [ə'laiv] lebendig; in Kraft, gültig; empfänglich (to für); lebhaft; belebt (with von).

**all** [ɔːl] 1. adj. all; ganz; jede(r, -s); for ~ that dessenungeachtet, trotzdem; 2. pron. alles; alle pl.; at ~ gar, überhaupt; not at ~ durchaus nicht; for ~ (that) I care meinetwegen; for ~ I know soviel ich weiß; 3. adv. ganz, völlig; ~ at once auf einmal; ~ the better desto besser; ~ but beinahe, fast; ~ in Am. F fertig, ganz erledigt; ~ right (alles) in Ordnung.

**all-American** [ɔːlə'merikən] rein amerikanisch; die ganzen USA vertretend.

**allay** [ə'lei] beruhigen; lindern.

**alleg|ation** [æle'geiʃən] unerwiesene Behauptung; **~e** [ə'ledʒ] behaupten; **~ed** angeblich.

**allegiance** [ə'liːdʒəns] Lehnspflicht f; (Untertanen)Treue f.

**alleviate** [ə'liːvieit] erleichtern, lindern.

**alley** ['æli] Allee f; Gäßchen n; Gang m; bsd. Am. schmale Zufahrtsstraße.

**alliance** [ə'laiəns] Bündnis n.

**allocat|e** ['æləkeit] zuteilen, anweisen; **~ion** [ælə'keiʃən] Zuteilung f.

**allot** [ə'lɔt] zuweisen, **~ment** [~t-mənt] Zuteilung f; Los n; Parzelle f.

**allow** [ə'lau] erlauben, bewilligen, gewähren; zugeben; ab-, anrechnen; vergüten; ~ for berücksichtigen; **~able** □ [ə'lauəbl] erlaubt, zulässig; **~ance** [~əns] Erlaubnis f; Bewilligung f; Taschengeld n, Zuschuß m; Vergütung f; Nachsicht f;

make ~ for s.th. et. in Betracht ziehen.

**alloy** 1. ['ælɔi] Legierung f; 2. [ə'lɔi] legieren; fig. verunedeln.

**all-red** ['ɔːl'red] rein britisch.

**all-round** ['ɔːl'raund] zu allem brauchbar; vielseitig.

**all-star** Am. ['ɔːl'stɑː] Sport u. thea.: aus den besten (Schau)Spielern bestehend.

**allude** [ə'luːd] anspielen (to auf acc.).

**allure** [ə'ljuə] (an-, ver)locken; **~ment** [~mənt] Verlockung f.

**allusion** [ə'luːʒən] Anspielung f.

**ally** 1. [ə'lai] (sich) vereinigen, verbünden (to, with mit); 2. ['ælai] Verbündete(r m) f, Bundesgenosse m; the Allies pl. die Alliierten pl.

**almanac** ['ɔːlmənæk] Almanach m.

**almighty** [ɔːl'maiti] 1. □ allmächtig; 2 ♀ Allmächtige(r) m.

**almond** ♀ ['ɑːmənd] Mandel f.

**almoner** ['ɑːmənə] Krankenhausfürsorger(in).

**almost** ['ɔːlmoust] fast, beinahe.

**alms** [ɑːmz] sg. u. pl. Almosen n; **~house** ['ɑːmzhaus] Armenhaus n.

**aloft** [ə'lɔft] (hoch) (dr)oben.

**alone** [ə'loun] allein; let od. leave ~ in Ruhe od. bleiben lassen; let ~ ... abgesehen von ...

**along** [ə'lɔŋ] 1. adv. weiter, vorwärts, her; mit, bei (sich); all ~ die ganze Zeit; ~ with zs. mit; get ~ with you! F scher dich weg!; 2. prp. entlang, längs; **~side** [~ŋ'said] Seite an Seite; neben.

**aloof** [ə'luːf] fern; weitab; stand ~ abseits stehen.

**aloud** [ə'laud] laut; hörbar.

**alp** [ælp] Alp(e) f; ♀s pl. Alpen pl.

**already** [ɔːl'redi] bereits, schon.

**also** ['ɔːlsou] auch; ferner.

**altar** ['ɔːltə] Altar m.

**alter** ['ɔːltə] (sich) (ver)ändern; ab-, umändern; **~ation** [ɔːltə'reiʃən] Änderung f (to an dat.).

**alternat|e** 1. ['ɔːltəːneit] abwechseln (lassen); alternating current ⚡ Wechselstrom m; 2. □ [ɔː'ləːnit] abwechselnd; 3. [~] Am. Stellvertreter m; **~ion** [ɔːltəː'neiʃən] Abwechslung f; Wechsel m; **~ive** [ɔː'ləːnə-tiv] 1. □ nur eine Wahl zwischen zwei Möglichkeiten lassend; 2. Alternative f; Wahl f; Möglichkeit f.

**although** [ɔːl'ðou] obgleich.

**altitude** ['æltitjuːd] Höhe f.

**altogether** [ɔːltə'geðə] im ganzen (genommen), alles in allem; gänzlich.

**aluminium** [ælju'minjəm] Aluminium n.

**aluminum** Am. [ə'luːminəm] = aluminium.

**always** ['ɔːlwəz] immer, stets.

**am** [æm; im Satz əm] 1. sg. pres. von be.

**amalgamate** [ə'mælgəmeit] amalgamieren; (sich) verschmelzen.

**amass** [ə'mæs] (an-, auf)häufen.

**amateur** ['æmətə:] Amateur *m*; Liebhaber *m*; Dilettant *m*.

**amaz|e** [ə'meiz] in Staunen setzen, verblüffen; **~ement** [~zmənt] Staunen *n*, Verblüffung *f*; **~ing** □ [~ziŋ] erstaunlich, verblüffend.

**ambassador** [æm'bæsədə] Botschafter *m*, Gesandte(r) *m*.

**amber** ['æmbə] Bernstein *m*.

**ambigu|ity** [æmbi'gju(:)iti] Zwei-, Vieldeutigkeit *f*; **~ous** □ [æm-'bigjuəs] zwei-, vieldeutig; doppelsinnig.

**ambitio|n** [æm'biʃən] Ehrgeiz *m*; Streben *n* (*of* nach); **~us** □ [~ʃəs] ehrgeizig; begierig (*of*, *for* nach).

**amble** ['æmbl] 1. Paßgang *m*; 2. im Paßgang gehen *od.* reiten; schlendern.

**ambulance** ['æmbjuləns] Feldlazarett *n*; Krankenwagen *m*; **~station** Sanitätswache *f*, Unfallstation *f*.

**ambus|cade** [æmbəs'keid], **~h** ['æmbuʃ] 1. Hinterhalt *m*; *be od. lie in ambush for s.o.* j-m auflauern; 2. auflauern (*dat.*); überfallen.

**ameliorate** [ə'mi:ljəreit] *v/t.* verbessern; *v/i.* besser werden.

**amend** [ə'mend] (sich) (ver)bessern; berichtigen; *Gesetz* (ab)ändern; **~ment** [~dmənt] Besserung *f*; 🕱 Berichtigung *f*; *parl.* Änderungsantrag *m*; *Am.* Zusatzartikel *m* zur Verfassung der USA; **~s** *sg.* (Schaden)Ersatz *m*.

**amenity** [ə'mi:niti] Annehmlichkeit *f*; Anmut *f*; *amenities pl.* angenehmes Wesen.

**American** [ə'merikən] 1. amerikanisch; **~ cloth** Wachstuch *n*; **~ plan** *Hotelzimmervermietung mit voller Verpflegung*; 2. Amerikaner(in); **~ism** [~nizəm] Amerikanismus *m*; **~ize** [~naiz] (sich) amerikanisieren.

**amiable** □ ['eimjəbl] liebenswürdig, freundlich.

**amicable** □ ['æmikəbl] freundschaftlich; gütlich.

**amid(st)** [ə'mid(st)] inmitten (*gen.*); (mitten) unter; mitten in (*dat.*).

**amiss** [ə'mis] verkehrt; übel; ungelegen; *take ~* übelnehmen.

**amity** ['æmiti] Freundschaft *f*.

**ammonia** [ə'mounjə] Ammoniak *n*.

**ammunition** [æmju'niʃən] Munition *f*.

**amnesty** ['æmnesti] 1. Amnestie *f* (*Straferlaß*); 2. begnadigen.

**among(st)** [ə'mʌŋ(st)] (mitten) unter, zwischen; [in *acc.*].

**amorous** □ ['æmərəs] verliebt (*of*).

**amount** [ə'maunt] 1. (*to*) sich belaufen (auf *acc.*); hinauslaufen (auf *acc.*); 2. Betrag *m*, (Gesamt-)

Summe *f*; Menge *f*; Bedeutung *f*, Wert *m*.

**amour** [ə'muə] Liebschaft *f*; **~-propre** Selbstachtung *f*; Eitelkeit *f*.

**ample** □ ['æmpl] weit, groß; geräumig; reichlich.

**ampli|fication** [æmplifi'keiʃən] Erweiterung *f*; *rhet.* weitere Ausführung *f*; *phys.* Verstärkung *f*; **~fier** ['æmplifaiə] *Radio:* Verstärker *m*; **~fy** [~fai] erweitern; verstärken; weiter ausführen; **~tude** [~itju:d] Umfang *m*, Weite *f*, Fülle *f*.

**amputate** ['æmpjuteit] amputieren.

**amuse** [ə'mju:z] amüsieren; unterhalten; belustigen; **~ment** [~z-mənt] Unterhaltung *f*; Zeitvertreib *m*.

**an** [æn, ən] *Artikel:* ein(e).

**an(a)emia** [ə'ni:mjə] Blutarmut *f*.

**an(a)esthetic** [ænis'θetik] 1. betäubend, Narkose...; 2. Betäubungsmittel *n*.

**analog|ous** □ [ə'næləgəs] analog, ähnlich; **~y** [~ədʒi] Ähnlichkeit *f*, Analogie *f*.

**analys|e** ['ænəlaiz] analysieren; zerlegen; **~is** [ə'næləsis] Analyse *f*.

**anarchy** ['ænəki] Anarchie *f*, Gesetzlosigkeit *f*; Zügellosigkeit *f*.

**anatom|ize** [ə'nætəmaiz] zergliedern; **~y** [~mi] Anatomie *f*; Zergliederung *f*, Analyse *f*.

**ancest|or** ['ænsistə] Vorfahr *m*, Ahn *m*; **~ral** [æn'sestrəl] angestammt; **~ress** ['ænsistris] Ahne *f*; **~ry** [~ri] Abstammung *f*; Ahnen *m/pl.*

**anchor** ['æŋkə] 1. Anker *m*; *at ~* vor Anker; 2. (ver)ankern; **~age** [~əridʒ] Ankerplatz *m*.

**anchovy** ['æntʃəvi] Sardelle *f*.

**ancient** ['einʃənt] 1. alt, antik; uralt; 2. *the ~s pl. hist.* die Alten, die antiken Klassiker.

**and** [ænd, ənd] und.

**anew** [ə'nju:] von neuem.

**angel** ['eindʒəl] Engel *m*; **~ic(al** □) [æn'dʒelik(əl)] engelgleich.

**anger** ['æŋgə] 1. Zorn *m*, Ärger *m* (*at* über *acc.*); 2. erzürnen, ärgern.

**angina** 🕱 [æn'dʒainə] Angina *f*, Halsentzündung *f*.

**angle** ['æŋgl] 1. Winkel *m*; *fig.* Standpunkt *m*; 2. angeln (*for* nach).

**Anglican** ['æŋglikən] 1. anglikanisch; *Am. a.* englisch; 2. Anglikaner(in).

**Anglo-Saxon** ['æŋglou'sæksən] 1. Angelsachse *m*; 2. angelsächsisch.

**angry** ['æŋgri] zornig, böse (*a.* 🕱) (*with s.o.*, *at s.th.* über, auf *acc.*).

**anguish** ['æŋgwiʃ] Pein *f*, (Seelen-) Qual *f*, Schmerz *m*.

**angular** □ ['æŋgjulə] winkelig; Winkel...; *fig.* eckig.

**animadver|sion** [ænimæd'və:ʃən]

Verweis *m*, Tadel *m*; ~t [~ə:t] tadeln, kritisieren.

**animal** ['æniməl] **1.** Tier *n*; **2.** tierisch.

**animat|e** ['ænimeit] beleben; beseelen; aufmuntern; ~ion [æni-'meiʃən] Leben *n* (und Treiben *n*), Lebhaftigkeit *f*, Munterkeit *f*.

**animosity** [æni'mɔsiti] Feindseligkeit *f*.

**ankle** ['æŋkl] Fußknöchel *m*.

**annals** ['ænlz] *pl.* Jahrbücher *n/pl.*

**annex 1.** [ə'neks] anhängen; annektieren; **2.** ['æneks] Anhang *m*; Anbau *m*; ~ation [ænek'seiʃən] Annexion *f*, Aneignung *f*; Einverleibung *f*.

**annihilate** [ə'naiəleit] vernichten; = *annul*.

**anniversary** [æni'və:səri] Jahrestag *m*; Jahresfeier *f*.

**annotat|e** ['ænouteit] mit Anmerkungen versehen; kommentieren; ~ion [ænou'teiʃən] Kommentieren *n*; Anmerkung *f*.

**announce** [ə'nauns] ankündigen; ansagen; ~ment [~smənt] Ankündigung *f*; Ansage *f*; *Radio*: Durchsage *f*; Anzeige *f*; ~r [~sə] *Radio*: Ansager *m*.

**annoy** [ə'nɔi] ärgern; belästigen; ~ance [ə'nɔiəns] Störung *f*; Plage *f*; Ärgernis *n*.

**annual** [ə'njuəl] **1.** □ jährlich; Jahres...; **2.** einjährige Pflanze; Jahrbuch *n*. [Rente *f*.)

**annuity** [ə'nju(:)iti] (Jahres-))

**annul** [ə'nʌl] für ungültig erklären, annullieren; ~ment [~lmənt] Aufhebung *f*.

**anodyne** ['ænoudain] **1.** schmerzstillend; **2.** schmerzstillendes Mittel.

**anoint** [ə'nɔint] salben.

**anomalous** □ [ə'nɔmələs] anomal, unregelmäßig, regelwidrig.

**anonymous** □ [ə'nɔniməs] anonym, ungenannt.

**another** [ə'nʌðə] ein anderer; ein zweiter; noch ein.

**answer** ['ɑ:nsə] **1.** *v/t. et.* beantworten; *j-m* antworten; entsprechen (*dat.*); *Zweck* erfüllen; *dem Steuer* gehorchen; *e-r Vorladung* Folge leisten; ~ *the bell od.* door (die Haustür) aufmachen; *v/i.* antworten (*to s.o.* j-m; *to a question* auf e-e Frage); entsprechen (*to dat.*); Erfolg haben; sich lohnen; ~ *for* einstehen für; bürgen für; **2.** Antwort *f* (*to* auf *acc.*); ~able □ [~ərəbl] verantwortlich.

**ant** [ænt] Ameise *f*.

**antagonis|m** [æn'tægənizəm] Widerstreit *m*; Widerstand *m*; Feindschaft *f*; ~t [~ist] Gegner(in).

**antagonize** [æn'tægənaiz] ankämpfen gegen; sich *j-n* zum Feind machen.

**antecedent** [ænti'si:dənt] **1.** □ vor-

hergehend; früher (*to* als); **2.** Vorhergehende(s) *n*.

**anterior** [æn'tiəriə] vorhergehend; früher (*to* als); vorder.

**ante-room** ['æntirum] Vorzimmer *n*.

**anthem** ['ænθəm] Hymne *f*.

**anti**|... ['ænti] Gegen...; gegen ... eingestellt *od.* wirkend; ~aircraft Fliegerabwehr...; ~biotic [~ibai-'ɔtik] Antibiotikum *n*.

**antic** ['æntik] Posse *f*; ~s *pl.* Mätzchen *n/pl.*; (tolle) Sprünge *m/pl.*

**anticipat|e** [æn'tisipeit] vorwegnehmen; zuvorkommen (*dat.*); voraussehen, ahnen; erwarten; ~ion [æntisi'peiʃən] Vorwegnahme *f*; Zuvorkommen *n*; Voraussicht *f*; Erwartung *f*; *in* ~ im voraus.

**antidote** ['æntidout] Gegengift *n*.

**antipathy** [æn'tipəθi] Abneigung *f*.

**antiqua|ry** ['æntikwəri] Altertumsforscher *m*; Antiquitätensammler *m*, -händler *m*; ~ted [~kweitid] veraltet, überlebt.

**antiqu|e** [æn'ti:k] **1.** □ antik, alt (-modisch); **2.** alter Kunstgegenstand; ~ity [æn'tikwiti] Altertum *n*; Vorzeit *f*.

**antiseptic** [ænti'septik] **1.** antiseptisch; **2.** antiseptisches Mittel.

**antlers** ['æntləz] *pl.* Geweih *n*.

**anvil** ['ænvil] Amboß *m*.

**anxiety** [æŋ'zaiəti] Angst *f*; *fig.* Sorge *f* (*for* um); ℱ Beklemmung *f*.

**anxious** □ ['æŋkʃəs] ängstlich, besorgt (*about* um, wegen); begierig, gespannt (*for* auf *acc.*); bemüht (*for* um).

**any** ['eni] **1.** *pron.* (irgend)einer; einige *pl.*; (irgend)welcher; (irgend) etwas; jeder (beliebige); *not* ~ keiner; **2.** *adv.* irgend(wie); ~body (irgend) jemand; jeder; ~how irgendwie; jedenfalls; ~one = anybody; ~thing (irgend) etwas, alles; ~ *but* alles andere als; ~way = anyhow; ohnehin; ~where irgendwo(hin); überall.

**apart** [ə'pɑ:t] einzeln; getrennt; für sich; beiseite; ~ *from* abgesehen von.

**apartheid** *pol.* [ə'pɑ:theit] Apartheid *f*, Rassentrennung(spolitik) *f*.

**apartment** [ə'pɑ:tmənt] Zimmer *n*, *Am. a.* Wohnung *f*; ~s *pl.* Wohnung *f*; ~ house *Am.* Mietshaus *n*.

**apathetic** [æpə'θetik] apathisch, gleichgültig.

**ape** [eip] **1.** Affe *m*; **2.** nachäffen.

**aperient** [ə'piəriənt] Abführmittel *n*.

**aperture** ['æpətjuə] Öffnung *f*.

**apiary** ['eipjəri] Bienenhaus *n*.

**apiculture** ['eipikʌltʃə] Bienenzucht *f*.

**apiece** [ə'pi:s] (für) das Stück; je.

**apish** □ ['eipiʃ] affig; äffisch.

**apolog|etic** [əpɔlə'dʒetik] (~ally) verteidigend; rechtfertigend; entschuldigend; ~ize [ə'pɔlədʒaiz] sich entschuldigen (for wegen; to bei); ~y [~dʒi] Entschuldigung f; F Notbehelf m.

apoplexy ['æpəpleksi] Schlag(anfall) m.

apostate [ə'pɔstit] Abtrünnige(r m)f.

apostle [ə'pɔsl] Apostel m.

apostroph|e [ə'pɔstrəfi] Anrede f; Apostroph m; ~ize [~faiz] anreden, sich wenden an (acc.).

appal [ə'pɔːl] erschrecken.

apparatus [æpə'reitəs] Apparat m, Vorrichtung f, Gerät n.

apparel [ə'pærəl] 1. Kleidung f; 2. (be)kleiden.

appar|ent □ [ə'pærənt] anscheinend; offenbar; ~ition [æpə'riʃən] Erscheinung f; Gespenst n.

appeal [ə'piːl] 1. (to) ₴ appellieren (an acc.); sich berufen (auf e-n Zeugen); sich wenden (an acc.); wirken (auf acc.); Anklang finden (bei); ~ to the country parl. Neuwahlen ausschreiben; 2. ₴ Revision f, Berufung(sklage) f; ₴ Rechtsmittel n; fig. Appell m (to an acc.); Wirkung f, Reiz m; ~ for mercy ₴ Gnadengesuch n; ~ing □ [~liŋ] flehend; ansprechend.

appear [ə'piə] (er)scheinen; sich zeigen; öffentlich auftreten; ~ance [~ərəns] Erscheinen n, Auftreten n; Äußere(s) n, Erscheinung f; Anschein m; ~s pl. äußerer Schein; to od. by all ~s allem Anschein nach.

appease [ə'piːz] beruhigen; beschwichtigen; stillen; mildern; beilegen.

appellant [ə'pelənt] 1. appellierend; 2. Appelant(in), Berufungskläger (-in).

append [ə'pend] anhängen; hinzu-, beifügen; ~age [~didʒ] Anhang m; Anhängsel n; Zubehör n, m; ~icitis [əpendi'saitis] Blinddarmentzündung f; ~ix [ə'pendiks] Anhang m; a. vermiform ~ ♀ Wurmfortsatz m, Blinddarm m.

appertain [æpə'tein] gehören (to zu).

appetite ['æpitait] (for) Appetit m (auf acc.); fig. Verlangen n (nach).

appetizing ['æpitaiziŋ] appetitanregend.

applaud [ə'plɔːd] applaudieren, Beifall spenden; loben.

applause [ə'plɔːz] Applaus m, Beifall m.

apple ['æpl] Apfel m; ~cart Apfelkarren m; upset s.o.'s ~ F j-s Pläne über den Haufen werfen; ~pie gedeckter Apfelkuchen; in ~ order F in schönster Ordnung; ~sauce Apfelmus n; Am. sl. Schmus m, Quatsch m.

appliance [ə'plaiəns] Vorrichtung f; Gerät n; Mittel n.

applica|ble ['æplikəbl] anwendbar

(to auf acc.); ~nt [~ənt] Bittsteller (-in); Bewerber(in) (for um); ~tion [æpli'keiʃən] (to) Auf-, Anlegung f (auf acc.); Anwendung f (auf acc.); Bedeutung f (für); Gesuch n (for um); Bewerbung f.

apply [ə'plai] v/t. (to) (auf)legen (auf acc.); anwenden (auf acc.); verwenden (für); ~ o.s. to sich widmen (dat.); v/i. (to) passen, sich anwenden lassen (auf acc.); gelten (für); sich wenden (an acc.); (for) sich bewerben (um); nachsuchen (um).

appoint [ə'pɔint] bestimmen; festsetzen; verabreden; ernennen (s.o. governor j-n zum ...); berufen (to auf e-n Posten); well ~ed gut eingerichtet; ~ment [~tmənt] Bestimmung f; Stelldichein n; Verabredung f; Ernennung f; Berufung f; Stelle f; ~s pl. Ausstattung f, Einrichtung f.

apportion [ə'pɔːʃən] ver-, zuteilen; ~ment [~nmənt] Verteilung f.

apprais|al [ə'preizəl] Abschätzung f; ~e [ə'preiz] abschätzen, taxieren.

apprecia|ble □ [ə'priːʃəbl] (ab-)schätzbar; merkbar; ~te [~ʃieit] v/t. schätzen; würdigen; dankbar sein für; v/i. im Werte steigen; ~tion [əpriːʃi'eiʃən] Schätzung f, Würdigung f; Verständnis n (of für); Einsicht f; Dankbarkeit f; Aufwertung f.

apprehen|d [æpri'hend] ergreifen; fassen, begreifen; befürchten; ~sion [~ʃən] Ergreifung f, Festnahme f; Fassungskraft f, Auffassung f; Besorgnis f; ~sive □ [~nsiv] schnell begreifend (of acc.); ängstlich; besorgt (of, for um, wegen; that daß).

apprentice [ə'prentis] 1. Lehrling m; 2. in die Lehre geben (to dat.); ~ship [~ʃip] Lehrzeit f; Lehre f.

approach [ə'prəutʃ] 1. v/i. näherkommen, sich nähern; v/t. sich nähern (dat.), herangehen od. herantreten an (acc.); 2. Annäherung f; fig. Herangehen n; Methode f; Zutritt m; Auffahrt f.

approbation [æprə'beiʃən] Billigung f, Beifall m.

appropriat|e 1. [ə'prouprieit] sich aneignen; verwenden; parl. bewilligen; 2. □ [~iit] (to) angemessen (dat.); passend (für); eigen (dat.); ~ion [əproupri'eiʃən] Aneignung f; Verwendung f.

approv|al [ə'pruːvəl] Billigung f, Beifall m; ~e [~uːv] billigen, anerkennen; (~ o.s. sich) erweisen als; ~ed □ bewährt.

approximate 1. [ə'prɔksimeit] sich nähern; 2. □ [~mit] annähernd; ungefähr; nahe.

apricot ['eiprikɔt] Aprikose f.

April ['eiprəl] April m.

**apron** ['eiprən] Schürze *f*; **~-string** Schürzenband *n*; *be tied to one's wife's (mother's)* ~*s fig.* unterm Pantoffel stehen (der Mutter am Rockzipfel hängen).

**apt** □ [æpt] geeignet, passend; be-gabt; ~ *to* geneigt zu; **~itude** ['æp-titju:d], **~ness** ['æptnis] Neigung *f* (*to* zu); Befähigung *f*.

**aquatic** [ə'kwætik] Wasserpflanze *f*; ~*s pl.* Wassersport *m*.

**aque|duct** ['ækwidʌkt] Aquädukt *m*, Wasserleitung *f*; **~ous** □ ['eikwiəs] wässerig.

**aquiline** ['ækwilain] Adler...; ge-bogen; ~ *nose* Adlernase *f*.

**Arab** ['ærəb] Araber(in); **~ic** [~bik] 1. arabisch; 2. Arabisch *n*.

**arable** ['ærəbl] pflügbar; Acker...

**arbit|er** ['a:bitə] Schiedsrichter *m*; *fig.* Gebieter *m*; **~rariness** [~trɛri-nis] Willkür *f*; **~ade** [~'keid] Arkade *f*; **~rary** [~trəri] willkürlich; eigenmächtig; **~rate** [~reit] entscheiden, schlichten; **~ration** [a:bi'treiʃən] Schieds-spruch *m*; Entscheidung *f*; **~rator** ɪ̃ ['a:bitreitə] Schiedsrichter *m*.

**arbo(u)r** ['a:bə] Laube *f*.

**arc** *ast.*, ⚡ *etc.* [a:k] (⚡ *Licht-*) Bogen *m*; **~ade** [~'keid] Arkade *f*; Bogen-, Laubengang *m*.

**arch**[1] [a:tʃ] 1. Bogen *m*; Gewölbe *n*; 2. (sich) wölben; überwölben.

**arch**[2] [~] erst; schlimmst; Haupt...; Erz...

**arch**[3] □ [~] schelmisch.

**archaic** [a:'keiik] (~*ally*) veraltet.

**archangel** ['a:keindʒəl] Erzengel *m*.

**archbishop** ['a:tʃ'biʃəp] Erzbischof *m*.

**archer** ['a:tʃə] Bogenschütze *m*; **~y** [~ri] Bogenschießen *n*.

**architect** ['a:kitekt] Architekt *m*; Urheber(in), Schöpfer(in); **~onic** [a:kitek'tɔnik] (~*ally*) architekto-nisch; *fig.* aufbauend; **~ure** ['a:ki-tektʃə] Architektur *f*, Baukunst *f*.

**archives** ['a:kaivz] *pl.* Archiv *n*.

**archway** ['a:tʃwei] Bogengang *m*.

**arc|-lamp** ['a:klæmp], **~-light** ⚡ Bogenlampe *f*.

**arctic** ['a:ktik] 1. arktisch, nördlich; Nord..., Polar...; 2. *Am.* wasser-dichter Überschuh.

**arden|cy** ['a:dənsi] Hitze *f*, Glut *f*; Innigkeit *f*; **~t** □ [~nt] *mst fig.* heiß, glühend; *fig.* feurig; eifrig.

**ardo(u)r** ['a:də] *fig.* Glut *f*; Eifer *m*.

**arduous** □ ['a:djuəs] mühsam; jäh.

**are** [a:; *im Satz a*] *pres. pl. u. 2. sg. von* be.

**area** ['ɛəriə] Areal *n*; (Boden-) Fläche *f*; Flächenraum *m*; Gegend *f*; Gebiet *n*; Bereich *m*.

**Argentine** ['a:dʒəntain] 1. argen-tinisch; 2. Argentinier(in); *the* ~ Argentinien *n*.

**argue** ['a:gju:] *v/t.* erörtern; be-weisen; begründen; einwenden; ~

*s.o. into* j-n zu *et.* bereden; *v/i.* streiten; Einwendungen machen.

**argument** ['a:gjumənt] Beweis (-grund) *m*; Streit(frage *f*) *m*; Er-örterung *f*; Thema *n* *m*; **~ation** [a:gjumen'teiʃən] Beweisführung *f*.

**arid** ['ærid] dürr, trocken (*a. fig.*).

**arise** [ə'raiz] [*irr.*] sich erheben (*a. fig.*); ent-, erstehen (*from* aus); **~n** [ə'rizn] *p.p von* arise.

**aristocra|cy** [æris'tɔkrəsi] Aristo-kratie *f* (*a. fig.*), Adel *m*; **~t** ['æris-təkræt] Aristokrat(in); **~tic(al** □)] [æristə'krætik(əl)] aristokratisch.

**arithmetic** [ə'riθmətik] Rechnen *n*.

**ark** [a:k] Arche *f*.

**arm**[1] [a:m] Arm *m*; Armlehne *f*; *keep s.o. at* ~*'s length* sich j-n vom Leibe halten; *infant in* ~*s* Säugling *m*.

**arm**[2] [~] 1. Waffe *f* (*mst pl.*); Waf-fengattung *f*; *be* (*all*) *up in* ~*s* in vollem Aufruhr sein; in Harnisch geraten; 2. (sich) (be)waffnen; (aus)rüsten; ⊕ armieren.

**armada** [a:'ma:də] Kriegsflotte *f*.

**arma|ment** ['a:məmənt] (Kriegs-aus)Rüstung *f*; Kriegsmacht *f*; ~ *race* Wettrüsten *n*; **~ture** ['a:mə-tjuə] Rüstung *f*; △, *phys.* Armatur *f*.

**armchair** ['a:m'tʃɛə] Lehnstuhl *m*, Sessel *m*.

**armistice** ['a:mistis] Waffenstill-stand *m* (*a. fig.*).

**armo(u)r** ['a:mə] 1. ✕ Rüstung *f*, Panzer *m* (*a. fig.*, *zo.*); 2. panzern; **~ed car** Panzerwagen *m*; **~y** [a:-məri] Rüstkammer *f* (*a. fig.*); *Am.* Rüstungsbetrieb *m*, Waffenfabrik *f*.

**armpit** ['a:mpit] Achselhöhle *f*.

**army** ['a:mi] Heer *n*, Armee *f*; *fig.* Menge *f*; ~ *chaplain* Militärgeist-liche(r) *m*.

**arose** [ə'rouz] *pret. von* arise.

**around** [ə'raund] 1. *adv.* rund-(her)um; *Am.* F hier herum; 2. *prp.* um ... her(um); *Am.* F unge-fähr, etwa (*bei Zahlenangaben*).

**arouse** [ə'rauz] aufwecken; *fig.* auf-rütteln; erregen.

**arraign** [ə'rein] vor Gericht stellen, anklagen; *fig.* rügen.

**arrange** [ə'reindʒ] (an)ordnen, *bsd.* ♪ einrichten; festsetzen; *Streit* schlichten; vereinbaren; erledigen; **~ment** [~dʒmənt] Anordnung *f*; Disposition *f*; Übereinkommen *n*; Vorkehrung *f*; ♪ Arrangement *n*.

**array** [ə'rei] 1. (Schlacht)Ordnung *f*; *fig.* Aufgebot *n*; 2. ordnen, auf-stellen; aufbieten; kleiden, putzen.

**arrear** [ə'riə] *mst pl.* Rückstand *m*, *bsd.* Schulden *f/pl.*

**arrest** [ə'rest] 1. Verhaftung *f*; Haft *f*; Beschlagnahme *f*; 2. verhaf-ten; beschlagnahmen; anhalten, hemmen.

**arriv|al** [ə'raivəl] Ankunft *f*; Auf-treten *n*; Ankömmling *m*; ~*s pl.* angekommene Personen *f/pl.*, Züge *m/pl.*, Schiffe *n/pl.*; ~e [ə'raiv] (an-)kommen, eintreffen; erscheinen; eintreten (*Ereignis*); ~ *at* erreichen (*acc.*).

arroga|nce ['ærəgəns] Anmaßung *f*; Überheblichkeit *f*; ~nt □ [~nt] anmaßend; überheblich; ~te ['ærougeit] sich *et.* anmaßen.

arrow ['ærou] Pfeil *m*; ~-head Pfeilspitze *f*; ~y ['æroui] pfeilartig.

arsenal ['a:sinl] Zeughaus *n*.

arsenic ['a:snik] Arsen(ik) *n*.

arson ½ [ɑ:sn] Brandstiftung *f*.

art [a:t] Kunst *f*; *fig.* List *f*; Kniff *m*; ~s *pl.* Geisteswissenschaften *f/pl.*; Faculty of ~s philosophische Fakultät *f*.

arter|ial [a:'tiəriəl] Pulsader...; ~ road Hauptstraße *f*; ~y ['a:təri] Arterie *f*, Pulsader *f*; *fig.* Verkehrsader *f*. [schmitzt.]

artful □ ['a:tful] schlau, ver-]

article ['a:tikl] Artikel *m*; *fig.* Punkt *m*; ~d *to* in der Lehre bei.

articulat|e 1. [a:'tikjuleit] deutlich (aus)sprechen; *Knochen* zs.-fügen; 2. □ [~lit] deutlich; gegliedert; ~ion [a:'tikju'leiʃən] deutliche Aussprache; *anat.* Gelenkfügung *f*.

artific|e ['a:tifis] Kunstgriff *m*, List *f*; ~ial [a:ti'fiʃəl] künstlich; Kunst...; ~ *person* ½ juristische Person.

artillery [a:'tiləri] Artillerie *f*; ~-man Artillerist *m*.

artisan [a:ti'zæn] Handwerker *m*.

artist ['a:tist] Künstler(in); ~e [a:'ti:st] Artist(in); ~ic(al) □ [a:-'tistik(əl)] künstlerisch; Kunst...

artless □ ['a:tlis] ungekünstelt, schlicht; arglos.

as [æz, əz] 1. *adv.* so; (ebenso) wie; (*in der Eigenschaft*) als; ~ *big* ~ so groß wie; ~ *well* ebensogut; auch; ~ *well* ~ sowohl...als auch; 2. *cj.* (so-) wie; ebenso; (*zu der Zeit*) als, während; da, weil, indem; sofern; ~ *it were* sozusagen; *sich* ~ *to* derart, daß; ~ *for*, ~ *to* was (an)betrifft; ~ *from* von...an.

ascend [ə'send] *v/i.* (auf-, empor-, hinauf)steigen; *zeitlich:* zurückgehen (*to* bis zu); *v/t.* be-, ersteigen; hinaufsteigen; *Fluß etc.* hinauffahren; ~ancy, ~ency [~dənsi] Überlegenheit *f*, Einfluß *m*; Herrschaft *f*.

ascension [ə'senʃən] Aufsteigen *n* (*bsd. ast.*); *Am. a.* Aufstieg *m* (*e-s Ballons etc.*); ♀ (*Day*) Himmelfahrt(stag *m*) *f*.

ascent [ə'sent] Aufstieg *m*; Besteigung *f*; Steigung *f*; Aufgang *m*.

ascertain [æsə'tein] ermitteln.

ascetic [ə'setik] (~ally) asketisch.

ascribe [ə'skraib] zuschreiben.

aseptic ⚕ [æ'septik] 1. aseptisch; 2. aseptisches Mittel.

ash¹ [æʃ] ♀ Esche *f*; Eschenholz *n*.

ash² (~), *mst. pl.* ~es ['æʃiz] Asche *f*; *Ash Wednesday* Aschermittwoch *m*.

ashamed [ə'ʃeimd] beschämt; *be* ~ *of* sich *e-r Sache od. j-s* schämen.

ash can *Am.* ['æʃkæn] = *dust-bin*.

ashen ['æʃn] Aschen...; aschfahl.

ashore [ə'ʃɔ:] am *od.* ans Ufer *od.* Land; *run* ~, *be driven* ~ stranden.

ash|-pan ['æʃpæn] Asch(en)kasten *m*; ~-tray Asch(en)becher *m*.

ashy ['æʃi] aschig; aschgrau.

Asiatic [eiʃi'ætik] 1. asiatisch; 2. Asiat(in).

aside [ə'said] 1. beiseite (*a. thea.*); abseits; seitwärts; ~ *from Am.* abgesehen von; 2. *thea.* Aparte *n*.

ask [a:sk] *v/t.* fragen (*s.th.* nach *et.*); verlangen (*of, from s.o.* von j-m); bitten (*s.o.* [*for*] *s.th.* j. um *et.*; *that darum, daß*); erbitten; ~ (*s.o.*) *a question* (j-m) e-e Frage stellen; *v/i.:* ~ *for* bitten um, fragen nach; *he* ~*ed for it od. for trouble* er wollte es ja so haben; *to be had for the* ~*ing* umsonst zu haben.

askance [əs'kæns], askew [əs'kju:] von der Seite, seitwärts; schief.

asleep [ə'sli:p] schlafend; in den Schlaf; eingeschlafen, *be* ~ schlafen; *fall* ~ einschlafen.

asparagus ♀ [əs'pærəgəs] Spargel *m*.

aspect ['æspekt] Äußere *n*; Aussicht *f*, Lage *f*; Aspekt *m*, Seite *f*, Gesichtspunkt *m*.

asperity [æs'periti] Rauheit *f*; Unebenheit *f*; *fig.* Schroffheit *f*.

asphalt ['æsfælt] 1. Asphalt *m*; 2. asphaltieren.

aspic ['æspik] Aspik *m*, Sülze *f*.

aspir|ant [əs'paiərənt] Bewerber (-in); ~ate *ling.* ['æspəreit] aspirieren; ~ation [æspə'reiʃən] Aspiration *f*; Bestrebung *f*; ~e [əs'paiə] streben, trachten (*to, after, at* nach).

ass [æs] Esel *m*.

assail [ə'seil] angreifen, überfallen (*a. fig.*); befallen (*Zweifel etc.*); ~ant [~lənt] Angreifer(in).

assassin [ə'sæsin] (Meuchel)Mörder(in); ~ate [~neit] (meuchlings) ermorden; ~ation [əsæsi'neiʃən] Meuchelmord *m*.

assault [ə'sɔ:lt] 1. Angriff *m* (*a. fig.*); 2. anfallen; ½ tätlich angreifen *od.* beleidigen; ✗ bestürmen (*a. fig.*).

assay [ə'sei] 1. (Erz-, Metall-)Probe *f*; 2. *v/t.* untersuchen; *v/i. Am.* Edelmetall enthalten.

assembl|age [ə'semblidʒ] (An-)Sammlung *f*; ⊕ Montage *f*; ~e [ə'sembl] (sich) versammeln; zs.-berufen; ⊕ montieren; ~y [~li] Versammlung *f*; Gesellschaft *f*; ⊕ Montage *f*; ~ *line* ⊕ Fließband *n*; ~ *man pol.* Abgeordnete(r) *m*.

**assent** [ə'sent] **1.** Zustimmung *f*; **2.** (*to*) zustimmen (*dat.*); billigen.

**assert** [ə'sə:t] (sich) behaupten; **~ion** [ə'sə:ʃən] Behauptung *f*; Erklärung *f*; Geltendmachung *f*.

**assess** [ə'ses] besteuern; zur Steuer veranlagen (*at* mit); **~able** □ [~əbl] steuerpflichtig; **~ment** [~smənt] (Steuer)Veranlagung *f*; Steuer *f*.

**asset** ['æset] † Aktivposten *m*; *fig.* Gut *n*, Gewinn *m*; **~s** *pl.* Vermögen *n*; † Aktiva *pl.*; ‡‡ Konkursmasse *f*.

**asseverate** [ə'sevəreit] beteuern.

**assiduous** □ [ə'sidjuəs] emsig, fleißig; aufmerksam.

**assign** [ə'sain] an-, zuweisen; bestimmen; zuschreiben; **~ation** [æsig'neiʃən] Verabredung *f*, Stelldichein *n*; = **~ment** [ə'sainmənt] An-, Zuweisung *f*; *bsd. Am.* Auftrag *m*; ‡‡ Übertragung *f*.

**assimilat|e** [ə'simileit] (sich) angleichen (*to*, *with dat.*); **~ion** [əsimi'leiʃən] Assimilation *f*, Angleichung *f*.

**assist** [ə'sist] *j-m* beistehen, helfen; unterstützen; **~ance** [~təns] Beistand *m*; Hilfe *f*; **~ant** [~nt] **1.** behilflich; **2.** Assistent(in).

**assize** ‡‡ [ə'saiz] (Schwur)Gerichtssitzung *f*; **~s** *pl.* periodisches Geschworenengericht.

**associa|te 1.** [ə'souʃieit] (sich) zugesellen (*with dat.*), (sich) vereinigen; Umgang haben (*with* mit); **2.** [~ʃiit] verbunden; **3.** [~] (*Amts*)Genosse *m*; Teilhaber *m*; **~tion** [əsousi'eiʃən] Vereinigung *f*, Verbindung *f*; *Handels- etc.* Gesellschaft *f*; Genossenschaft *f*; Verein *m*.

**assort** [ə'sɔ:t] *v/t.* sortieren, zs.-stellen; *v/i.* passen (*with* zu); **~ment** [~tmənt] Sortieren *n*; † Sortiment *n*, Auswahl *f*.

**assum|e** [ə'sju:m] annehmen; vorgeben; übernehmen; **~ption** [ə'sʌmpʃən] Annahme *f*; Übernahme *f*; *eccl.* 2 (*Day*) Mariä Himmelfahrt *f*.

**assur|ance** [ə'ʃuərəns] Zu-, Versicherung *f*; Zuversicht *f*; Sicherheit *f*; Gewißheit *f*; Selbstsicherheit *f*; Dreistigkeit *f*; **~e** [ə'ʃuə] (*Leben* ver)sichern; sicherstellen; **~ed 1.** (*adv.* **~edly** [~ʃridli]) sicher; dreist; **2.** Versicherte(r *m*) *f*.

**asthma** ['æsmə] Asthma *n*.

**astir** [ə'stə:] auf (den Beinen); in Bewegung, rege.

**astonish** [əs'tɔniʃ] in Erstaunen setzen; verwundern; befremden; *be* **~ed** erstaunt sein (*at* über *acc.*); **~ing** [~ʃiŋ] erstaunlich; **~ment** [~ʃmənt] (Er)Staunen *n*; Verwunderung *f*.

**astound** [əs'taund] verblüffen.

**astray** [əs'trei] vom (rechten) Wege

ab (*a. fig.*); irre; *go* **~** sich verlaufen, fehlgehen.

**astride** [əs'traid] mit gespreizten Beinen; rittlings (*of* auf *dat.*).

**astringent** ⚕ [əs'trindʒənt] **1.** □ zs.-ziehend; **2.** zs.-ziehendes Mittel.

**astro|logy** [əs'trɔlədʒi] Astrologie *f*; **~naut** ['æstrənɔ:t] Astronaut *m*, Raumfahrer *m*; **~nomer** [əs'trɔnəmə] Astronom *m*; **~nomy** [~mi] Astronomie *f*.

**astute** □ [əs'tju:t] scharfsinnig; schlau; **~ness** [~tnis] Scharfsinn *m*.

**asunder** [ə'sʌndə] auseinander; entzwei.

**asylum** [ə'sailəm] Asyl *n*.

**at** [æt; *unbetont* ət] *prp.* an; auf; aus; bei; für; in; mit; nach; über; um; von; vor; zu; **~** *school* in der Schule; **~** *the age of* im Alter von.

**ate** [et] *pret. von* eat 1.

**atheism** ['eiθiizəm] Atheismus *m*.

**athlet|e** ['æθli:t] (*bsd.* Leicht-)Athlet *m*; **~ic(al** □) [æθ'letik(əl)] athletisch; **~ics** *pl.* (*bsd.* Leicht-)Athletik *f*.

**Atlantic** [ət'læntik] **1.** atlantisch; **2.** *a.* **~** *Ocean* Atlantik *m*.

**atmospher|e** ['ætməsfiə] Atmosphäre *f* (*a. fig.*); **~ic(al** □) [ætməs-'ferik(əl)] atmosphärisch.

**atom** ⚛ ['ætəm] Atom *n* (*a. fig.*); **~ic** [ə'tɔmik] atomartig, Atom...; atomistisch; **~** *age* Atomzeitalter *n*; **~** *(a. atom)* bomb Atombombe *f*; **~** *pile* Atomreaktor *m*; **~ic-powered** durch Atomkraft betrieben; **~ize** ['ætəmaiz] in Atome auflösen; atomisieren; **~izer** [~zə] Zerstäuber *m*.

**atone** [ə'toun]: **~** *for* büßen für *et.*; **~ment** [~nmənt] Buße *f*; Sühne *f*.

**atroci|ous** □ [ə'trouʃəs] scheußlich, gräßlich; grausam; **~ty** [ə'trɔsiti] Scheußlichkeit *f*, Gräßlichkeit *f*; Grausamkeit *f*.

**attach** [ə'tætʃ] *v/t.* (*to.*) anheften (an, *acc.*), befestigen (an *dat.*); *Wert, Wichtigkeit etc.* beilegen (*dat.*); ‡‡ *j-n* verhaften; *et.* beschlagnahmen; **~** *o.s.* to sich anschließen an (*acc.*); **~ed**: **~** *to* gehörig zu; *j-m* zugetan, ergeben; **~ment** [~ʃmənt] Befestigung *f*; Bindung *f* (*to, for* an *acc.*); Anhänglichkeit *f* (*an acc.*), Neigung *f* (zu); Anhängsel *n* (*to gen.*); ‡‡ Verhaftung *f*; Beschlagnahme *f*.

**attack** [ə'tæk] **1.** angreifen (*a. fig.*); befallen (*Krankheit*); *Arbeit* in Angriff nehmen; **2.** Angriff *m*; ⚕ Anfall *m*; Inangriffnahme *f*.

**attain** [ə'tein] *v/t. Ziel* erreichen; *v/i.* **~** *to* gelangen zu; **~ment** [~nmənt] Erreichung *f*; *fig.* Aneignung *f*; **~s** *pl.* Kenntnisse *f/pl.*; Fertigkeiten *f/pl.*

**attempt** [ə'tempt] **1.** versuchen; **2.** Versuch *m*; Attentat *n*.

**attend** [ə'tend] *v/t.* begleiten; be-

dienen; pflegen; ⚡ behandeln; *j-m*
aufwarten; beiwohnen (*dat.*); *Vorlesung etc.* besuchen; *v/i.* achten,
hören (*to auf acc.*); anwesend sein
(*at bei*); ⁓ to erledigen; ⁓ance
[⁓dəns] Begleitung *f*; Aufwartung
*f*; Pflege *f*; ⚡ Behandlung *f*; Gefolge *n*; Anwesenheit *f* (*at bei*);
Besuch *m* (*der Schule etc.*); Be-
sucher(zahl *f*) *m/pl.*; Publikum *n*;
be in ⁓ zu Diensten stehen; ⁓ant
[⁓nt] 1. begleitend (*on, upon acc.*);
anwesend (*at bei*); 2. Diener(in);
Begleiter(in); Wärter(in); Besu-
cher(in) (*at gen.*); ⊕ Bedienungs-
mann *m*; ⁓s *pl.* Dienerschaft *f*.
attent|ion [ə'tenʃən] Aufmerksam-
keit *f* (*a. fig.*); ⁓! ✗ Achtung!;
⁓ive □ [⁓ntiv] aufmerksam.
attest [ə'test] bezeugen; beglaubigen; *bsd.* ✗ vereidigen.
attic ['ætik] Dachstube *f*. [dung *f*.]
attire [ə'taiə] 1. kleiden; 2. Klei-)
attitude ['ætitju:d] (Ein)Stellung *f*;
Haltung *f*; *fig.* Stellungnahme *f*.
attorney [ə'tɔ:ni] Bevollmächtig-
te(r) *m*; *Am.* Rechtsanwalt *m*;
power of ⁓ Vollmacht *f*; ⚡ *General*
Generalstaats- *od.* Kronanwalt *m*,
*Am.* Justizminister *m*.
attract [ə'trækt] anziehen, *Aufmerksamkeit* erregen; *fig.* reizen;
⁓ion [⁓kʃən] Anziehung(skraft) *f*;
*fig.* Reiz *m*; Zugartikel *m*; *thea.*
Zugstück *n*; ⁓ive [⁓ktiv] anziehend;
reizvoll; zugkräftig; ⁓iveness
[⁓vnis] Reiz *m*.
attribute 1. [ə'tribju(:)t] beimessen,
zuschreiben; zurückführen (*to auf
acc.*); 2. ['ætribju:t] Attribut *n*
(*a. gr.*), Eigenschaft *f*, Merkmal *n*.
attune [ə'tju:n] (ab)stimmen.
auburn ['ɔ:bən] kastanienbraun.
auction ['ɔ:kʃən] 1. Auktion *f*; *sell
by* ⁓, *put up for* ⁓ versteigern;
2. *mst* ⁓ off versteigern; ⁓eer
[ɔ:kʃə'niə] Auktionator *m*.
audaci|ous [ɔ:'deiʃəs] kühn; un-
verschämt; ⁓ty [ɔ:'dæsiti] Kühnheit *f*; Unverschämtheit *f*.
audible □ ['ɔ:dəbl] hörbar; Hör...
audience ['ɔ:djəns] Publikum *n*,
Zuhörerschaft *f*; Leserkreis *m*;
Audienz *f*; Gehör *n*; *give* ⁓ *to* Gehör schenken (*dat.*).
audit ['ɔ:dit] 1. Rechnungsprüfung
*f*; 2. *Rechnungen* prüfen; ⁓or [⁓tə]
Hörer *m*; Rechnungs-, Buchprüfer
*m*; ⁓orium [ɔ:di'tɔ:riəm] Hörsaal
*m*; *Am.* Vortrags-, Konzertsaal *m*.
auger ⊕ ['ɔ:gə] *großer* Bohrer.
aught [ɔ:t] (irgend) etwas; *for* ⁓ *I
care* meinetwegen; *for* ⁓ *I know*
soviel ich weiß.
augment [ɔ:g'ment] vergrößern;
⁓ation [ɔ:gmen'teiʃən] Vermeh-
rung *f*, Vergrößerung *f*; Zusatz *m*.
augur ['ɔ:gə] 1. Augur *m*; 2. weissagen, voraussagen (*well Gutes, ill*

Übles); ⁓y ['ɔ:gjuri] Prophezeiung *f*; An-, Vorzeichen *n*; Vor-
ahnung *f*.
August¹ ['ɔ:gəst] *Monat* August *m*.
august² □ [ɔ:'gʌst] erhaben.
aunt [ɑ:nt] Tante *f*.
auspic|e ['ɔ:spis] Vorzeichen *n*; ⁓s
*pl.* Auspizien *pl.*; Schirmherrschaft
*f*; ⁓ious □ [ɔ:s'piʃəs] günstig.
auster|e □ [ɔs'tiə] streng; herb;
hart; einfach; ⁓ity [ɔs'teriti]
Strenge *f*; Härte *f*; Einfachheit *f*.
Australian [ɔs'treiljən] 1. austra-
lisch; 2. Australier(in).
Austrian ['ɔstriən] 1. österreichisch;
2. Österreicher(in).
authentic [ɔ:'θentik] (⁓ally) authentisch; zuverlässig; echt.
author ['ɔ:θə] Urheber(in); Autor
(-in); Verfasser(in); ⁓itative □
[ɔ:'θɔritətiv] maßgebend; gebieterisch; zuverlässig; ⁓ity [ɔ:'θɔriti]
Autorität *f*; (Amts)Gewalt *f*, Vollmacht *f*; Einfluß *m* (*over auf acc.*);
Ansehen *n*; Glaubwürdigkeit *f*;
Quelle *f*; Fachmann *m*; Behörde *f*
(*mst pl.*); *on the* ⁓ *of auf j-s* Zeugnis
hin, ⁓ize ['ɔ:θəraiz] *j n* autorisieren,
bevollmächtigen; *et.* gutheißen;
⁓ship ['ɔ:θəʃip] Urheberschaft *f*.
autocar ['ɔ:touka:] Kraftwagen *m*.
autocra|cy [ɔ:'tɔkrəsi] Autokratie *f*;
⁓tic(al □) [ɔ:tə'krætik(əl)] auto-
kratisch, despotisch.
autogiro ⚡ ['ɔ:tou'dʒaiərou] Autogiro *n*, Tragschrauber *m*.
autograph ['ɔ:təgrɑ:f] Autogramm
*n*. [Restaurant *n*.]
automat ['ɔ:təmæt] Automaten-)
automat|ic [ɔ:tə'mætik] (⁓ally)
1. automatisch; ⁓ *machine* (Verkaufs)Automat *m*; 2. *Am.* Selbst-
ladepistole *f*, -gewehr *n*; ⁓ion
[⁓'meiʃən] Automation *f*; ⁓on *fig.*
[ɔ:'tɔmətən] Roboter *m*.
automobile *bsd. Am.* ['ɔ:təməbi:l]
Automobil *n*.
autonomy [ɔ:'tɔnəmi] Autonomie *f*.
autumn ['ɔ:təm] Herbst *m*; ⁓al □
[ɔ:'tʌmnəl] herbstlich; Herbst...
auxiliary [ɔ:g'ziljəri] helfend;
Hilfs...
avail [ə'veil] 1. nützen, helfen; ⁓
*o.s. of* sich *e-r S.* bedienen; 2. Nutzen *m*; *of no* ⁓ nutzlos; ⁓able □
[⁓ləbl] benutzbar; verfügbar; *pred.*
erhältlich, vorhanden; gültig.
avalanche ['ævəlɑ:nʃ] Lawine *f*.
avaric|e ['ævəris] Geiz *m*; Habsucht
*f*; ⁓ious □ [ævə'riʃəs] geizig; habgierig.
avenge [ə'vendʒ] rächen; *et.* ahn-
den; ⁓r [⁓dʒə] Rächer(in).
avenue ['ævinju:] Allee *f*; Pracht-
straße *f*; *fig.* Weg *m*, Straße *f*.
aver [ə'və:] behaupten.
average ['ævəridʒ] 1. Durchschnitt
*m*; ⚓ Havarie *f*; 2. □ durchschnittlich; Durchschnitts...; 3. durch-

schnittlich schätzen (at auf acc.); durchschnittlich betragen od. arbeiten etc.

**avers|e** □ [ə'vɔːs] abgeneigt (to, from dat.); widerwillig; **~ion** [ə'vɔːʃən] Widerwille m.

**avert** [ə'vɔːt] abwenden (a. fig.).

**aviat|ion** ✈ [eivi'eiʃən] Fliegen n; Flugwesen n; Luftfahrt f; **~or** ['eivieitə] Flieger m.

**avid** □ ['ævid] gierig (of nach; for auf acc.).

**avoid** [ə'vɔid] (ver)meiden; j-m ausweichen; ⚖ anfechten; ungültig machen; **~ance** [~dəns] Vermeidung f.

**avouch** [ə'vautʃ] verbürgen, bestätigen; = avow.

**avow** [ə'vau] bekennen, (ein)gestehen; anerkennen; **~al** [ə'vauəl] Bekenntnis n, (Ein)Geständnis n; **~edly** [ə'vauidli] eingestandenermaßen.

**await** [ə'weit] erwarten (a. fig.).

**awake** [ə'weik] 1. wach, munter; be ~ to sich e-r S. bewußt sein; 2. [irr.] v/t. (mst ~n [~kən]) (er-)wecken; v/i. erwachen; gewahr werden (to s.th. et.).

**award** [ə'wɔːd] 1. Urteil n, Spruch

m; Belohnung f; Preis m; 2. zuerkennen, Orden etc. verleihen.

**aware** [ə'wɛə]: be ~ wissen (of von od. acc.), sich bewußt sein (of gen.); become ~ of et. gewahr werden, merken.

**away** [ə'wei] (hin)weg; fort; immer weiter, darauflos; ~ back Am. f (schon) damals, weit zurück.

**awe** [ɔː] 1. Ehrfurcht f, Scheu f (of vor dat.); 2. (Ehr)Furcht einflößen (dat.).

**awful** □ ['ɔːful] ehrfurchtgebietend; furchtbar; f fig. schrecklich.

**awhile** [ə'wail] e-e Weile.

**awkward** □ ['ɔːkwəd] ungeschickt, unbeholfen; linkisch; unangenehm; dumm, ungünstig, unpraktisch.

**awl** [ɔːl] Ahle f, Pfriem m.

**awning** ['ɔːniŋ] Plane f; Markise f.

**awoke** [ə'wouk] pret. u. p.p. von awake 2.

**awry** [ə'rai] schief; fig. verkehrt.

**ax(e)** [æks] Axt f, Beil n.

**axis** ['æksis], pl. **axes** ['æksiːz] Achse f.

**axle** ⊕ ['æksl] a. **~-tree** (Rad-) Achse f, Welle f.

**ay(e)** [ai] Ja n; parl. Jastimme f; the ~s have it die Mehrheit ist dafür.

**azure** ['æʒə] azurn, azurblau.

# B

**babble** ['bæbl] 1. stammeln; (nach-) plappern; schwatzen; plätschern (Bach); 2. Geplapper n; Geschwätz n.

**baboon** zo. [bə'buːn] Pavian m.

**baby** ['beibi] 1. Säugling m, kleines Kind, Baby n; Am. sl. Süße f (Mädchen); 2. Baby...; Kinder...; klein; **~hood** [~ihud] frühe Kindheit.

**bachelor** ['bætʃələ] Junggeselle m; univ. Bakkalaureus m (Grad).

**back** [bæk] 1. Rücken m; Rückseite f; Rücklehne f; Hinterende n; Fußball: Verteidiger m; 2. adj. Hinter..., Rück...; hinter; rückwärtig; entlegen; rückläufig; rückständig; 3. adv. zurück; 4. v/t. mit e-m Rücken versehen; unterstützen; hinten anstoßen an (acc.); zurückbewegen; wetten od. setzen auf (acc.); † indossieren; v/i. sich rückwärts bewegen, zurückgehenod. zurückfahren; ~ alley Am. finstere Seitengasse; **~bite** ['bækbait] [irr. (bite)] verleumden; **~bone** Rückgrat n; **~er** ['bækə] Unterstützer (-in); † Indossierer m; Wetter(in); **~fire** mot. Frühzündung f; **~ground** Hintergrund m; ~ **number** alte Nummer (e-r Zeitung); **~**

**pedal** rückwärtstreten (Radfahren); **~ling brake** Rücktrittbremse f; **~side** Hinter-, Rückseite f; **~slapper** Am. [~slæpə] plump vertraulicher Mensch; **~slide** [irr. (slide)] rückfällig werden; **~stairs** Hintertreppe f; **~stop** Am. Baseball: Gitter n hinter dem Fänger; Schießstand: Kugelfang m; **~stroke** Rückenschwimmen n; **~talk** Am. freche Antworten; **~track** Am. f fig. e-n Rückzieher machen; **~ward** ['bækwəd] 1. adj. Rück(wärts)...; langsam, zurückgeblieben, rückständig; zurückhaltend; 2. adv. (a. **~wards** [~dz]) rückwärts, zurück; **~water** Stauwasser n; **~woods** pl. weit abgelegene Waldgebiete; fig. Provinz f; **~woodsman** Hinterwäldler m.

**bacon** ['beikən] Speck m.

**bacteri|ologist** [bæktiəri'ɔlədʒist] Bakteriologe m; **~um** [bæk'tiəriəm], pl. **~a** [~iə] Bakterie f.

**bad** □ [bæd] schlecht, böse, schlimm; falsch (Münze); faul (Schuld); he is ~ly off er ist übel dran; **~ly wounded** schwerverwundet; want **~ly** f dringend brauchen; be in ~ with Am. f in Ungnade bei.

**bade** [beid] pret. von bid 1.

**badge** [bædʒ] Ab-, Kennzeichen *n.*

**badger** ['bædʒə] **1.** *zo.* Dachs *m;* **2.** hetzen, plagen, quälen.

**badlands** *Am.* ['bædlændz] *pl.* Ödland *n.*

**badness** ['bædnis] schlechte Beschaffenheit; Schlechtigkeit *f.*

**baffle** ['bæfl] *j-n* verwirren; *Plan etc.* vereiteln, durchkreuzen.

**bag** [bæg] **1.** Beutel *m,* Sack *m;* Tüte *f;* Tasche *f;* ~ *and baggage* mit Sack und Pack; **2.** in e-n Beutel *etc.* tun, einsacken; *hunt.* zur Strecke bringen; (sich) bauschen.

**baggage** *Am.* ['bægidʒ] (Reise-) Gepäck *n;* ~ *car Am.* 🚂 Gepäckwagen *m;* ~ *check Am.* Gepäckschein *m.*

**bagpipe** ['bægpaip] Dudelsack *m.*

**bail** [beil] **1.** Bürge *m;* Bürgschaft *f;* Kaution *f; admit to* ~ 🔒 gegen Bürgschaft freilassen; **2.** bürgen für; ~ *out j-n* freibürgen; ✈ mit dem Fallschirm abspringen.

**bailiff** ['beilif] Gerichtsdiener *m;* (Guts)Verwalter *m;* Amtmann *m.*

**bait** [beit] **1.** Köder *m; fig.* Lockung *f;* **2.** *v/t.* Falle *etc.* beködern; *hunt.* hetzen; *fig.* quälen; reizen; *v/i.* rasten; einkehren.

**bak|e** [beik] **1.** backen; braten; *Ziegel* brennen; (aus)dörren; **2.** *Am.* gesellige Zusammenkunft; ~**er** ['beikə] Bäcker *m;* ~**ery** [~əri] Bäckerei *f;* ~**ing-powder** [~kiŋpaudə] Backpulver *n.*

**balance** ['bæləns] **1.** Waage *f;* Gleichgewicht *n* (*a. fig.*); Harmonie *f;* ✝ Bilanz *f,* Saldo *m,* Überschuß *m;* Restbetrag *m;* F Rest *m; a.* ~ *wheel* Unruh(e) *f der Uhr;* ~ *of power pol.* Kräftegleichgewicht *n;* ~ *of trade* (Außen-) Handelsbilanz *f;* **2.** *v/t.* (ab-, er)wägen; im Gleichgewicht halten; ausgleichen; ✝ bilanzieren; saldieren; *v/i.* balancieren; sich ausgleichen.

**balcony** ['bælkəni] Balkon *m.*

**bald** [bɔːld] kahl; *fig.* nackt; dürftig.

**bale** ✝ [beil] Ballen *m.*

**baleful** □ ['beilful] verderblich; unheilvoll.

**balk** [bɔːk] **1.** (Furchen)Rain *m;* Balken *m;* Hemmnis *n;* **2.** *v/t.* (ver-) hindern; enttäuschen; vereiteln; *v/i.* stutzen, scheuen.

**ball**[1] [bɔːl] **1.** Ball *m;* Kugel *f;* (Hand-, Fuß)Ballen *m;* Knäuel *m,* *n;* Kloß *m; Sport:* Wurf *m; keep the* ~ *rolling* das Gespräch in Gang halten; *play* ~ *Am.* F mitmachen; **2.** (sich) (zs.-)ballen.

**ball**[2] [~] Ball *m,* Tanzgesellschaft *f.*

**ballad** ['bæləd] Ballade *f;* Lied *n.*

**ballast** ['bæləst] **1.** Ballast *m;* 🚂 Schotter *m,* Bettung *f;* **2.** mit

Ballast beladen; 🚂 beschottern, betten.

**ball-bearing**(**s** *pl.*) ⊕ ['bɔːl-'beəriŋ(z)] Kugellager *n.*

**ballet** ['bælei] Ballett *n.*

**balloon** [bə'luːn] **1.** Ballon *m;* **2.** im Ballon aufsteigen; sich blähen; ~**ist** [~nist] Ballonfahrer *m.*

**ballot** ['bælət] **1.** Wahlzettel *m;* (geheime) Wahl; **2.** (geheim) abstimmen; ~ *for* losen um; ~**box** Wahlurne *f.*

**ball(-point) pen** ['bɔːl(pɔint)pen] Kugelschreiber *m.*

**ball-room** ['bɔːlrum] Ballsaal *m.*

**balm** [baːm] Balsam *m; fig.* Trost *m.*

**balmy** □ ['baːmi] balsamisch (*a. fig.*).

**baloney** *Am. sl.* [bə'louni] Quatsch *m.*

**balsam** ['bɔːlsəm] Balsam *m.*

**balustrade** [bæləs'treid] Balustrade *f,* Brüstung *f;* Geländer *n.*

**bamboo** [bæm'buː] Bambus *m.*

**bamboozle** F [bæm'buːzl] beschwindeln.

**ban** [bæn] **1.** Bann *m;* Acht *f;* (amtliches) Verbot; **2.** verbieten.

**banal** [bə'naːl] banal, abgedroschen.

**banana** [bə'naːnə] Banane *f.*

**band** [bænd] **1.** Band *n;* Streifen *m;* Schar *f;* ♪ Kapelle *f;* **2.** zs.-binden; ~ *o.s.* sich zs.-tun *od.* zs.-rotten.

**bandage** ['bændidʒ] **1.** Binde *f;* Verband *m;* **2.** bandagieren; verbinden.

**bandbox** ['bændbɔks] Hutschachtel *f.*

**bandit** ['bændit] Bandit *m.*

**band|-master** ['bændmaːstə] Kapellmeister *m;* ~**stand** Musikpavillon *m;* ~**wagon** *Am.* Wagen *m* mit Musikkapelle; *jump on the* ~ sich der erfolgversprechenden Sache anschließen.

**bandy** ['bændi] *Worte etc.* wechseln; ~**-legged** säbelbeinig.

**bane** [bein] Ruin *m;* ~**ful** □ ['beinful] verderblich.

**bang** [bæŋ] **1.** Knall *m;* Ponyfrisur *f;* **2.** dröhnend (zu)schlagen; ~**up** *Am. sl.* ['bæŋ'ʌp] Klasse, prima.

**banish** ['bæniʃ] verbannen; ~**ment** [~ʃmənt] Verbannung *f.*

**banisters** ['bænistəz] *pl.* Treppengeländer *n.*

**bank** [bæŋk] **1.** Damm *m;* Ufer *n;* (Spiel-, Sand-, Wolken- *etc.*)Bank *f;* ~ *of issue* Notenbank *f;* **2.** *v/t.* eindämmen; ✝ Geld auf die Bank legen; ✈ in die Kurve bringen; *v/i.* Bankgeschäfte machen; ein Bankkonto haben; ✈ in die Kurve gehen; ~ *on* sich verlassen auf (*acc.*); ~**bill** ['bæŋkbil] Bankwechsel *m; Am. s. banknote;* ~**er** [~kə] Bankier *m;* ~**ing** [~kiŋ] Bankgeschäft *n;* Bankwesen *n; attr.* Bank...; ~**note** Banknote *f;* Kassenschein *m;* ~

**rate** Diskontsatz *m*; ~rupt [~krəpt]
**1.** Bankrotteur *m*; **2.** bankrott;
**3.** bankrott machen; ~ruptcy
[~tsi] Bankrott *m*, Konkurs *m*.

**banner** ['bænə] Banner *n*; Fahne *f*.

**banns** [bænz] *pl.* Aufgebot *n*.

**banquet** ['bæŋkwit] **1.** Festmahl *n*;
**2.** *v/t.* festlich bewirten; *v/i.* tafeln.

**banter** ['bæntə] necken, hänseln.

**baptism** ['bæptizəm] Taufe *f*.

**baptist** ['bæptist] Täufer *m*.

**baptize** ['bæp'taiz] taufen.

**bar** [ba:] **1.** Stange *f*; Stab *m*;
Barren *m*; Riegel *m*; Schranke *f*;
Sandbank *f*; *fig.* Hindernis *n*; ✗
Spange *f*; ♪ Takt(strich) *m*; (Gerichts)Schranke *f*; *fig.* Urteil *n*;
Anwaltschaft *f*; Bar *f im Hotel etc.*;
**2.** verriegeln; (ver-, ab)sperren;
verwehren; einsperren; (ver)hin-
dern; ausschließen.

**barb** [ba:b] Widerhaken *m*; ~ed
wire Stacheldraht *m*.

**barbar|ian** [ba:'bɛəriən] **1.** bar-
barisch; **2.** Barbar(in); ~ous □
['ba:bərəs] barbarisch; roh; grausam.

**barbecue** ['ba:bikju:] **1.** großer
Bratrost; *Am.* Essen *n* (*im Freien*),
bei dem Tiere ganz gebraten
werden; **2.** im ganzen braten.

**barber** ['ba:bə] (Herren)Friseur *m*.

**bare** [bɛə] **1.** nackt, bloß; kahl; bar,
leer; arm, entblößt; **2.** entblößen;
~faced ['bɛəfeist] frech; ~foot,
~footed barfuß; ~headed bar-
häuptig; ~ly ['bɛəli] kaum.

**bargain** ['ba:gin] **1.** Geschäft *n*;
Handel *m*, Kauf *m*; vorteilhafter
Kauf; *a* (*dead*) ~ spottbillig; *it's a* ~!
F abgemacht!; *into the* ~ obendrein;
**2.** handeln, übereinkommen.

**barge** [ba:dʒ] Flußboot *n*, Lastkahn
*m*; Hausboot *n*; ~man ['ba:dʒmən]
Kahnführer *m*.

**bark¹** [ba:k] **1.** Borke *f*, Rinde *f*;
**2.** abrinden; *Haut* abschürfen.

**bark²** [~] **1.** bellen; **2.** Bellen *n*.

**bar-keeper** ['ba:ki:pə] Barbesitzer
*m*; Barkellner *m*.

**barley** ['ba:li] Gerste *f*; Graupe *f*.

**barn** [ba:n] Scheune *f*; *bsd. Am.*
(Vieh)Stall *m*; ~storm *Am. pol.*
['ba:nstɔ:m] herumreisen u. (Wahl-)
Reden halten.

**barometer** [bə'rɔmitə] Barometer *n*.

**baron** ['bærən] Baron *m*, Freiherr
*m*; ~ess [~nis] Baronin *f*.

**barrack(s** *pl.*) ['bærək(s)] (Miets-)
Kaserne *f*.

**barrage** ['bæra:ʒ] Staudamm *m*.

**barrel** ['bærəl] **1.** Faß *n*, Tonne *f*;
*Gewehr- etc.* Lauf *m*; ⊕ Trommel
*f*; Walze *f*; **2.** in Fässer füllen;
~organ ♪ Drehorgel *f*.

**barren** □ ['bærən] unfruchtbar;
dürr, trocken; tot (*Kapital*).

**barricade** [bæri'keid] **1.** Barrikade
*f*; **2.** verbarrikadieren; sperren.

**barrier** ['bæriə] Schranke *f* (*a. fig.*);
Barriere *f*, Sperre *f*; Hindernis
*n*.

**barrister** ['bæristə] (plädierender)
Rechtsanwalt, Barrister *m*.

**barrow¹** ['bærou] Trage *f*; Karre *f*.

**barrow²** [~] Hügelgrab *n*, Tumulus
*m*.

**barter** ['ba:tə] **1.** Tausch(handel)
*m*; **2.** tauschen (*for* gegen); F
schachern.

**base¹** [beis] gemein; unecht.

**base²** [~] **1.** Basis *f*; Grundlage *f*;
Fundament *n*; Fuß *m*; ✗ Base *f*;
Stützpunkt *m*; **2.** gründen, stützen.

**base|ball** ['beisbɔ:l] Baseball *m*;
~born von niedriger Abkunft;
unehelich; ~less ['beislis] grundlos;
~ment ['beismənt] Fundament *n*;
Kellergeschoß *n*.

**baseness** ['beisnis] Gemeinheit *f*.

**bashful** □ ['bæʃful] schüchtern.

**basic** ['beisik] (~ally) grundlegend;
Grund...; ✗ basisch.

**basin** ['beisn] Becken *n*; Schüssel *f*;
Tal-, Wasser-, Hafenbecken *n*.

**bas|is** ['beisis], *pl.* ~es ['beisi:z]
Basis *f*; Grundlage *f*; ✗, ♻ Stützpunkt *m*.

**bask** [ba:sk] sich sonnen (*a. fig.*).

**basket** ['ba:skit] Korb *m*; ~ball
Korbball(spiel *n*) *m*; ~ dinner, ~
supper *Am.* Picknick *n*.

**bass** ♪ [beis] Baß *m*.

**basso** ♪ ['bæsou] Baß(sänger) *m*.

**bastard** ['bæstəd] **1.** □ unehelich;
unecht; Bastard...; **2.** Bastard *m*.

**baste¹** [beist] *Braten* begießen;
durchprügeln.

**baste²** [~] lose nähen, (an)heften.

**bat¹** [bæt] Fledermaus *f*; *as blind
as a* ~ stockblind.

**bat²** [~] *Sport:* **1.** Schlagholz *n*;
Schläger *m*; **2.** *den Ball* schlagen.

**batch** [bætʃ] Schub *m* Brote (*a. fig.*);
Stoß *m* Briefe *etc.* (*a. fig.*).

**bate** [beit] verringern; verhalten.

**bath** [ba:θ] **1.** Bad *n*; ♿ chair Rollstuhl *m*; **2.** baden.

**bathe** [beið] baden.

**bathing** ['beiðiŋ] Baden *n*, Bad *n*;
*attr.* Bade...; ~suit Badeanzug *m*.

**bath|robe** *Am.* ['ba:θroub] Bade-
mantel *m*; ~room Badezimmer *n*;
~sheet Badelaken *n*; ~towel
Badetuch *n*; ~tub Badewanne *f*.

**batiste** ✝ [bæ'ti:st] Batist *m*.

**baton** ['bætən] Stab *m*; Taktstock
*m*.

**battalion** ✗ [bə'tæljən] Bataillon *n*.

**batten** ['bætn] **1.** Latte *f*; **2.** sich
mästen.

**batter** ['bætə] **1.** *Sport:* Schläger *m*;
Rührteig *m*; **2.** heftig schlagen;
verbeulen; ~ *down od. in* Tür einschlagen; ~y [~əri] Schlägerei *f*;
Batterie *f*; ⚡ Akku *m*; *fig.* Satz *m*;
*assault and* ~ ✗ tätlicher Angriff.

**battle** ['bætl] **1.** Schlacht *f* (*of* bei);

**2.** streiten, kämpfen; ~**-ax(e)**
Streitaxt *f*; F Xanthippe *f*; ~**-field**
Schlachtfeld *n*; ~**ments** [ˏlmənts]
*pl.* Zinnen *f/pl.*; ~**-plane** ⚔ Kriegs-
flugzeug *n*; ~**ship** ⚔ Schlacht-
schiff *n*.
**Bavarian** [bə'veəriən] **1.** bay(e)-
risch; **2.** Bayer(in).
**bawdy** ['bɔ:di] unzüchtig.
**bawl** [bɔ:l] brüllen; johlen, grölen;
~ out auf-, losbrüllen.
**bay**[1] [bei] **1.** rotbraun; **2.** Braune(r)
*m (Pferd)*.
**bay**[2] [ˏ] Bai *f*, Bucht *f*; Erker *m*.
**bay**[3] [ˏ] Lorbeer *m*.
**bay**[4] [ˏ] **1.** bellen, anschlagen;
**2.** stand at ~ sich verzweifelt
wehren; bring to ~ Wild etc. stellen.
**bayonet** ⚔ ['beiənit] **1.** Bajonett *n*;
**2.** mit dem Bajonett niederstoßen.
**bayou** *Am.* ['baiu:] sumpfiger
Nebenarm.
**bay window** ['bei'windou] Erker-
fenster *n*; *Am. sl.* Vorbau *m*
*(Bauch)*.
**baza(a)r** [bə'zɑ:] Basar *m*.
**be** [bi:, bi] [*irr.*] *v/i.* sein; there
is od. are es gibt; here you are again!
da haben wir's wieder!; ~ about beschäftigt sein mit; ~ at s.th. et.
vorhaben; ~ off aus sein; sich fortmachen; **2.** *v/aux.*: ~ reading beim
Lesen sein, gerade lesen; I am to
inform you ich soll Ihnen mitteilen;
**3.** *v/aux.* mit *p.p.* zur Bildung des
Passivs: werden.
**beach** [bi:tʃ] **1.** Strand *m*; **2.** ⚓ auf
den Strand setzen od. ziehen;
~**comber** ['bi:tʃkoumə] *fig.* Nichtstuer *m*.
**beacon** ['bi:kən] Blinklicht *n*;
Leuchtfeuer *n*, Leuchtturm *m*.
**bead** [bi:d] Perle *f*; Tropfen *m*;
Visier-Korn *n*; ~s *pl. a.* Rosenkranz *m*.
**beak** [bi:k] Schnabel *m*; Tülle *f*.
**beaker** ['bi:kə] Becher(glas *n*) *m*.
**beam** [bi:m] **1.** Balken *m*; Waage-
balken *m*; Strahl *m*; Glanz *m*;
Radio: Richtstrahl *m*; **2.** (aus-)
strahlen.
**bean** [bi:n] Bohne *f*; *Am. sl.* Birne *f*
*(Kopf)*; full of ~s F lebensprühend.
**bear**[1] [bɛə] Bär *m*; ✝ *sl.* Baissier *m*.
**bear**[2] [ˏ] [*irr.*] *v/t.* tragen; hervorbringen, gebären; Liebe etc. hegen;
ertragen; ~ down überwältigen; ~
out unterstützen, bestätigen; *v/i.*
tragen; fruchtbar od. trächtig sein;
leiden, dulden; ~ up standhalten,
fest bleiben; ~ (up)on einwirken auf
*(acc.)*; bring to ~ zur Anwendung
bringen, einwirken lassen, Druck
etc. ausüben.
**beard** [biəd] **1.** Bart *m*; ♀ Granne *f*;
**2.** *v/t.* j-m entgegentreten, trotzen.
**bearer** ['bɛərə] Träger(in); Über-
bringer(in), Wechsel-Inhaber(in).
**bearing** ['bɛəriŋ] (Er)Tragen *n*;

Betragen *n*; Beziehung *f*; Richtung *f*.
**beast** [bi:st] Vieh *n*, Tier *n*; Bestie
*f*; ~**ly** ['bi:stli] viehisch; scheußlich.
**beat** [bi:t] **1.** [*irr.*] *v/t.* schlagen;
prügeln; besiegen, *Am.* F j-m zuvorkommen; übertreffen; *Am.* F
betrügen; ~ it! *Am. sl.* hau ab!;
~ the band *Am.* F wichtig od.
großartig sein; ~ a retreat den
Rückzug antreten; ~ one's way *Am.*
F sich durchschlagen; ~ up auf-
treiben; *v/i.* schlagen; ~ about the
bush wie die Katze um den heißen
Brei herumgehen; **2.** Schlag *m*;
♪ Takt(schlag) *m*; Pulsschlag *m*;
Runde *f*, Revier *n* e-s Schutz-
mannes etc.; *Am.* sensationelle
Erstmeldung e-r Zeitung; **3.** F baff,
verblüfft; ~**en** ['bi:tn] *p.p. von*
beat 1; (aus)getreten (Weg).
**beatitude** [bi(:)'ætitju:d] (Glück-)
Seligkeit *f*.
**beatnik** ['bi:tnik] Beatnik *m*, junger
Antikonformist und Bohemien.
**beau** [bou] Stutzer *m*; Anbeter *m*.
**beautiful** □ ['bju:təful] schön.
**beautify** ['bju:tifai] verschönern.
**beauty** ♀ ['bju:ti] Schönheit *f*; Sleeping ♀ Dornrös-chen *n*; ~ parlo(u)r,
~ shop Schönheitssalon *m*.
**beaver** ['bi:və] Biber *m*; Biberpelz *m*.
**becalm** [bi'kɑ:m] beruhigen.
**became** [bi'keim] *pret. von* become.
**because** [bi'kɔz] weil; ~ of wegen.
**beckon** ['bekən] (j-m zu)winken.
**become** [bi'kʌm] [*irr.*] *v/i.* werden
(of aus); *v/t.* anstehen, ziemen
(*dat.*); sich schicken für; kleiden
(*Hut etc.*); ~**ing** □ [ˏmiŋ] passend;
schicklich; kleids.m.
**bed** [bed] **1.** Bett *n*; Lager *n* e-s
Tieres; ♪ Beet *n*; Unterlage *f*;
**2.** betten.
**bed-clothes** ['bedklouðz] *pl.* Bett-
wäsche *f*.
**bedding** ['bediŋ] Bettzeug *n*; Streu *f*.
**bedevil** [bi'devl] behexen; quälen.
**bedlam** ['bedləm] Tollhaus *n*.
**bed|rid(den)** ['bedrid(n)] bett-
lägerig; ~**room** Schlafzimmer *n*;
~**spread** Bett-, Tagesdecke *f*;
~**stead** Bettstelle *f*; ~**time** Schla-
fenszeit *f*.
**bee** [bi:] *zo.* Biene *f*; *Am.* nachbar-
liches Treffen; Wettbewerb *m*;
have a ~ in one's bonnet F e-e fixe
Idee haben.
**beech** ♀ [bi:tʃ] Buche *f*; ~**nut** Buch-
ecker *f*.
**beef** [bi:f] **1.** Rindfleisch *n*; **2.** *Am.*
F nörgeln; ~ tea Fleischbrühe *f*;
~**y** ['bi:fi] fleischig; kräftig.
**bee|hive** ['bi:haiv] Bienenkorb *m*,
-stock *m*; ~**keeper** Bienenzüchter
*m*; ~**line** kürzester Weg; make a
~ for *Am.* schnurstracks losgehen
auf (*acc.*).

**been** [bi:n, bin] *p.p. von* be.

**beer** [biə] Bier *n*; *small* ~ Dünnbier *n*. [Bete *f*.]

**beet** ♀ [bi:t] (Runkel)Rübe *f*,)

**beetle**[1] ['bi:tl] Käfer *m*.

**beetle**[2] [~] 1. überhängend; buschig (*Brauen*); 2. *v/i.* überhängen.

**beetroot** ['bi:tru:t] rote Rübe.

**befall** [bi'fɔ:l] [*irr. (fall)*] *v/t.* zustoßen (*dat.*); *v/i.* sich ereignen.

**befit** [bi'fit] sich schicken für.

**before** [bi'fɔ:] 1. *adv. Raum*: vorn; voran; *Zeit*: vorher, früher; schon (früher); 2. *cj.* bevor, ehe, bis; 3. *prp.* vor; ~**hand** vorher, zuvor; voraus (*with dat.*).

**befriend** [bi'frend] sich *j-m* freundlich erweisen.

**beg** [beg] *v/t. et.* erbetteln; erbitten (*of von*); *j-n* bitten; ~ *the question* um den Kern der Frage herumgehen; *v/i.* betteln; bitten; betteln gehen; sich gestatten.

**began** [bi'gæn] *pret. von* begin.

**beget** [bi'get] [*irr. (get)*] (er)zeugen.

**beggar** ['begə] 1. Bettler(in); F Kerl *m*; 2. zum Bettler machen; *fig.* übertreffen; *it* ~*s all description* es spottet jeder Beschreibung.

**begin** [bi'gin] [*irr.*] beginnen (*at* bei, mit); ~**ner** [~nə] Anfänger(in); ~**ning** [~niŋ] Beginn *m*, Anfang *m*.

**begone** [bi'gɔn] fort!, F pack dich!

**begot** [bi'gɔt] *pret. von* beget; ~**ten** [~tn] 1. *p.p. von* beget; 2. *adj.* erzeugt.

**begrudge** [bi'grʌdʒ] mißgönnen.

**beguile** [bi'gail] täuschen; betrügen (*of, out of* um); *Zeit* vertreiben.

**begun** [bi'gʌn] *p.p. von* begin.

**behalf** [bi'hɑ:f]: *on od. in* ~ *of* im Namen von; um … (*gen.*) willen.

**behav|e** [bi'heiv] sich benehmen; ~**io(u)r** [~vjə] Benehmen *n*, Betragen *n*.

**behead** [bi'hed] enthaupten.

**behind** [bi'haind] 1. *adv.* hinten, dahinter; zurück; 2. *prp.* hinter; ~**hand** zurück, im Rückstand.

**behold** [bi'hould] [*irr. (hold)*] 1. erblicken; 2. siehe (da)!; ~**en** [~dən] verpflichtet, verbunden.

**behoof** [bi'hu:f]: *to* (*for, on*) (*the*) ~ *of* in *j-s* Interesse, um *j-s* willen.

**behoove** *Am.* [bi'hu:v] = behove.

**behove** [bi'houv]: *it* ~*s s.o. to inf.* es ist *j-s* Pflicht, zu *inf.*

**being** ['bi:iŋ] (Da)Sein *n*; Wesen *n*; *in* ~ lebend; wirklich (vorhanden).

**belabo(u)r** F [bi'leibə] verbleuen.

**belated** [bi'leitid] verspätet.

**belch** [beltʃ] 1. rülpsen; ausspeien; 2. Rülpsen *n*; Ausbruch *m*.

**beleaguer** [bi'li:gə] belagern.

**belfry** ['belfri] Glockenturm *m*, -stuhl *m*. [2. Belgier(in).)

**Belgian** ['beldʒən] 1. belgisch;)

**belie** [bi'lai] Lügen strafen.

**belief** [bi'li:f] Glaube *m* (*in an acc.*).

**believable** [bi'li:vəbl] glaubhaft.

**believe** [bi'li:v] glauben (*in an acc.*); ~**r** [~və] Gläubige(r *m*) *f*.

**belittle** *fig.* [bi'litl] verkleinern.

**bell** [bel] Glocke *f*; Klingel *f*; ~**boy** *Am.* ['belbɔi] Hotelpage *m*.

**belle** [bel] Schöne *f*, Schönheit *f*.

**belles-lettres** ['bel'letr] *pl.* Belletristik *f*, schöne Literatur.

**bellhop** *Am. sl.* ['belhɔp] Hotelpage *m*.

**bellied** ['belid] bauchig.

**belligerent** [bi'lidʒərənt] 1. kriegführend; 2. kriegführendes Land.

**bellow** ['belou] 1. brüllen; 2. Gebrüll *n*; ~**s** *pl.* Blasebalg *m*.

**belly** ['beli] 1. Bauch *m*; 2. (sich) bauchen; (an)schwellen.

**belong** [bi'lɔŋ] (an)gehören; ~ *to* gehören *dat. od.* zu; sich gehören für; *j-m* gebühren; ~**ings** [~ŋiŋz] *pl.* Habseligkeiten *f/pl.*

**beloved** [bi'lʌvd] 1. geliebt; 2. Geliebte(r *m*) *f*.

**below** [bi'lou] 1. *adv.* unten; 2. *prp.* unter.

**belt** [belt] 1. Gürtel *m*; ✗ Koppel *n*; Zone *f*, Bezirk *m*; ⊕ Treibriemen *m*; 2. umgürten; ~ *out Am.* herausschmettern, loslegen (*singen*).

**bemoan** [bi'moun] betrauern, beklagen.

**bench** [bentʃ] Bank *f*; Richterbank *f*; Gerichtshof *m*; Arbeitstisch *m*.

**bend** [bend] 1. Biegung *f*, Kurve *f*; ⚓ Seemannsknoten *m*; 2. [*irr.*] (sich) biegen; *Geist etc.* richten (*to, on* auf *acc.*); (sich) beugen; sich neigen (*to* vor *dat.*).

**beneath** [bi'ni:θ] = below.

**benediction** [beni'dikʃən] Segen *m*.

**benefact|ion** [beni'fækʃən] Wohltat *f*; ~**or** ['benifæktə] Wohltäter *m*.

**beneficen|ce** [bi'nefisəns] Wohltätigkeit *f*; ~**t** □ [~nt] wohltätig.

**beneficial** □ [beni'fiʃəl] wohltuend; zuträglich; nützlich.

**benefit** ['benifit] 1. Wohltat *f*; Nutzen *m*, Vorteil *m*; Wohltätigkeitsveranstaltung *f*; (Wohlfahrts-) Unterstützung *f*; 2. nützen; begünstigen; Nutzen ziehen.

**benevolen|ce** [bi'nevələns] Wohlwollen *n*; ~**t** □ [~nt] wohlwollend; gütig, mildherzig.

**benign** □ [bi'nain] freundlich, gütig; zuträglich; ⚕ gutartig.

**bent** [bent] 1. *pret. u. p.p. von* bend 2; ~ *on* versessen auf (*acc.*); 2. Hang *m*; Neigung *f*.

**benzene** ⚗ ['benzi:n] Benzol *n*.

**benzine** ⚗ ['benzi:n] Benzin *n*.

**bequeath** [bi'kwi:ð] vermachen.

**bequest** [bi'kwest] Vermächtnis *n*.

**bereave** [bi'ri:v] [*irr.*] berauben.

**bereft** [bi'reft] *pret. u. p.p. von* bereave.

**beret** ['berei] Baskenmütze *f*.

**berry** ['beri] Beere f.

**berth** [bəːθ] **1.** ⚓ Ankergrund m; Koje f; fig. (gute) Stelle; **2.** vor Anker gehen.

**beseech** [bi'siːtʃ] [irr.] ersuchen; bitten; um et. bitten; flehen.

**beset** [bi'set] [irr. (set)] umgeben; bedrängen; verfolgen.

**beside** prp. [bi'said] neben; weitab von; ~ o.s. außer sich (with vor); ~ the point, ~ the question nicht zur Sache gehörig; ~s [dz] **1.** adv. außerdem; **2.** prp. abgesehen von, außer.

**besiege** [bi'siːdʒ] belagern.

**besmear** [bi'smiə] beschmieren.

**besom** ['biːzəm] (Reisig)Besen m.

**besought** [bi'sɔːt] pret. u. p.p. von beseech.

**bespatter** [bi'spætə] (be)spritzen.

**bespeak** [bi'spiːk] [irr. (speak)] vor-bestellen; verraten, (an)zeigen; bespoke tailor Maßschneider m.

**best** [best] **1.** adj. best; höchst; größt, meist; ~ man Brautführer m; **2.** adv. am besten, aufs beste; **3.** Beste(r m, -s n) f, Besten pl.; to the ~ of ... nach bestem ...; make the ~ of tun, was man kann, mit; at ~ im besten Falle.

**bestial** □ ['bestjəl] tierisch, viehisch.

**bestow** [bi'stou] geben, schenken, verleihen (on, upon dat.).

**bet** [bet] **1.** Wette f; **2.** [irr.] wetten; you ~ F sicherlich.

**betake** [bi'teik] [irr. (take)]: ~ o.s. to sich begeben nach; fig. s-e Zuflucht nehmen zu.

**bethink** [bi'θink] [irr. (think)]: ~ o.s. sich besinnen (of auf acc.); ~ o.s. to inf. sich in den Kopf setzen zu inf.

**betimes** [bi'taimz] beizeiten.

**betray** [bi'trei] verraten (a. fig.); verleiten; ~er [~eiə] Verräter(in).

**betrothal** [bi'trouðəl] Verlobung f.

**better** ['betə] **1.** adj. besser; he is ~, es geht ihm besser; **2.** Bessere(s) n; ~s pl. Höherstehenden pl.; Vorgesetzten pl.; get the ~ of die Oberhand gewinnen über (acc.); überwinden; **3.** adv. besser; mehr; so much the ~ desto besser; you had ~ go es wäre besser, wenn du gingest; **4.** v/t. (ver)bessern; v/i. sich bessern; ~ment [~əmənt] Verbesserung f.

**between** [bi'twiːn] (a. betwixt [bi'twikst]) **1.** adv. dazwischen; **2.** prp. zwischen, unter.

**bevel** ['bevəl] schräg, schief.

**beverage** ['bevəridʒ] Getränk n.

**bevy** ['bevi] Schwarm m; Schar f.

**bewail** [bi'weil] be-, wehklagen.

**beware** [bi'weə] sich hüten (of vor).

**bewilder** [bi'wildə] irremachen; verwirren; bestürzt machen; ~ment [~əmənt] Verwirrung f; Bestürzung f.

**bewitch** [bi'witʃ] bezaubern, behexen.

**beyond** [bi'jɔnd] **1.** adv. darüber hinaus; **2.** prp. jenseits, über (... hinaus); mehr als; außer.

**bi...** [bai] zwei...

**bias** ['baiəs] **1.** adj. u. adv. schief, schräg; **2.** Neigung f; Vorurteil n; **3.** beeinflussen; ~ed befangen.

**bib** [bib] (Sabber)Lätzchen n.

**Bible** ['baibl] Bibel f.

**biblical** □ ['biblikəl] biblisch; Bibel...

**bibliography** [bibli'ɔgrəfi] Bibliographie f.

**bicarbonate** /⚗ [bai'kɑːbənit] doppeltkohlensaures Natron.

**biceps** ['baiseps] Bizeps m.

**bicker** ['bikə] (sich) zanken; flakkern; plätschern; prasseln.

**bicycle** ['baisikl] **1.** Fahrrad n; **2.** radfahren, radeln.

**bid** [bid] **1.** [irr.] gebieten, befehlen; (ent)bieten; Karten: reizen; ~ fair versprechen; ~ farewell Lebewohl sagen; **2.** Gebot n, Angebot n; ~den ['bidn] p.p. von bid **1.**

**bide** [baid] [irr.]: ~ one's time den rechten Augenblick abwarten.

**biennial** [bai'eniəl] zweijährig.

**bier** [biə] (Toten)Bahre f.

**big** [big] groß; erwachsen; schwanger; F wichtig(tuerisch); ~ business Großunternehmertum n; ~ shot F hohes Tier; ~ stick Am. Macht (-entfaltung) f; talk ~ den Mund vollnehmen.

**bigamy** ['bigəmi] Doppelehe f.

**bigot** ['bigət] Frömmler(in); blinder Anhänger; ~ry [~tri] Frömmelei f.

**bigwig** F ['bigwig] hohes Tier (P.).

**bike** F [baik] (Fahr)Rad n.

**bilateral** □ [bai'lætərəl] zweiseitig.

**bile** [bail] Galle f (a. fig.).

**bilious** □ ['biljəs] gallig (a. fig.).

**bill¹** [bil] Schnabel m; Spitze f.

**bill²** [~] **1.** Gesetzentwurf m; Klage-, Rechtsschrift f; a. ~ of exchange Wechsel m; Zettel m; Am. Banknote f; ~ of fare Speisekarte f; ~ of lading Seefrachtbrief m, Konnossement n; ~ of sale Kaufvertrag m; ♀ of Rights englische Freiheitsurkunde (1689); Am. die ersten 10 Zusatzartikel zur Verfassung der USA; **2.** (durch Anschlag) ankündigen.

**billboard** Am. ['bilbɔːd] Anschlagbrett n.

**billfold** Am. ['bilfould] Brieftasche f für Papiergeld.

**billiards** ['biljədz] pl. od. sg. Billiard(spiel) n.

**billion** ['biljən] Billion f; Am. Milliarde f.

**billow** ['bilou] **1.** Woge f (a. fig.); **2.** wogen; ~y [~oui] wogend.

**billy** Am. ['bili] (Gummi)Knüppel m.

**bin** [bin] Kasten *m*, Behälter *m*.
**bind** [baind] [*irr.*] *v/t.* (an-, ein-, um-, auf-, fest-, ver)binden; verpflichten; *Handel* abschließen; *Saum* einfassen; *v/i.* binden; **~er** ['baində] Binder *m*; Binde *f*; **~ing** [**~**diŋ] **1.** bindend; **2.** Binden *n*; Einband *m*; Einfassung *f*.
**binocular** [bi'nɔkjulə] *mst* **~s** *pl.* Feldstecher *m*, Fern-, Opernglas *n*.
**biography** [bai'ɔgrəfi] Biographie *f*.
**biology** [bai'ɔlədʒi] Biologie *f*.
**biped** *zo.* ['baiped] Zweifüßer *m*.
**birch** [bə:tʃ] **1.** *♀* Birke *f*; (Birken-) Rute *f*; **2.** mit der Rute züchtigen.
**bird** [bə:d] Vogel *m*; **~'s-eye** ['bə:dzai]: **~** view Vogelperspektive *f*.
**birth** [bə:θ] Geburt *f*; Ursprung *m*; Entstehung *f*; Herkunft *f*; **bring to ~** entstehen lassen, veranlassen; **give ~ to** gebären, zur Welt bringen; **~ control** Geburtenregelung *f*; **~day** ['bə:θdei] Geburtstag *m*; **~place** Geburtsort *m*.
**biscuit** ['biskit] Zwieback *m*; Keks *m*, *n*; Biskuit *n* (*Porzellan*).
**bishop** ['biʃəp] Bischof *m*; Läufer *m* im *Schach*; **~ric** [**~**prik] Bistum *n*.
**bison** *zo.* ['baisn] Wisent *m*.
**bit** [bit] **1.** Bißchen *n*, Stückchen *n*; Gebiß *n am Zaum*; *Schlüssel*-Bart *m*; *a* (*little*) **~** ein (kleines) bißchen; **2.** zäumen; zügeln; **3.** *pret. von* bite 2.
**bitch** [bitʃ] Hündin *f*; V Hure *f*.
**bite** [bait] **1.** Beißen *n*; Biß *m*; Bissen *m*; *⊕* Fassen *n*; **2.** [*irr.*] (an)beißen; brennen (*Pfeffer*); schneiden (*Kälte*); *⊕* fassen; *fig.* verletzen.
**bitten** ['bitn] *p.p. von* bite 2.
**bitter** ['bitə] **1.** □ bitter; streng; *fig.* verbittert; **2.** **~s** *pl.* Magenbitter *m*.
**biz** F [biz] Geschäft *n*.
**blab** F [blæb] (aus)schwatzen.
**black** [blæk] **1.** □ schwarz; dunkel; finster; **~** eye blaues Auge; **2.** schwärzen; wichsen; **~** out verdunkeln; **3.** Schwarz *n*; Schwärze *f*; Schwarze(r *m*) *f* (*Neger*); **~amoor** ['blækəmuə] Neger *m*; **~berry** Brombeere *f*; **~bird** Amsel *f*; **~board** Wandtafel *f*; **~en** [**~**kən] *v/t.* schwärzen; *fig.* anschwärzen; *v/i.* schwarz werden; **~guard** ['blægɑ:d] **1.** Lump *m*, Schuft *m*; **2.** □ schuftig; **~head** *♣* Mitesser *m*; **~ing** [**~**kiŋ] Schuhwichse *f*; **~ish** [**~**iʃ] schwärzlich; **~jack 1.** *bsd. Am.* Totschläger *m* (*Instrument*); **2.** niederknüppeln; **~leg** Betrüger *m*; **~letter** *typ.* Fraktur *f*; **~mail 1.** Erpressung *f*; **2.** *j-n* erpressen; **~ market** schwarzer Markt; **~ness** [**~**knis] Schwärze *f*; **~out** Verdunkelung *f*; **~ pudding** Blutwurst *f*; **~smith** Grobschmied *m*.

**bladder** *anat.* ['blædə] Blase *f*.
**blade** [bleid] Blatt *n*, *♀* Halm *m*; *Säge-, Schulter- etc.* Blatt *n*; Propellerflügel *m*; Klinge *f*.
**blame** [bleim] **1.** Tadel *m*; Schuld *f*; **2.** tadeln; *be to ~ for* schuld sein an (*dat.*); **~ful** ['bleimful] tadelnswert; **~less** □ [**~**mlis] tadellos.
**blanch** [blɑ:ntʃ] bleichen; erbleichen (lassen); **~** over beschönigen.
**bland** □ [blænd] mild, sanft.
**blank** [blæŋk] **1.** □ blank; leer; unausgefüllt; unbeschrieben; *⊕* Blanko...; verdutzt; **~** *cartridge* *⚔* Platzpatrone *f*; **2.** Weiße *n*; Leere *f*; leerer Raum; Lücke *f*; unbeschriebenes Blatt, Formular *n*; Niete *f*.
**blanket** ['blæŋkit] **1.** Wolldecke *f*; *wet ~ fig.* Dämpfer *m*; Spielverderber *m*; **2.** (mit e-r Wolldecke) zudecken; **3.** *Am.* umfassend, Gesamt...
**blare** [blɛə] schmettern; grölen.
**blasphem|e** [blæs'fi:m] lästern (*against or acc.*); **~y** ['blæsfimi] Gotteslästerung *f*.
**blast** [blɑ:st] **1.** Windstoß *m*; Ton *m* *e-s Blasinstruments*; *⊕* Gebläse (-luft *f*) *n*; Luftdruck *m* *e-r Explosion*; *♀* Meltau *m*; **2.** (in die Luft) sprengen; zerstören (*a. fig.*); **~** (*it*)! verdammt; **~furnace** *⊕* ['blɑ:st'fə:nis] Hochofen *m*.
**blatant** □ ['bleitənt] lärmend.
**blather** *Am.* ['blæðə] schwätzen.
**blaze** [bleiz] **1.** Flamme(n *pl.*) *f*; Feuer *n*; **~s** *pl. sl.* Teufel *m*, Hölle *f*; heller Schein; *fig.* Ausbruch *m*; *go to ~s!* zum Teufel mit dir!; **2.** *v/i.* brennen, flammen, lodern; leuchten; *v/t.* **~** *abroad* ausposaunen; **~r** ['bleizə] Blazer *m*.
**blazon** ['bleizn] Wappen(kunde *f*) *n*.
**bleach** [bli:tʃ] bleichen; **~er** ['bli:tʃə] Bleicher(in); *mst* **~s** *pl. Am.* nichtüberdachte Zuschauerplätze.
**bleak** □ [bli:k] öde, kahl; rauh; *fig.* trüb, freudlos, finster.
**blear** [bliə] **1.** trüb; **2.** trüben; **~eyed** ['bliəraid] triefäugig.
**bleat** [bli:t] **1.** Blöken *n*; **2.** blöken.
**bleb** [bleb] Bläs-chen *n*, Pustel *f*.
**bled** [bled] *pret. u. p.p. von* bleed.
**bleed** [bli:d] [*irr.*] *v/i.* bluten; *v/t.* zur Ader lassen; *fig.* schröpfen; **~ing** ['bli:diŋ] **1.** Bluten *n*; Aderlaß *m*; **2.** *sl.* verflixt.
**blemish** ['blemiʃ] **1.** Fehler *m*; Makel *m*, Schande *f*; **2.** verunstalten; brandmarken.
**blench** [blentʃ] *v/i.* zurückschrecken; *v/t.* die Augen schließen vor.
**blend** [blend] **1.** [*irr.*] (sich) (ver-)mischen; *Wein etc.* verschneiden; **2.** Mischung *f*; *♣* Verschnitt *m*.
**blent** [blent] *pret. u. p.p. von* blend 1.
**bless** [bles] segnen; preisen; be-

glücken; ~ me! herrje!; ~ed □ [*pret. u. p.p.* blest; *adj.* 'blesid] glückselig; gesegnet; ~ing [~siŋ] Segen *m*.

**blew** [blu:] *pret. von* blow² *u.* blow³1.

**blight** [blait] **1.** ♀ Mehltau *m*; *fig.* Gifthauch *m*; **2.** vernichten.

**blind** □ [blaind] **1.** blind (*fig.* to gegen); geheim; nicht erkennbar; ~ alley Sackgasse *f*; ~ly *fig.* blindlings; **2.** Blende *f*; *Fenster*-Vorhang *m*, Jalousie *f*; *Am.* Versteck *n*; Vorwand *m*; **3.** blenden; verblenden (to gegen); abblenden; ~fold ['blaindfould] **1.** blindlings; **2.** j-m die Augen verbinden; ~worm Blindschleiche *f*.

**blink** [bliŋk] **1.** Blinzeln *n*; Schimmer *m*; **2.** v/i. blinzeln; blinken; schimmern; v/t. absichtlich übersehen; ~er ['bliŋkə] Scheuklappe *f*.

**bliss** [blis] Seligkeit *f*, Wonne *f*.

**blister** ['blistə] **1.** Blase *f* (*auf der Haut, im Lack*); Zugpflaster *n*; **2.** Blasen bekommen *od.* ziehen (auf *dat.*).

**blithe** □ *mst poet.* [blaið] lustig.

**blizzard** ['blizəd] Schneesturm *m*.

**bloat** [blout] aufblasen; aufschwellen; ~er ['bloutə] Bückling *m*.

**block** [blɔk] **1.** (*Häuser-, Schreib-etc.*)Block *m*; Klotz *m*; Druckstock *m*; Verstopfung *f*, Stockung *f*; **2.** formen; verhindern; ~ in entwerfen, skizzieren; *mst* ~ up (ab-, ver-) sperren; blockieren.

**blockade** [blɔ'keid] **1.** Blockade *f*; **2.** blockieren.

**block|head** ['blɔkhed] Dummkopf *m*; ~ letters Druckschrift *f*.

**blond(e** *f*) [blɔnd] **1.** blond; **2.** Blondine *f*.

**blood** [blʌd] Blut *n*; *fig.* Blut *n*; Abstammung *f*; in cold ~ kalten Blutes, kaltblütig; ~-curdling ['blʌdkə:dliŋ] haarsträubend; ~horse Vollblutpferd *n*; ~shed Blutvergießen *n*; ~shot blutunterlaufen; ~thirsty blutdürstig; ~vessel Blutgefäß *n*; ~y □ ['blʌdi] blutig; blutdürstig.

**bloom** [blu:m] **1.** Blüte *f*; Reif *m auf Früchten*; *fig.* Schmelz *m*; **2.** (er-) blühen (*a. fig.*).

**blossom** ['blɔsəm] **1.** Blüte *f*; **2.** blühen.

**blot** [blɔt] **1.** Klecks *m*; *fig.* Makel *m*; **2.** v/t. beklecksen, beflecken; (ab-) löschen; ausstreichen; v/i. klecksen.

**blotch** [blɔtʃ] Pustel *f*; Fleck *m*.

**blotter** ['blɔtə] Löscher *m*; *Am.* Protokollbuch *n*. [Löschpapier *n*.]

**blotting-paper** ['blɔtiŋpeipə]

**blouse** [blauz] Bluse *f*.

**blow**¹ [blou] Schlag *m*, Stoß *m*.

**blow**² [~] [*irr.*] blühen.

**blow**³ [~] **1.** v/i. blasen; wehen; schnaufen; ~ up in die Luft fliegen; v/t. (weg- *etc.*)blasen; wehen; ⚡

durchbrennen; ~ one's nose sich die Nase putzen; ~ up sprengen; **2.** Blasen *n*, Wehen *n*; ~er ['blouə] Bläser *m*.

**blown** [bloun] *p.p. von* blow² *und* blow³ 1.

**blow|-out** *mot.* ['blouaut] Reifenpanne *f*; ~pipe Gebläsebrenner *m*.

**bludgeon** ['blʌdʒən] Knüppel *m*.

**blue** [blu:] **1.** □ blau; F trüb, schwermütig; **2.** Blau *n*; **3.** blau färben; blauen; ~bird ['blu:bə:d] amerikanische Singdrossel; ~ laws *Am.* strenge (puritanische) Gesetze; ~s [blu:z] *pl.* Trübsinn *m*; ♪ Blues *m*.

**bluff** [blʌf] **1.** □ schroff; steil; derb; **2.** Steilufer *n*; Irreführung *f*; **3.** bluffen, irreführen.

**bluish** ['blu(:)iʃ] bläulich.

**blunder** ['blʌndə] **1.** Fehler *m*, Schnitzer *m*; **2.** e-n Fehler machen; stolpern; stümpern; verpfuschen.

**blunt** [blʌnt] **1.** □ stumpf (*a. fig.*); plump, grob, derb; **2.** abstumpfen.

**blur** [blə:] **1.** Fleck(en) *m*; *fig.* Verschwommenheit *f*; **2.** v/t. beflecken; verwischen; *Sinn* trüben.

**blush** [blʌʃ] **1.** Schamröte *f*; Erröten *n*; flüchtiger Blick; **2.** erröten; (sich) röten.

**bluster** ['blʌstə] **1.** Brausen *n*, Getöse *n*; Prahlerei *f*; **2.** brausen; prahlen.

**boar** [bɔ:] Eber *m*; *hunt.* Keiler *m*.

**board** [bɔ:d] **1.** (Anschlag)Brett *n*; Konferenztisch *m*; Ausschuß *m*; Gremium *n*; Behörde *f*; Verpflegung *f*; Pappe *f*; on ~ a train *Am.* in e-m Zug; ♀ of Trade Handelsministerium *n*; **2.** v/t. dielen, verschalen; beköstigen; an Bord gehen; ⚓ entern; *bsd. Am.* einsteigen in (*ein Fahr- od. Flugzeug*); v/i. in Kost sein; ~er ['bɔ:də] Kostgänger(in); Internatsschüler(in); ~ing-house ['bɔ:diŋhaus] Pension *f*; ~ing-school ['bɔ:diŋsku:l] Internatsschule *f*; ~walk *bsd. Am.* Strandpromenade *f*.

**boast** [boust] **1.** Prahlerei *f*; **2.** (of, about) sich rühmen (*gen.*), prahlen (mit); ~ful □ ['boustful] prahlerisch.

**boat** [bout] Boot *n*; Schiff *n*; ~ing ['boutiŋ] Bootfahrt *f*.

**bob** [bɔb] **1.** Quaste *f*; Ruck *m*; Knicks *m*; Schopf *m*; *sl.* Schilling *m*; **2.** v/t. Haar stutzen; ~bed hair Bubikopf *m*; v/i. springen, tanzen; knicksen.

**bobbin** ['bɔbin] Spule *f* (*a.* ⚡).

**bobble** *Am.* F ['bɔbl] Fehler *m*.

**bobby** *sl.* ['bɔbi] Schupo *m*, Polizist *m*.

**bobsleigh** ['bɔbslei] Bob(sleigh) *m* (*Rennschlitten*).

**bode**¹ [boud] prophezeien.

**bode**² [~] *pret. von* bide.

**bodice** ['bɔdis] Mieder n; Taille f.
**bodily** ['bɔdili] körperlich.
**body** ['bɔdi] Körper m, Leib m; Leichnam m; Körperschaft f; Hauptteil m; mot. Karosserie f; ✗ Truppenkörper m; **~-guard** Leibwache f.
**Boer** ['bouə] Bure m; attr. Buren...
**bog** [bɔg] 1. Sumpf m, Moor m; 2. im Schlamm versenken.
**boggle** ['bɔgl] stutzen; pfuschen.
**bogus** ['bougəs] falsch; Schwindel...
**boil** [bɔil] 1. kochen, sieden, (sich) kondensieren; 2. Sieden n; Beule f, Geschwür n; **~er** ['bɔilə] (Dampf-) Kessel m.
**boisterous** □ ['bɔistərəs] ungestüm; heftig, laut; lärmend.
**bold** □ [bould] kühn; keck, dreist; steil; typ. fett; make ~ sich erkühnen; **~ness** ['bouldnis] Kühnheit f; Keckheit f, Dreistigkeit f.
**bolster** ['boulstə] 1. Kopfkeil m; Unterlage f; 2. polstern; (unter-) stützen.
**bolt** [boult] 1. Bolzen m; Riegel m; Blitz(strahl) m; Ausreißen n; 2. adv. ~ upright kerzengerade; 3. v/t. verriegeln; F hinunterschlingen; sieben; v/i. eilen; durchgehen (Pferd) Am. pol. abtrünnig werden; **~er** ['boultə] Ausreißer(in).
**bomb** [bɔm] 1. Bombe f; 2. mit Bomben belegen.
**bombard** [bɔm'ba:d] bombardieren.
**bombastic** [bɔm'bæstik] schwülstig.
**bomb-proof** ['bɔmpru:f] bombensicher.
**bond** [bɔnd] Band n; Fessel f; Bündnis n; Schuldschein m; ↑ Obligation f; in ~ ✝ unter Zollverschluß; **~age** ['bɔndidʒ] Hörigkeit f; Knechtschaft f; **~(s)man** [~d(z)mən] Leibeigene(r) m.
**bone** [boun] 1. Knochen m; Gräte f; ~s pl. a. Gebeine n/pl.; ~ of contention Zankapfel m; make no ~s about F nicht lange fackeln mit; 2. die Knochen auslösen (aus); aus-, entgräten.
**bonfire** ['bɔnfaiə] Freudenfeuer n.
**bonnet** ['bɔnit] Haube f, Schute(nhut m) f; ⊕ (Motor)Haube f.
**bonus** ✝ ['bounəs] Prämie f; Gratifikation f; Zulage f.
**bony** ['bouni] knöchern; knochig.
**boob** Am. ['bu:b] Dummkopf m.
**booby** ['bu:bi] Tölpel m.
**book** [buk] 1. Buch n; Heft n; Liste f; Block m; 2. buchen; eintragen; Fahrkarte etc. lösen; e-n Platz etc. bestellen; Gepäck aufgeben; **~-burner** Am. F ['bukbə:nə] intoleranter Mensch; **~case** Bücherschrank m; **~ing-clerk** ['bukiŋklɑ:k] Schalterbeamt|e(r) m, -in f; **~ing-office** ['bukiŋɔfis] Fahrkartenausgabe f, -schalter m; thea.

Kasse f; **~ish** □ [~iʃ] gelehrt; **~keeping** Buchführung f; **~let** ['buklit] Büchlein n; Broschüre f; **~seller** Buchhändler m.
**boom¹** [bu:m] 1. ✝ Aufschwung m, Hochkonjunktur f, Hausse f; Reklamerummel m; 2. in die Höhe treiben od. gehen; für et. Reklame machen.
**boom²** [~] brummen; dröhnen.
**boon¹** [bu:n] Segen m, Wohltat f.
**boon²** [~] freundlich, munter.
**boor** fig. [buə] Bauer m, Lümmel m; **~ish** □ ['buəriʃ] bäuerisch, lümmel-, flegelhaft.
**boost** [hu:st] heben; verstärken (a. ⚡); Reklame machen.
**boot¹** [bu:t]: to ~ obendrein.
**boot²** [~] Stiefel m; Kofferraum m; **~black** Am. ['bu:tblæk] = shoeblack; **~ee** ['bu:ti:] Damen-Halbstiefel m.
**booth** [bu:ð] (Markt- etc.)Bude f; Wahlzelle f; Am. Fernsprechzelle f.
**boot|lace** ['bu:tleis] Schnürsenkel m; **~legger** Am. [~legə] Alkoholschmuggler m.
**booty** ['bu:ti] Beute f, Raub m.
**border** ['bɔ:də] 1. Rand m, Saum m; Grenze f, Einfassung f; Rabatte f; 2. einfassen; grenzen (upon an acc.).
**bore¹** [bɔ:] 1. Bohrloch n; Kaliber n; fig. langweiliger Mensch; Plage f; 2. bohren; langweilen; belästigen.
**bore²** [~] pret. von bear².
**born** [bɔ:n] p.p. von bear² gebären.
**borne** [bɔ:n] p.p. von bear² tragen.
**borough** ['bʌrə] Stadt(teil m) f; Am. a. Wahlbezirk m von New York City; municipal ~ Stadtgemeinde f.
**borrow** ['bɔrou] borgen, entleihen.
**bosom** ['buzəm] Busen m; fig. Schoß m.
**boss** F [bɔs] 1. Boss m, Chef m; bsd. Am. pol. (Partei)Bonze m; 2. leiten; **~y** Am. F ['bɔsi] tyrannisch; herrisch.
**botany** ['bɔtəni] Botanik f.
**botch** [bɔtʃ] 1. Flicken m; Flickwerk n; 2. flicken; verpfuschen.
**both** [bouθ] beide(s); ~ ... and sowohl ... als (auch).
**bother** F ['bɔðə] 1. Plage f; 2. (sich) plagen, (sich) quälen.
**bottle** ['bɔtl] 1. Flasche f; 2. auf Flaschen ziehen.
**bottom** ['bɔtəm] 1. Boden m, Grund m; Grundfläche f, Fuß m, Ende n; F Hintern m; fig. Wesen n, Kern m; at the ~ ganz unten; fig. im Grunde; 2. grundlegend, Grund...
**bough** [bau] Ast m, Zweig m.
**bought** [bɔ:t] pret. u. p.p von buy.
**boulder** ['bouldə] Geröllblock m.
**bounce** [bauns] 1. Sprung m, Rückprall m; F Aufschneiderei f; Auftrieb m; 2. (hoch)springen; F aufschneiden; **~r** ['baunsə] F Mordskerl m; Am. sl. Rausschmeißer m.

**bound¹** [baund] **1.** *pret. u. p.p von* *bind*; **2.** *adj.* verpflichtet; bestimmt, unterwegs (*for* nach).

**bound²** [⁓] **1.** Grenze *f*, Schranke *f*; **2.** begrenzen; beschränken.

**bound³** [⁓] **1.** Sprung *m*; **2.** (hoch-)springen; an-, abprallen.

**boundary** ['baundəri] Grenze *f*.

**boundless** □ ['baundlis] grenzenlos.

**bount|eous** ⁓ ['bauntiəs], **⁓iful** □ [⁓iful] freigebig; reichlich.

**bounty** ['baunti] Freigebigkeit *f*; Spende *f*; ✝ Prämie *f*.

**bouquet** ['bukei] Bukett *n*, Strauß *m*; Blume *f des Weines*.

**bout** [baut] *Fecht*-Gang *m*; *Tanz*-Tour *f*; ⚔ Anfall *m*; Kraftprobe *f*.

**bow¹** [bau] **1.** Verbeugung *f*; **2.** *v/i.* sich (ver)beugen; *v/t.* biegen; beugen.

**bow²** ⚓ [⁓] Bug *m*.

**bow³** [bou] **1.** Bogen *m*; Schleife *f*; **2.** geigen.

**bowdlerize** ['baudləraiz] *Text* von anstößigen Stellen reinigen.

**bowels** ['bauəlz] *pl.* Eingeweide *n*; *das* Innere; *fig.* Herz *n*.

**bower** ['bauə] Laube *f*.

**bowl¹** [boul] Schale *f*, Schüssel *f*; *Pfeifen*-Kopf *m*.

**bowl²** [⁓] **1.** Kugel *f*; **⁓s** *pl.* Bowling *n*; **2.** *v/t.* Ball *etc.* werfen; *v/i.* rollen; kegeln.

**box¹** [boks] Buchsbaum *m*; Büchse *f*, Schachtel *f*, Kasten *m*; Koffer *m*; ⊕ Gehäuse *n*; *thea.* Loge *f*; Abteilung *f*; **2.** in Kästen *etc.* tun.

**box²** [⁓] **1.** boxen; **2.**: ⁓ *on the ear* Ohrfeige *f*.

**Boxing-Day** ['boksiŋdei] zweiter Weihnachtsfeiertag.

**box|-keeper** ['bokski:pə] Logenschließer(in); **⁓-office** Theaterkasse *f*.

**boy** [boi] Junge *m*, junger Mann; Bursche *m* (*a. Diener*); **⁓-friend** Freund *m*; ⁓ *scout* Pfadfinder *m*; **⁓hood** ['boihud] Knabenalter *n*; **⁓ish** □ ['boiiʃ] knabenhaft; kindisch.

**brace** [breis] **1.** ⊕ Strebe *f*; Stützbalken *m*; Klammer *f*; Paar *n* (*Wild, Geflügel*); **⁓s** *pl.* Hosenträger *m/pl.*; **2.** absteifen; verankern; (an)spannen; *fig.* stärken.

**bracelet** ['breislit] Armband *n*.

**bracket** ['brækit] **1.** ⚒ Konsole *f*; Winkelstütze *f*; *typ.* Klammer *f*; *Leuchter*-Arm *m*; *lower income* ⁓ niedrige Einkommensstufe; **2.** einklammern; *fig.* gleichstellen.

**brackish** ['brækiʃ] brackig, salzig.

**brag** [bræg] **1.** Prahlerei *f*; **2.** prahlen. [**2.** □ prahlerisch.\]

**braggart** ['brægət] **1.** Prahler *m*;|

**braid** [breid] **1.** *Haar*-Flechte *f*; Borte *f*; Tresse *f*; **2.** flechten; mit Borte besetzen.

**brain** [brein] **1.** Gehirn *n*; Kopf *m* (*fig. mst* ⁓s = Verstand); **2.** *j-m* den Schädel einschlagen; **⁓-pan** ['brein-pæn] Hirnschale *f*; **⁓(s)** *trust* Am. [⁓n(z)trast] Expertenrat *m* (*mst pol.*); **⁓-wave** F Geistesblitz *m*.

**brake** [breik] **1.** ⊕ Bremse *f*; **2.** bremsen; **⁓(s)man** ✄ ['breik(s)-mən] Bremser *m*; *Am.* Schaffner *m*.

**bramble** ['bræmbl] Brombeerstrauch *m*.

**bran** [bræn] Kleie *f*.

**branch** [braːntʃ] **1.** Zweig *m*; Fach *n*; Linie *f des Stammbaumes*; Zweigstelle *f*; **2.** sich ver-, abzweigen.

**brand** [brænd] **1.** (Feuer)Brand *m*; Brandmal *n*; Marke *f*; Sorte *f*; **2.** einbrennen; brandmarken.

**brandish** ['brændiʃ] schwingen.

**bran(d)-new** ['bræn(d)'nju:] nagelneu.

**brandy** ['brændi] Kognak *m*; Weinbrand *m*.

**brass** [braːs] Messing *n*; F Unverschämtheit *f*; ⁓ *band* Blechblaskapelle *f*; ⁓ *knuckles pl. Am.* Schlagring *m*.

**brassière** ['bræsiə] Büstenhalter *m*.

**brave** [breiv] **1.** tapfer; prächtig; **2.** trotzen; mutig begegnen (*dat.*); **⁓ry** ['breivəri] Tapferkeit *f*; Pracht *f*.

**brawl** [brɔːl] **1.** Krakeel *m*, Krawall *m*; **2.** krakeelen, Krawall machen.

**brawny** ['brɔːni] muskulös.

**bray¹** [brei] **1.** Eselsschrei *m*; **2.** schreien; schmettern; dröhnen.

**bray²** [⁓] (zer)stoßen, zerreiben.

**brazen** □ ['breizˈn] bronzen; metallisch; *a.* **⁓-faced** unverschämt.

**Brazilian** [brəˈziljən] **1.** brasilianisch; **2.** Brasilianer(in).

**breach** [briːtʃ] **1.** Bruch *m*; *fig.* Verletzung *f*; ✗ Bresche *f*; **2.** *e-e* Bresche schlagen in (*acc.*).

**bread** [bred] Brot *n*; *know which side one's* ⁓ *is buttered* s-n Vorteil (er)kennen.

**breadth** [bredθ] Breite *f*, Weite *f*, Größe *f des Geistes*; *Tuch*-Bahn *f*.

**break** [breik] **1.** Bruch *m*; Lücke *f*; Pause *f*; Absatz *m*; ✝ *Am.* (Preis-)Rückgang *m*; *Tages*-Anbruch *m*; *a bad* ⁓ F *e-e* Dummheit; Pech *n*; *a lucky* ⁓ Glück *n*; **2.** [*irr.*] *v/t.* (zer)brechen; unterbrechen; übertreten; *Tier* abrichten; *Bank* sprengen; *Brief* erbrechen; *Tür* aufbrechen; abbrechen; *Vorrat* anbrechen; *Nachricht* schonend mitteilen; ruinieren; ⁓ *up* zerbrechen; auflösen; *v/i.* (zer)brechen; auslos-, an-, auf-, hervorbrechen; umschlagen (*Wetter*); ⁓ *away* sich losreißen; ⁓ *down* zs.-brechen; steckenbleiben; versagen; **⁓able** ['breikəbl] zerbrechlich; **⁓age** [⁓kidʒ] (*a.* ✝ *Waren*)Bruch *m*; **⁓down** Zs.-bruch *m*; Maschinen-

schaden *m*; *mot.* Pannc *f*; **~fast**
['brekfəst] 1. Frühstück *n*; 2. früh-
stücken; **~up** ['breik'ʌp] Verfall
*m*; Auflösung *f*; Schulschluß *m*;
**~water** ['~kwɔːtə] Wellenbrecher
*m*.

**breast** [brest] Brust *f*; Busen *m*;
Herz *n*; *make a clean ~ of s.th. et.*
offen gestehen; **~-stroke** ['brest-
strouk] Brustschwimmen *n*.

**breath** [breθ] Atem(zug) *m*; Hauch
*m*; *waste one's ~* s-e Worte verschwenden; **~e** [briːð] *v/i.* atmen;
*fig.* leben; *v/t.* (aus-, ein)atmen;
hauchen; flüstern; **~less** □ ['breθ-
lis] atemlos.

**bred** [bred] *pret. u. p.p. von*
*breed* 2.

**breeches** ['britʃiz] *pl.* Knie-, Reit-
hosen *f/pl.*

**breed** [briːd] 1. Zucht *f*; Rasse *f*;
Herkunft *f*; *Am.* Mischling *m bsd.*
*weiß-indianisch*; 2. [*irr.*] *v/t.* erzeugen; auf-, erziehen; züchten; *v/i.*
sich fortpflanzen; **~er** ['briːdə] Er-
zeuger(in); Züchter(in); **~ing** [~diŋ]
Erziehung *f*; Bildung *f*; (Tier-)
Zucht *f*.

**breeze** [briːz] Brise *f*; **~y** ['briːzi]
windig, luftig; frisch, flott.

**brethren** ['breðrin] *pl.* Brüder *m/pl.*

**brevity** ['breviti] Kürze *f*.

**brew** [bruː] 1. *v/t. u. v/i.* brauen;
zubereiten; *fig.* anzetteln; 2. Gebräu *n*; **~ery** ['bruəri] Brauerei *f*.

**briar** ['braiə] = *brier*.

**brib|e** [braib] 1. Bestechung(sgeld
*n*, -sgeschenk *n*) *f*; 2. bestechen;
**~ery** ['braibəri] Bestechung *f*.

**brick** [brik] 1. Ziegel(stein) *m*; *drop*
*a ~ sl.* ins Fettnäpfchen treten;
2. mauern; **~layer** ['brikleiə] Maurer *m*; **~works** *sg.* Ziegelei *f*.

**bridal** □ ['braidl] bräutlich; Braut-
...; *~ procession* Brautzug *m*.

**bride** [braid] Braut *f*, Neuvermählte
*f*; **~groom** ['braidgrum] Bräutigam
*m*, Neuvermählte(r) *m*; **~smaid**
[~dzmeid] Brautjungfer *f*.

**bridge** [bridʒ] 1. Brücke *f*; 2. e-e
Brücke schlagen über (*acc.*); *fig.*
überbrücken.

**bridle** ['braidl] 1. Zaum *m*; Zügel
*m*; 2. *v/t.* (auf)zäumen; zügeln; *v/i.*
*a. ~ up* den Kopf zurückwerfen;
**~path**, **~road** Reitweg *m*.

**brief** [briːf] 1. □ kurz, bündig; 2. ⚖
schriftliche Instruktion; *hold a ~*
*for* einstehen für; **~case** ['briːf-
keis] Aktenmappe *f*.

**brier** ⚘ ['braiə] Dorn-, Hagebutten-
strauch *m*, wilde Rose.

**brigade** ⚔ [bri'geid] Brigade *f*.

**bright** □ [brait] hell, glänzend, klar;
lebhaft; gescheit; **~en** ['braitn] *v/t.*
auf-, erhellen; polieren; aufheitern;
*v/i.* sich aufhellen; **~ness** [~nis]
Helligkeit *f*; Glanz *m*; Klarheit *f*;
Heiterkeit *f*; Aufgewecktheit *f*.

**brillian|ce**, **~cy** ['briljəns, ~si]
Glanz *m*; **~t** [~nt] 1. □ glänzend;
prächtig; 2. Brillant *m*.

**brim** [brim] 1. Rand *m*; Krempe *f*;
2. bis zum Rande füllen *od.* voll
sein; **~full**, **~-ful** ['brim'ful] ganz
voll; **~stone** † ['brimstən] Schwefel
*m*.

**brindle(d)** ['brindl(d)] scheckig.

**brine** [brain] Salzwasser *n*, Sole *f*.

**bring** [briŋ] [*irr.*] bringen; *j.* veranlassen; *Klage* erheben; *Grund etc.*
vorbringen; *~ about*, *~ to pass* zustande bringen; *~ down Preis* herabsetzen; *~ forth* hervorbringen; gebären; *~ home to j.* überzeugen; *~*
*round* wieder zu sich bringen; *~ up*
auf-, erziehen.

**brink** [briŋk] Rand *m*.

**brisk** □ [brisk] lebhaft, munter;
frisch; flink; belebend.

**bristl|e** ['brisl] 1. Borste *f*; 2. (sich)
sträuben; hochfahren, zornig wer-
den; *~ with fig.* starren von; **~ed**,
**~y** [~li] gesträubt; struppig.

**British** ['britiʃ] britisch; *the ~ pl.* die
Briten *pl.*; **~er** *bsd. Am.* [~ʃə] Ein-
wohner(in) Großbritanniens.

**brittle** ['britl] zerbrechlich, spröde.

**broach** [broutʃ] *Faß* anzapfen; vorbringen; *Thema* anschneiden.

**broad** □ [brɔːd] breit; weit; hell
(*Tag*); deutlich (*Wink etc.*); derb
(*Witz*); allgemein; weitherzig, liberal; **~cast** ['brɔːdkɑːst] 1. weitverbreitet; 2. [*irr.* (cast)] weit verbreiten; *Radio:* senden; 3. Rundfunk
(-sendung *f*) *m*; **~cloth** feiner
Wollstoff; **~-minded** großzügig.

**brocade** ⊹ [brə'keid] Brokat *m*.

**broil** [brɔil] 1. Lärm *m*, Streit *m*;
2. auf dem Rost braten; *fig.*
schmoren.

**broke** [brouk] 1. *pret. von break* 2;
2. *sl.* pleite, ohne e-n Pfennig; **~n**
['broukən] 1. *p.p. von break* 2; 2.:
*~ health* zerrüttete Gesundheit.

**broker** ['broukə] Altwarenhändler
*m*; Zwangsversteigerer *m*; Makler
*m*.

**bronc(h)o** *Am.* ['brɔŋkou] (halb-)
wildes Pferd; **~-buster** [~oubʌstə]
Zureiter *m*.

**bronze** [brɔnz] 1. Bronze *f*; 2. bronzen, Bronze...; 3. bronzieren.

**brooch** [broutʃ] Brosche *f*; Spange *f*.

**brood** [bruːd] 1. Brut *f*; *attr.*
Zucht...; 2. brüten (*a. fig.*); **~er**
*Am.* ['bruːdə] Brutkasten *m*.

**brook** [bruk] Bach *m*.

**broom** [brum] Besen *m*; **~stick**
['brumstik] Besenstiel *m*.

**broth** [brɔθ] Fleischbrühe *f*.

**brothel** ['brɔθl] Bordell *n*.

**brother** ['brʌðə] Bruder *m*; *~(s) and*
*sister(s)* Geschwister *pl.*; **~hood**
[~ʃhud] Bruderschaft *f*; **~-in-law**
[~ʃrinlɔ:] Schwager *m*; **~ly** [~əli]
brüderlich.

**brought** [brɔːt] *pret. u. p.p. von* bring.

**brow** [brau] (Augen)Braue *f*; Stirn *f*; Rand *m e-s Steilhanges*; **~beat** ['braubiːt] [*irr.* (*beat*)] einschüchtern; tyrannisieren.

**brown** [braun] 1. braun; 2. Braun *n*; 3. (sich) bräunen.

**browse** [brauz] 1. Grasen *n*; *fig.* Schmökern *n*; 2. grasen, weiden; *fig.* schmökern.

**bruise** [bruːz] 1. Quetschung *f*; 2. (zer)quetschen.

**brunt** [brʌnt] Hauptstoß *m*, (volle) Wucht *f*; *das* Schwerste.

**brush** [brʌʃ] 1. Bürste *f*; Pinsel *m*; *Fuchs*-Rute *f*; Scharmützel *n*; Unterholz *n*; 2. *v/t.* (ab-, aus)bürsten; streifen; *j.* abbürsten; ~ *up* wieder aufbürsten, *fig.* auffrischen; *v/i.* bürsten; (davon)stürzen; ~ *against s.o.* j. streifen; **~wood** ['brʌʃwud] Gestrüpp *n*, Unterholz *n*.

**brusque** [brusk] brüsk, barsch.

**Brussels sprouts** ♀ ['brʌslʹsprauts] *pl.* Rosenkohl *m*.

**brut|al** □ ['bruːtl] viehisch; roh, gemein; **~ality** [bruːʹtæliti] Brutalität *f*, Roheit *f*; **~e** [bruːt] 1. tierisch; unvernünftig; gefühllos; 2. Vieh *n*; F Untier *n*, Scheusal *n*.

**bubble** ['bʌbl] 1. Blase *f*; Schwindel *m*; 2. sieden; sprudeln.

**buccaneer** [bʌkəʹniə] Seeräuber *m*.

**buck** [bʌk] 1. *zo.* Bock *m*; Stutzer *m*; *Am. sl.* Dollar *m*; 2. *v/i.* bocken; ~ *for Am.* sich bemühen um; ~ *up* F sich zs.-reißen; *v/t. Am.* F sich stemmen gegen; *Am.* F die Oberhand gewinnen wollen über *et.*

**bucket** ['bʌkit] Eimer *m*, Kübel *m*.

**buckle** ['bʌkl] 1. Schnalle *f*; 2. *v/t.* (an-, auf-, um-, zu)schnallen; *v/i.* ⊕ sich (ver)biegen; ~ *to a task* sich ernsthaft an eine Aufgabe machen.

**buck|skin** *hunt.* ['bʌkʃot] Rehposten *m*; **~skin** Wildleder *n*.

**bud** [bʌd] 1. Knospe *f*; *fig.* Keim *m*; 2. *v/t.* ✔ veredeln; *v/i.* knospen.

**buddy** *Am.* F ['bʌdi] Kamerad *m*.

**budge** [bʌdʒ] (sich) bewegen.

**budget** ['bʌdʒit] Vorrat *m*; Staatshaushalt *m*; *draft* ~ Haushaltsplan *m*.

**buff** [bʌf] 1. Ochsenleder *n*; Lederfarbe *f*; 2. lederfarben.

**buffalo** *zo.* ['bʌfəlou] Büffel *m*.

**buffer** ⛴ ['bʌfə] Puffer *m*; Prellbock *m*.

**buffet¹** ['bʌfit] 1. Puff *m*, Stoß *m*, Schlag *m*; 2. puffen, schlagen; kämpfen.

**buffet²** [~] Büfett *n*; Anrichte *f*.

**buffet³** ['bufei] Büfett *n*, Theke *f*; Tisch *m* mit Speisen u. Getränken; Erfrischungsraum *m*.

**buffoon** [bʌʹfuːn] Possenreißer *m*.

**bug** [bʌg] Wanze *f*; *Am.* Insekt *n*, Käfer *m*; *Am. sl.* Defekt *m*, Fehler *m*; *big* ~ *sl.* hohes Tier.

**bugle** ['bjuːgl] Wald-, Signalhorn *n*.

**build** [bild] 1. [*irr.*] bauen; errichten; 2. Bauart *f*; Schnitt *m*; **~er** ['bildə] Erbauer *m*, Baumeister *m*; **~ing** [~diŋ] Erbauen *n*; Bau *m*, Gebäude *n*; *attr.* Bau...

**built** [bilt] *pret. u. p.p. von* build 1.

**bulb** [bʌlb] ♀ Zwiebel *f*, Knolle *f*; (Glüh)Birne *f*.

**bulge** [bʌldʒ] 1. (Aus)Bauchung *f*; Anschwellung *f*; 2. sich (aus)bauchen; (an)schwellen; hervorquellen.

**bulk** [bʌlk] Umfang *m*; Masse *f*; Hauptteil *m*; ⛴ Ladung *f*; *in* ~ lose; in großer Menge; **~y** ['bʌlki] umfangreich; unhandlich; ⛴ sperrig.

**bull¹** [bul] 1. Bulle *m*, Stier *m*; ✝ *sl.* Haussier *m*; 2. ✝ *die Kurse* treiben.

**bull²** [~] päpstliche Bulle.

**bulldog** ['buldɔg] Bulldogge *f*.

**bulldoze** *Am.* F ['buldouz] terrorisieren; ~**r** ⊕ [~zə] Bulldozer *m*, Planierraupe *f*.

**bullet** ['bulit] Kugel *f*, Geschoß *n*.

**bulletin** ['bulitin] Tagesbericht *m*; ~ *board Am.* Schwarzes Brett.

**bullion** ['buljən] Gold-, Silberbarren *m*; Gold-, Silberlitze *f*.

**bully** ['buli] 1. Maulheld *m*; Tyrann *m*; 2. prahlerisch; *Am.* F prima; 3. einschüchtern; tyrannisieren.

**bulwark** *mst fig.* ['bulwək] Bollwerk *n.*

**bum** *Am.* F [bʌm] 1. Nichtstuer *m*, Vagabund *m*; 2. *v/i.* nassauern.

**bumble-bee** ['bʌmblbiː] Hummel *f*.

**bump** [bʌmp] 1. Schlag *m*; Beule *f*; *fig.* Sinn *m* (of für); 2. (zs.-)stoßen; holpern; *Rudern:* überholen.

**bumper** ['bʌmpə] volles Glas (*Wein*) F *et.* Riesiges; *mot.* Stoßstange *f*; ~ *crop* Rekordernte *f*; ~ *house thea.* volles Haus.

**bun** [bʌn] Rosinenbrötchen *n*; *Haar*-Knoten *m*.

**bunch** [bʌntʃ] 1. Bund *n*; Büschel *n*; Haufen *m*; ~ *of grapes* Weintraube *f*; 2. (zs.-)bündeln; bauschen.

**bundle** ['bʌndl] 1. Bündel *n*, Bund *n*; 2. *v/t. a.* ~ *up* (zs.-)bündeln.

**bung** [bʌŋ] Spund *m*.

**bungalow** ['bʌŋgəlou] Bungalow *m* (*einstöckiges Haus*).

**bungle** ['bʌŋgl] 1. Pfuscherei *f*; 2. (ver)pfuschen.

**bunion** ⚕ ['bʌnjən] entzündeter Fußballen.

**bunk¹** *Am. sl.* [bʌŋk] Quatsch *m*.

**bunk²** [~] Schlafkoje *f*.

**bunny** ['bʌni] Kaninchen *n*.

**buoy** ⛴ [bɔi] 1. Boje *f*; 2. *Fahrwasser* betonnen; *mst* ~ *up fig.* aufrechterhalten; hebend; spannkräftig; *fig.* heiter; **~ant** □ ['bɔiənt] schwimmfähig; hebend; spannkräftig; *fig.* heiter.

**burden** ['bəːdn] 1. Last *f*; Bürde *f*; ⛴ Ladung *f*; ⛴ Tragfähigkeit *f*;

**2. beladen; belasten; ~some [~n-səm]** lästig; drückend.

**bureau [bjuə'rou]** Büro *n*, Geschäftszimmer *n*; Schreibpult *n*; *Am.* Kommode *f*; **~cracy [~'rɔ-krəsi]** Bürokratie *f*.

**burg** *Am.* F [bə:g] Stadt *f*.

**burgess ['bə:dʒis]** Bürger *m*.

**burglar ['bə:glə]** Einbrecher *m*; **~y [~əri]** Einbruch(sdiebstahl) *m*.

**burial ['beriəl]** Begräbnis *n*.

**burlesque [bə:'lesk] 1.** possenhaft; **2.** Burleske *f*, Posse *f*; **3.** parodieren.

**burly ['bə:li]** stämmig, kräftig.

**burn [bə:n] 1.** Brandwunde *f*; Brandmal *n*; **2.** *[irr.]* (ver-, an-)brennen; **~er [~'bə:nə]** Brenner *m*.

**burnish ['bə:niʃ]** polieren, glätten.

**burnt [bə:nt]** *pret. u. p.p. von* **burn 2**.

**burrow ['bʌrou] 1.** Höhle *f*, Bau *m*; **2.** (sich ein-, ver)graben.

**burst [bə:st] 1.** Bersten *n*; Krach *m*; Riß *m*; Ausbruch *m*; **2.** *[irr.]* *v/i.* bersten, platzen; zerspringen; explodieren; *~ from* sich losreißen von; *~ forth, ~ out* hervorbrechen; *~ into tears* in Tränen ausbrechen; *v/t.* (zer)sprengen.

**bury ['beri]** be-, vergraben; beerdigen; verbergen.

**bus** F [bʌs] (Omni)Bus *m*; **~ boy** *Am.* Kellnergehilfe *m*.

**bush [buʃ]** Busch *m*; Gebüsch *n*.

**bushel ['buʃl]** Scheffel *m* (*36,37 Liter*).

**bushy ['buʃi]** buschig.

**business ['biznis]** Geschäft *n*; Beschäftigung *f*; Beruf *m*; Angelegenheit *f*; Aufgabe *f*; ✝ Handel *m*; *~ of the day* Tagesordnung *f*; *on ~* geschäftlich; *have no ~ to inf.* nicht befugt sein zu *inf.*; *mind one's own ~* sich um s-e eigenen Angelegenheiten kümmern; **~ hours** *pl.* Geschäftszeit *f*; **~-like** geschäftsmäßig; sachlich; **~man** Geschäftsmann *m*; **~ tour, ~ trip** Geschäftsreise *f*.

**bust¹ [bʌst]** Büste *f*.

**bust²** *Am.* F [bʌst] Bankrott *m*.

**bustle ['bʌsl] 1.** Geschäftigkeit *f*; geschäftiges Treiben; **2.** *v/i.* (umher)wirtschaften; hasten; *v/t.* hetzen, jagen.

**busy** ☐ **['bizi] 1.** beschäftigt; geschäftig; fleißig (*at* bei, *an dat.*); lebhaft; *Am.* *teleph.* besetzt; **2.** (*mst* *~ o.s.* sich) beschäftigen (*with, in, at, about, ger.* mit).

**but [bʌt, bət] 1.** *cj.* aber, jedoch, sondern; *a. ~ that* wenn nicht; indessen; **2.** *prp.* außer; *the last ~ one* der vorletzte; *the next ~ one* der übernächste; *~ for* wenn nicht ... gewesen wäre; ohne; **3.** *nach Negation*: der (die *od.* das) nicht; *there is*

*no one ~ knows* es gibt niemand, der nicht wüßte; **4.** *adv.* nur; *~ just* soeben, eben erst; *~ now* erst jetzt; *all ~* fast, nahe daran; *nothing ~* nur; *I cannot ~ inf.* ich kann nur *inf.*

**butcher ['butʃə] 1.** Schlächter *m*, Fleischer *m*, Metzger *m*; *fig.* Mörder *m*; **2.** (*fig.* ab-, hin)schlachten; **~y [~əri]** Schlächterei *f*; Schlachthaus *n*.

**butler ['bʌtlə]** Butler *m*; Kellermeister *m*.

**butt [bʌt] 1.** Stoß *m*; *a. ~ end* (dikkes) Ende *e-s Baumes etc.*; Stummel *m*, Kippe *f*; *Gewehr*-Kolben *m*; Schießstand *m*; (End)Ziel *n*; *fig.* Zielscheibe *f*; **2.** (mit dem Kopf) stoßen.

**butter ['bʌtə] 1.** Butter *f*; F Schmeichelei *f*; **2.** mit Butter bestreichen; **~cup** Butterblume *f*; **~-fingered** tolpatschig; **~fly** Schmetterling *m*; **~y [~əri] 1.** butter(art)ig; Butter...; **2.** Speisekammer *f*.

**buttocks ['bʌtəks]** *pl.* Gesäß *n*.

**button ['bʌtn] 1.** Knopf *m*; Knospe *f*; **2.** an-, zuknöpfen.

**buttress ['bʌtris] 1.** Strebepfeiler *m*; *fig.* Stütze *f*; **2.** (unter)stützen.

**buxom ['bʌksəm]** drall, stramm.

**buy [bai]** *[irr.]* *v/t.* (an-, ein)kaufen (*from* bei); **~er [~'baiə]** (Ein)Käufer (-in).

**buzz [bʌz] 1.** Gesumm *n*; Geflüster *n*; *~ saw* *Am.* Kreissäge *f*; **2.** *v/i.* summen; surren; *~ about* herumschwirren, herumeilen.

**buzzard ['bʌzəd]** Bussard *m*.

**by [bai] 1.** *prp.* *Raum:* bei; an, neben; *Richtung:* durch, über; an (*dat.*) entlang *od.* vorbei; *Zeit:* an, bei; spätestens bis, bis zu; *Urheber, Ursache:* von, durch (*bsd. beim pass.*); *Mittel, Werkzeug:* durch, mit; *Art u. Weise:* bei; *Schwur:* bei; *Maß:* um, bei; *Richtschnur:* gemäß, bei; *~ the dozen* dutzendweise; *~ o.s.* allein; *~ land* zu Lande; *~ rail* per Bahn; *day ~ day* Tag für Tag; *~ twos* zu zweien; **2.** *adv.* dabei; vorbei; beiseite; *~ and ~* nächstens, bald; nach und nach; *~ the ~* nebenbei bemerkt; *~ and large* *Am.* im großen und ganzen; **3.** *adj.* Neben...; Seiten...; **~-election ['baiilekʃən]** Nachwahl *f*; **~-gone** vergangen; **~-law** Ortsstatut *n*; **~s** *pl.* Satzung *f*, Statuten *n/pl.*; **~-line** *Am.* Verfasserangabe *f zu e-m Artikel*; **~-name** Bei-, Spitzname *m*; **~-pass** Umgehungsstraße *f*; **~-path** Seitenpfad *m*; **~-product** Nebenprodukt *n*; **~-road** Seitenweg *m*; **~-stander** Zuschauer *m*; **~-street** Neben-, Seitenstraße *f*; **~-way** Seitenweg *m*; **~-word** Sprichwort *n*; Inbegriff *m*; *be a ~ for* sprichwörtlich bekannt sein wegen.

# C

cab [kæb] Droschke f, Mietwagen m, Taxi n; 🚂 Führerstand m.

cabbage ♀ ['kæbidʒ] Kohl m.

cabin ['kæbin] 1. Hütte f; ⚓ Kabine f, Kajüte f; Kammer f; 2. einpferchen; ~boy Schiffsjunge m; ~ cruiser ⚓ Kabinenkreuzer m.

cabinet ['kæbinit] Kabinett n, Ministerrat m; Schrank m, Vitrine f; (Radio)Gehäuse n; ~ council Kabinettssitzung f; ~-maker Kunsttischler m.

cable ['keibl] 1. Kabel n; ⚓ Ankertau n; 2. tel. kabeln; ~-car Kabine f, Gondel f; Drahtseilbahn f; ~gram [͵græm] Kabeltelegramm n.

cabman ['kæbmən] Droschkenkutscher m, Taxifahrer m.

caboose [kə'bu:s] ⚓ Kombüse f; Am. 🚂 Eisenbahnerwagen m am Güterzug.

cab-stand ['kæbstænd] Taxi-, Droschkenstand m.

cacao ♀ [kə'ka:ou] Kakaobaum m, -bohne f.

cackle ['kækl] 1. Gegacker n, Geschnatter n; 2. gackern, schnattern.

cad F [kæd] Prolet m; Kerl m.

cadaverous □ [kə'dævərəs] leichenhaft; leichenblaß.

cadence ♪ ['keidəns] Kadenz f; Tonfall m; Rhythmus m.

cadet [kə'det] Kadett m.

café ['kæfei] Café n.

cafeteria bsd. Am. [kæfi'tiəriə] Restaurant n mit Selbstbedienung.

cage [keidʒ] 1. Käfig m; Kriegsgefangenenlager n; ✕ Förderkorb m; 2. einsperren.

cagey □ bsd. Am. Γ ['keidʒi] gerissen, raffiniert.

cajole [kə'dʒoul] j-m schmeicheln; j-n beschwatzen.

cake [keik] 1. Kuchen m; Tafel f Schokolade, Riegel m Seife etc.; 2. zs.-backen.

calami|tous □ [kə'læmitəs] elend; katastrophal; ~ty [͵ti] Elend n, Unglück n; Katastrophe f.

calcify ['kælsifai] (sich) verkalken.

calculat|e ['kælkjuleit] v/t. kalkulieren; be-, aus-, errechnen; v/i. rechnen (on, upon auf acc.); Am. F vermuten; ~ion [kælkju'leiʃən] Kalkulation f, Berechnung f; Voranschlag m; Überlegung f.

caldron ['kɔ:ldrən] Kessel m.

calendar ['kælində] 1. Kalender m; Liste f; 2. registrieren.

calf [kɑ:f], pl. calves [kɑ:vz] Kalb n; Wade f; a. ~-leather ['kɑ:fleðə] Kalbleder n; ~skin Kalbfell n.

calibre ['kælibə] Kaliber n.

calico ✝ ['kælikou] Kaliko m.

call [kɔ:l] 1. Ruf m; teleph. Anruf m,

Gespräch n; fig. Berufung f (to in ein Amt; auf e-n Lehrstuhl); Aufruf m; Aufforderung f; Signal n; Forderung f; Besuch m; Nachfrage f (for nach); Kündigung f v. Geldern; on ~ ✝ auf Abruf; 2. v/t. (herbei-)rufen; (an)rufen; (ein)berufen; Am. Baseball: Spiel abbrechen; fig. berufen (to in ein Amt); nennen; wecken; Aufmerksamkeit lenken (to auf acc.); be ~ed heißen; ~ s.o. names j. beschimpfen, beleidigen; ~ down bsd. Am. F anpfeifen; ~ in Geld kündigen; ~ over Namen verlesen; ~ up aufrufen; teleph. anrufen; v/i. rufen; teleph. anrufen; vorsprechen (at an e-m Ort; on s.o. bei j-m); ~ at a port e-n Hafen anlaufen; ~ for rufen nach; et. fordern; abholen; to be (left till) ~ed for postlagernd; ~ on sich an j. wenden (for wegen); j. berufen, auffordern (to inf. zu); ~-box ['kɔ:lbɔks] Fernsprechzelle f; ~er ['kɔ:lə] teleph. Anrufer(in); Besucher(in).

calling ['kɔ:liŋ] Rufen n; Berufung f; Beruf m; ~ card Am. Visitenkarte f.

call-office ['kɔ:lɔfis] Fernsprechstelle f.

callous □ ['kæləs] schwielig; fig. dickfellig; herzlos.

callow ['kælou] nackt (ungefiedert); fig. unerfahren.

calm [kɑ:m] 1. □ still, ruhig; 2. (Wind)Stille f, Ruhe f; 3. (~ down sich) beruhigen; besänftigen.

calori|c phys. [kə'lɔrik] Wärme f, ~e phys. ['kæləri] Wärmeeinheit f.

column|iate [kə'lʌmnieit] verleumden; ~iution [kəlʌmni'eiʃən], ~y ['kæləmni] Verleumdung f.

calve [kɑ:v] kalben; ~s [kɑ:vz] pl. von calf.

cambric ✝ ['keimbrik] Batist m.

came [keim] pret. von come.

camel zo., ⚓ ['kæməl] Kamel n.

camera ['kæmərə] Kamera f; in ~ 🔨 unter Ausschluß der Öffentlichkeit.

camomile ♀ ['kæməmail] Kamille f.

camouflage ✕ ['kæmuflɑ:ʒ] 1. Tarnung f; 2. tarnen.

camp [kæmp] 1. Lager n; ✕ Feldlager n; ~ bed Feldbett n; 2. lagern; ~ out zelten.

campaign [kæm'pein] 1. Feldzug m; 2. e-n Feldzug mitmachen od. führen.

camphor ['kæmfə] Kampfer m.

campus Am. ['kæmpəs] Universitätsgelände n.

can[1] [kæn] [irr.] v/aux. können, fähig sein zu; dürfen.

can[2] [͵] 1. Kanne f; Am. Büchse f; 2. Am. in Büchsen konservieren.

Canadian [kə'neidjən] **1.** kanadisch; **2.** Kanadier(in).

canal [kə'næl] Kanal *m* (*a. ♗*).

canard [kæ'nɑːd] (Zeitungs)Ente *f.*

canary [kə'nɛəri] Kanarienvogel *m.*

cancel ['kænsəl] (durch)streichen; entwerten; absagen; *a.* ~ out *fig.* aufheben; be ~led ausfallen.

cancer *ast.*, ♋ ['kænsə] Krebs *m*; ~ous [~ərəs] krebsartig.

candid □ ['kændid] aufrichtig; offen.

candidate ['kændidit] Kandidat *m* (*for* für), Bewerber *m* (*for* um).

candied ['kændid] kandiert.

candle ['kændl] Licht *n*, Kerze *f*; *burn the* ~ *at both ends* mit s-n Kräften Raubbau treiben; ~stick Leuchter *m.*

cando(u)r ['kændə] Aufrichtigkeit *f.*

candy ['kændi] **1.** Kandis(zucker) *m*; *Am.* Süßigkeiten *f/pl.*; **2.** *v/t.* kandieren.

cane [kein] **1.** ♀ Rohr *n*; (Rohr-)Stock *m*; **2.** prügeln.

canine ['keinain] Hunde...

canker ['kæŋkə] ♋ Mundkrebs *m*; ♀ Brand *m.*

canned *Am.* [kænd] Büchsen...

cannery *Am.* ['kænəri] Konservenfabrik *f.*

cannibal ['kænibəl] Kannibale *m.*

cannon ['kænən] Kanone *f.*

cannot ['kænɔt] nicht können *etc.*; *s. can[1].*

canoe [kə'nuː] Kanu *n*; Paddelboot *n.*

canon ['kænən] Kanon *m*; Regel *f*; Richtschnur *f*; ~ize [~naiz] heiligsprechen.

canopy ['kænəpi] Baldachin *m*; *fig.* Dach *n*; ▲ Überdachung *f.*

cant[1] [kænt] **1.** Schrägung *f*; Stoß *m*; **2.** kippen; kanten.

cant[2] [~] **1.** Zunftsprache *f*; Gewäsch *n*; scheinheiliges Gerede; **2.** zunftmäßig *od.* scheinheilig reden.

can't F [kɑːnt] = cannot.

cantankerous F □ [kən'tæŋkərəs] zänkisch, mürrisch.

canteen [kæn'tiːn] ✕ Feldflasche *f*; Kantine *f*; ✕ Kochgeschirr *n*; Besteckkasten *m.*

canton **1.** ['kæntɔn] Bezirk *m*; **2.** ✕ [kən'tuːn] (sich) einquartieren.

canvas ['kænvəs] Segeltuch *n*; Zelt (-*e pl.*) *n*; Zeltbahn *f*; Segel *n/pl.*; *paint.* Leinwand *f*; Gemälde *n.*

canvass [~] **1.** (Stimmen)Werbung *f*; *Am. a.* Wahlnachprüfung *f*; **2.** *v/t.* erörtern; *v/i.* (Stimmen, *a.* Kunden) werben.

caoutchouc ['kautʃuk] Kautschuk *m.*

cap [kæp] **1.** Kappe *f*; Mütze *f*; Haube *f*; ⊕ Aufsatz *m*; Zündhütchen *n*; *set one's* ~ *at* sich *e-n Mann*

angeln (*Frau*); **2.** mit e-r Kappe *etc.* bedecken; *fig.* krönen; F übertreffen; die Mütze abnehmen.

capab|ility [keipə'biliti] Fähigkeit *f*; ~le □ ['keipəbl] fähig (*of* zu).

capaci|ous □ [kə'peiʃəs] geräumig; ~ty [kə'pæsiti] Inhalt *m*; Aufnahmefähigkeit *f*; *geistig* (*od.* ⊕ Leistungs)Fähigkeit *f* (*for ger.* zu *inf.*); Stellung *f*; *in my* ~ *as in* meiner Eigenschaft als.

cape[1] [keip] Kap *n*, Vorgebirge *n.*

cape[2] [~] Cape *n*, Umhang *m.*

caper ['keipə] **1.** Kapriole *f*, Luftsprung *m*; *cut* ~*s* = **2.** Kapriolen *od.* Sprünge machen.

capital ['kæpitl] **1.** □ Kapital...; todeswürdig, Todes...; hauptsächlich, Haupt...; vortrefflich; ~ *crime* Kapitalverbrechen *n*; ~ *punishment* Todesstrafe *f*; **2.** Hauptstadt *f*; Kapital *n*; *mst* ~ letter Großbuchstabe *m*; ~ism [~təlizəm] Kapitalismus *m*; ~ize [kə'pitəlaiz] kapitalisieren.

capitulate [kə'pitjuleit] kapitulieren (*to vor dat.*).

capric|e [kə'priːs] Laune *f*; ~ious □ [~iʃəs] kapriziös, launisch.

Capricorn *ast.* ['kæprikɔːn] Steinbock *m.*

capsize [kæp'saiz] *v/i.* kentern; *v/t.* zum Kentern bringen.

capsule ['kæpsjuːl] Kapsel *f.*

captain ['kæptin] Führer *m*; Feldherr *m*; ♣ Kapitän *m*; ✕ Hauptmann *m.*

caption ['kæpʃən] **1.** Überschrift *f*; Titel *m*; *Film:* Untertitel *m*; **2.** *v/t. Am.* mit Überschrift *etc.* versehen.

captious □ ['kæpʃəs] spitzfindig.

captiv|ate ['kæptiveit] *fig.* gefangennehmen, fesseln; ~e ['kæptiv] **1.** gefangen, gefesselt; **2.** Gefangene(r *m*) *f*; ~ity [kæp'tiviti] Gefangenschaft *f.*

capture ['kæptʃə] **1.** Eroberung *f*; Gefangennahme *f*; **2.** (ein)fangen; erobern; erbeuten; ♣ kapern.

car [kɑː] Auto *n*; (Eisenbahn-, Straßenbahn)Wagen *m*; Ballonkorb *m*; *Luftschiff*-Gondel *f*; Kabine *f* *e-s Aufzugs.*

caramel ['kærəmel] Karamel *m*; Karamelle *f.*

caravan ['kærəvæn] Karawane *f*; Wohnwagen *m.*

caraway ♀ ['kærəwei] Kümmel *m.*

carbine ['kɑːbain] Karabiner *m.*

carbohydrate ⚗ ['kɑːbou'haidreit] Kohle(n)hydrat *m.*

carbon ['kɑːbən] ⚗ Kohlenstoff *m*; ~ *copy* Brief-Durchschlag *m*; ~ *paper* Kohlepapier *n.*

carburet(t)or *mot.* ['kɑːbjuretə] Vergaser *m.*

car|case, *mst* ~cass ['kɑːkəs] (Tier-)Kadaver *m*; *Fleischerei:* Rumpf *m.*

card [kɑːd] Karte *f*; *have a* ~ *up*

*one's* sleeve et. in petto haben; ~**board** ['kɑːdɔːd] Kartonpapier *n*; Pappe *f*; ~ *box* Pappkarton *m*.

**cardigan** ['kɑːdigən] Wolljacke *f*.

**cardinal** □ ['kɑːdinl] **1.** Haupt...; hochrot; ~ *number* Grundzahl *f*; **2.** Kardinal *m*.

**card-index** ['kɑːdindeks] Kartei *f*.

**card-sharper** ['kɑːdʃɑːpə] Falschspieler *m*.

**care** [kɛə] **1.** Sorge *f*; Sorgfalt *f*, Obhut *f*, Pflege *f*; *medical* ~ ärztliche Behandlung; ~ *of (abbr.* c/o) ... per Adresse, bei ...; *take* ~ *of* acht(geb)en auf (*acc.*); *with* ~*!* Vorsicht!; **2.** Lust haben (*to inf.* zu); ~ *for* sorgen für; sich kümmern um; sich etwas machen aus; *I don't* ~*!* F meinetwegen!; *I couldn't* ~ *less* F es ist mir völlig egal; *well* ~*d-for* gepflegt. [bahn *f*; **2.** rasen.]

**career** [kə'riə] **1.** Karriere *f*; Lauf-]

**carefree** ['kɛəfriː] sorgenfrei.

**careful** □ ['kɛəful] besorgt (*for* um), achtsam (*of* auf *acc.*); vorsichtig; sorgfältig; ~**ness** [~lnis] Sorgsamkeit *f*; Vorsicht *f*; Sorgfalt *f*.

**careless** □ ['kɛəlis] sorglos; nachlässig; unachtsam; leichtsinnig; ~**ness** [~snis] Sorglosigkeit *f*; Nachlässigkeit *f*.

**caress** [kə'res] **1.** Liebkosung *f*; **2.** liebkosen; *fig.* schmeicheln.

**caretaker** ['kɛəteikə] Wärter(in); (Haus)Verwalter(in).

**care-worn** ['kɛəwɔːn] abgehärmt.

**carfare** *Am.* ['kɑːfɛə] Fahrgeld *n*.

**cargo** ⚓ ['kɑːgou] Ladung *f*.

**caricature** [kærikə'tjuə] **1.** Karikatur *f*; **2.** karikieren.

**carmine** ['kɑːmain] Karmin(rot) *n*.

**carn|al** □ ['kɑːnl] fleischlich; sinnlich; ~**ation** [kɑː'neiʃən] **1.** Fleischton *m*; ♀ Nelke *f*; **2.** blaßrot.

**carnival** ['kɑːnivəl] Karneval *m*.

**carnivorous** [kɑː'nivərəs] fleischfressend.

**carol** ['kærəl] **1.** Weihnachtslied *n*; **2.** Weihnachtslieder singen.

**carous|e** [kə'rauz] **1.** *a.* ~**al** [~əl] (Trink)Gelage *n*; **2.** zechen.

**carp** [kɑːp] Karpfen *m*.

**carpent|er** ['kɑːpintə] Zimmermann *m*; ~**ry** [~tri] Zimmerhandwerk *n*; Zimmermannsarbeit *f*.

**carpet** ['kɑːpit] **1.** Teppich *m*; *bring on the* ~ aufs Tapet bringen; **2.** mit e-m Teppich belegen; ~**bag** Reisetasche *f*; ~**bagger** [~tbægə] politischer Abenteurer.

**carriage** ['kærid3] Beförderung *f*, Transport *m*; Fracht *f*; Wagen *m*; Fuhr-, Frachtlohn *m*; Haltung *f*; Benehmen *n*; ~**drive** Anfahrt *f* (*vor e-m Hause*); ~**free**, ~**paid** frachtfrei; ~**way** Fahrbahn *f*.

**carrier** ['kæriə] Fuhrmann *m*; Spediteur *m*; Träger *m*; Gepäckträger *m*; ~**pigeon** Brieftaube *f*.

**carrion** ['kæriən] Aas *n*; *attr.* Aas...

**carrot** ['kærət] Mohrrübe *f*.

**carry** ['kæri] **1.** *v/t. wohin* bringen, führen, tragen (*a. v/i.*), fahren, befördern; (*bei sich*) haben; *Ansicht* durchsetzen; *Gewinn, Preis* davontragen; *Zahlen* übertragen; *Ernte, Zinsen* tragen; *Mauer etc.* weiterführen; *Benehmen* fortsetzen; *Antrag, Kandidaten* durchbringen; ✗ erobern; *be carried* angenommen werden (*Antrag*); durchkommen (*Kandidat*); ~ *the day* den Sieg davontragen; ~ *forward od. over* ♱ übertragen; ~ *on* fortsetzen, weiterführen; *Geschäft etc.* betreiben; ~ *out od. through* durchführen; **2.** Trag-, Schußweite *f*.

**cart** [kɑːt] **1.** Karren *m*; Wagen *m*; *put the* ~ *before the horse fig.* das Pferd beim Schwanz aufzäumen; **2.** karren, fahren; ~**age** ['kɑːtid3] Fahren *n*; Fuhrlohn *m*.

**carter** ['kɑːtə] Fuhrmann *m*.

**cartilage** ['kɑːtilid3] Knorpel *m*.

**carton** ['kɑːtən] Karton *m*.

**cartoon** [kɑː'tuːn] *paint.* Karton *m*; ⊕ Musterzeichnung *f*; Karikatur *f*; Zeichentrickfilm *m*; ~**ist** [~nist] Karikaturist *m*.

**cartridge** ['kɑːtrid3] Patrone *f*; ~**paper** Zeichenpapier *n*.

**cart-wheel** ['kɑːtwiːl] Wagenrad *n*; *Am.* Silberdollar *m*; *turn* ~*s* radschlagen.

**carve** [kɑːv] *Fleisch* vorschneiden, zerlegen; schnitzen; meißeln; ~**r** ['kɑːvə] (Bild)Schnitzer *m*; Vorschneider *m*; Vorlegemesser *n*.

**carving** ['kɑːviŋ] Schnitzerei *f*.

**cascade** [kæs'keid] Wasserfall *m*.

**case**[1] [keis] *m* Behälter *m*; Kiste *f*; Etui *n*; Gehäuse *n*; Schachtel *f*; Fach *n*; *typ.* Setzkasten *m*; **2.** (ein-) stecken; ver-, umkleiden.

**case**[2] [~] Fall *m* (*a. gr.*, ♟, ♚); *gr.* Kasus *m*; ♟ *a.* Kranke(r *m*) *f*; *Am.* F komischer Kauz; ♟♟ Schriftsatz *m*; Hauptargument *n*; Sache *f*, Angelegenheit *f*.

**case-harden** ⊕ ['keishɑːdn] hartgießen; ~**ed** *fig.* hartgesotten.

**case-history** ['keishistəri] Vorgeschichte *f*; Krankengeschichte *f*.

**casement** ['keismənt] Fensterflügel *m*; ~ *window* Flügelfenster *n*.

**cash** [kæʃ] **1.** Bargeld *n*, Kasse *f*; ~ *down, for* ~ gegen bar; ~ *on delivery* Lieferung *f* gegen bar; (*per*) Nachnahme *f*; ~ *register* Registrierkasse *f*; **2.** einkassieren, einlösen; ~**book** ['kæʃbuk] Kassabuch *n*; ~**ier** [kæˈʃiə] Kassierer(in).

**casing** ['keisiŋ] Überzug *m*, Gehäuse *n*, Futteral *n*; ⚓ Verkleidung *f*.

**cask** [kɑːsk] Faß *n*.

**casket** ['kɑːskit] Kassette *f*; *Am.* Sarg *m*.

**casserole** ['kæsəroul] Kasserolle *f.*

**cassock** *eccl.* ['kæsək] Soutane *f.*

**cast** [kɑːst] **1.** Wurf *m;* ⊕ Guß (-form *f*) *m;* Abguß *m,* Abdruck *m;* Schattierung *f,* Anflug *m;* Form *f,* Art *f;* ⚓ Auswerfen *n von Senkblei etc.; thea.* (Rollen)Besetzung *f;* **2.** [*irr.*] *v/t.* (ab-, aus-, hin-, um-, weg)werfen; *zo. Haut etc.* abwerfen; *Zähne etc.* verlieren; verwerfen; gestalten; ⊕ gießen; *a.* ~ *up* aus-, zs.-rechnen; *thea. Rolle* besetzen; *Rolle* übertragen (to *dat.*); *be* ~ *in a lawsuit* ⚖ e-n Prozeß verlieren; ~ *lots* losen (*for* um); ~ *in one's lot with s.o.* j-s Los teilen; *be* ~ *down* niedergeschlagen sein; *v/i.* sich gießen lassen; ⊕ sich (ver)werfen; ~ *about for* sinnen auf (*acc.*); sich *et.* überlegen.

**castanet** [kæstə'net] Kastagnette *f.*

**castaway** ['kɑːstəwei] **1.** verworfen, ⚓ schiffbrüchig; **2.** Verworfene(r *m*) *f;* Schiffbrüchige(r *m*) *f.*

**caste** [kɑːst] Kaste *f* (*a. fig.*).

**castigate** ['kæstigeit] züchtigen; *fig.* geißeln.

**cast iron** ['kɑːst'aiən] Gußeisen *n;* **cast-iron** gußeisern.

**castle** ['kɑːsl] Burg *f,* Schloß *n; Schach:* Turm *m.*

**castor**[1] ['kɑːstə]: ~ *oil* Rizinusöl *n.*

**castor**[2] [~] Laufrolle *f unter Möbeln;* (Salz-, Zucker- *etc.*) Streuer *m.*

**castrate** [kæs'treit] kastrieren.

**cast steel** ['kɑːststiːl] Gußstahl *m;* **cast-steel** aus Gußstahl.

**casual** □ ['kæʒjuəl] zufällig; gelegentlich; F lässig; ~**ty** [~lti] Unfall *m;* ✕ Verlust *m.*

**cat** [kæt] Katze *f;* ~ *burglar* Fassadenkletterer *m.*

**catalo|gue,** *Am.* ~**g** ['kætələg] **1.** Katalog *m; Am. univ.* Vorlesungsverzeichnis *n;* **2.** katalogisieren.

**catapult** ['kætəpʌlt] Schleuder *f;* ✂ Katapult *m, n.*

**cataract** ['kætərækt] Katarakt *m,* Wasserfall *m;* ✚ grauer Star.

**catarrh** [kə'tɑː] Katarrh *m;* Schnupfen *m.*

**catastrophe** [kə'tæstrəfi] Katastrophe *f.*

**catch** [kætʃ] **1.** Fang *m;* Beute *f, fig.* Vorteil *m;* ♪ Rundgesang *m;* Kniff *m;* ⊕ Haken *m,* Griff *m,* Klinke *f;* **2.** [*irr.*] *v/t.* fassen, F kriegen; fangen, ergreifen; ertappen; *Blick etc.* auffangen; *Zug etc.* erreichen; bekommen; sich *Krankheit* zuziehen, holen; *fig.* erfassen; ~ (*a*) *cold* sich erkälten; ~ *s.o.'s eye* j-m ins Auge fallen; ~ *up* auffangen; F *j.* unterbrechen; einholen; **3.** *v/i.* sich verfangen, hängenbleiben; fassen, einschnappen (*Schloß etc.*); ~ *on* F Anklang finden; *Am.* F kapieren; ~ *up with* ∴ einholen; ~**all** ['kætʃɔːl] *Am.*

**Platz** *m od.* Behälter *m* für alles mögliche (*a. fig. u. attr.*); ~**er** [~∫ə] Fänger(in); ~**ing** [~∫iŋ] packend; ✈ ansteckend; ~**line** Schlagzeile *f;* ~**word** Schlagwort *n;* Stichwort *n.*

**catechism** ['kætikizəm] Katechismus *m.*

**categor|ical** □ [kæti'gɔrikəl] kategorisch; ~**y** ['kætigəri] Kategorie *f.*

**cater** ['keitə]: ~ *for* Lebensmittel liefern für; *fig.* sorgen für; ~**ing** [~əriŋ] Verpflegung *f.*

**caterpillar** ['kætəpilə] *zo.* Raupe *f;* ⊕ Raupe(nschlepper *m*) *f.*

**catgut** ['kætgʌt] Darmsaite *f.*

**cathedral** [kə'θiːdrəl] Dom *m,* Kathedrale *f.*

**Catholic** ['kæθəlik] **1.** katholisch; **2.** Katholik(in).

**catkin** ♀ ['kætkin] Kätzchen *n.*

**cattish** *fig.* ['kætiʃ] falsch.

**cattle** ['kætl] Vieh *n;* ~**breeding** Viehzucht *f;* ~**plague** *vet.* Rinderpest *f.* [*catch* 2.]

**caught** [kɔːt] *pret. u. p.p. von*|

**ca(u)ldron** ['kɔːldrən] Kessel *m.*

**cauliflower** ♀ ['kɔliflauə] Blumenkohl *m.*

**caulk** ⚓ [kɔːk] kalfatern (*abdichten*).

**caus|al** □ ['kɔːzəl] ursächlich; ~**e** [kɔːz] **1.** Ursache *f,* Grund *m;* ⚖ Klage(grund *m*) *f;* Prozeß *m;* Angelegenheit *f,* Sache *f;* **2.** verursachen, veranlassen; ~**less** □ ['kɔːzlis] grundlos.

**causeway** ['kɔːzwei] Damm *m.*

**caustic** Ⓟ ['kɔːstik] (~*ally*) ätzend; *fig.* beißend, scharf.

**caution** ['kɔːʃən] **1.** Vorsicht *f;* Warnung *f;* Verwarnung *f;* ~ *money* Kaution *f;* **2.** warnen; verwarnen.

**cautious** □ ['kɔːʃəs] behutsam, vorsichtig; ~**ness** [~snis] Behutsamkeit *f,* Vorsicht *f.*

**cavalry** ✕ ['kævəlri] Reiterei *f.*

**cave** [keiv] **1.** Höhle *f;* **2.** *v/i.* ~ *in* einstürzen; klein beigeben.

**cavern** ['kævən] Höhle *f;* ~**ous** *fig.* [~nəs] hohl.

**cavil** ['kævil] **1.** Krittelei *f;* **2.** kritteln (*at, about an dat.*).

**cavity** ['kæviti] Höhle *f;* Loch *n.*

**cavort** *Am.* F [kə'vɔːt] sich aufbäumen, umherspringen.

**caw** [kɔː] **1.** krächzen; **2.** Krächzen *n.*

**cayuse** *Am.* F ['kaijuːs] kleines (Indianer)Pferd.

**cease** [siːs] *v/i.* (*from*) aufhören (mit), ablassen (von); *v/t.* aufhören mit; ~**less** □ ['siːslis] unaufhörlich.

**cede** [siːd] abtreten, überlassen.

**ceiling** ['siːliŋ] *Zimmer*-Decke *f; fig.* Höchstgrenze *f;* ~ *price* Höchstpreis *m.*

**celebrat|e** ['selibreit] feiern; ~**ed** gefeiert, berühmt (*for wegen*); ~**ion** [seli'breiʃən] Feier *f.*

**celebrity** [si'lebriti] Berühmtheit f.
**celerity** [si'leriti] Geschwindigkeit f.
**celery** ♧ ['seləri] Sellerie m, f.
**celestial** □ [si'lestjəl] himmlisch.
**celibacy** ['selibəsi] Ehelosigkeit f.
**cell** [sel] allg. Zelle f; ⚡ Element n.
**cellar** ['selə] Keller m.
**cement** [si'ment] 1. Zement m; Kitt m; 2. zementieren; (ver)kitten.
**cemetery** ['semitri] Friedhof m.
**censor** ['sensə] 1. Zensor m; 2. zensieren; **~ious** □ [sen'sɔ:riəs] kritisch; kritt(e)lig; **~ship** ['sensəʃip] Zensur f; Zensoramt n.
**censure** ['senʃə] 1. Tadel m; Verweis m; 2. tadeln.
**census** ['sensəs] Volkszählung f.
**cent** [sent] Hundert n; Am. Cent m = ¹/₁₀₀ Dollar; per ~ Prozent n.
**centenary** [sen'ti:nəri] Hundertjahrfeier f.
**centennial** [sen'tenjəl] 1. hundertjährig; 2. hundertjähriges Jubiläum.
**centi|grade** ['sentigreid]: 10 degrees ~ 10 Grad Celsius; **~metre**, Am. **~meter** Zentimeter n, m; **~pede** zo. [..ipi:d] Hundertfüßer m.
**central** □ ['sentrəl] zentral; **~heating** Zentralheizung f; ~ office, ⚡ ~ station Zentrale f; **~ize** [..laiz] zentralisieren.
**cent|re**, Am. **~er** ['sentə] 1. Zentrum n, Mittelpunkt m; 2. zentral; 3. (sich) konzentrieren; zentralisieren; zentrieren.
**century** ['sentʃuri] Jahrhundert n.
**cereal** ['siəriəl] 1. Getreide...; 2. Getreide(pflanze f) n; Hafer-, Weizenflocken f/pl.; Corn-flakes pl.
**cerebral** anat. ['seribrəl] Gehirn...
**ceremon|ial** [seri'mounjəl] 1. a. **~ious** □ [..jəs] zeremoniell; förmlich; 2. Zeremoniell n; **~y** ['seriməni] Zeremonie f; Feierlichkeit f; Förmlichkeit(en pl.) f.
**certain** □ ['sə:tn] sicher, gewiß; zuverlässig; bestimmt; gewisse(r, -s); **~ty** [..nti] Sicherheit f, Gewißheit f; Zuverlässigkeit f.
**certi|ficate** 1. [sə'tifikit] Zeugnis n, Schein m; ~ of birth Geburtsurkunde f; medical ~ ärztliches Attest; 2. [..keit] bescheinigen; **~fication** [sə:tifi'keiʃən] Bescheinigung f; **~fy** ['sə:tifai] et. bescheinigen; bezeugen; **~tude** [..itju:d] Gewißheit f.
**cessation** [se'seiʃən] Aufhören n.
**cession** ['seʃən] Abtretung f.
**cesspool** ['sespu:l] Senkgrube f.
**chafe** [tʃeif] v/t. reiben; wundreiben; erzürnen; v/i. sich scheuern; sich wundreiben; toben.
**chaff** [tʃɑ:f] 1. Spreu f; Häcksel n; F Neckerei f; 2. zu Häcksel schneiden; F necken.
**chaffer** ['tʃæfə] feilschen.

**chaffinch** ['tʃæfintʃ] Buchfink m.
**chagrin** ['ʃægrin] 1. Ärger m; 2. ärgern.
**chain** [tʃein] 1. Kette f; fig. Fessel f; ~ store bsd. Am. Kettenladen m, Zweiggeschäft n; 2. (an)ketten; fig. fesseln.
**chair** [tʃeə] Stuhl m; Lehrstuhl m; Vorsitz m; be in the ~ den Vorsitz führen; **~man** [tʃeəmən] Vorsitzende(r) m; Präsident m.
**chalice** ['tʃælis] Kelch m.
**chalk** [tʃɔ:k] 1. Kreide f; 2. mit Kreide (be)zeichnen; mst ~ up ankreiden; ~ out entwerfen.
**challenge** ['tʃælindʒ] 1. Herausforderung f; ⚔ Anruf m; bsd. ⚖ Ablehnung f; 2. herausfordern; anrufen; ablehnen; anzweifeln.
**chamber** ['tʃeimbə] parl., zo., ♧, ⊕, Am. Kammer f; **~s** pl. Geschäftsräume m/pl.; **~maid** Zimmermädchen n.
**chamois** ['ʃæmwa:] 1. Gemse f; a. **~leather** [oft a. 'ʃæmileðə] Wildleder n; 2. chamois (gelbbraun).
**champagne** [ʃæm'pein] Champagner m.
**champion** ['tʃæmpjən] 1. Vorkämpfer m, Verfechter m; Verteidiger m; Sport: Meister m; 2. verteidigen; kämpfen für; fig. stützen; 3. großartig; **~ship** Meisterschaft f.
**chance** [tʃɑ:ns] 1. Zufall m; Schicksal n; Glück(sfall m) n; Chance f; Aussicht f (of auf acc.); (günstige) Gelegenheit; Möglichkeit f; by ~ zufällig; take a ~, take one's ~ darauf ankommen lassen; 2. zufällig; gelegentlich; 3. v/i. geschehen; sich ereignen; ~ upon stoßen auf (acc.); v/t. F wagen.
**chancellor** ['tʃɑ:nsələ] Kanzler m.
**chancery** ['tʃɑ:nsəri] Kanzleigericht n; fig. in ~ in der Klemme.
**chandelier** [ʃændi'liə] Lüster m.
**chandler** ['tʃɑ:ndlə] Krämer m.
**change** [tʃeindʒ] 1. Veränderung f, Wechsel m, Abwechs(e)lung f; Tausch m; Wechselgeld n; Kleingeld n; 2. v/t. (ver)ändern; (aus-) wechseln, (aus-, ver)tauschen (for gegen); ~ trains umsteigen; v/i. sich ändern, wechseln; sich umziehen; **~able** □ ['tʃeindʒəbl] veränderlich; **~less** □ [..dʒlis] unveränderlich; **~ling** [..lin] Wechselbalg m; **~over** Umstellung f.
**channel** ['tʃænl] 1. Kanal m; Flußbett n; Rinne f; fig. Weg m; 2. furchen; aushöhlen.
**chant** [tʃɑ:nt] 1. (Kirchen)Gesang m; fig. Singsang m; 2. singen.
**chaos** ['keiɔs] Chaos n.
**chap¹** [tʃæp] 1. Riß m, Sprung m; 2. rissig machen od. werden.
**chap²** F [~] Bursche m, Kerl m, Junge m.

**chap**³ [..] Kinnbacken *m*; ..s *pl.* Maul *n*; ⊕ Backen *f/pl.*

**chapel** ['tʃæpəl] Kapelle *f*; Gottesdienst *m*.

**chaplain** ['tʃæplin] Kaplan *m*.

**chapter** ['tʃæptə] Kapitel *n*; *Am.* Orts-, Untergruppe *f* e-r *Vereinigung.*

**char** [tʃɑ:] verkohlen.

**character** ['kæriktə] Charakter *m*; Merkmal *n*; Schrift(zeichen *n*) *f*; Sinnesart *f*; Persönlichkeit *f*; Original *n*; *thea.,* Roman Person *f*; Rang *m*, Würde *f*; (*bsd.* guter) Ruf; Zeugnis *n*; ..istic [kæriktə'ristik] **1.** (..ally) charakteristisch (of für); **2.** Kennzeichen *n*; ..ize ['kæriktəraiz] charakterisieren.

**charcoal** ['tʃɑ:koul] Holzkohle *f*.

**charge** [tʃɑ:dʒ] **1.** Ladung *f*; *fig.* Last *f* (on für); Verwahrung *f*, Obhut *f*; Schützling *m*; Mündel *m*, *f*, *n*; Amt *n*, Stelle *f*; Auftrag *m*, Befehl *m*; Angriff *m*; Ermahnung *f*; Beschuldigung *f*, Anklage *f*; Preis *m*, Forderung *f*; ..s *pl.* ✝ Kosten *pl.*; be in ~ of *et.* in Verwahrung haben; mit *et.* beauftragt sein; für *et.* sorgen; *v/t.* laden; beladen, belasten; beauftragen; *j-m et.* einschärfen, befehlen; ermahnen; beschuldigen, anklagen (*with gen.*); zuschreiben (on, upon *dat.*); fordern, verlangen; an-, berechnen, in Rechnung stellen (*to dat.*); angreifen (*a. v/i.*); behaupten.

**chariot** *poet. od. hist.* ['tʃæriət] Streit-, Triumphwagen *m*.

**charitable** [ ] ['tʃæritəbl] mild(tätig), wohltätig.

**charity** ['tʃæriti] Nächstenliebe *f*; Wohltätigkeit *f*; Güte *f*; Nachsicht *f*; milde Gabe.

**charlatan** ['ʃɑ:lətən] Marktschreier *m*.

**charm** [tʃɑ:m] **1.** Zauber *m*; *fig.* Reiz *m*; **2.** bezaubern; *fig.* entzücken; ..ing □ ['tʃɑ:miŋ] bezaubernd.

**chart** [tʃɑ:t] **1.** ⏚ Seekarte *f*; Tabelle *f*; **2.** auf e-r Karte einzeichnen.

**charter** ['tʃɑ:tə] **1.** Urkunde *f*; Freibrief *m*; Patent *n*; Frachtvertrag *m*; **2.** privilegieren; ⏚, ✈ chartern, mieten.

**charwoman** ['tʃɑ:wumən] Putz-, Reinemachefrau *f*.

**chary** □ ['tʃɛəri] vorsichtig.

**chase** [tʃeis] **1.** Jagd *f*; Verfolgung *f*; gejagtes Wild; **2.** jagen, hetzen; Jagd machen auf (*acc.*).

**chasm** ['kæzəm] Kluft *f* (*a. fig.*); Lücke *f*.

**chaste** □ [tʃeist] rein, keusch, unschuldig; schlicht (*Stil*).

**chastise** [tʃæs'taiz] züchtigen.

**chastity** ['tʃæstiti] Keuschheit *f*.

**chat** [tʃæt] **1.** Geplauder *n*, Plauderei *f*; **2.** plaudern.

**chattels** ['tʃætlz] *pl. mst* goods and ~ Hab *n* und Gut *n*; Vermögen *n*.

**chatter** ['tʃætə] **1.** plappern; schnattern; klappern; **2.** Geplapper *n*; ..box F Plaudertasche *f*; ..er [..ərə] Schwätzer(in).

**chatty** ['tʃæti] gesprächig.

**chauffeur** ['ʃoufə] Chauffeur *m*.

**chaw** *sl.* [tʃɔ:] kauen; ~ up *Am. mst fig.* fix und fertig machen.

**cheap** ⏚ [tʃi:p] billig; *fig.* gemein; ..en ['tʃi:pən] (sich) verbilligen; *fig.* herabsetzen.

**cheat** [tʃi:t] **1.** Betrug *m*, Schwindel *m*; Betrüger(in); **2.** betrügen.

**check** [tʃek] **1.** Schach(stellung *f*) *n*; Hemmnis *n* (on für); Zwang *m*, Aufsicht *f*; Kontrolle *f* (on gen.); Kontrollmarke *f*; *Am.* (Gepäck-)Schein *m*; *Am.* ✝ = cheque; *Am.* Rechnung *f* im *Restaurant*; karierter Stoff; **2.** *v/i.* an-, innehalten; *Am.* e-n Scheck ausstellen; ~ in *Am.* (in e-m Hotel) absteigen; ~ out *Am.* das Hotel (*nach Bezahlung der Rechnung*) verlassen; *v/t.* hemmen, kontrollieren; nachprüfen; *Kleider* in der Garderobe abgeben; *Am. Gepäck* aufgeben; ..er ['tʃekə] Aufsichtsbeamte(r) *m*; ..s *pl. Am.* Damespiel *n*; ..ing-room [..kiŋrum] *Am.* Gepäckaufbewahrung *f*; ..mate **1.** Schachmatt *n*; **2.** matt setzen; ..up *Am.* scharfe Kontrolle.

**cheek** [tʃi:k] Backe *f*, Wange *f*; F Unverschämtheit *f*; ..y □ ['tʃi:ki] frech.

**cheer** [tʃiə] **1.** Stimmung *f*, Fröhlichkeit *f*; Hoch(ruf *m*) *n*; Beifall(sruf *m*); Speisen *f/pl.*, Mahl *n*; three ..s! dreimal hoch!; **2.** *v/t. a.* ~ up aufheitern; mit Beifall begrüßen; *a.* ~ on anspornen; *v/i.* hoch rufen; jauchzen; *a.* ~ up Mut fassen; ..ful □ ['tʃiəful] heiter; ..io F [..əri'ou] mach's gut!, tschüs!; prosit!; ..less □ [..lis] freudlos; ..y □ [..əri] heiter, froh.

**cheese** [tʃi:z] Käse *m*.

**chef** [ʃef] Küchenchef *m*.

**chemical** ['kemikəl] **1.** □ chemisch; **2.** ..s *pl.* Chemikalien *pl.*

**chemise** [ʃi'mi:z] (Frauen)Hemd *n*.

**chemist** ['kemist] Chemiker(in); Apotheker *m*; Drogist *m*; ..ry [..tri] Chemie *f*.

**cheque** ✝ [tʃek] Scheck *m*; crossed ~ Verrechnungsscheck *m*.

**chequer** ['tʃekə] **1.** *mst* ..s *pl.* Karomuster *n*; **2.** karieren; ..ed gewürfelt; *fig.* bunt.

**cherish** ['tʃeriʃ] hegen, pflegen.

**cherry** ['tʃeri] Kirsche *f*.

**chess** [tʃes] Schach(spiel) *n*; ..board [..esbɔ:d] Schachbrett *n*; ..man Schachfigur *m*.

**chest** [tʃest] Kiste *f*, Lade *f*; *anat.* Brustkasten *m*; ~ of drawers Kommode *f*.

**chestnut** ['tʃesnʌt] 1. ♀ Kastanie *f*; F alter Witz; 2. kastanienbraun.

**chevy** F ['tʃevi] 1. Hetzjagd *f*; Barlaufspiel *n*; 2. hetzen, jagen.

**chew** [tʃuː] kauen; sinnen; ~ the fact *od.* rag *Am. sl.* die Sache durchkauen; **~ing-gum** ['tʃu(ː)ɪŋgʌm] Kaugummi *m*.

**chicane** [ʃiˈkein] 1. Schikane *f*; 2. schikanieren.

**chicken** ['tʃikin] Hühnchen *n*, Küken *n*; **~-hearted** furchtsam, feige; **~-pox** ♂ [~pɔks] Windpocken *f/pl.*

**chid** [tʃid] *pret. u. p.p. von* chide; **~den** ['tʃidn] *p.p. von* chide.

**chide** *lit.* [tʃaid] [*irr.*] schelten.

**chief** [tʃiːf] 1. □ oberst; Ober..., Haupt...; hauptsächlich; ~ clerk Bürovorsteher *m*; 2. Oberhaupt *n*, Chef *m*; Häuptling *m*; ...-in-~ Ober...; **~tain** ['tʃiːftən] Häuptling *m*.

**chilblain** ['tʃilblein] Frostbeule *f*.

**child** [tʃaild] Kind *n*; from a ~ von Kindheit an; with ~ schwanger; **~birth** ['tʃaildbəːθ] Niederkunft *f*; **~hood** [~dhud] Kindheit *f*, ~ish □ [~diʃ] kindlich; kindisch; **~like** kindlich; **~ren** ['tʃildrən] *pl. v.* child.

**chill** [tʃil] 1. eisig, frostig; 2. Frost *m*, Kälte *f*; ♂ Fieberfrost *m*; Erkältung *f*; 3. *v/t.* erkalten lassen; abkühlen; *v/i.* erkalten; erstarren; **~y** ['tʃili] kalt, frostig.

**chime** [tʃaim] 1. Glockenspiel *n*; Geläut *n*; *fig.* Einklang *m*; 2. läuten; *fig.* harmonieren, übereinstimmen.

**chimney** ['tʃimni] Schornstein *m*; Rauchfang *m*; Lampen-Zylinder *m*; **~-sweep(er)** Schornsteinfeger *m*.

**chin** [tʃin] 1. Kinn *n*; take it on the ~ *Am.* F es standhaft ertragen; 2.: ~ *o.s. Am.* e-n Klimmzug machen.

**china** ['tʃainə] Porzellan *n*.

**Chinese** ['tʃaiˈniːz] 1. chinesisch; 2. Chinese(-n *pl.*) *m*, Chinesin *f*.

**chink** [tʃiŋk] Ritz *m*, Spalt *m*.

**chip** [tʃip] 1. Schnitzel *n*, Stückchen *n*; Span *m*; Glas- etc Splitter *m*; Spielmarke *f*; have a ~ on one's shoulder *Am.* F aggressiv sein; ~s *pl.* Pommes frites *pl.*; 2. *v/t.* schnitzeln; an-, abschlagen; *v/i.* abbröckeln; **~muck** ['tʃipmʌk], **~munk** [~ʌŋk] nordamerikanisches gestreiftes Eichhörnchen.

**chirp** [tʃəːp] 1. zirpen; zwitschern; 2. Gezirp *n*.

**chisel** ['tʃizl] 1. Meißel *m*; 2. meißeln; *sl.* (be)mogeln.

**chit-chat** ['tʃittʃæt] Geplauder *n*.

**chivalr|ous** □ ['ʃivəlrəs] ritterlich; **~y** [~ri] Ritterschaft *f*, Rittertum *n*; Ritterlichkeit *f*.

**chive** ♀ [tʃaiv] Schnittlauch *m*.

**chlor|ine** [~iːn] Chlor *n*; **~o-form** ['klɔrəfɔːm] 1. Chloroform *n*; 2. chloroformieren.

**chocolate** ['tʃɔkəlit] Schokolade *f*.

**choice** [tʃɔis] 1. Wahl *f*; Auswahl *f*; 2. □ auserlesen, vorzüglich.

**choir** ['kwaiə] Chor *m*.

**choke** [tʃouk] 1. *v/t.* (er)würgen, (a. *v/i.*) ersticken; ♀ (ab)drosseln; (ver)stopfen; *mst* ~ down hinunterwürgen; 2. Erstickungsanfall *m*; ⊕ Würgung *f*; *mot.* Choke *m*, Starterklappe *f*.

**choose** [tʃuːz] [*irr.*] (aus)wählen; ~ to *inf.* vorziehen zu *inf.*

**chop** [tʃɔp] 1. Hieb *m*; Kotelett *n*; **~s** *pl.* Maul *n*, Rachen *m*; ⊕ Backen *f/pl.*; 2. *v/t.* hauen, hacken; zerhacken; austauschen; *v/i.* wechseln; **~per** ['tʃɔpə] Hackmesser *n*; **~py** [~pi] unstet; unruhig (*See*); böig (*Wind*).

**choral** □ ['kɔːrəl] chormäßig; Chor...; **~(e)** ♪ [kɔˈrɑːl] Choral *m*.

**chord** [kɔːd] Saite *f*; Akkord *m*.

**chore** *Am.* [tʃɔː] Hausarbeit *f* (*mst pl.*).

**chorus** ['kɔːrəs] 1. Chor *m*; Kehrreim *m*; 2. im Chor singen *od.* sprechen.

**chose** [tʃouz] *pret. von* choose; **~n** ['tʃouzn] *p.p. von* choose.

**chow** *Am. sl.* [tʃau] Essen *n*.

**Christ** [kraist] Christus *m*.

**christen** ['krisn] taufen; **~ing** [~niŋ] Taufe *f*; *attr.* Tauf...

**Christian** ['kristjən] 1. □ christlich; ~ name Vor-, Taufname *m*; 2. Christ(in); **~ity** [kristiˈæniti] Christentum *n*.

**Christmas** ['krisməs] Weihnachten *n*.

**chromium** ['kroumjəm] Chrom *n* (*Metall*); **~-plated** verchromt.

**chronic** ['krɔnik] (~ally) chronisch (*mst* ♂), dauernd; *sl.* ekelhaft; **~le** [~kl] 1. Chronik *f*; 2. aufzeichnen.

**chronolog|ical** □ [krɔnəˈlɔdʒikəl] chronologisch; **~y** [krəˈnɔlədʒi] Zeitrechnung *f*; Zeitfolge *f*.

**chubby** F ['tʃʌbi] rundlich; pausbäckig; plump (*a. fig.*).

**chuck**[1] [tʃʌk] 1. Glucken *n*; my ~! mein Täubchen!; 2. glucken.

**chuck**[2] F [~] 1. schmeißen; 2. (Hinaus)Wurf *m*.

**chuckle** ['tʃʌkl] kichern, glucksen.

**chum** F [tʃʌm] 1. (Stuben)Kamerad *m*; 2. zs.-wohnen.

**chump** F [tʃʌmp] Holzklotz *m*.

**chunk** F [tʃʌŋk] Klotz *m*.

**church** [tʃəːtʃ] Kirche *f*; *attr.* Kirch(en)...; ~ service Gottesdienst *m*; **~warden** ['tʃəːtʃ'wɔːdn] Kirchenvorsteher *m*; **~yard** Kirchhof *m*.

**churl** [tʃəːl] Grobian *m*; Flegel *m*; **~ish** □ ['tʃəːliʃ] grob, flegelhaft.

**churn** [tʃəːn] 1. Butterfaß *n*; 2. buttern; aufwühlen.

**chute** [ʃuːt] Stromschnelle *f*; Gleit-, Rutschbahn *f*; Fallschirm *m*.

cider ['saidə] Apfelmost m.

cigar [si'gɑ:] Zigarre f.

cigarette [sigə'ret] Zigarette f; ~-case Zigarettenetui n.

cigar-holder [si'gɑ:houldə] Zigarrenspitze f.

cilia ['siliə] pl. (Augen)Wimpern f|pl.

cinch Am. sl. [sintʃ] sichere Sache.

cincture ['siŋktʃə] Gürtel m, Gurt m.

cinder ['sində] Schlacke f; ~s pl. Asche f; ℒella [sində'relə] Aschenbrödel n; ~-path Sport: Aschenbahn f.

cine-camera ['sini'kæmərə] Filmkamera f.

cinema ['sinəmə] Kino n; Film m.

cinnamon ['sinəmən] Zimt m.

cipher ['saifə] 1. Ziffer f; Null f (a. fig.); Geheimschrift f, Chiffre f; 2. chiffrieren; (aus)rechnen.

circle ['sə:kl] 1. Kreis m; Bekanntenetc. Kreis m; Kreislauf m; thea. Rang m; Ring m; 2. (um)kreisen.

circuit ['sə:kit] Kreislauf m; ⚡ Stromkreis m; Rundreise f; Gerichtsbezirk m; 📻 Rundflug m; short - ⚡ Kurzschluß m; ~ous □ [sə(:)'kju(:)itəs] weitschweifig; Um...

circular ['sə:kjulə] 1. □ kreisförmig; Kreis...; ~ letter Rundschreiben n; ~ note † Kreditbrief m; 2. Rundschreiben n; Laufzettel m.

circulat|e ['sə:kjuleit] v/i. umlaufen, zirkulieren; v/t. in Umlauf setzen; ~ing [~tiŋ]: ~ library Leihbücherei f; ~ion [sə:kju'leiʃən] Zirkulation f, Kreislauf m; fig. Umlauf m; Verbreitung f; Zeitungs-Auflage f.

circum|... ['sə:kəm] (her)um; ~ference [se'kʌmfərəns] (Kreis-)Umfang m, Peripherie f; ~jacent [sə:kəm'dʒeisənt] umliegend; ~location [~mlə'kju:ʃən] Umständlichkeit f; Weitschweifigkeit f; ~navigate [~m'nævigeit] umschiffen; ~scribe ['sə:kəmskraib] ⚡ umschreiben; fig. begrenzen; ~spect □ [~spekt] um-, vorsichtig; ~stance [~stəns] Umstand m (~s pl. a. Verhältnisse n/pl.); Einzelheit f; Umständlichkeit f; ~stantial □ [~'stænʃəl] umständlich; ~ evidence ⚡ Indizienbeweis m; ~vent [~m'vent] überlisten; vereiteln.

circus ['sə:kəs] Zirkus m; (runder) Platz.

cistern ['sistən] Wasserbehälter m.

cit|ation [sai'teiʃən] Vorladung f; Anführung f, Zitat n; Am. öffentliche Ehrung; ~e [sait] ⚡ vorladen; anführen; zitieren.

citizen ['sitizn] (Staats)Bürger(in); Städter(in); ~ship [~nʃip] Bürgerrecht n, Staatsangehörigkeit f.

citron ['sitrən] Zitrone f.

city ['siti] 1. Stadt f; the ℒ die City, das Geschäftsviertel; 2. städtisch, Stadt...; ℒ article Börsen-, Handelsbericht m; ~ editor Am. Lokalredakteur m; ~ hall Am. Rathaus n; ~ manager Am. Oberstadtdirektor m.

civic ['sivik] (staats)bürgerlich; städtisch; ~s sg. Staatsbürgerkunde f.

civil □ ['sivl] bürgerlich, Bürger...; zivil; ⚡ zivilrechtlich; höflich; ℒ Servant Verwaltungsbeamt|e(r) m, -in f; ℒ Service Staatsdienst m; ~ian ✕ [si'viljən] Zivilist m; ~ity [~liti] Höflichkeit f; ~ization [sivilai'zeiʃən] Zivilisation f, Kultur f; ~ize ['sivilaiz] zivilisieren.

clad [klæd] 1. pret. u. p.p. von clothe; 2. adj. gekleidet.

claim [kleim] 1. Anspruch m; Anrecht n (to auf acc.); Forderung f; Am. Parzelle f; 2. beanspruchen; fordern; sich berufen auf (acc.); ~ to be sich ausgeben für; ~ant ['kleimənt] Beanspruchende(r m) f; ⚡ Kläger m.

clairvoyant(e) [klɛə'vɔiənt] Hellseher(in).

clamber ['klæmbə] klettern.

clammy □ ['klæmi] feuchtkalt, klamm.

clamo(u)r ['klæmə] 1. Geschrei n, Lärm m; 2. schreien (for nach).

clamp ⊕ [klæmp] 1. Klammer f; 2. verklammern; befestigen.

clan [klæn] Clan m, Sippe f (a. fig.).

clandestine □ [klæn'destin] heimlich; Geheim...

clang [klæŋ] 1. Klang m, Geklirr n; 2. schallen; klirren (lassen).

clank [klæŋk] 1. Gerassel n, Geklirr n; 2. rasseln, klirren (mit).

clap [klæp] 1. Klatschen n; Schlag m, Klaps m; 2. schlagen (mit) klatschen; ~board Am. ['klæpbɔ:d] Schaltbrett n; ~trap Effekthascherei f.

claret ['klærət] roter Bordeaux; allg. Rotwein m; Weinrot n; sl. Blut n.

clarify ['klærifai] v/t. (ab)klären; fig. klären; v/i. sich klären.

clarity ['klæriti] Klarheit f.

clash [klæʃ] 1. Geklirr n; Zs.-stoß m; Widerstreit m; 2. klirren (mit); zs.-stoßen.

clasp [klɑ:sp] 1. Haken m, Klammer f; Schnalle f; Spange f; fig. Umklammerung f; Umarmung f; 2. v/t. an-, zuhaken; fig. umklammern; umfassen; v/i. festhalten; ~-knife ['klɑ:sp'naif] Taschenmesser n.

class [klɑ:s] 1. Klasse f; Stand m; (Unterrichts)Stunde f; Kurs m; Am. univ. Jahrgang m; 2. (in Klassen) einteilen, einordnen.

classic ['klæsik] Klassiker m; ~s

*pl.* die alten Sprachen; **~(al** □)
[**~**k(əl)] klassisch.

**classi|fication** [klæsifi'keiʃən] Klas-
sifizierung *f*, Einteilung *f*; **~fy**
['klæsifai] klassifizieren, einstufen.

**clatter** ['klætə] 1. Geklapper *n*;
2. klappern (mit); *fig.* schwatzen.

**clause** [klɔ:z] Klausel *f*, Bestimmung
*f*; *gr.* (Neben)Satz *m*.

**claw** [klɔ:] 1. Klaue *f*, Kralle *f*,
Pfote *f*; *Krebs*-Schere *f*; 2. (zer-)
kratzen; (um)krallen.

**clay** [klei] Ton *m*; *fig.* Erde *f*.

**clean** [kli:n] 1. *adj.* □ rein; sauber;
2. *adv.* rein, völlig; 3. reinigen (of
von); sich waschen lassen (*Stoff
etc.*); **~** up aufräumen; **~er** ['kli:nə]
Reiniger *m*; *mst* **~s** *pl.* (chemische)
Reinigung; **~ing** [**~**niŋ] Reinigung
*f*; **~liness** ['klenlinis] Reinlichkeit
*f*; **~ly** 1. *adv.* ['kli:nli] rein; sauber;
2. *adj.* ['klenli] reinlich; **~se** [klenz]
reinigen; säubern.

**clear** [kliə] 1. □ klar; hell, rein;
*fig.* rein (from von); frei (of von);
ganz, voll; ✝ rein, netto; 2. *v/t.*
er-, aufhellen; (auf)klären; reinigen (of, from von); *Wald* lichten,
roden; wegräumen (*a. ~ away od.*
off); *Hindernis* nehmen; *Rechnung*
bezahlen; ✝ (aus)klarieren; ver-
zollen; ✝ freisprechen; befreien;
rechtfertigen (from von); *v/i. a.* **~**
up sich aufhellen; sich verziehen;
**~ance** ['kliərəns] Aufklärung *f*;
Freilegung *f*; Räumung *f*; ✝ Abrechnung *f*; ♱, ✝ Verzollung *f*;
**~ing** [**~**riŋ] Aufklärung *f*; Lichtung
*f*, Rodung *f*; ✝ Ab-, Verrechnung
*f*; ♀ *House* Ab-, Verrechnungs-
stelle *f*.

**cleave**[1] [kli:v] (*irr.*) (*sich*) spalten;
*Wasser, Luft* (zer)teilen.

**cleave**[2] [**~**] *fig.* festhalten (*to an dat.*);
treu bleiben (*dat.*).

**cleaver** ['kli:və] Hackmesser *n*.

**clef** ♪ [klef] Schlüssel *m*.

**cleft** [kleft] 1. Spalte *f*; Sprung *m*,
Riß *m*; 2. *pret. u. p.p. von* cleave[1].

**clemen|cy** ['klemənsi] Milde *f*; **~t**
□ [**~**nt] mild.

**clench** [klentʃ] *Lippen etc.* fest zs.-
pressen; *Zähne* zs.-beißen; *Faust*
ballen; festhalten.

**clergy** ['klə:dʒi] Geistlichkeit *f*;
**~man** Geistliche(r) *m*.

**clerical** ['klerikəl] 1. □ geistlich;
Schreib(er)...; 2. Geistliche(r) *m*.

**clerk** [kla:k] Schreiber(in); Büro-
angestellte(r *m*) *f*; Sekretär(in); ✝
kaufmännische(r) Angestellte(r);
*Am.* Verkäufer(in); Küster *m*.

**clever** □ ['klevə] geschickt; gescheit.

**clew** [klu:] Knäuel *m*, *n*; = clue.

**click** [klik] 1. Knacken *n*; ⊕ Sperr-
haken *m*, -klinke *f*; 2. knacken; zu-,
einschnappen; klappen.

**client** ['klaiənt] Klient(in); Kund|e

*m*, -in *f*; **~ele** [kli:ãːn'teil] Kundschaft *f*.

**cliff** [klif] Klippe *f*; Felsen *m*.

**climate** ['klaimit] Klima *n*.

**climax** ['klaimæks] 1. *rhet.* Steigerung *f*; Gipfel *m*, Höhepunkt *m*;
2. (sich) steigern.

**climb** [klaim] (er)klettern, (er-)
klimmen, (er)steigen; **~er** ['klaimə]
Kletterer *m*, Bergsteiger(in); *fig.*
Streber(in); ♀ Kletterpflanze *f*;
**~ing** [**~**miŋ] Klettern *n*; *attr.*
Kletter...

**clinch** [klintʃ] 1. ⊕ Vernietung *f*;
Festhalten *n*; *Boxen:* Umklammerung *f*; 2. *v/t.* vernieten; festmachen; *s. clench*; *v/i.* festhalten.

**cling** [kliŋ] [*irr.*] (*to*) festhalten (an
*dat.*), sich klammern (an *acc.*);
sich (an)schmiegen (an *acc.*); *j-m*
anhängen.

**clinic** ['klinik] Klinik *f*; klinisches
Praktikum; **~al** □ [**~**kəl] klinisch.

**clink** [kliŋk] 1. Geklirr *n*; 2. klingen,
klirren (lassen); klimpern mit; **~er**
['kliŋkə] Klinker(stein) *m*.

**clip**[1] [klip] 1. Schur *f*; at one **~** *Am.*
F auf einmal; 2. ab-, aus-, beschnei-
den; *Schafe etc.* scheren.

**clip**[2] [**~**] Klammer *f*; Spange *f*.

**clipp|er** ['klipə] (*a. pair of*) **~s** *pl.*
Haarschneide-, Schermaschine *f*;
Klipper *m*; ♱ Schnellsegler *m*; ✈
Verkehrsflugzeug *n*; **~ings** [**~**piŋz]
*pl.* Abfälle *m/pl.*; *Zeitungs- etc.*
Ausschnitte *m/pl.*

**cloak** [klouk] 1. Mantel *m*; 2. *fig.* bemänteln, verhüllen; **~-room**
['kloukrum] Garderobe(nraum *m*) *f*;
Toilette *f*; ♱ Gepäckabgabe *f*.

**clock** [klɔk] Schlag-, Wand-Uhr *f*;
**~wise** ['klɔkwaiz] im Uhrzeiger-
sinn; **~work** Uhrwerk *n*; *like* **~**
wie am Schnürchen.

**clod** [klɔd] Erdklumpen *m*; *a.* **~-**
hopper (Bauern)Tölpel *m*.

**clog** [klɔg] 1. Klotz *m*; Holzschuh *m*,
Pantine *f*; 2. belasten; hemmen;
(sich) verstopfen.

**cloister** ['klɔistə] Kreuzgang *m*;
Kloster *n*.

**close** 1. □ [klous] geschlossen; verborgen; verschwiegen; knapp, eng;
begrenzt; nah, eng; bündig; dicht;
gedrängt; schwül; knickerig; ge-
nau; fest (*Griff*); **~** *by, ~* to dicht
bei; **~** fight, **~** quarters *pl.* Hand-
gemenge *n*, Nahkampf *m*; **~(ed)**
season, **~** time hunt. Schonzeit *f*;
*sail* **~** *to the wind fig.* sich hart an der
Grenze des Erlaubten bewegen;
2. [klouz] Schluß *m*; Abschluß *m*;
[klous] Einfriedung *f*; Hof *m*; 3.
[klouz] *v/t.* (ab-, ein-, ver-, zu-)
schließen; beschließen; *v/i.* (sich)
schließen; abschließen; handge-
mein werden; **~** *in* hereinbrechen
(*Nacht*); kürzer werden (*Tage*); **~**
*on* (*prp.*) sich schließen um, um-

fassen; ~ness ['klousnis] Genauigkeit f, Geschlossenheit f.
closet ['klɔzit] 1. Kabinett n;
(Wand)Schrank m; = water-~;
2.: be ~ed with mit j-m e-e geheime
Beratung haben. [nahme f.\
close-up ['klousʌp] Film: Großauf-\
closure ['klouʒə] Verschluß m; parl.
(Antrag m auf) Schluß m e-r Debatte.
clot [klɔt] 1. Klümpchen n; 2. zu
Klümpchen gerinnen (lassen).
cloth [klɔθ] Stoff m, Tuch n; Tisch-
tuch n; Kleidung f, Amts-Tracht f;
the ~ F der geistliche Stand; lay the
~ den Tisch decken; ~-binding
Leineneinband m; ~-bound in Leinen gebunden.
clothe [klouð] [irr.] (an-, be)kleiden;
einkleiden.
clothes [klouðz] pl. Kleider n/pl.;
Kleidung f; Anzug m; Wäsche f;
~-basket ['klouðzba:skit] Wasch-
korb m; ~-line Wäscheleine f; ~
peg Kleiderhaken m; Wäsche-
klammer f; ~-pin bsd. Am. Wäsche-
klammer f; ~-press Kleider-,
Wäscheschrank m.
clothier ['klouðiə] Tuch-, Kleider-
händler m.
clothing ['klouðiŋ] Kleidung f.
cloud [klaud] 1. Wolke f (a. fig.);
Trübung f; Schatten m; 2. (sich)
be~, umwölken (a. fig.); ~-burst
['klaudbə:st] Wolkenbruch m; ~less
□ [~dlis] wolkenlos; ~y □ [~di]
wolkig; Wolken...; trüb; unklar.
clout [klaut] Lappen m; F Kopf-
nuß f.
clove¹ [klouv] (Gewürz)Nelke f.
clove² [~] pret. von cleave¹; ~n
['klouvn] 1. p.p. von cleave¹; 2. adj.
gespalten.
clover ❧ ['klouvə] Klee m.
clown [klaun] Hanswurst m; Tölpel
m; ~ish □ ['klauniʃ] bäurisch;
plump; clownhaft.
cloy [klɔi] übersättigen, überladen.
club [klʌb] 1. Keule f; (Gummi-)
Knüppel m; Klub m; ~s pl. Karten:
Kreuz n; 2. v/t. mit e-r Keule
schlagen; v/i. sich zs.-tun; ~-foot
['klʌb'fut] Klumpfuß m.
clue [klu:] Anhaltspunkt m, Finger-
zeig m.
clump [klʌmp] 1. Klumpen m;
Baum-Gruppe f; 2. trampeln; zs.-
drängen.
clumsy □ ['klʌmzi] unbeholfen, ungeschickt; plump.
clung [klʌŋ] pret. u. p.p. von cling.
cluster ['klʌstə] 1. Traube f;
Büschel n; Haufen m; 2. büschel-
weise wachsen; (sich) zs.-drängen.
clutch [klʌtʃ] 1. Griff m; ⊕ Kupplung f; Klaue f; 2. (er)greifen.
clutter ['klʌtə] 1. Wirrwarr m;
2. durch-ea.-rennen; durch-ea.-
bringen.

coach [koutʃ] 1. Kutsche f; 🚋
Wagen m; Reisebus m; Einpauker
m; Trainer m; 2. in e-r Kutsche
fahren; (ein)pauken; trainieren;
~man ['koutʃmən] Kutscher m.
coagulate [kouˈægjuleit] gerinnen
(lassen).
coal [koul] 1. (Stein)Kohle f; carry
~s to Newcastle Eulen nach Athen
tragen; 2. ⚓ (be)kohlen.
coalesce [kouəˈles] zs.-wachsen;
sich vereinigen.
coalition [kouəˈliʃən] Verbindung f;
Bund m, Koalition f.
coal-pit ['koulpit] Kohlengrube f.
coarse □ [kɔ:s] grob; ungeschliffen.
coast [koust] 1. Küste f; bsd. Am.
Rodelbahn f; 2. die Küste entlangfahren; im Freilauf fahren; rodeln;
~er ['koustə] Am. Rodelschlitten;
⚓ Küstenfahrer m.
coat [kout] 1. Jackett n, Jacke f,
Rock m; Mantel m; Pelz m, Gefieder n; Überzug m; ~ of arms
Wappen(schild m, n) n; 2. überziehen; anstreichen; ~-hanger
['kouthæŋə] Kleiderbügel m; ~ing
['koutiŋ] Überzug m; Anstrich m;
Mantelstoff m.
coax [kouks] schmeicheln (dat.); beschwatzen (into zu).
cob [kɔb] kleines starkes Pferd;
Schwan m; Am. Maiskolben m.
cobbler ['kɔblə] Schuhmacher m;
Stümper m.
cobweb ['kɔbweb] Spinn(en)ge-
webe n.
cock [kɔk] 1. Hahn m; Anführer m;
Heuhaufen m; 2. a. ~ up aufrichten;
Gewehrhahn spannen.
cockade [kɔˈkeid] Kokarde f.
cockatoo [kɔkəˈtu:] Kakadu m.
cockboat ⚓ ['kɔkbout] Jolle f.
cockchafer ['kɔktʃeifə] Maikäfer m.
cock|-eyed sl. ['kɔkaid] schieläugig;
Am. blau (betrunken); ~-horse
Steckenpferd n.
cockney ['kɔkni] waschechter Londoner.
cockpit ['kɔkpit] Kampfplatz m für
Hähne; ⚓ Raumdeck n; ⚛ Führer-
raum m, Kanzel f.
cockroach zo. ['kɔkroutʃ] Schabe f.
cock|sure F ['kɔk'ʃuə] absolut
sicher; überheblich; ~tail Cocktail
m; ~y □ F ['kɔki] selbstbewußt;
frech.
coco ['koukou] Kokospalme f.
cocoa ['koukou] Kakao m.
coco-nut ['koukənʌt] Kokosnuß f.
cocoon [kəˈku:n] Seiden-Kokon m.
cod [kɔd] Kabeljau m.
coddle ['kɔdl] verhätscheln.
code [koud] 1. Gesetzbuch n; Kodex
m; Telegramm-, Signal-Schlüssel m;
2. chiffrieren.
codger F ['kɔdʒə] komischer Kauz.
cod-liver ['kɔdlivə]: ~ oil Lebertran
m.

**co-ed** *Am.* F ['kou'ed] Schülerin *f* e-r Koedukationsschule, *allg.* Studentin *f*.

**coerc|e** [kou'ə:s] (er)zwingen; **~ion** [kou'ə:ʃən] Zwang *m*.

**coeval** □ [kou'i:vəl] gleichzeitig; gleichalt(e)rig.

**coexist** ['kouig'zist] gleichzeitig bestehen.

**coffee** ['kɔfi] Kaffee *m*; **~-pot** Kaffeekanne *f*; **~-room** Speisesaal *m* e-s Hotels; **~-set** Kaffeeservice *n*.

**coffer** ['kɔfə] (Geld)Kasten *m*.

**coffin** ['kɔfin] Sarg *m*.

**cogent** □ ['koudʒənt] zwingend.

**cogitate** ['kɔdʒiteit] *v/i.* nachdenken; *v/t.* (er)sinnen.

**cognate** ['kɔgneit] verwandt.

**cognition** [kɔg'niʃən] Erkenntnis *f*.

**cognizable** ['kɔgnizəbl] erkennbar.

**coheir** ['kou'ɛə] Miterbe *m*.

**coheren|ce** [kou'hiərəns] Zs.-hang *m*; **~t** □ [~nt] zs.-hängend.

**cohesi|on** [kou'hi:ʒən] Kohäsion *f*; **~ve** [~i:siv] (fest) zs.-hängend.

**coiff|eur** [kwaː'fəː] Friseur *m*; **~ure** [~'fjuə] Frisur *f*.

**coil** [kɔil] 1. *a.* **~** *up* aufwickeln; (sich) zs.-rollen; 2. Rolle *f*, Spirale *f*; Wicklung *f*; ⚡ Spule *f*; Windung *f*; ⊕ (Rohr)Schlange *f*.

**coin** [kɔin] 1. Münze *f*; 2. prägen (*a. fig.*); münzen; **~age** ['kɔinidʒ] Prägung *f*; Geld *n*, Münze *f*.

**coincide** [kouin'said] zs.-treffen; übereinstimmen; **~nce** [kou'insidəns] Zs.-treffen *n*; *fig.* Übereinstimmung *f*.

**coke** [kouk] Koks *m* (*a. sl.* = Kokain); **1** *Am.* F Coca-Cola *n, f*.

**cold** [kould] 1. □ kalt; 2. Kälte *f*, Frost *m*; Erkältung *f*; **~ness** ['kouldnis] Kälte *f*.

**coleslaw** *Am.* ['koulslɔː] Krautsalat *m*.

**colic** 🧬 ['kɔlik] Kolik *f*.

**collaborat|e** [kə'læbəreit] zs.-arbeiten; zs.[kə'læbə'reiʃən] Zs.-, Mitarbeit *f*; *in* **~** gemeinsam.

**collaps|e** [kə'læps] 1. zs., einfallen; zs.-brechen; 2. Zs.-bruch *m*; **~ible** [~səbl] zs.-klappbar.

**collar** ['kɔlə] 1. Kragen *m*; Halsband *n*; Kum(me)t *n*; ⊕ Lager *n*; 2. beim Kragen packen; *Fleisch* zs.-rollen; **~-bone** Schlüsselbein *n*; **~-stud** Kragenknopf *m*.

**collate** [kɔ'leit] *Texte* vergleichen.

**collateral** [kɔ'lætərəl] 1. □ parallel laufend; Seiten..., Neben...; indirekt; 2. Seitenverwandte(r *m*) *f*.

**colleague** ['kɔliːg] Kolleg|e *m*, -in *f*.

**collect** 1. *eccl.* ['kɔlekt] Kollekte *f*; 2. *v/t.* [kə'lekt] (ein)sammeln; *Gedanken etc.* sammeln; einkassieren; abholen; *v/i.* sich (ver)sammeln; **~ed** □ *fig.* gefaßt; **~ion** [~kʃən] Sammlung *f*; Einziehung *f*; Sammel...; **~ive** [~ktiv] gesammelt; Sammel...; **~**

bargaining Tarifverhandlungen *f/pl.*; **~ively** [~vli] insgesamt; zs.-fassend; **~or** [~tə] Sammler *m*; Steuereinnehmer *m*; 🚋 Fahrkartenabnehmer *m*; ⚡ Stromabnehmer *m*.

**college** ['kɔlidʒ] College *n* (*Teil e-r Universität*); höhere Schule *od.* Lehranstalt *f*; Hochschule *f*; Akademie *f*; Kollegium *n*.

**collide** [kə'laid] zs.-stoßen.

**collie** ['kɔli] Collie *m*, schottischer Schäferhund.

**collier** ['kɔliə] Bergmann *m*; ⚓ Kohlenschiff *n*; **~y** ['kɔljəri] Kohlengrube *f*.

**collision** [kə'liʒən] Zs.-stoß *m*.

**colloquial** □ [kə'loukwiəl] umgangssprachlich, familiär.

**colloquy** ['kɔləkwi] Gespräch *n*.

**colon** *typ.* ['koulən] Doppelpunkt *m*.

**colonel** ✕ ['kəːnl] Oberst *m*.

**coloni|al** [kə'lounjəl] Kolonial...; **~alism** *pol.* [~lizəm] Kolonialismus *m*; **~ze** ['kɔlənaiz] kolonisieren; (sich) ansiedeln; besiedeln.

**colony** ['kɔləni] Kolonie *f*; Siedlung *f*.

**colossal** □ [kə'lɔsl] kolossal.

**colo(u)r** ['kʌlə] 1. Farbe *f*; *fig.* Färbung *f*; Anschein *m*; Vorwand *m*; **~s** *pl.* ✕ Fahne *f*, Flagge *f*; 2. *v/t.* färben; anstreichen; *fig.* beschönigen; *v/i.* sich (ver)färben; erröten; **~-bar** Rassenschranke *f*; **~ed** gefärbt, farbig; **~** *man* Farbige(r) *m*; **~ful** [~əful] farbenreich; -freudig; lebhaft; **~ing** [~əriŋ] Färbung *f*; Farbton *m*; *fig.* Beschönigung *f*; **~less** □ [~əlis] farblos; **~** **line** *bsd. Am.* Rassenschranke *f*.

**colt** [koult] Hengstfüllen *n*; *fig.* Neuling *m*.

**column** ['kɔləm] Säule *f*; *typ.* Spalte *f*; ✕ Kolonne *f*; **~ist** *Am.* [~mnist] Kolumnist *m*.

**comb** [koum] 1. Kamm *m*; ⊕ Hechel *f*; 2. *v/t.* kämmen; striegeln; *Flachs* hecheln.

**combat** ['kɔmbət] 1. Kampf *m*; *single* **~** Zweikampf *m*; 2. (be)kämpfen; **~ant** [~tənt] Kämpfer *m*.

**combin|ation** [kɔmbi'neiʃən] Verbindung *f*; *mst* **~s** *pl.* Hemdhose *f*; **~e** [kəm'bain] (sich) verbinden, vereinigen.

**combust|ible** [kəm'bʌstəbl] 1. brennbar; 2. **~s** *pl.* Brennmaterial *n*; *mot.* Betriebsstoff *m*; **~ion** [~tʃən] Verbrennung *f*.

**come** [kʌm] [*irr.*] kommen; *to* **~** künftig, kommend; **~** *about* sich zutragen; **~** *across* auf *j-n od. et.* stoßen; **~** *at* erreichen; **~** *by* vorbeikommen; zu *et.* kommen; **~** *down* herunterkommen (*a. fig.*); *Am.* F erkranken (*with an dat.*); **~** *for* abholen; **~** *off* davonkommen; losgehen (*Knopf*), ausfallen (*Haare etc.*); stattfinden;

~ *round* vorbeikommen (*bsd. zu Besuch*); wiederkehren; F zu sich kommen; *fig.* einlenken; ~ *to adv.* dazukommen; ♏ beidrehen; *prp.* betragen; ~ *up to* entsprechen (*dat.*); es *j-m* gleichtun; *Stand, Maß* erreichen; ~**back** ['kʌmbæk] Wiederkehr *f*, Comeback *n*; *Am. sl.* schlagfertige Antwort.

**comedian** [kə'miːdjən] Schauspieler(in); Komiker(in); Lustspieldichter *m*.

**comedy** ['kɔmidi] Lustspiel *n*.

**comeliness** ['kʌmlinis] Anmut *f*.

**comfort** ['kʌmfət] 1. Bequemlichkeit *f*; Behaglichkeit *f*; Trost *m*; *fig.* Beistand *m*; Erquickung *f*; 2. trösten; erquicken; beleben; ~**able** □ [~təbl] behaglich; bequem; tröstlich; ~**er** [~tə] Tröster *m*; *fig.* wollenes Halstuch; Schnuller *m*; *Am.* Steppdecke *f*; ~**less** □ [~tlis] unbehaglich; trostlos; ~ **station** *Am.* Bedürfnisanstalt *f*.

**comic(al** □) ['kɔmik(əl)] komisch; lustig, drollig.

**coming** ['kʌmiŋ] 1. kommend; künftig; 2. Kommen *n*.

**comma** ['kɔmə] Komma *n*.

**command** [kə'mɑːnd] 1. Herrschaft *f*, Beherrschung *f* (*a. fig.*); Befehl *m*; ✗ Kommando *n*; be (have) *at* ~ zur Verfügung stehen (haben); 2. befehlen; ✗ kommandieren; verfügen über (*acc.*); beherrschen; ~**er** [~də] Kommandeur *m*, Befehlshaber *m*; ♏ Fregattenkapitän *m*; ~**er-in-chief** [~rin-'tʃiːf] Oberbefehlshaber *m*; ~**ment** [~dmənt] Gebot *n*.

**commemorat|e** [kə'meməreit] gedenken (*gen.*), feiern; ~**ion** [kameˈmɔˈreiʃən] Gedächtnisfeier *f*.

**commence** [kə'mens] anfangen, beginnen; ~**ment** [~smənt] Anfang *m*.

**commend** [kə'mend] empfehlen;

**commensurable** □ [kə'menʃərəbl] vergleichbar (*with, to* mit).

**comment** ['kɔment] 1. Kommentar *m*; Erläuterung *f*; An-, Bemerkung *f*; 2. (*upon*) erläutern (*acc.*); sich auslassen (über *acc.*); ~**ary** ['kɔməntəri] Kommentar *m*; ~**ator** ['kɔmenteitə] Kommentator *m*; *Radio:* Berichterstatter *m*.

**commerc|e** ['kɔmə(ː)s] Handel *m*; Verkehr *m*; ~**ial** □ [kə'mɔːʃəl] 1. kaufmännisch; Handels..., Geschäfts...; gewerbsmäßig; ~ *traveller* Handlungsreisende(r) *m*; 2. *bsd. Am. Radio, Fernsehen:* kommerzielle (Werbe)Sendung.

**commiseration** [kəmizə'reiʃən] Mitleid *n* (*for* mit).

**commissary** ['kɔmisəri] Kommissar *m*; ✗ Intendanturbeamte(r) *m*.

**commission** [kə'miʃən] 1. Auftrag *m*; Übertragung *f von Macht etc.*;

Begehung *f e-s Verbrechens*; Provision *f*; Kommission *f*; (Offiziers-) Patent *n*; 2. beauftragen; bevollmächtigen; ✗ bestallen; ♏ in Dienst stellen; ~**er** [~ʃnə] Bevollmächtigte(r *m*) *f*; Kommissar *m*.

**commit** [kə'mit] anvertrauen; übergeben, überweisen; *Tat* begehen; bloßstellen; ~ (*o.s.* sich) verpflichten; ~ (*to prison*) in Untersuchungshaft nehmen; ~**ment** [~tmənt], ~**tal** [~tl] Überweisung *f*; Verpflichtung *f*; Verübung *f*; ~**tee** [~ti] Ausschuß *m*, Komitee *n*.

**commodity** [kə'mɔditi] Ware *f* (*mst pl.*), Gebrauchsartikel *m*.

**common** ['kɔmən] 1. □ (all)gemein; gewöhnlich; gemeinschaftlich; öffentlich; gemein (*niedrig*); ♀ *Council* Gemeinderat *m*; 2. Gemeindewiese *f*; *in* ~ gemeinsam; *in* ~ *with fig.* genau wie; ~**er** [~nə] Bürger *m*, Gemeine(r) *m*; Mitglied *n* des Unterhauses; ~ **law** Gewohnheitsrecht *n*; ♀ *Market* Gemeinsamer Markt; ~**place** 1. Gemeinplatz *m*; 2. gewöhnlich; F abgedroschen; ~**s** *pl.* das gemeine Volk; Gemeinschaftsverpflegung *f*; (*mst House of*) ♀ Unterhaus *n*; ~ *sense* gesunder Menschenverstand; ~**wealth** [~nwelθ] Gemeinwesen *n*, Staat *m*; *bsd.* Republik *f*; *the British* ♀ das Commonwealth.

**commotion** [kə'mouʃən] Erschütterung *f*; Aufruhr *m*; Aufregung *f*.

**communal** □ ['kɔmjunl] gemeinschaftlich; Gemeinde...

**commune** 1. [kə'mjuːn] sich vertraulich besprechen; 2. ['kɔmjuːn] Gemeinde *f*.

**communicat|e** [kə'mjuːnikeit] *v/t.* mitteilen; *v/i.* das Abendmahl nehmen, kommunizieren; in Verbindung stehen; ~**ion** [kəmjuːniˈkeiʃən] Mitteilung *f*; Verbindung *f*; ~**ive** [kə'mjuːnikətiv] gesprächig.

**communion** [kə'mjuːnjən] Gemeinschaft *f*; *eccl.* Kommunion *f*, Abendmahl *n*.

**communis|m** ['kɔmjunizəm] Kommunismus *m*; ~**t** [~ist] 1. Kommunist(in); 2. kommunistisch.

**community** [kə'mjuːniti] Gemeinschaft *f*; Gemeinde *f*; Staat *m*.

**commut|ation** [kɔmju(ː)'teiʃən] Vertauschung *f*; Umwandlung *f*; Ablösung *f*; ~ *ticket Am.* Zeitkarte *f*; ~**e** [kə'mjuːt] ablösen; *Strafe* (mildernd) umwandeln; *Am.* pendeln *im Arbeitsverkehr*.

**compact** 1. ['kɔmpækt] Vertrag *m*; 2. [kəm'pækt] *adj.* dicht, fest; knapp, bündig; *v/t.* fest verbinden.

**companion** [kəm'pænjən] Gefährt|e *m*, -in *f*; Gesellschafter(in); ~**able** [~nəbl] gesellig; ~**ship** [~nʃip] Gesellschaft *f*.

**company** ['kʌmpəni] Gesellschaft *f*; Kompanie *f*; Handelsgesellschaft *f*; Genossenschaft *f*; ⚓ Mannschaft *f*; *thea.* Truppe *f*; *have* ~ Gäste haben; *keep* ~ *with* verkehren mit.

**compar|able** □ ['kɔmpərəbl] vergleichbar; **~ative** [kəm'pærətiv] **1.** □ vergleichend; verhältnismäßig; **2.** *a.* ~ *degree gr.* Komparativ *m*; **~e** [~'pɛə] **1.:** *beyond* ~, *without* ~, *past* ~ unvergleichlich; **2.** *v/t.* vergleichen; gleichstellen (*to* mit); *v/i.* sich vergleichen (lassen); **~ison** [~'pærisn] Vergleich(ung *f*) *m*.

**compartment** [kəm'pɑːtmənt] Abteilung *f*; △ Fach *n*; ⚓ Abteil *n*.

**compass** ['kʌmpəs] **1.** Bereich *m*; ♪ Umfang *m*; Kompaß *m*; *oft pair of* ~*es pl.* Zirkel *m*; **2.** herumgehen um; einschließen; erreichen; planen.

**compassion** [kəm'pæʃən] Mitleid *n*; **~ate** □ [~nit] mitleidig.

**compatible** □ [kəm'pætəbl] vereinbar, verträglich; schicklich.

**compatriot** [kəm'pætriət] Landsmann *m*.

**compel** [kəm'pel] (er)zwingen.

**compensat|e** ['kɔmpenseit] *j-n* entschädigen; *et.* ersetzen; ausgleichen; **~ion** [kɔmpen'seiʃən] Ersatz *m*; Ausgleich(ung *f*) *m*; Entschädigung *f*; *Am.* Vergütung *f* (*Gehalt*).

**compère** ['kɔmpɛə] **1.** Conférencier *m*; **2.** ansagen (bei).

**compete** [kəm'piːt] sich mitbewerben (*for* um); konkurrieren.

**competen|ce, ~cy** ['kɔmpitəns, ~si] Befugnis *f*, Zuständigkeit *f*; Auskommen *n*; **~t** □ [~nt] hinreichend; (leistungs)fähig; fachkundig; berechtigt, zuständig.

**competit|ion** [kɔmpi'tiʃən] Mitbewerbung *f*; Wettbewerb *m*; ✝ Konkurrenz *f*; **~ive** [kəm'petitiv] wetteifernd; **~or** [~tə] Mitbewerber (-in); Konkurrent(in).

**compile** [kəm'pail] zs.-tragen, zs.-stellen (*from* aus); sammeln.

**complacen|ce, ~cy** [kəm'pleisns, ~si] Selbstzufriedenheit *f*.

**complain** [kəm'plein] (sich be-) klagen; **~ant** [~nənt] Kläger(in); **~t** [~nt] Klage *f*, Beschwerde *f*; ✚ Leiden *n*.

**complaisan|ce** [kəm'pleizəns] Gefälligkeit *f*; Entgegenkommen *n*; **~t** □ [~nt] gefällig; entgegenkommend.

**complement 1.** ['kɔmplimənt] Ergänzung *f*; volle Anzahl *f*; **2.** [~ment] ergänzen.

**complet|e** [kəm'pliːt] **1.** □ vollständig, ganz; vollkommen; **2.** vervollständigen; vervollkommnen; abschließen; **~ion** [~iːʃən] Vervollständigung *f*; Abschluß *m*; Erfüllung *f*.

**complex** ['kɔmpleks] **1.** □ zs.-gesetzt; *fig.* kompliziert; **2.** Gesamtheit *f*, Komplex *m*; **~ion** [kəm'plekʃən] Aussehen *n*; Charakter *m*, Zug *m*; Gesichtsfarbe *f*, Teint *m*; **~ity** [~ksiti] Kompliziertheit *f*.

**complian|ce** [kəm'plaiəns] Einwilligung *f*; Einverständnis *n*; *in* ~ *with* gemäß; **~t** □ [~nt] gefällig.

**complicate** ['kɔmplikeit] komplizieren, erschweren.

**complicity** [kəm'plisiti] Mitschuld *f* (*in an dat.*).

**compliment 1.** ['kɔmplimənt] Kompliment *n*; Schmeichelei *f*; Gruß *m*; **2.** [~ment] *v/t.* (*on*) beglückwünschen (zu); *j-m* Komplimente machen (über *acc.*); **~ary** [kɔmpli'mentəri] höflich.

**comply** [kəm'plai] sich fügen; nachkommen, entsprechen (*with dat.*).

**component** [kəm'pounənt] **1.** Bestandteil *m*; **2.** zs.-setzend.

**compos|e** [kəm'pouz] zs.-setzen; komponieren; verfassen; ordnen; beruhigen; *typ.* setzen; **~ed** □ ruhig, gesetzt; **~er** [~zə] Komponist(in); Verfasser(in); **~ition** [kɔmpə'ziʃən] Zs.-setzung *f*; Abfassung *f*; Komposition *f*; (Schrift-) Satz *m*; Aufsatz *m*; ✝ Vergleich *m*; **~t** ['kɔmpost] Kompost *m*; **~ure** [kəm'pouʒə] Fassung *f*, Gemütsruhe *f*.

**compound 1.** ['kɔmpaund] zs.-gesetzt; ~ *interest* Zinseszinsen *m/pl.*; **2.** Zs.-setzung *f*, Verbindung *f*; **3.** [kəm'paund] *v/t.* zs.-setzen; *Streit* beilegen; *v/i.* sich einigen.

**comprehend** [kɔmpri'hend] umfassen; begreifen, verstehen.

**comprehen|sible** □ [kɔmpri'hensəbl] verständlich; **~sion** [~ʃən] Verständnis *n*; Fassungskraft *f*; Umfang *m*; **~sive** □ [~nsiv] umfassend.

**compress** [kəm'pres] zs.-drücken; ~*ed air* Druckluft *f*; **~ion** [~ʃən] *phys.* Verdichtung *f*; ⊕ Druck *m*.

**comprise** [kəm'praiz] in sich fassen, einschließen, enthalten.

**compromise** ['kɔmprəmaiz] **1.** Kompromiß *m*, *n*; **2.** *v/t. Streit* beilegen; bloßstellen; *v/i.* e-n Kompromiß schließen.

**compuls|ion** [kəm'pʌlʃən] Zwang *m*; **~ory** [~səri] obligatorisch; Zwangs...; Pflicht...

**compunction** [kəm'pʌŋkʃən] Gewissensbisse *m/pl.*; Reue *f*; Bedenken *n*.

**comput|ation** [kɔmpju(ː)'teiʃən] (Be)Rechnung *f*; **~e** [kəm'pjuːt] (be-, er)rechnen; schätzen; **~er** [~tə] Computer *m*.

**comrade** ['kɔmrid] Kamerad *m*.

**con**[1] *abbr.* [kɔn] = *contra.*

**con²** *Am. sl.* [ˌ] **1.:** ~ *man* = *confidence man;* **2.** 'reinlegen *(betrügen).*

**conceal** [kən'siːl] verbergen; *fig.* verhehlen, verheimlichen, verschweigen.

**concede** [kən'siːd] zugestehen; einräumen; gewähren, nachgeben.

**conceit** [kən'siːt] Einbildung *f;* spitzfindiger Gedanke; übertriebenes sprachliches Bild; ~ed □ eingebildet *(of* auf *acc.).*

**conceiv|able** □ [kən'siːvəbl] denkbar; begreiflich; ~e [kən'siːv] *v/i.* empfangen *(schwanger werden);* sich denken *(of acc.); v/t.* Kind empfangen; sich denken; aussinnen.

**concentrate** ['kɔnsentreit] (sich) zs.-ziehen, (sich) konzentrieren.

**conception** [kən'sepʃən] Begreifen *n;* Vorstellung *f,* Begriff *m,* Idee *f; biol.* Empfängnis *f.*

**concern** [kən'səːn] **1.** Angelegenheit *f;* Interesse *n;* Sorge *f;* Beziehung *f* *(with* zu); ♰ Geschäft *n,* (industrielles) Unternehmen; **2.** betreffen, angehen, interessieren; ~ *o.s. about od.* for sich kümmern um; be ~ed in Betracht kommen; ~ed □ interessiert, beteiligt *(in an dat.);* bekümmert; ~ing *prp.* [ˌniŋ] betreffend, über, wegen, hinsichtlich.

**concert 1.** ['kɔnsət] Konzert *n;* **2.** [ˌsə(ː)t] Einverständnis *n;* **3.** [kən'səːt] sich einigen, verabreden; ~ed gemeinsam; ♪ mehrstimmig.

**concession** [kən'seʃən] Zugeständnis *n;* Erlaubnis *f.* [räumend.]

**concessive** □ [kən'sesiv] ein-

**conciliat|e** [kən'silieit] aus-, versöhnen; ausgleichen; ~or [ˌtə] Vermittler *m;* ~ory [ˌiətəri] versöhnlich, vermittelnd.

**concise** □ [kən'sais] kurz, bündig, knapp; ~ness [ˌsnis] Kürze *f.*

**conclude** [kən'kluːd] schließen, beschließen; abschließen; folgern; sich entscheiden; *to be* ~d Schluß folgt.

**conclusi|on** [kən'kluːʒən] Schluß *m,* Ende *n;* Abschluß *m;* Folgerung *f;* Beschluß *m;* ~ve □ [ˌuːsiv] schlüssig; endgültig.

**concoct** [kən'kɔkt] zs.-brauen; *fig.* aussinnen; ~ion [ˌkʃən] Gebräu *n; fig.* Erfindung *f.*

**concord** ['kɔŋkɔːd] Eintracht *f;* Übereinstimmung *f (a. gr.);* ♪ Harmonie *f;* ~ant □ [kən'kɔːdənt] übereinstimmend; einstimmig; ♪ harmonisch.

**concourse** ['kɔŋkɔːs] Zusammen-, Auflauf *m;* Menge *f; Am.* Bahnhofs-, Schalterhalle *f.*

**concrete 1.** ['kɔnkriːt] konkret; Beton...; **2.** [ˌ] Beton *m;* **3.** [kɔn'kriːt] *zu e-r Masse* verbinden; ['kɔnkriːt] betonieren.

**concur** [kən'kəː] zs.-treffen, zs.-wirken; übereinstimmen; ~rence [ˌ'kʌrəns] Zusammentreffen *n;* Übereinstimmung *f;* Mitwirkung *f.*

**concussion** [kən'kʌʃən]: ~ *of the brain* Gehirnerschütterung *f.*

**condemn** [kən'dem] verdammen; verurteilen; verwerfen; *Kranke* aufgeben; beschlagnahmen; ~ation [kɔndem'neiʃən] Verurteilung *f;* Verdammung *f;* Verwerfung *f.*

**condens|ation** [kɔnden'seiʃən] Verdichtung *f;* ~e [kən'dens] (sich) verdichten; ⊕ kondensieren; zs.-drängen; ~er [ˌsə] ⊕ Kondensator *m.*

**condescend** [kɔndi'send] sich herablassen; geruhen; ~sion [ˌnʃən] Herablassung *f.*

**condiment** ['kɔndimənt] Würze *f.*

**condition** [kən'diʃən] **1.** Zustand *m,* Stand *m;* Stellung *f,* Bedingung *f;* ~s *pl.* Verhältnisse *n/pl.;* **2.** bedingen; in e-n bestimmten Zustand bringen; ~al □ [ˌnl] bedingt *(on, upon* durch); Bedingungs...; ~ *clause gr.* Bedingungssatz *m;* ~ *mood gr.* Konditional *m.*

**condol|e** [kən'doul] kondolieren *(with dat.);* ~ence [ˌləns] Beileid *n.*

**conduc|e** [kən'djuːs] führen, dienen; ~ive [ˌsiv] dienlich, förderlich.

**conduct 1.** ['kɔndəkt] Führung *f;* Verhalten *n,* Betragen *n;* **2.** [kən'dʌkt] führen; ♪ dirigieren; ~ion [ˌkʃən] Leitung *f;* ~or [ˌktə] Führer *m;* Leiter *m;* Schaffner *m;* ♪ Dirigent *m;* ⚡ Blitzableiter *m.*

**conduit** ['kɔndit] (Leitungs-) Röhre *f.*

**cone** [koun] Kegel *m;* ♣ Zapfen *m.*

**confabulation** [kɔnfæbju'leiʃən] Plauderei *f.*

**confection** [kən'fekʃən] Konfekt *n;* ~er [ˌʃnə] Konditor *m;* ~ery [ˌəri] Konfekt *n;* Konditorei *f; bsd. Am.* Süßwarengeschäft *n.*

**confedera|cy** [kən'fedərəsi] Bündnis *n; the* ⚌ *bsd. Am.* die 11 Südstaaten *bei der Sezession* 1860—61; ~te **1.** [ˌrit] verbündet; **2.** [ˌ] Bundesgenosse *m;* **3.** [ˌreit] (sich) verbünden; ~tion [kɔnfedə'reiʃən] Bund *m,* Bündnis *n; the* ⚌ *bsd. Am.* die Staatenkonföderation *f* von 1781—1789.

**confer** [kən'fəː] *v/t.* übertragen, verleihen; *v/i.* sich besprechen; ~ence ['kɔnfərəns] Konferenz *f.*

**confess** [kən'fes] bekennen, gestehen; beichten; ~ion [ˌeʃən] Geständnis *n;* Bekenntnis *n;* Beichte *f;* ~ional [ˌnl] Beichtstuhl *m;* ~or [ˌesə] Bekenner *m;* Beichtvater *m.*

**confide** [kən'faid] *v/t.* anvertrauen; *v/i.* vertrauen *(in auf acc.);* ~nce ['kɔnfidəns] Vertrauen *n;* Zuversicht *f;* ~nce man Schwindler *m;*

Hochstapler *m*; ~nce trick Bauernfängerei *f*; ~nt □ [~nt] vertrauend; zuversichtlich; ~ntial □ [konfi'denʃəl] vertraulich.

confine [kən'fain] begrenzen; beschränken; einsperren; *be* ~*d* niederkommen (*of* mit); *be* ~*d to bed* das Bett hüten müssen; ~ment [~nmənt] Haft *f*; Beschränkung *f*; Entbindung *f*.

confirm [kən'fəːm] (be)kräftigen; bestätigen; konfirmieren; firmen; ~ation [konfə'meiʃən] Bestätigung *f*; *eccl.* Konfirmation *f*; *eccl.* Firmung *f*.

confiscat|e ['konfiskeit] beschlagnahmen; ~ion [konfis'keiʃən] Beschlagnahme *f*.

conflagration [konflə'greiʃən] gro [ßer Brand.]

conflict 1. ['konflikt] Konflikt *m*; 2. [kən'flikt] im Konflikt stehen.

conflu|ence ['konfluəns], ~x [~ʌks] Zs.-fluß *m*; Auflauf *m*; ~ent [~luənt] 1. zs.-fließend, zs.-laufend; 2. Zu-, Nebenfluß *m*.

conform [kən'fɔːm] (sich) anpassen; ~able □ [~məbl] (to) übereinstimmend (mit); entsprechend (*dat.*); nachgiebig (gegen); ~ity [~miti] Übereinstimmung *f*.

confound [kən'faund] vermengen; verwechseln; *j-n* verwirren; ~ *it!* F verdammt!; ~ed □ F verdammt.

confront [kən'frʌnt] gegenüberstellen; entgegentreten (*dat.*).

confus|e [kən'fjuːz] verwechseln; verwirren; ~ion [~uːʒən] Verwirrung *f*; Verwechs(e)lung *f*.

confut|ation [konfju:'teiʃən] Widerlegung *f*; ~e [kən'fjuːt] widerlegen.

congeal [kən'dʒiːl] erstarren (lassen); gerinnen (lassen).

congenial □ [kən'dʒiːnjəl] (geistes-)verwandt (*with dat.*); zusagend.

congenital [kən'dʒenitl] angeboren.

congestion [kən'dʒestʃən] (Blut-)Andrang *m*; Stauung *f*; *traffic* ~ Verkehrsstockung *f*.

conglomeration [kənglɔmə'reiʃən] Anhäufung *f*; Konglomerat *n*.

congratulat|e [kən'grætjuleit] beglückwünschen; *j-m* gratulieren; ~ion [kəngrætju'leiʃən] Glückwunsch *m*.

congregat|e ['kɔŋgrigeit] (sich) (ver)sammeln; ~ion [kɔŋgri'geiʃən] Versammlung *f*; *eccl.* Gemeinde *f*.

congress ['kɔŋgres] Kongreß *m*; ♀ Kongreß *m*, *gesetzgebende Körperschaft der USA*; ♀man, ♀woman *Am. pol.* Mitglied *n* des Repräsentantenhauses.

congruous □ ['kɔŋgruəs] angemessen (*to* für); übereinstimmend; folgerichtig.

conifer ['kounifə] Nadelholzbaum *m*.

conjecture [kən'dʒektʃə] 1. Mutmaßung *f*; 2. mutmaßen.

conjoin [kən'dʒɔin] (sich) verbinden; ~t ['kɔndʒɔint] verbunden.

conjugal □ ['kɔndʒugəl] ehelich.

conjugat|e *gr.* ['kɔndʒugeit] konjugieren, beugen; ~ion *gr.* [kɔndʒu'geiʃən] Konjugation *f*, Beugung *f*.

conjunction [kən'dʒʌŋkʃən] Verbindung *f*; Zs.-treffen *n*; *gr.* Konjunktion *f*.

conjunctivitis [kəndʒʌŋkti'vaitis] Bindehautentzündung *f*.

conjure[1] [kən'dʒuə] beschwören, inständig bitten.

conjur|e[2] ['kʌndʒə] *v/t.* beschwören; *et. wohin* zaubern; *v/i.* zaubern; ~er [~ərə] Zauber|er *m*, -in *f*; Taschenspieler(in); ~ing-trick [~riŋtrik] Zauberkunststück *n*; ~or [~rə] = *conjurer*.

connect [kə'nekt] (sich) verbinden; ⚡ schalten; ~ed □ verbunden; zs.-hängend (*Rede etc.*); *be* ~ *with* in Verbindung stehen mit *j-m*; ~ion [~kʃən] = *connexion*.

connexion [kə'nekʃən] Verbindung *f*; ⚡ Schaltung *f*; Anschluß *m* (*a.* ⛟, *📞*); Zs.-hang *m*; Verwandtschaft *f*.

connive [kə'naiv]: ~ *at* ein Auge zudrücken bei.

connoisseur [kɔni'səː] Kenner(in).

connubial □ [kə'njuːbjəl] ehelich.

conquer ['kɔŋkə] erobern; (be)siegen; ~or [~ərə] Eroberer *m*; Sieger *m*.

conquest ['kɔŋkwest] Eroberung *f*; Errungenschaft *f*; Sieg *m*.

conscience ['kɔnʃəns] Gewissen *n*.

conscientious □ [kɔnʃi'enʃəs] gewissenhaft; Gewissens...; ~ *objector* Kriegsdienstverweigerer *m* aus Überzeugung; ~ness [~nis] Gewissenhaftigkeit *f*.

conscious □ ['kɔnʃəs] bewußt; *be* ~ *of* sich bewußt sein (*gen.*); ~ness [~snis] Bewußtsein *n*.

conscript ⚔ ['kɔnskript] Wehrpflichtige(r) *m*; ~ion ⚔ [kən'skripʃən] Einberufung *f*.

consecrat|e ['kɔnsikreit] weihen, einsegnen; heiligen; widmen; ~ion [kɔnsi'kreiʃən] Weihung *f*, Einsegnung *f*; Heiligung *f*.

consecutive □ [kən'sekjutiv] aufea.-folgend; fortlaufend.

consent [kən'sent] 1. Zustimmung *f*; 2. einwilligen, zustimmen (*dat.*).

consequen|ce ['kɔnsikwəns] (to) Folge *f*, Konsequenz *f* (für); Wirkung *f*, Einfluß *m* (auf *acc.*); Bedeutung *f* (für); ~t [~nt] 1. folgend; 2. Folge(rung) *f*; ~tial □ [kɔnsi'kwenʃəl] sich ergebend (*on* aus); folgerichtig; wichtigtuerisch; ~tly ['kɔnsikwəntli] folglich, daher.

conserv|ation [kɔnsə(ː)'veiʃən] Erhaltung *f*; ~ative □ [kən'səːvətiv] 1. erhaltend (*of acc.*); konservativ; vorsichtig; 2. Konservative(r) *m*;

**~atory** [kən'sɔːvətri] Treib-, Gewächshaus *n*; ♪ Konservatorium *n*; **~e** [kən'sɔːv] erhalten.

**consider** [kən'sidə] *v/t.* betrachten; erwägen; überlegen; in Betracht ziehen; berücksichtigen; meinen, glauben; *v/i.* überlegen; *all things* **~ed** wenn man alles in Betracht zieht; **~able** □ [~ərəbl] ansehnlich, beträchtlich, ziemlich, (sehr) viel; **~ably** [~li] bedeutend, ziemlich, (sehr) viel; **~ate** □ [~rit] rücksichtsvoll; **~ation** [kənsidə'reiʃən] Betrachtung *f*, Erwägung *f*, Überlegung *f*; Rücksicht *f*; Wichtigkeit *f*; Entschädigung *f*; Entgelt *n*; *be under* **~** erwogen werden; in Betracht kommen; *on no* **~** unter keinen Umständen; **~ing** □ [kən'sidəriŋ] 1. *prp.* in Anbetracht (*gen.*); 2. **F** *adv.* den Umständen entsprechend.

**consign** [kən'sain] übergeben, überliefern; anvertrauen; **✝** konsignieren; **~ment ✝** [~nmənt] Übersendung *f*; Konsignation *f*.

**consist** [kən'sist] bestehen (*of* aus); in Einklang stehen (*with* mit); **~ence**, **~ency** [~təns, ~si] Festigkeit(sgrad *m*) *f*; Übereinstimmung *f*; Konsequenz *f*; **~ent** [~nt] fest; übereinstimmend, vereinbar (*with* mit); konsequent.

**consol|ation** [kɔnsə'leiʃən] Trost *m*; **~e** [kən'soul] trösten.

**consolidate** [kən'sɔlideit] festigen; *fig.* vereinigen; zs.-legen.

**consonan|ce** ['kɔnsənəns] Konsonanz *f*; Übereinstimmung *f*; **~t** [~nt] 1. □ übereinstimmend; 2. *gr.* Konsonant *m*, Mitlaut *m*.

**consort** ['kɔnsɔːt] Gemahl(in); ⚓ Geleitschiff *n*.

**conspicuous** □ [kən'spikjuəs] sichtbar; auffallend; hervorragend; *make o.s.* **~** sich auffällig benehmen.

**conspir|acy** [kən'spirəsi] Verschwörung *f*; **~ator** [~ətə] Verschwörer *m*; **~e** [~'spaiə] sich verschwören.

**constab|le** ['kʌnstəbl] Polizist *m*; Schutzmann *m*; **~ulary** [kən'stæbjuləri] Polizei(truppe) *f*.

**constan|cy** ['kɔnstənsi] Standhaftigkeit *f*; Beständigkeit *f*; **~t** □ [~nt] beständig, fest; unveränderlich; treu.

**consternation** [kɔnstə(:)'neiʃən] Bestürzung *f*.

**constipation** [kɔnsti'peiʃən] Verstopfung *f*.

**constituen|cy** [kən'stitjuənsi] Wählerschaft *f*; Wahlkreis *m*; **~t** [~nt] 1. wesentlich; Grund..., Bestand...; konstituierend; 2. wesentlicher Bestandteil; Wähler *m*.

**constitut|e** ['kɔnstitjuːt] ein-, errichten; ernennen; bilden, ausmachen; **~ion** [kɔnsti'tjuːʃən] Ein-, Errichtung *f*; Bildung *f*; Körper-

bau *m*; Verfassung *f*; **~ional** □ [~nl] konstitutionell; natürlich; verfassungsmäßig.

**constrain** [kən'strein] zwingen; *et.* erzwingen; **~t** [~nt] Zwang *m*.

**constrict** [kən'strikt] zs.-ziehen; **~ion** [~kʃən] Zs.-ziehung *f*.

**constringent** [kən'strindʒənt] zs.-ziehend.

**construct** [kən'strʌkt] bauen, errichten; *fig.* bilden; **~ion** [~kʃən] Konstruktion *f*; Bau *m*; Auslegung *f*; **~ive** [~ktiv] aufbauend, schöpferisch, konstruktiv, positiv; Bau...; **~or** [~tə] Erbauer *m*, Konstrukteur *m*.

**construe** [kən'struː] *gr.* konstruieren; auslegen, auffassen; übersetzen.

**consul** ['kɔnsəl] Konsul *m*; **~-general** Generalkonsul *m*; **~ate** [~sjulit] Konsulat *n* (*a. Gebäude*).

**consult** [kən'sʌlt] *v/t.* konsultieren, um Rat fragen; in *e-m Buch* nachschlagen; *v/i.* sich beraten; **~ation** [kɔnsəl'teiʃən] Konsultation *f*, Beratung *f*; Rücksprache *f*; **~** *hour* Sprechstunde *f*; **~ative** [kən'sʌltətiv] beratend.

**consume** [kən'sjuːm] *v/t.* verzehren; verbrauchen; vergeuden; **~r** [~mə] Verbraucher *m*; Abnehmer *m*.

**consummate** 1. □ [kən'sʌmit] vollendet; 2. [~sʌmeit] vollenden.

**consumpti|on** [kən'sʌmpʃən] Verbrauch *m*; ⚕ Schwindsucht *f*; **~ve** □ [~ptiv] verzehrend; ⚕ schwindsüchtig.

**contact** 1. ['kɔntækt] Berührung *f*; Kontakt *m*; **~** *lenses pl.* Haft-, Kontaktschalen *f/pl.*; 2. [kən'tækt] Fühlung nehmen mit.

**contagi|on** ⚕ [kən'teidʒən] Ansteckung *f*; Verseuchung *f*; Seuche *f*; **~ous** □ [~əs] ansteckend.

**contain** [kən'tein] (ent)halten, (um-)fassen; **~** *o.s.* an sich halten; **~er** [~nə] Behälter *m*; Großbehälter *m* (*im Frachtverkehr*).

**contaminat|e** [kən'tæmineit] verunreinigen; *fig.* anstecken, vergiften; verseuchen; **~ion** [kəntæmi'neiʃən] Verunreinigung *f*; (radioaktive) Verseuchung.

**contemplat|e** *fig.* ['kɔntempleit] betrachten; beabsichtigen; **~ion** [kɔntəm'pleiʃən] Betrachtung *f*; Nachsinnen *n*; **~ive** □ ['kɔntempleitiv] nachdenklich; [kən'templətiv] beschaulich.

**contempora|neous** □ [kəntempə-'reinjəs] gleichzeitig; **~ry** [kən-'tempərəri] 1. zeitgenössisch; gleichzeitig; 2. Zeitgenosse *m*, -in *f*.

**contempt** [kən'tempt] Verachtung *f*; **~ible** □ [~təbl] verachtenswert; **~uous** □ [~tjuəs] geringschätzig (*of* gegen); verächtlich.

**contend** [kən'tend] *v/i.* streiten; ringen (*for* um); *v/t.* behaupten.

**content** [kən'tent] 1. zufrieden; 2. befriedigen; ~ o.s. sich begnügen; 3. Zufriedenheit *f; to one's heart's* ~ nach Herzenslust; ['kɔntent] Umfang *m;* Gehalt *m;* ~s *pl. stofflicher* Inhalt; ~ed □ [kən'tentid] zufrieden; genügsam.

**contention** [kən'tenʃən] (Wort-) Streit *m;* Wetteifer *m.*

**contentment** [kən'tentmənt] Zufriedenheit *f,* Genügsamkeit *f.*

**contest** 1. ['kɔntest] Streit *m;* Wettkampf *m;* 2. [kən'test] (be)streiten; anfechten; um *et.* streiten. [*m.*]

**context** ['kɔntekst] Zusammenhang⌉

**contiguous** □ [kən'tigjuəs] anstoßend (*to* an *acc.*); benachbart.

**continent** ['kɔntinənt] 1. □ enthaltsam; mäßig; 2. Kontinent *m,* Erdteil *m;* Festland *n;* ~al [kɔnti'nentl] 1. □ kontinental; Kontinental...; 2. Kontinentaleuropäer(in).

**contingen|cy** [kən'tindʒənsi] Zufälligkeit *f;* Zufall *m;* Möglichkeit *f;* ~t [~nt] 1. □ zufällig; möglich (*to* bei); 2. ✕ Kontingent *n.*

**continu|al** □ [kən'tinjuəl] fortwährend, unaufhörlich; ~ance [~əns] (Fort)Dauer *f;* ~ation [kəntinju-'eiʃən] Fortsetzung *f;* Fortdauer *f;* ~ school Fortbildungsschule *f;* ~e [kən'tinju(:)] *v/t.* fortsetzen; beibehalten; *to be* ~d Fortsetzung folgt; *v/i.* fortdauern; fortfahren; ~ity [kɔnti'nju(:)iti] Kontinuität *f; Film:* Drehbuch *n; Radio:* verbindende Worte; ~ girl Skriptgirl *n;* ~ous □ [kən'tinjuəs] ununterbrochen.

**contort** [kən'tɔːt] verdrehen; verzerren; ~ion [~ɔːʃən] Verdrehung *f;* Verzerrung *f.*

**contour** ['kɔntuə] Umriß *m.*

**contra** ['kɔntrə] wider.

**contraband** [kɔntrə'bænd] Schmuggelware *f;* Schleichhandel *m; attr.* Schmuggel...

**contraceptive** [kɔntrə'septiv] 1. empfängnisverhütend; 2. empfängnisverhütendes Mittel.

**contract** 1. [kən'trækt] *v/t.* zs.-ziehen; sich *et.* zuziehen; *Schulden* machen; *Heirat etc.* (ab)schließen; *v/i.* einschrumpfen; e-n Vertrag schließen; sich verpflichten; 2. ['kɔntrækt] Kontrakt *m,* Vertrag *m;* ~ion [kən'trækʃən] Zs.-ziehung *f; gr.* Kurzform *f;* ~or [~ktə] Unternehmer *m;* Lieferant *m.*

**contradict** [kɔntrə'dikt] widersprechen (*dat.*); ~ion [~kʃən] Widerspruch *m;* ~ory □ [~ktəri] (sich) widersprechend.

**contrar|iety** [kɔntrə'raiəti] Widerspruch *m;* Widrigkeit *f;* ~y ['kɔntrəri] 1. entgegengesetzt; widrig; ~ to zuwider (*dat.*); gegen; 2. Gegenteil *n; on the* ~ im Gegenteil.

**contrast** 1. ['kɔntraːst] Gegensatz *m;* 2. [kən'traːst] *v/t.* gegenüberstellen; vergleichen; *v/i.* sich unterscheiden, abstechen (*with* von).

**contribut|e** [kən'tribju(:)t] beitragen, beisteuern; ~ion [kɔntri'bju:-ʃən] Beitrag *m;* ~or [kən'tribjutə] Beitragende(r *m*) *f;* Mitarbeiter(in) *an e-r Zeitung;* ~ory [~əri] beitragend.

**contrit|e** □ ['kɔntrait] reuevoll; ~ion [kən'triʃən] Zerknirschung *f.*

**contriv|ance** [kən'traivəns] Erfindung *f;* Plan *m;* Vorrichtung *f;* Kunstgriff *m;* Scharfsinn *m;* ~e [kən'traiv] *v/t.* ersinnen; planen; zuwegebringen; *v/i.* es fertig bringen (*to inf.* zu *inf.*); ~er [~və] Erfinder(in).

**control** [kən'troul] 1. Kontrolle *f,* Aufsicht *f;* Befehl *m;* Zwang *m;* Gewalt *f;* Zwangswirtschaft *f;* Kontrollvorrichtung *f;* Steuerung *f;* ~ board ⊕ Schaltbrett *n;* 2. einschränken; kontrollieren; beaufsichtigen; überwachen; beherrschen; (nach)prüfen; bewirtschaften; regeln; ✗ steuern (*a. fig. dat.*); ~ler [~lə] Kontrolleur *m,* Aufseher *m;* Leiter *m;* Rechnungsprüfer *m.*

**controver|sial** □ [kɔntrə'və:ʃəl] umstritten; streitsüchtig; ~sy ['kɔntrəvə:si] Streit(frage) *f m;* ~t [~ə:t] bestreiten.

**contumacious** □ [kɔntju(:)'meiʃəs] widerspenstig; ✗ ungehorsam.

**contumely** ['kɔntju(:)mli] Beschimpfung *f;* Schmach *f.*

**contuse** ✗ [kən'tju:z] quetschen.

**convalesce** [kɔnvə'les] genesen; ~nce [~sns] Genesung *f;* ~nt [~nt] 1. □ genesend; 2. Genesende(r *m*) *f.*

**convene** [kən'vi:n] (sich) versammeln; zs.-rufen; ✗ vorladen.

**convenien|ce** [kən'vi:njəns] Bequemlichkeit *f;* Angemessenheit *f;* Vorteil *m;* Klosett *n; at your earliest* ~ möglichst bald; ~t □ [~nt] bequem; passend; brauchbar.

**convent** ['kɔnvənt] (Nonnen)Kloster *n;* ~ion [kən'venʃən] Versammlung *f;* Konvention *f,* Übereinkommen *n,* Vertrag *m;* Herkommen *n;* ~ional [~nl] vertraglich; herkömmlich, konventionell.

**converge** [kən'və:dʒ] konvergieren, zs.-laufen (lassen).

**convers|ant** [kən'və:sənt] vertraut; ~ation [kɔnvə'seiʃən] Gespräch *n,* Unterhaltung *f;* ~ational [~nl] Unterhaltungs...; umgangssprachlich; ~e 1. [kən'və:s] umgekehrt; 2. [kən'və:s] sich unterhalten; ~ion [~ə:ʃən] Um-, Verwandlung *f;* ⊕, ⚯ Umformung *f; eccl.* Bekehrung *f; pol.* Meinungswechsel *m,* Übertritt *m;* ✝ Konvertierung *f;* Umstellung *f e-r Währung etc.*

convert 1. ['konvɔːt] Bekehrte(r *m*) *f*, Konvertit *m*; 2. [kən'vɔːt] (sich) um-, verwandeln; ⊕, ⚡ umformen; *eccl.* bekehren; † konvertieren; *Währung etc.* umstellen; **~er** ⊕, ⚡ [~tə] Umformer *m*; **~ible 1.** □ [~təbl] um-, verwandelbar; † konvertierbar; 2. *mot.* Kabrio(lett) *n*.

convey [kən'vei] befördern, bringen, schaffen; übermitteln; mitteilen; ausdrücken; übertragen; **~ance** [~eiəns] Beförderung *f*; † Spedition *f*; Übermittlung *f*; Verkehrsmittel *n*; Fuhrwerk *n*; Übertragung *f*; **~er**, **~or** ⊕ [~eiə] *a.* ~ belt Förderband *n*.

convict 1. ['konvikt] Sträfling *m*; 2. [kən'vikt] *j-n* überführen; **~ion** [~kʃən] ⚖ Überführung *f*; Überzeugung *f* (of von).

convince [kən'vins] überzeugen.

convivial □ [kən'viviəl] festlich; gesellig.

convocation [konvə'keiʃən] Einberufung *f*; Versammlung *f*.

convoke [kən'vouk] einberufen.

convoy ['konvɔi] 1. Geleit *n*; Geleitzug *m*; (Geleit)Schutz *m*; 2. geleiten.

convuls|ion [kən'vʌlʃən] Zuckung *f*, Krampf *m*; **~ive** □ [~lsiv] krampfhaft, -artig, konvulsiv.

coo [kuː] girren, gurren.

cook [kuk] 1. Koch *m*; Köchin *f*; 2. kochen; *Bericht etc.* frisieren; **~book** *Am.* ['kukbuk] Kochbuch *n*; **~ery** [~kəri] Kochen *n*; Kochkunst *f*; **~ie** *Am.* ['kuki] Plätzchen *n*; **~ing** [~iŋ] Küche *f* (*Kochweise*); **~y** *Am.* ['kuki] = cookie.

cool [kuːl] 1. □ kühl; *fig.* kaltblütig, gelassen; unverfroren; 2. Kühle *f*; 3. (sich) abkühlen.

coolness ['kuːlnis] Kühle *f* (*a. fig.*); Kaltblütigkeit *f*.

coon *Am.* F [kuːn] *zo.* Waschbär *m*; Neger *m*; (schlauer) Bursche.

coop [kuːp] 1. Hühnerkorb *m*; 2. ~ *up od. in* einsperren.

co-op F [kou'ɔp] = *co-operative* (*store*).

cooper ['kuːpə] Böttcher *m*, Küfer *m*.

co(-)operat|e [kou'ɔpəreit] mitwirken; zs.-arbeiten; **~ion** [kouɔpə-'reiʃən] Mitwirkung *f*; Zs.-arbeit *f*; **~ive** [kou'ɔpərətiv] zs.-wirkend; ~ *society* Konsumverein *m*; ~ *store* Konsum(vereinsladen) *m*; **~or** [~reitə] Mitarbeiter *m*.

co-ordinat|e 1. □ [kou'ɔːdnit] gleichgeordnet; 2. [~dineit] koordinieren, gleichordnen; auf-ea. einstellen; **~ion** [kouɔːdi'neiʃən] Gleichordnung *f*, -schaltung *f*.

copartner ['kou'pɑːtnə] Teilhaber *m*.

cope [koup]: ~ *with* sich messen mit, fertig werden mit.

copious □ ['koupjəs] reich(lich); weitschweifig, **~ness** [~snis] Fülle *f*.

copper¹ ['kɔpə] 1. Kupfer *n*; Kupfermünze *f*; 2. kupfern; Kupfer...

copper² *sl.* [~] Polyp *m* (*Polizist*).

coppice, copse ['kɔpis, kɔps] Unterholz *n*, Dickicht *n*.

copy ['kɔpi] 1. Kopie *f*; Nachbildung *f*; Abschrift *f*; Durchschlag *m*; Muster *n*; Exemplar *n* e-*s* Buches; Zeitungs-Nummer *f*; druckfertiges Manuskript; *fair od. clean* ~ Reinschrift *f*; 2. kopieren; abschreiben; nachbilden, nachahmen; **~book** Schreibheft *n*; **~ing** [~iiŋ] Kopier...; **~ist** [~ist] Abschreiber *m*; Nachahmer *m*; **~right** Verlagsrecht *n*, Copyright *n*.

coral ['kɔrəl] Koralle *f*.

cord [kɔːd] 1. Schnur *f*, Strick *m*; *anat.* Strang *m*; 2. (zu)schnüren, binden; **~ed** ['kɔːdid] gerippt.

cordial ['kɔːdjəl] 1. □ herzlich; herzstärkend; 2. (Magen)Likör *m*; **~ity** [kɔːdi'æliti] Herzlichkeit *f*.

cordon ['kɔːdn] 1. Postenkette *f*; 2. ~ *off* abriegeln, absperren.

corduroy ['kɔːdərɔi] Kord *m*; **~s** *pl.* Kordhosen *f/pl.*; ~ *road* Knüppeldamm *m*.

core [kɔː] 1. Kerngehäuse *n*; *fig.* Herz *n*; Kern *m*; 2. entkernen.

cork [kɔːk] 1. Kork *m*; 2. (ver)korken; **~ing** *Am.* F ['kɔːkiŋ] fabelhaft, prima; **~jacket** Schwimmweste *f*; **~screw** Kork(en)zieher *m*.

corn [kɔːn] 1. Korn *n*; Getreide *n*; *a. Indian* ~ *Am.* Mais *m*; ⚕ Hühnerauge *n*; 2. einpökeln.

corner ['kɔːnə] 1. Ecke *f*, Winkel *m*; Kurve *f*; *fig.* Enge *f*; † *Aufkäufer-Ring m*; 2. Eck...; 3. in die Ecke (*fig.* Enge) treiben; † aufkaufen; **~ed** ...eckig.

cornet ♪ ['kɔːnit] (kleines) Horn.

cornice △ ['kɔːnis] Gesims *n*.

corn|-juice *Am. sl.* ['kɔːndʒuːs] Maisschnaps *m*; ~ **pone** *Am.* ['kɔːnpoun] Maisbrot *n*; **~stalk** Getreidehalm *m*; *Am.* Maisstengel *m*; **~starch** *Am.* Maisstärke *f*.

coron|ation [kɔrə'neiʃən] Krönung *f*; **~er** ['kɔrənə] Leichenbeschauer *m*; **~et** [~nit] Adelskrone *f*.

corpor|al ['kɔːpərəl] 1. □ körperlich; 2. ✗ Korporal *m*; **~ation** [kɔːpə'reiʃən] Körperschaft *f*, Innung *f*, Zunft *f*; Stadtverwaltung *f*; *Am.* Aktiengesellschaft *f*.

corpse [kɔːps] Leichnam *m*.

corpulen|ce, **~cy** ['kɔːpjuləns, ~si] Beleibtheit *f*; **~t** [~nt] beleibt.

corral *Am.* [kɔː'rɑːl] 1. Einzäunung *f*; 2. zs.-pferchen, einsperren.

correct [kə'rekt] 1. *adj.* □ korrekt, richtig; 2. *v/t.* korrigieren; zurechtweisen; strafen; **~ion** [~kʃən] Berichtigung *f*; Verweis *m*; Strafe *f*;

Korrektur *f; house of* ~ Besserungsanstalt *f.*

**correlate** ['kɔrileit] in Wechselbeziehung stehen *od.* bringen.

**correspond** [kɔris'pɔnd] entsprechen (*with, to dat.*); korrespondieren; ~ence [~dəns] Übereinstimmung *f;* Briefwechsel *m;* ~ent [~nt] **1.** □ entsprechend; **2.** Briefschreiber(in); Korrespondent(in).

**corridor** ['kɔridɔ:] Korridor *m;* Gang *m;* ~ train D-Zug *m.*

**corrigible** □ ['kɔridʒəbl] verbesserlich; zu verbessern(d).

**corroborate** [kə'rɔbəreit] stärken; bestätigen.

**corro|de** [kə'roud] zerfressen; wegätzen; ~sion [~ouʒən] Ätzen *n,* Zerfressen *n;* ⊕ Korrosion *f;* Rost *m;* ~sive [~ousiv] **1.** □ zerfressend, ätzend; **2.** Ätzmittel *n.*

**corrugate** ['kɔrugeit] runzeln; ⊕ riefen; ~d iron Wellblech *n.*

**corrupt** [kə'rʌpt] **1.** □ verdorben; verderbt; bestechlich; **2.** *v/t.* verderben; bestechen; anstecken; *v/i.* (ver)faulen, verderben; ~ible □ [~təbl] verderblich; bestechlich; ~ion [~ʃən] Verderbnis *f,* Verdorbenheit *f;* Fäulnis *f;* Bestechung *f.*

**corsage** [kɔ:'sɑ:ʒ] Taille *f,* Mieder *n; Am.* Ansteckblume(n *pl.*) *f.*

**corset** ['kɔ:sit] Korsett *n.*

**coruscate** ['kɔrəskeit] funkeln.

**co-signatory** ['kou'signətəri] **1.** mitunterzeichnend; **2.** Mitunterzeichner *m.*

**cosmetic** [kɔz'metik] **1.** kosmetisch; **2.** Schönheitsmittel *n;* Kosmetik *f;* ~ian [kɔzme'tiʃən] Kosmetiker(in).

**cosmonaut** ['kɔzmənɔ:t] Kosmonaut *m,* Weltraumfahrer *m.*

**cosmopolit|an** [kɔzmə'pɔlitən], ~e [kɔz'mɔpəlait] **1.** kosmopolitisch; **2.** Weltbürger(in).

**cost** [kɔst] **1.** Preis *m;* Kosten *pl.;* Schaden *m; first od. prime* ~ Anschaffungskosten *pl.;* **2.** [*irr.*] kosten.

**cost|iness** ['kɔstlinis] Kostbarkeit *f;* ~y ['kɔstli] kostbar; kostspielig.

**costume** ['kɔstju:m] Kostüm *n;* Kleidung *f;* Tracht *f.*

**cosy** ['kouzi] **1.** □ behaglich, gemütlich; **2.** = *tea-cosy.*

**cot** [kɔt] Feldbett *n;* ⏚ Hängematte *f* mit Rahmen, Koje *f;* Kinderbett *n.*

**cottage** ['kɔtidʒ] Hütte *f;* kleines Landhaus, Sommerhaus *n;* ~ cheese *Am.* Quark(käse) *m;* ~ piano Piano *n;* ~r [~dʒə] Häusler *m;* Hüttenbewohner *m; Am.* Sommergast *m.*

**cotton** ['kɔtn] **1.** Baumwolle *f;* ⚕ Kattun *m; Näh-*Garn *n;* **2.** baumwollen; Baumwoll...; ~ wool Watte *f;* **3.** ⏚ sich vertragen; sich anschließen; ~-wood ⚘ *e-e* amerikanische Pappel.

**couch** [kautʃ] **1.** Lager *n;* Couch *f,* Sofa *n,* Liege *f;* Schicht *f;* **2.** *v/t.* Meinung *etc.* ausdrücken; Schriftsatz *etc.* abfassen; ⚔ Star stechen; *v/i.* sich (nieder)legen; versteckt liegen; kauern.

**cough** [kɔf] **1.** Husten *m;* **2.** husten.

**could** [kud] *pret. von can*[1].

**coulee** *Am.* ['ku:li] (trockenes) Bachbett.

**council** ['kaunsl] Rat(sversammlung *f*) *m;* ~(l)or [~silə] Ratsmitglied *n,* Stadtrat *m.*

**counsel** ['kaunsəl] **1.** Beratung *f;* Rat(schlag) *m;* ⚖ Anwalt *m;* ~ *for the defense* Verteidiger *m;* ~ *for the prosecution* Anklagevertreter *m;* **2.** *j-n* beraten; *j-m* raten; ~(l)or [~silə] Ratgeber(in); Anwalt *m; Am.* Rechtsbeistand *m.*

**count**[1] [kaunt] **1.** Rechnung *f;* Zahl *f;* ⚖ Anklagepunkt *m;* **2.** *v/t.* zählen; rechnen; dazurechnen; *fig.* halten für; *v/i.* zählen; rechnen; gelten (*for little* wenig).

**count**[2] [.] nichtbritischer Graf.

**count-down** ['kauntdaun] Countdown *m, n,* Startzählung *f* (*beim Raketenstart*).

**countenance** ['kauntinəns] **1.** Gesicht *n;* Fassung *f;* Unterstützung *f;* **2.** begünstigen, unterstützen.

**counter**[1] ['kauntə] Zähler *m,* Zählapparat *m;* Spielmarke *f;* Zahlpfennig *m;* Ladentisch *m;* Schalter *m.*

**counter**[2] [.] **1.** entgegen, zuwider (*to dat.*); Gegen...; **2.** Gegenschlag *m;* **3.** Gegenmaßnahmen treffen.

**counteract** [kauntə'rækt] zuwiderhandeln (*dat.*).

**counterbalance 1.** ['kauntəbæləns] Gegengewicht *n;* **2.** [kauntə'bæləns] aufwiegen; ⚖ ausgleichen.

**counter-espionage** ['kauntər'espiəna:ʒ] Spionageabwehr *f.*

**counterfeit** ['kauntəfit] **1.** □ nachgemacht; falsch, unecht; **2.** Nachahmung *f;* Fälschung *f;* Falschgeld *n;* **3.** nachmachen; fälschen; heucheln.

**counterfoil** ['kauntəfɔil] Kontrollabschnitt *m.*

**countermand** [kauntə'mɑ:nd] **1.** Gegenbefehl *m;* Widerruf *m;* **2.** widerrufen; abbestellen.

**counter-move** *fig.* ['kauntəmu:v] Gegenzug *m,* -maßnahme *f.*

**counterpane** ['kauntəpein] Bettdecke *f.*

**counterpart** ['kauntəpɑ:t] Gegenstück *n.*

**counterpoise** ['kauntəpɔiz] **1.** Gegengewicht *n;* **2.** das Gleichgewicht halten (*dat.*) (*a. fig.*), ausbalancieren.

**countersign** ['kauntəsain] **1.** Gegenzeichen *n;* ⚔ Losung(swort *n*) *f;* **2.** gegenzeichnen.

**countervail** ['kauntəveil] aufwiegen.

**countess** ['kauntis] Gräfin f.

**counting-house** ['kauntiŋhaus] Kontor n.

**countless** ['kauntlis] zahllos.

**countrified** ['kʌntrifaid] ländlich; bäurisch.

**country** ['kʌntri] 1. Land n; Gegend f; Heimatland n; 2. Land(s)..., ländlich; **~man** Landmann m (Bauer); Landsmann m; **~side** Gegend f; Land(bevölkerung f) n.

**county** ['kaunti] Grafschaft f, Kreis m; ~ seat Am. = ~ town Kreisstadt f.

**coup** [ku:] Schlag m, Streich m.

**couple** ['kʌpl] 1. Paar n; Koppel f; 2. (ver)koppeln; ⊕ kuppeln; (sich) paaren; **~r** [.lə] Radio: Koppler m.

**coupling** ['kʌpliŋ] Kupplung f; Radio: Kopplung f; attr. Kupplungs...

**coupon** ['ku:pɔn] Abschnitt m.

**courage** ['kʌridʒ] Mut m; **~ous** □ [kə'reidʒəs] mutig, beherzt.

**courier** ['kuriə] Kurier m, Eilbote m; Reiseführer m.

**course** [kɔːs] 1. Lauf m, Gang m; Weg m, ⚓, fig. Kurs m; Rennbahn f; Gang m (Speisen); Kursus m; univ. Vorlesung f; Ordnung f, Folge f; of ~ selbstverständlich; 2. v/t. hetzen; jagen; v/i. rennen.

**court** [kɔːt] 1. Hof m; Hofgesellschaft f; Gericht(shof m) n; General ♀ Am. gesetzgebende Versammlung; pay (one's) ~ to j-m den Hof machen; 2. j-m den Hof machen; werben um; **~day** ['kɔːtdei] Gerichtstag m; **~eous** □ ['kɔːtjəs] höflich; **~esy** ['kɔːtisi] Höflichkeit f; Gefälligkeit f; **~house** ['kɔːt-'haus] Gerichtsgebäude n; Am. a. Amtshaus n e-s Kreises; **~ier** ['kɔːtjə] Höfling m; **~ly** ['kɔːtli] höfisch; höflich; ~ martial ⚔ Kriegs-, Militärgericht n; **~-martial** ⚔ ['kɔːt'maːʃəl] vor ein Kriegs- od. Militärgericht stellen; ~ room Gerichtssaal m; **~ship** ['kɔːtʃip] Werbung f; **~yard** Hof m.

**cousin** ['kʌzn] Vetter m; Base f.

**cove** [kouv] 1. Bucht f; fig. Obdach n.

**covenant** ['kʌvinənt] 1. g's Vertrag m; Bund m; 2. v/t. geloben; v/i. übereinkommen.

**cover** ['kʌvə] 1. Decke f; Deckel m; Umschlag m; Hülle f; Deckung f; Schutz m; Dickicht n; Deckmantel m; Decke f, Mantel m (Bereifung); 2. (be-, zu)decken; einschlagen; einwickeln; verbergen, verdecken; schützen; ✝ zurücklegen; ✝ decken; mit e-r Schußwaffe zielen nach; ⚔ Gelände bestreichen; umfassen; fig. erfassen; Zeitung: berichten über (acc.); **~age** [.əridʒ]

Berichterstattung f (of über acc.); **~ing** [.riŋ] Decke f; Bett-Bezug m; Überzug m; Bekleidung f; Bedachung f.

**covert** 1. □ ['kʌvət] heimlich, versteckt; 2. □ ['kʌvə] Schutz m; Versteck n; Dickicht n.

**covet** ['kʌvit] begehren; **~ous** □ [.təs] (be)gierig; habsüchtig.

**cow**[1] [kau] Kuh f.

**cow**[2] [.] einschüchtern, ducken.

**coward** ['kauəd] 1. □ feig; 2. Feigling m; **~ice** [.dis] Feigheit f; **~ly** [.dli] feig(e).

**cow|boy** ['kaubɔi] Cowboy m (berittener Rinderhirt); **~catcher** Am. ⊜ Schienenräumer m.

**cower** ['kauə] kauern; sich ducken.

**cow|herd** ['kauhɜːd] Kuhhirt m; **~hide** 1. Rind(s)leder n; 2. peitschen; **~house** Kuhstall m.

**cowl** [kaul] Mönchskutte f; Kapuze f; Schornsteinkappe f.

**cow|man** ['kaumən] Melker m; Am. Viehzüchter m; **~puncher** Am. F ['kaupʌntʃə] Rinderhirt m; **~shed** Kuhstall m; **~slip** ♀ Schlüsselblume f; Am. Sumpfdotterblume f.

**coxcomb** ['kɔkskoum] Geck m.

**coxswain** ['kɔkswein, ⚓ mst 'kɔksn] Bootsführer m; Steuermann m.

**coy** □ [kɔi] schüchtern; spröde.

**crab** [kræb] Krabbe f, Taschenkrebs m; ⊕ Winde f; F Querkopf m.

**crab-louse** ['kræblaus] Filzlaus f.

**crack** [kræk] 1. Krach m; Riß m, Sprung m; F derber Schlag; Versuch m; Witz m; 2. F erstklassig; 3. v/t. (zer)sprengen; knallen mit et.; (auf)knacken; ~ a joke e-n Witz reißen; v/i. platzen, springen; knallen; umschlagen (Stimme); **~ed** geborsten; F verdreht; ~er ['krækə] Knallbonbon m; n; Schwärmer m; Am. Keks m (ungesüßt); **~le** [.kl] knattern, knistern; **~up** Zs.-stoß m; ✈ Bruchlandung f.

**cradle** ['kreidl] 1. Wiege f; Kindheit f (a. fig.); 2. (ein)wiegen.

**craft** [krɑːft] Handwerk n, Gewerbe n; Schiff(e pl.) n; Gerissenheit f; **~sman** ['krɑːftsmən] (Kunst)Handwerker m; **~y** □ ['krɑːfti] gerissen, raffiniert.

**crag** [kræg] Klippe f, Felsspitze f.

**cram** [kræm] (voll)stopfen; nudeln, mästen; F (ein)pauken.

**cramp** [kræmp] 1. Krampf m; ⊕ Klammer f; fig. Fessel f; 2. verkrampfen; einengen, hemmen.

**cranberry** ['krænbəri] Preiselbeere f.

**crane** [krein] 1. Kranich m; ⊕ Kran m; 2. (den Hals) recken; **~fly** zo. ['kreinflai] Schnake f.

**crank** [kræŋk] 1. Kurbel f; Schwengel m; Wortspiel n; Schrulle f; komischer Kauz; fixe Idee; 2. (an-)kurbeln; **~shaft** ⊕ ['kræŋkʃɑːft]

Kurbelwelle f; ~y [~ki] wacklig; launisch; verschroben.

**cranny** ['kræni] Riß m, Ritze f.

**crape** [kreip] Krepp m, Flor m.

**craps** Am. [kræps] pl. Würfelspiel.

**crash** [kræʃ] 1. Krach m (a. ✝); ✞ Absturz m; 2. v/i. krachen; einstürzen; ✞ abstürzen; mot. zs.-stoßen; fahren, fliegen, stürzen (into in, auf acc.); v/t. zerschmettern; 3. Am. F blitzschnell ausgeführt; ~-helmet ['kræʃhelmit] Sturzhelm m; ~-landing Bruchlandung f.

**crate** [kreit] Lattenkiste f.

**crater** ['kreitə] Krater m; Trichter m.

**crave** [kreiv] v/t. dringend bitten od. flehen um; v/i. sich sehnen.

**craven** ['kreivən] feig.

**crawfish** ['krɔ:fiʃ] 1. Krebs m; 2. Am. F sich drücken.

**crawl** [krɔ:l] 1. Kriechen n; 2. kriechen; schleichen; wimmeln; kribbeln; Schwimmen: kraulen; it makes one's flesh ~ man bekommt e-e Gänsehaut davon.

**crayfish** ['kreifiʃ] Flußkrebs m.

**crayon** ['kreiən] Zeichenstift m, bsd. Pastellstift m; Pastell(gemälde) n.

**craz|e** [kreiz] Verrücktheit f; F Fimmel m; be the ~ Mode sein; ~y □ ['kreizi] baufällig; verrückt (for, about nach).

**creak** [kri:k] knarren.

**cream** [kri:m] 1. Rahm m, Sahne f; Creme f; Auslese f; das Beste; 2. den Rahm abschöpfen; ~ery ['kri:məri] Molkerei f; Milchgeschäft n; ~y □ [~mi] sahnig.

**crease** [kri:s] 1. (Bügel)Falte f; 2. (sich) knittern; (sich) falten.

**creat|e** [kri(:)'eit] (er)schaffen; thea. e-e Rolle gestalten; verursachen; erzeugen; ernennen; ~ion [~'eiʃən] Schöpfung f; Ernennung f; ~ive [~'eitiv] schöpferisch; ~or [~tə] Schöpfer m; ~ure ['kri:tʃə] Geschöpf n; Kreatur f.

**creden|ce** ['kri:dəns] Glaube m; ~tials [kri'denʃəlz] pl. Beglaubigungsschreiben n; Unterlagen f/pl.

**credible** □ ['kredəbl] glaubwürdig; glaubhaft.

**credit** ['kredit] 1. Glaube(n) m; Ruf m, Ansehen n; Guthaben n; ✝ Kredit m; ✝ Kredit m; Einfluß m; Verdienst n, Ehre f; Am. Schule: (Anrechnungs)Punkt m; 2. j-m glauben; j-m trauen; ✝ gutschreiben; ~ s.o. with s.th. j-m et. zutrauen; ~able □ [~təbl] achtbar; ehrenvoll (to für); ~or [~tə] Gläubiger m.

**credulous** □ ['kredjuləs] leichtgläubig.

**creed** [kri:d] Glaubensbekenntnis n.

**creek** [kri:k] Bucht f; Am. Bach m.

**creel** [kri:l] Fischkorb m.

**creep** [kri:p] [irr.] kriechen; fig. (sich ein)schleichen; kribbeln; it makes my flesh ~ ich bekomme e-e Gänsehaut davon; ~er ['kri:pə] Kriecher(in); Kletterpflanze f.

**cremator|ium** [kremə'tɔ:riəm], bsd. Am. ~y ['krematəri] Krematorium n.

**crept** [krept] pret. u. p.p. von creep.

**crescent** ['kresnt] 1. zunehmend; halbmondförmig; 2. Halbmond m; ☾ City Am. New Orleans.

**cress** ♀ [kres] Kresse f.

**crest** [krest] Hahnen-, Berg- etc. Kamm m; Mähne f; Federbusch m; Heraldik: family ~ Familienwappen n; ~-fallen ['krestfɔ:lən] niedergeschlagen.

**crevasse** [kri'væs] (Gletscher)Spalte f; Am. Deichbruch m.

**crevice** ['krevis] Riß m, Spalte f.

**crew**[1] [kru:] Schar f; ♣, ✈ Mannschaft f.

**crew**[2] [~] pret. von crow 2.

**crib** [krib] 1. Krippe f; Kinderbett (-stelle f) n; F Schule: Klatsche f; bsd. Am. Behälter m; 2. einsperren; F mausen; F abschreiben.

**crick** [krik] Krampf m; ~ in the neck steifer Hals.

**cricket** ['krikit] zo. Grille f; Sport: Kricket n; not ~ F nicht fair.

**crime** [kraim] Verbrechen n.

**criminal** ['kriminl] 1. verbrecherisch; Kriminal..., Straf...; 2. Verbrecher(in); ~ity [krimi'næliti] Strafbarkeit f; Verbrechertum n.

**crimp** [krimp] kräuseln.

**crimson** ['krimzn] karmesin(rot).

**cringe** [krindʒ] sich ducken.

**crinkle** ['kriŋkl] 1. Windung f; Falte f; 2. (sich) winden; (sich) kräuseln.

**cripple** ['kripl] 1. Krüppel m; Lahme(r m) f; 2. verkrüppeln; fig. lähmen.

**cris|is** ['kraisis], pl. ~es [~si:z] Krisis f, Krise f, Wende-, Höhepunkt m.

**crisp** [krisp] 1. kraus; knusperig; frisch; klar; steif; 2. (sich) kräuseln; knusperig machen od. werden; 3. ~s pl., a. potato ~s pl. Kartoffelchips pl.

**criss-cross** ['kriskrɔs] 1. Kreuzzeichen n; 2. (durch)kreuzen.

**criteri|on** [krai'tiəriən], pl. ~a [~riə] Kennzeichen n, Prüfstein m.

**criti|c** ['kritik] Kritiker(in); ~cal □ [~kəl] kritisch; bedenklich; ~cism [~isizəm] Kritik f (of an dat.); ~cize [~saiz] kritisieren; beurteilen; tadeln; ~que [kri'ti:k] kritischer Essay; die Kritik.

**croak** [krouk] krächzen; quaken.

**crochet** ['krouʃei] 1. Häkelei f; 2. häkeln.

**crock** [krɔk] irdener Topf; **~ery** ['krɔkəri] Töpferware f.

**crocodile** zo. ['krɔkədail] Krokodil n.

**crone** F [kroun] altes Weib.

**crony** F ['krouni] alter Freund.

**crook** [kruk] **1.** Krümmung f; Haken m; Hirtenstab m; sl. Gauner m; **2.** (sich) krümmen; (sich) (ver)biegen; **~ed** ['krukid] krumm; bucklig; unehrlich; [krukt] Krück...

**croon** [kru:n] schmalzig singen; summen; **~er** ['kru:nə] Schnulzensänger m.

**crop** [krɔp] **1.** Kropf m; Peitschenstiel m; Reitpeitsche f; Ernte f; kurzer Haarschnitt; **2.** (ab-, be-) schneiden; (ab)ernten; Acker bebauen; ~ up fig. auftauchen.

**cross** [krɔs] **1.** Kreuz n (a. fig. Leiden); Kreuzung f; **2.** □ sich kreuzend; quer (liegend, laufend etc.); ärgerlich, verdrießlich; entgegengesetzt; Kreuz..., Quer...; **3.** v/t. kreuzen; durchstreichen; fig. durchkreuzen; überqueren; in den Weg kommen (dat.); ~ o.s. sich bekreuzigen; keep one's fingers ~ed den Daumen halten; v/i. sich kreuzen; **~-bar** ['krɔsba:] Fußball: Torlatte f; **~-breed** (Rassen)Kreuzung f; **~-country** querfeldein; **~-examination** Kreuzverhör n; **~-eyed** schieläugig; **~ing** [~siŋ] Kreuzung f; Übergang m; -fahrt f; **~-road** Querstraße f; **~-roads** pl. od. sg. Kreuzweg m; **~-section** Querschnitt m; **~wise** kreuzweise; **~word** (puzzle) Kreuzworträtsel n.

**crotchet** ['krɔtʃit] Haken m; ♪ Viertelnote f; wunderlicher Einfall.

**crouch** [krautʃ] **1.** sich ducken; **2.** Hockstellung f.

**crow** [krou] **1.** Krähe f; Krähen n; eat ~ Am. F zu Kreuze kriechen; **2.** [irr.] krähen; triumphieren; **~-bar** ['krouba:] Brecheisen n.

**crowd** [kraud] **1.** Haufen m, Menge f; Gedränge n; F Bande f; **2.** (sich) drängen; (über)füllen; wimmeln.

**crown** [kraun] **1.** Krone f; Kranz m; Gipfel m; Scheitel m; **2.** krönen; Zahn überkronen; to ~ all zu guter Letzt, zu allem Überfluß.

**cruci|al** □ ['kru:fjəl] entscheidend; kritisch; **~ble** ['kru:sibl] Schmelztiegel m; **~fixion** [kru:si'fikʃən] Kreuzigung f; **~fy** ['kru:sifai] kreuzigen.

**crude** □ [kru:d] roh; unfertig; unreif; unfein; grob; Roh...; grell.

**cruel** □ ['kruəl] grausam; hart; fig. blutig; **~ty** [~lti] Grausamkeit f.

**cruet** ['kru(:)it] (Essig-, Öl)Fläschchen n.

**cruise** ♣ [kru:z] **1.** Kreuzfahrt f, Seereise f; **2.** kreuzen; **~r** ['kru:zə]

♣ Kreuzer m; Jacht f; Am. Funkstreifenwagen m.

**crumb** [krʌm] **1.** Krume f; Brocken m; **2.** panieren; zerkrümeln; **~le** ['krʌmbl] (zer)bröckeln; fig. zugrunde gehen.

**crumple** ['krʌmpl] v/t. zerknittern; fig. vernichten; v/i. (sich) knüllen.

**crunch** [krʌntʃ] (zer)kauen; zermalmen; knirschen.

**crusade** [kru:'seid] Kreuzzug m (a. fig.); **~r** [~də] Kreuzfahrer m.

**crush** [krʌʃ] **1.** Druck m; Gedränge n; (Frucht)Saft m; Am. sl. Schwarm m; have a ~ on s.o. in j-n verliebt od. verschossen sein; **2.** v/t. (zer-, aus)quetschen; zermalmen; fig. vernichten; v/i. sich drängen; **~ barrier** ['krʌʃbæriə] Absperrgitter n.

**crust** [krʌst] **1.** Kruste f; Rinde f; Am. sl. Frechheit f; **2.** (sich) be-, überkrusten, verharschen; **~y** □ ['krʌsti] krustig; fig. mürrisch.

**crutch** [krʌtʃ] Krücke f.

**cry** [krai] **1.** Schrei m; Geschrei n; Ruf m; Weinen n; Gebell n; **2.** schreien; (aus)rufen; weinen; ~ for verlangen nach.

**crypt** [kript] Gruft f; **~ic** ['kriptik] verborgen, geheim.

**crystal** ['kristl] Kristall m, n; Am. Uhrglas n; **~line** [~təlain] kristallen; **~lize** [~aiz] kristallisieren.

**cub** [kʌb] **1.** Junge(s) n; Flegel m; Anfänger m; **2.** (Junge) werfen.

**cub|e** ⅋ [kju:b] Würfel m; Kubikzahl f; ~ root Kubikwurzel f; **~ic(al** □) ['kju:bik(əl)] würfelförmig; kubisch; Kubik...

**cuckoo** ['kuku:] Kuckuck m.

**cucumber** ['kju:kəmbə] Gurke f; as cool as a ~ fig. eiskalt, gelassen.

**cud** [kʌd] wiedergekäutes Futter; chew the ~ wiederkäuen; fig. überlegen.

**cuddle** ['kʌdl] v/t. (ver)hätscheln.

**cudgel** ['kʌdʒəl] **1.** Knüttel m; **2.** (ver)prügeln.

**cue** [kju:] Billard-Queue n; Stichwort n; Wink m.

**cuff** [kʌf] **1.** Manschette f; Handschelle f; (Ärmel-, Am. a. Hosen-) Aufschlag m; Faust-Schlag m; **2.** puffen, schlagen.

**cuisine** [kwi(:)'zi:n] Küche f (Art zu kochen).

**culminate** ['kʌlmineit] gipfeln.

**culpable** □ ['kʌlpəbl] strafbar.

**culprit** ['kʌlprit] Angeklagte(r m) f; Schuldige(r m) f, Missetäter(in).

**cultivat|e** ['kʌltiveit] kultivieren; an-, bebauen; ausbilden; pflegen; **~ion** [kʌlti'veiʃən] (An-, Acker)Bau m; Ausbildung f; Pflege f; Zucht f; **~or** ['kʌltiveitə] Landwirt m; Züchter m; ⚒ Kultivator m (Maschine).

**cultural** □ ['kʌltʃərəl] kulturell.
**culture** ['kʌltʃə] Kultur *f*; Pflege *f*; Zucht *f*; **~d** kultiviert.
**cumb|er** ['kʌmbə] überladen; belasten; **~ersome** [~əsəm], **~rous** □ [~brəs] lästig; schwerfällig.
**cumulative** □ ['kju:mjulətiv] (an-, auf)häufend; Zusatz...
**cunning** ['kʌniŋ] 1. □ schlau, listig; geschickt; *Am.* reizend; 2. List *f*, Schlauheit *f*; Geschicklichkeit *f*.
**cup** [kʌp] Becher *m*, Schale *f*, Tasse *f*; Kelch *m*; *Sport*: Pokal *m*; **~board** ['kʌbəd] (Speise- *etc.*)Schrank *m*.
**cupidity** [kju:(')piditi] Habgier *f*.
**cupola** ['kju:pələ] Kuppel *f*.
**cur** [kə:] Köter *m*; Schurke *m*, Halunke *m*.
**curable** ['kjuərəbl] heilbar.
**curate** ['kjuərit] Hilfsgeistliche(r) *m*.
**curb** [kə:b] 1. Kinnkette *f*; Kandare *f* (*a. fig.*); *a.* **~stone** ['kə:bstoun] Bordschwelle *f*; 2. an die Kandare nehmen (*a. fig.*); *fig.* zügeln; **~market** *Am. Börse*: Freiverkehr *m*; **~roof** Mansardendach *n*.
**curd** [kə:d] 1. Quark *m*; 2. (*mst* **~le** ['kə:dl]) gerinnen (lassen).
**cure** [kjuə] 1. Kur *f*; Heilmittel *n*; Seelsorge *f*; Pfarre *f*; 2. heilen; pökeln; räuchern; trocknen.
**curfew** ['kə:fju:] Abendglocke *f*; *pol.* Ausgehverbot *n*; **~bell** Abendglocke *f*.
**curio** ['kjuəriou] Rarität *f*; **~sity** [kjuəri'ɔsiti] Neugier *f*; Rarität *f*; **~us** □ ['kjuəriəs] neugierig; genau; seltsam, merkwürdig.
**curl** [kə:l] 1. Locke *f*; 2. (sich) kräuseln; (sich) locken; (sich) ringeln; **~y** ['kə:li] gekräuselt; lockig.
**currant** ['kʌrənt] Johannisbeere *f*; *a.* dried **~** Korinthe *f*.
**curren|cy** ['kʌrənsi] Umlauf *m*; ✝ Lauffrist *f*; Kurs *m*, Währung *f*; **~t** [~nt] 1. □ umlaufend; ✝ kursierend (*Geld*); allgemein (bekannt); laufend (*Jahr etc.*); 2. Strom *m* (*a. ⚡*); Strömung *f* (*a. fig.*); Luftzug *m*.
**curricul|um** [kə'rikjuləm], *pl.* **~a** [~lə] Lehr-, Stundenplan *m*; **~um vitae** [~m'vaiti:] Lebenslauf *m*.
**curry¹** ['kʌri] Curry *m*, *n*.
**curry²** [~] *Leder* zurichten; *Pferd* striegeln.
**curse** [kə:s] 1. Fluch *m*; 2. (ver)fluchen; strafen; **~d** □ ['kə:sid] verflucht.
**curt** □ [kə:t] kurz; knapp; barsch.
**curtail** [kə:'teil] beschneiden; *fig.* beschränken; kürzen (of um).
**curtain** ['kə:tn] 1. Vorhang *m*; Gardine *f*; 2. verhängen, verschleiern; **~lecture** F Gardinenpredigt *f*.
**curts(e)y** ['kə:tsi] 1. Knicks *m*; *m*; 2. knicksen (to vor).

**curvature** ['kə:vətʃə] (Ver)Krümmung *f*.
**curve** [kə:v] 1. Kurve *f*; Krümmung *f*; 2. (sich) krümmen; (sich) biegen.
**cushion** ['kuʃən] 1. Kissen *n*; Polster *n*; *Billard*-Bande *f*; 2. polstern.
**cuss** *Am.* F [kʌs] 1. Nichtsnutz *m*; 2. fluchen.
**custody** ['kʌstədi] Haft *f*; (Ob)Hut *f*.
**custom** ['kʌstəm] Gewohnheit *f*, Brauch *m*; Sitte *f*; Kundschaft *f*; **~s** *pl.* Zoll *m*; **~ary** □ [~məri] gewöhnlich, üblich; **~er** [~mə] Kund|e *m*, -in *f*; F Bursche *m*; **~-house** Zollamt *n*; **~-made** *Am.* maßgearbeitet.
**cut** [kʌt] 1. Schnitt *m*; Hieb *m*; Stich *m*; (Schnitt)Wunde *f*; Einschnitt *m*; Graben *m*; Kürzung *f*; Ausschnitt *m*; Wegabkürzung *f* (*mst* short-~); *Holz*-Schnitt *m*; *Kupfer*-Stich *m*; Schliff *m*; Schnitte *f*, Scheibe *f*; *Karten*-Abheben *n*; *Küche*: cold **~s** *pl.* Aufschnitt *m*; give *s.o.* the **~** (direct) F j. schneiden; 2. (*irr.*) *v/t.* schneiden; schnitzen; gravieren; ab-, an-, auf-, aus-, be-, durch-, zer-, zuschneiden; *Edelstein etc.* schleifen; *Karten* abheben; *j.* beim Begegnen schneiden; **~** teeth zahnen; **~** short *j.* unterbrechen; **~** back einschränken; **~** down fällen; mähen; beschneiden; *Preis* drücken; **~** out ausschneiden; *Am. Vieh* aussondern *aus der Herde*; *fig. j.* ausstechen; ✂ ausschneiden; be **~** out for das Zeug zu e-r S. haben; *v/i.* **~** in sich schneiden; 3. *adj.* geschnitten *etc.*, *s.* cut 2.
**cute** □ F [kju:t] schlau; *Am.* reizend.
**cuticle** ['kju:tikl] Oberhaut *f*; **~ scissors** *pl.* Hautschere *f*.
**cutlery** ['kʌtləri] Messerschmiedearbeit *f*; Stahlwaren *f/pl.*; Bestecke *n/pl.*
**cutlet** ['kʌtlit] Kotelett *n*; Schnitzel *n*.
**cut|-off** *Am.* ['kʌtɔ:f] Abkürzung *f* (*Straße*, *Weg*); **~out** *mot.* Auspuffklappe *f*; ⚡ Sicherung *f*; Ausschalter *m*; *Am.* Ausschneidebogen *m*, -bild *n*; **~purse** Taschendieb *m*; **~ter** ['kʌtə] Schneidende(r *m*) *f*; Schnitzer *m*; Zuschneider(in); *Film*: Cutter *m*; ⊕ Schneidezeug *n*, -maschine *f*; ⚓ Kutter *m*; *Am.* leichter Schlitten; **~throat** Halsabschneider *m*; Meuchelmörder *m*; **~ting** ['kʌtiŋ] 1. □ schneidend; scharf; ⊕ Schneid..., Fräs...; 2. Schneiden *n*; 🚂 *etc.* Einschnitt *m*; ♀ Steckling *m*; *Zeitungs*-Ausschnitt *m*; **~s** *pl.* Schnipsel *m*, *n/pl.*; ⊕ Späne *m/pl.*
**cycl|e** ['saikl] 1. Zyklus *m*; Kreis (-lauf) *m*; Periode *f*; ⊕ Arbeitsgang

*m*; Fahrrad *n*; 2. radfahren; ~ist [~list] Radfahrer(in).

**cyclone** ['saikloun] Wirbelsturm *m*.

**cylinder** ['silində] Zylinder *m*, Walze *f*; ⊕ Trommel *f*.

**cymbal** ♩ ['simbəl] Becken *n*.

**cynic** ['sinik] 1. *a*. ~al □ [~kəl] zynisch; 2. Zyniker *m*.

**cypress** ♣ ['saipris] Zypresse *f*.

**cyst** ♣ [sist] Blase *f*; Sackgeschwulst *f*; ~itis ♣ [sis'taitis] Blasenentzündung *f*.

**Czech** [tʃek] 1. Tschech|e *m*, -in *f*; 2. tschechisch.

**Czechoslovak** ['tʃekou'slouvæk] 1. Tschechoslowak|e *m*, -in *f*; 2. tschechoslowakisch.

# D

**dab** [dæb] 1. Klaps *m*; Tupf(en) *m*, Klecks *m*; 2. klapsen; (be)tupfen.

**dabble** ['dæbl] bespritzen; plätschern; (hinein)pfuschen.

**dad** F [dæd], ~dy F ['dædi] Papa *m*.

**daddy-longlegs** F *zo*. ['dædi'loŋlegz] Schnake *f*; *Am*. Weberknecht *m*.

**daffodil** ♣ ['dæfədil] gelbe Narzisse.

**daft** F [dɑːft] blöde, doof.

**dagger** ['dægə] Dolch *m*; be at ~s drawn *fig*. auf Kriegsfuß stehen.

**dago** *Am. sl.* ['deigou] *contp.* für *Spanier, Portugiese, mst Italiener.*

**daily** ['deili] 1. täglich; 2. Tageszeitung *f*.

**dainty** ['deinti] 1. □ lecker; zart, fein; wählerisch; 2. Leckerei *f*.

**dairy** ['dɛəri] Molkerei *f*, Milchwirtschaft *f*; Milchgeschäft *n*; ~ cattle Milchvieh *n*; ~man Milchhändler *m*.

**daisy** ♣ ['deizi] Gänseblümchen *n*.

**dale** [deil] Tal *n*.

**dall|iance** ['dæliəns] Trödelei *f*; Liebelei *f*; ~y ['dæli] vertrödeln; schäkern.

**dam** [dæm] 1. Mutter *f von Tieren*; Deich *m*, Damm *m*; 2. (ab)dämmen.

**damage** ['dæmidʒ] 1. Schaden *m*; ~s *pl.* ᵗᵗ Schadenersatz *m*; 2. (be-)schädigen.

**damask** ['dæməsk] Damast *m*.

**dame** [deim] Dame *f*; *sl*. Weib *n*.

**damn** [dæm] verdammen; verurteilen; ~ation [dæm'neiʃən] Verdammung *f*.

**damp** [dæmp] 1. feucht, dunstig; 2. Feuchtigkeit *f*, Dunst *m*; Gedrücktheit *f*; 3. *a*. ~en ['dæmpən] anfeuchten; dämpfen; niederdrükken; ~er [~pə] Dämpfer *m*.

**danc|e** [dɑːns] 1. Tanz *m*; Ball *m*; 2. tanzen (lassen); ~er ['dɑːnsə] Tänzer(in); ~ing [~siŋ] Tanzen *n*; *attr.* Tanz... [zahn *m*.]

**dandelion** ♣ ['dændilaiən] Löwen-]

**dandle** *sl.* ['dændl] wiegen, schaukeln.

**dandruff** ['dændrəf] (Kopf)Schuppen *f*/*pl.*

**dandy** ['dændi] 1. Stutzer *m*; F erstklassige Sache; 2. *Am*. F prima.

**Dane** [dein] Dän|e *m*, -in *f*.

**danger** ['deindʒə] Gefahr *f*; ~ous □ [~dʒrəs] gefährlich; ~signal 🚬 Notsignal *n*.

**dangle** ['dæŋgl] baumeln (lassen); schlenkern (mit); *fig*. schwanken.

**Danish** ['deiniʃ] dänisch.

**dank** [dæŋk] dunstig, feucht.

**Danubian** [də'njuːbjən] Donau...

**dapper** □ F ['dæpə] nett; behend.

**dapple** ['dæpl] sprenkeln; ~d scheckig; ~grey Apfelschimmel *m*.

**dar|e** [dɛə] *v/i*. es wagen; *v/t*. et. wagen; *j-n* herausfordern; *j-m* trotzen; ~e-devil ['dɛədevl] Draufgänger *m*; ~ing ['dɛəriŋ] 1. verwegen; 2. Verwegenheit *f*.

**dark** [dɑːk] 1. □ dunkel; brünett; schwerverständlich; geheim(nisvoll); trüb(selig); 2. Dunkel(heit *f*) *n*; before (after) ~ vor (nach) Einbruch der Dunkelheit; ♀ Ages *pl. das frühe Mittelalter*; ~en ['dɑːkən] (sich) (ver)dunkeln; (sich) verfinstern; ~ness ['dɑːknis] Dunkelheit *f*, Finsternis *f*; ~y F ['dɑːki] Schwarze(r *m*) *f*.

**darling** ['dɑːliŋ] 1. Liebling *m*; 2. Lieblings...; geliebt.

**darn** [dɑːn] stopfen; ausbessern.

**dart** [dɑːt] 1. Wurfspieß *m*; Wurfpfeil *m*; Sprung *m*, Satz *m*; ~s *pl*. Wurfpfeilspiel *n*; 2. *v/t*. schleudern; *v/i*. *fig*. schießen, (sich) stürzen.

**dash** [dæʃ] 1. Schlag *m*, (Zs.-)Stoß *m*; Klatschen *n*; Schwung *m*; Ansturm *m*; *fig*. Anflug *m*; Prise *f*; Schuß *m Rum etc*; Feder-Strich *m*; Gedankenstrich *m*; 2. *v/t*. schlagen, werfen, schleudern; zerschmettern; vernichten; (be)spritzen; vermengen; verwirren; *v/i*. stoßen, schlagen; stürzen; stürmen; jagen; ~board *mot.* ['dæʃbɔːd] Armaturenbrett *n*; ~ing ['dæʃiŋ] schneidig, forsch; flott, F fesch.

**dastardly** ['dæstədli] heimtückisch; feig.

**data** ['deitə] *pl., Am. a. sg.* Angaben

f/pl.; Tatsachen f/pl.; Unterlagen f/pl.; Daten pl.

**date** [deit] 1. ♀ Dattel f; Datum n; Zeit f; Termin m; Am. F Verabredung f; Freund(in); out of ~ veraltet, unmodern; up to ~ zeitgemäß, modern; auf dem laufenden; 2. datieren; Am. F sich verabreden.

**dative** gr. ['deitiv] a. ~ case Dativ m.

**daub** [dɔːb] (be)schmieren; (be-) klecksen.

**daughter** ['dɔːtə] Tochter f; ~-in-law [~ərinlɔː] Schwiegertochter f.

**daunt** [dɔːnt] entmutigen; ~less ['dɔːntlis] furchtlos, unerschrocken.

**daw** orn. [dɔː] Dohle f.

**dawdle** F ['dɔːdl] (ver)trödeln.

**dawn** [dɔːn] 1. Dämmerung f; fig. Morgenrot n; 2. dämmern, tagen; it ~ed upon him fig. es wurde ihm langsam klar.

**day** [dei] Tag m; oft ~s pl. (Lebens-) Zeit f; ~ off dienst-freier Tag; carry od. win the ~ den Sieg davontragen; the other ~ neulich; this ~ week heute in einer Woche; heute vor einer Woche; let's call it a ~ machen wir Schluß für heute; ~break ['deibreik] Tagesanbruch m; ~-labo(u)rer Tagelöhner m; ~-star Morgenstern m.

**daze** [deiz] blenden; betäuben.

**dazzle** ['dæzl] blenden; ⚓ tarnen.

**dead** [ded] 1. tot; unempfindlich (to für); matt (Farbe etc.); blind (Fenster etc.); erloschen (Feuer); schal (Getränk); tief (Schlaf); ♀ tot (Kapital etc.); ~ bargain Spottpreis m; ~ letter unzustellbarer Brief; ~ loss Totalverlust m; a ~ shot ein Meisterschütze; ~ wall blinde Mauer; ~ wood Reisig n; Am. Plunder m; 2. adv. gänzlich, völlig, total; durchaus; genau, (haar)scharf; ~ against gerade od. ganz und gar (ent)gegen; 3. the ~ der Tote; die Toten pl.; Totenstille f; in the ~ of winter im tiefsten Winter; in the ~ of night mitten in der Nacht; ~en ['dedn] abstumpfen; dämpfen; (ab)schwächen; ~-end Sackgasse f (a. fig.); ~-line Am. Sperrlinie f im Gefängnis; Schlußtermin m; Stichtag m; ~-lock Stockung f; fig. toter Punkt; ~ly [~li] tödlich.

**deaf** [def] taub; ~en ['defn] taub machen; betäuben.

**deal** [diːl] 1. Teil m; Menge f; Kartengeben n; F Geschäft n; Abmachung f; a good ~ ziemlich viel; a great ~ sehr viel; 2. [irr.] v/t. (aus-, ver-, zu)teilen; Karten geben; e-n Schlag versetzen; v/i. handeln (in mit e-r Ware); verfahren; verkehren; ~ with sich befassen mit, behandeln; ~er ['diːlə] Händler m; Kartengeber m; ~ing ['diːliŋ] mst

~s pl. Handlungsweise f; Verfahren n; Verkehr m; ~t [delt] pret. u p.p. von deal 2.

**dean** [diːn] Dekan m.

**dear** [diə] 1. □ teuer; lieb; 2. Liebling m; herziges Geschöpf; 3. o(h) ~!, ~ me! F du liebe Zeit!; ach herrje!

**death** [deθ] Tod m; Todesfall m; ~-bed ['deθbed] Sterbebett n; ~-duty Erbschaftssteuer f; ~less ['deθlis] unsterblich; ~ly [~li] tödlich; ~-rate Sterblichkeitsziffer f; ~-warrant Todesurteil n.

**debar** [di'bɑː] ausschließen; hindern.

**debarkation** [diːbɑːˈkeiʃən] Ausschiffung f.

**debase** [di'beis] verschlechtern; erniedrigen; verfälschen.

**debat|able** □ [di'beitəbl] strittig; umstritten; ~e [di'beit] 1. Debatte f; 2. debattieren; erörtern; überlegen.

**debauch** [di'bɔːtʃ] 1. Ausschweifung f; 2. verderben; verführen.

**debilitate** [di'biliteit] schwächen.

**debit** ♀ ['debit] 1. Debet n, Schuld f; 2. j-n belasten; debitieren.

**debris** ['debriː] Trümmer pl.

**debt** [det] Schuld f; ~or ['detə] Schuldner(in).

**debunk** ['diːˈbʌŋk] den Nimbus nehmen (dat.).

**début** ['deibuː] Debüt n.

**decade** ['dekeid] Jahrzehnt n.

**decadence** ['dekədəns] Verfall m.

**decamp** [di'kæmp] aufbrechen; ausreißen; ~ment [~pmənt] Aufbruch m.

**decant** [di'kænt] abgießen; umfüllen; ~er [~tə] Karaffe f.

**decapitate** [di'kæpiteit] enthaupten; Am. F fig. absägen (entlassen).

**decay** [di'kei] 1. Verfall m; Fäulnis f; 2. verfallen; (ver)faulen.

**decease** bsd. ʒʦ [di'siːs] 1. Ableben n; 2. sterben.

**deceit** [di'siːt] Täuschung f; Betrug m; ~ful □ [~tful] (be)trügerisch.

**deceive** [di'siːv] betrügen; täuschen; verleiten; ~r [~və] Betrüger(in).

**December** [di'sembə] Dezember m.

**decen|cy** ['diːsnsi] Anstand m; ~t □ [~nt] anständig; F annehmbar, nett.

**deception** [di'sepʃən] Täuschung f.

**decide** [di'said] (sich) entscheiden; bestimmen; ~d □ entschieden; bestimmt; entschlossen.

**decimal** ['desiməl] Dezimalbruch m; attr. Dezimal...

**decipher** [di'saifə] entziffern.

**decisi|on** [di'siʒən] Entscheidung f; ʒʦ Urteil n; Entschluß m; Entschlossenheit f; ~ve □ [di'saisiv] entscheidend; entschieden.

**deck** [dek] **1.** ⚓ Deck *n*; *Am.* Pack *m* Spielkarten; on ~ *Am.* F da(bei), bereit; **2.** *rhet.* schmücken; **~chair** ['dek'tʃɛə] Liegestuhl *m*.

**declaim** [di'kleim] vortragen; (sich er)eifern.

**declar|able** [di'klɛərəbl] steuer-, zollpflichtig; **~ation** [deklə'reiʃən] Erklärung *f*; Zoll-Deklaration *f*; **~e** [di'klɛə] (sich) erklären; behaupten; deklarieren.

**declension** [di'klenʃən] Abfall *m* (*Neigung*); Verfall *m*; *gr.* Deklination *f*.

**declin|ation** [dekli'neiʃən] Neigung *f*; Abweichung *f*; **~e** [di'klain] **1.** Abnahme *f*; Niedergang *m*; Verfall *m*; **2.** *v/t.* neigen, biegen; *gr.* deklinieren; ablehnen; *v/i.* sich neigen; abnehmen; verfallen.

**declivity** [di'kliviti] Abhang *m*.

**declutch** *mot.* ['di:'klʌtʃ] auskuppeln.

**decode** *tel.* ['di:'koud] entschlüsseln.

**decompose** [di:kəm'pouz] zerlegen; (sich) zersetzen; verwesen.

**decontrol** [di:kən'troul] *Waren, Handel* freigeben.

**decorat|e** ['dekəreit] (ver)zieren; schmücken; **~ion** [dekə'reiʃən] Verzierung *f*; Schmuck *m*; Orden(sauszeichnung *f*); **~** ♀ *Day Am.* Heldengedenktag *m*; **~ive** ['dekərətiv] dekorativ; Zier...; **~or** [~reitə] Dekorateur *m*, Maler *m*.

**decor|ous** □ ['dekərəs] anständig; **~um** [di'kɔ:rəm] Anstand *m*.

**decoy** [di'kɔi] **1.** Lockvogel *m* (*a. fig.*); Köder *m*; **2.** ködern; locken.

**decrease 1.** ['di:kri:s] Abnahme *f*; **2.** [di:'kri:s] (sich) vermindern.

**decree** [di'kri:] **1.** Dekret *n*, Verordnung *f*, Erlaß *m*; ⚖ Entscheid *m*; **2.** beschließen; verordnen, verfügen.

**decrepit** [di'krepit] altersschwach.

**decry** [di'krai] in Verruf bringen.

**dedicat|e** ['dedikeit] widmen; **~ion** [dedi'keiʃən] Widmung *f*.

**deduce** [di'dju:s] ableiten; folgern.

**deduct** [di'dʌkt] abziehen; **~ion** [~kʃən] Abzug *m*; † Rabatt *m*; Schlußfolgerung *f*.

**deed** [di:d] **1.** Tat *f*; Heldentat *f*; Urkunde *f*; **2.** *Am.* urkundlich übertragen (to auf *acc.*).

**deem** [di:m] *v/t.* halten für; *v/i.* denken, urteilen (of über *acc.*).

**deep** [di:p] **1.** □ tief; gründlich; schlau; vertieft; dunkel (*a. fig.*); verborgen; **2.** Tiefe *f*; *poet.* Meer *n*; **~en** ['di:pən] (sich) vertiefen; (sich) verstärken; **~freeze 1.** tiefkühlen; **2.** Tiefkühlfach *n*, -truhe *f*; **~ness** ['di:pnis] Tiefe *f*.

**deer** [diə] Rotwild *m*; Hirsch *m*.

**deface** [di'feis] entstellen; unkenntlich machen; ausstreichen.

**defalcation** [di:fæl'keiʃən] Unterschlagung *f*.

**defam|ation** [defə'meiʃən] Verleumdung *f*; **~e** [di'feim] verleumden; verunglimpfen.

**default** [di'fɔ:lt] **1.** Nichterscheinen *n* vor *Gericht*; Säumigkeit *f*; Verzug *m*; in ~ of which widrigenfalls; **2.** *s-n etc.* Verbindlichkeiten nicht nachkommen.

**defeat** [di'fi:t] **1.** Niederlage *f*, Besiegung *f*; Vereitelung *f*; **2.** ✕ besiegen; vereiteln; vernichten.

**defect** [di'fekt] Mangel *m*; Fehler *m*; **~ive** □ [~tiv] mangelhaft; unvollständig; fehlerhaft.

**defen|ce**, *Am.* **~se** [di'fens] Verteidigung *f*; Schutzmaßnahme *f*; witness for the ~ Entlastungszeuge *m*; **~celess**, *Am.* **~seless** [~slis] schutzlos, wehrlos.

**defend** [di'fend] verteidigen; schützen (from vor *dat.*); **~ant** [~dənt] Angeklagte(r *m*) *f*; Beklagte(r *m*) *f*; **~er** [~də] Verteidiger(in).

**defensive** [di'fensiv] Defensive *f*; *attr.* Verteidigungs...

**defer** [di'fə:] auf-, verschieben; *Am.* ✕ zurückstellen; sich fügen; nachgeben; payment on ~red terms Ratenzahlung *f*; **~ence** [ˈdefərəns] Ehrerbietung *f*; Nachgiebigkeit *f*; **~ential** □ [defə'renʃəl] ehrerbietig.

**defian|ce** [di'faiəns] Herausforderung *f*; Trotz *m*; **~t** □ [~nt] herausfordernd; trotzig.

**deficien|cy** [di'fiʃənsi] Unzulänglichkeit *f*; Mangel *m*; = deficit; **~t** [~nt] mangelhaft; unzureichend.

**deficit** ['defisit] Fehlbetrag *m*.

**defile 1.** ['di:fail] Engpaß *m*; **2.** [di'fail] *v/i.* vorbeiziehen; *v/t.* beflecken; schänden.

**defin|e** [di'fain] definieren; erklären; genau bestimmen; **~ite** □ ['definit] bestimmt; deutlich; genau; **~ition** [defi'niʃən] (Begriffs-)Bestimmung *f*; Erklärung *f*; **~itive** □ [di'finitiv] bestimmt; entscheidend; endgültig.

**deflect** [di'flekt] ablenken; abweichen.

**deform** [di'fɔ:m] entstellen, verunstalten; **~ed** verwachsen; **~ity** [~miti] Unförmigkeit *f*; Mißgestalt *f*.

**defraud** [di'frɔ:d] betrügen (of um).

**defray** [di'frei] *Kosten* bestreiten.

**defroster** *mot.* [di:'frɔstə] Entfroster *m*.

**deft** □ [deft] gewandt, flink.

**defunct** [di'fʌŋkt] verstorben.

**defy** [di'fai] herausfordern; trotzen.

**degenerate 1.** [di'dʒenəreit] entarten; **2.** □ [~rit] entartet.

**degrad|ation** [degrə'deiʃən] Absetzung *f*; **~e** [di'greid] *v/t.* absetzen; erniedrigen; demütigen.

**degree** [di'gri:] Grad *m*; *fig.* Stufe *f*,

Schritt *m*; Rang *m*, Stand *m*; *by* ~*s* allmählich; *in no* ~ in keiner Weise; *in some* ~ einigermaßen; *take one's* ~ sein Abschlußexamen machen.

**dehydrated** [di:'haidreitid] Trocken...

**deify** ['di:ifai] vergöttern; vergöttlichen.

**deign** [dein] geruhen; gewähren.

**deity** ['di:iti] Gottheit *f*.

**deject** [di'dʒekt] entmutigen; ~ed □ niedergeschlagen; ~ion [~kʃən] Niedergeschlagenheit *f*.

**delay** [di'lei] 1. Aufschub *m*; Verzögerung *f*; 2. *v/t.* aufschieben; verzögern; *v/i.* zögern; trödeln.

**delega|te** 1. ['deligeit] abordnen; übertragen; 2. [~git] Abgeordnete(*r m*) *f*; ~tion [deli'geiʃən] Abordnung *f*; *Am. parl. die* Kongreßabgeordneten *m/pl. e-s Staates.*

**deliberat|e** 1. [di'libəreit] *v/t.* überlegen, erwägen; *v/i.* nachdenken; beraten; 2. □ [~rit] bedachtsam; wohlüberlegt; vorsätzlich; ~ion [dilibə'reiʃən] Überlegung *f*; Beratung *f*; Bedächtigkeit *f*.

**delica|cy** ['delikəsi] Wohlgeschmack *m*; Leckerbissen *m*; Zartheit *f*; Schwächlichkeit *f*; Feinfühligkeit *f*; ~te [~kit] schmackhaft; lecker; zart; fein; schwach; heikel; empfindlich; feinfühlig; wählerisch; ~tessen [delikə'tesn] Feinkost(geschäft *n*) *f*.

**delicious** [di'liʃəs] köstlich.

**delight** [di'lait] 1. Lust *f*, Freude *f*, Wonne *f*; 2. entzücken; (sich) erfreuen (*in* an *dat.*); ~ *to inf.* Freude daran finden, zu *inf.*; ~ful □ [~tful] entzückend.                 [schildern.\

**delineate** [di'linieit] entwerfen;\

**delinquen|cy** [di'liŋkwənsi] Vergehen *n*; Kriminalität *f*; Pflichtvergessenheit *f*; ~t [~nt] 1. straffällig; pflichtvergessen; 2. Verbrecher(in).

**deliri|ous** □ [di'liriəs] wahnsinnig; ~um [~iəm] Fieberwahn *m*.

**deliver** [di'livə] befreien; über-, aus-, abliefern; *Botschaft* ausrichten; äußern; *Rede etc.* vortragen, halten; ⚓ entbinden; *Schlag* führen; werfen; ~ance [~ərəns] Befreiung *f*; (Meinungs)Äußerung *f*; ~er [~rə] Befreier(in); Überbringer(in); ~y [~ri] ⚓ Entbindung *f*; (Ab)Lieferung *f*; ✆ Zustellung *f*; Übergabe *f*; Vortrag *m*; Wurf *m*; *special* ~ Lieferung *f* durch Eilboten; ~y-truck, ~y-van Lieferwagen *m*.

**dell** [del] kleines Tal.

**delude** [di'lu:d] täuschen; verleiten.

**deluge** ['delju:dʒ] 1. Überschwemmung *f*; 2. überschwemmen.

**delus|ion** [di'lu:ʒən] Täuschung *f*, Verblendung *f*; Wahn *m*; ~ive □ [~u:siv] (be)trügerisch; täuschend.

**demand** [di'mɑ:nd] 1. Verlangen *n*; Forderung *f*; Bedarf *m*; ⚓ Nachfrage *f*; ⚓ Rechtsanspruch *m*; 2. verlangen, fordern; fragen (nach).

**demean** [di'mi:n]: ~ *o.s.* sich benehmen; sich erniedrigen; ~o(u)r [~nə] Benehmen *n*.

**demented** [di'mentid] wahnsinnig.

**demerit** [di:'merit] Fehler *m*.

**demesne** [di'mein] Besitz *m*.

**demi...** ['demi] Halb..., halb...

**demijohn** ['demidʒɔn] große Korbflasche, Glasballon *m*.

**demilitarize** ['di:'militəraiz] entmilitarisieren.

**demise** [di'maiz] 1. Ableben *n*; 2. vermachen.

**demobilize** [di:'moubilaiz] demobilisieren.

**democra|cy** [di'mɔkrəsi] Demokratie *f*; ~t ['deməkræt] Demokrat(in); ~tic(al □) [demə'krætik(əl)] demokratisch.

**demolish** [di'mɔliʃ] nieder-, abreißen; zerstören.

**demon** ['di:mən] Dämon *m*; Teufel *m*.

**demonstrat|e** ['demənstreit] anschaulich darstellen; beweisen; demonstrieren; ~ion [deməns'treiʃən] Demonstration *f*; anschauliche Darstellung; Beweis *m*; (Gefühls-)Äußerung *f*; ~ive □ [di'mɔnstrətiv] überzeugend; demonstrativ; ausdrucksvoll; auffällig, überschwenglich.

**demote** [di:'mout] degradieren.

**demur** [di'mə:] 1. Einwendung *f*; 2. Einwendungen erheben.

**demure** □ [di'mjuə] ernst; prüde.

**den** [den] Höhle *f*; Grube *f*; *sl.* Bude *f*.

**denial** [di'naiəl] Leugnen *n*; Verneinung *f*; abschlägige Antwort.

**denizen** [di'nizn] Bewohner *m*.

**denominat|e** [di'nɔmineit] (be-)nennen; ~ion [dinɔmi'neiʃən] Benennung *f*; Klasse *f*; Sekte *f*, Konfession *f*.

**denote** [di'nout] bezeichnen; bedeuten.

**denounce** [di'nauns] anzeigen; brandmarken; *Vertrag* kündigen.

**dens|e** □ [dens] dicht, dick (*Nebel*); beschränkt; ~ity ['densiti] Dichte *f*; Dichtigkeit *f*.

**dent** [dent] 1. Kerbe *f*; Beule *f*; 2. ver-, einbeulen.

**dent|al** ['dentl] Zahn...; ~ surgeon Zahnarzt *m*; ~ist [~tist] Zahnarzt *m*.

**denunciat|ion** [dinʌnsi'eiʃən] Anzeige *f*; Kündigung *f*; ~or [di'nʌnsieitə] Denunziant *m*.

**deny** [di'nai] verleugnen; verweigern, abschlagen; *j-n* abweisen.

**depart** [di'pɑ:t] *v/i.* abreisen, abfahren; abstehen, (ab)weichen;

verscheiden; ~ment [~tmənt] Abteilung f; Bezirk m; † Branche f; Am. Ministerium n; State ♀ Am. Außenministerium n; ~ store Warenhaus n; ~ure [~tʃə] Abreise f, ✈, ⚓ Abfahrt f; Abweichung f.

**depend** [di'pend]: ~ (up)on abhängen von; angewiesen sein auf (acc.); sich verlassen auf (acc.); it ~s F es kommt (ganz) darauf an; ~able [~dəbl] zuverlässig; ~ant [~ənt] Abhängige(r m) f; Angehörige(r m) f; ~ence [~dəns] Abhängigkeit f; Vertrauen n; ~ency [~si] Schutzgebiet n; ~ent [~ənt] 1. □ (on) abhängig (von); angewiesen (auf acc.); 2. Am. = dependant.

**depict** [di'pikt] darstellen; schildern.

**deplete** [di'pli:t] (ent)leeren; fig. erschöpfen.

**deplor|able** □ [di'plɔ:rəbl] beklagenswert; kläglich; jämmerlich; ~e [di'plɔ:] beklagen, bedauern.

**deponent** ⚖ [di'pounənt] vereidigter Zeuge.                [entvölkern.]

**depopulate** [di:'pɔpjuleit] (sich)]

**deport** [di'pɔ:t] Ausländer abschieben; verbannen; ~ o.s. sich benehmen; ~ment [~tmənt] Benehmen n.

**depose** [di'pouz] absetzen; ⚖ (eidlich) aussagen.

**deposit** [di'pɔzit] 1. Ablagerung f; Lager n; † Depot n; Bank-Einlage f; Pfand n; Hinterlegung f; 2. (nieder-, ab-, hin)legen; Geld einlegen, einzahlen; hinterlegen; (sich) ablagern; ~ion [depə'ziʃən] Ablagerung f; eidliche Zeugenaussage; Absetzung f; ~or [di'pɔzitə] Hinterleger m, Einzahler m; Kontoinhaber m.

**depot** ['depou] Depot n; Lagerhaus n; Am. Bahnhof m.

**deprave** [di'preiv] sittlich verderben.

**deprecate** ['deprikeit] ablehnen.

**depreciate** [di'pri:ʃeit] herabsetzen; geringschätzen; entwerten.

**depredation** [depri'deiʃən] Plünderung f.

**depress** [di'pres] niederdrücken; Preise etc. senken, drücken; bedrücken; ~ed fig. niedergeschlagen; ~ion [~eʃən] Senkung f; Niedergeschlagenheit f; † Flaute f, Wirtschaftskrise f; ✻ Schwäche f; Sinken n.

**deprive** [di'praiv] berauben; entziehen; ausschließen (of von).

**depth** [depθ] Tiefe f; attr. Tiefen...

**deput|ation** [depju(:)'teiʃən] Abordnung f; ~e [di'pju:t] abordnen; ~y ['depjuti] Abgeordnete(r m) f; Stellvertreter m, Beauftragte(r) m.

**derail** ⚙ [di'reil] v/i. entgleisen; v/t. zum Entgleisen bringen.

**derange** [di'reindʒ] in Unordnung bringen; stören; zerrütten; (mentally) ~d geistesgestört; a ~d stomach eine Magenverstimmung.

**derelict** ['derilikt] 1. verlassen; bsd. Am. nachlässig; 2. herrenloses Gut; Wrack n; ~ion [deri'likʃən] Verlassen n; Vernachlässigung f.

**deri|de** [di'raid] verlachen, verspotten; ~sion [di'riʒən] Verspottung f; ~sive □ [di'raisiv] spöttisch.

**deriv|ation** [deri'veiʃən] Ableitung f; Herkunft f; ~e [di'raiv] herleiten; Nutzen etc. ziehen (from aus).

**derogat|e** ['derəgeit] schmälern (from acc.); ~ion [derə'geiʃən] Beeinträchtigung f; Herabwürdigung f; ~ory □ [di'rɔgətəri] (to) nachteilig (dat., für); herabwürdigend.

**derrick** ['derik] ⊕ Drehkran m; ⚓ Ladebaum m; ✕ Bohrturm m.

**descend** [di'send] (her-, nieder)absteigen, herabkommen, sinken; ✹ niedergehen; ~ (up)on herfallen über (acc.); einfallen in (acc.); (ab)stammen; ~ant [~dənt] Nachkomme m.

**descent** [di'sent] Herabsteigen n; Abstieg m; Sinken n; Gefälle n; feindlicher Einfall; Landung f; Abstammung f; Abhang m.

**describe** [dis'kraib] beschreiben.

**description** [dis'kripʃən] Beschreibung f, Schilderung f; F Art f.

**descry** [dis'krai] wahrnehmen.

**desecrate** ['desikreit] entweihen.

**desegregate** Am. [di:'segrigeit] die Rassentrennung aufheben in (dat.).

**desert**[1] ['dezət] 1. verlassen; wüst, öde; Wüsten...; 2. Wüste f.

**desert**[2] [di'zə:t] v/t. verlassen; v/i. ausreißen; desertieren.

**desert**[3] [di'zə:t] Verdienst n.

**desert|er** [di'zə:tə] Fahnenflüchtige(r) m; ~ion [~ə:ʃən] Verlassen n; Fahnenflucht f.

**deserv|e** [di'zə:v] verdienen; sich verdient machen (of um); ~ing [~viŋ] würdig (of gen.); verdienstvoll.

**design** [di'zain] 1. Plan m; Entwurf m; Vorhaben n, Absicht f; Zeichnung f, Muster n; 2. ersinnen; zeichnen, entwerfen; planen; bestimmen.

**designat|e** ['dezigneit] bezeichnen; ernennen, bestimmen; ~ion [dezig'neiʃən] Bezeichnung f; Bestimmung f, Ernennung f.

**designer** [di'zainə] (Muster)Zeichner(in); Konstrukteur m.

**desir|able** □ [di'zaiərəbl] wünschenswert; angenehm; ~e [di'zaiə] 1. Wunsch m; Verlangen n; 2. verlangen, wünschen; ~ous □ [~ərəs] begierig.

**desist** [di'zist] abstehen, ablassen.

**desk** [desk] Pult n; Schreibtisch m.

**desolat|e** 1. ['desəleit] verwüsten; 2. □ [~lit] einsam; verlassen; öde; ~ion [desə'leiʃən] Verwüstung f; Einöde f; Verlassenheit f.

**despair** [dis'pɛə] 1. Verzweiflung f;

2. verzweifeln (of an *dat.*); ~ing □ [~riŋ] verzweifelt.

**despatch** [dis'pætʃ] = *dispatch*.

**desperat|e** *adj.* □ ['despərit] verzweifelt; hoffnungslos; F schrecklich; ~ion [despə'reiʃən] Verzweiflung *f*; Raserei *f*.

**despicable** □ ['despikəbl] verächtlich.

**despise** [dis'paiz] verachten.

**despite** [dis'pait] **1.** Verachtung *f*; Trotz *m*; Bosheit *f*; in ~ of zum Trotz, trotz; **2.** *prp. a.* ~ of trotz.

**despoil** [dis'poil] berauben (of *gen.*).

**despond** [dis'pɔnd] verzagen, verzweifeln; ~ency [~dənsi] Verzagtheit *f*; ~ent □ [~nt] verzagt.

**despot** ['despɔt] Despot *m*, Tyrann *m*; ~ism [~pətizəm] Despotismus *m*.

**dessert** [di'zə:t] Nachtisch *m*, Dessert *n*; *Am.* Süßspeise *f*.

**destin|ation** [desti'neiʃən] Bestimmung(sort *m*) *f*; ~e ['destin] bestimmen; ~y [~ni] Schicksal *n*.

**destitute** □ ['destitju:t] mittellos, notleidend; entblößt (of von).

**destroy** [dis'trɔi] zerstören, vernichten; töten; unschädlich machen; ~er [~ə] Zerstörer(in).

**destruct|ion** [dis'trʌkʃən] Zerstörung *f*; Tötung *f*; ~ive □ [~ktiv] zerstörend; vernichtend (of, to *acc.*); ~or [~tə] (Müll)Verbrennungsofen *m*.

**desultory** □ ['desəltəri] unstet; planlos; oberflächlich.

**detach** [di'tætʃ] losmachen, (ab-)lösen; absondern; ✕ (ab)kommandieren; ~ed einzeln (stehend); unbeeinflußt; ~ment [~ʃmənt] Loslösung *f*; Trennung *f*; ✕ Abteilung *f*.

**detail** ['di:teil] **1.** Einzelheit *f*; eingehende Darstellung; ✕ Kommando *n*; in ~ ausführlich; **2.** genau schildern; ✕ abkommandieren.

**detain** [di'tein] zurück-, auf-, abhalten; *j-n* in Haft behalten.

**detect** [di'tekt] entdecken; auffinden; ~ion [~kʃən] Entdeckung *f*; ~ive [~ktiv] Detektiv *m*; ~ story, ~ novel Kriminalroman *m*.

**detention** [di'tenʃən] Vorenthaltung *f*; Zurück-, Abhaltung *f*; Haft *f*.

**deter** [di'tə:] abschrecken (*from*).

**detergent** [di'tə:dʒənt] **1.** reinigend; **2.** Reinigungsmittel *n*.

**deteriorat|e** [di'tiəriəreit] (sich) verschlechtern; entarten; ~ion [ditiəriə'reiʃən] Verschlechterung *f*.

**determin|ation** [ditə:mi'neiʃən] Bestimmung *f*; Entschlossenheit *f*; Entscheidung *f*; Entschluß *m*; ~e [di'tə:min] *v/t.* bestimmen; entscheiden; veranlassen; *Strafe* festsetzen; beendigen; *v/i.* sich entschließen; ~ed entschlossen.

**deterrent** [di'terənt] **1.** abschreckend; **2.** Abschreckungsmittel *n*; *nuclear* ~ *pol.* atomare Abschreckung.

**detest** [di'test] verabscheuen; ~able □ [~təbl] abscheulich; ~ation [di:tes'teiʃən] Abscheu *m*.

**dethrone** [di'θroun] entthronen.

**detonate** ['detouneit] explodieren (lassen).

**detour, détour** ['deituə] **1.** Umweg *m*; Umleitung *f*; **2.** e-n Umweg machen.

**detract** [di'trækt]: ~ *from s.th. et.* beeinträchtigen, schmälern; ~ion [~kʃən] Verleumdung *f*; Herabsetzung *f*.

**detriment** ['detrimənt] Schaden *m*.

**deuce** [dju:s] Zwei *f im Spiel*; *Tennis:* Einstand *m*; F Teufel *m*; *the* ~! zum Teufel!

**devalu|ation** [di:vælju'eiʃən] Abwertung *f*; ~e [di:'vælju:] abwerten.

**devastat|e** ['devəsteit] verwüsten; ~ion [devəs'teiʃən] Verwüstung *f*.

**develop** [di'veləp] (sich) entwickeln; (sich) entfalten; (sich) erweitern; *Gelände* erschließen; ausbauen; *Am.* (sich) zeigen; ~ment [~pmənt] Entwicklung *f*, Entfaltung *f*; Erweiterung *f*; Ausbau *m*.

**deviat|e** ['di:vieit] abweichen; ~ion [di:vi'eiʃən] Abweichung *f*.

**device** [di'vais] Plan *m*; Kniff *m*; Erfindung *f*; Vorrichtung *f*; Muster *n*; Wahlspruch *m*; *leave s.o. to his own* ~s j. sich selbst überlassen.

**devil** ['devl] **1.** Teufel *m* (*a. fig.*); ⅌ Hilfsanwalt *m*; Laufbursche *m*; **2.** *v/t. Gericht* stark pfeffern; *Am.* plagen, quälen; ~ish [~liʃ] teuflisch; ~(t)ry [~l(t)ri] Teufelei *f*.

**devious** □ ['di:vjəs] abwegig.

**devise** [di'vaiz] **1.** ⅌ Vermachen *n*; Vermächtnis *n*; **2.** ersinnen; ⅌ vermachen.

**devoid** [di'vɔid] ~ of bar (*gen.*), ohne.

**devot|e** [di'vout] weihen, widmen; ~ed □ ergeben; zärtlich; ~ion [~ouʃən] Ergebenheit *f*; Hingebung *f*; Frömmigkeit *f*; ~s *pl.* Andacht *f*.

**devour** [di'vauə] verschlingen.

**devout** □ [di'vaut] andächtig; fromm; innig.

**dew** [dju:] **1.** Tau *m*; **2.** tauen; ~y ['dju:i] betaut; taufrisch.

**dexter|ity** [deks'teriti] Gewandtheit *f*; ~ous □ ['dekstərəs] gewandt.

**diabolic(al** □) [daiə'bɔlik(əl)] teuflisch.

**diagnose** ['daiəgnouz] diagnostizieren, erkennen.

**diagram** ['daiəgræm] graphische Darstellung; Schema *n*, Plan *m*.

**dial** ['daiəl] **1.** Sonnenuhr *f*; Zifferblatt *n*; *teleph.* Wähl(er)scheibe *f*; *Radio:* Skala *f*; **2.** *teleph.* wählen.

**dialect** ['daiəlekt] Mundart *f*.

dialo|gue, Am. a. ~g ['daiələg] Dialog m, Gespräch n.

dial-tone teleph. ['daiəltoun] Amtszeichen n.

diameter [dai'æmitə] Durchmesser m.

diamond ['daiəmənd] Diamant m; Rhombus m; Am. Baseball: Spielfeld n; Karten: Karo n.

diaper ['daiəpə] 1. Windel f; 2. Am. Baby trockenlegen, wickeln.

diaphragm ['daiəfræm] Zwerchfell n; opt. Blende f; teleph. Membran(e) f.

diarrh(o)ea ✠ [daiə'riə] Durchfall m.

diary ['daiəri] Tagebuch n.

dice [dais] 1. pl. von die²; 2. würfeln; ~-box ['daisbɔks] Würfelbecher m.

dick Am. sl. [dik] Detektiv m.

dicker Am. F ['dikə] (ver)schachern.

dick(e)y ['diki] 1. sl. schlecht, schlimm; 2. F Notsitz m; Hemdenbrust f; ~-bird Piepvögelchen n.

dictat|e 1. ['dikteit] Diktat n, Vorschrift f; Gebot n; 2. [dik'teit] diktieren; fig. vorschreiben; ~ion [~eiʃən] Diktat n; Vorschrift f; ~orship [~eitəʃip] Diktatur f.

diction ['dikʃən] Ausdruck(sweise f) m, Stil m; ~ary [~nri] Wörterbuch n.

did [did] pret. von do.

die¹ [dai] sterben, umkommen; untergehen; absterben; F schmachten; ~ away ersterben; verhallen (Ton); ~ out verlieren (Farbe); verlöschen (Licht); ~ down hinsiechen; (dahin)schwinden; erlöschen.

die² [~], pl. dice [dais] Würfel m; pl. dies [daiz] ⊕ Preßform f; Münz-Stempel m; lower ~ Matrize f.

die-hard ['daiha:d] Reaktionär m.

diet ['daiət] 1. Diät f; Nahrung f, Kost f; Landtag m; 2. v/t. Diät vorschreiben; beköstigen; v/i. diät leben.

differ ['difə] sich unterscheiden; anderer Meinung sein (with, from als); abweichen; ~ence ['difrəns] Unterschied m; Å, ✚ Differenz f; Meinungsverschiedenheit f; ~ent □ [~nt] verschieden; anders, andere(r, -s) (from als); ~entiate [difə'renʃieit] (sich) unterscheiden.

difficult □ ['difikəlt] schwierig; ~y [~ti] Schwierigkeit f.

diffiden|ce ['difidəns] Schüchternheit f; ~t □ [~nt] schüchtern.

diffus|e 1. fig. [di'fju:z] verbreiten; 2. □ [~u:s] weitverbreitet, zerstreut (bsd. Licht); weitschweifig; ~ion [~u:ʒən] Verbreitung f.

dig [dig] 1. (irr.] (um-, aus)graben; wühlen (in in dat.); 2. (Aus)Grabung(sstelle) f; ~s pl. F Bude f, Einzelzimmer n; F Stoß m, Puff m.

digest 1. [di'dʒest] v/t. ordnen; verdauen (a. fig. = überdenken; verwinden); v/i. verdaut werden;

2. ['daidʒest] Abriß m; Auslese f, Auswahl f; ⚖ Gesetzsammlung f; ~ible [di'dʒestəbl] verdaulich; ~ion [~tʃən] Verdauung f; ~ive [~tiv] Verdauungsmittel n.

digg|er ['digə] (bsd. Gold)Gräber m; sl. Australier m; ~ings F ['diginz] pl. Bude f (Wohnung); Am. Goldmine(n pl.) f.

dignif|ied □ ['dignifaid] würdevoll; würdig; ~y [~fai] Würde verleihen (dat.); (be)ehren; fig. adeln.

dignit|ary ['dignitəri] Würdenträger m; ~y [~ti] Würde f.

digress [dai'gres] abschweifen.

dike [daik] 1. Deich m; Damm m; Graben m; 2. eindeichen; eindämmen. [(lassen).]

dilapidate [di'læpideit] verfallen]

dilat|e [dai'leit] (sich) ausdehnen; Augen weit öffnen; ~ory □ ['dilətəri] aufschiebend; saumselig.

diligen|ce ['dilidʒəns] Fleiß m; ~t □ [~nt] fleißig, emsig.

dilute [dai'lju:t] 1. verdünnen; verwässern; 2. verdünnt.

dim [dim] 1. □ trüb; dunkel; matt; 2. (sich) verdunkeln; abblenden; (sich) trüben; matt werden.

dime Am. [daim] Zehncentstück n.

dimension [di'menʃən] Abmessung f; ~s pl. a. Ausmaß n.

dimin|ish [di'miniʃ] (sich) vermindern; abnehmen; ~ution [dimi'nju:ʃən] Verminderung f; Abnahme f; ~utive □ [di'minjutiv] winzig.

dimple ['dimpl] 1. Grübchen n; 2. Grübchen bekommen.

din [din] Getöse n, Lärm m.

dine [dain] (zu Mittag) speisen; bewirten; ~r ['dainə] Speisende(r m) f; (Mittags)Gast m; 🚍 bsd. Am. Speisewagen m; Am. Restaurant n.

dingle ['diŋgl] Waldschlucht f.

dingy [.] ['dindʒi] schmutzig.

dining-car 🚍 ['dainiŋka:] Speisewagen m; ~-room Speisezimmer n.

dinner ['dinə] (Mittag-, Abend-) Essen n; Festessen n; ~-jacket Smoking m; ~-pail Am. Essenträger m (Gerät); ~-party Tischgesellschaft f; ~-service, ~-set Tafelgeschirr n.

dint [dint] 1. Beule f; by ~ of kraft, vermöge (gen.); 2. ver-, einbeulen.

dip [dip] 1. v/t. (ein)tauchen; senken; schöpfen; abblenden; v/i. (unter)tauchen, untersinken; sich neigen; sich senken; 2. Eintauchen n; F kurzes Bad; Senkung f, Neigung f. [rie f.]

diphtheria ✠ [dif'θiəriə] Diphthe-]

diploma [di'ploumə] Diplom n; ~cy [~əsi] Diplomatie f; ~tic(al □) [diplə'mætik(əl)] diplomatisch; ~tist [di'ploumətist] Diplomat(in).

dipper ['dipə] Schöpfkelle f; Am. Great od. Big ♀ ast. der Große Bär.

**dire** ['daiə] gräßlich, schrecklich.

**direct** [di'rekt] 1. ☐ direkt; gerade; unmittelbar; offen, aufrichtig; deutlich; ~ current ∮ Gleichstrom m; ~ train durchgehender Zug; 2. adv. geradeswegs; = ~ly 3. richten; lenken, steuern; leiten; anordnen; j-n (an)weisen; Brief adressieren; ~ion [~kʃən] Richtung f; Gegend f; Leitung f; Anordnung f; Adresse f; Vorstand m; ~ion-finder [~nfaində] Radio: (Funk)Peiler m; Peil(funk)empfänger m; ~ion-indicator mot. Fahrtrichtungsanzeiger m; ⚡ Kursweiser m; ~ive [~ktiv] richtungweisend; leitend; ~ly [~tli] 1. adv. sofort; 2. cj. sobald, als.

**director** [di'rektə] Direktor m; Film: Regisseur m; board of ~s Aufsichtsrat m; ~ate [~ərit] Direktion f; ~y [~ri] Adreßbuch n; telephone ~ Telephonbuch n.

**dirge** [də:dʒ] Klage(lied n) f.

**dirigible** ['diridʒəbl] 1. lenkbar; 2. lenkbares Luftschiff.

**dirt** [də:t] Schmutz m; (lockere) Erde; ~-cheap F ['də:t'tʃi:p] spottbillig; ~y ['də:ti] 1. ☐ schmutzig (a. fig.); 2. beschmutzen; besudeln.

**disability** [disə'biliti] Unfähigkeit f.

**disable** [dis'eibl] (dienst-, kampf-) unfähig machen; ~d dienst-, kampfunfähig; körperbehindert; kriegsbeschädigt.

**disabuse** [disə'bju:z] e-s Besseren belehren (of über acc.).

**disadvantage** [disəd'va:ntidʒ] Nachteil m; Schaden m; ~ous [disædva:n'teidʒəs] nachteilig, ungünstig.

**disagree** [disə'gri:] nicht übereinstimmen; uneinig sein; nicht bekommen (with s.o. j-m); ~able ☐ [~riəbl] unangenehm; ~ment [~ri:mənt] Verschiedenheit f; Unstimmigkeit f; Meinungsverschiedenheit f.

**disappear** [disə'piə] verschwinden; ~ance [~ərəns] Verschwinden n.

**disappoint** [disə'pɔint] enttäuschen; vereiteln; j. im Stich lassen; ~ment [~tmənt] Enttäuschung f; Vereitelung f. [Mißbilligung f.)

**disapprobation** [disæprou'beiʃən]

**disapprov|al** [disə'pru:vəl] Mißbilligung f; ~e ['disə'pru:v] mißbilligen (of et.).

**disarm** [dis'a:m] v/t. entwaffnen (a. fig.); v/i. abrüsten; ~ament [~məmənt] Entwaffnung f; Abrüstung f.

**disarrange** ['dise'reindʒ] in Unordnung bringen, verwirren.

**disarray** ['disə'rei] 1. Unordnung f; 2. in Unordnung bringen.

**disast|er** [di'za:stə] Unglück(sfall m) n, Katastrophe f; ~rous ☐ [~trəs] unheilvoll; katastrophal.

25 SW E

**disband** [dis'bænd] entlassen; auflösen.

**disbelieve** ['disbi'li:v] nicht glauben.

**disburse** [dis'bə:s] auszahlen.

**disc** [disk] = disk.

**discard** 1. [dis'ka:d] Karten, Kleid etc. ablegen; entlassen; 2. ['diska:d] Karten: Abwerfen n; bsd. Am. Abfall(haufen) m.

**discern** [di'sə:n] unterscheiden; erkennen; beurteilen; ~ing ☐ [~niŋ] kritisch, scharfsichtig; ~ment [~nmənt] Einsicht f; Scharfsinn m.

**discharge** [dis'tʃa:dʒ] 1. v/t. ent-, ab-, ausladen; entlassen, entbinden; abfeuern; Flüssigkeit absondern; Amt versehen; Pflicht etc. erfüllen; Zorn etc. auslassen (on an dat.); Schuld tilgen; quittieren; Wechsel einlösen; entlassen; freisprechen; v/i. sich entladen; eitern; 2. Entladung f; Abfeuern n; Ausströmen n; Ausfluß m, Erter(ung f) m; Entlassung f; Entlastung f; Bezahlung f; Quittung f; Erfüllung f e-r Pflicht.

**disciple** [di'saipl] Schüler m; Jünger m.

**discipline** ['disiplin] 1. Disziplin f, Zucht f; Erziehung f; Züchtigung f; 2. erziehen; schulen; bestrafen.

**disclaim** [dis'kleim] (ab)leugnen; ablehnen; verzichten auf (acc.).

**disclose** [dis'klouz] aufdecken; erschließen, offenbaren, enthüllen.

**discolo(u)r** [dis'kʌlə] (sich) verfärben.

**discomfiture** [dis'kʌmfitʃə] Niederlage f; Verwirrung f; Vereitelung f.

**discomfort** [dis'kʌmfət] 1. Unbehagen n; 2. j-m Unbehagen verursachen.

**discompose** [diskəm'pouz] beunruhigen.

**disconcert** [diskən'sə:t] außer Fassung bringen; vereiteln.

**disconnect** ['diskə'nekt] trennen (a. ∮); ⊕ auskuppeln; ∮ ab-, ausschalten; ~ed ☐ zs.-hanglos.

**disconsolate** ☐ [dis'kɔnsəlit] trostlos.

**discontent** ['diskən'tent] Unzufriedenheit f; ~ed ☐ mißvergnügt, unzufrieden.

**discontinue** ['diskən'tinju(:)] aufgeben, aufhören mit; unterbrechen.

**discord** ['diskɔ:d], ~ance [dis'kɔ:dəns] Uneinigkeit f; ♪ Mißklang m.

**discount** ['diskaunt] 1. ♰ Diskont m; Abzug m, Rabatt m; 2. ♰ diskontieren; abrechnen; fig. absehen von; Nachricht mit Vorsicht aufnehmen; beeinträchtigen; ~enance [dis'kauntinəns] mißbilligen; entmutigen.

**discourage** [dis'kʌridʒ] entmutigen;

abschrecken; ~ment [~dʒmənt] Entmutigung f; Schwierigkeit f.

discourse [dis'kɔːs] 1. Rede f; Abhandlung f; Predigt f; 2. reden, sprechen; e-n Vortrag halten.

discourte|ous □ [dis'kɔːtjəs] unhöflich; ~sy [~tisi] Unhöflichkeit f.

discover [dis'kʌvə] entdecken; ausfindig machen; ~y [~əri] Entdeckung f.

discredit [dis'kredit] 1. schlechter Ruf; Unglaubwürdigkeit f; 2. nicht glauben; in Mißkredit bringen.

discreet □ [dis'kriːt] besonnen, vorsichtig; klug; verschwiegen.

discrepancy [dis'krepənsi] Widerspruch m; Unstimmigkeit f.

discretion [dis'kreʃən] Besonnenheit f, Klugheit f; Takt m; Verschwiegenheit f; Belieben n; age (od. years) of ~ Strafmündigkeit f (14 Jahre); surrender at ~ sich auf Gnade und Ungnade ergeben.

discriminat|e [dis'krimineit] unterscheiden; ~ against benachteiligen; ~ing □ [~tiŋ] unterscheidend; scharfsinnig; urteilsfähig; ~ion [diskrimi'neiʃən] Unterscheidung f; unterschiedliche (bsd. nachteilige) Behandlung; Urteilskraft f.

discuss [dis'kʌs] erörtern, besprechen; ~ion [~ʌʃən] Erörterung f.

disdain [dis'dein] 1. Verachtung f; 2. geringschätzen, verachten; verschmähen.

disease [di'ziːz] Krankheit f; ~d krank.

disembark ['disim'bɑːk] v/t. ausschiffen; v/i. landen, an Land gehen.

disengage ['disin'geidʒ] (sich) freimachen, (sich) lösen; ⊕ loskuppeln.

disentangle ['disin'tæŋgl] entwirren; fig. freimachen (from von).

disfavo(u)r ['dis'feivə] 1. Mißfallen n, Ungnade f; 2. nicht mögen.

disfigure [dis'figə] entstellen.

disgorge [dis'gɔːdʒ] ausspeien.

disgrace [dis'greis] 1. Ungnade f; Schande f; 2. in Ungnade fallen lassen; j-n entehren; ~ful □ [~sful] schimpflich.

disguise [dis'gaiz] 1. verkleiden; Stimme verstellen; verhehlen; 2. Verkleidung f; Verstellung f; Maske f.

disgust [dis'gʌst] 1. Ekel m; 2. anekeln; ~ing □ [~tiŋ] ekelhaft.

dish [diʃ] 1. Schüssel f, Platte f; Gericht n (Speise); the ~es das Geschirr; 2. anrichten; mst ~ up auftischen; ~-cloth ['diʃklɔθ] Geschirrspültuch n.

dishearten [dis'hɑːtn] entmutigen.

dishevel(l)ed [di'ʃevəld] zerzaust.

dishonest □ [dis'ɔnist] unehrlich, unredlich; ~y [~ti] Unredlichkeit f.

dishono(u)r [dis'ɔnə] 1. Unehre f,

Schande f; 2. entehren; schänden; Wechsel nicht honorieren; ~able □ [~ərəbl] entehrend; ehrlos.

dish|-pan Am. ['diʃpæn] Spülschüssel f; ~rag = dish-cloth; ~water Spülwasser n.

disillusion [disi'luːʒən] 1. Ernüchterung f, Enttäuschung f; 2. ernüchtern, enttäuschen.

disinclined ['disin'klaind] abgeneigt.

disinfect [disin'fekt] desinfizieren; ~ant [~tənt] Desinfektionsmittel n.

disintegrate [dis'intigreit] (sich) auflösen; (sich) zersetzen.

disinterested □ [dis'intristid] uneigennützig, selbstlos.

disk [disk] Scheibe f; Platte f; Schallplatte f; ~ brake mot. Scheibenbremse f; ~ jockey Ansager m e-r Schallplattensendung.

dislike [dis'laik] 1. Abneigung f; Widerwille m; 2. nicht mögen.

dislocate ['disləkeit] aus den Fugen bringen; verrenken; verlagern.

dislodge [dis'lɔdʒ] vertreiben, verjagen; umquartieren.

disloyal □ ['dis'lɔiəl] treulos.

dismal □ ['dizməl] trüb(selig); öde; trostlos, elend.

dismantl|e [dis'mæntl] abbrechen, niederreißen; ⚓ abtakeln; ⊕ demontieren; ~ing [~liŋ] Demontage f.

dismay [dis'mei] 1. Schrecken m; Bestürzung f; 2. v/t. erschrecken.

dismember [dis'membə] zerstükkeln.

dismiss [dis'mis] v/t. entlassen, wegschicken; ablehnen; Thema etc. fallen lassen; ⚖ abweisen; ~al [~səl] Entlassung f; Aufgabe f; ⚖ Abweichung f.

dismount ['dis'maunt] v/t. aus dem Sattel werfen; demontieren; ⊕ aus-ea.-nehmen; v/i. absteigen.

disobedien|ce [disə'biːdjəns] Ungehorsam m; ~t □ [~nt] ungehorsam.

disobey ['disə'bei] ungehorsam sein.

disoblige ['disə'blaidʒ] ungefällig sein gegen; kränken.

disorder [dis'ɔːdə] 1. Unordnung f; Aufruhr m; ⚕ Störung f; 2. in Unordnung bringen; stören; zerrütten; ~ly [~əli] unordentlich; ordnungswidrig; unruhig; aufrührerisch.

disorganize [dis'ɔːgənaiz] zerrütten.

disown [dis'oun] nicht anerkennen, verleugnen; ablehnen.

disparage [dis'pæridʒ] verächtlich machen, herabsetzen.

disparity [dis'pæriti] Ungleichheit f.

dispassionate □ [dis'pæʃnit] leidenschaftslos; unparteiisch.

**dispatch** [dis'pætʃ] **1.** (schnelle) Erledigung; (schnelle) Absendung; Abfertigung f; Eile f; Depesche f; **2.** (schnell) abmachen, erledigen (a. fig. = töten); abfertigen; (eilig) absenden.

**dispel** [dis'pel] vertreiben, zerstreuen.

**dispensa|ble** [dis'pensəbl] entbehrlich; **~ry** [~əri] Apotheke f; **~tion** [dispen'seiʃən] Austeilung f; Befreiung f (with von); göttliche Fügung.

**dispense** [dis'pens] v/t. austeilen; Gesetze handhaben; Arzneien anfertigen und ausgeben; befreien.

**disperse** [dis'pə:s] (sich) zerstreuen; auseinandergehen.

**dispirit** [di'spirit] entmutigen.

**displace** [dis'pleis] verschieben; absetzen; ersetzen; verdrängen.

**display** [dis'plei] **1.** Entfaltung f; Aufwand m; Schaustellung f; Schaufenster-Auslage f; **2.** entfalten; zur Schau stellen; zeigen.

**displeas|e** [dis'pli:z] j-m mißfallen; **~ed** ungehalten; **~ure** [~leʒə] Mißfallen n; Verdruß m.

**dispos|al** [dis'pouzəl] Anordnung f; Verfügung(srecht n) f; Beseitigung f; Veräußerung f; Übergabe f; **~e** [~ouz] v/t. (an)ordnen, einrichten; geneigt machen, veranlassen; v/i. **~ of** verfügen über (acc.); erledigen; verwenden; veräußern; unterbringen; beseitigen; **~ed** geneigt; ...gesinnt; **~ition** [dispə'ziʃən] Disposition f; Anordnung f; Neigung f; Sinnesart f; Verfügung f.

**dispossess** ['dispə'zes] (of) vertreiben (aus od. von); berauben (gen.).

**dispraise** [dis'preiz] tadeln.

**disproof** [dis'pru:f] Widerlegung f.

**disproportionate** □ [disprə'pɔ:-ʃnit] unverhältnismäßig.

**disprove** [dis'pru:v] widerlegen.

**dispute** [dis'pju:t] **1.** Streit(igkeit f) m; Rechtsstreit m; beyond (all) **~**, past **~** zweifellos; **2.** (be)streiten.

**disqualify** [dis'kwolifai] unfähig od. untauglich machen; für untauglich erklären.

**disquiet** [dis'kwaiət] beunruhigen.

**disregard** ['disri'ga:d] **1.** Nicht(be)achtung f; **2.** unbeachtet lassen.

**disreput|able** □ [dis'repjutəbl] schimpflich; verrufen; **~e** ['disri'pju:t] übler Ruf; Schande f.

**disrespect** ['disris'pekt] Nichtachtung f; Respektlosigkeit f; **~ful** □ [~tful] respektlos; unhöflich.

**disroot** [dis'ru:t] entwurzeln.

**disrupt** [dis'rʌpt] zerreißen; spalten.

**dissatis|faction** ['dissætis'fækʃən] Unzufriedenheit f; **~factory** [~fæktə-ri] unbefriedigend; **~fy** ['dis'sætis-fai] nicht befriedigen; j-m mißfallen.

**dissect** [di'sekt] zerlegen; zergliedern.

**dissemble** [di'sembl] v/t. verhehlen; v/i. sich verstellen, heucheln.

**dissen|sion** [di'senʃən] Zwietracht f, Streit m, Uneinigkeit f; **~t** [~nt] **1.** abweichende Meinung; Nichtzugehörigkeit f zur Staatskirche; **2.** andrer Meinung sein (from als).

**dissimilar** □ ['di'similə] (to) unähnlich (dat.); verschieden (von).

**dissimulation** [disimju'leiʃən] Verstellung f, Heuchelei f.

**dissipat|e** ['disipeit] (sich) zerstreuen; verschwenden; **~ion** [disi-'peiʃən] Zerstreuung f; Verschwendung f; ausschweifendes Leben.

**dissociate** [di'souʃieit] trennen; **~ o.s.** sich distanzieren, abrücken.

**dissoluble** [di'soljubl] (auf)lösbar.

**dissolut|e** □ ['disəlu:t] liederlich, ausschweifend; **~ion** [disə'lu:ʃən] Auflösung f; Zerstörung f; Tod m.

**dissolve** [di'zolv] v/t. (auf)lösen; schmelzen; v/i. sich auflösen; vergehen.

**dissonant** ['disənənt] ♪ mißtönend; abweichend; uneinig.

**dissuade** [di'sweid] j-m abraten.

**distan|ce** ['distəns] **1.** Abstand m, Entfernung f; Ferne f; Strecke f; Zurückhaltung f; at a **~** von weitem; in e-r gewissen Entfernung; weit weg; keep s.o. at a **~** j-m gegenüber reserviert sein; **2.** hinter sich lassen; **~t** □ [~nt] entfernt; fern; zurückhaltend; Fern...; **~ control** Fernsteuerung f.

**distaste** [dis'teist] Widerwille m; Abneigung f; **~ful** [~tful] widerwärtig; ärgerlich.

**distemper** [dis'tempə] Krankheit f (bsd. von Tieren); (Hunde)Staupe f.

**distend** [dis'tend] (sich) ausdehnen; (auf)blähen; (sich) weiten.

**distil** [dis'til] herabtröpfeln (lassen); ⚗ destillieren; **~lery** [~ləri] Branntweinbrennerei f.

**distinct** □ [dis'tiŋkt] verschieden; getrennt; deutlich, klar; **~ion** [~kʃən] Unterscheidung f; Unterschied m; Auszeichnung f; Rang m; **~ive** □ [~ktiv] unterscheidend; apart; kennzeichnend; bezeichnend.

**distinguish** [dis'tiŋgwiʃ] unterscheiden; auszeichnen; **~ed** berühmt, ausgezeichnet; vornehm.

**distort** [dis'tɔ:t] verdrehen; verzerren.

**distract** ['dis'trækt] ablenken; zerstreuen; beunruhigen; verwirren; verrückt machen; **~ion** [~kʃən] Zerstreutheit f; Verwirrung f; Wahnsinn m; Zerstreuung f.

**distraught** [dis'trɔ:t] verwirrt, bestürzt.

**distress** [dis'tres] **1.** Qual f; Elend n, Not f; Erschöpfung f; **2.** in Not

bringen; quälen; erschöpfen; ~ed
in Not befindlich; bekümmert; ~
*area* Notstandsgebiet *n.*

**distribut|e** [dis'tribju(:)t] verteilen;
einteilen; verbreiten; ~ion [distri-
'bju:ʃən] Verteilung *f*; *Film-*Ver-
leih *m*; Verbreitung *f*; Einteilung *f.*

**district** ['distrikt] Bezirk *m*; Gegend *f.*

**distrust** [dis'trʌst] **1.** Mißtrauen *n*;
**2.** mißtrauen (*dat.*); ~ful □ [~tful]
mißtrauisch; ~ (*of o.s.*) schüchtern.

**disturb** [dis'tə:b] beunruhigen; stören; ~ance [~bəns] Störung *f*; Unruhe *f*; Aufruhr *m*; ~ *of the peace*
ɡ̆ǯ öffentliche Ruhestörung; ~er
[~bə] Störenfried *m*, Unruhe-
stifter *m.*

**disunite** ['disju:'nait] (sich) trennen.

**disuse** ['dis'ju:z] nicht mehr gebrauchen.

**ditch** [ditʃ] Graben *m.*

**ditto** ['ditou] dito, desgleichen.

**divan** [di'væn] Diwan *m*; ~bed
[*oft* 'daivænbed] Bettcouch *f*, Liege *f.*

**dive** [daiv] **1.** (unter)tauchen; *vom
Sprungbrett* springen; e-n Sturzflug machen; eindringen in (*acc.*);
**2.** *Schwimmen*: Springen *n*; (Kopf-)
Sprung *m*; Sturzflug *m*; Keller-
lokal *n*; *Am.* F Kaschemme *f*; ~r
['daivə] Taucher *m.*

**diverge** [dai'və:dʒ] aus-ea.-laufen;
abweichen; ~nce [~dʒəns] Abweichung *f*; ~nt □ [~nt] (von-ea.-)ab-
weichend.

**divers** ['daivə(:)z] mehrere.

**divers|e** □ [dai'və:s] verschieden;
mannigfaltig; ~ion [~ə:ʃən] Ab-
lenkung *f*; Zeitvertreib *m*; ~ity
[~ə:siti] Verschiedenheit *f*; Man-
nigfaltigkeit *f.*

**divert** [dai'və:t] ablenken; *j-n* zerstreuen; unterhalten; *Verkehr* um-
leiten.

**divest** [dai'vest] entkleiden (*a. fig.*).

**divid|e** [di'vaid] **1.** *v/t.* teilen; tren-
nen; einteilen; A̸ dividieren (*by*
durch); *v/i.* sich teilen; zerfallen;
A̸ aufgehen; sich trennen *od.* auflösen; **2.** Wasserscheide *f*; ~end
['dividend] Dividende *f.*

**divine** [di'vain] **1.** □ göttlich; ~
*service* Gottesdienst *m*; **2.** Geist-
liche(r) *m*; **3.** weissagen; ahnen.

**diving** ['daiviŋ] Kunstspringen *n*;
*attr.* Taucher...

**divinity** [di'viniti] Gottheit *f*; Gött-
lichkeit *f*; Theologie *f.*

**divis|ible** □ [di'vizəbl] teilbar;
~ion [~iʒən] Teilung *f*; Trennung *f*;
Abteilung *f*; ✕, A̸ Division *f.*

**divorce** [di'vɔ:s] **1.** (Ehe)Scheidung
*f*; **2.** *Ehe* scheiden; sich scheiden
lassen.

**divulge** [dai'vʌldʒ] ausplaudern;
verbreiten; bekanntmachen.

**dixie** ✕ *sl.* ['diksi] Kochgeschirr *n*;

Feldkessel *m*; ♀ *Am.* die Südstaaten
*pl.*; ♀crat *Am. pol.* opponierender
Südstaatendemokrat.

**dizz|iness** ['dizinis] Schwindel *m*;
~y □ ['dizi] schwind(e)lig.

**do** [du:] [*irr.*] *v/t.* tun; machen;
(zu)bereiten; *Rolle, Stück* spielen;
~ *London sl.* London besichtigen;
*have done reading* fertig sein mit
Lesen; ~ *in* F um die Ecke bringen;
~ *into* übersetzen in; ~ *over* überstreifen, -ziehen; ~ *up* instand setzen; einpacken; *v/i.* tun; handeln;
sich benehmen; sich befinden; genügen; *that will* ~ das genügt;
*how* ~ *you* ~? guten Tag! *Wie geht's?*;
~ *well* s-e Sache gut machen; gute
Geschäfte machen; ~ *away with*
weg-, abschaffen; *I could* ~ *with* ...
ich könnte ... brauchen *od.* vertragen; ~ *without* fertig werden ohne;
~ *be quick* beeile dich doch; ~ *you
like London? — I* ~ gefällt Ihnen
London? — Ja.

**docil|e** ['dousail] gelehrig; fügsam;
~ity [dou'siliti] Gelehrigkeit *f.*

**dock**¹ [dɔk] stutzen; *fig.* kürzen.

**dock**² [~] **1.** ♻ Dock *n*; *bsd. Am.*
Kai *m*, Pier *m*; ɡ̆ǯ Anklagebank *f*;
**2.** ♻ docken.

**dockyard** ['dɔkja:d] Werft *f.*

**doctor** ['dɔktə] **1.** Doktor *m*; Arzt
*m*; **2.** Fverarzten; F*fig.* (ver)fälschen.

**doctrine** ['dɔktrin] Lehre *f*; Dogma
*n.*

**document 1.** ['dɔkjumənt] Urkunde
*f*; **2.** [~ment] beurkunden.

**dodge** [dɔdʒ] **1.** Seitensprung *m*;
Kniff *m*, Winkelzug *m*; **2.** *fig.* irre-
führen; ausweichen; Winkelzüge
machen; ~r ['dɔdʒə] Schieber(in);
*Am.* Hand-, Reklamezettel *m*; *Am.*
Maisbrot *n*, -kuchen *m.*

**doe** [dou] Hirschkuh *f*; Reh *n*;
Häsin *f.*

**dog** [dɔg] **1.** Hund *m*; Haken *m*,
Klammer *f*; **2.** nachspüren (*dat.*).

**dogged** □ ['dɔgid] verbissen.

**dogma** ['dɔgmə] Dogma *n*; Glau-
benslehre *f*; ~tic(al □) [dɔg'mæ-
tik(əl)] dogmatisch; bestimmt;
~tism ['dɔgmətizəm] Selbstherrlich-
keit *f.*

**dog's-ear** F ['dɔgziə] Eselsohr *n
im Buch.*

**dog-tired** F['dɔg'taiəd]hundemüde.

**doings** ['du(:)iŋz] *pl.* Dinge *n/pl.*;
Begebenheiten *f/pl.*; Treiben *n*;
Betragen *n.*

**dole** [doul] **1.** Spende *f*; F Erwerbs-
losenunterstützung *f*; **2.** verteilen.

**doleful** □ ['doulful] trübselig.

**doll** [dɔl] Puppe *f.*

**dollar** ['dɔlə] Dollar *m.*

**dolly** ['dɔli] Püppchen *n.*

**dolorous** ['dɔlərəs] schmerzhaft;
traurig.

**dolphin** ['dɔlfin] Delphin *m.*

**dolt** [doult] Tölpel *m.*

**domain** [də'mein] Domäne *f*; *fig.* Gebiet *n*; Bereich *m*.

**dome** [doum] Kuppel *f*; ⊕ Haube *f*; ⨯d gewölbt.

**Domesday Book** ['du:mzdei'buk] Reichsgrundbuch *n Englands*.

**domestic** [də'mestik] 1. (⨯ally) häuslich; inländisch; einheimisch; zahm; ⨯ *animal* Haustier *n*; 2. Dienstbote *m*; ⨯s *pl.* Haushaltsartikel *m/pl.*; ⨯**ate** [⨯keit] zähmen.

**domicile** ['dɔmisail] Wohnsitz *m*; ⨯d wohnhaft.

**domin|ant** ['dɔminənt] (vor)herrschend; ⨯**ate** [⨯neit] (be)herrschen; ⨯**ation** [dɔmi'neiʃən] Herrschaft *f*; ⨯**eer** [⨯'niə] (despotisch) herrschen; ⨯**eering** □ [⨯'əriŋ] herrisch, tyrannisch; überheblich.

**dominion** [də'minjən] Herrschaft *f*; Gebiet *n*; ♀ Dominion *n* (*im Brt. Commonwealth*).

**don** [dɔn] anziehen; *Hut* aufsetzen.

**donat|e** *Am.* [dou'neit] schenken; stiften; ⨯**ion** [⨯eiʃən] Schenkung *f*.

**done** [dʌn] 1. *p.p.* von *do*; 2. *adj.* abgemacht; fertig; gar *gekocht*.

**donkey** ['dɔŋki] *zo.* Esel *m*; *attr.* Hilfs...

**donor** ['dounə] (♨ *Blut*)Spender *m*.

**doom** [du:m] 1. Schicksal *n*, Verhängnis *n*; 2. verurteilen, verdammen.

**door** [dɔ:] Tür *f*, Tor *n*; *next* ⨯ nebenan; ⨯**handle** ['dɔ:hændl] Türgriff *m*; ⨯**keeper**, *Am.* ⨯**man** Pförtner *m*; Portier *m*; ⨯**way** Türöffnung *f*; Torweg *m*; ⨯**yard** *Am.* Vorhof *m*, Vorgarten *m*.

**dope** [doup] 1. Schmiere *f*; *bsd.* ✈ Lack *m*; Aufputschmittel *n*; Rauschgift *n*; *Am. sl.* Geheimtip *m*; 2. lackieren; *sl.* betäuben; aufpulvern; *Am. sl.* herauskriegen.

**dormant** *mst fig.* ['dɔ:mənt] schlafend, ruhend; unbenutzt; ✝ tot.

**dormer(-window)** ['dɔ:mə('windou)] Dachfenster *n*.

**dormitory** ['dɔ:mitri] Schlafsaal *m*; *bsd. Am.* Studenten(wohn)heim *n*.

**dose** [dous] 1. Dosis *f*, Portion *f*; 2. *j-m* e-e Medizin geben.

**dot** [dɔt] 1. Punkt *m*, Fleck *m*; 2. punktieren; tüpfeln; *fig.* verstreuen.

**dot|e** [dout]: ⨯ (*up*)*on* vernarrt sein in (*acc.*); ⨯**ing** ['doutiŋ] vernarrt.

**double** □ ['dʌbl] 1. doppelt; zu zweien; gekrümmt; zweideutig; 2. Doppelte(s) *n*; Doppelgänger(in) *f*; *Tennis:* Doppel(spiel) *n*; 3. *v/t.* verdoppeln; *a.* ⨯ *up* zs.-legen; *et.* umfahren, umsegeln; ⨯d *up* zs.-gekrümmt; *v/i.* sich verdoppeln; *a.* ⨯ *back* e-n Haken schlagen (*Hase*); ⨯**breasted** zweireihig (*Jackett*); ⨯**cross** *sl. Partner* betrügen; ⨯**dealing** Doppelzüngigkeit *f*; ⨯**edged** zweischneidig; ⨯**entry** doppelte Buchführung;

⨯**feature** *Am.* Doppelprogramm *n im Kino*; ⨯**header** *Am. Baseball:* Doppelspiel *n*; ⨯**park** *Am.* verboten in zweiter Reihe parken.

**doubt** [daut] 1. *v/i.* zweifeln; *v/t.* bezweifeln; mißtrauen (*dat.*); 2. Zweifel *m*; *no* ⨯ ohne Zweifel; ⨯**ful** □ ['dautful] zweifelhaft; ⨯**fulness** [⨯lnis] Zweifelhaftigkeit *f*; ⨯**less** ['dautlis] ohne Zweifel.

**douche** [du:ʃ] 1. Dusche *f*; Irrigator *m*; 2. duschen; spülen.

**dough** [dou] Teig *m*; ⨯**boy** *Am.* F ['douboi] Landser *m*; ⨯**nut** *Schmalzgebackenes.*

**dove** [dʌv] Taube *f*; *fig.* Täubchen *n*.

**dowel** ⊕ ['dauəl] Dübel *m*.

**down¹** [daun] Daune *f*; Flaum *m*; Düne *f*; ⨯s *pl.* Höhenrücken *m*.

**down²** [⨯] 1. *adv.* nieder; her-, hinunter, ab; abwärts; unten; *be* ⨯ *upon* F über *j-n* herfallen; 2. *prp.* herab, hinab, her-, hinunter; ⨯ *the river* flußabwärts; 3. *adj.* nach unten gerichtet; ⨯ *platform* Abfahrtsbahnsteig *m* (*London*); ⨯ *train* Zug *m* von London (fort); 4. *v/t.* niederwerfen; herunterholen; ⨯**cast** ['daunka:st] niedergeschlagen; ⨯**easter** *Am.* Neuengländer *m bsd. von Maine*; ⨯**fall** Fall *m*, Sturz *m*; Verfall *m*; ⨯**hearted** niedergeschlagen; ⨯**hill** bergab; ⨯**pour** Regenguß *m*; ⨯**right** □ 1. *adv.* geradezu, durchaus; völlig; 2. *adj.* ehrlich; plump (*Benehmen*); richtig, glatt (*Lüge etc.*); ⨯**stairs** die Treppe hinunter, (nach) unten; ⨯**stream** stromabwärts; ⨯**town** *bsd. Am.* Hauptgeschäftsviertel *n*; ⨯**ward(s)** ['daunwəd(z)] abwärts (gerichtet).

**downy** ['dauni] flaumig; *sl.* gerissen.

**dowry** ['dauəri] Mitgift *f* (*a. fig.*).

**doze** [douz] 1. dösen; 2. Schläfchen *n*.

**dozen** ['dʌzn] Dutzend *n*.

**drab** [dræb] gelblichgrau; eintönig.

**draft** [dra:ft] 1. Entwurf *m*; ✝ Tratte *f*; Abhebung *f*, ⨯ (Sonder-) Kommando *n*; Einberufung *f*; = *draught*; 2. entwerfen; aufsetzen; ⨯ abkommandieren; *Am.* einziehen; ⨯**ee** *Am.* ⨯ [⨯'ti:] Dienstpflichtige(r) *m*; ⨯**sman** ['dra:ftsmən] (technischer) Zeichner; Verfasser *m*, Entwerfer *m*.

**drag** [dræg] 1. Schleppnetz *n*; Schleife *f für Lasten*; Egge *f*; 2. *v/t.* schleppen, ziehen; *v/i.* (sich) schleppen, schleifen; (mit e-m Schleppnetz) fischen; [Libelle *f*.]

**dragon** ['drægən] Drache *m*; ⨯**fly**)

**drain** [drein] 1. Abfluß(graben *m*, -rohr *n*) *m*; F Schluck *m*; 2. *v/t.* entwässern; *Glas* leeren; *a.* ⨯ *off* abziehen; verzehren; *v/i.* ablaufen; ⨯**age** ['dreinidʒ] Abfluß *m*; Entwässerung(sanlage) *f*.

**drake** [dreik] Enterich *m*.

**dram** [dræm] Schluck *m*; *fig.* Schnaps *m*.

**drama** ['drɑ:mə] Drama *n*; **~tic** [drə'mætik] (*~ally*) dramatisch; **~tist** ['dræmətist] Dramatiker *m*; **~tize** [~taiz] dramatisieren.

**drank** [dræŋk] *pret. von* drink 2.

**drape** [dreip] 1. drapieren; in Falten legen; 2. *mst* **~s** *pl.* Vorhänge *m/pl.*; **~ry** ['dreipəri] Tuchhandel *m*; Tuchwaren *f/pl.*; Faltenwurf *m*.

**drastic** ['dræstik] (*~ally*) drastisch.

**draught** [drɑ:ft] Zug *m* (*Ziehen*; *Fischzug*; *Zugluft*; *Schluck*); ⊕ Tiefgang *m*; **~s** *pl.* Damespiel *n*; *s.* draft; **~ beer** Faßbier *n*; **~-horse** ['drɑ:fthɔ:s] Zugpferd *n*; **~sman** [~tsmən] Damestein *m*; = *draftsman*; **~y** [~ti] zugig.

**draw** [drɔ:] 1. [*irr.*] ziehen; an-, auf-, ein-, zuziehen; (sich) zs.-ziehen; in die Länge ziehen; dehnen; herausziehen, herauslocken; entnehmen; *Geld* abheben; anlocken, anziehen; abzapfen; ausfischen; *Geflügel* ausnehmen; zeichnen; entwerfen; *Urkunde* abfassen; unentschieden spielen; *Luft* schöpfen; **~ near** heranrücken; **~ out** in die Länge ziehen; **~ up** ab-, verfassen; **~ (up)on** ✝ (e-n Wechsel) ziehen auf (*acc.*); *fig.* in Anspruch nehmen; 2. Zug *m* (*Ziehen*); *Lotterie*: Ziehung *f*; Los *n*; *Sport*: unentschiedenes Spiel; F Zugstück *n*, -artikel *m*; **~back** ['drɔ:bæk] Nachteil *m*; Hindernis *n*; ✝ Rückzoll *m*; *Am.* Rückzahlung *f*; **~er** ['drɔ:ə] Ziehende(r *m*) *f*; Zeichner *m*; ✝ Aussteller *m*, Trassant *m*; [drɔ:] Schublade *f*; (*a pair of*) **~s** *pl.* (eine) Unterhose; (ein) Schlüpfer *m*; *mst* *chest of* **~s** Kommode *f*.

**drawing** ['drɔ:iŋ] Ziehen *n*; Zeichnen *n*; Zeichnung *f*; **~-account** Girokonto *n*; **~-board** Reißbrett *n*; **~-room** Gesellschaftszimmer *n*.

**drawn** [drɔ:n] 1. *p.p. von* draw 1; 2. *adj.* unentschieden; verzerrt.

**dread** [dred] 1. Furcht *f*; Schrecken *m*; 2. (sich) fürchten; **~ful** ☐ ['dredful] schrecklich; furchtbar.

**dream** [dri:m] 1. Traum *m*; 2. [*irr.*] träumen; **~er** ['dri:mə] Träumer (-in); **~t** [dremt] *pret. u. p.p. von* dream 2; **~y** ☐ ['dri:mi] träumerisch; verträumt.

**dreary** ☐ ['driəri] traurig; öde.

**dredge** [dredʒ] 1. Schleppnetz *n*; Bagger(maschine *f*) *m*; 2. (aus-) baggern.

**dregs** [dregz] *pl.* Bodensatz *m*, Hefe *f*.

**drench** [drentʃ] 1. (Regen)Guß *m*; 2. durchnässen; *fig.* baden.

**dress** [dres] 1. Anzug *m*; Kleidung *f*; Kleid *n*; 2. an-, ein-, zurichten; ✗ (sich) richten; zurechtmachen;

(sich) ankleiden; putzen; ✗ verbinden; frisieren; **~-circle** *thea.* ['dres'sə:kl] erster Rang; **~er** [~sə] Anrichte *f*; *Am.* Frisiertoilette *f*.

**dressing** ['dresiŋ] An-, Zurichten *n*; Ankleiden *n*; Verband *m*; Appretur *f*; *Küche*: Soße *f*; Füllung *f*; **~s** *pl.* ✗ Verbandzeug *n*; **~ down** Standpauke *f*; **~-gown** Morgenrock *m*; **~-table** Frisiertisch *m*.

**dress|maker** ['dresmeikə] Schneiderin *f*; **~-parade** Modenschau *f*.

**drew** ['dru:] *pret. von* draw 1.

**dribble** ['dribl] tröpfeln, träufeln (lassen); geifern; *Fußball*: dribbeln.

**dried** [draid] getrocknet; Dörr...

**drift** [drift] 1. (Dahin)Treiben *m*; *fig.* Lauf *m*; *fig.* Hang *m*; Zweck *m*; (Schnee-, Sand)Wehe *f*; 2. *v/t.* (zs.-)treiben, (zs.-)wehen; *v/i.* (dahin)treiben; sich anhäufen.

**drill** [dril] 1. Drillbohrer *m*; Furche *f*; ♪ Drill-, Sämaschine *f*; ✗ Exerzieren *n* (*a. fig.*); 2. bohren; ✗ (ein)exerzieren (*a. fig.*).

**drink** [driŋk] 1. Trunk *m*; (geistiges) Getränk; 2. [*irr.*] trinken.

**drip** [drip] 1. Tröpfeln *n*; Traufe *f*; 2. tröpfeln (lassen); triefen; **~-dry shirt** ['drip'drai ʃə:t] bügelfreies Hemd; **~ping** [~piŋ] Bratenfett *n*.

**drive** [draiv] 1. (Spazier)Fahrt *f*; Auffahrt *f*, Fahrweg *m*; ⊕ Antrieb *m*; *fig.* (Auf)Trieb *m*; Drang *m*; Unternehmen *n*, Feldzug *m*; *Am.* Sammelaktion *f*; 2. [*irr.*] *v/t.* (an-, ein)treiben; *Geschäft* betreiben; fahren; lenken; zwingen; vertreiben; *v/i.* treiben; fahren; **~ at** hinzielen auf.

**drive-in** *Am.* ['draiv'in] 1. *mst attr.* Auto...; **~ cinema** Autokino *n*; 2. Autokino *n*; Autorestaurant *n*.

**drivel** ['drivl] 1. geifern; faseln; 2. Geifer *m*; Faselei *f*.

**driven** ['drivn] *p.p. von* drive 2.

**driver** ['draivə] Treiber *m*; *mot.* Fahrer *m*, Chauffeur *m*; 🚂 Führer *m*.

**driving| licence** ['draiviŋ laisəns] Führerschein *m*; **~ school** Fahrschule *f*.

**drizzle** ['drizl] 1. Sprühregen *m*; 2. sprühen, nieseln.

**drone** [droun] 1. *zo.* Drohne *f*; *fig.* Faulenzer *m*; 2. summen; dröhnen.

**droop** [dru:p] *v/t.* sinken lassen; *v/i.* schlaff niederhängen; den Kopf hängen lassen; (ver)welken; schwinden.

**drop** [drɔp] 1. Tropfen *m*; Fruchtbonbon *m*, *n*; Fall *m*; Falltür *f*; *thea.* Vorhang *m*; *get* (*have*) *the* **~** *on Am.* F zuvorkommen; 2. *v/t.* tropfen (lassen); niederlassen; fallen lassen; *Brief* einwerfen; *Fahrgast* absetzen; senken; **~** *s.o. a few lines pl.* j-m ein paar Zeilen schreibeu; v/i. tropfen; (herab)fallen; um-, hinsinken; ~ in unerwartet kommen.

**dropsy** ♂ ['drɒpsi] Wassersucht f.

**drought** [draut], **drouth** [drauθ] Trockenheit f, Dürre f.

**drove** [drouv] 1. Trift f Rinder; Herde f (a. fig.); 2. pret. von drive 2.

**drown** [draun] v/t. ertränken; überschwemmen; fig. übertäuben; übertönen; v/i. ertrinken.

**drows|e** [drauz] schlummern, schläfrig sein od. machen; ~y ['drauzi] schläfrig; einschläfernd.

**drudge** [drʌdʒ] 1. fig. Sklave m, Packesel m, Kuli m; 2. sich (ab-)placken.

**drug** [drʌg] 1. Droge f, Arzneiware f; Rauschgift n; unverkäufliche Ware; 2. mit (schädlichen) Zutaten versetzen; Arznei od. Rauschgift geben (dat.) od. nehmen; ~gist ['drʌgist] Drogist m; Apotheker m; ~store Am. Drugstore m.

**drum** [drʌm] 1. Trommel f; Trommelfell n; 2. trommeln; ~mer ['drʌmə] Trommler m; bsd. Am. F Vertreter m.

**drunk** [drʌŋk] 1. p.p. von drink 2; 2. adj. (be)trunken; get ~ sich betrinken; ~ard ['drʌŋkəd] Trinker m, Säufer m; ~en adj. [~kən] (be-)trunken.

**dry** [drai] 1. □ trocken; herb (Wein); F durstig; F antialkoholisch; ~ goods pl. Am. F Kurzwaren f/pl.; 2. Am. F Alkoholgegner m; 3. trocknen; dörren; ~ up austrocknen; verdunsten; ~-clean ['drai'kli:n] chemisch reinigen; ~-nurse Kinderfrau f.

**dual** □ ['dju(:)əl] doppelt; Doppel...

**dubious** □ ['dju:bjəs] zweifelhaft.

**duchess** ['dʌtʃis] Herzogin f.

**duck** [dʌk] 1. zo. Ente f; Am. sl. Kerl m; Verbeugung f; Ducken n; (Segel)Leinen n; F Liebling m; 2. (unter)tauchen; (sich) ducken; Am. j-m ausweichen.

**duckling** ['dʌkliŋ] Entchen n.

**dude** Am. [dju:d] Geck m; ~ ranch Am. Vergnügungsfarm f.

**dudgeon** ['dʌdʒən] Groll m.

**due** [dju:] 1. schuldig; gebührend; gehörig; fällig; in ~ time zur rechten Zeit; be ~ to j-m gebühren; herrühren od. kommen von; be ~ to inf. sollen, müssen; Am. im Begriff sein zu; 2. adv. ✈ gerade; genau; 3. Schuldigkeit f; Recht n, Anspruch m; Lohn m; mst ~s pl. Abgabe(n pl.) f, Gebühr(en pl.) f; Beitrag m. 2. sich duellieren.}

**duel** ['dju(:)əl] 1. Zweikampf m;}

**dug** [dʌg] pret. u. p.p. von dig 1.

**duke** [dju:k] Herzog m; ~dom ['dju:kdəm] Herzogtum n; Herzogswürde f.

**dull** [dʌl] 1. □ dumm; träge;

schwerfällig; stumpf(sinnig); matt (Auge etc.); schwach (Gehör); langweilig; teilnahmslos; dumpf; trüb; ✝ flau; 2. stumpf machen; fig. abstumpfen; (sich) trüben; ~ness ['dʌlnis] Stumpfsinn m; Dummheit f; Schwerfälligkeit f; Mattheit f; Langweiligkeit f; Teilnahmslosigkeit f; Trübheit f; Flauheit f.

**duly** adv. ['dju:li] gehörig; richtig.

**dumb** □ [dʌm] stumm; sprachlos; Am. F doof, blöd; ~founded [dʌm'faundid] sprachlos; ~waiter ['dʌm'weitə] Drehtisch m; Am. Speisenaufzug m.

**dummy** ['dʌmi] Attrappe f; Schein m, Schwindel m; fig. Strohmann m; Statist m; attr. Schein...; Schwindel...

**dump** [dʌmp] 1. v/t. auskippen; Schutt etc. abladen; Waren zu Schleuderpreisen ausführen; v/i. hinplumpsen; 2. Klumpen m; Plumps m; Schuttabladestelle f; ⚔ Munitionslager n; ~ing ✝ ['dʌmpiŋ] Schleuderausfuhr f; ~s pl.. (down) in the ~ F niedergeschlagen.

**dun** [dʌn] mahnen, drängen.

**dunce** [dʌns] Dummkopf m.

**dune** [dju:n] Düne f.

**dung** [dʌŋ] 1. Dung m; 2. düngen.

**dungeon** ['dʌndʒən] Kerker m.

**dunk** Am. F [dʌŋk] (ein)tunken.

**dupe** [dju:p] anführen, täuschen.

**duplex** ⊕ ['dju:pleks] attr. Doppel...; Am Zweifamilienhaus n.

**duplic|ate** 1. ['dju:plikit] doppelt; 2. [~] Duplikat n; 3. [~keit] doppelt ausfertigen; ~ity [dju(:)'plisiti] Doppelzüngigkeit f.

**dura|ble** □ ['djuərəbl] dauerhaft. ~tion [djuə'reiʃən] Dauer f.

**duress(e)** [djuə'res] Zwang m.

**during** prp ['djuəriŋ] während.

**dusk** [dʌsk] Halbdunkel n, Dämmerung f, ~y □ ['dʌski] dämmerig, düster (a. fig.); schwärzlich.

**dust** [dʌst] 1. Staub m; 2. abstauben; bestreuen; ~bin ['dʌstbin] Mülleimer m; ~ bowl Am Sandstaubu. Dürregebiet n im Westen der USA; ~-cart Müllwagen m; ~er [~tə] Staublappen m, -wedel m; Am. Staubmantel m; ~-jacket Am. Schutzumschlag m e-s Buches; ~man Müllabfuhrmann m; ~y □ [~ti] staubig.

**Dutch** [dʌtʃ] 1. holländisch; ~ treat Am. F getrennte Rechnung; 2. Holländisch n; the ~ die Holländer pl.

**duty** ['dju:ti] Pflicht f, Ehrerbietung f; Abgabe f, Zoll m; Dienst m; off ~ dienstfrei; ~-free zollfrei.

**dwarf** [dwɔ:f] 1. Zwerg m; 2. in der Entwicklung hindern; verkleinern.

**dwell** [dwel] [irr.] wohnen; verweilen (on, upon bei); ~ (up)on bestehen auf (acc.); ~ing ['dweliŋ] Wohnung f.

**dwelt** [dwelt] *pret. u. p.p. von* dwell.
**dwindle** ['dwindl] (dahin)schwinden, abnehmen; (herab)sinken.
**dye** [dai] **1.** Farbe *f; of deepest ~ fig.* schlimmster Art; **2.** färben.
**dying** ['daiiŋ] **1.** □ sterbend; Sterbe...; **2.** Sterben *n.*

**dynam|ic** [dai'næmik] dynamisch, kraftgeladen; **~ics** [~ks] *mst sg.* Dynamik *f;* **~ite** ['dainəmait] **1.** Dynamit *n;* **2.** mit Dynamit sprengen.
**dysentery** ⚕ ['disntri] Ruhr *f.*
**dyspepsia** ⚕ [dis'pepsiə] Verdauungsstörung *f.*

# E

**each** [i:tʃ] jede(r, -s); **~** other einander, sich.
**eager** □ ['i:gə] (be)gierig; eifrig; **~ness** ['i:gənis] Begierde *f;* Eifer *m.*
**eagle** ['i:gl] Adler *m; Am.* Zehndollarstück *n;* **~-eyed** scharfsichtig.
**ear** [iə] Ähre *f;* Ohr *n;* Öhr *n,* Henkel *m;* keep an ~ to the ground *bsd. Am.* aufpassen, was die Leute sagen *od.* denken; **~-drum** ['iə-drʌm] Trommelfell *n.*
**earl** [ə:l] *englischer* Graf.
**early** ['ə:li] früh; Früh...; Anfangs...; erst; bald(ig); *as ~ as* schon in *(dat.).* [nen.]
**ear-mark** ['iəma:k] (kenn)zeich-
**earn** [ə:n] verdienen; einbringen.
**earnest** ['ə:nist] **1.** □ ernst(lich, -haft); ernstgemeint; **2.** Ernst *m.*
**earnings** ['ə:niŋz] Einkommen *n.*
**ear|piece** *teleph.* ['iəpi:s] Hörmuschel *f;* **~shot** Hörweite *f.*
**earth** [ə:θ] **1.** Erde *f;* Land *n;* **2.** *v/t.* ⚡ erden; **~en** ['ə:θən] irden; **~enware** [~nweə] **1.** Töpferware *f;* Steingut *n;* **2.** irden; **~ing** ⚡ ['ə:θiŋ] Erdung *f;* **~ly** ['ə:θli] irdisch; **~quake** Erdbeben *n;* **~worm** Regenwurm *m.*
**ease** [i:z] **1.** Bequemlichkeit *f,* Behagen *n;* Ruhe *f;* Ungezwungenheit *f;* Leichtigkeit *f; at ~* bequem, behaglich; **2.** *v/t.* erleichtern; lindern; beruhigen; bequem(er) machen; *v/i.* sich entspannen *(Lage).*
**easel** ['i:zl] Staffelei *f.*
**easiness** ['i:zinis] = ease 1.
**east** [i:st] **1.** Ost(en *m);* Orient *m; the ♀ Am.* die Oststaaten *der USA;* **2.** Ost...; östlich; ostwärts.
**Easter** ['i:stə] Ostern *n; attr.* Oster...
**easter|ly** ['i:stəli] östlich; Ost...; nach Osten; **~n** [~ən] = easterly; orientalisch; **~ner** [~nə] Ostländer (-in); Oriental|e *m,* -in *f; ♀ Am.* Oststaatler(in).
**eastward(s)** ['i:stwəd(z)] ostwärts.
**easy** ['i:zi] □ leicht; bequem; frei von Schmerzen; ruhig; willig; ungezwungen; *in ~ circumstances* wohlhabend; *on ~ street Am.* in guten Verhältnissen; *take it ~!* immer mit der Ruhe!; **~ chair** Klubsessel *m;* **~-going** *fig.* bequem.

**eat** [i:t] **1.** [*irr.*] essen; (zer)fressen; **2.** **~s** *pl. Am. sl.* Essen *n,* Eßwaren *f/pl.;* **~ables** ['i:təblz] *pl.* Eßwaren *f/pl.;* **~en** ['i:tn] *p.p. von* eat 1.
**eaves** [i:vz] *pl.* Dachrinne *f,* Traufe *f;* **~drop** ['i:vzdrɔp] (er)lauschen; horchen.
**ebb** [eb] **1.** Ebbe *f; fig.* Abnahme *f;* Verfall *m;* **2.** verebben; *fig.* abnehmen, sinken; **~-tide** ['eb'taid] Ebbe *f.*
**ebony** ['ebəni] Ebenholz *n.*
**ebullition** [ebə'liʃən] Überschäumen *n;* Aufbrausen *n.*
**eccentric** [ik'sentrik] **1.** exzentrisch; *fig.* überspannt; **2.** Sonderling *m.*
**ecclesiastic** [ikli:zi'æstik] Geistliche(r) *m;* **~al** □ [~kəl] geistlich, kirchlich.
**echo** ['ekou] **1.** Echo *n;* **2.** widerhallen; *fig.* echoen, nachsprechen.
**eclipse** [i'klips] **1.** Finsternis *f;* **2.** (sich) verfinstern, verdunkeln.
**econom|ic(al** □) [i:kə'nɔmik(əl)] haushälterisch; wirtschaftlich; Wirtschafts...; **~ics** [~ks] *sg.* Volkswirtschaft(slehre) *f;* **~ist** [i(:)'kɔnəmist] Volkswirt *m;* **~ize** [~maiz] sparsam wirtschaften (mit); **~y** [~mi] Wirtschaft *f;* Wirtschaftlichkeit *f;* Einsparung *f; political ~* Volkswirtschaft(slehre) *f.*
**ecsta|sy** ['ekstəsi] Ekstase *f,* Verzückung *f;* **~tic** [eks'tætik] (~ally) verzückt.
**eddy** ['edi] **1.** Wirbel *m;* **2.** wirbeln.
**edge** [edʒ] **1.** Schneide *f;* Schärfe *f;* Rand *m;* Kante *f; Tisch-Ecke f; be on ~* nervös sein; *have the ~ on s.o. bsd. Am.* F j-m über sein; **2.** schärfen; (um)säumen; (sich) drängen; **~ways, ~wise** ['edʒweiz, 'edʒwaiz] seitwärts; von der Seite.
**edging** ['edʒiŋ] Einfassung *f;* Rand|
**edgy** ['edʒi] scharf; F nervös. [*m.*]
**edible** ['edibl] eßbar.
**edict** ['i:dikt] Edikt *n.*
**edifice** ['edifis] Gebäude *n.*
**edifying** □ ['edifaiiŋ] erbaulich.
**edit** ['edit] *Text* herausgeben, redigieren; *Zeitung* als Herausgeber leiten; **~ion** [i'diʃən] *Buch-*Ausgabe *f;* Auflage *f;* **~or** ['editə] Herausgeber *m;* Redakteur *m;* **~orial**

[edi'tɔ:riəl] Leitartikel *m*; *attr.* Redaktions...; **~orship** ['editəʃip] Schriftleitung *f*, Redaktion *f*.

**educat|e** ['edju(:)keit] erziehen; unterrichten; **~ion** [edju(:)'keiʃən] Erziehung *f*; (Aus)Bildung *f*; Erziehungs-, Schulwesen *n*; *Ministry of* ♀ Unterrichtsministerium *n*; **~ional** □ [~nl] erzieherisch; Erziehungs...; ～ Bildungs...; **~or** ['edju:keitə] Erzieher *m*.

**eel** [i:l] Aal *m*.

**efface** [i'feis] auslöschen; *fig.* tilgen.

**effect** [i'fekt] **1.** Wirkung *f*; Folge *f*; ⊕ Leistung *f*; **~s** *pl.* Effekten *pl.*; Habseligkeiten *f/pl.*; *be of* ～ Wirkung haben; *take* ～ in Kraft treten; *in* ～ in der Tat; *to the* ～ des Inhalts; **2.** bewirken, ausführen; **~ive** [~tiv] wirkend; wirksam; eindrucksvoll; wirklich vorhanden; ⊕ nutzbar; ～ *date* Tag *m* des Inkrafttretens; **~ual** □ [~tjuəl] wirksam, kräftig.

**effeminate** □ [i'feminit] verweichlicht; weibisch.

**effervesce** [efə'ves] (auf)brausen; **~nt** [~nt] sprudelnd, schäumend.

**effete** [e'fi:t] verbraucht; entkräftet.

**efficacy** ['efikəsi] Wirksamkeit *f*, Kraft *f*.

**efficien|cy** [i'fiʃənsi] Leistung(sfähigkeit) *f*; ～ *expert Am.* Rationalisierungsfachmann *m*; **~t** □ [~nt] wirksam; leistungsfähig; tüchtig.

**efflorescence** [ɔflɔ:'resns] Blütezeit *f*; ♔ Beschlag *m*.

**effluence** ['efluəns] Ausfluß *m*.

**effort** ['efət] Anstrengung *f*, Bemühung *f* (*at* um); Mühe *f*.

**effrontery** [e'frʌntəri] Frechheit *f*.

**effulgent** □ [e'fʌldʒənt] glänzend.

**effus|ion** [i'fju:ʒən] Erguß *m*; **~ive** □ [~:siv] überschwenglich.

**egg¹** [eg] *mst* ～ *on* aufreizen.

**egg²** [~] Ei *n*; *put all one's* ～*s in one basket* alles auf eine Karte setzen; *us sure as* ～*s is* ～*s* F todsicher; **~-cup** ['egkʌp] Eierbecher *m*; **~head** *Am. sl.* Intellektuelle(r) *m*.

**egotism** ['egoutizəm] Selbstgefälligkeit *f*.

**egregious** *iro.* □ [i'gri:dʒəs] ungeheuer.

**egress** ['i:grəs] Ausgang *m*; Ausweg *m*.

**Egyptian** [i'dʒipʃən] **1.** ägyptisch; **2.** Ägypter(in).

**eider** ['aidə]: ～ *down* Eiderdaunen *f/pl.*; Daunendecke *f*.

**eight** [eit] **1.** acht; **2.** Acht *f*; *behind the* ～ *ball Am.* in der (die) Klemme; **~een** ['ei'ti:n] achtzehn; **~eenth** [~nθ] achtzehnt; **~fold** ['eitfould] achtfach; **~h** [eitθ] **1.** achte(r, -s); **2.** Achtel *n*; **~hly** ['eitθli] achtens; **~ieth** ['eitiiθ] achtzigste(r, -s); **~y** ['eiti] achtzig.

**either** ['aiðə] **1.** *adj. u. pron.* einer

*von beiden*; beide; **2.** *cj.* ～ ... *or* entweder ... oder; *not* (...) ～ auch nicht.

**ejaculate** [i'dʒækjuleit] *Worte, Flüssigkeit* ausstoßen.

**eject** [i(:)'dʒekt] ausstoßen; vertreiben, ausweisen; entsetzen (*e-s Amtes*).

**eke** [i:k]: ～ *out* ergänzen; verlängern; sich mit *et.* durchhelfen.

**el** *Am.* F [el] = elevated railroad.

**elaborat|e 1.** □ [i'læbərit] sorgfältig ausgearbeitet; kompliziert; **2.** [~reit] sorgfältig ausarbeiten; **~eness** [~ritnis], **~ion** [ilæbə'reiʃən] sorgfältige Ausarbeitung.

**elapse** [i'læps] verfließen, verstreichen.

**elastic** [i'læstik] **1.** (～*ally*) dehnbar; spannkräftig; **2.** Gummiband *n*; **~ity** [elæs'tisiti] Elastizität *f*, Dehnbarkeit *f*; Spannkraft *f*.

**elate** [i'leit] (er)heben, ermutigen, froh erregen; stolz machen; **~d** in gehobener Stimmung, freudig erregt (*at über acc.*; *with durch*).

**elbow** ['elbou] **1.** Ellbogen *m*; Biegung *f*; ⊕ Knie *n*; *at one's* ～ nahe, bei der Hand; *out at* ～*s fig.* heruntergekommen; **2.** mit dem Ellbogen (weg)stoßen; ～ *out* verdrängen; ～ *grease* F Armschmalz *n* (*Kraftanstrengung*).

**elder** ['eldə] **1.** älter; **2.** der, die Ältere; (Kirchen)Älteste(r) *m*; ♀ Holunder *m*; **~ly** [~əli] ältlich.

**eldest** ['eldist] älteste(r, -s).

**elect** [i'lekt] **1.** (aus)gewählt; **2.** (aus~, er)wählen; ～*ion* [~kʃən] Wahl *f*; **~ive** [~ktiv] **1.** □ wählend; gewählt; Wahl...; *Am.* fakultativ; **2.** *Am.* Wahlfach *n*; **~or** [~tə] Wähler *m*; *Am.* Wahlmann *m*; Kurfürst *m*; **~oral** [~ərəl] Wahl...; Wähler...; ～ *college Am.* Wahlmänner *m/pl.*; **~orate** [~rit] Wähler(schaft *f*) *m/pl.*

**electric|al** □ [i'lektrik(əl)] elektrisch; Elektro...; *fig.* faszinierend; **~al engineer** Elektrotechniker *m*; ～ **blue** stahlblau; ～ **chair** elektrischer Stuhl; **~ian** [ilek'triʃən] Elektriker *m*; **~ity** [~isiti] Elektrizität *f*.

**electri|fy** [i'lektrifai], **~ze** [~raiz] elektrifizieren; elektrisieren.

**electro|cute** [i'lektrəkju:t] auf dem elektrischen Stuhl hinrichten; durch elektrischen Strom töten; **~metallurgy** Elektrometallurgie *f*.

**electron** [i'lektrən] Elektron *n*; **~-ray tube** magisches Auge.

**electro|plate** [i'lektroupleit] galvanisch versilbern; **~type** galvanischer Druck; Galvano *n*.

**elegan|ce** ['eligəns] Eleganz *f*; Anmut *f*; **~t** □ [~nt] elegant; geschmackvoll; *Am.* erstklassig.

**element** ['elimənt] Element *n*; Urstoff *m*; (Grund)Bestandteil *m*; **~s** *pl.* Anfangsgründe *m/pl.*; **~al** □

[eli'mentl] elementar; wesentlich; ⁓ary [⁓təri] **1.** ☐ elementar; Anfangs...; ⁓ *school* Volks-, Grundschule *f;* **2.** *elementaries pl.* Anfangsgründe *m/pl.*

**elephant** ['elifənt] Elefant *m.*

**elevat|e** ['eliveit] erhöhen; *fig.* erheben; ⁓ed erhaben; ⁓ (*railroad*) *Am.* Hochbahn *f;* ⁓ion [eli'veiʃən] Erhebung *f,* Erhöhung *f;* Höhe *f;* Erhabenheit *f;* ⁓or ⊕ ['eliveitə] Aufzug *m; Am.* Fahrstuhl *m;* ⚡ Höhenruder *n;* (*grain*) ⁓ *Am.* Getreidespeicher *m.*

**eleven** [i'levn] **1.** elf; **2.** Elf *f;* ⁓th [⁓nθ] elfte(r, -s).

**elf** [elf] Elf(e *f*) *m,* Kobold *m;* Zwerg *m.*

**elicit** [i'lisit] hervorlocken, herausholen.

**eligible** ☐ ['elidʒəbl] geeignet, annehmbar; passend.

**eliminat|e** [i'limineit] aussondern, ausscheiden; ausmerzen; ⁓ion [ilimi'neiʃən] Aussonderung *f;* Ausscheidung *f.*

**élite** [ei'li:t] Elite *f;* Auslese *f.*

**elk** *zo.* [elk] Elch *m.*

**ellipse** ⚹ [i'lips] Ellipse *f.*

**elm** ⚘ [elm] Ulme *f,* Rüster *f.*

**elocution** [elə'kju:ʃən] Vortrag(skunst, -sweise *f*) *m.*

**elongate** ['i:lɔŋgeit] verlängern.

**elope** [i'loup] entlaufen, durchgehen.

**eloquen|ce** ['eləkwəns] Beredsamkeit *f;* ⁓t ☐ [⁓nt] beredt.

**else** [els] sonst, andere(r, -s), weiter; ⁓where ['elswɛə] anderswo(hin).

**elucidat|e** [i'lu:sideit] erläutern; ⁓ion [ilu:si'deiʃən] Aufklärung *f.*

**elude** [i'lu:d] geschickt umgehen; ausweichen, sich entziehen (*dat.*).

**elus|ive** [i'lu:siv] schwer faßbar; ⁓ory [⁓səri] trügerisch.

**emaciate** [i'meiʃieit] abzehren, ausmergeln.

**emanat|e** ['eməneit] ausströmen; ausgehen (*from* von); ⁓ion [emə'neiʃən] Ausströmen *n; fig.* Ausstrahlung *f.*

**emancipat|e** [i'mænsipeit] emanzipieren, befreien; ⁓ion [imænsi'peiʃən] Emanzipation *f;* Befreiung *f.*

**embalm** [im'ba:m] (ein)balsamieren; *be* ⁓ed *in* fortleben in (*dat.*).

**embankment** [im'bæŋkmənt] Eindämmung *f;* Deich *m;* (Bahn-) Damm *m;* Uferstraße *f,* Kai *m.*

**embargo** [em'ba:gou] (Hafen-, Handels)Sperre *f,* Beschlagnahme *f.*

**embark** [im'ba:k] (sich) einschiffen (*for* nach); *Geld* anlegen; sich einlassen (*in, on, upon* in, auf *acc.*).

**embarrass** [im'bærəs] (be)hindern; verwirren; in (Geld)Verlegenheit bringen; verwickeln; ⁓ing ☐ [⁓siŋ]

unangenehm; unbequem; ⁓ment [⁓smənt] (Geld)Verlegenheit *f;* Schwierigkeit *f.*

**embassy** ['embəsi] Botschaft *f;* Gesandtschaft *f.*

**embed** [im'bed] (ein)betten, lagern.

**embellish** [im'beliʃ] verschönern; ausschmücken. [Asche.]

**embers** ['embəz] *pl.* glühende]

**embezzle** [im'bezl] unterschlagen; ⁓ment [⁓lmənt] Unterschlagung *f.*

**embitter** [im'bitə] verbittern.

**emblazon** [im'bleizən] mit e-m Wappenbild bemalen; *fig.* verherrlichen.

**emblem** ['embləm] Sinnbild *n;* Wahrzeichen *n.*

**embody** [im'bɔdi] verkörpern; vereinigen; einverleiben (*in dat.*).

**embolden** [im'bouldən] ermutigen.

**embolism** ⚕ ['embɔlizəm] Embolie *f.*

**embosom** [im'buzəm] ins Herz schließen; ⁓ed *with* umgeben von.

**emboss** [im'bɔs] bossieren; *mit dem Hammer* treiben.

**embrace** [im'breis] **1.** (sich) umarmen; umfassen; *Beruf etc.* ergreifen; *Angebot* annehmen; **2.** Umarmung *f.*

**embroider** [im'brɔidə] sticken; ausschmücken; ⁓y [⁓əri] Stickerei *f.*

**embroil** [im'brɔil] (in Streit) verwickeln; verwirren.

**emendation** [i:men'deiʃən] Verbesserung *f.*

**emerald** ['emərəld] Smaragd *m.*

**emerge** [i'mə:dʒ] auftauchen; hervorgehen; sich erheben; sich zeigen; ⁓ncy [⁓dʒənsi] unerwartetes Ereignis; Notfall *m; attr.* Not...; ⁓ brake Notbremse *f;* ⁓ call Notruf *m;* ⁓ exit Notausgang *m;* ⁓ man *Sport:* Ersatzmann *m;* ⁓nt [⁓nt] auftauchend, entstehend; ⁓ countries Entwicklungsländer *n/pl.*

**emersion** [i(:)'mə:ʃən] Auftauchen *n.*

**emigra|nt** ['emigrənt] **1.** auswandernd; **2.** Auswanderer *m;* ⁓te [⁓reit] auswandern; ⁓tion [emi'greiʃən] Auswanderung *f.*

**eminen|ce** ['eminəns] (An)Höhe *f;* Auszeichnung *f;* hohe Stellung; Eminenz *f* (*Titel*); ⁓t ☐ [⁓nt] *fig.* ausgezeichnet, hervorragend; ⁓tly [⁓tli] ganz besonders.

**emissary** ['emisəri] Emissär *m.*

**emit** [i'mit] von sich geben; aussenden, ausströmen; ☦ ausgeben.

**emolument** [i'mɔljumənt] Vergütung *f;* ⁓s *pl.* Einkünfte *pl.*

**emotion** [i'mouʃən] (Gemüts)Bewegung *f;* Gefühl(sregung *f*) *n;* Rührung *f;* ⁓al ☐ [⁓nl] gefühlsmäßig, gefühlvoll, gefühlsbetont; ⁓less [⁓nlis] gefühllos, kühl.

**emperor** ['empərə] Kaiser *m.*

**empha|sis** ['emfəsis] Nachdruck *m*; **~size** [~saiz] nachdrücklich betonen; **~tic** [im'fætik] (~ally) nachdrücklich; ausgesprochen.

**empire** ['empaiə] (Kaiser)Reich *n*; Herrschaft *f*; *the British* ♀ das britische Weltreich.

**empirical** □ [em'pirikəl] erfahrungsgemäß.

**employ** [im'plɔi] **1.** beschäftigen, anstellen; an-, verwenden, gebrauchen; **2.** Beschäftigung *f*; *in the ~ of* angestellt bei; **~ee** [emplɔi'i:] Angestellte(r *m*) *f*; Arbeitnehmer(in); **~er** [im'plɔiə] Arbeitgeber *m*; ✝ Auftraggeber *m*; **~ment** [~imənt] Beschäftigung *f*; Arbeit *f*; *~ agency* Stellenvermittlungsbüro *n*; ♀ *Exchange* Arbeitsamt *n*.

**empower** [im'pauə] ermächtigen; befähigen.

**empress** ['empris] Kaiserin *f*.

**empt|iness** ['emptinis] Leere *f*; Hohlheit *f*; **~y** □ ['empti] **1.** leer; *fig.* hohl; **2.** (sich) (aus-, ent)leeren.

**emul|ate** ['emjuleit] wetteifern mit; nacheifern, es gleichtun (*dat.*); **~ation** [emju'leiʃən] Wetteifer *m*.

**enable** [i'neibl] befähigen, es *j-m* ermöglichen; ermächtigen.

**enact** [i'nækt] verfügen, verordnen; *Gesetz* erlassen; *thea.* spielen.

**enamel** [i'næməl] **1.** Email(le *f*) *n*, (Zahn)Schmelz *m*; Glasur *f*; Lack *m*; **2.** emaillieren; glasieren.

**enamo(u)r** [i'næmə] verliebt machen; **~ed of** verliebt in.

**encamp** ✗ [in'kæmp] (sich) lagern. **encase** [in'keis] einschließen.

**enchain** [in'tʃein] anketten; fesseln.

**enchant** [in'tʃɑːnt] bezaubern; **~ment** [~tmənt] Bezauberung *f*; Zauber *m*; **~ress** [~tris] Zauberin *f*.

**encircle** [in'səːkl] einkreisen.

**enclos|e** [in'klouz] einzäunen; einschließen; beifügen; **~ure** [~ou3ə] Einzäunung *f*; eingehegtes Grundstück; Bei-, Anlage *f zu e-m Brief*.

**encompass** [in'kʌmpəs] umgeben.

**encore** *thea.* [ɔŋ'kɔː] **1.** um e-e Zugabe bitten; **2.** Zugabe *f*.

**encounter** [in'kauntə] **1.** Begegnung *f*; Gefecht *n*; **2.** begegnen (*dat.*); auf *Schwierigkeiten etc.* stoßen; mit *j-m* zs.-stoßen.

**encourage** [in'kʌridʒ] ermutigen; fördern; **~ment** [~dʒmənt] Ermutigung *f*; Unterstützung *f*.

**encroach** [in'kroutʃ] (*on, upon*) eingreifen, eindringen (*in acc.*); beschränken (*acc.*); mißbrauchen (*acc.*); **~ment** [~ʃmənt] Ein-, Übergriff *m*.

**encumb|er** [in'kʌmbə] belasten; (be)hindern; **~rance** [~brəns] Last *f*; *fig.* Hindernis *n*; Schuldenlast *f*; *without ~* ohne (Familien)Anhang.

**encyclop(a)edia** [ensaiklou'piːdjə]

Enzyklopädie *f*, Konversationslexikon *n*.

**end** [end] **1.** Ende *n*; Ziel *n*, Zweck *m*; *no ~ of* unendlich viel(e), unzählige; *in the ~* am Ende, auf die Dauer; *on ~* aufrecht; *stand on ~* zu Berge stehen; *to no ~* vergebens; *go off the deep ~* *fig.* in die Luft gehen; *make both ~s meet* gerade auskommen; **2.** enden, beend(ig)en.

**endanger** [in'deindʒə] gefährden.

**endear** [in'diə] teuer machen; **~ment** [~əmənt] Liebkosung *f*, Zärtlichkeit *f*.

**endeavo(u)r** [in'devə] **1.** Bestreben *n*, Bemühung *f*; **2.** sich bemühen.

**end|ing** ['endiŋ] Ende *n*; Schluß *m*; *gr.* Endung *f*; **~less** □ ['endlis] endlos, unendlich; ⊕ ohne Ende.

**endorse** [in'dɔːs] ✝ indossieren; *et.* vermerken (*on auf der Rückseite e-r Urkunde*); gutheißen; **~ment** [~smənt] Aufschrift *f*; ✝ Indossament *n*.

**endow** [in'dau] ausstatten; **~ment** [~aumənt] Ausstattung *f*; Stiftung *f*.

**endue** *fig.* [in'djuː] (be)kleiden.

**endur|ance** [in'djuərəns] (Aus-) Dauer *f*; Ertragen *n*; **~e** [in'djuə] (aus)dauern; ertragen.

**enema** ✗ ['enimə] Klistier(spritze *f*) *n*.

**enemy** ['enimi] **1.** Feind *m*; *the* ♀ der Teufel; **2.** feindlich.

**energ|etic** [enə'dʒetik] (~ally) energisch; **~y** ['enədʒi] Energie *f*.

**enervate** ['enəːveit] entnerven.

**enfeeble** [in'fiːbl] schwächen.

**enfold** [in'fould] einhüllen; umfassen.

**enforce** [in'fɔːs] erzwingen; aufzwingen (*upon dat.*); bestehen auf (*dat.*); durchführen; **~ment** [~smənt] Erzwingung *f*; Geltendmachung *f*; Durchführung *f*.

**enfranchise** [in'fræntʃaiz] das Wahlrecht verleihen (*dat.*); *Sklaven* befreien.

**engage** [in'geidʒ] *v/t.* anstellen; verpflichten; mieten; in Anspruch nehmen; ✗ angreifen; *be ~d* verlobt sein (*to mit*); beschäftigt sein (*in mit*); besetzt sein; *~ the clutch* einkuppeln; *v/i.* sich verpflichten, versprechen, garantieren; sich beschäftigen (*in mit*); ✗ angreifen; ⊕ greifen (*Zahnräder*); **~ment** [~dʒmənt] Verpflichtung *f*; Verlobung *f*; Verabredung *f*; Beschäftigung *f*; ✗ Gefecht *n*; Einrücken *n e-s Ganges etc.*

**engaging** □ [in'geidʒiŋ] einnehmend.

**engender** *fig.* [in'dʒendə] erzeugen.

**engine** ['endʒin] Maschine *f*, Motor *m*; ⊕ Lokomotive *f*; **~-driver** Lokomotivführer *m*.

**engineer** [endʒi'niə] **1.** Ingenieur *m*,

Techniker *m*; Maschinist *m*; *Am.*
Lokomotivführer *m*; ✗ Pionier *m*;
**2.** Ingenieur sein; bauen; **~ing**
[~əriŋ] **1.** Maschinenbau *m*; Inge-
nieurwesen *n*; **2.** technisch; Ingenieur...

**English** ['iŋgliʃ] **1.** englisch; **2.** Englisch *n*; the ~ *pl.* die Engländer *pl.*;
*in plain ~ fig.* unverblümt; **~man**
Engländer *m*.

**engrav|e** [in'greiv] gravieren, ste-
chen; *fig.* einprägen; **~er** [~və]
Graveur *m*; **~ing** [~viŋ] (Kupfer-,
Stahl)Stich *m*; Holzschnitt *m*.

**engross** [in'grous] an sich ziehen;
ganz in Anspruch nehmen.

**engulf** *fig.* [in'gʌlf] verschlingen.

**enhance** [in'haːns] erhöhen.

**enigma** [i'nigmə] Rätsel *n*; **~tic(al**
□) [enig'mætik(əl)] rätselhaft.

**enjoin** [in'dʒɔin] auferlegen (*on j-m*).

**enjoy** [in'dʒɔi] sich erfreuen an
(*dat.*); genießen; *did you ~ it?* hat
es Ihnen gefallen?; *~ o.s.* sich amüsieren; *I ~ my dinner* es schmeckt
mir; **~able** [~iəbl] genußreich, erfreulich; **~ment** [~imənt] Genuß
*m*, Freude *f*.

**enlarge** [in'laːdʒ] (sich) erweitern,
ausdehnen; vergrößern; **~ment**
[~dʒmənt] Erweiterung *f*; Vergrößerung *f*.

**enlighten** [in'laitn] *fig.* erleuchten;
*j-n* aufklären; **~ment** [~nmənt]
Aufklärung *f*.

**enlist** [in'list] *v/t.* ✗ anwerben; gewinnen; *~ed men pl. Am.* ✗ Unter-
offiziere *pl.* und Mannschaften *pl.*;
*v/i.* sich freiwillig melden.

**enliven** [in'laivn] beleben.

**enmity** ['enmiti] Feindschaft *f*.

**ennoble** [i'noubl] adeln; veredeln.

**enorm|ity** [i'nɔːmiti] Ungeheuer-
lichkeit *f*; **~ous** □ [~məs] ungeheuer.

**enough** [i'nʌf] genug.

**enquire** [in'kwaiə] = *inquire*.

**enrage** [in'reidʒ] wütend machen;
**~d** wütend (*at* über *acc.*).

**enrapture** [in'ræptʃə] entzücken.

**enrich** [in'ritʃ] be-, anreichern.

**enrol(l)** [in'roul] *in e-e Liste* eintragen; ✗ anwerben; aufnehmen;
**~ment** [~lmənt] Eintragung *f*; bsd.
✗ Anwerbung *f*, Einstellung *f*;
Aufnahme *f*; Verzeichnis *n*; Schü-
ler-, Studenten-, Teilnehmerzahl *f*.

**ensign** ['ensain] Fahne *f*; Flagge *f*;
Abzeichen *n*; ♣ *Am.* ['ensn] Leutnant *m* zur See.

**enslave** [in'sleiv] versklaven; **~ment**
[~vmənt] Versklavung *f*.

**ensnare** *fig.* [in'snɛə] verführen.

**ensue** [in'sjuː] folgen, sich ergeben.

**ensure** [in'ʃuə] sichern.

**entail** [in'teil] **1.** zur Folge haben;
als unveräußerliches Gut vererben;
**2.** (Übertragung *f* als) unveräußerliches Gut.

**entangle** [in'tæŋgl] verwickeln; **~-**
**ment** [~lmənt] Verwicklung *f*; ✗
*Draht*-Verhau *m*.

**enter** ['entə] *v/t.* (ein)treten in (*acc.*);
betreten; einsteigen, einfahren *etc.*
in (*acc.*); eindringen in (*acc.*); eintragen, ✝ buchen; *Protest* einbringen; aufnehmen; melden; *~ s.o. at
school* j-n zur Schule anmelden; *v/i.*
eintreten; sich einschreiben; *Sport:*
sich melden; aufgenommen werden;
*~ into fig.* eingehen auf (*acc.*); *~*
(*up*)*on Amt etc.* antreten; sich einlassen auf (*acc.*).

**enterpris|e** ['entəpraiz] Unterneh-
men *n*; Unternehmungslust *f*;
**~ing** □ [~ziŋ] unternehmungslustig.

**entertain** [entə'tein] unterhalten;
bewirten; in Erwägung ziehen;
*Meinung etc.* hegen; **~er** [~nə] Gastgeber *m*; Unterhaltungskünstler *m*;
**~ment** [~nmənt] Unterhaltung *f*;
Bewirtung *f*; Fest *n*, Gesellschaft *f*.

**enthral(l)** *fig.* [in'θrɔːl] bezaubern.

**enthrone** [in'θroun] auf den Thron
setzen.

**enthusias|m** [in'θjuːziæzəm] Be-
geisterung *f*; **~t** [~æst] Schwärmer
(-in); **~tic** [inθjuːzi'æstik] (**~ally**)
begeistert (*at, about* von).

**entice** [in'tais] (ver)locken; **~-**
**ment** [~smənt] Verlockung *f*, Reiz
*m*.

**entire** □ [in'taiə] ganz; vollständig;
ungeteilt; **~ly** [~əli] völlig; lediglich; **~ty** [~əti] Gesamtheit *f*.

**entitle** [in'taitl] betiteln; berechtigen.

**entity** ['entiti] Wesen *n*; Dasein *n*.

**entrails** ['entreilz] *pl.* Eingeweide
*n/pl.*; Innere(s) *n*.

**entrance** ['entrəns] Ein-, Zutritt *m*;
Einfahrt *f*, Eingang *m*; Einlaß *m*.

**entrap** [in'træp] (ein)fangen; verleiten.

**entreat** [in'triːt] bitten, ersuchen;
*et.* erbitten; **~y** [~ti] Bitte *f*, Gesuch *n*.

**entrench** ✗ [in'trentʃ] (mit *od.* in
Gräben) verschanzen.

**entrust** [in'trʌst] anvertrauen (*s. th.
to s.o.* j-m *et.*); betrauen.

**entry** ['entri] Eintritt *m*; Eingang
*m*; ⚖ Besitzantritt *m* (*on, upon
gen.*); Eintragung *f*; *Sport:* Meldung *f*; *~ permit* Einreisegenehmi-
gung *f*; *~ book-keeping by double
(single) ~* doppelte (einfache) Buchführung.

**enumerate** [i'njuːməreit] aufzäh-
len.

**enunciate** [i'nʌnsieit] verkünden;
*Lehrsatz* aufstellen; aussprechen.

**envelop** [in'veləp] einhüllen; einwickeln; umgeben; einkreisen;
**~e** ['enviloup] Briefumschlag *m*; **~-**
**ment** [in'veləpmənt] Umhüllung *f*.

**envi|able** □ ['enviəbl] beneidens-
wert; **~ous** □ [~iəs] neidisch.

**environ** [in'vaiərən] umgeben; ~-ment [ˌnmənt] Umgebung *f e-r Person*; ~s ['environz] *pl.* Umgebung *f e-r Stadt.*

**envisage** [in'vizidʒ] sich *et.* vorstellen.

**envoy** ['envɔi] Gesandte(r) *m*; Bote *m.*

**envy** ['envi] 1. Neid *m*; 2. beneiden.

**epic** ['epik] 1. episch; 2. Epos *n.*

**epicure** ['epikjuə] Feinschmecker *m.*

**epidemic** [epi'demik] 1. (~ally) seuchenartig; ~ *disease* = 2. Seuche *f.*

**epidermis** [epi'də:mis] Oberhaut *f.*

**epilepsy** ['epilepsi] Epilepsie *f.*

**epilogue** ['epilɔg] Nachwort *n.*

**episcopa|cy** [i'piskəpəsi] bischöfliche Verfassung; ~l [ˌəl] bischöflich; ~te [ˌpit] Bischofswürde *f*; Bistum *n.*

**epist|le** [i'pisl] Epistel *f*; ~olary [ˌstələri] brieflich; Brief...

**epitaph** ['epitɑ:f] Grabschrift *f.*

**epitome** [i'pitəmi] Auszug *m*, Abriß *m.*

**epoch** ['i:pɔk] Epoche *f.*

**equable** □ ['ekwəbl] gleichförmig, gleichmäßig; *fig.* gleichmütig.

**equal** ['i:kwəl] 1. □ gleich, gleichmäßig; ~ *to fig.* gewachsen (*dat.*); 2. Gleiche(r *m*) *f*; 3. gleichen (*dat.*); ~ity [i(:)'kwɔliti] Gleichheit *f*; ~ization [i:kwəlai'zeiʃən] Gleichstellung *f*; Ausgleich *m*; ~ize ['i:kwəlaiz] gleichmachen, gleichstellen; ausgleichen.

**equanimity** [i:kwə'nimiti] Gleichmut *m.*

**equat|ion** [i'kweiʃən] Ausgleich *m*; Å Gleichung *f*; ~or [ˌeitə] Äquator *m.*

**equestrian** [i'kwestriən] Reiter *m.*

**equilibrium** [i:kwi'libriəm] Gleichgewicht *n*; Ausgleich *m.*

**equip** [i'kwip] ausrüsten; ~ment [ˌpmənt] Ausrüstung *f*; Einrichtung *f.*

**equipoise** ['ekwipɔiz] Gleichgewicht *n*; Gegengewicht *n.*

**equity** ['ekwiti] Billigkeit *f*; *equities pl.* † Aktien *f/pl.*

**equivalent** [i'kwivələnt] 1. gleichwertig; gleichbedeutend (*to* mit); 2. Äquivalent *n*, Gegenwert *m.*

**equivoca|l** □ [i'kwivəkəl] zweideutig, zweifelhaft; ~te [ˌkeit] zweideutig reden.

**era** ['iərə] Zeitrechnung *f*; -alter *n.*

**eradicate** [i'rædikeit] ausrotten.

**eras|e** [i'reiz] ausradieren, ausstreichen; auslöschen; ~er [ˌzə] Radiergummi *m*; ~ure [i'reiʒə] Ausradieren *n*; radierte Stelle.

**ere** [eə] 1. *cj.* ehe, bevor; 2. *prp.* vor.

**erect** [i'rekt] 1. □ aufrecht; 2. aufrichten; *Denkmal etc.* errichten; aufstellen; ~ion [ˌkʃən] Auf-, Errichtung *f*; Gebäude *n.*

**eremite** ['erimait] Einsiedler *m.*

**ermine** *zo.* ['ə:min] Hermelin *n.*

**erosion** [i'rouʒən] Zerfressen *n*; Auswaschung *f.*

**erotic** [i'rɔtik] 1. erotisch; 2. erotisches Gedicht; ~ism [ˌisizəm] Erotik *f.*

**err** [ə:] (sich) irren; fehlen, sündigen.

**errand** ['erənd] Botengang *m*, Auftrag *m*; ~boy Laufbursche *m.*

**errant** □ ['erənt] (umher)irrend.

**errat|ic** [i'rætik] (~ally) wandernd; unberechenbar; ~um [e'rɑ:təm], *pl.* ~a [ˌtə] Druckfehler *m.*

**erroneous** □ [i'rounjəs] irrig.

**error** ['erə] Irrtum *m*, Fehler *m*; ~s excepted Irrtümer vorbehalten.

**erudit|e** □ ['eru(:)dait] gelehrt; ~ion [eru(:)'diʃən] Gelehrsamkeit *f.*

**erupt** [i'rʌpt] ausbrechen (*Vulkan*); durchbrechen (*Zähne*); ~ion [ˌpʃən] Vulkan-Ausbruch *m*; ♣ Hautausschlag *m.*

**escalat|ion** [eskə'leiʃən] Eskalation *f* (*stufenweise Steigerung*); ~or ['eskəleitə] Rolltreppe *f.*

**escap|ade** [eskə'peid] toller Streich; ~e [is'keip] 1. entschlüpfen, entgehen; entkommen, entrinnen; entweichen; *j-m* entfallen; 2. Entrinnen *n*; Entweichen *n*; Flucht *f.*

**eschew** [is'tʃu:] (ver)meiden.

**escort** 1. ['eskɔ:t] Eskorte *f*; Geleit *n*; 2. [is'kɔ:t] eskortieren, geleiten.

**escutcheon** [is'kʌtʃən] Wappenschild *m*, *n*; Namensschild *n.*

**especial** [is'peʃəl] besonder; vorzüglich; ~ly [ˌli] besonders.

**espionage** [espiə'nɑ:ʒ] Spionage *f.*

**espresso** [es'presou] Espresso *m* (*Kaffee*); ~ bar, ~ café Espressobar *f.*

**espy** [is'pai] erspähen.

**esquire** [iə'kwaiə] Landedelmann *m*, Gutsbesitzer *m*; *auf Briefen*: John Smith Esq. Herrn J. S.

**essay** 1. [e'sei] versuchen; probieren; 2. ['esei] Versuch *m*; Aufsatz *m*, kurze Abhandlung, Essay *m*, *n.*

**essen|ce** ['esns] Wesen *n et-r Sache*; Extrakt *m*; Essenz *f*; ~tial [i'senʃəl] 1. □ (*to* für) wesentlich; wichtig; 2. Wesentliche(s) *n.*

**establish** [is'tæbliʃ] festsetzen; errichten, gründen; einrichten; einsetzen; ~ *o.s.* sich niederlassen; *Led Church* Staatskirche *f*; ~ment [ˌʃmənt] Festsetzung *f*; Gründung *f*; Er-, Einrichtung *f*; (*bsd. großer*) Haushalt; Anstalt *f*; Firma *f.*

**estate** [is'teit] Grundstück *n*; Grundbesitz *m*, Gut *n*; Besitz *m*; (Konkurs)Masse *f*, Nachlaß *m*; Stand *m*; *real* ~ Liegenschaften *pl.*; *housing* ~ Wohnsiedlung *f*; ~ *agent* Grundstücksmakler *m*; ~ *car* Kombiwagen *m*; ~ *duty* Nachlaßsteuer *f.*

**esteem** [is'ti:m] 1. Achtung *f*, Ansehen n (with bei); 2. (hoch)achten, (hoch)schätzen; erachten für.

**estimable** ['estiməbl] schätzenswert.

**estimat|e** 1. ['estimeit] (ab)schätzen; veranschlagen; 2. [‿mit] Schätzung f; (Vor)Anschlag m; **‿ion** [esti'meiʃən] Schätzung f; Meinung f; Achtung f.

**estrange** [is'treindʒ] entfremden.

**estuary** ['estjuəri] (den Gezeiten ausgesetzte) weite Flußmündung.

**etch** [etʃ] ätzen, radieren.

**etern|al** [i(:)'təːnl] immerwährend, ewig; **‿ity** [‿niti] Ewigkeit f.

**ether** ['iːθə] Äther m; **‿eal** [i(:)'θiəriəl] ätherisch (a fig.).

**ethic|al** [ˈeθikəl] sittlich, ethisch; **‿s** [‿ks] sg. Sittenlehre f, Ethik f.

**etiquette** [eti'ket] Etikette f.

**etymology** [eti'mɔlədʒi] Etymologie f, Wortableitung f.

**Eucharist** ['juːkərist] Abendmahl n.

**euphemism** ['juːfimizəm] beschönigender Ausdruck.

**European** [juərə'pi(ː)ən] 1. europäisch; 2. Europäer(in).

**evacuate** [i'vækjueit] entleeren; evakuieren; Land etc. räumen.

**evade** [i'veid] (geschickt) ausweichen (dat.); umgehen.

**evaluate** [i'væljueit] zahlenmäßig bestimmen, auswerten; berechnen.

**evanescent** [iːvə'nesnt] (ver)schwindend. [evangelisch.]

**evangelic|al** [iːvæn'dʒelik(ə)l]/

**evaporat|e** [i'væpəreit] verdunsten, verdampfen (lassen); **‿ion** [ivæpə-'reiʃən] Verdunstung f, Verdampfung f.

**evasi|on** [i'veiʒən] Umgehung f; Ausflucht f; **‿ve** [i'veisiv] ausweichend; be ‿ ausweichen.

**eve** [iːv] Vorabend m; Vortag m; on the ‿ of unmittelbar vor (dat.), am Vorabend (gen.).

**even** ['iːvən] 1. adj. ☐ eben, gleich; gleichmäßig; ausgeglichen; glatt; gerade (Zahl); unparteiisch; get ‿ with s.o. fig. mit j-m abrechnen; 2. adv. selbst, sogar, auch; not ‿ nicht einmal; ‿ though, ‿ if wenn auch; 3. ebnen, glätten; gleichstellen; **‿-handed** unparteiisch.

**evening** ['iːvniŋ] Abend m; ‿ dress Gesellschaftsanzug m; Frack m, Smoking m; Abendkleid n.

**evenness** ['iːvənnis] Ebenheit f; Geradheit f; Gleichmäßigkeit f; Unparteilichkeit f; Seelenruhe f.

**evensong** ['iːvənsɔŋ] Abendgottesdienst m.

**event** [i'vent] Ereignis n; Vorfall m; fig. Ausgang m; sportliche Veranstaltung; athletic ‿s pl. Leichtathletikwettkämpfe m/pl.; at all ‿s auf alle Fälle; in the ‿ of im Falle (gen.); **‿ful** [‿tful] ereignisreich.

**eventual** ☐ [i'ventjuəl] etwaig, möglich; schließlich; **‿ly** am Ende; im Laufe der Zeit; gegebenenfalls.

**ever** ['evə] je, jemals; immer; ‿ so noch so (sehr); as soon as ‿ I can sobald ich nur irgend kann; ‿ after, ‿ since von der Zeit an; ‿ and anon von Zeit zu Zeit; for ‿ für immer, auf ewig; Briefschluß: yours ‿ stets Dein ...; **‿glade** Am. Sumpfsteppe f; **‿green** 1. immergrün; 2. immergrüne Pflanze; **‿lasting** ☐ [evə-'laːstiŋ] ewig; dauerhaft; **‿more** ['evə'mɔː] immerfort.

**every** ['evri] jede(r, ‿s); alle(s); ‿ now and then dann und wann; ‿ one of them jeder von ihnen; ‿ other day einen Tag um den anderen, jeden zweiten Tag; **‿body** jeder (-mann); **‿day** Alltags...; **‿one** jeder(mann); **‿thing** alles; **‿where** überall.

**evict** [i(ː)'vikt] exmittieren; ausweisen.

**eviden|ce** ['evidəns] 1. Beweis(material n) m; ✠ Zeugnis n; Zeuge m; in ‿ als Beweis; deutlich sichtbar; 2. beweisen; **‿t** ☐ [‿nt] augenscheinlich, offenbar, klar.

**evil** ['iːvl] 1. ☐ übel, schlimm, böse; the ♀ One der Böse (Teufel); 2. Übel n, Böse(s) n; **‿-minded** ['iːvl'maindid] übelgesinnt, boshaft.

**evince** [i'vins] zeigen, bekunden.

**evoke** [i'vouk] (herauf)beschwören.

**evolution** [iːvə'luːʃən] Entwicklung f; ✕ Entfaltung f e-r Formation.

**evolve** [i'vɔlv] (sich) entwickeln.

**ewe** [juː] Mutterschaf n.

**ex** [eks] prp. ✝ ab Fabrik etc.; Börse: ohne; aus.

**ex-...** [‿] ehemalig, früher.

**exact** [ig'zækt] 1. ☐ genau; pünktlich; 2. Zahlung eintreiben; fordern; **‿ing** [‿tiŋ] streng, genau; **‿itude** [‿jitjuːd], **‿ness** [‿nis] Genauigkeit f; Pünktlichkeit f.

**exaggerate** [ig'zædʒəreit] übertreiben.

**exalt** [ig'zɔːlt] erhöhen, erheben; verherrlichen; **‿ation** [egzɔːl'teiʃən] Erhöhung f, Erhebung f; Höhe f; Verzückung f.

**exam** Schul-sl. [ig'zæm] Examen n.

**examin|ation** [igzæmi'neiʃən] Examen n; Prüfung f; Untersuchung f; Vernehmung f; **‿e** [ig'zæmin] untersuchen; prüfen, verhören.

**example** [ig'zaːmpl] Beispiel n; Vorbild n, Muster n; for ‿ zum Beispiel.

**exasperate** [ig'zaːspəreit] erbittern; ärgern; verschlimmern.

**excavate** ['ekskəveit] ausgraben, ausheben, ausschachten.

**exceed** [ik'siːd] überschreiten; übertreffen; zu weit gehen; **‿ing** ☐ [‿diŋ] übermäßig; **‿ingly** [‿ŋli] außerordentlich, überaus.

**excel** [ik'sel] *v/t.* übertreffen; *v/i.* sich auszeichnen; **~lence** ['eksələns] Vortrefflichkeit *f;* hervorragende Leistung; Vorzug *m;* **~lency** [~si] Exzellenz *f;* **~lent** □ [~nt] vortrefflich.

**except** [ik'sept] **1.** ausnehmen; *et.* einwenden; **2.** *prp.* ausgenommen, außer; **~ for** abgesehen **von;** **~ing** *prp.* [~tiŋ] ausgenommen; **~ion** [~pʃən] Ausnahme *f;* Einwendung *f (to gegen);* **by way of ~** ausnahmsweise; **take ~ to** Anstoß nehmen an (*dat.*); **~ional** [~nl] außergewöhnlich; **~ionally** [~ʃnəli] un-, außergewöhnlich.

**excerpt** ['eksə:pt] Auszug *m.*

**excess** [ik'ses] Übermaß *n;* Überschuß *m;* Ausschweifung *f; attr.* Mehr...; **~ fare** Zuschlag *m;* **~ luggage** Übergewicht *n (Gepäck);* **~ postage** Nachgebühr *f;* **~ive** □ [~siv] übermäßig, übertrieben.

**exchange** [iks'tʃeindʒ] **1.** (aus-, ein-, um)tauschen *(for gegen);* wechseln; **2.** (Aus-, Um)Tausch *m; (bsd.* Geld)Wechsel *m; a.* **bill of ~** Wechsel *m; a.* **♀ Börse** *f;* Fernsprechamt *n;* **foreign ~(s pl.)** Devisen *f/pl.;* **(rate of) ~** Wechselkurs *m.*

**exchequer** [iks'tʃekə] Schatzamt *n;* Staatskasse *f;* **Chancellor of the ♀** (britischer) Schatzkanzler, Finanzminister *m.*

**excise**[1] ['eksaiz] indirekte Steuer; Verbrauchssteuer *f.*

**excise**[2] [~] (her)ausschneiden.

**excit|able** [ik'saitəbl] reizbar; **~e** [ik'sait] er-, anregen; reizen; **~ement** [~tmənt] Auf-, Erregung *f;* Reizung *f;* **~ing** [~tiŋ] erregend.

**exclaim** [iks'kleim] ausrufen; eifern.

**exclamation** [eksklə'meiʃən] Ausruf(ung *f*) *m;* **~s pl.** Geschrei *n;* **note of ~, point of ~, ~ mark** Ausrufezeichen *n.*

**exclude** [iks'klu:d] ausschließen.

**exclusi|on** [iks'klu:ʒən] Ausschließung *f,* Ausschluß *m;* **~ve** □ [~u:siv] ausschließlich; sich abschließend; **~ of** abgesehen von, ohne.

**excommunicat|e** [ekskə'mju:nikeit] exkommunizieren; **~ion** ['ekskəmju:ni'keiʃən] Kirchenbann *m.*

**excrement** ['ekskrimənt] Kot *m.*

**excrete** [eks'kri:t] ausscheiden.

**excruciat|e** [iks'kru:ʃieit] martern; **~ing** □ [~tiŋ] qualvoll.

**exculpate** ['ekskʌlpeit] entschuldigen; rechtfertigen; freisprechen *(from von).*

**excursion** [iks'kə:ʃən] Ausflug *m;* Abstecher *m.*

**excursive** □ [eks'kə:siv] abschweifend.

**excus|able** □ [iks'kju:zəbl] entschuldbar; **~e 1.** [iks'kju:z] ent-

schuldigen; **~ s.o. s.th.** j-m et. erlassen; **2.** [~u:s] Entschuldigung *f.*

**exeat** ['eksiæt] *Schule etc.;* Urlaub *m.*

**execra|ble** □ ['eksikrəbl] abscheulich; **~te** ['eksikreit] verwünschen.

**execut|e** ['eksikju:t] ausführen; vollziehen; **♪** vortragen; hinrichten; *Testament* vollstrecken; **~ion** [eksi'kju:ʃən] Ausführung *f;* Vollziehung *f;* (Zwangs)Vollstreckung *f;* Hinrichtung *f;* **♪** Vortrag *m;* **put od. carry a plan into ~** e-n Plan ausführen *od.* verwirklichen; **~ioner** [~ʃnə] Scharfrichter *m;* **~ive** [ig'zekjutiv] **1.** □ vollziehend; **~ committee** Vorstand *m;* **2.** vollziehende Gewalt; *Am. Staats*-Präsident *m;* **†** Geschäftsführer *m;* **~or** [~tə] (Testaments)Vollstrecker *m.*

**exemplary** [ig'zempləri] vorbildlich.

**exemplify** [ig'zemplifai] durch Beispiele belegen; veranschaulichen.

**exempt** [ig'zempt] **1.** befreit, frei; **2.** ausnehmen, befreien.

**exercise** ['eksəsaiz] **1.** Übung *f;* Ausübung *f; Schule:* Übungsarbeit *f;* Leibesübung *f;* **take ~** sich Bewegung machen; *Am.* **~s pl.** Feierlichkeit(en *f) f;* **✗** Manöver *n;* **2.** üben; ausüben; (sich) Bewegung machen; exerzieren.

**exert** [ig'zə:t] *Einfluß etc.* ausüben; **~ o.s.** sich anstrengen *od.* bemühen; **~ion** [~ə:ʃən] Ausübung *f etc.*

**exhale** [eks'heil] ausdünsten, ausatmen; aushauchen; *Gefühlen* Luft machen.

**exhaust** [ig'zɔ:st] **1.** erschöpfen; entleeren; auspumpen; **2.** ⊕ Abgas *n,* Abdampf *m;* Auspuff *m;* **~ box** Auspufftopf *m;* **~ pipe** Auspuffrohr *n;* **~ed** erschöpft *(a. fig.);* vergriffen *(Auflage);* **~ion** [~tʃən] Erschöpfung *f;* **~ive** □ [~tiv] erschöpfend.

**exhibit** [ig'zibit] **1.** ausstellen; zeigen, darlegen; aufweisen; **2.** Ausstellungsstück *n;* Beweisstück *n;* **~ion** [eksi'biʃən] Ausstellung *f;* Darlegung *f;* Zurschaustellung *f;* Stipendium *n.*

**exhilarate** [ig'ziləreit] erheitern.

**exhort** [ig'zɔ:t] ermahnen.

**exigen|ce, -cy** ['eksidʒəns, ~si] dringende Not; Erfordernis *n;* **~t** [~nt] dringlich; anspruchsvoll.

**exile** ['eksail] **1.** Verbannung *f,* Exil *n;* Verbannte(r *m) f;* **2.** verbannen.

**exist** [ig'zist] existieren, vorhanden sein; leben; **~ence** [~təns] Existenz *f,* Dasein *n,* Vorhandensein *n;* Leben *n;* **in ~** = **~ent** [~nt] vorhanden.

**exit** ['eksit] **1.** Abgang *m;* Tod *m;* Ausgang *m;* **2.** *thea.* (geht) ab.

**exodus** ['eksədəs] Auszug *m.*

**exonerate** [ig'zɔnəreit] *fig.* entla-

sten, entbinden, befreien; rechtfertigen.

**exorbitant** □ [ig'zɔ:bitənt] maßlos,
übermäßig.

**exorci|se**, **~ze** ['eksɔ:saiz] *Geister*
beschwören, austreiben (*from* aus);
befreien (*of* von).

**exotic** [eg'zɔtik] ausländisch, exotisch; fremdländisch.

**expan|d** [iks'pænd] (sich) ausbrei-
ten; (sich) ausdehnen; (sich) erweitern; *Abkürzungen* (voll) ausschreiben; freundlich *od.* heiter
werden; **~se** [~ns], **~sion** [~nʃən]
Ausdehnung *f*; Weite *f*; Breite *f*;
**~sive** □ [~nsiv] ausdehnungsfähig;
ausgedehnt, weit; *fig.* mitteilsam.

**expatiate** [eks'peiʃieit] sich weit-
läufig auslassen (*on* über *acc.*).

**expatriate** [eks'pætrieit] ausbür-
gern.

**expect** [iks'pekt] erwarten; F annehmen; *be ~ing* ein Kind erwarten; **~ant** [~tənt] 1. erwartend (*of
acc.*); ~ *mother* werdende Mutter;
2. Anwärter *m*; **~ation** [ekspek-
'teiʃən] Erwartung *f*; Aussicht *f*.

**expectorate** [eks'pektəreit] *Schleim
etc.* aushusten, auswerfen.

**expedi|ent** [iks'pi:djənt] 1. □
zweckmäßig; berechnend; 2. Mit-
tel *n*; (Not)Behelf *m*; **~tion** [ekspi-
'diʃən] Eile *f*; ✕ Feldzug *m*; (For-
schungs)Reise *f*; **~tious** □ [~ʃəs]
schnell, eilig, flink.

**expel** [iks'pel] (hin)ausstoßen; vertreiben, verjagen; ausschließen.

**expen|d** [iks'pend] *Geld* ausgeben;
aufwenden; verbrauchen; **~diture**
[~ditʃə] Ausgabe *f*; Aufwand *m*;
**~se** [iks'pens] Ausgabe *f*; Kosten
*pl.*; **~s** *pl.* Unkosten *pl.*; Auslagen
*f/pl.*; *at the* ~ *of* auf Kosten (*gen.*);
*at any* ~ um jeden Preis; *go to the*
~ *of* Geld ausgeben für; **~se account**
Spesenrechnung *f*; **~sive** □ [~siv]
kostspielig, teuer.

**experience** [iks'piəriəns] 1. Erfahrung *f*; Erlebnis *n*; 2. erfahren, erleben; **~d** erfahren.

**experiment** 1. [iks'perimənt] Versuch *m*; 2. [~iment] experimentie-
ren; **~al** □ [eksperi'mentl] Versuchs...; erfahrungsmäßig.

**expert** ['ekspə:t] 1. □ [*pred.* eks-
'pə:t] erfahren, geschickt; fach-
männisch; 2. Fachmann *m*; Sach-
verständige(r *m*) *f*.

**expiate** ['ekspieit] büßen, sühnen.

**expir|ation** [ekspai'reiʃən] Ausat-
mung *f*; Ablauf *m*, Ende *n*; **~e**
[iks'paiə] ausatmen; verscheiden;
ablaufen; † verfallen; erlöschen.

**explain** [iks'plein] erklären, erläutern; *Gründe* auseinandersetzen; ~
*away* wegdiskutieren.

**explanat|ion** [eksplə'neiʃən] Erklä-
rung *f*; Erläuterung *f*; **~ory** □
[iks'plænətəri] erklärend.

**explicable** ['eksplikəbl] erklärlich.

**explicit** □ [iks'plisit] deutlich.

**explode** [iks'ploud] explodieren (lassen); ausbrechen; platzen (*with*
vor).

**exploit** 1. ['eksplɔit] Heldentat *f*;
2. [iks'plɔit] ausbeuten; **~ation**
[eksplɔi'teiʃən] Ausbeutung *f*.

**explor|ation** [eksplɔ:'reiʃən] Er-
forschung *f*; **~e** [iks'plɔ:] erforschen; **~er** [~ɔ:rə] (Er)Forscher *m*;
Forschungsreisende(r) *m*.

**explosi|on** [iks'plouʒən] Explosion
*f*; Ausbruch *m*; **~ve** [~ousiv] 1. □
explosiv; 2. Sprengstoff *m*.

**exponent** [eks'pounənt] Exponent
*m*; Vertreter *m*.

**export** 1. [eks'pɔ:t] ausführen;
2. ['ekspɔ:t] Ausfuhr(artikel *m*) *f*;
**~ation** [ekspɔ:'teiʃən] Ausfuhr *f*.

**expos|e** [iks'pouz] aussetzen; *phot.*
belichten; ausstellen; entlarven;
bloßstellen; **~ition** [ekspə'ziʃən]
Ausstellung *f*; Erklärung *f*.

**expostulate** [iks'pɔstjuleit] protestieren; ~ *with j-m* Vorhaltungen
machen.

**exposure** [iks'pouʒə] Aussetzen *n*;
Ausgesetztsein *n*; Aufdeckung *f*;
Enthüllung *f*, Entlarvung *f*; *phot.*
Belichtung *f*; Bild *n*; Lage *f e-s
Hauses*; ~ *meter* Belichtungsmesser
*m*.      (legen.)

**expound** [iks'paund] erklären, aus-

**express** [iks'pres] 1. □ ausdrücklich, deutlich; Expreß...; Eil...; ~
*company Am.* Transportfirma *f*;
~ *highway* Schnellverkehrsstraße *f*;
2. Eilbote *m*; *a.* ~ *train* Schnellzug
*m*; *by* ~ = 3. *adv.* durch Eilboten;
als Eilgut; 4. äußern, ausdrücken;
auspressen; **~ion** [~eʃən] Ausdruck
*m*; **~ive** □ [~esiv] ausdrückend (*of
acc.*); ausdrucksvoll; **~ly** [~sli] ausdrücklich, eigens; **~way** *Am.* Autobahn *f*.      (eignen.)

**expropriate** [eks'prouprieit] ent-

**expulsi|on** [iks'pʌlʃən] Vertreibung
*f*; **~ve** [~lsiv] (aus)treibend.

**expunge** [eks'pʌndʒ] streichen.

**expurgate** ['ekspə:geit] säubern.

**exquisite** □ ['ekskwizit] auserlesen,
vorzüglich; fein; heftig, scharf.

**extant** [eks'tænt] (noch) vorhanden.

**extempor|aneous** □ [ekstempə-
'reinjəs], **~ary** [iks'tempərəri], **~e**
[eks'tempəri] aus dem Stegreif
(vorgetragen).

**extend** [iks'tend] *v/t.* ausdehnen;
ausstrecken; erweitern; verlängern;
*Gunst etc.* erweisen; ✕ (aus)schwär-
men lassen; *v/i.* sich erstrecken.

**extensi|on** [iks'tenʃən] Ausdehnung
*f*; Erweiterung *f*; Verlängerung *f*;
Aus-, Anbau *m*; *teleph.* Nebenan-
schluß *m*; ~ *cord ⚡* Verlängerungs-
schnur *f*; *University ♀* Volkshochschule *f*; **~ve** □ [~nsiv] ausgedehnt,
umfassend.

**extent** [iks'tent] Ausdehnung *f*, Weite *f*, Größe *f*, Umfang *m*; Grad *m*; to the ~ of bis zum Betrage von; to some ~ einigermaßen.

**extenuate** [eks'tenjueit] abschwächen, mildern, beschönigen.

**exterior** [eks'tiəriə] 1. äußerlich; Außen...; außerhalb; 2. Äußere(s) *n*; *Film:* Außenaufnahme *f*.

**exterminate** [eks'tə:mineit] ausrotten, vertilgen.

**external** [eks'tə:nl] 1. □ äußere(r, -s), äußerlich; Außen...; 2. ~s *pl.* Äußere(s) *n*; *fig.* Äußerlichkeiten *f|pl.*

**extinct** [iks'tiŋkt] erloschen; ausgestorben.

**extinguish** [iks'tiŋgwiʃ] (aus)löschen; vernichten.

**extirpate** ['ekstə:peit] ausrotten; ⚔ *Organ etc.* entfernen.

**extol** [iks'tol] erheben, preisen.

**extort** [iks'tɔ:t] erpressen; abnötigen (*from dat.*); ~ion [~'tɔ:ʃən] Erpressung *f*.

**extra** ['ekstrə] 1. Extra...; außer...; Neben...; Sonder...; ~ pay Zulage *f*; 2. *adv.* besonders; außerdem; 3. *et.* Zusätzliches; Zuschlag *m*; **Extrablatt** *n*; *thea., Film:* Statist(in).

**extract** 1. ['ekstrækt] Auszug *m*; 2. [iks'trækt] (heraus)ziehen; herauslocken; ab-, herleiten; ~ion [~kʃən] (Heraus)Ziehen *n*; Herkunft *f*.

**extradit|e** ['ekstrədait] *Verbrecher* ausliefern (lassen); ~ion [ekstrə-'diʃən] Auslieferung *f*.

**extraordinary** □ [iks'trɔ:dnri]

außerordentlich; Extra...; ungewöhnlich; envoy ~ außerordentlicher Gesandter.

**extra student** ['ekstrə'stju:dənt] Gasthörer(in).

**extravagan|ce** [iks'trævigəns] Übertriebenheit *f*; Überspanntheit *f*; Verschwendung *f*, Extravaganz *f*; ~t □ [~nt] übertrieben, überspannt; verschwenderisch; extravagant.

**extrem|e** [iks'tri:m] 1. □ äußerst, größt, höchst; sehr streng; außergewöhnlich; 2. Äußerste(s) *n*; Extrem *n*; höchster Grad; ~ity [~remi-ti] Äußerste(s) *n*; höchste Not; äußerste Maßnahme; extremities *pl.* Gliedmaßen *pl.*

**extricate** ['ekstrikeit] herauswinden, herausziehen; befreien; ⚙ entwickeln.

**extrude** [eks'tru:d] ausstoßen.

**exuberan|ce** [ig'zju:bərəns] Überfluß *m*; Überschwenglichkeit *f*; ~t □ [~nt] reichlich; üppig; überschwenglich.

**exult** [ig'zʌlt] frohlocken.

**eye** [ai] 1. Auge *n*; Blick *m*; Öhr *n*; Öse *f*; up to the ~s in work bis über die Ohren in Arbeit; with an ~ to mit Rücksicht auf (*acc.*); mit der Absicht zu; 2. ansehen; mustern; ~ball ['aibɔ:l] Augapfel *m*; ~brow Augenbraue *f*; ~d ...äugig; ~glass Augenglas *n*; (a pair of) ~es *pl.* (ein) Kneifer; (e-e) Brille; ~lash Augenwimper *f*; ~lid Augenlid *n*; ~sight Augen(licht *n*) *pl.*; Sehkraft *f*; ~witness Augenzeug|e *m*, -in *f*.

# F

**fable** ['feibl] Fabel *f*; Mythen *pl.*, Legenden *pl.*; Lüge *f*.

**fabric** ['fæbrik] Bau *m*, Gebäude *n*; Struktur *f*; Gewebe *n*, Stoff *m*; ~ate [~keit] fabrizieren (*mst fig.* = erdichten, fälschen).

**fabulous** □ ['fæbjuləs] legendär; sagen-, fabelhaft.

**façade** ⚠ [fə'sɑ:d] Fassade *f*.

**face** [feis] 1. Gesicht *n*; Anblick *m*; *fig.* Stirn *f*, Unverschämtheit *f*; (Ober)Fläche *f*; Vorderseite *f*; Zifferblatt *n*; ~ to ~ with Auge in Auge mit; save one's ~ das Gesicht wahren; on the ~ of it auf den ersten Blick; set one's ~ against sich gegen *et.* stemmen; 2. *v/t.* ansehen; gegenüberstehen (*dat.*); (hinaus)gehen auf (*acc.*); die Stirn bieten (*dat.*); einfassen; ⚠ bekleiden; *v/i.* ~ about sich umdrehen; ~cloth ['feiskloθ] Waschlappen *m*.

**facetious** □ [fə'si:ʃəs] witzig.

**facil|e** ['fæsail] leicht; gewandt; ~itate [fə'siliteit] erleichtern; ~ity [~ti] Leichtigkeit *f*; Gewandtheit *f*; mst facilities *pl.* Erleichterung(en *pl.*) *f*, Möglichkeit(en *pl.*) *f*, Gelegenheit(en *pl.*) *f*.

**facing** ['feisiŋ] ⊕ Verkleidung *f*; ~s *pl. Schneiderei:* Besatz *m*.

**fact** [fækt] Tatsache *f*; Wirklichkeit *f*; Wahrheit *f*; Tat *f*. [keit *f.*]

**faction** ['fækʃən] Partei *f*; Uneinig-]

**factitious** □ [fæk'tiʃəs] künstlich.

**factor** ['fæktə] *fig.* Umstand *m*, Moment *n*, Faktor *m*; Agent *m*; Verwalter *m*; ~y [~əri] Fabrik *f*.

**faculty** ['fækəlti] Fähigkeit *f*; Kraft *f*; *fig.* Gabe *f*; *univ.* Fakultät *f*.

**fad** F *fig.* [fæd] Steckenpferd *n*.

**fade** [feid] (ver)welken (lassen), verblassen; schwinden; *Radio:* ~ in einblenden.

**fag** F [fæg] v/i. sich placken; v/t. erschöpfen, mürbe machen.

**fail** [feil] 1. v/i. versagen, mißlingen, fehlschlagen; versäumen; versiegen; nachlassen; Bankrott machen; durchfallen (*Kandidat*); he ~ed to do es mißlang ihm zu tun; he cannot ~ to er muß (einfach); v/t. im Stich lassen, verlassen, versäumen; 2. without ~ unfehlbar; ~ing ['feiliŋ] Fehler m, Schwäche f; ~ure [~ljə] Fehlen n; Ausbleiben n; Fehlschlag m; Mißerfolg m; Verfall m; Versäumnis n; Bankrott m; Versager m (P.).

**faint** [feint] 1. □ schwach, matt; 2. schwach werden; in Ohnmacht fallen (with vor); 3. Ohnmacht f; ~hearted □ ['feint'ha:tid] verzagt.

**fair¹** [fɛə] 1. adj. gerecht, ehrlich, anständig, fair; ordentlich; schön (*Wetter*); günstig (*Wind*); reichlich; blond; hellhäutig; freundlich; sauber, in Reinschrift; schön (*Frau*); 2. adv. gerecht, ehrlich, anständig, fair; in Reinschrift; direkt.

**fair²** [~] (Jahr)Markt m, Messe f. **fair|ly** ['fɛəli] ziemlich; völlig; ~ness ['fɛənis] Schönheit f; Blondheit f; Gerechtigkeit f; Redlichkeit f; Billigkeit f; ~way ⚓ Fahrwasser n.

**fairy** ['fɛəri] Fee f; Zauberin f; Elf(e f) m; ~land Feen-, Märchenland n; ~tale Märchen n.

**faith** [feiθ] Glaube m; Vertrauen n; Treue f; ~ful □ ['feiθful] treu; ehrlich; yours ~ly Ihr ergebener; ~less □ ['feiθlis] treulos; ungläubig.

**fake** sl. [feik] 1. Schwindel m; Fälschung f; Schwindler m; 2. a. ~ up fälschen.

**falcon** ['fɔ:lkən] Falke m.

**fall** [fɔ:l] 1. Fall(en n) m; Sturz m; Verfall m; Einsturz m; Am. Herbst m; Sinken n der Preise etc.; Fällen n; Wasserfall m (mst pl.); Senkung f, Abhang m; 2. [irr.] fallen; ab-, einfallen; sinken; sich legen (*Wind*); in e-n Zustand verfallen; ~ back zurückweichen; ~ back (up)on zurückkommen auf; ~ ill od. sick krank werden; ~ in love with sich verlieben in (acc.); ~ out sich entzweien; sich zutragen; ~ short knapp werden (of an dat.); ~ short of zurückbleiben hinter (dat.); ~ to sich machen an (acc.).

**fallacious** □ [fə'leiʃəs] trügerisch.

**fallacy** ['fæləsi] Täuschung f.

**fallen** ['fɔ:lən] p.p. von fall 2.

**fall guy** Am. sl. ['fɔ:l'gai] der Lackierte, der Dumme.

**fallible** □ ['fæləbl] fehlbar.

**falling** ['fɔ:liŋ] Fallen n; ~ sickness

**Fallsucht** f; ~ star Sternschnuppe f.

**fallow** ['fælou] zo. falb; ⚔ brach (-liegend).

**false** □ [fɔ:ls] falsch; ~hood ['fɔ:lshud], ~ness [~snis] Falschheit f.

**falsi|fication** ['fɔ:lsifi'keiʃən] (Ver-)Fälschung f; ~fy ['fɔ:lsifai] (ver-)fälschen; ~ty [~iti] Falschheit f.

**falter** ['fɔ:ltə] schwanken; stocken (*Stimme*); stammeln; fig. zaudern.

**fame** [feim] Ruf m, Ruhm m; ~d [~md] berühmt (for wegen).

**familiar** [fə'miljə] 1. □ vertraut; gewohnt; familiär; 2. Vertraute(r m) f; ~ity [fəmili'æriti] Vertrautheit f; (plumpe) Vertraulichkeit; ~ize [fə'miljəraiz] vertraut machen.

**family** ['fæmili] 1. Familie f; 2. Familien..., Haus...; in the ~ way in anderen Umständen; ~ allowance Kinderzulage f; ~ tree Stammbaum m.

**fami|ne** ['fæmin] Hungersnot f; Mangel m (of an dat.); ~sh [~iʃ] (aus-, ver)hungern.

**famous** □ ['feiməs] berühmt.

**fan¹** [fæn] 1. Fächer m; Ventilator m; 2. (an)fächeln; a. ~ fig. entfachen.

**fan²** F [~] Sport- etc. Fanatiker m, Liebhaber m; Radio: Bastler m; ...narr m, ...fex m.

**fanatic** [fə'nætik] 1. a. ~al □ [~kəl] fanatisch; 2. Fanatiker(in).

**fanciful** □ ['fænsiful] phantastisch.

**fancy** ['fænsi] 1. Phantasie f; Einbildung(skraft) f; Schrulle f; Vorliebe f; Liebhaberei f; 2. Phantasie...; Liebhaber...; Luxus...; Mode...; ~ ball Maskenball m; ~ goods pl. Modewaren f/pl.; 3. sich einbilden; Gefallen finden an (dat.); just ~! denken Sie nur!; ~work feine Handarbeit, Stickerei f.

**fang** [fæŋ] Fangzahn m; Giftzahn m.

**fantas|tic** [fæn'tæstik] (~ally) phantastisch; ~y ['fæntəsi] Phantasie f.

**far** [fɑ:] 1. adj. fern, entfernt; weit; 2. adv. fern; weit; (sehr) viel; as ~ as bis; in so ~ as insofern als; ~away ['fɑ:rəwei] weit entfernt.

**fare** [fɛə] 1. Fahrgeld n; Fahrgast m; Verpflegung f, Kost f; 2. gut leben; he ~d well es (er)ging ihm gut; ~well ['fɛə'wel] 1. lebe(n Sie) wohl!; 2. Abschied m, Lebewohl n.

**far|-fetched** fig. ['fɑ:'fetʃt] weit hergeholt, gesucht; ~ gone F fertig (todkrank, betrunken etc.).

**farm** [fɑ:m] 1. Bauernhof m, -gut n, Gehöft n, Farm f; Züchterei f; chicken ~ Hühnerfarm f; 2. (ver-)pachten; Land bewirtschaften; ~er ['fɑ:mə] Landwirt m; Pächter m; ~hand Landarbeiter(in); ~house Bauern-, Gutshaus n; ~ing ['fɑ:miŋ]

**1.** Acker...; landwirtschaftlich; **2.** Landwirtschaft *f*; ~**stead** Gehöft *n*; ~**yard** Wirtschaftshof *m e-s Bauernguts.*

**far-off** ['fɑːɔːf] entfernt, fern; ~**sighted** *fig.* weitblickend.

**farthe|r** ['fɑːðə] *comp. von far*; ~**st** ['fɑːðist] *sup. von far.*

**fascinat|e** ['fæsineit] bezaubern; ~**ion** [fæsi'neiʃən] Zauber *m*, Reiz *m*.

**fashion** ['fæʃən] Mode *f*; Art *f*; feine Lebensart; Form *f*; Schnitt *m*; *in (out of)* ~ (un)modern; **2.** gestalten; *Kleid* machen; ~**able** □ ['fæʃnəbl] modern, elegant.

**fast**[1] [fɑːst] schnell; fest; treu; waschecht; flott; *be* ~ vorgehen (*Uhr*).

**fast**[2] [~] **1.** Fasten *n*; **2.** fasten.

**fasten** ['fɑːsn] *v/t.* befestigen; anheften; fest (zu)machen; zubinden; *Augen etc.* heften (*on, upon* auf *acc.*); *v/i.* schließen (*Tür*); ~ *upon fig.* sich klammern an (*acc.*); ~**er** [~nə] Verschluß *m*; Klammer *f*.

**fastidious** □ [fæs'tidiəs] anspruchsvoll, heikel, wählerisch, verwöhnt.

**fat** [fæt] **1.** □ fett; dick; fettig; **2.** Fett *n*; **3.** fett machen *od.* werden; mästen.

**fatal** □ ['feitl] verhängnisvoll (*to* für); Schicksals...; tödlich; ~**ity** [fə'tæliti] Verhängnis *n*; Unglücks-, Todesfall *m*; Todesopfer *n*.

**fate** [feit] Schicksal *n*; Verhängnis *n*.

**father** ['fɑːðə] **1.** Vater *m*; **2.** der Urheber sein von; ~**hood** [~əhud] Vaterschaft *f*; ~**-in-law** [~ərinlɔː] Schwiegervater *m*; ~**less** [~əlis] vaterlos; ~**ly** [~li] väterlich.

**fathom** ['fæðəm] **1.** Klafter *f* (*Maß*); ⊕ Faden *m*; **2.** ⊕ loten; *fig.* ergründen; ~**less** [~mlis] unergründlich.

**fatigue** [fə'tiːg] **1.** Ermüdung *f*; Strapaze *f*; **2.** ermüden; strapazieren.

**fat|ness** ['fætnis] Fettigkeit *f*; Fettheit *f*; ~**ten** ['fætn] fett machen *od.* werden; mästen; *Boden* düngen.

**fatuous** □ ['fætjuəs] albern.

**faucet** *Am.* ['fɔːsit] (Zapf)Hahn *m*.

**fault** [fɔːlt] Fehler *m*; Defekt *m*; Schuld *f*; *find* ~ *with et.* auszusetzen haben an (*dat.*); *be at* ~ auf falscher Fährte sein; ~**finder** ['fɔːltfaində] Nörgler *m*; ~**less** □ [~tlis] fehlerfrei, tadellos; ~**y** □ [~ti] mangelhaft.

**favo(u)r** ['feivə] **1.** Gunst(bezeigung) *f*; Gefallen *m*; Begünstigung *f*; *in* ~ *of* zugunsten von *od. gen.*; *do s.o. a* ~ j-m e-n Gefallen tun; **2.** begünstigen; beehren; ~**able** □ [~ərəbl] günstig; ~**ite** [~rit] Günstling *m*; Liebling *m*; *Sport:* Favorit *m*; *attr.* Lieblings...

**fawn**[1] [fɔːn] **1.** *zo.* (Dam)Kitz *n*; Rehbraun *n*; **2.** (Kitze) setzen.

**fawn**[2] [~] schwänzeln (*Hund*); kriechen (*upon* vor).

**faze** *bsd. Am.* F [feiz] durcheinanderbringen.

**fear** [fiə] **1.** Furcht *f* (*of* vor *dat.*); Befürchtung *f*; Angst *f*; **2.** (be-) fürchten; sich fürchten vor (*dat.*); ~**ful** □ ['fiəful] furchtsam; furchtbar; ~**less** □ ['fiəlis] furchtlos.

**feasible** ['fiːzəbl] ausführbar.

**feast** [fiːst] **1.** Fest *n*; Feiertag *m*; Festmahl *n*, Schmaus *m*; **2.** *v/t.* festlich bewirten; *v/i.* sich ergötzen; schmausen. [stück *n*.]

**feat** [fiːt] (Helden)Tat *f*; Kunst-

**feather** ['feðə] **1.** Feder *f*; *a.* ~*s* Gefieder *n*; *show the white* ~ F sich feige zeigen; *in high* ~ in gehobener Stimmung; **2.** mit Federn schmücken; ~**bed** **1.** *Feder*-Unterbett *n*; **2.** verwöhnen; ~**brained**, ~**headed** unbesonnen; albern; ~**ed** be-, gefiedert; ~**y** [~əri] feder(art)ig.

**feature** ['fiːtʃə] **1.** (Gesichts-, Grund-, Haupt-, Charakter)Zug *m*; (charakteristisches) Merkmal; *Radio:* Feature *n*; *Am.* Bericht *m*, Artikel *m*; ~*s pl.* Gesicht *n*; Charakter *m*; **2.** kennzeichnen; sich auszeichnen durch; groß aufziehen; *Film:* in der Hauptrolle zeigen; ~ **film** Haupt-, Spielfilm *m*.

**February** ['februəri] Februar *m*.

**fecund** ['fiːkənd] fruchtbar.

**fed** [fed] *pret. u. p.p. von feed* 2.

**federa|l** ['fedərəl] Bundes...; ~**lize** [~laiz] (sich) verbünden; ~**tion** [fedə'reiʃən] Staatenbund *m*; Vereinigung *f*; Verband *m*.

**fee** [fiː] **1.** Gebühr *f*; Honorar *n*; Trinkgeld *n*; **2.** bezahlen.

**feeble** □ ['fiːbl] schwach.

**feed** [fiːd] **1.** Futter *n*; Nahrung *f*; Fütterung *f*; ⊕ Zuführung *f*, Speisung *f*; **2.** [*irr.*] *v/t.* füttern; speisen (*a.* ⊕), nähren; weiden; *Material etc.* zuführen; *be fed up with et.* satt haben; *well fed* wohlgenährt; *v/i.* (fr)essen; sich nähren; ~**er** ['fiːdə] Fütterer *m*; *Am.* Viehmäster *m*; Esser(in) *m*; ~**er road** Zubringer(straße *f*) *m*; ~**ing-bottle** ['fiːdiŋbɔtl] Saugflasche *f*.

**feel** [fiːl] **1.** [*irr.*] (sich) fühlen; befühlen; empfinden; sich anfühlen; *I* ~ *like doing* ich möchte am liebsten tun; **2.** Gefühl *n*; Empfindung *f*; ~**er** ['fiːlə] Fühler *m*; ~**ing** ['fiːliŋ] **1.** □ (mit)fühlend; gefühlvoll; **2.** Gefühl *n*; Meinung *f*.

**feet** [fiːt] *pl. von foot* 1.

**feign** [fein] heucheln; vorgeben.

**feint** [feint] Verstellung *f*; Finte *f*.

**felicit|ate** [fi'lisiteit] beglückwünschen; ~**ous** □ [~təs] glücklich; ~**y** [~ti] Glück(seligkeit *f*) *n*.

**fell** [fel] **1.** *pret. von fall* 2; **2.** niederschlagen; fällen.

**felloe** ['felou] (Rad)Felge f.
**fellow** ['felou] Gefährt|e m, -in f,
Kamerad(in); Gleiche(r, -s); Gegenstück n; univ. Fellow m, Mitglied n e-s College; Bursche m,
Mensch m; attr. Mit...; old ~ F
alter Junge; the ~ of a glove der
andere Handschuh; **~country-**
**man** Landsmann m; **~ship** [~ouʃip]
Gemeinschaft f; Kameradschaft f;
Mitgliedschaft f.
**felly** ['feli] (Rad)Felge f.
**felon** ♣ ['felən] Verbrecher m; **~y**
[~ni] Kapitalverbrechen n.
**felt**¹ [felt] pret. u. p.p. von feel 1.
**felt**² [~] 1. Filz m; 2. (be)filzen.
**female** ['fi:meil] 1. weiblich;
2. Weib n; zo. Weibchen n.
**feminine** □ ['feminin] weiblich;
weibisch.
**fen** [fen] Fenn n, Moor n; Marsch f.
**fence** [fens] 1. Zaun m; Fechtkunst
f; sl. Hehler(nest n) m; sit on the ~
abwarten; 2. v/t. a. ~ in ein-, umzäunen; schützen; v/i. fechten; sl.
hehlen.
**fencing** ['fensiŋ] Einfriedung f;
Fechten n; attr. Fecht...
**fend** [fend]: ~ off abwehren; **~er**
['fendə] Schutzvorrichtung f;
Schutzblech n; Kamingitter n,
-vorsetzer m; Stoßfänger m.
**fennel** ♣ ['fenl] Fenchel m.
**ferment** 1. ['fɔ:ment] Ferment n;
Gärung f; 2. [fə(:)'ment] gären
(lassen); **~ation** [fə:men'teiʃən]
Gärung f.
**fern** ♣ [fɔ:n] Farn(kraut n) m.
**feroci|ous** □ [fə'rouʃəs] wild; grausam; **~ty** [fə'rɔsiti] Wildheit f.
**ferret** ['ferit] 1. zo. Frettchen n;
fig. Spürhund m; 2. (umher)stöbern; ~ out aufstöbern.
**ferry** ['feri] 1. Fähre f; 2. übersetzen; **~boat** Fährboot n, Fähre
f; **~man** Fährmann m.
**fertil|e** □ ['fɔ:tail] fruchtbar; reich
(of, in an dat.); **~ity** [fɔ:'tiliti]
Fruchtbarkeit f (a. fig.); **~ize**
['fɔ:tilaiz] fruchtbar machen; befruchten; düngen; **~izer** [~zə]
Düngemittel n.
**ferven|cy** ['fɔ:vənsi] Glut f; Inbrunst f; **~t** □ [~nt] heiß; inbrünstig, glühend; leidenschaftlich.
**fervo(u)r** ['fɔ:və] Glut f; Inbrunst f.
**festal** □ ['festl] festlich.
**fester** ['festə] eitern; verfaulen.
**festiv|al** ['festəvəl] Fest n; Feier f;
Festspiele n/pl.; **~e** □ [~tiv] festlich; **~ity** [fes'tiviti] Festlichkeit f.
**festoon** [fes'tu:n] Girlande f.
**fetch** [fetʃ] holen; Preis erzielen;
Seufzer ausstoßen; **~ing** □ F
['fetʃiŋ] reizend.
**fetid** □ ['fetid] stinkend.
**fetter** ['fetə] 1. Fessel f; 2. fesseln.
**feud** [fju:d] Fehde f; Leh(e)n n;

**~al** □ ['fju:dl] lehnbar; Lehns...;
**~alism** [~dəlizəm] Lehnswesen n.
**fever** ['fi:və] Fieber n; **~ish** □
[~əriʃ] fieb(e)rig; fig. fieberhaft.
**few** [fju:] wenige; a ~ ein paar;
quite a ~, a good ~ e-e ganze Menge.
**fiancé** [fi'ɑ̃:nsei] Verlobte(r) m; **~e**
[~] Verlobte f.
**fiat** ['faiæt] Befehl m; ~ money Am.
Papiergeld n (ohne Deckung).
**fib** F [fib] 1. Flunkerei f, Schwindelei f; 2. schwindeln, flunkern.
**fib|re**, Am. **~er** ['faibə] Faser f;
Charakter m; **~rous** □ ['faibrəs]
faserig.
**fickle** ['fikl] wankelmütig; unbeständig; **~ness** [~lnis] Wankelmut
m.
**fiction** ['fikʃən] Erfindung f; Roman-, Unterhaltungsliteratur f; **~al**
□ [~nl] erdichtet; Roman...
**fictitious** □ [fik'tiʃəs] erfunden.
**fiddle** F ['fidl] 1. Geige f, Fiedel f;
2. fiedeln; tändeln; **~r** [~lə] Geiger
(-in); **~stick** Fiedelbogen m; **~s!**
fig. dummes Zeug!
**fidelity** [fi'deliti] Treue f; Genauigkeit f.
**fidget** F ['fidʒit] 1. nervöse Unruhe;
2. nervös machen od. sein; **~y** [~ti]
nervös.
**fie** [fai] pfui! [kribbelig.]
**field** [fi:ld] Feld n; (Spiel)Platz m;
Arbeitsfeld n; Gebiet n; Bereich m;
hold the ~ das Feld behaupten;
**~day** ['fi:lddei] ✕ Felddienstübung f; Parade f; fig. großer Tag;
Am. (Schul)Sportfest n; Am. Exkursionstag m; **~ events** pl. Sport:
Sprung- u. Wurfwettkämpfe m/pl.;
**~glass(es** pl.) Feldstecher m; **~of-**
**ficer** Stabsoffizier m; **~sports** pl.
Jagen n u. Fischen n.
**fiend** [fi:nd] böser Feind, Teufel m;
**~ish** □ ['fi:ndiʃ] teuflisch, boshaft.
**fierce** □ [fiəs] wild; grimmig;
**~ness** ['fiəsnis] Wildheit f; Grimm
m.
**fiery** □ ['faiəri] feurig; hitzig.
**fif|teen** ['fif'ti:n] fünfzehn; **~teenth**
[~nθ] fünfzehnte(r, -s); **~th** [fifθ]
1. fünfte(r, -s); 2. Fünftel n; **~thly**
['fifθli] fünftens; **~tieth** ['fiftiiθ]
fünfzigste(r, -s); **~ty** [~ti] fünfzig;
**~ty-fifty** F halb und halb.
**fig** [fig] Feige f; F Zustand m.
**fight** [fait] 1. Kampf m; Kampflust
f; show ~ sich zur Wehr setzen;
2. [irr.] v/t. bekämpfen; erkämpfen;
v/i. kämpfen, sich schlagen; **~er**
['faitə] Kämpfer m, Streiter m; ✕
Jagdflugzeug n; **~ing** ['faitiŋ]
Kampf m.
**figurative** □ ['figjurətiv] bildlich.
**figure** ['figə] 1. Figur f; Gestalt f;
Ziffer f; Preis m; be good at ~s gut
im Rechnen sein; 2. v/t. abbilden;
darstellen; sich ~ vorstellen; beziffern; ~ up od. out berechnen; v/i.
erscheinen; e-e Rolle spielen (as)

als); ~ on *Am. et.* überdenken;
~skating [~ɔskeitiŋ] Eiskunst-
lauf *m*.

**filament** ['filəmənt] Faden *m*, Faser
*f*; ♀ Staubfaden *m*; ≠ Glüh-, Heiz-
faden *m*.

**filbert** ♀ ['filbə(:)t] Haselnuß *f*.

**filch** [filtʃ] stibitzen (*from dat.*).

**file¹** [fail] **1.** Akte *f*, Ordner *m*;
Ablage *f*; Reihe *f*; ✗ Rotte *f*; *on*
~ bei den Akten; **2.** *v/t.* aufreihen;
*Briefe etc.* einordnen; ablegen; einreichen; *v/i.* hinter-ea. marschieren.

**file²** [~] **1.** Feile *f*; **2.** feilen.

**filial** □ ['filjəl] kindlich, Kindes...

**filibuster** ['filibʌstə] **1.** *Am.* Ob-
struktion(spolitiker *m*) *f*; **2.** *Am.*
Obstruktion treiben.

**fill** [fil] **1.** (sich) füllen; an-, aus-, erfüllen; *Am. Auftrag* ausführen;
~ *in Formular* ausfüllen; **2.** Fülle *f*,
Genüge *f*; Füllung *f*.

**fillet** ['filit] Haarband *n*; Lenden-
braten *m*; Roulade *f*; *bsd.* ♣ Band *n*.

**filling** ['filiŋ] Füllung *f*; ~ *station*
*Am.* Tankstelle *f*.

**fillip** ['filip] Nasenstüber *m*.

**filly** ['fili] (Stuten)Füllen *n*; *fig.*
wilde Hummel.

**film** [film] **1.** Häutchen *n*; Mem-
bran(e) *f*; Film *m*; Trübung *f des*
*Auges*; Nebelschleier *m*; *take od.*
*shoot a* ~ e-n Film drehen; **2.** (sich)
verschleiern; (ver)filmen.

**filter** ['filtə] **1.** Filter *m*; **2.** filtern.

**filth** [filθ] Schmutz *m*; ~y □ ['filθi]
schmutzig; *fig.* unflätig.

**filtrate** ['filtreit] filtrieren.

**fin** [fin] Flosse *f* (*a. sl.* = Hand).

**final** ['fainl] **1.** □ letzte(r, -s);
endlich; schließlich; End...; endgültig; **2.** Schlußprüfung *f*; *Sport:*
Schlußrunde *f*, Endspiel *n*.

**financ|e** [fai'næns] **1.** Finanzwesen
*n*; ~s *pl.* Finanzen *pl.*; **2.** *v/t.* finan-
zieren; *v/i.* Geldgeschäfte machen;
~ial □ [~nʃəl] finanziell; ~ier
[~nsiə] Finanzmann *m*; Geldgeber
*m*.

**finch** *orn.* [fintʃ] Fink *m*.

**find** [faind] **1.** [*irr.*] finden; (an-)
treffen; auf-, herausfinden; *schuldig*
*etc.* befinden; beschaffen; versorgen; *all found* freie Station; **2.** Fund
*m*; ~ings ['faindiŋz] *pl.* Befund *m*;
Urteil *n*.

**fine¹** □ [fain] **1.** schön; fein; ver-
feinert; rein; spitz, dünn, scharf;
geziert; vornehm; **2.** *adv.* gut, bestens.

**fine²** [~] **1.** Geldstrafe *f*; **2.** zu e-r
Geldstrafe verurteilen.

**fineness** ['fainnis] Fein-, Zart-,
Schönheit *f*, Eleganz *f*; Genauigkeit *f*.

**finery** ['fainəri] Glanz *m*; Putz *m*;
Staat *m*.

**finger** ['fiŋgə] **1.** Finger *m*; **2.** be-
tasten, (herum)fingern an (*dat.*);

~language Zeichensprache *f*;
~nail Fingernagel *m*; ~print
Fingerabdruck *m*.

**fini|cal** □ ['finikəl], ~cking [~kiŋ],
~kin [~in] geziert; wählerisch.

**finish** ['finiʃ] **1.** *v/t.* beenden, vollenden; fertigstellen; abschließen; vervollkommnen; erledigen; *v/i.* enden; **2.** Vollendung *f*, letzter
Schliff (*a. fig.*); Schluß *m*.

**finite** □ ['fainait] endlich, begrenzt.

**fink** *Am. sl.* [fiŋk] Streikbrecher *m*.

**Finn** [fin] Finn|e *m*, -in *f*; ~ish
['finiʃ] finnisch.

**fir** [fə:] (Weiß)Tanne *f*; Fichte *f*;
~cone ['fə:koun] Tannenzapfen *m*.

**fire** ['faiə] **1.** Feuer *n*; *on* ~ in Brand,
in Flammen; **2.** *v/t.* an-, entzünden;
*fig.* anfeuern; abfeuern; *Ziegel etc.*
brennen; F 'rausschmeißen (*ent-*
*lassen*); heizen; *v/i.* Feuer fangen
(*a. fig.*); feuern; ~alarm ['faiər-
əlɑ:m] Feuermelder *m*; ~brigade
Feuerwehr *f*; ~bug *Am.* F Brandstifter *m*; ~cracker Frosch *m*
(*Feuerwerkskörper*); ~department
*Am.* Feuerwehr *f*; ~engine ['faiər-
endʒin] (Feuer)Spritze *f*; ~escape
[~riskeip] Rettungsgerät *n*; Not-
treppe *f*; ~extinguisher [~rik-
stiŋwiʃə] Feuerlöscher *m*; ~man
Feuerwehrmann *m*; Heizer *m*;
~place Herd *m*; Kamin *m*; ~plug
Hydrant *m*; ~proof feuerfest;
~screen Ofenschirm *m*; ~side
Herd *m*; Kamin *m*; ~station
Feuerwache *f*; ~wood Brennholz *n*;
~works *pl.* Feuerwerk *n*.

**firing** ['faiəriŋ] Heizung *f*; Feuerung *f*.

**firm** [fə:m] **1.** □ fest; derb; standhaft; **2.** Firma *f*; ~ness ['fə:mnis]
Festigkeit *f*.

**first** [fə:st] **1.** *adj.* erste(r, -s); be-
ste(r, -s); **2.** *adv.* erstens; zuerst;
~ *of all* an erster Stelle; zu aller-
erst; **3.** Erste(r, -s); ~ *of exchange*
♣ Primawechsel *m*; *at* ~ zuerst,
anfangs; *from the* ~ von Anfang
an; ~born ['fə:stbɔ:n] erstgeboren;
~ class **1.** Klasse (*e-s Verkehrsmit-*
*tels*); ~class erstklassig; ~ly [~tli]
erstlich; erstens; ~ name Vorname *m*; Beiname *m*; ~papers *Am.*
vorläufige Einbürgerungspapiere;
~rate ersten Ranges; erstklassig.

**firth** [fə:θ] Förde *f*; (Flut)Mün-
dung *f*.

**fish** [fiʃ] **1.** Fisch(e *pl.*) *m*; F Kerl *m*;
**2.** fischen, angeln; haschen; ~bone
['fiʃboun] Gräte *f*.

**fisher** ['fiʃə], ~man Fischer *m*;
~y [~əri] Fischerei *f*.

**fishing** ['fiʃiŋ] Fischen *n*; ~line
Angelschnur *f*; ~tackle Angel-
gerät *n*. [händler *m*.]

**fishmonger** ['fiʃmʌŋgə] Fisch-

**fiss|ion** ⚛ ['fiʃən] Spaltung *f*; ~ure
['fiʃə] Spalt *m*; Riß *m*.

**fist** [fist] Faust *f*; F Klaue *f*; **.icuffs** ['fistikʌfs] *pl.* Faustschläge *m*/*pl.*

**fit¹** [fit] **1.** □ geeignet, passend; tauglich; *Sport:* in (guter) Form; bereit; **2.** *v*/*t.* passen für *od. dat.*; anpassen, passend machen; befähigen; geeignet machen (*for,* to für, zu); *a.* ~ on anprobieren; ausstatten; ~ out ausrüsten; ~ up einrichten; montieren; *v*/*i.* passen; sich schikken; sitzen (*Kleid*); **3.** Sitz *m* (*Kleid*).

**fit²** [~] Anfall *m*; ♫ Ausbruch *m*; Anwandlung *f*; *by* ~s *and starts* ruckweise; *give s.o. a* ~ j-n hochbringen; j-m e-n Schock versetzen.

**fit|ful** □ ['fitful] ruckartig; *fig.* unstet; **.ness** ['fitnis] Schicklichkeit *f*; Tauglichkeit *f*; **.ter** ['fitə] Monteur *m*; Installateur *m*; **.ting** ['fitiŋ] **1.** passend; **2.** Montage *f*; Anprobe *f*; ~s *pl.* Einrichtung *f*; Armaturen *f*/*pl.*

**five** [faiv] **1.** fünf; **2.** Fünf *f*.

**fix** [fiks] **1.** *v*/*t.* befestigen, anheften; fixieren; *Augen etc.* heften, richten; fesseln; aufstellen; bestimmen, festsetzen; *bsd. Am.* richten, *Bett etc.* machen; ~ *o.s.* sich niederlassen; ~ up in Ordnung bringen, arrangieren; *v*/*i.* fest werden; ~ on sich entschließen für; **2.** F Klemme *f*; *Am.* Zustand *m*; ~ed fest; bestimmt; starr; **.ing** ['fiksiŋ] Befestigen *n*; Instandsetzen *n*; Fixieren *n*; Aufstellen *n*, Montieren *n*; Besatz *m*, Versteifung *f*; *Am.* ~s *pl.* Zubehör *n*, Extraausrüstung *f*; **.ture** [~stʃə] fest angebrachtes Zubehörteil, feste Anlage; Inventarstück *n*; *lighting* ~ Beleuchtungskörper *m*.

**fizz** [fiz] **1.** zischen, sprudeln; **2.** Zischen *n*; F Schampus *m* (*Sekt*).

**flabbergast** F ['flæbəgɑːst] verblüffen; *be* ~ed baff *od.* platt sein.

**flabby** □ ['flæbi] schlaff, schlapp.

**flag** [flæg] **1.** Flagge *f*; Fahne *f*; Fliese *f*; Schwertlilie *f*; **2.** beflaggen; durch Flaggen signalisieren; mit Fliesen belegen; ermatten; mutlos werden; **.day** ['flægdei] Opfertag *m*; *Flag Day Am.* Tag *m* des Sternenbanners (*14. Juni*).

**flagitious** □ [flə'dʒiʃəs] schändlich.

**flagrant** □ ['fleigrənt] abscheulich; berüchtigt; offenkundig.

**flag|staff** ['flægstɑːf] Fahnenstange *f*; **.stone** Fliese *f*.

**flair** [flɛə] Spürsinn *m*, feine Nase.

**flake** [fleik] **1.** Flocke *f*; Schicht *f*; **2.** (sich) flocken; abblättern.

**flame** [fleim] **1.** Flamme *f*, Feuer *n*; *fig.* Hitze *f*; **2.** flammen, lodern.

**flank** [flæŋk] **1.** Flanke *f*; Weiche *f der Tiere*; **2.** flankieren.

**flannel** ['flænl] Flanell *m*; Waschlappen *m*; ~s *pl.* Flanellhose *f*.

**flap** [flæp] **1.** (Ohr)Läppchen *n*;

Rockschoß *m*; *Hut*-Krempe *f*; Klappe *f*; Klaps *m*; (Flügel)Schlag *m*; **2.** *v*/*t.* klatschen(d schlagen); *v*/*i.* lose herabhängen; flattern.

**flare** [flɛə] **1.** flackern; sich nach außen erweitern, sich bauschen; ~ up aufflammen; *fig.* aufbrausen; **2.** flackerndes Licht; Lichtsignal *n*.

**flash** [flæʃ] **1.** aufgedonnert; unecht; Gauner...; **2.** Blitz *m*; *fig.* Aufblitzen *n*; *bsd. Am. Zeitung:* kurze Meldung; *in a* ~ im Nu; ~ *of wit* Geistesblitz *m*; **3.** (auf)blitzen; auflodern (lassen); *Blick etc.* werfen; flitzen; funken, telegraphieren; *it* ~ed *on me* mir kam plötzlich der Gedanke; **.back** ['flæʃbæk] *Film:* Rückblende *f*; **.light** *phot.* Blitzlicht *n*; Blinklicht *n*; Taschenlampe *f*; **.y** □ [~ʃi] auffallend.

**flask** [flɑːsk] Taschen-, Reiseflasche *f*.

**flat** [flæt] **1.** □ flach, platt; schal; ♫ flau; klar; glatt; *♪* um e-n halben Ton erniedrigt; ~ *price* Einheitspreis *m*; **2.** *adv.* glatt; völlig; *fall* ~ danebengehen; *sing* ~ zu tief singen; **3.** Fläche *f*, Ebene *f*; Flachland *n*; Untiefe *f*; (Miet)Wohnung *f*; *♪* B *n*; F Simpel *m*; *mot. sl.* Plattfuß *m*; **.foot** ['flætfut] Plattfuß *m*; *Am. sl.* Polyp *m* (*Polizist*); **.footed** plattfüßig; *Am.* F *fig.* stur, eisern; **.iron** Plätteisen *n*; **.ness** [~tnis] Flachheit *f*; Plattheit *f*; ♫ Flauheit *f*; **.ten** [~tn] (sich) ab-, verflachen.

**flatter** ['flætə] schmeicheln (*dat.*); **.er** [~ərə] Schmeichler(in); **.y** [~ri] Schmeichelei *f*.

**flavo(u)r** ['fleivə] **1.** Geschmack *m*; Aroma *n*; Blume *f* (*Wein*); *fig.* Beigeschmack *m*; Würze *f*; **2.** würzen; **.less** [~lis] geschmacklos, fad.

**flaw** [flɔː] **1.** Sprung *m*, Riß *m*; Fehler *m*; ♫ Bö *f*; **2.** zerbrechen; beschädigen; **.less** □ ['flɔːlis] fehlerlos.

**flax** ♫ [flæks] Flachs *m*, Lein *m*.

**flay** [flei] die Haut abziehen (*dat.*).

**flea** [fliː] Floh *m*.

**fled** [fled] *pret. u. p.p. von* flee.

**fledge** [fledʒ] *v*/*i.* flügge werden; *v*/*t.* befiedern; **.(e)ling** ['fledʒliŋ] Küken *n* (*a. fig.*); Grünschnabel *m*.

**flee** [fliː] [*irr.*] fliehen; meiden.

**fleece** [fliːs] **1.** Vlies *n*; **2.** scheren; prellen; **.y** ['fliːsi] wollig.

**fleer** [fliə] höhnen (*at* über *acc.*).

**fleet** [fliːt] **1.** □ schnell; **2.** Flotte *f*; **⚥** *Street* die (Londoner) Presse.

**flesh** [fleʃ] **1.** *lebendiges* Fleisch; *fig.* Fleisch(eslust *f*) *n*; **2.** *hunt.* Blut kosten lassen; **.ly** ['fleʃli] fleischlich; irdisch; **.y** [~ʃi] fleischig; fett.

**flew** [fluː] *pret. von* fly 2.

**flexib|ility** [fleksə'biliti] Biegsamkeit *f*; **.le** □ ['fleksəbl] flexibel, biegsam; *fig.* anpassungsfähig.

**flick** [flik] schnippen; schnellen.

**flicker** ['flikə] **1.** flackern; flattern; flimmern; **2.** Flackern *n*, Flimmern *n*; Flattern *n*; *Am.* Buntspecht *m*.

**flier** ['flaiə] = *flyer*.

**flight** [flait] Flucht *f*; Flug *m* (*a. fig.*); Schwarm *m*; ⚔, ✗ Kette *f*; (~ *of stairs* Treppen)Flucht *f*; *put to* ~ in die Flucht schlagen; **~y** □ ['flaiti] flüchtig; leichtsinnig.

**flimsy** ['flimzi] dünn, locker; schwach; *fig.* fadenscheinig.

**flinch** [flintʃ] zurückweichen; zukken.

**fling** [fliŋ] **1.** Wurf *m*; Schlag *m*; *have one's* ~ sich austoben; **2.** [*irr.*] *v/i.* eilen; ausschlagen (*Pferd*); *fig.* toben; *v/t.* werfen, schleudern; ~ *o.s.* sich stürzen; ~ *open* aufreißen.

**flint** [flint] Kiesel *m*; Feuerstein *m*.

**flip** [flip] **1.** Klaps *m*; Ruck *m*; **2.** schnippen; klapsen; (umher-) flitzen.

**flippan|cy** ['flipənsi] Leichtfertigkeit *f*; **~t** □ [~nt] leichtfertig; vorlaut.

**flirt** [flə:t] **1.** Kokette *f*; Weiberheld *m*; **2.** flirten, kokettieren; = *flip* 2; **~ation** [flə:'teiʃən] Flirt *m*.

**flit** [flit] flitzen; wandern; umziehen.

**flivver** *Am. sl.* ['flivə] **1.** Nuckelpinne *f* (*billiges Auto*); **2.** mißlingen.

**float** [flout] **1.** Schwimmer *m*; Floß *n*; Plattformwagen *m*; **2.** *v/t.* überfluten; flößen; tragen (*Wasser*); ⚓ flott machen, *fig.* in Gang bringen; ✝ gründen; verbreiten; *v/i.* schwimmen, treiben; schweben; umlaufen.

**flock** [flɔk] **1.** Herde *f* (*a. fig.*); Schar *f*; **2.** sich scharen; zs.-strömen.

**floe** [flou] (treibende) Eisscholle.

**flog** [flɔg] peitschen; prügeln.

**flood** [flʌd] **1.** *a.* ~*tide* Flut *f*; Überschwemmung *f*; **2.** überfluten, überschwemmen; **~gate** ['flʌdgeit] Schleusentor *n*; **~light** ⚡ Flutlicht *n*.

**floor** [flɔ:] **1.** Fußboden *m*; Stock (-werk *n*) *m*; ✓ Tenne *f*; ~ *leader Am.* Fraktionsvorsitzende(r) *m*; ~ *show* Nachtklubvorstellung *f*; *take the* ~ das Wort ergreifen; **2.** dielen; zu Boden schlagen; verblüffen; **~cloth** ['flɔ:klɔθ] Putzlappen *m*; **~ing** ['flɔ:riŋ] Dielung *f*; Fußboden *m*; **~lamp** Stehlampe *f*; **~walker** *Am.* ['flɔ:wɔ:kə] = *shopwalker*.

**flop** [flɔp] **1.** schlagen; flattern; (hin)plumpsen (lassen); *Am.* versagen; **2.** Plumps *m*; Versager *m*; **~house** *Am. sl.* Penne *f*.

**florid** □ ['flɔrid] blühend.

**florin** ['flɔrin] Zweischillingstück *n*.

**florist** ['flɔrist] Blumenhändler *m*.

**floss** [flɔs] Florettseide *f*.

**flounce¹** [flauns] Volant *m*.

**flounce²** [~] stürzen; zappeln.

**flounder¹** *ichth.* ['flaundə] Flunder *f*.

**flounder²** [~] sich (ab)mühen.

**flour** ['flauə] (feines) Mehl.

**flourish** ['flʌriʃ] **1.** Schnörkel *m*; Schwingen *n*; ♩ Tusch *m*; *v/i.* blühen, gedeihen; *v/t.* schwingen.

**flout** [flaut] (ver)spotten.

**flow** [flou] **1.** Fluß *m*; Flut *f*; **2.** fließen, fluten; wallen.

**flower** ['flauə] **1.** Blume *f*; Blüte *f* (*a. fig.*); Zierde *f*; **2.** blühen; **~pot** Blumentopf *m*; **~y** [~əri] blumig.

**flown** [floun] *p.p. von fly* 2.

**flubdub** *Am. sl.* ['flʌbdʌb] Geschwätz *n*.

**fluctuat|e** ['flʌktjueit] schwanken; **~ion** [flʌktju'eiʃən] Schwankung *f*.

**flu(e)** *F* [flu:] = *influenza*.

**flue** [flu:] Kaminrohr *n*; Heizrohr *n*.

**fluen|cy** *fig.* ['flu:(:)ənsi] Fluß *m*; **~t** □ [~nt] fließend, geläufig (*Rede*).

**fluff** [flʌf] **1.** Flaum *m*; Flocke *f*; *fig.* Schnitzer *m*; **2.** *Kissen* aufschütteln; *Federn* aufplustern (*Vogel*); **~y** ['flʌfi] flaumig; flockig.

**fluid** ['flu:(:)id] **1.** flüssig; **2.** Flüssigkeit *f*.

**flung** [flʌŋ] *pret. u. p.p. von fling* 2.

**flunk** *Am.* *F* *fig.* [flʌŋk] durchfallen (lassen).

**flunk(e)y** ['flʌŋki] Lakai *m*.

**fluorescent** [fluə'resnt] fluoreszierend.

**flurry** ['flʌri] Nervosität *f*; Bö *f*; *Am. a.* (Regen)Schauer *m*; Schneegestöber *n*.

**flush** [flʌʃ] **1.** ⊕ in gleicher Ebene; reichlich; (über)voll; **2.** Erröten *n*; Übermut *m*; Fülle *f*; Wachstum *n*; *fig.* Blüte *f*; Spülung *f*; *Karten:* Flöte *f*; **3.** über-, durchfluten; (aus)spülen; strömen; sprießen (lassen); erröten (machen); übermütig machen; aufjagen.

**fluster** ['flʌstə] **1.** Aufregung *f*; **2.** *v/t.* aufregen.

**flute** [flu:t] **1.** ♩ Flöte *f*; Falte *f*; **2.** (auf der) Flöte spielen; riefeln; fälteln.

**flutter** ['flʌtə] **1.** Geflatter *n*; Erregung *f*; *F* Spekulation *f*; **2.** *v/t.* aufregen; *v/i.* flattern.

**flux** [flʌks] *fig.* Fluß *m*; ✗ Ausfluß *m*.

**fly** [flai] **1.** *zo.* Fliege *f*; Flug *m*; *Am. Baseball:* hochgeschlagener Ball; Droschke *f*; **2.** [*irr.*] (*a. fig.*) fliegen (lassen); entfliehen (*Zeit*); ⚑ führen; *Flagge* hissen; fliehen; ~ *überfliegen*; ~ *at* herfallen über; ~ *into a passion od. rage* in Zorn geraten.

**flyer** ['flaiə] Flieger *m*; Renner *m*; *take a* ~ *Am.* *F* Vermögen riskieren.

**fly-flap** ['flaiflæp] Fliegenklatsche *f*.

**flying** ['flaiiŋ] fliegend; Flug...; ~ *squad* Überfallkommando *n*.

**fly|-over** ['flaiouvə] (Straßen)Überführung *f*; **~weight** *Boxen:* Fliegengewicht *n*; **~wheel** Schwungrad *n*.

**foal** [foul] 1. Fohlen *n*; 2. fohlen.

**foam** [foum] 1. Schaum *m*; 2. schäumen; **~y** ['foumi] schaumig.

**focus** ['foukəs] 1. Brennpunkt *m*; 2. (sich) im Brennpunkt vereinigen; *opt.* einstellen (*a. fig.*); konzentrieren.

**fodder** ['fɔdə] (Trocken)Futter *n*.

**foe** *poet.* [fou] Feind *m*, Gegner *m*.

**fog** [fɔg] 1. (dichter) Nebel; *fig.* Umnebelung *f*; *phot.* Schleier *m*; 2. *mst fig.* umnebeln; *phot.* verschleiern.

**fogey** F ['fougi]: *old ~* komischer alter Kauz.

**foggy** □ ['fɔgi] neb(e)lig; *fig.* nebelhaft.

**fogy** *Am.* ['fougi] = *fogey*.

**foible** *fig.* ['fɔibl] Schwäche *f*.

**foil**[1] [fɔil] Folie *f*; Hintergrund *m*.

**foil**[2] [~] 1. vereiteln; 2. Florett *n*.

**fold**[1] [fould] 1. Schafhürde *f*; *fig.* Herde *f*; 2. einpferchen.

**fold**[2] [~] 1. Falte *f*; Falz *m*; 2. ...fach, ...fältig; 3. *v/t.* falten; falzen; *Arme* kreuzen; *~* (*up*) einwickeln; *v/i.* sich falten; *Am.* F eingehen; **~er** ['fouldə] Mappe *f*, Schnellhefter *m*; Faltprospekt *m*.

**folding** ['fouldiŋ] zs.-legbar; Klapp...; **~bed** Feldbett *n*; **~boat** Faltboot *n*; **~door**(s *pl.*) Flügeltür *f*; **~screen** spanische Wand; **~seat** Klappsitz *m*.

**foliage** ['fouliidʒ] Laub(werk) *n*.

**folk** [fouk] *pl.* Leute *pl.*; **~s** *pl.* Leute *pl.* (F *a. Angehörige*); **~lore** ['foukbɔ:] Volkskunde *f*; Volkssagen *f/pl.*; **~song** Volkslied *n*.

**follow** ['fɔlou] folgen (*dat.*); folgen auf (*acc.*); be~, verfolgen; *s-m Beruf etc.* nachgehen; **~er** [~ouə] Nachfolger(in); Verfolger(in); Anhänger(in); **~ing** [~ouiŋ] Anhängerschaft *f*, Gefolge *n*.

**folly** ['fɔli] Torheit *f*; Narrheit *f*.

**foment** [fou'ment] *j-m* warme Umschläge machen; *Unruhe* stiften.

**fond** [fɔnd] zärtlich; vernarrt (*of* in *acc.*); *be ~ of* gern haben, lieben; **~le** ['fɔndl] liebkosen; streicheln; (ver)hätscheln; **~ness** [~dnis] Zärtlichkeit *f*; Vorliebe *f*.

**font** [fɔnt] Taufstein *m*; *Am.* Quelle *f*.

**food** [fu:d] Speise *f*, Nahrung *f*; Futter *n*; Lebensmittel *n/pl.*; **~stuff** ['fu:dstʌf] Nahrungsmittel *n*.

**fool** [fu:l] 1. Narr *m*, Tor *m*; Hanswurst *m*; *make a ~ of s.o.* j-n zum Narren halten; *make a ~ of o.s.* sich lächerlich machen; 2. *Am.* F närrisch, dumm; 3. *v/t.* narren; prellen (*out of* um *et.*); *~ away* F vertrödeln; *v/i.* albern; (herum)spielen; *~* (*a*)*round bsd. Am.* Zeit vertrödeln.

**fool|ery** ['fu:ləri] Torheit *f*; **~hardy**

□ ['fu:lhɑ:di] tollkühn; **~ish** □ ['fu:liʃ] töricht; **~ishness** [~ʃnis] Torheit *f*; **~proof** kinderleicht.

**foot** [fut] 1. *pl.* **feet** [fi:t] Fuß *m* (*a. Maß*); Fußende *n*; ✗ Infanterie *f*; *on ~ zu* Fuß; im Gange, in Gang; 2. *v/t. mst ~ up* addieren; *~ the bill* F die Rechnung bezahlen; *v/i. ~ it* zu Fuß gehen; **~board** ['futbɔ:d] Trittbrett *n*; **~boy** Page *m*; **~fall** Tritt *m*, Schritt *m*; **~gear** Schuhwerk *n*; **~hold** fester Stand; *fig.* Halt *m*.

**footing** ['futiŋ] Halt *m*, Stand *m*; Grundlage *f*, Basis *f*; Stellung *f*; fester Fuß; Verhältnis *n*; ✗ Zustand *m*; Endsumme *f*; *be on a friendly ~ with s.o.* ein gutes Verhältnis zu j-m haben; *lose one's ~* ausgleiten.

**foot|lights** *thea.* ['futlaits] *pl.* Rampenlicht(er *pl.*) *n*; Bühne *f*; **~man** Diener *m*; **~passenger** Fußgänger (-in); **~path** Fußpfad *m*; **~print** Fußstapfe *f*, -spur *f*; **~sore** fußkrank; **~step** Fußstapfe *f*, Spur *f*; **~stool** Fußbank *f*; **~wear** = *footgear*.

**fop** [fɔp] Geck *m*, Fatzke *m*.

**for** [fɔ:, fɔr, fə] 1. *prp. mst* für; *Zweck, Ziel, Richtung:* zu; nach; *warten, hoffen etc.* auf (*acc.*); *sich sehnen etc.* nach; *Grund, Anlaß:* aus, vor (*dat.*), wegen; *Zeitdauer: ~ three days etc.* Tage (lang); *seit drei Tagen; Entfernung: I walked ~ a mile* ich ging eine Meile (weit); *Austausch:* (an-) statt; *in der Eigenschaft als; I ~ one* ich zum Beispiel; *~ sure* sicher!, gewiß!; 2. *cj.* denn.

**forage** ['fɔridʒ] 1. Futter *n*; 2. (nach Futter) suchen.

**foray** ['fɔrei] räuberischer Einfall.

**forbear**[1] [fɔː'bɛə] [*irr.* (*bear*)] *v/t.* unterlassen; *v/i.* sich enthalten (*from gen.*); Geduld haben.

**forbear**[2] ['fɔːbɛə] Vorfahr *m*.

**forbid** [fə'bid] [*irr.* (*bid*)] verbieten; hindern; **~ding** □ [~diŋ] abstoßend.

**force** [fɔ:s] 1. *mst* Kraft *f*, Gewalt *f*; Nachdruck *m*; Zwang *m*; Heer *n*; Streitmacht *f*; *the ~* die Polizei; *armed ~s pl.* Streitkräfte *f/pl.*; *come* (put) *in ~* in Kraft treten (setzen); 2. zwingen, nötigen; erzwingen; aufzwingen; Gewalt antun (*dat.*); beschleunigen; aufbrechen; künstlich reif machen; *~ open* aufbrechen; **~d:** *~ landing* Notlandung *f*; *~ loan* Zwangsanleihe *f*; *~ march* Eilmarsch *m*; **~ful** □ ['fɔ:sful] kräftig; eindringlich.

**forceps** ⚕ ['fɔ:seps] Zange *f*.

**forcible** [ ] ['fɔ:səbl] gewaltsam; Zwangs...; eindringlich; wirksam.

**ford** [fɔ:d] 1. Furt *f*; 2. durchwaten.

**fore** [fɔ:] 1. *adv.* vorn; 2. Vorderteil *m*, *n*; *bring* (come) *to the ~* zum

Vorschein bringen (kommen); **3.** *adj.* vorder; Vorder...; ~**bode** [fɔ:-'boud] vorhersagen; ahnen; ~**boding** [~diŋ] (böses) Vorzeichen; Ahnung *f*; ~**cast** ['fɔ:ka:st] **1.** Vorhersage *f*; **2.** [*irr.* (*cast*)] vorhersehen; voraussagen; ~**father** Vorfahr *m*; ~**finger** Zeigefinger *m*; ~**foot** Vorderfuß *m*; ~**go** [fɔ:'gou] [*irr.* (*go*)] vorangehen; ~**gone** [fɔ:-'gɔn, *adj.* 'fɔ:gɔn] von vornherein feststehend; ~ *conclusion* Selbstverständlichkeit *f*; ~**ground** Vordergrund *m*; ~**head** ['fɔrid] Stirn *f*.

**foreign** ['fɔrin] fremd; ausländisch; auswärtig; ~**er** [~nə] Ausländer(in), Fremde(r *m*) *f*; ♀ **Office** Außenministerium *n*; ~ *policy* Außenpolitik *f*; ~ **trade** Außenhandel *m*.

**fore|knowledge** ['fɔ:'nɔlidʒ] Vorherwissen *n*; ~**leg** ['fɔ:leg] Vorderbein *n*; ~**lock** Stirnhaar *n*; *fig.* Schopf *m*; ~**man** ⚖ Obmann *m*; Vorarbeiter *m*, (Werk)Meister *m*; ⚒ Steiger *m*; ~**most** vorderst, erst; ~**name** Vorname *m*; ~**noon** Vormittag *m*; ~**runner** Vorläufer *m*, Vorbote *m*, ~**see** [fɔ:'si:] [*irr.* (*see*)] vorhersehen; ~**shadow** ankündigen; ~**sight** ['fɔ:sait] Voraussicht *f*; Vorsorge *f*.

**forest** ['fɔrist] **1.** Wald *m* (*a. fig.*), Forst *m*; **2.** aufforsten.

**forestall** [fɔ:'stɔ:l] *et.* vereiteln; *j-m* zuvorkommen.

**forest|er** ['fɔristə] Förster *m*; Waldarbeiter *m*; ~**ry** [~tri] Forstwirtschaft *f*; Waldgebiet *n*.

**fore|taste** ['fɔ:teist] Vorgeschmack *m*; ~**tell** [fɔ:'tel] [*irr.* (*tell*)] vorhersagen; vorbedeuten; ~**thought** ['fɔ:θɔ:t] Vorbedacht *m*; ~**woman** Aufseherin *f*; Vorarbeiterin *f*; ~**word** Vorwort *n*.

**forfeit** ['fɔ:fit] **1.** Verwirkung *f*; Strafe *f*, Pfand *n*; **2.** verwirken; einbüßen; ~**able** [~təbl] verwirkbar.

**forge¹** [fɔ:dʒ] *mst* ~ *ahead* sich vor(wärts)arbeiten.

**forge²** [~] **1.** Schmiede *f*; **2.** schmieden (*fig. ersinnen*); fälschen; ~**ry** ['fɔ:dʒəri] Fälschung *f*.

**forget** [fə'get] [*irr.*] vergessen; ~**ful** □ [~tful] vergeßlich; ~**-me-not** ♀ Vergißmeinnicht *n*.

**forgiv|e** [fə'giv] [*irr.* (*give*)] vergeben, verzeihen; *Schuld* erlassen; ~**eness** [~vnis] Verzeihung *f*; ~**ing** □ [~viŋ] versöhnlich; nachsichtig.

**forgo** [fɔ:'gou] [*irr.* (*go*)] verzichten auf (*acc.*); aufgeben.

**forgot** [fə'gɔt] *pret. von* forget; ~**ten** [~tn] *p.p. von* forget.

**fork** [fɔ:k] **1.** Gabel *f*; **2.** (sich) gabeln; ~**lift** ['fɔ:klift] Gabelstapler *m*.

**forlorn** [fɔ:'lɔ:n] verloren, verlassen.

**form** [fɔ:m] **1.** Form *f*; Gestalt *f*; Formalität *f*; Formular *n*; (Schul-) Bank *f*; *Schul-*Klasse *f*; Kondition

*f*; geistige Verfassung; **2.** (sich) formen, (sich) bilden, gestalten; ⚔ (sich) aufstellen.

**formal** □ ['fɔ:məl] förmlich; formell; äußerlich; ~**ity** [fɔ:'mæliti] Förmlichkeit *f*, Formalität *f*.

**formati|on** [fɔ:'meiʃən] Bildung *f*; ~**ve** ['fɔ:mətiv] bildend; gestaltend; ~ *years pl.* Entwicklungsjahre *n/pl.*

**former** ['fɔ:mə] vorig, früher; ehemalig, vergangen; erstere(r, -s); jene(r, -s); ~**ly** [~əli] ehemals, früher.

**formidable** □ ['fɔ:midəbl] furchtbar, schrecklich; ungeheuer.

**formula** ['fɔ:mjulə] Formel *f*; ⚕ Rezept *n*; ~**te** [~leit] formulieren.

**forsake** [fə'seik] [*irr.*] aufgeben; verlassen; ~**n** [~kən] *p.p. von* forsake.

**forsook** [fə'suk] *pret. von* forsake.

**forsooth** *iro.* [fə'su:θ] wahrlich.

**forswear** [fɔ:'sweə] [*irr.* (*swear*)] abschwören.     [werk *n*) *f*.\]

**fort** ⚔ [fɔ:t] Fort *n*, Festungs-)

**forth** [fɔ:θ] vor(wärts), voran; heraus, hinaus, hervor; weiter, fort(an); ~**coming** [fɔ:θ'kʌmiŋ] erscheinend; bereit; bevorstehend; F entgegenkommend; ~**with** ['fɔ:θ'wiθ] sogleich.

**fortieth** ['fɔ:tiiθ] **1.** vierzigste(r, -s); Vierzigstel *n*.

**forti|fication** [fɔ:tifi'keiʃən] Befestigung *f*; ~**fy** ['fɔ:tifai] ⚔ befestigen; *fig.* (ver)stärken; ~**tude** [~itju:d] Seelenstärke *f*; Tapferkeit *f*.

**fortnight** ['fɔ:tnait] vierzehn Tage.

**fortress** ['fɔ:tris] Festung *f*.

**fortuitous** □ [fɔ:'tju(:)itəs] zufällig.

**fortunate** ['fɔ:tʃnit] glücklich; ~**ly** [~tli] glücklicherweise.

**fortune** ['fɔ:tʃən] Glück *n*; Schicksal *n*; Zufall *m*; Vermögen *n*; ~**teller** Wahrsager(in).

**forty** ['fɔ:ti] **1.** vierzig; ~**niner** *Am. kalifornischer Goldsucher von 1849*; ~ *winks pl.* F Nickerchen *n*; **2.** Vierzig *f*.

**forward** ['fɔ:wəd] **1.** *adj.* vorder; bereit(willig); fortschrittlich; vorwitzig, keck; **2.** *adv.* vor(wärts); **3.** *Fußball.* Stürmer *m*; **4.** (be)fördern; (ab-, ver)senden.

**forwarding-agent** ['fɔ:wədiŋei-dʒənt] Spediteur *m*.

**foster** ['fɔstə] **1.** *fig.* nähren, pflegen; ~ *up* aufziehen; **2.** Pflege...

**fought** [fɔ:t] *pret. u. p.p. von* fight 2.

**foul** [faul] **1.** □ widerwärtig; schmutzig (*a. fig.*); unehrlich; regelwidrig; übelriechend; faul, verdorben; widrig; schlecht (*Wetter*); *fall* ~ *of* mit *dem Gesetz* in Konflikt kommen; **2.** Zs.-stoß *m*; *Sport:* regelwidriges Spiel; *through fair and* ~ durch dick und dünn; **3.** be-, verschmutzen; (sich) verwickeln.

**found** [faund] **1.** *pret. u. p.p. von* find 1; **2.** (be)gründen; stiften; ⊕ gießen.

**foundation** [faun'deiʃən] Gründung *f*; Stiftung *f*; Fundament *n*.

**founder** ['faundə] **1.** (Be)Gründer (-in), Stifter(in); Gießer *m*; **2.** *v/i.* scheitern; lahmen.

**foundling** ['faundliŋ] Findling *m*.

**foundry** ⊕ ['faundri] Gießerei *f*.

**fountain** ['fauntin] Quelle *f*; Springbrunnen *m*; **~-pen** Füllfederhalter *m*.

**four** [fɔː] **1.** vier; **2.** Vier *f*; *Sport:* Vierer *m*; **~-flusher** *Am. sl.* ['fɔː-'flʌʃə] Hochstapler *m*; **~-square** viereckig; *fig.* unerschütterlich; **~-stroke** *mot.* Viertakt...; **~teen** ['fɔː'tiːn] vierzehn; **~teenth** [~nθ] vierzehnte(r, -s); **~th** [fɔːθ] **1.** vierte(r, -s); **2.** Viertel *n*; **~thly** ['fɔːθli] viertens.

**fowl** [faul] Geflügel *n*; Huhn *n*; Vogel *m*; **~ing-piece** ['fauliŋpiːs] Vogelflinte *f*.

**fox** [fɔks] **1.** Fuchs *m*; **2.** überlisten; **~glove** ♀ ['fɔksglʌv] Fingerhut *m*; **~y** ['fɔksi] fuchsartig; schlau.

**fraction** ['frækʃən] Bruch(teil) *m*.

**fracture** ['fræktʃə] **1.** (*bsd.* Knochen)Bruch *m*; **2.** brechen.

**fragile** ['frædʒail] zerbrechlich.

**fragment** ['frægmənt] Bruchstück *n*.

**fragran|ce** ['freigrəns] Wohlgeruch *m*, Duft *m*; **~t** □ [~nt] wohlriechend.

**frail** □ [freil] ge-, zerbrechlich; schwach; **~ty** *fig.* ['freilti] Schwäche *f*.

**frame** [freim] **1.** Rahmen *m*; Gerippe *n*; Gerüst *n*; (Brillen)Gestell *n*; Körper *m*; (An)Ordnung *f*; *phot.* (Einzel)Bild *n*; ✗ Frühbeetkasten *m*; **~ of mind** Gemütsverfassung *f*; **2.** bilden, formen, bauen; entwerfen; (ein)rahmen; sich entwickeln; **~-house** ['freimhaus] Holzhaus *n*; **~-up** *bsd. Am.* F abgekartetes Spiel; **~work** ⊕ Gerippe *n*; Rahmen *m*; *fig.* Bau *m*.

**franchise** ⚖ ['fræntʃaiz] Wahlrecht *n*; Bürgerrecht *n*; *bsd. Am.* Konzession *f*.

**frank** [fræŋk] **1.** □ frei(mütig), offen; **2.** *Brief* maschinell frankieren.

**frankfurter** ['fræŋkfətə] Frankfurter Würstchen.

**frankness** ['fræŋknis] Offenheit *f*.

**frantic** ['fræntik] (~ally) wahnsinnig.

**fratern|al** □ [frə'təːnl] brüderlich; **~ity** [~niti] Brüderlichkeit *f*; Brüderschaft *f*; *Am. univ.* Verbindung *f*.

**fraud** [frɔːd] Betrug *m*; F Schwindel *m*; **~ulent** □ ['frɔːdjulənt] betrügerisch.

**fray** [frei] **1.** (sich) abnutzen; (sich) durchscheuern; **2.** Schlägerei *f*.

**frazzle** *bsd. Am.* F ['fræzl] **1.** Fetzen *m/pl.*; **2.** zerfetzen.

**freak** [friːk] Einfall *m*, Laune *f*.

**freckle** ['frekl] Sommersprosse *f*.

**free** [friː] **1.** □ *allg.* frei; freigebig (of mit); freiwillig; *he is ~ to inf.* es steht ihm frei, zu *inf.*; **~ and easy** zwanglos; sorglos; *make ~* sich Freiheiten erlauben; *set ~* freilassen; **2.** befreien; freilassen, *et.* freimachen; **~booter** ['friːbuːtə] Freibeuter *m*; **~dom** ['friːdəm] Freiheit *f*; freie Benutzung; Offenheit *f*; Zwanglosigkeit *f*; (plumpe) Vertraulichkeit; **~ of a city** (Ehren-)Bürgerrecht *n*; **~holder** Grundeigentümer *m*; **~man** freier Mann; Vollbürger *m*; **~mason** Freimaurer *m*; **~wheel** Freilauf *m*.

**freez|e** [friːz] (*irr.*) *v/i.* (ge)frieren; erstarren; *v/t.* gefrieren lassen; **~er** ['friːzə] Eismaschine *f*; Gefriermaschine *f*; Gefriertruhe *f*; **~ing** □ [~ziŋ] eisig; **~ point** Gefrierpunkt *m*.

**freight** [freit] **1.** Fracht(geld *n*) *f*; *attr. Am.* Güter...; **2.** be-, verfrachten; **~-car** *Am.* ['freitkaː] Güterwagen *m*; **~ train** *Am.* Güterzug *m*.

**French** [frentʃ] **1.** französisch; *take ~ leave* heimlich weggehen; **~ window** Balkon-, Verandatür *f*; **2.** Französisch *n*; *the ~ pl.* die Franzosen *pl.*; **~man** ['frentʃmən] Franzose *m*.

**frenz|ied** ['frenzid] wahnsinnig; **~y** [~zi] Wahnsinn *m*.

**frequen|cy** ['friːkwənsi] Häufigkeit *f*; ⚡ Frequenz *f*; **~t 1.** □ [~nt] häufig; **2.** [fri'kwent] (oft) besuchen.

**fresh** □ [freʃ] frisch; neu; unerfahren; *Am.* F frech; **~ water** Süßwasser *n*; **~en** ['freʃn] frisch machen *od.* werden; **~et** [~ʃit] Hochwasser *n*; *fig.* Flut *f*; **~man** *univ.* Student *m* im ersten Jahr; **~ness** [~ʃnis] Frische *f*; Neuheit *f*; Unerfahrenheit *f*; **~water** Süßwasser...; **~ college** *Am.* drittrangiges College.

**fret** [fret] **1.** Aufregung *f*; Ärger *m*; ♩ Bund *m*, Griffleiste *f*; **2.** zerfressen; (sich) ärgern; (sich) grämen; **~ away**, **~ out** aufreiben.

**fretful** □ ['fretful] ärgerlich.

**fret-saw** ['fretsɔː] Laubsäge *f*.

**fretwork** ['fretwəːk] (geschnitztes) Gitterwerk; Laubsägearbeit *f*.

**friar** ['fraiə] Mönch *m*.

**friction** ['frikʃən] Reibung *f* (*a. fig.*).

**Friday** ['fraidi] Freitag *m*.

**fridge** F [fridʒ] Kühlschrank *m*.

**friend** [frend] Freund(in); Bekannte(r *m*) *f*; **~ly** ['frendli] freund(schaft)lich; **~ship** [~dʃip] Freundschaft *f*.

**frigate** ⚓ ['frigit] Fregatte *f*.

**frig(e)** F [fridʒ] = *fridge*.

**fright** [frait] Schreck(en) *m*; *fig.*
Vogelscheuche *f*; **~en** ['fraitn] erschrecken; **~ed** *at od. of* bange vor
(*dat.*); **~ful** □ [**~**tful] schrecklich.

**frigid** □ ['fridʒid] kalt, frostig.

**frill** [fril] Krause *f*, Rüsche *f*.

**fringe** [frindʒ] 1. Franse *f*; Rand *m*;
*a.* **~s** *pl.* Ponyfrisur *f*; 2. mit Fran-
sen besetzen.

**frippery** ['fripəri] Flitterkram *m*.

**Frisian** ['friziən] friesisch.

**frisk** [frisk] 1. Luftsprung *m*;
2. hüpfen; *sl. nach Waffen etc.* durchsuchen; **~y** □ ['friski] munter.

**fritter** ['fritə] 1. Pfannkuchen *m*,
Krapfen *m*; 2.: **~** *away* verzetteln.

**frivol|ity** [fri'vɔliti] Frivolität *f*,
Leichtfertigkeit *f*; **~ous** □ ['fri-
vələs] nichtig; leichtfertig.

**frizzle** ['frizl] *a.* **~** *up* (sich) kräuseln; *Küche*: brutzeln.

**fro** [frou]: *to and* **~** hin und her.

**frock** [frɔk] Kutte *f*; *Frauen-*Kleid
*n*; Kittel *m*; Gehrock *m*.

**frog** [frɔg] Frosch *m*.

**frolic** ['frɔlik] 1. Fröhlichkeit *f*;
Scherz *m*; 2. scherzen, spaßen;
**~some** □ [**~**ksəm] lustig, fröhlich.

**from** [frɔm; frəm] *von* aus,
von ... her; von ... (an); aus, vor,
wegen; nach, gemäß; *defend* **~**
schützen vor (*dat.*); **~** *amidst* mitten aus.

**front** [frʌnt] 1. Stirn *f*; Vorderseite
*f*; X Front *f*; Hemdbrust *f*; Strandpromenade *f*; Kühnheit *f*, Frech-
heit *f*; *in* **~** vorn; *in* **~** *of räumlich*
vor; 2. Vorder...; 3. *a.* **~** *on*, **~**
*towards* die Front haben nach;
gegenüberstehen, gegenübertreten
(*dat.*); **~al** ['frʌntl] Stirn...; Front-
...; Vorder...; **~** *door* Haustür *f*;
**~ier** [**~**tjə] Grenze *f, bsd. Am. hist.*
*Grenze zum Wilden Westen; attr.*
Grenz...; **~iersman** [**~**əzmən]
Grenzbewohner *m*; *fig.* Pionier *m*;
**~ispiece** [**~**tispi:s] △ Vorderseite *f*;
*typ.* Titelbild *n*; **~** *man fig.* Aus-
hängeschild *n*; **~page** *Zeitung:*
Titelseite *f*; **~wheel drive** *mot.*
Vorderradantrieb *m*.

**frost** [frɔst] 1. Frost *m*; *a.* hoar **~**,
white **~** Reif *m*; 2. (mit Zucker)
bestreuen; glasieren; mattieren;
**~ed** *glass* Milchglas *n*; **~bite** ❄
['frɔstbait] Erfrierung *f*; **~y** □
[**~**ti] frostig; bereift.

**froth** [frɔθ] 1. Schaum *m*; 2. schäumen; zu Schaum schlagen; **~y** □
['frɔθi] schaumig; *fig.* seicht.

**frown** [fraun] 1. Stirnrunzeln *n*;
finsterer Blick; 2. *v/i.* die Stirn
runzeln; finster blicken.

**frow|sty** □ ['frausti], **~zy** ['frauzi]
moderig; schlampig.

**froze** [frouz] *pret. von freeze;* **~n**
['frouzn] 1. *p.p. von freeze;* 2. *adj.*
(eis)kalt; (ein)gefroren.

**frugal** □ ['fru:gəl] mäßig; sparsam.

**fruit** [fru:t] 1. Frucht *f*; Früchte *pl.*;
Obst *n*; 2. Frucht tragen; **~erer**
['fru:tərə] Obsthändler *m*; **~ful** □
[**~**tful] fruchtbar; **~less** □ [**~**tlis]
unfruchtbar.

**frustrat|e** [frʌs'treit] vereiteln;
enttäuschen; **~ion** [**~**eiʃən] Vereitelung *f*; Enttäuschung *f*.

**fry** [frai] 1. Gebratene(s) *n*; Fisch-
brut *f*; 2. braten, backen; **~ing-pan**
['fraiiŋpæn] Bratpfanne *f*.

**fuchsia** ♀ ['fju:ʃə] Fuchsie *f*.

**fudge** [fʌdʒ] 1. F zurechtpfuschen;
2. Unsinn *m*; Weichkaramelle *f*.

**fuel** [fjuəl] 1. Brennmaterial *n*;
Betriebs-, *mot.* Kraftstoff *m*; 2. *mot.*
tanken.

**fugitive** ['fju:dʒitiv] 1. flüchtig
(*a. fig.*); 2. Flüchtling *m*.

**fulfil(l)** [ful'fil] erfüllen; vollziehen;
**~ment** [**~**mənt] Erfüllung *f*.

**full** [ful] 1. □ *allg.* voll; Voll...;
vollständig, völlig; reichlich; ausführlich; *of* **~** *age* volljährig; 2. *adv.*
völlig, ganz; genau; 3. Ganze(s) *n*;
Höhepunkt *m*; *in* **~** völlig; ausführlich; *to the* **~** vollständig; **~**
**blooded** ['ful'blʌdid] vollblütig;
kräftig; reinrassig; **~dress** Gesellschaftsanzug *m*; **~dress** ['fuldres]
förmell, Gala...; *Am.* ausführlich;
**~fledged** ['ful'fledʒd] flügge; voll
ausgewachsen; **~** *stop* Punkt *m*.

**ful(l)ness** ['fulnis] Fülle *f*.

**full-time** ['fultaim] vollbeschäftigt;
Voll...

**fulminate** *fig.* ['fʌlmineit] wettern.

**fumble** ['fʌmbl] tasten; fummeln.

**fume** [fju:m] 1. Dunst *m*, Dampf *m*;
2. rauchen; aufgebracht sein.

**fumigate** ['fju:migeit] ausräuchern,
desinfizieren.

**fun** [fʌn] Scherz *m*, Spaß *m*; *make*
*of* sich lustig machen über (*acc.*).

**function** ['fʌŋkʃən] 1. Funktion *f*;
Beruf *m*; Tätigkeit *f*; Aufgabe *f*;
Feierlichkeit *f*; 2. funktionieren;
**~ary** [**~**ʃnəri] Beamte(r) *m*; Funk-
tionär *m*.

**fund** [fʌnd] 1. Fonds *m*; **~s** *pl.*
Staatspapiere *n/pl.*; Geld(mittel
*n/pl.*) *n*; Vorrat *m*; 2. *Schuld* fun-
dieren; *Geld* anlegen.

**fundamental** □ [fʌndə'mentl]
1. grundlegend; Grund...; 2. **~s** *pl.*
Grundlage *f*, -züge *m/pl.*, -begriffe
*m/pl.*

**funer|al** ['fju:nərəl] Beerdigung *f*;
*attr.* Trauer..., Begräbnis...; **~eal** □
[fju(:)'niəriəl] traurig, düster.

**fun-fair** ['fʌnfeə] Rummelplatz
*m*.

**funicular** [fju(:)'nikjulə] 1. Seil...;
2. *a.* **~** *railway* (Draht)Seilbahn *f*.

**funnel** ['fʌnl] Trichter *m*; Rauchfang *m*; ⚓, 🚂 Schornstein *m*.

**funnies** *Am.* ['fʌniz] *pl.* Comics *pl.*
(*primitive Bildserien*).

**funny** □ ['fʌni] spaßig, komisch.

**fur** [fə:] **1.** Pelz *m*; Belag *m der Zunge*; Kesselstein *m*; ~s *pl.* Pelzwaren *pl.*; **2.** mit Pelz besetzen *od.* füttern.

**furbish** ['fə:biʃ] putzen, polieren.

**furious** ['fjuəriəs] wütend; wild.

**furl** [fə:l] zs.-rollen; zs.-klappen.

**furlough** ⚔ ['fə:lou] Urlaub *m*.

**furnace** ['fə:nis] Schmelz-, Hochofen *m*; (Heiz)Kessel *m*; Feuerung *f*.

**furnish** ['fə:niʃ] versehen (*with* mit); *et.* liefern; möblieren; ausstatten.

**furniture** ['fə:nitʃə] Möbel *pl.*, Einrichtung *f*; Ausstattung *f*; sectional ~ Anbaumöbel *pl.*

**furrier** ['fʌriə] Kürschner *m*.

**furrow** ['fʌrou] **1.** Furche *f*; **2.** furchen.

**further** ['fə:ðə] **1.** *adj. u. adv.* ferner, weiter; **2.** fördern; ~ance [~ərəns] Förderung *f*; ~more [~ə'mɔ:] ferner, überdies; ~most [~əmoust] weitest.

**furthest** ['fə:ðist] = *furthermost.*

**furtive** □ ['fə:tiv] verstohlen.

**fury** ['fjuəri] Raserei *f*, Wut *f*; Furie *f*.

**fuse** [fju:z] **1.** (ver)schmelzen; ⚡ durchbrennen; ausgehen (*Licht*); ⚔ mit Zünder versehen; **2.** ⚡ (Schmelz)Sicherung *f*; ⚔ Zünder *m*.

**fuselage** ['fju:zila:ʒ] (Flugzeug-) Rumpf *m*.

**fusion** ['fju:ʒən] Schmelzen *n*; Verschmelzung *f*, Fusion *f*; ~ **bomb** ⚔ Wasserstoffbombe *f*.

**fuss** F [fʌs] **1.** Lärm *m*; Wesen *n*, Getue *n*; **2.** viel Aufhebens machen (*about* um, von); (sich) aufregen.

**fusty** ['fʌsti] muffig; *fig.* verstaubt.

**futile** ['fju:tail] nutzlos, nichtig.

**future** ['fju:tʃə] **1.** (zu)künftig; **2.** Zukunft *f*; *gr.* Futur *n*, Zukunft *f*; ~s *pl.* † Termingeschäfte *n/pl.*

**fuzz** [fʌz] **1.** feiner Flaum; Fussel *f*; **2.** fusseln, (zer)fasern.

# G

**gab** F [gæb] Geschwätz *n*; *the gift of the* ~ ein gutes Mundwerk.

**gabardine** ['gæbədi:n] Gabardine *m* (*Wollstoff*).

**gabble** ['gæbl] **1.** Geschnatter *n*, Geschwätz *n*; **2.** schnattern, schwatzen.

**gaberdine** ['gæbədi:n] Kaftan *m*; = *gabardine.*

**gable** ['geibl] Giebel *m*.

**gad** F [gæd]: ~ *about* sich herumtreiben.

**gadfly** *zo.* ['gædflai] Bremse *f*.

**gadget** *sl.* ['gædʒit] Dings *n*, Apparat *m*; Kniff *m*, Pfiff *m*.

**gag** [gæg] **1.** Knebel *m*; Witz *m*; **2.** knebeln; *pol.* mundtot machen.

**gage¹** [geidʒ] Pfand *n*.

**gage²** [~] = *gauge.*

**gaiety** ['geiəti] Fröhlichkeit *f*.

**gaily** ['geili] *adv. von gay.*

**gain** [gein] **1.** Gewinn *m*; Vorteil *m*; **2.** *v/t.* gewinnen; erreichen; bekommen; *v/i.* vorgehen (*Uhr*); ~ in zunehmen an (*acc.*); ~ful □ ['geinful] einträglich.

**gait** [geit] Gang(art *f*) *m*; Schritt *m*.

**gaiter** ['geitə] Gamasche *f*.

**gal** *Am. sl.* [gæl] Mädel *n*.

**gale** [geil] Sturm *m*; steife Brise.

**gall** [gɔ:l] **1.** Galle *f*; 𝔰 Wolf *m*; Pein *f*; *bsd. Am. sl.* Frechheit *f*; **2.** wundreiben; ärgern.

**gallant** ['gælənt] **1.** □ stattlich; tapfer; galant, höflich; **2.** Kavalier *m*; **3.** galant sein; ~ry [~tri] Tapferkeit *f*; Galanterie *f*.

**gallery** ['gæləri] Galerie *f*; Empore *f*.

**galley** ['gæli] ⚓ Galeere *f*; ⚓ Kombüse *f*; ~proof Korrekturfahne *f*.

**gallon** ['gælən] Gallone *f* (*4,54 Liter, Am. 3,78 Liter*).

**gallop** ['gæləp] **1.** Galopp *m*; **2.** galoppieren (lassen).

**gallows** ['gælouz] *sg.* Galgen *m*.

**galore** [gə'lɔ:] in Menge.

**gamble** ['gæmbl] (um Geld) spielen; **2.** F Glücksspiel *n*; ~r [~lə] Spieler(in).

**gambol** ['gæmbəl] **1.** Luftsprung *m*; **2.** (fröhlich) hüpfen, tanzen.

**game** [geim] **1.** Spiel *n*; Scherz *m*; Wild *n*; **2.** F entschlossen; furchtlos; **3.** spielen; ~keeper ['geimki:pə] Wildhüter *m*; ~licence Jagdschein *m*; ~ster ['geimstə] Spieler(in).

**gander** ['gændə] Gänserich *m*.

**gang** [gæŋ] **1.** Trupp *m*; Bande *f*; **2.** ~ *up* sich zs.-rotten *od.* zs.-tun; ~board ⚓ ['gæŋbɔ:d] Laufplanke *f*.

**gangster** *Am.* ['gæŋstə] Gangster *m*.

**gangway** ['gæŋwei] (Durch)Gang *m*; ⚓ Fallreep *n*; ⚓ Laufplanke *f*.

**gaol** [dʒeil], ~**bird** ['dʒeilbə:d], ~**er** ['dʒeilə] *s. jail etc.*

**gap** [gæp] Lücke *f*; Kluft *f*; Spalte *f*.

**gape** [geip] gähnen; klaffen; gaffen.

**garage** ['gæra:ʒ] **1.** Garage *f*; Autowerkstatt *f*; **2.** *Auto* einstellen.

**garb** [gɑ:b] Gewand *n*, Tracht *f*.

**garbage** ['gɑ:bidʒ] Abfall *m*;

Schund *m*; ~ *can Am*. Mülltonne *f*;
~ *pail* Mülleimer *m*.
**garden** ['gɑːdn] **1.** Garten *m*;
**2.** Gartenbau treiben; ~er [~nə]
Gärtner(in); ~ing [~niŋ] Gartenarbeit *f*.
**gargle** ['gɑːgl] **1.** gurgeln; **2.** Gurgelwasser *n*.
**garish** ☐ ['geəriʃ] grell, auffallend.
**garland** ['gɑːlənd] Girlande *f*.
**garlic** ♀ ['gɑːlik] Knoblauch *m*.
**garment** ['gɑːmənt] Gewand *n*.
**garnish** ['gɑːniʃ] garnieren; zieren.
**garret** ['gærət] Dachstube *f*.
**garrison** ⚔ ['gærisn] **1.** Besatzung
*f*; Garnison *f*; **2.** mit e-r Besatzung
belegen.                           [haft.\
**garrulous** ☐ ['gærʊləs] schwatz-\
**garter** ['gɑːtə] Strumpfband *n*; *Am*.
Socken-, Strumpfhalter *m*.
**gas** [gæs] **1.** Gas *n*; *Am*. = *gasoline*;
**2.** *v/t*. vergasen; *v/i*. F faseln; ~eous
['geizjəs] gasförmig.
**gash** [gæʃ] **1.** klaffende Wunde;
Hieb *m*; Riß *m*; **2.** tief (ein)schneiden in (*acc*.).
**gas|-light** ['gæslait] Gasbeleuchtung *f*; ~meter Gasuhr *f*; ~o-
lene, ~oline *Am. mot.* ['gæsəliːn]
Benzin *n*.
**gasp** [gɑːsp] **1.** Keuchen *n*; **2.** keuchen; nach Luft schnappen.
**gas|sed** [gæst] gasvergiftet; ~stove
['gæs'stouv] Gasofen *m*, -herd *m*;
~works ['gæswəːks] *sg*. Gaswerk
*n*, -anstalt *f*.
**gat** *Am. sl.* [gæt] Revolver *m*.
**gate** [geit] Tor *n*; Pforte *f*; Sperre *f*;
~man ☞ ['geitmən] Schrankenwärter *m*; ~way Tor(weg *m*) *n*,
Einfahrt *f*.
**gather** ['gæðə] **1.** *v/t*. (ein-, ver-)
sammeln; ernten; pflücken; schließen (*from aus*); *zs*.-ziehen; kräuseln; ~ *speed* schneller werden; *v/i*.
sich (ver)sammeln; sich vergrößern; ✿ u. fig. reifen; **2.** Falte *f*;
~ing [~riŋ] Versammlung *f*; Zs.-
kunft *f*.
**gaudy** ☐ ['gɔːdi] grell; protzig.
**gauge** [geidʒ] **1.** (Normal)Maß *n*;
Maßstab *m*; ⊕ Lehre *f*; ⚌ Spurweite *f*; Meßgerät *n*; **2.** eichen;
(aus)messen; *fig*. abschätzen.
**gaunt** ☐ [gɔːnt] hager; finster.
**gauntlet** ['gɔːntlit] *fig*. Fehdehandschuh *m*; *run the* ~ Spießruten laufen.
**gauze** [gɔːz] Gaze *f*.
**gave** [geiv] *pret. von* give.
**gavel** *Am*. ['gævl] Hammer *m* des
*Versammlungsleiters od. Auktionators*.
**gawk** F [gɔːk] Tölpel *m*; ~y [gɔː'ki]
tölpisch.
**gay** ☐ [gei] lustig, heiter; bunt, lebhaft, glänzend.
**gaze** [geiz] **1.** starrer *od*. aufmerksamer Blick; **2.** starren.

**gazette** [gə'zet] **1.** Amtsblatt *n*;
**2.** amtlich bekanntgeben.
**gear** [giə] **1.** ⊕ Getriebe *n*; *mot*.
Gang *m*; Mechanismus *m*; Gerät *n*;
*in* ~ mit eingelegtem Gang; in Betrieb; *out of* ~ im Leerlauf; außer
Betrieb; *landing* ~ ✈ Fahrgestell *n*;
*steering* ~ ⏚ Ruderanlage *f*; *mot*.
Lenkung *f*; **2.** einschalten; ⊕
greifen; ~ing ['giəriŋ] (Zahnrad-)
Getriebe *n*; Übersetzung *f*; ~
lever, *bsd. Am*. ~shift Schalthebel
*m*.
**gee** [dʒiː] **1.** *Kindersprache*: Hottehü
*n* (*Pferd*); **2.** *Fuhrmannsruf*: hü!
hott!; *Am*. nanu!, so was!
**geese** [giːs] *pl. von* goose.
**gem** [dʒem] Edelstein *m*; Gemme *f*;
*fig*. Glanzstück *n*.
**gender** *gr*. ['dʒendə] Genus *n*,
Geschlecht *n*.
**general** ['dʒenərəl] **1.** ☐ allgemein;
gewöhnlich; Haupt..., General...;
~ *election* allgemeine Wahlen; **2.** ⚔
General *m*; Feldherr *m*; ~ity
[dʒenə'ræliti] Allgemeinheit *f*; *die*
große Masse; ~ize ['dʒenərəlaiz]
verallgemeinern; ~ly [~li] im allgemeinen, überhaupt; gewöhnlich.
**generat|e** ['dʒenəreit] erzeugen;
~ion [dʒenə'reiʃən] (Er)Zeugung *f*;
Generation *f*; Menschenalter *n*;
~or ['dʒenəreitə] Erzeuger *m*; ⊕
Generator *m*; *bsd. Am. mot*. Lichtmaschine *f*.
**gener|osity** [dʒenə'rɔsiti] Großmut
*f*; Großzügigkeit *f*; ~ous ☐
['dʒenərəs] großmütig, großzügig.
**genial** ☐ ['dʒiːnjəl] freundlich; anregend; gemütlich (*Person*); heiter.
**genitive** *gr*. ['dʒenitiv] *a*. ~ *case*
Genitiv *m*.
**genius** ['dʒiːnjəs] Geist *m*; Genie *n*.
**gent** F [dʒent] Herr *m*.
**genteel** ☐ [dʒen'tiːl] vornehm; elegant.
**gentile** ['dʒentail] **1.** heidnisch,
nichtjüdisch; **2.** Heid|e *m*, -in *f*.
**gentle** ☐ ['dʒentl] sanft, mild;
zahm; leise, sacht; vornehm; ~man
Herr *m*; Gentleman *m*; ~manlike,
~manly [~li] gebildet; vornehm;
~ness [~nis] Sanftheit *f*; Milde *f*;
Güte *f*, Sanftmut *f*.
**gentry** ['dʒentri] niederer Adel;
gebildete Stände *m/pl*.
**genuine** ☐ ['dʒenjuin] echt; aufrichtig.
**geography** [dʒi'ɔgrəfi] Geographie
*f*.
**geology** [dʒi'ɔlədʒi] Geologie *f*.
**geometry** [dʒi'ɔmitri] Geometrie *f*.
**germ** [dʒəːm] **1.** Keim *m*; **2.** keimen.
**German¹** ['dʒəːmən] **1.** deutsch;
**2.** Deutsche(r *m*) *f*; Deutsch *n*.
**german²** ['dʒəːmən] *brother* ~ leiblicher
Bruder; ~e [dʒəː'mein] (*to*) verwandt (mit); entsprechend (*dat*.).
**germinate** ['dʒəːmineit] keimen.

**gesticulat|e** ['dʒes'tikjuleit] gestikulieren; ~**ion** [dʒestikju'leiʃən] Gebärdenspiel n.

**gesture** ['dʒestʃə] Geste f, Gebärde f.

**get** [get] [irr.] v/t. erhalten, bekommen, F kriegen; besorgen; holen; bringen; erwerben; verdienen; ergreifen, fassen; (veran)lassen; mit adv. mst bringen, machen; have got haben; ~ one's hair cut sich das Haar schneiden lassen; ~ by heart auswendig lernen; v/i. gelangen, geraten, kommen; gehen; werden; ~ ready sich fertig machen; ~ about auf den Beinen sein; ~ abroad bekannt werden; ~ ahead vorwärtskommen; ~ at (heran-)kommen an ... (acc.); zu et. kommen; ~ away wegkommen; sich fortmachen; ~ in einsteigen; ~ on with s.o. mit j-m auskommen; ~ out aussteigen; ~ to hear (know, learn) erfahren; ~ up aufstehen; ~-up ['getʌp] Aufmachung f; Am. F Unternehmungsgeist m.

**ghastly** ['gɑːstli] gräßlich; schrecklich; (toten)bleich; gespenstisch.

**gherkin** ['gəːkin] Gewürzgurke f.

**ghost** [goust] Geist m, Gespenst n; fig. Spur f; ~**like** ['goustlaik], ~**ly** [~li] geisterhaft.

**giant** ['dʒaiənt] 1. riesig; 2.Riese m.

**gibber** ['dʒibə] kauderwelschen; ~**ish** ['gibəriʃ] Kauderwelsch n.

**gibbet** ['dʒibit] 1. Galgen m; 2. hängen.

**gibe** [dʒaib] verspotten, aufziehen.

**giblets** ['dʒiblits] pl. Gänseklein n.

**gidd|iness** ['gidinis] ⚓ Schwindel m; Unbeständigkeit f; Leichtsinn m; ~**y** □ ['gidi] schwind(e)lig; leichtfertig; unbeständig; albern.

**gift** [gift] Gabe f; Geschenk n; Talent n; ~**ed** ['giftid] begabt.

**gigantic** [dʒai'gæntik] (~ally) riesenhaft, riesig, gigantisch.

**giggle** ['gigl] 1. kichern; 2. Gekicher n.

**gild** [gild] [irr.] vergolden; verschönen; ~**ed** youth Jeunesse f dorée.

**gill** [gil] ichth. Kieme f; ⚥ Lamelle f.

**gilt** [gilt] 1. pret. u. p.p. von gild; 2. Vergoldung f.

**gimmick** Am. sl. ['gimik] Trick m.

**gin** [dʒin] Gin m (Wacholderschnaps); Schlinge f; ⊕ Entkörnungsmaschine f.

**ginger** ['dʒindʒə] 1. Ingwer m; Lebhaftigkeit f; 2. ~ up in Schwung bringen; 3. hellrot, rötlich-gelb; ~**bread** Pfefferkuchen m; ~**ly** [~əli] zimperlich; sachte.

**gipsy** ['dʒipsi] Zigeuner(in).

**gird** [gəːd] sticheln; [irr.] (um)gürten; umgeben.

**girder** ⊕ ['gəːdə] Tragbalken m.

**girdle** ['gəːdl] 1. Gürtel m; Hüfthalter m, -gürtel m; 2. umgürten.

**girl** [gəːl] Mädchen n; ♀ **Guide** ['gəːlgaid] Pfadfinderin f; ~**hood** ['gəːlhud] Mädchenzeit f; Mädchenjahre n/pl.; ~**ish** □ ['gəːliʃ] mädchenhaft; ~**y** Am. F ['gəːli] mit spärlich bekleideten Mädchen (Magazin, Varieté etc.).

**girt** [gəːt] pret. u. p.p. von gird.

**girth** [gəːθ] (Sattel)Gurt m; Umfang m.

**gist** [dʒist] das Wesentliche.

**give** [giv] [irr.] v/t. geben; ab-, übergeben; her-, hingeben; überlassen; zum besten geben; schenken; gewähren; von sich geben; ergeben; ~ birth to zur Welt bringen; ~ away verschenken; F verraten; ~ forth von sich geben; herausgeben; ~ in einreichen; ~ up Geschäft etc. aufgeben; j-n ausliefern; v/i. mst ~ in nachgeben; weichen; ~ into, ~ (up)on hinausgehen auf (acc.) (Fenster etc.); ~ out aufhören; versagen; ~ **and take** [givən'teik] (Meinungs)Austausch m; Kompromiß m, n; ~**away** Preisgabe f; ~ show od. program bsd. Am. Radio, Fernsehen: öffentliches Preisraten; ~**n** ['givn] 1. p.p. von give; 2. ~ to ergeben (dat.).

**glaci|al** □ ['gleisjəl] eisig; Eis...; Gletscher...; ~**er** ['glæsjə] Gletscher m.

**glad** □ [glæd] froh, erfreut; erfreulich; ~**ly** gern; ~**den** ['glædn] erfreuen.

**glade** [gleid] Lichtung f; Am. sumpfige Niederung.

**gladness** ['glædnis] Freude f.

**glair** [glɛə] Eiweiß n.

**glamo|rous** ['glæmərəs] bezaubernd; ~**(u)r** ['glæmə] 1. Zauber m, Glanz m, Reiz m; 2. bezaubern.

**glance** [glɑːns] 1. Schimmer m, Blitz m; flüchtiger Blick; 2. hinweggleiten; mst ~ off abprallen; blitzen; glänzen; ~ at flüchtig ansehen; anspielen auf (acc.).

**gland** anat. [glænd] Drüse f.

**glare** [glɛə] 1. grelles Licht; wilder, starrer Blick; 2. grell leuchten; wild blicken; (at an)starren.

**glass** [glɑːs] 1. Glas n; Spiegel m; Opern-, Fernglas n; Barometer n; (a pair of) ~es pl. (eine) Brille; 2. gläsern; Glas...; 3. verglasen; ~**case** ['glɑːskeis] Vitrine f; Schaukasten m; ~**house** Treibhaus n; ⚔ sl. Bau m; ~**y** [~si] gläsern; glasig.

**glaze** [gleiz] 1. Glasur f; 2. v/t. verglasen; glasieren; polieren; v/i. trüb(e) od. glasig werden (Auge); ~**ier** ['gleizjə] Glaser m.

**gleam** [gliːm] 1. Schimmer m, Schein m; 2. schimmern.

**glean** [gli:n] v/t. sammeln; v/i. Ähren lesen.

**glee** [gli:] Fröhlichkeit f; mehrstimmiges Lied; ~ club Gesangverein m.

**glen** [glen] Bergschlucht f.

**glib** □ [glib] glatt, zungenfertig.

**glid|e** [glaid] 1. Gleiten n; ⚡ Gleitflug m; 2. (dahin)gleiten (lassen); e-n Gleitflug machen; ~er ['glaidə] Segelflugzeug n.

**glimmer** ['glimə] 1. Schimmer m; min. Glimmer m; 2. schimmern.

**glimpse** [glimps] 1. flüchtiger Blick (of auf acc.); Schimmer m; flüchtiger Eindruck; 2. flüchtig (er)blicken.

**glint** [glint] 1. blitzen, glitzern; 2. Lichtschein m.

**glisten** ['glisn], **glitter** ['glitə] glitzern, glänzen.

**gloat** [glout]: ~ (up)on od. over sich weiden an (dat.).

**globe** [gloub] (Erd)Kugel f; Globus m.

**gloom** [glu:m], **~iness** ['glu:minis] Düsterkeit f, Dunkelheit f; Schwermut f; ~y □ ['glu:mi] dunkel, düster; schwermütig; verdrießlich.

**glori|fy** ['glɔ:rifai] verherrlichen; **~ous** □ [~iəs] herrlich; glorreich.

**glory** ['glɔ:ri] 1. Ruhm m; Herrlichkeit f, Pracht f; Glorienschein m; 2. frohlocken; stolz sein.

**gloss** [glɔs] 1. Glosse f, Bemerkung f; Glanz m; 2. Glossen machen (zu); Glanz geben (dat.); ~ over beschönigen.

**glossary** ['glɔsəri] Wörterverzeichnis n.

**glossy** □ ['glɔsi] glänzend, blank.

**glove** [glʌv] Handschuh m.

**glow** [glou] 1. Glühen n; Glut f; 2. glühen.

**glower** ['glauə] finster blicken.

**glow-worm** ['glouwə:m] Glühwürmchen n.

**glucose** ['glu:kous] Traubenzucker m.

**glue** [glu:] 1. Leim m; 2. leimen.

**glum** □ [glʌm] mürrisch.

**glut** [glʌt] überfüllen.

**glutinous** □ ['glu:tinəs] klebrig.

**glutton** ['glʌtn] Unersättliche(r m) f; Vielfraß m; **~ous** □ [~əs] gefräßig; **~y** [~ni] Gefräßigkeit f.

**G-man** Am. F ['dʒi:mæn] FBI-Agent m.

**gnarl** [nɑ:l] Knorren m, Ast m.

**gnash** [næʃ] knirschen (mit).

**gnat** [næt] (Stech)Mücke f.

**gnaw** [nɔ:] (zer)nagen; (zer)fressen.

**gnome** [noum] Erdgeist m, Gnom m.

**go** [gou] 1. [irr.] allg. gehen, fahren; vergehen (Zeit); werden; führen (to nach); sich wenden (to an); funktionieren, arbeiten; passen; kaputtgehen; let ~ loslassen; ~

shares teilen; ~ to od. and see besuchen; ~ at losgehen auf (acc.); ~ between vermitteln (zwischen); ~ by sich richten nach; ~ for gehen nach, holen; ~ for a walk, etc. einen Spaziergang etc. machen; ~ in for an examination e-e Prüfung machen; ~ on weitergehen; fortfahren; ~ through durchgehen; durchmachen; ~ without sich behelfen ohne; 2. F Mode f; Schwung m, Schneid m; on the ~ auf den Beinen; im Gange; it is no ~ es geht nicht; in one ~ auf Anhieb; have a ~ at es versuchen mit.

**goad** [goud] 1. Stachelstock m; fig. Ansporn m; 2. fig. anstacheln.

**go-ahead** F ['gouəhed] 1. zielstrebig; unternehmungslustig; 2. bsd. Am. F Erlaubnis f zum Weitermachen.

**goal** [goul] Mal n; Ziel n; Fußball: Tor n; **~keeper** ['goulki:pə] Torwart m.

**goat** [gout] Ziege f, Geiß f.

**gob** [gɔb] V Schleimklumpen m; F Maul n; Am. F Blaujacke f (Matrose).

**gobble** ['gɔbl] gierig verschlingen; **~dygook** Am. sl. [~ldiguk] Amts-, Berufsjargon m; Geschwafel n; **~r** [~lə] Vielfraß m; Truthahn m.

**go-between** ['goubitwi:n] Vermittler(in).

**goblet** ['gɔblit] Kelchglas n; Pokal m.

**goblin** ['gɔblin] Kobold m, Gnom m.

**god**, eccl. ♀ [gɔd] Gott m; fig. Abgott m; **~child** ['gɔdtʃaild] Patenkind n; **~dess** [~ɔdis] Göttin f; **~father** Pate m; **~head** Gottheit f; **~less** ['gɔdlis] gottlos; **~like** gottähnlich; göttlich; **~ly** [~li] gottesfürchtig; fromm; **~mother** Patin f.

**go-getter** Am. sl. ['gou'getə] Draufgänger m.

**goggle** ['gɔgl] 1. glotzen; 2. **~s** pl. Schutzbrille f.

**going** ['gouiŋ] 1. gehend; im Gange (befindlich); be ~ to inf. im Begriff sein zu inf., gleich tun wollen od. werden; 2. Gehen n; Vorwärtskommen n; Straßenzustand m; Geschwindigkeit f, Leistung f; **~s-on** F [~ŋz'ɔn] pl. Treiben n.

**gold** [gould] 1. Gold n; 2. golden; **~digger** Am. ['goulddigə] Goldgräber m; **~en** mst fig. [~dən] golden, goldgelb; **~finch** zo. Stieglitz m; **~smith** Goldschmied m.

**golf** [gɔlf] 1. Golf(spiel) n; 2. Golf spielen; **~course** ['gɔlfkɔ:s], **~links** pl. Golfplatz m.

**gondola** ['gɔndələ] Gondel f.

**gone** [gɔn] 1. p.p. von go 1; 2. adj. fort; F futsch; vergangen; tot; F hoffnungslos.

**good** [gud] 1. allg. gut; artig; gütig;

⚓ zahlungsfähig; gründlich; ~ at geschickt in (dat.); 2. Gute(s) n; Wohl n, Beste(s) n; ~s pl. Waren f/pl.; Güter n/pl.; that's no ~ das nützt nichts; for ~ für immer; ~by(e) 1. [gud'bai] Lebewohl n; 2. ['gud'bai] (auf) Wiedersehen!; ♀ Friday Karfreitag m; ~ly ['gudli] anmutig, hübsch; fig. ansehnlich; ~natured gutmütig; ~ness [~nis] Güte f; das Beste; thank ~! Gott sei Dank!; ~will Wohlwollen n; ⚓ Kundschaft f; ⚓ Firmenwert m.

**goody** ['gudi] Bonbon m, n.

**goon** Am. sl. [gu:n] bestellter Schläger bsd. für Streik; Dummkopf m.

**goose** [gu:s], pl. **geese** [gi:s] Gans f (a. fig.); Bügeleisen n.

**gooseberry** ['guzbəri] Stachelbeere f.

**goose|-flesh** ['gu:sfleʃ], Am. ~-pimples pl. fig. Gänsehaut f.

**gopher** bsd. Am. ['goufə] Erdeichhörnchen n.

**gore** [gɔ:] 1. (geronnenes) Blut; Schneiderei: Keil m; 2. durchbohren, aufspießen.

**gorge** [gɔ:dʒ] 1. Kehle f, Schlund m; enge (Fels)Schlucht; 2. (ver-)schlingen; (sich) vollstopfen.

**gorgeous** □ ['gɔ:dʒəs] prächtig.

**gory** □ ['gɔ:ri] blutig.

**gospel** ['gɔspəl] Evangelium n.

**gossip** ['gɔsip] 1. Geschwätz n; Klatschbase f; 2. schwatzen.

**got** [gɔt] pret. u. p.p. von get.

**Gothic** ['gɔθik] gotisch; fig. barbarisch.

**gotten** Am. ['gɔtn] p.p. von get.

**gouge** [gaudʒ] 1. ⊕ Hohlmeißel m; 2. ausmeißeln; Am. F betrügen.

**gourd** ⚘ [guəd] Kürbis m.

**gout** ⚕ [gaut] Gicht f.

**govern** ['gʌvən] v/t. regieren, beherrschen; lenken, leiten; v/i. herrschen; ~ess [~nis] Erzieherin f; ~ment ['gʌvnmənt] Regierung(s-form) f; Leitung f; Herrschaft f (of über acc.); Ministerium n; Statthalterschaft f; attr. Staats...; ~mental [gʌvn'mentl] Regierungs...; ~or ['gʌvənə] Gouverneur m; Direktor m, Präsident m; F Alte(r) m (Vater, Chef).

**gown** [gaun] 1. (Frauen)Kleid n; Robe f, Talar m; 2. kleiden.

**grab** F [græb] 1. grapsen; an sich reißen, packen; 2. plötzlicher Griff; ⊕ Greifer m; ~-bag bsd. Am. Glückstopf m.

**grace** [greis] 1. Gnade f; Gunst f; (Gnaden)Frist f; Grazie f, Anmut f; Anstand m; Zier(de) f; Reiz m; Tischgebet n; Your ♀ Euer Gnaden; 2. zieren, schmücken; begünstigen, auszeichnen; ~ful □ ['greisful] anmutig; ~fulness [~nis] Anmut f.

**gracious** □ ['greiʃəs] gnädig.

**gradation** [grə'deiʃən] Abstufung f.

**grade** [greid] 1. Grad m, Rang m; Stufe f; Qualität f; bsd. Am. = gradient; Am. Schule: Klasse f, Note f; make the ~ Am. Erfolg haben; ~ crossing bsd. Am. schienengleicher Bahnübergang; ~(d) school bsd. Am. Grundschule f; 2. abstufen; einstufen; ⊕ planieren.

**gradient** ⚞ etc. ['greidjənt] Steigung f.

**gradua|l** □ ['grædjuəl] stufenweise, allmählich; ~te 1. [~ueit] graduieren; (sich) abstufen; die Abschlußprüfung machen; promovieren; 2. univ. [~uit] Graduierte(r m) f; ~tion [grædju'eiʃən] Gradeinteilung f; Abschlußprüfung f; Promotion f.

**graft** [grɑ:ft] 1. ⚘ Pfropfreis n; Am. Schiebung f; 2. ⚘ pfropfen; ⚕ verpflanzen; Am. fig. schieben.

**grain** [grein] (Samen)Korn n; Getreide n; Gefüge n; fig. Natur f; Gran n (Gewicht).

**gram** [græm] = gramme.

**gramma|r** ['græmə] Grammatik f; ~r-school höhere Schule, Gymnasium m; Am. a. Mittelschule f; ~tical □ [grə'mætikəl] grammati(kali)sch.

**gramme** [græm] Gramm n.

**granary** ['grænəri] Kornspeicher m.

**grand** □ [grænd] 1. fig. großartig; erhaben; groß; Groß..., Haupt...; ♀ Old Party Am. Republikanische Partei; ~ stand Sport: (Haupt-)Tribüne f; 2. ♪ a. ~ piano Flügel m; Am. sl. tausend Dollar pl.; ~child ['græntʃaild] Enkel(in); ~eur [~ndʒə] Größe f, Hoheit f; Erhabenheit f; ~father Großvater m.

**grandiose** □ ['grændious] großartig.

**grand|mother** ['grænmʌðə] Großmutter f; ~parents [~npeərənts] pl. Großeltern pl.

**grange** [greindʒ] Gehöft n; Gut n; Am. Name für Farmerorganisation f.

**granny** F ['græni] Oma f.

**grant** [grɑ:nt] 1. Gewährung f; Unterstützung f; Stipendium n; 2. gewähren, bewilligen; verleihen; zugestehen; ⚞ übertragen; take for ~ed als selbstverständlich annehmen.

**granul|ate** ['grænjuleit] (sich) körnen; ~e [~ju:l] Körnchen n.

**grape** [greip] Weinbeere f, -traube f; ~fruit ⚘ ['greipfru:t] Pampelmuse f.

**graph** [græf] graphische Darstellung; ~ic(al □) ['græfik(əl)] graphisch; anschaulich; graphic arts pl. Graphik f; ~ite min. [~fait] Graphit m.

**grapple** ['græpl] entern; packen; ringen.

**grasp** [grɑ:sp] 1. Griff *m*; Bereich *m*; Beherrschung *f*; Fassungskraft *f*; 2. (er)greifen, packen; begreifen.

**grass** [grɑ:s] Gras *n*; Rasen *m*; *send to* ~ auf die Weide schicken; ~**hopper** ['grɑ:shɔpə] Heuschrecke *f*; ~ **roots** *pl. Am. pol. die* landwirtschaftlichen Bezirke, *die* Landbevölkerung; ~**widow(er)** F Strohwitwe(r *m*) *f*; ~**si**] grasig; Gras...

**grate** [greit] 1. (Kamin)Gitter *n*; (Feuer)Rost *m*; 2. (zer)reiben; mit *et.* knirschen; *fig.* verletzen.

**grateful** □ ['greitful] dankbar.

**grater** ['greitə] Reibeisen *n*.

**grati|fication** [grætifi'keiʃən] Befriedigung *f*; Freude *f*; ~**fy** ['grætifai] erfreuen; befriedigen.

**grating** ['greitiŋ] 1. □ schrill; unangenehm; 2. Gitter(werk) *n*.

**gratitude** ['grætitju:d] Dankbarkeit *f*.

**gratuit|ous** □ [grə'tju(:)itəs] unentgeltlich; freiwillig; ~**y** [~ti] Abfindung *f*; Gratifikation *f*; Trinkgeld *n*.

**grave** [greiv] 1. □ ernst; (ge)wichtig; gemessen; 2. Grab *n*; 3. [*irr.*] *mst fig.* (ein)graben; ~**digger** ['greivdigə] Totengräber *m*.

**gravel** ['grævəl] 1. Kies *m*; *s* Harngrieß *m*; 2. mit Kies bedecken.

**graven** ['greivən] *p.p. von* grave 3.

**graveyard** ['greivjɑ:d] Kirchhof *m*.

**gravitation** [grævi'teiʃən] Schwerkraft *f*; *fig.* Hang *m*.

**gravity** ['græviti] Schwere *f*; Wichtigkeit *f*; Ernst *m*; Schwerkraft *f*.

**gravy** *bsd. Am.* ['greivi] Fleischsaft *m*, Bratensoße *f*.

**gray** *bsd. Am.* [grei] Am. [grei] grau.

**graze** [greiz] 1. (ab)weiden; (ab)grasen; streifen, schrammen.

**grease** 1. [gri:s] Fett *n*; Schmiere *f*; 2. [gri:z] (be)schmieren.

**greasy** □ ['gri:zi] fettig; schmierig.

**great** □ [greit] *allg.* groß; Groß...; F großartig, ~**coat** ['greit'kout] Überzieher *m*; ~**grandchild** Urenkel(in); ~**grandfather** Urgroßvater *m*; ~**ly** [~tli] sehr; ~**ness** [~tnis] Größe *f*; Stärke *f*.

**greed** [gri:d] Gier *f*, ~**y** □ ['gri:di] (be)gierig (*of, for* nach); habgierig.

**Greek** [gri:k] 1. griechisch; 2. Griech|e *m*, -in *f*; Griechisch *n*.

**green** [gri:n] 1. □ grün (*a. fig.*); frisch (*Fisch etc.*); neu; Grün...; 2. Grün *n*; Rasen *m*; Wiese *f*; ~*s pl.* frisches Gemüse; ~**back** *Am.* ['gri:nbæk] Dollarnote *f*; ~**grocer** Gemüsehändler(in); ~**grocery** Gemüsehandlung (*f*); ~**horn** Grünschnabel *m*; ~**house** Gewächshaus *n*; ~**ish** [~niʃ] grünlich; ~**sickness** Bleichsucht *f*.

**greet** [gri:t] (be)grüßen; ~**ing** ['gri:tiŋ] Begrüßung *f*; Gruß *m*.

**grenade** ⚔ [gri'neid] Granate *f*.

**grew** [gru:] *pret. von* grow.

**grey** [grei] 1. □ grau; 2. Grau *n*; 3. grau machen *od.* werden; ~**hound** ['greihaund] Windhund *m*.

**grid** [grid] Gitter *n*; 📻, *f* Netz *n*; *Am. Fußball:* Spielfeld *n*; ~**iron** ['gridaiən] (Brat)Rost *m*.

**grief** [gri:f] Gram *m*, Kummer *m*; *come to* ~ zu Schaden kommen.

**griev|ance** ['gri:vəns] Beschwerde *f*; Mißstand *m*; ~**e** [gri:v] kränken; (sich) grämen; ~**ous** □ ['gri:vəs] kränkend, schmerzlich; schlimm.

**grill** [gril] 1. grillen; braten (*a. fig.*); 2. Bratrost *m*, Grill *m*; gegrilltes Fleisch; *a.* ~**room** Grillroom *m*.

**grim** □ [grim] grimmig; schrecklich.

**grimace** [gri'meis] 1. Fratze *f*, Grimasse *f*; 2. Grimassen schneiden.

**grim|e** [graim] Schmutz *m*; Ruß *m*; ~**y** □ ['graimi] schmutzig; rußig.

**grin** [grin] 1. Grinsen *n*; 2. grinsen.

**grind** [graind] 1. [*irr.*] (zer)reiben; mahlen; schleifen; Leierkasten *etc.* drehen; *fig.* schinden; mit *den Zähnen* knirschen; 2. Schinderei *f*; ~**stone** ['graindstoun] Schleif-, Mühlstein *m*.

**grip** [grip] 1. packen, fassen (*a. fig.*); 2. Griff *m*; Gewalt *f*; Herrschaft *f*; *Am.* = gripsack.

**gripe** [graip] Griff *m*; ~**s** *pl.* Kolik *f*; *bsd. Am.* Beschwerden *f/pl.*

**gripsack** *Am.* ['gripsæk] Handtasche *f*, -köfferchen *f*.

**grisly** ['grizli] gräßlich, schrecklich.

**gristle** ['grisl] Knorpel *m*.

**grit** [grit] 1. Kies *m*; Sand(stein) *m*; *fig.* Mut *m*; 2. knirschen (mit).

**grizzly** ['grizli] 1. grau; 2. Graubär *m*.

**groan** [groun] seufzen, stöhnen.

**grocer** ['grousə] Lebensmittelhändler *m*; ~**ies** [~əriz] *pl.* Lebensmittel *n/pl.*; ~**y** [~ri] Lebensmittelgeschäft *n*.

**groceteria** *Am.* [grousi'tiəriə] Selbstbedienungsladen *m*.

**groggy** ['grɔgi] taumelig; wackelig.

**groin** *anat.* [grɔin] Leistengegend *f*.

**groom** [grum] 1. Reit-, Stallknecht *m*; Bräutigam *m*; 2. pflegen; *Am. pol. Kandidaten* lancieren.

**groove** [gru:v] 1. Rinne *f*, Nut *f*; *fig.* Gewohnheit *f*; 2. nuten, falzen.

**grope** [group] (be)tasten, tappen.

**gross** [grous] 1. □ dick; grob; derb; † Brutto...; 2. Gros *n* (*12 Dutzend*); *in the* ~ im ganzen.

**grotto** ['grɔtou] Grotte *f*.

**grouch** *Am.* F [grautʃ] 1. quengeln, meckern; 2. Griesgram *m*; schlechte Laune; ~**y** ['grautʃi] quenglig.

**ground**[1] [graund] 1. *pret. u. p.p. von* **grind** 1; 2. ~ **glass** Mattglas *n.*

**ground**[2] [graund] 1. *mst* Grund *m*; Boden *m*; Gebiet *n*; Spiel- etc. Platz *m*; Beweg- etc. Grund *m*; ∮ Erde *f*; ~s *pl.* Grundstück *n*, Park(s *pl.*) *m*, Gärten *m/pl.*; Kaffee-Satz *m*; on the ~(s) of auf Grund (*gen.*); stand od. hold od. keep one's ~ sich behaupten; 2. niederlegen; (be)gründen; j-m die Anfangs-gründe beibringen; ∮ erden; ~**floor** ['graund'flɔ:] Erdgeschoß *n*; ~**hog** [~dhɔg] *bsd. Am.* Murmel-tier *n*; ~**less** □ [~dlis] grundlos; ~**staff** ⚓ Bodenpersonal *n*; ~**work** Grundlage *f.*

**group** [gru:p] 1. Gruppe *f*; 2. (sich) gruppieren.

**grove** [grouv] Hain *m*; Gehölz *n.*

**grovel** *mst fig.* ['grɔvl] kriechen.

**grow** [grou] [*irr.*] *v/i.* wachsen; werden; *v/t.* ∮ anpflanzen, an-bauen; ~**er** ['grouə] Bauer *m*; Züchter *m.*

**growl** [graul] knurren, brummen; ~**er** ['graulə] *fig.* Brummbär *m*; *Am. sl.* Bierkrug *m.*

**grow|n** [groun] 1. *p.p. von* **grow**; 2. *adj.* erwachsen; bewachsen; ~**n-up** ['grounʌp] 1. erwachsen; 2. Erwachsene(r *m*) *f*; ~**th** [grouθ] Wachstum *n*; (An)Wachsen *n*; Ent-wicklung *f*; Wuchs *m*; Gewächs *n*, Erzeugnis *n.*

**grub** [grʌb] 1. Raupe *f*, Larve *f*, Made *f*; *contp.* Prolet *m*; 2. graben; sich abmühen; ~**by** [grʌbi] schmie-rig.

**grudge** [grʌdʒ] 1. Groll *m*; 2. miß-gönnen; ungern geben *od.* tun *etc.*

**gruel** [gruəl] Haferschleim *m.*

**gruff** □ [grʌf] grob, schroff, barsch.

**grumble** ['grʌmbl] murren; (g)rol-len; ~**r** *fig.* [~lə] Brummbär *m.*

**grunt** [grʌnt] grunzen.

**guarant|ee** [gærən'ti:] 1. Bürge *m*; = **guaranty**; 2. bürgen für; ~**or** [~'tɔ:] Bürge *m*; ~**y** ['gærənti] Bürg-schaft *f*, Garantie *f*; Gewähr *f.*

**guard** [gɑ:d] 1. Wacht *f*; ✗ Wache *f*; Wächter *m*, Wärter *m*; ⚙ Schaffner *m*; Schutz(vorrichtung *f*) *m*; ~s *pl.* Garde *f*; be on (off) one's ~ (nicht) auf der Hut sein; 2. *v/t.* bewachen, (be)schützen (*from vor dat.*); *v/i.* sich hüten (*against vor dat.*); ~**ian** ['gɑ:djən] Hüter *m*, Wächter *m*; ⚙ Vormund *m*; *attr.* Schutz...; ~**ianship** [~nʃip] Obhut *f*; Vor-mundschaft *f.*

**guess** [ges] 1. Vermutung *f*; 2. ver-muten; (er)raten; *Am.* denken.

**guest** [gest] Gast *m*; ~**house** ['gesthaus] (Hotel)Pension *f*, Fremden-heim *n*; ~**room** Gast-, Fremden-zimmer *n.*

**guffaw** [gʌ'fɔ:] schallendes Ge-lächter.

**guidance** ['gaidəns] Führung *f*; (An)Leitung *f.*

**guide** [gaid] 1. Führer *m*; ⊕ Füh-rung *f*; *attr.* Führungs...; 2. leiten; führen; lenken; ~**book** ['gaidbuk] Reiseführer *m*; ~**post** Wegweiser *m.*

**guild** [gild] Gilde *f*, Innung *f*; ⊕**hall** ['gild'hɔ:l] Rathaus *n* (*Lon-don*).

**guile** [gail] Arglist *f*; ~**ful** □ ['gailful] arglistig; ~**less** □ ['gaillis] arglos.

**guilt** [gilt] Schuld *f*; Strafbarkeit *f*; ~**less** □ ['giltlis] schuldlos; un-kundig; ~**y** □ [~ti] schuldig; straf-bar.

**guinea** ['gini] Guinee *f* (*21 Schil-ling*); ~**pig** Meerschweinchen *n.*

**guise** [gaiz] Erscheinung *f*, Gestalt *f*; Maske *f.*

**guitar** ♪ [gi'tɑ:] Gitarre *f.*

**gulch** *Am.* [gʌlʃ] tiefe Schlucht.

**gulf** [gʌlf] Meerbusen *m*, Golf *m*; Abgrund *m*; Strudel *m.*

**gull** [gʌl] 1. Möwe *f*; Tölpel *m*; 2. übertölpeln; verleiten (*into zu*).

**gullet** ['gʌlit] Speiseröhre *f*; Gur-gel *f.*

**gulp** [gʌlp] Schluck *m*; Schlucken *n.*

**gum** [gʌm] 1. *a.* ~s *pl.* Zahnfleisch *n*; Gummi *n*; Klebstoff *m*; ~s *pl. Am.* Gummischuhe *m/pl.*; 2. gummie-ren; zukleben.

**gun** [gʌn] 1. Gewehr *n*; Flinte *f*; Geschütz *n*, Kanone *f*; *Am.* Re-volver *m*; big ~ F *fig.* hohes Tier; 2. *Am.* auf die Jagd gehen; ~**boat** ['gʌnbout] Kanonenboot *n*; ~**licence** Waffenschein *m*; ~**man** *Am.* Gangster *m*; ~**ner** ✗ ⚓ ['gʌnə] Kanonier *m*; ~**powder** Schießpulver *n*; ~**smith** Büchsen-macher *m.*

**gurgle** ['gə:gl] gluckern, gur-geln.

**gush** [gʌʃ] 1. Guß *m*; *fig.* Erguß *m*; 2. (sich) ergießen, schießen (*from aus*); *fig.* schwärmen; ~**er** ['gʌʃə] *fig.* Schwärmer(in); Ölquelle *f.*

**gust** [gʌst] Windstoß *m*, Bö *f.*

**gut** [gʌt] Darm *m*; ♪ Darmsaite *f*; ~s *pl.* Eingeweide *n/pl.*; das In-nere; *fig.* Mut *m.*

**gutter** ['gʌtə] Dachrinne *f*; Gosse *f* (*a. fig.*), Rinnstein *m.*

**guy** [gai] 1. Halteseil *n*; F Vogel-scheuche *f*; *Am.* F Kerl *m*; 2. ver-ulken.

**guzzle** ['gʌzl] saufen; fressen.

**gymnas|ium** [dʒim'neizjəm] Turn-halle *f*, -platz *m*; ~**tics** [~'næstiks] *pl.* Turnen *n*; Gymnastik *f.*

**gypsy** *bsd. Am.* ['dʒipsi] = **gipsy**.

**gyrate** [dʒaiə'reit] kreisen; wir-beln.

**gyroplane** ['dʒaiərəplein] Hub-schrauber *m.*

# H

**haberdasher** ['hæbədæʃə] Kurz-
warenhändler *m*; *Am.* Herrenarti-
kelhändler *m*; ~y [~əri] Kurzwaren
(-geschäft *n*) *f/pl.*; *Am.* Herren-
artikel *m/pl.*

**habit** ['hæbit] 1. (An)Gewohnheit
*f*; Verfassung *f*; Kleid(ung *f*) *n*;
*fall od.* get into bad ~s schlechte
Gewohnheiten annehmen; 2. (an-)
kleiden; ~able [~təbl] bewohnbar;
~ation [hæbi'teiʃən] Wohnung *f*.

**habitual** □ [hə'bitjuəl] gewohnt,
gewöhnlich; Gewohnheits...

**hack** [hæk] 1. Hieb *m*; Einkerbung
*f*; Miet-, Arbeitspferd *n* (*a. fig.*);
*a.* ~ writer literarischer Lohn-
schreiber *m*; 2. (zer)hacken.

**hackneyed** *fig.* ['hæknid] abgedroschen.

**had** [hæd] *pret. u. p.p. von* have.

**haddock** ['hædək] Schellfisch *m*.

**h(a)emorrhage** ['heməridʒ] Blut-
sturz *m*.

**hag** [hæg] (*mst fig.* alte) Hexe.

**haggard** □ ['hægəd] verstört; hager.

**haggle** ['hægl] feilschen, schachern.

**hail** [heil] 1. Hagel *m*; Anruf *m*;
2. (nieder)hageln (lassen); anrufen;
(be)grüßen; ~ *from* stammen aus;
~stone ['heilstoun] Hagelkorn *n*;
~storm Hagelschauer *m*.

**hair** [hɛə] Haar *n*; ~breadth
['hɛəbredθ] Haaresbreite *f*; ~cut
Haarschnitt *m*; ~do *Am.* Frisur *f*;
~dresser (*bsd.* Damen)Friseur *m*;
~drier [~draiə] Trockenhaube *f*;
Fön *m*; ~less ['hɛəlis] ohne Haare,
kahl; ~pin Haarnadel *f*; ~raising
['hɛəreiziŋ] haarsträubend; ~split-
ting Haarspalterei *f*; ~y ['hɛəri]
haarig.

**hale** [heil] gesund, frisch, rüstig.

**half** [hɑːf] 1. *pl.* **halves** [hɑːvz]
Hälfte *f*; by halves nur halb; go
halves halbpart machen, teilen
2. halb; ~ a crown eine halbe
Krone; ~back ['hɑːf'bæk] *Fußball:* Läufer *m*; ~breed ['hɑːf-
briːd] Halbblut *n*; ~caste Halbblut *n*; ~hearted □ ['hɑːf'hɑːtid]
lustlos, lau; ~length Brustbild *n*;
~penny ['heipni] halber Penny;
~time ['hɑːf'taim] *Sport:* Halb-
zeit *f*; ~way halbwegs; ~witted
einfältig, idiotisch.

**halibut** *ichth.* ['hælibət] Heilbutt *m*.

**hall** [hɔːl] Halle *f*; Saal *m*; Vorraum
*m*; Flur *m*; Diele *f*; Herren-, Gutshaus *n*; *univ.* Speisesaal *m*; ~ *of
residence* Studentenwohnheim *n*.

**halloo** [hə'luː] (hallo) rufen.

**hallow** ['hælou] heiligen, weihen;
♈mas [~oumæs] Allerheiligenfest *n*.

**halo** ['heilou] *ast.* Hof *m*; Heiligenschein *m*.

**halt** [hɔːlt] 1. Halt(estelle *f*) *m*;
Stillstand *m*; 2. (an)halten; *mst fig.*
hinken; schwanken.

**halter** ['hɔːltə] Halfter *f*; Strick *m*.

**halve** [hɑːv] halbieren; ~s [hɑːvz]
*pl. von half* 1.

**ham** [hæm] Schenkel *m*; Schinken
*m*.

**hamburger** *Am.* ['hæmbəːgə] Frikadelle *f*; mit Frikadelle belegtes
Brötchen.

**hamlet** ['hæmlit] Weiler *m*.

**hammer** ['hæmə] 1. Hammer *m*;
2. (be)hämmern.

**hammock** ['hæmək] Hängematte *f*.

**hamper** ['hæmpə] 1. Geschenk-,
Eßkorb *m*; 2. verstricken; behin-
dern.

**hamster** *zo.* ['hæmstə] Hamster *m*.

**hand** [hænd] 1. Hand *f* (*a. fig.*);
Handschrift *f*; Handbreite *f*;
(Uhr)Zeiger *m*; Mann *m*, Arbeiter
*m*; *Karten:* Blatt *n*; at ~ bei der
Hand; nahe bevorstehend; *at first* ~
aus erster Hand; *a good* (poor) ~ *at*
(un)geschickt in (*dat.*); ~ *and glove*
ein Herz und eine Seele; *change* ~s
den Besitzer wechseln; *lend a* ~
(mit) anfassen; *off* ~ aus dem Handgelenk *od.* Stegreif; *on* ~ ✝ vorrätig, auf Lager; *bsd. Am.* zur
Stelle, bereit; *on one's* ~s auf dem
Halse; *on the one* ~ einerseits; *on
the other* ~ andererseits; ~ *to* ~
Mann gegen Mann; *come to* ~
sich bieten; einlaufen (*Briefe*); 2.
reichen; ~ *about* herumreichen; ~
*down* vererben; ~ *in* einhändigen;
~ *over* aushändigen; ~bag
['hændbæg] Handtasche *f*; ~bill
Hand-, Reklamezettel *m*;
~brake ⊕ Handbremse *f*; ~cuff
Handfessel *f*; ~ful ['~dful] Hand-
voll *f*; F Plage *f*; ~glass Hand-
spiegel *m*; Leselupe *f*.

**handicap** ['hændikæp] 1. Handikap
*n*; Vorgaberennen *n*, Vorgabespiel
*n*; (Extra)Belastung *f*; 2. (extra)
belasten; beeinträchtigen.

**handi|craft** ['hændikrɑːft] Hand-
werk *n*; Handfertigkeit *f*; ~crafts-
man Handwerker *m*; ~work Handarbeit *f*; Werk *n*.

**handkerchief** ['hæŋkətʃi(ː)f] Taschentuch *n*; Halstuch *n*.

**handle** ['hændl] 1. Griff *m*; Stiel *m*;
Henkel *m*; Pumpen- *etc.* Schwengel
*m*; *fig.* Handhabe *f*; fly off the ~ F
platzen vor Wut; 2. anfassen; handhaben; behandeln; ~bar Lenk-
stange *f e-s Fahrrades*.

**hand|-luggage** ['hændlʌgidʒ]
Handgepäck *n*; ~made handgear-
beitet; ~me-downs *Am.* F *pl.* Fer-
tigkleidung *f*; getragene Kleider *pl.*;
~rail Geländer *n*; ~shake Hände-

druck *m*; ~some □ ['hænsəm] ansehnlich; hübsch; anständig; ~work Handarbeit *f*; ~writing Handschrift *f*; ~y □ ['hændi] geschickt; handlich; zur Hand.

hang [hæŋ] 1. [*irr.*] *v/t.* hängen; auf-, einhängen; verhängen; (*pret. u. p.p. mst ~ed*) (er)hängen; hängen lassen; *Tapete* ankleben; *v/i.* hängen; schweben; sich neigen; ~ *about* (*Am. around*) herumlungern; sich an *j-n* hängen; ~ *back* sich zurückhalten; ~ *on* sich klammern an (*acc.*); *fig.* hängen an (*dat.*); 2. Hang *m*; Fall *m e-r Gardine etc.*; F Wesen *n*; F *fig.* Kniff *m*; Dreh *m*.

hangar ['hæŋə] Flugzeughalle *f*.

hang-dog ['hæŋdɔg] Armesünder...

hanger ['hæŋə] Aufhänger *m*; Hirschfänger *m*; ~on *fig.* [~ər'ɔn] Klette *f*.

hanging ['hæŋiŋ] 1. Hänge...; 2. ~s *pl.* Behang *m*; Tapeten *f/pl.*

hangman ['hæŋmən] Henker *m*.

hang-nail ✍ ['hæŋneil] Niednagel *m*.

hang-over *sl.* ['hæŋouvə] Katzenjammer *m*, Kater *m*.

hanker ['hæŋkə] sich sehnen.

hap|hazard ['hæp'hæzəd] 1. Zufall *m*; *at ~* aufs Geratewohl; 2. zufällig; ~less □ ['hæplis] unglücklich.

happen ['hæpən] sich ereignen, geschehen; *he ~ed to be at home er war zufällig zu Hause; ~ (up)on* zufällig treffen auf (*acc.*); ~ *in Am.* F hereinschneien; ~ing ['hæpniŋ] Ereignis *n*.

happi|ly ['hæpili] glücklicherweise; ~ness [~inis] Glück(seligkeit *f*) *n*.

happy □ ['hæpi] *allg.* glücklich; beglückt; erfreut; erfreulich; geschickt; treffend; F angeheitert; ~-go-lucky F unbekümmert.

harangue [hə'ræŋ] 1. Ansprache *f*, Rede *f*; 2. *v/t.* feierlich anreden.

harass ['hærəs] belästigen, quälen.

harbo(u)r ['ha:bə] 1. Hafen *m*; Zufluchtsort *m*; 2. (be)herbergen; *Rache etc.* hegen; ankern; ~age [~əridʒ] Herberge *f*; Zuflucht *f*.

hard [ha:d] 1. *adj. allg.* hart; schwer; mühselig; streng; ausdauernd; fleißig; heftig; *Am.* stark (*Spirituosen*); ~ *of hearing* schwerhörig; 2. *adv.* stark; tüchtig; mit Mühe; ~ *by* nahe bei; ~ *up* in Not; ~-boiled ['ha:d'bɔild] hartgesotten; *Am.* gerissen; ~ *cash* Bargeld *n*; klingende Münze; ~en ['ha:dn] härten; hart machen *od.* werden; (sich) abhärten; *fig.* (sich) verhärten; ✝ sich festigen (*Preise*); ~headed nüchtern denkend; ~hearted □ hartherzig; ~ihood ['ha:dihud] Kühnheit *f*; ~iness [~inis] Widerstandsfähigkeit *f*, Härte *f*; ~ly ['ha:dli] kaum; streng;

mit Mühe; ~ness ['ha:dnis] Härte *f*; Schwierigkeit *f*; Not *f*; ~pan *Am.* harter Boden, *fig.* Grundlage *f*; ~ship ['ha:dʃip] Bedrängnis *f*, Not *f*; Härte *f*; ~ware Eisenwaren *f/pl.*; ~y □ ['ha:di] kühn; widerstandsfähig, hart; abgehärtet; winterfest (*Pflanze*).

hare [hεə] Hase *m*; ~bell ⚘ ['hεəbel] Glockenblume *f*; ~-brained zerfahren; ~lip *anat.* ['hεə'lip] Hasenscharte *f*.

hark [ha:k] horchen (*to* auf *acc.*).

harlot ['ha:lət] Hure *f*.

harm [ha:m] 1. Schaden *m*; Unrecht *n*, Böse(s) *n*; 2. beschädigen, verletzen; schaden, Leid zufügen (*dat.*); ~ful □ ['ha:mful] schädlich; ~less □ ['ha:mlis] harmlos; unschädlich.

harmon|ic [ha:'mɔnik] (~ally), ~ious □ [ha:'mounjəs] harmonisch; ~ize ['ha:mənaiz] *v/t.* in Einklang bringen; *v/i.* harmonieren; ~y [~ni] Harmonie *f*.

harness ['ha:nis] 1. Harnisch *m*; Zug-Geschirr *n*; *die in ~ in den Sielen sterben; 2. anschirren; bändigen; *Wasserkraft* nutzbar machen.

harp [ha:p] 1. Harfe *f*; 2. Harfe spielen; ~ (*up*)*on* herumreiten auf (*dat.*). [2. harpunieren.]

harpoon [ha:'pu:n] 1. Harpune *f*;]

harrow ✍ ['hærou] 1. Egge *f*; 2. eggen, *fig.* quälen, martern.

harry ['hæri] plündern; quälen.

harsh □ [ha:ʃ] rauh; herb; grell; streng; schroff; barsch.

hart *zo.* [ha:t] Hirsch *m*.

harvest ['ha:vist] 1. Ernte(zeit) *f*; Ertrag *m*; 2. ernten; einbringen.

has [hæz] 3. *sg. pres. von* have.

hash [hæʃ] 1. gehacktes Fleisch; *Am.* F Essen *n*, Fraß *m*; *fig.* Mischmasch *m*; 2. (zer)hacken.

hast|e [heist] Eile *f*; Hast *f*; *make ~* (sich be)eilen; ~en ['heisn] (sich be)eilen; *j-n* antreiben; *et.* beschleunigen; ~y □ ['heisti] (vor)eilig; hastig; hitzig, heftig.

hat [hæt] Hut *m*.

hatch [hætʃ] 1. Brut *f*, Hecke *f*; ⚓, ☇ Luke *f*; *serving ~* Durchreiche *f*; 2. (aus)brüten (*a. fig.*).

hatchet ['hætʃit] Beil *n*.

hatchway ⚓ ['hætʃwei] Luke *f*.

hat|e [heit] 1. Haß *m*; 2. hassen; ~ful □ ['heitful] verhaßt; abscheulich; ~red ['heitrid] Haß *m*.

haught|iness ['hɔ:tinis] Stolz *m*; Hochmut *m*; ~y □ ['hɔ:ti] stolz; hochmütig.

haul [hɔ:l] 1. Ziehen *n*; (Fisch-)Zug *m*; *Am.* Transport(weg) *m*; 2. ziehen; schleppen; transportieren; ⚒ fördern; ⚓ abdrehen; ~ *down one's flag* die Flagge streichen; *fig.* sich geschlagen geben.

**haunch** [hɔ:ntʃ] Hüfte *f*; Keule *f von Wild.*

**haunt** [hɔ:nt] **1.** Aufenthaltsort *m*; Schlupfwinkel *m*; **2.** oft besuchen; heimsuchen; verfolgen; spuken in (*dat.*).

**have** [hæv] [*irr.*] *v/t.* haben; bekommen; *Mahlzeit* einnehmen; lassen; ~ to do tun müssen; *I* ~ *my hair cut* ich lasse mir das Haar schneiden; *he will* ~ *it that* ... er behauptet, daß ...; *I had better go* es wäre besser, wenn ich ginge; *I had rather go* ich möchte lieber gehen; ~ *about one* bei *od.* an sich haben; ~ *on* anhaben; ~ *it out with* sich auseinandersetzen mit; *v/aux.* haben; *bei v/i. oft* sein; ~ *come* gekommen sein.

**haven** ['heivn] Hafen *m* (*a. fig.*).

**havoc** ['hævək] Verwüstung *f*; *make* ~ *of*, *play* ~ *with od. among* verwüsten; übel zurichten.

**haw** ♀ [hɔ:] Hagebutte *f*.

**Hawaiian** [ha:'waiiən] **1.** hawaiisch; **2.** Hawaiier(in).

**hawk** [hɔ:k] **1.** Habicht *m*; Falke *m*; **2.** sich räuspern; hausieren mit.

**hawthorn** ♀ ['hɔ:θɔ:n] Weißdorn *m*.

**hay** [hei] **1.** Heu *n*; **2.** heuen; ~**cock** ['heikɔk] Heuhaufen *m*; ~**fever** Heuschnupfen *m*; ~**loft** Heuboden *m*; ~**maker** *bsd.* Am. K.o.-Schlag *m*; ~**rick** = haycock; ~**seed** *bsd. Am.* F Bauerntölpel *m*; ~**stack** = haycock.

**hazard** ['hæzəd] **1.** Zufall *m*; Gefahr *f*, Wagnis *n*; Hasard(spiel) *n*; **2.** wagen; ~**ous** □ [~dəs] gewagt.

**haze** [heiz] **1.** Dunst *m*; **2.** ♣ *u. Am.* schinden; F schurigeln.

**hazel** ['heizl] **1.** ♀ Hasel(staude) *f*; **2.** nußbraun; ~**nut** Haselnuß *f*.

**hazy** □ ['heizi] dunstig; *fig.* unklar.

**H-bomb** ⚔ ['eitʃbɔm] H-Bombe *f*, Wasserstoffbombe *f*.

**he** [hi:] **1.** er; ~ *who* derjenige, welcher; **2.** Mann *m*; *zo.* Männchen *n*; **3.** *adj. in Zssgn:* männlich, ...männchen *n*; ~**goat** Ziegenbock *m*.

**head** [hed] **1.** *allg.* Kopf *m* (*a. fig.*); Haupt *n* (*a. fig.*); *nach Zahlwort:* Mann *m* (*a. pl.*); Stück *n* (*a. pl.*); Leiter(in); Chef *m*; Kopfende *n e-s Bettes etc.*; Kopfseite *f e-r Münze*; Gipfel *m*; Quelle *f*; *Schiffs*-Vorderteil *n*; Hauptpunkt *m*, Abschnitt *m*; Überschrift *f*; *come to a* ~ eitern (*Geschwür*); *fig.* sich zuspitzen, zur Entscheidung kommen; *get it into one's* ~ *that* ... es sich in den Kopf setzen, daß; ~ *over heels* Hals über Kopf; **2.** erst; Ober...; Haupt...; **3.** *v/t.* (an)führen; an der Spitze von *et.* stehen; vorausgehen (*dat.*); mit e-r Überschrift versehen; ~ *off* ablenken; *v/i.* ♣ zusteuern (*for auf acc.*); *Am.* entspringen (*Fluß*); ~**ache** ['hedeik] Kopfweh *n*; ~

**dress** Kopfputz *m*; Frisur *f*; ~**gear** Kopfbedeckung *f*; Zaumzeug *n*; ~**ing** ['hediŋ] Brief-, Titelkopf *m*, Rubrik *f*; Überschrift *f*, Titel *m*; *Sport:* Kopfball *m*; ~**land** ['hedlənd] Vorgebirge *n*; ~**light** *mot.* Scheinwerfer(licht *n*) *m*; ~**line** Überschrift *f*; Schlagzeile *f*; ~*s pl. Radio:* das Wichtigste in Kürze; ~**long 1.** *adj.* ungestüm; **2.** *adv.* kopfüber; ~**master** Direktor *m e-r Schule*; ~**phone** *Radio:* Kopfhörer *m*; ~**quarters** *pl.* ⚔ Hauptquartier *n*; Zentral(stell)e *f*; ~**strong** halsstarrig; ~**waters** *pl.* Quellgebiet *n*; ~**way** Fortschritt(e *pl.*) *m*; *make* ~ vorwärtskommen; ~**word** Stichwort *n e-s Wörterbuchs*; ~**y** □ ['hedi] ungestüm; voreilig; zu Kopfe steigend.

**heal** [hi:l] heilen; ~ *up* zuheilen.

**health** [helθ] Gesundheit *f*; ~**ful** □ ['helθful] gesund; heilsam; ~**resort** Kurort *m*; ~**y** □ ['helθi] gesund.

**heap** [hi:p] **1.** Haufe(n) *m*; **2.** *a.* ~ *up* (auf)häufen; überhäufen.

**hear** [hiə] [*irr.*] hören; erfahren; anhören, *j-m* zuhören; erhören; *Zeugen* verhören; *Lektion* abhören; ~**d** [hə:d] *pret. u. p.p. von hear*; ~**er** ['hiərə] (Zu)Hörer(in); ~**ing** [~riŋ] Gehör *n*; Audienz *f*; *t⅞* Verhör *n*; Hörweite *f*; ~**say** Hörensagen *n*.

**hearse** [hə:s] Leichenwagen *m*.

**heart** [hɑ:t] *allg.* Herz *n* (*a. fig.*); Innere(s) *n*; Kern *m*; *fig.* Schatz *m*; *by* ~ auswendig; *out of* ~ mutlos; *lay to* ~ sich zu Herzen nehmen; *lose* ~ den Mut verlieren; *take* ~ sich ein Herz fassen; ~**ache** ['hɑ:teik] Kummer *m*; ~**break** Herzeleid *n*; ~**breaking** □ [~kiŋ] herzzerbrechend; ~**broken** gebrochenen Herzens; ~**burn** Sodbrennen *n*; ~**en** ['hɑ:tn] ermutigen; ~**failure** ⚕ Herzversagen *n*; ~**felt** innig, tief empfunden.

**hearth** [hɑ:θ] Herd *m* (*a. fig.*).

**heart|less** □ ['hɑ:tlis] herzlos; ~**rending** ['hɑ:trendiŋ] herzzerreißend; ~ *transplant* Herzverpflanzung *f*; ~**y** □ ['hɑ:ti] □ herzlich; aufrichtig; gesund; herzhaft.

**heat** [hi:t] **1.** *allg.* Hitze *f*; Wärme *f*; Eifer *m*; *Sport:* Gang *m*, einzelner Lauf; *zo.* Läufigkeit *f*; **2.** heizen; (sich) erhitzen (*a. fig.*); ~**er** ⊕ ['hi:tə] Erhitzer *m*; Ofen *m*.

**heath** [hi:θ] Heide *f*; ♀ Heidekraut *n*.

**heathen** ['hi:ðən] **1.** Heid|e *m*, -in *f*; **2.** heidnisch.

**heather** ['heðə] Heide(kraut *n*) *f*.

**heat|ing** ['hi:tiŋ] Heizung *f*; *attr.* Heiz...; ~ *lightning Am.* Wetterleuchten *n*.

**heave** [hi:v] **1.** Heben *n*; Übelkeit *f*;

2. [*irr.*] *v/t.* heben; schwellen; *Seufzer* ausstoßen; *Anker* lichten; *v/i.* sich heben, wogen, schwellen.

**heaven** ['hevn] Himmel *m*; **~ly** [~nli] himmlisch.

**heaviness** ['hevinis] Schwere *f*, Druck *m*; Schwerfälligkeit *f*; Schwermut *f*.

**heavy** □ ['hevi] *allg.* schwer; schwermütig; schwerfällig; trüb; drückend; heftig (*Regen etc.*); unwegsam (*Straße*); Schwer...; **~ current** ⚡ Starkstrom *m*; **~ handed** ungeschickt; **~-hearted** niedergeschlagen; **~-weight** *Boxen*: Schwergewicht *n*.

**heckle** ['hekl] durch Zwischenfragen in die Enge treiben.

**hectic** ⚕ ['hektik] hektisch (*auszehrend*; *sl.* fieberhaft erregt).

**hedge** [hedʒ] 1. Hecke *f*; 2. *v/t.* einhegen, einzäunen; umgeben; **~ up** sperren; *v/i.* sich decken; sich nicht festlegen; **~hog** *zo.* ['hedʒhɔg] Igel *m*; *Am.* Stachelschwein *n*; **~row** Hecke *f*.

**heed** [hiːd] 1. Beachtung *f*, Aufmerksamkeit *f*; *take ~ of*, *give ed.* *pay ~ to* achtgeben auf (*acc.*), beachten; 2. beachten, achten auf (*acc.*); **~less** □ ['hiːdlis] unachtsam; unbekümmert (*of* um).

**heel** [hiːl] 1. Ferse *f*; Absatz *m*; *Am. sl.* Lump *m*; *head over ~s* Hals über Kopf; *down at ~* mit schiefen Absätzen; *fig.* abgerissen; schlampig; 2. mit e-m Absatz versehen; **~ed** *Am.* F finanzstark; **~er** *Am. sl. pol.* ['hiːlə] Befehlsempfänger *m*.

**heft** [heft] Gewicht *n*; *Am.* F Hauptteil *m*.

**heifer** ['hefə] Färse *f* (*junge Kuh*).

**height** [hait] Höhe *f*; Höhepunkt *m*; **~en** ['haitn] erhöhen; vergrößern.

**heinous** □ ['heinəs] abscheulich.

**heir** [ɛə] Erbe *m*; *~ apparent* rechtmäßiger Erbe; **~ess** ['ɛəris] Erbin *f*; **~loom** ['ɛəluːm] Erbstück *n*.

**held** [held] *pret. u. p.p. von* hold 2.

**helibus** *Am.* F ['helibʌs] Lufttaxi *n*.

**helicopter** ✈ ['helikɔptə] Hubschrauber *m*.

**hell** [hel] Hölle *f*; *attr.* Höllen...; *what the ~ ...?* F was zum Teufel ...?; *raise ~* Krach machen; **~bent** ['helbent] *Am. sl.* unweigerlich entschlossen; **~ish** □ ['heliʃ] höllisch.

**hello** ['he'lou] hallo!

**helm** ⚓ [helm] (Steuer)Ruder *n*.

**helmet** ['helmit] Helm *m*.

**helmsman** ⚓ ['helmzmən] Steuermann *m*.

**help** [help] 1. *allg.* Hilfe *f*; (Hilfs-)Mittel *n*; (Dienst)Mädchen *n*; 2. *v/t.* (ab)helfen (*dat.*); unterlassen; *bei Tisch* geben, reichen;

*~ o.s.* sich bedienen, zulangen; *I could not ~ laughing* ich konnte nicht umhin zu lachen; *v/i.* helfen, dienen; **~er** ['helpə] Helfer(in), Gehilf|e *m*, -in *f*; **~ful** □ [~pful] hilfreich; nützlich; **~ing** [~piŋ] Portion *f*; **~less** □ [~plis] hilflos; **~lessness** [~snis] Hilflosigkeit *f*; **~mate**, **~meet** Gehilf|e *m*, -in *f*; Gattin *f*.

**helter-skelter** ['heltə'skeltə] holterdiepolter.

**helve** [helv] Stiel *m*, Griff *m*.

**Helvetian** [hel'viːʃjən] Helvetier (-in); *attr.* Schweizer...

**hem** [hem] 1. Saum *m*; 2. *v/t.* säumen; *~ in* einschließen; *v/i.* sich räuspern.

**hemisphere** ['hemisfiə] Halbkugel *f*.

**hem-line** ['hemlain] *Kleid:* Saum *m*.

**hemlock** ♀ ['hemlɔk] Schierling *m*; **~-tree** Schierlingstanne *f*.

**hemp** [hemp] Hanf *m*.

**hemstitch** ['hemstitʃ] Hohlsaum *m*.

**hen** [hen] Henne *f*; *Vogel*-Weibchen *n*.

**hence** [hens] weg; hieraus; daher; von jetzt an; *a year ~* heute übers Jahr; **~forth** ['hens'fɔːθ], **~forward** [~ɔː'wəd] von nun an.

**hen|-coop** ['henkuːp] Hühnerstall *m*; **~pecked** unter dem Pantoffel (stehend).

**hep** *Am. sl.* [hep]: *to be ~ to* kennen; **~cat** *Am. sl.* ['hepkæt] Eingeweihte(r *m*) *f*; Jazzfanatiker(in).

**her** [hə:, hə] sie; ihr; ihr(e).

**herald** ['herəld] 1. Herold *m*; 2. (sich) ankündigen; *~ in* einführen; **~ry** [~dri] Wappenkunde *f*, Heraldik *f*.

**herb** [hə:b] Kraut *n*; **~age** ['hə:bidʒ] Gras *n*; Weide *f*; **~ivorous** [hə:-'bivərəs] pflanzenfressend.

**herd** [hə:d] 1. Herde *f* (*a. fig.*); 2. *v/t.* Vieh hüten; *v/i. a. ~ together* in e-r Herde leben; zs.-hausen; **~er** ['hə:də], **~sman** ['hə:dzmən] Hirt *m*.

**here** [hiə] hier; hierher; *~'s to ...!* auf das Wohl von ...!

**here|after** [hiər'ɑ:ftə] 1. künftig; 2. Zukunft *f*; **~by** ['hiə'bai] hierdurch.

**heredit|ary** [hi'reditəri] erblich; Erb...; **~y** [~ti] Erblichkeit *f*.

**here|in** ['hiər'in] hierin; **~of** [hiər-'ɔv] hiervon.

**heresy** ['herəsi] Ketzerei *f*.

**heretic** ['herətik] Ketzer(in).

**here|tofore** ['hiətu'fɔ:] bis jetzt; ehemals; **~upon** ['hiərə'pɔn] hierauf; **~with** hiermit.

**heritage** ['heritidʒ] Erbschaft *f*.

**hermit** ['hə:mit] Einsiedler *m*.

**hero** ['hiərou] Held *m*; **~ic(al** □) [hi'rouik(əl)] heroisch; heldenhaft;

Helden...; ~ine ['herouin] Heldin f; ~ism [~izəm] Heldenmut m, -tum n.

heron zo. ['herən] Reiher m.

herring ichth. ['heriŋ] Hering m.

hers [hə:z] der (die, das) ihrige; ihr.

herself [hə:'self] (sie, ihr, sich) selbst; sich; of ~ von selbst; by ~ allein.

hesitat|e ['heziteit] zögern, un-schlüssig sein; Bedenken tragen; ~ion [hezi'teiʃən] Zögern n; Un-schlüssigkeit f; Bedenken n.

hew [hju:] [irr.] hauen, hacken; ~n [hju:n] p.p. von hew.

hey [hei] ei!; hei!; he!, heda!

heyday ['heidei] 1. heisa!; oho!; 2. fig. Höhepunkt m, Blüte f.

hi [hai] hi!, heda!; hallo!

hicc|ough, ~up ['hikʌp] 1 Schluk-ken m; 2. schlucken; den Schluk-ken haben.

hid [hid] pret. u. p.p. von hide 2; ~den ['hidn] p.p. von hide 2.

hide [haid] 1. Haut f; 2. [irr.] (sich) verbergen, verstecken; ~-and-seek ['haidənd'si:k] Versteckspiel n.

hidebound fig. ['haidbaund] eng-herzig.

hideous □ ['hidiəs] scheußlich.

hiding ['haidiŋ] F Tracht f Prügel; Verbergen n; ~-place Versteck n.

hi-fi Am. ['hai'fai] = high-fidelity.

high [hai] 1. adj. □ allg. hoch; vor-nehm; gut, edel (Charakter); stolz; hochtrabend; angegangen (Fleisch); extrem; stark; üppig, flott (Leben); Hoch...; Ober...; with a ~ hand arrogant, anmaßend; in ~ spirits in gehobener Stimmung, guter Lau-ne; ~ life die vornehme Welt; ~ time höchste Zeit; ~ words heftige Worte; 2. meteor. Hoch n; bsd. Am. für Zssgn wie high school, etc.; 3. adv. hoch; sehr, mächtig; ~ball Am. ['haibɔ:l] Whisky m mit Soda; ~-bred vornehm erzogen; ~-brow F 1. Intellektuelle(r m) f; 2. betont intellektuell; ~-class erstklassig; ~-fidelity mit höchster Wieder-gabetreue, Hi-Fi; ~-grade hoch-wertig; ~-handed anmaßend; ~-land ['hailənd] Hochland n; ~-lights pl. fig. Höhepunkte m/pl.; ~ly ['haili] hoch; sehr; speak ~ of s.o. j-n loben; ~-minded hochher-zig; ~ness ['hainis] Höhe f; fig. Hoheit f; ~-pitched schrill (Ton); steil (Dach); ~-power: ~ station Großkraftwerk n; ~-road Land-straße f; ~ school höhere Schule; ~-strung überempfindlich; ~ tea frühes Abendessen mit Tee u. Fleisch etc.; ~-water Hochwasser n; ~way Landstraße f; fig. Weg m; ~ code Straßenverkehrsordnung f; ~wayman Straßenräuber m.

hike F [haik] 1. wandern; 2. Wan-

derung f; bsd. Am. F Erhöhung f (Preis etc.); ~r ['haikə] Wanderer m.

hilarious □ [hi'lɛəriəs] ausgelassen.

hill [hil] Hügel m, Berg m; ~billy Am. F ['hilbili] Hinterwäldler m; ~ock ['hilək] kleiner Hügel; ~side ['hil'said] Hang m; ~y ['hili] hüge-lig.

hilt [hilt] Griff m (bsd. am Degen).

him [him] ihn; ihm; den, dem(je-nigen); ~self [him'self] (er, ihm, ihn, sich) selbst; sich; of ~ von selbst; by ~ allein.

hind¹ zo. [haind] Hirschkuh f.

hind² [~] Hinter...; ~er 1. ['haində] hintere(r, -s); Hinter...; 2. ['hində] v/t. hindern (from an dat.); hem-men; ~most ['haindmoust] hin-terst, letzt.

hindrance ['hindrəns] Hindernis n.

hinge [hindʒ] 1. Türangel f; Schar-nier n; fig. Angelpunkt m; 2. ~ upon fig. abhängen von.

hint [hint] 1. Wink m; Anspielung f; 2. andeuten; anspielen (at auf acc.).

hinterland ['hintəlænd] Hinterland n. [butte f.]

hip [hip] anat. Hüfte f; ♀ Hage-]

hippopotamus zo. [hipə'pɔtəməs] Flußpferd n.

hire ['haiə] 1. Miete f; Entgelt m, n, Lohn m; 2. mieten; j-n anstellen; ~ out vermieten.

his [hiz] sein(e); der (die, das) sei-nige.

hiss [his] v/i. zischen; zischeln; v/t. a. ~ off auszischen, auspfeifen.

histor|ian [his'tɔ:riən] Historiker m; ~ic(al □) [his'tɔrik(əl)] histo-risch, geschichtlich; Geschichts...; ~y ['histəri] Geschichte f.

hit [hit] 1. Schlag m, Stoß m; fig. (Seiten)Hieb m; (Glücks)Treffer m; thea., ♪ Schlager m; 2. [irr.] schlagen, stoßen; treffen; auf et. stoßen; Am. F eintreffen in (dat.) ~ s.o. a blow j-m e-n Schlag ver-setzen; ~ it off with F sich vertragen mit; ~ (up)on (zufällig) kommen od. stoßen od. verfallen auf (acc.).

hitch [hitʃ] 1. Ruck m; ♣ Knoten m; fig. Haken m, Hindernis n; 2 rük-ken; (sich) festmachen, festhaken; hängenbleiben; rutschen; ~-hike F ['hitʃhaik] per Anhalter fahren.

hither lit. ['hiðə] hierher; ~to bisher.

hive [haiv] 1. Bienenstock m; Bienenschwarm m; fig. Schwarm m; 2. ~ up aufspeichern; zs.-woh-nen.

hoard [hɔ:d] 1. Vorrat m, Schatz m; 2. a. ~ up aufhäufen; horten.

hoarfrost ['hɔ:'frɔst] (Rauh)Reif m.

hoarse □ [hɔ:s] heiser, rauh.

hoary ['hɔ:ri] (alters)grau.

hoax [houks] 1. Täuschung f; Falschmeldung f; 2. foppen.

hob [hɔb] = hobgoblin; raise ~ bsd. Am. F Krach schlagen.

**hobble** ['hɔbl] 1. Hinken n, Humpeln n; F Klemme f, Patsche f; 2. v/i. humpeln, hinken (a. fig.); v/t. an den Füßen fesseln.

**hobby** ['hɔbi] fig Steckenpferd n, Hobby n; ~-horse Steckenpferd n; Schaukelpferd n.

**hobgoblin** ['hɔbgɔblin] Kobold m.

**hobo** Am. sl. ['houbou] Landstreicher m.

**hock¹** [hɔk] Rheinwein m.

**hock²** zo. [.] Sprunggelenk n.

**hod** [hɔd] Mörteltrog m.

**hoe** ⚹ [hou] 1. Hacke f; 2. hacken.

**hog** [hɔg] 1. Schwein n (a. fig.); 2. Mähne stutzen; mot. drauflos rasen; ~gish [] ['hɔgiʃ] schweinisch; gefräßig.

**hoist** [hɔist] 1. Aufzug m; 2. hochziehen, hissen.

**hokum** sl. ['houkəm] Mätzchen n/pl.; Kitsch m; Humbug m.

**hold** [hould] 1. Halten n; Halt m, Griff m; Gewalt f, Einfluß m; ⚓ Lade-, Frachtraum m; catch (od. get, lay, take, seize) ~ of erfassen, ergreifen; sich aneignen; keep ~ of festhalten; 2. [irr.] v/t. allg. halten; fest-, aufhalten; enthalten; fig. behalten; Versammlung etc. abhalten; (inne)haben; Ansicht vertreten; Gedanken etc. hegen; halten für; glauben; behaupten; ~ one's ground, ~ one's own sich behaupten; ~ the line teleph. am Apparat bleiben; ~ on et. (an s-m Platz fest)halten; ~ over aufschieben; ~ up aufrecht halten; (unter-) stützen; aufhalten; (räuberisch) überfallen; v/i. (fest)halten; gelten; sich bewähren; standhalten; ~ forth Reden halten; ~ good od. true gelten; sich bestätigen; ~ off sich fernhalten; ~ on ausharren; fortdauern; sich festhalten; teleph. am Apparat bleiben; ~ to festhalten an (dat.); ~ up sich (aufrecht) halten; ~er ['houldə] Pächter m; Halter m (Gerät); Inhaber(in) (bsd. ✝); ~ing [.diŋ] Halten n; Halt m; Pachtgut n; Besitz m; ~ company Dachgesellschaft f; ~-over Am. Rest m; ~-up Raubüberfall m; Stauung f, Stockung f.

**hole** [houl] 1. Loch n; Höhle f; F fig. Klemme f; pick ~s in bekritteln; 2. aushöhlen; durchlöchern.

**holiday** ['hɔlədi] Feiertag m; freier Tag; ~s pl. Ferien pl., Urlaub m; ~-maker Urlauber(in).

**holler** Am. F ['hɔlə] laut rufen.

**hollow** ['hɔlou] 1. [] hohl; leer; falsch; 2. Höhle f, (Aus)Höhlung f; Land-Senke f; 3. aushöhlen.

**holly** ♀ ['hɔli] Stechpalme f.

**holster** ['houlstə] Pistolentasche f.

**holy** ['houli] heilig; ♀ Thursday Gründonnerstag m; ~ water Weihwasser n; ♀ Week Karwoche f.

**homage** ['hɔmidʒ] Huldigung f; do od. pay od. render ~ huldigen (to dat.).

**home** [houm] 1. Heim n; Haus n, Wohnung f; Heimat f; Mal n; at ~ zu Hause; 2. adj. (ein)heimisch, inländisch; wirkungsvoll; tüchtig (Schlag etc.); ♀ Office Innenministerium n; ~ rule Selbstregierung f; ♀ Secretary Innenminister m; ~ trade Binnenhandel m; 3. adv. heim, nach Hause; an die richtige Stelle; gründlich; hit od. strike ~ den rechten Fleck treffen; ♀ Counties die Grafschaften um London; ~ economics Am. Hauswirtschaftslehre f; ~-felt ['houmfelt] tief empfunden; ~-less [houmlis] heimatlos; ~like anheimelnd, gemütlich; ~ly [.li] anheimelnd; häuslich; fig. hausbacken; schlicht; anspruchslos; reizlos; ~-made selbstgemacht, Hausmacher...; ~sickness Heimweh n; ~stead Anwesen n; ~ team Sport: Gastgeber m/pl.; ~ward(s) ['houmwəd(z)] heimwärts (gerichtet); Heim...; ~work Hausaufgabe(n pl.) f, Schularbeiten f/pl.

**homicide** ['hɔmisaid] Totschlag m; Mord m; Totschläger(in).

**homogeneous** [] [hɔmə'dʒi:njəs] homogen, gleichartig.

**hone** ⊕ [houn] 1. Abziehstein m; 2. Rasiermesser abziehen.

**honest** [] ['ɔnist] ehrlich, rechtschaffen; aufrichtig; echt; ~y [.ti] Ehrlichkeit f, Rechtschaffenheit f; Aufrichtigkeit f.

**honey** ['hʌni] Honig m; fig. Liebling m; ~comb [.ikoum] (Honig-) Wabe f; ~ed [.hʌnid] honigsüß; ~moon 1. Flitterwochen f/pl.; 2. die Flitterwochen verleben.

**honk** mot. [hɔŋk] hupen, tuten.

**honky-tonk** Am. sl. ['hɔŋkitɔŋk] Spelunke f.

**honorary** ['ɔnərəri] Ehren...; ehrenamtlich.

**hono(u)r** ['ɔnə] 1. Ehre f; Achtung f; Würde f; fig. Zierde f; Your ♀ Euer Gnaden; 2. (be)ehren; ✝ honorieren; ~able [] ['ɔnərəbl] ehrenvoll; redlich; ehrbar; ehrenwert.

**hood** [hud] 1. Kapuze f; mot. Verdeck n; Am. (Motor)Haube f; ⊕ Kappe f; 2. mit e-r Kappe etc. bekleiden; ein-, verhüllen.

**hoodlum** Am. F ['hu:dləm] Strolch m.

**hoodoo** bsd. Am. ['hu:du:] Unglücksbringer m; Pech n (Unglück).

**hoodwink** ['hudwiŋk] täuschen.

**hooey** Am. sl. ['hu:i] Quatsch m.

**hoof** [hu:f] Huf m; Klaue f.

**hook** [huk] 1. (bsd. Angel)Haken m; Sichel f; by ~ or by crook so oder so;

**2.** (sich) (zu-, fest)haken; angeln (*a. fig.*); ~y ['huki] **1.** hakig; **2.**: *play* ~ *Am. sl.* (die Schule) schwänzen.

**hoop** [hu:p] **1.** *Faß-* etc. Reif(en) *m*; ⊕ Ring *m*; **2.** *Fässer* binden.

**hooping-cough** ['hu:piŋkɔf] Keuchhusten *m*.

**hoot** [hu:t] **1.** Geschrei *n*; **2.** *v/i.* heulen; johlen; *mot.* hupen; *v/t.* auspfeifen, auszischen.

**Hoover** ['hu:və] **1.** Staubsauger *m*; **2.** (mit e-m Staubsauger) saugen.

**hop** [hɔp] **1.** ♣ Hopfen *m*; Sprung *m*; F Tanzerei *f*; **2.** hüpfen, springen (über *acc.*).

**hope** [houp] **1.** Hoffnung *f*; **2.** hoffen (*for* auf *acc.*); ~ *in* vertrauen auf (*acc.*); ~**ful** □ ['houpful] hoffnungsvoll; ~**less** □ ['houplis] hoffnungslos; verzweifelt.

**horde** [hɔ:d] Horde *f*.

**horizon** [hə'raizn] Horizont *m*.

**horn** [hɔ:n] Horn *n*; Schalltrichter *m*; *mot.* Hupe *f*; ~s *pl.* Geweih *n*; ~ *of plenty* Füllhorn *n*.

**hornet** *zo.* ['hɔ:nit] Hornisse *f*.

**horn|swoggle** *Am. sl.* ['hɔ:nswɔgl] *j-n* 'reinlegen; ~y ['hɔ:ni] hornig; schwielig.

**horr|ible** □ ['hɔrəbl] entsetzlich; scheußlich; ~**id** [ ['hɔrid] gräßlich, abscheulich; schrecklich; ~**ify** [~ifai] erschrecken; entsetzen; ~**or** ['hɔrə] Entsetzen *n*, Schauder *m*; Schrecken *m*; Greuel *m*.

**horse** [hɔ:s] *zo.* Pferd *n*; Reiterei *f*; Bock *m*, Gestell *n*; ~**back** ['hɔ:sbæk]: *on* ~ zu Pferde; ~**hair** Roßhaar *n*; ~**laugh** F wieherndes Lachen; ~**man** Reiter *m*; ~**manship** [~nʃip] Reitkunst *f*; ~ **opera** *Am.* drittklassiger Wildwestfilm; ~**power** Pferdestärke *f*; ~**radish** Meerrettich *m*; ~**shoe** Hufeisen *n*.

**horticulture** ['hɔ:tikʌltʃə] Gartenbau *m*.

**hose** [houz] Schlauch *m*; Strumpfhose *f*; *coll.* Strümpfe *m/pl.*

**hosiery** ['houʒəri] Strumpfwaren *f/pl.*

**hospitable** □ ['hɔspitəbl] gastfrei.

**hospital** ['hɔspitl] Krankenhaus *n*; ✠ Lazarett *n*; ~**ity** [hɔspi'tæliti] Gastfreundschaft *f*, Gastlichkeit *f*.

**host** [houst] Wirt *m*; Gastgeber *m*; Gastwirt *m*; *fig.* Heer *n*; Schwarm *m*; *eccl.* Hostie *f*.

**hostage** ['hɔstidʒ] Geisel *m, f*.

**hostel** ['hɔstəl] Herberge *f*; *univ.* Studenten(wohn)heim *n*.

**hostess** ['houstis] Wirtin *f*; Gastgeberin *f*; = *air* ~.

**hostil|e** ['hɔstail] feindlich (gesinnt); ~**ity** [hɔs'tiliti] Feindseligkeit *f* (*to* gegen).

**hot** [hɔt] heiß; scharf; beißend; hitzig, heftig; eifrig; warm (*Speise, Fährte*); *Am. sl.* falsch (*Scheck*); gestohlen; radioaktiv; ~**bed** ['hɔtbed] Mistbeet *n*; *fig.* Brutstätte *f*.

**hotchpotch** ['hɔtʃpɔtʃ] Mischmasch *m*; Gemüsesuppe *f*. [chen.\]

**hot dog** F ['hɔt 'dɔg] heißes Würst-\]

**hotel** [hou'tel] Hotel *n*.

**hot|head** ['hɔthed] Hitzkopf *m*; ~**house** Treibhaus *n*; ~**pot** Irish Stew *n*; ~ **rod** *Am. sl. mot.* frisiertes altes Auto; ~**spur** Hitzkopf *m*.

**hound** [haund] **1.** Jagd-, Spürhund *m*; *fig.* Hund *m*; **2.** jagen, hetzen

**hour** ['auə] Stunde *f*; Zeit *f*, Uhr *f*; ~**ly** ['auəli] stündlich.

**house 1.** [haus] *allg.* Haus *n*; the ♀ das Unterhaus; die Börse; **2.** [hauz] *v/t.* unterbringen; *v/i.* hausen; ~**agent** ['hauseidʒənt] Häusermakler *m*; ~**breaker** ['hausbreikə] Abbrucharbeiter *m*; ~**hold** Haushalt *m*; *attr.* Haushalts...; Haus...; ~**holder** Hausherr *m*; ~**keeper** Haushälterin *f*; ~**keeping** Haushaltung *f*; ~**maid** Hausmädchen *n*; ~**warming** ['hauswɔ:miŋ] Einzugsfeier *f*; ~**wife** ['hauswaif] Hausfrau *f*; ['hʌzif] Nähtäschchen *n*; ~**wifery** ['hauswifəri] Haushaltung *f*; ~**work** Haus(halts)arbeiten *f/pl.*

**housing** ['hauziŋ] Unterbringung *f*; Wohnung *f*; ~ *estate* Wohnsiedlung *f*.

**hove** [houv] *pret. u. p.p. von heave* 2.

**hovel** ['hɔvəl] Schuppen *m*; Hütte *f*.

**hover** ['hɔvə] schweben; lungern; *fig.* schwanken; ~**craft** Luftkissenfahrzeug *n*.

**how** [hau] wie; ~ *do you do? Begrüßungsformel bei der Vorstellung*; ~ *about ...?* wie steht's mit ...? ~**ever** [hau'evə] **1.** *adv.* wie auch (immer); wenn auch noch so ...; **2.** *cj.* jedoch.

**howl** [haul] **1.** heulen, brüllen; **2.** Geheul *n*; ~**er** ['haulə] Heuler *m*; *sl.* grober Fehler.

**hub** [hʌb] (Rad)Nabe *f*; *fig.* Mittel-, Angelpunkt *m*.

**hubbub** ['hʌbʌb] Tumult *m*, Lärm *m*.

**hub(by)** F ['hʌb(i)] (Ehe)Mann *m*.

**huckleberry** ♣ ['hʌklberi] amerikanische Heidelbeere.

**huckster** ['hʌkstə] Hausierer(in).

**huddle** ['hʌdl] **1.** *a.* ~ *together* (sich) zs.-drängen, zs.-pressen; ~ (*o.s.*) *up* sich zs.-kauern; **2.** Gewirr *n*, Wirrwarr *m*. [*cry* Zetergeschrei *n*.\]

**hue** [hju:] Farbe *f*; Hetze *f*; ~ *and*\]

**huff** [hʌf] **1.** üble Laune; **2.** *v/t.* grob anfahren; beleidigen; *v/i.* wütend werden; schmollen.

**hug** [hʌg] **1.** Umarmung *f*; **2.** an sich drücken, umarmen; *fig.* festhalten an (*dat.*); sich dicht am *Weg etc.* halten.

**huge** □ ['hju:dʒ] ungeheuer, riesig; ~**ness** ['hju:dʒnis] ungeheure Größe.

**hulk** *fig.* [hʌlk] Klotz *m*.

**hull** [hʌl] 1. ♣ Schale f; Hülse f; ⚓ Rumpf m; 2. enthülsen; schälen.

**hullabaloo** [hʌləbə'luː] Lärm m.

**hullo** ['hʌ'lou] hallo (bsd. teleph.).

**hum** [hʌm] summen; brumme(l)n; make things ～ F Schwung in die Sache bringen.

**human** ['hjuːmən] 1. ☐ menschlich; ～ly nach menschlichem Ermessen; 2. F Mensch m; ～e ☐ [hju(ː)'mein] human, menschenfreundlich; ～itarian [hju(ː)mæni'teəriən] 1. Menschenfreund m; 2. menschenfreundlich; ～ity [hju(ː)'mæniti] menschliche Natur; Menschheit f; Humanität f; ～kind ['hjuːmən'kaind] Menschengeschlecht n.

**humble** ['hʌmbl] 1. ☐ demütig; bescheiden; 2. erniedrigen; demütigen.

**humble-bee** ['hʌmblbiː] Hummel f.

**humbleness** ['hʌmblnis] Demut f.

**humbug** ['hʌmbʌg] 1. (be)schwindeln; 2. Schwindel m.

**humdinger** Am. sl. [hʌm'diŋə] Mordskerl m, -sache f.

**humdrum** ['hʌmdrʌm] eintönig.

**humid** ['hjuːmid] feucht, naß; ～ity [hju(ː)'miditi] Feuchtigkeit f.

**humiliat|e** [hju(ː)'milieit] erniedrigen, demütigen; ～ion [hju(ː)mili'eiʃən] Erniedrigung f, Demütigung f.

**humility** [hju(ː)'militi] Demut f.

**humming** F ['hʌmiŋ] mächtig, gewaltig; ～bird zo. Kolibri m.

**humorous** ☐ ['hjuːmərəs] humoristisch, humorvoll; spaßig.

**humo(u)r** ['hjuːmə] 1. Laune f, Stimmung f; Humor m; das Spaßige; ✂ hist. Körpersaft m; out of ～ schlecht gelaunt; 2. j-m s-n Willen lassen; eingehen auf (acc.).

**hump** [hʌmp] 1. Höcker m, Buckel m; 2. krümmen; ärgern, verdrießen; ～ o.s. Am. sl. sich dranhalten; ～back ['hʌmpbæk] = humpback.

**hunch** [hʌntʃ] 1. Höcker m; großes Stück; Am. F Ahnung f; 2. a. ～ out, ～ up krümmen; ～back ['hʌntʃbæk] Bucklige(r m) f.

**hundred** ['hʌndrəd] 1. hundert; 2. Hundert n; ～th [～dθ] 1. hundertste; 2. Hundertstel n; ～weight englischer Zentner (50,8 kg).

**hung** [hʌŋ] 1. pret. u. p.p. von hang 1; 2. adj. abgehangen (Fleisch).

**Hungarian** [hʌŋ'gɛəriən] 1. ungarisch; 2. Ungar(in); Ungarisch n.

**hunger** ['hʌŋgə] 1. Hunger m (a. fig.; for nach); 2. v/i. hungern (for, after nach); v/t. durch Hunger zwingen (into zu).

**hungry** ☐ ['hʌŋgri] hungrig.

**hunk** F ['hʌŋk] dickes Stück.

**hunt** [hʌnt] 1. Jagd f (for nach); Jagd(revier n r) f; Jagd(gesellschaft) f; 2. jagen; Revier bejagen; hetzen; ～ out od. up aufspüren; ～ for, ～ after

Jagd machen auf (acc.); ～er ['hʌntə] Jäger m; Jagdpferd n; ～ing [～tiŋ] Jagen n; Verfolgung f; attr. Jagd...; ～ing-ground Jagdrevier n; ～sman [～tsmən] Jäger m; Rüdemann m (Meutenführer).

**hurdle** ['həːdl] Hürde f (a. fig.); ～r [～lə] Hürdenläufer(in); ～race Hürdenrennen n.

**hurl** [həːl] 1. Schleudern n; 2. schleudern; Worte ausstoßen.

**hurricane** ['hʌrikən] Orkan m.

**hurried** ☐ ['hʌrid] eilig; übereilt.

**hurry** ['hʌri] 1. (große) Eile, Hast f; be in a ～ es eilig haben; not ... in a ～ F nicht so bald, nicht so leicht; 2. v/t. (an)treiben; drängen; et. beschleunigen; eilig schicken od. bringen; v/i. eilen, hasten; ～ up sich beeilen.

**hurt** [həːt] 1. Verletzung f; Schaden m; 2. [irr.] verletzen (a. fig.); weh tun (dat.); schaden (dat.).

**husband** ['hʌzbənd] 1. (Ehe)Mann m; 2. haushalten mit; verwalten; ～man Landwirt m; ～ry [～dri] Landwirtschaft f, Ackerbau m.

**hush** [hʌʃ] 1. still!; 2. Stille f; 3. v/t. zum Schweigen bringen; beruhigen; Stimme dämpfen; ～ up vertuschen; v/i. still sein; ～money ['hʌʃmʌni] Schweigegeld n.

**husk** [hʌsk] 1. ♣ Hülse f, Schote f; Schale f (a. fig.); 2. enthülsen; ～y ['hʌski] 1. ☐ hülsig; trocken; heiser; F stramm, stämmig; 2. F stämmiger Kerl.

**hussy** ['hʌsi] Flittchen n; Range f.

**hustle** ['hʌsl] 1. v/t. (an)rempeln; stoßen; drängen; v/i. (sich) drängen; eilen; bsd. Am. mit Hochdruck arbeiten; 2. Hochbetrieb m; Rührigkeit f; ～ and bustle Gedränge und Gehetze n.

**hut** [hʌt] Hütte f; ✗ Baracke f.

**hutch** [hʌtʃ] Kasten m; bsd. Kaninchen-Stall m (a. fig.); Trog m.

**hyacinth** ♣ ['haiəsinθ] Hyazinthe f.

**hyaena** zo. [hai'iːnə] Hyäne f.

**hybrid** ⚕ ['haibrid] Bastard m, Mischling m; Kreuzung f; attr. Bastard...; Zwitter...; ～ize [～daiz] kreuzen.

**hydrant** ['haidrənt] Hydrant m.

**hydro|** ⚕ ['haidrou] Wasser...; ～carbon Kohlenwasserstoff m; ～chloric acid [～'klɔrikæsid] Salzsäure f; ～gen [～ridʒən] Wasserstoff m; ～gen bomb Wasserstoffbombe f; ～pathy [hai'drɔpəθi] Wasserheilkunde f, Wasserkur f; ～phobia [haidrə'foubjə] Wasserscheu f; ✗ Tollwut f; ～plane ['haidrouplein] Wasserflugzeug n; (Motor)Gleitboot n, Rennboot n.

**hyena** zo. [hai'iːnə] Hyäne f.

**hygiene** ['haidʒiːn] Hygiene f.

**hymn** [him] 1. Hymne f; Lobgesang m; Kirchenlied n; 2. preisen.

**hyphen** ['haifən] **1.** Bindestrich *m*; **2.** mit Bindestrich schreiben *od.* verbinden; **~ated** [~neitid] mit Bindestrich geschrieben; **~** *Americans pl.* Halb-Amerikaner *m/pl.* (*z. B. German-Americans*). [ren.\
**hypnotize** ['hipnətaiz] hypnotisie-\
**hypo|chondriac** [haipou'kɔndriæk] Hypochonder *m*; **~crisy** [hi'pɔ-

krəsi] Heuchelei *f*; **~crite** ['hipə-krit] Heuchler(in); Scheinheilige(r *m*) *f*; **~critical** □ [hipə'kritikəl] heuchlerisch; **~thesis** [hai'pɔθisis] Hypothese *f*.
**hyster|ia** [his'tiəriə] Hysterie *f*; **~ical** □ [~'terikəl] hysterisch; **~ics** [~ks] *pl.* hysterischer Anfall; *go into ~* hysterisch werden.

# I

**I** [ai] ich.
**ice** [ais] **1.** Eis *n*; **2.** gefrieren lassen; *a.* **~ *up*** vereisen; *Kuchen* mit Zuk-kerguß überziehen; in Eis kühlen; **~age** ['aiseidʒ] Eiszeit *f*; **~berg** ['aisbəːg] Eisberg *m* (*a. fig.*); **~bound** eingefroren; **~box** Eis-schrank *m*; *Am. a.* Kühlschrank *m*; **~cream** Speiseeis *n*; **~floe** Eis-scholle *f*.
**icicle** ['aisikl] Eiszapfen *m*.
**icing** ['aisiŋ] Zuckerguß *m*; Ver-eisung *f*.
**icy** □ ['aisi] eisig (*a. fig.*); vereist.
**idea** [ai'diə] Idee *f*; Begriff *m*; Vorstellung *f*; Gedanke *m*; Mei-nung *f*; Ahnung *f*; Plan *m*; **~l** [~əl] **1.** □ ideell; eingebildet; ideal; **2.** Ideal *n*.
**identi|cal** □ [ai'dentikəl] identisch, gleich(bedeutend); **~fication** [aidentifi'keiʃən] Identifizierung *f*; Ausweis *m*; **~fy** [ai'dentifai] identi-fizieren; ausweisen; erkennen; **~ty** [~iti] Identität *f*; Persönlichkeit *f*, Eigenart *f*; **~ card** Personalaus-weis *m*, Kennkarte *f*; **~ disk** ✕ Er-kennungsmarke *f*.
**ideological** □ [aidiə'lɔdʒikəl] ideo-logisch.
**idiom** ['idiəm] Idiom *n*; Mundart *f*; Redewendung *f*.
**idiot** ['idiət] Idiot(in), Schwach-sinnige(r *m*) *f*; **~ic** [idi'ɔtik] (**~ally**) blödsinnig.
**idle** ['aidl] **1.** □ müßig, untätig; träg, faul; unnütz; nichtig; **~** *hours pl.* Mußestunden *f/pl.*; **2.** *v/t. mst* **~** *away* vertrödeln; *v/i.* faulenzen; ⊕ leer laufen; **~ness** ['aidlnis] Muße *f*; Trägheit *f*; Nichtigkeit *f*; **~r** ['aidlə] Müßiggänger(in).
**idol** ['aidl] Idol *n*, Götzenbild *n*; *fig.* Abgott *m*; **~atrous** □ [ai'dɔlə-trəs] abgöttisch; **~atry** [~ri] Ab-götterei *f*; Vergötterung *f*; **~ize** ['aidəlaiz] vergöttern.
**idyl(l)** ['idil] Idyll(e *f*) *n*.
**if** [if] **1.** wenn, falls; ob; **2.** Wenn *n*; **~fy** *Am.* F ['ifi] zweifelhaft.
**ignit|e** [ig'nait] (sich) entzünden; zünden; **~ion** [ig'niʃən] ⚙ Entzün-dung *f*; *mot.* Zündung *f*.

**ignoble** □ [ig'noubl] unedel; niedrig, gemein.
**ignominious** □ [ignə'miniəs] schändlich, schimpflich.
**ignor|ance** ['ignərəns] Unwissen-heit *f*; **~ant** [~nt] unwissend; un-kundig; **~e** [ig'nɔː] ignorieren, nicht beachten; ⚖ verwerfen.
**ill** [il] **1.** *adj. u. adv.* übel, böse; schlimm, schlecht; krank; *adv.* kaum; *fall ~*, *be taken ~* krank wer-den; **2.** Übel *n*; Übel(s) *n*, Böse(s) *n*.
**ill-advised** □ ['iləd'vaizd] schlecht beraten; unbesonnen, unklug; **~bred** ungebildet, ungezogen; **~ breeding** schlechtes Benehmen.
**illegal** □ [i'liːgəl] ungesetzlich.
**illegible** □ [i'ledʒəbl] unleserlich.
**illegitimate** □ [ili'dʒitimit] illegi-tim; unrechtmäßig; unehelich.
**ill-favo(u)red** ['il'feivəd] häßlich; **~humo(u)red** übellaunig.
**illiberal** □ [i'libərəl] engstirnig; intolerant; knauserig.
**illicit** □ [i'lisit] unerlaubt.
**illiterate** □ [i'litərit] **1.** ungelehrt, ungebildet; **2.** Analphabet(in).
**ill-judged** ['il'dʒʌdʒd] unklug, un-vernünftig; **~mannered** unge-zogen; mit schlechten Umgangs-formen; **~natured** □ boshaft, bös-artig.
**illness** ['ilnis] Krankheit *f*.
**illogical** □ [i'lɔdʒikəl] unlogisch.
**ill-starred** ['il'staːd] unglücklich; **~tempered** schlecht gelaunt; **~timed** ungelegen; **~treat** miß-handeln.
**illuminat|e** [i'ljuːmineit] be-, er-leuchten (*a. fig.*); erläutern; auf-klären; **~ing** [~tiŋ] Leucht...; *fig.* aufschlußreich; **~ion** [ilju:mi'nei-ʃən] Er-, Beleuchtung *f*; Erläute-rung *f*; Aufklärung *f*.
**ill-use** ['il'juːz] mißhandeln.
**illus|ion** [i'luːʒən] Illusion *f*, Täu-schung *f*; **~ive** [i'luːsiv], **~ory** □ [~səri] illusorisch, täuschend.
**illustrat|e** ['iləstreit] illustrieren; erläutern; bebildern; **~ion** ['iləs-'treiʃən] Erläuterung *f*; Illustra-tion *f*; **~ive** □ ['iləstreitiv] erläu-ternd.

**illustrious** □ [i'lʌstriəs] berühmt.

**ill will** ['il'wil] Feindschaft *f*.

**image** ['imidʒ] Bild *n*; Standbild *n*; Ebenbild *n*; Vorstellung *f*; **~ry** [~dʒəri] Bilder *n/pl.*; Bildersprache *f*, Metaphorik *f*.

**imagin|able** □ [i'mædʒinəbl] denkbar; **~ary** [~əri] eingebildet; **~ation** [imædʒi'neiʃən] Einbildung(skraft) *f*; **~ative** □ [i'mædʒinətiv] ideen-, einfallsreich; **~e** [i'mædʒin] sich *et.* einbilden *od.* vorstellen *od.* denken.

**imbecile** □ ['imbisi:l] 1. geistesschwach; 2. Schwachsinnige(r *m*) *f*.

**imbibe** [im'baib] einsaugen; *fig.* sich zu eigen machen.

**imbue** [im'bju:] (durch)tränken; tief färben; *fig.* erfüllen.

**imitat|e** ['imiteit] nachahmen; imitieren; **~ion** [imi'teiʃən] 1. Nachahmung *f*; 2. künstlich, Kunst...

**immaculate** □ [i'mækjulit] unbefleckt, rein; fehlerlos.

**immaterial** □ [imə'tiəriəl] unkörperlich; unwesentlich (*to* für).

**immature** [imə'tjuə] unreif.

**immeasurable** □ [i'meʒərəbl] unermeßlich.

**immediate** □ [i'mi:djət] unmittelbar; unverzüglich, sofortig; **~ly** [~tli] 1. *adv.* sofort; 2. *cj.* gleich nachdem.

**immense** □ [i'mens] ungeheuer.

**immerse** [i'mə:s] (ein-, unter)tauchen; *fig.* **~ o.s.** *in* sich versenken *od.* vertiefen in (*acc.*).

**immigra|nt** ['imigrənt] Einwanderer(in); **~te** [~greit] *v/i.* einwandern; *v/t.* ansiedeln (*into* in *dat.*); **~tion** [imi'greiʃən] Einwanderung *f*.

**imminent** □ ['iminənt] bevorstehend, drohend.

**immobile** [i'moubail] unbeweglich.

**immoderate** □ [i'modərit] maßlos.

**immodest** □ [i'modist] unbescheiden; unanständig.

**immoral** □ [i'morəl] unmoralisch.

**immortal** □ [i'mo:tl] 1. □ unsterblich; 2. Unsterbliche(r *m*) *f*; **~ity** [imo:'tæliti] Unsterblichkeit *f*.

**immovable** [i'mu:vəbl] 1. □ unbeweglich; unerschütterlich; 2. **~s** *pl.* Immobilien *f*.

**immun|e** **~** *s* *u. fig.* [i'mju:n] immun, gefeit (*from* gegen); **~ity** [~niti] Immunität *f*, Freiheit *f* (*from* von); Unempfänglichkeit *f* (für).

**immutable** □ [i'mju:təbl] unveränderlich.

**imp** [imp] Teufelchen *n*; Schelm *m*.

**impact** ['impækt] (Zs.-)Stoß *m*; Anprall *m*; Einwirkung *f*.

**impair** [im'pɛə] schwächen; (ver-)mindern; beeinträchtigen.

**impart** [im'pɑ:t] verleihen; weitergeben.

**impartial** [im'pɑ:ʃəl] unparteiisch; **~ity** ['impɑ:ʃi'æliti] Unparteilichkeit *f*, Objektivität *f*.

**impassable** □ [im'pɑ:səbl] ungangbar, unpassierbar.

**impassible** □ [im'pæsibl] unempfindlich; gefühllos (*to* gegen).

**impassioned** [im'pæʃənd] leidenschaftlich.

**impassive** □ [im'pæsiv] unempfindlich; teilnahmslos; heiter.

**impatien|ce** [im'peiʃəns] Ungeduld *f*; **~t** □ [~nt] ungeduldig.

**impeach** [im'pi:tʃ] anklagen (*of, with gen.*); anfechten, anzweifeln.

**impeccable** □ [im'pekəbl] sündlos; makellos, einwandfrei.

**impede** [im'pi:d] (ver)hindern.

**impediment** [im'pedimənt] Hindernis *n*.

**impel** [im'pel] (an)treiben.

**impend** [im'pend] hängen, schweben; bevorstehen, drohen.

**impenetrable** □ [im'penitrəbl] undurchdringlich; *fig.* unergründlich; *fig.* unzugänglich (*to dat.*).

**impenitent** □ [im'penitənt] unbußfertig, verstockt.

**imperative** □ [im'perətiv] 1. □ notwendig, dringend, unbedingt erforderlich; befehlend; gebieterisch; *gr.* imperativisch; 2. Befehl *m*; *a.* **~ mood** *gr.* Imperativ *m*, Befehlsform *f*. [unmerklich.]

**imperceptible** □ [impə'septəbl]

**imperfect** □ [im'pə:fikt] 1. □ unvollkommen; unvollendet; 2. *a.* **~ tense** *gr.* Imperfekt *n*.

**imperial** □ [im'piəriəl] kaiserlich; Reichs...; majestätisch; großartig; **~ism** [~lizəm] Imperialismus *m*, Weltmachtpolitik *f*.

**imperil** [im'peril] gefährden.

**imperious** □ [im'piəriəs] gebieterisch, anmaßend; dringend.

**imperishable** □ [im'periʃəbl] unvergänglich.

**impermeable** □ [im'pə:mjəbl] undurchdringlich, undurchlässig.

**impersonal** □ [im'pə:snl] unpersönlich.

**impersonate** [im'pə:səneit] verkörpern; *thea.* darstellen.

**impertinen|ce** [im'pə:tinəns] Unverschämtheit *f*; Nebensächlichkeit *f*; **~t** □ [~nt] unverschämt; ungehörig; nebensächlich.

**imperturbable** □ [impə(:)'tə:bəbl] unerschütterlich.

**impervious** □ [im'pə:vjəs] unzugänglich (*to* für); undurchlässig.

**impetu|ous** □ [im'petjuəs] ungestüm, heftig; **~s** ['impitəs] Antrieb *m*.

**impiety** [im'paiəti] Gottlosigkeit *f*.

**impinge** [im'pindʒ] *v/i.* (ver)stoßen (*on, upon, against* gegen).

**impious** □ ['impiəs] gottlos; pietätlos; frevelhaft.

**implacable** □ [im'plækəbl] unversöhnlich, unerbittlich.

**implant** [im'plɑ:nt] einpflanzen.

**implement 1.** ['implimənt] Werkzeug *n*; Gerät *n*; **2.** [͜ment] ausführen.

**implicat|e** ['implikeit] verwickeln; in sich schließen; **∼ion** [impli'keiʃən] Verwick(e)lung *f*; Folgerung *f*.

**implicit** □ [im'plisit] mit eingeschlossen; blind (*Glaube etc.*).

**implore** [im'plɔː] (an-, er)flehen.

**imply** [im'plai] mit einbegreifen, enthalten; bedeuten; andeuten.

**impolite** □ [impə'lait] unhöflich.

**impolitic** □ [im'pɔlitik] unklug.

**import 1.** ['impɔːt] Bedeutung *f*; Wichtigkeit *f*; Einfuhr *f*; **∼s** *pl.* Einfuhrwaren *f/pl.*; **2.** [im'pɔːt] einführen; bedeuten; **∼ance** [͜təns] Wichtigkeit *f*; **∼ant** □ [͜nt] wichtig; wichtigtuerisch; **∼ation** [impɔː-'teiʃən] Einfuhr(waren *f/pl.*) *f*.

**importun|ate** □ [im'pɔːtjunit] lästig; zudringlich; **∼e** [im'pɔːtjuːn] dringend bitten; belästigen.

**impos|e** [im'pouz] *v/t.* auf(er)legen, aufbürden (*on, upon dat.*); *v/i.* **∼ upon** *j-m* imponieren; *j-n* täuschen; **∼ition** [impə'ziʃən] Auf(er)legung *f*; Steuer *f*; Strafarbeit *f*; Betrügerei *f*.

**impossib|ility** [impɔsə'biliti] Unmöglichkeit *f*; **∼le** □ [im'pɔsəbl] unmöglich.

**impost|or** [im'pɔstə] Betrüger *m*; **∼ure** [͜tʃə] Betrug *m*.

**impoten|ce** [im'potəns] Unfähigkeit *f*; Machtlosigkeit *f*; **∼t** □ [͜nt] unvermögend, machtlos, schwach.

**impoverish** [im'pɔvəriʃ] arm machen; *Boden* auslaugen.

**impracticable** □ [im'præktikəbl] undurchführbar; unwegsam.

**impractical** [im'præktikəl] unpraktisch; theoretisch; unnütz.

**imprecate** ['imprikeit] *Böses* herabwünschen (*upon auf acc.*).

**impregn|able** □ [im'pregnəbl] uneinnehmbar; unüberwindlich; **∼ate** ['impregneit] schwängern; 🜚 sättigen; ⊕ imprägnieren.

**impress 1.** ['impres] (Ab-, Ein-) Druck *m*; *fig.* Stempel *m*; **2.** [im-'pres] eindrücken, prägen; *Kraft etc.* übertragen; *Gedanken etc.* einprägen (*on dat.*); *j-n* beeindrucken; *j-n mit et.* erfüllen; **∼ion** [͜eʃən] Eindruck *m*; *typ.* Abdruck *m*; Abzug *m*; Auflage *f*; *be under the ∼ that* den Eindruck haben, daß; **∼ive** □ [͜esiv] eindrucksvoll.

**imprint 1.** [im'print] aufdrücken, prägen; *fig.* einprägen (*on, in dat.*); **2.** ['imprint] Eindruck *m*; Stempel *m* (*a. fig.*); *typ.* Druckvermerk *m*.

**imprison** [im'prizn] inhaftieren; **∼ment** [͜nment] Haft *f*; Gefängnis (-strafe *f*) *n*.

**improbable** □ [im'prɔbəbl] unwahrscheinlich.

**improper** □ [im'prɔpə] ungeeignet, unpassend; falsch; unanständig.

**impropriety** [imprə'praiəti] Ungehörigkeit *f*; Unanständigkeit *f*.

**improve** [im'pruːv] *v/t.* verbessern; veredeln; aus-, benutzen; *v/i.* sich (ver)bessern; **∼ upon** vervollkommnen; **∼ment** [͜vmənt] Verbesserung *f*, Vervollkommnung *f*; Fortschritt *m* (*on, upon gegenüber dat.*).

**improvise** ['imprəvaiz] improvisieren.

**imprudent** □ [im'pruːdənt] unklug.

**impuden|ce** ['impjudəns] Unverschämtheit *f*, Frechheit *f*; **∼t** □ [͜nt] unverschämt, frech.

**impuls|e** ['impʌls], **∼ion** [im'pʌl-ʃən] Impuls *m*, (An)Stoß *m*; *fig.* (An)Trieb *m*; **∼ive** □ [͜lsiv] (an-) treibend; *fig.* impulsiv; rasch (handelnd).

**impunity** [im'pjuːniti] Straflosigkeit *f*; *with ∼* ungestraft.

**impure** □ [im'pjuə] unrein (*a. fig.*); unkeusch.

**imput|ation** [impju(ː)'teiʃən] Beschuldigung *f*; **∼e** [im'pjuːt] zurechnen, beimessen; *zur Last legen*.

**in** [in] **1.** *prp. allg.* in (*dat.*); *engS.*: (*∼ the morning, ∼ number, ∼ itself, professor ∼ the university*) an (*dat.*); (*∼ the street, ∼ English*) auf (*dat.*); (*∼ this manner*) auf (*acc.*); (*coat ∼ velvet*) aus; (*∼ Shakespeare, ∼ the daytime, ∼ crossing the road*) bei; (*engaged ∼ reading, ∼ a word*) mit; (*∼ my opinion*) nach; (*rejoice ∼ s.th.*) über (*acc.*); (*∼ the circumstances, ∼ the reign of, one ∼ ten*) unter (*dat.*); (*cry out ∼ alarm*) vor (*dat.*); (*grouped ∼ tens, speak ∼ reply, ∼ excuse, ∼ honour of*) zu; *∼ 1949* im Jahre 1949; *∼ that ... insofern als, weil*; **2.** *adv.* drin(nen); herein; hinein; *be ∼ for et. zu erwarten haben*; *e-e Prüfung etc.* vor sich haben; *I be well ∼ with sich gut mit j-m stehen*; **3.** *adj.* hereinkommend; Innen...

**inability** [inə'biliti] Unfähigkeit *f*.

**inaccessible** □ [inæk'sesəbl] unzugänglich. [unrichtig.)

**inaccurate** □ [in'ækjurit] ungenau;]

**inactiv|e** □ [in'æktiv] untätig, 🜚 lustlos; 🜚 unwirksam; **∼ity** [inæk-'tiviti] Untätig-, Lustlosigkeit *f*.

**inadequate** □ [in'ædikwit] unangemessen; unzulänglich.

**inadmissible** □ [inəd'misəbl] unzulässig.

**inadvertent** □ [inəd'vəːtənt] unachtsam; unbeabsichtigt, versehentlich.

**inalienable** □ [in'eiljənəbl] unveräußerlich.

**inane** □ [i'nein] *fig.* leer; albern.

**inanimate** □ [in'ænimit] leblos; *fig.* unbelebt; geistlos, langweilig.

**inapproachable** [inə'proutʃəbl] unnahbar, unzugänglich.

**inappropriate** □ [inə'proupriit] unangebracht, unpassend.

**inapt** □ [in'æpt] ungeeignet, untauglich; ungeschickt; unpassend.

**inarticulate** □ [inɑ:'tikjulit] undeutlich; schwer zu verstehen(d); undeutlich sprechend.

**inasmuch** [inəz'mʌtʃ]: ~ *as* insofern als. [merksam.)

**inattentive** □ [inə'tentiv] unauf-)

**inaudible** □ [in'ɔ:dəbl] unhörbar.

**inaugura|l** [i'nɔ:gjurəl] Antrittsrede *f*; *attr.* Antritts...; ~te [~reit] (feierlich) einführen, einweihen; beginnen; ~tion [inɔ:gju'reiʃən] Einführung *f*, Einweihung *f*; ♀ *Day Am.* Amtseinführung *f* des neugewählten Präsidenten der USA.

**inborn** ['in'bɔ:n] angeboren.

**incalculable** □ [in'kælkjuləbl] unberechenbar; unzählig.

**incandescent** [inkæn'desnt] weiß glühend; Glüh...

**incapa|ble** □ [in'keipəbl] unfähig, ungeeignet (*of* zu); ~citate [inkə-'pæsiteit] unfähig machen; ~city [~ti] Unfähigkeit *f*.

**incarnate** [in'kɑ:nit] Fleisch geworden; *fig.* verkörpert.

**incautious** □ [in'kɔ:ʃəs] unvorsichtig.

**incendiary** [in'sendjəri] **1.** brandstifterisch; *fig.* aufwieglerisch; **2.** Brandstifter *m*; Aufwiegler *m*.

**incense**[1] ['insens] Weihrauch *m*.

**incense**[2] [in'sens] in Wut bringen.

**incentive** [in'sentiv] Antrieb *m*.

**incessant** □ [in'sesnt] unaufhörlich.

**incest** ['insest] Blutschande *f*.

**inch** [intʃ] Zoll *m* (*2,54 cm*); *fig. ein* bißchen; *by* ~es allmählich; *every* ~ ganz (u. gar).

**inciden|ce** ['insidəns] Vorkommen *n*; Wirkung *f*; ~t [~nt] **1.** (*to*) vorkommend (bei), eigen (*dat.*); **2.** Zu-, Vor-, Zwischenfall *m*; Nebenumstand *m*; ~tal □ [insi'dentl] zufällig, gelegentlich; Neben...; *be* ~ *to* gehören zu; ~ly nebenbei.

**incinerate** [in'sinəreit] einäschern; Müll verbrennen.

**incis|e** [in'saiz] einschneiden; ~ion [in'siʒən] Einschnitt *m*; ~ive □ [in'saisiv] (ein)schneidend, scharf; ~or [~aizə] Schneidezahn *m*.

**incite** [in'sait] anspornen, anregen; anstiften; ~ment [~tmənt] Anregung *f*; Ansporn *m*; Anstiftung *f*.

**inclement** [in'klemənt] rauh.

**inclin|ation** [inkli'neiʃən] Neigung *f* (*a. fig.*); ~e [in'klain] **1.** *v/i.* sich neigen (*a. fig.*); ~ *to fig.* zu *et.* neigen; *v/t.* neigen; geneigt machen; **2.** Neigung *f*, Abhang *m*.

**inclos|e** [in'klouz], ~ure [~ouʒə] *s.* enclose, enclosure.

**inclu|de** [in'klu:d] einschließen; enthalten; ~sive □ [~u:siv] einschließlich; alles einbegriffen; *be* ~ *of* einschließen; ~ *terms pl.* Pauschalpreis *m*.

**incoheren|ce**, ~cy [inkou'hiərəns, ~si] Zs.-hangslosigkeit *f*; Inkonsequenz *f*; ~t □ [~nt] unzs.-hängend; inkonsequent.

**income** ['inkəm] Einkommen *n*; ~-tax Einkommensteuer *f*.

**incommode** [inkə'moud] belästigen.

**incommunica|do** *bsd. Am.* [inkəmju:ni'kɑ:dou] ohne Verbindung mit der Außenwelt; ~tive □ [inkə'mju:nikətiv] nicht mitteilsam, verschlossen.

**incomparable** □ [in'kɔmpərəbl] unvergleichlich.

**incompatible** □ [inkəm'pætəbl] unvereinbar; unverträglich.

**incompetent** □ [in'kɔmpitənt] unfähig; unzuständig, unbefugt.

**incomplete** □ [inkəm'pli:t] unvollständig; unvollkommen.

**incomprehensible** □ [inkəmpri-'hensəbl] unbegreiflich.

**inconceivable** □ [inkən'si:vəbl] unbegreiflich, unfaßbar.

**incongruous** □ [in'kɔŋgruəs] nicht übereinstimmend; unpassend.

**inconsequent** □ [in'kɔnsikwənt] inkonsequent, folgewidrig; ~ial [inkɔnsi'kwenʃəl] unbedeutend; = *inconsequent.*

**inconsidera|ble** □ [inkən'sidərəbl] unbedeutend; ~te □ [~rit] unüberlegt; rücksichtslos.

**inconsisten|cy** [inkən'sistənsi] Unvereinbarkeit *f*; Inkonsequenz *f*; ~t □ [~nt] unvereinbar; widerspruchsvoll; inkonsequent.

**inconsolable** □ [inkən'souləbl] untröstlich.

**inconstant** □ [in'kɔnstənt] unbeständig; veränderlich.

**incontinent** □ [in'kɔntinənt] unmäßig; ausschweifend.

**inconvenien|ce** [inkən'vi:njəns] **1.** Unbequemlichkeit *f*; Unannehmlichkeit *f*; **2.** belästigen; ~t □ [~nt] unbequem; ungelegen; lästig.

**incorporat|e 1.** [in'kɔ:pəreit] einverleiben (*into dat.*); sich (ver)einigen; *als Mitglied* aufnehmen; ⅌⅔ *als Körperschaft* eintragen; **2.** [~rit] einverleibt; vereinigt; ~ed (amtlich) eingetragen; ~ion [inkɔ:pə'reiʃən] Einverleibung *f*; Verbindung *f*. [fehlerhaft; ungehörig.)

**incorrect** □ [inkə'rekt] unrichtig;)

**incorrigible** □ [in'kɔridʒəbl] unverbesserlich.

**increas|e 1.** [in'kri:s] *v/i.* zunehmen; sich vergrößern *od.* vermehren; *v/t.* vermehren, vergrößern; erhöhen; **2.** ['inkri:s] Zunahme *f*; Vergrößerung *f*; Zuwachs *m*; ~ingly [in'kri:siŋli] zunehmend, immer (*mit folgendem comp.*); ~ *difficult* immer schwieriger.

**incredible** □ [in'kredəbl] unglaublich.

**incredul|ity** [inkri'dju:liti] Unglaube *m*; **~ous** ☐ [in'kredjuləs] ungläubig, skeptisch.

**incriminate** [in'krimineit] beschuldigen; belasten.

**incrustation** [inkrʌs'teiʃən] Verkrustung *f*; Kruste *f*; ⊕ Belag *m*.

**incub|ate** ['inkjubeit] (aus)brüten; **~ator** [~tə] Brutapparat *m*.

**inculcate** ['inkʌlkeit] einschärfen (*upon dat.*).

**incumbent** [in'kʌmbənt] obliegend; *be ~ on s.o.* j-m obliegen.

**incur** [in'kə:] sich *et.* zuziehen; geraten in (*acc.*); *Verpflichtung* eingehen; *Verlust* erleiden.

**incurable** [in'kjuərəbl] **1.** ☐ unheilbar; **2.** Unheilbare(r *m*) *f*.

**incurious** ☐ [in'kjuəriəs] gleichgültig, uninteressiert.

**incursion** [in'kə:ʃən] *feindlicher* Einfall.

**indebted** [in'detid] verschuldet; *fig.* (zu Dank) verpflichtet.

**indecen|cy** [in'di:snsi] Unanständigkeit *f*; **~t** ☐ [~nt] unanständig.

**indecis|ion** [indi'siʒən] Unentschlossenheit *f*; **~ve** [~'saisiv] nicht entscheidend; unbestimmt.

**indecorous** ☐ [in'dekərəs] unpassend; ungehörig.

**indeed** [in'di:d] **1.** *adv.* in der Tat, tatsächlich; wirklich; allerdings; **2.** *int.* so?; nicht möglich!

**indefatigable** ☐ [indi'fætigəbl] unermüdlich.

**indefensible** ☐ [indi'fensəbl] unhaltbar.

**indefinite** ☐ [in'definit] unbestimmt; unbeschränkt; ungenau.

**indelible** ☐ [in'delibl] untilgbar.

**indelicate** [in'delikit] unfein; taktlos.

**indemni|fy** [in'demnifai] sicherstellen; *j-m* Straflosigkeit zusichern; entschädigen; **~ty** [~iti] Sicherstellung *f*; Straflosigkeit *f*; Entschädigung *f*.

**indent 1.** [in'dent] einkerben, auszacken; eindrücken; ▓ *Vertrag* mit Doppel ausfertigen; **~ upon** *s.o.* for *s.th.* ✝ et. bei j-m bestellen; **2.** ['indent] Kerbe *f*; Vertiefung *f*; ✝ Auslandsauftrag *m*; = *indenture*; **~ation** [inden'teiʃən] Einkerbung *f*; Einschnitt *m*; **~ure** [in'dentʃə] **1.** Vertrag *m*; Lehrbrief *m*; **2.** vertraglich verpflichten.

**independen|ce** [indi'pendəns] Unabhängigkeit *f*; Selbständigkeit *f*; Auskommen *n*; ♀ *Day* Am. Unabhängigkeitstag *m* (*4. Juli*); **~t** ☐ [~nt] unabhängig; selbständig.

**indescribable** ☐ [indis'kraibəbl] unbeschreiblich.

**indestructible** ☐ [indis'trʌktəbl] unzerstörbar.

**indeterminate** ☐ [indi'tə:minit] unbestimmt.

**index** ['indeks] **1.** (An)Zeiger *m*; Anzeichen *n*; Zeigefinger *m*; Index *m*; (Inhalts-, Namen-, Sach)Verzeichnis *n*; **2.** *Buch* mit e-m Index versehen.

**Indian** ['indjən] **1.** indisch; indianisch; **2.** Inder(in); *a. Red ~* Indianer(in); **~ corn** Mais *m*; **~ file:** *in ~* im Gänsemarsch; **~ pudding** *Am.* Maismehlpudding *m*; **~ summer** Altweiber-, Nachsommer *m*.

**Indiarubber** ['indjə'rʌbə] Radiergummi *m*.

**indicat|e** ['indikeit] (an)zeigen; hinweisen auf (*acc.*); andeuten; **~ion** [indi'keiʃən] Anzeige *f*; Anzeichen *n*; Andeutung *f*; **~ive** [in'dikətiv] *a. ~ mood* gr. Indikativ *m*; **~or** ['indikeitə] Anzeiger *m* (*a.* ⊕); *mot.* Blinker *m*.

**indict** [in'dait] anklagen (*for* wegen); **~ment** [~tmənt] Anklage *f*.

**indifferen|ce** [in'difrəns] Gleichgültigkeit *f*; **~t** ☐ [~nt] gleichgültig (*to* gegen); unparteiisch; (nur) mäßig; unwesentlich; unbedeutend.

**indigenous** [in'didʒinəs] eingeboren, einheimisch.

**indigent** ☐ ['indidʒənt] arm.

**indigest|ible** ☐ [indi'dʒestəbl] unverdaulich; **~ion** [~tʃən] Verdauungsstörung *f*, Magenverstimmung *f*.

**indign|ant** ☐ [in'dignənt] entrüstet, empört, ungehalten; **~ation** [indig'neiʃən] Entrüstung *f*; **~ity** [in'digniti] Beleidigung *f*.

**indirect** ☐ [indi'rekt] indirekt; nicht direkt; *gr. a.* abhängig.

**indiscre|et** ☐ [indis'kri:t] unbesonnen; unachtsam; indiskret; **~tion** [~reʃən] Unachtsamkeit *f*; Unbesonnenheit *f*; Indiskretion *f*.

**indiscriminate** ☐ [indis'kriminit] unterschieds-, wahllos.

**indispensable** ☐ [indis'pensəbl] unentbehrlich, unerläßlich.

**indispos|ed** [indis'pouzd] unpäßlich; abgeneigt; **~ition** [indispə'ziʃən] Abneigung *f* (*to* gegen); Unpäßlichkeit *f*.

**indisputable** ☐ [indis'pju:təbl] unbestreitbar, unstreitig.

**indistinct** ☐ [indis'tiŋkt] undeutlich; unklar.

**indistinguishable** ☐ [indis'tiŋgwiʃəbl] nicht zu unterscheiden(d).

**indite** [in'dait] ab-, verfassen.

**individual** [indi'vidjuəl] **1.** ☐ persönlich, individuell; besondere(r, -s); einzeln; Einzel...; **2.** Individuum *n*; **~ism** [~lizəm] Individualismus *m*; **~ist** [~ist] Individualist *m*; **~ity** [individju'æliti] Individualität *f*.

**indivisible** ☐ [indi'vizəbl] unteilbar.

**indolen|ce** ['indələns] Trägheit *f*;

~t □ [~nt] indolent, träge, lässig; ⚕
schmerzlos.

**indomitable** □ [in'dɔmitəbl] unbezähmbar.

**indoor** ['indɔː] im Hause (befindlich); Haus..., Zimmer..., Sport:
Hallen...; ~s ['in'dɔːz] zu Hause;
im od. ins Haus.

**indorse** [in'dɔːs] = endorse etc.

**induce** [in'djuːs] veranlassen;
~ment [~smənt] Anlaß m, Antrieb
m.

**induct** [in'dʌkt] einführen; ~ion
[~kʃən] Einführung f, Einsetzung f
in Amt, Pfründe; ⚡ Induktion f.

**indulge** [in'dʌldʒ] nachsichtig sein
gegen j-n; j-m nachgeben; ~ with
j-n erfreuen mit; ~ (o.s.) in s.th. sich
et. gönnen; sich e-r S. hin- od. ergeben; ~nce [~dʒəns] Nachsicht f;
Nachgiebigkeit f; Sichgehenlassen
n; Vergünstigung f; ~nt □ [~nt]
nachsichtig.

**industri|al** □ [in'dʌstriəl] gewerbe-
treibend, gewerblich; industriell;
Gewerbe...; Industrie...; ~ area
Industriebezirk m; ~ estate Indu-
striegebiet n e-r Stadt; ~ school
Gewerbeschule f; ~alist [~list]
Industrielle(r) m; ~alize [~laiz]
industrialisieren; ~ous □ [~iəs]
fleißig.

**industry** ['indəstri] Fleiß m; Gewerbe n; Industrie f.

**inebriate 1.** [i'niːbrieit] betrunken
machen; **2.** [~iit] Trunkenbold m.

**ineffable** □ [in'efəbl] unaussprechlich.

**ineffect|ive** [ini'fektiv], ~ual □
[~tjuəl] unwirksam, fruchtlos.

**inefficient** □ [ini'fiʃənt] wirkungs-
los; (leistungs)unfähig.

**inelegant** □ [in'eligənt] unelegant,
geschmacklos.

**ineligible** □ [in'elidʒəbl] nicht
wählbar; ungeeignet; bsd. ✕ untauglich.

**inept** □ [i'nept] unpassend; albern.

**inequality** [ini(:)'kwɔliti] Ungleichheit f; Ungleichmäßigkeit f; Unebenheit f.

**inequitable** □ [in'ekwitəbl] unbillig.

**inert** □ [i'nəːt] träge; ~ia [i'nəːʃjə],
~ness [i'nəːtnis] Trägheit f.

**inescapable** [inis'keipəbl] unent-
rinnbar.

**inessential** ['ini'senʃəl] unwesentlich (to für).

**inestimable** □ [in'estiməbl] unschätzbar.

**inevitab|le** □ [in'evitəbl] unver-
meidlich; ~ly [~li] unweigerlich.

**inexact** □ [inig'zækt] ungenau.

**inexcusable** □ [iniks'kjuːzəbl] un-
entschuldbar.

**inexhaustible** □ [inig'zɔːstəbl] unerschöpflich; unermüdlich.

**inexorable** □ [in'eksərəbl] unerbittlich.

**inexpedient** □ [iniks'piːdjənt] unzweckmäßig, unpassend.

**inexpensive** □ [iniks'pensiv] nicht
teuer, billig, preiswert.

**inexperience** [iniks'piəriəns] Unerfahrenheit f; ~d [~st] unerfahren.

**inexpert** □ [ineks'pəːt] unerfahren.

**inexplicable** □ [in'eksplikəbl] unerklärlich.

**inexpressi|ble** □ [iniks'presəbl]
unaussprechlich; ~ve [~siv] aus-
druckslos.

**inextinguishable** □ [iniks'tiŋgwi-
ʃəbl] unauslöschlich.

**inextricable** □ [in'ekstrikəbl] un-
entwirrbar.

**infallible** □ [in'fæləbl] unfehlbar.

**infam|ous** □ ['infəməs] ehrlos;
schändlich; verrufen; ~y [~mi] Ehr-
losigkeit f; Schande f; Nieder-
tracht f.

**infan|cy** ['infənsi] Kindheit f; ⚖
Minderjährigkeit f; ~t [~nt] Säugling m; (kleines) Kind; Minder-
jährige(r m) f.

**infanti|le** ['infəntail], ~ne [~ain]
kindlich; Kindes..., Kinder...; kindisch.

**infantry** ✕ ['infəntri] Infanterie f.

**infatuate** [in'fætjueit] betören; ~d
vernarrt (with in acc.).

**infect** [in'fekt] anstecken (a. fig.);
infizieren, verseuchen, verpesten;
~ion [~kʃən] Ansteckung f; ~ious
□ [~ʃəs], ~ive [~ktiv] ansteckend;
Ansteckungs...

**infer** [in'fəː] folgern, schließen;
~ence ['infərəns] Folgerung f.

**inferior** [in'fiəriə] **1.** untere(r, -s)
minderwertig; ~ to niedriger od.
geringer als; untergeordnet (dat.);
unterlegen (dat.); **2.** Geringere(r m)
f; Untergebene(r m) f; ~ity [infiəri-
'ɔriti] geringerer Wert od. Stand;
Unterlegenheit f; Minderwertig-
keit f.

**infern|al** □ [in'fəːnl] höllisch; ~o
[~nou] Inferno n, Hölle f.

**infertile** [in'fəːtail] unfruchtbar.

**infest** [in'fest] heimsuchen; verseuchen; fig. überschwemmen.

**infidelity** [infi'deliti] Unglaube m;
Untreue f (to gegen).

**infiltrate** ['infiltreit] v/t. durchdringen; v/i. durchsickern, eindringen.

**infinite** □ ['infinit] unendlich.

**infinitive** [in'finitiv] a. ~ mood gr.
Infinitiv m, Nennform f.

**infinity** [in'finiti] Unendlichkeit f.

**infirm** □ [in'fəːm] kraftlos, schwach;
~ary [~məri] Krankenhaus n; ~ity
[~miti] Schwäche f (a. fig.); Ge-
brechen n.

**inflame** [in'fleim] entflammen (mst
fig.); (sich) entzünden (a. fig. u. ⚕).

**inflamma|ble** □ [in'flæməbl] ent-
zündlich; feuergefährlich; ~tion
[inflə'meiʃən] Entzündung f; ~tory

[in'flæmətəri] entzündlich; *fig.* aufrührerisch; hetzerisch; Hetz...

**inflat|e** [in'fleit] aufblasen, aufblähen (*a. fig.*); **~ion** [~eiʃən] Aufblähung *f*; ✝ Inflation *f*; *fig.* Aufgeblasenheit *f*.

**inflect** [in'flekt] biegen; *gr.* flektieren, beugen.

**inflexi|ble** □ [in'fleksəbl] unbiegsam; *fig.* unbeugsam; **~on** [~kʃən] Biegung *f*; *gr.* Flexion *f*, Beugung *f*; Modulation *f*.

**inflict** [in'flikt] auferlegen; zufügen; *Hieb* versetzen; *Strafe* verhängen; **~ion** [~kʃən] Auferlegung *f*; Zufügung *f*; Plage *f*.

**influen|ce** ['influəns] 1. Einfluß *m*; 2. beeinflussen; **~tial** *f* [influ-'enʃəl] einflußreich.

**influenza** 𝔰 [influ'enzə] Grippe *f*.

**influx** ['inflʌks] Einströmen *n*; *fig.* Zufluß *m*, (Zu)Strom *m*.

**inform** [in'fɔ:m] *v/t.* benachrichtigen, unterrichten (*of* von); *v/i.* anzeigen (*against* s.o. j.); **~al** □ [~ml] formlos, zwanglos; **~ality** [infɔ:-'mæliti] Formlosigkeit *f*; Formfehler *m*; **~ation** [infə'meiʃən] Auskunft *f*; Nachricht *f*, Information *f*; **~ative** [in'fɔ:mətiv] informatorisch; lehrreich; mitteilsam; **~er** [in'fɔ:mə] Denunziant *m*; Spitzel *m*.

**infrequent** [in'fri:kwənt] selten.

**infringe** [in'frindʒ] *a.* ~ *upon* *Vertrag etc.* verletzen; übertreten.

**infuriate** [in'fjuərieit] wütend machen.

**infuse** [in'fju:z] einflößen; aufgießen.

**ingen|ious** □ [in'dʒi:njəs] geist-, sinnreich; erfinderisch; raffiniert; genial; **~uity** [indʒi'nju(:)iti] Genialität *f*; **~uous** □ [in'dʒenjuəs] freimütig; unbefangen, naiv.

**ingot** ['ingət] *Gold- etc.* Barren *m*.

**ingrati|ate** [in'greiʃieit]: ~ *o.s.* sich beliebt machen (*with* bei); **~tude** [~rætitju:d] Undankbarkeit *f*.

**ingredient** [in'gri:djənt] Bestandteil *m*.

**ingrowing** ['ingrouiŋ] nach innen wachsend; eingewachsen.

**inhabit** [in'hæbit] bewohnen; **~able** [~təbl] bewohnbar; **~ant** [~ənt] Bewohner(in), Einwohner(in).

**inhal|ation** [inhə'leiʃən] Einatmung *f*; **~e** [in'heil] einatmen.

**inherent** □ [in'hiərənt] anhaftend; innewohnend, angeboren (*in dat.*).

**inherit** [in'herit] (er)erben; **~ance** [~təns] Erbteil *n*, Erbe *n*; Erbschaft *f*; *biol.* Vererbung *f*.

**inhibit** [in'hibit] (ver)hindern; verbieten; zurückhalten; **~ion** [inhi-'biʃən] Hemmung *f*; Verbot *n*.

**inhospitable** □ [in'hɔspitəbl] ungastlich, unwirtlich.

**inhuman** □ [in'hju:mən] unmenschlich.

**inimical** □ [i'nimikəl] feindlich; schädlich.

**inimitable** □ [i'nimitəbl] unnachahmlich.

**iniquity** [i'nikwiti] Ungerechtigkeit *f*; Schlechtigkeit *f*.

**initia|l** [i'niʃəl] 1. □ Anfangs...; anfänglich; 2. Anfangsbuchstabe *m*; **~te** 1. [~ʃiit] Eingeweihte(r *m*) *f*; 2. [~ieit] beginnen; anbahnen; einführen, einweihen; **~tion** [iniʃi-'eiʃən] Einleitung *f*; Einführung *f*, Einweihung *f*; ~ *fee* *bsd. Am.* Aufnahmegebühr *f* (*Vereinigung*); **~tive** [i'niʃiətiv] Initiative *f*; einleitender Schritt; Entschlußkraft *f*; Unternehmungsgeist *m*; Volksbegehren *n*; **~tor** [~ieitə] Initiator *m*, Urheber *m*.

**inject** [in'dʒekt] einspritzen; **~ion** [~kʃən] Injektion *f*, Spritze *f*.

**injudicious** □ [indʒu(:)'diʃəs] unverständig, unklug, unüberlegt.

**injunction** [in'dʒʌŋkʃən] gerichtliche Verfügung *f*; ausdrücklicher Befehl.

**injur|e** [in'dʒə] (be)schädigen; schaden (*dat.*); verletzen; beleidigen; **~ious** [in'dʒuəriəs] schädlich; ungerecht; beleidigend; **~y** ['indʒəri] Unrecht *n*; Schaden *m*; Verletzung *f*; Beleidigung *f*.

**injustice** [in'dʒʌstis] Ungerechtigkeit *f*; Unrecht *n*.

**ink** [iŋk] 1. Tinte *f*; *mst printer's* ~ Druckerschwärze *f*; *attr.* Tinten...; 2. (mit Tinte) schwärzen; beklecksen.

**inkling** ['iŋkliŋ] Andeutung *f*; dunkle *od.* leise Ahnung.

**ink|pot** ['iŋkpɔt] Tintenfaß *n*; **~stand** Schreibzeug *n*; **~y** ['iŋki] tintig; Tinten...; tintenschwarz.

**inland** 1. ['inlənd] inländisch; Binnen...; 2. [~] Landesinnere(s) *n*, Binnenland *n*; 3. [in'lænd] landeinwärts.

**inlay** 1. [in'lei] [*irr.* (*lay*)] einlegen; 2. ['inlei] Einlage *f*; Einlegearbeit *f*.

**inlet** ['inlet] Bucht *f*; Einlaß *m*.

**inmate** [in'meit] Insasse *m*, -in *f*; Hausgenoss|e *m*, -in *f*.

**inmost** ['inmoust] innerst.

**inn** [in] Gasthof *m*, Wirtshaus *n*.

**innate** □ [i'neit] angeboren.

**inner** ['inə] inner, inwendig; geheim; **~most** innerst; geheimst.

**innervate** ['inə:veit] Nervenkraft geben (*dat.*); kräftigen.

**innings** ['iniŋz] *Sport:* Dransein *n*.

**innkeeper** ['iŋki:pə] Gastwirt(in).

**innocen|ce** ['inəsns] Unschuld *f*; Harmlosigkeit *f*; Einfalt *f*; **~t** [~nt] 1. □ unschuldig; harmlos; 2. Unschuldige(r *m*) *f*; Einfältige(r *m*) *f*.

**innocuous** □ [i'nɔkjuəs] harmlos.

**innovation** [inou'veiʃən] Neuerung *f*.

**innoxious** □ [i'nɔkʃəs] unschädlich.

innuendo [inju(:)'endou] Andeutung f.

innumerable ☐ [i'nju:mərəbl] unzählbar, unzählig.

inoccupation ['inɔkju'peiʃən] Beschäftigungslosigkeit f.

inoculate [i'nɔkjuleit] (ein)impfen.

inoffensive [inə'fensiv] harmlos.

inofficial [inə'fiʃəl] inoffiziell.

inoperative [in'ɔpərətiv] unwirksam.

inopportune ☐ [in'ɔpətju:n] unangebracht, zur Unzeit.

inordinate [i'nɔ:dinit] unmäßig.

in-patient ['inpeiʃənt] Krankenhauspatient m, stationärer Patient.

inquest ['inkwest] Untersuchung f; coroner's ~ Leichenschau f.

inquir|e [in'kwaiə] fragen, sich erkundigen (of bei j-m); ~ into untersuchen; ~ing ☐ [~əriŋ] forschend; ~y [~ri] Erkundigung f, Nachfrage f; Untersuchung f; Ermittlung f.

inquisit|ion [inkwi'ziʃən] Untersuchung f; ~ive ☐ [in'kwizitiv] neugierig; wißbegierig.

inroad ['inroud] feindlicher Einfall; Ein-, Übergriff m.

insan|e ☐ [in'sein] wahnsinnig; ~ity [in'sæniti] Wahnsinn m.

insatia|ble ☐ [in'seiʃəbl], ~te [~ʃiit] unersättlich (of nach).

inscribe [in'skraib] ein-, auf-, beschreiben; beschriften; fig. einprägen (in, on dat.); Buch widmen.

inscription [in'skripʃən] In-, Aufschrift f; ✝ Eintragung f.

inscrutable ☐ [in'skru:təbl] unerforschlich, unergründlich.

insect ['insekt] Insekt n; ~icide [in'sektisaid] Insektengift n.

insecure ☐ [insi'kjuə] unsicher.

insens|ate ☐ [in'senseit] gefühllos, unvernünftig; ~ible ☐ [~səbl] unempfindlich; bewußtlos; unmerklich; gleichgültig; ~itive [~sitiv] unempfindlich.

inseparable ☐ [in'sepərəbl] untrennbar; unzertrennlich.

insert 1. [in'sə:t] einsetzen, einschalten, einfügen; (hinein)stecken; Münze einwerfen; inserieren; 2. ['insə:t] Bei-, Einlage f; ~ion [in'sə:ʃən] Einsetzung f, Einfügung f, Eintragung f; Einwurf m e-r Münze; Anzeige f, Inserat n.

inshore ⚓ ['in'ʃɔ:] an od. nahe der Küste (befindlich); Küsten...

inside [in'said] 1. Innenseite f; Innere(s) n; turn ~ out umkrempeln; auf den Kopf stellen; 2. adj. inner, inwendig; Innen...; 3. adv. im Innern; 4. prp. innerhalb.

insidious ☐ [in'sidiəs] heimtückisch.

insight ['insait] Einsicht f, Einblick m.

insignia [in'signiə] pl. Abzeichen n/pl., Insignien pl.

insignificant [insig'nifikənt] bedeutungslos; unbedeutend.

insincere ☐ [insin'siə] unaufrichtig.

insinuat|e [in'sinjueit] unbemerkt hineinbringen; zu verstehen geben; andeuten; ~ion [insinju'eiʃən] Einschmeichelung f; Anspielung f, Andeutung f; Wink m.

insipid [in'sipid] geschmacklos, fad.

insist [in'sist]: ~ (up)on bestehen auf (dat.); dringen auf (acc.); ~ence [~təns] Bestehen n; Beharrlichkeit f; Drängen n; ~ent ☐ [~nt] beharrlich; eindringlich.

insolent ☐ ['insələnt] unverschämt.

insoluble ☐ [in'sɔljubl] unlöslich.

insolvent [in'sɔlvənt] zahlungsunfähig. [keit f.\

insomnia [in'sɔmniə] Schlaflosig-\

insomuch [insou'mʌtʃ]: ~ that dermaßen od. so sehr, daß.

inspect [in'spekt] untersuchen, prüfen, nachsehen; ~ion [~kʃən] Prüfung f, Untersuchung f; Inspektion f; ~or [~ktə] Aufsichtsbeamte(r) m.

inspir|ation [inspə'reiʃən] Einatmung f; Eingebung f; Begeisterung f; ~e [in'spaiə] einatmen; fig. eingeben, erfüllen; j-n begeistern.

install [in'stɔ:l] einsetzen; (sich) niederlassen; ⊕ installieren; ~ation [instə'leiʃən] Einsetzung f; ⊕ Installation f, Einrichtung f; ⚡ etc. Anlage f.

instal(l)ment [in'stɔ:lmənt] Rate f; Teil-, Ratenzahlung f; (Teil)Lieferung f; Fortsetzung f.

instance ['instəns] Ersuchen n; Beispiel n; (besonderer) Fall; ✝ Instanz f; for ~ zum Beispiel.

instant ☐ ['instənt] 1. dringend; sofortig; on the 10th ~ am 10. dieses Monats; 2. Augenblick m; ~aneous ☐ [instən'teinjəs] augenblicklich; Moment...; ~ly ['instəntli] sogleich.

instead [in'sted] dafür; ~ of anstatt.

instep ['instep] Spann m.

instigat|e ['instigeit] anstiften; aufhetzen; ~or [~tə] Anstifter m, Hetzer m.

instil(l) [in'stil] einträufeln; fig. einflößen (into dat.).

instinct ['instiŋkt] Instinkt m; ~ive ☐ [in'stiŋktiv] instinktiv.

institut|e ['institju:t] 1. Institut n; 2. einsetzen, stiften, einrichten, verordnen; ~ion [insti'tju:ʃən] Einsetzung f, Einrichtung f; An-, Verordnung f; Satzung f; Institut(ion f) n; Gesellschaft f; Anstalt f; ~ional [~nl] Instituts..., Anstalts...

instruct [in'strʌkt] unterrichten; belehren; j-n anweisen; ~ion [~kʃən] Vorschrift f; Unterweisung f; Anweisung f; ~ive ☐ [~ktiv] lehrreich; ~or [~tə] Lehrer m; Ausbilder m; Am. univ. Dozent m.

instrument ['instrumənt] Instru-

**ment** *n*, Werkzeug *n* (*a. fig.*); z't
Urkunde *f*; **~al** □ [instru'mentl]
als Werkzeug dienend; dienlich; *♪*
Instrumental...; **~ality** [instrumen-
'tæliti] Mitwirkung *f*, Mittel *n*.

**insubordinat|e** [insə'bɔːdnit] auf-
sässig; **~ion** ['insəbɔːdi'neiʃən] Auf-
lehnung *f*.

**insubstantial** [insəb'stænʃəl] unwirklich; gebrechlich.

**insufferable** □ [in'sʌfərəbl] unerträglich, unausstehlich.

**insufficient** □ [insə'fiʃənt] unzulänglich, ungenügend.

**insula|r** □ ['insjulə] Insel...; *fig.*
engstirnig; **~te** [~leit] isolieren;
**~tion** [insju'leiʃən] Isolierung *f*.

**insult** 1. ['insʌlt] Beleidigung *f*;
2. [in'sʌlt] beleidigen.

**insupportable** □ [insə'pɔːtəbl] unerträglich, unaussstehlich.

**insur|ance** [in'ʃuərəns] Versiche-
rung *f*; *attr.* Versicherungs...;
**~ance policy** Versicherungspolice
*f*, -schein *m*; **~e** [in'ʃuə] versichern.

**insurgent** [in'sɔːdʒənt] 1. aufrührerisch; 2. Aufrührer *m*.

**insurmountable** □ [insə(ː)'maun-
təbl] unübersteigbar, *fig.* unüberwindlich.

**insurrection** [insə'rekʃən] Aufstand
*m*, Empörung *f*.

**intact** [in'tækt] unberührt; unversehrt.

**intangible** □ [in'tændʒəbl] unfühl-
bar; unfaßbar; unantastbar.

**integ|ral** □ ['intigrəl] ganz, voll-
ständig; wesentlich; **~rate** [~reit]
ergänzen; zs.-tun; einfügen; **~rity**
[in'tegriti] Vollständigkeit *f*; Redlichkeit *f*, Integrität *f*.

**intellect** ['intilekt] Verstand *m*;
*konkr. die* Intelligenz; **~ual** [inti-
'lektjuəl] 1. □ intellektuell; Ver-
standes...; geistig; verständig; 2. In-
tellektuelle(r *m*) *f*.

**intelligence** [in'telidʒəns] Intelligenz *f*; Verstand *m*; Verständnis *n*;
Nachricht *f*, Auskunft *f*; **~ department** Nachrichtendienst *m*.

**intellig|ent** [in'telidʒənt] intelli-
gent; klug; **~ible** □ [~dʒəbl] verständlich (*to* für).

**intempera|nce** [in'tempərəns] Un-
mäßigkeit *f*; Trunksucht *f*; **~te**
[~rit] unmäßig; zügellos; unbe-
herrscht; trunksüchtig.

**intend** [in'tend] beabsichtigen, wollen; **~ for** bestimmen für *od.* zu;
**~ed** 1. absichtlich; beabsichtigt, *a.*
zukünftig; 2. F Verlobte(r *m*) *f*.

**intense** □ [in'tens] intensiv; ange-
strengt; heftig; kräftig (*Farbe*).

**intensify** [in'tensifai] (sich) verstärken *od.* steigern.

**intensity** [in'tensiti] Intensität *f*.

**intent** [in'tent] 1. □ gespannt; bedacht; beschäftigt (*on* mit); 2. Absicht *f*; Vorhaben *n*; *to all* **~s and**

*purposes* in jeder Hinsicht; **~ion**
[~nʃən] Absicht *f*; Zweck *m*; **~ional**
□ [~nl] absichtlich; **~ness** [~ntnis]
gespannte Aufmerksamkeit; Eifer
*m*.

**inter** [in'tɔː] beerdigen, begraben.

**inter...** ['intə(ː)] zwischen; Zwischen...; gegenseitig, einander.

**interact** [intər'ækt] sich gegenseitig
beeinflussen.

**intercede** [intə(ː)'siːd] vermitteln.

**intercept** [intə(ː)'sept] ab-, auffangen; abhören; aufhalten; unterbrechen; **~ion** [~pʃən] Ab-, Auffangen *n*; Ab-, Mithören *n*; Unterbrechung *f*; Aufhalten *n*.

**intercession** [intə'seʃən] Fürbitte
*f*; **~or** [~esə] Fürsprecher *m*.

**interchange** 1. [intə(ː)'tʃeindʒ] *v/t.*
austauschen, auswechseln; *v/i.* abwechseln; 2. ['intə(ː)'tʃeindʒ] Austausch *m*; Abwechs(e)lung *f*.

**intercourse** ['intə(ː)kɔːs] Verkehr *m*.

**interdict** 1. [intə(ː)'dikt] untersagen,
verbieten (*s.th. to s.o.* j-m et.; *s.o.
from doing* j-m zu tun); 2. ['intə(ː)-
dikt], **~ion** [intə(ː)'dikʃən] Verbot
*n*; Interdikt *n*.

**interest** ['intrist] 1. Interesse *n*;
Anziehungskraft *f*; Bedeutung *f*;
Nutzen *m*; ✝ Anteil *m*, Beteiligung
*f*, Kapital *n*; Zins(en *pl.*) *m*; **~s** *pl.*
Interessenten *m/pl.*, Kreise *m/pl.*;
*take an* **~** *in* sich interessieren für;
*return a blow with* **~** noch heftiger
zurückschlagen; *banking* **~s** *pl.*
Bankkreise *m/pl.*; 2. *allg.* interessieren (*in* für *et.*); **~ing** [~tiŋ]
interessant.

**interfere** [intə'fiə] sich einmischen
(*with* in *acc.*); vermitteln; (*ea.*)
stören; **~nce** [~ərəns] Einmischung
*f*; Beeinträchtigung *f*; Störung *f*.

**interim** ['intərim] 1. Zwischenzeit
*f*; 2. vorläufig; Interims...

**interior** [in'tiəriə] 1. □ inner; inner-
lich; Innen...; **~ decorator** Innen-
architekt *m*; Maler *m*, Tapezierer
*m*; 2. Innere(s) *n*; Interieur *n*; *pol.*
innere Angelegenheiten; *Depart-
ment of the* **♀** *Am.* Innenministerium *n*.

**interjection** [intə(ː)'dʒekʃən] Ausruf *m*.

**interlace** [intə(ː)'leis] *v/t.* durch-
flechten, -weben; *v/i.* sich kreuzen.

**interlock** [intə(ː)'lɔk] in-ea.-greifen;
in-ea.-schlingen; in-ea.-haken.

**interlocut|ion** [intə(ː)lou'kjuːʃən]
Unterredung *f*; **~or** [~ɔ(ː)'lɔkjutə]
Gesprächspartner *m*.

**interlope** [intə(ː)'loup] sich ein-
drängen; **~r** ['intə(ː)loupə] Eindringling *m*.

**interlude** ['intə(ː)luːd] Zwischen-
spiel *n*; Zwischenzeit *f*; **~s of bright
weather** zeitweilig schön.

**intermarriage** [intə(ː)'mæridʒ]
Mischehe *f*.

**intermeddle** [intə(:)'medl] sich ein-mischen (*with, in* in *acc.*).

**intermedia|ry** [intə(:)'mi:djəri] **1.** = *intermediate;* vermittelnd; **2.** Vermittler *m;* **~te** □ [**~ət**] in der Mitte liegend; Mittel..., Zwi-schen...; **~range ballistic missile** Mittelstreckenrakete *f;* **~ school** *Am.* Mittelschule *f.*

**interment** [in'tə:mənt] Beerdi-gung *f.*

**interminable** □ [in'tə:minəbl] end-los, unendlich.

**intermingle** [intə(:)'miŋgl] (sich) vermischen.

**intermission** [intə(:)'miʃən] Aus-setzen *n,* Unterbrechung *f;* Pause *f.*

**intermit** [intə(:)'mit] unterbrechen, aussetzen; **~tent** □ [**~tənt**] aus-setzend; **~ fever** 🌡 Wechselfieber *n.*

**intermix** [intə(:)'miks] (sich) ver-mischen.

**intern**[1] [in'tə:n] internieren.

**intern**[2] ['intə:n] Assistenzarzt *m.*

**internal** □ [in'tə:nl] inner(lich); inländisch.

**international** □ [intə(:)'næʃənl] international; **~ law** Völkerrecht *n.*

**interphone** ['intəfoun] Hausteile-phon *n; Am.* 🚗 Bordsprechanlage *f.*

**interpolate** [in'tə:pouleit] ein-schieben.

**interpose** [intə(:)'pouz] *v/t. Veto* einlegen; *Wort* einwerfen; *v/i.* dazwischentreten; vermitteln.

**interpret** [in'tə:prit] auslegen, er-klären, interpretieren; (ver)dol-metschen; darstellen; **~ation** [intə:-pri'teiʃən] Auslegung *f;* Darstel-lung *f;* **~er** [in'tə:pritə] Ausleger (-in); Dolmetscher(in); Interpret (-in).

**interrogat|e** [in'terəgeit] (be-, aus-) fragen; verhören; **~ion** [intərə-'geiʃən] (Be-, Aus)Fragen *n,* Ver-hör(en) *n;* Frage *f; note od. mark od. point of* **~** Fragezeichen *n;* **~ive** □ [intə'rɔgətiv] fragend; Frage...

**interrupt** [intə'rʌpt] unterbrechen; **~ion** [**~pʃən**] Unterbrechung *f.*

**intersect** [intə(:)'sekt] (sich) schnei-den; **~ion** [**~kʃən**] Durchschnitt *m;* Schnittpunkt *m; Straßen- etc.* Kreuzung *f.*

**intersperse** [intə(:)'spə:s] einstreu-en; untermengen, durchsetzen.

**interstate** *Am.* [intə(:)'steit] zwi-schenstaatlich.

**intertwine** [intə(:)'twain] verflech-ten.

**interval** ['intəvəl] Zwischenraum *m;* Pause *f; (Zeit)*Abstand *m.*

**interven|e** [intə(:)'vi:n] dazwischen-kommen; sich einmischen; ein-schreiten; dazwischenliegen; **~tion** [**~'venʃən**] Dazwischenkommen *n;* Einmischung *f;* Vermitt(e)lung *f.*

**interview** ['intəvju:] **1.** Zusammen-kunft *f,* Unterredung *f;* Interview *n;* **2.** interviewen.

**intestine** [in'testin] **1.** inner; **2.** Darm *m;* **~s** *pl.* Eingeweide *n/pl.*

**intima|cy** ['intiməsi] Intimität *f,* Vertraulichkeit *f;* **~te 1.** [**~meit**] bekanntgeben; zu verstehen geben; **2.** □ [**~mit**] intim; **3.** [**~**] Vertrau-te(r *m*) *f;* **~tion** [inti'meiʃən] An-deutung *f,* Wink *m;* Ankündigung *f.*

**intimidate** [in'timideit] einschüch-tern.

**into** *prp.* ['intu, *vor Konsonant* 'intə] in (*acc.*), in ... hinein.

**intolera|ble** □ [in'tɔlərəbl] uner-träglich; **~nt** □ [**~ənt**] unduldsam, intolerant.

**intonation** [intou'neiʃən] Anstim-men *n; gr.* Intonation *f,* Tonfall *m.*

**intoxica|nt** [in'tɔksikənt] **1.** berau-schend; **2.** berauschendes Getränk; **~te** [**~keit**] berauschen (*a. fig.*); **~tion** [intɔksi'keiʃən] Rausch *m* (*a. fig.*).

**intractable** □ [in'træktəbl] un-lenksam, störrisch; schwer zu bän-digen(d).

**intransitive** □ *gr.* [in'trænsitiv] intransitiv.

**intrastate** *Am.* [intrə'steit] inner-staatlich.

**intrench** [in'trentʃ] = *entrench.*

**intrepid** [in'trepid] unerschrocken.

**intricate** □ ['intrikit] verwickelt.

**intrigue** [in'tri:g] **1.** Ränkespiel *n,* Intrige *f;* (Liebes)Verhältnis *n;* **2.** *v/i.* Ränke schmieden, intrigie-ren; ein (Liebes)Verhältnis haben; *v/t.* neugierig machen; **~r** [**~gə**] Intrigant(in).

**intrinsic(al** □) [in'trinsik(əl)] in-ner(lich); wirklich, wahr.

**introduc|e** [intrə'dju:s] einführen (*a. fig.*); bekannt machen (*to* mit), vorstellen (*to j-m*); einleiten; **~tion** [**~'dʌkʃən**] Einführung *f;* Einlei-tung *f;* Vorstellung *f; letter of* **~** Empfehlungsschreiben *n;* **~tory** [**~ktəri**] einleitend, einführend.

**introspection** [introu'spekʃən] Selbstprüfung *f;* Selbstbetrach-tung *f.*

**introvert 1.** [introu'və:t] einwärts-kehren; **2.** *psych.* ['introuvə:t] nach innen gekehrter Mensch.

**intru|de** [in'tru:d] hineinzwängen; (sich) ein- *od.* aufdrängen; **~der** [**~də**] Eindringling *m;* **~sion** [**~'u:-ʒən**] Eindringen *n;* Auf-, Zudring-lichkeit *f;* **~sive** □ [**~'u:siv**] zu-dringlich.

**intrust** [in'trʌst] = *entrust.*

**intuition** [intju(:)'iʃən] unmittel-bare Erkenntnis, Intuition *f.*

**inundate** ['inʌndeit] überschwem-men.

**inure** [i'njuə] gewöhnen (*to an acc.*).

**invade** [in'veid] eindringen in, einfallen in (*acc.*); *fig.* befallen; **~r** [~də] Angreifer *m*; Eindringling *m*.

**invalid**[1] ['invəli:d] **1.** dienstunfähig; kränklich; **2.** Invalide *m*.

**invalid**[2] [in'vælid] (rechts)ungültig; **~ate** [~deit] entkräften; ⚖ ungültig machen; [~schätzbar.]

**invaluable** □ [in'væljuəbl] un-]

**invariab|le** □ [in'veəriəbl] unveränderlich; **~ly** [~li] ausnahmslos.

**invasion** [in'veiʒən] Einfall *m*, Angriff *m*, Invasion *f*; Eingriff *m*; ⚔ Anfall *m*.

**invective** [in'vektiv] Schmähung *f*, Schimpfrede *f*, Schimpfwort *n*.

**inveigh** [in'vei] schimpfen (*against* über, auf *acc.*).

**inveigle** [in'vi:gl] verleiten.

**invent** [in'vent] erfinden; **~ion** [~nʃən] Erfindung(sgabe) *f*; **~ive** □ [~ntiv] erfinderisch; **~or** [~tə] Erfinder(in); **~ory** [~'inventri] **1.** Inventar *n*; Inventur *f*; **2.** inventarisieren.

**invers|e** □ ['in'və:s] umgekehrt; **~ion** [in'və:ʃən] Umkehrung *f*; *gr.* Inversion *f*.

**invert** [in'və:t] umkehren; umstellen; **~ed commas** *pl.* Anführungszeichen *n/pl.*

**invest** [in'vest] investieren, anlegen; bekleiden; ausstatten; umgeben (*with* von); ✗ belagern.

**investigat|e** [in'vestigeit] erforschen; untersuchen; nachforschen; **~ion** [investi'geiʃən] Erforschung *f*; Untersuchung *f*; Nachforschung *f*; **~or** [in'vestigeitə] Untersuchende(*r m*) *f*.

**invest|ment** ✝ [in'vestmənt] Kapitalanlage *f*; Investition *f*; **~or** [~tə] Geldgeber *m*.

**inveterate** [in'vetərit] eingewurzelt.

**invidious** □ [in'vidiəs] verhaßt; gehässig; beneidenswert.

**invigorate** [in'vigəreit] kräftigen.

**invincible** □ [in'vinsəbl] unbesiegbar; unüberwindlich.

**inviola|ble** □ [in'vaiələbl] unverletzlich; **~te** [~lit] unverletzt.

**invisible** [in'vizəbl] unsichtbar.

**invit|ation** [invi'teiʃən] Einladung *f*, Aufforderung *f*; **~e** [in'vait] einladen; auffordern; (an)locken.

**invoice** ✝ ['invɔis] Faktura *f*, Warenrechnung *f*.

**invoke** [in'vouk] anrufen; zu Hilfe rufen (*acc.*); sich berufen auf (*acc.*); *Geist* heraufbeschwören.

**involuntary** □ [in'vɔləntəri] unfreiwillig; unwillkürlich.

**involve** [in'vɔlv] verwickeln, hineinziehen; in sich schließen, enthalten; mit sich bringen; **~ment** [~vmənt] Verwicklung *f*; (*bsd.* Geld)Schwierigkeit *f*.

**invulnerable** □ [in'vʌlnərəbl] unverwundbar; *fig.* unanfechtbar.

**inward** ['inwəd] **1.** □ inner(lich); **2.** *adv. mst* **~s** einwärts; nach innen; **3.** **~s** *pl.* Eingeweide *n/pl.*

**iodine** ['aiədi:n] Jod *n*.

**IOU** ['aiou'ju:] ( = *I owe you*) Schuldschein *m*.

**irascible** □ [i'ræsibl] jähzornig.

**irate** [ai'reit] zornig, wütend.

**iridescent** [iri'desnt] schillernd.

**iris** ['aiəris] *anat.* Regenbogenhaut *f*, Iris *f*; ♀ Schwertlilie *f*.

**Irish** ['aiəriʃ] **1.** irisch; **2.** Irisch *n*; *the* **~** *pl.* die Iren *pl.*; **~man** Ire *m*.

**irksome** ['ə:ksəm] lästig, ermüdend.

**iron** ['aiən] **1.** Eisen *n*; *a. flat-*~ Bügeleisen *n*; **~s** *pl.* Fesseln *f/pl.*; *strike while the* **~** *is hot fig.* das Eisen schmieden, solange es heiß ist; **2.** eisern (*a. fig.*); Eisen...; **3.** bügeln; in Eisen legen; **~-bound** eisenbeschlagen; felsig; unbeugsam; **~clad 1.** gepanzert; **2.** Panzerschiff *n*; **~curtain** *pol.* eiserner Vorhang; **~-hearted** *fig.* hartherzig.

**ironic(al** □) [ai'rɔnik(əl)] ironisch, spöttisch.

**iron|ing** ['aiəniŋ] Plätten *n*, Bügeln *n*; *attr.* Plätt..., Bügel...; **~ lung** ⚔ eiserne Lunge; **~monger** Eisenhändler *m*; **~mongery** [~əri] Eisenwaren *f/pl.*; **~mo(u)ld** Rostfleck *m*; **~work** schmiedeeiserne Arbeit; **~works** *mst sg.* Eisenhütte *f*.

**irony**[1] ['aiən] eisenartig, -haltig.

**irony**[2] ['aiərəni] Ironie *f*.

**irradiant** [i'reidjənt] strahlend (*with* vor *Freude etc.*).

**irradiate** [i'reidieit] bestrahlen (*a.* ✍); *fig.* aufklären; strahlen lassen.

**irrational** [i'ræʃəl] unvernünftig.

**irreclaimable** □ [iri'kleiməbl] unverbesserlich.

**irrecognizable** □ [i'rekəgnaizəbl] nicht (wieder)erkennbar.

**irreconcilable** □ [i'rekənsailəbl] unversöhnlich; unvereinbar.

**irrecoverable** □ [iri'kʌvərəbl] unersetzlich; unwiederbringlich.

**irredeemable** □ [iri'di:məbl] unkündbar; nicht einlösbar; unersetzlich.

**irrefutable** □ [i'refjutəbl] unwiderleglich, unwiderlegbar.

**irregular** □ [i'regjulə] unregelmäßig, regelwidrig; ungleichmäßig.

**irrelevant** □ [i'relivənt] nicht zur Sache gehörig; unzutreffend; unerheblich; belanglos (*to* für).

**irreligious** □ [iri'lidʒəs] gottlos.

**irremediable** □ [iri'mi:djəbl] unheilbar; unersetzlich.

**irremovable** □ [iri'mu:vəbl] nicht entfernbar; unabsetzbar.

**irreparable** □ [i'repərəbl] nicht wieder gutzumachen(d).

**irreplaceable** [iri'pleisəbl] unersetzlich.

**irrepressible** □ [iri'presəbl] ununterdrückbar; unbezähmbar.

**irreproachable** □ [iri'proutʃəbl] einwandfrei, untadelig.
**irresistible** □ [iri'zistəbl] unwiderstehlich.
**irresolute** □ [i'rezəluːt] unentschlossen.
**irrespective** □ [iris'pektiv] (*of*) rücksichtslos (gegen); ohne Rücksicht (auf *acc.*); unabhängig (von).
**irresponsible** □ [iris'pɔnsəbl] unverantwortlich; verantwortungslos.
**irretrievable** □ [iri'triːvəbl] unwiederbringlich, unersetzlich; nicht wieder gutzumachen(d).
**irreverent** □ [i'revərənt] respektlos, ehrfurchtslos.
**irrevocable** □ [i'revəkəbl] unwiderruflich; unabänderlich, endgültig.
**irrigate** [i'irigeit] bewässern.
**irrita|ble** □ ['iritəbl] reizbar; **.nt** [..ənt] Reizmittel *n*; **.te** [..teit] reizen; ärgern; **.ting** □ [..tiŋ] aufreizend; ärgerlich (*Sache*); **.tion** [iri'teiʃən] Reizung *f*; Gereiztheit *f*, Ärger *m*.
**irrupt|ion** [i'rʌpʃən] Einbruch *m* (*mst fig.*); **.ive** [..ptiv] (her)einbrechend.
**is** [iz] *3. sg. pres. von* be.
**island** ['ailənd] Insel *f*; Verkehrsinsel *f*; **.er** [..də] Inselbewohner(in).
**isle** [ail] Insel *f*; **.t** ['ailit] Inselchen *n*.
**isolat|e** ['aisəleit] absondern; isolieren; **.ed** abgeschieden; **.ion** [aisə'leiʃən] Isolierung *f*, Absonderung *f*; **~ ward** ♂ Isolierstation *f*; **.ionist** *Am. pol.* [..ʃnist] Isolationist *m*.
**issue** ['isjuː, *Am.* 'iʃuː] 1. Heraus-

kommen *n*, Herausfließen *n*; Abfluß *m*; Ausgang *m*; Nachkommen (-schaft *f*) *m/pl.*; *fig.* Ausgang *m*, Ergebnis *n*; Streitfrage *f*; Ausgabe *f* v. *Material etc.*, Erlaß *m v. Befehlen*; Ausgabe *f*, Exemplar *n*; Nummer *f e-r Zeitung*; **~** in *law* Rechtsfrage *f*; be *at* **~** uneinig sein; *point at* **~** strittiger Punkt; 2. *v/i.* herauskommen; herkommen, entspringen; endigen (*in* in *acc.*); *v/t.* von sich geben; *Material etc.* ausgeben; *Befehl* erlassen; *Buch* herausgeben.
**isthmus** ['isməs] Landenge *f*.
**it** [it] 1. es; *nach prp.* da... (*z.B. by* **~** dadurch; *for* **~** dafür); 2. das gewisse Etwas.
**Italian** [i'tæljən] 1. italienisch; 2. Italiener(in); Italienisch *n*.
**italics** *typ.* [i'tæliks] Kursivschrift *f*.
**itch** [itʃ] 1. ♂ Krätze *f*; Jucken *n*; Verlangen *n*; 2. jucken; be **~**ing to *inf.* darauf brennen, zu *inf.*; *have an* **~**ing palm raffgierig sein; **.ing** ['itʃiŋ] Jucken *n*; *fig.* Gelüste *n*.
**item** ['aitem] 1. desgleichen; 2. Einzelheit *f*, Punkt *m*; Posten *m*; (Zeitungs)Artikel *m*; **.ize** [..maiz] einzeln angeben *od.* aufführen.
**iterate** ['itəreit] wiederholen.
**itiner|ant** □ [i'tinərənt] reisend; umherziehend; Reise...; **.ary** [ai'tinərəri] Reiseroute *f*; -plan *m*; Reisebericht *m*; *attr.* Reise...
**its** [its] sein(e); dessen, deren.
**itself** [it'self] (es, sich) selbst; sich; *of* **~** von selbst; *in* **~** in sich, an sich; *by* **~** für sich allein, besonders.
**ivory** ['aivəri] Elfenbein *n*.
**ivy** ♀ ['aivi] Efeu *m*.

# J

**jab** F [dʒæb] 1. stechen; stoßen; 2. Stich *m*, Stoß *m*.
**jabber** ['dʒæbə] plappern.
**jack** [dʒæk] 1. Hebevorrichtung *f*, *bsd.* Wagenheber *m*; Malkugel *f beim Bowlspiel*; ♣ Gösch *f*, kleine Flagge; *Karten:* Bube *m*; 2. *a.* **~** *up* aufbocken. [Handlanger *m.*]
**jackal** ['dʒækɔːl] *zo.* Schakal *m*; *fig.*|
**jack|ass** ['dʒækæs] Esel *m* (*a. fig.*); **.boots** Reitstiefel *m/pl.*; hohe Wasserstiefel *m/pl.*; **.daw** *orn.* Dohle *f*.
**jacket** ['dʒækit] Jacke *f*; ⊕ Mantel *m*; Schutzumschlag *m e-s Buches*.
**jack|-knife** ['dʒæknaif] (großes) Klappmesser *n*; **♀ of all trades** Hansdampf in allen Gassen; **2 of all work** Faktotum *n*; **.pot** *Poker:* Einsatz *m*; hit the **~** *Am.* F großes Glück haben.
**jade** [dʒeid] (Schind)Mähre *f*, Klepper *m*; *contp.* Frauenzimmer *n*.

**jag** [dʒæg] Zacken *m*; *sl.* Sauferei *f*; **.ged** ['dʒægid] zackig; gekerbt; *bsd. Am. sl.* voll (*betrunken*).
**jaguar** *zo.* ['dʒægjuə] Jaguar *m*.
**jail** [dʒeil] 1. Kerker *m*; 2. einkerkern; **.bird** ['dʒeilbəːd] F Knastbruder *m*; Galgenvogel *m*; **.er** ['dʒeilə] Kerkermeister *m*.
**jalop(p)y** *bsd. Am.* F *mot.*, ⚡ [dʒə'lɔpi] Kiste *f*.
**jam**[1] [dʒæm] Marmelade *f*.
**jam**[2] [..] 1. Gedränge *n*; ⊕ Hemmung *f*; *Radio:* Störung *f*; *traffic* **~** Verkehrsstockung *f*; be *in a* **~** *sl.* in der Klemme sein; 2. (sich) (fest-, ver)klemmen; pressen, quetschen; versperren; *Radio:* stören; **~** the brakes mit aller Kraft bremsen.
**jamboree** [dʒæmbə'riː] (*bsd.* Pfadfinder)Treffen *n*; *sl.* Vergnügen *n*, Fez *m*.

**jangle** ['dʒæŋgl] schrillen (lassen); laut streiten, keifen.

**janitor** ['dʒænitə] Portier m.

**January** ['dʒænjuəri] Januar m.

**Japanese** [dʒæpə'ni:z] 1. japanisch; 2. Japaner(in); Japanisch n; the ~ pl. die Japaner pl.

**jar** [dʒɑ:] 1. Krug m; Topf m; Glas n; Knarren n, Mißton m; Streit m; mißliche Lage; 2. knarren; unangenehm berühren; erzittern (lassen); streiten.

**jaundice** ['dʒɔ:ndis] Gelbsucht f; ~d [~st] gelbsüchtig; fig. neidisch.

**jaunt** [dʒɔ:nt] 1. Ausflug m, Spritztour f; 2. e-n Ausflug machen; ~y □ ['dʒɔ:nti] munter; flott.

**javelin** ['dʒævlin] Wurfspeer m.

**jaw** [dʒɔ:] 1. Kinnbacken m, Kiefer m; ~s pl. Rachen m; Maul n; Schlund m; ⊕ Backen f/pl.; ~-bone ['dʒɔ:boun] Kieferknochen m.

**jay** orn. [dʒei] Eichelhäher m; ~walker Am. F ['dʒeiwɔ:kə] achtlos die Straße überquerender Fußgänger.

**jazz** [dʒæz] 1. Jazz m; 2. F grell.

**jealous** □ ['dʒeləs] eifersüchtig; besorgt (of um); neidisch; ~y [~si] Eifersucht f; Neid m.

**jeans** [dʒi:nz] pl. Jeans pl., Niet(en)-hose f.

**jeep** [dʒi:p] Jeep m.

**jeer** [dʒiə] 1. Spott m, Spötterei f; 2. spotten (at über acc.); (ver-)höhnen.

**jejune** □ [dʒi'dʒu:n] nüchtern, fad.

**jelly** ['dʒeli] 1. Gallert(e f) n; Gelee n; 2. gelieren; ~-fish zo. Qualle f.

**jeopardize** ['dʒepədaiz] gefährden.

**jerk** [dʒə:k] 1. Ruck m; (Muskel-)Krampf m; 2. rucken od. zerren (an dat.); schnellen; schleudern; ~water Am. ['dʒə:kwɔ:tə] 1. ⓦ Nebenbahn f; 2. F klein, unbedeutend; ~y ['dʒə:ki] 1. □ ruckartig; holperig; 2. Am. luftgetrocknetes Rindfleisch.

**jersey** ['dʒə:zi] Wollpullover m; wollenes Unterhemd.

**jest** [dʒest] 1. Spaß m; 2. scherzen; ~er ['dʒestə] Spaßmacher m.

**jet** [dʒet] 1. (Wasser-, Gas)Strahl m; Strahlrohr n; ⊕ Düse f; Düsenflugzeug n; Düsenmotor m; 2. hervorsprudeln; ~-propelled ['dʒetprəpeld] mit Düsenantrieb.

**jetty** ⚓ ['dʒeti] Mole f; Pier m.

**Jew** [dʒu:] Jude m; attr. Juden...

**jewel** ['dʒu:əl] Juwel m, n; ~(l)er [~lə] Juwelier m; ~(le)ry [~lri] Juwelen pl., Schmuck m.

**Jew|ess** ['dʒu(:)is] Jüdin f; ~ish ['dʒu(:)iʃ] jüdisch.

**jib** ⚓ [dʒib] Klüver m.

**jibe** Am. F [dʒaib] zustimmen.

**jiffy** F ['dʒifi] Augenblick m.

**jig-saw** ['dʒigsɔ:] Laubsägema-

**schine** f; ~ puzzle Zusammensetzspiel n.

**jilt** [dʒilt] 1. Kokette f; 2. Liebhaber versetzen.

**Jim** [dʒim]: ~ Crow Am. Neger m; Am. Rassentrennung f.

**jingle** ['dʒiŋgl] 1. Geklingel n; 2. klingeln, klimpern (mit).

**jitney** Am. sl. ['dʒitni] 5-Cent-Stück n; billiger Omnibus.

**jive** Am. sl. [dʒaiv] heiße Jazzmusik; Jazzjargon m.

**job** [dʒɔb] 1. (Stück n) Arbeit f; Sache f, Aufgabe f; Beruf m; Stellung f; by the ~ stückweise; im Akkord; ~ lot F Ramschware f; ~ work Akkordarbeit f; 2. v/t. Pferd etc. (ver)mieten; ✝ vermitteln; v/i. im Akkord arbeiten; Maklergeschäfte machen; ~ber ['dʒɔbə] Akkordarbeiter m; Makler m; Schieber m.

**jockey** ['dʒɔki] 1. Jockei m; 2. prellen.

**jocose** □ [dʒə'kous] scherzhaft, spaßig.

**jocular** □ ['dʒɔkjulə] lustig; spaßig.

**jocund** □ ['dʒɔkənd] lustig, fröhlich.

**jog** [dʒɔg] 1. Stoß(en n) m; Rütteln n; Trott m; 2. v/t. (an)stoßen, (auf-)rütteln; v/i. mst ~ along, ~ on dahintrotten, dahinschlendern.

**John** [dʒɔn]: ~ Bull John Bull (der Engländer); ~ Hancock Am. F Friedrich Wilhelm m (Unterschrift).

**join** [dʒɔin] 1. v/t. verbinden, zs.-fügen (to mit); sich vereinigen mit, sich gesellen zu; eintreten in (acc.); ~ battle den Kampf beginnen; ~ hands die Hände falten; sich die Hände reichen (a. fig.); v/i. sich verbinden, sich vereinigen; ~ in mitmachen bei; ~ up Soldat werden; 2. Verbindung(sstelle) f.

**joiner** ['dʒɔinə] Tischler m; ~y [~əri] Tischlerhandwerk n; Tischlerarbeit f.

**joint** [dʒɔint] 1. Verbindung(sstelle) f; Scharnier n; anat. Gelenk n; ♀ Knoten m; Braten m; Am. sl. Spelunke f; put out of ~ verrenken; 2. □ gemeinsam; Mit...; ~ heir Miterbe m; ~ stock ✝ Aktienkapital n; 3. zs.-fügen; zerlegen; ~ed ['dʒɔintid] gegliedert; Glieder...; ~-stock ✝ Aktien...; ~ company Aktiengesellschaft f.

**jok|e** [dʒouk] 1. Scherz m, Spaß m; practical ~ Streich m; 2. v/i. scherzen; schäkern; v/t. necken (about mit); ~er ['dʒoukə] Spaßvogel m; Karten: Joker m; Am. versteckte Klausel; ~y □ ['dʒouki] spaßig.

**jolly** ['dʒɔli] lustig, fidel; F nett.

**jolt** [dʒoult] 1. stoßen, rütteln; holpern; 2. Stoß m; Rütteln n.

**Jonathan** ['dʒɔnəθən]: Brother ~ der Amerikaner.

**josh** *Am. sl.* [dʒɔʃ] **1.** Ulk *m*; **2.** aufziehen, auf die Schippe nehmen.

**jostle** ['dʒɔsl] **1.** anrennen; zs.-stoßen; **2.** Stoß *m*; Zs.-Stoß *m*.

**jot** [dʒɔt] **1.** Jota *n*, Pünktchen *n*; **2.** ~ down notieren.

**journal** ['dʒəːnl] Journal *n*; Tagebuch *n*; Tageszeitung *f*; Zeitschrift *f*; ⊕ Wellenzapfen *m*; ~ism ['dʒəːnəlizəm] Journalismus *m*.

**journey** ['dʒəːni] **1.** Reise *f*; Fahrt *f*; **2.** reisen; ~man Geselle *m*.

**jovial** □ ['dʒouvjəl] heiter; gemütlich.

**joy** [dʒɔi] Freude *f*; Fröhlichkeit *f*; ~ful □ ['dʒɔiful] freudig; erfreut; fröhlich; ~less □ ['dʒɔilis] freudlos; unerfreulich; ~ous □ ['dʒɔiəs] freudig, fröhlich.

**jubil|ant** ['dʒuːbilənt] jubilierend, frohlockend; ~ate [~leit] jubeln; ~ee [~liː] Jubiläum *n*.

**judge** [dʒʌdʒ] **1.** Richter *m*; Schiedsrichter *m*; Beurteiler(in), Kenner(in); **2.** *v/i.* urteilen (*of* über *acc.*); *v/t.* richten; aburteilen; beurteilen (*by* nach); ansehen als.

**judg(e)ment** ['dʒʌdʒmənt] Urteil *n*; Urteilsspruch *m*; Urteilskraft *f*; Einsicht *f*; Meinung *f*; *göttliches* (Straf)Gericht; *Day of* ⚖, ⚖ *Day* Jüngstes Gericht.

**judicature** ['dʒuːdikətʃə] Gerichtshof *m*; Rechtspflege *f*.

**judicial** □ [dʒuː(ː)'diʃəl] gerichtlich; Gerichts...; kritisch; unparteiisch.

**judicious** □ [dʒuː(ː)'diʃəs] verständig, klug; ~ness [~snis] Einsicht *f*.

**jug** [dʒʌg] Krug *m*, Kanne *f*.

**juggle** ['dʒʌgl] **1.** Trick *m*; Schwindel *m*; **2.** jonglieren (*a. fig.*); verfälschen; betrügen; ~r [~lə] Jongleur *m*; Taschenspieler(in).

**Jugoslav** ['juːgouˈslɑːv] **1.** Jugoslaw|e *m*, -in *f*; **2.** jugoslawisch.

**juic|e** [dʒuːs] Saft *m*; *sl. mot.* Sprit *m*, Gas *n*; ~y □ ['dʒuːsi] saftig; F interessant. [sikautomat *m.*]

**juke-box** *Am.* F ['dʒuːkbɔks] Mu-

**julep** ['dʒuːlep] *süßes* (Arznei)Getränk; *bsd. Am.* alkoholisches Eisgetränk.

**July** [dʒuː(ː)'lai] Juli *m*.

**jumble** ['dʒʌmbl] **1.** Durcheinander *n*; **2.** *v/t.* durch-ea.-werfen; ~sale Wohltätigkeitsbasar *m*.

**jump** [dʒʌmp] **1.** Sprung *m*; ~s *pl.*

nervöses Zs.-fahren; *high* (*long*) ~ Hoch- (Weit)Sprung *m*; *get* (*have*) *the* ~ *on Am.* F zuvorkommen; **2.** *v/i.* (auf)springen; ~ *at* sich stürzen auf (*acc.*); ~ *to conclusions* übereilte Schlüsse ziehen; *v/t.* hinwegspringen über (*acc.*); überspringen; springen lassen; ~er ['dʒʌmpə] Springer *m*; Jumper *m*; ~y [~pi] nervös.

**junct|ion** ['dʒʌŋkʃən] Verbindung *f*; Kreuzung *f*; 🚂 Knotenpunkt *m*; ~ure [~ktʃə] Verbindungspunkt *m*, -stelle *f*; (kritischer) Zeitpunkt; *at this* ~ bei diesem Stand der Dinge.

**June** [dʒuːn] Juni *m*.

**jungle** ['dʒʌŋgl] Dschungel *m, n, f*.

**junior** ['dʒuːnjə] **1.** jünger (*to* als); *Am. univ.* der Unterstufe (angehörend); ~ *high school Am.* Oberschule *f* mit Klassen 7, 8, 9; **2.** Jüngere(r *m*) *f*; *Am.* (Ober)Schüler *m od.* Student *m* im 3. Jahr; F Kleine(r) *m*.

**junk** [dʒʌŋk] ♣ Dschunke *f*; Plunder *m*, alter Kram.

**junket** ['dʒʌŋkit] Quarkspeise *f*; *Am.* Party *f*; Vergnügungsfahrt *f*.

**juris|diction** [dʒuəris'dikʃən] Rechtsprechung *f*; Gerichtsbarkeit *f*; Gerichtsbezirk *m*; ~prudence ['dʒuərispruːdəns] Rechtswissenschaft *f*.

**juror** ['dʒuərə] Geschworene(r) *m*.

**jury** ['dʒuəri] *die* Geschworenen *pl.*; Jury *f*, Preisgericht *n*; ~man Geschworene(r) *m*.

**just** [dʒʌst] **1.** *adj.* gerecht; rechtschaffen; **2.** *adv.* richtig; genau; (so)eben; nur; ~ *now* eben *od.* gerade jetzt.

**justice** ['dʒʌstis] Gerechtigkeit *f*; Richter *m*; Recht *n*; Rechtsverfahren *n*; *court of* ~ Gericht(shof) *n*.

**justification** [dʒʌstifiˈkeiʃən] Rechtfertigung *f*.

**justify** ['dʒʌstifai] rechtfertigen.

**justly** [ dʒʌstli] mit Recht.

**justness** ['dʒʌstnis] Gerechtigkeit *f*, Billigkeit *f*; Rechtmäßigkeit *f*; Richtigkeit *f*.

**jut** [dʒʌt] *a.* ~ *out* hervorragen.

**juvenile** ['dʒuːvinail] **1.** jung, jugendlich; Jugend...; **2.** junger Mensch.

# K

**kale** [keil] (*bsd.* Kraus-, Grün)Kohl *m*; *Am. sl.* Moos *n* (*Geld*).

**kangaroo** [kæŋɡə'ru:] Känguruh *n*.

**keel** ⚓ [ki:l] 1. Kiel *m*; 2. ~ *over* kieloben legen *od.* liegen; umschlagen.

**keen** □ [ki:n] scharf (*a. fig.*); eifrig, heftig; stark, groß (*Appetit etc.*); ~ *on* F scharf *od.* erpicht auf *acc.*; *be* ~ *on hunting* ein leidenschaftlicher Jäger sein; **~-edged** ['ki:ned3d] scharfgeschliffen; **~ness** ['ki:nnis] Schärfe *f*; Heftigkeit *f*; Scharfsinn *m*.

**keep** [ki:p] 1. (Lebens)Unterhalt *m*; *for* ~*s* F für immer; 2. [*irr.*] *v/t. allg.* halten; behalten; unterhalten; (er-)halten; einhalten; (ab)halten; *Buch, Ware etc.* führen; *Bett etc.* hüten; fest-, aufhalten; (bei)behalten; (auf)bewahren; ~ *s.o. company* j-m Gesellschaft leisten; ~ *company with* verkehren mit; ~ *one's temper* sich beherrschen; ~ *time* richtig gehen (*Uhr*); ♪, ✗ Takt, Schritt halten; ~ *s.o. waiting* j-n warten lassen; ~ *away* fernhalten; ~ *s.th. from s.o.* j-m et. vorenthalten; ~ *in* zurückhalten; *Schüler* nachsitzen lassen; ~ *on Kleid* anbehalten, *Hut* aufbehalten; ~ *up* aufrechterhalten; (*Mut*) bewahren; in Ordnung halten; hindern, zu Bett zu gehen; aufbleiben lassen; ~ *it up* (es) durchhalten; *v/i.* sich halten, bleiben; F sich aufhalten; ~ *doing* immer wieder tun; ~ *away* sich fernhalten; ~ *from* sich enthalten (*gen.*); ~ *off* sich fernhalten; ~ *on talking* fortfahren zu sprechen; ~ *to* sich halten an (*acc.*); ~ *up* sich aufrecht halten; sich aufrechterhalten; ~ *up with* Schritt halten mit; ~ *up with the Joneses* es den Nachbarn gleichtun.

**keep|er** ['ki:pə] Wärter *m*, Wächter *m*, Aufseher *m*; Verwalter *m*; Inhaber *m*; **~ing** ['ki:piŋ] Verwahrung *f*; Obhut *f*; Gewahrsam *m*, *n*; Unterhalt *m*; *be in* (*out of*) ~ *with* ... (nicht) übereinstimmen mit ...; **~sake** ['ki:pseik] Andenken *n*.

**keg** [keg] Fäßchen *n*.

**kennel** ['kenl] Gosse *f*, Rinnstein *m*; Hundehütte *f*, -zwinger *m*.

**kept** [kept] *pret. u. p.p. von* keep 2.

**kerb** [kə:b], **~stone** ['kə:bstoun] = curb *etc.*

**kerchief** ['kə:tʃif] (Kopf)Tuch *n*.

**kernel** ['kə:nl] Kern *m* (*a. fig.*); *Hafer-, Mais- etc.* Korn *n*.

**kettle** ['ketl] Kessel *m*; **~drum** ♪ Kesselpauke *f*.

**key** [ki:] 1. Schlüssel *m* (*a. fig.*); ⚠ Schlußstein *m*; ⊕ Keil *m*; Schraubenschlüssel *m*; *Klavieretc.* Taste *f*; ♩ Taste *f*, Druck-

knopf *m*; ♪ Tonart *f*; *fig.* Ton *m*; 2. ~ *up* ♪ stimmen; erhöhen; *fig.* in erhöhte Spannung versetzen; **~board** ['ki:bɔ:d] Klaviatur *f*, Tastatur *f*; **~hole** Schlüsselloch *n*; **~man** Schlüsselfigur *f*; **~money** Ablösung *f* (*für e-e Wohnung*); **~note** ♪ Grundton *m*; **~stone** Schlußstein *m*; *fig.* Grundlage *f*.

**kibitzer** /*m.* F ['kibitsə] Kiebitz *m*, Besserwisser *m*.

**kick** [kik] 1. (Fuß)Tritt *m*; Stoß *m*; Schwung *m*; F Nervenkitzel *m*; *get a* ~ *out of* F Spaß finden an (*dat.*); 2. *v/t.* (mit dem Fuß) stoßen *od.* treten; *Fußball:* schießen; ~ *out* F hinauswerfen; *v/i.* (hinten) ausschlagen; stoßen (*Gewehr*); sich auflehnen; ~ *in with Am. sl.* Geld 'reinbuttern; ~ *off Fußball:* anstoßen; **~back** *bsd. Am.* F ['kikbæk] Rückzahlung *f*; **~er** ['kikə] Fußballspieler *m*.

**kid** [kid] 1. Zicklein *n*; *sl.* Kind *n*; Ziegenleder *n*; 2. *sl.* foppen; **~dy** *sl.* ['kidi] Kind *n*; ~ *glove* Glacéhandschuh *m* (*a. fig.*); **~-glove** sanft, zart.

**kidnap** ['kidnæp] entführen; **~(p)er** [~pə] Kindesentführer *m*, Kidnapper *m*.

**kidney** ['kidni] *anat.* Niere *f*; F Art *f*; ~ *bean* ♀ weiße Bohne.

**kill** [kil] 1. töten (*a. fig.*); *fig.* vernichten; *parl.* zu Fall bringen; ~ *off* abschlachten; ~ *time* die Zeit totschlagen; 2. Tötung *f*; Jagdbeute *f*; **~er** ['kilə] Totschläger *m*; **~ing** ['kiliŋ] 1. ☐ mörderisch; F komisch; 2. *Am.* F finanzieller Volltreffer.

**kiln** [kiln] Brenn-, Darrofen *m*.

**kilo|gram(me)** ['kiləgræm] Kilogramm *n*; **~metre**, *Am.* **~meter** Kilometer *m*.

**kilt** [kilt] Kilt *m*, Schottenrock *m*.

**kin** [kin] (Bluts)Verwandtschaft *f*.

**kind** [kaind] 1. ☐ gütig, freundlich; 2. Art *f*, Gattung *f*, Geschlecht *n*; Art und Weise *f*; *pay in* ~ in Naturalien zahlen; *fig.* mit gleicher Münze heimzahlen.

**kindergarten** ['kindəga:tn] Kindergarten *m*.

**kind-hearted** ['kaind'ha:tid] gütig.

**kindle** ['kindl] anzünden; (sich) entzünden (*a. fig.*).

**kindling** ['kindliŋ] Kleinholz *n*.

**kind|ly** ['kaindli] freundlich; günstig; **~ness** [~dnis] Güte *f*, Freundlichkeit *f*; Gefälligkeit *f*.

**kindred** ['kindrid] 1. verwandt, gleichartig; 2. Verwandtschaft *f*.

**king** [kiŋ] König *m* (*a. fig. u. Schach, Kartenspiel*); **~dom** ['kiŋdəm] Königreich *n*; *bsd.* ♀, *zo.* Reich *n*, Gebiet *n*; *eccl.* Reich *n* Gottes; **~like**

['kiŋlaik], ~ly [~li] königlich; ~size F ['kiŋsaiz] überlang, übergroß.

kink [kiŋk] Schlinge f, Knoten m; fig. Schrulle f, Fimmel m.

kin|ship ['kinʃip] Verwandtschaft f; ~sman ['kinzmən] Verwandte(r) m.

kipper ['kipə] Räucherhering m Bückling m; sl. Kerl m.

kiss [kis] 1. Kuß m; 2. (sich) küssen.

kit [kit] Ausrüstung f (a. ✕ u. Sport); Handwerkszeug n, Werkzeug n; ~bag ['kitbæg] ✕ Tornister m; Seesack m; Reisetasche f.

kitchen ['kitʃin] Küche f; ~ette [kitʃi'net] Kochnische f; ~garden ['kitʃin'gɑːdn] Gemüsegarten m.

kite [kait] Papier-Drachen m.

kitten ['kitn] Kätzchen n.

Klan Am. [klæn] Ku-Klux-Klan m; ~sman ['klænzmən] Mitglied n des Ku-Klux-Klan.

knack [næk] Kniff m, Dreh m; Geschicklichkeit f. [Rucksack m.]

knapsack ['næpsæk] Tornister m;]

knave [neiv] Schurke m; Kartenspiel: Bube m; ~ry ['neivəri] Gaunerei f.

knead [niːd] kneten; massieren.

knee [niː] Knie n; ⊕ Kniestück n; ~cap ['niːkæp] Kniescheibe f; ~deep bis an die Knie (reichend); ~joint Kniegelenk n; ~l [niːl] [irr.] knien (to vor dat.).

knell [nel] Totenglocke f.

knelt [nelt] pret. u. p.p. von kneel.

knew [njuː] pret. von know.

knicker|bockers ['nikəbɔkəz] pl. Knickerbocker pl., Kniehosen f/pl.; ~s F ['nikəz] pl. Schlüpfer m; = knickerbockers.

knick-knack ['niknæk] Spielerei f; Nippsache f.

knife [naif] 1. pl. knives [naivz] Messer n; 2. schneiden; (er)stechen.

knight [nait] 1. Ritter m; Springer m im Schach; 2. zum Ritter schlagen; ~errant ['nait'erənt] fahrender Ritter; ~hood ['naithud] Rittertum n; Ritterschaft f; ~ly ['naitli] ritterlich.

knit [nit] [irr.] stricken; (ver)knüp-

fen; (sich) eng verbinden; ~ the brows die Stirn runzeln; ~ting ['nitiŋ] Stricken n; Strickzeug n; attr. Strick...

knives [naivz] pl. von knife 1.

knob [nɔb] Knopf m; Buckel m; Brocken m.

knock [nɔk] 1. Schlag m; Anklopfen n; mot. Klopfen n; 2. v/i. klopfen; pochen; stoßen; schlagen; ~ about F sich herumtreiben; v/t. klopfen, stoßen, schlagen; Am. sl. bekritteln, schlechtmachen; ~ about herumstoßen, übel zurichten; ~ down niederschlagen; Auktion: zuschlagen; ⊕ aus-ea.-nehmen; be ~ed down überfahren werden; ~ off aufhören mit; F zs.-hauen (schnell erledigen); Summe abziehen; ~ out Boxen: k.o. schlagen; ~er ['nɔk] Klopfende(r) m; Türklopfer m; Am. sl. Kritikaster m; ~kneed ['nɔk-niːd] x-beinig; fig. hinkend; ~out Boxen: Knockout m, K.o. m; sl. tolle Sache od. Person.

knoll[1] [noul] kleiner Erdhügel.

knoll[2] [~] (bsd. zu Grabe) läuten.

knot [nɔt] 1. Knoten m; Knorren m; Seemeile f; Schleife f, Band n (a. fig.); Schwierigkeit f; 2. (ver)knoten, (ver)knüpfen (a. fig.); Stirn runzeln; verwickeln; ~ty ['nɔti] knotig; knorrig; fig. verwickelt.

know [nou] [irr.] wissen; (er)kennen; erfahren; ~ French Französisch können; come to ~ erfahren; get to ~ kennenlernen; ~ one's business, ~ the ropes, ~ a thing or two, ~ what's what sich auskennen, Erfahrung haben; you ~ (am Ende des Satzes) nämlich; ~ing □ ['nouiŋ] erfahren; klug; schlau; verständnisvoll; wissentlich; ~ledge ['nɔlidʒ] Kenntnis(se pl.) f; Wissen n; to my ~ meines Wissens; ~n [noun] p.p. von know; come to be ~ bekannt werden; make ~ bekanntmachen.

knuckle ['nʌkl] 1. Knöchel m; 2. ~ down, ~ under nachgeben.

Kremlin ['kremlin] der Kreml.

Ku-Klux-Klan Am. ['kjuːklʌks-'klæn] Geheimbund in den USA.

# L

label ['leibl] 1. Zettel m, Etikett n; Aufschrift f; Schildchen n; Bezeichnung f; 2. etikettieren, beschriften; fig. abstempeln (as als).

laboratory [lə'bɔrətəri] Laboratorium n; ~ assistant Laborant(in).

laborious □ [lə'bɔːriəs] mühsam; arbeitsam; schwerfällig (Stil).

labo(u)r ['leibə] 1. Arbeit f; Mühe

f; (Geburts)Wehen f/pl.; Arbeiter m/pl.; Ministry of ♀ Arbeitsministerium n; hard ~ Zwangsarbeit f; 2. Arbeiter...; Arbeits...; 3. v/i. arbeiten; sich abmühen; ~ under leiden unter (dat.), zu kämpfen haben mit; v/t. ausarbeiten; ~ed schwerfällig (Stil); mühsam (Atem etc.); ~er [~ərə] ungelernter Arbeiter; ♀ Exchange Arbeitsamt n; Labour

Party *pol.* Labour Party *f*; **labor union** *Am.* Gewerkschaft *f*.

lace [leis] 1. Spitze *f*; Borte *f*; Schnur *f*; 2. (zu)schnüren; mit Spitze *etc.* besetzen; *Schnur* durch-, einziehen; ~ (*into*) *s.o.* j-n verprügeln.

lacerate ['læsəreit] zerreißen; *fig.* quälen.

lack [læk] 1. Fehlen *n*, Mangel *m*; 2. *v/t.* ermangeln (*gen.*); he ~s *money* es fehlt ihm an Geld; *v/i.* be ~ing fehlen, mangeln; **~-lustre** ['lækʌstə] glanzlos, matt.

laconic [lə'kɔnik] (~ally) lakonisch, wortkarg, kurz und prägnant.

lacquer ['lækə] 1. Lack *m*; 2. lakkieren.

lad [læd] Bursche *m*, Junge *m*.

ladder ['lædə] Leiter *f*; Laufmasche *f*; **~-proof** maschenfest (*Strumpf etc.*).

laden ['leidn] beladen.

lading ['leidiŋ] Ladung *f*, Fracht *f*.

ladle ['leidl] 1. Schöpflöffel *m*, Kelle *f*; 2. ~ out *Suppe* austeilen.

lady ['leidi] Dame *f*; Lady *f*; Herrin *f*; ~ doctor Ärztin *f*; **~bird** Marienkäfer *m*; **~like** damenhaft; **~-love** Geliebte *f*; **~ship** [~ʃip]: *her* ~ die gnädige Frau; *Your* ♀ gnädige Frau, Euer Gnaden.

lag [læg] 1. zögern; *a.* ~ *behind* zurückbleiben; 2. Verzögerung *f*.

lager (beer) ['lɑ:gə(biə)] Lagerbier *n*.

laggard ['lægəd] Nachzügler *m*.

lagoon [lə'gu:n] Lagune *f*.

laid [leid] *pret. u. p.p. von* lay³ 2; ~ *up* bettlägerig (*with* mit, wegen).

lain [lein] *p.p. von* lie² 2.

lair [lɛə] Lager *n* e-s *wilden Tieres.*

laity ['leiiti] Laien *m/pl.*

lake [leik] See *m*; rote Pigmentfarbe.

lamb [læm] 1. Lamm *n*; 2. lammen.

lambent ['læmbənt] leckend; züngelnd (*Flamme*); funkelnd.

lamb|kin ['læmkin] Lämmchen *n*; **~like** lammfromm.

lame [leim] 1. ☐ lahm (*a. fig.* = *mangelhaft*); 2. lähmen.

lament [lə'ment] 1. Wehklage *f*; 2. (be)klagen; trauern; **~able** ☐ ['læməntəbl] beklagenswert; kläglich; **~ation** [læmən'teiʃən] Wehklage *f*.

lamp [læmp] Lampe *f*; *fig.* Leuchte *f*.

lampoon [læm'pu:n] 1. Schmähschrift *f*; 2. schmähen.

lamp-post ['læmppoust] Laternenpfahl *m*.

lampshade ['læmpʃeid] Lampenschirm *m*.

lance [lɑ:ns] 1. Lanze *f*; Speer *m*; 2. ⚕ aufschneiden; **~-corporal** ✠ ['lɑ:ns'kɔ:pərəl] Gefreite(r) *m*.

land [lænd] 1. Land *n*; Grundstück *n*; *by* ~ auf dem Landweg; **~s** *pl.*

Ländereien *f/pl.*; 2. landen; ⚓ löschen; *Preis* gewinnen; **~-agent** ['lændeidʒənt] Grundstücksmakler *m*; Gutsverwalter *m*; **~ed** grundbesitzend; Land..., Grund...; **~holder** Grundbesitzer(in).

landing ['lændiŋ] Landung *f*; Treppenabsatz *m*; Anlegestelle *f*; **~field** ✈ Landebahn *f*; **~-gear** Fahrgestell *n*; **~-stage** Landungsbrücke *f*.

land|lady ['lænleidi] Vermieterin *f*, Wirtin *f*; **~lord** [~lɔ:d] Vermieter *m*; Wirt *m*; Haus-, Grundbesitzer *m*; **~-lubber** ⚓ *contp.* Landratte *f*; **~mark** Grenz-, Markstein *m* (*a. fig.*); Wahrzeichen *n*; **~owner** Grundbesitzer(in); **~scape** ['lænskeip] Landschaft *f*; **~slide** [~slaid] Erdrutsch *m* (*a. pol.*); *a Democratic* ~ ein Erdrutsch zugunsten der Demokraten; **~slip** *konkr.* Erdrutsch *m*.

lane [lein] Feldweg *m*; Gasse *f*; Spalier *n*; *mot.* Fahrbahn *f*, Spur *f*.

language ['læŋgwidʒ] Sprache *f*; *strong* ~ Kraftausdrücke *m/pl.*

languid ☐ ['læŋgwid] matt; träg.

languish ['læŋgwiʃ] matt werden; schmachten; dahinsiechen.

languor ['læŋgə] Mattigkeit *f*; Schmachten *n*; Stille *f*.

lank [læŋk] schmächtig, dünn; schlicht; **~y** ☐ ['læŋki] schlaksig.

lantern ['læntən] Laterne *f*; **~-slide** Dia(positiv) *n*, Lichtbild *n*.

lap [læp] 1. Schoß *m*; ⊕ Vorstoß *m*; Runde *f*; 2. über-ea.-legen; (ein)hüllen; (auf)lecken; schlürfen; plätschern (gegen) (*Wellen*).

lapel [lə'pel] Aufschlag *m am Rock.*

lapse [læps] 1. Verlauf *m der Zeit*; Verfallen *n*; Versehen *n*; 2. (ver)fallen; verfließen; fehlen.

larceny ✠ ['lɑ:sni] Diebstahl *m*.

larch ♀ [lɑ:tʃ] Lärche *f*.

lard [lɑ:d] 1. (Schweine)Schmalz *n*; 2. spicken (*a. fig.*); **~er** ['lɑ:də] Speisekammer *f*.

large ☐ [lɑ:dʒ] groß; weit; reichlich; weitherzig; flott; Groß-...; *at* ~ auf freiem Fuß; ausführlich; als Ganzes; **~ly** ['lɑ:dʒli] zum großen Teil, weitgehend; **~-minded** weitherzig; **~ness** ['lɑ:dʒnis] Größe *f*; Weite *f*; **~-sized** groß(formatig).

lariat *Am.* ['læriət] Lasso *n, m.*

lark [lɑ:k] *orn.* Lerche *f*; *fig.* Streich *m*.

larkspur ♀ ['lɑ:kspə:] Rittersporn *m*.

larva *zo.* ['lɑ:və] Larve *f*, Puppe *f*.

larynx *anat.* ['læriŋks] Kehlkopf *m*.

lascivious ☐ [lə'siviəs] lüstern.

lash [læʃ] 1. Peitsche(nschnur) *f*; Hieb *m*; Wimper *f*; 2. peitschen; *fig.* geißeln; (an)treiben; anbinden.

lass, ~ie [læs, 'læsi] Mädchen *n*.

lassitude ['læsitju:d] Mattigkeit *f*, Abgespanntheit *f*; Desinteresse *n*.

**last¹** [lɑːst] **1.** adj. letzt; vorig; äußerst; geringst; ~ but one vorletzt; ~ night gestern abend; **2.** Letzte(r m, -s n) f; Ende n; at ~ zuletzt, endlich; **3.** adv. zuletzt; ~, but not least nicht zuletzt.

**last²** [~] dauern; halten (Farbe); ausreichen; ausdauern.

**last³** [~] (Schuhmacher)Leisten m.

**lasting** □ ['lɑːstiŋ] dauerhaft; beständig.

**lastly** ['lɑːstli] zuletzt, schließlich.

**latch** [lætʃ] **1.** Klinke f, Drücker m; Druckschloß n; **2.** ein-, zuklinken.

**late** [leit] spät; (kürzlich)verstorben; ehemalig; jüngst; at (the) ~st spätestens; as ~ as noch (in dat.); of ~ letzthin; ~r on später; be ~ (zu) spät kommen; ~ly ['leitli] kürzlich.

**latent** □ ['leitənt] verborgen, latent; gebunden (Wärme etc.).

**lateral** □ ['lætərəl] seitlich; Seiten...

**lath** [lɑːθ] **1.** Latte f; **2.** belatten.

**lathe** ⊕ [leið] Drehbank f; Lade f.

**lather** ['lɑːðə] **1.** (Seifen)Schaum m; **2.** v/t. einseifen; v/i. schäumen.

**Latin** ['lætin] **1.** lateinisch; **2.** Latein n.

**latitude** ['lætitjuːd] Breite f; fig. Umfang m, Weite f; Spielraum m.

**latter** ['lætə] neuer; der (die, das) letztere; ~ly [~əli] neuerdings.

**lattice** ['lætis] a. ~-work Gitter n.

**laud** [lɔːd] loben, preisen; ~able □ ['lɔːdəbl] lobenswert, löblich.

**laugh** [lɑːf] **1.** Gelächter n, Lachen n; **2.** lachen; ~ at j-n auslachen; he ~s best who ~s last wer zuletzt lacht, lacht am besten; ~able □ ['lɑːfəbl] lächerlich; ~ter ['lɑːftə] Gelächter n, Lachen n.

**launch** [lɔːntʃ] **1.** ⊕ Stapellauf m; Barkasse f; **2.** vom Stapel laufen lassen; Boot aussetzen; schleudern (a. fig.); Schläge versetzen; Rakete starten, abschießen; fig. in Gang bringen; ~ing-pad ['lɔːntʃiŋpæd] (Raketen)Abschußrampe f.

**launderette** [lɔːndə'ret] Selbstbedienungswaschsalon m.

**laund|ress** [lɔːndris] Wäscherin f; ~ry [~ri] Waschanstalt f; Wäsche f.

**laurel** ♀ ['lɔrəl] Lorbeer m (a. fig.).

**lavatory** ['lævətəri] Waschraum m; Toilette f; public ~ Bedürfnisanstalt f.

**lavender** ♀ ['lævində] Lavendel m.

**lavish** ['læviʃ] **1.** □ freigebig, verschwenderisch; **2.** verschwenden.

**law** [lɔː] Gesetz n; (Spiel)Regel f; Recht(swissenschaft f) n; Gericht(sverfahren) n; go to ~ vor Gericht gehen; lay down the ~ den Ton angeben; ~-abiding ['lɔːəbaidiŋ] friedlich; ~-court Gericht(shof m) n; ~ful □ ['lɔːful] gesetzlich; gültig; ~less □ ['lɔːlis] gesetzlos; ungesetzlich; zügellos.

**lawn** [lɔːn] Rasen(platz) m; Batist m.

**law|suit** ['lɔːsjuːt] Prozeß m; ~yer ['lɔːjə] Jurist m; (Rechts)Anwalt m.

**lax** □ [læks] locker; schlaff (a. fig.); lasch; ~ative ♀ ['læksətiv] **1.** abführend; **2.** Abführmittel n.

**lay¹** [lei] pret. von lie² 2.

**lay²** [~] weltlich; Laien...

**lay³** [~] **1.** Lage f, Richtung f; **2.** [irr.] v/t. legen; umlegen; Plan etc. ersinnen; stellen, setzen; Tisch decken; lindern; besänftigen; auferlegen; Summe wetten; ~ before s.o. j-m vorlegen; ~ in einlagern, sich eindecken mit; ~ low niederwerfen; ~ open darlegen; ~ out auslegen; Garten etc. anlegen; ~ up Vorräte hinlegen, sammeln; be laid up ans Bett gefesselt sein; ~ with belegen mit; v/i. (Eier) legen; a. ~ a wager wetten.

**lay-by** ['leibai] Park-, Rastplatz m an e-r Fernstraße.

**layer** ['leiə] Lage f, Schicht f.

**layman** ['leimən] Laie m.

**lay|off** ['leiɔːf] Arbeitsunterbrechung f; ~out Anlage f; Plan m.

**lazy** □ ['leizi] faul.

**lead¹** [led] Blei n; ⊕ Lot n, Senkblei n; typ. Durchschuß m.

**lead²** [liːd] **1.** Führung f; Leitung f; Beispiel n; thea. Hauptrolle f; Kartenspiel: Vorhand f; ⚡ Leitung f; Hunde-Leine f; **2.** [irr.] v/t. (an-)führen, leiten; bewegen (zu tun); Karte ausspielen; ~ on (ver)locken; v/i. vorangehen; ~ off den Anfang machen; ~ up to überleiten zu.

**leaden** ['ledn] bleiern (a. fig.); Blei...

**leader** ['liːdə] (An)Führer(in), Leiter(in); Erste(r) m; Leitartikel m; ~ship [~ʃip] Führerschaft f.

**leading** ['liːdiŋ] **1.** leitend; Leit...; Haupt...; **2.** Leitung f, Führung f.

**leaf** [liːf], pl. leaves [liːvz] Blatt n; Tür- etc. Flügel m; Tisch-Platte f; ~let ['liːflit] Blättchen n; Flug-, Merkblatt n; ~y ['liːfi] belaubt.

**league** [liːg] **1.** Liga f (a. hist. u. Sport); Bund m; mst poet. Meile f; **2.** (sich) verbünden.

**leak** [liːk] **1.** Leck n; **2.** leck sein; tropfen; ~ out durchsickern; ~age ['liːkidʒ] Lecken n; ♀ Leckage f; Verlust m (a. fig.), Schwund m; Durchsickern n; ~y ['liːki] leck; undicht.

**lean** [liːn] **1.** [irr.] (sich) (an)lehnen; (sich) stützen; (sich) (hin)neigen; **2.** mager; **3.** mageres Fleisch.

**leant** [lent] pret. u. p.p. von lean 1.

**leap** [liːp] **1.** Sprung m; **2.** [irr.] (über)springen; ~t [lept] pret. u. p.p. von leap 2.; ~-year ['liːpjɑː] Schaltjahr n.

**learn** [lɜːn] [irr.] lernen; erfahren, hören; ~ from ersehen aus; ~ed ['lɜːnid] gelehrt; ~er ['lɜːnə] Anfänger(in); **~ing** ['lə:niŋ] Lernen n; Gelehrsamkeit f; **~t** [lə:nt] pret. u. p.p. von learn.

**lease** [li:s] 1. Verpachtung f, Vermietung f; Pacht f, Miete f; Pacht-, Mietvertrag m; 2. (ver-) pachten, (ver)mieten.

**leash** [li:ʃ] 1. Koppelleine f; Koppel f (3 Hunde etc.); 2. koppeln.

**least** [li:st] 1. adj. kleinst, geringst; wenigst, mindest; 2. adv. a. ~ of all am wenigsten; at ~ wenigstens; 3. das Mindeste, das Wenigste; to say the ~ gelinde gesagt.

**leather** ['leðə] 1. Leder n (fig.Haut); 2. a. ~n ledern; Leder...

**leave** [li:v] 1. Erlaubnis f; a. ~ of absence Urlaub m; Abschied m; 2. [irr.] v/t. (ver)lassen; zurück-, hinterlassen; übriglassen; überlassen; ~ off aufhören (mit); Kleid ablegen; v/i. ablassen; weggehen, abreisen (for nach).

**leaven** ['levn] Sauerteig m; Hefe f.

**leaves** [li:vz] pl. von leaf; Laub n.

**leavings** ['li:viŋz] pl. Überbleibsel n/pl.

**lecherous** ['letʃərəs] wollüstig.

**lecture** ['lektʃə] 1. Vorlesung f, Vortrag m; Strafpredigt f; 2. v/i. Vorlesungen od. Vorträge halten; v/t. abkanzeln; **~r** [~ərə] Vortragende(r m) f; univ. Dozent(in).

**led** [led] pret. u. p.p. von lead[2] 2.

**ledge** [ledʒ] Leiste f; Sims m, n; Riff n.

**ledger** † ['ledʒə] Hauptbuch n.

**leech** zo. [li:tʃ] Blutegel m; fig. Schmarotzer m.

**leek** ♀ [li:k] Lauch m, Porree m.

**leer** [liə] 1. (lüsterner od. finsterer) Seitenblick; 2. schielen (at nach).

**lees** [li:z] pl. Bodensatz m, Hefe f.

**lee|ward** ♣ ['li:wəd] leewärts; **~way** ['li:wei] ♣ Abtrift f; make up ~ fig. Versäumtes nachholen.

**left**[1] [left] pret. u. p.p. von leave 2.

**left**[2] [~] 1. link(s); 2. Linke f; **~-handed** □ ['left'hændid] linkshändig; linkisch.

**left|-luggage office** ['left'lʌgidʒ'ɔfis] Gepäckaufbewahrung(sstelle) f; **~overs** pl. Speisereste m/pl.

**leg** [leg] Bein n; Keule f; (Stiefel-) Schaft m; ⚓ Schenkel m; pull s.o.'s ~ j-n auf den Arm nehmen (hänseln).

**legacy** ['legəsi] Vermächtnis n.

**legal** □ ['li:gəl] gesetzlich; rechtsgültig; juristisch; Rechts...; **~ize** [~laiz] rechtskräftig machen; beurkunden.

**legation** [li'geiʃən] Gesandtschaft f.

**legend** ['ledʒənd] Legende f; **~ary** [~dəri] legendär, sagenhaft.

**leggings** ['leginz] pl. Gamaschen f/pl.

**legible** □ ['ledʒəbl] leserlich.

**legionary** ['li:dʒənəri] Legionär m.

**legislat|ion** [ledʒis'leiʃən] Gesetz-

gebung f; **~ive** ['ledʒislətiv] gesetzgebend; **~or** [~leitə] Gesetzgeber m.

**legitima|cy** [li'dʒitiməsi] Rechtmäßigkeit f; **~te** 1. [~meit] legitimieren; 2. [~mit] rechtmäßig.

**leisure** ['leʒə] Muße f; at your ~ wenn es Ihnen paßt; **~ly** [~əli] gemächlich.

**lemon** ['lemən] Zitrone f; **~ade** [lemə'neid] Limonade f; ~ squash Zitronenwasser n.

**lend** [lend] [irr.] (ver-, aus)leihen; Hilfe gewähren.

**length** [leŋθ] Länge f; Strecke f; (Zeit)Dauer f; at ~ endlich, zuletzt; go all ~s aufs Ganze gehen; **~en** ['leŋθən] (sich) verlängern, (sich) ausdehnen; **~wise** [~θwaiz] der Länge nach; **~y** □ [~θi] sehr lang.

**lenient** □ ['li:njənt] mild, nachsichtig.

**lens** opt. [lenz] Linse f.

**lent**[1] [lent] pret. u. p.p. von lend.

**Lent**[2] [~] Fasten pl., Fastenzeit f.

**leopard** ['lepəd] Leopard m.

**lepr|osy** ⚕ ['leprəsi] Aussatz m, Lepra f; **~ous** [~əs] aussätzig.

**less** [les] 1. adj. u. adv. kleiner, geringer; weniger; 2. prp. minus.

**lessen** ['lesn] v/t. vermindern, schmälern; v/i. abnehmen.

**lesser** ['lesə] kleiner; geringer.

**lesson** ['lesn] Lektion f; Aufgabe f; (Unterrichts)Stunde f; Lehre f; **~s** pl. Unterricht m.

**lest** [lest] damit nicht, daß nicht.

**let** [let] [irr.] lassen; vermieten, verpachten; ~ alone in Ruhe lassen; geschweige denn; ~ down j-n im Stich lassen; ~ go loslassen; ~ in einweihen in (acc.); ~ off abschießen; j-n laufen lassen; ~ out hinauslassen; ausplaudern; vermieten; ~ up aufhören.

**lethal** □ ['li:θəl] tödlich; Todes...

**lethargy** [le'θadʒi] Lethargie f.

**letter** ['letə] 1. Buchstabe m; Type f; Brief m; ~s pl. Literatur f, Wissenschaft f; attr. Brief...; to the ~ buchstäblich; 2. beschriften, betiteln; **~box** Briefkasten m; **~card** Kartenbrief m; **~carrier** Am. Briefträger m; **~case** Brieftasche f; **~cover** Briefumschlag m; **~ed** (literarisch) gebildet; **~file** Briefordner m; **~ing** [~əriŋ] Beschriftung f; **~press** Kopierpresse f.

**lettuce** ♀ ['letis] Lattich m, Salat m.

**leuk(a)emia** ⚕ [lju:'ki:miə] Leukämie f.

**levee**[1] ['levi] Morgenempfang m.

**levee**[2] Am. [~] Uferdamm m.

**level** ['levl] 1. waag(e)recht, eben; gleich; ausgeglichen; my ~ best mein möglichstes; ~ crossing ⚑ schienengleicher Übergang; 2. ebe-

ne Fläche; (gleiche) Höhe, Niveau
n, Stand m; fig. Maßstab m; Was-
serwaage f; sea ~ Meeresspiegel m;
on the ~ F offen, aufrichtig; 3. v/t.
gleichmachen, ebnen; fig. anpassen;
richten, zielen mit; ~ up erhöhen;
v/i. ~ at, against zielen auf (acc.);
~-headed vernünftig, nüchtern.

**lever** ['li:və] Hebel m; Hebestange f;
~age [~əridჳ] Hebelkraft f.

**levity** ['leviti] Leichtfertigkeit f.

**levy** ['levi] 1. Erhebung f von Steuern; ✕ Aushebung f; Aufgebot n;
2. Steuern erheben; ✕ ausheben.

**lewd** □ [lu:d] liederlich, unzüchtig.

**liability** [laiə'biliti] Verantwortlich-
keit f; ✕ Haftpflicht f; Verpflichtung f; fig. Hang m; liabilities pl.
Verbindlichkeiten f/pl., † Passiva
pl.

**liable** □ ['laiəbl] verantwortlich;
haftpflichtig; verpflichtet; ausge-
setzt (to dat.); be ~ to neigen zu.

**liar** ['laiə] Lügner(in).

**libel** ['laibəl] 1. Schmähschrift f;
Verleumdung f; 2. schmähen; verunglimpfen.

**liberal** ['libərəl] 1. □ liberal (a.
pol.); freigebig; reichlich; freisin-
nig; 2. Liberale(r) m; ~ity [libə-
'ræliti] Freigebigkeit f; Freisinnig-
keit f.

**liberat|e** ['libəreit] befreien; frei-
lassen; ~ion [libə'reiʃən] Befreiung
f; ~or ['libəreitə] Befreier m.

**libertine** ['libə(:)tain] Wüstling m.

**liberty** ['libəti] Freiheit f; take
liberties sich Freiheiten erlauben;
be at ~ frei sein.

**librar|ian** [lai'brɛəriən] Bibliothe-
kar(in); ~y ['laibrəri] Bibliothek f.

**lice** [lais] pl. von louse.

**licen|ce**, Am. ~se ['laisəns] 1. Li-
zenz f; Erlaubnis f; Konzession f;
Freiheit f; Zügellosigkeit f; driving
~ Führerschein m; 2. lizenzieren,
berechtigen; et. genehmigen; ~see
[laisən'si:] Lizenznehmer m.

**licentious** □ [lai'senʃəs] unzüchtig;
ausschweifend.

**lichen** ♀, ✳ ['laikən] Flechte f.

**lick** [lik] 1. Lecken n; Salzlecke f;
F Schlag m; 2. (be)lecken; F verdreschen; übertreffen; ~ the dust
im Staub kriechen; fallen; geschlagen werden; ~ into shape zurecht-
stutzen.

**licorice** ['likəris] Lakritze f.

**lid** [lid] Deckel m; (Augen)Lid n.

**lie¹** [lai] 1. Lüge f; give s.o. the ~
j-n Lügen strafen; 2. lügen.

**lie²** [~] 1. Lage f; 2. [irr.] liegen; ~ by
still-, brachliegen; ~ down sich niederlegen; ~ in wait for j-m auflauern; let sleeping dogs ~ fig. daran
rühren wir lieber nicht; ~-down
[lai'daun] Nickerchen n; have
a ~ sich gründlich ausschlafen.

**lien** ⚖ ['liən] Pfandrecht n.

**lieu** [lju:]: in ~ of (an)statt.

**lieutenant** [lef'tenənt; ⚓ le'tenənt;
Am. lu:'tenənt] Leutnant m; Statthalter m; ~-commander ⚓ Korvet-
tenkapitän m.

**life** [laif], pl. **lives** [laivz] Leben n;
Menschenleben n; Lebensbeschrei-
bung f; for ~ auf Lebenszeit; for
one's ~, for dear ~ ums (liebe) Leben; to the ~ naturgetreu; ~ sentence lebenslängliche Zuchthausstrafe; ~ assurance Lebensversicherung f; ~belt ['laifbelt] Ret-
tungsgürtel m; ~boat Rettungs-
boot n; ~guard Leibwache f;
Badewärter m am Strand; ~ insurance Lebensversicherung f; ~
jacket ⚓ Schwimmweste f; ~less
□ ['laiflis] leblos; matt (a. fig.);
~like lebenswahr; ~long lebens-
länglich; ~preserver Am. ['laif-
prizə:və] Schwimmgürtel m; Totschläger m (Stock mit Bleikopf);
~time Lebenszeit f.

**lift** [lift] 1. Heben n; phys., ✈ Auftrieb m; fig. Erhebung f; Fahrstuhl
m; give s.o. a ~ j-m helfen; j-n (im
Auto) mitnehmen; 2. v/t. (auf)he-
ben; erheben; beseitigen; sl. klauen,
stehlen; v/i. sich heben.

**ligature** ['ligətʃuə] Binde f; ✳
Verband m.

**light¹** [lait] 1. Licht n (a. fig.); Fenster n; Aspekt m, Gesichtspunkt
m; Feuer n; Glanz m; fig. Leuchte
f; ~s pl. Fähigkeiten f/pl.; will you
give me a ~ darf ich Sie um Feuer
bitten; put a ~ to anzünden; 2. licht,
hell; blond; 3. [irr.] v/t. oft ~ up
be-, erleuchten; anzünden; v/i.
mst ~ up aufleuchten; ~ out Am. sl.
schnell losziehen, abhauen.

**light²** [~] 1. adj. □ u. adv. leicht
(a. fig.); ~ current ⚡ Schwachstrom
m; make ~ of et. leicht nehmen;
2. ~ (up)on stoßen od. fallen auf
(acc.), geraten an (acc.); sich niederlassen auf (dat.).

**lighten** ['laitn] blitzen; (sich) erhellen; leichter machen; (sich) erleichtern.

**lighter** ['laitə] Anzünder m; (Taschen)Feuerzeug n; ⚓ L(e)ichter m.

**light|-headed** ['lait'hedid] wirr im
Kopf, irr; ~-hearted [~'ha:tid]
leichtherzig; fröhlich; ~house
['laithaus] Leuchtturm m.

**lighting** ['laitiŋ] Beleuchtung f;
Anzünden n.

**light|-minded** ['lait'maindid] leicht-
sinnig; ~ness ['laitnis] Leichtigkeit
f; Leichtsinn m.

**lightning** ['laitniŋ] Blitz m; ~ bug
Am. zo. Leuchtkäfer m; ~conduc-
tor, ~rod ⚡ Blitzableiter m.

**light-weight** ['laitweit] Sport:
Leichtgewicht n.

**like** [laik] 1. gleich; ähnlich; wie;
such ~ dergleichen; feel ~ F sich

aufgelegt fühlen zu *et.*; ~ *that so; what is he ~?* wie sieht er aus?; wie ist er?; 2. Gleiche *m, f, n;* ~*s pl.* Neigungen *f/pl.; his* ~ seinesgleichen; *the* ~ der-, desgleichen; 3. mögen, gern haben; *how do you* ~ *London?* wie gefällt Ihnen L.?; *I should* ~ *to know* ich möchte wissen.

like|lihood ['laiklihud] Wahrscheinlichkeit *f*; ~ly ['laikli] wahrscheinlich; geeignet; *he is* ~ *to die* er wird wahrscheinlich sterben.

like|n ['laikən] vergleichen (*to* mit); ~ness ['laiknis] Ähnlichkeit *f*; (Ab-) Bild *n*; Gestalt *f*; ~wise ['laikwaiz] gleich-, ebenfalls.

liking ['laikiŋ] (*for*) Neigung *f* (für, zu), Gefallen *n* (an *dat.*).

lilac ['lailək] 1. lila; 2. ♀ Flieder *m*.

lily ♀ ['lili] Lilie *f*; ~ *of the valley* Maiglöckchen *n*; ~-white schneeweiß.

limb [lim] *Körper*-Glied *n*; Ast *m*.

limber ['limbə] 1. biegsam, geschmeidig; 2.: ~ *up* (sich) lockern.

lime [laim] Kalk *m*; Vogelleim *m*; ♀ Limone *f*; ♀ Linde *f*; ~light ['laimlait] Kalklicht *n*; *thea.* Scheinwerfer(licht *n*) *m*; *fig.* Mittelpunkt *m* des öffentlichen Interesses.

limit ['limit] 1. Grenze *f*; *in (off)* ~*s* Zutritt gestattet (verboten) (*to* für); *that is the* ~! F das ist der Gipfel!; das ist (doch) die Höhe!; *go the* ~ *Am.* F bis zum Äußersten gehen; 2. begrenzen; beschränken (*to* auf *acc.*); ~ation [limi'teiʃən] Begrenzung *f*, Beschränkung *f*; *fig.* Grenze *f*; 🕱 Verjährung *f*; ~ed: ~ (*liability*) *company* Gesellschaft *f* mit beschränkter Haftung; ~ *in time* befristet; ~less □ [~tlis] grenzenlos.

limp [limp] 1. hinken; 2. Hinken *n*; 3. schlaff; weich.

limpid □ ['limpid] klar, durchsichtig.

line [lain] 1. Linie *f*; Reihe *f*, Zeile *f*; Vers *m*; Strich *m*; Falte *f*, Furche *f*; (*Menschen*)Schlange *f*; Folge *f*; Verkehrsgesellschaft *f*; Eisenbahnlinie *f*; Strecke *f*; *tel.* Leitung *f*; Branche *f*, Fach *n*; Leine *f*, Schnur *f*; Äquator *m*; Richtung *f*; ✕ Linie(ntruppe) *f*; Front *f*; ~*s pl.* Richtlinien *f/pl.*; Grundlage *f*; ~ *of conduct* Lebensweise *f*; *hard* ~*s pl.* hartes Los, Pech *n*; *in* ~ *with* in Übereinstimmung mit; *stand in* ~ Schlange stehen; *draw the* ~ *fig.* nicht mehr mitmachen; *hold the* ~ *teleph.* am Apparat bleiben; 2. *v/t.* liniieren; aufstellen; *Weg etc.* säumen, einfassen; *Kleid* füttern; ~ *out* entwerfen; *v/i.* ~ *up* sich auf-, anstellen.

linea|ge ['liniidʒ] Abstammung *f*; Familie *f*; Stammbaum *m*; ~l □ [~iəl] gerade, direkt (*Nachkomme* *etc.*); ~ment [~əmənt] (Gesichts-) Zug *m*; ~r ['liniə] geradlinig.

linen ['linin] 1. Leinen *n*, Leinwand *f*; Wäsche *f*; 2. leinen; ~-closet, ~-cupboard Wäscheschrank *m*; ~-draper [~ndreipə] Weißwarenhändler *m*, Wäschegeschäft *n*.

liner ['lainə] Linienschiff *n*, Passagierdampfer *m*; Verkehrsflugzeug *n*.

linger ['liŋgə] zögern; (ver)weilen; sich aufhalten; sich hinziehen; dahinsiechen; ~ *at*, ~ *about* sich herumdrücken an od. bei (*dat.*).

lingerie ['lɛ̃:nʒəri:] Damenunterwäsche *f*. [Einreibemittel *n*.]

liniment ⚕ ['linimənt] Liniment *n*,]

lining ['lainiŋ] *Kleider- etc.* Futter *n*; Besatz *m*; ⊕ Verkleidung *f*.

link [liŋk] 1. *Ketten*-Glied *n*, Gelenk *n*; Manschettenknopf *m*; *fig.* Bindeglied *n*; 2. (sich) verbinden.

links [liŋks] *pl.* Dünen *f/pl.*; *a. golf*~ Golf(spiel)platz *m*.

linseed ['linsi:d] Leinsame(n) *m*; ~ *oil* Leinöl *n*.

lion ['laiən] Löwe *m*; *fig.* Größe *f*, Berühmtheit *f*; ~ess [~nis] Löwin *f*.

lip [lip] Lippe *f*; Rand *m*; *sl.* Unverschämtheit *f*; ~-stick ['lipstik] Lippenstift *m*.

liquefy ['likwifai] schmelzen.

liquid ['likwid] 1. flüssig; ✝ liquid; klar (*Luft etc.*); 2. Flüssigkeit *f*.

liquidat|e ['likwideit] ✝ liquidieren; bezahlen; ~ion [likwi'deiʃən] Abwicklung *f*, Liquidation *f*.

liquor ['likə] Flüssigkeit *f*; Alkohol *m*, alkoholisches Getränk.

liquorice ['likəris] Lakritze *f*.

lisp [lisp] 1. lispeln; 2. Lispeln *n*.

list [list] 1. Liste *f*, Verzeichnis *n*; Leiste *f*; Webkante *f*; 2. (in e-e Liste) eintragen; verzeichnen.

listen ['lisn] (*to*) lauschen, horchen (auf *acc.*); anhören (*acc.*), zuhören (*dat.*); hören (auf *acc.*); ~ *in teleph., Radio*: (mit)hören (*to* *acc.*); ~er [~nə] Zuhörer(in); *a.* ~-*in* (Rundfunk)Hörer(in).

listless □ ['listlis] gleichgültig; lustlos.

lists [lists] *pl.* Schranken *f/pl.*

lit [lit] *pret. u. p.p. von light[1]* 3.

literal □ ['litərəl] buchstäblich; am Buchstaben klebend; wörtlich.

litera|ry □ ['litərəri] literarisch; Literatur...; Schrift...; ~ture [~ritʃə] Literatur *f*.

lithe [laið] geschmeidig, wendig.

lithography [li'θɔgrəfi] Lithographie *f*, Steindruck *m*.

litigation [liti'geiʃən] Prozeß *m*.

lit|re, *Am.* ~er ['li:tə] Liter *n, m*.

litter ['litə] 1. Sänfte *f*; Tragbahre *f*; Streu *f*; Abfall *m*; Unordnung *f*; Wurf *m junger Tiere*; 2. ~ *down* mit Streu versehen; ~ *up* in Unordnung bringen; *Junge* werfen; ~-basket, ~-bin Abfallkorb *m*.

**little** ['litl] 1. *adj.* klein; gering(fügig); wenig; *a ~ one* ein Kleines (*Kind*); 2. *adv.* wenig; 3. Kleinigkeit *f*; *a ~* ein bißchen; *~ by ~* nach und nach; *not a ~* nicht wenig.

**live** 1. [liv] *allg.* leben; wohnen; *~ to see erleben*; *~ s.th down* et. durch guten Lebenswandel vergessen machen; *~ through durchmachen, durchstehen, überleben*; *~ up to s-m Ruf* gerecht werden, *s-n Grundsätzen* gemäß leben; *Versprechen halten*; 2. [laiv] lebendig; richtig; aktuell; glühend; ✗ scharf (*Munition*); ⚡ stromführend; *Radio*. Direkt..., *Original...*; **~lihood** ['laivlihud] Unterhalt *m*; **~liness** [~inis] Lebhaftigkeit *f*; **~ly** ['laivli] lebhaft; lebendig; aufregend; schnell; bewegt.

**liver** *anat.* ['livə] Leber *f*.

**livery** ['livəri] Livree *f*; (Amts-)Tracht *f*; *at ~* in Futter (*stehen etc.*).

**live|s** [laivz] *pl. von life*; **~-stock** ['laivstɔk] Vieh(bestand *m*) *n*.

**livid** ['livid] bläulich; fahl; F wild.

**living** ['liviŋ] 1. lebend(ig); *the ~ image of* das genaue Ebenbild *gen.*; 2. Leben *n*; Lebensweise *f*; Lebensunterhalt *m*; *eccl.* Pfründe *f*; **~-room** Wohnzimmer *n*.

**lizard** *zo.* ['lizəd] Eidechse *f*.

**load** [loud] 1. Last *f*; Ladung *f*; 2. (be)laden; *fig.* überhäufen; überladen; **~ing** ['loudiŋ] Laden *n*; Ladung *f*, Fracht *f*; *attr.* Lade...

**loaf** [louf] 1. *pl.* **loaves** [louvz] *Brot*-Laib *m*; (Zucker)Hut *m*; 2. herumlungern.

**loafer** ['loufə] Bummler *m*.

**loam** [loum] Lehm *m*, Ackerkrume *f*.

**loan** [loun] 1. Anleihe *f*, Darlehen *n*; Leihen *n*; Leihgabe *f*; *on ~* leihweise; 2. *bsd. Am.* ausleihen.

**loath** ☐ [louθ] abgeneigt; **~e** [louð] sich ekeln vor (*dat.*); verabscheuen; **~ing** ['louðiŋ] Ekel *m*; **~some** ☐ ['louðsəm] ekelhaft; verhaßt.

**loaves** [louvz] *pl. von loaf* 1.

**lobby** ['lɔbi] 1. Vorhalle *f*; *parl.* Wandelgang *m*; *thea.* Foyer *n*; 2. *parl.* *s-n* Einfluß geltend machen.

**lobe** *anat.*, ♀ [loub] Lappen *m*.

**lobster** ['lɔbstə] Hummer *m*.

**local** ☐ ['loukəl] 1. örtlich; Orts...; lokal; *~ government* Gemeindeverwaltung *f*; 2. *Zeitung* Lokalnachricht *f*; *~ train* Vorortzug *m*; F Wirtshaus *n* (am Ort); **~ity** [lou'kæliti] Örtlichkeit *f*; Lage *f*; **~ize** ['loukəlaiz] lokalisieren.

**locat|e** [lou'keit] *v/t.* versetzen, verlegen, unterbringen; ausfindig machen; *Am.* an-, festlegen; *be ~d* gelegen sein; wohnen; *v/i.* sich niederlassen; **~ion** [~eiʃən] Lage *f*; Niederlassung *f*; *Am.* Anweisung *f* von Land; angewiesenes Land; Ort

*m*; *Film*: Gelände *n* für Außenaufnahmen.

**loch** *schott.* [lɔk] See *m*; Bucht *f*.

**lock** [lɔk] 1. *Tür-, Gewehr- etc.* Schloß *n*; Schleuse(nkammer) *f*; ⚙ Sperrvorrichtung *f*; Stauung *f*; Locke *f*; Wollflocke *f*; 2. (ver-)schließen (*a. fig.*), absperren; sich verschließen lassen; ⊕ blockieren, sperren; greifen; umschließen; *~ s.o. in* j-n einsperren; *~ up weg-schließen*; abschließen; einsperren; *Geld* fest anlegen.

**lock|er** ['lɔkə] Schrank *m*, Kasten *m*; **~et** ['lɔkit] Medaillon *n*; **~-out** Aussperrung *f* *von Arbeitern*; **~smith** Schlosser *m*; **~-up** 1. Haftzelle *f*; ✝ zinslose Kapitalanlage; 2. verschließbar.

**loco** *Am. sl.* ['loukou] verrückt.

**locomot|ion** [loukə'mouʃən] Fortbewegung(sfähigkeit) *f*; **~ive** ['loukəmoutiv] 1. sich fortbewegend; beweglich; 2. *a. ~ engine* Lokomotive *f*.

**locust** ['loukəst] *zo.* Heuschrecke *f*; ♀ unechte Akazie.

**lode|star** ['loudsta:] Leitstern *m* (*a. fig.*); **~stone** Magnet(eisenstein) *m*.

**lodg|e** [lɔdʒ] 1. Häus-chen *n*; (Forst-, Park-, Pförtner)Haus *n*; Portierloge *f*; *Freimaurer*-Loge *f*; 2. *v/t.* beherbergen, aufnehmen; *Geld* hinterlegen; *Klage* einreichen; *Hieb* versetzen; *v/i.* (*bsd. zur Miete*) wohnen; logieren; **~er** ['lɔdʒə] (Unter)Mieter(in); **~ing** ['lɔdʒiŋ] Unterkunft *f*; **~s** *pl.* möbliertes Zimmer; Wohnung *f*.

**loft** [lɔ:ft] (Dach)Boden *m*; Empore *f*; **~y** ☐ ['lɔfti] hoch; erhaben; stolz.

**log** [lɔg] Klotz *m*; Block *m*; gefällter Baumstamm; ⚓ Log *n*; **~-cabin** ['lɔgkæbin] Blockhaus *n*; **~gerhead** ['lɔgəhed]: *be at ~s* sich in den Haaren liegen; **~-house**, **~-hut** Blockhaus *n*.

**logic** ['lɔdʒik] Logik *f*; **~al** ☐ [~kəl] logisch.

**logroll** *bsd. Am. pol.* ['lɔgroul] (sich gegenseitig) in die Hände arbeiten.

**loin** [lɔin] Lende(nstück *n*) *f*.

**loiter** ['lɔitə] trödeln, schlendern.

**loll** [lɔl] (sich) strecken; (sich) rekeln; *~ about* herumlungern.

**lone|liness** ['lounlinis] Einsamkeit *f*; **~ly** ☐ ['lounli], **~some** ☐ ['lounsəm] einsam.

**long**[1] [lɔŋ] 1. Länge *f*; *before ~* binnen kurzem; *for ~* lange; *take ~* lange brauchen *od.* dauern; 2. *adj.* lang; langfristig; langsam; *in the ~ run* am Ende; auf die Dauer; *be ~* lange dauern *od.* brauchen; 3. *adv.* lang(e); *so ~!* bis dann! (*auf Wiedersehen*); *(no) ~er* (nicht) länger *od.* mehr.

**long²** [ˌ] sich sehnen (*for* nach).
**long|-distance**['lɔŋ'distəns]Fern...,
Weit...; **˜evity** [lɔn'dʒeviti] Lang-
lebigkeit *f;* langes Leben; **˜hand**
['lɔŋhænd] Langschrift *f.*
**longing** ['lɔŋiŋ] 1. [ sehnsüchtig;
2. Sehnsucht *f;* Verlangen *n.*
**longitude** *geogr.* ['lɔndʒitjuːd] Länge *f.*
**long|-shore-man** ['lɔŋʃɔːmən] Ha-
fenarbeiter*m;* **˜-sighted**['lɔŋ'saitid]
weitsichtig; **˜-standing** seit langer
Zeit bestehend, alt; **˜-suffering** 1.
langmütig; 2. Langmut *f;* **˜-term**
['lɔŋtəːm] langfristig; **˜-winded** □
['lɔŋ'windid] langatmig.
**look** [luk] 1. Blick *m;* Anblick *m;*
*oft* ˜*s pl.* Aussehen *n;* *have a* ˜ *at*
*s.th.* sich et. ansehen; *I don't like*
*the* ˜ *of it* es gefällt mir nicht; 2.*v/i.*
sehen, blicken (*at, on* auf *acc.,*
nach); zusehen, *daß od. wie* ...; nachsehen, *wer etc.* ...; *krank etc.* aussehen; *nach e-r Richtung* liegen;
˜ *after* sehen nach, sich kümmern
um; versorgen; nachsehen, nachblicken (*dat.*); ˜ *at* ansehen; ˜ *for*
erwarten; suchen; ˜ *forward to* sich
freuen auf (*acc.*); ˜ *in* als Besucher
hereinschauen (*on* bei); ˜ *into* prüfen; erforschen; ˜ *on* zuschauen
(*dat.*); betrachten (*as* als); liegen zu,
gehen auf (*acc.*) (*Fenster*); ˜ *out*
vorsehen; ˜ (*up*)*on fig.* ansehen (*as*
als); *v/t.* ˜ *disdain* verächtlich
blicken; ˜ *over* et. durchsehen; *j-n*
mustern; ˜ *up et.* nachschlagen.
**looker-on** ['lukər'ɔn] Zuschauer(in).
**looking-glass** ['lukiŋglɑːs] Spiegel
*m.*
**look-out** ['luk'aut] Ausguck *m,*
Ausblick *m,* Aussicht *f* (*a. fig.*);
*that is my* ˜ F das ist meine Sache.
**loom** [luːm] 1. Webstuhl *m;* 2. undeutlich zu sehen sein, sich ab-
zeichnen.
**loop** [luːp] 1. Schlinge *f,* Schleife *f,*
Öse *f;* 2. *v/t.* in Schleifen legen;
schlingen; *v/i.* e-e Schleife machen;
sich winden; **˜hole** ['luːphoul]
Guck-, Schlupfloch *n;* ✕ Schieß-
scharte *f.*
**loose** [luːs] 1. □ *allg.* lose, locker;
schlaff; weit; frei; un-zs.-hängend;
ungenau; liederlich; 2. lösen; aufbinden; lockern; **˜n** ['luːsn] (sich)
lösen, (sich) lockern.
**loot** [luːt] 1. plündern; 2. Beute *f.*
**lop** [lɔp] *Baum* beschneiden; stutzen; schlaff herunterhängen (lassen); **˜-sided** ['lɔp'saidid] schief;
einseitig.
**loquacious** □ [lou'kweiʃəs] geschwätzig.
**lord** [lɔːd] Herr *m;* Gebieter *m;*
Magnat *m;* Lord *m;* the ♀ der Herr
(*Gott*); *my* ˜ [mi'lɔːd] Mylord,
Euer Gnaden; *the* ♀'s *Prayer* das
Vaterunser; *the* ♀'s *Supper* das

Abendmahl; **˜ly** ['lɔːdli] vornehm,
edel; großartig; hochmütig; **˜ship**
['lɔːdʃip] Lordschaft *f* (*Titel*).
**lore** [lɔː] Lehre *f,* Kunde *f.*
**lorry** ['lɔri] Last(kraft)wagen *m,*
LKW *m;* ⚙ Lore *f.*
**lose** [luːz] [*irr.*] *v/t.* verlieren; vergeuden; verpassen; abnehmen; ˜
*o.s.* sich verirren; *v/i.* verlieren;
nachgehen (*Uhr*).
**loss** [lɔs] Verlust *m;* Schaden *m;*
*at a* ˜ in Verlegenheit; außerstande.
**lost** [lɔst] *pret. u. p.p. von* lose; *be* ˜
verlorengehen; verschwunden sein;
*fig.* versunken sein; **˜-property office**
Fundbüro *n.*
**lot** [lɔt] Los *n* (*a. fig.*); Anteil *m;*
♈ Partie *f;* Posten *m;* F Menge *f;*
Parzelle *f;* *Am. Film:* Ateliorge-
lände *n; a* ˜ *of people* F eine Menge
Leute; *draw* ˜*s* losen; *fall to s.o.'s* ˜
j-m zufallen.
**loth** □ [louθ] *s.* loath.
**lotion** ['louʃən] (Haut)Wasser *n.*
**lottery** ['lɔtəri] Lotterie *f.*
**loud** □ [laud] laut (*a. adv.*); *fig.*
schreiend, grell; **˜-speaker** ['laud-
'spiːkə] Lautsprecher *m.*
**lounge** [laundʒ] 1. sich rekeln; faulenzen; 2. Bummel *m;* Wohnzimmer *n,* -diele *f;* Gesellschaftsraum
*m* e-s *Hotels; thea.* Foyer *n;* Chaiselongue *f;* **˜-chair** ['laundʒ'tʃeə]
Klubsessel *m;* **˜-suit** Straßenanzug
*m.*
**lour** ['lauə] finster blicken *od.* aussehen; die Stirn runzeln.
**lous|e** [laus], *pl.* lice [lais] Laus *f;*
**˜y** ['lauzi] verlaust; lausig; Lause...
**lout** [laut] Tölpel *m,* Lümmel *m.*
**lovable** □ ['lʌvəbl] liebenswürdig,
liebenswert.
**love** [lʌv] 1. Liebe *f* (*of, a. for, to,*
*towards* zu); Liebschaft *f;* Ange-
betete *f;* Liebling *m* (*als Anrede*);
liebe Grüße *m/pl.; Sport:* nichts, null;
*attr.* Liebes...; *give od.* send one's
˜ *to s.o.* j-n freundlichst grüßen
(lassen); *in* ˜ *with* verliebt in (*acc.*);
*fall in* ˜ *with* sich verlieben in (*acc.*);
*make* ˜ *to* werben um; 2. lieben;
gern haben; ˜ *to do* gern tun;
**˜-affair** ['lʌvəfeə] Liebschaft *f;*
**˜ly** ['lʌvli] lieblich; entzückend;
reizend; **˜r** ['lʌvə] Liebhaber *m;*
*fig.* Verehrer(in), Liebhaber(in).
**loving** □ ['lʌviŋ] liebevoll.
**low¹** [lou] 1. niedrig; tief; gering;
leise; *fig.* niedergeschlagen;
schwach; gemein; ˜*est bid* Mindest-
gebot *n;* 2. *meteor.* Tief(druckgebiet) *n; bsd. Am.* Tiefstand *m,*
-punkt *m.*
**low²** [ˌ] brüllen, muhen (*Rind*).
**low-brow** F ['loubrau] 1. geistig anspruchslos, spießig; 2. Spießer *m,*
Banause *m.*
**lower¹** ['louə] 1. niedriger; tiefer;
geringer; leiser; untere(r, -s); Un-

ter...; 2. *v/t.* nieder-, herunterlassen; senken; erniedrigen; abschwächen; *Preis etc.* herabsetzen; *v/i.* fallen, sinken.

**lower²** ['lɔuə] *s. lour.*

**low|land** ['lɔulənd] Tiefland *n;* **~liness** ['lɔulinis] Demut *f;* **~ly** ['lɔuli] demütig; bescheiden; **~ necked** (**tief**) ausgeschnitten (*Kleid*); **~-spirited** niedergeschlagen. [Treue *f.*\]

**loyal** □ ['lɔiəl] treu; **~ty** [~lti]\]

**lozenge** ['lɔzindʒ] Pastille *f.*

**lubber** ['lʌbə] Tölpel *m,* Stoffel *m.*

**lubric|ant** ['lu:brikənt] Schmiermittel *n;* **~ate** [~keit] schmieren; **~ation** [lu:bri'keiʃən] Schmieren *n,* ⊕ Ölung *f.*

**lucid** □ ['lu:sid] leuchtend, klar.

**luck** [lʌk] Glück(sfall *m*) *n;* Geschick *n; good* **~** Glück *n; bad* **~,** *hard* **~,** *ill* **~** Unglück *n,* Pech *n; worse* **~** unglücklicherweise; **~ily** ['lʌkili] glücklicherweise, zum Glück; **~y** □ ['lʌki] glücklich; *Glücks...; be* **~** Glück haben.

**lucr|ative** □ ['lu:krətiv] einträglich; **~e** ['lu:kə] Gewinn(sucht *f*) *m.*

**ludicrous** □ ['lu:dikrəs] lächerlich.

**lug** [lʌg] zerren, schleppen.

**luge** [lu:ʒ] **1.** Rodelschlitten *m;* **2.** rodeln.

**luggage** ['lʌgidʒ] Gepäck *n;* **~-carrier** Gepäckträger *m am Fahrrad;* **~-office** 🚋 Gepäckschalter *m;* **~-rack** Gepäcknetz *n;* **~-ticket** Gepäckschein *m.*

**lugubrious** □ [lu:'gju:briəs] traurig.

**lukewarm** ['lu:kwɔ:m] lau (*a. fig.*).

**lull** [lʌl] **1.** einlullen; (sich) beruhigen; **2.** (Wind)Stille *f;* Ruhepause *f.*

**lullaby** ['lʌləbai] Wiegenlied *n.*

**lumbago** ♪ [lʌm'beigou] Hexenschuß *m.*

**lumber** ['lʌmbə] **1.** Bau-, Nutzholz *n;* Gerümpel *n;* **2.** *v/t. a.* **~ up** vollstopfen; *v/i.* rumpeln, poltern; sich (dahin)schleppen; **~er** [~ərə], **~jack,** **~man** Holzfäller *m,* -arbeiter *m;* **~-mill** Sägewerk *n;* **~-room** Rumpelkammer *f;* **~-yard** Holzplatz *m,* -lager *n.*

**lumin|ary** ['lu:minəri] Himmelskörper *m;* Leuchtkörper *m; fig.* Leuchte *f;* **~ous** □ [~nəs] leuchtend; Licht...; Leucht...; *fig.* lichtvoll.

**lump** [lʌmp] **1.** Klumpen *m; fig.* Klotz *m;* Beule *f;* Stück *n* Zucker *etc.; in the* **~** in Bausch und Bogen; **~ sugar** Würfelzucker *m;* **~ sum**

Pauschalsumme *f;* **2.** *v/t.* zs.-werfen, zs.-fassen; *v/i.* Klumpen bilden; **~ish** ['lʌmpiʃ] schwerfällig; **~y** □ [~pi] klumpig.

**lunacy** ['lu:nəsi] Wahnsinn *m.*

**lunar** ['lu:nə] Mond...

**lunatic** ['lu:nətik] **1.** irr-, wahnsinnig; **2.** Irre(r *m*) *f;* Wahnsinnige(r *m*) *f;* Geistesgestörte(r *m*) *f;* **~ asylum** Irrenhaus *n,* -anstalt *f.*

**lunch**|(**eon**) [lʌntʃ, 'lʌntʃən] **1.** Lunch *m,* Mittagessen *n;* zweites Frühstück; **2.** zu Mittag essen; *j-m* ein Mittagessen geben; **~-hour** Mittagszeit *f,* -pause *f.*

**lung** *anat.* [lʌŋ] Lunge(nflügel *m*) *f; the* **~s** *pl.* die Lunge.

**lunge** [lʌndʒ] **1.** *Fechten:* Ausfall *m;* **2.** *v/i.* ausfallen (*at gegen*); (dahin-)stürmen; *v/t.* stoßen.

**lupin(e)** ♀ ['lu:pin] Lupine *f.*

**lurch** [lə:tʃ] **1.** taumeln, torkeln; **2.:** *leave in the* **~** im Stich lassen.

**lure** [ljuə] **1.** Köder *m; fig.* Lockung *f;* **2.** ködern, (an)locken.

**lurid** ['ljuərid] unheimlich; erschreckend, schockierend; düster, finster.

**lurk** [lə:k] lauern; versteckt liegen.

**luscious** □ ['lʌʃəs] köstlich; üppig; süß(lich), widerlich.

**lust** [lʌst] (sinnliche) Begierde; *fig.* Gier *f,* Sucht *f.*

**lust|re,** *Am.* **~er** ['lʌstə] Glanz *m;* Kronleuchter *m;* **~rous** □ [~trəs] glänzend.

**lusty** □ ['lʌsti] rüstig; *fig.* lebhaft, kräftig.

**lute¹** ♪ [lu:t] Laute *f.*

**lute²** [~] **1.** Kitt *m;* **2.** (ver)kitten.

**Lutheran** ['lu:θərən] lutherisch.

**luxate** ♣ ['lʌkseit] verrenken.

**luxur|iant** □ [lʌg'zjuəriənt] üppig; **~ious** □ [~iəs] luxuriös, üppig; **~y** ['lʌkʃəri] Luxus *m,* Üppigkeit *f;* Luxusartikel *m;* Genußmittel *n.*

**lyceum** [lai'siəm] Vortragsraum *m; bsd. Am.* Volkshochschule *f.*

**lye** [lai] Lauge *f.*

**lying** ['laiiŋ] **1.** *p.pr. von lie¹ 2 u. lie²* **2;** **2.** *adj.* lügnerisch; **~-in** [~ŋ'in] Wochenbett *n;* **~** *hospital* Entbindungsheim *n.*

**lymph** ♣ [limf] Lymphe *f.*

**lynch** [lintʃ] lynchen; **~-law** ['lintʃlɔ:] Lynchjustiz *f.*

**lynx** *zo.* [liŋks] Luchs *m.*

**lyric** ['lirik] **1.** lyrisch; **2.** lyrisches Gedicht; **~s** *pl.* (Lied)Text *m* (*bsd. e-s Musicals*); Lyrik *f;* **~al** □ [~kəl] lyrisch, gefühlvoll; schwärmerisch, begeistert.

# M

**ma'am** [mæm] Majestät f (*Anrede für die Königin*); Hoheit f (*Anrede für Prinzessinnen*); F [məm] gnä' Frau f (*von Dienstboten verwendete Anrede*).

**macaroni** [mækə'rouni] Makkaroni *pl.*

**macaroon** [mækə'ru:n] Makrone f.

**machin|ation** [mæki'neiʃən] Anschlag m; ~s *pl.* Ränke *pl.*; ~e [mə'ʃi:n] 1. Maschine f; Mechanismus m (a. *fig.*); 2. maschinell herstellen *od.* (be)arbeiten; ~e-made maschinell hergestellt; ~ery [~nəri] Maschinen f/pl.; Maschinerie f; ~ist [~nist] Maschinist m; Maschinennäherin f.

**mackerel** *ichth.* ['mækrəl] Makrele f.

**mackinaw** *Am.* ['mækinɔ:] Stutzer m (*Kleidungsstück*).

**mackintosh** ['mækintɔʃ] Regenmantel m.

**mad** □ [mæd] wahnsinnig; toll (-wütig); *fig.* wild; F wütend; go ~ verrückt werden; drive ~ verrückt machen.

**madam** ['mædəm] gnädige Frau, gnädiges Fräulein (*Anrede*).

**mad|cap** ['mædkæp] 1. toll; 2. Tollkopf m; Wildfang m; ~den ['mædn] toll *od.* rasend machen.

**made** [meid] *pret. u. p.p. von* make 1.

**made-up** ['meid'ʌp] zurechtgemacht; erfunden; fertig; ~ clothes *pl.* Konfektion f.

**mad|house** ['mædhaus] Irrenhaus n; ~man Wahnsinnige(r) m; ~ness ['mædnis] Wahnsinn m; (Toll)Wut f.

**magazine** [mægə'zi:n] Magazin n; (Munitions)Lager n; Zeitschrift f.

**maggot** *zo.* ['mægət] Made f.

**magic** ['mædʒik] 1. a. ~al □ [~kəl] magisch; Zauber...; 2. Zauberei f; *fig.* Zauber m; ~ian [me'dʒiʃən] Zauberer m.

**magistra|cy** ['mædʒistrəsi] Richteramt n; *die* Richter m/pl.; ~te [~rit] (Polizei-, Friedens)Richter m.

**magnanimous** □ [mæg'næniməs] großmütig.

**magnet** ['mægnit] Magnet m; ~ic [mæg'netik] (~ally) magnetisch.

**magni|ficence** [mæg'nifisns] Pracht f, Herrlichkeit f; ~ficent □ [~nt] prächtig, herrlich; ~fy ['mægnifai] vergrößern; ~tude [~itju:d] Größe f, Wichtigkeit f.

**magpie** *orn.* ['mægpai] Elster f.

**mahogany** [mə'hɔgəni] Mahagoni (-holz) n.

**maid** [meid] *lit.* Mädchen n; (Dienst)Mädchen n; old ~ alte

Jungfer; ~ of all work Mädchen n für alles; ~ of honour Ehren-, Hofdame f.

**maiden** ['meidn] 1. = maid; 2. jungfräulich; unverheiratet; *fig.* Jungfern..., Erstlings...; ~ name Mädchenname m e-r Frau; ~head Jungfräulichkeit f; ~hood [~hud] Mädchenjahre n/pl.; ~ly [~nli] jungfräulich, mädchenhaft.

**mail¹** [meil] (Ketten)Panzer m.

**mail²** [~] 1. Post(dienst m) f; Post(sendung) f; 2. *Am.* mit der Post schicken, aufgeben; ~able *Am.* ['meiləbl] postversandfähig; ~bag Briefträger-, Posttasche f; Postsack m; ~box bsd. *Am.* Briefkasten m; ~ carrier *Am.* Briefträger m; ~man *Am.* Briefträger m; ~-order firm, bsd. *Am.* ~-order house (Post)Versandgeschäft n.

**maim** [meim] verstümmeln.

**main** [mein] 1. Haupt..., hauptsächlich; by ~ force mit voller Kraft; 2. Hauptrohr n, -leitung f; ~s *pl.* ≠ (Strom)Netz n; in the ~ in der Hauptsache, im wesentlichen; ~land ['meinlənd] Festland n; ~ly [~li] hauptsächlich; ~spring Uhrfeder f; *fig.* Haupttriebfeder f; ~stay ⚓ Großstag n; *fig.* Hauptstütze f 2 **Street** *Am.* Hauptstraße f; 2 **Streeter** *Am.* Kleinstadtbewohner m.

**maintain** [men'tein] (aufrecht)erhalten; beibehalten; (unter)stützen; unterhalten; behaupten.

**maintenance** ['meintinəns] Erhaltung f; Unterhalt m; ⊕ Wartung f.

**maize** ♃ [meiz] Mais m.

**majestic** [mə'dʒestik] (~ally) majestätisch; ~y ['mædʒisti] Majestät f; Würde f, Hoheit f.

**major** ['meidʒə] 1. größer; wichtig(er); mündig; ♩ Dur n; ~ key Dur-Tonart f; ~ league *Am.* Baseball: Oberliga f; 2. ⚔ Major m; Mündige(r m) f; *Am. univ.* Hauptfach n; ~-general ⚔ Generalmajor m; ~ity [mə'dʒɔriti] Mehrheit f; Mündigkeit f; Majorsrang m.

**make** [meik] 1. [*irr.*] *v/t. allg.* machen; verfertigen, fabrizieren; bilden; (aus)machen; ergeben; (veran)lassen; gewinnen, verdienen; sich erweisen als, abgeben; *Regel etc.* aufstellen; *Frieden etc.* schließen; *e-e Rede* halten; ~ good wieder gutmachen; wahr machen; *do you* ~ *one of us?* machen Sie mit?; ~ port ⚓ den Hafen anlaufen; ~ way vorwärtskommen; ~ into verarbeiten zu; ~ out ausfindig machen; erkennen; verstehen; entziffern; *Rechnung etc.* ausstellen; ~ over übertragen; ~ up ergänzen; vervoll-

ständigen; zs.-stellen; bilden, ausmachen; *Streit* beilegen; zurechtmachen, schminken; = ~ *up for*
*(v/i.)*; ~ *up one's mind* sich entschließen; *v/i.* sich begeben;
gehen; ~ *away with* beseitigen;
*Geld* vertun; ~ *for* zugehen auf
*(acc.)*; sich aufmachen nach; ~ *off*
sich fortmachen; ~ *up* sich zurechtmachen; sich schminken; ~ *up for*
nach-, aufholen; für *et.* entschädigen; 2. Mach-, Bauart *f*; Bau *m des*
*Körpers*; Form *f*; Fabrikat *n*, Erzeugnis *n*; ~**believe** ['meikbili:v]
Schein *m*, Vorwand *m*, Verstellung
*f*; ~**r** ['meikə] Hersteller *m*; ♀
Schöpfer *m* (*Gott*); ~**shift** 1. Notbehelf *m*; 2. behelfsmäßig; ~**up**
*typ.* Umbruch *m*; *fig.* Charakter *m*;
Schminke *f*, Make-up *n*.

**maladjustment** ['mælə'dʒʌstmənt]
mangelhafte Anpassung.

**maladministration** ['mælədmi-
nis'treiʃən] schlechte Verwaltung.

**malady** ['mælədi] Krankheit *f*.

**malcontent** ['mælkəntent] 1. unzufrieden; 2. Unzufriedene(r) *m*.

**male** [meil] 1. männlich; 2. Mann
*m*; *zo.* Männchen *n*.

**malediction** [mæli'dikʃən] Fluch
*m*.

**malefactor** ['mælifæktə] Übeltäter
*m*.

**malevolen|ce** [mə'levələns] Bös-
willigkeit *f*; ~**t** □ [~nt] böswillig.

**malice** ['mælis] Bosheit *f*; Groll *m*.

**malicious** □ [mə'liʃəs] boshaft;
böswillig; ~**ness** [~snis] Bosheit *f*.

**malign** [mə'lain] 1. □ schädlich;
2. verleumden; ~**ant** □ [mə-
'lignənt] böswillig; ❀ bösartig;
~**ity** [~niti] Bosheit *f*; Schadenfreude *f*; *bsd.* ❀ Bösartigkeit *f*.

**malleable** ['mæliəbl] hämmerbar;
*fig.* geschmeidig.

**mallet** ['mælit] Schlegel *m*.

**malnutrition** ['mælnju(:)'triʃən]
Unterernährung *f*.

**malodorous** □ [mæ'loudərəs] übelriechend.

**malpractice** ['mæl'præktis] Übel-
tat *f*; ❀ falsche Behandlung.

**malt** [mɔ:lt] Malz *n*.

**maltreat** [mæl'tri:t] schlecht behandeln; mißhandeln.

**mam(m)a** [mə'mɑ:] Mama *f*.

**mammal** ['mæməl] Säugetier *n*.

**mammoth** ['mæməθ] riesig.

**mammy** F ['mæmi] Mami *f*; *Am.*
farbiges Kindermädchen *n*.

**man** [mæn, *in Zssgn* ...mən] 1. *pl.*
**men** [men] Mann *m*; Mensch(en
*pl.*) *m*; Menschheit *f*; Diener *m*;
*Schach*: Figur *f*; Damestein *m*;
2. männlich; 3. ⚔, ⚓ bemannen;
~ *o.s.* sich ermannen.

**manage** ['mænidʒ] *v/t.* handhaben;
verwalten, leiten; *Menschen, Tiere*
lenken; mit *j-m* fertig werden; *et.*

fertigbringen; ~ *to inf.* es fertigbringen, zu *inf.*; *v/i.* die Aufsicht
haben, die Geschäfte führen; auskommen; F es schaffen; ~**able** □
[~dʒəbl] handlich; lenksam; ~**ment**
[~dʒmənt] Verwaltung *f*, Leitung *f*;
Direktion *f*, Geschäftsführung *f*;
geschickte Behandlung; ~**r** [~dʒə]
Leiter *m*, Direktor *m*; Regisseur *m*;
Manager *m*; ~**ress** [~əres] Leiterin
*f*, Direktorin *f*.

**managing** ['mænidʒiŋ] geschäfts-
führend; Betriebs...; ~ *clerk* Ge-
schäftsführer *m*, Prokurist *m*.

**mandat|e** ['mændeit] Mandat *n*;
Befehl *m*; Auftrag *m*; Vollmacht *f*;
~**ory** [~dətəri] befehlend.

**mane** [mein] Mähne *f*.

**maneuver** [mə'nu:və] = *ma-*
*noeuvre*.

**manful** □ ['mænful] mannhaft.

**mange** *vet.* [meindʒ] Räude *f*.

**manger** ['meindʒə] Krippe *f*.

**mangle** ['mæŋgl] 1. Wringmaschine
*f*; Wäschemangel *f*; 2. mangeln;
wringen; zerstückeln; *fig.* verstümmeln.

**mangy** ['meindʒi] räudig; *fig.*
schäbig.

**manhood** ['mænhud] Mannesalter
*n*; Männlichkeit *f*; die Männer *m/pl.*

**mania** ['meinjə] Wahnsinn *m*;
Sucht *f*, Manie *f*; ~**c** ['meiniæk]
1. Wahnsinnige(r *m*) *f*; 2. wahnsinnig.

**manicure** ['mænikjuə] 1. Maniküre
*f*; 2. manikۈren.

**manifest** ['mænifest] 1. □ offenbar;
2. ♣ Ladungsverzeichnis *n*; 3. *v/t.*
offenbaren; kundtun; ~**ation**
[mænifes'teiʃən] Offenbarung *f*;
Kundgebung *f*; ~**o** [mæni'festou]
Manifest *n*.

**manifold** □ ['mænifould] 1. mannigfaltig; 2. vervielfältigen.

**manipulat|e** [mə'nipjuleit] (ge-
schickt) handhaben; ~**ion** [mæni-
pju'leiʃən] Handhabung *f*, Behandlung *f*, Verfahren *n*; Kniff *m*.

**man|kind** [mæn'kaind] die Mensch-
heit; ['mænkaind] die Männer *pl.*;
~**ly** ['mænli] männlich; mannhaft.

**manner** ['mænə] Art *f*, Weise *f*;
Stil(art *f*) *m*; Manier *f*; ~*s pl.* Manieren *f/pl.*, Sitten *f/pl.*; *in a* ~
gewissermaßen; ~**ed** [~əd] ...gear-
tet; gekünstelt; ~**ly** [~əli] manier-
lich, gesittet.

**manoeuvre**, *Am. a.* **maneuver**
[mə'nu:və] 1. Manöver *n* (*a. fig.*);
2. manövrieren (lassen).

**man-of-war** ⚓ ['mænəv'wɔ:]
Kriegsschiff *n*.

**manor** ['mænə] Rittergut *n*; *lord of*
*the* ~ Gutsherr *m*; ~**house** Herr-
schaftshaus *n*, Herrensitz *m*; Schloß
*n*.

**manpower** ['mænpauə] Men-
schenpotential *n*; Arbeitskräfte *f/pl.*

**man-servant** ['mænsəːvənt] Diener *m*.

**mansion** ['mænʃən] (herrschaftliches) Wohnhaus.

**manslaughter** ['mænslɔːtə] Totschlag *m*, fahrlässige Tötung.

**mantel|piece** ['mæntlpiːs], **~shelf** Kaminsims *m*, -platte *f*.

**mantle** ['mæntl] 1. Mantel *m*; *fig.* Hülle *f*; Glühstrumpf *m*; 2. *v/t.* verhüllen; *v/i.* sich röten (*Gesicht*).

**manual** ['mænjuəl] 1. □ Hand...; mit der Hand (gemacht); 2. Handbuch *n*.                [brik *f*.]

**manufactory** [mænjuˈfæktəri] Fa-

**manufactur|e** [mænjuˈfæktʃə] 1. Fabrikation *f*; Fabrikat *n*; 2. fabrizieren; verarbeiten; **~er** [~ərə] Fabrikant *m*; **~ing** [~riŋ] Fabrik...; Gewerbe...; Industrie...

**manure** [məˈnjuə] 1. Dünger *m*; 2. düngen.

**manuscript** ['mænjuskript] Manuskript *n*; Handschrift *f*.

**many** ['meni] 1. viele; **~** *a* **manche(r, ~s)**; *be one too* **~** *for s.o.* j-m überlegen sein; 2. Menge *f*; *a good* **~,** *a great* **~** ziemlich viele, sehr viele.

**map** [mæp] 1. (Land)Karte *f*; 2. aufzeichnen; **~** *out* planen; einteilen.

**maple** ♀ ['meipl] Ahorn *m*.

**mar** [maː] schädigen; verderben.

**maraud** [məˈrɔːd] plündern.

**marble** ['maːbl] 1. Marmor *m*; Murmel *f*; 2. marmorn.

**March**¹ [maːtʃ] März *m*.

**march**² [~] 1. Marsch *m*; Fortschritt *m*; Gang *m* der *Freignisse etc.*; 2. marschieren (lassen); *fig.* vorwärtsschreiten.

**marchioness** ['maːʃənis] Marquise *f*.

**mare** [meə] Stute *f*; **~'s** *nest fig.* Schwindel *m*; (Zeitungs)Ente *f*.

**marg|arine** [maːdʒəˈriːn], *a.* **~e** F [maːdʒ] Margarine *f*.

**margin** ['maːdʒin] Rand *m*; Grenze *f*; Spielraum *m*; Verdienst-, Gewinn-, Handelsspanne *f*; **~al** □ [~nl] am Rande (befindlich); Rand...; **~** *note* Randbemerkung *f*.

**marine** [məˈriːn] Marineinfanterist *m*; Marine *f*; *paint.* Seestück *n*; *attr.* See...; Marine...; Schiffs...; **~r** ['mærinə] Seemann *m*.

**marital** □ ['mæritl] ehelich, Ehe...

**maritime** ['mæritaim] an der See liegend *od.* lebend; See...; Küsten-...; Schiffahrt(s)...

**mark**¹ [maːk] Mark *f* (*Geldstück*).

**mark**² [~] 1. Marke *f*, Merkmal *n*, Zeichen *n*; ✝ Preiszettel *m*; Fabrik-, Schutzmarke *f*; (Körper)Mal *n*; Norm *f*; *Schule:* Zensur *f*, Note *f*, Punkt *m*; *Sport:* Startlinie *f*; Ziel *n*; *a man of* **~** ein Mann von Bedeutung; *fig. up to the* **~** auf der Höhe;

*beside the* **~,** *wide of the* **~** den Kern der Sache verfehlend; unrichtig; 2. *v/t.* (be)zeichnen, markieren; *Sport:* anschreiben; kennzeichnen; be(ob)achten; sich *et.* merken; **~** *off* abtrennen; **~** *out* bezeichnen; abstecken; **~** *time* auf der Stelle treten; *v/i.* achtgeben; **~ed** □ auffallend; merklich; ausgeprägt.

**market** ['maːkit] 1. Markt(platz) *m*; Handel *m*; ✝ Absatz *m*; *in the* **~** auf dem Markt; *play the* **~** *Am. sl.* an der Börse spekulieren; 2. *v/t.* auf den Markt bringen, verkaufen; *v/i.* einkaufen gehen; **~able** □ [~təbl] marktfähig, -gängig; **~ing** [~tiŋ] ✝ Marketing *n*, Absatzpolitik *f*; Marktbesuch *m*.

**marksman** ['maːksmən] (guter) Schütze.

**marmalade** ['maːməleid] Orangenmarmelade *f*.

**maroon** [məˈruːn] 1. kastanienbraun; 2. *auf e-r einsamen Insel* aussetzen; 3. Leuchtrakete *f*.

**marquee** [maːˈkiː] (großes) Zelt.

**marquis** [maːˈkiː] Marquis *m*.

**marriage** ['mæridʒ] Heirat *f*, Ehe (-stand *m*) *f*; Hochzeit *f*; *civil* **~** standesamtliche Trauung; **~able** [~dʒəbl] heiratsfähig; **~** *articles pl.* Ehevertrag *m*; **~** *lines pl.* Trauschein *m*; **~** *portion* Mitgift *f*.

**married** ['mærid] verheiratet; ehelich; Ehe...; **~** *couple* Ehepaar *n*.

**marrow** ['mærou] Mark *n*; *fig.* Kern *m*, Beste(s) *n*; **~y** [~oui] markig.

**marry** ['mæri] *v/t.* (ver)heiraten; *eccl.* trauen; *v/i.* (sich ver)heiraten.

**marsh** [maːʃ] Sumpf *m*, Morast *m*.

**marshal** ['maːʃəl] 1. Marschall *m*; *hist.* Hofmarschall *m*; Zeremonienmeister *m*; *Am.* Bezirkspolizeichef *m*; Leiter *m* der Feuerwehr; 2. ordnen; führen; *zs.*-**stellen**.

**marshy** ['maːʃi] sumpfig.

**mart** [maːt] Markt *m*; Auktionsraum *m*.

**marten** *zo.* ['maːtin] Marder *m*.

**martial** □ ['maːʃəl] kriegerisch; Kriegs...; **~** *law* Stand-, Kriegsrecht *n*.

**martyr** ['maːtə] 1. Märtyrer(in) (*to gen.*); 2. (zu Tode) martern.

**marvel** ['maːvel] 1. Wunder *n*; 2. sich wundern; **~lous** □ ['maːviləs] wunderbar, erstaunlich.

**mascot** ['mæskət] Maskottchen *n*.

**masculine** ['maːskjulin] männlich.

**mash** [mæʃ] 1. Gemisch *n*; Maische *f*; Mengfutter *n*; 2. mischen; zerdrücken; (ein)maischen; **~ed** *potatoes pl.* Kartoffelbrei *m*.

**mask** [maːsk] 1. Maske *f*; 2. maskieren; *fig.* verbergen; tarnen; **~ed:** **~** *ball* Maskenball *m*.

**mason** ['meisn] Steinmetz *m*; Maurer *m*; Freimaurer *m*; **~ry** [~nri] Mauerwerk *n*.

masque [maːsk] Maskenspiel n.

masquerade [mæskə'reid] 1. Maskenball m; Verkleidung f; 2. fig. sich maskieren.

mass [mæs] 1. eccl. Messe f; Masse f; Menge f; ~ meeting Massenversammlung f; 2. (sich) (an)sammeln.

massacre ['mæsəkə] 1. Blutbad n; 2. niedermetzeln.

massage ['mæsaːʒ] 1. Massage f; 2. massieren.

massif ['mæsiːf] (Gebirgs)Massiv n.

massive ['mæsiv] massiv; schwer.

mast ⚓ [maːst] Mast m.

master ['maːstə] 1. Meister m; Herr m (a. fig.); Gebieter m; Lehrer m; Kapitän m e-s Handelsschiffs; Anrede: (junger) Herr; univ. Rektor m e-s College; ♀ of Arts Magister m Artium; ♀ of Ceremonies Conférencier m; 2. Meister...; fig. führend; 3. Herr sein od. werden über (acc.); Sprache etc. meistern, beherrschen; ~-builder Baumeister m; ~ful □ [~ful] herrisch; meisterhaft; ~key Hauptschlüssel m; ~ly [~əli] meisterhaft; ~piece Meisterstück n; ~ship [~əʃip] Meisterschaft f; Herrschaft f; Lehramt n; ~y [~əri] Herrschaft f; Vorrang m; Oberhand f; Meisterschaft f; Beherrschung f.

masticate ['mæstikeit] kauen.

mastiff ['mæstif] englische Dogge.

mat [mæt] 1. Matte f; Deckchen n; Unterlage f; 2. fig. bedecken; (sich) verflechten; 3. mattiert, matt.

match¹ [mætʃ] Streichholz n.

match² [~] 1. Gleiche(r m, -s n) f; Partie f; Wettspiel n, -kampf m; Heirat f; be a ~ for j-m gewachsen sein; meet one's ~ s-n Meister finden; 2. v/t. anpassen; passen zu; et. Passendes finden od. geben zu; es aufnehmen mit; verheiraten; well ~ed zs.-passend; v/i. zs.-passen; to ~ dazu passend; ~less □ ['mætʃlis] unvergleichlich, ohnegleichen; ~maker Ehestifter(in).

mate¹ [meit] Schach: matt (setzen).

mate² [~] 1. Gefährt|e m, -in f; Kamerad(in); Gatt|e m, -in f; Männchen n, Weibchen n von Tieren; Gehilf|e m, -in f; ⚓ Maat m; 2. (sich) verheiraten; (sich) paaren.

material □ [mə'tiəriəl] 1. materiell; körperlich; materialistisch; wesentlich; 2. Material n, Stoff m; Werkstoff m; writing ~s pl. Schreibmaterial(ien pl.) n.

matern|al □ [mə'təːnl] mütterlich; Mutter...; mütterlicherseits; ~ity [~niti] Mutterschaft f; Mütterlichkeit f; mst ~ hospital Entbindungsanstalt f.

mathematic|ian [mæθimə'tiʃən] Mathematiker m; ~s [~'mætiks] mst sg. Mathematik f.

matriculate [mə'trikjuleit] (sich) immatrikulieren (lassen).

matrimon|ial □ [mætri'mounjəl] ehelich; Ehe...; ~y ['mætriməni] Ehe(stand m) f.

matrix ['meitriks] Matrize f.

matron ['meitrən] Matrone f; Hausmutter f; Oberin f.

matter ['mætə] 1. Materie f, Stoff m; ⚕ Eiter m; Gegenstand m; Ursache f; Sache f; Angelegenheit f, Geschäft n; printed ~ ⚘ Drucksache f; what's the ~? was gibt es?; what's the ~ with you? was fehlt Ihnen?; no ~ es hat nichts zu sagen; no ~ who gleichgültig wer; ~ of course Selbstverständlichkeit f; for that ~, for the ~ of that was dies betrifft; ~ of fact Tatsache f; 2. von Bedeutung sein; it does not ~ es macht nichts; ~-of-fact tatsächlich; sachlich.

mattress ['mætris] Matratze f.

matur|e [mə'tjuə] 1. □ reif; reiflich; † fällig; 2. reifen; zur Reife bringen; † fällig werden; ~ity [~əriti] Reife f; † Fälligkeit f.

maudlin □ ['mɔːdlin] rührselig.

maul [mɔːl] beschädigen; fig. heruntermachen; roh umgehen mit.

Maundy Thursday eccl. ['mɔːndi 'θəːzdi] Gründonnerstag m.

mauve [mouv] 1. Malvenfarbe f; 2. hellviolett.

maw [mɔː] Tier-Magen m; Rachen m.

mawkish □ ['mɔːkiʃ] rührselig, sentimental.

maxim ['mæksim] Grundsatz m; ~um [~məm] Höchstmaß n, -stand m, -betrag m; attr. Höchst...

May¹ [mei] Mai m.

may² [~] [irr.] mag, kann, darf.

maybe Am. ['meibiː] vielleicht.

may|-beetle zo. ['meibiːtl], ~bug Maikäfer m.

May Day ['meidei] der 1. Mai.

mayor [mɛə] Bürgermeister m.

maypole ['meipoul] Maibaum m.

maz|e [meiz] Irrgarten m, Labyrinth n; fig. Wirrnis f; in a ~ = ~ed [meizd] bestürzt, verwirrt; ~y □ ['meizi] labyrinthisch; wirr.

me [miː, mi] mich; mir; F ich.

mead [miːd] Met m; poet. = meadow.

meadow ['medou] Wiese f.

meag|re, Am. ~er □ ['miːgə] mager, dürr; dürftig.

meal [miːl] Mahl(zeit f) n; Mehl n.

mean¹ □ [miːn] gemein, niedrig, gering; armselig; knauserig.

mean² [~] 1. mittler, mittelmäßig; Durchschnitts...; in the ~ time inzwischen; 2. Mitte f; ~s pl. (Geld-) Mittel n/pl.; (a. sg.) Mittel n; by all ~s jedenfalls; by no ~s keineswegs; by ~s of mittels (gen.).

mean³ [~] [irr.] meinen; beabsichtigen; bestimmen; bedeuten; ~ *well* (*ill*) es gut (schlecht) meinen.

**meaning** ['mi:niŋ] **1.** □ bedeutsam; **2.** Sinn *m*, Bedeutung *f*; **~less** [‚ɔlis] bedeutungslos; sinnlos.

**meant** [ment] *pret. u. p.p. von* **mean³**.

**mean|time** ['mi:n'taim], **~while** mittlerweile, inzwischen.

**measles** ⚕ ['mi:zlz] *sg.* Masern *pl.*

**measure** ['meʒə] **1.** Maß *n*; ♪ Takt *m*; Maßregel *f*; ~ *of capacity* Hohlmaß *n*; *beyond* ~ über alle Maßen; *in a great* ~ großenteils; *made to* ~ nach Maß gemacht; **2.** (ab-, aus-, ver)messen; *j-m* Maß nehmen; ~ *up Am.* heranreichen; **~less** □ [‚ɔlis] unermeßlich; **~ment** [‚ɔmənt] Messung *f*; Maß *n*.

**meat** [mi:t] Fleisch *n*; *fig.* Gehalt *m*; ~ *tea* frühes Abendessen mit Tee; **~y** ['mi:ti] fleischig; *fig.* gehaltvoll.

**mechanic** [mi'kænik] Handwerker *m*; Mechaniker *m*; **~al** □ [‚ɔkəl] mechanisch; Maschinen...; **~ian** [mekə'niʃən] Mechaniker *m*; **~s** [mi'kæniks] *mst sg.* Mechanik *f*.

**mechan|ism** ['mekənizəm] Mechanismus *m*; **~ize** [‚ɔnaiz] mechanisieren; ✗ motorisieren.

**medal** ['medl] Medaille *f*; Orden *m*.

**meddle** ['medl] sich einmischen (*with, in* in *acc.*); **~some** [‚ɔlsəm] zu-, aufdringlich.

**mediaeval** □ [medi'i:vəl] mittelalterlich.

**media|l** □ ['mi:djəl], **~n** [‚ɔn] Mittel..., in der Mitte (befindlich).

**mediat|e** ['mi:dieit] vermitteln; **~ion** [mi:di'eiʃən] Vermittlung *f*; **~or** ['mi:dieitə] Vermittler *m*.

**medical** □ ['medikəl] medizinisch, ärztlich; ~ *certificate* Krankenschein *m*, Attest *n*; ~ *evidence* ärztliches Gutachten; ~ *man* Arzt *m*, Mediziner *m*; ~ *supervision* ärztliche Aufsicht.

**medicate** ['medikeit] medizinisch behandeln; mit Arzneistoff versehen; **~d** *bath* medizinisches Bad.

**medicin|al** □ [me'disinl] medizinisch; heilend, heilsam; **~e** ['medsin] Medizin *f*.

**medieval** □ [medi'i:vəl] = *mediaeval*.

**mediocre** ['mi:dioukə] mittelmäßig.

**meditat|e** ['mediteit] *v/i.* nachdenken, überlegen; *v/t.* sinnen auf (*acc.*); erwägen; **~ion** [medi'teiʃən] Nachdenken *n*; innere Betrachtung; **~ive** □ ['meditətiv] nachdenklich, meditativ.

**Mediterranean** [meditə'reinjən] Mittelmeer *n*; *attr.* Mittelmeer...

**medium** ['mi:djəm] **1.** Mitte *f*; Mittel *n*; Vermittlung *f*; Medium *n*; *Lebens*-Element *n*; **2.** mittler; Mittel..., Durchschnitts...

**medley** ['medli] Gemisch *n*; ♪ Potpourri *n*.

**meek** □ [mi:k] sanft-, demütig; **~ness** ['mi:knis] Sanft-, Demut *f*.

**meerschaum** ['miəʃəm] Meerschaum(pfeife *f*) *m*.

**meet¹** [mi:t] passend; schicklich.

**meet²** [‚ɔ] [*irr.*] *v/t.* treffen; begegnen (*dat.*); abholen; stoßen auf *den Gegner*; Wunsch *etc.* befriedigen; *e-r Verpflichtung* nachkommen; *Am. j-m* vorgestellt werden; *go to* ~ *s.o.* j-m entgegengehen; *v/i.* sich treffen; zs.-stoßen; sich versammeln; ~ *with* stoßen auf (*acc.*); erleiden; **~ing** ['mi:tiŋ] Begegnung *f*; (Zs.-)Treffen *n*, Versammlung *f*; Tagung *f*.

**melancholy** ['melənkəli] **1.** Schwermut *f*; **2.** melancholisch.

**meliorate** ['mi:ljəreit] (sich) verbessern.

**mellow** ['melou] **1.** □ mürbe; reif; weich; mild; **2.** reifen (lassen); weich machen *od.* werden; (sich) mildern.

**melo|dious** □ [mi'loudjəs] melodisch; **~dramatic** [meloudrə'mætik] melodramatisch; **~dy** ['melədi] Melodie *f*; Lied *n*.

**melon** ♀ ['melən] Melone *f*.

**melt** [melt] (zer)schmelzen; *fig.* zerfließen; *Gefühl* erweichen.

**member** ['membə] (Mit)Glied *n*; *parl.* Abgeordnete(r *m*) *f*; **~ship** [‚ɔʃip] Mitgliedschaft *f*; Mitgliederzahl *f*.

**membrane** ['membrein] Membran(e) *f*, Häutchen *n*. [*n*.\

**memento** [mi'mentou] Andenken *n*.

**memo** ['mi:mou] = *memorandum*.

**memoir** ['memwa:] Denkschrift *f*; **~s** *pl.* Memoiren *pl.*

**memorable** □ ['memərəbl] denkwürdig.

**memorandum** [memə'rændəm] Notiz *f*; *pol.* Note *f*; Schriftsatz *m*.

**memorial** [mi'mɔ:riəl] Denkmal *n*; Gedenkzeichen *n*; Denkschrift *f*, Eingabe *f*; *attr.* Gedächtnis..., Gedenk...

**memorize** ['meməraiz] auswendig lernen, memorieren.

**memory** ['meməri] Gedächtnis *n*; Erinnerung *f*; Andenken *n*; *commit to* ~ dem Gedächtnis einprägen; *in* ~ *of* zum Andenken an (*acc.*).

**men** [men] *pl. von man 1*; Mannschaft *f*.

**menace** ['menəs] **1.** (be)drohen; **2.** Gefahr *f*; Drohung *f*.

**mend** [mend] **1.** *v/t.* (ver)bessern; ausbessern, flicken; besser machen; ~ *one's ways* sich bessern; *v/i.* sich bessern; **2.** Flicken *m*; *on the* ~ auf dem Wege der Besserung.

**mendacious** □ [men'deiʃəs] lügnerisch, verlogen.

**mendicant** ['mendikənt] **1.** bettelnd; Bettel...; 2. Bettler *m*; Bettel-mönch *m*.

**menial** *contp.* ['mi:njəl] **1.** □ knechtisch; niedrig; **2.** Knecht *m*; Lakai *m*.

**meningitis** ♀ [menin'dʒaitis] Hirnhautentzündung *f*, Meningitis *f*.

**mental** □ ['mentl] geistig; Geistes...; ~ **arithmetic** Kopfrechnen *n*; **~ity** [men'tæliti] Mentalität *f*.

**mention** ['menʃən] **1.** Erwähnung *f*; **2.** erwähnen; *don't* ~ *it!* bitte!

**menu** ['menju:] Speisenfolge *f*, Menü *n*; Speisekarte *f*.

**mercantile** ['mə:kəntail] kaufmännisch; Handels...

**mercenary** ['mə:sinəri] **1.** □ feil, käuflich; gedungen; gewinnsüchtig; **2.** ✕ Söldner *m*.

**mercer** ['mə:sə] Seidenwaren-, Stoffhändler *m*.

**merchandise** ['mə:tʃəndaiz] Ware(n *pl.*) *f*.

**merchant** ['mə:tʃənt] **1.** Kaufmann *m*; *Am.* (Klein)Händler *m*; **2.** Handels..., Kaufmanns...; *law* ~ Handelsrecht *n*; **~man** Handelsschiff *n*.

**merci|ful** □ ['mə:siful] barmherzig; **~less** □ [~ilis] unbarmherzig.

**mercury** ['mə:kjuri] Quecksilber *n*.

**mercy** ['mə:si] Barmherzigkeit *f*; Gnade *f*; *be at s.o.'s* ~ in j-s Gewalt sein.

**mere** [miə] rein, lauter; bloß; **~ly** ['miəli] bloß, lediglich, allein.

**meretricious** □ [meri'triʃəs] aufdringlich; kitschig.

**merge** [mə:dʒ] verschmelzen (*in* mit); **~r** ['mə:dʒə] Verschmelzung *f*.

**meridian** [mə'ridiən] *geogr.* Meridian *m*; *fig.* Gipfel *m*; *attr.* Mittags...

**merit** ['merit] **1.** Verdienst *n*; Wert *m*; Vorzug *m*; *bsd.* ɪ̃ ~*s pl.* Hauptpunkte *m/pl.*, Wesen *n e-r Sache*; *make a* ~ *of* als Verdienst ansehen; **2.** *fig.* verdienen; **~orious** □ [meri'tɔːriəs] verdienstvoll.

**mermaid** ['mə:meid] Nixe *f*.

**merriment** ['merimənt] Lustigkeit *f*; Belustigung *f*.

**merry** □ ['meri] lustig, fröhlich; *make* ~ lustig sein; ~ **andrew** Hanswurst *m*; **~go-round** Karussell *n*; **~making** [~imeikiŋ] Lustbarkeit *f*.

**mesh** [meʃ] **1.** Masche *f*; *fig.* oft ~*es pl.* Netz *n*; *be in* ~ ⊕ (in-ea.-)greifen; **2.** in e-m Netz fangen.

**mess**[1] [mes] **1.** Unordnung *f*; Schmutz *m*, F Schweinerei *f*; F Patsche *f*; *make a* ~ *of* verpfuschen; **2.** *v/t.* in Unordnung bringen; verpfuschen; *v/i.* ~ *about* F herummurksen.

**mess**[2] [~] Kasino *n*, Messe *f*.

**message** ['mesidʒ] Botschaft *f*; *go on a* ~ e-e Besorgung machen.

**messenger** ['mesindʒə] Bote *m*.

**Messieurs**, *mst* **Messrs.** ['mesəz] (die) Herren *m/pl.*; Firma *f*.

**met** [met] *pret. u. p.p. von* meet[2].

**metal** ['metl] **1.** Metall *n*; Schotter *m*; **2.** beschottern; **~lic** [mi'tælik] (~*ally*) metallisch; Metall...; **~lurgy** [me'tælədʒi] Hüttenkunde *f*.

**metamorphose** [metə'mɔːfouz] verwandeln, umgestalten.

**metaphor** ['metəfə] Metapher *f*.

**meteor** ['mi:tjə] Meteor *m* (*a. fig.*); **~ology** [mi:tjə'rɔlədʒi] Meteorologie *f*, Wetterkunde *f*.

**meter** ['mi:tə] Messer *m*, Zähler *m*; *Am.* = metre.

**methinks** † [mi'θiŋks] mich dünkt.

**method** ['meθəd] Methode *f*; Art u. Weise *f*; Verfahren *n*; Ordnung *f*, System *n*; **~ic(al** □) [mi'θɔdik(əl)] methodisch.

**methought** [mi'θɔ:t] *pret. von* methinks.

**meticulous** □ [mi'tikjuləs] peinlich genau.

**met|re**, *Am.* **~er** ['mi:tə] Meter *n*, *m*; Versmaß *n*.

**metric** ['metrik] (~*ally*) metrisch; ~ *system* Dezimalsystem *n*.

**metropoli|s** [mi'trɔpəlis] Hauptstadt *f*, Metropole *f*; **~tan** [metrə'pɔlitən] hauptstädtisch.

**mettle** ['metl] Feuereifer *m*, Mut *m*; *be on one's* ~ sein Bestes tun.

**mews** [mju:z] Stallung *f*; *daraus entstandene* Garagen *f/pl. od.* Wohnhäuser *n/pl.*

**Mexican** ['meksikən] **1.** mexikanisch; **2.** Mexikaner(in).

**miaow** [mi(:)'au] miauen; mauzen.

**mice** [mais] *pl. von* mouse.

**Michaelmas** ['miklməs] Michaelis (-tag *m*) *n* (29. September).

**micro...** ['maikrou] klein..., Klein...

**micro|phone** ['maikrəfoun] Mikrophon *n*; **~scope** Mikroskop *n*.

**mid** [mid] mittler; Mitt(el)...; *in* ~ *air* mitten in der Luft; *in* ~ *winter* mitten im Winter; **~day** ['middei] **1.** Mittag *m*; **2.** mittägig; Mittags...

**middle** ['midl] **1.** Mitte *f*; Hüften *f/pl.*; **2.** mittler; Mittel...; ♀ *Ages pl.* Mittelalter *n*; **~aged** von mittlerem Alter; **~class** Mittelstands-...; ~ *class*(es *pl.*) Mittelstand *m*; **~man** Mittelsmann *m*; ~ *name* zweiter Vorname *m*; **~sized** mittelgroß; **~weight** *Boxen:* Mittelgewicht *n*.

**middling** ['midliŋ] mittelmäßig; leidlich; Mittel...

**middy** F ['midi] = midshipman.

**midge** [midʒ] Mücke *f*; **~t** ['midʒit] Zwerg *m*, Knirps *m*.

**mid|land** ['midlənd] **1.** binnenländisch; **2.** *the* ♀s *pl.* Mittelengland *n*; **~most** mittelste(r, -s); **~night** Mitternacht *f*; **~riff** ['midrif] Zwerchfell *n*; **~shipman** Leutnant *m* zur See; *Am.* Oberfähnrich *m* zur See; **~st** [midst] Mitte *f*; *in the* ~ *of* inmitten (*gen.*); **~summer**

Sommersonnenwende *f*; Hochsommer *m*; ~way 1. halber Weg; *Am.* Schaubudenstraße *f*; 2. *adj.* in der Mitte befindlich; 3. *adv.* auf halbem Wege; ~wife Hebamme *f*; ~wifery ['midwifəri] Geburtshilfe *f*; ~winter Wintersonnenwende *f*; Mitte *f* des Winters.

mien [mi:n] Miene *f*.

might [mait] 1. Macht *f*, Gewalt *f*, Kraft *f*; with ~ and main mit aller Gewalt; 2. *pret. von* may²; ~y □ ['maiti] mächtig, gewaltig.

migrat|e [mai'greit] (aus)wandern; ~ion [~ei∫ən] Wanderung *f*; ~ory ['maigrətəri] wandernd; Zug...

mild □ [maild] mild, sanft; gelind.

mildew ♀ ['mildju:] Mehltau *m*.

mildness ['maildnis] Milde *f*.

mile [mail] Meile *f* (1609.33 m).

mil(e)age ['mailidʒ] Laufzeit *f in Meilen*, Meilenstand *m* e-s Autos; Kilometergeld *n*.

milestone ['mailstoun] Meilenstein *m*.

milit|ary ['militəri] 1. □ militärisch; Kriegs...; ⚥ Government Militärregierung *f*; 2. *das* Militär; ~ia [mi'li∫ə] Land-, Bürgerwehr *f*.

milk [milk] 1. Milch *f*; it's no use crying over spilt ~ geschehen ist geschehen; 2. *v/t.* melken; *v/i.* Milch geben; ~maid ['milkmeid] Melkerin *f*; Milchmädchen *n*; ~man Milchmann *m*; ~powder Milchpulver *n*; ~shake Milchmischgetränk *n*; ~sop Weichling *m*; ~y ['milki] milchig; Milch...; ⚥ Way Milchstraße *f*.

mill¹ [mil] 1. Mühle *f*; Fabrik *f*, Spinnerei *f*; 2. mahlen; ⊕ fräsen; *Geld* prägen; *Münze* rändeln.

mill² *Am.* [~] 1/1000 Dollar *m*.

millepede *zo.* ['milipi:d] Tausendfüß(l)er *m*.

miller ['milə] Müller *m*; ⊕ Fräsmaschine *f*.

millet ♀ ['milit] Hirse *f*.

milliner ['milinə] Putzmacherin *f*, Modistin *f*; ~y [~əri] Putz-, Modewaren(geschäft *n*) *pl*.

million ['miljən] Million *f*; ~aire [miljə'nɛə] Millionär(in); ~th ['miljənθ] 1. millionste(r, -s); 2. Millionstel *n*.

mill|-pond ['milpɔnd] Mühlteich *m*; ~stone Mühlstein *m*.

milt [milt] Milch *f der Fische*.

mimic ['mimik] 1. mimisch; Schein...; 2. Mime *m*; 3. nachahmen, nachäffen; ~ry [~kri] Nachahmung *f*; *zo.* Angleichung *f*.

mince [mins] 1. *v/t.* zerhacken; he does not ~ matters er nimmt kein Blatt vor den Mund; *v/i.* sich zieren; 2. *a.* ~d meat Hackfleisch *n*; ~meat ['minsmi:t] e-e Tortenfüllung; ~pie Torte *f* aus mincemeat; ~r [~sə] Fleischwolf *m*.

mincing-machine ['minsiŋmə∫i:n] = mincer.

mind [maind] 1. Sinn *m*; Gemüt *n*; Geist *m*, Verstand *m*; Meinung *f*; Absicht *f*; Neigung *f*, Lust *f*; Gedächtnis *n*; Sorge *f*; to my ~ meiner Ansicht nach; out of one's ~, not in one's right ~ von Sinnen; change one's ~ sich anders besinnen; bear s.th. in ~ (immer) an et. denken; have (half) a ~ to (beinahe) Lust haben zu; have s.th. on one's ~ et. auf dem Herzen haben; make up one's ~ sich entschließen; 2. merken *od.* achten auf (*acc.*); sich kümmern um; etwas (einzuwenden) haben gegen; ~! gib acht!; never ~! macht nichts!; ~ the step! Achtung, Stufe!; I don't ~ (it) ich habe nichts dagegen; do you ~ if I smoke? stört es Sie, wenn ich rauche?; would you ~ taking off your hat? würden Sie bitte den Hut abnehmen?; ~ your own business! kümmern Sie sich um Ihre Angelegenheiten!; ~ful □ ['maindful] (of) eingedenk (*gen.*); achtsam (auf *acc.*).

mine¹ [main] 1. der (die, das) meinige; mein; 2. die Mein(ig)en *pl*.

mine² [~] 1. Bergwerk *n*, Grube *f*; *fig.* Fundgrube *f*; ✕ Mine *f*; 2. *v/i.* graben, minieren; *v/t.* graben; ✕ fördern; ✕ unterminieren; ✕ verminen; ~r ['mainə] Bergmann *m*.

mineral ['minərəl] 1. Mineral *n*; ~s *pl.* Mineralwasser *n*; 2. mineralisch.

mingle ['miŋgl] (ver)mischen; sich mischen *od.* mengen (with unter).

miniature ['minjət∫ə] 1. Miniatur (-gemälde *n*) *f*; 2. in Miniatur; Miniatur...; Klein...; ~ camera Kleinbildkamera *f*.

minikin ['minikin] 1. winzig; geziert; 2. Knirps *m*.

minim|ize ['minimaiz] möglichst klein machen; *fig.* verringern; ~um [~məm] Minimum *n*; Mindestmaß *n*; Mindestbetrag *m*; *attr.* Mindest...

mining ['mainiŋ] Bergbau *m*; *attr.* Berg(bau)...; Gruben...

minion ['minjən] Günstling *m*; *fig.* Lakai *m*.

miniskirt ['miniskə:t] Minirock *m*.

minister ['ministə] 1. Diener *m*; *fig.* Werkzeug *n*; Geistliche(r) *m*; Minister *m*; Gesandte(r) *m*; 2. *v/t.* darreichen; *v/i.* dienen; Gottesdienst halten.

ministry ['ministri] geistliches Amt; Ministerium *n*; Regierung *f*.

mink *zo.* [miŋk] Nerz *m*.

minor ['mainə] 1. kleiner, geringer, weniger bedeutend; ♪ Moll; A ~ A-moll *n*; 2. Minderjährige(r *m*) *f*; *Am. univ.* Nebenfach *n*; ~ity [mai'nɔriti] Minderheit *f*; Unmündigkeit *f*.

minster ['minstə] Münster *n*.

minstrel ['minstrəl] Minnesänger m; ~s pl. Negersänger m/pl.

mint [mint] 1. ♀ Minze f; Münze f; fig. Goldgrube f; a ~ of money e-e Menge Geld; 2. münzen, prägen.

minuet ♪ [minju'et] Menuett n.

minus ['mainəs] 1. prp. weniger; F ohne; 2. adj. negativ.

minute 1. □ [mai'nju:t] sehr klein, winzig; unbedeutend; sehr genau; 2. ['minit] Minute f; Augenblick m; ~s pl. [mai'nju:tnis] Kleinheit f; Genauigkeit f.

mirac|le ['mirəkl] Wunder n; ~ulous □ [mi'rækjuləs] wunderbar.

mirage ['mira:ʒ] Luftspiegelung f.

mire ['maiə] 1. Sumpf m; Kot m, Schlamm m; 2. mit Schlamm od. Schmutz bedecken.

mirror ['mirə] 1. Spiegel m; 2. (wider)spiegeln (a. fig.).

mirth [mə:θ] Fröhlichkeit f; ~ful □ ['mə:θful] fröhlich; ~less □ ['mə:θlis] freudlos.

miry ['maiəri] kotig.

mis... [mis] miß..., übel, falsch.

misadventure ['misəd'ventʃə] Mißgeschick n, Unfall m.

misanthrop|e ['mizənθroup], ~ist [mi'zænθrəpist] Menschenfeind m.

misapply ['misə'plai] falsch anwenden. [mißverstehen.]

misapprehend ['misæpri'hend]]

misappropriate ['misə'prouprieit] unterschlagen, veruntreuen.

misbehave ['misbi'heiv] sich schlecht benehmen.

misbelief ['misbi'li:f] Irrglaube m.

miscalculate ['miskælkjuleit] falsch (be)rechnen.

miscarr|iage [mis'kæridʒ] Mißlingen n; Verlust m v. Briefen; Fehlgeburt f; ~ of justice Fehlspruch m; ~y [~ri] mißlingen; verlorengehen (Brief); fehlgebären.

miscellan|eous □ [misi'leinjəs] ge-, vermischt; vielseitig; ~y [mi-'seləni] Gemisch n; Sammelband m.

mischief ['mistʃif] Schaden m, Unfug m; Mutwille m, Übermut m; ~-maker Unheilstifter(in).

mischievous □ ['mistʃivəs] schädlich; boshaft, mutwillig.

misconceive ['miskən'si:v] falsch auffassen od. verstehen.

misconduct 1. [mis'kɔndəkt] schlechtes Benehmen; Ehebruch m; schlechte Verwaltung; 2. ['miskən-'dʌkt] schlecht verwalten; ~ o.s. sich schlecht benehmen; e-n Fehltritt begehen.

misconstrue ['miskən'stru:] mißdeuten.

miscreant ['miskriənt] Schurke m.

misdeed ['mis'di:d] Missetat f.

misdemeano(u)r ᶻ̆ᶻ [misdi'mi:nə] Vergehen n.

misdirect ['misdi'rekt] irreleiten; an die falsche Adresse richten.

misdoing ['misdu(:)iŋ] Vergehen n (mst pl.).

mise en scène thea. ['mi:zã:n'sein] Inszenierung f.

miser ['maizə] Geizhals m.

miserable □ ['mizərəbl] elend; unglücklich, erbärmlich.

miserly ['maizəli] geizig, filzig.

misery ['mizəri] Elend n, Not f.

misfit ['misfit] schlecht passendes Stück (Kleid, Stiefel etc.); Einzelgänger m, Eigenbrötler m.

misfortune [mis'fɔ:tʃən] Unglück(sfall m) n; Mißgeschick n.

misgiving [mis'giviŋ] böse Ahnung, Befürchtung f.

misguide ['mis'gaid] irreleiten.

mishap ['mishæp] Unfall m; mot. Panne f.

misinform ['misin'fɔ:m] falsch unterrichten. [deuten.]

misinterpret ['misin'tə:prit] miß-]

mislay [mis'lei] (irr. (lay)) verlegen.

mislead [mis'li:d] (irr. (lead)) irreführen; verleiten.

mismanage ['mis'mænidʒ] schlecht verwalten.

misplace ['mis'pleis] falsch stellen, verstellen; verlegen; falsch anbringen.

misprint 1. [mis'print] verdrucken; 2. ['mis'print] Druckfehler m.

misread ['mis'ri:d] (irr. (read)) falsch lesen od. deuten.

misrepresent['misrepri'zent]falsch darstellen, verdrehen.

miss¹ [mis] mst ♀ Fräulein n.

miss² [~] 1. Verlust m; Fehlschuß m, -stoß m, -wurf m; 2. v/t. (ver-) missen; verfehlen; verpassen; auslassen; übersehen; überhören; v/i. fehlen (nicht treffen); fehlgehen.

misshapen ['mis'ʃeipən] verunstaltet; mißgestaltet.

missile ['misail] (Wurf)Geschoß n; Rakete f.

missing ['misiŋ] fehlend; ✗ vermißt; be ~ fehlen; vermißt werden.

mission ['miʃən] Sendung f; Auftrag m; Berufung f, Lebensziel n; Gesandtschaft f; eccl., pol. Mission f; ~ary ['miʃnəri] Missionar m; attr. Missions...

missive ['misiv] Sendschreiben n.

mis-spell ['mis'spel] (irr. (spell)) falsch buchstabieren od. schreiben.

mis-spend ['mis'spend] (irr. (spend)) falsch verwenden; vergeuden.

mist [mist] 1. Nebel m; 2. (um)nebeln; sich trüben; beschlagen.

mistake [mis'teik] 1. (irr. (take)) sich irren in (dat.), verkennen; mißverstehen; verwechseln (for mit); be ~n sich irren; 2. Irrtum m; Versehen n; Fehler m; ~n □ [~kən] irrig, falsch (verstanden).

**mister** ['mistə] Herr m (abbr. **Mr.**).
**mistletoe** & ['misltou] Mistel f.
**mistress** ['mistris] Herrin f; Hausfrau f; Lehrerin f; Geliebte f; Meisterin f.
**mistrust** ['mis'trʌst] **1.** mißtrauen (dat.); **2.** Mißtrauen n; **~ful** □ [~tful] mißtrauisch.
**misty** □ ['misti] neb(e)lig; unklar.
**misunderstand** ['misʌndə'stænd] [irr. (stand)] mißverstehen; **~ing** [~diŋ] Mißverständnis n.
**misus|age** [mis'ju:zidʒ] Mißbrauch m; Mißhandlung f; **~e 1.** ['mis'ju:z] mißbrauchen, mißhandeln; **2.** [~u:s] Mißbrauch m.
**mite** [mait] zo. Milbe f; Heller m; fig. Scherflein n; Knirps m.
**mitigate** ['mitigeit] mildern, lindern (a. fig.).
**mit|re,** Am. **~er** ['maitə] Bischofsmütze f.
**mitt** [mit] Baseball-Handschuh m; F Boxhandschuh m; = **mitten.**
**mitten** ['mitn] Fausthandschuh m; Halbhandschuh m (ohne Finger); Am. sl. Tatze f (Hand).
**mix** [miks] (sich) (ver)mischen; verkehren (with mit); **~ed** gemischt; fig. zweifelhaft; **~ up** durch-ea.bringen; be **~ed up** with in e-e S. verwickelt sein; **~ture** ['mikstʃə] Mischung f.
**moan** [moun] **1.** Stöhnen n; **2.** stöhnen.
**moat** [mout] Burg-, Stadtgraben m.
**mob** [mɔb] **1.** Pöbel m; **2.** anpöbeln.
**mobil|e** ['moubail] beweglich; ✗ mobil; **~ization** [moubilai'zeiʃən] Mobilmachung f; **~ize** ✗ ['moubilaiz] mobil machen.
**moccasin** ['mɔkəsin] weiches Leder; Mokassin m (Schuh).
**mock** [mɔk] **1.** Spott m; **2.** Schein...; falsch, nachgemacht; **3.** v/t. verspotten; nachmachen; täuschen; v/i. spotten (at über acc.); **~ery** ['mɔkəri] Spötterei f, Gespött n; Äfferei f.
**mocking-bird** orn. ['mɔkiŋbə:d] Spottdrossel f.
**mode** [moud] Art und Weise f; (Erscheinungs)Form f; Sitte f, Mode f.
**model** ['mɔdl] **1.** Modell n; Muster n; fig. Vorbild n; Vorführdame f; attr. Muster...; **2.** modellieren; (ab)formen; fig. modeln, bilden.
**moderat|e 1.** □ ['mɔdərit] (mittel-)mäßig; **2.** [~reit] (sich) mäßigen; **~ion** [mɔdə'reiʃən] Mäßigung f; Mäßigkeit f.
**modern** ['mɔdən] modern, neu; **~ize** [~ə(:)naiz] (sich) modernisieren.
**modest** □ ['mɔdist] bescheiden; anständig; **~y** [~ti] Bescheidenheit f.
**modi|fication** [mɔdifi'keiʃən] Ab-,

Veränderung f; Einschränkung f; **~fy** ['mɔdifai] (ab)ändern; mildern.
**mods** [mɔdz] pl. Halbstarke m/pl.
**modulate** ['mɔdjuleit] modulieren.
**moiety** ['mɔiəti] Hälfte f; Teil m.
**moist** [mɔist] feucht, naß; **~en** ['mɔisn] be-, anfeuchten; **~ure** ['mɔistʃə] Feuchtigkeit f.
**molar** ['moulə] Backenzahn m.
**molasses** [mə'læsiz] Melasse f; Sirup m.
**mole¹** zo. [moul] Maulwurf m.
**mole²** [~] Muttermal n.
**mole³** [~] Mole f, Hafendamm m.
**molecule** ['mɔlikju:l] Molekül n.
**molehill** ['moulhil] Maulwurfshügel m; make a mountain out of a **~** aus e-r Mücke e-n Elefanten machen.
**molest** [mou'lest] belästigen.
**mollify** ['mɔlifai] besänftigen.
**mollycoddle** ['mɔlikɔdl] **1.** Weichling m, Muttersöhnchen n; **2.** verzärteln.
**molten** ['moultən] geschmolzen.
**moment** ['moumənt] Augenblick m; Bedeutung f; = momentum; **~ary** □ [~təri] augenblicklich; vorübergehend; **~ous** □ [mou'mentəs] (ge)wichtig, bedeutend; **~um** phys. [~təm] Moment n; Triebkraft f.
**monarch** ['mɔnək] Monarch(in) f; **~y** [~ki] Monarchie f.
**monastery** ['mɔnəstəri] (Mönchs-)Kloster n.
**Monday** ['mʌndi] Montag m.
**monetary** ['mʌnitəri] Geld...
**money** ['mʌni] Geld n; ready **~** Bargeld n; **~-box** Sparbüchse f; **~-changer** [~itʃeindʒə] (Geld-)Wechsler m; **~-order** Postanweisung f.
**monger** ['mʌŋgə] ...händler m, ...krämer m.
**mongrel** ['mʌŋgrəl] Mischling m, Bastard m; attr. Bastard...
**monitor** ['mɔnitə] ⊕ Monitor m; (Klassen)Ordner m.
**monk** [mʌŋk] Mönch m.
**monkey** ['mʌŋki] **1.** zo. Affe m (a. fig.); ⊕ Rammblock m; put s.o.'s **~** up F j-n auf die Palme bringen; **~ business** Am. sl. fauler Zauber; **2.** F (herum)albern; **~ with** herummurksen an (dat.); **~-wrench** ⊕ Engländer m (Schraubenschlüssel); throw a **~** in s.th. Am. sl. et. über den Haufen werfen.
**monkish** ['mʌŋkiʃ] mönchisch.
**mono|...** ['mɔnou] ein(fach)...; **~cle** ['mɔnɔkl] Monokel n; **~gamy** [mɔ'nɔgəmi] Einehe f; **~logue**, Am. **~log** ['mɔnələg] Monolog m; **~polist** [mə'nɔpəlist] Monopolist m; **~polize** [~laiz] monopolisieren, fig. an sich reißen; **~poly** [~li] Monopol n (of auf acc.); **~tonous** □ [~ɔtnəs] monoton, eintönig; **~tony** [~ni] Monotonie f.

monsoon [mɔn'suːn] Monsun *m*.

monster ['mɔnstə] Ungeheuer *n* (*a. fig.*); Monstrum *n*; *attr.* Riesen...

monstro|sity [mɔns'trɔsiti] Ungeheuer(lichkeit *f*) *n*; ~us □ ['mɔnstrəs] ungeheuer(lich); gräßlich.

month [mʌnθ] Monat *m*; *this day* ~ heute in e-m Monat; ~ly ['mʌnθli] 1. monatlich; Monats...; 2. Monatsschrift *f*.

monument ['mɔnjumənt] Denkmal *n*; ~al □ [mɔnju'mentl] monumental; Gedenk...; großartig.

mood [muːd] Stimmung *f*, Laune *f*; ~y □ ['muːdi] launisch; schwermütig; übellaunig.

moon [muːn] 1. Mond *m*; *once in a blue* ~ F alle Jubeljahre einmal; 2. *mst* ~ *about* F herumdösen; ~light ['muːnlait] Mondlicht *n*, ~schein *m*; ~lit mondhell; ~struck mondsüchtig.

Moor¹ [muə] Maure *m*; Mohr *m*.

moor² [~] Ödland *n*, Heideland *n*.

moor³ ♣ [~] (sich) vertäuen; ~ings ♣ ['muəriŋz] *pl.* Vertäuungen *f/pl.*

moose *zo.* [muːz] *a.* ~-deer *amerikanischer* Elch.

moot [muːt] ~ *point* Streitpunkt *m*.

mop [mɔp] 1. Mop *m*; (Haar)Wust *m*; 2. auf~, abwischen.

mope [moup] den Kopf hängen lassen.

moral ['mɔrəl] 1. □ Moral...; moralisch; 2. Moral *f*; Nutzanwendung *f*; ~*s pl.* Sitten *f/pl.*; ~e [mɔ'raːl] *bsd.* ⚔ Moral *f*, Haltung *f*; ~ity [mə'ræliti] Moralität *f*; Sittlichkeit *f*, Moral *f*; ~ize ['mɔrəlaiz] moralisieren.

morass [mə'ræs] Morast *m*, Sumpf *m*.

morbid □ ['mɔːbid] krankhaft.

more [mɔː] mehr; *once* ~ noch einmal, wieder; *so much od. all the* ~ um so mehr; *no* ~ nicht mehr.

morel ♣ [mɔ'rel] Morchel *f*.

moreover [mɔː'rouvə] überdies, weiter, ferner.

morgue [mɔːg] Leichenschauhaus *n*; Archiv *n*.

moribund ['mɔribʌnd] im Sterben (liegend), dem Tode geweiht.

morning ['mɔːniŋ] Morgen *m*; Vormittag *m*; *tomorrow* ~ morgen früh; ~ dress Tagesgesellschaftsanzug *m*. [*m*) *f*.\

moron ['mɔːrɔn] Schwachsinnige(r)

morose □ [mə'rous] mürrisch.

morph|ia ['mɔːfjə], ~ine ['mɔːfiːn] Morphium *n*.

morsel ['mɔːsəl] Bissen *m*; Stückchen *n*, *das* bißchen.

mortal ['mɔːtl] 1. □ sterblich; tödlich; Tod(es)...; 2. Sterbliche(r *m*) *f*; ~ity [mɔː'tæliti] Sterblichkeit *f*.

mortar ['mɔːtə] Mörser *m*; Mörtel *m*.

mortgag|e ['mɔːgidʒ] 1. Pfandgut *n*; Hypothek *f*; 2. verpfänden, ~ee [mɔːgə'dʒiː] Hypothekengläubiger *m*; ~er ['mɔːgidʒə], ~or [mɔːgə'dʒɔː] Hypothekenschuldner *m*.

mortician *Am.* [mɔː'tiʃən] Leichenbestatter *m*.

morti|fication [mɔːtifi'keiʃən] Kasteiung *f*; Kränkung *f*; ~fy ['mɔːtifai] kasteien; kränken.

morti|se, ~ce ⊕ ['mɔːtis] Zapfenloch *n*.

mortuary ['mɔːtjuəri] Leichenhalle *f*.

mosaic [mə'zeiik] Mosaik *n*.

mosque [mɔsk] Moschee *f*.

mosquito *zo.* [məs'kiːtou] Moskito *m*. [moosig.\

moss [mɔs] Moos *n*; ~y ['mɔsi]\

most [moust] 1. *adj.* □ meist; 2. *adv.* meist, am meisten; höchst; 3. *das* meiste; die meisten; Höchste(s) *n*; *at* (*the*) ~ höchstens; *make the* ~ *of* möglichst ausnutzen; ~ly ['moustli] meistens.

moth [mɔθ] Motte *f*; ~-eaten ['mɔθiːtn] mottenzerfressen.

mother ['mʌðə] 1. Mutter *f*; 2. bemuttern; ~ country Vaterland *n*; Mutterland *n*; ~hood [~hud] Mutterschaft *f*; ~-in-law [~rinlɔː] Schwiegermutter *f*; ~ly [~li] mütterlich; ~-of-pearl [~rəv'pəːl] Perlmutter *f*; ~-tongue Muttersprache *f*.

motif [mou'tiːf] (Leit)Motiv *n*.

motion ['mouʃən] 1. Bewegung *f*; Gang *m* (*a.* ⊕); *parl.* Antrag *m*; 2. *v/t.* durch Gebärden auffordern *od.* andeuten; *v/i.* winken; ~less [~nlis] bewegungslos; ~ picture Film *m*.

motivate ['moutiveit] motivieren, begründen.

motive ['moutiv] 1. bewegend; 2. Motiv *n*, Beweggrund *m*; 3. veranlassen; ~less [~vlis] grundlos.

motley ['mɔtli] (bunt)scheckig.

motor ['moutə] 1. Motor *m*; treibende Kraft; Automobil *n*; ✗ Muskel *m*; 2. motorisch, bewegend; Motor...; Kraft...; Auto...; 3. (im) Auto fahren; ~-assisted [~ərə'sistid] mit Hilfsmotor; ~ bicycle, ~bike = *motor cycle*; ~ boat Motorboot *n*; ~ bus Autobus *m*; ~cade *Am.* [~əkeid] Autokolonne *f*; ~-car Auto(mobil) *n*; ~ coach Reisebus *m*; ~ cycle Motorrad *n*; ~ing [~əriŋ] Autofahren *n*; ~ist [~rist] Kraftfahrer(in); ~ize [~raiz] motorisieren; ~ launch Motorbarkasse *f*; ~-road, ~way Autobahn *f*.

mottled ['mɔtld] gefleckt.

mo(u)ld [mould] 1. Gartenerde *f*; Schimmel *m*, Moder *m*; (Guß-) Form *f* (*a. fig.*); Abdruck *m*; Art *f*; 2. formen, gießen (*on, upon* nach).

mo(u)lder ['mouldə] zerfallen.

mo(u)lding Δ ['mouldiŋ] Fries m.

mo(u)ldy ['mouldi] schimm(e)lig, dumpfig, mod(e)rig.

mo(u)lt [moult] (fig. sich) mausern.

mound [maund] Erdhügel m, -wall m.

mount [maunt] 1. Berg m; Reitpferd n; 2. v/i. (empor)steigen; aufsteigen (Reiter); v/t. be-, ersteigen; beritten machen; montieren; aufziehen, aufkleben; Edelstein fassen.

mountain ['mauntin] 1. Berg m; ~s pl. Gebirge n; 2. Berg..., Gebirgs...; ~eer [maunti'niə] Bergbewohner(in); Bergsteiger(in); ~ous ['mauntinəs] bergig, gebirgig.

mountebank ['mauntibæŋk]Marktschreier m, Scharlatan m.

mourn [mɔ:n] (be)trauern; ~er ['mɔ:nə] Leidtragende(r m) f; ~ful □ ['mɔ:nful] Trauer...; traurig; ~ing ['mɔ:niŋ] Trauer f; attr. Trauer... [Maus f.]

mouse [maus], pl. mice [mais]

moustache [məs'ta:ʃ] Schnurrbart m.

mouth [mauθ], pl. ~s [mauðz]Mund m; Maul n; Mündung f; Öffnung f; ~ful ['mauθful] Mundvoll m; ~ organ Mundharmonika f; ~piece Mundstück n; fig. Sprachrohr n.

move [mu:v] 1. v/t. allg. bewegen; in Bewegung setzen; (weg)rücken; (an)treiben; Leidenschaft erregen; seelisch rühren; beantragen; heaven and earth Himmel und Hölle in Bewegung setzen; v/i. sich (fort)bewegen; sich rühren; Schach: ziehen; (um)ziehen (Mieter); ~ for s.th. et. beantragen; ~ in einziehen; ~ on weitergehen; ~ out ausziehen; 2. Bewegung f; Schach: Zug m; fig. Schritt m; on the ~ in Bewegung; make a ~ die Tafel aufheben; ~ment ['mu:vmənt] Bewegung f; ♪ Tempo n; ♪ Satz m; ⊕ (Geh-)Werk n.

movies F ['mu:viz] pl. Kino n.

moving □ ['mu:viŋ] bewegend; beweglich; ~ staircase Rolltreppe f.

mow [mou] [irr.] mähen; ~er ['mouə] Mäher(in); Mähmaschine f; ~ing machine ['mouiŋməʃi:n] Mähmaschine f; ~n [moun] p.p. von mow.

much [mʌtʃ] 1. adj. viel; 2. adv. sehr; viel; bei weitem; fast; ~ as I would like so gern ich möchte; I thought as ~ das dachte ich mir; make ~ of viel Wesens machen von; I am not ~ of a dancer ich bin kein großer Tänzer.

muck [mʌk] Mist m (F a. fig.); ~rake ['mʌkreik] 1. Mistgabel f; = ~r; 2. im Schmutz wühlen; ~raker [~kə] Am. Korruptionsschnüffler m.

mucus ['mju:kəs] (Nasen)Schleim m.

mud [mʌd] Schlamm m; Kot m; ~dle ['mʌdl] 1. v/t. verwirren; a. ~ up, ~ together durcheinanderbringen; F benebeln; v/i. stümpern; ~ through F sich durchwursteln; 2. Wirrwarr m; F Wurstelei f; ~dy ['mʌdi] schlammig; trüb; ~guard Kotflügel m.

muff [mʌf] Muff m.

muffin ['mʌfin] Muffin n (heißes Teegebäck).

muffle ['mʌfl] oft ~ up ein-, umhüllen, umwickeln; Stimme etc. dämpfen; ~r [~lə] Halstuch n; Boxhandschuh m; mot. Auspufftopf m.

mug [mʌg] Krug m; Becher m.

muggy ['mʌgi] schwül.

mugwump Am. iro. ['mʌgwʌmp] großes Tier (Person); pol. Unabhängige(r) m.

mulatto [mju(:)'lætou] Mulatt|e m, -in f.

mulberry ['mʌlbəri] Maulbeere f.

mule [mju:l] Maultier m, -esel m; störrischer Mensch; ~teer [mju:li-'tiə] Maultiertreiber m.

mull[1] [mʌl] Mull m.

mull[2] [~]: ~ over überdenken.

mulled [mʌld] ~ wine Glühwein m.

mulligan Am. F ['mʌligən] Eintopf m aus Resten.

mullion ['mʌliən] Fensterpfosten m.

multi|farious □ [mʌlti'feəriəs] mannigfaltig; ~form [~'mʌltifɔ:m] vielförmig; ~ple [~ipl] 1. vielfach; 2. Vielfache(s) n; ~plication [mʌltipli'keiʃən] Vervielfältigung f, Vermehrung f; Multiplikation f; compound (simple) ~ Großes (Kleines) Einmaleins n; ~ table Einmaleins n; ~plicity [~i'plisiti] Vielfalt f; ~ply ['mʌltiplai] (sich) vervielfältigen; multiplizieren; ~tude [~itju:d] Vielheit f, Menge f; ~tudinous [mʌlti-'tju:dinəs] zahlreich.

mum [mʌm] still.

mumble ['mʌmbl] murmeln, nuscheln; mummeln (mühsam essen).

mummery contp. ['mʌməri] Mummenschanz m.

mummify ['mʌmifai] mumifizieren.

mummy[1] ['mʌmi] Mumie f.

mummy[2] [~] Mami f, Mutti f.

mumps ⅌ [mʌmps] sg. Ziegenpeter m, Mumps m.

munch [mʌntʃ] mit vollen Backen (fr)essen, mampfen.

mundane □ ['mʌndein] weltlich.

municipal □ [mju(:)'nisipəl] städtisch, Gemeinde..., Stadt...; ~ity [mju(:)nisi'pæliti] Stadtbezirk m; Stadtverwaltung f.

munificen|ce [mju(:)'nifisns] Freigebigkeit f; ~t [~nt] freigebig.

munitions [mju(:)'niʃənz] pl. Munition f.

mural ['mjuərəl] Mauer...

murder ['mə:də] 1. Mord m; 2. (er-)

morden; *fig.* verhunzen; **~er** [~ərə]
Mörder *m*; **~ess** [~ris] Mörderin *f*;
**~ous** □ [~rəs] mörderisch.
**murky** □ ['mə:ki] dunkel, finster.
**murmur** ['mə:mə] 1. Gemurmel *n*;
Murren *n*; 2. murmeln; murren.
**murrain** ['mʌrin] Viehseuche *f*.
**musc|le** ['mʌsl] 1. Muskel *m*; 2. **~ in**
*Am. sl.* sich rücksichtslos eindrän-
gen; **~le-bound** mit Muskelkater;
be **~** Muskelkater haben; **~ular**
['mʌskjulə] Muskel...; muskulös.
**Muse**[1] [mju:z] Muse *f*.
**muse**[2] [~] (nach)sinnen, grübeln.
**museum** [mju:(ˈ)ziəm] Museum *n*.
**mush** [mʌʃ] Brei *m*, Mus *n*; *Am.*
Polenta *f*, Maisbrei *m*.
**mushroom** ['mʌʃrum] 1. Pilz *m*,
*bsd.* Champignon *m*; 2. rasch wachsen; **~** *up* in die Höhe schießen.
**music** ['mju:zik] Musik *f*; Musik-
stück *n*; Noten *f/pl.*; set to **~** ver-
tonen; **~al** □ [~kəl] musikalisch;
Musik...; wohlklingend; **~ box**
Spieldose *f*; **~ box** *Am.* Spieldose *f*;
**~-hall** Varieté(theater) *n*; **~ian**
[mju:(ˈ)ziʃən] Musiker(in); **~stand**
Notenständer *m*; **~stool** Klavier-
stuhl *m*.
**musk** [mʌsk] Moschus *m*, Bisam *m*;
**~-deer** *zo.* ['mʌsk'diə] Moschus-
tier *n*.
**musket** ['mʌskit] Muskete *f*.
**musk-rat** *zo.* ['mʌskræt] Bisamratte *f*.
**muslin** ['mʌzlin] Musselin *m*.
**musquash** ['mʌskwoʃ] Bisamratte *f*;
Bisampelz *m*.
**muss** *bsd. Am.* F [mʌs] Durcheinander *n*.
**mussel** ['mʌsl] (Mies)Muschel *f*.
**must**[1] [mʌst] 1. muß(te); darf;
durfte; *I* **~** *not* ich darf nicht; 2.
Muß *n*.
**must**[2] [mʌst] Schimmel *m*, Moder *m*.

**must**[3] [~] Most *m*.
**mustach|e** *Am.* [məsˈtæʃ], **~io** *Am.*
[məsˈtɑ:ʃou] = *moustache*.
**mustard** ['mʌstəd] Senf *m*.
**muster** ['mʌstə] 1. ✕ Musterung *f*;
*fig.* Heerschau *f*; 2. ✕ mustern;
aufbieten, aufbringen.
**musty** ['mʌsti] mod(e)rig, muffig.
**muta|ble** □ ['mju:təbl] verän-
derlich; wankelmütig; **~tion** [mju(:)-
'teiʃən] Veränderung *f*.
**mute** [mju:t] 1. □ stumm; 2. Stum-
me(r *m*) *f*; Statist(in); 3. dämpfen.
**mutilate** ['mju:tileit] verstümmeln.
**mutin|eer** [mju:ti'niə] Meuterer *m*;
**~ous** □ ['mju:tinəs] meuterisch;
**~y** [~ni] 1. Meuterei *f*; 2. meu-
tern.
**mutter** ['mʌtə] 1. Gemurmel *n*;
Gemurre *n*; 2. murmeln; murren.
**mutton** ['mʌtn] Hammelfleisch *n*;
*leg of* **~** Hammelkeule *f*; **~ chop**
Hammelkotelett *n*.
**mutual** □ ['mju:tjuəl] gegenseitig;
gemeinsam.
**muzzle** ['mʌzl] 1. Maul *n*, Schnauze
*f*; Mündung *f* e-r *Feuerwaffe*;
Maulkorb *m*; 2. e-n Maulkorb anlegen (*dat.*); *fig.* den Mund stopfen
(*dat.*).
**my** [mai] mein(e).
**myrrh** ♀ [mə:] Myrrhe *f*.
**myrtle** ♀ ['mə:tl] Myrte *f*.
**myself** [mai'self] (ich) selbst; mir;
mich; *by* **~** allein.
**myster|ious** □ [mis'tiəriəs] ge-
heimnisvoll, mysteriös; **~y** ['mistəri]
Mysterium *n*; Geheimnis *n*; Rätsel
*n*.
**mysti|c** ['mistik] 1. *a.* **~cal** □
[~kəl] mystisch, geheimnisvoll; 2.
Mystiker *m*; **~fy** [~ifai] mystifizie-
ren, täuschen.
**myth** [miθ] Mythe *f*, Mythos *m*,
Sage *f*.

# N

**nab** *sl.* [næb] schnappen, erwischen.
**nacre** ['neikə] Perlmutter *f*.
**nadir** ['neidiə] *ast.* Nadir *m* (*Fuß-
punkt*); *fig.* tiefster Stand.
**nag** [næg] 1. F Klepper *m*; 2. *v/i.*
nörgeln, quengeln; *v/t.* bekritteln.
**nail** [neil] 1. (Finger-, Zehen)Nagel
*m*; ⊕ Nagel *m*; *zo.* Kralle *f*, Klaue
*f*; 2. (an-, fest)nageln; *Augen etc.*
heften (*to auf acc.*); **~-scissors**
['neilsizəz] *pl.* Nagelschere *f*; **~-
varnish** Nagellack *m*.
**naïve** □ [nɑːˈiːv], **naive** □ [neiv]
naiv; ungekünstelt.
**naked** □ ['neikid] nackt, bloß; kahl;
*fig.* unverhüllt; *poet.* schutzlos;

**~ness** [~dnis] Nacktheit *f*, Blöße *f*;
Kahlheit *f*; Schutzlosigkeit *f*; *fig.*
Unverhülltheit *f*.
**name** [neim] 1. Name *m*; Ruf *m*;
*of od. by the* **~** *of ...* namens ...;
*call s.o.* **~s** j-n beschimpfen; 2. (be-)
nennen; erwähnen; ernennen; **~
less** □ ['neimlis] namenlos; unbekannt; **~ly** [~li] nämlich; **~-plate**
Namens-, Tür-, Firmenschild *n*;
**~sake** ['neimseik] Namensvetter *m*.
**nanny** ['næni] Kindermädchen *n*;
**~-goat** Ziege *f*.
**nap** [næp] 1. Tuch-Noppe *f*; Schläfchen *n*; *have od. take a* **~** ein
Nickerchen machen; 2. schlummern.

**nape** [neip] *mst* ~ *of the neck* Genick *n.*

**nap|kin** ['næpkin] Serviette *f*; Windel *f*; *mst sanitary* ~ *Am.* Monatsbinde *f*; ~**py** F ['næpi] Windel *f*.

**narcosis** ♯ [nɑː'kousis] Narkose *f.*

**narcotic** [nɑː'kɔtik] 1. (~*ally*) narkotisch; **2.** Betäubungsmittel *n.*

**narrat|e** [næ'reit] erzählen; ~**ion** [~ei∫ən] Erzählung *f*; ~**ive** ['nærətiv] 1. □ erzählend; 2. Erzählung *f*; ~**or** [næ'reitə] Erzähler *m.*

**narrow** ['nærou] 1. eng, schmal, beschränkt; knapp (*Mehrheit, Entkommen*); engherzig; 2. ~**s** *pl.* Engpaß *m*; Meerenge *f*; 3. (sich) verengen; beschränken; einengen; *Maschen* abnehmen; ~**chested** schmalbrüstig; ~**minded** □ engherzig; ~**ness** [~ounis] Enge *f*; Beschränktheit *f* (*a. fig.*); Engherzigkeit *f.*

**nary** *Am.* F ['nεəri] kein.

**nasal** □ ['neizəl] nasal; Nasen...

**nasty** □ ['nɑːsti] schmutzig; garstig; eklig, widerlich; häßlich; unflätig; ungemütlich.

**natal** ['neitl] Geburts...

**nation** ['nei∫ən] Nation *f*, Volk *n.*

**national** □ ['næ∫ənl] 1. □ national; Volks..., Staats...; 2. Staatsangehörige(r *m*) *f*; ~**ity** [næ∫ə'næliti] Nationalität *f*; ~**ize** ['næ∫nəlaiz] naturalisieren, einbürgern; verstaatlichen.

**nation-wide** ['nei∫ənwaid] die ganze Nation umfassend.

**native** ['neitiv] 1. □ angeboren; heimatlich, Heimat...; eingeboren; einheimisch; ~ *language* Muttersprache *f*; 2. Eingeborene(r *m*) *f*; ~**born** (im Lande) geboren, einheimisch.

**nativity** [nə'tiviti] Geburt *f.*

**natter** F ['nætə] plaudern.

**natural** □ ['næt∫rəl] natürlich; *engS.*: angeboren; ungezwungen; unehelich (*Kind*); ~ *science* Naturwissenschaft *f*; ~**ist** [~list] Naturalist *m*; Naturforscher *m*; Tierhändler *m*; ~**ize** [~laiz] einbürgern; ~**ness** [~lnis] Natürlichkeit *f.*

**nature** ['neit∫ə] Natur *f.*

**naught** [nɔːt] Null *f*; *set at* ~ für nichts achten; ~**y** □ ['nɔːti] unartig.

**nause|a** ['nɔːsjə] Übelkeit *f*; Ekel *m*; ~**ate** ['nɔːsieit] *v/i.* Ekel empfinden; *v/t.* verabscheuen; *be* ~*d* sich ekeln; ~**ous** □ ['nɔːsjəs] ekelhaft.

**nautical** ['nɔːtikəl] nautisch; See...

**naval** ⚔ ['neivəl] See..., Marine...; ~ *base* Flottenstützpunkt *m.*

**nave**[1] ⚙ [neiv] (Kirchen)Schiff *n.*

**nave**[2] [~] Rad-Nabe *f.*

**navel** ['neivəl] Nabel *m*; Mitte *f.*

**naviga|ble** □ ['nævigəbl] schiffbar; fahrbar; lenkbar; ~**te** [~geit] *v/i.* schiffen, fahren; *v/t. See etc.* befahren; steuern; ~**tion** [nævi'gei∫ən]

Schiffahrt *f*; Navigation *f*; ~**tor** ['nævigeitə] Seefahrer *m.*

**navy** ['neivi] (Kriegs)Marine *f.*

**nay** † [nei] nein; nein vielmehr.

**near** [niə] 1. *adj.* nahe; gerade (*Weg*); nahe verwandt; verwandt; vertraut; genau; knapp; knauserig; ~ *at hand* dicht dabei; 2. *adv.* nahe; 3. *prp.* nahe (*dat.*), nahe bei *od.* an; 4. sich nähern (*dat.*); ~**by** ['niəbai] in der Nähe (gelegen); nah; ~**ly** ['niəli] nahe; fast, beinahe; genau; ~**ness** ['niənis] Nähe *f*; ~**sighted** kurzsichtig.

**neat** □ [niːt] nett; niedlich; geschickt; ordentlich; sauber; rein; ~**ness** ['niːtnis] Nettigkeit *f*; Sauberkeit *f*; Zierlichkeit *f.*

**nebulous** □ ['nebjuləs] neblig.

**necess|ary** □ ['nesisəri] 1. notwendig; unvermeidlich; 2. *mst necessaries pl.* Bedürfnisse *n/pl.*; ~**itate** [ni'sesiteit] *et.* erfordern; zwingen; ~**ity** [~ti] Notwendigkeit *f*; Zwang *m*; Not *f.*

**neck** [nek] 1. (*a. Flaschen*)Hals *m*; Nacken *m*, Genick *n*; Ausschnitt *m* (*Kleid*); ~ *and* ~ Kopf an Kopf; ~ *or nothing* F alles oder nichts; 2. *sl.* sich abknutschen; ~**band** ['nekbænd] Halsbund *m*; ~**erchief** ['nekət∫if] Halstuch *n*; ~**lace** ['neklis], ~**let** [~lit] Halskette *f*; ~**tie** Krawatte *f.*

**necromancy** ['nekroumænsi] Zauberei *f.*

**née** [nei] *bei Frauennamen:* geborene.

**need** [niːd] 1. Not *f*; Notwendigkeit *f*; Bedürfnis *n*; Mangel *m*, Bedarf *m*; *be od. stand in* ~ *of* brauchen; 2. nötig haben, brauchen; bedürfen (*gen.*); müssen; ~**ful** ['niːdful] notwendig.

**needle** ['niːdl] 1. Nadel *f*; Zeiger *m*; 2. nähen; *bsd. Am.* irritieren; anstacheln.

**needless** □ ['niːdlis] unnötig.

**needle|woman** ['niːdlwumən] Näherin *f*; ~**work** Handarbeit *f.*

**needy** □ ['niːdi] bedürftig, arm.

**nefarious** □ [ni'fεəriəs] schändlich.

**negat|e** [ni'geit] verneinen; ~**ion** [~ei∫ən] Verneinung *f*; Nichts *n*; ~**ive** ['negətiv] 1. □ negativ; verneinend; 2. Verneinung *f*; *phot.* Negativ *n*; 3. ablehnen.

**neglect** [ni'glekt] 1. Vernachlässigung *f*; Nachlässigkeit *f*; 2. vernachlässigen; ~**ful** □ [~tful] nachlässig.

**negligen|ce** ['neglidʒəns] Nachlässigkeit *f*; ~**t** □ [~nt] nachlässig.

**negligible** □ ['neglidʒəbl] nebensächlich; unbedeutend.

**negotia|te** [ni'gou∫ieit] verhandeln (*über acc.*); zustande bringen; bewältigen; *Wechsel* begeben; ~**tion** [nigou∫i'ei∫ən] Begebung *f e-s Wechsels etc.*; Ver-, Unterhandlung *f*; Bewältigung *f*; **~tor** [ni'gouʃieitə] Unterhändler *m*.

**negr|ess** ['ni:gris] Negerin *f*; **~o** [~rou], *pl*. **~oes** Neger *m*.

**neigh** [nei] 1. Wiehern *n*; 2. wiehern.

**neighbo(u)r** ['neibə] Nachbar(in); Nächste(r *m*) *f*; **~hood** [~əhud] Nachbarschaft *f*; **~ing** [~əriŋ] benachbart; **~ly** [~əli] nachbarlich, freundlich; **~ship** [~əʃip] Nachbarschaft *f*.

**neither** ['naiðə] 1. keiner (von beiden); 2. **~** ... *nor* ... weder ... noch ...; *not* ... **~** auch nicht.

**nephew** ['nevju(:)] Neffe *m*.

**nerve** [nə:v] 1. Nerv *m*; Sehne *f*; *Blatt*-Rippe *f*; Kraft *f*, Mut *m*; Dreistigkeit *f*; *get on one's* **~s** e-m auf die Nerven gehen; 2. kräftigen; ermutigen; **~less** [' 'nə:vlis] kraftlos.

**nervous** □ ['nə:vəs] Nerven...; nervig, kräftig; nervös; **~ness** [~snis] Nervigkeit *f*; Nervosität *f*.

**nest** [nest] 1. Nest *n* (*a. fig.*); 2. nisten; **~le** ['nesl] *v/i*. (sich ein-) nisten; sich (an)schmiegen; *v/t*. schmiegen.

**net¹** [net] 1. Netz *n*; 2. mit e-m Netz fangen *od*. umgeben.

**net²** [~] 1. netto; Rein...; 2. netto einbringen.

**nether** ['neðə] nieder; Unter...

**nettle** ['netl] 1. ♀ Nessel *f*; 2. ärgern.

**network** ['netwə:k] (Straßen-, Kanal- *etc*.)Netz *n*; Sendergruppe *f*.

**neurosis** ♫ [njuə'rousis] Neurose *f*.

**neuter** ['nju:tə] 1. geschlechtslos; 2. geschlechtsloses Tier; *gr*. Neutrum *n*.

**neutral** ['nju:trəl] 1. neutral; unparteiisch; 2. Neutrale(r *m*) *f*; Null(punkt *m*) *f*; Leerlauf(stellung *f*) *m*; **~ity** [nju:(:)'træliti] Neutralität *f*; **~ize** ['nju:trəlaiz] neutralisieren.

**neutron** *phys*. ['nju:trɔn] Neutron *n*.

**never** ['nevə] nie(mals); gar nicht; **~more** [~'mɔ:] nie wieder; **~theless** [nevəðə'les] nichtsdestoweniger.

**new** [nju:] neu; frisch; unerfahren; **~comer** ['nju:'kʌmə] Ankömmling *m*; **~ly** ['nju:li] neulich; neu.

**news** [nju:z] *mst. sg*. Neuigkeit(en *pl*.) *f*, Nachricht(en *pl*.) *f*; **~agent** ['nju:zeidʒənt] Zeitungshändler *m*; **~boy** Zeitungsausträger *m*; **~butcher** *Am. sl*. Zeitungsverkäufer *m*; **~cast** *Radio*: Nachrichten *f/pl*.; **~monger** Neuigkeitskrämer *m*; **~paper** Zeitung *f*; *attr*. Zeitungs...; **~print** Zeitungspapier *n*; **~reel** *Film*: Wochenschau *f*; **~room** Lesezimmer *n*; *Am. Zeitung*: Nachrichtenredaktion *f*; **~stall**, *Am*. **~stand** Zeitungskiosk *m*.

**new year** ['nju:'jə:] *das* neue Jahr; *New Year's Day* Neujahr(stag *m*) *n*; *New Year's Eve* Silvester *m*.

**next** [nekst] 1. *adj*. nächst; **~** *but one der* übernächste; **~** *door to fig*. beinahe; **~** *to* nächst (*dat*.); 2. *adv*. zunächst, gleich darauf; nächstens.

**nibble** ['nibl] *v/t*. knabbern an (*dat*.); *v/i*. **~** *at* nagen *od*. knabbern an (*dat*.); (*herum*)kritteln an (*dat*.).

**nice** □ [nais] fein; wählerisch; peinlich (genau); heikel; nett; niedlich; hübsch; **~ly** ['naisli] F (sehr) gut; **~ty** ['naisiti] Feinheit *f*; Genauigkeit *f*; Spitzfindigkeit *f*.

**niche** [nitʃ] Nische *f*.

**nick** [nik] 1. Kerbe *f*; *in the* **~** *of time* gerade zur rechten Zeit; 2. (ein)kerben; *sl. j-n* schnappen.

**nickel** ['nikl] 1. *min*. Nickel *m* (*Am. a. Fünfcentstück*); 2. vernickeln.

**nick-nack** ['niknæk] = *knickknack*.

**nickname** ['nikneim] 1. Spitzname *m*; 2. e-n Spitznamen geben (*dat*.).

**niece** [ni:s] Nichte *f*.

**nifty** *Am. sl*. ['nifti] elegant; stinkend.

**niggard** ['nigəd] Geizhals *m*; **~ly** [~dli] geizig, knauserig; karg.

**nigger** F *mst contp*. ['nigə] Nigger *m* (*Neger*); **~** *in the woodpile Am. sl. der* Haken an der Sache.

**night** [nait] Nacht *f*; Abend *m*; *by* **~**, *in the* **~**, *at* **~** nachts; **~cap** ['naitkæp] Nachtmütze *f*; Nachttrunk *m*; **~club** Nachtlokal *n*; **~dress** (Damen)Nachthemd *n*; **~fall** Einbruch *m* der Nacht; **~gown** = *night-dress*; **~ingale** *orn*.['naitiŋgeil] Nachtigall *f*; **~ly** ['naitli] nächtlich; jede Nacht; **~mare** Alptraum *m*; **~shirt** (Herren)Nachthemd *n*; **~spot** *Am*. Nachtlokal *n*; **~y** ['naiti] F (Damen- *od*. Kinder)Nachthemd *n*.

**nil** [nil] *bsd. Sport*: nichts, null.

**nimble** □ ['nimbl] flink, behend.

**nimbus** ['nimbəs] Nimbus *m*, Heiligenschein *m*; Regenwolke *f*.

**nine** [nain] 1. neun; 2. Neun *f*; **~pins** ['nainpinz] *pl*. Kegel(spiel *n*) *m/pl*.; **~teen** ['nain'ti:n] neunzehn; **~ty** ['nainti] neunzig.

**ninny** F ['nini] Dummkopf *m*.

**ninth** [nainθ] 1. neunte(r, -s); 2. Neuntel *n*; **~ly** ['nainθli] neuntens.

**nip** [nip] 1. Kniff *m*; scharfer Frost; Schlückchen *n*; 2. zwicken; schneiden (*Kälte*); *sl*. flitzen; nippen; **~** *in the bud im* Keime ersticken.

**nipper** ['nipə] Krebsschere *f*; (*a pair of*) **~s** *pl*. (eine) (Kneif)Zange.

**nipple** ['nipl] Brustwarze *f*.

**Nisei** *Am*. ['ni:'sei] (*a. pl*.) Japaner *m*, geboren in den USA.

**nit|re**, *Am*. **~er** ♫ ['naitə] Salpeter *m*.

**nitrogen** ['naitridʒən] Stickstoff *m*.

**no** [nou] **1.** *adj.* kein; *in* ~ *time* im Nu; ~ *one* keiner; **2.** *adv.* nein; nicht; ~ Nein *n.*

**nobility** [nou'biliti] Adel *m* (*a. fig.*).

**noble** ['noubl] **1.** adlig; edel, vornehm; vortrefflich; **2.** Adlige(r *m*) *f*; ~**man** Adlige(r) *m*; ~**minded** edelmütig; ~**ness** [~lnis] Adel *m*; Würde *f*.

**nobody** ['noubədi] niemand.

**nocturnal** [nɔk'tə:nl] Nacht...

**nod** [nɔd] **1.** nicken, schlafen; (sich) neigen; ~*ding acquaintance* oberflächliche Bekanntschaft; **2.** Nicken *n*; Wink *m*.

**node** [noud] Knoten *m* (*a. & u. ast.*); *&* Überbein *n.*

**noise** [nɔiz] **1.** Lärm *m*; Geräusch *n*; Geschrei *n*; *big* ~ *bsd. Am.* F großes Tier (*Person*); **2.** ~ *abroad* ausschreien; ~**less** □ ['nɔizlis] geräuschlos.

**noisome** ['nɔisəm] schädlich; widerlich.

**noisy** □ ['nɔizi] geräuschvoll, lärmend; aufdringlich (*Farbe*).

**nomin|al** □ ['nɔminl] nominell, (nur) dem Namen nach (vorhanden); namentlich; ~ *value* Nennwert *m*; ~**ate** [~neit] ernennen; zur Wahl vorschlagen; ~**ation** [nɔmi-'neiʃən] Ernennung *f*; Vorschlagsrecht *n.*

**nominative** ['nɔminətiv] *a.* ~ *case gr.* Nominativ *m.*

**non** [nɔn] *in Zssgn:* nicht, un..., Nicht...

**nonage** ['nounidʒ] Minderjährigkeit *f.*

**non-alcoholic** ['nɔnælkə'hɔlik] alkoholfrei.

**nonce** [nɔns]: *for the* ~ nur für diesen Fall.

**non-commissioned** ['nɔnkə'miʃənd] nicht bevollmächtigt; ~ *officer* × Unteroffizier *m.*

**non-committal** ['nɔnkə'mitl] unverbindlich.

**non-compliance** ['nɔnkəm'plaiəns] Zuwiderhandlung *f*, Verstoß *m.*

**non-conductor** *≠* ['nɔnkəndʌktə] Nichtleiter *m.*

**nonconformist** ['nɔnkən'fɔ:mist] Dissident(in), Freikirchler(in).

**nondescript** ['nɔndiskript] unbestimmbar; schwer zu beschreiben(d).

**none** [nʌn] **1.** keine(r, -s); nichts; **2.** keineswegs, gar nicht; ~ *the less* nichtsdestoweniger.

**nonentity** [nɔ'nentiti] Nichtsein *n*; Unding *n*; Nichts *n*; *fig.* Null *f.*

**non-existence** ['nɔnig'zistəns] Nicht(da)sein *n.*

**non-fiction** ['nɔn'fikʃən] Sachbücher *n/pl.*

**nonpareil** ['nɔnpərəl] Unvergleichliche(r *m*, -s *n*) *f.*

**non-party** ['nɔn'pa:ti] parteilos.

**non-performance** ×️ ['nɔnpə-'fɔ:məns] Nichterfüllung *f.*

**nonplus** ['nɔn'plʌs] **1.** Verlegenheit *f*; **2.** in Verlegenheit bringen.

**non-resident** ['nɔn'rezidənt] nicht im Haus *od.* am Ort wohnend.

**nonsens|e** ['nɔnsəns] Unsinn *m*; ~**ical** [nɔn'sensikəl] unsinnig.

**non-skid** ['nɔn'skid] rutschfest.

**non-smoker** ['nɔn'smoukə] Nichtraucher *m.*

**non-stop** 🚌, ✈️ ['nɔn'stɔp] durchgehend; Ohnehalt...

**non-union** ['nɔn'ju:njən] nicht organisiert (*Arbeiter*).

**non-violence** ['nɔn'vaiələns] (Politik *f der*) Gewaltlosigkeit *f.*

**noodle** ['nu:dl] Nudel *f.*

**nook** [nuk] Ecke *f*, Winkel *m.*

**noon** [nu:n] Mittag *m*; *attr.* Mittags...; ~**day** ['nu:ndei], ~**tide**, ~**time** = *noon.*

**noose** [nu:s] **1.** Schlinge *f*; **2.** (mit der Schlinge) fangen; schlingen.

**nope** *Am.* F [noup] nein.

**nor** [nɔ:] noch; auch nicht.

**norm** [nɔ:m] Norm *f*, Regel *f*; Muster *n*; Maßstab *m*; ~**al** □ ['nɔ:məl] normal; ~**lize** [~laiz] normalisieren; normen.

**north** [nɔ:θ] **1.** Nord(en *m*); **2.** nördlich; Nord..., ~**east** ['nɔ:θ'i:st] **1.** Nordost *m*; **2.** *a.* ~**eastern** [~tən] nordöstlich; ~**erly** ['nɔ:ðəli], ~**ern** [~ən] nördlich; Nord..., ~**erner** [~ən] Nordländer(in); *Am. 2* Nordstaatler(in); ~**ward** ['nɔ:θwəd(z)] *adv.* nördlich; nordwärts; ~**west** ['nɔ:θ'west] **1.** Nordwest *m*; **2.** *a.* ~**western** [~tən] nordwestlich.

**Norwegian** [nɔ:'wi:dʒən] **1.** norwegisch; **2.** Norweger(in); Norwegisch *n.*

**nose** [nouz] **1.** Nase *f*; Spitze *f*; Schnauze *f*; **2.** *v/t.* riechen; ~ *one's way* vorsichtig fahren; *v/i.* schnüffeln; ~**dive** ✈️ ['nouzdaiv] Sturzflug *m*; ~**gay** ['nouzgei] Blumenstrauß *m.*

**nostalgia** [nɔs'tældʒiə] Heimweh *n*, Sehnsucht *f.*

**nostril** ['nɔstril] Nasenloch *n*, Nüster *f.*

**nostrum** ['nɔstrəm] Geheimmittel *n*; Patentlösung *f.*

**nosy** F ['nouzi] neugierig.

**not** [nɔt] nicht.

**notable** ['noutəbl] **1.** □ bemerkenswert; **2.** angesehene Person.

**notary** ['noutəri] *oft* ~ *public* Notar *m.* [*f.*)

**notation** [nou'teiʃən] Bezeichnung *f.*

**notch** [nɔtʃ] **1.** Kerbe *f*, Einschnitt *m*; Scharte *f*; *Am.* Engpaß *m*, Hohlweg *m*; **2.** einkerben.

**note** [nout] **1.** Zeichen *n*; Notiz *f*; Anmerkung *f*; Briefchen *n*; (*bsd.* Schuld)Schein *m*; Note *f*; Ton *m*; Ruf *m*; Beachtung *f*; *take* ~*s* sich

Notizen machen; 2. be(ob)achten; besonders erwähnen; a. ~ down notieren; mit Anmerkungen versehen; ~book ['noutbuk] Notizbuch n; ~d bekannt; berüchtigt; ~paper Briefpapier n; ~worthy beachtenswert.

**nothing** ['nʌθiŋ] 1. nichts; 2. Nichts n; Null f; for ~ umsonst; good for ~ untauglich; bring (come) to ~ zunichte machen (werden).

**notice** ['noutis] 1. Notiz f; Nachricht f, Bekanntmachung f; Kündigung f; Warnung f; Beachtung f; at short ~ kurzfristig; give ~ that bekanntgeben, daß; give a week's ~ acht Tage vorher kündigen; take ~ of Notiz nehmen von; without ~ fristlos; 2. bemerken; be(ob)achten; ~able □ [~səbl] wahrnehmbar; bemerkenswert.

**noti|fication** [noutifi'keiʃən] Anzeige f; Meldung f; Bekanntmachung f; ~fy ['noutifai] et. anzeigen, melden; bekanntmachen.

**notion** ['nouʃən] Begriff m, Vorstellung f; Absicht f; ~s pl. Am. Kurzwaren f/pl.

**notorious** □ [nou'tɔːriəs] all-, weltbekannt; notorisch; berüchtigt.

**notwithstanding** prp. [nɔtwiθ'stændiŋ] ungeachtet, trotz (gen.).

**nought** [nɔːt] Null f, Nichts n.

**noun** gr. [naun] Hauptwort n.

**nourish** ['nʌriʃ] (er)nähren; fig. hegen; ~ing [~iŋ] nahrhaft; ~ment [~ʃmənt] Nahrung(smittel n) f.

**novel** ['nɔvəl] 1. neu; ungewöhnlich; 2. Roman m; ~ist [~list] Romanschriftsteller(in), Romancier m; ~ty [~lti] Neuheit f.

**November** [nou'vembə] November m.

**novice** ['nɔvis] Neuling m; eccl. Novize m, f.

**now** [nau] 1. nun, jetzt; eben; just ~ soeben; ~ and again od. then dann u. wann; 2. cj. a. ~ that nun da.

**nowadays** ['nauədeiz] heutzutage.

**nowhere** ['nouwɛə] nirgends.

**noxious** □ ['nɔkʃəs] schädlich.

**nozzle** ['nɔzl] ⊕ Düse f; Tülle f.

**nuance** [nju(ː)'ɑ̃ːns] Nuance f, Schattierung f.

**nub** [nʌb] Knubbe(n m) f; Am. F springender Punkt in e-r Sache.

**nucle|ar** ['njuːkliə] Kern...; ~ reactor Kernreaktor m; ~ research (Atom-) Kernforschung f; ~us [~iəs] Kern m.

**nude** [njuːd] 1. nackt; 2. paint. Akt m.

**nudge** F [nʌdʒ] 1. j-n heimlich anstoßen; 2. Rippenstoß m.

**nugget** ['nʌgit] (bsd. Gold)Klumpen m.

**nuisance** ['njuːsns] Mißstand m;

Ärgernis n; Unfug m; fig. Plage f; what a ~! wie ärgerlich!; make o.s. od. be a ~ lästig fallen.

**null** [nʌl] nichtig; nichtssagend; ~ and void null u. nichtig; ~ify ['nʌlifai] zunichte machen; aufheben, ungültig machen; ~ity [~iti] Nichtigkeit f, Ungültigkeit f.

**numb** [nʌm] 1. starr; taub (empfindungslos); 2. starr od. taub machen; erd erstarrt.

**number** ['nʌmbə] 1. Nummer f; (An)Zahl f; Heft n, Lieferung f, Nummer f e-s Werkes; without ~ zahllos; in ~ an der Zahl; 2. zählen; numerieren; ~less [~lis] zahllos; ~plate mot. Nummernschild n.

**numera|l** ['njuːmərəl] 1. Zahl...; 2. Ziffer f; ~tion [njuːmə'reiʃən] Zählung f; Numerierung f.

**numerical** □ [njuː(ː)'merikəl] zahlenmäßig; Zahl...

**numerous** □ ['njuːmərəs] zahlreich.

**numskull** F ['nʌmskʌl] Dummkopf m.

**nun** [nʌn] Nonne f; orn. Blaumeise f.

**nunnery** ['nʌnəri] Nonnenkloster n.

**nuptial** ['nʌpʃəl] 1. Hochzeits..., Ehe...; 2. ~s pl. Hochzeit f.

**nurse** [nəːs] 1. Kindermädchen n, Säuglingsschwester f; a. wet-Amme f; (Kranken)Pflegerin f, (Kranken)Schwester f; at ~ in Pflege; put out to ~ in Pflege geben; 2. stillen, nähren; großziehen; pflegen; hätscheln; ~ling ['nəːsliŋ] Säugling m; Pflegling m; ~maid ['nəːsmeid] Kindermädchen n; ~ry ['nəːsri] Kinderzimmer n; ✶ Pflanzschule f; ~ rhymes pl. Kinderlieder n/pl., -reime m/pl.; ~ school Kindergarten m; ~ slopes pl. Ski: Idiotenhügel m/pl.

**nursing** ['nəːsiŋ] Stillen n; (Kranken)Pflege f; ~ bottle Saugflasche f; ~ home Privatklinik f.

**nursling** ['nəːsliŋ] = nurseling.

**nurture** ['nəːtʃə] 1. Pflege f; Erziehung f; 2. aufziehen; nähren.

**nut** [nʌt] Nuß f; ⊕ (Schrauben-) Mutter f; sl. verrückter Kerl; ~s pl. Nußkohle f; ~cracker ['nʌtkrækə] Nußknacker m; ~meg ['nʌtmeg] Muskatnuß f.

**nutriment** ['njuːtrimənt] Nahrung f.

**nutri|tion** [njuː(ː)'triʃən] Ernährung f; Nahrung f; ~tious [~əs], ~tive □ ['njuːtritiv] nahrhaft; Ernährungs...

**nut|shell** ['nʌtʃel] Nußschale f; in a ~ in aller Kürze; ~ty ['nʌti] nußreich; nußartig; sl. verrückt.

**nylon** ['nailən] Nylon n; ~s pl. Nylonstrümpfe m/pl.

**nymph** [nimf] Nymphe f.

# O

o [ou] 1. oh!; ach!; 2. (in Telefon-
nummern) Null f.
oaf [ouf] Dummkopf m; Tölpel m.
oak [ouk] Eiche f.
oar [ɔ:] 1. Ruder n; 2. rudern;
~sman ['ɔ:zmən] Ruderer m.
oas|is [ou'eisis], pl. ~es [ou'eisi:z]
Oase f (a. fig.).
oat [out] mst ~s pl. Hafer m; feel
one's ~s Am. F groß in Form sein;
sich wichtig vorkommen; sow one's
wild ~s sich austoben.
oath [ouθ], pl. ~s [ouðz] Eid m;
Schwur m; Fluch m; take (make,
swear) an ~ e-n Eid leisten, schwören.
oatmeal ['outmi:l] Haferflocken
f/pl.
obdurate ☐ ['ɔbdjurit] verstockt.
obedien|ce [ə'bi:djəns] Gehorsam
m; ~t ☐ [~nt] gehorsam.
obeisance [ou'beisəns] Ehrerbietung f; Verbeugung f; do ~ huldigen.
obesity [ou'bi:siti] Fettleibigkeit f.
obey [ə'bei] gehorchen (dat.); Befehl etc. befolgen, Folge leisten
(dat.).
obituary [ə'bitjuəri] Totenliste f;
Todesanzeige f; Nachruf m;
attr. Todes..., Toten...
object 1. ['ɔbdʒikt] Gegenstand m;
Ziel n, fig. Zweck m; Objekt n (a.
gr.); 2. [əb'dʒekt] v/t. einwenden
(to gegen); v/i. et. dagegen haben
(to ger. daß).
objection [əb'dʒekʃən] Einwand m;
~able ☐ [~ʃnəbl] nicht einwandfrei; unangenehm.
objective [əb'dʒektiv] 1. ☐ objektiv,
sachlich; 2. ✗ Ziel n.
object-lens opt. ['ɔbdʒiktlenz] Objektiv n.
obligat|ion [ɔbli'geiʃən] Verpflich-
tung f; ✝ Schuldverschreibung f;
be under (an) ~ to s.o. j-m zu Dank
verpflichtet sein; be under ~ to inf.
die Verpflichtung haben, zu inf.;
~ory ☐ [ɔ'bligətəri] verpflichtend;
verbindlich.
oblig|e [ə'blaidʒ] (zu Dank) ver-
pflichten; nötigen; ~ s.o. j-m e-n
Gefallen tun; much ~d sehr verbunden; danke bestens; ~ing ☐
[~dʒiŋ] verbindlich, hilfsbereit,
gefällig.
oblique ☐ [ə'bli:k] schief, schräg.
obliterate [ə'blitəreit] auslöschen,
tilgen (a. fig.); Schrift ausstreichen;
Briefmarken entwerten.
obliv|ion [ə'bliviən] Vergessen(heit
f) n; ~ous ☐ [~iəs] vergeßlich.
oblong ['ɔblɔŋ] länglich; recht-
eckig.
obnoxious ☐ [əb'nɔkʃəs] anstößig;
widerwärtig, verhaßt.

30*

obscene ☐ [əb'si:n] unanständig.
obscur|e ☐ [əb'skjuə] 1. ☐ dunkel
(a. fig.); unbekannt; 2. verdunkeln;
~ity [~əriti] Dunkelheit f (a. fig.);
Unbekanntheit f; Niedrigkeit f der
Geburt.
obsequies ['ɔbsikwiz] pl. Leichen-
begängnis n, Trauerfeier f.
obsequious ☐ [əb'si:kwiəs] unterwürfig (to gegen).
observ|able ☐ [əb'zə:vəbl] be-
merkbar; bemerkenswert; ~ance
[~əns] Befolgung f; Brauch m;
~ant ☐ [~nt] beobachtend; achtsam; ~ation [ɔbzə(:)'veiʃən]
Beobachtung f; Bemerkung f;
attr. Beobachtungs...; Aussichts...;
~atory [əb'zə:vətri] Sternwarte f;
~e [əb'zə:v] v/t. be(ob)achten;
acht(geb)en auf (acc.); bemerken;
v/i. sich äußern.
obsess [əb'ses] heimsuchen, quälen;
~ed by od. with besessen von; ~ion
[~eʃən] Besessenheit f.
obsolete ['ɔbsəli:t] veraltet.
obstacle ['ɔbstəkl] Hindernis n.
obstina|cy ['ɔbstinəsi] Hartnäckig-
keit f; ~te ☐ [~nit] halsstarrig;
eigensinnig; hartnäckig.
obstruct [əb'strʌkt] verstopfen,
versperren; hindern; ~ion [~kʃən]
Verstopfung f; Hemmung f; Hindernis n; ~ive ☐ [~ktiv] hinderlich.
obtain [əb'tein] v/t. erlangen, erhalten, erreichen, bekommen; v/i.
sich erhalten (haben); ~able ✝
[~nəbl] erhältlich.
obtru|de [əb'tru:d] (sich) aufdrän-
gen (on dat.); ~sive ☐ [~usiv] aufdringlich.                [schwerfällig.)
obtuse ☐ [əb'tju:s] stumpf(sinnig);)
obviate ['ɔbvieit] vorbeugen (dat.).
obvious ☐ ['ɔbviəs] offensichtlich,
augenfällig, einleuchtend.
occasion [ə'keiʒən] 1. Gelegenheit
f; Anlaß m; Veranlassung f; F (fest-
liches) Ereignis; on the ~ anläßlich (gen.); 2. veranlassen; ~al ☐
[~nl] gelegentlich; Gelegenheits...
occident ['ɔksidənt] Westen m;
Okzident m, Abendland n; ~al ☐
[ɔksi'dentl] abendländisch, westlich.
occult ☐ [ɔ'kʌlt] geheim, verborgen;
magisch, okkult.
occup|ant ['ɔkjupənt] Besitzergrei-
fer(in); Bewohner(in); ~ation[ɔkju-
'peiʃən] Besitz(ergreifung f) m; ✗
Besetzung f; Beruf m; Beschäftigung f; ~y ['ɔkjupai] einnehmen,
in Besitz nehmen, ✗ besetzen; besitzen; innehaben; in Anspruch
nehmen; beschäftigen.
occur [ə'kə:] vorkommen; sich ereignen; it ~red to me es fiel mir ein;
~rence [ə'kʌrəns] Vorkommen n;
Vorfall m, Ereignis n.

**ocean** ['ouʃən] Ozean *m*, Meer *n*.

**o'clock** [ə'klɔk] Uhr (*bei Zeitangaben*); five ~ fünf Uhr.

**October** [ɔk'toubə] Oktober *m*.

**ocul|ar** □ ['ɔkjulə] Augen...; ~**ist** [~list] Augenarzt *m*.

**odd** □ [ɔd] ungerade (*Zahl*); einzeln; und einige *od.* etwas darüber; überzählig; gelegentlich; sonderbar, merkwürdig; ~**ity** ['ɔditi] Seltsamkeit *f*; ~**s** [ɔdz] *oft sg.* (Gewinn)Chancen *f/pl.*; Wahrscheinlichkeit *f*; Vorteil *m*; Vorgabe *f*, Handikap *n*; Verschiedenheit *f*; Unterschied *m*; Streit *m*; be at ~ with s.o. mit j-m im Streit sein; nicht übereinstimmen mit j-m; ~ and ends Reste *m/pl.*; Krimskrams *m*.

**ode** [oud] Ode *f* (*Gedicht*).

**odious** □ ['oudjəs] verhaßt; ekelhaft.

**odo(u)r** ['oudə] Geruch *m*; Duft *m*.

**of** *prp.* [ɔv, əv] *allg.* von; *Ort*: bei (*the battle* ~ *Quebec*); um (*cheat s.o.* ~ *s.th.*); aus (~ *charity*); vor (*dat.*) (*afraid* ~); auf (*acc.*) (*proud* ~); über (*acc.*) (*ashamed* ~); nach (*smell* ~ *roses; desirous* ~); an (*acc.*) (*think* ~ *s.th.*); *nimble* ~ *foot* leichtfüßig.

**off** [ɔːf, ɔf] **1.** *adv.* weg; ab; herunter; aus (*vorbei*); *Zeit:* hin (*3 months* ~); ~ *and on* ab und an; hin und her; *be* ~ fort sein, weg sein; *engS.:* (weg)gehen; zu sein (*Hahn etc.*); aus sein; *well etc.* ~ *gut etc.* daran; **2.** *prp.* von ... (weg, ab, herunter); frei von, ohne; unweit(*gen.*); neben; ♣ auf der Höhe von; **3.** *adj.* entfern(t)er; abseitsliegend; Neben...; *arbeits*~, dienstfrei; † *shade* Fehlfarbe *f*; **4.** *int.* weg!, fort!, raus!

**offal** ['ɔfəl] Abfall *m*; Schund *m*; ~**s** *pl.* Fleischerei: Innereien *f/pl.*

**offen|ce**, *Am.* ~**se** [ə'fens] Angriff *m*; Beleidigung *f*, Kränkung *f*; Ärgernis *n*, Anstoß *m*; Vergehen *n*.

**offend** [ə'fend] *v/t.* beleidigen, verletzen; ärgern; *v/i.* sich vergehen; ~**er** [~də] Übel-, Missetäter(in); Straffällige(r *m*) *f*; *first* ~ noch nicht Vorbestrafte(r *m*) *f*.

**offensive** [ə'fensiv] **1.** □ beleidigend; anstößig; ekelhaft; Neben-siv..., Angriffs...; **2.** Offensive *f*.

**offer** ['ɔfə] **1.** Angebot *n*, Anerbieten *n*; ~ *of marriage* Heiratsantrag *m*; **2.** *v/t.* anbieten; *Preis, Möglichkeit etc.* bieten; *Gebet, Opfer* darbringen; versuchen; zeigen; *Widerstand* leisten; *v/i.* sich bieten; ~**ing** ['ɔfəriŋ] Opfer *n*; Anerbieten *n*, Angebot *n*.

**off-hand** ['ɔːf'hænd] aus dem Handgelenk *od.* Stegreif, unvorbereitet; ungezwungen, frei.

**office** ['ɔfis] Büro *n*; Geschäftsstelle

*f*; Ministerium *n*; Amt *n*, Pflicht *f*; ~**s** *pl.* Hilfe *f*; *booking*-~ Schalter *m*; *box*-~ (*Theater- etc.*)Kasse *f*; *Divine* ♀ Gottesdienst *m*; ~**r** [~sə] Beamt|e(r) *m*, -in *f*; ✗ Offizier *m*.

**official** [ə'fiʃəl] **1.** □ offiziell, amtlich; Amts...; **2.** Beamte(r) *m*.

**officiate** [ə'fiʃieit] amtieren.

**officious** □ [ə'fiʃəs] aufdringlich, übereifrig; offiziös, halbamtlich.

**off|-licence** ['ɔːflaisəns] Schankrecht *n* über die Straße; ~**print** Sonderdruck *m*; ~**set** ausgleichen; ~**shoot** Sproß *m*; Ausläufer *m*; ~**side** ['ɔːf'said] *Sport:* abseits; ~**spring** ['ɔːfspriŋ] Nachkomme(n-schaft *f*) *m*; Ergebnis *n*.

**often** ['ɔːfn] oft(mals), häufig.

**ogle** [ougl] liebäugeln (mit).

**ogre** ['ougə] Menschenfresser *m*.

**oh** [ou] oh!; ach!

**oil** [ɔil] **1.** Öl *n*; Erdöl *n*, Petroleum *n*; **2.** ölen; (*a. fig.*) schmieren; ~**cloth** ['ɔilklɔθ] Wachstuch *n*; ~**skin** Öl(einwand *f*; ~**s** *pl.* Ölzeug *n*; ~**y** □ ['ɔili] ölig (*a. fig.*); fettig; schmierig (*a. fig.*).

**ointment** ['ɔintmənt] Salbe *f*.

**O.K., okay** F ['ou'kei] **1.** richtig, stimmt!; gut, in Ordnung; **2.** annehmen, gutheißen.

**old** [ould] alt; altbekannt; althergebracht; erfahren; ~ *age* (das) Alter; *days of* ~ alte Zeiten *f/pl.*; ~**-age** ['ouldeidʒ] Alters...; ~**-fashioned** ['ould'fæʃənd] altmodisch; altväterlich; ♀ *Glory* Sternenbanner *n*; ~**ish** ['ouldiʃ] ältlich.

**olfactory** *anat.* [ɔl'fæktəri] Geruchs...

**olive** ['ɔliv] ♀ Olive *f*; Olivgrün *n*.

**Olympic Games** [ou'limpik 'geimz] Olympische Spiele *pl.*

**ominous** □ ['ɔminəs] unheilvoll.

**omission** [ou'miʃən] Unterlassung *f*; Auslassung *f*.

**omit** [ou'mit] unterlassen; auslassen.

**omnipoten|ce** [ɔm'nipətəns] Allmacht *f*; ~**t** □ [~nt] allmächtig.

**omniscient** □ [ɔm'nisiənt] allwissend.

**on** [ɔn] **1.** *prp. mst* auf; *engS.:* an (~ *the wall*, ~ *the Thames*); auf ... (los), nach ... (hin) (*march* ~ *London*); auf ... (hin) (~ *his authority*); *Zeit:* an (~ *the 1st of April*); (gleich) nach, bei (~ *his arrival*); über (*acc.*) (*talk* ~ *a subject*); nach (~ *this model*); *get* ~ *a train bsd. Am.* in e-n Zug einsteigen; ~ *hearing it* als ich *etc.* es hörte; **2.** *adv.* darauf; auf (*keep one's hat* ~), an (*have a coat* ~); voraus, vorwärts; weiter (*and so* ~); *be* ~ im Gange sein; auf sein (*Hahn etc.*); an sein (*Licht etc.*); **3.** *int.* drauf!, ran!

**once** [wʌns] **1.** *adv.* einmal; einst (-mals); *at* ~ (so)gleich, sofort; zugleich; ~ for all ein für allemal; ~ in a while dann und wann; this ~ dieses eine Mal; 2. cj. a. ~ that so bald.

**one** [wʌn] **1.** ein; einzig; eine(r), ein; eins; man; ~ day eines Tages; **2.** Eine(r) m; Eins f; the little ~s pl. die Kleinen pl.; ~ another einander; at ~ einig; ~ by ~ einzeln; l for ~ ich für meinen Teil.

**onerous** □ ['ɔnərəs] lästig.

**one|self** [wʌn'self] (man) selbst, sich; **~-sided** □ ['wʌn'saidid] einseitig; **~-way** ['wʌnwei]: ~ street Einbahnstraße f.

**onion** ['ʌnjən] Zwiebel f.

**onlooker** ['ɔnlukə] Zuschauer(in).

**only** ['ounli] **1.** adj. einzig; **2.** adv. nur; bloß; erst; ~ yesterday erst gestern; **3.** cj. ~ (that) nur daß.

**onrush** ['ɔnrʌʃ] Ansturm m.

**onset** ['ɔnset], **onslaught** ['ɔnslɔ:t] Angriff m; bsd. fig. Anfall m; Anfang m.

**onward** ['ɔnwəd] **1.** adj. fortschreitend; **2.** a. ~s adv. vorwärts, weiter.

**ooze** [u:z] **1.** Schlamm m; **2.** v/i. (durch)sickern; ~ away schwinden; v/t. ausströmen, ausschwitzen.

**opaque** □ [ou'peik] undurchsichtig.

**open** ['oupən] **1.** □ allg. offen; geöffnet, auf; frei (Feld etc.); öffentlich; offenstehend, unentschieden; aufrichtig; zugänglich (to dat.); aufgeschlossen (to gegenüber); mild (Wetter); **2.** in the ~ (air) im Freien; come out into the ~ fig. an die Öffentlichkeit treten; **3.** v/t. öffnen; eröffnen (a. fig.); v/i. sich öffnen; anfangen; ~ into führen in (acc.) (Tür etc.); ~ on to hinausgehen auf (acc.) (Fenster etc.); ~ out sich ausbreiten; **~-air** ['oupn'ɛə] im Freien (stattfindend), Freilicht..., Frei-(luft)...; **~-armed** ['oupn'ɑ:md] herzlich, warm; **~er** ['oupnə] (Er-)Öffner(in); (Dosen)Öffner m; **~-eyed** ['oupn'aid] wach; mit offenen Augen; aufmerksam; **~-handed** ['oupn'hændid] freigebig, großzügig; **~-hearted** ['oupnə'hɑ:tid] offen(herzig), aufrichtig; **~ing** ['oupniŋ] (Er)Öffnung f; Gelegenheit f; attr. Eröffnungs...; **~-minded** fig. ['oupn'maindid] aufgeschlossen. [pl.) Opernglas n.|

**opera** ['ɔpərə] Oper f; **~-glass(es**

**operat|e** ['ɔpəreit] v/t. ⚙ operieren; bsd. Am. in Gang bringen; Maschine bedienen; Unternehmen leiten; v/i. (ein)wirken; sich auswirken; arbeiten; ⚙, ✈ operieren, ⚙ operieren; **~ion** [ɔpə'reiʃən] Wirkung f; Tätigkeit f; ⚙, ✈, ✗, ⊕ Operation f; be in ~ in Betrieb sein; in Kraft sein; **~ive** ['ɔpərətiv] **1.** □ wirksam, tätig; praktisch; ✈ operativ; **2.** Arbeiter m; **~or** [~reitə] Operateur m; Telephonist(in); ⊕ Maschinist m.

**opin|e** [ou'pain] meinen; **~ion** [ə'pinjən] Meinung f; Ansicht f; Stellungnahme f; Gutachten n; in my ~ meines Erachtens.

**opponent** [ə'pounənt] Gegner m.

**opportun|e** □ ['ɔpətju:n] passend; rechtzeitig; günstig; **~ity** [ɔpə'tju:niti] (günstige) Gelegenheit.

**oppos|e** [ə'pouz] entgegen-, gegenüberstellen; bekämpfen; **~ed** entgegengesetzt; be ~ to gegen ... sein; **~ite** ['ɔpəzit] **1.** □ gegenüberliegend; entgegengesetzt; **2.** prp. u. adv. gegenüber; **3.** Gegenteil n; **~ition** [ɔpə'ziʃən] Gegenüberstehen n; Widerstand m; Gegensatz m; Widerspruch m, -streit m; ✝ Konkurrenz f; Opposition f.

**oppress** [ə'pres] be-, unterdrücken; **~ion** [~eʃən] Unterdrückung f; Druck m; Bedrängnis f; Bedrücktheit f; **~ive** □ [~esiv] (be)drückend; gewaltsam.

**optic** ['ɔptik] Augen..., Seh...; = **~al** □ [~kəl] optisch; **~ian** [ɔp'tiʃən] Optiker m.

**optimism** ['ɔptimizəm] Optimismus m.

**option** ['ɔpʃən] Wahl(freiheit) f; ✝ Vorkaufsrecht n, Option f; **~al** □ [~nl] freigestellt, wahlfrei.

**opulence** ['ɔpjuləns] Reichtum m.

**or** [ɔ:] oder; ~ else sonst, wo nicht.

**oracular** □ [ɔ'rækjulə] orakelhaft.

**oral** □ ['ɔ:rəl] mündlich; Mund...

**orange** ['ɔrindʒ] **1.** Orange(farbe) f; Apfelsine f; **2.** orangefarben; **~ade** ['ɔrindʒ'eid] Orangenlimonade f.

**orat|ion** [ɔ:'reiʃən] Rede f; **~or** ['ɔrətə] Redner m; **~ory** [~əri] Redekunst f, Rhetorik f; Kapelle f.

**orb** [ɔ:b] Ball m; fig. Himmelskörper m; poet. Augapfel m; **~it** ['ɔ:bit] **1.** Planetenbahn f; Kreis-, Umlaufbahn f; Auge(nhöhle f) n; **2.** sich in e-r Umlaufbahn bewegen.

**orchard** ['ɔ:tʃəd] Obstgarten m.

**orchestra** ♪ ['ɔ:kistrə] Orchester n.

**orchid** ♀ ['ɔ:kid] Orchidee f.

**ordain** [ɔ:'dein] an-, verordnen; bestimmen; Priester ordinieren.

**ordeal** fig. [ɔ:'di:l] schwere Prüfung.

**order** ['ɔ:də] **1.** Ordnung f; Anordnung f; Befehl m; Regel f; ✝ Auftrag m; Zahlungsanweisung f; Klasse f, Rang m; Orden m (a. eccl.); take (holy) ~s in den geistlichen Stand treten; in ~ to inf. um zu inf.; in ~ that damit; make to ~ auf Bestellung anfertigen; standing ~s pl. parl. Geschäftsordnung f; **2.** (an)ordnen; befehlen; ✝ bestellen; j-n beordern; **~ly** ['ɔ:dəli] **1.** ordentlich; ruhig; regelmäßig; **2.** ✗ Ordonnanz f; ✗ Bursche m; Krankenpfleger m.

**ordinal** ['ɔ:dinl] **1.** Ordnungs...; **2.** a. ~ number Ordnungszahl f.

**ordinance** ['ɔ:dinəns] Verordnung f.

**ordinary** □ ['ɔ:dnri] gewöhnlich.

**ordnance** ⚔, ⚓ ['ɔ:dnəns] Artillerie f, Geschütze n/pl.; Feldzeugwesen n.

**ordure** ['ɔ:djuə] Kot m, Schmutz m.

**ore** [ɔ:] Erz n.

**organ** ['ɔ:gən] ♪ Orgel f; Organ n; **~grinder** [~ngraində] Leierkastenmann m; **~ic** [ɔ:'gænik] (~ally) organisch; **~ization** [ɔ:gənai'zeiʃən] Organisation f; **~ize** ['ɔ:gənaiz] organisieren; **~izer** [~zə] Organisator(in).

**orgy** ['ɔ:dʒi] Ausschweifung f.

**orient** ['ɔ:riənt] 1. Osten m; Orient m, Morgenland n; 2. orientieren; **~al** [ɔ:ri'entl] 1. □ östlich; orientalisch; 2. Oriental|e m, -in f; **~ate** ['ɔ:rienteit] orientieren.

**orifice** ['ɔrifis] Mündung f; Öffnung f.

**origin** ['ɔridʒin] Ursprung m; Anfang m; Herkunft f.

**original** [ə'ridʒənl] 1. □ ursprünglich; originell; Original...; ♦ Stamm...; 2. Original n; **~ity** [əridʒi'næliti] Originalität f; **~ly** [ə'ridʒnəli] originell; ursprünglich, zuerst, anfangs, anfänglich.

**originat|e** [ə'ridʒineit] v/t. hervorbringen, schaffen; v/i. entstehen; **~or** [~tə] Urheber m.

**ornament** 1. ['ɔ:nəmənt] Verzierung f; fig. Zierde f; 2. [~ment] verzieren; schmücken; **~al** [ɔ:nə'mentl] zierend; schmückend.

**ornate** □ [ɔ:'neit] reich verziert; überladen.

**orphan** ['ɔ:fn] 1. Waise f; 2. a. **~ed** verwaist; **~age** [~nidʒ] Waisenhaus n.

**orthodox** □ ['ɔ:θədɔks] rechtgläubig; üblich; anerkannt.

**oscillate** ['ɔsileit] schwingen; fig. schwanken.

**osier** ♀ ['ouʒə] Korbweide f.

**osprey** orn. ['ɔspri] Fischadle · m.

**ossify** ['ɔsifai] verknöchern.

**ostensible** □ [ɔs'tensəbl] angeblich.

**ostentatio|n** [ɔstən'teiʃən] Zurschaustellung f; Protzerei f; **~us** □ [~ʃəs] prahlend, prahlerisch.

**ostler** ['ɔslə] Stallknecht m.

**ostracize** ['ɔstrəsaiz] verbannen; ächten.

**ostrich** orn. ['ɔstritʃ] Strauß m.

**other** ['ʌðə] andere(r, -s); the ~ day neulich; the ~ morning neulich morgens; every ~ day einen Tag; um den anderen, jeden zweiten Tag; **~wise** ['ʌðəwaiz] anders; sonst.

**otter** zo. ['ɔtə] Otter(pelz) m.

**ought** [ɔ:t] sollte; you ~ to have done it Sie hätten es tun sollen.

**ounce** [auns] Unze f (= 28,35 g).

**our** ['auə] unser; **~s** ['auəz] der (die, das) unsrige; unsere(r, -s); pred. unser; **~selves** [auə'selvz] wir selbst; uns (selbst).

**oust** [aust] verdrängen, vertreiben, hinauswerfen; e-s Amtes entheben.

**out** [aut] 1. adv. aus; hinaus, heraus; draußen; außerhalb; (bis) zu Ende; be ~ with böse sein mit; ~ and ~ durch und durch; ~ and about wieder auf den Beinen; way ~ Ausgang m; 2. Am. F Ausweg m; the ~s pl. parl. die Opposition; 3. ♦ übernormal, Über... (Größe); 4. prp. ~ of aus, aus ... heraus; außerhalb; außer; aus, von.

**out|balance** [aut'bæləns] schwerer wiegen als; **~bid** [~'bid] [irr. (bid)] überbieten; **~board** ['autbɔ:d] Außenbord...; **~break** [~breik] Ausbruch m; **~building** [~bildiŋ] Nebengebäude n; **~burst** [~bə:st] Ausbruch m; **~cast** [~ka:st] 1. ausgestoßen; 2. Ausgestoßene(r m) f; **~come** [~kʌm] Ergebnis n; **~cry** [~krai] Aufschrei m, Schrei m der Entrüstung; **~dated** [aut'deitid] zeitlich überholt; **~distance** [~'distəns] überholen; **~do** [~'du:] [irr. (do)] übertreffen; **~door** adj. ['autdɔ:], **~doors** adv. [~'dɔ:z] Außen...; draußen, außer dem Hause; im Freien.

**outer** ['autə] äußer; Außen...; **~most** ['automoust] äußerst.

**out|fit** ['autfit] Ausrüstung f, Ausstattung f; Am. Haufen m, Trupp m, (Arbeits)Gruppe f; **~going** [~gouiŋ] 1. weg-, abgehend; 2. Ausgehen n; **~s** pl. Ausgaben f/pl.; **~grow** [aut'grou] [irr. (grow)] herauswachsen aus; hinauswachsen über (acc.); **~house** ['authaus] Nebengebäude n; Am. Außenabort m.

**outing** ['autiŋ] Ausflug m, Tour f.

**out|last** [aut'lɑ:st] überleben; **~law** ['autlɔ:] 1. Geächtete(r m) f; 2. ächten; **~lay** [~lei] Geld-Auslage(n pl.) f; **~let** [~let] Auslaß m; Ausgang m; Abfluß m; **~line** [~lain] 1. Umriß m; Überblick m; Skizze f; 2. umreißen; skizzieren; **~live** [aut'liv] überleben; **~look** ['autluk] Ausblick m (a. fig.); Auffassung f; **~lying** [~laiiŋ] entlegen; **~match** [aut'mætʃ] weit übertreffen; **~number** [~'nʌmbə] an Zahl übertreffen; **~patient** ♨ ['autpeiʃənt] ambulanter Patient; **~post** [~poust] Vorposten m; **~pouring** [~pɔ:riŋ] Erguß m (a. fig.); **~put** [~put] Produktion f, Ertrag m.

**outrage** ['autreidʒ] 1. Gewalttätigkeit f; Attentat n; Beleidigung f; 2. gröblich verletzen; Gewalt antun (dat.); **~ous** [aut'reidʒəs] abscheulich; empörend; gewalttätig.

**out|reach** [aut'ri:tʃ] weiter reichen als; **~right** [adj. 'autrait, adv. aut'rait] gerade heraus; völlig; **~run** [~'rʌn] [irr. (run)] schneller laufen als; hinausgehen über (acc.); **~set**

['autset] Anfang *m*; Aufbruch *m*; **shine** [aut'ʃain] [*irr. (shine)*] überstrahlen; **side** ['aut'said] 1. Außenseite *f*; *fig.* Äußerste(s) *n*; *at* the~höchstens; 2. außen...; außenstehend; äußerst (*Preis*); 3. (nach) (dr)außen; 4. *prp.* außerhalb; **sider** [~də] Außenseiter(in), -stehende(r *m*) *f*; **size** [~saiz] Übergröße *f*; **skirts** [~ska:ts] *pl.* Außenbezirke *m/pl.*, (Stadt)Rand *m*; **smart** *Am.* ⌐ [aut'sma:t] übervorteilen; **spoken** [~'spoukən] freimütig; **spread** ['aut'spred] ausgestreckt, ausgebreitet; **standing** [aut'stændiŋ] hervorragend (*a. fig.*); ausstehend (*Schuld*); offenstehend (*Frage*); **stretched** ['autstretʃt] = outspread; **strip** [aut'strip] überholen (*a. fig.*).

**outward** ['autwəd] 1. äußer(lich); nach (dr)außen gerichtet; 2. *adv. mst* ~s auswärts, nach (dr)außen; **ly** [~dli] äußerlich; an der Oberfläche.

**out|weigh** [aut'wei] überwiegen; **wit** [~'wit] überlisten; **worn** ['autwo:n] erschöpft; *fig.* abgegriffen; überholt.

**oval** ['ouvəl] 1. oval; 2. Oval *n*.

**oven** ['ʌvn] Backofen *m*.

**over** ['ouvə] 1. *adv.* über; hin-, herüber; drüben; vorbei; übermäßig; darüber; von Anfang bis zu Ende; noch einmal; ~ *and above* neben, zusätzlich zu; (*all*) ~ *again* noch einmal (von vorn); ~ *against* gegenüber (*dat.*); *all* ~ ganz und gar; ~ *and* ~ *again* immer wieder; *read* ~ durchlesen; 2. *prp.* über; *all* ~ *the town* durch die ganze *od.* in der ganzen Stadt.

**over|act** ['ouvər'ækt] übertreiben; **all** [~ro:l] 1. Arbeitsanzug *m*, -kittel *m*; Kittel(schürze *f*) *m*; 2. gesamt, Gesamt...; **awe** [ouvər'o:] einschüchtern; **balance** □ [~'bæləns] 1. Übergewicht *n*; 2. umkippen; überwiegen; **bearing** [~'bɛəriŋ] anmaßend; **board** ⚓ ['ouvəbɔ:d] über Bord; **cast** [~ka:st] bewölkt; **charge** [~'tʃa:dʒ] 1. überladen; überfordern; 2. Überladung *f*; Überforderung *f*; **coat** [~kout] Mantel *m*; **come** [ouvə'kʌm] [*irr. (come)*] überwinden, überwältigen; **crowd** [~'kraud] überfüllen; **do** [~'du:] [*irr. (do)*] zu viel tun; übertreiben; zu sehr kochen; überanstrengen; **draw** ['ouvə'drɔ:] [*irr. (draw)*] übertreiben; † *Konto* überziehen; **dress** [~'dres] (sich) übertrieben anziehen; **due** [~'dju:] (über)fällig; **eat** [~'i:t] [*irr. (eat)*]: ~ *o.s.* sich überessen; **flow** 1. [ouvə'flou] [*irr. (flow)*] *v/t.* überfluten; *v/i.* überfließen; 2. ['ouvəflou] Überschwemmung *f*; Überfüllung *f*; **grow**

[~'grou] [*irr. (grow)*] *v/t.* überwuchern; *v/i.* zu sehr wachsen; **hang** 1. [~'hæŋ] [*irr. (hang)*] *v/t.* über (*acc.*) hängen; *v/i.* überhängen; 2. [~hæŋ] Überhang *m*; **haul** [ouvə'hɔ:l] überholen; **head** 1. *adv.* ['ouvə'hed] (dr)oben; 2. *adj.* [~hed] Ober...; † allgemein (*Unkosten*); 3. ~s *pl.* † allgemeine Unkosten *pl.*; **hear** [ouvə'hiə] [*irr. (hear)*] belauschen; **joyed** [~'dʒɔid] überglücklich; **lap** [~'læp] *v/t.* übergreifen auf (*acc.*); überschneiden; *v/i.* ineinandergreifen, überlappen; **lay** [~'lei] [*irr. (lay)*] belegen; ⊕ überlagern; **leaf** [ouvə'li:f] umseitig; **load** [~'loud] überladen; **look** [ouvə'luk] übersehen; beaufsichtigen; **master** [~'ma:stə] überwältigen; **much** ['ouvə'mʌtʃ] zu viel; **night** [~'nait] 1. am Vorabend; über Nacht; 2. Nacht...; nächtlich; Übernachtungs...; **pay** [~'pei] [*irr. (pay)*] zu viel bezahlen für; **peopled** [ouvə'pi:pld] übervölkert; **plus** ['ouvəplʌs] Überschuß *m*; **power** [ouvə'pauə] überwältigen; **rate** ['ouvə'reit] überschätzen; **reach** [ouvə'ri:tʃ] übervorteilen; ~ *o.s.* sich übernehmen; **ride** *fig.* [~'raid] [*irr. (ride)*] sich hinwegsetzen über (*acc.*); umstoßen; **rule** [~'ru:l] überstimmen; ⅍ verwerfen; **run** [~'rʌn] [*irr. (run)*] überrennen; überziehen; überlaufen; bedecken; **sea** ['ouvə'si:] [*irr.*] 1. *a.* ~s überseeisch; Übersee...; 2. ~s *in od.* nach Übersee; **see** [~'si:] [*irr. (see)*] beaufsichtigen; **seer** [~siə] Aufseher *m*; **shadow** [ouvə'ʃædou] überschatten; **sight** ['ouvəsait] Versehen *n*; **sleep** [~'sli:p] [*irr. (sleep)*] verschlafen; **state** [~'steit] übertreiben; **statement** [~'tmənt] Übertreibung *f*; **strain** 1. [~'strein] (sich) überanstrengen; *fig.* übertreiben; 2. [~strein] Überanstrengung *f*.

**overt** ['ouvə:t] offen(kundig).

**over|take** [ouvə'teik] [*irr. (take)*] einholen; *j-n* überraschen; **tax** ['ouvə'tæks] zu hoch besteuern; *fig.* überschätzen; übermäßig in Anspruch nehmen; **throw** 1. [ouvə'θrou] [*irr. (throw)*] (um)stürzen (*a. fig.*); vernichten; 2. ['ouvəθrou] Sturz *m*; Vernichtung *f*; **time** [~taim] Überstunden *f/pl.*

**overture** ['ouvətjuə] ♪ Ouvertüre *f*; Vorspiel *n*; Vorschlag *m*, Antrag *m*.

**over|turn** [ouvə'tə:n] (um)stürzen; **value** ['ouvə'vælju:] zu hoch einschätzen; **weening** [ouvə'wi:niŋ] eingebildet; **weight** ['ouvəweit] Übergewicht *n*; **whelm** [ouvə'welm] überschütten (*a. fig.*); überwältigen; **work** ['ouvə'wə:k] 1.

Überarbeitung *f*; 2. [*irr.* (*work*)] sich überarbeiten; **~wrought** [**~**ˈrɔːt] überarbeitet; überreizt.

**owe** [ou] *Geld, Dank etc.* schulden, schuldig sein; verdanken.

**owing** [ˈouiŋ] schuldig; **~** *to* infolge.

**owl** *orn.* [aul] Eule *f*.

**own** [oun] 1. eigen; richtig; einzig, innig geliebt; 2. *my* **~** mein Eigentum; *a house of one's* **~** ein eigenes Haus; *hold one's* **~** standhalten;

3. besitzen; zugeben; anerkennen; sich bekennen (*to zu*).

**owner** [ˈounə] Eigentümer(in); **~ship** [ˈounəʃip] Eigentum(srecht) *n*.

**ox** [ɔks], *pl.* **oxen** [ˈɔksən] Ochse *m*; Rind *n*.

**oxid|ation** ⚗ [ɔksiˈdeiʃən] Oxydation *f*, Oxydierung *f*; **~e** [ˈɔksaid] Oxyd *n*; **~ize** [ˈɔksidaiz] oxydieren.

**oxygen** ⚗ [ˈɔksidʒən] Sauerstoff *m*.

**oyster** [ˈɔistə] Auster *f*.

**ozone** ⚗ [ˈouzoun] Ozon *n*.

# P

**pace** [peis] 1. Schritt *m*; Gang *m*; Tempo *n*; 2. *v/t.* abschreiten; *v/i.* (einher)schreiten; (im) Paß gehen.

**pacific** [pəˈsifik] (**~**ally) friedlich; the ♀ (*Ocean*) der Pazifik, der Pazifische od. Stille Ozean; **~ation** [pæsifiˈkeiʃən] Beruhigung *f*.

**pacify** [ˈpæsifai] beruhigen.

**pack** [pæk] 1. Pack(en) *m*; Paket *n*; Ballen *m*; Spiel *n Karten*; Meute *f*; Rotte *f*, Bande *f*; Packung *f*; 2. *v/t.* oft **~** *up* (zs.-, ver-, ein)packen; *a.* **~** *off* fortjagen; *Am.* F (bei sich) tragen (*als Gepäck etc.*); bepacken, vollstopfen; ⊕ dichten; *v/i.* oft **~** *up* packen; sich packen (lassen); **~age** [ˈpækidʒ] Pack *m*, Ballen *m*; *bsd. Am.* Paket *n*; Packung *f*; Frachtstück *n*; **~er** [ˈpækə] Packer(in); *Am.* Konservenfabrikant *m*; **~et** [ˈpækit] Paket *n*; Päckchen *n*; *a.* **~-boat** Postschiff *n*.

**packing** [ˈpækiŋ] Packen *n*; Verpackung *f*; **~ house** *Am.* (*bsd.* Fleisch)Konservenfabrik *f*.

**packthread** [ˈpækθred] Bindfaden *m*.

**pact** [pækt] Vertrag *m*, Pakt *m*.

**pad** [pæd] 1. Polster *n*; *Sport:* Beinschutz *m*; Schreibblock *m*; Stempelkissen *n*; (Abschuß)Rampe *f*; 2. (aus)polstern; **~ding** [ˈpædiŋ] Polsterung *f*; *fig.* Lückenbüßer *m*.

**paddle** [ˈpædl] 1. Paddel(ruder) *n*; ♣ (Rad)Schaufel *f*; 2. paddeln; planschen; **~wheel** Schaufelrad *n*.

**paddock** [ˈpædək] (Pferde)Koppel *f*; *Sport:* Sattelplatz *m*.

**padlock** [ˈpædlɔk] Vorhängeschloß *n*.

**pagan** [ˈpeigən] 1. heidnisch; 2. Heid|e *m*, -in *f*.

**page¹** [peidʒ] 1. *Buch*-Seite *f*; *fig.* Buch *n*; 2. paginieren.

**page²** [**~**] 1. (Hotel)Page *m*; *Am.* Amtsdiener *m*; 2. *Am.* (durch e-n Pagen) holen lassen.

**pageant** [ˈpædʒənt] historisches Festspiel; festlicher Umzug.

**paid** [peid] *pret. u. p.p. von* pay 2.

**pail** [peil] Eimer *m*.

**pain** [pein] 1. Pein *f*, Schmerz *m*; Strafe *f*; **~**s *pl.* Leiden *n/pl.*; Mühe *f*; *on od. under* **~** *of death* bei Todesstrafe; *be in* **~** leiden; *take* **~**s sich Mühe geben; 2. *j-m* weh tun; **~ful** [ˈpeinful] schmerzhaft, schmerzlich; peinlich; mühevoll; **~less** ] [ˈpeinlis] schmerzlos; **~staking** ] [ˈpeinzteikiŋ] fleißig.

**paint** [peint] 1. Farbe *f*; Schminke *f*; Anstrich *m*; 2. (be)malen; anstreichen; (sich) schminken; **~brush** [ˈpeintbrʌʃ] Malerpinsel *m*; **~er** [**~**tə] Maler(in); **~ing** [**~**tiŋ] Malen *n*; Malerei *f*; Gemälde *n*.

**pair** [pɛə] 1. Paar *n*; *a* **~** *of scissors* eine Schere; 2. (sich) paaren; zs.-passen; *a.* **~** *off* paarweise weggehen.

**pal** *sl.* [pæl] Kumpel *m*, Kamerad *m*.

**palace** [ˈpælis] Palast *m*.

**palatable** ] [ˈpælətəbl] schmackhaft. [schmack *m* (*a. fig.*).]

**palate** [ˈpælit] Gaumen *m*; Ge-}

**pale¹** [peil] 1. ] blaß, bleich; fahl; **~** *ale* helles Bier; 2. er(bleichen.

**pale²** [**~**] Pfahl *m*; *fig.* Grenzen *f/pl.*

**paleness** [ˈpeilnis] Blässe *f*.

**palisade** [pæliˈseid] 1. Palisade *f*; Staket *n*; **~**s *pl. Am.* Steilufer *n*; 2. umpfählen.

**pall** [pɔːl] schal werden; **~** (*up*)*on j-n* langweilen.

**pallet** [ˈpælit] Strohsack *m*.

**palliat|e** [ˈpælieit] bemänteln; lindern; **~ive** [**~**iətiv] Linderungsmittel *n*.

**pall|id** □ [ˈpælid] blaß; **~idness** [**~**dnis], **~or** [ˈpælə] Blässe *f*.

**palm** [pɑːm] 1. Handfläche *f*; ♀ Palme *f*; 2. in der Hand verbergen; **~** *s.th. off upon s.o.* j-m et. andrehen; **~-tree** [ˈpɑːmtriː] Palme *f*.

**palpable** □ [ˈpælpəbl] fühlbar; *fig.* handgreiflich, klar, eindeutig.

**palpitat|e** [ˈpælpiteit] klopfen (*Herz*); **~ion** [pælpiˈteiʃən] Herzklopfen *n*.

**palsy** ['pɔ:lzi] **1.** Lähmung *f*; *fig.* Ohnmacht *f*; **2.** *fig.* lähmen.

**palter** ['pɔ:ltə] sein Spiel treiben.

**paltry** □ ['pɔ:ltri] erbärmlich.

**pamper** ['pæmpə] verzärteln.

**pamphlet** ['pæmflit] Flugschrift *f.*

**pan** [pæn] Pfanne *f*; Tiegel *m.*

**pan...** [~] all..., gesamt...; pan..., Pan...

**panacea** [pænə'siə] Allheilmittel *n.*

**pancake** ['pænkeik] Pfannkuchen *m*; ~ **landing** ✶ Bumslandung *f.*

**pandemonium** *fig.* [pændi'mounjəm] Hölle(nlärm *m) f.*

**pander** ['pændə] **1.** Vorschub leisten (*to dat.*); kuppeln; **2.** Kuppler *m.*

**pane** [pein] (Fenster)Scheibe *f.*

**panegyric** [pæni'dʒirik] Lobrede *f.*

**panel** ['pænl] **1.** ⚙ Fach *n*; Tür-Füllung *f*; ⚖ Geschworenen(liste *f) m/pl.*; Diskussionsteilnehmer *m/pl.*; Kassenarztliste *f*; **2.** täfeln.

**pang** [pæŋ] plötzlicher Schmerz, Weh *n*; *fig.* Angst *f*, Qual *f.*

**panhandle** ['pænhændl] **1.** Pfannenstiel *m*; *Am.* schmaler Fortsatz *e-s Staatsgebiets*; **2.** *Am.* F betteln.

**panic** ['pænik] **1.** panisch; **2.** Panik *f.*

**pansy** ♀ ['pænzi] Stiefmütterchen *n.*

**pant** [pænt] *nach Luft* schnappen; keuchen; klopfen (*Herz*); lechzen (*for, after* nach).

**panther** *zo.* ['pænθə] Panther *m.*

**panties** F ['pæntiz] (Damen)Schlüpfer *m*; (Kinder)Hös-chen *n.*

**pantry** ['pæntri] Vorratskammer *f.*

**pants** [pænts] *pl.* Hose *f*; † lange Unterhose.

**pap** [pæp] Brei *m.*

**papa** [pə'pɑ:] Papa *m.*

**papal** □ ['peipəl] päpstlich.

**paper** ['peipə] **1.** Papier *n*; Zeitung *f*; Prüfungsaufgabe *f*; Vortrag *m*; Aufsatz *m*; ~**s** *pl.* (Ausweis)Papiere *n/pl.*; **2.** tapezieren; ~**back** Taschenbuch *n*, Paperback *n*; ~**bag** Tüte *f*; ~**clip** Büroklammer *f*; ~**fastener** Musterklammer *f*; ~**hanger** Tapezierer *m*; ~**mill** Papierfabrik *f*; ~**weight** Briefbeschwerer *m.*

**pappy** ['pæpi] breiig.

**par** [pɑ:] ✝ Nennwert *m*, Pari *n*; *at ~* zum Nennwert; *be on a ~ with* gleich *od.* ebenbürtig sein (*dat.*).

**parable** ['pærəbl] Gleichnis *n.*

**parachut|e** ['pærəʃuːt] Fallschirm *m*; ~**ist** [~tist] Fallschirmspringer(in).

**parade** [pə'reid] **1.** ✗ (Truppen-)Parade *f*; Zurschaustellung *f*; Promenade *f*; (Um)Zug *m*; *programme ~ Radio:* Programmvorschau *f*; *make a ~ of et.* zur Schau stellen; **2.** ✗ antreten (lassen); ✗ vorbeimarschieren (lassen); zur Schau stellen; ~**ground** ✗ Exerzier-, Paradeplatz *m.*

**paradise** ['pærədais] Paradies *n.*

**paragon** ['pærəgən] Vorbild *n*; Muster *n.*

**paragraph** ['pærəgrɑːf] Absatz *m*; Paragraph(zeichen *n) m*; kurze Zeitungsnotiz.

**parallel** ['pærəlel] **1.** parallel; **2.** Parallele *f* (*a. fig.*); Gegenstück *n*; Vergleich *m*; *without (a)* ~ ohnegleichen; **3.** vergleichen; entsprechen; gleichen; parallel laufen (mit).

**paraly|se** ['pærəlaiz] lähmen; *fig.* unwirksam machen; ~**sis** ✗ ['rælisis] Paralyse *f*, Lähmung *f.*

**paramount** ['pærəmaunt] oberst, höchst, hervorragend; größer, höher stehend (*to* als).

**parapet** ['pærəpit] ✗ Brustwehr *f*; Brüstung *f*; Geländer *n.*

**paraphernalia** [pærəfə'neiljə] *pl.* Ausrüstung *f*; Zubehör *n*, *m.*

**parasite** ['pærəsait] Schmarotzer *m.*

**parasol** [pærə'sɔl] Sonnenschirm *m.*

**paratroops** ✗ ['pærətruːps] Luftlandetruppen *f/pl.*

**parboil** ['pɑːbɔil] ankochen.

**parcel** ['pɑːsl] **1.** Paket *n*; Parzelle *f*; **2.** ~ *out* aus-, aufteilen.

**parch** [pɑːtʃ] rösten, (aus)dörren.

**parchment** ['pɑːtʃmənt] Pergament *n.*

**pard** *Am. sl.* [pɑːd] Partner *m.*

**pardon** ['pɑːdn] **1.** Verzeihung *f*; ⚖ Begnadigung *f*; **2.** verzeihen; *j.* begnadigen; ~**able** □ [~nəbl] verzeihlich.

**pare** [pɛə] (be)schneiden (*a. fig.*); schälen.

**parent** ['pɛərənt] Vater *m*, Mutter *f*; *fig.* Ursache *f*; ~**s** *pl.* Eltern *pl.*; ~**age** [~tidʒ] Herkunft *f*; ~**al** [pə'rentl] elterlich.

**parenthe|sis** [pə'renθisis], *pl.* ~**ses** [~siːz] Einschaltung *f*; *typ.* (runde) Klammer.

**paring** ['pɛəriŋ] Schälen *n*, Abschneiden *n*; ~**s** *pl.* Schalen *f/pl.*, Schnipsel *m/pl.*

**parish** ['pæriʃ] **1.** Kirchspiel *n*, Gemeinde *f*; **2.** Pfarr...; Gemeinde...; ~ *council* Gemeinderat *m*; ~**ioner** [pə'riʃənə] Pfarrkind *n*, Gemeindemitglied *n.*

**parity** ['pæriti] Gleichheit *f.*

**park** [pɑːk] **1.** Park *m*, Anlagen *f/pl.*; Naturschutzgebiet *n*; *mst car-*~ Parkplatz *m*; **2.** *mot.* parken; ~**ing** *mot.* ['pɑːkiŋ] Parken *n*; ~**ing lot** Parkplatz *m*; ~**ing meter** Parkuhr *f.*

**parlance** ['pɑːləns] Ausdrucksweise *f.*

**parley** ['pɑːli] **1.** Unterhandlung *f*; **2.** unterhandeln; sich besprechen.

**parliament** ['pɑːləmənt] Parlament *n*; ~**arian** [pɑːləmen'tɛəriən] Parlamentarier(in); ~**ary** □ [pɑːlə'mentəri] parlamentarisch; Parlaments...

parlo(u)r ['pɑːlə] Wohnzimmer n; Empfangs-, Sprechzimmer n; beauty ~ bsd. Am. Schönheitssalon m; ~ car 👑 Am. Salonwagen m; ~maid Stubenmädchen n.

parochial □ [pə'roukjəl] Pfarr...; Gemeinde...; fig. engstirnig, beschränkt.

parole [pə'roul] 1. ♩ mündlich; 2. ✕ Parole f; Ehrenwort n; put on ~ = 3. ♩ bsd. Am. bedingt freilassen.

parquet ['pɑːkei] Parkett(fußboden m) n; Am. thea. Parkett n.

parrot ['pærət] 1. orn. Papagei m (a. fig.); 2. (nach)plappern.

parry ['pæri] abwehren, parieren.

parsimonious □ [pɑːsi'mounjəs] sparsam, karg; knauserig.

parsley ♧ ['pɑːsli] Petersilie f.

parson ['pɑːsn] Pfarrer m; ~age [~nidʒ] Pfarrei f; Pfarrhaus n.

part [pɑːt] 1. Teil m; Anteil m; Partei f; thea., fig. Rolle f; ♩ Einzel-Stimme f; Gegend f; a man of ~s ein fähiger Mensch; take ~ in s.th. an e-r Sache teilnehmen; take in good (bad) ~ gut (übel) aufnehmen; for my (own) ~ meinerseits; in ~ teilweise; on the ~ of von seiten (gen.); on my ~ meinerseits; 2. adv. teils; 3. v/t. (ab-, ein-, zer)teilen; Haar scheiteln; ~ company sich trennen (with von); v/i sich trennen (with von); scheiden

partake [pɑː'teik] [irr (take)] teilnehmen, teilhaben; ~ of Mahlzeit einnehmen; grenzen an (acc.).

partial □ ['pɑːʃəl] Teil ~ teilweise; partiell; parteiisch; eingenommen (to von, für); ~ity [pɑːʃi'æliti] Parteilichkeit f; Vorliebe f

particip|ant [pɑː'tisipənt] Teilnehmer(in); ~ate [~peit] teilnehmen; ~ation [pɑːtisi'peiʃən] Teilnahme f.

participle gr. ['pɑːtsipl] Partizip n, Mittelwort n.

particle ['pɑːtikl] Teilchen n.

particular [pə'tikjulə] 1. □ mst besonder; einzeln; Sonder...; genau; eigen; wählerisch; 2. Einzelheit f; Umstand m, in ~ insbesondere; ~ity [pətikju'læriti] Besonderheit f; Ausführlichkeit f, Eigenheit f; ~ly [pə'tikjulɑːli] besonders.

parting ['pɑːtiŋ] 1. Trennung f; Teilung f; Abschied m; Haar-Scheitel m; ~ of the ways bsd. fig. Scheideweg m; 2. Abschieds...

partisan [pɑːti'zæn] Parteigänger (-in); ✕ Partisan m; attr. Partei...

partition [pɑː'tiʃən] 1. Teilung f; Scheidewand f; Verschlag m, Fach n; 2. mst ~ off (ab)teilen.

partly ['pɑːtli] teilweise, zum Teil.

partner ['pɑːtnə] 1. Partner(in); 2. (sich) zs.-tun mit, zs.-arbeiten mit; ~ship [~ʃip] Teilhaber-, Part-

nerschaft f; ♱ Handelsgesellschaft f.

part-owner ['pɑːtounə] Miteigentümer(in).

partridge orn. ['pɑːtridʒ] Rebhuhn n.

part-time ['pɑːttaim] 1. adj. Teilzeit..., Halbtags...; 2. adv. halbtags.

party ['pɑːti] Partei f; ✕ Trupp m, Kommando n; Party f, Gesellschaft f; Beteiligte(r) m; co. Type f, Individuum n; ~ line pol. Parteilinie f, -direktive f.

pass [pɑːs] 1. Paß m, Ausweis m; Passierschein m; Bestehen n e-s Examens; univ. gewöhnlicher Grad; (kritische) Lage; Fußball: Paß m; Bestreichung f, Strich m; (Gebirgs-) Paß m, Durchgang m; Karten: Passen n; free ~ Freikarte f; 2. v/i. passieren, geschehen; hingenommen werden; Karten: passen; (vorbei)gehen, (vorbei)kommen, (vorbei)fahren; vergehen (Zeit); sich verwandeln; angenommen werden (Banknoten); bekannt sein; vergehen; aussterben; a. ~ away sterben; durchkommen (Gesetz; Prüfling); ~ for gelten als; ~ out statten gehen; ~ out F ohnmächtig werden; come to ~ geschehen; bring to ~ bewirken; v/t. vorbeigehen od. vorbeikommen od. vorbeifahren an (dat.); passieren; kommen od. fahren durch; verbringen; reichen, geben; Bemerkung machen, von sich geben; Banknoten in Umlauf bringen; Gesetz durchbringen, annehmen; Prüfling durchkommen lassen; Prüfung bestehen; (hinaus-) gehen über (acc.); Urteil abgeben; Meinung äußern; bewegen; streichen mit; Ball zuspielen; Truppen vorbeimaschieren lassen; ~able □ ['pɑːsəbl] passierbar; gangbar, gültig (Geld); leidlich.

passage ['pæsidʒ] Durchgang m, Durchfahrt f; Überfahrt f; Durchreise f; Korridor m, Gang m; Weg m; Annahme f e-s Gesetzes; ♩ Passage f; Text-Stelle f; bird of ~ Zugvogel m.

passbook ♱ ['pɑːsbuk] Sparbuch n.

passenger ['pæsindʒə] Passagier m, Fahr-, Fluggast m, Reisende(r m) f.

passer-by ['pɑːsə'bai] Vorübergehende(r m) f, Passant(in).

passion ['pæʃən] Leidenschaft f; (Gefühls)Ausbruch m; Zorn m; ♀ eccl. Passion f; be in a ~ zornig sein; in ~ im Affekt; ♀ Week eccl. Karwoche f; ~ate □ [~nit] leidenschaftlich.

passive □ ['pæsiv] passiv (a. gr.); teilnahmslos; untätig.

passport ['pɑːspɔːt] (Reise)Paß m.

password ✕ ['pɑːswɔːd] Losung f.

past [pɑːst] 1. adj. vergangen; gr. Vergangenheits...; früher; for some *time* ~ seit einiger Zeit; ~ *tense gr.* Vergangenheit *f*; 2. *adv.* vorbei; 3. *prp.* nach, über; über ... *(acc.)* hinaus; an ... *(dat.)* vorbei; *half* ~ two halb drei; ~ *endurance* unerträglich; ~ *hope* hoffnungslos; 4. Vergangenheit *f (a. gr.).*

**paste** [peist] 1. Teig *m*; Kleister *m*; Paste *f*; 2. (be)kleben; **~board** ['peistbɔːd] Pappe *f*; *attr.* Papp...

**pastel** [pæs'tel] Pastell(bild) *n.*

**pasteurize** ['pæstəraiz] pasteurisieren, keimfrei machen.

**pastime** ['paːstaim] Zeitvertreib *m.*

**pastor** ['paːstə] Pastor *m*; Seelsorger *m*; **~al** □ [.ərəl] Hirten...; pastoral.

**pastry** ['peistri] Tortengebäck *n*, Konditorwaren *f/pl.*; Pasteten *f/pl.*; **~-cook** Pastetenbäcker *m*, Konditor *m.*

**pasture** ['paːstʃə] 1. Vieh-Weide *f*; Futter *n*; 2. (ab)weiden.

**pat** [pæt] 1. Klaps *m*; Portion *f* Butter; 2. tätscheln; klopfen; 3. gelegen, gerade recht; bereit.

**patch** [pætʃ] 1. Fleck *m*; Flicken *m*; Stück *n* Land; ✗ Pflaster *n*; 2. flikken; **~work** ['pætʃwəːk] Flickwerk *n.*

**pate** F [peit] Schädel *m.*

**patent** ['peitənt, *Am.* 'pætənt] 1. offenkundig; patentiert; Patent...; *letters* ~ ['pætənt] *pl.* Patent *n*; ~ *leather* Lackleder *n*; 2. Patent *n*; Privileg *n*, Freibrief *m*; ~ *agent* Patentanwalt *m*; 3. patentieren; **~ee** [peitən'tiː] Patentinhaber *m.*

**patern|al** [pə'təːnl] väterlich; **~ity** [.niti] Vaterschaft *f.*

**path** [paːθ], *pl.* **~s** [paːðz] Pfad *m*; Weg *m.*

**pathetic** [pə'θetik] (~ally) pathetisch; rührend, ergreifend.

**pathos** ['peiθɔs] Pathos *n.*

**patien|ce** ['peiʃəns] Geduld *f*; Ausdauer *f*; Patience *f (Kartenspiel)*; **~t** [.nt] 1. □ geduldig; 2. Patient(in).

**patio** *Am.* ['pætiou] Innenhof *m*, Patio *m.*

**patrimony** ['pætriməni] väterliches Erbteil.

**patriot** ['peitriət] Patriot(in).

**patrol** ✗ [pə'troul] 1. Patrouille *f*, Streife *f*; ~ *wagon Am.* Polizeigefangenenwagen *m*; 2. (ab)patrouillieren; **~man** [.lmæn] patrouillierender Polizist; Pannenhelfer *m e-s Automobilclubs.*

**patron** ['peitrən] (Schutz)Patron *m*; Gönner *m*; Kunde *m*; **~age** ['pætrənidʒ] Gönnerschaft *f*; Kundschaft *f*; Schutz *m*; **~ize** [.naiz] beschützen; begünstigen; Kunde sein bei; gönnerhaft behandeln.

**patter** ['pætə] *v/i.* platschen; trappeln; *v/t.* (her)plappern.

**pattern** ['pætən] 1. Muster *n* (*a.*

*fig.*); Modell *n*; 2. formen *(after,* on nach).

**paunch** ['pɔːntʃ] Wanst *m.*

**pauper** ['pɔːpə] Fürsorgeempfänger(in); **~ize** [.əraiz] arm machen.

**pause** [pɔːz] 1. Pause *f*; 2. pausieren.

**pave** [peiv] pflastern; *fig.* Weg bahnen; **~ment** ['peivmənt] Bürgersteig *m*, Gehweg *m*; Pflaster *n.*

**paw** [pɔː] 1. Pfote *f*, Tatze *f*; 2. scharren; F befingern; rauh behandeln.

**pawn** [pɔːn] 1. Bauer *m im Schach*; Pfand *n*; *in od. at* ~ verpfändet; 2. verpfänden; **~broker** ['pɔːnbroukə] Pfandleiher *m*; **~shop** Leihhaus *n.*

**pay** [pei] 1. (Be)Zahlung *f*; Sold *m*, Lohn *m*; 2. *[irr.] v/t.* (be)zahlen; (be)lohnen; sich lohnen für; *Ehre etc. erweisen; Besuch abstatten;* ~ *attention od. heed to* achtgeben auf *(acc.)*; ~ *down* bar bezahlen; ~ *off* j-n bezahlen u. entlassen; *j-n* voll auszahlen; *v/i.* zahlen; sich lohnen; ~ *for* (für) *et.* bezahlen; **~able** ['peiəbl] zahlbar; fällig; **~day** Zahltag *m*; **~ee** † [pei'iː] Zahlungsempfänger *m*; **~ing** ['peiiŋ] lohnend; **~master** Zahlmeister *m*; **~ment** ['peimənt] (Be)Zahlung *f*; Lohn *m*, Sold *m*; **~off** Abrechnung *f (a. fig.); Am.* F Höhepunkt *m*; **~roll** Lohnliste *f.*

**pea** ♀ [piː] Erbse *f.*

**peace** [piːs] Frieden *m*, Ruhe *f*; *at* ~ friedlich; **~able** □ ['piːsəbl] friedliebend, friedlich; **~ful** □ ['piːsful] friedlich; **~maker** Friedensstifter(in).

**peach** ♀ [piːtʃ] Pfirsich(baum) *m.*

**pea|cock** *orn.* ['piːkɔk] Pfau(hahn) *m*; **~hen** *orn.* ['piːhen] Pfauhenne *f.*

**peak** [piːk] Spitze *f*; Gipfel *m*; Mützen-Schirm *m*; *attr.* Spitzen...; Höchst...; **~ed** [piːkt] spitz.

**peal** [piːl] 1. Geläut *n*; Glockenspiel *n*; Dröhnen *n*; ~ *s of laughter* dröhnendes Gelächter; 2. erschallen (lassen); laut verkünden; dröhnen.

**peanut** ['piːnʌt] Erdnuß *f.*

**pear** ♀ [pɛə] Birne *f.*

**pearl** [pɔːl] 1. Perle *f (a. fig.); attr.* Perl(en)...; 2. tropfen, perlen; **~y** ['pɔːli] perlenartig.

**peasant** ['pezənt] 1. Bauer *m*; 2. bäuerlich; **~ry** [.tri] Landvolk *n.*

**peat** [piːt] Torf *m.*

**pebble** ['pebl] Kiesel(stein) *m.*

**peck** [pek] 1. Viertelscheffel *m* (9,087 *Liter*); *fig.* Menge *f*; 2. pikken, hacken *(at* nach).

**peculate** ['pekjuleit] unterschlagen.

**peculiar** □ [pi'kjuːljə] eigen(tümlich); besonder; seltsam; **~ity** [pikjuːli'æriti] Eigenheit *f*; Eigentümlichkeit *f.*

**pecuniary** [pi'kjuːnjəri] Geld...

**pedagog|ics** [pedə'gɔdʒiks] *mst sg.*

Pädagogik f; ~ue ['pedəgɔg] Pädagoge m; Lehrer m.
pedal ['pedl] 1. Pedal n; 2. Fuß...;
3. Radfahren: fahren, treten.
pedantic [pi'dæntik] (~ally) pedantisch.
peddle ['pedl] hausieren (mit); ~r
Am. [.lə] = pedlar.
pedestal ['pedistl] Sockel m (a. fig.).
pedestrian [pi'destriən] 1. zu Fuß;
nüchtern; 2. Fußgänger(in); ~
crossing Fußgängerübergang m.
pedigree ['pedigri:] Stammbaum m.
pedlar ['pedlə] Hausierer m.
peek [pi:k] 1. spähen, gucken, lugen;
2. flüchtiger Blick.
peel [pi:l] 1. Schale f; Rinde f; 2. a.
~ off v/t. (ab)schälen; Kleid abstreifen; v/i. sich (ab)schälen.
peep [pi:p] 1. verstohlener Blick;
Piepen n; 2. (verstohlen) gucken;
a. ~ out (hervor(gucken (a. fig.);
piepen; ~hole ['pi:phoul] Guckloch n.
peer [piə] 1. spähen, lugen; ~ at
angucken; 2. Gleiche(r m) f; Pair
m; ~less □ ['piəlis] unvergleichlich.
peevish □ ['pi:viʃ] verdrießlich.
peg [peg] 1. Stöpsel m, Dübel m,
Pflock m; Kleider-Haken m; ♩
Wirbel m; Wäsche-Klammer f; fig.
Aufhänger m; take s.o. down a ~ or
two j-n demütigen; 2. festpflöcken;
Grenze abstecken; ~ away od.
along F darauflosarbeiten; ~top
['pegtɔp] Kreisel m.
pelican orn. ['pelikən] Pelikan m.
pellet ['pelit] Kügelchen n; Pille f;
Schrotkorn n.
pell-mell ['pel'mel] durcheinander.
pelt [pelt] 1. Fell n; † rohe Haut;
2. v/t. bewerfen; v/i. niederprasseln.
pelvis anat. ['pelvis] Becken n.
pen [pen] 1. (Schreib)Feder f;
Hürde f; 2. schreiben; [irr.] einpferchen.
penal □ ['pi:nl] Straf...; strafbar;
~ code Strafgesetzbuch n; ~ servitude Zuchthausstrafe f; ~ize ['pi:nəlaiz] bestrafen; ~ty ['penlti]
Strafe f; Sport: Strafpunkt m; ~ area
Fußball: Strafraum m; ~ kick Fußball: Freistoß m.
penance ['penəns] Buße f.
pence [pens] pl. von penny.
pencil ['pensl] 1. Bleistift m; 2. zeichnen; (mit Bleistift) anzeichnen od.
anstreichen; Augenbrauen nachziehen; ~sharpener Bleistiftspitzer
m.
pendant ['pendənt] Anhänger m.
pending ['pendiŋ] 1. ⚖ schwebend;
2. prp. während; bis zu.
pendulum ['pendjuləm] Pendel n.
penetra|ble □ ['penitrəbl] durchdringbar; ~te [.reit] durchdringen;
ergründen; eindringen (in acc.);
vordringen (to bis zu); ~tion [peni-

'treiʃən] Durch-, Eindringen n;
Scharfsinn m; ~tive □ ['penitrətiv]
durchdringend (a. fig.); eindringlich; scharfsinnig.
pen-friend ['penfrend] Brieffreund
(-in).
penguin orn. ['peŋgwin] Pinguin m.
penholder ['penhouldə] Federhalter m.
peninsula [pi'ninsjulə] Halbinsel f.
peniten|ce ['penitəns] Buße f, Reue
f; ~t 1. □ reuig, bußfertig; 2. Büßer(in); ~tiary [peni'tenʃəri] Besserungsanstalt f; Am. Zuchthaus n.
pen|knife ['pennaif] Taschenmesser
n; ~man Schönschreiber m;
Schriftsteller m; ~name Schriftstellername m, Pseudonym n.
pennant ♧ ['penənt] Wimpel m.
penniless □ ['penilis] ohne Geld.
penny ['peni], pl. mst pence [pens]
(englischer) Penny (1/12 Schilling);
Am. Cent m; Kleinigkeit f; ~weight
englisches Pennygewicht (1 1/2
Gramm).
pension ['penʃən] 1. Pension f,
Ruhegehalt n; 2. oft ~ off pensionieren; ~ary [.nəri, .nə]
Pensionär(in).
pensive □ ['pensiv] gedankenvoll.
pent [pent] pret. u. p.p. von pen 2;
~up aufgestaut (Zorn etc.).
Pentecost ['pentikɔst] Pfingsten n.
penthouse ['penthaus] Schutzdach
n; Dachwohnung f auf e-m Hochhaus.
penu|rious □ [pi'njuəriəs] geizig;
~ry ['penjuri] Armut f; Mangel m.
people ['pi:pl] 1. Volk n, Nation f;
coll. die Leute pl.; man; 2. bevölkern.
pepper ['pepə] 1. Pfeffer m; 2. pfeffern; ~mint ♧ Pfefferminze f; ~y
□ [.əri] pfefferig; fig. hitzig.
per [pə:] per, durch, für; laut; je.
perambulat|e [pə'ræmbjuleit]
(durch)wandern; bereisen; ~or
['præmbjuleitə] Kinderwagen m.
perceive [pə'si:v] (be)merken, wahrnehmen; empfinden; erkennen.
per cent [pə'sent] Prozent n.
percentage [pə'sentidʒ] Prozentsatz
m; Prozente n/pl.; fig. Teil m.
percept|ible □ [pə'septəbl] wahrnehmbar; ~ion [.pʃən] Wahrnehmung(svermögen n) f; Erkenntnis
f; Auffassung(skraft) f.
perch [pə:tʃ] 1. ichth. Barsch m;
Rute f (5,029 m); (Sitz)Stange f für
Vögel; 2. (sich) setzen; sitzen.
perchance [pə'tʃɑ:ns] zufällig; vielleicht.
percolate ['pə:kəleit] durchtropfen,
durchsickern (lassen); sickern.
percussion [pə:'kʌʃən] Schlag m;
Erschütterung f; ♪ Abklopfen n.
perdition [pə:'diʃən] Verderben n.
peregrination[perigri'neiʃən]Wanderschaft f; Wanderung f.

**peremptory** □ [pə'remptəri] bestimmt; zwingend; rechthaberisch.
**perennial** □ [pə'renjəl] dauernd; immerwährend; ♀ perennierend.
**perfect 1.** ['pə:fikt] □ vollkommen; vollendet; gänzlich, völlig; **2.** [„] *a.* ~ *tense gr.* Perfekt *n*; **3.** [pə-'fekt] vervollkommnen; vollenden; **„ion** [„kʃən] Vollendung *f*; Vollkommenheit *f*; *fig.* Gipfel *m*.
**perfidious** □ [pə:'fidiəs] treulos (*to* gegen), verräterisch.
**perfidy** ['pə:fidi] Treulosigkeit *f*.
**perforate** ['pə:fəreit] durchlöchern.
**perforce** [pə'fɔ:s] notgedrungen.
**perform** [pə'fɔ:m] verrichten; ausführen; tun; *Pflicht etc.* erfüllen; *thea.*, ♪ aufführen, spielen, vortragen (*a. v/i.*); **„ance** [„məns] Verrichtung *f*; *thea.* Aufführung *f*; Vortrag *m*; Leistung *f*; **„er** [„mə] Vortragende(r *m*) *f*.
**perfume 1.** ['pə:fju:m] Wohlgeruch *m*; Parfüm *n*; **2.** [pə'fju:m] parfümieren; **„ry** [„məri] Parfümerie(n *pl.*) *f*.
**perfunctory** □ [pə'fʌŋktəri] mechanisch; oberflächlich.
**perhaps** [pə'hæps, præps] vielleicht.
**peril** ['peril] **1.** Gefahr *f*; **2.** gefährden; **„ous** □ [„ləs] gefährlich.
**period** ['piəriəd] Periode *f*; Zeitraum *m*; *gr.* Punkt *m*; langer Satz; (Unterrichts)Stunde *f*; *mst* ~*s pl.* ♀ Periode *f*; **„ic** [piəri'ɔdik] periodisch; **„ical** [„kəl] **1.** □ periodisch; **2.** Zeitschrift *f*.
**perish** ['periʃ] umkommen, zugrunde gehen; **„able** □ [„ʃəbl] vergänglich; leicht verderblich; **„ing** □ [„ʃiŋ] vernichtend, tödlich.
**periwig** ['periwig] Perücke *f*.
**perjur|e** ['pə:dʒə]: ~ *o.s.* falsch schwören; **„y** [„əri] Meineid *m*.
**perk** F [pə:k] *v/i. mst* ~ *up* selbstbewußt auftreten; sich wieder erholen; *v/t.* recken; ~ *o.s.* (*up*) sich putzen.
**perky** □ ['pə:ki] keck, dreist; flott.
**perm** F [pə:m] **1.** Dauerwelle *f*; **2.** *j-m* Dauerwellen machen.
**permanen|ce** ['pə:mənəns] Dauer *f*; **„t** □ [„nt] dauernd, ständig; dauerhaft; Dauer...; ~ *wave* Dauerwelle *f*.
**permea|ble** □ ['pə:mjəbl] durchlässig; **„te** ['pə:mieit] durchdringen; eindringen.
**permissi|ble** □ [pə'misəbl] zulässig; **„on** [„ʃən] Erlaubnis *f*.
**permit 1.** [pə'mit] erlauben, gestatten; **2.** ['pə:mit] Erlaubnis *f*, Genehmigung *f*; Passierschein *m*.
**pernicious** □ [pə:'niʃəs] verderblich; ♀ bösartig.
**perpendicular** □ [pə:pən'dikjulə] senkrecht; aufrecht; steil.
**perpetrate** ['pə:pitreit] verüben.
**perpetu|al** □ [pə'petjuəl] fort-

während, ewig; **„ate** [„ueit] verewigen.
**perplex** [pə'pleks] verwirren; **„ity** [„siti] Verwirrung *f*.
**perquisites** ['pə:kwizits] *pl.* Nebeneinkünfte *pl.*
**persecut|e** ['pə:sikju:t] verfolgen; **„ion** [pə:si'kju:ʃən] Verfolgung *f*; **„or** ['pə:sikju:tə] Verfolger *m*.
**persever|ance** [pə:si'viərəns] Beharrlichkeit *f*, Ausdauer *f*; **„e** [pə:-si'viə] beharren; aushalten.
**persist** [pə'sist] beharren (*in auf dat.*); **„ence**, **„ency** [„təns, „si] Beharrlichkeit *f*; **„ent** □ [„nt] beharrlich.
**person** ['pə:sn] Person *f* (*a. gr.*); Persönlichkeit *f*; *thea.* Rolle *f*; **„age** [„nidʒ] Persönlichkeit *f*; *thea.* Charakter *m*; **„al** □ [„nl] persönlich (*a. gr.*); *attr.* Personal...; Privat...; eigen; **„ality** [pə:sə'næliti] Persönlichkeit *f*; *personalities pl.* persönliche Bemerkungen *f/pl.*; **„ate** ['pə:səneit] darstellen; sich ausgeben für; *fig.* [pə:'sənifai] verkörpern; **„nel** [pə:sə'nel] Personal *n*.
**perspective** [pə'spektiv] Perspektive *f*; Ausblick *m*, Fernsicht *f*.
**perspex** ['pə:speks] Plexiglas *n*.
**perspicuous** □ [pə'spikjuəs] klar.
**perspir|ation** [pə:spə'reiʃən] Schwitzen *n*; Schweiß *m*; **„e** [pəs-'paiə] (aus)schwitzen.
**persua|de** [pə'sweid] überreden; überzeugen; **„sion** [„eiʒən] Überredung *f*; Überzeugung *f*; Glaube *m*; **„sive** □ [„eisiv] überredend, überzeugend.     [weis.\
**pert** □ [pə:t] keck, vorlaut, nase-\
**pertain** [pə:'tein] (*to* gehören (*dat. od. zu*); betreffen (*acc.*).
**pertinacious** □ [pə:ti'neiʃəs] hartnäckig, zäh.
**pertinent** □ ['pə:tinənt] sachdienlich, -gemäß; zur Sache gehörig.
**perturb** [pə'tə:b] beunruhigen; stören.
**perus|al** [pə'ru:zəl] sorgfältige Durchsicht *f*; **„e** [„u:z] durchlesen; prüfen.
**pervade** [pə:'veid] durchdringen.
**pervers|e** □ [pə'və:s] verkehrt; ♂ pervers; eigensinnig; vertrackt (*Sache*); **„ion** [„ʃən] Verdrehung *f*; Abkehr *f*; **„ity** [„siti] Verkehrtheit *f*; ♂ Perversität *f*; Eigensinn *m*.
**pervert 1.** [pə'və:t] verdrehen; verführen; **2.** ♂ ['pə:və:t] perverser Mensch.
**pessimism** ['pesimizəm] Pessimismus *m*.
**pest** [pest] Pest *f*, Plage *f*; Schädling *m*; **„er** ['pestə] belästigen.
**pesti|ferous** □ ['pesti'fərəs] krankheiterregend; **„lence** ['pestiləns] Seuche *f*, *bsd.* Pest *f*; **„lent** [„nt] gefährlich; *co.* verdammt; **„lential**

□ [pesti'lenʃəl] pestartig; verderbenbringend.

**pet** [pet] **1.** üble Laune; zahmes Tier; Liebling *m*; **2.** Lieblings...; ~ *dog* Schoßhund *m*; ~ *name* Kosename *m*; **3.** (ver)hätscheln; knutschen.

**petal** ♀ ['petl] Blütenblatt *n*.

**petition** [pi'tiʃən] **1.** Bitte *f*; Bittschrift *f*, Eingabe *f*; **2.** bitten, ersuchen; e-e Eingabe machen.

**petrify** ['petrifai] versteinern.

**petrol** *mot.* ['petrəl] Benzin *n*; ~ station Tankstelle *f*.

**petticoat** ['petikout] Unterrock *m*.

**pettish** □ ['petiʃ] launisch.

**petty** □ ['peti] klein, geringfügig.

**petulant** ['petjulənt] gereizt.

**pew** [pju:] Kirchensitz *m*, -bank *f*.

**pewter** ['pju:tə] Zinn(gefäße *n/pl.*) *n*.

**phantasm** ['fæntæzəm] Trugbild *n*.

**phantom** ['fæntəm] Phantom *n*, Trugbild *n*; Gespenst *n*.

**Pharisee** ['færisi:] Pharisäer *m*.

**pharmacy** ['fɑ:məsi] Pharmazie *f*; Apotheke *f*.  [Phasen.)

**phase** [feiz] Phase *f*; ~d [feizd] in)

**pheasant** *orn.* ['feznt] Fasan *m*.

**phenomen|on** [fi'nɔminən], *pl.* ~a [~nə] Phänomen *n*, Erscheinung *f*.

**phial** ['faiəl] Phiole *f*. Fläschchen *n*.

**philander** [fi'lændə] flirten.

**philanthropist** [fi'lænθrəpist] Menschenfreund(in).

**philolog|ist** [fi'lɔlədʒist] Philolog|e *m*, -in *f*; ~y [~dʒi] Philologie *f*.

**philosoph|er** [fi'lɔsəfə] Philosoph *m*; ~ize [~faiz] philosophieren; ~y [~fi] Philosophie *f*.

**phlegm** [flem] Schleim *m*; Phlegma *n*.

**phone** F [foun] *s. telephone.*

**phonetics** [fou'netiks] *pl.* Phonetik *f*, Lautbildungslehre *f*.

**phon(e)y** *Am. sl.* ['founi] **1.** Fälschung *f*; Schwindler *m*; **2.** unecht.

**phosphorus** ['fɔsfərəs] Phosphor *m*.

**photograph** ['foutəgrɑːf] **1.** Photographie *f* (*Bild*); **2.** photographieren; ~er [fə'tɔgrəfə] Photograph (-in); ~y [~fi] Photographie *f*.

**phrase** [freiz] **1.** (Rede)Wendung *f*, Redensart *f*, Ausdruck *m*; **2.** ausdrücken.

**physic|al** □ ['fizikəl] physisch; körperlich; physikalisch; ~ *education*, ~ *training* Leibeserziehung *f*; ~ian [fi'ziʃən] Arzt *m*; ~ist ['fizisist] Physiker *m*; ~s [~iks] *sg.* Physik *f*.

**physique** [fi'zi:k] Körperbau *m*.

**piano** ['pjænou] Klavier *n*.

**piazza** [pi'ætsə] Piazza *f*, (Markt-) Platz *m*; *Am.* große Veranda.

**pick** [pik] Auswahl *f*; = *pickaxe*; **2.** auf-, wegnehmen; pflücken; (herum)stochern; *in der Nase* bohren; abnagen; *Schloß* knacken; *Streit* suchen; auswählen; (auf-) picken; bestehlen; ~ *out* auswählen;

heraussuchen; ~ *up* aufreißen, aufbrechen; aufnehmen, auflesen; sich *e-e Fremdsprache* aneignen; erfassen; (*im Auto*) mitnehmen, abholen; *Täter* ergreifen; gesund werden; ~-a-back ['pikəbæk] huckepack; ~axe Spitzhacke *f*.

**picket** ['pikit] **1.** Pfahl *m*; ⚔ Feldwache *f*; Streikposten *m*; **2.** einpfählen; an e-n Pfahl binden; mit Streikposten besetzen.

**picking** ['pikiŋ] Picken *n*, Pflücken *n*; Abfall *m*; *mst* ~s *pl.* Nebengewinn *m*.

**pickle** ['pikl] **1.** Pökel *m*; Eingepökelte(s) *n*, Pickles *pl.*; F mißliche Lage; **2.** (ein)pökeln; ~d *herring* Salzhering *m*.

**pick|lock** ['piklɔk] Dietrich *m*; ~pocket Taschendieb *m*; ~up Ansteigen *n*; Tonabnehmer *m*; Kleinlieferwagen *m*; *sl.* Straßenbekanntschaft *f*.

**picnic** ['piknik] Picknick *n*.

**pictorial** [pik'tɔ:riəl] **1.** □ malerisch; illustriert; **2.** Illustrierte *f*.

**picture** ['piktʃə] **1.** Bild *n*, Gemälde *n*; *et.* Bildschönes; ~s *pl.* F Kino *n*; *attr.* Bilder...; *put s.o. in the* ~ j. ins Bild setzen, j. informieren; **2.** (aus-) malen; sich *et.* ausmalen; ~ postcard Ansichtskarte *f*; ~sque [piktʃə'resk] malerisch.

**pie** [pai] Pastete *f*; Obsttorte *f*.

**piebald** ['paibɔ:ld] (bunt)scheckig.

**piece** [pi:s] **1.** Stück *n*; Geschütz *n*; Gewehr *n*; Teil *n* e-s *Services*; *Schach- etc.* Figur *f*; *a* ~ *of advice* ein Rat; *a* ~ *of news* e-e Neuigkeit; *of a* ~ gleichmäßig; *give s.o. a* ~ *of one's mind* j-m gründlich die Meinung sagen; *take to* ~s zerlegen; **2.** *a.* ~ *up* flicken, ausbessern; ~ together zs.-stellen, -setzen, -stücken, -flicken; ~ *out* ausfüllen; ~meal ['pi:smi:l] stückweise; ~work Akkordarbeit *f*.

**pieplant** *Am.* ['paiplɑ:nt] Rhabarber *m*.

**pier** [piə] Pfeiler *m*; Wellenbrecher *m*; Pier *m*, *f*, Hafendamm *m*, Mole *f*, Landungsbrücke *f*.

**pierce** [piəs] durchbohren; durchdringen; eindringen (*in acc.*).

**piety** ['paiəti] Frömmigkeit *f*; Pietät *f*.

**pig** [pig] Ferkel *n*; Schwein *n*.

**pigeon** ['pidʒin] Taube *f*; ~hole **1.** Fach *n*; **2.** in ein Fach legen.

**pig|headed** ['pig'hedid] dickköpfig; ~iron ['pigaiən] Roheisen *n*; ~skin Schweinsleder *n*; ~sty ['pigstai] Schweinestall *m*; ~tail (Haar)Zopf *m*.

**pike** [paik] ⚔ Pike *f*; Spitze *f*; *ichth.* Hecht *m*; Schlagbaum *m*; gebührenpflichtige Straße.

**pile** [pail] **1.** (Scheiter)Haufen *m*; Stoß *m* (*Holz*); großes Gebäude; ⚡ Batterie *f*; Pfahl *m*; Haar *n*;

Noppe *f*; ~*s pl.* &#x263F; Hämorrhoiden *f/pl.*; (*atomic*) ~ *phys.* Atommeiler *m*, Reaktor *m*; 2. *oft* ~ *up*, ~ *on* auf-, anhäufen, aufschichten.

**pilfer** ['pilfə] mausen, stibitzen.

**pilgrim** ['pilgrim] Pilger *m*; ~**age** [~midʒ] Pilgerfahrt *f*.

**pill** [pil] Pille *f*.

**pillage** ['pilidʒ] 1. Plünderung *f*; 2. plündern.

**pillar** ['pilə] Pfeiler *m*, Ständer *m*; Säule *f*; ~**box** Briefkasten *m*.

**pillion** *mot.* ['piljən] Soziussitz *m*.

**pillory** ['piləri] 1. Pranger *m*; 2. an den Pranger stellen; anprangern.

**pillow** ['pilou] (Kopf)Kissen *n*; ~**case**, ~**slip** (Kissen)Bezug *m*,

**pilot** ['pailət] 1. &#x2114; Pilot *m*; ⨁ Lotse *m*; *fig.* Führer *m*; 2. lotsen, steuern; ~**balloon** Versuchsballon *m*.

**pimp** [pimp] 1. Kuppler(in); 2. kuppeln.

**pin** [pin] 1. (Steck-, Krawatten-, Hut- *etc.*)Nadel *f*; Reißnagel *m*; Pflock *m*; ♪ Wirbel *m*; Kegel *m*; 2. (an)heften; befestigen; *fig.* festnageln.

**pinafore** ['pinəfɔ:] Schürze *f*.

**pincers** ['pinsəz] *pl.* Kneifzange *f*.

**pinch** [pintʃ] 1. Kniff *m*; Prise *f* (*Tabak etc.*); Druck *m*, Not *f*; 2. *v/t.* kneifen, zwicken; F klauen; *v/i.* drücken; in Not sein; knausern.

**pinch-hit** *Am.* ['pintʃhit] einspringen (*for* für).

**pincushion** ['pinkuʃin] Nadelkissen *n*.

**pine** [pain] 1. &#x2663; Kiefer *f*, Föhre *f*; 2. sich abhärmen; sich sehnen, schmachten; ~**apple** &#x2663; ['painæpl] Ananas *f*; ~**cone** Kiefernzapfen *m*.

**pinion** ['pinjən] 1. Flügel(spitze *f*) *m*; Schwungfeder *f*; ⨁ Ritzel *n* (*Antriebsrad*); 2. die Flügel beschneiden (*dat.*); *fig.* fesseln.

**pink** [piŋk] 1. &#x2663; Nelke *f*; Rosa *n*; *fig.* Gipfel *m*; 2. rosa(farben).

**pin-money** ['pinmʌni] Nadelgeld *n*.

**pinnacle** ['pinəkl] △ Zinne *f*, Spitztürmchen *n*; (Berg)Spitze *f*; *fig.* Gipfel *m*.

**pint** [paint] Pinte *f* (*0,57 od. Am. 0,47 Liter*).

**pioneer** [paiə'niə] 1. Pionier *m* (*a.* &#x2694;); 2. den Weg bahnen (für).

**pious** ['paiəs] fromm, religiös; pflichtgetreu.

**pip** [pip] *vet.* Pips *m*; *sl.* miese Laune; Obstkern *m*; Auge *n auf Würfeln etc.*; &#x2694; Stern *m* (*Rangabzeichen*).

**pipe** [paip] 1. Rohr *n*, Röhre *f*; Pfeife *f* (*a.* ♪); Flöte *f*; Lied *n e-s Vogels*; Luftröhre *f*; Pipe *f* (*Weinfaß = 477,3 Liter*); 2. pfeifen; quieken; ~**layer** ['paipleiə] Rohrleger *m*; *Am. pol.* Drahtzieher *m*;

~**line** Ölleitung *f*, Pipeline *f*; ~**r** ['paipə] Pfeifer *m*.

**piping** ['paipiŋ] 1. pfeifend; schrill (*Stimme*); ~ *hot* siedend heiß; 2. Rohrnetz *n*; *Schneiderei*: Paspel *f*.

**piquant** □ ['pi:kənt] pikant.

**pique** [pi:k] 1. Groll *m*; 2. *j-n* reizen; ~ *o.s. on* sich brüsten mit.

**piracy** ['paiərəsi] Seeräuberei *f*; Raubdruck *m von Büchern*; ~**te** [~rit] 1. Seeräuber(schiff *n*) *m*; Raubdrucker *m*; 2. unerlaubt nachdrucken.

**pistol** ['pistl] Pistole *f*.

**piston** ⨁ ['pistən] Kolben *m*; ~**rod** Kolbenstange *f*; ~**stroke** Kolbenhub *m*.

**pit** [pit] 1. Grube *f* (*a.* &#x2695;, *anat.*); &#x2697; Miete *f*; *thea.* Parterre *n*; Pockennarbe *f*; (Tier)Falle *f*; *Am. Börse*: Maklerstand *m*; *Am. Obst*-Stein *m*; 2. &#x2698; einmieten; mit Narben bedecken.

**pitch** [pitʃ] 1. Pech *n*; Stand(platz) *m*; Tonhöhe *f*; Grad *m*, Stufe *f*; Steigung *f*, Neigung *f*; Wurf *m*; ⛴ Stampfen *n*; 2. *v/t.* werfen; schleudern; Zelt *etc.* aufschlagen; ♪ stimmen (*a. fig.*); ~ *too high fig.* Ziel *etc.* zu hoch stecken; *v/i.* &#x2695; (sich) lagern; fallen; ⛴ stampfen; ~ *into* F herfallen über (*acc.*).

**pitcher** ['pitʃə] Krug *m*.

**pitchfork** ['pitʃfɔ:k] Heu-, Mistgabel *f*; ♪ Stimmgabel *f*.

**piteous** □ ['pitiəs] kläglich.

**pitfall** ['pitfɔ:l] Fallgrube *f*, Falle *f*.

**pith** [piθ] Mark *n*; *fig.* Kern *m*; Kraft *f*; ~**y** □ ['piθi] markig, kernig.

**pitiable** □ ['pitiəbl] erbärmlich.

**pitiful** □ ['pitifl] mitleidig; erbärmlich, jämmerlich (*a. contp.*).

**pitiless** □ ['pitilis] unbarmherzig.

**pittance** ['pitəns] Hungerlohn *m*.

**pity** ['piti] 1. Mitleid *n* (*on* mit); *it is a* ~ es ist schade; 2. bemitleiden.

**pivot** ['pivət] 1. ⨁ Zapfen *m*; (Tür-) Angel *f*; *fig.* Drehpunkt *m*; 2. sich drehen (*on, upon* um). [verrückt.]

**pixilated** *Am.* F ['piksileitid] leicht]

**placable** □ ['plækəbl] versöhnlich.

**placard** ['plækɑ:d] 1. Plakat *n*; 2. anschlagen; mit e-m Plakat bekleben.

**place** [pleis] 1. Platz *m*; Ort *m*; Stadt *f*; Stelle *f*; Stätte *f*; Stellung *f*; Aufgabe *f*; Anwesen *n*, Haus *n*, Wohnung *f*; ~ *of delivery* &#x2709; Erfüllungsort *m*; *give* ~ *to j-m* Platz machen; *in* ~ *of* an Stelle (*gen.*); *out of* ~ fehl am Platz; 2. stellen, legen, setzen; *j-n* anstellen; Auftrag erteilen; *I can't place him fig.* ich weiß nicht, wo ich ihn hintun soll (*identifizieren*).

**placid** □ ['plæsid] sanft; ruhig.

**plagiarism** ['pleidʒjərizəm] Plagiat *n*; ~**ize** [~raiz] abschreiben.

**plague** [pleig] 1. Plage *f*; Seuche *f*; Pest *f*; 2. plagen, quälen.
**plaice** *ichth.* [pleis] Scholle *f*.
**plaid** [plæd] *schottisches* Plaid.
**plain** [plein] 1. ˘ flach, eben; klar; deutlich; rein; einfach, schlicht; unscheinbar; offen, ehrlich; einfarbig; 2. *adv.* klar, deutlich; 3. Ebene *f*, Fläche *f*; *bsd. Am.* Prärie *f*; **~-clothes man** ['pleinklouðz mən] Geheimpolizist *m*; **~ dealing** ehrliche Handlungsweise; **~-dealing** ehrlich.
**plainsman** ['pleinzmən] Flachlandbewohner *m*; *Am.* Präriebewohner *m*.
**plaint|iff** ɡ̇ʒ ['pleintif] Kläger(in); **~ive** □ [~iv] traurig, klagend.
**plait** [plæt, *Am.* pleit] 1. *Haar- etc.* Flechte *f*; Zopf *m*; 2. flechten.
**plan** [plæn] 1. Plan *m*; 2. e-n Plan machen von *od.* zu; *fig.* planen.
**plane** [plein] 1. flach, eben; 2. Ebene *f*, Fläche *f*; ⚒ Tragfläche *f*; Flugzeug *n*; *fig.* Stufe *f*; ⊕ Hobel *m*; 3. ebnen; (ab)hobeln; ⚒ fliegen.
**plank** [plæŋk] 1. Planke *f*, Bohle *f*, Diele *f*; *Am. pol.* Programmpunkt *m*; 2. dielen; verschalen; **~ down** *sl., Am.* F Geld auf den Tisch legen.
**plant** [plɑːnt] 1. Pflanze *f*; ⊕ Anlage *f*; Fabrik *f*; 2. (an-, ein)pflanzen (*a. fig.*); (auf)stellen; anlegen; *Schlag* verpassen; bepflanzen; besiedeln; **~ation** [plæn'teiʃən] Pflanzung *f* (*a. fig.*); Plantage *f*; Besiedelung *f*; **~er** ['plɑːntə] Pflanzer *m*.
**plaque** [plɑːk] Platte *f*; Gedenktafel *f*.
**plash** [plæʃ] platschen.
**plaster** ['plɑːstə] 1. *pharm.* Pflaster *n*; ⊕ Putz *m*; *mst* **~ of Paris** Gips *m*, Stuck *m*; 2. bepflastern; verputzen.
**plastic** ['plæstik] 1. (**~ally**) plastisch; Plastik...; 2. *oft* **~s** *pl.* Plastik(material) *n*, Kunststoff *m*.
**plat** [plæt] *s.* plait; *s.* plot 1.
**plate** [pleit] 1. *allg.* Platte *f*; Bild-Tafel *f*; Schild *n*; *Kupfer*-Stich *m*; Tafelsilber *n*; Teller *m*; *Am. Baseball*: (Schlag)Mal *n*; ⊕ Grobblech *n*; 2. plattieren; ☓, ⚓ panzern.
**platform** ['plætfɔːm] Plattform *f*; *geogr.* Hochebene *f*; ⛟ Bahnsteig *m*; *Am. bsd.* Plattform *f am Wagenende*; Rednerbühne *f*; *pol.* Parteiprogramm *n*; *bsd. Am. pol.* Aktionsprogramm *n im Wahlkampf*.
**platinum** *min.* ['plætinəm] Platin *n*.
**platitude** *fig.* ['plætitjuːd] Plattheit *f*.
**platoon** ☓ [plə'tuːn] Zug *m*.
**plat(t)en** ['plætən] (Schreibmaschinen)Walze *f*.
**platter** ['plætə] (Servier)Platte *f*.
**plaudit** ['plɔːdit] Beifall *m*.
**plausible** □ ['plɔːzəbl] glaubhaft.

**play** [plei] 1. Spiel *n*; Schauspiel *n*; ⊕ Spiel *n*, Gang *m*; Spielraum *m*; 2. spielen; ⊕ laufen; **~ upon** einwirken auf (*acc.*); **~ off** *fig.* ausspielen (*against* gegen); **~ed out** erledigt; **~-bill** ['pleibil] Theaterzettel *m*; **~-book** *thea.* Textbuch *n*; **~-boy** Playboy *m*; **~er** ['pleiə] (Schau)Spieler(in); **~-piano** elektrisches Klavier; **~fellow** Spielgefährt|e *m*, -in *f*; **~ful** ◑ [~ful] spielerisch, scherzhaft; **~goer** ['pleigouə] Theaterbesucher(in); **~ground** Spielplatz *m*; Schulhof *m*; **~house** Schauspielhaus *n*; *Am.* Miniaturhaus *n für Kinder*; **~mate** *s.* playfellow; **~thing** Spielzeug *n*; **~wright** Bühnenautor *m*, Dramatiker *m*.
**plea** [pliː] ɡ̇ʒ Einspruch *m*; Ausrede *f*; Gesuch *n*; **on the ~ of** *od.* **that** unter dem Vorwand (*gen.*) *od.* daß.
**plead** [pliːd] *v/i.* plädieren; **~ for** für *j*-n sprechen; sich einsetzen für; **~ guilty** sich schuldig bekennen; *v/t.* Sache vertreten; als Beweis anführen; **~er** ɡ̇ʒ ['pliːdə] Verteidiger *m*; **~ing** □ [~diŋ] Schriftsatz *m*.
**pleasant** □ ['pleznt] angenehm; erfreulich; **~ry** [~tri] Scherz *m*, Spaß *m*.
**please** [pliːz] *v/i.* gefallen; belieben; *if you ~* iro. stellen Sie sich vor; **~ come in!** bitte, treten Sie ein!; *v/t. j*-m gefallen, angenehm sein; befriedigen; **~ yourself** tun Sie, was Ihnen gefällt; **be ~d to do et.** gerne tun; **be ~d with** Vergnügen haben an (*dat.*); **~d** erfreut; zufrieden.
**pleasing** □ ['pliːziŋ] angenehm.
**pleasure** ['pleʒə] Vergnügen *n*, Freude *f*; Belieben *n*; *attr.* Vergnügungs...; *at* **~** nach Belieben; **~-ground** (Vergnügungs)Park *m*.
**pleat** [pliːt] 1. (Plissee)Falte *f*; 2. fälteln, plissieren.
**pledge** [pledʒ] 1. Pfand *n*; Zutrinken *n*; Gelöbnis *n*; 2. verpfänden; *j*-m zutrinken; **he ~d himself** er gelobte.
**plenary** ['pliːnəri] Voll...
**plenipotentiary** [plenipə'tenʃəri] Bevollmächtigte(r *m*) *f*. [reichlich.)
**plenteous** □ *poet.* ['plentjəs] voll,)
**plentiful** □ ['plentiful] reichlich.
**plenty** ['plenti] 1. Fülle *f*, Überfluß *m*; **~ of** reichlich; 2. F reichlich.
**pliable** □ ['plaiəbl] biegsam; *fig.* geschmeidig, nachgiebig.
**pliancy** ['plaiənsi] Biegsamkeit *f*.
**pliers** ['plaiəz] *pl.* (*a pair of* **~** *pl.* eine) (Draht-, Kombi)Zange.
**plight** [plait] 1. *Ehre, Wort* verpfänden; verloben; 2. Gelöbnis *n*; Zustand *m*, (Not)Lage *f*.
**plod** [plɔd] *a.* **~ along**, **~ on** sich dahinschleppen; sich plagen, schuften.

**plot** [plɔt] **1.** Platz *m*; Parzelle *f*; Plan *m*; Komplott *n*, Anschlag *m*; Intrige *f*; Handlung *f* e-s Dramas etc.; **2.** v/t. aufzeichnen; planen, anzetteln; v/i. intrigieren.

**plough**, *Am. mst* **plow** [plau] **1.** Pflug *m*; **2.** pflügen; (a. fig.) furchen; **~man** ['plauman] Pflüger *m*; **~share** ['plauʃεə] Pflugschar *f*.

**pluck** [plʌk] **1.** Mut *m*, Schneid *m*, *f*; Innereien *f/pl.*; Zug *m*, Ruck *m*; **2.** pflücken; *Vogel* rupfen (a. fig.); reißen; **~** *at* zerren an; **~** *up courage* Mut fassen; **~y** F[̣], ['plʌki] mutig.

**plug** [plʌg] **1.** Pflock *m*; Dübel *m*; Stöpsel *m*; *f* Stecker *m*; Zahn-Plombe *f*; Priem *m* (*Tabak*); *Am. Radio:* Reklamehinweis *m*; alter Gaul; **~** socket Steckdose *f*; **2.** v/t. zu-, verstopfen; *Zahn* plombieren; stöpseln; *Am.* F *im Rundfunk etc.* Reklame machen für *et.*

**plum** [plʌm] Pflaume *f*; Rosine *f* (a. fig.).

**plumage** ['plu:midʒ] Gefieder *n*.

**plumb** [plʌm] **1.** lotrecht; gerade; richtig; **2.** (Blei)Lot *n*; **3.** v/t. lotrecht machen; loten; sondieren (a. fig.); F Wasser- od. Gasleitungen legen in; v/i. F als Rohrleger arbeiten; **~er** ['plʌmə] Klempner *m*, Installateur *m*; **~ing** [~min] Klempnerarbeit *f*; Rohrleitungen *f/pl.*

**plume** [plu:m] **1.** Feder *f*; Federbusch *m*; **2.** mit Federn schmücken; *die Federn* putzen; **~** *o.s. on* sich brüsten mit.

**plummet** ['plʌmit] Senkblei *n*.

**plump** [plʌmp] **1.** adj. drall, prall, mollig; F □ glatt (*Absage etc.*); **2.**(hin)plumpsen (lassen); **3.** Plumps *m*; **4.** F adv. geradewegs.

**plum pudding** ['plʌm'pudiŋ] Plumpudding *m*.

**plunder** ['plʌndə] **1.** Plünderung *f*; Raub *m*, Beute *f*; **2.** plündern.

**plunge** [plʌndʒ] **1.** (Unter)Tauchen *n*; (Kopf)Sprung *m*; Sturz *m*; *make od.* take the **~** den entscheidenden Schritt tun; **2.** (unter-)tauchen; (sich) stürzen (*into in acc.*); *Schwert etc.* stoßen; *f* stampfen.

**plunk** [plʌŋk] v/t. *Saite* zupfen; et. hinplumpsen lassen, hinwerfen; v/i. (hin)plumpsen, fallen.

**pluperfect** gr. ['plu:'pə:fikt] Plusquamperfekt *n*.

**plural** gr. ['pluərəl] Plural *m*, Mehrzahl *f*; **~ity** [pluə'ræliti] Vielheit *f*, Mehrheit *f*; Mehrzahl *f*.

**plus** [plʌs] **1.** prp. plus; **2.** adj. positiv; **3.** Plus *n*; Mehr *n*.

**plush** [plʌʃ] Plüsch *m*.

**ply** [plai] **1.** Lage *f* *Tuch etc.*; Strähne *f*; *fig.* Neigung *f*; **2.** v/t. fleißig anwenden; *j-m* zusetzen, *j-n* überhäufen; v/i. regelmäßig fahren; **~wood** ['plaiwud] Sperrholz *n*.

**pneumatic** [nju(:)'mætik] **1.** (**~ally**) Luft...; pneumatisch; **2.** Luftreifen *m*.

**pneumonia** &[nju(:)'mounjə] Lungenentzündung *f*.

**poach** [poutʃ] wildern; *Erde* zertreten; **~ed eggs** *pl.* verlorene Eier *n/pl.*

**poacher** ['poutʃə] Wilddieb *m*.

**pock** & [pɔk] Pocke *f*, Blatter *f*.

**pocket** ['pɔkit] **1.** Tasche *f*; *f* Luft-Loch *n*; **2.** einstecken (a. fig.); *Am. pol.* Gesetzesvorlage nicht unterschreiben; *Gefühl* unterdrücken; **3.** Taschen...; **~book** Notizbuch *n*; Brieftasche *f*; *Am.* Geldbeutel *m*; Taschenbuch *n*.

**pod** ♀ [pɔd] Hülse *f*, Schale *f*, Schote *f*.

**poem** ['pouim] Gedicht *n*.

**poet** ['pouit] Dichter *m*; **~ess** [~tis] Dichterin *f*; **~ic(al** □) [pou'etik(əl)] dichterisch; **~ics** [~ks] sg. Poetik *f*; **~ry** ['pouitri] Dichtkunst *f*; Dichtung *f*, coll. Dichtungen *f/pl.*

**poignan|cy** ['pɔinənsi] Schärfe *f*; **~t** [~nt] scharf; *fig.* eindringlich.

**point** [pɔint] **1.** Spitze *f*; Pointe *f*; Landspitze *f*; *gr.*, Â, *phys. etc.* Punkt *m*; Fleck *m*, Stelle *f*; ⚓ Kompaßstrich *m*; Auge *n auf Karten etc.*; Grad *m*; (springender) Punkt; Zweck *m*; *fig.* Eigenschaft *f*; **~s** *pl.* ⚙ Weichen *f/pl.*; **~** *of view* Stand-, Gesichtspunkt *m*; *the* **~** *is that ...* die Sache ist die, daß ...; *make a* **~** *of s.th.* auf *et.* bestehen; *in* **~** *of* in Hinsicht auf (*acc.*); *off od. beside the* **~** nicht zur Sache (gehörig); *on the* **~** *of ger.* im Begriff zu *inf.*; *win on* **~s** nach Punkten siegen; *to the* **~** zur Sache (gehörig); **2.** v/t. (zu)spitzen; *oft* **~** *out* zeigen, hinweisen auf (*acc.*); punktieren; **~** *at Waffe etc.* richten auf (*acc.*); v/i. **~** *at* weisen auf (*acc.*); **~** *to* nach e-r Richtung weisen; **~ed** □ ['pɔintid] spitz(ig), Spitz...; *fig.* scharf; **~er** [~tə] Zeiger *m*; Zeigestock *m*; Hühnerhund *m*; **~less** [~tlis] stumpf; witzlos; zwecklos.

**poise** [pɔiz] **1.** Gleichgewicht *n*; Haltung *f*; **2.** v/t. im Gleichgewicht erhalten; *Kopf etc.* tragen, halten; v/i. schweben.

**poison** ['pɔizn] **1.** Gift *n*; **2.** vergiften; **~ous** □ [~nəs] giftig (a. fig.).

**poke** [pouk] **1.** Stoß *m*, Puff *m*; **2.** v/t. stoßen; schüren; *Nase etc. in et.* stecken; **~** *fun at* sich über *j-n* lustig machen; v/i. stoßen; stochern.

**poker** ['poukə] Feuerhaken *m*.

**poky** ['pouki] eng; schäbig; erbärmlich. [*m.*]

**polar** ['poulə] polar; **~** *bear* Eisbär[ ]

**Pole**[1] [poul] Pole *m*, Polin *f*.

**pole**[2] [~] Pol *m*; Stange *f*, Mast *m*; Deichsel *f*; (Sprung)Stab *m*.

**polecat** zo. ['poulkæt] Iltis m; Am. Skunk m.

**polemic** [pɔ'lemik], a. ~al □ [~kəl] polemisch; feindselig.

**pole-star** ['poulstɑː] Polarstern m; fig. Leitstern m.

**police** [pə'liːs] 1. Polizei f; 2. überwachen; ~man Polizist m; ~office Polizeipräsidium n; ~officer Polizeibeamte(r) m, Polizist m; ~station Polizeiwache f.

**policy** ['pɔlisi] Politik f; (Welt-) Klugheit f; Police f; Am. Zahlenlotto n.

**polio(myelitis)** 🌸 ['pouliou(maiə'laitis)] spinale Kinderlähmung.

**Polish¹** ['poulif] polnisch.

**polish²** ['pɔlif] 1. Politur f; fig. Schliff m; 2. polieren; fig. verfeinern.

**polite** □ [pə'lait] artig, höflich; fein; ~ness [~tnis] Höflichkeit f.

**politic** □ ['pɔlitik] politisch; schlau; ~al □ [pə'litikəl] politisch; staatlich; Staats..; ~ian [pɔli'tifən] Politiker m; ~s ['pɔlitiks] oft sg. Staatswissenschaft f, Politik f.

**polka** ['pɔlkə] Polka f; ~ dot Am. Punktmuster n auf Stoff.

**poll** [poul] 1. Wählerliste f; Stimmenzählung f; Wahl f; Stimmenzahl f; Umfrage f; co. Kopf m; 2. v/t. Stimmen erhalten; v/i. wählen; ~book ['poulbuk] Wählerliste f.

**pollen** 🌸 ['pɔlin] Blütenstaub m.

**polling-district** ['poulindistrikt] Wahlbezirk m.

**poll-tax** ['poultæks] Kopfsteuer f.

**pollute** [pə'luːt] beschmutzen, beflecken; entweihen.

**polyp|(e)** zo. ['pɔlip], ~us 🌸 [~pəs] Polyp m.

**pommel** ['pʌml] 1. Degen-, Sattel-Knopf m; 2. knuffen, schlagen.

**pomp** [pɔmp] Pomp m, Gepränge n.

**pompous** □ ['pɔmpəs] prunkvoll; hochtrabend; pompös.

**pond** [pɔnd] Teich m, Weiher m.

**ponder** ['pɔndə] v/t. erwägen; v/i. nachdenken; ~able [~ərəbl] wägbar; ~ous □ [~rəs] schwer(fällig).

**pontiff** ['pɔntif] Hohepriester m; Papst m.

**pontoon** ✕ [pɔn'tuːn] Ponton m; ~bridge Schiffsbrücke f.

**pony** ['pouni] Pony n, Pferdchen n.

**poodle** ['puːdl] Pudel m.

**pool** [puːl] 1. Teich m; Pfütze f, Lache f; (Schwimm)Becken n; (Spiel)Einsatz m; ✝ Ring m, Kartell n; ~ room Am. Billardspielhalle f; Wettannahmestelle f; 2. ✝ zu e-m Ring vereinigen; Gelder zs.-werfen.

**poop** ⚓ [puːp] Heck n; Achterhütte f.

**poor** □ [puə] arm(selig); dürftig; schlecht; ~house ['puəhaus] Armenhaus n; ~law ⚖ Armenrecht

n; ~ly [~li] 1. adj. unpäßlich; 2. adv. dürftig; ~ness ['puənis] Armut f.

**pop¹** [pɔp] 1. Knall m; ✝ Sprudel m; ✝ Schampus m; 2. v/t. knallen lassen; Am. Mais rösten; schnell wohin tun, stecken; v/i. puffen, knallen; mit adv. huschen; ~ in hereinplatzen.

**pop²** F [~] 1. populär, beliebt; 2. Schlager m; volkstümliche Musik.

**pop³** Am. F [~] Papa m, alter Herr.

**popcorn** Am. ['pɔpkɔːn] Puffmais m.

**pope** [poup] Papst m.

**poplar** 🌸 ['pɔplə] Pappel f.

**poppy** 🌸 ['pɔpi] Mohn m; ~cock Am. F Quatsch m.

**popu|lace** ['pɔpjuləs] Pöbel m; ~lar □ [~lə] Volks...; volkstümlich, populär; ~larity [pɔpju'læriti] Popularität f.

**populat|e** ['pɔpjuleit] bevölkern; ~ion [pɔpju'leifən] Bevölkerung f.

**populous** □ ['pɔpjuləs] volkreich.

**porcelain** ['pɔːslin] Porzellan n.

**porch** [pɔːtf] Vorhalle f, Portal n; Am. Veranda f.

**porcupine** zo. ['pɔːkjupain] Stachelschwein n.

**pore** [pɔː] 1. Pore f; 2. fig. brüten.

**pork** [pɔːk] Schweinefleisch n; ~barrel Am. sl. ['pɔːkbærəl] politisch berechnete Geldzuwendung der Regierung; ~y F ['pɔːki] 1. fett, dick; 2. Am. = porcupine.

**porous** □ ['pɔːrəs] porös.

**porpoise** ichth. ['pɔːpəs] Tümmler m.

**porridge** ['pɔridʒ] Haferbrei m.

**port** [pɔːt] 1. Hafen m; ⚓ (Pfort-, Lade)Luke f; ⚓ Backbord n; Portwein m; 2. ⚓ das Ruder nach der Backbordseite umlegen.

**portable** ['pɔːtəbl] transportabel.

**portal** ['pɔːtl] Portal n, Tor n.

**portend** [pɔː'tend] vorbedeuten.

**portent** ['pɔːtent] (bsd. üble) Vorbedeutung; Wunder n; ~ous □ [pɔː'tentəs] unheilvoll; wunderbar.

**porter** ['pɔːtə] Pförtner m; (Gepäck)Träger m; Porterbier n.

**portion** ['pɔːfən] 1. (An)Teil m; Portion f Essen; Erbteil n; Aussteuer f; fig. Los n; 2. teilen; ausstatten.

**portly** ['pɔːtli] stattlich.

**portmanteau** [pɔːt'mæntou] Handkoffer m. [nis n.]

**portrait** ['pɔːtrit] Porträt n, Bild-]

**portray** [pɔː'trei] (ab)malen, porträtieren; schildern; ~al [~eiəl] Porträtieren n; Schilderung f.

**pose** [pouz] 1. Pose f; 2. (sich) in Positur setzen; F sich hinstellen (as als); Frage aufwerfen.

**posh** sl. [pɔf] schick, erstklassig.

**position** [pə'zifən] Lage f, Stellung f (a. fig.); Stand m; fig. Standpunkt m.

**positive** ['pɔzətiv] **1.** ☐ bestimmt, ausdrücklich; feststehend, sicher; unbedingt; positiv; überzeugt; rechthaberisch; **2.** *das* Bestimmte; *gr.* Positiv *m*; *phot.* Positiv *n*.

**possess** [pə'zes] besitzen; beherrschen; *fig.* erfüllen; ~ o.s. of *et.* in Besitz nehmen; ~ed besessen; ~ion [~eʃən] Besitz *m*; *fig.* Besessenheit *f*; ~ive *gr.* [~esiv] **1.** besitzanzeigend; ~ *case* Genitiv *m*; **2.** Possessivpronomen *n*, besitzanzeigendes Fürwort; Genitiv *m*; ~or [~sə] Besitzer *m*.

**possib|ility** [pɔsə'biliti] Möglichkeit *f*; ~le ['pɔsəbl] möglich; ~ly [~li] möglicherweise, vielleicht; *if I* ~ *can* wenn ich irgend kann.

**post** [poust] **1.** Pfosten *m*; Posten *m*; Stelle *f*, Amt *n*; Post *f*; ~ *exchange Am.* ✗ Einkaufsstelle *f*; **2.** *v/t.* Plakat *etc.* anschlagen; postieren; eintragen; zur Post geben; per Post senden; ~ *up j-n* informieren; *v/i.* (dahin)eilen.

**postage** ['poustidʒ] Porto *n*; ~ stamp Briefmarke *f*.

**postal** ☐ ['poustəl] **1.** postalisch; Post...; ~ *order* Postanweisung *f*; **2.** *a.* ~ card *Am.* Postkarte *f*.

**postcard** ['poustkɑ:d] Postkarte *f*.

**poster** ['poustə] Plakat *n*, Anschlag *m*.

**posterior** [pɔs'tiəriə] **1.** ☐ später (to als); hinter; **2.** Hinterteil *n*.

**posterity** [pɔs'teriti] Nachwelt *f*; Nachkommenschaft *f*.

**post-free** ['poust'fri:] portofrei.

**post-graduate** ['poust'grædjuit] **1.** nach beendigter Studienzeit; **2.** Doktorand *m*.

**post-haste** ['poust'heist] eilig(st).

**posthumous** ☐ ['pɔstjuməs] nachgeboren; hinterlassen.

**post|man** ['poustmən] Briefträger *m*; ~mark **1.** Poststempel *m*; **2.** abstempeln; ~master Postamtsvorsteher *m*.

**post-mortem** ['poust'mɔ:tem] **1.** nach dem Tode; **2.** Leichenschau *f*.

**post|(-)office** ['poustɔtis] Postamt *n*; ~ box Post(schließ)fach *n*; ~-paid frankiert.

**postpone** [poust'poun] ver-, aufschieben; ~ment [~nmənt] Aufschub *m*. [tum *n*.]

**postscript** ['pousskript] Postskrip-

**postulate 1.** ['pɔstjulit] Forderung *f*; **2.** [~leit] fordern; (als gegeben) voraussetzen.

**posture** ['pɔstʃə] **1.** Stellung *f*, Haltung *f des Körpers*; **2.** (sich) zurechtstellen; posieren.

**post-war** ['poust'wɔ:] Nachkriegs...

**posy** ['pouzi] Blumenstrauß *m*.

**pot** [pɔt] **1.** Topf *m*; Kanne *f*; Tiegel *m*; **2.** in e-n Topf tun; einlegen.

**potation** [pou'teiʃən] *mst* ~s *pl.* Trinken *n*, Zecherei *f*; Trunk *m*.

**potato** [pə'teitou], *pl.* ~es Kartoffel *f*.

**pot-belly** ['pɔtbeli] Schmerbauch *m*.

**poten|cy** ['poutənsi] Macht *f*; Stärke *f*; ~t [~nt] mächtig; stark; ~tial [po'tenʃəl] **1.** potentiell; möglich; **2.** Leistungsfähigkeit *f*.

**pother** ['pɔðə] Aufregung *f*.

**pot|-herb** ['pɔthə:b] Küchenkraut *n*; ~house Kneipe *f*.

**potion** ['pouʃən] (Arznei)Trank *m*.

**potter**[1] ['pɔtə]: ~ *about* herumwerkeln.

**potter**[2] [~] Töpfer *m*; ~y [~əri] Töpferei *f*; Töpferware(n *pl.*) *f*.

**pouch** [pautʃ] **1.** Tasche *f*; Beutel *m*; **2.** einstecken; (sich) beuteln.

**poulterer** ['poultərə] Geflügelhändler *m*.

**poultice** 🌣 ['poultis] Packung *f*.

**poultry** ['poultri] Geflügel *n*.

**pounce** [pauns] **1.** Stoß *m*, Sprung *m*; **2.** sich stürzen (on, upon auf *acc.*).

**pound** [paund] **1.** Pfund *n*; ~ (sterling) Pfund *n* Sterling (*abbr.* £ = *20 shillings*); Pfandstall *m*; Tierasyl *n*; **2.** (zer)stoßen; stampfen; schlagen.

**pounder** ['paundə] ...pfünder *m*.

**pour** [pɔ:] *v/t.* gießen, schütten; ~ *out* Getränk eingießen; *v/i.* sich ergießen, strömen; *it never rains but it ~s fig.* ein Unglück kommt selten allein.

**pout** [paut] **1.** Schmollen *n*; **2.** *v/t.* Lippen aufwerfen; *v/i.* schmollen.

**poverty** ['pɔvəti] Armut *f*.

**powder** ['paudə] **1.** Pulver *n*; Puder *m*; **2.** pulverisieren; (sich) pudern; bestreuen; ~box Puderdose *f*.

**power** ['pauə] Kraft *f*; Macht *f*, Gewalt *f*; 𝄢 Vollmacht *f*; ⚖ Potenz *f*; *in* ~ an der Macht, im Amt; ~current Starkstrom *m*; ~ful ['pauəful] mächtig, kräftig, wirksam; ~less ['pauəlis] macht-, kraftlos; ~plant *s.* power-station; ~politics *oft sg.* Machtpolitik *f*; ~station Kraftwerk *n*.

**powwow** ['pauwau] Medizinmann *m*; *Am.* F Versammlung *f*.

**practica|ble** ☐ ['præktikəbl] ausführbar; gangbar (*Weg*); brauchbar; ~l ☐ [~əl] praktisch; tatsächlich; eigentlich; sachlich; ~ *joke* Schabernack *m*; ~lly [~li] so gut wie.

**practice** ['præktis] **1.** Praxis *f*; Übung *f*; Gewohnheit *f*; Brauch *m*; Praktik *f*; *put into* ~ in die Praxis umsetzen; **2.** *Am.* = practise.

**practise** [~] *v/t.* in die Praxis umsetzen; ausüben; betreiben; üben; *v/i.* (sich) üben; praktizieren; ~ *upon j-s Schwäche* ausnutzen; ~d geübt (*P.*).

practitioner [præk'tiʃnə] a. general ~ praktischer Arzt; Rechtsanwalt m.

prairie Am. ['preəri] Grasebene f; Prärie f; ~-schooner Am. Planwagen m.

praise [preiz] 1. Preis m, Lob n; 2. loben, preisen.

praiseworthy ☐ ['preizwə:ði] lobenswert.

pram F [præm] Kinderwagen m.

prance [prɑːns] sich bäumen; paradieren; einherstolzieren.

prank [præŋk] Possen m, Streich m.

prate [preit] 1. Geschwätz n; 2. schwatzen, plappern.

prattle ['prætl] s. prate.

pray [prei] beten; (er)bitten; bitte! prayer [preə] Gebet n; Bitte f; oft ~s pl. Andacht f; Lord's ♀ Vaterunser n; ~-book ['preəbuk] Gebetbuch n.

pre... [priː; pri] vor(her)...; Vor...; früher.

preach [priːtʃ] predigen; ~er ['priːtʃə] Prediger(in).

preamble [priː'æmbl] Einleitung f.

precarious ☐ [pri'kɛəriəs] unsicher.

precaution [pri'kɔːʃən] Vorsicht(smaßregel) f; ~ary [~ʃnəri] vorbeugend.

precede [pri(ː)'siːd] voraus-, vorangehen (dat.); ~nce, ~ncy [~dəns, ~si] Vortritt m, Vorrang m; ~nt ['presidənt] Präzedenzfall m.

precept ['priːsept] Vorschrift f, Regel f; ~or [pri'septə] Lehrer m.

precinct ['priːsiŋkt] Bezirk m, bsd. Am. Wahlbezirk m, -kreis m; ~s pl. Umgebung f; Bereich m; Grenze f; pedestrian ~ Fußgängerzone f.

precious ['preʃəs] 1. ☐ kostbar; edel; F arg, gewaltig, schön; 2. F adv. recht, äußerst.

precipi|ce ['presipis] Abgrund m; ~tate 1. [pri'sipiteit] (hinab)stürzen; ⚗ fällen; überstürzen; 2. [~tit] übereilt, hastig; 3. [~] ⚗ Niederschlag m; ~tation [prisipi-'teiʃən] Sturz m; Überstürzung f, Hast f; ⚗ Niederschlag(en n) m; ~tous ☐ [pri'sipitəs] steil, jäh.

précis ['preisiː] gedrängte Übersicht, Zs.-fassung f.

precis|e ☐ [pri'sais] genau; ~ion [~'siʒən] Genauigkeit f; Präzision f.

preclude [pri'kluːd] ausschließen; vorbeugen (dat.); j-n hindern.

precocious ☐ [pri'kouʃəs] frühreif; altklug.

preconceive ['priːkən'siːv] vorher ausdenken; ~d vorgefaßt (Meinung).

preconception ['priːkən'sepʃən] vorgefaßte Meinung. [m.]

precursor [pri(ː)'kɔːsə] Vorläufer/ predatory ['predətəri] räuberisch.

predecessor ['priːdisesə] Vorgänger m.

predestin|ate [pri(ː)'destineit] vorherbestimmen; ~ed [~nd] auserkoren.

predetermine ['priːdi'tə:min] vorher festsetzen; vorherbestimmen.

predicament [pri'dikəmənt] (mißliche) Lage.

predicate 1. ['predikeit] aussagen; 2. gr. [~kit] Prädikat n, Satzaussage f.

predict [pri'dikt] vorhersagen; ~ion [~kʃən] Prophezeiung f.

predilection [priːdi'lekʃən] Vorliebe f.

predispos|e ['priːdis'pouz] vorher geneigt od. empfänglich machen (to für); ~ition [~spə'ziʃən] Geneigtheit f; bsd. ⚕ Anfälligkeit f (to für).

predomina|nce [pri'dɔminəns] Vorherrschaft f; Übergewicht n; Vormacht(stellung) f; ~nt ☐ [~nt] vorherrschend; ~te [~neit] die Oberhand haben; vorherrschen.

pre-eminent ☐ [pri(ː)'eminənt] hervorragend.

pre-emption [pri(ː)'empʃən] Vorkauf(srecht n) m.

pre-exist ['priːig'zist] vorher dasein.

prefabricate ['priː'fæbrikeit] vorfabrizieren.

preface ['prefis] 1. Vorrede f, Vorwort n, Einleitung f; 2. einleiten.

prefect ['priːfekt] Präfekt m; Schule: Vertrauensschüler m, Klassensprecher m.

prefer [pri'fə:] vorziehen; Gesuch etc. vorbringen; Klage einreichen; befördern; ~able ☐ ['prefərəbl] (to) vorzuziehen(d) (dat.); vorzüglicher (als); ~ably [~li] vorzugsweise; besser; ~ence [~rəns] Vorliebe f; Vorzug m; ~ential ☐ [prefə'renʃəl] bevorzugt; Vorzugs-...; ~ment [pri'fə:mənt] Beförderung f.

prefix ['priːfiks] Präfix n, Vorsilbe f.

pregnan|cy ['pregnənsi] Schwangerschaft f; fig. Fruchtbarkeit f; Bedeutungsreichtum m; ~t ☐ [~nt] schwanger; fig. fruchtbar, inhaltsvoll.

prejud|ge ['priː'dʒʌdʒ] vorher (ver-) urteilen; ~ice ['predʒudis] 1. Voreingenommenheit f; Vorurteil n; Schaden m; 2. voreinnehmen; benachteiligen; e-r S. Abbruch tun; ~d (vor)eingenommen; ~icial ☐ [predʒu'diʃəl] nachteilig.

prelate ['prelit] Prälat m.

preliminary [pri'liminəri] 1. ☐ vorläufig; einleitend; Vor...; 2. Einleitung f.

prelude ['prelju:d] Vorspiel n.

premature ☐ [premə'tjuə] fig. frühreif; vorzeitig; vorschnell.

premeditat|e [pri(ː)'mediteit] vorher überlegen; ~ion [pri(ː)medi-'teiʃən] Vorbedacht m.

**premier** ['premjə] 1. erst; 2. Premierminister m.

**premises** ['premisiz] pl. (Gebäude pl. mit) Grundstück n, Anwesen n; Lokal n.

**premium** ['pri:mjəm] Prämie f; Anzahlung f; ✝ Agio n; Versicherungsprämie f; Lehrgeld n; at a ~ über pari; sehr gesucht.

**premonition** [pri:mə'niʃən] Warnung f; (Vor)Ahnung f.

**preoccup|ied** [pri(:)'ɔkjupaid] in Gedanken verloren; ~y [~pai] vorher in Besitz nehmen; ausschließlich beschäftigen; in Anspruch nehmen.

**prep** F [prep] = preparation, preparatory school.

**preparat|ion** [prepə'reiʃən] Vorbereitung f; Zubereitung f; ~ory □ [pri'pærətəri] vorbereitend; ~ (school) Vorschule f.

**prepare** [pri'pɛə] v/t. vorbereiten; zurechtmachen; (zu)bereiten; (aus-)rüsten; v/i. sich vorbereiten; sich anschicken; ~d □ bereit.

**prepay** ['pri:'pei] [irr. (pay)] vorausbezahlen; frankieren.

**prepondera|nce** [pri'pondərəns] Übergewicht n; ~nt □ [~nt] überwiegend; ~te [~reit] überwiegen.

**preposition** gr. [prepə'ziʃən] Präposition f, Verhältniswort n.

**prepossess** [pri:pə'zes] günstig stimmen; ~ing □ [~siŋ] einnehmend.

**preposterous** [pri'pɔstərəs] widersinnig, albern; grotesk.

**prerequisite** ['pri:'rekwizit] Vorbedingung f, Voraussetzung f.

**prerogative** [pri'rɔgətiv] Vorrecht n.

**presage** ['presidʒ] 1. Vorbedeutung f; Ahnung f; 2. vorbedeuten; ahnen; prophezeien.

**prescribe** [pris'kraib] vorschreiben; ✻ verschreiben.

**prescription** [pris'kripʃən] Vorschrift f, Verordnung f; ✻ Rezept n.

**presence** ['prezns] Gegenwart f; Anwesenheit f; Erscheinung f; ~ of mind Geistesgegenwart f.

**present¹** ['preznt] 1. □ gegenwärtig; anwesend, vorhanden; jetzig; laufend (Jahr etc.); vorliegend (Fall etc.); ~ tense gr. Präsens n; 2. Gegenwart f, gr. a. Präsens n; Geschenk n; at ~ jetzt; for the ~ einstweilen.

**present²** [pri'zent] präsentieren; (dar)bieten; (vor)zeigen; j-n vorstellen; vorschlagen; (über)reichen; (be)schenken.

**presentation** [prezen'teiʃən] Dar-, Vorstellung f; Ein-, Überreichung f; Schenkung f; Vorzeigen n, Vorlage f.

**presentiment** [pri'zentimənt] Vorgefühl n, Ahnung f.

**presently** ['prezntli] sogleich, bald (darauf), alsbald; Am. zur Zeit.

**preservati|on** [prezə(:)'veiʃən] Bewahrung f, Erhaltung f; ~ve [pri-'zə:vətiv] 1. bewahrend; 2. Schutz-, Konservierungsmittel n.

**preserve** [pri'zə:v] 1. bewahren, behüten; erhalten; einmachen; Wild hegen; 2. hunt. Gehege n (a. fig.); mst ~s pl. Eingemachte(s) n. [ren (over bei).]

**preside** [pri'zaid] den Vorsitz füh-]

**presiden|cy** ['prezidənsi] Vorsitz m; Präsidentschaft f; ~t [~nt] Präsident m, Vorsitzende(r) m; Am. ✝ Direktor m.

**press** [pres] 1. Druck m der Hand; (Wein- etc.)Presse f; die Presse (Zeitungen); Druckerei f; Verlag m; Druck(en n) m; a. printing~ Druckerpresse f; Menge f; fig. Druck m, Last f, Andrang m; Schrank m; 2. v/t. (aus)pressen; drücken; lasten auf (dat.); (be)drängen; dringen auf (acc.); aufdrängen (on dat.); bügeln; be ~ed for time es eilig haben; v/i. drücken; (sich) drängen; ~ for sich eifrig bemühen um; ~ on weitereilen; ~(up)on eindringen auf (acc.); ~ agency Nachrichtenbüro n; ~ agent Reklameagent m; ~ button Druckknopf m; ~ing □ ['presiŋ] dringend; ~ure ['preʃə] Druck m (a. fig.); Drang(sal f) m.

**prestige** [pres'ti:ʒ] Prestige n.

**presum|able** □ [pri'zju:məbl] vermutlich; ~e [pri'zju:m] v/t. annehmen; vermuten; voraussetzen; v/i. vermuten; sich erdreisten; anmaßend sein; ~ (up)on pochen auf (acc.); ausnutzen, mißbrauchen.

**presumpt|ion** [pri'zʌmpʃən] Mutmaßung f; Wahrscheinlichkeit f; Anmaßung f; ~ive □ [~ptiv] mutmaßlich; ~uous □ [~tjuəs] überheblich; vermessen.

**presuppos|e** [pri:sə'pouz] voraussetzen; ~ition [pri:sʌpə'ziʃən] Voraussetzung f.

**preten|ce, Am. ~se** [pri'tens] Vortäuschung f; Vorwand m; Schein m, Verstellung f.

**pretend** [pri'tend] vorgeben; vortäuschen; heucheln; Anspruch erheben (to auf acc.); ~ed □ angeblich.

**pretension** [pri'tenʃən] Anspruch m (to auf acc.); Anmaßung f.

**preterit(e)** gr. ['pretərit] Präteritum n, Vergangenheitsform f.

**pretext** ['pri:tekst] Vorwand m.

**pretty** ['priti] 1. □ hübsch, niedlich; nett; 2. adv. ziemlich.

**prevail** [pri'veil] die Oberhand haben od. gewinnen; (vor)herrschen; maßgebend od. ausschlaggebend sein; ~ (up)on s.o. j-n dazu bewegen, et. zu tun; ~ing □ [~liŋ] (vor)herrschend.

**prevalent** □ ['prevələnt] vorherrschend, weit verbreitet.

**prevaricate** [pri'værikeit] Ausflüchte machen.

**prevent** [pri'vent] verhüten, *e-r S.* vorbeugen; *j-n* hindern; ~ion [~n-Jən] Verhinderung *f*; Verhütung *f*; ~ive [~ntiv] **1.** □ vorbeugend; **2.** Schutzmittel *n*.

**preview** ['pri:'vju:] Vorschau *f*; Vorbesichtigung *f*.

**previous** □ ['pri:vjəs] vorhergehend; vorläufig; Vor...; ~ **to** vor (*dat.*); ~ly [~sli] vorher, früher.

**pre-war** ['pri:'wɔ:] Vorkriegs...

**prey** [prei] **1.** Raub *m*, Beute *f*; *beast of* ~ Raubtier *n*; *bird of* ~ Raubvogel *m*; *be a* ~ *to* geplagt werden von; **2.** ~ (*up*)*on* rauben, plündern; fressen; *fig.* nagen an (*dat.*).

**price** [prais] **1.** Preis *m*; Lohn *m*; **2.** *Waren* auszeichnen; die Preise festsetzen für; (ab)schätzen; ~less ['praislis] unschätzbar; unbezahlbar.

**prick** [prik] **1.** Stich *m*; Stachel *m* (*a. fig.*); **2.** *v/t.* (durch)stechen; *fig.* peinigen; *a.* ~ *out* Muster punktieren; ~ *up one's ears* die Ohren spitzen; *v/i.* stechen; ~le ['prikl] Stachel *m*, Dorn *m*; ~ly [~li] stachelig.

**pride** [praid] **1.** Stolz *m*; Hochmut *m*; *take* ~ *in* stolz sein auf (*acc.*); **2.** ~ *o.s.* sich brüsten (*on, upon* mit).

**priest** [pri:st] Priester *m*.

**prig** [prig] Tugendbold *m*, selbstgerechter Mensch; Pedant *m*.

**prim** □ [prim] steif; zimperlich.

**prima|cy** ['praiməsi] Vorrang *m*; ~rily [~rili] in erster Linie; ~ry □ [~ri] **1.** ursprünglich; hauptsächlich; Ur..., Anfangs..., Haupt...; Elementar...; höchst; *č*, *♂* Primär...; **2.** *a.* ~ *meeting Am.* Wahlversammlung *f*; ~ry **school** Elementar~, Grundschule *f*.

**prime** [praim] **1.** □ erst; wichtigst; Haupt...; vorzüglich(st); ~ *cost* † Selbstkosten *pl.*; ~ *minister* Ministerpräsident *m*; ~ *number* Primzahl *f*; **2.** *fig.* Blüte(zeit) *f*; Beste(s) *n*; höchste Vollkommenheit; **3.** *v/t.* vorbereiten; *Pumpe* anlassen; instruieren; F vollaufen lassen (*betrunken machen*); *paint.* grundieren.

**primer** ['praimə] Fibel *f*, Elementarbuch *n*. [lich; Ur...]

**primeval** [prai'mi:vəl] uranfäng-

**primitive** ['primitiv] **1.** □ erst, ursprünglich; Stamm...; primitiv; **2.** *gr.* Stammwort *n*.

**primrose** ♀ ['primrouz] Primel *f*.

**prince** [prins] Fürst *m*; Prinz *m*; ~ss [prin'ses, *vor npr.* 'prinses] Fürstin *f*; Prinzessin *f*.

**principal** ['prinsəpl] **1.** □ erst, hauptsächlich(st); Haupt...; ~ *parts pl. gr.* Stammformen *f/pl. des vb.*;

**2.** Hauptperson *f*; Vorsteher *m*; *bsd. Am.* (Schul)Direktor *m*, Rektor *m*; † Chef *m*; ⚖ Hauptschuldige(r) *m*; † Kapital *n*; ~ity [prinsi'pæliti] Fürstentum *n*.

**principle** ['prinsəpl] Prinzip *n*; Grund(satz) *m*; Ursprung *m*; *on* ~ grundsätzlich, aus Prinzip.

**print** [print] **1.** Druck *m*; (Finger-*etc.*)Abdruck *m*; bedruckter Kattun, Druckstoff *m*; Stich *m*; *phot.* Abzug *m*; *Am.* Zeitungsdrucksache *f*; *out of* ~ vergriffen; **2.** (ab-, auf-, be)drucken; *phot.* kopieren; *fig.* einprägen (*on dat.*); in Druckbuchstaben schreiben; ~er ['printə] (Buch)Drucker *m*.

**printing** ['printiŋ] Druck *m*; Drucken *n*; *phot.* Abziehen *n*, Kopieren *n*; ~ink Druckerschwärze *f*; ~office (Buch)Druckerei *f*; ~press Druckerpresse *f*.

**prior** ['praiə] **1.** früher, älter (*to* als); **2.** *adv.* ~ *to* vor (*dat.*); **3.** *eccl.* Prior *m*; ~ity [prai'ɔriti] Priorität *f*; Vorrang *m*; Vorfahrtsrecht *f*.

**prism** ['prizəm] Prisma *n*.

**prison** ['prizn] Gefängnis *n*; ~er [~nə] Gefangene(r *m*) *f*, Häftling *m*; *take s.o.* ~ j-n gefangennehmen.

**privacy** ['praivəsi] Zurückgezogenheit *f*; Geheimhaltung *f*.

**private** ['praivit] **1.** □ privat; Privat...; persönlich; vertraulich; geheim; *žč* (gewöhnlicher) Soldat; *in* ~ privatim; im geheimen.

**privation** [prai'veiʃən] Mangel *m*, Entbehrung *f*.

**privilege** ['privilidʒ] **1.** Privileg *n*; Vorrecht *n*; **2.** bevorrechten.

**privy** ['privi] **1.** □ ~ *to* eingeweiht in (*acc.*); ♀ *Council* Staatsrat *m*; ♀ *Councillor* Geheimer Rat; ♀ *Seal* Geheimsiegel *n*; **2.** *žč* Mitinteressent *m* (*to an dat.*); Abort *m*.

**prize** [praiz] **1.** Preis *m*, Prämie *f*; ⚓ Beute *f*; (Lotterie)Gewinn *m*; **2.** preisgekrönt, Preis...; **3.** (hoch)-schätzen; aufbrechen (*öffnen*); ~fighter ['praizfaitə] Berufsboxer *m*.

**pro** [prou] für.

**probab|ility** [prɔbə'biliti] Wahrscheinlichkeit *f*; ~le □ ['prɔbəbl] wahrscheinlich.

**probation** [prə'beiʃən] Probe *f*, Probezeit *f*; *žč* Bewährungsfrist *f*; ~ *officer* Bewährungshelfer *m*.

**probe** [proub] **1.** *ℱ* Sonde *f*; *fig.* Untersuchung *f*; *lunar* ~ Mondsonde *f*; **2.** *a.* ~ *into* sondieren; untersuchen.

**probity** ['proubiti] Redlichkeit *f*.

**problem** ['prɔbləm] Problem *n*; ♫ Aufgabe *f*; ~atic(al □) [~'ætik(əl)] problematisch, zweifelhaft. [*n*; Handlungsweise *f*.]

**procedure** [prə'si:dʒə] Verfahren

**proceed** [prə'si:d] weitergehen; fortfahren; vor sich gehen; vorgehen; *univ.* promovieren; ~ *from von od.* aus *et.* kommen; ausgehen von; ~ *to* zu *et.* übergehen; ~ing [~diŋ] Vorgehen *n*; Handlung *f*; ~s *pl.* ᵼᵼ Verfahren *n*; Verhandlungen *f/pl.*, (Tätigkeits)Bericht *m*; ~s ['prousi:dz] *pl.* Ertrag *m*, Gewinn *m*.

**process** ['prouses] **1.** Fortschreiten *n*, Fortgang *m*; Vorgang *m*; Verlauf *m der Zeit*; Prozeß *m*, Verfahren *n*; *in* ~ im Gange; *in* ~ *of construction* im Bau (befindlich); **2.** gerichtlich belangen; ⊕ bearbeiten; ~ion [prə'seʃən] Prozession *f*.

**proclaim** [prə'kleim] proklamieren; erklären; ausrufen.

**proclamation** [prɔklə'meiʃən] Proklamation *f*; Bekanntmachung *f*; Erklärung *f*.

**proclivity** [prə'kliviti] Neigung *f*.

**procrastinate** [prou'kræstineit] zaudern.

**procreate** ['proukrieit] (er)zeugen.

**procuration** [prɔkjuə'reiʃən] Vollmacht *f*; ✝ Prokura *f*; ~or ['prɔkjuəreitə] Bevollmächtigte(r) *m*.

**procure** [prə'kjuə] *v/t.* be-, verschaffen; *v/i.* Kuppelei treiben.

**prod** [prɔd] **1.** Stich *m*; Stoß *m*; *fig.* Ansporn *m*; **2.** stechen; stoßen; *fig.* anstacheln.

**prodigal** ['prɔdigəl] **1.** ⬚ verschwenderisch; *the* ~ *son* der verlorene Sohn; **2.** Verschwender(in)

**prodigious** ⬚ [prə'didʒəs] erstaunlich, ungeheuer; ~y ['prɔdidʒi] Wunder *n* (*a. fig.*); Ungeheuer *n*; *oft infant* ~ Wunderkind *n*

**produce 1.** [prə'djuːs] vorbringen, vorführen, vorlegen, beibringen; hervorbringen; produzieren, erzeugen; *Zinsen etc.* (ein)bringen; ♉ verlängern; *Film etc* herausbringen; **2.** ['prɔdjuːs] (Natur)Erzeugnis(se *pl.*) *n*, Produkt *n*, Ertrag *m*; ~r [prə'djuːsə] Erzeuger *m*, Hersteller *m*; *Film:* Produzent *m*; *thea.* Regisseur *m*.

**product** ['prɔdʌkt] Produkt *n*, Erzeugnis *n*; ~ion [prə'dʌkʃən] Hervorbringung *f*; Vorlegung *f*, Beibringung *f*; Produktion *f*, Erzeugung *f*; *thea.* Herausbringen *n*; Erzeugnis *n*; ~ive ⬚ [~ktiv] schöpferisch; produktiv, erzeugend; ertragreich; fruchtbar; ~iveness [~vnis], ~ivity [prɔdʌk'tiviti] Produktivität *f*.

**prof** *Am.* F [prɔf] Professor *m*.

**profanation** [prɔfə'neiʃən] Entweihung *f*; ~e [prə'fein] **1.** profan; weltlich; uneingeweiht; gottlos; **2.** entweihen; ~ity [~'fæniti] Gottlosigkeit *f*; Fluchen *n*.

**profess** [prə'fes] (sich) bekennen (zu); erklären; *Reue etc.* bekunden; *Beruf* ausüben; lehren; ~ed ⬚ erklärt; angeblich; Berufs...; ~ion

[~eʃən] Bekenntnis *n*; Erklärung *f*; Beruf *m*; ~ional [~nl] **1.** ⬚ Berufs...; Amts...; berufsmäßig; freiberuflich; ~ men Akademiker *m/pl.*; **2.** Fachmann *m*; *Sport:* Berufsspieler *m*; Berufskünstler *m*; ~or [~esə] Professor *m*.

**proffer** ['prɔfə] **1.** anbieten; **2.** Anerbieten *n*.

**proficiency** [prə'fiʃənsi] Tüchtigkeit *f*; ~t [~nt] **1.** ⬚ tüchtig; bewandert; **2.** Meister *m*.

**profile** ['proufail] Profil *n*.

**profit** ['prɔfit] **1.** Vorteil *m*, Nutzen *m*, Gewinn *m*; **2.** *v/t. j-m* Nutzen bringen; *v/i.* ~ *by* Nutzen ziehen aus; ausnutzen; ~able ⬚ [~təbl] nützlich, vorteilhaft, einträglich; ~eer [prɔfi'tiə] **1.** Schiebergeschäfte machen; **2.** Profitmacher *m*, Schieber *m*; ~-sharing ['prɔfitʃɛəriŋ] Gewinnbeteiligung *f*.

**profligate** ['prɔfligit] **1.** ⬚ liederlich; **2.** liederlicher Mensch.

**profound** ⬚ [prə'faund] tief; tiefgründig; gründlich; *fig.* dunkel.

**profundity** [prə'fʌnditi] Tiefe *f*.

**profuse** ⬚ [prə'fjuːs] verschwenderisch; übermäßig, überreich; ~ion *fig* [~'uːʒən] Überfluß *m*.

**progenitor** [prou'dʒenitə] Vorfahr *m*, Ahn *m*; ~y ['prɔdʒini] Nachkommen(schaft *f*) *m/pl.*; Brut *f*.

**prognosis** ⚕ [prɔg'nousis], *pl.* ~es [~siːz] Prognose *f*.

**prognostication** [prəgnɔsti'keiʃən] Vorhersage *f*.

**program(me)** ['prougræm] Programm *n*.

**progress 1.** ['prougres] Fortschritt(e *pl.*) *m*; Vorrücken *n* (*a.* ✕); Fortgang *m*; *in* ~ im Gang; **2.** [prə'gres] fortschreiten; ~ion [~'greʃən] Fortschreiten *n*; ♉ Reihe *f*; ~ive [~'sesiv] **1.** ⬚ fortschreitend; fortschrittlich; **2.** *pol.* Fortschrittler *m*.

**prohibit** [prə'hibit] verbieten; verhindern; ~ion [proui'biʃən] Verbot *n*; Prohibition *f*; ~ionist [~ʃnist] *bsd. Am.* Prohibitionist *m*; ~ive [prə'hibitiv] verbietend; Sperr...; unerschwinglich.

**project 1.** ['prɔdʒekt] Projekt *n*; Vorhaben *n*, Plan *m*; **2.** [prə'dʒekt] *v/t.* planen; (ent)werfen; ♉ projizieren; *v/i.* vorspringen; ~ile ['prɔdʒiktail] Projektil *n*, Geschoß *n*; ~ion [prə'dʒekʃən] Werfen *n*; Entwurf *m*; Vorsprung *m*; ♉, *ast., phot.* Projektion *f*; ~or [~ktə] ✝ Gründer *m*; *opt.* Projektor *m*.

**proletarian** [proule'tɛəriən] **1.** proletarisch; **2.** Proletarier(in).

**prolific** [prə'lifik] (~ally) fruchtbar.

**prolix** ⬚ ['prouliks] weitschweifig.

**prologue**, *Am. a.* ~g ['proulɔg] Prolog *m*.

**prolong** [prə'lɔŋ] verlängern.

**promenade** [prɔmi'nɑːd] **1.** Promenade f; **2.** promenieren.

**prominent** □ ['prɔminənt] hervorragend (a. fig.); fig. prominent.

**promiscuous** □ [prə'miskjuəs] unordentlich, verworren; gemeinsam; unterschiedslos.

**promis|e** ['prɔmis] **1.** Versprechen n; fig. Aussicht f; **2.** versprechen; **~ing** □ [~siŋ] vielversprechend; **~sory** [~səri] versprechend; ~ note † Eigenwechsel m.

**promontory** ['prɔməntri] Vorgebirge n.

**promot|e** [prə'mout] et. fördern; j-n befördern; bsd. Am. Schule: versetzen; parl. unterstützen; † gründen; bsd. Am. Verkauf durch Werbung steigern; **~ion** [~ouʃən] Förderung f; Beförderung f; † Gründung f.

**prompt** [prɔmpt] **1.** □ schnell; bereit(willig); sofortig; pünktlich; **2.** j-n veranlassen; Gedanken eingeben; j-m vorsagen, soufflieren; **~er** ['prɔmptə] Souffleu|r m, -se f; **~ness** [~tnis] Schnelligkeit f; Bereitschaft f.

**promulgate** ['prɔməlgeit] verkünden, verbreiten.

**prone** □ [proun] mit dem Gesicht nach unten (liegend); hingestreckt; ~ to fig. geneigt od. neigend zu.

**prong** [prɔŋ] Zinke f; Spitze f.

**pronoun** gr. ['prounaun] Pronomen n, Fürwort n.

**pronounce** [prə'nauns] aussprechen; verkünden; erklären (für).

**pronto** Am. F ['prɔntou] sofort.

**pronunciation** [prɔnʌnsi'eiʃən] Aussprache f.

**proof** [pruːf] **1.** Beweis m; Probe f, Versuch m; typ. Korrekturbogen m; typ., phot. Probeabzug m; **2.** fest; in Zssgn: ...fest, ...dicht, ...sicher; **~-reader** typ. ['pruːfriːdə] Korrektor m.

**prop** [prɔp] **1.** Stütze f (a. fig.); **2.** a. ~ up (unter)stützen.

**propaga|te** ['prɔpəgeit] (sich) fortpflanzen; verbreiten; **~tion** [prɔpə'geiʃən] Fortpflanzung f; Verbreitung f.

**propel** [prə'pel] (vorwärts-, an-) treiben; **~ler** [~lə] Propeller m, (Schiffs-, Luft)Schraube f.

**propensity** [prə'pensiti] Neigung f.

**proper** □ ['prɔpə] eigen(tümlich); eigentlich; passend, richtig; anständig; **~ty** [~əti] Eigentum n, Besitz m, Vermögen n; Eigenschaft f.

**prophe|cy** ['prɔfisi] Prophezeiung f; **~sy** [~sai] prophezeien.

**prophet** ['prɔfit] Prophet m.

**propi|tiate** [prə'piʃieit] günstig stimmen, versöhnen; **~tious** □ [~ʃəs] gnädig; günstig.

**proportion** [prə'pɔːʃən] **1.** Verhältnis n; Gleichmaß n; (An)Teil m; ~s pl. (Aus)Maße n/pl.; **2.** in ein Verhältnis bringen; **~al** □ [~nl] im Verhältnis (to zu); **~ate** □ [~ʃnit] angemessen.

**propos|al** [prə'pouzl] Vorschlag m; (a. Heirats)Antrag m; Angebot n; Plan m; **~e** [~ouz] v/t. vorschlagen; e-n Toast ausbringen auf (acc.); ~ to o.s. sich vornehmen; v/i. beabsichtigen; anhalten (to um); **~ition** [prɔpə'ziʃən] Vorschlag m, Antrag m; Behauptung f; Problem n.

**propound** [prə'paund] Frage etc. vorlegen; vorschlagen.

**propriet|ary** [prə'praiətəri] Eigentümer..., Eigentums...; Besitz(er)...; gesetzlich geschützt (a. Arzneimittel); **~or** [~tə] Eigentümer m; **~y** [~ti] Richtigkeit f; Schicklichkeit f; the proprieties pl. die Anstandsformen f/pl. [m.]

**propulsion** ⊕ [prə'pʌlʃən] Antrieb]

**prorate** Am. [prou'reit] anteilmäßig verteilen.

**prosaic** [prou'zeiik] (~ally) fig. prosaisch (nüchtern, trocken).

**proscribe** [prous'kraib] ächten.

**proscription** [prous'kripʃən] Achtung f; Acht f; Verbannung f.

**prose** [prouz] **1.** Prosa f. **2.** prosaisch.

**prosecut|e** ['prɔsikjuːt] (a. gerichtlich) verfolgen; Gewerbe etc. betreiben; verklagen; **~ion** [prɔsi'kjuːʃən] Verfolgung f e-s Plans etc.; Betreiben n e-s Gewerbes etc.; gerichtliche Verfolgung; **~or** zⁿⁱ ['prɔsikjuːtə] Kläger m; Anklagevertreter m; public ~ Staatsanwalt m.

**prospect 1.** ['prɔspekt] Aussicht f (a. fig.); Anblick m; † Interessent m; **2.** [prə'spekt] ⚒ schürfen, bohren (for nach Öl); **~ive** □ [~tiv] vorausblickend; voraussichtlich; **~us** [~təs] (Werbe)Prospekt m.

**prosper** ['prɔspə] v/i. Erfolg haben, gedeihen, blühen; v/t. begünstigen, segnen; **~ity** [prɔs'periti] Gedeihen n; Wohlstand m; Glück n; fig. Blüte f; **~ous** □ ['prɔspərəs] glücklich, gedeihlich; fig. blühend; günstig.

**prostitute** ['prɔstitjuːt] **1.** Dirne f; **2.** zur Dirne machen; (der Schande) preisgeben, feilbieten (a. fig.).

**prostrat|e 1.** ['prɔstreit] hingestreckt; erschöpft; daniederliegend; demütig; gebrochen; **2.** [prɔs'treit] niederwerfen; fig. niederschmettern; entkräften; **~ion** [~eiʃən] Niederwerfung f; Fußfall m; fig. Demütigung f; Entkräftung f.

**prosy** fig. ['prouzi] prosaisch; langweilig.

**protagonist** [prou'tægənist] thea. Hauptfigur f; fig. Vorkämpfer(in).

**protect** [prə'tekt] (be)schützen; **~ion** [~kʃən] Schutz m; Wirtschaftsschutz m, Schutzzoll m; **~ive**

[„ktiv] schützend; Schutz...; ~ duty Schutzzoll m; ~or [„tə] (Be)Schützer m; Schutz-, Schirmherr m; ~orate [„ərit] Protektorat n.

**protest 1.** ['proutest] Protest m; Einspruch m; **2.** [prə'test] beteuern; protestieren; reklamieren.

**Protestant** ['prɔtistənt] **1.** protestantisch; **2.** Protestant(in).

**protestation** [proutes'teiʃən] Beteuerung f; Verwahrung f.

**protocol** ['proutəkɔl] **1.** Protokoll n; **2.** protokollieren.

**prototype** ['proutətaip] Urbild n; Prototyp m, Modell n.

**protract** [prə'trækt] in die Länge ziehen, hinziehen.

**protru|de** [prə'tru:d] (sich) (her-)vorstrecken; (her)vorstehen, (her-) vortreten (lassen); ~sion [„u:ʒən] Vorstrecken n; (Her)Vorstehen n, (Her)Vortreten n.

**protuberance** [prə'tju:bərəns] Hervortreten n; Auswuchs m, Höcker m.

**proud** ☐ [praud] stolz (of auf acc.).

**prove** [pru:v] v/t. be-, er-, nachweisen; prüfen; erleben, erfahren; v/i. sich herausstellen od. erweisen (als); ausfallen; ~n ['pru:vən] erwiesen; bewährt.

**provenance** ['prɔvinəns] Herkunft f.

**provender** ['prɔvində] Futter n.

**proverb** ['prɔvəb] Sprichwort n.

**provide** [prə'vaid] v/t. besorgen, beschaffen, liefern; bereitstellen; versehen, versorgen; ⚕ vorsehen, festsetzen; v/i. (vor)sorgen; ~d (that) vorausgesetzt, daß; sofern.

**providen|ce** ['prɔvidəns] Vorsehung f; Voraussicht f; Vorsorge f; ~t ☐ [„nt] vorausblickend; vorsorglich; haushälterisch; ~tial ☐ [prɔvi'denʃəl] durch die göttliche Vorsehung bewirkt; glücklich.

**provider** [prə'vaidə] Ernährer m der Familie; Lieferant m.

**provinc|e** ['prɔvins] Provinz f; fig. Gebiet n; Aufgabe f; ~ial [prə'vinʃəl] **1.** provinziell; kleinstädtisch; **2.** Provinzbewohner(in).

**provision** [prə'viʒən] Beschaffung f; Vorsorge f; ⚕ Bestimmung f; Vorkehrung f, Maßnahme f; Vorrat m; ~s pl. Proviant m, Lebensmittel pl.; ~al ☐ [„nl] provisorisch.

**proviso** [prə'vaizou] Vorbehalt m.

**provocat|ion** [prɔvə'keiʃən] Herausforderung f; ~ive [prə'vɔkətiv] herausfordernd; (auf)reizend.

**provoke** [prə'vouk] auf-, anreizen; herausfordern.

**provost** ['prɔvəst] Leiter m e-s College; schott. Bürgermeister m; ✕ [prə'vou]: ~ marshal Kommandeur m der Militärpolizei.

**prow** ⚓ [prau] Bug m, Vorschiff n.

**prowess** ['prauis] Tapferkeit f.

**prowl** [praul] **1.** v/i. umherstreifen; v/t. durchstreifen; **2.** Umherstreifen n; ~ car Am. ['praulka:] Streifenwagen m der Polizei.

**proximity** [prɔk'simiti] Nähe f.

**proxy** ['prɔksi] Stellvertreter m; Stellvertretung f; Vollmacht f; by ~ in Vertretung.

**prude** [pru:d] Prüde f, Spröde f; Zimperliese f.

**pruden|ce** ['pru:dəns] Klugheit f, Vorsicht f; ~t ☐ [„nt] klug, vorsichtig.

**prud|ery** ['pru:dəri] Prüderie f, Sprödigkeit f, Zimperlichkeit f; ~ish ☐ [„diʃ] prüde, zimperlich, spröde.

**prune** [pru:n] **1.** Backpflaume f; **2.** ✁ beschneiden (a. fig.); a. ~ away, ~ off wegschneiden.

**prurient** ☐ ['pruəriənt] geil, lüstern.

**pry** [prai] **1.** neugierig gucken; ~ into s-e Nase stecken in (acc.); ~ open aufbrechen; ~ up hochheben; **2.** Hebel(bewegung f) m.

**psalm** [sa:m] Psalm m.

**pseudo|...** ['psju:dou] Pseudo...; falsch; ~nym [„dənim] Deckname m.

**psychiatr|ist** [sai'kaiətrist] Psychiater m (Nervenarzt); ~y [„ri] Psychiatrie f.

**psychic(al** ☐) ['saikik(əl)] psychisch, seelisch.

**psycholog|ical** ☐ [saikə'lɔdʒikəl] psychologisch; ~ist [sai'kɔlədʒist] Psycholog|e m, -in f; ~y [„dʒi] Psychologie f (Seelenkunde).

**pub** F [pʌb] Kneipe f, Wirtschaft f.

**puberty** ['pju:bəti] Pubertät f.

**public** ['pʌblik] **1.** ☐ öffentlich; staatlich, Staats...; allbekannt; ~ spirit Gemeinsinn m; **2.** Publikum n; Öffentlichkeit f; ~an [„kən] Gastwirt m; ~ation [pʌbli'keiʃən] Bekanntmachung f; Veröffentlichung f; Verlagswerk n; monthly ~ Monatsschrift f; ~ house Wirtshaus n; ~ity [pʌb'lisiti] Öffentlichkeit f; Propaganda f, Reklame f, Werbung f; ~ library Volksbücherei f; ~ relations pl. Verhältnis n zur Öffentlichkeit; Public Relations pl.; ~ school Public School f, Internatsschule f.

**publish** ['pʌbliʃ] bekanntmachen, veröffentlichen; Buch etc. herausgeben, verlegen; ~ing house Verlag m; ~er [„ʃə] Herausgeber m, Verleger m; ~s pl. Verlag(sanstalt f) m.

**pucker** ['pʌkə] **1.** Falte f; **2.** falten; Falten werfen; runzeln.

**pudding** ['pudiŋ] Pudding m; Süßspeise f; Auflauf m; Wurst f; black ~ Blutwurst f.

**puddle** ['pʌdl] Pfütze f.

**pudent** ['pju:dənt] verschämt.

**puerile** ☐ ['pjuərail] kindisch.

**puff** [pʌf] **1.** Hauch m; Zug m beim

*Rauchen*; (Dampf-, Rauch)Wölkchen *n*; Puderquaste *f*; (aufdringliche) Reklame; 2. *v/t.* (auf)blasen, pusten; paffen; anpreisen; ~ out sich (auf)blähen; ~ up *Preise* hochtreiben; ~ed up *fig.* aufgeblasen; ~ed eyes geschwollene Augen; *v/i.* paffen; pusten; **~-paste** ['pʌfpeist] Blätterteig *m*; **~y** ['pʌfi] böig; kurzatmig; geschwollen; dick; bauschig.

**pug** [pʌg], **~-dog** ['pʌgdɔg] Mops *m*.

**pugnacious** [pʌg'neiʃəs] kämpferisch; kampflustig; streitsüchtig.

**pug-nose** ['pʌgnouz] Stupsnase *f*.

**puissant** ['pju(ː)isnt] mächtig.

**puke** [pjuːk] (sich) erbrechen.

**pull** [pul] 1. Zug *m*; Ruck *m*; *typ.* Abzug *m*; Ruderpartie *f*; Griff *m*; Vorteil *m*; 2. ziehen; zerren; reißen; zupfen; pflücken; rudern; ~ about hin- u. herzerren; ~ down niederreißen; ~ in einfahren (*Zug*); ~ off zustande bringen; *Preis* eringen; ~ out heraus-, hinausfahren; ausscheren; ~ round wiederherstellen; ~ through *j-n* durchbringen; ~ o.s. together sich zs.-nehmen; ~ up *Wagen* anhalten; halten; ~ up with, ~ up to einholen.

**pulley** ⊕ ['puli] Rolle *f*; Flaschenzug *m*; Riemenscheibe *f*.

**pull|-over** ['pulouvə] Pullover *m*; **~-up** Halteplatz *m*, Raststätte *f*.

**pulp** [pʌlp] Brei *m*; *Frucht-, Zahn*-Mark *n*; ⊕ Papierbrei *m*; *a.* ~ *magazine Am.* Schundillustrierte *f*.

**pulpit** ['pulpit] Kanzel *f*.

**pulpy** □ ['pʌlpi] breiig; fleischig.

**puls|ate** [pʌl'seit] pulsieren; schlagen; **~e** [pʌls] Puls(schlag) *m*.

**pulverize** ['pʌlvəraiz] *v/t.* pulverisieren; *v/i.* zu Staub werden.

**pumice** ['pʌmis] Bimsstein *m*.

**pump** [pʌmp] 1. Pumpe *f*; Pumps *m*; 2. pumpen; F *j-n* aushorchen.

**pumpkin** ♀ ['pʌmpkin] Kürbis *m*.

**pun** [pʌn] 1. Wortspiel *n*; 2. ein Wortspiel machen.

**Punch¹** [pʌntʃ] Kasperle *n*, *m*.

**punch²** [~] 1. ⊕ Punze(n *m*) *f*, Locheisen *n*, Locher *m*; Lochzange *f*; (Faust)Schlag *m*; Punsch *m*; 2. punzen, durchbohren; lochen; knuffen, puffen; *Am.* Vieh treiben, hüten.

**puncher** ['pʌntʃə] Locheisen *n*; Locher *m*; F Schläger *m*; *Am.* Cowboy *m*.

**punctilious** [pʌŋk'tiliəs] peinlich (genau), spitzfindig; förmlich.

**punctual** □ ['pʌŋktjuəl] pünktlich; **~ity** [pʌŋktju'æliti] Pünktlichkeit *f*.

**punctuat|e** ['pʌŋktjueit] (inter-)punktieren; *fig.* unterbrechen; **~ion** *gr.* [pʌŋktju'eiʃən] Interpunktion *f*.

**puncture** ['pʌŋktʃə] 1. Punktur *f*,

Stich *m*; Reifenpanne *f*; 2. (durch-)stechen; platzen (*Luftreifen*).

**pungen|cy** ['pʌndʒənsi] Schärfe *f*; **~t** [~nt] stechend, beißend, scharf.

**punish** ['pʌniʃ] (be)strafen; **~able** □ [~ʃəbl] strafbar; **~ment** [~ʃmənt] Strafe *f*, Bestrafung *f*.

**punk** *Am.* [pʌŋk] Zunderholz *n*; Zündmasse *f*; F *fig.* Mist *m*, Käse *m*.

**puny** □ ['pjuːni] winzig; schwächlich.

**pupa** *zo.* ['pjuːpə] Puppe *f*.

**pupil** ['pjuːpl] *anat.* Pupille *f*; Schüler(in); Mündel *m*, *n*.

**puppet** ['pʌpit] Marionettef (*a. fig.*); **~-show** Puppenspiel *n*.

**pup(py)** [pʌp, 'pʌpi] Welpe *m*, junger Hund; *fig.* Laffe *m*, Schnösel *m*.

**purchase** ['pəːtʃəs] 1. (An-, Ein-) Kauf *m*; Erwerb(ung *f*) *m*; Anschaffung *f*; ⊕ Hebevorrichtung *f*; *fig.* Ansatzpunkt *m*; make ~s Einkäufe machen; 2. kaufen; *fig.* erkaufen; anschaffen; ⊕ aufwinden; **~r** [~sə] Käufer(in).

**pure** □ [pjuə] *allg.* rein; *engS.*: lauter; echt; gediegen; theoretisch; **~-bred** *Am.* ['pjuəbred] reinrassig.

**purgat|ive** ⚕ ['pəːgətiv] 1. abführend; 2. Abführmittel *n*; **~ory** [~təri] Fegefeuer *n*.

**purge** [pəːdʒ] 1. ⚕ Abführmittel *n*; *pol.* Säuberung *f*; 2. *mst fig.* reinigen; *pol.* säubern; ⚕ abführen.

**purify** ['pjuərifai] reinigen; läutern.

**Puritan** ['pjuəritən] 1. Puritaner (-in); 2. puritanisch.

**purity** ['pjuəriti] Reinheit *f* (*a. fig.*).

**purl** [pəːl] murmeln (*Bach*).

**purlieus** ['pəːljuːz] *pl.* Umgebung *f*.

**purloin** [pəː'lɔin] entwenden.

**purple** ['pəːpl] 1. purpurn, purpurrot; 2. Purpur *m*; 3. (sich) purpurn färben.

**purport** ['pəːpət] 1. Sinn *m*; Inhalt *m*; 2. besagen; beabsichtigen; vorgeben.

**purpose** ['pəːpəs] 1. Vorsatz *m*; Absicht *f*, Zweck *m*; Entschlußkraft *f*; for the ~ of ger. um zu *inf.*; on ~ absichtlich; to the ~ zweckdienlich; to no ~ vergebens; 2. vorhaben, bezwecken; **~ful** □ [~sful] zweckmäßig; absichtlich; zielbewußt; **~less** □ [~slis] zwecklos; ziellos; **~ly** [~li] vorsätzlich.

**purr** [pəː] schnurren (*Katze*).

**purse** [pəːs] 1. Börse *f*, Geldbeutel *m*; Geld(preis *m*) *n*; *public* ~ Staatssäckel *m*; 2. *oft* ~ up Mund spitzen; *Stirn* runzeln; *Augen* zs.-kneifen.

**pursuan|ce** [pə'sju(ː)əns] Verfolgung *f*; in ~ of zufolge (*dat.*); **~t** □ [~nt]: ~ to zufolge, gemäß, entsprechend (*dat.*).

**pursue** [pə'sjuː] verfolgen (*a. fig.*); streben nach; *e-m Beruf etc.* nachgehen; fortsetzen, fortfahren; **~er**

[~ju(:)ə] Verfolger(in); ~it [~ju:t] Verfolgung *f*; *mst* ~s *pl.* Beschäftigung *f*.

**purvey** [pə:'vei] *Lebensmittel* liefern; ~or [~eiə] Lieferant *m*.

**pus** [pʌs] Eiter *m*.

**push** [puʃ] 1. (An-, Vor)Stoß *m*; Schub *m*; Druck *m*; Notfall *m*; Energie *f*; Unternehmungsgeist *m*; Elan *m*; 2. stoßen; schieben; drängen; *Knopf* drücken; (an)treiben; *a.* ~ through durchführen; *Anspruch etc.* durchdrücken; ~ *s.th.* on *s.o.* j-m et. aufdrängen; ~ one's way sich durch- *od.* vordrängen; ~ along, ~ on, ~ forward weitermachen, -gehen, -fahren *etc.*; ~**button** ⚡ ['puʃbʌtn] Druckknopf *m*; ~**over** *Am. fig.* Kinderspiel *n*; leicht zu beeinflussender Mensch.

**pusillanimous** □ [pju:si'læniməs] kleinmütig.

**puss** [pus] Kätzchen *n*, Katze *f* (*a. fig.* = *Mädchen*); ~**y** ['pusi], *a.* ~-cat Miezе *f*; Kätzchen *n*; ~**yfoot** *Am.* F leisetreten, sich zurückhalten.

**put** [put] (*irr.*) *v/t.* setzen, legen, stellen, stecken, tun, machen; *Frage* stellen, vorlegen; werfen; ausdrücken, sagen; ~ *about Gerüchte etc.* verbreiten; ⚓ wenden; ~ *across sl.* drehen, schaukeln; ~ *back* zurückstellen; ~ *by Geld* zurücklegen; ~ *down* niederlegen, -setzen, -werfen; aussteigen lassen; notieren; zuschreiben (*to dat.*); unterdrücken; ~ *forth Kräfte* aufbieten; *Knospen etc.* treiben; ~ *forward Meinung etc.* vorbringen; ~ *o.s. forward* sich hervortun; ~ *in* hinein-, hereinst(r)ecken; *Anspruch* erheben; *Gesuch* einreichen; *Urkunde* vorlegen; anstellen; ~ *off* auf-, verschieben; vertrösten; abbringen; hindern; *fig.* ablegen; ~ *on Kleid* anziehen *Hut* aufsetzen; *fig.* annehmen; an-, einschalten;

vergrößern; ~ *on airs* sich aufspielen; ~ *on weight* zunehmen; ~ *out* ausmachen, (aus)löschen; verrenken; (her)ausstrecken; verwirren; *j-m* Ungelegenheiten bereiten; *Kraft* aufbieten; *Geld* ausleihen; ~ *right in* Ordnung bringen; ~ *through teleph.* verbinden (to mit); ~ *to* hinzufügen; ~ *to death* hinrichten; ~ *to the rack od. torture auf die Folter spannen; ~ *up* aufstellen *etc.*; errichten, bauen; *Waren* anbieten; *Miete* erhöhen; ver-, wegpacken; *Widerstand* leisten; *Kampf* liefern; *Gäste* unterbringen; *Bekanntmachung* anschlagen; *v/i.* ~ *off*, ~ *out*, ~ *to sea* ⚓ auslaufen; ~ *in* ⚓ einlaufen; ~ *up at* einkehren *od.* absteigen in (*dat.*); ~ *up for* sich bewerben um; ~ *up with* sich gefallen lassen; sich abfinden mit.

**putrefy** ['pju:trifai] (ver)faulen.

**putrid** □ ['pju:trid] faul, verdorben; *sl.* scheußlich, saumäßig, ~**ity** [pju:'triditi] Fäulnis *f*.

**putty** ['pʌti] 1. Kitt *m*; 2. kitten.

**puzzle** ['pʌzl] 1. schwierige Aufgabe, Rätsel *n*; Verwirrung *f*; Geduldspiel *n*; 2. *v/t.* irremachen; *j-m* Kopfzerbrechen machen; ~ *out* austüfteln; *v/i.* sich den Kopf zerbrechen; ~**headed** konfus.

**pygm|(a)ean** [pig'mi:ən] zwerghaft; ~**y** ['pigmi] Zwerg *m*; *attr.* zwerghaft.

**pyjamas** [pə'dʒɑ:məz] *pl.* Schlafanzug *m*.

**pyramid** ['pirəmid] Pyramide *f*; ~**al** □ [pi'ræmidl] pyramidal.

**pyre** ['paiə] Scheiterhaufen *m*.

**pyrotechnic|(al** □) ['pairou'teknik(əl)] pyrotechnosch, Feuerwerks...; ~**s** *pl.* Feuerwerk *n* (*a. fig.*).

**Pythagorean** [paiθægə'ri(:)ən] 1.pythagoreisch; 2. Pythagoreer *m*.

**pyx** *eccl.* [piks] Monstranz *f*.

# Q

**quack** [kwæk] 1. Quaken *n*; Scharlatan *m*; Quacksalber *m*, Kurpfuscher *m*; Marktschreier *m*; 2. quacksalberisch; 3. quaken; quacksalbern (*an dat.*); ~**ery** ['kwækəri] Quacksalberei *f*.

**quadrangle** ['kwɔdræŋgl] Viereck *n*; Innenhof *m* *e-s College*.

**quadrennial** □ [kwɔ'dreniəl] vierjährig; vierjährlich.

**quadru|ped** ['kwɔdruped] Vierfüßer *m*; ~**ple** [~pl] 1. □ vierfach; 2. (sich) vervierfachen; ~**plets** [~lits] *pl.* Vierlinge *m/pl.*

**quagmire** ['kwægmaiə] Sumpf (-land *n*) *m*, Moor *n*.

**quail[1]** *orn.* [kweil] Wachtel *f*.

**quail[2]** [~] verzagen; beben.

**quaint** □ [kweint] anheimelnd, malerisch; putzig; seltsam.

**quake** [kweik] 1. beben, zittern (*with*, *for* vor *dat.*); 2. Erdbeben *n*.

**Quaker** ['kweikə] Quäker *m*.

**quali|fication** ['kwɔlifi'keiʃən] (erforderliche) Befähigung; Einschränkung *f*; *gr.* nähere Bestimmung; ~**fy** ['kwɔlifai] *v/t.* befähigen; (be-) nennen; *gr.* näher bestimmen; ein-

schränken, mäßigen; mildern; *v/i.*
seine Befähigung nachweisen; **~ty**
[~iti] Eigenschaft *f*, Beschaffenheit
*f*; ✝ Qualität *f*; vornehmer Stand.

**qualm** [kwɔːm] plötzliche Übelkeit;
Zweifel *m*; Bedenken *n*.

**quandary** ['kwɔndəri] verzwickte
Lage, Verlegenheit *f*.

**quantity** ['kwɔntiti] Quantität *f*,
Menge *f*; großer Teil.

**quantum** ['kwɔntəm] Menge *f*,
Größe *f*, Quantum *n*; Anteil *m*.

**quarantine** ['kwɔrəntiːn] 1. Quarantäne *f*; 2. unter Quarantäne
stellen.

**quarrel** ['kwɔrəl] 1. Zank *m*, Streit
*m*; 2. (sich) zanken, streiten; **~-
some** □ [~ɪsəm] zänkisch; streitsüchtig.

**quarry** ['kwɔri] 1. Steinbruch *m*;
*fig.* Fundgrube *f*; (Jagd)Beute *f*;
2. *Steine* brechen; *fig.* stöbern.

**quart** [kwɔːt] Quart *n* (*1,136 l*).

**quarter** ['kwɔːtə] 1. Viertel *n*, vierter Teil; *bsd.* Viertelstunde *f*; Vier-
teljahr *n*, Quartal *n*; Viertelzentner
*m*; *Am.* 25 Cent; Keule *f*, Viertel *n*
*e-s geschlachteten Tieres*; Stadtvier-
tel *n*; (Himmels)Richtung *f*, Gegend *f*; ✕ Gnade *f*, Pardon *m*; **~s**
*pl.* Quartier *n* (*a.* ✕), Unterkunft *f*;
*fig.* Kreise *m/pl.*; *live in close* **~s**
beengt wohnen; *at close* **~s** dicht
aufeinander; *come to close* **~s** hand-
gemein werden; 2. vierteln, vier-
teilen; beherbergen; ✕ einquartieren; **~back** *Am. Sport:* Abwehr-
spieler *m*; **~day** Quartalstag *m*;
**~deck** Achterdeck *n*; **~ly** [~əli]
1. vierteljährlich; 2. Vierteljahres-
schrift *f*; **~master** ✕ Quartiermei-
ster *m*.            [*n*.\

**quartet(te)** ♪ [kwɔːˈtet] Quartett\

**quarto** ['kwɔːtou] Quart(format) *n*.

**quash** ♎ [kwɔʃ] aufheben, verwerfen; unterdrücken.

**quasi** ['kwɑːzi(ː)] gleichsam, sozusagen; Quasi..., Schein...

**quaver** ['kweivə] 1. Zittern *n*; ♪
Triller *m*; 2. mit zitternder Stimme
sprechen *od.* singen; trillern.

**quay** [kiː] Kai *m*; Uferstraße *f*.

**queasy** □ ['kwiːzi] empfindlich
(*Magen, Gewissen*); heikel, mäkelig; ekelhaft.

**queen** [kwiːn] Königin *f*; **~ bee**
Bienenkönigin *f*; **~like** ['kwiːnlaik];
**~ly** [~li] wie eine Königin, königlich.

**queer** [kwiə] sonderbar, seltsam;
wunderlich; komisch; homo-
sexuell.

**quench** [kwentʃ] *fig. Durst etc.* löschen, stillen; kühlen; *Aufruhr*
unterdrücken.

**querulous** □ ['kwerʊləs] quengelig,
mürrisch, verdrossen.

**query** ['kwiəri] 1. Frage(zeichen *n*)
*f*; 2. (be)fragen; (be-, an)zweifeln.

**quest** [kwest] 1. Suche(*n n*) *f*, Nach-
forschen *n*; 2. suchen, forschen.

**question** ['kwestʃən] 1. Frage *f*;
Problem *n*; Untersuchung *f*; Streitfrage *f*; Zweifel *m*; Sache *f*, Angelegenheit *f*; *beyond* (*all*) **~** ohne
Frage; *in* **~** fraglich; *call in* **~** anzweifeln; *that is out of the* **~** das
steht außer *od.* kommt nicht in
Frage; 2. befragen; bezweifeln;
**~able** □ [~nəbl] fraglich; fragwürdig; **~er** [~nə] Fragende(r *m*) *f*;
**~-mark** Fragezeichen *n*; **~naire**
[kwestiə'neə] Fragebogen *m*.

**queue** [kjuː] 1. Reihe *f v. Personen
etc.*, Schlange *f*; Zopf *m*; 2. *mst* **~
up** (in e-r Reihe) anstehen, Schlange
stehen.

**quibble** ['kwibl] 1. Wortspiel *n*;
Spitzfindigkeit *f*; Ausflucht *f*; 2. *fig.*
ausweichen; scharf witzeln.

**quick** [kwik] 1. schnell, rasch; voreilig; lebhaft; gescheit; beweglich;
lebendig; scharf (*Gehör etc.*); 2. lebendes Fleisch; *the* **~** die Leben-
den; *to the* **~** (bis) ins Fleisch; *fig.*
(bis) ins Herz, tief; *cut s.o. to the* **~**
j-n aufs empfindlichste kränken; **~en**
['kwikən] *v/t.* beleben; beschleunigen; *v/i.* aufleben; sich regen; **~ly**
[~kli] schnell, rasch; **~ness** [~knis]
Lebhaftigkeit *f*; Schnelligkeit *f*;
Voreiligkeit *f*; Schärfe *f des Ver-
standes etc.*; **~sand** Triebsand *m*;
**~set** ♣ Setzling *m*, *bsd.* Hagedorn
*m*; *a.* **~ hedge** lebende Hecke; **~-
sighted** scharfsichtig; **~silver** *min.*
Quecksilber *n*; **~witted** schlag-
fertig.

**quid**[1] [kwid] Priem *m* (*Kautabak*).

**quid**[2] *sl.* [~] Pfund *n* Sterling.

**quiescen|ce** [kwai'esns] Ruhe *f*,
Stille *f*; **~t** □ [~nt] ruhend; *fig.*
ruhig, still.

**quiet** ['kwaiət] 1. □ ruhig, still;
2. Ruhe *f*; *on the* **~** (*sl.* on the q.t.)
unter der Hand, im stillen; 3. *a.* **~
down** (sich) beruhigen; **~ness**
[~tnis], **~ude** ['kwaiitjuːd] Ruhe *f*,
Stille *f*.

**quill** [kwil] 1. Federkiel *m*; *fig.* Feder *f*; Stachel *m des Igels etc.*;
2. rund fälteln; **~ing** ['kwilin]
Rüsche *f*, Krause *f*; **~pen** Gänse-
feder *f zum Schreiben*.

**quilt** [kwilt] 1. Steppdecke *f*;
2. steppen; wattieren.

**quince** ♣ [kwins] Quitte *f*.

**quinine** *pharm.* [kwi'niːn, *Am.*
'kwainain] Chinin *n*.

**quinquennial** □ [kwiŋ'kweniəl]
fünfjährig; fünfjährlich.

**quinsy** ♨ ['kwinzi] Mandelentzündung *f*.

**quintal** ['kwintl] (Doppel)Zentner
*m*.

**quintessence** [kwin'tesns] Quint-
essenz *f*, Kern *m*, Inbegriff *m*.

**quintuple** ['kwintjupl] 1. □ fünffach; 2. (sich) verfünffachen; ~ts [⸚lits] pl. Fünflinge m/pl.

quip [kwip] Stich(elei f) m; Witz (-wort n) m; Spitzfindigkeit f.

quirk [kwəːk] Spitzfindigkeit f; Witz(elei f) m; Kniff m; Schnörkel m; Eigentümlichkeit f; △ Hohlkehle f.

quisling ['kwizliŋ] Quisling m, Kollaborateur m.

quit [kwit] 1. v/t. verlassen; aufgeben; Am. aufhören (mit); vergelten; Schuld tilgen; v/i. aufhören; ausziehen (Mieter); give notice to ~ kündigen; 2. quitt; frei, los.

quite [kwait] ganz, gänzlich; recht; durchaus; ~ a hero ein wirklicher Held; ~ (so)!, ~ that! ganz recht; ~ the thing F große Mode.

quittance ['kwitəns] Quittung f.

quitter Am. F ['kwitə] Drückeberger m.

quiver¹ ['kwivə] zittern, beben.

quiver² [~] Köcher m.

quiz [kwiz] 1. Prüfung f, Test m; Quiz n; belustigter Blick; 2. (aus-) fragen; prüfen; necken, foppen; anstarren, beäugen; ~zical □ ['kwizikəl] spöttisch; komisch.

quoit [kɔit] Wurfring m; ~s pl. Wurfringspiel n.

Quonset Am. ['kwɔnsit] a. ~ hut Wellblechbaracke f.

quorum parl. ['kwɔːrəm] beschlußfähige Mitgliederzahl.

quota ['kwoutə] Quote f, Anteil m, Kontingent n.

quotation [kwou'teiʃən] Anführung f, Zitat n; ✝ Preisnotierung f; Kostenvoranschlag m; ~-marks pl. Anführungszeichen n/pl.

quote [kwout] anführen, zitieren; ✝ berechnen, notieren (at mit).

quotient Ⱥ ['kwouʃənt] Quotient m.

quoth † [kwouθ]: ~ I sagte ich; ~ he sagte er.

quotidian [kwɔ'tidiən] (all)täglich.

# R

rabbi ['ræbai] Rabbiner m.

rabbit ['ræbit] Kaninchen n.

rabble ['ræbl] Pöbel(haufen) m.

rabid □ ['ræbid] tollwütig (Tier); fig. wild, wütend.

rabies vet. ['reibiːz] Tollwut f.

raccoon [rə'kuːn] - racoon.

race [reis] 1. Geschlecht n, Stamm m; Rasse f, Schlag m; Lauf m (a. fig.); Wettrennen n; Strömung f; ~s pl. Pferderennen n; 2. rennen; rasen; um die Wette laufen (mit); ⊕ leer laufen; ~-course ['reiskɔːs] Rennbahn f, -strecke f; ~-horse Rennpferd n; ~r ['reisə] Rennpferd n; Rennboot n; Rennwagen)

racial ['reiʃəl] Rassen... [m.]

racing ['reisiŋ] Rennsport m; attr. Renn...

rack [ræk] 1. Gestell n; Kleiderständer m; Gepäcknetz n; Raufe f, Futtergestell n; Folter(bank) f; go to ~ and ruin völlig zugrunde gehen; 2. strecken; foltern, quälen (a. fig.); ~ one's brains sich den Kopf zermartern.

racket ['rækit] 1. Tennis-Schläger m; Lärm m; Trubel m; Am. F Schwindel(geschäft n) m; Strapaze f; 2. lärmen; sich amüsieren; ~eer Am. [ræki'tiə] Erpresser m; ~eering Am. [~əriŋ] Erpresserwesen n; ~y ['rækiti] Gassenjunge m.

racoon zo. [rə'kuːn] Waschbär m.

racy □ ['reisi] kraftvoll, lebendig; stark; würzig; urwüchsig.

radar ['reidə] Radar(gerät) n.

radian|ce, ~cy ['reidjəns, ~si] Strahlen n; ~t □ [~nt] strahlend, leuchtend.

radiat|e ['reidieit] (aus)strahlen; strahlenförmig ausgehen; ~ion [reidi'eiʃən] (Aus)Strahlung f; ~or ['reidieitə] Heizkörper m; mot. Kühler m.

radical ['rædikəl] 1. □ Wurzel..., Grund...; gründlich; eingewurzelt; pol. radikal; 2. pol. Radikale(r m) f.

radio ['reidiou] 1. Radio n; Funk (-spruch) m; ~ drama, ~ play Hörspiel n; ~ set Radiogerät n; 2. funken; ~(-)active radioaktiv; ~graph [~ougraːf] 1. Röntgenbild n; 2. ein Röntgenbild machen von; ~-telegram Funktelegramm n; ~-therapy Strahlen-, Röntgentherapie f.

radish ♀ ['rædiʃ] Rettich m; (red) ~ Radieschen n.

radius ['reidjəs] Radius m.

raffle ['ræfl] 1. Tombola f, Verlosung f; 2. verlosen.

raft [raːft] 1. Floß n; 2. flößen; ~er ['raːftə] ⊕ (Dach)Sparren m.

rag¹ [ræg] Lumpen m; Fetzen m; Lappen m.

rag² sl. [~] 1. Unfug m; Radau m; 2. Unfug treiben (mit); j-n aufziehen; j-n beschimpfen; herumtollen, Radau machen.

ragamuffin ['rægəmʌfin] Lumpenkerl m; Gassenjunge m.

rage [reidʒ] 1. Wut f, Zorn m, Raserei f; Sucht f, Gier f (for nach); Manie f; Ekstase f; it is all the ~ es ist allgemein Mode; 2. wüten, rasen.

**rag-fair** ['rægfɛə] Trödelmarkt m.

**ragged** □ ['rægid] rauh; zottig; zackig; zerlumpt.

**ragman** ['rægmən] Lumpensammler m.

**raid** [reid] 1. (feindlicher) Überfall, Streifzug m; (Luft)Angriff m; Razzia f; 2. einbrechen in (acc.); überfallen.

**rail¹** [reil] schimpfen.

**rail²** [⌣] 1. Geländer n; Stange f; 🚋 Schiene f; off the ~s entgleist; fig. in Unordnung; by ~ per Bahn; 2. a. ~ in, ~ off mit e-m Geländer umgeben.

**railing** ['reiliŋ], a. ~s pl. Geländer n; Staket n.

**raillery** ['reiləri] Spötterei f.

**railroad** Am. ['reilroud] Eisenbahn f. [~man Eisenbahner m.\
**railway** ['reilwei] Eisenbahn f;}

**rain** [rein] 1. Regen m; 2. regnen; ~bow ['reinbou] Regenbogen m; ~coat Regenmantel m; ~fall Regenmenge f; ~proof 1. regendicht; 2. Regenmantel m; ~y □ ['reini] regnerisch; Regen...; a ~ day fig. Notzeiten f/pl.

**raise** [reiz] oft ~ up heben; (oft fig.) erheben; errichten; erhöhen (a. fig.); Geld etc. aufbringen; Anleihe aufnehmen; verursachen; fig. erwecken; anstiften; züchten, ziehen; Belagerung etc. aufheben.

**raisin** ['reizn] Rosine f.

**rake** [reik] 1. Rechen m, Harke f; Wüstling m; Lebemann m; 2. v/t (zs.-)harken; zs.-scharren; fig. (durch)stöbern; ~off Am. sl. ['reikɔːf] Schwindelprofit m.

**rakish** □ ['reikiʃ] schnittig, liederlich, ausschweifend; verwegen; salopp.

**rally** ['ræli] 1. Sammeln n; Treffen n; Am. Massenversammlung f; Erholung f; mot. Rallye f; 2. (sich ver)sammeln; sich erholen; necken.

**ram** [ræm] 1. zo., ast. Widder m; ⊕, 🚢 Ramme f; 2. (fest)rammen; 🚢 rammen.

**rambl|e** ['ræmbl] 1. Streifzug m; 2. umherstreifen; abschweifen; ~er [⌣lə] Wanderer m; ♀ Kletterrose f; ~ing [⌣liŋ] weitläufig.

**ramify** ['ræmifai] (sich) verzweigen.

**ramp** [ræmp] Rampe f; ~ant □ ['ræmpənt] wuchernd; fig. zügellos.

**rampart** ['ræmpaːt] Wall m.

**ramshackle** ['ræmʃækl] wack(e)lig.

**ran** [ræn] pret. von run 1.

**ranch** [raːntʃ, Am. ræntʃ] Ranch f, Viehfarm f; ~er ['raːntʃə, Am. 'ræntʃə], ~man Rancher m, Viehzüchter m; Farmer m.

**rancid** □ ['rænsid] ranzig.

**ranco(u)r** ['ræŋkə] Groll m, Haß m.

**random** ['rændəm] 1. at ~ aufs Geratewohl, blindlings; 2. ziel-, wahllos; zufällig.

**rang** [ræŋ] pret. von ring 2.

**range** [reindʒ] 1. Reihe f; (Berg-)Kette f; ♣ Kollektion f, Sortiment n; Herd m; Raum m; Umfang m, Bereich m; Reichweite f; Schußweite f; (ausgedehnte) Fläche; Schießstand m; 2. v/t. (ein)reihen, ordnen; Gebiet etc. durchstreifen; 🚢 längs et. fahren; v/i. in e-r Reihe od. Linie stehen; (umher-)streifen; sich erstrecken, reichen; ~r ['reindʒə] Förster m; Aufseher m e-s Parks; Am. Förster m; ✕ Nahkampfspezialist m.

**rank** [ræŋk] 1. Reihe f, Linie f; ✕ Glied n; Klasse f; Rang m, Stand m; the ~s pl., the ~ and file die Mannschaften f/pl.; fig. die große Masse; 2. v/t. (ein)reihen, (ein-)ordnen; v/i. sich reihen, sich ordnen; gehören (with zu); e-e Stelle einnehmen (above über dat.); ~ as gelten als; 3. üppig; ranzig; stinkend.

**rankle** fig. ['ræŋkl] nagen.

**ransack** ['rænsæk] durchwühlen, durchstöbern, durchsuchen; ausrauben.

**ransom** ['rænsəm] 1. Lösegeld n; Auslösung f; 2. loskaufen; erlösen.

**rant** [rænt] 1. Schwulst m; 2. Phrasen dreschen; mit Pathos vortragen.

**rap** [ræp] 1. Klaps m; Klopfen n; fig. Heller m; 2. schlagen, klopfen.

**rapaci|ous** □ [rə'peiʃəs] raubgierig; ~ty [rə'pæsiti] Raubgier f.

**rape** [reip] 1. Raub m; Entführung f; Notzucht f, Vergewaltigung f; ♀ Raps m; 2. rauben; vergewaltigen.

**rapid** ['ræpid] 1. □ schnell, reißend, rapid(e); steil; 2. ~s pl. Stromschnelle(n pl.) f; ~ity [rə'piditi] Schnelligkeit f.

**rapprochement** pol. [ræ'prɔʃmãːŋ] Wiederannäherung f.

**rapt** [ræpt] entzückt; versunken; ~ure ['ræptʃə] Entzücken n; go into ~s in Entzücken geraten.

**rare** □ [rɛə] selten; phys. dünn.

**rarebit** ['rɛəbit]: Welsh ~ geröstete Käseschnitte.

**rarefy** ['rɛərifai] (sich) verdünnen.

**rarity** ['rɛəriti] Seltenheit f; Dünnheit f.

**rascal** ['raːskəl] Schuft m; co. Gauner m; ~ity [raːs'kæliti] Schurkerei f; ~ly ['raːskəli] schuftig; erbärmlich.

**rash¹** □ [ræʃ] hastig, vorschnell; übereilt; unbesonnen; waghalsig.

**rash²** 🚑 [⌣] Hautausschlag m.

**rasher** ['ræʃə] Speckschnitte f.

**rasp** [raːsp] 1. Raspel f; 2. raspeln; j-m weh(e) tun; kratzen; streiten.

**raspberry** ['raːzbəri] Himbeere f.

**rat** [ræt] zo. Ratte f; pol. Überläufer m; smell a ~ Lunte od. den Braten riechen; ~s! Quatsch!

**rate** [reit] 1. Verhältnis n, Maß n,

Satz *m*; Rate *f*; Preis *m*, Gebühr *f*; Taxe *f*; (Gemeinde)Abgabe *f*, Steuer *f*; Grad *m*, Rang *m*; *bsd.* ⚓ Klasse *f*; Geschwindigkeit *f*; at any ~ auf jeden Fall; ~ of exchange (Umrechnungs)Kurs *m*; ~ of interest Zinsfuß *m*; 2. (ein)schätzen; besteuern; ~ among rechnen, zählen zu (*dat.*); ausschelten.

**rather** ['rɑːðə] eher, lieber; vielmehr; besser gesagt; ziemlich; ~! F und ob!; I had od. would ~ do ich möchte lieber tun.

**ratify** ['rætifai] ratifizieren.

**rating** ['reitiŋ] Schätzung *f*; Steuersatz *m*; ⚓ Dienstgrad *m*; ⚓ (Segel-) Klasse *f*; Matrose *m*; Schelte(n *n*) *f*.

**ratio** ℞ *etc.* ['reiʃiou] Verhältnis *n*.

**ration** ['ræʃən] 1. Ration *f*, Zuteilung *f*; 2. rationieren.

**rational** ☐ ['ræʃənl] vernunftgemäß, vernünftig, (a. ℞) rational; ~ity [ræʃə'næliti] Vernunft(mäßigkeit) *f*; ~ize ['ræʃnəlaiz] rationalisieren; wirtschaftlich gestalten.

**rat race** ['ræt 'reis] sinnlose Hetze; rücksichtsloses Aufstiegsstreben.

**ratten** ['rætn] sabotieren.

**rattle** ['rætl] 1. Gerassel *n*; Geklapper *n*; Geplapper *n*; Klapper *f*; (Todes)Röcheln *n*; 2. rasseln (mit); klappern; plappern; röcheln; ~ off herunterrasseln; ~brain, ~pate Hohl-, Wirrkopf *m*; ~snake Klapperschlange *f*; ~trap *fig.* Klapperkasten *m* (*Fahrzeug*).

**rattling** ['rætliŋ] 1. *adj.* rasselnd; *fig.* scharf (*Tempo*); 2. *adv.* sehr, äußerst.

**raucous** ☐ ['rɔːkəs] heiser, rauh.

**ravage** ['rævidʒ] 1. Verwüstung *f*; 2. verwüsten; plündern.

**rave** [reiv] rasen, toben; schwärmen (about, of von).

**ravel** ['rævəl] *v/t.* verwickeln; ~ (out) auftrennen; *fig.* entwirren; *v/i. a.* ~ out ausfasern, aufgehen.

**raven** *orn.* ['reivn] Rabe *m*.

**raven|ing** ['rævniŋ], ~ous ☐ ['rævinəs] gefräßig; heißhungrig; raubgierig.

**ravine** [rə'viːn] Hohlweg *m*; Schlucht *f*.

**ravings** ['reiviŋz] *pl.* Delirien *n/pl.*

**ravish** ['ræviʃ] entzücken; vergewaltigen; rauben; ~ing ☐ [~iŋ] hinreißend, entzückend; ~ment [~ʃmənt] Schändung *f*; Entzücken *n*.

**raw** ☐ [rɔː] roh; Roh...; wund; rauh (*Wetter*); ungeübt, unerfahren; ~boned [~rɔːbound] knochig, hager; ~ hide Rohleder *m*.

**ray** [rei] Strahl *m*; *fig.* Schimmer *m*.

**rayon** ['reiən] Kunstseide *f*.

**raze** [reiz] *Haus etc.* abreißen; *Festung* schleifen; tilgen.

**razor** ['reizə] Rasiermesser *n*; Ra-

sierapparat *m*; ~blade Rasierklinge *f*; ~edge *fig. des Messers* Schneide *f*, kritische Lage.

**razz** *Am. sl.* [ræz] aufziehen.

**re...** [riː] wieder...; zurück...; neu...; um...

**reach** [riːtʃ] 1. Ausstrecken *n*; Griff *m*; Reichweite *f*; Fassungskraft *f*, Horizont *m*; Flußstrecke *f*; beyond ~, out of ~ unerreichbar; within easy ~ leicht erreichbar; 2. *v/i.* reichen; langen, greifen; sich erstrecken; *v/t.* (hin-, her)reichen, (hin-, her)langen; ausstrecken; erreichen.

**react** [riː'ækt] reagieren (to auf *acc.*); (ein)wirken (on, upon auf *acc.*); sich auflehnen (against gegen).

**reaction** [riː'ækʃən] Reaktion *f* (*a. pol.*); ~ary [~ʃnəri] 1. reaktionär; 2. Reaktionär(in).

**reactor** *phys.* [riː'æktə] Reaktor *m*.

**read** 1. [riːd] [*irr.*] lesen; deuten; (an)zeigen (*Thermometer*); studieren; sich *gut etc.* lesen; lauten; ~ to *s.o.* j-m vorlesen; 2. [red] *pret. u. p.p.* von I; 3. [~] *adj.* belesen; ~able ☐ ['riːdəbl] lesbar; leserlich; lesenswert; ~er ['riːdə] (Vor)Leser(in); *typ.* Korrektor *m*; Lektor *m*; *univ.* Dozent *m*; Lesebuch *n*.

**readi|ly** ['redili] *adv.* gleich, leicht; gern; ~ness [~inis] Bereitschaft *f*; Bereitwilligkeit *f*; Schnelligkeit *f*.

**reading** ['riːdiŋ] Lesen *n*; Lesung *f* (*a. parl.*); Stand *m* des *Thermometers*; Belesenheit *f*; Lektüre *f*; Lesart *f*; Auffassung *f*; *attr.* Lese...

**readjust** ['riːə'dʒʌst] wieder in Ordnung bringen; wieder anpassen; ~ment [~tmənt] Wiederanpassung *f*; Neuordnung *f*.

**ready** ☐ ['redi] bereit, fertig; bereitwillig; im Begriff (to do zu tun); schnell; gewandt; leicht; zur Hand; ✝ bar; ~ for use gebrauchsfertig; make od. get ~ (sich) fertig machen; ~made fertig, Konfektions...

**reagent** ℞ [riː'eidʒənt] Reagens *n*.

**real** ☐ [riəl] wirklich, tatsächlich, real; echt; ~ estate Grundbesitz *m*, Immobilien *f/pl.*; ~ism ['riəlizəm] Realismus *m*; ~istic [riə'listik] (~ally) realistisch; sachlich; wirklichkeitsnah; ~ity [riː'æliti] Wirklichkeit *f*; ~ization [riəlai'zeiʃən] Verwirklichung *f*; Erkenntnis *f*; ✝ Realisierung *f*; ~ize ['riəlaiz] sich klarmachen; erkennen; verwirklichen; realisieren, zu Geld machen; ~ly [~li] wirklich, in der Tat.

**realm** [relm] Königreich *n*; Reich *n*.

**realt|or** *Am.* ['riəltə] Grundstücksmakler *m*; ~y ⚖ [~ti] Grundeigentum *n*.

**reap** [riːp] *Korn* schneiden; *Feld*

**mähen**; *fig.* ernten; **~er** ['riːpə] Schnitter(in); Mähmaschine *f*.

**reappear** ['riːə'piə] wieder erscheinen.

**rear** [riə] **1.** *v/t.* auf-, großziehen; züchten; *v/i.* sich aufrichten; **2.** Rück-, Hinterseite *f*; *mot.*, ⚓ Heck *n*; ✕ Nachhut *f*; *at the ~ of, in (the) ~ of* hinter (*dat.*); **3.** Hinter..., Nach...; **~ wheel drive** Hinterradantrieb *m*; **~admiral** ⚓ ['riə-'ædmərəl] Konteradmiral *m*; **~guard** ✕ Nachhut *f*; **~lamp** *mot.* Schlußlicht *n*.

**rearm** ['riː'ɑːm] (wieder)aufrüsten; **~ament** [~məmənt] Aufrüstung *f*.

**rearmost** ['riəmoust] hinterst.

**rearward** ['riəwəd] **1.** *adj.* rückwärtig; **2.** *adv. a.* **~s** rückwärts.

**reason** ['riːzn] **1.** Vernunft *f*; Verstand *m*; Recht *n*, Billigkeit *f*; Ursache *f*, Grund *m*; *by ~* of wegen; *for this ~* aus diesem Grund; *listen to ~* Vernunft annehmen; *it stands to ~* that es leuchtet ein, daß; **2.** *v/i.* vernünftig denken; schließen; urteilen; argumentieren; *v/t. a. ~ out* durchdenken; *~ away* fortdisputieren; *~ s.o. into (out of) s.th.* j-m et. ein- (aus)reden; **~able** □ [~nəbl] vernünftig; billig; angemessen; leidlich.

**reassure** [riːə'ʃuə] wieder versichern; (wieder) beruhigen.

**rebate** ['riːbeit] ✝ Rabatt *m*, Abzug *m*; Rückzahlung *f*.

**rebel 1.** ['rebl] Rebell *m*; Aufrührer *m*; **2.** [~] rebellisch; **3.** [ri'bel] sich auflehnen; **~lion** [~ljən] Empörung *f*; **~lious** [~jəs] — *rebel 2*.

**rebirth** ['riː'bəːθ] Wiedergeburt *f*.

**rebound** [ri'baund] **1.** zurückprallen; **2.** Rückprall *m*, Rückschlag *m*.

**rebuff** [ri'bʌf] **1.** Zurück-, Abweisung *f*; **2.** zurück-, abweisen.

**rebuild** ['riː'bild] [*irr.* (*build*)] wieder (auf)bauen.

**rebuke** [ri'bjuːk] **1.** Tadel *m*; **2.** tadeln.

**rebut** [ri'bʌt] zurückweisen.

**recall** [ri'kɔːl] **1.** Zurückrufung *f*; Abberufung *f*; Widerruf *m*; *beyond ~, past ~* unwiderruflich; **2.** zurückrufen; ab(be)rufen; (sich) erinnern an (*acc.*); widerrufen; ✝ Kapital kündigen.

**recapitulate** [riːkə'pitjuleit] kurz wiederholen, zs.-fassen.

**recapture** ['riː'kæptʃə] wieder (gefangen)nehmen; ✕ zurückerobern.

**recast** ['riː'kɑːst] [*irr.* (*cast*)] ⊕ umgießen; umformen, neu gestalten.

**recede** [ri(ː)'siːd] zurücktreten.

**receipt** [ri'siːt] **1.** Empfang *m*; Eingang *m v.* Waren; Quittung *f*; (Koch)Rezept *n*; **~s** *pl.* Einnahmen *f/pl.*; **2.** quittieren.

**receiv|able** [ri'siːvəbl] annehmbar; ✝ noch zu fordern(d), ausstehend;

**~e** [ri'siːv] empfangen; erhalten; bekommen; aufnehmen; annehmen; anerkennen; **~ed** anerkannt; **~er** [~və] Empfänger *m*; *teleph.* Hörer *m*; Hehler *m*; *Steuer- etc.* Einnehmer *m*; *official ~* ⚖ Masseverwalter *m*.

**recent** □ ['riːsnt] neu; frisch; modern; *~ events* die jüngsten Ereignisse *n/pl.*; **~ly** [~tli] neulich, vor kurzem.

**receptacle** [ri'septəkl] Behälter *m*.

**reception** [ri'sepʃən] Aufnahme *f* (*a. fig.*), (*a.* Radio)Empfang *m*; Annahme *f*; **~ist** [~nist] Empfangsdame *f*, -herr *m*; **~room** Empfangszimmer *n*.

**receptive** □ [ri'septiv] empfänglich, aufnahmefähig (*of* für).

**recess** [ri'ses] Pause *f*; *bsd. parl.* Ferien *pl.*; (entlegener) Winkel; Nische *f*; *~es pl. fig.* Tiefe(n *pl.*) *f*; **~ion** [~eʃən] Zurückziehen *n*, Zurücktreten *n*; ✝ Konjunkturrückgang *m*, rückläufige Bewegung.

**recipe** ['resipi] Rezept *n*.

**recipient** [ri'sipiənt] Empfänger(in).

**reciproc|al** [ri'siprəkəl] wechsel-, gegenseitig; **~ate** [~eit] *v/i.* sich erkenntlich zeigen; ⊕ sich hin- und herbewegen; *v/t.* Glückwünsche etc. erwidern; ✝ Konjunkturrückgang; **~ity** [resi'prositi] Gegenseitigkeit *f*.

**recit|al** [ri'saitl] Bericht *m*; Erzählung *f*; ♪ (Solo)Vortrag *m*, Konzert *n*; **~ation** [resi'teiʃən] Hersagen *n*; Vortrag *m*; **~e** [ri'sait] vortragen; aufsagen; berichten.

**reckless** □ ['reklis] unbekümmert; rücksichtslos; leichtsinnig.

**reckon** ['rekən] *v/t.* rechnen; *a. ~ for, ~ as* schätzen als, halten für; *~ up* zs.-zählen; *v/i.* rechnen; denken; vermuten; *~ (up)on* sich verlassen auf (*acc.*); **~ing** ['rekniŋ] Rechnen *n*; (Ab-, Be)Rechnung *f*.

**reclaim** [ri'kleim] wiedergewinnen; *j-n* bessern; zivilisieren; urbar machen.

**recline** [ri'klain] (sich) (zurück-) lehnen; *~ upon fig.* sich stützen auf.

**recluse** [ri'kluːs] Einsiedler(in).

**recogni|tion** [rekəg'niʃən] Anerkennung *f*; Wiedererkennen *n*; **~ze** ['rekəgnaiz] anerkennen; (wieder-) erkennen.

**recoil** [ri'kɔil] **1.** zurückprallen; **2.** Rückstoß *m*, -lauf *m*.

**recollect[1]** [rekə'lekt] sich erinnern an (*acc.*).

**re-collect[2]** ['riː'kə'lekt] wieder sammeln; *~ o.s.* sich fassen.

**recollection** [rekə'lekʃən] Erinnerung *f* (*of* an *acc.*); Gedächtnis *n*.

**recommend** [rekə'mend] empfehlen; **~ation** [rekəmen'deiʃən] Empfehlung *f*; Vorschlag *m*.

**recompense** ['rekəmpens] **1.** Belohnung *f*, Vergeltung *f*; Ersatz *m*;

2. belohnen, vergelten; entschädigen; ersetzen.

**reconcil|e** ['rekənsail] aus-, versöhnen; in Einklang bringen; schlichten; **~iation** [rekənsili'eiʃən] Ver-, Aussöhnung f.

**recondition** ['ri:kən'diʃən] wieder herrichten; ⊕ überholen.

**reconn|aissance** ✕ [ri'kɔnisəns] Aufklärung f, Erkundung f; fig. Übersicht f; **~oitre**, Am. **~oiter** [rekə'nɔitə] erkunden, auskundschaften.

**reconsider** ['ri:kən'sidə] wieder erwägen; nochmals überlegen.

**reconstitute** ['ri:'kɔnstitju:t] wiederherstellen.

**reconstruct** ['ri:kəns'trʌkt] wieder-aufbauen; **~ion** [~kʃən] Wiederaufbau m, Wiederherstellung f.

**reconvert** ['ri:kən'və:t] umstellen.

**record 1.** ['rekɔ:d] Aufzeichnung f; ᵗᵗ Protokoll n; schriftlicher Bericht; Ruf m, Leumund m; Wiedergabe f; Schallplatte f; Sport: Rekord m; place on ~ schriftlich niederlegen; ♀ Office Staatsarchiv n; off the ~ Am. inoffiziell; 2. [ri'kɔ:d] auf-, verzeichnen; auf Schallplatte etc. aufnehmen; **~er** [~də] Registrator m; Stadtrichter m; Aufnahmegerät n; Tonbandgerät n; ♪ Blockflöte f; **~ing** [~diŋ] Radio: Aufzeichnung f, Aufnahme f; **~player** Plattenspieler m.

**recount** [ri'kaunt] erzählen.

**recoup** [ri'ku:p] j-n entschädigen (for für); et. wieder einbringen.

**recourse** [ri'kɔ:s] Zuflucht f; have ~ to s-e Zuflucht nehmen zu.

**recover** [ri'kʌvə] v/t. wiedererlangen, wiederfinden; wieder einbringen, wiedergutmachen; Schulden etc. eintreiben; be ~ed wiederhergestellt sein; v/i. sich erholen; genesen; **~y** [~əri] Wiedererlangung f; Wiederherstellung f; Genesung f; Erholung f.

**recreat|e** ['rekrieit] v/t. erfrischen; v/i. a. ~ o.s. sich erholen; **~ion** [rekri'eiʃən] Erholung(spause) f.

**recrimination** [rikrimi'neiʃən] Gegenbeschuldigung f; Gegenklage f.

**recruit** [ri'kru:t] 1. Rekrut m; fig. Neuling m; 2. erneuern, ergänzen; Truppe rekrutieren; ✕ Rekruten ausheben; sich erholen.

**rectangle** ⅄ ['rektæŋgl] Rechteck n.

**recti|fy** ['rektifai] berichtigen; verbessern; ⅄, Radio: gleichrichten; **~tude** [~itju:d] Geradheit f.

**rector** ['rektə] Pfarrer m; Rektor m; **~y** [~əri] Pfarre(i) f; Pfarrhaus n.

**recumbent** □ [ri'kʌmbənt] liegend.

**recuperate** [ri'kju:pəreit] wiederherstellen; sich erholen.

**recur** [ri'kə:] zurück-, wiederkehren (to zu), zurückkommen (to auf acc.); ~ to j-m wieder einfallen; **~rence**

[ri'kʌrəns] Wieder-, Rückkehr f; **~rent** □ [~nt] wiederkehrend.

**red** [red] 1. rot; ~ heat Rotglut f; ~ herring Bückling m; ~ tape Amtsschimmel m; 2. Rot n; (bsd. pol.) Rote(r m) f; be in the ~ Am. F in Schulden stecken.

**red|breast** ['redbrest] a. robin ~ Rotkehlchen n; **~cap** Militärpolizist m; Am. Gepäckträger m; **~den** ['redn] (sich) röten; erröten; **~dish** ['rediʃ] rötlich.

**redecorate** ['ri:'dekəreit] Zimmer renovieren (lassen).

**redeem** [ri'di:m] zurück-, loskaufen; ablösen; Versprechen einlösen; büßen; entschädigen für; erlösen; **₂er** eccl. [~mə] Erlöser m, Heiland m.

**redemption** [ri'dempʃən] Rückkauf m; Auslösung f; Erlösung f.

**red|-handed** ['red'hændid]: catch od. take s.o. ~ j-n auf frischer Tat ertappen; **~head** Rotschopf m; Hitzkopf m; **~headed** rothaarig; **~hot** rotglühend; fig. hitzig; ₂ Indian Indianer(in); **~letter day** Festtag m; fig. Freuden-, Glückstag m; **~ness** ['rednis] Röte f.

**redolent** ['redoulənt] duftend.

**redouble** [ri'dʌbl] (sich) verdoppeln.

**redoubt** ✕ [ri'daut] Redoute f; **~able** rhet. [~təbl] fürchterlich.

**redound** [ri'daund]: ~ to beitragen od. gereichen od. führen zu.

**redress** [ri'dres] 1. Abhilfe f; Wiedergutmachung f; ᵗᵗ Entschädigung f; 2. abhelfen (dat.); wiedergutmachen.

**red|-tapism** ['red'teipizəm] Bürokratismus m; **~tapist** [~ist] Bürokrat m.

**reduc|e** [ri'dju:s] fig. zurückführen, bringen (to auf, in acc., zu); verwandeln (to in acc.); verringern, vermindern; einschränken; Preise herabsetzen; (be)zwingen; ⅄, ᴋ reduzieren; ♂ einrenken; ~ to writing schriftlich niederlegen; **~tion** [ri'dʌkʃən] Reduktion f; Verwandlung f; Herabsetzung f, (Preis)Nachlaß m, Rabatt m; Verminderung f; Verkleinerung f; ♂ Einrenkung f.

**redundant** □ [ri'dʌndənt] überflüssig; übermäßig; weitschweifig.

**reed** [ri:d] Schilfrohr n; Rohrflöte f.

**re-education** ['ri:edju(:)'keiʃən] Umschulung f, Umerziehung f.

**reef** [ri:f] (Felsen)Riff n; ᚦ Reff n.

**reefer** ['ri:fə] Seemannsjacke f; Am. sl. Marihuana-Zigarette f.

**reek** [ri:k] 1. Rauch m, Dampf m; Dunst m; 2. rauchen, dampfen (with von); unangenehm riechen.

**reel** [ri:l] 1. Haspel f; (Garn-, Film)Rolle f, Spule f; 2. v/t. haspeln; wickeln, spulen; v/i. wirbeln; schwanken; taumeln.

**re-elect** ['riːi'lekt] wiederwählen.

**re-enter** [riː'entə] wieder eintreten (in *acc.*).

**re-establish** ['riːis'tæbliʃ] wiederherstellen.

**refection** [ri'fekʃən] Erfrischung *f*.

**refer** [ri'fɔː]: ~ to ver-, überweisen **an** (*acc.*); sich beziehen auf (*acc.*); **erwähnen** (*acc.*); zuordnen (*dat.*); befragen (*acc.*), nachschlagen in (*dat.*); zurückführen auf (*acc.*), zuschreiben (*dat.*); ~**ee** [refə'riː] Schiedsrichter *m*; *Boxen*: Ringrichter *m*; ~**ence** ['refrəns] Referenz *f*, Empfehlung *f*, Zeugnis *n*; Verweisung *f*; Bezugnahme *f*; Anspielung *f*; Beziehung *f*; Auskunft (-geber *m*) *f*; in *od.* with ~ to in betreff (*gen.*), in bezug auf (*acc.*); ~ **book** Nachschlagewerk *n*; ~ **library** Handbibliothek *f*; ~ **number** Aktenzeichen *n*; **make** ~ **to** et. erwähnen.

**referendum** [refə'rendəm] Volksentscheid *m*.

**refill** 1. ['riːfil] Nachfüllung *f*; Ersatzfüllung *f*; 2. ['riː'fil] (sich) wieder füllen, auffüllen.

**refine** [ri'fain] (sich) verfeinern *od.* veredeln; ⊕ raffinieren; (sich) läutern (*a. fig.*); klügeln; ~ (up)on et. verfeinern, verbessern; ~**ment** [~nmənt] Verfeinerung *f*, Vered(e)-lung *f*; Läuterung *f*; Feinheit *f*, Bildung *f*; Spitzfindigkeit *f*; ~**ry** [~nəri] ⊕ Raffinerie *f*; *metall.* (Eisen)Hütte *f*.

**refit** ⚓ ['riː'fit] *v/t.* ausbessern; neu ausrüsten; *v/i.* ausgebessert werden.

**reflect** [ri'flekt] *v/t.* zurückwerfen, reflektieren; zurückstrahlen, widerspiegeln (*a. fig.*); zum Ausdruck bringen; *v/i.* ~ (up)on nachdenken über (*acc.*); sich abfällig äußern über (*acc.*); ein schlechtes Licht werfen auf (*acc.*); ~**ion** [~kʃən] Zurückstrahlung *f*, Widerspiegelung *f*; Reflex *m*; Spiegelbild *n*; Überlegung *f*; Gedanke *m*; abfällige Bemerkung; Makel *m*; ~**ive** ☐ [~ktiv] zurückstrahlend; nachdenklich.

**reflex** ['riːfleks] 1. Reflex...; 2.Widerschein *m*, Reflex *m* (*a. physiol.*).

**reflexive** ☐ [ri'fleksiv] zurückwirkend; *gr.* reflexiv, rückbezüglich.

**reforest** ['riː'fɔrist] aufforsten.

**reform**[1] [ri'fɔːm] 1. Verbesserung *f*, Reform *f*; 2. verbessern, reformieren; (sich) bessern.

**re-form**[2] ['riː'fɔːm] (sich) neu bilden; ⚔ sich wieder formieren.

**reform|ation** [refə'meiʃən] Umgestaltung *f*; Besserung *f*; *eccl.* ♀ Reformation *f*; ~**atory** [ri'fɔːmətəri] 1. bessernd; 2. Besserungsanstalt *f*; ~**er** [ri'fɔːmə] *eccl.* Reformator *m*; *bsd. pol.* Reformer *m*.

**refract|ion** [ri'frækʃən] Strahlenbrechung *f*; ~**ory** ☐ [~ktəri] widerspenstig; hartnäckig; ⊕ feuerfest.

**refrain** [ri'frein] 1. sich enthalten (*from gen.*), unterlassen (*from acc.*); 2. Kehrreim *m*, Refrain *m*.

**refresh** [ri'freʃ] (sich) erfrischen; auffrischen; ~**ment** [~ʃmənt] Erfrischung *f* (*a. Getränk etc.*).

**refrigerat|e** [ri'fridʒəreit] kühlen; ~**or** [~tə] Kühlschrank *m*, -raum *m*; ~ **car** Kühlwagen *m*.

**refuel** ['riː'fjuəl] tanken.

**refuge** ['refjuːdʒ] Zuflucht(sstätte) *f*; *a.* street-~ Verkehrsinsel *f*; ~**e** [refju(ː)'dʒiː] Flüchtling *m*; ~ **camp** Flüchtlingslager *n*.

**refulgent** [ri'fʌldʒənt] strahlend.

**refund** [riː'fʌnd] zurückzahlen.

**refurbish** ['riː'fəːbiʃ] aufpolieren.

**refusal** [ri'fjuːzəl] abschlägige Antwort; (Ver)Weigerung *f*; Vorkaufsrecht *n* (of auf *acc.*).

**refuse**[1] [ri'fjuːz] *v/t.* verweigern; abweisen, ablehnen; scheuen vor (*dat.*); *v/i.* sich weigern; scheuen (*Pferd*). [fall *m*, Müll *m*.)

**refuse**[2] ['refjuːs] Ausschuß *m*; Ab-)

**refute** [ri'fjuːt] widerlegen.

**regain** [ri'gein] wiedergewinnen.

**regal** ['riːgəl] königlich; Königs...

**regale** [ri'geil] *v/t.* festlich bewirten; *v/i.* schwelgen (on in *dat.*).

**regard** [ri'gɑːd] 1. fester Blick; (Hoch)Achtung *f*, Rücksicht *f*; Beziehung *f*; with ~ to im Hinblick auf (*acc.*); kind ~**s** herzliche Grüße; 2. ansehen; (be)achten; betrachten; betreffen; as ~**s** ... was ... anbetrifft; ~**ing** [~diŋ] hinsichtlich (*gen.*); ~**less** ☐ [~dlis]: ~ of ohne Rücksicht auf (*acc.*).

**regenerate** 1. [ri'dʒenəreit] (sich) erneuern; (sich) regenerieren; (sich) neu bilden; 2. [~rit] wiedergeboren.

**regent** ['riːdʒənt] 1. herrschend; 2. Regent *m*.

**regiment** ⚔ ['redʒimənt] 1. Regiment *n*; 2. [~ment] organisieren; ~**als** ⚔ [redʒi'mentlz] *pl.* Uniform*f*.

**region** [ riːdʒən] Gegend *f*, Gebiet *n*; *fig.* Bereich *m*; ~**al** ☐ [~nl] örtlich; Orts...

**register** ['redʒistə] 1. Register *n*, Verzeichnis *n*; ⊕ Schieber *m*, Ventil *n*; ♪ Register *n*; Zählwerk *n*; *cash* Registrierkasse *f*; 2. registrieren *od.* eintragen (lassen); (an-)zeigen, auf-, verzeichnen; *Postsache* einschreiben (lassen), *Gepäck* aufgeben; sich *polizeilich* melden.

**registr|ar** [redʒis'trɑː] Registrator *m*; Standesbeamte(r) *m*; ~**ation** [~reiʃən] Eintragung *f*; ~ **fee** Anmeldegebühr *f*; ~**y** ['redʒistri] Eintragung *f*; Registratur *f*; Register *n*; ~ **office** Standesamt *n*.

**regress, ~ion** ['riːgres, ri'greʃən] Rückkehr *f*; *fig.* Rückgang *m*.

**regret** [ri'gret] 1. Bedauern *n*; Schmerz *m*; 2. bedauern; *Verlust* beklagen; **~ful** □ [~tful] bedauernd; **~fully** [~li] mit Bedauern; **~table** □ [~təbl] bedauerlich.

**regular** □ ['regjulə] regelmäßig; regelrecht, richtig; ordentlich; pünktlich; ✕ regulär; **~ity** [regju'læriti] Regelmäßigkeit *f*; Richtigkeit *f*, Ordnung *f*.

**regulat|e** ['regjuleit] regeln, ordnen; regulieren; **~ion** [regju'leiʃən] 1. Regulierung *f*; Vorschrift *f*, Bestimmung *f*; 2. vorschriftsmäßig.

**rehash** *fig.* ['ri:'hæʃ] 1. wieder durchkauen *od.* aufwärmen; 2. Aufguß *m*.

**rehears|al** [ri'hə:səl] *thea.*, ♪ Probe *f*; Wiederholung *f*; **~e** [ri'hə:s] *thea.* proben; wiederholen; aufsagen.

**reign** [rein] 1. Regierung *f*; *fig.* Herrschaft *f*; 2. herrschen, regieren.

**reimburse** [ri:im'bə:s] *j-n* entschädigen; *Kosten* wiedererstatten.

**rein** [rein] 1. Zügel *m*; 2. zügeln.

**reindeer** *zo.* ['reindiə] Ren(tier)*n*.

**reinforce** [ri:in'fɔ:s] verstärken; **~ment** [~smənt] Verstärkung *f*.

**reinstate** ['ri:in'steit] wieder einsetzen; wieder instand setzen.

**reinsure** ['ri:in'ʃuə] rückversichern.

**reiterate** [ri:'itəreit] (dauernd) wiederholen.

**reject** [ri'dʒekt] ver-, wegwerfen; ablehnen, ausschlagen; zurückweisen; **~ion** [~kʃən] Verwerfung *f*; Ablehnung *f*; Zurückweisung *f*.

**rejoic|e** [ri'dʒɔis] *v/t.* erfreuen; *v/i.* sich freuen (*at, in* über *acc.*); **~ing** [~siŋ] 1. □ freudig; 2. *oft* **~s** *pl.* Freude(nfest *n*) *f*.

**rejoin** ['ri:'dʒɔin] (sich) wieder vereinigen (mit); wieder zurückkehren zu; [ri'dʒɔin] erwidern.

**rejuvenate** [ri'dʒu:vineit] verjüngen. [entzünden.]

**rekindle** ['ri:'kindl] (sich) wieder]

**relapse** [ri'læps] 1. Rückfall *m*; 2. zurückfallen, rückfällig werden.

**relate** [ri'leit] *v/t.* erzählen; in Beziehung bringen; *v/i.* sich beziehen (*to* auf *acc.*); **~d** verwandt (*to* mit).

**relation** [ri'leiʃən] Erzählung *f*; Beziehung *f*; Verhältnis *n*; Verwandtschaft *f*; Verwandte(r *m*) *f*; *in* ~ *to* in bezug auf (*acc.*); **~ship** [~nʃip] Verwandtschaft *f*; Beziehung *f*.

**relative** ['relətiv] 1. □ bezüglich (*to gen.*); *gr.* relativ; verhältnismäßig; entsprechend; 2. *gr.* Relativpronomen *n*; Verwandte(r *m*) *f*.

**relax** [ri'læks] (sich) lockern; mildern; nachlassen (in *dat.*); (sich) entspannen, ausspannen; milder werden; **~ation** [ri:læk'seiʃən] Lokkerung *f*; Nachlassen *n*; Entspannung *f*, Erholung *f*.

**relay**[1] 1. [ri'lei] frisches Gespann; Ablösung *f*; ['ri:'lei] ⚡ Relais *n*; *Radio*: Übertragung *f*; 2. [~] *Radio*: übertragen.

**re-lay**[2] ['ri:'lei] *Kabel etc.* neu verlegen.

**relay-race** ['ri:leireis] *Sport*: Staffellauf *m*.

**release** [ri'li:s] 1. Freilassung *f*; *fig.* Befreiung *f*; Freigabe *f*; *Film*: *oft first* ~ Uraufführung *f*; ⊕, *phot.* Auslöser *m*; 2. freilassen; erlösen; freigeben; *Recht* aufgeben, übertragen; *Film* uraufführen; ⊕ auslösen.

**relegate** ['religeit] verbannen; verweisen (*to an acc.*).

**relent** [ri'lent] sich erweichen lassen; **~less** □ [~tlis] unbarmherzig.

**relevant** ['relivənt] sachdienlich; zutreffend; wichtig, erheblich.

**reliab|ility** [rilaiə'biliti] Zuverlässigkeit *f*; **~le** □ [ri'laiəbl] zuverlässig.

**reliance** [ri'laiəns] Ver-, Zutrauen *n*; Verlaß *m*.

**relic** ['relik] Überrest *m*; Reliquie *f*; **~t** [~kt] Witwe *f*.

**relief** [ri'li:f] Erleichterung *f*; (angenehme) Unterbrechung; Unterstützung *f*; ✕ Ablösung *f*; ✕ Entsatz *m*; Hilfe *f*; △ *etc.* Relief *n*; ~ *works pl.* Notstandsarbeiten *f/pl.*

**relieve** [ri'li:v] erleichtern; mildern, lindern; *Arme etc.* unterstützen; ✕ ablösen; ✕ entsetzen; ꜗ (ab)helfen (*dat.*); befreien; hervortreten lassen; (angenehm) unterbrechen.

**religion** [ri'lidʒən] Religion *f*; Ordensleben *n*; *fig.* Ehrensache *f*.

**religious** □ [ri'lidʒəs] Religions...; religiös; *eccl.* Ordens...; gewissenhaft.

**relinquish** [ri'liŋkwiʃ] aufgeben; verzichten auf (*acc.*); loslassen.

**relish** ['reliʃ] 1. (Bei)Geschmack *m*; Würze *f*; Genuß *m*; 2. gern essen; Geschmack finden an (*dat.*); schmackhaft machen.

**reluctan|ce** [ri'lʌktəns] Widerstreben *n*; *bsd. phys.* Widerstand *m*; **~t** □ [~nt] widerstrebend, widerwillig.

**rely** [ri'lai]: ~ (*up*)*on* sich verlassen (auf *acc.*), bauen auf (*acc.*).

**remain** [ri'mein] 1. (ver)bleiben; übrigbleiben; 2. **~s** *pl.* Überbleibsel *n/pl.*, Überreste *m/pl.*; sterbliche Reste *m/pl.*; **~der** [~ndə] Rest *m*.

**remand** [ri'mɑ:nd] 1. ꜗ in die Untersuchungshaft) zurückschikken; 2. (Zurücksendung *f* in die) Untersuchungshaft *f*; *prisoner on* ~ Untersuchungsgefangene(r *m*) *f*; ~ *home* Jugendstrafanstalt *f*.

**remark** [ri'mɑ:k] 1. Beachtung *f*; Bemerkung *f*; 2. *v/t.* bemerken; *v/i.* sich äußern; **~able** □ [~kəbl] bemerkenswert; merkwürdig.

**remedy** ['remidi] 1. (Heil-, Hilfs-, Gegen-, Rechts)Mittel *n*; (Ab-)Hilfe *f*; 2. heilen; abhelfen (*dat.*).

**rememb|er** [ri'membə] sich erinnern an (*acc.*); denken an (*acc.*); beherzigen; ~ me to her grüße sie von mir; **~rance** [~brəns] Erinnerung *f*; Gedächtnis *n*; Andenken *n*; **~s** *pl.* Empfehlungen *f/pl.*, Grüße *m/pl.*

**remind** [ri'maind] erinnern (*of* an *acc.*); **~er** [~də] Mahnung *f*.

**reminiscen|ce** [remi'nisns] Erinnerung *f*; **~t** □ (~nt) (sich) erinnernd.

**remiss** □ [ri'mis] schlaff, (nach-)lässig; **~ion** [~iʃən] Sünden-Vergebung *f*; Erlassung *f v.* Strafe etc.; Nachlassen *n*.

**remit** [ri'mit] *Sünden* vergeben; *Schuld etc.* erlassen; nachlassen in (*dat.*); überweisen; **~tance** [~təns] (Geld)Sendung *f*; ✝ Rimesse *f*.

**remnant** ['remnənt] (Über)Rest *m*.

**remodel** ['ri:'mɔdl] umbilden.

**remonstra|nce** [ri'mɔnstrəns] Vorstellung *f*, Einwendung *f*; **~te** [~treit] Vorstellungen machen (*on* über *acc.*; *with* s.o. j-m); einwenden.

**remorse** [ri'mɔ:s] Gewissensbisse *m/pl.*; **~less** □ [~slis] hart(herzig).

**remote** □ [ri'mout] entfernt, entlegen; **~ness** [~tnis] Entfernung *f*.

**remov|al** [ri'mu:vəl] Entfernen *n*; Beseitigung *f*; Umzug *m*; Entlassung *f*; ~ van Möbelwagen *m*; **~e** [~u:v] 1. *v/t.* entfernen; wegräumen, wegrücken; beseitigen; entlassen; *v/i.* (aus-, um-, ver)ziehen; 2. Entfernung *f*; Grad *m*; *Schule:* Versetzung *f*; Abteilung *f* e-r *Klasse*; **~er** [~və] (Möbel)Spediteur *m*.

**remunerat|e** [ri'mju:nəreit] (be-)lohnen; entschädigen; **~ive** □ [~rətiv] lohnend.

**Renaissance** [rə'neisəns] Renaissance *f*.

**renascen|ce** [ri'næsns] Wiedergeburt *f*; Renaissance *f*; **~t** [~nt] wieder wachsend.

**rend** [rend] [*irr.*] (zer)reißen.

**render** ['rendə] wieder-, zurückgeben; *Dienst etc.* leisten; *Ehre etc.* erweisen; *Dank* abstatten; übersetzen; ♪ vortragen; darstellen, interpretieren; *Grund* angeben; ✝ *Rechnung* überreichen; übergeben; machen (zu); *Fett* auslassen; **~ing** [~əriŋ] Wiedergabe *f*; Interpretation *f*; Übersetzung *f*, Wiedergabe *f*; △ Rohbewurf *m*.

**rendition** [ren'diʃən] Wiedergabe *f*.

**renegade** ['renigeid] Abtrünnige(r *m*) *f*.

**renew** [ri'nju:]erneuern; **~al** [~u:(:)əl] Erneuerung *f*.

**renounce** [ri'nauns] entsagen (*dat.*); verzichten auf (*acc.*); verleugnen.

**renovate** ['renouveit] erneuern.

**renown** [ri'naun] Ruhm *m*, Ansehen *n*; **~ed** [~nd] berühmt, namhaft.

**rent¹** [rent] 1. *pret. u. p.p. von* rend; 2. Riß *m*; Spalte *f*.

**rent²** [rent] 1. Miete *f*; Pacht *f*; 2. (ver)mieten, (ver)pachten; **~al** ['rentl] (Einkommen *n* aus) Miete *f* od. Pacht *f*

**renunciation** [rinʌnsi'eiʃən] Entsagung *f*; Verzicht *m* (*of* auf *acc.*).

**repair¹** [ri'pɛə] 1. Ausbesserung *f*, Reparatur *f*; **~s** *pl.* Instandsetzungsarbeiten *f/pl.*; ~ shop Reparaturwerkstatt *f*; *in good* ~ in gutem (baulichen) Zustand, gut erhalten; *out of* ~ baufällig; 2. reparieren, ausbessern; erneuern; wiedergutmachen.

**repair²** [~] ~ to sich begeben nach.

**reparation** [repə'reiʃən] Ersatz *m*; Entschädigung *f*; *make* ~s *pol.* Reparationen leisten.

**repartee** [repa:'ti:] schlagfertige Antwort, Schlagfertigkeit *f*.

**repast** [ri'pa:st] Mahl(zeit *f*) *n*.

**repay** [ri:'pei] [*irr.* (*pay*)] *et.* zurückzahlen; *fig* erwidern; *et.* vergelten; *j-n* entschädigen; **~ment** [~eimənt] Rückzahlung *f*.

**repeal** [ri'pi:l] 1. Aufhebung *f von Gesetzen*; 2. aufheben, widerrufen.

**repeat** [ri'pi:t] 1. (sich) wiederholen; aufsagen; nachliefern; aufstoßen (*Essen*); 2. Wiederholung *f*; *oft* order Nachbestellung *f*; ♪ Wiederholungszeichen *n*.

**repel** [ri'pel] zurückstoßen, zurücktreiben, zurückweisen; *fig.* abstoßen.

**repent** [ri'pent] bereuen; **~ance** [~təns] Reue *f*; **~ant** [~nt] reuig.

**repercussion** [ri:pə'kʌʃən] Rückprall *m*, *fig.* Rückwirkung *f*.

**repertory** ['repətəri] *thea.* Repertoire *n*, *fig* Fundgrube *f*.

**repetition** [repi'tiʃən] Wiederholung *f*, Aufsagen *n*; Nachbildung *f*.

**replace** [ri'pleis] wieder hinstellen od. einsetzen; ersetzen; an *j-s* Stelle treten; **~ment** [~smənt] Ersatz *m*.

**replant** ['ri:'pla:nt] umpflanzen.

**replenish** [ri'pleniʃ] wieder auffüllen; **~ment** [~ʃmənt] Auffüllung *f*; Ergänzung *f*.

**replete** [ri'pli:t] angefüllt, voll.

**replica** ['replikə] Nachbildung *f*.

**reply** [ri'plai] 1. antworten, erwidern · to auf *acc.*); 2. Erwiderung *f*.

**report** [ri'pɔ:t] 1. Bericht *m*; Gerücht *n*; *guter* Ruf; Knall *m*; *school* ~ (Schul)Zeugnis *n*; 2. berichten (*über acc.*); (sich) melden; anzeigen; **~er** [~tə] Berichterstatter(in).

**repos|e** [ri'pouz] 1. *allg.* Ruhe *f*; 2. *v/t* ausruhen; (aus)ruhen lassen; ~ trust etc. in Vertrauen etc. setzen auf (acc.); v/i. a. ~ o.s. (sich) ausruhen; ruhen; beruhen (on auf dat.); ~itory [ri'pozitəri] Verwahrungsort m; Warenlager n; fig. Fundgrube f.

**reprehend** [repri'hend] tadeln.

**represent** [repri'zent] darstellen; verkörpern; thea. aufführen; schildern; bezeichnen (as als); vertreten; ~ation [repriːzən'teiʃən] Darstellung f; thea. Aufführung f; Vorstellung f; Vertretung f; ~ative □ [repri'zentətiv] 1. dar-, vorstellend (of acc.); vorbildlich; (stell)vertretend; parl. repräsentativ; typisch; 2. Vertreter(in); House of ~s Am. parl. Repräsentantenhaus n.

**repress** [ri'pres] unterdrücken; ~ion [~eʃən] Unterdrückung f.

**reprieve** [ri'priːv] 1. (Gnaden)Frist f; Aufschub m; 2. j-m Aufschub od. eine Gnadenfrist gewähren.

**reprimand** ['reprimaːnd] 1. Verweis m; 2. j-m e-n Verweis geben.

**reprisal** [ri'praizəl] Repressalie f.

**reproach** [ri'proutʃ] 1. Vorwurf m; Schande f; 2. vorwerfen (s.o. with s.th. j-m et.); Vorwürfe machen; ~ful □ [~sful] vorwurfsvoll.

**reprobate** ['reproubeit] 1. verkommen, verderbt; 2. verkommenes Subjekt; 3. mißbilligen; verdammen.

**reproduc|e** [riːprə'djuːs] wiedererzeugen; (sich) fortpflanzen; wiedergeben, reproduzieren; ~tion [~'dakʃən] Wiedererzeugung f; Fortpflanzung f; Reproduktion f.

**reproof** [ri'pruːf] Vorwurf m, Tadel m.

**reprov|al** [ri'pruːvəl] Tadel m, Rüge f; ~e [~uːv] tadeln, rügen.

**reptile** zo. ['reptail] Reptil n.

**republic** [ri'pʌblik] Republik f; ~an [~kən] 1. republikanisch; 2. Republikaner(in).

**repudiate** [ri'pjuːdieit] nicht anerkennen; ab-, zurückweisen.

**repugnan|ce** [ri'pʌgnəns] Abneigung f, Widerwille m; ~t □ [~nt] abstoßend; widerwärtig.

**repuls|e** [ri'pʌls] 1. Zurück-, Abweisung f; 2. zurück-, abweisen; ~ive □ [~siv] abstoßend; widerwärtig.

**reput|able** □ ['repjutəbl] achtbar; ehrbar, anständig; ~ation [repju(:)-'teiʃən] (bsd. guter) Ruf, Ansehen n; ~e [ri'pjuːt] 1. Ruf m; 2. halten für; ~ed vermeintlich; angeblich.

**request** [ri'kwest] 1. Gesuch n, Bitte f; Ersuchen n; † Nachfrage f; by ~, on ~ auf Wunsch; in (great) ~ (sehr) gesucht, begehrt; ~ stop Bedarfshaltestelle f; 2. um et. bitten od. ersuchen; j-n bitten; et. erbitten.

**require** [ri'kwaiə] verlangen, fordern; brauchen, erfordern; ~d er-

forderlich; ~ment [~əmənt] (An-) Forderung f; Erfordernis n.

**requisit|e** ['rekwizit] 1. erforderlich; 2. Erfordernis n; Bedarfs-, Gebrauchsartikel m; toilet ~s pl. Toilettenartikel m/pl.; ~ion [rekwi-'ziʃən] 1. Anforderung f; ✕ Requisition f; 2. anfordern; ✕ requirieren.

**requital** [ri'kwaitl] Vergeltung f.

**requite** [ri'kwait] j-m et. vergelten.

**rescind** [ri'sind] aufheben.

**rescission** [ri'siʒən] Aufhebung f.

**rescue** ['reskjuː] 1. Rettung f; (⚔ gewaltsame) Befreiung; 2. retten; (⚔ gewaltsam) befreien.

**research** [ri'səːtʃ] Forschung f; Untersuchung f; Nachforschung f; ~er [~ʃə] Forscher m.

**resembl|ance** [ri'zembləns] Ähnlichkeit f (to mit); ~e [ri'zembl] gleichen, ähnlich sein (dat.).

**resent** [ri'zent] übelnehmen; ~ful □ [~tful] übelnehmerisch; ärgerlich; ~ment [~tmənt] Ärger m; Groll m.

**reservation** [rezə'veiʃən] Vorbehalt m; Am. Indianerreservation f; Vorbestellung f von Zimmern etc.

**reserve** [ri'zəːv] 1. Vorrat m; † Rücklage f; Reserve f (a. fig., ✕); Zurückhaltung f, Verschlossenheit f; Vorsicht f; Vorbehalt m; Sport: Ersatzmann m; 2. aufbewahren, aufsparen; vorbehalten; zurücklegen; Platz etc. reservieren; ~d □ fig. zurückhaltend, reserviert.

**reservoir** ['rezəvwaː] Behälter m für Wasser etc.; Sammel-, Staubecken n; fig. Reservoir n.

**reside** [ri'zaid] wohnen; (orts)ansässig sein; ~ in innewohnen (dat.); ~nce ['rezidəns] Wohnen n; Ortsansässigkeit f; (Wohn)Sitz m; Residenz f; ~ permit Aufenthaltsgenehmigung f; ~nt [~nt] 1. wohnhaft; ortsansässig; 2. Ortsansässige(r m) f, Einwohner(in).

**residu|al** [ri'zidjuəl] übrigbleibend; ~e ['rezidjuː] Rest m; Rückstand m; ⚖ Reinnachlaß f.

**resign** [ri'zain] v/t. aufgeben; Amt niederlegen; überlassen; ~ o.s. to sich ergeben in (acc.), sich abfinden mit; v/i. zurücktreten; ~ation [rezig'neiʃən] Rücktritt m; Ergebung f; Entlassungsgesuch n; ~ed □ ergeben, resigniert.

**resilien|ce** [ri'ziliəns] Elastizität f; ~t [~nt] elastisch, fig. spannkräftig.

**resin** ['rezin] 1. Harz n; 2. harzen.

**resist** [ri'zist] widerstehen (dat.); sich widersetzen (dat.); ~ance [~təns] Widerstand m; attr. Widerstands...; line of least ~ Weg m des geringsten Widerstands; ~ant [~nt] widerstehend; widerstandsfähig.

**resolut|e** □ ['rezoluːt] entschlossen; ~ion [rezə'luːʃən] (Auf)Lösung f;

**resolve** [ri'zɔlv] **1.** v/t. auflösen; fig. lösen; Zweifel etc. beheben; entscheiden; v/i. a. ~ o.s. sich auflösen; beschließen; ~ (up)on sich entschließen zu; **2.** Entschluß m; Am. Beschluß m; ~d □ entschlossen.

**resonan|ce** [ˈreznəns] Resonanz f; ~t [~nt] nach-, widerhallend.

**resort** [riˈzɔːt] **1.** Zuflucht f; Besuch m; Aufenthalt(sort) m; Erholungsort m; health ~ Kurort m; seaside ~ Seebad n; summer ~ Sommerfrische f; **2.** ~ to oft besuchen; seine Zuflucht nehmen zu. [sen).]

**resound** [riˈzaund] widerhallen (las-)

**resource** [riˈsɔːs] natürlicher Reichtum; Hilfsquelle f, -mittel n; Zuflucht f; Findigkeit f; Zeitvertreib m, Entspannung f; ~ful □ [~sful] findig.

**respect** [risˈpekt] **1.** Rücksicht f (to, of auf acc.); Beziehung f; Achtung f; ~s pl. Empfehlungen f/pl.; **2.** v/t. (hoch)achten; Rücksicht nehmen auf (acc.); betreffen; ~able □ [~təbl] achtbar; ansehnlich; anständig; bsd. ✝ solid; ~ful □ [~tful] ehrerbietig; yours ~ly hochachtungsvoll; ~ing [~tiŋ] hinsichtlich (gen.); ~ive □ [~iv] jeweilig; we went to our ~ places wir gingen jeder an seinen Platz; ~ively [~vli] beziehungsweise; je.

**respirat|ion** [respəˈreiʃən] Atmen n; Atemzug m; ~or [ˈrespəreitə] Atemfilter m; ⚔ Atemgerät n; Gasmaske f.

**respire** [risˈpaiə] atmen; aufatmen.

**respite** [ˈrespait] Frist f; Stundung f.

**resplendent** □ [risˈplendənt] glänzend.

**respond** [risˈpɔnd] antworten, erwidern; ~ to reagieren auf (acc.).

**response** [risˈpɔns] Antwort f, Erwiderung f; fig. Reaktion f.

**responsi|bility** [rispɔnsəˈbiliti] Verantwortlichkeit f; Verantwortung f; ✝ Zahlungsfähigkeit f; ~ble [risˈpɔnsəbl] verantwortlich; verantwortungsvoll; ✝ zahlungsfähig.

**rest** [rest] **1.** Rest m; Ruhe f; Rast f; Schlaf m; fig. Tod m; Stütze f; Pause f; **2.** v/i. ruhen; rasten; schlafen; (sich) lehnen, sich stützen (on auf acc.); ~ (up)on fig. beruhen auf (dat.); in e-m Zustand bleiben; v/t. (aus)ruhen lassen; stützen.

**restaurant** [ˈrestərɔ̃ː, ~rɔnt] Gaststätte f.

**rest-cure** ⚕ [ˈrestkjuə] Liegekur f.

**restful** [ˈrestful] ruhig, geruhsam.

**resting-place** [ˈrestiŋpleis] Ruheplatz m, -stätte f.

**restitution** [restiˈtjuːʃən] Wiederherstellung f; Rückerstattung f.

**restive** □ [ˈrestiv] widerspenstig.

**restless** [ˈrestlis] ruhelos; rastlos; unruhig; ~ness [~snis] Ruhelosigkeit f; Rastlosigkeit f; Unruhe f.

**restorat|ion** [restəˈreiʃən] Wiederherstellung f; Wiedereinsetzung f; Rekonstruktion f, Nachbildung f; ~ive [risˈtɔrətiv] **1.** stärkend; **2.** Stärkungsmittel n.

**restore** [risˈtɔː] wiederherstellen; wiedereinsetzen (to in acc.); wiedergeben; ~ to health wieder gesund machen.

**restrain** [risˈtrein] zurückhalten (from von); in Schranken halten; unterdrücken; einsperren; ~t [~nt] Zurückhaltung f; Beschränkung f, Zwang m; ∠wangshaft f.

**restrict** [risˈtrikt] be-, einschränken; ~ion [~kʃən] Be-, Einschränkung f; Vorbehalt m.

**result** [riˈzʌlt] **1.** Ergebnis n, Folge f, Resultat n; **2.** folgen, sich ergeben (from aus); ~ in hinauslaufen auf (acc.), zur Folge haben.

**resum|e** [riˈzjuːm] wiedernehmen, -erlangen; wiederaufnehmen; zs.-fassen; ~ption [riˈzʌmpʃən] Zurücknahme f; Wiederaufnahme f.

**resurgent** [riˈsəːdʒənt] sich wiedererhebend, wieder aufkommend.

**resurrection** [rezəˈrekʃən] Wiederaufleben n; ⚰ eccl. (Wieder)Auferstehung f.

**resuscitate** [risˈʌsiteit] wiedererwecken, wiederbeleben.

**retail 1.** [ˈriːteil] Einzelhandel m; by ~ im Einzelverkauf; **2.** [~] Einzelhandels. ~ Detail...; **3.** [riːˈteil] im kleinen verkaufen; ~er [~lə] Einzelhändler(in).

**retain** [riˈtein] behalten (a. fig.); zurück-, festhalten; beibehalten; Anwalt nehmen.

**retaliat|e** [riˈtælieit] v/t. Unrecht vergelten, v/i sich rächen; ~ion [ritæliˈeiʃən] Vergeltung f.

**retard** [riˈtɑːd] verzögern; aufhalten; verspäten.

**retention** [riˈtenʃən] Zurück-, Behalten n; Beibehaltung f.

**reticent** [ˈretisənt] verschwiegen; schweigsam; zurückhaltend.

**retinue** [ˈretinjuː] Gefolge n.

**retir|e** [riˈtaiə] v/t. zurückziehen; pensionieren; v/i. sich zurückziehen; zurück-, abtreten; in den Ruhestand treten; ~ed □ zurückgezogen; im Ruhestand (lebend); entlegen; pay Pension f; ~ement [~əmənt] Sichzurückziehen n; Aus-, Rücktritt m; Ruhestand m; Zurückgezogenheit f; ~ing [~əriŋ] zurückhaltend; schüchtern; ~ pension Ruhegehalt n.

**retort** [riˈtɔːt] **1.** Erwiderung f; 🝪 Retorte f; **2.** erwidern.

**retouch** [ˈriːˈtʌtʃ] et. überarbeiten; phot. retuschieren.

**retrace** [ri'treis] zurückverfolgen; ~ one's steps zurückgehen.

**retract** [ri'trækt] (sich) zurückziehen; ⊕ einziehen; widerrufen.

**retread** ['ri:tred] 1. *Reifen* runderneuern; 2. runderneuerter Reifen.

**retreat** [ri'tri:t] 1. Rückzug *m*; Zurückgezogenheit *f*; Zuflucht(sort *m*) *f*; ✗. Zapfenstreich *m*; *beat a ~ fig.* es aufgeben; 2. sich zurückziehen; *fig.* zurücktreten.

**retrench** [ri'trentʃ] (sich) einschränken; kürzen; *Wort etc.* streichen; ✗ verschanzen.

**retribution** [retri'bju:ʃən] Vergeltung *f*.

**retrieve** [ri'tri:v] wiederbekommen; wiederherstellen; wiedergutmachen; *hunt.* apportieren.

**retro|...** ['retrou] (zu)rück...; **~active** [retrou'æktiv] rückwirkend; **~grade** ['retrougreid] 1. rückläufig; 2. zurückgehen; **~gression** [retrou'greʃən] Rück-, Niedergang *m*; **~spect** ['retrouspekt] Rückblick *m*; **~spective** ☐ [retrou'spektiv] zurückblickend; rückwirkend.

**retry** ⚖ ['ri:'trai] *Prozeß* wiederaufnehmen.

**return** [ri'tə:n] 1. Rückkehr *f*; Wiederkehr *f*; *parl.* Wiederwahl *f*; *oft* ~*s pl.* ✝ Gewinn *m*, Ertrag *m*; Umsatz *m*; ⚾ Rückfall *m*; Rückgabe *f*, Rückzahlung *f*; Vergeltung *f*; Erwiderung *f*; Gegenleistung *f*; Dank *m*; *amtlicher* Bericht; Wahlergebnis *n*; Steuererklärung *f*; ₣ Rückfahrkarte *f*; *attr.* Rück...; *many happy ~s of the day* herzliche Glückwünsche zum Geburtstag; *in* ~ dafür; *als Ersatz (for* für); *by* ~ *(of post)* postwendend; ~ *ticket* Rückfahrkarte *f*; 2. *v/i.* zurückkehren; wiederkehren; *v/t.* zurückgeben; zurücktun; zurückzahlen; zurücksenden; *Dank* abstatten; erwidern; berichten, angeben; *parl.* wählen; *Gewinn* abwerfen.

**reunification** *pol.* ['ri:ju:nifi'keiʃən] Wiedervereinigung *f*.

**reunion** ['ri:'ju:njən] Wiedervereinigung *f*; Treffen *n*, Zs.-kunft *f*.

**reval|orization** ✝ [ri:vælərai'zeiʃən] Aufwertung *f*; **~uation** [~ju-'eiʃən] Neubewertung *f*.

**revamp** ⊕ ['ri:'væmp] vorschuhen; *Am.* ✝ aufmöbeln; erneuern.

**reveal** [ri'vi:l] enthüllen; offenbaren; **~ing** [~liŋ] aufschlußreich.

**revel** ['revl] 1. Lustbarkeit *f*; Gelage *n*; 2. ausgelassen sein; schwelgen; zechen.

**revelation** [revi'leiʃən] Enthüllung *f*; Offenbarung *f*.

**revel|(l)er** ['revlə] Feiernde(r *m*) *f*; Zecher *m*; **~ry** [~lri] Gelage *n*; Lustbarkeit *f*; Rummel *m*; Orgie *f*.

**revenge** [ri'vendʒ] 1. Rache *f*;

*Sport:* Revanche *f*; 2. rächen; **~ful** ☐ [~dʒful] rachsüchtig; **~r** [~dʒə] Rächer(in).

**revenue** ['revinju:] Einkommen *n*; **~s** *pl.* Einkünfte *pl.*; ~ *board*, ~ *office* Finanzamt *n*.

**reverberate** [ri'və:bəreit] zurückwerfen; zurückstrahlen; widerhallen.

**revere** [ri'viə] (ver)ehren; **~nce** ['revərəns] 1. Verehrung *f*; Ehrfurcht *f*; 2. (ver)ehren; **~nd** [~nd] 1. ehrwürdig; 2. Geistliche(r) *m*.

**reverent(ial)** ☐ ['revərənt, revə-'renʃəl] ehrerbietig, ehrfurchtsvoll.

**reverie** ['revəri] Träumerei *f*.

**revers|al** [ri'və:səl] Umkehrung *f*; Umschwung *m*; ⚖ Umstoßung *f*; ⊕ Umsteuerung *f*; **~e** [~ə:s] 1. Gegenteil *n*; Kehrseite *f*; Rückschlag *m*; 2. ☐ umgekehrt; Rück(wärts)...; ~ *(gear) mot.* Rückwärtsgang *m*; ~ *side* linke Stoff-Seite; 3. umkehren, umdrehen; *Urteil* umstoßen; ⊕ umsteuern; **~ion** [~ə:ʃən] Umkehrung *f*; Rück(wärts)...; ⚖ Heimfall *m*; *biol.* Rückartung *f*.

**revert** [ri'və:t] um-, zurückkehren; *biol.* zurückarten; *Blick* wenden.

**review** [ri'vju:] 1. Nachprüfung *f*; ⚖ Revision *f*; ✗ Parade *f*; Rückblick *m*; Überblick *m*; Rezension *f*; Zeitschrift *f*; *pass s.th. in* ~ *et.* Revue passieren lassen; 2. (über-, nach)prüfen; zurückblicken auf *(acc.)*; überblicken; ✗ besichtigen; rezensieren; **~er** [~u(:)ə] Rezensent *m*. [*fen.*]

**revile** [ri'vail] schmähen, beschimp-]

**revis|e** [ri'vaiz] überarbeiten, durchsehen, revidieren; **~ion** [ri'viʒən] Revision *f*; Überarbeitung *f*.

**reviv|al** [ri'vaivəl] Wiederbelebung *f*; Wiederaufleben *n*, Wiederaufblühen *n*; Erneuerung *f*; *fig.* Erweckung *f*; **~e** [~aiv] wiederbeleben; wieder aufleben (lassen); erneuern; wieder aufblühen.

**revocation** [revə'keiʃən] Widerruf *m*; Aufhebung *f*.

**revoke** [ri'vouk] *v/t.* widerrufen; *v/i. Karten:* nicht bedienen.

**revolt** [ri'voult] 1. Revolte *f*, Empörung *f*, Aufruhr *m*; 2. *v/i.* sich empören; abfallen; *v/t. fig.* abstoßen.

**revolution** [revə'lu:ʃən] Umwälzung *f*, Umdrehung *f*; *pol.* Revolution *f*; **~ary** [~ʃnəri] 1. revolutionär; 2. *a.* **~ist** [~ʃnist] Revolutionär(in); **~ize** [~ʃnaiz] aufwiegeln; umgestalten.

**revolv|e** [ri'vɔlv] *v/i.* sich drehen *(about, round* um); *v/t.* umdrehen; *fig.* erwägen; **~ing** [~viŋ] sich drehend; Dreh...

**revue** *thea.* [ri'vju:] Revue *f*; Kabarett *n*.

**revulsion** [ri'vʌlʃən] *fig.* Umschwung *m*; ⚕ Ableitung *f*.

**reward** [ri'wɔ:d] **1.** Belohnung f; Vergeltung f; **2.** belohnen; vergelten.

**rewrite** ['ri:'rait] [*irr.* (*write*)] neu (*od.* um)schreiben.

**rhapsody** ['ræpsədi] Rhapsodie f; *fig.* Schwärmerei f; Wortschwall m.

**rhetoric** ['retərik] Rhetorik f.

**rheumatism** ♣ ['ru:mətizəm] Rheumatismus m.

**rhubarb** ♀ ['ru:bɑ:b] Rhabarber m.

**rhyme** [raim] **1.** Reim m (*to* auf *acc.*); Vers m; *without ~ or reason* ohne Sinn u. Verstand; **2.** (sich) reimen.

**rhythm** ['riðəm] Rhythmus m; **~ic(al** □) ['riðmik(əl)] rhythmisch.

**Rialto** *Am.* [ri'æltou] Theaterviertel n e-r Stadt, *bsd.* in *New York.*

**rib** [rib] **1.** Rippe f; **2.** rippen; *sl.* aufziehen, necken.

**ribald** ['ribəld] lästerlich; unflätig; **~ry** [~dri] Zoten f/pl.; derbe Späße m/pl.

**ribbon** ['ribən] Band n; Streifen m; **~s** pl. Fetzen m/pl.; Zügel m/pl.; **~ building, ~ development** Reihenbau m.

**rice** [rais] Reis m.

**rich** [ritʃ] reich (*in an dat.*); reichlich; prächtig, kostbar; ergiebig, fruchtbar; voll (*Ton*); schwer (*Speise, Wein, Duft*); satt (*Farbe*); **~es** ['ritʃiz] pl. Reichtum m, Reichtümer m/pl.; **~ness** [~nis] Reichtum m; Fülle f.

**rick** ⸱ [rik] (Heu)Schober m.

**ricket|s** ♣ ['rikits] sg. *od.* pl. Rachitis f; **~y** [~ti] rachitisch; wack(e)lig (*Möbel*).

**rid** [rid] [*irr.*] befreien, frei machen (*of* von); *get ~ of* loswerden.

**ridden** [ˈridn] **1.** p.p. *von* ride 2; **2.** *in Zssgn:* bedrückt *od.* geplagt von .

**riddle** ['ridl] **1.** Rätsel n; grobes Sieb, 2. sieben; durchlöchern.

**ride** [raid] **1.** Ritt m; Fahrt f; Reitweg m; **2.** [*irr.*] v/i. reiten; rittlings sitzen; fahren; treiben; schweben; liegen; *v/t. Pferd etc.* reiten; *Land* durchreiten; **~r** ['raidə] Reiter(in); Fahrende(r m) f.

**ridge** [ridʒ] **1.** (Gebirgs)Kamm m, Grat m, ▵ First m; ⸱ Rain m; **2.** (sich) furchen.

**ridicul|e** ['ridikju:l] **1.** Hohn m, Spott m; **2.** lächerlich machen; **~ous** [ri'dikjuləs] lächerlich.

**riding** ['raidiŋ] Reiten n; *attr.* Reit... { **~ with** voll von.}

**rife** [raif] häufig; vorherrschend; }

**riff-raff** ['rifræf] Gesindel n.

**rifle** ['raifl] **1.** Gewehr n; **2.** (aus)plündern; **~man** ⚔ Schütze m.

**rift** [rift] Riß m, Sprung m; Spalte f.

**rig**[1] [rig] **1.** Markt etc. manipulieren; **2.** Schwindelmanöver n.

**rig**[2] [~] **1.** ⚓ Takelung f; F Aufma-chung f; **2.** auftakeln; **~ s.o. out** j-n versorgen *od.* ausrüsten; j-n herausputzen *od.* herrichten; **~ging** ⚓ ['rigiŋ] Takelage f.

**right** [rait] **1.** □ recht; richtig; recht (*Ggs.* left); *be ~* recht haben; *all ~!* alles in Ordnung!; ganz recht!; *put od. set ~* in Ordnung bringen; berichtigen; **2.** *adv.* recht, richtig; gerade; direkt; ganz (und gar); *~ away* sogleich;; *~ on* geradeaus; **3.** Recht n; Rechte f, rechte Seite *od.* Hand; *the ~s and wrongs* der wahre Sachverhalt; *by ~ of* auf Grund (*gen.*); *on od. to the ~* rechts; *~ of way* Wegerecht n; Vorfahrt(s-recht n) f; **4.** j-m Recht verschaffen; *et.* in Ordnung bringen; ⚓ (sich) aufrichten; **~-down** ['rait'daun] regelrecht, ausgemacht; wirklich; **~eous** □ ['raitʃəs] rechtschaffen; **~ful** □ ['raitful] recht(mäßig); gerecht.

**rigid** □ ['ridʒid] starr; *fig. a.* streng, hart; **~ity** [ri'dʒiditi] Starrheit f; Strenge f, Härte f.

**rigmarole** ['rigməroul] Geschwätz n.

**rigor** ♣ ['raigə] Fieberfrost m.

**rigo(u)r** ['rigə] Strenge f, Härte f.

**rigorous** □ ['rigərəs] streng, rigoros.

**rim** [rim] **1.** Felge f; Radkranz m; Rand m; **2.** rändern; einfassen.

**rime** [raim] Reim m; Rauhreif m.

**rind** [raind] Rinde f, Schale f; Speck-Schwarte f.

**ring**[1] [riŋ] **1.** Klang m; Geläut(e) n; Klingeln n; Rufzeichen n; Anruf m; *give s.o. a ~* j-n anrufen; **2.** [*irr.*] läuten; klingen (lassen); erschallen (*with* von); *~ again* widerhallen; *~ off teleph.* das Gespräch beenden; *~ the bell* klingeln; *~ s.o. up* j-n *od.* bei j-m anrufen.

**ring**[2] [~] **1.** Ring m; Kreis m; **2.** beringen; *mst ~ in, ~ round, ~ about* umringen; **~leader** ['riŋli:də] Rädelsführer m; **~let** [~lit] (Ringel)Locke f.

**rink** [riŋk] Eisbahn f; Rollschuhbahn f.

**rinse** [rins] *oft ~ out* (aus)spülen.

**riot** ['raiət] **1.** Tumult m; Aufruhr m; Orgie f (*a. fig.*); *run ~* durchgehen; (sich aus)toben; **2.** Krawall machen, im Aufruhr sein; toben; schwelgen; **~er** [~tə] Aufrührer(in); Randalierer m; **~ous** □ [~təs] aufrührerisch; lärmend; liederlich (*Leben*).

**rip** [rip] **1.** Riß m; **2.** (auf)trennen; (auf-, zer)reißen; (dahin)sausen.

**ripe** [raip] reif; **~n** ['raipən] reifen; **~ness** ['raipnis] Reife f.

**ripple** ['ripl] **1.** kleine Welle; Kräuselung f; Geriesel n; **2.** (sich) kräuseln; rieseln.

**rise** [raiz] **1.** (An-, Auf)Steigen n;

Anschwellen *n*; (Preis-, Gehalts-) Erhöhung *f*; *fig.* Aufstieg *m*; Steigung *f*; Anhöhe *f*; Ursprung *m*; *take (one's)* ~ entstehen; entspringen; **2.** [*irr.*] sich erheben, aufstehen; die Sitzung schließen; steigen; aufsteigen (*a. fig.*); auferstehen; aufgehen (*Sonne, Samen*); anschwellen; sich empören; entspringen (*Fluß*); ~ *to* sich *e-r Lage* gewachsen zeigen; ~**n** ['rizn] *p.p. von* rise 2; ~**r** ['raizə]: early ~ Frühaufsteher(in).

**rising** ['raiziŋ] **1.** (Auf)Steigen *n*; Steigung *f*; *ast.* Aufgang *m*; Aufstand *m*; **2.** heranwachsend (*Generation*).

**risk** [risk] **1.** Gefahr *f*, Wagnis *n*; † Risiko *n*; *run the* ~ Gefahr laufen; **2.** wagen, riskieren; ~**y** □ ['riski] gefährlich, gewagt.

**rit|e** [rait] Ritus *m*, Brauch *m*; ~**ual** ['ritjuəl] **1.** rituell; **2.** Ritual *n*.

**rival** ['raivəl] **1.** Nebenbuhler(in); Rivale *m*; **2.** rivalisierend; † Konkurrenz...; **3.** wetteifern (mit); ~**ry** [~lri] Rivalität *f*; Wetteifer *m*.

**rive** [raiv] [*irr.*] (sich) spalten; ~**n** ['rivn] *p.p. von* rive.

**river** ['rivə] Fluß *m*; Strom *m* (*a. fig.*); ~**side 1.** Flußufer *n*; **2.** am Wasser (gelegen).

**rivet** ['rivit] **1.** ⊕ Niet(e *f*) *m*; **2.** (ver)nieten; *fig.* heften (to an *acc.*; on, upon auf *acc.*); fesseln.

**rivulet** ['rivjulit] Bach *m*, Flüßchen *n*.

**road** [roud] Straße *f* (*a. fig.*), Weg *m*; *Am.* railroad; *mst* ~**s** *pl.* ⚓ Reede *f*; ~**stead** ⚓ ['roudsted] Reede *f*; ~**ster** [~tə] Roadster *m*, offener Sportwagen; ~**way** Fahrbahn *f*

**roam** [roum] *v/i.* umherstreifen, wandern; *v/t.* durchstreifen.

**roar** [rɔː] **1.** brüllen; brausen, tosen, donnern; **2.** Gebrüll *n*; Brausen *n*; Krachen *n*, Getöse *n*; brüllendes Gelächter.

**roast** [roust] **1.** rösten, braten; **2.** geröstet; gebraten; ~ *meat* Braten *m*.

**rob** [rɔb] (be)rauben; ~**ber** ['rɔbə] Räuber *m*; ~**bery** [~əri] Raub (-überfall) *m*, Räuberei *f*.

**robe** [roub] (Amts)Robe *f*, Talar *m*; (Staats)Kleid *n*; *Am.* Morgenrock *m*.

**robin** *orn.* ['rɔbin] Rotkehlchen *n*.

**robust** [rə'bʌst] robust, kräftig.

**rock** [rɔk] **1.** Felsen *m*; Klippe *f*; Gestein *n*; Zuckerstange *f*; ~ *crystal* Bergkristall *m*; **2.** schaukeln; (ein)wiegen.

**rocker** ['rɔkə] Kufe *f*; *Am.* Schaukelstuhl *m*; Rocker *m*, Halbstarke(r) *m*.

**rocket** ['rɔkit] Rakete *f*; *attr.* Ra-

keten...; ~**-powered** mit Raketenantrieb; ~**ry** [~tri] Raketentechnik*f*.

**rocking-chair** ['rɔkiŋtʃeə] Schaukelstuhl *m*.

**rocky** ['rɔki] felsig; Felsen...

**rod** [rɔd] Rute *f*; Stab *m*; ⊕ Stange *f*; Meßrute *f* (5½ *yards*); *Am. sl.* Pistole *f*.

**rode** [roud] *pret. von* ride 2.

**rodent** ['roudənt] Nagetier *n*.

**rodeo** *Am.* [rou'deiou] Rodeo *m*; Zusammentreiben *n*; Cowboyturnier *n*.

**roe**[1] [rou] Reh *n*.

**roe**[2] *ichth.* [rou] *a.* hard ~ Rogen *m*; soft ~ Milch *f*.

**rogu|e** [roug] Schurke *m*; Schelm *m*; ~**ish** ['rougiʃ] schurkisch; schelmisch.

**roister** ['rɔistə] krakeelen.

**role, rôle** *thea.* [roul] Rolle *f* (*a. fig.*).

**roll** [roul] **1.** Rolle *f*; ⊕ Walze *f*; Brötchen *n*, Semmel *f*; Verzeichnis *n*; Urkunde *f*; (Donner)Rollen *n*; (Trommel)Wirbel *m*; ⚓ Schlingern *n*; **2.** *v/t.* rollen; wälzen; walzen; *Zigarette* drehen; ~ *up* zs.- rollen; einwickeln; *v/i.* rollen; sich wälzen; wirbeln (*Trommel*); ⚓ schlingern; ~**-call** ['roulkɔːl] Appell *m*; ~**er** ['roulə] Rolle *f*, Walze *f*; Sturzwelle *f*; ~ *coaster Am.* Achterbahn *f*; ~ *skate* Rollschuh *m*.

**rolliking** ['rɔlikiŋ] übermütig.

**rolling** ['rouliŋ] rollend; Roll..., Walz...; *mill* ⊕ Walzwerk *n*.

**Roman** ['roumən] **1.** römisch; **2.** Römer(in); *mst typ.* Antiqua *f*.

**romance**[1] [rə'mæns] **1.** (Ritter-, Vers)Roman *m*; Abenteuer-, Liebesroman *m*, Romanze *f* (*a. fig.*); *fig.* Märchen *n*; Romantik *f*; **2.** *fig.* aufschneiden.

**Romance**[2] *ling.* [~]: ~ *languages* romanische Sprachen *f/pl.*

**romancer** [rə'mænsə] Romanschreiber(in), Aufschneider(in).

**Romanesque** [roumə'nesk] **1.** romanisch **2.** romanischer Baustil.

**romantic** [rə'mæntik] (~ally) romantisch; ~**ism** [~sizəm] Romantik *f*; ~**ist** [~ist] Romantiker(in).

**romp** [rɔmp] **1.** Range *f*, Wildfang *m*; Balgerei *f*; **2.** sich balgen, tollen; ~**er(s)** [~pə(z)] Spielanzug *m*.

**rood** [ruːd] ⚓ Kruzifix *n*; Viertelmorgen *m* (10,117 Ar).

**roof** [ruːf] **1.** Dach *n*; ~ *of the mouth* Gaumen *m*; **2.** *a.* ~ *over* überdachen; ~**ing** ['ruːfiŋ] **1.** Bedachung*f*; **2.** Dach..., felt Dachpappe *f*.

**rook** [ruk] **1.** *Schach* Turm *m*; *fig.* Gauner *m*; *orn.* Saatkrähe *f*; **2.** betrügen.

**room** [rum] **1.** Raum *m*; Platz *m*; Zimmer *n*; Möglichkeit *f*; ~**s** *pl.* Wohnung *f*; *in my* ~ an meiner Stelle; **2.** *Am.* wohnen; ~**er** ['rumə] *bsd. Am.* Untermieter(in); ~ing-house ['ruminhaus] *bsd. Am.* Miets-, Logierhaus *n*; ~mate Stubenkamerad *m*; ~y □ ['rumi] geräumig.

**roost** [ru:st] **1.** Schlafplatz *m e-s Vogels*; Hühnerstange *f*; Hühnerstall *m*; **2.** sich (zum Schlaf) niederhocken; *fig.* übernachten; ~er ['ru:stə] Haushahn *m*.

**root** [ru:t] **1.** Wurzel *f*; **2.** (ein)wurzeln; (auf)wühlen; ~ *for Am. sl.* Stimmung machen für; ~ out ausrotten; ~ out *od.* up ausgraben; ~ed ['ru:tid] eingewurzelt; ~er *Am. sl.* ['ru:tə] Fanatiker *m für et.*

**rope** [roup] **1.** Tau *n*, Seil *n*; Strick *m*; Schnur *f Perlen etc.*; *be at the end of one's ~* F mit s-m Latein zu Ende sein; *know the ~s* sich auskennen; **2.** mit e-m Seil befestigen *od. (mst ~ in od. off od. out)* absperren; anseilen; ~way ['roupwei] Seilbahn *f*.

**ropy** ['roupi] klebrig, zähflüssig.

**rosary** *eccl.* ['rouzəri] Rosenkranz *m*.

**rose**[1] [rouz] ♀ Rose *f*; (Gießkannen)Brause *f*; Rosenrot *n*.

**rose**[2] [~] *pret. von* rise *2*.

**rosebud** ['rouzbʌd] Rosenknospe *f*; *Am.* hübsches Mädchen; Debütantin *f*.

**rosin** ['rɔzin] (Geigen)Harz *n*.

**rostrum** ['rɔstrəm] Rednertribüne *f*.

**rosy** □ ['rouzi] rosig.

**rot** [rɔt] **1.** Fäulnis *f*; *sl.* Quatsch *m*; **2.** *v/t.* faulen lassen; Quatsch machen mit *j-m*; *v/i.* verfaulen, vermodern.

**rota|ry** ['routəri] drehend; Rotations...; ~te [rou'teit] (sich) drehen, (ab)wechseln; ~tion [~'eiʃən] Umdrehung *f*; Kreislauf *m*; Abwechs(e)lung *f*; ~tory ['routətəri] *s.* rotary; abwechselnd.

**rote** [rout]: *by ~* auswendig.

**rotten** □ ['rɔtn] verfault faul(ig); mod(e)rig; morsch *(alle a. fig.)*; *sl.* saumäßig, dreckig.

**rotund** [~] [rou'tʌnd] rund; voll *(Stimme)*; hochtrabend.

**rouge** [ru:ʒ] **1.** Rouge *n*; Silberputzmittel *n*; **2.** Rouge auflegen (auf *acc.*).

**rough** [rʌf] **1.** □ rauh; roh; grob; *fig.* ungehobelt; ungefähr *(Schätzung)*; ~ *and ready grob (gearbeitet)*; Not..., Behelfs... ~ *copy* roher Entwurf; **2.** Rauhe *n*, Grobe *n*; Lümmel *m*; **3.** (an-, auf)rauhen; ~ *it* sich mühsam durchschlagen; ~cast ['rʌfkɑ:st] **1.** ⊕ Rohputz *m*; **2.** unfertig; **3.** ⊕ roh verputzen; roh entwerfen; ~ *werden* ~neck *Am. sl.* Rabauke *m*; ~ness [~nis] rauhe Beschaffenheit *f*; Grobheit *f*; ~shod: *ride ~ over* rücksichtslos behandeln.

**round** [raund] **1.** □ rund; voll *(Stimme etc.)*; flott *(Gangart)*; abgerundet *(Stil)*; unverblümt; ~ *game* Gesellschaftsspiel *n*; ~ *trip* Rundreise *f*; **2.** *adv.* rund-, ringsum(her); *a.* ~ *about* in der Runde; *all* ~ ringsum; *fig.* ohne Unterschied; *all the year* ~ das ganze Jahr hindurch; **3.** *prp.* um ... herum; **4.** Rund *n*, Kreis *m*; Runde *f*; Kreislauf *m*; (Leiter)Sprosse *f*; Rundgesang *m*; *Lach- etc.*Salve *f*; *100* ~*s* ✕ 100 Schuß; **5.** *v/t.* runden; herumgehen *od.* herumfahren um; ~ *off* abrunden; ~ *up* einkreisen; *v/i.* sich runden; sich umdrehen; ~about ['raundəbaut] **1.** umschweifig; **2.** Umweg *m*; Karussell *n*; Kreisverkehr *m*; ~ish [~diʃ] rundlich; ~up Einkreisung *f*; Razzia *f*.

**rous|e** [rauz] *v/t.* wecken; ermuntern; aufjagen; (auf)reizen; ~ *o.s.* sich aufraffen; *v/i.* aufwachen; ~ing ['rauziŋ] brausend *(Beifall etc.)*.

**roustabout** *Am.* ['raustəbaut] ungelernter *(mst Hafen)*Arbeiter.

**rout** [raut] **1.** Rotte *f*; wilde Flucht; *a.* ~ *put to* ~ vernichtend schlagen; **2.** aufwühlen.

**route** [ru:t, ✕ *a.* raut] Weg *m*; ✕ Marschroute *f*.

**routine** [ru:'ti:n] **1.** Routine *f*; **2.** üblich; Routine...

**rove** [rouv] umherstreifen, umherwandern.

**row**[1] [rou] **1.** Reihe *f*; Ruderfahrt *f*; **2.** rudern.

**row**[2] F [rau] **1.** Spektakel *m*; Krach *m*; Schlägerei *f*; **2.** ausschimpfen.

**row-boat** ['roubout] Ruderboot *n*.

**rower** ['rouə] Ruder|er *m*, -in *f*.

**royal** □ ['rɔiəl] königlich; prächtig; ~ty [~lti] Königtum *n*, -reich *n*; Königswürde *f*; königliche Persönlichkeit; Tantieme *f*.

**rub** [rʌb] **1.** Reiben *n*; Schwierigkeit *f*; *fig.* Stichelei *f*; Unannehmlichkeit *f*; **2.** *v/t.* reiben; (ab)wischen; (wund)scheuern; schleifen; ~ *down* abreiben; ~ *in* einreiben; *fig.* betonen; ~ *off* abreiben; ~ *out* auslöschen; ~ *up* auffrischen; verreiben; *v/i.* sich reiben; *fig.* ~ *along od. through* sich durchschlagen.

**rubber** ['rʌbə] **1.** Gummi *m, m*; Radiergummi *m*; Masseur *m*; Wischtuch *n*; *Whist* Robber *m*; ~*s pl. Am.* Gummischuhe *m/pl.*; **2.** Gummi...; ~ *check Am. sl.* geplatzter Scheck; ~neck *Am. sl.* **1.** Gaffer(in); **2.** sich den Hals verrenken; mithören; ~ *stamp* Gummistempel *m*; *Am.* F *fig.* Nachbeter *m*; ~-stamp automatisch gutheißen.

**rubbish** ['rʌbiʃ] Schutt *m*; Abfall *m*; Kehricht *m*; *fig.* Schund *m*; Unsinn *m*.

**rubble** ['rʌbl] Schutt *m*.

**rube** *Am. sl.* [ru:b] Bauernlümmel *m.*

**ruby** ['ru:bi] Rubin(rot *n*) *m.*

**rucksack** ['ruksæk] Rucksack *m.*

**rudder** ['rʌdə] ⚓ (Steuer)Ruder *n*; ✈ Seitenruder *n.*

**rudd|iness** ['rʌdinis] Röte *f*; **~y** ['rʌdi] rot; rotbäckig.

**rude** □ [ru:d] unhöflich; unanständig; heftig, unsanft; ungebildet; einfach, kunstlos; robust; roh.

**rudiment** *biol.* ['ru:dimənt] Ansatz *m*; **~s** *pl.* Anfangsgründe *m/pl.*

**rueful** □ ['ru:ful] reuig; traurig.

**ruff** [rʌf] Halskrause *f.*

**ruffian** ['rʌfjən] Rohling *m*; Raufbold *m*; Schurke *m.*

**ruffle** ['rʌfl] 1. Krause *f*, Rüsche *f*; Kräuseln *n*; *fig.* Unruhe *f*; 2. kräuseln; zerdrücken; zerknüllen; *fig.* aus der Ruhe bringen; stören.

**rug** [rʌg] (Reise-, Woll)Decke *f*; Vorleger *m*, Brücke *f*; **~ged** □ ['rʌgid] rauh (*a. fig.*); uneben; gefurcht.

**ruin** [ruin] 1. Ruin *m*, Zs.-bruch *m*; Untergang *m*; *mst* **~s** *pl.* Ruine(n *pl.*) *f*, Trümmer *pl.*; 2. ruinieren; zugrunde richten; zerstören; verderben, **~ous** □ ['ruinəs] ruinenhaft, verfallen; verderblich, ruinös.

**rul|e** [ru:l] 1. Regel *f*; Vorschrift *f*; Ordnung *f*; Satzung *f*; Herrschaft *f*; Lineal *n*; *as a* **~** in der Regel; **~(s)** *of the road* Straßenverkehrsordnung *f*; 2. *v/t.* regeln; leiten; beherrschen; verfügen; liniieren; **~ out** ausschließen; *v/i.* herrschen; **~er** ['ru:lə] Herrscher(in); Lineal *n.*

**rum** [rʌm] Rum *m*; *Am.* Alkohol *m.*

**Rumanian** [ru(:)'meinjən] 1. rumänisch; 2. Rumän|e *m*, -in *f*; Rumänisch *n.*

**rumble** ['rʌmbl] 1. Rumpeln *n*; *a.* **~-seat** *Am. mot.* Notsitz *m*; *Am.* F Fehde *f* zwischen Gangsterbanden; 2. rumpeln, rasseln; grollen (*Donner*).

**rumina|nt** ['ru:minənt] 1. wiederkäuend; 2. Wiederkäuer *m*; **~te** [**~**neit] wiederkäuen; *fig.* nachsinnen.

**rummage** ['rʌmidʒ] 1. Durchsuchung *f*; Ramsch *m*, Restwaren *f/pl.*; 2. *v/t.* durchsuchen, durchstöbern, durchwühlen; *v/i.* wühlen.

**rumo(u)r** ['ru:mə] 1. Gerücht *n*; 2. (als Gerücht) verbreiten; *it is* **~ed** es geht das Gerücht. [*m.*]

**rump** *anat.* [rʌmp] Steiß *m*; Rumpf *f*

**rumple** ['rʌmpl] zerknittern; zerren, (zer)zausen.

**rum-runner** *Am.* ['rʌmrʌnə] Alkoholschmuggler *m.*

**run** [rʌn] 1. [*irr.*] *v/i. allg.* laufen; rennen (*Mensch, Tier*); eilen; zerlaufen (*Farbe etc.*); umgehen (*Gerücht etc.*); lauten (*Text*); gehen (*Melodie*); † sich stellen (*Preis*); *across s.o.* j-m in die Arme laufen;

**~** *away* davonlaufen; **~** *down* ablaufen (*Uhr etc.*); *fig.* herunterkommen; **~** *dry* aus-, vertrocknen; **~** *for parl.* kandidieren für; **~** *into* geraten in (*acc.*); werden zu; j-m in die Arme laufen; **~** *low* zur Neige gehen; **~** *mad* verrückt werden; **~** *off* weglaufen; **~** *on* fortfahren; **~** *out*, **~** *short* zu Ende gehen; **~** *through* durchmachen; durchlesen; **~** *to* sich belaufen auf (*acc.*); sich entwickeln zu; **~** *up* to sich belaufen auf (*acc.*); *v/t.* Strecke durchlaufen; Weg einschlagen; laufen lassen; Hand etc. gleiten lassen; stecken, stoßen; transportieren; Flut ergießen; Geschäft betreiben, leiten; *hunt.* verfolgen, hetzen; um die Wette rennen mit; schmuggeln; heften; **~** *the blockade* die Blockade brechen; **~** *down* umrennen; zur Strecke bringen; *fig.* schlecht machen; herunterwirtschaften; *be* **~** *down* abgearbeitet sein; **~** *errands* Botengänge machen; **~** *in mot.* einfahren; F *Verbrecher* einbuchten; **~** *off* ablaufen lassen; **~** *out* hinausjagen; **~** *over* überfahren; *Text* überfliegen; **~** *s.o.* *through* j-n durchbohren; **~** *up Preis, Neubau etc.* emportreiben; *Rechnung etc.* auflaufen lassen; 2. Laufen *n*, Rennen *n*, Lauf *m*; Verlauf *m*; Fahrt *f e-s Schiffes*; Reihe *f*; Folge *f*; Serie *f*; Reise *f*, Ausflug *m*; † Andrang *m*; Ansturm *m*; *Am.* Bach *m*; *Am.* Laufmasche *f*; Vieh-Trift *f*; freie Benutzung *f*; Art *f*, Schlag *m*; *the common* **~** die große Masse; *have a* **~** *of 20 nights thea.* 20mal nacheinander gegeben werden; *in the long* **~** auf die Dauer, am Ende; *in the short* **~** fürs nächste.

**run|about** *mot.* ['rʌnəbaut] kleiner (Sport)Wagen; **~away** Ausreißer *m.*

**rune** [ru:n] Rune *f.*

**rung[1]** [rʌŋ] *p.p. von ring* 2.

**rung[2]** [**~**] (Leiter)Sprosse *f* (*a. fig.*).

**run-in** ['rʌn'in] *Sport:* Einlauf *m*; *Am.* F Krach *m*, Zs.-stoß *m* (*Streit*).

**run|let** ['rʌnlit], **~nel** ['rʌnl] Rinnsal *n*; Rinnstein *m.*

**runner** ['rʌnə] Läufer *m*; Bote *m*; (Schlitten)Kufe *f*; Schieber *m am Schirm*; ♀ Ausläufer *m*; **~-up** [**~**ər'ʌp] *Sport:* Zweitbeste(r *m*) *f*, Zweite(r *m*) *f.*

**running** ['rʌniŋ] 1. laufend; *two days* **~** zwei Tage nacheinander; **~** *hand* Kurrentschrift *f*; 2. Rennen *n*; **~-board** Trittbrett *n.*

**runt** [rʌnt] *zo.* Zwergrind *n*; *fig.* Zwerg *m*; *attr.* Zwerg...

**runway** ['rʌnwei] ✈ Rollbahn *f*; *hunt.* Wechsel *m*; Holzrutsche *f*; *watching* Ansitzjagd *f.*

**rupture** ['rʌptʃə] 1. Bruch *m* (*a.* ⚕); 2. brechen; sprengen.

**rural** □ ['ruərəl] ländlich; Land...

**ruse** [ru:z] List *f*, Kniff *m*.
**rush** [rʌʃ] **1.** ♀ Binse *f*; Jagen *n*, Hetzen *n*, Stürmen *n*; (An)Sturm *m*; Andrang *m*; ✝ stürmische Nachfrage; ~ *hour(s pl.*) Hauptverkehrszeit *f*; **2.** *v/i.* stürzen, jagen, hetzen, stürmen; ~ *at* sich stürzen auf (*acc.*); ~ *into print et.* überstürzt veröffentlichen; *v/t.* jagen, hetzen; drängen; ✂ *u. fig.* stürmen; *sl.* neppen.
**russet** [rʌsit] braunrot; grob.
**Russian** [rʌʃən] **1.** russisch; **2.** Russ|e *m*, -in *f*; Russisch *n*.
**rust** [rʌst] **1.** Rost *m*; **2.** (ver-, ein-) rosten (lassen) (*a. fig.*).

**rustic** [rʌstik] **1.** (~*ally*) ländlich; bäurisch; Bauern...; **2.** Bauer *m*.
**rustle** [rʌsl] **1.** rascheln (mit *od.* in *dat.*); rauschen; *Am.* F sich ranhalten; *Vieh* stehlen; **2.** Rascheln *n*.
**rust|less** [rʌstlis] rostfrei; ~**y** [rʌsti] rostig; eingerostet (*a. fig.*); verschossen (*Stoff*); rostfarben.
**rut** [rʌt] Wagenspur *f*; *bsd. fig.* ausgefahrenes Geleise; *hunt.* Brunst *f*, Brunft *f*.
**ruthless** ☐ [ru:θlis] unbarmherzig; rücksichts-, skrupellos.
**rutted** [rʌtid] ausgefahren (*Weg*).
**rutty** [rʌti] ausgefahren (*Weg*).
**rye** ♀ [rai] Roggen *m*.

# S

**sable** [seibl] Zobel(pelz) *m*; Schwarz *n*. [**2.** sabotieren.)
**sabotage** [sæbɔta:ʒ] **1.** Sabotage *f*;)
**sabre** [seibə] Säbel *m*.
**sack** [sæk] **1.** Plünderung *f*; Sack *m*; *Am.* Tüte *f*; Sackkleid *n*; Sakko *m*, *n*; *give* (*get*) *the* ~ F entlassen (werden); den Laufpaß geben (bekommen); **2.** plündern; einsacken; F rausschmeißen; *j-m* den Laufpaß geben; ~**cloth** [sækklɔθ], ~**ing** [sækiŋ] Sackleinwand *f*.
**sacrament** *eccl.* [sækrəmənt] Sakrament *n*.
**sacred** ☐ [seikrid] heilig; geistlich.
**sacrifice** [sækrifais] **1.** Opfer *n*; *at* *a* ~ ✝ mit Verlust; **2.** opfern; ✝ mit Verlust verkaufen.
**sacrilege** [sækrilidʒ] Kirchenraub *m*, -schändung *f*; Sakrileg *n*; ~**ious** ☐ [sækri'lidʒəs] frevelhaft.
**sad** ☐ [sæd] traurig; jämmerlich, kläglich; schlimm, arg; dunkel.
**sadden** [sædn] (sich) betrüben.
**saddle** [sædl] **1.** Sattel *m*; **2.** satteln; *fig.* belasten; ~**r** [~lə] Sattler *m*.
**sadism** [sædizəm] Sadismus *m*.
**sadness** [sædnis] Traurigkeit *f*, Trauer *f*, Schwermut *f*.
**safe** [seif] **1.** ☐ *allg.* sicher; unversehrt; zuverlässig; **2.** Safe *m*, *n*, Geldschrank *m*; Speiseschrank *m*; ~**blower** *Am.* [seifblouə] Geldschrankknacker *m*; ~ **conduct** freies Geleit; Geleitbrief *m*; ~**guard** **1.** Schutz *m*; **2.** sichern, schützen.
**safety** [seifti] Sicherheit *f*; ~**belt** *mot.* Sicherheitsgurt *m*; ~ **island** Verkehrsinsel *f*; ~**lock** Sicherheitsschloß *n*; ~**pin** Sicherheitsnadel *f*; ~ **razor** Rasierapparat *m*.
**saffron** [sæfrən] Safran(gelb *n*) *m*.
**sag** [sæg] durchsacken; ⊕ durchhängen; ⚓ (ab)sacken (*a. fig.*).

**sagaci|ous** ☐ [sə'geiʃəs] scharfsinnig; ~**ty** [sə'gæsiti] Scharfsinn *m*.
**sage** [seidʒ] **1.** ☐ klug, weise; **2.** Weise(r) *m*; ♀ Salbei *m*, *f*.
**said** [sed] *pret. u. p.p. von* say **1.**
**sail** [seil] **1.** Segel *n*; Fahrt *f*; Windmühlenflügel *m*; (Segel-) Schiff(e *pl.*) *n*; *set* ~ in See stechen; **2.** *v/i.* (ab)segeln, fahren; *fig.* schweben; *v/t.* befahren; *Schiff* führen; ~**boat** *Am.* [seilbout] Segelboot *n*; ~**er** [seilə] Segler *m* (*Schiff*); ~**ing-ship** [seiliŋʃip], ~**ing-vessel** [~vesl] Segelschiff *n*; ~**or** [seilə] Seemann *m*, Matrose *m*; *be a good* (*bad*) ~ (nicht) seefest sein; ~**plane** Segelflugzeug *n*.
**saint** [seint] **1.** Heilige(r *m*) *f*; [*vor npr. snt*] Sankt...; **2.** heiligsprechen; ~**ly** [seintli] *adj.* heilig, fromm.
**saith** ✝ *od. poet.* [seθ] *3. sg. pres. von* say **1.**
**sake** [seik]: *for the* ~ *of* um ... (*gen.*) willen; *for my* ~ meinetwegen; *for God's* ~ um Gottes willen.
**salad** [sæləd] Salat *m*.
**salary** [sæləri] **1.** Besoldung *f*; Gehalt *n*; **2.** besolden; ~**earner** [~ɔ:nə] Gehaltsempfänger(in).
**sale** [seil] (Aus)Verkauf *m*; Absatz *m*; Auktion *f*; *for* ~, *on* ~ zum Verkauf, zu verkaufen, verkäuflich.
**sal(e)able** [seiləbl] verkäuflich.
**sales|man** [seilzmən] Verkäufer *m*; ~**woman** Verkäuferin *f*.
**salient** ☐ [seiljənt] vorspringend; *fig.* hervorragend, hervortretend; Haupt...
**saline** [seilain] salzig; Salz...
**saliva** [sə'laivə] Speichel *m*.
**sallow** [sælou] blaß; gelblich.
**sally** [sæli] **1.** ✕ Ausbruch *m*; witziger Einfall; **2.** *a.* ~ *out* ✕ ausbrechen; ~ *forth*, ~ *out* sich aufmachen.
**salmon** *ichth.* [sæmən] Lachs *m*, Salm *m*.

saloon [sə'lu:n] Salon m; (Gesellschafts)Saal m; erste Klasse auf Schiffen; Am. Kneipe f.

salt [sɔ:lt] 1. Salz n; fig. Würze f; old ~ alter Seebär; 2. salzig; gesalzen; Salz...; Pökel...; 3. (ein)salzen; pökeln; ~-cellar ['sɔ:ltselə] Salzfäßchen n; ~petre, Am. ~peter [˛tpi:tə] Salpeter m; ~-water Salzwasser...; ~y [˛ti] salzig.

salubrious □ [sə'lu:briəs], salutary ⌈: ['sæljutəri] heilsam, gesund.

salut|ation [sælju(:)'teiʃən] Gruß m, Begrüßung f; Anrede f; ~e [sə-'lu:t] 1. Gruß m; co. Kuß m; ✕ Salut m; 2. (be)grüßen; ✕ salutieren.

salvage ['sælvidʒ] 1. Bergung(sgut n) f; Bergegeld n; 2. bergen.

salvation [sæl'veiʃən] Erlösung f; (Seelen)Heil n; fig. Rettung f; ⦵ Army Heilsarmee f.

salve¹ [sælv] retten, bergen.

salve² [sa:v] 1. Salbe f; fig. Balsam m; 2. mst fig. (ein)salben; beruhigen.

salvo ['sælvou] Vorbehalt m; ✕ Salve f (fig. Beifall).

same [seim]: the ~ der-, die-, dasselbe; all the ~ trotzdem; it is all the ~ to me es ist mir (ganz) gleich.

samp Am. [sæmp] grobgemahlener Mais.

sample ['sa:mpl] 1. Probe f, Muster n; 2. bemustern; (aus)probieren.

sanatorium [sænə'tɔ:riəm] (bsd. Lungen)Sanatorium n; Luftkurort m.

sanct|ify ['sæŋktifai] heiligen, weihen; ~imonious □ [sæŋkti'mounjəs] scheinheilig; ~ion ['sæŋkʃən] 1. Sanktion f; Bestätigung f; Genehmigung f; Zwangsmaßnahme f; 2. bestätigen, genehmigen; ~ity [˛ktiti] Heiligkeit f; ~uary [˛tjuəri] Heiligtum n; das Allerheiligste; Asyl n, Freistätte f.

sand [sænd] 1. Sand m; ~s pl. Sand (-massen f/pl.) m; Sandwüste f; Sandbank f; 2. mit Sand bestreuen.

sandal ['sændl] Sandale f.

sand|-glass ['sændgla:s] Sanduhr f; ~hill Sanddüne f; ~piper orn. Flußuferläufer m.

sandwich ['sænwidʒ] 1. Sandwich n; 2. a. ~ in einlegen, einklemmen.

sandy ['sændi] sandig; sandfarben.

sane [sein] geistig gesund; vernünftig (Antwort etc.).

sang [sæŋ] pret. von sing.

sanguin|ary □ ['sæŋgwinəri] blutdürstig; blutig; ~e [˛win] leichtblütig; zuversichtlich; vollblütig.

sanitarium Am. [sæni'teəriəm] = sanatorium.

sanitary □ ['sænitəri] Gesundheits...; gesundheitlich; ⊕ Sanitär...; ~ towel Damenbinde f.

sanit|ation [sæni'teiʃən] Gesund-

heitspflege f; sanitäre Einrichtung; ~y ['sæniti] gesunder Verstand.

sank [sæŋk] pret. von sink 1.

Santa Claus [sæntə'klɔ:z] Nikolaus m.

sap [sæp] 1. ♀ Saft m; fig. Lebenskraft f; ✕ Sappe f; 2. untergraben (a. fig.); sl. büffeln; ~less ['sæplis] saft-, kraftlos; ~ling [˛liŋ] junger Baum; fig Grünschnabel m.

sapphire min. ['sæfaiə] Saphir m.

sappy ['sæpi] saftig; fig. kraftvoll.

sarcasm ['sa:kæzm] bitterer Spott.

sardine ichth. [sa:'di:n] Sardine f.

sash [sæʃ] Schärpe f; Fensterrahmen m. [befenster n.]

sash-window ['sæʃwindou] Schie-]

sat [sæt] pret. u. p.p. von sit.

Satan ['seitən] Satan m.

satchel ['sætʃəl] Schulmappe f.

sate [seit] (über)sättigen.

sateen [sæ'ti:n] Satin m.

satellite ['sætəlait] Satellit(enstaat) m.

satiate ['seiʃieit] (über)sättigen.

satin ['sætin] Seidensatin m.

satir|e ['sætaiə] Satire f; ~ist ['sætərist] Satiriker m; ~ize [˛raiz] verspotten.

satisfaction [sætis'fækʃən] Befriedigung f; Genugtuung f; Zufriedenheit f; Sühne f; Gewißheit f.

satisfactory □ [sætis'fæktəri] befriedigend, zufriedenstellend.

satisfy ['sætisfai] befriedigen; genügen (dat.); zufriedenstellen; überzeugen; Zweifel beheben.

saturate ⚗ u. fig. ['sætʃəreit] sättigen.

Saturday ['sætədi] Sonnabend m, Samstag m.

saturnine ['sætə:nain] düster, finster.

sauce [sɔ:s] 1. (oft kalte) Soße; Am. Kompott n; fig. Würze f; F Frechheit f; 2. würzen; F frech werden zu j-m; ~-boat ['sɔ:sbout] Soßenschüssel f; ~pan Kochtopf m; Kasserolle f; ~r ['sɔ:sə] Untertasse f.

saucy □ F ['sɔ:si] frech; dreist.

saunter ['sɔ:ntə] 1. Schlendern n; Bummel m; 2. (umher)schlendern; bummeln.

sausage ['sɔsidʒ] Wurst f.

savage ['sævidʒ] 1. □ wild; roh, grausam; 2. Wilde(r m) f; fig. Barbar m; ~ry [˛dʒəri] Wildheit f; Barbarei f.

savant ['sævənt] Gelehrte(r) m.

save [seiv] 1. retten; erlösen; bewahren; (er)sparen; schonen; 2. rhet. prp. u. cj. außer; ~ for bis auf (acc.); ~ that nur daß.

saver ['seivə] Retter(in); Sparer(in).

saving ['seiviŋ] 1. □ sparsam; 2. Rettung f; ~s pl. Ersparnisse f/pl.

savings|-bank ['seiviŋzbæŋk] Sparkasse f; ~-deposit Spareinlage f.

savio(u)r ['seivjə] Retter *m*; *Saviour eccl.* Heiland *m*.

savo(u)r ['seivə] **1.** Geschmack *m*; *fig.* Beigeschmack *m*; **2.** *fig.* schmecken, riechen (*of* nach).

savo(u)ry¹ □ ['seivəri] schmackhaft; appetitlich; pikant.

savo(u)ry² ♀ [~] Bohnenkraut *n*.

saw¹ [so:] *pret. von* see.

saw² [~] Spruch *m*.

saw³ [~] **1.** [*irr.*] sägen; **2.** Säge *f*; ~dust ['so:dʌst] Sägespäne *m/pl.*; ~mill Sägewerk *n*; ~n [so:n] *p.p. von* saw³ **1.**

Saxon ['sæksn] **1.** sächsisch; *ling. oft* germanisch; **2.** Sachse *m*, Sächsin *f*.

say [sei] **1.** [*irr.*] sagen; hersagen; berichten; ~ grace das Tischgebet sprechen; *that is to* ~ das heißt; *you don't* ~ *so!* was Sie nicht sagen!; *I* ~ sag(en Sie) mal; ich muß schon sagen; *he is said to be ...* er soll ... sein; *no sooner said than done* gesagt, getan; **2.** Rede *f*, Wort *n*; *it is my* ~ *now* jetzt ist die Reihe zu reden an mir; *have a* od. *some* (no) ~ *in s.th. et.* (nichts) zu sagen haben bei et.; ~ing ['seiiŋ] Rede *f*; Redensart *f*; Ausspruch *m*; *it goes without* ~ es versteht sich von selbst.

scab [skæb] ♂, ♀ Schorf *m*; *vet.* Räude *f*; *sl.* Streikbrecher *m*.

scabbard ['skæbəd] Säbel-Scheide*f*.

scabrous ['skeibrəs] heikel.

scaffold ['skæfəld] (Bau)Gerüst *n*; Schafott *n*; ~ing [~diŋ] (Bau)Gerüst *n*.

scald [sko:ld] **1.** Verbrühung *f*; **2.** verbrühen; *Milch* abkochen.

scale¹ [skeil] **1.** Schuppe *f*; Kesselstein *m*; ♂ Zahnstein *m*; Waagschale *f*; (*a pair of*) ~s *pl.* (eine) Waage; **2.** (sich) abschuppen, ablösen; ⊕ *Kesselstein* abklopfen; ♂ *Zähne* vom Zahnstein reinigen; wiegen.

scale² [~] **1.** Stufenleiter *f*; ♪ Tonleiter *f*; Skala *f*; Maßstab *m*; *fig.* Ausmaß *n*; **2.** ersteigen; ~ *up* (*down*) maßstabsgetreu vergrößern (verkleinern).

scallop ['skɔləp] **1.** *zo.* Kammuschel *f*; ⊕ Langette *f*; **2.** ausbogen.

scalp [skælp] **1.** Kopfhaut *f*; Skalp *m*; **2.** skalpieren.

scaly ['skeili] schuppig; voll Kesselstein.

scamp [skæmp] **1.** Taugenichts *m*; **2.** pfuschen; ~er ['skæmpə] **1.** (umher)tollen; hetzen; **2.** *fig.* Hetzjagd *f*.

scan [skæn] *Verse* skandieren; absuchen; *fig.* überfliegen.

scandal ['skændl] Skandal *m*; Ärgernis *n*; Schande *f*; Klatsch *m*; ~ize [~dəlaiz] Anstoß erregen bei *j-m*; ~ous [~ləs] skandalös, anstößig; schimpflich; klatschhaft.

**Scandinavian** [skændi'neivjən]

**1.** skandinavisch; **2.** Skandinavier (-in).

scant *lit.* [skænt] **1.** knapp, kärglich; **2.** knausern mit, sparen an (*dat.*); ~y □ ['skænti] knapp, spärlich, kärglich, dürftig.

scape|goat ['skeipgout] Sündenbock *m*; ~grace [~greis] Taugenichts *m*.

scar [ska:] **1.** Narbe *f*; *fig.* (Schand-) Fleck *m*, Makel *m*; Klippe *f*; **2.** *v/t.* schrammen; *v/i.* vernarben.

scarc|e [skeəs] knapp; rar; selten; ~ely ['skeəsli] kaum; ~ity [~siti] Mangel *m*; Knappheit *f*; Teuerung *f*.

scare [skeə] **1.** er-, aufschrecken; verscheuchen; ~d verstört; ängstlich; **2.** Panik *f*; ~crow ['skeəkrou] Vogelscheuche *f* (*a. fig.*); ~head (-ing) Riesenschlagzeile *f*.

scarf [ska:f], *pl.* ~s, scarves [~fs, ska:vz] Schal *m*; Hals-, Kopftuch *n*; Krawatte *f*; ✂ Schärpe *f*.

scarlet ['ska:lit] **1.** Scharlach(rot *n*) *m*; **2.** scharlachrot; ~ *fever* ♂ Scharlach *m*; ~ *runner* ♀ Feuerbohne *f*.

scarred [ska:d] narbig.

scarves [ska:vz] *pl. von* scarf.

scathing *fig.* ['skeiðiŋ] vernichtend.

scatter ['skætə] (sich) zerstreuen; aus-, verstreuen; (sich) verbreiten.

scavenger ['skævindʒə] Straßenkehrer *m*.

scenario [si'na:riou] *Film:* Drehbuch *n*.

scene [si:n] Szene *f*; Bühne(nbild *n*) *f*; Schauplatz *m*; ~s *pl.* Kulissen *f/pl.*; ~ry ['si:nəri] Szenerie *f*; Bühnenausstattung *f*; Landschaft*f*.

scent [sent] **1.** (Wohl)Geruch *m*; Duft *m*; Parfüm *n*; *hunt.* Witterung(svermögen *n*) *f*; Fährte *f*; **2.** wittern; parfümieren; ~less ['sentlis] geruchlos.

sceptic ['skeptik] Skeptiker(in); ~al □ [~kəl] skeptisch.

scept|re, *Am.* ~er ['septə] Zepter *n*.

schedule ['ʃedju:l, *Am.* 'skedju:l] **1.** Verzeichnis *n*; Tabelle *f*; *Am.* Fahrplan *m*; *on* ~ fahrplanmäßig; **2.** auf-, verzeichnen; festsetzen.

scheme [ski:m] **1.** Schema *n*; Zs.-stellung *f*; Plan *m*; **2.** *v/t.* planen; *v/i.* Pläne machen; Ränke schmieden.

schism ['sizəm] (Kirchen)Spaltung *f*.

scholar ['skɔlə] Gelehrte(r) *m*; *univ.* Stipendiat *m*; † Schüler(in); ~ly *adj.* [~əli] gelehrt; ~ship [~ʃip] Gelehrsamkeit *f*; Wissenschaftlichkeit *f*; *univ.* Stipendium *n*.

scholastic [skə'læstik] **1.** (~ally) *phls.* scholastisch; schulmäßig; Schul...; **2.** *phls.* Scholastiker *m*.

school [sku:l] **1.** Schwarm *m*; Schule *f* (*a. fig.*); *univ.* Fakultät *f*;

Disziplin *f*; Hochschule *f*; *at ~ auf od.* in der Schule; **2.** schulen, erziehen; **~boy** ['sku:lbɔi] Schüler *m*; **~fellow** Mitschüler(in); **~girl** Schülerin *f*; **~ing** [~liŋ] (Schul-)Ausbildung *f*; **~master** Lehrer *m* (*bsd. e-r höheren Schule*); **~mate** Mitschüler(in); **~mistress** Lehrerin *f* (*bsd. e-r höheren Schule*); **~teacher** (*bsd.* Volksschul)Lehrer (-in).

**schooner** ['sku:nə] ⚓ Schoner *m*; *Am.* großes Bierglas; **=** prairie-schooner.

**science** ['saiəns] Wissenschaft *f*; Naturwissenschaft(en *pl.*) *f*; Technik *f*.

**scientific** [saiən'tifik] (*~ally*) (*engS.* natur)wissenschaftlich; kunstgerecht.

**scientist** ['saiəntist] (*bsd.* Natur-)Wissenschaftler *m*.

**scintillate** ['sintileit] funkeln.

**scion** ['saiən] Sproß *m*, Sprößling *m*.

**scissors** ['sizəz] *pl.* (*a pair of ~ pl.* eine) Schere.

**scoff** [skɔf] **1.** Spott *m*; **2.** spotten.

**scold** [skould] **1.** zänkisches Weib; **2.** (aus)schelten, schimpfen.

**scon(e)** [skɔn] weiches Teegebäck.

**scoop** [sku:p] **1.** Schaufel *f*, Schippe *f*; Schöpfeimer *m*, **~kelle** *f*; F Coup *m*, gutes Geschäft; F Exklusivmeldung *f*; **2.** (aus)schaufeln; einscheffeln.

**scooter** ['sku:tə] (Kinder)Roller *m*; Motorroller *m*.

**scope** [skoup] Bereich *m*; *geistiger* Gesichtskreis; Spielraum *m*.

**scorch** [skɔ:tʃ] *v/t.* versengen, verbrennen; *v/i.* F (dahin)rasen.

**score** [skɔ:] **1.** Kerbe *f*; Zeche *f*, Rechnung *f*; 20 Stück; *Sport*: Punktzahl *f*; (Tor)Stand *m*; Grund *m*; ♪ Partitur *f*; **~s of** viele; *four ~* achtzig; *run up ~s* Schulden machen; *on the ~ of* wegen (*gen.*); **2.** (ein)kerben; anschreiben; *Sport*: (Punkte) machen; *Fußball*: ein Tor schießen; gewinnen; instrumentieren; *Am.* F scharfe Kritik üben an (*dat.*).

**scorn** [skɔ:n] **1.** Verachtung *f*; Spott *m*; **2.** verachten; verschmähen; **~ful** □ ['skɔ:nful] verächtlich.

**Scotch** [skɔtʃ] **1.** schottisch; **2.** Schottisch *n*; *the ~* die Schotten *pl.*; **~man** ['skɔtʃmən] Schotte *m*.

**scot-free** ['skɔt'fri:] straflos.

**Scots** [skɔts], **~man** ['skɔtsmən] **=** Scotch(man).

**scoundrel** ['skaundrəl] Schurke *m*.

**scour** ['skauə] *v/t.* scheuern; reinigen; durchstreifen, absuchen; *v/i.* eilen.

**scourge** [skə:dʒ] **1.** Geißel *f*; **2.** geißeln.

**scout** [skaut] **1.** Späher *m*, Kundschafter *m*; ⚓ Aufklärungsfahrzeug

*n*; ✈ Aufklärer *m*; *mot.* Mitglied *n* der Straßenwacht; (*Boy*) ♀ Pfadfinder *m*; **~ party** ✕ Spähtrupp *m*; **2.** (aus)kundschaften, spähen; verächtlich zurückweisen.

**scowl** [skaul] **1.** finsteres Gesicht; **2.** finster blicken.

**scrabble** ['skræbl] (be)kritzeln; scharren; krabbeln.

**scrag** *fig.* [skræg] Gerippe *n* (*dürrer Mensch etc.*)

**scramble** ['skræmbl] **1.** klettern; sich balgen (*for* um); **~d eggs** *pl.* Rührei *n*; **2.** Kletterei *f*; Balgerei *f*.

**scrap** [skræp] **1.** Stückchen *n*; (Zeitungs)Ausschnitt *m*, Bild *n* *zum Einkleben*; Altmaterial *n*; Schrott *m*; **~s** *pl.* Reste *m/pl.*; **2.** ausrangieren; verschrotten; **~-book** ['skræpbuk] Sammelalbum *n*.

**scrap|e** [skreip] **1.** Kratzen *n*, Scharren *n*; Kratzfuß *m*; Not *f*, Klemme *f*; **2.** schrap(p)en; (ab)schaben; (ab)kratzen; scharren; (entlang)streifen; **~er** ['skreipə] Kratzeisen *n*.

**scrap|-heap** ['skræphi:p] Abfall-, Schrotthaufen *m*; **~-iron** Alteisen *n*, Schrott *m*.

**scratch** [skrætʃ] **1.** Schramme *f*; *Sport* Startlinie *f*; **2.** zs.-gewürfelt; Zufalls...; *Sport*: ohne Vorgabe; **3.** (zer)kratzen; (zer)schrammen; *parl. u. Sport*: streichen; **~ out** ausstreichen.

**scrawl** [skrɔ:l] **1.** kritzeln; **2.** Gekritzel *n*.

**scrawny** *Am.* F ['skrɔ:ni] dürr.

**scream** [skri:m] **1.** Schrei *m*; Gekreisch *n*; *he is a ~* F er ist zum Schreien komisch; **2.** schreien, kreischen.

**screech** [skri:tʃ] *s.* scream; **~owl** *orn.* ['skri:tʃaul] Käuzchen *n*.

**screen** [skri:n] **1.** Wand-, Ofenschutzschirm *m*; *fig.* Schleier *m*; (Film)Leinwand *f*; *der* Film; Sandsieb *n*; (Fliegen)Gitter *n*; **2.** (ab)schirmen, (be)schützen; ✕ tarnen; auf die Leinwand zeigen; verfilmen; (durch)sieben; **~ play** Drehbuch *n*; Fernsehfilm *m*.

**screw** [skru:] **1.** Schraube *f*; ✕ Propeller *m*; **2.** (fest)schrauben; *fig.* bedrängen; ver-, umdrehen; **~ up** festschrauben; **~ up one's courage** Mut fassen; **~ball** *Am. sl.* ['skru:bɔ:l] komischer Kauz; **~-driver** Schraubenzieher *m*; **~-jack** Wagenheber *m*; **~-propeller** Schiffs-, Flugzeugschraube *f*.

**scribble** ['skribl] **1.** Gekritzel *n*; **2.** kritzeln. [*skimp etc.*]

**scrimp** [skrimp], **~y** ['skrimpi] =]

**scrip** † [skrip] Interimsschein(e *pl.*) *m*.

**script** [skript] Schrift *f*; Schreibschrift *f*; Manuskript *n*; *Film*: Drehbuch *n*.

**Scripture** ['skriptʃə] *mst the Holy* ~s *pl.* die Heilige Schrift.

**scroll** [skroul] Schriftrolle *f*, Liste*f*; ⚓ Schnecke *f*; Schnörkel *m*.

**scrub** [skrʌb] **1.** Gestrüpp *n*; Zwerg *m*; *Am. Sport:* zweite (Spieler-) Garnitur; **2.** schrubben, scheuern.

**scrubby** ['skrʌbi] struppig; schäbig.

**scrup|le** ['skru:pl] **1.** Skrupel *m*, Zweifel *m*, Bedenken *n*; **2.** Bedenken haben; ~ulous □ [~pjuləs] (allzu) bedenklich; gewissenhaft; ängstlich.

**scrutin|ize** ['skru:tinaiz] (genau) prüfen; ~y [~ni] forschender Blick; genaue (*bsd.* Wahl)Prüfung.

**scud** [skʌd] **1.** (Dahin)Jagen *n*; (da-hintreibende) Wolkenfetzen *m/pl.*; Bö *f*; **2.** eilen, jagen; gleiten.

**scuff** [skʌf] schlurfen, schlorren.

**scuffle** ['skʌfl] **1.** Balgerei *f*, Rauferei *f*; **2.** sich balgen, raufen.

**scull** ⚓ [skʌl] **1.** kurzes Ruder; **2.** rudern, skullen.

**scullery** ['skʌləri] Spülküche *f*.

**sculptor** ['skʌlptə] Bildhauer *m*.

**sculpture** ['skʌlptʃə] **1.** Plastik *f*; Bildhauerkunst *f*, Skulptur *f*; **2.** (heraus)meißeln, formen.

**scum** *fig.* [skʌm] (Ab)Schaum *m*.

**scurf** [skə:f] (Haut)Schuppen *f/pl.*

**scurrilous** ['skɜriləs] gemein.

**scurry** ['skʌri] hasten, rennen.

**scurvy**[1] ⚕ ['skə:vi] Skorbut *m*.

**scurvy**[2] [~] (hunds)gemein.

**scuttle** ['skʌtl] **1.** Kohlenbehälter *m*; **2.** eilen; *fig.* sich drücken.

**scythe** ⚒ [saið] Sense *f*.

**sea** [si:] See *f*, Meer *n* (*a. fig.*); hohe Welle; *at* ~ auf See; *fig.* ratlos; ~**board** ['si:bɔ:d] Küste(nge-biet *n*) *f*; ~**coast** Küste *f*; ~**faring** ['si:fɛəriŋ] seefahrend; ~**food** eßbare Seefische *m/pl.*; Meeresfrüchte *pl.*; ~**going** Hochsee...; ~**gull** (See)Möwe *f*.

**seal** [si:l] **1.** *zo.* Seehund *m*, Robbe *f*; Siegel *n*; Stempel *m*; Bestätigung *f*; **2.** versiegeln; *fig.* besiegeln; ~ *up* (fest) verschließen; ⚓ abdichten.

**sea-level** ['si:levl] Meeresspiegel *m*.

**sealing-wax** ['si:liŋwæks] Siegellack *m*.

**seam** [si:m] **1.** Saum *m*; (*a.* ⊕) Naht *f*; ⊕ Fuge *f*; *geol.* Flöz *n*; Narbe *f*; **2.** schrammen; furchen.

**seaman** ['si:mən] Seemann *m*, Matrose *m*.

**seamstress** ['semstris] Näherin *f*.

**sea|-plane** ['si:plein] Wasserflugzeug *n*; ~**power** Seemacht *f*.

**sear** [siə] **1.** dürr, welk; **2.** austrocknen, versengen; ⚕ brennen; *fig.* verhärten.

**search** [sə:tʃ] **1.** Suchen *n*, Forschen *n*; Unter-, Durchsuchung *f*; *in* ~ *of* auf die Suche nach; **2.** *v/t.* durch-, untersuchen; ⚕ sondieren; erfor-

schen; durchdringen; *v/i.* suchen, forschen (*for* nach); ~ *into* ergründen; ~**ing** □ ['sə:tʃiŋ] forschend, prüfend; eingehend (*Prüfung etc.*); ~**light** (Such)Scheinwerfer *m*; ~**warrant** ⚖️ Haussuchungsbefehl *m*.

**sea|-shore** ['si:'ʃɔ:] Seeküste *f*; ~**sick** seekrank; ~**side** Strand *m*, Küste *f*; ~ *place*, ~ *resort* Seebad *n*; *go to the* ~ an die See gehen.

**season** ['si:zn] **1.** Jahreszeit *f*; (rechte) Zeit; Saison *f*; F *für* ~**-ticket**; *cherries are in* ~ jetzt ist Kirschenzeit; *out of* ~ zur Unzeit; *with the compliments of the* ~ mit den besten Wünschen zum Fest; **2.** *v/t.* reifen (lassen); würzen; abhärten (*to gegen*); *v/i.* ablagern; ~**able** □ [~nəbl] zeitgemäß; rechtzeitig; ~**al** □ ['si:zənl] Saison...; periodisch; ~**ing** ['si:zniŋ] Würze *f*; ~**-ticket** ⚖️ Zeitkarte *f*; *thea.* Abonnement *n*.

**seat** [si:t] **1.** Sitz *m* (*a. fig.*); Sessel *m*, Stuhl *m*, Bank *f*; (Sitz)Platz *m*; Landsitz *m*; Gesäß *n*; Schauplatz *m*; **2.** (hin)setzen; e-n Hosenboden einsetzen in (*acc.*); fassen, Sitzplätze haben für; ~*ed* sitzend; ...*sitzig; be* ~*ed* sitzen; sich setzen; ~**-belt** ⚓ ['si:tbelt] Sicherheitsgurt *m*.

**sea|-urchin** *zo.* ['si:'ə:tʃin] Seeigel *m*; ~**ward** ['si:wəd] **1.** *adj.* seewärts gerichtet; **2.** *adv. a.* ~*s* seewärts; ~**weed** ⚒ (See)Tang *m*; ~**worthy** seetüchtig.

**secede** [si'si:d] sich trennen.

**secession** [si'seʃən] Lossagung *f*; Abfall *m*; ~**ist** [~ʃnist] Abtrünnige(r *m*) *f*.

**seclu|de** [si'klu:d] abschließen, absondern; ~**ded** einsam; zurückgezogen; abgelegen; ~**sion** [~u:ʒən] Abgeschlossen-, Abgeschiedenheit *f*.

**second** ['sekənd] **1.** □ zweite(r, -s); nächste(r, -s); geringer (*to als*); *on* ~ *thoughts* bei genauerer Überlegung; **2.** Zweite(r, -s); Sekundant *m*; Beistand *m*; Sekunde *f*; ~*s pl.* Waren *pl.* zweiter Wahl; **3.** sekundieren (*dat.*); unterstützen; ~**ary** □ [~dəri] sekundär; untergeordnet; Neben...; Hilfs...; Sekundär...; ~**ary school** höhere Schule; weiterführende Schule; ~**-hand** aus zweiter Hand; gebraucht; antiquarisch; ~**ly** [~dli] zweitens; ~**-rate** zweiten Ranges; zweitklassig.

**secre|cy** ['si:krisi] Heimlichkeit *f*; Verschwiegenheit *f*; ~**t** [~it] **1.** □ geheim; Geheim...; verschwiegen; verborgen; **2.** Geheimnis *n*; *in* ~ insgeheim; *be in the* ~, *be taken into the* ~ eingeweiht sein.

**secretary** ['sekrətri] Schriftführer *m*; Sekretär(in) *f*; 2 *of State* Staatssekretär *m*, Minister *m*; *Am.* Außenminister *m.*

**secret|e** [si'kri:t] verbergen; absondern; **~ion** [~i:ʃən] Absonderung *f*; **~ive** [~i:tiv] *fig.* verschlossen; geheimtuerisch.

**section** ['sekʃən] ⚓ Sektion *f*; (Durch)Schnitt *m*; Teil *m*; Abschnitt *m*, Paragraph *m*; *typ.* Absatz *m*; Abteilung *f*; Gruppe *f.*

**secular** □ ['sekjulə] weltlich.

**secur|e** [si'kjuə] **1.** □ sicher; **2.** (sich *et.*) sichern; schützen; festmachen; **~ity** [~əriti] Sicherheit *f*; Sorglosigkeit *f*; Gewißheit *f*; Schutz *m*; Kaution *f*; *securities pl.* Wertpapiere *n/pl.*

**sedan** [si'dæn] Limousine *f*; *a.* **~-chair** Sänfte *f.*

**sedate** □ [si'deit] gesetzt; ruhig.

**sedative** *mst* ⚕ ['sedətiv] **1.** beruhigend; **2.** Beruhigungsmittel *n.*

**sedentary** □ ['sedntəri] sitzend; seßhaft.

**sediment** ['sedimənt] (Boden)Satz *m*; *geol.* Ablagerung *f.*

**sediti|on** [si'diʃən] Aufruhr *m*; **~ous** □ [~ʃəs] aufrührerisch.

**seduc|e** [si'dju:s] verführen; **~tion** [si'dʌkʃən] Verführung *f*; **~tive** □ [~ktiv] verführerisch.

**sedulous** □ ['sedjuləs] emsig.

**see¹** [si:] [*irr.*] *v/i.* sehen; *fig.* einsehen; *I* ~ ich verstehe; ~ *about* s.th. sich um et. kümmern; ~ *through* s.o. *od.* s.th. j-n *od.* et. durchschauen; ~ *to* achten auf (*acc.*); *v/t.* sehen; beobachten; einsehen; sorgen (*daß* et. *geschieht*); besuchen; *Arzt* aufsuchen; ~ *s.o. home* j-n nach Hause begleiten; ~ *off* Besuch etc. wegbringen; ~ *out* Besuch hinausbegleiten; *et.* zu Ende erleben; ~ s.th. *through* et. durchhalten; ~ s.o. *through* j-m durchhelfen; *live to* ~ erleben.

**see²** [~] (erz)bischöflicher Stuhl.

**seed** [si:d] **1.** Same(n) *m*, Saat(gut *n*) *f*; (Obst)Kern *m*; Keim *m* (*a. fig.*); *go od. run to* ~ in Samen schießen; *fig.* herunterkommen; **2.** *v/t.* (be-)säen; entkernen; *v/i.* in Samen schießen; **~less** [si'dlis] kernlos (*Obst*); **~ling** ✿ [~liŋ] Sämling *m*; **~y** ['si:di] schäbig; F elend.

**seek** [si:k] [*irr.*] suchen (nach); begehren; trachten nach.

**seem** [si:m] (er)scheinen; **~ing** □ ['si:miŋ] anscheinend; scheinbar; **~ly** ['si:mli] schicklich.

**seen** [si:n] *p.p. von* see¹.

**seep** [si:p] durchsickern, tropfen.

**seer** ['si:(:)ə] Scher(in), Prophet(in).

**seesaw** ['si:sɔ:] **1.** Wippen *n*; Wippe *f*, Wippschaukel *f*; **2.** wippen; *fig.* schwanken.

**seethe** [si:ð] sieden, kochen.

**segment** ['segmənt] Abschnitt *m.*

**segregat|e** ['segrigeit] absondern,

trennen; **~ion** [segri'geiʃən] Absonderung *f*; Rassentrennung *f.*

**seiz|e** [si:z] ergreifen, fassen; mit Beschlag belegen; *fig.* erfassen; *a.* ~ *upon* sich *e-r S. od. j-s* bemächtigen; **~ure** ['si:ʒə] Ergreifung *f*; ⚖ Beschlagnahme *f*; ⚕ plötzlicher Anfall.

**seldom** *adv.* ['seldəm] selten.

**select** [si'lekt] **1.** auswählen, auslesen, aussuchen; **2.** auserwählt; erlesen; ausgesucht; **~ion** [~ʃən] Auswahl *f*, Auslese *f*; **~man** *Am.* Stadtrat *m in den Neuenglandstaaten.*

**self** [self] **1.** *pl.* **selves** [selvz] Selbst *n*, Ich *n*; Persönlichkeit *f*; **2.** *pron.* selbst; † *od.* F = *myself etc.*; **3.** *adj.* ✿ einfarbig; **~-centered** ['self-'sentəd] egozentrisch; **~-command** Selbstbeherrschung *f*; **~-conceit** Eigendünkel *m*; **~-conceited** dünkelhaft; **~-confidence** Selbstvertrauen *n*; **~-conscious** befangen, gehemmt; **~-contained** (in sich) abgeschlossen; *fig.* verschlossen; **~-control** Selbstbeherrschung *f*; **~-defence**, *Am.* **~-defense** Selbstverteidigung *f*; *in* ~ in (der) Notwehr; **~-denial** Selbstverleugnung *f*; **~-employed** selbständig (*Handwerker etc.*); **~-evident** selbstverständlich; **~-government** Selbstverwaltung *f*, Autonomie *f*; **~-indulgent** bequem; zügellos; **~-interest** Eigennutz *m*; **~ish** □ [~fiʃ] selbstsüchtig; **~-possession** Selbstbeherrschung *f*; **~-reliant** [~fri'laiənt] selbstsicher; **~-righteous** selbstgerecht; **~-seeking** [~f'si:kiŋ] eigennützig; **~-willed** eigenwillig.

**sell** [sel] [*irr.*] *v/t.* verkaufen (*a. fig.*); *Am.* aufschwatzen; *v/i.* handeln; gehen (*Ware*); ~ *off*, ~ *out* † ausverkaufen; **~er** [~elə] Verkäufer *m*; *good etc.* ~ † gut etc. gehende Ware.

**selves** [selvz] *pl. von* self ¹.

**semblance** ['sembləns] Anschein *m*; Gestalt *f.*

**semi|...** ['semi] halb...; Halb...; **~colon** Strichpunkt *m*; **~-detached house** Doppelhaus(hälfte *f*) *n*; **~-final** *Sport:* Vorschlußrunde *f.*

**seminary** ['seminəri] (Priester)Seminar *n*; *fig.* Schule *f.*

**sempstress** ['sempstris] Näherin *f.*

**senate** ['senit] Senat *m.*

**senator** ['senətə] Senator *m.*

**send** [send] [*irr.*] senden, schicken; (*mit adj. od. p.pr.*) machen; ~ *for* kommen lassen, holen (lassen); ~ *forth* aussenden; veröffentlichen; ~ *in* einsenden; einreichen; ~ *up* in die Höhe treiben; ~ *word* mitteilen.

**senil|e** ['si:nail] greisenhaft, senil; **~ity** [si'niliti] Greisenalter *n.*

**senior** ['si:njə] **1.** älter; dienstälter; Ober...; ~ *partner* † Chef *m*; **2.** Ältere(r) *m*; Dienstältere(r) *m*;

Senior m; he is my ~ by a year er ist ein Jahr älter als ich; **~ity** [si:ni-'ɔriti] höheres Alter od. Dienstalter.

**sensation** [sen'seiʃən] (Sinnes-) Empfindung f, Gefühl n; Eindruck m; Sensation f; **~al** □ [~nl] Empfindungs...; sensationell.

**sense** [sens] 1. allg. Sinn m (of für); Empfindung f, Gefühl n; Verstand m; Bedeutung f; Ansicht f; in (out of) one's ~ bei (von) Sinnen; bring s.o. to his ~s j-n zur Vernunft bringen; make ~ Sinn haben (S.); talk ~ vernünftig reden; 2. spüren.

**senseless** □ ['senslis] sinnlos; bewußtlos; gefühllos; **~ness** [~snis] Sinnlosigkeit f; Bewußt-, Gefühllosigkeit f.

**sensibility** [sensi'biliti] Sensibilität f, Empfindungsvermögen n; Empfindlichkeit f; **sensibilities** pl. Empfindsamkeit f, Zartgefühl n.

**sensible** □ ['sensəbl] verständig, vernünftig; empfänglich (of für); fühlbar; be ~ of sich e-r S. bewußt sein; et. empfinden.

**sensitive** □ ['sensitiv] empfindlich (to für); Empfindungs...; feinfühlig; **~eness** [~vnis], **~ity** [sensi-'tiviti] Empfindlichkeit f (to für).

**sensual** □ ['sensjuəl] sinnlich.

**sensuous** □ ['sensjuəs] sinnlich; Sinnes...; sinnenfreudig.

**sent** [sent] pret. u. p.p. von send.

**sentence** ['sentəns] 1. ½ Urteil n; gr. Satz m; serve one's ~ s-e Strafe absitzen; 2. verurteilen.

**sententious** □ [sen'tenʃəs] sentenziös; salbungsvoll; salbaderisch.

**sentient** ['senʃənt] empfindend.

**sentiment** ['sentimənt] (seelische) Empfindung, Gefühl n; Meinung f; s. sentimentality; **~al** □ [senti'mentl] empfindsam; sentimental; **~ality** [sentimen'tæliti] Sentimentalität f.

**sentinel** ['sentinl], **~ry** [~tri] Schildwache f, Posten m.

**separable** □ ['sepərəbl] trennbar; **~te** 1. □ ['seprit] (ab)getrennt, gesondert, besonder, separat, für sich; 2. ['sepəreit] (sich) trennen; (sich) absondern; (sich) scheiden; **~tion** [sepə'reiʃən] Trennung f, Scheidung f.

**sepsis** ⚕ ['sepsis] Sepsis f, Blutvergiftung f. [m.]

**September** [səp'tembə] September]

**septic** ⚕ ['septik] septisch.

**sepulchral** [si'pʌlkrəl] Grab...; Toten...; fig. düster; **~chre** Am. **~cher** ['sepəlkə] Grab(stätte f) n; **~ture** [~ltʃə] Begräbnis n.

**sequel** ['si:kwəl] Folge f; Nachspiel n; (Roman)Fortsetzung f.

**sequence** ['si:kwəns] Aufeinander-, Reihenfolge f; Film: Szene f; ~ of tenses gr. Zeitenfolge f; **~t** [~nt] aufeinanderfolgend.

**sequestrate** ½ [si'kwestreit] Eigentum einziehen; beschlagnahmen.

**serenade** [seri'neid] 1. ♪ Serenade f, Ständchen n; 2. j-m ein Ständchen bringen.

**serene** □ [si'ri:n] klar, heiter; ruhig; **~ity** [si'reniti] Heiterkeit f; Ruhe f.

**serf** [sə:f] Leibeigene(r m) f, Hörige(r m) f; fig. Sklave m.

**sergeant** ['sa:dʒənt] ✕ Feldwebel m, Wachtmeister m; (Polizei)Wachtmeister m.

**serial** □ ['siəriəl] 1. fortlaufend, reihenweise, Serien...; Fortsetzungs...; 2. Fortsetzungsroman m.

**series** ['siəri:z] sg. u. pl. Reihe f; Serie f; Folge f; biol. Gruppe f.

**serious** □ ['siəriəs] allg. ernst; ernsthaft, ernstlich; be ~ es im Ernst meinen; **~ness** [~snis] Ernst (-haftigkeit f) m.

**sermon** ['sə:mən] (iro. Straf)Predigt f.

**serpent** ['sə:pənt] Schlange f; **~ine** [~tain] schlangengleich, -förmig; Serpentinen...

**serum** ['siərəm] Serum n.

**servant** ['sə:vənt] Diener(in); a. domestic ~ Dienstbote m, Bedienstete(r m) f; Dienstmädchen n.

**serve** [sə:v] 1. v/t. dienen (dat.); Zeit abdienen; bedienen; Speisen reichen; Speisen auftragen; behandeln; nützen, dienlich sein (dat.); Zweck erfüllen; Tennis: angeben; (it) ~ him right (das) geschieht ihm recht; s. sentence; ~ out et. austeilen; v/i. dienen (a. ✕; as, for als, zu); bedienen; nützen, zweckmäßig sein; ~ at table servieren; 2. Tennis: Aufschlag m.

**service** ['sə:vis] 1. Dienst m; Bedienung f; Gefälligkeit f; a. divine ~ Gottesdienst m; Betrieb m; Verkehr m; Nutzen m; Gang m von Speisen; Service n; ½ Zustellung f; Tennis Aufschlag m; be at s.o.'s ~ j-m zu Diensten stehen; 2. ⊕ warten, pflegen; **~able** □ [~səbl] dienlich, nützlich; benutzbar; strapazierfähig; ~ station Tankstelle f; Werkstatt f.

**servile** □ ['sə:vail] sklavisch (a. fig.); unterwürfig; kriecherisch; **~ity** [sə:'viliti] Unterwürfigkeit f, Kriecherei f.

**serving** ['sə:viŋ] Portion f.

**servitude** ['sə:vitju:d] Knechtschaft f; Sklaverei f.

**session** ['seʃən] (a. Gerichts)Sitzung f; be in ~ tagen.

**set** [set] 1. irr. v/t. setzen; stellen; legen; zurechtstellen, (ein)richten, ordnen; Aufgabe, Wecker stellen; Messer abziehen; Edelstein fassen; festsetzen; erstarren lassen; Haar legen; ⚕ Knochenbruch einrichten; ~ s.o. laughing j-n zum Lachen bringing; ~ *an example* ein Beispiel geben; ~ *sail* Segel setzen; ~ *one's teeth* die Zähne zs.-beißen; ~ *aside* beiseite stellen *od.* legen; *fig.* verwerfen; ~ *at ease* beruhigen; ~ *at rest* beruhigen; *Frage* entscheiden; ~ *store by* Wert legen auf (*acc.*); ~ *forth* darlegen; ~ *off* hervorheben; anrechnen; ~ *up* auf-, er-, einrichten; aufstellen; *j-n* etablieren; *v/i. ast.* untergehen; gerinnen, fest werden; laufen (*Flut etc.*); sitzen (*Kleid etc.*); ~ *about s.th.* sich an et. machen; ~ *about s.o.* F über j-n herfallen; ~ *forth* aufbrechen; ~ *off* aufbrechen; ~ *(up)on* anfangen; angreifen; ~ *out* aufbrechen; ~ *to* sich daran machen; ~ *up* sich niederlassen; ~ *up for* sich aufspielen als; 2. fest; starr; festgesetzt, bestimmt; vorgeschrieben; ~ *(up)on* versessen auf (*acc.*); ~ *with* besetzt mit; *Barometer:* ~ *fair* beständig; *hard* ~ in großer Not; ~ *speech* wohlüberlegte Rede; 3. Reihe *f*, Folge *f*, Serie *f*, Sammlung *f*, Satz *m*; Garnitur *f*; Service *n*; *Radio-* Gerät *n*; † Kollektion *f*; Gesellschaft *f*; Sippschaft *f*; ✗ Setzling *m*; *Tennis:* Satz *m*; Neigung *f*, Richtung *f*; Sitz *m* *e-s Kleides etc.*; *poet.* Untergang *m der Sonne*; *thea.* Bühnenausstattung *f*.

**set|-back** ['sɛtbæk] *fig.* Rückschlag *m*; **~-down** *fig.* Dämpfer *m*; **~-off** Kontrast *m*; *fig.* Ausgleich *m*.

**settee** [sɛ'tiː] *kleines* Sofa.

**setting** ['sɛtɪŋ] Setzen *n*; Einrichten *n*; Fassung *f e-s Edelsteins*; Lage *f*; Schauplatz *m*; Umgebung *f*; *thea.* Ausstattung *f*; *fig.* Umrahmung *f*; ♪ Komposition *f*; (*Sonnen- etc.*) Untergang *m*; ⊕ Einstellung *f*.

**settle** ['sɛtl] 1. Sitzbank *f*; 2. *v/t.* (fest)setzen; *Kind etc.* versorgen, ausstatten; *j-n* etablieren; regeln; *Geschäft* abschließen, abmachen, erledigen; *Frage* entscheiden; *Rechnung* begleichen; ordnen; beruhigen; *Streit* beilegen; *Rente* aussetzen; ansiedeln; *Land* besiedeln; *v/i.* sich senken (*Haus*); *oft* ~ *down* sich niederlassen; *a.* ~ *in* sich einrichten; sich legen (*Wut etc.*); beständig werden (*Wetter*); sich entschließen; ~ *down to* sich widmen (*dat.*); **~d** fest; beständig; *auf Rechnungen:* bezahlt; **~ment** ['~lmənt] Erledigung *f*; Übereinkunft *f*; (Be)Siedlung *f*; ⚖ (Eigentums)Übertragung *f*; **~r** ['~lə] Siedler *m*.

**set|-to** F ['sɛt'tuː] Kampf *m*; Schlägerei *f*; **~up** F Aufbau *m*; *Am. sl.* abgekartete Sache.

**seven** ['sɛvn] 1. sieben; 2. Sieben *f*; **~teen(th)** ['~n'tiːn(θ)] siebzehn (-te[r, -s]); **~th** ['~nθ] 1. □ sieben(n)te(r, -s); 2. Sieb(en)tel *n*; **~thly**

[~θli] sieb(en)tens; **~tieth** [~ntiiθ] siebzigste(r, -s); **~ty** [~ti] 1. siebzig; 2. Siebzig *f*.

**sever** ['sɛvə] (sich) trennen; (auf-) lösen; zerreißen.

**several** □ ['sɛvrəl] mehrere, verschiedene; einige; einzeln; besonder; getrennt; **~ly** [~li] besonders, einzeln.

**severance** ['sɛvərəns] Trennung *f*.

**sever|e** □ [si'viə] streng; rauh (*Wetter*); hart (*Winter*); scharf (*Tadel*); ernst (*Mühe*); heftig (*Schmerz etc.*); schlimm, schwer (*Unfall etc.*); **~ity** [si'vɛriti] Strenge *f*, Härte *f*; Schwere *f*; Ernst *m*.

**sew** [sou] [*irr.*] nähen; heften.

**sewage** ['sjuː(:)idʒ] Abwasser *n*.

**sewer¹** ['souə] Näherin *f*.

**sewer²** ['sjuə] Abwasserkanal *m*; **~age** [~əridʒ] Kanalisation *f*.

**sew|ing** ['souiŋ] Nähen *n*; Näherei *f*; *attr.* Näh...; **~n** [soun] *p.p. von* sew.

**sex** [sɛks] Geschlecht *n*.

**sexton** ['sɛkstən] Küster *m*, Totengräber *m*.

**sexual** □ ['sɛksjuəl] geschlechtlich; Geschlechts...; sexuell; Sexual...

**shabby** □ ['ʃæbi] schäbig; gemein.

**shack** *Am.* [ʃæk] Hütte *f*, Bude *f*.

**shackle** ['ʃækl] 1. Fessel *f* (*fig. mst pl.*); 2. fesseln.

**shade** [ʃeid] 1. Schatten *m*, Dunkel *n* (*a. fig.*); *Lampen- etc.* Schirm *m*; Schattierung *f*; *Am.* Rouleau *n*; *fig.* Spur *f*, Kleinigkeit *f*; 2. beschatten; verdunkeln (*a. fig.*); abschirmen; schützen; schattieren; ~ *away*, ~ *off* allmählich übergehen (*luuuwn*) (*into* in *acc.*).

**shadow** ['ʃædou] 1. Schatten *m* (*a. fig.*); Phantom *n*; Spur *f*, Kleinigkeit *f*; 2. beschatten; (*mst* ~ *forth od. out*) andeuten; versinnbildlichen; *j-n* beschatten, überwachen; **~y** [~oui] schattig, dunkel; schattenhaft; wesenlos.

**shady** ['ʃeidi] schattenspendend; schattig; dunkel; F zweifelhaft.

**shaft** [ʃɑːft] Schaft *m*; Stiel *m*; Pfeil *m* (*a. fig.*); *poet.* Strahl *m*; ⊕ Welle *f*; Deichsel *f*; ✗ Schacht *m*.

**shaggy** ['ʃægi] zottig.

**shake** [ʃeik] 1. [*irr.*] *v/t.* schütteln, rütteln; erschüttern; ~ *down* herunterschütteln; *Stroh etc.* hinschütten; ~ *hands* sich die Hände geben *od.* schütteln; ~ *up* Bett aufschütteln; *fig.* aufrütteln; *v/i.* zittern, beben, wackeln, wanken (*with* vor *dat.*); ♪ trillern; 2. Schütteln *n*; Erschütterung *f*; Beben *n*; ♪ Triller *m*; **~down** ['ʃeik'daun] 1. Notlager *n*; *Am. sl.* Erpressung *f*; 2. *adj.:* ~ *cruise* ⚓ Probefahrt *f*; **~hands** *pl.* Händedruck *m*; **~n** ['ʃeikən] 1. *p.p. von* shake 1; 2. *adj.* erschüttert.

**shaky** □ ['ʃeiki] wack(e)lig (*a. fig.*); (sch)wankend; zitternd, zitterig.

**shall** [ʃæl] [*irr.*] *v/aux.* soll; werde.

**shallow** ['ʃælou] 1. seicht; flach; *fig.* oberflächlich; 2. Untiefe *f*; 3. (sich) verflachen.

**sham** [ʃæm] 1. falsch; Schein...; 2. Trug *m*; Täuschung *f*; Schwindler(in); 3. *v/t.* vortäuschen; *v/i.* sich verstellen; simulieren; ~ *ill* (-*ness*) sich krank stellen.

**shamble** ['ʃæmbl] watscheln; ~s *pl. od. sg.* Schlachthaus *n*; *fig.* Schlachtfeld *n*.

**shame** [ʃeim] 1. Scham *f*; Schande *f*; *for* ~!, ~ *on you!* pfui, schäm dich!; *put to* ~ beschämen; 2. beschämen; *j-m* Schande machen; ~**faced** □ ['ʃeimfeist] schamhaft, schüchtern; ~**ful** □ [~ful] schändlich, beschämend; ~**less** □ ['ʃeimlis] schamlos.

**shampoo** [ʃæm'puː] 1. Shampoo *n*; Haarwäsche *f*; 2. *Haare* waschen.

**shamrock** ['ʃæmrɔk] Kleeblatt *n*.

**shank** [ʃæŋk] (Unter)Schenkel *m*; ⊕ Stiel *m*; (⚓ Anker)Schaft *m*.

**shanty** ['ʃænti] Hütte *f*, Bude *f*.

**shape** [ʃeip] 1. Gestalt *f*, Form *f* (*a. fig.*); Art *f*; 2. *v/t.* gestalten, formen, bilden; anpassen (*to dat.*); *v/i.* sich entwickeln; ~**d** ...förmig; ~**less** □ ['ʃeiplis] formlos; ~**ly** [~li] wohlgestaltet.

**share** [ʃɛə] 1. (An)Teil *m*; Beitrag *m*; ✝ Aktie *f*; ⚒ Kux *m*; *have a* ~ *in* teilhaben an (*dat.*); *go* ~ *s* teilen; 2. *v/t.* teilen; *v/i.* teilhaben (*in dat.*); ~**cropper** *Am.* ['ʃɛəkrɔpə] *kleiner* Farmpächter; ~**holder** ✝ Aktionär(in).

**shark** [ʃɑːk] *ichth.* Hai(fisch) *m*; Gauner *m*; *Am. sl.* Kanone *f* (*Experte*).

**sharp** [ʃɑːp] 1. □ *allg.* scharf (*a. fig.*); spitz; schneidend, stechend; schrill; hitzig; schnell; pfiffig, schlau, gerissen; C ⚐ ♪ Cis *n*; 2. *adv.* ♪ zu hoch; F pünktlich; *look* ~! (mach) schnell!; 3. ♪ Kreuz *n*; durch ein Kreuz erhöhte Note; F Gauner *m*; ~**en** ['ʃɑːpən] (ver-) schärfen; spitzen; ~**ener** ['ʃɑːpə] *Messer-*Schärfer *m*; *Bleistift-*Spitzer *m*; ~**er** ['ʃɑːpə] Gauner *m*; ~**ness** ['ʃɑːpnis] Schärfe *f* (*a. fig.*); ~**set** ['ʃɑːp'set] hungrig; erpicht; ~**sighted** scharfsichtig; ~**witted** scharfsinnig.

**shatter** ['ʃætə] zerschmettern, zerschlagen; *Nerven etc.* zerrütten.

**shave** [ʃeiv] 1. [*irr.*] (sich) rasieren; (ab)schälen; haarscharf vorbeigehen *od.* vorbeifahren *od.* vorbeikommen an (*dat.*); 2. Rasieren *n*, Rasur *f*; *have a* ~ sich rasieren (lassen); *a close* ~ ein Entkommen mit knapper Not; ~**n** ['ʃeivn] *p.p. von* shave 1.

**shaving** ['ʃeiviŋ] 1. Rasieren *n*; ~s *pl.* (*bsd.* Hobel)Späne *m/pl.*; 2. Rasier...

**shawl** [ʃɔːl] Schal *m*, Kopftuch *n*.

**she** [ʃiː] 1. sie; 2. Sie *f*; *zo.* Weibchen *n*; 3. *adj. in Zssgn:* weiblich, ...weibchen *n*; ~**dog** Hündin *f*.

**sheaf** [ʃiːf], *pl.* **sheaves** [ʃiːvz] Garbe *f*; Bündel *n*.

**shear** [ʃiə] 1. [*irr.*] scheren; *fig.* rupfen; 2. ~s *pl.* große Schere.

**sheath** [ʃiːθ] Scheide *f*; ~**e** [ʃiːð] (in die Scheide) stecken; einhüllen; ⊕ bekleiden, beschlagen.

**sheaves** [ʃiːvz] *pl. von* sheaf.

**shebang** *Am. sl.* [ʃə'bæŋ] Bude *f*, Laden *m*.

**shed**[1] [ʃed] [*irr.*] aus-, vergießen; verbreiten; *Blätter etc.* abwerfen.

**shed**[2] [~] Schuppen *m*; Stall *m*.

**sheen** [ʃiːn] Glanz *m* (*bsd. Stoff*).

**sheep** [ʃiːp] Schaf(e *pl.*) *n*; Schafleder *n*; ~**cot** ['ʃiːpkɔt] = *sheepfold*; ~**dog** Schäferhund *m*; ~**fold** Schafhürde *f*; ~**ish** □ ['ʃiːpiʃ] blöd(e), einfältig; ~**man** *Am.* Schafzüchter *m*; ~**skin** Schaffell *n*; Schafleder *n*; F Diplom *n*.

**sheer** [ʃiə] rein; glatt; *Am.* hauchdünn; steil; senkrecht; direkt.

**sheet** [ʃiːt] Bett-, Leintuch *n*, Laken *n*; (*Glas- etc.*)Platte *f*; ⊕ ...blech *n*; Blatt *n*, Bogen *m Papier*; weite Fläche (*Wasser etc.*); ⚓ Schot(e) *f*; *the rain came down in* ~s es regnete in Strömen; ~ *iron* Eisenblech *n*; ~ *lightning* ['ʃiːtlaitniŋ] Wetterleuchten *n*.

**shelf** [ʃelf], *pl.* **shelves** [ʃelvz] Brett *n*, Regal *n*, Fach *n*; Riff *n*; *on the* ~ *fig.* ausrangiert.

**shell** [ʃel] 1. Schale *f*, Hülse *f*, Muschel *f*; Gehäuse *n*; Gerippe *n e-s Hauses*; ⚔ Granate *f*; 2. schälen, enthülsen; ⚔ bombardieren; ~**fire** ['ʃelfaiə] Granatfeuer *n*; ~**fish** *zo.* Schalentier *n*; ~**proof** bombensicher.

**shelter** ['ʃeltə] 1. Schuppen *m*; Schutz-, Obdach *n*; *fig.* Schutz *m*, Schirm *m*; 2. *v/t.* (be)schützen; (be)schirmen; Zuflucht gewähren (*dat.*); *v/i. a. take* ~ Schutz suchen.

**shelve** [ʃelv] mit Brettern *od.* Regalen versehen; auf ein Brett stellen; *fig.* zu den Akten legen; *fig.* beiseite legen; sich allmählich neigen.

**shelves** [ʃelvz] *pl. von* shelf.

**shenanigan** *Am.* F [ʃi'nænigən] Gaunerei *f*; Humbug *m*.

**shepherd** ['ʃepəd] 1. Schäfer *m*, Hirt *m*; 2. (be)hüten; leiten.

**sherbet** ['ʃəːbət] Brauselimonade *f*; (*Art*) (Speise)Eis *n*.

**shield** [ʃiːld] 1. (Schutz)Schild *m*; Wappenschild *n*; 2. (be)schirmen (*from vor dat.*, gegen).

**shift** [ʃift] 1. Veränderung *f*, Verschiebung f, Wechsel m; Notbehelf m; List f, Kniff m; Ausflucht f; (Arbeits)Schicht f; make ~ es möglich machen (to inf. zu inf.); sich behelfen; sich durchschlagen; 2. v/t. (ver-, weg)schieben; (ab)wechseln; verändern; Platz, Szene verlegen, verlagern; v/i. wechseln; sich verlagern; sich behelfen; ~ for o.s. sich selbst helfen; ~less □ ['ʃiftlis] hilflos; faul; ~y □ [~ti] fig. gerissen; unzuverlässig.

**shilling** ['ʃiliŋ] englischer Schilling.

**shin** [ʃin] 1. a. ~-bone Schienbein n; 2. ~ up hinaufklettern.

**shine** [ʃain] 1. Schein m; Glanz m; 2. [irr.] v/i. scheinen; leuchten; fig. glänzen, strahlen; v/t. blank putzen.

**shingle** ['ʃiŋgl] Schindel f; Am. F (Aushänge)Schild n; Strandkiesel m/pl.; ~s pl. ♀ Gürtelrose f.

**shiny** □ ['ʃaini] blank, glänzend.

**ship** [ʃip] 1. Schiff n; Am. F Flugzeug n; 2. an Bord nehmen od. bringen; verschiffen, versenden; ♣ heuern; ~board ['ʃipbɔ:d]: on ~ ♣ an Bord, ~ment ['ʃipmənt] Verschiffung f; Versand m; Schiffsladung f; ~owner Reeder m; ~ping ['ʃipiŋ] Verschiffung f; Schiffe n/pl., Flotte f; attr. Schiffs...; Verschiffungs..., Verlade...; ~wreck 1. Schiffbruch m; 2. scheitern (lassen); ~wrecked schiffbrüchig; ~yard Schiffswerft f.    [schaft f.]

**shire** ['ʃaiə, in Zssgn ...ʃiə] Graf-}

**shirk** [ʃə:k] sich drücken (um et.); ~er ['ʃə:kə] Drückeberger m.

**shirt** [ʃə:t] Herrenhemd n; a. ~-waist Am. Hemdbluse f; ~-sleeve ['ʃə:tsliːv] 1. Hemdsärmel m; 2. hemdsärmelig; informell; ~ diplomacy bsd. Am. offene Diplomatie.

**shiver** ['ʃivə] 1. Splitter m; Schauer m; 2. zersplittern; schau(d)ern; (er)zittern; frösteln; ~y [~əri] fröstelnd.

**shoal** [ʃoul] 1. Schwarm m, Schar f; Untiefe f; 2. flacher werden; 3. seicht.

**shock** [ʃɔk] 1. Garbenhaufen m; (Haar)Schopf m; Stoß m; Anstoß m; Erschütterung f, Schlag m; ♀ (Nerven)Schock m; 2. a. fig. verletzen; empören, Anstoß erregen bei; erschüttern; ~ing □ ['ʃɔkiŋ] anstößig; empörend; haarsträubend.

**shod** [ʃɔd] pret. u. p.p. von shoe 2.

**shoddy** ['ʃɔdi] 1. Reißwolle f; fig. Schund m; Am. Protz m; 2. falsch; minderwertig; Am. protzig.

**shoe** [ʃuː] 1. Schuh m; Hufeisen n; 2. [irr.] beschuhen; beschlagen; ~black ['ʃuːblæk] Schuhputzer m; ~blacking Schuhwichse f; ~horn Schuhanzieher m; ~lace Schnürsenkel m; ~maker Schuhmacher m; ~string Schnürsenkel m.

**shone** [ʃɔn] pret. u. p.p. von shine 2.

**shook** [ʃuk] pret. von shake 1.

**shoot** [ʃuːt] 1. fig. Schuß m; ♀ Schößling m; 2. [irr.] v/t. (ab-)schießen; erschießen; werfen, stoßen; Film aufnehmen, drehen; fig. unter e-r Brücke etc. hindurchschießen, über et. hinwegschießen; ♀ treiben; ~ (ein)spritzen; v/i. schießen; stechen (Schmerz); daherschießen; stürzen; a. ~ forth ausschlagen; ~ ahead vorwärtsschießen; ~er ['ʃuːtə] Schütze m.

**shooting** ['ʃuːtiŋ] 1. Schießen n; Schießerei f; Jagd f; Film: Dreharbeiten f/pl.; 2. stechend (Schmerz); ~-gallery Schießstand m, -bude f; ~-range Schießplatz m; ~ star Sternschnuppe f.

**shop** [ʃɔp] 1. Laden m, Geschäft n; Werkstatt f, Betrieb m; talk ~ fachsimpeln; 2. mst go ~ping einkaufen gehen; ~assistant ['ʃɔpəsistənt] Verkäufer(in); ~keeper Ladeninhaber(in); ~lifter ['ʃɔpliftə] Ladendieb m; ~man Ladengehilfe m; ~per ['ʃɔpə] Käufer(in); ~ping ['ʃɔpiŋ] Einkaufen n; attr. Einkaufs...; ~ centre Einkaufszentrum n; ~steward Betriebsrat m; ~walker ['ʃɔpwɔːkə] Aufsichtsherr m, -dame f; ~window Schaufenster n.

**shore** [ʃɔː] 1. Küste f, Ufer n; Strand m; Stütze f; on ~ an Land; 2. ~ up abstützen.

**shorn** [ʃɔːn] p.p. von shear 1.

**short** [ʃɔːt] 1. adj. kurz (a. fig.); klein; knapp; mürbe (Gebäck); wortkarg; in ~ kurz(um); ~ of knapp an (dat.); 2. adv. ~ of abgesehen von; come od. fall ~ of et. nicht erreichen; run ~ (of) ausgehen (Vorräte); stop ~ of zurückschrecken vor (dat.); ~age ['ʃɔːtidʒ] Fehlbetrag m; Gewichtsverlust m; Knappheit f; ~coming Unzulänglichkeit f; Fehler m; Mangel m; ~ cut Abkürzungsweg m; ~dated ♣ auf kurze Sicht; ~en ['ʃɔːtn] v/t. ab-, verkürzen; v/i. kürzer werden; ~ening [~niŋ] Backfett n; ~hand Kurzschrift f; ~ typist Stenotypistin f; ~ly ['ʃɔːtli] adv. kurz; bald; ~ness ['ʃɔːtnis] Kürze f; Mangel m; ~sighted kurzsichtig; ~term kurzfristig; ~winded kurzatmig.

**shot** [ʃɔt] 1. pret. u. p.p. von shoot 2; 2. Schuß m; Geschoß n, Kugel f; Schrot(korn) n; Schußweite f; Schütze m; Sport: Stoß m, Schlag m, Wurf m; phot., Film: Aufnahme f; ♀ Spritze f; have a ~ at et. versuchen; not by a long ~ F noch lange nicht; big ~ F großes Tier; ~-gun ['ʃɔtgʌn] Schrotflinte f; ~ marriage Am. F Mußheirat f.

**should** [ʃud, ʃəd] pret. von shall.

shoulder ['ʃouldə] 1. Schulter f (a.
v. Tieren; fig. Vorsprung); Achsel f;
2. auf die Schulter od. fig. auf sich
nehmen; ✕ schultern; drängen;
~blade anat. Schulterblatt n; ~
strap ˋTräger m am Kleid; ✕
Schulter-, Achselstück n.

shout [ʃaut] 1. lauter Schrei od. Ruf;
Geschrei n; 2. laut schreien.

shove [ʃʌv] 1. Schub m, Stoß m;
2. schieben, stoßen.

shovel ['ʃʌvl] 1. Schaufel f; 2. schau-
feln.

show [ʃou] 1. [irr.] v/t. zeigen; ausstellen; erweisen; beweisen; ~ in
hereinführen; ~ off zur Geltung
bringen; ~ out hinausgeleiten; ~
round herumführen; ~ up hinauf-
führen; entlarven; v/i. a. ~ up sich
zeigen; zu sehen sein; ~ up angeben, prahlen, sich aufspielen;
2. Schau(stellung) f; Ausstellung f;
Auf-, Vorführung f; Anschein m;
on ~ zu besichtigen; ~ business
['ʃoubiznis] Unterhaltungsindustrie
f; Schaugeschäft n; ~-case Schaukasten m, Vitrine f; ~-down Aufdecken n der Karten (bsd. Am. a.
fig.); fig. Kraftprobe f.

shower ['ʃauə] 1. (Regen)Schauer
m; Dusche f; fig. Fülle f; 2. v/t.
herabschütten (a. fig.); überschüt-
ten; v/i. sich ergießen; ~y ['ʃauəri]
regnerisch.

show|n [ʃoun] p.p. von show 1; ~-
room ['ʃourum] Ausstellungsraum
m; ~-window Schaufenster n; ~y
☐ ['ʃoui] prächtig; protzig.

shrank [ʃræŋk] pret. von shrink.

shred [ʃred] 1. Stückchen n;
Schnitz(el n) m; Fetzen m (a. fig.);
2. [irr.] (zer)schnitzeln; zerfetzen.

shrew [ʃru:] zänkisches Weib.

shrewd ☐ [ʃru:d] scharfsinnig;
schlau.

shriek [ʃri:k] 1. (Angst)Schrei m;
Gekreisch n; 2. kreischen, schreien.

shrill [ʃril] 1. ☐ schrill, gellend;
2. schrillen, gellen; schreien.

shrimp [ʃrimp] zo. Krabbe f; fig.
Knirps m.                      [m.]

shrine [ʃrain] Schrein m; Altar]

shrink [ʃriŋk] [irr.] (ein-, zs.-)
schrumpfen (lassen); einlaufen;
sich zurückziehen; zurückschrek-
ken (from, at vor dat.); ~age
['ʃriŋkidʒ] Einlaufen n, Zs.-
schrumpfen n; Schrumpfung f; fig.
Verminderung f.

shrivel ['ʃrivl] einschrumpfen (lassen).

shroud [ʃraud] 1. Leichentuch n;
fig. Gewand n; 2. in ein Leichentuch einhüllen; fig. hüllen.

Shrove|tide ['ʃrouvtaid] Fast-
nachtszeit f; ~Tuesday Fastnachts-
dienstag m.

shrub [ʃrʌb] Strauch m; Busch m;
~bery['ʃrʌbəri] Gebüsch n.

shrug [ʃrʌg] 1. (die Achseln) zucken;
2. Achselzucken n.

shrunk [ʃrʌŋk] p.p. von shrink; ~en
['ʃrʌŋkən] adj. (ein)geschrumpft.

shuck bsd. Am. [ʃʌk] 1. Hülse f,
Schote f; ~s! F Quatsch!; 2. enthülsen.

shudder ['ʃʌdə] 1. schaudern; (er-)
beben; 2. Schauder m.

shuffle ['ʃʌfl] 1. schieben; Karten:
mischen; schlurfen; Ausflüchte
machen; ~ off von sich schieben;
abstreifen; 2. Schieben n; Mischen
n; Schlurfen n; Ausflucht f; Schiebung f.

shun [ʃʌn] (ver)meiden.

shunt [ʃʌnt] 1. ∰ Rangieren n; ∰
Weiche f; ⚡ Nebenschluß m; 2. ∰
rangieren; ⚡ nebenschließen; fig.
verschieben.

shut [ʃʌt] [irr.] (sich) schließen; zumachen; ~ down Betrieb schließen;
~ up ein-, verschließen; einsperren;
~ up! F halt den Mund!; ~ter
['ʃʌtə] Fensterladen m; phot. Verschluß m.

shuttle ['ʃʌtl] 1. ⊕ Schiffchen n;
Pendelverkehr m; 2. pendeln.

shy [ʃai] 1. ☐ scheu; schüchtern;
2. (zurück)scheuen (at vor dat.).

shyness ['ʃainis] Schüchternheit f;
Scheu f.

shyster sl., bsd. Am. ['ʃaistə] gerissener Kerl; Winkeladvokat m.

Siberian [sai'biəriən] 1. sibirisch;
2. Sibirier(in).

sick [sik] krank (of an dat.; with vor
dat.); übel; überdrüssig; be ~ for
sich sehnen nach; be ~ of genug
haben von; go ~, report ~ sich
krank melden; ~-benefit ['sik-
benifit] Krankengeld n; ~en ['sikn]
v/i. krank werden; kränkeln; ~ at
sich ekeln vor (dat.); v/t. krank
machen; anekeln.

sickle ['sikl] Sichel f.

sick|-leave ['sikli:v] Krankheits-
urlaub m; ~ly [~li] kränklich;
schwächlich; bleich, blaß; ungesund (Klima); ekelhaft; matt (Lächeln); ~ness ['siknis] Krankheit f;
Übelkeit f.

side [said] 1. allg. Seite f; ~ by ~
Seite an Seite; take ~ with Partei
ergreifen für; 2. Seiten...; Neben...;
3. Partei ergreifen (with für);
~board ['saidbɔ:d] Anrichte(tisch
m) f, Sideboard n; ~car mot.
Beiwagen m; ~d ...seitig; ~light
Streiflicht n; ~long 1. adv. seitwärts; 2. adj. seitlich; Seiten...;
~-stroke Seitenschwimmen n;
~-track 1. ∰ Nebengleis n; 2. auf
ein Nebengleis schieben; bsd. Am
fig. aufschieben; beiseite schieben;
~walk bsd. Am. Bürgersteig m;
~ward(s) [~wəd(z)], ~ways seitlich; seitwärts.

siding ∰ ['saidiŋ] Nebengleis n.

**sidle** ['saidl] seitwärts gehen.
**siege** [si:dʒ] Belagerung f; lay ~ to belagern.
**sieve** [siv] 1. Sieb n; ~ (durch-)sieben.
**sift** [sift] sieben; fɪ sichten; prüfen.
**sigh** [sai] 1. Seutze m; 2. seufzen; sich ~ehnen (after, for nach).
**sight** [sait] 1. Sehvermögen n, Sehkraft f; fig. Auge n; Anblick m; Visier n; Sicht f ~s pl. Sehenswürdigkeiten f/pl.; at ~, a. on ~ beim Anblick; ʃ vom Blatt; ♥ nach Sicht; catch ~ oʃ rblicken, zu Gesicht bekommen; lose ~ oʃ aus den Augen verlieren; within ~ in Sicht; know by ~ vom Sehen kennen; 2. ~ichten; (n)v sieren; ~ed ['saitid] ...sichtig; ~y 'saitli] ansehnlich, stattlich; ~seeing ['saitsi:iŋ] Besichtigung f von Sehenswürdigkeiten ~seer Tourist(in).
**sign** [sain 1. Zeichnen n; Wink m; Schild n; in ~ of zum Zeichen (gen.); 2. v/i. winken. Z..chen geben; v/t. (unter)zeichnen unterschreiben.
**signal** ['signl] 1. Signal n; Zeichen n; 2. ~ bemer enswer außerordentlich, 3. ~ nalisieren ~ize [~nəlaiz] uszeichnen; = signal 3.
**signat|ory** ['signətə 1. Unterzeichner m; 2. un erze chnend; ~ powers pl. Signatarmächt f/pl.; ~ure [~nitʃə Signatur ʃ; Unterschrift ʃ; ~ un Radio Kennmelodie f.
**sign|board** ['sainbo:d] (Aushänge-)Schild n ~er 'sainə] Unterzeichner(in).
**signet** ['signit Siege. n.
**signific|ance** [sig'nifikəns Bedeutung ʃ; ~ant ~ nti] bedeutsam; bezeichnend (o. ür); ~ation signifi'keiʃən] Bedeutung ʃ.
**signify** 'signifai beze chnen andeuten; kundg-ben. bedeuten.
**signpost** 'sainpous Wegweiser m.
**silence** ['sailəns] 1. (Still)Schweigen n; Stille ʃ, Ruhe ʃ Ruhe pu od. reduce to ~ = z. zum Schweigen bringen; ~ɪ ~ə ⊕ Sch dämpfer m; mot. Auspuff op m.
**silent** ʃ 'sailənt til]; schweigend; schweigsam; tumm: ~ ortner ♥ stiller Teilh.ber
**silk** [silk] Seide n; ttr. Seiden... ~en ʃ ['silkən] eiden. ~stocking Am. vornehm; ~worm Seidenraupe f; ~y ʃ ~y si d(enart)ig.
**sill** [sil] Schwell ʃ; Fensterbrett n.
**silly** ʃ ['sili] albern; ör cht.
**silt** [silt] 1. Schlamm m; ~ mst ~ up verschlammen.
**silver** ['silvə] 1. Silber n; 2. silbern; Silber...; 3. versilbern; silberig od. silberweiß werden (l ssen); ~ware Am. Tafelsilber n; ~y ~əri silberglänzend; silberhell.

**similar** ☐ ['similə] ähnlich, gleich; ~ity [simi'læriti] Ähnlichkeit ʃ.
**simile** ['simili] Gleichnis n.
**similitude** [si'militju:d] Gestalt ʃ; Ebenbild n; Gleichnis n.
**simmer** ['simə] sieden od. brodeln (lassen); fig. kochen, gären (Gefühl, Aufstand); ~ down ruhig(er) werden.
**simper** ['simpə] 1 einfältiges Lächeln; 2. einfälti; lächeln.
**simple** ☐ 'simpl] einfach; schlicht; einfältig; arglos; ~hearted, ~minded arglos. naiv; ~ton [~ltən] Einfaltspinsel m.
**simpli|city** [sim'plisiti] Einfachheit ʃ; Klarheit ʃ; Schlichtheit ʃ; Einfalt ʃ; ~fication [simplifi'keiʃən] Vereinfachung ʃ; ~fy ['simplifai] vereinfachen.
**simply** ['simpli] einfach; bloß.
**simulat** ['simjuleit] vortäuschen; (er)heucheln; sich tarnen als.
**simultaneous** ☐ [siməl'teinjəs] gleichzeitig.
**sin** [sin] 1. Sünde ʃ; 2. sündigen.
**since** [sins] 1. prp. eit; 2. adv. seitdem; 3. cj. seit(dem) da (ja).
**sincer|e** ☐ [sin'siə. autrichtig; Yours ~ly Ihr ergebener; ~ity [~'seriti] Aufrichtigkeit ʃ.
**sinew** ['sinju: Sehne ʃ; fig. mst. ~s pl. Nerven(kraʃt ʃ) m/pl.; Seele ʃ; ~y [~ju(:)i] sehnig; nervig, .tark.
**sinful** ☐ 'sinful] sündig, sündhaft, böse.
**sing** [siŋ] irr. singen; besingen; ~ to s.o. j-m vor ingen.
**singe** [sindʒ] (ver)sengen.
**inger** ['sinə Sänger(in).
**singing** ['siŋiŋ] Gesang m Singen n; ~ bird Singvoge m.
**single** 'ngl] 1. ☐ einzig; einzeln; Einzel...; einfach ledig unverheiratet; book-k eping by ~ entry einfache Buchführun; ~ file Gänsemarsch m; ~ n einfache Fahrkarte; mst ~s sg. Tennis Einze n; 3. ~ out auswähle. aussuchen; ~breasted einreihig Jacke etc.); ~en ned ⚡ einmotorig; ~handed eigenhändig, allein. ~hearted ☐, ~minded ☐ au richtig; zielstrebig; ~t [~lit Unterhemd n; ~track eingleisig.
**ingular** ['siŋ uəj 1. ☐ einzigartig; eigenartı; sonderb r; 2. a. ~ number ; Singu m m Einzahl ʃ; ~ity [singju'læri.t] Einzigartigkeit ʃ; Sonderbarkeit ʃ.
**sini ter** ☐ 'sinistə]unhe lvoll; böse.
**sink** [siŋk] 1. irr. v/i. sinken; nieder- unter- versinken; sich senken; eindringen; iegen; v/t. (ver)senken; Brunnen bohren; Geld festlegen; Namen etc. .ugeben; 2. Ausguß m; .ing ʃ siŋk n] (Ver-)Sinken n; Versenken n; ♣ Schwäche(gefühl n) ʃ; Senkung ʃ; ♥

Tilgung *f*; ~ fund (Schulden)Tilgungsfonds *m*.

**sinless** ['sinlis] sündenlos, -frei.

**sinner** ['sinə] Sünder(in).

**sinuous** □ ['sinjuəs] gewunden.

**sip** [sip] 1. Schlückchen *n*; 2. schlürfen; nippen; langsam trinken.

**sir** [sə:] Herr *m*; ♀ Sir (*Titel*).

**sire** ['saiə] *mst poet.* Vater *m*; Vorfahr *m*; *zo.* Vater(tier *n*) *m*.

**siren** ['saiərin] Sirene *f*.

**sirloin** ['sə:lɔin] Lendenstück *n*.

**sissy** *Am.* ['sisi] Weichling *m*.

**siste** ['sistə] (*a.* Ordens-, Ober-) Schwester *f*; ~hood [~hud] Schwesternschaft *f*; ~in-law [~ɔrinlɔ:] Schwägerin *f*; ~ly [~əli] schwesterlich.

**sit** [sit] [*irr.*] *v/i.* sitzen; Sitzung halten, tagen; *fig.* liegen; ~ down sich setzen; ~ up aufrecht sitzen; aufbleiben; *v/t.* setzen; sitzen auf (*dat.*).

**site** [sait] Lage *f*; (Bau)Platz *m*.

**sitting** ['sitiŋ] Sitzung *f*; ~-room Wohnzimmer *n*.

**situated** ['sitjueitid] gelegen; be ~ liegen, gelegen sein; ~ion [sitju-'eiʃən] Lage *f*; Stellung *f*.

**six** [siks] 1. sechs; 2. Sechs *f*; ~teen ['siks'ti:n] sechzehn. ~teenth [~nθ] sechzehnte(r, -s); ~th [siksθ] 1. sechste(r, -s); ~ Sechstel *n*; ~thly ['siksθli] sechstens; ~tieth [~stiiθ] sechzigste(r, -s); ~ty [~ti] 1. sechzig; 2. Sechzig *f*.

**size** [saiz] 1. Größe *f*; Format *n*; 2. nach de Größe ordnen; ~ up F *j-n* abschätzen. ~d ~on Größe.

**siz(e)able** ['saizəbl] ziemlich groß

**sizzle** ['sizl] ~schen~ nistern. brutz~ng sizzling hot glühend heiß.

**skate** [skeit] 1. Schlittschuh *m*; roller~ Rollschuh *m*. ~ Schlittsch od. Rollschuh ~uten ~r 'skeitə] Schlittschuh- Rollschuhläufer(in).

**skedaddle** [ski'dædl] abhauen.

**skeesick** *Am.* ['ki:ziks] Nichtsnutz *n*

**~kein** [skein] Strähne *f*. Docke *f*.

**skeleton** ['skelitn] Skelett *n*; Gerippe *n*; ⚙ ~ tell *atr* Skelet....; ✕ Stamm. ~key Nachschlüssel *m*.

**skeptic** ['skeptik] *sceptic*

**sketch** [sketʃ] 1. Skizze *f*; Entwurf *m*; Umriß *m*; ~ skizzieren, entwerfen.

**ski** [ski:, ʃi:] 1. *pl.* ~s ki Ski *m*, Ski *m*; 2. Schi *od.* Ski laufen.

**skid** [skid] 1. Hemmschuh *m*, Bremsklotz *m* ✈ (Gleit)Kufe *f*; Rutsche *m* *mo.* schleudern *n*; 2. *v/i* hemmen ... ins schleudern

**skidoo** [ski'du:] *Am.* sk du phauen.

**skier** ['ski: ~ Schi~ Ski uter(in).

**skiing** ['ski: ~] Schi~ Skilaufen *n*.

**skilful** □ ['skilful] geschickt; kundig.

**skill** [skil] Geschicklichkeit *f*, Fertigkeit *f*; ~ed [skild] geschickt; gelernt; ~ worker Facharbeiter *m*.

**skillful** *Am.* ['skilful] *s. skilful.*

**skim** [skim] 1. abschöpfen; abrahmen; dahingleiten über (*acc.*); *Buch* überfliegen: ~ through durchblättern; 2. ~ milk Magermilch *f*.

**skimp** [skimp] *j-n* knapp halten; sparen (mit *et.*); ~y □ ['skimpi] knapp, dürftig.

**skin** [skin] 1. Haut *f*; Fell *n*; Schale *f*; 2. *v/t* (ent)h.uten; abbalgen; schälen; ~ off ² abstreifen; *v/i. a.* ~ over zuheilen; ~deep ['skin'di:p] (nur) oberflächlich; ~flint Knicker *m*; ~ny [~ni] mager.

**skip** [skip] 1. Sprung *m*; 2. *v/i.* hüpfen. springen; seilhüpfen; *v/t.* überspringen.

**skipper** ['skipə] ♣ Schiffer *m*; ♣, ✕. *Sport.* Kapitän *m*.

**skirmish** ['skə:miʃ] 1. ✕ Scharmützel *n*; 2. plänkeln.

**skirt** [skə:t] 1. (Damen)Rock *m*; (Rock)Schoß *m*; *oft* ~s *pl.* Rand *m*, Saum *m*; 2. umsäumen; (sich) entlangziehen (an *dat.*); entlangfahren; ~ing-board ['skə:tiŋbɔ:d] Scheuerleiste *f*.

**skit** [skit] Stichelei *f*; Satire *f*; ~tish □ ['skitiʃ] ungebärdig.

**skittle** ['skitl] Kegel *m*; *play (at)* ~s Kegel schieben; ~alley Kegelbahn *f*. [Gemeinheit *f*.]

**skulduggery** *Am.* F [skʌl'dʌgəri]]

**skulk** [skʌlk] schleichen; sich verstecken, lauern; sich drücken; ~er ['skʌlkə] Drückeberger *m*.

**skull** [skʌl] Schädel *m*.

**sky** [skai] *oft* skies *pl.* Himmel *m*; ~lark ['skaila:k] 1. *orn.* Feldlerche *f*; 2. Ulk treiben; ~light Oberlicht *n*; Dachtenster *n*; ~line Horizont *m*; Silhouette *f*; ~rocket F emporschnellen; ~scraper Wolkenkratzer *m*; ~ward(s) ['skaiwəd(z)] himmelwarts.

**slab** [slæb] Platte *f*; Scheibe *f*; Fliese *f*.

**slack** [slæk] 1. schlaff; locker; (nach)lässig; ✝ flau; 2. ♣ Lose *n* (*loses Tauende*); ✝ Flaute *f*; Kohlengrus *m*; 3. slacken; = slake; ~en ['slækən] schlaff machen *od.* werden; verringern; nachlassen; (sich) lockern, (sich) entspannen; (sich) verlangsamen; ~s *pl.* (lange) Hose.

**slag** [slæg] Schlacke *f*.

**slain** [slein] *p.p. von slay.*

**slake** [sleik] *Durst, Kalk* löschen; *fig.* stillen.

**slam** [slæm] 1. Zuschlagen *n*; Knall *m*; ~ *Tür etc.* zuschlagen, zuknallen; *et. auf den Tisch etc.* knallen.

**slander** ['sla:ndə] 1. Verleumdung *f*; 2. verleumden; ~ous □ [~rəs] verleumderisch.

**slang** [slæŋ] 1. Slang *m*; Berufssprache *f*; lässige Umgangssprache; 2. *j-n* wüst beschimpfen.

**slant** [slɑːnt] 1. schräge Fläche; Abhang *m*; Neigung *f*; *Am.* Standpunkt *m*; 2. schräg legen *od.* liegen; sich neigen; **~ing** *adj.*, □ ['slɑːntiŋ], **~wise** *adv.* [˷twaiz] schief, schräg.

**slap** [slæp] 1. Klaps *m*, Schlag *m*; 2. klapsen; schlagen; klatschen; **~jack** *Am.* ['slæpdʒæk] *Art* Pfannkuchen *m*; **~stick** (Narren)Fritsche *f*; *a.* ~ comedy *thea.* Posse *f*, Burleske *f*.

**slash** [slæʃ] 1. Hieb *m*; Schnitt *m*; Schlitz *m*; 2. (auf)schlitzen; schlagen, hauen; verreißen (*Kritiker*).

**slate** [sleit] 1. Schiefer *m*; Schiefertafel *f*; *bsd. Am.* Kandidatenliste *f*; 2. mit Schiefer decken; heftig kritisieren; *Am.* F für *e-n* Posten vorschlagen; **~pencil** ['sleit'pensl] Griffel *m*.

**slattern** ['slætə(ː)n] Schlampe *f*.

**slaughter** ['slɔːtə] 1. Schlachten *n*; Gemetzel *n*; 2. schlachten; niedermetzeln; **~house** Schlachthaus *n*.

**Slav** [slɑːv] 1. Slawe *m*, -in *f*; 2. slawisch.

**slave** [sleiv] 1. Sklav|e *m*, -in *f* (*a. fig.*); 2. F sich placken, schuften.

**slaver** ['slævə] 1. Geifer *m*, Sabber *m*; 2. (be)geifern, F (be)sabbern.

**slav|ery** ['sleivəri] Sklaverei *f*; F Plackerei *f*; **~ish** [˷viʃ] sklavisch.

**slay** *rhet.* [slei] [*irr.*] erschlagen; töten.

**sled** [sled] = sledge 1.

**sledge**[1] [sledʒ] 1. Schlitten *m*; 2. Schlitten fahren.

**sledge**[2] [˷] *a.* **~hammer** Schmiedehammer *m*.

**sleek** [sliːk] 1. □ glatt, geschmeidig; 2. glätten; **~ness** ['sliːknis] Glätte *f*.

**sleep** [sliːp] 1. [*irr.*] *v/i* schlafen; ~ (up)on *od.* over *et.* beschlafen; *v/t.* *j-n* für die Nacht unterbringen; ~ away Zeit verschlafen; 2. Schlaf *m*; go to ~ einschlafen; **~er** ['sliːpə] Schläfer(in), Schwelle *f*, Schlafwagen *m*; **~ing** [˷piŋ] schlafend; Schlaf..., **~ing Beauty** Dornröschen *n*; **~ing-car(riage)** Schlafwagen *m*; **~ing partner** stiller Teilhaber, **~less** [˷plis] schlaflos; **~walker** Schlafwandler(in); **~y** [˷pi] schläfrig; verschlafen.

**sleet** [sliːt] 1. Graupelregen *m*; 2. graupeln; **~y** ['sliːti] graupelig.

**sleeve** [sliːv] Ärmel *m*; Muffe *f*; **~link** ['sliːvliŋk] Manschettenknopf *m*.

**sleigh** [slei] 1. (*bsd.* Pferde)Schlitten *m*; 2. (im) Schlitten fahren.

**sleight** [slait]: **~of-hand** Taschenspielerei *f*; Kunststück *n*.

**slender** □ ['slendə] schlank; schmächtig; schwach; dürftig.

**slept** [slept] *pret. u. p.p. von* sleep 1.

**sleuth** [sluːθ], **~hound** ['sluːθhaund] Blut-, Spürhund *m* (*a. fig.*).

**slew** [sluː] *pret. von* slay.

**slice** [slais] 1. Schnitte *f*, Scheibe *f*, Stück *n*; Teil *m*, *n*; 2. (in) Scheiben schneiden; aufschneiden.

**slick** F [slik] 1. *adj.* glatt; *fig.* raffiniert; 2. *adv.* direkt; 3. *a.* ~ paper *Am. sl.* vornehme Zeitschrift; **~er** *Am.* F ['slikə] Regenmantel *m*; gerissener Kerl.

**slid** [slid] *pret. u. p.p. von* slide 1.

**slide** [slaid] 1. [*irr.*] gleiten (lassen); rutschen; schlittern; ausgleiten; geraten (*into in acc.*); let things ~ die Dinge laufen lassen; 2. Gleiten *n*; Rutsche *f*; ⊕ Schieber *m*; Diapositiv *n*; *a.* land~ Erdrutsch *m*; **~rule** ['slaidruːl] Rechenschieber *m*.

**slight** [slait] 1. □ schmächtig; schwach; gering, unbedeutend; 2. Geringschätzung *f*; 3. geringschätzig behandeln; unbeachtet lassen.

**slim** [slim] 1. □ schlank; dünn; schmächtig; dürftig; *sl.* schlau, gerissen; 2. *e-e* Schlankheitskur machen.

**slim|e** [slaim] Schlamm *m*; Schleim *m*; **~y** ['slaimi] schlammig; schleimig.

**sling** [sliŋ] 1. Schleuder *f*; Tragriemen *m*; ✠ Schlinge *f*, Binde *f*; Wurf *m*; 2. [*irr.*] schleudern; aufhängen; *a.* ~ up hochziehen.

**slink** [sliŋk] [*irr.*] schleichen.

**slip** [slip] 1. [*irr.*] *v/i* schlüpfen, gleiten, rutschen; ausgleiten; *~ away* entschlüpfen; sich ersehen; *v/t.* schlüpfen *od.* gleiten lassen, loslassen; entschlüpfen, entgleiten (*dat.*); *~ in* Bemerkung dazwischenwerfen; *into* hineinstecken *od.* hineinschieben in (*acc.*); *~ on, off* Kleid über-, (ab)streifen; *have ped s.o.'s* memory *j-m* entfallen sein, 2. (Aus)Gleiten *n*; Fehltritt *m* (*a. fig.*); Versehen *n*; (Flüchtigkeits)Fehler *m*; Verstoß *m*; Streifen *m*, Zettel *m*, Unterkleid *n*; *a.* **~way** ⚓ Helling *f*; (Kissen)Überzug *m*, *s pl.* Badehose *f*; *give s.o. the* *j-m* entwischen, **~per** ['slipə] Pantoffel *m*, Hausschuh *m*; **~pery** [˷əri] schlüpfrig, **~shod** [˷ʃɔd] schlampig, nachlässig; **~t** [slipt] *pret. u. p.p. von* slip 1.

**slit** [slit] 1. Schlitz *m*; Spalte *f*; 2. [*irr.*] (auf-, zer)schlitzen.

**sliver** [ˈslivə] Splitter *m*.

**slobber** [ˈslɔbə] 1. Sabber *m*; Gesabber *n*; 2. F (be)sabbern.

**slogan** [ˈslougən] Schlagwort *n*, Losung *f*; (Werbe)Slogan *m*.

**sloop** ⚓ [sluːp] Schaluppe *f*.

**slop** [slɔp] **1.** Pfütze *f*; ~s *pl.* Spül-, Schmutzwasser *n*; Krankenspeise *f*; **2.** *v/t.* verschütten; *v/i.* überlaufen.

**slope** [sloup] **1.** (Ab)Hang *m*; Neigung *f*; **2.** schräg legen; ⊕ abschrägen; abfallen; schräg verlaufen; (sich) neigen.

**sloppy** □ [ˈslɔpi] naß, schmutzig; schlampig; F labb(e)rig; rührselig.

**slops** [slɔps] *pl.* billige Konfektionskleidung; ⚓ Kleidung *f* u. Bettzeug *n*.

**slot** [slɔt] Schlitz *m*.

**sloth** [slouθ] Faulheit *f*; *zo.* Faultier *n*.

**slot-machine** [ˈslɔtməʃiːn] (Warenod. Spiel)Automat *m*.

**slouch** [slautʃ] **1.** faul herumhängen; F herumlatschen; **2.** schlaffe Haltung; ~ *hat* Schlapphut *m*.

**slough**[1] [slau] Sumpf(loch *n*) *m*.

**slough**[2] [slʌf] *Haut* abwerfen.

**sloven** [ˈslʌvn] unordentlicher Mensch; F Schlampe *f*; **~ly** [~nli] liederlich.

**slow** [slou] **1.** □ langsam (*of* in *dat.*); schwerfällig; lässig; *be* ~ nachgehen (*Uhr*); **2.** *adv.* langsam; **3.** *oft* ~ *down od. up od. off v/t.* verlangsamen; *v/i.* langsam(er) werden *od.* gehen *od.* fahren; **~coach** [ˈsloukoutʃ] Langweiler *m*; altmodischer Mensch; **~motion picture** Zeitlupenaufnahme *f*; **~worm** *zo.* Blindschleiche *f*.

**sludge** [slʌdʒ] Schlamm *m*; Matsch *m*.

**slug** [slʌg] **1.** Stück *n* Rohmetall; *zo.* Wegschnecke *f*; *Am.* F (Faust-)Schlag *m*; **2.** *Am.* F hauen.

**slugg**|**ard** [ˈslʌgəd] Faulenzer(in); **~ish** □ [~giʃ] träge, faul.

**sluice** [sluːs] **1.** Schleuse *f*; **2.** ausströmen (lassen); ausspülen; waschen.

**slum** [slʌm] schmutzige Gasse; ~s *pl.* Elendsviertel *n*, Slums *pl.*

**slumber** [ˈslʌmbə] **1.** *a.* ~s *pl.* Schlummer *m*; **2.** schlummern.

**slump** [slʌmp] *Börse:* **1.** fallen, stürzen; **2.** (Kurs-, Preis)Sturz *m*.

**slung** [slʌŋ] *pret. u. p.p. von* sling 2.

**slunk** [slʌŋk] *pret. u. p.p. von* slink.

**slur** [sləː] **1.** Fleck *m*; *fig.* Tadel *m*; ♪ Bindebogen *m*; **2.** *v/t. oft* ~ *over* übergehen; ♪ *Töne* binden.

**slush** [slʌʃ] Schlamm *m*; Matsch *m*; F Kitsch *m*.

**slut** [slʌt] F Schlampe *f*; Nutte *f*.

**sly** □ [slai] schlau, verschmitzt; hinterlistig; *on the* ~ heimlich.

**smack** [smæk] **1.** (Bei)Geschmack *m*; Prise *f Salz etc.*; *fig.* Spur *f*; Schmatz *m*; Schlag *m*, Klatsch *m*, Klaps *m*; **2.** schmecken (*of* nach); e-n Beigeschmack haben; klatschen, knallen (mit); schmatzen (mit); *j-m* e-n Klaps geben.

**small** [smɔːl] **1.** *allg.* klein; unbe-

deutend; *fig.* kleinlich; niedrig; wenig; *feel* ~, *look* ~ sich gedemütigt fühlen; *the* ~ *hours* die frühen Morgenstunden *f/pl.*; *in a* ~ *way* bescheiden; **2.** dünner Teil; ~s *pl.* F Leibwäsche *f*; ~ *of the back anat.* Kreuz *n*; **~arms** [ˈsmɔːlɑːmz] *pl.* Handfeuerwaffen *f/pl.*; ~ **change** Kleingeld *n*; *fig.* triviale Bemerkungen *f/pl.*; **~ish** [~liʃ] ziemlich klein; **~pox** 🜊 [~lpɔks] Pocken *f/pl.*; ~ **talk** Plauderei *f*; **~time** *Am.* F unbedeutend.

**smart** [smɑːt] **1.** □ scharf; gewandt; geschickt; gescheit; gerissen; schmuck, elegant, adrett; forsch; ~ *aleck Am.* F Neunmalkluge(r) *m*; **2.** Schmerz *m*; **3.** schmerzen; leiden; **~money** [ˈsmɑːtmʌni] Schmerzensgeld *n*; **~ness** [~tnis] Klugheit *f*; Schärfe *f*; Gewandtheit *f*; Gerissenheit *f*; Eleganz *f*.

**smash** [smæʃ] **1.** *v/t.* zertrümmern; *fig.* vernichten; (zer)schmettern; *v/i.* zerschellen; zs.-stoßen; *fig.* zs.-brechen; **2.** Zerschmettern *n*; Krach *m*; Zs.-bruch *m* (*a.* ✝); *Tennis:* Schmetterball *m*; **~up** [ˈsmæʃʌp] Zs.-stoß *m*; Zs.-bruch *m*.

**smattering** [ˈsmætəriŋ] oberflächliche Kenntnis.

**smear** [smiə] **1.** (be)schmieren; *fig.* beschmutzen; **2.** Schmiere *f*; Fleck *m*.

**smell** [smel] **1.** Geruch *m*; **2.** [*irr.*] riechen (*of* nach *et.*); *a.* ~ *at* riechen an (*dat.*); **~y** [ˈsmeli] übelriechend.

**smelt**[1] [smelt] *pret. u. p.p. von* smell 2.

**smelt**[2] [~] schmelzen.

**smile** [smail] **1.** Lächeln *n*; **2.** lächeln.

**smirch** [sməːtʃ] besudeln.

**smirk** [sməːk] grinsen.

**smite** [smait] [*irr.*] schlagen; heimsuchen; *schwer* treffen; quälen.

**smith** [smiθ] Schmied *m*.

**smithereens** [ˌsmiðəˈriːnz] *pl.* Stücke *n/pl.*, Splitter *m/pl*, Fetzen *m/pl.*

**smithy** [ˈsmiði] Schmiede *f*.

**smitten** [ˈsmitn] **1.** *p.p. von* smite; **2.** *adj.* ergriffen; betroffen; *fig.* hingerissen (*with* von).

**smock** [smɔk] **1.** fälteln; **2.** Kittel *m*; **~frock** [ˈsmɔkˈfrɔk] Bauernkittel *m*.

**smog** [smɔg] Smog *m*, Gemisch *n* von Nebel und Rauch.

**smoke** [smouk] **1.** Rauch *m*; *have a* ~ (eine) rauchen; **2.** rauchen; dampfen; (aus)räuchern; **~dried** [ˈsmoukdraid] geräuchert; ~ [~kə] Raucher *m*; 🚃 F Raucherwagen *m*, **-abteil** *n*; **~stack** 🚢, ⚙ Schornstein *m*.

**smoking** [ˈsmoukiŋ] Rauchen *n*; *attr.* Rauch(er)...; **~compartment** 🚃 Raucherabteil *n*.

**smoky** □ ['smouki] rauchig; verräuchert. [der.]

**smolder** *Am.* ['smouldə] = smoul-

**smooth** [smu:ð] 1. □ glatt; *fig.* fließend; mild; schmeichlerisch; 2. glätten; ebnen (*a. fig.*); plätten; mildern; *a.* ~ over, ~ away *fig.* wegräumen; ~ness ['smu:ðnis] Glätte *f.*

**smote** [smout] *pret. von* smite.

**smother** ['smʌðə] ersticken.

**smoulder** ['smouldə] schwelen.

**smudge** [smʌdʒ] 1. (be)schmutzen; (be)schmieren; 2. Schmutzfleck *m.*

**smug** [smʌg] selbstzufrieden.

**smuggle** ['smʌgl] schmuggeln; ~r [~lə] Schmuggler(in).

**smut** [smʌt] Schmutz *m*; Ruß(fleck) *m*; Zoten *f/pl.*; 2. beschmutzen.

**smutty** □ ['smʌti] schmutzig.

**snack** [snæk] Imbiß *m*; ~-bar ['snækba:], ~-counter Snackbar *f*, Imbißstube *f.*

**snaffle** ['snæfl] Trense *f.*

**snag** [snæg] (Ast-, Zahn)Stumpf *m*; *fig.* Haken *m*; *Am.* Baumstumpf *m* (*bsd. unter Wasser*).

**snail** *zo.* [sneil] Schnecke *f.*

**snake** *zo.* [sneik] Schlange *f.*

**snap** [snæp] 1. Schnappen *n*, Biß *m*; Knack(s) *m*; Knall *m*; *fig.* Schwung *m*, Schmiß *m*; Schnappschloß *n*; *phot.* Schnappschuß *m*; cold ~ Kältewelle *f*; 2. *v/i.* schnappen (*at* nach); zuschnappen (*Schloß*); krachen; knacken; (zer)brechen; knallen; schnauzen; ~ *at s.o.* j-n anschnauzen; ~ *into it! Am. sl.* mach schnell!, Tempo!; ~ *out of it! Am. sl.* hör auf damit!; komm, komm!; *v/t.* (er)schnappen; (zu)schnappen lassen; *phot.* knipsen; zerbrechen; ~ *out Wort* hervorstoßen; ~ *up* wegschnappen; ~-fastener ['snæpfa:snə] Druckknopf *m*; ~pish □ [~piʃ] bissig; schnippisch; ~py [~pi] bissig; F flott; ~shot Schnappschuß *m*, Photo *n*, Momentaufnahme *f.*

**snare** [snɛə] 1. Schlinge *f*; 2. fangen; *fig.* umgarnen.

**snarl** [sna:l] 1. knurren; murren; 2. Knurren *n*; Gewirr *n.*

**snatch** [snætʃ] 1. schneller Griff; Ruck *m*; Stückchen *n*; 2. schnappen; ergreifen; an sich reißen; nehmen; ~ *at* greifen nach.

**sneak** [sni:k] 1. *v/i.* schleichen; F petzen; *v/t.* F stibitzen; 2. Schleicher *m*; F Petzer *m*; ~ers ['sni:kəz] *pl.* F leichte Segeltuchschuhe *m/pl.*

**sneer** [sniə] 1. Hohnlächeln *n*; Spott *m*; 2. hohnlächeln; spotten; spötteln.

**sneeze** [sni:z] 1. niesen; 2. Niesen *n.*

**snicker** ['snikə] kichern; wiehern.

**sniff** [snif] schnüffeln; schnuppern; riechen; die Nase rümpfen.

**snigger** ['snigə] kichern.

**snip** [snip] 1. Schnitt *m*; Schnipsel *m*, *n*; 2. schnippeln, schnipseln; knipsen.

**snipe** [snaip] 1. *orn.* (Sumpf-) Schnepfe *f*; 2. ✗ aus dem Hinterhalt (ab)schießen; ~r ✗ ['snaipə] Scharf-, Heckenschütze *m.*

**snivel** ['snivl] schniefen; schluchzen; plärren.

**snob** [snɔb] Großtuer *m*; Snob *m*; ~bish □ ['snɔbiʃ] snobistisch.

**snoop** *Am.* [snu:p] 1. *fig.* (herum-) schnüffeln; 2. Schnüffler(in).

**snooze** F [snu:z] 1. Schläfchen *n*; 2. dösen.

**snore** [snɔ:] schnarchen.

**snort** [snɔ:t] schnauben, schnaufen.

**snout** [snaut] Schnauze *f*; Rüssel *m.*

**snow** [snou] 1. Schnee *m*; 2. (be-) schneien; be ~ed under *fig.* erdrückt werden; ~bound ['snoubaund] eingeschneit; ~-capped, ~-clad, ~-covered schneebedeckt; ~-drift Schneewehe *f*; ~drop Schneeglöckchen *n*; ~y ['snoui] schneeig; schneebedeckt, verschneit; schneeweiß.

**snub** [snʌb] 1. schelten, anfahren; 2. Verweis *m*; ~-nosed ['snʌbnouzd] stupsnasig.

**snuff** [snʌf] 1. Schnuppe *f* e-r *Kerze*; Schnupftabak *m*; 2. *a.* take ~ schnupfen; *Licht* putzen; ~le ['snʌfl] schnüffeln; näseln.

**snug** [snʌg] geborgen; behaglich; eng anliegend; ~gle ['snʌgl] (sich) schmiegen *od.* kuscheln (*to an acc.*).

**so** [sou] so; deshalb; also; *I hope* ~ ich hoffe es; *are you tired,* ~ *I am* bist du müde? Ja; *you are tired,* ~ *am I* du bist müde, ich auch; ~ *far* bisher.

**soak** [souk] *v/t.* einweichen; durchnässen; (durch)tränken; auf-, einsaugen; *v/i.* weichen; durchsickern.

**soap** [soup] 1. Seife *f*; soft ~ Schmierseife *f*; 2. (ein)seifen ~-box ['soupbɔks] Seifenkiste *f*; improvisierte Rednertribüne; ~y □ ['soupi] seifig; *fig.* unterwürfig.

**soar** [sɔ:] sich erheben, sich aufschwingen; schweben; ✈ segelfliegen.

**sob** [sɔb] 1. Schluchzen *n*; 2. schluchzen.

**sober** ['soubə] 1. □ nüchtern; 2. (sich) ernüchtern; ~ness [~nis], **sobriety** [sou'braiəti] Nüchternheit *f.*

**so-called** ['sou'kɔ:ld] sogenannt.

**soccer** F ['sɔkə] (Verbands)Fußball *m* (*Spiel*).

**sociable** ['souʃəbl] 1. □ gesellig; gemütlich; 2. geselliges Beisammensein.

**social** ['souʃəl] 1.□ gesellschaftlich; gesellig; sozial(istisch), Sozial...; ~ *insurance* Sozialversicherung *f*; ~ *services pl.* Sozialeinrichtungen *f/pl.*; 2. geselliges Beisammensein;

**~ism** [~lizəm] Sozialismus *m*; **~ist** [~ist] 1. Sozialist(in); 2. *a*. **~istic** [souʃə'listik] (~ally) sozialistisch; **~ize** ['souʃəlaiz] sozialisieren; verstaatlichen.

**society** [sə'saiəti] Gesellschaft *f*; Verein *m*, Klub *m*.

**sociology** [sousi'ɔlədʒi] Sozialwissenschaft *f*.

**sock** [sɔk] Socke *f*; Einlegesohle *f*.

**socket** ['sɔkit] (Augen-, Zahn)Höhle *f*; (Gelenk)Pfanne *f*; ⊕ Muffe *f*; ≠ Fassung *f*; ≠ Steckdose *f*.

**sod** [sɔd] 1. Grasnarbe *f*; Rasen (-stück *n*) *m*; 2. mit Rasen bedecken.

**soda** ['soudə] Soda *f*, *n*; **~fountain** Siphon *m*; *Am.* Erfrischungshalle *f*, Eisdiele *f*.

**sodden** ['sɔdn] durchweicht; teigig.

**soft** [sɔft] 1. □ *allg.* weich; *engS.*: mild; sanft; sacht, leise; zart, zärtlich; weichlich; F einfältig; ~ **drink** F alkoholfreies Getränk; 2. *adv.* weich; 3. F Trottel *m*; **~en** ['sɔfn] weich machen; (sich) erweichen; mildern; **~-headed** schwachsinnig; **~-hearted** gutmütig.

**soggy** ['sɔgi] durchnäßt; feucht.

**soil** [sɔil] 1. Boden *m*, Erde *f*; Fleck *m*; Schmutz *m*; 2. (be)schmutzen; beflecken.

**sojourn** ['sɔdʒəːn] 1. Aufenthalt *m*; 2. sich aufhalten.

**solace** ['sɔləs] 1. Trost *m*; 2. trösten.

**solar** ['soulə] Sonnen...

**sold** [sould] *pret. u. p.p. von* sell.

**solder** ['sɔldə] 1. Lot *n*; 2. löten.

**soldier** ['souldʒə] Soldat *m*; **~like**, **~ly** [~li] soldatisch; **~y** [~əri] Militär *n*.

**sole¹** □ [soul] alleinig, einzig; ~ **agent** Alleinvertreter *m*.

**sole²** [~] 1. Sohle *f*; 2. besohlen.

**solemn** □ ['sɔləm] feierlich; ernst; **~ity** [sə'lemniti] Feierlichkeit *f*; Steifheit *f*; **~ize** ['sɔləmnaiz] feiern; feierlich vollziehen.

**solicit** [sə'lisit] (dringend) bitten; ansprechen, belästigen; **~ation** [səlisi'teiʃən] dringende Bitte; **~or** [sə'lisitə] ⚖️ Anwalt *m*; *Am.* Agent *m*, Werber *m*; **~ous** □ [~təs] besorgt; ~ **of** begierig nach; ~ **to** *inf.* bestrebt zu *inf.*; **~ude** [~tjuːd] Sorge *f*, Besorgnis *f*; Bemühung *f*.

**solid** ['sɔlid] 1. □ fest; dauerhaft, haltbar; derb; massiv; ⚖️ körperlich, Raum...; *fig.* gediegen; solid; triftig; solidarisch; *a* ~ **hour** e-e volle Stunde; 2. (fester) Körper; **~arity** [sɔli'dæriti] Solidarität *f*; **~ify** [sə'lidifai] (sich) verdichten; **~ity** [~iti] Solidität *f*; Gediegenheit *f*.

**soliloquy** [sə'liləkwi] Selbstgespräch *n*, Monolog *m*.

**solit|ary** □ ['sɔlitəri] einsam; einzeln; einsiedlerisch; **~ude** [~tjuːd]

Einsamkeit *f*; Verlassenheit *f*; Öde *f*.

**solo** ['soulou] Solo *n*; ✈ Alleinflug *m*; **~ist** [~ouist] Solist(in).

**solu|ble** ['sɔljubl] löslich; (auf)lösbar; **~tion** [sɔ'luːʃən] (Auf)Lösung *f*; ⊕ Gummilösung *f*.

**solve** [sɔlv] lösen; **~nt** ['sɔlvənt] 1. (auf)lösend; ✝ zahlungsfähig; 2. Lösungsmittel *n*.

**somb|re**, *Am.* **~er** □ ['sɔmbə] düster.

**some** [sʌm, səm] irgendein; etwas; einige, manche *pl.*; *Am.* F prima; ~ 20 *miles* etwa 20 Meilen; *in* ~ *degree*, *to* ~ *extent* einigermaßen; **~body** ['sʌmbədi] jemand; ~ **day** eines Tages; **~how** irgendwie; ~ *or other* so oder so; **~one** jemand.

**somersault** ['sʌməsɔːlt] Salto *m*; Rolle *f*, Purzelbaum *m*; *turn a* ~ e-n Purzelbaum schlagen.

**some|thing** ['sʌmθiŋ] (irgend) etwas; ~ *like* so etwas wie, so ungefähr; **~time** 1. einmal, dereinst; 2. ehemalig; **~times** manchmal; **~what** etwas, ziemlich; **~where** irgendwo(hin).

**somniferous** □ [sɔm'nifərəs] einschläfernd.

**son** [sʌn] Sohn *m*.

**song** [sɔŋ] Gesang *m*; Lied *n*; Gedicht *n*; *for an old* ~ *an old* ~ *für* e-n Pappenstiel; **~bird** ['sɔŋbəːd] Singvogel *m*; **~ster** ['sɔŋstə] Singvogel *m*; Sänger *m*.

**sonic** ['sɔnik] Schall...

**son-in-law** ['sʌninlɔː] Schwiegersohn *m*.

**sonnet** ['sɔnit] Sonett *n*.

**sonorous** □ [sə'nɔːrəs] klangvoll.

**soon** [suːn] bald; früh; gern; *as od. so* ~ *as* sobald als *od.* wie; **~er** ['suːnə] eher; früher; lieber; *no* ~ ... *than* kaum ... als; *no* ~ *said than done* gesagt, getan.

**soot** [sut] 1. Ruß *m*; 2. verrußen.

**sooth** [suːθ]: *in* ~ in Wahrheit, fürwahr; **~e** [suːð] beruhigen; mildern; **~sayer** ['suːθseiə] Wahrsager(in).

**sooty** □ ['suti] rußig.

**sop** [sɔp] 1. eingeweichter Brocken; *fig.* Bestechung *f*; 2. eintunken.

**sophist|icate** [sə'fistikeit] verdrehen; verfälschen; **~icated** kultiviert, raffiniert; intellektuell; blasiert; hochentwickelt, kompliziert; **~ry** ['sɔfistri] Spitzfindigkeit *f*.

**sophomore** *Am.* ['sɔfəmɔː] Student *m* im zweiten Jahr.

**soporific** [soupə'rifik] 1. (~ally) einschläfernd; 2. Schlafmittel *n*.

**sorcer|er** ['sɔːsərə] Zauberer *m*; **~ess** [~ris] Zauberin *f*; Hexe *f*; **~y** [~ri] Zauberei *f*.

**sordid** □ ['sɔːdid] schmutzig, schäbig (*bsd. fig.*).

**sore** [sɔː] 1. □ schlimm, entzündet;

wund; weh; empfindlich; ~ *throat* Halsweh *n*; 2. wunde Stelle; **~head** *Am.* F ['sɔːhed] 1. mürrischer Mensch; 2. enttäuscht.

**sorrel** ['sɔrəl] 1. rötlichbraun (*bsd.* *Pferd*); 2. Fuchs *m* (*Pferd*).

**sorrow** ['sɔrou] 1. Sorge *f*; Kummer *m*, Leid *n*; Trauer *f*; 2. trauern; sich grämen; **~ful** □ ['sɔrəful] traurig, betrübt; elend.

**sorry** □ ['sɔri] betrübt, bekümmert; traurig; (*I am*) (*so*) ~*!* es tut mir (sehr) leid; Verzeihung!; *I am ~ for him* er tut mir leid; *we are ~ to say* wir müssen leider sagen.

**sort** [sɔːt] 1. Sorte *f*, Art *f*; *what ~ of* was für; *of a ~*, *of ~s* F so was wie; ~ *of* F gewissermaßen; *out of* ~*s* F unpäßlich; verdrießlich; 2. sortieren; ~ *out* (aus)sondern.

**sot** [sɔt] Trunkenbold *m*.

**sough** [sau] 1. Sausen *n*; 2. rauschen.

**sought** [sɔːt] *pret. u. p.p. von* seek.

**soul** [soul] Seele *f* (*a. fig.*).

**sound** [saund] 1. □ *allg.* gesund; ganz; vernünftig; gründlich; fest; † sicher; *fig.* gültig; 2. Ton *m*, Schall *m*, Laut *m*, Klang *m*; *fig.* Sonde *f*; Meerenge *f*; Fischblase *f*; 3. (er)tönen, (er)klingen; erschallen (lassen); sich *gut etc.* anhören; sondieren; *fig.* loten; *fig.* abhorchen; **~film** ['saundfilm] Tonfilm *m*; **~ing** [~diŋ] Lotung *f*; ~*s pl.* lotbare Wassertiefe; **~less** □ [~dlis] lautlos; **~ness** [~dnis] Gesundheit *f*; **~proof** schalldicht; **~track** *Film*: Tonspur *f*; **~wave** Schallwelle *f*.

**soup¹** [suːp] Suppe *f*.

**soup²** *Am. sl. mot.* [~] 1. Stärke *f*; 2. ~ *up Motor* frisieren.

**sour** ['sauə] 1. □ sauer; *fig.* bitter; mürrisch; 2. *v/t.* säuern; *fig.* ver~, erbittern; *v/i.* sauer (*fig.* bitter) werden.

**source** ['sɔːs] Quelle *f*; Ursprung *m*.

**sour|ish** □ ['sauərif] säuerlich; **~ness** ['sauənis] Säure *f*; *fig.* Bitterkeit *f*.

**souse** [saus] eintauchen; (mit Wasser) begießen; *Fisch etc.* einlegen, einpökeln.

**south** [sauθ] 1. Süd(en *m*); 2. Süd...; südlich; **~east** ['sauθ'iːst] 1. Südosten *m*; 2. *a.* **~eastern** [sauθ'iːstən] südöstlich.

**souther|ly** ['sʌðəli], **~n** [~ən] südlich; Süd...; **~ner** [~nə] Südländer(in), *Am.* Südstaatler(in).

**southernmost** ['sʌðənmoust] südlichst.

**southpaw** *Am.* ['sauθpɔː] *Baseball:* Linkshänder *m*.

**southward(s)** *adv.* ['sauθwəd(z)] südwärts, nach Süden.

**south|-west** ['sauθ'west] 1. Südwesten *m*; 2. südwestlich; **~wester** [sauθ'westə] Südwestwind

*m*; *fig.* Südwester *m*; **~westerly**, **~western** südwestlich.

**souvenir** ['suːvəniə] Andenken *n*.

**sovereign** ['sɔvrin] 1. □ höchst; unübertrefflich; unumschränkt; 2. Herrscher(in); Sovereign *m* (*20-Schilling-Stück*); **~ty** [~rənti] Oberherrschaft *f*, Landeshoheit *f*.

**soviet** ['souviet] Sowjet *m*; *attr.* Sowjet...

**sow¹** [sau] *zo.* Sau *f*, (Mutter-)Schwein *n*; *fig.* Sau *f*, Massel *f*.

**sow²** [sou] [*irr.*] (aus)säen, ausstreuen; besäen; **~n** [soun] *p.p. von* sow².

**spa** [spaː] Heilbad *n*; Kurort *m*.

**space** [speis] 1. (Welt)Raum *m*; Zwischenraum *m*; Zeitraum *m*; 2. *typ.* sperren; **~craft** ['speiskraːft], **~ship** Raumschiff *n*; **~suit** Raumanzug *m*.

**spacious** □ ['speifəs] geräumig; weit, umfassend.

**spade** [speid] Spaten *m*; *Kartenspiel* Pik *n*.

**span¹** [spæn] 1. Spanne *f*; Spannweite *f*; *Am.* Gespann *n*; 2. (um-, über)spannen; (aus)messen.

**span²** [~] *pret. von* spin 1.

**spangle** ['spæŋgl] 1. Flitter *m*; 2. (mit Flitter) besetzen; *fig.* übersäen.

**Spaniard** ['spænjəd] Spanier(in).

**Spanish** ['spæniʃ] 1. spanisch; 2. Spanisch *n*.

**spank** F [spæŋk] 1. verhauen; 2. Klaps *m*; **~ing** ['spæŋkiŋ] 1. □ schnell, scharf; 2. F Haue *f*, Tracht *f* Prügel.

**spanner** *⊕* ['spænə] Schraubenschlüssel *m*.

**spar** [spaː] 1. *⊕* Spiere *f*; *≯* Holm *m*; 2. boxen; *fig.* sich streiten.

**spare** [spɛə] 1. □ spärlich, sparsam; mager; überzählig; überschüssig; Ersatz...; Reserve...; ~ *hours* Mußestunden *f/pl.*; ~ *room* Gastzimmer *n*; ~ *time* Freizeit *f*; 2. *⊕* Ersatzteil *m*, *n*; 3. (ver)schonen; erübrigen; entbehren; (übrig)haben für; (er)sparen; sparen mit.

**sparing** □ ['spɛəriŋ] sparsam.

**spark** [spaːk] 1. Funke(n) *m*; *fig.* flotter Kerl; Galan *m*; 2. Funken sprühen; **~(ing)-plug** *mot.* ['spaːk(iŋ)plʌg] Zündkerze *f*.

**sparkle** ['spaːkl] 1. Funke(n) *m*; Funkeln *n*; *fig.* sprühendes Wesen; 2. funkeln; blitzen; schäumen; *sparkling wine* Schaumwein *m*.

**sparrow** *orn.* ['spærou] Sperling *m*, Spatz *m*; **~hawk** *orn.* Sperber *m*.

**sparse** □ [spaːs] spärlich, dünn.

**spasm** *≯* ['spæzəm] Krampf *m*; **~odic(al** □) *≯* [spæz'mɔdik(əl)] krampfhaft, -artig; *fig.* sprunghaft.

**spat¹** [spæt] (Schuh)Gamasche *f*.

**spat²** [~] *pret. u. p.p. von* spit² 2.

**spatter** ['spætə] (be)spritzen.

**spawn** [spɔːn] **1.** Laich *m*; *fig. contp.* Brut *f*; **2.** laichen; *fig.* aushecken.

**speak** [spiːk] [*irr.*] *v/i.* sprechen; reden; ~ out, ~ up laut sprechen; offen reden; ~ to *j-n* od. mit *j-m* sprechen; *v/t.* (aus)sprechen; äußern; **~-easy** *Am. sl.* ['spiːkiːzi] Flüsterkneipe *f* (*ohne Konzession*); **~er** [~kə] Sprecher(in), Redner(in); *parl.* Vorsitzende(r) *m*; **~ing-trumpet** [~kiŋtrʌmpit] Sprachrohr *n*.

**spear** [spiə] **1.** Speer *m*, Spieß *m*; Lanze *f*; **2.** (auf)spießen.

**special** ['speʃəl] **1.** □ besonder; Sonder...; speziell; Spezial...; **2.** Hilfspolizist *m*; Sonderausgabe *f*; Sonderzug *m*; *Am.* (Tages)Spezialität *f*; **~ist** [~list] Spezialist *m*; **~ity** [speʃi'æliti] Besonderheit *f*; Spezialfach *n*; † Spezialität *f*; **~ize** ['speʃəlaiz] besonders anführen; (sich) spezialisieren; **~ty** [~lti] *s. speciality*.

**specie** ['spiːʃiː] Metall-, Hartgeld *n*; **~s** [~iːz] *pl. u. sg.* Art *f*, Spezies *f*.

**speci|fic** [spi'sifik] (**~ally**) spezifisch; besonder; bestimmt; **~fy** ['spesifai] spezifizieren, einzeln angeben; **~men** [~imin] Probe *f*, Exemplar *n*.

**specious** □ ['spiːʃəs] blendend, bestechend; trügerisch; Schein...

**speck** [spek] **1.** Fleck *m*; Stückchen *n*; **2.** flecken; **~le** ['spekl] **1.** Fleckchen *n*; **2.** flecken, sprenkeln.

**spectacle** ['spektəkl] Schauspiel *n*; Anblick *m*; (*a pair of*) **~s** *pl.* (eine) Brille.

**spectacular** [spek'tækjulə] **1.** □ eindrucksvoll; auffallend, spektakulär; **2.** *Am.* F Galarevue *f*.

**spectator** [spek'teitə] Zuschauer *m*.

**spect|ral** □ ['spektrəl] gespenstisch; **~re**, *Am.* **~er** [~tə] Gespenst *n*.

**speculat|e** ['spekjuleit] grübeln, nachsinnen; † spekulieren; **~ion** [spekju'leiʃən] theoretische Betrachtung; Grübelei *f*; † Spekulation *f*; **~ive** □ ['spekjulətiv] grüblerisch; theoretisch; † spekulierend; **~or** [~leitə] Denker *m*; † Spekulant *m*.

**sped** [sped] *pret. u. p.p. von* speed 2.

**speech** [spiːtʃ] Sprache *f*; Rede *f*, Ansprache *f*; *make a* ~ e-e Rede halten; **~-day** ['spiːtʃdei] *Schule:* (Jahres)Schlußfeier *f*; **~less** □ [~ʃlis] sprachlos.

**speed** [spiːd] **1.** Geschwindigkeit *f*; Schnelligkeit *f*; Eile *f*; ⊕ Drehzahl *f*; **2.** [*irr.*] *v/i.* schnell fahren, rasen; ~ up (*pret. u. p.p. ~ed*) die Geschwindigkeit erhöhen; *v/t. j-m* Glück verleihen; befördern; ~ up (*pret. u. p.p. ~ed*) beschleunigen; **~-limit** ['spiːdlimit] Geschwindigkeitsbegrenzung *f*; **~ometer** *mot.*

---

[spi'dɔmitə] Geschwindigkeitsmesser *m*, Tachometer *n*; **~way** Motorradrennbahn *f*; *bsd. Am.* Schnellstraße *f*; **~y** □ [~di] schnell.

**spell** [spel] **1.** (Arbeits)Zeit *f*, ⊕ Schicht *f*; Weilchen *n*; Zauber (-spruch) *m*; **2.** abwechseln mit *j-m*; [*irr.*] buchstabieren; richtig schreiben; bedeuten; **~binder** *Am.* ['spelbaində] fesselnder Redner; **~bound** *fig.* (fest)gebannt; **~er** *bsd. Am.* [~ə] Fibel *f*; **~ing** [~liŋ] Rechtschreibung *f*; **~ing-book** Fibel *f*.

**spelt** [spelt] *pret. u. p.p. von* spell 2.

**spend** [spend] [*irr.*] verwenden; (*Geld*) ausgeben; verbrauchen; verschwenden; verbringen; ~ *o.s.* sich erschöpfen; **~thrift** ['spendθrift] Verschwender *m*.

**spent** [spent] **1.** *pret. u. p.p. von* spend; **2.** *adj.* erschöpft, matt.

**sperm** [spəːm] Same(n) *m*.

**spher|e** [sfiə] Kugel *f*; Erd-, Himmelskugel *f*; *fig.* Sphäre *f*; (Wirkungs)Kreis *m*; Bereich *m*; *fig.* Gebiet *n*; **~ical** □ ['sferikəl] sphärisch; kugelförmig.

**spice** [spais] **1.** Gewürz(e *pl.*) *n*; *fig.* Würze *f*; Anflug *m*; **2.** würzen.

**spick and span** ['spikən'spæn] frisch u. sauber; schmuck; funkelnagelneu.

**spicy** □ ['spaisi] würzig; pikant.

**spider** *zo.* ['spaidə] Spinne *f*.

**spiel** *Am. sl.* [spiːl] Gequassel *n*.

**spigot** ['spigət] (Faß)Zapfen *m*.

**spike** [spaik] **1.** Stift *m*; Spitze *f*; Dorn *m*; Stachel *m*; *Sport:* Laufdorn *m*; *mot.* Spike *m*; ♀ Ähre *f*; **2.** festnageln; mit *eisernen* Stacheln versehen.

**spill** [spil] **1.** [*irr.*] *v/t.* verschütten; vergießen; F Reiter etc. abwerfen; schleudern; *v/i.* überlaufen; **2.** F Sturz *m*.

**spilt** [spilt] *pret. u. p.p. von* spill 1; *cry over* ~ milk über et. jammern, was doch nicht zu ändern ist.

**spin** [spin] **1.** [*irr.*] spinnen (*a.fig.*); wirbeln; sich drehen; *Münze* hochwerfen; sich et. ausdenken; erzählen; ≫ trudeln; ~ *along* dahinsausen; ~ *s.th.* out et. in die Länge ziehen; **2.** Drehung *f*; Spritztour *f*; ≫ Trudeln *n*.

**spinach** ♀ ['spinidʒ] Spinat *m*.

**spinal** *anat.* ['spainl] Rückgrat...; ~ *column* Wirbelsäule *f*; ~ *cord*, ~ *marrow* Rückenmark *n*.

**spindle** ['spindl] Spindel *f*.

**spin-drier** ['spindraiə] Wäscheschleuder *f*.

**spine** [spain] *anat.* Rückgrat *n*; Dorn *m*; (Gebirgs)Grat *m*; (Buch-) Rücken *m*.

**spinning|-mill** ['spiniŋmil] Spinnerei *f*; **~-wheel** Spinnrad *n*.

**spinster** ['spinstə] unverheiratete Frau; (alte) Jungfer.

**spiny** ['spaini] dornig.

**spiral** ['spaiərəl] 1. ☐ spiralig; ~ staircase Wendeltreppe f; 2. Spirale f; fig. Wirbel m.

**spire** ['spaiə] Turm-, Berg- etc. Spitze f; Kirchturm(spitze f) m.

**spirit** ['spirit] 1. allg. Geist m; Sinn m; Temperament n, Leben n; Mut m; Gesinnung f; Spiritus m; Sprit m, Benzin n; ~s pl. Spirituosen pl.; high (low) ~s pl. gehobene (gedrückte) Stimmung; 2. ~ away od. off wegzaubern; ~ed ☐ geistvoll; temperamentvoll; mutig; ~less ☐ [~tlis] geistlos; temperamentlos; mutlos.

**spiritual** ☐ ['spiritjuəl] geistig; geistlich; geistvoll; ~ism [~lizəm] Spiritismus m.

**spirituous** ['spiritjuəs] alkoholisch.

**spirt** [spə:t] (hervor)spritzen.

**spit**[1] [spit] 1. Bratspieß m; Landzunge f; 2. aufspießen.

**spit**[2] [~] 1. Speichel m; F Ebenbild n; 2. [irr.] (aus)spucken; fauchen; sprühen (fein regnen).

**spite** [spait] 1. Bosheit f; Groll m; in ~ of trotz (gen.); 2. ärgern; kränken; ~ful ☐ ['spaitful] boshaft, gehässig.

**spitfire** ['spitfaiə] Hitzkopf m.

**spittle** ['spitl] Speichel m, Spucke f.

**spittoon** [spi'tu:n] Spucknapf m.

**splash** [splæʃ] 1. Spritzfleck m; P(l)atschen n; 2. (be)spritzen; p(l)atschen; planschen; (hin)klecksen.

**splay** [splei] 1. Ausschrägung f; 2. auswärts gebogen; 3. v/t. ausschrägen; v/i. ausgeschrägt sein; ~foot ['spleifut] Spreizfuß m.

**spleen** [spli:n] anat. Milz f; üble Laune, Ärger m.

**splend|id** ☐ ['splendid] glänzend, prächtig, herrlich; ~o(u)r [~də] Glanz m, Pracht f, Herrlichkeit f.

**splice** [splais] (ver)spleißen.

**splint** [splint] 1. Schiene f; 2. schienen; ~er ['splintə] 1. Splitter m; 2. (zer)splittern.

**split** [split] 1. Spalt m, Riß m; fig. Spaltung f; 2. gespalten; 3. [irr.] v/t. (zer)spalten; zerreißen; (sich) et. teilen; ~ hairs Haarspalterei treiben; ~ one's sides with laughter sich totlachen; v/i. sich spalten; platzen; ~ting ['splitiŋ] heftig, rasend (Kopfschmerz).

**splutter** ['splʌtə] s. sputter.

**spoil** [spoil] 1. oft ~s pl. Beute f, Raub m; fig. Ausbeute f; Schutt m; ~s pl. pol. bsd. Am. Futterkrippe f; 2. [irr.] (be)rauben; plündern; verderben; verwöhnen; Kind verziehen; ~sman Am. pol. ['spoilzmən] Postenjäger m; ~sport Spielver-

derber(in); ~s system Am. pol. Futterkrippensystem n.

**spoilt** [spoilt] pret. u. p.p. von spoil 2.

**spoke** [spouk] 1. pret. von speak; 2. Speiche f; (Leiter)Sprosse f; ~n ['spoukən] p.p. von speak; ~sman [~ksmən] Wortführer m.

**sponge** [spʌndʒ] 1. Schwamm m; 2. v/t. mit e-m Schwamm (ab)wischen; ~ up aufsaugen; v/i. schmarotzen; ~-cake ['spʌndʒ'keik] Biskuitkuchen m; ~r F fig. [~dʒə] Schmarotzer(in).

**spongy** ['spʌndʒi] schwammig.

**sponsor** ['sponsə] 1. Pate m; Bürge m; Förderer m; Auftraggeber m für Werbesendungen; 2. Pate stehen bei; fördern; ~ship [~ʃip] Paten-, Gönnerschaft f.

**spontane|ity** [spontə'ni:iti] Freiwilligkeit f; eigener Antrieb; ~ous ☐ [spon'teinjəs] freiwillig, von selbst (entstanden); Selbst...; spontan; unwillkürlich; unvermittelt.

**spook** [spu:k] Spuk m; ~y ['spu:ki] geisterhaft, Spuk...

**spool** [spu:l] 1. Spule f; 2. spulen.

**spoon** [spu:n] 1. Löffel m; 2. löffeln; ~ful ['spu:nful] Löffelvoll m.

**sporadic** [spə'rædik] (~ally) sporadisch, verstreut.

**spore** ♀ [spɔ:] Spore f, Keimkorn n.

**sport** [spɔ:t] 1. Sport m; Spiel n; fig. Spielball m; Scherz m; sl. feiner Kerl; ~s pl. allg. Sport m; Sportfest n; 2. v/i. sich belustigen; spielen; v/t. F protzen mit; ~ive ☐ ['spɔ:tiv] lustig; scherzhaft; ~sman [~tsmən] Sportler m.

**spot** [spot] 1. allg. Fleck m; Tupfen m; Makel m; Stelle f; & Leberfleck m; & Pickel m; Tropfen m; a ~ of F etwas; on the ~ auf der Stelle; sofort; 2. sofort liefer- od. zahlbar; 3. (be)flecken; ausfindig machen; erkennen; ~less ☐ ['spotlis] fleckenlos; ~light thea. Scheinwerfer (-licht n) m; ~ter [~tə] Beobachter m; Am. Kontrolleur m; ~ty [~ti] fleckig.

**spouse** [spauz] Gatte m; Gattin f.

**spout** [spaut] 1. Tülle f; Strahlrohr n; (Wasser)Strahl m; 2. (aus)spritzen; F salbadern.

**sprain** [sprein] 1. Verstauchung f; 2. verstauchen.

**sprang** [spræŋ] pret. von spring 2.

**sprat** ichth. [spræt] Sprotte f.

**sprawl** [sprɔ:l] sich rekeln, ausgestreckt daliegen; ♀ wuchern.

**spray** [sprei] 1. zerstäubte Flüssigkeit; Sprühregen m; Gischt m; Spray m, n; = sprayer; 2. zerstäuben; et. besprühen; ~er ['spreiə] Zerstäuber m.

**spread** [spred] 1. [irr.] v/t. a. ~ out ausbreiten; (aus)dehnen; verbreiten; belegen; Butter etc. aufstreichen; Brot etc. bestreichen; ~ the *table* den Tisch decken; *v/i.* sich aus- *od.* verbreiten; 2. Aus-, Verbreitung *f*; Spannweite *f*; Fläche *f*; *Am. Bett-* etc. Decke *f*; *Brot*-Aufstrich *m*; F Festschmaus *m*.

**spree** F [spri:] Spaß *m*, Jux *m*; Zechgelage *n*; Orgie *f*; *Kauf-* etc. Welle *f*.

**sprig** [sprig] Sproß *m*, Reis *n* (*a. fig.*); ⊕ Zwecke *f*, Stift *m*.

**sprightly** ['spraitli] lebhaft, munter.

**spring** [spriŋ] 1. Sprung *m*, Satz *m*; (Sprung)Feder *f*; Federkraft *f*, Elastizität *f*; Triebfeder *f*; Quelle *f*, *fig.* Ursprung *m*; Frühling *m*; 2. [*irr.*] *v/t.* springen lassen; (zer-) sprengen; *Wild* aufjagen; ~ *a leak* ⚓ leck werden; ~ *a surprise on s.o.* j-n überraschen; *v/i.* springen; entspringen; ♀ sprießen; ~ *up* aufkommen (*Ideen* etc.); ~-**board** ['spriŋbɔ:d] Sprungbrett *n*; ~ **tide** Springflut *f*; ~**tide**, ~**time** Frühling(szeit *f*) *m*; ~**y** □ [~ŋi] federnd.

**sprinkl|e** ['spriŋkl] (be)streuen; (be)sprengen; ~**er** [~lə] Berieselungsanlage *f*; Rasensprenger *m*; ~**ing** [~liŋ] Sprühregen *m*; *a* ~ *of* ein wenig, ein paar.

**sprint** [sprint] *Sport:* 1. sprinten; spurten; 2. Sprint *m*; Kurzstreckenlauf *m*; Endspurt *m*; ~**er** ['sprintə] Sprinter *m*, Kurzstreckenläufer *m*.

**sprite** [sprait] Geist *m*, Kobold *m*.

**sprout** [spraut] 1. sprießen, wachsen (lassen); 2. ♀ Sproß *m*; (*Brussels*) ~*s pl.* Rosenkohl *m*.

**spruce**[1] □ [spru:s] schmuck, nett.

**spruce**[2] ♀ [~] *a.* ~ *fir* Fichte *f*, Rottanne *f*.

**sprung** [sprʌŋ] *pret.* (~) *u. p.p. von* spring 2.

**spry** [sprai] munter, flink.

**spun** [spʌn] *pret. u. p.p. von* spin 1.

**spur** [spə:] 1. Sporn *m* (*a. zo.*, ♀); *fig.* Ansporn *m*; Vorsprung *m*, Ausläufer *m* *e-s Berges*; *on the* ~ *of the moment* der Eingebung des Augenblicks folgend; spornstreichs; 2. (an)spornen.

**spurious** □ ['spjuəriəs] unecht, gefälscht.

**spurn** [spə:n] verschmähen, verächtlich zurückweisen.

**spurt** [spə:t] 1. alle s-e Kräfte zs.-nehmen; *Sport:* spurten; *s. spirt*; 2. plötzliche Anstrengung, Ruck *m*; *Sport:* Spurt *m*.

**sputter** ['spʌtə] 1. Gesprudel *n*; 2. (hervor)sprudeln; spritzen.

**spy** [spai] 1. Späher(in); Spion(in); 2. (er)spähen; erblicken; spionieren; ~**glass** ['spaiglɑ:s] Fernglas *n*; ~**hole** Guckloch *n*.

**squabble** ['skwɔbl] 1. Zank *m*, Kabbelei *f*; 2. (sich) zanken.

**squad** [skwɔd] Rotte *f*, Trupp *m*; ~**ron** ['skwɔdrən] ✕ Schwadron *f*; ✈ Staffel *f*; ⚓ Geschwader *n*.

**squalid** □ ['skwɔlid] schmutzig, armselig.

**squall** [skwɔ:l] 1. ⚓ Bö *f*; Schrei *m*; ~*s pl.* Geschrei *n*; 2. schreien.

**squalor** ['skwɔlə] Schmutz *m*.

**squander** ['skwɔndə] verschwenden.

**square** [skwɛə] 1. □ viereckig; quadratisch; rechtwinklig; eckig; passend, stimmend; in Ordnung; direkt; quitt, gleich; ehrlich, offen; F altmodisch, spießig; ~ *measure* Flächenmaß *n*; ~ *mile* Quadratmeile *f*; 2. Quadrat *n*; Viereck *n*; *Schach*-Feld *n*; öffentlicher Platz; Winkelmaß *n*; F altmodischer Spießer; 3. *v/t.* viereckig machen; einrichten (*with* nach), anpassen (*dat.*); ♱ be-, ausgleichen; *v/i.* passen (*with* zu); übereinstimmen; ~-**built** ['skwɛə'bilt] vierschrötig; ~ **dance** Quadrille *f*; ~-**toes** *sg.* F Pedant *m*.

**squash**[1] [skwɔʃ] 1. Gedränge *n*; Fruchtsaft *m*; Platsch(en *n*) *m*; Rakettspiel *n*; 2. (zer-, zs.-)quetschen; drücken.

**squash**[2] ♀ [~] Kürbis *m*.

**squat** [skwɔt] 1. kauernd; untersetzt; 2. hocken, kauern; ~**ter** ['skwɔtə] *Am.* Schwarzsiedler *m*; *Australien:* Schafzüchter *m*.

**squawk** [skwɔ:k] 1. kreischen, schreien; 2. Gekreisch *n*, Geschrei *n*.

**squeak** [skwi:k] quieken, quietschen.

**squeal** [skwi:l] quäken; gell schreien; quieken.

**squeamish** □ ['skwi:miʃ] empfindlich; mäkelig; heikel; penibel.

**squeeze** [skwi:z] 1. (sich) drücken, (sich) quetschen; auspressen; *fig.* (be)drängen; 2. Druck *m*; Gedränge *n*; ~ *f* ['skwi:zə] Presse *f*.

**squelch** F [skweltʃ] zermalmen.

**squid** *zo.* [skwid] Tintenfisch *m*.

**squint** [skwint] schielen; blinzeln.

**squire** ['skwaiə] 1. Gutsbesitzer *m*; (Land)Junker *m*; *Am.* F (Friedens-) Richter *m*; 2. *e-e Dame* begleiten.

**squirm** F [skwə:m] sich winden.

**squirrel** *zo.* ['skwirəl, *Am.* 'skwə:rəl] Eichhörnchen *n*.

**squirt** [skwə:t] 1. Spritze *f*; Strahl *m*; F Wichtigtuer *m*; 2. spritzen.

**stab** [stæb] 1. Stich *m*; 2. *v/t.* (er-) stechen; *v/i.* stechen (*at* nach).

**stabili|ty** [stə'biliti] Stabilität *f*; Standfestig-, Beständigkeit *f*; ~**ze** ['steibilaiz] stabilisieren (*a.* ✈).

**stable**[1] □ ['steibl] stabil, fest.

**stable**[2] [~] 1. Stall *m*; 2. einstallen.

**stack** [stæk] 1. ♂ (Heu-, Stroh-, Getreide)Schober *m*; Stapel *m*; Schornstein(reihe *f*) *m*; Regal *n*; ~*s pl. Am.* Hauptmagazin *n* *e-r*

*Bibliothek*; F Haufen *m*; **2.** aufstapeln.

**stadium** ['steidjəm] *Sport*: Stadion *n*, Sportplatz *m*, Kampfbahn *f*.

**staff** [sta:f] **1.** Stab *m* (*a.* ✕), Stock *m*; Stütze *f*; ♪ Notensystem *n*; Personal *n*; Belegschaft *f*; Beamten-, Lehrkörper *m*; **2.** (mit Personal, Beamten *od.* Lehrern) besetzen.

**stag** *zo.* [stæg] Hirsch *m*.

**stage** [steidʒ] **1.** Bühne *f*, Theater *n*; *fig.* Schauplatz *m*; Stufe *f*, Stadium *n*; Teilstrecke *f*, Etappe *f*; Haltestelle *f*; Gerüst *n*, Gestell *n*; **2.** inszenieren; **~coach** ['steidʒkoutʃ] Postkutsche *f*; **~craft** dramatisches Talent; Theatererfahrung *f*; **~ direction** Bühnenanweisung *f*; **~ fright** Lampenfieber *n*; **~ manager** Regisseur *m*.

**stagger** ['stægə] **1.** *v/i.* (sch)wanken, taumeln; *fig.* stutzen; *v/t.* ins Wanken bringen; staffeln; **2.** Schwanken *n*; Staffelung *f*.

**stagna|nt** □ ['stægnənt] stehend (*Wasser*); stagnierend; stockend; träg; ♥ still; **~te** [~neit] stocken.

**staid** [steid] gesetzt, ruhig.

**stain** [stein] **1.** Fleck(en) *m* (*a. fig.*); Beize *f*; **2.** fleckig machen; *fig.* beflecken; beizen, färben; **~ed glass** buntes Glas; **~less** □ ['steinlis] ungefleckt; *fig.* fleckenlos; rostfrei.

**stair** [stɛə] Stufe *f*; **~s** *pl.* Treppe *f*, Stiege *f*; **~case** ['stɛəkeis], **~way** Treppe(nhaus *n*) *f*.

**stake** [steik] **1.** Pfahl *m*; Marterpfahl *m*; (Spiel)Einsatz *m* (*a. fig.*); **~s** *pl.* Pferderennen: Preis *m*; Rennen *n*; *pull up* **~s** *Am.* F abhauen; *be at* **~** auf dem Spiel stehen; **2.** (um)pfählen; auts Spiel setzen; **~ out**, **~ off** abstecken.

**stale** □ [steil] alt; schal, abgestanden; verbraucht (*Luft*); fad.

**stalk** [sto:k] **1.** Stengel *m*, Stiel *m*; Halm *m*; *hunt.* Pirsch *f*; **2.** *v/i.* einherstolzieren; heranschleichen; *hunt.* pirschen; *v/t.* beschleichen.

**stall** [sto:l] **1.** (Pferde)Box *f*; (Verkaufs)Stand *m*, Marktbude *f*; *thea.* Sperrsitz *m*; **2.** *v/t.* einstallen; *Motor* abwürgen; *v/i. mot.* aussetzen.

**stallion** ['stæljən] Hengst *m*.

**stalwart** □ ['sto:lwət] stramm, stark.

**stamina** ['stæminə] Ausdauer *f*.

**stammer** ['stæmə] **1.** stottern, stammeln; **2.** Stottern *n*.

**stamp** [stæmp] **1.** (Auf)Stampfen *n*; ⊕ Stampfe(r *m*) *f*; Stempel *m* (*a. fig.*); (Brief)Marke *f*; Gepräge *n*; Art *f*; **2.** (auf)stampfen; prägen; stanzen; (ab)stempeln (*a. fig.*); frankieren.

**stampede** [stæm'pi:d] **1.** Panik *f*, wilde Flucht; **2.** *v/i.* durchgehen; *v/t.* in Panik versetzen.

**stanch** [sta:ntʃ] **1.** hemmen; stillen; **2.** □ fest; zuverlässig; treu.

**stand** [stænd] **1.** [*irr.*] *v/i. allg.* stehen; sich befinden; beharren; *mst* **~** *still* stillstehen, stehenbleiben; bestehen (bleiben); **~** *against j-m* widerstehen; **~** *aside* beiseite treten; **~** *back* zurücktreten; **~** *by* dabeistehen; *fig.* (fest) stehen zu; helfen; bereitstehen; **~** *for* kandidieren für; bedeuten; eintreten für; F sich *et.* gefallen lassen; **~** *in* einspringen; **~** *in with* sich gut stellen mit; **~** *off* zurücktreten (von); **~** *off!* weg da!; **~** *on* (*fig.* be)stehen auf; **~** *out* hervorstehen; sich abheben (*against* gegen); standhalten (*dat.*); **~** *over* stehen *od.* liegen bleiben; **~** *pat Am.* F stur bleiben; **~** *to* bleiben bei; **~** *up* aufstehen; sich erheben; **~** *up for* eintreten für; **~** *up to* sich zur Wehr setzen gegen; standhalten (*dat.*); **~** *upon* (*fig.* be)stehen auf (*dat.*); *v/t.* (hin)stellen; aushalten, (v)ertragen; über sich ergehen lassen; F spendieren; **2.** Stand *m*; Standplatz *m*; Bude *f*; Standpunkt *m*; Stillstand *m*; Ständer *m*; Tribüne *f*; *bsd. Am.* Zeugenstand *m*; *make a od.* one's **~** *against* standhalten (*dat.*).

**standard** ['stændəd] **1.** Standarte *f*, Fahne *f*; Standard *m*, Norm *f*; Regel *f*, Maßstab *m*; Niveau *n*; Stufe *f*; Münzfuß *m*; Währung *f*; Ständer *m*, Mast *m*; **2.** maßgebend; Normal...; **~ize** [~daiz] norm(ier)en.

**stand-by** ['stændbai] Beistand *m*.

**standee** [stæn'di:] Stehende(r) *m*; *Am.* Stehplatzinhaber *m*.

**standing** ['stændiŋ] **1.** □ stehend; fest; (be)ständig; **~** *orders pl. parl.* Geschäftsordnung *f*; **2.** Stellung *f*, Rang *m*, Ruf *m*; Dauer *f*; *of long* **~** *alt*; **~room** Stehplatz *m*.

**stand|off** *Am.* ['stændo:f] Unentschieden *n*; Dünkel *m*; **~offish** [~'o:fiʃ] zurückhaltend; **~patter** *Am. pol.* [stænd'pætə] sturer Konservativer; **~point** ['stændpoint] Standpunkt *m*; **~still** Stillstand *m*; **~up:** **~** *collar* Stehkragen *m*.

**stank** [stæŋk] *pret. von stink* 2.

**stanza** ['stænzə] Stanze *f*; Strophe *f*.

**staple**[1] ['steipl] Haupterzeugnis *n*; Hauptgegenstand *m*; *attr.* Haupt...

**staple**[2] [~] Krampe *f*; Heftklammer *f*.

**star** [sta:] **1.** Stern *m*; *thea.* Star *m*; **~s** *and Stripes pl. Am.* Sternenbanner *n*; **2.** mit Sternen schmücken; *thea.*, *fig.* die Hauptrolle spielen.

**starboard** ⚓ ['sta:bəd] **1.** Steuerbord *n*; **2.** *Ruder* steuerbord legen.

**starch** [sta:tʃ] **1.** (Wäsche)Stärke *f*; *fig.* Steifheit *f*; **2.** stärken.

**stare** [stɛə] **1.** Starren *n*; Staunen *n*; starrer Blick; **2.** starren, staunen.

**stark** [stɑːk] **1.** *adj.* starr; bar, völlig (*Unsinn*); **2.** *adv.* völlig.

**starlight** ['stɑːlait] Sternenlicht *n.*

**starling** *orn.* ['stɑːliŋ] Star *m.*

**starlit** ['stɑːlit] sternenklar.

**star|ry** ['stɑːri] Stern(en)...; gestirnt; **~-spangled** ['stɑːspæŋgld] sternenbesät; ♀ Banner *Am.* Sternenbanner *n.*

**start** [stɑːt] **1.** Auffahren *n*, Stutzen *n*; Ruck *m*; *Sport:* Start *m*; Aufbruch *m*; Anfang *m*; *fig.* Vorsprung *m*; get the ~ of s.o. j-m zuvorkommen; **2.** *v/i.* aufspringen, auffahren; stutzen; *Sport:* starten; abfahren; aufbrechen; *mot.* anspringen; anfangen (*on* mit; *doing* zu tun); *v/t.* in Gang bringen; *mot.* anlassen; *Sport:* starten (lassen); aufjagen; *fig.* anfangen; veranlassen (*doing* zu tun); **~er** ['stɑːtə] *Sport:* Starter *m*; Läufer *m*; *mot.* Anlasser *m.*

**startl|e** ['stɑːtl] (er-, auf)schrecken; **~ing** [~liŋ] bestürzend, überraschend, aufsehenerregend.

**starv|ation** [stɑː'veiʃən] (Ver)Hungern *n*, Hungertod *m*; *attr.* Hunger...; **~e** [stɑːv] verhungern (lassen); *fig.* verkümmern (lassen).

**state** [steit] **1.** Zustand *m*; Stand *m*; Staat *m*; *pol. mst* ♀ Staat *m*; *attr.* Staats...; *in* ~ feierlich; **2.** angeben; darlegen, darstellen; feststellen; melden; *Regel etc.* aufstellen; ♀ **Department** *Am. pol.* Außenministerium *n*; **~ly** ['steitli] stattlich; würdevoll; erhaben; **~ment** [~tmənt] Angabe *f*; Aussage *f*; Darstellung *f*; Feststellung *f*; Aufstellung *f*; ♀ (~ *of account* Konto-) Auszug *m*; **~room** Staatszimmer *n*; ♣ Einzelkabine *f*; **~side** *Am.* F **1.** *adj.* USA-..., Heimat...; **2.** *adv.:* go ~ heimkehren; **~sman** [~smən] Staatsmann *m.*

**static** ['stætik] statisch, Ruhe...

**station** ['steiʃən] **1.** Stand(ort) *m*; Stelle *f*; Stellung *f*; ✕, ♣, ☒ Station *f*; Bahnhof *m*; Rang *m*, Stand *m*; **2.** aufstellen, postieren, stationieren; **~ary** ☐ [~ʃnəri] stillstehend; feststehend; **~ery** [~] Schreibwaren *f/pl.*; **~-master** ☒ Stationsvorsteher *m*; **~ wagon** *Am.* mot. Kombiwagen *m.*

**statistics** [stə'tistiks] *pl.* Statistik *f.*

**statu|ary** ['stætjuəri] Bildhauer(-kunst *f*) *m*; **~e** [~ju:] Standbild *n*, Plastik *f*, Statue *f.*

**stature** ['stætʃə] Statur *f*, Wuchs *m.*

**status** ['steitəs] Zustand *m*; Stand *m.*

**statute** ['stætjuːt] Statut *n*, Satzung *f*; (Landes)Gesetz *n.*

**staunch** [stɔːntʃ] *s.* stanch.

**stave** [steiv] **1.** Faßdaube *f*; Strophe *f*; **2.** [*irr.*] *mst* ~ *in* ein Loch schlagen in (*acc.*); ~ *off* abwehren.

**stay** [stei] **1.** ♣ Stag *n*; ⊕ Strebe *f*; Stütze *f*; Aufschub *m*; Aufenthalt *m*; **~s** *pl.* Korsett *n*; **2.** bleiben; wohnen; (sich) aufhalten; Ausdauer haben; hemmen; aufschieben; *Hunger* vorläufig stillen; stützen; **~er** ['steiə] *Sport:* Steher *m.*

**stead** [sted] Stelle *f*, Statt *f*; **~fast** ☐ ['stedfəst] fest, unerschütterlich; standhaft; unverwandt (*Blick*).

**steady** ['stedi] **1.** ☐ (be)ständig; stetig; sicher; fest; ruhig; gleichmäßig; unerschütterlich; zuverlässig; **2.** stetig *od.* sicher machen *od.* werden; (sich) festigen; stützen; (sich) beruhigen; **3.** *Am.* F feste Freundin, fester Freund.

**steal** [stiːl] **1.** [*irr.*] *v/t.* stehlen (*a. fig.*); *v/i.* sich stehlen *od.* schleichen; **2.** *Am.* Diebstahl *m.*

**stealth** [stelθ] Heimlichkeit *f*; *by* ~ heimlich; **~y** ☐ ['stelθi] verstohlen.

**steam** [stiːm] **1.** Dampf *m*; Dunst *m*; *attr.* Dampf...; **2.** *v/i.* dampfen; ~ *up* beschlagen (*Glas*); *v/t.* ausdünsten; dämpfen; **~er** ♣ ['stiːmə] Dampfer *m*; **~y** ☐ [~mi] dampfig; dampfend; dunstig.

**steel** [stiːl] **1.** Stahl *m*; **2.** stählern; Stahl...; **3.** (ver)stählen.

**steep** [stiːp] **1.** steil, jäh; F toll; **2.** einweichen; einlegen; eintauchen; tränken; *fig.* versenken.

**steeple** ['stiːpl] Kirchturm *m*; **~-chase** *Sport:* Hindernisrennen *n.*

**steer¹** [stiə] junger Ochse.

**steer²** [~] steuern; **~age** ♣ ['stiəridʒ] Steuerung *f*; Zwischendeck *n*; **~ing-wheel** [~riŋwiːl] Steuerrad *n*; *mot.* Lenkrad *n*; **~sman** ♣ [~zmən] Rudergänger *m.*

**stem** [stem] **1.** (Baum-, Wort)Stamm *m*; Stiel *m*; Stengel *m*; ♣ Vordersteven *m*; **2.** *Am.* (ab)stammen (*from* von); sich stemmen gegen, ankämpfen gegen.

**stench** [stentʃ] Gestank *m.*

**stencil** ['stensl] Schablone *f*; *typ.* Matrize *f*. [graph(in).\

**stenographer** [ste'nɔgrəfə] Steno-\

**step¹** [step] **1.** Schritt *m*, Tritt *m*; *fig.* Strecke *f*; Fußstapfe *f*; (Treppen)Stufe *f*; Trittbrett *n*; **~s** *pl.* Trittleiter *f*; **2.** *v/i.* schreiten; treten, gehen; ~ *out* ausschreiten; *v/t.* ~ *off*, ~ *out* abschreiten; ~ *up* ankurbeln.

**step²** [~] *in Zssgn* Stief...; **~father** ['stepfɑːðə] Stiefvater *m*; **~mother** Stiefmutter *f.*

**steppe** [step] Steppe *f.*

**stepping-stone** *fig.* ['stepiŋstoun] Sprungbrett *n.*

**steril|e** ['sterail] unfruchtbar; steril; **~ity** [ste'riliti] Sterilität *f*; **~ize** ['sterilaiz] sterilisieren.

**sterling** ['stəːliŋ] vollwertig, echt; gediegen; ♱ Sterling *m* (*Währung*).

**stern** [stəːn] **1.** ☐ ernst; finster, streng, hart; **2.** ♣ Heck *n*; **~ness**

['stə:nnis] Ernst *m*; Strenge *f*;
~-post ⚓ Hintersteven *m*.
**stevedore** ⚓ ['sti:vidɔ:] Stauer *m*.
**stew** [stju:] 1. schmoren, dämpfen;
2. Schmorgericht *n*; F Aufregung *f*.
**steward** [stjuəd] Verwalter *m*; ⚓,
✈ Steward *m*; (Fest)Ordner *m*;
~ess ⚓, ✈ ['stjuədis] Stewardeß *f*.
**stick** [stik] 1. Stock *m*; Stecken *m*;
Stab *m*; (Besen- *etc*.)Stiel *m*; Stange
*f*; F Klotz *m* (*unbeholfener Mensch*);
~s *pl*. Kleinholz *n*; the ~s *pl*. Am. F
die hinterste Provinz; 2. [*irr*.] *v*/*i*.
stecken (bleiben); haften; kleben
(to an *dat*.); ~ at nothing vor nichts
zurückscheuen; ~ out, ~ up hervorstehen; F standhalten; ~ to bleiben
bei; *v*/*t*. (ab)stechen; (an)stecken,
(an)heften; (an)kleben; F ertragen;
~ing-plaster ['stikiŋplɑ:stə] Heftpflaster *n*.
**sticky** □ ['stiki] kleb(e)rig; zäh.
**stiff** □ [stif] steif; starr; hart; fest;
mühsam; stark (*Getränk*); be bored
~ F zu Tode gelangweilt sein; keep
a ~ upper lip die Ohren steifhalten;
~en ['stifn] (sich) (ver)steifen;
~-necked [~'nekt] halsstarrig.
**stifle** ['staifl] ersticken (a. *fig*.).
**stigma** ['stigmə] (Brand-, Schand-)
Mal *n*; Stigma *n*; ~tize [~ətaiz]
brandmarken.
**stile** [stail] Zauntritt *m*, Zaunüber-
gang *m*.
**still** [stil] 1. *adj*. still; 2. *adv*. noch
(immer); 3. *cj*. doch, dennoch;
4. stillen; beruhigen; 5. Destillier-
apparat *m*; ~-born ['stilbɔ:n] tot-
geboren; ~ life Stilleben *n*; ~ness
Stille *f*, Ruhe *f*.
**stilt** [stilt] Stelze *f*; ~ed ['stiltid]
gespreizt, hochtrabend, geschraubt.
**stimul|ant** ['stimjulənt] 1. ✈ stimu-
lierend; 2. ✈ Reizmittel *n*; Genuß-
mittel *n*; Anreiz *m*; ~ate [~leit]
(an)reizen; anregen; ~ation [stimju-
'leiʃən] Reizung *f*, Antrieb *m*; ~us
['stimjuləs] Antrieb *m*; Reizmittel *n*.
**sting** [stiŋ] 1. Stachel *m*; Stich *m*;
Biß *m*; *fig*. Schärfe *f*; Antrieb *m*;
2. [*irr*.] stechen; brennen; schmerzen; (an)treiben.
**sting|iness** ['stindʒinis] Geiz *m*; ~y
□ ['stindʒi] geizig; knapp, karg.
**stink** [stiŋk] 1. Gestank *m*; 2. [*irr*.]
*v*/*i*. stinken; *v*/*t*. verstänkern.
**stint** [stint] 1. Einschränkung *f*;
Arbeit *f*; 2. knausern mit; einschränken; *j-n* knapp halten.
**stipend** ['staipend] Gehalt *n*.
**stipulat|e** ['stipjuleit] *a*. ~ for aus-
bedingen, ausmachen, vereinbaren;
~ion [stipju'leiʃən] Abmachung *f*;
Klausel *f*, Bedingung *f*.
**stir** [stə:] 1. Regung *f*; Bewegung *f*;
Rühren *n*; Aufregung *f*; Aufsehen
*n*; 2. (sich) rühren; umrühren, bewegen; aufregen; ~ up aufrühren;
aufrütteln.

34*

**stirrup** ['stirəp] Steigbügel *m*.
**stitch** [stitʃ] 1. Stich *m*; Masche *f*;
Seitenstechen *n*; 2. nähen; heften.
**stock** [stɔk] 1. (Baum)Strunk *m*;
Pfropfunterlage *f*; Griff *m*, Kolben
*m* *e-s Gewehrs*; Stamm *m*, Herkunft *f*; Rohstoff *m*; (Fleisch-,
Gemüse)Brühe *f*; Vorrat *m*, (Waren)Lager *n*; (Wissens)Schatz *m*;
*a*. live~ Vieh(bestand *m*) *n*; ✝
Stammkapital *n*; Anleihekapital *n*; ~s
*pl*. Effekten *pl*.; Aktien *f/pl*.; Staatspapiere *n/pl*.; ~s *pl*. ⚓ Stapel *m*; in
(out of) ~ (nicht) vorrätig; take ~ ✝
Inventur machen; take ~ of *fig*. sich
klarwerden über (*acc*.); 2. vorrätig;
ständig; gängig; Standard...; 3. versorgen; *Waren* führen; ✝ vorrätig
haben.
**stockade** [stɔ'keid] Staket *n*.
**stock|-breeder** ['stɔkbri:də] Vieh-
züchter *m*; ~broker ✝ Börsen-
makler *m*; ~exchange ✝ Börse *f*;
~farmer Viehzüchter *m*; ~holder
✝ Aktionär(in).
**stockinet** [stɔki'net] Trikot *n*.
**stocking** ['stɔkiŋ] Strumpf *m*.
**stock|jobber** ✝ ['stɔkdʒɔbə] Börsen-
makler *m*; ~market ✝ Börse *f*;
~still unbeweglich; ~taking Inventur *f*; ~y ['stɔki] stämmig.
**stog|ie, ~y** Am. ['stougi] billige
Zigarre.
**stoic** ['stouik] 1. stoisch; 2. Stoiker
*m*.
**stoker** ['stoukə] Heizer *m*.
**stole** [stoul] *pret. von* steal 1; ~n
['stoulən] *p.p. von* steal 1.
**stolid** □ ['stɔlid] schwerfällig,
gleichmütig; stur.
**stomach** ['stʌmək] 1. Magen *m*;
Leib *m*, Bauch *m*; *fig*. Lust *f*; 2. verdauen, vertragen; *fig*. ertragen.
**stomp** Am. [stɔmp] (auf)stampfen.
**stone** [stoun] 1. Stein *m*; (Obst-)
Kern *m*; *Gewichtseinheit von 6,35 kg*;
2. steinern; Stein...; 3. steinigen;
entsteinen; ~blind ['stoun'blaind]
stockblind; ~dead mausetot;
~ware [~nwɛə] Steingut *n*.
**stony** ['stouni] steinig; *fig*. steinern.
**stood** [stud] *pret. u. p.p. von* stand 1.
**stool** [stu:l] Schemel *m*; ✈ Stuhlgang *m*; ~pigeon Am. ['stu:l-
pidʒin] Lockvogel *m*; Spitzel *m*.
**stoop** [stu:p] 1. *v*/*i*. sich beugen;
sich erniedrigen *od*. herablassen;
krumm gehen; *v*/*t*. neigen; 2. ge-
beugte Haltung; *Am*. Veranda *f*.
**stop** [stɔp] 1. *v*/*t*. anhalten; hindern;
aufhören; ~ up (ver)stopfen;
*Zahn* plombieren; (ver)sperren;
*Zahlung* einstellen; *Lohn* einbehal-
ten; *v*/*i*. stehenbleiben; aufhören;
halten; F bleiben; ~ dead, ~ short
plötzlich anhalten; ~ over Halt-
machen; 2. (Ein)Halt *m*; Pause *f*;
Hemmung *f*; ⊕ Anschlag *m*; Aufhören *n*, Ende *n*; Haltestelle *f*; *mst*

*full ~ gr.* Punkt *m*; **~gap** ['stɔpgæp] Notbehelf *m*; **~page** [~pidʒ] Verstopfung *f*; (Zahlungs- *etc.*)Einstellung *f*; Sperrung *f*; (Lohn)Abzug *m*; Aufenthalt *m*; ⊕ Hemmung *f*; Betriebsstörung *f*; (Verkehrs-) Stockung *f*; **~per** [~pə] Stöpsel *m*; **~ping** ⚓ [~piŋ] Plombe *f*.

**storage** ['stɔ:ridʒ] Lagerung *f*, Aufbewahrung *f*; Lagergeld *n*.

**store** [stɔ:] **1.** Vorrat *m*; *fig.* Fülle *f*; Lagerhaus *n*; *Am.* Laden *m*; **~s** *pl.* Kauf-, Warenhaus *n*; *in ~* vorrätig, auf Lager; **2.** *a. ~ up* (auf)speichern; (ein)lagern; versorgen; **~house** Lagerhaus *n*; *fig.* Schatzkammer *f*; **~keeper** Lagerverwalter *m*; *Am.* Ladenbesitzer *m*.

**stor(e)y** ['stɔ:ri] Stock(werk *n*) *m*.

**storeyed** ['stɔ:rid] mit ... Stockwerken, ...stöckig.

**storied** [~] *s.* storeyed.

**stork** [stɔ:k] Storch *m*.

**storm** [stɔ:m] **1.** Sturm *m*; Gewitter *n*; **2.** stürmen; toben; **~y** ['stɔ:mi] stürmisch.

**story** ['stɔ:ri] Geschichte *f*; Erzählung *f*; Märchen *n*; *thea.* Handlung *f*; F Lüge *f*; *short ~* Kurzgeschichte *f*.

**stout** [staut] **1.** □ stark, kräftig; derb; dick; tapfer; **2.** Starkbier *n*.

**stove** [stouv] **1.** Ofen *m*; Herd *m*; **2.** *pret. u. p.p. von* stave 2.

**stow** [stou] (ver)stauen, packen; **~away** ⚓ ['stouəwei] blinder Passagier.

**straddle** ['strædl] (die Beine) spreizen; rittlings sitzen auf (*dat.*); *Am. fig.* es mit beiden Parteien halten; schwanken.

**straggl|e** ['strægl] verstreut *od.* einzeln liegen; umherstreifen; bummeln; *fig.* abschweifen; ♃ wuchern; **~ing** □ [~liŋ] weitläufig, lose.

**straight** [streit] **1.** *adj.* gerade; *fig.* aufrichtig, ehrlich; glatt (*Haar*); *Am.* pur, unverdünnt; *Am. pol.* hundertprozentig; *put ~ in* Ordnung bringen; **2.** *adv.* gerade(wegs); geradeaus; direkt; sofort; *~ away* sofort; *~ out* rundheraus; **~en** ['streitn] gerade machen *od.* werden; *~ out in* Ordnung bringen; **~forward** □ [streit'fɔ:wəd] gerade; ehrlich, redlich.

**strain** [strein] **1.** Abstammung *f*; Art *f*; ⊕ Spannung *f*; (Über)Anstrengung *f*; starke Inanspruchnahme (*on gen.*); Druck *m*; ⚕ Zerrung *f*; Ton *m*; **~s** *pl.* ♩ Weise *f*; Hang *m* (*of zu*); **2.** *v/t.* (an)spannen; (über)anstrengen; überspannen; ⊕ beanspruchen; ♩ zerren; durchseihen; *v/i.* sich spannen; sich anstrengen; sich abmühen (*after um*); zerren (*at an dat.*); **~er** ['streinə] Durchschlag *m*; Filter *m*; Sieb *n*.

**strait** [streit] (*in Eigennamen* ~s *pl.*)

Meerenge *f*, Straße *f*; **~s** *pl.* Not (-lage) *f*; *~ jacket* Zwangsjacke *f*; **~ened** ['streitnd] dürftig; in Not.

**strand** [strænd] **1.** Strand *m*; Strähne *f* (*a. fig.*); **2.** auf den Strand setzen; *fig.* stranden (lassen).

**strange** □ [streindʒ] fremd (*a. fig.*); seltsam; **~r** ['streindʒə] Fremde(r) *m.*

**strangle** ['stræŋgl] erwürgen.

**strap** [stræp] **1.** Riemen *m*; Gurt *m*; Band *n*; **2.** an-, festschnallen; mit Riemen peitschen. [List *f*.]

**stratagem** ['strætidʒəm] (Kriegs-)

**strateg|ic** [strə'ti:dʒik] (~ally) strategisch; **~y** ['strætidʒi] Kriegskunst *f*, Strategie *f*.

**strat|um** *geol.* ['strɑ:təm], *pl* **~a** [~tə] Schicht *f* (*a. fig.*), Lage *f*.

**straw** [strɔ:] **1.** Stroh(halm *m*) *n*; **2.** Stroh...; *~ vote Am.* Probeabstimmung *f*; **~berry** ['strɔ:bəri] Erdbeere *f*.

**stray** [strei] **1.** irregehen; sich verirren; abirren; umherschweifen; **2.** *a. ~ed* verirrt; vereinzelt; **3.** verirrtes Tier.

**streak** [stri:k] **1.** Strich *m*, Streifen *m*; *fig.* Ader *f*, Spur *f*; kurze Periode; *~ of lightning* Blitzstrahl *m*; **2.** streifen; jagen, F Eilzustreak

**stream** [stri:m] **1.** Bach *m*; Strom *m*; Strömung *f*, *f*; *v/i.* strömen; triefen; flattern; *v/t.* strömen lassen; ausströmen; **~er** ['stri:mə] Wimpel *m*; *fig.* (fliegendes) Band; Lichtstrahl *m*; *typ.* Schlagzeile *f*.

**street** [stri:t] Straße *f*; **~car** *Am.* ['stri:tkɑ:] Straßenbahn(wagen *m*) *f*.

**strength** [streŋθ] Stärke *f*, Kraft *f*; *on the ~ of auf* ... hin, auf Grund (*gen.*); **~en** ['streŋθən] *v/t.* stärken; kräftigen; bestärken; *v/i.* erstarken.

**strenuous** □ ['strenjuəs] rührig, emsig; eifrig; anstrengend.

**stress** [stres] **1.** Druck *m*; Nachdruck *m*; Betonung *f* (*a. gr.*); *fig.* Schwergewicht *n*; Ton *m*; *psych.* Stress *m*; **2.** betonen.

**stretch** [stretʃ] **1.** *v/t.* strecken; (aus)dehnen; *mst ~ out* ausstrecken; (an)spannen; *fig.* überspannen; *Gesetz* zu weit auslegen; *v/i.* sich (er-)strecken; sich dehnen (lassen); **2.** Strecken *n*; Dehnung *f*; (An-) Spannung *f*; Übertreibung *f*; Überschreitung *f*; Strecke *f*, Fläche *f*; **~er** ['stretʃə] Tragbahre *f*; Streckvorrichtung *f*.

**strew** [stru:] [*irr.*] (be)streuen; **~n** [~u:n] *p.p. von* strew.

**stricken** ['strikən] *p.p. von* strike 2; **2.** *adj.* ge~, betroffen.

**strict** [strikt] streng; genau; **~ly** *speaking* strenggenommen; **~ness** ['striktnis] Genauigkeit *f*; Strenge *f*.

**stridden** ['stridn] *p.p. von* stride 1.

**stride** [straid] **1.** [*irr.*] *v/t.* über-, durchschreiten; **2.** (weiter) Schritt.

**strident** □ ['straidnt] kreischend.
**strife** [straif] Streit m, Hader m.
**strike** [straik] 1. Streik m; (Öl-, Erz)Fund m; fig. Treffer m; ✗ (Luft)Angriff m auf ein Einzelziel; Am. Baseball: Verlustpunkt m; be on ∼ streiken; 2. [irr.] v/t. treffen, stoßen; schlagen; gegen od. auf (acc.) schlagen od. stoßen; stoßen od. treffen auf (acc.); Flagge etc. streichen; Ton anschlagen; auffallen (dat.); ergreifen; Handel abschließen; Streichholz, Licht anzünden; Wurzel schlagen; Pose annehmen; Bilanz ziehen; ∼ up ♪ anstimmen; Freundschaft schließen; v/i. schlagen; ⚓ auf Grund stoßen; streiken; ∼ home (richtig) treffen; ∼r ['straikə] Streikende(r) m.
**striking** □ ['straikiŋ] Schlag...; auffallend; eindrucksvoll; treffend.
**string** [striŋ] 1. Schnur f; Bindfaden m; Band n; Am. F Bedingung f; (Bogen)Sehne f; ♩ Faser f; ♩ Saite f; Reihe f, Kette f; ∼s pl. ♩ Saiteninstrumente n/pl., Streicher m/pl.; pull the ∼s der Drahtzieher sein; 2. [irr.] spannen; aufreihen; besaiten (a. fig.), bespannen; (ver-, zu)schnüren; Bohnen abziehen; Am. sl. j-n verkohlen; be strung up angespannt od. erregt sein; ∼band♩ ['striŋbænd] Streichorchester n.
**stringent** □ ['strindʒənt] streng, scharf; bindend, zwingend; knapp.
**stringy** ['striŋi] faserig; zäh.
**strip** [strip] 1. entkleiden (a. fig.); (sich) ausziehen; abziehen; fig. entblößen, berauben; ⊕ auseinandernehmen; ⚓ abtakeln; a. ∼ off ausziehen, abstreifen; 2. Streifen m.
**stripe** [straip] Streifen m; ✗ Tresse f.
**stripling** ['stripliŋ] Bürschchen n.
**strive** [straiv] [irr.] streben; sich bemühen; ringen (for um); ∼n ['strivn] p.p. von strive.
**strode** [stroud] pret. von stride 1.
**stroke** [strouk] 1. Schlag m (a. 🏊); Streich m; Stoß m; Strich m; ∼ of luck Glücksfall m; 2. streiche(l)n.
**stroll** [stroul] 1. schlendern; umherziehen; 2. Bummel m, Spaziergang m; ∼er ['stroulə] Bummler(in), Spaziergänger(in); Am. (Falt)Sportwagen m.
**strong** □ [strɔŋ] allg. stark; kräftig; energisch, eifrig; fest; schwer (Speise etc.); ∼box ['strɔŋbɔks] Stahlkassette f; ∼hold Festung f; fig. Bollwerk n; ∼room Stahlkammer f; ∼willed eigenwillig.
**strop** [strɔp] 1. Streichriemen m: 2. Messer abziehen.
**strove** [strouv] pret. von strive.
**struck** [strʌk] pret. u. p.p. von strike 2.
**structure** ['strʌktʃə] Bau(werk n) m; Struktur f, Gefüge n; Gebilde n.

**struggle** ['strʌgl] 1. sich (ab)mühen; kämpfen, ringen; sich sträuben; 2. Kampf m; Ringen n; Anstrengung f.
**strung** [strʌŋ] pret. u. p.p. von string 2.
**strut** [strʌt] 1. v/i. stolzieren; v/t. ⊕ abstützen; 2. Stolzieren n; ⊕ Strebe(balken m) f; Stütze f.
**stub** [stʌb] 1. (Baum)Stumpf m; Stummel m; Am. Kontrollabschnitt m; 2. (aus)roden; sich den Fuß stoßen.
**stubble** ['stʌbl] Stoppel(n pl.) f.
**stubborn** □ ['stʌbən] eigensinnig; widerspenstig; stur; hartnäckig.
**stuck** [stʌk] pret. u. p.p. von stick 2; ∼up ['stʌk'ʌp] F hochnäsig.
**stud** [stʌd] 1. (Wand)Pfosten m; Ziernagel m; Knauf m; Manschetten-, Kragenknopf m; Gestüt n; 2. beschlagen; besetzen; ∼book ['stʌdbuk] Gestütbuch n.
**student** ['stju:dənt] Student(in).
**studied** □ ['stʌdid] einstudiert; gesucht; gewollt.
**studio** ['stju:diou] Atelier n; Studio n; Radio: Aufnahme-, Senderaum m.
**studious** □ ['stju:djəs] fleißig; bedacht; bemüht; geflissentlich.
**study** ['stʌdi] 1. Studium n; Studier-, Arbeitszimmer n; paint. etc. Studie f; be in a brown ∼ versunken sein; 2. (ein)studieren; sich et. genau ansehen; sich bemühen um.
**stuff** [stʌf] 1. Stoff m; Zeug n; fig. Unsinn m; 2. v/t. (voll-, aus)stopfen; ∼ed shirt Am. sl. Fatzke m; v/i. sich vollstopfen; ∼ing ['stʌfiŋ] Füllung f; ∼y □ [∼fi] dumpf(ig), muffig, stickig; fig. verärgert.
**stultify** ['stʌltifai] lächerlich machen, blamieren; et. hinfällig machen.
**stumble** ['stʌmbl] 1. Stolpern n; Fehltritt m; 2. stolpern; straucheln; ∼ upon stoßen auf (acc.).
**stump** [stʌmp] 1. Stumpf m, Stummel m; 2. v/t. F verblüffen; Am. F herausfordern; ∼ the country als Wahlredner im Land umherziehen; v/i. (daher)stapfen; ∼y □ ['stʌmpi] gedrungen; plump.
**stun** [stʌn] betäuben (a. fig.).
**stung** [stʌŋ] pret. u. p.p. von sting 2.
**stunk** [stʌŋk] pret. u. p.p. von stink 2.
**stunning** □ F ['stʌniŋ] toll, famos.
**stunt**[1] F [stʌnt] Kraft-, Kunststück n; (Reklame)Trick m; Sensation f.
**stunt**[2] [stʌnt] ⊕ im Wachstum hindern; ∼ed ['stʌntid] verkümmert.
**stup|efy** ['stju:pifai] fig. betäuben; verblüffen; verdummen; ∼endous □ [stju(:)'pendəs] erstaunlich; ∼id □ ['stju:pid] dumm, einfältig, stumpfsinnig; blöd; ∼idity [stju(:)'piditi] Dummheit f; Stumpfsinn m; ∼or ['stju(:)pə] Erstarrung f, Betäubung f.

sturdy ['stə:di] derb, kräftig, stark; stämmig; stramm; handfest.

stutter ['stʌtə] 1. stottern; 2. Stottern n.

sty[1] [stai] Schweinestall m, Koben m.

sty[2], stye [~] Gerstenkorn n am Auge.

style [stail] 1. Stil m; Mode f; Betitelung f; 2. (be)nennen, betiteln.

stylish □ ['stailiʃ] stilvoll; elegant; ~ness [~ʃnis] Eleganz f.

stylo F ['stailou], ~graph [~ləgrɑːf] Tintenkuli m.

suave □ [swɑːv] verbindlich; mild.

sub... [sʌb] mst Unter..., unter...; Neben...; Hilfs...; fast ...

subdeb Am. F [sʌb'deb] Backfisch m, junges Mädchen.

subdivision ['sʌbdiviʒən] Unterteilung f; Unterabteilung f.

subdue [səb'djuː] unterwerfen; bezwingen; bändigen; unterdrücken, verdrängen; dämpfen.

subject ['sʌbdʒikt] 1. unterworfen; untergeben, abhängig; untertan; unterliegend (to dat.); be ~ to neigen zu; 2. adv. ~ to vorbehaltlich (gen.); 3. Untertan m, Staatsangehörige(r m) f; phls., gr. Subjekt n; a. ~ matter Thema n, Gegenstand m; 4. [səb'dʒekt] unterwerfen; fig. aussetzen; ~ion [~kʃən] Unterwerfung f. [chen.]

subjugate ['sʌbdʒugeit] unterjo-

subjunctive gr. [səb'dʒʌnktiv] a. ~ mood Konjunktiv m.

sub|lease ['sʌb'liːs], ~let [irr. (let)] untervermieten.

sublime □ [sə'blaim] erhaben.

submachine-gun ['sʌbmə'ʃiːngʌn] Maschinenpistole f.

submarine ['sʌbməriːn] 1. unterseeisch; 2. ♣ Unterseeboot n.

submerge [səb'məːdʒ] untertauchen; überschwemmen.

submission [səb'miʃən] Unterwerfung f; Unterbreitung f; ~ive □ [~isiv] unterwürfig.

submit [səb'mit] (sich) unterwerfen; anheimstellen; unterbreiten, einreichen; fig. sich fügen od. ergeben (to in acc.).

subordinate 1. □ [sə'bɔːdnit] untergeordnet; untergeben; ~ clause gr. Nebensatz m; 2. [~] Untergebene(r m) f; 3. [~dineit] unterordnen.

suborn ✝ [sʌ'bɔːn] verleiten.

subscribe [səb'skraib] v/t. Geld stiften (to für); Summe zeichnen; s-n Namen setzen (to unter acc.); unterschreiben mit; v/i. ~ to Zeitung etc. abonnieren; e-r Meinung zustimmen, et. unterschreiben; ~r [~bə] (Unter)Zeichner(in); Abonnent(in); teleph. Teilnehmer(in).

subscription [səb'skripʃən] (Unter-)Zeichnung f; Abonnement n.

subsequent □ ['sʌbsikwent] folgend; später; ~ly hinterher.

subservient □ [səb'səːvjənt] dienlich; dienstbar; unterwürfig.

subsid|e [səb'said] sinken, sich senken; fig. sich setzen; sich legen (Wind); ~ into verfallen in (acc.); ~iary [~'sidjəri] 1. □ Hilfs...; Neben...; untergeordnet; 2. Tochtergesellschaft f; Filiale f; ~ize ['sʌbsidaiz] mit Geld unterstützen; subventionieren; ~y [~di] Beihilfe f; Subvention f.

subsist [səb'sist] bestehen; leben (on, by von); ~ence [~təns] Dasein n; (Lebens)Unterhalt m.

substance ['sʌbstəns] Substanz f; Wesen n; fig. Hauptsache f; Inhalt m; Wirklichkeit f; Vermögen n.

substantial □ [səb'stænʃəl] wesentlich; wirklich; kräftig; stark; solid; vermögend; namhaft (Summe).

substantiate [səb'stænʃieit] beweisen, begründen, dartun.

substantive gr. ['sʌbstəntiv] Substantiv n, Hauptwort n.

substitut|e ['sʌbstitjuːt] 1. an die Stelle setzen od. treten (for von); unterschieben (for statt); 2. Stellvertreter m; Ersatz m; ~ion [sʌbsti'tjuːʃən] Stellvertretung f; Ersatz m.

subterfuge ['sʌbtəfjuːdʒ] Ausflucht f.

subterranean □ [sʌbtə'reinjən] unterirdisch.

sub-title ['sʌbtaitl] Untertitel m.

subtle □ ['sʌtl] fein(sinnig); subtil; spitzfindig; ~ty [~lti] Feinheit f.

subtract ♣ [səb'trækt] abziehen, subtrahieren.

subtropical ['sʌb'trɔpikəl] subtropisch.

suburb ['sʌbəːb] Vorstadt f, Vorort m; ~an [sə'bəːbən] vorstädtisch.

subvention [sʌb'venʃən] 1. Subvention f; 2. subventionieren.

subver|sion [sʌb'vəːʃən] Umsturz m; ~sive [~əsiv] zerstörend (of acc.); subversiv; ~t [~əːt] (um-)stürzen; untergraben.

subway ['sʌbwei] (bsd. Fußgänger-) Unterführung f; Am. Untergrundbahn f.

succeed [sək'siːd] Erfolg haben; glücken, gelingen; (nach)folgen (dat.); ~ to übernehmen; erben.

success [sək'ses] Erfolg m; ~ful □ [~sful] erfolgreich; ~ion [~eʃən] (Nach-, Erb-, Reihen)Folge f; Nachkommenschaft f; in ~ nacheinander; ~ive [~esiv] aufeinanderfolgend; ~or [~sə] Nachfolger(in). [fen.]

succo(u)r ['sʌkə] 1. Hilfe f; 2. hel-

succulent □ ['sʌkjulənt] saftig.

succumb [sə'kʌm] unter-, erliegen.

such [sʌtʃ] solch(er, -e, -es); derartig; so groß; ~ a man ein solcher Mann; ~ as die, welche.

**suck** [sʌk] **1.** (ein)saugen; saugen an (*dat.*); aussaugen; lutschen; **2.** Saugen *n*; ~er ['sʌkə] Saugorgan *n*; ♀ Wurzelsproß *m*; *Am.* Einfaltspinsel *m*; ~le ['sʌkl] säugen, stillen; ~ling [~liŋ] Säugling *m*.

**suction** ['sʌkʃən] (An)Saugen *n*; Sog *m*; *attr.* Saug...

**sudden** □ ['sʌdn] plötzlich; *all of a* ~ ganz plötzlich.

**suds** [sʌdz] *pl.* Seifenlauge *f*; Seifenschaum *m*; ~y *Am.* ['sʌdzi] schaumig, seifig.

**sue** [sju:] *v/t.* verklagen; ~ *out* erwirken; *v/i.* nachsuchen (*for* um); klagen.

**suède** [sweid] (feines) Wildleder.

**suet** [sjuit] Nierenfett *n*; Talg *m*.

**suffer** ['sʌfə] *v/i.* leiden (*from* an *dat.*); *v/t.* erleiden, erdulden, (zu-)lassen; ~ance [~ərəns] Duldung *f*; ~er [~rə] Leidende(r *m*) *f*; Dulder(in); ~ing [~riŋ] Leiden *n*.

**suffice** [sə'fais] genügen; ~ *it to say* es sei nur gesagt.

**sufficien|cy** [sə'fiʃənsi] genügende Menge; Auskommen *n*; ~t [~nt] genügend, ausreichend.

**suffix** *gr.* ['sʌfiks] **1.** anhängen; **2.** Nachsilbe *f*, Suffix *n*.

**suffocate** ['sʌfəkeit] ersticken.

**suffrage** ['sʌfridʒ] (Wahl)Stimme *f*; Wahl-, Stimmrecht *n*.

**suffuse** [sə'fju:z] übergießen; überziehen.

**sugar** ['ʃugə] **1.** Zucker *m*; **2.** zuckern; ~basin, *Am.* ~bowl Zuckerdose *f*; ~cane ♀ Zuckerrohr *n*; ~coat überzuckern, versüßen; ~y [~əri] zuckerig; zuckersüß.

**suggest** [sə'dʒest] vorschlagen, anregen; nahelegen; vorbringen; *Gedanken* eingeben; andeuten; denken lassen an (*acc.*); ~ion [~tʃən] Anregung *f*; Rat *m*, Vorschlag *m*; Suggestion *f*; Eingebung *f*; Andeutung *f*; ~ive □ [~tiv] anregend; andeutend (*of acc.*); gehaltvoll; zweideutig.

**suicide** ['sjuisaid] **1.** Selbstmord *m*; Selbstmörder(in); **2.** *Am.* Selbstmord begehen.

**suit** [sju:t] **1.** (Herren)Anzug *m*; (Damen)Kostüm *n*; Anliegen *n*; (Heirats)Antrag *m*; *Karten:* Farbe *f*; ♯♯ Prozeß *m*; **2.** *v/t.* j-m passen, zusagen, bekommen; j-n kleiden; j-m stehen, passen zu (*Kleidungsstück etc.*); ~ *oneself* tun, was e-m beliebt; ~ *s.th. to* et. anpassen (*dat.*); *be* ~*ed* geeignet sein (*for* für), passen (*to* zu); *v/i.* passen; ~able □ ['sju:təbl] passend, geeignet; entsprechend; ~case (Hand)Koffer *m*; ~e [swi:t] Gefolge *n*; (Reihen)Folge *f*; ♪ Suite *f*; *a.* ~ *of rooms* Zimmerflucht *f*; Garnitur *f*, (Zimmer)Einrichtung *f*; ~or ['sju:tə] Freier *m*; ♯♯ Kläger(in).

**sulk** [sʌlk] schmollen, bocken; ~iness ['sʌlkinis] üble Laune; ~s *pl.* = *sulkiness*; ~y ['sʌlki] **1.** verdrießlich; launisch; schmollend; **2.** *Sport:* Traberwagen *m*, Sulky *n*.

**sullen** □ ['sʌlən] verdrossen, mürrisch.

**sully** ['sʌli] *mst fig.* beflecken.

**sulphur** ♫ ['sʌlfə] Schwefel *m*; ~ic [sʌl'fjuərik] Schwefel...

**sultriness** ['sʌltrinis] Schwüle *f*.

**sultry** □ ['sʌltri] schwül; *fig.* heftig, hitzig.

**sum** [sʌm] **1.** Summe *f*; Betrag *m*; *fig.* Inbegriff *m*, Inhalt *m*; Rechenaufgabe *f*; *do* ~*s* rechnen; **2.** *mst* ~ *up* zs.-rechnen; zs.-fassen.

**summar|ize** ['sʌməraiz] (kurz) zs.-fassen; ~y [~ri] **1.** □ kurz (zs.-gefaßt); ♯♯ Schnell...; **2.** (kurze) Inhaltsangabe, Auszug *m*.

**summer** ['sʌmə] Sommer *m*; ~ *resort* Sommerfrische *f*; ~ *school* Ferienkurs *m*; ~ly [~əli], ~y [~əri] sommerlich.

**summit** ['sʌmit] Gipfel *m* (*a. fig.*).

**summon** ['sʌmən] auffordern; (be-)rufen; ♯♯ vorladen; *Mut etc.* aufbieten; ~s Aufforderung *f*; ♯♯ Vorladung *f*.

**sumptuous** □ ['sʌmptjuəs] kostbar.

**sun** [sʌn] **1.** Sonne *f*; *attr.* Sonnen...; **2.** (sich) sonnen; ~bath Sonnenbad *n*; ~beam Sonnenstrahl *m*; ~burn Sonnenbräune *f*; Sonnenbrand *m*.

**Sunday** ['sʌndi] Sonntag *m*.

**sun|dial** ['sʌndaiəl] Sonnenuhr *f*; ~down Sonnenuntergang *m*.

**sundr|ies** ['sʌndriz] *pl. bsd.* ♦ Verschiedene(s) *n*; Extraausgaben *f/pl.*; ~y [~ri] verschiedene.

**sung** [sʌŋ] *pret. u. p.p. von sing*.

**sun-glasses** ['sʌnglɑ:siz] *pl.* (*a pair of* ~ *pl.* eine) Sonnenbrille *f*.

**sunk** [sʌŋk] *pret. u. p.p. von sink* 1.

**sunken** ['sʌŋkən] **1.** *p.p. von sink* 1; **2.** *adj.* versunken; *fig.* eingefallen.

**sun|ny** □ ['sʌni] sonnig; ~rise Sonnenaufgang *m*; ~set Sonnenuntergang *m*; ~shade Sonnenschirm *m*; ~shine Sonnenschein *m*; ~stroke ♯ Sonnenstich *m*.

**sup** [sʌp] zu Abend essen.

**super** F ['sju:pə] erstklassig, prima, super.

**super|...** ['sju:pə] Über..., über...; Ober..., ober...; Groß...; ~abundant □ [sju:pərə'bʌndənt] überreichlich; überschwenglich; ~annuate [~ə'rænjueit] pensionieren; ~d ausgedient; veraltet (*S.*).

**superb** □ [sju:(:)'pə:b] prächtig; herrlich.

**super|charger** *mot.* ['sju:pətʃɑ:dʒə] Kompressor *m*; ~cilious [sju:pə-

'siliəs] hochmütig; **~ficial** □ [~ə'fiʃəl] oberflächlich; **~fine** ['sju:pə'fain] extrafein; **~fluity** [sju:pə-flu(:)iti] Überfluß *m*; **~fluous** □ [sju(:)'pə:fluəs] überflüssig; **~heat** ⊕ [sju:pə'hi:t] überhitzen; **~human** □ [~'hju:mən] übermenschlich; **~impose** ['sju:pərim'pouz] darauf-, darüberlegen; **~induce** [~rin'dju:s] noch hinzufügen; **~intend** [sju:prin'tend] die Oberaufsicht haben über (*acc.*); überwachen; **~intendent** [~dənt] 1. Leiter *m*, Direktor *m*; (Ober)Aufseher *m*, Inspektor *m*; 2. aufsichtführend.

**superior** [sju(:)'piəriə] 1. □ ober; höher(stehend); vorgesetzt; besser, hochwertiger; überlegen (*to dat.*); vorzüglich; 2. Höherstehende(r *m*) *f*, *bsd.* Vorgesetzte(r *m*) *f*; *eccl.* Obere(r) *m*; *mst* Lady ♀, Mother ♀ *eccl.* Oberin *f*; **~ity** [sju(:)piəri'ɔriti] Überlegenheit *f*.

**super|lative** [sju(:)'pɔ:lətiv] 1. □ höchst; überragend; 2. *a.* ~ degree *gr.* Superlativ *m*; **~market** Supermarkt *m*; **~natural** □ [sju:pə'nætʃrəl] übernatürlich; **~numerary** [~'nju:mərəri] 1. überzählig; 2. Überzählige(r *m*) *f*; *thea.* Statist (-in); **~scription** [~'skripʃən] Über-, Aufschrift *f*; **~sede** [~'si:d] ersetzen; verdrängen; absetzen; *fig.* überholen; **~sonic** *phys.* ['sju:pə'sonik] Überschall...; **~stition** [sju:pə'stiʃən] Aberglaube *m*; **~stitious** □ [~ʃəs] abergläubisch; **~vene** [~'vi:n] noch hinzukommen; unerwartet eintreten; **~vise** ['sju:pəvaiz] beaufsichtigen, überwachen; **~vision** [sju:pə'viʒən] (Ober)Aufsicht *f*; Beaufsichtigung *f*; **~visor** ['sju:pəvaizə] Aufseher *m*, Inspektor *m*.

**supper** ['sʌpə] Abendessen *n*; *the (Lord's)* ♀ das Heilige Abendmahl.

**supplant** [sə'pla:nt] verdrängen.

**supple** ['sʌpl] geschmeidig (machen).

**supplement** 1. ['sʌplimənt] Ergänzung *f*; Nachtrag *m*; (Zeitungs-*etc.*)Beilage *f*; 2. [~ment] ergänzen; **~al** □ [sʌpli'mentl], **~ary** [~təri] Ergänzungs...; nachträglich; Nachtrags...

**suppliant** ['sʌpliənt] 1. □ demütig bittend, flehend; 2. Bittsteller(in).

**supplicat|e** ['sʌplikeit] demütig bitten, anflehen; **~ion** [sʌpli'keiʃən] demütige Bitte.

**supplier** [sə'plaiə] Lieferant(in).

**supply** [sə'plai] 1. liefern; *e-m* Mangel abhelfen; *e-e Stelle* ausfüllen; vertreten; ausstatten, versorgen; ergänzen; 2. Lieferung *f*; Versorgung *f*; Zufuhr *f*; Vorrat *m*; Bedarf *m*; Angebot *n*; (Stell)Vertretung *f*; *mst supplies pl. parl.* Etat *m*.

**support** [sə'pɔ:t] 1. Stütze *f*; Hilfe *f*; ⊕ Träger *m*; Unterstützung *f*; Lebensunterhalt *m*; 2. (unter)stützen, unterhalten, sorgen für (*Familie etc.*); aufrechterhalten; (v)ertragen.

**suppose** [sə'pouz] annehmen; voraussetzen; vermuten; *he is* ~*d to do* er soll tun; ~ *we go* gehen wir; *wie wär's, wenn wir gingen.*

**supposed** □ [sə'pouzd] vermeintlich; **~ly** [~zidli] vermutlich.

**supposition** [sʌpə'ziʃən] Voraussetzung *f*; Annahme *f*; Vermutung *f*.

**suppress** [sə'pres] unterdrücken; **~ion** [~eʃən] Unterdrückung *f*.

**suppurate** ['sʌpjuəreit] eitern.

**suprem|acy** [sju'preməsi] Oberhoheit *f*; Vorherrschaft *f*; Überlegenheit *f*; Vorrang *m*; **~e** □ [sju(:)'pri:m] höchst; oberst; Ober...; größt.

**surcharge** [sɔ:'tʃɑ:dʒ] 1. überladen; Zuschlag *od.* Nachgebühr erheben von *j-m*; 2. ['sɔ:tʃɑ:dʒ] Überladung *f*; (Straf)Zuschlag *m*; Nachgebühr *f*; Überdruck *m auf Briefmarken*.

**sure** □ [ʃuə] *allg.* sicher; *to be* ~!, ~ *enough*!, *Am.* ~! F sicher(lich)!; **~ly** ['ʃuəli] sicherlich; **~ty** ['ʃuəti] Bürge *m*.

**surf** [sɔ:f] Brandung *f*.

**surface** ['sɔ:fis] 1. (Ober)Fläche *f*; ⚒ Tragfläche *f*; 2. ⚓ auftauchen (*U-Boot*).

**surf|-board** ['sɔ:fbɔ:d] Wellenreiterbrett *n*; **~-boat** Brandungsboot *n*.

**surfeit** ['sɔ:fit] 1. Übersättigung *f*; Ekel *m*; 2. (sich) überladen.

**surf-riding** ['sɔ:fraidiŋ] *Sport*: Wellenreiten *n*.

**surge** [sɔ:dʒ] 1. Woge *f*; 2. wogen.

**surg|eon** ['sɔ:dʒən] Chirurg *m*; **~ery** [~əri] Chirurgie *f*; Sprechzimmer *n*; ~ *hours pl.* Sprechstunde(n *pl.*) *f*.

**surgical** □ ['sɔ:dʒikəl] chirurgisch.

**surly** □ ['sɔ:li] mürrisch; grob.

**surmise** 1. ['sɔ:maiz] Vermutung *f*; Argwohn *m*; 2. [sɔ:'maiz] vermuten; argwöhnen.

**surmount** [sɔ:'maunt] übersteigen; überragen; *fig.* überwinden.

**surname** ['sɔ:neim] Zu-, Nachname *m*.

**surpass** *fig.* [sɔ:'pɑ:s] übersteigen, übertreffen; **~ing** [~siŋ] überragend.

**surplus** ['sɔ:pləs] 1. Überschuß *m*, Mehr *n*; 2. überschüssig; Über...

**surprise** [sə'praiz] 1. Überraschung *f*; ⚔ Überrump(e)lung *f*; 2. überraschen; ⚔ überrumpeln.

**surrender** [sə'rendə] 1. Übergabe *f*, Ergebung *f*; Kapitulation *f*; Aufgeben *n*; 2. *v/t.* übergeben; aufgeben; *v/i. a.* ~ *o.s.* sich ergeben.

**surround** [sə'raund] umgeben; ⚔

umzingeln; ~ing [~diŋ] umliegend; ~ings pl. Umgebung f.

**surtax** ['sɔːtæks] Steuerzuschlag m.

**survey** 1. [sɔ'vei] überblicken; mustern; begutachten; surv. vermessen; 2. ['sɔːvei] Überblick m (a. fig.); Besichtigung f; Gutachten n; surv. Vermessung f; ~or [sə(ː)-'veiə] Land-, Feldmesser m.

**surviv|al** [sə'vaivəl] Über-, Fortleben n; Überbleibsel n; ~e [~aiv] überleben; noch leben; fortleben; am Leben bleiben; bestehen bleiben; ~or [~və] Überlebende(r m) f.

**suscept|ible** ☐ [sə'septəbl], ~ive [~tiv] empfänglich (of, to für); empfindlich (gegen); be ~ of et. zulassen.

**suspect** 1. [səs'pekt] (be)argwöhnen; in Verdacht haben, verdächtigen; vermuten, befürchten; 2. ['sʌspekt] Verdächtige(r m) f; 3. [~] = ~ed [səs'pektid] verdächtig.

**suspend** [səs'pend] (auf)hängen; aufschieben; in der Schwebe lassen; Zahlung einstellen; aussetzen; suspendieren, sperren; ~ed schwebend; ~er [~də] Strumpf-, Sockenhalter m; ~s pl. Am. Hosenträger m/pl.

**suspens|e** [səs'pens] Ungewißheit f; Unentschiedenheit f; Spannung f; ~ion [~nʃən] Aufhängung f; Aufschub m; Einstellung f; Suspendierung f, Amtsenthebung f; Sperre f; ~ion bridge Hängebrücke f; ~ive ☐ [~nsiv] aufschiebend.

**suspici|on** [səs'piʃən] Verdacht m; Argwohn m; fig. Spur f; ~ous ☐ [~ʃəs] argwöhnisch; verdächtig.

**sustain** [səs'tein] stützen; fig. aufrechterhalten; aushalten; erleiden; ⟐⟐ anerkennen; ~ed anhaltend; ununterbrochen.

**sustenance** ['sʌstinəns] (Lebens-) Unterhalt m; Nahrung f.

**svelte** [svelt] schlank (Frau).

**swab** [swɔb] 1. Aufwischmop m; ⚕ Tupfer m; ⚕ Abstrich m; 2. aufwischen.

**swaddl|e** ['swɔdl] Baby wickeln; ~ing-clothes mst fig. [~liŋklouðz] pl. Windeln f/pl.

**swagger** ['swægə] 1. stolzieren; prahlen, renommieren; 2. F elegant.

**swale** Am. [sweil] Mulde f, Niederung f.

**swallow** ['swɔlou] 1. orn. Schwalbe f; Schlund m; Schluck m; 2. (hinunter-, ver)schlucken; fig. Ansicht etc. begierig aufnehmen.

**swam** [swæm] pret. von swim 1.

**swamp** [swɔmp] 1. Sumpf m; 2. überschwemmen (a. fig.); versenken; ~y ['swɔmpi] sumpfig.

**swan** [swɔn] Schwan m.

**swank** sl. [swæŋk] 1. Angabe f,

Protzerei f; 2. angeben, protzen; ~y ['swæŋki] protzig, angeberisch.

**swap** F [swɔp] 1. Tausch m; 2. (ver-, aus)tauschen.

**sward** [swɔːd] Rasen m.

**swarm** [swɔːm] 1. Schwarm m; Haufe(n) m, Gewimmel n; 2. schwärmen; wimmeln (with von).

**swarthy** ☐ ['swɔːði] dunkelfarbig.

**swash** [swɔʃ] plan(t)schen.

**swat** [swɔt] Fliege klatschen.

**swath** ↗ [swɔːθ] Schwade(n m) f.

**swathe** [sweið] (ein)wickeln.

**sway** [swei] 1. Schaukeln n; Einfluß m; Herrschaft f; 2. schaukeln; beeinflussen; beherrschen.

**swear** [swɛə] [irr.] (be)schwören; fluchen; ~ s.o. in j-n vereidigen.

**sweat** [swet] 1. Schweiß m; by the ~ of one's brow im Schweiße seines Angesichts; all of a ~ F in Schweiß gebadet (a. fig.); 2. [irr.] v/i. schwitzen; v/t. (aus)schwitzen; in Schweiß bringen; Arbeiter ausbeuten; ~er ['swetə] Sweater m, Pullover m; Trainingsjacke f; fig. Ausbeuter m; ~y [~ti] schweißig; verschwitzt.

**Swede** [swiːd] Schwed|e m, -in f.

**Swedish** ['swiːdiʃ] 1. schwedisch; 2. Schwedisch n.

**sweep** [swiːp] 1. [irr.] fegen (a. fig.), kehren; fig. streifen; bestreichen (a. ✕); (majestätisch) (dahin)rauschen; 2. (fig. Dahin)Fegen n; Kehren n; Schwung m; Biegung f; Spielraum m, Bereich m; Schornsteinfeger m; make a clean ~ reinen Tisch machen (of mit); ~er ['swiːpə] (Straßen)Feger m; Kehrmaschine f; ~ing ☐ [~piŋ] weitgehend; schwungvoll; ~ings pl. Kehricht m, Müll m.

**sweet** [swiːt] 1. ☐ süß; lieblich; freundlich; frisch; duftend; have a ~ tooth ein Leckermaul sein; 2. Liebling m; Süßigkeit f, Bonbon m, n; Nachtisch m; ~en ['swiːtn] (ver)süßen; ~heart Liebling m, Liebste(r m) f; ~ish [~tiʃ] süßlich; ~meat Bonbon m, n; kandierte Frucht; ~ness [~tnis] Süßigkeit f; Lieblichkeit f; ~ pea ♀ Gartenwicke f.

**swell** [swel] 1. [irr.] v/i. (an)schwellen; sich blähen; sich (aus)bauchen; v/t. (an)schwellen lassen; aufblähen; 2. F fein; sl. prima; 3. Anschwellen n; Schwellung f; ⚓ Dünung f; F feiner Herr; ~ing ['sweliŋ] Geschwulst f.

**swelter** ['sweltə] vor Hitze umkommen.

**swept** [swept] pret. u. p.p. von sweep 1.

**swerve** [swəːv] 1. (plötzlich) abbiegen; 2. (plötzliche) Wendung f.

**swift** ☐ [swift] schnell, eilig, flink; ~ness ['swiftnis] Schnelligkeit f.

**swill** [swil] 1. Spülicht *n*; Schweinetrank *m*; 2. spülen; saufen.

**swim** [swim] 1. [*irr.*] (durch-)schwimmen; schweben; *my head* ~s mir schwindelt; 2. Schwimmen *n*; *be in the* ~ auf dem laufenden sein; ~ming ['swimiŋ] 1. Schwimmen *n*; 2. Schwimm...; ~bath (*bsd.* Hallen)Schwimmbad *n*; ~pool Schwimmbecken *n*; ~suit Badeanzug *m*.

**swindle** ['swindl] 1. (be)schwindeln; 2. Schwindel *m*.

**swine** [swain] Schwein(e *pl.*) *n*.

**swing** [swiŋ] 1. [*irr.*] schwingen, schwanken; ~ baumeln; (sich) schaukeln; schwenken; sich drehen; 2. Schwingen *n*; Schwung *m*; Schaukel *f*; Spielraum *m*; *in full* ~ in vollem Gange; ~door ['swiŋdɔ:] Drehtür *f*.

**swinish** □ ['swaini∫] schweinisch.

**swipe** [swaip] 1. aus vollem Arm schlagen; 2. starker Schlag.

**swirl** [swə:l] 1. (herum)wirbeln, strudeln; 2. Wirbel *m*, Strudel *m*.

**Swiss** [swis] 1. schweizerisch, Schweizer...; 2. Schweizer(in); *the* ~ *pl.* die Schweizer *m/pl.*

**switch** [swit∫] 1. Gerte *f*; Weiche *f*; Schalter *m*; falscher Zopf; 2. peitschen; rangieren; (um-)schalten; *fig.* wechseln, überleiten; ~ *on* (*off*) ein- (aus)schalten; ~board ['swit∫bɔ:d] Schaltbrett *n*, -tafel *f*.

**swivel** ⊕ ['swivl] Drehring *m*; *attr.* Dreh...

**swollen** ['swoulən] *p.p. von* swell 1.

**swoon** [swu:n] 1. Ohnmacht *f*; 2. in Ohnmacht fallen.

**swoop** [swu:p] 1. ~ *down on od. upon* (herab)stoßen auf (*acc.*) (*Raubvogel*); überfallen; 2. Stoß *m*.

**swop** F [swɔp] *s.* swap.

**sword** [sɔ:d] Schwert *n*, Degen *m*.

**swordsman** ['sɔ:dzmən] Fechter *m*.

**swore** [swɔ:] *pret. von* swear.

**sworn** [swɔ:n] *p.p. von* swear.

**swum** [swʌm] *p.p. von* swim 1.

**swung** [swʌŋ] *pret. u. p.p. von* swing 1.

**sycamore** ♀ ['sikəmɔ:] Bergahorn *m*; *Am.* Platane *f*.

**sycophant** ['sikəfənt] Kriecher *m*.

**syllable** ['siləbl] Silbe *f*.

**syllabus** ['siləbəs] (*bsd.* Vorlesungs-)Verzeichnis *n*; (*bsd.* Lehr)Plan *m*.

**sylvan** ['silvən] waldig, Wald...

**symbol** ['simbəl] Symbol *n*, Sinnbild *n*; ~ic(al □) [sim'bɔlik(əl)] sinnbildlich; ~ism ['simbəlizəm] Symbolik *f*.

**symmetr|ical** □ [si'metrikəl] ebenmäßig; ~y ['simitri] Ebenmaß *n*.

**sympath|etic** [simpə'θetik] (~ally) mitfühlend; sympathisch; ~ *strike* Sympathiestreik *m*; ~ize ['simpəθaiz] sympathisieren, mitfühlen; ~y [~θi] Sympathie *f*, Mitgefühl *n*.

**symphony** ♪ ['simfəni] Symphonie *f*.

**symptom** ['simptəm] Symptom *n*.

**synchron|ize** ['siŋkrənaiz] *v/i.* gleichzeitig sein; *v/t.* als gleichzeitig zs.-stellen; *Uhren* auf-ea. abstimmen; *Tonfilm*: synchronisieren; ~ous □ [~nəs] gleichzeitig.

**syndicate** 1. ['sindikit] Syndikat *n*; 2. [~keit] zu e-m Syndikat verbinden.

**synonym** ['sinənim] Synonym *n*; ~ous □ [si'nɔniməs] sinnverwandt.

**synop|sis** [si'nɔpsis], *pl.* ~ses [~si:z] zs.-fassende Übersicht.

**syntax** *gr.* ['sintæks] Syntax *f*.

**synthe|sis** ['sinθisis], *pl.* ~ses [~si:z] Synthese *f*, Verbindung *f*; ~tic(al □) [sin'θetik(əl)] synthetisch.

**syringe** ['sirindʒ] 1. Spritze *f*; 2. (be-, ein-, aus)spritzen.

**syrup** ['sirəp] Sirup *m*.

**system** ['sistim] System *n*; Organismus *m*, Körper *m*; Plan *m*, Ordnung *f*; ~atic [sisti'mætik] (~ally) systematisch.

# T

**tab** [tæb] Streifen *m*; Schildchen *n*; Anhänger *m*; Schlaufe *f*, Aufhänger *m*; F Rechnung *f*, Konto *n*.

**table** ['teibl] 1. Tisch *m*, Tafel *f*; Tisch-, Tafelrunde *f*; Tabelle *f*, Verzeichnis *n*; *Bibel*: Gesetzestafel *f*; *s.* ~land; *at* ~ bei Tisch; *turn the* ~s den Spieß umdrehen (*on gegen*); 2. auf den Tisch legen; tabellarisch anordnen.

**tableau** ['tæblou], *pl.* ~x [~ouz] lebendes Bild.

**table|-cloth** ['teiblklɔθ] Tischtuch *n*; ~land Tafelland *n*, Plateau *n*,

Hochebene *f*; ~linen Tischwäsche *f*; ~spoon Eßlöffel *m*.

**tablet** ['tæblit] Täfelchen *n*; (Gedenk)Tafel *f*; (Schreib- *etc.*)Block *m*; Stück *n* Seife; Tablette *f*.

**table-top** ['teibltɔp] Tischplatte *f*.

**taboo** [tə'bu:] 1. tabu, unantastbar; verboten; 2. Tabu *n*; Verbot *n*; 3. verbieten.

**tabulate** ['tæbjuleit] tabellarisch ordnen.

**tacit** □ ['tæsit] stillschweigend; ~urn □ [~tə:n] schweigsam.

**tack** [tæk] 1. Stift *m*, Zwecke *f*;

Heftstich *m*; ⚓ Halse *f*; ⚓ Gang *m*
*beim Lavieren*; *fig.* Weg *m*; **2.** *v/t.*
(an)heften; *fig.* (an)hängen; *v/i.* ⚓
wenden; *fig.* lavieren.

**tackle** ['tækl] **1.** Gerät *n*; ⚓ Takel-,
Tauwerk *n*; ⊕ Flaschenzug *m*;
**2.** (an)packen; in Angriff nehmen;
fertig werden mit; *j-n* angehen (*for*
um).

**tacky** ['tæki] klebrig; *Am.* F schäbig.

**tact** [tækt] Takt *m*, Feingefühl *n*;
**~ful** □ ['tæktful] taktvoll.

**tactics** ['tæktiks] Taktik *f*.

**tactless** □ ['tæktlis] taktlos.

**tadpole** *zo.* ['tædpoul] Kaulquappe*f*.

**taffeta** ['tæfitə] Taft *m*.

**taffy** *Am.* ['tæfi] = toffee; F Schmus
*m*, Schmeichelei *f*.

**tag** [tæg] **1.** (Schnürsenkel)Stift *m*;
Schildchen *n*, Etikett *n*; Redensart
*f*, Zitat *n*; Zusatz *m*; loses Ende;
Fangen *n* (*Kinderspiel*); **2.** etikettieren, auszeichnen; anhängen (*to*,
*onto* an *acc.*); ~ *after* herlaufen hinter (*dat.*); ~ *together* an-ea.-reihen.

**tail** [teil] **1.** Schwanz *m*; Schweif *m*;
hinteres Ende, Schluß *m*; ~*s* *pl.*
Rückseite *f* e-r Münze; F Frack *m*;
*turn* ~ davonlaufen; ~*s* up in Hoch-
stimmung; **2.** ~ *after* s.o. j-m nach-
laufen; ~ s.o. *Am.* j-n beschatten; ~
*away*, ~ *off* abflauen, sich verlieren;
zögernd enden; ~-*coat* ['teil'kout]
Frack *m*; ~-**light** *mot. etc.* ['teillait]
Rück-, Schlußlicht *n*.

**tailor** ['teilə] **1.** Schneider *m*;
**2.** schneidern; ~-**made** Schneider..., Maß...

**taint** [teint] **1.** Flecken *m*, Makel *m*;
⚕ Ansteckung *f*; *fig. krankhafter*
Zug; Verderbnis *f*; **2.** beflecken;
verderben; ⚕ anstecken.

**take** [teik] **1.** (*irr.*) *v/t.* nehmen; an-,
ab-, auf-, ein-, fest-, hin-, weg-
nehmen; (weg)bringen; *Speise* (zu
sich) nehmen; *Maßnahme*, *Gelegenheit* ergreifen; *Eid*, *Gelübde*, *Examen* ablegen; *phot.* aufnehmen; *et.
gut etc.* aufnehmen; *Beleidigung*
hinnehmen; fassen, ergreifen; fangen; *fig.* fesseln; sich *e-e Krankheit*
holen; erfordern; brauchen; *Zeit*
dauern; auffassen; halten, ansehen
(*for* für); I ~ *it that* ich nehme an,
daß; ~ *breath* verschnaufen; ~ *comfort* sich trösten; ~ *compassion* on
Mitleid empfinden mit; sich erbarmen (*gen.*); ~ *counsel* beraten; ~ *a
drive* e-e Fahrt machen; ~ *fire* Feuer
fangen; ~ *in hand* unternehmen; ~
*hold of* ergreifen; ~ *pity* on Mitleid
haben mit; ~ *place* stattfinden;
spielen (*Handlung*); ~ *a seat* Platz
nehmen; ~ *a walk* e-n Spaziergang
machen; ~ *my word for it* verlaß
dich drauf; ~ *about* herumführen;
~ *along* mitnehmen; ~ *down* her-
unternehmen; notieren; ~ *for* halten für; ~ *from* j-m wegnehmen;

abziehen von; ~ *in enger* machen;
*Zeitung* halten; aufnehmen (*als
Gast etc.*); einschließen; verstehen;
erfassen; F *j-n* reinlegen; ~ *off* ab-,
wegnehmen; *Kleid* ausziehen, *Hut*
abnehmen; ~ *on* an-, übernehmen;
*Arbeiter etc.* einstellen; *Fahrgäste*
zusteigen lassen; ~ *out* heraus-, entnehmen; *Fleck* entfernen; *j-n* ausführen; *Versicherung* abschließen; ~
*to pieces* auseinandernehmen; ~
*up* aufnehmen; sich *e-r S.* annehmen; *Raum*, *Zeit* in Anspruch nehmen; *v/i.* wirken, ein-, anschlagen;
gefallen, ziehen; ~ *after* j-m nachschlagen; ~ *off* abspringen; ⚓ aufsteigen, starten; ~ *on* F Anklang
finden; ~ *over* die Amtsgewalt übernehmen; ~ *to* liebgewinnen; *fig.*
sich verlegen auf (*acc.*); Zuflucht
nehmen zu; sich ergeben (*dat.*); ~
*up* F sich bessern (*Wetter*); ~ *up
with* sich anfreunden mit; *that
won't* ~ *with me* das verfängt bei
mir nicht; **2.** Fang *m*; *Geld*-Ein-
nahme *f*; *Film:* Szene(naufnahme)
*f*; ~-**in** F ['teik'in] Reinfall *m*; ~-**n**
['teikən] *p.p.* von tale 1; be ~ besetzt sein; be ~ *with* entzückt sein
von; be ~ *ill* krank werden; ~-**off**
['teik:f] Karikatur *f*; Absprung *m*;
⚓ Start *m*.

**taking** ['teikiŋ] **1.** □ F anziehend,
fesselnd, einnehmend; ansteckend;
**2.** (An-, Ab-, Auf-, Ein-, Ent-,
Hin-, Weg- *etc.*)Nehmen *n*; Inbe-
sitznahme *f*; ⚔ Einnahme *f*; F Aufregung *f*; ~*s* *pl.* ✝ Einnahme *f*/*pl.*

**tale** [teil] Erzählung *f*, Geschichte *f*;
Märchen *n*, Sage *f*; *it tells its own* ~
es spricht für sich selbst; ~-**bearer**
['teilbeərə] Zuträger(in).

**talent** ['tælənt] Talent *n*, Begabung
*f*, Anlage *f*; ~-**ed** [_tid] talentvoll,
begabt.

**talk** [tɔːk] **1.** Gespräch *n*; Unterredung *f*; Plauderei *f*; Vortrag *m*;
Geschwätz *n*; **2.** sprechen, reden
(*von et.*); plaudern; ~-**ative** □ ['tɔː-
kətiv] gesprächig, geschwätzig; ~-**er**
['tɔːkə] Schwätzer(in); Sprechen-
de(r *m*) *f*.

**tall** [tɔːl] groß, lang, hoch; F übertrieben, unglaublich; *that's a* ~
*order* F das ist ein bißchen viel
verlangt.

**tallow** ['tælou] ausgelassener Talg.

**tally** ['tæli] **1.** Kerbholz *n*; Gegenstück *n* (of *zu*); Kennzeichen *n*;
**2.** übereinstimmen.

**talon** *orn.* ['tælən] Kralle *f*, Klaue
*f*.

**tame** [teim] **1.** □ zahm; folgsam;
harmlos; lahm, fad(e); **2.** (be)zäh-
men, bändigen.

**Tammany** *Am.* ['tæməni] New
Yorker Demokraten-Vereinigung.

**tamper** ['tæmpə]: ~ *with* sich (unbefugt) zu schaffen machen mit;

*j-n* zu bestechen suchen; *Urkunde* fälschen.

**tan** [tæn] **1.** Lohe *f*; Lohfarbe *f*; (Sonnen)Bräune *f*; **2.** lohfarben; **3.** gerben; bräunen.

**tang** [tæŋ] Beigeschmack *m*; *scharfer* Klang; ♀ Seetang *m*.

**tangent** ['tændʒənt] Å Tangente *f*; *fly od.* go off at a ~ vom Gegenstand abspringen.

**tangerine** ♀ [tændʒə'ri:n] Mandarine *f*.

**tangible** □ ['tændʒəbl] fühlbar, greifbar (*a. fig.*); klar.

**tangle** ['tæŋgl] **1.** Gewirr *n*; Verwicklung *f*; **2.** (sich) verwirren, verwickeln.

**tank** [tæŋk] **1.** Zisterne *f*, Wasserbehälter *m*; ⊕, ✗ Tank *m*; **2.** tanken. [(Bier)Krug *m*.)

**tankard** ['tæŋkəd] Kanne *f*, *bsd.*)

**tanner** ['tænə] Gerber *m*; ~y [~əri] Gerberei *f*.

**tantalize** ['tæntəlaiz] quälen.

**tantamount** ['tæntəmaunt] gleichbedeutend (mit).

**tantrum** F ['tæntrəm] Koller *m*.

**tap** [tæp] **1.** leichtes Klopfen; (Wasser-, Gas-, Zapf)Hahn *m*; Zapfen *m*; Schankstube *f*; F Sorte *f*; ~*s pl.* *Am.* ✗ Zapfenstreich *m*; **2.** pochen, klopfen, tippen (auf, an, gegen *acc.*); an-, abzapfen; ~**dance** ['tæpda:ns] Stepptanz *m*.

**tape** [teip] schmales Band; *Sport:* Zielband *n*; *tel.* Papierstreifen *m*; Tonband *n*; red ~ Bürokratismus *m*; ~**measure** ['teipmeʒə] Bandmaß *n*.

**taper** ['teipə] **1.** dünne Wachskerze; **2.** *adj.* spitz (zulaufend); schlank; **3.** *v/i.* spitz zulaufen; *v/t.* zuspitzen.

**tape| recorder** ['teiprikɔ:də] Tonbandgerät *n*; ~ **recording** Tonbandaufnahme *f*.

**tapestry** ['tæpistri] Gobelin *m*.

**tapeworm** ['teipwə:m] Bandwurm*m*.

**tap-room** ['tæprum] Schankstube*f*.

**tar** [ta:] **1.** Teer *m*; **2.** teeren.

**tardy** □ ['ta:di] langsam; spät.

**tare** ✝ [tɛə] Tara *f*.

**target** ['ta:git] (Schicß)Scheibe *f*; *fig.* Ziel(scheibe *f*) *n*; Ziel(leistung *f*) *n*; Soll *n*; ~ *practice* Scheibenschießen *n*.

**tariff** ['tærif] (*bsd.* Zoll)Tarif *m*.

**tarnish** ['ta:niʃ] **1.** *v/t.* ⊕ trüb *od.* blind machen; *fig.* trüben; *v/i.* trüb werden, anlaufen; **2.** Trübung *f*; Belag *m*.

**tarry**[1] *lit.* ['tæri] säumen, zögern; verweilen.

**tarry**[2] ['ta:ri] teerig.

**tart** [ta:t] **1.** □ sauer, herb; *fig.* scharf, schroff; **2.** (Obst)Torte *f*; *sl.* Dirne *f*.

**tartan** ['ta:tən] Tartan *m*; Schottentuch *n*; Schottenmuster *n*.

**task** [ta:sk] **1.** Aufgabe *f*; Arbeit *f*; take to ~ zur Rede stellen; **2.** beschäftigen; in Anspruch nehmen.

**tassel** ['tæsəl] Troddel *f*, Quaste *f*.

**taste** [teist] **1.** Geschmack *m*; (Kost)Probe *f*; Lust *f* (for zu); **2.** kosten, schmecken; versuchen; genießen; ~**ful** □ ['teistful] geschmackvoll; ~**less** □ [~tlis] geschmacklos.

**tasty** □ F ['teisti] schmackhaft.

**ta-ta** ['tæ'ta:] auf Wiedersehen!

**tatter** ['tætə] **1.** zerfetzen; **2.** ~*s pl.* Fetzen *m/pl.*

**tattle** ['tætl] **1.** schwatzen; tratschen; **2.** Geschwätz *n*; Tratsch *m*.

**tattoo** [tə'tu:] **1.** ✗ Zapfenstreich *m*; Tätowierung *f*; **2.** *fig.* trommeln; tätowieren.

**taught** [tɔ:t] *pret. u. p.p. von* teach.

**taunt** [tɔ:nt] **1.** Stichelei *f*, Spott *m*; **2.** verhöhnen, verspotten.

**taut** ⊕ [tɔ:t] steif, straff; schmuck.

**tavern** ['tævən] Schenke *f*.

**tawdry** □ ['tɔ:dri] billig; kitschig.

**tawny** ['tɔ:ni] lohfarben.

**tax** [tæks] **1.** Steuer *f*, Abgabe *f*; *fig.* Inanspruchnahme *f* (*on, upon gen.*); **2.** besteuern; *fig.* stark in Anspruch nehmen; ✗ *Kosten* schätzen; auf e-e harte Probe stellen; *j-n* zur Rede stellen; ~ *s.o.* with *s.th.* j-n e-r S. beschuldigen; ~**ation** [tæk'seiʃən] Besteuerung *f*; Steuer(n *pl.*) *f*; *bsd.* ✗ Schätzung *f*.

**taxi** F ['tæksi] **1.** = ~*cab*; **2.** mit e-m Taxi fahren; ✈ rollen; ~**cab** Taxi *n*, (Auto)Droschke *f*.

**taxpayer** ['tækspeiə] Steuerzahler *m*.

**tea** [ti:] Tee *m*; high ~, meat ~ frühes Abendbrot mit Tee.

**teach** [ti:tʃ] [*irr.*] lehren, unterrichten, *j-m* et. beibringen; ~**able** □ ['ti:tʃəbl] gelehrig; lehrbar; ~**er** [~ʃə] Lehrer(in); ~**in** [~ʃ'in] (politische) Diskussion *als Großveranstaltung.*

**tea|-cosy** ['ti:kouzi] Teewärmer *m*; ~**cup** Teetasse *f*; storm in a ~ *fig.* Sturm *m* im Wasserglas; ~**kettle** Wasserkessel *m*.

**team** [ti:m] Team *n*, Arbeitsgruppe *f*; Gespann *n*; *bsd. Sport:* Mannschaft *f*; ~**ster** ['ti:mstə] Gespannführer *m*; *Am.* LKW-Fahrer *m*; ~**work** Zusammenarbeit *f*, Teamwork *n*; Zusammenspiel *n*.

**teapot** ['ti:pɔt] Teekanne *f*.

**tear**[1] [tɛə] **1.** [*irr.*] zerren, (zer)reißen; rasen, stürmen; **2.** Riß *m*.

**tear**[2] [tiə] Träne *f*.

**tearful** □ ['tiəful] tränenreich.

**tea-room** ['ti:rum] Tearoom *m*. Teestube *f*, Café *n*.

**tease** [ti:z] **1.** necken, hänseln; quälen; **2.** Necker *m*; Quälgeist *m*.

**teat** [ti:t] Zitze *f*; Brustwarze *f*; (Gummi)Sauger *m*.

**technic|al** □ ['teknikəl] technisch; gewerblich, Gewerbe...; fachlich, Fach...; **~ality** [tekni'kæliti] technische Eigentümlichkeit *od.* Einzelheit; Fachausdruck *m*; **~ian** [tek'niʃən] Techniker(in).

**technique** [tek'ni:k] Technik *f*, Verfahren *n*.

**technology** [tek'nɔlədʒi] Gewerbekunde *f*; *school of* ~ Technische Hochschule.

**teddy boy** F ['tedibɔi] Halbstarke(r) *m*.

**tedious** □ ['ti:djəs] langweilig, ermüdend; weitschweifig.

**tee** [ti:] *Sport:* Mal *n*, Ziel *n*; *Golf:* Abschlagmal *n*.

**teem** [ti:m] wimmeln, strotzen (*with* von).

**teens** [ti:nz] *pl.* Lebensjahre *n/pl.* von 13—19.

**teeny** F ['ti:ni] winzig.

**teeth** [ti:θ] *pl. von* tooth; **~e** [ti:ð] zahnen.

**teetotal(l)er** [ti:'toutlə] Abstinenzler(in).

**telecast** ['telika:st] **1.** Fernsehsendung *f*; **2.** [*irr.* (*cast*)] im Fernsehen übertragen.

**telecourse** *Am.* F ['telikɔ:s] Fernsehlehrgang *m*.

**telegram** ['teligræm] Telegramm *n*.

**telegraph** ['teligra:f] **1.** Telegraph *m*; **2.** Telegraphen...; **3.** telegraphieren; **~ic** [teli'græfik] (**~ally**) telegraphisch; telegrammäßig (*Stil*); **~y** [ti'legrəfi] Telegraphie *f*.

**telephon|e** ['telifoun] **1.** Telephon *n*, Fernsprecher *m*; **2.** telephonieren; anrufen; **~e booth** Telephonzelle *f*; **~ic** [teli'fɔnik] (**~ally**) telephonisch; **~y** [ti'lefəni] Fernsprechwesen *n*.

**telephoto** *phot.* ['teli'foutou] *a.* ~ *lens* Teleobjektiv *n*.

**teleprinter** ['teli,printə] Fernschreiber *m*.

**telescope** ['teliskoup] **1.** *opt.* Fernrohr *n*; **2.** (sich) ineinanderschieben.

**teletype** ['telitaip] Fernschreiber *m*.

**televis|e** ['telivaiz] im Fernsehen übertragen; **~ion** [~viʒən] Fernsehen *n*; *watch* ~ fernsehen; **~ion set**, **~or** [~vaizə] Fernsehapparat *m*.

**tell** [tel] [*irr.*] *v/t.* zählen; sagen; erzählen; erkennen; ~ *s.o. to do s.th.* j-m sagen, er solle et. tun; ~ *off* abzählen; auswählen; F abkanzeln; *v/i.* erzählen (*of, about* von); (aus)plaudern; sich auswirken; sitzen (*Hieb etc.*); **~er** ['telə] (Er)Zähler *m*; **~ing** □ ['teliŋ] wirkungsvoll; **~tale** ['telteil] **1.** Klatschbase *f*; ⊕ Anzeiger *m*; **2.** *fig.* verräterisch.

**temerity** [ti'meriti] Unbesonnenheit *f*, Verwegenheit *f*.

**temper** ['tempə] **1.** mäßigen, mildern; *Kalk etc.* anrühren; *Stahl* anlassen; **2.** ⊕ Härte(grad *m*) *f*;

(Gemüts)Ruhe *f*, Gleichmut *m*; Temperament *n*, Wesen *n*; Stimmung *f*; Wut *f*; *lose one's* ~ in Wut geraten; **~ament** [~ərəmənt] Temperament *n*; **~amental** □ [tempərə'mentl] anlagebedingt; launisch; **~ance** ['tempərəns] Mäßigkeit *f*; Enthaltsamkeit *f*; **~ate** □ [~rit] gemäßigt; zurückhaltend; maßvoll; mäßig; **~ature** [~pritʃə] Temperatur *f*.

**tempest** ['tempist] Sturm *m*; Gewitter *n*; **~uous** □ [tem'pestjəs] stürmisch; ungestüm.

**temple** ['templ] Tempel *m*; *anat.* Schläfe *f*.

**tempor|al** □ ['tempərəl] zeitlich; weltlich; **~ary** □ [~əri] zeitweilig; vorläufig; vorübergehend; Not...; (Aus)Hilfs..., Behelfs...; **~ize** [~raiz] Zeit zu gewinnen suchen.

**tempt** [tempt] *j-n* versuchen; verleiten; verlocken; **~ation** [temp'teiʃən] Versuchung *f*; Reiz *m*; **~ing** □ ['temptiŋ] verführerisch.

**ten** [ten] **1.** zehn; **2.** Zehn *f*.

**tenable** ['tenəbl] haltbar (*Theorie etc.*); verliehen (*Amt.*).

**tenaci|ous** □ [ti'neiʃəs] zäh; festhaltend (*of an dat.*); gut (*Gedächtnis*); **~ty** [ti'næsiti] Zähigkeit *f*; Festhalten *n*; Verläßlichkeit *f des Gedächtnisses.

**tenant** ['tenənt] Pächter *m*; Mieter *m*.

**tend** [tend] *v/i.* (*to*) gerichtet sein (auf *acc.*); hinstreben (zu); abzielen (auf *acc.*); neigen (zu); *v/t.* pflegen; hüten; ⊕ bedienen; **~ance** ['tendəns] Pflege *f*; Bedienung *f*; **~ency** [~si] Richtung *f*; Neigung *f*; Zweck *m*.

**tender** ['tendə] **1.** □ zart; weich; empfindlich; heikel (*Thema*); zärtlich; **2.** Angebot *n*; Kostenanschlag *m*; 🚃, ⚓ Tender *m*; *legal* ~ gesetzliches Zahlungsmittel; **3.** anbieten; *Entlassung* einreichen; **~foot** *Am.* F Neuling *m*, Anfänger *m*; **~loin** *bsd. Am.* Filet *n*; *Am.* berüchtigtes Viertel; **~ness** [~ənis] Zartheit *f*; Zärtlichkeit *f*.

**tendon** *anat.* ['tendən] Sehne *f*.

**tendril** ♀ ['tendril] Ranke *f*.

**tenement** ['tenimənt] Wohnhaus *n*; (*bsd. Am.*)Wohnung *f*; ~ *house* Mietshaus *n*.

**tennis** ['tenis] Tennis(spiel) *n*; ~ *court* Tennisplatz *m*.

**tenor** ['tenə] Fortgang *m*, Verlauf *m*; Inhalt *m*; ♪ Tenor *m*.

**tens|e** [tens] **1.** *gr.* Zeit(form) *f*, Tempus *n*; **2.** ⊕ gespannt (*a. fig.*); straff; **~ion** ['tenʃən] Spannung *f*.

**tent** [tent] **1.** Zelt *n*; **2.** zelten.

**tentacle** *zo.* ['tentəkl] Fühler *m*; Fangarm *m e-s Polypen*.

**tentative** □ ['tentətiv] versuchend; Versuchs...; **~ly** versuchsweise.

**tenth** [tenθ] **1.** zehnte(r, -s); **2.** Zehntel n; **~ly** ['tenθli] zehntens.

**tenuous** □ ['tenjuəs] dünn; zart, fein; dürftig.

**tenure** ['tenjuə] Besitz(art f, -dauer f) m.

**tepid** □ ['tepid] lau(warm).

**term** [tə:m] **1.** (bestimmte) Zeit, Frist f, Termin m; Zahltag m; Amtszeit f; ♩♩ Sitzungsperiode f; Semester n, Quartal n, Trimester n, Tertial n; Å, phls. Glied n; (Fach-)Ausdruck m, Wort n, Bezeichnung f; Begriff m; **~s** pl. Bedingungen f/pl.; Beziehungen f/pl.; be on good (bad) **~s** with gut (schlecht) stehen mit; come to **~s**, make **~s** sich einigen (als); **2.** (be)nennen; bezeichnen (als).

**termagant** ['tə:məgənt] **1.** □ zanksüchtig; **2.** Zankteufel m (Weib).

**termina|l** ['tə:minl] **1.** □ End...; letzt; **~ly** terminweise; **2.** Endstück n; ♂ Pol m; Am. ⬛ Endstation f; **~te** [~neit] begrenzen; (be)endigen; **~tion** [tə:mi'neiʃən] Beendigung f; Ende n; gr. Endung f.

**terminus** ['tə:minəs] Endstation f.

**terrace** ['terəs] Terrasse f; Häuserreihe f; **~-house** Reihenhaus n; **~d** [~st] terrassenförmig.

**terrestrial** □ [ti'restriəl] irdisch; Erd...; bsd. zo., ♧ Land...

**terrible** □ ['terəbl] schrecklich.

**terri|fic** [tə'rifik] (**~ally**) fürchterlich, schrecklich; F ungeheuer, großartig; **~fy** ['terifai] v/t. erschrecken.

**territor|ial** [teri'tɔ:riəl] **1.** □ territorial; Land...; Bezirks...; ♀ Army, ♀ Force Territorialarmee f; **2.** ✗ Angehörige(r) m der Territorialarmee; **~y** ['teritəri] Territorium n, (Hoheits-, Staats)Gebiet n.

**terror** ['terə] Schrecken m, Entsetzen n; **~ize** [~raiz] terrorisieren.

**terse** □ [tə:s] knapp; kurz u. bündig.

**test** [test] **1.** Probe f; Untersuchung f; (Eignungs)Prüfung f; Test m; ♁ Reagens n; **2.** probieren, prüfen, testen.

**testament** ['testəmənt] Testament n.

**testicle** anat. ['testikl] Hode(n m) [m, f.

**testify** ['testifai] (be)zeugen; (als Zeuge) aussagen (on über acc.).

**testimon|ial** [testi'mounjəl] (Führungs)Zeugnis n; Zeichen n der Anerkennung; **~y** ['testiməni] Zeugnis n; Beweis m.

**test-tube** ♁ ['testtju:b] Reagenzglas n.

**testy** □ ['testi] reizbar, kribbelig.

**tether** ['teðə] **1.** Haltestrick m; fig. Spielraum m; at the end of one's **~** fig. am Ende s-r Kraft; **2.** anbinden.

**text** [tekst] Text m; Bibelstelle f;

**~book** ['tekstbuk] Leitfaden m, Lehrbuch n.

**textile** ['tekstail] **1.** Textil..., Web...; **2.** **~s** pl. Webwaren f/pl., Textilien pl.

**texture** ['tekstʃə] Gewebe n; Gefüge n.

**than** [ðæn, ðən] als.

**thank** [θæŋk] **1.** danken (dat.); **~** you, bei Ablehnung no, **~** you danke; **2.** **~s** pl. Dank m; **~s!** vielen Dank!; danke (schön)!; **~s** to dank (dat.); **~ful** □ ['θæŋkful] dankbar; **~less** □ [~klis] undankbar; **~giving** [~ksgivin] Danksagung f; Dankfest n; ♀ (Day) bsd. Am. (Ernte)Dankfest n.

**that** [ðæt, ðət] **1.** pl. those [ðouz] pron. jene(r, -s); der, die, das; der-, die-, das(jenige); welche(r, -s); **2.** cj. daß; damit.

**thatch** [θætʃ] **1.** Dachstroh n; Strohdach n; **2.** mit Stroh decken.

**thaw** [θɔ:] **1.** Tauwetter n; (Auf-)Tauen n; **2.** (auf)tauen.

**the** [ði:; vor Vokalen ði; vor Konsonanten ðə] **1.** art. der, die, das; **2.** adv. desto, um so; **~** ... **~** ... je ... desto ...

**theat|re**, Am. **~er** ['θiətə] Theater n; fig. (Kriegs)Schauplatz m; **~ric(al** □) [θi'ætrik(əl)] Theater...; theatralisch.

**thee** Bibel, poet. [ði:] dich; dir.

**theft** [θeft] Diebstahl m.

**their** [ðeə] ihr(e); **~s** [~z] der (die, das) ihrige od. ihre.

**them** [ðem, ðəm] sie (acc. pl.); ihnen.

**theme** [θi:m] Thema n; Aufgabe f.

**themselves** [ðem'selvz] sie (acc. pl.) selbst; sich selbst.

**then** [ðen] **1.** adv. dann; damals; da; by **~** bis dahin; inzwischen; every now and **~** alle Augenblicke; there and **~** sogleich; now **~** nun denn; **2.** cj. denn, also, folglich; **3.** adj. damalig.

**thence** lit. [ðens] daher; von da.

**theolog|ian** [θiə'loudʒjən] Theologe m; **~y** [θi'ɔlədʒi] Theologie f.

**theor|etic(al** □) [θiə'retik(əl)] theoretisch; **~ist** ['θiərist] Theoretiker m; **~y** [~ri] Theorie f.

**therap|eutic** [θerə'pju:tik] **1.** (**~ally**) therapeutisch; **2.** **~s** mst. sg. Therapeutik f; **~y** ['θerəpi] Therapie f, Heilbehandlung f.

**there** [ðeə] da, dort; darin; dorthin; na!; **~** is, **~** are es gibt, es ist, es sind; **~about(s)** ['ðeərəbaut(s)] da herum; so ungefähr; **~after** [ðeər'ɑ:ftə] danach; **~by** ['ðeə'bai] dadurch, damit; **~fore** ['ðeəfɔ:] darum, deswegen; deshalb, daher; **~upon** ['ðeərə'pɔn] darauf(hin); **~with** [ðeə'wið] damit.

**thermal** ['θə:məl] **1.** □ Thermal...; phys. Wärme...; **2.** Aufwind m.

**thermo|meter** [θə'mɔmitə] Thermometer *n*; ♀s ['θə:məs] *a.* ~ *flask*, ~ *bottle* Thermosflasche *f*.

**these** [ðiːz] *pl. von* this.

**thes|is** ['θiːsis], *pl.* ~es ['θiːsiːz] These *f*; Dissertation *f*.

**they** [ðei] sie (*pl.*).

**thick** [θik] 1. □ *allg.* dick; dicht; trüb; legiert (*Suppe*); heiser; dumm; *pred.* F dick befreundet; ~ *with* dicht besetzt mit; 2. dickster Teil; *fig.* Brennpunkt *m*; *in the* ~ *of* mitten in (*dat.*); ~en ['θikən] (sich) verdicken; (sich) verstärken; legieren; (sich) verdichten; ~et ['θikit] Dickicht *n*; ~headed dumm; ~ness ['θiknis] Dicke *f*, Stärke *f*; Dichte *f*; ~set dicht (gepflanzt); untersetzt; ~skinned *fig.* dickfellig.

**thief** [θiːf], *pl.* **thieves** [θiːvz] Dieb(in); **thieve** [θiːv] stehlen.

**thigh** [θai] (Ober)Schenkel *m*.

**thimble** ['θimbl] Fingerhut *m*.

**thin** [θin] 1. □ *allg.* dünn; leicht; mager; spärlich, dürftig; schwach; fadenscheinig (*bsd. fig.*); 2. verdünnen; (sich) lichten; abnehmen.

**thine** *Bibel, poet.* [ðain] dein; der (die, das) deinige *od.* deine.

**thing** [θiŋ] Ding *n*; Sache *f*; Geschöpf *n*; ~s *pl.* Sachen *f/pl.*; die Dinge *n/pl.* (*Umstände*); *the* ~ F das Richtige; richtig; die Hauptsache; ~s *are going better* es geht jetzt besser.

**think** [θiŋk] [*irr.*] *v/i.* denken (*of an acc.*); nachdenken; sich besinnen; meinen, glauben; gedenken (*to inf.* zu *inf.*); *v/t.* (sich) *et.* denken; halten für; ~ *much etc. of* viel *etc.* halten von; ~ *s.th. over* (sich) *et.* überlegen, über *et.* nachdenken.

**third** [θə:d] 1. dritte(r, -s); 2. Drittel *n*; ~ly ['θə:dli] drittens; ~rate ['θə:d'reit] drittklassig.

**thirst** [θə:st] 1. Durst *m*; 2. dürsten; ~y □ ['θə:sti] durstig; dürr (*Boden*).

**thirt|een** ['θə:'tiːn] dreizehn; ~eenth ['θə:'tiːnθ] dreizehnte(r, -s); ~ieth ['θə:tiiθ] dreißigste(r, -s); ~y ['θə:ti] dreißig.

**this** [ðis], *pl.* **these** [ðiːz] diese(r, -s); ~ *morning* heute morgen.

**thistle** ♣ ['θisl] Distel *f*.

**thong** [θɔŋ] (Leder-, Peitschen-) Riemen *m*.

**thorn** ♣ [θɔːn] Dorn *m*; ~y ['θɔːni] dornig, stach(e)lig; beschwerlich.

**thorough** □ ['θʌrə] vollkommen; vollständig; vollendet; gründlich; ~ly *a.* durchaus; ~bred Vollblüter *m*; *attr.* Vollblut...; ~fare Durchgang *m*; Durchfahrt *f*; Hauptverkehrsstraße *f*; ~going gründlich; tatkräftig.

**those** [ðouz] *pl. von* that 1.

**thou** *Bibel, poet.* [ðau] du.

**though** [ðou] obgleich, obwohl,

wenn auch; zwar; aber, doch; freilich; *as* ~ als ob.

**thought** [θɔːt] 1. *pret. u. p.p. von* think; 2. Gedanke *m*; (Nach)Denken *n*; *on second* ~s nach nochmaliger Überlegung; ~ful □ ['θɔːtful] gedankenvoll, nachdenklich; rücksichtsvoll (*of gegen*); ~less □ ['θɔːtlis] gedankenlos; unbesonnen; rücksichtslos (*of gegen*).

**thousand** ['θauzənd] 1. tausend; 2. Tausend *n*; ~th [~ntθ] 1. tausendste(r, -s); 2. Tausendstel *n*.

**thrash** [θræʃ] (ver)dreschen, (ver-) prügeln; (hin und her) schlagen; *s. thresh*; ~ing ['θræʃiŋ] Dresche *f*, Tracht *f* Prügel; *s. threshing*.

**thread** [θred] 1. Faden *m* (*a. fig.*); Zwirn *m*, Garn *n*; ⊕ (Schrauben-) Gewinde *n*; 2. einfädeln; sich durchwinden (*durch*); durchziehen; ~bare ['θredbeə] fadenscheinig.

**threat** [θret] Drohung *f*; ~en ['θretn] (be-, an)drohen; ~ening [~niŋ] bedrohlich.

**three** [θriː] 1. drei; 2. Drei *f*; ~fold ['θriːfould] dreifach; ~pence ['θrepəns] Dreipence(stück *n*) *m/pl.*; ~score ['θriː'skɔː] sechzig.

**thresh** [θreʃ] ⚊ (aus)dreschen; *s. thrash*; ~ out *fig.* durchdreschen; ~er ['θreʃə] Drescher *m*; Dreschmaschine *f*; ~ing [~ʃiŋ] Dreschen *n*; ~ing-machine Dreschmaschine *f*.

**threshold** ['θreʃhould] Schwelle *f*.

**threw** [θruː] *pret. von* throw 1.

**thrice** [θrais] dreimal.

**thrift** [θrift] Sparsamkeit *f*, Wirtschaftlichkeit *f*; ~less □ ['θriftlis] verschwenderisch; ~y □ [~ti] sparsam; *poet.* gedeihend.

**thrill** [θril] 1. *v/t.* durchdringen, durchschauern; *fig.* packen, aufwühlen; aufregen; *v/i.* (er)beben; 2. Schauer *m*; Beben *n*; aufregendes Erlebnis; Sensation *f*; ~er F ['θrilə] Reißer *m*, Thriller *m*, Schauerroman *m*, Schauerstück *n*; ~ing [~liŋ] spannend.

**thrive** [θraiv] [*irr.*] gedeihen; *fig.* blühen; Glück haben; ~n ['θrivn] *p.p. von* thrive.

**throat** [θrout] Kehle *f*; Hals *m*; Gurgel *f*; Schlund *m*; *clear one's* ~ sich räuspern.

**throb** [θrɔb] 1. pochen, klopfen, schlagen; pulsieren; 2. Pochen *n*; Schlagen *n*; Pulsschlag *m*.

**throes** [θrouz] *pl.* Geburtswehen *f/pl.* [Thrombose *f.*]

**thrombosis** ⚕ [θrɔm'bousis]

**throne** [θroun] Thron *m*.

**throng** [θrɔŋ] 1. Gedränge *n*; Menge *f*, Schar *f*; 2. sich drängen (in *dat.*); anfüllen *etc.*

**throstle** *orn.* ['θrɔsl] Drossel *f*.

**throttle** ['θrɔtl] 1. erdrosseln; ⊕ (ab)drosseln; 2. ⊕ Drosselklappe *f*.

**through** [θru:] 1. durch; 2. Durch-
gangs...; durchgehend; **~out**
[θru(:)'aut] 1. *prp.* überall in (*dat.*);
2. *adv.* durch u. durch, ganz und
gar, durchweg.

**throve** [θrouv] *pret. von* thrive.

**throw** [θrou] 1. [*irr.*] (ab)werfen,
schleudern; *Am.* F *Wettkampf etc.*
betrügerisch verlieren; würfeln; ⊕
schalten; ~ off (die Jagd) beginnen;
~ over aufgeben; ~ up in die Höhe
werfen; erbrechen; *fig.* hinwerfen;
2. Wurf *m*; **~n** [θroun] *p.p. von*
throw 1.

**thru** *Am.* [θru:] = through.

**thrum** [θrʌm] klimpern (auf *dat.*).

**thrush** *orn.* [θrʌʃ] Drossel *f*.

**thrust** [θrʌst] 1. Stoß *m*; Vorstoß
*m*; ⊕ Druck *m*, Schub *m*; 2. [*irr.*]
stoßen; ~ *o.s.* into sich drängen in
(*acc.*); ~ *upon s.o.* j-m aufdrängen.

**thud** [θʌd] 1. dumpf aufschlagen,
F bumsen; 2. dumpfer (Auf)Schlag,
F Bums *m*.

**thug** [θʌg] Strolch *m*.

**thumb** [θʌm] 1. Daumen *m*; Tom ♀
Däumling *m im Märchen*; 2. *Buch
etc.* abgreifen; ~ *a lift* per Anhalter
fahren; **~tack** *Am.* ['θʌmtæk]
Reißzwecke *f*.

**thump** [θʌmp] 1. F Bums *m*; F Puff
*m*; 2. *v/t.* F bumsen *od.* pochen auf
(*acc.*) *od.* gegen; F knuffen, puffen;
*v/i.* F (auf)bumsen.

**thunder** ['θʌndə] 1. Donner *m*;
2. donnern; **~bolt** Blitz *m* (*u.* Donner *m*); **~clap** Donnerschlag *m*;
**~ous** □ [~ərəs] donnernd; **~storm**
Gewitter *n*; **~struck** wie vom
Donner gerührt.

**Thursday** ['θə:zdi] Donnerstag *m*.

**thus** [ðʌs] so; also, somit.

**thwart** [θwɔ:t] 1. durchkreuzen;
hintertreiben; 2. Ruderbank *f*.

**thy** *Bibel, poet.* [ðai] dein(e).

**tick¹** *zo.* [tik] Zecke *f*.

**tick²** [~] 1. Ticken *n*; (Vermerk-)
Häkchen *n*; 2. *v/i.* ticken; *v/t.* an-
haken; ~ off abhaken.

**tick³** [~] Inlett *n*; Matratzenbezug *m*.

**ticket** ['tikit] 1. Fahrkarte *f*, -schein
*m*; Flugkarte *f*; Eintrittskarte *f*;
(Straf)Zettel *m*; (Preis- *etc.*)Schild-
chen *n*; *pol.* (Wahl-, Kandidaten-)
Liste *f*; 2. etikettieren, *Ware* auszeichnen; **~machine** Fahrkarten-
automat *m*; ~ **office**, ~ **window**
*bsd. Am.* Fahrkartenschalter *m*.

**tick|le** ['tikl] kitzeln (*a. fig.*); **~ish**
□ [~liʃ] kitzlig; heikel.

**tidal** ['taidl]: ~ **wave** Flutwelle *f*.

**tide** [taid] 1. Gezeit(en *pl.*) *f*; Ebbe *f*
und Flut *f*; *fig.* Strom *m*, Flut *f*; *in
Zssgn: rechte* Zeit; *high* ~ Flut *f*;
*low* ~ Ebbe *f*; 2. ~ over *fig.* hinweg-
kommen *od. j-m* hinweghelfen über
(*acc.*).

**tidings** ['taidiŋz] *pl. od. sg.* Neuig-
keiten *f/pl.*, Nachrichten *f/pl.*

**tidy** ['taidi] 1. ordentlich, sauber,
reinlich; F ganz schön, beträchtlich
(*Summe*); 2. Behälter *m*; Abfallkorb
*m*; 3. *a.* ~ up zurechtmachen; ordnen; aufräumen.

**tie** [tai] 1. Band *n* (*a. fig.*); Schleife *f*;
Krawatte *f*, Schlips *m*; Bindung *f*;
*fig.* Fessel *f*, Verpflichtung *f*; *Sport*:
Punkt-, *parl.* Stimmengleichheit *f*;
*Sport*: Entscheidungsspiel *n*; ⊞
*Am.* Schwelle *f*; 2. *v/t.* (ver)binden;
~ **down** *fig.* binden (*to an acc.*); ~
up zu-, an-, ver-, zs.-binden; *v/i.*
*Sport*: punktgleich sein.

**tier** [tiə] Reihe *f*; Rang *m*.

**tie-up** ['taiʌp] (Ver)Bindung *f*; ✝
Fusion *f*; Stockung *f*; *bsd. Am.*
Streik *m*.

**tiffin** ['tifin] Mittagessen *n*.

**tiger** ['taigə] *zo.* Tiger *m*; *Am.* F
Beifallsgebrüll *m*.

**tight** [tait] 1. □ dicht; fest; eng;
knapp (sitzend); straff, prall;
knapp; F beschwipst; *be in a* ~
*place od. corner* F in der Klemme
sein; 2. *adv.* fest; *hold* ~ festhalten;
**~en** ['taitn] *a.* ~ up (sich) zs.-ziehen;
*Gürtel* enger schnallen; **~fisted**
knick(e)rig; **~ness** ['taitnis] Festigkeit *f*, Dichtigkeit *f*; Straffheit *f*;
Knappheit *f*; Enge *f*; Geiz *m*; **~s**
[taits] *pl.* Trikot *n*.

**tigress** ['taigris] Tigerin *f*.

**tile** [tail] 1. (Dach)Ziegel *m*; Kachel
*f*; Fliese *f*; 2. mit Ziegeln *etc.*
decken; kacheln; fliesen.

**till¹** [til] Laden(tisch)kasse *f*.

**till²** [~] 1. *prp.* bis (zu); 2. *cj.* bis.

**till³** 🖋 [~] bestellen, bebauen; **~age**
['tilidʒ] (Land)Bestellung *f*; Ackerbau *m*; Ackerland *n*.

**tilt** [tilt] 1. Plane *f*; Neigung *f*,
Kippe *f*; Stoß *m*; Lanzenbrechen *n*
(*a. fig.*); 2. kippen; ~ *against* anrennen gegen.

**timber** ['timbə] 1. (Bau-, Nutz-)
Holz *n*; Balken *m*; Baumbestand
*m*, Bäume *m/pl.*; 2. zimmern.

**time** [taim] 1. Zeit *f*; Mal *n*; Takt
*m*; Tempo *n*; ~ *and again* immer
wieder; *at a* ~ zugleich; *for the* ~
*being* einstweilen; *have a good* ~
es gut haben; sich amüsieren; *in*
~, *on* ~ zur rechten Zeit, rechtzeitig; 2. zeitlich festsetzen; zeitlich abpassen; die Zeitdauer messen; **~hono(u)red** ['taimɔnəd] alt-
ehrwürdig; **~ly** ['taimli] (recht)zei-
tig; **~piece** Uhr *f*; **~sheet** An-
wesenheitsliste *f*; **~table** Termin-
kalender *m*; Fahr-, Stundenplan *m*.

**tim|id** □ ['timid], **~orous** □ ['ti-
mərəs] furchtsam; schüchtern.

**tin** [tin] 1. Zinn *n*; Weißblech *n*;
(Konserven)Büchse *f*; 2. verzinnen;
in Büchsen einmachen, eindosen.

**tincture** ['tiŋktʃə] 1. Farbe *f*; Tinktur *f*; *fig.* Anstrich *m*; 2. färben.

**tinfoil** ['tin'fɔil] Stanniol *n*.

tinge [tindʒ] 1. Färbung *f*; *fig.* Anflug *m*, Spur *f*; 2. färben; *fig.* e-n Anstrich geben (*dat.*).

tingle ['tiŋgl] klingen; prickeln.

tinker ['tiŋkə] basteln (*at an dat.*).

tinkle ['tiŋkl] klingeln (mit).

tin|-opener ['tinoupnə] Dosenöffner *m*; ~-plate Weißblech *n*.

tinsel ['tinsəl] Flitter(werk *n*) *m*; Lametta *n*.

tin-smith ['tinsmiθ] Klempner *m*.

tint [tint] 1. Farbe *f*; (Farb)Ton *m*, Schattierung *f*; 2. färben; (ab-)tönen.

tiny ['taini] winzig, klein.

tip [tip] 1. Spitze *f*; Mundstück *n*; Trinkgeld *n*; Tip *m*, Wink *m*; leichter Stoß; Schuttabladeplatz *m*; 2. mit e-r Spitze versehen; (um-)kippen; *j-m* ein Trinkgeld geben; *a.* ~ off *j-m* e-n Wink geben.

tipple ['tipl] zechen, picheln.

tipsy ['tipsi] angeheitert.

tiptoe ['tiptou] 1. auf Zehenspitzen gehen; 2. on ~ auf Zehenspitzen.

tire¹ ['taiə] (Rad-, Auto)Reifen *m*.

tire² [~] ermüden, müde machen *od.* werden; ~d □ müde; ~less □ ['taiəlis] unermüdlich; ~some □ ['taiəsəm] ermüdend; lästig.

tiro ['taiərou] Anfänger *m*.

tissue ['tisju:, *Am.* 'tiʃu:] Gewebe *n*; ~paper Seidenpapier *n*.

tit¹ [tit] = teat.

tit² *orn.* [~] Meise *f*.

titbit ['titbit] Leckerbissen *m*.

titillate ['titileit] kitzeln.

title ['taitl] 1. (Buch-, Ehren)Titel *m*; Überschrift *f*; ♯♭ Anspruch *m*; 2. betiteln; ~d *bsd.* ad(e)lig.

titmouse *orn.* ['titmaus] Meise *f*.

titter ['titə] 1. kichern; 2. Kichern *n*.

tittle ['titl] Pünktchen *n*; *fig.* Tüttelchen *n*; ~-tattle [~tlætl] Schnickschnack *m*.

to [tu:, tu, tə] *prp.* zu (*a. adv.*); gegen, nach, an, in, auf; bis zu, bis an (*acc.*); um zu; für; ~ me *etc.* mir *etc.*; *I weep* ~ *think of it* ich weine, wenn ich daran denke; *here's* ~ *you!* auf Ihr Wohl!, Prosit!

toad *zo.* [toud] Kröte *f*; ~stool ['toudstu:l] (größerer Blätter)Pilz; Giftpilz *m*; ~y *f* ['toudi] 1. Speichellecker *m*; 2. *fig.* vor *j-m* kriechen.

toast [toust] 1. Toast *m*, geröstetes Brot; Trinkspruch *m*; 2. toasten, rösten; *fig.* wärmen, trinken auf (*acc.*).

tobacco [tə'bækou] Tabak *m*; ~nist [~kənist] Tabakhändler *m*.

toboggan [tə'bɔgən] 1. Toboggan *m*; Rodelschlitten *m*; 2. rodeln.

today [tə'dei] heute. [teln.)

toddle ['tɔdl] unsicher gehen; zot-)

toddy ['tɔdi] *Art* Grog *m*.

to-do F [tə'du:] Lärm *m*, Aufheben *n*.

toe [tou] 1. Zehe *f*; Spitze *f*; 2. mit den Zehen berühren.

toff|ee, ~y ['tɔfi] Sahnebonbon *m*, *n*, Toffee *n*.

together [tə'geðə] zusammen; zugleich; nacheinander.

toil [tɔil] 1. schwere Arbeit; Mühe *f*, F Plackerei *f*; 2. sich plagen.

toilet ['tɔilit] Toilette *f*; ~-paper Toilettenpapier *n*; ~-table Frisiertoilette *f*. [*n*.)

toils [tɔilz] *pl.* Schlingen *f/pl.*, Netz)

toilsome □ ['tɔilsəm] mühsam.

token ['toukən] Zeichen *n*; Andenken *n*, Geschenk *n*; ~ *money* Notgeld *n*; *in* ~ *of* zum Zeichen (*gen.*).

told [tould] *pret. u. p.p. von* tell.

tolera|ble □ ['tɔlərəbl] erträglich; ~nce [~əns] Duldsamkeit *f*; ~nt □ [~nt] duldsam (*of gegen*); ~te [~reit] dulden; ertragen; ~tion [tɔlə'reiʃən] Duldung *f*.

toll [toul] 1. Zoll *m* (*a. fig.*); Wege-, Brücken-, Marktgeld *n*; *fig.* Tribut *m*; ~ *of the road die* Verkehrsopfer *n/pl.*; 2. läuten; ~-bar ['toulbɑ:], ~-gate Schlagbaum *m*.

tomato ♀ [tə'mɑ:tou, *Am.* tə'meitou], *pl.* ~es Tomate *f*.

tomb [tu:m] Grab(mal) *n*.

tomboy ['tɔmbɔi] Range *f*.

tombstone ['tu:mstoun] Grabstein *m*.

tom-cat ['tɔm'kæt] Kater *m*.

tomfool ['tɔm'fu:l] Hansnarr *m*.

tomorrow [tə'mɔrou] morgen.

ton [tʌn] Tonne *f* (*Gewichtseinheit*).

tone [toun] 1. Ton *m*; Klang *m*; Laut *m*; *out of* ~ verstimmt; 2. e-n Ton geben (*dat.*); stimmen; *paint.* abtönen; ~ *down* (*sich*) abschwächen, mildern.

tongs [tɔŋz] *pl.* (*a pair of* ~ *pl.* eine) Zange.

tongue [tʌŋ] Zunge *f*; Sprache *f*; Landzunge *f*; (Schuh)Lasche *f*; *hold one's* ~ den Mund halten; ~-tied ['tʌŋtaid] sprachlos; schweigsam; stumm.

tonic ['tɔnik] 1. (~*ally*) tonisch; ♪ stärkend; 2. ♪ Grundton *m*; ♪ Stärkungsmittel *n*, Tonikum *n*.

tonight [tə'nait] heute abend *od.* nacht.

tonnage ♣ ['tʌnidʒ] Tonnengehalt *m*; Lastigkeit *f*; Tonnengeld *n*.

tonsil *anat.* ['tɔnsl] Mandel *f*; ~itis ♯ [tɔnsi'laitis] Mandelentzündung *f*.

too [tu:] zu, allzu; auch, noch dazu.

took [tuk] *pret. von* take 1.

tool [tu:l] Werkzeug *n*, Gerät *n*; ~-bag ['tu:lbæg], ~-kit Werkzeugtasche *f*.

toot [tu:t] 1. blasen, tuten; 2. Tuten *n*.

tooth [tu:θ] *pl.* teeth [ti:θ] Zahn *m*; ~ache ['tu:θeik] Zahnschmerzen *pl.*; ~-brush Zahnbürste *f*; ~less □

['tu:θlis] zahnlos; ~-paste Zahn-
pasta f; ~pick Zahnstocher m;
~some □ ['tu:θsəm] schmackhaft.
**top** [tɔp] 1. oberstes Ende; Ober-
teil n; Gipfel m (a. fig.); Wipfel m;
Kopf m e-r Seite; mot. Am. Verdeck n; fig. Haupt n, Erste(r) m;
Stiefel-Stulpe f; Kreisel m; at the
~ of one's voice aus voller Kehle;
on ~ obenauf; obendrein; 2. ober(er,
-e, -es); oberst; höchst; 3. oben
bedecken; fig. überragen; vorangehen in (dat.); als erste(r) stehen
auf e-r Liste; ~-boots ['tɔp'bu:ts]
pl. Stulpenstiefel m/pl.
**toper** ['toupə] Zecher m.
**tophat** F ['tɔp'hæt] Zylinderhut m.
**topic** ['tɔpik] Gegenstand m, Thema
n; ~al □ [~kəl] lokal; aktuell.
**topmost** ['tɔpmoust] höchst, oberst.
**topple** ['tɔpl] (um)kippen.
**topsyturvy** □ ['tɔpsi'tə:vi] auf den
Kopf gestellt; das Oberste zuunterst; drunter und drüber.
**torch** [tɔ:tʃ] Fackel f; electric ~
Taschenlampe f; ~light ['tɔ:tʃlait]
Fackelschein m; ~ procession Fak-
kelzug m.
**tore** [tɔ:] pret. von tear[1] 1.
**torment** 1. ['tɔ:ment] Qual f,
Marter f; 2. [tɔ:'ment] martern,
quälen.
**torn** [tɔ:n] p.p. von tear[1] 1.
**tornado** [tɔ:'neidou], pl. ~es Wirbelsturm m, Tornado m.
**torpedo** [tɔ:'pi:dou], pl. ~es 1. Torpedo m; 2. ⚓ torpedieren (a. fig.).
**torp|id** □ ['tɔ:pid] starr; apathisch;
träg; ~idity [tɔ:'piditi], ~or ['tɔ:pə]
Erstarrung f, Betäubung f.
**torrent** ['tɔrənt] Sturz-, Gießbach
m; (reißender) Strom; ~ial □
[tɔ'renʃəl] gießbachartig; strömend;
fig. ungestüm.
**torrid** ['tɔrid] brennend heiß.
**tortoise** zo. ['tɔ:təs] Schildkröte f.
**tortuous** □ ['tɔ:tjuəs] gewunden.
**torture** ['tɔ:tʃə] 1. Folter f, Marter f,
Tortur f; 2. foltern, martern.
**toss** [tɔs] 1. Werfen n, Wurf m;
Zurückwerfen n (Kopf); 2. a.
~ about (sich) hin und her werfen;
schütteln; (mit adv.) werfen; a. ~
up hochwerfen; ~ off Getränk hin-
unterstürzen; Arbeit hinhauen; a.
~ up losen (for um); ~-up ['tɔsʌp]
Losen n; fig. etwas Zweifelhaftes.
**tot** F [tɔt] Knirps m (kleines Kind).
**total** ['toutl] 1. □ ganz, gänzlich;
total; gesamt; 2. Gesamtbetrag m;
3. sich belaufen auf (acc.); sum-
mieren; ~itarian [toutæli'tɛəriən]
totalitär; ~ity [tou'tæliti] Gesamtheit f.
**totter** ['tɔtə] wanken, wackeln.
**touch** [tʌtʃ] 1. (sich) berühren; anrühren, anfassen; stoßen an (acc.);
betreffen; fig. rühren; erreichen; ♩
anschlagen; a bit ~ed fig. ein biß-

chen verrückt; ~ at ⚓ anlegen in
(dat.); ~ up auffrischen; retuschieren; 2. Berührung f; Gefühl(s-
sinn m) n; Anflug m, Zug m; Fertigkeit f; ♩ Anschlag m; (Pinsel-)
Strich m; ~-and-go ['tʌtʃən'gou]
gewagte Sache; it is ~ es steht auf
des Messers Schneide; ~ing [~ʃiŋ]
rührend; ~stone Prüfstein m;
~y [~ʃi] empfindlich; heikel.
**tough** [tʌf] zäh (a. fig.); schwer,
hart; grob, brutal, übel; ~en [~tʌfn]
zäh machen od. werden; ~ness
[~nis] Zähigkeit f.
**tour** [tuə] 1. (Rund)Reise f, Tour
(-nee) f; conducted ~ Führung f;
Gesellschaftsreise f; 2. (be)reisen;
~ist ['tuərist] Tourist(in); ~ agency,
~ bureau, ~ office Reisebüro n; ~
season Reisezeit f. [n.]
**tournament** ['tuənəmənt] Turnier.]
**tousle** ['tauzl] (zer)zausen.
**tow** [tou] 1. Schleppen n; take in
~ ins Schlepptau nehmen; 2. (ab-)
schleppen; treideln; ziehen.
**toward(s)** [tə'wɔ:d(z)] gegen; nach
... zu, auf ... (acc.) zu; (als Beitrag)
zu.
**towel** ['tauəl] 1. Handtuch n; 2. abreiben; ~-rack Handtuchhalter m.
**tower** ['tauə] 1. Turm m; fig. Hort
m, Bollwerk n; 2. sich erheben;
~ing [ˈtauəriŋ] (turm)hoch; rasend (Wut).
**town** [taun] 1. Stadt f; 2. Stadt...;
städtisch; ~ clerk Stadtsyndikus m;
~ council Stadtrat m (Versammlung); ~ councillor Stadtrat m
(Person); ~ hall Rathaus n; ~sfolk
['taunzfouk] pl. Städter pl.; ~ship
['taunʃip] Stadtgemeinde f; Stadt-
gebiet n; ~sman ['taunzmən]
(Mit)Bürger m; ~speople [~zpi:pl]
pl. = townsfolk.
**toxi|c(al** □) ['tɔksik(əl)] giftig;
Gift...; ~n [~in] Giftstoff m.
**toy** [tɔi] 1. Spielzeug n; Tand m;
~s pl. Spielwaren f/pl.; 2. Spiel-
(zeug)...; Miniatur...; Zwerg...;
3. spielen; ~-book ['tɔibuk] Bilder-
buch n.
**trace** [treis] 1. Spur f (a. fig.);
Strang m; 2. nachspüren (dat.); fig.
verfolgen; herausfinden; (auf-)
zeichnen; (durch)pausen.
**tracing** ['treisiŋ] Pauszeichnung f.
**track** [træk] 1. Spur f; Sport: Bahn
f; Rennstrecke f; Pfad m; Gleis
n; ~ events pl. Laufdisziplinen f/pl.;
2. nachspüren (dat.); verfolgen; ~
down, ~ out aufspüren.
**tract** [trækt] Fläche f, Strecke f,
Gegend f; Traktat n, Abhandlung f.
**tractable** □ ['træktəbl] lenk-, füg-
sam.
**tract|ion** ['trækʃən] Ziehen n, Zug
m; ~ engine Zugmaschine f; ~or ⊕
[~ktə] Trecker m, Traktor m.

**trade** [treid] 1. Handel *m*; Gewerbe *n*; Handwerk *n*; *Am.* Kompensationsgeschäft *n*; 2. Handel treiben; handeln; ~ **on** ausnutzen; ~ **mark** ♱ Warenzeichen *n*, Schutzmarke *f*; ~ **price** Händlerpreis *m*; ~**r** ['treidə] Händler *m*; ~**sman** [~dzmən] Geschäftsmann *m*; ~ **union** Gewerkschaft *f*; ~ **wind** ⚓ Passatwind *m*.

**tradition** [trə'diʃən] Tradition *f*, Überlieferung *f*; ~**al** ☐ [~nl] traditionell.

**traffic** ['træfik] 1. Verkehr *m*; Handel *m*; 2. handeln (*in* mit); ~ **jam** Verkehrsstauung *f*; ~ **light** Verkehrsampel *f*.

**traged|ian** [trə'dʒi:djən] Tragiker *m*; *thea.* Tragöd|e *m*, -in *f*; ~**y** ['trædʒidi] Tragödie *f*.

**tragic(al** ☐) ['trædʒik(əl)] tragisch.

**trail** [treil] 1. *fig.* Schweif *m*; Schleppe *f*; Spur *f*; Pfad *m*; 2. *v/t.* hinter sich (her)ziehen; verfolgen; *v/i.* (sich) schleppen; ⚘ kriechen; ~ **blazer** *Am.* Bahnbrecher *m*; ~**er** ['treilə] (Wohnwagen)Anhänger *m*; ⚘ Kriechpflanze *f*; *Film:* Vorschau *f*.

**train** [trein] 1. (Eisenbahn)Zug *m*; *allg.* Zug *m*; Gefolge *n*; Reihe *f*, Folge *f*, Kette *f*; Schleppe *f am Kleid*; 2. erziehen; schulen; abrichten; ausbilden; trainieren; (sich) üben; ~**ee** [trei'ni:] in der Ausbildung Begriffene(r) *m*; ~**er** ['treinə] Ausbilder *m*; Trainer *m*.

**trait** [trei] (Charakter)Zug *m*.

**traitor** ['treitə] Verräter *m*.

**tram** [træm] *s.* ~*-car*, ~*ways* ~*-car* ['træmka:] Straßenbahnwagen *m*.

**tramp** [træmp] 1. Getrampel *n*; Wanderung *f*; Tramp *m*, Landstreicher *m*; 2. trampeln, treten; (durch)wandern; ~**le** ['træmpl] (zer)trampeln.

**tramway** ['træmwei] Straßenbahn *f*.

**trance** [tra:ns] Trance *f*.

**tranquil** ☐ ['træŋkwil] ruhig; gelassen; ~(l)ity [træŋ'kwiliti] Ruhe *f*; Gelassenheit *f*; ~(l)ize ['træŋkwilaiz] beruhigen; ~(l)izer [~zə] Beruhigungsmittel *n*.

**transact** [træn'zækt] abwickeln, abmachen; ~**ion** [~kʃən] Verrichtung *f*; Geschäft *n*, Transaktion *f*; ~**s** *pl.* (Tätigkeits)Bericht(e *pl.*) *m*.

**transalpine** ['trænz'ælpain] transalpin(isch).

**transatlantic** ['trænzət'læntik] transatlantisch, Transatlantik...

**transcend** [træn'send] überschreiten, übertreffen; hinausgehen über (*acc.*); ~**ence**, ~**ency** [~dəns, ~si] Überlegenheit *f*; *phls.* Transzendenz *f*.

**transcribe** [træns'kraib] abschreiben; *Kurzschrift* übertragen.

**transcript** ['trænskript], ~**ion**

[træns'kripʃən] Abschrift *f*; Umschrift *f*.

**transfer** 1. [træns'fə:] *v/t.* übertragen; versetzen, verlegen; *v/i.* übertreten; *Am.* umsteigen; 2. ['trænsfə(:)] Übertragung *f*; ♱ Transfer *m*; Versetzung *f*, Verlegung *f*; *Am.* Umsteigefahrschein *m*; ~**able** [træns'fərəbl] übertragbar.

**transfigure** [træns'figə] umgestalten; verklären.

**transfix** [træns'fiks] durchstechen; ~**ed** *fig.* versteinert, starr (*with* vor *dat.*).

**transform** [træns'fɔ:m] umformen; um-, verwandeln; ~**ation** [trænsfə'meiʃən] Umformung *f*; Um-, Verwandlung *f*.

**transfus|e** [træns'fju:z] ⚕ *Blut etc.* übertragen; *fig.* einflößen; *fig.* durchtränken; ~**ion** [~u:ʒən] (*bsd.* ⚕ Blut)Übertragung *f*, Transfusion *f*.

**transgress** [træns'gres] *v/t.* überschreiten; übertreten, verletzen; *v/i.* sich vergehen; ~**ion** [~eʃən] Überschreitung *f*; Übertretung *f*; Vergehen *n*; ~**or** [~esə] Übertreter *m*.

**transient** ['trænziənt] 1. = *transitory*; 2. *Am.* Durchreisende(r *m*) *f*.

**transit** ['trænsit] Durchgang *m*; Durchgangsverkehr *m*.

**transition** [træn'siʒən] Übergang *m*.

**transitive** ☐ *gr.* ['trænsitiv] transitiv.

**transitory** ☐ ['trænsitəri] vorübergehend; vergänglich, flüchtig.

**translat|e** [træns'leit] übersetzen, übertragen; überführen; *fig.* umsetzen; ~**ion** [~eiʃən] Übersetzung *f*, Übertragung *f*; *fig.* Auslegung *f*; ~**or** [~eitə] Übersetzer(in).

**translucent** [trænz'lu:snt] durchscheinend; *fig.* hell.

**transmigration** [trænzmai'greiʃən] (Aus)Wanderung *f*; Seelenwanderung *f*.

**transmission** [trænz'miʃən] Übermittlung *f*; *biol.* Vererbung *f*; *phys.* Fortpflanzung *f*; *mot.* Getriebe *n*; *Radio:* Sendung *f*.

**transmit** [trænz'mit] übermitteln, übersenden; übertragen; senden; *biol.* vererben; *phys.* fortpflanzen; ~**ter** [~tə] Übermittler(in); *tel. etc.* Sender *m*.

**transmute** [trænz'mju:t] um-, verwandeln.

**transparent** ☐ [træns'pɛərənt] durchsichtig (*a. fig.*).

**transpire** [træns'paiə] ausdünsten, ausschwitzen; *fig.* durchsickern.

**transplant** [træns'plɑ:nt] um-, verpflanzen; ~**ation** [trænsplɑ:n'teiʃən] Verpflanzung *f*.

**transport** 1. [træns'pɔ:t] fortschaffen, befördern, transportieren; *fig.* hinreißen; 2. ['trænspɔ:t] Fortschaffen n; Beförderung f; Transport m; Verkehr m; Beförderungsmittel n; Transportschiff n; Verzückung f; *be in* ~s außer sich sein; **~ation** [trænspɔ'teiʃən] Beförderung f, Transport m.

**transpose** [træns'pouz] versetzen, umstellen; ♪ transponieren.

**transverse** □ ['trænzvə:s] quer laufend; Quer...

**trap** [træp] 1. Falle f (*a. fig.*); Klappe f; 2. (in e-r Falle) fangen, in die Falle locken; *fig.* ertappen; **~door** ['træpdɔ:] Falltür f; *thea.* Versenkung f.

**trapeze** [trə'pi:z] Zirkus: Trapez n.

**trapper** ['træpə] Trapper m, Fallensteller m, Pelzjäger m.

**trappings** *fig.* ['træpiŋz] *pl.* Schmuck m, Putz m.

**traps** F [træps] *pl.* Siebensachen *pl.*

**trash** [træʃ] Abfall m; *fig.* Plunder m; Unsinn m, F Blech n; Kitsch m; **~y** □ ['træʃi] wertlos, kitschig.

**travel** ['trævl] 1. *v/i.* reisen; sich bewegen; wandern; *v/t.* bereisen; 2. *das* Reisen; ⊕ Lauf m; ~s *pl.* Reisen f/pl.; **~(l)er** [~lə] Reisende(r) m; ~'s cheque (*Am. check*) Reisescheck m.

**traverse** ['trævə(:)s] 1. Durchquerung f; 2. (über)queren; durchqueren; *fig.* durchkreuzen.

**travesty** ['trævisti] 1. Travestie f; Karikatur f; 2. travestieren; verulken.

**trawl** [trɔ:l] 1. (Grund)Schleppnetz n; 2. mit dem Schleppnetz fischen; **~er** ['trɔ:lə] Trawler m.

**tray** [trei] (Servier)Brett n, Tablett n; Ablage f; *pen*-~ Federschale f.

**treacher|ous** □ ['tretʃərəs] verräterisch, treulos; (heim)tückisch; trügerisch; **~y** [~ri] Verrat m, Verräterei f, Treulosigkeit f; Tücke f.

**treacle** ['tri:kl] Sirup m.

**tread** [tred] 1. *[irr.]* treten; schreiten; 2. Tritt m, Schritt m; Lauffläche f; **~le** ['tredl] Pedal n; Tritt m; **~mill** Tretmühle f.

**treason** ['tri:zn] Verrat m; **~able** □ [~nəbl] verräterisch.

**treasure** ['treʒə] 1. Schatz m, Reichtum m; ~ trove Schatzfund m; 2. *Schätze* sammeln, aufhäufen; **~r** [~ərə] Schatzmeister m, Kassenwart m.

**treasury** ['treʒəri] Schatzkammer f; (*bsd.* Staats)Schatz m; ♀ **Bench** *parl.* Ministerbank f; ♀ **Board**, *Am.* ♀ **Department** Finanzministerium m.

**treat** [tri:t] 1. *v/t.* behandeln; betrachten; ~ *s.o. to s.th.* j-m et. spendieren; *v/i.* ~ *of* handeln von; ~ *with* unterhandeln mit j-m; 2. Vergnügen n; *school* ~ Schulausflug m; *it is my* ~ F es geht auf meine Rechnung; **~ise** ['tri:tiz] Abhandlung f;

**~ment** [~tmənt] Behandlung f; ♣ Kur f; *follow-up* ~ ♣ Nachkur f; **~y** ['tri:ti] Vertrag m.

**treble** ['trebl] 1. □ dreifach; 2. Dreifache(s) n; ♪ Diskant m, Sopran m; 3. (sich) verdreifachen.

**tree** [tri:] Baum m.

**trefoil** ♀ ['trefɔil] Klee m.

**trellis** ['trelis] 1. ✗ Spalier n; 2. vergittern; ✗ am Spalier ziehen.

**tremble** ['trembl] zittern.

**tremendous** □ [tri'mendəs] schrecklich, furchtbar; F kolossal, riesig.

**tremor** ['tremə] Zittern n, Beben n.

**tremulous** □ ['tremjuləs] zitternd, bebend.

**trench** [trentʃ] 1. (Schützen)Graben m; Furche f; 2. *v/t.* mit Gräben durchziehen; ✗ umgraben; ~ (*up*)*on* eingreifen in (*acc.*); **~ant** □ ['trentʃənt] scharf.

**trend** [trend] 1. Richtung f; *fig.* Lauf m; *fig.* Strömung f; Tendenz f; 2. sich erstrecken, laufen.

**trepidation** [trepi'deiʃən] Zittern n, Beben n; Bestürzung f.

**trespass** ['trespəs] 1. Übertretung f; 2. unbefugt eindringen (*on, upon* in *acc.*); über Gebühr in Anspruch nehmen; **~er** ⚖ [~sə] Rechtsverletzer m; Unbefugte(r m) f.

**tress** [tres] Haarlocke f, -flechte f.

**trestle** ['tresl] Gestell n, Bock m.

**trial** ['traiəl] Versuch m; Probe f, Prüfung f (*a. fig.*); Plage f; ⚖ Verhandlung f, Prozeß m; *on* ~ auf Probe; vor Gericht; *give s.o. a* ~ es mit j-m versuchen; ~ *run* Probefahrt f.

**triang|le** ['traiæŋgl] Dreieck n; **~ular** □ [trai'æŋgjulə] dreieckig.

**tribe** [traib] Stamm m; Geschlecht n; *contp.* Sippe f; ♀, *zo.* Klasse f.

**tribun|al** [trai'bju:nl] Richterstuhl m; Gericht(shof m) n; **~e** ['tribju:n] Tribun m; Tribüne f.

**tribut|ary** ['tribjutəri] 1. □ zinspflichtig; *fig.* helfend; Neben...; 2. Nebenfluß m; **~e** [~ju:t] Tribut m (*a. fig.*), Zins m; Anerkennung f.

**trice** [trais]: *in a* ~ im Nu.

**trick** [trik] 1. Kniff m, List f, Trick m; Kunstgriff m, -stück n; Streich m; Eigenheit f; 2. betrügen; herausputzen; **~ery** ['trikəri] Betrügerei f.

**trickle** ['trikl] tröpfeln, rieseln.

**trick|ster** ['trikstə] Gauner m; **~y** □ [~ki] verschlagen; F heikel; verzwickt, verwickelt.

**tricycle** ['traisikl] Dreirad n.

**trident** ['traidənt] Dreizack m.

**trifl|e** ['traifl] 1. Kleinigkeit f; Lappalie f; *a* ~ ein bißchen, ein wenig, etwas; 2. *v/i.* spielen, spaßen; *v/t.* ~ *away* verschwenden; **~ing** □ [~liŋ] geringfügig; unbedeutend.

**trig** [trig] 1. hemmen; 2. schmuck.

**trigger** ['trigə] Abzug *m am Gewehr*; *phot.* Auslöser *m*.

**trill** [tril] 1. Triller *m*; gerolltes R; 2. trillern; *bsd.* das R rollen.

**trillion** ['triljən] Trillion *f*; *Am.* Billion *f*.

**trim** [trim] 1. □ ordentlich; schmuck; gepflegt; 2. (richtiger) Zustand; Ordnung *f*; 3. zurechtmachen; (~ *up* aus)putzen, schmükken; besetzen; stutzen; beschneiden; ✂, ⚓ trimmen; **~ming** ['trimin] *mst* **~s** *pl.* Besatz *m*, Garnierung *f*.

**Trinity** *eccl.* ['triniti] Dreieinigkeit *f*.

**trinket** ['triŋkit] wertloses Schmuckstück; **~s** *pl.* F Kinkerlitzchen *pl.*

**trip** [trip] 1. Reise *f*, Fahrt *f*; Ausflug *m*, Spritztour *f*; Stolpern *n*, Fallen *n*; Fehltritt *m* (*a. fig.*); *fig.* Versehen *n*, Fehler *m*; 2. *v/i.* trippeln; stolpern; e-n Fehltritt tun (*a. fig.*); *fig.* e-n Fehler machen; *v/t. a.* ~ *up* j-m ein Bein stellen (*a. fig.*).

**tripartite** ['trai'pu:tait] dreiteilig.

**tripe** [traip] Kaldaunen *f/pl.*

**triple** □ ['tripl] dreifach; **~ts** [~lits] *pl.* Drillinge *m/pl.*

**triplicate** 1. ['triplikit] dreifach; 2. [~keit] verdreifachen.

**tripod** ['traipɔd] Dreifuß *m*; *phot.* Stativ *n*.

**tripper** F ['tripə] Ausflügler(in).

**trite** □ [trait] abgedroschen, platt.

**triturate** ['trit∫ureit] zerreiben.

**triumph** ['traiəmf] 1. Triumph *m*, Sieg *m*; 2. triumphieren; **~al** [trai-'æmfəl] Sieges..., Triumph...; **~ant** □ [~ənt] triumphierend.

**trivial** □ ['triviəl] bedeutungslos; unbedeutend; trivial; alltäglich.

**trod** [trɔd] *pret. von* tread 1; **~den** ['trɔdn] *p.p. von* tread 1.

**troll** [troul] (vor sich hin)trällern.

**troll(e)y** ['trɔli] Karren *m*; Draisine *f*; Servierwagen *m*; ⚡ Kontaktrolle *f* *es Oberleitungsfahrzeugs*; *Am.* Straßenbahnwagen *m*; **~ bus** O(ber-leitungs)bus *m*. [Hure *f*.]

**trollop** ['trɔləp] F Schlampe *f*.

**trombone** ♪ [trɔm'boun] Posaune *f*.

**troop** [tru:p] 1. Truppe *f*; Schar *f*; ✕ (Reiter)Zug *m*; 2. sich scharen, sich sammeln; ~ *away*, ~ *off* abziehen; **~ing** the colour(s) ✕ Fahnenparade *f*; **~er** ✕ ['tru:pə] Kavallerist *m*.

**trophy** ['troufi] Trophäe *f*.

**tropic** ['trɔpik] Wendekreis *m*; **~s** *pl.* Tropen *pl.*; **~(al** □) [~k(ə)l] tropisch.

**trot** [trɔt] 1. Trott *m*, Trab *m*; 2. traben (lassen).

**trouble** ['trʌbl] 1. Unruhe *f*; Störung *f*; Kummer *m*, Not *f*; Mühe *f*; Plage *f*; Unannehmlichkeiten *f/pl.*; ask *od.* look for ~ sich (selbst) Schwierigkeiten machen; das

Schicksal herausfordern; take (the) ~ sich (die) Mühe machen; 2. stören, beunruhigen, belästigen; quälen, plagen; Mühe machen (*dat.*); (sich) bemühen; ~ *s.o.* for j-n bemühen um; **~man**, **~shooter** *Am.* F Störungssucher *m*; **~some** □ [~ʃsəm] beschwerlich, lästig.

**trough** [trɔf] (Futter)Trog *m*; Backtrog *m*, Mulde *f*.

**trounce** F [trauns] *j-n* verhauen.

**troupe** *thea.* [tru:p] Truppe *f*.

**trousers** ['trauzəz] *pl.* (a pair of ~ *pl.* eine) (lange) Hose; Hosen *f/pl.*

**trousseau** ['tru:sou] Aussteuer *f*.

**trout** *ichth.* [traut] Forelle(n *pl.*) *f*.

**trowel** ['trauəl] Maurerkelle *f*.

**truant** ['tru(:)ənt] 1. müßig; 2. Schulschwänzer *m*; *fig.* Bummler *m*.

**truce** [tru:s] Waffenstillstand *m*.

**truck** [trʌk] 1. (offener) Güterwagen; Last(kraft)wagen *m*, Lkw *m*; Transportkarren *m*; Tausch (-handel) *m*; Verkehr *m*; Naturallohnsystem *n*; *Am.* Gemüse *n*; 2. (ver)tauschen; **~farm** *Am.* ['trʌkfa:m] Gemüsegärtnerei *f*.

**truckle** ['trʌkl] zu Kreuze kriechen.

**truculent** □ ['trʌkjulənt] wild, roh.

**trudge** [trʌdʒ] wandern; sich (dahin)schleppen, mühsam gehen.

**true** [tru:] wahr; echt, wirklich; treu; genau; richtig; it is ~ gewiß, freilich, zwar; come ~ sich bewahrheiten; in Erfüllung gehen; ~ to nature naturgetreu.

**truism** ['tru(:)izəm] Binsenwahrheit *f*.

**truly** ['tru:li] wirklich; wahrhaft; aufrichtig; genau; treu; Yours ~ Hochachtungsvoll.

**trump** [trʌmp] 1. Trumpf *m*; 2. (über)trumpfen; ~ *up* erdichten; **~ery** ['trʌmpəri] Plunder *m*.

**trumpet** ['trʌmpit] 1. Trompete *f*; 2. trompeten; *fig.* ausposaunen.

**truncheon** ['trʌnt∫ən] (Polizei-)Knüppel *m*; Kommandostab *m*.

**trundle** ['trʌndl] rollen.

**trunk** [trʌŋk] (Baum)Stamm *m*; Rumpf *m*; Rüssel *m*; *großer* Koffer; **~call** *teleph.* ['trʌŋkɔ:l] Ferngespräch *n*; **~exchange** *teleph.* Fernamt *n*; **~line** ⚡ Hauptlinie *f*; *teleph.* Fernleitung *f*; **~s** [trʌŋks] *pl.* Turnhose *f*; Badehose *f*; Herrenunterhose *f*.

**trunnion** ⊕ ['trʌnjən] Zapfen *m*.

**truss** [trʌs] 1. Bündel *n*, Bund *n*; ⚕ Bruchband *n*; ⚖ Binder *m*, Gerüst *n*; 2. (zs.-)binden; △ stützen.

**trust** [trʌst] 1. Vertrauen *n*; Glaube *m*; Kredit *m*; Pfand *n*; Verwahrung *f*; ⚖ Treuhand *f*; † Ring *m*, Trust *m*; ~ company Treuhandgesellschaft *f*; in ~ zu treuen Händen; 2. *v/t.* (ver)trauen (*dat.*); anvertrauen, übergeben (*s.o. with s.th., s.th. to s.o.* j-m et.); zuversichtlich hoffen;

v/i. vertrauen (in, to auf acc.); ⁓ee [trʌs'ti:] Sach-, Verwalter m; ⁓ Treuhänder m; ⁓ful □ ['trʌstful], ⁓ing □ [⁓tiŋ] vertrauensvoll; ⁓worthy [⁓twəːδi] vertrauenswürdig; zuverlässig.

**truth** [tru:θ], pl. ⁓s [tru:δz] Wahrheit f; Wirklichkeit f; Wahrhaftigkeit f; Genauigkeit f; ⁓ful □ ['tru:θful] wahrhaft(ig).

**try** [trai] **1.** versuchen; probieren; prüfen; ⁒ verhandeln über et. od. gegen j-n; vor Gericht stellen; aburteilen; die Augen etc. angreifen; sich bemühen od. bewerben; ⁓ on Kleid anprobieren; **2.** Versuch m; ⁓ing □ ['traiiŋ] anstrengend; kritisch.

**Tsar** [za:] Zar m.

**T-shirt** ['ti:ʃəːt] kurzärmeliges Sporthemd.

**tub** [tʌb] **1.** Faß n, Zuber m; Kübel m; Badewanne f; F (Wannen)Bad n.

**tube** [tju:b] Rohr n; (Am. bsd. Radio)Röhre f; Tube f; (Luft-)Schlauch m; Tunnel m; F (Londoner) Untergrundbahn f.

**tuber** ⚕ ['tju:bə] Knolle f; ⁓culosis [tju(:)bəːkju'lousis] Tuberkulose f.

**tubular** □ ['tju:bjulə] röhrenförmig.

**tuck** [tʌk] **1.** Falte f; Abnäher m; **2.** ab-, aufnähen; packen, stecken; ⁓ up hochschürzen, aufkrempeln; in e-e Decke etc. einwickeln.

**Tuesday** ['tju:zdi] Dienstag m.

**tuft** [tʌft] Büschel n, Busch m; (Haar)Schopf m.

**tug** [tʌg] **1.** Zug m, Ruck m; ⚓ Schlepper m; fig. Anstrengung f; **2.** ziehen, zerren; ⚓ schleppen; sich mühen.

**tuition** [tju(:)'iʃən] Unterricht m; Schulgeld n.

**tulip** ⚘ ['tju:lip] Tulpe f.

**tumble** ['tʌmbl] **1.** v/i. fallen, purzeln; taumeln; sich wälzen; v/t. werfen; zerknüllen; **2.** Sturz m; Wirrwarr m; ⁓down baufällig; ⁓r [⁓lə] Becher m; orn. Tümmler m.

**tumid** □ ['tju:mid] geschwollen.

**tummy** F ['tʌmi] Bäuchlein n, Magen m.

**tumo(u)r** ⚚ ['tju:mə] Tumor m.

**tumult** ['tju:mʌlt] Tumult m; ⁓uous □ [tju(:)'mʌltjuəs] stürmisch.

**tun** [tʌn] Tonne f, Faß n.

**tuna** ichth. ['tu:nə] Thunfisch m.

**tune** [tju:n] **1.** Melodie f, Weise f; ♪ Stimmung f (a. fig.); in ⁓ (gut-) gestimmt; out of ⁓ verstimmt; **2.** stimmen (a. fig.); ⁓ in Radio: einstellen; ⁓ out Radio: ausschalten; ⁓ up die Instrumente stimmen; fig. Befinden etc. heben; mot. die Leistung erhöhen; ⁓ful □ ['tju:nful] melodisch; ⁓less □ [⁓nlis] unmelodisch.

**tunnel** ['tʌnl] **1.** Tunnel m; ⚒

Stollen m; **2.** e-n Tunnel bohren (durch).

**tunny** ichth. ['tʌni] Thunfisch m.

**turbid** ['təːbid] trüb; dick.

**turb|ine** ⊕ ['təːbin] Turbine f; ⁓o-jet ['təːbou'dʒet] Strahlturbine f; ⁓o-prop [⁓ou'prɔp] Propellerturbine f.

**turbot** ichth. ['təːbət] Steinbutt m.

**turbulent** □ ['təːbjulənt] unruhig; ungestüm; stürmisch, turbulent.

**tureen** [təˈriːn] Terrine f.

**turf** [təːf] **1.** Rasen m; Torf m; Rennbahn f; Rennsport m; **2.** mit Rasen bedecken; ⁓y ['təːfi] rasenbedeckt.

**turgid** □ ['təːdʒid] geschwollen.

**Turk** [təːk] Türk|e m, -in f.

**turkey** ['təːki] orn. Truthahn m, -henne f, Pute(r m) f; Am. sl. thea., Film: Pleite f, Versager m.

**Turkish** ['təːkiʃ] türkisch.

**turmoil** ['təːmɔil] Aufruhr m, Unruhe f; Durcheinander n.

**turn** [təːn] **1.** v/t. drehen; (um)wenden, umkehren; lenken; verwandeln; abbringen; abwehren; übertragen; bilden; drechseln; verrückt machen; ⁓ a corner um eine Ecke biegen; ⁓ s.o. against j-n aufhetzen gegen; ⁓ aside abwenden; ⁓ away abwenden; abweisen; ⁓ down umbiegen; Gas etc. kleinstellen; Decke etc. zurückschlagen; ablehnen; ⁓ off ableiten (a. fig.); hinauswerfen; wegjagen; ⁓ off (on) ab- (an)drehen, ab- (ein)schalten; ⁓ out hinauswerfen; Fabrikat herausbringen; Gas etc. ausdrehen; ⁓ over umwenden; fig. übertragen; ✝ umsetzen; überlegen; ⁓ up nach oben richten; hochklappen; umwenden; Hose etc. auf-, umschlagen; Gas etc. aufdrehen; v/i. sich (um)drehen; sich wenden; sich verwandeln; umschlagen (Wetter etc.); Christ, grau etc. werden; a. ⁓ sour sauer werden (Milch); ⁓ about sich umdrehen; ⁓ back zurückkehren; ⁓ in einkehren; F zu Bett gehen; ⁓ off abbiegen; ⁓ on sich drehen um; ⁓ out ausfallen, ausgehen; sich herausstellen als; ⁓ to sich zuwenden (dat.), sich wenden an (acc.); werden zu; ⁓ up auftauchen; ⁓ upon sich wenden gegen; **2.** (Um)Drehung f; Biegung f; Wendung f; Neigung f; Wechsel m; Gestalt f, Form f; Spaziergang m; Reihe(nfolge) f; Dienst(leistung f) m; F Schreck m; at every ⁓ auf Schritt und Tritt; by od. in ⁓s der Reihe nach, abwechselnd; it is my ⁓ ich bin an der Reihe; take ⁓s mit-ea. abwechseln; does it serve your ⁓? entspricht das Ihren Zwecken?; ⁓coat ['təːnkout] Abtrünnige(r) m; ⁓er ['təːnə] Drechsler *m*; ~ery [~əri] Drechslerei *f*; Drechslerarbeit *f*.

**turning** ['tə:niŋ] Drechseln *n*; Wendung *f*; Biegung *f*; Straßenecke *f*; (Weg)Abzweigung *f*; Querstraße *f*; ~point *fig.* Wendepunkt *m.*

**turnip** ♀ ['tə:nip] (*bsd.* weiße) Rübe.

**turn|key** ['tə:nki:] Schließer *m*; ~out ['tə:n'aut] Ausstaffierung *f*; Arbeitseinstellung *f*; † Gesamtproduktion *f*; ~over ['tə:nouvə] † Umsatz *m*; Verschiebung *f*; ~pike Schlagbaum *m*; (gebührenpflichtige) Schnellstraße; ~stile Drehkreuz *n*. [pentin *n*.]

**turpentine** ⚕ ['tə:pəntain] Ter-)

**turpitude** ['tə:pitju:d] Schändlichkeit *f*.

**turret** ['tʌrit] Türmchen *n*; ✂, ⚓ Panzerturm *m*; ⚓ Kanzel *f*.

**turtle** ['tə:tl] *zo.* Schildkröte *f*; *orn. mst* ~dove Turteltaube *f*.

**tusk** [tʌsk] Fangzahn *m*; Stoßzahn *m*; Hauer *m*.

**tussle** ['tʌsl] **1.** Rauferei *f*, Balgerei *f*; **2.** raufen, sich balgen.

**tussock** ['tʌsək] Büschel *n*.

**tut** [tʌt] ach was!; Unsinn!

**tutelage** ['tju:tilidʒ] ⚖ Vormundschaft *f*; Bevormundung *f*.

**tutor** ['tju:tə] **1.** (Privat-, Haus-) Lehrer *m*; *univ.* Tutor *m*; *Am.univ.* Assistent *m* mit Lehrauftrag; ⚖ Vormund *m*; **2.** unterrichten; schulen, erziehen; *fig.* beherrschen; ~ial [tju(:)'tɔ:riəl] *univ.* Unterrichtsstunde *f* e-s *Tutors*; *attr.* Lehrer...; Tutoren...

**tuxedo** *Am.* [tʌk'si:dou] Smoking *m.*

**TV** ['ti:'vi:] Fernsehen *n*; Fernsehapparat *m*; *attr.* Fernseh...

**twaddle** ['twɔdl] **1.** Geschwätz *n*; **2.** schwatzen, quatschen.

**twang** [twæŋ] **1.** Schwirren *n*; *mst* nasal ~ näselnde Aussprache; **2.** schwirren (lassen); klimpern; näseln.

**tweak** [twi:k] zwicken.

**tweet** [twi:t] zwitschern.

**tweezers** ['twi:zəz] *pl.* (a pair of ~ *pl.* eine) Pinzette.

**twelfth** [twelfθ] **1.** zwölfte(r, -s); **2.** Zwölftel *n*; 2-night ['twelfθnait] Dreikönigsabend *m.*

**twelve** [twelv] zwölf.

**twent|ieth** ['twentiiθ] **1.** zwanzigste(r, -s); **2.** Zwanzigstel *n*; ~y [~ti] zwanzig.

**twice** [twais] zweimal.

**twiddle** ['twidl] (sich) drehen; mit *et.* spielen.

**twig** [twig] Zweig *m*, Rute *f*.

**twilight** ['twailait] Zwielicht *n*; Dämmerung *f* (*a. fig.*).

**twin** [twin] **1.** Zwillings...; doppelt; **2.** Zwilling *m*; ~engined ⚓ ['twinendʒind] zweimotorig.

**twine** [twain] **1.** Bindfaden *m*,

Schnur *f*; Zwirn *m*; **2.** zs.-drehen; verflechten; (sich) schlingen *od.* winden; umschlingen, umranken.

**twinge** [twindʒ] Zwicken *n*; Stich *m*; bohrender Schmerz.

**twinkle** ['twiŋkl] **1.** funkeln, blitzen; huschen; zwinkern; **2.** Funkeln *n*, Blitzen *n*; (Augen)Zwinkern *n*, Blinzeln *n.*

**twirl** [twə:l] **1.** Wirbel *m*; **2.** wirbeln.

**twist** [twist] **1.** Drehung *f*; Windung *f*; Verdrehung *f*; Verdrehtheit *f*; Neigung *f*; (Gesichts)Verzerrung *f*; Garn *n*; Kringel *m*, Zopf *m* (*Backwaren*); **2.** (sich) drehen *od.* winden; zs.-drehen; verdrehen, verziehen, verzerren.

**twit** *fig.* [twit] *j-n* aufziehen.

**twitch** [twitʃ] **1.** zupfen (an *dat.*); zucken; **2.** Zupfen *n*; Zuckung *f.*

**twitter** ['twitə] **1.** zwitschern; **2.** Gezwitscher *n*; be in a ~ zittern.

**two** [tu:] **1.** zwei; in ~ entzwei; put ~ and ~ together sich et. zs.-reimen; **2.** Zwei *f*; in ~s zu zweien; ~bit *Am.* F ['tu:bit] 25-Cent...; *fig.* unbedeutend, klein...; ~edged ['tu:-'edʒd] zweischneidig; ~fold ['tu:-fould] zweifach; ~pence ['tʌpəns] zwei Pence; ~penny ['tʌpni] zwei Pence wert; ~piece ['tu:pi:s] zweiteilig; ~seater *mot.* ['tu:'si:tə] Zweisitzer *m*; ~storey ['tu:stɔ:ri], ~storied zweistöckig; ~stroke *mot.* Zweitakt...; ~way Doppel...; ~ adapter ⚡ Doppelstecker *m*; ~ traffic Gegenverkehr *m.*

**tycoon** *Am.* F [tai'ku:n] Industriekapitän *m*, Industriemagnat *m.*

**tyke** [taik] Köter *m*; Kerl *m.*

**type** [taip] Typ *m*; Urbild *n*; Vorbild *n*; Muster *n*; Art *f*; Sinnbild *n*; *typ.* Type *f*, Buchstabe *m*; true to ~ artecht; set in ~ setzen; ~write ['taiprait] (*irr.* write) (mit der) Schreibmaschine schreiben; ~writer Schreibmaschine *f*; ~ ribbon Farbband *n.*

**typhoid** ⚗ ['taifoid] **1.** typhös; ~ fever = **2.** (Unterleibs)Typhus *m.*

**typhoon** [tai'fu:n] Taifun *m.*

**typhus** ⚗ ['taifəs] Flecktyphus *m.*

**typi|cal** □ ['tipikəl] typisch; richtig; bezeichnend, kennzeichnend; ~fy [~ifai] typisch sein für; versinnbildlichen; ~st ['taipist] *a.* shorthand ~ Stenotypistin *f.*

**tyrann|ic(al** □) [ti'rænik(əl)] tyrannisch; ~ize ['tirənaiz] tyrannisieren; ~y [~ni] Tyrannei *f.*

**tyrant** ['taiərənt] Tyrann(in).

**tyre** ['taiə] s. tire 1.

**tyro** ['taiərou] s. tiro.

**Tyrolese** [tirə'li:z] **1.** Tiroler(in); **2.** tirolisch, Tiroler...

**Tzar** [zɑ:] Zar *m.*

# U

**ubiquitous** □ [ju(:)'bikwitəs] allgegenwärtig, überall zu finden(d).

**udder** ['ʌdə] Euter *n*.

**ugly** □ ['ʌgli] häßlich; schlimm.

**ulcer** ♫ ['ʌlsə] Geschwür *n*; (Eiter-) Beule *f*; ~ate ♫ [~əreit] eitern (lassen); ~ous ♫ [~rəs] geschwürig.

**ulterior** □ [ʌl'tiəriə] jenseitig; *fig.* weiter; tiefer liegend, versteckt.

**ultimate** □ ['ʌltimit] letzt; endlich; End...; ~ly [~tli] zu guter Letzt.

**ultimat|um** [ʌlti'meitəm], *pl. a.* ~a [~tə] Ultimatum *n*.

**ultimo** † ['ʌltimou] vorigen Monats.

**ultra** ['ʌltrə] übermäßig; Ultra..., ultra...; ~**fashionable** ['ʌltrə'fæʃənəbl] hypermodern; ~**modern** hypermodern.

**umbel** ♀ ['ʌmbəl] Dolde *f*.

**umbrage** ['ʌmbridʒ] Anstoß *m* (*Ärger*); Schatten *m*.

**umbrella** [ʌm'brelə] Regenschirm *m*; *fig.* Schirm *m*, Schutz *m*; ⚔ Abschirmung *f*. ·

**umpire** ['ʌmpaiə] 1. Schiedsrichter *m*; 2. Schiedsrichter sein.

**un...** [ʌn] un...; Un...; ent...; nicht...

**unabashed** ['ʌnə'bæʃt] unverfroren; unerschrocken.

**unabated** ['ʌnə'beitid] unvermindert. [stande.]

**unable** ['ʌn'eibl] unfähig, außer-]

**unaccommodating** ['ʌnə'kɔmədeitiŋ] unnachgiebig.

**unaccountable** □ ['ʌnə'kauntəbl] unerklärlich; seltsam; nicht zur Rechenschaft verpflichtet.

**unaccustomed** ['ʌnə'kʌstəmd] ungewohnt; ungewöhnlich.

**unacquainted** ['ʌnə'kweintid]: ~ *with* unbekannt mit, *e-r S* unkundig.

**unadvised** □ ['ʌnəd'vaizd] unbedacht; unberaten.

**unaffected** □ ['ʌnə'fektid] unberührt; ungerührt; ungekünstelt.

**unaided** ['ʌn'eidid] ohne Unterstützung; (ganz) allein; bloß (*Auge*).

**unalter|able** □ [ʌn'ɔːltərəbl] unveränderlich; ~ed ['ʌn'ɔːltəd] unverändert.

**unanim|ity** [juːnə'nimiti] Einmütigkeit *f*; ~ous □ [juː(ː)'næniməs] einmütig, einstimmig.

**unanswer|able** □ [ʌn'ɑːnsərəbl] unwiderleglich; ~ed ['ʌn'ɑːnsəd] unbeantwortet.

**unapproachable** □ [ʌnə'proutʃəbl] unzugänglich.

**unapt** □ [ʌn'æpt] ungeeignet.

**unashamed** □ ['ʌnə'ʃeimd] schamlos.

**unasked** ['ʌn'ɑːskt] unverlangt; ungebeten.

**unassisted** □ ['ʌnə'sistid] ohne Hilfe *od.* Unterstützung.

**unassuming** □ ['ʌnə'sjuːmiŋ] anspruchslos, bescheiden.

**unattached** ['ʌnə'tætʃt] nicht gebunden; ungebunden, ledig, frei.

**unattractive** □ [ʌnə'træktiv] wenig anziehend, reizlos; uninteressant.

**unauthorized** ['ʌn'ɔːθəraizd] unberechtigt, unbefugt.

**unavail|able** ['ʌnə'veiləbl] nicht verfügbar; ~ing [~liŋ] vergeblich.

**unavoidable** □ [ʌnə'vɔidəbl] unvermeidlich.

**unaware** ['ʌnə'wɛə] ohne Kenntnis; *be* ~ *of et.* nicht merken; ~s [~əz] unversehens, unvermutet; versehentlich.

**unbacked** ['ʌn'bækt] ohne Unterstützung; ungedeckt (*Scheck*).

**unbag** ['ʌn'bæg] aus dem Sack holen *od.* lassen.

**unbalanced** ['ʌn'bælənst] nicht im Gleichgewicht befindlich; unausgeglichen; geistesgestört.

**unbearable** □ [ʌn'bɛərəbl] unerträglich.

**unbeaten** ['ʌn'biːtn] ungeschlagen; unbetreten (*Weg*).

**unbecoming** □ ['ʌnbi'kʌmiŋ] unkleidsam; unziemlich, unschicklich.

**unbeknown** F ['ʌnbi'noun] unbekannt.

**unbelie|f** ['ʌnbi'liːf] Unglaube *m*; ~**vable** [ʌnbi'liːvəbl] unglaublich; ~**ving** □ ['ʌnbi'liːviŋ] ungläubig.

**unbend** ['ʌn'bend] [*irr.* (*bend*)] (sich) entspannen; freundlich werden, auftauen; ~ing [~diŋ] unbiegsam; *fig.* unbeugsam.

**unbias(s)ed** □ ['ʌn'baiəst] vorurteilsfrei, unbefangen, unbeeinflußt.

**unbid(den)** ['ʌn'bid(n)] ungeheißen, unaufgefordert; ungebeten.

**unbind** ['ʌn'baind] [*irr.* (*bind*)] losbinden, befreien; lösen.

**unblushing** □ [ʌn'blʌʃiŋ] schamlos. [boren.]

**unborn** ['ʌn'bɔːn] (noch) unge-]

**unbosom** [ʌn'buzəm] offenbaren.

**unbounded** □ [ʌn'baundid] unbegrenzt; schrankenlos.

**unbroken** □ ['ʌn'broukən] ungebrochen; unversehrt; ununterbrochen.

**unbutton** ['ʌn'bʌtn] aufknöpfen.

**uncalled-for** [ʌn'kɔːldfɔː] ungerufen; unverlangt (*S.*); unpassend.

**uncanny** □ [ʌn'kæni] unheimlich.

**uncared-for** ['ʌn'kɛədfɔː] unbeachtet, vernachlässigt.

**unceasing** □ [ʌn'siːsiŋ] unaufhörlich.

**unceremonious** □ ['ʌnseri'mounjəs] ungezwungen; formlos.

**uncertain** □ [ʌn'səːtn] unsicher; ungewiß; unbestimmt; unzuverlässig; **~ty** [~nti] Unsicherheit *f*.

**unchallenged** ['ʌn'tʃælindʒd] unangefochten.

**unchang|eable** □ [ʌn'tʃeindʒəbl] unveränderlich, unwandelbar; **~ed** ['ʌn'tʃeindʒd] unverändert; **~ing** [~'ʌn'tʃeindʒiŋ] unveränderlich.

**uncharitable** □ [ʌn'tʃæritəbl] lieblos; unbarmherzig; unfreundlich.

**unchecked** ['ʌn'tʃekt] ungehindert.

**uncivil** □ ['ʌn'sivl] unhöflich; **~ized** [~vilaizd] unzivilisiert.

**unclaimed** ['ʌn'kleimd] nicht beansprucht (*bsd. Brief*).

**unclasp** ['ʌn'klɑːsp] auf-, loshaken, auf-, losschnallen; aufmachen.

**uncle** ['ʌŋkl] Onkel *m*.

**unclean** □ ['ʌn'kliːn] unrein.

**unclose** ['ʌn'klouz] (sich) öffnen.

**uncomely** ['ʌn'kʌmli] reizlos; unpassend.

**uncomfortable** □ [ʌn'kʌmfətəbl] unbehaglich, ungemütlich; unangenehm.

**uncommon** □ [ʌn'kɔmən] ungewöhnlich.

**uncommunicative** □ ['ʌnkə'mjuːnikətiv] wortkarg, schweigsam.

**uncomplaining** □ ['ʌnkəm'pleiniŋ] klaglos; ohne Murren; geduldig.

**uncompromising** □ [ʌn'kɔmprəmaiziŋ] kompromißlos.

**unconcern** ['ʌnkən'səːn] Unbekümmertheit *f*; Gleichgültigkeit *f*; **~ed** □ [~nd] unbekümmert; unbeteiligt.

**unconditional** □ ['ʌnkən'diʃənl] unbedingt; bedingungslos.

**unconfirmed** ['ʌnkən'fəːmd] unbestätigt; *eccl.* nicht konfirmiert.

**unconnected** ['ʌnkə'nektid] unverbunden.

**unconquer|able** □ [ʌn'kɔŋkərəbl] unüberwindlich; **~ed** ['ʌn'kɔŋkəd] unbesiegt.

**unconscionable** □ [ʌn'kɔnʃnəbl] gewissenlos; F unverschämt, übermäßig.

**unconscious** □ [ʌn'kɔnʃəs] unbewußt; bewußtlos; **~ness** [~snis] Bewußtlosigkeit *f*.

**unconstitutional** □ ['ʌnkɔnsti'tjuːʃənl] verfassungswidrig.

**uncontroll|able** □ [ʌnkən'trouləbl] unkontrollierbar; unbändig; **~ed** ['ʌnkən'trould] unbeaufsichtigt; *fig.* unbeherrscht.

**unconventional** □ ['ʌnkən'venʃənl] unkonventionell; ungezwungen.

**unconvinc|ed** [ʌnkən'vinst] nicht überzeugt; **~ing** [~siŋ] nicht überzeugend.

**uncork** ['ʌn'kɔːk] entkorken.

**uncount|able** □ [ʌn'kauntəbl] unzählbar; **~ed** [~tid] ungezählt.

**uncouple** ['ʌn'kʌpl] loskoppeln.

**uncouth** □ [ʌn'kuːθ] ungeschlacht.

**uncover** [ʌn'kʌvə] aufdecken, freilegen; entblößen.

**unct|ion** ['ʌŋkʃən] Salbung *f* (*a. fig.*); Salbe *f*; **~uous** □ ['ʌŋktjuəs] fettig, ölig; *fig.* salbungsvoll.

**uncult|ivated** ['ʌn'kʌltiveitid], **~ured** [~tʃəd] unkultiviert.

**undamaged** ['ʌn'dæmidʒd] unbeschädigt.

**undaunted** □ [ʌn'dɔːntid] unerschrocken.

**undeceive** ['ʌndi'siːv] *j-n* aufklären.

**undecided** □ ['ʌndi'saidid] unentschieden; unentschlossen.

**undefined** □ ['ʌndi'faind] unbestimmt; unbegrenzt.

**undemonstrative** □ ['ʌndi'mɔnstrətiv] zurückhaltend.

**undeniable** □ ['ʌndi'naiəbl] unleugbar; unbestreitbar.

**under** ['ʌndə] 1. *adv.* unten; darunter; 2. *prp.* unter; 3. *adj.* unter; *in Zssgn:* unter...; Unter...; mangelhaft ...; **~bid** [~'bid] [*irr.* (bid)] unterbieten; **~brush** [~brʌʃ] Unterholz *n*; **~carriage** ✕ (Flugzeug)Fahrwerk *n*; *mot.* Fahrgestell *n*; **~clothes**, **~clothing** Unterkleidung *f*, Unterwäsche *f*; **~cut** [~'kʌt] Preise unterbieten; **~dog** [~dɔg] Unterlegene(r) *m*; Unterdrückte(r) *m*; **~done** [~'dʌn] nicht gar; **~estimate** [~r'estimeit] unterschätzen; **~fed** [~'fed] unterernährt; **~go** [ʌndə'gou] [*irr.* (go)] erdulden; sich unterziehen (*dat.*); **~graduate** [~'grædjuit] Student (-in); **~ground** ['ʌndəgraund] 1. unterirdisch; Untergrund...; 2. Untergrundbahn *f*; **~growth** Unterholz *n*; **~hand** unter der Hand; heimlich; **~lie** [ʌndə'lai] [*irr.* (lie)] zugrunde liegen (*dat.*); **~line** [~'lain] unterstreichen; **~ling** ['ʌndəliŋ] Untergeordnete(r) *m*; **~mine** [ʌndə'main] unterminieren; *fig.* untergraben; schwächen; **~most** ['ʌndəmoust] unterst; **~neath** [ʌndə'niːθ] 1. *prp.* unter (-halb); 2. *adv.* unten; darunter; **~pin** [~'pin] untermauern; **~plot** ['ʌndəplɔt] Nebenhandlung *f*; **~privileged** [~'privilidʒd] benachteiligt; **~rate** [ʌndə'reit] unterschätzen; **~secretary** ['ʌndə'sekrətəri] Unterstaatssekretär *m*; **~sell** ✝ [~'sel] [*irr.* (sell)] *j-n* unterbieten; *Ware* verschleudern; **~signed** [~saind] Unterzeichnete(r) *m*; **~sized** [~'saizd] zu klein; **~staffed** [ʌndə'stɑːft] unterbesetzt; **~stand** [~'stænd] [*irr.* (stand)] *allg.* verstehen; sich verstehen auf (*acc.*); (als sicher) annehmen; auffassen; (sinngemäß) ergänzen; *make o.s. understood* sich verständlich machen; *an understood thing* e-e abgemachte Sache; **~standable** [~dəbl] verständlich; **~standing** [~diŋ]

Verstand *m*; Einvernehmen *n*; Verständigung *f*; Abmachung *f*; Voraussetzung *f*; **~state** ['ʌndə'steit] zu gering angeben; abschwächen; **~statement** Unterbewertung *f*; Understatement *n*, Untertreibung *f*; **~take** [ʌndə'teik] [*irr.* (*take*)] unternehmen; übernehmen; sich verpflichten; **~taker** ['ʌndəteikə] Bestattungsinstitut *n*; **~taking** [ʌndə'teikiŋ] Unternehmung *f*; Verpflichtung *f*; ['ʌndəteikiŋ] Leichenbestattung *f*; **~tone** leiser Ton; **~value** [~'vælju:] unterschätzen; **~wear** [~wɛə] Unterkleidung *f*, Unterwäsche *f*; **~wood** Unterholz *n*; **~write** [*irr.* (*write*)] *Versicherung* abschließen; **~writer** Versicherer *m*.

**undeserv|ed** □ ['ʌndi'zə:vd] unverdient; **~ing** [~viŋ] unwürdig.

**undesigned** □ ['ʌndi'zaind] unbeabsichtigt; absichtslos.

**undesirable** ['ʌndi'zairəbl] **1.** □ unerwünscht; **2.** unerwünschte Person.

**undeviating** □ [ʌn'di:vieitiŋ] unentwegt.

**undignified** □ [ʌn'dignifaid] würdelos.

**undisciplined** [ʌn'disiplind] zuchtlos, undiszipliniert; ungeschult.

**undisguised** □ ['ʌndis'gaizd] unverkleidet; unverhohlen.

**undisputed** □ ['ʌndis'pju:tid] unbestritten.

**undo** ['ʌn'du:] [*irr.* (*do*)] aufmachen; (auf)lösen; ungeschehen machen, aufheben; vernichten; **~ing** [~u(:)iŋ] Aufmachen *n*; Ungeschehenmachen *n*; Vernichtung *f*; Verderben *n*; **~ne** ['ʌn'dʌn] erledigt, vernichtet.

**undoubted** □ [ʌn'dautid] unzweifelhaft, zweifellos.

**undreamt** □ [ʌn'dremt]: **~of** ungeahnt.

**undress** ['ʌn'dres] **1.** (sich) entkleiden *od.* ausziehen; **2.** Hauskleid *n*; **~ed** unbekleidet; unangezogen; nicht zurechtgemacht.

**undue** □ ['ʌn'dju:] ungebührlich; übermäßig; † noch nicht fällig.

**undulat|e** ['ʌndjuleit] wogen; wallen; wellig sein; **~ion** [ʌndju'leiʃən] wellenförmige Bewegung.

**undutiful** □ ['ʌn'dju:tiful] ungehorsam, pflichtvergessen.

**unearth** [ʌn'ə:θ] ausgraben; *fig.* aufstöbern; **~ly** [ʌn'ə:θli] überirdisch.

**uneas|iness** [ʌn'i:zinis] Unruhe *f*; Unbehagen *n*; **~y** □ [ʌn'i:zi] unbehaglich; unruhig; unsicher.

**uneducated** □ ['ʌn'edjukeitid] unerzogen; ungebildet.

**unemotional** □ ['ʌni'mouʃənl] leidenschaftslos; passiv; nüchtern.

**unemploy|ed** ['ʌnim'plɔid] **1.** un-

beschäftigt; arbeitslos; unbenutzt; **2.**: the **~** *pl.* die Arbeitslosen *pl.*; **~ment** [~ɔimənt] Arbeitslosigkeit *f*.

**unending** □ [ʌn'endiŋ] endlos.

**unendurable** □ ['ʌnin'djuərəbl] unerträglich.

**unengaged** ['ʌnin'geidʒd] frei.

**unequal** □ ['ʌn'i:kwəl] ungleich; nicht gewachsen (**to** *dat.*); **~(l)ed** [~ld] unvergleichlich, unerreicht.

**unerring** □ ['ʌn'ə:riŋ] unfehlbar.

**unessential** □ ['ʌni'senʃəl] unwesentlich, unwichtig (**to** für).

**uneven** □ ['ʌn'i:vən] uneben; ungleich(mäßig); ungerade (*Zahl*).

**uneventful** □ ['ʌni'ventful] ereignislos; ohne Zwischenfälle.

**unexampled** [ʌnig'zɑ:mpld] beispiellos.

**unexceptionable** □ [ʌnik'sepʃnəbl] untadelig; einwandfrei.

**unexpected** □ ['ʌniks'pektid] unerwartet.

**unexplained** ['ʌniks'pleind] unerklärt.

**unfading** □ [ʌn'feidiŋ] nicht welkend; unvergänglich; echt (*Farbe*).

**unfailing** □ [ʌn'feiliŋ] unfehlbar; nie versagend; unerschöpflich; *fig.* treu.

**unfair** □ ['ʌn'fɛə] unehrlich; unfair; ungerecht.

**unfaithful** □ ['ʌn'feiθful] un(ge)treu, treulos; nicht wortgetreu.

**unfamiliar** ['ʌnfə'miljə] unbekannt; ungewohnt.

**unfasten** ['ʌn'fɑ:sn] aufmachen; lösen; **~ed** unbefestigt, lose.

**unfathomable** □ [ʌn'fæðəməbl] unergründlich.

**unfavo(u)rable** □ ['ʌn'feivərəbl] ungünstig.

**unfeeling** □ [ʌn'fi:liŋ] gefühllos.

**unfilial** □ ['ʌn'filjəl] respektlos, pflichtvergessen (*Kind*).

**unfinished** □ [ʌn'finiʃt] unvollendet; unfertig.

**unfit 1.** □ ['ʌn'fit] ungeeignet, unpassend; **2.** [ʌn'fit] untauglich machen.

**unfix** ['ʌn'fiks] losmachen, lösen.

**unfledged** ['ʌn'fledʒd] ungcfiedert; (noch) nicht flügge; *fig.* unreif.

**unflinching** □ [ʌn'flintʃiŋ] fest entschlossen, unnachgiebig.

**unfold** ['ʌn'fould] (sich) entfalten *od.* öffnen; [ʌn'fould] klarlegen; enthüllen.

**unforced** □ ['ʌn'fɔ:st] ungezwungen.

**unforeseen** ['ʌnfɔ:'si:n] unvorhergesehen.

**unforgettable** □ ['ʌnfə'getəbl] unvergeßlich.

**unforgiving** ['ʌnfə'giviŋ] unversöhnlich.

**unforgotten** ['ʌnfə'gɔtn] unvergessen.

**unfortunate** [ʌn'fɔ:tʃnit] **1.** □ unglücklich; 2. Unglückliche(r m) f; **~ly** [~tli] unglücklicherweise, leider.

**unfounded** □ ['ʌn'faundid] unbegründet; grundlos.

**unfriendly** ['ʌn'frendli] unfreundlich; ungünstig.

**unfurl** [ʌn'fə:l] entfalten, aufrollen.

**unfurnished** ['ʌn'fə:niʃt] unmöbliert.

**ungainly** [ʌn'geinli] unbeholfen, plump.

**ungenerous** □ ['ʌn'dʒenərəs] uncdelmütig; nicht freigebig.

**ungentle** □ ['ʌn'dʒentl] unsanft.

**ungodly** □ [ʌn'gɔdli] gottlos.

**ungovernable** □ [ʌn'gʌvənəbl] unlenksam; zügellos, unbändig.

**ungraceful** □ ['ʌn'greisful] ungraziös, ohne Anmut; unbeholfen.

**ungracious** □ ['ʌn'greiʃəs] ungnädig; unfreundlich.

**ungrateful** □ [ʌn'greitful] undankbar.

**unguarded** □ ['ʌn'gɑ:did] unbewacht; unvorsichtig; ungeschützt.

**unguent** ['ʌŋgwənt] Salbe f.

**unhampered** ['ʌn'hæmpəd] ungehindert.               [schön.]

**unhandsome** □ [ʌn'hænsəm] un-)

**unhandy** □ [ʌn'hændi] unhandlich; ungeschickt; unbeholfen.

**unhappy** □ [ʌn'hæpi] unglücklich.

**unharmed** ['ʌn'hɑ:md] unversehrt.

**unhealthy** □ [ʌn'helθi] ungesund.

**unheard-of** [ʌn'hə:dɔv] unerhört.

**unheed|ed** ['ʌn'hi:did] unbeachtet, unbewacht; **~ing** [~diŋ] sorglos.

**unhesitating** □ [ʌn'heziteitiŋ] ohne Zögern; unbedenklich.

**unholy** [ʌn'houli] unheilig; gottlos.

**unhono(u)red** ['ʌn'ɔnəd] ungeehrt; uneingelöst (Pfand, Scheck).

**unhook** ['ʌn'huk] auf-, aushaken.

**unhoped-for** [ʌn'houptfɔ:] unverhofft.

**unhurt** ['ʌn'hə:t] unverletzt.

**unicorn** ['ju:nikɔ:n] Einhorn n.

**unification** [ju:nifi'keiʃən] Vereinigung f; Vereinheitlichung f.

**uniform** ['ju:nifɔ:m] 1. □ gleichförmig, gleichmäßig; einheitlich; 2. Dienstkleidung f; Uniform f; 3. uniformieren; **~ity** [ju:ni'fɔ:miti] Gleichförmigkeit f, Gleichmäßigkeit f.

**unify** ['ju:nifai] verein(ig)en; vereinheitlichen.

**unilateral** □ ['ju:ni'lætərəl] einseitig.

**unimagina|ble** □ [ʌni'mædʒinəbl] undenkbar; **~tive** □ ['ʌni'mædʒinətiv] einfallslos.

**unimportant** □ ['ʌnim'pɔ:tənt] unwichtig.

**unimproved** ['ʌnim'pru:vd] nicht kultiviert, unbebaut (Land); unverbessert.

**uninformed** ['ʌnin'fɔ:md] nicht unterrichtet.

**uninhabit|able** ['ʌnin'hæbitəbl] unbewohnbar; **~ed** [~tid] unbewohnt.

**uninjured** ['ʌn'indʒəd] unbeschädigt, unverletzt.

**unintelligible** □ ['ʌnin'telidʒəbl] unverständlich.

**unintentional** □ ['ʌnin'tenʃənl] unabsichtlich.

**uninteresting** □ ['ʌn'intristiŋ] uninteressant.

**uninterrupted** □ ['ʌnintə'rʌptid] ununterbrochen.

**union** ['ju:njən] Vereinigung f; Verbindung f; Union f, Verband m; Einigung f; Einigkeit f; Verein m, Bund m; univ. (Debattier)Klub m; Gewerkschaft f; **~ist** [~nist] Gewerkschaftler m; **♀ Jack** Union Jack m (britische Nationalflagge); **~ suit** Am. Hemdhose f.

**unique** □ [ju:'ni:k] einzigartig, einmalig.

**unison** ♪ u. fig. ['ju:nizn] Einklang m.

**unit** ['ju:nit] Einheit f; ♣ Einer m; **~e** [ju:'nait] (sich) vereinigen, verbinden; **~ed** vereinigt, vereint; **~y** ['ju:niti] Einheit f; Einigkeit f.

**univers|al** □ [ju:ni'və:səl] allgemein; allumfassend; Universal..., Welt...; **~ality** [ju:nivə:'sæliti] Allgemeinheit f; umfassende Bildung, Vielseitigkeit f; **~e** ['ju:nivə:s] Weltall n, Universum n; **~ity** [ju:ni'və:siti] Universität f.

**unjust** □ ['ʌn'dʒʌst] ungerecht; **~ifiable** □ [ʌn'dʒʌstifaiəbl] nicht zu rechtfertigen(d), unverantwortlich.

**unkempt** ['ʌn'kempt] ungepflegt.

**unkind** □ [ʌn'kaind] unfreundlich.

**unknow|ing** □ ['ʌn'nouiŋ] unwissend; unbewußt; **~n** [~oun] 1. unbekannt; unbewußt; **~ to me** ohne mein Wissen; 2. Unbekannte(r m, -s n) f.

**unlace** ['ʌn'leis] aufschnüren.

**unlatch** ['ʌn'lætʃ] aufklinken.

**unlawful** □ ['ʌn'lɔ:ful] ungesetzlich; weitS. unrechtmäßig.

**unlearn** ['ʌn'lə:n] (irr. (learn)) verlernen.

**unless** [ən'les] wenn nicht, außer wenn; es sei denn, daß.

**unlike** ['ʌn'laik] 1. adj. □ ungleich; 2. prp. anders als; **~ly** [ʌn'laikli] unwahrscheinlich.

**unlimited** [ʌn'limitid] unbegrenzt.

**unload** ['ʌn'loud] ent-, ab-, ausladen; Ladung löschen.

**unlock** ['ʌn'lɔk] aufschließen; Waffe entsichern; **~ed** unverschlossen.

**unlooked-for** [ʌn'luktfɔ:] unerwartet.

**unloose**, **~n** ['ʌn'lu:s, ʌn'lu:sn] lösen, losmachen.

**unlov|ely** ['ʌn'lʌvli] reizlos, unschön; **~ing** □ [~viŋ] lieblos.

**unlucky** □ [ʌn'lʌki] unglücklich.

unmake ['ʌn'meik] [irr. (make)] vernichten; rückgängig machen; umbilden; Herrscher absetzen.

unman ['ʌn'mæn] entmannen.

unmanageable □ [ʌn'mænidʒəbl] unlenksam, widerspenstig.

unmarried ['ʌn'mærid] unverheiratet, ledig.

unmask ['ʌn'mɑːsk] (sich) demaskieren; fig. entlarven.

unmatched ['ʌn'mætʃt] unerreicht; unvergleichlich.

unmeaning □ [ʌn'miːniŋ] nichtssagend.

unmeasured [ʌn'meʒəd] ungemessen; unermeßlich.

unmeet ['ʌn'miːt] ungeeignet.

unmentionable □ [ʌn'menʃnəbl] nicht zu erwähnen(d), unnennbar.

unmerited ['ʌn'meritid] unverdient.

unmindful □ [ʌn'maindful] unbedacht; sorglos; ohne Rücksicht.

unmistakable □ ['ʌnmis'teikəbl] unverkennbar; unmißverständlich.

unmitigated [ʌn'mitigeitid] ungemildert; richtig; fig. Erz...

unmolested ['ʌnmou'lestid] unbelästigt.

unmounted ['ʌn'mauntid] unberitten; nicht gefaßt (Stein); unaufgezogen (Bild); unmontiert.

unmoved ['ʌn'muːvd] unbewegt, ungerührt.

unnamed ['ʌn'neimd] ungenannt.

unnatural □ [ʌn'nætʃrəl] unnatürlich. [nötig.)

unnecessary □ [ʌn'nesisəri] un-

unneighbo(u)rly ['ʌn'neibəli] nicht gutnachbarlich.

unnerve ['ʌn'nəːv] entnerven.

unnoticed ['ʌn'noutist] unbemerkt.

unobjectionable □ ['ʌnəb'dʒekʃnəbl] einwandfrei.

unobserv|ant □ ['ʌnəb'zəːvənt] unachtsam; ~ed □ [~vd] unbemerkt.

unobtainable ['ʌnəb'teinəbl] unerreichbar.

unobtrusive □ ['ʌnəb'truːsiv] unaufdringlich, bescheiden.

unoccupied ['ʌn'ɔkjupaid] unbesetzt; unbewohnt; unbeschäftigt.

unoffending ['ʌn'fendiŋ] harmlos.

unofficial □ ['ʌn'fiʃəl] nichtamtlich, inoffiziell.

unopposed ['ʌnə'pouzd] ungehindert.

unostentatious □ ['ʌnɔstən'teiʃəs] anspruchslos; unauffällig; schlicht.

unowned ['ʌn'ound] herrenlos.

unpack ['ʌn'pæk] auspacken.

unpaid ['ʌn'peid] unbezahlt; unbelohnt; & unfrankiert.

unparalleled ['ʌn'pærəleld] beispiellos, ohnegleichen.

unperceived □ ['ʌnpə'siːvd] unbemerkt.

unperturbed ['ʌnpə(ː)'təːbd] ruhig, gelassen.

unpleasant □ [ʌn'pleznt] unangenehm; unerfreulich; ~ness [~tnis] Unannehmlichkeit f.

unpolished ['ʌn'pɔliʃt] unpoliert; fig. ungebildet.

unpolluted ['ʌnpə'luːtid] unbefleckt.

unpopular □ ['ʌn'pɔpjulə] unpopulär, unbeliebt; ~ity ['ʌnpɔpju-'læriti] Unbeliebtheit f.

unpracti|cal □ ['ʌn'præktikəl] unpraktisch; ~sed, Am. ~ced [ʌn-'præktist] ungeübt.

unprecedented □ [ʌn'presidəntid] beispiellos; noch nie dagewesen.

unprejudiced □ [ʌn'predʒudist] unbefangen, unvoreingenommen.

unpremeditated □ ['ʌnpri'mediteitid] unbeabsichtigt.

unprepared □ ['ʌnpri'pɛəd] unvorbereitet.

unpreten|ding □ ['ʌnpri'tendiŋ], ~tious □ [~nʃəs] anspruchslos.

unprincipled [ʌn'prinsəpld] ohne Grundsätze; gewissenlos.

unprivileged [ʌn'priviildʒd] sozial benachteiligt; arm.

unprofitable □ [ʌn'prɔfitəbl] unnütz.

unproved ['ʌn'pruːvd] unerwiesen.

unprovided ['ʌnprə'vaidid] nicht versehen (with mit); ~ for unversorgt, mittellos.

unprovoked □ ['ʌnprə'voukt] ohne Grund.

unqualified □ ['ʌn'kwɔlifaid] ungeeignet; unberechtigt; [ʌn'kwɔlifaid] unbeschränkt.

unquestion|able □ [ʌn'kwestʃənəbl] unzweifelhaft, fraglos; ~ed [~nd] ungefragt; unbestritten.

unquote ['ʌn'kwout] Zitat beenden.

unravel [ʌn'rævəl] (sich) entwirren; enträtseln.

unready □ ['ʌn'redi] nicht bereit od. fertig; unlustig, zögernd.

unreal □ ['ʌn'riəl] unwirklich; ~istic ['ʌnriə'listik] (~ally) wirklichkeitsfremd, unrealistisch.

unreasonable □ [ʌn'riːznəbl] unvernünftig; grundlos; unmäßig.

unrecognizable □ [ʌn'rekəgnaizəbl] nicht wiederzuerkennen(d).

unredeemed □ ['ʌnri'diːmd] unerlöst; uneingelöst; ungemildert.

unrefined ['ʌnri'faind] ungeläutert; fig. ungebildet. [dankenlos.)

unreflecting □ ['ʌnri'flektiŋ] ge-

unregarded ['ʌnri'gɑːdid] unbeachtet; unberücksichtigt.

unrelated ['ʌnri'leitid] ohne Beziehung (to zu).

unrelenting □ ['ʌnri'lentiŋ] erbarmungslos; unerbittlich.

unreliable ['ʌnri'laiəbl] unzuverlässig.

**unrelieved** ☐ ['ʌnri'li:vd] ungelindert; ununterbrochen.

**unremitting** ☐ [ʌnri'mitiŋ] unablässig, unaufhörlich; unermüdlich.

**unrepining** ☐ ['ʌnri'painiŋ] klaglos; unverdrossen.

**unrequited** ☐ ['ʌnri'kwaitid] unerwidert; unbelohnt.

**unreserved** ☐ ['ʌnri'zə:vd] rückhaltlos; unbeschränkt; ohne Vorbehalt.

**unresisting** ☐ ['ʌnri'zistiŋ] widerstandslos.

**unresponsive** ['ʌnris'pɔnsiv] unempfänglich (to für).

**unrest** ['ʌn'rest] Unruhe f.

**unrestrained** ☐ ['ʌnris'treind] ungehemmt; unbeschränkt.

**unrestricted** ☐ ['ʌnris'triktid] uneingeschränkt.

**unriddle** ['ʌn'ridl] enträtseln.

**unrighteous** ☐ ['ʌn'raitʃəs] ungerecht; unredlich.

**unripe** ['ʌn'raip] unreif.

**unrival(l)ed** ['ʌn'raivəld] unvergleichlich, unerreicht, einzigartig.

**unroll** ['ʌn'roul] ent-, aufrollen.

**unruffled** ['ʌn'rʌfld] glatt; ruhig.

**unruly** [ʌn'ru:li] ungebärdig.

**unsafe** ☐ ['ʌn'seif] unsicher.

**unsal(e)able** ['ʌn'seiləbl] unverkäuflich.

**unsanitary** ['ʌn'sænitəri] unhygienisch.

**unsatisfactory** ☐ ['ʌnsætis'fæktəri] unbefriedigend; unzulänglich; **~ied** ['ʌn'sætisfaid] unbefriedigt; **~ying** [~ʌiiŋ] = unsatisfactory.

**unsavo(u)ry** ☐ ['ʌn'seivəri] unappetitlich (a. fig.), widerwärtig.

**unsay** ['ʌn'sei] [irr. (say)] zurücknehmen, widerrufen.

**unscathed** ['ʌn'skeiðd] unversehrt.

**unschooled** ['ʌn'sku:ld] ungeschult; unverbildet.

**unscrew** ['ʌn'skru:] v/t. ab-, los-, aufschrauben; v/i. sich abschrauben lassen.

**unscrupulous** ☐ [ʌn'skru:pjuləs] bedenkenlos; gewissenlos; skrupellos.

**unsearchable** ☐ [ʌn'sə:tʃəbl] unerforschlich; unergründlich.

**unseason|able** ☐ [ʌn'si:znəbl] unzeitig; fig. ungelegen; **~ed** ['ʌn'si:znd] nicht abgelagert (Holz); fig. nicht abgehärtet; ungewürzt.

**unseat** ['ʌn'si:t] des Amtes entheben; abwerfen.

**unseemly** [ʌn'si:mli] unziemlich.

**unseen** ['ʌn'si:n] ungesehen; unsichtbar.

**unselfish** ☐ ['ʌn'selfiʃ] selbstlos, uneigennützig; **~ness** [~ʃnis] Selbstlosigkeit f.

**unsettle** ['ʌn'setl] in Unordnung bringen; verwirren; erschüttern; **~d** nicht festgesetzt; unbeständig; ✝ unbezahlt; unerledigt; ohne festen Wohnsitz; unbesiedelt.

**unshaken** ['ʌn'ʃeikən] unerschüttert; unerschütterlich.

**unshaven** ['ʌn'ʃeivn] unrasiert.

**unship** ['ʌn'ʃip] ausschiffen.

**unshrink|able** ['ʌn'ʃriŋkəbl] nicht einlaufend (Stoff); **~ing** ☐ [ʌn'ʃriŋkiŋ] unverzagt.

**unsightly** [ʌn'saitli] häßlich.

**unskil|(l)ful** ☐ ['ʌn'skilful] ungeschickt; **~led** [~ld] ungelernt.

**unsoci|able** [ʌn'souʃəbl] ungesellig; **~al** [~al] ungesellig; unsozial.

**unsolder** ['ʌn'sɔldə] los-, ablöten.

**unsolicited** ['ʌnsə'lisitid] nicht gefragt (S.); unaufgefordert (P.).

**unsolv|able** ['ʌn'sɔlvəbl] unlösbar; **~ed** [~vd] ungelöst.

**unsophisticated** ['ʌnsə'fistikeitid] unverfälscht; ungekünstelt; unverdorben, unverbildet.

**unsound** ☐ ['ʌn'saund] ungesund; verdorben; wurmstichig; morsch; nicht stichhaltig (Beweis); verkehrt.

**unsparing** ☐ [ʌn'spɛəriŋ] freigebig; schonungslos, unbarmherzig.

**unspeakable** ☐ [ʌn'spi:kəbl] unsagbar; unsäglich.

**unspent** ['ʌn'spent] unverbraucht; unerschöpft.

**unspoil|ed, ~t** ['ʌn'spɔilt] unverdorben; unbeschädigt; nicht verzogen (Kind).

**unspoken** ['ʌn'spoukən] ungesagt; **~of** unerwähnt.

**unstable** ☐ ['ʌn'steibl] nicht (stand)fest; unbeständig; unstet(ig); labil.

**unsteady** ☐ ['ʌn'stedi] unstet(ig), unsicher; schwankend; unbeständig; unsolid; unregelmäßig.

**unstrained** ['ʌn'streind] unfiltriert; fig. ungezwungen.

**unstrap** ['ʌn'stræp] los-, abschnallen.

**unstressed** ['ʌn'strest] unbetont.

**unstring** ['ʌn'striŋ] [irr. (string)] Saite entspannen.

**unstudied** ['ʌn'stʌdid] ungesucht, ungekünstelt, natürlich.

**unsubstantial** ☐ ['ʌnsəb'stænʃəl] wesenlos; gegenstandslos; inhaltlos; gehaltlos; dürftig.

**unsuccessful** ☐ ['ʌnsək'sesful] erfolglos, ohne Erfolg.

**unsuitable** ☐ ['ʌn'sju:təbl] unpassend; unangemessen.

**unsurpassed** ['ʌnsə(:)'pa:st] unübertroffen.

**unsuspect|ed** ['ʌnsəs'pektid] unverdächtig; unvermutet; **~ing** [~tiŋ] nichts ahnend; arglos.

**unsuspicious** ☐ ['ʌnsəs'piʃəs] nicht argwöhnisch, arglos.

unswerving ☐ [ʌn'swəːviŋ] unentwegt.

untangle ['ʌn'tæŋgl] entwirren.

untarnished ['ʌn'tɑːniʃt] unbefleckt; ungetrübt.

unteachable ['ʌn'tiːtʃəbl] unbelehrbar (P.); unlehrbar (S.).

untenanted ['ʌn'tənəntid] unvermietet, unbewohnt.

unthankful ☐ ['ʌn'θæŋkful] undankbar.

unthink|able [ʌn'θiŋkəbl] undenkbar; ~ing ☐ ['ʌn'θiŋkiŋ] gedankenlos.

unthought ['ʌn'θɔːt] unbedacht; ~-of unvermutet.

unthrifty ☐ ['ʌn'θrifti] verschwenderisch; nicht gedeihend.

untidy ☐ [ʌn'taidi] unordentlich.

untie ['ʌn'tai] aufbinden, aufknüpfen; Knoten etc. lösen; j-n losbinden.

until [ən'til] 1. prp. bis; 2. cj. bis (daß); not ~ erst wenn od. als.

untimely [ʌn'taimli] unzeitig; vorzeitig; ungelegen.                    [lich.

untiring ☐ [ʌn'taiəriŋ] unermüd-)

unto ['ʌntu] = to.

untold ['ʌn'tould] unerzählt; ungezählt; unermeßlich, unsäglich.

untouched ['ʌn'tʌtʃt] unberührt; fig. ungerührt; phot. unretuschiert.

untried ['ʌn'traid] unversucht; unerprobt; g͟t noch nicht verhört.

untrod, ~den ['ʌn'trɔd, ~dn] unbetreten.

untroubled ['ʌn'trʌbld] ungestört.

untrue ☐ ['ʌn'truː] unwahr; untreu.

untrustworthy ☐ ['ʌn'trʌstwəːði] unzuverlässig, nicht vertrauenswürdig.

unus|ed ['ʌn'juːzd] ungebraucht; [~uːst] nicht gewöhnt (to an acc.; zu inf.); ~ual ☐ [ʌn'juːʒuəl] ungewöhnlich; ungewohnt.

unutterable ☐ [ʌn'ʌtərəbl] unaussprechlich.

unvarnished fig. ['ʌn'vɑːniʃt] ungeschminkt.

unvarying ☐ [ʌn'vɛəriiŋ] unveränderlich.

unveil [ʌn'veil] entschleiern, enthüllen.

unversed ['ʌn'vəːst] unbewandert, unerfahren (in in dat.).

unvouched ['ʌn'vautʃt] a. ~-for unverbürgt, unbezeugt.

unwanted ['ʌn'wɔntid] unerwünscht.

unwarrant|able ☐ [ʌn'wɔrəntəbl] unverantwortlich; ~ed [~tid] unberechtigt; ['ʌn'wɔrəntid] unverbürgt.

unwary ☐ [ʌn'wɛəri] unbedachtsam.

unwelcome [ʌn'welkəm] unwillkommen.

unwholesome ['ʌn'houlsəm] ungesund; schädlich.

unwieldy ☐ [ʌn'wiːldi] unhandlich; ungefüge; sperrig.

unwilling ☐ ['ʌn'wiliŋ] un-, widerwillig, abgeneigt.

unwind ['ʌn'waind] [irr. (wind)] auf-, loswickeln; (sich) abwickeln.

unwise ☐ ['ʌn'waiz] unklug.

unwitting ☐ ['ʌn'witiŋ] unwissentlich; unbeabsichtigt.

unworkable ['ʌn'wəːkəbl] undurchführbar; ⊕ nicht betriebsfähig.

unworthy ☐ [ʌn'wəːði] unwürdig.

unwrap ['ʌn'ræp] auswickeln, auspacken, aufwickeln.

unwrought ['ʌn'rɔːt] unbearbeitet; roh; Roh...

unyielding ☐ [ʌn'jiːldiŋ] unnachgiebig.

up [ʌp] 1. adv. (her-, hin)auf; aufwärts, empor; oben; auf(gestanden); aufgegangen (Sonne); hoch; abgelaufen, um (Zeit); Am. Baseball: am Schlag; ~ and about wieder auf den Beinen; be hard ~ in Geldschwierigkeiten sein; ~ against a task e-r Aufgabe gegenüber; ~ to bis (zu); it is ~ to me to do es ist an mir, zu tun; what are you ~ to there? was macht ihr da? what's ~? sl. was ist los? 2. prp. hinauf; ~ the river flußaufwärts; 3. adj.: ~ train Zug m nach der Stadt; 4.: the ~s and downs das Auf und Ab, die Höhen und Tiefen des Lebens; 5. F (sich) erheben; hochfahren; hochtreiben.

up|-and-coming Am. F ['ʌpən'kʌmiŋ] unternehmungslustig; ~braid [ʌp'breid] schelten; ~bringing ['ʌpbriŋiŋ] Erziehung f; ~country ['ʌp'kʌntri] landeinwärts (gelegen); ~heaval [ʌp'hiːvəl] Umbruch m; ~hill [ʌp'hil] bergan; mühsam; ~hold [ʌp'hould] [irr. (hold)] aufrecht(er)halten; stützen; ~holster [ʌp'~lstə] Möbel (auf)polstern; Zimmer dekorieren; ~holsterer [~ərə] Tapezierer m, Dekorateur m, Polsterer m; ~holstery [~ri] Polstermöbel n/pl.; Möbelstoffe m/pl.; Tapezierarbeit f.

up|keep ['ʌpkiːp] Instandhaltung(s-kosten pl.) f; Unterhalt m; ~land ['ʌpland] Hoch-, Oberland n; ~lift 1. [ʌp'lift] (empor-, er)heben; 2. ['ʌplift] Erhebung f; fig. Aufschwung m.

upon [ə'pɔn] = on.

upper ['ʌpə] ober; Ober...; ~most oberst, höchst.

up|raise [ʌp'reiz] erheben; ~rear [ʌp'riə] aufrichten; ~right 1. ☐ ['ʌp'rait] aufrecht; ~ piano ♪ Klavier n; fig. ['ʌprait] rechtschaffen; 2. Pfosten m; Ständer m; ~rising [ʌp'raiziŋ] Erhebung f, Aufstand m.

uproar ['ʌprɔː] Aufruhr m; ~ious ☐ [ʌp'rɔːriəs] tobend; tosend.

**up|root** [ʌp'ruːt] entwurzeln; (her-) ausreißen; **~set** [ʌp'set] [*irr.* (set)] umwerfen; (um)stürzen; außer Fassung *od.* in Unordnung bringen; stören; verwirren; *be ~* außer sich sein; **~shot** ['ʌpʃɔt] Ausgang *m*; **~side** ['ʌpsaid] *adv.*: ~ *down* das Oberste zuunterst; verkehrt; **~stairs** [ʌp'stɛəz] die Treppe hinauf, (nach) oben; **~start** ['ʌpstɑːt] Emporkömmling *m*; **~state** *Am.* ['ʌp'steit] Hinterland *n e-s* Staates; **~stream** ['ʌp'striːm] fluß-, stromaufwärts; **~-to-date** ['ʌptə'deit] modern, neuzeitlich; **~town** ['ʌp'taun] im *od.* in den oberen Stadtteil; *Am.* im Wohn- *od.* Villenviertel; **~turn** [ʌp'təːn] nach oben kehren; **~ward(s)** ['ʌpwəd(z)] aufwärts (gerichtet).

**uranium** [juə'reinjəm] Uran *n*.

**urban** ['əːbən] städtisch; Stadt...; **~e** □ [əː'bein] höflich; gebildet.

**urchin** ['əːtʃin] Bengel *m*.

**urge** [əːdʒ] 1. *oft* ~ *on* j-n drängen, (an)treiben; dringen in *j-n*; dringen auf *et.*; *Recht* geltend machen; 2. Drang *m*; **~ncy** ['əːdʒənsi] Dringlichkeit *f*; Drängen *n*; **~nt** □ [~nt] dringend; dringlich; eilig.

**urin|al** ['juərinl] Harnglas *n*; Bedürfnisanstalt *f*; **~ate** [~neit] urinieren; **~e** [~] Urin *m*, Harn *m*.

**urn** [əːn] Urne *f*; Tee- *etc.* Maschine *f*.

**us** [ʌs, əs] uns; *of* ~ unser.

**usage** ['juːzidʒ] Brauch *m*, Gepflogenheit *f*; Sprachgebrauch *m*; Behandlung *f*, Verwendung *f*, Gebrauch *m*.

**usance** † ['juːzəns] Wechselfrist *f*.

**use** 1. [juːs] Gebrauch *m*; Benutzung *f*; Verwendung *f*; Gewohnheit *f*, Übung *f*; Brauch *m*; Nutzen *m*; (*of*) *no* ~ unnütz, zwecklos; *have no* ~ *for* keine Verwendung haben

für; *Am.* F nicht mögen; 2. [juːz] gebrauchen; benutzen, ver-, anwenden; behandeln; ~ *up* ver-, aufbrauchen; *I ~d to do* ich pflegte zu tun, früher tat ich; **~d** [juːzd] gewöhnt (*to an acc.*); gewohnt (*to zu od. acc.*); **~ful** □ ['juːsful] brauchbar; nützlich; Nutz...; **~less** □ ['juːslis] nutz-, zwecklos, unnütz.

**usher** ['ʌʃə] 1. Türhüter *m*, Pförtner *m*; Gerichtsdiener *m*; Platzanweiser *m*; 2. *mst.* ~ *in* (hin)einführen, anmelden; **~ette** [ʌʃə'ret] Platzanweiserin *f*.

**usual** □ ['juːʒuəl] gewöhnlich; üblich; gebräuchlich.

**usurer** ['juːʒərə] Wucherer *m*.

**usurp** [juː'zəːp] sich *et.* widerrechtlich aneignen, an sich reißen; **~er** [~pə] Usurpator *m*.

**usury** ['juːʒuri] Wucher(zinsen *pl.*) *m*.

**utensil** [juː(ː)'tensl] Gerät *n*; Geschirr *n*.

**uterus** *anat.* ['juːtərəs] Gebärmutter *f*.

**utility** [juː(ː)'tiliti] 1. Nützlichkeit *f*, Nutzen *m*; *public* ~ öffentlicher Versorgungsbetrieb; 2. Gebrauchs..., Einheits...

**utiliz|ation** [juːtilai'zeiʃən] Nutzbarmachung *f*; Nutzanwendung *f*; **~e** ['juːtilaiz] sich *et.* zunutze machen.

**utmost** ['ʌtmoust] äußerst.

**Utopian** [juː'toupjən] 1. utopisch; 2. Utopist(in), Schwärmer(in).

**utter** ['ʌtə] 1. □ *fig.* äußerst; völlig, gänzlich; 2. äußern; *Seufzer etc.* ausstoßen, von sich geben; *Falschgeld etc.* in Umlauf setzen; **~ance** ['ʌtərəns] Äußerung *f*, Ausdruck *m*; Aussprache *f*; **~most** ['ʌtəmoust] äußerst.

**uvula** *anat.* ['juːvjulə] Zäpfchen *n*.

# V

**vacan|cy** ['veikənsi] Leere *f*; leerer *od.* freier Platz; Lücke *f*; offene Stelle; **~t** □ [~nt] leer (*a. fig.*); frei (*Zeit, Zimmer*); offen (*Stelle*); unbesetzt, vakant (*Amt*).

**vacat|e** [və'keit, *Am.* 'veikeit] räumen; *Stelle* aufgeben, aus *e-m* Amt scheiden; **~ion** [və'keiʃən, *Am.* vei'keiʃən] 1. (Schul)Ferien *pl.*; *bsd. Am.* Urlaub *m*; Räumung *f*; Niederlegung *f e-s* Amtes; 2. *Am.* Urlaub machen; **~ionist** *Am.* [~nist] Ferienreisende(r *m*) *f*.

**vaccin|ate** ['væksineit] impfen;

**~ation** [væksi'neiʃən] Impfung *f*; **~e** ['væksiːn] Impfstoff *m*.

**vacillate** ['væsileit] schwanken.

**vacu|ous** □ ['vækjuəs] *fig.* leer, geistlos; **~um** *phys.* [~uəm] Vakuum *n*; ~ *cleaner* Staubsauger *m*; ~ *flask*, ~ *bottle* Thermosflasche *f*.

**vagabond** ['vægəbɔnd] 1. vagabundierend; 2. Landstreicher *m*.

**vagary** ['veigəri] wunderlicher Einfall, Laune *f*, Schrulle *f*.

**vagrant** ['veigrənt] 1. wandernd; *fig.* unstet; 2. Landstreicher *m*, Vagabund *m*; Strolch *m*.

**vague** □ [veig] unbestimmt; unklar.

**vain** □ [vein] eitel, eingebildet; leer; nichtig; vergeblich; *in ~* vergebens, umsonst; **~glorious** □ [vein'glɔ:riəs] prahlerisch.

**vale** [veil] *poet. od. in Namen:* Tal *n.*

**valediction** [væli'dikʃən] Abschied(sworte *n/pl.*) *m.*

**valentine** ['væləntain] Valentinsschatz *m,* -gruß *m* (*am Valentinstag, 14. Februar, erwählt; gesandt.*).

**valerian** ♀ [və'liəriən] Baldrian *m.*

**valet** ['vælit] 1. (Kammer)Diener *m;* 2. Diener sein bei *j-m; j-n* bedienen.

**valetudinarian** ['vælitju:di'neəriən] 1. kränklich; 2. kränklicher Mensch; Hypochonder *m.*

**valiant** □ ['væljənt] tapfer.

**valid** □ ['vælid] triftig, richtig, stichhaltig; (rechts)gültig; *be ~* gelten; **~ity** [və'liditi] Gültigkeit *f;* Triftig-, Richtigkeit *f.*

**valise** [və'li:z] Reisetasche *f;* ✕ Tornister *m.*

**valley** ['væli] Tal *n.*

**valo(u)r** ['vælə] Tapferkeit *f.*

**valuable** ['væljuəbl] 1. □ wertvoll; 2. *~s pl.* Wertsachen *f/pl.*

**valuation** [vælju'eiʃən] Abschätzung *f;* Taxwert *m.*

**value** ['vælju:] 1. Wert *m;* Währung *f; give (get) good ~ (for one's money)* ♀ reell bedienen (bedient werden); 2. (ab)schätzen; *fig.* schätzen; **~less** [~julis] wertlos.

**valve** [vælv] Klappe *f;* Ventil *n; Radio:* Röhre *f.*

**vamoose** *Am. sl.* [və'mu:s] *v/i.* abhauen; *v/t.* räumen (*verlassen*).

**vamp** F [væmp] 1. Vamp *m* (*verführerische Frau*); 2. neppen.

**vampire** ['væmpaiə] Vampir *m.*

**van** [væn] Möbelwagen *m;* Lieferwagen *m;* ⛉ Pack-, Güterwagen *m;* ✕ Vorhut *f.*

**vane** [vein] Wetterfahne *f;* (Windmühlen-, Propeller)Flügel *m.*

**vanguard** ✕ ['vænga:d] Vorhut *f.*

**vanilla** ♀ [və'nilə] Vanille *f.*

**vanish** ['væniʃ] (ver)schwinden.

**vanity** ['væniti] Eitelkeit *f,* Einbildung *f;* Nichtigkeit *f; ~ bag* Kosmetiktäschchen *n.*

**vanquish** ['væŋkwiʃ] besiegen.

**vantage** ['va:ntidʒ] *Tennis:* Vorteil *m;* **~ground** günstige Stellung.

**vapid** □ ['væpid] schal; fad(e).

**vapor|ize** ['veipəraiz] verdampfen, verdunsten (lassen); **~ous** □ [~rəs] dunstig; nebelhaft.

**vapo(u)r** ['veipə] Dunst *m;* Dampf *m.*

**varia|ble** □ ['veəriəbl] veränderlich; **~nce** [~əns] Veränderung *f;* Uneinigkeit *f; be at ~* uneinig sein; (sich) widersprechen; *set at ~* entzweien; **~nt** [~nt] 1. abweichend; 2. Variante *f;* **~tion** [veəri'eiʃən]

**Abänderung** *f;* Schwankung *f;* Abweichung *f;* ♪ Variation *f.*

**varicose** ✿ ['værikous] Krampfader(n)...; *~ vein* Krampfader *f.*

**varie|d** □ ['veərid] verschieden, verändert, mannigfaltig; **~gate** [~igeit] bunt gestalten; **~ty** [və'raiəti] Mannigfaltigkeit *f,* Vielzahl *f; biol.* Abart *f;* ✟ Auswahl *f;* Menge *f; ~ show* Varietévorstellung *f; ~ theatre* Varieté(theater) *n.*

**various** □ ['veəriəs] verschiedene, mehrere; mannigfaltig; verschiedenartig.     [Racker.)

**varmint** *sl.* ['va:mint] *kleiner)*

**varnish** ['va:niʃ] 1. Firnis *m,* Lack *m; fig.* (äußerer) Anstrich; 2. firnissen, lackieren; *fig.* beschönigen.

**vary** ['veəri] (sich) (ver)ändern; wechseln (mit *et.*); abweichen.

**vase** [va:z] Vase *f.*

**vassal** ['væsəl] Vasall *m; attr.* Vasallen...

**vast** □ [va:st] ungeheuer, gewaltig, riesig, umfassend, weit.

**vat** [væt] Faß *n;* Bottich *m;* Kufe *f.*

**vaudeville** *Am.* ['voudəvil] Varieté *n.*

**vault** [vɔ:lt] 1. Gewölbe *n;* Wölbung *f;* Stahlkammer *f;* Gruft *f; bsd. Sport:* Sprung *m; wine-~* Weinkeller *m;* 2. (über)wölben; *bsd. Sport:* springen (über *acc.*).

**vaulting-horse** ['vɔ:ltiŋhɔ:s] *Turnen:* Pferd *n.*

**vaunt** *lit.* [vɔ:nt] (sich) rühmen.

**veal** [vi:l] Kalbfleisch *n; roast ~* Kalbsbraten *m.*

**veer** [viə] (sich) drehen.

**vegeta|ble** ['vedʒitəbl] 1. Pflanzen..., pflanzlich; 2. Pflanze *f; mst ~s pl.* Gemüse *n;* **~rian** [vedʒi'teəriən] 1. Vegetarier(in); 2. vegetarisch; **~te** ['vedʒiteit] vegetieren; **~tive** □ [~tətiv] vegetativ; wachstumsfördernd.

**vehemen|ce** ['vi:iməns] Heftigkeit *f;* Gewalt *f;* **~t** □ [~nt] heftig; ungestüm.

**vehicle** ['vi:ikl] Fahrzeug *n,* Beförderungsmittel *n; fig.* Vermittler *m,* Träger *m;* Ausdrucksmittel *n.*

**veil** [veil] 1. Schleier *m;* Hülle *f;* 2. (sich) verschleiern (*a. fig.*).

**vein** [vein] Ader *f* (*a. fig.*); Anlage *f;* Neigung *f;* Stimmung *f.*

**velocipede** [vi'lɔsipi:d] *Am.* (Kinder)Dreirad *n; hist.* Veloziped *n.*

**velocity** [vi'lɔsiti] Geschwindigkeit *f.*

**velvet** ['velvit] 1. Samt *m; hunt.* Bast *m;* 2. Samt...; samten; **~y** [~ti] samtig.

**venal** ['vi:nl] käuflich, feil.

**vend** [vend] verkaufen; **~er, ~or** ['vendə, ~dɔ:] Verkäufer *m,* Händler *m.*

**veneer** [vi'niə] 1. Furnier *n;* 2. furnieren; *fig.* bemänteln.

venera|ble □ ['venərəbl] ehrwürdig; ~te [~reit] (ver)ehren; ~tion [venə'reiʃən] Verehrung f.

venereal [vi'niəriəl] Geschlechts...

Venetian [vi'ni:ʃən] 1. venetianisch; ~ blind (Stab)Jalousie f; 2. Venetianer(in).

vengeance ['vendʒəns] Rache f; with a ~ F und wie, ganz gehörig.

venial □ ['vi:njəl] verzeihlich.

venison ['venzn] Wildbret n.

venom ['venəm] (bsd. Schlangen-) Gift n; fig. Gift n; Gehässigkeit f; ~ous □ [~məs] giftig.

venous ['vi:nəs] Venen...; venös.

vent [vent] 1. Öffnung f; Luft-, Spundloch n; Auslaß m; Schlitz m, give ~ to e-m Zorn etc. Luft machen; 2. fig. Luft machen (dat.).

ventilat|e ['ventileit] ventilieren, (be-, ent-, durch)lüften; fig. erörtern; ~ion [venti'leiʃən] Ventilation f, Lüftung f; fig. Erörterung f; ~or ['ventileitə] Ventilator m.

ventral anat. ['ventrəl] Bauch...

ventriloquist [ven'triləkwist] Bauchredner m.

ventur|e ['ventʃə] 1. Wagnis n; Risiko n; Abenteuer n; Spekulation f; at a ~ auf gut Glück; 2. (sich) wagen; riskieren; ~esome □ [~əsəm], ~ous □ [~ərəs] verwegen, kühn.

veracious [ve'reiʃəs] wahrhaft.

verb gr. [və:b] Verb(um) n, Zeitwort n; ~al □ ['və:bəl] wörtlich; mündlich; ~iage ['və:biidʒ] Wortschwall m; ~ose □ [və:'bous] wortreich.                    [reif.)

verdant □ ['və:dənt] grün; fig. un-)

verdict ['və:dikt] ½½ (Urteils-) Spruch m der Geschworenen; fig. Urteil n; bring in od. return a ~ of guilty auf schuldig erkennen.

verdigris ['və:digris] Grünspan m.

verdure ['və:dʒə] Grün n.

verge [və:dʒ] 1. Rand m, Grenze f; on the ~ of am Rande (gen.); dicht vor (dat.); 2. sich (hin)neigen; ~ (up)on grenzen an (acc.).

veri|fy ['verifai] (nach)prüfen; beweisen; bestätigen; ~similitude [verisi'militju:d] Wahrscheinlichkeit f; ~table □ ['veritəbl] wahr (-haftig).

vermic|elli [və:mi'seli] Fadennudeln f/pl.; ~ular [və:'mikjulə] wurmartig.

vermilion [və'miljən] 1. Zinnoberrot n; 2. zinnoberrot.

vermin ['və:min] Ungeziefer n; hunt. Raubzeug n; fig. Gesindel n; ~ous [~nəs] voller Ungeziefer.

vernacular [və'nækjulə] 1. □ einheimisch; Volks...; 2. Landes-, Muttersprache f; Jargon m.

versatile □ ['və:sətail] wendig.

verse [və:s] Vers(e pl.) m; Strophe f; Dichtung f; ~d [və:st] bewandert.

versify ['və:sifai] v/t. in Verse bringen; v/i. Verse machen.

version ['və:ʃən] Übersetzung f; Fassung f, Darstellung f; Lesart f.

versus bsd. ½½ ['və:səs] gegen.

vertebra anat. ['və:tibrə], pl. ~e [~ri:] Wirbel m.

vertical □ ['və:tikəl] vertikal, senkrecht.

vertig|inous □ [və:'tidʒinəs] schwindlig; schwindelnd (Höhe); ~o ['və:tigou] Schwindel(anfall) m.

verve [veəv] Schwung m, Verve f.

very ['veri] 1. adv. sehr; the ~ best das allerbeste; 2. adj. wirklich; eben; bloß; the ~ same ebenderselbe; in the ~ act auf frischer Tat; gerade dabei; the ~ thing gerade das; the ~ thought der bloße Gedanke; the ~ stones sogar die Steine; the veriest rascal der größte Schuft.

vesicle ['vesikl] Bläschen n.

vessel ['vesl] Gefäß n (a. anat., ⚓, fig.); ⚓ Fahrzeug n, Schiff n.

vest [vest] 1. Unterhemd n; Weste f; 2. v/t. bekleiden (with mit); j-n einsetzen (in in acc.); et. übertragen (in s.o. j-m); v/i. verliehen werden.

vestibule ['vestibju:l] Vorhof m (a. anat.); Vorhalle f; Hausflur m; bsd. Am. ⚓ Korridor m zwischen zwei D-Zug-Wagen; ~ train D-Zug m.

vestige ['vestidʒ] Spur f.

vestment ['vestmənt] Gewand n.

vestry ['vestri] eccl. Sakristei f; Gemeindevertretung f; Gemeindesaal m; ~man Gemeindevertreter m.

vet F [vet] 1. Tierarzt m; Am. ⚔ Veteran m; 2. co. verarzten; gründlich prüfen.

veteran ['vetərən] 1. ausgedient; erfahren; 2. Veteran m.

veterinary ['vetərinəri] 1. tierärztlich; 2. a. ~ surgeon Tierarzt m.

veto ['vi:tou] 1. pl. ~es Veto n; 2. sein Veto einlegen gegen.

vex [veks] ärgern; schikanieren; ~ation [vek'seiʃən] Verdruß m; Ärger(nis n) m; ~atious [~ʃəs] ärgerlich.

via [vaiə] über, via.

viaduct ['vaiədʌkt] Viadukt m, Überführung f.

vial ['vaiəl] Phiole f, Fläschchen n.

viand ['vaiənd] mst. ~s pl. Lebensmittel n/pl.

vibrat|e [vai'breit] vibrieren; zittern; ~ion [~eiʃən] Schwingung f, Zittern n, Vibrieren n, Erschütterung f.

vicar eccl. ['vikə] Vikar m; ~age [~əridʒ] Pfarrhaus n.

vice[1] [vais] Laster n; Fehler m; Unart f; ⊕ Schraubstock m.

vice[2] prp. ['vaisi] an Stelle von.

vice[3] [vais] F Stellvertreter m; attr. Vize..., Unter...; ~roy ['vaisrɔi] Vizekönig m.

**vice versa** ['vaisi'vɔːsə] umgekehrt.

**vicinity** [vi'siniti] Nachbarschaft f; Nähe f.

**vicious** □ ['viʃəs] lasterhaft; bösartig; boshaft; fehlerhaft.

**vicissitude** [vi'sisitjuːd] Wandel m; Wechsel m; ~s pl. Wechselfälle m/pl.

**victim** ['viktim] Opfer n; ~ize [~maiz] (hin)opfern; fig. j-n hereinlegen.

**victor** ['viktə] Sieger m; 2ian hist. [vik'tɔːriən] Viktorianisch; ~ious □ [~iəs] siegreich; Sieges...; ~y ['viktəri] Sieg m.

**victual** ['vitl] 1. (sich) verpflegen od. verproviantieren; 2. mst ~s pl. Lebensmittel n/pl., Proviant m; ~(l)er [~lə] Lebensmittellieferant m.

**video** ['vidiou] Fernseh...

**vie** [vai] wetteifern.

**Viennese** [vie'niːz] 1. Wiener(in); 2. Wiener..., wienerisch.

**view** [vjuː] 1. Sicht f, Blick m; Besichtigung f; Aussicht f (of auf acc.); Anblick m; Ansicht f (a. fig.); Absicht f; at first ~ auf den ersten Blick; in ~ sichtbar, zu sehen; in ~ of im Hinblick auf (acc.); fig. angesichts (gen.); on ~ zu besichtigen; with a ~ to inf. od. of ger. in der Absicht zu inf.; have (keep) in ~ im Auge haben (behalten); 2. ansehen, besichtigen; fig. betrachten; ~er ['vjuːə] Betrachter(in), Zuschauer (-in); ~less ['vjuːlis] ohne eigene Meinung; poet. unsichtbar; ~point Gesichts~, Standpunkt m.

**vigil** ['vidʒil] Nachtwache f; ~ance [~ləns] Wachsamkeit f; ~ant □ [~nt] wachsam.

**vigo|rous** □ ['vigərəs] kräftig; energisch; nachdrücklich; ~(u)r ['vigə] Kraft f; Vitalität f; Nachdruck m.

**viking** ['vaikiŋ] 1. Wiking(er) m; 2. wikingisch, Wikinger...

**vile** □ [vail] gemein; abscheulich.

**vilify** ['vilifai] verunglimpfen.

**village** ['vilidʒ] Dorf n; ~ green Dorfanger m, -wiese f; ~r [~dʒə] Dorfbewohner(in).

**villain** ['vilən] Schurke m, Schuft m, Bösewicht m; ~ous □ [~nəs] schurkisch; F scheußlich; ~y [~ni] Schurkerei f.

**vim** F [vim] Schwung m, Schneid m.

**vindicat|e** ['vindikeit] rechtfertigen (from gegen); verteidigen; ~ion [vindi'keiʃən] Rechtfertigung f.

**vindictive** □ [vin'diktiv] rachsüchtig.

**vine** ♀ [vain] Wein(stock) m, Rebe f; ~gar ['vinigə] (Wein)Essig m; ~growing ['vaingrouiŋ] Weinbau m; ~yard ['vinjəd] Weinberg m.

**vintage** ['vintidʒ] 1. Weinlese f; (Wein)Jahrgang m; 2. klassisch; erlesen; altmodisch; ~ car mot. Veteran m; ~r [~dʒə] Winzer m.

**viola** ♪ [vi'oulə] Bratsche f.

**violat|e** ['vaiəleit] verletzen; Eid etc. brechen; vergewaltigen, schänden; ~ion [vaiə'leiʃən] Verletzung f; (Eid- etc.)Bruch m; Vergewaltigung f, Schändung f.

**violen|ce** ['vaiələns] Gewalt(samkeit, -tätigkeit) f; Heftigkeit f; ~t □ [~nt] gewaltsam; gewalttätig; heftig.

**violet** ♀ ['vaiəlit] Veilchen n.

**violin** ♪ [vaiə'lin] Violine f, Geige f.

**V.I.P., VIP** ['viːai'piː] F hohes Tier.

**viper** zo. ['vaipə] Viper f, Natter f.

**virago** [vi'rɑːgou] Zankteufel m.

**virgin** ['vəːdʒin] 1. Jungfrau f; 2. a. ~al □ [~nl] jungfräulich; Jungfern...; ~ity [vəː'dʒiniti] Jungfräulichkeit f.

**viril|e** ['virail] männlich; Mannes...; ~ity [vi'riliti] Männlichkeit f.

**virtu** [vəː'tuː]: article of ~ Kunstgegenstand m; ~al □ ['vəːtjuəl] eigentlich; ~ally [~li] praktisch; ~e ['vəːtjuː] Tugend f; Wirksamkeit f; Vorzug m, Wert m; in od. by ~ of kraft, vermöge (gen.); make a ~ of necessity aus der Not e-e Tugend machen; ~osity [vəːtju'ɔsiti] Virtuosität f; ~ous □ ['vəːtjuəs] tugendhaft.

**virulent** □ ['virulənt] giftig; 🗡 virulent; fig. bösartig.

**virus** 🗡 ['vaiərəs] Virus n; fig. Gift n.

**visa** ['viːzə] Visum n, Sichtvermerk m; ~ed [~əd] mit e-m Sichtvermerk od. Visum versehen.

**viscose** 🝆 ['viskous] Viskose f; ~ silk Zellstoffseide f.

**viscount** ['vaikaunt] Vicomte m; ~ess [~tis] Vicomtesse f.

**viscous** □ ['viskəs] zähflüssig.

**vise** Am. [vais] Schraubstock m.

**visé** ['viːzei] = visa.

**visib|ility** [vizi'biliti] Sichtbarkeit f; Sichtweite f; ~le □ ['vizəbl] sichtbar; fig. (er)sichtlich; pred. zu sehen (S.); zu sprechen (P.).

**vision** ['viʒən] Sehvermögen n, Sehkraft f; fig. Seherblick m; Vision f, Erscheinung f; ~ary ['viʒnəri] 1. phantastisch; 2. Geisterseher(in); Phantast(in).

**visit** ['vizit] 1. v/t. besuchen; besichtigen; fig. heimsuchen; et. vergelten, v/i. ~le~ Besuche machen; Am. sich unterhalten, plaudern (with mit); 2. Besuch m; ~ation [vizi'teiʃən] Besuch m; Besichtigung f; Heimsuchung f; ~or ['vizitə] Besucher(in), Gast m; Inspektor m.

**vista** ['vistə] Durchblick m; Rück- od. Ausblick m.

**visual** □ ['vizjuəl] Seh...; Gesichts...; ~ize [~laiz] (sich) vor Augen stellen, sich ein Bild machen von.

**vital** □ ['vaitl] 1. Lebens...; lebenswichtig, wesentlich; lebensgefährlich; ~ parts pl. = **2.** ~s pl. lebenswichtige Organe n/pl.; edle Teile m/pl.; ~ity [vai'tæliti] Lebenskraft f; Vitalität f; ~ize ['vaitəlaiz] beleben.

**vitamin(e)** ['vitəmin] Vitamin n.
**vitiate** ['viʃieit] verderben; beeinträchtigen; hinfällig (z̄ z̄ ungültig) machen.
**vitreous** □ ['vitriəs] Glas...; gläsern.
**vituperate** [vi'tju:pəreit] schelten; schmähen, beschimpfen.
**vivaci|ous** □ [vi'veiʃəs] lebhaft; ~ty [vi'væsiti] Lebhaftigkeit f.
**vivid** □ ['vivid] lebhaft, lebendig.
**vivify** ['vivifai] (sich) beleben.
**vixen** ['viksn] Füchsin f; zänkisches Weib.
**vocabulary** [və'kæbjuləri] Wörterverzeichnis n; Wortschatz m.
**vocal** □ ['voukəl] stimmlich; Stimm...; gesprochen; laut; ♪ Vokal..., Gesang...; klingend; gr. stimmhaft; ~ist [~list] Sänger(in); ~ize [~laiz] (gr. stimmhaft) aussprechen; singen.
**vocation** [vou'keiʃən] Berufung f; Beruf m; ~al □ [~nl] beruflich; Berufs...
**vociferate** [vou'sifəreit] schreien.
**vogue** [voug] Beliebtheit f; Mode f.
**voice** [vɔis] **1.** Stimme f; active (passive) ~ gr. Aktiv n (Passiv n); give ~ to Ausdruck geben (dat.); **2.** äußern, ausdrücken; gr. stimmhaft aussprechen.
**void** [vɔid] **1.** leer; z̄ z̄ ungültig; ~ of frei von; arm an (dat.); ohne; **2.** Leere f; Lücke f; **3.** entleeren; ungültig machen, aufheben.
**volatile** ['vɔlətail] ♬ flüchtig (a. fig.); flatterhaft.
**volcano** [vɔl'keinou] pl. ~es Vulkan m.
**volition** [vou'liʃən] Wollen n; Wille(nskraft f) m.
**volley** ['vɔli] **1.** Salve f; (Geschoß etc.)Hagel m; fig. Schwall m; Tennis: Flugball m; **2.** mst ~ out e-n Schwall von Worten etc. von sich geben; Salven abgeben; fig. hageln; dröhnen; ~-ball Sport: Volleyball m, Flugball m.
**volt** ⚡ [voult] Volt n; ~age ⚡ ['voultidʒ] Spannung f; ~meter ⚡ Volt-, Spannungsmesser m.
**volub|ility** [vɔlju'biliti] Redegewandtheit f; ~le □ ['vɔljubl] (rede-)gewandt.
**volum|e** ['vɔljum] Band m e-s Buches; Volumen n; fig. Masse f,

große Menge; (bsd. Stimm)Umfang m; ~ of sound Radio: Lautstärke f; ~inous □ [və'lju:minəs] vielbändig; umfangreich, voluminös.
**volunt|ary** □ ['vɔləntəri] freiwillig; willkürlich; ~eer [vɔlən'tiə] **1.** Freiwillige(r m) f; attr. Freiwilligen...; **2.** v/i. freiwillig dienen; sich freiwillig melden; sich erbieten; v/t. anbieten; sich e-e Bemerkung erlauben.
**voluptu|ary** [və'lʌptjuəri] Wollüstling m; ~ous □ [~uəs] wollüstig; üppig.
**vomit** ['vɔmit] **1.** (sich) erbrechen; fig. (aus)speien, ausstoßen; **2.** Erbrochene(s) n; Erbrechen n.
**voraci|ous** □ [və'reiʃəs] gefräßig; gierig; ~ty [vɔ'ræsiti] Gefräßigkeit f; Gier f.
**vort|ex** ['vɔ:teks] pl. mst ~ices ['vɔ:tisi:z] Wirbel m, Strudel m (mst fig.).
**vote** [vout] **1.** (Wahl)Stimme f; Abstimmung f; Stimmrecht n; Beschluß m, Votum n; ~ of no confidence Mißtrauensvotum n; cast a ~ (s)eine Stimme abgeben; take a ~ on s.th. über et. abstimmen; **2.** v/t. stimmen für; v/i. (ab)stimmen; wählen; ~ for stimmen für; F für et. sein; et. vorschlagen; ~r ['voutə] Wähler(in).
**voting** ['voutiŋ] Abstimmung f; attr. Wahl...; ~ machine Stimmenzählmaschine f; ~-paper Stimmzettel m; ~-power Stimmrecht n.
**vouch** [vautʃ] verbürgen; ~ for bürgen für; ~er ['vautʃə] Beleg m, Unterlage f; Gutschein m; Zeuge m; ~safe [vautʃ'seif] gewähren; geruhen.
**vow** [vau] **1.** Gelübde n; (Treu-)Schwur m; **2.** v/t. geloben.
**vowel** gr. ['vauəl] Vokal m, Selbstlaut m.
**voyage** ['vɔidʒ] **1.** längere (See-, Flug)Reise; **2.** reisen, fahren, ~r ['vɔiədʒə] (See)Reisende(r m) f.
**vulgar** ['vʌlgə] **1.** □ gewöhnlich, gemein, vulgär, pöbelhaft; ~ tongue Volkssprache f; **2.**: the ~ der Pöbel; ~ism [~rizəm] vulgärer Ausdruck; ~ity [vʌl'gæriti] Gemeinheit f; ~ize ['vʌlgəraiz] gemein machen; erniedrigen; populär machen.
**vulnerable** □ ['vʌlnərəbl] verwundbar; fig. angreifbar.
**vulpine** ['vʌlpain] Fuchs...; fuchsartig; schlau, listig.
**vulture** orn. ['vʌltʃə] Geier m.
**vying** ['vaiiŋ] wetteifernd.

# W

**wacky** *Am. sl.* ['wæki] verrückt.
**wad** [wɔd] **1.** (Watte)Bausch *m*; Polster *n*; Pfropf(en) *m*; Banknotenbündel *n*; **2.** wattieren; polstern; zs.-pressen; zustopfen; **~ding** ['wɔdiŋ] Wattierung *f*; Watte *f*.
**waddle** ['wɔdl] watscheln, wackeln.
**wade** [weid] *v/i.* waten; *fig.* sich hindurcharbeiten; *v/t.* durchwaten.
**wafer** ['weifə] Waffel *f*; Oblate *f*; *eccl.* Hostie *f*.
**waffle** ['wɔfl] **1.** Waffel *f*; **2.** F quasseln.
**waft** [wɑ:ft] **1.** wehen, tragen; **2.** Hauch *m*.
**wag** [wæg] **1.** wackeln (mit); wedeln (mit); **2.** Schütteln *n*; Wedeln *n*; Spaßvogel *m*.
**wage¹** [weidʒ] *Krieg* führen.
**wage²** [~] *mst* **~s** *pl.* Lohn *m*; **~-earner** ['weidʒə:nə] Lohnempfänger *m*.
**wager** ['weidʒə] **1.** Wette *f*; **2.** wetten.
**waggish** □ ['wægiʃ] schelmisch.
**waggle** F ['wægl] wackeln (mit).
**wag(g)on** ['wægən] (Roll-, Güter-) Wagen *m*; **~er** [~nə] Fuhrmann *m*.
**wagtail** *orn.* ['wægteil] Bachstelze *f*.
**waif** [weif] herrenloses Gut; Strandgut *n*; Heimatlose(r *m*) *f*.
**wail** [weil] **1.** (Weh)Klagen *n*; **2.** (weh)klagen.
**wainscot** ['weinskɔt] (Holz)Täfelung *f*.
**waist** [weist] Taille *f*; schmalste Stelle; ♣ Mitteldeck *n*; **~coat** ['weiskout] Weste *f*; **~line** ['weistlain] *Schneiderei*: Taille *f*.
**wait** [weit] **1.** *v/i.* warten (*for* auf *acc.*); *a.* ~ *at* (*Am. on*) table bedienen, servieren; ~ (*up*)on *j-n* bedienen; *j-n* besuchen; ~ *and see* abwarten; *v/t.* abwarten; mit *dem Essen* warten (*for* auf *j-n*); **2.** Warten *n*, Aufenthalt *m*; lie in ~ for *s.o.* *j-m* auflauern; **~er** ['weitə] Kellner *m*; Tablett *n*.
**waiting** ['weitiŋ] Warten *n*; Dienst *m*; *in* ~ diensttuend; **~-room** Wartezimmer *n*; ♛ *etc.* Wartesaal *m*.
**waitress** ['weitris] Kellnerin *f*.
**waive** [weiv] verzichten auf (*acc.*), aufgeben; **~r** ⚖ ['weivə] Verzicht *m*.
**wake** [weik] **1.** ♣ Kielwasser *n* (*a. fig.*); Totenwache *f*; Kirmes *f*; **2.** [*irr.*] *v/i. a.* ~ *up* aufwachen; *v/t. a.* ~ *up* (auf)wecken; erwecken; *fig.* wachrufen; **~ful** □ ['weikful] wachsam; schlaflos; **~n** ['weikən] *s.* wake 2.
**wale** *bsd. Am.* [weil] Strieme *f*.
**walk** [wɔ:k] **1.** *v/i.* (zu Fuß) gehen; spazierengehen; wandern; Schritt gehen; ~ *out* F streiken; ~ *out on sl.*

im Stich lassen; *v/t.* führen; *Pferd* Schritt gehen lassen; begleiten; (durch)wandern; umhergehen auf *od.* in (*dat.*); **2.** (Spazier)Gang *m*; Spazierweg *m*; ~ *of life* Lebensstellung *f*, Beruf *m*; **~er** ['wɔ:kə] Fuß-, Spaziergänger(in).
**walkie-talkie** ⚔ ['wɔ:ki'tɔ:ki] tragbares Sprechfunkgerät.
**walking** ['wɔ:kiŋ] Spaziergehen *n*, Wandern *n*; *attr.* Spazier...; Wander...; ~ **papers** *pl. Am.* F Entlassung(spapiere *n/pl.*) *f*; Laufpaß *m*; **~-stick** Spazierstock *m*; **~-tour** (Fuß)Wanderung *f*.
**walk|-out** *Am.* ['wɔ:kaut] Ausstand *m*; **~-over** Kinderspiel *n*, leichter Sieg.
**wall** [wɔ:l] **1.** Wand *f*; Mauer *f*; **2.** mit Mauern umgeben; ~ *up* zumauern.
**wallet** ['wɔlit] Ränzel *n*; Brieftasche *f*.
**wallflower** *fig.* ['wɔ:lflauə] Mauerblümchen *n*.
**wallop** F ['wɔləp] *j-n* verdreschen.
**wallow** ['wɔlou] sich wälzen.
**wall|-paper** ['wɔ:lpeipə] Tapete *f*; **~-socket** ⚡ Steckdose *f*.
**walnut** ⚘ ['wɔ:lnət] Walnuß(baum *m*) *f*.
**walrus** *zo.* ['wɔ:lrəs] Walroß *n*.
**waltz** [wɔ:ls] **1.** Walzer *m*; **2.** Walzer tanzen.
**wan** □ [wɔn] blaß, bleich, fahl.
**wand** [wɔnd] (Zauber)Stab *m*.
**wander** ['wɔndə] wandern; umherschweifen, umherwandern; *fig.* abschweifen; irregehen; phantasieren.
**wane** [wein] **1.** abnehmen (*Mond*); *fig.* schwinden; **2.** Abnehmen *n*.
**wangle** *sl.* ['wæŋgl] *v/t.* deichseln, hinkriegen; *v/i.* mogeln.
**want** [wɔnt] **1.** Mangel *m* (*of* an *dat.*); Bedürfnis *n*; Not *f*; **2.** *v/i.*: be ~*ing* fehlen; es fehlen lassen (*in* an *dat.*); unzulänglich sein; ~ *for* Not leiden an (*dat.*); *it* ~*s of* es fehlt an (*dat.*); *v/t.* bedürfen (*gen.*), brauchen; nicht haben; wünschen, (haben) wollen; *it* ~*s s.th.* es fehlt an et. (*dat.*); *he* ~*s energy* es fehlt ihm an Energie; ~*ed* gesucht; **~-ad** F ['wɔntæd] Kleinanzeige *f*; Stellenangebot *n*, -gesuch *n*.
**wanton** ['wɔntən] **1.** □ geil; üppig; mutwillig; **2.** Dirne *f*; **3.** umhertollen.
**war** [wɔ:] **1.** Krieg *m*; *attr.* Kriegs...; *make* ~ Krieg führen (*upon* gegen); **2.** (ea. wider)streiten.
**warble** ['wɔ:bl] trillern; singen.
**ward** [wɔ:d] **1.** Gewahrsam *m*; Vormundschaft *f*; Mündel *n*; Schützling *m*; Gefängniszelle *f*; Abteilung *f*, Station *f*, Krankenzimmer *n*;

(Stadt)Bezirk *m*; ⊕ Einschnitt *m im Schlüsselbart*; 2. ~ off abwehren; **~en** ['wɔ:dn] Aufseher *m*; (Luftschutz)Wart *m*; *univ.* Rektor *m*; **~er** ['wɔ:də] (Gefangenen)Wärter *m*; **~robe** ['wɔ:droub] Garderobe *f*; Kleiderschrank *m*; ~ *trunk* Schrankkoffer *m*.

**ware** [weə] Ware *f*; Geschirr *n*.

**warehouse** 1. ['weəhaus] (Waren-) Lager *n*; Speicher *m*; 2. [~auz] auf Lager bringen, einlagern.

**war|fare** ['wɔ:feə] Krieg(führung*f*) *m*; **~head** ⚔ Sprengkopf *m ɐ-r Rakete etc.*

**wariness** ['weərinis] Vorsicht *f*.

**warlike** ['wɔ:laik] kriegerisch.

**warm** [wɔ:m] 1. □ warm (*a. fig.*); heiß; *fig.* hitzig; 2. F Erwärmung *f*; 3. *v/t. a.* ~ up (auf-, an-, er)wärmen; *v/i. a.* ~ up warm werden, sich erwärmen; **~th** [wɔ:mθ] Wärme *f*.

**warn** [wɔ:n] warnen (*of, against* vor *dat.*); verwarnen; ermahnen; verständigen; **~ing** ['wɔ:niŋ] (Ver-) Warnung *f*; Mahnung *f*; Kündigung *f*.

**warp** [wɔ:p] *v/i.* sich verziehen (*Holz*); *v/t. fig.* verdrehen, verzerren; beeinflussen; *j-n* abbringen (*from* von).

**warrant** ['wɔrənt] 1. Vollmacht *f*; Rechtfertigung *f*; Berechtigung *f*; 𝄐 (Vollziehungs)Befehl *m*; Berechtigungsschein *m*; ~ *of arrest* 𝄐 Haftbefehl *m*; 2. bevollmächtigen; *j-n* berechtigen; *et.* rechtfertigen; verbürgen; ✝ garantieren; **~y** [~ti] Garantie *f*; Berechtigung *f*.

**warrior** ['wɔriə] Krieger *m*.

**wart** [wɔ:t] Warze *f*; Auswuchs *m*.

**wary** □ ['weəri] vorsichtig, behutsam; wachsam.

**was** [wɔz, wəz] 1. *und 3. sg. pret. von* be; *pret. pass. von* be; *he* ~ *to have come* er hätte kommen sollen.

**wash** [wɔʃ] 1. *v/t.* waschen; (um-) spülen; ~ up abwaschen, spülen; *v/i.* sich waschen (lassen); waschecht sein (*a. fig.*); spülen, schlagen (*Wellen*); 2. Waschen *n*; Wäsche *f*; Wellenschlag *m*; Spülwasser *n*; *contp.* Gewäsch *n*; *mouth-*~ Mundwasser *n*; **~able** ['wɔʃəbl] waschbar; **~basin** Waschbecken *n*; **~cloth** Waschlappen *m*; **~er** ['wɔʃə] Wäscherin *f*; Waschmaschine *f*; ⊕ Unterlagscheibe *f*; **~erwoman** Waschfrau *f*; **~ing** ['wɔʃiŋ] 1. Waschen *n*; Wäsche *f*; ~s *pl.* Spülicht *n*; 2. Wasch...; **~ing-up** Abwaschen *n*; **~rag** *bsd. Am.* Waschlappen *m*; **~y** ['wɔʃi] wässerig.

**wasp** [wɔsp] Wespe *f*.

**wastage** ['weistidʒ] Abgang *m*, Verlust *m*; Vergeudung *f*.

**waste** [weist] 1. wüst, öde; unbebaut; überflüssig; Abfall...; *lay* ~ verwüsten; ~ *paper* Altpapier *n*; 2. Verschwendung *f*, Vergeudung *f*; Abfall *m*; Einöde *f*, Wüste *f*; 3. *v/t.* verwüsten; verschwenden; verzehren; *v/i.* verschwendet werden; **~ful** □ ['weistful] verschwenderisch; **~-paper-basket** [weist'peipə:skit] Papierkorb *m*; **~pipe** ['weistpaip] Abflußrohr *n*.

**watch** [wɔtʃ] 1. Wache *f*; Taschenuhr *f*; 2. *v/i.* wachen; ~ *for* warten auf (*acc.*); ~ *out* F aufpassen; *v/t.* bewachen; beobachten; achtgeben auf (*acc.*); Gelegenheit abwarten; **~dog** ['wɔtʃdɔg] Wachhund *m*; **~ful** □ [~ʃful] wachsam, achtsam; **~maker** Uhrmacher *m*; **~man** (Nacht)Wächter *m*; **~word** Losung *f*.

**water** ['wɔ:tə] 1. Wasser *n*; Gewässer *n*; *drink the* ~s Brunnen trinken; 2. *v/t.* bewässern; (be-) sprengen; (be)gießen; mit Wasser versorgen; tränken; verwässern (*a. fig.*); *v/i.* wässern (*Mund*); tränen (*Augen*); Wasser einnehmen; **~closet** (Wasser)Klosett *n*; **~colo(u)r** Aquarell(malerei *f*) *n*; **~course** Wasserlauf *m*; **~cress** 🌿 Brunnenkresse *f*; **~fall** Wasserfall *m*; **~front** Ufer *n*, *bsd. Am.* städtisches Hafengebiet; **~ga(u)ge** ⊕ Wasserstands(an)zeiger *m*; Pegel *m*.

**watering** ['wɔ:təriŋ]: **~can** Gießkanne *f*; **~place** Wasserloch *n*; Tränke *f*; Bad(eort *m*) *n*; Seebad *n*; **~pot** Gießkanne *f*.

**water|-level** ['wɔ:təlevl] Wasserspiegel *m*; Wasserstand(slinie *f*) *m*; ⊕ Wasserwaage *f*; **~man** Fährmann *m*; Bootsführer *m*; Ruderer *m*; **~proof** 1. wasserdicht; 2. Regenmantel *m*; 3. imprägnieren; **~shed** Wasserscheide *f*; Stromgebiet *n*; **~side** 1. Fluß-, Seeufer *n*; 2. am Wasser (gelegen); **~tight** wasserdicht; *fig.* unangreifbar; **~way** Wasserstraße *f*; **~works** *oft sg.* Wasserwerk *n*; **~y** [~əri] wässerig.

**watt** ⚡ [wɔt] Watt *n*.

**wattle** ['wɔtl] 1. Flechtwerk *n*; 2. aus Flechtwerk herstellen.

**wave** [weiv] 1. Welle *f*; Woge *f*; Winken *n*; 2. *v/t.* wellig machen, wellen; schwingen; schwenken; ~ *s.o. aside* j-n beiseite winken; *v/i.* wogen; wehen, flattern; winken; **~length** *phys.* ['weivleŋθ] Wellenlänge *f*.

**waver** ['weivə] (sch)wanken; flakkern.

**wavy** ['weivi] wellig; wogend.

**wax**[1] [wæks] 1. Wachs *n*; Siegellack *m*; Ohrenschmalz *n*; 2. wachsen; bohnern.

**wax**[2] [~] [*irr.*] zunehmen (*Mond*).

**wax|en** *fig.* ['wæksən] wächsern; **~y** □ [~si] wachsartig; weich.

**way** [wei] 1. *mst* Weg *m*; Straße *f*;

Art u. Weise *f*; *eigene* Art; Strecke *f*; Richtung *f*; ✠ Gegend *f*; ⚓ Fahrt *f*; *fig.* Hinsicht *f*; Zustand *m*; ⚓ Heiling *f*; ~ in Eingang *m*; ~ out Ausgang *m*; *fig.* Ausweg *m*; right of ~ ⚓ Wegerecht *n*; *bsd. mot.* Vorfahrt(srecht *n*) *f*; *this* ~ hierher, hier entlang; *by the* ~ übrigens; *by* ~ *of* durch; *on the* ~, *on one's* ~ unterwegs; *out of the* ~ ungewöhnlich; *under* ~ in Fahrt; *give* ~ zurückgehen; *mot.* die Vorfahrt lassen (to *dat.*); nachgeben; abgelöst werden (to von); sich hingeben (to *dat.*); *have one's* ~ s-n Willen haben; *lead the* ~ vorangehen; **2.** *adv.* weit; **~bill** ['weibil] Frachtbrief *m*; **~farer** ['weifεərə] Wanderer *m*; **~lay** [wei'lei] [*irr.* (lay)] *j-m* auflauern; **~side 1.** Wegrand *m*; **2.** am Wege; ~ **station** *Am.* Zwischenstation *f*; **~train** *Am.* Bummelzug *m*; **~ward** □ ['weiwəd] starrköpfig, eigensinnig.

**we** [wi:, wi] wir.

**weak** □ [wi:k] schwach; schwächlich; dünn (*Getränk*); **~en** ['wi:kən] *v/t.* schwächen; *v/i.* schwach werden; **~ling** ['wi:kliŋ] Schwächling *m*; **~ly** [⸱li] schwächlich; **~minded** ['wi:k'maindid] schwachsinnig; **~ness** ['wi:knis] Schwäche *f*.

**weal** [wi:l] Wohl *n*; Strieme *f*.

**wealth** [welθ] Wohlstand *m*; Reichtum *m*; *fig.* Fülle *f*; **~y** □ ['welθi] reich; wohlhabend.

**wean** [wi:n] entwöhnen; ~ *s.o. from s.th.* j-m et. abgewöhnen.

**weapon** ['wepən] Waffe *f*.

**wear** [wεə] **1.** [*irr.*] *v/t.* am Körper tragen; zur Schau tragen; *a.* ~ *away*, ~ *down*, ~ *off*, ~ *out* abnutzen, abtragen, verbrauchen; erschöpfen; ermüden; zermürben; *v/i.* sich *gut etc.* tragen od. halten; *a.* ~ *off* od. *out* sich abnutzen od. abtragen; *fig.* sich verlieren; ~ *on* vergehen; **2.** Tragen *n*; (Be)Kleidung *f*; Abnutzung *f*; *for hard* ~ strapazierfähig; *the worse for* ~ abgetragen; ~ **and tear** Verschleiß *m*.

**wear|iness** ['wiərinis] Müdigkeit *f*; Ermüdung *f*; *fig.* Überdruß *m*; **~isome** □ [⸱isəm] ermüdend; langweilig; **~y** ['wiəri] **1.** □ müde; *fig.* überdrüssig; ermüdend; anstrengend; **2.** ermüden.

**weasel** *zo.* ['wi:zl] Wiesel *n*.

**weather** ['weðə] **1.** Wetter *n*, Witterung *f*; **2.** *v/t.* dem Wetter aussetzen; ⚓ *Sturm* abwettern; *fig.* überstehen; *v/i.* verwittern; **~beaten** vom Wetter mitgenommen; **~bureau** Wetteramt *n*; **~chart** Wetterkarte *f*; **~forecast** Wetterbericht *m*, -vorhersage *f*; **~worn** verwittert.

**weav|e** ['wi:v] [*irr.*] weben; wirken; flechten; *fig.* ersinnen, erfinden;

sich schlängeln; **~er** ['wi:və] Weber *m*.

**weazen** ['wi:zn] verhutzelt.

**web** [web] Gewebe *n*; *orn.* Schwimmhaut *f*; **~bing** ['webiŋ] Gurtband *n*.

**wed** [wed] heiraten; *fig.* verbinden (to mit); **~ding** ['wediŋ] **1.** Hochzeit *f*; **2.** Hochzeits...; Braut...; Trau...; **~ring** Ehe-, Trauring *m*.

**wedge** [wedʒ] **1.** Keil *m*; **2.** (ver-)keilen; *a.* ~ *in* (hin)einzwängen.

**wedlock** ['wedlɔk] Ehe *f*.

**Wednesday** ['wenzdi] Mittwoch *m*.

**wee** [wi:] klein, winzig; *a* ~ *bit* ein klein wenig.

**weed** [wi:d] **1.** Unkraut *n*; **2.** jäten; säubern (*of* von); ~ *out* ausmerzen; **~killer** ['wi:dkilə] Unkrautvertilgungsmittel *n*; **~s** *pl. mst* widow's ~ Witwenkleidung *f*; **~y** ['wi:di] voll Unkraut, verkrautet; *fig.* lang aufgeschossen.

**week** [wi:k] Woche *f*; *this day* ~ heute im od. vor e-r Woche; **~day** ['wi:kdei] Wochentag *m*; **~end** ['wi:k'end] Wochenende *n*; **~ly** ['wi:kli] **1.** wöchentlich; **2.** *a.* ~ *paper* Wochenblatt *n*, Wochen(zeit)-schrift *f*.

**weep** [wi:p] [*irr.*] weinen; tropfen; **~ing** ['wi:piŋ] Trauer...; ~ *willow* ♀ Trauerweide *f*.

**weigh** [wei] *v/t.* (ab)wiegen, *fig.* ab-, erwägen; ~ *anchor* ⚓ den Anker lichten; ~ *ed down* niedergebeugt; *v/i.* wiegen (*a. fig.*); ausschlaggebend sein; ~ (*up*)*on* lasten auf (*dat.*).

**weight** [weit] **1.** Gewicht *n* (*a.fig.*); Last *f* (*a. fig.*); *fig.* Bedeutung *f*; Wucht *f*; **2.** beschweren; *fig.* belasten; **~y** □ ['weiti] (ge)wichtig; wuchtig.

**weir** [wiə] Wehr *n*; Fischreuse *f*.

**weird** [wiəd] Schicksals...; unheimlich; F sonderbar, seltsam.

**welcome** ['welkəm] **1.** willkommen; *you are* ~ *to inf.* es steht Ihnen frei, zu *inf.*; (*you are*) ~! gern geschehen!, bitte sehr!; **2.** Willkomm(en *n*) *m*; **3.** willkommen heißen; *fig.* begrüßen.

**weld** ⊕ [weld] (zs.-)schweißen.

**welfare** ['welfεə] Wohlfahrt *f*; ~ **centre** Fürsorgeamt *n*; ~ **state** Wohlfahrtsstaat *m*; ~ **work** Fürsorge *f*, Wohlfahrtspflege *f*; ~ **worker** Fürsorger(in).

**well¹** [wel] **1.** Brunnen *m*; *fig.* Quelle *f*; ⊕ Bohrloch *n*; Treppen-, Aufzugs-, Licht-, Luftschacht *m*; **2.** quellen.

**well²** [⸱] **1.** wohl; gut; ordentlich, gründlich; gesund; ~ *off* in guten Verhältnissen, wohlhabend; *I am not* ~ mir ist nicht wohl; **2.** *int.* nun!, F na!; **~being** ['wel'bi:iŋ] Wohl(sein) *n*; **~born** von guter

Herkunft; **~-bred** wohlerzogen; **~-defined** deutlich, klar umrissen; **~-favo(u)red** gut aussehend; **~-intentioned** wohlmeinend; gut gemeint; **~ known**, **~-known** bekannt; **~-mannered** mit guten Manieren; **~-nigh** ['welnai] beinahe; **~ timed** rechtzeitig; **~-to-do** ['weltə'du:] wohlhabend; **~-wisher** Gönner m, Freund m; **~-worn** abgetragen; *fig.* abgedroschen.

**Welsh** [welʃ] **1.** walisisch; **2.** Walisisch n; the **~** *pl.* die Waliser *pl.*; **~ rabbit** überbackene Käseschnitte.

**welt** [welt] ⊕ Rahmen m, *Schuh*-Rahmen m; Einfassung f; Strieme f.

**welter** ['weltə] **1.** rollen, sich wälzen; **2.** Wirrwarr m, Durcheinander n.

**wench** [wentʃ] Mädchen n; Dirne f.

**went** [went] *pret. von* go 1.

**wept** [wept] *pret. u. p.p. von* weep.

**were** [wəː, wə] **1.** *pret. pl. u.* **2.** *sg. von* be; **2.** *pret. pass. von* be; **3.** *subj. pret. von* be.

**west** [west] **1.** West (en m); **2.** West...; westlich; westwärts; **~erly** ['westəli], **~ern** [~ən] westlich; **~erner** [~nə] *Am.* Weststaatler(in); Abendländer(in); **~ward(s)** [~twəd(z)] westwärts.

**wet** [wet] **1.** naß, feucht; *Am.* den Alkoholhandel gestattend; **2.** Nässe f; Feuchtigkeit f; **3.** [*irr.*] naß machen, anfeuchten.

**wetback** *Am. sl.* ['wetbæk] illegaler Einwanderer *aus Mexiko.*

**wether** ['weðə] Hammel m.

**wet-nurse** ['wetnəːs] Amme f.

**whack** F [wæk] **1.** verhauen; **2.** Hieb m.

**whale** [weil] Wal m; **~bone** ['weilboun] Fischbein n; **~-oil** Tran m; **~r** ['weilə] Walfischfänger m.

**whaling** ['weiliŋ] Walfischfang m.

**wharf** [wɔːf], *pl. a.* **wharves** [wɔːvz] Kai m, Anlegeplatz m.

**what** [wɔt] **1.** was; das, was; *know* **~'s ~** Bescheid wissen; **2.** was?; wie?; wieviel?; welch(er, -e, -es)?; was für ein(e)?; **~ about ...?** wie steht's mit ...?; **~ for?** wozu?; **~ of it?** was ist denn dabei?; **~ next?** was sonst noch?; *iro.* was denn noch alles?; **~ a blessing!** was für ein Segen!; **3.** **~ with ... ~ with ...** teils durch ... teils durch ...; **~-(so)ever** [wɔt(sou)'evə] was *od.* welcher auch (immer).

**wheat** ♀ [wiːt] Weizen m.

**wheedle** ['wiːdl] beschwatzen; **~ s.th. out of s.o.** j-m et. abschwatzen.

**wheel** [wiːl] **1.** Rad n; Steuer n; *bsd. Am.* F Fahrrad n; Töpferscheibe f; Drehung f; ✕ Schwenkung f; **2.** rollen, fahren, schieben; sich drehen; sich umwenden; ✕ schwenken; F radeln; **~barrow**

['wiːlbærou] Schubkarren m; **~ chair** Rollstuhl m; **~ed** mit Rädern; fahrbar; **...räd(e)rig.**

**wheeze** [wiːz] schnaufen, keuchen.

**whelp** [welp] **1.** *zo.* Welpe m; *allg.* Junge(s) n; F Balg m, n *(ungezogenes Kind)*; **2.** (Junge) werfen.

**when** [wen] **1.** wann?; **2.** wenn; als; während *od.* da doch; und da.

**whence** [wens] woher, von wo.

**when(so)ever** [wen(sou)'evə] immer *od.* jedesmal wenn; sooft (als).

**where** [wɛə] wo; wohin; **~about(s) 1.** ['wɛərə'hauts] wo herum?; **2.** [~əbauts] Aufenthalt m; **~as** [~r'æz] wohingegen, während (doch); **~at** [~'æt] wobei, worüber, worauf; **~by** [wɛə'bai] wodurch; **~fore** ['wɛəfɔː] weshalb; **~in** [wɛər'in] worin; **~of** [~r'ɔv] wovon; **~upon** [~rə'pɔn] worauf(hin); **~ver** [~r'evə] wo(hin) (auch) immer; **~withal** ['wɛəwiðɔːl] Erforderliche(s) n; Mittel n/pl.

**whet** [wet] wetzen, schärfen; anstacheln.

**whether** ['weðə] ob; **~ or no** so oder so.

**whetstone** ['wetstoun] Schleifstein m.

**whey** [wei] Molke f.

**which** [witʃ] **1.** welche(r, -s)?; **2.** der, die, das; was; **~ever** [~ʃ'evə] welche(r, -s) (auch) immer.

**whiff** [wif] **1.** Hauch m; Zug m *beim Rauchen*; Zigarillo m; **2.** paffen.

**while** [wail] **1.** Weile f; Zeit f; *for a* **~** e-e Zeitlang; *worth* **~** der Mühe wert; **2.** *mst* **~ away** Zeit verbringen; **3.** *a.* **whilst** [wailst] während.

**whim** [wim] Schrulle f, Laune f.

**whimper** ['wimpə] wimmern.

**whim|sical** □ ['wimzikəl] wunderlich; **~sy** ['wimzi] Grille f, Laune f.

**whine** [wain] winseln; wimmern.

**whinny** ['wini] wiehern.

**whip** [wip] **1.** *v/t.* peitschen; geißeln (*a. fig.*); j-n verprügeln; schlagen (F *a. fig.*); umsäumen; werfen; reißen; *~ in parl.* zs.-trommeln; *~ on Kleidungsstück* überwerfen; *~ up* antreiben; aufraffen; *v/i.* springen, flitzen; **2.** Peitsche f; Geißel f.

**whippet** *zo.* ['wipit] Whippet m *(kleiner englischer Rennhund).*

**whipping** ['wipiŋ] Prügel *pl.*; **~-top** Kreisel m.

**whippoorwill** *orn.* ['wipuəwil] Ziegenmelker m.

**whirl** [wəːl] **1.** wirbeln; (sich) drehen; **2.** Wirbel m, Strudel m; **~pool** ['wəːlpuːl] Strudel m; **~wind** Wirbelwind m.

**whir(r)** [wəː] schwirren.

**whisk** [wisk] **1.** Wisch m; Staubwedel m; *Küche:* Schneebesen m; Schwung m; **2.** *v/t.* (ab-, weg)wischen, (ab-, weg)fegen; wirbeln (mit); schlagen; *v/i.* huschen, flitzen; **~er** ['wiskə] Barthaar *n*; *mst ~s pl.* Backenbart *m*.

**whisper** ['wispə] **1.** flüstern; **2.** Geflüster *n*.

**whistle** ['wisl] **1.** pfeifen; **2.** Pfeife *f*; Pfiff *m*; F Kehle *f*; **~-stop** *Am.* 🚄 Haltepunkt *m*; *fig.* Kaff *n*; *pol.* kurzes Auftreten *e-s Kandidaten im Wahlkampf.*

**Whit** [wit] *in Zssgn:* Pfingst...

**white** [wait] **1.** *allg.* weiß; rein; F anständig; weiß...; **2.** Weiß(e) *n*; Weiße(r *m*) *f* (*Rasse*); **~-collar** ['wait'kɔlə] geistig, Kopf..., Büro...; *~ workers pl.* Angestellte *pl.*; **~ heat** Weißglut *f*; **~ lie** fromme Lüge; **~n** ['waitn] weiß machen *od.* werden; bleichen; **~ness** [~nis] Weiße *f*; Blässe *f*; **~wash 1.** Tünche *f*; **2.** weißen; *fig.* rein waschen.

**whither** *lit.* ['wiðə] wohin.

**whitish** ['waitiʃ] weißlich.

**Whitsun** ['witsn] Pfingst...; **~tide** Pfingsten *pl.*

**whittle** ['witl] schnitze(l)n; **~ away** verkleinern, schwächen.

**whiz(z)** [wiz] zischen, sausen.

**who** [hu:, hu] **1.** welche(r, -s); der, die, das; **2.** wer?

**whodun(n)it** *sl.* [hu:'dʌnit] Krimi (-nalroman, -nalfilm) *m*.

**whoever** [hu(:)'evə] wer auch immer.

**whole** [houl] **1.** □ ganz; heil, unversehrt; *made out of ~ cloth Am.* F frei erfunden; **2.** Ganze(s) *n*; (*up*)*on the ~ im ganzen; im allgemeinen*; **~-hearted** □ ['houl'ha:tid] aufrichtig; **~-meal bread** ['houlmi:l bred] Vollkorn-, Schrotbrot *n*; **~sale 1.** *mst ~ trade* Großhandel *m*; **2.** Großhandels...; En-gros...; *fig.* Massen...; *~ dealer* = **~saler** [~lə] Großhändler *m*; **~some** □ [~səm] gesund.

**wholly** *adv.* ['houlli] ganz, gänzlich.

**whom** [hu:m] *acc. von* who.

**whoop** [hu:p] **1.** Schrei *m*, Geschrei *n*; **2.** laut schreien; *~ it up Am. sl.* laut feiern; **~ee** *Am.* F ['wupi:] Freudenfest *n*; *make ~ auf die Pauke hauen*; **~ing-cough** 🩺 ['hu:-piŋkɔf] Keuchhusten *m*.

**whore** [hɔ:] Hure *f*.

**whose** [hu:z] *gen. von* who.

**why** [wai] **1.** warum, weshalb; *~ so?* wieso?; **2.** ei!, ja!; (je) nun.

**wick** [wik] Docht *m*.

**wicked** □ ['wikid] *moralisch* böse, schlimm; **~ness** [~dnis] Bosheit *f*.

**wicker** ['wikə] aus Weide geflochten; Weiden...; Korb...; *~ basket* Weidenkorb *m*; *~ chair* Korbstuhl *m*.

**wicket** ['wikit] Pförtchen *n*; *Kricket:* Dreistab *m*, Tor *n*; **~-keeper** Torhüter *m*.

**wide** [waid] *a.* □ *u. adv.* weit; ausgedehnt; weitgehend; großzügig;

breit; weitab; *~ awake* völlig (*od.* hell)wach; aufgeweckt (*schlau*); *3 feet ~ 3 Fuß breit*; **~n** ['waidn] (sich) erweitern; **~-open** ['waid'ou-pən] weit geöffnet; *Am. sl.* großzügig *in der Gesetzesdurchführung*; **~-spread** weitverbreitet, ausgedehnt.

**widow** ['widou] Witwe *f*; *attr.* Witwen...; **~er** [~ouə] Witwer *m*.

**width** [widθ] Breite *f*, Weite *f*.

**wield** *lit.* [wi:ld] handhaben.

**wife** [waif], *pl.* **wives** [waivz] (Ehe-) Frau *f*; Gattin *f*; Weib *n*; **~ly** ['waifli] fraulich.

**wig** [wig] Perücke *f*.

**wigging** F ['wigiŋ] Schelte *f*.

**wild** [waild] **1.** □ wild; toll; unbändig; abenteuerlich; planlos; *run ~ wild (auf)wachsen; talk ~* (wild) darauflos reden; *~ for od. about (ganz)* verrückt nach; **2.** *mst ~s pl.* Wildnis *f*; **~cat** ['waildkæt] **1.** *zo.* Wildkatze *f*; *Am.* Schwindelunternehmen *n*; *bsd. Am.* wilde Ölbohrung; **2.** wild (*Streik*); Schwindel...; **~erness** ['wildənis] Wildnis *f*, Wüste *f*; Einöde *f*; **~fire:** *like ~ wie ein Lauffeuer.*

**wile** [wail] List *f*; *mst ~s pl.* Tücke *f*.

**wil(l)ful** □ ['wilful] eigensinnig; vorsätzlich.

**will** [wil] **1.** Wille *m*; Wunsch *m*; Testament *n*; *of one's own free ~ aus freien Stücken*; **2.** [*irr.*] *v/aux.:* *he ~ come er wird kommen; er kommt gewöhnlich; I ~ do it ich will es tun*; **3.** wollen; durch Willenskraft zwingen; entscheiden; ⚖️ vermachen.

**willing** □ ['wiliŋ] willig, bereit (*-willig*); *pred.* gewillt (*to inf. zu*); **~ness** [~ŋnis] (Bereit)Willigkeit *f*.

**will-o'-the-wisp** ['wiləðwisp] Irrlicht *n*.

**willow** ♣ ['wilou] Weide *f*.

**willy-nilly** ['wili'nili] wohl oder übel.

**wilt** [wilt] (ver)welken.

**wily** □ ['waili] schlau, verschmitzt.

**win** [win] **1.** [*irr.*] *v/t.* gewinnen; erringen; erlangen, erreichen; *j-n dazu bringen (to do zu tun)*; *~ s.o. over j-n für sich gewinnen*; *v/i.* gewinnen; siegen; **2.** *Sport:* Sieg *m*.

**wince** [wins] (zs.-)zucken.

**winch** [wintʃ] Winde *f*; Kurbel *f*.

**wind¹** [wind, *poet.a.* waind] **1.** Wind *m*; Atem *m*, Luft *f*; 🩺 Blähung *f*; ♪ Blasinstrumente *n/pl.*; **2.** wittern; außer Atem bringen; verschnaufen lassen.

**wind²** [waind] [*irr.*] *v/t.* winden; wickeln; *Horn* blasen; *~ up Uhr* aufziehen; *Geschäft* abwickeln; ♱ liquidieren; *v/i.* sich winden; sich schlängeln.

**wind|bag** ['windbæg] Schwätzer *m*; **~fall** Fallobst *n*; Glücksfall *m*.

winding ['waindiŋ] 1. Windung f;
2. □ sich windend; ~ stairs pl.
Wendeltreppe f; ~sheet Leichentuch n.

wind-instrument ♪ ['windinstru-
mənt] Blasinstrument n.

windlass ⊕ ['windləs] Winde f.

windmill ['winmil] Windmühle f.

window ['windou] Fenster n;
Schaufenster n; ~dressing Schau-
fensterdekoration f; fig. Aufma-
chung f, Mache f; ~shade Am.
Rouleau n; ~shopping Schau-
fensterbummel m.

wind|pipe ['windpaip] Luftröhre f;
~screen, Am. ~shield mot.
Windschutzscheibe f; ~ wiper
Scheibenwischer m.

windy □ ['windi] windig (a. fig.
inhaltlos); geschwätzig.

wine [wain] Wein m; ~press
['wainpres] Kelter f.

wing [wiŋ] 1. Flügel m (a. ✗ u. ⚙);
Schwinge f; F co. Arm m; mot.
Kotflügel m; ✈ Tragfläche f; ✗,
✗ Geschwader n; ~s pl. Kulissen
f/pl.; take ~ weg-, auffliegen; on
the ~ im Fluge; 2. fig. beflügeln;
fliegen.

wink [wiŋk] 1. Blinzeln n, Zwinkern
n; not get a ~ of sleep kein Auge
zutun; s. forty; 2. blinzeln, zwinkern (mit); ~ at ein Auge zudrücken bei et.; j-m zublinzeln.

winn|er ['winə] Gewinner(in), Sie-
ger(in); ~ing ['winiŋ] 1. □ einnehmend, gewinnend; 2. ~s pl.
Gewinn m.

winsome ['winsəm] gefällig, einnehmend.

wint|er ['wintə] 1. Winter m;
2. überwintern; ~ry [~tri] winter-
lich; fig. frostig.

wipe [waip] (ab-, auf)wischen; reinigen; (ab)trocknen; ~ out weg-
wischen; (aus)löschen; fig. vernichten; tilgen.

wire ['waiə] 1. Draht m; Leitung f;
F Telegramm n; pull the ~s der
Drahtzieher sein; s-e Beziehungen
spielen lassen; 2. (ver)drahten; telegraphieren; ~drawn ['waiədrɔːn]
spitzfindig; ~less ['waiəlis] 1. □
drahtlos; Funk...; 2. a. ~ set Radio
(-apparat m) n; on the ~ im Rundfunk; 3. funken; ~netting ['waiə-
'netiŋ] Drahtgeflecht n.

wiry □ ['waiəri] drahtig, sehnig.

wisdom ['wizdəm] Weisheit f;
Klugheit f; ~ tooth Weisheitszahn
m.

wise [waiz] 1. □ weise, verständig;
klug; erfahren; ~ guy Am. sl.
Schlauberger m; 2. Weise f, Art f.

wise-crack F ['waizkræk] 1. witzige
Bemerkung f; 2. witzeln.

wish [wiʃ] 1. wünschen; wollen; ~
for (sich) et. wünschen; ~ well (ill)
wohl- (übel)wollen; 2. Wunsch m;

~ful □ ['wiʃful] sehnsüchtig; ~
thinking Wunschdenken n.

wisp [wisp] Wisch m; Strähne f.

wistful □ ['wistful] sehnsüchtig.

wit [wit] 1. Witz m; a. ~s pl. Verstand m; witziger Kopf; be at one's
~'s end mit s-r Weisheit zu Ende
sein; keep one's ~s about one e-n
klaren Kopf behalten; 2.: to ~ nämlich, das heißt.

witch [witʃ] Hexe f, Zauberin f;
~craft ['witʃkrɑːft], ~ery [~ʃəri]
Hexerei f; ~hunt pol. Hexenjagd
f (Verfolgung politisch verdächtiger
Personen).

with [wið] mit; nebst; bei; von;
durch; vor (dat.); ~ it sl. schwer
auf der Höhe.

withdraw [wið'drɔː] [irr. (draw)]
v/t. ab-, ent-, zurückziehen; zurücknehmen; Geld abheben; v/i.
sich zurückziehen; abtreten; ~al
[~ɔːəl] Zurückziehung f; Rückzug
m.

wither ['wiðə] v/i. (ver)welken;
verdorren; austrocknen; v/t. welk
machen.

with|hold [wið'hould] [irr. (hold)]
zurückhalten; et. vorenthalten; ~in
[wi'ðin] 1. adv. lit. im Innern,
drin(nen); zu Hause; 2. prp. in(ner-
halb); ~ doors im Hause; ~ call in
Rufweite; ~out [wi'ðaut] 1. adv. lit.
(dr)außen; äußerlich; 2. prp. ohne;
lit. außerhalb; ~stand [wið'stænd]
[irr. (stand)] widerstehen (dat.).

witness ['witnis] 1. Zeug|e m, -in f;
bear ~ Zeugnis ablegen (to für; of
von); in ~ of zum Zeugnis (gen.);
2. (be)zeugen; Zeuge sein von et.;
~box, Am. ~ stand Zeugenstand
m.

wit|ticism ['witisizəm] Witz m;
~ty □ ['witi] witzig; geistreich.

wives [waivz] pl. von wife.

wiz Am. sl. [wiz] Genie n; ~ard
['wizəd] Zauberer m; Genie n.

wizen(ed) ['wizn(d)] schrump(e)lig.

wobble ['wɔbl] schwanken; wackeln.

woe [wou] Weh n, Leid n; ~ is me!
wehe mir!; ~begone ['woubigɔn]
jammervoll; ~ful □ ['wouful]
jammervoll, traurig, elend.

woke [wouk] pret. u. p.p. von wake 2;
~n ['woukən] p.p. von wake 2.

wold [would] (hügeliges) Heidland.

wolf [wulf] 1. zo. pl. wolves
[wulvz] Wolf m; 2. verschlingen;
~ish □ ['wulfiʃ] wölfisch; Wolfs...

woman ['wumən], pl. women ['wi-
min] 1. Frau f; Weib n; 2. weiblich;
~ doctor Ärztin f; ~ student Studentin f; ~hood [~hud] die
Frauen f/pl.; Weiblichkeit f; ~ish
□ [~niʃ] weibisch; ~kind [~n-
'kaind] Frauen(welt f) f/pl.; ~like
[~nlaik] fraulich; ~ly [~li] weiblich.

womb [wuːm] anat. Gebärmutter f;
Mutterleib m; fig. Schoß m.

**women** ['wimin] *pl. von* woman; ⟨folk(s), ⟨kind die Frauen f/pl.; F Weibervolk *n*.

**won** [wʌn] *pret. u. p.p. von* win 1.

**wonder** ['wʌndə] **1.** Wunder *n*; Verwunderung *f*; **2.** sich wundern; gern wissen mögen, sich fragen; ⟨ful □ [⟨əful] wunderbar, -voll; ⟨ing □ [⟨əriŋ] staunend, verwundert.

**won't** [wount] = will not.

**wont** [⟨] **1.** *pred.* gewohnt; be ⟨ to *inf.* pflegen zu *inf.*; **2.** Gewohnheit *f*; ⟨ed ['wountid] gewohnt.

**woo** [wu:] werben um; locken.

**wood** [wud] Wald *m*, Gehölz *n*; Holz *n*; Faß *n*; ♪ Holzblasinstrument (-e *pl.*) *n*; touch ⟨! unberufen!; ⟨chuck *zo.* ['wudtʃʌk] Waldmurmeltier *n*; ⟨cut Holzschnitt *m*; ⟨cutter Holzfäller *m*; *Kunst*: Holzschneider *m*; ⟨ed ['wudid] bewaldet; ⟨en ['wudn] hölzern (*a. fig.*); Holz...; ⟨man Förster *m*; Holzfäller *m*; ⟨pecker *orn.* ['wudpekə] Specht *m*; ⟨sman ['wudzmən] *s.* woodman; ⟨wind ♪ Holzblasinstrument *n*; *oft* ⟨s *pl.* ♪ Holzbläser *m/pl.*; ⟨work Holzwerk *n*; ⟨y ['wudi] waldig; holzig.

**wool** [wul] Wolle *f*; ⟨gathering ['wulgæðəriŋ] Geistesabwesenheit *f*; ⟨(l)en ['wulin] **1.** wollen; Woll-...; **2.** ⟨s *pl.* Wollsachen f/pl.; ⟨(l)y ['wuli] **1.** wollig; Woll...; belegt (*Stimme*); verschwommen; **2.** woollies *pl.* F Wollsachen f/pl.

**word** [wə:d] **1.** *mst* Wort *n*; *engS.*: Vokabel *f*; Nachricht *f*; ✗ Losung(swort *n*) *f*; Versprechen *n*; Befehl *m*; Spruch *m*; ⟨s *pl.* Wörter *n/pl.*; Worte *n/pl.*; *fig.* Wortwechsel *m*; Text *m* e-s Liedes; have a ⟨ with mit j-m sprechen; **2.** (in Worten) ausdrücken, (ab)fassen; ⟨ing ['wə:diŋ] Wortlaut *m*; Fassung *f*; ⟨splitting Wortklauberei *f*.

**wordy** □ ['wə:di] wortreich; Wort...

**wore** [wɔ:] *pret. von* wear 1.

**work** [wə:k] **1.** Arbeit *f*; Werk *n*; *attr.* Arbeits...; ⟨s *pl.* ⊕ (Uhr-, Feder)Werk *n*; ✗ Befestigungen *pl.*; ⟨s *sg.* Werk *n*, Fabrik *f*; ⟨ of art Kunstwerk *n*; at ⟨ bei der Arbeit; be in ⟨ Arbeit haben; be out of ⟨ arbeitslos sein; set to ⟨, set od. go about one's ⟨ an die Arbeit gehen; ⟨s council Betriebsrat *m*; **2.** [*a. irr.*] *v/i.* arbeiten (*a. fig.*); wirken; gären; sich *hindurch- etc.* arbeiten; ⟨ at arbeiten an (*dat.*); ⟨ out herauskommen (*Summe*); *v/t.* (be)arbeiten; arbeiten lassen; betreiben; *Maschine etc.* bedienen; (be)wirken; ausrechnen, *Aufgabe* lösen; ⟨ one's way sich durcharbeiten; ⟨ off abarbeiten; *Gefühl* abreagieren; ✝ abstoßen; ⟨ out ausarbeiten; lösen;

ausrechnen; ⟨ up hochbringen; aufregen; verarbeiten (into zu).

**work|able** □ ['wə:kəbl] bearbeitungs-, betriebsfähig; ausführbar; ⟨aday ['⟨ədei] Alltags...; ⟨day Werktag *m*; ⟨er ['wə:kə] Arbeiter (-in); ⟨house Armenhaus *n*; *Am.* Besserungsanstalt *f*, Arbeitshaus *n*.

**working** ['wə:kiŋ] **1.** Bergwerk *n*; Steinbruch *m*; Arbeits-, Wirkungsweise *f*; **2.** arbeitend; Arbeits...; Betriebs...; ⟨class Arbeiter...; ⟨day Werk-, Arbeitstag *m*; ⟨ hours *pl.* Arbeitszeit *f*.

**workman** ['wə:kmən] Arbeiter *m*; Handwerker *m*; ⟨like [⟨nlaik] kunstgerecht; ⟨ship [⟨nʃip] Kunstfertigkeit *f*.

**work|out** *Am.* F ['wə:kaut] *mst Sport*: (Konditions)Training *n*; Erprobung *f*; ⟨shop Werkstatt *f*; ⟨woman Arbeiterin *f*.

**world** [wə:ld] *allg.* Welt *f*; a ⟨ of e-e Unmenge (von); bring (come) into the ⟨ zur Welt bringen (kommen); think the ⟨ of alles halten von; ⟨ling ['wə:ldliŋ] Weltkind *n*.

**worldly** ['wə:ldli] weltlich; Welt...; ⟨wise [⟨i'waiz] weltklug.

**world|-power** *pol.* ['wə:ldpauə] Weltmacht *f*; ⟨wide weltweit; weltumspannend; Welt...

**worm** [wə:m] **1.** Wurm *m* (*a. fig.*); **2.** *ein Geheimnis* entlocken (out of dat.); ⟨ o.s. sich schlängeln; *fig.* sich einschleichen (into in *acc.*); ⟨eaten ['wə:mi:tn] wurmstichig.

**worn** [wɔ:n] *p.p. von* wear 1; ⟨out ['wɔ:n'aut] abgenutzt; abgetragen; verbraucht (*a. fig.*); müde, erschöpft; abgezehrt; verhärmt.

**worry** ['wʌri] **1.** (sich) beunruhigen; (sich) ärgern; sich sorgen; sich aufregen; bedrücken; zerren, (ab)würgen; plagen, quälen; **2.** Unruhe *f*; Sorge *f*; Ärger *m*; Qual *f*, Plage *f*; Quälgeist *m*.

**worse** [wə:s] schlechter; schlimmer; ⟨ luck! leider!; um so schlimmer!; from bad to ⟨ vom Regen in die Traufe; ⟨n ['wə:sn] (sich) verschlechtern.

**worship** ['wə:ʃip] **1.** Verehrung *f*; Gottesdienst *m*; Kult *m*; **2.** verehren; anbeten; den Gottesdienst besuchen; ⟨(p)er [⟨pə] Verehrer (-in); Kirchgänger(in).

**worst** [wə:st] **1.** schlechtest; ärgst; schlimmst; **2.** überwältigen.

**worsted** ['wustid] Kammgarn *n*.

**worth** [wə:θ] **1.** wert; ⟨ reading lesenswert; **2.** Wert *m*; Würde *f*; ⟨less □ ['wə:θlis] wertlos; unwürdig; ⟨while ['wə:θ'wail] der Mühe wert; ⟨y □ ['wə:ði] würdig.

**would** [wud] [*pret. von* will 2] wollte; würde; möchte; pflegte; ⟨be ['wudbi:] angeblich, soge-

nannt; möglich, potentiell; Pseu-
do...

**wound**[1] [wu:nd] **1.** Wunde *f*, Ver-
wundung *f*, Verletzung *f*; *fig.*
Kränkung *f*; **2.** verwunden, verletzen (*a. fig.*).

**wound**[2] [waund] *pret. u. p.p. von*
*wind* 2.

**wove** [wouv] *pret. von* weave; **~n**
['wouvən] *p.p. von* weave.

**wow** *Am.* [wau] **1.** *int.* Mensch!;
toll!; **2.** *sl.* Bombenerfolg *m*.

**wrangle** ['ræŋgl] **1.** streiten, (sich)
zanken; **2.** Streit *m*, Zank *m*.

**wrap** [ræp] **1.** *v/t.* (ein)wickeln; *fig.*
einhüllen; *be* **~ped up** *in* gehüllt sein
in (*acc.*); ganz aufgehen in (*dat.*);
*v/i.* **~ up** sich einhüllen; **2.** Hülle *f*;
*engS.:* Decke *f*; Schal *m*; Mantel
*m*; **~per** ['ræpə] Hülle *f*, Umschlag
*m*; *a. postal* **~** Streifband *n*; **~ping**
['ræpiŋ] Verpackung *f*.

**wrath** *lit.* [rɔ:θ] Zorn *m*, Grimm *m*.

**wreak** [ri:k] *Rache* üben, *Zorn* auslassen (*upon* an *j-m*).

**wreath** [ri:θ], *pl.* **~s** [ri:ðz] (Blu-
men)Gewinde *n*; Kranz *m*; Girlande *f*; Ring *m*, Kreis *m*; Schneewehe *f*; **~e** [ri:ð] [*irr.*] *v/t.* (um-)
winden; *v/i.* sich ringeln.

**wreck** [rek] **1.** ⏚ Wrack *n*; Trümmer *pl.*; Schiffbruch *m*; *fig.* Untergang *m*; **2.** zum Scheitern (⚓ Entgleisen) bringen; zertrümmern;
vernichten; *be* **~ed** ⏚ scheitern;
Schiffbruch erleiden; **~age** ['rekidʒ]
Trümmer *pl.*; Wrackteile *n/pl.*; **~ed**
schiffbrüchig; ruiniert; **~er** ['rekə]
⏚ Bergungsschiff *n*, -arbeiter *m*;
Strandräuber *m*; Abbrucharbeiter
*m*; *Am. mot.* Abschleppwagen *m*;
**~ing** ['rekiŋ] Strandraub *m*; **~ com-**
**pany** *Am.* Abbruchfirma *f*; **~ ser-**
**vice** *Am. mot.* Abschlepp-, Hilfs-
dienst *m*.

**wren** *orn.* [ren] Zaunkönig *m*.

**wrench** [rentʃ] **1.** drehen; reißen;
entwinden (*from s.o.* j-m); verdrehen (*a. fig.*); verrenken; **~ open** auf-
reißen; **2.** Ruck *m*; Verrenkung *f*;
*fig.* Schmerz *m*; ⊕ Schraubenschlüssel *m*.

**wrest** [rest] reißen; verdrehen; ent-
reißen; **~le** ['resl] ringen (mit);
**~ling** ['resliŋ] Ringkampf *m*, Ringen
*n*.

**wretch** [retʃ] Elende(r *m*) *f*; Kerl *m*.

**wretched** ☐ ['retʃid] elend.

**wriggle** ['rigl] sich winden *od.*
schlängeln; **~** *out of* sich drücken
von *et.*

**wright** [rait] ...macher *m*, ...bauer *m*.

**wring** [riŋ] [*irr.*] *Hände* ringen;
(aus)wringen; pressen; *Hals* umdrehen; abringen (*from s.o.* j-m);
**~** *s.o.'s heart* j-m zu Herzen gehen.

**wrinkle** ['riŋkl] **1.** Runzel *f*; Falte *f*;
Wink *m*; Trick *m*; **2.** (sich) runzeln.

**wrist** [rist] Handgelenk *n*; **~** *watch*
Armbanduhr *f*; **~band** ['ristbænd]
Bündchen *n*, (Hemd)Manschette *f*.

**writ** [rit] Erlaß *m*; (gerichtlicher)
Befehl; *Holy* ⚡ Heilige Schrift.

**write** [rait] [*irr.*] schreiben; **~** *down*
auf-, niederschreiben; ausarbeiten;
hervorheben; **~r** ['raitə] Schreiber
(-in); Verfasser(in); Schriftsteller
(-in).

**writhe** [raið] sich krümmen.

**writing** ['raitiŋ] Schreiben *n*; Aufsatz *m*; Werk *n*; Schrift *f*; Schrift-
stück *n*; Urkunde *f*; Stil *m*; *attr.*
Schreib...; *in* **~** schriftlich; **~-case**
Schreibmappe *f*; **~-desk** Schreibtisch *m*; **~-paper** Schreibpapier *n*.

**written** ['ritn] **1.** *p.p. von* write;
**2.** *adj.* schriftlich.

**wrong** [rɔŋ] **1.** ☐ unrecht; verkehrt,
falsch; *be* **~** unrecht haben; in Unordnung sein; falsch gehen (*Uhr*);
*go* **~** schiefgehen; *on the* **~** *side of*
*sixty* über die 60 hinaus; **2.** Unrecht *n*; Beleidigung *f*; **3.** unrecht
tun (*dat.*); ungerecht behandeln;
**~doer** ['rɔŋ'du:ə] Übeltäter(in); **~-**
**ful** ☐ ['rɔŋful] ungerecht; unrechtmäßig.

**wrote** [rout] *pret. von* write.

**wrought** [rɔ:t] *pret. u. p.p. von*
work 2; **~** *iron* Schmiedeeisen *n*;
**~-iron** ['rɔ:t'aiən] schmiedeeisern;
**~-up** erregt.

**wrung** [rʌŋ] *pret. u. p.p. von* wring.

**wry** ☐ [rai] schief, krumm, verzerrt.

# X, Y

**Xmas** ['krisməs] = *Christmas.*

**X-ray** ['eks'rei] **1.** **~s** *pl.* Röntgen-
strahlen *m/pl.*; **2.** Röntgen...;
**3.** durchleuchten, röntgen.

**xylophone** ♪ ['zailəfoun] Xylophon
*n*.

**yacht** ⏚ [jɔt] **1.** (Motor)Jacht *f*;
Segelboot *n*; **2.** auf e-r Jacht fah-
ren; segeln; **~club** ['jɔtklʌb]
Segel-, Jachtklub *m*; **~ing** ['jɔtiŋ]
Segelsport *m*; *attr.* Segel...

**Yankee** F ['jæŋki] Yankee *m* (*Ameri-*
*kaner, bsd. der Nordstaaten*).

**yap** [jæp] kläffen; F quasseln.

**yard** [jɑ:d] Yard *n*, *englische* Elle
(= 0,914 m); ⏚ Rah(e) *f*; Hof *m*;
(Bau-, Stapel)Platz *m*; *Am.* Garten
*m* (*um das Haus*); **~measure**

['jɑːdmeʒə], **~stick** Yardstock *m*, **~maß** *n*.

**yarn** [jɑːn] **1.** Garn *n*; F Seemannsgarn *n*; abenteuerliche Geschichte; **2.** F erzählen.

**yawl** ⚓ [jɔːl] Jolle *f*.

**yawn** [jɔːn] **1.** gähnen; **2.** Gähnen *n*.

**ye** †, *prov.*, *co.* [jiː] ihr.

**yea** †, *prov.* [jei] **1.** ja; **2.** Ja *n*.

**year** [jəː] Jahr *n*; **~ly** ['jəːli] jährlich.

**yearn** [jəːn] sich sehnen, verlangen; **~ing** ['jəːniŋ] **1.** Sehnen *n*, Sehnsucht *f*; **2.** □ sehnsüchtig.

**yeast** [jiːst] Hefe *f*; Schaum *m*.

**yegg(man)** *Am. sl.* ['jeg(mən)] Stromer *m*; Einbrecher *m*.

**yell** [jel] **1.** (gellend) schreien; aufschreien; **2.** (gellender) Schrei; anfeuernder Ruf.

**yellow** ['jelou] **1.** gelb; F hasenfüßig (*feig*); Sensations...; Hetz...; **2.** Gelb *n*; **3.** (sich) gelb färben; **~ed** vergilbt; **~ fever** 🌡 Gelbfieber *n*; **~ish** [~ouiʃ] gelblich.

**yelp** [jelp] **1.** Gekläff *n*; **2.** kläffen.

**yen** *Am. sl.* [jen] brennendes Verlangen.

**yeoman** ['joumən] freier Bauer.

**yep** *Am.* F [jep] ja.

**yes** [jes] **1.** ja; doch; **2.** Ja *n*.

**yesterday** ['jestədi] gestern.

**yet** [jet] **1.** *adv.* noch; bis jetzt; schon; sogar; *as* ~ bis jetzt; *not* ~ noch nicht; **2.** *cj.* (je)doch, dennoch, trotzdem.

**yew** ♣ [juː] Eibe *f*, Taxus *m*.

**yield** [jiːld] **1.** *v/t.* hervorbringen, liefern; ergeben; *Gewinn* (ein)bringen; gewähren; übergeben; zugestehen; *v/i.* ↗ tragen; sich fügen; nachgeben; **2.** Ertrag *m*; **~ing** □ ['jiːldiŋ] nachgebend; *fig.* nachgiebig.

**yip** *Am.* F [jip] jaulen.

**yod|el, ~le** ['joudl] **1.** Jodler *m*; **2.** jodeln.

**yoke** [jouk] **1.** Joch *n* (*a. fig.*); Paar *n* (Ochsen); Schultertrage *f*; **2.** an-, zs.-spannen; *fig.* paaren (to mit).

**yolk** [jouk] (Ei)Dotter *m*, *n*, Eigelb *n*.

**yon** [jɔn], **~der** *lit.* ['jɔndə] **1.** jene(r, -s); jenseitig; **2.** dort drüben.

**yore** [jɔː]: *of* ~ ehemals, ehedem.

**you** [juː, ju] ihr; du, Sie; man.

**young** [jʌŋ] **1.** □ jung; *von Kindern a.* klein; **2.** (Tier)Junge(s) *n*; (Tier)Junge *pl.*; *with* ~ trächtig; **~ster** ['jʌŋstə] Junge *m*.

**your** [jɔː] euer(e); dein(e), Ihr(e); **~s** [jɔːz] der (die, das) eurige, deinige, Ihrige; euer; dein, Ihr; **~self** [jɔː'self], *pl.* **~selves** [~lvz] (du, ihr, Sie) selbst; dich, euch, Sie (selbst), sich (selbst); *by* ~ allein.

**youth** [juːθ], *pl.* **~s** [juːðz] Jugend *f*; Jüngling *m*; ~ *hostel* Jugendherberge *f*; **~ful** □ ['juːθful] jugendlich.

**yule** *lit.* [juːl] Weihnacht *f*.

# Z

**zeal** [ziːl] Eifer *m*; **~ot** ['zelət] Eiferer *m*; **~ous** □ [~əs] eifrig; eifrig bedacht (*for auf acc.*); innig, heiß.

**zebra** *zo.* ['ziːbrə] Zebra *n*; **~ crossing** Fußgängerüberweg *m*.

**zenith** ['zeniθ] Zenit *m*; *fig.* Höhepunkt *m*.

**zero** ['ziərou] Null *f*; Nullpunkt *m*.

**zest** [zest] **1.** Würze *f* (*a. fig.*); Lust *f*, Freude *f*; Genuß *m*; **2.** würzen.

**zigzag** ['zigzæg] Zickzack *m*.

**zinc** [ziŋk] **1.** *min.* Zink *n*; **2.** verzinken.

**zip** [zip] Schwirren *n*; F Schwung *m*; **~-fastener** ['zipfɑːsnə], **~per** ['zipə] Reißverschluß *m*.

**zodiac** *ast.* ['zoudiæk] Tierkreis *m*.

**zone** [zoun] Zone *f*; *fig.* Gebiet *n*.

**Zoo** F [zuː] Zoo *m*.

**zoolog|ical** □ [zouə'lɔdʒikəl] zoologisch; **~y** [zou'ɔlədʒi] Zoologie *f*.

# Alphabetical List of the German Irregular Verbs

## Infinitive — Preterite — Past Participle

backen - backte (buk) - gebacken
bedingen - bedang (bedingte) - bedungen (*conditional*: bedingt)
befehlen - befahl - befohlen
beginnen - begann - begonnen
beißen - biß - gebissen
bergen - barg - geborgen
bersten - barst - geborsten
bewegen - bewog - bewogen
biegen - bog - gebogen
bieten - bot - geboten
binden - band - gebunden
bitten - bat - gebeten
blasen - blies - geblasen
bleiben - blieb - geblieben
bleichen - blich - geblichen
braten - briet - gebraten
brauchen - brauchte - gebraucht (*v/aux.* brauchen)
brechen - brach - gebrochen
brennen - brannte - gebrannt
bringen - brachte - gebracht
denken - dachte - gedacht
dreschen - drosch - gedroschen
dringen - drang - gedrungen
dürfen - durfte - gedurft (*v/aux.* dürfen)
empfehlen - empfahl - empfohlen
erlöschen - erlosch - erloschen
erschrecken - erschrak - erschrocken
essen - aß - gegessen
fahren - fuhr - gefahren
fallen - fiel - gefallen
fangen - fing - gefangen
fechten - focht - gefochten
finden - fand - gefunden
flechten - flocht - geflochten
fliegen - flog - geflogen
fliehen - floh - geflohen
fließen - floß - geflossen
fressen - fraß - gefressen
frieren - fror - gefroren
gären - gor (*esp. fig.* gärte) - gegoren (*esp. fig.* gegärt)
gebären - gebar - geboren
geben - gab - gegeben
gedeihen - gedieh - gediehen
gehen - ging - gegangen
gelingen - gelang - gelungen
gelten - galt - gegolten
genesen - genas - genesen
genießen - genoß - genossen
geschehen - geschah - geschehen
gewinnen - gewann - gewonnen

gießen - goß - gegossen
gleichen - glich - geglichen
gleiten - glitt - geglitten
glimmen - glomm - geglommen
graben - grub - gegraben
greifen - griff - gegriffen
haben - hatte - gehabt
halten - hielt - gehalten
hängen - hing - gehangen
hauen - haute (hieb) - gehauen
heben - hob - gehoben
heißen - hieß - geheißen
helfen - half - geholfen
kennen - kannte - gekannt
klingen - klang - geklungen
kneifen - kniff - gekniffen
kommen - kam - gekommen
können - konnte - gekonnt (*v/aux.* können)
kriechen - kroch - gekrochen
laden - lud - geladen
lassen - ließ - gelassen (*v/aux.* lassen)
laufen - lief - gelaufen
leiden - litt - gelitten
leihen - lieh - geliehen
lesen - las - gelesen
liegen - lag - gelegen
lügen - log - gelogen
mahlen - mahlte - gemahlen
meiden - mied - gemieden
melken - melkte (molk) - gemolken (gemelkt)
messen - maß - gemessen
mißlingen - mißlang - mißlungen
mögen - mochte - gemocht (*v/aux.* mögen)
müssen - mußte - gemußt (*v/aux.* müssen)
nehmen - nahm - genommen
nennen - nannte - genannt
pfeifen - pfiff - gepfiffen
preisen - pries - gepriesen
quellen - quoll - gequollen
raten - riet - geraten
reiben - rieb - gerieben
reißen - riß - gerissen
reiten - ritt - geritten
rennen - rannte - gerannt
riechen - roch - gerochen
ringen - rang - gerungen
rinnen - rann - geronnen
rufen - rief - gerufen
salzen - salzte - gesalzen (gesalzt)
saufen - soff - gesoffen

saugen - sog - gesogen
schaffen - schuf - geschaffen
schallen - schallte (scholl) - ge-
schallt (*for erschallen a.* erschol-
len)
scheiden - schied - geschieden
scheinen - schien - geschienen
schelten - schalt - gescholten
scheren - schor - geschoren
schieben - schob - geschoben
schießen - schoß - geschossen
schinden - schund - geschunden
schlafen - schlief - geschlafen
schlagen - schlug - geschlagen
schleichen - schlich - geschlichen
schleifen - schliff - geschliffen
schließen - schloß - geschlossen
schlingen - schlang - geschlungen
schmeißen - schmiß - geschmissen
schmelzen - schmolz - geschmolzen
schneiden - schnitt - geschnitten
schrecken - schrak - † geschrocken
schreiben - schrieb - geschrieben
schreien - schrie - geschrie(e)n
schreiten - schritt - geschritten
schweigen - schwieg - geschwiegen
schwellen - schwoll - geschwollen
schwimmen - schwamm - ge-
schwommen
schwinden - schwand - geschwun-
den
schwingen - schwang - geschwun-
gen
schwören - schwor - geschworen
sehen - sah - gesehen
sein - war - gewesen
senden - sandte - gesandt
sieden - sott - gesotten
singen - sang - gesungen
sinken - sank - gesunken
sinnen - sann - gesonnen
sitzen - saß - gesessen
sollen - sollte - gesollt (*v/aux.* sollen)
spalten - spaltete - gespalten (ge-
spaltet)
speien - spie - gespie(e)n
spinnen - spann - gesponnen
sprechen - sprach - gesprochen

sprießen - sproß - gesprossen
springen - sprang - gesprungen
stechen - stach - gestochen
stecken - steckte (stak) - gesteckt
stehen - stand - gestanden
stehlen - stahl - gestohlen
steigen - stieg - gestiegen
sterben - starb - gestorben
stieben - stob - gestoben
stinken - stank - gestunken
stoßen - stieß - gestoßen
streichen - strich - gestrichen
streiten - stritt - gestritten
tragen - trug - getragen
treffen - traf - getroffen
treiben - trieb - getrieben
treten - trat - getreten
triefen - triefte (troff) - getrieft
trinken - trank - getrunken
trügen - trog - getrogen
tun - tat - getan
verderben - verdarb - verdorben
verdrießen - verdroß - verdrossen
vergessen - vergaß - vergessen
verlieren - verlor - verloren
verschleißen - verschliß - ver-
schlissen
verzeihen - verzieh - verziehen
wachsen - wuchs - gewachsen
wägen - wog (↖ wägte) - gewogen
(↖ gewägt)
waschen - wusch - gewaschen
weben - wob - gewoben
weichen - wich - gewichen
weisen - wies - gewiesen
wenden - wandte - gewandt
werben - warb - geworben
werden - wurde - geworden (worden*)
werfen - warf - geworfen
wiegen - wog - gewogen
winden - wand - gewunden
wissen - wußte - gewußt
wollen - wollte - gewollt (*v/aux.* wollen)
wringen - wrang -gewrungen
ziehen - zog - gezogen
zwingen - zwang - gezwungen

* only in connexion with the past participles of other verbs, *e.g. er ist gesehen worden* he has been seen.

# Alphabetical List of the English Irregular Verbs

## Infinitive — Preterite — Past Participle

Irregular forms marked with asterisks (*) can be exchanged for the regular forms.

abide (*bleiben*) - abode* - abode*
arise (*sich erheben*) - arose - arisen
awake (*erwachen*) - awoke - awoke*
be (*sein*) - was - been
bear (*tragen; gebären*) - bore - getragen: borne - *geboren*: born
beat (*schlagen*) - beat - beat(en)
become (*werden*) - became - become
beget (*zeugen*) - begot - begotten
begin (*anfangen*) - began - begun
bend (*beugen*) - bent - bent
bereave (*berauben*) - bereft* - bereft*
beseech (*ersuchen*) - besought - besought
bet (*wetten*) - bet* - bet*
bid ([*ge*]*bieten*) - bade, bid - bid(den)
bide (*abwarten*) - bode* - bided
bind (*binden*) - bound - bound
bite (*beißen*) - bit - bitten
bleed (*bluten*) - bled - bled
blend (*mischen*) - blent* - blent*
blow (*blasen; blühen*) - blew - blown
break (*brechen*) - broke - broken
breed (*aufziehen*) - bred - bred
bring (*bringen*) - brought - brought
build (*bauen*) - built - built
burn (*brennen*) - burnt* - burnt*
burst (*bersten*) - burst - burst
buy (*kaufen*) - bought - bought
cast (*werfen*) - cast - cast
catch (*fangen*) - caught - caught
chide (*schelten*) - chid - chid(den)
choose (*wählen*) - chose - chosen
cleave ([*sich*] *spalten*) cleft, clove* - cleft, cloven*
cling (*sich* [*an*]*klammern*) - clung - clung
clothe ([*an-, be*]*kleiden*) - clad* - clad*
come (*kommen*) - came - come
cost (*kosten*) - cost - cost
creep (*kriechen*) - crept - crept
crow (*krähen*) - crew* - crowed
cut (*schneiden*) - cut - cut
deal (*handeln*) - dealt - dealt
dig (*graben*) - dug - dug
do (*tun*) - did - done
draw (*ziehen*) - drew - drawn
dream (*träumen*) - dreamt* - dreamt*
drink (*trinken*) - drank - drunk
drive (*treiben; fahren*) - drove - driven
dwell (*wohnen*) - dwelt - dwelt

eat (*essen*) - ate, eat - eaten
fall (*fallen*) - fell - fallen
feed (*füttern*) - fed - fed
feel (*fühlen*) - felt - felt
fight (*kämpfen*) - fought - fought
find (*finden*) - found - found
flee (*fliehen*) - fled - fled
fling (*schleudern*) - flung - flung
fly (*fliegen*) - flew - flown
forbid (*verbieten*) - forbade - forbidden
forget (*vergessen*) - forgot - forgotten
forsake (*aufgeben; verlassen*) - forsook - forsaken
freeze ([*ge*]*frieren*) - froze - frozen
get (*bekommen*) - got - got, *Am.* gotten
gild (*vergolden*) - gilt* - gilt*
gird ([*um*]*gürten*) - girt* - girt*
give (*geben*) - gave - given
go (*gehen*) - went - gone
grave ([*ein*]*graben*) - graved - graven*
grind (*mahlen*) - ground - ground
grow (*wachsen*) - grew - grown
hang (*hängen*) - hung - hung
have (*haben*) - had - had
hear (*hören*) - heard - heard
heave (*heben*) - hove* - hove*
hew (*hauen, hacken*) - hewed - hewn*
hide (*verbergen*) - hid - hid(den)
hit (*treffen*) - hit - hit
hold (*halten*) - held - held
hurt (*verletzen*) - hurt - hurt
keep (*halten*) - kept - kept
kneel (*knien*) - knelt* - knelt*
knit (*stricken*) - knit* - knit*
know (*wissen*) - knew - known
lay (*legen*) - laid - laid
lead (*führen*) - led - led
lean ([*sich*] [*an*]*lehnen*) - leant* - leant*
leap ([*über*]*springen*) - leapt* - leapt*
learn (*lernen*) - learnt* - learnt*
leave (*verlassen*) - left - left
lend (*leihen*) - lent - lent
let (*lassen*) - let - let
lie (*liegen*) - lay - lain
light (*anzünden*) - lit* - lit*
lose (*verlieren*) - lost - lost
make (*machen*) - made - made
mean (*meinen*) - meant - meant
meet (*begegnen*) - met - met
mow (*mähen*) - mowed - mown*

**pay** *(zahlen)* - paid - paid
**pen** *(einpferchen)* - pent - pent
**put** *(setzen, stellen)* - put - put
**read** *(lesen)* - read - read
**rend** *([zer]reißen)* - rent - rent
**rid** *(befreien)* - rid\* - rid\*
**ride** *(reiten)* - rode - ridden
**ring** *(läuten)* - rang - rung
**rise** *(aufstehen)* - rose - risen
**rive** *([sich] spalten)* - rived - riven\*
**run** *(laufen)* - ran - run
**saw** *(sägen)* - sawed - sawn\*
**say** *(sagen)* - said - said
**see** *(sehen)* - saw - seen
**seek** *(suchen)* - sought - sought
**sell** *(verkaufen)* - sold - sold
**send** *(senden)* - sent - sent
**set** *(setzen)* - set - set
**sew** *(nähen)* - sewed - sewn\*
**shake** *(schütteln)* - shook - shaken
**shave** *([sich] rasieren)* - shaved - shaven\*
**shear** *(scheren)* - sheared - shorn
**shed** *(ausgießen)* - shed - shed
**shine** *(scheinen)* - shone - shone
**shoe** *(beschuhen)* - shod - shod
**shoot** *(schießen)* - shot - shot
**show** *(zeigen)* - showed - shown\*
**shred** *([zer]schnitzeln, zerfetzen)* - shred\* - shred\*
**shrink** *(einschrumpfen)* - shrank - shrunk
**shut** *(schließen)* - shut - shut
**sing** *(singen)* - sang - sung
**sink** *(sinken)* - sank - sunk
**sit** *(sitzen)* - sat - sat
**slay** *(erschlagen)* - slew - slain
**sleep** *(schlafen)* - slept - slept
**slide** *(gleiten)* - slid - slid
**sling** *(schleudern)* - slung - slung
**slink** *(schleichen)* - slunk - slunk
**slip** *(schlüpfen, gleiten)* - slipt\* - slipt\*
**slit** *(schlitzen)* - slit - slit
**smell** *(riechen)* - smelt\* - smelt\*
**smite** *(schlagen)* - smote - smitten, smote
**sow** *([aus]säen)* - sowed - sown\*
**speak** *(sprechen)* - spoke - spoken
**speed** *(eilen)* - sped\* - sped\*
**spell** *(buchstabieren)* - spelt\* - spelt\*
**spend** *(ausgeben)* - spent - spent

**spill** *(verschütten)* - spilt\* - spilt\*
**spin** *(spinnen)* - spun - spun
**spit** *([aus]spucken)* - spat - spat
**split** *(spalten)* - split - split
**spoil** *(verderben)* - spoilt\* - spoilt\*
**spread** *(verbreiten)* - spread - spread
**spring** *(springen)* - sprang - sprung
**stand** *(stehen)* - stood - stood
**stave** *(den Boden einschlagen)* - stove\* - stove\*
**steal** *(stehlen)* - stole - stolen
**stick** *(stecken)* - stuck - stuck
**sting** *(stechen)* - stung - stung
**stink** *(stinken)* - stank - stunk
**strew** *([be]streuen)* - strewed - strewn\*
**stride** *(über-, durchschreiten)* - strode - stridden
**strike** *(schlagen)* - struck - struck
**string** *(spannen)* - strung - strung
**strive** *(streben)* - strove - striven
**swear** *(schwören)* - swore - sworn
**sweat** *(schwitzen)* - sweat\* - sweat\*
**sweep** *(fegen)* - swept - swept
**swell** *([an]schwellen)* - swelled - swollen
**swim** *(schwimmen)* - swam - swum
**swing** *(schwingen)* - swung - swung
**take** *(nehmen)* - took - taken
**teach** *(lehren)* - taught - taught
**tear** *(ziehen)* - tore - torn
**tell** *(sagen)* - told - told
**think** *(denken)* - thought - thought
**thrive** *(gedeihen)* - throve\* - thriven\*
**throw** *(werfen)* - threw - thrown
**thrust** *(stoßen)* - thrust - thrust
**tread** *(treten)* - trod - trodden
**wake** *(wachen)* - woke\* - woke(n)\*
**wax** *(zunehmen)* - waxed - waxen\*
**wear** *([Kleider] tragen)* - wore - worn
**weave** *(weben)* - wove - woven
**weep** *(weinen)* - wept - wept
**wet** *(nässen)* - wet\* - wet\*
**win** *(gewinnen)* - won - won
**wind** *(winden)* - wound - wound
**work** *(arbeiten)* - wrought\* - wrought\*
**wreathe** *([um]winden)* - wreathed - wreathen\*
**wring** *([aus]wringen)* - wrung - wrung
**write** *(schreiben)* - wrote - written

# German Proper Names

**Aachen** ['ɑ:xən] n Aachen, Aix-la-Chapelle.

**Adenauer** ['ɑ:dənauər] *first chancellor of the German Federal Republic.*

**Adler** ['ɑ:dlər] *Austrian psychologist.*

**Adria** ['ɑ:dria] *f* Adriatic Sea.

**Afrika** ['ɑ:frika] n Africa.

**Ägypten** [ɛ'gyptən] n Egypt.

**Albanien** [al'bɑ:njən] n Albania.

**Algerien** [al'ge:rjən] n Algeria.

**Algier** ['alʒi:r] n Algiers.

**Allgäu** ['algɔy] n Al(l)gäu (*region of Bavaria*).

**Alpen** ['alpən] *pl.* Alps *pl.*

**Amerika** [a'me:rika] n America.

**Anden** ['andən] *pl.* the Andes *pl.*

**Antillen** [an'tilən] *f/pl.* Antilles *pl.*

**Antwerpen** [ant'verpən] n Antwerp.

**Apenninen** [ape'ni:nən] *m/pl.* the Apennines *pl.*

**Argentinien** [argen'ti:njən] n Argentina, the Argentine.

**Ärmelkanal** ['ɛrməlkanɑ:l] *m* English Channel.

**Asien** ['ɑ:zjən] n Asia.

**Athen** [a'te:n] n Athens.

**Äthiopien** [ɛti'o:pjən] Ethiopia.

**Atlantik** [at'lantik] *m* Atlantic.

**Australien** [au'strɑ:ljən] n Australia.

**Bach** [bax] *German composer.*

**Baden-Württemberg** ['bɑ:dən-'vyrtəmbork] *n Land of the German Federal Republic.*

**Barlach** ['barlax] *German sculptor.*

**Basel** ['bɑ:zəl] n Bâle, Basle.

**Bayern** ['baiərn] n Bavaria (*Land of the German Federal Republic*).

**Becher** ['beçər] *German poet.*

**Beckmann** ['bekman] *German painter.*

**Beethoven** ['be:tho:fən] *German composer.*

**Belgien** ['belgjən] n Belgium.

**Belgrad** ['belgrɑ:t] n Belgrade.

**Berg** [berk] *Austrian composer.*

**Berlin** [ber'li:n] n Berlin.

**Bermuda-Inseln** [ber'mu:da'ɪnzəln] *f/pl.* Bermudas *pl.*

**Bern** [bern] n Bern(e).

**Bismarck** ['bismark] *German statesman.*

**Bloch** [blɔx] *German philosopher.*

**Böcklin** ['bœkli:n] *German painter.*

**Bodensee** ['bo:dənze:] *m* Lake of Constance.

**Böhm** [bø:m] *Austrian conductor.*

**Böhmen** ['bø:mən] n Bohemia.

**Böll** [bœl] *German author.*

**Bonn** [bɔn] *n capital of the German Federal Republic.*

**Brahms** [brɑ:ms] *German composer.*

**Brandt** [brant] *German politician.*

**Brasilien** [bra'zi:ljən] n Brazil.

**Braunschweig** ['braunʃvaik] n Brunswick.

**Brecht** [brɛçt] *German dramatist.*

**Bremen** ['bre:mən] *n Land of the German Federal Republic.*

**Bruckner** ['bruknər] *Austrian composer.*

**Brüssel** ['brysəl] n Brussels.

**Budapest** ['bu:dapest] n Budapest.

**Bukarest** ['bu:karest] n Bucharest.

**Bulgarien** [bul'gɑ:rjən] n Bulgaria.

**Calais** [ka'lɛ] n: Straße von ~ Straits of Dover.

**Calvin** [kal'vi:n] *Swiss religious reformer.*

**Chile** ['tʃi:lə] n Chile.

**China** ['çi:na] n China.

**Christus** ['kristus] *m* Christ.

**Daimler** ['daimlər] *German inventor.*

**Dänemark** ['dɛ:nəmark] n Denmark.

**Deutschland** ['dɔytʃlant] n Germany.

**Diesel** ['di:zəl] *German inventor.*

**Döblin** [dø'bli:n] *German author.*

**Dolomiten** [dolo'mi:tən] *pl.* the Dolomites *pl.*

**Donau** ['do:nau] *f* Danube.

**Dortmund** ['dɔrtmunt] n industrial city in West Germany.

**Dresden** ['dre:sdən] n capital of Saxony.

**Dublin** ['dʌblin] n Dublin.

**Dünkirchen** ['dy:nkirçən] n Dunkirk.

**Dürer** ['dy:rər] *German painter.*

**Dürrenmatt** ['dyrənmat] *Swiss dramatist.*

**Düsseldorf** ['dysəldɔrf] n capital of North Rhine-Westphalia.

**Ebert** ['e:bərt] *first president of the Weimar Republic.*

**Egk** [ɛk] *German composer.*

**Eichendorff** ['aiçəndɔrf] *German poet.*

**Eiger** ['aigər] *Swiss mountain.*

**Einstein** ['ainʃtain] *German physicist.*

**Elbe** ['ɛlbə] *f German river.*

**Elsaß** ['ɛlzas] *n* Alsace.

**Engels** ['ɛŋəls] *German philosopher.*

England ['ɛŋlant] n England.
Essen ['esən] n industrial city in West Germany.
Europa [ɔʏ'ro:pa] n Europe.

Feldberg ['fɛltbɛrk] German mountain.
Finnland ['finlant] n Finland.
Florenz [flo'rɛnts] n Florence.
Fontane [fɔn'ta:nə] German author.
Franken ['fraŋkən] n Franconia.
Frankfurt ['fraŋkfurt] n Frankfurt.
Frankreich ['fraŋkraiç] n France.
Freud [frɔʏt] Austrian psychologist.
Frisch [friʃ] Swiss author.

Garmisch ['garmiʃ] n health resort in Bavaria.
Genf [gɛnf] n Geneva; ~er See m Lake of Geneva.
Genua ['ge:nua] n Genoa.
Gibraltar [gi'braltar] n Gibraltar.
Goethe ['gø:tə] German poet.
Grass [gras] German author.
Graubünden [grau'byndən] n the Grisons.
Griechenland ['gri:çənlant] n Greece.
Grillparzer ['grilpartsər] Austrian dramatist.
Grönland ['grø:nlant] n Greenland.
Gropius ['gro:pjus] German architect.  [Great Britain.]
Großbritannien[gro:sbri'tanjən]n
Großglockner [gro:s'glɔknər] Austrian mountain.
Grünewald ['gry:nəvalt] German painter.

Haag [ha:k] Den ~ The Hague.
Habsburg hist. ['ha:psburk] n Hapsburg (German dynasty).
Hahn [ha:n] German chemist.
Hamburg ['hamburk] n Land of the German Federal Republic.
Händel ['hɛndəl] Handel (German composer).
Hannover [ha'no:fər] n Hanover (capital of Lower Saxony).
Hartmann ['hartman] German composer.
Harz [ha:rts] m Harz Mountains pl.
Hauptmann ['hauptman] German dramatist.
Haydn ['haidən] Austrian composer.
Hegel ['he:gəl] German philosopher.
Heidegger ['haidegər] German philosopher.
Heidelberg ['haidəlbɛrk] n university town in West Germany.
Heine ['hainə] German poet.
Heinemann ['hainəman] president of the German Federal Republic.
Heisenberg ['haizənbɛrk] German physicist.
Heißenbüttel ['haisənbytəl] German poet.
Helgoland ['hɛlgolant] n Heligoland.

Helsinki ['hɛlziŋki] n Helsinki.
Henze ['hɛntsə] German composer.
Hesse ['hɛsə] German poet.
Hessen ['hɛsən] n Hesse (Land of the German Federal Republic).
Heuß [hɔʏs] first president of the German Federal Republic.
Hindemith ['hindəmit] German composer.
Hohenzollern hist. [ho:ən'tsɔlərn] n German dynasty.
Hölderlin ['hœldərli:n] German poet.
Holland ['hɔlant] n Holland.

Indien ['indjən] n India.
Inn [in] m affluent of the Danube.
Innsbruck ['insbruk] n capital of the Tyrol.
Irak [i'ra:k] m Iraq, a. Irak.
Irland ['irlant] n Ireland.
Island ['i:slant] n Iceland.
Israel ['israɛl] n Israel.
Italien [i'ta:ljən] n Italy.

Japan ['ja:pan] n Japan.
Jaspers ['jaspərs] German philosopher.
Jesus ['je:zus] m Jesus.
Jordanien [jɔr'da:njən] n Jordan.
Jugoslawien [jugo'sla:vjən]n Yugoslavia.
Jung [juŋ] Swiss psychologist.
Jungfrau ['juŋfrau] f Swiss mountain.

Kafka ['kafka] Czech poet.
Kanada ['kanada] n Canada.
Kant [kant] German philosopher.
Karajan ['ka:rajan] Austrian conductor.
Karlsruhe [karls'ru:ə] n city in South-Western Germany.
Kärnten ['kɛrntən] n Carinthia.
Kassel ['kasəl] n Cassel.
Kästner ['kɛstnər] German author.
Kiel [ki:l] n capital of Schleswig-Holstein.
Kiesinger ['ki:ziŋər] German politician.
Klee [kle:] German painter.
Kleist [klaist] German poet.
Klemperer ['klɛmpərər] German conductor.
Koblenz ['ko:blɛnts] n Coblenz, Koblenz.
Kokoschka [ko'kɔʃka] German painter.
Köln [kœln] n Cologne.
Kolumbien [ko'lumbjən] n Columbia.
Kolumbus [ko'lumbus] m Columbus.
Königsberg ['kø:niçsbɛrk] n capital of East Prussia.
Konstanz ['kɔnstants] n Constance.
Kopenhagen [kopən'ha:gən] n Copenhagen.
Kordilleren [kɔrdil'je:rən] f/pl. the Cordilleras pl.

**Kreml** ['kre:məl] *m the* Kremlin.

**Leibniz** ['laɪbnits] *German philosopher.*
**Leipzig** ['laɪptsiç] *n* Leipsic.
**Lessing** ['lesiŋ] *German poet.*
**Libanon** ['li:banɔn] *m* Lebanon.
**Liebig** ['li:biç] *German chemist.*
**Lissabon** ['lisabɔn] *n* Lisbon.
**London** ['lɔndɔn] *n* London.
**Lothringen** ['lo:trɪŋən] *n* Lorraine.
**Lübeck** ['ly:bɛk] *n city in West Germany.*
**Luther** ['lutər] *German religious reformer.*
**Luxemburg** ['luksəmburk] *n* Luxemb(o)urg.
**Luzern** [lu'tsern] *n* Lucerne.

**Maas** [mɑ:s] *f* Meuse.
**Madrid** [ma'drit] *n* Madrid.
**Mahler** ['mɑ:lər] *Austrian composer.*
**Mailand** ['maɪlant] *n* Milan.
**Main** [maɪn] *m German river.*
**Mainz** [maɪnts] *n* Mayence *(capital of Rhineland-Palatinate).*
**Mann** [man] *name of three German authors.*
**Marokko** [ma'rɔko] *n* Morocco.
**Marx** [marks] *German philosopher.*
**Matterhorn** ['matərhɔrn] *Swiss mountain.*
**Meißen** ['maɪsən] *n* Meissen.
**Meitner** ['maɪtnər] *German female physicist.*
**Memel** ['me:məl] *f frontier river in East Prussia.*
**Menzel** ['mentsəl] *German painter.*
**Mexiko** ['meksiko] *n* Mexico.
**Mies van der Rohe** ['mi:sfandər-'ro:ə] *German architect.*
**Mittelamerika** ['mitəlʔa'me:rika] *n* Central America.
**Mitteleuropa** ['mitəlʔɔʏ'ro:pa] *n* Central Europe.
**Mittelmeer** ['mitəlme:r] *n* Mediterranean (Sea).
**Moldau** ['mɔldau] *f Bohemian river.*
**Mörike** ['mø:rikə] *German poet.*
**Mosel** ['mo:zəl] *f* Moselle.
**Mössbauer** ['mœsbauər] *German physicist.*
**Moskau** ['mɔskau] *n* Moscow.
**Mozart** ['mo:tsart] *Austrian composer.*
**München** ['mynçən] *n* Munich *(capital of Bavaria).*

**Neapel** [ne'a:pəl] *n* Naples.
**Neisse** ['naɪsə] *f German river.*
**Neufundland** [nɔʏ'funtlant] *n* Newfoundland.
**Neuseeland** [nɔʏ'ze:lant] *n* New Zealand.
**Niederlande** ['ni:dərlandə] *n/pl. the* Netherlands *pl.*
**Niedersachsen** ['ni:dərzaksən] *n* Lower Saxony *(Land of the German Federal Republic).*

**Nietzsche** ['ni:tʃə] *German philosopher.*
**Nil** [ni:l] *m* Nile.
**Nordamerika** ['nɔrtʔa'me:rika] *n* North America.
**Nordrhein-Westfalen** ['nɔrtraɪnvest'fa:lən] *n* North Rhine-Westphalia *(Land of the German Federal Republic).*
**Nordsee** ['nɔrtze:] *f* German Ocean, North Sea.
**Norwegen** ['nɔrve:gən] *n* Norway.
**Nürnberg** ['nyrnbɛrk] *n* Nuremberg.

**Oder** ['o:dər] *f German river.*
**Orff** [ɔrf] *German composer.*
**Oslo** ['ɔslo] *n* Oslo.
**Ostasien** ['ɔst'a:zjən] *n* Eastern Asia.
**Ostende** [ɔst'ɛndə] *n* Ostend.
**Österreich** ['ø:stəraɪç] *n* Austria.
**Ostsee** ['ɔstze:] *f* Baltic.

**Palästina** [palɛ'sti:na] *n* Palestine.
**Paris** [pa'ri:s] *n* Paris.
**Persien** ['perzjən] *n* Persia.
**Pfalz** [pfalts] *f* Palatinate.
**Philippinen** [fili'pi:nən] *f/pl.* Philippines *pl.,* Philippine Islands *pl.*
**Planck** [plaŋk] *German physicist.*
**Polen** ['po:lən] *n* Poland.
**Pommern** ['pɔmərn] *n* Pomerania.
**Portugal** ['pɔrtugal] *n* Portugal.
**Prag** [prɑ:g] *n* Prague.
**Preußen** *hist.* ['prɔʏsən] *n* Prussia.
**Pyrenäen** [pyre'nɛ:ən] *pl.* Pyrenees *pl.*

**Regensburg** ['re:gənsburk] *n* Ratisbon.
**Reykjavik** ['raɪkjavi:k] *n* Reykjavik.
**Rhein** [raɪn] *m* Rhine.
**Rheinland-Pfalz** ['raɪnlant'pfalts] *n* Rhineland-Palatinate *(Land of the German Federal Republic).*
**Rilke** ['rilkə] *Austrian poet.*
**Rom** [ro:m] *n* Rome.
**Röntgen** ['rœntgən] *German physicist.*
**Ruhr** [ru:r] *f German river;* **Ruhrgebiet** ['ru:rgəbi:t] *n industrial centre of West Germany.*
**Rumänien** [ru'mɛ:njən] *n* Ro(u)mania.
**Rußland** ['ruslant] *n* Russia.

**Saale** ['za:lə] *f German river.*
**Saar** [za:r] *f affluent of the Moselle;* **Saarbrücken** [za:r'brykən] *n capital of the Saar;* **Saarland** ['za:rlant] *n* Saar *(Land of the German Federal Republic).*
**Sachsen** ['zaksən] *n* Saxony.
**Scherchen** ['ʃerçən] *Swiss conductor.*
**Schiller** ['ʃilər] *German poet.*
**Schlesien** ['ʃle:zjən] *n* Silesia.
**Schleswig-Holstein** ['ʃle:sviç'hɔl-

ʃtaɪn] n Land of the German Federal Republic.

**Schönberg** [ˈʃøːnbɛrk] Austrian composer.

**Schottland** [ˈʃɔtlant] n Scotland.

**Schubert** [ˈʃuːbərt] Austrian composer.

**Schumann** [ˈʃuːman] German composer.

**Schwaben** [ˈʃvaːbən] n Swabia.

**Schwarzwald** [ˈʃvartsvalt] m Black Forest.

**Schweden** [ˈʃveːdən] n Sweden.

**Schweiz** [ʃvaɪts] f: die ~ Switzerland.

**Sibirien** [ziˈbiːrjən] n Siberia.

**Siemens** [ˈziːmɛns] German inventor.

**Sizilien** [ziˈtsiːljən] n Sicily.

**Skandinavien** [skandiˈnaːvjən] n Scandinavia.

**Sofia** [ˈzɔfja] n Sofia.

**Sowjetunion** [zɔˈvjetʔunjoːn] f the Soviet Union.

**Spanien** [ˈʃpaːnjən] n Spain.

**Spitzweg** [ˈʃpitsveːk] German painter.

**Spranger** [ˈʃpraŋər] German philosopher.

**Steiermark** [ˈʃtaɪərmark] f Styria.

**Stifter** [ˈʃtiftər] Austrian author.

**Stockholm** [ˈʃtɔkhɔlm] n Stockholm.

**Storm** [ʃtɔrm] German poet.

**Strauß** [ʃtraʊs] Austrian composer.

**Strauss** [ʃtraʊs] German composer.

**Stresemann** [ˈʃtreːzəman] German statesman.

**Stuttgart** [ˈʃtutgart] n capital of Baden-Württemberg.

**Südamerika** [zyːtʔaˈmeːrika] n South America.

**Sudan** [zuˈdaːn] m S(o)udan.

**Syrien** [ˈzyːrjən] n Syria.

**Themse** [ˈtɛmzə] f Thames.

**Thoma** [ˈtoːma] German author.

**Thüringen** [ˈtyːriŋən] n Thuringia.

**Tirana** [tiˈraːna] n Tirana.

**Tirol** [tiˈroːl] n the Tyrol.

**Trakl** [ˈtraːkəl] Austrian poet.

**Tschechoslowakei** [tʃɛçoslovaˈkaɪ] f: die ~ Czechoslovakia.

**Türkei** [tyrˈkaɪ] f: die ~ Turkey.

**Ungarn** [ˈuŋgarn] n Hungary.

**Ural** [uˈraːl] m Ural (Mountains pl.).

**Vatikan** [vatiˈkaːn] m the Vatican.

**Venedig** [veˈneːdiç] n Venice.

**Vereinigte Staaten** [vərˈaɪnɪçtə ˈʃtaːtən] m/pl. the United States pl.

**Vierwaldstätter See** [fiːrˈvaltʃtɛtər ˈzeː] m Lake of Lucerne.

**Wagner** [ˈvaːgnər] German composer.

**Wankel** [ˈvaŋkəl] German inventor.

**Warschau** [ˈvarʃaʊ] n Warsaw.

**Weichsel** [ˈvaɪksəl] f Vistula.

**Weiß** [vaɪs] German dramatist.

**Weizsäcker** [ˈvaɪtszɛkər] German physicist.

**Werfel** [ˈvɛrfəl] Austrian author.

**Weser** [ˈveːzər] f German river.

**Westdeutschland** pol. [ˈvɛstdɔʏtʃlant] n West Germany.

**Wien** [viːn] n Vienna.

**Wiesbaden** [ˈviːsbaːdən] n capital of Hesse.

**Zeppelin** [ˈtsɛpəliːn] German inventor.

**Zuckmayer** [ˈtsukmaɪər] German dramatist.

**Zweig** [tsvaɪg] Austrian author.

**Zürich** [ˈtsyːriç] n Zurich.

**Zypern** [ˈtsyːpərn] n Cyprus.

# German Abbreviations

**a. a. O.** *am angeführten Ort* in the place cited, *abbr.* loc. cit., l. c.
**Abb.** *Abbildung* illustration.
**Abf.** *Abfahrt* departure, *abbr.* dep.
**Abg.** *Abgeordnete* Member of Parliament, *etc.*
**Abk.** *Abkürzung* abbreviation.
**Abs.** *Absatz* paragraph; *Absender* sender.
**Abschn.** *Abschnitt* paragraph, chapter. [dept.]
**Abt.** *Abteilung* department, *abbr.*
**a. D.** *außer Dienst* retired.
**Adr.** *Adresse* address.
**AG** *Aktiengesellschaft* joint-stock company, *Am.* (stock) corporation.
**allg.** *allgemein* general.
**a. M.** *am Main* on the Main.
**Ank.** *Ankunft* arrival.
**Anm.** *Anmerkung* note.
**a. O.** *an der Oder* on the Oder.
**a. Rh.** *am Rhein* on the Rhine.
**Art.** *Artikel* article.
**atü** *Atmosphärenüberdruck* atmospheric excess pressure.
**Aufl.** *Auflage* edition.

**b.** *bei* at; with; *with place names:* near, *abbr.* nr; care of, *abbr.* c/o.
**Bd.** *Band* volume, *abbr.* vol.; **Bde.** *Bände* volumes, *abbr.* vols.
**beil.** *beiliegend* enclosed.
**Bem.** *Bemerkung* note, comment, observation.
**bes.** *besonders* especially.
**betr.** *betreffend, betrifft, betreffs* concerning, respecting, regarding.
**Betr.** *Betreff, betrifft letter:* subject, re. [reference to.]
**bez.** *bezahlt* paid; *bezüglich* with
**Bez.** *Bezirk* district.
**Bhf.** *Bahnhof* station.
**bisw.** *bisweilen* sometimes, occasionally.
**BIZ** *Bank für Internationalen Zahlungsausgleich* Bank for International Settlements.
**Bln.** *Berlin* Berlin.
**BRD** *Bundesrepublik Deutschland* Federal Republic of Germany.
**BRT** *Bruttoregistertonnen* gross register tons.
**b. w.** *bitte wenden* please turn over, *abbr.* P.T.O.
**bzw.** *beziehungsweise* respectively.

**C** *Celsius* Celsius, *abbr.* C.
**ca.** *circa, ungefähr, etwa* about, approximately, *abbr.* c.
**cbm** *Kubikmeter* cubic met|re, *Am.* -er.

**ccm** *Kubikzentimeter* cubic centimet|re, *Am.* -er, *abbr.* c.c.
**CDU** *Christlich-Demokratische Union* Christian Democratic Union.
**cm** *Zentimeter* centimet|re, *Am.* -er.
**Co.** *Kompagnon* partner; *Kompanie* Company.
**CSU** *Christlich-Soziale Union* Christian Social Union.

**d. Ä.** *der Ältere* senior, *abbr.* sen.
**DB** *Deutsche Bundesbahn* German Federal Railway.
**DDR** *Deutsche Demokratische Republik* German Democratic Republic.
**DGB** *Deutscher Gewerkschaftsbund* Federation of German Trade Unions.
**dgl.** *dergleichen, desgleichen* the like.
**d. Gr.** *der Große* the Great.
**d. h.** *das heißt* that is, *abbr.* i. e.
**d. i.** *das ist* that is, *abbr.* i. e.
**DIN, Din** *Deutsche Industrie-Norm* (-en) German Industrial Standards.
**Dipl.** *Diplom* diploma.
**d. J.** *dieses Jahres* of this year; *der Jüngere* junior, *abbr.* jr, jun.
**DM** *Deutsche Mark* German Mark.
**d. M.** *dieses Monats* instant, *abbr.* inst.
**do.** *dito* ditto, *abbr.* do.
**d. O.** *der (die, das) Obige* the above-mentioned.
**dpa, DPA** *Deutsche Presse-Agentur* German Press Agency.
**Dr.** *Doktor* Doctor, *abbr.* Dr; ~ **jur.** *Doktor der Rechte* Doctor of Laws (LL.D.); ~ **med.** *Doktor der Medizin* Doctor of Medicine (M.D.); ~ **phil.** *Doktor der Philosophie* Doctor of Philosophy (D. ph[il]., Ph. D.); ~ **theol.** *Doktor der Theologie* Doctor of Divinity (D. D.).
**DRK** *Deutsches Rotes Kreuz* German Red Cross.
**dt(sch).** *deutsch* German.
**Dtz., Dtzd.** *Dutzend* dozen.
**d. Verf.** *der Verfasser* the author.

**ebd.** *ebenda* in the same place.
**ed.** *edidit* = *hat (es) herausgegeben.*
**eig., eigtl.** *eigentlich* properly.
**einschl.** *einschließlich* including, inclusive, *abbr.* incl.
**entspr.** *entsprechend* corresponding.
**Erl.** *Erläuterung* explanation, (explanatory) note.
**ev.** *evangelisch* Protestant.
**e. V.** *eingetragener Verein* registered association, incorporated, *abbr.* inc.

**evtl.** *eventuell* perhaps, possibly.
**EWG** *Europäische Wirtschaftsgemeinschaft* European Economic Community, *abbr.* EEC.
**exkl.** *exklusive* except(ed), not included.
**Expl.** *Exemplar* copy.

**Fa.** *Firma* firm; *letter*: Messrs.
**FDGB** *Freier Deutscher Gewerkschaftsbund* Free Federation of German Trade Unions.
**FDP** *Freie Demokratische Partei* Liberal Democratic Party.
**FD(-Zug)** *Fernschnellzug* long-distance express.
**ff.** *sehr fein* extra fine; *folgende Seiten* following pages.
**Forts.** *Fortsetzung* continuation.
**Fr.** *Frau* Mrs.
**frdl.** *freundlich* kind.
**Frl.** *Fräulein* Miss.

**g** *Gramm* gram(me).
**geb.** *geboren* born; *geborene ...* née; *gebunden* bound.
**Gebr.** *Gebrüder* Brothers.
**gef.** *gefällig(st)* kind(ly).
**gegr.** *gegründet* founded.
**geh.** *geheftet* stitched.
**gek.** *gekürzt* abbreviated.
**Ges.** *Gesellschaft* association, company; society. [registered.]
**ges. gesch.** *gesetzlich geschützt*
**gest.** *gestorben* deceased.
**gez.** *gezeichnet* signed, *abbr.* sgd.
**GmbH** *Gesellschaft mit beschränkter Haftung* limited liability company, *abbr.* Ltd., *Am.* closed corporation under German law.

**ha** *Hektar* hectare.
**Hbf.** *Hauptbahnhof* central *or* main station.
**Hbg.** *Hamburg* Hamburg.
**h. c.** *honoris causa* = *ehrenhalber academic title*: honorary.
**Hr., Hrn.** *Herr(n)* Mr.
**hrsg.** *herausgegeben* edited, *abbr.* ed.
**Hrsg.** *Herausgeber* editor, *abbr.* ed.

**i.** *im, in* in.
**i. A.** *im Auftrage* for, by order, under instruction.
**i. allg.** *im allgemeinen* in general, generally speaking.
**i. Durchschn.** *im Durchschnitt* on an average.
**inkl.** *inklusive, einschließlich* inclusive.
**i. J.** *im Jahre* in the year.
**Ing.** *Ingenieur* engineer.
**Inh.** *Inhaber* proprietor.
**'Interpol** *Internationale Kriminalpolizei-Kommission* International Criminal Police Commission, *abbr.* ICPC.
**i. V.** *in Vertretung* by proxy, as a substitute.

**Jb.** *Jahrbuch* annual.
**jr., jun.** *junior, der Jüngere* junior *abbr.* jr, jun.

**Kap.** *Kapitel* chapter.
**kath.** *katholisch* Catholic.
**Kfm.** *Kaufmann* merchant.
**kfm.** *kaufmännisch* commercial.
**Kfz.** *Kraftfahrzeug* motor vehicle.
**kg** *Kilogramm* kilogram(me).
**KG** *Kommanditgesellschaft* limited partnership.
**Kl.** *Klasse* class; *school*: form.
**km** *Kilometer* kilomet|re, *Am.* -er.
**'Kripo** *Kriminalpolizei* Criminal Investigation Department, *abbr.* CID.
**Kto.** *Konto* account, *abbr.* a/c.
**kW** *Kilowatt* kilowatt, *abbr.* kw.
**kWh** *Kilowattstunde* kilowatt hour.

**l** *Liter* lit|re, *Am.* -er.
**LDP** *Liberal-Demokratische Partei* Liberal Democratic Party.
**lfd.** *laufend* current, running.
**lfde. Nr.** *laufende Nummer* consecutive number.
**Lfg., Lfrg.** *Lieferung* delivery; instalment, part.
**Lit.** *Literatur* literature.
**Lkw.** *Lastkraftwagen* lorry, truck.
**lt.** *laut* according to.

**m** *Meter* met|re, *Am.* -er.
**m. A. n.** *meiner Ansicht nach* in my opinion.
**M. d. B.** *Mitglied des Bundestages* Member of the Bundestag.
**m. E.** *meines Erachtens* in my opinion.
**MEZ** *mitteleuropäische Zeit* Central European Time.
**mg** *Milligramm* milligram(me[s]), *abbr.* mg.
**Mill.** *Million(en)* million(s).
**mm** *Millimeter* millimet|re, *Am.* -er.
**möbl.** *möbliert* furnished.
**MP** *Militärpolizei* Military Police.
**mtl.** *monatlich* monthly.
**m. W.** *meines Wissens* as far as I know.

**N** *Nord(en)* north.
**nachm.** *nachmittags* in the afternoon, *abbr.* p. m.
**n. Chr.** *nach Christus* after Christ, *abbr.* A. D.
**n. J.** *nächstes Jahres* of next year.
**n. M.** *nächsten Monats* of next month.
**No., Nr.** *Numero, Nummer* number, *abbr.* N°.
**NS** *Nachschrift* postscript, *abbr.* P. S.

**O** *Ost(en)* east.
**o. B.** *ohne Befund ♣* without findings.
**od.** *oder* or.

**OEZ** *osteuropäische Zeit* time of the East European zone.

**OHG** *Offene Handelsgesellschaft* ordinary partnership.

**o. J.** *ohne Jahr* no date.

**p. Adr.** *per Adresse* care of, *abbr.* c/o.

**Pf** *Pfennig German coin*: pfennig.

**Pfd.** *Pfund German weight*: pound.

**PKW, Pkw.** *Personenkraftwagen* (motor) car.

**P. P.** *praemissis praemittendis* omitting titles, to whom it may concern.

**p.p., p.pa., ppa.** *per procura* per proxy, *abbr.* per pro.

**Prof.** *Professor* professor.

**PS** *Pferdestärke(n)* horse-power, *abbr.* H.P., h.p.; *postscriptum, Nachschrift* postscript, *abbr.* P.S.

**qkm** *Quadratkilometer* square kilomet|re, *Am.* -er.     [*Am.* -er.|
**qm** *Quadratmeter* square met|re,|

**Reg. Bez.** *Regierungsbezirk* administrative district.

**Rel.** *Religion* religion.

**resp.** *respektive* respectively.

**S** *Süd(en)* south.

**S.** *Seite* page.

**s.** *siehe* see, *abbr.* v., vid. (= vide).

**s. a.** *siehe auch* see also.

**Sa.** *Summa, Summe* sum, total.

**s. d.** *siehe dies* see this.

**SED** *Sozialistische Einheitspartei Deutschlands* United Socialist Party of Germany.

**sen.** *senior,* der *Ältere* senior.

**sm** *Seemeile* nautical mile.

**s. o.** *siehe oben* see above.

**sog.** *sogenannt* so-called.

**SPD** *Sozialdemokratische Partei Deutschlands* Social Democratic Party of Germany.

**St.** *Stück* piece; *Sankt* Saint.

**St(d).** **Stde.** *Stunde* hour, *abbr.* h.

**Str.** *Straße* street, *abbr.* St.

**s. u.** *siehe unten* see below.

**s. Z.** *seinerzeit* at that time.

**t** *Tonne* ton.

**tägl.** *täglich* daily, per day.

**Tel.** *Telephon* telephone; *Telegramm* wire, cable.

**TH** *Technische Hochschule* technical university or college.

**u.** *und* and.

**u. a.** *und andere(s)* and others; *unter anderem or anderen* among other things, inter alia.

**u. ä.** *und ähnliche(s)* and the like.

**U.A.w.g.** *Um Antwort wird gebeten* an answer is requested, *répondez s'il vous plaît, abbr.* R.S.V.P.

**u. dgl. (m.)** *und dergleichen (mehr)* and the like.

**u. d. M.** *unter dem Meeresspiegel* below sea level; **ü. d. M.** *über dem Meeresspiegel* above sea level.

**UdSSR** *Union der Sozialistischen Sowjetrepubliken* Union of Soviet Socialist Republics.

**u. E.** *unseres Erachtens* in our opinion.     [following.|

**u. f., u. ff.** *und folgende* and the|

**UKW** *Ultrakurzwelle* ultra-short wave, very high frequency, *abbr.* VHF.

**U/min.** *Umdrehungen in der Minute* revolutions per minute, *abbr.* r.p.m.

**urspr.** *ursprünglich* original(ly).

**US(A)** *Vereinigte Staaten (von Amerika)* United States (of America).

**usw.** *und so weiter* and so on, *abbr.* etc.     [stances permitting.|
**u. U.** *unter Umständen* circum-|

**v.** *von, vom* of; from; by.

**V** *Volt* volt; *Volumen* volume.

**V.** *Vers* line, verse.

**v. Chr.** *vor Christus* before Christ, *abbr.* B. C.

**VEB** *Volkseigener Betrieb* People's Own Undertaking.

**Verf., Vf.** *Verfasser* author.

**Verl.** *Verlag* publishing firm; *Verleger* publisher.

**vgl.** *vergleiche* confer, *abbr.* cf.

**v.g.u.** *vorgelesen, genehmigt, unterschrieben* read, confirmed, signed.

**v. H.** *vom Hundert* per cent.

**v. J.** *vorigen Jahres* of last year.

**v. M.** *vorigen Monats* of last month.

**vorm.** *vormittags* in the morning, *abbr.* a. m.; *vormals* formerly.

**Vors.** *Vorsitzender* chairman.

**v. T.** *vom Tausend* per thousand.

**VW** *Volkswagen* Volkswagen, People's Car.

**W** *West(en)* west; *Watt* watt(s).

**WE** *Wärmeeinheit* thermal unit.

**WEZ** *westeuropäische Zeit* Western European time (Greenwich time).

**WGB** *Weltgewerkschaftsbund* World Federation of Trade Unions, *abbr.* WFTU.

**Wwe.** *Witwe* widow.

**Z.** *Zahl* number; *Zeile* line.

**z.** *zu, zum, zur* at; to.

**z. B.** *zum Beispiel* for instance, *abbr.* e. g.

**z. H(d).** *zu Händen* attention of, to be delivered to, care of, *abbr.* c/o.

**z. S.** *zur See* of the navy.

**z. T.** *zum Teil* partly.

**Ztg.** *Zeitung* newspaper.

**Ztr.** *Zentner* centner.

**Ztschr.** *Zeitschrift* periodical.

**zus.** *zusammen* together.

**zw.** *zwischen* between; among.

**z. Z(t).** *zur Zeit* at the time, at present, for the time being.

# American and British Proper Names

Aberdeen [æbə'diːn] *Stadt in Schottland.*

Africa ['æfrikə] Afrika *n.* [*U.S.A.*]

Alabama [ælə'bæmə] *Staat der*

Alaska [ə'læskə] *Staat der U.S.A.*

Albania [æl'beinjə] Albanien *n.*

Alberta [æl'bəːtə] *Provinz in Kanada.* [*U.S.A.*]

Alleghany ['æligeini] *Gebirge in*

Alsace ['ælsæs] Elsaß *n.*

America [ə'merikə] Amerika *n.*

Antilles [æn'tiliːz] *die* Antillen.

Appalachians [æpə'leitʃənz] *die* Appalachen (*Gebirge in U.S.A.*).

Arizona [æri'zounə] *Staat der U.S.A.* [*U.S.A.*]

Arkansas ['ɑːkənsɔː] *Staat der*

Arlington ['ɑːliŋtən] *Nationalfriedhof bei Washington.*

Ascot ['æskət] *Stadt in England.*

Asia ['eiʃə] Asien *n.*

Athens ['æθinz] Athen *n.*

Australia [ɔs'treiljə] Australien *n.*

Austria ['ɔstriə] Österreich *n.*

Avon ['eivən] *Fluß in England.*

Azores [ə'zɔːz] *die* Azoren.

Bacon ['beikən] *engl. Philosoph.*

Bahamas [bə'hɑːməz] *die* Bahamainseln.

Balmoral [bæl'mɔrəl] *Königsschloß in Schottland.*

Bedford(shire) ['bedfəd(ʃiə)] *Grafschaft in England.*

Belfast [bel'fɑːst] *Hauptstadt von Nordirland.*

Belgium ['beldʒəm] Belgien *n.*

Belgrade [bel'greid] Belgrad *n.*

Ben Nevis [ben'nevis] *höchster Berg in Großbritannien.*

Berkshire ['bɑːkʃiə] *Grafschaft in England.*

Bermudas [bə'mjuːdəz] *die* Bermudainseln.

Bern(e) [bəːn] Bern *n.*

Birmingham ['bəːmiŋəm] *Industriestadt in England* [Biskaya.]

Biscay ['biskei] *Bay of ∼ Golf m von*

Boston ['bɔstən] *Stadt in U.S.A.*

Bournemouth ['bɔːnməθ] *Seebad in England.*

Brighton ['braitn] *Seebad in England.* [land.]

Bristol ['bristl] *Hafenstadt in Eng-*

Britten ['britn] *engl. Komponist.*

Brooklyn ['bruklin] *Stadtteil von New York.*

Brussels ['brʌslz] Brüssel *n.*

Bucharest ['bjuːkərest] Bukarest *n.*

Buckingham(shire)['bʌkiŋəm(ʃiə)] *Grafschaft in England.*

Budapest ['bjuːdə'pest] Budapest *n.*

Bulgaria [bʌl'geəriə] Bulgarien *n.*

Burns [bəːnz] *schott. Dichter.*

Byron ['baiərən] *engl. Dichter.*

California [kæli'fɔːnjə] Kalifornien *n (Staat der U.S.A.*).

Cambridge ['keimbridʒ] *engl. Universitätsstadt; Stadt in U.S.A.; a. ∼shire* ['∼ʃiə] *Grafschaft in England.*

Canada ['kænədə] Kanada *n.*

Canary Islands [kə'neəri 'ailəndz] *die* Kanarischen Inseln.

Canberra ['kænbərə] *Hauptstadt von Australien.* [*England.*]

Canterbury ['kæntəbəri] *Stadt in*

Capetown ['keiptaun] Kapstadt *n.*

Cardiff ['kɑːdif] *Hauptstadt von Wales.*

Carinthia [kə'rinθiə] Kärnten *n.*

Carlyle [kɑː'lail] *engl. Autor.*

Carolina [kærə'lainə]: North ∼ Nordkarolina *n (Staat der U.S.A.*); South ∼ Südkarolina *n (Staat der U.S.A.*).

Ceylon [si'lɔn] Ceylon *n.*

Chamberlain ['tʃeimbəlin, ∼lein] *Name mehrerer brit. Staatsmänner.*

Cheshire ['tʃeʃə] *Grafschaft in England.*

Chicago [ʃi'kɑːgou, *Am.* ʃi'kɔːgou] *Industriestadt in U.S.A.*

China ['tʃainə] China *n.* [*mann.*]

Churchill ['tʃəːtʃil] *brit. Staats-*

Cleveland ['kliːvlənd] *Industrie- und Hafenstadt in U.S.A.*

Clyde [klaid] *Fluß in Schottland.*

Coleridge ['koulridʒ] *engl. Dichter.*

Colorado [kɔlə'rɑːdou] *Staat der U.S.A.*

Columbia [kə'lʌmbiə] *Fluß in U.S.A.; Bundesdistrikt der U.S.A.*

Connecticut [kə'netikət] *Staat der U.S.A.*

Constance ['kɔnstəns]: *Lake of ∼* Bodensee *m.*

Cooper ['kuːpə] *amer. Autor.*

Copenhagen [koupn'heigən] Kopenhagen *n.* [dilleren.]

Cordilleras [kɔːdi'ljeərəz] *die* Kor-

Cornwall ['kɔːnwəl] *Grafschaft in England.*

Coventry ['kɔvəntri] *Industriestadt in England.* [*mann.*]

Cromwell ['krɔmwəl] *engl. Staats-*

Cumberland ['kʌmbələnd] *Grafschaft in England.*

Cyprus ['saiprəs] Zypern *n.*

Czecho-Slovakia ['tʃekouslou'vækiə] *die* Tschechoslowakei.

**Dakota** [dəˈkoutə]: *North ~ Nord-dakota n (Staat der U.S.A.); South ~ Süddakota n (Staat der U.S.A.).*
**Defoe** [dəˈfou] *engl. Autor.*
**Delaware** [ˈdeləwɛə] *Staat der U.S.A.*
**Denmark** [ˈdenmaːk] *Dänemark n.*
**Derby(shire)** [ˈdaːbi(ʃə)] *Grafschaft in England.*
**Detroit** [dəˈtrɔit] *Industriestadt in U.S.A.*
**Devon(shire)** [ˈdevn(ʃiə)] *Grafschaft in England.*
**Dickens** [ˈdikinz] *engl. Autor.*
**Dorset(shire)** [ˈdɔːsit(ʃiə)] *Graf-schaft in England.* [land.)
**Dover** [ˈdouvə] *Hafenstadt in Eng-*
**Downing Street** [ˈdauniŋ ˈstriːt] *Straße in London mit der Amts-wohnung des Prime Minister.*
**Dublin** [ˈdʌblin] *Hauptstadt von Ir-land.*
**Dunkirk** [dʌnˈkəːk] *Dünkirchen n.*
**Durham** [ˈdʌrəm] *Grafschaft in England.*

**Edinburgh** [ˈedinbərə] *Edinburg n.*
**Edison** [ˈedisn] *amer. Erfinder.*
**Egypt** [ˈiːdʒipt] *Ägypten n.*
**Eire** [ˈɛərə] *Republik Irland.*
**Eisenhower** [ˈaizənhauə] *Präsident der U.S.A.*
**Eliot** [ˈeljət] *engl. Dichter.*
**Emerson** [ˈeməsn] *amer. Philosoph.*
**England** [ˈiŋglənd] *England n.*
**Epsom** [ˈepsəm] *Stadt in England.*
**Erie** [ˈiəri] *Lake ~ Eriesee m.*
**Essex** [ˈesiks] *Grafschaft in England.*
**Eton** [ˈiːtn] *berühmte Public School.*
**Europe** [ˈjuərəp] *Europa n.*

**Falkland Islands** [ˈfɔːlklənd ˈailəndz] *die Falklandinseln.*
**Faulkner** [ˈfɔːknə] *amer. Autor.*
**Finland** [ˈfinlənd] *Finnland n.*
**Florida** [ˈflɔridə] *Staat der U.S.A.*
**Flushing** [ˈflʌʃiŋ] *Vlissingen n.*
**France** [fraːns] *Frankreich n.*
**Franklin** [ˈfræŋklin] *amer. Staats-mann und Physiker.*

**Galsworthy** [ˈgɔːlzwəːði] *engl. Au-tor.*
**Geneva** [dʒiˈniːvə] *Genf n; Lake of ~ Genfer See m.*
**Georgia** [ˈdʒɔːdʒiə] *Staat der U.S.A.*
**Germany** [ˈdʒəːməni] *Deutschland n.* [nist.)
**Gershwin** [ˈgəːʃwin] *amer. Kompo-)*
**Gibraltar** [dʒiˈbrɔːltə] *Gibraltar n.*
**Glasgow** [ˈglaːsgou] *Hafenstadt in Schottland.*
**Gloucester** [ˈglɔstə] *Stadt in Eng-land; a. ~shire [ˈ~ʃiə] Grafschaft in England.*
**Great Britain** [ˈgreit ˈbritn] *Groß-britannien n.*
**Greece** [griːs] *Griechenland n.*

**Greene** [griːn] *engl. Autor.*
**Greenland** [ˈgriːnlənd] *Grönland n.*
**Greenwich** [ˈgrinidʒ] *Vorort von London.*
**Guernsey** [ˈgəːnzi] *Kanalinsel.*

**Hague** [heig]: *The ~ Den Haag.*
**Hampshire** [ˈhæmpʃiə] *Grafschaft in England.*
**Harlem** [ˈhaːlem] *Stadtteil von New York.*
**Harrow** [ˈhærou] *berühmte Public School.*
**Harvard University** [ˈhaːvəd juːniˈvəːsiti] *amer. Universität.*
**Harwich** [ˈhæridʒ] *Hafenstadt in England.*
**Hawaii** [haːˈwaii] *Staat der U.S.A.*
**Hebrides** [ˈhebridiːz] *die Hebriden.*
**Helsinki** [ˈhelsiŋki] *Helsinki n.*
**Hemingway** [ˈhemiŋwei] *amer. Au-tor.*
**Hereford(shire)** [ˈherifəd(ʃiə)] *Grafschaft in England.*
**Hertford(shire)** [ˈhaːtfəd(ʃiə)] *Grafschaft in England.*
**Hollywood** [ˈhɔliwud] *Filmstadt in Kalifornien, U.S.A.*
**Houston** [ˈjuːstən] *Stadt in U.S.A.*
**Hudson** [ˈhʌdsn] *Fluß in U.S.A.*
**Hull** [hʌl] *Hafenstadt in England.*
**Hume** [hjuːm] *engl. Philosoph.*
**Hungary** [ˈhʌŋgəri] *Ungarn n.*
**Huntingdon(shire)** [ˈhʌntiŋdən (-ʃiə)] *Grafschaft in England.* [m.)
**Huron** [ˈhjuərən]: *Lake ~ Huronsee)*
**Huxley** [ˈhʌksli] *engl. Autor.*

**Iceland** [ˈaislənd] *Island n.*
**Idaho** [ˈaidəhou] *Staat der U.S.A.*
**Illinois** [iliˈnɔi] *Staat der U.S.A.*
**India** [ˈindjə] *Indien n.*
**Indiana** [indiˈænə] *Staat der U.S.A.*
**Iowa** [ˈaiouə] *Staat der U.S.A.*
**Irak, Iraq** [iˈraːk] *Irak m.*
**Iran** [iˈraːn] *Iran m.*
**Ireland** [ˈaislənd] *Irland n.*
**Irving** [ˈəːviŋ] *amer. Autor.*
**Italy** [ˈitəli] *Italien n.*

**Jefferson** [ˈdʒefəsn] *Präsident der U.S.A., Verfasser der Unabhängig-keitserklärung von 1776.*
**Johnson** [ˈdʒɔnsn] *1. engl. Autor; 2. Präsident der U.S.A.*

**Kansas** [ˈkænzəs] *Staat der U.S.A.*
**Kashmir** [kæʃˈmiə] *Kaschmir n.*
**Keats** [kiːts] *engl. Dichter.*
**Kennedy** [ˈkenidi] *Präsident der U.S.A.; ~ Airport Flughafen von New York.*
**Kent** [kent] *Grafschaft in England.*
**Kentucky** [kenˈtʌki] *Staat der U.S.A.*
**Kipling** [ˈkipliŋ] *engl. Dichter.*
**Klondike** [ˈklɔndaik] *Fluß und Land-schaft in Kanada und Alaska.*
**Kremlin** [ˈkremlin] *der Kreml.*

**Labrador** ['læbrədɔ:] *Halbinsel Nordamerikas.*

**Lancashire** ['læŋkəʃiə] *Grafschaft in England.*

**Lancaster** ['læŋkəstə] *Name zweier Städte in England und U.S.A.; s. Lancashire.* [*land.*]

**Leeds** [li:dz] *Industriestadt in Eng-*

**Leicester** ['lestə] *Stadt in England; a. ~shire* ['~ʃiə] *Grafschaft in England.*

**Lincoln** ['liŋkən] **1.** *Präsident der U.S.A.; 2. a. ~shire* ['~ʃiə] *Grafschaft in England.*

**Lisbon** ['lizbən] *Lissabon n.*

**Liverpool** ['livəpu:l] *Hafen- und Industriestadt in England.*

**Locke** [lɔk] *engl. Philosoph.*

**London** ['lʌndən] *London n.*

**Los Angeles** [lɔs 'ændʒili:z] *Stadt in U.S.A.* [*U.S.A.*]

**Louisiana** [lu:izi'ænə] *Staat der*

**Lucerne** [lu:'sə:n]: *Lake of ~ Vierwaldstätter See m.*

**Luxemburg** ['lʌksəmbə:g] *Luxemburg n.*

**Madrid** [mə'drid] *Madrid n.*

**Maine** [mein] *Staat der U.S.A.*

**Malta** ['mɔ:ltə] *Malta n.*

**Manchester** ['mæntʃistə] *Industriestadt in England.*

**Manhattan** [mæn'hætən] *Stadtteil von New York.* [*Kanada.*]

**Manitoba** [mæni'toubə] *Provinz in*

**Maryland** ['mɛərilənd, Am. 'merilənd] *Staat der U.S.A.*

**Massachusetts** [mæsə'tʃu:sits] *Staat der U.S.A.*

**Melbourne** ['məlbən] *Stadt in Australien.*

**Miami** [mai'æmi] *Badeort in Florida, U.S.A.*

**Michigan** ['miʃigən] *Staat der U.S.A.; Lake ~ Michigansee m.*

**Middlesex** ['midlseks] *Grafschaft in England.*

**Miller** ['milə] *amer. Dramatiker.*

**Milton** ['miltən] *engl. Dichter.*

**Milwaukee** [mil'wɔ:ki:] *Stadt in U.S.A.*

**Minneapolis** [mini'æpəlis] *Stadt in U.S.A.* [*U.S.A.*]

**Minnesota** [mini'soutə] *Staat der*

**Mississippi** [misi'sipi] *Strom und Staat der U.S.A.*

**Missouri** [mi'zuəri] *Fluß und Staat der U.S.A.*

**Monmouth(shire)** ['mɔnməθ(ʃiə)] *Grafschaft in England.*

**Monroe** [mən'rou] *Präsident der U.S.A.* [*U.S.A.*]

**Montana** [mɔn'tænə] *Staat der*

**Montgomery** [mənt'gɔməri] *brit. Feldmarschall.*

**Montreal** [mɔntri'ɔ:l] *Stadt in Kanada.*

**Moore** [muə] *engl. Bildhauer.*

**Moscow** ['mɔskou] *Moskau n.*

**Nebraska** [ni'bræskə] *Staat der U.S.A.*

**Nelson** ['nelsn] *engl. Admiral.*

**Netherlands** ['neðələndz] *die Niederlande.*

**Nevada** [ne'va:də] *Staat der U.S.A.*

**New Brunswick** [nju: 'brʌnzwik] *Provinz in Kanada.*

**Newcastle** ['nju:ka:sl] *Hafenstadt in England.* [*von Indien.*]

**New Delhi** [nju: 'deli] *Hauptstadt*

**New England** [nju: 'iŋglənd] *Neuengland n.* [*Neufundland n.*]

**Newfoundland** [nju:fənd'lænd]

**New Hampshire** [nju: 'hæmpʃiə] *Staat der U.S.A.*

**New Jersey** [nju: 'dʒə:si] *Staat der U.S.A.*

**New Mexico** [nju: 'meksikou] *Neumexiko n (Staat der U.S.A.).*

**New Orleans** [nju: 'ɔ:liəns] *Hafenstadt in U.S.A.*

**Newton** ['nju:tn] *engl. Physiker.*

**New York** ['nju: 'jɔ:k] *Stadt und Staat der U.S.A.*

**New Zealand** [nju: 'zi:lənd] *Neuseeland n.*

**Niagara** [nai'ægərə] *Niagara m.*

**Nixon** ['niksn] *Präsident der U.S.A.*

**Norfolk** ['nɔ:fək] *Grafschaft in England.*

**Northampton** [nɔ:'θæmptən] *Stadt in England; a. ~shire* ['~ʃiə] *Grafschaft in England.*

**Northumberland** [nɔ:'θʌmbələnd] *Grafschaft in England.*

**Norway** ['nɔ:wei] *Norwegen n.*

**Nottingham** ['nɔtiŋəm] *Stadt in England; a. ~shire* ['~ʃiə] *Grafschaft in England.*

**Nova Scotia** ['nouvə 'skouʃə] *Provinz in Kanada.*

**Ohio** [ou'haiou] *Staat der U.S.A.*

**O'Neill** [ou'ni:l] *amer. Dramatiker.*

**Ontario** [ɔn'tɛəriou] *Provinz in Kanada; Lake ~ Ontariosee m.*

**Oregon** ['ɔrigən] *Staat der U.S.A.*

**Orkney Islands** ['ɔ:kni 'ailəndz] *die Orkneyinseln.*

**Osborne** ['ɔzbən] *engl. Dramatiker.*

**Oslo** ['ɔzlou] *Oslo n.*

**Ostend** [ɔs'tend] *Ostende n.*

**Ottawa** ['ɔtəwə] *Hauptstadt von Kanada.*

**Oxford** ['ɔksfəd] *engl. Universitätsstadt; a. ~shire* ['~ʃiə] *Grafschaft in England.*

**Pakistan** [pa:kis'ta:n] *Pakistan n.*

**Paris** ['pæris] *Paris n.*

**Pearl Harbour** ['pə:l 'ha:bə] *Hafenstadt auf Hawaii.*

**Pennsylvania** [pensil'veinjə] *Pennsylvanien n (Staat der U.S.A.).*

**Philadelphia** [filə'delfjə] *Stadt in U.S.A.*

**Philippines** ['filipi:nz] *die Philippinen.*

**Pittsburg(h)** ['pitsbə:g] *Stadt in U.S.A.*

**Plymouth** ['pliməθ] *Hafenstadt in England.*

**Poe** [pou] *amer. Autor.*

**Poland** ['poulənd] Polen *n.*

**Portsmouth** ['pɔ:tsməθ] *Hafenstadt in England.*

**Portugal** ['pɔ:tjugəl] Portugal *n.*

**Prague** [prɑ:g] Prag *n.*

**Purcell** ['pə:sl] *engl. Komponist.*

**Quebec** [kwi'bek] *Provinz und Stadt in Kanada.*

**Reykjavik** ['reikjəvi:k] Reykjavik *n.*

**Rhode Island** [roud 'ailənd] *Staat der U.S.A.*

**Rocky Mountains** ['rɔki 'mauntinz] *Gebirge in U.S.A.*

**Rome** [roum] Rom *n.*

**Roosevelt** ['rouzəvelt] *Name zweier Präsidenten der U.S.A.* [*School.*]

**Rugby** ['rʌgbi] *berühmte Public*

**Rumania** [ru:'meinjə] Rumänien *n.*

**Russell** ['rʌsl] *engl. Philosoph.*

**Russia** ['rʌʃə] Rußland *n.*

**Rutland(shire)** ['rʌtlənd(ʃiə)] *Grafschaft in England.*

**San Francisco** [sænfrən'siskou] *Hafenstadt in U.S.A.*

**Saskatchewan** [səs'kætʃiwən] *Provinz von Kanada.*

**Scandinavia** [skændi'neivjə] Skandinavien *n.*

**Scotland** ['skɔtlənd] Schottland *n.*

**Shakespeare** ['ʃeikspiə] *engl. Dichter.*

**Shaw** [ʃɔ:] *engl. Dramatiker.*

**Shelley** ['ʃeli] *engl. Dichter.*

**Shetland Islands** ['ʃetlənd 'ailəndz] *die Shetlandinseln.*

**Shropshire** ['ʃrɔpʃiə] *Grafschaft in England.*

**Snowdon** ['snoudn] *Berg in Wales.*

**Sofia** ['soufjə] Sofia *n.*

**Somerset(shire)** ['sʌməsit(ʃiə)] *Grafschaft in England.*

**Southhampton** [sauθ'æmptən] *Hafenstadt in England.*

**Spain** [spein] Spanien *n.*

**Stafford(shire)** ['stæfəd(ʃiə)] *Grafschaft in England.*

**Stevenson** ['sti:vnsn] *engl. Autor.*

**St. Lawrence** [snt'lɔrəns] *der St. Lorenz-Strom.*

**St. Louis** [snt'luis] *Industriestadt in U.S.A.*

**Stockholm** ['stɔkhoum] Stockholm*)*

**Stratford** ['strætfəd]: *~-on-Avon Geburtsort Shakespeares.*

**Suffolk** ['sʌfək] *Grafschaft in England.* [rcr See *m.*]

**Superior** [sju:'piəriə]: *Lake ~ Obe-*

**Surrey** ['sʌri] *Grafschaft in England.*

**Sussex** ['sʌsiks] *Grafschaft in England.*

**Sweden** ['swi:dn] Schweden *n.*

**Swift** [swift] *engl. Autor.*

**Switzerland** ['switsələnd] die Schweiz. [*tralien.*]

**Sydney** ['sidni] *Hafenstadt in Aus-*

**Tennessee** [tene'si] *Staat der U.S.A.*

**Tennyson** ['tenisn] *engl. Dichter.*

**Texas** ['teksəs] *Staat der U.S.A.*

**Thackeray** ['θækəri] *engl. Autor.*

**Thames** [temz] Themse *f.*

**Tirana** [ti'rɑ:nə] Tirana *n.* [*nada.*]

**Toronto** [tə'rɔntou] *Stadt in Ka-*

**Toynbee** ['tɔinbi] *engl. Historiker.*

**Trafalgar** [trə'fælgə] *Vorgebirge bei Gibraltar.* [*U.S.A.*]

**Truman** ['tru:mən] *Präsident der*

**Turkey** ['tə:ki] die Türkei.

**Twain** [twein] *amer. Autor.*

**Tyrol** ['tirəl] Tirol *n.*

**United States of America** [ju:'nai-tid 'steitsəvə'merikə] *die* Vereinigten Staaten von Amerika.

**Utah** ['ju:tɑ:] *Staat der U.S.A.*

**Vancouver** [væn'ku:və] *Stadt in Kanada.*

**Vermont** [və:'mɔnt] *Staat der*

**Vienna** [vi'enə] Wien *n.* [*U.S.A.*]

**Virginia** [və'dʒinjə] Virginien *n* (*Staat der U.S.A.*); West ~ *Staat der U.S.A.*

**Wales** [weilz] Wales *n.*

**Warsaw** ['wɔ:sɔ:] Warschau *n.*

**Warwick(shire)** ['wɔrik(ʃiə)] *Grafschaft in England.*

**Washington** ['wɔʃiŋtən] 1. *Präsident der U.S.A.*; 2. *Staat der U.S.A.*; 3. *Bundeshauptstadt der U.S.A.*

**Wellington** ['weliŋtən] *Hauptstadt von Neuseeland.*

**Westmoreland** ['westmələnd] *Grafschaft in England.*

**White House** ['wuit 'haus] *das* Weiße Haus.

**Whitman** ['witmən] *amer. Dichter.*

**Wilson** ['wilsn] 1. *Präsident der U.S.A.*; 2. *brit. Premier.*

**Wiltshire** ['wiltʃiə] *Grafschaft in England.*

**Wimbledon** ['wimbldən] *Vorort von London.* [*Kanada.*]

**Winnipeg** ['winipeg] *Stadt in*

**Wisconsin** [wis'kɔnsin] *Staat der U.S.A.*

**Worcester** ['wustə] *Industriestadt in England*; *a.* ~shire ['~ʃiə] *Grafschaft in England.*

**Wordsworth** ['wə:dzwə:θ] *engl. Dichter.*

**Yale University** ['jeil ju:ni'və:siti] *amer. Universität.*

**York** [jɔ:k] *Stadt in England*; *a.* ~shire ['~ʃiə] *Grafschaft in England.*

**Yugoslavia** ['ju:gou'slɑ:vjə] Jugoslawien *n.*

# American and British Abbreviations

**abbr.** *abbreviated* abgekürzt; *abbreviation* Abk., Abkürzung *f.*

**A.B.C.** *American Broadcasting Company* Amer. Rundfunkgesellschaft *f.*

**A.C.** *alternating current* Wechselstrom *m.*

**A.E.C.** *Atomic Energy Commission* Atomenergie-Kommission *f.*

**AFL-CIO** *American Federation of Labor & Congress of Industrial Organizations* (größter amer. Gewerkschaftsverband).

**A.F.N.** *American Forces Network* (Rundfunkanstalt der amer. Streitkräfte).

**Ala.** *Alabama.*

**Alas.** *Alaska.*

**a.m.** *ante meridiem* (lateinisch = *before noon*) vormittags.

**A.P.** *Associated Press* (amer. Nachrichtenbüro).

**A.R.C.** *American Red Cross* Amer. Rotes Kreuz.

**Ariz.** *Arizona.*

**Ark.** *Arkansas.*

**arr.** *arrival* Ank., Ankunft *f.*

**B.A.** *Bachelor of Arts* Bakkalaureus *m* der Philosophie.

**B.B.C.** *British Broadcasting Corporation* Brit. Rundfunkgesellschaft *f.*

**B.E.A.** *British European Airways* Brit.-Europäische Luftfahrtgesellschaft.

**Beds.** *Bedfordshire.*

**Benelux** *Belgium, Netherlands, Luxemburg* (Zollunion).

**Berks.** *Berkshire.*

**B.F.N.** *British Forces Network* (Sender der brit. Streitkräfte in Deutschland) *m* des Rechts.

**B.L.** *Bachelor of Law* Bakkalaureus

**B.M.** *Bachelor of Medicine* Bakkalaureus *m* der Medizin.

**B.O.A.C.** *British Overseas Airways Corporation* Brit. Übersee-Luftfahrtgesellschaft *f.*

**B.R.** *British Railways.*

**Br(it).** *Britain* Großbritannien *n*; *British* britisch.

**B.S.** *Bachelor of Science* Bakkalaureus *m* der Naturwissenschaften.

**Bucks.** *Buckinghamshire.*

**C.** *Celsius, centigrade.*

**c.** *cent(s)* Cent *m*; *circa* ca., ungefähr, zirka; *cubic* Kubik...

**Cal(if).** *California.*

**Cambs.** *Cambridgeshire.*

**Can.** *Canada* Kanada *n*; *Canadian* kanadisch.

**cf.** *confer* vgl., vergleiche.

**Ches.** *Cheshire.*

**C.I.C.** *Counter Intelligence Corps* (Spionageabwehrdienst der U.S.A.).

**C.I.D.** *Criminal Investigation Department* (brit. Kriminalpolizei).

**Co.** *Company* Gesellschaft *f*; *County* Grafschaft *f*, Kreis *m.*

**c/o** *care of* p.A., per Adresse, bei.

**Col(o).** *Colorado.*

**Conn.** *Connecticut.*

**cp.** *compare* vgl., vergleiche.

**Cumb.** *Cumberland.*

**cwt.** *hundredweight* (etwa 1) Zentner *m.*

**d.** *penny, pence.*

**D.C.** *direct current* Gleichstrom *m*; *District of Columbia* (mit der amer. Hauptstadt Washington).

**Del.** *Delaware.*

**dep.** *departure* Abf., Abfahrt *f.*

**Dept.** *Department* Abt., Abteilung *f.*

**Derby.** *Derbyshire.*

**Devon.** *Devonshire.*

**Dors.** *Dorsetshire.*

**Dur(h).** *Durham.*

**dz.** *dozen* Dutzend *n* od. *pl.*

**E.** *east* Ost(en *m*); *eastern* östlich; *English* englisch.

**E.C.** *East Central* (London) Mitte-Ost (Postbezirk).

**ECOSOC** *Economic and Social Council* Wirtschafts- und Sozialrat *m* (U.N.).

**Ed., ed.** *edition* Auflage *f*; *edited* hrsg., herausgegeben; *editor* Hrsg., Herausgeber *m.*

**E.E.C.** *European Economic Community* EWG, Europäische Wirtschaftsgemeinschaft.

**E.F.T.A.** *European Free Trade Association* EFTA, Europäische Freihandelsgemeinschaft od. -zone.

**e.g.** *exempli gratia* (lateinisch = *for instance*) z.B., zum Beispiel.

**Enc.** *enclosure(s)* Anlage(n *pl.*) *f.*

**Ess.** *Essex.*

**F.** *Fahrenheit.*

**f.** *fathom(s)* Faden *m*, Klafter *f, m, n*; *feminine* weiblich; *foot, pl.* feet Fuß *m* od. *pl.*; *following* folgend.

**F.A.O.** *Food and Agricultural Organization* Organisation *f* für Ernährung und Landwirtschaft (U.N.).

**FBI** *Federal Bureau of Investigation* (Bundeskriminalamt der U.S.A.).

**fig.** *figure(s)* Abb., Abbildung(en *pl.*) *f.*

**Fla.** *Florida.*

**F.O.** *Foreign Office* brit. Auswärtiges Amt.

**fr.** *franc(s)* Frank(en *pl.*) *m.*

**ft.** *foot, pl.* feet Fuß *m* od. *pl.*

**g.** *gramme* g, Gramm *n*; *guinea* Guinee *f* (*21 Schilling*).

**Ga.** *Georgia*.

**gal.** *gallon* Gallone *f*.

**G.A.T.T.** *General Agreement on Tariffs and Trade* Allgemeines Zoll- und Handelsabkommen.

**G.B.** *Great Britain* Großbritannien *n*.

**G.I.** *government issue* von der Regierung ausgegeben; Staatseigentum *n*; *fig. der* amer. Soldat.

**Glos.** *Gloucestershire*.

**G.P.O.** *General Post Office* Haupt-\
**gr.** *gross* brutto. [postamt *n*.\
**Gt.Br.** *Great Britain* Großbritannien *n*.

**h.** *hour(s)* Std., Stunde(n *pl.*) *f*.

**Hants.** *Hampshire*.

**H.C.** *House of Commons* Unterhaus *n*.

**Heref.** *Herefordshire*.

**Herts.** *Hertfordshire*.

**hf.** *half* halb.

**H.I.** *Hawaiian Islands*.

**H.L.** *House of Lords* Oberhaus *n*.

**H.M.** *His (Her) Majesty* Seine (Ihre) Majestät.

**H.M.S.** *His (Her) Majesty's Service* Dienst *m*, & Dienstsache *f*; *His (Her) Majesty's Ship* Seiner (Ihrer) Majestät Schiff *n*.

**H.O.** *Home Office* brit. Innenministerium *n*. [stärke *f*.\
**H.P., h.p.** *horse-power* PS, Pferde-\
**H.Q., Hq.** *Headquarters* Stab(squartier *n*) *m*, Hauptquartier *n*.

**H.R.** *House of Representatives* Repräsentantenhaus *n* (*der U.S.A.*).

**H.R.H.** *His (Her) Royal Highness* Seine (Ihre) Königliche Hoheit *f*.

**Hunts.** *Huntingdonshire*.

**Ia.** *Iowa*.

**I.C.B.M.** *intercontinental ballistic missile* interkontinentaler ballistischer Flugkörper.

**I.D.** *Intelligence Department* Nachrichtenamt *n*.

**Id(a).** *Idaho*. [d.h., das heißt.\
**i.e.** *id est* (*lateinisch = that is to say*)\
**Ill.** *Illinois*.

**I.M.F.** *International Monetary Fund* Weltwährungsfonds *m*.

**in.** *inch(es)* Zoll *m od. pl.* [gen.\
**Inc.** *Incorporated* (amtlich) eingetra-\
**Ind.** *Indiana*.

**I.O.C.** *International Olympic Committee* Internationales Olympisches Komitee.

**Ir.** *Ireland* Irland *n*; *Irish* irisch.

**I.R.C.** *International Red Cross* Internationales Rotes Kreuz.

**J.P.** *Justice of the Peace* Friedensrichter *m*.

**Kan(s).** *Kansas*.

**k.o.** *knock(ed) out Boxen:* k.o. (ge-) schlagen; *fig.* erledigen (erledigt).

**Ky.** *Kentucky*.

**£** *pound sterling* Pfund *n* Sterling.

**La.** *Louisiana*.

**Lancs.** *Lancashire*. [wicht).\
**lb.** *pound(s)* Pfund *n od. pl.* (Ge-\
**L.C.** *letter of credit* Kreditbrief\
**Leics.** *Leicestershire*. [m.\
**Lincs.** *Lincolnshire*.

**LP** *long-playing* Langspiel...(*Platte*).

**L.P.** *Labour Party* (*brit. Arbeiterpartei*). [tung.\
**Ltd.** *limited* mit beschränkter Haf-\

**m.** *male* männlich; *metre* m, Meter *n*; *m*; *mile* Meile *f*; *minute* Min., Minute *f*. [Philosophie.\
**M.A.** *Master of Arts* Magister *m* der\
**Mass.** *Massachusetts*.

**M.D.** *Medicinae Doctor* (*lateinisch = Doctor of Medicine*) Dr. med., Doktor *m* der Medizin.

**Md.** *Maryland*.

**Me.** *Maine*.

**mi.** *mile* Meile *f*.

**Mich.** *Michigan*.

**Middx.** *Middlesex*.

**Minn.** *Minnesota*.

**Miss.** *Mississippi*.

**Mo.** *Missouri*.

**M.O.** *money order* Postanweisung *f*.

**Mon.** *Monmouthshire*.

**Mont.** *Montana*.

**MP, M.P.** *Member of Parliament* Parlamentsabgeordnete *m*; *Military Police* Militärpolizei *f*.

**m.p.h.** *miles per hour* Stundenmei-\
**Mr** *Mister* Herr *m*. [len *pl*.\
**Mrs** *Mistress* Frau *f*.

**Mt.** *Mount* Berg *m*.

**N.** *north* Nord(en *m*); *northern* nörd-\
**n.** *noon* Mittag *m*. lich.\
**NASA** *National Aeronautics and Space Administration* (*amer. Luftfahrt- und Raumforschungsbehörde*).

**NATO** *North Atlantic Treaty Organization* Nordatlantikpakt-Organisation *f*.

**N.C.** *North Carolina*.

**N.D(ak).** *North Dakota*.

**Neb(r).** *Nebraska*.

**Nev.** *Nevada*.

**N.H.** *New Hampshire*.

**N.H.S.** *National Health Service* Nationaler Gesundheitsdienst (*brit. Krankenversicherung*).

**N.J.** *New Jersey*.

**N.M(ex).** *New Mexico*.

**Norf.** *Norfolk*.

**Northants.** *Northamptonshire*.

**Northumb.** *Northumberland*.

**Notts.** *Nottinghamshire*.

**nt.** *net* netto.

**N.Y.** *New York*. [York.\
**N.Y.C.** *New York City* Stadt *f* New\

**O.** *Ohio*; *order* Auftrag *m*.

**O.A.S.** *Organization of American States* Organisation *f* amerikanischer Staaten.

**O.E.E.C.** *Organization of European Economic Co-operation* Organisation *f* für europäische wirtschaftliche Zusammenarbeit.
**Okla.** *Oklahoma.*
**Ore(g).** *Oregon.*
**Oxon.** *Oxfordshire.*

**Pa.** *Pennsylvania.*
**P.A.A.** *Pan-American Airways* Pan-amer. Luftfahrtgesellschaft *f.*
**P.C.** *police constable* Schutzmann *m.*
**p.c.** *per cent* %, Prozent *n od. pl.*
**pd.** *paid* bezahlt.
**P.E.N.**, *mst* **PEN Club** *Poets, Playwrights, Editors, Essayists, and Novelists* Pen-Club *m, (Internationale Vereinigung von Dichtern, Dramatikern, Redakteuren, Essayisten und Romanschriftstellern).*
**Penn(a).** *Pennsylvania.*
**Ph.D.** *Philosophiae Doctor (lateinisch = Doctor of Philosophy)* Dr. phil., Doktor *m* der Philosophie.
**p.m.** *post meridiem (lateinisch = after noon)* nachmittags, abends.
**P.O.** *Post Office* Postamt *n; postal order* Postanweisung *f.*
**P.O.B.** *Post Office Box* Postschließfach *n.*
**P.S.** *Postscript* P.S., Nachschrift *f.*
**P.T.O.**, *p.t.o. please turn over* b.w., bitte wenden.
**PX** *Post Exchange (Verkaufsläden der amer. Streitkräfte).*

**R.A.F.** *Royal Air Force* Königlich-Brit. Luftwaffe *f.*
**Rd.** *Road* Straße *f.*
**ref(c).** *(In) reference (to)* (in) Bezug *m* (auf); Empfehlung *f.*
**regd.** *registered* eingetragen; *&* eingeschrieben. [tonne *f.*\
**reg. tn.** *register ton* RT, Register-\
**resp.** *respective(ly)* bzw., beziehungsweise.
**ret.** *retired* i.R., im Ruhestand.
**Rev.** *Reverend* Ehrwürden.
**R.I.** *Rhode Island.* Marine *f.*\
**R.N.** *Royal Navy* Königlich-Brit.\
**R.R.** *Railroad Am.* Eisenbahn *f.*
**Rutland.** *Rutlandshire.*
**Ry.** *Railway* Eisenbahn *f.*

**S.** *south* Süd(en *m); southern* südlich.
**s.** *second(s)* Sek., Sekunde(n *pl.) f; shilling(s)* Schilling *m od. pl.*
**$** *dollar* Dollar *m.*
**S.A.** *South Africa* Südafrika *n; South America* Südamerika *n.*
**Salop** *Shropshire.*
**S.C.** *South Carolina; Security Council* Sicherheitsrat *m (U.N.).*
**S.D(ak).** *South Dakota.*
**SEATO** *South East Asia Treaty Organization* Südostasienpakt-Organisation *f.*
**sh.** *shilling(s)* Schilling *m od. pl.*
**Soc.** *society* Gesellschaft *f;* Verein *m.*

**Som.** *Somersetshire.*
**Sq.** *Square* Platz *m.*
**sq.** *square* ... Quadrat...
**Staffs.** *Staffordshire.*
**St(.)** *Saint* ... Sankt ...; *Station* Bahnhof *m; Street* Straße *f.*
**Suff.** *Suffolk.*
**suppl.** *supplement* Nachtrag *m.*
**Sur.** *Surrey.*
**Suss.** *Sussex.*

**t.** *ton(s)* Tonne(n *pl.) f.*
**Tenn.** *Tennessee.*
**Tex.** *Texas.*
**T.M.O.** *telegraph money order* telegraphische Geldanweisung.
**T.O.** *Telegraph (Telephone) Office* Telegraphen- (Fernsprech)amt *n*
**T.U.** *Trade(s) Union(s)* Gewerkschaft(en *pl.) f.*
**T.U.C.** *Trade(s) Union Congress* brit. Gewerkschaftsverband *m.*

**U.K.** *United Kingdom* Vereinigtes Königreich *(England, Schottland, Wales und Nordirland).*
**U.N.** *United Nations* Vereinte Nationen *pl.*
**UNESCO** *United Nations Educational, Scientific, and Cultural Organization* Organisation *f* der Vereinten Nationen für Wissenschaft, Erziehung und Kultur.
**U.N.S.C.** *United Nations Security Council* Sicherheitsrat *m* der Vereinten Nationen.
**U.P.I.** *United Press International (amer. Nachrichtenagentur).*
**U.S.(A.)** *United States (of America)* Vereinigte Staaten *pl.* (von Ame-\
**Ut.** *Utah.* [rika.)\

**Va.** *Virginia.*
**vol(s).** *volume(s)* Band *m* (Bände\
**Vt.** *Vermont.* [*pl.*).\
**V.T.O.(L.)** *vertical take-off (and landing) (aircraft)* Senkrechtstart(er) *m.*

**W.** *west* West(en *m);* western west-\
**War.** *Warwickshire.* [lich.\
**Wash.** *Washington.*
**W.C.** *West Central (London)* Mitte-West *(Postbezirk).*
**W.F.T.U.** *World Federation of Trade Unions* Weltgewerkschaftsbund *m.*
**W.H.O.** *World Health Organization* Weltgesundheitsorganisation *f (U.N.).*
**W.I.** *West Indies* Westindien *n.*
**Wilts.** *Wiltshire.*
**Wis.** *Wisconsin.*
**Worcs.** *Worcestershire.*
**wt.** *weight* Gewicht *n.*
**W.Va.** *West Virginia.*
**Wyo.** *Wyoming.*

**yd.** *yard(s)* Elle(n *pl.) f.*
**Yorks.** *Yorkshire.*

# German Weights and Measures

## I. Linear Measure

**1 mm**  *Millimeter* millimet|re, *Am.* -er = 0.039 inch

**1 cm**  *Zentimeter* centimet|re, *Am.* -er = 10 mm = 0.394 inch

**1 m**  *Meter* met|re, *Am.* -er = 100 cm = 1.094 yards = 3.281 feet

**1 km**  *Kilometer* kilomet|re, *Am.* -er = 1000 m = 0.621 mile

**1 sm**  *Seemeile* nautical mile = 1852 m

## II. Square Measure

**1 mm²**  *Quadratmillimeter* square millimet|re, *Am.* -er = 0.002 square inch

**1 cm²**  *Quadratzentimeter* square centimet|re, *Am.* -er = 100 mm² = 0.155 square inch

**1 m²**  *Quadratmeter* square met|re, *Am.* -er = 10000 cm² = 1.196 square yards = 10.764 square feet

**1 a**  *Ar* are = 100 m² = 119.599 square yards

**1 ha**  *Hektar* hectare = 100 a = 2.471 acres

**1 km²**  *Quadratkilometer* square kilomet|re, *Am.* -er = 100 ha = 247.11 acres = 0.386 square mile

## III. Cubic Measure

**1 cm³**  *Kubikzentimeter* cubic centimet|re, *Am.* -er = 1000 mm³ = 0.061 cubic inch

**1 m³**  *Kubikmeter* cubic met|re, *Am.* -er = 1000000 cm³ = 35.315 cubic feet = 1.308 cubic yards

**1 RT**  *Registertonne* register ton = 2,832 m³ = 100 cubic feet

## IV. Measure of Capacity

**1 l**  *Liter* lit|re, *Am.* -er = 1.760 pints = *U.S.* 1.057 liquid quarts *or* 0.906 dry quart

**1 hl**  *Hektoliter* hectolit|re, *Am.* -er = 100 l = 2.75 bushels = *U.S.* 26.418 gallons

## V. Weight

**1 g**  *Gramm* gram(me) = 15.432 grains

**1 Pfd.**  *Pfund* pound (German) = 500 g = 1.102 pounds avdp.

**1 kg**  *Kilogramm* kilogram(me) = 1000 g = 2.205 pounds avdp. = 2.679 pounds troy

**1 Ztr.**  *Zentner* centner = 100 Pfd. = 0.984 hundredweight = 1.102 *U.S.* hundredweights

**1 dz**  *Doppelzentner* = 100 kg = 1.968 hundredweights = 2.204 *U.S.* hundredweights

**1 t**  *Tonne* ton = 1000 kg = 0.984 long ton = *U.S.* 1.102 short tons

# American and British Weights and Measures

## 1. Linear Measure

**1 inch (in.)** = 2,54 cm
**1 foot (ft)**
= 12 inches = 30,48 cm
**1 yard (yd)**
= 3 feet = 91,439 cm
**1 perch (p.)**
= 5$^1/_2$ yards = 5,029 m
**1 mile (m.)**
= 1,760 yards = 1,609 km

## 2. Nautical Measure

**1 fathom (f., fm)**
= 6 feet = 1,829 m
**1 nautical mile**
= 6,080 feet = 1853,18 m

## 3. Square Measure

**1 square inch (sq. in.)**
= 6,452 cm$^2$
**1 square foot (sq. ft)**
= 144 square inches
= 929,029 cm$^2$
**1 square yard (sq. yd)**
= 9 square feet = 8361,26 cm$^2$
**1 square perch (sq. p.)**
= 30$^1/_4$ square yards = 25,293m$^2$
**1 rood**
= 40 square perches = 10,117 a
**1 acre (a.)** = 4 roods = 40,47 a
**1 square mile**
= 640 acres = 258,998 ha

## 4. Cubic Measure

**1 cubic inch (cu. in.)**
= 16,387 cm$^3$
**1 cubic foot (cu. ft)**
= 1,728 cubic inches = 0,028 m$^3$
**1 cubic yard (cu. yd)**
= 27 cubic feet = 0,765 m$^3$
**1 register ton (reg. ton)**
= 100 cubic feet = 2,832 m$^3$

## 5. Measure of Capacity
### Dry and Liquid Measure

**1 British** *or* **imperial gill (gl, gi.)**
= 0,142 l
**1 British** *or* **imperial pint (pt)**
= 4 gills = 0,568 l
**1 British** *or* **imperial quart (qt)**
= 2 pints = 1,136 l
**1 British** *or* **imp. gallon (imp. gal.)**
= 4 imperial quarts = 4,546 l

### Dry Measure

**1 British** *or* **imperial peck (pk)**
= 2 imperial gallons = 9,092 l
**1 Brit.** *or* **imp. bushel (bu., bus.)**
= 8 imperial gallons = 36,366 l

**1 Brit.** *or* **imp. quarter (qr)**
= 8 imperial bushels = 290,935 l

### Liquid Measure

**1 Brit.** *or* **imp. barrel (bbl, bl)**
= 36 imperial gallons = 163,656 l

\*

**1 U.S. dry pint** = 0,551 l
**1 U.S. dry quart**
= 2 dry pints = 1,101 l
**1 U.S. dry gallon**
= 4 dry quarts = 4,405 l
**1 U.S. peck**
= 2 dry gallons = 8,809 l
**1 U.S. bushel**
= 8 dry gallons = 35,238 l
**1 U.S. gill** = 0,118 l
**1 U.S. liquid pint**
= 4 gills = 0,473 l
**1 U.S. liquid quart**
= 2 liquid pints = 0,946 l
**1 U.S. liquid gallon**
= 8 liquid pints = 3,785 l
**1 U.S. barrel**
= 3$^1/_2$ liquid gallons = 119,228 l
**1 U.S. barrel petroleum**
= 42 liquid gallons = 158,97 l

## 6. Avoirdupois Weight

**1 grain (gr.)** = 0,065 g
**1 dram (dr.)**
= 27.344 grains = 1,772 g
**1 ounce (oz.)**
= 16 drams = 28,35 g
**1 pound (lb.)**
= 16 ounces = 453,592 g
**1 quarter (qr)**
= 28 pounds = 12,701 kg
(*U.S.A.* 25 pounds
= 11,339 kg)
**1 hundredweight (cwt.)**
= 112 pounds
= 50,802 kg (*U.S.A.* 100 pounds
= 45,359 kg)
**1 ton (t.)**
(*a.* long ton) = 20 hundredweights = 1016,05 kg (*U.S.A.*,
*a.* short ton, = 907,185 kg)
**1 stone (st.)** = 14 pounds = 6,35 kg

## 7. Troy Weight

**1 grain** = 0,065 g
**1 pennyweight (dwt.)**
= 24 grains = 1,555 g
**1 ounce**
= 20 pennyweights = 31,103 g
**1 pound** = 12 ounces = 373,242 g